American Constitutionalism

Volume II **Rights and Liberties**

Howard Gillman
University of Southern California

Mark A. Graber
University of Maryland

Keith E. Whittington
Princeton University

New York Oxford
Oxford University Press

Oxford University Press is a department of the University of Oxford. It furthers the University's objective of excellence in research, scholarship, and education by publishing worldwide.

Oxford New York
Auckland Cape Town Dar es Salaam Hong Kong Karachi
Kuala Lumpur Madrid Melbourne Mexico City Nairobi
New Delhi Shanghai Taipei Toronto

With offices in
Argentina Austria Brazil Chile Czech Republic France Greece
Guatemala Hungary Italy Japan Poland Portugal Singapore
South Korea Switzerland Thailand Turkey Ukraine Vietnam

Copyright © 2013 by Oxford University Press, Inc.

For titles covered by Section 112 of the US Higher Education Opportunity Act, please visit www.oup.com/us/he for the latest information about pricing and alternate formats.

Published by Oxford University Press.
198 Madison Avenue, New York, NY 10016
http://www.oup.com

Oxford is a registered trademark of Oxford University Press

All rights reserved. No part of this publication may be reproduced, stored in a retrieval system, or transmitted, in any form or by any means, electronic, mechanical, photocopying, recording, or otherwise, without the prior permission of Oxford University Press.

ISBN 978-0-19-975135-8
9 8 7 6 5 4 3 2

Printed in the United States of America
on acid-free paper

Brief Contents

Contents

Appendices

Topical Outline of Volume II

Tables, Figures, and Illustrations

Preface

This textbook pioneers a new approach to American constitutionalism. Our target audience consists of professors, students, and readers interested in researching, teaching, and learning about constitutional politics in the United States. This preface explains four crucial features of the material that follows.

- We discuss *all important debates* in American constitutional history.
- We include readings from *all prominent participants* in these constitutional debates.
- We organize these constitutional debates by *historical era*.
- Chapter introductions clearly lay out the *political and legal contexts*.

Our goal is to familiarize readers with the central constitutional issues that have excited Americans over the years—and that are still vigorously debated in our time. We hope to break the habit of equating American constitutionalism with the decisions of the Supreme Court of the United States. Constitutionalism in the United States covers more topics, is more complex, and is more interesting than one would gather from merely reading essays by judges in law reports.

American Constitutionalism is directed at all persons who hope to become sophisticated observers and informed participants in a constitutional regime, not just the very few who make arguments before federal judges or the extraordinary few who become federal judges. Our text provides readers with the materials they need to form educated opinions on the fundamental questions of American constitutionalism.

Constitutional norms pervade all of American politics, and all of us participate in that constitutional politics. The very vocabulary that ordinary Americans use when talking politics reflects the language chosen by long-dead framers. When we think that government is treating us unfairly, we complain that we have been denied "the equal protection of the laws." We insist or deny that national health care is a legitimate exercise of the congressional power under Article I "to regulate commerce among the several states." We debate whether the individual mandate in the Affordable Health Care Act of 2010 is a "necessary and proper" exercise of the constitutional power "to lay and collect Taxes and provide for the general welfare of the United States."

Sophisticated observers and informed participants need a different introduction to American constitutionalism than lawyers practicing before the Supreme Court. Both should be exposed to such judicial landmarks as *McCulloch v. Maryland* (1819), the decision that defined the scope of national powers, and *Brown v. Board of Education* (1954), the decision that declared unconstitutional the laws that mandated racial segregation in public schools. For this reason, *American Constitutionalism* includes generous selections from the most important cases decided by the Supreme Court of the United States.

Participants in constitutional politics should be familiar with important constitutional issues that are *not* being litigated, and may never have been litigated, before the Supreme Court. They should know the basic arguments for and against presidential power to initiate military action in foreign countries, even if that constitutional question has not been decided by the Supreme Court. Sophisticated observers should be aware of the ways in which Supreme Court rulings may be consequences of previous constitutional choices made by other constitutional authorities. The *Brown* decision, for example, occurred only after Presidents Roosevelt, Truman, and Eisenhower had packed the federal courts with racial liberals who believed Jim Crow unconstitutional.

American Constitutionalism provides the tools and resources for this more comprehensive perspective on

American constitutional politics. If our goal is to understand American constitutionalism, then we should be open to the full range of the American constitutional experience. If our goal is to engage the fundamental questions that have roiled American politics and understand the dynamics of constitutional development, then we must widen our point of view. We must incorporate the constitutional politics underlying landmark Supreme Court decisions, and we must include landmark constitutional decisions made by elected officials and state courts. *American Constitutionalism* offers these materials.

Constitutional arguments are as much the stuff of politics as the pork barrel and the log roll. The interplay of legal principles, moral values, partisan interests, and historical developments is a central feature of our constitutional system. Basic constitutional institutions provide normative and procedural frameworks that allow political debate and decision making to move forward in ways that political winners and losers alike usually consider legitimate. At the same time, preexisting constitutional commitments confer advantages on some political movements and partisan coalitions relative to others.

With the materials that follow we hope to provide an understanding of how constitutionalism actually works in the United States. We reject the simple view that constitutionalism has nothing to do with politics—and the equally simple view that constitutionalism is nothing more than a dressed-up version of ordinary politics. American constitutionalism is a distinctive form of politics with distinctive goals and modes of justification. Understanding the interplay between all the different elements of constitutional law and politics is a precondition for any realistic assessment of how American constitutionalism actually works, how that system of governance should work, and how our political order might work better.

All Important Constitutional Debates

American Constitutionalism covers the major constitutional controversies that have excited Americans from the Colonial Era to the present. Readings range from protests that the Stamp Act violated the unwritten English Constitution to the arguments made in the contemporary controversy over "enhanced" methods of interrogating suspected terrorists. Along the way, we include the constitutional debates over the Bill of Rights, the Louisiana Purchase, the Emancipation Proclamation, Prohibition, women's suffrage, the New Deal, and presidential power to order troops into foreign countries.

When determining what materials to include, we looked to the impact of the controversy on American constitutional development. We devote space to the constitutional disputes over the annexation of Texas and the proposed Human Life Amendment. Both debates were central to the constitutional politics of the time and provide foundations for contemporary constitutional politics. We spend less time on technical legal questions primarily of interest to lawyers with a federal courts practice. We believe that scarce space in a textbook aimed at providing a deeper understanding of the workings of our constitutional system is better spent covering such issues as the N.A.A.C.P.'s litigation strategy for defeating segregation than the precise details of the Supreme Court's commercial speech jurisprudence."

All Important Constitutional Participants

American Constitutionalism examines the contributions of all Americans to important constitutional debates. These contributions include the judicial opinions in such landmark Supreme Court cases as *Marbury v. Madison* (1803) and *Roe v. Wade* (1973). The major contributions to important constitutional debates also include the arguments that lawyers made before the Supreme Court, the judicial opinions and legal arguments in lower federal court and state court cases, presidential speeches and opinions of the attorney general, congressional debates and legislative reports, party manifestos, pamphlets produced by interest groups, and scholarly commentaries. A comprehensive education in American constitutionalism should include Salmon Chase's argument that Congress had no constitutional power to pass a fugitive slave act, the prominent state court decisions interpreting provisions in state bills of rights, President Nixon's veto of the War Powers Resolution, the congressional debates over the ratification of the post–Civil War Amendments, and the Margold Report outlining the NAACP's strategy during the 1930s and 1940s for securing a Supreme Court decision that ended the policy of "separate but equal."

We include these materials because we recognize that American constitutionalism takes shape in the legislative and executive branches of government, as well as in the judiciary. Constitutional provisions and principles are elaborated within the national government, by state and local officials, and on the streets and in meeting places throughout the United States. Constitutional meaning is determined by government officials, party platforms, campaign speeches, legal treatises, and newspaper articles.

Our emphasis on all participants is closely related to our concern with presenting all major constitutional debates. Consider the constitutional issues raised by national expansion and presidential war-making powers. These matters were debated and settled by elected officials. We would only skim the surface of the constitutional controversies raised during the contemporary War on Terror if we limited materials to Supreme Court rulings. Even when courts make constitutional rulings, those rulings are typically preceded and structured by constitutional politics outside the judiciary. The Supreme Court in *Planned Parenthood v. Casey* (1992) refrained from overruling *Roe v. Wade* in part because pro-choice Democrats in 1986 were able to prevent President Reagan from appointing Robert Bork, a vigorous critic of *Roe*, to the Supreme Court. The Supreme Court in *McCulloch v. Maryland* declared that congressional decisions made during the preceding decade had partly settled questions about the constitutionality of the national bank. Elected officials often decide the fate of judicial decisions once they are handed down. If we pay too much attention to *Brown v. Board of Education* (1954), we will overlook the crucial role that the Civil Rights Act of 1964 played in securing desegregation. If we concentrate too narrowly on the words of the Court in *Brown*, we miss the equally significant and diverse words of Harry Truman, Dwight Eisenhower, the Southern Manifesto, and Martin Luther King, Jr.

Historical Organization

American Constitutionalism is organized historically. The text respects the traditional pedagogical division of constitutionalism into two courses: the first on the structures of government and the second on rights and liberties. Within each volume, we divide American constitutional development into ten relatively distinct and stable political regimes: Colonial (before 1776), Founding (1776–1791), Early National (1791–1828), Jacksonian (1829–1860), Civil War/Reconstruction (1861–1876), Republican (1877–1932), New Deal/Great Society (1933–1968), Liberalism Divided (1969–1980), Reagan (1981–1993), and Contemporary (1994–present). These ten eras are characterized by important constitutional stabilities that mark each period off from previous and later eras.

Constitutional questions about secession and slavery were settled by the Civil War. Americans during the Jacksonian Era bitterly debated the constitutional issues associated with national territorial expansion, banking, and internal improvements. Americans after Reconstruction were far more concerned with national power to regulate railroads and drinking. New Dealers temporarily settled the constitutional questions over national power to regulate the economy that divided Americans from 1876 to 1932. Many of these issues reemerged in new forms during the Contemporary Era. *Brown v. Board of Education* was hotly contested during the New Deal and Great Society. Americans after 1968 celebrated *Brown* and debated whether that decision supported or undermined affirmative action.

Approaching American constitutionalism historically provides a sound framework for understanding crucial episodes in American constitutional politics. Consider struggles over constitutional authority. Thomas Jefferson, Andrew Jackson, Abraham Lincoln, and Franklin Roosevelt maintained that the president, when making constitutional decisions, should not always be bound by past Supreme Court decisions. Other presidents have accepted judicial rulings as authoritative. Our period divisions enable readers to see patterns in this cycle of presidential assertion and deference.

The historical approach also enables students to see vital connections between different constitutional issues. Debates over slavery ranged from the scope of the federal power to regulate the interstate slave trade under the interstate commerce clause to whether the Sixth Amendment gave alleged fugitive slaves the right to a jury trial. The movement for racial equality during the 1950s and 1960s challenged existing constitutional understandings of the First Amendment, constitutional criminal procedure, cruel and unusual punishment, equal protection, the scope of federal power over interstate commerce, and state power to regulate interstate commerce in the absence of federal power. We risk losing the vital connections between constitutional provisions when we cabin American constitutionalism into artificial doctrinal categories and treat them as timeless abstractions.

The Political and Legal Contexts

In all these ways, *American Constitutionalism* provides readers with information about the political and legal contexts in which constitutional controversies arise, are debated, and are settled. A concise introduction to each chapter identifies the central features of American constitutional politics during a particular era. These crucial elements are both political and legal.

The *political elements* include the most important partisan coalitions that fought for electoral supremacy, the main interests that supported those coalitions, the positions that those coalitions took on the most important issues that divided Americans, and the extent to which one coalition was more successful than others at gaining control of the national government. The *Dred Scott* decision (1857), which declared that Congress could not ban slavery in American territories, articulated the constitutional commitments of the Jacksonian Democrats, who largely controlled the national government from 1828 to 1860.

The *legal elements* include the most important schools of constitutional and legal thought in a particular era. They include the general principles that most people believed best justified the constitutional order, what governing authorities thought the best methods for interpreting the Constitution, and the available precedents that could be invoked to justify future constitutional developments. New Deal liberals, when justifying extensive government regulation of the national economy, relied heavily on notions of a "living Constitution" that had become increasingly prominent in legal thought during the early twentieth century.

Pedagogical Framework

The context presented in chapter introductions is part of a consistent pedagogical framework:

- An opening chapter lays out the basic concepts essential to understanding rights and liberties, and the constitutional politics of rights and liberties. This chapter also provides an essential introduction to students unfamiliar with basic principles of constitutional interpretation and constitutional authority.
- Each historical chapter is divided into a consistent set of topical sections.
- After the period introduction, sections within each subsequent chapter summarize the major issues. Each section begins with a bulleted list of major developments, for ease of reference and to facilitate understanding.
- All readings are prefaced with explanatory headnotes, and all headnotes to court cases end with questions. We believe that this more effectively creates engaged readers and engaged citizens.
- Period illustrations, such as political cartoons, further suggest controversies and contexts.
- Tables throughout the volume summarize key issues and court cases.
- All chapters end with suggested readings.

We hope that the materials provided here allow readers to think about questions of constitutional interpretation and what the various texts mean, but also to think about questions of constitutional design and practice. If resolving fundamental disputes were merely a matter of consulting a neutral referee, such as a Supreme Court, whose authority was acknowledged by all players, then constitutional politics would be a simple matter of appeals, decisions, and essays in law books. Because our system does not work in this way, we have written this book.

For ease of use, the readings in the text are modernized, and we generally use modern terminology to refer to political and constitutional concepts. Since U.S. Supreme Court cases can now be easily found, we have generally cited them only by party names and decision date. We provide footnote citations to state cases only when they are not otherwise identified in excerpts. To help readers distinguish references to U.S. Supreme Court cases and state cases we have added state identifiers to the decision dates when we mention state cases; e.g., *Smith v. Jones* (MD 1823). All excerpts from presidential speeches and party platforms are taken from the terrific "American Presidency Project" at the University of California, Santa Barbara. These materials can be found at http://www.presidency.ucsb.edu/index.php. All quotations from *The Federalist Papers* are taken from *The Federalist: A Collection of Essays, Written in Favour of the New Constitution, as Agreed Upon by the Federal Convention, September 17, 1787, in two volumes* (New York: J. and A. McLean, 1788).

Supplements

However hard we tried, two volumes alone could not have space for all the participants in all the debates without growing so large as to be both costly and intimidating. While we have kept chapters flexible so that instructors can skip around, we nonetheless took a further step: we have made many more readings available on the Web, as part of the extensive supplements available with this book at www.oup.com/us/Gillman.

We also make available correlation guides to match our coverage to more traditional sequences. We wish to make our unusual range of coverage suitable to *any* class. Yet we also hope in this way to make the transition to a new approach easier. We believe that a historical organization best reflects the lived experience of the political actors who challenged existing constitutional practices and the constitutional authorities who determined the validity of those challenges.

Acknowledgments

American Constitutionalism was inspired by and is for our teachers and our students. Walter Murphy, Sanford Levinson, Mark Tushnet, Stephen Elkin, Lou Fisher, Bruce Ackerman, Martin Shapiro, and Rogers Smith are foremost among our many teachers. From them and others we learned that American constitutionalism was about the construction of a political regime and not limited to close analysis of a few Supreme Court opinions. Leslie Goldstein, Judith Baer, Gary Jacobsohn, H. W. Perry, Gordon Silverstein, Paul Frymer, Julie Novkov, George Lovell, Daniel Carpenter, Cornell Clayton, Michael McCann, Barry Friedman, Jack Balkin, Randy Barnett, Douglas Reed, Steve Griffin, Karen Orren, Pamela Brandwein, Kevin McMahon, Tom Keck, Keith Bybee, Shep Melnick, Ken Kersch, Ron Kahn, Stephen Skowronek, and many others have simultaneously been our teachers and students. For the past quarter-century we have participated in a common project devoted to elaborating new constitutional histories, new constitutional theories, and new constitutional visions all aimed at exploring the ways in which the study of American constitutional politics might differ from the study of constitutional law. We are particularly grateful for the opportunities to teach and learn from Kim Scheppele, Ran Hirschl, Gary Jacobsohn, Leslie Goldstein, and Thomas Ginsburg, who have consistently reminded us that we can understand American constitutionalism only by understanding constitutionalism outside of the United States. Over the past decade, we have welcomed Mariah Zeisberg, Tom Clark, Bradley Hays, Steve Simon, Beau Breslin, Doug Edlin, Helen Knowles, David Erdos, Justin Crowe, David Glick, and Emily Zackin to this constitutionalist fellowship. Each of these talented scholars has been tolerant of our foibles while diligently pointing out the many mistakes made in the initial elaboration of this new American constitutionalism. Finally, we should acknowledge the debt we owe to our students at Princeton University, the University of Southern California, and the University of Maryland. They will inherit American constitutionalism, if not *American Constitutionalism*. From them, we have learned that less is often more. We have experienced firsthand the hunger in younger Americans for ways to better understand and reform the American constitutional order.

The three of us owe a special debt of gratitude to the many persons who directly assisted the actual writing of *American Constitutionalism*. The list of friends and colleagues who responded promptly when we asked for advice about such matters as executive privilege in the Jacksonian Era or Sunday laws in the 1920s is probably longer than this volume, if that can be imagined. Nevertheless, we ought to single out Rogers Smith and Sandy Levinson for being particularly helpful with their comments and assistance. A legion of research assistants worked diligently finding cases, making tables, correcting typos, and inserting periods. They include Deborah Beim, David Bridge, Benjamin Bruins, Jonathan Cheng, Colleen Clary, Ina Cox, Danny Frost, Wandaly Fernandez, David Glick, Abigail Graber, Ayana Mayberry, April Morton, David Myers, Herschel Nachlis, Benjamin Newton, David Nohe, Amanda Radke, Jennifer Ratcliff, Jessica Rebarber, Edward Reilly, Ryan Palmer, Clara Shaw, Michael Sullivan, Thaila Sundaresan, Jeff Tessin, and Katie Zuber.

Many friends and colleagues helped us test earlier iterations of *American Constitutionalism*. Each of them provided vital encouragement to us at initial stages of the project, but also gave us plain hard truths about the difficult choices we needed to make in order to bring this book to market. We thank them profusely for their counsel, as well as their students, whose comments on earlier editions we did our best to incorporate in the later volumes.

This project would not exist if not for Jennifer Carpenter and John Haber, our editors at Oxford University Press. They combined consistent encouragement, meticulous editing, and the patience of Job. Most important, they kept the faith that what we had to say mattered if said right and clearly. Other members of Oxford University Press, most notably Shelby Peak and Maegan Sherlock, demonstrated the same standard of exemplary professionalism and friendship. Sarah Vogelsong was a fabulous and copyeditor. Sue McCarty provided first-rate help on the references.

We must also thank the many reviewers who closely examined each chapter to ensure its scholarly integrity and suitability to their course in constitutional law: Christopher W. Bonneau, University of Pittsburgh; Jennifer Bowie, George Mason University; Daniel Breen, Brandeis University; Rose Corrigan, Drexel University; McKinzie Craig, Texas A&M University; John P. Feldmeier, Wright State University; Michael P. Fix, Georgia State University; Louis Gordon, California State University, San Bernardino; Hans J. Hacker, Arkansas State University; Charles Hersch, Cleveland State University; Jeffrey D. Hockett, University of Tulsa; Melvin C. Laracey, The University of Texas at San Antonio; Mark C. Miller, Clark University; Wayne D. Moore, Virginia Polytechnic Institute and State University; Paul Nolette, Marquette University; Adam W. Nye, The Pennsylvania State University; Rogers M. Smith, University of Pennsylvania; Isaac Unah, The University of North Carolina at Chapel Hill; Teena Wilhelm, University of Georgia; Martha T. Zingo.

Still others have class-tested drafts of this text with their students: Emily Zackin, Hunter College, and Helen Knowles, Whitman College.

Before, during, and after writing this book, we drew inspiration from our families, who seem appropriately amused with our fascination for American constitutional development. Mark Graber wishes to extend his love and appreciation to his mother, Anita Wine Graber, and his spouse, Julia Bess Frank, and children—Naomi, Abigail, and Rebecca. Keith Whittington thanks Tracey and Taylor for their great patience and love. Howard Gillman thanks Ellen, Arielle, and Danny. The good news for our families is that, if they are reading this, the volume is finally done. The bad news is that we are probably still down in the basement, obsessed by some other project on which we have already missed a deadline.

Part 1 **Themes**

Chapter 1

Introduction to Rights and Liberties

The Declaration of Independence declares:

> We hold these truths to be self-evident, that all Men are created equal, that they are endowed by their Creator with certain unalienable Rights, that among these are Life, Liberty, and the pursuit of Happiness.—That to secure these Rights, Governments are instituted among Men, deriving their just Powers from the Consent of the Governed.

With these words, Thomas Jefferson articulated a national commitment to protecting freedom. Previous political regimes in the West had been dedicated to world conquest, the promotion of the one true religion, or the enrichment of a few noble families. Constitutional government in the United States would be different. The regime announced by the Declaration of Independence and established by the Constitution of the United States aspires to "secure the Blessings of Liberty to ourselves and our Posterity."

Americans have renewed these vows throughout their history. "Four score and seven years ago," Abraham Lincoln's Gettysburg Address begins, "our fathers brought forth on this continent, a new nation, conceived in Liberty, and dedicated to the proposition that all men are created equal." Republicans and Democrats at the turn of the twenty-first century agree that protecting fundamental rights and liberties is a core concern of American constitutionalism. President George W. Bush's first inaugural address told the "story of a new world that became a friend and liberator of the old, a story of the slave-holding society that became a servant of freedom." Eight years later, President Barack Obama's inaugural address called on Americans "to carry forward that precious gift, that noble idea, passed on from generation to generation: the God-given promise that all are equal, all are free, and all deserve a chance to pursue their full measure of happiness."

Many constitutional commentators, inspired by the American example, insist that all constitutional systems are united by a common commitment to human rights. One prominent political thinker claims that constitutionalism is "a system of protected freedom for the individual."[1] The structure of constitutional institutions, the powers of the national government, and federalism are institutional vehicles for securing fundamental rights. "Constitutionalism does not reject democratic processes," a leading text proclaims, "it treats them as means—necessary, but insufficient—to achieve what it considers the ultimate substantive purposes of the political order, which might be protecting individual liberty, promoting virtue, or something else."[2] When people vote for governing officials, these officials are more likely to respect popular liberties. When power is divided between different governments and different governmental institutions, factions bent on establishing majority or minority tyranny find themselves facing insuperable difficulties in gaining the necessary control over political institutions.

I. Constitutional Rights

Constitutional rights and liberties in the United States can be divided into four rough categories:

1. Individual rights

1. Giovanni Sartori, "Constitutionalism: A Preliminary Discussion," *American Political Science Review* 56 (1962): 853–54.

2. Walter F. Murphy, James E. Fleming, Sotirios A. Barber, and Stephen Macedo, *American Constitutional Interpretation*, 4th ed. (New York: Foundation Press, 2008), 54.

2. Political rights
3. Equality rights
4. Procedural rights

Many constitutional provisions protect more than one kind of right. What kind of rights Americans understand a particular constitutional clause to protect changes over time.

Individual rights limit the extent to which national and state officials may regulate personal behavior. Article I, Section 10 prohibits states from interfering with freely made contractual obligations. Neither Congress nor state legislatures, proponents of legal abortion assert, may pass a law forbidding a woman from terminating a pregnancy. The Supreme Court in *Sherbert v. Verner* (1963) ruled that government officials may pass laws restricting the free exercise of religion only when the regulation is justified by a compelling interest.

Political rights grant persons powers to influence state and national policy making. The First Amendment protects the right to criticize public officials. Opponents of common campaign finance regulations believe that government officials may not pass laws restricting the sums that contributors may spend supporting the candidate of their choice. The Supreme Court in *Harper v. Virginia State Board of Elections* (1966) ruled that state governments could not condition the right to vote on the payment of a poll tax.

Equality rights guarantee all persons the same government benefits and burdens that are provided to other similarly situated persons. The Fifteenth Amendment prohibits state laws that deny the ballot to an otherwise qualified person of color. Proponents of same-sex marriage believe that a person who by state law is entitled to marry a man has a constitutional right to marry a similarly situated woman. In *United States v. Virginia* (1996) the Supreme Court ruled that the Virginia Military Institute was constitutionally obligated to admit women who satisfied that institution's physical and academic standards for men.

Procedural rights ensure that persons are given a fair hearing before the state is permitted to take away any of the above rights. The Fifth Amendment declares that defendants in criminal trials cannot be compelled to testify against themselves. Critics of presidential power in wartime insist that only Congress can suspend the right of habeas corpus. *Duncan v. Louisiana* (1968) held that persons tried for criminal offenses in a state court have the right to a jury trial.

These individual, political, equality, and procedural rights are usually understood as *limits* on government power. The most important constitutional provisions on civil liberties are phrased in the negative. The First Amendment declares, "Congress shall make no law respecting an establishment of religion." The Fourteenth Amendment asserts, "No State shall . . . deny to any person within its jurisdiction the equal protection of the laws." In the United States, government action, not inaction, is constitutionally suspect. A government whose officials never passed or enforced any law could not violate the above constitutional restrictions on government power. Americans would hardly enjoy any liberties if national officials made no effort to combat crime or rebuff foreign invasion. Still, while the general system of constitutional freedom requires a government strong enough to prevent private or foreign invasion of various rights, the Constitution rarely mandates that government officials take specific actions that enhance liberty.

The Constitution of the United States is increasingly distinctive in its emphasis on negative liberties, or freedoms from government. Many new constitutions in other countries require that the government provide specific goods or services for all citizens. The Constitution of South Africa declares that "everyone has the right to have access to adequate housing" and that "the state must take reasonable legislative and other measures, within its available resources, to achieve the progressive realisation of this right." Some commentators think that American constitutional provisions, when properly interpreted, also protect what are called *positive rights*.[3] Whether the Constitution guarantees such rights and whether those rights are judicially enforceable is controversial.

A single constitutional provision or specific constitutional clause may protect more than one kind of right. Constitutional protections for freedom of speech presently guarantee the freedom to advocate that Congress reduce the minimum wage (a political right) and the freedom to urge your buddy to buy your car

---

3. See Sotirios A. Barber, *Welfare and the Constitution* (Princeton, NJ: Princeton University Press, 2005). For a classic statement of the alternative position, see *Jackson v. City of Joliet*, 715 F.2d 1200, 1203 (7th Cir. 1983) (specifically, "The Constitution is a charter of negative rather than positive liberties").

for $500 (an individual right). The Supreme Court at different times in history has declared that the due process clauses of the Fifth and Fourteenth Amendments protect the right to marry (an individual right), the right to vote without paying a poll tax (a political right), the right to attend desegregated schools (an equality right), and the right to a court-appointed lawyer during a criminal trial (a procedural right). Political movements and interest groups often assert that their cherished freedoms fit more than one category of right. Pro-choice advocates insist that restrictions on abortion violate a woman's individual right to decide whether to become a parent and her equality right to participate in public life on the same terms as a man. Abolitionists insisted that slavery violated the liberty and equality rights of persons of color.

Constitutional liberties often migrate over time from being considered as one kind of right to being considered as another. During the nineteenth century, the freedom of association was most often understood as an individual right: the right to combine with others for any lawful purpose. That liberty is presently treated as a political right: the freedom of expressive association, a right that enables persons to combine with others for the purpose of communicating particular messages to the general public. The First Amendment during the first half of the nineteenth century was understood as protecting a political right, but during the second half was seen as protecting an individual right. Contemporary Americans debate whether the free exercise clause is best conceptualized as an individual right to engage in various religious activities free from government restriction or an equality right to be free from discrimination based on one's religious beliefs.

II. Connections

Constitutional rights are connected in at least three ways.

1. Functional connections. Some rights help secure other rights.
2. Political connections. Political parties, political movements, and interest groups often champion various rights and liberties.
3. Principled connections. Constitutional thinkers often insist that numerous rights and liberties are aspects of more general constitutional principles.

No constitutional right or clause is an island, with a history or justification that is completely separate from that of other constitutional rights and clauses. We cannot understand how Americans understood free speech in 1791, 1868, or 2010 unless we understand the various connections that Americans at different times made between the First Amendment and other constitutional provisions

Functional Connections. Particular rights are both intrinsic goods and vital means for protecting other rights. Procedural rights enable persons to better secure other freedoms. American colonists believed that the right to trial by jury helped guarantee free speech and property rights. Having juries determine whether a publication was seditious or a private dwelling was illegally searched, they insisted, was the most effective means for preventing government censorship or invasions of private homes. New Deal liberals maintained that as long as democratic rights were respected, government could be trusted to protect other rights. "Freedom of thought and speech," Justice Benjamin Cardozo declared in *Palko v. Connecticut* (1937), "is the matrix, the indispensable condition, of nearly every other form of freedom." Justice Robert Jackson in *Railway Express Agency v. New York* (1949) connected equality rights and individual rights. He asserted,

> There is no more effective practical guaranty against arbitrary and unreasonable government than to require that the principles of law which officials would impose upon a minority must be imposed generally. Conversely, nothing opens the door to arbitrary action so effectively as to allow those officials to pick and choose only a few to whom they will apply legislation and thus to escape the political retribution that might be visited upon them if larger numbers were affected.

Political Connections. Different rights are connected by politics. Political parties, political movements, and interest groups typically pursue a variety of rights policies. A political coalition may simultaneously fight for gun rights and against capital punishment partly to mobilize more supporters, partly to better secure the interests of group members, and partly because many group members make principled connections between gun rights and capital punishment. The 1856 Republican Party platform declared, "It is both the right and the imperative duty of Congress to prohibit in the Territories those twin relics of barbarism—Polygamy, and Slavery." The present Republican Party rallies supporters behind a platform that includes assertions that the First Amendment permits voluntary school prayer, the Second Amendment protects an individual right to bear arms, the Eighth Amendment does not prohibit capital punishment, and the Fourteenth Amendment bans any use of race in the law school admissions process. Political movements and interest groups similarly take positions on numerous rights and liberties issues. To promote racial equality, the civil rights movement of the 1950s and 1960s championed the right of attorneys to solicit clients for cases challenging Jim Crow practices, the right to protest near government buildings, the right to have a fair trial, the right to marry the person of one's choice, and the right to a desegregated education. Contemporary Christian conservatives combine appeals that the free speech clause of the First Amendment does not protect pornography with claims that the free exercise clause protects the right of parents to homeschool their children.

Principled Connections. Rights are connected by their broader underlying principles. Prominent constitutional conservatives at the turn of the twentieth century believed that the Constitution protected "the right of the citizen to be free in the enjoyment of all his faculties."[4] Justice James McReynolds in *Meyer v. Nebraska* (1923) maintained that this general principle encompassed "the right of the individual to contract, to engage in any of the common occupations of life, to acquire useful knowledge, to marry, establish a home and bring up children, to worship God according to the dictates of his own conscience, and generally to enjoy those privileges long recognized at common law as essential to the orderly pursuit of happiness by free men." New Deal liberals believed that the constitutional commitment to democracy justified judicial activism on behalf of a very different set of constitutional rights and liberties. Justice Harlan Fiske Stone's influential Footnote Four in *United States v. Carolene Products Co.* (1938) insisted that justices prevent elected officials from interfering with political rights or violating the equality rights of "discrete and insular minorities." Rights may be connected by principles of constitutional interpretation. Justice Antonin Scalia insists that the Constitution protects an individual right to bear arms, but not the right to terminate a pregnancy, because he thinks that the persons responsible for the Second Amendment intended to protect an individual right to use a gun in self-defense, but that the persons responsible for the Fourteenth Amendment did not intend to protect abortion rights.

III. Sources

The rights Americans enjoy stem from five uncontroversial and two controversial sources. The uncontroversial sources are:

1. The Constitution of the United States
2. Federal laws
3. State constitutions
4. State laws
5. Judge-made common law

The Fifth Amendment to the Constitution of the United States declares, "No person . . . shall be compelled in any criminal case to be a witness against himself." The Voting Rights Act of 1975 forbids states from requiring prospective voters to take a literacy test. Article 46 of the constitution of Maryland states, "Equality of rights under the law shall not be abridged or denied because of sex." State laws routinely give residents the right to attend free public schools. Before the Civil War many common law judges in the United States followed the rule of *Somerset v. Stewart* (1773), which held that slavery had no legal existence unless plainly sanctioned by the Constitution or legislation. Americans agree that all these texts and decisions are legitimate sources of rights and liberties. They disagree only on their proper interpretation.

The controversial sources of American liberties and rights are:

1. Natural law
2. Customary international law, or the law of nations

Justice Johnson in *Fletcher v. Peck* (1810) asserted, "I do not hesitate to declare that a State does not possess the power of revoking its own grants. But I do it on a general principle, on the reason and nature of things: a principle which will impose laws even on the deity." Justice Joseph Story invoked what he believed was the

4. *Allgeyer v. Louisiana*, 165 U.S. 578, 589 (1897).

customary practice of all civilized nations when ruling in *La Jeune Eugenie* (1822) that "the [international slave] trade [is] an offence against the universal law of society."[5] Nevertheless, while no constitutional decision maker questions that constitutions, legislation, and common law decisions are valid sources for rights, disputes exist over whether constitutional decision makers may rely on natural law or the law of nations. Justice James Iredell in *Calder v. Bull* (1798) insisted that courts should not rely on natural law when making decisions because "the ideas of natural justice are regulated by no fixed standard." Chief Justice John Marshall rejected Joseph Story's claim that federal courts could rely on the law of nations as opposed to the law of particular nations when adjudicating claims arising from the international slave trade. "As no nation can prescribe a rule for others," he wrote in *The Antelope* (1825), "none can make a law of nations and this traffic remains lawful to those whose governments have not forbidden it."

Hierarchy among Sources of Rights. A clear hierarchy exists among the uncontroversial sources of rights and liberties. Constitutional law is higher than statutory law. Statutory law is higher than all forms of judge-made common law. All federal laws are a higher legal authority than state constitutions or state law. No lower legal authority may pass a law that contradicts a higher legal authority. If the Constitution of the United States grants women the right to terminate a pregnancy, then Congress cannot constitutionally pass a federal law declaring that unborn children have an absolute right to life. No state may ban abortion by constitutional decree or legislative edict. If Congress passes a law forbidding race discrimination in employment, then no state may ratify a state constitutional provision or pass a state law that permits employers to hire only white workers.

The place of natural law and the law of nations in the American constitutional hierarchy is less clear. General agreement presently exists that constitutional provisions are a higher legal authority than natural law or the law of nations. If a constitutional provision plainly declared, "Women have an absolute right to abortion under all circumstances," then even the most committed pro-life thinkers would not claim a right under American law to substitute what they might think was natural law or the law of nations for this plain constitutional provision.[6] Some commentators insist that ambiguous constitutional provisions should be interpreted in a manner consistent with natural law or the law of nations. Whether capital punishment is "cruel and unusual" in this view partly depends on the status of the death penalty in moral philosophy or customary international law. Other commentators vigorously reject such claims, insisting that ambiguous constitutional provisions should be interpreted in light of practices at the time those provisions were ratified or in light of subsequent constitutional precedents in the United States.[7]

Federal Statutes and State Constitutional Law. Congress and state officials may provide additional protections for rights and liberties beyond those found in the Constitution of the United States, as long as those additional rights and liberties are consistent with higher legal authorities. If the Supreme Court rules that the Fourteenth Amendment does not protect same-sex marriage, the Supreme Court of New Jersey may legally rule that the constitution of New Jersey protects same-sex marriage. State justices in New Jersey may announce this state constitutional right to same-sex marriage even when the words of the relevant clause in the New Jersey Constitution are identical to the wording of the U.S. Constitution. When the Supreme Court declares that the Constitution does not require states to respect a particular right, states are free to choose whether to protect that right.

Such divergences between federal and state constitutional law are common. Less than five years after the U.S. Supreme Court ruled in *Gregg v. Georgia* (1976) that the "cruel *and* unusual punishment" clause of the Eighth Amendment did not prohibit capital punishment, the Supreme Judicial Court of Massachusetts ruled in *District Attorney for Suffolk District v. Watson* (1980) that capital punishment was inconsistent with the "cruel *or* unusual punishment" clause of the state constitution. Had the Constitution of the United States

5. *La Jeune Eugenie*, 26 F. Cas. 832 (C.C.D. Mass. 1822).

6. Of course, a decision maker might believe the duty to decide according to the natural law or the law of nations was a higher *ethical* obligation than the duty to decide what was legal under the American Constitution.

7. For a flavor of this debate, see the essays in Antonin Scalia, *A Matter of Interpretation: Federal Courts and the Law* (Princeton, NJ: Princeton University Press, 1998).

mandated that murder be punished by death, the Massachusetts court could not have outlawed capital punishment under the state constitution.

Because we cannot understand constitutional practice in the United States unless we understand both federal and state practice, *American Constitutionalism* includes a healthy dose of state constitutional debates and decisions. Throughout much of American history, the only constitutional decisions on specific issues were state constitutional decisions. Nineteenth-century debates on the freedom of religion took place almost entirely within state legislatures and state courts. At present, whether a same-sex couple has a constitutional right to marry is primarily an issue of state constitutional law. Federal constitutional decisions are often shaped by previous state constitutional decisions. Justice George Sutherland's opinion in *Powell v. Alabama* (1932) relied heavily on state constitutional decisions when it asserted that the due process clause of the Fourteenth Amendment protected the right to counsel in a state criminal trial. State constitutional decision makers have often recognized rights rejected by federal constitutional decision makers. Dismayed by the increasing conservatism of the Supreme Court during the 1970s, Justice Brennan called on state judges to adopt more liberal interpretations of state constitutional provisions protecting the rights of criminal suspects.[8] Some state courts responded, whereas others have preferred to interpret state constitutional rights consistent with Supreme Court interpretations of federal constitutional rights.

State constitutional decisions, we should emphasize, are only law within the state where the decision was made. The Massachusetts decision declaring that capital punishment violates the constitution of Massachusetts has no legal status in Virginia or any other state. A Virginia justice who thought the Massachusetts decision well reasoned could decide to interpret the constitution of Virginia as also prohibiting capital punishment. Most state decisions we include in this book have either influenced other state courts or were typical of state court decisions at the time. Nevertheless, while justices on the Supreme Court of Virginia must act in a manner consistent with all federal law and past Virginia precedents, they have no more legal obligation to follow a Massachusetts court decision than they have to adopt the rules announced in a French court, a proposal made in a law review article, or the comments of a person on the street.

8. William J. Brennan, Jr., "State Constitutions and the Protection of Individual Rights," *Harvard Law Review* 90 (1977): 489.

IV. Constitutional Interpretation

The text of the U.S. Constitution plainly resolves some matters while leaving others open for debate and investigation. The president, Article II plainly states, must be at least thirty-five years old. No one seriously claims that the best high school newspaper editor in the nation is constitutionally eligible to be the next president of the United States. However, the constitutional status of federal laws imposing capital punishment is harder to discern. The Eighth Amendment forbids "cruel and unusual punishments" without specifying what punishments are cruel and unusual. The amendment also fails to elaborate any elements of a cruel and unusual punishment. Constitutional decision makers and commentators have developed six approaches for interpreting such constitutional provisions.[9]

Originalism. Historical or originalist arguments maintain that constitutional provisions mean what they meant when they were ratified. Thomas Jefferson advised Supreme Court Justice William Johnson, "On every question of construction, carry ourselves back to the time when the Constitution was adopted, recollect the spirit manifested in the debates, and instead of trying what meaning may be squeezed out of the text, or invented against it, conform to the probable one in which it was passed."[10] Proponents of originalism sometimes refer to the original *intentions* underlying constitutional provisions, but most now emphasize original *meanings*. As Randy Barnett describes the original meaning approach, "Each word must be interpreted the way a normal speaker of English would have read it when it was enacted."[11] What matters is the public meaning of the constitutional text at

9. There is no single typology of methods of constitutional interpretation, but a useful discussion of some common forms of constitutional argument can be found in Philip Bobbitt, *Constitutional Fate* (New York: Oxford University Press, 1982), 3–119.

10. Thomas Jefferson, "To William Johnson, June 12, 1823," in *The Writings of Thomas Jefferson*, ed. Paul Leicester Ford (New York: G.P. Putnam's Sons, 1899), 10:231.

11. Randy E. Barnett, *Restoring the Lost Constitution* (Princeton, NJ: Princeton University Press, 2004), xiii.

the time the provision was ratified—not private understandings between particular framers, specific goals or applications the framers had in mind, or what that constitutional language might mean in the present. That most framers expected George Washington to be the first president has no bearing on the proper interpretation of the provisions in Article II discussing the constitutional qualifications for that office.

Originalism takes different forms. Some originalists focus on practices at the time a constitutional provision was ratified. They think *Roe v. Wade* (1973) wrongly decided because bans on abortion were common when Congress proposed the Fourteenth Amendment. Other originalists claim that contemporary constitutional interpreters are bound only to act on their best understanding of constitutional principles when interpreting such phrases as "equal protection of the law." In this view, whether the Fourteenth Amendment outlaws sex segregation in public schools depends on whether such policies are consistent with the constitutional commitment to equality and not on whether the framers of the Fourteenth Amendment consciously intended to forbid such policies.[12]

Textualism. Textualist arguments emphasize the specific language of the Constitution. This includes the relationship among the terms used, as well as the common meaning of those terms. Justice Joseph Story was a leading nineteenth-century champion of textualism. In Story's view, interpreters should look only to "what is written," not to "scattered documents" and "probable guesses" about what those who adopted the Constitution meant. "It is obvious, that there can be no security to the people in any constitution of government," he wrote, "if they are not to judge of it by the fair meaning of the words of the text."[13] Leslie Goldstein, a leading contemporary textualist, adopts a similar position. She believes that "it is inappropriate for judges to strike down statutes on the basis of anything other than a principle fairly inferable from the constitutional text (although such principle need not have been present in the conscious minds of the framers)."[14]

Textualists dispute the best ways of reading the Constitution. Some textualists place constitutional language in a historical context, looking to usages at the time that constitutional words were ratified. They make use of eighteenth-century dictionaries when interpreting the meaning of "commerce" in the interstate commerce clause. Other textualists focus on the language without regard to any particular historical context. They are willing to use modern dictionaries. When determining whether secularism is a religion for First Amendment purposes, these textualists look to the contemporary meaning of "religion" without worrying whether people in 1791 relied on similar definitions.

Doctrinalism. Doctrinal arguments resolve contemporary controversies by interpreting past precedents. Rather than focus on the constitutional text or what various provisions meant when adopted, doctrinalism emphasizes what government officials, particularly judges, have said about the Constitution over time. The Constitution is interpreted in light of previous constitutional decisions or precedents. Doctrinal arguments often rely on drawing analogies to previous constitutional decisions. If the justices have declared that the Constitution protects the right to burn the flag of the United States, then the justices should declare that the Constitution protects the right to burn a map of the United States or the Texas state flag. All three cases treat burning certain objects as a form of political speech.

Precedents do not have the same binding force as text. The doctrine of *stare decisis* states that courts should generally adhere to the principles laid down in previous rulings. Nevertheless, *stare decisis* is not absolute. Constitutional decision makers may overrule precedents they believe to have been wrongly decided. During the New Deal the Supreme Court overruled several past decisions limiting congressional power to regulate the economy. When declaring a right to same-sex intimacy in *Lawrence v. Texas* (2003), the Court overruled *Bowers v. Hardwick* (1986), which had decided that states had the power to prohibit sexual relations between adults of the same sex.

Structuralism. Structural arguments rely on the general principles that best explain the structure of and

12. Compare Jack Balkin, *Living Originalism* (Cambridge, MA: Harvard University Press, 2011) with Robert Bork, *The Tempting of America: The Political Seduction of the Law* (New York: Free Press, 1989).

13. Joseph Story, *Commentaries on the Constitution of the United States* (Boston: Hillard, Gray, 1833), 1:391.

14. Leslie Friedman Goldstein, *In Defense of the Text* (Savage, MD: Rowman & Littlefield, 1991), 3.

relationships between governing institutions. Structural arguments, Charles Black claims, provide an "inference from the structures and relationships created by the Constitution in all its parts or in some principal part."[15] Such basic principles as the "separation of powers," "democracy," or "federalism" are not stated explicitly in the constitutional text. Nevertheless, those principles help us understand the constitutional institutions established by Articles I, II, and III. When determining whether the president should have a line-item veto, a structuralist looks at the general principles underlying the separation of powers. Structuralists decide whether states may constitutionally regulate interstate commerce on the basis of their understanding of the constitutional commitment to federalism.

Justice Scalia's opinion in *Printz v. United States* (1997) is a good example of a structural argument. *Printz* struck down a federal requirement that local officials implement a federal gun control regulation. Scalia acknowledged that "there is no constitutional text speaking to this precise question," but he insisted that Congress could not mandate that state officials enforce federal laws. He began with a general principle. Scalia declared that the Constitution "contemplates that a State's government will represent and remain accountable to its own citizens." He then applied that principle to the issue before the court. Preventing the federal government from "impress[ing] into its service—at no cost to itself" the police officers to whom local citizens have assigned other tasks, Scalia concluded, is essential to maintaining a "healthy balance of power between the States and the Federal Government."

Prudentialism. Prudential arguments examine the costs and benefits of different constitutional policies. Justice Robert Jackson made a prudential argument in a dissent in *Terminiello v. City of Chicago* (1949) when he criticized a decision protecting speakers who directed abusive language at their audience. "If the Court does not temper its doctrinaire logic with a little practical wisdom," Jackson warned, "it will convert the constitutional Bill of Rights into a suicide pact." Given several plausible interpretations of the Constitution, prudentialists claim, decision makers should choose the interpretation that will produce the best consequences.

15. Charles L. Black, Jr., *Structure and Relationship in Constitutional Law* (Baton Rouge: Louisiana State University Press, 1969), 7.

Aspirationalism. Aspirational arguments interpret constitutional provisions in light of the fundamental principles of justice underlying the Constitution. Ronald Dworkin, the leading proponent of aspirationalism, insists that constitutional decision makers have an obligation to make the Constitution "the best it can be."[16] They do so, he believes, by discerning what general principles best justify American constitutional practice. They then determine whether particular governmental practices are consistent with that normative commitment. Justice William Brennan, a longtime leader of the liberal wing of the Court, was a vocal advocate of the aspirationalist approach. In his view, the "Constitution is a sublime oration on the dignity of man, a bold commitment by a people to the ideal of libertarian dignity protected through law." Constitutional interpreters, Brennan believed, should interpret constitutional provisions in light of these aspirations.[17] Justice Anthony Kennedy's opinion in *Lawrence v. Texas* (2003) provides a good example of an aspirationalist argument. As Scalia did in *Printz*, Kennedy began with a general principle. "In our tradition the State is not omnipresent in the home," he wrote. From these principles, Kennedy deduced that government could not prohibit consenting adults from engaging in private homosexual acts.

V. Constitutional Decision Making

Scholars debate whether any theory of constitutional decision making actually influences constitutional practice. Legitimate constitutional arguments may exist for practically any policy. Two prominent law professors claim, "The range of permissible constitutional arguments now extends so far that a few workable ones are always available in a pinch."[18] Both proponents and opponents of abortion, health care, or federal aid to cities, in this view, can make intellectually respectable constitutional arguments for their

16. Ronald Dworkin, *Law's Empire* (Cambridge, MA: Harvard University Press, 1986), 53.

17. William J. Brennan, "The Constitution of the United States: Contemporary Ratification," *South Texas Law Review* 27 (1986): 433, 438.

18. Pamela S. Karlan and Daniel R. Ortiz, "Constitutional Farce," in *Constitutional Stupidities, Constitutional Tragedies*, ed. William N. Eskridge, Jr. and Sanford Levinson (New York: New York University Press, 1998), 180.

preferred policy. Worse, political actors may not make good-faith efforts to interpret the Constitution when they know the best interpretation is inconsistent with their policy preferences. Conservatives charge liberal pro-choice advocates with manufacturing a right to abortion out of thin jurisprudential air. Liberals charge conservatives with grossly distorting precedent in *Bush v. Gore* (2000) in order to hand George W. Bush the 2000 presidential election.

Lawyers and political scientists have developed four different models for thinking about the way judges and other constitutional authorities reach decisions. The attitudinal and strategic models claim that justices are far more concerned with policy than with law. The legal model claims that constitutional decision makers place greater emphasis on legal criteria than proponents of the attitudinal or strategic model recognize. Historical institutionalists seek to combine the best insights of the legal, attitudinal, and strategic models of constitutional decision making.

The Attitudinal Model. Many prominent political scientists point to evidence that constitutional arguments do not constrain constitutional decision makers. Jeffrey Segal and Harold Spaeth, the two leading proponents of the attitudinal model of judicial decision making, insist that Supreme Court decisions are based almost entirely on policy preferences. "Justices," they write, "make decisions by considering the facts of the case in light of their ideological attitudes and values."[19] Segal, Spaeth, and other attitudinalists note that Supreme Court justices are particularly well positioned to act on their ideology and values. Unlike legislators, they cannot easily be held accountable for their decisions by voters or other political actors. Unlike lower court judges, their decisions are not reviewed by other courts and cannot easily be overturned. The cases that reach the Supreme Court are precisely those in which the law is unclear and political values might matter. As a result, justices are likely to decide cases in a manner consistent with their political values.

Proponents of the attitudinal model point out that justices routinely form conservative and liberal voting blocs. These blocs hold together across a range of issues and legal contexts. The same justices who consistently cast liberal votes in free speech cases also cast liberal votes in cases concerning federalism and the meaning of the commerce clause. If they know that the Roberts Court voted 5–4 on some case, that Justice Ruth Bader Ginsburg was in the majority and Justice Clarence Thomas was in the minority, court watchers (and students taking constitutional law classes) can normally predict with a high degree of accuracy how the other seven justices voted.

Figure 1-1 illustrates how some political scientists assess and represent the political ideologies of the justices, in this case by using voting behavior in 1974 to align the justices from most liberal on the left to most conservative on the right. With this tool we can see who the swing voters on the Court were and which justices tended to vote together. We can also see the potential impact on the Court's behavior when a justice at one location on the spectrum is replaced by a justice who occupies a very different spot. For example, in 1975 Justice Douglas was replaced by John Paul Stevens, who voted just to the left of Stewart. Trading a strong liberal for a centrist meant that the Court would hand down more conservative decisions after 1975.

The Strategic Model. The strategic model suggests that justices seek to achieve their policy preferences by adjusting their behavior to take into account the behavior of other actors. Constitutional decision makers vote and write strategically, rather than sincerely. Persons engage in sincere voting when they vote solely on the basis of their personal preferences. An opponent of the death penalty votes sincerely when voting to declare all death sentences unconstitutional. Persons engage in sophisticated voting or vote strategically when they vote in ways they believe will achieve the most feasible policy. An opponent of the death penalty might strategically sign an opinion holding that capital punishment may be constitutionally imposed, but only when the condemned person was represented at trial by a criminal defense specialist, if this were the practical alternative the justice believed would result in the fewest executions.

The strategic model recognizes that justices need the cooperation of colleagues on the bench, lower court judges, legislators, executive branch officials, and ultimately the citizenry to achieve policy and legal goals. Governing officials implement judicial decisions, appoint like-minded justices to the bench, and preserve the constitutional and statutory foundations

19. Jeffrey A. Segal and Harold J. Spaeth, *The Supreme Court and the Attitudinal Model Revisited* (New York: Cambridge University Press, 2002), 110.

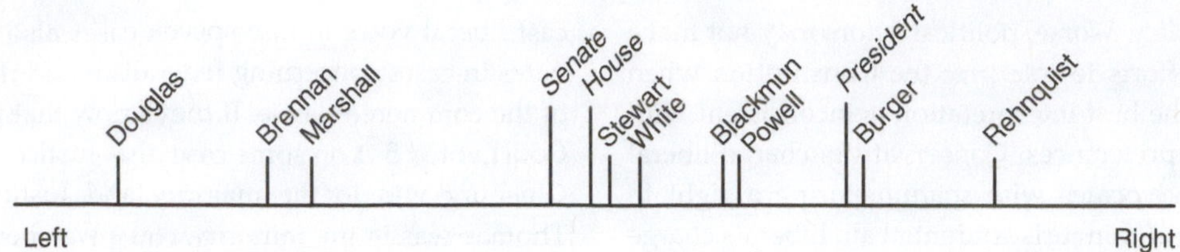

Figure 1-1 Left-Right Distribution of Justices, Congress, and President in 1974.

Note: House and Senate placement reflect the median members of the chamber.

Sources: Lee Epstein, Andrew D. Martin, Jeffrey A. Segal, and Chad Westerland, "Judicial Common Space," http://epstein.law.northwestern.edu/research/JCS.html; Keith T. Poole, "Common Space Scores, Congress 75-108," http://voteview.com/basic.htm.

of judicial independence. Justices interested in making good policy must make accommodations to win that cooperation. As Lee Epstein and Jack Knight observe:

> If their objective is to see their favored policies become the law of the land, they must take into account the preferences of other actors and the actions they expect them to take. Failing to do so may have undesirable consequences: Congress could replace their most preferred position with their least, or the public may refuse to comply with a ruling, in which case their policy fails to take on the force of law.[20]

When justices act too far outside the political mainstream, they invite backlash. After the justices in *Furman v. Georgia* (1972) declared all laws imposing the death penalty unconstitutional, two-thirds of the states passed new death penalty statutes. As a result, more people were executed during the 1980s than during the 1960s. Perhaps a more strategically minded justice would have made a narrower ruling in the *Furman* case. Such a ruling might have prohibited William Furman from being executed but would not have declared all death penalty laws unconstitutional.

The Legal Model. Proponents of the legal model believe that history, text, and precedent influence constitutional decision makers, even when these sources do not provide answers to all constitutional questions.[21] They point out that American constitutional history is littered with instances in which law constrained constitutional decision making. Before joining the Supreme Court, Felix Frankfurter was a prominent proponent of free speech rights. Frankfurter was also committed to judicial restraint. When on the Court, he often voted to sustain what he thought were unwise legislative decisions regulating speech. Justice Scalia is a conservative, but he voted with liberal justices on the Court in *Texas v. Johnson* (1989) to strike down laws prohibiting flag burning, and his dissenting opinion in *Hamdi v. Rumsfeld* (2004) declared unconstitutional the indefinite detention of an American citizen. Whether these votes were consistent with Scalia's policy preferences is doubtful. The better explanation of these liberal votes is that Scalia believed they were consistent with his commitment to deciding cases in a manner consistent with the original intentions of the framers.

Elected officials are also motivated by their beliefs about the best interpretation of the Constitution, even when those beliefs clash with cherished policy preferences. Abraham Lincoln believed that slavery was an atrocious evil, but he also thought that the Constitution did not allow Congress to interfere with slavery in the states. Lincoln similarly recognized the constitutional authority of the fugitive slave clause. Free-state citizens, he claimed throughout his career, were constitutionally obliged to return fugitive slaves to their masters.

Historical Institutionalism. The historical institutionalist school of political science insists that these three models take too narrow a perspective on constitutional decision making.[22] Constitutional authorities are

20. Lee Epstein and Jack Knight, *The Choices Justices Make* (Washington, DC: CQ Press, 1998), 14–15.

21. For an extended discussion, see Lief Carter and Thomas Burke, *Reason in Law*, 8th ed. (New York: Longman, 2009) and Howard Gillman, "What's Law Got to Do With It? Judicial Behavioralists Test the 'Legal Model' of Judicial Decision Making," *Law and Social Inquiry* 26 (2001): 465.

22. For an extended discussion, see Rogers M. Smith, "Historical Institutionalism and the Study of Law," in *The Oxford Handbook of Law and Politics*, ed. Keith E. Whittington, R. Daniel Kelemen, and Gregory A. Caldeira (New York: Oxford University Press, 2008), 46.

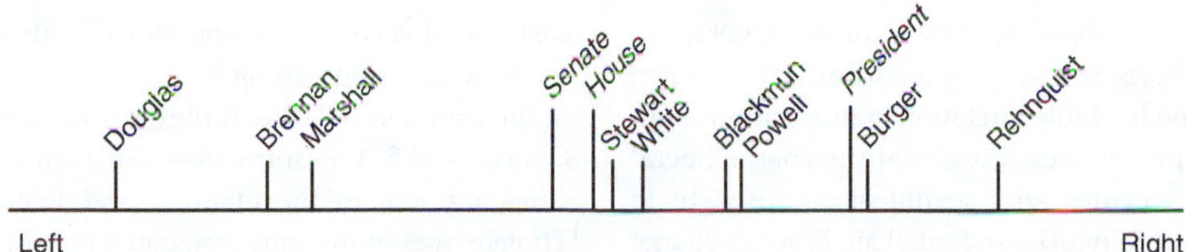

Figure 1-1 Left-Right Distribution of Justices, Congress, and President in 1974.

Note: House and Senate placement reflect the median members of the chamber.

Sources: Lee Epstein, Andrew D. Martin, Jeffrey A. Segal, and Chad Westerland, "Judicial Common Space," http://epstein.law.northwestern.edu/research/JCS.html; Keith T. Poole, "Common Space Scores, Congress 75-108," http://voteview.com/basic.htm.

of judicial independence. Justices interested in making good policy must make accommodations to win that cooperation. As Lee Epstein and Jack Knight observe:

> If their objective is to see their favored policies become the law of the land, they must take into account the preferences of other actors and the actions they expect them to take. Failing to do so may have undesirable consequences: Congress could replace their most preferred position with their least, or the public may refuse to comply with a ruling, in which case their policy fails to take on the force of law.[20]

When justices act too far outside the political mainstream, they invite backlash. After the justices in *Furman v. Georgia* (1972) declared all laws imposing the death penalty unconstitutional, two-thirds of the states passed new death penalty statutes. As a result, more people were executed during the 1980s than during the 1960s. Perhaps a more strategically minded justice would have made a narrower ruling in the *Furman* case. Such a ruling might have prohibited William Furman from being executed but would not have declared all death penalty laws unconstitutional.

The Legal Model. Proponents of the legal model believe that history, text, and precedent influence constitutional decision makers, even when these sources do not provide answers to all constitutional questions.[21] They point out that American constitutional history is littered with instances in which law constrained constitutional decision making. Before joining the Supreme Court, Felix Frankfurter was a prominent proponent of free speech rights. Frankfurter was also committed to judicial restraint. When on the Court, he often voted to sustain what he thought were unwise legislative decisions regulating speech. Justice Scalia is a conservative, but he voted with liberal justices on the Court in *Texas v. Johnson* (1989) to strike down laws prohibiting flag burning, and his dissenting opinion in *Hamdi v. Rumsfeld* (2004) declared unconstitutional the indefinite detention of an American citizen. Whether these votes were consistent with Scalia's policy preferences is doubtful. The better explanation of these liberal votes is that Scalia believed they were consistent with his commitment to deciding cases in a manner consistent with the original intentions of the framers.

Elected officials are also motivated by their beliefs about the best interpretation of the Constitution, even when those beliefs clash with cherished policy preferences. Abraham Lincoln believed that slavery was an atrocious evil, but he also thought that the Constitution did not allow Congress to interfere with slavery in the states. Lincoln similarly recognized the constitutional authority of the fugitive slave clause. Free-state citizens, he claimed throughout his career, were constitutionally obliged to return fugitive slaves to their masters.

Historical Institutionalism. The historical institutionalist school of political science insists that these three models take too narrow a perspective on constitutional decision making.[22] Constitutional authorities are

20. Lee Epstein and Jack Knight, *The Choices Justices Make* (Washington, DC: CQ Press, 1998), 14–15.

21. For an extended discussion, see Lief Carter and Thomas Burke, *Reason in Law*, 8th ed. (New York: Longman, 2009) and Howard Gillman, "What's Law Got to Do With It? Judicial Behavioralists Test the 'Legal Model' of Judicial Decision Making," *Law and Social Inquiry* 26 (2001): 465.

22. For an extended discussion, see Rogers M. Smith, "Historical Institutionalism and the Study of Law," in *The Oxford Handbook of Law and Politics*, ed. Keith E. Whittington, R. Daniel Kelemen, and Gregory A. Caldeira (New York: Oxford University Press, 2008), 46.

preferred policy. Worse, political actors may not make good-faith efforts to interpret the Constitution when they know the best interpretation is inconsistent with their policy preferences. Conservatives charge liberal pro-choice advocates with manufacturing a right to abortion out of thin jurisprudential air. Liberals charge conservatives with grossly distorting precedent in *Bush v. Gore* (2000) in order to hand George W. Bush the 2000 presidential election.

Lawyers and political scientists have developed four different models for thinking about the way judges and other constitutional authorities reach decisions. The attitudinal and strategic models claim that justices are far more concerned with policy than with law. The legal model claims that constitutional decision makers place greater emphasis on legal criteria than proponents of the attitudinal or strategic model recognize. Historical institutionalists seek to combine the best insights of the legal, attitudinal, and strategic models of constitutional decision making.

The Attitudinal Model. Many prominent political scientists point to evidence that constitutional arguments do not constrain constitutional decision makers. Jeffrey Segal and Harold Spaeth, the two leading proponents of the attitudinal model of judicial decision making, insist that Supreme Court decisions are based almost entirely on policy preferences. "Justices," they write, "make decisions by considering the facts of the case in light of their ideological attitudes and values."[19] Segal, Spaeth, and other attitudinalists note that Supreme Court justices are particularly well positioned to act on their ideology and values. Unlike legislators, they cannot easily be held accountable for their decisions by voters or other political actors. Unlike lower court judges, their decisions are not reviewed by other courts and cannot easily be overturned. The cases that reach the Supreme Court are precisely those in which the law is unclear and political values might matter. As a result, justices are likely to decide cases in a manner consistent with their political values.

Proponents of the attitudinal model point out that justices routinely form conservative and liberal voting blocs. These blocs hold together across a range of issues and legal contexts. The same justices who consistently cast liberal votes in free speech cases also cast liberal votes in cases concerning federalism and the meaning of the commerce clause. If they know that the Roberts Court voted 5–4 on some case, that Justice Ruth Bader Ginsburg was in the majority and Justice Clarence Thomas was in the minority, court watchers (and students taking constitutional law classes) can normally predict with a high degree of accuracy how the other seven justices voted.

Figure 1-1 illustrates how some political scientists assess and represent the political ideologies of the justices, in this case by using voting behavior in 1974 to align the justices from most liberal on the left to most conservative on the right. With this tool we can see who the swing voters on the Court were and which justices tended to vote together. We can also see the potential impact on the Court's behavior when a justice at one location on the spectrum is replaced by a justice who occupies a very different spot. For example, in 1975 Justice Douglas was replaced by John Paul Stevens, who voted just to the left of Stewart. Trading a strong liberal for a centrist meant that the Court would hand down more conservative decisions after 1975.

The Strategic Model. The strategic model suggests that justices seek to achieve their policy preferences by adjusting their behavior to take into account the behavior of other actors. Constitutional decision makers vote and write strategically, rather than sincerely. Persons engage in sincere voting when they vote solely on the basis of their personal preferences. An opponent of the death penalty votes sincerely when voting to declare all death sentences unconstitutional. Persons engage in sophisticated voting or vote strategically when they vote in ways they believe will achieve the most feasible policy. An opponent of the death penalty might strategically sign an opinion holding that capital punishment may be constitutionally imposed, but only when the condemned person was represented at trial by a criminal defense specialist, if this were the practical alternative the justice believed would result in the fewest executions.

The strategic model recognizes that justices need the cooperation of colleagues on the bench, lower court judges, legislators, executive branch officials, and ultimately the citizenry to achieve policy and legal goals. Governing officials implement judicial decisions, appoint like-minded justices to the bench, and preserve the constitutional and statutory foundations

19. Jeffrey A. Segal and Harold J. Spaeth, *The Supreme Court and the Attitudinal Model Revisited* (New York: Cambridge University Press, 2002), 110.

neither automatons who leave all personal considerations out of their decisions nor single-minded policy entrepreneurs. Rather, historical institutionalists hold that judges and others try to make the best decision from a value or policy perspective that is permitted by legal texts, history, and precedent.

Historical institutionalists are interested in why people with particular policy preferences and constitutional visions have constitutional authority at a particular time. Rather than ask what particular Supreme Court justices thought about pornography or originalism, they ask why obscenity issues arose during the time period when those particular justices were on the Court. This approach explains constitutional decisions as consequences of their political, historical, ideological, and institutional contexts. The liberalism of the Warren Court, for instance, was deeply rooted in the liberalism of the New Deal and Great Society coalition that dominated American politics from 1932 to 1968. Liberals staffed the Supreme Court because liberals controlled the branches of the national government that appointed and confirmed Supreme Court justices. Constitutional decisions in the nineteenth century were as rooted in political and social contexts. When sustaining laws mandating racial segregation in *Plessy v. Ferguson* (1896) Justice Henry Billings Brown wrote, "Legislation is powerless to eradicate racial instincts, or to abolish distinctions based upon physical differences." His decision was rooted in the common assumption of the time that "stateways cannot change folkways."

Both historical and institutional factors influence constitutional practice. History creates some constitutional options while foreclosing others. Consider the reason why states at present may not violate free speech rights. An initial reading of the Constitution might suggest that the provision in the Fourteenth Amendment prohibiting states from abridging the "privileges and immunities" of American citizens provides the best grounds for declaring unconstitutional state restrictions on free speech. A series of precedents dating from the *Slaughter-House Cases* (1873) foreclosed that constitutional basis for protecting political dissent. During the early twentieth century a different line of precedents interpreted the due process clause of the Fourteenth Amendment as protecting fundamental rights. For this reason, free speech advocates at present speak of "due process" rather than "privileges and immunities" when challenging the constitutionality of state measures that restrict expression. Institutional positions similarly influence constitutional perspectives. Justices are more familiar with the criminal process than are other governing officials. Perhaps for this reason, judges have historically cared more about the rights of criminal suspects than have elected officials. Judges are also, unsurprisingly, more committed to the constitutional powers of the federal courts than are legislators or members of the executive branch.

VI. Constitutional Authority

Controversy rages over which governing institutions are authorized to settle constitutional disputes about whether constitutional rights and liberties provisions have been correctly interpreted. In principle, any of the three branches of government could act as the ultimate interpreter of the Constitution. Prominent Americans before the Civil War insisted that individual states had the power to determine whether national legislation was constitutional. After the Civil War, most persons abandoned claims that states, the national executive, or the national legislature had the power to settle constitutional disputes. Judicial review, the judicial power to declare laws unconstitutional, is now entrenched. How that power can be justified and how courts should exercise that power remains unsettled.

Judicial Supremacy. Most Americans support judicial supremacy, the view that the Supreme Court is the institution authorized to resolve disputes over the Constitution. With few exceptions, Supreme Court justices have aggressively asserted that their institution has the final authority to determine what the Constitution means. Judicial supremacy includes the judicial powers to ignore unconstitutional acts when resolving specific cases and to establish principles that bind all other actors. When state officials in Arkansas questioned the correctness of *Brown v. Board of Education* (1954), Chief Justice Earl Warren treated them to a stern civics lecture. "The federal judiciary is supreme in the exposition of the law of the Constitution," he stated in *Cooper v. Aaron* (1958), "and that principle has . . . been respected by this Court and the Country as a permanent and indispensable feature of our constitutional system."

Proponents claim that judicial supremacy is a necessary ingredient of constitutionalism. If the Constitution is fundamental law, they believe, then the primary responsibility for interpreting the Constitution should be vested in the institution responsible for interpreting the law, the judiciary. Justice Kennedy recently asserted, "If Congress could define its own powers by altering the Fourteenth Amendment's meaning, no longer would the Constitution be 'superior paramount law, unchangeable by ordinary means.'"[23]

Departmentalism. Departmentalists believe that all federal institutions have an equal right to interpret the Constitution. Departmentalists favor judicial review, the judicial power to make constitutional decisions that bind the particular parties before the court. Proponents of departmentalism, however, reject the position that elected officials must always adhere to the principles that justices announce in those decisions. They maintain that judicial supremacy subverts constitutionalism by inviting politicians to ignore their constitutional responsibilities and allowing unchecked judges to warp constitutional principles through abuse and misinterpretation.

Throughout American history, prominent political leaders have asserted an equal right to constitutional authority. James Madison explained, "As the legislative, executive, and judicial departments are coordinate, and each equally bound to support the Constitution, it follows that each must, in the exercise of its functions, be guided by the text of the Constitution according to its own interpretation of it."[24] President Lincoln vigorously denied that his administration had a constitutional obligation to respect *Dred Scott v. Sandford* (1857), which ruled that the federal government could not ban slavery in the territories. "The candid citizen must confess that if the policy of the government . . . is to be irrevocably fixed by decisions of the Supreme Court," he contended in his first inaugural address, "the people will have ceased to be their own rulers." Lincoln thought that his administration was bound by the legal decision in the court case between Dred Scott and John Sanford.[25] Lincoln admitted that his government could not forcibly free Dred Scott if the courts held that he was legally enslaved. But the government did not have to accept the "political rule" that the Supreme Court had laid down in the case. When in power, Republicans did not hesitate to ban slavery in the federal territories and the District of Columbia.

The Politics of Constitutional Authority. For more than two hundred years American constitutionalism has witnessed ongoing contests over constitutional authority. Sometimes these struggles pit judges against elected officials. More often, elected officials empower courts to declare constitutional meanings. They staff courts with justices willing to declare constitutional limits on government power, they pass laws facilitating constitutional challenges to federal and state laws, and they pass vague legislation that may force courts to make policy in the guise of statutory or constitutional interpretation. Presidents do not nominate individuals to the Supreme Court who are pledged to always uphold laws against constitutional challenge. Elected officials have various reasons for supporting judicial power. National government officials may want to keep local political majorities in line. Political moderates may want to avoid difficult decisions that divide their political supporters. Party leaders with a tenuous hold on elected office may want the insurance that courts will protect some of their interests when they are out of power.

Struggles for constitutional authority do not end when the judiciary speaks. Justices do not enforce their decrees. Elected officials often do not comply with constitutional orders in cases they believe to have been wrongly decided. "Where there is local hostility to change," political scientist Gerald Rosenberg's study of judicial power concludes, "court orders will be ignored." In his view, "community pressure, violence or threats of violence, and lack of market response all serve to curtail actions to implement court decisions."[26] Many famous judicial decisions declaring laws unconstitutional had almost no immediate consequences. Ten years after *Brown v. Board of Education* was decided, less than 2 percent of African-American children in the Deep South were attending integrated schools.[27] Judicial decisions prohibiting state-organized prayer in public schools had little immediate effect on the

23. *City of Boerne v. Flores*, 521 U.S. 507, 529 (1997).

24. James Madison, "To Mr. ___, 1834," in *Letters and Other Writings of James Madison*, vol. 4 (Philadelphia: J. B. Lippincott, 1867), 349.

25. Note that the Supreme Court reporter misspelled John Sanford's name when the decision was handed down, which is why his proper name is different than the name used in the case.

26. Gerald N. Rosenberg, *The Hollow Hope: Can Courts Bring About Social Change?*, 2nd ed. (Chicago: University of Chicago Press, 2008), 337.

27. Rosenberg, *Hollow Hope*, 50.

incidence of that religious practice in schools across the United States.[28]

Judicial decisions shape but do not end political struggles over constitutional meaning. Political movements hardly ever fold their tents after sustaining judicial defeats. The Republican Party after *Dred Scott* remained committed to prohibiting slavery in the territories. Contemporary pro-life forces remain committed to reversing Supreme Court decisions prohibiting bans on abortion. Contemporary pro-choice forces remain committed to reversing Supreme Court decisions sustaining regulations on abortion. Constitutional conflicts are settled politically, not legally. Constitutional politics come to an end only when the political forces backing the losing side are slaughtered (see the Civil War), concede defeat, or lose political interest in the issue.

While conflict is a normal feature of American constitutionalism, it is important not to overlook the tendencies toward convergence or consensus on many constitutional questions. Many political scientists argue that judicial decisions are (almost) as consistent with majoritarian sentiments as decisions made by other governing officials. A half century ago Robert Dahl observed that "it would appear . . . somewhat unrealistic to suppose that a Court whose members are recruited in the fashion of Supreme Court Justices would long hold to norms of Right or Justice substantially at odds with the rest of the political elite."[29] As Justice Benjamin Cardozo observed, the "great tides and currents which engulf the rest of men do not turn aside in their course and pass the judges by."[30] Figure 1-2 maps the overall liberal tendency of public opinion and the liberalism of Supreme Court decisions in the latter half of the twentieth century.[31] The Court followed the public's more conservative mood in the 1970s, although judicial decisions did not turn as sharply in a more liberal direction as public opinion did in the late 1980s and early 1990s. One scholar has argued that this tendency to follow "majoritarian impulses" pervades almost the entire history of judicial decision making on civil rights and liberties.[32]

28. Kenneth M. Dolbeare and Phillip E. Hammond, *The School Prayer Decisions* (Chicago: University of Chicago Press, 1971).

29. Robert A. Dahl, "Decision making in a Democracy: The Supreme Court as a National Policy Maker," *Journal of Public Law* 6 (1957):291.

30. Benjamin N. Cardozo, *The Nature of the Judicial Process* (New Haven: Yale University Press, 1921), 168.

31. See also Kevin T. McGuire and James A. Stimson, "The Least Dangerous Branch Revisited: New Evidence on Supreme Court Responsiveness to Public Preferences," *Journal of Politics* 66 (2004):1018.

VII. Scope

Constitutional rights and liberties restrict the power of different people and may not be in force in all places. Three significant limits have been placed on the scope of different constitutional provisions.

1. With the exception of the Thirteenth Amendment, constitutional rights provisions only restrict the actions of government officials.
2. Some constitutional provisions—most notably, Article I, Section 9 and the Bill of Rights—limit only federal power. Other constitutional provisions—most notably, Article I, Section 10 and the Fourteenth Amendment—limit only state power.
3. Whether and to what extent federal officials must respect the liberties set out in the Bill of Rights when they are governing American territories and acting in foreign countries is controversial.

Contrary to popular understanding, the First Amendment does not give Americans the right to object to all interferences with their religious freedom. Imagine that Flintstone prevents Rubble from attending midnight mass. Whether a constitutional violation has taken place depends on whether Flintstone is a governing official; where his offending action took place; and, if Flintstone is a federal official acting on foreign soil, whether Rubble is an American citizen.

State Action. Virtually all constitutional protections for individual, political, equality, and procedural rights limit only government officials. Private parties need not honor constitutional rights unless they are required to do so by federal or state statute. Congress may not abridge the freedom of speech. Your grandmother may. A state university may not condition admissions on political affiliation or religious belief. Temple Emanuel or Holy Trinity may. With the exception of the Thirteenth Amendment, which forbids both private persons and government officials from enslaving

32. Michael J. Klarman, "Rethinking the Civil Rights and Civil Liberties Revolutions," *Virginia Law Review* 82 (1996):1.

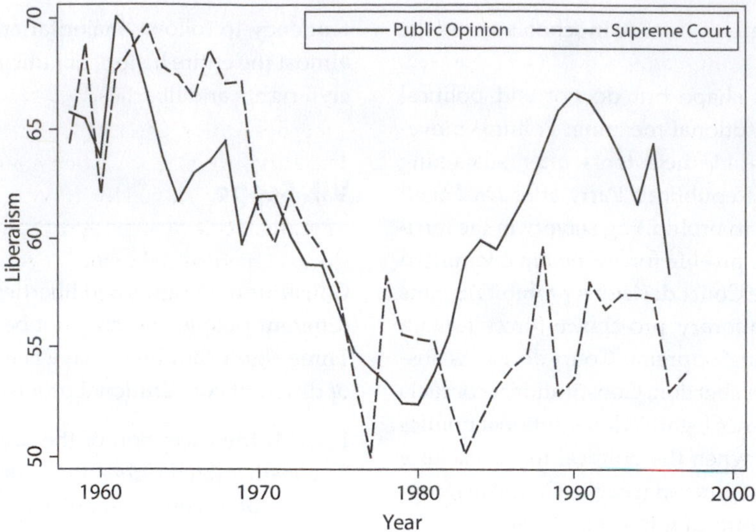

Figure 1-2 The Supreme Court and Public Opinion, 1957–97

Note: The two series are a public mood score and a percentage of Supreme Court decisions that ruled in a liberal direction in cases reversing lower courts across three issue domains. Both series are scaled to public mood for presentation.

Source: Kevin T. McGuire, "The Least Dangerous Branch Revisited" [replication data], http://www.unc.edu/~kmcguire/data.opinion.zip.

others, ordinary citizens have no *constitutional* obligation to respect fundamental rights and liberties. Constitutional rights are largely protections against state officials. Unless persons can demonstrate what is called "state action," they have no constitutional claim. Your classmates do not violate the equal protection clause when they choose not to associate with persons of a different race, religious belief system, or political affiliation. Your parents are not constitutionally required to permit you to vote on when your curfew should be—they may have different curfews for you and your siblings, and they may send you to your room without a hearing when they believe you have violated that curfew. However, federal law may require private persons to respect various rights. The Civil Rights Act of 1964 forbids employers from discriminating on the ground of race or gender. Still, in virtually all cases, private persons in the United States are obligated to respect fundamental rights only if a state or federal statute imposes that obligation.

The distinction between state actions subject to constitutional norms and private actions that are not regulated by the Constitution is often not as obvious as in the above examples. Consider whether a neighborhood watch group that is trained by government officials and has regular contact with the police violates the Fourth Amendment when members search a private house without a warrant. When a professor with a grant from the federal government discriminates on the basis of race when hiring a research assistant, is that state action or merely private bias? These and related problems have been the subject of ongoing disputes for more than 150 years.

Federalism. Most constitutional rights limit only particular government actors. Article I, Section 10 declares, "No state shall . . . pass any . . . Law impairing the Obligation of Contracts." The Constitution does not lay any analogous restriction on federal power. The Supreme Court in *Barron v. Baltimore* (1833) ruled that the first ten amendments to the Constitution limited only the powers of the national government. If, before the Civil War, the constitution of Pennsylvania did not have an establishment clause, then the Pennsylvania legislature was free to declare Congregationalism, Unitarianism, or Islam to be the state religion. This difference between constitutional restrictions on the federal government and constitutional restrictions on state governments was extremely important for most of American history. During the twentieth century, however, the Supreme Court slowly began ruling that the due process clause of the Fourteenth Amendment obligated states to respect most, but not all, of the liberties in the Bill of Rights. Differences remain, but with respect to such fundamental rights as free speech, freedom of religion, and the right to an attorney, the federal and state obligations are now the same. Nevertheless, what clause a government actor violates depends on who employs that official. If your home is illegally searched by the local police, that search violates the Fourteenth Amendment. If your home is illegally searched by the Federal Bureau of Investigation, that search violates the Fourth Amendment.

Extraterritoriality. No strong consensus exists on whether the Bill of Rights restricts federal officials acting in American territories or foreign countries. In a series of decisions at the turn of the twentieth century that have become known as the *Insular Cases* (1900–04), a narrow judicial majority ruled that Congress must respect the liberties set out in the Bill of Rights when governing territories that are being prepared for statehood, but that the national legislature need not respect those liberties when governing territories held for other reasons. In practice, this meant that persons living in the Territory of Oklahoma had greater constitutional rights than persons living in Puerto Rico or the Philippines, which were obtained from Spain after the Spanish-American War (1898). Whether federal officials acting in foreign countries must respect constitutional rights and liberties presently depends on whether an American citizen is claiming a rights violation, where the claimed rights violation took place, and the practicality of recognizing the right. Judicial majorities balancing these factors have extended habeas corpus rights to suspected terrorists detained in Guantanamo Bay,[33] ruled that American civilians living on military bases have rights to a jury trial,[34] but determined that German nationals in custody of the Army after World War II might be tried by a military commission.[35]

VIII. Constitutional History

Contemporary American constitutional politics, constitutional culture, and constitutional education are preoccupied with constitutional rights and liberties. Most citizens are familiar with various rights-oriented interest groups such as the American Civil Liberties Union (ACLU), the National Association for the Advancement of Colored People (NAACP), the National Organization of Women (NOW), and the National Rifle Association (NRA). Far fewer interest groups are devoted to the powers and structure of government. *Law and Order* and other primetime favorites regularly feature controversies over the rights of criminal suspects or persons in same-sex relationships. We do not know of a major movie or episode of a popular television show that highlights disputes over the commerce clause, the legislative veto, or the Tenth Amendment. Constitutional law classes reflect the popular hold of civil liberties on the American constitutional mind. The most widely used text in law schools for the past quarter century devotes at least three times as many pages to liberties issues than to structure of government issues.[36] Two-volume works on constitutional law often sneak property rights under the heading of government powers in order to produce texts of approximately equal length.

This common understanding that students of American constitutionalism should devote themselves primarily to examining particular rights and liberties is a phenomenon of the last half-century. Constitutional politics, culture, and education before the New Deal were more concerned with delineating the powers of the national government. In the most liberal reading possible, only 10 percent of Joseph Story's *Commentaries on the Constitution of the United States* (1833) is devoted to interpreting the explicit rights protecting provisions of the Constitution. Thomas Cooley's *General Principles of Constitutional Law* (1880), a popular text of the late nineteenth century, devotes about 40 percent of the work to constitutional rights and liberties. Cooley discusses constitutional protections for free speech and equality, but they are hardly given the place of pride in his textbook. That Story, Cooley, and others did not devote as many pages as contemporary textbook writers to constitutional rights and liberties does not mean they were less concerned with protecting fundamental freedoms. Rather, how Americans have conceptualized the "blessings of liberty" has changed dramatically over time.

33. *Boumediene v. Bush*, 553 U.S. 723 (2008).

34. *Reid v. Covert*, 354 U.S. 1 (1957).

35. *Johnson v. Eisentrager*, 339 U.S. 763 (1950).

36. Kathleen M. Sullivan and Gerald Gunther, *Constitutional Law*, 17th ed. (New York: Foundation Press, 2010).

Prominent framers and American constitutional thinkers before the New Deal insisted that limited government guaranteed the blessings of liberty. During the debates over ratification, Federalists declared that specific constitutional protections for such rights as free speech were unnecessary, because the national government was granted no power to regulate political dissent. "Everything which is not given is reserved,"[37] James Wilson declared. Liberty was conceptualized as an absence of government power. When persons claimed that a particular action violated the freedom of speech or the liberty of contract, constitutional decision makers first examined the justification for the government action. If the decision maker concluded that government was pursuing the public good, then the restriction on the right was sustained. Some constitutional decision makers during the nineteenth century demanded more evidence than others that rights restricting actions fostered the public good. Many state and federal judges carefully scrutinized legislation to make sure that elected officials were pursuing the public interest and not using the language of the common good as a pretext for granting boons to particular individuals or a particular class of citizens. Still, what we would study today under the heading of "civil liberties," Americans before the New Deal often studied under the heading of "government powers."

Most contemporary Americans, conservative and liberal, insist that people enjoy the blessings of liberty only when government does not restrict certain behaviors, unless the benefit to the public very clearly outweighs the harm to the individual rights holder. The Supreme Court in *United States v. Virginia* (1996) insisted that gender discriminations must have a "very persuasive justification." Free speech, Justice Holmes famously declared in *Schenck v. United States* (1919), may be abridged only when there is a "clear and present danger." With rare exception, individuals do not have an absolute right to be free from certain government regulations. Government may discriminate on the basis of race and restrict other freedoms when a sufficiently compelling reason justifies doing so. Nevertheless, the mere demonstration that government is pursuing a legitimate constitutional end is no longer sufficient to justify restraints on what have become known as preferred freedoms. "Individual rights are political trumps," Ronald Dworkin declares.[38] Much modern civil liberties debate is over what freedoms should enjoy this high standard of protection and how strong the government justification for restriction must be.

The differences between contemporary claims about a woman's right to abortion and late-nineteenth-century claims about the liberty of contract illustrate this evolution in American thinking about rights and liberties. Abortion is presently a preferred freedom. Government must have a compelling or very important justification for banning abortion. Regulations must not unduly burden the pregnant woman. This right is not absolute. The government interest in protecting future human life justifies some regulation. Nevertheless, the existence of a legitimate government interest does not justify any regulation. In particular, the legitimate government interest in potential life is not sufficiently compelling to justify a ban on abortion in the first two trimesters of the pregnancy. The debate over economic freedoms before the New Deal had a different structure. Proponents of the freedom of contract insisted that government did not have any legitimate reason for interfering with bargains between particular employees and employers or for favoring one particular class (say, bakers) over another (people who employed bakers). Proponents of minimum wages and maximum hour laws responded that these regulations served such legitimate government purposes as public health. The entire debate was over whether these progressive regulations were legitimate exercises of government power or pretexts for arbitrarily benefiting some people at the expense of others. Neither the majority nor the dissenting opinions in *Lochner v. New York* (1905) or any other important pre–New Deal cases on the liberty of contract asserted that the proper way to resolve the constitutional controversy over minimum wage and maximum hour laws was to balance the government interest in regulation with the individual interest in being free from official restraint.[39]

---

37. Merrill Jensen, ed., *The Documentary History of the Ratification of the Constitution* (Stevens Point, WI: State Historical Society of Wisconsin, 1976), 2:167–68.

38. Ronald M. Dworkin, *Taking Rights Seriously* (Cambridge, MA: Harvard University Press, 1978), xi.

39. See Howard Gillman, *The Constitution Besieged: The Rise and Demise of Lochner Era Police Powers Jurisprudence* (Durham: Duke University Press, 1993).

IX. Constitutional Politics

Politics determine what constitutional rights and liberties government officials respect. Contests between political parties often determine who gets what liberties from government. The debate over the Alien and Sedition Acts in 1798 was shaped more by conflicts between Federalists and Jeffersonians than by proponents and opponents of broad free speech rights. The fate of abortion rights depends on electoral struggles between pro-choice Democrats and pro-life Republicans. Elected officials often make crucial rights decisions. Free-state legislatures before the Civil War consistently refused to pass laws restricting anti-slavery speech, even though such restrictions were probably consistent with contemporaneous judge-made constitutional law. The Civil Rights Act of 1964 was as responsible as *Brown v. Board of Education* for desegregating American education. Constitutional battles over rights on the local level are often as fierce as constitutional battles in national politics. Nineteenth-century debates over the constitutional status of Catholic schools took place almost entirely within particular states and cities. Before the ratification of the Eighteenth Amendment (1919), whether one had a constitutional right to drink depended almost entirely on state constitutions, state law, and state judicial decisions.

The constitutional politics of rights and liberties has three distinctive features:

1. The somewhat lesser role of political parties
2. The heightened role of political movements and interest groups
3. The heightened role of courts

These features are related. Interest groups and courts play a greater role in the constitutional politics of rights and liberties than in the constitutional politics of powers and structures partly because political parties play a somewhat lesser role.

Political Parties. Major party platforms throughout American history have usually placed greater emphasis on foreign and economic policy issues than on constitutional questions about individual rights. Major political parties typically stress foreign and economic policy for two reasons. First, more voters in national elections cast their ballots on the basis of economic and foreign policy than cast them on the basis of individual rights. One poll taken just days before the 2008 national election found that more than 90 percent of all potential voters thought that the economy, the war in Iraq, health care, and terrorism were the most important issues facing the country.[40] Few mentioned same-sex marriage or the constitutional rights of criminal suspects. For these reasons, neither the Democrats nor the Republicans had reason to focus their energies on rights and liberties issues of less salience to crucial voters. Second, rights issues often crosscut the dominant lines of partisan difference. Attitudes about slavery before the Civil War reflected the difference between the North and the South, not Whigs and Jacksonians. The Roosevelt coalition during the New Deal included both the most fervent proponents and the most fervent opponents of racial equality. Badly divided on rights issues, most major political parties prefer to focus public attention on the economic and government powers issues that unite their supporters.

Political Movements and Interest Groups. Political movements and interest groups often replace parties as the most important advocates of particular rights and liberties. The National Woman Suffrage Association (NWSA) and the American Woman Suffrage Association (AWSA) were the groups most responsible for putting the rights of women on the national agenda during the late nineteenth century. Much contemporary civil rights litigation is sponsored by such groups as the ACLU, the NAACP, and the NRA. At times, interest groups form alliances with political parties. Most pro-choice groups at present reliably support Democrats. Most pro-life groups are reliable Republican supporters. Other interest groups, such as the American Bar Association, prefer to maintain a nonpartisan reputation.

The greater influence of interest groups on the constitutional politics of rights and liberties helps explain the greater influence of courts. Parties focus their attention on controlling the elected branches of government, confident that control of the judiciary will follow from control of Congress and the White House. Most major interest groups lobby elected officials extensively, but they also take advantage of the opportunities that partisan politics create for successful litigation. As already noted, rights issues often divide dominant political coalitions. When partisan coalitions are internally

40. CNN Politics, "Election Center 2008: Issue Tracker," http://www.cnn.com/ELECTION/2008/issues/.

divided over questions as diverse as slavery, abortion, and Prohibition, elected officials often seek to foist these issues on the courts as a way of avoiding responsibility for contested issues. These partisan incentives create opportunities for both interest group litigation campaigns and judicial policy making. Politicians who may be unwilling to repeal laws banning birth control may not hinder and may even facilitate interest groups seeking a judicial decision announcing a constitutional right to use contraception. Justices are freer to hand down controversial decisions on the constitutional status of slavery in American territories, the freedom of contract, or segregated schools when divided political coalitions do not have the ability to challenge courts. Interest groups often find litigation cheaper than national campaigns. Opponents of affirmative action or school prayer who litigate must convince five of the nine justices on the Supreme Court. In contrast, opponents of affirmative action or school prayer who lobby must convince the president and majorities in both houses of Congress.

Two important problems stem from the increased role of courts in determining constitutional rights and liberties. The first problem is democratic. From *Dred Scott v. Sandford* (1857) to contemporary cases on same-sex marriage, numerous important civil liberties decisions have been made by justices who enjoy life tenure. Even when evidence shows that the justices acted with the blessing of the president or important members of Congress, many commentators question whether such important rulings should be made by unelected officials. Whether a woman should have a right to an abortion, in this view, should be determined by our elected officials, even if many elected officials prefer that courts take responsibility for resolving that matter. The second is a problem of implementation. Alexander Hamilton pointed out in *Federalist* 78 that "the judiciary . . . has no influence over either the sword or the purse . . . and must ultimately depend upon the aid of the executive arm even for the efficacy of its judgments." Throughout history, elected officials have ignored court rulings they have thought constitutionally wrong. Free states often refused to implement court rulings on fugitive slaves. Fifty years after the Supreme Court in *Engel v. Vitale* (1962) declared unconstitutional voluntary prayer in public schools, one still hears homages to God over the loudspeaker before big football games in rural America.

We have tried to capture these constitutional politics. The introduction to each chapter in this book highlights where the parties stood on the major civil liberties issues of the day, which parties controlled what governing institutions, struggles to staff the federal judiciary with persons committed to particular rights and liberties, and the most important interest groups of a particular time period. When we consider particular issues or cases, we note whether the U.S. government took a particular position, the interest groups involved in the constitutional struggle, and the consequences of particular decisions. This approach enables us to capture some crucial features of American constitutional politics that lie behind the words of judicial decisions. We cannot understand why the Supreme Court during the 1960s suddenly began adjudicating many cases involving the constitutional rights of the poor until we realize that the Legal Services Organization and other poverty rights groups for the first time in American history had the funding necessary to litigate claims of constitutional wrong on behalf of the poor.[41] We may not be able to understand why Justice O'Connor became more accepting of affirmative action in *Grutter v. Bollinger* (2003) unless we realize that the Chamber of Commerce and the military groups normally associated with conservative positions, had become more accepting of affirmative action.

What constitutional provisions mean and how constitutions operate is inevitably forged within an historical and political context. We cannot understand *Brown v. Board of Education* unless we understand how the Soviet Union was exploiting Jim Crow for propaganda purposes in third-world countries to undermine the United States, as well as the increased importance of the African-American vote in northern states. Richard Nixon's southern strategy and the popularization of the birth control pill explain why *Roe v. Wade* was decided in 1973, not 1873, and why the Republican Party soon adopted a pro-life platform. Students who understand these historical and political forces, as well as the dominant political and legal ideas of particular eras, will gain a better perspective on both the American constitutional past and how history, politics, and ideas structure the contemporary American constitutional regime. More broadly, we hope readers of the pages that follow will recognize that we cannot understand the constitutional law of rights and liberties unless we

41. See Susan E. Lawrence, *The Poor in Court: The Legal Services Program and Supreme Court Decision Making* (Princeton, NJ: Princeton University Press, 1990).

understand the constitutional politics and history of rights and liberties.

Suggested Readings

Abraham, Henry Julian. *Justices, Presidents, and Senators: A History of the U.S. Supreme Court Appointments from Washington to Bush II* (Lanham, MD: Rowman & Littlefield, 2008).

Ackerman, Bruce A. *We the People: Transformations* (Cambridge, MA: Harvard University Press, 1998).

Amar, Akhil Reed. *America's Constitution: A Biography* (New York: Random House, 2005).

Amar, Akhil Reed. *The Bill of Rights: Creation and Reconstruction* (New Haven, CT: Yale University Press, 1998).

Amar, Akhil Reed. *The Constitution and Criminal Procedure: First Principles* (New Haven, CT: Yale University Press, 1997).

Baer, Judith A., and Leslie Friedman Goldstein. *The Constitutional and Legal Rights of Women: Cases in Law and Social Change*, 3rd ed. (New York: Oxford University Press, 2006).

Balkin, Jack M. *Living Originalism* (Cambridge, MA: Harvard University Press, 2011).

Banner, Stuart. *The Death Penalty: An American History* (Cambridge, MA: Harvard University Press, 2002).

Barber, Sotorios A. *On What the Constitution Means* (Baltimore, MD: Johns Hopkins University Press, 1983).

Barnett, Randy. *Restoring the Lost Constitution: The Presumption of Liberty* (Princeton, NJ: Princeton University Press, 2004).

Bedau, Hugo Adam. *The Death Penalty in America*, 3rd ed. (New York: Oxford University Press, 1982).

Bickel, Alexander M. *The Least Dangerous Branch: The Supreme Court at the Bar of Politics* (Indianapolis: Bobbs-Merrill, 1962).

Bobbitt, Philip. *Constitutional Fate: Theory of the Constitution* (New York: Oxford University Press, 1982).

Bodenhamer, David J. *Fair Trial: Rights of the Accused in American History* (New York: Oxford University Press, 1992).

Brandwein, Pamela. *Reconstructing Reconstruction: The Supreme Court and the Production of Historical Truth* (Durham, NC: Duke University Press, 1999).

Clayton, Cornell W., and Howard Gillman, eds. *Supreme Court Decision Making: New Institutionist Approaches* (Chicago: University of Chicago Press, 1999).

Cornell, Saul. *A Well-Regulated Militia: the Founding Fathers and the Origins of Gun Control in America* (New York: Oxford University Press, 2006).

Curtis, Michael Kent. *Free Speech, "The People's Darling Privilege": Struggles for Freedom of Expression in American History* (Durham, NC: Duke University Press, 2000).

Dahl, Robert A. "Decision Making in a Democracy: The Supreme Court as a National Policymaker," *Journal of Public Law* 6 (1957):279–95.

Devins, Neal, and Louis Fisher. *The Democratic Constitution* (New York: Oxford University Press, 2004).

Dinan. John J. *The American State Constitutional Tradition* (Lawrence: University Press of Kansas, 2006).

Dworkin, Ronald. *Taking Rights Seriously* (Cambridge, MA: Harvard University Press, 1977).

Ely, James W., Jr. *The Guardian of Every Other Right: A Constitutional History of Property Rights*, 3rd ed. (New York: Oxford University Press, 2008).

Ely, John Hart. *Democracy and Distrust: A Theory of Judicial Review* (Cambridge, MA: Harvard University Press, 1980).

Engel, Stephen M. *American Politicians Confront the Court: Opposition Politics and Changing Responses to Judicial Power* (New York: Cambridge University Press, 2011).

Epp, Charles. *The Rights Revolution: Lawyers, Activists, and Supreme Courts in Comparative Perspectives* (Chicago: University of Chicago Press, 1998).

Epstein, Lee, and Jack Knight. *The Choices Justices Make.* Washington, DC: CQ Press, 1998).

Feldman, Stephen M. *Free Expression and Democracy in America: A History* (Chicago: University of Chicago Press, 2008).

Fisher, Louis. *Constitutional Dialogues: Interpretation as Political Process* (Princeton, NJ: Princeton University Press, 1988).

Fisher, Louis. *Religious Liberty in America: Political Safeguards* (Lawrence: University Press of Kansas, 2002).

Fleming, James E. *Securing Constitutional Democracy: The Case of Autonomy* (Chicago: University of Chicago Press, 2006).

Friedman, Barry. *The Will of the People: How Public Opinion Has Influenced the Supreme Court and Shaped the Meaning of the Constitution* (New York: Farrar, Straus and Giroux, 2009).

Gardner, James A. *Interpreting State Constitutions: A Jurisprudence of Function in a Federal System* (Chicago: University of Chicago Press, 2005).

Goldstein, Leslie Friedman. *In Defense of the Text: Democracy and Constitutional Theory* (Savage, MD: Rowman & Littlefield, 1991).

Graber, Mark A. "The Non-Majoritarian Problem: Legislative Deference to the Judiciary," *Studies in American Political Development* 7 (1993):35-73.

Griffin, Stephen. *American Constitutionalism: From Theory to Politics* (Princeton, NJ: Princeton University Press, 1996).

Helmholz, R. M., Charles M. Gray, John H. Langbein, and Eben Moglen. *The Privilege against Self-Incrimination: Its Origins and Development* (Chicago: University of Chicago Press, 1997).

Horowitz, Donald L. *The Courts and Social Policy* (Washington, DC: Brookings Institution Press, 1977).

Kahn, Ronald, and Ken I. Kersch, eds. *The Supreme Court and American Political Development* (Lawrence: University Press of Kansas, 2006).

Kairys, David, ed. *The Politics of Law: A Progressive Critique*, 3rd ed. (New York: Basic, 1998).

Keck, Thomas M. "Party, Policy or Duty: Why Does the Supreme Court Invalidate Federal Statues?" *American Political Science Review* 101 (2007):321–38.

Kersch, Ken I. *Constructing Civil Liberties: Discontinuities in the Development of American Constitutional Law* (New York: Cambridge University Press, 2004).

Kettner, James H. *The Development of American Citizenship, 1608–1870* (Chapel Hill: University of North Carolina Press, 1978).

Keyssar, Alexander. *The Right to Vote: The Contested History of Democracy in the United States* (New York: Basic, 2000).

Klarman, Michael J. *From Jim Crow to Civil Rights: The Supreme Court and the Struggle for Civil Rights* (New York: Oxford University Press, 2004).

Klinkner, Philip A., and Rogers M. Smith. *The Unsteady March: The Rise and Decline of Racial Equality in America* (Chicago: University of Chicago Press, 1999).

Kramer, Larry D. *The People Themselves: Popular Constitutionalism and Judicial Review* (New York: Oxford University Press, 2004).

Kyvig, David E. *Explicit and Authentic Acts: Amending the U.S. Constitution, 1776–1995* (Lawrence: University Press of Kansas, 1996).

Levinson, Sanford. *Constitutional Faith* (Princeton, NJ: Princeton University Press, 2011).

McCloskey, Robert G., and Sanford Levinson. *The American Supreme Court*, 5th ed. (Chicago: University of Chicago Press, 2010).

Moore, Wayne D. *Constitutional Rights and Powers of the People* (Princeton, NJ: Princeton University Press, 1996).

Nieman, Donald G. *Promises to Keep: African-Americans and the Constitutional Order, 1776 to the Present* (New York: Oxford University Press, 1991).

Neuman, Gerald L. *Strangers to the Constitution: Immigrants, Borders, and Fundamental Law* (Princeton, NJ: Princeton University Press, 1996).

Peretti, Terri Jennings. *In Defense of a Political Court* (Princeton, NJ: Princeton University Press, 2001).

Posner, Richard A. *Overcoming Law* (Cambridge, MA: Harvard University Press, 1995).

Powe, Lucas A., Jr. *American Broadcasting and the First Amendment* (Berkeley: University of California Press, 1987).

Powe, Lucas A., Jr. *The Supreme Court and the American Elite* (Cambridge, MA: Harvard University Press, 2009).

Rosenberg, Gerald N. *The Hollow Hope: Can Courts Bring about Social Change?*, 2nd ed. (Chicago: University of Chicago Press, 2008).

Scalia, Antonin. *A Matter of Interpretation: Federal Courts and the Law* (Princeton, NJ: Princeton University Press, 1997).

Segal, Jeffrey A., and Harold J. Spaeth. *The Supreme Court and the Attitudinal Model Revisited* (New York: Cambridge University Press, 2002).

Silverstein, Gordon. *Law's Allure: How Law Shapes, Constrains, Saves, and Kills Politics* (New York: Cambridge University Press, 2009).

Smith, Rogers M. *Civic Ideals: Conflicting Visions of Citizenship in U.S. History* (New Haven, CT: Yale University Press, 1997).

Smith, Rogers M. *Liberalism and American Constitutional Law* (Cambridge, MA: Harvard University Press, 1985).

Sunstein, Cass A. *One Case at a Time: Judicial Minimalism on the Supreme Court* (Cambridge, MA: Harvard University Press, 1999).

Tushnet, Mark. *Taking the Constitution Away from the Courts* (Princeton, NJ: Princeton University Press, 1999).

Tushnet, Mark. *Why the Constitution Matters* (New Haven, CT: Yale University Press, 2010).

VanBurkelo, Sandra F. *"Belonging to the World": Women's Rights and American Constitutional Culture* (New York: Oxford University Press, 2001).

Waldron, Jeremy. *Law and Disagreement* (New York: Oxford University Press, 1999).

Wert, Justin J. *Habeas Corpus in America: The Politics of Individual Rights* (Lawrence: University Press of Kansas, 2011).

Whittington, Keith E. *Constitutional Construction: Divided Powers and Constitutional Meaning* (Cambridge, MA: Harvard University Press, 1999).

Whittington, Keith E. *Constitutional Interpretation: Textual Meaning, Original Intent, and Judicial Review* (Lawrence: University Press of Kansas, 1999).

Whittington, Keith E. *Political Foundations of Judicial Supremacy: The President, the Supreme Court, and Constitutional Leadership in U.S. History* (Princeton, NJ: Princeton University Press, 2007).

Wunder, John R. *"Retained by the People": A History of American Indians and the Bill of Rights* (New York: Oxford University Press, 1994).

Yalof, David. *Pursuit of Justices: Presidential Politics and the Pursuit of Supreme Court Nominations* (Chicago: University of Chicago Press, 1999).

Zietlow, Rebecca E. *Enforcing Equality: Congress, the Constitution and the Protection of Individual Rights* (New York: New York University Press, 2006).

Part 2 **Development**

Chapter 2

Colonial Era: Before 1776

I. Introduction

The American revolutionaries marched backward into the American Revolution.[1] When justifying their complaints against England and the British Parliament, such colonial leaders as Patrick Henry and Samuel Adams demanded that Americans have ancient rights restored, not new rights granted. The pamphlets American revolutionaries wrote, the resolutions they made, and the speeches they gave vigorously maintained that they were being denied the hard-won, well-established liberties of native-born Englishmen. James Otis of Massachusetts in 1764 spoke of "our rights as men and freeborn British subjects."[2] Benjamin Franklin and John Adams insisted that "the Colonists do not deserve to be deprived of the native right of Britons, the right of being taxed only by representatives chosen by themselves."[3] When the colonies urged residents of Quebec to send representatives to the Continental Congress, they presented themselves as the defenders of the longstanding English Constitution. Their "Appeal to the Inhabitants of Quebec" declared that existing constitutional protections for rights were sufficient to "defy time, tyranny, treachery, internal, and foreign wars."[4]

These constant appeals to rights recognized "from time immemorial" masked claims that most Englishmen regarded as revolutionary. What Otis, Franklin, Adams, and other colonists described as well-established liberties were consequences of recent political struggles over fundamental freedoms. During the 170 years between the first settlement of the Jamestown Colony (1607) and the Declaration of Independence (1776), both Great Britain and the colonies experienced violent contests over what constituted the rights of Englishmen. These struggles left one English king (Charles I) without his head, undermined royal authority in the colonies, inspired Parliament to pass the English Bill of Rights, influenced judicial decisions declaring common law protections for fundamental rights, and provided political support for novel liberal and republican theories about the purpose of constitutional government. John Locke, the most prominent English liberal thinker of the period, insisted on a limited government whose primary purpose was to protect individual rights. James Harrington and other republican thinkers of the period maintained that government should foster both political participation and civic virtue. American colonists borrowed from both liberal and republican thinkers when claiming that the British government was becoming a corrupt tyranny.

Factions (Parties and Interest Groups). Constitutional politics during the Colonial Era was structured by competition among factions. Political alliances in England at the time the colonies were settled were based largely on relationships between powerful families and individuals. Colonial politics during most of the sixteenth and seventeenth centuries similarly consisted of struggles for power between families, rather than contests over political principles. Parties united by policy commitments first developed in England. By the seventeenth century clear differences had emerged between

1. Quentin Skinner, *Visions of Politics: Regarding Method* (New York: Cambridge University Press, 2002), 149–50.

2. James Otis, *The Rights of the British Colonies Asserted and Proved*, in *Tracts of the American Revolution*, ed. Merrill Jensen (Indianapolis: Bobbs-Merrill, 1978), 24.

3. Daniel Leonard and John Adams, *Massachusettensis and Novanglus*, in *Tracts of the American Revolution*, 307.

4. *Journals of the American Congress: From 1774 to 1788* (Washington, DC: Way and Gideon), 1:41.

the Whigs, who favored greater parliamentary power, and Tories, who favored preserving more royal power. Members of these parties began coordinating their political actions and distributing the rewards of political success to fellow partisans.

Two factional and partisan struggles in Great Britain had enduring consequences for Americans. The first was the English Civil War and the Glorious Revolution. During the 1640s Parliament rebelled against King Charles I. That rebellion ended with the execution of the king in 1649. Forty years later, after the reigning monarch King James II fled the realm, Parliament adopted the English Bill of Rights. That proclamation established parliamentary supremacy and asserted that Englishmen had certain fundamental rights that future kings had to respect. The second struggle was between the Court and Country movements. The dominant Court movement, which was based in the Whig Party and included most of England's mercantile community, sought to centralize power in Parliament in ways that better enabled Great Britain to become a modern state. Members of the Country movement, which included many Tories, dissident Whigs, and the rural nobility insisted that centralization corrupted politics and threatened traditional English liberties. Prominent notables who identified with the Country movement, such as John Wilkes, Peter Trenchard, and John Gordon, penned numerous essays on free speech and other rights.

The English Civil War and subsequent factional struggles in England shaped colonial understandings of fundamental rights and liberties. Americans were aware of the political upheavals taking place in England during the seventeenth century. They assumed that the liberties asserted in the 1689 English Bill of Rights belonged to them as English colonists. Prominent

Box 2-1 A Partial Cast of Characters of the Colonial Era

Roger Williams	▪ Puritan ▪ Separationist, who favored complete separation of church and state ▪ Fled England in 1630 ▪ Convicted of sedition for questioning legitimacy of colonial charter ▪ Exiled from Massachusetts Bay Colony in 1636 ▪ Founded Rhode Island Colony on separationist principles in 1643
John Witherspoon	▪ Presbyterian ▪ Advocate of a public morality rooted in natural law ▪ Early advocate of American independence ▪ President of the College of New Jersey (now Princeton University) ▪ Taught James Madison ▪ Signer of the Declaration of Independence ▪ Anti-Federalist opponent of constitutional ratification
William Penn	▪ Converted to Quakerism ▪ Became the most prominent writer defending the Quaker faith ▪ Arrested for violating laws against Quaker meetings and publishing without a license ▪ Founded Pennsylvania as a Quaker haven in 1681 ▪ Drafted the Frame of Government of Pennsylvania, which included guarantees for religious liberty
James Otis	▪ Patriot ▪ Lawyer who argued against the legality of general writs of assistance before Massachusetts colonial court ▪ Wrote prominent pamphlets on limits of parliamentary authority over colonies ▪ Early proponent of judicial review

colonial politicians adopted the Country movement's critique of the English government. Frequently citing Wilkes, Trenchard, and Gordon, Americans claimed that English politics had been corrupted by the shift toward centralization. This corruption explained the tendency of Parliament to violate the traditional rights of English subjects residing in the colonies. Americans also cheered when Wilkes and other members of the Country movement condemned political parties. The more English politics became a struggle between Whigs and Tories for control of the government, the more Americans became convinced that governing officials in Great Britain no longer had the republican independence necessary for good governance.

Courts. Colonists looked more to juries than judges to protect their fundamental rights. The colonists regarded royally appointed judges as instruments of royal power. Juries were the bulwark of individual freedom. The colonists celebrated such English decisions as *Bushell's Case* (1670), which held that a judge could not imprison juries for declaring a defendant not guilty. A New York jury in *Zenger's Case* (1735) ignored the charge given by a royally appointed judge and protected the right of a printer to publish criticisms of the royal governor.

Judicial review was at most a gleam in the eye of a few justices and political activists. Lord Edward Coke (1552–1634) asserted in *Dr. Bonham's Case* (1610), "The common law will control acts of parliament, and sometimes adjudge them to be utterly void."[5] Some colonists insisted that *Bonham's Case* established the precedential foundations for English courts to declare unconstitutional parliamentary edicts mandating the use of general warrants and other actions thought to violate what colonists believed were their constitutional rights as Englishmen. These pleas to the judiciary fell on deaf ears. No British or colonial court ever declared unconstitutional a law the colonists claimed violated their constitutional rights. William Blackstone expressed conventional English wisdom when he rejected judicial power to overturn legislation. His *Commentaries on the Laws of England* declared, "If the parliament will positively enact a thing to be done which is unreasonable, I know of no power in the ordinary forms of the constitution, that is vested with authority to control it."[6]

Constitutional Thought. American colonists were influenced by developments in English political thought during the seventeenth and eighteenth centuries. The English Civil War and Glorious Revolution inspired two novel perspectives on the purpose of constitutional government. Liberalism was the first. John Locke and other liberal thinkers claimed that society was based on a social contract between free persons in a state of nature. The purpose of the government created by this contract was to protect certain natural rights, most notably life, liberty, and property. Republicanism was the second. James Harrington and other seventeenth-century republican thinkers understood freedom as self-government. Constitutions guaranteed that all citizens had the opportunity to participate in the political processes that determined what liberties were protected.

Most fundamental controversies in the Colonial Era were over which institution had the power to pass legislation regulating behavior. The English Bill of Rights limited only royal power to abridge rights. English liberty was protected as long as Parliament determined whether the public good required increased taxation or restrictions on free speech rights. Many Americans insisted that the principles underlying the English Bill of Rights supported their position that the rights of Englishmen in the colonies could be restricted only by institutions in which the colonists were represented. This is the meaning of the slogan, "No Taxation without Representation." Other colonists advanced the more novel (for the time) position that no government official could violate certain natural rights. Such leading proponents of religious freedom as Roger Williams, the founder of Rhode Island Colony, insisted, "All Civil States with their Officers of justice" are "not Judges, Governours or *Defenders* of the Spiritual or Christian state and Worship."[7]

The dominant trends of colonial constitutional thinking during the eighteenth century increasingly diverged from the dominant trends of English constitutional thinking. William Blackstone (1723–80) and other influential English legal commentators

5. *Dr. Bonham's Case*, (1610), 77 Eng. Rep. 646 (K.B.) 652; 8 Co. Rep. 107 a, 118 a.

6. William Blackstone, *Blackstone's Commentaries on the Laws of England*, ed. St. George Tucker (Philadelphia: William Young Birch and Abraham Small, 1803), 1:90–91.

7. Roger Williams, *The Bloudy Tenent* (London: n.p., 1644).

of the eighteenth century insisted on parliamentary supremacy. Committed to a modern understanding of law as man-made, they believed that the national legislature was legally and constitutionally free to decide whether to maintain, modify, or abolish the traditional rights of English citizens. Rights were limits on the monarch, not the legislature. If rights originated in a parliamentary statute, then Parliament should be free to repeal that statute. In contrast, James Otis, John Adams, and most American legal commentators insisted that rights were rooted in natural law. Committed to the traditional understanding of rights as antecedent to government, the persons responsible for the American Revolution insisted that government existed to protect preexisting liberties and was not free to alter those rights and liberties as officials saw fit.

The differences between English and American conceptions of fundamental rights explain the conflicts over the parliamentary edicts that inspired the American Revolution. For most English officials, Parliament was merely exercising legitimate sovereign powers when authorizing customs officials to use writs of assistance or increasing tax burdens on the colonists. The colonists could not claim that their rights as Englishmen had been violated by any parliamentary decree because Parliament was the institution that determined what constituted the rights of Englishmen at any particular time. Most colonists insisted that these parliamentary and royal edicts violated preexisting property rights and the right to trial by jury. No English authority, they said, had the right to deprive an Englishman of his property without due process. A revolution was therefore necessary to restore their traditional natural rights.

The constitutional controversies that rocked the colonies during the mid-eighteenth century were not only between colonists and Parliament, but also among colonists themselves. Many Americans endorsed the English view that "liberty" meant only liberty consistent with the laws enacted by Parliament. While some Americans, most notably Roger Williams, maintained that government should not interfere with religious matters, other Americans remained committed to traditional state religious establishments. Once Americans secured their independence, these disputes over rights would have to be resolved.

Legacies. The political and legal controversies discussed in this chapter have shaped the development of American constitutionalism for more than two hundred years. The rights and liberties enumerated in the constitutions Americans ratified after the Revolution were those rights and liberties that had been contested in England and the colonies immediately prior to the Revolution. Americans explicitly declared that persons had constitutional rights to religious freedom because they had experienced religious intolerance before and after immigrating to the Americas. The U.S. Constitution did not provide explicit protection for what Theodore Sedgewick, a member of the First Congress, declared was the "right to wear his hat if he pleased; that he might get up when he pleased, and go to bed when he thought proper,"[8] because no governing authority in the Colonial Era sought to restrict that freedom. Had the colonial experience been different during the 1760s, Americans would have enumerated different rights in the 1780s.

When Americans consider the meaning of such constitutional provisions as the freedom of speech or the due process clause of the Fifth and Fourteenth Amendments, they often turn to earlier decisions made in England or the colonies. After the First Amendment was ratified, Americans cited the *Zenger* trial in defense of the proposition that persons had a right to speak the truth about public officials. Contemporary judicial opinions discussing the meaning of the Fourth Amendment begin with *Wilkes v. Wood* (1763) and other English precedents decided in the mid-eighteenth century.

The different ways in which English and American authorities thought about rights influenced institutional development in each regime. If, as eighteenth-century English commentators thought, rights are man-made, then entrusting legislatures with the power to determine the rights of citizens is appropriate. Rights at any given time are what most people want rights to be. But if, as many Americans thought, rights are inherent in human nature, then elected officials have no power to violate the fundamental rights of man. This line of thinking suggests that some institution other than a popularly elected legislature might be better suited to ensure that governing officials act in a manner consistent with human rights. Although only a few colonists suggested that the judiciary might be that institution, the seeds for judicial authority were

8. *Annals of Congress*, 1st Cong., 1st Sess., (August 15, 1789), 759.

Table 2-1 Major Rights and Liberties Issues and Statements of the Colonial Era

Major Political Issues	Major Constitutional Issues
English Civil War and Glorious Revolution	Magna Carta (1215)
Foundation of Plymouth Colony	English Bill of Rights (1689)
Foundation of Virginia Colony	Relationship Between Church and State
Growth of Religious Diversity	Prior Restraint of Publications
Maryland Toleration Act of 1649	Seditious Libel
English Restrictions on Quakers	Military Exemptions for Quakers
Rise of Slavery	*Somerset v. Stewart* (1773)
Liberal and Republican Political Thought	Criticism of General Search Warrants
Rights of Representation	Debate over Confessions Extracted through Coercion
Independence of Colonies	Juries decide Facts and Law
	New Conception of Constitutionalism

planted in the American understanding of rights and liberties before the Revolution.

II. Foundations

MAJOR DEVELOPMENTS

- First statutory declarations of fundamental rights
- Rise of liberal and republican political thought
- Debates over rights of representation

The American revolutionaries who demanded their rights engaged in practices that were both centuries old and novel. From at least 1215, the year the Magna Carta was written and signed, Englishmen had demanded that their king respect their rights. Over the years these rights became embodied in such parliamentary enactments as the English Bill of Rights (1689) and such common law judicial decisions as *Wilkes v. Wood* (1763). What changed was who demanded rights. Throughout much of English history, kings, aristocrats, and religious elites were the only persons who insisted that they had fundamental rights and liberties. The Magna Carta was a peace treaty between King John I and rebellious English barons. No prominent person at Runnymede, where that enactment was sealed, thought that the Magna Carta limited aristocrats' power to rule over ordinary people. Over time more and more English subjects insisted that they also had fundamental rights, and by the time the colonies were settled legal authorities recognized that the principles of the Magna Carta limited royal power over all persons, not just persons with a title. Over the next 150 years liberal and republican political thinkers popularized claims that government was the product of a social contract in which all rulers promised to protect the fundamental rights of all people.

English authorities and prominent colonists disputed the parties to that social contract. Most English political thinkers regarded the social contract as being between the king and the people. Rights were limits on royal power, not limits on the power of the people's representatives in Parliament. The king could not censor speech, but Parliament could pass laws punishing those who advocated what the majority believed to be bad ideas. American political thinkers challenged two elements of English constitutional thought. First, they insisted that a Parliament in which the American colonies were not represented could not make binding law for American colonists. Second, they began to think of the social contract as binding popular majorities as well as the king. All citizens, in this view, were parties to the social contract. This meant that all governing institutions had to protect fundamental rights.

A. Sources

The English Constitution to which American colonists appealed in the eighteenth century was different from the Constitution to which Americans appeal in the twenty-first century. The English Constitution was (and still is) unwritten. That constitution consists of the series of laws, judicial decisions, and customary practices that make up the fundamental laws of England.

The English Bill of Rights is part of the English Constitution even though that enactment was passed by normal parliamentary procedures. Eighteenth-century English judges did not believe that they could determine whether parliamentary laws were inconsistent with their nation's constitution. Judges might strain to interpret laws as being consistent with what they believed to be fundamental constitutional principles, but the English Constitution was and is not judicially enforceable. English judges did not and do not declare laws unconstitutional.

British subjects and American colonists revered the English Constitution. George III insisted, "The pride, the glory of Britain, and the direct end of its constitution is political liberty."[9] Properly interpreted, both subjects and colonists insisted, the constitution of England guaranteed to all British subjects their natural rights. Colonial leaders had faith that "the natural absolute personal rights of individuals" were "the very basis of all municipal laws."[10] English lawyers regarded the common law as animated by "right reason." That courts could not declare unconstitutional a legislative enactment did not mean that common law rights were not fundamental. The proper remedies to government violation of the English Constitution were protest and rebellion, not a litigation campaign.

The American colonists looked to three particular sources for their constitutional rights and liberties. The first was English decrees, most notably the Magna Carta (1215), the Petition of Right (1628), and the English Bill of Rights (1689). These enactments established due process rights and the right not to be taxed without consent. The second was common law decisions handed down during the late seventeenth and eighteenth centuries. Such decisions as *Ex parte Bushell* (1670) and *Wilkes v. Wood* (1763) established the right to trial by jury and forbade general warrants. Colonial charters and laws were a third source of rights. The Connecticut Charter (1662) asserted, "That all, and every the Subjects of Us, . . . shall have and enjoy all Liberties and Immunities . . . as if they . . . were born within the realm of England." The Charter of Rhode Island and Providence Plantations (1663) guaranteed religious freedom. The Massachusetts Body of Liberties (1641) forbade "cruel and unusual punishments."

The American colonists believed that the rights declared by various English decrees, common law decisions, and colonial charters were *constitutional* rights, even if they were not written down in a distinctive constitutional text or judicially enforceable. When colonists complained that Parliament was violating their rights, they typically complained that Parliament was violating their *constitutional* rights. "If she would strip us of all the advantages derived to us from the English constitution," one colonist declared, "why should we desire to continue our connection?"[11] James Otis insisted that the basic rights of the American colonists were "founded on the principles of liberty and the British constitution." Furthermore, he claimed, "By this constitution, every man in the dominion is a free man," and "no parts of his Majesty's dominion can be taxed without their consent."[12]

Constitutions and Amendments

The English Bill of Rights (1689)

The middle of the seventeenth century was a time of great political turmoil in England. In 1640 Parliament and King Charles I took up arms against each other. That struggle ended in 1649 with Parliament victorious and King Charles beheaded. For the next eleven years, from 1649 to 1660, Great Britain was ruled by a protectorate under the authority of Oliver Cromwell, the leader of the parliamentary forces during the English Civil War. The monarchy was restored to power in 1660 (the Restoration) after Cromwell died and a badly divided Parliament invited Charles II, the son of Charles I, to occupy the throne. Charles II ruled from 1660 until his death in 1685. The throne then passed to his brother, James II, who, as a Catholic ruler in a country with an established Protestant church, quickly proved unacceptable to prominent English elites. James also attempted to restore many monarchial privileges that had been lost after the execution of Charles I. Protestant political leaders quickly mobilized. In 1688 James fled the country before an imminent invasion led by William of Orange and his wife

9. Gordon S. Wood, *The Radicalism of the American Revolution* (New York: Alfred A. Knopf, 1992), 14.

10. Bernard Bailyn, *The Ideological Origins of the American Revolution* (Cambridge, MA: Harvard University Press, 1967), 78.

11. William Goddard (?), *The Constitutional Courant*, in *Tracts of the American Revolution* (see note 2), 91.

12. Otis, *Rights of the British Colonies*, 22, 39.

Mary, who was James's daughter. This event became known as the Glorious Revolution. In 1689 Parliament confirmed the rule of William and Mary by passing An Act Declaring the Rights and Liberties of the Subject and Settling the Succession of the Crown. This measure is better known as the English Bill of Rights.

The English Bill of Rights sharply limits royal power to violate rights. Few provisions, however, limit parliamentary power. Why is this so? What protection did English citizens have in 1700 against parliamentary violations of rights?

Whereas the late King James the Second, by the assistance of diverse evil counselors, judges and ministers employed by him, did endeavour to subvert and extirpate the Protestant religion and the laws and liberties of this kingdom;

By assuming and exercising a power of dispensing with and suspending of laws and the execution of laws without consent of Parliament;

By committing and prosecuting diverse worthy prelates for humbly petitioning to be excused from concurring to the said assumed power;

By issuing and causing to be executed a commission under the great seal for erecting a court called the Court of Commissioners for Ecclesiastical Causes;

By levying money for and to the use of the Crown by pretence of prerogative for other time and in other manner than the same was granted by Parliament;

By raising and keeping a standing army within this kingdom in time of peace without consent of Parliament, and quartering soldiers contrary to law;

By causing several good subjects being Protestants to be disarmed at the same time when papists were both armed and employed contrary to law;

By violating the freedom of election of members to serve in Parliament;

By prosecutions in the Court of King's Bench for matters and causes cognizable only in Parliament, and by divers other arbitrary and illegal courses;

And whereas of late years partial corrupt and unqualified persons have been returned and served on juries in trials, and particularly diverse jurors in trials for high treason which were not freeholders;

And excessive bail hath been required of persons committed in criminal cases to elude the benefit of the laws made for the liberty of the subjects;

And excessive fines have been imposed;

And illegal and cruel punishments inflicted;

And several grants and promises made of fines and forfeitures before any conviction or judgment against the persons upon whom the same were to be levied;

All which are utterly and directly contrary to the known laws and statutes and freedom of this realm;

. . .

. . . The . . . Lords Spiritual and Temporal and Commons, pursuant to their respective letters and elections, being now assembled in a full and free representative of this nation . . . do . . . for the vindicating and asserting their ancient rights and liberties declare

That the pretended power of suspending the laws or the execution of laws by regal authority without consent of Parliament is illegal;

That the pretended power of dispensing with laws or the execution of laws by regal authority, as it hath been assumed and exercised of late, is illegal;

That the commission for erecting the late Court of Commissioners for Ecclesiastical Causes, and all other commissions and courts of like nature, are illegal and pernicious;

That levying money for or to the use of the Crown by pretence of prerogative, without grant of Parliament, for longer time, or in other manner than the same is or shall be granted, is illegal;

That it is the right of the subjects to petition the king, and all commitments and prosecutions for such petitioning are illegal;

That the raising or keeping a standing army within the kingdom in time of peace, unless it be with consent of Parliament, is against law;

That the subjects which are Protestants may have arms for their defence suitable to their conditions and as allowed by law;

That election of members of Parliament ought to be free;

That the freedom of speech and debates or proceedings in Parliament ought not to be impeached or questioned in any court or place out of Parliament;

That excessive bail ought not to be required, nor excessive fines imposed, nor cruel and unusual punishments inflicted;

That jurors ought to be duly impanelled and returned, and jurors which pass upon men in trials for high treason ought to be freeholders;

That all grants and promises of fines and forfeitures of particular persons before conviction are illegal and void;

And that for redress of all grievances, and for the amending, strengthening and preserving of the laws, Parliaments ought to be held frequently.

Massachusetts Body of Liberties (1641)

The Massachusetts Body of Liberties, written primarily by Puritan minister Nathaniel Ward, was the first legal code for the Massachusetts Bay Colony. The document combines what appear to be very modern liberties with more seventeenth-century concerns. Massachusetts was a Christian Commonwealth. How does Christianity influence the rights included in the text and the rights not included? Compare the Massachusetts Body of Liberties with the bills of rights (state and federal) discussed in the next chapter. What are the most significant similarities and omissions? What explains those similarities and omissions?

. . .

1. No man's life shall be taken away, no man's honour or good name shall be stained, no man's person shall be arrested, restrained, banished, dismembered, nor any ways punished, no man shall be deprived of his wife or children, no man's goods or estate shall be taken away from him, nor any way damaged under colour of law or Countenance of Authority, unless it be by virtue or equity of some express law of the Country warranting the same, established by a general Court and sufficiently published, or in case of the defect of a law in any particular case by the word of God. . . .

2. Every person within this Jurisdiction, whether Inhabitant or foreigner shall enjoy the same justice and law, that is general for the plantation. . . .

. . .

8. No man's Cattle or goods . . . shall be . . . taken for any public use or service, unless it be by warrant grounded upon some act of the general Court,[13] nor without such reasonable prices and hire as the ordinary rates of the Country do afford. . . .

. . .

12. Every man whether Inhabitant or foreigner, free or not free shall have liberty to come to any public Court, Council, or Town meeting, and either by speech or writing to move any lawful, seasonable, and material question, or to present any necessary motion, complaint, petition, Bill or information, whereof that meeting hath proper cognizance, so it be done in convenient time, due order, and respective manner.

. . .

16. Every Inhabitant that is a house holder shall have free fishing and fowling in any great ponds and Bay, Coves and Rivers. . . .

17. Every man of or within this Jurisdiction shall have free liberty . . . to remove both himself, and his family at their pleasure out of the same. . . .

18. No man's person shall be restrained or imprisoned by any authority whatsoever, before the law hath sentenced him thereto, if he can put in sufficient security . . . for his appearance, and good behavior in the mean time, unless it be in Crimes Capital, and Contempts in open Court. . . .

. . .

26. Every man that finds himself unfit to plead his own cause in any Court shall have Liberty to employ any man against whom the Court doth not except, to help him, Provided he give him no fee or reward for his pains. This shall not exempt the party himself from Answering such Questions in person as the Court shall . . . demand of him.

. . .

29. In all actions at law it shall be the liberty of the plaintiff and defendant by mutual consent to choose whether they will be tried by the Bench or by a Jury. . . . The like liberty shall be granted to all persons in Criminal cases.

. . .

42. No man shall be twice sentenced by Civil Justice for one and the same Crime, offence, or Trespass.

43. No man shall be beaten with above 40 stripes, nor shall any true gentleman, nor any man equal to a gentleman be punished with whipping, unless his crime be very shameful, and his course of life vicious and profligate.

. . .

45. No man shall be forced by Torture to confess any Crime against himself nor any other unless it be in some Capital case, where he is first fully convicted by clear and sufficient evidence to be guilty, After which if the cause be of that nature, that it is very apparent there be other conspirators, or confederates with him, Then he may be tortured, yet not with such Tortures as be Barbarous and inhumane.

46. For bodily punishments we allow amongst us none that are inhumane Barbarous or cruel.

13. The General Court was the main governing body in seventeenth-century Massachusetts. As was common at that time, the institution combined legislative and judicial functions.

. . .

58. Civil authority hath power and liberty to see the peace, ordinances and Rules of Christ observed in every church according to his word. . . .

. . .

65. No custom or prescription shall ever prevail amongst us . . . that can be proved to be morally sinful by the word of god.

. . .

67. It is the constant liberty of the free men of this plantation to choose yearly at the Court of Election out of the freemen all the General officers of this Jurisdiction. . . .

. . .

70. All Freemen called to give any advise, vote, verdict, or sentence in any Court, Council, or Civil Assembly, shall have full freedom to do it according to their true Judgments and Consciences, so it be done orderly and inoffensively for the manner.

. . .

80. Every married woman shall be free from bodily correction or stripes by her husband, unless it be in his own defense upon her assault. . . .

. . .

89. If any people of other Nations professing the true Christian Religion shall flee to us from the tyranny or oppression of their persecutors, or from famine, wars, or the like necessary and compulsory cause, They shall be entertained and succored amongst us, according to that power and prudence, god shall give us.

. . .

91. There shall never be any bond slavery . . . amongst us unless it be lawful Captives taken in just wars, and such strangers as willingly sell themselves or are sold to us. . . .

. . .

All the people of god within this Jurisdiction who are not in a church way, and be orthodox in Judgment, and not scandalous in life, shall have full liberty to gather themselves into a Church Estate. Provided they do it in a Christian way, with due observation of the rules of Christ revealed in his word.

B. Principles

Political thinking about the purpose of government changed dramatically between the time the first colonies were settled and the American Revolution in 1776. When the first colonies were established during the early 1600s most political leaders and political thinkers assumed that God vested kings and priests with the right to rule. Kings and their deputies were expected to promote prosperity and the true religion. Should they fail, God and God alone held them accountable. Royal subjects had no right to chastise or criticize wayward rulers. Outside of a few members of the nobility, people had no right to influence governmental decisions and no rights that they could enforce against government in this life. "We have our authority from God," John Winthrop informed the Plymouth Colony in his "Little Speech on Liberty."[14] This consensus was unraveling as Winthrop was speaking. Two related developments in political thought challenged assertions about the divine right of kings and the rights of citizens. The first was liberalism. The second was republicanism.

Liberalism. Political liberals in the seventeenth and eighteenth centuries believed that government existed to protect individual rights. Thomas Hobbes and other English liberal philosophers maintained that government was a social contract between all inhabitants of a community. People agreed to a common ruler, usually a king, on the condition that the ruler protected their life, liberty, and property. Government officials who failed to protect life, liberty, and property forfeited their right to rule. Those they offended need not wait for God's justice in the afterlife. Citizens had the right to rebel against any monarch or governor who consistently refused to respect their liberties. Locke, the most influential political liberal of the seventeenth century, claimed in his Second Treatise on Government that these rights were derived from natural law. He claimed, "MEN being, as has been said, by nature, all free, equal, and independent, no one can be put out of this estate, and subjected to the political power of another, without his own consent."[15] More commonly, English liberals assumed that government was obligated to respect certain time-honored rights set out in the Magna Carta and the English Bill of Rights.

14. John Winthrop, *The History of New England from 1630 to 1649*, ed. James Savage (Boston: Little, Brown and Company, 1853), 2:280.

15. John Locke, *Two Treatises on Government* (London: R. Butler, 1821), 269.

Republicanism. Republican thinkers in the seventeenth and eighteenth centuries emphasized the importance of political participation and civic virtue. Such thinkers as James Harrington and Jean-Jacques Rousseau asserted that people were free to the extent that they were self-governing. Republicans believed that the most fundamental liberty people enjoyed was the right to participate in the political process. Maximillian Petty, a seventeenth-century English radical, declared, "We judge that all inhabitants that have not lost their birthright should have an equal voice in elections."[16] Consider the famous expression, "No Taxation without Representation." The colonists who made this assertion were not objecting to exorbitant taxation. That would be a liberal claim. Rather, they insisted that people could be taxed only with the permission of their elected representatives. Republican political thought is more concerned with the processes by which political decisions are made than with the substance of those decisions. Classical republicans are also more concerned with promoting the public good than with individual rights. Gordon Wood notes, "Liberty was realized when the citizens were virtuous—that is, willing to sacrifice their private interests for the sake of the community, including serving in public office without pecuniary rewards."[17]

Liberalism and Republicanism. Liberalism and republicanism rarely exist in pure form. Both in the Colonial Era and at present, political thinkers typically appeal to both liberal and republican values. Consider the common claim in late colonial America that representation is the best means for protecting individual rights. That assertion mixes republican means and liberal ends. Representative government is republican because citizens participate in the lawmaking process. Representative government is liberal because representatives elected by the people are unlikely to violate rights.

The leading liberal and republican thinkers during the seventeenth and eighteenth centuries agreed that rights holders could be limited by nationality, religion, race, gender, class, and other characteristics. The English Bill of Rights discusses the rights of Englishmen. Whether colonists enjoyed those rights was contested. Frenchmen and Spaniards had to look elsewhere for their liberties. John Locke's influential *Letter Concerning Toleration* limited religious freedom to members of Protestant sects. Most classical liberal and republican thinkers believed that women and persons of color were incapable of exercising certain fundamental rights. Many believed that only property holders could exercise certain rights.

C. Scope

American colonists enjoyed the rights of Englishmen. The common law was clear on this point. Chief Justice Edward Coke stated in *Calvin's Case* (1608) that English subjects who moved to English territory retained the same rights they had enjoyed in England. He wrote, "In the case of . . . conquest, . . . the King's subjects . . . are capable of lands in the kingdom or country conquered, and may maintain any real action, and have the like privileges and benefits there, as they may have in England."[18] William Blackstone elaborated on this point in his *Commentaries on the Laws of England.* Blackstone noted that English laws might have to be modified in light of the particular circumstances of the English territory. Nevertheless, English privileges traveled with settlers as they crossed the Atlantic.

> If an uninhabited country be discovered and planted by English subjects, all the English laws then in being, which are the birthright of every subject, are immediately there in force. But this must be understood with very many and very great restrictions. Such colonists carry with them only so much of the English law as is applicable to their own situation and the condition of an infant colony; such, for instance, as the general rules of inheritance, and of protection from personal injuries.[19]

Blackstone questioned whether the American colonies were previously uninhabited, but most English authorities agreed that Englishmen who moved to England's colonies in the Americas did not surrender their rights as Englishmen. Immigrants enjoyed the same rights and privileges. When the colonies naturalized settlers from France, Germany, and other European countries,

16. *Sources and Debates in English History, 1485–1715,* eds. Newton Key and Robert Bucholz, 2nd ed. (San Francisco: Wiley-Blackwell, 2009), 189.

17. Wood, *Radicalism,* 104.

18. *Calvin's Case,* (1608) 77 Eng. Rep. 377, 398 (K.B.); 7 Co. Rep. 1 a, 17 b.

19. Blackstone, *Commentaries,* 1:107.

those persons gained the same rights they would have obtained had they been naturalized in England.

The disputes that eventually led to the American Revolution were over how to apply the principle that persons residing in the colonies had the same rights as English subjects. King George III, his ministers, and the parliamentary majority in the 1760s and 1770s insisted that English subjects throughout the realm enjoyed the same rights when all were governed by Parliament. American revolutionaries insisted that English subjects throughout the realm were treated equally when all were governed by a local legislature.

English legal authorities maintained that people in both London and Boston had to pay whatever taxes Parliament thought appropriate. That no colonist could vote for any representative in Parliament was of no legal or constitutional significance. Very few English subjects who resided in England during the eighteenth century voted in parliamentary elections. Parliament was expected to represent the interests of all English subjects, whether or not they voted, and no matter where they resided. The political theory of the time regarded American colonists, as well as Englishmen without the vote, as virtually represented in Parliament. People are virtually represented in a legislature when governing officials can be trusted to consider their interests fairly. Thomas Whatley, the member of Parliament most responsible for the Stamp Act of 1765, relied on the principle of virtual representation when defending the right of Parliament to tax the colonies. He asserted,

> The fact is, that the inhabitants of the colonies are represented in Parliament; they do not indeed choose the members of that assembly; neither are nine tenths of the people of *Britain* electors; for the right of election is annexed to certain species of property, to peculiar franchises, and to inhabitancy in some particular places; but these descriptions comprehend only a very small part of the land, the property, and the people of this island . . . . Women and persons under age be their property ever so large, and all of it freehold, have [no vote]. The merchants of *London*, a numerous and respectable body of men, whose opulence exceeds all that *America* could collect . . . are all in the same Circumstances; none of them choose their representatives; and yet are they not represented in Parliament? Is their vast property subject to taxes without their consent? Are they all arbitrarily bound by laws to which they have not agreed? The colonies are in exactly the same Situation; All British Subjects are really in the same; none are actually, all are virtually represented in Parliament; for every Member of Parliament sits in the House not as a representative of his own constituents, but as one of that august Assembly by which all the commons of *Great Britain* are represented.[20]

By the 1750s and 1760s many prominent colonists were no longer satisfied with being virtually represented in Parliament. Such revolutionaries as Patrick Henry in Virginia and Samuel Adams in Massachusetts insisted that the right of Englishmen to be taxed only with their consent meant that the colonies either had to be represented in Parliament or could be taxed only by the local colonial legislature. In 1768 Adams drafted a protest on behalf of the colonial legislature in Massachusetts explicitly asserting that the Stamp Act and other taxes imposed by Parliament violated the right of English subjects in the colonies to be taxed only with the consent of their representatives. The Massachusetts Circular Letter of February 11, 1768, declared,

> It is moreover their humble opinion, which they express with the greatest deference to the wisdom of the Parliament that the acts made there imposing duties of the people of this province with the sole & express purpose of raising a revenue, are infringements of their natural & constitutional rights because as they are not represented in the British Parliament, His Majesty's Commons in Britain, by those acts, grant their property without their consent.
>
> The House further are of the opinion that their constituents considering their local circumstances cannot by any possibility be represented in the Parliament, & that it will forever be impracticable that they should be equally represented there & consequently not at all; being separated by an ocean of a thousand leagues: and that his Majesty's royal predecessors for this reason were graciously pleased to form a subordinate legislature here that their sub-

20. Excerpt taken from Thomas Whately, *The Regulations Lately Made concerning the Colonies, and the Taxes Imposed upon Them, Considered*, 3rd ed. (London: J. Wilkie, 1775), 101–10.

jects might enjoy the unalienable right of a representation. . . .[21]

This debate over representation extended far beyond taxation. Proponents of the English Constitution at the time of the American Revolution believed that fundamental rights were protected by the combination of parliamentary sovereignty and strict restrictions on the power of the king. Parliament could take property, limit speech, and restrict other rights because the presumption was that a national legislature in which all subjects were represented would limit rights only when doing so promoted the public good. If the colonies could not be said to be represented in Parliament, then English legislation restricting any right of English subjects in the colonies was inconsistent with the fundamental rights of Englishmen.

III. Individual Rights

MAJOR DEVELOPMENTS

- Establishment of the principle that government cannot take private property without compensation
- Increased recognition of the freedom of religion
- Development of the right to bear arms
- Substantial morals regulation

Englishmen and American colonists believed that government should protect individual rights. The persons who instigated the English Civil War and the American Revolution insisted that rebellion was justified because governing authorities had violated fundamental liberties. Nevertheless, individual rights claims in the seventeenth and eighteenth centuries differed from many rights claims at the turn of the twenty-first century. Contemporary Americans tend to conceive of rights as limits on all government officials. No government official may violate our freedom of speech or interfere with our intimate affairs. By contrast, the English Bill of Rights conceptualized rights as limits only against *executive* action or abuse. The king could not levy taxes, disarm good citizens, or interfere with debate in Parliament, but Parliament could tax citizens as representatives saw fit. Elected officials could adopt other restrictions on individual action that the people's representatives thought contributed to the public good.

Contemporary Americans conceive of rights as trumps against public policy. Speech rights may be restricted only when the offending expression presents a grave threat to the general public. Colonial Americans believed that no one had a right to injure others. A general consensus existed on the truth of the common law maxim *"sic utere tuo ut alienum non laedas"*—"so use your own so as not to harm that of another." If Parliament or a colonial legislature thought that some use of property or a particular form of religious conduct threatened any public harm, they could prohibit that use of property or religious conduct. Harm was understood very broadly. No prominent colonist found legislation enforcing common notions of morality to be constitutionally problematic.

A. Property

Colonial Americans and their British counterparts believed that government in a free society provided substantial protection for property rights. English political theorists and the American colonists maintained that property guaranteed independence. Persons who owned land or freeholds were self-sustaining, able to earn a living without relying on other persons. "Liberty," Americans proclaimed, "consists in an independency upon the will of another," and a slave was a person "who depends upon the will of another for the enjoyment of his life and property."[22] Confident that only property holders were truly free, American colonies restricted the franchise to persons who owned property—often, considerable property. Few explicit protections for property rights were thought necessary when colonial legislatures tended to be composed of those local notables who owned the most property.

Englishmen and American colonists on the eve of the American Revolution believed that persons had three fundamental property rights:

1. Government could not confiscate property.
2. Government could take property for a public purpose only when government paid the fair value of that property to the original property holder.

21. Excerpt taken from Harry Alonzo Cushing, ed., *The Writings of Samuel Adams* (New York: G. P. Putnam's Sons, 1904), 1:184–88.

22. Wood, *Radicalism*, 179.

3. Government could not tax a person without the consent of that person as manifested by the people's representatives.

William Blackstone elaborated on these property rights in his *Commentaries on the Laws of England*. The section on property stated,

> The third absolute right, inherent in every Englishman, is that of property: which consists in the free use, enjoyment, and disposal of all his acquisitions, without any control or diminution, save only by the laws of the land. . . . Upon this principle the great charter [Magna Carta] has declared that no freeman shall be disseised, or divested, of his freehold, or of his liberties, or free customs, but by the judgment of his peers, or by the law of the land. . . . So great moreover is the regard of the law for private property, that it will not authorize the least violation of it; no, not even for the general good of the whole community. If a new road, for instance, were to be made through the grounds of a private person, it might perhaps be extensively beneficial to the public; but the law permits no man, or set of men, to do this without consent of the owner of the land. In vain may it be urged, that the good of the individual ought to yield to that of the community; for it would be dangerous to allow any private man, or even any public tribunal, to be the judge of this common good, and to decide whether it be expedient or no. Besides, the public good is in nothing more essentially interested, than in the protection of every individual's private rights, as modeled by the municipal law. In this and similar cases the legislature alone can, and indeed frequently does, interpose, and compel the individual to acquiesce. But how does it interpose and compel? Not by absolutely stripping the subject of his property in an arbitrary manner; but by giving him a full indemnification and equivalent for the injury thereby sustained. The public is now considered as an individual, treating with an individual for an exchange. All that the legislature does is to oblige the owner to alienate his possessions for a reasonable price; and even this is an exertion of power, which the legislature indulges with caution, and which nothing but the legislature can perform. Nor is this the only instance in which the law of the land has postponed even public necessity to the sacred and inviolable rights of private property. For no subject of England can be constrained to pay any aids or taxes, even for the defence of the realm or the support of government, but such as are imposed by his own consent, or that of his representatives in parliament.[23]

Contract. English subjects and American colonists during the seventeenth and first half of the eighteenth centuries did not speak of rights to contract. Parliament in 1677 recognized the increasing importance of contracts in public life by passing the Statute of Frauds. This measure, which is still valid law in many states, declares that judges may enforce certain kinds of agreements between persons only when those bargains appear in writing. Still, contract law and contract rights remained relatively undeveloped on the eve of the American Revolution. Blackstone spent only four pages of his multi-volume treatise discussing contracts, and that discussion focused on marriage contracts. Few prominent persons spoke of distinctive contract rights or liberties. What future generations would consider contract rights were either regarded as a species of property rights or ignored by eighteenth-century common law treatise writers.

B. RELIGION

Both England and the colonies were wracked by religious disputes during the seventeenth century and the first part of the eighteenth century. Conventional wisdom in 1600 maintained that government should advance the one true religion. In England this meant the Anglican, or Episcopalian, Church. Government officials appointed Anglican ministers, paid their salaries, sponsored Anglican religious ceremonies, and required all subjects to worship God in a manner consistent with Anglican doctrines. Blackstone's *Commentaries* detailed the numerous offenses against religion that proponents of the union between the English state and the Anglican Church demanded government officials punish. Over the next 150 years, prominent voices challenged this union. Some, like the Puritans who founded the Massachusetts Bay Colony, believed wholeheartedly in the union of church and state but thought that England had established the wrong church. They left England because they were

23. Blackstone, *Commentaries*, 2:138–39.

convinced that their version of Protestantism was the one true religion that ought to be established. Other religious dissenters accepted establishment but called for some tolerance for religious dissenters in order to preserve the peace. The Maryland Toleration Act declared that government should not "molest" any form of private Christian worship. John Locke, Roger Williams, William Penn, and their followers went further. They insisted that government and government officials had no business advancing the one true religion. Religion, in their view, was a private matter between God and an individual's conscience.

These struggles were eventually settled in favor of an increased commitment to greater religious freedoms in both England and the American colonies.

- The colonies on the eve of the American Revolution provided far less support for religion and mandated far less religious observance than had been the case during the years when they were first being established.
- American colonists were increasingly likely to tolerate all major Protestant sects, although many colonies still imposed significant disabilities on Catholics and Jews.
- A few colonies, most notably Rhode Island, recognized the right to free exercise of religion.
- American colonists debated whether the freedom of conscience required that government give special exemptions to members of such sects as the Quakers, who had religious objections to taking certain oaths and bearing arms.

These developments reflected the increased influence of liberal ideas on colonial politics, changes in Protestant religious commitments, and the brute fact of religious diversity in the colonies. Such political liberals as John Locke insisted that religion was a private affair. Locke's *Letter on Toleration* maintained that government ought to be concerned with protecting rights, not promoting religious observance. Roger Williams, a devout Protestant, reached the same conclusion for more sectarian reasons. His 1644 book *The Bloudy Tenent* asserted that religious coercion was inconsistent with religious obligations. Religious diversity made establishments difficult. In sharp contrast to England in 1600, most American colonies by 1750 lacked a religious majority capable of maintaining a strong union between a particular religious sect and the state. Tolerance was as much a pragmatic political necessity as a deeply felt commitment. Many arguments for religious toleration, in both England and the colonies, emphasized the costs of religious warfare.

Establishment

Proponents of the traditional union between church and state maintained that government should promote religious belief, and that widespread religious faith was necessary to ensure a virtuous citizenry. Government and church cooperated to maintain and spread the one true religion. "Christianity," William Blackstone claimed, "is a part of the laws of England."[24] The Virginia colony required that all ministers preach consistently with the "doctrines, rights, and religion now professed and established within the realme of England." Massachusetts in the seventeenth century was governed by a religious theocracy, whose members punished all conduct inconsistent with their conception of Christianity. The godly citizens of Salem, Massachusetts, in 1692 executed nineteen men and women for allegedly practicing witchcraft. Other colonies were also self-consciously Christian commonwealths. Consider the Agreement of the Settlers at Exeter in New Hampshire (1639):

> Whereas it hath pleased the Lord to move the Heart of our dread Sovereign Charles by the Grace of God King &c. to grant License and Liberty to sundry of his subjects to plant themselves in the Western parts of America. We his loyal Subjects Brethern of the Church in Exeter situate and lying upon the River Pascataqua with other Inhabitants there, considering with ourselves the holy Will of God and o'er own Necessity that we should not live without wholesome Laws and Civil Government among us of which we are altogether destitute; do in the name of Christ and in the sight of God combine ourselves together to erect and set up among us such Government as shall be to our best discerning agreeable to the Will of God professing ourselves Subjects to our Sovereign Lord King Charles according to the Liberties of our English Colony of Massachusetts, and binding of ourselves solemnly by the Grace and Help of Christ and in His Name and fear to submit ourselves to such Godly and Christian Laws as

24. Blackstone, *Commentaries*, 5:59.

Illustration 2-1 Sir William Blackstone

Source: Samuel Bellin, engraver (1799–1893), *Sir William Blackstone.* Emmet Collection, Miriam and Ira D. Wallach Division of Art, Prints and Photographs, The New York Public Library, Astor, Lenox and Tilden Foundations.

> are established in the realm of England to our best Knowledge, and to all other such Laws which shall upon good grounds be made and enacted among us according to God that we may live quietly and peaceably together in all godliness and honesty.[25]

The union of church and state in colonial America had two elements. *Establishment* was the first. States paid the salaries of religious ministers, built churches, and sponsored religious activities. *Conformity* was the second. State laws required persons to worship God in particular ways and behave in a manner consistent with Christian religious doctrine. During the seventeenth century most states had a favored religious sect. Virginia favored the Church of England. Massachusetts was dominated by Puritans (Congregationalists). By the eve of the American Revolution multiple establishments were more common. All towns in a state sponsored a church, but popular majorities determined the favored sect. In some communities everyone was taxed to support a church, but persons chose what church received their taxes.

Liberal ideas slowly weakened these unions between church and state. Proponents of *separation* insisted that the government had no business financing or sponsoring religious activities. Led by Roger Williams, separationists claimed that the union between the church and the state corrupted both the church and the state. Proponents of *toleration* insisted that people be free to practice the religion of their choice. Toleration was consistent with a mild establishment. Some colonies provided assistance for some religions while permitting persons to practice other religions in private.

The union between church and state on the eve of the American Revolution was far weaker than when

25. Yale Law School, Lillian Goldman Law Library, Avalon Project, http://avalon.law.yale.edu/17th_century/nh06.asp.

the colonies were first settled. Most colonies retained established churches. Colonial governments gave those religious institutions far less support than had been provided in the seventeenth century or was provided in most European countries. Many states supported more than one church. Pennsylvania, Delaware, Rhode Island, and New Jersey either did not have an established church or did not direct any tax money to religious institutions. Still, Americans generally understood themselves to be living in a Christian commonwealth. Blasphemy was universally considered to be a crime, and the criminal law enforced biblical injunctions. John Witherspoon, a prominent colonial minister and revolutionary, reflected the views of most colonists in his sermons emphasizing how state support for religion was necessary to maintain the moral foundations of a good regime.

William Blackstone, Of Offences Against God and Religion (1773)[26]

William Blackstone championed the traditional union of church and state. Government, he insisted, had the obligation to teach religious doctrine and punish religious dissenters. What reasons does Blackstone give for maintaining the union between church and state? What policies does he believe necessary to maintain that union? Blackstone emphasizes the suppression of Catholics (papists)—a hostility shared by many American Protestants of the period. What, from Blackstone's perspective, is the main threat that Catholicism presents to the political regime? Finally, Blackstone notes a "difference between tolerance and establishment." What is that difference? Why does he think that this difference is important?

. . .

First then, such crimes and misdemeanors, as more immediately offend Almighty God, by openly transgressing the precepts of religion either natural or revealed. . . .

. . . [T]he first is that of apostacy, or a total renunciation of christianity, by embracing either a false religion, or no religion at all. . . . Doubtless the preservation of christianity, as a national religion, is, abstracted from it's own intrinsic truth, of the utmost consequence to the civil state. . . . The belief of a future state of rewards and punishments, the entertaining just ideas of the moral attributes of the supreme being, and a firm persuasion that he superintends and will finally compensate every action in human life . . . these are the grand foundation of all judicial oaths; . . . all moral evidence therefore, all confidence in human veracity, must be weakened by irreligion, and overthrown by infidelity. Wherefore all affronts to christianity, or endeavors to depreciate it's efficacy, are highly deserving of human punishment. . . .

. . .

Another species of offences against religion are those which affect the established church. . . .

. . . [F]irst, of the offence of reviling the ordinances of the church. This is a crime of a much grosser nature than the other of mere non-conformity: since it carries with it the utmost indecency, arrogance, and ingratitude: indecency, by setting up private judgment in opposition to public; arrogance, by treating with contempt and rudeness what has at least a better chance to be right, than the singular notions of any particular man; and ingratitude, by denying that indulgence and liberty of conscience to the members of the national church. . . . Nor can their continuance to this time be thought too severe and intolerant; when we consider, that they are leveled at an offence, to which men cannot now be prompted by any laudable motive; not even by a mistaken zeal for reformation: since from political reasons . . . [it] would now be extremely unadvisable to make any alterations in the service of the church. . . . And therefore the virulent declamations of peevish or opinionated men on topics so often refuted, and of which the preface to the liturgy is itself a perpetual refutation, can be calculated for no other purpose, than merely to disturb the consciences, and poison the minds of the people.

Non-conformity to the worship of the church is the other, or negative branch of this offence. . . . [U]ndoubtedly all persecution and oppression of weak consciences, on the score of religious persuasions, are highly unjustifiable upon every principle of natural reason, civil liberty, or found religion. But care must be taken not to carry this indulgence into such extremes, as may endanger the national church: there is always a difference to be made between toleration and establishment.

Non-conformists are of two sorts: first, such as absent themselves from the divine worship in the

26. Excerpted from Blackstone, *Commentaries*, 4:42–43.

established church . . . and attend the service of no other persuasion. These . . . forfeit one shilling to the poor every lord's day they so absent themselves, and . . . to the king if they continue such default for a month together. . . .

The second species of non-conformists are those who offend through a mistaken or perverse zeal. Such were esteemed by our laws, enacted since the time of the reformation, to be papists and protestant dissenters. . . . [T]he laws against the former are much more severe. . . . [T]he principles of the papists being deservedly looked upon to be subversive of the civil government, but not those of the protestant dissenters. As to the papists, their tenets are undoubtedly calculated for the introduction of all slavery, both civil and religious. . . . He is bound indeed to protect the established church, by admitting none but it's genuine members to offices of trust and emolument: for, if every sect was to be indulged in a free communion of civil employments, the idea of a national establishment would at once be destroyed, and the Episcopal church would be no longer the church of England. . . .

As to papists, . . . [i]f once they could be brought to renounce the supremacy of the pope, they might quietly enjoy their seven sacraments, their purgatory, and auricular confession; their worship of relics and images; nay even their transubstantiation. But while they acknowledge a foreign power, superior to the sovereignty of the kingdom, they cannot complain if the laws of that kingdom will not treat them upon the footing of good subjects. . . .

In order the better to secure the established church against perils from non-conformists of all denominations . . . there are . . . two bulwarks erected; called the corporation and test acts. By the former . . . no person can be legally elected to any office relating to the government . . . unless, within a twelve month before, he has received the sacrament of the lord's supper according to the rites of the church of England: and he is also enjoined to take the oaths of allegiance and supremacy at the same time that he takes the oath of office. . . . The other, called the test act, directs all officers civil and military to take the oaths and make the declaration against transubstantiation . . . , and also within the same time to receive the sacrament of the lord's supper. . . .

The fourth species of offences therefore, more immediately against God and religion, is that of blasphemy against the Almighty, by denying his being or providence; or by contumelious reproaches of our Saviour Christ. Whither also may be referred all profane scoffing at the holy scripture, or exposing it to contempt and ridicule. These are offences punishable at common law by fine and imprisonment, or other infamous corporal punishment: christianity is part of the laws of England.

Somewhat allied to this, though in an inferior degree, is the offence of profane and common swearing and cursing. . . .

A sixth species of offences against God and religion . . . is . . . the offence of witchcraft. . . . To deny the possibility, nay, actual existence, of witchcraft and sorcery, is at once flatly to contradict the revealed word of God. . . . But all executions for this dubious crime are now at an end. . . . And accordingly it is with us enacted by statute . . . that no prosecution shall for the future be carried on against any person for conjuration, witchcraft, sorcery, or enchantment. . . .

Profanation of the lord's day, or sabbath-breaking, is a ninth offence against God and religion, punished by the municipal laws of England. For, besides the notorious indecency and scandal, of permitting any secular business to be publicly transacted on that day, in a country professing christianity, and the corruption of morals which usually follows it's profanation, the keeping one day in seven holy, as a time of relaxation and refreshment as well as for public worship, is of admirable service to a state, considered merely as a civil institution. It humanizes by the help of conversation and society the manners of the lower classes; which would otherwise degenerate into a sordid ferocity. . . ; it enables the industrious workman to pursue his occupation in the ensuing week with health and cheerfulness: it imprints on the minds of the people that sense of their duty to God, so necessary to make them good citizens. . . .

John Locke, A Letter Concerning Toleration (1689)[27]

John Locke was a leading proponent of disestablishment, the view that government should not support religion. His influential Letter Concerning Toleration *gave both religious and nonreligious reasons for separating the church and the state. Locke insisted that Jesus Christ rejected the union of church*

27. Excerpted from John Locke, *A Letter Concerning Toleration* (n.p.: J. Brook, 1796).

and state. He also maintained that state support for religion and religious coercion are inconsistent with liberal political principles. What are those liberal political principles? Why does Locke think these principles justify the separation of church and state? Locke insists that some religious doctrines should not be tolerated. Is this lack of toleration consistent with his liberal perspective? Does Locke maintain that Catholics, who believe in papal authority, should not be tolerated? Locke argues that religious persons have an obligation to obey all laws that have secular purposes, even if those laws burden religious practice. How does he justify that conclusion?

...

I esteem that toleration to be the chief characteristic mark of the true Church. . . .

. . . The business of true religion is . . . not instituted in order to the erecting of an external pomp, nor to the obtaining of ecclesiastical dominion, nor to the exercising of compulsive force, but to the regulating of men's lives, according to the rules of virtue and piety. . . . For it is impossible that those should sincerely and heartily apply themselves to make other people Christians, who have not really embraced the Christian religion in their own hearts. If the Gospel and the apostles may be credited, no man can be a Christian without charity and without that faith which works, not by force, but by love. Now, I appeal to the consciences of those that persecute, torment, destroy, and kill other men upon pretence of religion, whether they do it out of friendship and kindness towards them or no? . . .

...

The toleration of those that differ from others in matters of religion is so agreeable to the Gospel of Jesus Christ, and to the genuine reason of mankind, that it seems monstrous for men to be so blind as not to perceive the necessity and advantage of it in so clear a light. . . . [T]hat none may impose either upon himself or others, by the pretences of loyalty and obedience to the prince, or of tenderness and sincerity in the worship of God; I esteem it above all things necessary to distinguish exactly the business of civil government from that of religion and to settle the just bounds that lie between the one and the other. . . .

The commonwealth seems to me to be a society of men constituted only for the procuring, preserving, and advancing their own civil interests.

Civil interests I call life, liberty, health, and indolence of body; and the possession of outward things, such as money, lands, houses, furniture, and the like.

It is the duty of the civil magistrate, by the impartial execution of equal laws, to secure unto all the people in general and to every one of his subjects in particular the just possession of these things belonging to this life. . . .

Now that the whole jurisdiction of the magistrate reaches only to these civil concernments, and that all civil power, right and dominion, is bounded and confined to the only care of promoting these things; and that it neither can nor ought in any manner to be extended to the salvation of souls, these following considerations seem unto me abundantly to demonstrate.

First, because the care of souls is not committed to the civil magistrate, any more than to other men. It is not committed unto him, I say, by God; because it appears not that God has ever given any such authority to one man over another as to compel anyone to his religion. Nor can any such power be vested in the magistrate by the consent of the people, because no man can so far abandon the care of his own salvation as blindly to leave to the choice of any other, whether prince or subject, to prescribe to him what faith or worship he shall embrace. For no man can, if he would, conform his faith to the dictates of another. All the life and power of true religion consist in the inward and full persuasion of the mind; and faith is not faith without believing. . . .

In the second place, the care of souls cannot belong to the civil magistrate, because his power consists only in outward force; but true and saving religion consists in the inward persuasion of the mind, without which nothing can be acceptable to God. . . .

. . . Magistracy does not oblige him to put off either humanity or Christianity; but it is one thing to persuade, another to command; one thing to press with arguments, another with penalties. . . . Every man has commission to admonish, exhort, convince another of error, and, by reasoning, to draw him into truth; but to give laws, receive obedience, and compel with the sword, belongs to none but the magistrate. And, upon this ground, I affirm that the magistrate's power extends not to the establishing of any articles of faith, or forms of worship, by the force of his laws. For laws are of no force at all without penalties, and penalties in this case are absolutely impertinent, because they are not proper to convince the mind. . . .

...

. . . [N]o private person has any right in any manner to prejudice another person in his civil enjoyments because he is of another church or religion. All the rights and franchises that belong to him as a man, or as a denizen, are inviolably to be preserved to him. These are not the business of religion. No violence nor injury is to be offered him, whether he be Christian or Pagan. . . . If any man err from the right way, it is his own misfortune, no injury to thee; nor therefore art thou to punish him in the things of this life because thou supposest he will be miserable in that which is to come.

. . . [T]he civil government can give no new right to the church, nor the church to the civil government. So that, whether the magistrate join himself to any church, or separate from it, the church remains always as it was before—a free and voluntary society. It neither requires the power of the sword by the magistrate's coming to it, nor does it lose the right of instruction and excommunication by his going from it. . . .

. . .

You will say . . . if some congregations should have a mind to sacrifice infants, or (as the primitive Christians were falsely accused) lustfully pollute themselves in promiscuous uncleanness, or practice any other such heinous enormities, is the magistrate obliged to tolerate them, because they are committed in a religious assembly? I answer: No. These things are not lawful in the ordinary course of life, nor in any private house; and therefore neither are they so in the worship of God, or in any religious meeting. But, indeed, if any people congregated upon account of religion should be desirous to sacrifice a calf, I deny that that ought to be prohibited by a law. Meliboeus, whose calf it is, may lawfully kill his calf at home, and burn any part of it that he thinks fit. For no injury is thereby done to any one, no prejudice to another man's goods. And for the same reason he may kill his calf also in a religious meeting. . . . But if peradventure such were the state of things that the interest of the commonwealth required all slaughter of beasts should be forborne for some while, in order to the increasing of the stock of cattle that had been destroyed by some extraordinary murrain, who sees not that the magistrate, in such a case, may forbid all his subjects to kill any calves for any use whatsoever? Only it is to be observed that, in this case, the law is not made about a religious, but a political matter; nor is the sacrifice, but the slaughter of calves, thereby prohibited.

By this we see what difference there is between the Church and the Commonwealth. Whatsoever is lawful in the Commonwealth cannot be prohibited by the magistrate in the Church. Whatsoever is permitted unto any of his subjects for their ordinary use, neither can nor ought to be forbidden by him to any sect of people for their religious uses. . . .

. . .

. . . [T]here is absolutely no such thing under the Gospel as a Christian commonwealth. There are, indeed, many cities and kingdoms that have embraced the faith of Christ, but they have retained their ancient form of government, with which the law of Christ hath not at all meddled. He, indeed, hath taught men how, by faith and good works, they may obtain eternal life; but He instituted no commonwealth. He prescribed unto His followers no new and peculiar form of government, nor put He the sword into any magistrate's hand, with commission to make use of it in forcing men to forsake their former religion and receive His.

. . .

. . . [T]he magistrate ought not to forbid the preaching or professing of any speculative opinions in any Church because they have no manner of relation to the civil rights of the subjects. If a Roman Catholic believe that to be really the body of Christ which another man calls bread, he does no injury thereby to his neighbor. If a Jew do not believe the New Testament to be the Word of God, he does not thereby alter anything in men's civil rights. If a heathen doubt of both Testaments, he is not therefore to be punished as a pernicious citizen. The power of the magistrate and the estates of the people may be equally secure whether any man believe these things or no. I readily grant that these opinions are false and absurd. But the business of laws is not to provide for the truth of opinions, but for the safety and security of the commonwealth and of every particular man's goods and person. And so it ought to be. For the truth certainly would do well enough if she were once left to shift for herself. She seldom has received and, I fear, never will receive much assistance from the power of great men, to whom she is but rarely known and more rarely welcome. . . .

. . .

. . . [N]o opinions contrary to human society, or to those moral rules which are necessary to the preservation of civil society, are to be tolerated by the magistrate. . . .

Another more secret evil, but more dangerous to the commonwealth, is when men arrogate to themselves, and to those of their own sect, some peculiar prerogative covered over with a specious show of deceitful words, but in effect opposite to the civil right of the community. . . . These, therefore, and the like, who attribute unto the faithful, religious, and orthodox, that is, in plain terms, unto themselves, any peculiar privilege or power above other mortals, in civil concernments; or who upon pretence of religion do challenge any manner of authority over such as are not associated with them in their ecclesiastical communion, I say these have no right to be tolerated by the magistrate; as neither those that will not own and teach the duty of tolerating all men in matters of mere religion. . . .

Again: That Church can have no right to be tolerated by the magistrate which is constituted upon such a bottom that all those who enter into it do thereby ipso facto deliver themselves up to the protection and service of another prince. . . .

Lastly, those are not at all to be tolerated who deny the being of a God. Promises, covenants, and oaths, which are the bonds of human society, can have no hold upon an atheist. The taking away of God, though but even in thought, dissolves all; besides also, those that by their atheism undermine and destroy all religion, can have no pretence of religion whereupon to challenge the privilege of a toleration. As for other practical opinions, though not absolutely free from all error, if they do not tend to establish domination over others, or civil impunity to the Church in which they are taught, there can be no reason why they should not be tolerated. . . .

Roger Williams, **The Bloudy Tenent** (1644)[28]

Roger Williams (1603?–83) is considered the founder of religious freedom in the United States. Shortly after his 1631 arrival in the Massachusetts Bay Colony Williams sided with those Puritans who insisted on a complete separation with the Anglican Church. Unlike other separationists who favored the union of a more purified church and state, Williams concluded that any union of church and state was inconsistent with Christian doctrine. Exiled from Massachusetts in 1635, Williams settled in what is now Providence, Rhode Island. Eventually he founded the Rhode Island Colony, which was committed to a complete separation of church and state. The 1663 Charter of Rhode Island declared,

> *No person within the said colony, at any time hereafter, shall be any ways molested, punished, disquieted, or called in question, for any differences in opinion in matters of religion, and do not actually disturb the civil peace of our said colony; but that all and every person and persons may, from time to time, and at all times hereafter, freely and fully have and enjoy his and their own judgments and consciences, in matters of religious concernments.*

The Bloudy Tenent *was published in London while Williams was trying to convince English authorities to grant Rhode Island a charter. The book was considered so radical that Parliament ordered every copy burned. Nevertheless,* The Bloudy Tenent *had substantial influence throughout the colonies. Consider when you read the introduction whether Williams is best conceptualized as a political liberal or a liberal Protestant. Which of his arguments might appeal to a contemporary secular citizen? Which are based entirely on religious doctrine?*

First, That the blood of so many hundred thousand souls of *Protestants* and *Papists,* spilt in the *Wars* of *present* and *former Ages,* for their respective *Consciences,* is not *required* nor *accepted* by *Jesus Christ* the *Prince* of *Peace.*

Secondly, Pregnant *Scriptures* and *Arguments* are throughout the Work proposed against the *Doctrine* of *persecution* for *cause* of *Conscience.*

. . .

Fourthly, The *Doctrine of persecution* for cause of *Conscience,* is proved guilty of all the *blood* of the *Souls* crying for *vengeance* under the *Altar.*

Fifthly, All *Civil States* with their *Officers* of *justice* in their respective *constitutions* and *administrations* are proved *essentially Civil,* and therefore not *Judges, Governours* or *Defenders* of the *Spiritual or Christian state* and *Worship.*

Sixly, It is the will and command of *God,* that (since the coming of his Son the *Lord Jesus)* a *permission* of the most *Paganish, Jewish, Turkish,* or *Antichristian consciences* and *worships,* be granted to *all* men in all *Nations* and *Countries:* and they are only to *be fought* against with that *Sword* which is only (in *Soul matters) able* to *conquer,* to wit, the *Sword of Gods Spirit,* the *Word* of *God.*

. . .

Eightly, *God* requires not a *uniformity* of *Religion* to be *enacted* and *enforced* in any *civil state;* which enforced uniformity (sooner or later) is the greatest occasion of

28. Excerpted from Roger Williams, *The Bloudy Tenent* (London: 1644).

civil War, ravishing of *conscience, persecution* of *Christ Jesus* in his servants, and of the *hypocrisy* and *destruction* of *millions* of *souls.*

Ninthly, In holding an enforced *uniformity* of *Religion* in a *civil state,* we must necessarily *disclaim* our desires and hopes of the *Jews conversion* to *Christ.*

Tenthly, An enforced *uniformity* of *Religion* throughout a *Nation* or *civil state,* confounds the *Civil* and *Religious,* denies the principles of Christianity and civility, and that *Jesus Christ* is come in the Flesh.

Eleventhly, The permission of other *consciences* and *worships* then a state professes, only can (according to God) procure a firm and lasting *peace,* (good *assurance* being taken according to the *wisdom* of the *civil state* for *uniformity* of *civil obedience* from all sorts.)

Twelfthly, lastly, true *civility* and *Christianity* may both flourish in a *state* or *Kingdom,* notwithstanding the *permission* of diverse and contrary *consciences,* either of *Jew* or *Gentile.*

John Witherspoon, The Dominion of Providence Over the Passions of Men (1776)[29]

John Witherspoon (1723–84) was a Presbyterian minister, the president of the College of New Jersey (later Princeton University), and the mentor of James Madison. He was an early proponent of independence, a member of the Second Continental Congress, and a signer of the Declaration of Independence. Witherspoon was one of many ministers who preached for independence from the pulpit. "The Dominion of Providence over the Passions of Men" is his most famous sermon. Witherspoon in this address claims divine support for American independence while emphasizing the religious foundations for organized government. Why does Witherspoon believe that religious belief provides a crucial foundation for political orders? Is he correct to think that all political orders require a virtuous citizenry? If he is correct, was there an eighteenth-century substitute for religion? As was the case with many political thinkers in the late eighteenth century, Witherspoon did not believe that government should establish a particular sect. How broad is his ecumenicism? Based on the passages below, do you believe that Witherspoon would tolerate Catholics? Jews? Members of other non-Protestant sects?

29. Excerpted from John Witherspoon, *The Dominion of Providence over the Passions of Men* (Philadelphia: R. Aitken, 1776).

Suffer me to recommend to you an attention to the public interest of religion, or in other words, zeal for the glory of God and the good of others. . . . Nothing is more certain than that a general profligacy and corruption of manners make a people ripe for destruction. A good form of government may hold the rotten materials together for some time, but beyond a certain pitch, even the best constitution will be ineffectual, and slavery must ensue. On the other hand, when the manners of a nation are pure, when true religion and internal principles maintain their vigor, the attempts of the most powerful enemies to oppress them are commonly baffled and disappointed. This will be found equally certain, whether we consider the great principles of God's moral government, or the operation and influence of natural causes.

What follows from this? That he is the best friend to American liberty, who is most sincere and active in promoting true and undefiled religion, and who sets himself with the greatest firmness to bear down profanity and immorality of every kind. Whoever is an avowed enemy to God, I scruple not to call him an enemy to his country. Do not suppose, my brethren, that I mean to recommend a furious and angry zeal for the circumstances of religion, or the contentions of one sect with another about their peculiar distinctions. I do not wish you to oppose any body's religion, but every body's wickedness. Perhaps there are few surer marks of the reality of religion, than when a man feels himself more joined in spirit to a true holy person of a different denomination, than to an irregular liver of his own. It is therefore your duty in this important and critical season to exert yourselves, every one in his proper sphere, to stem the tide of prevailing vice, to promote the knowledge of God, the reverence of his name and worship, and obedience to his laws.

. . .

. . . Magistrates, ministers, parents, heads of families, and those whom age has rendered venerable, are called to use their authority and influence for the glory of God and the good of others. Bad men themselves discover an inward conviction of this, for they are often liberal in their reproaches of persons of grave characters or religious profession, if they bear with patience the profanity of others. Instead of enlarging on the duty of men in authority in general, I must particularly recommend this matter to those who have the command of soldiers enlisted for the defense of their country. The cause is sacred, and the champions for it ought to be holy. Nothing is more grieving to the heart of a good man, than to hear from those who are going to the field, the horrid sound of cursing and blasphemy; it cools the ardor of his prayers, as well as abates his confidence and hope in God. Many more circumstances affect me in such a case, than I can enlarge upon, or indeed easily enumerate at present; the glory of God, the interest of the deluded sinner, going like a devoted victim, and imprecating vengeance on his own head, as well as the cause itself committed to his care. We have sometimes taken the liberty to forebode the downfall of the British empire, from the corruption and degeneracy of the people. Unhappily the British soldiers have been distinguished among all the nations in Europe, for the most shocking profanity. Shall we then pretend to emulate them in this internal distinction, or rob them of the horrid privilege? God forbid. Let the officers of the army in every degree remember, that as military subjection, while it lasts, is the most complete of any, it is in their power greatly to restrain, if not wholly to banish, this flagrant enormity.

. . . True religion is nothing else but an inward temper and outward conduct suited to your state and circumstances in providence at any time. And as peace with God and conformity to him, adds to the sweetness of created comforts while we possess them, so in times of difficulty and trial, it is in the man of piety and inward principle, that we may expect to find the uncorrupted patriot, the useful citizen, and the invincible soldier. God grant that in America true religion and civil liberty may be inseparable, and that the unjust attempts to destroy the one, may in the issue tend to the support and establishment of both. . . .

Free Exercise

Colonial Americans frequently persecuted members of minority religious sects. The first colonies sponsored religious activities and legally mandated that all persons practice the favored religion. Tolerance was interpreted as evidence of weak religious commitment. Nathaniel Ward asserted, "He that is willing to tolerate any Religion, or discrepant way of Religion, besides his own, unless it be in matters merely indifferent, either doubts of his own, or is not sincere in it."[30]

Government in the seventeenth century had two means for enforcing religious conformity. First, the law compelled persons to attend specific religious services and prohibited the religious practices of rival sects. Virginia in 1611 passed laws requiring all persons to attend church. Massachusetts in the seventeenth century executed alleged witches and confessed Quakers. Second, the colonies imposed secular burdens on members of disfavored religions. Many colonies compelled voters or officeholders to take an oath that they believed in the divinity of Jesus Christ. Some colonies insisted that officeholders swear that they rejected elements of the Catholic faith. One common oath required public officials to declare, "I do believe that there is not any transubstantiation in the Sacrament of the Lord's Supper, or in the Elements of Bread and Wine, at or after the Consecration thereof, by any person whatever."

Proponents of religious toleration criticized these restrictions. The most common attack on religious conformity in the seventeenth century was rooted in religious belief. Roger Williams and John Locke believed that true Christianity was inconsistent with both state support for religion and religious coercion. William Penn, the Quaker who founded the Pennsylvania Colony, maintained that laws requiring religious conformity violated God's law. Penn's essay "The Great Case of Liberty of Conscience" asserted, "the Imposition, Restraint, and Persecution, for Matters relating to Conscience, directly invade the Divine Prerogative, and Divest the Almighty of a Due, proper to none besides himself."[31]

Religious and liberal arguments for the freedom of conscience gained numerous adherents during the Colonial Era. A few colonies, most notably Pennsylvania and Rhode Island, rejected all explicit legal burdens on religious exercise. Others colonies passed laws that either lightened the burdens on members of disfavored religions or increased the number of sects whose practices were tolerated. The Maryland Toleration Act of 1649 declared that all forms of Christian worship were legal. By the middle of the eighteenth century, most persons in the colonies no longer feared for their lives when they practiced their religion privately.

30. Nathaniel Ward, *The Simple Cobler of Aggawam in America* (Salem, MA: Salem Press Company, 1906), 8.

31. William Penn, *The Select Works of William Penn*, 3rd ed. (London: James Phillips, 1782), 12.

Maryland Toleration Act (1649)[32]

Maryland was originally founded as a safe haven for Catholics, who faced significant persecution in England. The Calvert family, who secured the colonial charter from King Charles I, hoped that Maryland would be a place where Catholics and Protestants could live peacefully together. The Maryland Toleration Act expressed this hope. The measure was the first statutory enactment protecting freedom of conscience in Anglo-American history. The Toleration Act was short-lived. The ordinance was repealed within ten years, revived, and then permanently abandoned by the end of the seventeenth century. In the early eighteenth century the Maryland legislature established the Church of England and prohibited Catholics from voting or holding office.

When reading the Maryland Toleration Act, notice what is tolerated and what is not tolerated. What is the difference between acceptable and unacceptable religious behavior? How would Marylanders in the seventeenth century justify that distinction? What are the differences between the Maryland Toleration Act and the understanding of toleration proposed by William Penn or Roger Williams?

. . .

That whatsoever person or persons within this Province and the Islands thereunto belonging shall from henceforth blaspheme God, that is Curse him, or deny our Saviour Jesus Christ to be the son of God, or shall deny the holy Trinity the father son and holy Ghost, or the Godhead of any of the said Three persons of the Trinity or the Unity of the Godhead, or shall use or utter any reproachful Speeches, words or language concerning the said Holy Trinity, or any of the said three persons thereof, shall be punished with death and confiscation or forfeiture of all his or her lands and goods to the Lord Proprietary and his heires.

. . .

And be it further likewise Enacted by the Authority and consent aforesaid That every person and persons within this Province that shall at any time hereafter prophane the Sabbath or Lords day called Sunday by frequent swearing, drunkennes or by any uncivil or disorderly recreation, or by working on that day when absolute necessity doth not require it shall for every such first offence forfeit 2s 6d sterling or the value thereof, and for the second offence 5s sterling or the value thereof, and for the third offence and soe for every time he shall offend in like manner afterwards 10s sterling or the value thereof. . . .

And whereas the enforcing of the conscience in matters of Religion hath frequently fallen out to be of dangerous Consequence in those commonwealthes where it hath been practised, And for the more quiet and peaceable governement of this Province, and the better to preserve mutual Love and amity amongst the Inhabitants thereof, Be it Therefore also by the Lord Proprietary with the advise and consent of this Assembly Ordeyned and enacted . . . that no person or persons whatsoever within this Province, or the Islands, Ports, Harbors, Creekes, or havens thereunto belonging professing to believe in Jesus Christ, shall from henceforth be any ways troubled, Molested or discountenanced for or in respect of his or her religion nor in the free exercise thereof within this Province or the Islands thereunto belonging nor any way compelled to the belief or exercise of any other Religion against his or her consent, so as they be not unfaithful to the Lord Proprietary, or molest or conspire against the civil Governement established or to be established in this Province under him or his heirs. And that all and every person and persons that shall presume Contrary to this Act and the true intent and meaning thereof directly or indirectly either in person or estate willfully to wrong, disturb, trouble or molest any person whatsoever within this Province professing to believe in Jesus Christ or in respect of his or her religion or the free exercise thereof within this Province other than is provided for in this Act that such person or persons so offending, shall be compelled to pay treble damages to the party so wronged or molested, . . . or if the partie so offending as aforesaid shall refuse or be unable to recompense the party so wronged . . . then such Offender shall be severely punished by public whipping and imprisonment. . . .

Legal Exemptions for Religious Believers

As the colonies became more tolerant, new questions arose about whether the freedom of conscience entitled religious believers to exemptions from some secular duties. In one view, persons enjoy religious freedom as long as no laws explicitly prohibit their religion or impose secular burdens on persons who practice

32. Excerpted from *A Law of Maryland Concerning Religion* (London: 1690).

their religion. In his *Letter Concerning Toleration*, Locke insisted that religious believers had an obligation to obey laws that had legitimate secular reasons. He believed that the freedom of religion is violated only by such laws as "No one shall attend midnight mass" or "No Jew shall hold land or be a member of the state legislature." In another view, persons enjoy religious freedoms only when the laws do not impose unnecessary burdens on their religious practice. Religious people ought to be exempt from secular laws unless an exemption would pose serious social harms. Proponents of this view claim that the freedom of religion is violated by such laws as "No person under eighteen shall be allowed to drink alcohol" if that law does not permit children to drink small amounts of wine during religious ceremonies.

The most important political controversy that tested the meaning of religious toleration in colonial America was over whether Quakers and other religious pacifists should be required to perform military service. Many colonies and towns passed laws requiring all men (or all white men) to serve in the local militia. These measures promoted self-defense, a secular governmental purpose. Relationships with Native American tribes in many colonies were tense. A French invasion was possible. Quakers and other religious pacifists claimed exemptions from these laws because they believed that God forbade all military action. Laws requiring religious believers to behave in ways they believed forbidden by divine sanction, Quakers and their supporters maintained, violated the freedom of conscience.

Conflicts over whether religious pacifists should have an exemption from military service were particularly intense in Pennsylvania.[33] The Quaker founders of the Pennsylvania Colony insisted that the state have no militia. As more non-Quakers settled Pennsylvania, they complained that the anti-militia policy was both an establishment of the Quaker sect and a foolish policy in light of Native American and French threats to the western part of the state. In response to these demands Benjamin Franklin proposed that the state establish a militia, but that military service be voluntary. His letter to the state legislature insisted that granting religious exemptions was the only policy that satisfied all the rights of religious conscience at stake in the controversy over militia service.

> Whereas this Province was first settled by . . . the People called Quakers, who, though they do not, as the World is now circumstanced, condemn the Use of Arms in others, yet are principled against bearing Arms themselves; and to make any Law to compel them thereto against their Consciences, would not only be to violate a Fundamental in our Constitution, and be a direct Breach of our Charter of Privileges, but would also in Effect be to commence Persecution against all that Part of the Inhabitants of the Province: And for them by any Law to compel others to bear Arms, and exempt themselves, would be inconsistent and partial. Yet forasmuch as by the general Toleration and Equity of our Laws, great Numbers of People of other religious Denominations are come among us, who are under no such Restraint, some of whom have been disciplined in the Art of War, and conscientiously think it their Duty to fight in Defense of their Country, their Wives, their Families and Estates, and such have an equal Right to Liberty of Conscience with others. . . . And whereas the Governor hath frequently recommended it to the Assembly, that in preparing and passing a Law for such Purposes, they should have a due Regard to scrupulous and tender Consciences, which cannot be done where compulsive Means are used to force Men into Military Service; therefore as we represent all the People of the Province, and are composed of Members of different religious Persuasions, we do not think it reasonable that any should, through a Want of legal Powers, be in the least restrained from doing what they judge it their Duty to do for their own Security and the Public Good.[34]

Conflict over the Pennsylvania militia intensified on the eve of the American Revolution. Many Pennsylvanians demanded that the colonial legislature pass a compulsory conscription law. In their view, Quakers should not receive what they believed was special treatment. One pamphlet declared,

33. The material in this paragraph and all quotations not otherwise cited are taken from Ellis M. West, "The Right to Religion-Based Exemptions in Early America: The Case of Conscientious Objection to Conscription," *Journal of Law and Religion* 10, no. 2 (1993/94): 367–401.

34. Benjamin Franklin, *The Works of Benjamin Franklin*, ed. Jared Sparks, rev. ed. (Philadelphia: Childs & Peterson, 1840), 3: 78–80.

> We cannot alter the Opinion we have ever held with Regard to those parts of the Charter [granting religious freedom] . . . , that they relate only to an Exemption from any Acts of Uniformity in Worship, and from paying towards the Support of other religious Establishments, than those to which the Inhabitants of this Province respectively belong. We know of no Distinctions of Sects, when we meet our Fellow Citizens on Matters of Public Concern, and ask those conscientiously scrupulous against bearing Arms, to contribute toward the Experience of our Opposition, not because of their *religious Persuasion*, but because the general Defence of the Province demands it.

Prominent Quakers insisted that such measures violated their religious freedoms. One resolution insisted that the "liberty of conscience . . . was not limited to the Acts of Public Worship only." "To wrest the Enjoyment of the Same from any Body," other Quakers declared, "must be Sacrilege [and e]xcite divine Vengeance, and must be void in Effect." The matter was finally resolved just before Americans declared independence. In 1776 the Pennsylvania state legislature passed a law that permitted Quakers and others not to serve in the militia as long as they paid a sum of money to the state.

C. GUNS

English subjects and American colonists believed that they had a right to be armed. The English Bill of Rights asserted, "The subjects which are Protestants may have arms for their defence suitable to their conditions and as allowed by law." Blackstone claimed that the right of self-defense entailed the right to bear arms. His *Commentaries* declared that Englishmen had the right "of having arms for their defense, suitable to their condition and degree, and such as are allowed by law." This liberty, Blackstone continued, "under due restrictions," was derived from "the natural right of resistance and self-preservation, when the sanctions of society and laws are found insufficient to restrain the violence of oppression."[35] John Adams, when defending the soldiers accused of the Boston Massacre, stated, "The inhabitants had a right to arm themselves at that time, for their defence."[36]

This right to bear arms was often derived from a civic obligation to serve in the local militia. Most Americans on the eve of the Revolution believed that the community was best defended by an armed citizenry, not a professional army. One contemporary commentator observes, "Citizens had both a right and an obligation to arm themselves so that they might participate in a militia."[37] Pennsylvania was one of many jurisdictions that linked gun rights and opposition to a standing army. The first state constitution stated, "The people have a right to bear arms for the defense of themselves and the state; and as standing armies in the time of peace are dangerous to liberty, they ought not be kept up." Consistent with this obligation, some communities required men of a certain age to maintain weapons in good condition and prohibited persons not eligible for militia service, such as free persons of color, from bearing arms.

Both English and colonial practice suggest that the right to bear arms might serve three other important purposes besides militia service. The first was protection. Life on the American frontier was dangerous. Colonists believed that arms were needed to thwart attacks from Native Americans and common criminals. Thomas Jefferson anticipated claims made by many contemporary proponents of gun rights when he asserted, "Laws forbidding people to bear arms are of this nature; they only disarm those who are neither inclined nor determined to commit crimes and political tyrants."[38] Colonists wanted protection against vicious rulers. "It is a natural right which the people have reserved to themselves, confirmed by the [English] Bill of Rights," the *New York Journal* stated in 1769, "to keep arms for their own defense."[39] Other colonists maintained that weapons were necessary means for hunting, a vital source of food in early America. Joyce Lee Malcolm notes that riots took place in seventeenth-century England when laws aiming to prevent the killing of too many wild animals disarmed English citizens.[40]

35. Blackstone, *Commentaries*, 1:139.

36. Frederic Kidder and John Adams, *History of the Boston Massacre, March 5, 1770* (Albany, NY: Joel Munsell, 1870), 237.

37. Saul Cornell, *A Well-Regulated Militia: The Founding Fathers and the Origins of Gun Control in America* (New York: Oxford University Press, 2006), 17.

38. Thomas Jefferson, *The Commonplace Book of Thomas Jefferson*, ed. Gilbert Chinard (Baltimore, MD: Johns Hopkins University Press, 1926), 314.

39. *New York Journal*, April 13, 1769, at 1, col. 3.

40. Joyce Lee Malcolm, *To Keep and Bear Arms: The Origins of an Anglo-American Right* (Cambridge, MA: Harvard University Press, 1994), 11–15.

D. Personal Freedom and Public Morality

Governing authorities during the colonial era believed that the state should regulate morality. "Adultery, fornication, uncleanliness, lasciviousness, idolatry, and such-like things" were among the "immoralities" that John Locke in his *Letter Concerning Toleration* urged government to "root out."[41] Blackstone maintained that government should prosecute "open and notorious lewdness: either by frequenting houses of ill fame, . . . or by some grossly scandalous and public indecency," as well as drunkenness. These were offenses against "religion and morality." The *Commentaries* also stated that abortion performed after quickening was a crime. "Life is the immediate gift of God," Blackstone wrote,

> a right inherent by nature in every individual; and it begins in contemplation of law as soon as an infant is able to stir in the mother's womb. For if a woman is quick with child, and by a potion, or otherwise, kills it in her womb; or if any one beat her, whereby the child dies in her body, and she is delivered of a dead child; this, though not murder, was by the ancient law homicide or manslaughter. But at present it is not looked upon in quite so atrocious a light, though it remains a very heinous misdemeanor.[42]

Two hundred years later, pro-choice activists noted that Blackstone said nothing about abortion before quickening. This is correct, but neither Blackstone nor any other common law authority maintained that persons had a right to terminate a pregnancy at any time. Blackstone did recognize a right to marry if at the time when the marriage contract was made the persons involved were willing to contract, able to contract, and did contract to marry according to existing legal rules.[43]

Prominent persons living in the seventeenth and eighteenth centuries thought that laws regulating morality served two public purposes. The first was religious. Blackstone and other proponents of the union of church and state insisted that Christian commonwealths prohibit such Christian sins as gambling, drunkenness, and the expression of sexuality outside of marriage. The second purpose was secular. Republican political thinkers of the time believed that free governments could be maintained only if the citizenry was virtuous. John Witherspoon declared, "Nothing is more certain than that a general profligacy and corruption of manners make a people ripe for destruction." This virtue could be maintained only if the laws prevented persons from gambling and limited human sexuality to traditional marriage. Many republicans also worried about the population's military prowess. Morality laws, Locke believed, were necessary to "increase" the "inward strength" of the society "against foreign invasions."

Political and legal commentary in the Colonial Era nevertheless planted some seeds for the development of greater individual choice on moral matters. Locke and Blackstone emphasized that government could regulate individual behavior only when doing so advanced the public good. Blackstone wrote,

> Political therefore, or civil, liberty . . . is no other than natural liberty so far restrained by human laws (and no farther) as is necessary and expedient for the general advantage of the public. Hence we may collect that the law, which restrains a man from doing mischief to his fellow citizens, though it diminishes the natural, increases the civil liberty of mankind: but every wanton and causeless restraint of the will of the subject, whether practiced by a monarch, a nobility, or a popular assembly, is a degree of tyranny. Nay, that even laws themselves, whether made with or without our consent, if they regulate and constrain our conduct in matters of mere indifference, without any good end in view, are laws destructive of liberty: whereas if any public advantage can arise from observing such precepts, the control of our private inclinations, in one or two particular points, will conduce to preserve our general freedom in others of more importance; by supporting that state, of society, which alone can secure our independence.[44]

Locke suggested that individuals might have quite broad privacy rights on matters that Blackstone described as "matters of mere indifference." Locke's *Letter Concerning Toleration* argued that government

41. Locke, *A Letter Concerning Toleration*, 8.

42. Blackstone, *Commentaries*, 1:125–26.

43. Blackstone, *Commentaries*, 1:421.

44. Blackstone, *Commentaries*, 1:121–22.

should not prohibit self-regarding acts, acts that have no consequences to other people.

> Laws provide, as much as is possible, that the goods and health of subjects be not injured by the fraud and violence of others; they do not guard them from the negligence or ill-husbandry of the possessors themselves. No man can be forced to be rich or healthful whether he will or no. Nay, God Himself will not save men against their wills. . . . But now, if I be marching on with my utmost vigour in that way which, according to the sacred geography, leads straight to Jerusalem, why am I beaten and ill-used by others because, perhaps, I wear not buskins; because my hair is not of the right cut; because, perhaps, I have not been dipped in the right fashion; because I eat flesh upon the road, or some other food which agrees with my stomach; because I avoid certain by-ways, which seem unto me to lead into briars or precipices; because, amongst the several paths that are in the same road, I choose that to walk in which seems to be the straightest and cleanest; because I avoid to keep company with some travellers that are less grave and others that are more sour than they ought to be; or, in fine, because I follow a guide that either is, or is not, clothed in white, or crowned with a mitre?[45]

Both Blackstone and Locke were firmly convinced that gambling, promiscuity, and similar acts harmed the public. When, however, some Americans came to the conclusion that these were actually "matters of mere indifference," they could point to seventeenth- and eighteenth-century legal sources for arguments that these morality laws violated individual rights.

IV. Democratic Rights

MAJOR DEVELOPMENTS

- No prior restraints on free speech
- Debate over seditious libel, the crime of criticizing the government
- Property restrictions on voting and officeholding
- Citizenship and allegiance determined by place of birth

45. Locke, *A Letter Concerning Toleration*, 28.

The American regime during the Colonial Era began making the transition from a monarchy to a republic. In a monarchy, kings and nobles rule over their subjects. Power is inherited and, in this period, rooted in divine sanction. King George III was entitled to rule England because he was the eldest son of King George II and because God authorized his family, the Hanovers, to rule the land. Subjects who criticized the king or his chosen ministers undermined the public peace and challenged divine authority. In a republic, representatives govern citizens. Power is gained through election and rooted in the consent of the people. Patrick Henry had the right to cast a vote in the Virginia House of Burgesses because he was elected as a representative by his fellow citizens. Citizens who criticized their representatives were simply engaging in self-government.

None of the colonies were pure republican regimes on the eve of the American Revolution. Until the Declaration of Independence, Americans acknowledged the authority of the king of England. Voting and speech rights were limited. No colony met contemporary democratic standards, even when considering only the status of white men. Instead, the leading champions of republican government during the mid-eighteenth century hoped to establish a more natural aristocracy. This natural aristocracy would foster government by the most virtuous citizens rather than government by people who happened to be born into noble families. Prominent American elites regarded free speech and voting rights as a means for helping society identify those persons who could best govern. This desire to create a "republic of virtue" explains popular limits on participation rights. All colonies restricted voting to property holders on the ground that poorer citizens lacked the independence and capacities necessary to identify and select the best rulers. In colonial America, the liberty to speak did not include a license to say anything about any topic. Persons had to prove they spoke the truth with good motives. Unsurprisingly, Americans who criticized the distant English Parliament found this standard easier to meet than Americans who criticized members of the local legislature.

As you read the materials in this section, consider the extent to which Americans during the Colonial Era made the transition from a monarchical society to a republican one. How did prominent colonists in 1750 justify the rights they thought most important for republican government? What are the differences between the political rights colonial elites asserted and the political rights claimed by contemporary American citizens?

A. Free Speech

The Colonial Era witnessed frequent controversies over free speech in both Great Britain and the Americas. The most important disputes were over who determined what speech could be restricted. During the seventeenth century English legal authorities debated whether persons should be permitted to publish books or pamphlets freely, or if they should be required to first obtain a license from the king or a representative of the throne. During the eighteenth century American colonists debated whether a judge or a jury should determine whether an author was guilty of criminal libel.

Free speech disputes concerned the opinions persons could express as well as which governing officials could limit speech. English common law recognized the crime of seditious libel, or speaking ill of the king or government. Truth was not a defense against this charge. Eighteenth-century proponents of free speech in both England and the colonies sought greater protection for expression rights. In their view, persons had the right to criticize government officials as long as they spoke truthfully and with good motives.

Prior Restraint. The first major free speech controversy in Anglo-American history concerned the Licensing Acts of 1643 and 1662. These measures required all persons to obtain official permission before publishing any material. The crucial provision of the Licensing Act of 1662 declared: "No private person . . . shall at any time hereafter print . . . any Book or Pamphlet . . . unless the same Book or Pamphlet . . . shall be first lawfully licensed and authorized to be printed." A licenser approving a book for publication had to attest that the manuscript did not criticize Christianity or the government. Licensers or censors did not have to provide an official explanation when they refused to give a book or pamphlet their (literal) stamp of approval. If a king's minister found a children's book such as *Pat the Bunny* to be offensively sweet, he could refuse to issue a license. Authors who published unlicensed books would be imprisoned.

Prominent English political thinkers and writers vigorously protested the licensing laws. John Milton, the author of *Paradise Lost*, wrote the most famous attack on this form of censorship. His pamphlet *Areopatigica* (1644) is the seminal statement in Anglo-American history on the importance of free speech rights. Milton emphasized the value of free speech for discovering truths. The pamphlet's best-known passage states, "Though all the winds of doctrine were let loose to play upon the earth, so Truth be in the field, we do injuriously by licensing and prohibiting to misdoubt her strength. Let her and Falsehood grapple; who ever knew Truth put to the worse in a free and open encounter?"[46]

Milton and other critics of the licensing laws were successful in their resistance. When the Licensing Act expired in 1694, Parliament refused to renew it. By the middle of the eighteenth century both English and American authorities agreed that freedom of the press meant that government could not pass what became known as prior restraints on speech. A prior restraint is an official action that forbids a person from either publishing or uttering some opinion. If Congress passes a law that requires persons speaking about pollution to first obtain the permission of the Environmental Protection Agency, that is a prior restraint on speech. If Congress passes a law imposing a $500 fine on any person who publishes a book on the environment, however, that law is not a prior restraint on speech. The rule against prior restraints forbids government efforts to *prevent* speech, not government efforts to punish people for speaking.

Prominent legal authorities on the eve of the American Revolution insisted that the right to free speech was limited to this right against prior restraint. William Blackstone took this position in his *Commentaries*:

> The liberty of the press is indeed essential to the nature of a free state: but this consists in laying no previous restraints upon publications, and not in freedom from censure for criminal matter when published. Every freeman has an undoubted right to lay what sentiments he pleases before the public: to forbid this, is to destroy the freedom of the press: but if he publishes what is improper, mischievous, or illegal, he must take the consequence of his own temerity. To subject the press to the restrictive power of a licenser, as was formerly done, . . . is to subject all freedom of sentiment to the prejudices of one man, and make him the arbitrary and

46. John Milton, *Areopagitica* (London: A. Millar, 1738), 51.

> infallible judge of all controverted points in learning, religion, and government. But to punish (as the law does at present) any dangerous or offensive writings, which, when published, shall on a fair and impartial trial be adjudged of a pernicious tendency, is necessary for the preservation of peace and good order, of government and religion, the only solid foundations of civil liberty. Thus the will of individuals is still left free; the abuse only of that free will hereby laid upon freedom, of thought or enquiry: liberty of private sentiment is still left; the disseminating, or making public, of bad sentiments, destructive of the ends of society, is the crime which society corrects.[47]

When reading this passage, consider why Blackstone believes that prior restraints are wrong, but that government should be free to punish any harmful speech after publication. Are juries and judges better able to determine harm than executive officials?

Seditious Libel. Blackstone and most eighteenth-century English lawyers believed that government had the power to punish any speech that had a "pernicious tendency." They had no doubt that government could aggressively punish seditious libel, the crime of criticizing the king, the government, or government officials. Such criticisms, whether true or false, were thought to threaten the public peace and undermine the political order. Blackstone wrote,

> [L]ibels . . . are malicious defamations of any person, and especially a magistrate, [that] provoke him to wrath, or expose him to public hatred, contempt, and ridicule. The direct tendency of these libels is the breach of the public peace, by stirring up the objects of them to revenge, and perhaps to bloodshed. . . . [I]t is immaterial with respect to the essence of a libel, whether the matter of it be true or false; since the provocation, and not the falsity, is the thing to be punished criminally. . . . [I]n a criminal prosecution, the tendency which all libels have to create animosities, and to disturb the public peace, is the sole consideration of the law. And therefore, in such prosecutions, the only facts to be considered are, first, the making or publishing of the book or writing; and secondly, whether the matter be criminal: and, if both these points are against the defendant, the offence against the public is complete.[48]

Seditious libel had two crucial elements. First, truth was not a defense against the charge. A prosecutor who demonstrated that a printer had published an essay that was critical of the government had proved seditious libel. Second, the jury decided only whether the defendant had published the offending work. Judges determined whether the work was defamatory, a criticism of the government or a government official.

Prominent English dissenters and many American colonists criticized the crime of seditious libel, with John Trenchard and Thomas Gordon being the most notable critics. Writing under the pseudonym "Cato," they published more than one hundred essays between 1720 and 1723 attacking what they perceived to be the increasing corruption of English politics. Their most influential essay, "Of Freedom of Speech," contended that seditious libel was inconsistent with English freedom.

> Without freedom of thought, there can be no such thing as wisdom; and no such thing as public liberty, without freedom of speech: Which is the right of every man, as far as by it he does not hurt and control the right of another; and this is the only check which it ought to suffer, the only bounds which it ought to know.
>
> . . .
>
> That men ought to speak well of their governors, is true, while their governors deserve to be well spoken of; but to do public mischief, without hearing of it, is only the prerogative and felicity of tyranny: A free people will be showing that they are so, by their freedom of speech.
>
> The administration of government is nothing else, but the attendance of the trustees of the people upon the interest and affairs of the people. And as it is the part and business of the people, for whose sake alone all public matters are, or ought to be, transacted, to see whether they be well or ill transacted; so it is the interest, and ought to be the ambition, of all honest magistrates, to have their deeds openly examined, and publicly scanned.[49]

47. Blackstone, *Commentaries*, 5:151–52.

48. Blackstone, *Commentaries*, 5:149–50.

49. John Trenchard and Thomas Gordon, *Cato's Letters* (London: W. Wilkins, 1723), 1:98.

Trenchard and Gordon had more influence in the colonies than in England. Many colonists regarded their essays as documenting disturbing political trends in Great Britain that threatened American liberties. The essay on freedom of speech was particularly influential. Magistrates who punished good-faith criticisms, colonists thought, were more interested in holding power than in governing for the republican good.

The colonists soon had an opportunity to test the legal meaning of free speech. John Peter Zenger was arrested for seditious libel after he published an article criticizing the royal governor. His lawyer, Andrew Hamilton, relied heavily on "Cato's Letters" when arguing to the jury that persons could not be punished for making true criticisms of government officials. Hamilton was successful: his arguments ultimately convinced the jury to find Zenger not guilty. After the Zenger trial, royal authorities abandoned prosecutions for seditious libel in the colonies.

Free speech rights remained precarious. Persons who criticized unpopular royal governors could trust local juries to find them not guilty. Colonial legislatures, however, often imprisoned for contempt persons who criticized their actions. As a result, when declaring independence, Americans could point to both an emerging tradition of dissent and an ongoing tradition of repression.[50] This tension persisted during the years of the Revolution. Loyalists discovered that they were not nearly as free to criticize popular legislative acts as Zenger was to criticize an unpopular royal governor.

The Open Press (and Commercial Speech). Some scholars contend that colonial printers had different rights and responsibilities than does the contemporary media.[51] Contemporary newspapers wield complete editorial control over what they publish. The *New York Times* is free to decide whether to publish your commentary on the most recent Supreme Court decision. In contrast, many colonial printers did not see themselves as enjoying the same editorial judgment. They saw their press as a public convenience, analogous to a ferry or an inn. Proprietors of all three had an obligation to serve all people willing to pay a reasonable fee for the service and behave responsibly. If someone wished to publish some political commentary and that commentary did not violate the law, the printer was expected to publish it. Benjamin Franklin articulated this position in his *Apology for Printers.* In that commentary, Franklin contended that he had a responsibility to print a wide variety of opinions.

> Printers are educated in the Belief, that when Men differ in Opinion, both Sides ought equally to have the Advantage of being heard by the Publick; and that when Truth and Error have fair Play, the former is always an overmatch for the latter: Hence they chearfully serve all contending Writers that pay them well, without regarding on which side they are of the Question in Dispute.
>
> . . .
>
> Being thus continually employ'd in serving all Parties, Printers naturally acquire a vast Unconcernedness as to the right or wrong Opinions contain'd in what they print; regarding it only as the Matter of their daily labour: They print things full of Spleen and Animosity, with the utmost Calmness and Indifference, and without the least Ill-will to the Persons reflected on; who nevertheless unjustly think the Printer as much their Enemy as the Author, and join both together in their resentment.
>
> That it is unreasonable to imagine Printers approve of every thing they print, and to censure them on any particular thing accordingly; since in the way of their Business they print such great variety of things opposite and contradictory. It is likewise as unreasonable what some assert, That Printers ought not to print any Thing but what they approve; since if all of that Business should make such a Resolution, and abide by it, an End would thereby be put to Free Writing, and the World would afterwards have nothing to read but what happen'd to be the Opinions of Printers.[52]

The *Zenger* Trial (1733–34)[53]

John Peter Zenger was the publisher of the New York Weekly Journal. *From 1733 to 1734 the* Weekly Journal

50. Stephan M. Feldman, *Free Expression and Democracy in America: A History* (Chicago: University of Chicago Press, 2008), 3.

51. Robert W.T. Martin, *The Free and Open Press: The Founding of American Democratic Press Liberty, 1640-1800* (New York: New York University Press, 2001).

52. Benjamin Franklin, *The Autobiography and other Writing on Politics, Economics, and Virtue*, ed. Alan Houston (New York: Cambridge University Press, 2004), 160.

53. Excerpted from John Peter Zenger, *A Brief Narrative of the Case and Trial of John Peter Zenger* (London: 1738).

Illustration 2-2 Andrew Hamilton Defending John Peter Zenger in Court
Source: Library of Congress, Prints and Photographs Division, Washington, DC 20540 USA.

published articles criticizing William Crosby, the royal governor of New York. One essay complained that the people of New York "think, as matters now stand, that their liberties and properties are precarious, and that slavery is likely to be entailed on them and their posterity if some past things be not amended, and this they collect from many past proceedings." That essay was most likely penned by James Alexander, a prominent opponent of the royal government and a patron of the Weekly Journal. *Unable to prove that Alexander wrote the offending articles, Governor Crosby had Zenger arrested and charged with seditious libel.*

Crosby's actions were consistent with early-eighteenth-century legal practice. Seditious libel was the common law crime of bringing the government into contempt. The prosecution had to prove only that the defendant had published material that defamed or criticized a public official. Truth was not a defense. "The greater the truth, the greater the libel," lawyers believed. The trial judge determined whether the publication was defamatory; the jury had only to decide whether the defendant published the offending matter. For these reasons, Zenger had every reason to believe he would be imprisoned. He published the Weekly Journal. *The essays he published were defamatory.*

Zenger's champions insisted that the concept of seditious libel was inconsistent with the freedom of speech. Benjamin Franklin, then publishing a newspaper in Philadelphia, arranged for Zenger to be defended by Andrew Hamilton, a prominent colonial lawyer. At trial, Hamilton urged the jury to find Zenger not guilty if they believed that the Weekly Journal *had published true criticisms of the royal governor. Persons, Hamilton claimed, were free to speak the truth about government as long as they had good motives for raising their concerns. The trial judge, James Delancy, rejected this interpretation of the common law and frequently informed the jury that they were only to determine publication. These instructions seemed to seal Zenger's fate. Nevertheless, the jury came back almost immediately with a verdict of not guilty.*

The Zenger trial was the most important free speech dispute in colonial America. After the verdict was handed down, James Alexander published a widely circulated account of the trial. Many colonial Americans agreed with Hamilton that truth for good motives could not be prosecuted. Nevertheless, official law continued to maintain that publication was the only element of libel. Political dissenters before the Revolution criticized government at their risk.

The Zenger trial highlighted the close connection between the right to a jury and free speech during the eighteenth century. When local juries rather than royally appointed judges determined law, all persons who obtained a jury trial were in practice free to make popular criticisms of governing officials. Not surprisingly, colonists who criticized locally elected officials were less likely to regard the petit jury as a bulwark of freedom.

When you read the excerpts below, compare how the prosecution and defense define free speech. What reasons does each give for its broader and narrower conceptions of that right? Who should decide the meaning of free speech? What are the advantages and disadvantages of having juries determine that law?

Case for the Prosecution (RICHARD BRADLEY)

. . . [L]ibeling has always been discouraged as a thing that tends to create differences among men, ill blood among the people, and oftentimes great bloodshed between the party libeling and the party libeled.

. . .

. . . [A]s Mr. Hamilton has confessed the printing and publishing of these libels, I think the jury must find a verdict for the king. For supposing they were true, the law says that they are not the less libelous for that. Nay, indeed the law says their being true is an aggravation of the crime.

. . .

. . . That by government we were protected in our lives, religion, and properties; and for these reasons great care had always been taken to prevent everything that might tend to scandalize magistrates and others concerned in the administration of the government, especially the supreme magistrate. And that there were many instances of very severe judgments, and of punishments, inflicted upon such as had attempted to bring the government into contempt by publishing false and scurrilous libels against it, or by speaking evil and scandalous words of men in authority, to the great disturbance of the public peace. . . .

. . . [L]ibel [is] a malicious defamation of any person, expressed either in printing or writing, signs or pictures, to asperse the reputation of one that is alive, or the memory of one that is dead. If he is a private man, the libeler deserves a severe punishment, but if it is against a magistrate or other public person, it is a greater offense. For this concerns not only the breach of the peace but the scandal of the government. What greater scandal of government can there be than to have corrupt or wicked magistrates appointed by the king to govern his subjects? A greater imputation to the state there cannot be than to suffer such corrupt men to sit in the sacred seat of justice, or to have any meddling in or concerning the administration of justice. . . .

. . .

Mr. HAMILTON: Summation for Zenger

. . .

. . . [I]t is natural, it is a privilege, I will go farther, it is a right, which all free men claim, that they are entitled to complain when they are hurt. They have a right publicly to remonstrate against the abuses of power in the strongest terms, to put their neighbors upon their guard against the craft or open violence of men in authority, and to assert with courage the sense they have of the blessings of liberty, the value they put upon it, and their resolution at all hazards to preserve it as one of the greatest blessings heaven can bestow.

. . .

But to proceed. I beg leave to insist that the right of complaining or remonstrating is natural; that the restraint upon this natural right is the law only; and that those restraints can only extend to what is false. For as it is truth alone that can excuse or justify any man for complaining of a bad administration, I as frankly agree that nothing ought to excuse a man who raises a false charge or accusation even against a private person, and that no manner of allowance ought to be made to him who does so against a public magistrate.

Truth ought to govern the whole affair of libels. And yet the party accused runs risk enough even then; for if he fails in proving every title of what he has written, and to the satisfaction of the court and jury too, he may find to his cost that when the prosecution is set on foot by men in power it seldom wants friends to favor it.

. . .

There is heresy in law as well as in religion, and both have changed very much. We well know that it is not two centuries ago that a man would have been burned as a heretic for owning such opinions in matters of religion as are publicly written and printed at this day. They were fallible men, it seems, and we take the liberty not only to differ from them in religious opinions, but to condemn them and their opinions too. I must presume that in taking these freedoms in thinking and speaking about matters of faith or religion, we are in the right; for although it is said that there are very great liberties of this kind taken in New York, yet I have heard of no information preferred by Mr. Attorney for any offenses of this sort. From which I think it is pretty clear that in New York a man may make very free with his God, but he must take a special care what he says of his governor.

It is agreed upon by all men that this is a reign of liberty. While men keep within the bounds of truth I hope they may with safety both speak and write their sentiments of the conduct of men in power, I mean of that part of their conduct only which affects the liberty or property of the people under their administration. Were this to be denied, then the next step may make them slaves; for what notions can be entertained of slavery beyond that of suffering the greatest injuries and oppressions without the liberty of complaining, or if they do, to be destroyed, body and estate, for so doing?

It is said and insisted on by Mr. Attorney that government is a sacred thing; that it is to be supported and reverenced; that it is government that protects our persons and estates, prevents treasons, murders, robberies, riots, and all the train of evils that overturns kingdoms and states and ruins particular persons. And if those in the administration, especially the supreme magistrate, must have all their conduct censured by private men, government cannot subsist. This is called a licentiousness not to be tolerated. It is said that it brings the rulers of the people into contempt, and their authority not to be regarded, and so in the end the laws cannot be put into execution.

These, I say, and such as these, are the general topics insisted upon by men in power and their advocates. But I wish it might be considered at the same time how often it has happened that the abuse of power has been the primary cause of these evils, and that it was the injustice and oppression of these great men that has commonly brought them into contempt with the people. The craft and art of such men is great, and who that is the least acquainted with history or law can be ignorant of the specious pretenses that have often been made use of by men in power to introduce arbitrary rule, and to destroy the liberties of a free people?

. . .

Gentlemen: The danger is great in proportion to the mischief that may happen through our too great credulity. A proper confidence in a court is commendable, but as the verdict, whatever it is, will be yours, you ought to refer no part of your duty to the discretion of other persons. If you should be of the opinion that there is no falsehood in Mr. Zenger's papers, you will, nay pardon me for the expression, you ought, to say so—because you do not know whether others—I mean the Court—may be of that opinion. It is your right to do so, and there is much depending upon your resolution as well as upon your integrity.

But to conclude: the question before the Court and you, Gentlemen of the jury, is not of small or private concern. It is not the cause of one poor printer, nor of New York alone, which you are now trying. No! It may in its consequence affect every free man that lives under a British government on the main of America. It is the best cause. It is the cause of liberty. And I make no doubt but your upright conduct this day will not only entitle you to the love and esteem of your fellow citizens, but every man who prefers freedom to a life of slavery will bless and honor you as men who have baffled the attempt of tyranny, and by an impartial and uncorrupt verdict have laid a noble foundation for securing to ourselves, our posterity, and our neighbors, that to which nature and the laws of our country have given us a right—the liberty both of exposing and opposing arbitrary power (in these parts of the world at least) by speaking and writing truth.

B. VOTING

The right to vote in the colonies varied by community and by election. The king appointed the royal governor in most colonies and the royal governor often appointed judges. As was the case in England, membership in the legislature was determined by election. As was also the case in England, the franchise was sharply limited.

Property requirements were common in both England and the colonies. Persons without property were thought to lack the necessary independence and virtues for exercising the suffrage. Blackstone asserted,

> The true reason of requiring any qualification, with regard to property, in voters, is to exclude such persons as are in so mean a situation that they are

> esteemed to have no will of their own. If these persons had votes, they would be tempted to dispose of them under some undue influence or other. This would give a great, an artful, or a wealthy man, a larger share in elections than is consistent with general liberty. If it were probable that every man would give his vote freely and without influence of any kind, then, upon the true theory and genuine principles of liberty, every member of the community, however poor, should have a vote in electing those delegates, to whose charge is committed the disposal of his property, his liberty, and his life. But, since that can hardly be expected in persons of indigent fortunes, or such as are under the immediate dominion of others, all popular states have been obliged to establish certain qualifications; whereby some, who are suspected to have no will of their own, are excluded from voting, in order to set other individuals, whose wills may be supposed independent, more thoroughly upon a level with each other.[54]

Property qualifications determined those persons who were eligible to be elected to the colonial legislature. Many colonies enacted onerous property qualifications for membership in the upper house of the local legislature and somewhat less restrictive property qualifications for membership in the lower house.

Colonists were often disenfranchised on the basis of gender, race, or religion. Most colonies disenfranchised women, although women did vote in some elections. Most, but not all, southern colonies limited the ballot to white persons. Religious restrictions were common. Catholics were deprived of the vote in five colonies. Jews were disenfranchised in four. Some colonies required officeholders to swear a religious oath that effectively barred most non-Protestants from sitting in the legislature.

C. Citizenship

Most American colonists believed that they were subjects of the English king. The members of the First Continental Congress in 1774 described themselves as "his majesty's loyal subjects." The Virginia resolutions establishing a Committee of Correspondence in 1773 referred to "his Majesty's faithful subjects in this colony." The American colonists were subjects of the king according to the common law, because they were born in the king's dominions or naturalized. This principle that birth determines allegiance was famously articulated in *Calvin's Case* (1608), in which Chief Judge Edward Coke asserted that any person born in England or an English territory was a subject of the king of England. The common law permitted persons to renounce that allegiance only with the permission of the king.

English subjects had rights as well as responsibilities. A person born in England or English territory, *Calvin's Case* held, enjoyed all the rights of Englishmen. Americans seized on this common law principle when tensions with Great Britain began to mount. The colonists were persons born on English soil who had retained their allegiance to the English king. As such, they had the same rights as persons living in Great Britain.

54. Blackstone, *Commentaries*, 2:169–70.

V. Equality

MAJOR DEVELOPMENTS

- Increased demands for equality under law
- The establishment of slavery in the colonies and the principle *"in favorem libertatis"* in the common law
- Traditional gender roles maintained

Great Britain was not an egalitarian society on the eve of the American Revolution. The king had different rights and responsibilities than the nobility. Nobles had different rights and responsibilities than ordinary people. Men had different rights and responsibilities than women. Protestants had different rights and responsibilities than Catholics. The headings for Blackstone's *Commentaries* capture the various inequalities of the English regime. Different chapters discuss the rights of "Individuals," "the King," "the Military," "Master and Servant," and "Husband and Wife." Blackstone never speaks of any person having a right to be treated equally with other persons. The rights of persons in eighteenth-century England depended on their status, and that status was often determined at birth. Arbitrary rule was common and accepted. The king could shower gifts upon court favorites without having to explain why they were more worthy of government beneficence than others.

American colonists took for granted some long-standing inequalities, rejected others, and added some new forms of status hierarchy. Every colony maintained traditional gender roles. Many, but not all, gave Protestants far more rights than they did Catholics and Jews. The colonists, however, rejected the traditional English aristocracy. When colonial Americans demanded equality before the law, they meant that no person should have special legal rights because they were born to a noble family.

The colonists were less egalitarian than the English when making racial distinctions. English law in the seventeenth and eighteenth centuries did not sharply discriminate against persons of color, in large part because hardly any Africans (or Asians) resided in England. Efforts to establish slavery in England failed, partly because of an important legal decision, *Somerset v. Stewart* (1773), which denied any common law right to hold a person as a slave. The American colonists, in contrast, established slavery by statutory decree during the seventeenth century. By 1750 most Africans residing in the colonies were enslaved. Those who were not enslaved suffered heavy legal disabilities. Prominent Englishmen regarded this combination of anti-aristocratic sentiment and slaveholding as hypocritical. "How is it that we hear the loudest yelps for liberty among the drivers of negroes?" a leading English essayist complained in 1775.[55]

Edmund Morgan suggested possible connections between this anti-aristocratic sentiment and American slavery. He wrote:

> The small planter's small take in human property placed him on the same side of the fence as the large man, whom he regularly elected to protect his interests. Virginia's small farmers could perceive a common identity with the large, because there was one. . . . Neither was a slave. And both were equal in not being slaves.[56]

Is this analysis correct?

55. James Boswell, *Life of Johnson* (London: Henry Frowde, 1904), 2:154.

56. Edmund S. Morgan, *American Slavery, American Freedom: The Ordeal of Colonial Virginia* (New York: W. W. Norton & Co, 1975), 381.

A. Equality Under Law

Colonial Americans understood equality to mean that (1) they should have the same rights as British subjects who resided in England, (2) government should not establish an aristocracy in which nobles acquired special political and legal rights at birth, and (3) government officials should not give special favors to privileged citizens. This "rage for equality" was not universal. Colonial American law governing race, gender, and Native American issues was inegalitarian, to say the least. The initial American demands for equality are best characterized as the demands of the local propertied elite for the same status as the native propertied elite in England. Still, egalitarian rhetoric proved hard to restrain. The egalitarian claims made by colonial notables were soon employed by ordinary Americans demanding the same rights and privileges as these notables.

Equal to Other British Subjects. Prominent colonists insisted that the king should not discriminate between residents of Great Britain and Englishmen who resided in the Americas. Thomas Jefferson began *A Summary View of the Rights of British America* (1774) by "reminding" King George III "that our ancestors, before their emigration to America, were the free inhabitants of the British dominions in Europe." Instead of experiencing "equal and impartial legislation," Jefferson complained, the colonists were the victims of "arbitrary acts." Parliamentary edicts repeatedly denied the colonists rights and privileges possessed by persons residing in England. *A Summary View* insisted that such policies violated the equal rights of American colonists in one of two ways: "Either . . . justice is not the same in America as in Britain," Jefferson stated, "or else . . . the British parliament pays less regard to it here than there." Jefferson concluded the pamphlet by insisting that all American grievances could be resolved if Parliament recognized that English residents of the colonies had the same rights as English residents in Great Britain: "The whole art of government consists in the art of being honest. Only aim to do your duty, and mankind will give you credit where you fail. No longer persevere in sacrificing the rights of one part of the empire to the inordinate desires of another; but deal out to all equal and impartial right."[57]

57. Jefferson, *A Summary View of the Rights of British America*, in *Tracts of the American Revolution* (see note 2), 256–76 passim.

No Nobility. Most foreign observers regarded the colonies as unparalleled egalitarian societies in large part because no American aristocracy ever developed. All eighteenth-century European countries had persons of various noble ranks. These were the barons, dukes, and earls that one encounters in old movies and romance novels. Nobles enjoyed special political and legal privileges. In Great Britain, certain nobles had the right to sit in the House of Lords. Criminal procedure was often different when a lord was on trial. Analogous practices either never existed in the colonies or were soon abandoned. No one had a right to sit in a colonial legislature because of his birth (or because he purchased a title). No one gained any special legal privileges because he was the oldest son of a person with special privileges. The colonial principle of equality under law entitled persons to be judged by their individual characteristics, not by their birth status. Birth status often indirectly influenced rights. If South Carolina had a property qualification for voting and you inherited property from your parents, you could vote. Still, a person who gained the same property holdings through his efforts gained the same right to vote. If you wasted your estate, you would lose the right to vote.

Americans on the eve of the Revolution took pride in their commitment to "a natural aristocracy." In the new world, fame and power reflected virtue, not birth. American colonists condemned a regime in which "all power might center on one family," and in which public office "like a precious jewel will be handed down from father to son."[58] The Virginia Declaration of Rights declared: "No Man or set of Men are entitled to exclusive or separate Emoluments or Privileges from the Community, but in Consideration of public Services; which not being descendible, or hereditary, the Ideal of man born a Magistrate, a Legislator, or a Judge is unnatural and absurd." Equality under law meant equality of opportunity. People were judged by their public services, not by titles gained by distant ancestors.

Patronage. Colonial Americans condemned the increasing practice of patronage in Great Britain, such as government ministers who, in order to gain support for their political programs, either appointed political allies to prominent positions or passed legislation that gave special privileges to specific groups or people. In *A Summary View of the Rights of British America*, Jefferson damned one offensive measure as having "little connection with British convenience, except that of accommodating his majesty's ministers and favourites with the sale of a lucrative and easy office."[59] He and other American leaders regarded such instances of patronage "as 'corruption,' as attempts by great men and their power-hungry minions to promote their private interests at the expense of the public good."[60] Republican ideology demanded that the public good be the only criterion for legislation and other government acts.

Americans soon transformed this eighteenth-century opposition to private-regarding policies into an opposition to "class legislation." The constitutional commitment to equality before the law required that legislation have a public purpose and not, as the hated English laws did, be motivated by the desire to benefit one class of persons (English supporters of George III) at the expense of another (American colonists).

B. Race

Human bondage flourished in the American colonies. Virginians by 1619 were purchasing Africans to work their lands. Whether these workers were initially slaves is not entirely clear. Some historical evidence indicates that the first blacks in the colonies were treated similarly to white indentured servants. By the 1660s colonial law clearly sanctioned slavery. By 1700 every colony had laws mandating permanent enslavement.

The increased colonial commitment to liberal political thought threatened slavery. During the seventeenth and early eighteenth centuries few persons questioned the morality of human bondage. The colonial tendency to rely on liberal notions of natural rights when protesting against various parliamentary edicts, however, inspired some persons to view domestic practices in light of those values. If all persons had a natural right to life, liberty, and property, then slavery was a worse violation of natural law than taxation without representation. Such arguments were more frequently heard in the northern colonies, whose economies depended less on slavery. Many Quakers in the middle South

58. Wood, *The Radicalism of the American Revolution*, 181.

59. Jefferson, *A Summary View*, 263.

60. Wood, *Radicalism*, 174–75.

were also influenced by the beliefs that liberalism and slavery were inconsistent.

The growing anti-slavery movement in England and the colonies received a dramatic boost in 1773 when Lord Mansfield decided *Somerset v. Stewart*. During the seventeenth and eighteenth centuries some merchants imported into England slaves they had purchased in the West Indies or the American colonies. By the 1760s England had a significant black population whose legal status was unclear. *Somerset v. Stewart* resolved that uncertainty. Lord Mansfield insisted that slavery was so odious to basic natural law principles that property in human beings could exist legally only in places where statutory law explicitly stated that one human being could own another. A person claiming a right to hold a slave had to point to an explicit law that legalized slavery. He could not rely on the common law of property or any other common law doctrine. Because Parliament had never passed a law making slavery legal in England, this decision meant that no person could be legally held as a slave in that country.

Somerset had no direct effect on enslaved persons of color in the New World. In 1773 statutes existed in all colonies (and the West Indies) legalizing human bondage. Masters could point to specific rules that entitled them to possess other human beings.

Still, many colonists worried that *Somerset* might undermine American slavery. Consider the problem of fugitive slaves. If a slave from Virginia ran away to New Jersey and New Jersey had no explicit law on the status of fugitive slaves, the principle of *Somerset* suggested that New Jersey should treat that fugitive as free. More generally, *Somerset* suggested that ambiguous statutory and constitutional provisions should be interpreted in a manner consistent with the Latin maxim, "*In favorem libertatis*" ("In favor of liberty"). Judges relying on this principle assume that the law favors freedom unless such an interpretation is impossible. Given the informality of much colonial law, such an interpretive practice had significant emancipatory consequences.

The status of free blacks in colonial America was ambiguous and varied by colony. Most southern colonies enacted regulations sharply restricting the rights of freed slaves or persons of color who were born free. In 1668 Virginia passed laws mandating that free blacks "ought not in all respects . . . be admitted to a full fruition of the exemptions and immunities of the English."[61] Nevertheless, some blacks voted and were considered citizens in some states. Northern colonies placed fewer restrictions on free blacks. Whether this practice reflected a genuine commitment to racial equality or was simply the consequence of blacks being too few in number to attract much legislative concern was for the future to determine.

Somerset v. Stewart, 20 Howell's 1 (1772)

Charles Stewart brought his slave, James Somerset, to England in 1769. Two years later Stewart attempted to ship Somerset back to the West Indies. English abolitionists thwarted this effort by obtaining a writ of habeas corpus on Somerset's behalf. Somerset was being illegally detained, they declared, because slavery did not exist in England.[62]

Lord Mansfield's decision freeing Somerset is one of the most important rulings in Anglo-American judicial history. Abolitionists were thrilled that Mansfield insisted that slavery could exist only by positive law. Somerset *seems to hold that a court must declare an alleged slave free unless a statute clearly mandates enslavement. American abolitionists soon declared that "In favorem libertatis" was both a common law and a constitutional principle.*

Consider the following questions as you read the short paragraph below and later discussions of slavery. What exactly did Somerset *hold? Was the decision the great triumph for freedom that abolitionists proclaimed, or was the ruling narrower? What impact did* Somerset *have on American constitutional law? Is "In favorem libertatis" a constitutional principle? Did that principle survive the abolition of slavery?*

Transcript of LORD MANSFIELD'S Judgment

The cause returned is, the slave absented himself, and departed from his master's service, and refused to return and serve him during his stay in England; whereupon, by his master's orders, he was put on board the ship by force, and there detained in secure custody, to

61. Rogers Smith, *Civic Ideals: Contested Visions of Citizenship in U.S. History* (New Haven: Yale University Press, 1999), 65.

62. For a good discussion of *Somerset*, see George Van Cleve, "Forum: Somerset's Case Revisited: Somerset's Case and Its Antecedents in Imperial Perspective," *Law and History Review* 24, no. 3 (2006).

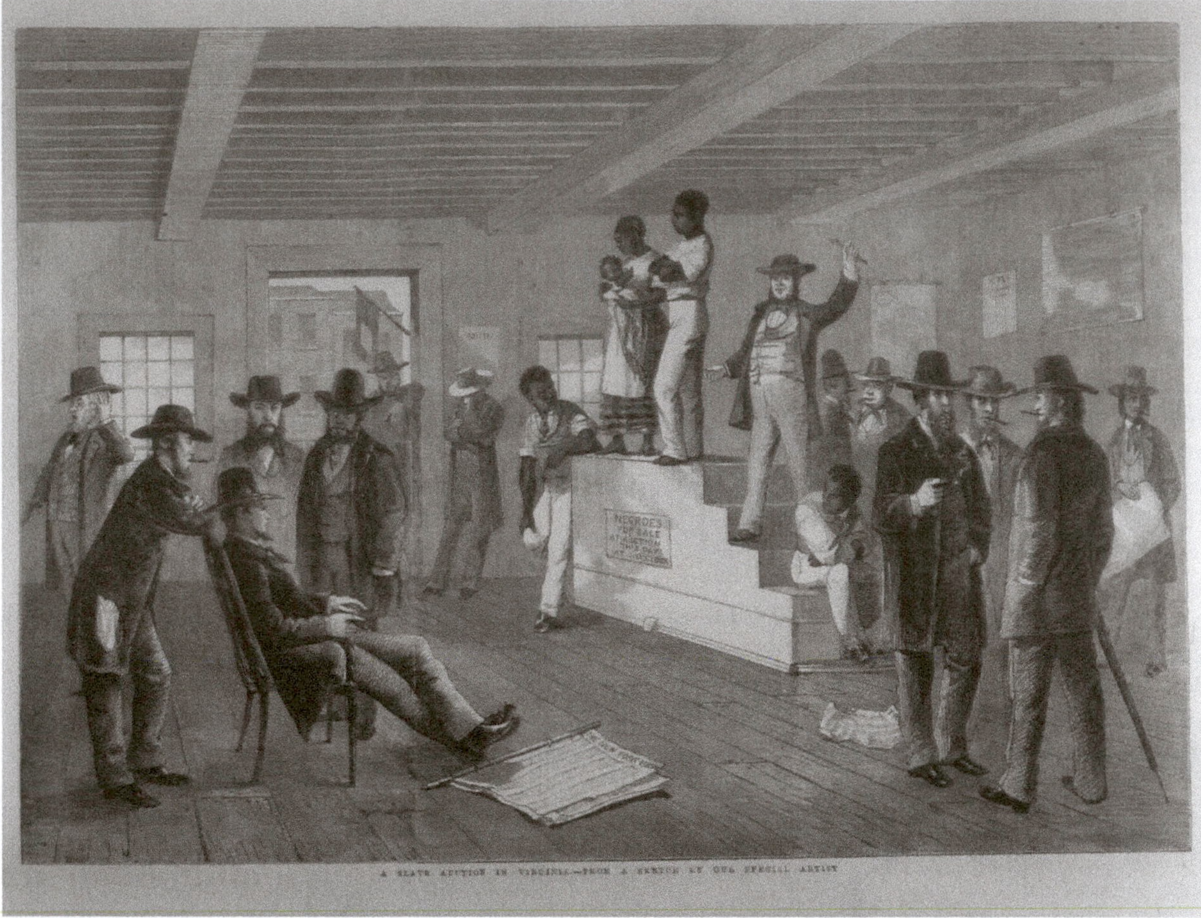

Illustration 2-3 A Slave Auction in Virginia

Source: Illustrated London News, February 16, 1861, Valentine Richmond History Center.

be carried out of the kingdom and sold. So high an act of dominion must derive its authority, if any such it has, from the law of the kingdom where executed. A foreigner cannot be imprisoned here on the authority of any law existing in his own country: the power of a master over his servant is different in all countries, more or less limited or extensive; the exercise of it therefore must always be regulated by the laws of the place where exercised. The state of slavery is of such a nature, that it is incapable of now being introduced by Courts of Justice upon mere reasoning or inferences from any principles, natural or political; it must take its rise from positive law; the origin of it can in no country or age be traced back to any other source: immemorial usage preserves the memory of positive law long after all traces of the occasion; reason, authority, and time of its introduction are lost; and in a case so odious as the condition of slaves must be taken strictly, the power claimed by this return was never in use here; no master ever was allowed here to take a slave by force to be sold abroad because he had deserted from his service, or for any other reason whatever; we cannot say the cause set forth by this return is allowed or approved of by the laws of this kingdom, therefore the man must be discharged.

C. Gender

Men and women had very different legal rights and duties in colonial America. Women in most colonies could not vote, hold public office, engage in most professions, or serve on juries. Women who attempted to engage in traditional male activities were often severely sanctioned. Consider the experience of Anne Hutchinson. Hutchinson, who had religious training, held religious meetings in her house during the 1630s. At these meetings she commented on religious texts and the sermons given in the local Puritan church. For these actions Hutchinson was excommunicated and forced to leave Massachusetts. Her accusers insisted that by commenting on the religious and political affairs of the colony, Hutchinson had "stepped out of [her] place." The charges against her declared, "You have rather been a Husband than a Wife and a preacher than a Hearer, and a Magistrate than a Subject." [63] Another woman who attempted to preach in Puritan Massachusetts was eventually executed for witchcraft.

The most fundamental right of women in colonial America was to decide on a marriage partner. Once that choice was made, the married woman was subordinated to her husband. John Winthrop, the first leader of the Massachusetts Bay Colony, asserted, "The woman's own choice . . . makes . . . a man her husband; yet being so chosen, he is her lord."[64] A husband controlled virtually all of his wife's legal affairs. The common law considered a married woman to be a "feme covert." Blackstone offered the conventional description of this term and the rights of women under common law in his *Commentaries*:

> By marriage, the husband and wife are one person in law: that is, the very being or legal existence of the woman is suspended during the marriage, or at least is incorporated and consolidated into that of the husband: under whose wing, protection, and cover, she performs every thing; and is therefore called in our law-french a feme-covert; is said to be covert-baron, or under the protection and influence of her husband, her baron, or lord; and her condition during her marriage is called her coverture. Upon this principle, of a union of person in husband and wife, depend almost all the legal rights, duties, and disabilities, that either of them acquire by the marriage. . . . For this reason, a man cannot grant any thing to his wife, or enter into covenant with her: for the grant would be to suppose her separate existence: . . . and therefore it is also generally true, that all compacts made between husband and wife, when single, are voided by the intermarriage. . . . The husband is bound to provide his wife with necessaries by law, as much as himself; and if the contracts debts for them, he is obliged to pay them. . . . If the wife be indebted before marriage, the husband is bound afterwards to pay the debt; for he has adopted her and her circumstances together. If the wife be injured in her person or her property, she can bring no action for redress without her husband's concurrence, and in his name, as well as her own: neither can she be sued, without making the husband a defendant. There is indeed one case where the wife shall sue and be sued as a feme sole, viz. where the husband has abjured the realm, or is banished: for then he is dead in law. . . .
>
> . . .
>
> The husband also (by the old law) might give his wife moderate correction. For, as he is to answer for her misbehaviour, the law thought it reasonable to entrust him with this power of restraining her, by domestic chastisement, in the same moderation that a man is allowed to correct his servants or children. . . . But this power of correction was confined within reasonable bounds; and the husband was prohibited to use any violence to his wife. . . .
>
> But, with us, . . . this power of correction began to be doubted: and a wife may now have security of the peace against her husband; or, in return, a husband against his wife. Yet the lower rank of people, who were always fond of the old common law, still claim and exert their ancient privilege: and the courts of law will still permit a husband to restrain a wife of her liberty, in case of any gross misbehavior.
>
> These are the chief legal effects of marriage during the coverture; upon which we may observe, that even the disabilities, which the wife lies under, are for the most part intended for her protection and benefit. So great a favourite is the female sex of the laws of England.[65]

Contemporary feminists sum up these principles by noting that under common law, the husband and wife were one person, and that person was the husband. What reason might Blackstone have for nevertheless

63. Sandra F. Van Burkeo, *"Belonging to the World": Women's Rights and American Constitutional Culture* (New York: Oxford University Press, 2001), 7.

64. Winthrop, *History of New England*, 2:281.

65. Blackstone, *Commentaries*, 1:430–33.

thinking that the "female sex" was the "great favourite" of the "laws of England"?

D. Native Americans

The legal status of Native Americans was unclear throughout the Colonial Era. Rogers Smith observes, "it remained ambiguous whether the British home authorities, the colonists, and the tribes themselves viewed the tribes' status as conquered British subjects, voluntary subjects, semi-independent 'protected' nations, or as truly independent nations joined with the British empire via certain treaty agreements."[66] These different statuses mattered. Whether Native Americans had rights under English law or rights as English subjects depended on whether they were or could become ordinary members of the colonies. At some times and in some places American colonists and British authorities made serious attempts to work out these complex legal questions. Too often, colonists treated Native Americans as having no rights that European settlers had to respect.

VI. Criminal Justice

MAJOR DEVELOPMENTS

- Development of due process and habeas corpus
- Strict limits on general warrants
- Development of the right against coercive confessions and testimony under oath
- Emphasis on the right to trial by jury and jury nullification
- Beginnings of the right to counsel

The rights of persons accused of crime have an ancient lineage in the common law. The most famous sentence in the Magna Carta (1215) asserts, "No free man shall be seized or imprisoned, or stripped of his rights or possessions, or outlawed or exiled, or deprived of his standing in any other way, nor will we proceed with force against him, or send others to do so, except by the lawful judgment of his equals or by the law of the land." By the Colonial Era these words were understood as requiring due process of law in criminal cases. Persons accused of crimes could be convicted and sentenced only if the government followed certain rules during the investigation and prosecution of the offense. One study of colonial laws and practices found a general consensus that criminal defendants enjoyed the following:

1. No search or seizure without warrant
2. Right to reasonable bail
3. Confessions out of court invalid
4. Right to have cause determined with reasonable speed
5. Grand jury indictment in capital cases
6. Right to know the charges
7. Straighforward pleading with double jeopardy barred
8. Right to challenge the jurors
9. Process to compel witnesses for the defense
10. Right to confront accusers
11. Trial by jury
12. Limitation of punishment to the convict: no corruption of blood or forfeiture
13. No cruel or unusual punishment
14. Equal protection of the law: dependent classes—women, children, and servants—have access to the courts
15. Equal execution of the law: no capricious mitigation or application of penalties
16. Limited right of appeal[67]

By the time the *Mayflower* landed on Plymouth Rock in 1620, a general consensus existed that prosecutors had to prove that a criminal defendant was guilty of the charged offense. As early as the 1400s the chief justice of England asserted, "One would much rather that twenty guilty persons should escape the punishment of death, than that one innocent person should be condemned, and suffer capitally."[68]

This long list of rights better described colonial theory than it did actual processes that were followed when persons were suspected or accused of criminal offenses. Investigations and trials during the seventeenth and eighteenth centuries were rarely conducted according to legal formalities. Colonial America had fewer public prosecutors, fewer police officers, and far fewer defense attorneys than was the case in the United States during the nineteenth century. Most criminal

66. Smith, *Civic Ideals*, 62.

67. David J. Bodenhamer, *Fair Trial: Rights of the Accused in American History* (New York: Oxford University Press, 1992), 19.

68. Ibid., 13.

trials consisted of the accused being hauled up in front of the judge, a quick judicial survey of the evidence, a conviction, and the sentence. Few defendants knew or exercised their rights, and few judges were interested in protecting defendants' rights. The point of the criminal process was to identify and punish guilty people. Criminal trials took place only when a person of significant political interest was charged with violating the law. John Peter Zenger had a jury trial, complete with all legal formalities, when he was accused of seditious libel by the royal governor, because his trial was of great political interest to local political elites. Very few thieves in New York had a similar legal experience.

Colonial Americans connected the rights of persons accused of crimes with more substantive liberties.[69] Many rights we presently associate with the criminal process were in the eighteenth century means for preventing the discovery or prosecution of certain crimes. Zenger was guilty of seditious libel as seditious libel was defined at the time of his trial. His right to a jury trial, however, made convicting him for criticizing an unpopular royal governor nearly impossible. John Wilkes (the defendant in *Wilkes v. Wood* [1763]) was also guilty of seditious libel, but his ability to forbid government officials from searching his papers prevented them from proving he had written the incriminating pamphlets (that everyone knew he had written). Heresy was difficult to detect when persons could not be compelled to incriminate themselves. If royal officials could not easily search a private dwelling for Greek idols or force people to testify that they worshiped the Greek gods, they could not obtain the necessary evidence to prosecute those persons for worshiping Greek gods.

The jury trial was the most important procedural right that protected substantive liberties. Juries in the seventeenth and eighteenth centuries often determined both the facts and the law of a case. Some judges instructed juries that they could decide what conduct was legal. More often, juries disregarded judicial instructions when acquitting defendants who had violated the letter of an unpopular law. Colonial juries, by deciding the law and facts of a case, prevented government officials appointed by English authorities from passing and enforcing onerous measures. Many colonial juries refused to convict smugglers, for example, because most colonists enjoyed illegally imported goods. This practice, known as jury nullification, provided persons with a practical right to perform any action that their neighbors believed should be lawful. In eighteenth-century Massachusetts, jury nullification provided persons with the practical right to import rum from the Caribbean. Today, jury nullification might provide students in a college town with the practical right to use some recreational drugs.

When determining the scope of such rights as trial by jury, colonial Americans looked to English practice. Two sources were particularly important. The first were the treatises on English law written by notable English lawyers and judges. The most popular of these were Justice Edward Coke's *Institutes of the Laws of England* (1628–44) and Blackstone's *Commentaries on the Laws of England* (1765–69). The second source was cases decided by English judges during the seventeenth and eighteenth centuries. Many cases, most notably *Wilkes v. Wood* (1763) and *Entick v. Carrington* (1765), protected the rights of criminal suspects accused of political offenses. Reports of these judicial decisions were widely circulated in the colonies. Colonial leaders often treated these rulings as authoritative statements on the rights of Americans suspected of crimes.

A. Due Process and Habeas Corpus

Common law protections for people suspected of crimes were shaped by English politics. The origins of due process lie in a royal concession to nobles upset by high taxes. The writ of habeas corpus originally enabled the king to ensure that local aristocrats respected royal prerogatives. Both due process and habeas corpus were transformed into instruments of individual liberty during the seventeenth century. Struggles between the king and Parliament broadened the rights of all persons suspected of crimes.

Due Process. Most American colonists and English legal authorities regarded the Magna Carta as the foundation of their liberty. During the last part of the twelfth and first part of the thirteenth centuries, English monarchs raised taxes considerably to finance crusades, other military adventures, and an increasingly lavish royal court. Prominent English barons objected to these financial sacrifices. In 1215 King John I forestalled a full-scale revolt by making a series of commitments to the nobility that became known as the Magna

69. William J. Stuntz, "The Substantive Origins of Criminal Procedure," *Yale Law Journal* 105 (1995): 393, 411–19.

Carta. Section 39 of this document would become the most influential concession. That provision asserted, "No free man shall be seized or imprisoned, or stripped of his rights or possessions, or outlawed or exiled, or deprived of his standing in any other way, nor will we proceed with force against him, or send others to do so, except by the lawful judgment of his equals or by the law of the land." As originally understood, the Magna Carta only limited royal power over the English aristocracy. Over time, however, the charter was interpreted as the foundation for the rights of all English citizens. Section 39 came to stand for the principle that persons could be punished only if a jury determined that they had violated some preexisting law.

By the sixteenth century the Magna Carta's phrase "by law of the land" had become equated with the concept of "due process of law." The leading treatise on the common law at the time the colonies were first settled, Edward Coke's *Institutes of the Laws of England*, made that link explicit when asserting that due process was a fundamental right of all English subjects. Coke declared, "The true sense and exposition of ['by the law of the land' was] . . . without due process of law; . . . it be contained in the great charter, that no man be taken, imprisoned, or put out of his free-hold without process of the law; that is, by indictment or presentment of good and lawful men."[70] Persons could be imprisoned in a manner consistent with due process, the *Institutes* maintained, only if they violated "the common law, statute law, or the customs of England." Persons could be prosecuted only for violating a preexisting law. Coke insisted that due process also required that the indictment or presentment be sufficiently clear to enable the accused person to know the charges against him and give that person a chance to make a defense. He declared, "No man ought to be put from his livelihood without answer." Finally, due process entailed the right to a jury trial. A person could be deprived of his property or liberty, Coke wrote, only by "the lawful judgment [or] verdict of his equals."[71]

Coke made another important contribution to the development of due process when deciding *Bonham's Case* (1610). Thomas Bonham was charged with the unlawful practice of medicine and was subsequently convicted and fined by the Royal College of Medicine. According to parliamentary law, the Royal College of Medicine had the right to keep half the imposed fine. Coke ruled that practice illegal. The most famous passage of his opinion in *Bonham* declared,

> The censors cannot be judges, ministers, and parties; judges to give sentence or judgment; ministers to make summons; and parties to have the moiety of the forfeiture. . . . And it appears in our books, that in many cases, the common law will control Acts of Parliament, and sometimes adjudge them to be utterly void: for when an Act of Parliament is against common right and reason, or repugnant, or impossible to be performed, the common law will control it, and adjudge such Act to be void.[72]

Bonham's Case came to stand for two important principles. The first was that due process requires an impartial judge and jury. The Royal College could not legally judge whether Thomas Bonham was guilty because members had a financial interest in the outcome. The second was that justices could declare parliamentary laws unconstitutional. The national legislature, Coke ruled, could not abolish by statute fundamental due process rights.

English and colonial authorities disputed the significant of *Bonham*. English legal practice soon rejected judicial power to ignore parliamentary statutes. As discussed in Volume I, English law by the late eighteenth century was committed to parliamentary supremacy. No English court was authorized to challenge parliamentary legislation restricting the rights of criminal suspects or the rights of any other persons. *Bonham* had more influence in the colonies. Colonial critics of parliamentary taxes and impositions cited Coke's opinion when calling on royal judges to ignore statutes that the colonists believed violated their fundamental rights. James Otis in 1764 pointed to *Bonham* when asking a royal court to forbid the use of general search warrants that had been authorized by legislation. His argument stated,

> It is hoped it will not be considered a new doctrine, that even the authority of the Parliament of Great-Britain is circumscribed by certain bounds, which if exceeded, their acts become those of mere power without right, and consequently void. The judges of England have declared in favor of these sentiments

70. Edward Coke, *The Second Part of the Institutes of the Laws of England* (London: W. Clarke and Sons, 1809), 2:50.

71. Ibid., 2:46–47.

72. *Bonham's Case*, at 118 a.

> when they expressly declare, that acts of Parliament against natural equity are void. That acts against the fundamental principles of the British constitution are void.[73]

Habeas Corpus. "Habeas corpus" is Latin for "you have the body." Writs of habeas corpus require jailers to explain to courts why they have the legal authority to detain a named person. Habeas corpus proceedings are jurisdictional. The only issue in a habeas corpus proceeding is whether the jailer or legal authority has the power to detain a person for a particular offense. Habeas corpus does not determine whether the detained person is guilty of that offense. Consider the fate of a peasant in fourteenth-century England who has been detained by a local lord for illegally hunting in the forest. The peasant in a habeas corpus proceeding could not claim that he was innocent of the offense—that claim was reserved for the trial court. The peasant could claim only that the local lord did not have the power to punish people for hunting in that forest. This claim addresses jurisdiction, or the legal authority of the jailer.

The writ of habeas corpus dates from the late twelfth century.[74] During the thirteenth, fourteenth, fifteenth, and sixteenth centuries, habeas corpus was an instrument of royal power. Royal justices used the writ to take cases from local courts to ensure that local aristocrats were behaving in a manner consistent with royal edicts and royal concerns. A king might use a writ of habeas corpus to make sure that his rules were governing who hunted in the local forest. The persons most often protected by habeas corpus were royal officials and royal favorites, who sought the writ after being charged with offenses in local courts by local nobles.

The modern writ of habeas corpus took shape in the early seventeenth century. During the mid-1620s King Charles I raised revenues without consulting Parliament. Persons who refused to pay his unpopular duties and taxes were imprisoned. Habeas corpus was initially ineffective. Royal justices in *Darnel's Case* (1627–28) refused to grant a writ of habeas corpus to persons languishing in jail for refusing to make forced loans to the king. Parliament, frustrated with the king, reacted vigorously. In 1628 that legislative body passed the Petition of Right. This measure declared that the king could not raise revenues without the consent of Parliament. Any person imprisoned for failing to pay an illegal tax, the Petition of Right provided, had the right to habeas corpus. The crucial provision stated,

> [W]hereas it is declared and enacted by a statute made in the time of the reign of King Edward I, . . . that no tallage or aid shall be laid or levied by the king or his heirs in this realm, without the good will and assent of the archbishops, bishops, earls, barons, knights, burgesses, and other the freemen of the commonalty of this realm; and by authority of parliament holden in the five-and-twentieth year of the reign of King Edward III, it is declared and enacted, that from thenceforth no person should be compelled to make any loans to the king against his will . . . by which statutes before mentioned, and other the good laws and statutes of this realm, your subjects have inherited this freedom, that they should not be compelled to contribute to any tax, tallage, aid, or other like charge not set by common consent, in parliament.
>
> Yet nevertheless of late divers commissions directed to sundry commissioners in several counties, with instructions, have issued; by means whereof your people have been in divers places assembled, and required to lend certain sums of money unto your Majesty, and many of them, upon their refusal so to do . . . have been therefore imprisoned, confined, and sundry other ways molested and disquieted . . . against the laws and free custom of the realm.
>
> And whereas also by the statute called "The Great Charter of the Liberties of England," it is declared and enacted, that no freeman may be taken or imprisoned or be disseized of his freehold or liberties, or his free customs, or be outlawed or exiled, or in any manner destroyed, but by the lawful judgment of his peers, or by the law of the land.
>
> And in the eight-and-twentieth year of the reign of King Edward III, it was declared and enacted by authority of parliament, that no man, of what estate or condition that he be, should be put out of his land or tenements, nor taken, nor imprisoned, nor disinherited nor put to death without being brought to answer by due process of law.
>
> . . .

73. James Otis, *The Rights of the British Colonies Asserted and Proved* (London: J. Almon, 1764), 106–13.

74. Justin J. Wert, *Habeas Corpus in America: The Politics of Individual Rights* (Lawrence: University Press of Kansas, 2011).

And whereas of late great companies of soldiers and mariners have been dispersed into divers counties of the realm, and the inhabitants against their wills have been compelled to receive them into their houses, and there to suffer them to sojourn against the laws and customs of this realm, and to the great grievance and vexation of the people.

. . .

They do therefore humbly pray your most excellent Majesty, that no man hereafter be compelled to make or yield any gift, loan, benevolence, tax, or such like charge, without common consent by act of parliament; and that none be called to make answer, or take such oath, or to give attendance, or be confined, or otherwise molested or disquieted concerning the same or for refusal thereof; and that no freeman, in any such manner as is before mentioned, be imprisoned or detained.

Fifty years later Parliament expanded the writ of habeas corpus. The Habeas Corpus Act of 1679 prevented executive officials from using various subterfuges to prevent persons from seeking that writ. The measure required governing officials to produce the body of any person seeking a writ of habeas corpus before a judge within three days. Such tactics as removing a prisoner from the country were forbidden. If the jailer could not demonstrate that the person was being detained because he had violated or was suspected of violating the laws of the land, then the judge was authorized to free the detainee. The Habeas Corpus Act of 1679 asserted,

> Whereas great delays have been used by . . . Officers to whose Custody any of the Kings Subjects have been committed for criminal or supposed criminal matters in making returns of Writs of Habeas Corpus to them . . . contrary to their duty and the known laws of the land whereby many of the Kings Subjects have been and hereafter may be long detained in prison in such cases where by law they are bailable to their great charge and vexation. For the prevention whereof and the more speedy relief of all persons imprisoned for any such criminal or supposed criminal matters be it enacted . . . that whensoever any person or persons shall bring any Habeas Corpus directed unto any Sheriff. . . or other Person . . . for any person in his or their custody said officer . . . shall within three days . . . bring or cause to be brought the body of the party so committed or restrained unto or before the Lord Chancellor or . . . the Judges or Barons of the said Court from whence the said Writ shall issue or unto and before such other . . . persons before whom the said Writ is made returnable . . . , and shall certify the true causes of his Detainer or Imprisonment unless the commitment of the said party be in any place beyond the distance of twenty miles from the place or places where such Court or Person is or shall be residing and if beyond the distance of twenty miles and not above one hundred miles then within the space of ten days and if beyond the distance of one hundred miles then within the space of twenty days.
>
> And if any person or persons shall be or stand committed or detained as aforesaid for any Crime unless for Treason or Felony plainly expressed in the Warrant of Commitment, it shall and may be lawful to and for the person or persons so committed or detained by legal Process or any one his or their behalf to appeal or complain to . . . any one of His Majesties Justices . . . and the said . . . Justices . . . are hereby authorized. . . to award and grant an Habeas Corpus.

Blackstone described the Habeas Corpus Act of 1679 as "another Magna Carta." His *Commentaries* asserted,

> The glory of the English law consist[s] in clearly defining the times, the causes, and the extent, when, wherefore, and to what degree, the imprisonment of the subject may be lawful. This induces an absolute necessity of expressing upon every commitment the reason for which it is made; that the court upon an habeas corpus may examine into it's validity; and according to the circumstances of the case may discharge, admit to bail, or remand the prisoner.[75]

The extent to which American colonists enjoyed habeas corpus is unclear.[76] Colonial courts in the eighteenth century sometimes issued the writ. Judges based these decisions on the common law right of habeas corpus or claims that Englishmen living in the colonies enjoyed the benefits of the Habeas Corpus Act. Nevertheless, when colonial legislatures passed laws explicitly authorizing courts to issue writs of

75. Blackstone, *Commentaries*, 4:133.

76. This paragraph relies on Michael O'Neill, "On Reforming the Federal Writ of Habeas Corpus," *Seton Hall Law Review* 26 (1996): 1493.

habeas corpus, those measures were disallowed by the Privy Council in England. Such decisions angered colonists. When the royal governor of Massachusetts refused to authorize habeas corpus, Cotton Mather, the leading intellectual in New England at the turn of the eighteenth century, declared, "We are slaves."

B. Search and Seizure

The common law sharply limited official power to search private residences. William Pitt (1708–78), a prominent English politician and prime minister, poetically expressed this right to privacy when he stated, "The poorest man may, in his cottage, bid defiance to all the forces of the Crown. It may be frail; its roof may shake; the wind may blow through it; the storm may enter; the rain may enter; but the King of England may not enter; all his forces dare not cross the threshold of the ruined tenement."[77] Both public officials and private persons who conducted searches without warrants took grave risks. If they found evidence of a crime, the evidence would be admitted at the resulting criminal trial. If a public official or private person failed to find incriminating evidence, they could be sued for trespass. The reasonableness of their search was not a legal defense. If every person living in your apartment complex swore that you had illegal drugs in your room and a police officer conducted a warrantless search on that basis, eighteenth-century law permitted you to sue the police officer for trespass if no illegal goods were discovered. Damages could be significant.

Governing officials could claim immunity from lawsuits only if they first obtained a search warrant from a local magistrate. The common law rules that governed search warrants were strict. *Wilkes v. Wood* (1763) ruled that general search warrants were invalid. *Entick v. Carrington* (1765) ruled that a warrant to search for private papers was invalid. Government could search only for illegal, usually stolen, goods. Warrants were valid only if they specified what illegal goods were being searched for and where those illegal goods were located.

American colonists celebrated *Wilkes v. Wood* and *Entick v. Carrington* as declarations of the fundamental rights of all English subjects. Applying those cases in prerevolutionary America, however, was not straightforward. *Wilkes* and *Entick* raised questions about common law rights. The sole issue in those cases was the conditions under which the common law authorized a judge to issue a warrant. Crown officials conducting search and seizures in the colonies acted on the basis of parliamentary statutes authorizing general warrants, not on the basis of judicially authorized warrants. English authorities claimed that this made a difference. Persons had rights against arbitrary executive action, in their view, but not against the people's representatives in Parliament. James Otis in the *Writs of Assistance Case* (1761) claimed that this difference did not make a difference. He maintained that general warrants were invalid, whether issued by judges or authorized by the legislature. Otis was unsuccessful. Royal justices in the colonies authorized writs of assistance that enabled crown officials to search the residence of anyone suspected of smuggling. The judicial practice of issuing general warrants was one of the first grievances that eventually moved Americans to demand their independence.

Entick v. Carrington, 19 Howell's State Trials 1029 (1765)

John Entick was the author of several pamphlets criticizing the English government. Under English law at the time, any writing that defamed a government official was criminal libel, and persons who penned such works could be criminally punished. Lord Halifax, the secretary of state, issued a warrant in 1762 authorizing his agents to seize all of Entick's writings. Led by Nathan Carrington, the agents searched Entick's house for four hours. They carried away more than one hundred pamphlets. Entick responded by suing Carrington for trespass. Carrington claimed that a person with a valid warrant could not be sued for trespass. Entick replied that Lord Halifax had no power to issue a general warrant that authorized persons to search homes for evidence of criminal libel. The jury delivered a special verdict, deciding that if the warrant were invalid, Carrington should be required to pay three hundred pounds in damages. Lord Chief Judge Camden was asked to determine whether the warrant was valid.

Chief Judge Camden ruled that the warrant was illegal. Entick, he declared, was entitled to damages. Pay careful attention to two features of this opinion. First, Camden distinguishes between searches for papers and searches for stolen goods.

---

77. Henry Brougham, *The Critical and Miscellaneous Writings of Henry Lord Brougham* (Philadelphia: Lea & Blanchard, 1841), 1:264.

What is that distinction? Why the different rules? Do you agree? Second, Camden condemns seditious libel while seemingly preventing that crime from being prosecuted. During the eighteenth century, most political essays were anonymous or written under pseudonyms. When Alexander Hamilton, James Madison, and John Jay wrote The Federalist Papers, *they used the name "Publius." If, after* Entick v. Carrington, *the government could not search private homes for papers, how likely was it that they would be able to prove that private persons who used pseudonyms were guilty of seditious libel?*

LORD CHIEF JUDGE CAMDEN'S Judgment

[T]he defendants . . . are under a necessity to maintain the legality of the warrants, under which they have acted, and to shew that the secretary of state in the instance now before us, had a jurisdiction to seize the defendants' papers. If he had no such jurisdiction, the law is clear, that the officers are as much responsible for the trespass as their superior.

This, though it is not the most difficult, is the most interesting question in the cause; because if this point should be determined in favor of the jurisdiction, the secret cabinets and bureaus of every subject in this kingdom will be thrown open to the search and inspection of a messenger, whenever the secretary of state shall think fit to charge, or even to suspect, a person to be the author, printer, or publisher of a seditious libel.

. . .

This power, so claimed by the secretary of state, is not supported by one single citation from any law book extant. . . .

If honestly exerted, it is a power to seize that man's papers, who is charged upon oath to be the author or publisher of a seditious libel; if oppressively, it acts against every man, who is so described in the warrant, though he be innocent.

It is executed against the party, before he is heard or even summoned; and the information, as well as the informers, is unknown.

. . .

If this injury falls upon an innocent person, he is as destitute of remedy as the guilty: and the whole transaction is so guarded against discovery, that if the officer should be disposed to carry off a bank bill he may do it with impunity, since there is no man capable of proving either the taker or the thing taken.

. . .

The great end, for which men entered into society, was to secure their property. That right is preserved sacred and incommunicable in all instances, where it has not been taken away or abridged by some public law for the good of the whole. The cases where this right of property is set aside by private law, are various. Distresses, executions, forfeitures, taxes etc are all of this description; wherein every man by common consent gives up that right, for the sake of justice and the general good. By the laws of England, every invasion of private property, be it ever so minute, is a trespass. No man can set his foot upon my ground without my license, but he is liable to an action, though the damage be nothing; which is proved by every declaration in trespass, where the defendant is called upon to answer for bruising the grass and even treading upon the soil. If he admits the fact, he is bound to show by way of justification, that some positive law has empowered or excused him. The justification is submitted to the judges, who are to look into the books; and if such a justification can be maintained by the text of the statute law, or by the principles of common law. If no excuse can be found or produced, the silence of the books is an authority against the defendant, and the plaintiff must have judgment.

According to this reasoning, it is now incumbent upon the defendants to show the law by which this seizure is warranted. If that cannot be done, it is a trespass.

Papers are the owner's goods and chattels: they are his dearest property; and are so far from enduring a seizure, that they will hardly bear an inspection; and though the eye cannot by the laws of England be guilty of a trespass, yet where private papers are removed and carried away, the secret nature of those goods will be an aggravation of the trespass, and demand more considerable damages in that respect. Where is the written law that gives any magistrate such a power? I can safely answer, there is none; and therefore it is too much for us without such authority to pronounce a practice legal, which would be subversive of all the comforts of society.

But though it cannot be maintained by any direct law, yet it bears a resemblance, as was urged, to the known case of search and seizure for stolen goods.

I answer that the difference is apparent. In the one, I am permitted to seize my own goods, which are placed in the hands of a public officer, till the felon's conviction shall entitle me to restitution. In the other, the party's own property is seized before and without conviction, and he has no power to reclaim his goods, even after his innocence is cleared by acquittal.

. . .

Observe too the caution with which the law proceeds in this singular case. There must be a full charge upon oath of a theft committed. The owner must swear that the goods are lodged in such place. He must attend at the execution of the warrant to shew them to the officer, who must see that they answer the description. And, lastly, the owner must abide the event at his peril; for if the goods are not found, he is a trespasser; and the officer being an innocent person, will be always a ready a convenient witness against him.

. . .

On the contrary, in the case before us nothing is described, nor distinguished. No charge is requisite to prove that the party has any criminal papers in his custody; no person present to separate or select; no person to prove in the owner's behalf the officer's misbehavior. . . .

. . .

To search, seize, and carry away all the papers of the subject upon the first warrant; that such a right should have existed from the time whereof the memory of man runneth not to the contrary, and never yet have found a place in any book of law is incredible. But if so strange a thing could be supposed, I do not see, how we could declare the law upon such evidence.

. . .

If the power of search is to follow the right of seizure, every body sees the consequence. He that has it or has had it in his custody; he that has published, copied or maliciously reported it, may fairly be under a reasonable suspicion of having the thing in his custody, and consequently become the object of the search warrant. If libels may be seized it ought to be laid down with precision, when, where, upon what charge, against whom, by what magistrate, and in what stage of the prosecution. All these particulars must be explained and proved to be law, before this general proposition can be established.

As therefore no authority in our book can be produced to support such a doctrine, . . . I cannot be persuaded that such a power can be justified by the common law.

. . .

It is then said, that it is necessary for the ends of government to lodge such a power with a state officer; and that it is better to prevent the publication before than to punish the offender afterwards. I answer, if the legislature be of that opinion, they will revive the Licensing Act. But if they have not done that I conceive they are not of that opinion. And with respect to the argument of state necessity, or a distinction that has been aimed at between state offenses and others, the common law does not understand that kind of reasoning, nor do our books take notice of any such distinctions.

. . .

It is very certain that the law obligeth no man to accuse himself; because the necessary means of compelling self-accusation, falling upon the innocent as well as the guilty, would be both cruel and unjust; and it should seem, that search for evidence is disallowed upon the same principle. There too the innocent would be confounded with the guilty.

. . .

I have now taken notice of every thing that has been urged upon the present point; and upon the whole we are all of opinion, that the warrant to seize and carry away the party's papers in the case of a seditious libel, is illegal and void. . . .

C. Interrogations

General agreement existed among English and colonial legal authorities that persons could not be compelled to testify against themselves. At a minimum this meant that governing authorities could not torture persons to gain confessions. Common law practice suggested that the right against compelled testimony had three other functions. First, persons had a right not to answer inappropriate questions, even when their questioning did not involve torture or compulsion. Second, requiring persons to confess their crimes under oath or in public violated their right to conscience. Third, prosecutors in an adversary system of criminal justice had an obligation to make their case for conviction without relying on the defendant for incriminating evidence.[78]

Torture. Colonial Americans rejected torture as a means for extracting confessions. A leader of the Plymouth Colony, when asked how far a magistrate might go to extract a confession, responded,

78. This section relies heavily on R. H. Helmholz, Charles M. Gray, John H. Langbein, and Eben Moglen, *The Privilege against Self-Incrimination: Its Origins and Development* (Chicago: University of Chicago Press, 1997). All quotes in the text are taken from that source.

> I conceive that a magistrate is bound, by careful examination of circumstances & weighing of probabilities, to sift the accused; and by force of argument to draw him to an acknowledgment of the truth. But he may not extract a confession of a capital crime from a suspected person by any violent means, whether it be by oath imposed, or by any punishment inflicted or threatened to be inflicted, for he may draw forth an acknowledgement of a crime from a fearful innocent. If guilty, he shall be compelled to be his own accuser, when no other can, which is against the rule of justice.

Colonial magistrates found nothing improper in interrogating criminal suspects. John Winthrop, the governor of the Plymouth Colony, asserted that "when one witness or strong presumptions do point out the offender, there the judge may examine him strictly, and he is bound to answer directly." Winthrop rejected only unduly coercive means of interrogation. "Examination by oath or torture in criminal cases," he stated, "is generally denied to be lawful."[79] The Massachusetts Body of Liberties permitted interrogators to employ violence to gain confessions in one circumstance. People could be tortured after their conviction when doing so might reveal their confederates in crime. Salem authorities during the infamous witch trials (1692) revived the common law practice of "peine forte et dure" (hard and forceful punishment) for persons who refused to plead either guilty or not guilty. Such persons had increasingly heavy weights placed on their chest until they pleaded or suffocated. No instance of this practice has been recorded as occurring in the colonies after the turn of the eighteenth century.

Privacy and Confessions under Oath. Winthrop and his peers refused to require persons suspected of crimes to answer questions under oath. Colonial Americans believed that forcing a criminal suspect to swear to tell the truth was a form of violence. Criminals might be too tempted to commit perjury, and by doing so, they risked their immortal soul. Everyone agreed that confession was good for the soul. Confessions under oath, however, were thought to be private matters.

The controversy over the "oath ex officio" highlights the connection that Anglo-American legal authorities made between the right not to testify against oneself and privacy. This oath was used by religious authorities in England during the sixteenth and seventeenth centuries. Members of the Star Chamber, a special tribunal established by Queen Elizabeth I to root out heresy, made extensive use of sworn testimony. Members of the Star Chamber made persons swear to tell the truth in response to any interrogation. This was the oath ex officio. The person was then asked various questions, often about their religious or political beliefs. Punishment followed if what they expressed was heretical or seditious. Opponents of the oath ex officio and the Star Chamber raised several objections to this practice. Many common people did not understand the intricacies of religious doctrine. Under oath they might unknowingly confess to holding beliefs that governing officials thought heretical (imagine trying to state every tenet of your religious faith, knowing that you will be tortured if you make a mistake). Prominent legal authorities questioned whether persons should be punished for their private beliefs. Edward Coke contended, "No free man should be compelled to answer for his secret thoughts and opinions."[80] No good reason existed for punishing a person who never publicly expressed or acted on privately held unorthodox beliefs about Jesus Christ.

The controversy over the oath ex officio came to a head during the 1630s and 1640s after John Lilburne (1614–57) was imprisoned by the Star Chamber. Lilburne was a prominent religious and political dissident. During his questioning he bluntly refused to take the oath ex officio or to answer any questions about his religious beliefs. He informed his interrogators,

> I am not willing to answer you to any more of these questions, because I see you go about by this examination to ensnare me; for, seeing the things for which I am imprisoned cannot be proved against me, you will get other matter out of my examination; and therefore, if you will not ask me about the thing laid to my charge, I shall answer no more; . . . and of any other matter that you have to accuse me of, I know it is warrantable by the law of God, and I think by the law of the land, that I may stand upon my just defence and not answer to your interrogatories.[81]

79. Winthrop, *History of New England*, 2:56.

80. For more on this strand of thought, see Stuntz, "Substantive Origins," 411–19.

81. *Lilburne's Case*, 3 State Trials 1315, 1318 (1637).

Illustration 2-4 Governor John Winthrop

Source: Charles W. Sharpe, engraver, *Jo. Winthrop, Governor of Massachusetts, 1630–49*. Emmet Collection, Miriam and Ira D. Wallach Division of Art, Prints and Photographs, The New York Public Library, Astor, Lenox and Tilden Foundations.

The Star Chamber condemned Lilburne in 1638. Three years later, the House of Commons declared the verdict "illegal and against the liberty of the subject." Later that year, Parliament abolished the Star Chamber. By the late seventeenth century, the oath ex officio had been abandoned.[82]

Improper Questions. Some colonial sources suggest that persons at the time had the right not to respond when governing officials engaged in "fishing expeditions." Governor John Winthrop insisted that criminal suspects answer questions only when strong extrinsic evidence supported their guilt. He thought that no one was obligated to answer questions in absence of such evidence. "If there be only light suspicion," Winthrop informed the magistrates of Massachusetts, "then the judge is not to press him to answer . . . , but he may be silent, and call for his accusers."[83] One historian concludes that "officials in the seventeenth century and earlier were expected to have probable cause before asking suspects to respond under oath to incriminating evidence."[84]

The Adversary System. The right to remain silent may have been an element of the adversary system of criminal justice that was emerging in the eighteenth century. As criminal trials became contests between prosecutors and defense attorneys, legal authorities insisted that the government prove guilt without any help from the defendant. The defendant's right to remain silent was a right not to provide the prosecution with any evidence

82. See John H. Wigmore, "The Privilege against Self-Crimination: Its History," *Harvard Law Review* 15 (1902): 1610.

83. Winthrop, *History of New England*, 2:56.

84. Albert W. Alschuler, "A Peculiar Privilege in Historical Perspective," in *Privilege against Self-Incrimination* (see note 78), 186.

that might point toward conviction. Some sources suggest that colonists opposed using confessions as the primary evidence of guilt. John Winthrop and other governing officials in the seventeenth century did not believe that persons could be questioned about crimes unless extrinsic evidence pointed to their culpability. The rule that a person could be questioned only after other evidence pointed to his or her guilt meant that the prosecution could not rely solely on confessions to secure criminal convictions.

Stronger claims about the relationship between the right against self-incrimination and the adversary system are anachronistic. Until the turn of the eighteenth century, criminal defendants were required to represent themselves at trial. Very few had defense lawyers on the eve of the Revolution. A criminal defendant who lacked a defense attorney could not remain silent. To do so would forfeit his right to make a defense.

D. JURIES AND LAWYERS

The right to trial by jury and the right to an attorney were well established in both English and American law on the eve of the American Revolution. By 1776 the right to a jury trial had assumed contemporary form. Persons accused of serious crimes could be punished only if a jury voted to convict. The right to an attorney in the Colonial Era was quite different from contemporary practice. Americans at the turn of the twenty-first century recognize the right of a person accused of crime to be defended by a court-appointed attorney paid for by the government. The colonists recognized only the right of a person accused of a crime to hire a defense attorney.

Juries. The jury trial was a staple of common law justice. That procedure dates from the Assize of Clarendon (1166), which established the manner in which the king's ministers would bring the king's justice to the entire realm. When the royal officials or "court" entered a township, they assembled twenty-four men who were thought to be trustworthy. Those men were asked who had broken the king's law. The practice gradually evolved into what we call the grand jury, the institution that indicts persons suspected of committing crimes. Over time, English kings made use of a petit jury. This group of twelve persons determines whether persons charged with crimes by the grand jury are guilty.

Both Englishmen and colonial Americans regarded the jury as the leading bulwark of rights. In a series of important cases, most notably the trial of William Penn in England and the trial of John Peter Zenger in the colonies, juries thwarted unpopular prosecutions. In the Penn trial, a jury refused to convict William Penn of unlawful assembly for preaching Quaker gospel in public. The trial judge imprisoned the jury for refusing to convict, but the jurors in *Bushell's Case* (1670) were freed on a writ of habeas corpus. *Bushell's Case* immediately came to stand for the principle that judges could not interfere with a jury verdict. If a jury declared a person not guilty, neither the jury nor the defendant could be punished.

Juries in the Colonial Era often judged both fact and law. Juries were expected to find such facts as whether the defendant had published the offending criticism of a government official, whether the killing was done in self-defense, or whether the goods were illegally smuggled. Many prominent lawyers insisted that juries also had the right to determine the relevant law. In this view, a jury could determine both whether the defendant had published a criticism of a public official and whether that criticism was protected by the common law. Most judges in both England and the colonies opposed this claimed jury power to determine the law. Nevertheless, jury nullification was quite common. When popular defendants were charged with violating unpopular laws, many juries simply refused to convict. This capacity for nullifying unpopular laws explains why American colonists far preferred rule by local juries to decisions made by royally appointed judges.

Attorneys. The right to counsel developed more slowly in colonial America than the right to a jury. English law until the late seventeenth century required persons to defend themselves. Conventional wisdom maintained that innocent persons did not need assistance at trial. Reform was slow. The Treason Act of 1695 gave accused traitors the right "to make . . . full Defense, by Counsel learned in the Law." Gradually, a series of decisions and statutes permitted defense counsel to play a more active role in all felony cases. Defense counsel did not become a regular participant in English criminal trials until the nineteenth century.

The American colonies retained the traditional suspicion of lawyers but were more liberal than the English on the right to retain counsel. Massachusetts in the seventeenth century gave persons a right to employ counsel as long as counsel was not paid. By the eve of the American Revolution the law in most colonies permitted most criminal defendants to be represented by an attorney if they could afford such representation. This right to counsel was nevertheless the least important right associated with the criminal defense process. Americans celebrated such decisions as *Entick v. Carrington*, *Wilkes v. Wood*, and *Bushell's Case*. No similar canonical ruling on the right to counsel was handed down by an English or colonial judge during the seventeenth and eighteenth centuries.

The Trial of William Penn and Bushell's Case (1670)[85]

William Penn (1644–1718) was a prominent English Quaker who, with other Quakers, frequently preached on the streets of London. The English government arrested Penn for disturbing the peace. At his trial Penn and his co-defendant William Mead pleaded not guilty. Penn urged the jury to ignore the indictment and respect his right to preach. The jury agreed. At first, the jurors asserted that Penn was guilty only of speaking, and not of disturbing the peace. The trial judge insisted that the jury give a more specific verdict. When the jurors refused, they were imprisoned. Eventually the jurors declared that Penn and Mead were not guilty. The trial judge responded by returning the jurors to prison. Edward Bushell and his fellow jurors sought a writ of habeas corpus on the ground that they could not be imprisoned merely because the judge disagreed with their verdict.

In Bushell's Case, *Judge Vaughns granted the writ. In his view, the right to trial by jury meant the right to have the jurors freely determine whether the defendant was innocent or guilty. This right could not be exercised if jurors were subject to punishment.* Bushell's Case *became the leading colonial precedent for the right to a jury trial. How far does this precedent go? Does* Bushell *establish the right of a jury to find facts or the right of the jury to decide on both the facts and the law?*

The Trial of William Penn

. . .

RECORDER: You have heard what the Indictment is, It is for preaching to the people, and drawing a

85. Excerpted from William Penn, *The People's Ancient and Just Liberties Asserted, in the Trial of William Penn and William Mead* (London: 1670).

Illustration 2-5 The Arrest of William Penn

Source: Annie Cole Cady, *The American Continent and Its inhabitants before Its Discovery by Columbus: Also the Story of Its Invasion by Spain, France, and England, a Unique History* (Philadelphia: Gebbie, 1890). / Picture Collection, The New York Public Library, Astor, Lenox and Tilden Foundations.

tumultuous company after them, and Mr. Penn was speaking; if they should not be disturbed, you see they will go on; there are three or four witnesses that have proved this, that he did preach there; that Mr. Mead did allow of it: after this you have heard by substantial witnesses what is said against them: now we are upon the matter of fact, which you are to keep to, and observe, as what hath been fully sworn at your peril.

. . .

WILLIAM PENN: I appeal to the jury who are my Judges, and this great assembly, whether the proceedings of the court are not most arbitrary, and void of all law, in offering to give the jury their charge in the absence of the prisoners; I say it is directly opposite to, and destructive of the undoubted right of every English prisoner.

. . .

CLERK: Look upon the prisoners at the bar; how say you? Is William Penn Guilty of the matter whereof he stands indicted in manner and form, or Not Guilty?

FOREMAN: Guilty of speaking in Grace-church street.

COURT: Is that all?

FOREMAN: That is all I have in commission.

RECORDER: You had as good say nothing.

MAYOR: Was it not an unlawful assembly? You mean he was speaking to a tumult of people there?

FOREMAN: My Lord, This is all I had in commission.

. . .

RECORDER: The law of England will not allow you to part till you have given in your Verdict.

JURY: We have given in our Verdict, and we can give in no other.

[*The next day*]

. . .

CLERK: What say you? Look upon the prisoners: Is William Penn Guilty in manner and form, as he stands indicted, or Not Guilty?

FOREMAN: Here is our Verdict; . . . "We the jurors, hereafter named, do find William Penn to be Guilty of speaking or preaching to an assembly, met together in Grace Church Street, the 14th of August last, 1670, And that William Mead is Not Guilty of the said Indictment."

. . .

RECORDER: Gentlemen, you shall not be dismissed till we have a verdict that the court will accept; and you shall be locked up, without meat, drink, fire, and tobacco; you shall not think thus to abuse the court; we will have a verdict, by the help of God, or you shall starve for it.

PENN: My jury, who are my judges, ought not to be thus menaced; their verdict should be free, and not compelled; the bench ought to wait upon them, but not forestall them. I do desire that justice may be done me, and that the arbitrary resolves of the bench may not be made the measure of my jury's verdict. . . . The agreement of 12 men is a verdict in law, and such a one being given by the jury, I require the clerk of the peace to record it, as he will answer it at his peril. And if the jury bring in another verdict contradictory to this, I affirm they are perjured men in law; And looking upon the jury, said, You are Englishmen, mind your privilege, give not away your right.

RECORDER: Gentlemen, You must be contented with your hard fate, let your patience overcome it; for the court is resolved to have a verdict, and that before you can be dismissed.

[*The next day*]

CLERK: What say you? Look upon the prisoners at the bar; is William Penn guilty of the matter whereof he stands indicted, in manner and form as aforesaid, or Not Guilty?

FOREMAN: William Penn is Guilty of speaking in Gracechurch-Street.

MAYOR: To an unlawful assembly?

FOREMAN: No, my lord, we give no other verdict than what we gave last night; we have no other verdict to give.

PENN: It is intolerable that my jury should he thus menaced: Is this according to the fundamental laws? Are not they my proper judges by the Great Charter of England? What hope is there of ever having justice done, when juries are threatened, and their verdicts rejected? I am concerned to speak, and grieved to see such arbitrary proceedings. Did not the lieutenant of the Tower render one of them worse than a felon? And do you not plainly seem to condemn such for factious fellows, who answer not your ends? Unhappy are those juries, who are threatened to be fined, and starved, and ruined, if they give not in Verdicts contrary to their consciences.

[*The next day*]

CLERK: How say you? is William Penn Guilty, &c. or Not Guilty.

FOREMAN: Not Guilty.

. . .

OBSERVER: They hauled the prisoners into the Bale-dock, and from thence sent them to Newgate, for non-payment of their fines; and so were their Jury. But the Jury were afterwards discharged upon an Habeas Corpus, returnable in the Common-Pleas, where their commitment was adjudged illegal.

Case of the Imprisonment of Edward Bushell for Alleged Misconduct as a Juryman

Opinion of CHIEF JUSTICE VAUGHN

. . .

Another fault in the return is, that the jurors are not said to have acquitted the persons indicted, against full and manifest evidence corruptly, and knowing the said evidence to be full and manifest against the persons indicted, for how manifest soever the evidence was, if it were not manifest to them, and that they believed it such, it was not a finable fault, nor deserving imprisonment, upon which difference the law of punishing jurors for false verdicts principally depends.

. . .

I would know whether any thing be more common, than for two men students, barristers, or judges, to deduce contrary and opposite conclusions out of the same case in law? And is here any difference that two men should infer distinct conclusions from the same testimony? Is any thing more known than that the same author, and place in that author, is forcibly urged to maintain contrary conclusions, and the decision hard, which is in the right? Is any thing more frequent in the controversies of religion, than to press the same text for opposite tenets? How then comes it to pass that two persons may, not apprehend with reason and honesty, what a witness, or many, say, to prove in the understanding of one plainly one thing, but in the apprehension of the other, clearly the contrary thing? Must therefore one of these merit fine and imprisonment, because he doth that which he cannot otherwise do, preserving his oath and integrity? And this often is the case of the judge and jury.

I conclude therefore, That this return, charging the prisoners to have acquitted Penn and Mead, against full and manifest evidence, first and next, without saying that they did know and believe that Evidence to be full and manifest against the indicted persons, is no cause of fine or imprisonment.

. . .

We come now to the next part of the Return, viz. "That the jury acquitted those indicted against the direction of the court in matter of law, openly given and declared to them in court."

. . .

[I]f the judge, from the evidence, shall by his own judgment first resolve upon any trial what the fact is, and so knowing the fact, shall then resolve what the law is, and order the jury penally to find accordingly, what either necessary or convenient use can be fancied of juries, or to continue trials by them at all?

. . .

. . . [T]he judge cannot fine the jury for going against their evidence or direction of the court, without other misdemeanor.

. . .

But the reasons are, I conceive, most clear, that the judge could not, nor can fine and imprison the jury in such cases.

Without a fact agreed, it is as impossible for a judge, or any other, to know the law relating to that fact or direct concerning it, as to know an accident that hath no subject.

Hence it follows, that the judge can never direct what the law is in any matter controverted, without first knowing the fact; and then it follows, that without his previous knowledge of the fact, the jury cannot go against his direction in law, for he could not direct.

But the judge, *quâ* judge, cannot know the fact possibly but from the evidence which the jury have, but (as will appear) he can never know what evidence the jury have, and consequently he cannot know the matter of fact, nor punish the jury for going against their evidence, when he cannot know what their evidence is.

It is true, if the jury were to have no other evidence for the fact, but what is deposed in court, the judge might know their evidence, and the fact from it, equally as they, and so direct what the law were in the case, though even then the judge and jury might honestly differ in the result from the evidence, as well as two judges may, which often happens.

But the evidence which the jury have of the fact is much other than that: for,

1. Being returned of the vicinage, whence the cause of action ariseth, the law supposeth them thence to have sufficient knowledge to try the matter in issue (and so they must) though no evidence were given on either side in court, but to this evidence the judge is a stranger.

2. They may have evidence from their own personal knowledge, by which they may be assured, and sometimes are, that what is deposed in court, is absolutely false: but to this the judge is a stranger, and he knows no more of the fact than he hath learned in court, and perhaps by false depositions, and consequently knows nothing.

3. The jury may know the witnesses to be stigmatized and infamous, which may be unknown to the parties, and consequently to the court.

4. In many cases the jury are to have view necessarily, in many, by consent, for their better information; to this evidence likewise the judge is a stranger.

. . .

A man cannot see by anothers eye, nor hear by anothers ear, no more can a man conclude or infer the thing to be resolved by anothers understanding or reasoning; and though the verdict be right the jury give, yet they being not assured it is so from their own understanding, are forsworn, at least *in foro conscientiæ*. . . .

E. Punishments

Crime and punishment repulsed and fascinated people living in the seventeenth and eighteenth centuries. Numerous crimes were punished by death. Relying heavily on biblical command, the Massachusetts Body of Liberties declared the following to be capital offenses.

> If any man after legal conviction shall have or worship any other god, but the lord god, he shall be put to death.
>
> If any man or woman be a witch, (that is hath or consulted with a familiar spirit,) They shall be put to death.
>
> If any person shall Blaspheme the name of god, the father, Son or Holy Ghost, with direct, express, presumptuous or high handed blasphemy, or shall curse god in the like manner, he shall be put to death.
>
> If any person commit any willful murder, which is manslaughter, committed upon premeditated malice, hatred, or Cruelty, . . . he shall be put to death.
>
> If any person slay an other suddenly in his anger or Cruelty of passion, he shall be put to death.
>
> If any person shall slay an other through guile, either by poisoning or other such devilish practice, he shall be put to death.
>
> If any man or woman shall lye with any beast or brute creature by Carnal Copulation, They shall surely be put to death. And the beast shall be slain, and buried and not eaten.
>
> If any man lies with [a man] as he lies with a woman, both of them have committed abomination, they both shall surely be put to death.
>
> If any person commit Adultery with a married or [engaged] wife, the Adulterer and Adulteress shall surely be put to death.
>
> If any man steals a man . . . , he shall surely be put to death.
>
> If any man rise up by false witness, wittingly and of purpose to take away any man's life, he shall be put to death.

This list was humane by English standards. English law punished more than one hundred crimes by death.

Punishments in the seventeenth and eighteenth centuries were severe. Most legal elites opposed cruelty, but what constituted cruelty was considerably different from contemporary standards. Consider Blackstone's notions of what constituted legitimate punishments, sanctions he insisted did "honour to English law":

> Some [offenses] are capital, which extend to the life of the offender, and consist generally in being hanged by the neck till dead; though in very atrocious crimes other circumstances of terror, pain, or disgrace are superadded: as, in treasons of all kings, being drawn or dragged to the place of execution; in high treason affecting the king's person or government, emboweling alive, beheading, and

quartering; and in murder, a public dissection. And, in case of any treason committed by a female, the judgment is to be burned alive. But the humanity of the English nation has authorized, by a tacit consent, an almost general mitigation of such part of these judgments as favour of torture or cruelty: a sledge or hurdle being usually allowed to such traitors as are condemned to be drawn; and there being very few instances (and those accidental or by negligence) of any person's being emboweled or burned, till previously deprived of sensation by strangling. Some punishments consist in exile or banishment, by abjuration of the realm, or transportation to the American colonies: others in loss of liberty, by perpetual or temporary imprisonment. Some extend to confiscation, by forfeiture of lands . . . : others induce a disability, of holding offices or employments, being heirs, executors, and the like. Some, though rarely, occasion a mutilation or dismembering, by cutting off the hand or ears: others fix a lasting stigma on the offender, by slitting the nostrils, or branding in the hand or face. Some are merely pecuniary, by stated or discretionary fines: and lastly there are others, that consist principally in their ignominy, though most of them are mixed with some degree of corporal pain; and these are inflicted chiefly for crimes, which arise from indigence, or which render even opulence disgraceful. Such as whipping, hard labour in the house of correction, the pillory, the stocks, and the ducking-stool.

Disgusting as this catalogue may seem, it will afford pleasure to an English reader, and do honour to the English law, to compare it with that shocking apparatus of death and torment, to be met with in the criminal codes of almost every other nation in Europe.[86]

Suggested Readings

Bailyn, Bernard. *The Ideological Origins of the American Republic* (Cambridge, MA: Harvard University Press, 1967).

Bilder, Mary Sarah. *The Transatlantic Constitution: Colonial Legal Culture and the Empire* (Cambridge, MA: Harvard University Press, 2004).

Bodenhamer, David J. *Fair Trial: Rights of the Accused in American History* (New York: Oxford University Press, 1992)

Breen, T. H. *American Insurgents, American Patriots: The Revolution of the People* (New York: Hill and Wang, 2010).

Greene, Jack P. *Peripheries and Center: Constitutional Development in the Extended Polities of the British Empire and the United States, 1607–1788* (Athens: University of Georgia Press, 1986).

Hamburger, Philip. *Law and Judicial Duty* (Cambridge, MA: Harvard University Press, 2008).

Helmholz, R. H., Charles M. Gray, John H. Langbein, Eben Moglen, Henry E. Smith, and Albert W. Alschuler. *The Privilege against Self-Incrimination: Its Origins and Development* (Chicago: University of Chicago Press, 1997).

Kammen, Michael G. *Spheres of Liberty: Changing Perceptions of Liberty in American Culture* (Madison: University of Wisconsin Press, 1986).

Lutz, Donald S. *The Origins of American Constitutionalism* (Baton Rouge: Louisiana State University Press, 1988).

Maier, Pauline. *American Scripture: Making the Declaration of Independence* (New York: Vintage, 1997).

McIlwain, Charles Howard. *The American Revolution: A Constitutional Interpretation* (New York: Macmillan, 1923).

McLaughlin, Andrew C. *The Foundations of American Constitutionalism* (New York: New York University Press, 1932).

Morgan, Edmund. *The Birth of the Republic, 1763–89* (Chicago: University of Chicago Press, 1956).

Pocock, J. G. A., ed. *Three British Revolutions: 1641, 1688, 1776* (Princeton, NJ: Princeton University Press, 1980).

Reid, Thomas Phillip. *The Constitutional History of the American Revolution*, 4 vols. (Madison: University of Wisconsin Press, 1986–1993).

Russell, Elmer Beecher. *The Review of American Colonial Legislation by the King in Council* (New York: Columbia University Press, 1915).

Smith, Joseph Henry. *Appeals to the Privy Council from the American Plantations* (New York: Columbia University Press, 1950).

Stoner, James R. *The Common Law and Liberal Theory: Coke, Hobbes, and the Origins of American Constitutionalism* (Lawrence: University Press of Kansas, 1992).

86. Blackstone, *Commentaries*, 4:370–71.

Chapter 3

The Founding Era: 1776–1791

I. Introduction

Americans began their national existence by declaring that "all men are created equal, that they are endowed by their creator with certain inalienable rights, [and] that among these are life, liberty and the pursuit of Happiness." The purpose of government, the Declaration of Independence continued, was "to secure these rights." Americans learned over the next fifteen years that declaring fundamental rights in the abstract was easier than defining these liberties or devising government institutions that secured those freedoms. Both during and immediately after the Revolution, the newly independent states faced disputes over the precise applications of the right to a jury trial, the right to free speech, and the right to religious liberty. Bitter conflicts arose over what governing arrangements best protected generally agreed-upon rights. Controversies raged over whether rights were best protected in a smaller or larger republic, whether a life-tenured institution such as the judiciary had a special responsibility for protecting rights, whether constitutional documents ought to include an explicit guarantee of rights, and, if so, what rights ought to be enumerated.

Founding Era Americans contested the value of enumerating rights in a constitution. Some state constitutions contained a bill of rights. Others did not. Often, the rights enumerated were haphazard.[1] Some state constitutions included a right to free speech; others did not. No evidence suggests that the presence or absence of particular rights in state constitutions reflected carefully considered views about the importance of the right in question. The original U.S. Constitution did not include a bill of rights, although the text did enumerate some liberties. Federalists claimed that such an enumeration was unnecessary. Prominent advocates of ratification insisted that the federal government lacked the powers necessary to violate fundamental rights and that a well-designed government could be trusted to protect fundamental rights, even when those rights were not explicitly enumerated.

Concerned with popular support for the Constitution, James Madison and other Federalists promised to pass a bill of rights during the First Congress. Madison honored that commitment, proposing an early version in late spring 1789. That proposal, in substantially revised form, was ratified in 1791. Few Americans in the Founding Era celebrated the significance of those constitutional amendments. Madison himself described the Bill of Rights as "not altogether useless." He and other Federalists remained more concerned with the structure of the national government than with the precise enumeration of constitutional liberties.

Factions (Parties and Interest Groups). National constitutional politics was shaped by the debate between Federalists and anti-Federalists. Federalists favored a strong national government with sufficient powers to promote national interests. Anti-Federalists favored a more limited government that lacked the power to oppress ordinary citizens. Federalists tended to be more affluent than anti-Federalists and more involved in commercial activities. The precise composition of each faction varied from state to state.

The Federalists and anti-Federalists who debated whether to ratify the Constitution were not parties in a modern sense. Neither faction had an organizational structure. Neither existed before the ratification debates, and the alliances formed during those debates

1. Leonard W. Levy, *Origins of the Bill of Rights* (New Haven: Yale University Press, 1999), 186.

Box 3-1 A Partial Cast of Characters of the Founding Era

George Mason	■ Virginia anti-Federalist ■ Virginia revolutionary active in protesting parliamentary violations of the British constitution ■ Drafted Virginia Declaration of Rights and state constitution in 1776 ■ Member of Philadelphia Convention that drafted U.S. Constitution ■ Opposed ratification of U.S. Constitution in Virginia convention because of absence of a bill of rights ■ Helped draft amendment proposals in Virginia convention that became basis for the Bill of Rights
James Madison	■ Virginia Federalist ■ Managed the passage of the Virginia Statute for Religious Freedom ■ Leading figure in the Philadelphia constitutional convention ■ An author of the *Federalist* essays supporting ratification ■ Authored the Bill of Rights ■ Advocated a moderate form of strict constructionism in constitutional interpretation ■ Secretly authored the Virginia Resolutions of 1798 ■ Helped create the Jeffersonian Republican Party ■ Secretary of state for Republican Thomas Jefferson (1801–09) ■ President of the United States (1809–17)
Benjamin Franklin	■ Pennsylvania Federalist ■ Advocate of closer union of the British colonies in North America ■ First postmaster general of the United States ■ Signer of the Declaration of Independence ■ American ambassador to France during the Revolution ■ Pennsylvania delegate to the Philadelphia constitutional convention ■ President of Pennsylvania (1785–88)
John Adams	■ Massachusetts Federalist ■ Leading patriot defending colonial rights against Britain before Revolution ■ Leading advocate for independence in Continental Congress ■ Primary American ambassador to Great Britain during the Revolution and Confederation period ■ Drafted Massachusetts Constitution of 1780 ■ First vice president of the United States (1789–97) ■ President of the United States (1797–1801)
Benjamin Rush	■ Pennsylvania Federalist ■ Signer of the Declaration of Independence ■ Member of the Pennsylvania state ratification convention for U.S. Constitution ■ Founder of Dickinson College ■ Advocate of government support for the distribution and reading of the Bible ■ Anti-slavery advocate ■ Prison reformer and opponent of capital punishment

quickly disintegrated. By the end of the Founding Era, James Madison and Alexander Hamilton, two of the authors of *The Federalist Papers*, were the leaders of rival factions in the national government.

Courts. Some Americans in the Founding Era suggested that courts might limit the incidence of minority or majority tyranny. Alexander Hamilton in *Federalist* 78 claimed that a federal judiciary would provide additional protection for individual rights. Nevertheless, in 1787 the framers focused on the structure of governing institutions as the primary device for limiting government and protecting individual rights.

The possibility of judicial review played a greater role during the debates over the Bill of Rights. During the Virginia ratification convention, George Mason and Patrick Henry celebrated potential judicial power to declare laws unconstitutional in speeches criticizing the lack of textual protections for individual liberties in the original Constitution.[2] "In the arguments in favor of a declaration of rights you omit one which has a great weight with me," Jefferson wrote Madison, "the legal check which it puts into the hands of the judiciary." Madison, when introducing the Bill of Rights in Congress, asserted, "If they are incorporated into the constitution, independent tribunals of justice will consider themselves in a peculiar manner the guardians of those rights." Proponents of a bill of rights also emphasized how enumerating liberties would provide civic education in fundamental principles. Constitutions taught people about their rights. The anti-Federalist Brutus stated that "a full declaration of rights" should have been included in the original version of the Constitution because "the principles . . . upon which the social compact is founded, ought to have been clearly and precisely stated."[3]

Constitutional Thought. The most important constitutional debates between 1776 and 1791 were over what government institutions best protected individual rights. Many Americans initially believed that regular elections and fair criminal trials sufficed to secure a free regime. Local majority rule guaranteed the selection of governing officials who would govern consistently and share broad understandings of justice. Trial by jury enabled local citizens to check the rare elected official bent on restricting popular rights. Majority rule was also consistent with the common understanding that rights could be limited when doing so was in the public interest. Americans in the late eighteenth century believed that restrictions on liberties that served the public good did not violate fundamental rights. No one had a right to use property in ways that harmed others. Most framers thought that government authorities could restrict speech and limit voting rights when such measures served common social interests.

During the 1780s such luminaries as James Madison, Alexander Hamilton, and George Washington became convinced that different government institutions were needed to protect liberty. In their view, constitutions should forestall both majority and minority tyranny. Madison and others feared that majority factions would redistribute property and repress religious heretics. The Constitution alleviated this threat to liberty by establishing a strong federal government with the power to prevent majority tyranny in the states and instituting a separation of powers within that federal government to prevent majority tyranny at the national level.

Most persons responsible for the U.S. Constitution were classical liberals. They agreed that constitutions protected individual rights, and they were committed to a liberal republic that would provide protection against external enemies, preserve domestic peace, and promote commercial prosperity. Unlike the founders of many previous regimes, the American founders rejected such nonliberal ends as achieving global domination or spreading the one true religion.

The 1780s saw substantial popular disagreement over the application of liberal rights. Virginians engaged in a vigorous debate over religious freedom. Ordinary citizens challenged inherited restrictions on voting. Some framers insisted that slavery was inconsistent with the principle that "all men are created equal." Abigail Adams suggested that this principle might also include women. Some of these voices were faint in the 1780s, but they became louder over time.

Legacies. The founding generation bequeathed to their descendants a set of enumerated rights and a set of institutions designed to protect those rights. Future

---

2. Merrill Jensen, ed., *The Documentary History of the Ratification of the Constitution* (Madison: State Historical Society of Wisconsin, 1978), 10:1219, 1361.

3. Brutus, "Essays of Brutus," in *The Anti-Federalist: Writings by the Opponents of the Constitution*, ed. Herbert Storing (Chicago: University of Chicago Press, 1981), 117.

Table 3-1 Ratification of the U.S. Constitution by State

State	Convention Majority	Ratification Date	Final Vote (%)
Delaware	Federalist	Dec. 7, 1787	100
Pennsylvania	Federalist	Dec. 12, 1787	67
New Jersey	Federalist	Dec. 19, 1787	100
Georgia	Federalist	Jan. 2, 1788	100
Connecticut	Federalist	Jan. 9, 1788	76
Massachusetts	Anti-Federalist	Feb. 6, 1788	53
Maryland	Federalist	April 28, 1788	85
South Carolina	Federalist	May 23, 1788	67
New Hampshire	Anti-Federalist	June 21, 1788	55
Constitution meets Article VII requirement for ratification			
Virginia	Evenly split	June 25, 1788	53
New York	Anti-Federalist	July 26, 1788	53
George Washington inaugurated as first president April 30, 1789 Bill of Rights passed by Congress Sept. 25, 1789			
North Carolina	Federalist	Nov. 21, 1789	71
Rhode Island	Anti-Federalist	May 29, 1790	52

generations of Americans determined what rights state and federal governments protected by interpreting the constitutional provisions ratified during the 1780s. When controversies broke out in 1798, 1917, and 1969 over government power to regulate political dissent, all parties turned to the protections for free speech that the founders had placed in the state and federal constitutions. The constitutional politics responsible for protecting these rights and liberties were also established by the founders. Supreme Court justices from 1789 to the present have been appointed according to the rules laid out in Article III of the U.S. Constitution. Presidential candidates who promise to ban abortion or support gun control must gain office according to the rules laid down in Article II, as modified by the Twelfth Amendment.

Many constitutional arguments over the next two hundred years relied on the original understanding or meaning of constitutional provisions. Some commentators insist that the Constitution should be interpreted in light of the specific rights that Americans in 1791 thought they were protecting. Whether the Eighth Amendment prohibits punishing armed robbery by death depends on whether late-eighteenth-century legal authorities thought punishing armed robbery by death was cruel and unusual. Others insist that the Constitution should be interpreted in light of the more general principles underlying the constitutional provisions ratified in the late eighteenth century. Whether the Eighth Amendment prohibits punishing armed robbery by death depends on whether that sanction is cruel and unusual, not on whether late-eighteenth-century legal authorities thought it cruel and unusual.

Some Americans ask whether the framers are worthy of this attention. Most celebrate the founding generation as having a remarkable capacity for propounding timeless insights into constitutional governance. In the Gettysburg Address, Abraham Lincoln credited the framers for bringing "forth . . . a new nation, conceived in liberty, and dedicated to the proposition that all men are created equal." Jack Rakove suggests that "the meditations about popular government that we encounter" when we read *The Federalist Papers* and other original commentaries on the Constitution "remain more profound than those that the ordinary politics of our endless democratic present usually sustain."[4] A few condemn this national rever-

4. Jack N. Rakove, *Original Meanings* (New York: Vintage, 1997), 368.

Illustration 3-1 Behold! A Fabric Now to Freedom Rear'd.
Allegorical James Trenchard engraving celebrating the ratification of the U.S. Constitution and the union of the thirteen states.

Source: Trenchard, James, b. 1747, engraver. Library of Congress Prints and Photographs Division Washington, DC 20540, USA.

ence for what they perceive as white, male propertied elites. In a controversial bicentennial address, Thurgood Marshall described the Constitution as "defective from the start, requiring several amendments, a civil war, and momentous social transformation to attain the system of constitutional government, and its respect for the individual freedoms and human rights, we hold as fundamental today."[5] Paul Brest claims that references

5. Thurgood Marshall, "The Constitution's Bicentennial: Commemorating the Wrong Document?" *Vanderbilt Law Review* 40 (1987): 1338.

to the framers in contemporary constitutional debates are analogous to "having a remote ancestor who came over on the *Mayflower*."[6]

II. Foundations

MAJOR DEVELOPMENTS

- Debates over the value of enumerating rights in a constitution
- Ratification of bills of rights in state constitutions
- Ratification of the Bill of Rights in the federal Constitution

Americans after the Revolution established written constitutions. The U.S. Constitution and the constitutions of the several states were embodied in specific texts. Those texts could be ratified only by a specific process at a specific time. Specific rules determined how constitutional texts could be amended.

Americans believed that a written constitution was superior to the unwritten English constitution. Written constitutions were clearer. By writing down their fundamental laws, the founders believed that they had established firm limitations on government power. A "written constitution," St. George Tucker declared in *Kamper v. Hawkins*, is "not an 'ideal thing, but a real existence: it can be produced in a visible form:' its principles can be ascertained from the living letter, not from obscure reasoning or deductions only."[7] English authorities questioned whether past practice supported an absolute prohibition on general warrants. Americans could point to the language in the Fourth Amendment that states, "No Warrants shall issue, but upon probable cause, . . . and particularly describing the place to be searched, and the persons or things to be seized." Written constitutions were less subject to alteration by ordinary politics than unwritten constitutions. By establishing a written constitution with specific rules for amendment, Americans believed that they had prevented elected officials from changing fundamental laws without approval from the people. Parliament claimed the authority to determine what speech was constitutionally protected. Congress had no similar power to alter unilaterally the First Amendment to the Constitution.

6. Paul Brest, "The Misconceived Quest for the Original Understanding," *Boston University Law Review* 60 (1980): 234.

7. *Kamper v. Hawkins*, 3 Va. 20, 78–79 (VA 1793).

Founding Era Americans confronted two questions when writing constitutions. The first question was what to write. Federalists insisted that writing down the structure and powers of government institutions provided sufficient protections for rights and liberties. Enumerating rights was unnecessary and might be counterproductive. Anti-Federalists insisted that government officials were less likely to ride roughshod over fundamental liberties when the Constitution contained a bill of rights. Americans ratified the Bill of Rights in 1791, but many Federalists remained skeptical that "parchment barriers" provided adequate protections for rights. The second question was whether the Constitution was the sole source of fundamental rights and liberties. Many prominent political actors during the Founding Era insisted that government officials had obligations to respect natural rights and the law of nations, even if those laws and rights were not specifically enumerated in the Constitution.

A. Sources

Americans established numerous new constitutional protections for rights. State constitutions included either a bill of rights or various provisions protecting fundamental rights. The Bill of Rights was added to the national Constitution in 1791. Section 14 of the Northwest Ordinance guaranteed the fundamental liberties of persons living in the Northwest Territories. These documents, combined with the post–Civil War Amendments to the federal Constitution, provide the legal foundations for fundamental rights in the United States.

Bills of rights and related enactments in the late eighteenth century were outcomes of political struggles over how consensual rights were best protected. Most Americans agreed that government should protect property rights, free speech, the right to a jury trial, and habeas corpus. With the important exceptions of religious freedom and slavery, few substantial disputes broke out between 1776 and 1791 over the substance of these rights. Federalists and anti-Federalists debated the institutional practices that best secured rights against oppressive government actions. Most Federalists believed that well-designed governmental institutions were the best constitutional means for preventing government oppression. Anti-Federalists insisted that the federal Constitution needed more explicit protections for fundamental rights.

The anti-Federalists won this debate, but the scope and significance of their victory was contested. In 1791 Americans ratified ten amendments that provided explicit protections for some rights. The Ninth Amendment stated that citizens had rights that were not specifically enumerated in the Constitution. Nevertheless, what role state and federal bills of rights would play in constitutional politics remained unclear. Many Federalists supported the Bill of Rights only because they believed that hortatory expressions of rights were likely to have little effect on political decisions. Others expected that the Bill of Rights would remind both citizens and public officials that government should protect fundamental rights, but have little legal authority. Thomas Jefferson was one of the very few public figures who anticipated that a bill of rights might provide courts with powerful tools to limit government.

Constitutions were not the only source of fundamental rights during the Founding Era. Many political activists insisted that government officials had obligations to protect natural rights, regardless of whether those rights were specifically enumerated in the relevant constitutional text. James Varnum in *Trevett v. Weeden* (RI 1786) maintained, "The Judges, and all others, are bound by the laws of nature in preference to any human laws, because they were ordained by God himself anterior to any civil or political institutions."[8] Several judges claimed that the law of nations bound state governments. Judge James Duane in *Rutgers v. Waddington* (NY 1784) asserted, "By our excellent constitution, the common law is declared to be part of the law of the land; and the *jus gentium* [law of nations] is a branch of the common law."

Constitutions and Amendments

State Constitutions. State constitutions framed and ratified during the 1770s and 1780s took very different approaches to enumerating fundamental rights. Pennsylvania, Massachusetts, North Carolina, and Maryland prefaced their state constitutions with long declarations of rights. The Virginia legislature enacted a separate declaration of rights. Georgia, South Carolina, New Jersey, and New York enumerated some fundamental rights, but not others. New York and New Jersey enumerated only a few rights; New Hampshire and Delaware failed to enumerate any. Rhode Island and Connecticut did not adopt state constitutions during the Founding Era at all. In general, the framers of state constitutions typically listed the rights they thought most needed protection, but why some rights were included and others excluded remains a mystery.

These state bills of rights and constitutional provisions were directed at all elected officials and ordinary citizens. Many clauses assert general principles, not specific liberties. The Virginia Declaration of Rights proclaims, "All men are by nature equally free and independent." These maxims were expected to guide legislatures and executives, but not serve as legal standards for judicial decisions. Rights provisions were often phrased as exhortations rather than legal commands. The constitution of Pennsylvania asserts, "The freedom of the press *ought* not to be restrained." The First Amendment to the Constitution of the United States more decisively declares, "Congress *shall* make no law . . . abridging the freedom of speech." Few precedents in the 1770s support claims that the liberties set out in bills of rights were judicially enforceable. Citizens protected constitutional rights by voting offending officials out of office.

The Federal Constitution. The federal Constitution that Americans drafted and ratified from 1787 to 1789 contained very few provisions that explicitly protected individual rights. Article I, Section 9 forbade Congress from suspending the writ of habeas corpus "unless in Cases of Rebellion or Invasion," passing bills of attainder, or making ex post facto laws. Article I, Section 10 declared that states could not pass bills of attainder, ex post facto laws, or laws "impairing the Obligation of Contract." A writ of habeas corpus (Latin for "produce the body") requires government officials to explain in court why their detention of the person named in the writ is lawful. A bill of attainder is a law that declares a specific person guilty of a crime. Congress, therefore, may not enact a measure declaring that you or your worst enemy has committed treason or seditious libel. An ex post facto law is a bill that penalizes behavior that was legal when the action took place. Government officials may pass laws prohibiting persons from consuming fatty foods, but government officials may not punish persons who consumed fatty foods before the bill was passed. The contracts clause prohibits debtor relief laws. Congress may not forbid banks from collecting money owed from student loans.

8. James M. Varnum, *The Case, Trevett v. Weeden* in *Bernard* in *The Bill of Rights: A Documentary History*, ed. Bernard Schwartz (New York: Chelsea House Publishers, 1971), 424.

The Bill of Rights. Many Americans objected to the constitutional failure to provide explicit protections for freedom of speech, the free exercise of religion, and trial by jury. A few members of the framing convention insisted on the addition of a bill of rights. Concern with that omission intensified during the ratification debates. Participants in this dispute focused more on how the Constitution should protect rights than on the rights the Constitution should protect. General consensus existed on the principles announced by the Declaration of Independence. Americans agreed that all persons had certain inalienable rights, such as the right to free speech. Federalists and anti-Federalists debated whether enumerating those specific rights was a waste of good parchment or an important means for securing those natural and social rights.

Prominent Federalists insisted that specific constitutional protections for individual rights were dangerous, useless, and confusing. No one could list all natural rights. Worse, a partial listing of rights implied that government could violate those rights that were omitted. A constitution that did not specify rights to engage in common recreational activities might allow officials the power to forbid people from playing card games or softball. Besides, Federalists insisted, the federal government was one of enumerated powers, and rights were protected by the absence of federal power. No need existed to specify that the government could not censor the press because no constitutional provision gave Congress the power to censor the press. Experience had taught many Federalists that constitutional texts did not restrain officials bent on unconstitutional usurpations. Roger Sherman informed New Englanders, "No bill of rights ever yet bound the supreme power longer than the honey moon of a new married couple, unless the rulers were interested in preserving the rights."[9] Federalists believed that a constitution could not adequately define fundamental rights. "What signifies a declaration that 'the liberty of the press shall be inviolably preserved?'" Alexander Hamilton asked in *Federalist* 84. "What is the liberty of the press? Who can give it any definition which would not leave the utmost latitude for evasion?"

Prominent proponents of ratification maintained that the best way to prevent government power from violating rights was by careful design of government institutions. "All observations founded upon the danger of usurpation," Hamilton wrote, "ought to be referred to the composition and structure of the government, not to the nature or extent of its powers." Federalists repeatedly declared that elections protected popular liberties far more effectively than what they derisively referred to as "parchment barriers." Roger Sherman of Connecticut maintained that making officials "dependent on the suffrage of the people for their appointment to, and continuance in office" was "a much greater security than a declaration of rights, or restraining clauses upon paper."[10] In *Federalist* 10, Madison insisted that the best protection for religious freedom was a large republic. Such a regime would encompass so many religious sects that no particular sect or combination of sects would have the political capacity to oppress other sects.

Anti-Federalists vigorously disputed contentions that republican governments could forego written protections for basic rights. The national government, in their view, was given substantial power to violate such fundamental liberties as the freedom of speech. Anti-Federalists saw such provisions as the "necessary and proper clause" of Article I, Section 8 as a grant of near-unlimited power to national officials. They feared that government officials would abuse these powers unless the Constitution enumerated fundamental freedoms. Brutus declared,

> The powers, rights, and authority, granted to the general government by this constitution, are as complete, with respect to every object to which they extend, as that of any state government—It reaches to every thing which concerns human happiness—Life, liberty, and property, are under its control. There is the same reason, therefore, that the exercise of power, in this case, should be restrained within proper limits [by a bill of rights].[11]

The anti-Federalist concern with a bill of rights created a political opening for such moderate Federalists as James Madison. Most anti-Federalists were less interested in provisions protecting the freedom of speech and similar rights than with amendments that weakened national power. Madison addressed the former, but not the latter, concern when he proposed the Bill of Rights. He drafted amendments that provided textual protections for various rights, but did not significantly limit federal powers. This political strategy

9. Jensen, *Documentary History*, 2:433.

10. Jensen, *Documentary History*, 14:387.

11. Brutus, "Essays of Brutus," 119.

culminated in the ratification of a bill of rights that few persons in the late eighteenth century celebrated. Many anti-Federalists insisted that the amendments ratified did little to limit overbearing federal power. Representative Elbridge Gerry of Massachusetts complained, "The amendments proposed by Congress . . . will not . . . serve any other purposes than to reconcile those who had no adequate idea of the essential defects of the Constitution."[12] Representative Benjamin Goodhue of Massachusetts declared, "We have at last gone through the wearisome business of amendments to the great joy of I believe every member of the House. . . . God grant it may have the effects which are desired and that we may never hear any more of it."[13]

State Bills of Rights

The Virginia Declaration of Rights and the Pennsylvania Constitution's Declaration of Rights are typical of the lengthy enumerations of rights that appear in some early state constitutions. What do these declarations have in common? What are their differences? How do they differ from the more famous Bill of Rights in the U.S. Constitution or the English Bill of Rights? What explains the differences between state declarations of rights and the federal Bill of Rights?

Virginia Declaration of Rights (1776)

I. That all men are by nature equally free and independent, and have certain inherent rights, of which, when they enter into a state of society, they cannot, by any compact, deprive or divest their posterity; namely, the enjoyment of life and liberty, with the means of acquiring and possessing property, and pursuing and obtaining happiness and safety.

II. That all power is vested in, and consequently derived from, the people; that magistrates are their trustees and servants, and at all times amenable to them.

III. That government is, or ought to be, instituted for the common benefit, protection, and security of the people, nation or community; of all the various modes and forms of government that is best, which is capable of producing the greatest degree of happiness and safety and is most effectually secured against the danger of maladministration; and that, whenever any government shall be found inadequate or contrary to these purposes, a majority of the community hath an indubitable, unalienable, and indefeasible right to reform, alter or abolish it, in such manner as shall be judged most conducive to the public weal.

IV. That no man, or set of men, are entitled to exclusive or separate emoluments or privileges from the community, but in consideration of public services; which, not being descendible, neither ought the offices of magistrate, legislator, or judge be hereditary.

V. That the legislative and executive powers of the state should be separate and distinct from the judicative; and, that the members of the two first may be restrained from oppression by feeling and participating the burthens of the people, they should, at fixed periods, be reduced to a private station, return into that body from which they were originally taken, and the vacancies be supplied by frequent, certain, and regular elections in which all, or any part of the former members, to be again eligible, or ineligible, as the laws shall direct.

VI. That elections of members to serve as representatives of the people in assembly ought to be free; and that all men, having sufficient evidence of permanent common interest with, and attachment to, the community have the right of suffrage and cannot be taxed or deprived of their property for public uses without their own consent or that of their representatives so elected, nor bound by any law to which they have not, in like manner, assented, for the public good.

VII. That all power of suspending laws, or the execution of laws, by any authority without consent of the representatives of the people is injurious to their rights and ought not to be exercised.

VIII. That in all capital or criminal prosecutions a man hath a right to demand the cause and nature of his accusation, to be confronted with the accusers and witnesses, to call for evidence in his favor, and to a speedy trial by an impartial jury of his vicinage, without whose unanimous consent he cannot be found guilty, nor can he be compelled to give evidence against himself; that no man be deprived of his liberty except by the law of the land or the judgement of his peers.

IX. That excessive bail ought not to be required, nor excessive fines imposed; nor cruel and unusual punishments inflicted.

12. Elbridge Gerry to John Wendell, September 14, 1789, in Helen E. Veit, Kenneth R. Bowling and Charlene Bangs Bickford, *Creating the Bill of Rights: The Documentary Record from the First Federal Congress* (Baltimore, MD: Johns Hopkins University Press, 1991), 294.

13. Benjamin Goodhue to the Salem Insurance Offices, August 23, 1789 in *Creating the Bill of Rights*, 286.

X. That general warrants, whereby any officer or messenger may be commanded to search suspected places without evidence of a fact committed, or to seize any person or persons not named, or whose offense is not particularly described and supported by evidence, are grievous and oppressive and ought not to be granted.

XI. That in controversies respecting property and in suits between man and man, the ancient trial by jury is preferable to any other and ought to be held sacred.

XII. That the freedom of the press is one of the greatest bulwarks of liberty and can never be restrained but by despotic governments.

XIII. That a well regulated militia, composed of the body of the people, trained to arms, is the proper, natural, and safe defense of a free state; that standing armies, in time of peace, should be avoided as dangerous to liberty; and that, in all cases, the military should be under strict subordination to, and be governed by, the civil power.

XIV. That the people have a right to uniform government; and therefore, that no government separate from, or independent of, the government of Virginia, ought to be erected or established within the limits thereof.

XV. That no free government, or the blessings of liberty, can be preserved to any people but by a firm adherence to justice, moderation, temperance, frugality, and virtue and by frequent recurrence to fundamental principles.

XVI. That religion, or the duty which we owe to our Creator and the manner of discharging it, can be directed by reason and conviction, not by force or violence; and therefore, all men are equally entitled to the free exercise of religion, according to the dictates of conscience; and that it is the mutual duty of all to practice Christian forbearance, love, and charity towards each other.

A Declaration of the Rights of the Inhabitants of Pennsylvania (1776)

I. That all men are born equally free and independent, and have certain natural, inherent and inalienable rights, amongst which are, the enjoying and defending life and liberty, acquiring, possessing and protecting property, and pursuing and obtaining happiness and safety.

II. That all men have a natural and unalienable right to worship Almighty God according to the dictates of their own consciences and understanding:

III. That the people of this State have the sole, exclusive and inherent right of governing and regulating the internal police of the same.

IV. That all power being originally inherent in, and consequently derived from, the people; therefore all officers of government, whether legislative or executive, are their trustees and servants, and at all times accountable to them.

V. That government is, or ought to be, instituted for the common benefit, protection and security of the people, nation or community; and not for the particular emolument or advantage of any single man, family, or sort of men, who are a part only of that community, And that the community hath an indubitable, unalienable and indefeasible right to reform, alter, or abolish government in such manner as shall be by that community judged most conducive to the public weal.

VI. That those who are employed in the legislative and executive business of the State, may be restrained from oppression, the people have a right, at such periods as they may think proper, to reduce their public officers to a private station, and supply the vacancies by certain and regular elections.

VII. That all elections ought to be free; and that all free men having a sufficient evident common interest with, and attachment to the community, have a right to elect officers, or to be elected into office.

VIII. That every member of society hath a right to be protected in the enjoyment of life, liberty and property, and therefore is bound to contribute his proportion towards the expence of that protection, and yield his personal service when necessary, or an equivalent thereto: But no part of a man's property can be justly taken from him, or applied to public uses, without his own consent, or that of his legal representatives: Nor can any man who is conscientiously scrupulous of bearing arms, be justly compelled thereto, if he will pay such equivalent, nor are the people bound by any laws, but such as they have in like manner assented to, for their common good.

IX. That in all prosecutions for criminal offences, a man hath a right to be heard by himself and his council, to demand the cause and nature of his accusation, to be confronted with the witnesses, to call for evidence in his favour, and a speedy public trial, by an impartial jury of the country, without the unanimous consent of which jury he cannot be found guilty; nor can he be compelled to give evidence against himself; nor can any man be justly deprived of his liberty except by the laws of the land, or the judgment of his peers.

X. That the people have a right to hold themselves, their houses, papers, and possessions free from search and seizure, and therefore warrants without oaths or affirmations first made, affording a sufficient foundation for them, and whereby any officer or messenger may be commanded or required to search suspected places, or to seize any person or persons, his or their property, not particularly described, are contrary to that right, and ought not to be granted.

XI. That in controversies respecting property, and in suits between man and man, the parties have a right to trial by jury, which ought to be held sacred.

XII. That the people have a right to freedom of speech, and of writing, and publishing their sentiments; therefore the freedom of the press ought not to be restrained.

XIII. That the people have a right to bear arms for the defence of themselves and the state; and as standing armies in the time of peace are dangerous to liberty, they ought not to be kept up; And that the military should be kept under strict subordination to, and governed by, the civil power.

XIV. That a frequent recurrence to fundamental principles, and a firm adherence to justice, moderation, temperance, industry, and frugality are absolutely necessary to preserve the blessings of liberty, and keep a government free: The people ought therefore to pay particular attention to these points in the choice of officers and representatives, and have a right to exact a due and constant regard to them, from their legislatures and magistrates, in the making and executing such laws as are necessary for the good government of the state.

XV. That all men have a natural inherent right to emigrate from one state to another that will receive them, or to form a new state in vacant countries, or in such countries as they can purchase, whenever they think that thereby they may promote their own happiness.

XVI. That the people have a right to assemble together, to consult for their common good, to instruct their representatives, and to apply to the legislature for redress of grievances, by address, petition, or remonstrance.

The Drafting Debates over the National Bill of Rights (1787)[14]

The framers paid very little attention to explicit constitutional protections for individual rights during the drafting convention in Philadelphia. Debate focused on the structure and powers of the national government. The southern demand that free states return fugitive slaves was the constitutional rights provision that garnered the most attention during the summer of 1787. Just before the convention adjourned, George Mason of Virginia urged fellow delegates to include a bill of rights or provide other specific protections for fundamental rights. This demand was rebuffed without debate. The motion for a Bill of Rights was defeated by a 10–0 vote. Massachusetts abstained. New York and Rhode Island were absent. A later motion to include constitutional protection for the press was defeated by a 7–4 vote. Massachusetts, Maryland, Virginia, and South Carolina voted for the motion. New York and Rhode Island were not present. When Mason later published his reasons for refusing to endorse the Constitution, he emphasized this omission.

The following excerpts constitute almost the entire debate over the inclusion of a bill of rights in the Constitution during the framing convention. Why did the framers spend so little energy on this question? Was this a political mistake?

Records of the Federal Constitution, September 12, 1787

GEORGE MASON (Virginia)

He wished the plan had been prefaced with a Bill of Rights, & would second a Motion if made for the purpose. It would give great quiet to the people. . . .

ROGER SHERMAN (Connecticut)

[He] was for securing the rights of the people where requisite. The State Declarations of Rights are not repealed by this Constitution; and being in force are sufficient—There are many cases where juries are proper which cannot be discriminating. The Legislature may be safely trusted.

14. Excerpted from Max Farrand, ed., *The Records of the Federal Convention of 1787* (New Haven, CT: Yale University Press, 1911).

GEORGE MASON

The Laws of the U.S. are to be paramount to State Bill of Rights.

Records of the Federal Convention, September 14, 1787

CHARLES PINCKNEY (South Carolina) and ELBRIDGE GERRY (Massachusetts)

[Pinkney and Gerry] moved to insert a declaration "that the liberty of the Press should be inviolably observed."

ROGER SHERMAN

It is unnecessary—The power of Congress does not extend to the Press.

George Mason, "Objections to This Constitution of Government"

There is no Declaration of Rights and the laws of the general government being paramount to the laws and constitution of the several States, the Declaration of Rights in the separate States are no security.

The Ratification Debates over the National Bill of Rights

Participants in the debates over whether to ratify the Constitution expressed more concern with the omission of a bill of rights than the persons who framed the Constitution. The most important anti-Federalist writings condemned the drafting convention's failure to provide explicit constitutional protections for such liberties as the freedom of speech and religion. Such leading Federalists as James Wilson and Alexander Hamilton defended this omission. They insisted that a bill of rights was unnecessary in a popular government with strictly enumerated powers.

Debate was particularly intense in Pennsylvania, where James Wilson and John Smilie engaged in an early and influential exchange over whether the Constitution should provide specific guarantees for fundamental rights. Wilson and his Federalist allies gained a majority for ratification at the state convention. Smilie and other Pennsylvania allies then issued a public dissent that attacked the absence of a constitutional bill of rights. Confronted with these anti-Federalist criticisms in the closely contested New York ratifying convention, Alexander Hamilton in Federalist *84 penned the classic Federalist defense for the constitutional failure to include a bill of rights.*

As the debates wore on, some Federalists moved toward a compromise position. James Madison in his correspondence with Thomas Jefferson indicated that he was not opposed to a bill of rights, even though he did not think such provisions particularly important. Many state ratification conventions approved the Constitution with the understanding that amendments protecting fundamental rights would swiftly be added. Virginia, New York, Massachusetts, South Carolina, New Hampshire, and North Carolina proposed amendments when voting to ratify the Constitution.

As you read the materials below, consider the following questions. To what extent was the debate over the Bill of Rights a debate over what rights the Constitution should protect or a debate over how the Constitution should protect rights? How did the different participants in the debate believe a bill of rights would function? Did the Federalists have an effective answer to anti-Federalist concerns that the federal government could exercise Article I powers to curtail rights? Did Hamilton and Wilson believe that the federal government would never censor the press, or that any censorship would be for a legitimate government purpose (and hence not violate the freedom of the press)? To what extent were anti-Federalists concerned with individual rights or government powers? To what extent would that distinction make little sense to the participants in the ratification debates over the Bill of Rights?

The Pennsylvania Ratification Debates (October 28, 1787)[15]

JAMES WILSON

I cannot say, Mr. President, what were the reasons of every member of that Convention for not adding a bill of rights. I believe the truth is, that such an idea never entered the mind of many of them. . . . A proposition to adopt a measure that would have supposed that we were throwing into the general government every power not expressly reserved by the people, would have been spurned at, in that house, with the greatest indignation. Even in a single government, if the powers of the people rest on the same establishment as is expressed in this Constitution, a bill of rights is by no means a necessary measure. In a government possessed of enumerated powers, such a measure would be not only unnecessary, but preposterous and dangerous. Whence comes this notion

15. Excerpted from Jonathan Elliot, ed., *The Debates in the Several State Conventions on the Adoption of the Federal Constitution as Recommended by the General Convention at Philadelphia in 1787*, 2nd ed. (Washington, DC: Jonathan Elliot, 1836), 2:408–09.

that in the United States there is no security without a bill of rights? Have the citizens of South Carolina no security for their liberties? They have no bill of rights. Are the citizens on the eastern side of the Delaware less free, or less secured in their liberties, than those on the western side? The state of New Jersey has no bill of rights. The state of New York has no bill of rights. The states of Connecticut and Rhode Island have no bill of rights. I know not whether I have exactly enumerated the states who have not thought it necessary to add *a bill of rights* to their constitutions; but this enumeration, sir, will serve to show by experience, as well as principle, that, even in single governments, a bill of rights is not an essential or necessary measure. But in a government consisting of enumerated powers, such as is proposed for the United States, a bill of rights would not only be unnecessary, but, in my humble judgment, highly imprudent. In all societies, there are many powers and rights which cannot be particularly enumerated. A bill of rights annexed to a constitution is *an enumeration of the powers* reserved. If we attempt an enumeration, every thing that is not enumerated is presumed to be given. The consequence is, that an imperfect enumeration would throw all implied power into the scale of the government, and the rights of the people would be rendered incomplete. On the other hand, an imperfect enumeration of the powers of government reserves all implied power to the people; and by that means the constitution becomes incomplete. But of the two, it is much safer to run the risk on the side of the constitution; for an omission in the enumeration of the powers of government is neither so dangerous nor important as an omission in the enumeration of the rights of the people. . . .

November 28, 1787[16]
JOHN SMILIE

The arguments which have been urged, Mr. President, have not, in my opinion, satisfactorily shown that a bill of rights would have been an improper, nay, that it is not a necessary appendage to the proposed system. . . . [T]he members of the federal convention were themselves convinced, in some degree, of the expediency and propriety of a bill of rights, for we find them expressly declaring that the writ of habeas corpus and the trial by jury of criminal cases shall not be suspended or infringed. How does this indeed agree with the maxim that whatever is not given is reserved? Does it not rather appear from the reservation of these two articles that everything else, which is not specified, is included in the powers delegated to the government? This, Sir, must prove the necessity of a full and explicit declaration of rights; and when we further consider the extensive, and undefined powers vested in the administrators of this system, when we consider the system itself as a great political compact between the governors and the governed, a plain, strong, and accurate criterion by which the people might at once determine when, and in what instance their rights were violated, is a preliminary, without which, this plan ought not to be adopted. So loosely, so inaccurately are the powers which are enumerated in this constitution defined, that it will be impossible, without a test of that kind, to ascertain the limits of authority, and to declare when government has degenerated into oppression. In that event the contest will arise between the people and the rulers: "You have exceeded the powers of your office, you have oppressed us," will be the language of the suffering citizen. The answer of the government will be short—"We have not exceeded our power; you have no test by which you can prove it." Hence, Sir, it will be impracticable to stop the progress of tyranny, for there will be no check but the people and their exertions must be futile and uncertain; since it will be difficult, indeed, to communicate to them the violation that has been committed, and their proceedings will be neither systematical nor unanimous. It is said, however, that the difficulty of framing a bill of rights was insurmountable; but, Mr. President, I cannot agree in this opinion. Our experience, and the numerous precedents before us, would have furnished a very sufficient guide. At present there is no security even for the rights of conscience, and under the sweeping force of the sixth article, every principle of a bill of rights, every stipulation for the most sacred and invaluable privileges of man, are left at the mercy of government.

The Address and Reasons of Dissent of the Minority of the Convention of Pennsylvania to Their Constituents (1787)[17]

. . . We offered our objections to the convention, and opposed those parts of the plan, which, in our opinion,

16. John Bach McMaster and Frederick D. Stone, eds., *Pennsylvania and the Federal Constitution, 1787–1788*, (Lancaster: Historical Society of Pennsylvania, 1888), 1:254–56.

17. McMaster and Stone, *Pennsylvania and the Federal Constitution*, 2:461–82.

would be injurious to you, in the best manner we were able; and closed our arguments by offering the following propositions to the convention.

1. The right of conscience shall be held inviolable, and neither the legislative, executive nor judicial powers of the United States shall have authority to alter, abrogate, or infringe any part of the constitution of the several states, which provide for the preservation of liberty in matters of religion.

2. That in controversies respecting property, and in suits between man and man, trial by jury shall remain as heretofore, as well in the federal courts, as in those of the several states.

3. That in all capital and criminal prosecutions, a man has a right to demand the cause and nature of his accusation, as well in the federal courts, as in those of the several states; to be heard by himself and his counsel, to be confronted with the accusers and witnesses; to call for evidence in his favor, and a speedy trial by an impartial jury of his vicinage, without whose unanimous consent, he cannot be found guilty, nor can he be compelled to give evidence against himself; and that no man be deprived of his liberty, except by the law of the land or the judgment of his peers.

4. That excessive bail ought not to be required, nor excessive fines imposed, nor cruel nor unusual punishments inflicted.

5. That warrants unsupported by evidence, whereby any officer or messenger may be commanded or required to search suspected places, or to seize any person or persons, his or their property, not particularly described, are grievous and oppressive, and shall not be granted either by the magistrates of the federal government or others.

6. That the people have a right to the freedom of speech, of writing and publishing their sentiments, therefore, the freedom of the press shall not be restrained by any law of the United States.

7. That the people have a right to bear arms for the defence of themselves and their own state, or the United States, or for the purpose of killing game; and no law shall be passed for disarming the people or any of them, unless for crimes committed, or real danger of public injury from individuals; and as standing armies in the time of peace are dangerous to liberty, they ought not to be kept up: and that the military shall be kept under strict subordination to and be governed by the civil powers.

8. The inhabitants of the several states shall have liberty to fowl and hunt in seasonable times, on the lands they hold, and on all other lands in the United States not inclosed, and in like manner to fish in all navigable waters, and others not private property, without being restrained therein by any laws to be passed by the legislature of the United States.

9. That no law shall be passed to restrain the legislatures of the several states from enacting laws for imposing taxes, except imposts and duties upon goods imported or exported, and postage on letters shall be levied by the authority of Congress.

10. That the house of representatives be properly increased in number; that elections shall remain free; that the several states shall have power to regulate the elections for senators and representatives, without being controled either directly or indirectly by any interference on the part of the Congress, and that elections of representatives be annual.

11. That the power of organizing, arming and disciplining the militia (the manner of disciplining the militia to be prescribed by Congress) remain with the individual states, and that Congress shall not have authority to call or march any of the militia out of their own state, without the consent of such state, and for such length of time only as such state shall agree.

That the sovereignty, freedom and independency of the several states shall be retained, and every power, jurisdiction and right which is not by this constitution expressly delegated to the United States in Congress assembled.

. . .

The first consideration that this review suggests, is the omission of a *BILL* of *RIGHTS*, ascertaining and fundamentally establishing those unalienable and personal rights of men, without the full, free, and secure enjoyment of which there can be no liberty, and over which it is not necessary for a good government to have the control. The principal of which are the rights of conscience, personal liberty by the clear and unequivocal establishment of the writ of habeas *corpus*, jury trial in criminal and civil cases, by an impartial jury of the vicinage or county, with the common law proceedings, for the safety of the accused in criminal prosecutions, and the liberty of the press, that scourge of tyrants, and the grand bulwark of every other liberty and privilege; the stipulations heretofore made in favor of them in the state constitutions, are entirely superceded by this constitution. . . .

Alexander Hamilton, The Federalist, *No. 84*

. . .

The most considerable of the remaining objections is that the plan of the convention contains no bill of rights. . . .

. . . The Constitution proposed by the convention contains . . . a number of such provisions.

. . .

The establishment of the writ of habeas corpus, the prohibition of ex-post-facto laws, and of TITLES OF NOBILITY . . . are perhaps greater securities to liberty and republicanism than [the Constitution of New York] contains. The creation of crimes after the commission of the fact, or, in other words, the subjecting of men to punishment for things which, when they were done, were breaches of no law, and the practice of arbitrary imprisonments, have been, in all ages, the favorite and most formidable instruments of tyranny. . . .

Nothing need be said to illustrate the importance of the prohibition of titles of nobility. This may truly be denominated the corner-stone of republican government; for so long as they are excluded, there can never be serious danger that the government will be any other than that of the people.

. . .

It has been several times truly remarked that bills of rights are, in their origin, stipulations between kings and their subjects, abridgements of prerogative in favor of privilege, reservations of rights not surrendered to the prince. Such was MAGNA CHARTA . . . , the PETITION OF RIGHT . . . (and) the Declaration of Right . . . in 1688, (which was) . . . afterwards thrown into the form of an act of parliament called the Bill of Rights. It is evident, therefore, that, according to their primitive signification, they have no application to constitutions professedly founded upon the power of the people, and executed by their immediate representatives and servants. Here, in strictness, the people surrender nothing; and as they retain every thing they have no need of particular reservations. "WE, THE PEOPLE of the United States, to secure the blessings of liberty to ourselves and our posterity, do ORDAIN and ESTABLISH this Constitution for the United States of America." Here is a better recognition of popular rights, than volumes of those aphorisms which make the principal figure in several of our State bills of rights, and which would sound much better in a treatise of ethics than in a constitution of government.

. . .

I go further, and affirm that bills of rights, in the sense and to the extent in which they are contended for, are not only unnecessary in the proposed Constitution, but would even be dangerous. They would contain various exceptions to powers not granted; and, on this very account, would afford a colorable pretext to claim more than were granted. For why declare that things shall not be done which there is no power to do? Why, for instance, should it be said that the liberty of the press shall not be restrained, when no power is given by which restrictions may be imposed? I will not contend that such a provision would confer a regulating power; but it is evident that it would furnish, to men disposed to usurp, a plausible pretense for claiming that power. They might urge with a semblance of reason, that the Constitution ought not to be charged with the absurdity of providing against the abuse of an authority which was not given, and that the provision against restraining the liberty of the press afforded a clear implication, that a power to prescribe proper regulations concerning it was intended to be vested in the national government. This may serve as a specimen of the numerous handles which would be given to the doctrine of constructive powers, by the indulgence of an injudicious zeal for bills of rights.

On the subject of the liberty of the press, . . . I contend, that whatever has been said about it in that of any other State, amounts to nothing. What signifies a declaration, that "the liberty of the press shall be inviolably preserved"? What is the liberty of the press? Who can give it any definition which would not leave the utmost latitude for evasion? I hold it to be impracticable; and from this I infer, that its security, whatever fine declarations may be inserted in any constitution respecting it, must altogether depend on public opinion, and on the general spirit of the people and of the government. And here, after all, as is intimated upon another occasion, must we seek for the only solid basis of all our rights.

. . . The truth is, after all the declamations we have heard, that the Constitution is itself, in every rational sense, and to every useful purpose, A BILL OF RIGHTS. The several bills of rights in Great Britain form its Constitution, and conversely the constitution of each

State is its bill of rights. And the proposed Constitution, if adopted, will be the bill of rights of the Union. Is it one object of a bill of rights to declare and specify the political privileges of the citizens in the structure and administration of the government? This is done in the most ample and precise manner in the plan of the convention. . . . Is another object of a bill of rights to define certain immunities and modes of proceeding, which are relative to personal and private concerns? This we have seen has also been attended to, in a variety of cases, in the same plan. . . .

Thomas Jefferson and James Madison, Correspondence (1787–89)[18]

Thomas Jefferson to James Madison, December 20, 1787

. . . I will now add what I do not like. First the omission of a bill of rights providing clearly & without the aid of sophisms for freedom of religion, freedom of the press, protection against standing armies, restriction against monopolies, the eternal & unremitting force of the habeas corpus laws, and trials by jury in all matters of fact triable by the laws of the land & not by the law of nations. To say, as Mr. Wilson does, that a bill of rights was not necessary because all is reserved in the case of the general government which is not given, while in the particular ones all is given which is not reserved, might do for the audience to whom it was addressed, but is surely . . . opposed by strong inferences from the body of the instrument, as well as from the omission of the clause of our present confederation which had declared that in express terms. . . . Let me add that a bill of rights is what the people are entitled to against every government on earth, general or particular, & what no just government should refuse, or rest on inferences.

James Madison to Thomas Jefferson, October 17, 1788

. . .

My own opinion has always been in favor of a bill of rights; provided that it be so framed as not to imply powers not meant to be included in the enumeration. At the same time I have never thought the omission a material defect, nor been anxious to supply it even by subsequent amendment, for any other reason than that it is anxiously desired by others. I have favored it because I suppose it might be of use, and if properly executed could not be of disservice.

I have not viewed it in an important light—

1. because I conceive that in a certain degree . . . the rights in question are reserved by the manner in which the federal powers are granted.

2. because there is great reason to fear that a positive declaration of some of the most essential rights could not be obtained in the requisite latitude. I am sure that the rights of conscience in particular, if submitted to public definition would be narrowed much more than they are ever likely to be by an assumed power.

3. because the limited powers of the federal Government and the jealousy of the subordinate Governments, afford a security which has not existed in the case of the State Governments, and exists in no other.

4. because experience proves the inefficiency of a bill of rights on those occasions when its controul is most needed. Repeated violations of these parchment barriers have been committed by overbearing majorities in every State. In Virginia I have seen the bill of rights violated in every instance where it has been opposed to a popular current. Notwithstanding the explicit provision contained in that instrument for the rights of Conscience, it is well known that a religious establishment would have taken place in that State, if the Legislative majority had found as they expected, a majority of the people in favor of the measure; and I am persuaded that if a majority of the people were now of one sect, the measure would still take place. . . .

Wherever the real power in a government lies, there is the danger of oppression. In our Governments the real power lies in the majority of the Community, and the invasion of private rights is chiefly to be apprehended, not from acts of Government contrary to the sense of its constituents, but from acts in which the Government is the mere instrument of the major number of the Constituents. The difference so far as it relates to the point in question—the efficacy of a bill of rights in controlling abuses of power—lies in this: that in a monarchy the latent force of the nation is superior to that of the Sovereign, and a solemn charter of popular rights must have a great effect, as a standard for trying the validity of public acts, and a signal for rousing & uniting the superior force of the community; whereas in a popular Government, the political and physical power may be considered as vested in the same hands, that is in a majority of the

---

18. Excerpted from James Morton Smith, ed., *The Republic of Letters: The Correspondence between Thomas Jefferson and James Madison 1776-1826* (New York: W. W. Norton, 1995) 1:512, 564–65, 587–88.

people, and, consequently the tyrannical will of the Sovereign is not [to] be controlled by the dread of an appeal to any other force within the community. What use then it may be asked can a bill of rights serve in popular Governments? I answer the two following which, though less essential than in other Governments, sufficiently recommend the precaution: 1. The political truths declared in that solemn manner acquire by degrees the character of fundamental maxims of free Government, and as they become incorporated with the national sentiment, counteract the impulses of interest and passion. 2. Although it be generally true as above stated that the danger of oppression lies in the interested majorities of the people rather than in usurped acts of the Government, yet there may be occasions on which the evil may spring from the latter source; and on such, a bill of rights will be good ground for an appeal to the sense of the community. . . .

Supposing a bill of rights to be proper. . . . I am inclined to think that absolute restrictions in cases that are doubtful, or where emergencies may overrule them, ought to be avoided. The restrictions however strongly marked on paper will never be regarded when opposed to the decided sense of the public, and after repeated violations in extraordinary cases they will lose even their ordinary efficacy. Should a Rebellion or insurrection alarm the people as well as the Government, and a suspension of the Habeas Corpus be dictated by the alarm, no written prohibitions on earth would prevent the measure. . . .

Thomas Jefferson to James Madison, March 15, 1789

. . .

[Y]our thoughts on the subject of the Declaration of rights in the letter of Oct. 17. I have weighted with great satisfaction. . . . [I]n the arguments in favor of a declaration of rights you omit one which has a great weight with me, the legal check which it puts into the hands of the judiciary. This is a body, which if rendered independent, & kept strictly to their own department merits great confidence for their learning & integrity. . . .

I cannot refrain from making short answers to the objections which your letter states to have been missed.

1. That the rights in question are reserved by the manner in which the federal powers are granted. Answer. . . . [A] constitutive act which leaves some precious article unnoticed, and raises implications against others, a declaration of rights becomes necessary by way of supplement. This is the case of our new federal constitution. This instrument forms us into one state as to certain objects, and gives us a legislative & executive body for these objects. It should therefore guard us against their abuses of power within the field submitted to them.

2. A positive declaration of some essential rights could not be obtained in the requisite latitude. Answer. Half a loaf is better than no bread. If we cannot secure all our rights, let us secure what we can.

3. The limited powers of the federal government & jealousy of the subordinate governments afford a security which exists in no other instance. Answer. The first member of this seems resolvable into the 1st. objection before stated. The jealousy of the subordinate governments is a precious reliance. But observe that those governments are only agents. They must have principles furnished them whereon to found their opposition. The declaration of rights will be the text whereby they will try all the acts of the federal government. In this view it is necessary to the federal government also: as by the same text they may try the opposition of the subordinate governments.

4. Experience proves the inefficacy of a bill of rights. True. But though it is not absolutely efficacious under all circumstances, it is of great potency always, and rarely inefficacious. A brace the more will often keep up the building which would have fallen with that brace the less. There is a remarkable difference between the characters of the inconveniencies which attend a Declaration of rights, & those which attend the want of it. The inconveniences of the Declaration are that it may cramp government in it's useful exertions. But the evil of this is shortlived, moderate, & reparable. The inconveniencies of the want of a Declaration are permanent, afflicting & irreparable: they are in constant progression from bad to worse. The executive in our governments is not the sole, it is scarcely the principal object of my jealousy. The tyranny of the legislatures is the most formidable dread at present, and will be for long years. . . .

The First Congress Debates the Bill of Rights (June 8, 1789)[19]

Members of the First Congress were reluctant to consider constitutional amendments protecting specific liberties.

19. *Annals of Congress*, 1st Cong., 1st Sess., 424–26, 431–44.

William Smith of South Carolina, John Jackson of Georgia, and others insisted that representatives in 1789 had more important tasks. Amendment, in their view, should take place only after experience demonstrated a government propensity to violate rights.

James Madison was persistent. Concerned that North Carolina and Rhode Island had not yet ratified the Constitution, that substantial opposition to the Constitution remained in states that had ratified, and that he might have electoral trouble in Virginia if promises about an eventual bill of rights were not kept, Madison eventually persuaded many skeptical congressmen to consider, frame, and propose twelve amendments. The original first amendment, which concerned the ratio of representatives to population, was rejected by the states. The original second amendment declared, "No Law, varying the compensation for the services of the Senators and Representatives, shall take effect, until an election of Representatives shall have intervened." That provision became the Twenty-Seventh Amendment in 1992. The other ten amendments were ratified between 1789 and 1791 by the required supermajority. They are now known as the Bill of Rights.

Madison limited amendments to textual declarations of fundamental rights. He proposed constitutional protections for state violations of free speech, trial by jury, and other liberties. Madison recommended a more general clause, which later became the Ninth Amendment, which stated that the constitutional list of rights did not exhaust the rights retained by the people. Virginia and other states recommended numerous amendments adjusting the structure and powers of the national government. Madison proposed none of these changes. With the exception of a proposed constitutional amendment permitting localities to instruct their representatives, no amendment on the structure of government was debated when the First Congress considered the Bill of Rights. This pleased Madison. He informed political allies that rights could be enumerated only if such provisions did not alter basic constitutional practices. What would become the Bill of Rights, he stated, "aims at the two-fold object of removing the fears of the discontented, and of avoiding all such alterations as would . . . displease the adverse side. . . ."[20]

We do not know many details about the actual debates over the Bill of Rights.[21] *The Senate in 1789 did not keep an official journal. The debate in the House was remarkably sparse. We do know that Congress rejected outright Madison's proposal for an amendment limiting state power to violate fundamental rights. Congress changed the text of the other amendments Madison proposed. Consider the difference between Madison's suggested amendment, "The civil rights of none shall be abridged on account of religious belief or worship, nor shall any national religion be established, nor shall the full and equal rights of conscience be in any manner, or on any pretext infringed" and the final Constitutional declaration, "Congress shall make no law respecting an establishment of religion, or prohibiting the free exercise thereof." Americans have debated for more than two centuries whether these and other changes altered the substance of the rights protected or are merely stylistic flourishes.*

Federalists rarely considered the implications of particular language choices. Congressmen brushed aside questions about the meaning and application of proposed constitutional provisions. Some representatives raised questions about whether proposed constitutional protections for religious freedoms required exemptions for those with religious scruples against military combat. No record exists that reveals whether these concerns were resolved. For many Federalists, constitutional politics, not constitutional law, remained the primary line of defense against abusive official actions. Fundamental freedoms were secured when well-constructed constitutional processes privileged the selection of governing officials who had the combination of abilities and interests necessary to recognize the fundamental liberties of their fellow citizens and act on that judgment. The constitutional rights set out in the Bill of Rights merely guided the judgment process.

Prominent supporters of the Bill of Rights expressed concern with substantive issues only when anti-Federalists proposed amendments aimed at adjusting the constitutional politics that Federalists thought best protected fundamental rights. Federalist willingness to accommodate their political opponents came to an abrupt halt when Thomas Tudor Tucker moved that the House of Representatives add "to instruct their representatives" to what became the First Amendment. The right of instruction was a right to dictate how a representative should vote on an issue. This power gave local authorities increased control over national legislation. Critics of the

---

20. James Madison to Samuel Johnson, June 21, 1789, in *The Writings of James Madison* (New York: G.P. Putnam's Sons, 1900-1910), 5:409.

21. Virtually all known materials are ably collected in Veit et al., *Creating the Bill of Rights.*

original Constitution regarded a right to instruct representatives as central to a popular regime. "Instruction and representation in a republic," John Page declared, "appear to me to be inseparably connected." The leading proponents of the Bill of Rights vigorously rejected this effort to change the nature of constitutional representation. Theodore Sedgwick insisted that congressmen were "representatives of the great body of the people" of "the whole Union." If national legislators began regarding themselves as representing a particular state or district, he stated, "the greatest security the people have for their rights and privileges is destroyed." Roger Sherman condemned instructions for interfering with the "duty of a good representative to inquire what measures are most likely to promote the general welfare."[22] *These comments expressed two core Federalist commitments. First, legislation aimed at the common good did not violate fundamental rights. Second, the best way to secure the common good was to design an electoral system that enabled particularly virtuous persons to deliberate about the general welfare.*

As you read the following excerpts, consider the following questions. What were Madison's reasons for proposing the Bill of Rights? What legal and political changes did he believe the Bill of Rights made to the constitutional order? How, if at all, should the politics of the Bill of Rights influence their subsequent interpretation? To what extent should the framers be understood as enacting specific rules, general principles whose elucidation would be left to future generations, or a set of platitudes designed to appease the legally naive?

WILLIAM LOUGHTON SMITH (South Carolina)

. . . [I]t must appear extremely impolitic to go into the consideration of amending the Government, before it has begun to operate. Certainly, upon reflection, it must appear to be premature.

JAMES JACKSON (Georgia)

I am of opinion we ought not be in a hurry with respect to altering the constitution. . . . If I agree to alternations in the mode of administering the Government, I shall like to stand on the sure ground of experience, and not be treading air. What experience have we had of the good or bad qualities of this constitution? . . .

Let the constitution have a fair trial; let it be examined by experience, discover by that test what its errors are, and then talk of amending; but to attempt it now is doing it at a risk, which is certainly imprudent.

JAMES MADISON (Virginia)

. . . It appears to me that this house is bound by every motive of prudence, not to let the first session pass over without proposing to the state legislatures some things to be incorporated into the constitution, as will render it as acceptable to the whole people of the United States, as it has been found acceptable to a majority of them. I wish, among other reasons why something should be done, that those who have been friendly to the adoption of this constitution, may have the opportunity of proving to those who were opposed to it, that they were as sincerely devoted to liberty and a republican government, as those who charged them with wishing the adoption of this constitution in order to lay the foundation of an aristocracy or despotism. It will be a desirable thing to extinguish from the bosom of every member of the community any apprehensions, that there are those among his countrymen who wish to deprive them of the liberty for which they valiantly fought and honorably bled. And if there are amendments desired, of such a nature as will not injure the constitution, and they can be ingrafted so as to give satisfaction to the doubting part of our fellow citizens; the friends of the federal government will evince that spirit of deference and concession for which they have hitherto been distinguished.

. . .

. . . I should be unwilling to see a door opened for a re-consideration of the whole structure of the government, for a re-consideration of the principles and the substance of the powers given; because I doubt, if such a door was opened, if we should be very likely to stop at that point which would be safe to the government itself: But I do wish to see a door opened to consider, so far as to incorporate those provisions for the security of rights, against which I believe no serious objection has been made by any class of our constituents, such as would be likely to meet with the concurrence of two-thirds of both houses, and the approbation of three-fourths of the state legislatures. . . .

. . .

The amendments which have occurred to me, proper to be recommended by congress to the state legislatures, are these:

22. The quotes in this paragraph can be found at ibid., 163, 164, 172.

First. That there be prefixed to the constitution a declaration—That all power is originally vested in, and consequently derived from the people.

That government is instituted, and ought to be exercised for the benefit of the people; which consists in the enjoyment of life and liberty, with the right of acquiring and using property, and generally of pursuing and obtaining happiness and safety.

That the people have an indubitable, unalienable, and indefeasible right to reform or change their government, whenever it be found adverse or inadequate to the purposes of its institution.

. . .

Fourthly. That in article 1st, section 9, between clauses 3 and 4, be inserted these clauses, to wit, The civil rights of none shall be abridged on account of religious belief or worship, nor shall any national religion be established, nor shall the full and equal rights of conscience be in any manner, or on any pretext infringed.

The people shall not be deprived or abridged of their right to speak, to write, or to publish their sentiments; and the freedom of the press, as one of the great bulwarks of liberty, shall be inviolable.

The people shall not be restrained from peaceably assembling and consulting for their common good; nor from applying to the legislature by petitions, or remonstrances for redress of their grievances.

The right of the people to keep and bear arms shall not be infringed; a well armed, and well regulated militia being the best security of a free country: but no person religiously scrupulous of bearing arms, shall be compelled to render military service in person.

No soldier shall in time of peace be quartered in any house without the consent of the owner; nor at any time, but in a manner warranted by law.

No person shall be subject, except in cases of impeachment, to more than one punishment, or one trial for the same offence; nor shall be compelled to be a witness against himself; nor be deprived of life, liberty, or property without due process of law; nor be obliged to relinquish his property, where it may be necessary for public use, without a just compensation.

Excessive bail shall not be required, nor excessive fines imposed, nor cruel and unusual punishments inflicted.

The rights of the people to be secured in their persons, their houses, their papers, and their other property from all unreasonable searches and seizures, shall not be violated by warrants issued without probable cause, supported by oath or affirmation, or not particularly describing the places to be searched, or the persons or things to be seized.

In all criminal prosecutions, the accused shall enjoy the right to a speedy and public trial, to be informed of the cause and nature of the accusation, to be confronted with his accusers, and the witnesses against him; to have a compulsory process for obtaining witnesses in his favor; and to have the assistance of counsel for his defence.

The exceptions here or elsewhere in the constitution, made in favor of particular rights, shall not be so construed as to diminish the just importance of other rights retained by the people; or as to enlarge the powers delegated by the constitution; but either as actual limitations of such powers, or as inserted merely for greater caution.

Fifthly. That in article 1st, section 10, between clauses 1 and 2, be inserted this clause, to wit:

No state shall violate the equal rights of conscience, or the freedom of the press, or the trial by jury in criminal cases.

Sixthly. That article 3d, section 2, be annexed to the end of clause 2d, these words to wit: but no appeal to such court shall be allowed where the value in controversy shall not amount to ___ dollars: nor shall any fact triable by jury, according to the course of common law, be otherwise re-examinable than may consist with the principles of common law.

Seventhly. That in article 3d, section 2, the third clause be struck out, and in its place be inserted the clauses following, to wit:

The trial of all crimes (except in cases of impeachments, and cases arising in the land or naval forces, or the militia when on actual service in time of war or public danger) shall be by an impartial jury of freeholders of the vicinage, with the requisite of unanimity for conviction, of the right of challenge, and other accustomed requisites; and in all crimes punishable with loss of life or member, presentment or indictment by a grand jury, shall be an essential preliminary, provided that in cases of crimes committed within any county which may be in possession of an enemy, or in which a general insurrection may prevail, the trial may by law be authorized in some other county of the same state, as near as may be to the seat of the offence.

. . .

Eighthly. That immediately after article 6th, be inserted, as article 7th, the clauses following, to wit:

The powers delegated by this constitution, are appropriated to the departments to which they are respectively distributed: so that the legislative department shall never exercise the powers vested in the executive or judicial; nor the executive exercise the powers vested in the legislative or judicial; nor the judicial exercise the powers vested in the legislative or executive departments.

The powers not delegated by this constitution, nor prohibited by it to the states, are reserved to the States respectively.

. . .

The first of these amendments, relates to what may be called a bill of rights; I will own that I never considered this provision so essential to the federal constitution, as to make it improper to ratify it, until such an amendment was added; at the same time, I always conceived, that in a certain form and to a certain extent, such a provision was neither improper nor altogether useless. I am aware, that a great number of the most respectable friends to the government and champions for republican liberty, have thought such a provision, not only unnecessary, but even improper, nay, I believe some have gone so far as to think it even dangerous. . . .

. . . I am inclined to believe, if once bills of rights are established in all the states as well as the federal constitution, we shall find that although some of them are rather unimportant, yet, upon the whole, they will have a salutary tendency.

. . .

In our government it is, perhaps, less necessary to guard against the abuse in the executive department than any other; because it is not the stronger branch of the system, but the weaker: It therefore must be leveled against the legislative, for it is the most powerful, and most likely to be abused, because it is under the least control; hence, so far as a declaration of rights can tend to prevent the exercise of undue power, it cannot be doubted but such declaration is proper. But I confess that I do conceive, that in a government modified like this of the United States, the great danger lies rather in the abuse of the community than in the legislative body. The prescriptions in favor of liberty, ought to be leveled against that quarter where the greatest danger lies, namely, that which possesses the highest prerogative of power: But this is not found in either the executive or legislative departments of government, but in the body of the people, operating by the majority against the minority.

It may be thought all paper barriers against the power of the community, are too weak to be worthy of attention. I am sensible they are not so strong as to satisfy gentlemen of every description who have seen and examined thoroughly the texture of such a defence; yet, as they have a tendency to impress some degree of respect for them, to establish the public opinion in their favor, and rouse the attention of the whole community, it may be one mean to control the majority from those acts to which they might be otherwise inclined.

. . . It has been said that in the federal government [constitutional declarations of rights] are unnecessary, because the powers are enumerated, and it follows that all that are not granted by the constitution are retained: that the constitution is a bill of powers, the great residuum being the rights of the people; and therefore a bill of rights cannot be so necessary as if the residuum was thrown into the hands of the government. I admit that these arguments are not entirely without foundation; but they are not conclusive to the extent which has been supposed. It is true the powers of the general government are circumscribed; they are directed to particular objects; but even if government keeps within those limits, it has certain discretionary powers with respect to the means, which may admit of abuse to a certain extent. . . ; because in the constitution of the United States there is a clause granting to Congress the power to make all laws which shall be necessary and proper for carrying into execution all the powers vested in the government of the United States, or in any department or officer thereof; this enables them to fulfill every purpose for which the government was established. Now, may not laws be considered necessary and proper by Congress, for it is them who are to judge of the necessity and propriety to accomplish those special purposes which they may have in contemplation, which laws in themselves are neither necessary or proper; as well as improper laws could be enacted by the state legislatures, for fulfilling the more extended objects of those governments. I will state an instance which I think in point, and proves that this might be the case. The general government has a right to pass all laws which shall be necessary to collect its revenue; the means for enforcing the collection are within the direction of the legislature: may not general warrants be considered necessary for this purpose, as well as for some purposes which it was supposed at the framing of their constitutions the state governments had in view. . . .

. . .

It has been objected also against a bill of rights, that, by enumerating particular exceptions to the grant of power, it would disparage those rights which were not placed in that enumeration, and it might follow by implication, that those rights which were not singled out, were intended to be assigned into the hands of the general government, and were consequently insecure. This is one of the most plausible arguments I have ever heard urged against the admission of a bill of rights into this system; but, I conceive, that may be guarded against. I have attempted it, as gentlemen may see by turning to the last clause of the 4th resolution.

It has been said, that it is unnecessary to load the constitution with this provision, because it was not found effectual in the constitution of the particular states. It is true, there are a few particular states in which some of the most valuable articles have not, at one time or other, been violated; but does it not follow but they may have, to a certain degree, a salutary effect against the abuse of power. If they are incorporated into the constitution, independent tribunals of justice will consider themselves in a peculiar manner the guardians of those rights; they will be an impenetrable bulwark against every assumption of power in the legislative or executive; they will be naturally led to resist every encroachment upon rights expressly stipulated for in the constitution by the declaration of rights. Beside this security, there is a great probability that such a declaration in the federal system would be enforced; because the state legislatures will jealously and closely watch the operations of this government, and be able to resist with more effect every assumption of power than any other power on earth can do; and the greatest opponents to a federal government admit the state legislatures to be sure guardians of the people's liberty. . . .

JAMES JACKSON

The more I consider the subject of amendments, the more I am convinced it is improper. I revere the rights of my constituents as much as any gentleman in Congress, yet I am against inserting a declaration of rights in the constitution, and that for some of the reasons referred to by [Madison]. If such an addition is not dangerous or improper, it is at least unnecessary: that is a sufficient reason for not entering into the subject at a time when there are urgent calls for our attention to important business. Let me ask gentlemen, what reason there is for the suspicions which are to be removed by this measure? Who are the Congress, that such apprehensions should be entertained of them? Do we not belong to the mass of the people? Is there not a single right that, if infringed, will not affect us and our connections as much as any other person? Do we not return at the expiration of two years into private life? And is not this a security against encroachments? . . .

The Law of Nations

The law of nations consists of understandings about how civilized nations behave. Customary international law is "that system of right and justice that ought to prevail between nations or sovereign states."[23] Customary international law binds all political regimes, with or without their consent. Governments have an obligation to obey the law of nations, because these practices are rooted in principles of justice thought to be universal.

The law of nations protects certain individual rights. Spies could be hanged, eighteenth-century statesmen agreed, but captured soldiers who wore the uniform of their country had the right to be released when hostilities ended. Legal authorities determined what rights customary international law protects by looking for "a general and consistent practice of states followed by them from a sense of legal obligation."[24] Jefferson thought the "principles of the law of nations" were ascertained by examining "the Declarations, Stipulations and Practices of every civilized nation."[25]

Americans in the Founding Era believed that states and the national government should respect the law of nations. "The Law of Nations," John Jay stated in 1790, is "part of the laws of this, and of every civilized nation."[26] In *Rutgers v. Waddington* (NY 1784), a New York court ruled that the law of nations was part of the law of New York. The persons responsible for the federal Constitution reached similar conclusions. Article I, Section 8 of the Constitution empowers Congress to "define and punish . . . Offences against the Law of Nations." Alexander Hamilton extolled this power

---

23. Emmerich de Vattel, *Law of Nations*, ed. Joseph Chitty (Philadelphia: T. & J. W. Johnson, 1867), viii.

24. *Restatement (Third) of the Foreign Relations Law of the United States* §102(2) (1987).

25. Jefferson to Pinckney, May 7, 1793, in *The Writings of Thomas Jefferson*, ed. Paul Leicester Ford (New York: G. P. Putnam's Sons, 1904-5), 7:314.

26. John Jay, "Charge to the Grand Jury for the District of New York," *New Hampshire Gazette*, April 4, 1790.

to "aid and support" international law. "[F]or want of this authority," he stated, "the faith of the United States may be broken, their reputation sullied, and their peace interrupted by the negligence or misconception of any particular state."[27] Several prominent framers insisted that international laws were a higher authority than national laws. The "law of nations," a Virginia Federalist maintained, is "superior to any act or law of any nation."[28]

Prominent statesmen provided three different justifications for the legal obligation to respect rights protected by the law of nations.

1. Natural law. Every nation must respect the law of nations.
2. Positive law. The federal and state constitutions created an obligation to respect the law of nations.
3. Natural law as a default rule. Nations must respect the law of nations unless national laws explicitly reject that obligation.

Americans from 1776 to 1791 did not clearly distinguish between these justifications for recognizing the law of nations. That task was left for future generations.

Rutgers v. Waddington, New York Mayor's Court (1784)[29]

Elizabeth Rutgers owned a brewery in New York City. She left the city in 1776 after New York was captured by English forces. English authorities authorized James Waddington and several merchants to take possession of her brewery. Waddington and his business associates occupied the property for the rest of the American Revolution. In 1783 the restored New York legislature passed the Trespass Act, which permitted New Yorkers to sue those who had taken possession of their property during the American Revolution. The state law forbade defendants from claiming that a military order justified their actions. Rutgers immediately sued Waddington for damages. Alexander Hamilton, who was Waddington's lawyer, insisted that the Trespass Act violated the law of nations. Under the law of nations, belligerent forces may occupy abandoned property, and those authorized by military order to possess abandoned property may not be subsequently sued for trespass. Hamilton maintained that the New York Constitution of 1777 incorporated the law of nations, and that the Mayor's Court should declare the Trespass Act void for that reason.

The New York court declared that Waddington had a right under the law of nations to occupy the brewery. The New York Constitution, Major James Duane ruled, incorporated the law of nations, and that law of nations permitted Waddington to occupy abandoned property during a war if he had proper military authorization. What reasons does Duane give for claiming that New York must respect rights protected by the law of nations? Are these reasons sound? Would Rutgers v. Waddington *be correctly decided under the national Constitution?*

. . .

The truth is, that the law of nations is a noble and most important institution: The rights of sovereigns, and the happiness of the human race, are promoted by its maxims and concerned for its vindication.

We hitherto have not been so loudly called upon to form and inculcate an extensive knowledge of this interesting science; but now since we are placed in a new situation, as one of the nations of the earth, it is become an indispensable obligation. We profess to revere the rights of human nature; at every hazard and expense we have vindicated, and successfully established them in our land! and we cannot but reverence a law which is their chief guardian—a law which inculcates as a first principle—that the amiable precepts of the law of nature, are as obligatory on nations in their mutual intercourse, as they are on individuals in their conduct towards each other; and that every nation is bound to contribute all in its power to the happiness and perfection of others! What more eminently distinguishes the refined and polished nations of Europe, from the piratical states of Barbary, than a *respect* or a *contempt* for this law. Books therefore which treat of the law of nations have always been received with avidity and applause.

. . .

. . . By our excellent constitution, the common law is declared to be part of the law of the land; and the *jus gentium* [law of nations] is a branch of the common law. . . .

. . .

Indeed if we should not recognize the law of nations, neither ought the benefit of that law to be extended to us: and it would follow that our *commerce*,

27. John C. Hamilton, ed., *The Works of Alexander Hamilton* (New York: C. S. Francis, 1851), 2:274.

28. Elliot, *Debates*, 3:502.

29. Excerpted from Anonymous, *Arguments and Judgment of the Mayor's Court of the City of New York, in a Cause between Elizabeth Rutgers and Joshua Waddington* (New York: Samuel Loudon, 1784).

and our *persons*, in foreign parts, would be unprotected by the great sanctions, which it has enjoined.

. . .

We have in some measure anticipated another question, which was much debated at the hearing—

Whether the courts of justice ought to be governed by the *statute*, where it clearly militated against the law of nations.

. . .

The supremacy of the Legislature need not be called into question; if they think fit *positively* to enact a law, there is no power which can control them. When the main object of such a law is clearly expressed, and the intention manifest, the Judges are not at liberty, altho' it appears to them to be *unreasonable*, to reject it: for this were to set the *judicial* above the legislative, which would be subversive of all government.

But when a law is expressed in *general words*, and some *collateral matter*, which happens to arise from those general words is *unreasonable*, there the Judges are in decency to conclude, that the consequences were not foreseen by the Legislature; and therefore they are at liberty to expound the statute by *equity*, and only *quoad hoc* [to this extent] to disregard it.

B. Principles

Political elites in the Founding Era favored republican government. They believed that republics were committed to the following principles.

1. The people are the source of all political authority.
2. The purpose of government is to protect natural rights and advance the public good.
3. All government officials, not just the king (or chief executive), must respect natural rights.
4. The most important rights that government protects are life, liberty, and property.
5. Government may regulate behavior when doing so promotes the public good. No one may harm others or act contrary to the public good.
6. All political decisions are made by the people's elected representatives or by persons appointed by the people's elected representatives.
7. A well-designed republic follows procedures for staffing the government that privilege the selection of particularly virtuous persons with the probity to protect private rights and the wisdom to identify the public good.
8. A well-designed republic follows procedures for making laws that limit temptations for self-seeking behavior and provide incentives for representatives to protect private rights and seek the common good.

These principles differ from contemporary notions of democratic government. Most of the framers believed in the existence of a common good that was not simply an aggregation of individual interests. Numerous constitutional provisions were designed to prevent legislation that advanced the interests of one social group at the expense of another. Most of the framers believed that some people had more capacity to govern than others, and that constitutions should be designed to ensure the election of the best-qualified governors, as opposed to the most popular citizens. The persons responsible for the Constitution had no conception of electoral competition between political parties as being central to a democracy or vital for maintaining governmental accountability.

Thomas Jefferson, Declaration of Independence (1776)

The Declaration of Independence provided the theoretical justification for the American Revolution. King George III, Thomas Jefferson declared, had violated the fundamental rights of American colonists. The English people had done nothing to prevent those rights violations. This combination of tyranny and indifference provided legitimate grounds for the colonial decision to declare independence.

Jefferson's claim that "all men are created equal" echoes arguments made in John Locke's Second Treatise on Government. *What similarities do you detect in the reasoning? Do you detect important differences as well? Jefferson's complaints against King George III also echo seventeenth- and eighteenth-century English complaints against Charles I and other monarchs. Compare the Declaration of Independence to the English Bill of Rights (1689). To what extent did Jefferson accuse George III of repeating the crimes of Charles I? What new offenses does the Declaration include? What is the relationship between the Declaration and the American Bill of Rights? To what extent were Americans in 1776 and Americans in 1791 concerned with the same rights and the same threats to rights?*

. . .

We hold these truths to be self-evident, that all men are created equal, that they are endowed by their Creator with certain unalienable rights, that among these are life, liberty and the pursuit of happiness. That to secure these rights, governments are instituted among men, deriving their just powers from the consent of the governed. That whenever any form of government becomes destructive to these ends, it is the right of the people to alter or to abolish it, and to institute new government, laying its foundation on such principles and organizing its powers in such form, as to them shall seem most likely to effect their safety and happiness. . . . The history of the present King of Great Britain is a history of repeated injuries and usurpations, all having in direct object the establishment of an absolute tyranny over these states. To prove this, let facts be submitted to a candid world.

. . .

He has dissolved representative houses repeatedly, for opposing with manly firmness his invasions on the rights of the people.

. . .

He has made judges dependent on his will alone, for the tenure of their offices, and the amount and payment of their salaries.

He has erected a multitude of new offices, and sent hither swarms of officers to harass our people, and eat out their substance.

He has kept among us, in times of peace, standing armies without the consent of our legislature.

. . .

He has combined with others [Parliament] to subject us to a jurisdiction foreign to our constitution, and unacknowledged by our laws; giving his assent to their acts of pretended legislation:

For quartering large bodies of armed troops among us:

. . .

For imposing taxes on us without our consent:

For depriving us in many cases, of the benefits of trial by jury:

. . .

For suspending our own legislatures, and declaring themselves invested with power to legislate for us in all cases whatsoever.

. . . He has excited domestic insurrections amongst us, and has endeavored to bring on the inhabitants of our frontiers, the merciless Indian savages, whose known rule of warfare, is undistinguished destruction of all ages, sexes and conditions.[30]

. . .

Nor have we been wanting in attention to our British brethren. We have warned them from time to time of attempts by their legislature to extend an unwarrantable jurisdiction over us. We have reminded them of the circumstances of our emigration and settlement here. We have appealed to their native justice and magnanimity, and we have conjured them by the ties of our common kindred to disavow these usurpations, which, would inevitably interrupt our connections and correspondence. They too have been deaf to the voice of justice and of consanguinity. We must, therefore, acquiesce in the necessity, which denounces our separation, and hold them, as we hold the rest of mankind, enemies in war, in peace friends.

We, therefore, the representatives of the United States of America, in General Congress, assembled, appealing to the Supreme Judge of the world for the rectitude of our intentions, do, in the name, and by the authority of the good people of these colonies, solemnly publish and declare, that these united colonies are, and of right ought to be free and independent states; that they are absolved from all allegiance to the British Crown, and that all political connection between them and the state of Great Britain, is and ought to be totally dissolved. . . .

---

30. At this point, Jefferson penned an attack on the international slave trade.

> [H]e has waged cruel war against human nature itself, violating it's most sacred rights of life & liberty in the persons of a distant people who never offended him, captivating & carrying them to slavery in another hemisphere, or to incur miserable death in their transportations thither. This piratical warfare, the opprobrium of infidel powers, is the warfare of the Christian king of Great Britain. determined to keep open a market where MEN should be bought & sold, he has prostituted his negative for suppressing every legislative attempt to prohibit or to restrain this execrable commerce and that this assemblage of horrors might want no fact of distinguished die, he is now exciting those very people to rise in arms against us, and to purchase that liberty of which he has deprived them, by murdering the people upon whom he also obtruded them; thus paying off former crimes which he urges them to commit against the lives of another.

Congress voted to delete this passage.

Illustration 3-2 James Madison

Source: Edwin, David, 1776–1841, engraver; Sully, Thomas, 1783–1872, artist. Library of Congress Prints and Photographs Division Washington, DC 20540, USA.

James Madison, The Federalist, No. 10

Federalist *10 is presently considered the most important analysis of the founding era concerning how republican governments protect rights. In it, Madison distinguishes republics from democracies, elaborates the purposes of republic government, and explains why the institutions set out in the proposed Constitution will promote republican commitments to private right and the common good. Few framers agreed with Madison's claim that larger polities were more likely than smaller polities to protect rights.*[31] *Nevertheless,* Federalist *10 articulates the broad Federalist consensus that republican ends are better secured by constitutional design than by textual guarantees. Extended republics with religious diversity, Madison contends, are more likely than small, religiously homogenous republics to protect religious freedoms, no matter what language each uses in their respective constitutional texts.*

When reading the selection below, consider the following questions. How does Madison think a well-designed republic protects private rights and promotes the public interest? Is his republican scheme sound? Do Madisonian institutions remain good means for protecting private rights and promoting the public interest? What sort of office seekers are privileged by the constitutional rules for staffing the national government? What sorts of policies are privileged by the constitutional rules for making laws? If you wanted a better class of officeholders, how might you change the constitutional rules?

AMONG the numerous advantages promised by a well constructed Union, none deserves to be more accurately developed than its tendency to break and

31. Larry D. Kramer, "Madison's Audience," *Harvard Law Review* 112 (1999): 611.

control the violence of faction. . . . Complaints are everywhere heard from our most considerate and virtuous citizens, . . . that our governments are too unstable, that the public good is disregarded in the conflicts of rival parties, and that measures are too often decided, not according to the rules of justice and the rights of the minor party, but by the superior force of an interested and overbearing majority. However anxiously we may wish that these complaints had no foundation, the evidence, of known facts will not permit us to deny that they are in some degree true. . . .

By a faction, I understand a number of citizens, whether amounting to a majority or a minority of the whole, who are united and actuated by some common impulse of passion, or of interest, adverse to the rights of other citizens, or to the permanent and aggregate interests of the community.

. . .

There are . . . two methods of removing the causes of faction: the one, by destroying the liberty which is essential to its existence; the other, by giving to every citizen the same opinions, the same passions, and the same interests.

It could never be more truly said than of the first remedy, that it was worse than the disease. Liberty is to faction what air is to fire, an aliment without which it instantly expires. But it could not be less folly to abolish liberty, which is essential to political life, because it nourishes faction, than it would be to wish the annihilation of air, which is essential to animal life, because it imparts to fire its destructive agency.

The second expedient is as impracticable as the first would be unwise. As long as the reason of man continues fallible, and he is at liberty to exercise it, different opinions will be formed. . . . The diversity in the faculties of men, from which the rights of property originate, is not less an insuperable obstacle to a uniformity of interests. The protection of these faculties is the first object of government. From the protection of different and unequal faculties of acquiring property, the possession of different degrees and kinds of property immediately results; and from the influence of these on the sentiments and views of the respective proprietors, ensures a division of the society into different interests and parties.

The latent causes of faction are thus sown in the nature of man. . . . [T]he most common and durable source of factions has been the various and unequal distribution of property. Those who hold and those who are without property have ever formed distinct interests in society. Those who are creditors, and those who are debtors, fall under a like discrimination. A landed interest, a manufacturing interest, a mercantile interest, a moneyed interest, with many lesser interests, grow up of necessity in civilized nations, and divide them into different classes, actuated by different sentiments and views. The regulation of these various and interfering interests forms the principal task of modern legislation, and involves the spirit of party and faction in the necessary and ordinary operations of the government.

. . .

It is in vain to say that enlightened statesmen will be able to adjust these clashing interests, and render them all subservient to the public good. Enlightened statesmen will not always be at the helm. . . .

. . .

If a faction consists of less than a majority, relief is supplied by the republican principle, which enables the majority to defeat its sinister views by regular vote. . . . When a majority is included in a faction, the form of popular government, on the other hand, enables it to sacrifice to its ruling passion or interest both the public good and the rights of other citizens. To secure the public good and private rights against the danger of such a faction, and at the same time to preserve the spirit and the form of popular government, is then the great object to which our inquiries are directed. . . .

. . .

. . . [A] pure democracy, by which I mean a society consisting of a small number of citizens, who assemble and administer the government in person, can admit of no cure for the mischiefs of faction. A common passion or interest will, in almost every case, be felt by a majority of the whole; a communication and concert result from the form of government itself; and there is nothing to check the inducements to sacrifice the weaker party or an obnoxious individual. Hence it is that such democracies have ever been spectacles of turbulence and contention; have ever been found incompatible with personal security or the rights of property; and have in general been as short in their lives as they have been violent in their deaths. . . .

A republic, by which I mean a government in which the scheme of representation takes place, opens a different prospect, and promises the cure for which we are seeking. . . .

The two great points of difference between a democracy and a republic are: first, the delegation of the government, in the latter, to a small number of citizens elected by the rest; secondly, the greater number of citizens, and greater sphere of country, over which the latter may be extended.

The effect of the first difference is, on the one hand, to refine and enlarge the public views, by passing them through the medium of a chosen body of citizens, whose wisdom may best discern the true interest of their country, and whose patriotism and love of justice will be least likely to sacrifice it to temporary or partial considerations. Under such a regulation, it may well happen that the public voice, pronounced by the representatives of the people, will be more consonant to the public good than if pronounced by the people themselves, convened for the purpose. . . .

. . . [A]s each representative will be chosen by a greater number of citizens in the large than in the small republic, it will be more difficult for unworthy candidates to practice with success the vicious arts by which elections are too often carried; and the suffrages of the people being more free, will be more likely to centre in men who possess the most attractive merit and the most diffusive and established characters.

. . .

The other point of difference is, the greater number of citizens and extent of territory which may be brought within the compass of republican than of democratic government; and it is this circumstance principally which renders factious combinations less to be dreaded in the former than in the latter. The smaller the society, the fewer probably will be the distinct parties and interests composing it; the fewer the distinct parties and interests, the more frequently will a majority be found of the same party; and the smaller the number of individuals composing a majority, and the smaller the compass within which they are placed, the more easily will they concert and execute their plans of oppression. Extend the sphere, and you take in a greater variety of parties and interests; you make it less probable that a majority of the whole will have a common motive to invade the rights of other citizens; or if such a common motive exists, it will be more difficult for all who feel it to discover their own strength, and to act in unison with each other. . . .

. . .

The influence of factious leaders may kindle a flame within their particular States, but will be unable to spread a general conflagration through the other States. A religious sect may degenerate into a political faction in a part of the Confederacy; but the variety of sects dispersed over the entire face of it must secure the national councils against any danger from that source. A rage for paper money, for an abolition of debts, for an equal division of property, or for any other improper or wicked project, will be less apt to pervade the whole body of the Union than a particular member of it; in the same proportion as such a malady is more likely to taint a particular county or district, than an entire State. . . .

C. Scope

The founders did not clarify three questions about which governing officials were limited by the Bill of Rights and when those governing officials were limited.

1. Were state governments limited by the provisions in the Bill of Rights?
2. Was the federal government limited by the provisions in the Bill of Rights when making laws for American territories?
3. Were federal officials limited by the provisions in the Bill of Rights when they acted in foreign territory?

Madison's original Bill of Rights included a provision declaring, "No state shall violate the equal rights of conscience, or the freedom of the press, or the trial by jury in criminal cases." The congressional decision to reject that provision suggests a general understanding that the first ten amendments limited only federal power. No one suggested otherwise during the framing debates. No prominent framer discussed whether the Bill of Rights limited federal power in American territories or federal power overseas. These issues, ignored in the 1790s, became important during the early nineteenth century.

III. Individual Rights

MAJOR DEVELOPMENTS

- State courts declare legislative takings unconstitutional
- First constitutional protections for contract rights
- Greater emphasis on religious freedom

The Preface to the Constitution of the United States promises that Americans will enjoy the "blessings of liberty." These blessings include various private property rights, the freedom of religion, the right to bear arms, and free speech. During the Founding Era, general agreement existed on paradigmatic rights violations. Government could not confiscate property, execute Baptists, or disarm the local militia. Nevertheless, Americans from 1776 to 1791 did little to spell out the precise contours of most individual rights. Members of the First Congress did not discuss at length the meaning of various provisions in the Bill of Rights. As a result, this limited debate did not settle the rights controversies of the 1780s. Some representatives in the First Congress asked whether the free exercise clause gave religious pacifists a right to avoid military service, but neither the brief debate that followed nor the text of the First Amendment clearly answered their concern.

Americans in the Founding Era agreed that "the blessings of liberty" could be restricted when the common good justified regulation. Legal authorities commonly distinguished between liberty and license, acts inconsistent with the public welfare, safety, health, or morality. No person in the late eighteenth century had a right to harm himself, other people, or the community. "Every one," a New England minister declared, "must be required to do all he can that tends to the highest good of the state."[32] During the Revolution, many communities confiscated privately owned horses and weapons in order to provide the Continental Army with necessary supplies. Compensation for these confiscations was almost always inadequate and sometimes not paid at all.

Government could constitutionally restrict liberty only when doing so promoted the common good. Public officials violated liberty rights when they regulated private behavior or property solely to serve the interests of particular persons or classes. Taxation was a legitimate means for providing the money necessary to build local roads. However, government could not tax the wealthy solely to redistribute their assets to the poor. Unsurprisingly, whether an act furthered the common good or merely served private interests was hotly contested during the Founding Era.

32. Willi Paul Adams, *The First American Constitutions: Republican Ideology and the Making of the State Constitutions in the Revolutionary Era* (Lanham, MD: Rowman & Littlefield, 2001), 217.

A. Property

The persons responsible for the national and state constitutions during the Founding Era were committed to protecting property rights. Influential framers asserted that "property was certainly the principal object of Society" (John Rutledge), that the "one great object of Government is personal protection and the security of property" (Alexander Hamilton), and that "property must be secured or liberty cannot exist" (John Adams).[33] Charles Beard's *An Economic Interpretation of the Constitution of the United States* (1913) ignited a major controversy by claiming that large property holders and land speculators drafted and ratified the Constitution in order the protect their wealth. Subsequent research demonstrated that the Beard thesis was exaggerated, if not wrongheaded.[34] Nevertheless, no one disputes that the founders believed that written constitutions were vital means for securing private property.

The U.S. Constitution provided three direct protections for property rights:

1. The Fifth Amendment states, "No person shall . . . be deprived of life, liberty, or property, without due process of law."
2. The Fifth Amendment also states, "nor shall private property be taken for public use, without just compensation."
3. Article I, Section 10 states, "No State shall . . . make any Thing but gold and silver Coin a Tender in Payment of Debts" or "pass any . . . Law impairing the Obligation of Contracts."

Many state constitutions included a due process clause, a takings clause, or clauses aimed at protecting similar rights. Some state constitutions prohibited entails, legal devices that allowed aristocrats to ensure that their large holdings could not be broken up into smaller estates. By forbidding entails and related

33. James W. Ely, Jr., *The Guardian of Every Other Right: A Constitutional History of Property Rights*, 3rd ed. (New York: Oxford University Press, 2008), 43.

34. Charles Beard, *An Economic Interpretation of the Constitution of the United States* (New York: Macmillan, 1913). For responses, see Robert E. Brown, *Charles Beard and the Constitution* (Princeton, NJ: Princeton University Press, 1956); Forrest McDonald, *We the People* (Chicago: University of Chicago Press, 1958); D. W. Brogan, "The Quarrel over Charles Austin Beard and the American Constitution," *Economic History Review* 18 (1965): 199; Robert A. McGuire, *To Form a More Perfect Union* (New York: Oxford University Press, 2003).

common law practices, Founding Era constitutionalists thought they were enabling more citizens to acquire property and preventing a permanent class of large landholders from forming.

Property qualifications for voting were an important indirect constitutional protection for property rights. All states in 1790 required that persons own some property in order to vote. The Constitution of the United States incorporates these requirements by making the right to vote for a member of the House of Representatives conditional on the right to vote in certain state elections. If a person does not meet the property requirements to vote for a member of the lower house of the Maryland legislature, then that person has no constitutional right to vote in a federal election. Federalists were confident that a legislature composed of representatives elected by property holders did not need further written limitations on their power to regulate property. Such officials could be trusted to regulate property only when the regulation was consistent with the interests of most property holders.

Contracts

Contracts and commercial paper played an increasingly prominent role in economic life during the late eighteenth century. The commercial revolution that was underway in England and the United States created a new class of entrepreneurs whose wealth lay in stocks, bonds, and debts. These holdings needed constitutional protection. When Madison in 1786 described the "improper and wicked project[s]" that threatened new forms of property, he was referring to the "rage for paper money, for an abolition of debts." Paper money and an abolition of debts, Federalists agreed, transferred property (the debt) from A (the creditor) to B (the debtor) without due process of law.

Article I, Section 10 provides two constitutional protections for creditors. First, by preventing states from printing paper money (which causes inflation), the Constitution requires borrowers to pay their debts in currency worth approximately what the currency was worth when the loan was made. Second, the contracts clause, which forbids states from passing legislation that "impair(s) the obligation of contract," prevents local governments from freeing borrowers from their legal obligation to pay their debts.

Leading Federalists expected the contracts clause to provide crucial protections for property. Madison asserted that the provision was a "bulwark in favor of personal security and private rights." Charles Pinckney of South Carolina declared that the contracts clause was "the soul of the Constitution." "No more shall paper money, no more shall tender-laws, drive their commerce from our shores," he stated, "and darken the American name in every country where it is known." Anti-Federalists feared that the contracts clause was one of many constitutional provisions that favored the formation of a wealthy aristocracy. Luther Martin of Maryland complained that states would not long be able "to prevent the *wealthy creditor* and the *monied man* from *totally* destroying the *poor* though even *industrious debtor*."[35]

Takings and Due Process

Americans in the Founding Era agreed that the due process clause forbade government from taking Blackacre Estate from A and giving it to B. Government could take Blackacre from A only if that taking advanced the common good. Furthermore, government had to compensate the original owner when property was taken for public purposes.

The most common constitutional dispute in the Founding Era was over what constituted taking from A and giving to B. Suppose both A and B claimed a valid title to Blackacre. Could a legislature resolve that dispute in favor of A? Several state courts rejected that legislative power. *Bayard v. Singleton* (NC 1787) and *Bowman v. Middleton* (SC 1792) held that juries were the appropriate constitutional institution for resolving disputes over property. Legislation resolving land disputes unconstitutionally took property without due process of law because persons had a constitutional right to have a jury determine whether their title to the property was valid. The South Carolina Court of Common Pleas in *Bowman* declared, "It was against common right, as well as against Magna Charta, to take away the freehold of one man, and vest it in another; and that too, to the prejudice of third persons, without any compensation, or even a trial by a jury of the country, to determine the right in question."[36]

---

35. Ely, *The Guardian of Every Other Right*, 50–51.
36. *Bowman v. Middleton*, 1 Bay 252 (SC 1792).

Bayard v. Singleton, 1 N.C. 5 (1787)

Singleton purchased land from North Carolina that state officials had confiscated from Samuel Cornell during the Revolution. After the land was confiscated, Cornell sold his interest in the property to the Bayard family. In 1786 the Bayard family sued Singleton to regain possession of the land. Singleton claimed his title was valid because North Carolina law permitted the legislature to confiscate the estates of all loyalists and Cornell had declared allegiance to Great Britain. Singleton also pointed to a 1785 North Carolina law that required state courts to dismiss any lawsuit in which the plaintiffs were seeking to recover lands under the Confiscation Act. The Bayards claimed that both the North Carolina confiscation law and the law requiring that confiscation lawsuits be dismissed violated constitutional property rights.

The Supreme Court of North Carolina attempted to persuade the parties to compromise. During this delay, the judges were summoned by the state legislature and asked to explain why they had not dismissed the case. Dissatisfied with the judicial response, North Carolina officials charged the judges with disregarding a legislative act and making remarks that were derogatory of legislative authority. Found guilty of these charges, the judges were nevertheless discharged without penalty, since they had not actually been found guilty of malpractice in office. Singleton then renewed his motion to dismiss the case.

The Supreme Court of North Carolina declared unconstitutional the state law requiring the lawsuit to be dismissed. Constitutional rights to property, the court ruled, included the constitutional right to have property claims tried by a jury. How do the justices connect property rights and the right to a jury? Why did they believe that this connection is important?

Opinion of JUDGES ASHE, WILLIAMS, and SPENCER

. . .

That by the constitution every citizen had undoubtedly a right to a decision of his property by a trial by jury. For that if the Legislature could take away this right, and require him to stand condemned in his property without a trial, it might with as much authority require his life to be taken away without a trial by jury, and that he should stand condemned to die, without the formality of any trial at all: that if the members of the General Assembly could do this, they might with equal authority, not only render themselves the Legislators of the State for life, without any further election of the people, from thence transmit the dignity and authority of legislation down to their heirs male forever.

But that it was clear, that no act they could pass, could by any means repeal or alter the constitution, because if they could do this, they would at the same instant of time, destroy their own existence as a Legislature, and dissolve the government thereby established. Consequently the constitution (which the judicial power was bound to take notice of as much as of any other law whatever), standing in full force as the fundamental law of the land, notwithstanding the act on which the present motion was grounded, the same act must of course, in that instance, stand as abrogated and without any effect.

B. Religion

Most Americans were committed to protecting some religious freedoms. The First Amendment declares, "Congress shall make no law . . . prohibiting the free exercise" of religion. Many state constitutions included similar provisions protecting religious belief. Such clauses were no longer controversial by 1790. Americans in the Founding Era agreed that persons ought to be free to act according to their religious convictions in private.

The First Amendment also declares, "Congress shall make no law respecting an establishment of religion." Establishment clauses were more controversial. Many states in 1790 had established churches, even though popular support for establishment was weakening. A number of states constitutionally prohibited religious establishments. Some commentators today maintain that the establishment clause of the U.S. Constitution was intended to protect federalism, not individual rights. The establishment clause, in this view, protects state religious establishments and state decisions to forego a religious establishment from federal interference. Congress left Massachusetts free to establish the Congregational Church, Virginia free to establish the Anglican Church, and Pennsylvania free to have no establishment.[37]

The difference between Article VI of the U.S. Constitution and many state constitutions demonstrates

37. Akhil Reed Amar, *The Bill of Rights: Creation and Reconstruction* (New Haven: Yale University Press, 1998), 32–33.

the clear influence that federalism exerted on the idea of religious freedom. Persons of all religious faiths are eligible to hold all federal offices. Article VI asserts, "No religious Test shall ever be required as a Qualification to any Office or public Trust under the United States." This provision was controversial. Anti-Federalists feared that a "godless constitution" lacked the moral foundations necessary to maintain republican government. In contrast, many state constitutions imposed religious tests. The Delaware Constitution required all officeholders to take the following oath: "I, [name], do profess faith in God the Father, and in Jesus Christ His only Son, and in the Holy Ghost, one God, blessed for evermore; and I do acknowledge the holy scriptures of the Old and New Testament to be given by divine inspiration." The constitution of South Carolina declared that all executive branch officials in the state must be of "the Protestant religion" and required all voters to "acknowledge . . . the being of a God." Some state constitutions forbade members of the clergy from holding public office. The constitution of New York stated, "And whereas the ministers of the gospel are, by their profession, dedicated to the service of God and the care of souls, and ought not to be diverted from the great duties of their function; therefore, no minister of the gospel, or priest of any denomination whatsoever, shall, at any time hereafter, under any presence or description whatever, be eligible to, or capable of holding, any civil or military office or place within this State."

Proponents of religious freedom in the Founding Era relied heavily on religious arguments to support disestablishment and the freedom of conscience. James Madison claimed that state support for religion was "adverse to the diffusion of the light of Christianity."[38] Many Baptists insisted that God had ordained the separation of church and state. Isaac Backus, an influential Baptist minister in Massachusetts, urged Massachusetts officials to follow God's law by including the freedom of conscience in the state constitution:

> As God is the only worthy object of all religious worship, and nothing can be true religion but a voluntary obedience unto his revealed will, of which each rational soul has an equal right to judge for itself, every person has an unalienable right to act in all religious affairs according to the full persuasion of his own mind, where others are not injured thereby, And civil rules are so far from having any right to empower any person or persons, to judge for others in such affairs, and to enforce their judgments with the sword, that their power ought to be exerted to protect all persons and societies, within their jurisdiction from being injured or interrupted in the free enjoyment of this right.[39]

No consensus formed on the precise meaning of free exercise or establishment. Congress did not debate the particulars of any provision in the Bill of Rights at length. No one answered when Representative Egbert Benson of New York asked whether the free exercise clause required Congress to grant exemptions to persons with religious scruples against military service. We know that the precise wording of the religion

Table 3-2 Selected State Constitutional Provisions Regarding Religion, 1800

State	Established Church	Religious Test for Legislators
Vermont	Prohibited	Prohibited
New Hampshire	Yes	Protestant
Massachusetts	Yes	Protestant
Connecticut	Yes	None
Rhode Island	Prohibited	None
New York	Prohibited	Protestant
New Jersey	Prohibited	Protestant
Pennsylvania	Prohibited	Christian/Jewish
Delaware	Prohibited	Prohibited
Maryland	None	Christian
Virginia	None	None
North Carolina	Prohibited	Protestant
South Carolina	Prohibited	Protestant
Georgia	Prohibited	None
Tennessee	Prohibited	Prohibited
Kentucky	Prohibited	Prohibited

Source: John K. Wilson, "Religion under the State Constitutions, 1776–1800," *Journal of Church and State* 4 (1990): 753.

38. Madison, *Writings*, 2:189.

39. Isaac Backus, "A Declaration of the Rights, of the Inhabitants of the State of Massachusetts-Bay, in New-England," in *A Documentary History of Religion in America to 1877*, 3rd ed., ed. Eadwin Gaustad and Mark A. Noll (Grand Rapids, MI: Wm. B. Eerdmans, 2003), 238.

clauses changed during congressional debate, but we do not know why the final language was accepted and other phrases rejected.

Establishment

The framers made a self-conscious decision to reject a national religious establishment. The federal Constitution makes no reference to God or a divine being, does not empower government to assist religion, and explicitly prohibits the use of any religious oath as a condition for public office. Religious tests for office, many Federalists thought, more often disrupted the civic peace than fostered moral virtue. This commitment to disestablishment provoked debate during the ratification process. Some anti-Federalists believed that no republican government could exist without religious support. Others were concerned because, before the Bill of Rights was ratified, they thought the Constitution did not protect local churches from federal interference.

State constitutions were more sectarian. Eleven of the thirteen states had some form of establishment when the Constitution was ratified, and most required religious tests for office. Virginians abandoned an official state religion only after a bitter debate. During the 1780s James Madison and Thomas Jefferson engaged in a lengthy campaign for religious freedom in the state. Their opponents included Patrick Henry and other Virginia elites who favored maintaining the official status of the Anglican Church. That struggle ended with the passage of the Virginia Act for Religious Freedom, the law that disestablished the Anglican Church.

South Carolina Constitution of 1778, Section 38

The vast majority of states during the Founding Era established churches. Some states established a particular Protestant sect. The Anglican (Episcopal) Church was the established church of Virginia until the late 1780s. More often, states supported all Protestant sects. The South Carolina Constitution of 1778 provided the legal foundation for a multiple establishment. All Protestants were entitled to state support and assistance. Catholics and Jews had a right to practice their religion, but had no right to state support. Under this constitution, churches were required to elect their ministers. This provision expressed the conventional eighteenth-century Protestant fear that Catholics, whose priests were chosen by cardinals and bishops, were less fit to be republican citizens than Protestants, whose ministers were chosen by the local congregation.

The creation of the federal Constitution led to changes in some state practices. When South Carolina ratified a new constitution in 1790 it removed all religious tests for office-holders and deleted the intricate code of beliefs specified in Article 38 of the 1778 constitution. Charles Pinckney, governor and president of the state constitutional convention, had been a leading proponent of the prohibition of religious tests oaths in Article VI, section 3 of the federal Constitution. Article VIII, section 1 of the 1790 state constitution also guaranteed the free exercise of religion "without discrimination or preference."

That all persons and religious societies who acknowledge that there is one God, and a future state of rewards and punishments, and that God is publicly to be worshipped, shall be freely tolerated. The Christian Protestant religion shall be deemed, and is hereby constituted and declared to be, the established religion of this State. That all denominations of Christian Protestants in this State, demeaning themselves peaceably and faithfully, shall enjoy equal religious and civil privileges. . . . And that whenever fifteen or more male persons, not under twenty-one years of age, professing the Christian Protestant religion, and agreeing to unite themselves in a society for the purposes of religious worship, they shall, (on complying with the terms hereinafter mentioned,) be, and be constituted a church, and be esteemed and regarded in law as of the established religion of the State, and on a petition to the legislature shall be entitled to be incorporated and to enjoy equal privileges. . . . But that previous to the establishment and incorporation of the respective societies of every denomination as aforesaid, and in order to entitle them thereto, each society so petitioning shall have agreed to and subscribed in a book the following five articles, without which no agreement nor union of men upon presence of religion shall entitle them to be incorporated and esteemed as a church of the established religion of this State:

1st. That there is one eternal God, and a future state of rewards and punishments.
2d. That God is publicly to be worshipped.
3d. That the Christian religion is the true religion
4th. That the holy scriptures of the Old and New Testaments are of divine inspiration, and are the rule of faith and practice.

5th. That it is lawful and the duty of every man being thereunto called by those that govern, to bear witness to the truth.

And that every inhabitant of this State, when called to make an appeal to God as a witness to truth, shall be permitted to do it in that way which is most agreeable to the dictates of his own conscience. And that the people of this State may forever enjoy the right of electing their own pastors or clergy, and at the same time that the State may have sufficient security for the due discharge of the pastoral office, by those who shall be admitted to be clergymen, no person shall officiate as minister of any established church who shall not have been chosen by a majority of the society to which he shall minister, or by persons appointed by the said majority, to choose and procure a minister for them. . . . No person shall disturb or molest any religious assembly; nor shall use any reproachful, reviling, or abusive language against any church, that being the certain way of disturbing the peace, and of hindering the conversion of any to the truth, by engaging them in quarrels and animosities, to the hatred of the professors, and that profession which otherwise they might be brought to assent to. . . . No person shall, by law, be obliged to pay towards the maintenance and support of a religious worship that he does not freely join in, or has not voluntarily engaged to support. . . .

The Virginia Debate over Religious Assessments

The Virginia debate over religious assessments was the most important controversy concerning religious establishments that took place in the United States between the Revolution and the ratification of the Bill of Rights. The controversy began in 1784 when Patrick Henry proposed that all citizens be taxed to support Christian instruction. Henry's bill sought a multiple establishment, similar to that instituted in South Carolina, under which taxpayers could designate which Christian church they wished to support. Quakers and Mennonites could make other religious uses of the assessment. James Madison and Thomas Jefferson vigorously opposed state support for religious instruction. In 1785 Madison drafted the "Memorial and Remonstrance against Religious Assessments." That pamphlet was widely circulated and is generally credited with being responsible for the defeat of Henry's proposal. In 1786 the Virginia legislature passed "An Act for Establishing Religious Freedom." Thomas Jefferson, who drafted that bill, insisted that his tombstone mention only that he was the author of the Declaration of Independence, the founder of the University of Virginia, and the person responsible for the bill establishing religious freedom in Virginia.

Consider the following when reading the materials below. Do Madison and Jefferson reject Henry's claim that religious belief is vital to a republican state? Are their arguments for religious freedom more secular or as religious as the arguments that Roger Williams and William Penn made for religious freedom in the seventeenth century? To what extent is the dispute between Madison/Jefferson and Henry over the proper place of religion in a liberal state? To what extent is their dispute over the best means for promoting Christianity? Suppose that Henry had proposed the following. "All persons shall be taxed $5 to pay for after-school activities. All persons may designate which after-school activities they support." If some Virginians decided their taxes should go toward religious instruction, would Madison and Jefferson have opposed that proposed bill?

A Bill Establishing a Provision for Teachers of the Christian Religion (1784)[40]

Whereas the general diffusion of Christian knowledge hath a natural tendency to correct the morals of men, restrain their vices, and preserve the peace of society; which cannot be effected without a competent provision for learned teachers, who may be thereby enabled to devote their time and attention to the duty of instructing such citizens, as from their circumstances and want of education, cannot otherwise attain such knowledge; and it is judged that such provision may be made by the Legislature, without counteracting the liberal principle heretofore adopted and intended to be preserved by abolishing all distinctions of preeminence amongst the different societies or communities of Christians;

Be it therefore enacted by the General Assembly, That for the support of Christian teachers, _____ per centum on the amount, or _____ in the pound on the sum payable for tax on the property within this Commonwealth, is hereby assessed, and shall be paid by every person chargeable with the said tax at the time the same shall become due. . . .

40. Excerpt taken from *A Bill Establishing a Provision for Teachers of the Christian Religion* (Richmond, VA: n.p., 1784).

And be it enacted, That for every sum so paid, the Sheriff or Collector shall give a receipt, expressing therein to what society of Christians the person from whom he may receive the same shall direct the money to be paid. . . .

And be it further enacted, That the money to be raised by virtue of this Act, shall be by the Vestries, Elders, or Directors of each religious society, appropriated to a provision for a Minister or Teacher of the Gospel of their denomination, or the providing places of divine worship, and to none other use whatsoever, except in the denominations of Quakers and Menonists, who may receive what is collected from their members, and place it in their general fund, to be disposed of in a manner which they shall think best calculated to promote their particular mode of worship.

James Madison, "Memorial and Remonstrance against Religious Assessments"[41] (1785)

. . .

. . . [W]e hold it for a fundamental and undeniable truth, "that religion or the duty which we owe to our Creator and the manner of discharging it, can be directed only by reason and conviction, not by force or violence." The Religion then of every man must be left to the conviction and conscience of every man; and it is the right of every man to exercise it as these may dictate. This right is in its nature an unalienable right. It is unalienable, because the opinions of men, depending only on the evidence contemplated by their own minds cannot follow the dictates of other men: It is unalienable also, because what is here a right towards men, is a duty towards the Creator. It is the duty of every man to render to the Creator such homage and such only as he believes to be acceptable to him. This duty is precedent, both in order of time and in degree of obligation, to the claims of Civil Society. Before any man can be considered as a member of Civil Society, he must be considered as a subject of the Governor of the Universe: And if a member of Civil Society, do it with a saving of his allegiance to the Universal Sovereign. We maintain therefore that in matters of Religion, no man's right is abridged by the institution of Civil Society and that Religion is wholly exempt from its cognizance. True it is, that no other rule exists, by which any question which may divide a Society, can be ultimately determined, but the will of the majority; but it is also true that the majority may trespass on the rights of the minority.

. . .

. . . Who does not see that the same authority which can establish Christianity, in exclusion of all other Religions, may establish with the same ease any particular sect of Christians, in exclusion of all other Sects? That the same authority which can force a citizen to contribute three pence only of his property for the support of any one establishment, may force him to conform to any other establishment in all cases whatsoever?

. . . [T]he Bill violates the equality which ought to be the basis of every law, and which is more indispensible, in proportion as the validity or expediency of any law is more liable to be impeached. If "all men are by nature equally free and independent," all men are to be considered as entering into Society on equal conditions; as relinquishing no more, and therefore retaining no less, one than another, of their natural rights. Above all are they to be considered as retaining an "equal title to the free exercise of Religion according to the dictates of Conscience." Whilst we assert for ourselves a freedom to embrace, to profess and to observe the Religion which we believe to be of divine origin, we cannot deny an equal freedom to those whose minds have not yet yielded to the evidence which has convinced us. If this freedom be abused, it is an offence against God, not against man: To God, therefore, not to man, must an account of it be rendered. . . .

. . . [T]he Bill implies either that the Civil Magistrate is a competent Judge of Religious Truth; or that he may employ Religion as an engine of Civil policy. The first is an arrogant pretension falsified by the contradictory opinions of Rulers in all ages, and throughout the world: the second an unhallowed perversion of the means of salvation.

. . . [T]he establishment proposed by the Bill is not requisite for the support of the Christian Religion. To say that it is, is a contradiction to the Christian Religion itself, for every page of it disavows a dependence on the powers of this world: it is a contradiction to fact; for it is known that this Religion both existed and flourished, not only without the support of human laws, but in spite of every opposition from them, and not only during the period of miraculous aid, but long

41. Madison, *Writings*, 2:183.

after it had been left to its own evidence and the ordinary care of Providence. . . .

. . . [E]xperience witnessed that ecclesiastical establishments, instead of maintaining the purity and efficacy of Religion, have had a contrary operation. During almost fifteen centuries has the legal establishment of Christianity been on trial. What have been its fruits? More or less in all places, pride and indolence in the Clergy, ignorance and servility in the laity, in both, superstition, bigotry and persecution. . . .

. . . [T]he establishment in question is not necessary for the support of Civil Government. If it be urged as necessary for the support of Civil Government only as it is a means of supporting Religion, and it be not necessary for the latter purpose, it cannot be necessary for the former. If Religion be not within the cognizance of Civil Government how can its legal establishment be necessary to Civil Government? What influence in fact have ecclesiastical establishments had on Civil Society? In some instances they have been seen to erect a spiritual tyranny on the ruins of the Civil authority; in many instances they have been seen upholding the thrones of political tyranny: in no instance have they been seen the guardians of the liberties of the people. . . .

. . . [T]he proposed establishment is a departure from the generous policy, which, offering an Asylum to the persecuted and oppressed of every Nation and Religion, promised a lustre to our country, and an accession to the number of its citizens. . . .

. . .

. . . [I]t will destroy that moderation and harmony which the forbearance of our laws to intermeddle with Religion has produced among its several sects. Torrents of blood have been split in the old world, by vain attempts of the secular arm, to extinguish Religious discord, by proscribing all difference in Religious opinion. Time has at length revealed the true remedy. Every relaxation of narrow and rigorous policy, wherever it has been tried, has been found to assauge the disease. . . .

. . . [T]he policy of the Bill is adverse to the diffusion of the light of Christianity. . . . Instead of Levelling as far as possible, every obstacle to the victorious progress of Truth, the Bill with an ignoble and unchristian timidity would circumscribe it with a wall of defence against the encroachments of error.

. . .

. . . [F]inally, "the equal right of every citizen to the free exercise of his Religion according to the dictates of conscience" is held by the same tenure with all our other rights. If we recur to its origin, it is equally the gift of nature; if we weigh its importance, it cannot be less dear to us; if we consult the "Declaration of those rights which pertain to the good people of Virginia, as the basis and foundation of Government," it is enumerated with equal solemnity, or rather studied emphasis. Either the, we must say, that the Will of the Legislature is the only measure of their authority; and that in the plenitude of this authority, they may sweep away all our fundamental rights; or, that they are bound to leave this particular right untouched and sacred: Either we must say, that they may control the freedom of the press, may abolish the Trial by Jury, may swallow up the Executive and Judiciary Powers of the State; nay that they may despoil us of our very right of suffrage, and erect themselves into an independent and hereditary Assembly or, we must say, that they have no authority to enact into the law the Bill under consideration.

An Act for Establishing Religious Freedom (1786)[42]

Whereas, Almighty God hath created the mind free; that all attempts to influence it by temporal punishments or burdens, or by civil incapacitations tend only to beget habits of hypocrisy and meanness, and are a departure from the plan of the holy author of our religion, who being Lord, both of body and mind yet chose not to propagate it by coercions on either, . . . that the impious presumption of legislators and rulers, . . . who, being themselves but fallible and uninspired men have assumed dominion over the faith of others, setting up their own opinions and modes of thinking as the only true and infallible, and as such endeavoring to impose them on others, hath established and maintained false religions over the greatest part of the world and through all time; that to compel a man to furnish contributions of money for the propagation of opinions which he disbelieves is sinful and tyrannical; that even the forcing him to support this or that teacher of his own religious persuasion is depriving him of the comfortable liberty of giving his contributions to the particular pastor, whose

42. B. L. Rayner, *Sketches of the Life, Writings, and Opinions of Thomas Jefferson* (New York: A. Francis and W. Boardman, 1832), 159–60.

morals he would make his pattern, and whose powers he feels most persuasive to righteousness . . . ; that our civil rights have no dependence on our religious opinions any more than our opinions in physics or geometry, that therefore the proscribing any citizen as unworthy the public confidence, by laying upon him an incapacity of being called to offices of trust and emolument, unless he profess or renounce this or that religious opinion, is depriving him injuriously of those privileges and advantages, to which, in common with his fellow citizens, he has a natural right, that it tends only to corrupt the principles of that very Religion it is meant to encourage, by bribing with a monopoly of worldly honours and emoluments those who will externally profess and conform to it; . . . that to suffer the civil magistrate to intrude his powers into the field of opinion and to restrain the profession or propagation of principles on supposition of their ill tendency is a dangerous fallacy which at once destroys all religious liberty because he being of course judge of that tendency will make his opinions the rule of judgment and approve or condemn the sentiments of others only as they shall square with or differ from his own; that it is time enough for the rightful purposes of civil government, for its officers to interfere when principles break out into overt acts against peace and good order; and finally, that Truth is great, and will prevail if left to herself, that she is the proper and sufficient antagonist to error, and has nothing to fear from the conflict, unless by human interposition disarmed of her natural weapons free argument and debate, errors ceasing to be dangerous when it is permitted freely to contradict them: Be it enacted by General Assembly that no man shall be compelled to frequent or support any religious worship, place, or ministry whatsoever, nor shall be enforced, restrained, molested, or burdened in his body or goods, nor shall otherwise suffer on account of his religious opinions or belief, but that all men shall be free to profess, and by argument to maintain, their opinions in matters of Religion, and that the same shall in no wise diminish, enlarge or affect their civil capacities. And though we well know that this Assembly elected by the people for the ordinary purposes of Legislation only, have no power to restrain the acts of succeeding Assemblies constituted with powers equal to our own, and that therefore to declare this act irrevocable would be of no effect in law; yet we are free to declare, and do declare that the rights hereby asserted, are of the natural rights of mankind, and that if any act shall be hereafter passed to repeal the present or to narrow its operation, such act will be an infringement of natural right.

Free Exercise

Americans did not draw sharp distinctions between establishment and free exercise issues. The central debate of the framing period—the extent to which states could compel religious worship—raised both establishment issues (could the state require a particular form of religious worship?) and free exercise issues (could individuals be forced to worship God in a particular way?). Americans did confront ongoing issues with whether religious pacifists should be exempted from laws requiring able-bodied men to serve in the militia. The framers of the Bill of Rights recognized this matter but do not appear to have reached a definite conclusion on it.

House Debate over Conscientious Objectors (1789)[43]

Madison's proposed bill of rights included the following clause: "No person religiously scrupulous of bearing arms, shall be compelled to render military service in person." This provision was one of the few debated in the First Congress. Many representatives favored granting religious pacifists exemptions from military service. Nevertheless, Madison's proposal was rejected. Consider the significance of this deletion when reading the following excerpts from that debate. Was the clause dropped because representatives rejected the right to an exemption or because the clause was thought unnecessary? How should this debate over military exemptions for religious pacifists influence controversies over whether religious believers have rights to exemptions from other general laws that burden their religious practices?

REPRESENTATIVE JAMES JACKSON (Georgia)

[He] did not expect that all the people of the United States would turn Quaker or Moravians [religious sects that had conscientious objection to military service]; consequently one part would have to defend the other in case of invasion. Now this, in his opinion, was

43. *Annals of Congress*, 1st Cong., 1st Sess., 750–51, 766–67.

unjust, unless the constitution secured an equivalent: for this reason he moved to amend the clause, by inserting at the end of it, "upon paying an equivalent, to be established by law."

REPRESENTATIVE ROGER SHERMAN (Connecticut)

[H]e did not see an absolute necessity for a clause of this kind. We do not live under an arbitrary Government, said he, and the States, respectively, will have the government of the militia, unless when called into actual service.

REPRESENTATIVE EGBERT BENSON (New York)

No man can claim this indulgence of right. It may be a religious persuasion, but it is no natural right, and therefore ought to be left to the discretion of the Government. If this stands part of the constitution, it will be a question before the Judiciary on every regulation you make with respect to the organization of the militia, . . . whether it comports with this declaration or not.

REPRESENTATIVE THOMAS SCOTT (Pennsylvania)

[He] objected to the clause in the sixth amendment, "No person religiously scrupulous shall be compelled to bear arms." He observed that if this becomes part of the constitution, such persons can neither be called upon for their services, nor can an equivalent be demanded. . . . I conceive it, said he, to be a legislative right altogether. There are many sects I know, who are religiously scrupulous in this respect; I do not mean to deprive them of any indulgence the law affords; my design is to guard against those who are of no religion. It has been urged that religion is on the decline; if so, the argument is more strong in my favor, for when the time comes that religion shall be discarded, the generality of persons will have recourse to these pretexts to get excused from bearing arms.

REPRESENTATIVE ELIAS BOUDINOT (New Jersey)

Can any dependence, said he, be placed in men who are conscientious in this respect? Or what justice can there be in compelling them to bear arms, when, according to their religious principles, they would rather die than use them. . . . I hope that in establishing this Government, we may show the world that proper care is taken that the Government may not interfere with the religious sentiments of any person.

C. Guns

The Second Amendment to the U.S. Constitution declares, "A well regulated Militia, being necessary to the security of a free State, the right of the people to keep and bear Arms, shall not be infringed." This amendment explicitly connects the right to bear arms with militia service. During the ratification debates, anti-Federalists insisted that the Constitution gave Congress the power to disband all state militias. The national legislature, they feared, was empowered to raise a large professional army capable of violating fundamental rights. George Mason, the leading opponent of ratification in Virginia, expressed these concerns when he declared,

> There are various ways of destroying the militia. A standing army may be perpetually established in their stead. I abominate and detest the idea of a government, where there is a standing army. The militia may be here destroyed by that method which has been practiced in other parts if the world before; that is, by rendering useless—by disarming them. . . .
>
> No man has a greater regard for the military gentlemen than I have. . . . But when once a standing army is established in any country, the people lose their liberty. When, against a regular and disciplined army, yeomanry are the only defence,—yeomanry, unskilled and unarmed,—what chance is there for preserving freedom.[44]

The Second Amendment places the institution of state militia on a constitutional foundation. By preventing national officials from disarming the local citizens who constitute the local militia, the Constitution maintains state militia as a vital protection for local liberties. Or so most Americans in 1791 believed.

The Bill of Rights does not explicitly connect the right to bear arms with three other important eighteenth-century concerns: protection against criminals, protection against oppressive government officials, and hunting. Many state constitutions recognized a right to use weapons in self-defense. Article XIII of the Virginia Declaration of Rights asserts, "The people have a right to bear arms for the defence of themselves

44. David E. Young, ed., *The Origin of the Second Amendment: A Documentary History of the Bill of Rights 1787–1792*, 2nd ed. (Ontonagon, MI: Golden Oak Books, 1995), 400.

and the state." Some anti-Federalists wanted state constitutions and the federal Constitution to include specific protections for hunting. The dissenting minority in Pennsylvania proposed a constitutional amendment stating, "That the people have a right to bear arms for the defence of themselves and their own state, or the United States, or for the purpose of killing game and no law shall be passed for disarming the people or any of them, unless for crimes committed, or real danger of public injury from individuals."

Whether the framers thought the Second Amendment protected these freedoms is controversial. Consider the brief comments by Tench Coxe of Pennsylvania. Shortly after Madison introduced the Bill of Rights in Congress, Coxe contributed an article to the Philadelphia *Federal Gazette* that commented on the language that became the Second Amendment. He stated,

> As civil rulers, not having their duty to the people, duly before them, may attempt to tyrannize, and as the military forces which shall be occasionally raised to defend our country, might pervert their power to the injury of their fellow citizens, the people are confirmed by the next article in their right to keep and bear their private arms.[45]

All parties in contemporary debates over the Second Amendment claim that this passage supports their position. Does the reference to "private arms" suggest that the Bill of Rights protects an individual right to self-defense? Does the context of the quote suggest that private arms are expected to be used only in the state militia or a similar institution?[46]

D. Personal Freedom and Public Morality

The Ninth Amendment declares, "The enumeration in the Constitution, of certain rights, shall not be construed to deny or disparage others retained by the people." During the ratification debates, Federalists claimed that a complete enumeration of rights was impossible. James Iredell informed the North Carolina ratifying convention, "Let any one make what collection or enumeration of rights he pleases, I will immediately mention twenty or thirty more rights not contained in it."[47] Iredell and others correctly observed that no one can list every possible fundamental right and attempting to do so would make the Constitution unwieldy. The Ninth Amendment alleviated this fear of an incomplete enumeration.

When considering what rights the Ninth Amendment might protect, consider the rights that Federalists mentioned when asserting that no enumeration could include all possible liberties.[48] Noah Webster (of *Webster's Dictionary* fame) suggested that a complete enumeration of liberties would include a provision declaring, "Congress shall never restrain any inhabitant of America from eating and drinking, at seasonable times, or prevent his lying on his left side, in a long winter's night, or even on his back, when he is fatigued by lying on his right." Other Federalists added to this enumeration the right to marry, the right to bury the dead, the right to wear (or not wear) a beard, the right to make clothes, the right to wear a hat, and the right to choose one's bedtime. Some Federalists pointed out the tendency of popular conceptions of rights to change over time. Edmund Pendleton of Virginia thought that proposed bills of rights failed to anticipate that "in the progress of things, [we may] discover some great and Important [right], which we don't now think of."[49]

IV. Democratic Rights

MAJOR DEVELOPMENTS

- Debates over whether free speech rights were limited to prior restraints
- Property qualifications for voting and office holding
- Failure to define clearly the conditions for American citizenship

45. Tench Cox, "A Pennsylvania," in Young, *Origin of the Second Amendment*, 671.

46. The bibliography of Saul Cornell, ed., *Whose Right to Bear Arms Did the Second Amendment Protect?* (New York: Bedford/St. Martin's, 2000) includes a good selection of the leading works on all sides of the debate over the original meaning of the Second Amendment.

47. Elliot, *Debates*, 4:167.

48. This section relies heavily on Terry Brennan, "Natural Rights and the Constitution: The Original 'Original Intent,'" *Harvard Journal of Law and Public Policy* 15 (1992): 965.

49. David John Mays, ed., *The Letters and Papers of Edmund Pendleton, 1734–1803* (Charlottesville: University of Virginia Press, 1967), 2:533.

The American founders intended to establish a constitutional republic. In *Federalist* 10 James Madison emphasized that republican government "promise[d] the cure" for faction, the disease that proved fatal for all democratic governments. Republican institutions, he believed, encouraged the selection of virtuous rulers who would protect individual rights and pursue the common good. In a democracy, which Madison defined as a regime in which people met as a whole to determine laws and policies, policy reflected only what a majority of ordinary people thought good at a particular time.

Most Federalists shared Madison's analysis of the best form of popular government, even though many more often used *republic* and *democracy* as synonyms. The persons responsible for the Constitution were more inclined to view elections as a means for empowering a natural aristocracy who would govern wisely than as a means for facilitating government by popular opinion. Committed to popular government, the framers recognized the value of free speech, voting rights, and citizenship. Nevertheless, proponents of a constitutional republic in the late eighteenth century were more inclined than contemporary democrats to limit expression, suffrage, and citizenship when they thought that restrictions on these liberties promoted the public good.

Keep Madison's distinction between republican and democratic government in mind when you read the material in this section. Some contemporary thinkers maintain that eighteenth-century restrictions on democratic rights reflect the limited experience that Madison and others had with popular government. "Wise as the framers were," Robert Dahl writes, "they were necessarily limited by their profound ignorance."[50] Others interpret late-eighteenth-century restrictions on democratic rights as consistent with republican political commitments. Stephen Feldman suggests that republican forms of government permit political participation to be "subordinated . . . to the pursuit of the common good." This common good, in the Founding Era, was invoked to support the exclusion of persons of different races, religions, or ethnicities.[51] To what extent do the following materials support claims that Americans in the Founding Era were democrats, immature democrats, republicans, or something else?

A. Free Speech

Americans in the Founding Era were constitutionally committed to free speech. The First Amendment to the Constitution of the United States declares, "Congress shall make no law . . . abridging the freedom of speech, or of the press; or the right of the people peaceably to assemble, and to petition the Government for a redress of grievances." State constitutions contained similar provisions. The constitution of Massachusetts asserted, "The liberty of the press is essential to the security of freedom in a State; it ought not, therefore, to be restricted in this commonwealth." Some states had no explicit constitutional protection for free speech. This absence seems better explained by the Federalist belief that enumerated rights served little purpose than by any hostility to free speech.

Americans in the late eighteenth century disputed what speech merited constitutional protection. The parties in *Respublica v. Oswald* (PA 1788) debated whether constitutional protections for free speech were limited to prior restraints. The state prosecutor in Pennsylvania insisted that government was constitutionally free to punish expression after publication. Eleazar Oswald maintained that the Pennsylvania Constitution forbade censoring libels before publication and punishing libels after publication. Legal commentators proposed different theories of free speech. In 1788 James Wilson informed the Pennsylvania Ratification Convention that "what is meant by the liberty of the press is, that there should be no antecedent restraint upon it; but that every author is responsible when he attacks the security or welfare of the government, or the safety, character and property of the individual."[52] Three years later, Wilson gave a broader definition of free speech. He believed the "citizen under a free government has a right to think, to speak, to write, to print, and to publish freely, but with decency and truth, concerning public men, public bodies, and public measures."[53] Americans championed more libertarian understandings of free speech rights when they wished to speak

50. Robert A. Dahl, *How Democratic Is the American Constitution?* (New Haven, CT: Yale University Press, 2001), 7. See also Sanford Levinson, *Our Undemocratic Constitution: Where the Constitution Goes Wrong (and How We the People Can Correct It)* (New York: Oxford University Press, 2006).

51. Stephen M. Feldman, *Free Expression and Democracy in America: A History* (Chicago: University of Chicago Press, 2008), 5.

52. Elliot, *Debates*, 2:420.

53. James DeWitt Andrews, ed., *The Works of James Wilson* (Chicago: Callaghan and Co., 1896), 2:287.

than when they wished to prevent others from speaking. The same advocates of revolution in Boston who condemned English authorities for prosecuting the radical *Boston Gazette* later attempted to silence "the scandalous license of the tory presses."[54]

Some contemporary commentators believe that the First Amendment was a federalism provision, similar to the establishment clause. Congress was given no power to restrict any speech, even speech that no good republican thinker thought of any value. States would determine what expression was constitutionally protected.[55]

Most Americans in the Founding Era rejected Blackstone's claim that government could punish seditious libel. As noted in Chapter 2, seditious libel is criticism, true or false, of government officials. Consider the 1789 correspondence between John Adams and William Cushing, the chief justice of the Massachusetts Supreme Judicial Court. Cushing was concerned with the proper interpretation of the free speech clause in the Massachusetts Constitution. His letter maintained that republican governments provided constitutional protection for true comments about government.

> Judge Blackstone says . . . the liberty of the press consists in laying no *previous* restraints upon publication, and not in freedom from censure for criminal matter, when published. . . .
>
> But the words of our article understood according to plain English, make no such distinction, and must exclude *subsequent* restraints, as much as *previous* restraints. In other words, if all men are restrained by the fear of jails, scourges and loss of ears from examining the conduct of persons in administration and where their conduct is illegal, tyrannical and tending to overthrow the Constitution and introduce slavery, are so restrained from declaring it to the public *that* will be as effectual a restraint as any *previous* restraint whatever.
>
> . . . This liberty of publishing truth can never effectually injure a good government, or honest administrators; but it may save a state from the necessity of a revolution, as well as bring one about, when it is necessary.

Adams endorsed Cushing's view that constitutional protections for free speech encompassed a right to publish the truth. His reply to Cushing emphasized the distinctive role speech played in a republican regime,

> The difficult and important question is whether the Truth of words can be admitted by the court to be given in evidence to the jury, upon a plea of not guilty. In England I suppose it is settled. But it is a serious Question whether our Constitution is not at present so different as to render the innovation necessary? Our chief magistrates and Senators &c are annually eligible by the people [Adams is talking about the constitution of Massachusetts]. How are their characters and conduct to be known to their constituents but by the press? If the press is to be stopped and the people kept in Ignorance we had much better have the first magistrate and Senators hereditary. I am therefore very clear . . . it would be safest to admit evidence to the jury of the Truth of accusations, and if the jury found them true and that they were published for the Public good, they would readily acquit.[56]

Neither Cushing nor Adams thought false speech merited protection. People had a right to speak in a republican regime, but only if they spoke responsibly.

Benjamin Franklin provided an interesting perspective on the republican distinction between liberty, speech consistent with the public good, and license (harmful speech) when offering a distinctive remedy for abuses of the press. Franklin drew a line between responsible and irresponsible speech.

> If by the *Liberty of the Press* were understood merely the Liberty of discussing the Propriety of Public Measures and political opinions, let us have as much of it as you please: But if it means the Liberty of affronting, calumniating, and defaming one another, I for my part, own myself willing to part with my Share of it when our Legislators shall please so to alter the Law, and shall cheerfully consent to exchange my *Liberty* of Abusing others for the *Privilege* of not being abused myself.[57]

54. Feldman, *Free Expression*, 50–51.

55. Lucas A. Powe, *The Fourth Estate and the Constitution* (Berkeley: University of California Press, 1991), 48-49.

56. "William Cushing and John Adams Support Truth as a Defense," in *Freedom of the Press from Zenger to Jefferson*, ed. Leonard W. Levy (Chapel Hill: Carolina Academic Press, 1966), 150–51, 153.

57. "Ben Franklin Censures Abuses of the Press," in ibid., 156.

Franklin suggested that extralegal remedies were an appropriate response to irresponsible speech:

> My proposal is, to leave the liberty of the press untouched, to be exercised in its full extent, force, and vigor; but to permit the *liberty of the cudgel* to go with it. . . . Thus, my fellow-citizens, if an impudent writer attacks your reputation, dearer to you perhaps than your life, and puts his name to the charge, you may go to him openly and break his head. . . . [I]f the public should ever happen to be affronted, *as it ought to be*, with the conduct of such writers, I would not advise proceeding immediately to these extremities; but that we should in moderation content ourselves with tarring and feathering, and tossing them in a blanket.[58]

The liberty of speech championed by Adams and the liberty of the cudgel championed by Franklin rely heavily on juries to identify free speech rights and wrongs. Adams thought that juries should determine whether criticisms of government officials were true. Jury trials, he maintained, prevented government officials from silencing critics of public policies that ordinary citizens believed violated private rights or did not promote the common good. Franklin thought that juries should determine whether criticisms of private figures were abusive. Persons who exercised the liberty of the cudgel after being criticized in the press had a right to a jury trial. The jury would consider whether the criticism was abusive when considering whether the assault was justified. Ordinary persons would not convict defendants whom they believed were merely protecting their honor. Jones is free to criticize Smith, in this view, only if Jones is confident that a local jury will side with him should Smith react violently to the criticism.

Respublica v. Oswald, 1 U.S. 319 (1788)

Eleazer Oswald was the publisher of the Independent Gazetteer. *In 1788 Andrew Browne sued Oswald in a Pennsylvania court for libel. On July 1, 1788, Justice Bryan conducted a preliminary hearing on the lawsuit. Later that day, Oswald published his version of that proceeding and his view of the case. The crucial passage stated,*

> *Enemies I have had in the legal profession, and it may perhaps add to the hopes of malignity, that this action is instituted in the Supreme Court of Pennsylvania. However, if former prejudices should be found to operate against me on the bench, it is with a jury of my country, properly elected and empanelled, a jury of freemen and independent citizens, I must rest the suit. . . . The doctrine of libels being a doctrine incompatible with law and liberty, and at once destructive of the privileges of a free country in the communication of our thoughts, has not hitherto gained any footing in Pennsylvania: and the vile measures formerly taken to lay me by the heels on this subject only brought down obloquy upon the conductors themselves. I may well suppose the same love of liberty yet pervades my fellow citizens, and that they will not allow the freedom of the press to be violated upon any refined pretence, which oppressive ingenuity or courtly study can invent.*

Oswald was charged with contempt of court for publishing such commentary about an ongoing judicial proceeding. He responded that his essay was protected by the free speech clause of the Pennsylvania Constitution.

Chief Justice McKean of the Supreme Court of Pennsylvania ruled that Oswald was guilty of contempt. His opinion concluded that libel was not protected by the Pennsylvania Constitution and that people have no constitutional right to comment on judicial proceedings. How does McKean interpret the freedom of speech? Does he admit any protection other than immunity from prior restraints?

Oswald appealed to the state legislature. After debate, the state legislature condemned the judicial ruling. The legislature resolved,

> *That the proceedings of the supreme court against Mr. Eleazer Oswald, in punishing him by fine and imprisonment, at their discretion, for a constructive or implied contempt, not, committed in the presence of the court, nor against any officer, or order thereof, but for writing and publishing improperly, or indecently, respecting a cause depending before the supreme court, and respecting some of the judges of said court, was an unconstitutional exercise of judicial power, and sets an alarming precedent, of the most dangerous consequence, to the citizens of this commonwealth.*

How does this resolution differ from McKean's understanding of the constitutional meaning of free speech? What light does Oswald *cast on the original meaning of constitutional protections for free speech?*

58. Ibid., 158.

CHIEF JUSTICE MCKEAN

. . . Mr. Oswald's address . . . was intended to prejudice the public mind upon the merits of the cause, by propagating an opinion that Browne was the instrument of a party to persecute and destroy the defendant; that he acted under the particular influence of Dr. Rush, whose brother is a judge of this court; and, in short, that from the ancient prejudices of all the judges, the defendant did not stand a chance of a fair trial. Assertions and imputations of this kind are certainly calculated to defeat and discredit the administration of justice. Let us, therefore, enquire, first, whether they ought to be considered as a contempt of the court. . . .

. . . [L]ibelling is a great crime, whatever sentiments may be entertained by those who live by it. With respect to the heart of the libeller, it is more dark and base than that of the assassin, or than he who commits a midnight arson. It is true, that I may never discover the wretch who has burned my house, or set fire to my barn; but these losses are easily repaired, and bring with them no portion of ignominy or reproach. But the attacks of the libeller admit not of this consolation: the injuries which are done to character and reputation seldom can be cured, and the most innocent man may in a moment be deprived of his good name, upon which, perhaps, he depends for all the prosperity, and all the happiness of his life. . . . But shall such things be transacted with impunity in a free country, and among an enlightened people? Let every honest man make this appeal to his heart and understanding, and the answer must be no!

What then is the meaning of the Bill of Rights, and the Constitution of Pennsylvania, when they declare, "That the freedom of the press shall not be restrained," and "that the printing presses shall be free to every person who undertakes to examine the proceedings of the legislature, or any part of the government?" However ingenuity may torture the expressions, there can be little doubt of the just sense of these sections: they give to every citizen a right of investigating the conduct of those who are entrusted with the public business; and they effectually preclude any attempt to fetter the press by the institution of a licenser. . . .

But is there any thing in the language of the constitution (much less in its spirit and intention) which authorizes one man to impute crimes to another, for which the law has provided the mode of trial, and the degree of punishment? Can it be presumed that the slanderous words, which, when spoken to a few individuals, would expose the speaker to punishment, become sacred by the authority of the constitution, when delivered to the public through the more permanent and dissusive medium of the press? Or, will it be said, that the constitutional right to examine the proceedings of government, extends to warrant an anticipation of the acts of the legislature, or the judgments of the court? and not only to authorize a candid commentary upon what has been done, but to permit every endeavour to bias and intimidate with respect to matters still in suspense? The futility of any attempt to establish a construction of this sort, must be obvious to every intelligent mind.

The true liberty of the press is amply secured by permitting every man to publish his opinions; but it is due to the peace and dignity of society to enquire into the motives of such publications, and to distinguish between those which are meant for use and reformation, and with an eye solely to the public good, and those which are intended merely to delude and defame. To the latter description, it is impossible that any good government should afford protection and impunity. If then, the liberty of the press is regulated by any just principle, there can be little doubt, that he, who attempts to raise a prejudice against his antagonist, in the minds of those that must ultimately determine the dispute between them; who, for that purpose, represents himself as a persecuted man, and asserts that his judges are influenced by passion and prejudice, willfully seeks to corrupt the source, and to dishonor the administration of justice. Such is evidently the object and tendency of Mr. Oswald's address to the public. . . . Upon the whole, we consider the publication in question, as having the tendency which has been ascribed to it, that of prejudicing the public (a part of whom must hereafter be summoned as jurors) with respect to the merits of a cause depending in this court, and of corrupting the administration of justice: We are, therefore, unanimously of opinion, on the first point, that it amounts to a contempt.

Oswald's Protest to the State Legislature

. . .

Mr. Lewis, as a member of the house, then delivered a very elaborate argument, in vindication of the conduct of the judges. . . .

He began with stating the inestimable character of true liberty, which is equally endangered by tyranny on the one hand, and by licentiousness upon the other. He said, it did not consist in the uncontrolled power of doing whatever the will might prompt an individual to attempt; but, while it was independent of arbitrary and despotic rule, it was happily regulated by the laws and constitution of the state. . . .

He then commented upon the origin, nature, and purposes of a state of society, which, he said, was principally formed to protect the rights of individuals; and, of those rights, he pathetically described the right of enjoying a good name, to be the most important and most precious. He observed, that the injuries which could be done to any other property, might be repaired; but reputation was not only the most valuable, but, likewise, the most delicate of human possessions. It was the most difficult to acquire; when acquired, it was the most difficult to preserve; and when lost, it was never to be regained. . . . But this evil is effectually removed, when we consider the bill of rights as precluding any attempt to restrain the press, and not as authorizing insidious falsehoods and anonymous abuse. The right of publication, like every other right, has its natural and necessary boundary; for, though the law allows a man the free use of his arm, or the possession of a weapon, yet it does not authorize him to plunge a dagger in the breast of an inoffensive neighbor.

. . .[Mr. Lewis] engaged in a long and ingenious disquisition upon the nature of what is called the liberty of the press. . . . On the one hand, it is not subject to the tyranny of previous restraints, and, on the other, it affords no sanction to ribaldry and slander; so true it is, that to censure the licentiousness, is to maintain the liberty of the press. . . . Here, then, is to be discerned the genuine meaning of this section in the bill of rights, which an opposite construction would prostitute to the most ignoble purposes. Every man may publish what he pleases; but, it is at his peril, if he publishes any thing which violates the rights of another, or interrupts the peace and order of society; as every man may keep poisons in his closet, but who will assert that he may vend them to the public for cordials? . . .

It has been asserted, however, that Mr. Oswald's address was of a harmless texture; that is was no abuse of the right of publication, to which, as a citizen, he was entitled; and, in short, that in considering it as a contempt of the court, the judges have acted tyrannically, illegally, and unconstitutionally. But let us divest the subject of these high-sounding epithets, and the reverse of this assertion will be evident to every candid and unprejudiced mind: For, such publications are certainly calculated to draw the administration of justice from the proper tribunals; and in their place to substitute newspaper altercations, in which the most skilful writer will generally prevail against all the merits of the case. But it is moreover the duty of the judges to protect suitors, not only from personal violence, but from insidious attempts, to undermine their claims to law and justice. . . .

. . .

Mr. Findley, a member from Westmoreland, rose, and delivered his sentiments, with great ability and precision . . . asserted the right of every man to publish his sentiments on public proceedings; and having urged the danger of permitting the judges, by implication, to punish for offences against themselves (observing, that if it was a contempt to write, it was also a contempt to speak of a cause depending in the courts) he concluded with intimating, that he should take an opportunity of submitting a resolution to the house, which might serve to avert the pernicious consequences of allowing the case of Mr. Oswald to grow into precedent. . . .

B. Voting

The American Revolution inspired ordinary citizens to fight more vigorously for voting rights. Poorer citizens, who had been barred from voting during the Colonial Era, claimed that the principles that justified separation from England should be more rigorously applied in domestic politics. If a Parliament in which no Americans were represented had no authority outside of England, they reminded political leaders in the states, what right did a legislature chosen only by large property holders have to make laws for citizens denied the ballot? Persons seeking an expanded suffrage declared, "No man can be bound by a law that he has not given his consent to, either by his person, or legal representative."[59] Many Revolutionary War veterans insisted that they had earned the right to vote by their service to the country. One newspaper editorial demanded the ballot be given to "every man who pays his shot and bears his lot."[60]

---

59. Ronald M. Peters, Jr., *The Massachusetts Constitution of 1780: A Social Compact* (Amherst, MA: University of Massachusetts Press, 1974), 131.

60. This paragraph and the next borrow heavily from Alexander Keyssar, *The Right to Vote: The Contested History of Democracy in the United States* (New York: Basic, 2000), 3–25.

Federalists repudiated these democratic challenges to their republican commitments. They defended the traditional view that persons who lacked sufficient property lacked the capacities necessary to vote. John Adams stated, "Men in general in every Society, who are wholly destitute of Property, are also too little acquainted with public Affairs to form a Right Judgment, and too dependent upon other Men to have a Will of their own."[61] James Madison agreed. He informed the constitutional convention in Philadelphia,

> The freeholders of the Country would be the safest depositories of Republican liberty. In future times a great majority of the people will not only be without landed, but any other sort of, property. These will either combine under the influence of their common situation; in which case, the rights of property & the public liberty will not be secure in their hands; or which is more probable, they will become tools of opulence & ambition, in which case there will be equal danger on another side.[62]

Proponents of voting rights enjoyed limited success during the Founding Era. Most states reduced property qualifications, and Vermont abandoned wealth qualifications completely. Most states limited the ballot to free white men, but women were allowed to vote in New Jersey and free African-Americans voted in some states. The U.S. Constitution incorporated these state legal developments. Article I, Section 4 entitles any person to vote in a federal election who, by state law, may vote for a member of the house in the state legislature with the most members (states tended to have higher property qualifications for the upper, smaller house of the state legislature). State laws extending or narrowing the suffrage would have the same consequences for state and federal elections.

Many Federalists favored greater restrictions on the right to vote in federal elections. At the constitutional convention, Gouverneur Morris proposed a freehold qualification for voting. After a short debate, that proposal was decisively defeated by a 7-1 vote. Nevertheless, when governing the Northwest Territories, Congress imposed strict freehold qualifications for both electors and representatives. Section 9 of the Northwest Ordinance declared,

> That no person be eligible or qualified to act as a representative unless he shall have been a citizen of one of the United States three years, and be a resident in the district, or unless he shall have resided in the district three years; and, in either case, shall likewise hold in his own right, in fee simple, two hundred acres of land within the same; Provided, also, That a freehold in fifty acres of land in the district, having been a citizen of one of the states, and being resident in the district, or the like freehold and two years residence in the district, shall be necessary to qualify a man as an elector of a representative.

61. John Adams to James Sullivan, May 26, 1776, in *Papers of John Adams*, ed. Robert J. Taylor, Mary-Jo Kline, Gregg L. Lint and Celeste Walker (Cambridge, MA: Belknap Press of Harvard University Press, 1977), 1:395.

62. Farrand, *Records of the Federal Convention*, 2:203–04.

John Adams and Benjamin Franklin on Universal Male Suffrage

The vast majority of the Revolutionary War leadership believed that the establishment of some property qualifications was a vital means for preserving property rights. John Adams was a particularly vigorous defender of this inherited wisdom. Adams insisted that suffrage restrictions ensured that voters had the interests, capacities, and independence necessary to choose the most qualified representatives. Benjamin Franklin was one of the few well-known political actors who favored giving most men the right to vote. He criticized proposals for a freehold requirement in Pennsylvania. In sharp contrast to Adams, Franklin questioned whether property holders had any more capacity to govern than less economically fortunate citizens.

As you read these excerpts, consider how Franklin responds to the Adams argument. Is Adams correct to think that a regime that values property must impose some property qualifications on voters? Is Franklin committed to republican notions of private right and the common good, or are his values more democratic? What are those values? Keep these excerpts in mind when you read the section on gender equality. Does Franklin give any reasons for denying the ballot to women?

John Adams, Letter to James Sullivan (May 26, 1776)

. . .

It is certain in Theory, that the only moral Foundation of Government is the Consent of the People. But to what an Extent Shall We carry this Principle?

Illustration 3-3 Uncle Sam's Thanksgiving Dinner

Thomas Nast's Reconstruction-era cartoon celebrates the expectation of "universal suffrage" after the ratification of the Fourteenth Amendment. Before the Civil War, Nast had often taken a more pessimistic view of how universal suffrage actually worked, frequently depicting the ignorance of voters and the corruption of the electoral process in a mass democracy. Many framers in 1787 had similar fears of ordinary people voting.

Source: Uncle Sam's Thanksgiving Dinner by Thomas Nast, November 20, 1869. Harper's Weekly. Image provided by The Ohio State University Billy Ireland Cartoon Library & Museum.

Shall We Say, that every Individual of the Community, old and young, male and female, as well as rich and poor, must consent, expressly to every Act of Legislation? No, you will Say. This is impossible. How then does the Right arise in the Majority to govern the Minority, against their Will? Whence arises the Right of the Men to govern Women, without their Consent? Whence the Right of the old to bind the Young, without theirs.

But let us first Suppose, that the whole Community of every Age, Rank, Sex, and Condition, has a Right to vote. This Community, is assembled—a Motion is made and carried by a Majority of one Voice. The Minority will not agree to this. Whence arises the Right of the Majority to govern, and the Obligation of the Minority to obey? from Necessity, you will Say, because there can be no other Rule. But why exclude Women? You will Say, because their Delicacy renders them unfit for Practice and Experience, in the great Business of Life, and the hardy Enterprises of War, as well as the arduous Cares of State. Besides, their attention is so much engaged with the necessary Nurture of their Children, that Nature has made them fittest for domestic Cares. And Children have not Judgment or Will of their own. True. But will not these Reasons apply to others? Is it not equally true, that Men in general in every Society, who are wholly destitute of Property, are also too little acquainted with public Affairs to form a Right Judgment, and too dependent upon other Men to have a Will of their own? If this is a Fact, if you give to every Man, who has no Property, a Vote, will you not make a fine encouraging Provision for Corruption by your fundamental Law? Such is the Frailty of the human Heart, that very few Men, who have no Property, have any Judgment of their own. They talk and vote as they are directed by Some Man of Property, who has attached their Minds to his Interest.

. . .

. . . Power always follows Property. . . . We may advance one Step farther and affirm that the Balance of Power in a Society, accompanies the Balance of Property in Land. The only possible Way then of preserving the Balance of Power on the side of equal Liberty and public Virtue, is to make the Acquisition of Land easy to every Member of Society: to make a Division of the Land into Small Quantities, So that the Multitude may be possessed of landed Estates. If the Multitude is possessed of the Balance of real Estate, the Multitude will have the Balance of Power, and in that Case the Multitude will take Care of the Liberty, Virtue, and Interest of the Multitude in all Acts of Government.

. . .

The Same Reasoning, which will induce you to admit all Men, who have no Property, to vote, with those who have, for those Laws, which affect the Person will prove that you ought to admit Women and Children: for generally Speaking, Women and Children, have as good Judgment, and as independent Minds as those Men who are wholly destitute of Property: these last being to all Intents and Purposes as much dependent upon others, who will please to feed, cloth, and employ them, as Women are upon their Husbands, or Children on their Parents.

. . .

Depend upon it, sir, it is dangerous to open So fruitful a Source of Controversy and Altercation, as would be opened by attempting to alter the Qualifications of Voters. There will be no End of it. New Claims will arise. Women will demand a Vote. Lads from 12 to 21 will think their Rights not enough attended to, and every Man, who has not a Farthing, will demand an equal Voice with any other in all Acts of State. It tends to confound and destroy all Distinctions, and prostrate all Ranks, to one common Level.

Benjamin Franklin, Queries and Remarks Respecting Alterations in the Constitution of Pennsylvania (1789)[63]

. . . What is the Proportion of Freemen possessing Lands and Houses of one thousand Pounds Value compared to that of Freemen whose Possessions are inferior? Are they as one to ten? Are they even as one to twenty? I should doubt whether they are as one to fifty. If this Minority is to choose a Body expressly to control that which is to be chosen by the great Majority of the Freemen, what have this great Majority done to forfeit so great a Portion of their Right in Elections? Why is this Power of Control, contrary to the Spirit of all Democracies, to be vested in a Minority, instead of a Majority? Then is it intended or is it not that the Rich should have a Vote in the Choice of Members for the lower House, while those of inferior Property are deprived of the Right of voting for Members of the upper House? And why should the upper House, chosen by a Minority have equal Power with the lower, chosen by a Majority? Is it supposed that Wisdom is the necessary Concomitant of Riches, and that one Man worth a thousand Pound must have as much Wisdom as twenty, who have each only 999? And why is Property to be represented at all?. . . Private Property . . . is a Creature of Society and is subject to the Calls of that Society whenever its Necessities shall require it, even to its last Farthing; its Contributions therefore to the public Exigencies are not to be considered as conferring a Benefit on the Public, entitling the Contributors to the Distinctions of Honor and Power; but as the Return of an Obligation previously received or the Payment of a just Debt. The Combinations of Civil Society are not like those of a Set of Merchants who club their Property in different Proportions for Building and Freighting a Ship, and may therefore have some Right to vote in the Disposition of the Voyage in a greater or less Degree according to their respective Contributions; but the important Ends of Civil Society are the personal Securities of Life and Liberty; these remain the same in every Member of the Society, and the poorest continues to have an equal Claim to them with the most opulent, whatever Difference Time, Chance or Industry may occasion in their Circumstances. On these Considerations I am sorry to see the Signs this Paper I have been considering affords of a Disposition among some of our People to commence an Aristocracy, by giving the Rich a Predominancy in Government, a Choice peculiar to themselves in one half the Legislature, to be proudly called the UPPER House, and the other Branch chosen by the Majority of the People degraded by the Denomination of the LOWER, and giving to this *upper House* a Permanency of four Years, and but two to the *lower*. . . .

63. Excerpted from Jared Sparks, ed., *Works of Benjamin Franklin* (Boston: Hillard, Gray and Company, 1840), 5:167.

The Debate over Property Qualifications (1787)[64]

Members of the federal constitutional convention sharply disputed the merits of property qualifications. James Madison and Gouverneur Morris of Pennsylvania insisted that preventing poor persons from casting ballots preserved republican government. Others, most notably Benjamin Franklin, questioned the merits and prudence of national restrictions on voting rights. After a brief debate, the convention rejected national freehold qualifications by a 7-1 vote. The U.S. Constitution gives persons a right to vote in federal elections if they meet whatever qualifications their home state imposes for voting for representatives in the lower house of the state legislature.

Notice the emphasis most framers placed on land. George Mason pointed out that a freehold qualification bars very wealthy individuals from voting if their wealth is not vested in land. What reason might people in the Founding Era have had for disenfranchising merchants and other "monied" men?

GOUVERNEUR MORRIS (Pennsylvania) moved . . . that some other provision might be substituted [for Article IV, Section 1] which would restrain the right of suffrage to freeholders.

. . .

JAMES WILSON (Pennsylvania). . . . It was difficult to form any uniform rule of qualifications for all the States. . . .

OLIVER ELLSWORTH (Connecticut). . . . The right of suffrage was a tender point. . . . The people will not readily subscribe to the National Constitution, if it should subject them to be disfranchised. The States are the best Judges of the circumstances and temper of their own people.

. . .

JOHN DICKINSON (Delaware). . . . He considered [freeholders] as the best guardians of liberty; And the restriction of the right to them as a necessary defence against the dangerous influence of those multitudes without property & without principle, with which our Country like all others, will in time abound. . . .

GOUVERNEUR MORRIS (Pennsylvania). . . . Give the votes to people who have no property, and they will sell them to the rich who will be able to buy them. . . . The time is not distant when this Country will abound with mechanics & manufacturers who will receive their bread from employers. Will such men be the secure & faithful Guardians of liberty? Will they be the impregnable barrier against aristocracy? . . . Children do not vote. Why? Because they want prudence, because they have no will of their own. The ignorant & the dependent can be as little trusted with the public interest. . . .

GEORGE MASON (Virginia). . . . [E]very man having evidence of attachment to & permanent common interest with the Society ought to share in all its rights & privileges. Was this qualification restrained to freeholders? Does no other kind of property but land evidence a common interest in the proprietor? Ought the merchant, the monied man, the parent of a number of children whose fortunes are to be pursued in their own (Country), to be viewed as suspicious characters, and unworthy to be trusted with the common rights of their fellow Citizens.

JAMES MADISON (Virginia). . . . [T]he freeholders of the Country would be the safest depositories of Republican liberty. In future times a great majority of the people will not only be without landed, but any other sort of, property. These will either combine under the influence of their common situation; in which case, the rights of property & the public liberty will not be secure in their hands; or which is more probable, they will become tools of opulence & ambition, in which case there will be equal danger on another side. . . .

BENJAMIN FRANKLIN (Pennsylvania). . . . We should not depress the virtue & public spirit of our common people; of which they displayed a great deal during the war, and which contributed principally to the favorable issue of it. . . . He did not think that the elected had any right in any case to narrow the privileges of the electors. . . .

. . .

JOHN RUTLEDGE (South Carolina) thought the idea of restraining the right of suffrage to the freeholders a very unadvised one. It would create differences among the people & make enemies of all those who should be excluded.

C. Citizenship

Americans during the Founding Era were transformed from subjects to citizens. Before 1776, residents of the colonies were subjects of Great Britain. As Englishmen, they owed allegiance to the king. After 1776, Americans were citizens of their home state and, per-

64. Excerpted from Farrand, *Records*, 2:201–06.

haps, the United States. As republican citizens, they owed allegiance to their fellow citizens and elected representatives.

The transition from subject to citizen raised several important questions.

1. Did the transition occur on July 4, 1776, when the United States officially declared independence?
2. Did all former subjects of the English monarch automatically become American citizens, or was the transition more complicated?
3. What were the distinguishing marks of an American citizen?

Americans self-consciously determined when the transition from subject to citizen took place. In *Respublica v. Chapman* (PA 1781), the Supreme Court of Pennsylvania acknowledged that residents of the newly independent states had the right to reserve a short time period for determining whether to become American citizens or retain their allegiance to Great Britain. Other states adopted similar policies. Americans from 1776 to 1791 did not attempt to determine who was eligible for American citizenship. The Constitution of the United States does not explicitly set out the conditions for American citizenship or the distinctive rights of an American citizen.

American Identity

Americans conceptualized the distinguishing features of an American citizen in two different ways. The first was idealistic. Americans were committed to liberal or republican understandings of rights and liberties. J. Hector Crevecoeur championed this vision of Americanism in *Letters from an American Farmer* (1782). He wrote,

> *He* is an American, who leaving behind him all his ancient prejudices and manners, receives new ones from the new mode of life he has embraced, the new government he obeys, and the new rank he holds. He becomes an American by being received in the broad lap of our great *Alma Mater*. Here individuals of all nations are melted into a new race of men, whose labours and posterity will one day cause great changes in the world. . . . The American is a new man, who acts upon new principles; he must therefore entertain new ideas, and form new opinions.[65]

65. J. Hector Crevecoeur, *Letters from an American Farmer* (New York: Signet, 1963), 64.

The second way of conceptualizing Americanism was ethno-centric. Americans shared important racial, ethnic, and religious characteristics. John Jay championed this vision of Americanism in *Federalist* 2. He wrote,

> With equal pleasure I have as often taken notice that Providence has been pleased to give this one connected country to one united people—a people descended from the same ancestors, speaking the same language, professing the same religion, attached to the same principles of government, very similar in their manners and customs, and who, by their joint counsels, arms, and efforts, fighting side by side throughout a long and bloody war, have nobly established general liberty and independence.

Many Americans combined these perspectives. They claimed that European Protestants were racially and religiously more committed than other people to republican and liberal principles.

V. Equality

MAJOR DEVELOPMENTS

- Rejection of aristocracy
- The federal Constitution protects slavery, but Massachusetts declares human bondage unconstitutional
- Consensus that gender distinctions are based on real differences between men and women

Americans are born equal. The Declaration of Independence proclaims, "All men are created equal," and many state constitutions repeat this language. The Virginia Declaration of Rights asserts:

> That all men are by nature equally free and independent, and have certain inherent rights, of which, when they enter into a state of society, they cannot, by any compact, deprive or divest their posterity; namely, the enjoyment of life and liberty, with the means of acquiring and possessing property, and pursuing and obtaining happiness and safety.

Neither the Constitution of the United States nor the Bill of Rights included a similar clause. Nevertheless, in 1789 all prominent framers believed that Americans were constitutionally committed to republican equality. "Equality," a national consensus maintained, "ought to be the basis of every law."[66]

This professed commitment to equality coexisted with the preservation of remarkable inequalities. The U.S. Constitution rejects a hereditary aristocracy. Article I, Section 9 asserts, "No Title of Nobility shall be granted by the United States." In every state, however, men had different rights than women, white persons had different rights than persons of color, persons with more property had different rights than persons with less property, and so on. Americans maintained that such legal distinctions were justified because they reflected "real differences" between people. Seventeenth-century laws that permitted only nobles to hunt in the forest violated egalitarian norms, because every good republican knew that no real difference existed between nobles and ordinary citizens. Laws that limited militia service to white men were justified, however, because most prominent Americans were certain that the distinctive characteristics of white men made them more qualified for militia service than women or persons of color.

Some Americans invoked the egalitarian rhetoric of the American Revolution when challenging existing status hierarchies. Proponents of voting rights asserted that an egalitarian society should adopt universal male suffrage. Anti-slavery advocates insisted that the constitutional commitment to equality entailed a commitment to emancipation. Some women suggested that no real differences between men and women could justify common gender discriminations.

Consider the relationship between the egalitarian rhetoric of the Founding Era and conventional forms of discrimination during the late eighteenth century. Did such stirring phrases as "all men are created equal" do little more than change the dominant justifications for various inequalities? To what extent do you believe that this rhetoric inspired less fortunate Americans to demand greater rights? To what extent do you believe that the constitutional commitment to equality influenced American attitudes toward persons of color, women, and Native Americans?

66. James Madison, *The Mind of the Founder: Sources of the Political Thought of James Madison*, ed. Marvin Meyers (Indianapolis: Bobbs-Merrill, 1973), 10–11.

A. Equality Under Law

Americans maintained that regimes committed to equality under law respect three principles.[67]

1. No one has legal right *solely* because of his or her status.
2. Government has a right to regulate whenever doing so promotes the common good.
3. Laws that treat persons differently must be based on real distinctions between the groups involved and cannot be efforts to favor one group at the expense of another.

Federalists sought to realize these ideals by designing constitutional institutions that could not be captured by interest groups. Madison articulated this commitment to a faction-free society when he told Jefferson that the U.S. Constitution fashioned a government that "may be sufficiently neutral between different parts of the Society to control one part from invading the rights of another, and at the same time sufficiently controlled itself, from setting up an interest adverse to that of the entire society."[68] If, as Madison hoped, national institutions were controlled by either a virtuous elite or less-virtuous representatives who had institutional incentives to pursue the common good, national laws would make distinctions between persons only when doing so was in the public interest and when the distinctions were rooted in real differences between the affected classes. Madison also thought that representation would promote equality by connecting the interests of government officials with the interests of their constituents. In *Federalist* 57, he asserted,

> I will add, as a fifth circumstance in the situation of the House of Representatives, restraining them from oppressive measures, that they can make no law which will not have its full operation on themselves and their friends, as well as on the great mass of the society. This has always been deemed one of the strongest bonds by which human policy can connect the rulers and

67. For more elaboration on the themes in this brief subsection, see Howard Gillman, *The Constitution Besieged: The Rise and Demise of Lochner Era Police Powers Jurisprudence* (Durham, NC: Duke University Press, 1993).

68. Madison to Jefferson, October 24, 1787, *The Republic of Letters*, 1:502.

> the people together. It creates between them that communion of interests and sympathy of sentiments, of which few governments have furnished examples; but without which every government degenerates into tyranny. If it be asked, what is to restrain the House of Representatives from making legal discriminations in favor of themselves and a particular class of the society? I answer: the genius of the whole system; the nature of just and constitutional laws; and above all, the vigilant and manly spirit which actuates the people of America, a spirit which nourishes freedom, and in return is nourished by it.

When representatives and their friends are required to pay taxes, for example, taxes are unlikely to be onerous.

State constitutions provided more explicit protections for equality under the law. Many prohibited laws granting special rights to specific citizens. The Massachusetts Constitution of 1780 declared, "No man, nor corporation, or association of men, have any other title to obtain advantages, or particular and exclusive privileges, distinct from those of the community, than what arises from the consideration of services rendered to the public." The Maryland and North Carolina Constitutions explicitly forbade the state legislature from granting monopolies.

B. Race

Heated debates over slavery occurred in the constitutional convention. Some northerners, inspired by revolutionary rhetoric, maintained that slavery was an evil that ought to be abolished as soon as possible. Gouverneur Morris described human bondage as "a nefarious practice, . . . the curse of heaven on the States where it prevailed."[69] Slaveholders from South Carolina and Georgia aggressively defended the practice. Charles Pinckney informed the convention, "If slavery be wrong, it is justified by the example of all the world."[70] Many delegates insisted that slavery was wrong but maintained that anti-slavery constitutional provisions were unnecessary or unwise. They thought that human bondage was likely to die a natural death or that compromise was necessary to achieve a national union. "Let us not intermeddle," Oliver Ellsworth of Connected advised. He thought that "poor laborers [would] soon be so plenty as to render slavery useless."[71]

The resulting bargaining over human bondage provided slaveholders with important constitutional protections. Some guarantees were substantive. Article I, Section 2 declares that slaves count as three-fifths of a person when determining how seats are allocated in the House of Representatives. If South Carolina had one million citizens and one million slaves, then the state had 1.6 million persons for apportionment purposes. Article I, Section 9 forbids Congress from banning the international slave trade until 1808. Article IV, Section 2 requires all states to return fugitive slaves. Other constitutional protections were institutional. The framers designed every government institution with the balance of power between the slave and (soon-to-be) free states in mind. Because of the common assumption that southern states would grow faster than northern states, most political elites believed that Articles I, II, and III guaranteed that the slave states would have the power to prevent any anti-slavery measure from becoming law.

Controversy still rages over whether the final Constitution is best characterized as pro-slavery or anti-slavery. Those who think that the Constitution favored slaveholders point to various clauses that they believe provided powerful protections for human bondage. Charles Cotesworth Pinckney celebrated a pro-slavery Constitution when he informed the South Carolina ratification convention, "We have a security that the general government can never emancipate [slaves,] because no such authority is vested."[72] Those who think that Abraham Lincoln correctly celebrated the Constitution for placing slavery "on a course of ultimate extinction"[73] point out that the text never employs the word "slave." Madison implied that the framers were committed to securing abolition in the long run when he declared that members of the drafting convention "thought it

69. Farrand, *Records*, 2:221.

70. Ibid., 2:371.

71. Ibid.

72. Elliot, *Debates*, 4:268.

73. Abraham Lincoln, *Political Debates between Abraham Lincoln and Stephen A. Douglas in the Celebrated Campaign of 1858 in Illinois* (Cleveland, OH: O. S. Hubbell and Co., 1895), 2.

wrong to admit in the Constitution that there could be property in men."[74]

Americans made some racial progress during the Founding Era. Some northern states freed slaves. *Commonwealth v. Jennison* (MA 1783) effectively ended slavery in Massachusetts. Other states adopted measures that gradually abolished slavery. Pennsylvania passed a post-nati ("born after") law that freed all children of slaves once they reached a certain age. Several southern states eased burdens on manumission. Some slave state citizens thought that such laws, which enabled slaveholders to voluntarily free their slaves, were the first step toward a more general abolition.

These trends toward emancipation and liberal manumission were not accompanied by any tendency to increase the rights of free blacks. At the time the Constitution was ratified, free blacks were permitted to vote in some states. Nevertheless, all states discriminated on the basis of race. White Americans were confident that such discriminations were based on real differences between the races. Thomas Jefferson insisted that the phrase "all men are created equal" encompassed persons of color. Nevertheless, his *Notes on Virginia* expressed the conventional wisdom that whites and blacks were too different to share the same civic space.

Commonwealth v. Jennison (1783)[75]

After Nathaniel Jennison beat Quock Walker, Walker sued Jennison for battery. Jennison moved to dismiss the suit because Walker was his slave. Under common law, masters had the right to beat their slaves and apprentices, but not their servants or employees. A jury found that Walker was free and awarded him fifty pounds in damages. Shortly thereafter, Jennison was indicted for assaulting Walker. Jennison again claimed that he had the right to discipline his slave. The prosecution responded that slavery no longer existed in Massachusetts, because the "free and equal" clause of the 1780 Massachusetts Constitution had legally emancipated slaves in the state.

Chief Justice William Cushing accepted the prosecution's arguments when rejecting Jennison's defense that he had a right to beat his slave. He contended that Jennison beat a free man because all slaves in Massachusetts were emancipated by the constitution of 1780. Compare Commonwealth v. Jennison *to* Somerset v. Stewart *(1773). What are the main similarities and differences in the opinions? Would Lord Mansfield have endorsed Justice Cushing's opinion?*

The impact of Jennison *is controversial. A general consensus exists that the opinion dealt a mortal blow to slavery in Massachusetts. Some commentators think that Justice Cushing's decision played an important role in the emancipation process. Others claim that slavery was for all practical purposes moribund when* Jennison *was decided. Similar questions about the impact of judicial decisions recur throughout this text. When thinking about* Jennison, *consider whether judicial decisions are capable of playing major roles in fights for civil liberties, or whether they are effective only when most influential persons have abandoned the practice under constitutional attack.*

Chief Justice William Cushing declared that "every subject is entitled to liberty." After Jennison, *was Walker a citizen of Massachusetts?*

. . .

. . . It is true, without investigating the rights of Christians to hold Africans in perpetual servitude, that they had been considered by some of the Province laws as actually existing among us; but nowhere do we find it expressly established. . . . But whatever sentiments have formerly prevailed or slid in upon us by the example of others on the subject, they can no longer exist. Sentiments more favorable to the natural rights of mankind, and to that innate desire of liberty, which heaven, without regard to complexion or shape, has planted in the human breast—have prevailed since the glorious struggle for our rights began. And these sentiments led the framers of our constitution of government—by which the people of this Commonwealth have solemnly bound themselves to each other—to declare—that all men are born free and equal; and that every subject is entitled to liberty, and to have it guarded by the laws, as well as his life and property. In short, without resorting to implication in constructing the constitution, slavery is in my judgment effectively abolished as it can be by the granting of rights and privileges wholly incompatible and repugnant to its existence. The court are therefore fully of opinion that perpetual servitude can no longer be tolerated in

74. Farrand, *Records*, 2:417.

75. Excerpted from *Proceedings of the Massachusetts Historical Society* (Boston: Massachusetts Historical Society, 1875), 292.

our government, and that liberty can only be forfeited by some criminal conduct or relinquished by personal consent or contract.

Thomas Jefferson, Notes on the State of Virginia (1787)[76]

Thomas Jefferson embodied the American ambivalence toward slavery. A slaveholder who had several children with his slave mistress, Jefferson also penned a series of powerful anti-slavery appeals. Most Americans in the late eighteenth century shared Jefferson's abstract anti-slavery sentiments and his commitment to white supremacy. Prominent framers who lived north of South Carolina frequently asserted that slavery was an evil. Slaveholders in Virginia confessed that they hated the practice. "There is not a man living who wishes more sincerely than I do," said George Washington, "to see a plan adopted for the abolition of [slavery.]"[77] Most Americans were also unprepared to live in a multiracial society. One delegate to a southern ratification convention maintained, "It is impossible for us to be happy if, after manumission, they are to stay among us."[78]

Jefferson's Notes on the State of Virginia *reflects both these anti-slavery and racist themes. Jefferson condemned both human bondage and a multiracial society. Herbert Storing claimed that, although Jefferson acknowledged that all persons had a fundamental right to be free, he contended that no one has a fundamental right to be an American citizen.[79] Does this explain Jefferson's beliefs? What other reasons might explain Jefferson's combination of anti-slavery convictions and racism?*

. . . Why [after emancipating all slaves] not retain and incorporate the blacks into the state. . . . Deep rooted prejudices entertained by the whites; ten thousand recollections, by the blacks, of the injuries they have sustained; new provocations; the real distinctions which nature has made; and many other circumstances, will divide us into parties, and produce convulsions which will probably never end but in the extermination of the one or the other race.—To these objections, which are political, may be added others, which are physical and moral. The first difference which strikes us is that of color. . . . And is this difference of no importance? Is it not the foundation of a greater or less share of beauty in the two races? Are not the fine mixtures of red and white, the expressions of every passion by greater or less suffusions of color in the one, preferable to that eternal monotony, which reigns in the countenances, that immoveable veil of black which covers all the emotions of the other race? . . . They seem to require less sleep. A black, after hard labor through the day, will be induced by the slightest amusements to sit up till midnight, or later, though knowing he must be out with the first dawn of the morning. They are at least as brave, and more adventuresome. . . . Comparing them by their faculties of memory, reason, and imagination, it appears to me, that in memory they are equal to the whites; in reason much inferior, as I think one could scarcely be found capable of tracing and comprehending the investigations of Euclid; and that in imagination they are dull, tasteless, and anomalous. . . . [N]ever yet could I find that a black had uttered a thought above the level of plain narration; never see even an elementary trait of painting or sculpture. In music they are more generally gifted than the whites with accurate ears for tune and time. . . .

. . . Notwithstanding these considerations which must weaken their respect for the laws of property, we find among them numerous instances of the most rigid integrity, and as many as among their better instructed masters, of benevolence, gratitude, and unshaken fidelity. . . . This unfortunate difference of colour, and perhaps of faculty, is a powerful obstacle to the emancipation of these people. Many of their advocates, while they wish to vindicate the liberty of human nature, are anxious also to preserve its dignity and beauty. Some of these, embarrassed by the question "What further is to be done with them?" join themselves in opposition with those who are actuated by sordid avarice only. Among the Romans emancipation required but one effort. The slave, when made free, might mix with, without staining the blood of his master. But with us a second is necessary, unknown to history. When freed, he is to be removed beyond the reach of mixture.

---

76. Excerpted from Thomas Jefferson, *The Writings of Thomas Jefferson*, ed. Paul Leicester Ford (G.P. Putnam's Sons: New York, 1894), 3:244–46, 250, 267–68.

77. George Washington to Robert Morris, April 12, 1786, in *The Writings of George Washington*, ed. Jared Sparks (Boston: Russell, Odiorne, and Metcalf & Hilliard, Gray & Co., 1835), 9:159.

78. Elliot, *Debates*, 4:101.

79. Herbert J. Storing, "Slavery and the Moral Foundations of the American Republic," *in Slavery and Its Consequences*, ed. Robert A. Goldwin and Art Kaufman (Washington, D.C.: American Enterprise Institute, 1988), 59.

. . .

. . . There must doubtless be an unhappy influence on the manners of our people produced by the existence of slavery among us. The whole commerce between master and slave is a perpetual exercise of the most boisterous passions, the most unremitting despotism on the one part, and degrading submissions on the other. . . And can the liberties of a nation be thought secure when we have removed their only firm basis, a conviction in the minds of the people that these liberties are of the gift of God? That they are not to be violated but with his wrath? Indeed I tremble for my country when reflect that God is just: that his justice cannot sleep for ever: that considering numbers, nature and natural means only, a revolution of the wheel of fortune, an exchange of situation, is among possible events: that it may become probable by supernatural interference! The Almighty has no attribute which can take side with us in such a contest.—But it is impossible to be temperate and to pursue this subject through the various considerations of policy, of morals, of history natural and civil. We must be contented to hope they will force their way into every one's mind. I think a change already perceptible, since the origin of the present revolution. The spirit of the master is abating, that of the slave rising from the dust, his condition mollifying, the way I hope preparing, under the auspices of heaven, for a total emancipation, and that this is disposed, in the order of events, to be with the consent of the masters, rather than by their extirpation.

C. Gender

The egalitarian principles that inspired the American Revolution had little practical influence on gender equality. "American judges and lawyers sometimes gave thought to the implications of republicanism for women," one study points out, "but . . . they ultimately refused to meddle with tradition."[80] The Revolutionary War created opportunities for women to become more involved in political and economic life than had previously been possible. Sandra Van Burkleo notes, "Women joined in processions, circulated petitions, supplied troops with food 'liberated' from shops, cooked and sewed, harassed Loyalist women, made ammunition, boycotted tea and other British goods, donned homespun, published inspirational poetry, occasionally took men's places on the front lines, spied, and eagerly talked politics at the dinner table."[81] Inspired by these efforts, Samuel Adams informed his spouse that he saw "no Reason why a Man may not communicate his political opinions to his wife, if he pleases."[82] Nevertheless, prominent men resisted efforts to obliterate what they thought were natural gender differences. Consider Isaac Backus, a leader in the struggle for religious freedom in Massachusetts. His Christian principles required the female members of his congregation "to keep silent in the church." Natural rights were for one sex only. The Creator gave "liberty to all men . . . opposing women to men, sex to sex."[83] The U.S. Constitution made no mention of gender, and state constitutions framed in the Founding Era limited the vote to male inhabitants who met other qualifications. New Jersey was the only state in 1791 that permitted women to vote.

80. Sandra F. VanBurkleo, *"Belonging to the World": Women's Rights and American Constitutional Culture* (New York: Oxford University Press, 2001), 37.

John Adams and Abigail Adams, **Correspondence on Women's Rights** (1776)[84]

The following correspondence between John and Abigail Adams demonstrates how the egalitarian rhetoric of the American Revolution was invoked to support women's rights, as well as the practical limits on such advocacy. Unlike many men of the Founding Era, John Adams regarded his wife as a valued political advisor. When John was in Philadelphia representing Massachusetts in the Continental Congress, he relied on Abigail to provide him with intelligence on local events. Much of their correspondence dealt with important questions of war and politics. In early spring 1776, Abigail turned her attention to gender. She suggested that the principles underlying the American Revolution supported greater rights for women. John refused to take these claims seriously.

Abigail Adams employs standard liberal justifications when asserting women's rights. What was Abigail asking for when she told John he should "remember the ladies"?

81. Ibid., 47.

82. Ibid.

83. Ibid., 37, 39, 47.

84. Charles Francis Adams, ed., *Familiar Letters of John Adams, and His Wife Abigail Adams* (New York: Hurd and Houghton, 1876), 150.

Was John's response consistent with the liberal commitments of the late eighteenth century? Could he have defended existing restrictions on woman's rights?

Abigail Adams to John Adams, March 31, 1776

. . .

I have sometimes been ready to think that the passion for Liberty cannot be Equally Strong in the Breasts of those who have been accustomed to deprive their fellow Creatures of theirs. Of this I am certain that it is not founded upon that generous and christian principal of doing to others as we would that others should do unto us.

. . .

. . . I long to hear that you have declared an independancy—and by the way in the new Code of Laws which I suppose it will be necessary for you to make I desire you would Remember the Ladies, and be more generous and favorable to them than your ancestors. Do not put such unlimited power into the hands of the Husbands. Remember all Men would be tyrants if they could. If particular care and attention is not paid to the Ladies we are determined to foment a Rebellion, and will not hold ourselves bound by any Laws in which we have no voice, or Representation.

That your Sex are Naturally Tyrannical is a Truth so thoroughly established as to admit of no dispute, but such of you as wish to be happy willingly give up the harsh title of Master for the more tender and endearing one of Friend. Why then, not put it out of the power of the vicious and the Lawless to use us with cruelty and indignity with impunity. Men of Sense in all Ages abhor those customs which treat us only as the vassals of your Sex. Regard us then as Beings placed by providence under your protection and in imitation of the Supreme Being make use of that power only for our happiness.

Illustration 3-4 A Society of the Patriotic Ladies at Edenton in North Carolina

This satirical British cartoon depicts the launch of a boycott of English tea and clothing organized by the women of Edenton, North Carolina, in 1774.

Source: Robert Sayer and John Bennett (Firm), publisher; Dawe, Philip, artist. Library of Congress Prints and Photographs Division Washington, DC 20540, USA.

John Adams to Abigail Adams, April 14, 1776

. . .

As to your extraordinary Code of Laws, I cannot but laugh. We have been told that our Struggle has loosened the bands of Government every where. That Children and Apprentices were disobedient—that schools and Colleges were grown turbulent—that Indians slighted their Guardians and Negroes grew insolent to their Masters. But your Letter was the first Intimation that another Tribe more numerous and powerful than all the rest were grown discontented.—This is rather too coarse a Compliment but you are so saucy, I wont blot it out.

Depend upon it, We know full better than to repeal our Masculine systems. Although they are in full Force, you know they are little more than Theory. We dare not exert our Power in its full Latitude. We are obliged to go fair, and softly, and in Practice you know. We are the subjects. We have only the Name of Masters, and rather than give up this, which would completely subject us to the Despotism of the Petticoat, I hope General Washington, and all our brave Heroes would fight. I am sure every good Politician would plot, as long as he would against Despotism, Empire, Monarchy, Aristocracy, Oligarchy, or Ochlocracy.—A fine Story indeed. I begin to think the Ministry as deep as they are wicked. After stirring up Tories, Landjobbers, Trimmers, Bigots, Canadians, Indians, Negroes, Hanoverians, Hessians, Russians, Irish Roman Catholics, Scotch Renegades, at last they have stimulated the [ladies] to demand new Privileges and threaten to rebel.

Abigail Adams to John Adams, May 7, 1776

. . .

I cannot say that I think you very generous to the Ladies, for whilst you are proclaiming peace and good will to Men, Emancipating all nations, you insist upon retaining an absolute power over Wives. But you must remember that arbitrary power is like most other things which are very hard, very liable to be broken—and not withstanding all your wise Laws and Maxims we have it in our power not only to free ourselves but to subdue our Masters, and without violence throw both your natural and legal authority at our feet.

D. Native Americans

Native Americans attracted more political than constitutional attention. Americans from 1776 to 1791 negotiated a series of treaties with Native American tribes, broke several treaties, and engaged in frequent hostilities with tribal warriors. Still, the founding documents of American constitutionalism made little direct reference to the precise legal status of Native Americans living on soil claimed by the United States.

The fragmentary evidence suggests that Native Americans were considered a subordinate people with a different legal status than foreign visitors, aliens, or slaves. The commerce clause in Article I, Section 8 gave Congress the power "to regulate Commerce with foreign Nations, and among the several States, and with the Indian Tribes." This implies that tribes differ from both states and foreign nations, but the Constitution does not clarify *how* they differ. The Northwest Ordinance treats Native Americans as neither people of the United States nor citizens of foreign nations. Section 14, Article 3 declares:

> The utmost good faith shall always be observed towards the Indians; their lands and property shall never be taken from them without their consent; and, in their property, rights, and liberty, they shall never be invaded or disturbed, unless in just and lawful wars authorized by Congress; but laws founded in justice and humanity, shall from time to time be made for preventing wrongs being done to them, and for preserving peace and friendship with them.

Little evidence exists that Native Americans enjoyed any constitutional rights in 1791. Whether anyone had a legal obligation to observe "the utmost good faith" toward Native Americans was doubtful. No prominent American maintained that Congress had to adhere to the Bill of Rights when regulating Native Americans.

VI. Criminal Justice

MAJOR DEVELOPMENTS

- New constitutional protections for habeas corpus, due process, and other rights
- More emphasis on the right to a jury trial than on the right to an attorney
- The birth of the movement to abolish capital punishment

Americans established written constitutional protections for persons suspected or convicted of criminal offenses. Article I, Section 9 declares, "The privilege of the Writ of Habeas Corpus shall not be suspended, unless when in Cases of Rebellion or Invasion the public Safety may require it." Article III, Section 2 guarantees jury trials in federal courts for persons accused of crimes. The Bill of Rights offers protections against unreasonable searches and seizures, forbids general warrants, prohibits the practices of compelling persons to testify against themselves or trying a person twice for the same offense, requires grand juries, mandates due process of law, demands speedy and public trials before an impartial jury, insists that criminal defendants be informed of the charges against them, provides persons accused of crimes with the opportunity to confront their accusers and subpoena witnesses to testify on their behalf, grants criminal defendants the right to have a lawyer, and bans barbaric punishments. State constitutions provided similar guarantees for persons suspected or convicted of crimes. The precise rights protected and the precise language used to protect those rights varied from state to state. This variation more often reflected local idiosyncrasies than it did fundamental differences over what constituted fair criminal procedure.

A few controversies took place between 1776 and 1791 over constitutional criminal procedure. State courts debated when persons had the right to a jury trial and state legislatures considered reducing the number of crimes punishable by death. With those exceptions, judges did not issue major decisions on state criminal procedure, and elected officials did not issue new edicts on what constituted a fair trial. Participants in constitutional conventions rarely discussed at any length the precise meaning of such phrases as "cruel and unusual punishment" or "due process of law."

This lack of debate presents challenges to those interested in determining what procedures Americans thought necessary for a fair trial. Often, historians and lawyers must rely on primary sources from 1770 or 1810 when analyzing how Americans in 1791 understood the warrant requirement or constitutional provisions forbidding persons from being compelled to testify against themselves. This is often problematic. Attitudes toward crime and punishment evolved during the late eighteenth century. Many legal authorities questioned the use of the death penalty for many, if not all, crimes. Others insisted that criminal sanctions should aim to rehabilitate offenders. Popular understandings of a fair criminal trial were influenced by changes in the ways crimes were detected, prosecuted, and punished. The late eighteenth century witnessed increases in prosecutors, police officers, defense lawyers, and penitentiaries. When the Bill of Rights was ratified, Americans were only partly able to grasp the significance of these developments for constitutional criminal procedure.

The extent to which conceptions of a fair criminal trial were in flux can be exaggerated. No legal authority thought that persons making arrests had to give *Miranda* warnings. The vast majority of Americans thought capital punishment an appropriate sanction for murder. Liberal understandings of crime and the criminal process were only beginning to gain social acceptance. How these new ideas and changing practices should influence constitutional criminal procedure was for future generations to determine.

A. Due Process and Habeas Corpus

Americans inherited from Great Britain a constitutional commitment to due process of law and habeas corpus. General agreement existed on what constituted due process. Criminal defendants had a right to notice of the charges against them and the opportunity to respond to those charges. Americans also agreed on the basic contours of habeas corpus. Persons detained by a government official had the right to a judicial proceeding that determined whether they were being lawfully confined.

By inadvertence or intention, the federal Constitution failed to clarify whether *federal* habeas corpus was a constitutional or statutory right. Article I, Section 9 of the Constitution declares that Congress may not suspend the writ of habeas corpus unless there is an invasion, rebellion, or public emergency. Nowhere does the Constitution affirmatively empower federal courts to issue writs of habeas corpus. Article III grants Congress the power to regulate federal jurisdiction in general but does not explicitly mention congressional power over habeas proceedings. Some commentators interpret these constitutional provisions as limiting federal power to prevent state courts from issuing writs of habeas corpus, while leaving Congress to determine when federal courts may issue the habeas writ.[85]

85. See William F. Duker, *A Constitutional History of Habeas Corpus* (Westport, CT: Greenwood, 1980).

B. Search and Seizure

The Fourth Amendment to the U.S. Constitution of declares, "The right of the people to be secure in their persons, houses, papers, and effects, against unreasonable searches and seizures, shall not be violated, and no Warrants shall issue, but upon probable cause, supported by Oath or affirmation, and particularly describing the place to be searched, and the persons or things to be seized." Most state constitutions contained similar provisions. The 1786 constitution of Vermont states,

> That the people have a right to hold themselves, their houses, papers and possessions, free from search or seizure: and therefore warrants, without oaths or affirmations first made, affording sufficient foundation for them, and whereby any officer or messenger may be commanded or required to search suspected places, or to seize any person or persons, his, her or their property not particularly described, are contrary to that right, and ought not to be granted.

Americans believed that constitutional prohibitions on unreasonable searches and general warrants incorporated the principles asserted in *Wilkes v. Wood* (1763) and *Entick v. Carrington* (1765). General warrants that granted the warrant holder discretion to determine where the search would take place and what goods could be searched for were invalid. Victims had the right to receive monetary damages in a trespass suit against those who engaged in illegal searches. The exclusionary rule was a nineteenth-century innovation, unknown to the framers.

Constitutional decision makers expressed particular contempt for general warrants. Many states' constitutional provisions demanded that search warrants specify the place to be searched and the thing for which the warrant holder was searching. The constitution of North Carolina declared, "That general warrants—whereby an officer or messenger may be commanded to search suspected places, without evidence of the fact committed, or to seize any person or persons, not named, whose offences are not particularly described, and supported by evidence—are dangerous to liberty, and ought not to be granted." Several states passed statutes outlawing general warrants. In Connecticut, general warrants were forbidden by the judicial decree in *Frisbie v. Butler* (CT 1787). Josiah Butler obtained a warrant authorizing a constable to "search all suspected places and persons" that Butler thought "proper, to find his lost pork." The Superior Court of Connecticut declared illegal warrants that cast the net so widely. The Court's opinion declared,

> Although it is the duty of a justice of the peace granting a search warrant (in doing which he acts judicially) to limit the search to such particular place or places, as he, from the circumstances, shall judge there is reason to suspect; and the arrest to such person or persons as the goods shall be found with: And the warrant in the present case, being general, to search all places, and arrest all persons, the complainant should suspect, is clearly illegal.[86]

C. Interrogations

The Fifth Amendment declares, "No person . . . shall be compelled in any criminal case to be a witness against himself." Several state constitutions contain similar provisions. The constitution of Pennsylvania asserts, "Nor can [the defendant in a criminal prosecution] be compelled to give evidence against himself." General agreement existed that persons suspected of crimes could not be required to testify under oath. Historians debate whether the Fifth Amendment was thought to provide criminal suspects with other constitutional protections.

Commentators offer two distinctive analyses of Founding Era thought on the Fifth Amendment. Some insist that constitutional provisions prohibiting compelled testimony restricted only improper questioning. Confessions could not be forced by torture or the threat of divine punishment (the oath), but a magistrate could interrogate criminal suspects when evidence pointed to their guilt. Albert Alschuler states, "The self-incrimination clause neither mandated an accusatorial system nor afforded defendants a right to remain silent. It focused on improper methods of gaining information from criminal suspects."[87] Others insist that constitutional provisions prohibiting compelled testimony

86. *Frisbie v. Butler*, 1 Kirby 213 (Conn. 1787).

87. Albert W. Alschuler, "A Peculiar Privilege in Historical Perspective," in *The Privilege against Self-Incrimination: Its Origins and Development*, ed. R. H. Helmholz, Charles M. Gray, John H. Langbein, Eben Moglen, Henry E. Smith, and Albert Alschuler (Chicago: University of Chicago Press, 1997), 192.

protected a right to remain silent. This constitutional commitment to an adversarial system gave defendants an absolute right to not cooperate with prosecutors and others who were seeking to prove them guilty of criminal offenses. Leonard Levy writes, "The Fifth Amendment reflected the . . . judgment that in a free society, based on respect for the individual, the determination of guilt or innocence, by just procedures, in which the accused made no unwilling contribution to his conviction, was more important than punishing the guilty."[88]

No good evidence exists on what methods persons thought would compel testimony from suspected criminals. The rack and similar forms of torture were obviously unconstitutional. Still, legal authorities regularly engaged in interrogation practices that seem coercive by contemporary standards. *Commonwealth v. Dillon* (1792) suggests that Founding Era legal authorities thought interrogations that risked extorting unreliable confessions to be unconstitutional, but perceived any confession that rang true to be proper. *Dillon* also suggests that juries were empowered to ignore any confession that they believed was a consequence of improper questioning.

Commonwealth of Pennsylvania v. Dillon, 4 U.S. 116 (1792)

Dillon, a twelve-year-old boy, was suspected of burning down several stables. After being arrested, he was interrogated by the major of Philadelphia, several "respectable" citizens, and prison officials. Dillon's interrogators threatened him with a stay in the local dungeon unless he confessed. They promised good food, clothing, and shelter if Dillon admitted to arson. After a full day of questioning, Dillon acknowledged his guilt. At trial, his defense attorney argued that the jury should not consider any confession gained by such questioning and threats. The prosecution claimed that the confession should be considered because no reason existed to think that Dillon confessed falsely or that improper methods were used to obtain his confession.

The Supreme Court of Pennsylvania ruled that the jury could consider the confession if they believed it to be true. The justices concluded that the confession was admissible, even if the method of obtaining it was objectionable. Dillon *permits juries to decide whether a confession is false. Ultimately, the jury found Dillon not guilty. Might this have been an instance when the jury decided that a confession obtained by objectionable means should not be considered, even if true? Alternatively, consider the possibility that the jury did not find Dillon guilty because the punishment for arson was death and jury members thought the punishment excessive in this case.*

. . . The confession was freely and voluntarily made, was fairly and openly received, before the mayor; and, therefore, it was regularly read in evidence. But still, it has been urged, that it was thus apparently well made before the mayor, in consequence of improper measures previously pursued with the boy. The interference of the inspectors of the prison was certainly irregular. . . . The manner in which he was urged, though not threatened, by the citizens who visited him, may, likewise, be objectionable. But is it reasonable to infer, that all the prisoner's confessions were falsely made under the influence of those occurrences? Consider the nature of the offence. It cannot be openly perpetrated; for, it would be instantly prevented; and if it is secretly perpetrated, how, generally speaking, can the offender be detected, but by his own declarations? If such declarations are *voluntarily* made, all the world will agree, that they furnish the strongest evidence, of imputed guilt. The hope of mercy actuates almost every criminal, who confesses his crime; and merely that he cherishes the hope, is no reason, in morality, nor in law, to disbelieve him. The true point for consideration, therefore, is, whether the prisoner has falsely declared himself guilty of a capital offence? If there is ground even to suspect, that he has done so, God forbid, that his life should be the sacrifice! While, therefore, on the one hand, it is remarked, that all the stables set on fire, were in the neighborhood of his master's house; that he has, in part, communicated the facts to another boy; that his conduct had excited the attention and suspicion of a girl, who knew him; and that he expressed no wish to retract the statement, which he has given: the jury will, on the other hand, remember, that if they entertain a doubt upon the subject, it is their duty to pronounce an acquittal. Though it is their province to administer justice, and not to bestow mercy; and though it is better not to err at all; yet, in a doubtful case, an error on the side of mercy is safer, is more venial, than error on the side of rigid justice.

88. Leonard W. Levy, *Origins of the Fifth Amendment: The Right Against Self-Incrimination* (New York: Macmillan Publishing, Co., 1986), 432.

D. Juries and Lawyers

Americans agreed that persons suspected of a crime had a right to a jury trial but disputed whether access to defense counsel merited constitutional protection. The U.S. Constitution recognizes both the right to a jury trial and the right to an attorney. The Sixth Amendment declares, "In all criminal prosecutions, the accused shall enjoy the right to a speedy and public trial, by an impartial jury of the State and district wherein the crime shall have been committed, . . . and to have the Assistance of Counsel for his defence." Every state constitution that included a declaration of rights guaranteed the right to a jury trial. The constitution of New Jersey stated, "The inestimable right of trial by jury shall remain confirmed as a part of the law of this Colony, without repeal, forever." Very few state constitutions protected the right to be represented by counsel. Defense counsel was a relatively new phenomenon in the eighteenth century. Many Americans believed that innocent persons suspected of crime should defend themselves. The constitution of Georgia recognized only this right to self-defense, stating,

> No person shall be allowed to plead in the courts of law in this State, except those who are authorized so to do by the house of assembly; and if any person so authorized shall be found guilty of malpractice before the house of assembly, they shall have power to suspend them. This is not intended to exclude any person from that inherent privilege of every *freeman*, the liberty to plead his own cause.

The jury trial was the foundation of other constitutional rights. Constitutional law connected the right to a jury to the following:

1. Private property rights (*Bayard v. Singleton*; *Bowman v. Middleton*)
2. Contract rights (*Trevett v. Weeden*)
3. Free speech rights (*Zenger's Case*)
4. Rights against unreasonable searches and seizures (*Wilkes v. Wood*; *Entick v. Carrington*)
5. Rights against compelled confessions and harsh punishments (*Commonwealth v. Dillon*).

The first state law declared unconstitutional by a state court was frequently a state statute limiting the right to a jury. Cases striking down state restrictions on jury trials include *Holmes v. Watson* (NJ 1780; seizure of loyalist property), *The Ten Pound Note Cases* (NH 1786–87; property rights), *Trevett v. Weeden* (RI 1786; contract rights), *Bayard v. Singleton* (NC 1787; property rights), and *Bowman v. Middleton* (SC 1792). State restrictions on jury trials, New Hampshire justices insisted, "were unconstitutional and unjust."[89]

Judicial decisions protecting the right to a jury trial facilitated jury review of the substantive criminal law for violations of fundamental rights. Juries decided both the facts and the law of the case. Members of a jury were empowered to determine whether a person accused of being a public drunk was actually drunk in public, as well as whether the law against public drunkenness was consistent with community norms. The highest court in Connecticut ruled that a jury verdict could not be overturned for "mistak[ing] the law or the evidence, for by the practice of this state, they are judges of both." In 1791 Justice James Wilson of the U.S. Supreme Court declared, "Verdicts in criminal cases, generally determine the question of law, as well as the question of fact."[90] Juries often decided cases on legal grounds, even when instructed to give a verdict on the facts. Zenger was found not guilty even though the judge informed the jury that they were to determine only publication, and not whether the publication was libelous.

E. Punishments

The American founders placed constitutional restrictions on the punishments that legislatures and judges could impose on persons found guilty of criminal offenses. The Eighth Amendment to the U.S. Constitution declares, "Nor [shall] cruel and unusual punishments [be] inflicted." Many, but not all, state constitutions included similar provisions. The Delaware Declaration of Rights and Fundamental Rules states, "Nor [shall] cruel *or* unusual punishments [be] inflicted." The principles underlying these provisions were uncontroversial. No record exists of them being debated either during a state constitutional convention or during discussions over the Bill of Rights.

---

89. For more details on the close connection between the right to a jury trial and the rise of judicial review, see William Michael Treanor, "Judicial Review before *Marbury*," *Stanford Law Review* 58 (2005): 455.

90. *Witter v. Brewster*, Kirby 422, 423 (CT 1788); Bird Wilson, ed., *Works of James Wilson* (Philadelphia: Bronson and Chauncey, 1804), 2:387.

What constituted a cruel and unusual punishment was controversial. Many late-eighteenth-century political thinkers championed liberal theories of crime and punishment. Inspired by such works as Cesar Beccaria's *Of Crimes and Punishment* (1764), prominent Americans advocated penal reform. Two reforms in particular were popular. First, public officials sought to make punishments better fit offenses. The Pennsylvania Constitution of 1776 called on the state legislature to pass laws making "punishments . . . in general more proportionate to the crimes." Second, Americans emphasized the rehabilitation of criminal offenders. Robert Turnbull declared, "We know that there are in every man . . . some few sparks of honor, a certain consciousness of the intrinsic nature of moral goodness, which though they be latent and apparently extinguished, yet may at any time be kindled and roused into action by the application of proper stimulus."[91] Jefferson spoke of "so many who, if reformed, might be restored sound members to society."[92] Reformers thought that both proportionality and rehabilitation could be best achieved by a relatively new institution: the penitentiary. Criminals no longer needed to be executed, some proponents of liberal theories of criminal justice proclaimed. They could be retrained.

James Wilson elaborated on these Enlightenment themes when explaining the virtues of milder punishments. Restraint was pragmatic, whereas "barbarous" punishments perversely enabled criminals to escape any punishment. Juries preferred finding known criminals not guilty to subjecting them to excessive punishment. Sanctions were more likely to be imposed when punishments were less severe.

> When, on the other hand, punishments are moderate and mild, every one will, from a sense of interest and of duty, take his proper part in detecting, in exposing, in trying, and in passing sentence on crimes. The consequence will be, that criminals will seldom elude the vigilance, or baffle the energy, of public justice.

Restraint was the hallmark of a civilized society. "A nation broke to cruel punishments," Wilson concluded, "becomes dastardly and contemptible."[93]

The influence of liberal theory on criminal sanctions can easily be exaggerated. Criminal sanctions became milder, but they were still severe, even cruel, by contemporary standards. Jefferson proposed punishing men guilty of "rape, polygamy, or sodomy" with "castration" and women "by cutting thro' the cartilage of her nose, a hole of one half inch diameter at least."[94] Less "enlightened" framers endorsed more painful sanctions.

Americans began debating the death penalty late in the Founding Era. Capital punishment had long been imposed for many crimes. The Puritan settlers in Massachusetts relied heavily on the Bible when determining appropriate sanctions, and the Bible demands the death sentence for both violent and nonviolent crimes. The common law imposed capital punishment for crimes ranging from murder to ordinary theft. Inspired by liberal thinking, some legislatures and prominent elites sought to reduce the incidence of capital punishment. Pennsylvania limited capital punishment to treason, murder, rape, and arson.[95] Thomas Jefferson proposed imposing capital punishment only for murder. Benjamin Rush and Benjamin Franklin urged fellow citizens to abolish executions.

Benjamin Rush, On Punishing Murder by Death (1792)[96]

Benjamin Rush was a signer of the Declaration of Independence. He was a leading political activist, a prominent physician, and a close friend of many of the founding fathers. He was also one of the first prominent Americans to call for the abolition of capital punishment. The following excerpt outlines his reasons for thinking that a liberal republic should not punish murder by death.

When reading this essay, think about possible connections between liberal theories of government and liberal theories of punishment. To what extent is Rush a classical liberal, influenced by such liberal thinkers as John Locke? To what extent

91. David J. Bodenhamer, *Fair Trial: Rights of the Accused in American History* (New York: Oxford University Press, 1992), 58.

92. Thomas Jefferson, "A Bill for Proportioning Crimes and Punishments in Cases Heretofore Capital," in *The Papers of Thomas Jefferson*, ed. Julian P. Boyd (Princeton, NJ: Princeton University Press), 2:492.

93. Wilson, *Works*, 3:360.

94. Ibid., 497.

95. Bodenhamer, *Fair Trial*, 57.

96. Excerpted from Dagobert D. Runes, ed., *The Selected Writings of Benjamin Rush* (New York: Philosophical Library, 1947).

is he better described as a religious liberal similar to Roger Williams? Rush claims that "capital punishments are the natural offspring of monarchical governments." Why does he make this claim? Is he correct that republicans are committed to milder forms of punishment?

The punishment of murder by death, is contrary to reason, and to the order and happiness of society.

It lessens the horror of taking away human life, and thereby tends to multiply murders.

It produces murder, by its influence upon people who are tired of life, and who, from a supposition, that murder is a less crime than suicide, destroy a life (and often that of a near connexion) and afterwards deliver themselves up to justice, that they may escape from their misery by means of a halter.

The punishment of murder by death, multiplies murders, from the difficulty it creates of convicting persons who are guilty of it. Humanity, revolting at the idea of the severity and certainty of a capital punishment, often steps in, and collects such evidence in favour of a murderer, as screens him from justice altogether, or palliates his crime into manslaughter. If the punishment of murder consisted in long confinement, and hard labor, it would be proportioned by the measure of our feelings of justice, and every member of society would be a watchman or a magistrate, to apprehend a destroyer of human life, and to bring him to punishment.

. . .

III. The punishment of murder by death, is contrary to divine revelation. . . .

. . .

I cannot take leave of this subject without remarking that capital punishments are the natural offspring of monarchical governments. Kings believe that they possess their crowns by a *divine* right: no wonder, therefore, they assume the divine power of taking away human life. Kings consider their subjects as their property: no wonder, therefore, they shed their blood with as little emotion as men shed the blood of their sheep or cattle. But the principles of republican governments speak a very different language. They teach us the absurdity of the divine origin of kingly power. They approximate the extreme ranks of men to each other. They restore man to his God—to society—and to himself. They revive and establish the relations of fellow-citizen, friend, and brother. They appreciate human life, and increase public and private obligations to preserve it. They consider human sacrifices as no less offensive to the sovereignty of the people, than they are to the majesty of heaven. They view the attributes of government, like the attributes of the Deity, as infinitely more honoured by destroying evil by means of *merciful* than by exterminating punishments. The United States have adopted these peaceful and benevolent forms of government. It becomes them therefore to adopt their mild and benevolent principles. An execution in a republic is like a human sacrifice in religion. It is an offering to monarchy, and to that malignant being, who has been styled a murderer from the beginning, and who delights equally in murder, whether it be perpetrated by the cold, but vindictive arm of the law, or by the angry hand of private revenge.

Suggested Readings

Adams, Willi Paul. *The First American Constitutions: Republican Ideology and the Making of the State Constitutions in the Revolutionary Era* (Chapel Hill: University of North Carolina Press, 1980).

Beard, Charles A. *An Economic Interpretation of the Constitution of the United States* (New York: Free Press, 1935).

Gibson, Alan Ray. *Understanding the Founding: The Crucial Questions* (Lawrence: University Press of Kansas, 2007).

Gillespie, Michael Allen, and Michael Lienesch, eds. *Ratifying the Constitution* (Lawrence: University Press of Kansas, 1989).

Kramick, Isaac, and R. Laurence Moore. *The Godless Constitution: The Case against Religious Correctness* (New York: W. W. Norton & Company, 1996).

Kruman, Marc. *Between Liberty and Authority: State Constitution Making in Revolutionary America* (Chapel Hill: University of North Carolina Press, 1997).

Lutz, Donald S. *Popular Consent and Popular Control: Whig Political Theory in the Early State Constitution* (Baton Rouge: Louisiana State University Press, 1980).

McDonald, Forrest. *Novus Ordo Sectorum: The Intellectual Origins of the Constitution* (Lawrence: University Press of Kansas, 1985).

McDonald, Forrest. *We the People: The Economic Origins of the Constitution* (Chicago: University of Chicago Press, 1958).

Maier, Paul. *Ratification: The People Debate the Constitution, 1787–1788* (New York: Simon and Schuster, 2010).

Morgan, Edmund. *The Birth of the Republic, 1763–89* (Chicago: University of Chicago Press, 1956).

Morgan, Edmund S. *Inventing the People: The Rise of Popular Sovereignty in America* (New York: W. W. Norton, 1988).

Nedelsky, Jennifer. *Private Property and the Limits of American Constitutionalism: The Madisonian Framework and Its Legacy* (Chicago: University of Chicago Press, 1994).

Rakove, Jack N. *Original Meanings: Politics and Ideas in the Making of the Constitution* (New York: Knopf, 1996).

Tsesis, Alexander. *For Liberty and Equality: The Life and Times of the Declaration of Independence* (New York: Oxford University Press, 2012).

Wood, Gordon S. *The Creation of the American Republic, 1776–1787* (Chapel Hill: University of North Carolina Press, 1969).

Chapter 4

The Early National Era: 1791–1828

I. Introduction

The ink was hardly dry on the Bill of Rights when Americans discovered that inscribing liberties in a national constitution did not necessarily generate a consensus on the scope or meaning of those liberties. Bitter debates immediately broke out over the nature of American citizenship, the place of natural law in constitutional decision making, and the right to criticize national officials. Federalists insisted that the Alien and Sedition Acts of 1798 were constitutional means for preventing disloyal citizens and immigrants from subverting the new republic, while Jeffersonians insisted that these measures were unconstitutional efforts to suppress political opposition. In 1820 northerners and southerners discovered that no bisectional consensus existed on either the general constitutional status of slavery in the new republic or whether slaveholders had a constitutional right to bring their human property into the territories.

During the debates that took place over the Alien and Sedition Acts, the Missouri Compromise, and other rights controversies, Americans disputed both the specific meaning of constitutional provisions and the general principles underlying specific provisions. In the controversy over the Alien and Sedition Acts, Federalists insisted that the common law of England provided the proper standard for determining the constitutional meaning of free speech. Jeffersonians insisted that the constitutional meaning of free speech was derived from the distinctive features of the American commitment to a constitutional republic.

Few controversies over rights were decisively resolved. More often, partisans on both sides staked out positions that were subject to continued disputes in Jacksonian America and beyond. Participants in the controversies over African-American citizenship and slavery in the 1850s elaborated on arguments first made in Congress during the debates over the Missouri Compromise (1819–21). Early National Era debates over the role of religion in public discourse have remained vibrant through the twenty-first century.

Parties. The constitutional politics of rights and liberties was fairly disorganized during the Early National Era. Party competition existed only from 1791 to 1808. From 1808 until 1828 political competition largely occurred between two different Jeffersonian factions, National Republicans and Old Republicans. Federalists and National Republicans, more often than Jeffersonians and Old Republicans, favored laws limiting political participation, promoting religious establishments, and maintaining vested property rights. There were more rights controversies between shifting coalitions of Jeffersonians than between two distinctive national parties.

The Early National Era witnessed a dramatic change in partisan control of the government. From 1789 until 1801 Federalists controlled all three branches of the national government. From 1801 until 1828 Jeffersonians controlled all elected branches of the national government. By 1812 Jeffersonian appointees held a majority on the Supreme Court. This change in partisan control explains why many studies of American politics refer to the "Federalist Era" and the "Jeffersonian Era," rather than the "Early National Era."

The transition from Federalist to Jeffersonian rule had far less consequences for constitutional rights than either Federalists or Jeffersonians anticipated. Most rights issues in the Early National Era were local and influenced by the distinctive structures of local politics. The most important national rights debates after 1801

Box 4-1 A Partial Cast of Characters of the Early National Era

Thomas Jefferson	■ Republican ■ Author of the Declaration of Independence ■ Drafter of the Virginia Statute of Religious Liberty ■ Secretary of state to Federalist George Washington (1790–93) ■ Vice president to Federalist John Adams (1797–1801) ■ President of the United States (1801–09) ■ Founder of the Jeffersonian Republican Party ■ Secret author of the Kentucky Resolution of 1798 ■ Leading political proponent of "strict constructionism" in constitutional interpretation
John Marshall	■ Federalist ■ Secretary of state to Federalist John Adams (1800–01) ■ Chief justice of the United States (1801–35), appointed by John Adams after the election of 1800 ■ Leading judicial proponent of broad, nationalist interpretation of the Constitution ■ Author of most of the Court's important constitutional opinions in the early republic
Joseph Story	■ National Republican ■ Massachusetts speaker of the house (1811) ■ Associate justice of the U.S. Supreme Court (1812–45) ■ Harvard law professor ■ Madison's fourth choice to fill a vacancy on the Supreme Court; opposed by Jefferson, who regarded Story as too much of a Federalist ■ Close ally of John Marshall and a leading treatise writer in the early republic

were over slavery. That matter divided Americans by section, not by partisanship. The National Republican wing of the Jeffersonian coalition, which included James Madison and John Quincy Adams, held views on property rights and related issues that were quite similar to earlier Federalist positions.

Interest Groups. Neither permanent nor national interest groups formed during the Early National Era. Few rights issues attracted the sustained national attention necessary for the formation of national interest groups. Most rights and liberties issues interested only political activists in a few states, even when they raised questions about the U.S. Constitution. During the 1830s, Whigs praised and Jacksonians scorned the Supreme Court's decision in *Dartmouth College v. Woodward* (1819), which ruled that the contracts clause protected rights granted by corporate characters. During the Early National Era that decision attracted almost no interest outside of New England. Social movements or interest groups also played little role in early American constitutional politics. People often responded to particular grievances by forming a committee in a particular town or county. These associations rarely survived the particular incident that initially gave them life.

Courts. Judges played a greater role adjudicating questions of constitutional right. The Supreme Court asserted its right to declare laws unconstitutional in *Marbury v. Madison* (1803). By the end of the Early National Era, most state supreme courts had asserted the power to declare state laws unconstitutional, frequently in cases involving jury trials or property rights.

The Supreme Court in the Early National Era was dominated by John Marshall, a Federalist judicial appointee who served as chief justice from 1801 until 1835. Although Republicans gained control of the national government in 1801, most Republican judicial

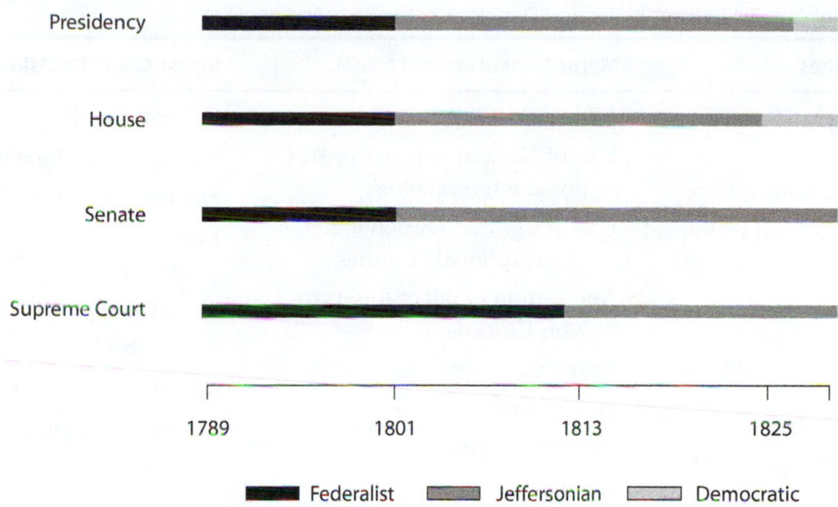

Figure 4-1 Partisan Control of the U.S. Government, 1789–1828

appointees identified with the more nationalist wing of the Jeffersonian coalition. The result was an enduring majority coalition of Federalists and National Republicans that was committed to extending national power and protecting vested property rights. The Marshall Court did not make many civil rights and liberties decisions during the Early National Era. Nevertheless, such cases as *Fletcher v. Peck* (1810) demonstrated a judicial willingness to make aggressive use of the contracts clause to promote property rights and restrict state legislatures. Many state courts, particularly when controlled by similar Federalist/National Republican alliances, relied on state due process or takings clauses to provide protection for vested property rights

Most constitutional controversies over rights and liberties took place in local legislative settings. Alas, in most cases, no record was ever made of the debates, the records were lost in fires many years ago, or they remain undiscovered in someone's attic.

Constitutional Thought. The central jurisprudential debate of the Early National Era was over the role of natural law in constitutional decision making. Many constitutional decision makers relied heavily on broad principles when assessing rights and liberties claims. Justice Samuel Chase in *Calder v. Bull* (1798) claimed, "An ACT of the Legislature (for I cannot call it a law) contrary to the great first principles of the social compact, cannot be considered a rightful exercise of legislative authority." Other constitutional decision makers insisted that interpretation be confined to the words of the constitutional text. Justice James Iredell in the same case insisted, "The Court cannot pronounce [a law] to be void, merely because it is, in their judgment, contrary to the principles of natural justice."

Legacies. The Early National Era marked the beginning of constitutional politics in the United States. During the 1790s both Federalists and Jeffersonians perceived their rivals as betraying the original Constitution. Federalists insisted that politics was not the proper forum for determining the constitutional meaning of free speech or what constituted "impairing the obligation of contract." Jeffersonians saw a return to monarchy behind every Federalist pronouncement. While the rhetoric of constitutional betrayal remains a staple of American political discourse, ordinary constitutional politics became less heated over time. Many political elites recognized, often grudgingly, that persons could in good faith dispute the meaning of particular constitutional provisions. Constitutional disagreement became a legitimate subject for ordinary politics rather than an automatic threat to regime stability. The Missouri Compromise demonstrated that when the constitutional disagreement was significant,the foundations of the national polity shook. Nevertheless, Americans by 1828 disagreed peacefully about the constitutional rights of religious dissenters, gun holders, and criminal suspects.

The practice of constitutional interpretation was the most important legacy that Americans of the Early National Era left to their descendants. Constitutional decision makers initially resolved disputes by referring to natural law, without focusing on specific

Table 4-1 Major Rights and Liberties Issues and Decisions of the Early National Era

Major Political Issues	Major Constitutional Issues	Major Court Decisions
Relations with England and France	Adoption of Bill of Rights	*Calder v. Bull* (1798)
Party Competition	Role of Natural Law in Constitutional Interpretation	*Marbury v. Madison* (1803)
Alien and Sedition Acts of 1798	Role of Courts in Resolving Constitutional Disputes	*Fletcher v. Peck* (1810)
Judiciary Act of 1801 and its Repeal	Application of Bill of Rights to Non-Citizens	*Dartmouth College v. Woodward* (1819)
Louisiana Purchase	Religious Liberty	*United States v. Callendar* (C.C.D. Va. 1800)
Yazoo Land Scandal	Free Speech	*United States v. Burr* (C.C.Va. 1807)
Burr Conspiracy	Property Rights	*Commonwealth v. Griffith* (MA 1823)
War of 1812	Contract Clause	*Johnson v. McIntosh* (1823)
"Era of Good Feelings"	Voting Rights	
Weakening Property Qualifications for Voting	Animus Against Class Legislation	
Democratization of Legislatures	Rights of Slaveowners	
Missouri Compromise	Citizenship Status of Free Blacks	
	Definition of Treason	
	Role of Judges versus Juries in Determining the Law	

constitutional provisions. Justice William Johnson in *Fletcher v. Peck* (1810) asserted that he would base his decision on "general principle, on the reason and nature of things." Supreme Court Joseph Story referred to natural law at great length when discussing the legal status of the international slave trade. By the beginning of the Jacksonian Era, such expressions were appearing less frequently in mainstream American constitution discourse. Rather than pointing to natural law, constitutional decision makers spoke of precedent or common understandings at the time constitutional provisions were ratified. Why this transformation took place is not clear. The increased role of courts in constitutional decision making may explain the growing American tendency to make legal arguments for rights rather than rely on natural law. Americans may also have relied more on legal discourse after discovering that they did not agree on how to apply natural law to specific circumstances. Finally, the turn from natural law to constitutional law may have been rhetorical. Constitutional opinions that refer to precedent and history may mask decisions based on contested judgments about natural law and good policy.

Americans in the Early National Era left a more specific legacy to the next generation. Courts gained increased power to resolve rights controversies. State and federal tribunals declared unconstitutional laws they believed interfered with vested property rights. Judges made a surprising number of decisions protecting rights in cases involving guns, religion, and persons suspected of crimes. Although pockets of legislative resistance existed, most Americans by 1830 had concluded that the federal judiciary was the appropriate institution for resolving constitutional disputes over land rights. Many political elites, satisfied with judicial performance in cases involving ordinary property, considered whether courts might be the proper forum to resolve broad national disputes over the constitutional status of human property. This hunch that the federal judiciary was particularly well suited for determining whether persons had a constitutional right to bring slavery into the territories helped structure constitutional politics in the Jacksonian Era.

II. Foundations

MAJOR DEVELOPMENTS

- Decline of reasoning based on natural law in constitutional decision making
- Greater influence of courts in constitutional decision making

- Debate over the status of the slave trade in customary international law

In 1789 Americans began their novel experiment with written constitutional protections for fundamental rights. The United States was the first constitutional republic in world history. No other political regime had ever established written limitations on all government officials. As a result, Americans could not refer to the experience of any other country when determining how to implement a written constitution.

Governing authorities were immediately confronted with basic questions about the sources, principles, and scope of constitutional rights and liberties. Americans did not settle any of these matters. Constitutional decision makers eventually subordinated natural law and the law of nations to written constitutional provisions. Justices gained increased authority to settle constitutional disputes. Prominent officials insisted that Congress did not have unlimited power when governing American territories. All these resolutions were tentative. All were challenged during the Early National Era and remained contested afterwards.

A. Sources

Americans became increasingly committed to establishing positive law protections for fundamental rights. Founding Era state constitutions often either lacked a bill of rights or included a haphazard listing of liberties. In contrast, every state admitted to the Union between 1791 and 1828 placed a bill of rights in the state constitution. The number of rights enumerated increased. The Alabama Declaration of Rights (1819) contained twice as many provisions as the Virginia Declaration of Rights (1776). Little was left to the imagination.

This increased tendency to enumerate rights in the state constitution coincided with a decreased tendency for legal authorities to rely primarily on natural law or the law of nations when imposing limits on government power. Many constitutional decisions and arguments in the Founding Era relied exclusively on natural law. Constitutional decisions and arguments in the Early National Era more frequently pointed to specific constitutional language, such as "due process of law." References to natural law decreased, while references to past legal precedents and practices at the time of ratification increased.

Natural Law

Justices from 1789 to 1829 did not initially agree on whether constitutional provisions provided the only legal grounds for striking down federal and state laws. Several decisions that were handed down suggest that natural law was an independent basis for judicial action. The South Carolina Court of Common Pleas made no mention of a specific constitutional provision when striking down a state law in *Bowman v. Middleton* (SC 1792). Justice William Johnson's concurring opinion in *Fletcher v. Peck* (1810) relied on "general principle, on the reason and nature of things." Justice Samuel Chase in *Calder v. Bull* (1798) declared, "I cannot subscribe to the omnipotence of a State Legislature, or that it is absolute and without control; although its authority should not be expressly restrained by the Constitution, or fundamental law, of the State." Other justices questioned references to natural law. "It is true, that some speculative jurists have held, that a legislative act against natural justice must, in itself, be void," Justice James Iredell claimed in *Calder*, "but I cannot think that, under such a government, any Court of Justice would possess a power to declare it so."

These references to natural law became fewer and fewer as the Early National Era progressed. Several explanations exist for the increased judicial tendency to rely on the constitutional text. The justices may have found little need to make independent references to natural law. In most cases, they could reach a desired result by citing constitutional language and interpreting that language in a manner consistent with natural law principles. The specter of slavery hovered over early efforts to rely on natural law, because most Americans of the period believed that slavery was inconsistent with natural law. If natural law were an independent source for judicial decisions, judicial recourse to it might compel justices to make a politically charged ruling that federal courts were not prepared to make from 1789 to 1829.

Calder v. Bull, 3 U.S. 386 (1798)

Norman Morrison wrote a will that left his estate to his grandson, Caleb Bull. In 1793 the Court of Probate for Hartford, Connecticut, concluded that the will was void. The Connecticut legislature two years later passed a law setting aside that decree and granting a new hearing. At this second hearing, the court approved Morrison's will. The Calder family, who stood to inherit under the first probate decision, appealed that decision to the Supreme Court of the United States. The Calders maintained that the state decree setting aside the first probate ruling was an ex post facto law, prohibited by the constitution of Connecticut and the Constitution of the United States.

The Supreme Court unanimously rejected that claim. All four justices who heard the case agreed that the ex post facto clause banned only retrospective criminal laws and not laws adjusting property rights. Over the course of this case, Justices Samuel Chase and James Iredell engaged in an important debate over the role of natural law in constitutional decision making. Iredell asserted that courts had no business striking down laws solely on the ground that the legislation was inconsistent with natural justice. Chase asserted that no people empowered a legislature to violate certain fundamental rights. Chase did not state clearly whether he believed that fundamental law provided a standard that justices should use when interpreting the Constitution (i.e., the presumption exists that a constitution does not give the legislature power to violate fundamental rights) or whether he believed that fundamental law provided an independent ground for judicial decisions to void legislation (i.e., courts should void laws that violate fundamental rights, even when the Constitution explicitly sanctions that violation). Which interpretation do you believe is correct? Should judicial power include the power to set aside clearly unjust laws?[1]

JUSTICE CHASE delivered the opinion of the Court.

. . . I cannot subscribe to the omnipotence of a State Legislature, or that it is absolute and without control; although its authority should not be expressly restrained by the Constitution, or fundamental law, of the State. The people of the United States erected their Constitutions, or forms of government, to establish justice, to promote the general welfare, to secure the blessings of liberty; and to protect their persons and property from violence. The purposes for which men enter into society will determine the nature and terms of the social compact; and as they are the foundation of the legislative power, they will decide what are the proper objects of it: The nature, and ends of legislative power will limit the exercise of it. This fundamental principle flows from the very nature of our free Republican governments, that no man should be compelled to do what the laws do not require; nor to refrain from acts which the laws permit. There are acts which the Federal, or State, Legislature cannot do, without exceeding their authority. There are certain vital principles in our free Republicans governments, which will determine and over-rule an apparent and flagrant abuse of legislative power; as to authorize manifest injustice by positive law; or to take away that security for personal liberty, or private property, for the protection whereof the government was established. An ACT of the Legislature (for I cannot call it a law) contrary to the great first principles of the social compact, cannot be considered a rightful exercise of legislative authority. The obligation of a law in governments established on express compact, and on republican principles, must be determined by the nature of the power, on which it is founded. A few instances will suffice to explain what I mean. A law that punished a citizen for an innocent action, or, in other words, for an act, which, when done, was in violation of no existing law; a law that destroys, or impairs, the lawful private contracts of citizens; a law that makes a man a Judge in his own cause; or a law that takes property from A. and gives it to B: It is against all reason and justice, for a people to entrust a Legislature with SUCH powers; and, therefore, it cannot be presumed that they have done it. The genius, the nature, and the spirit, of our State Governments, amount to a prohibition of such acts of legislation; and the general principles of law and reason forbid them. The Legislature may enjoin, permit, forbid, and punish; they may declare new crimes; and establish rules of conduct for all its citizens in future cases; they may command what is right, and prohibit what is wrong; but they cannot change innocence into guilt; or punish innocence as a crime; or violate the right of an antecedent lawful private contract; or the right of private property. To maintain that our Federal, or State, Legislature possesses such powers, if they had not been expressly restrained; would, in my opinion, be a political heresy, altogether inadmissible in our free republican governments. . . .

JUSTICE IREDELL, concurring in part.

. . . It is true, that some speculative jurists have held, that a legislative act against natural justice must, in itself, be void; but I cannot think that, under such a government, any Court of Justice would possess a power to declare it so. . . .

1. See Douglas E. Edlin, *Judges and Unjust Laws: Common Law Constitutionalism and the Foundations of Judicial Review* (Ann Arbor: University of Michigan Press, 2008).

> ... [I]t has been the policy of all the American states, which have, individually, framed their state constitutions since the revolution, and of the people of the United States, when they framed the Federal Constitution, to define with precision the objects of the legislative power, and to restrain its exercise within marked and settled boundaries. If any act of Congress, or of the Legislature of a state, violates those constitutional provisions, it is unquestionably void; though, I admit, that as the authority to declare it void is of a delicate and awful nature, the Court will never resort to that authority, but in a clear and urgent case. If, on the other hand, the Legislature of the Union, or the Legislature of any member of the Union, shall pass a law, within the general scope of their constitutional power, the Court cannot pronounce it to be void, merely because it is, in their judgment, contrary to the principles of natural justice. The ideas of natural justice are regulated by no fixed standard: the ablest and the purest men have differed upon the subject; and all that the Court could properly say, in such an event, would be, that the Legislature (possessed of an equal right of opinion) had passed an act which, in the opinion of the judges, was inconsistent with the abstract principles of natural justice. There are then but two lights, in which the subject can be viewed: 1st. If the Legislature pursue the authority delegated to them, their acts are valid. 2d. If they transgress the boundaries of that authority, their acts are invalid. In the former case, they exercise the discretion vested in them by the people, to whom alone they are responsible for the faithful discharge of their trust: but in the latter case, they violate a fundamental law, which must be our guide, whenever we are called upon as judges to determine the validity of a legislative act.

The Law of Nations

Constitutional authorities in the new republic thought that all sovereign nations were obligated to respect international law. Justice James Wilson in *Ware v. Hylton* (1796) proclaimed, "When the United States declared their independence they were bound to receive the law of nations, in its modern state of purity and refinement." "The Law of Nations," John Jay agreed, was "part of the laws of this, and of every civilized nation."[2] The precise contours of this obligation were unclear. Justices on the early Supreme Court believed that they should enforce international law when state and federal law were silent. No judge determined whether international law provided sufficient grounds for voiding an inconsistent federal or state law.

The international slave trade provoked particularly heated disputes over the place of international law in the American legal system. In 1808 Congress passed laws prohibiting Americans from importing African slaves into the United States. Most European nations had adopted similar bans on the international slave trade. Some Americans claimed that international law gave naval officers the right to condemn any vessel engaged in the international slave trade, even if that vessel was not licensed by the United States. Normally, one nation has no legal power to enforce the laws of another country or insist that persons on foreign soil obey the domestic laws of that jurisdiction. Nevertheless, prominent Americans insisted that two reasons justified the enforcement of prohibitions on the international slave trade. First, that trade violated the law of nature, the natural right of persons to be free. Second, that trade violated the law of nations, the customary practices of civilized countries.

Joseph Story, acting as a circuit court judge in *La Jeune Eugenie* (1822), condemned the international slave trade as violating both the law of nature and the law of nations. Three years later, the Supreme Court in *The Antelope* (1825) ruled that federal courts could not declare that the international slave trade violated the law of nations. Chief Justice Marshall's opinion declared,

> Whatever might be the answer of a moralist to this question, a jurist must search for its legal solution, in those principles of action which are sanctioned by the usages, the national acts, and the general assent, of that portion of the world of which he considers himself as a part, and to whose law the appeal is made. If we resort to this standard as the test of international law, the question, as has already been observed, is decided in favour of the legality of the trade. Both Europe and America embarked in it; and for nearly two centuries, it was carried on without opposition, and without censure. A jurist could not say, that a practice thus supported was illegal, and that those engaged in it might be punished, either personally, or by deprivation of property.

2. John Jay, "Charge to the Grand Jury for the District of New York," *New Hampshire Gazette*, April 4, 1790.

United States v. The La Jeune Eugenie, 26 F. Cas. 832 (C.C.D. Mass. 1822)

On May 17, 1821, Captain Robert F. Stockton, a navy officer in command of the Alligator, *captured the* La Jeune Eugenie, *a schooner suspected of being engaged in the slave trade. The ship's registry declared that the owners were French. Stockton suspected fraud—that Americans intending to profit by the slave trade actually owned the ship. U.S. authorities moved immediately to confiscate the ship and the ship's cargo of slaves. Federal attorneys pointed to a federal law prohibiting persons from importing slaves into the United States. Subsequent legislation forbade any American citizen or ship from participating in the slave trade. The ship's owners, however, claimed that French citizens acting in international waters did not have to obey American law.*

Justice Joseph Story concluded that actual ownership was not legally relevant. The cargo of slaves was forfeit even if La Jeune Eugenie *was French. Federal officials, in his view, had the power under international law to prevent the international slave trade.* La Jeune Eugenie *raises important questions about rights claims under domestic, international, and natural law. Given that the U.S. Constitution gives Congress the power to permit the international slave trade, on what basis does Story conclude that the slave trade is inconsistent with fundamental principles of American constitutionalism (or does he make that claim)? Story believes in a living law of nations—that is, that the principles of international law change over time. How do such changes occur? Does Story think that American constitutionalism evolves in a similar manner? Suppose that in 1800, when the slave trade was legal in the United States, a French navy officer had captured an American ship engaged in the slave trade. Would the principle of* La Jeune Eugenie *entitle the French to condemn the ship?*

La Jeune Eugenie *highlights common notions of search and seizure before the Civil War. Federal officials engaged in searches at sea at their peril. If they found evidence of lawbreaking, the search was legal. If not, they could be sued. "In such a case you do not acquire a right of search which justifies your encroachment upon the private concerns of a foreign ship," Story wrote, "but nevertheless, having a right to seize for breach of your own laws, you may seize at your peril; and if the case turns out to be innocent, you are responsible for damages; if guilty, you are justified by the event."*

STORY, Circuit Justice.

. . .

. . . [T]he first question naturally arising out of the asserted facts is, whether the African slave trade be prohibited by the law of nations; for, if it be so, it will not, I presume, be denied, that confiscation of the property ought to follow; for that is the proper penalty denounced by that law for any violation of its precepts; and the same reasons, which enforce that penalty ordinarily, apply with equal force to employment in this trade. . . .

I shall take up no time in the examination of the history of slavery, or of the question, how far it is consistent with the natural rights of mankind. That it may have a lawful existence, at least by way of punishment for crimes, will not be doubted by any persons, who admit the general right of society to enforce the observance of its laws by adequate penalties. That it has existed in all ages of the world, and has been tolerated by some, encouraged by others, and sanctioned by most, of the enlightened and civilized nations of the earth in former ages, admits of no reasonable question. That it has interwoven itself into the municipal institutions of some countries, and forms the foundation of large masses of property in a portion of our own country, is known to all of us. Sitting, therefore, in an American court of judicature, I am not permitted to deny, that under some circumstances it may have a lawful existence; and that the practice may be justified by the condition, or wants, of society, or may form a part of the domestic policy of a nation. It would be unbecoming in me here to assert, that the state of slavery cannot have a legitimate existence, or that it stands condemned by the unequivocal testimony of the law of nations. But this concession carries us but a very short distance towards the decision of this cause. It is not, as the learned counsel for the government have justly stated, on account of the simple fact, that the traffic necessarily involves the enslavement of human beings, that it stands reprehended by the present sense of nations; but that it necessarily carries with it a breach of all the moral duties, of all the maxims of justice, mercy and humanity, and of the admitted rights, which independent Christian nations now hold sacred in their intercourse with each other. What is the fact as to the ordinary, nay, necessary course, of this trade? It begins in corruption, and plunder, and kidnapping. It creates and stimulates unholy wars for the purpose of making captives. It desolates whole villages and provinces for the purpose of seizing the young, the feeble, the defenceless, and the innocent. It breaks down all the ties of parent, and children, and family, and country. It shuts up all sympathy for human suffering and sorrows. It manacles the inoffensive females and the starving infants. It forces the brave to untimely death in defence of their humble homes and firesides, or drives them to despair and self-immolation. It stirs up the worst passions of the human soul, darkening the spirit of revenge, sharpening the greediness of avarice, brutalizing the selfish, envenoming the cruel, famishing the weak, and crushing to death the broken-hearted. This is but the beginning of the evils. Before the unhappy captives arrive at the destined market, where the traffic ends, one quarter part at least in the ordinary course of events perish in cold blood under the inhuman, or thoughtless treatment of their oppressors. Strong as these expressions may seem, and dark as is the colouring of this statement, it is short of the real calamities inflicted by this traffic. All the wars, that have desolated Africa for the last three centuries, have had their origin in the slave trade. The blood of thousands of her miserable children has stained her shores, or quenched the dying embers of her desolated towns, to glut the appetite of slave dealers. The ocean has received in its deep and silent bosom thousands more, who have perished from disease and want during their passage from their native homes to the foreign colonies. . . . It is of this traffic, thus carried on, and necessarily carried on, beginning in lawless wars, and rapine, and kidnapping, and ending in disease, and death, and slavery,—it is of this traffic in the aggregate of its accumulated wrongs, that I would ask, if it be consistent with the law of nations? . . .

Now the law of nations may be deduced, first, from the general principles of right and justice, applied to the concerns of individuals, and thence to the relations and duties of nations; or, secondly, in things indifferent or questionable, from the customary observances and recognitions of civilized nations; or, lastly, from the conventional or positive law, that regulates the intercourse between states. What, therefore, the law of nations is, does not rest upon mere theory, but may be considered as modified by practice, or ascertained by the treaties of nations at different periods. It does not follow, therefore, that because a principle cannot be found settled by the consent or practice of nations at one time, it is to be concluded, that at no subsequent period the principle can be considered as incorporated into the public code of nations. Nor is it to be admitted, that no principle belongs to the law of nations, which is not universally recognised, as such, by all civilized communities, or even by those constituting, what may be called, the Christian states of Europe. Some doctrines, which we, as well as Great Britain, admit to belong to the law of nations, are of but recent origin and application, and have not, as yet, received any public or general sanction in other nations; and yet they are founded in such a just view of the duties and rights of nations, belligerent and neutral, that we have not hesitated to enforce them by the penalty of confiscation. There are other doctrines, again, which have met the decided hostility of some of the European states, enlightened as well as powerful, such as the right of search, and the rule, that free ships do not make free goods, which, nevertheless, both Great Britain and the United States maintain, and in my judgment with unanswerable arguments, as settled rules in the law of prize, and scruple not to apply them to the ships of all other nations. And yet, if the general custom of nations in modern times, or even in the present age, recognized an opposite doctrine, it could not, perhaps, be affirmed, that that practice did not constitute a part, or, at least, a modification, of the law of nations. But I think it may be unequivocally affirmed, that every doctrine, that may be fairly deduced by correct reasoning from the rights and duties of nations, and the nature of moral obligation, may theoretically be said to exist in the law of nations; and unless it be relaxed or waived by the consent of nations, which may be evidenced by their general practice and customs, it may be enforced by a court of justice, whenever it arises in judgment. And I may go farther and say, that no practice whatsoever can obliterate the fundamental distinction between right and wrong, and that every nation is at liberty to apply to another the correct principle, whenever both nations by their public acts recede from such practice, and admits the injustice or cruelty of it.

Now in respect to the African slave trade, such as it has been described to be, and in fact is, in its origin, progress, and consummation, it cannot admit of serious question, that it is founded in a violation of some of the first principles, which ought to govern nations. It is repugnant to the great principles of Christian duty, the dictates of natural religion, the obligations of good faith and morality, and the eternal maxims of social justice. When any trade can be truly said to have these ingredients, it is impossible, that it can be consistent with any system of law, that purports to rest on the authority of reason or revelation. And it is sufficient to stamp any trade as interdicted by public law, when it can be justly affirmed, that it is repugnant to the general principles of justice and humanity. Now there is scarcely a single maritime nation of Europe, that has not in the most significant terms, in the most deliberate and solemn conferences, acts, or treaties, acknowledged the injustice and inhumanity of this trade; and pledged itself to promote its abolition. . . . Our own country, too, has firmly and earnestly pressed forward in the same career. The trade has been reprobated and punished, as far as our authority extended, from a very early period of the government; and by a very recent statute, to mark at once its infamy and repugnance to the law of nations, it has been raised in the catalogue of public crimes to the bad eminence of piracy. I think, therefore, that I am justified in saying, that at the present moment the traffic is vindicated by no nation, and is admitted by almost all commercial nations as incurably unjust and inhuman. It appears to me, therefore, that in an American court of judicature, I am bound to consider the trade an offence against the universal law of society and in all cases, where it is not protected by a foreign government, to deal with it as an offence carrying with it the penalty of confiscation. . . .

B. Principles

Rights in the American constitutional republic differed from rights in the English constitutional monarchy. Rights in a constitutional monarchy limited only the power of the king, whereas rights in a constitutional republic limited all governing officials. This difference created an enforcement problem. Parliament was responsible for ensuring that English monarchs respected the constitutional limits on their power. If, however, rights limited all governing officials, including the national legislature, what institution ensured that Congress respected constitutional limits? What governing institution had the authority to settle disputes over whether a particular policy violated constitutional rights? If Congress passed a bill restricting political criticism, did any other institution have the power to declare that bill unconstitutional?

Over time, more political actors claimed that the federal judiciary was the proper forum for resolving disputes over constitutional rights and liberties. Thomas Jefferson in the Kentucky Resolutions insisted that the states retained the authority to determine the meaning of constitutional provisions. "As in all other cases of compact among powers having no common judge," he wrote, "each party has an equal right to judge for itself."[3] The Massachusetts legislature responded to this problem by insisting on judicial supremacy. The state legislature was "persuaded that the decision of all cases in law and equity arising under the Constitution of the United States, and the construction of all laws made in pursuance thereof, are exclusively vested by the people in the judicial courts of the United States."[4] Shortly thereafter, the Supreme Court in *Marbury v. Madison* (1803) asserted the judicial power to declare laws unconstitutional. "It is emphatically the province and duty of the judicial department to say what the law is," John Marshall's unanimous opinion decreed.

As time passed, state courts also became more effective participants in constitutional politics. Increasingly, officials and citizens looked to judicial doctrine when determining state and federal constitutional standards for civil rights and liberties. Local judges routinely resolved disputes over constitutional rights. By the end of the Early National Era, most of the original states had begun to develop lines of precedents on the meaning of state constitutional protections for property rights and persons suspected of criminal offenses.

However, judicial review was not a firmly established principle at the end of the Early National Era. Most major national controversies over civil liberties were settled outside of the federal courts. States often ignored federal court rulings and state judiciaries struggled to exercise independent constitutional authority. When the Supreme Court of Kentucky challenged the state legislature too aggressively, elected officials in that state established a new judicial system. Nevertheless, by 1828, the courts had partly remade republican constitutionalism. Constitutional rights and liberties were increasingly understood as legal limitations on official power that were enforceable in courts of law.

Marbury v. Madison, 5 U.S. 137 (1803)

Shortly before leaving the presidency, John Adams nominated William Marbury as a justice of the peace for the District of Columbia. The Senate confirmed his appointment the day before Thomas Jefferson took office. Marbury's judicial

3. Thomas Jefferson, *The Writings of Thomas Jefferson*, ed. Paul Leicester Ford (New York: G.P. Putnam's Sons, 1896), 7:292.

4. "Response of the Senate of the Commonwealth of Massachusetts to the Virginia Legislature's Resolution Condemning the Alien and Sedition Laws," February 9, 1799, reported in supplement to *Niles' Weekly Register*, 43:3.

commission was signed and sealed but not delivered during the haste and confusion that marked the last hours of the Adams administration. Jefferson, outraged by these last-minute appointments, ordered that the leftover commissions remain undelivered. In December 1801 Marbury asked the Supreme Court for a writ of mandamus ordering Jefferson's secretary of state, James Madison, to deliver his commission. The central issue of the Marbury *litigation was thought to be whether the justices could order the executive to deliver the commission, not whether the justices had the power to declare laws unconstitutional.*

The Supreme Court unanimously ruled that the justices lacked jurisdiction to resolve Marbury's claim because the case was improper brought under the Court's "original jurisdiction" (meaning it was the first court to hear the case) rather than its "appellate jurisdiction" (meaning the case was being appealed from other court). John Marshall's opinion first interpreted Section 13 of the Judiciary Act of 1789 as vesting the Court with the power to issue a writ of mandamus in cases of original jurisdiction, and then maintained that the federal statute unconstitutionally gave the court original jurisdiction in circumstances under which Article III limited judicial power to appellate jurisdiction. Marbury *was the first time that the U.S. Supreme Court explicitly justified the judicial power to declare federal laws unconstitutional. As you read, consider how persuasive Marshall's argument is. How else might judicial review be defended? Consider what power Marshall is defending. Some scholars insist that Marshall meant to assert a judicial power to declare unconstitutional only laws affecting the judiciary. Others insist that the judicial power in* Marbury *is limited to clearly unconstitutional laws. Debate exists over whether Marshall meant to assert that justices may interpret the Constitution when deciding cases or whether he meant to assert that the Supreme Court had the power to announce the constitutional principles that should guide the entire government. Which interpretation of* Marbury *do you think best?*

Marbury *asserts a special judicial power to protect individual rights. Do federal courts have a special institutional obligation to enforce the rights provisions in the Constitution? Might judicial power to protect constitutional rights also weaken legislative and executive commitments to protecting rights? Consider the following comment on institutional capacity to protect fundamental rights.*

> *During a republican regime, which . . . predominated throughout the nineteenth century, rights were secured primarily through representative institutions and the political process, particularly through the passage of legislative statutes. . . . Not until the middle of the twentieth century can we identify the emergence of a judicialist regime, which was instituted primarily through changes in the realm of thought and which holds that rights are best protected through judicial enforcement of bills of rights.*[5]

CHIEF JUSTICE MARSHALL delivered the opinion of the Court.

. . .

The question, whether an act, repugnant to the constitution, can become the law of the land, is a question deeply interesting to the United States; but, happily, not of an intricacy proportioned to its interest. It seems only necessary to recognize certain principles, supposed to have been long and well established, to decide it.

That the people have an original right to establish, for their future government, such principles as, in their opinion, shall most conduce to their own happiness, is the basis, on which the whole American fabric has been erected. The exercise of this original right is a very great exertion; nor can it, nor ought it to be frequently repeated. The principles, therefore, so established, are deemed fundamental. And as the authority, from which they proceed, is supreme, and can seldom act, they are designed to be permanent.

This original and supreme will organizes the government, and assigns, to different departments, their respective powers. It may either stop here; or establish certain limits not to be transcended by those departments.

The government of the United States is of the latter description. The powers of the legislature are defined, and limited; and that those limits may not be mistaken, or forgotten, the constitution is written. To what purpose are powers limited, and to what purpose is that limitation committed to writing, if these limits may, at any time, be passed by those intended to be restrained? The distinction, between a government with limited and unlimited powers, is abolished, if those limits do not confine the persons on whom they are imposed, and if acts prohibited and acts allowed, are of equal obligation. It is a proposition too plain to be contested, that the constitution controls any legislative act repugnant to it; or, that the legislature may alter the constitution by an ordinary act.

Between these alternatives there is no middle ground. The constitution is either a superior, paramount law, unchangeable by ordinary means, or it is on a level

5. John J. Dinan, *Keeping the People's Liberties: Legislators, Citizens, and Judges as Guardians of Rights* (Lawrence: University of Kansas Press, 1998), xi.

with ordinary legislative acts, and like other acts, is alterable when the legislature shall please to alter it.

If the former part of the alternative be true, then a legislative act contrary to the constitution is not law: if the latter part be true, then written constitutions are absurd attempts, on the part of the people, to limit a power, in its own nature illimitable.

Certainly all those who have framed written constitutions contemplate them as forming the fundamental and paramount law of the nation, and consequently the theory of every such government must be, that an act of the legislature, repugnant to the constitution, is void.

This theory is essentially attached to a written constitution, and is consequently to be considered, by this court, as one of the fundamental principles of our society. It is not therefore to be lost sight of in the further consideration of this subject.

If an act of the legislature, repugnant to the constitution, is void, does it, notwithstanding its invalidity, bind the courts, and oblige them to give it effect? Or, in other words, though it be not law, does it constitute a rule as operative as if it was a law? This would be to overthrow in fact what was established in theory; and would seem, at first view, an absurdity too gross to be insisted on. It shall, however, receive a more attentive consideration.

It is emphatically the province and duty of the judicial department to say what the law is. Those who apply the rule to particular cases, must of necessity expound and interpret that rule. If two laws conflict with each other, the courts must decide on the operation of each.

So if a law be in opposition to the constitution; if both the law and the constitution apply to a particular case, so that the court must either decide that case conformably to the law, disregarding the constitution; or conformably to the constitution, disregarding the law; the court must determine which of these conflicting rules governs the case. This is of the very essence of judicial duty.

If then the courts are to regard the constitution; and the constitution is superior to any ordinary act of the legislature; the constitution, and not such ordinary act, must govern the case to which they both apply.

Those then who controvert the principle that the constitution is to be considered, in court, as a paramount law, are reduced to the necessity of maintaining that courts must close their eyes on the constitution, and see only the law.

This doctrine would subvert the very foundation of all written constitutions. It would declare that an act, which, according to the principles and theory of our government, is entirely void; is yet, in practice, completely obligatory. It would declare, that if the legislature shall do what is expressly forbidden, such act, notwithstanding the express prohibition, is in reality effectual. It would be giving to the legislature a practical and real omnipotence, with the same breath which professes to restrict their powers within narrow limits. It is prescribing limits, and declaring that those limits may be passed at pleasure.

That it thus reduces to nothing what we have deemed the greatest improvement on political institutions—a written constitution—would of itself be sufficient, in America, where written constitutions have been viewed with so much reverence, for rejecting the construction. But the peculiar expressions of the constitution of the United States furnish additional arguments in favor of its rejection.

The judicial power of the United States is extended to all cases arising under the constitution.

Could it be the intention of those who gave this power, to say that, in using it, the constitution should not be looked into? That a case arising under the constitution should be decided without examining the instrument under which it arises?

This is too extravagant to be maintained.

In some cases then, the constitution must be looked into by the judges. And if they can open it at all, what part of it are they forbidden to read, or to obey?

There are many other parts of the constitution which serve to illustrate this subject.

It is declared that "no tax or duty shall be laid on articles exported from any state." Suppose a duty on the export of cotton, of tobacco, or of flour; and a suit instituted to recover it. Ought judgment to be rendered in such a case? Ought the judges to close their eyes on the constitution, and only see the law.

The constitution declares that "no bill of attainder or ex post facto law shall be passed."

If, however, such a bill should be passed and a person should be prosecuted under it; must the court condemn to death those victims whom the constitution endeavors to preserve?

"No person," says the constitution, "shall be convicted of treason unless on the testimony of two witnesses to the same overt act, or on confession in open court."

Here the language of the constitution is addressed especially to the courts. It prescribes, directly for them, a rule of evidence not to be departed from. If the legislature should change that rule, and declare one witness, or a confession out of court, sufficient for conviction, must the constitutional principle yield to the legislative act?

From these, and many other selections which might be made, it is apparent, that the framers of the constitution contemplated that instrument, as a rule for the government of courts, as well as of the legislature.

Why otherwise does it direct the judges to take an oath to support it? This oath certainly applies, in an especial manner, to their conduct in their official character. How immoral to impose it on them, if they were to be used as the instruments, and the knowing instruments, for violating what they swear to support!

. . .

It is also not entirely unworthy of observation, that in declaring what shall be the supreme law of the land, the constitution itself is first mentioned; and not the laws of the United States generally, but those only which shall be made in pursuance of the constitution, have that rank.

Thus, the particular phraseology of the constitution of the United States confirms and strengthens the principle, supposed to be essential to all written constitutions, that a law repugnant to the constitution is void; and that courts, as well as other departments, are bound by that instrument.

C. Scope

Americans considered but failed to resolve permanently three important questions about the scope of the Bill of Rights.

1. Did the Bill of Rights limit state power?
2. Did the Bill of Rights limit federal power in the territories?
3. Did the Bill of Rights protect aliens?

A few state courts briefly considered the first question, dividing on whether the Bill of Rights limited state power. Congress briefly considered but did not decide whether the Bill of Rights limited federal power to govern American territories acquired by the Louisiana Purchase.[6] More extensive debates over the constitutional rights of aliens were also inconclusive.

6. See Sarah H. Cleveland, "Powers Inherent in Sovereignty: Indians, Aliens, Territories and the Nineteenth Century Origins of Plenary Power of Foreign Affairs," *Texas Law Review* 81 (2002): 171–81.

III. Individual Rights

MAJOR DEVELOPMENTS

- Use of due process and takings clauses to protect property rights
- Debates over whether the United States is a Christian country
- First decisions on the constitutional meaning of the right to bear arms

Government was a regular presence in the lives of most Americans during the Early National Era. State and local officials built roads, regulated the numerous mills springing up along the rivers, punished drunkenness, and forbade people from carrying concealed weapons. Proponents of these measures insisted that they advanced the common good. Opponents insisted that government officials were violating constitutional rights to property, religion, personal choice, or guns. Many persons affected by state regulations brought lawsuits against the government. For the first time, courts were asked to determine the proper balance between individual rights and the common good.

When reading about the constitutional controversies discussed in this section, consider the relationship between individual rights and the common good. Previous chapters have detailed how people in the Colonial and Founding Eras did not ordinarily think that persons had a right to act in any way that harmed another person or was inconsistent with the public interest. To what extent did this principle remain vibrant during the Early National Era? Do you detect any changes in what legal authorities thought constituted the common good or individual right? Do you detect any changes in the way that legal authorities understood the relationship between the common good and individual right? How did the increased participation of the courts influence the constitutional relationships between the common good and individual right?

A. Property

Americans during the Early National Era struggled to determine which government regulations unconstitutionally took property from A and gave it to B. All constitutional decision makers agreed that government could not play favorites. Unlike the king of England, the governor of Tennessee was constitutionally prohibited from giving an estate to his mistress or raising taxes on towns suspected of being loyal to a different political faction. As government regulations became routine and commercial practices changed, controversies arose over whether new forms of regulation were legitimate efforts to secure the common good or unconstitutional attempts to enrich some citizens at the expense of others. By the 1820s, courts had become the forum for settling many constitutional controversies over property rights. Justice Story in *Wilkinson v. Leland* (1829) declared, "Government can scarcely be deemed to be free, where the rights of property are left solely dependent upon the will of a legislative body, without any restraint. The fundamental maxims of a free government seem to require that the rights of personal liberty and private property should be held sacred." Most early-nineteenth-century judges claimed that courts should prevent government from redistributing property and ensure that all government regulations promoted the public good. When you read the materials below, consider whether that is a fair characterization of judicial behavior. How did justices characterize the public interest and private rights when disputes over property arose?

Contracts

Federal courts relied almost exclusively on the contracts clause when policing individual rights violations in the states. Disputes over the meaning of the contracts clause were the most enduring constitutional debates in the Early National Era and reflected the deep concern over the stability of property that animated many Americans who pushed for the formation of a stronger national government during the 1780s. Americans in the Founding Era expected that the contracts clause would prevent states from passing debtor relief laws or legislation requiring creditors to forgive past debts. They were not disappointed. Bankruptcy issues came before the Marshall Court in *Sturgeis v. Crowninshield* (1819) and *Ogden v. Saunders* (1827). The justices in those cases ruled that states could pass bankruptcy laws that regulated only those contracts made after the statute was enacted. If you declared bankruptcy in 2010 and the bankruptcy law in your state was passed in 2005, then that statute determined whether you had to pay debts you contracted in 2007 (*Ogden*), but not whether you had to pay debts you contracted in 2003 (*Sturgis*).

The most important contracts clause cases concerned state land grants and corporate charters. The federal government and states frequently granted lands to investors and settlers. Governments granted corporate charters that permitted entrepreneurs to build roads, establish banks, and engage in other enterprises. The corporate form was valuable, because most corporations enjoy limited liability. Persons harmed by the corporation may sue for corporate assets, but they may not normally receive damages directly from the individual persons who formed or invested in the corporation. Imagine that the defective toaster you bought from the Acme Corporation starts a fire that destroys your house. You want to sue Acme for $1 million, but the Acme Corporation only has $100,000 in assets. Limited liability means that you cannot normally collect damages from Acme shareholders, Acme management, or Acme workers. Corporate charters promise investors other benefits in addition to limited liability. States often promise that a corporation will not be taxed or will enjoy exemptions from certain laws. Unsurprisingly, state governments during the Early National Era frequently sought to rescind land grants and corporate charters that legislators thought contained unfavorable terms. When state governments made such attempts, investors claimed that the state action violated the contracts clause. Their lawyers asserted that state grants and corporate charters were as much contracts as were private agreements to sell a horse.

The Supreme Court supported private investors in two important decisions. *Fletcher v. Peck* (1810) ruled that state land grants were contracts subject to contracts clause strictures. *Dartmouth College v. Woodward* (1819) determined that corporate charters were contracts for constitutional purposes. In the latter case, the Marshall Court held that nonprofit corporate charters had the same constitutional status as for-profit corporate charters. Both *Fletcher* and *Dartmouth*, if broadly interpreted, provide powerful limitations on state capacity to redistribute land and regulate business enterprises.

The first Marshall Court cases on property rights suggest a certain ambiguity in the source of the limits on government power. Chief Justice Marshall concluded his *Fletcher* opinion by declaring that "the state of Georgia was restrained, either by general principles which are common to our free institutions, or by the particular provisions of the constitution of the United States." This claim is similar to Justice Chase's assertion in *Calder v. Bull* (1798) that certain natural rights are judicially enforceable, even in the absence of a specific constitutional provision. Justice Johnson's concurrence in *Fletcher* invoked "a general principle, on the reason and nature of things; a principle which will impose laws even on the Deity."

Cases decided in the Marshall Court over time placed more emphasis on constitutional provisions and less emphasis on natural law. The *Dartmouth College* case and other decisions handed down during the 1820s relied exclusively on the contracts clause. Constitutional authorities nevertheless regarded the obligation of contracts as rooted in natural justice, even if judicial power was increasingly seen as grounded in the constitutional text.

An investor-friendly contracts clause jurisprudence developed during the first third of the nineteenth century. These decisions help explain why many business elites became firm supporters of judicial power. Federal courts, Daniel Webster and his business-friendly allies were convinced, could be trusted to protect property rights against democratic legislatures. Courts, in their view, were the national institution that had the special capacity to secure the liberties of affluent Americans, a minority that elites thought needed special judicial protection from popular majorities. Table 4-2 illustrates how contract clause cases were an important part of the early Supreme Court's work, but later declined as the justices limited the scope of that constitutional provision.

Table 4-2 Selection of U.S. Supreme Court Cases Reviewing State Laws under the Contracts Clause

Case	Vote	Outcome	Decision
Fletcher v. Peck, 10 U.S. (6 Cranch) 187 (1810)	4-1	Struck down	Legislature cannot rescind grants once the rights have vested
New Jersey v. Wilson, 11 U.S. (7 Cranch) 164 (1812)	7-0	Struck down	Legislature cannot revoke tax immunity that was part of a land grant to a Native American tribe
Dartmouth College v. Woodward, 17 U.S. (4 Wheat.) 518 (1819)	6-1	Struck down	A corporate charter is a contract that cannot be altered by the state
Sturges v. Crowninshield, 17 U.S. (4 Wheat.) 122 (1819)	7-0	Struck down	States cannot adopt a bankruptcy law that retroactively applies to preexisting contracts
Green v. Biddle, 21 U.S. (8 Wheat.) 1 (1823)	6-1	Struck down	States cannot violate an interstate compact regarding land titles
Ogden v. Saunders, 25 U.S. (12 Wheat.) 213 (1827)	4-3	Upheld	States may adopt a bankruptcy law that prospectively applies to new contracts
Mason v. Haile, 25 U.S. (12 Wheat.) 370 (1827)	6-1	Upheld	States may alter remedies for enforcing contracts by discharging individuals from debtors prison
Charles River Bridge v. Warren Bridge, 36 U.S. (11 Pet.) 420 (1837)	5-2	Upheld	Charters and grants should be construed strictly so as not to impair future legislative discretion
Bronson v. Kinzie, et al., 42 U.S. (1 How.) 311 (1843)	6-1	Struck down	State law that substantially alters available remedies impairs the obligation of contracts
Gelpcke v. City of Dubuque, 68 U.S. (1 Wall.) 175 (1863)	9-1	Struck down	Municipal bonds are valid contracts even if a state court later determines that the city did not have legal authority to issue the bonds
Von Hoffman v. City of Quincy, 71 U.S. (4 Wall.) 535 (1866)	9-0	Struck down	A state cannot withdraw from a city the taxation power necessary to repay bonds

(*Continued*)

Table 4-2 *(Continued)*

Case	Vote	Outcome	Decision
Pennsylvania College Cases, 80 U.S. (13 Wall.) 190 (1871)	9-0	Upheld	A state may amend, alter, or repeal any corporate charters granted after the adoption of a general reservation statute
Beer Company v. Massachusetts, 97 U.S. 25 (1877)	9-0	Upheld	Legislature has no power to contract away its police powers, and so alcohol prohibition is a valid regulation of a corporation chartered to manufacture alcohol
Stone v. Mississippi, 101 U.S. 814 (1880)	9-0	Upheld	The granting of a 25-year charter to a lottery company does not preclude a state from subsequently banning the sale of lottery tickets either through legislation or constitutional amendment
City of Cleveland v. Cleveland City Railway Company, 194 U.S. 517 (1904)	8-0	Struck down	A city ordinance lowering streetcar fares violates a corporate charter that specified a five-cent fare
Home Building & Loan Association v. Blaisdell, 290 U.S. 398 (1934)	5-4	Upheld	States can exercise police powers to modify mortgage remedies in an economic emergency
W.B. Worthen Co. v. Thomas, 292 U.S. 426 (1934)	9-0	Struck down	State law protecting insurance benefits from debt collectors cannot be justified as an emergency measure
United States Trust Co. v. New Jersey, 431 U.S. 1 (1977)	4-3	Struck down	The repeal of a bi-state agreement that blocked the ability of a rail line to subsidize passengers by spending bond reserves is invalid
Allied Structural Steel Co. v. Spannaus, 438 U.S. 234 (1978)	5-3	Struck down	A state statute requiring companies to pay pensions to all long-term employees if a plant closes or a pension plan is terminated, regardless of the terms of the employment contract, is invalid
Exxon Corp. v. Eagerton, 462 U.S. 176 (1983)	9-0	Upheld	A statutory provision that oil and gas severance tax cannot be passed on to consumers, regardless of existing contracts allowing pass-throughs, is valid as a generally applicable statute
Energy Reserves Group v. Kansas Power & Light, 459 U.S. 400 (1983)	9-0	Upheld	A state may alter contracts to set price levels on natural gas if doing so serves a significant public purpose and is a reasonable means for accomplishing that goal
Keystone Bituminous Coal Association v. DeBenedictis, 480 U.S. 470 (1987)	5-4	Upheld	A state may alter land titles on mining rights if doing so serves a substantial public interest and the state itself is not a contracting party

Fletcher v. Peck, 10 U.S. 87 (1810)

John Peck of Massachusetts sold fifteen thousand acres of land along the Yazoo River to Robert Fletcher of New Hampshire. Fletcher immediately sued Peck in federal court, claiming that the title to the land Peck sold was defective. Georgia owned the disputed lands when the Constitution was ratified. In 1795 the Georgia legislature granted some 35 million acres of Yazoo lands, making up most of what is now Alabama and Mississippi, to four companies for little more than a penny per acre. Evidence soon emerged that the entire legislature had been bribed, and members were turned out in the next election. The new Georgia legislature repealed the land grant in 1796. Fletcher claimed that the repeal divested Peck of his title, since by law the title had reverted back to Georgia. Peck claimed that he had good title to the Yazoo property because he had purchased the lands unaware of the original corrupt bargain. Under the common law, Peck asserted, buyers acquire good title when they are not aware that the seller gained the property fraudulently (this is called being a "holder in due course").

The Yazoo affair sparked a national controversy. Many "innocent" land purchasers, rebuffed by the Georgia legislature, turned to Congress with requests for reimbursement. When Thomas Jefferson assumed the presidency, he appointed a commission to investigate the scandal. Jefferson and his political ally James Madison hoped to encourage persons to settle the western frontier by establishing the principle that democratic governments respected vested property rights. More radical Jeffersonians opposed any government assistance for land speculators who were benefiting from a corrupt bargain.

Many investors thought that the courts provided a better forum for resolving their rights to the Yazoo lands. Fletcher v. Peck *was a collusive suit. Peck and Fletcher structured their transaction to maximize the chance of getting the Supreme Court to decide whether Georgia could constitutionally repeal the land grant. The case quickly attracted top legal and political talent. Future justice Joseph Story, future president John Quincy Adams, federal constitutional convention delegate Luther Martin, and Congressman Robert Harper participated. Peck won at trial, and the verdict was appealed to the Supreme Court of the United States.*

The Marshall Court unanimously held that the Georgia law rescinding the land grant unconstitutionally deprived the third-party purchasers of their property. Chief Justice Marshall's opinion declared that land grants were contracts. Therefore, laws rescinding land grants impaired the obligation of contracts. When reading this case, consider the following questions. On what basis does Chief Justice Marshall find that a state grant of land is a contract? What theory of constitutional interpretation does he employ? Is his execution of that theory sound? Consider the references to general principles discussed in the introduction to the section on the contracts clause. Is Fletcher v. Peck *an appropriate instance of natural justice? Would your opinion be different if there had been no fraud or bribery in the original transaction?*

The Supreme Court's decision in Fletcher *did not end the controversy. Resolution did not come until 1814, when Congress paid $5 million to acquire the disputed territory and settle all the private legal claims.*

CHIEF JUSTICE MARSHALL, delivered the opinion of the court as follows:.

. . .

The lands in controversy vested absolutely in James Gunn and others, the original grantees, by the conveyance of the governor, made in pursuance of an act of assembly to which the legislature was fully competent. Being thus in full possession of the legal estate, they, for a valuable consideration, conveyed portions of the land to those who were willing to purchase. If the original transaction was infected with fraud, these purchasers did not participate in it, and had no notice of it. They were innocent. Yet the legislature of Georgia has involved them in the fate of the first parties to the transaction, and, if the act be valid, has annihilated their rights also.

. . .

It is not intended to speak with disrespect of the legislature of Georgia, or of its acts. Far from it. The question is a general question, and is treated as one. For although such powerful objections to a legislative grant, as are alleged against this, may not again exist, yet the principle, on which alone this rescinding act is to be supported, may be applied to every case to which it shall be the will of any legislature to apply it. The principle is this; that a legislature may, by its own act, divest the vested estate of any man whatever, for reasons which shall, by itself, be deemed sufficient. . . . [T]hose who purchased parts of [the granted land] were not stained by that guilt which infected the original transaction. Their case is not distinguishable from the ordinary case of purchasers of a legal estate without knowledge of any secret fraud which might have led to the emanation of the original grant. According to the well known course of equity, their rights could not be affected by such fraud. Their situation was the same, their title was the same, with that of every other member of the community who holds land by regular conveyances from the original patentee.

Is the power of the legislature competent to the annihilation of such title, and to a resumption of the property thus held?

The principle asserted is, that one legislature is competent to repeal any act which a former legislature was competent to pass; and that one legislature cannot abridge the powers of a succeeding legislature.

The correctness of this principle, so far as respects general legislation, can never be controverted. But, if an act be done under a law, a succeeding legislature cannot undo it. The past cannot be recalled by the most absolute power. Conveyances have been made, those conveyances have vested legal estates, and, if those estates may be seized by the sovereign authority, still, that they originally vested is a fact, and cannot cease to be a fact.

When, then, a law is in its nature a contract, when absolute rights have vested under that contract, a repeal of the law cannot divest those rights; and the act of annulling them, if legitimate, is rendered so by a power applicable to the case of every individual in the community.

It may well be doubted whether the nature of society and of government does not prescribe some limits to the legislative power; and, if any be prescribed, where are they to be found, if the property of an individual, fairly and honestly acquired, may be seized without compensation. . . .

The validity of this rescinding act, then, might well be doubted, were Georgia a single sovereign power. But Georgia cannot be viewed as a single, unconnected, sovereign power, on whose legislature no other restrictions are imposed than may be found in its own constitution. She is a part of a large empire; she is a member of the American union; and that union has a constitution the supremacy of which all acknowledge, and which imposes limits to the legislatures of the several states, which none claim a right to pass. The constitution of the United States declares that no state shall pass any bill of attainder, ex post facto law, or law impairing the obligation of contracts.

Does the case now under consideration come within this prohibitory section of the constitution?

In considering this very interesting question, we immediately ask ourselves what is a contract? Is a grant a contract?. . .

If, under a fair construction of the constitution, grants are comprehended under the term contracts, is a grant from the state excluded from the operation of the provision? Is the clause to be considered as inhibiting the state from impairing the obligation of contracts between two individuals, but as excluding from that inhibition contracts made with itself?

The words themselves contain no such distinction. They are general, and are applicable to contracts of every description. If contracts made with the state are to be exempted from their operation, the exception must arise from the character of the contracting party, not from the words which are employed.

Whatever respect might have been felt for the state sovereignties, it is not to be disguised that the framers of the constitution viewed, with some apprehension, the violent acts which might grow out of the feelings of the moment; and that the people of the United States, in adopting that instrument, have manifested a determination to shield themselves and their property from the effects of those sudden and strong passions to which men are exposed. The restrictions on the legislative power of the states are obviously founded in this sentiment; and the constitution of the United States contains what may be deemed a bill of rights for the people of each state.

No state shall pass any bill of attainder, ex post facto law, or law impairing the obligation of contracts.

A bill of attainder may affect the life of an individual, or may confiscate his property, or may do both. In this form the power of the legislature over the lives and fortunes of individuals is expressly restrained. What motive, then, for implying, in words which import a general prohibition to impair the obligation of contracts, an exception in favour of the right to impair the obligation of those contracts into which the state may enter?

The state legislatures can pass no ex post facto law. An ex post facto law is one which renders an act punishable in a manner in which it was not punishable when it was committed. Such a law may inflict penalties on the person, or may inflict pecuniary penalties which swell the public treasury. The legislature is then prohibited from passing a law by which a man's estate, or any part of it, shall be seized for a crime which was not declared, by some previous law, to render him liable to that punishment. Why, then, should violence be done to the natural meaning of words for the purpose of leaving to the legislature the power of seizing, for public use, the estate of an individual in the form of a law annulling the title by which he holds that estate? The court can perceive no sufficient grounds for making this distinction. . . .

JUSTICE JOHNSON, concurring.

In this case I entertain, on two points, an opinion different from that which has been delivered by the court.

I do not hesitate to declare that a state does not possess the power of revoking its own grants. But I do it on a general principle, on the reason and nature of things: a principle which will impose laws even on the deity.

A contrary opinion can only be maintained upon the ground that no existing legislature can abridge the powers of those which will succeed it. To a certain extent this is certainly correct; but the distinction lies between power and interest, the right of jurisdiction and the right of soil.

. . . When the legislature have once conveyed their interest or property in any subject to the individual, they have lost all control over it; have nothing to act upon; it has passed from them; is vested in the individual; becomes intimately blended with his existence, as essentially so as the blood that circulates through his system. The government may indeed demand of him the one or the other, not because they are not his, but because whatever is his is his country's. . . .

Takings and Due Process

Americans in the Early National Era did not make sharp distinctions between due process rights and rights against uncompensated takings. Before the Civil War, the paradigmatic due process violation was a law that redistributed property from A to B without reason. Whether a state judge adjudicating such claims focused on due process, takings, the contracts clause of the federal Constitution, or some combination of the three, depended partly on the language used in the state constitution and partly on the judge. Many property rights decisions in the early republic consisted of little more than a paragraph, but some judges with national followings preferred long, complex expositions on both constitutional specifics and general constitutional principles.

Courts adjudicated three different property claims. First, persons claimed that government officials had unconstitutionally decided a property dispute between two persons. *Bowman v. Middleton* (SC 1792) determined that juries should settle disputes over land titles.[7] Second, persons claimed that government officials had unconstitutionally rescinded a land grant. *Fletcher v. Peck* (1810) decided that state laws rescinding land grants violated the contracts clause of the U.S. Constitution. *University of North Carolina v. Foy* (NC 1805) ruled that state rescissions violated due process rights. Third, persons claimed that state regulations reduced the worth of their property. *Callender v. Marsh* (MA 1823) held that a state could be considered to have taken property unconstitutionally only when the state physically occupied the property.[8] Judges debated what constituted a physical occupation. In one instance, a court may have ruled that a taking could occur without physical occupation. In *Crenshaw & Crenshaw v. The Slate River Company* (VA 1828), Virginia judges decided that the state could not pass laws requiring mill owners to make expensive improvements and to allow persons free passage through their land.[9]

National constitutional decision makers rarely considered due process and takings questions. *Brown v. United States* (1814) was the most important federal court decision that discussed whether the national government violated property rights. Chief Justice Marshall ruled that the president could not unilaterally confiscate property during wartime. His opinion concluded, "The power of confiscating enemy property is in the legislature, and that the legislature has not yet declared its will to confiscate property which was within our territory at the declaration of war." Had Congress passed a law authorizing the president to confiscate property during the War of 1812, *Brown* indicates that the court would have found that Congress did not violate the constitutional rights of property holders.

University of North Carolina v. Foy, 5 N.C. 58 (1805)

In 1789 the North Carolina legislature gave the University of North Carolina land that the trustees could sell to fund the educational mission of the school. Eleven years later the state legislature passed a law divesting the university of the property not yet sold. Soon after, the North Carolina legislature granted Foy some land originally given to the university in 1789. The trustees brought a lawsuit against Foy, claiming that the university retained title to the disputed property. The trustees claimed that the legislative attempt to repeal the 1789 land grant deprived them of property without due process of law. Foy claimed that the due process clause limited the power of executives and judges, but not legislatures.

7. *Bowman v. Middleton*, 1 Bay 252 (SC 1792).

8. *Callender v. Marsh*, 18 Mass. 418 (1823).

9. *Crenshaw & Crenshaw v. The Slate River Company*, 27 Va. 245 (1828).

The Supreme Court of North Carolina ruled that the repeal was unconstitutional. Judge Locke declared that the due process clause of the state constitution limited all governing officials and that corporations had the same property rights as individuals. University of North Carolina v. Foy *was one of the first precedents holding that due process provided substantive limits on legislation. Why does Judge Locke think that the due process clause has substantive content? What legislative enactments does he believe are inconsistent with due process of law?*

JUDGE LOCKE delivered the opinion of the Court.

. . .

But one great and important reason which influences us in deciding this question, is the 10th section of the bill of rights, which declares "that no freeman ought to be taken, imprisoned, or disseized of his freehold, liberties or privileges, or outlawed or exiled, or in any manner destroyed or deprived of his life, liberty or property, but by the law of the land."—It has been yielded on the part of the defendants that if the Legislature had vested an individual with the property in question, this section of the bill of rights would restrain them from depriving him of such right: but it is denied that this section has any operation on corporations whose members are mere naked Trustees, and have no interest in the donation, and especially on a corporation erected for a public purpose. It is also insisted that the term, "Law of the Land," does not impose any restrictions on the Legislature, who are capable of making the Law of the Land, and was only intended to prevent abuses in the other branches of government. That this clause was intended to secure to corporations as well as to individuals the rights therein enumerated, seems clear from the word *"liberties,"* which peculiarly signifies those privileges and rights which corporations have by virtue of the instruments which incorporate them, and is certainly used in this clause in contradistinction to the word *"liberty,"* which refers to the personal liberty of the citizen. We therefore infer that by this clause the legislature are as much restrained from affecting the property of corporations, as they are that of a private individual. . . . It is evident the framers of the constitution intended the provision as a restraint upon some branch of the government, either the Executive, Legislative, or Judicial. To suppose it applicable to the executive would be absurd on account of the limited powers conferred on that officer; and from the subjects enumerated in that clause, no danger could be apprehended, from the Executive Department, that being entrusted with the exercise of no powers by which the principles thereby intended to be secured could be affected. To apply it to the Judiciary, would, if possible, be still more idle, if the Legislature can make the *"Law of the Land."* For the Judiciary are only to expound and enforce the law and have no discretionary powers enabling them to judge of the propriety or impropriety of laws. They are bound, whether agreeable to their ideas of justice or not, to carry into effect the acts of the legislature as far as they are binding or do not contravene the constitution. If then this clause is applicable to the legislature alone, and was intended as a restraint on their acts, . . . Let us next enquire, what will be the operation which this clause will or ought to have on the present question. It seems to us to warrant a belief that members of a corporation as well as individuals shall not be so deprived of their liberties or property, unless by a trial by Jury in a court of Justice, according to the known and established rules of decision, derived from the common law, and such acts of the Legislature as are consistent with the constitution—and although the Trustees are a corporation established for public purposes, yet their property is as completely beyond the control of the Legislature, as the property of individuals or that of any other corporation. Indeed, it seems difficult to conceive of a corporation established for merely private purposes. In every institution of that kind, the ground of the establishment is some public good or purpose intended to be promoted; but in many, the members thereof have a private interest, coupled with the public object. In this case, the trustees have no private interest beyond the general good: yet we conceive that circumstance will not make the property of the Trustees subject to the arbitrary will of the Legislature. The property vested in the Trustees must remain for the uses intended for the University, until the Judiciary of the country in the usual and common form, pronounce them guilty of such acts, as will, in law, amount to a forfeiture of their rights or a dissolution of their body. . . .

JUDGE HALL, dissenting. . . .

B. Religion

Constitutional debates over religion changed subtly after federal and state constitutions were ratified. Americans during the Colonial and Founding Eras debated the place of religion in a Christian commonwealth. Roger Williams, James Madison, and other proponents of religious freedom provided Christian justifications for disestablishment and the liberty of conscience. Americans during the Early National Era debated the place of religion in a constitutional republic where the vast majority of citizens were Christians. Proponents of religious freedom gave secular justifications for their preferred practices. Many proponents of test oaths and laws banning blasphemy provided more secular reasons for maintaining what had formerly been viewed of as laws protecting and promoting Christianity. Americans in 1829 were still living in a Christian society. Whether American culture or American law could be described as Christian, however, was controversial, and would become even more controversial during the Second Great Awakening, the religious revival that took place in Jacksonian America.

Establishment

Americans debated whether to retain any religious establishments. Some constitutional decision makers insisted that "Christianity . . . is the law of our land."[10] They believed that Christian religious establishments were necessary means for fostering a virtuous republican citizenry. Other Americans sought to build a "wall of separation" between church and state. Led by Thomas Jefferson, they maintained that combining government and religion corrupted both.

Proponents of religious disestablishment gained strength after the Constitution was ratified. Most states repealed constitutional provisions requiring that officeholders be devout Christians. Several abjured financial support for religious institutions. Successful champions of these reforms increasingly relied on secular arguments. Opponents of test oaths in the Massachusetts Constitutional Convention insisted, "It was an established principle that acts, not opinions, were the subject of laws." Thomas Jefferson's famous "Letter to the Danbury Baptists" placed more emphasis on the liberal principle that government should regulate only action than on the Christian principle that expressions of faith should be sincere.

American presidents during the Early National Era disagreed over whether they should issue Thanksgiving proclamations and call for special days of prayer. George Washington accepted a congressional request to "recommend . . . a day of public thanksgiving and prayer." John Adams on several occasions established a "day of solemn humiliation, fasting, and prayer." His proclamations were explicitly Christian. Adams called on "the citizens of these States [to] . . . offer their devout addresses to the Father of Mercies, . . . beseeching Him at the same time, of His infinite grace, through the Redeemer of the World, freely to remit all our offenses, and to incline us by His Holy Spirit to that sincere repentance and reformation which may afford us reason to hope for his inestimable favor and heavenly benediction." Thomas Jefferson refused to issue proclamations establishing Thanksgiving Day or days of prayers. He thought that the president had "no authority to direct the religious exercises of his constituents."[11]

Religion retained a strong presence in the states. Official proceedings often began with prayer. Most states retained blasphemy laws, which state judges sustained on secular grounds. *People v. Ruggles* (NY 1811) declared that persons could be punished for blasphemy because insulting God threatened the public peace.[12]

Thomas Jefferson, Letter to the Danbury Baptists (1802)[13]

Thomas Jefferson fought to limit the influence of politics on religious affairs. In contrast to Federalists, who believed state support for religion to be crucial for maintaining public morality, Jefferson and his supporters worried that state establishments fostered European religious persecutions. Chapter Three discusses his responsibility for the bill that established religious freedom in Virginia. During the election of 1800, Jefferson wrote a letter to his friend Benjamin Rush asserting, "The Congregationalist and Episcopalian clergy in the United States entertained a very favorable

10. *Updegraph v. Commonwealth,* 11 Serg. & Rawle 394, 409 (Pa. 1824).

11. Thomas Jefferson to Rev. Samuel Miller, in *The Works of Thomas Jefferson,* ed. Paul Leicester Ford (New York: G. P. Putnam's Sons, 1904-5), 11:7.

12. *People v. Ruggles,* 8 Johns. R. 290 (NY 1811).

13. Excerpt from Thomas Jefferson, *The Writings of Thomas Jefferson,* ed. H.A. Washington (Washington, DC: Taylor & Maury, 1854), 8:133.

hope of obtaining an establishment of a particular form of Christianity thro' the US." Jefferson promised to defeat such schemes. He informed Rush that he had "sworn upon the altar of god, eternal hostility against every form of tyranny over the mind of man."[14]

Jefferson expressed similar commitments to religious liberty when serving as president. Responding to a congratulatory letter from members of the Baptist Church in Connecticut, he penned the famous phrase "a wall of separation between Church and State." This phrase is often repeated in debates over the meaning of the establishment clause. Consider these words in the broader context of the letter to the Danbury Baptists. What did Jefferson mean by "a wall of separation between Church and State"? Was he merely making a literary allusion? Does that phrase or his letter provide any clear principles that help resolve contemporary debates over prayer at school graduations or school choice programs?

Believing with you that religion is a matter which lies solely between Man & his God, that he owes account to none other for his faith or his worship, that the legitimate powers of government reach actions only, & not opinions, I contemplate with sovereign reverence that act of the whole American people which declared that their legislature should "make no law respecting an establishment of religion, or prohibiting the free exercise thereof," thus building a wall of separation between Church & State. Adhering to this expression of the supreme will of the nation in behalf of the rights of conscience, I shall see with sincere satisfaction the progress of those sentiments which tend to restore to man all his natural rights, convinced he has no natural right in opposition to his social duties....

Massachusetts Debates Test Oaths (1820–21)[15]

The 1780 Massachusetts Constitution required that all elected officials be Christians. Members of the executive and legislative branches took the following oath: "I . . . do declare that I believe the Christian religion, and have a firm persuasion of its truth." In 1820 Massachusetts held a convention to consider revising the original constitution. The delegates proposed fourteen amendments, nine of which were ratified by the people. One of these amendments modified the religious oath so that after 1820, members of the executive and legislative branches of government would only be required to express a belief in God. The new oath of office was: "I . . . do solemnly swear, that I will bear true faith and allegiance to the Commonwealth of Massachusetts and will support the constitution thereof. So help me, God." Quakers were permitted to take a modified oath.

The debate over religious oaths in the Massachusetts Constitutional Convention was vigorous. Proponents of the 1780 oath insisted that a Christian people had the right to limit officeholders to believing Christians. Opponents insisted that the oath fostered hypocrisy and was inconsistent with republican commitments to equality. When reading the excerpts from the debates below, consider the changing place of religion in the American constitutional democracy. What different relationships do advocates draw between Christianity and the Constitution? Did any speaker think the people of Massachusetts likely to elect non-Christians to public office? If not, what explains the vigor with which the test oath was debated?

DANIEL WEBSTER of Boston

. . . In the first place; have the People a right, if in their judgment, the security of their Government and its due administration demand it to require a declaration of belief in the Christian Religion as a qualification or condition of office? . . . By the fundamental principles of popular and elective Government, all office is in the free gift of the people. They may grant, or they may withhold it at pleasure; and it may be for them, and them only, to decide whether they will grant office, it for them to decide, also on what terms, and with what conditions, they will grant it. Nothing is more unfounded than the notion that any man has a right to an office. This must depend on the choice of others, and consequently on the opinions of others, in relations to his fitness and qualifications for office. No man can be said to have a right to that, which others may withhold from him, at pleasure....

This qualification has nothing to do with any man's conscience. If he dislike the conditions, he may decline the office....

However clear the right may be . . . the expediency of retaining the declaration is a more difficult question.

14. Thomas Jefferson to Benjamin Rush, September 23, 1800, in *The Papers of Thomas Jefferson*, ed. Barbara Oberg (Princeton, NJ: Princeton University Press, 2005), 32:166–68.

15. Excerpted from *Journal of Debates and Proceedings in the Convention of Delegates Chosen to Revise the Constitution of Massachusetts* (Boston: Office of the Daily Advertiser, 1853).

It is said not to be necessary, because, in this Commonwealth, ninety-nine out of every hundred of the inhabitants profess to believe in the Christian religion. It is sufficiently certain, therefore, that persons of this description, and not others, will ordinarily be chosen to places of public trust. . . .

This qualification is made applicable only to the Executive and the members of the Legislature. It would not be easy, perhaps, to say why it should not be extended to the Judiciary, if it were thought necessary for any office. There can be no office, in which the sense of religious responsibility is more necessary than in that of a Judge; especially of those judges who pass, in the last resort, on the lives, liberty and property of every man. . . . [L]egislation is in its nature general. Laws usually affect the whole society, and, if mischievous or unjust, the whole society is alarmed, and seeks their repeal. The judiciary power, on the other hand, acts directly on individuals. The injured may suffer, without sympathy, or the hopes of redress. The last hope of the innocent, under accusation, and in distress, is the integrity of the judges. If this fail, all fails; and there is no remedy on this side the bar of Heaven. Of all places, therefore, there is none, which so imperatively demands that he who occupies it should be under the fear of God, and above all other fear, as the situation of a Judge.

JAMES PRINCE of Boston

. . . I submit the following positions, first, admitting the right (which, however, I do not) of the citizens when forming a social compact to prescribe such terms as a majority may deem expedient and proper, yet I hold it to be unjust to introduce a principle into the compact which while it provides that the individual shall afford his personal aid and risk his life for the common defense and yield up all his property (if need be) for the maintenance of the government and its laws; yet virtually precludes him from participating in any of the advantages resulting from offices, or from any share in the administration of the government, because he differs on a subject with which society has but a doubtful right to interfere; although in point of morality and strength of intellect he shines as "a star of the first magnitude."

Secondly, I hold that this act of injustice toward the individual is neither politic nor expedient; first, because . . . it may deprive society of talent, and moral excellence, which should always be secured and cherished as one of the best means of preserving the prosperity of the Commonwealth; and secondly, while it may thus exclude men possessing such useful and amiable qualifications, yet it is no effectual safeguard whereby to keep out ambitious unprincipled men from office, or a seat in the public counsels.

And, I moreover hold, that the cause of Christianity doth not require such a qualification to support it. This religion is founded on a rock and supported by a power which humanity cannot affect—it does not want the secular arm to defend it—its divine origin, and its own intrinsic merit, ever have been, and ever will be, its firmest support. What have the powers of the world to do with such a religion? Experience has demonstrated that when left to the umpire of reason and the aid of arguments, it has triumphed the most brilliantly over the attacks of infidelity. . . .

I verily believe in forming or revising the social compact, we ought wholly to exclude every principle which by possible construction may interfere with the consciences of men, thereby leaving them and their religions opinions where alone they ought to be left "to him who searcheth the heart and knows our inmost thoughts. Whether the individual has or has not formed a correct religious opinion is nothing to us, as civilians. . . .

Reverend JOSEPH TUCKERMAN of Chelsea

. . . The constitution declares every man to be eligible to all the high offices of the state, on the condition of certain prescribed qualifications. Yet if there was any probability that any people of color would be elected to fill either of these offices, he presumed that no doubt would be felt, either as to the right, or the propriety, of their exclusion. There would, without doubt, be a provision in the constitution for their exclusion; or, it would be required, that these offices should be holden only by the white inhabitants of the commonwealth. And if, as is without doubt a fact, ninety-five out of hundred of the people of this commonwealth are in their faith Christian, it seems to be as unquestionable as any one of the rights of a people, to require that their rulers shall, in the faith be Christians. . . .

. . .

On the question of the propriety of the test, he said, his objections were still more solemn. Either the religion of Jesus Christ is from God, or it is not. Either we are accountable to God for all our means and opportunities of advancing the interests of this religion, or we are not. If our religion be from God, and if it be our duty, by all means which are consistent with its spirit, to promote its progress, it is a question on which we ought to pause, whether we shall open the door of office indiscriminately to those who believe, and to those who reject this revelation of God's will. We all know the descending influence of example. If men should be elevated to high and responsible stations, who are enemies of Christianity, may we not look with some apprehension to the consequences. . . . Sir, we owe it to God, to Christ, and to our own souls, to do what we may for the extension and security, of our faith as Christians; and to give our influence, whatever it may be, to the election of magistrates, who will make laws, and administer justice, in the spirit of Christianity. . . .

HENRY A. S. DEARBORN of Roxbury

. . . [T]he test was an unjust exaction and a violation of the unalienable rights of the people. He referred to the opinion of the learned, pious and illustrious Locke, that it was not the business of religion to interfere with the civil government. It was an established principle that acts, not opinions, were the subject of laws. Political opinions were not subject to a test; why should those upon religion be subject to any? They had no right to compel a man to throw open the portals of his mind and discover his religious sentiments. He trusted such oppression would not prevail in the free and enlightened country. There was no authority for it in the scriptures. . . .

Blasphemy. Most Americans did not believe that blasphemy—speech insulting to (the Christian) religion—was constitutionally protected. Judges in both New York and Pennsylvania sustained without any difficulty the convictions of persons who made disparaging remarks about Jesus Christ or Christianity. In *People v. Ruggles* (NY 1811), Chief Justice James Kent provided a secular justification for punishing profane comments by insisting that blasphemy "tends to corrupt the morals of the people, and to destroy good order."[16] The judges on the Supreme Court of Pennsylvania asserted that Christianity had special legal status. Justice Duncan in *Updegraph v. Commonwealth* (PA 1824) stated,

> This is the Christianity which is the law of our land, and I do not think it will be an invasion of any man's right of private judgment, or of the most extended privilege of propagating his sentiments with regard to religion, in the manner which he thinks most conclusive. If from a regard to decency and the good order of society, profane swearing, breach of the Sabbath, and blasphemy, are punishable by civil magistrates, these are not punished as sins or offences against God, but crimes injurious to, and having a malignant influence on society; for it is certain, that by these practices, no one pretends to prove any supposed truths, detect any supposed error, or advance any sentiment whatever.[17]

Some prominent Americans maintained that blasphemy prosecutions were inconsistent with religious liberty. John Adams complained about the *Ruggles* decision in a letter to Thomas Jefferson. He wrote,

> We think ourselves possessed or at least we boast that we are so of Liberty of conscience on all subjects and of the right of free inquiry and private judgment, in all cases and yet how far are we from these exalted privileges in fact. There exists I believe throughout the whole Christian world a law which makes it blasphemy to deny or to doubt the divine inspiration of all the books of the old and new Testaments from Genesis to Revelations. . . . Now, what free inquiry, when a writer must surely encounter the risk of fine or imprisonment for adducing any argument for investigation into the divine authority of those books? . . . I think such laws a great embarrassment, great obstructions to the improvement of the human mind. . . . The substance and essence of Christianity as I understand it is eternal and unchangeable and will bear examination forever but it has been mixed with extraneous ingredients, which I think will not bear examination and they ought to be separated.[18]

Jefferson agreed with Adams. He described judicial claims that "Christianity is a part of the common law" as "usurpation." "The proof of the contrary," he wrote, is "that the common law existed while the Anglo-Saxons were yet Pagans, at a time when they had never yet heard the name of Christ pronounced."[19]

16. *People v. Ruggles*, 8 Johns. R. 290 N.Y. (1811).

17. *Updegraph v. Commonwealth*, 11 Serg. & Rawle 394 Pa. (1824).

18. John Adams to Thomas Jefferson, January 23, 1825, in *The Adams-Jefferson Letters*, ed. Lester J. Cappon (Chapel Hill: University of North Carolina Press, 1988), 607–8.

19. Thomas Jefferson, *Memoir, Correspondence, and Miscellanies from The Papers of Thomas Jefferson*, ed. Thomas Jefferson Randolph (Charlottesville, VA: F. Carr and Co., 1829), 4:397.

Free Exercise

By the early nineteenth century, a national consensus had formed that government should permit people to worship (or not worship) God in private according to their personal religious beliefs. George Washington's "Letter to the Jews of Newport" asserted that "all possess alike liberty of conscience" in the United States. Proponents of religious establishments agreed that government should not regulate private religious life. One champion of test oaths in the Massachusetts Constitutional Convention maintained, "He would have no sect preferred, no restraint upon the consciences, opinions, or even caprices of men."[20]

The same consensus did not exist on rights to exemptions from otherwise valid laws. The majority of state court decisions concluded that the principle of freedom of conscience did not entitle persons to violate state laws that interfered with cherished religious practices. *Commonwealth v. Wolf* (PA 1817) is a typical instance in which state courts rejected claims that religious minorities had rights to exemptions from state laws aimed at secular goods.[21] *People v. Phillips* (NY 1813) is an important exception to the general tendency of courts to reject claims for religious exemptions.[22] In that case, a New York court declared that priests had a right not to reveal confessions. The relatively small number of cases that considered whether religious believers had constitutional rights to exemptions do not permit clear conclusions on whether *Phillips* represents a strong strand of Early National Era thinking or is best understood as an aberrant decision.

George Washington, Letter to the Jews of Newport (1790)[23]

George Washington favored religious liberty. During the campaign to ratify the Bill of Rights, Washington promoted the freedom of conscience. The nation's small Jewish population was particularly concerned with the fate of religious liberty in the United States. When Washington visited Newport, Rhode Island, Moses Seixas, a leader of the local Jewish community, wrote him a letter stating:

> *Deprived as we heretofore have been of the invaluable rights of free Citizens, we now (with a deep sense of gratitude to the Almighty disposer of all events) behold a Government, erected by the Majesty of the People—a Government, which to bigotry gives no sanction, to persecution no assistance—but generously affording to All liberty of conscience, and immunities of Citizenship: deeming every one, of whatever Nation, tongue, or language, equal parts of the great governmental Machine.*[24]

Washington's "Letter to the Jews of Newport" responded to Seixas's concerns by stating that European-style religious persecution would not take place in the United States. Persons would not be forced to swear allegiance to Jesus Christ. Jewish children would not be taken from their parents to be raised as Christians. Washington's assertion that Jews enjoyed religious freedom sent a signal to the entire nation that private religious beliefs were not the public business of the state. What else does this letter maintain? Consider Washington's letter in light of other materials in this chapter. Is the claim that "Christianity was part of the common law of the United States" inconsistent with any claim Washington makes in his "Letter to the Jews of Newport"?

. . .

The citizens of the United States of America have a right to applaud themselves for having given to mankind examples of an enlarged and liberal policy—a policy worthy of imitation. All possess alike liberty of conscience and immunities of citizenship.

It is now no more that toleration is spoken of as if it were the indulgence of one class of people that another enjoyed the exercise of their inherent natural rights, for, happily, the Government of the United States, which gives to bigotry no sanction, to persecution no assistance, requires only that they who live under its protection should demean themselves as good citizens in giving it on all occasions their effectual support.

. . . May the children of the stock of Abraham who dwell in this land continue to merit and enjoy the good will of the other inhabitants—while every one shall sit in safety under his own vine and fig tree and there shall be none to make him afraid.

20. *Journal of Debates and Proceedings*, 93.

21. *Commonwealth v. Wolf*, 3 Serg. & R. 48 (Sup. Ct. Penn. 1817).

22. *People v. Phillips*, Court of General Sessions, City of New York (June 14, 1813).

23. Excerpted from W. W. Abbott and Dorothy Twohig, eds., *The Papers of George Washington, Presidential Series* (Charlottesville, VA: University Press of Virginia, 1987), 6:284–86.

24. Samuel M. Schmucker, *A History of the Modern Jews* (Philadelphia: Quaker City, 1867), 324.

May the father of all mercies scatter light, and not darkness, upon our paths, and make us all in our several vocations useful here, and in His own due time and way everlastingly happy.

Commonwealth v. Wolf, 1817 W.L. 1768 (PA 1817)

Abraham Wolf was a Jewish tradesman who lived in Philadelphia. In keeping with Jewish law, Wolf refrained from working on Saturday and instead worked on Sunday. His work habits violated a Pennsylvania law that forbade persons from working on "the Lord's day" unless the work was necessary or they were performing charitable acts. Wolf was arrested, convicted, and fined $4. He appealed his conviction to the Supreme Court of Pennsylvania.

The Supreme Court of Pennsylvania had little difficulty sustaining the Pennsylvania law. Justice Yeates emphasized that Jews might be obligated to rest on Saturday, but nothing in the Jewish religion required adherents to work on Sunday. Justice Yeates had no hesitation in interpreting Jewish law. Is it constitutionally appropriate for a judge to interpret religious law? Should justices determine what constitute religious obligations? Can justices avoid such questions if they are expected to assess claims regarding religious liberty?

JUSTICE YEATES delivered the opinion of the Court.

. . .

The defendant's counsel has not contended that the prohibition of work on Sunday, immediately opposes the received doctrine of the Jews, as disclosed in the five books of Moses: but has asserted, that there may be persons of that religious persuasion, who may suppose, that the command in the decalogue, "six days shalt thou labor and do all that thou hast to do," imperiously binds them to work six days in each week; and firmly believing Saturday to be the day set apart for rest, they can only cease to work on that day, consistently with their ideas of religious duty. It has also been urged that there may be others who may make it a point of conscience to show, by plain, open, unequivocal acts, that the Christian institution of Sunday is abhorrent to their minds.

To this we answer that we have never heard of the fourth commandment having received this construction by any persons who profess to believe either in the Old or New Testament. And that the Jewish Talmud, containing the traditions of that people, and the Rabbinical constitutions and explications of their law asserts no such doctrine. The true meaning of the command is uniformly supposed to be, that we should abstain from our usual labor the one-seventh part of our time, and devote the same to the worship of the Deity and the exercise of our religious duties. Upon this subject the sense of the adherents to the Mosaic dispensation is strongly evinced by the religious holidays which they keep at the proper seasons.

Laws cannot be administered in any civilized government unless the people are taught to revere the sanctity of an oath, and look to a future state of rewards and punishments for the deeds of this life. It is of the utmost moment, therefore, that they should be reminded of their religious duties at stated periods; and the laboring part of the community must feel the institution of a day of rest as peculiarly adapted to invigorate their bodies for fresh exertions of activity. A wise policy would naturally lead to the formation of laws calculated to subserve those salutary purposes. The invaluable privilege of the rights of conscience secured to us by the constitution of the commonwealth, was never intended to shelter those persons, who, out of mere caprice, would directly oppose those laws for the pleasure of showing their contempt and abhorrence of the religious opinions of the great mass of the citizens.

C. Guns

Many early-nineteenth-century Americans revered guns. Men commonly carried guns for self-defense and as part of their obligation to serve in the militia. Proponents of state rights celebrated the Second Amendment for ensuring the integrity of a state militia capable of defending against a potentially oppressive national government. St. George Tucker, the most important Jeffersonian constitutional treatise writer, described the "right to bear arms" protected by the Second Amendment as "the true palladium of liberty." He continued:

> The right of self defence is the first law of nature: in most governments it has been the study of rulers to confine this right within the narrowest limits possible. Wherever standing armies are kept up, and the right of the people to keep and bear arms is, under any colour or pretext whatsoever, prohibited, liberty, if not already annihilated, is on the brink of destruction.[25]

25. St. George Tucker, *Blackstone's Commentaries: With Notes of Reference* (Union, NJ: Lawbook Exchange, 1996), 1:300 (appendix).

Many elected officials feared guns. Private violence plagued towns and cities. As a result, states and localities, concerned with crime rates, passed bans on concealed weapons. The preface to the Louisiana concealed weapons law worried about "assassinations and attempts to commit the same" that "have of late been of such frequent occurrences as to become a subject of serious alarm to the peaceable and well disposed inhabitants of the state."[26] Gun owners challenged these measures as violating their constitutional right to bear arms.

The first major constitutional decision in American history on the right to bear arms protected the rights of gun owners. In *Bliss v. Commonwealth* (KY 1822), the Supreme Court of Kentucky declared a concealed weapon ban unconstitutional. "Whatever restrains the full and complete exercise of that right," the justices declared, "is forbidden by the explicit language in the constitution."

26. Saul Cornell, *The Other Founders: Anti-Federalism and the Dissenting Tradition in America, 1788–1828* (Chapel Hill: University of North Carolina Press, 1999), 141.

Bliss v. Commonwealth, 2 Litt. 90, (KY 1822)

Bliss appeared in public with a ceremonial sword sheathed in his cane. He was arrested and indicted under a Kentucky law that forbade persons from carrying concealed weapons. At trial, Bliss was found guilty and fined $100. He appealed to the Court of Appeals of Kentucky on the ground that the state law violated the state constitutional right to bear arms.

The court of appeals agreed with Bliss that the law was unconstitutional. The justices ruled that the state constitution forbade any legislation regulating the right to bear arms. On what basis does the court reach this conclusion? The Kentucky Constitution in 1822 granted persons the right to "bear arms in defense of themselves and the state." This language differs from the Second Amendment to the

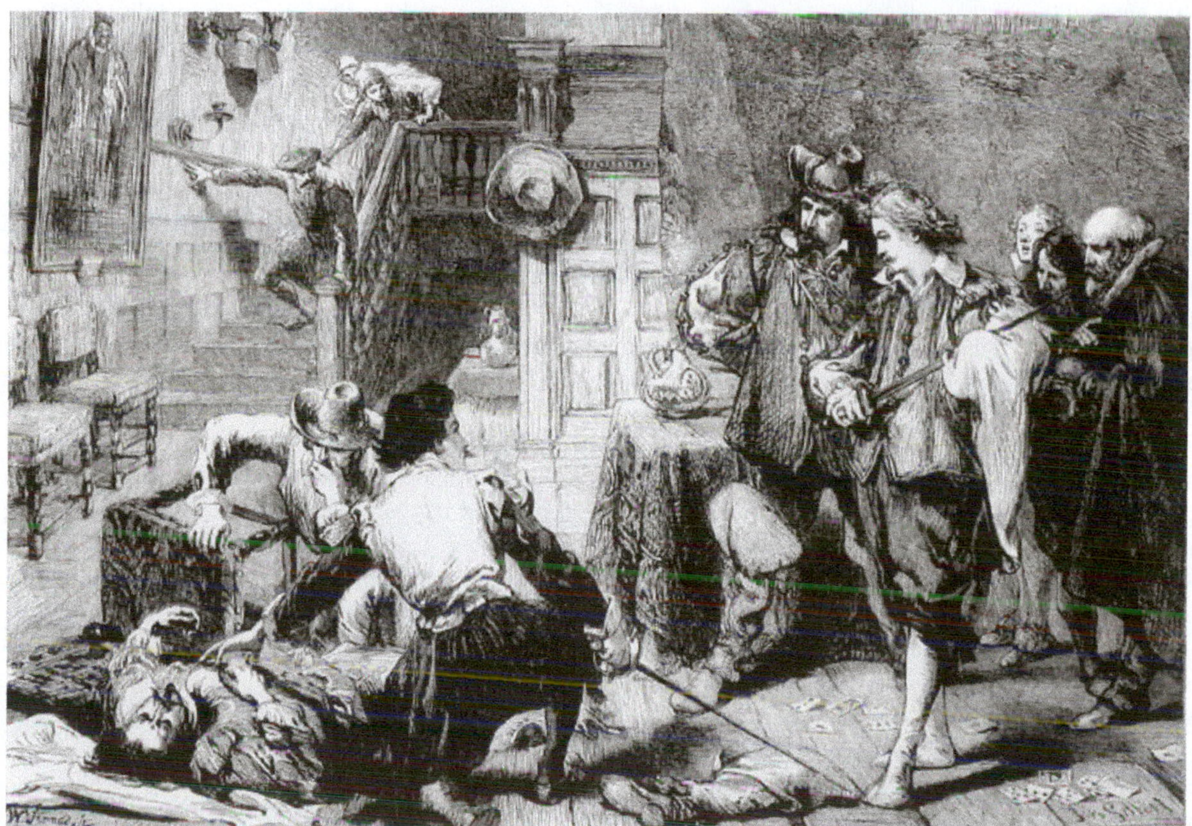

Illustration 4-1 A Tavern Brawl

Source: John Gilbert, "A Tavern Brawl," *Illustrated London News*, June 18, 1864. Manuscript, Archives, and Rare Book Library, Emory University.

U.S. Constitution, which is prefaced by a reference to state militias. Does the Court of Appeals of Kentucky provide any hint about whether the precise wording of the constitutional right to bear arms influenced the judicial decision in Bliss?

[The Constitution of Kentucky] provides, "that the right of the citizens to bear arms in defense of themselves and the state, shall not be questioned."

The provision contained in this section, perhaps, is as well calculated to secure to the citizens the right to bear arms in defense of themselves and the state, as any that could have been adopted by the makers of the constitution. If the right be assailed, immaterial through what medium, whether by an act of the legislature or in any other form, it is equally opposed to the comprehensive import of the section. The legislature is nowhere expressly mentioned in the section; but the language employed is general, without containing any expression restricting its import to any particular department of government; and in the twenty-eighth section of the same article of the constitution, it is expressly declared, "that every thing in that article is excepted out of the general powers of government, and shall forever remain inviolate; and that all laws contrary thereto, or contrary to the constitution, shall be void."

. . .

That the provisions of the act in question do not import an entire destruction of the right of the citizens to bear arms in defense of themselves and the state, will not be controverted by the court; for though the citizens are forbid wearing weapons concealed in the manner described in the act, they may, nevertheless, bear arms in any other admissible form. But to be in conflict with the constitution, it is not essential that the act should contain a prohibition against bearing arms in every possible form—it is the right to bear arms in defense of the citizens and the state, that is secured by the constitution, and whatever restrains the full and complete exercise of that right, though not an entire destruction of it, is forbidden by the explicit language of the constitution.

Not merely all legislative acts, which purport to take it away; but all which diminish or impair it as it existed when the constitution was formed, are void.

If, therefore, the act in question imposes any restraint on the right, immaterial what appellation may be given to the act, whether it be an act regulating the manner of bearing arms or any other, the consequence, in reference to the constitution, is precisely the same, and its collision with that instrument equally obvious.

And can there be entertained a reasonable doubt but the provisions of the act import a restraint on the right of the citizens to bear arms? The court apprehends not. The right existed at the adoption of the constitution; it had then no limits short of the moral power of the citizens to exercise it, and it in fact consisted in nothing else but in the liberty of the citizens to bear arms. Diminish that liberty, therefore, and you necessarily restrain the right; and such is the diminution and restraint, which the act in question most indisputably imports, by prohibiting the citizens wearing weapons in a manner which was lawful to wear them when the constitution was adopted. In truth, the right of the citizens to bear arms, has been as directly assailed by the provisions of the act, as though they were forbid carrying guns on their shoulders, swords in scabbards, or when in conflict with an enemy, were not allowed the use of bayonets; and if the act be consistent with the constitution, it can not be incompatible with that instrument for the legislature, by successive enactments, to entirely cut off the exercise of the right of the citizens to bear arms. For, in principle, there is no difference between a law prohibiting the wearing concealed arms, and a law forbidding the wearing such as are exposed; and if the former be unconstitutional, the latter must be so likewise. . . .

D. Personal Freedom and Public Morality

Family and morals laws were not constitutionalized during the Early National Era. No significant constitutional debates took place over whether persons had a right to marry, use birth control, terminate pregnancies, or have sexual relationships outside of marriage. Few major federal or state constitutional decisions or debates seem to have taken place over whether government could regulate such personal habits as drinking or gambling. Legislation dictating who could marry whom, for example, was not subject to constitutional challenge before 1829. Courts had little difficulty sustaining statutes banning obscenity as legitimate means for ensuring a decent moral climate.

IV. Democratic Rights

MAJOR DEVELOPMENTS

- Federalists pass, but Jeffersonians fail to renew, the Alien and Sedition Acts

- States weaken property qualifications for voting
- Federalists and Jeffersonians debate expatriation

Intense partisan conflicts broke out during the Early National Era over democratic rights. Federalists and their successors believed that constitutional politics in the United States should be modeled on English constitutional politics, abandoning only a hereditary monarch and aristocracy. They proposed national sedition laws, sought to maintain a restricted suffrage, and maintained that a person's political allegiance was determined by birth. Jeffersonians championed a more inclusive constitutional politics. They sought to expand free speech rights, reduce qualifications for voting, and provide greater opportunities for people to choose their political allegiance.

Jeffersonians enjoyed varying degrees of success in implementing their more democratic agenda. Voting became more egalitarian between 1789 and 1829. Property qualifications were replaced with less onerous taxpaying requirements or else were abandoned completely. The national government abandoned speech restrictions after 1801. Jeffersonians refused to renew the Sedition Act of 1798, Jefferson pardoned all persons convicted under that Federalist measure, and Madison resisted temptations during the War of 1812 to pass a new sedition law. State constitutional law rarely reflected the libertarian sentiments that Jeffersonians articulated when discussing national constitutional standards. Local constitutional authorities frequently punished libel, blasphemy, and obscenity. Few constitutional questions about citizenship were firmly resolved. Jeffersonians criticized Federalist judicial decisions claiming that persons had no right to expatriation, but the extent to which citizens of the United States had a constitutional right to emigrate remained unsettled.

The constitutional politics of democratic rights raises important questions about the relationship between ideology and interests. When reading the materials below, try to explain Federalist behavior in the years after the Constitution was ratified. Interest, at first glance, seems paramount. The Sedition Act of 1798 was a Federalist attempt to silence critics. Federalists opposed allowing poorer people to vote because most poor persons voted for Jeffersonians. The Federalists, however, are the only partisan coalition in American history that has disappeared solely because of insufficient popular support. Could their elitist constitutional vision explain why they could not make the necessary adjustments demanded by public opinion that political parties must make to survive in a constitutional democracy?

A. Free Speech

The Early National Era witnessed bitter national and state controversies over free speech. Political leaders routinely perceived what we might think of as normal political criticism as attempts to undermine government. The Federalists who controlled the national government from 1789 to 1801 were particularly prone to interpret political dissent as sedition. Most Federalists believed that ordinary persons should limit their political participation to electing virtuous people to run the government. Private political organizations and commentary were illegitimate attempts to interfere with the people's elected representatives. Many Jeffersonian state officials were equally as sensitive to political criticism. Just as Federalists saw Jacobins (the most extreme faction of the French Revolution) behind every criticism of the Washington and Adams administrations, so too were many Jeffersonians sure that adverse commentary on Thomas Jefferson or James Madison was rooted in a secret desire to restore monarchy to the United States.

National controversies over free speech were more partisan than local controversies. Federalists believed that sedition laws were a vital means of ensuring respect for the national government. Jeffersonians insisted that the national government had no power to pass a sedition law, and that sedition laws violated the First Amendment. After Jefferson took office, Federalists proposed and Jeffersonians rejected a measure that would have extended the Sedition Act of 1798. Federalists and Jeffersonians in the states were less principled. Local elected officials of all persuasions restricted political criticism.

Most governing authorities believed that persons had a constitutional right to make true criticisms of government for good reasons. The Sedition Act of 1798 considered truth a valid defense in sedition prosecutions. Such influential state court decisions as *People v. Croswell* (NY 1804) endorsed the truth defense. Some commentators went further. James Madison insisted that political opinions were constitutionally protected. Tunis Wortman, the author of the first book-length study on free speech published in the United States, condemned any restriction on free speech. His *Treatise Concerning Political Enquiry and the Liberty of the Press* maintained:

> The formation of general opinion upon correct and salutary principles, requires the unbiased exercise of individual intellect; neither prejudice, authority, or terror, should be suffered to impede the liberty of discussion; no due influence should tyrannize over mind; every man should be left to the independent exercise of his reflection; all should be permitted to communicate their ideas with the energy and ingenuousness of truth.[27]

Madison was guided by these libertarian sentiments when he refused to call for a sedition law during the War of 1812. State judges were less libertarian. Local officials punished political commentators after juries determined that they had not published the truth for good reasons. Many states refused to recognize truth as a defense when private figures were defamed. *Commonwealth v. Clap* (MA 1808) declared,

> The publication of a libel maliciously and with intent to defame, whether it be true or not, is clearly an offence against law, on sound principles, which must be adhered to, so long as the restraint of all tendencies to the breach of the public peace, and to private animosity and revenge, is salutary to the commonwealth.[28]

States also prohibited obscenity. In *Commonwealth v. Sharpless* (PA 1815), the Supreme Court of Pennsylvania stated, "Actions of *public indecency* [are] always indictable, as tending to corrupt the public morals."[29]

The Sedition Act (1798)

Political tensions increased during the 1790s. Newspapers were filled with scandalous, often anonymous gossip and opinion about political leaders. Few commentators practiced any restraint when commenting on political opponents. The president of Yale asserted that Thomas Jefferson would have "the bible cast into a bonfire, . . . our wives and daughters the victims of legal prostitution."[30] *Jefferson described Washington and Adams as "apostates who have gone over to [English] heresies, men who were Samsons in the field and Solomons in the council, but who have had their heads shorn by that harlot England."*[31] *New forms of political organization further heated up the political environment. Thomas Jefferson and James Madison organized an anti-administration faction in both Congress and the states. George Washington denounced Democratic-Republican clubs for their scrutiny and often-harsh criticism of government officials. War with France became increasingly likely. Americans were outraged when the French foreign minister demanded bribes before meeting with an American delegation sent to negotiate a new peace treaty (the so-called XYZ Affair). With anti-French passions peaking, Federalists in Congress and the Adams administration hoped to put an end to the "factions" dividing the nation and encouraging foreign enemies.*

These tensions culminated in the Sedition Act of 1798, which cracked down on speech and writings that brought the government into contempt. In keeping with Colonial and Founding Era practice, Federalists permitted truth as a defense. The Sedition Act also required that a jury determine whether a piece of writing was seditious. Federalists claimed that the law was a constitutional means for maintaining support for the government. Harrison Otis stated, "Every independent Government has a right to preserve and defend itself against injuries and outrages which endanger its existence."[32]

Adams administration officials implemented the Sedition Act immediately. The resulting prosecutions and convictions shut down several prominent Jeffersonian newspapers. Matthew Lyon of Vermont, a Jeffersonian representative in Congress, was one victim of the legislation. Sentenced to prison for criticizing the Adams administration, he became a popular hero and easily won reelection.

Jeffersonians conducted a public campaign against the Sedition Act, with the Virginia and Kentucky Resolutions of 1798 being the most visible and significant protests. These resolutions, secretly penned by James Madison and Thomas

---

27. Tunis Wortman, *A Treatise Concerning Political Enquiry and the Liberty of the Press* (New York: George Forman, 1800), 121.

28. *Commonwealth v. Clap*, 4 Mass. 163, 169 (1808).

29. *Commonwealth v. Sharpless*, 2 Serg. & Rawle 91 (Pa. 1815).

30. Stephen M. Feldman, *Free Expression and Democracy in America: A History* (Chicago: University of Chicago Press, 2008), 78.

31. Thomas Jefferson, *The Writings of Thomas Jefferson*, ed. Paul Leicester Ford (New York: G. P. Putnam's Sons, 1896), 7:76.

32. *Annals of Congress*, 5th Cong., 2nd Sess. (1798), 2:2145–48.

Illustration 4-2 Republican Matthew Lyon and Federalist Roger Griswold Fighting on the Floor of the U.S. House of Representatives

Vermont Republican Matthew Lyon (holding the tongs) and Connecticut Federalist Roger Griswold (holding the cane) fighting on the floor of the U.S. House of Representatives. A vote to expel Lyon from his seat in the House of Representatives for having insulted Griswold was unsuccessful. Lyon was prosecuted and convicted of violating the Sedition Act of 1798, but his constituents reelected him to office in the 1798 elections while he was serving his sentence.

Source: [Philadelphia], 1798. Library of Congress Prints and Photographs Division, Washington, DC.

Jefferson, condemned both the Sedition Act and other Federalist measures. One year later, James Madison submitted a report to the Virginia Legislature that elaborated both federalism and free speech criticisms of Federalist policy. States, he insisted, had reserved the power to determine when seditious speech should be punished. Going beyond the reigning free speech orthodoxy, Madison declared that constitutional republicans must protect opinion, as well as true criticisms of public officials.

The Virginia and Kentucky Resolutions and Madison's Report became celebrated touchstones of Jeffersonian political ideology and constitutional thought. Their immediate influence on free speech practice is less certain. When Jefferson assumed the presidency, he and his political allies in Congress refused to extend the Sedition Act after its expiration in 1800. This refusal suggests a commitment to free speech principles. Nevertheless, many Jeffersonians in the states, often with Jefferson's permission, prosecuted Federalists who made what they believed were unfair criticisms of Republican politicians and policies. This suggests that the principles of federalism were the more practical grounds for criticizing the Sedition Act.

When reading the following materials, think about the following interpretation of how Federalists understood popular government:

> *Federalists claimed the people "deliberated" only via their representatives in the legislature and therefore that only*

the legislature could authoritatively declare what public opinion was or fully participate in the political deliberations of the polity. The "representative" quality of political debate justified Federalist repression. The modern system of political deliberation, in which the people "discuss" politics via the mass media and political organizations, the Federalists argued, only empowers nonrepresentative minorities. Instead, if popular participation is restricted to the right of petition and election, methods that inform and motivate representatives without intruding directly into political deliberations, the whole people can participate equally in debate via their representatives.[33]

Does this passage explain why Federalists supported the Sedition Act (and condemned private political clubs), even when Thomas Jefferson was president? How did Federalists understand political participation in a constitutional republic? How did opponents of the Sedition Act understand the role of political participation in a constitutional republic?

The Report of a Select Committee on the Petitions Praying for a Repeal of the Alien and Sedition Laws (1799)[34]

. . .

[A] law to punish false, scandalous, and malicious writings against the Government, with the intent to stir up sedition, is a law necessary for carrying into effect the power vested by the Constitution in the Government of the United States, and in the departments and officers thereof, and, consequently, such a law as Congress may pass; because the direct tendency of such writings is to obstruct the acts of the Government by exciting opposition to them, to endanger its existence by rendering it odious and contemptible in the eyes of the people, and to produce seditious combinations against the laws, the power to punish which has never been questioned; because it would be manifestly absurd to suppose that a Government might punish sedition, and yet be void of power to prevent it by punishing those acts which plainly and necessarily lead to it; and, because, under the general power to make all laws proper and necessary for carrying into effect the powers vested by the Constitution in the Government of the United States, Congress has passed many laws for which no express provision can be found in the Constitution, and the constitutionality of which has never been questioned, such as the first section of the act now under consideration for punishing seditious combinations. . . .

. . . [T]he liberty of the press consists not in a license for every man to publish what he pleases without being liable for punishment, if he should abuse this license to the injury of others, but in a permission to publish, without previous restraint, whatever he may think proper, being answerable to the public and individuals, for any abuse of this permission to their prejudice. In like manner, as the liberty speech does not authorize a man to speak malicious slanders against his neighbor, nor the liberty of action justify him in going, by violence, into another man's house, or in assaulting any person whom he may meet in the streets. In the several States the liberty of the press has always been understood in this manner, and no other. . . .

. . .

. . . [H]ad the Constitution intended to prohibit Congress from legislating at all on the subject of the press, which is the construction whereon the objections to this law are founded, it would have used the same expressions as in that part of the clause which relates to religion and religious laws; whereas, the words are wholly different: "Congress," says the Constitution, . . . "shall make no law respecting the establishment of religion, or prohibiting the free exercise thereof, or abridging the freedom of speech or the press." Here it is manifest that the Constitution intended to prohibit Congress from legislating on all the subjects of religious establishments, and the prohibition is made in the most express terms. Had the same intention prevailed respecting the press, the same expressions would have been used, and Congress would have been "prohibited from passing a law respecting the press." They are not, however, "prohibited" from legislating at all on the subject, but merely from abridging the liberty of the press. . . . Its liberty, according to the well known and universally admitted definition, consists in permission to publish, without previous restraint upon the press, but subject to punishment afterwards for improper publications. A law, therefore, to impose previous restraint upon the press, and not one to inflict punishment on wicked and malicious publications,

---

33. James P. Martin, "When Repression Is Democratic and Constitutional: The Federalist Theory of Representation and the Sedition Act of 1798," *University of Chicago Law Review* 66 (1999): 117.

34. Excerpted from *Annals of Congress*, 5th Cong., 3rd Sess. (1799), 2986–90.

would be a law to abridge the liberty of the press, and, as such, unconstitutional.

James Madison, Virginia Report of 1799[35]

. . .

The freedom of the press under the common law; is, in the defences of the sedition-act, made to consist in an exemption from all *previous* restraint on printed publications, by persons authorized to inspect and prohibit them. It appears to the committee, that this idea of the freedom of the press, can never be admitted to be the American idea of it: since a law inflicting penalties on printed publications, would have a similar effect with a law authorizing a previous restraint on them. . . .

In the British government, the danger of encroachments on the rights of the people, is understood to be confined to the executive magistrate. . . . Hence . . . all the ramparts for protecting the rights of the people, such as the magna charta, their bill of rights, etc., are not reared against the parliament, but against the royal prerogative. . . . Under such a government as this, an exemption of the press from previous restraint by licensers appointed by the king, is all the freedom that can be secured to it.

In the United States, the case is altogether different. The people, not the government, possess the absolute sovereignty. The legislature, no less than the executive, is under limitations of power. Encroachments are regarded as possible from the one, as well as from the other. Hence, in the United States, the great and essential rights of the people are secured against legislative, as well as against executive ambition. . . .

The state of the press, therefore, under the common law, cannot, in this point of view, be the standard of its freedom in the United States.

. . .

The nature of governments elective, limited, and responsible, in all their branches, may well be supposed to require a greater freedom of animadversion than might be tolerated by the genius of such a government as that of Great Britain. In the latter, it is a maxim, that the king . . . can do no wrong. . . . In the United States, the executive magistrates are not held to be infallible, nor the legislatures to be omnipotent; and both being elective, are both responsible. Is it not natural and necessary, under such different circumstances, that a different degree of freedom, in the use of the press, should be contemplated?

. . .

The practice of America must be entitled to much more respect. In every state, probably, in the Union, the press has exerted a freedom in canvassing the merits and measures of public men, of every description, which has not been confined to the strict limits of the common law. On this footing, the freedom of the press has stood; on this footing it yet stands. . . .

. . .

Is then the federal government, it will be asked, destitute of every authority for restraining the licentiousness of the press, and for shielding itself against the libelous attacks which may be made on those who administer it?

The Constitution alone can answer the question. If no such power be expressly delegated, and it be not both necessary and proper to carry into execution an express power; above all, if it be expressly forbidden by a declaratory amendment to the Constitution, the answer must be, that the federal government is destitute of all such authority.

. . .

Let it be recollected, lastly, that the right of electing members of the government, constitutes more particularly the essence of a free and responsible government. The value and efficacy of this right, depends on the knowledge of the comparative merits and demerits of the candidates for public trust; and on the equal freedom, consequently, of examining and discussing these merits and demerits of the candidates respectively. It has been seen, that a number of important elections will take place whilst the act is in force. . . . Should there happen, then, as is extremely probable in relation to some or other of the branches of the government, to be competitions between those who are and those who are not, members of the government, what will be the situations of the competitors? Not equal; because the characters of the former will be covered by the "sedition-act" from animadversions exposing them to disrepute among the people; whilst the latter may be exposed to contempt and hatred of the people, without violation of the act. What will be the situation of the people? Not free; because they will be compelled to

35. Excerpted from *The Virginia Report of 1799–1800, Touching the Alien and Sedition Laws* (Richmond, VA: J. W. Randolph, 1850), 210–27.

make their election between competitors, whose pretensions they are not permitted, by the act, equally to examine, to discuss, and to ascertain. And from both situations, will not those in power derive an undue advantage for continuing themselves in it; which by impairing the right of election, endangers the blessings of the government founded on it?

People v. Croswell, 3 Johns. Cas. 337 (N.Y. Sup. 1804)

Harry Croswell was the publisher of The Wasp, *a newspaper in Hudson, New York. On September 9, 1802, Croswell declared that Thomas Jefferson paid another journalist, James Thompson Callender, to write articles claiming that George Washington was a "traitor" and John Adams a "hoary-headed incendiary." Jefferson's supporters in New York immediately arrested Croswell and charged him with criminal libel. During his trial, Croswell sought to call Callender to the stand. Croswell claimed that Callender would testify that Jefferson had paid him to publish remarks critical of Presidents Washington and Adams. The judge refused to allow that testimony on the ground that truth was not a defense to libel. The trial judge also ruled that whether the publication was libelous was a matter of law, and that the jury could determine only whether Croswell published the offending article. According to the common law, the trial judge claimed, publications that cast aspersions on the character of public men were libelous, whether those aspersions were true or false. Croswell appealed to the Supreme Court of New York.*

People v. Croswell *reprised the Sedition Act debates, but with many main characters playing very different roles. Local Jeffersonians prosecuted a critic of a government official. President Jefferson knew and approved their effort to silence Harry Croswell. Alexander Hamilton, the titular leader of the Federalist Party, served as Croswell's attorney. Judge James Kent, who wrote the opinion overruling the trial judge, was a leading Federalist jurist who supported the Sedition Act. James Callender in the 1790s was a Jeffersonian and a victim of Sedition Act prosecutions. During the early 1800s, he became a critic. We know Callender today as the journalist who first reported that Jefferson fathered children by his slave, Sally Hemings.*

The Supreme Court of New York reversed the trial court. Justice Kent ruled that the jury had a right to determine whether a publication was libelous, and that true statements about public officials are not libelous under the common law and constitution of New York. Kent drew a close connection between free speech rights and the right to a trial by jury. In what ways are jury trials vital safeguards of free speech? In what ways might jury trials be a threat to free speech? Kent insisted that Croswell *was consistent with the Federalist defense of the Sedition Act. How does he reach this conclusion? Do you think that the result in* Croswell *is best explained by jurisprudence or by New York politics at the turn of the nineteenth century?*

JUSTICE KENT delivered the opinion of the Court.

The criminality of the charge in the indictment consisted in a malicious and seditious intention. . . . There can be no crime without an evil mind. . . . The simple act of publication, which was all that was left to the jury, in the present case, was not, in itself, criminal. It is the application to times, persons and circumstances; it is the particular intent and tendency that constitute the libel. Opinions and acts may be innocent under one set of circumstances, and criminal under another. This application to circumstances, and this particular intent, are as much matters of fact, as the printing and publishing. . . . Where an act, innocent in itself, becomes criminal, when done with a particular intent, that intent is the material fact to constitute the crime. . . . And I think there cannot be a doubt, that the mere publication of a paper is not, per se, criminal; for otherwise, the copying of the indictment by the clerk, or writing a friendly and admonitory letter to a father, on the vices of his son, would be criminal. The intention of the publisher, and every circumstance attending the act must, therefore, be cognisable by the jury, as questions of fact. And if they are satisfied that the publication is innocent; that it has no mischievous or evil tendency; that the mind of the writer was not in fault; that the publication was inadvertent, or from any other cause, was no libel, how can they conscientiously pronounce the defendant guilty, from the mere fact of publication? A verdict of guilty, embraces the whole charge upon the record, and are the jury not permitted to take into consideration the only thing that constitutes the crime, which is the malicious intent? According to the doctrine laid down at the trial, all that results from a verdict of guilty is, that the defendant has published a certain paper, and that it applies to certain persons, according to the innuendoes; but whether the paper be lawful or unlawful; whether it be criminal, or innocent, or meritorious; whether the intent was wicked or virtuous, are matters of law which do not belong to the jury, but are reserved for the determination of the court. . . . To deny to the jury the right of judging of the intent and tendency of the act, is to take away the substance, and with it the value and security of this mode of trial. It is to transfer the exclusive cognisance of crimes from the jury to the court, and to give the judges the absolute control of the press. . . .

If the criminal intent be, in this case, an inference of law, the right of the jury is still the same. In every criminal case, upon the plea of not guilty, the jury may, and indeed they must, unless they choose to find a special verdict, take upon themselves the decision of the law, as well as the fact, and bring in a verdict as comprehensive as the issue; because, in every such case, they are charged with the deliverance of the defendant from the crime of which he is accused. . . .

. . .

As a libel is a defamatory publication, made with a malicious intent, the truth or falsehood of the charge may, in many cases, be a very material and pertinent consideration with the jury, in order to ascertain that intent. There can be no doubt that it is competent for the defendant to rebut the presumption of malice, drawn from the fact of publication; and it is consonant to the general theory of evidence, and the dictates of justice, that the defendant should be allowed to avail himself of every fact and circumstance that may serve to repel that presumption. And what can be a more important circumstance than the truth of the charge, to determine the goodness of the motive in making it, if it be a charge against the competency or purity of a character in public trust, or of a candidate for public favour, or a charge of actions in which the community have an interest, and are deeply concerned? To shut out wholly the inquiry into the truth of the accusation, is to abridge essentially the means of defence. It is to weaken the arm of the defendant, and to convict him, by means of a presumption, which he might easily destroy by proof that the charge was true, and that, considering the nature of the accusation, the circumstances and time under which it was made, and the situation of the person implicated, his motive could have been no other than a pure and disinterested regard for the public welfare. At the same time, this doctrine will not go to tolerate libels upon private character, or the circulation of charges for seditious and wicked ends, or to justify exposing to the public eye one's personal defects or misfortunes. The public have no concern with, nor are they injured by, such information, and the truth of the charge would rather aggravate than lessen the baseness and evil tendency of the publication. It will, therefore, still remain, in every case, a question for the jury, what was the intent and tendency of the paper, and how far the truth, in the given case, has been used for commendable, or abused for malicious purposes.

. . .

That falsehood is a material ingredient in a public libel, is a doctrine not without precedent in former times; it has always been asserted, and occasionally admitted, by the English courts. In this country it has taken firmer root, and in regard to the measures of government, and the character and qualifications of candidates for public trust, it is considered as the vital support of the liberty of the press.

. . .

. . . [W]hatever may be our opinion on the English law, there is another and a very important view of the subject to be taken, and that is with respect to the true standard of the freedom of the American press. In England, they have never taken notice of the press in any parliamentary recognition of the principles of the government, or of the rights of the subject, whereas the people of this country have always classed the freedom of the press among their fundamental rights. . . .

I am far from intending that these authorities mean, by the freedom of the press, a press wholly beyond the reach of the law, for this would be emphatically Pandora's box, the source of every evil. And yet the house of delegates in Virginia, by their resolution of the 7th January, 1800, and which appears to have been intended for the benefit and instruction of the union, came forward as the advocates of a press totally unshackled, and declare, in so many words, that "the baneful tendency of the sedition act was but little diminished by the privilege of giving in evidence the truth of the matter contained in political writings." They seem also to consider it as the exercise of a pernicious influence, and as striking at the root of free discussion, to punish, even for a false and malicious writing, published with intent to defame those who administer the government. If this doctrine was to prevail, the press would become a pest, and destroy the public morals. Against such a commentary upon the freedom of the American press, I beg leave to enter my protest. The founders of our governments were too wise and too just, ever to have intended, by the freedom of the press, a right to circulate falsehood as well as truth, or that the press should be the lawful vehicle of malicious defamation, or an engine for evil and designing men, to cherish, for mischievous purposes, sedition, irreligion, and impurity. Such an abuse of the press would be incompatible with the existence and good order of civil society. The true rule of law is, that the intent and tendency of the publication is, in every instance, to be the substantial inquiry on the trial, and that the truth is admissible in evidence, to explain that intent, and not in every instance to justify it. I adopt, in this case, as perfectly correct, the comprehensive and accurate definition of one of the counsel at the bar, that the liberty of the press consists in the right to publish, with impunity, truth, with good motives, and for justifiable ends, whether it respects government, magistracy, or individuals.

JUSTICE THOMPSON, concurred.

CHIEF JUSTICE LEWIS, concurred.

. . .

. . . [I]t ever has been invariably, and still is, the law of England, that the truth cannot be given in evidence, as a justification in a criminal prosecution for a libel, at common law. Nay, I might almost venture to say, there is not a single dictum in the books to the contrary.

. . .

On the trial of John Peter Zenger, in this state, under its colonial government, the same rule of law was laid down by Chief Justice Delancey. . . .

. . .

This leads me to the consideration of the question next in importance, which is, whether the intention of the defendant, in publishing the libel with which he is charged, ought to have been submitted to the inquiry of the jury, as a fact on which his guilt or innocence depended. The intent is certainly an ingredient in the constitution of every offence. But it is, as certainly, in many cases, though not in all, an inference of law deduced from facts. Where an act, in itself criminal, is performed without lawful excuse, there the criminal intent is an inference of law. . . .

. . .

It has been urged, that to deny a jury the right of deciding on the law and the fact, in all cases of criminal prosecution, is contrary to the spirit and genius of our government. But how, has not been attempted to be shown. In England, where the judges are appointed by the crown, and juries form a substantial barrier between the prerogatives of that crown and the liberties of the people, the reasons for extending the powers of the latter are certainly much stronger than with us, where the judges are, in effect, appointed by the people themselves, and amenable to them for any misconduct. . . .

. . .

JUSTICE LIVINGSTON, concurred. . . .

B. Voting

Between 1789 and 1828, Americans moved toward universal white male suffrage. As Figures 4-2a and 4-2b illustrate, property qualifications were abandoned as the Early National Era progressed. Congress in 1811 permitted all taxpayers who lived in the Northwest Territories to vote in territorial elections. Many states similarly reformed their suffrage laws. A growing consensus emerged that productive persons who paid taxes were as good republican citizens as persons who owned land. Some states eliminated property qualifications entirely.

Americans exercised their voting rights during this period. Local elections in the 1790s were often marked by low turnout, as contests between local notables failed to inspire most citizens. Increased political organization and less deferential politics raised turnout levels. By the time Andrew Jackson took office in 1829, most people who could legally vote exercised their right to cast a ballot.

Numerous partisan struggles took place over voting rights. Federalists and their successors insisted that property qualifications and a restricted suffrage were vital means for protecting property rights and promoting the public good. One representative to the Massachusetts Constitutional Convention declared, "It was . . . wholly inequitable in its nature, that men without a dollar should, in any way, determine the rights of property."[36] Jeffersonians responded that men who fought in the Revolution and against the British during the War of 1812 ought to have access to the ballot. Many linked taxation to representation. "[T]here ought to be a representation on the foundation of equality," another representative responded. "This could not be, so long as any people, who are taxed, do not vote."[37]

---

36. *Journal of Debates and Proceedings in the Convention of Delegates Chosen to Revise the Constitution of Massachusetts* (Boston: Boston Daily Advertiser), 247.

37. Ibid., 124.

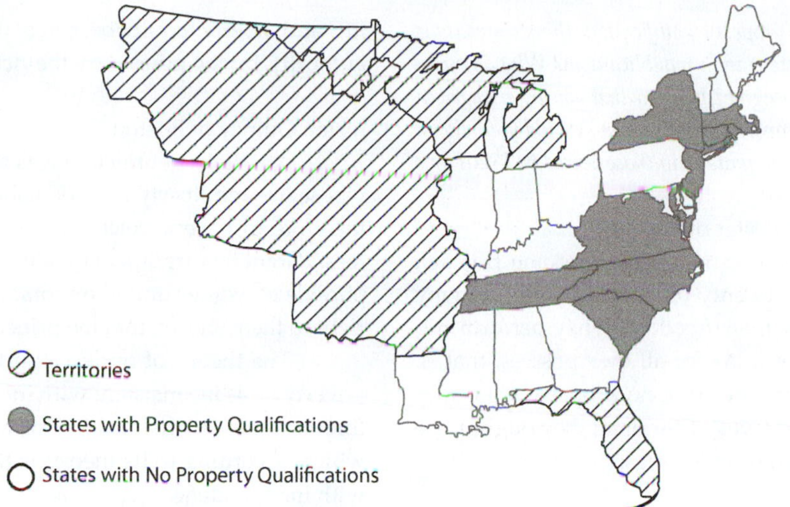

Figure 4-2a Property Qualifications for Suffrage, 1820

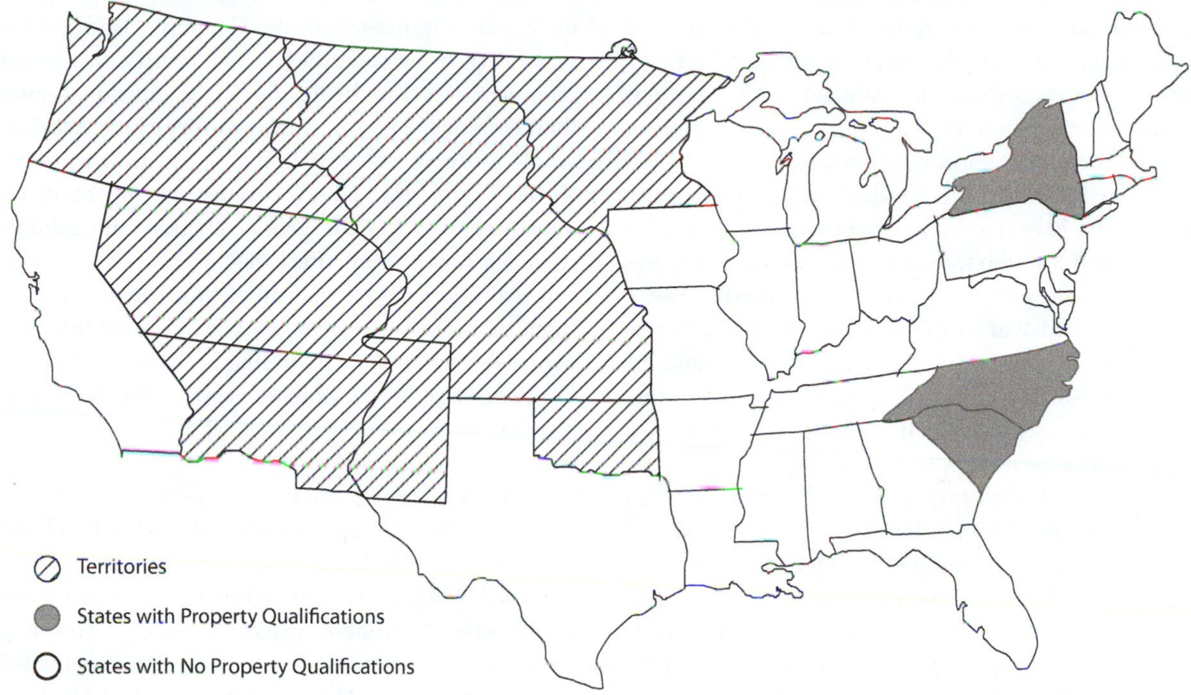

Figure 4-2b Property Qualifications for Suffrage, 1850

Massachusetts Debates Property Qualifications (1820)[38]

In 1820 Massachusetts held a convention to revise the state constitution. Such constitutional conventions were common in the early nineteenth century and throughout American history. State constitutions in the United States are regularly amended, revised, and replaced. Many constitutional conventions in the Early National Era considered suffrage reform. Debates were particularly lively in Massachusetts. The Massachusetts Constitution of 1780 limited voting in state senate elections to persons with a freehold worth 60 pounds and required that voters in elections for the lower house be property holders. Many delegates believed those qualifications too restrictive. They preferred either a taxpayer qualification or no economic qualification. The convention eventually substituted a taxpayer qualification for the property qualification.

Many participants in the debate over voting qualifications relied heavily on arguments drawn from republican principles.

38. Ibid., 247–57.

Why do proponents of property qualifications think restrictions on the suffrage consistent with republicanism? Why do opponents of restrictions disagree? Imagine that you are engaged in an argument about property qualifications. Would you rely on similar or different arguments than those voiced in 1820?

Reverend Edmund Foster of Littleton

. . . Men in this Commonwealth become freemen when they arrive at twenty-one years of age; and why oblige them to buy their freedom? They perform militia duty—they pay a tax for all they possess, that is, their polls. . . . Men who have no property are put in the situation of the slaves of Virginia; they ought to be saved from the degrading feelings.

Warren Dutton of Boston

. . . He thought it expedient to retain the [freehold] qualification in the constitution. It was in the nature of a privilege, and, as such, it was connected with many virtues, which conduced to the good order of society. It was a distinction to be sought for; it was the reward of good conduct. It encouraged industry, economy and prudence; it elevated the standard of all our civil institutions, and gave dignity and importance to those who chose, and those who were chosen. It acted as a stimulus to exertion to acquire what it was a distinction to possess. He maintained that in this country, where the means of subsistence were so abundant, and the demand for labor so great, every man of sound body could acquire the necessary qualification. If he failed to do this, it must be, ordinarily, because he was indolent or vicious. . . . He also considered it as unreasonable, that a man who had no property should act indirectly upon the property of others. If gentlemen would look to the statute book, to the business of the Legislature, or to the courts of law, how much of all that was done, would be found to relate to the rights of property. It lay at the foundation of the social state, it was the spring of all action and all employment. It was therefore . . . wholly inequitable in its nature, that men without a dollar should, in any way, determine the rights of property, or have any concern in its appropriation. He also contended, that the principle of the resolution was anti-republican. It greatly increased the number of voters and those of a character must liable to be improperly influenced or corrupted. . . .

George Blake of Boston

. . . Life was as dear to a poor man as to a rich man; so was liberty. Every subject therefore, involving only life and liberty, could be acted upon, with as good authority, by the poor as by the rich. . . .

Josiah Quincy of Boston

. . . [Mr. Blake's] principle was this. . . . "Every man, whose life and liberty is made liable to the laws, ought therefore to have a voice, in the choice of his legislators." Grant this argument to be just. Is it not equally applicable to women and to minors? . . . The denial of this right to them shows, that the principle is not just. . . .

. . . The theory of our constitution is, that extreme poverty . . . is inconsistent with independence. It therefore assumes a qualification of a very low amount, which, according to its theory, is the lowest consistent with independence. . . .

. . . Everything indicates that the destinies of the country will eventuate in the establishment of a great manufacturing interest in the Commonwealth. There is nothing in the condition of our country, to prevent manufacturers from being absolutely dependent upon their employers, here as they are everywhere else. The whole body of every manufacturing establishment, therefore, are dead votes, counted by the head, by their employer. Let the gentlemen from the country consider, how it may affect their rights, liberties and properties, if in every county of this Commonwealth there should arise . . . one, two, or three manufacturing establishments, each sending . . . from one to eight hundred votes to the polls depending on the will of one employer.

Holder Slocum of Dartmouth

. . . Taxation and representation should go hand and hand. Take this text and apply it to the men who are excluded by this qualification from the rights of voting. Who are they? The laboring parts of society? How long have they been fettered? Forty years? Who achieved our independence? This class of men. And shall we then disenfranchise them? I hope not. . . . If a man was a Newton or a Locke, if he is poor, he may stand by and see his liberties voted away. Suppose an invasion should happen—these men would be obliged to come forward in defense of their country. He felt conscientiously bound to give them the right of voting. . . .

C. Citizenship

Americans in the Early National Era had difficulty determining who was a citizen and whether citizenship could voluntarily be relinquished. Federalists maintained that the Constitution incorporated the common law principle that allegiance was determined by birth. Jeffersonians advocated citizenship practices that permitted white men to choose their allegiance.

Some citizenship problems were unique to the Early National Era. Congress engaged in extensive debate over the citizenship status of William Smith, a South Carolina native who resided abroad during the American Revolution. Other citizenship debates were more enduring. Americans left unsettled questions about expatriation, the status of citizens in the territories, the citizenship status of African-Americans, and the constitutional rights of aliens.

The Alien Friends Act (1798)[39]

Federalists in the late 1790s proposed giving the president the power to deport any alien whom he suspected "of being dangerous to the peace and safety of the United States." Such a power would allow the president to act unilaterally. Aliens had no right to a trial or even a hearing. Jeffersonians claimed that the president did not have the power to deport alien friends, subjects of foreign countries not at war with the United States. They also insisted that the proposed Alien Friends Act of 1798 violated constitutional rights to due process and a jury trial. Federalists responded that the measure was a constitutional exercise of the war power and that only citizens had constitutional rights. Federalists and Jeffersonians also disputed whether deportation was a criminal punishment subject to the constitutional rules for criminal procedure. After a short debate, the measure passed by a 46-40 vote. No alien was ever deported under the Alien Friends Act, but many probably muted their criticisms of Federalist policies.

The Alien Friends Act raises questions about whether the Bill of Rights is limited to American citizens. Why did Federalists believe that aliens did not have a right to trial by jury? Why did Jeffersonians think that aliens had a right to trial by jury? Were Jeffersonians and Federalists reasoning from different constitutional premises, or did they merely reach different conclusions from common premises? Most aliens were more sympathetic toward Jeffersonian positions. To what extent do you believe that partisanship rather than principle underlay the debate over the Alien Friends Act?

REPRESENTATIVE ALBERT GALLATIN (Pennsylvania, Jeffersonian)

. . .

. . . He knew the rights of aliens are limited; but if we can dispense with the law towards them, we may also do it with respect to citizens. The trial by jury does not speak of citizens but of persons. . . .

Again, with respect to the writ of habeas corpus, what do gentlemen say? They say it is only to prevent any man from being imprisoned in an arbitrary manner: and that, as the present bill describes the cases in which a man is liable to arrest and imprisonment; it cannot be a suspension of that law; that is to say the writ of habeas corpus is designed to prevent arbitrary imprisonment, or what the gentleman calls illegal imprisonment; but according to this doctrine, if you give, by law, the power to the President of arbitrary imprisonment, that power being thus given by law, is on that account no longer illegal nor arbitrary. That was the kind of security which citizens might expect to derive from the clause of the Constitution which related to the writ of habeas corpus. That privilege was to be done away by a legal distinction.

By the [fifth] amendment to our Constitution, it is provided that "no person shall be deprived of life, liberty, or property, without due process of law." According to the doctrine of the gentleman, Congress may give, by law, the power to the President, or anyone else, to deprive a citizen of his liberty or property, and the act of giving that power by law, will be called the due process of law contemplated by the Constitution.

. . .

. . . [T]he States and the State Judiciary . . . must, consider the law as a mere nullity, they must declare it to be unconstitutional. . . .

REPRESENTATIVE HARRISON GRAY OTIS (Massachusetts, Federalist)

. . .

. . . [Mr. Gallatin] proceeds upon the very erroneous hypothesis, that aliens are parties to our Constitution, that it was made for their benefit as well as our own and that they may claim equal rights and privileges with our own citizens. But upon reading the Constitution, he found that "we, the people of the United States," were the only parties concerned in making that instrument. He found nothing in it which bound us to fraternize with the whole world. On the contrary, the power was expressly given to Congress to decide on

39. Excerpted from *Annals of Congress*, 5th Cong. (June 19–21, 1798), 8:1981–82, 2018–19.

what terms foreigners should become entitled to the immunities of citizens; until they are thus entitled they cannot complain of any breach of our Constitution. . . . [T]he citizens have rights paramount to the Constitution and the laws; but foreigners enjoy no rights except those which are derived from the Constitution and the laws. The sovereign authority of a nation may, undoubtedly, forbid the entrance of foreigners, and, consequently prescribe their conditions of admission. . . .

. . .

It had been earnestly contended that the right of trial by jury had been extended by the Constitution to all persons without distinction, to aliens as well as citizens. To this he might reply, that the persons contemplated in that instrument were those only who were concerned in making that compact—the people of the United States; and that it was through mere courtesy and humanity that this, as well as other advantages, were made common to aliens. . . .

V. Equality

MAJOR DEVELOPMENTS

- Strong animus against class legislation
- State courts rule that free African-Americans are not citizens of the United States
- The Supreme Court rules that Native Americans are not protected by the Bill of Rights

Americans during the Early National Era faced the challenge of implementing constitutional commitments to the proposition that "all men are created equal" in a society marked by substantial inequalities. Many Americans invoked egalitarian values when challenging legal practices they believed gave special privileges to some citizens or imposed special burdens on others. Jeffersonians made egalitarian claims when weakening religious establishments or undermining property qualifications for voting. State courts invoked constitutional commitments to equality when striking down local regulations that judges believed unfairly provided special advantages to some citizens or unique disabilities to others. Radicals suggested that these constitutional commitments to equality justified emancipating slaves, giving women political rights, and improving the status of Native Americans. Most Americans were more complacent. They thought that laws treating people differently on the basis of race, gender, or ethnicity were justified by real differences between white males, on the one hand, and women, blacks, and Native Americans on the other. Many liberalizing trends from the Founding Era slowed, stalled, or were reversed during the early years of the American republic.

A. Equality Under Law

Jeffersonian Republicans celebrated a constitutional commitment to equality under law. They believed that such Federalist proposals as the national bank were inconsistent with constitutional requirements that government not give special privileges to any class of citizens. Thomas Jefferson's first inaugural address declared that government should "entertain[] a due sense of our equal right to the use of our own faculties, to the acquisitions of our own industry, to honor and confidence from our fellow-citizens, resulting not from birth, but from our actions and their sense of them." Jefferson called on his fellow citizens to support "Equal and exact justice to all men, of whatever state or persuasion, religious or political."

Jeffersonian decision makers developed constitutional doctrines that facilitated this commitment to "equal and exact justice to all men." Several state courts declared unconstitutional legislation that judges believed arbitrarily distinguished between equal citizens. *Holden v. James* (MA 1814) voided a Massachusetts law that granted specific persons exemptions from state laws. "An act conferring upon any one citizen, privileges to the prejudice of another, and which is not applicable to others, in like circumstances," the Supreme Court of Vermont in *Ward v. Bernard* (VT 1815) agreed, "does not enter into the idea of municipal law, having no relation to the community in general."[40]

Holden v. James, 11 Mass. 396 (1814)

Moses Holden believed that he was entitled to some money from the estate of Amos Ranger. Eleazer James, the adminis-

40. *Ward v. Bernard,* 1 Aik. 121 (VT 1815).

trator of that estate, disagreed. Massachusetts law permitted lawsuits against an administrator of an estate only within four years of the person taking that office. Such a restriction is called a statute of limitations and remains quite common. The purpose of such statutes is to prevent people from bringing lawsuits long after the details of events are forgotten. James became the administrator of the Ranger estate in December 1806. In 1813, the Massachusetts legislature passed a law that suspended the statute of limitations only with respect to the claim Holden had against James. James insisted that the legislature had no power to pass that law. In his view, the Massachusetts Constitution permitted elected officials to repeal the statute of limitations, but they could not pass a law granting a specific person an exemption from an otherwise general law.

The Supreme Judicial Court of Massachusetts declared unconstitutional Holden's exemption from the statute of limitations. Justice Jackson ruled that legislation exempting one person from a legal requirement unconstitutionally gave "special privileges" to a particular individual. His opinion emphasizes the differences between the American and English forms of government. What are those differences? How did Jackson's conception of those differences influence his opinion?

JUSTICE JACKSON, delivered the opinion of the Court.

. . .

The principles of our government are widely different [from England] in this particular. Here the sovereign and absolute power resides in the people; and the legislature can only exercise what is delegated to them according to the constitution. It is obvious that the exercise of the power in question would be equally oppressive to the subject, and subversive of his right to protection, "according to standing laws," whether exercised by one man or by a number of men. It cannot be supposed that the people, when adopting this general principle from the *English* bill of rights, and inserting it in our constitution, intended to bestow, by implication, on the General Court one of the most odious and oppressive prerogatives of the ancient kings of *England*. It is manifestly contrary to the first principles of civil liberty and natural justice, and to the spirit of our constitution and laws, that any one citizen should enjoy privileges and advantages which are denied to all others under like circumstances; or that any one should be subjected to losses, damages, suits, or actions, from which all others, under like circumstances, are exempted.

There is no doubt that the legislature may suspend a law, or the execution or operation of a law, whenever they shall think it expedient. But in such case, the law thus suspended will have no effect or operation whatever during the time for which it is so suspended. . . . So the privilege and benefit of the writ of *habeas corpus* may be suspended by the legislature, under the circumstances mentioned in the constitution. But it was never supposed that it could be suspended as to certain individuals by name, and left to be enjoyed by all the other citizens. . . .

B. Race

The United States became a more racially stratified society during the Early National Era. When the Constitution was ratified, most political elites believed that slavery was a necessary evil and hoped that human bondage would eventually disappear. Few thought seriously about the legal and constitutional status of free blacks. Some Americans in the following years insisted that governing authorities promote emancipation and treat free blacks as equal citizens. Far more political elites articulated explicit constitutional commitments to white supremacy. Constitutional decision makers maintained that real racial differences justified keeping blacks in bondage, required that any program for emancipation be combined with measures for returning freed slaves to Africa, and supported laws denying fundamental rights to free persons of color. The Jeffersonians who were most likely to invoke egalitarian norms in debates between different groups of white persons were, if anything, more racist than more elitist Federalists.

Three federal laws encapsulate the legal and constitutional status of free blacks. The First Congress in 1790 indicated that black citizens were undesirable by limiting naturalization to "free white person[s]." The Fugitive Slave Act of 1793 permitted slaveholders to recover alleged runaways merely by obtaining a certificate from a local magistrate. Congress refused to provide blacks alleged to be slaves with any procedural protections. White persons' property rights trumped black persons' rights to due process and freedom. The Missouri Compromise in 1820 recognized that slavery was likely to be an enduring institution. Congress sought to maintain a permanent balance between the slave and free states by permitting slavery in territories south of the 36°30′ parallel line (the southern border of Missouri) and banning slavery in the territories north of that line. Slaveholders in 1820 insisted they had a constitutional right to bring slaves into American territories. Many supported the final compromise only because they believed the northern regions of the Louisiana Purchase unlikely to be settled for the foreseeable future.

Slavery: The Rights of Masters

Slaveholders during the Early National Era adjusted their constitutional arguments, shifting from arguments about limited national powers to arguments about constitutional rights to possess slaves. National debates over slavery between 1789 and 1819 focused on legislative powers. Congress, representatives concluded in 1791, had no power to emancipate slaves in existing states. During the Missouri Compromise debates, representatives from the southern states for the first time asserted constitutional rights to slaveholding. Some southern members of Congress claimed that the due process clause protected their right to bring slaves into American territories. Others claimed that the constitutional commitment to equality entitled slaveholders and non-slaveholders to bring their cherished properties into the territories. The Missouri Compromise, which prohibited slavery in some territories but not others, did not settle the status of these constitutional claims.

Congressional Debate over the Missouri Compromise (1818–21)[41]

Sectional tensions intensified in 1818 when the people of the Missouri Territory petitioned Congress for admission into the Union. Representative James Tallmadge of New York proposed that Missouri be admitted only if the state agreed to pass laws mandating the gradual emancipation of slavery. Several days later, Representative John Taylor of New York proposed banning slavery in the Arkansas Territory. In the days and months that followed, many Americans feared that

41. *Annals of Congress*, 16th Cong., 1st Sess. (1820), 35:993–98, and 36:1467–70.

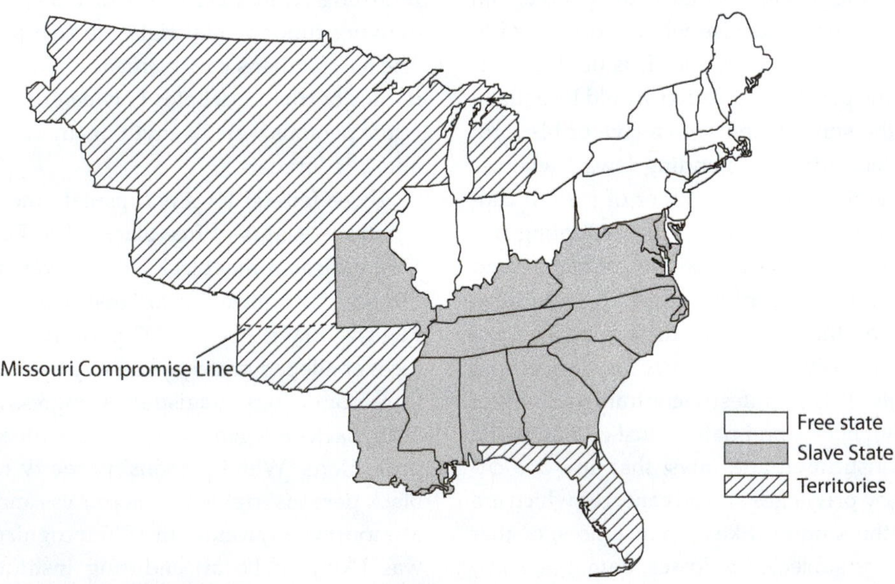

Figure 4-3 Missouri Compromise: Slave States, Free States, and Territories

the quarrels over these proposals would destroy the national union.

Congress eventually reached a series of compromises. Both Missouri and Maine were admitted to the Union at the same time. Their joint admission maintained the balance in the Senate between the free and slave states. Many people thought this equality to be a vital procedural guarantee for slavery, since slaveholders, by voting as a bloc, could prevent any perceived anti-slavery measure from becoming law. Free and slave state representatives also agreed to divide the remaining territories. The Missouri Compromise prohibited slavery in the Louisiana Territory north of latitude 36°30′, the southern border of Missouri. Slavery remained legal in territories below that line.

Participants in the Missouri controversy bitterly disputed whether persons had a constitutional right to bring slaves into the territories. Representatives from the free states pointed to Article IV, Section 3 of the Constitution, which states, "The Congress shall have Power to dispose of and make all needful Rules and Regulations respecting the Territory . . . belonging to the United States." They interpreted this clause as empowering the national legislature to ban slavery in American territories. Thomas Morril of New Hampshire stated, "Congress have a right and power to prohibit slavery in every territory within its dominion."[42] *Southern representatives claimed that the Constitution recognized the right to bring slaves into territories. "I have an equal right with my worthy friend from Pennsylvania," Richard Johnson of Kentucky declared, "to remove with my property (slaves and all) to Missouri, a common property, purchased with the money of the whole people."*[43]

Below are two brief excerpts from the debate over the Missouri Compromise. What arguments did Alexander Smyth of Virginia make in favor of the right to bring slaves into the territories? What is the relationship between those arguments and various arguments made about property and equality during the Early National Era? Why did Timothy Fuller of Massachusetts insist that Congress had the power to ban slavery in the territories? Whose definition of "republicanism" is most consistent with American constitutional understandings in 1820?

Many Americans soon regarded the Missouri Compromise as sacred legislation. What is the significance of the Missouri Compromise? Does the Compromise establish the principle that Congress may abolish slavery in all territories or only in some territories? Most southerners voted for the compromise only because they believed the northern territories unlikely to be settled in the foreseeable future. That assumption was mistaken. Does this indicate only that southern representatives made a bargain that turned out badly? Might the Missouri Compromise stand for the principle that slavery could be prohibited in territories only when southerners agreed to waive perceived constitutional rights to settle those regions?

REPRESENTATIVE ALEXANDER SMYTH (Virginia, Republican)

. . .

Has the power to legislate over slavery been delegated to the United States? It has not. Has it been prohibited to the States? It has not. Then it is reserved to the States, respectively, or to the people. . . . And any attempt by Congress to deprive them of this reserved power, will be unjust, tyrannical, unconstitutional, and void.

The only condition that may constitutionally be annexed to the admission of a new State is, that its constitution shall be republican. . . .

. . .

The people of each of the States who adopted the Constitution, except Massachusetts, owned slaves, yet they certainly considered their own constitutions to be republican. . . .

The Constitution recognizes the right to the slave property, and it thereby appears that it was intended, by the Convention and by the people, that that property should be secure.

. . .

. . . [T]he adoption of the proposition on your table[44] . . . would be a direct violation of the Constitution, which provides that "no person shall be deprived of property without due process of law; nor shall private property be taken for public use without just compensation." If you cannot take property even for public use, without just compensation, you certainly have not power to take it away for the purpose of annihilation, without compensation. . . . You cannot force the people to give up their property. You cannot force a portion of the people to emancipate their slaves.

42. *Annals of Congress*, 16th Cong., 1st Sess. (1820), 35:137–38.

43. *Annals of Congress*, 16th Cong., 1st Sess. (1820), 35:351–52.

44. Smyth is referring to the proposed emancipation of slaves in Missouri. Other slaveholders made the same argument with respect to the emancipation of slaves in the territories.

. . .

. . . It is a principle of the Constitution that no advantage shall be given to some of the States over others. . . . It is a sacred duty of Congress to do equal and impartial justice to every part of the Union.

. . . If $15,000,000 of the money raised by taxes paid by the whole people, are appropriated to purchase a territory, is it just to exclude there from the inhabitants of a part of the States? The inhabitants of the slave-holding States being slaveholders, you exclude them, if you exclude their slaves, as effectually as you would exclude married men by a law that children and married women should not come into the territory. . . .

Shall the slaveholders be declared incapable of holding any share of the territory purchased with the money of the whole people? Have they not contributed their full proportion of the money paid for the territory? . . .

REPRESENTATIVE TIMOTHY FULLER (Massachusetts, Republican)[45]

. . .

. . . If we proclaim the glorious truth, that "all men are born free and equal" in our constitutions, and, while acting under them, forge the chains of millions of our unoffending species, can we expect to escape derision and contempt? . . .

. . .

. . . [N]othing is more easily demonstrated, than that the establishment of slavery is a direct violation of the very first principle of republican government—political equality. . . . While they remain territories, . . . we may prohibit slavery by an act of legislation; our power being equivalent by the third section, fourth article, to that of the State Legislature. . . .

. . .

The authority of the General Government over the Territories, while they remain such, is very extensive; "to make all needful rules and regulations respecting them," comprehending legislative and executive jurisdiction. . . .

. . .

[Fuller then emphasized the provision in the Northwest Ordinance prohibiting slavery in the northwest territories as proof that Congress had the power to ban slavery in the territories acquired by the Louisiana Purchase.]

45. *Annals of Congress*, 16th Cong., 1st Sess. (1820), 36:1467–70.

Slavery and Free Blacks

National constitutional law and the constitutional laws of many states assumed that blacks were slaves. The Fugitive Slave Act of 1793 allowed masters the same right to recover runaway slaves as the common law gave owners to recapture runaway horses. Legal authorities in the free states routinely rejected claims by persons of color that slave catchers had violated their rights. "It is very obvious that slaves are not parties to the constitution," Chief Justice Parker of the Supreme Judicial Court of Massachusetts asserted in *Commonwealth v. Griffith* (MA 1823). When a judge in Virginia insisted that masters should have the burden of proof in freedom suits, that decision was quickly reversed in *Hudgins v. Wright* (VA 1806). Responding to claims that the "free and equal" clause in the Virginia Declaration of Rights compelled a presumption of freedom, Judge Tucker stated in *Hudgins*,

> The first clause of the Bill of Rights, which was notoriously framed with a cautious eye to this subject, and was meant to embrace the case of free citizens, or aliens only; and not by a side wind to overturn the rights of property, and give freedom to those very people whom we have been compelled from imperious circumstances to retain, generally, in the same state of bondage that they were in at the revolution, in which they had no *concern*, *agency* or *interest*.[46]

Commonwealth v. Griffith, 2 Pick. 11 (MA 1823)

Camillus Griffith was a slave catcher. In 1823 he travelled to New Bedford, Massachusetts, to recapture a slave named Randolph. Acting without a warrant, Griffith entered Randolph's property, seized him, and confined him before bringing him before a magistrate. Local authorities indicted Griffin for assault, battery, and false imprisonment. Griffith claimed that his acts were legal under federal law, which permitted slaves to be seized without a warrant. After being convicted by the trial court, Griffith appealed to the Supreme Judicial Court of Massachusetts.

46. *Hudgins v. Wright*, 11 Va. (1 Hen. & M.) 134 (Sup. Ct. App. 1806).

The Supreme Judicial Court reversed the conviction. Chief Justice Parker declared that slaves had no constitutional rights because they were not parties to the Constitution. How did Parker know that Randolph was a slave? Did Parker give Randolph any opportunity to challenge Griffith's conclusion? On what basis does Parker conclude that slaves have no constitutional rights? Is this reading of the Constitution correct?

CHIEF JUSTICE PARKER delivered the opinion of the Court.

. . .

This brings the case to a single point, whether the statute of the United States giving power to seize a slave without a warrant is constitutional. It is difficult in a case like this, for persons who are not inhabitants of slaveholding States, to prevent prejudice from having too strong an effect on their minds. We must reflect, however, that the constitution was made with some States in which it would not occur to the mind, to inquire whether slaves were property. It was a very serious question, when they came to make the constitution, what should be done with their slaves. They might have kept aloof from the constitution. That instrument was a compromise. It was a compact by which all are bound. We are to consider then what was the intention of the constitution. The words of it were used out of delicacy, so as not to offend some in the convention whose feelings were abhorrent to slavery; but we there entered into an agreement that slaves should be considered as property. Slavery would still have continued if no constitution had been made.

The constitution does not prescribe the mode of reclaiming a slave, but leaves it to be determined by Congress. It is very clear, that it was not intended that application should be made to the executive authority of the State. It is said that the act which Congress has passed on this subject, is contrary to the amendment of the constitution, securing the people in their persons and property against seizures &c., without a complaint upon oath. But all the parts of the instrument are to be taken together. It is very obvious that slaves are not parties to the constitution, and the amendment has relation to the parties.

But it is said, that when a seizure is made, it should be made conformably to our laws. This does not follow from the constitution, and the act of Congress says that the person to whom the service is due may *seize* &c. Whether the statute is a harsh one, is not for us to determine. But it is objected, that a person may in this summary manner seize a freeman. It may be so, but this would be attended with mischievous consequences to the person making the seizure, and a *habeas corpus* would lie to obtain the release of the person seized. We do not perceive that the statute is unconstitutional, and we think that the defence is well made out.

JUSTICE THACHER, dissenting.

Though I agree to many things said by the *Chief Justice*, I do not entirely coincide with him. I am not disposed to question the constitutionality of the statute, but I think it intended that the seizures should be made in conformity to the laws of the several States, and not in violation of the laws of any one of them. The laws here do not recognise a slave. Every person here is a freeman, and entitled to all the privileges of a freeman; one of which is, to be secure against all seizures &c., without a complaint upon oath. I admit that in the southern States they may seize a slave without a warrant, because it is according to the laws of those States. But it does not follow that the same may be done here. I think it is the intention of the statute, that the seizure of a slave here shall be by process of law here. The complaint should not state that Randolph was a slave, for our law knows no such creature, but that he was a person held to service by the laws of Virginia. I admit that Congress might prescribe a new mode of apprehending a fugitive from service, which should supersede our law. In the case before the Court, the defendant, in my opinion, violated the law of our State. . . .

Free Blacks

Most white Americans believed that free blacks were neither national nor state citizens. State courts in Virginia and Kentucky declared that free blacks were not state citizens. "The numerous restrictions imposed on this class of people in our Statute Book, many of which are inconsistent with the letter and spirit of the Constitution, both of this State and of the United States, as respects the free whites," the General Court of Virginia declared in *Aldridge v. Commonwealth* (VA 1824), "demonstrate, that, here, those instruments have not been considered to extend equally to both classes of our population."[47] William Wirt, U.S. attorney general

47. *Aldridge v. Commonwealth*, 4 Va. 447 (VA 1824).

under President Monroe, issued an influential opinion asserting that free African-Americans were not citizens of the United States. Wirt declared,

> I am of the opinion that the constitution, by the description of "citizens of the United States," intended those only who enjoyed the full and equal privileges of white citizens in the State of their residence. If this be correct, . . . then free people of color in Virginia are not citizens of the United States.[48]

Congressional Debate over the Missouri Compromise and Black Citizenship (1820)[49]

Members of Congress debated the citizenship status of free blacks when considering the constitutionality of a provision in the proposed Missouri Constitution that would forbid free blacks and mulattoes from entering the state. Some free state representatives insisted that this provision violated Article IV, Section 2 of the U.S. Constitution, which declares, "The Citizens of each State shall be entitled to all Privileges and Immunities of Citizens in the several States." A free black citizen of Massachusetts, they claimed, had a constitutional right to travel to Missouri. Slave state representatives asserted that free blacks were not American citizens. Charles Pinckney of South Carolina insisted that when the Constitution was ratified, "There did not then exist such a thing in the Union as a black or colored citizen."[50] Congress voted to admit Missouri on the condition that that state not violate the constitutional rights of any American citizen. When Missouri barred free blacks, the national legislature did nothing.

The two speeches excerpted below present the major arguments for and against black citizenship. Joseph Hemphill of Pennsylvania and Louis McLane of Delaware agreed that free blacks enjoyed some state rights and were subject to some discriminations. Each reached different conclusions from these facts. Why does Hemphill conclude that persons who enjoy some rights are state citizens? How does he explain racial discriminations in the free states? Why does McLane conclude that persons who are subject to some discriminations are not state citizens? How does he explain the rights that free blacks enjoyed in some states?

48. William Wirt, "Rights of Free Negroes in Virginia," 1 Ops. Atty. Gen. 506 (1821).

49. *Annals of Congress*, 16th Cong., 2nd Sess. (1820), 37:596–606, 614–26.

50. *Annals of Congress*, 16th Cong., 2nd Sess. (1820), 37:1134.

REPRESENTATIVE JOSEPH HEMPHILL (Pennsylvania, Federalist)

. . .

Discriminations are familiar to us, in the several States, both as to political and civil rights; but it never was believed that they effected a total extinguishment of citizenship. Some citizens are entitled to vote, and others are not. Some are exempted from serving in the militia, or on juries, for various reasons; and this throws an unequal burden on the rest of the community. . . .

. . . Females are also citizens, but they by no means fall within the given definition, particularly in the sense in which it is intended to operate on political rights.

. . .

. . . [P]revious to the adoption of the Constitution of the United States, each State had the unquestionable right of saying who should compose its own citizens; and if, at the adoption of the Constitution of the United States, free negroes and mulattoes were citizens of any one State in the Union, the Federal Constitution gave to such citizens all the privileges and immunities of the citizens in the several States.

. . .

[*Representative Hemphill proceeded to point out that free blacks voted in many states when the Constitution was ratified and were still voting in some states in 1820.*]

When our different constitutions were formed, this class of people lived among us, not in the character of foreigners; they were connected with no other nation—this was their native country, and as dear to them as to us. Thousands of them were free born, and they composed a part of the people in the several States. They were identified with the nation, and its wealth consisted, in part, of their labor. They had fought for their country, and were righteously included in the principles of the Declaration of Independence. This was their condition when the Constitution of the United States was framed, and that high instrument does not cast the least shade of doubt upon any of their rights or privileges. . . .

They have a right to pursue their own happiness, in as high a degree as any other class of people. Their situation is similar to others, in relation to the acquirement of property, and the various pursuits of industry. They are entitled to the same rights of religion and protection, and are subjected to the same punishments. They are enumerated in the census. They can be taxed, and made liable to militia duty; they are denied none of the privileges contained in the bill of rights. . . .

When they enjoy all these rights, civil and religious, equally with the white people; and when they all flow from the same constitutions and laws, without any especial designation or reference to them, I have a curiosity to learn upon what principle any right can be singled out, as one of which they are to be deprived.

. . .

It is, however, wholly unnecessary, on this occasion, to trouble ourselves in drawing nice lines of distinction as to the propriety or power of abridging the common rights in regard to this class of people; for no one can gravely accede to the proposition, that a citizen can be denied the privilege of residing on the soil of his citizenship, when he has committed no offense; that he can be held in a state of exile without being branded with any mark of disgrace. . . .

REPRESENTATIVE LOUIS MCLANE (Delaware, Federalist)

. . .

. . . [T]he free negroes and mulattoes in the United States are not that description of citizens contemplated by the Constitution of the United States as entitled to Federal Rights.

I do not mean, sir, to deny that these people have certain rights. . . . But their rights are of a local nature, dependent upon the gratuitous favor of the municipal authority of the States, and liable to be curtailed or enlarged by those authorities; they are limited to the State granting them, and confer no claim to similar privileges and immunities purely federal. . . . The State authority may confer the right of citizenship within their State upon aliens and Indians; but it was never imagined that they would therefore be the subjects of federal rights. Nor could the Constitution have intended to refer to any description of persons whose privileges were matters of grace from the local municipality. For I take it to be clear, that no person can claim federal immunities who cannot claim, as a matter of right, the privileges of a citizen in the State of which he is a resident. . . .

. . . [A] person, to be a "citizen" under one Government, must be a member of the civil community, and entitled as matter of right to equal advantages in that community. . . . A State . . . may regulate the right of suffrage, and extend it to such only of its members as possess a freehold property; but it could not extend it to one freeholder and not to another; much less could it say that a citizen should not acquire a freehold; for it is the inherent right of every citizen to exert his mental and physical powers in the pursuit of happiness and for the acquisition of property, and to have his acquisitions protected. Our political system is founded upon this principle of equal rights in the members of the community, and any State regulation which would interfere with them would be unconstitutional. It follows, therefore, that those only are "citizens" who can claim these advantages as a matter of right; all others, and those whose privileges depend upon the grace or favor of the local authority fall under the denomination of inhabitants and aliens, holding their rights at the will of the Government under which they live. . . .

Of the two last of these classes [inhabitants and permanent inhabitants], I consider the Indians and free negroes and mulattoes of the United States. The "laws and custom" nowhere give them the right of participating in all the advantages of society. Their actual advantages vary in almost every State, in some they are dealt out more liberally, in others with a sparing hand; in none are they complete. In some States they cannot be witnesses against the whites; in others they cannot be jurors; in none are they allowed to hold offices or to intermarry with the whites. . . . If they were citizens these disabilities could not be imposed upon them, but for some personal defect. The real truth is, sir, that they are nowhere considered as members of the civil society, but as inhabitants of the country, holding their rights at the will of the local authority.

. . .

I will not stop to notice . . . the stale argument from the abstract doctrines announced in the Declaration of Independence. . . . Broad as they appear, every one knows they were limited. They did not include the slaves, nor the Indians, because they referred only to those who were members of our civil community; and, if my position be correct, for the same reason they had no allusion to the free negroes in the country. It is impossible they could have had, when in those States in which these declarations are the fullest, free negroes were expressly excluded from the advantages of their naturalization laws.

. . . It is said, too, that in one or two States they are allowed to vote, and some have voted. But I have shown you that the right to vote is no test of citizenship; it is dependent on legislative favor, in part, and may be conferred on aliens and others, and taken away again, if it be not founded on the claim of citizenship; and therefore, if the free negroes only exercise it as a matter of grace merely, it gives them no claim to Federal immunities.

. . .

All freemen have the capacity to be witnesses, jurors, and to serve in the militia; but, in most of the States, these are denied to free negroes by the municipal laws. . . . Why cannot a free negro be a witness against a white man, as a foreigner or an Indian may? It is because the custom of society, having drawn a discrimination between the white and the black, disparaging to the latter, the law deems it safe and wise to deprive him of the means of gratifying feelings which such a condition might engender. . . . In no State of the Union is intermarriage between white and black permitted. . . . [T]his fact proves the entire argument. It not only shows that these people are not members of the civil community, but that they can never become so, because the strong sense of the community is against it; it closes the only legitimate avenue to their amalgamation; it strengthens and sanctifies the moral feelings of society; it keeps the black man forever without its bosom, and perpetuates its discrimination. . . .

. . .

I am an enemy to slavery; if I had the power, and could do so consistently with the safety of the white population, I would wipe it out of our history; but I never will agree to put the white and black population upon an equality, or to destroy the features of both, by the vain attempt to amalgamate one with the other. . . . [B]etween these descriptions of men, reason and nature have drawn a line of discrimination which never can be effaced, till both shall be compelled to yield to the law of force.

. . . It is unreasonable to conclude that the Constitution ever meant to alter the condition of the black population, or to interfere with the municipal authorities over them, so as to place all the States at the mercy of a dissolute, heterogeneous population of any one. Can it be supposed that the States would ever have entered into the Union upon the principle of allowing the free negroes in New York or Massachusetts to be placed upon an equal footing with the whites, in States whose safety required them to deny similar privileges to their own native free negroes? . . . The Constitution was the work of States composed of a white population, and designed to secure their interests chiefly; and to such of these who had perfect rights in one State, it guarantied the immunities in any other. It was intended to make the United States a common country for such as were full members of the particular States. At the time, too, the condition of the free blacks was known to be as I have already described it; they were known to be a distinct class everywhere, and the creatures of local and municipal policy; certainly of an inferior order, and enjoying such rights as the policy of the particular State might think proper to confer. They were everywhere considered as inhabitants merely, who had not attained to the condition of citizens, and enjoyed only partially the privileges appertaining to the former class. . . .

Amy v. Smith, 1 Litt. 326 (KY 1822)

William Smith physically assaulted Amy, a woman of color. Amy promptly sued him for assault and battery, trespass, and false imprisonment. Smith claimed that he had a legal right to beat his slaves. Such claims and defenses were typical in freedom suits: Persons of color alleged they had been beaten; defendants admitted the beating but claimed they had a right to beat their slave. The judicial ruling on whether an assault took place by necessity settled whether the plaintiff was lawfully enslaved.

Amy v. Smith *was more complex than the conventional freedom suit. Amy claimed that she had become free when she resided in Pennsylvania. In 1780 Pennsylvania had passed a law providing for the gradual emancipation of all slaves in that state. Before she left Pennsylvania for Kentucky, Amy insisted, she met Pennsylvania's statutory conditions for freedom. In 1808, however, Kentucky had passed a law requiring all persons claiming freedom under Pennsylvania law to bring their freedom suit within two years. Persons who failed to bring a claim by 1810 lost their right to challenge their enslavement. Amy filed her lawsuit in the 1820s. She claimed that the Kentucky statute of limitations violated the state constitutional right of citizens to have access to courts for redress of wrongs. Smith insisted that Amy had no constitutional rights in Kentucky. Even if free, he declared, Amy was not a state citizen.*

The Court of Appeals of Kentucky ruled that Amy was not a citizen and therefore did not have the right to access to Kentucky courts. The judicial majority insisted that citizens were those who enjoyed the highest privileges of the state. On what ground does the court justify that decision? How does the court explain why women and children are not citizens? Why does the dissenting opinion reject those conclusions? How do the different justices conceive of citizenship?

Opinion of the Court

. . .

Before we can determine whether she was a citizen, or not, of either of those states, it is necessary to ascertain what it is that constitutes a citizen. In England, birth in the country was alone sufficient to make any one a subject. Even a villain or a slave, born within the king's allegiance is, according to the principles of the common law, a subject; but it never can be admitted that he is a citizen. . . . It is, in fact, not the place of a man's birth, but the rights and privileges he may be entitled to enjoy, which make him a citizen. The term, citizen, is derived from the Latin word, *civis,* and in its primary sense signifies one who is vested with the freedom and privileges of a city. . . . In England, a citizen is not only entitled to all the local privileges of the city to which he belongs but he has also the right of electing and being elected to parliament, which is itself rather an extraordinary privilege, since it does not belong to every class of subjects. . . .

. . .

When the term came to be applied to the inhabitants of a state, it necessarily carried with it the same signification, with reference to the privileges of the state, which had been implied by it with reference to the privileges of a city, when it was applied to the inhabitants of the city; and it is in this sense, that the term, citizen, is believed to be generally, if not universally understood in the United States. This, indeed, evidently appears to be the sense in which the term is used in the clause of the constitution which is under consideration; for the terms, "privileges and immunities," which are expressive of the object intended to be secured to the citizens of each state, in every other, plainly import, according to the best usages of our language, something more than those ordinary rights of personal security and property, which, by the courtesy of all civilized nations, are extended to the citizens or subjects of other countries, while they reside among them.

No one can, therefore, in the correct sense of the term, be a citizen of a state, who is not entitled, upon the terms prescribed by the institutions of the state, to all the rights and privileges conferred by those institutions upon the highest class of society. It is true, that females and infants do not personally possess those rights and privileges, in any state in the Union; but they are generally dependent upon adult males through whom they enjoy the benefits of those rights and privileges; and it is a rule of common law, as well as of common sense, that females and infants should, in this respect, partake of the quality of those adult males who belong to the same class and condition in society, and of course they will or will not be citizens, as the adult males of the same class are or are not so. Nor do we mean to say, that it is necessary, even for an adult male to be a citizen, that he should be in the actual enjoyment of all those rights and privileges which belong to a citizen. He may not only not be in the actual enjoyment of those rights and privileges, but he may even not possess those qualifications, of property, of age, or of residence, which most of the states prescribe as requisites to the enjoyment of some of their highest privileges and immunities, and yet be a citizen; but, to be a citizen, it is necessary, that he should be entitled to the enjoyment of those privileges and immunities, upon the same terms upon which they are conferred upon other citizens; and unless he is so entitled, he can not, in the proper sense of the term, be a citizen.

It results, then, that the plaintiff can not have been a citizen, either of Pennsylvania or of Virginia, unless she belonged to a class of society, upon which, by the institutions of the states, was conferred a right to enjoy all the privileges and immunities appertaining to the state. That this was the case, there is no evidence in the record to show, and the presumption is against it. Free negroes and mulattoes are, almost everywhere, considered and treated as a degraded race of people; insomuch so, that, under the constitution and laws of the United States, they can not become citizens of the United States.

. . .

Prior to the adoption of the constitution of the United States, each state had a right to make citizens of any persons they pleased; but as the federal constitution does not authorize any but white persons to become citizens of the United States, it furnishes a presumption that none other were then citizens of any state; which presumption will stand, until repelled by positive testimony. . . .

The honorable BENJAMIN MILLS dissented. . . .

. . .

. . . The American colonies brought with them the common, and not the civil law; and each state, at the revolution, adopted either more or less of it, and not one of them exploded the principle, that the place of birth conferred citizenship. Indeed, the very argument, that being born in England makes a subject, shows that being born here makes a citizen. . . . But let the position be assumed, that none are citizens but those entitled to the highest honors of the state, and it follows that no person, who is not a white male, and has not resided here for six years, and is not of the age of thirty-five years, can be a citizen; for such must be the qualifications of our chief magistrate. . . . Can it, then, be compatible with the spirit or letter of the constitution of the United States, to say, and that by construction, that when it speaks of "citizen" of a state, it only intends one-eighth of its population; that the aristocracy of each state alone, is embraced—their rights secured; while nothing is secured by its provisions to the great mass, the full seven-eighths of the whole? Such a construction is much too limited, and if applied to that instrument, or to the constitution of our own state, it will be found that the rights of the few, and not the many, are protected by them.

We will here take occasion to mention the case of white females and infants. They, being not entitled to political advancement, can not be citizens. The only answer given to this, is, that they are represented by the citizen males, such as their husbands, fathers or guardians. But what becomes of the widows and maids of mature age, and of the unprotected orphan? They have no such representative, and therefore are not citizens. . . .

. . .

The mistake on this subject must arise from not attending to a sensible distinction between political and civil rights. The latter constitutes the citizen, while the former are not necessary ingredients. A state may deny all her political rights to an individual, and yet he may be a citizen. The rights of office and suffrage are political purely, and are denied by some or all the states, to part of their population, who are still citizens. A citizen, then, is one who owes to the government, allegiance, service, and money by way of taxation, and to whom the government in turn, grants and guarantees liberty of person and of conscience, the right of acquiring and possessing property, of marriage and the social relations, of suit and defense, and security in person, estate and reputation. These, with some others which might be enumerated, being guaranteed and secured by government, constitute a citizen. . . .

C. Gender

Americans during the Early National Era became committed to "separate spheres" for men and women. Proponents of "separate spheres" insisted that men and women were equal republican citizens, but that perceived natural differences between the sexes justified giving each different rights and responsibilities. Men were responsible for public affairs; women were responsible for private affairs. Supreme Court Justice James Wilson expressed the emerging conventional wisdom when he declared:

> You have, indeed, heard much of public government and public law: but these things were not made for themselves: they were made for something better; and of that something better, you form the better part—I mean society—I mean particularly domestic society: there the lovely and accomplished woman shines with superior luster.[51]

Married women remained *femes covert*, women whose legal status was determined entirely by their spouse's status. *Martin v. Commonwealth* (MA 1805) held that married men could suffer legal consequences for fleeing the United States during the American Revolution, but married women, who had an obligation to follow their husbands, could not.

Voices for greater gender equality could be heard. In 1792 Mary Wollstonecraft published *A Vindication of the Rights of Women*, which many feminists consider the first important defense of women's rights. Wollstonecraft was English, but her arguments circulated in the United States. American proponents of greater gender equality often championed increased educational opportunities for women. Some educated women demanded political rights. Priscilla Mason, one of the first graduates of the Young Ladies Academy in Philadelphia, called for "equal participation in honor and office." Mason believed that women and men were different, but that gender differences supported greater female participation in public life:

> But supposing now that we possessed all the talents of the orator, in the highest perfection; where shall we find a theater for the display of them? The Church, the Bar, and the Senate are shut against us. Who shut them? Man; despotic man, first made us incapable of the duty, and then forbid us the exercise. Let us by suitable education, qualify ourselves for those high departments—they will open before us.[52]

---

51. James Wilson, *The Works of James Wilson*, ed. James DeWitt Andrews (Chicago: Callaghan and Co., 1896), 1:30–31.

52. Priscilla Mason, "Salutatory Oration," in *The Rise and Progress of the Young Ladies Academy of Philadelphia* (Philadelphia: Stewart and Cochran, 1794), 90–93.

Martin v. Commonwealth, 1 Mass. 347 (1805)

William and Anna Martin were loyalists who fled the United States in 1776, never to return. The attorney general of Massachusetts immediately filed a lawsuit to have the Martin lands forfeited to the state. Massachusetts law permitted state officials to confiscate the property of any loyalist who left the state during the Revolution. The state's supreme judicial court allowed the confiscation, and Massachusetts took possession in 1781. Twenty years later, James Martin, Anna Martin's son and heir, challenged that decision, claiming that the state statute did not permit forfeiture of the interest a women had in various properties. As a "feme covert," a wife, James Martin argued, could not be charged with violating her duties to the state of Massachusetts. Anna Martin had both a legal and a moral duty to follow her husband, William Martin, when he left the United States.

The Supreme Judicial Court of Massachusetts agreed that Anna Martin did not forfeit her property interests when she left the United States. Justice Sedgwick maintained that the Massachusetts legislature did not intend to confiscate lands from women who merely followed their husbands. Although Martin *was based on an interpretation of Massachusetts law, note how the justices refer to broader principles. Anna Martin could not have violated her duty to Massachusetts, they claimed, because married women had no distinctive duties to Massachusetts. On what basis do the justices reach that conclusion? Consider* Martin *in light of James Wilson's discussion of separate spheres. How might Wilson have resolved* Martin*? How would you have decided* Martin v. Commonwealth*?*

JUSTICE THACHER, delivered the opinion of the Court. . . .

JUSTICE SEDGWICK, concurring.

. . .

By the record before us, it appears that *William Martin* and *Anna Martin*, the father and mother of the plaintiff in error, are *jointly* charged with the several acts which are alleged in the libel of the *Attorney-General* as incurring the forfeiture for which he sued; that since the 19th day of April, 1775, they had levied war and conspired to levy war against the provinces, or colonies, or *United States;* that they had adhered to the king of *Great Britain*, his fleets and armies, and had given to them aid and comfort; that, since that time, they had, without the permission of the legislative or executive authority of any of the *United States*, withdrawn themselves therefrom into parts and places under the acknowledged authority of the king of *Great Britain:* all these are charged as done jointly by the husband and wife; and we are called upon, by matter apparent on the record, and by one of the errors expressly assigned, to say whether a *feme-covert*, for *any* of these acts, *performed with her husband*, is within the intention of the statute; and I think that she is not. In construing statutes, the great object is to discover from the words, the subject matter, the mischiefs contemplated, and the remedies proposed, what was the true meaning and design of the legislature. In the relation of husband and wife, the law makes, in her behalf, such an allowance for the authority of the husband, and her duty of obedience, that guilt is not imputed to her for actions performed jointly by them, unless of the most heinous and aggravated nature. For instance; the law says, whoever steals shall be punished, and yet if a wife participates in a theft with her husband she is not punishable. Innumerable other instances might be given. She is exempted from punishment, not because she is not within the letter of the law, if she had sufficient will to be considered as acting voluntarily and as a moral agent, but because she is viewed in such a state of subjection, and so under the control of her husband, that she acts merely as his instrument, and that no guilt is imputable to her. Compare this with the case under consideration. In a case of great political interest, in which men of great powers and equal integrity, as is said by the *Attorney-General*, divided; and where a *feme-covert* is not expressly included, shall we suppose her to be so by general words? Can we believe that a wife, for so respecting the understanding of her husband as to submit her own opinions to his, on a subject so all-important as this, should lose her own property, and forfeit the inheritance of her children? Was she to be considered as criminal because she permitted her husband to elect his own and her place of residence? Because she did not, in violation of her marriage vows, rebel against the will of her husband? So hard and cruel a construction against the general and known principles of law on this subject, could be justified by none but strong and unequivocal expressions. So far is this from being the case in this statute, that it seems to me there are no words by which it can fairly be understood that such was the intention of the legislature; but the contrary. The preamble of the statute has described the persons whom it intended to bring within it. It is that member who "withdraws himself from the jurisdiction of the government, and thereby deprives it of the benefit of his personal services." A *wife* who left the country in the company of her husband did not *withdraw* herself; but was, if I may so express it, withdrawn by him. She did not deprive the government of the benefit of her personal services; she had none to render; none were exacted of her. "The member who so withdraws, incurs," says the preamble, "the forfeiture of all his property, rights, and liberties, holden under and derived from that constitution of government, to the support of which he has refused to afford his aid and assistance." Can any one believe it was the intention of the legislature to demand of *femes-covert* their *aid and assistance* in the support of their constitution of government? The preamble then goes on to particularize the violation of our rights by our former sovereign, and proceeds to declare that it thereupon "became the indispensable duty of all the *people* of said states forthwith to unite in defence of their common freedom, and *by arms* to oppose the fleets and armies of the said king; yet, nevertheless, divers of the *members* of this, and of the other *United States* of *America*, evilly disposed, or regardless of their duty towards their country, did withdraw themselves," &c. Now it is unquestionably true that the *members* here spoken of as "evilly disposed" are included in the *people* abovementioned. What then was the duty of these evilly-disposed persons, for a violation of which they were to be cut off from the community to which they had belonged, and rendered aliens to it? It was "to unite in defence of their common freedom, and *by arms* to oppose" an invading enemy. And can it be supposed to have been the intention of the legislature to exact the performance of this duty from *wives*, in opposition to the will and command of their husbands? Can it be believed that a humane and just legislature ever intended that wives should be subjected to the horrid alternative of, either, on the one hand, separating from their husbands and disobeying them, or, on the other, of sacrificing their property? It is impossible for me to suppose that such was ever their intention. The conclusion of the preamble speaks of those who withdrew as thereby "aiding or giving encouragement and countenance to the operations" of the enemy. Were *femes-covert*, accompanying their husbands, thus considered by the legislature? I believe not. So far from believing that *wives* are within the statute, for any acts by them done jointly with their husbands, that a fair construction of the whole *act* together, does, to my judgment, clearly exclude them. . . .

D. Native Americans

Governing authorities in the United States almost immediately determined that Native Americans were not protected by the Bill of Rights. Many congressional statutes passed during the Early National Era denied to tribal members the liberties set out in the first ten amendments to the Constitution. Some statutes declared that Native Americans accused of crimes could be convicted by trials that did not meet the standards of the Fifth and Sixth Amendments. In 1800 Congress restricted Native American speech. The Act for the Preservation of the Peace with Indian Tribes prohibited "any citizen or other person" from "alienat[ing], or attempt[ing] to alienate the confidence of the Indians from the government of the United States." Judicial decisions ignored the Bill of Rights when Native American property rights were challenged. In *Johnson v. McIntosh* (1823), Chief Justice John Marshall evaluated tribal rights to property under the law of nations, not the due process or takings clause of the Fifth Amendment. State courts reached similar conclusions. *Goodell v. Jackson* (NY 1823) bluntly declared that Native Americans "have never been regarded as citizens or members of our body politic, within the contemplation of the constitution."[53]

Johnson v. McIntosh, 21 U.S. 543 (1823)

On October 18, 1775, the Piankeshaw Tribe sold to William Johnson and other investors a large tract of land in what is now Illinois. On July 20, 1818, the United States sold the same land to William McIntosh. Johnson's heirs claimed that the U.S. government had no power to sell the land they had legally acquired from the Piankeshaws. McIntosh asserted that Native Americans lacked the legal title necessary to sell the contested land. After the federal district court in Illinois upheld McIntosh's property claim, Johnson's heirs appealed to the U.S. Supreme Court.

The Supreme Court in Johnson v. McIntosh *unanimously held that the United States had title to the land in question. Chief Justice Marshall insisted that by rights of discovery and conquest, the Europeans who settled North America acquired title to all land. At no point in* Johnson *did Marshall consider the Bill of Rights to be relevant. The first paragraph of his opinion declared that questions about*

53. *Goodell v. Jackson*, 20 Johns. 693 (NY 1823).

Native American land claims depended on "the law of nations" and the "principles . . . which our own government has adopted." What was the relevant law of nations? What were the relevant "principles" of the American government? Marshall suggests that when one Christian country conquers another Christian country, existing property rights are not disturbed. What reasons does he give for rejecting this principle with respect to Native Americans? Do these reasons explain why Marshall thought the Bill of Rights was not applicable to Native Americans?

CHIEF JUSTICE MARSHALL delivered the opinion of the Court.

. . .

As the right of society, to prescribe those rules by which property may be acquired and preserved is not, and cannot be drawn into question; as the title to lands, especially, is and must be admitted to depend entirely on the law of the nation in which they lie; it will be necessary, in pursuing this inquiry, to examine, not singly those principles of abstract justice, which the Creator of all things has impressed on the mind of his creature man, and which are admitted to regulate, in a great degree, the rights of civilized nations, whose perfect independence is acknowledged; but those principles also which our own government has adopted in the particular case, and given us as the rule for our decision.

On the discovery of this immense continent, the great nations of Europe were eager to appropriate to themselves so much of it as they could respectively acquire. . . . But, as they were all in pursuit of nearly the same object, it was necessary, in order to avoid conflicting settlements, and consequent war with each other, to establish a principle, which all should acknowledge as the law by which the right of acquisition, which they all asserted, should be regulated as between themselves. This principle was, that discovery gave title to the government by whose subjects, or by whose authority, it was made, against all other European governments, which title might be consummated by possession.

The exclusion of all other Europeans, necessarily gave to the nation making the discovery the sole right of acquiring the soil from the natives, and establishing settlements upon it. It was a right with which no Europeans could interfere. It was a right which all asserted for themselves, and to the assertion of which, by others, all assented.

Those relations which were to exist between the discoverer and the natives, were to be regulated by themselves. The rights thus acquired being exclusive, no other power could interpose between them.

In the establishment of these relations, the rights of the original inhabitants were, in no instance, entirely disregarded; but were necessarily, to a considerable extent, impaired. They were admitted to be the rightful occupants of the soil, with a legal as well as just claim to retain possession of it, and to use it according to their own discretion; but their rights to complete sovereignty, as independent nations, were necessarily diminished, and their power to dispose of the soil at their own will, to whomsoever they pleased, was denied by the original fundamental principle, that discovery gave exclusive title to those who made it.

While the different nations of Europe respected the right of the natives, as occupants, they asserted the ultimate dominion to be in themselves; and claimed and exercised, as a consequence of this ultimate dominion, a power to grant the soil, while yet in possession of the natives. These grants have been understood by all, to convey a title to the grantees, subject only to the Indian right of occupancy.

. . .

The United States, then, have unequivocally acceded to that great and broad rule by which its civilized inhabitants now hold this country. They hold, and assert in themselves, the title by which it was acquired. They maintain, as all others have maintained, that discovery gave an exclusive right to extinguish the Indian title of occupancy, either by purchase or by conquest; and gave also a right to such a degree of sovereignty, as the circumstances of the people would allow them to exercise.

The power now possessed by the government of the United States to grant lands, resided, while we were colonies, in the crown, or its grantees. The validity of the titles given by either has never been questioned in our Courts. It has been exercised uniformly over territory in possession of the Indians. The existence of this power must negative the existence of any right which may conflict with, and control it. An absolute title to lands cannot exist, at the same time, in different persons, or in different governments. An absolute, must be an exclusive title, or at least a title which excludes all others not compatible with it. All our institutions recognise the absolute title of the crown, subject only to the Indian right of occupancy, and recognise the absolute title of the crown to extinguish that right. This is incompatible with an absolute and complete title in the Indians.

. . .

The title by conquest is acquired and maintained by force. The conqueror prescribes its limits. Humanity, however, acting on public opinion, has established, as a general rule, that the conquered shall not be wantonly oppressed, and that their condition shall remain as eligible as is compatible with the objects of the conquest. Most usually, they are incorporated with the victorious nation, and become subjects or citizens of the government with which they are connected. The new and old members of the society mingle with each other; the distinction between them is gradually lost, and they make one people. Where this incorporation is practicable, humanity demands, and a wise policy requires, that the rights of the conquered to property should remain unimpaired; that the new subjects should be governed as equitably as the old, and that confidence in their security should gradually banish the painful sense of being separated from their ancient connexions, and united by force to strangers.

. . .

But the tribes of Indians inhabiting this country were fierce savages, whose occupation was war, and whose subsistence was drawn chiefly from the forest. To leave them in possession of their country, was to leave the country a wilderness; to govern them as a distinct people, was impossible, because they were as brave and as high spirited as they were fierce, and were ready to repel by arms every attempt on their independence.

What was the inevitable consequence of this state of things? The Europeans were under the necessity either of abandoning the country, and relinquishing their pompous claims to it, or of enforcing those claims by the sword, and by the adoption of principles adapted to the condition of a people with whom it was impossible to mix, and who could not be governed as a distinct society, or of remaining in their neighbourhood, and exposing themselves and their families to the perpetual hazard of being massacred.

. . .

That law which regulates, and ought to regulate in general, the relations between the conqueror and conquered, was incapable of application to a people under such circumstances. The resort to some new and different rule, better adapted to the actual state of things, was unavoidable. . . .

However extravagant the pretension of converting the discovery of an inhabited country into conquest may appear; if the principle has been asserted in the first instance, and afterwards sustained; if a country has been acquired and held under it; if the property of the great mass of the community originates in it, it becomes the law of the land, and cannot be questioned. So, too, with respect to the concomitant principle, that the Indian inhabitants are to be considered merely as occupants, to be protected, indeed, while in peace, in the possession of their lands, but to be deemed incapable of transferring the absolute title to others. However this restriction may be opposed to natural right, and to the usages of civilized nations, yet, if it be indispensable to that system under which the country has been settled, and be adapted to the actual condition of the two people, it may, perhaps, be supported by reason, and certainly cannot be rejected by Courts of justice. . . .

VI. Criminal Justice

MAJOR DEVELOPMENTS

- The Supreme Court narrowly defines treason
- State courts permit constables and private persons to make warrantless arrests and search private places for illegal goods on the condition that they may be sued for false imprisonment and trespass if the victim of their search is innocent
- Judges and juries dispute whether juries in criminal trials may determine the law as well as the facts

Americans were determined to establish a republican system of criminal justice. The national and state bills of rights promised a criminal process structured by formal procedures and respect for individual rights. Keeping these promises proved harder than placing good language in constitutional texts. Due process was difficult to achieve in a society with few professional police officers, fewer prosecutors, and even fewer defense attorneys. Most criminal defendants were tried almost immediately after arrest in proceedings that lacked most constitutional formalities. Americans were tempted to short-circuit constitutional rights during the major criminal trials that took place between 1789 and 1828. Persons tried for violating the Sedition Act of 1798 and the alleged members of the Burr conspiracy accused the national government of running roughshod over constitutional rights in their attempt to gain politically motivated convictions.

Few precedents were fixed in stone. Federal courts decided very few criminal cases and hardly any state criminal case attracted national attention. With the exception of the treason trials of former Vice President Aaron Burr, during which Chief Justice Marshall fashioned enduring precedents on federal power to issue writs of habeas corpus and on the definition of treason, Americans more often created frameworks for debating constitutional criminal procedure than established constitutional rules that bound subsequent generations.

Questions about constitutional criminal justice occupied the national stage only during two major political trials. The first were the trials of persons accused of violating the Sedition Act of 1798. During these trials Jeffersonians accused Federalists of violating the constitutional rights of criminal defendants in order to imprison critics of Federalist officeholders. The second trials were of persons accused of being members of the Burr conspiracy, a plot allegedly aimed at securing the independence of the Western states under the leadership of former Vice President Burr. During these trials Federalists regularly accused President Thomas Jefferson of violating the constitutional rights of criminal defendants in order to imprison his political rivals.

Partisan politics explains much maneuvering during these court cases, but a consensus formed on some constitutional rules. The Federalists who passed the Sedition Act recognized the right to have a jury determine whether a criminal defendant had spoken truthfully about public officials. After Aaron Burr and his confederates were arrested, a Jeffersonian-dominated House of Representatives refused to pass legislation suspending habeas corpus.

A. Due Process and Habeas Corpus

The Supreme Court in *Ex parte Bollman* (1807) forged a subtle link between habeas corpus and due process. Chief Justice John Marshall freed two alleged participants in the Burr conspiracy because he determined that Jefferson did not have sufficient evidence to prove that the two had committed treason. In effect, *Bollman* held that government officials cannot imprison or detain people on the ground that they have committed a crime when no evidence exists that they have actually committed the crime in question. The due process clause does not permit people to be tried or convicted of crimes in the absence of sufficient evidence. If a person is imprisoned for a crime for which the government does not have sufficient evidence, then that person can obtain a writ of habeas corpus to vindicate their due process right. Future generations debated what other due process rights could be vindicated by habeas corpus appeals.

Habeas Corpus. The most important debate over habeas corpus took place after General Andrew Jackson declared martial law in New Orleans on December 16, 1814.[54] Fearful of British spies, Jackson required every able-bodied man to defend the city and imposed martial law throughout the district.. Many individuals were arrested for disobeying his commands. These arrests continued after the battle of New Orleans ended on January 8, 1815. On March 3, state senator Louis Louaillier sharply criticized Jackson's action in a local paper, stating, "It is high time the laws should resume their empire; that the citizens of this State should return to the full enjoyment of their rights." Jackson ordered that Louaillier be arrested. When federal district Judge Dominick Hall ordered Jackson to justify Louaillier's detention, Jackson promptly had Hall arrested. Jackson explained his actions as follows:

> Martial law, being established, applies . . . to all persons who remain within the sphere of its operations, and claims exclusive jurisdiction of all offenses which aim at the disorganization and ruin of the army over which it extends. To a certain extent it is believed, it makes every man a soldier; to defend the spot where chance or choice has placed him, and to make him liable for any misconduct calculated to weaken his defence. . . . Decide with the accused, no army can be safe, no general can command. Disaffection and disobedience, anarchy and confusion, must take the place of order and subordination—defeat and shame, of victory and triumph.

Once martial law was lifted, Judge Hall almost immediately cited Jackson for contempt of court and fined him $1000. Members of the Madison administration

54. The following materials, including the quotations, are taken from Matthew Warshauer, *Andrew Jackson and the Politics of Martial Law: Nationalism, Civil Liberties, and Partisanship* (Knoxville: University of Tennessee Press, 2006), 19–46.

questioned Jackson's decision to suspend martial law. Secretary of War Alexander Dallas asserted:

> The military power is clearly defined, and carefully limited by the Constitution and laws of the United States; but the experience of the best regulated Governments teaches us, that exigencies may sometimes arise, when . . . "Constitutional forms must be suspended, for the permanent preservation of Constitutional rights." . . . If, therefore, [an American Commander] undertake to suspend the writ of Habeas Corpus, to restrain the liberty of the Press, to inflect military punishments, upon the citizens who are not military men, and generally to supersede the functions of the civil magistrate, he may be justified by the law of necessity, while he has the merit of saving his country, but he cannot resort to the established law of the land, for the means of vindication.

How do you interpret this claim? Was Dallas censuring or supporting Jackson? What should Jackson have done? Should Jackson's status as a very popular war hero have influenced Dallas?

Due Process. Criminal trials in the early nineteenth century were similar in theory and practice to criminal trials during the Colonial and Founding Eras. In theory, all parties were committed to due process of law. All criminal defendants had a constitutional right to notice of the charges against them and an opportunity to rebut those charges. *United States v. Gooding* (1827) suggests that the prosecution in a criminal trial bears the burden of proof. In rendering an opinion in this case, Justice Joseph Story wrote, "The general rule of our jurisprudence is, that the party accused need not establish his innocence; but it is for the government itself to prove his guilt, before it is entitled to a verdict or conviction." In practice, most criminal trials remained brief and informal. Some evidence suggests that many trial judges made sincere efforts to enforce constitutional norms. Still, with rare exceptions, persons suspected of crimes did not have the knowledge or resources necessary to assert or realize their right to due process.

B. Search and Seizure

Early search and seizure cases explored the conditions under which any person could search and arrest persons suspected of crimes. Very few communities had professional police forces. Town constables had no more privileges than ordinary citizens. *Mayo v. Wilson* (1817) treated as reasonable any search that successfully identified a criminal. Persons who made false arrests were subject to lawsuits. Under this rule, you are free to physically detain a movie star whom you see shoplifting. If, however, he or she was given the merchandise by management, you can be sued. As the Supreme Court of New Hampshire said in *Mayo*, "He who arrests upon suspicion must take care that his cause of suspicion be such, as will bear the test, for otherwise he may be punishable for false imprisonment."

Mayo v. Wilson, 1 N.H. 53 (1817)

James Wilson and Simeon Dodge were constables in Francestown, New Hampshire. On Sunday, March 3, 1816, they stopped Solomon Mayo, who was travelling in a sleigh loaded with commercial goods. Mayo sued Wilson and Dodge for trespass and false arrest because they did not have an arrest warrant, insisting that the state constitution permitted arrests only when persons had a warrant from a magistrate. Wilson and Dodge claimed they did not need a warrant because New Hampshire law permitted them to arrest any person suspected of traveling unnecessarily on Sunday.

Chief Justice Richardson claimed that the search was constitutional. His opinion ruled that the New Hampshire Constitution should be interpreted according to the common law, which permitted persons to make arrests without warrants under certain conditions. What were those conditions? Chief Justice Richardson declares that any person may arrest a person they see engaging in a crime. May private persons make arrests in other circumstances? What did the New Hampshire court think is the point of the warrant requirement?

CHIEF JUSTICE RICHARDSON delivered the opinion of the Court.

. . .

By the 15th article of the bill of rights prefixed to the constitution of this state, it is declared that "no subject shall be arrested, imprisoned, despoiled or deprived of his property, immunities or privileges, put out of the protection of the law, exiled, or deprived of his life, liberty or estate, but by the judgment of his peers, or the law of the land." By the 19th article of the same bill of rights, it is declared "that every subject hath a right to be secure from all unreasonable searches and seizures of his person, his house, his papers and all his possessions. Therefore all warrants to search suspected places, or arrest a person for examination or trial in prosecutions, for criminal matters are contrary to this right, if the cause or foundation of them be not previously supported by oath or affirmation." . . . And we have no doubt that the phrase *by the law of the land* in our constitution, means the same thing as *by due process of law.*

. . .

There is a sound and safe rule for the construction of statutes, which it is believed will enable us to determine with great certainty, the true meaning of these clauses in the constitution, and that is, if a statute make use of a word, the meaning of which is well known at common law, the word shall be understood in the statute, in the same sense it was understood at common law. . . . The clause in our constitution now under consideration happens to be a literal translation from *Magna Carta.* . . . The phrase "per legem terræ" [by the law of the land] in Magna Carta, has a meaning as fixed and as well determined as any phrase known in the common law. The makers of the constitution having adopted a phrase from Magna Carta, the meaning of which in that instrument was so well known must be intended to have used it in the same sense in which it has always been understood to have been used there. . . . [P]rocess of law for the purpose of an arrest is two fold, either by the king's writ, or by what is called a warrant in law. . . . [A] warrant in law is again two fold, *viz.* 1. a warrant in deed by authority of a legal magistrate, or 2. that which each private person is invested with and may exercise. [The following are] the cases where the law warrants a private person to arrest and imprison another. 1. If a man is present when another commits treason, felony or notorious breach of the peace, he has a right instantly to arrest and commit him, lest he should escape. 2. If an affray be made to the breach of the peace, any present may during the continuance of the affray by warrant in law restrain any of the offenders, but if the affray be over there must be an express warrant. 3. If one man dangerously wound another, any person may arrest him, that he be safely kept, till it be known whether the person shall die or not. 4. Suspicion also, when it is violent and strong is in many cases a good cause of imprisonment, but he who arrests upon suspicion must take care that his cause of suspicion be such, as will bear the test, for otherwise he may be punishable for false imprisonment. 5. A watchman may arrest a night walker at unseasonable hours by the common law. But with respect to persons arrested by private authority, there must be an information on oath before a magistrate, and a commitment thereon in a reasonable time, which is esteemed twenty-four hours, otherwise the person is to be no longer detained. . . . It seems clear that an arrest if authorized by the statute or common law, though without writ or warrant in deed, has always been considered in *England* as warranted *per legem terræ*, by due process of law, within the meaning of *magna carta,* and we have no doubt, that any arrest here authorized by our common or statute law must be considered an arrest by the law of the land, by due process, within the meaning of our constitution. We think that the 15th article in our bill of rights, was not intended to abridge the power of the legislature, but to assert the right of every citizen to be secure from all arrests not warranted by law.

. . .

The second article of the bill of rights declares, that all men have certain natural, essential, inherent rights, among which are the enjoying and defending life and liberty, and acquiring, possessing and defending property; but the third article declares, that, when men enter into a state of society, they surrender up some of their natural rights to that society. All society is founded upon the principle, that each individual shall submit to the will of the whole. When we become members of society, then, we surrender our natural right, to be governed by our own wills in every case, where our own wills would lead us counter to the general will. We agree to conform our actions to the rules prescribed by the whole, and we agree to pay the forfeiture, which the general will may impose upon the violation of those rules, whether it be the loss of property, of liberty, or of life. Upon this agreement rests all legitimate government, and the general will duly expressed is alone law. The people of this state have formed a constitution in which they have agreed upon the manner in which the public will shall be expressed, and upon the extent, to which individuals shall surrender their natural rights: and the people being the fountain of all power, and the constitution their will duly expressed, it is clear that the constitution is a part of the law of the land paramount to all other laws.

By the constitution, the power to declare the general will is confided to a general court. "Full power and authority are hereby given and granted to said general court from time to time to make, ordain and establish all manner of wholesome and reasonable laws, statutes, ordinances, directions and instructions, either with penalties or without, so as the same be not repugnant or contrary to this constitution." The people of this state seem to have been extremely anxious that their natural rights should be surrendered only to the will of the whole, or in other words, to the law. It is therefore declared in the 12th article of the bill of rights that the inhabitants of this state are not controlable by any other laws than those to which they or their representative body have given their assent. The constitution is a part of the law of the land, made by the people themselves, and the constitution having declared that all laws which had been adopted and approved, and usually practised on in the courts of law should remain and be in force until altered by the legislature, the common and statute law in force before the adoption of the constitution may be considered as adopted and made by the people themselves. It is clear then that the people of this state are controlable only by the constitution, by the common and statute law adopted by the constitution and not altered, and by laws made by the general court in pursuance of the constitution. The last clause in the 15th article of the bill of rights only asserts the same thing. No subject shall be arrested, &c. but by the judgment of his peers or the law of the land. This clause may be thus analized. 1. No subject shall be arrested but by the law of the land: that is, by due process of law warranted by the constitution, by the common law adopted by the constitution and not altered, or by statutes made in pursuance of the constitution. Thus if the house of representatives were to commit or arrest a person for a contempt in their presence, it would be by process of law, expressly warranted by the constitution. If this court were to arrest a person for a contempt in its presence, it would be by process of law warranted by the common law adopted by the constitution. When an individual is arrested for travelling on Sunday, it is by process warranted by a statute made in pursuance of the constitution.

. . .

In giving a construction to the 19th article of the bill of rights it must be recollected that by the common law, which the constitution adopts, in certain cases of open and manifest guilt, and in some cases of strong suspicion an arrest might be made without a warrant, but in all other cases, a warrant founded upon a complaint under oath was required. In the cases where an arrest was permitted without a warrant, such an arrest was no more unreasonable and no more dangerous to personal liberty, than an arrest by a warrant, because it was not permitted but in cases where there was strong evidence of guilt.

The 19th article of the bill of rights does not seem intended to restrain the legislature from authorizing arrests without warrant, but to guard against the abuse of warrants issued by magistrates.

On the whole we are clearly of opinion that the act in question is not unconstitutional and that the plea is good.

C. Interrogations

Americans conducted criminal investigations and interrogations during the Early National Era much as they had done in the Founding and Colonial Eras. Criminal investigation remained largely informal and often private. A general consensus existed that persons could not be forced to answer under oath any questions that might incriminate or embarrass them. Supreme Court Justice James Iredell spoke for most Americans when in *United States v. Gooseley* (n.d.) he asserted that a witness under oath was "not bound to tell anything that might tend to criminate himself."[55] Confessions gained without oaths were admitted when judges determined that they were probably true. The Supreme Court of Pennsylvania in *State v. Guild* (PA 1828) maintained, "The question must turn, not on the possibility, but the presence of influence; not whether influence once existed, but, whether it continued to exert its force."[56]

D. Juries and Lawyers

Americans in the Early National Era loved juries a bit less than they had during the Colonial and Founding Eras. Most Americans who lived between 1789 and 1829 considered the jury trial the most important bulwark against tyranny. *Zylstra v. Corporation of City of Charleston* (SC 1794) gave the right to a jury trial "a rank among the first of those which belong to us as freemen."[57] Some elites were less certain. Prominent Federalist judges proposed limiting the traditional

---

55. *United States v. Gooseley*, 25 F. Cas. 1363, 1364 (C.C.D. Va.).

56. *State v. Guild*, 10 N.J.L. 163 (Sup. Ct. 1828).

57. *Zylstra v. Corporation of City of Charleston*, 1 S.C.L. (1 Bay), 382, 391–92 (S. C. Ct. Com. Pl. 1794).

role of the jury. Justice Samuel Chase in *United States v. Callender* (1800) opposed attempts to have the jury determine the constitutionality of the Sedition Act. Rejecting Andrew Hamilton's argument in the *Zenger* trial, Chase asserted, "The petit jury have no right to decide on the constitutionality of the statute on which the [defendant] is indicted."

Few Americans waxed as eloquent on lawyers as they did on juries. Still, the right to counsel gained ground. Political elites concluded that the rare criminal defendant who could afford an attorney had a right to hire that attorney. Zephaniah Swift, the leading constitutional commentator in Connecticut, regarded the right to counsel as a modern, liberal innovation. He asserted,

> Our ancestors, when they first enacted their laws respecting crimes, influenced by the illiberal principles which they had imbibed in their native country, denied counsel to prisoners to plead for them to anything but points of law. It is manifest that there is as much necessity for counsel to investigate matters of fact, as points of law, if truth is to be discovered.
>
> The legislature has become so thoroughly convinced of the impropriety and injustice of shackling and restricting a prisoner with respect to his defence, that they have abolished all those odious laws, and every person when he is accused of a crime, is entitled to every possible privilege in making his defence, and manifesting his innocence, by the instrumentality of counsel, and the testimony of witnesses.[58]

Swift in this passage was discussing the right to hire an attorney. Legal aid for persons who could not afford a lawyer was almost unheard of and not considered a constitutional right.

United States v. Callender, 25 F. Cas. 239 (C.C.D. Va. 1800)

James Callender was charged with violating the Sedition Act after he made such claims as: "The reign of Mr. Adams has been one continued tempest of malignant passions." During the course of the trial, his counsel asserted that the Sedition Act was unconstitutional and that juries had the right to determine the constitutionality of federal laws. Justice Samuel Chase immediately interrupted. Chase ruled that juries were not empowered to decide the constitutionality of legislation. That task was reserved for judicial determination.

The colloquy between Callender's defense attorneys and the judges highlight increasing controversies over the role of the jury in a criminal trial. During the eighteenth century, most Americans celebrated the right of juries to determine both law and fact. Federalists questioned whether juries should retain this power. In their view, professional judges were better suited to determine the law of a case than were amateur juries. Professional judges might also be more committed to upholding national laws than local juries. Jeffersonians disagreed. They regarded the jury as the best protection against federal oppression.

Compare how Callender's lawyers and Justice Chase understand the respective roles of judge and jury in a criminal trial. What do each see as the virtues of judges and juries? How do those virtues influence their understanding of their proper roles in a criminal trial? What are the vices and virtues of having juries determine the constitutionality of federal statutes?

Argument of GEORGE NICHOLAS:

First, that a law contrary to the constitution is void; and, secondly, that the jury have a right to consider the law and the fact. First, it seems to be admitted on all hands, that, when the legislature exercise a power not given them by the constitution, the judiciary will disregard their acts. The second point, that the jury have a right to decide the law and the fact, appears to me equally clear. In the exercise of the power of determining law and fact, a jury cannot be controlled by the court. . . .

. . . [I]f an act of congress contravene the constitution of the United States, a jury have a right to say that it is null, and that they will not give the efficacy of a law to an act which is void in itself; believing it to be contrary to the constitution, they will not convict any man of a violation of it; if this jury believed that the sedition act is not a law of the land, they cannot find the defendant guilty. The constitution secures to every man a fair and impartial trial by jury, in the district where the fact shall have been committed: and to preserve this sacred right unimpaired, it should never be interfered with. If ever a precedent is established, that the court can control the jury so as to prevent them from finding a general verdict, their important right, without which

58. Zephaniah Swift, *A System of Laws of the State of Connecticut* (Windham, CT: John Byrne, 1796), 2:398–99.

every other right is of no value, will be impaired, if not absolutely destroyed. Juries are to decide according to the dictates of conscience and the laws of the country, and to control them would endanger the right of this most invaluable mode of trial.

Opinion of JUSTICE CHASE:

. . .

. . . The petit jury, to discharge their duty, must first inquire, whether the traverser committed all or any of the facts alleged in the indictment to have been done by him, some time before the indictment. If they find that he did commit all or any of the said facts, their next inquiry is, whether the doing such facts have been made criminal and punishable by the statute of the United States, on which the traverser is indicted. . . . By this provision, I understand that a right is given to the jury to determine what the law is in the case before them; and not to decide whether a statute of the United States produced to them, is a law or not, or whether it is void, under an opinion that it is unconstitutional, that is, contrary to the constitution of the United States. . . . It is one thing to decide what the law is, on the facts proved, and another and a very different thing, to determine that the statute produced is no law. . . .

. . . Was it ever intended, by the framers of the constitution, or by the people of America, that it should ever be submitted to the examination of a jury, to decide what restrictions are expressly or impliedly imposed by it on the national legislature? I cannot possibly believe that congress intended, by the statute, to grant a right to a petit jury to declare a statute void. . . .

. . . If a petit jury can rightfully exercise this power over one statute of congress, they must have an equal right and power over any other statute, and indeed over all the statutes; for no line can be drawn, no restriction imposed on the exercise of such power; it must rest in discretion only. If this power be once admitted, petit jurors will be superior to the national legislature, and its laws will be subject to their control. The power to abrogate or to make laws nugatory, is equal to the authority of making them. The evident consequences of this right in juries will be, that a law of congress will be in operation in one state and not in another. A law to impose taxes will be obeyed in one state, and not in another, unless force be employed to compel submission. The doing certain acts will be held criminal, and punished in one state, and similar acts may be held innocent, and even approved and applauded in another. The effects of the exercise of this power by petit jurors may be readily conceived. It appears to me that the right now claimed has a direct tendency to dissolve the union of the United States, on which, under Divine Providence, our political safety, happiness, and prosperity depend.

. . .

[T]he judicial power of the United States is the only proper and competent authority to decide whether any statute made by congress (or any of the state legislatures) is contrary to, or in violation of, the federal constitution. . . . No position can be more clear than that all the federal judges are bound by the solemn obligation of religion, to regulate their decisions agreeably to the constitution of the United States, and that it is the standard of their determination in all cases that come before them. I believe that it has been the general and prevailing opinion in all the Union, that the power now wished to be exercised by a jury, properly belonged to the federal courts. . . . It is now contended, that the constitutionality of the laws of congress should be submitted to the decision of a petit jury. May I ask, whence this change of opinion? I declare that the doctrine is entirely novel to me, and that I never heard of it before my arrival in this city. It appears to me to be not only new, but very absurd and dangerous, in direct opposition to, and a breach of the constitution. . . . It must be evident, that decisions in the district or circuit courts of the United States will be uniform, or they will become so by the revision and correction of the supreme court; and thereby the same principles will pervade all the Union; but the opinions of petit juries will very probably be different in different states.

The decision of courts of justice will not be influenced by political and local principles, and prejudices. If inferior courts commit error, it may be rectified; but if juries make mistakes, there can be no revision or control over their verdicts, and therefore, there can be no mode to obtain uniformity in their decisions. Besides, petit juries are under no obligation by the terms of their oath, to decide the constitutionality of any law; their determination, therefore, will be extra judicial. . . .

E. Punishments

Constitutional authorities interpreted "cruel and unusual punishment" provisions in state constitutions by looking at common law practice. Controversies broke out over how to determine the common law. Some constitutional decision makers interpreted the common and constitutional law to be relatively unchanging. The Supreme Court of Virginia in *Commonwealth v. Wyatt* (VA 1828) permitted a convicted person to be repeatedly whipped on the ground that whipping was not unknown to the common law. "The punishment of offences by stripes is certainly odious," the justices decreed, "but cannot be said to be *unusual*."[59] Other constitutional decision makers interpreted the common and constitutional law to be more capable of growth. In *James v. Commonwealth* (PA 1825), the Supreme Court of Pennsylvania looked to more recent common law developments when determining that ducking women in the river was an unconstitutional punishment. "[T]his customary ancient punishment for ducking scolds," the justices stated, "was never adopted, and therefore, is not the common law of Pennsylvania."

James v. Commonwealth, 12 Serg. & Rawle 220 (PA 1825)

Nancy James was convicted by a trial court in Philadelphia of being a common scold. The court ordered that she "be placed in a certain engine of correction, called a cucking or ducking-stool . . . and being so placed therein, to be plunged three times into the water." James appealed this judgment, claiming that ducking women in the river violated both the Constitution of the United States and the Pennsylvania Constitution.

The Supreme Court of Pennsylvania determined that ducking violated the state constitution. How does Justice Duncan reach that conclusion? To what extent does he rely on English common law? To what extent does he rely on contemporary practice in Pennsylvania? Do you read James v. Commonwealth *as consistent with a living constitution or with claims that constitutional rights are determined by practice at the time that constitutional rights are ratified?*

JUSTICE DUNCAN delivered the opinion of the Court.

The judgment was, "that the defendant be placed in a ducking or cucking-stool, and be plunged three times in the water." This sentence, we are informed, has created much ferment and excitement in the public mind; it is considered as a cruel, unusual, unnatural and ludicrous judgment; but whatever prejudices may exist against it, still, if it be the law of the land, the court must pronounce judgment for it. But, as it is revolting to humanity, and is of that description that only could have been invented in an age of barbarism, we ought to be well persuaded, either that it is the appropriate judgment of the common law, or is inflicted by some positive law; and that that common law or statutory provision has been adopted here, and is now in force. . . .

It must strike all, as a peculiar feature of this offence, that it is of the feminine gender, that it degraded woman to a mere *thing*, to a *nuisance*, and does not consider her as a person. But this is not to be wondered at, when we reflect on the general degraded state of woman, when this punishment was introduced; she was, in some respects, the servant or slave of the husband; so that he might correct her with a stick as thick as his own thumb. . . .

. . .

The instances are numerous of statutes being repealed in fact—a kind of silent legislation. As to the abrogation of statutes by *"non user,"* there may rest some doubt; for myself, I own, my opinion is, that *"non user"* may be such as to render them obsolete, when their objects vanish or their reason ceases. The common law (and this is but a customary punishment), what is it, but common usage? The long desuetude of any law amounts to its repeal. . . . It certainly requires very strong grounds to presume a law obsolete, yet as the whole community includes as well the legislative power as its subjects, total disuse of any civil institution for ages past, may afford just and rational objections against disrespected and superannuated ordinances. . . .

. . .

I do not know that all the members of the court agree with me in the conclusion, as to the abrogation of this punishment in England, by disuse; but in the inquiry most important, there is no difference of opinion. We all agree in this, that this customary ancient punishment for ducking scolds, was never adopted, and therefore, is not the common law of Pennsylvania.

. . .

It is not true, that our ancestors brought with them all the common-law offences. . . . Our ancestors, when they emigrated, took with them such of the English principles as were convenient for the situation in which they were about to place themselves. By degrees, as circumstances demanded, we adopted the English usages, or substituted others better suited to our wants; until,

59. *Commonwealth v. Wyatt*, 6 Rand. 694 (VA 1828).

before the revolution, we had formed a system of our own, founded, in general, on the English constitution, but not without considerable variation; and in nothing was the variation greater, than in the trial and punishment of crimes. . . .

Here, all our legislation has been opposed to this punishment; judicial decisions there are none. . . .

. . . Since 1782, until the last case in the mayor's court, forty years ran round, and there has been no instance of this punishment. There has been one of an acquittal; that case, therefore, proves nothing.

. . .

In coming to the conclusion, that the ducking-stool is not the punishment of scolds, I do not take into consideration the humane provisions of the constitutions of the United States and of this state, as to cruel and unusual punishments, further than they show the sense of the whole community. If the reformation of the culprit, and prevention of the crime, be the just foundation and object of all punishments, nothing could be further removed from these salutary ends, than the infliction in question. It destroys all personal respect; the women thus punished would scold on for life, and the exhibition would be far from being beneficial to the spectators. What a spectacle would it exhibit! what a congregation of the idle and disordely, of black and white spirits! and the day would produce more *scolding,* in this polite city, than would otherwise take place in a year. The city is rescued from this ignominious and odious show, and the state from the opprobrium of the continuance of so barbarous an institution; which would pluck from the brow of our legislators, that diadem of humanity, which the civilized world has awarded. The courts of our sister states of New York and Massachusetts, governed by the same common law as we are, have declared that this strange and ludicrous punishment no longer exists with them. . . .

F. Infamous Crimes and Criminals

The Burr Trial

The first "trial of the century" in U.S. history took place after former Vice President Aaron Burr was arrested on January 16, 1807, in Natchez, Mississippi, and accused of treason. Aaron Burr was the most notorious politician of the early republic. During the 1790s he was a senator from New York, a member of the New York legislature, and Jefferson's "running mate" in the 1796 and 1800 presidential election. We place "running mate" in quotes because presidential electors before 1804 cast their ballots for two persons. When every member of the Jefferson majority in 1800 cast their ballots for Jefferson and Burr, the presidential election was officially tied. Republicans assumed that Burr would defer to Jefferson. He did not. Worse, Burr said nothing when prominent Federalists urged fellow partisans to support him for the presidency. This effort failed, and after some very nervous moments, the House of Representatives chose Jefferson. For not stepping aside, Burr became a political outcast among Republicans. As his vice-presidential term was ending, Burr sought elective office in New York but was thwarted by Alexander Hamilton. The Federalist leader publicly declared that Burr was a scoundrel who had engaged in "despicable" conduct. Burr challenged Hamilton to a duel. On July 11, 1804, Burr mortally wounded the former secretary of the treasury and Federalist leader. This ruined Burr's political standing among Federalists

Seeking to recoup his financial and political fortunes, Burr went to the American West, which was then Kentucky, Louisiana, and Mississippi. What Burr did between 1805 and 1806 is not clear. We know that he raised money to organize a group of armed men. President Jefferson was convinced that Burr intended to deploy those men to separate the American West from the rest of the United States—a crime that would be considered treason. Other evidence indicates that Burr intended to attack Spanish territories in Central America—a violation of American neutrality laws. Burr claimed that he intended only to attack Spanish territories in the event of a war between the United States and Spain, an act that might have been legal. One commentator suggests that, anticipating the movie and Broadway hit *The Producers*, Burr planned to pocket the money raised for vague plots that he knew were flights of fancy.[60]

Burr was arrested in 1807 and charged with treason. Many leading political luminaries participated in his trial. President Jefferson helped direct the prosecution, and Caesar Rodney, the attorney general of the United States, ran the prosecution. Burr was defended by a dream team of the early American bar. His

60. Peter Charles Hoffer, *The Treason Trials of Aaron Burr* (Lawrence: University Press of Kansas, 2008), 191.

lawyers included Charles Lee, a prominent Federalist attorney who had previously argued *Marbury v. Madison*; Luther Martin, a former member of the drafting convention of 1787; and John Randolph, a former Jeffersonian leader in the House of Representatives. Burr's trial was presided over by Chief Justice John Marshall in his capacity as circuit court judge. Jefferson and Marshall had a longstanding feud that predated Jefferson's presidency and Marshall's assumption of the chief justiceship. The events of the Burr trial increased the antipathy between the two.

The Burr treason trials consisted of two distinct legal proceedings. The first, *Ex parte Bollman* (1807), was a habeas corpus proceeding held before the Supreme Court of the United States. The Court concluded:

1. The Supreme Court may issue writs of habeas corpus only when authorized by federal legislation.
2. Conspiracy to commit treason is not treason as defined in the Constitution.

The second proceeding, *United States v. Burr*, was the treason trial of Aaron Burr that took place in the federal circuit court of Virginia with Chief Justice Marshall presiding. The Supreme Court in that case concluded:

1. A defendant in a criminal case has a constitutional right to have the court issue a subpoena to the president of the United States.
2. Judges determine when witnesses may refuse to answer questions on the ground that the answer may incriminate them.
3. The Sixth Amendment permits the seating of a juror who has formed an opinion about the case as long as the juror's mind is open to reaching a contrary conclusion.
4. The prosecution in a treason trial must prove the actual use of military force.
5. Hearsay evidence violates the confrontation clause of the Sixth Amendment.

In part because Chief Justice Marshall resolved most issues against the government, Burr's confederates were released and Burr was found not guilty.

As you read the materials below, consider whether Marshall applied neutral principles of law to fend off politically motivated convictions or acted as a partisan interested in weakening the Jefferson administration. Jefferson, after the trial ended, suggested that Congress might consider impeaching the chief justice. Did that attempt have any merit?

United States v. Burr, 25 F. Cas. 30 (C.C.Va. 1807)

The prosecution in the Burr trial called several witnesses who described what had happened on Blennerhasset Island on December 9, 1806. This testimony was crucial. The indictment charged Burr with assembling men in that spot for the purpose of levying war against the United States. Burr's lawyers insisted that this testimony was inadmissible. Burr could not constitutionally be found guilty of treason, they declared, because no witness saw Burr on Blennerhasset Island on December 9, 1806, and no witness could testify that any military force was used at that time and place. The prosecution agreed that no witness placed Burr on Blennerhasset Island and that no military force was used at that time and place. Nevertheless, prosecuting attorneys contended that the evidence was relevant because the men assembled on Blennerhasset Island were part of a conspiracy to wage war against the United States. Treason, in their view, could be committed without Burr's actual presence or an actual demonstration of military force.

Chief Justice Marshall ruled inadmissible the evidence of what happened on Blennethasset Island. He insisted that the constitutional definition of treason required the prosecution to prove an actual use or show of military force. If the men on Blennerhasset Island were merely planning an attack, they might be guilty of conspiracy, but not treason. What reasons did Marshall give for concluding that a conspiracy to commit treason is not treason? Marshall maintained that the opinions in Burr *and* Ex parte Bollman *(1807) are consistent. In* Bollman, *Marshall ruled that a person not present when the treasonous act occurred could be constitutionally prosecuted for treason. Is this consistent with his* Burr *opinion?*

CHIEF JUSTICE MARSHALL delivered the opinion of the Court.

. . .

. . . [W]e should probably all concur in the declaration that war could not be levied without the employment and exhibition of force. War is an appeal from reason to the sword; and he who makes the appeal evidences the fact by the use of the means. His intention to go to war may be proved by words; but the actual going to war is a fact which is to be proved by open deed. The end is to be effected by force; and it would seem that in cases where no declaration is to be made, the state of actual war could only be created by the employment of force, or being in a condition to employ it. But the term, having been adopted by our constitution, must be understood in that sense in which it was universally received in this country when the constitution was framed. The sense in which it was received is to be collected from the most approved authorities of that nation from which we have borrowed the term. Lord Coke says that levying war against the king was treason at the common law. "A compassing or conspiracy to levy war, he adds, is no treason, for there must be a levying of war in fact." . . .

. . .

But it is said all these authorities have been overruled by the decision of the supreme court in the case of [*Ex parte Bollman* (1807)]. . . . In the case of the *United States against Bollman and Swartwout*, there was no evidence that even two men had ever met for the purpose of executing the plan in which those persons were charged with having participated. It was, therefore, sufficient for the court to say that unless men were assembled, war could not be levied. That case was decided by this declaration. The court might indeed have defined the species of assemblage which would amount to levying of war; but, as this opinion was not a treatise on treason, but a decision of a particular case, expressions of doubtful import should be construed in reference of the case itself, and the mere omission to state that a particular circumstance was necessary to the consummation of the crime ought not to be construed into a declaration that the circumstance was unimportant. General expressions ought not to be considered as overruling settled principles, without a direct declaration to that effect. After these preliminary observations, the court will proceed to examine the opinion which has occasioned them.

The first expression in it bearing on the present question is, "To constitute that specific crime for which the prisoner now before the court has been committed, war must be actually levied against the United States. However flagitious may be the crime of conspiracy to subvert by force the government of our country, such conspiracy is not treason. To conspire to levy war and actually to levy war are distinct offences. The first must be brought into operation by the assemblage of men for a purpose treasonable in itself, or the fact of levying war cannot have been committed." Although it is not expressly stated that the assemblage of men for the purpose of carrying into operation the treasonable intent which will amount to levying war must be an assemblage in force, yet it is fairly to be inferred from the context; and nothing like dispensing with force appears in this paragraph. The expressions are, "to constitute the crime, war must be actually levied." A conspiracy to levy war is spoken of as "a conspiracy to subvert by force the government of our country." Speaking in general terms of an assemblage of men for this or for any other purpose, a person would naturally be understood as speaking of an assemblage in some degree adapted to the purpose. An assemblage to subvert by force the government of our country, and amounting to a levying of war, should be an assemblage in force. . . . "A body of men actually assembled, in order to effect by force a treasonable purpose," must be a body assembled with such appearance of force as would warrant the opinion that they were assembled for the particular purpose. An assemblage to constitute an actual levying of war should be an assemblage with such appearance of force as would justify the opinion that they met for the purpose. . . .

. . .

That opinion [in *Ex parte Bollman*] is, that an individual may be guilty of treason "who has not appeared in arms against his country; that if war be actually levied, that is, if a body of men be actually assembled for the purpose of effecting by force a treasonable object, all those who perform any part, however minute, or however remote from the scene of action, and who are actually leagued in the general conspiracy, are to be considered as traitors." This opinion does not touch the case of a person who advises or procures an assemblage, and does nothing further. The advising, certainly, and perhaps the procuring, is more in the nature of a conspiracy to levy war than of the actual levying of war. According to the opinion, it is not enough to be leagued in the conspiracy, and that war be levied, but it is also necessary to perform a part: that part is the act of levying war. That part, it is true, may be minute, it may not be the actual appearance in arms, and it may be remote from the scene of action, that is, from the place where the army is assembled; but it must be a part, and that part must be performed by a person who is leagued in the conspiracy. This part, however minute or remote, constitutes the overt act of which alone the person who performs it can be convicted. The opinion does not declare that the person who has performed this remote and minute part may be indicted for a part which was, in truth, performed by others, and convicted on their overt acts. It amounts to this and nothing more, that when war is actually levied, not only those who bear arms, but those also who are leagued in the conspiracy, and who perform the various distinct parts which are necessary for the prosecution of war, do, in the sense of the constitution, levy war. . . .

It is, then, the opinion of the court that this indictment can be supported only by testimony which proves the accused to have been actually or constructively present when the assemblage took place on Blennerhassett's Island; or by the admission of the doctrine that he who procures an act may be indicted as having performed that act.

It is further the opinion of the court that there is no testimony whatever which tends to prove that the accused was actually or constructively present when that assemblage did take place; indeed, the contrary is most apparent. . . .

. . . The present indictment charges the prisoner with levying war against the United States, and alleges an overt act of levying war. That overt act must be proved, according to the mandates of the constitution and of the act of congress, by two witnesses. It is not proved by a single witness. The presence of the accused has been stated to be an essential component part of the overt act in this indictment, unless the common law principle respecting accessories should render it unnecessary; and there is not only no witness who has proved his actual or legal presence, but the fact of his absence is not controverted. The counsel for the prosecution offer to give in evidence subsequent transactions at a different place and in a different state, in order to prove—what? The overt act laid in the indictment? That the prisoner was one of those who assembled at Blennerhassett's Island? No: that is not alleged. It is well known that such testimony is not competent to establish such a fact. The constitution and law require that the fact should be established by two witnesses; not by the establishment of other facts from which the jury might reason to this fact. The testimony, then, is not relevant. . . .

. . . No testimony relative to the conduct or declarations of the prisoner elsewhere, and subsequent to the transaction on Blennerhassett's Island, can be admitted; because such testimony, being in its nature merely corroborative and incompetent to prove the overt act in itself, is irrelevant until there be proof of the overt act by two witnesses. This opinion does not comprehend the proof by two witnesses that the meeting on Blennerhassett's Island was procured by the prisoner. On that point the court for the present withholds its opinion for reasons which have been already assigned; and as it is understood from the statements made on the part of the prosecution that no such testimony exists, if there be such let it be offered, and the court will decide upon it.

Suggested Readings

Banning, Lance. *The Sacred Fire of Liberty: James Madison and the Founding of the American Republic* (Ithaca, NY: Cornell University Press, 1995).

Cornell, Saul. *The Other Founders: Anti-Federalism and the Dissenting Tradition in America, 1788–1828* (Chapel Hill: University of North Carolina Press, 1999).

Currie, David P. *The Constitution in Congress: The Federalist Period, 1789–1801* (Chicago: University of Chicago Press, 2001).

Currie, David P. *The Constitution in Congress: The Jeffersonians* (Chicago: University of Chicago Press, 2001).

Elkins, Stanley, and Eric McKitrick. *The Age of Federalism: The Early American Republic, 1788–1800* (New York: Oxford University Press, 2001).

Hoffer, Peter Charles. *The Treason Trials of Aaron Burr* (Lawrence: University Press of Kansas, 2008).

Levy, Leonard W. *Emergence of a Free Press* (New York: Oxford University Press, 1985).

Magrath, C. Peter. *Yazoo: Law and Politics in the New Republic: The Case of* Fletcher v. Peck (New York: W. W. Norton & Company, 1967).

Mayer, David N. *The Constitutional Thought of Thomas Jefferson* (Charlottesville: University of Virginia Press, 1994).

Newmyer, R. Kent. *John Marshall and the Heroic Age of the Supreme Court* (Baton Rouge: Louisiana State University Press, 2002).

Rosenfeld, Richard N. *American Aurora: A Democratic-Republican Returns* (New York: St. Martin's Griffin, 1997).

Van Cleve, George. *A Slaveholder's Union: Slavery, Politics, and the Constitution in the Early American Republic* (Chicago: University of Chicago Press, 2010).

White, G. Edward. *The Marshall Court and Cultural Change, 1815–1835* (New York: Oxford University Press, 1988).

Chapter 5

The Jacksonian Era: 1829–1860

I. Introduction

Americans experienced a democratic revolution between 1828 and 1860. Jacksonians proclaimed that the Constitution of the United States was committed to democracy and equality. The 1844 Democratic Party platform spoke of such "cardinal principles in the democratic faith" as "a clear reliance upon the intelligence, patriotism, and the discriminating justice of the American masses." In an 1832 veto message, President Andrew Jackson declared, "If [government] would confine itself to equal protection, and, as Heaven does its rains, shower its favors alike on the high and the low, the rich and the poor, it would be an unqualified blessing."

The most important constitutional controversies over rights in Jacksonian America were over what constitutional commitments to democracy and equality meant in practice. Senator Stephen Douglas of Illinois insisted that the constitutional commitment to democracy justified granting the settlers in every American territory the power to decide whether to permit slavery. Abraham Lincoln responded that this conception of popular sovereignty violated the more important constitutional commitment to human equality. Other political actors, championing such causes as temperance, nativism, and women's suffrage, pointed to the dual Jacksonian commitments to democracy and equality when justifying their preferred policies.

Middle- and lower-middle-class white men were the primary beneficiaries of the Jacksonian constitutional commitments to democracy and equality. Most states adopted (near) universal male suffrage. State courts declared laws that gave special privileges to some men unconstitutional. The same constitutional decision makers often informed women, free persons of color, Native Americans, and (sometimes) aliens that real differences between them and white Americans justified imposing distinct liabilities on the basis of gender, race, and ethnicity.

Parties. The first mass political parties in American history organized during the Jacksonian Era. By 1838 two political parties, the Whigs and the Democrats, competed throughout the country. Democrats and Whigs battled as equals in state and congressional elections, but Democrats won six of the eight presidential elections held between 1828 and 1856. Democrats then used their control over the White House to gain control of the federal judiciary. Roger Taney, chief justice of the United States from 1836 to 1864, was a member of Andrew Jackson's cabinet before being appointed to the Court. A majority of justices on the Supreme Court from 1835 until the 1860s were Democratic appointees with substantial experience in electoral politics.

In national elections, Democrats and Whigs emphasized issues of government power. Whigs favored a national bank, high tariffs, and internal improvements. Jacksonians maintained that all these policies were either unconstitutional or unsound. The parties also disputed some national rights and liberties issues. Democrat demands that Native American tribes be removed to regions west of the Mississippi triumphed over Whig opposition. Northern Whigs were more anti-slavery than northern Jacksonians. When slavery was debated during the 1840s and 1850s, however, section was more important than partisan identities.

During the 1850s the Whigs collapsed and the Republican Party was organized. Unlike either Democrats or Whigs, Republicans took a firm anti-slavery stand. Policies such as banning slavery in the territories, Abraham Lincoln and his political allies insisted,

Figure 5-1 Partisan Control of the U.S. Government, 1829–60

placed slavery "on a course of ultimate extinction."[1] Unlike either Democrats or Whigs, Republicans ignored the other rights issues that wracked antebellum America. They refused to be identified with either temperance or nativist movements, although the party platform in 1856 condemned Mormon polygamy in the territories.

Slavery issues dominated the constitutional rights agenda of Jacksonian America. Constitutional debates over slavery included the free speech rights of anti-slavery advocates, whether Congress was bound by the Bill of Rights when regulating slavery in the territories, whether laws prohibiting slavery in the territories violated the property rights of slaveholders, whether fugitive slaves had rights to habeas corpus and jury trials, and whether free persons of color were state and national citizens. These debates over slavery influenced and were influenced by other constitutional rights and liberties controversies. Anti-slavery advocates abandoned schemes for a gradual emancipation in favor of immediatism after witnessing the tragic consequences of Native American removal in the 1830s. The movement for women's rights began when anti-slavery women were barred from participating in an anti-slavery conference.

Other constitutional controversies over rights arose more often in state and local settings than in national politics. Whigs before the Civil War emphasized Protestant moral virtues and favored government support for Protestant religion, as well as various measures directly or indirectly aimed at Catholics. Many, influenced by a religious revival known as the Second Great Awakening, supported temperance, if not prohibition. Jacksonians favored more limited government and cultural diversity, at least with respect to white citizens. Local Democrats sided with Catholics and immigrants against mainstream and evangelical Protestants who wished to curb their drinking and gambling habits. Whigs favored property qualifications for voters; Democrats championed universal male suffrage. These local politics generated diverse policies on personal freedoms, guns, religion, and the rights of criminal suspects. States adopted different policies toward drinking, different state counties instituted different temperance policies, and those policies changed over time.

Interest Groups. Jacksonian democracy spawned numerous political movements. Americans organized to abolish slavery, emancipate women, prohibit drinking, limit immigration, and advance numerous other causes. Such public interest groups as the American Temperance Society and the American Anti-Slavery Society established chapters in many states. Women played a major role in many political movements. Social reform movements such as the temperance crusade, which sought to reform American drinking habits, were deeply religious.

1. Abraham Lincoln, *Political Debates between Abraham Lincoln and Stephen A. Douglas in the Celebrated Campaign of 1858 in Illinois* (Cleveland, OH: O. S. Hubbell and Co., 1895), 2.

Box 5-1 A Partial Cast of Characters of the Jacksonian Era

Andrew Jackson	■ Democrat ■ Brief political career in Tennessee ■ Popular military leader in War of 1812 and Seminole wars in Georgia and Spanish Florida ■ Lost controversial presidential election of 1824 that was settled in the House of Representatives ■ President of the United States (1829–37) ■ Leader of the Democratic Party ■ Advocate of presidential power, nationalism, popular democracy, and strict constructionism
Roger Taney	■ Democrat ■ Entered politics as a Maryland Federalist ■ U.S. attorney general under Democrat Andrew Jackson (1831–33) ■ Authored important presidential papers, including Bank Veto message ■ U.S. secretary of treasury under Jackson (1833–34) ■ Nomination as associate justice defeated by Whig Senate; confirmed as chief justice by Democratic Senate to succeed John Marshall (1836–64) ■ Advocate of states' rights and strict constructionism; known as a defender of slave interests, especially as author of *Dred Scott* decision
Daniel Webster	■ Whig ■ Began career as Massachusetts Federalist ■ Member of the U.S. House of Representatives (1813–17, 1823–27) ■ Member of U.S. Senate (1827–41, 1845–50) ■ Whig candidate for president in 1836 ■ U.S. secretary of state under several Whig presidents (1841–43, 1850–52) ■ Leading Supreme Court litigator and advocate of property rights, national union, and broad construction of congressional powers
Lemuel Shaw	■ Whig ■ Member of Massachusetts state legislature (1811–14, 1820–22, 1829) ■ Member of Massachusetts state constitutional convention of 1820 ■ Chief justice of the Massachusetts Supreme Court (1830–60) ■ Decided many influential race- and slavery-related cases ■ Provided a significant early definition of the police power
Benjamin R. Curtis	■ Whig ■ Student of Justice Joseph Story and protégé of Daniel Webster ■ Argued a prominent anti-slavery case in the Supreme Judicial Court of Massachusetts ■ Member of Massachusetts state legislature (1849–51) ■ Associate justice of U.S. Supreme Court (1851–57) ■ Authored key dissent in *Dred Scott* case ■ Critic of presidential power during Lincoln administration ■ Served as chief counsel to President Andrew Johnson during his impeachment

(*Continued*)

Box 5-1 *(Continued)*

Elizabeth Cady Stanton	▪ Social activist ▪ Organizer of Seneca Falls Conference of 1848 ▪ Author of Declaration of Sentiments urging women's rights ▪ Founder of Women's State Temperance Society in 1852 ▪ Advocate of universal suffrage after the Civil War ▪ Founder of National Woman Suffrage Association in 1869

The French visitor Alexis de Tocqueville famously commented in *Democracy in America* on the American propensity for forming associations whenever confronted with political problems. He wrote:

> In no country in the world has the principle of association been more successfully used, or applied to a greater multitude of objects, than in America. . . .
>
> . . . If some public pleasure is concerned, an association is formed to give more splendor and regularity to the entertainment. Societies are formed to resist evils which are exclusively of a moral nature, as to diminish the vice of intemperance. In the United States, associations are established to promote the public safety, commerce, industry, morality, and religion. There is no end which the human will despairs of attaining through the combined power of individuals united into a society.[2]

These political movements were distinct from the major national political parties of Jacksonian America. Prominent members of both major parties served on the national board of the American Temperance Society. The American Anti-Slavery Society remained suspicious of the Republican Party, a coalition that many abolitionists regarded as far too moderate. Frequently, members of political movements formed third parties, which sometimes siphoned crucial votes away from Democrats and Whigs. The Free Soil and Liberty Parties were anti-slavery. The American Party was anti-immigrant.

Courts. Slavery was the only rights issue that received substantial national judicial attention during the Jacksonian Era. Moderate Jacksonian and Whig leaders sought to promote the courts as the proper forum for resolving such bitterly divisive issues as the procedures for recovering fugitive slaves and the status of slavery in the territories. The resulting Supreme Court

Illustration 5-1 Woman's Holy War
Voluntary temperance in the consumption of alcohol and the legal prohibition of the sale and possession of alcohol were among the popular causes pursued by new social movements and interest groups beginning in the early decades of the nineteenth century. Many of these reform organizations were inspired by religion and led by women. The laws that emerged from these efforts raised a variety of new constitutional questions on issues ranging from property rights to criminal processes.

Source: New York: Published by Currier & Ives, c. 1874. Library of Congress Prints and Photographs Division, Washington, DC 20540, USA.

2. Alexis de Tocqueville, *Democracy in America*, ed. Francis Bowen (Cambridge, MA: Sever and Francis, 1862), 1:242–43.

Table 5-1 Major Rights and Liberties Issues and Decisions of the Jacksonian Era

Major Political Issues	Major Constitutional Issues	Major Court Decisions
Rise of Mass Political Parties	State Courts Restrict "Class Legislation"	*Barron v. Baltimore* (1833)
Attacks on Special Privileges	Applicability of Federal Bill of Rights to the States and Territories	*Proprietors of the Charles River Bridge v. Proprietors of the Warren Bridge* (1837)
Second Great Awakening	Decline of Contract Clause Restrictions on States	*Roberts v. City of Boston* (MA 1849)
Slavery	Due Process Protections for Property Rights	*Commonwealth v. Anthes* (MA 1855)
Mexican War	Debate Over Right to Drink	*Wynehamer v. People* (NY 1856)
Abolitionism	Fugitive Slave Clause	*Dred Scott v. Sandford* (1857)
Fugitive Slave Act of 1850	Religious Liberty	*Ableman v. Booth* (1859)
Native American Removal	Funding for Parochial School	
Temperance	Debate Over Anti-Slavery Petitions and Speech	
Nativism	Suffrage and Property Qualifications	
Women's Rights Movement	Scope of Search and Seizure Powers	
	Limits on Power of Juries to Decide Questions of Law	

decisions in *Prigg v. Pennsylvania* (1842), which sustained the Fugitive Slave Act of 1793, and *Dred Scott v. Sandford* (1857), which declared unconstitutional the Missouri Compromise, expressed the pro-slavery and racist constitutional principles that were shared by many, although not all, Jacksonian Era elites.

Democrats and Whigs preferred to resolve most rights issues, and even some slavery issues, outside of federal courts. No federal court adjudicated the right to petition Congress to free slaves in the District of Columbia or the right to mail abolitionist pamphlets. During controversies over nativism, immigration, and temperance, federal courts resolved only relatively peripheral issues. Congress determined whether the post office could deliver abolitionists' pamphlets in the South and whether Michigan could permit aliens to vote in federal elections. Women directed their demands for equality toward elected officials, not judges. State and local officials determined whether Catholic schools could receive public funds.

State courts played a more important role in resolving rights and liberties questions. After state legislatures passed measures limiting religious freedom, curbing anti-slavery advocacy, prohibiting concealed weapons, or mandating prayer in school, opponents often turned to local courts for redress. Many state courts played activist roles, striking down legislation as violating civil rights clauses in the state constitution. Both Democrats and Whigs could become judicial activists, depending on the issue before the court.

Constitutional Thought. Democrats and Whigs refined a distinctive nineteenth-century framework for thinking about constitutional rights and liberties. Americans from the Founding Era until the New Deal treated what contemporary Americans consider constitutional rights claims as issues of government powers. Constitutional decision makers considering official actions restricting religious liberty or property rights first assessed whether the contested regulation (a) served some legitimate government purpose to promote the health, safety, and morality of the community as a whole (the definition of the states' inherent "police powers") and (b) was not merely an arbitrary (unjustifiable) attempt to bestow special burdens or benefits on particular groups. If they concluded that a law limiting drinking protected the public health, the legislation was constitutional. If they determined that state officials had acted with the purpose of restricting liberty or sought to benefit one class at the expense of another, the law was declared unconstitutional. This practice was not uniform. Nevertheless, constitutional decision makers were far more likely to understand rights as the residuum of legitimate government power than as a trump against otherwise legitimate government power.[3]

Legacies. The Jacksonian Era witnessed the birth of a distinctive American constitutional politics. While many social movements and public interest groups that flourished before the Civil War have not survived, their influence on the constitutional politics of rights and liberties has become an enduring feature of the American constitutional order. From the Jacksonian Era to the present, social movements and public interest groups have had substantial influence on constitutional debates over most rights and liberties. National elections are usually fought over the economy or foreign policy. Social movements championing abolitionism, prohibition, women's suffrage, the freedom of the press, and the right to bear arms ensure that controversies over rights and liberties are always on the national and local agendas.

The thirty years before the Civil War introduced Americans to the politics of "rum, Romanism, and rebellion." Northern Whigs, later Republicans, favored temperance, believed government should inculcate Protestant virtues, and condemned rights violations in the South. Democrats opposed temperance ("rum"), championed the rights of Catholics ("Romanism"), and tended to support the South on racial issues ("rebellion"). Although the Civil War eventually ended slavery, the basic cultural cleavages that formed in the Jacksonian Era structured constitutional politics for the rest of the nineteenth century.

The Jacksonian Era is often viewed as a vital negative reference point in American constitutionalism. Americans claim that such Colonial, Founding, and Early National Era landmarks as the *Zenger Case*, the Virginia Statute of Religious Freedom, and *Marbury v. Madison* (1803) provided important foundations for enduring constitutional practices. Americans more often regard such constitutional decisions as *Barron v. Baltimore* (1833), which ruled that the states are not bound by the federal Bill of Rights, and *Dred Scott* as mistaken precedents that required later constitutional corrections. The Republicans who framed the post–Civil War Amendments were determined to create a constitutional order that did not repeat such injustices of the Jacksonian Era as slavery, bans on anti-slavery speech, and Native American removal. This anti-slavery opposition to the dominant lines of Jacksonian constitutionalism before the Civil War helps explain the constitutional choices that Republicans made after peace was established in 1865.

3. See Howard Gillman, *The Constitution Besieged: The Rise and Demise of Lochner Era Police Powers Jurisprudence* (Durham: Duke University Press, 1993).

II. Foundations

MAJOR DEVELOPMENTS

- Broad celebration of constitutional liberties
- Disputes over the constitutional status of slavery
- Bill of Rights limits only the federal government

Jacksonians were a generation removed from the persons responsible for the U.S. Constitution. Such political leaders as George Washington, Thomas Jefferson, James Madison, and John Marshall interpreted the texts that they helped frame or ratify, and close personal relationships formed during the 1770s and 1780s sometimes eased the partisan tensions that developed during the Early National Era. Besides John Quincy Adams, no prominent Jacksonian Era political leader participated in the American Revolution, helped frame the Constitution, or had close ties to the framers. The politicians and judges who debated the constitutional status of slavery in the territories were not present at the nation's creation. Andrew Jackson and Henry Clay had no shared experiences on which they could draw when partisan conflicts threatened to disrupt alliances between national political leaders.

Americans in the Jacksonian Era regarded the Constitution framed and ratified by the previous generation as binding. Democrats, Whigs, and Republicans celebrated the Constitution as the embodiment of the good republic. Some prominent abolitionists scorned the framing generation for making illicit compromises with evil, but their voices were drowned out by mainstream politicians who insisted that such compromises were necessary to maintain the Union and other abolitionists who insisted that the framers had committed the United States to the eventual abolition of slavery.

Members of the Jacksonian generation did not agree on why the U.S. Constitution should be venerated. All parties to constitutional debates highlighted certain features of the constitutional past while downplaying, if not ignoring, others. Prominent Democrats emphasized the more democratic elements of American constitutionalism. Prominent Whigs stressed the republican commitments to a virtuous citizenry. Republicans highlighted the more anti-slavery strands of American constitutionalism. Pro-slavery advocates pointed to such provisions as the fugitive slave clause, which they claimed demonstrated a special constitutional commitment to human bondage.

A. Sources

Americans in the Jacksonian Era inherited from the Early National Era a commitment to constitutional foundations for rights and liberties. Constitutional decision makers pointed to specific provisions in federal and state constitutions when justifying their rulings. References to natural law or fundamental principles as independent sources of rights and liberties largely, although not completely, disappeared from legal discourse.

Most political elites perceived no fundamental conflict between the Constitution and natural law. Democrats, Whigs, and Republicans agreed that the Constitution promoted justice and prosperity. Andrew Jackson's "Farewell Address" asserted,

> Our Constitution is no longer a doubtful experiment; and, at the end of nearly a half a century, we find that it has preserved unimpaired the liberties of the people, secured the rights of property, and that our country has improved and is flourishing beyond any former example in the history of nations.

Abraham Lincoln declared, "Don't interfere with anything in the Constitution. That must be maintained, for it is the only safeguard of our liberties."[4] Those Democrats and Whigs who thought slavery evil rationalized constitutional protections for human bondage as vital means for forming a more perfect Union.

Some northern abolitionists challenged this complacent view that slavery was a necessary constitutional evil. William Lloyd Garrison condemned the Constitution as committing the country to preserving injustice. In 1843 he successfully persuaded the American Anti-Slavery Society to pass a resolution stating, "The compact which exists between the North and the South is a covenant with death and an agreement with hell; involving both parties in atrocious criminality, and should be immediately annulled."[5] On July 4, 1854, Garrison publicly burned a copy of the Constitution.[6] Wendell Phillips detailed the abolitionist critique of the Constitution in *The Constitution, a Pro-Slavery Compact*. That work asserted that the framers committed the United States to protecting slavery for as long as slaveholders sought constitutional protection.

Other anti-slavery advocates celebrated a Constitution they interpreted as either outlawing slavery or placing slavery on "a course of ultimate extinction." Many argued that federal statutes protecting slavery were unconstitutional. Frederick Douglass was a leading champion of this view. His works "denied that the Constitution guarantees the right to hold property in man."[7]

B. Principles

The Democrats and the Whigs were the two major national parties during most of the Jacksonian Era. The national party platforms of each coalition focused on national powers. Democrats opposed the national bank, federally funded internal improvements, and protective tariffs. Whigs favored these measures. Democrats and Whigs in the states more often disputed rights and liberties. Whigs favored using government power to improve citizens and foster a uniform, Protestant culture; Democrats opposed such Whig initiatives as common schools and temperance laws. Whigs supported nativism and limiting voting rights; Democrats championed the rights of (white) immigrants and an expanded suffrage. Northern Whigs were far more inclined than northern Democrats to support the rights of women, blacks, and Native Americans.

During the 1850s party competition between Democrats and Republicans replaced party competition between Democrats and Whigs. Most Republicans, including Abraham Lincoln, were former Whigs. Nevertheless, the political realignment of the 1850s was based

4. Abraham Lincoln, *Collected Works of Abraham Lincoln*, ed. Roy P. Basler (New Brunswick, NJ: Rutgers University Press, 1953), 2:366.

5. Wendell Phillips Garrison and Francis Jackson Garrison, *William Lloyd Garrison, 1805–1879, The Story of his Life Told by his Children* (New York: Century Co., 1889), 3:88.

6. Henry Mayer, *All on Fire: William Lloyd Garrison and the Abolition of Slavery* (New York: St. Martin's Griffin, 1998), 444–445.

7. Frederick Douglass, *Selected Speeches and Writings*, ed. Philip S. Foner (Chicago: Chicago Review Press, 2000), 380.

on a change in the basis of partisan competition, not a change in party labels. Democrats and Republicans primarily fought over slavery. Republicans insisted that slavery be prohibited in all American territories, blamed slaveholders for civil rights violations in the Territory of Kansas, and demanded that Kansas enter the Union as a free state. Democrats maintained that the Constitution gave slaveholders the right to bring their slaves into American territories and blamed abolitionists for the violence that took place in Kansas during the 1850s. Most Democrats, although not all, believed that Kansas should enter the Union as a slave state.

C. Scope

Americans in the Jacksonian Era disputed the scope of the first ten amendments to the U.S. Constitution. The best-known controversy was over whether the federal Bill of Rights limited the power of state governments. The more important controversy was over whether the Bill of Rights limited congressional power in the territories. By 1860 a consensus had been reached. The Supreme Court in *Barron v. Baltimore* (1833) ruled that states had no constitutional obligation to respect the liberties set out in the first ten amendments to the Constitution. The Supreme Court in *Dred Scot v. Sandford* (1857) ruled that when governing territories, Congress had to respect the liberties set out in the first ten amendments. This consensus about the scope of the Bill of Rights in the states (no) and territories (yes) was not universal. Several state supreme courts suggested that states should respect the liberties set out in the Bill of Rights, either because these liberties were fundamental or because the federal Constitution bound both states and Congress. Chief Justice Joseph Henry Lumpkin of the Supreme Court of Georgia asserted in *Campbell v. State* (GA 1852), "The rights which the [first ten amendments to the Constitution of the United States] were designed to protect, were too sacred to be violated by any republican tribunal, legislative or judicial."[8] Antislavery advocates complained that *Barron* left local officials in the South free to muzzle anti-slavery speech. These antebellum concerns resurfaced after the Civil War when Americans revisited the status of the Bill of Rights in the states and territories.

8. *Campbell v. State*, 11 Ga. 353 (1852).

Incorporation

Barron v. Baltimore, 32 U.S. 243 (1833)

John Barron and John Craig owned a wharf on the Baltimore Harbor. Baltimore adopted a commercial development plan that required officials to divert several local streams. These internal improvements lowered the water level on the Barron and Craig property. When their wharf became useless, Barron sued for damages. He claimed that the city took property from him in violation of the due process clause of the Fifth Amendment. The city responded that localities had the right to divert streams as part of general police powers and that the Fifth Amendment of the federal Constitution limited only national power. Barron was awarded compensation at trial, but the state court of appeals reversed the ruling. Barron appealed this decision to the Supreme Court of the United States, claiming that both the national government and local authorities were limited by the Fifth Amendment.

The Supreme Court unanimously rejected Barron's appeal. Chief Justice Marshall's opinion held that the Bill of Rights limited only federal power, and that local governments only had to respect whatever rights were found in the relevant state constitution. If the constitution of Maryland did not have a due process clause or Maryland courts did not interpret the due process clause of the state constitution as protecting Barron or a similarly situated person, then the local action was constitutional. What reasons does Marshall give for this ruling? Do you believe the ruling sound? When thinking about this decision, you might consider that, after Andrew Jackson was elected president in 1828, the Supreme Court consistently found state actions to be constitutional. Compare Barron *to such cases as* Fletcher v. Peck *(1810), when the Supreme Court declared a state law unconstitutional. How do you explain the different result in* Barron*? Does* Barron *present a different legal issue, one that merits a different legal result? Was the Marshall Court far more deferential to states after 1828 because the judges feared political backlash in the wake of the Jacksonian states-rights revolution?*

CHIEF JUSTICE MARSHALL delivered the opinion of the Court.

. . .

The constitution was ordained and established by the people of the United States for themselves, for their own government, and not for the government of the individual states. Each state established a constitution for itself, and, in that constitution, provided such limitations and restrictions on the powers of its particular government as its judgment dictated. The people of the United States framed such a government for the United States as they supposed best adapted to their situation, and best calculated to promote their interests. The powers they conferred on this government were to be exercised by itself; and the limitations on power, if expressed in general terms, are naturally, and, we think, necessarily applicable to the government created by the instrument. They are limitations of power granted in the instrument itself; not of distinct governments, framed by different persons and for different purposes.

If these propositions be correct, the fifth amendment must be understood as restraining the power of the general government, not as applicable to the states. In their several constitutions they have imposed such restrictions on their respective governments as their own wisdom suggested; such as they deemed most proper for themselves. It is a subject on which they judge exclusively, and with which others interfere no farther than they are supposed to have a common interest.

. . .

The ninth section having enumerated, in the nature of a bill of rights, the limitations intended to be imposed on the powers of the general government, the tenth proceeds to enumerate those which were to operate on the state legislatures. These restrictions are brought together in the same section, and are by express words applied to the states. "No state shall enter into any treaty," etc. Perceiving that in a constitution framed by the people of the United States for the government of all, no limitation of the action of government on the people would apply to the state government, unless expressed in terms; the restrictions contained in the tenth section are in direct words so applied to the states.

. . .

Had the people of the several states, or any of them, required changes in their constitutions; had they required additional safeguards to liberty from the apprehended encroachments of their particular governments: the remedy was in their own hands, and would have been applied by themselves. A convention would have been assembled by the discontented state, and the required improvements would have been made by itself. The unwieldy and cumbrous machinery of procuring a recommendation from two-thirds of congress, and the assent of three-fourths of their sister states, could never have occurred to any human being as a mode of doing that which might be effected by the state itself. Had the framers of these amendments intended them to be limitations on the powers of the state governments, they would have imitated the framers of the original constitution, and have expressed that intention. Had congress engaged in the extraordinary occupation of improving the constitutions of the several states by affording the people additional protection from the exercise of power by their own governments in matters which concerned themselves alone, they would have declared this purpose in plain and intelligible language.

. . .

We are of opinion that the provision in the fifth amendment to the constitution, declaring that private property shall not be taken for public use without just compensation, is intended solely as a limitation on the exercise of power by the government of the United States, and is not applicable to the legislation of the states. . . .

III. Individual Rights

MAJOR DEVELOPMENTS

- Decline of contracts clause and rise of due process protections for property rights
- Struggles between Protestants and Catholics over religious freedom
- Debate over whether the right to bear arms was limited to militia service
- Debate over whether temperance laws violated individual rights

Jacksonian Era Americans applied an inherited framework for thinking about individual constitutional rights to a bewildering array of new circumstances. Founding and Early National Era precedents established that government officials could regulate individuals whenever restraints promoted the common good and did not benefit one class of persons at the expense of another. Technological, cultural, and political developments exerted pressure on this understanding of individual rights. The transportation revolution created demands for new regulations on property that accommodated perceived needs for trains and canals. Moral crusaders inspired by the Second Great Awakening passed laws regulating drinking, gambling, and such hotbeds of sin as bowling alleys. Many Protestants insisted that state support for Christianity was necessary to maintain the private virtues essential for republican government. Government officials responded to urban crime waves with gun control laws.

Opponents challenged the constitutionality of all these laws. The resulting debates raised constitutional questions about what constituted the public good and the relationships between the public good and new regulations.

A. Property

The constitutional politics and law of property rights were altered subtly during the Jacksonian Era. During the Early National Era federal courts relying on the contracts clause of the national Constitution provided the most important protections for economic freedom. *Proprietors of the Charles River Bridge v. Proprietors of the Warren Bridge* (1837) weakened contract clause protections for property holders. That decision held that courts should construe contractual ambiguities in bargains between state officials and private parties in favor of state power. State courts, by comparison, protected property rights more aggressively during the Jacksonian Era than they had during the Early National Era. State judges, relying on the takings and due process clauses of state constitutions, restricted state power to pass internal improvements, build roads, and adjust property rights. The vast majority of cases protecting property rights before 1828 prohibited government from passing laws that divested people of their entire right to a particular piece of property. During the Jacksonian Era, some state courts interpreted state constitutional provisions as limiting state regulations of property and economic freedom, even when those regulations left persons with nominal title to their land or possessions.

Contracts

The role of the contracts clause as a valuable protection for property rights and economic freedoms declined during the Jacksonian Era. Such Early National Era cases as *Fletcher v. Peck* (1810) and *Dartmouth College v. Woodward* (1819) established that state grants and corporate charters were contracts that states could not alter at will. These rulings were some of the central accomplishments of the Federalist/National Republican–inspired Marshall Court. During the thirty years before the Civil War, the Supreme Court under Chief Justice Roger Taney limited those precedents. *Proprietors of the Charles River Bridge v. Proprietors of the Warren Bridge* (1837) ruled that local officials could pass any law that did not explicitly violate a provision in a state land grant or corporate charter. *West River Bridge Co. v. Dix* (1848) ruled that states could take property granted by a previous state contract, as long as the state paid adequate compensation.

Contract clause litigation remained vibrant. Economic hard times during the late 1830s and early 1840s put pressure on local legislatures to relieve distressed debtors. Federal courts usually sustained the resulting state laws. Nevertheless, the contracts clause retained some bite. In *Piqua Branch of State Bank of Ohio v. Knoop* (1853), the Supreme Court declared unconstitutional an Ohio law that required bank assets to be taxed at the same rate as other personal property in the state. That measure, Justice John McLean's majority opinion asserted, abridged a provision in the bank's corporate charter that mandated a 6 percent tax on all bank profits. McLean placed particular emphasis on the charter's provision that the 6 percent fee was "in lieu of all taxes to which the company . . . would otherwise be subject." He declared: "Every valuable privilege given by the charter, and which conduced to an acceptance of it and an organization under it is a contract which cannot be changed by the legislature, where the power to do so is not reserved in the charter."Supreme Court justices treated the contracts clause as limiting both federal and state power, even though Article I, Section 9 is directed only at the states. *Rice v. Minnesota & N.W.R. Co.* (1861) held that neither the federal nor the state governments could renege on land grants. Justice Nathan Clifford's majority opinion asserted, "If the legal effect of the act of Congress . . . was to grant to the Territory a beneficial interest in the lands [in dispute], then it is equally clear that it was not competent for Congress to pass the repealing act, and divest the title." Justice Nelson's dissent in that case agreed with Justice Clifford's assumption of a federal contracts clause. After citing *Fletcher v. Peck* for the proposition that "[i]t is well settled in this court that grants [of land], when made by the Legislature of a State cannot be recalled," Nelson asserted, "we do not perceive any reason why the inviolability of the same class of grants should be less when made by the legislative power of the General Government."

Proprietors of the Charles River Bridge v. Proprietors of the Warren Bridge, 36 U.S. 420 (1837)

In 1785 the Massachusetts legislature granted a charter to the proprietors of the Charles River Bridge Company. That corporate charter authorized the company to build a bridge over the Charles River and collect tolls for forty years. In

1792 a new charter was issued to the Charles River Bridge Company extending the right to collect tolls until 1856. In 1828 the Massachusetts legislature, responding to increased transportation needs, authorized the Warren Bridge Company to build a second bridge across the Charles River. The proprietors of the Warren Bridge were permitted to collect tolls for no more than six years before turning the bridge over to the state. The proprietors of the Charles River Bridge sued to block the opening of the Warren Bridge. They claimed that the charter that Massachusetts gave to the Warren Bridge Company deprived them of the promised benefits of collecting tolls for forty years and thus impaired the state obligations in their corporate charter. After a divided state court ruled in favor of the Warren Bridge, the proprietors of the Charles River Bridge appealed that decision to the Supreme Court of the United States.

The Supreme Court by a 5-2 vote sustained the Massachusetts law incorporating the Warren Bridge Company. Chief Justice Taney's opinion held that the contracts clause protected exclusive privileges only when those exclusive privileges were explicitly written in the corporate charter. His conclusion articulates the Jacksonian antipathy to private privilege and monopoly. Why does Chief Justice Taney reach this conclusion? Why does Justice Story disagree? Both Taney and Story insisted that their interpretation of the contracts clause promoted economic growth. Who is right? Should such considerations influence the proper interpretation of the contracts clause?

CHIEF JUSTICE TANEY delivered the opinion of the Court.

. . .

. . . It is well settled by the decisions of this Court, that a state law may be retrospective in its character, and may divest vested rights; and yet not violate the constitution of the United States, unless it also impairs the obligation of a contract. . . .

. . . [The plaintiff] must show that the state had entered into a contract with them, or those under whom they claim, not to establish a free bridge at the place where the Warren Bridge is erected. Such, and such only, are the principles upon which the plaintiffs in error can claim relief in this case.

. . .

. . . The act of incorporation is silent in relation to the contested power. . . .

. . . [T]he object and end of all government is to promote the happiness and prosperity of the community by which it is established; and it can never be assumed, that the government intended to diminish its power of accomplishing the end for which it was created. And in a country like ours, free, active, and enterprising, continually advancing in numbers and wealth; new channels of communication are daily found necessary, both for travel and trade; and are essential to the comfort, convenience, and prosperity of the people. A state ought never to be presumed to surrender this power, because, like the taxing power, the whole community have an interest in preserving it undiminished. And when a corporation alleges, that a state has surrendered for seventy years, its power of improvement and public accommodation, in a great and important line of travel, along which a vast number of its citizens must daily pass; the community have a right to insist . . . "that its abandonment ought not to be presumed, in a case, in which the deliberate purpose of the state to abandon it does not appear." The continued existence of a government would be of no great value, if by implications and presumptions, it was disarmed of the powers necessary to accomplish the ends of its creation; and the functions it was designed to perform, transferred to the hands of privileged corporations. . . .

. . .

Indeed, the practice and usage of almost every state in the Union, old enough to have commenced the work of internal improvement, is opposed to the doctrine contended for on the part of the plaintiffs in error. Turnpike roads have been made in succession, on the same line of travel; the later ones interfering materially with the profits of the first. These corporations have, in some instances, been utterly ruined by the introduction of newer and better modes of transportation, and travelling. In some cases, rail roads have rendered the turnpike roads on the same line of travel so entirely useless, that the franchise of the turnpike corporation is not worth preserving. Yet in none of these cases have the corporations supposed that their privileges were invaded, or any contract violated on the part of the state. . . .

. . . How far must the new improvement be distant from the old one? How near may you approach without invading its rights in the privileged line? If this Court should establish the principles now contended for, what is to become of the numerous rail roads established on the same line of travel with turnpike companies; and which have rendered the franchises of the turnpike corporations of no value? Let it once be understood that such charters carry with them these implied contracts, and give this unknown and undefined property in a line of travelling; and you will soon find the old turnpike corporations awakening from their sleep, and calling upon this Court to put down the improvements which have taken their place. The millions of property which have been invested in rail roads and canals, upon lines of travel which had been before occupied by turnpike corporations, will be put in jeopardy. We shall be thrown back to the improvements of the last century, and obliged to stand still, until the claims of the old turnpike corporations shall be satisfied; and they shall consent to permit these states to avail themselves of the lights of modern science, and to partake of the benefit of those improvements which are now adding to the wealth and prosperity, and the convenience and comfort, of every other part of the civilized world. . . .

. . .

JUSTICE McLEAN, concurring. . . .

JUSTICE STORY, dissenting.

. . .

. . . [I]t has been argued, and the argument has been pressed in every form which ingenuity could suggest, that if grants of this nature are to be construed liberally, as conferring any exclusive rights on the grantees, it will interpose an effectual barrier against all general improvements of the country. For myself, I profess not to feel the cogency of this argument; either in its general application to the grant of franchises, or in its special application to the present grant. . . . For my own part, I can conceive of no surer plan to arrest all public improvements, founded on private capital and enterprise, than to make the outlay of that capital uncertain, and questionable both as to security, and as to productiveness. No man will hazard his capital in any enterprise, in which, if there be a loss, it must be borne exclusively by himself; and if there be success, he has not the slightest security of enjoying the rewards of that success for a single moment. . . .

. . . The prohibition [against a new bridge] arises by natural, if not by necessary implication. It would be against the first principles of justice to presume that the legislature reserved a right to destroy its own grant. That was the doctrine in *Fletcher v. Peck* [1810] . . . in this Court: and in other cases turning upon the same great principle of political and constitutional duty and right. Can the legislature have power to do that indirectly, which it cannot do directly? If it cannot take away, or resume the franchise itself, can it take away its whole substance and value? If the law will create an implication that the legislature shall not resume its own grant, is it not equally as natural and as necessary an implication, that the legislature shall not do any act directly to prejudice its own grant, or to destroy its value?

. . .

To sum up, then, the whole argument on this head; I maintain, that, upon the principles of common reason and legal interpretation, the present grant carries with it a necessary implication that the legislature shall do no act to destroy or essentially to impair the franchise; that . . . there is an implied agreement that the state will not grant another bridge between Boston and Charlestown, so near as to draw away the custom from the old one; and . . . that there is an implied agreement of the state to grant the undisturbed use of the bridge and its tolls, so far as respects any acts of its own, or of any persons acting under its authority. In other words, the state, impliedly, contracts not to resume its grant, or to do any act to the prejudice or destruction of its grant. . . . I maintain, that under the principles of the common law, there exists no more right in the legislature of Massachusetts, to erect the Warren Bridge, to the ruin of the franchise of the Charles River Bridge, than exists to transfer the latter to the former, or to authorize the former to demolish the latter. If the legislature does not mean in its grant to give any exclusive rights, let it say so, expressly; directly; and in terms admitting of no misconstruction. The grantees will then take at their peril, and must abide the results of their overweening confidence, indiscretion, and zeal. . . .

Takings

The transportation revolution challenged inherited understandings of the takings clauses in state constitutions. A long constitutional tradition maintained that government could not take land from one private person and give that land to another private person. During the 1820s and afterwards, government increasingly took private lands to build roads and railroad tracks. Quite frequently government gave that land to private persons or privately owned railroad companies. Some states gave private railroads the power to determine when the government would use the power of eminent domain. Proponents insisted that government could take land from A and give it to B as long as the previous owners were fairly compensated and the takings had a public purpose. Opponents insisted that government could use the takings power only when the state intended to take title to the condemned property.

Constitutional decision makers concluded that government could transfer ownership of land from one private party to another only when the first party was fairly compensated and the taking helped the state achieve a public purpose. *Beekman v. The Saratoga and Schenectady Railroad Co.* (NY 1831) permitted railroads to exercise the power of eminent domain because the judges agreed that railroads served a public purpose. "Upon the . . . principle of public benefit, not only the agents of the government," the judicial majority on the Chancery Court of New York declared, "but also individuals and corporate bodies, have been authorized to take private property for the purpose of making public highways, turnpike roads and canals." *Taylor v. Porter & Ford* (NY 1843) limited *Beekman* to instances when the taking was done for the benefit of the public. Justice Bronson asserted, "There is no provision in the constitution that just compensation shall be made to the owner when his property is taken for private purposes."

Beekman v. The Saratoga and Schenectady Railroad Company, 3 Paige Ch. 45 (NY 1831)

New York State in 1831 passed a law incorporating the Saratoga and Schenectady Railroad Company. The law permitted the railroad company to appropriate private land for a railroad between Saratoga Springs and Schenectady, provided that the company compensated owners for the fair value of their property. Beekman objected when the company had the state condemn his land. He asked the Chancery Court of New York for an injunction to restrain the state from exercising the power of eminent domain, claiming that New York could not vest a private company with the power of eminent domain. The Saratoga and Schenectady Railroad Company responded that eminent domain could be used to give land to a private company as long as the exercise of eminent domain had a public purpose.

The Chancery Court declared the New York statute constitutional. Chancellor Reuben Hyde Walworth's opinion asserted that states could use the power of eminent domain to transfer the property of one private owner to another private owner as long as the transfer had a public purpose and just compensation was made. How does Chancellor Walworth justify that decision? Is that decision consistent with previous understandings of the takings clause, or was the takings clause "updated" in light of the transportation revolution? After Beekman, *what constitutes a public use for constitutional purposes?*

THE CHANCELLOR

. . .

. . . It is admitted that the complainant held the land in fee; and probably under a title derived from the crown, to the rights of which the people have now succeeded. A law declaring the grant from the crown void, and divesting his title on that ground, would impair the obligation of the contract. But it was no part of the contract between the crown and its grantees or their assigns, that the property should not be taken for public use, upon paying a fair compensation therefor, whenever the public interest or necessities required that it should be so taken. All separate interests of individuals in property are held of the government under this tacit agreement or implied reservation. Notwithstanding the grant to individuals, the *eminent domain,* the highest and most exact idea of property, remains in the government, or in the aggregate body of the people in their sovereign capacity; and they have a right to resume the possession of the property, in the manner directed by the constitution and laws of the state, whenever the public interest requires it. This right of resumption may be exercised not only where the safety, but also where the interest or even the expediency of the state is concerned; as where the land of the individual is wanted for a road, canal or other public improvement. The only restriction upon this power, in cases where the public or the inhabitants of any particular section of the state have an interest in the contemplated improvement as citizens merely, is that the property shall not be taken for the public use without just compensation to the owner, and in the mode prescribed by law. The right of *eminent domain* does not, however, imply a right in the sovereign power to take the property of one citizen and transfer it to another, even for a full compensation, where the public interest will be in no way promoted by such transfer. And if the legislature should attempt thus to transfer the property of one individual to another, where there could be no pretence of benefit to the public by such exchange, it would probably be a violation of the contract by which the land was granted by the government to the individual, or to those under whom he claimed title, and repugnant to the constitution of the United States. But if the public interest can be in any way promoted by the taking of private property, it must rest in the wisdom of the legislature to determine whether the benefit to the public will be of sufficient importance to render it expedient for them to exercise the right of *eminent domain,* and to authorize an interference with the private rights of individuals for that purpose. It is upon this principle that the legislatures of several of the states have authorized the condemnation of the lands of individuals for mill sites, where, from the nature of the country, such mill sites could not be obtained for the accommodation of the inhabitants without overflowing the lands thus condemned. Upon the same principle of public benefit, not only the agents of the government, but also individuals and corporate bodies, have been authorized to take private property for the purpose of making public highways, turnpike roads and canals; of erecting and constructing wharves and basins; of establishing ferries; of draining swamps and marshes; and of bringing water to cities and villages. In all such cases the object of the legislative grant of power, is the public benefit derived from the contemplated improvement, whether such improvement is to be effected directly by the agents of the government, or through the medium of corporate bodies, or of individual enterprise. . . .

It is objected, however, that a railroad differs from other public improvements, and particularly from turnpikes and canals, because travelers cannot use it with their own carriages, and farmers cannot transport their produce in their own vehicles; that the company in this case, are under no obligation to accommodate the public with transportation; and that they are unlimited in the amount of tolls which they are authorized to take. If the making of a railroad will enable the traveler to go from one place to another without the expense of a carriage and horses, he derives a greater benefit from the improvement than if he was compelled to travel with his own conveyance over a turnpike road at the same expense. And if a mode of conveyance has been discovered by which the farmer can procure his produce to be transported to market at half the expense which it would cost him to carry it there with his own wagon and horses, there is no reason why the public should not enjoy the benefit of the discovery. And if any individual is so unreasonable as to refuse to have the railroad made through his lands, for a fair compensation, the legislature may lawfully appropriate a portion of his property for this public benefit, or may authorize an individual or a corporation thus to appropriate it, upon paying a just compensation to the owner of the land for the damage sustained. The objection that the corporation is under no legal obligation to transport produce or passengers upon this road, and at a reasonable expense, is unfounded in fact. The privilege of making a road and taking tolls thereon is a franchise, as much as the establishment of a ferry or a public wharf and taking tolls for the use of the same. The public have an interest in the use of the railroad, and the owners may be prosecuted for the damages sustained, if they should refuse to transport an individual, or his property, without any reasonable excuse, upon being paid the usual rate of fare. The legislature may also, from time to time, regulate the use of the franchise and limit the amount of toll which it shall be lawful to take, in the same manner as they may regulate the amount of tolls to be taken at a ferry, or for grinding at a mill, unless they have deprived themselves of that power by a legislative contract with the owners of the road. . . .

Taylor v. Porter & Ford, 4 Hill 140 (NY 1843)

Porter and Ford owned property in Milton, New York. In 1840 they applied for a permit to build a private road connecting their property to the town center. Under New York law the commissioners of highways reviewed applications for private roads. If a road was approved, the commissioners summoned a jury of six freeholders to determine what damages building the road caused to other properties. The applicants were required to pay those damages before building the road. The commissioners approved the proposed Porter and Ford road. Following New York law, they required Porter and Ford to pay compensation to the persons over whose land the road would be built. Taylor was one of those landholders. When Porter and Ford started to lay out their private road, he sued them for trespass. Porter and Ford claimed that the commissioner of the highways had given them the right to build. Taylor claimed that the New York law authorizing people building private roads to take land violated the constitution of New York.

The Supreme Court of New York ruled that the state legislature had no power to take land to build private roads, even when compensation was paid. Justice Bronson's majority opinion asserted that the New York law violated both the due process and takings clauses of the state constitution. Why does he reach that conclusion? A decade before Taylor, *New York judges in* Beekman *permitted railroad companies to exercise the power of eminent domain, How is* Taylor *different from* Beekman? *Chief Justice Nelson's dissent observes that the New York law on building private roads predated the state constitution. Is* Taylor *an example of living constitutionalism, or were New Yorkers mistaken about their state constitution for more than seventy years?*

JUSTICE BRONSON delivered the opinion of the Court.

. . .

The right to take private property for *public* purposes is one of the inherent attributes of sovereignty, and exists in every independent government. Private interests must yield to public necessity. But even this right of eminent domain cannot be exercised without making just compensation to the owner of the property. And thus, what would otherwise be a burden upon a single individual, has been made to fall equally upon every member of the state. But there is no provision in the constitution that just compensation shall be made to the owner when his property is taken for *private* purposes; and if the power exists to take the property of one man without his consent and transfer it to another, it may be exercised without any reference to the question of compensation. The power of making bargains for individuals has not been delegated to any branch of the government, and if the title of A. can, without his fault, be transferred to B., it may as well be done without as with a consideration. . . . .

Under our form of government the legislature is not supreme. It is only one of the organs of that absolute sovereignty which resides in the whole body of the people. Like other departments of the government, it can only exercise such powers as have been delegated to it; and when it steps beyond that boundary, its acts, like those of the most humble magistrate in the state who transcends his jurisdiction, are utterly void. Where, then, shall we find a delegation of power to the legislature to take the property of A. and give it to B., either with or without compensation? Only one clause of the constitution can be cited in support of the power, and that is the first section of the first article, where the people have declared that "the legislative power of this state shall be vested in a senate and assembly." . . . The security of life, liberty and property, lies at the foundation of the social compact; and to say that this grant of "legislative power" includes the right to attack private property, is equivalent to saying that the people have delegated to their servants the power of defeating one of the great ends for which the government was established. If there was not one word of qualification in the whole instrument, I should feel great difficulty in bringing myself to the conclusion that the clause under consideration had clothed the legislature with despotic power; and such is the extent of their authority if they can take the property of A., either with or without compensation, and give it to B. "The legislative power of this state" does not reach to such an unwarrantable extent. Neither life, liberty nor property, except when forfeited by crime, or when the latter is taken for public use, falls within the scope of the power. Such, at least, are my present impressions.

But the question does not necessarily turn on the section granting legislative power. The people have added negative words, which should put the matter at rest. "No member of this state shall be disfranchised, or deprived of any of the rights or privileges secured to any citizen thereof, unless *by the law of the land,* or the judgment of his peers." . . . The meaning of the section then seems to be, that no member of the state shall be disfranchised, or deprived of any of his rights or privileges, unless the matter shall be adjudged against him upon trial had according to the course of the common law. It must be ascertained judicially that he has forfeited his privileges, or that some one else has a superior title to the property he possesses, before either of them can be taken from him. It cannot be done by mere legislation.

But if there can be a doubt upon the first section of the seventh article, there can, I think, be none that the seventh section of the same article covers the case. "No person shall be deprived of life, liberty, or property, *without due process of law;* nor shall private property be taken for public use, without just compensation." . . . Mr. Senator Tracy said, the words should be construed "as equivalent to a constitutional declaration, that private property, without the consent of the owner, shall be taken *only* for the public use, and then only upon a just compensation." . . .

. . .

. . . I am of opinion that a private road cannot be laid out without the consent of the owner of the land over which it passes.

JUSTICE COWEN, concurring. . . .

CHIEF JUSTICE NELSON, dissenting.

I cannot concur in the opinion that the statute authorizing the laying out of private roads is unconstitutional and void. It was first enacted by the colonial legislature in 1772, and has been in force in the colony and state ever since—a period of about seventy years. . . . Its constitutionality has never before, so far as I know, been doubted.

. . .

It is said the laying out of a private road over the land of another is an appropriation of the property for *private* and not for *public* purposes, and therefore a violation of the spirit of that clause in the constitution which forbids the taking of it for public use without making just compensation. . . . I am far from disputing the existence of the rule itself. Private property cannot be taken for strictly private purposes without the consent of the owner, whether compensation be provided or not. But I deny that the statute authorizing the laying out of private ways is at all in conflict with the general rule. The construction of roads and bridges is a power belonging to all governments, in the exercise of which every citizen or subject is deeply concerned. Works of this nature are indispensable to the prosperity of a country. They must begin with its earliest settlement and keep pace with its advancement in population, in commerce and social enjoyment. So intimately are they interwoven with individual enterprise and the public welfare, that their establishment and regulation have hitherto been regarded as an essential branch of internal police; the first to be attended to, and the last to be neglected. Private roads in the settlement of a country are often as necessary for the accommodation of the inhabitants, as those of a public nature. Thoroughfares and highways cannot be made to traverse every part of the territory, so as to reach the dwellings of all who need their use. And what must be the unavoidable result, if the power to lay out private roads under public authority be denied? We have in this state about eight hundred towns, and I doubt not there may be an average of some two or three private roads in each, accommodating probably four thousand or more inhabitants. Is not the public interest concerned that they shall have access to our highways and thoroughfares? If it be refused them, how are they to discharge the various duties enjoined by law, or enjoy the privileges which the law was intended to secure to them? With what propriety can they be called on to work upon the highways, to serve in the militia, as jurors, or as public officers, when they cannot leave their possessions without committing a trespass?

Due Process

Constitutional decision makers in the Jacksonian Era frequently used the due process or law of the land clauses in state constitutions to protect property rights and economic freedoms. State court justices spoke of due process when declaring unconstitutional laws that deprived people of public offices (*Hoke v. Henderson* [NC 1833]), laws that deprived settlers of preexisting land rights (*Wally's Heirs v. Kennedy* [TN 1831]), laws that gave married women control over their property (*White v. White* [NY 1849]), and laws that restricted the manufacture and sale of intoxicating liquors (*Wynehamer v. People* [NY 1856]). Constitutional decision makers usually sustained state regulations of property and economic activity. Nevertheless, judicial rulings that state laws violated due process rights to property were neither rare nor confined to a particular state court or judge.

Due process incorporated equal protection and takings concerns The Supreme Court of Tennessee in *Wally's Heirs v. Kennedy* yoked due process and equal protection together when declaring that the "'law of the land,' means a general public law, equally binding upon every member of the community."[9] Many takings cases used due process as an alternative ground for declaring a state law unconstitutional. *Hoke v. Henderson* yoked due process and takings together when declaring, "A legislative act, which deprives one person of a right and vests it in another, is not a 'law of the land' within the meaning of the bill of rights."[10]

The leading proponents and opponents of slavery made extensive use of substantive due process claims, the claim that due process protected particular property and liberty rights. Justice Taney's opinion in *Dred Scott v. Sandford* (1857) maintained that federal laws prohibiting slavery in the territories deprived slaveholders of their property without due process of law. Prominent abolitionists insisted that federal laws sanctioning slavery in the territories deprived persons of color of their liberty without due process of law. These claims were not invented out of thin air for use in slavery controversies. Both pro-slavery and anti-slavery advocates relied on due process arguments that were well developed in state courts.

9. *Wally's Heirs v. Kennedy*, 2 Yerg. 544 (Tenn. 1831).
10. *Hoke v. Henderson*, 15 N.C. 1 (1833).

Wynehamer v. People, 2 Parker Crim. Rep. 490 (NY 1856)

Thomas Toynbee was arrested for selling a glass of brandy to a customer. This act violated a New York law that declared, "Intoxicating liquor, except as hereinafter provided, shall not be sold, or kept for sale, or with intent to be sold, by any person, for himself or any other person." Toynbee was convicted and required to pay a $50 fine. Toynbee's sentence was reversed by the Supreme Court of New York, which declared the ban on intoxicating beverages unconstitutional. The state appealed that decision to the New York Court of Appeals. The Court of Appeals combined Toynbee's case with that of James Wynehamer, whose conviction for selling intoxicating liquors had been affirmed by a different lower state court.

The New York Court of Appeals confirmed the supreme court's ruling in Wynehamer's case and declared unconstitutional the legislative ban on selling intoxicating liquors. Justice Comstock insisted that the New York law violated property rights protected by the due process clause of the state constitution. What were those property rights? How do the judges distinguish between laws that regulate property and laws that confiscate property? Do you find that distinction convincing? Suppose evidence came to light in 1850 that intoxicating beverages caused heart disease. Would the New York law be constitutional?

JUSTICE COMSTOCK delivered the opinion of the Court.

. . .

. . . It is . . . universally admitted that when this law was passed, intoxicating liquors, to be used as a beverage, were *property* in the most absolute and unqualified sense of the term; and as such, as much entitled to the protection of the constitution as lands, houses, or chattels of any description. From the earliest ages they have been produced and consumed as a beverage, and have constituted an article of great importance in the commerce of the world. In this country, the right of property in them was never, so far as I know, for an instant questioned. In this state, they were bought and sold like other property; they were seized and sold upon legal process for the payment of debts; they were, like other goods, the subject of actions at law, and, when the owner died, their value constituted a fund for the benefit of his creditors, or went to his children and kindred, according to law or the will of the deceased. . . .

It may be said, it is true, that intoxicating drinks are a species of property which performs no beneficent part in the political, moral, or social economy of the world. It may even be urged, and I will admit, demonstrated with reasonable certainty, that the abuses to which it is liable are so great that the people of this state can dispense with its very existence, not only without injury to their aggregate interests, but with absolute benefit. The same can be said, although, perhaps, upon less palpable grounds, of other descriptions of property. Intoxicating beverages are by no means the only article of admitted property and of lawful commerce in this state, against which arguments of this sort may be directed. But if such arguments can be allowed to subvert the fundamental idea of property, then there is no private right entirely safe, because there is no limitation upon the absolute discretion of the legislature, and the guarantees of the constitution are a mere waste of words.

. . .

These observations appear to me quite elementary, yet they seem to be necessary in order to exclude the discussion of extraneous topics. They lead us directly to the conclusion that all property is alike in the characteristic of inviolability. If the legislature has no power to confiscate and destroy property in general, it has no such power over any particular species. There may be, and there doubtless are, reasons of great urgency for regulating the trade in intoxicating drinks, as well as in other articles of commerce. In establishing such regulations merely, the legislature may proceed upon such views of policy, of economy, or morals, as may be addressed to its discretion. The whole field of discussion is open, when the legislature, keeping within its acknowledged powers, seeks to regulate and restrain a traffic, the general lawfulness of which is admitted; but when the simplest question is propounded, whether it can confiscate and *destroy* property lawfully acquired by the citizen in intoxicating liquors, then we are to remember that all property is equally sacred in the view of the constitution, and therefore that speculations as to its chemical or scientific qualities, or the mischief engendered by its abuse, have very little to do with the inquiry. Property, if protected by the constitution from such legislation as that we are now considering, is protected because *it is property* innocently acquired under existing laws, and not upon any theory which even so much as opens the question of its utility. If intoxicating liquors are property, the constitution does not permit a legislative estimate to be made of its usefulness with a view to its destruction. In a word, that which belongs to the citizen in the sense of property, and as such has to him a commercial value, cannot be pronounced worthless or pernicious, and so destroyed or deprived of its essential attributes.

. . .

We must be allowed to know, what is known by all persons of common intelligence, that intoxicating liquors are produced for sale and consumption as a beverage; that such has been their primary and principal use in all ages and countries; and that it is this use which has imparted to them, in this state, more than ninety-nine hundredths of their commercial value. It must follow that any scheme of legislation which, aiming at the destruction of this use, makes the keeping or sale of them as a beverage, in any quantity, and by any person, a criminal offence—which declares them a public nuisance—which subjects them to seizure and physical destruction, and denies a legal remedy, if they are taken by lawless force or robbery, must be deemed in every beneficial sense, to deprive the owner of the enjoyment of his property.

. . .

I am brought, therefore, to a more particular consideration of the limitations of power contained in the fundamental law: "No member of this state shall be disfranchised or deprived of any of the rights or privileges secured to any citizen thereof, unless by the law of the land, or the judgment of his peers. No person shall be deprived of life, liberty or property, without due process of law; nor shall private property be taken for public use without just compensation." . . .

No doubt, it seems to me, can be admitted of the meaning of these provisions. To say, as has been suggested, that the law of the land, or "due process of law," may mean the very act of legislation which deprives the citizen of his rights, privileges, or property, leads to a simple absurdity. The constitution would then mean, that no person shall be deprived of his property or rights, unless the legislature shall pass a law to effectuate the wrong, and this would be throwing the restraint entirely away.

The true interpretation of these constitutional phrases is, that where rights are acquired by the citizen under the existing law, there is no power in any branch of the government to take them away; but where they are held contrary to the existing law, or are forfeited by its violation, then they may be taken from him—not by an act of the legislature, but in the due administration of the law itself, before the judicial tribunals of the state. The cause or occasion for depriving the citizen of his supposed rights must be found in the law as it is, or, at least, it cannot be *created* by a legislative act which aims at their destruction. Where rights of property are admitted to exist, the legislature cannot say they shall exist no longer; nor will it make any difference although a process and a tribunal are appointed to execute the sentence. If this is the "law of the land," and "due process of law," within the meaning of the constitution, then the legislature is omnipotent. It may, under the same interpretation pass a law to take away the liberty or life without a pre-existing cause, appointing judicial and executive agencies to execute its will. Property is placed, by the constitution, in the same category with liberty and life.

. . .

Material objects . . . are property, in the true sense, because they are impressed by the laws and usages of society with certain qualities, among which are, fundamentally, the right of the occupant or owner to use and enjoy them exclusively, and his absolute power to sell and dispose of them; and as property consists in the artificial impression of these qualities upon material things, so, whatever removes the impression destroys the notion of property, although the things themselves may remain physically untouched.

. . .

The statute under consideration, without reference to its provisions for the seizure and physical destruction of intoxicating liquors, by force of its prohibitions alone, sweeps them from the commerce of the state, and thus annihilates the quality of sale, which makes them valuable to the owner. This is destructive of the notion of property.

. . .

Unless, therefore, the right of property in liquor is denied altogether, and this has never been done, or unless they can be distinguished from every other species of property, and this has not been attempted, the act cannot stand consistently with the constitution. The provisions of the constitution should receive a beneficent and liberal interpretation, where the fundamental rights of the citizen are concerned. . . .

. . .

JUSTICE T. A. JOHNSON, dissenting:

. . .

That intemperance, pauperism and crime are evils, with which the government is necessarily compelled to deal, none will deny. In the judgment of the legislative bodies, by which this statute was enacted, one great source of all these great, oppressive and dangerous evils was the traffic in intoxicating liquors. So injurious, in their opinion, has this traffic become under existing restrictions, in its consequences upon the community, that it ought to be subjected to still more rigorous and extensive restrictions and prohibitions, and impressed with additional features of criminality. If the legislature had the power to enact a law to accomplish this end, the right to choose the means best calculated to effect it was necessarily vested in it; unless, indeed, the use of such means is forbidden by the constitution. . . . The argument is, that the value of property as an article of trade is an essential element of it as property, and that to the extent to which the restriction or prohibition diminishes its value for such purposes, to the same extent the owner is deprived of his property, although neither the title nor the possession of such owner is in any respect interfered with; and that this is accomplished by the operation of the act, independent of any trial or judgment, in other words, without due process of law. Is not this a strained and unwarrantable construction and application of this provision of the constitution? Clearly it is. This provision has no application whatever to a case where the market value of property is incidentally diminished by the operation of a statute passed for an entirely different object, and a purpose in itself legitimate, and which in no respect affects the title, possession, personal use or enjoyment of the owner. Such a construction would prohibit all regulations by the legislature, and all restrictions upon the internal trade and commerce of the state; it would place the right of traffic above every other right, and render it independent of the power of the government. "Deprived" is there used in its ordinary and popular sense, and relates simply to divesting of, forfeiting, alienating, taking away property. It applies to property in the same sense that it does to life and liberty, and no other. . . .

. . .

A distinction has been attempted to be drawn between the power to restrict, by way of regulation, and the power to prohibit. But this distinction, if there be one, is altogether too narrow and uncertain to serve as the test of the rightful exercise of a power like that of making laws for the government of a state. The right to restrict and regulate includes that of prohibition. . . .

This whole controversy, so far as it involves any question of principle, is narrowed down to a struggle for the right of the individual to traffic, in whatever the law adjudges to be property, at his discretion, irrespective of consequences, over the right of government to control and restrict it within limits compatible with the public welfare and security. Everything beyond this is merged in considerations of expediency. This right of the owner to traffic in his property never was, since the institution of society, a right independent of the control of government. It is a right surrendered necessarily to the government, by every one when he enters into society and becomes one of its members. A government which does not possess the power to make all needful regulations in respect to its internal trade and commerce, to impose such restrictions upon it as may be deemed necessary for the good of all, and even to prohibit and suppress entirely any particular traffic which is found to be injurious and demoralizing in its tendencies and consequences, is no government. It must lack that essential element of sovereignty, indispensably necessary to render it capable of accomplishing the primary object for which governments are instituted, that of affording security, protection and redress to all interests and all classes and conditions of persons within their limits. . . .

B. Religion

The Jacksonian Era was a time of substantial religious ferment. During these years Christianity and unconventional religious practices became more salient in the lives of many Americans. Baptists, Methodists, and Presbyterians all gained converts. New nondenominational churches came into existence. Entirely new religious movements and utopian communities were founded, with the most prominent being the Mormons, the Millerite movement (which gave rise to the Seventh Day Adventists and Jehovah's Witnesses), and the Oneida Community. The United States also experienced significant Catholic immigration, primarily from Ireland.

Increased religious diversity altered American constitutional politics and religious fervor gave rise to various moral reform movements. Religious Americans formed associations dedicated to Sabbath-keeping, temperance, the suppression of gambling and prostitution, prison and asylum reform, the destruction of slavery, and women's rights. Proponents of nativism and school reform often allied closely with moral reform movements. National political parties kept their distance, but both major political parties relied heavily on ethnic and religious groups in many localities to build their organizations and voting base. Whigs absorbed many evangelical Protestants. Most Catholics became Democrats. Whigs became the party of moral reform, whereas Democrats often campaigned on the freedom of religion.

Constitutional arguments and issues evolved when Americans confronted religious diversity. Such proponents of religious freedom in the Colonial, Framing, and Early National Eras as Roger Williams and James Madison relied heavily on Protestant religious principles when defending the separation of church and state. Prominent proponents of religious freedom during the 1830s more often relied on the secular claim that the Constitution gave government no right to interfere in religious affairs. Americans in the Colonial, Founding, and Early National Eras debated whether government should provide financial support for Protestant sects and exclude non-Christians from political privileges. In 1833 Massachusetts became the last state to abandon financial support of churches, ending formal religious establishment in the United States. Americans in the Jacksonian Era debated whether such practices as Bible reading in schools and such practices as hiring legislative chaplains inculcated republican virtues or were illegitimate efforts to promote Protestant religious beliefs.

Catholics were the focus of many important constitutional debates over religion. Many nativists questioned whether Catholics could be good republican citizens. Samuel Morse declared, "Popery is also a political, a despotic system, which we must repel as altogether incompatible with the existence of freedom."[11] Proponents of religious diversity regarded these anti-Catholic polemics as "a direct attack upon the Constitution itself," and "beneath criticism."[12] Catholics objected to the widespread practice of reading from the King James Bible in public schools. Protestants objected to Catholic calls for states to fund parochial schools.

Establishment

Controversy swirled over whether the United States was a Christian nation. Protestant leaders demanded a greater religious presence in both public life and the public schools. Lyman Beecher, a prominent leader of the Second Great Awakening, insisted that "[Protestant] religious education and moral principle" were necessary to preserve republican institutions.[13] Senator George Badger declared that the framers "did not intend to spread over all the public authorities and the whole public action of the nation the dead and revolting spectacle of atheistical apathy."[14] Many Democrats (and Catholics) challenged these sentiments. William Leggett stated that official thanksgiving days were inconsistent with the constitutional commitment to "perfect free trade in religion." He believed it was a matter of "regret that even this single exception should exist to that rule of entire separation of the affairs of state from those of the church...."[15] Jacksonian opponents of establishment relied more on constitutional principles than on Christian tenets. The Constitution, not God, some Americans suggested, mandated the strict separation of church and state. One collection of critics petitioning against congressional chaplains declared, "No ecclesiastical authority has been delegated to the National Legislature."[16]

Free Exercise

The Jacksonian Era witnessed the development of a distinctive free exercise claim. The most important free exercise controversies in the Founding and Early National Eras were over whether religious believers had a right to exemption from secular state laws. Quakers, for ex-

11. Samuel F. B. Morse, *Foreign Conspiracy against the Liberties of the United States*, 7th Ed. (New York: American and Foreign Christian Union, 1855), 112.

12. Philip Phillips, "On the Religious Proscription of Catholics," July 4, 1855, reprinted in *The American Jewish Archives*, October 1959, 182.

13. Lyman Beecher, *A Plea for the West* (Cincinnati, OH: Truman and Smith, 1815), 23.

14. The Reports of Committees of the Senate of the United States for the Second Session of the Thirty-Second Congress, 1852–53 (Washington: Robert Armstrong, 1853), 4.

15. William Leggett, *A Collection of the Political Writings of William Leggett*, ed. Theodore Sedgwick, Jr. (New York: Taylor & Dodd, 1840), 2:115.

16. "Remonstrance Against the Appointment of Chaplains to Congress, by Inhabitants of Livingston County, Kentucky," Executive Documents, 23rd Cong., 1st Sess. (1833), 141.

ample, claimed the right not to engage in military service. Many free exercise controversies in the Jacksonian Era were over whether religious believers had a right to exemption from laws they believed inconsistent with the separation of church and state. These challenges combined establishment and free exercise arguments in ways that are difficult to disentangle. *Donahue v. Richards* (ME 1854) raised questions about whether public schools could require students to read from the King James Bible and, if they could, whether Catholic students had a free exercise right to be excused from that exercise.[17] The controversy over Sunday mail raised questions about whether the government could forbear from delivering the mail on the Christian day of rest and, if not, whether Christian postmasters had a free exercise right to not work on Sundays.

Constitutional authorities before the Civil War generally rejected free exercise claims. The Supreme Judicial Court of Massachusetts in *Commonwealth v. Kneeland* (MA 1838) insisted that laws against blasphemy promoted the public peace and protected the sanctity of oaths.[18] School board members maintained that Bible reading promoted general moral principles, and that attacks on "popery" in the textbooks used in public schools accurately depicted history. No state court found that religious believers had a right to be exempt from general state laws. Congress did, however, permit religious postmasters to not work on Sundays.

Illustration 5-2 Tilden's Wolf at the Door

In this 1876 cartoon by Thomas Nast, schoolmaster Uncle Sam helps defend the school door from Democratic presidential candidate Samuel Tilden's "wolf," the Roman Catholic Church. Political support for government funding of parochial schools and accommodation of Catholic concerns in government-run schools often divided along partisan lines, and the conflicts that began with large-scale Irish immigration in the 1830s continued until well after the Civil War.

Source: Thomas Nast, "Tilden's Wolf at the Door," *Harper's Weekly*, September 16, 1876. Provided courtesy of HarpWeek.

Catholics and Protestants Debate Funding for Parochial Schools in New York City (1840)

New York City was a flash point in the debate over the creation of "common," or public, schools. Public schools in the city required that students read from the King James Bible and often taught history in ways that placed Roman Catholicism in a bad light. Catholics who objected to these practices established private religious schools. Many Catholic leaders insisted that the state provide the same funding for those parochial schools as government did for Protestant-dominated public schools.

Catholic Bishop John Hughes (1797–1864) arrived in New York just as these debates were heating up. He quickly became a leading champion for Catholic immigrants and state funding for parochial schools. Hughes condemned such practices as requiring that students read from the King James Bible and taxing Catholic parents to support the common schools, because, he claimed, both interfered with the ability of Catholics to freely practice their religion. The Roman Catholic community of New York on July 27, 1840, passed resolutions condemning the constitutionality of New York City public education. The crucial paragraphs declared,

> *Whereas, The wisdom and liberality of the Legislature of this State did provide, at the public expense, for the education of the poor children of the State, without injury or detriment to the civil and religious rights vested in their parents or guardians by the laws of nature and of the land; and, whereas, the administration of that system, as now conducted, is such that the parents or*

17. *Donahue v. Richards*, 38 Me. 376 (1854).

18. *Commonwealth v. Kneeland*, 37 Mass. 206 (1838).

guardians of Catholic children cannot allow them to frequent such schools without doing violence to these rights of conscience which the Constitution secures equal and inviolable to all citizens, viz.: They cannot allow their children to be brought up under a system which proposes to shut the door against Christianity, under the pretext of excluding sectarianism, and which yet has not the merit of being true to its bad promise;

And, whereas, Catholics who are the least wealthy, and most in need of the education intended by the bounty of the State, are those cut off from the benefit of funds to which they are obliged to contribute, and constrained either to contribute new funds for the purposes of education among themselves, or else to see their children brought up under a system of free-thinking and practical irreligion, or else to see them left in that ignorance which they dread, and which it was the benevolent and wise intention of the Legislature to remove; therefore,

Resolved, That the operation of the common school system, as the same is now administered, is a violation of our civil and religious rights.

Mainstream Protestants challenged these assertions. The Public School Society of New York City, the leading proponent of existing public school practices, insisted that Catholics were bent on violating the state constitution. The trustees of the society declared that proposals to fund private Catholic schools violated fundamental constitutional principles:

Unconstitutional—because in our State charter, and in our statute-book, the common school fund is appropriated to and for the benefit and support of common schools only and exclusively; and we deem it self-evident that no school can be so called, unless opened to all classes and descriptions of citizens, and conducted on a system to which none can reasonably object. Such is not the case with the Catholic schools. The peculiar sectarian tenets of that faith are part, and by them thought to be an essential part of the course of instruction; and hence all unbelievers in Catholic doctrines are unwilling, and may with good reason object, to send their children to such schools.

Unconstitutional—because it is utterly at variance with the letter and spirit of our chartered rights, and with the genius of our political institutions, that the community should be taxed to support an establishment in which sectarian dogmas are inculcated, whether that establishment be a school or a church.[19]

19. William Oland Bourne, *History of the Public School Society of the City of New York* (New York: Wm. Wood & Co., 1870), 180.

The Public School Society successfully prevented Catholic schools from receiving state funds. Governor William Seward's proposal to divide state funds between public and private schools failed. Instead, the New York legislature passed a law forbidding state funding for religious instruction or for schools where religion was taught. This had little effect on the status quo. Proponents of New York public schools denied that Bible reading was religious instruction.

The following two excerpts summarize the Catholic and Protestant positions on the constitutional issues raised by New York City school practices. All parties agreed that religious education is vital to student development. Their dispute was over whether public schools engage in sectarian religious instruction. Why does Bishop Hughes believe New York practice in 1840 to be unconstitutional? Why does Hughes call for funding for Catholic schools instead of removing Protestant practices from public schools? On what grounds do the Protestant pastors dispute Catholic charges? Why do they claim that the public schools are nonsectarian?

John Hughes, Speech on the School Question[20]

. . .

[A] Catholic could not conscientiously approve this system, if he were an enlightened Catholic, and understood his duty to his God and the principles of his religion, and remembered that education comprehended the mysterious development of the young mind, with its three-fold faculties of will, memory, and understanding. The inculcation of knowledge is only part of an enlightened system of education; a training of the WILL is as necessary as the cultivation of the other faculties of the mind, and as the Common School system is in this respect deficient, he repeated that a parent who understood that system, and had a knowledge of his religion and of his own responsibility, would never submit to it. The Catholic primitive, continuous, perpetual church never recognized the principles of leaving the mind of a child without religious culture until it grew up. . . . Therefore, he said, this common school system was Protestant, but it was not the system Catholics could adopt with their children, because they gave religious instruction to their children as a duty which

20. Excerpted from John Hughes, *Complete Works of the Most Rev. John Hughes*, ed. Lawrence Kehoe (New York: Lawrence Kehoe, 1866), 1:41.

was imperative, while Protestants were independent of religious education, and were of opinion that it was best to have religion to come at some uncertain period, when a change of heart would occur, and a person was to "join the church." . . .

He contended for the right of conscience, and for the sacred right of every man to educate his own children; and when these are the consequences that follow this system of Common School education, he asked if it were just to tax such a man for its support, while its tendency was to draw away the mind of his child from the religion which he professed and which he desired to teach him. The question was a simple one, and he was sure they would see but very little difference between it and the question of tithes for the support of the Protestant church in England and Ireland. To be sure, in those countries they had not excluded the Catholics from the churches: they said, our churches are open; we have provided them expressly for your benefit; if you don't come, it is your own fault; but whether you come or not, you must give us your money. . . . He did not ask for the Catholics anything that was not just; that was not constitutional. All laws of the country—all constitutional laws—are necessarily founded on the principle which secures to every man his religious rights, and if any law trenches on that right, he asserted that it was not, and could not be constitutional. . . .

. . .

Let there be granted to the Catholics a fair and just proportion of the funds appropriated for the Common Schools, provided the Catholics will do with it the same thing that is done in the Common Schools, and leave no reason to complain that the system is not followed. If they will do that they will take away the Catholic's cause of anxiety for his children.

The Pastors of the Methodist Episcopal Church, To the Honorable the Common Council of the City of New York[21]

. . .

It must be manifest to the Common Council, that, if the Roman Catholic claims are granted, all the other Christian denominations will urge their claims for a similar appropriation, and that the money raised for education by a general tax will be solely applied to the purposes of proselytism, through the medium of sectarian schools. But if this were done, would it be the price of peace? Or would it not throw the apple of discord into the whole Christian community, should we agree in the division of the spoils? Would each sect be satisfied with the portion allotted to it? . . . But, when all the Christian sects shall be satisfied with their individual share of the public fund, what is to become of those children whose parents belong to none of these sects, and who cannot conscientiously allow them to be educated in the peculiar dogmas of any one of them? . . . We are sorry that the reading of the Bible in the public schools, without note or commentary, is offensive to them; but we cannot allow the Holy Scriptures to be accompanied with their notes and commentaries, and to be put into the hands of the children who may hereafter be the rulers and legislators of our beloved country; because, among other bad things taught in these commentaries, is to be found the lawfulness of murdering heretics, and the unqualified submission, in all matters of conscience, to the Roman Catholic Church.

. . .

If all are to be released from taxation when they cannot conscientiously derive any benefit from the disbursement of the money collected, what will be done for the Society of Friends, and other sects who are opposed to war under all circumstances? Many of these, besides the tax paid on all foreign goods thus consumed, pay direct duties at the Custom House, which go to the payment of the army and to purchase the munitions of war. And even when the Government finds it necessary to lay direct war taxes, these conscientious sects are compelled to pay their proportion, on the ground that the public defence requires it. So, it is believed, the public interest requires the education of the whole rising generation; because it would be unsafe to commit the public liberty, and the perpetuation of our republican institutions, to those whose ignorance of their nature and value would render them careless of their preservation, or the easy dupes of artful innovators; and hence every citizen is required to contribute in proportion to his means to the public purpose of universal education.

The Roman Catholics complain that books have been introduced into the public schools which are injurious to them as a body. It is allowed, however, that the passages in these books to which such reference is made are chiefly, if not entirely, historical; and we put

21. Excerpted from Bourne, *History*, 198–201.

it to the candor of the Common Council to say, whether any history of Europe for the last ten centuries could be written which could either omit to mention the Roman Catholic Church, or mention it without recording historical facts unfavorable to that Church? . . .

History itself, then, must be falsified for their accommodation; and yet they complain that the system of education adopted in the public schools does not teach the sinfulness of lying. They complain that no religion is taught in these schools, and declare that any, even the worst form of Christianity, would be better than none: and yet they object to the reading of the Holy Scriptures, which are the only foundation of all true religion. Is it not plain, then, that they will not be satisfied with any thing short of the total abandonment of public school instruction, or the appropriation of such portion of the public fund as they may claim to their own sectarian purposes? . . .

C. Guns

Jacksonians closely tied the right to bear arms with citizenship. In *Dred Scott v. Sandford* (1857), Chief Justice Roger Taney insisted that state laws in the eighteenth century prohibiting persons of color from serving in the militia or bearing arms demonstrated that the framers believed that free persons of color were not American citizens. Constitutional commentators linked gun rights with a citizen's obligation to serve in the militia. Supreme Court Justice Joseph Story declared that "the importance" of the Second Amendment "will scarcely be doubted." He added:

> The militia is the natural defence of a free country against sudden foreign invasions, domestic insurrections, and domestic usurpations of power by rulers. It is against sound policy for a free people to keep up large military establishments and standing armies in time of peace, both from the enormous expenses, with which they are attended, and the facile means, which they afford to ambitious and unprincipled rulers, to subvert the government, or trample upon the rights of the people. The right of the citizens to keep, and bear arms has justly been considered, as the palladium of the liberties of a republic; since it offers a strong moral check against the usurpation and arbitrary power of rulers.[22]

Other commentators insisted that citizens enjoyed a fundamental right to self-defense. American abolitionists maintained that persons of color were citizens who had the right to use weapons to protect themselves and their families. Joel Tiffany declared, "The right to keep and bear arms also implies the right to use them if necessary in self defense."[23]

Americans did not agree on the relationship between the right to bear arms, militia service, and self-defense. The Supreme Court of Arkansas in *State v. Buzzard* (AR 1842) limited the bearing of arms to militia service. Other state courts connected the bearing of arms with self-defense. *Nunn v. State* (GA 1846) spoke of a citizen's "natural right of self-defense, or of his constitutional right to keep and bear arms." Race influenced gun rights.[24] State constitutions and statutes limited militia service and the bearing of arms to free white citizens. *State v. Newsom* (NC 1844) held that free persons of color were not among the "people" whom the constitution of North Carolina declared "have a right to bear arms for the defense of the State."[25]

State v. Buzzard, 4 Ark. 18 (1842)

Buzzard was indicted for carrying a concealed weapon. At trial he successfully moved to have the indictment quashed on the ground that the Arkansas law banning concealed weapons violated the right to bear arms protected by the state and federal constitutions. The state appealed this decision to the Supreme Court of Arkansas.

The Supreme Court of Arkansas ruled that the state concealed-weapons law did not abridge the right to bear arms. The judicial opinions in Buzzard *represent the most extensive antebellum discussion on the relationship between the right to bear arms, militia service, and self-defense. How would you describe the differences between the majority opinions and the dissent? Do the judges dispute basic constitutional principles, methods of constitutional interpretation, or applications of shared principles? Do the justices simply have different values? Are the judges engaged in a good-faith dispute over the meaning of constitutional principles, or do some opinions smuggle illegitimate nonlegal principles into constitutional interpretation?*

---

22. Joseph Story, *Commentaries on the Constitution of the United States*, abridged ed. (Boston: Hilliary, Gray and Company, 1833), 708.

23. Joel Tiffany, *A Treatise on the Unconstitutionality of American Slavery* (1849) (reprint Miami: Mnemosyne, 1969), 117–118.

24. *Nunn v. State*, 1 Kelley 243 (GA 1846).

25. *State v. Newsom*, 27 N.C. (5 Ired.) 250 (1844).

Contemporary constitutional commentators dispute whether the result of State v. Buzzard *reflects a general sentiment in Jacksonian America that the right to bear arms was limited to militia service.* State v. Buzzard *is the precedent of choice for contemporary Americans who champion a narrow reading of Second Amendment. Nevertheless, other Jacksonian cases connect the right to bear arms to self-defense. The Supreme Court of Louisiana in* State v. Chandler *(LA 1850) spoke of persons' right to "a manly and noble defence of themselves" when construing the state constitutional right to bear arms.*[26] *Contemporary champions of broad gun rights insist that such cases as* Chandler *are more reflective of constitutional opinion before the Civil War.*

CHIEF JUSTICE RINGO

...

... [I]t may not be without utility to inquire for what object the right to keep and bear arms is retained exempt from all legal regulation or control, if in fact it has been so retained, as urged in the argument for the appellee. Is it to enable each member of the community to protect and defend by individual force his private rights against every illegal invasion, or to obtain redress in like manner for injuries thereto committed by persons acting contrary to law? Certainly not; because, according to the fundamental principles of government, such rights are created, limited, and defined by law, or retained subject to be regulated and controlled thereby; and the laws alone are and must be regarded as securing to every individual the quiet enjoyment of every right with which he is invested; thus affording to all persons, through the agency of the public authorities to whom their administration and execution are confided, ample redress for every violation thereof. And to these authorities every person is, in most cases, bound to resort, for the security of his private rights, as well as the redress of all injuries thereto. . . .

...

. . . [T]he government possesses, in my opinion, ample power to inhibit, by law, all such acts and practices of individuals, as affect, injuriously, the private rights of others, tend to disturb domestic tranquility, or the peace and good order of society, militate against the common interests, impair the means of common defence, or sap the free institutions of the country; and to enforce the observance of such laws by adequate penalties, the character and quantum of which, in most respects, depend exclusively upon the will and judgment of the Legislature.

If these general powers of the government are restricted in regard to the right to keep and bear arms, the limitation, to whatever extent it may exist, will be better understood, and more clearly seen, when the object for which the right is supposed to have been retained, is stated. That object could not have been to protect or redress by individual force, such rights as are merely private and individual, as has been already, it is believed, sufficiently shown: consequently, the object must have been to provide an additional security for the public liberty and the free institutions of the state, as no other important object is perceived, which the reservation of such right could have been designed to effect. Besides which, the language used appears to indicate distinctly that this, and this alone, was the object for which the article under consideration was adopted. And it is equally apparent, that a well regulated militia was considered by the people as the best security a free state could have, or at least, the best within their power to provide. But it was also well understood that the militia, without arms, however well disposed, might be unable to resist, successfully, the effort of those who should conspire to overthrow the established institutions of the country, or subjugate their common liberties; and therefore, to guard most effectually against such consequences, and enable the militia to discharge this most important trust, so reposed in them, and for this purpose only, it is conceived the right to keep and bear arms was retained, and the power which, without such reservation, would have been vested in the government, to prohibit, by law, their keeping and bearing arms for any purpose whatever was so far limited or withdrawn; which conclusion derives additional support from the well-known fact that the practice of maintaining a large standing army in times of peace had been denounced and repudiated by the people of the United States as an institution dangerous to civil liberty and a free State, which produced at once the necessity of providing some adequate means for the security and defense of the state, more congenial to civil liberty and republican government. And it is confidently believed that the people designed and expected to accomplish this object by the adoption of the article under consideration, which would forever invest them with a legal right to keep and bear arms for that purpose; but it surely was not designed to operate

26. *State v. Chandler*, 5 La. Ann. 489 (1850).

as an immunity to those who should so keep or bear their arms as to injure or endanger the private rights of others, or in any manner prejudice the common interests of society.

. . .

Suppose a portion of the community consider their private rights invaded by some act or exercise of authority on the part of the government, which they consider as unauthorized, can they, by virtue of any legal right with which they are invested, either prevent or redress such injury by private force? In my opinion they cannot; their private rights being in this, as in most other cases, committed, as it were, to the care and custody of the law, and to it, so long as our civil liberties and republican institutions remain unimpaired, they are bound to look for protection as well as redress; both of which the government is under a positive obligation to provide. . . .

JUSTICE LACY

. . . I take the expressions "a well regulated militia being necessary for the security of a free State," and the terms "common defense," to be the reasons assigned for the granting of the right, and not a restriction or limitation upon the right itself, or the perfect freedom of its exercise. The security of the state is the constitutional reason for the guaranty. But when was it contended before that the reason given for the establishment of a right or its uninterrupted enjoyment not only limited the right itself, but restrained it to a single specific object? . . . According to the rule laid down in [the majority's] interpretation of this clause, I deem the right to be valueless and not worth preserving; for the State unquestionably possesses the power, without the grant, to arm the militia and direct how they shall be employed in cases of invasion or domestic insurrection. If this be the meaning of the Constitution, why give that which is no right in itself and guarantees a privilege that is useless? This construction, according to the views I entertain, takes the arms out of the hands of the people, and places them in the hands of the Legislature, with no restraint or limitation whatever upon their power, except their own free will and sovereign pleasure. Are great affirmative grants of political powers to be determined by this technical rule of verbal criticism? If so, its rigid application to other portions of the Constitution would erase from its pages many of its most important and salutary provisions. Such a principle, I apprehend, should never be recognized or adopted by any judicial tribunal in determining the inherent and original rights of the citizen. It goes to abridge instead of enlarging the constitutional guarantees of personal liberty.

. . . I deny that any just or free government upon earth has the power to disarm its citizens and to take from them the only security and ultimate hope that they have for the defense of their liberties and their rights. I deny this, not only upon constitutional grounds, but upon the immutable principles of natural and equal justice that all men have a right to, and which to deprive them of amounts to tyranny and oppression. Can it be doubted, that if the Legislature, in moments of high political excitement or of revolution, were to pass an act disarming the whole population of the State, that such an act would be utterly void, not only because it violated the spirit and tenor of the Constitution, but because it invaded the original rights of natural justice? Now, if they are private and not public arms, the Constitution guarantees the right of keeping and bearing them.

. . . A man's arms are his private property: how, then, can he be legally deprived of them? If they can forbid him, under the penalty of fine and imprisonment, to keep them concealed or exposed about his person, or on his own premises, although their unrestrained use may be necessary for all the purposes of his ordinary business and of personal defense, then certainly the right of keeping and bearing arms according to his own discretion, is infringed and violated, and his own free will in the management of this property abridged and destroyed.

. . . I maintain that the simple fact of a man's keeping and bearing private arms, whether concealed or exposed, is an act innocent of itself, and its freedom secured from all legislative interference. The act being innocent and allowed, can not be made penal, or prohibited by law. The existence and freedom of a right is one thing, and the culpable and criminal use of it another and a wholly different thing. A right, in itself innocent and guaranteed by law, can not be made illegal or punished as a crime; and the error into which the court has fallen in the present instance, seems to me to result from confounding these two things, which are wholly separate and independent of each other.

. . . I maintain that the act is not only lawful, but expressly secured by the Constitution, and of course cannot be controlled by ordinary legislation. I admit that, if a man uses his arms improperly, or in an unlawful manner, then it is competent for the Legislature to punish him for the improper and illegal use of them; and it is right to do so; for every one is bound so to exercise his own rights, as not to prejudice those of others. The Legislature, in doing this, does not punish an innocent act, but an unwarrantable one; it does not abridge a natural and constitutional right, or in any manner interfere with its freedom. It merely punishes an unlawful use of a right; and it can do that only when the party has committed, with his own arms, unauthorized aggression upon the person or property of another. . . .

Sic utere tuo, non lædas alienum ["so use your own so as not to harm that of another"] is a maxim that runs through the whole body of the English common law, and pervades every part of our entire system of jurisprudence. . . . The application of this governing rule in the construction of laws, demonstrates and explains the reasons why it would be unlawful so to keep arms and ammunition of any kind, as to endanger the lives or property of others; and it solves the supposed difficulty, that if there is no limitation or restriction of the power of keeping and bearing arms, then the State has no authority to disarm a criminal for any offense whatever. When a citizen breaks his covenant with his government, he forfeits the protection of her laws; and of course this supercedes or destroys many of his municipal rights and political franchises, which he otherwise would be entitled to receive at her hands.

. . . By far the most important and largest of the rights of the Constitution appertain exclusively to the person of the citizen, and concern the inherent rights of life, liberty and property. Many of these rights lie behind the Constitution, and existed antecedent to its formation and its adoption. They are embodied in its will, and organized by its power, to give them greater sanctity and effect. They are written that they may be understood and remembered; and then declared inviolate and supreme, because they cannot be weakened or invaded without doing the government and citizen manifest injustice and wrong. Among these rights, I hold, is the privilege of the people to keep and to bear their private arms for the necessary defense of their person, habitation and property, or for any useful or innocent purpose whatever. We derive this right from our Anglo-Saxon ancestors, and under the form of that government it has ever been regarded as sacred and inviolable. It is of great antiquity and of invaluable price. Its necessary operation, in times of convulsion and of revolution, has been the only means by which public liberty or the security of free States has been vindicated and maintained. Here, the principles of equal and natural justice, as well as the obvious meaning and spirit of the Constitution, have placed it above legislative interference. To forbid a citizen, under the penalty of fine and imprisonment, to carry his own private arms about his person, in any manner that he may think proper for his security or safety, is, in my opinion, an unauthorized attempt to abridge a constitutional privilege, and therefore I hold the law in question to be of no effect.

D. Personal Freedom and Public Morality

Americans regulated sexual morality without constitutional qualms. Very few radicals aside, a general consensus existed that sexual activity could be heavily regulated and confined to marriage. The Supreme Judicial Court of Massachusetts in *Parton v. Hervey* (MA 1854) declared,

> In regulating the intercourse of the sexes, by giving its highest sanctions to the contract of marriage, and rendering it, as far as possible, inviolable, the law looks, beyond the welfare of the individual and a class, to the general interests of society; and seeks, in the exercise of a wise and sound policy, to chasten and refine this intercourse, and to guard against the manifold evils which would result from illicit cohabitation.[27]

Drinking raised bitterly contested issues of public morality during the mid-eighteenth century. Temperance brought together a broad coalition of supporters. Women were concerned about the sobriety of their husbands; native Protestants were concerned about the sobriety of Catholic immigrants; businessmen were concerned about the sobriety of their workers. Temperance societies first relied on moral suasion and community pressure. When those seemed inadequate, reformers turned to legal regulation and eventually prohibition. As detailed in Table 5-2, the American Temperance Society persuaded many state legislatures, particularly in the Northeast, to pass laws restricting or prohibiting the sale of alcohol. Other Americans, who resented these intrusions on both their businesses and their private lives, insisted that these laws violated numerous constitutional rights.[28]

---

27. *Parton v. Hervey*, 1 Gray 119 (Mass. 1854).

28. John Compton has recently argued that property rights may have trumped the public good in morals cases more often than conventional wisdom suggests. See John W. Compton, "A Moral Revolution: Evangelical Reform and the Transformation of American Constitutionalism, 1830-1937" (Ph.D. Dissertation, UCLA, 2011)

Table 5-2 Major State Statutes in First Wave of Alcohol Prohibition

State	Adoption	Type	Fate
Massachusetts	1838	No liquor sales in quantities smaller than 15 gallons	Repealed, 1840
Rhode Island	1838	Local option licensing law	Replaced, 1853
Mississippi	1839	No liquor sales in quantities smaller than 1 gallon	Repealed, 1842
Vermont	1844	Local option for prohibition	Replaced, 1850
Pennsylvania	1846	Local option for prohibition	Struck down, 1847
Delaware	1847	Local option for prohibition	Struck down, 1847
Maine	1851	Statutory prohibition	Repealed, 1856
Massachusetts	1852	Statutory prohibition	Repealed, 1868
Rhode Island	1853	Statutory prohibition	Struck down and modified, 1854; replaced, 1863
Michigan	1853	Statutory prohibition	Struck down, 1854
Indiana	1853	Statutory prohibition	Struck down, 1855
Connecticut	1854	Statutory prohibition	Replaced, 1872
Minnesota	1854	Statutory prohibition for Sioux Indian territory	Replaced, 1887
Delaware	1855	Statutory prohibition	Replaced, 1857
Iowa	1855	Statutory prohibition	Struck down and modified, 1857; replaced, 1858
Indiana	1855	Statutory prohibition	Repealed, 1857
Nebraska	1855	Statutory prohibition	Repealed, 1858
Michigan	1855	No liquor sales in quantities smaller than 5 gallons	Repealed, 1875
New York	1855	Statutory prohibition	Replaced, 1857
New Hampshire	1855	Alcohol can only be kept and sold by town liquor agents	Repealed, 1903

Source: Ernest Hurst Cherrington, *Standard Encyclopedia of the Alcohol Problem*, 6 vols. (Westerville, Ohio: American Issue Publishing Co., 1925).

Most direct constitutional attacks on temperance laws failed. *People v. Gallagher* (MI 1856) is one prominent an example of a state court decision sustaining state power to restrict alcoholic beverages. Judge Johnson insisted that courts must defer to the legislative judgment that "intemperance was an evil, . . . very much aggravated by the unrestricted traffic of intoxicating liquors."[29] The Supreme Court of Delaware reached the same conclusion. If owners had a constitutional right to sell alcoholic beverages, the justices concluded,

> the sovereignty of the State would be robbed of nearly all its police power, and the individual right to dispose of his property would be above the right of the public to be protected in their morals, health, peace or safety. Poisonous drugs; unwholesome food; infected goods; demoralizing books or prints; combustible and explosive substances; dangerous animals; and every species of property could be held and transferred at the will of the owner. . . . The right

29. *People v. Gallagher*, 4 Mich. 244 (1856).

to sell it is conferred by law and may be taken away by law, or its use prohibited in any specified form which is deemed to be injurious or demoralizing.[30]

IV. Democratic Rights

MAJOR DEVELOPMENTS

- Debate over anti-slavery petitions and speech
- Near-universal white male suffrage
- Greater recognition of expatriation rights

Jacksonians revered democracy. The dominant coalition enthusiastically called themselves "Democrats" or "the Democracy"—a label that has stuck for almost two hundred years. The *Democratic Review* was a leading journal of the period. John L. O'Sullivan, the owner of that periodical, declared that "the first principle of democracy" was "an abiding confidence in the virtue, intelligence, and full capacity for self-government, of the great mass of our people, our industrious, honest, manly, intelligent millions of freemen."[31]

These democratic sentiments inaugurated a new era of constitutional politics. Political elites of the Founding and Early National Eras maintained that governing should be done by a "natural aristocracy" chosen by a voting system designed to privilege the "best persons." Jacksonians rejected this elitist politics. Their constitution was unashamedly "democratic." Andrew Jackson expressed this sensibility when he declared in his First Annual Message to Congress, "[The] duties of all public offices are, or at least admit of being made, so plain and simple that men of intelligence may readily qualify themselves for their performance."

Jacksonians fell far short of their democratic ideals. Most Americans favored silencing anti-slavery advocates by legal or extralegal means. States removed economic qualifications for voting but often added new restrictions aimed at limiting the political power of new immigrants. Nonwhites were routinely denied citizenship and the rights associated with citizenship. Whether the United States would have scored higher on a contemporary democratic index in 1860 than in 1828 is doubtful. Certainly the improvement would not be substantial.

Americans both expanded and narrowed understandings of popular government during this era. From the perspective of native white men uninterested in slavery, the Jacksonian Era fulfilled the democratic promise of the Constitution. By the 1850s, most states had instituted near-universal white male suffrage, vigorous political debate was taking place on the issues dividing Jacksonians from Whigs, and white men enjoyed a broad set of rights associated with citizenship. Jacksonian democracy was largely confined to these white men. Jackson and his successors built on past precedents that understood the United States as a white man's country, rather than on those that emphasized a constitutional commitment to the rights of all persons.

When reading the materials below, consider two issues. First, is the Jacksonian tendency to increase the democratic rights of white males in any way connected to the Jacksonian tendency to reject the democratic rights of persons of color or those who championed their causes? Second, what is the relationship between the politics and law of democratic rights during the Jacksonian Era? To what extent were Jacksonians animated by a coherent theory of democracy, at least for white males? To what extent did constitutional decision makers simply want their supporters to have more rights?

A. Free Speech

Free speech rights in Jacksonian America varied according to the subject. Persons spoke freely on matters that divided Democrats from Whigs. Americans vigorously debated the merits of the national bank and internal improvements. Americans opposed to the Mexican War suffered no legal consequences when they called President Polk a liar and the military conflict a "senseless quest for more room."[32] Anti-slavery advocacy, however, bore the brunt of censorship. Prominent abolitionists after 1830 insisted on the immediate emancipation of all slaves. Slaveholders decried such advocacy as inciting slave rebellions. Political moderates decried such advocacy as threatening the union.

30. *State v. Allmond*, 7 Del. 612 (1858).

31. John L. O'Sullivan, "An Introductory Statement of the Democratic Principle," in *Social Theories of Jacksonian Democracy: Representative Writings of the Period 1825–1850*, ed. Joseph L. Blau (New York: Liberal Arts Press, 1954), 22.

32. Frederick Merk, "Dissent in the Mexican War," *Proceedings of the Massachusetts Historical Society* 81 (1969):48–50.

Illustration: 5-3 Election Day in New York
This illustration from a London newspaper depicts election day in New York City in 1864 at two polling stations, one located in the "aristocratic quarter" and the other in the "dirty and unwholesome districts" of the city. Although paid partisan "shoulder-hitters" who "traveled on their muscle" could be seen circulating in the crowd of wealthy male voters, the lower-class crowd voted next to the local liquor store under the watchful eye of a heavy police presence.

Source: "Election Day in New York," *Illustrated London News*, December 3, 1864. Manuscript, Archives, and Rare Book Library, Emory University.

Slaveholders and their political (usually Democratic Party) allies had various means for silencing anti-slavery speech.

- Anti-abolitionist mobs in the North destroyed abolitionist presses and murdered one abolitionist editor
- Anti-abolitionist post officers refused to deliver anti-slavery pamphlets
- Anti-abolitionist members of Congress refused to consider anti-slavery petitions
- Anti-abolitionist state legislators proposed criminalizing anti-slavery advocacy

These efforts enjoyed mixed success. Mob violence failed to suppress abolitionist journals. Congress passed vague legislation regulating the post office that some presidents interpreted as prohibiting postmasters from delivering anti-slavery materials. From 1836 until 1844 Congress tabled all anti-slavery petitioners. Southern states criminalized anti-slavery advocacy, and *State v. Worth* (NC 1860) held that one such statute was constitutional.[33] Northern states refused to censor abolitionists.

Efforts to silence abolitionists often backfired. Many northerners who were not particularly concerned with the plight of African-American slaves were distressed when their white neighbors were arrested or attacked for speaking out against slavery. Anti-slavery advocates in the North found that they could organize mass support for their cause by placing greater emphasis on how slave owner demands for national censorship violated the rights of white citizens. The motto of the anti-slavery Free Soil Party was "Free Soil, Free Speech, Free Labor and Free Men." The Republican Party's 1856 platform complained that "the freedom of speech and of the press has been abridged."

Congress Debates Incendiary Publications in the Mail (1836)

The first constitutional controversy over abolitionist speech arose when the American Anti-Slavery Society in 1835 mailed abolitionist pamphlets to prominent southern citizens. Amos Kendall (1789–1869), the U.S. postmaster general, informed local postmasters that they had no obligation to deliver abolitionist literature, even though no law existed on the subject. "Without claiming for the General Government the power to pass laws prohibiting the discussions of any sort, as a means of protecting States from domestic violence," he wrote, "it may be safely assumed, that the United States have no right through their officers or departments, knowingly to be instrumental in producing, within the several States, the very mischief which the Constitution commands them to repress."[34] Both Kendall and President Jackson immediately urged Congress to pass a law legally banning anti-slavery literature from the mails.

33. *State v. Worth*, 52 N.C. 488 (1860).

34. "Report of the Postmaster General," House Documents, Twenty-Fourth Congress, First Session (1835), Appendix 9.

Illustration 5-4 New Method of Assorting the Mail, as Practiced by Southern Slave-Holders, or Attack on the Post Office, Charleston, SC
Depiction of an 1835 mob entering a post office and burning abolitionist literature in Charleston, South Carolina. The mob was led by former governor Robert Y. Hayne. No arrests were made. Virginia responded the next year by passing a state law requiring federal postmasters to report the arrival of any abolitionist literature to the local justice of the peace, who was charged with the duty of immediately burning any materials that he deemed to be dangerous.

Source: [Boston?], 1835. Library of Congress, Prints and Photographs Division, Washington, DC 20540, USA.

Two controversies erupted when Jackson made that proposal. One controversy was over federalism. Senator John C. Calhoun (1782–1850) of South Carolina insisted that the federal government had no power to determine what literature could be mailed. He thought the federal government should prohibit only material that was banned in the recipient state. The other controversy was over free speech. Representative Hiland Hall (1795–1885) claimed that Congress could not constitutionally exclude anti-slavery speech from the mails. These legislative divisions prevented Congress from taking a clear stand on the controversy over abolitionist pamphlets. The Post Office Act of 1836 asserted that postmasters could not "unlawfully" refuse to deliver the mail but did not specify what constituted an unlawful refusal. Many Jacksonian postmaster generals interpreted that law as prohibiting postmasters from delivering anti-slavery literature in states where that literature was prohibited.

Consider the relationship between the postal power and free speech when reading the materials below. How do the participants in this debate conceptualize that relationship? Is the debate over whether the post office may refuse to deliver literature that is not protected by the First Amendment? Does the post office have to mail literature that is protected by the First Amendment? How do the various participants in the debate conceptualize the First Amendment?

Report from the Select Committee on the Circulation of Incendiary Publications (John C. Calhoun)[35]

. . .

The Select Committee fully concur with the President . . . as to the character and tendency of the papers, which have been attempted to be circulated in the South, through the mail, and participate with him in the indignant regret, which he expresses at conduct so destructive of the peace and harmony of the country, and repugnant to the Constitution, and the dictates of humanity and religion. They also concur in the hope that, if the strong tone of disapprobation which these unconstitutional and wicked attempts have called forth, does not arrest them, the non-slaveholding States will be prompt to exercise their power to suppress them, as far as their authority extends. But while they agree with the President as to the evil and its highly dangerous tendency, and the necessity of arresting it, they have not been able to assent to the measure of redress which he recommends; that Congress should pass a law prohibiting under severe penalty the transmission of incendiary publications, though the mail, intended to instigate the slaves to insurrection.

After the most careful and deliberate investigation, they have been constrained to adopt the conclusion that Congress has not the power to pass such a law: that it would be a violation of one of the most sacred provisions of the Constitution, and subversive of reserved powers essential to the preservation of the domestic institutions of the slaveholding states. . . .

. . . [The Committee] refer to the amended Article of the Constitution which . . . provides that Congress shall pass no law, which shall abridge the liberty of the press, a provision, which interposes . . . an insuperable objection to the measure recommended by the President. . . .

. . . Madison, in his celebrated report to the Virginia Legislature in 1799, against the Alien and Sedition Law, . . . conclusively settled the principle that Congress has no right, in any form, or in any manner, to interfere with the freedom of the press. . . .

. . . Assuming [the Sedition Act] to be unconstitutional . . . which no one now doubts, it will not be difficult to show that if, instead of inflicting punishment for publishing, the act had inflicted punishment for circulating through the mail, for the same offense, it would have been equally unconstitutional. The one would have abridged the freedom of the press as effectually as the other. The object of publishing is circulation, and to prohibit circulation is, in effect, to prohibit publication. They have both a common object. The communication of sentiments and opinions to the public, and the prohibition of one may as effectually suppress such communication, as the prohibition of the other, and, of course, would as effectually interfere with the freedom of the press, and be equally unconstitutional.

. . . [I]f it be admitted, that Congress has the right to discriminate in reference to their character, what papers shall, or what shall not be transmitted by the mail, [that] would subject the freedom of the press, on all subjects, political, moral, and religious, completely to its will and pleasure. . . .

. . .

. . . Nothing is more clear, than that the admission of the right on the part of Congress to determine what papers are incendiary, and as such to prohibit their circulation through the mail, necessarily involves the right to determine, what are not incendiary and to enforce their circulation. Nor is it less certain, that to admit such a right would be virtually to clothe Congress with the power to abolish slavery, by giving it the means of breaking down all the barriers which the slave holding States have erected for the protection of their lives and property. It would give Congress without regard to the prohibitory laws of the States the authority to open the gates to the flood of incendiary publications, which are ready to break into those States, and to punish all, who dare resist, as criminals. Fortunately, Congress has no such right. The internal peace and security of the States are under the protection of the States themselves, to the entire exclusion of all authority and control on the part of Congress. It belongs to them, and not to Congress, to determine what is, or is not, calculated to disturb their peace and security, and of course in the case under consideration, it belongs to the Slave holding States to determine, what is incendiary and intended to incite to insurrection, and to adopt such defensive measures, as may be necessary for their security, with unlimited means of carrying them into effect, except such as may be expressly inhibited to the States by the Constitution.

. . .

35. Sen. Doc. 118, 24th Cong., 1st Sess. (1836), reprinted in *The Papers of John C. Calhoun*, Clyde N. Wilson ed., vol. XIII (Columbia: University of South Carolina Press, 1980), 53-60.

If, consequently, the right to protect her internal peace and security belongs to a State, the general Government is bound to respect the measures adopted by her for that purpose, and to cooperate in their execution, as far as its delegated powers may admit, or the measure may require. Thus, in the present case, the slave-holding States having the unquestionable right to pass all such laws as may be necessary to maintain the existing relation between master and slave, in those States, their right, of course, to prohibit the circulation of any publication, or any intercourse, calculated to disturb or destroy that relation is incontrovertible. In the execution of the measures, which may be adopted by the States for this purpose, the powers of Congress over the mail, and of regulating commerce with foreign nations and between the States, may require cooperation on the part of the general Government; and it is bound, in conformity with the principle established, to respect the laws of the State in their exercise, and so to modify its acts, as not only not to violate those of the States, but, as far as practicable, to cooperate in their execution.

. . .

Regarding [the above principle] as established . . . the Committee . . . have prepared a Bill . . . prohibiting under penalty of fine and dismissal from office, any Deputy Postmaster, in any State, Territory or District, from knowingly receiving and putting into the mail, any letter, packet, pamphlet, paper, or pictorial representation, directed to any Post office or person in a State, Territory or District, by the laws of which the circulation is forbidden. . . .

Report of the Minority of the Committee on Post Offices and Post Roads on the President's Message[36]

. . .

. . . [T]he establishment of a censorship over all publications . . . must necessarily operate with extreme harshness. . . . In order to make the law effectual, a censor must be appointed in the vicinity of every printing press, whose duty it would be to examine every number of every periodical, and every edition of all other publications, for which a mail circulation was sought, and certify their fitness for such circulation to the postmasters. . . . One of the obvious legal effects of this mode of legislation would be to transfer the power of determining a publisher's right to circulate, and also his right of property in the publications, from a jury of his peers to the summary discretion of any one of many thousand individuals. The medium of mail circulation has become so useful and important to the press of the country, and would be so trammeled and obstructed by the previous submission of all matters to be transmitted to the tribunal of a licenser, that this species of censorship could be scarcely less exceptionable and oppressive than a censorship that should extend to the restraint of the actual printing of publications. On the whole, a law of this description would be in such direct opposition to all the preconceived opinions of the People of this country, so abhorrent to their notions of the principles of civil liberty, and so utterly destructive of the freedom of the press, that the undersigned will not permit themselves seriously to apprehend that, under any possible circumstances, such a law can ever find a place on our statute book. . . .

The second mode of legislation [is] prohibiting the circulation by mail of such publications as the States shall prohibit. . . . If one State has a right to call on Congress to enact laws to prevent the effect of a mail circulation of publications within its limits, any other State has the same right; and if the judgment of one State is to be received as evidence of the evil tendency of particular publications, the judgment of every other State must have the same force, and impose the same obligation on Congress. A statute, therefore, founded on this principle, would provide that it should be an offense against the United States for any person to send through the mail into any State any publication the circulation of which might be prohibited by the laws of such State. A statute of this description would not only punish the citizen of Massachusetts before the federal court in his State for sending publications by mail on the subject of slavery into Georgia, but would also punish the citizen of Georgia, before the federal court in his State, for sending a publication on any subject into Massachusetts, that subject, whatever it might be, having previously come under the interdict of the law of Massachusetts. . . . One State might prohibit the

---

36. *Register of the Debates in Congress*, 24th Cong., 1st Sess. (1836), 2944; also appears as "Proposed Report by Mr. Hall (of Vt.) on Incendiary Publications," *National Intelligencer*, April 8, 1836 at 2. See Richard John, "Highland Hall's 'Report on Incendiary Publications,' A Forgotten Nineteenth-Century Defense of the Freedom of the Press," 41 *American Journal of Legal History* 94 (1997).

dissemination of the Catholic doctrine; another, that of the Protestant; one that of one political sentiment, and another that of its opposite. . . .

. . .

We are then thrown back on the question of what authority Congress possesses over "incendiary publications," by the grants of power contained in the Constitution, under the restrictions on the exercise of those powers found in that instrument? . . . The mode which this species of legislation provides, for executing the judgment which the Government forms of the character of publications, is most exceptionable and alarming. It does not, like other statutes, provide for the trial and punishment of the actual offender, but for the manual seizure and destruction of the article which it judges to be offensive. It deprives the citizen of his right of trial by jury to determine the fact of the unlawfulness of the publication, and takes from him his property without any "process of law" whatever. In this respect it is a direct violation of the fifth article of the amendment to the constitution. It is a censorship of the Press, committed to this summary discretion of any single Post Master—a censorship exercised in secret and upon evidence which can only be reached by an inquisitorial scrutiny into the contents of the mails, which must at once destroy all confidence in this security for any purpose. It is believed that a law with such odious features could not long be tolerated by any free people.

. . . The minority have not been able to come to the conclusion that Congress possesses the constitutional power to restrain the mail circulation of the publications specified in the message. On the contrary, they believe that any legislation for that purpose would come in direct conflict with that clause in the Constitution which prohibits Congress from making any law "abridging the freedom of speech or of the press." . . . The meaning of the term abridge is not qualified in the Constitution by the specification of any particular degree beyond which the liberty of the press is not permitted to be diminished. The slightest contraction or lessening of that liberty is forbidden. Nor does the Constitution point out any particular mode by which the freedom of the press may not be abridged. All modes of abridgment whatever are excluded, whether by the establishment of a censorship, the imposition of punishments, a tax on the promulgation of obnoxious opinions, or by any other means which can be devised to give a legislative preference, either in publication or circulation, to one sentiment emanating from the press, over that of another. Otherwise, the clause, by being susceptible of evasion, would be nugatory and useless. It was not against particular forms of legislation but to secure the substance of the freedom of the press, that the clause was made a part of the Constitution. The object of publication is circulation. The mere power to print, without the liberty to circulate, would be utterly valueless. The Post Office power, which belongs to the General Government, is an exclusive power. Under that power Congress has the entire control of the whole regular circulation of the country. Neither a State nor individuals, in opposition to the will of Congress, can establish or carry on the business of such circulation. A power, therefore, in Congress to judge of the moral, religious, political, or physical tendency of publications, and to deny the medium of mail circulation to those it deemed of an obnoxious character, would not only enable Congress to abridge the freedom of the press, but absolutely and completely to destroy it. . . .

. . .

. . . The prohibition of "incendiary publications" from mail circulation is not within the legitimate scope of the post office power; the power of proscribing them not being at all necessary to the safe, convenient, or expeditious transportation of the mail. . . . A law to prevent their circulation would be founded in erroneous and unconstitutional principles. Under cover of providing for the convenient transportation of the mail, and of preventing its use for evil purposes, it would assume a power in Congress to judge of the tendency of opinions emanating from the press; a power to discriminate between packages, not in reference to their bulk or form, but in relation to the sentiments they might be designed to inculcate. One class of opinions, meeting the approbation of Congress, is permitted a free circulation; another class of opinions, which Congress denominate "dangerous, seditious, and incendiary," is prohibited. . . . The People of the United States never intended that the Government of the Union should exercise over the press the power of discriminating between true and erroneous opinions, of determining that this sentiment was patriotic, that seditious and incendiary, and therefore wisely prohibited Congress all power over the subject. The minority of the committee respectfully submit to the House that Congress does not possess the constitutional power to distinguish from other publications, of like size and form, the "incendiary publications" specified in the

Message of the President, or in any way to restrain their mail circulation.

B. Voting

Democrats and Whigs vigorously disputed voting rights. Many Democrats insisted that all free white male inhabitants should have the right to vote. A "democrat," they believed, was "one who favors universal suffrage."[37] Many Whigs insisted that only citizens who owned property should cast ballots, or that government should be structured in ways that gave property holders extra representatives. Judge Abel P. Upshur (1790–1844) of Virginia maintained, "If men enter into the social compact upon unequal terms; if one man brings into the partnership, his rights of person alone, and another brings into it, equal rights of person and all the rights of property beside, can they be said to have an equal interest in the common stock?"[38]

Democrats won struggles over voting rights when the focus of the debate was the rights of native-born Americans. Whigs and nativists were more successful when attempting to restrict the rights of noncitizens and immigrants. Most states abandoned both property and taxpaying requirements for voting. Most, but not all, states limited voting to citizens. Many adopted voting registration statutes to prevent fraud (and possibly limit immigrant voting). State courts declared these laws constitutional. Chief Justice Shaw in *Capen v. Foster* (MA 1832), declared registration laws "a reasonable and convenient regulation of the mode of exercising the right of voting."[39]

By 1860 most Americans were committed to universal male suffrage. Nevertheless, for every voting restriction Jacksonians abandoned, they added a new one. Registration requirements, first pioneered during the Jacksonian Era, became permanent features of the American constitutional landscape.

Legislators apportioned legislatures by both geography and population. As the population moved west and new towns sprang up, legislators were not always quick to change electoral boundaries to recognize these communities. Battles over how to conduct elections were often heated, partisan, and sometimes played out in state constitutional conventions called to restructure the legislature. Disputes over how the Rhode Island legislature was elected led to armed clashes in 1842 between the incumbent government and reformers. In most states, the move toward more fair apportionment of legislatures was less violent. Until the twentieth century, the courts stayed on the sidelines while such political battles played themselves out.

Virginia Debates Property Qualifications and Apportionment (1829–30)[40]

The Virginia Constitutional Convention of 1829–30 focused on voting rights. Two issues dominated the agenda. The most important was the apportionment of representatives to the state legislature. The original state constitution, by counting slaves as persons for purposes of representation, sharply increased the percentage of representatives from the slave-rich eastern part of the state. Western delegates insisted that representation be apportioned by the number of eligible voters, not total persons in a county. The other issue was the right to vote. The existing state constitution required that voters have a freehold worth at least $50. Many Virginians insisted that all taxpayers should have a right to vote. Both reapportionment and voting rights pitted the more affluent eastern counties of the state against the less affluent western counties.

The delegates compromised on both issues. Virginians allocated representatives by voters but relied on an 1820 census that did not fully capture relative population increases in the western counties. The freehold qualification was cut in half but not eliminated.

The continued malapportionment of the Virginia legislature was consequential. Three years later Virginia held another constitutional convention with slavery as a main item on the agenda. Western representatives proposed a gradual emancipation. Their proposal was narrowly defeated. Had representation in Virginia in 1833 been allocated entirely on the basis of the voting population, Virginia might have taken the first constitutional steps toward becoming a free state.

37. Alexander Keyssar, *The Right to Vote: The Contested History of Democracy in the United States* (New York: Basic Books, 2001), 27.

38. Abel P. Upshur, "Speech Before the Convention," 27 October 1829, quoted in Erik S. Root, *All Honor to Jefferson? The Virginia Slavery Debates and the Positive Good Thesis* (Lanham: Lexington Books, 2008), 85.

39. *Capen v. Foster*, 12 Pick. 485 (MA 1832).

40. *Proceedings and Debates of the Virginia State Convention, 1829–1830* (Richmond: Ritchie & Cook, 1830).

Consider the new political alignments in Jacksonian America when reading the excerpts below. James Madison, James Monroe, and John Marshall were political opponents during the Early National Era. Each opposed the Jacksonian revolution. Each supported property qualifications for voting and apportionment. Why did these former political rivals unite in the late 1820s? Do you note important differences and similarities between Jacksonian arguments for an expanded franchise and the arguments made during the Early National Era? To what extent did slavery influence arguments made in Virginia?

JOHN COOKE of Fredrick

. . .

[The Virginia Declaration of Rights] declares . . . in the first place, "that all power is vested in, and consequently derived from, *the people.*"

. . .

. . . Taking first the insulated proposition, that "all men are, by nature, *equally* free"; I pronounce it to be a great practical truth; a self-evident proposition; the primary postulate of the science of Government. Sir, what does this proposition mean, but that no *one* man is born with a natural right to control any *other* man; that no one man comes into the world with a mark on him, to designate him as possessing superior rights to any other man; that neither God nor nature recognize, in anticipation, the distinctions of bond and free, of despot and slave; but that these distinctions are artificial; are the work of man; are the result of fraud or violence. And who is so bold as to deny this simple truth?

. . .

But it is said, that if it be true that "all men are by nature equally free," then all men, all women, and all children, are entitled to equal shares of political power; in other words, that they are all entitled to the right of suffrage, which is, practically, political power.

. . . The framers of that instrument . . . did not *express* the self-evident truth that the Creator of the Universe, to render woman more fit for the sphere in which He intended her to act, had made her weak and timid, in comparison with man, and had thus placed her under his *control,* as well as under his protection. That children, also, from the immaturity of their bodies and their minds, are under a like control. . . . [N]ature herself had therefore pronounced, on women and children, a sentence of incapacity to exercise political power. They did not say all this; and why? Because to the universal sense of all mankind, these were self-evident truths. They meant, therefore, this, and no more: that all the members of a community, of mature reason, and free agents by situation, are originally and by nature, *equally* entitled to the exercise of political power, or a voice in the Government.

. . . In affirming and declaring the *jus majoris* to be the law of all free communities, they did but declare the simple and obvious truth, that the essential character of a free Government, of a Government whose movements are regulated by numbers, involves the *necessity* of a submission by the *minority* to the *majority.* . . .

. . .

The Bill of Rights declared, that *the people* are the only legitimate source and fountain *of* political power.—The resolution of the Committee affirms this doctrine, by proposing, that in apportioning representation, or political power, regard shall be had to *the people* exclusively. Not to wealth, not to overgrown sectional interests, not to the supposed rights of the counties; but to the white population; to *the people* only. The Bill of Rights asserts the political equality of the citizens.—The resolution proposes to give to that principle a practical existence in our Government, by abolishing the inveterate abuse *of* the *equal* representation of *unequal* counties, and equalizing, as nearly as may be, the electoral districts throughout the Commonwealth, on the basis of free white population alone.

The Bill of Rights [of Virginia] pronounces the *jus majoris* to be the law of all free communities, by attributing to the majority of a community, the power to reform, alter or abolish, at its will and pleasure, the very Government itself, and consequently the lesser power of deciding, without appeal, in all matters of *ordinary legislation.*—The resolution proposes to give practical effect to the *jus majoris,* by making each Delegate the representative of an *equal number* of the people, so that the voice of a majority of the Delegates, will be the voice of a majority of the people. It proposes, in short, to establish that beautiful harmony between our theoretical principles and our practical regulation; the want of which, has been, for fifty years, the reproach of Virginia. . . .

JAMES MADISON of Orange

. . . [P]ersons now and property are the two great subjects on which Governments are to act; and that the rights of persons, and the rights of property, are the objects, for the protection of which Government was instituted. These rights cannot well be separated. The personal right to acquire property, which is a natural right, gives to property, when acquired, a right to protection, as a social right. The essence of Government is power; and power, lodged as it must be in human hands, will ever be liable to abuse. . . . In republics, the great danger is, that the majority may not sufficiently respect the rights of the minority. Some gentlemen, consulting the purity and generosity of their own minds, without adverting to the lessons of experience, would find a security against that danger, in our social feelings; in a respect for character; in the dictates of the monitor within; in the interests of individuals; in the aggregate interests of the community. But man is known to be a selfish, as well as a social being. Respect for character, though often a salutary restraint, is but too often overruled by other motives. When numbers of men act in a body, respect for character is often lost, just in proportion as it is necessary to control what is not right. We all know that conscience is not a sufficient safe-guard; and besides, that conscience itself may be deluded; may be misled, by an unconscious bias, into acts which an enlightened conscience would forbid. As to the permanent interest of individuals in the aggregate interests of the community, and in the proverbial maxim, that honesty is the best policy, present temptation is often found to be an overmatch for those considerations. These favorable attributes of the human character are all valuable, as auxiliaries; but they will not serve as a substitute for the coercive provision belonging to Government and Law. They will always, in proportion as they prevail, be favorable to a mild administration of both: but they can never be relied on as a guaranty of the rights of the minority against a majority disposed to take unjust advantage of its power. The only effectual safeguard to the rights of the minority, must be laid in such a basis and structure of the Government itself, as may afford, in a certain degree, directly or indirectly, a defensive authority in behalf of a minority having right on its side.

To come more nearly to the subject before the Committee, viz.: that peculiar feature in our community, which calls for a peculiar division in the basis of our government, I mean the colored part of our population. It is apprehended, if the power of the Commonwealth shall be in the hands of a majority, who have no interest in this species of property, that, from the facility with which it may be oppressed by excessive taxation, injustice may be done to its owners. It would seem, therefore, if we can incorporate that interest into the basis of our system, it will be the most apposite and effectual security that can be devised. Such an arrangement is recommended to me by many very important considerations. It is due to justice; due to humanity; due to truth; to the sympathies of our nature; in fine, to our character as a people, both abroad and at home, that they should be considered, as much as possible, in the light of human beings, and not as mere property. As such, they are acted upon by our laws, and have an interest in our laws. They may be considered as making a part, though a degraded part, of the families to which they belong. The Federal number [three-fifths], as it is called, is particularly recommended to attention in forming a basis of Representation, by its simplicity, its certainty, its stability, and its permanency.

C. Citizenship

Most Americans combined robust and restrictive conceptions of citizenship. Democrats insisted that citizenship entailed numerous liberties, including the right to bear arms and the right to vote. Most denied that free persons of color or Native Americans were citizens. Northern Whigs were more inclined to extend citizenship to free persons of color and Native Americans but less inclined to think that citizenship entailed a robust set of rights.

V. Equality

MAJOR DEVELOPMENTS

- Courts restrict "class legislation"
- Constitutional decision makers reject African-American and Native American citizenship
- The movement for women's rights is organized

Jacksonians held a powerful but restrictive conception of equality. Constitutional decision makers often scrutinized very strictly legislation and legislative proposals that they believed treated one class of persons differently from another class of persons. *Wally's Heirs v. Kennedy* (TN 1831) insisted, "The rights of every individual must stand or fall by the same rule or *law* that governs every other member of the body politic."[41]

41. *Wally's Heirs*, 2 Yerg. 554 (TN 1831).

This equality was confined to white men. A few radicals aside, most Democrats and Whigs endorsed rules or laws for woman, persons of color, and Native Americans that differed from those that governed every other member of the body politic. Persons of color, in particular, were regarded as legally inferior to whites. Roger Taney's opinion in *Dred Scott v. Sandford* (1857) infamously asserted that African-Americans, free or enslaved, "had no rights which the white man was bound to respect."

When reading the materials in this section, consider the relationship between the powerful and restrictive elements of constitutional equality. What are the connections between these elements? Does ideology help explain why Jacksonians were so sensitive to equality when evaluating legal differences between different classes of white men and so unconcerned with equality when considering racial or gender differences? How did Jacksonian conceptions of equality influence the arguments that proponents of racial and gender equality before the Civil War made when objecting to slavery, racism, and separate spheres?

A. Equality Under Law

Jacksonians hated class legislation, which they insisted, unjustifiably provided special benefits to or imposed distinctive burdens on only one group of citizens. President Andrew Jackson's Farewell Address attacked the "spirit of monopoly and thirst for exclusive privileges." Jackson had earlier condemned the Bank of the United States for "enab[ing] one class of society . . . to act injuriously upon the interests of all the others and to exercise more that its just proportion of influence in political affairs. . . . Men who love liberty desire nothing but equal rights and equal laws." The *Evening Post*, an important Jacksonian periodical, proclaimed that "the functions of Government . . . are . . . restricted to the making of *general laws*, uniform and universal in their operation."[42] The Supreme Court of Tennessee in *Wally's Heirs v. Kennedy* (TN 1831) declared:

> The clause, "law of the land," means a general public law, equally binding upon every member of the community. The rights of every individual must stand or fall by the same rule or law, that governs every other member of the body politic, or land, under similar circumstances; and every partial, or private law, which directly proposes to destroy or affect individual rights, or does the same thing by affording remedies leading to similar consequences, is unconstitutional and void.[43]

B. Race

Race and slavery presented numerous bitterly contested civil liberties issues. Some disputes raised questions about the constitutional powers of national and state officials. The Supreme Court in *Prigg v. Pennsylvania* (1842) ruled that Congress had the power to pass a fugitive slave law. Other disputes raised questions about constitutional rights and liberties. Pro-slavery and anti-slavery activists disputed whether alleged fugitive slaves had a constitutional right to a jury trial in the state where they were apprehended. Most disputes raised constitutional questions about the powers of the national government, federalism, and individual rights. Whether Congress could prohibit slavery in the territories depended on whether such regulations deprived slaveholders of their property without due process of law and whether federal bans on human bondage were legitimate exercises of Article IV, Section 3's command that "the Congress shall have Power to dispose of and make all needful Rules and Regulations respecting the Territory or other Property belonging to the United States."

Four developments structured the constitutional politics of slavery. The first was the dramatic increase in free state populations. Contrary to original expectations, the population of the northwestern states grew substantially more rapidly than the population of the southwestern states. One immediate consequence of this demographic development was that both houses of Congress had free state majorities after 1850. Many southerners had good reason for fearing that the free states would soon have permanent control over all national institutions. The second development was the continued entrenchment of slavery in most slave states. Such border states as Delaware aside, no southern state was likely to emancipate slaves in the foreseeable future. George Washington and the founding generation of Virginians often asserted that slavery

42. "True Functions of Government," *Evening Post*, November 21, 1834.

43. *Wally's Heirs*, 2 Yerg. 544 (TN 1831).

was a necessary evil that they hoped would some day disappear. Southern Jacksonians more often asserted that slavery was a positive good that promoted white civilization. Third, a growing anti-slavery movement demanded that the national government pass legislation promoting emancipation. More radical abolitionists, led by William Lloyd Garrison, insisted that slavery be abolished immediately. More moderate anti-slavery advocates, led first by William Seward and later by Abraham Lincoln, insisted that slavery be abolished in all territories. Federal measures that confined slavery to existing states, they believed, fostered the eventual emancipation of all slaves. The fourth development that structured the constitutional politics of slavery was westward expansion. More territory gained by the Louisiana Purchase was settled and the United States acquired new southwestern territories after the Mexican War. The free and slave states competed vigorously, often violently, for control over these territories. All parties knew that extra slave or free states would alter political power in Congress.

The constitutional politics of slavery unfolded in two stages. From 1828 to 1845 debates focused on abolitionist speech. These controversies included whether states and the federal government could restrict anti-slavery expression, whether the post office had an obligation to deliver anti-slavery tracts, and whether Congress was obligated to receive anti-slavery petitions. After 1845 debates focused on the consequences of westward expansion and settlement. Toward the end of the Mexican War Congressman David Wilmot of Pennsylvania asked Congress to ban slavery in all territories acquired from Mexico. The Wilmot Proviso divided Americans both between and within sections. Southerners split into those who insisted that Congress had no power to ban slavery in any territory and those who would accept as a compromise the extension of the Missouri Compromise line to the Pacific Ocean. Northerners split into those who believed that Congress had no power to permit slavery in any territory; those who believed that Congress could decide whether to permit slavery in the territories; and those who believed, as a constitutional or practical matter, that the people of each territory should decide whether slavery was permitted in their jurisdiction.

The Compromise of 1850 adopted a policy that became known as *popular sovereignty*. The New Mexico and Utah Territories were organized without any reference to slavery. This omission left the status of human bondage to the local populace. Congress in 1854 widened the scope for popular sovereignty when passing the Kansas-Nebraska Act. That measure repealed the Missouri Compromise, which had prohibited human bondage in Kansas and Nebraska. Both the Compromise of 1850 and the Kansas-Nebraska Act provided expedited appeals to the U.S. Supreme Court for any lawsuit raising questions about the constitutional status of slavery. While some politicians maintained that this decision to foist the problem of slavery on the federal courts provided a neutral arbiter for divisive sectional questions, many northerners were suspicious. By the 1850s the northern white population was almost double the southern white population. Nevertheless, because of federal statues that located five of the nine federal circuit courts entirely within the slave states and the practice of having one Supreme Court justice represent each of the federal circuits, the Supreme Court before the Civil War had a southern majority.

Americans before the Civil War debated the constitutional status of free blacks as well as the constitutional status of slavery. Constitutional decision makers usually concluded that free blacks were not citizens under the national and state constitutions. Some western states prohibited free blacks from becoming residents. States such as Massachusetts that did not attach racial conditions to citizenship were nevertheless ambivalent on whether race provided legitimate grounds for distinguishing between state citizens. In *Roberts v. City of Boston* (MA 1849), the Supreme Judicial Court of Massachusetts ruled that Boston could constitutionally segregate city schools. The segregation ordinance was almost immediately repealed, in large part because many local officials believed the measure unconstitutional.

Dred Scott v. Sandford (1857) sought to resolve questions about the status of free blacks and the status of slavery in the territories. Chief Justice Taney ruled that former slaves could not become national citizens and that Congress had no power to ban slavery in the territories. Hopes that a judicial ruling would settle these controversies were soon dashed. The controversy over Kansas statehood aggravated latent tensions between northern and southern Democrats. On the eve of the 1860 presidential election, southern Democrats demanded that Congress enact a slave code for the territories. Northern Democrats offered as a compromise a proposal to have the matter adjudicated by the Supreme Court. When that compromise was rejected, the Democratic Party divided—a division that ensured that Abraham Lincoln won the 1860 presidential election. Shortly after Lincoln gained the White House, six slave states seceded from the Union.

Slavery: The Rights of Masters

The constitutional status of slavery in the territories was the most contentious issue dividing North from South. Congress practically ceased to function as a deliberative body after Congressman David Wilmot of Pennsylvania in 1846 proposed that the national government prohibit human bondage in any territory acquired by the United States as a consequence of the Mexican War. The Wilmot Proviso stated:

> That, as an express and fundamental condition to the acquisition of any territory from the Republic of Mexico by the United States, by virtue of any treaty which may be negotiated between them, and to the use by the Executive of the moneys herein appropriated, neither slavery nor involuntary servitude shall ever exist in any part of said territory, except for crime, whereof the party shall first be duly convicted.

The northern-dominated House of Representatives passed that measure. The more southern-leaning Senate refused to endorse the Proviso. Temporary harmony was restored by the Compromise of 1850, which admitted California as a free state, organized the New Mexico Territories without any reference to slavery, and established new procedures for recovering fugitive slaves. The bill organizing the New Mexico Territory also expressed a bipartisan hope that the Supreme Court might determine the precise constitutional status of slavery in the territories. The Kansas-Nebraska Act contained a similar provision expediting judicial review of any legal dispute over slavery in those territories. The Supreme Court did not disappoint mainstream politicians eager to remove slavery issues from the political agenda.

Illustration 5-5 Chief Justice Roger Taney

Source: Library of Congress Prints and Photographs Division, Washington, DC 20540, USA.

Dred Scott v. Sandford, 60 U.S. 393 (1857)

John Emerson's hypochondria was responsible for the most infamous case in American judicial history. Emerson was an army surgeon who complained of health problems wherever he was posted. He could not stomach Rock Island, Illinois, nor a stint in Louisiana, nor, finally, a posting at Fort Snelling in Minnesota Territory. Emerson was accompanied on his travels by Dred Scott, his slave. While Emerson served at Fort Snelling, Dred Scott married Harriet Robinson, another slave.[44] In 1838 Emerson returned to Missouri with both Dred and Harriet Scott as slaves. When Emerson died, Irene and John Sanford (misspelled in the case name) inherited the Scotts.

During the late 1840s the Scotts sued Sanford in state court, claiming that their previous residence in a free state and a free territory emancipated them. The case initially presented fairly simple state law issues. Both free and slave states during the early nineteenth century made a distinction between residence and sojourning. Slaves who resided in free states with their masters were emancipated. Slaves who traveled through free states with their masters

44. Lea VanderVelde, *Mrs. Dred Scott: A Life on Slavery's Frontier* (New York: Oxford University Press, 2009).

remained slaves. Had Missouri applied these conventional rules, the Scotts would have won their freedom suit, because Emerson had resided in both a free state and a free territory. State constitutional law, however, was in flux. Several northern state courts had abandoned the residence/sojourning distinction. In Commonwealth v. Aves (MA 1836), *Chief Justice Lemuel Shaw of the Supreme Judicial Court of Massachusetts ruled that slaves travelling with their masters were free the instant they entered that state. In response the Missouri Supreme Court in Dred Scott's case ruled that slavery reattached whenever a slaveholder returned with his slaves from a free state or territory, no matter how long the northern stay.*

The Scotts re-filed their freedom lawsuit in federal court, hoping that a federal judge might treat their claims under federal common law rather than state law.[45] *This move changed the legal claims open to both parties. Sanford claimed that Dred Scott could not sue in federal court because Dred Scott was not a citizen under Article III. If a slave or a former slave could not be an American citizen, then Scott and Sanford did not meet the diversity of citizenship requirement for federal jurisdiction. The federal district court did not rule on this matter, claiming that the issue of citizenship had been waived. The trial court instead supported the state court ruling that slavery reattached when the Scotts returned to Missouri.*[46] *When Scott appealed that decision, Sanford added as alternative ground for judgment the claim that Scott did not become free in Minnesota because the congressional ban on slavery in that territory was unconstitutional.*

The Supreme Court by a 7-2 vote ruled that Scott was a slave. Chief Justice Taney's opinion for the Court declared that former slaves could not constitutionally become American citizens and that Congress could not ban slavery in American territories. Almost every facet of the Dred Scott *decision was and continues to be controversial. Consider Justice Taney's decision to rule on the constitutionality of the Missouri Compromise after he declared that former slaves, because they were not citizens of the United States, could not bring lawsuits in federal court. Was this, as many northerners charged, a judicially inappropriate effort to discuss the merits of a case in which the Court declined jurisdiction? Or, as Taney insisted, was the discussion of the Missouri Compromise an alternative ground for rejecting jurisdiction? Virtually all commentators agree that the* Dred Scott *ruling is wrong as a matter of constitutional law.*[47] *Do you agree with this assessment? To what extent is what is wrong with Dred Scott only what is wrong with slavery and racism? Could a person who believed in slavery and racism find Chief Justice Taney's arguments constitutionally plausible? If Taney is wrong, is he wrong because he used the wrong method of constitutional interpretation or because he misapplied the right method of constitutional interpretation? What method does Taney use? Is he an originalist, or does he implicitly reject originalism? What methods do the dissents use? Is the argument between the dissenting and majority opinions an argument about method or application of method?*

Justice Benjamin Curtis's dissent is considered a masterpiece of legal writing. Curtis concludes that Congress could decide whether to ban slavery in the territories. He asserts that free blacks are American citizens only if the state in which they were born treats free blacks as citizens. Very few states did so in 1856. Justice John McLean's dissent maintains that Congress is constitutionally obligated to ban slavery in the territories and that all free persons of color born in the United States are American citizens. What explains why Curtis took the more narrow position? Which position is constitutionally correct? If you were on the Taney Court, would you write a narrower or a broader dissent?

Most legal commentators believe that Dred Scott *helped cause the Civil War. Robert McCloskey declared that the Taney Court tragically "imagined that a flaming political issue could be quenched by calling it a 'legal' issue and deciding it judicially."*[48] *Both northern and southern Democrats, however, rallied around the* Dred Scott *decision in the spring and summer of 1857. Democrats gained votes at the expense of Republicans in every northern election held between March and September of that year. They fractured in the late fall over Kansas statehood. Did* Dred Scott *nevertheless aggravate sectional tensions by increasing Republican militancy or providing another barrier between northern and southern Democrats when the controversy*

45. This argument relies heavily on *Tyson v. Swift*, 41 U.S. 1 (1842). In *Tyson*, the justices ruled that when resolving diversity cases, federal courts not need rely on the law of the state in which the contested action took place.

46. Several justices in *Dred Scott* refused to consider the citizenship issue on that grounds.

47. The seminal expression of the scholarly consensus is Don E. Fehrenbacher, *The Dred Scott Case: Its Significance in American Law and Politics* (New York: Oxford University Press, 1978). But also see Mark A. Graber, *Dred Scott and the Problem of Constitutional Evil* (New York: Cambridge University Press, 2006).

48. Robert McCloskey, *The American Supreme Court*, 4th ed., rev. Sanford Levinson (Chicago: University of Chicago Press, 2005), 62.

over Kansas statehood emerged? Is the real lesson of the 1850s that no American institution was able to fashion a successful compromise over slavery?

CHIEF JUSTICE TANEY delivered the opinion of the court.

. . .

The words "people of the United States" and "citizens" are synonymous terms, and mean the same thing. They both describe the political body who . . . form the sovereignty, and who hold the power and conduct the Government through their representatives. . . . The question before us is, whether [former slaves and their descendants] compose a portion of this people, and are constituent members of this sovereignty? We think they are not, and that they are not included, and were not intended to be included, under the word "citizens" in the Constitution, and can therefore claim none of the rights and privileges which that instrument provides for and secures to citizens of the United States. On the contrary, they were at that time considered as a subordinate and inferior class of beings, who had been subjugated by the dominant race, and, whether emancipated or not, yet remained subject to their authority, and had no rights or privileges but such as those who held the power and the Government might choose to grant them.

. . .

In discussing this question, we must not confound the rights of citizenship which a State may confer within its own limits, and the rights of citizenship as a member of the Union. It does not by any means follow, because he has all the rights and privileges of a citizen of a State, that he must be a citizen of the United States. . . . For, previous to the adoption of the Constitution of the United States, every State had the undoubted right to confer on whomsoever it pleased the character of citizen, and to endow him with all its rights. But this character of course was confined to the boundaries of the State, and gave him no rights or privileges in other States beyond those secured to him by the laws of nations and the comity of States. . . . Each State may still confer them upon an alien, or any one it thinks proper, or upon any class or description of persons; yet he would not be a citizen in the sense in which that word is used in the Constitution of the United States, nor entitled to sue as such in one of its courts, nor to the privileges and immunities of a citizen in the other States. . . . The Constitution has conferred on Congress the right to establish a uniform rule of naturalization, and this right is evidently exclusive. . . . Consequently, no State, since the adoption of the Constitution, can by naturalizing an alien invest him with the rights and privileges secured to a citizen of a State under the Federal Government. . . .

. . .

It is true, every person, and every class and description of persons, who were at the time of the adoption of the Constitution recognized as citizens in the several States, became also citizens of this new political body; but none other; it was formed by them, and for them and their posterity, but for no one else. . . .

. . .

In the opinion of the court, the legislation and histories of the times, and the language used in the Declaration of Independence, show, that neither the class of persons who had been imported as slaves, nor their descendants, whether they had become free or not, were then acknowledged as a part of the people, nor intended to be included in the general words used in that memorable instrument.

. . .

They had for more than a century before been regarded as beings of an inferior order, and altogether unfit to associate with the white race, either in social or political relations; and so far inferior, that they had no rights which the white man was bound to respect; and that the negro might justly and lawfully be reduced to slavery for his benefit. . . .

. . .

The language of the Declaration of Independence is equally conclusive:

. . .

It . . . say[s]: "We hold these truths to be self-evident: that all men are created equal; that they are endowed by their Creator with certain unalienable rights; that among them is life, liberty, and the pursuit of happiness; that to secure these rights, Governments are instituted, deriving their just powers from the consent of the governed."

The general words above quoted would seem to embrace the whole human family, and if they were used in a similar instrument at this day would be so understood. But it is too clear for dispute, that the enslaved African race were not intended to be included, and formed no part of the people who framed and adopted this declaration; for if the language, as understood in that day, would embrace them, the conduct of the distinguished men who framed the Declaration of Independence would have been utterly and flagrantly inconsistent with the principles they asserted; and instead of the sympathy of mankind, to which they so confidently appealed, they would have deserved and received universal rebuke and reprobation.

. . .

. . . [W]hen we look to the condition of this race in the several States at the time, it is impossible to believe that these rights and privileges were intended to be extended to them. . . .

By the laws of New Hampshire, collected and finally passed in 1815, no one was permitted to be enrolled in the militia of the State, but free white citizens; and the same provision is found in a subsequent collection of the laws, made in 1855. Nothing could more strongly mark the entire repudiation of the African race. The alien is excluded, because, being born in a foreign country, he cannot be a member of the community until he is naturalized. But why are the African race, born in the State, not permitted to share in one of the highest duties of the citizen? The answer is obvious; he is not, by the institutions and laws of the State, numbered among its people. He forms no part of the sovereignty of the State, and is not therefore called on to uphold and defend it.

. . .

Undoubtedly, a person may be a citizen, that is, a member of the community who form the sovereignty, although he exercises no share of the political power, and is incapacitated from holding particular offices. Women and minors, who form a part of the political family, cannot vote; and when a property qualification is required to vote or hold a particular office, those who have not the necessary qualification cannot vote or hold the office, yet they are citizens.

So, too, a person may be entitled to vote by the law of the State, who is not a citizen even of the State itself. And in some of the States of the Union foreigners not naturalized are allowed to vote. And the State may give the right to free negroes and mulattoes, but that does not make them citizens of the State, and still less of the United States. And the provision in the Constitution giving privileges and immunities in other States, does not apply to them.

. . .

No one, we presume, supposes that any change in public opinion or feeling, in relation to this unfortunate race, in the civilized nations of Europe or in this country, should induce the court to give to the words of the Constitution a more liberal construction in their favor than they were intended to bear when the instrument was framed and adopted. Such an argument would be altogether inadmissible in any tribunal called on to interpret it. If any of its provisions are deemed unjust, there is a mode prescribed in the instrument itself by which it may be amended; but while it remains unaltered, it must be construed now as it was understood at the time of its adoption. It is not only the same in words, but the same in meaning, and delegates the same powers to the Government, and reserves and secures the same rights and privileges to the citizen; and as long as it continues to exist in its present form, it speaks not only in the same words, but with the same meaning and intent with which it spoke when it came from the hands of its framers, and was voted on and adopted by the people of the United States. Any other rule of construction would abrogate the judicial character of this court, and make it the mere reflex of the popular opinion or passion of the day. This court was not created by the Constitution for such purposes. Higher and graver trusts have been confided to it, and it must not falter in the path of duty.

. . .

The act of Congress, upon which the plaintiff relies [as the basis of his freedom claim], declares that slavery and involuntary servitude, except as a punishment for crime, shall be forever prohibited in all that part of the territory ceded by France . . . which lies north of thirty-six degrees thirty minutes north latitude, and not included within the limits of Missouri. . . .

The counsel for the plaintiff has laid much stress upon that article in the Constitution which confers on Congress the power "to dispose of and make all needful rules and regulations respecting the territory or other property belonging to the United States"; but, in the judgment of the court, that provision has no bearing on the present controversy, and the power there given, whatever it may be, is confined, and was intended to be confined, to the territory which at that time belonged to, or was claimed by, the United States, and was within their boundaries as settled by the treaty with Great Britain, and can have no influence upon a territory afterwards acquired from a foreign Government. . . .

. . .

. . . [T]he power of Congress over the person or property of a citizen can never be a mere discretionary power under our Constitution and form of Government. The powers of the Government and the rights and privileges of the citizen are regulated and plainly defined by the Constitution itself. And when the Territory becomes a part of the United States, the Federal Government enters into possession in the character impressed upon it by those who created it. It enters upon it with its powers over the citizen strictly defined, and limited by the Constitution, from which it derives its own existence, and by virtue of which alone it continues to exist and act as a Government and sovereignty. . . .

. . .

For example, no one, we presume, will contend that Congress can make any law in a Territory respecting the establishment of religion, or the free exercise thereof, or abridging the freedom of speech or of the press, or the right of the people of the Territory peaceably to assemble, and to petition the Government for the redress of grievances.

. . .

. . . [T]he rights of property are united with the rights of person, and placed on the same ground by the fifth amendment to the Constitution, which provides that no person shall be deprived of life, liberty, and property, without due process of law. And an act of Congress which deprives a citizen of the United States of his liberty or property, merely because he came himself or brought his property into a particular Territory of the United States, and who had committed no offence against the laws, could hardly be dignified with the name of due process of law.

. . .

It seems, however, to be supposed, that there is a difference between property in a slave and other property, and that different rules may be applied to it in expounding the Constitution of the United States. . . .

. . . [N]o laws or usages of other nations, or reasoning of statesmen or jurists upon the relations of master and slave, can enlarge the powers of the Government, or take from the citizens the rights they have reserved. And if the Constitution recognizes the right of property of the master in a slave, and makes no distinction between that description of property and other property owned by a citizen, no tribunal, acting under the authority of the United States, whether it be legislative, executive, or judicial, has a right to draw such a distinction, or deny to it the benefit of the provisions and guarantees which have been provided for the protection of private property against the encroachments of the Government.

. . . [T]he right of property in a slave is distinctly and expressly affirmed in the Constitution. . . . [N]o word can be found in the Constitution which gives Congress a greater power over slave property, or which entitles property of that kind to less protection that property of any other description. The only power conferred is the power coupled with the duty of guarding and protecting the owner in his rights.

Upon these considerations, it is the opinion of the court that the act of Congress which prohibited a citizen from holding and owning property of this kind in the territory of the United States north of the line therein mentioned, is not warranted by the Constitution, and is therefore void; and that neither Dred Scott himself, nor any of his family, were made free by being carried into this territory; even if they had been carried there by the owner, with the intention of becoming a permanent resident. . . .

JUSTICE WAYNE, concurring. . . .
JUSTICE NELSON, concurring. . . .
JUSTICE DANIEL, concurring. . . .
JUSTICE CAMPBELL, concurring. . . .
JUSTICE CATRON, concurring. . . .
JUSTICE McLEAN, dissenting. . . .
JUSTICE GRIER, concurring. . . .

JUSTICE CURTIS, dissenting. . . .

. . .

To determine whether any free persons, descended from Africans held in slavery, were citizens of the United States under the Confederation, and consequently at the time of the adoption of the Constitution of the United States, it is only necessary to know whether any such persons were citizens of either of the States under the Confederation, at the time of the adoption of the Constitution.

Of this there can be no doubt. At the time of the ratification of the Articles of Confederation, all free native-born inhabitants of the States of New Hampshire, Massachusetts, New York, New Jersey, and North Carolina, though descended from African slaves, were not only citizens of those States, but such of them as had the other necessary qualifications possessed the franchise of electors, on equal terms with other citizens.

. . .

. . . I shall not enter into an examination of the existing opinions of that period respecting the African race, nor into any discussion concerning the meaning of those who asserted, in the Declaration of Independence, that all men are created equal; that they are endowed by their Creator with certain inalienable rights; that among these are life, liberty, and the pursuit of happiness. My own opinion is, that a calm comparison of these assertions of universal abstract truths, and of their own individual opinions and acts, would not leave these men under any reproach of inconsistency; that the great truths they asserted on that solemn occasion, they were ready and anxious to make effectual, wherever a necessary regard to circumstances, which no statesman can disregard without producing more evil than good, would allow; and that it would not be just to them, nor true in itself, to allege that they intended to say that the Creator of all men had endowed the white race, exclusively, with the great natural rights which the Declaration of Independence asserts. . . .

. . .

. . .[M]y opinion is, that, under the Constitution of the United States, every free person born on the soil of a State, who is a citizen of that State by force of its Constitution or laws, is also a citizen of the United States.

. . .

It has been often asserted that the Constitution was made exclusively by and for the white race. It has already been shown that in five of the thirteen original States, colored persons then possessed the elective franchise, and were among those by whom the Constitution was ordained and established. If so, it is not true, in point of fact, that the Constitution was made exclusively by the white race. And that it was made exclusively for the white race is, in my opinion, not only an assumption not warranted by anything in the Constitution, but contradicted by its opening declaration, that it was ordained and established by the people of the United States, for themselves and their posterity. And as free colored persons were then citizens of at least five States, and so in every sense part of the people of the United States, they were among those for whom and whose posterity the Constitution was ordained and established.

. . . [C]itizenship, under the Constitution of the United States, is not dependent on the possession of any particular political or even of all civil rights; and any attempt so to define it must lead to error. To what citizens the elective franchise shall be confided, is a question to be determined by each State, in accordance with its own views of the necessities or expediencies of its condition. What civil rights shall be enjoyed by its citizens, and whether all shall enjoy the same, or how they may be gained or lost, are to be determined in the same way.

. . .

It has been urged that the words "rules and regulations" are not appropriate terms in which to convey authority to make laws for the government of the territory.

But it must be remembered that this is a grant of power to the Congress—that it is therefore necessarily a grant of power to legislate—and, certainly, rules and regulations respecting a particular subject, made by the legislative power of a country, can be nothing but laws. Nor do the particular terms employed, in my judgment, tend in any degree to restrict this legislative power. . . .

. . .

If, then, this clause does contain a power to legislate respecting the territory, what are the limits of that power?

To this I answer, that, in common with all the other legislative powers of Congress, it finds limits in the express prohibitions on Congress not to do certain things; that, in the exercise of the legislative power, Congress cannot pass an ex post facto law or bill of attainder; and so in respect to each of the other prohibitions contained in the Constitution.

Besides this, the rules and regulations must be needful. But undoubtedly the question whether a particular rule or regulation be needful, must be finally determined by Congress itself. Whether a law be needful, is a legislative or political, not a judicial, question. Whatever Congress deems needful is so, under the grant of power.

. . .

But it is insisted, that whatever other powers Congress may have respecting the territory of the United States, the subject of negro slavery forms an exception.

The Constitution declares that Congress shall have power to make "*all* needful rules and regulations" respecting the territory belonging to the United States.

There is nothing in the context which qualifies the grant of power. The regulations must be "respecting the territory." An enactment that slavery may or may not exist there, is a regulation respecting the territory. Regulations must be needful; but it is necessarily left to the legislative discretion to determine whether a law be needful. No other clause of the Constitution has been referred to at the bar, or has been seen by me, which imposes any restriction or makes any exception concerning the power of Congress to allow or prohibit slavery in the territory belonging to the United States.

. . .

This provision [in the Northwest Ordinance banning slavery] shows that it was then understood Congress might make a regulation prohibiting slavery, and that Congress might also allow it to continue to exist in the Territory; and accordingly, when, a few days later, Congress passed the act of May 20th, 1790 [which permitted slavery in the southwest territories].

. . .

[With respect to policy arguments for permitting slavery in the territory], this court has no concern. One or the other may be justly entitled to guide or control the legislative judgment upon what is a needful regulation. The question here is, whether they are sufficient to authorize this court to insert into this clause of the Constitution an exception of the exclusion or allowance of slavery, not found therein, nor in any other part of that instrument. To engraft on any instrument a substantive exception not found in it, must be admitted to be a matter attended with great difficulty. And the difficulty increases with the importance of the instrument, and the magnitude and complexity of the interests involved in its construction. To allow this to be done with the Constitution, upon reasons purely political, renders its judicial interpretation impossible—because judicial tribunals, as such, cannot decide upon political considerations. Political reasons have not the requisite certainty to afford rules of juridical interpretation. They are different in different men. They are different in the same men at different times. And when a strict interpretation of the Constitution, according to the fixed rules which govern the interpretation of laws, is abandoned, and the theoretical opinions of individuals are allowed to control its meaning, we have no longer a Constitution; we are under the government of individual men, who for the time being have power to declare what the Constitution is, according to their own views of what it ought to mean. When such a method of interpretation of the Constitution obtains, in place of a republican Government, with limited and defined powers, we have a Government which is merely an exponent of the will of Congress; or what, in my opinion, would not be preferable, an exponent of the individual political opinions of the members of this court.

. . .

I confess myself unable to perceive any difference whatever between my own opinion of the general extent of the power of Congress and the opinion of the majority of the court, save that I consider it derivable from the express language of the Constitution, while they hold it to be silently implied from the power to acquire territory. Looking at the power of Congress over the Territories as of the extent just described, what positive prohibition exists in the Constitution, which restrained Congress from enacting a law in 1820 to prohibit slavery north of thirty-six degrees thirty minutes north latitude?

The only one suggested is that clause in the fifth article of the amendments of the Constitution which declares that no person shall be deprived of his life, liberty, or property, without due process of law. . . .

Slavery, being contrary to natural right, is created only by municipal law.

. . .

. . . [T]hey who framed and adopted the constitution were aware that persons held to service under the laws of a State are property only to the extent and under the conditions fixed by those laws; that they must cease to be available as property, when their owners voluntarily place them permanently within another jurisdiction, where no municipal laws on the subject of slavery exist; and that, being aware of these principles, and having said nothing to interfere with or displace them, or to compel Congress to legislate in any particular manner on the subject, and having empowered Congress to make all needful rules and regulations respecting the territory of the United States, it was their intention to leave to the discretion of Congress what regulations, if any, should be made concerning slavery therein. Moreover, if the right exists, what are its limits, and what are its conditions? If citizens of the United States have the right to take their slaves to a Territory, and hold them there as slaves, without regard to the laws of the Territory, I suppose this right is not to be restricted to the citizens of slaveholding States. A citizen of a State which does not tolerate slavery can hardly be denied the power of doing the same thing.

Nor, in my judgment, will the position, that a prohibition to bring slaves into a Territory deprives any one of his property without due process of law, bear examination.

. . .

And if a prohibition of slavery in a Territory in 1820 violated this principle, . . . the ordinance of 1787 also violated it; and what power had, I do not say the Congress of the Confederation alone, but the Legislature of Virginia, of the Legislature of any or all the States of the Confederacy, to consent to such a violation? . . . It was certainly understood by the Convention which framed the Constitution, and has been so understood ever since, that, under the power to regulate commerce, Congress could prohibit the importation of slaves; and the exercise of the power was restrained till 1808. A citizen of the United States owns slaves in Cuba, and brings them to the United States, where they are set free by the legislation of Congress. Does this legislation deprive him of his property without due process of law? If so, what becomes of the laws prohibiting the slave trade? If not, how can similar regulation respecting a Territory violate the fifth amendment of the Constitution? . . .

Free Blacks

Roberts v. City of Boston, 59 Mass. 198 (1849)

Sarah Roberts, a five-year-old African-American, applied to attend the Boston primary school nearest her place of residence. Her application was rejected. The school committee insisted that Roberts attend one of the two schools that Boston maintained for children of color. After negotiations between the free black community of Boston and the school board failed, Benjamin Roberts, Sarah's father, filed a lawsuit claiming that racially separate schools violated the state constitutional commitment to equality. The school committee asserted by resolution that "the continuance of the separate schools for colored children, and the regular attendance of all such children upon the schools, is not only legal and just, but is best adapted to promote the education of that class of our population." After the trial court rejected his contention, Roberts appealed to the Supreme Judicial Court of Massachusetts. Charles Sumner, a leading abolitionist and later a senator from Massachusetts, argued the case for the Roberts family.

The African-American community proved more successful in legislative and electoral politics than in judicial politics. The Supreme Judicial Court of Massachusetts rejected the Roberts lawsuit. Chief Justice Lemuel Shaw agreed that free blacks had a constitutional right to equal treatment but nevertheless insisted that the school committee made a reasonable decision when mandating racial segregation in the Boston public schools. Proponents of school desegregation in Massachusetts did not abandon their cause after that judicial defeat. In 1854 the Free Soil Party won a dramatic victory in the state election. The next year Free Soil majorities in the Massachusetts legislature passed a law outlawing racial segregation in public schools.[49]

When reading the excerpts from the Sumner argument and the Shaw opinion, keep in mind that Massachusetts was one of the few states in Jacksonian America in which free blacks were state citizens. For this reason many persons after the Civil War insisted that Roberts *was a precedent that cast light on the citizenship rights guaranteed by the Fourteenth Amendment. Should the Fourteenth Amendment be read in light of Chief Justice Shaw's claim that segregated schools are consistent with constitutional equality? Should the Fourteenth Amendment be read in light of the subsequent decision of the Massachusetts legislature that segregated education violated the Massachusetts constitution?*

Mr. SUMNER argued as follows:—

1. According to the spirit of American institutions, and especially of the constitution of Massachusetts . . . all men, without distinction of color or race, are equal before the law.

. . .

4. The exclusion of colored children from the public schools, which are open to white children, is a source of practical inconvenience to them and their parents, to which white persons are not exposed, and is, therefore, a violation of equality.

5. The separation of children in the public schools of Boston, on account of color or race, is in the nature of caste, and is a violation of equality.

6. . . . The regulations and by-laws of municipal corporations must be reasonable, or they are inoperative

49. For the full details of the struggle for desegregated schools in Jacksonian Massachusetts, see J. Morgan Kousser, "'The Supremacy of Equal Rights': The Struggle against Racial Discrimination in Antebellum Massachusetts and the Foundations of the Fourteenth Amendment," *Northwestern Law Review* 82 (1988): 941.

and void. . . . So, the regulations and by-laws of the school committee must be reasonable; and their discretion must be exercised in a reasonable manner. The discrimination made by the school committee of Boston, on account of color, is not legally reasonable. A colored person may occupy any office connected with the public schools, from that of governor, or secretary of the board of education, to that of member of a school committee, or teacher in any public school, and as a voter he may vote for members of the school committee. It is clear, that the committee may classify scholars, according to age and sex, for these distinctions are inoffensive, and recognized as legal or according to their moral and intellectual qualifications, because such a power is necessary to the government of schools. But the committee cannot assume, without individual examination, that an entire race possess certain moral or intellectual qualities, which render it proper to place them all in a class by themselves.

But it is said, that the committee, in thus classifying the children, have not violated any principle of equality, inasmuch as they have provided a school with competent instructors for the colored children, where they enjoy equal advantages of instruction with those enjoyed by the white children. To this there are several answers: 1st, The separate school for colored children is not one of the schools established by the law relating to public schools, and having no legal existence, cannot be a legal equivalent. 2d. It is not in fact an equivalent. It is the occasion of inconveniences to the colored children, to which they would not be exposed if they had access to the nearest public schools; it inflicts upon them the stigma of caste; and although the matters taught in the two schools may be precisely the same, a school exclusively devoted to one class must differ essentially, in its spirit and character, from that public school known to the law, where all classes meet together in equality. 3d. Admitting that it is an equivalent, still the colored children cannot be compelled to take it. They have an equal right with the white children to the general public schools.

7. . . . Slavery was abolished in Massachusetts, by virtue of the declaration of rights in our constitution, without any specific words of abolition in that instrument, or in any subsequent legislation. . . . The same words, which are potent to destroy slavery, must be equally potent against any institution founded on caste. . . . If there should be any doubt in this case, the court should incline in favor of equality; as every interpretation is always made in favor of life and liberty. . . .

The fact, that the separation of the schools was originally made at the request of the colored parents, cannot affect the rights of the colored people, or the powers of the school committee. The separation of the schools, so far from being for the benefit of both races, is an injury to both. It tends to create a feeling of degradation in the blacks, and of prejudice and uncharitableness in the whites.

CHIEF JUSTICE SHAW delivered the opinion of the Court.

. . .

The great principle, advanced by the learned and eloquent advocate of the plaintiff, is, that by the constitution and laws of Massachusetts, all persons without distinction of age or sex, birth or color, origin or condition, are equal before the law. This, as a broad general principle, such as ought to appear in a declaration of rights, is perfectly sound; it is not only expressed in terms, but pervades and animates the whole spirit of our constitution of free government. But, when this great principle comes to be applied to the actual and various conditions of persons in society, it will not warrant the assertion, that men and women are legally clothed with the same civil and political powers, and that children and adults are legally to have the same functions and be subject to the same treatment; but only that the rights of all, as they are settled and regulated by law, are equally entitled to the paternal consideration and protection of the law, for their maintenance and security. What those rights are, to which individuals, in the infinite variety of circumstances by which they are surrounded in society, are entitled, must depend on laws adapted to their respective relations and conditions.

Conceding, therefore, in the fullest manner, that colored persons, the descendants of Africans, are entitled by law, in this commonwealth, to equal rights, constitutional and political, civil and social, the question then arises, whether the regulation in question, which provides separate schools for colored children, is a violation of any of these rights.

. . .

The power of general superintendence vests a plenary authority in the [school] committee to arrange, classify, and distribute pupils, in such a manner as they think best adapted to their general proficiency and welfare. If it is thought expedient to provide for very young children, it may be, that such schools may be kept exclusively by female teachers, quite adequate to their instruction, and yet whose services may be obtained at a cost much lower than that of more highly-qualified male instructors. So if they should judge it expedient to have a grade of schools for children from seven to ten, and another for those from ten to fourteen, it would seem to be within their authority to establish such schools. So to separate male and female pupils into different schools. It has been found necessary, that is to say, highly expedient, at times, to establish special schools for poor and neglected children, who have passed the age of seven, and have become too old to attend the primary school, and yet have not acquired the rudiments of learning, to enable them to enter the ordinary schools. If a class of youth, of one or both sexes, is found in that condition, and it is expedient to organize them into a separate school, to receive the special training, adapted to their condition, it seems to be within the power of the superintending committee, to provide for the organization of such special school.

. . .

In the absence of special legislation on this subject, the law has vested the power in the committee to regulate the system of distribution and classification; and when this power is reasonably exercised, without being abused or perverted by colorable pretences, the decision of the committee must be deemed conclusive. The committee, apparently upon great deliberation, have come to the conclusion, that the good of both classes of schools will be best promoted, by maintaining the separate primary schools for colored and for white children, and we can perceive no ground to doubt, that this is the honest result of their experience and judgment.

It is urged, that this maintenance of separate schools tends to deepen and perpetuate the odious distinction of caste, founded in a deep-rooted prejudice in public opinion. This prejudice, if it exists, is not created by law, and probably cannot be changed by law. Whether this distinction and prejudice, existing in the opinion and feelings of the community, would not be as effectually fostered by compelling colored and white children to associate together in the same schools, may well be doubted; at all events, it is a fair and proper question for the committee to consider and decide upon, having in view the best interests of both classes of children placed under their superintendence, and we cannot say, that their decision upon it is not founded on just grounds of reason and experience, and in the results of a discriminating and honest judgment. . . .

C. Gender

Women more vociferously demanded equal rights during the later part of the Jacksonian Era. If, as the Supreme Court of Tennessee insisted in *Wally's Heirs v. Kennedy* (TN 1831), "the rights of every individual must stand or fall by the same rule or law that governs every other member of the body politic," then, many early feminists claimed, women ought to be governed by the same rule or law that governed men. The first major women's rights convention was held at Seneca Falls, New York, in 1848. That convention adopted a Declaration of Sentiments that demanded that women be granted "immediate admission to all the rights and privileges which belong to them as citizens of the United States."[50] The Seneca Falls convention was immediately followed by other women's rights conventions. Participants in these conventions called for the right to vote, the right to economic equality, and the right to more equitable treatment in marriage.

The early women's rights movement enjoyed more success in legislative settings than in courtrooms. Many state legislatures liberalized previous restrictions on married women owning property. Some states passed laws granting women more rights to the custody of their children after divorce. Judges were less moved by pleas for gender equality. In *White v. White* (NY 1849), New York judges declared that a married women's property act could not be applied retroactively. In *Shanks v. DuPont* (1830), the Supreme Court upheld the traditional position that women's citizenship followed their husbands' citizenship.

Men were particularly illiberal when women demanded greater political rights. Elizabeth Cady Stanton, Lucretia Mott, and other feminist leaders successfully placed gender issues on the agendas of state constitutional conventions. Nevertheless, suffrage rights were at most briefly debated before being resoundingly rejected. Few women voted before the

50. Rogers M. Smith, *Civic Ideals: Conflicting Visions of Citizenship in U.S. History* (New Haven: Yale University Press, 1999), 232.

Civil War. Communities that permitted women to vote typically restricted the ballot to local matters. Members of the Kansas Constitutional Convention of 1859 expressed the consensus view when concluding, "The [political] rights of women are safe in present hands."[51]

Elizabeth Cady Stanton, **Keynote Address, Seneca Falls Convention** (July 19, 1848)[52]

The Seneca Falls Convention was the first important gathering for women's rights held in the United States. Individual women had demanded political equality before 1848. Abigail Adams was among the many women who criticized the male monopoly on political power. Women did not organize to demand rights, however, during the Founding and Early National Eras. Gender politics in the United States changed after an international anti-slavery conference in London refused to seat a delegation of abolitionist women from the United States. Outraged, Elizabeth Cady Stanton and Lucretia Mott resolved to create a women's movement. Their goal was to obtain for women the same equal political and economic rights that radical abolitionists demanded for persons of color.

Compare Elizabeth Cady Stanton's "Keynote Address" to the other Jacksonian readings in this chapter. To what extent might all the arguments below be described as conventional Jacksonian demands for equality, with the only difference being that the equality demanded is between men and women rather than between different classes of men? To what extent do Stanton and her political supporters make different kinds of equality arguments to justify gender equality?

. . .

. . . [W]e are assembled to protest against a form of government existing without the consent of the governed—to declare our right to be free as man is free, to be represented in the government which we are taxed to support, to have such disgraceful laws as give man the power to chastise and imprison his wife, to take the wages which she earns, the property which she inherits, and, in case of separation, the children of her love; laws which make her the mere dependent on his bounty. It is to protest against such unjust laws as these that we are assembled today, and to have them, if possible, forever erased from our statute books, deeming them a shame and a disgrace to a Christian republic in the nineteenth century. We have met to uplift woman's fallen divinity upon an even pedestal with man's. And, strange as it may seem to many, we now demand our right to vote according to the declaration of the government under which we live.

This right no one pretends to deny. We need not prove ourselves equal to Daniel Webster to enjoy this privilege, for the ignorant Irishman in the ditch has all the civil rights he has. We need not prove our muscular power equal to this same Irishman to enjoy this privilege, for the most tiny, weak, ill-shaped stripling of twenty-one has all the civil rights of the Irishman. We have no objection to discuss the question of equality, for we feel that the weight of argument lies wholly with us, but we wish the question of equality kept distinct from the question of rights, for the proof of the one does not determine the truth of the other. All white men in this country have the same rights, however they may differ in mind, body, or estate.

The right is ours. The question now is: how shall we get possession of what rightfully belongs to us? We should not feel so sorely grieved if no man who had not attained the full stature of a Webster, Clay, Van Buren, or Gerrit Smith [a noted abolitionist] could claim the right of the elective franchise. But to have drunkards, idiots, horse-racing, rum-selling rowdies, ignorant foreigners, and silly boys fully recognized, while we ourselves are thrust out from all the rights that belong to citizens, it is too grossly insulting to the dignity of woman to be longer quietly submitted to.

. . .

Verily, the world waits the coming of some new element, some purifying power, some spirit of mercy and love. The voice of woman has been silenced in the state, the church, and the home, but man cannot fulfill his destiny alone, he cannot redeem his race unaided. There are deep and tender chords of sympathy and love in the hearts of the downfallen and oppressed that woman can touch more skillfully than man.

The world has never yet seen a truly great and virtuous nation, because in the degradation of woman the very fountains of life are poisoned at their source. It is vain to look for silver and gold from mines of copper and lead.

51. *Kansas Constitutional Convention, a reprint of the Proceedings and Debates of the Convention which Framed the Constitution of Kansas at Wyandotte in July,* July 14, 1859 (Topeka, KS: Kansas State Printing Plant, 1920), 169.

52. Excerpted from *Address of Mrs. Elizabeth Cady Stanton: Delivered at Seneca Falls and Rochester, NY, July 19th and August 2d, 1848* (New York: R. J. Johnston, 1870).

. . .

We do not expect our path will be strewn with the flowers of popular applause, but over the thorns of bigotry and prejudice will be our way, and on our banners will beat the dark storm clouds of opposition from those who have entrenched themselves behind the stormy bulwarks of custom and authority, and who have fortified their position by every means, holy and unholy. But we will steadfastly abide the result. Unmoved we will bear it aloft. Undauntedly we will unfurl it to the gale, for we know that the storm cannot rend from it a shred, that the electric flash will but more clearly show to us the glorious words inscribed upon it, "Equality of Rights."

D. Native Americans

Native Americans did not fare well in Jacksonian America, to say the least. Congress in 1830 passed the Indian Removal Act, which permitted the federal government, after pressuring tribes to sell lands, to remove most Native Americans from the southeast to west of the Mississippi. More than four thousand Cherokees died along the "Trail of Tears" when making the trek from Georgia to Oklahoma. Federal officials consistently ruled that Native Americans were not citizens of the United States and were therefore not entitled as a matter of constitutional right to any protections set out in federal or state constitutions. Attorney General Caleb Cushing claimed that "the Indians are the *subjects* of the United States, and therefore are not, in mere right of home-birth, citizens of the United States."[53] Constitutional decision makers before the Civil War regarded Native Americans as an alien race. In *United States v. Rogers* (1846), the Supreme Court of the United States provided racial justifications for a ruling that white persons could not acquire the legal status of Native Americans. William Rogers was indicted for the murder of Jacob Nicholson. Under American law federal courts did not have jurisdiction over crimes committed by Native Americans on tribal lands in the territories. Rogers claimed that he had become a Native American. Chief Justice Taney quickly brushed aside the claim that a person could change races:

And we think it very clear, that a white man who at mature age is adopted in an Indian tribe does not thereby become an Indian, and was not intended to be embraced in the exception above mentioned. He may by such adoption become entitled to certain privileges in the tribe, and make himself amenable to their laws and usages. Yet he is not an Indian; and the exception is confined to those who by the usages and customs of the Indians are regarded as belonging to their race. It does not speak of members of a tribe, but of the race generally,—of the family of Indians; and it intended to leave them both, as regarded their own tribe, and other tribes also, to be governed by Indian usages and customs.

Taney further concluded: "Whatever obligations the prisoner may have taken upon himself by becoming a Cherokee by adoption, his responsibility to the laws of the United States remained unchanged and undiminished. He was still a white man, of the white race, and therefore not within the exception in the act of Congress."

The Removal Debates (1830)[54]

Jacksonian efforts to remove Native Americans from Georgia and other southeastern states led to one of the greatest tragedies in American history. Presidents during the Early National Era sought to assimilate Native Americans. Congress in the early nineteenth century regularly funded missionaries, who were expected to teach Native Americans agriculture and convert them to Christianity. These efforts were both partly successful and controversial. By the 1820s the Cherokees in Georgia had abandoned many traditional tribal practices, adopted a constitution similar to the Constitution of the United States, and increasingly resembled a conventional American community. Georgia and other southern states bitterly resented federal policies aimed at "mainstreaming" Native Americans. In 1829 and 1830 Georgia passed laws declaring sovereignty over Cherokee lands, forbidding whites from living among the Cherokees without a state license, outlawing all Cherokee political organizations, prohibiting contracts between whites and Cherokees, and forbidding Cherokees from testifying against white persons in civil or criminal trials. President Jackson

53. *Official Opinions of the Attorneys General of the United States*, C. C. Andrews ed., vol. VII (Washington: W.H. & O.H. Morrison, 1871), 749.

54. *Register of Debates*, 21st Cong., 1st Sess. (1830), 1081–1103; 309–20.

and Democrats in Congress supported such state assertions of sovereignty over Native American soil.

The Cherokees triumphed in their initial conflict with Georgia. Samuel Worcester, a local missionary, refused to obtain the required license. He was arrested, convicted, and sentenced to four years in prison. Anti-Jacksonians were incensed at what they perceived to be a violation of religious freedoms. The Boston Daily Advertiser *questioned whether "the Christian people of the United States [would] give their sanction . . . to the conduct of a President who treats the ministers of the Christian religion with open outrage."*[55] *The Supreme Court in* Worcester v. Georgia *(1832) declared that Georgia's effort to assert sovereignty over Native American soil violated treaties the United States had signed with the Cherokees. John Marshall's majority opinion rejected claims that Native American rights could be subordinated to the power of state governments. He declared, "The Indian nations had always been considered as distinct, independent communities, retaining their original natural rights."*

Worcester *was a hollow victory. Although the decision struck down* state *efforts to limit the rights of Native Americans who lived on land granted to them by treaties, the justices gave Native Americans no rights against the national government. This distinction was important. In sharp contrast to the presidents of the Early National Era, President Andrew Jackson supported state efforts to assert control over Native American lands. He did little to implement* Worcester. *More important, Jackson and his congressional allies sponsored the Indian Removal Act of 1830. This law authorized federal officials to purchase Cherokee lands and remove the Cherokees to Oklahoma. In theory the decision to sell was voluntary. When Cherokee leadership refused to sell, however, Georgia jailed tribal officials and negotiated a treaty with a rival group willing to accept removal. The resulting treaty was accepted by a one-vote margin in the Senate. In 1838 federal troops helped remove the Cherokees from Georgia. Four thousand persons died on the trek from Georgia to the western territories.*

The following excerpts are from the 1830 congressional debate over Native American removal. Debate focused on several issues. The most important was whether the United States or Georgia had the power to deal with the Cherokees. Participants also debated whether the Cherokees had natural rights to soil and other natural rights that white persons had to respect. On what basis does Representative Wilde deny that Native Americans have natural rights to soil? Why does Senator Frelinghuysen disagree? How do these men's attitudes toward Native Americans influence their understanding of Native American rights?

The removal debate had important ramifications for American constitutional development. Many anti-slavery advocates abandoned colonization plans after seeing how the forced removal of the Cherokees decimated that tribe. William Lloyd Garrison and others first insisted on the immediate abolition of slavery after witnessing how the demand to open Cherokee lands led to a human rights tragedy. Later, during the debates over the Fourteenth Amendment, Republicans referred to the removal debates as demonstrating the need to provide constitutional limitations on state power to violate fundamental rights.[56]

REPRESENTATIVE RICHARD HENRY WILDE (Georgia, Democrat)

. . .

. . . Our ancestors seem to have made the true distinction, when by law they declared that Indians had property in the lands they possessed and improved, by subduing them, inferring they had no property in land not subdued by them: this distinction was founded on the law of nature, which has ever required that labor be bestowed upon a thing common, in order to make it individual property. Europeans, in fact, have ever considered our Indians as capable of property in a fish or wild beast, because capable of bestowing on either that labor necessary and adequate to appropriate to oneself property from the common stock; but they have never considered them capable of property in lands generally, because generally incapable of subduing them from a wilderness to a cultivated states, and in this respect wholly unlike Europeans.

. . .

To take measures to preserve the Indians, is to take measures to preserve so much barbarity, helplessness, and want, to the exclusion of so much industry and thriftiness. No personal injustice should be, or is tolerated; but the laws which have for their end to keep up the existence of large bodies of half clad barbarians, who will not, or cannot sustain themselves by the arts of civilized life, are laws to prevent comfort and improvement from taking the place of misery and want. The object of true humanity is not blindly to better the

55. Ronald N. Satz, *American Indian Policy in the Jacksonian Era* (Norman: University of Oklahoma Press, 2002), 50.

56. The discussion in this paragraph is heavily influenced by Gerard M. Magliocca, "The Cherokee Removal and the Fourteenth Amendment," *Duke Law Journal* 53 (2003): 875.

condition of a given individual, whether he will be bettered or not, but to put a happier individual in the place of a less happy one. If it can be done by changing the nature of the latter, it is well; if it cannot, leave him to the operation of his character and habits. Do not resist the order of Providence, which is carrying him away; and, when he is gone, a civilized man will step into his place, and your end is attained. . . .

. . .

The fundamental principle [of the Cherokee Constitution] is, that the land is to remain common and inalienable. This, of itself, is barbarism. Separate property in land is the basis of civilized society. Have not all the efforts of all our Presidents to civilize the Indians assumed this principle?

. . .

What is the scope and spirit of these laws [on Cherokee removal]? Simply to restore the full blooded Cherokees, the great bulk of the nation, to their free will, and leave them to decide for themselves whether they will emigrate or not, unawed by the power, and exempted from the cruelty of those who have in fact enslaved them.

. . .

The provision, with respect to Indian evidence [in the Georgia code that forbade Indians from testifying against white persons] . . . was in truth, a relaxation of the common law rule of evidence. By what form of adjuration will you bind the conscience of an Indian? Will you swear him on the Old or the New Testament, on the Koran or the Shaster? Sir, he believes in none of these. Under what circumstances does he conceive himself under an obligation to tell the truth, and nothing but the truth? After his conjurors have performed their superstitious rites, and he has drank the black drink, and assembled at the council fire, then, and not till then, does he come under that obligation. Then, and not till then, has he involved the vengeance of his deities upon the guilt of perjury. Sir, can you perform these ceremonies in a court of justice? Can such a man be made a witness there?

. . .

When gentlemen talk of preserving the Indians, what is it that they mean to preserve? Is it their mode of life? No. You intended to convert them from hunters to agriculturalists or herdsmen. Is it their barbarous laws and customs? No. You propose to furnish them with a code, and prevail upon them to adopt habits like your own. Their language? No. You intend to supersede their imperfect jargon, by teaching them your own rich, copious, energetic tongue. Their religion? No. You intend to convert them from their miserable and horrible superstitions to the mild and cheering doctrines of Christianity.

What is it, then, that constitutes the Indian individuality—the identity of that race which gentlemen are so anxious to preserve? Is it the more copper color of the skin, which marks them—according to our prejudices, at least—an inferior—a conquered—a degraded race? . . .

SENATOR THEODORE FRELINGHUYSEN (New Jersey, Anti-Jacksonian)

. . .

. . . I believe, sir, it is not now seriously denied that the Indians are men, endowed with kindred faculties and powers with ourselves; that they have a place in human sympathy, and are justly entitled to a share in the common bounties of a benign Providence. And, with this conceded, I ask in what code of the law of nations, or by what process of abstract deduction, their rights have been extinguished?

. . . However mere human policy, or the law of power, or the tyrant's plea of expediency, may have found it convenient at any or in all times to recede from the unchangeable principles of eternal justice, no argument can shake the political maxim, that, where the Indian always has been, he enjoys an absolute right still to be, in the free exercise of his own modes of thought, government, and conduct.

In the light of natural law, can a reason for a distinction exist in the mode of enjoying that which is my own? If I use it for hunting, may another take it because he needs it for agriculture? I am aware that some writers have, by a system of artificial reasoning, endeavored to justify, or rather excuse the encroachments made upon Indian territory; and they denominate these abstractions the law of nations, and, in this ready way, the question is dispatched. Sir, as we trace the sources of this law, we find its authority to depend either upon the conventions or common consent of nations. And when, permit me to inquire, were the Indian tribes ever consulted on the establishment of such a law? Whoever represented them or their interests in any Congress of nations, to confer upon the public rules of intercourse, and the proper foundations of dominion and property? The plain matter of fact is, that all these partial doctrines have resulted from the selfish plans and pursuits of more enlightened nations; and it is not matter for any great wonder, that they should so largely partake of a mercenary and exclusive spirit toward the claim of the Indians.

It is, however, admitted, sir, that when the increase of population and the wants of mankind demand the cultivation of the earth, a duty is thereby devolved upon the proprietors of large and uncultivated regions, of devoting them to such useful purposes. But such appropriations are to be obtained by fair contract, and for reasonable compensation. It is, in such a case, the duty of the proprietor to sell: we may properly address his reason to induce him; but we cannot rightfully compel the cession of his lands, or take them by violence, if his consent be withheld. . . .

. . .

. . . The last section [of the Georgia Cherokee Code] declares, "that no Indian, or descendant of any Indian, residing within the Creek or Cherokee nations of Indians, shall be deemed a competent witness in any Court of this State, to which a white person may be a party. . . ." It did not suffice to rob these people of the last vestige of their own political rights and liberties; the work was not complete until they were shut out of the protection of Georgia laws. For, sir, after the first day of June next, a gang of lawless white men may break into the Cherokee country, plunder their habitations, murder the mother with the children, and all in the sight of the wretched husband and father, and no law of Georgia will reach the atrocity. It is vain to tell us, sir, that murder may be traced by circumstantial probabilities. The charge against this State is, you have, by force and violence, stripped these people of the protection of their government, and now refuse to cast over them the shield of your own. The outrage of the deed is, that you leave the poor Indian helpless and defenseless, and in this cruel way hope to banish him from his home. Sir, if this law be enforced, I do religiously believe that it will awaken tones of feeling that will go up to God, and call down the thunders of his wrath.

. . .

. . . And, sir, weigh a moment the considerations that address us on behalf of the Cherokees especially. Prompted and encouraged by our counsels, they have in good earnest resolved to become men, rational, educated, Christian men; and they have succeeded beyond our most sanguine hopes. They have established a regular constitution of civil government, republican in its principles. Wise and beneficent laws are enacted; the people acknowledge their authority, and feel their obligation. A printing press, conducted by one of the nation, circulates a weekly newspaper, printed partly in English and partly in the Cherokee language—schools flourish in many of their settlements—Christian temples, to the God of the Bible, are frequented by respectful, devout, and many sincere worshippers. . . .

VI. Criminal Justice

MAJOR DEVELOPMENTS

- Alleged fugitive slaves denied jury trials
- Judges wrest power to determine the law from juries
- First decisions on right to counsel

Americans in the Jacksonian Era faced conflicting pressures when considering the rights of persons suspected and convicted of criminal offenses. Most persons wanted a criminal justice system that punished persons who had committed what all agreed were moral wrongs. The law of self-incrimination emphasized the likelihood of a confession being true or false. Professional police officers and urban residents put pressure on courts to reduce due process protections for persons accused of ordinary crimes. Controversies over constitutional criminal procedure also erupted as part of more fundamental controversies over substantive criminal offenses. Free and slave state citizens disagreed vehemently over whether alleged fugitive slaves and those who assisted fugitive slaves were entitled to jury trials and habeas corpus. Justices hostile to temperance laws often protecting the rights of persons accused of possessing, selling or drinking intoxicating liquor. Such decisions as *Fisher v. McGirr* (MA 1854), which protected persons suspected of storing alcoholic beverages from intrusive searches, enabled Jacksonians to protect the right to drink without overturning temperance laws.

When reading the materials in this section, pay careful attention to the crimes or acts of wrongdoing alleged. Consider whether the constitutional decision on criminal procedure would have been different if a different crime had been charged. To what extent do you believe that constitutional decision makers were committed to protecting the procedural rights of persons who might be guilty of any criminal offense?

To what extent were constitutional decision makers influenced by their attitudes toward particular substantive crimes? Did the decisions below make certain crimes more difficult to detect or prosecute? To what extent did legal and constitutional changes in the Jacksonian Era make other crimes easier to detect and prosecute?

A. Due Process and Habeas Corpus

During the Jacksonian Era Americans debated whether fugitive slaves and persons who assisted fugitive slaves merited strong due process and habeas corpus protections, while agreeing that ordinary criminals enjoyed only a bare procedural minimum of these protections at their trials. Bitter sectional debates broke out over whether the Fugitive Slave Acts of 1793 and 1850 provided sufficient constitutional protections to alleged fugitive slaves. Equally bitter sectional debates broke out over whether state courts could issue writs of habeas corpus to federal officials on behalf of alleged fugitive slaves and those accused of helping them escape North. No analogous debates broke out over whether persons accused of ordinary crimes merited the same substantial constitutional protections. Sherman Booth became a household name after he helped spirit Joshua Glover, an alleged fugitive slave, from a Wisconsin prison to Canada. Whether the mayor of Hagerstown, Maryland, remembered Eliza Shafer the day after fining her for "lewd" behavior is doubtful.

"Ordinary" Crimes. Due process protections were sparse before the Civil War. Most petty criminals hauled up before justices experienced summary procedures. Trial judges offered some protections for persons suspected of crimes. State appellate courts reversed convictions in particularly egregious cases. Nevertheless, few judges were willing to free people whom they believed to be guilty of wrongdoing. Such treatise writers as Supreme Court Justice Story equated due process as shorthand for the other constitutional rights of persons suspected of crime. Criminal defendants who could not complain of some other constitutional violation could not complain that their due process rights were violated.

Due process rights were often modified when urban centers felt pressure to quickly process a high number of criminal cases. Consider *Shafer v. Mumma* (MD 1861). Eliza Shafer was fined by the mayor of Hagerstown, Maryland, for being a "lewd woman." The Supreme Court of Maryland in a short opinion brushed aside her demand for the full panoply of protections constitutionally due persons accused of crimes. The justices reasoned,

> It would be next to, if not quite impossible for a large city like Baltimore to preserve order within its limits, preserve the streets free from interruption, indeed to do most of the thousand things necessary to be done, to carry on its various and indispensable operations, if in every case it were a necessary preliminary that the offender should be regularly prosecuted by presentment, indictment, and trial. It has always been understood that, under the police power, persons disturbing the public peace, persons guilty of a nuisance, or obstructing the public highways, and the like offences, may be summarily arrested and fined, without any infraction of that part of the Constitution which apportions the administration of the judicial power, strictly as such. We regard the power conferred on the corporation of Hagerstown, to summarily punish persons of the description the appellant, Elmira, is admitted to have been, as falling directly within the definition of a police regulation.[57]

Ordinary criminals rarely made use of habeas corpus. The Force Act of 1833 gave federal courts the power to issue writs of habeas corpus to persons detained by states for enforcing national laws. This measure provided protections for customs officials who attempted to collect tariffs in South Carolina, but not to such victims of summary procedures as Eliza Shafer. In the antebellum South, writs of habeas corpus were sometimes used by slaveholders to recover slaves.

Fugitive Slaves. Jacksonians sharply contested the due process and habeas corpus rights of persons alleged to be fugitive slaves. The Fugitive Slave Acts of 1793 and 1850 provided no significant protections to persons of color alleged to be runaways. J. J. Crittenden, the attorney general under Millard Fillmore, expressed mainstream Jacksonian and Whig views when he declared that Congress could enact summary procedures for identifying fugitive slaves and returning them to their southern owners. The procedures Congress required

57. *Shafer v. Mumma*, 17 Md. 331 (1861).

in 1850 merely required a slaveholder to provide a certificate to a local federal commissioner alleging that a particular person of color was an escaped slave. The alleged slave was not allowed to contest this claim, at least in the state in which that person was found. Charles Sumner, a prominent senator and abolitionist, articulated the mainstream anti-slavery view when he insisted that the Fugitive Slave Acts violated due process and habeas corpus rights.

The constitutional debates over fugitive slaves were further complicated by northern personal liberties laws. These measures required a trial by jury and provided other procedural protections for persons accused of being fugitive slaves. Proponents of these measures insisted that states had the right to protect free residents of color. Opponents insisted that personal liberties laws unconstitutionally interfered with slaveholder rights and were inconsistent with the Fugitive Slave Acts of 1793 and 1850.

Anti-slavery activists resisted efforts to remove fugitive slaves by legal and extralegal means. Violent threats were common. Some intimidated slave owners chose not to pursue their claims. Anti-slavery advocates in Boston staged a prison break that freed those persons claimed to be fugitive slaves before they could be returned south. President Franklin Pierce ordered federal troops to Boston to ensure that Anthony Burns, a fugitive slave, was returned to Virginia. Northerners who engaged in these rescue missions insisted that they were vindicating constitutional rights in the streets. Southerners and northern conservatives complained that mob violence was impairing the constitutional rights of slaveholders.

Federal and state courts reached different conclusions when adjudicating fugitive slave cases. New York judges in *Jack v. Mary Martin* (NY 1835) insisted that the due process clause of the New York Constitution guaranteed persons of color the right to have a jury determine whether they were an escaped slave. In a series of cases beginning with *In re Booth* (WI 1854), the Supreme Court of Wisconsin declared unconstitutional the Fugitive Slave Law of 1850 and ruled that state courts could issue writs of habeas corpus to persons in federal prisons accused of violating that law. Federal courts (and most state courts) rejected these contentions. The Supreme Court in *Prigg v. Pennsylvania* (1842) declared that the Fugitive Slave Act of 1793 did not violate the constitutional rights of alleged fugitives. The Supreme Court in *Ableman v. Booth* (1858) ruled that state courts could not issue writs of habeas corpus to federal officials and sustained the Fugitive Slave Act of 1850. These decisions did not end the constitutional debate. Wisconsin officials in 1859 passed resolutions nullifying *Ableman v. Booth*. On the eve of the Civil War, the practical right of a slaveholder to recapture a fugitive slave depended more on the skill of the slave catcher and local attitudes in northern communities than on judicial opinions in legal reports.

The Booth Cases (1854–58)

Sherman Booth was an anti-slavery journalist who lived in Milwaukee, Wisconsin. In March 1854 Booth helped a fugitive slave, Joshua Glover, break out of prison and escape to Canada. On May 26 Booth was arrested by a federal commissioner for violating the Fugitive Slave Act of 1850. Booth immediately asked the Supreme Court of Wisconsin for a writ of habeas corpus. Booth's petition asserted that he was being illegally detained by federal officials, because the Fugitive Slave Act was unconstitutional. Justice Abram Smith granted the writ and his decision was later affirmed by the Supreme Court of Wisconsin (Booth I). *The justices in* Booth I *ruled that state courts could issue writs of habeas corpus to persons being detained by a federal commissioner because federal commissioners had no authority to determine whether a federal law was constitutional. The state court justices then determined that the Fugitive Slave Act of 1850 was unconstitutional and issued the writ. On July 8 a federal grand jury indicted Booth for aiding and abetting the escape of Joshua Glover. Two days later a federal district judge issued an arrest warrant. Booth again asked the Supreme Court of Wisconsin for a writ of habeas corpus. This time the Wisconsin Supreme Court* (Booth II) *unanimously rejected his petition. Unlike federal commissioners, the state justices reasoned, federal courts were authorized by the Constitution of the United States to make an independent determination of whether the Fugitive Slave Act of 1850 was unconstitutional. At his federal court trial Booth was found guilty of helping Joshua Glover escape from federal marshals but was not found guilty of violating the Fugitive Slave Act of 1850. Once more Booth appealed to the Wisconsin Supreme Court for a writ of habeas corpus. This time, the court* (Booth III) *unanimously granted the writ. All three judges insisted that federal courts had jurisdiction only over federal crimes. Helping someone escape from a federal marshal was not a federal crime, they noted, in the crucial absence of evidence that Booth had helped an escaped slave escape from a federal marshal. Federal authorities in Wisconsin appealed this decision to the Supreme Court of the United States.*

Roger Taney, writing for a unanimous Court in Ableman v. Booth, *reversed the Supreme Court of Wisconsin's decision. State courts, he declared, had no power to issue a writ of habeas corpus to a person in federal custody on the ground that federal courts had misinterpreted federal law or the federal Constitution.*

The Taney Court decision did not bring the Booth affair to a halt. The Wisconsin Supreme Court refused to retract the writ of habeas corpus. The Wisconsin legislature passed a resolution nullifying Ableman v. Booth. *Nevertheless, Booth was rearrested. He remained in prison long after his thirty-day sentence ended because he refused to pay the $1000 fine. President James Buchanan pardoned Booth on his last day in office. Litigation over the escape of Joshua Glover did not end until the closing days of the Civil War.*[58]

The follow pages excerpt Justice Smith's initial decision to grant the writ of habeas corpus and the opinion of the Supreme Court of the United States in Ableman v. Booth. *Consider first the questions that these materials raise about habeas corpus. The Wisconsin Supreme Court claims a right to issue writs of habeas corpus to persons imprisoned by a federal commissioner. Why do they make that claim? Does the Taney Court in* Ableman *dispute that claim, or is* Ableman *directed only at the authority of state courts to question persons detained by federal judges? Consider questions about the Fugitive Slave Act of 1850. Why do Justices Smith and Whiton consider that law unconstitutional?*

In re Booth [Booth I], 3 Wis. 1 (1854)

JUSTICE SMITH

. . .

. . . [T]he States will never submit to the assumption, that United States commissioners have the power to hear and determine upon the rights and liberties of their citizens, and issue process to enforce their adjudications, which is beyond the examination or review of the state judiciary. They will cheerfully submit to the exercise of all power and authority by the federal judiciary, which is delegated to that department by the federal constitution; but they have a right to insist, and they will insist that the state judiciary shall be and remain supreme in all else, and that the functions of the federal judiciary within the territory of the states shall be exercised by the officers designated or provided for by the constitution of the United States, and that they shall not be transferred to subordinate and irresponsible functionaries, holding their office at the will of the federal courts, doing their duty and obeying their mandates, for which neither the one nor the other is responsible.

. . .

. . . [T]he *status* of the fugitive is essentially different in this state, from his *status* or condition in the state from whence he fled. In the latter, he remained subject to all the disabilities of his class, though he may have escaped from the domicil or premises of his master. Here, he is entitled to the full and complete protection of our laws; as much so as any other human being, so long as he is unclaimed. He may sue and be sued; he may acquire and hold property; he is, to all intents and purposes, a free man, until a lawful claim is made for him; and this claim must be made by the person to whom his service or labor is due, under the laws of the state from which he escaped. No one else can interfere with him. If no *claim* is set up to his service or labor by the person to whom his service or labor is due, there is no power or authority, or person on earth, that can derive any advantage from his former condition, or assert it, to his prejudice. So long as the owner does not choose to assert his *claim*, the cottage of the fugitive in Wisconsin is as much his castle—his property, liberty and person are as much the subject of legal protection, as those of any other person. Our legal tribunals are as open to his complaint or appeal, as to that of any other man. He *may* never be claimed; and if not, he would remain forever free, and transmit freedom to his posterity born on our soil.

. . .

We have seen how the power of legislation was granted to congress in respect to public records, etc. We have seen that no such power is granted in respect to the surrender of fugitives from labor, and that it was not even asked for; and from the known temper and scruples of the national convention, we may safely affirm, that had it been asked it would not have been granted, and had it been granted, no union could have been formed upon such a basis. The history of the times fully justifies this conclusion. Can it be supposed

58. Readers interested in all the bloody details should consult H. Robert Baker, *The Rescue of Joshua Glover: A Fugitive Slave, the Constitution, and the Coming of the Civil War* (Athens: Ohio University Press, 2006).

for a moment, that had the framers of the constitution imagined, that under this provision the federal government would assume to override the state authorities, appoint subordinate tribunals in every county in every state, invested with jurisdiction beyond the reach or inquiry of the state judiciary, to multiply executive and judicial officers *ad infinitum,* wholly independent of, and irresponsible to the police regulations of the state, and that the whole army and navy of the union could be sent into a state, without the request, and against the remonstrance of the legislature thereof; nay, even that under its operation, the efficacy of the writ of habeas corpus could be destroyed, if the privileges thereof were not wholly suspended; if the members of the convention had dreamed that they were incorporating such a power into the constitution, does any one believe, that it would have been adopted without opposition and without debate? And if these results had suggested themselves to the states on its adoption, would it have been passed by them, *sub silentio,* jealous as they were of state rights and state sovereignty? The idea is preposterous. The union would never have been formed upon such a basis. It is an impeachment of historic truth, to assert it.

. . .

. . . But it may be asked, how are the rights here stipulated and guaranteed, to be enforced? I answer, that every state officer, executive, legislative and judicial, who takes an oath to support the constitution of the United States, is bound to provide for, and aid in their enforcement, according to the true intent and meaning of the constitution. . . .

. . .

To my mind, therefore, it is apparent that congress has no constitutional power to legislate on this subject. It is equally apparent, that the several states can pass no laws, nor adopt any regulations, by which the fugitive may be discharged from service. . . .

. . .

The clause as finally adopted reads, "but shall be delivered up on claim of the party *to whom such service or labor is* DUE." Here is a fact to be ascertained, before the fugitive can be legally delivered up, viz: that his service or labor is really due to the party who claims him. How is the fact to be ascertained? . . . What authority shall determine it? Clearly the authority of the state whose duty it is to deliver up the fugitive when the fact is determined. Until the issue which the constitution itself creates, is decided, the *person* is entitled to the protection of the laws of the state. When the issue is determined against the fugitive, then the constitutional compact rises above the laws and regulations of the state, and to the former the latter must yield.

. . . The law of 1850, by providing for a trial of the constitutional issue, between the *parties* designated thereby, by officers not recognized by any constitution, state or national, is unconstitutional and void.

It has been already said, that until the claim of the owner be interposed, the fugitive in this state is, to all intents and purposes, a free man.

. . . Therefore the trial thereof must not only be had before a judicial tribunal, but whether proceedings be commenced by the fugitive to resist the claimant, or by the claimant to enforce, and establish his claim, it would seem that either party would be entitled to a jury. . . .

. . .

Again, the constitution provides that no person shall be deprived of life, liberty or property, without *due process of law.* This last phrase has a distinct technical meaning, viz: regular judicial proceedings, according to the course of the common law, or by a regular suit commenced and prosecuted according to the forms of law. An essential requisite is due process to bring the party into court. It is in accordance with the first principles of natural law. Every person is entitled to his "day in court," to be legally notified of the proceedings taken against him, and duly summoned to defend. The passing of judgment upon any person without his "day in court"; without due process, or its equivalent, is contrary to the law of nature, and of the civilized world, and without the express guaranty of the constitution, it would be implied as a fundamental condition of all civil governments. But the tenth section of the act of 1850, expressly nullifies this provision of the constitution. It provides that the claimant may go before any court of record, or judge, in vacation, and without process, make proof of the escape, and the owing of service or labor; whereupon a record is made of the matters proved, and a general description of the person alleged to have escaped; a transcript of such record made out and attested by the clerk with the seal of the court, being exhibited to the judge or commissioner, must be taken and held to be conclusive evidence of the fact of escape, and that service or labor is due to the party mentioned in the record, and *may* be held sufficient evidence of the identity of the person escaping.

Here is a palpable violation of the constitution. Can that be said to be by due *process* of law which is without process altogether? Here the *status* or condition of the person is instantly changed in his absence, without process, without notice, without opportunity, to meet or examine the witnesses against him, or rebut their testimony. A record is made, which is conclusive against him, "in any state or territory in which he may be found." It is not a process to bring the person before the court in which the record is made up, but it is to all intents and purposes, a judgment of the court or judge, which commits the person absolutely to the control and possession of the claimant, to be taken whithersoever he pleases, to be dragged from a state where the legal presumption is in favor of his freedom, to any state or territory where the legal presumption is against his freedom. . . .

Ableman v. Booth, 62 U.S. 506 (1858)

CHIEF JUSTICE TANEY delivered the opinion of the court.

. . .

. . . [N]o one will suppose that a Government which has now lasted nearly seventy years, enforcing its laws by its own tribunals, and preserving the union of the States, could have lasted a single year, or fulfilled the high trusts committed to it, if offences against its laws could not have been punished without the consent of the State in which the culprit was found.

. . . [N]o State can authorize one of its judges or courts to exercise judicial power, by *habeas corpus* or otherwise, within the jurisdiction of another and independent Government. And although the State of Wisconsin is sovereign within its territorial limits to a certain extent, yet that sovereignty is limited and restricted by the Constitution of the United States. And the powers of the General Government, and of the State, although both exist and are exercised within the same territorial limits, are yet separate and distinct sovereignties, acting separately and independently of each other, within their respective spheres. And the sphere of action appropriated to the United States is as far beyond the reach of the judicial process issued by a State judge or a State court, as if the line of division was traced by landmarks and monuments visible to the eye. . . .

. . . The Constitution was not formed merely to guard the States against danger from foreign nations, but mainly to secure union and harmony at home; for if this object could be attained, there would be but little danger from abroad; and to accomplish this purpose, it was felt by the statesmen who framed the Constitution, and by the people who adopted it, that it was necessary that many of the rights of sovereignty which the States then possessed should be ceded to the General Government; and that, in the sphere of action assigned to it, it should be supreme, and strong enough to execute its own laws by its own tribunals, without interruption from a State or from State authorities. And it was evident that anything short of this would be inadequate to the main objects for which the Government was established; and that local interests, local passions or prejudices, incited and fostered by individuals for sinister purposes, would lead to acts of aggression and injustice by one State upon the rights of another, which would ultimately terminate in violence and force, unless there was a common arbiter between them, armed with power enough to protect and guard the rights of all, by appropriate laws, to be carried into execution peacefully by its judicial tribunals.

. . .

We do not question the authority of State court, or judge, who is authorized by the laws of the State to issue the writ of *habeas corpus*, to issue it in any case where the party is imprisoned within its territorial limits, provided it does not appear, when the application is made, that the person imprisoned is in custody under the authority of the United States. The court or judge has a right to inquire, in this mode of proceeding, for what cause and by what authority the prisoner is confined within the territorial limits of the State sovereignty. And it is the duty of the marshal, or other person having the custody of the prisoner, to make known to the judge or court, by a proper return, the authority by which he holds him in custody. This right to inquire by process of *habeas corpus*, and the duty of the officer to make a return, grows, necessarily, out of the complex character of our Government, and the existence of two distinct and separate sovereignties within the same territorial space, each of them restricted in its powers, and each within its sphere of action, prescribed by the Constitution of the United States, independent of the other. But, after the return is made, and the State judge or court judicially apprized that the party is in custody under the authority of the United States, they can proceed no further. They then know that the prisoner is within the dominion and jurisdiction of another

Government, and that neither the writ of *habeas corpus*, nor any other process issued under State authority, can pass over the line of division between the two sovereignties. He is then within the dominion and exclusive jurisdiction of the United States. If he has committed an offence against their laws, their tribunals alone can punish him. If he is wrongfully imprisoned, their judicial tribunals can release him and afford him redress. . . . No State judge or court, after they are judicially informed that the party is imprisoned under the authority of the United States, has any right to interfere with him, or to require him to be brought before them. . . .

B. Search and Seizure

The constitutional law of search and seizure in Jacksonian America depended partly on the crime being investigated. Many cities and towns established professional police forces. The expansion of the criminal law and the rise of professional police forces during the Jacksonian Era initiated a lengthy process of working out detailed constitutional rules for how searches could be conducted. Police officers sought to relax previous constitutional understandings that permitted constables to be sued for trespass whenever a warrantless search failed to generate evidence of criminal conduct. State courts proved sympathetic to these claims. In *Rohan v. Sawin* (MA 1850), the Supreme Judicial Court of Massachusetts declared that innocent persons subject to warrantless arrests could not sue police officers for damages if the police officer had probable cause for making the arrest. The Supreme Judicial Court in *Commonwealth v. Dana* (MA 1841) provided another boon to law enforcement professionals when permitting prosecutors to introduce in criminal trials evidence that had been unconstitutionally obtained by government officials. Massachusetts justices were more sympathetic to defendants' rights when cases involving state bans on intoxicating liquors came before the court. In *Fisher v. McGirr* (MA 1854), the justices declared unconstitutional a Massachusetts law that authorized government officials to search private residences for illegal alcoholic beverages.[59]

59. *Fisher v. McGirr*, 67 Mass. 1 (1854).

Rohan v. Sawin, 59 Mass. 281 (1850)

Charles Sawin, a constable in Boston, believed that Edward Rohan had knowingly received stolen goods. Sawin arrested Rohan without a warrant and imprisoned him for fifteen hours. Rohan was subsequently released by a magistrate, who found insufficient evidence to charge him with a felony. Rohan then sued Sawin for trespass. He claimed that police officers could arrest persons without a warrant only when the person was guilty of a criminal offence or when the arrest was justified by public necessity. Sawin responded that police officers could make warrantless arrests whenever they had probable cause for thinking crimes had been committed. The trial judge instructed the jury that they could find Sawin not liable only if Rohan was guilty of receiving stolen goods or "there was an immediate necessity for the arrest." The jury found for Rohan. Sawin appealed that verdict to the Supreme Judicial Court of Massachusetts.

The Supreme Judicial Court of Massachusetts reversed the lower court's decision. They ruled that Sawin only needed probable cause to make a warrantless arrest. Justice Dewey's opinion claims that the common law distinguishes between arrests by civilians, which require an actual crime, and arrests by police officers, which may be made on probable cause. Other state supreme courts also adopted this rule. What is the source of the distinction between private and official arrests? Reread the search and seizure cases from the Early National and Colonial Eras. Was Justice Dewey following precedent, making new law, or doing a little of both?

JUSTICE DEWEY delivered the opinion of the Court.

. . .

Peace-officers without warrant may arrest suspected felons. . . . [A] constable, having reasonable cause to suspect that a felony has been actually committed, is justified in arresting the party suspected, although it afterwards appear that no felony has been committed. . . .

. . .

It has been sometimes contended, that an arrest of this character, without a warrant, was a violation of the great fundamental principles of our national and state constitutions, forbidding unreasonable searches and arrests, except by warrant founded upon a complaint made under oath. Those provisions doubtless had another and different purpose, being in restraint of general warrants to make searches, and requiring warrants to issue only upon a complaint made under

Table 5-3 Some Landmark Cases in the Development of the Power of Search and Seizure

Case	Court	Decision
Writ of Assistance Case (1761)	Massachusetts Colony Superior Court	General search warrants are legal
Frisbie v. Butler, 1 Kirby 213 (CT 1787)	Connecticut Superior Court	General search warrants are illegal
Commonwealth v. Griffith, 19 Mass. 11 (1823)	Supreme Judicial Court of Massachusetts	Slaves are not entitled to Fourth Amendment protection
Commonwealth v. Dana, 43 Mass. 329 (1841)	Supreme Judicial Court of Massachusetts	Search warrants can be issued for contraband, such as illegal lottery tickets, and unconstitutionally sezied evidence is admissible at trial
Commonwealth v. Lottery Tickets, 5 Cush. 369 (MA 1850)	Supreme Judicial Court of Massachusetts	Valid search warrants must rest on a firmer basis than the mere "belief" that contraband is present
Riley v. Johnston, 13 Ga. 260 (1853)	Georgia Supreme Court	If an illegal search is conducted as a result of a bad warrant, then the proper remedy is a civil suit against the person who secured the warrant; if the process for issuing the warrant was faulty, then the judge can be sued for trespass
Fisher v. McGirr, 1 Gray 1 (MA 1854)	Supreme Judicial Court of Massachusetts	Search warrants resulting directly in forfeiture of contraband alcohol without additional criminal proceedings are invalid
Ex parte Jackson, 96 U.S. 727 (1878)	U.S. Supreme Court	Sealed packages in the mail may only be opened with a warrant
Boyd v. United States, 116 U.S. 616 (1886)	U.S. Supreme Court	Tax collectors' requirement that a business produce its books is a constitutional search requiring a warrant
Alexis Delafoile v. State, 54 N.J.L. 381 (1892)	New Jersey Court of Appeals	Officers in one part of a private dwelling may not, even with a reasonable belief that criminal liquor sales are taking place, forcibly enter another part of the dwelling without a warrant
State v. Slamon, 73 Vt. 212 (1901)	Vermont Supreme Court	When executing a search warrant for stolen goods, officers may not seize correspondence found in an office
Wilson v. United States, 221 U.S. 361 (1911)	U.S. Supreme Court	Corporations have limited Fourth Amendment rights, but corporate officers must produce specific, relevant business documents on demand to government administrators with adequate statutory authority
Weeks v. United States, 232 U.S. 383 (1914)	U.S. Supreme Court	Federal government may not use illegally obtained evidence in trials; such evidence is excluded
Hester v. United States, 265 U.S. 57 (1924)	U.S. Supreme Court	Fourth Amendment protections do not extend to "open fields"
Carroll v. United States, 267 U.S. 132 (1925)	U.S. Supreme Court	Officers may stop and search a car for illegal alcohol without a search warrant
Marron v. United States, 275 U.S. 192 (1927)	U.S. Supreme Court	As an incident of arrest, officers may seize evidence of a crime on the premises even if that evidence is not described in a search warrant

(*Continued*)

Table 5-3 *(Continued)*

Case	Court	Decision
Olmstead v. United States, 277 U.S. 438 (1928)	U.S. Supreme Court	Wiretapping a telephone is not a constitutionally defined search and does not require a warrant
Wolf v. Colorado, 338 U.S. 25 (1949)	U.S. Supreme Court	Fourteenth Amendment does not require that states exclude illegally obtained evidence from trial
Mapp v. Ohio, 367 U.S. 643 (1961)	U.S. Supreme Court	Fourteenth Amendment requires states to adopt the exclusionary rule for illegally obtained evidence
Katz v. United States, 389 U.S. 347 (1967)	U.S. Supreme Court	Individuals have a reasonable expectation of privacy in their phone conversations, and warrantless wiretaps are invalid
Warden v. Hayden, 387 U.S. 294 (1967)	U.S. Supreme Court	Police may conduct a warrantless entry and search if the exigencies of the situation demand it to protect lives
Terry v. Ohio, 392 U.S. 1 (1968)	U.S. Supreme Court	An officer may "stop and frisk" a suspicious person for weapons
Chimel v. California, 395 U.S. 752 (1969)	U.S. Supreme Court	Searches incident to arrest must be limited to the area under the immediate control of the suspect
Wyman v. James, 400 U.S. 309 (1971)	U.S. Supreme Court	Fourth Amendment does not apply to the mandatory home visit of a welfare caseworker
United States v. Leon, 468 U.S. 897 (1984)	U.S. Supreme Court	There is a "good faith" exception to the exclusionary rule for mistakenly issued search warrants
Arizona v. Hicks, 480 U.S. 321 (1987)	U.S. Supreme Court	Warrantless seizures must be limited to evidence that is in plain view of where an officer has a right to be
National Treasury Employees Union v. Von Raab, 489 U.S. 656 (1989)	U.S. Supreme Court	Mandatory drug testing for selected Customs Service employees does not violate the Fourth Amendment
California v. Hodari D, 499 U.S. 621 (1991)	U.S. Supreme Court	Drugs abandoned during a police chase are not protected by the Fourth Amendment
Vernonia School District 47J v. Acton, 515 U.S. 646 (1995)	U.S. Supreme Court	Random drug testing of student athletes in public school is a reasonable intrusion on individual privacy
United States v. Simons, 206 F.3d 392 (4th Cir., 2000)	Fourth Circuit U.S. Court of Appeals	No reasonable expectation of privacy for Internet activity in workplace, and so warrantless search of hard drive is valid
Bond v. United States, 529 U.S. 334 (2000)	U.S. Supreme Court	Border Patrol agents may not give a "hard feel" of the carry-on bags of bus passengers
Indianapolis v. Edmond, 531 U.S. 32 (2000)	U.S. Supreme Court	Highway roadblocks and warrantless vehicle searches for narcotics are unrelated to highway safety and violate the Fourth Amendment
Kyllo v. United States, 533 U.S. 27 (2001)	U.S. Supreme Court	Use of a thermal-imaging device to examine a home is a constitutional search and requires a warrant
Samson v. California, 547 U.S. 843 (2005)	U.S. Supreme Court	Parolees do not have a reasonable expectation of privacy and may be subject to warrantless searches
United States v. Jones, 565 U.S. __ (2012)	U.S. Supreme Court	The attachment of a GPS tracking device to a motor vehicle constitutes a search and requires a warrant

oath. They do not conflict with the authority of constables or other peace-officers, or private persons under proper limitations, to arrest without warrant those who have committed felonies. The public safety, and the due apprehension of criminals, charged with heinous offences, imperiously require that such arrests should be made without warrant by officers of the law. As to the right appertaining to private individuals to arrest without a warrant, it is a much more restricted authority, and is confined to cases of the actual guilt of the party arrested; and the arrest can only be justified by proving such guilt. But as to constables, and other peace-officers, acting officially, the law clothes them with greater authority, and they are held to be justified, if they act, in making the arrest, upon probable and reasonable grounds for believing the party guilty of a felony; and this is all that is necessary for them to show, in order to sustain a justification of an arrest, for the purpose of detaining the party to await further proceedings under a complaint on oath and a warrant thereon. It was not necessary, therefore, in the present case, for the defendant to establish the actual guilt of the plaintiff of the offence imputed to him. It was only necessary to show, that upon the representation made to him of the commission of a felony, and the other circumstances coming to his knowledge, he had reasonable ground to suspect the plaintiff of having committed the crime of receiving stolen goods, knowing them to be stolen.

But the presiding judge further ruled, that if the defendant had reasonable ground to suspect the plaintiff of having committed the crime of receiving stolen goods, knowing them to be stolen, the defendant would not be justified in making the arrest, unless there was an immediate necessity therefor, arising from the danger, that the plaintiff would otherwise escape, or secrete the stolen property, before a warrant could be procured against him.

. . . We do not find, however, any authority for thus restricting a constable in the exercise of his authority to arrest for a felony without a warrant. The probability of an escape, or not, if the party is not forthwith arrested, ought to have its proper effect upon the mind of the officer, in deciding whether he will arrest without a warrant; but it is not a matter upon which a jury is to pass, in deciding upon the right of the officer to arrest. The question of reasonable necessity for an immediate arrest, in order to prevent the escape of the party charged with the felony, is one that the officer must act upon, under his official responsibility, and not a question to be reviewed elsewhere.

. . .

The result is, that the court are of opinion, that the jury should have been instructed, that if they were satisfied upon the evidence, that at the time of the arrest and imprisonment, the defendant had reasonable grounds to suspect the plaintiff of the crime of receiving or aiding in the concealment of any stolen goods or property, knowing them to be stolen, and the defendant, acting on such belief, as a constable or other peace-officer, arrested and detained the plaintiff, for the purpose of securing him to answer to a complaint for such offence, the defendant would be justified in making an arrest, and detaining him a reasonable time for that purpose, without a warrant.

Commonwealth v. Dana, 43 Mass. 329 (1841)

On January 4, 1841, Jacob C. Tallant, a Boston constable, obtained a warrant to search the office of Elisha W. Dana, whom he suspected of illegally conducting a lottery. The search was successful: Tallant discovered five hundred tickets to the School Fund Lottery, a benefit for public schools in Rhode Island. Dana was immediately arrested and indicted. Dana objected to the admission of the lottery tickets at trial, claiming that the admission violated his state constitutional rights. After the trial judge overruled the objection, Dana was convicted. He appealed that conviction to the Supreme Judicial Court of Massachusetts.

The Supreme Judicial Court of Massachusetts sustained the conviction. Justice Wilde's opinion declared that the search was constitutional and that the lottery tickets could be admitted into evidence even if the search was unconstitutional. Commonwealth v. Dana *is the first case in which courts determined whether trial judges were required to exclude illegally seized evidence. Why did the issue not come before judges until 1841? Justice Wilde claims that his decision is consistent with* Entick v. Carrington *(1765). Why does he make that claim? Is he correct?*

JUSTICE WILDE

. . .

The question is, whether the search for and the seizure of the defendant's papers and property, directed by the warrant in this case, were an unreasonable search and seizure. The defendant's counsel maintain that such searches and seizures are utterly inconsistent with the plainest principles of the common law, and the natural rights of mankind. That the right to search for and seize private papers is unknown to the common law is most conclusively shown by the able opinion of Lord Camden, in the case of *Entick v. Carrington* [1765]. . . .

. . .

With the fresh recollection of those stirring discussions, and of the revolution which followed them, the article in the Bill of Rights, respecting searches and seizures, was framed and adopted. This article does not prohibit all searches and seizures of a man's person, his papers, and possessions; but such only as are "unreasonable," and the foundation of which is "not previously supported by oath or affirmation." The legislature were not deprived of the power to authorize search warrants for probable causes, supported by oath or affirmation, and for the punishment or suppression of any violation of law. The law, therefore, authorizing search warrants in certain cases, is in no respect inconsistent with the declaration of rights.

We are also of the opinion, that the warrant in this case is in conformity with all the requisitions of the statute and the declaration of rights. The complaint is under oath, and alleges a probable cause to authorize the search and seizure. The articles seized are described, and the place in which they were concealed is designated, with sufficient certainty. There could be no difficulty in ascertaining, by inspection, the articles which the officer was directed to seize. . . .

. . .

Again, it has been urged, that the seizure of the lottery tickets and materials for a lottery, for the purpose of using them as evidence against the defendant, is virtually compelling him to furnish evidence against himself, in violation of another article in the declaration of rights. But the right of search and seizure does not depend on the question whether the papers or property seized were intended to be used in evidence against the offender or not. The possession of lottery tickets with the intent to sell them was a violation of law. The defendant's possession, therefore, was unlawful, and the tickets were liable to seizure as belonging to the *corpus delicti*, or for the purpose of preventing any further violations of law.

In cases of the seizure of stolen goods on search warrants, the goods have almost in all cases been given in evidence against the offender, and no one I apprehend ever supposed that a seizure for that purpose was a violation of the declaration of rights; and in this respect there is no distinction between the seizure of stolen goods and the seizure of lottery tickets.

There is another conclusive answer to all these objections. Admitting that the lottery tickets and materials were illegally seized, still this is no legal objection to the admission of them in evidence. If the search warrant were illegal, or if the officer serving the warrant exceeded his authority, the party on whose complaint the warrant issued, or the officer, would be responsible for the wrong done; but this is no good reason for excluding the papers seized as evidence, if they were pertinent to the issue, as they unquestionably were. When papers are offered in evidence, the court can take no notice how they were obtained, whether lawfully or unlawfully; nor would they form a collateral issue to determine that question.

C. Interrogations

The Jacksonian conception of an involuntary confession was both more and less protective of criminal defendants than are contemporary conceptions. Confessions were inadmissible only if unreliable. If a reliable confession were extracted by some means other than torture, most courts permitted the admission to be used as evidence against the criminal defendant. *Miranda* warnings were more than one hundred years in the future. Nevertheless, Jacksonians found some confessions that are admissible at present to be unreliable. Plea bargaining—when persons plead guilty to a lesser charge in return for not being prosecuted for a more serious crime—is routine in the United States today. Antebellum constitutional decision makers were more suspicious of this process. *People v. McMahon* (NY 1857) expressed the conventional understanding that confessions were unreliable if induced by promises of leniency or a lesser sentence. Justice Selden declared:

> However slight the threat or small the inducement thus held out, the statement will be excluded as not voluntary. It is plain therefore that, in such cases at least, by voluntary is meant, proceeding from the spontaneous suggestion of the party's own mind, free from the influence of any extraneous disturbing cause.[60]

60. *People v. McMahon*, 15 N.Y. 384 (1857).

D. Juries and Lawyers

The increased professionalization of the criminal justice process influenced the right to a jury and the right to an attorney. Judges, more confident of their legal knowledge, wrested control over the law from juries. Most states adopted the rule of *Commonwealth v. Anthes* (MA 1855), which held that the jury in a criminal trial should determine only the facts. The law was for judges to pronounce. State appellate courts during the mid-nineteenth century placed more emphasis on the right to an attorney. As more states and localities employed professional prosecutors, more jurisdictions insisted that criminal defendants be represented by attorneys. *State v. Cummings* (LA 1850) noted how "often the greatest injustice and oppression occurred"when persons accused of crime defended themselves in court."[61]

Juries. Contests between judges and juries over the content of the criminal law intensified during the mid-nineteenth century. Some struggles reflected differences over the substance of the criminal law. Judicial elites were far more inclined to support temperance measures than were many jurors. Federally appointed judges and magistrates were far more likely to support slave catchers than were northern juries. Charles Sumner condemned the Fugitive Slave Act of 1850 for not requiring a jury trial for persons who claimed to be free, because he expected that free state jurors would nullify the hated federal law. Other struggles were rooted in the increased professionalization of the bench. Judges in the mid-nineteenth century understood law as a science that required specialized legal training. Chief Justice Lemuel Shaw in *Anthes* insisted that only expert judges could provide the legal certainty necessary to maintain a government of laws.

Lawyers. Lawyers played an increasingly prominent role in criminal trials during the second half of the Jacksonian Era. New state constitutions recognized the right to have the assistance of counsel at trial. The Supreme Court of Wisconsin was one of several tribunals that exercised a common law power to appoint counsel for indigent criminal defendants. *Dane County v. Smith* (WI 1861) declared,

> It may be said that the rights of the prisoner, who is so poor as to be unable to secure the services of counsel, may safely be entrusted to the care and protection of the court and the public prosecutor. But a slight experience in judicial affairs will demonstrate the fallacy of that position, and show that, however vigilant the court might be, or however upright and conscientious the prosecutor, it would, as a general practice, be most unsafe and hazardous. The antagonism and conflict of opposing and experienced minds, each anxious and active to detect and expose the defects and weaknesses in the cause of the other, are, in general, absolutely essential to the discovery and establishment of legal truth; and more particularly is this true of the investigation of extensive and complicated questions of fact, such as are often presented in the prosecution of public offenders. And, however criminal trials may have been heretofore, or are now, conducted elsewhere, this kind of ex parte trial would, at this time and in this country, be generally considered extremely partial and discreditable.[62]

Several states passed constitutional amendments or statutes requiring appointment of counsel for indigent defendants. State courts established new precedents on the meaning of the right to counsel. *Cummings* held that persons had a right to the assistance of counsel throughout the entire trial. The Supreme Court of Louisiana in *State v. Ferris* (LA 1862) determined that the constitutional right to counsel included "a reasonable time for preparation." Justice Voorhies declared,

> The law in securing to them the assistance of counsel did not intend to extend a barren right, for of what avail would be the privilege of counsel to have free access to the prisoner at all reasonable hours, if on the spur of the moment, without an opportunity of studying the case, the former should be compelled to enter into the investigation of the cause.[63]

Commonwealth v. Anthes, 5 Gray 185 (MA 1855)

Philip Anthes was indicted for selling intoxicating liquors. His attorney asked the trial judge to instruct the jury that jurors could determine whether the Massachusetts temperance laws were constitutional. Defense counsel claimed that

61. *State v. Cummings*, 5 La. Ann. 330 (1850).

62. *Dane County v. Smith*, 13 Wis. 585 (1861).

63. *State v. Ferris*, 16 La. Ann. 424 (1862).

such an instruction was required by a Massachusetts statute that gave the jury the power "to decide at their discretion, by a general verdict, both the fact and the law involved in the issue." The trial judge ruled that the jury had the power to interpret the Massachusetts laws, but not the power to determine whether the laws were constitutional. Anthes was convicted. He appealed that verdict to the Supreme Judicial Court of Massachusetts on the ground that the trial court's decision to forbid the jury from determining whether the temperance laws were constitutional deprived him of his right to trial by jury.

The Supreme Judicial Court of Massachusetts by a 4–2 vote ruled that juries had no authority to determine the meaning of state laws or whether state laws were constitutional. Three judges declared that the Massachusetts statute did not give the jury the power to determine the law and that any statute that vested this power in the jury was unconstitutional. Justice Bigelow declared that the Massachusetts law did vest the jury with the power to determine the law and, for that reason, was unconstitutional. Justices Dewey and Thomas maintained that the Massachusetts law vested juries with the power to determine the law, and that this was a constitutional exercise of legislative power.

When reading the excerpts below, focus on the constitutional issues. Why does Chief Justice Shaw believe that judges should have the exclusive power to determine the law? Why does Judge Thomas disagree? To what extent do the judges adopt different methods of constitutional interpretation or apply the same method differently? Anthes *was a prohibition case. Might attitudes toward state temperance laws influence attitudes toward juries (lower-middle-class jurors were probably not very sympathetic to laws limiting drinking)? Suppose Massachusetts passed laws forbidding juries from determining the law. Would Justices Dewey and Thomas think those laws unconstitutional? What do you think?*

CHIEF JUSTICE SHAW delivered the opinion of the court.

. . .

Such then is the nature and character of a criminal prosecution in every system of jurisprudence; it necessarily embraces two questions: first, whether there is such a law as the indictment assumes; and next, whether the accused has violated it.

The one requires the most accurate and complete knowledge both of the written and unwritten law, and, in America, an equally thorough and practical knowledge of constitutional law, as they are to be derived from records and adjudged cases, ancient and modern, and books of acknowledged authority in which they are embodied, from statutes, and from the constitutions of the United States and the state in which the case arises, and adjudications thereon.

The other is a question of fact, to be decided by competent evidence, to be weighed and considered in reference to its tendency to prove the acts charged to have been done by the defendant; and the question is, are these facts true? The adjudication of this question, in addition to the integrity and impartiality requisite to the decision of both, requires experience, practical knowledge of affairs, and a quick and accurate discernment of the motives, reasons and intentions by which persons in various circumstances are actuated.

. . .

In my opinion, it is for the judges to adjudicate, (using the term in the sense above stated,) to adjudicate finally, upon the whole question of law, and for a jury to adjudicate upon the whole question of fact.

. . .

[A]n adjudication in matter of law, especially if made by a court of last resort, is regarded as a precedent, and affords a rule of decision for the same court and for all other courts, judges and magistrates, very strong, if not absolutely binding and conclusive, in all subsequent cases depending on the same facts, and involving the same principles. . . .

It is from the consideration that the adjudications of courts of last resort, in matters of law, are regarded as rules of law, and that it is necessary to the freedom of the citizen, and the peace and good order of society, that all rules of law should be certain and uniform, that the necessity has been felt of establishing one court, and one only, of last resort, be it called superior court, supreme judicial court, or court of errors. . . .

If it be asked why such adjudication of a court of last resort should have such effect, the answer, it appears to me, is this: It is necessary to the security of public and private rights, to the liberty of the subject, and the safety of the community, that there be an authoritative exposition, as well as an authoritative enactment of all laws, especially all penal laws; that, as far as possible, they should be declared, published and known; and the adjudications of the highest court, or court of last resort, are conclusive, because there is no power under the Constitution and laws, by which they can be reversed or altered.

. . .

And in my judgment the true glory and excellence of the trial by jury is this; that the power of deciding fact and law is wisely divided; that the authority to decide questions of law is placed in a body well qualified, by a suitable course of training, to decide all questions of law; and another body, well qualified for the duty, is charged with deciding all questions of fact, definitively; and whilst each, within its own sphere, performs the duty entrusted to it, such a trial affords the best possible security for a safe administration of justice and the security of public and private rights.

. . .

Nor can the jury be punished, because their verdict is against evidence; because it is impossible for the judge to know the evidence; it is not his province to weigh evidence, decide on the credit of witnesses, and draw inferences, and therefore on such general verdict the court cannot know that the verdict was not given upon the evidence, which it is the province of the jury alone to consider and decide, according to its influence on their own minds and judgments. . . .

. . .

A . . . leading idea which pervades the whole system—Preamble, Declaration of Rights and Frame of Government [of the Massachusetts Constitution]—is the absolute necessity to the peace, harmony and tranquillity of the citizens of a free government that the laws under which they live be fixed and settled.

. . .

Art[icle]. 30. . . . "In the government of this commonwealth, the legislative department shall never exercise the executive and judicial powers, or either of them; the executive shall never exercise the legislative and judicial powers, or either of them; the judicial shall never exercise the legislative and executive powers, or either of them; TO THE END IT MAY BE A GOVERNMENT OF LAWS AND NOT OF MEN."

. . .

. . . I think the result is, that the Constitution most sedulously endeavors to provide for a government of fixed, permanent laws:

That this certainty depends in a great measure upon having a steady, fixed and uniform interpretation of the laws and administration of justice, including all questions of the constitutionality and validity of legislative enactments of the legislature of the State or of the United States:

That the better to secure this certainty and uniformity, the constitution provided for a distinct judicial department with whom this power was to be deposited, and by which alone and exclusively it was to be exercised:

That this was committed not to one judge or set of judges, but to a judicial department, constituted, as such department had ever been under the prior governments of Massachusetts, of one superior or supreme court, and as many subordinate courts and judges as the public exigencies might require, and to operate as such a department must operate in systems following more or less closely the common law, which is, that the judge holding a jury trial, in a criminal case, will declare the law of that case to the jury, subject, if the jury convict, to be revised by the highest legal tribunal, so that the law may be ultimately and definitively decided by the tribunal of last resort having jurisdiction coextensive with the commonwealth:

. . .

The founders of our constitution understood, what every reflecting person must understand, from the nature of the law, in its fundamental principles, and in its comprehensive details, that it is a science, requiring a long course of preparatory training, of profound study and active practice, to be expected of no one who has not dedicated his life to its pursuit; they well understood that no safe system of jurisprudence could be established, that no judiciary department of government could be constituted, without bringing into its service jurists thus trained and qualified. The judiciary department was intended to be permanent and coextensive with the other departments of government, and, as far as practicable, independent of them; and therefore it is not competent for the legislature to take the power of deciding the law from this judiciary department, and vest it in other bodies of men, juries, occasionally and temporarily called to attend courts, for the performance of very important duties indeed, but duties very different from those of judges, and requiring different qualifications. . . .

JUSTICE BIGELOW, concurring. . . .

JUSTICE THOMAS, dissenting.

. . .

[T]he rightful power of the jury is but this: Having heard the evidence admitted by the court, the arguments of counsel and the instructions of the court, if the jury cannot see, are not convinced of the existence of both elements necessary to a verdict of guilty, to wit, first, that there is such a law as the Commonwealth has charged the defendant with violating; and, secondly, that the facts proved against him bring him within its scope and purview, they may, if they do not choose to find the facts specially, return a verdict of acquittal; a power that has always existed, and with respect to which there has been but one controversy, and that is, whether the power may be rightfully used. The effect of the statute is to declare that, in favor of the defendant, it may be rightfully used.

. . .

The gist, the substance, of this trial by jury, so far as the criminal law was concerned, was this: On the trial of a subject on a criminal charge, an issue between him and his sovereign, the question of his guilt or innocence should be determined by a free, independent body of his fellow subjects, and not by the judges or other officers appointed by the crown. . . .

. . .

Whatever may be said of the relative fitness, in other respects, of judge or jury to determine the matters involved in a criminal issue, on the question of mere impartiality there can be no preference for the judge over the jury. . . .

. . .

I begin with [John Adams] . "It was never yet disputed or doubted that a general verdict, given under the direction of the court in point of law, was a legal determination of the issue. Therefore the jury have a power of deciding an issue upon a general verdict. And, if they have, is it not an absurdity to suppose that the law would oblige them to find a verdict according to the direction of the court, against their own opinion, judgment and conscience?" . . .

. . .

In our Convention of 1788, called to act upon the adoption of the Constitution of the United States, Theophilus Parsons, in discussing the objection to the Constitution, that it had no Bill of Rights, closes with this language: "But, sir, the people themselves have it in their power effectually to resist usurpation, without being driven to an appeal to arms. An act of usurpation is not obligatory; it is not law; and any man may be justified in his resistance. Let him be considered as a criminal by the general government. Yet only his own fellow citizens can convict him; they are his jury; and if they pronounce him innocent, not all the powers of congress can hurt him; and innocent they will certainly pronounce him, if the supposed law he resisted was an act of usurpation." . . .

. . .

These citations speak, I believe, the general opinion of our early jurists. They show that, if this doctrine as to the right of the jury be an error, it is, in this country at least, an old one, the error of many of our wisest and most conservative judges and statesmen. . . .

. . .

Another fact is, the long well settled usage, in the Commonwealth and in the Province, in criminal trials, for counsel to read authorities and argue fully questions of law to the jury; a usage which can be predicated only on the right of the jury to consider and weigh what was argued; counsel having no legal right to address an argument to a tribunal that cannot hear and determine.

. . .

As matter of theory, the system of trial by jury is open to much criticism; but practically, and in the long run, it works well. The subject has found his safety in it. His common law rights have grown out of it, and been secured by it. It is, in fact, the conservative power of a free government. It conserves its freedom. . . .

The law is indeed a science, a complicated science; its range as wide as that of human interests and passions. To administer it wisely, a man must give to it the strength of life. It seems therefore anomalous, at first view, that men coming from the ordinary pursuits of life, and with no previous training, should be called upon to decide questions of law. But reflection relieves, if it does not remove the difficulty. In the first place, it is conceded that the jury must take the law and apply it to the facts. To do this intelligently and justly, they must, to some extent, understand it. . . .

JUSTICE DEWEY, dissenting. . . .

E. Punishments

Persons convicted of crimes were often punished severely. *State v. McCauley* (CA 1860) articulated the conventional judicial view that punishments were cruel and unusual only if "of a barbarous character, and unknown to the common law."[64] *McCauley* sustained a state law mandating convict labor. Other cases sustained flogging and banishment. Judges typically discussed only the method of punishment, not whether the punishment was excessive. The Supreme Judicial Court of Massachusetts in *Commonwealth v. Hutchings* (MA 1855) asserted, "The question whether

64. *State v. McCauley*, 15 Cal. 429 (1860).

the punishment is too severe, and disproportionate to the offence, is for the legislature to determine."[65]

Some state legislatures were more lenient than state courts. Michigan (1846), Rhode Island (1852), and Wisconsin (1853) abolished capital punishment. During the Michigan legislative debates, opponents of state executions maintained that the death penalty violated the fundamental right to life. Legislators in all three states were influenced by recent executions of possibly innocent persons. States that did not abolish the death penalty often reduced the number of crimes punishable by death. Many adopted a distinction between first- and second-degree murder primarily for the purpose of enabling juries to convict guilty persons without fear of sending them to be executed.

Suggested Readings

Allen, Austin. *Origins of the Dred Scott Case: Jacksonian Jurisprudence and the Supreme Court, 1837–1857* (Athens: University of Georgia Press, 2006).

Baker, H. Robert. *The Rescue of Joshua Glover: A Fugitive Slave, the Constitution, and the Coming of the Civil War* (Athens: Ohio University Press, 2006).

Currie, David P. *The Constitution in Congress: Democrats and Whigs, 1829–1861* (Chicago: University of Chicago Press, 2005).

Currie, David P. *The Constitution in Congress: Descent into the Maelstrom, 1829–1861* (Chicago: University of Chicago Press, 2005).

Fehrenbacher, Don E. *The Dred Scott Case: Its Significance in American Law and Politics* (New York: Oxford University Press, 1978).

Graber, Mark A. *Dred Scott and the Problem of Constitutional Evil* (New York: Cambridge University Press, 2006).

Graber, Mark A. "Resolving Political Questions into Judicial Questions: Tocqueville's Thesis Revisited," *Constitutional Commentary* 16 (2004):485.

Howe, Daniel Walker. *The Political Culture of the American Whigs* (Chicago: University of Chicago Press, 1979).

Kutler, Stanley I. *Privilege and Creative Destruction: The Charles River Bridge Case* (Baltimore, MD: Johns Hopkins University Press, 1989).

Magliocca, Gerald N. *Andrew Jackson and the Constitution: The Rise and Fall of Generational Regimes* (Lawrence: University Press of Kansas, 2007).

Newmyer, R. Kent. *The Supreme Court under Marshall and Taney* (New York: Thomas Y. Crowell Company, 1968).

Norgren, Jill. *The Cherokee Cases: The Confrontation of Law and Politics* (New York: McGraw-Hill, 1996).

Novak, William J. *The People's Welfare: Law and Regulation in Nineteenth-Century America* (Chapel Hill: University of North Carolina Press, 1996).

Richards, Leonard I. *The Slave Power: The Free North and Southern Domination, 1780–1860* (Baton Rouge: Louisiana State University Press, 2000).

Scalia, Laura J. *America's Jeffersonian Experiment: Remaking State Constitutions, 1820–1850* (De Kalb: Northern Illinois University Press, 1999).

Swisher, Carl B. *Roger B. Taney* (New York: Macmillan, 1936).

Swisher, Carl B. *The Taney Period* (New York: Macmillan, 1974).

Whittington, Keith E. "The Road Not Taken: *Dred Scott*, Constitutional Law, and Political Questions," *Journal of Politics* 63 (2001):365-91.

Wiecek, William M. *The Sources of Antislavery Constitutionalism in America, 1760–1848* (Ithaca, NY: Cornell University Press).

65. *Commonwealth v. Hutchings*, 5 Gray 482 (Mass. 1855).

Chapter 6

The Civil War and Reconstruction: 1861–1876

I. Introduction

Americans during the Civil War and Reconstruction experienced sustained national controversies over rights and liberties. Republicans, Democrats, slaveholders, abolitionists, and ordinary citizens debated the constitutional status of slavery; the constitutionality of restrictions on property, speech, and habeas corpus rights during the Civil War; the merits of proposed constitutional amendments in the wake of the Civil War; the constitutionality of military rule in the South after the Civil War; and the constitutional meaning of the post–Civil War Amendments. Some controversies raised questions about whether constitutional norms remained the same in both wartime and peacetime. Could criticism of the president that was constitutionally protected in peacetime be prohibited once hostilities began? Other controversies raised questions about the "new birth of freedom" that Abraham Lincoln promised in his Gettysburg Address. Prominent Americans disputed the constitutional commitments entailed by the abolition of slavery and the fundamental rights entailed by American citizenship. Democrats and Republicans fought over the scope of congressional power to protect former slaves granted by three new constitutional amendments. The Supreme Court was asked, in light of these amendments, to reconsider the ruling in *Barron v. Baltimore* (1833) that the first ten amendments to the Constitution did not limit state power.

Federal actions during the Civil War and Reconstruction were unprecedented, but their enduring constitutional significance remained unclear as federal troops were removed from the South after the presidential election in 1876. Many Republicans insisted that they had successfully corrected the original Constitution's inadequate protections for fundamental rights and liberties. They believed that Americans had finally established the constitutional and statutory foundation for realizing the founding commitment to the "proposition that all men are created equal." Many southerners and northern Democrats claimed that the Lincoln administration and the Reconstruction Congress had violated fundamental constitutional freedoms of war critics and former slaveholders. They hoped for a return to the "Constitution as it was," minus slavery.

Parties. National parties divided over rights and liberties. The Democratic Party during the Civil War vigorously opposed Lincoln administration policies restricting individual rights. The party platform in 1864 condemned

> the subversion of the civil by military law in States not in insurrection; the arbitrary military arrest, imprisonment, trial, and sentence of American citizens in States where civil law exists in full force; the suppression of freedom of speech and of the press; the denial of the right of asylum; the open and avowed disregard of State rights; the employment of unusual test-oaths; and the interference with and denial of the right of the people to bear arms in their defense.

Four years later, Democrats complained about Republican policy during Reconstruction. The party platform in 1868 declared that the majority party

> has nullified . . . the right of trial by jury; it has abolished the habeas corpus, that most sacred writ of liberty; it has overthrown the freedom of speech and of the press; it has substituted arbitrary seizures and arrests, and military trials and secret star-chamber

> inquisitions, for the constitutional tribunals; it has disregarded in time of peace the right of the people to be free from searches and seizures; it has entered the post and telegraph offices, and even the private rooms of individuals, and seized their private papers and letters without any specific charge or notice of affidavit, as required by the organic law.

Republicans maintained that the Lincoln administration took constitutional steps during the Civil War to preserve the republic and abolish slavery. Their 1864 party platform asserted,

> We approve and indorse, as demanded by the emergency and essential to the preservation of the nation and as within the provisions of the Constitution, the measures and acts which [President Lincoln] has adopted to defend the nation against its open and secret foes; that we approve, especially, the Proclamation of Emancipation, and the employment as Union soldiers of men heretofore held in slavery; and that we have full confidence in his determination to carry these and all other Constitutional measures essential to the salvation of the country into full and complete effect.

Military rule during Reconstruction, Republicans stated, was necessary to maintain the rights and liberties gained during the Civil War. The party platform in 1872 asserted,

> We hold that Congress and the President have only fulfilled an imperative duty in their measures for the suppression of violent and treasonable organizations in certain lately rebellious regions, and for the protection of the ballot-box, and therefore they are entitled to the thanks of the nation.

Neither party united on all civil liberties issues. Republicans divided over whether the party should transform the constitutional order or seek only to prohibit slavery. More radical Republicans proposed confiscating Confederate property with a minimum of judicial procedure. Abraham Lincoln and more conservative Republicans rejected these proposals. Many Republicans, including members of Lincoln's cabinet, opposed suspending habeas corpus and declaring martial law during the Civil War. Lincoln thought such measures were constitutional means for ensuring national security. War Democrats supported some restrictions on civil liberties. Peace Democrats maintained that Lincoln was a tyrant bent on subverting longstanding constitutional freedoms.

During Reconstruction bitter disputes divided radical, moderate, and conservative Republicans. Radical Republicans demanded constitutional amendments and federal statutes that guaranteed full political and economic equality for former slaves. Thaddeus Stevens, the leader of the most radical faction in the House of Representatives, coined the slogan "Forty Acres and a Mule" when championing laws that would confiscate southern plantations and give the land to freed persons of color. More conservative Republicans thought sufficient emancipation combined with some equal protection guarantees. Their constitutional vision foresaw no change to the economic order other than the abolition of slavery.

Republicans won every national election held between 1860 and 1872. Abraham Lincoln was elected in 1860 and 1864. Ulysses Grant won the 1868 and 1872 presidential elections. Republicans gained majorities in both houses of Congress in 1860, when the vast majority of southern representatives resigned their seats. They maintained their majorities until 1874, when Democrats gained control of the House of Representatives. Republican majorities in Congress were augmented after the Civil War when Congress refused to seat Democrats representing southern states who could not take an oath that they had been loyal to the Union. The loyalty oath in conjunction with other Reconstruction measures left such states as South Carolina either unrepresented in Congress or represented by Republicans appointed by local military authorities.

Democrats nevertheless influenced constitutional politics, particularly during Reconstruction. Abraham Lincoln selected a loyal southern Democrat, Senator Andrew Johnson of Tennessee, to be his running mate in 1864. When Lincoln was assassinated in 1865 Johnson assumed the presidency. Johnson was a white supremacist who fought Republican efforts to promote black citizenship and racial equality. His vetoes of the Freedmen's Bureau Act and the Civil Rights Act of 1866 slowed the pace of Reconstruction, even though he was eventually forced to accept and implement federal legislation.

Interest Groups. With one important and controversial exception, interest groups played little role in the constitutional politics of the Civil War and Reconstruction. The Republican Party was the major vehicle for securing emancipation and the rights of former slaves. Slaveholders in the South worked through conventional politics to secure their ends. The most

Box 6-1 A Partial Cast of Characters of the Civil War and Reconstruction

Abraham Lincoln	■ Whig and Republican ■ Representative from Illinois (1847–49) ■ President of the United States (1861–65), assassinated 1865 ■ Known for his dedication to preserving the Union and his success in leading the North to victory in the Civil War ■ Anti-slavery advocate and author of the Emancipation Proclamation
Charles Sumner	■ Free Soiler and Republican ■ Radical abolitionist senator from Massachusetts (1851–74) ■ Cofounder of Free Soil Party ■ Helped galvanize northern public opinion against the expansion of slavery in the antebellum period and led efforts to take a hard-line view against the South during the war and Reconstruction ■ Leading proponent of racial equality
Samuel F. Miller	■ Whig and Republican ■ Native of Kentucky, later resident of Iowa ■ Associate justice of the U.S. Supreme Court (1862–90) ■ Served on the electoral commission that decided the presidential election of 1876 ■ Supporter of national power to fight the Civil War and regulate the economy ■ Favored a restricted reading of the Reconstruction amendments
Edgar Cowan	■ Republican ■ Pennsylvania lawyer ■ U.S. senator from Pennsylvania (1861–67) ■ Conservative who broke with the GOP on most Reconstruction issues ■ Nominated by President Andrew Johnson to be ambassador to Austria, but not confirmed by Senate

important nongovernmental organization during Reconstruction was the Ku Klux Klan, which sought to restore white supremacy through terror and violence rather than by litigation and political mobilization. The constitutional politics of the 1870s often centered on the extent to which the federal government had the power to suppress Klan violence. Federal attorneys relying on the Enforcement Acts of 1870 and 1871 were able to win prosecutions that severely weakened the Klan in South Carolina. Nevertheless, the Supreme Court in later cases, most notably *United States v. Cruikshank* (1876), ruled that the federal government could not normally prosecute Klan vigilantes and other violent white supremacists unless they proved specific intent to interfere with a narrow set of federal rights.

Courts. The Supreme Court remained passive during the Civil War but provided some support for conservative constitutional visions during Reconstruction. Federal constitutional questions about rights and liberties raised between 1861 and 1865 were resolved by Congress and the president, not federal courts. The Supreme Court joined the fray only after Robert E. Lee surrendered at Appomattox and the Confederacy collapsed. In *Ex parte Milligan* (1865) the justices declared that President Lincoln had unconstitutionally declared martial law during the Civil War. Over the next several years the justices declared several minor Reconstruction laws unconstitutional. They did not issue any ruling directly addressing the constitutionality of military rule in the South. During the 1870s the Supreme Court handed down several decisions that narrowed the scope of the post–Civil War Amendments and congressional power to enforce those amendments. The *Slaughter-House Cases* (1873) held that the basic liberties set out in the Bill of Rights were not among the privileges and immunities of U.S. citizens that the Fourteenth Amendment declared states could no longer abridge. In *United States v. Cruikshank* (1876) the justices overturned a jury verdict against the perpetrators of a massacre of former slaves on the ground that the indictment for murder did not accuse the white supremacists of violating a specific federal right.

History and politics help explain why a court whose majority was appointed by Republicans was conservative on racial issues. The Jacksonian holdovers from the Taney Court consistently supported Democratic opposition to Reconstruction whenever doing so was politically feasible. They were often joined by such War Democrats as Stephen Field, whom Lincoln appointed to the bench in an effort to promote national unity. Furthermore, prominent northern elites quickly tired of Reconstruction. During the 1870s many preferred reconciliation with the South and the promotion of business enterprise to racial equality. The elite Republicans on the federal bench shared the northern elite weariness with Civil War issues. Chief Justice Salmon Chase, appointed in 1864, was the only Lincoln appointee to the Supreme Court affiliated with the most anti-slavery wing of the Republican Party. When Chase died in 1873 and was replaced by Chief Justice Morrison Waite, a railroad lawyer, no powerful voice for racial equality remained on the highest bench.

Constitutional Thought. The Civil War was the first sustained occasion Americans had for considering constitutional questions about rights and liberties during wartime. Justice David Davis in *Ex parte Milligan* (1866) eloquently stated that Americans retain their liberties in full when the United States is involved in military hostilities. His opinion asserted,

> The Constitution of the United States is a law for rulers and people, equally in war and in peace, and covers with the shield of its protection all classes of men, at all times, and under all circumstances. No doctrine, involving more pernicious consequences, was ever invented by the wit of man than that any of its provisions can be suspended during any of the great exigencies of government.

Table 6-1 Major Rights and Liberties Issues and Decisions of the Civil War and Reconstruction

Major Political Issues	Major Constitutional Issues	Major Court Decisions
Rise of the Republican Party	"New Birth of Freedom" or Mere Elimination of Slavery?	*Ex parte Merryman* (1861)
Purposes of the Civil War	Role of Courts During Wartime	*Ex parte Milligan* (1866)
Military Draft	Suspension of Habeas Corpus	*Cummings v. Missouri* (1867)
War	Suppression of Free Speech	*Ex parte McCardle* (1869)
Martial Law	Confiscation	*Slaughter-House Cases* (1873)
Reconstruction of South	Emancipation	*Bradwell v. Illinois* (1873)
Black Civil Rights	Federal Protections for Civil Rights	*Minor v. Happersett* (1874)
The New Departure	Martial Law versus Civil Authority	*United States v. Cruikshank* (1876)
Ku Klux Klan	Post-Civil War Amendments	
End of Reconstruction	Test Oaths	
	Right of Former Slaves to Own Guns	
	Suffrage	
	Rights Entailed by American Citizenship	
	Attacks on "Unequal and Partial Legislation"	
	Post-War Debates on School Segregation	

While Abraham Lincoln never acknowledged that he had violated constitutional rights, he insisted that such violations were justified in wartime. His message to Congress on July 4, 1861, claimed,

> The whole of the laws which were required to be faithfully executed were being resisted and failing of execution in nearly one-third of the States. Must they be allowed to finally fail of execution, even had it been perfectly clear that by the use of the means necessary to their execution some single law, made in such extreme tenderness of the citizen's liberty that practically it relieves more of the guilty than of the innocent, should to a very limited extent be violated? To state the question more directly, are all the laws but one to go unexecuted, and the Government itself go to pieces lest that one be violated? Even in such a case, would not the official oath be broken if the Government should be overthrown when it was believed that disregarding the single law would tend to preserve it?

Legacies. The Thirteenth, Fourteenth, and Fifteenth Amendments are the most important constitutional legacies of the Civil War. Before the Civil War slavery was legal in many states, overt racial discrimination was rampant, and, following the Supreme Court's ruling in *Barron v. Baltimore* (1833), states were constitutionally responsible for protecting fundamental freedoms. The Reconstruction Amendments abolished slavery, forbade overt racial discrimination, and prohibited states from violating certain fundamental freedoms. Some commentators think that these amendments perfected the Constitution of 1789, because the Reconstruction Congress made constitutionally explicit what Abraham Lincoln insisted were the original anti-slavery commitments of the constitutional order. Other commentators regard the Reconstruction Amendments as fashioning an entirely different constitutional regime. In this transformed constitutional order Americans gained new fundamental rights and new institutional means for protecting those fundamental rights.

Americans then and now dispute the nature of the constitutional commitments made from 1861 to 1876. President Johnson and Republicans in Congress fought over whether the Thirteenth Amendment permitted Congress to establish relief agencies for newly freed slaves. Contemporary debates over affirmative action, guns, gay marriage, and other liberties require Americans to ask such questions as, "What was the Civil War about?", "To what extent did the Reconstruction Amendments alter fundamental constitutional commitments?", and "What is entailed by the constitutional commitment to abolishing slavery and securing racial equality?"

The precise meaning of these new constitutional commitments was neither legally nor politically established in 1876. The Supreme Court in the *Slaughter-House Cases* (1873) narrowed the privileges and immunities clause of the Fourteenth Amendment. Few authoritative decisions interpreted the other provisions in the Fourteenth Amendment, the Thirteenth Amendment, or the Fifteenth Amendment. The post–Civil War Amendments were imposed on the former slave states during a time when, inspired in large part by the heroics of African-American troops during the Civil War, northerners experienced an unprecedented wave of sentiment for racial equality. How those constitutional commitments were interpreted after that northern enthusiasm for racial equality faded and federal troops were no longer present in the South was for the constitutional politics of the late nineteenth century to determine.

II. Foundations

MAJOR DEVELOPMENTS

- Debate over the constitutional amendments necessary to realize the fruits of the Civil War
- Debate over the meaning of racial equality
- The Supreme Court rules that the new amendments do not require states to respect the liberties enumerated in the Bill of Rights

The Thirteenth, Fourteenth, and Fifteenth Amendments were the first significant textual changes to the Constitution of the United States. Americans transformed a Constitution that had been designed to accommodate slavery and was arguably for white persons only into one that prohibited slavery and mandated some form of racial equality. The precise transformation was controversial in 1865 and remains controversial today. Consider the Thirteenth Amendment. Americans during the Civil War and Reconstruction did not agree on what the Constitution should say about slavery. The Crittenden Commission in 1860 recommended amendments that entrenched slavery. Americans in 1865, after an intense political struggle, adopted a constitutional amendment prohibiting slavery. No agreement exists, then or now, on the precise meaning of that amendment or the extent to which emancipating all slaves fundamentally changed the nature of the American constitutional regime.

When reading the materials below, consider two very different perspectives on the reconstructed constitutional order. Some commentators insist that the Constitution of 1868 was radically different in principle than the Constitution of 1789. Bruce Ackerman speaks of "the quantum leap the Republicans . . . made in nationalizing the protection of individual rights against state abridgement." The most fundamental constitutional question, he asserts, "was no longer whether state sovereignty was more important than individual rights, but which individual rights were sufficiently fundamental to warrant national protection."[1] Other commentators insist that, aside from freeing slaves and ensuring persons of color equal protection of the law, the post–Civil War Amendments left intact basic constitutional structures concerning rights and liberties. When rejecting a claim that the Fourteenth Amendment gave federal courts the power to declare unconstitutional state laws that violated fundamental rights, Justice Samuel Miller's majority opinion in the *Slaughter-House Cases* (1873) asserted,

> These consequences are so serious, so far-reaching and pervading, so great a departure from the structure and spirit of our institutions; when the effect is to fetter and degrade the State governments by subjecting them to the control of Congress, in the exercise of powers heretofore universally conceded to them of the most ordinary and fundamental character; when in fact it radically changes the whole theory of the relations of the State and Federal governments to each other and of both these governments to the people; the argument has a force that is irresistible, in the absence of language which expresses such a purpose too clearly to admit of doubt.
>
> We are convinced that no such results were intended by the Congress which proposed these amendments, nor by the legislatures of the States which ratified them.

Whose perspective on the post–Civil War Amendments is more accurate? To what extent did Americans do little more than abolish slavery and declare that free persons of color were citizens? To what extent did the Constitutions of 1789 and 1868 protect different liberties? To what extent were those constitutions animated by different principles?

A. Sources

Americans during the Civil War and Reconstruction Era ratified a new pro-slavery Constitution of the Confederacy, rejected proposed amendments that would have entrenched slavery in the Constitution of the United States, and adopted three new amendments to that Constitution. These amendments abolished slavery, committed the United States to racial equality and equality under law, protected certain fundamental rights, and outlawed racial discrimination in voting. No other era in American history has witnessed such important proposals for change and actual changes to the constitutional text.

Customary international law remained a vital source for interpreting both constitutional rights and constitutional powers. The Supreme Court in *The Prize Cases* (1863) relied heavily on international law when determining the validity of Lincoln's decision to blockade southern ports. The Lincoln administration honored international law principles when refraining from imprisoning sailors who ran the Union blockade. A military commission in 1864 ruled that "forfeiture of ship and cargo and loss of wages are the only penalty imposed by the law of nations for breach of blockage."[2]

Constitutions and Amendments

Debates over the Thirteenth Amendment (1864–65)[3]

The Thirteenth Amendment to the Constitution of the United States prohibits slavery and gives Congress the

1. Bruce Ackerman, *We the People: Foundations* (Cambridge, MA: Harvard University Press, 1991), 82.

2. Mark E. Neely, Jr., *The Fate of Liberty: Abraham Lincoln and Civil Liberties* (New York: Oxford University Press, 1991), 144.

3. *Congressional Globe*, 38th Cong., 1st Sess. (1864), 1439–90.

Illustration 6-1 The First Vote

Source: Waud, Alfred R. (Alfred Rudolph), 1828–1891, artist, 1867 November 16. Library of Congress, Prints and Photographs Division, Washington, DC 20540, USA.

power to implement this constitutional commitment to freedom. The text declares,

1. *Neither slavery nor involuntary servitude, except as a punishment for crime whereof the party shall have been duly convicted, shall exist within the United States, or any place subject to their jurisdiction.*
2. *Congress shall have power to enforce this article by appropriate legislation.*

The Thirteenth Amendment passed both houses of Congress in late January 1865 and was ratified by a sufficient number of states before the end of that year.

Anti-slavery advocates overcame numerous political difficulties in working toward the ratification of the Thirteenth Amendment. Whether Americans would write a constitutional amendment abolishing slavery was not a foregone conclusion at the end of the Civil War. Democrats were leery. How southern states could be induced to ratify was uncertain. The House of Representatives in 1864 failed to give a proposed Thirteenth Amendment the necessary two-thirds majority. The Lincoln administration made substantial use of patronage when securing a successful vote in 1865. New Jersey, Kentucky, and Delaware voted to reject the Thirteenth Amendment, and rumors persist today that the final votes for the amendment were procured by bribery. Many southern states ratified on the condition that the amendment be narrowly interpreted.

Two distinctive debates took place when Americans considered a constitutional amendment prohibiting slavery. Republicans debated the scope of the proposed Thirteenth Amendment. Charles Sumner, Frederick Douglass, and other radical Republicans sought to include guarantees for specific rights, most notably equality under law. Sumner proposed a constitutional amendment that stated, "Everywhere within the limits of the United States, and of each State or Territory thereof, all persons are equal before the law, so that no person can hold another as a slave." Republican moderates rejected this language. Some insisted that Congress had the power to guarantee newly freed slaves equality under the law. Others preferred leaving the amendment ambiguous. Democrats debated whether to support the Thirteenth Amendment.

Proponents insisted that the Democratic Party would not be viable in the North until the party took a strong anti-slavery stand. Montgomery Blair, a former Democrat and member of Lincoln's cabinet, advised party leaders that "by giving up the past, [and] considering slavery extinct," they could "make an issue upon which not only the Democracy of the North and South may unite against the abolitionists, but on which the larger portion of the Republicans will join us in sustaining the exclusive right of Gov[ernment] of the white race." Opponents believed that the amendment promoted a racial amalgamation inconsistent with what they perceived to be the original constitutional commitment to white supremacy. Celebrating "the Constitution as it is," pro-slavery Democrats declared that persons of color were incapable of living as free persons in a republican society. Joel Barlow, a prominent journalist, asserted that "to free" slaves "would be an act of cruelty."[4]

Consider this mixture of principle and politics when reading the excerpts below. What principles best explain ratification? What did different proponents of the Thirteenth Amendment think the abolition of slavery entailed? To what extent did Republicans dispute basic principles and to what extent did party disputes concern the language that best expressed those principles? How did politics influence the language and ratification of the Thirteenth Amendment? Would you have insisted on a more strongly worded amendment or settled for the language most likely to be ratified?

SENATOR JAMES HARLAN (Republican, Iowa)

. . .

. . . I ask whence the origin of the title to the services of the adult offspring of the slave mother? Or is it not manifest that there is no just title? Is it not a mere usurpation without any known mode of justification, under any existing code of laws, human or divine?

If it cannot be thus justified, is it a desirable institution? If the supposed owner had no title, is it the duty of the nation to maintain the usurped claim of the master to the services of his slaves? Are the incidents of slavery sufficiently desirable to justify such policy? Some of the incidents of slavery may be stated as follows: it necessarily abolishes the conjugal relation. . . . [T]he prohibition of the conjugal relation is a necessary incident of slavery, and that slavery cannot or would not be maintained in the absence of such a regulation.

The existence of this institution therefore requires the existence of a law that annuls the law of God establishing the relation of man and wife, which is taught by the churches to be a sacrament as holy in its nature and its design as the eucharist itself. If informed that in these Christian States of the Union men were prohibited by positive statute law from partaking of the emblems of the broken body and shed blood of the Saviour, what Senator could hesitate to vote for their repeal and future inhibition? And yet here one of these holy sacraments that we are taught to regard with the most sacred feelings, equally holy, instituted by the Author of our being, deemed to be necessary for the preservation of virtue in civil society, is absolutely inhibited by the statute laws of the States where slavery exists. The conjugal relation is abrogated among four million human beings, who are thus driven to heterogeneous intercourse like the beasts of the field, the most of whom are natives of these Christian States. If you continue slavery you must continue this necessary incident of its existence.

Another incident is the abolition practically of the parental relation, robbing the offspring of the care and attention of his parents, severing a relation which is universally cited as the emblem of the relation sustained by the Creator to the human family. And yet, according to the matured judgment of the slave States, this guardianship of the parent over his own children must be abrogated to secure the perpetuity of slavery.

But again, it abolishes necessarily the relation of person to property. It declares the slave to be incapable of acquiring and holding property, and that this disability shall extend to his offspring from generation to generation throughout the coming age. We sometimes shed tears over the misfortunes of men, and when by flood or storm or fire they are robbed of their earthly possessions contributions are made to enable them to start again in their accustomed business pursuits; but the Senator who votes to perpetuate slavery votes not only to sweep away every shred of property that four million people can possibly hold, but he votes to destroy their capacity to acquire and hold it and to impose this disability on their posterity forever. . . .

But it also necessarily, as an incident of its continuance, deprives all those held to be slaves of a status in court. Having no rights to maintain and no legal wrongs to redress, they are held to be incapable of

4. Michael Vorenberg, *Final Freedom: The Civil War, the Abolition of Slavery and the Thirteenth Amendment* (New York: Cambridge University Press, 2001), 78–79. The discussion in the introduction to this reading relies heavily on Vorenberg's work.

bringing a suit in the courts of the United States; a disability as it seems to me that ought to shock the sensibilities of any Christian statesman. Robbed of all their rights, and then robbed of their capacity to complain of wrongs; robbed of the power to appear before impartial tribunals for the redress of any grievances, however severe!

As an incident of this condition, they are robbed of the right to testify; and, as if to put the cap on this climax of gigantic iniquity, they are denied the right to human sympathy. . . .

. . .

And then another incident of this institution is the suppression of the freedom of speech and of the press, not only among those down-trodden people themselves but among the white race. Slavery cannot exist where its merits can be freely discussed; hence in the slave States it becomes a crime to discuss its claims for protection or the wisdom of its continuance. Its continuance also requires perpetuity of the ignorance of its victims. It is therefore made a felony to teach slaves to read and write.

It also precludes the practical possibility of maintaining schools for the education of those of the white race who have not the means to provide for their own mental culture. It consequently degrades the white as well as African race. It also impoverishes the State, as is manifest by a comparison of the relative wealth, population, and prosperity of the free and slave States of the Union.

. . .

If I am right in my conclusions that slavery as it exists in this country cannot be justified by human reason, has no foundation at common law, and is not supported by the positive municipal laws of the States, nor by the divine law, and that none of its incidents are desirable, and that its abolition would injure no one, and will do no wrong, but will secure unity of purpose, unity of action, and military strength here at home, and the support of the strong nations of the world, as it seems to me, the Senate of the United States ought not to hesitate to take the action necessary to enable the people of the States to terminate its existence forever. . . .

SENATOR CHARLES SUMNER (Republican, Massachusetts)

. . .

There is nothing in the Constitution on which slavery can rest, or find any the least support. Even on the face of that instrument, it is an outlaw; but if we look further at its provisions we find at least four distinct sources of power, which, if executed, must render slavery impossible, while the preamble makes them all vital for freedom: first, the power to provide for the common defense and welfare; secondly, the power to raise armies and maintain navies; thirdly, the power to guaranty to every State a republican form of government; and fourthly, the power to secure liberty to every person restrained without due process of law. But all these provisions are something more than powers; they are duties also. And yet we are constantly and painfully reminded in this Chamber that pending measures against slavery are unconstitutional. Sir, this is an immense mistake. Nothing against slavery can be unconstitutional. It is only hesitation which is unconstitutional.

And yet slavery still exists—in defiance of all these requirements of the Constitution; nay, more, in defiance of reason and justice, which can never be disobeyed with impunity—it exists, the perpetual spoiler of human rights and disturber of the public peace, degrading master as well as slave, corrupting society, weakening government, impoverishing the very soil itself, and impairing the natural resources of the country. Such an outrage, so offensive in every respect, not only to the Constitution, but also to the whole system of order by which the universe is governed, is plainly a national nuisance, which, for the general welfare and in the name of justice, ought to be abated. But at this moment, when it menaces the national life, it will not be enough to treat slavery merely as a nuisance; for it is much more. It is a public enemy and traitor wherever it shows itself, to be subdued, in the discharge of solemn guaranties of Government and of personal rights, and in the exercise of unquestionable and indefeasible rights of self-defence. . . . But whether regarded as national nuisance or as public enemy and traitor, it is obnoxious to the same judgment, and must be abolished.

If, in abolishing slavery, any injury were done to the just interests of any human being or to any rights of any kind, there might be something "to give us pause," even against these irresistible requirements. But nothing of the kind can ensue. No just interests and no rights can suffer. It is the rare felicity of such an act, as well outside as inside the rebel States, that, while striking a blow at the rebellion, and assuring future tranquillity, so that the Republic shall no longer be a house divided against itself, it will add at once to the value of the whole fee simple wherever slavery exists, will secure individual rights, and will advance civilization itself.

...

Again, we are brought by learned Senators to the Constitution, which requires that there shall be "just compensation" where "private property" is taken for public use. But plainly on the present occasion the requirement of the Constitution is absolutely inapplicable, for there is no "private property" to take. Slavery is but a bundle of barbarous pretensions, from which certain persons are to be released. . . .

...

. . . The people must be summoned to confirm the whole work. It is for them to put the cap-stone upon the sublime structure. An amendment of the Constitution may do what courts and Congress decline to do, or, even should they act, it may cover their action with its panoply. Such an amendment in any event will give completeness and permanence to emancipation, and bring the Constitution into avowed harmony with the Declaration of Independence. Happy day, long wished for, destined to gladden those beatified spirits who have labored on earth to this end, but died without the sight.

...

Let me say frankly that I should prefer a form of expression different from that which has the sanction of the committee. . . . I know nothing better than these words:

> All persons are equal before the law, so that no person can hold another as a slave; and the Congress shall have power to make all laws necessary and proper to carry this declaration into effect everywhere within the United States and the jurisdiction thereof.

The words in the latter part supersede all questions as to the applicability of the declaration to States. But the distinctive words in this clause assert the equality of all persons before the law. . . .

...

It will be felt at once that this expression, "equality before the law," gives precision to that idea of human rights which is enunciated in our Declaration of Independence. The sophistries of [John C.] Calhoun . . . are all overthrown by this simple statement. . . .

SENATOR LAZARUS POWELL (Democrat, Kentucky)

...

I do not believe it was ever designed by the founders of our Government that the Constitution of the United States should be so amended as to destroy property. I do not believe it is the province of the Federal Government to say what is or what is not property. Its province is to guard, protect, and secure, rather than to destroy. If you admit the principle contended for by the gentlemen who urge this amendment, logic would lead them to the conclusion that the General Government could, by an amendment to its Constitution, regulate every domestic matter in the States. If it, by constitutional amendment, can regulate the relation of master and servant, it certainly can, on the same principle, make regulations concerning the relation of parent and child, husband and wife, and guardian and ward. If it has the right to strike down property in slaves, it certainly would have a right to strike down property in horses, to make a partition of the land, and to say that none shall hold land in any State in the Union in fee simple. . . .

...

But it is said slavery is the cause of the war, and because it is the cause of the war it must die. If that is the kind of logic on which honorable Senators act they could destroy almost everything that is pure, good, and holy in the world. The blessed religion of our Saviour has been the pretext of more wars perhaps than any other subject. Why not strike down the Christian religion because it has been the subject-matter about which throats have been cut, cities sacked, and empires overthrown? There have been furious wars about territory and territorial boundaries, and there will continue to be such wars as long as the cupidity of man prompts him to make conquests. Why not destroy all tenure in land? Ferocious wars have been waged about women. In Homeric verse we have the historical record of a ten years' contest for frail Helen. Why not destroy the loveliest of God's handiwork. . . .

. . . I desire the Union to be restored, restored as it was with the Constitution as it is; and I verily believe that if you pass this amendment to the Constitution it will be the most effective disunion measure that could be passed by Congress. . . .

...

. . . You seem to care for nothing but the negro. That seems to be your sole desire. You seem to be inspired by no other wish than to elevate the negro to

Table 6-2a Passage and Ratification of the Fourteenth Amendment, U.S. Senate Vote (June 8, 1866)

Party	Ayes	Nays
Republican	32	3
Democratic	0	7
Union	1	1
Total	33	11

equality and give him liberty. . . . I believe this government was made by white men and for white men; and if it is ever preserved it must be preserved by white men. . . . I would ask the Senators who are so zealous for the negro to point me to a place on the earth where he has been so civilized, so humanized, so christianized, so well cared for as he is in a state of slavery in the United States of America. He has existed, I suppose, as long as the other peoples of the earth; but if you were today to strike from existence everything that the woolly-headed negro has given to art, to science, to the mechanic arts, to literature, or to any of the industrial pursuits, the world would not miss it. He is an inferior man in his capacity, and no fanaticism can raise him to the talent of the Caucasian race. The white man is his superior, and will be so whether you call him a slave or an equal. It has ever been so, and I can see no reason why the history of all the past should be reversed. . . .

Debates over the Fourteenth Amendment (1866)[5]

The bipartisan coalition that secured the Thirteenth Amendment fractured when considering the Fourteenth Amendment. Republicans were outraged by southern behavior immediately after the Civil War. Most former slave states passed Black Codes. These laws prohibited persons of color from engaging in many occupations and exercising such political rights as serving on juries and voting. Southern Unionists were also persecuted and denied fundamental rights. While most Republicans believed that the Thirteenth Amendment gave Congress the power to outlaw these rights violations, party members agreed that a more specific constitutional amendment was necessary to secure greater racial equality. Democrats aggressively challenged Republican efforts to reconstruct the South. Party members, even those who supported the Thirteenth Amendment, insisted that southern practices after the Civil War reflected an enduring constitutional commitment to white supremacy.

Politics and principle freely mixed during the debates over the Fourteenth Amendment. Republicans feared that a reconstructed South might provide the Democratic Party with the votes necessary to return that coalition to national power. Such an outcome was likely if former slaves, who were being denied the ballot, counted as full persons for purposes of apportioning representatives in Congress. Many Democrats believed that their party could make substantial inroads in the North by running as the party committed to rule by white men.

The Republican Party internally divided over the text and scope of an appropriate constitutional amendment. After the elections of 1864 and 1866, party members enjoyed the majorities necessary to ratify the constitutional amendment of their choice but could not agree on principles or language. Such radical Republicans as Thaddeus Stevens and Charles Sumner favored a package of constitutional amendments and statutes that would grant persons of color the same political, civil, and economic rights as white persons enjoyed. They championed a Fourteenth Amendment that declared:

Congress shall have power to make all laws necessary and proper to secure all citizens of the United States, in

Table 6-2b Passage and Ratification of the Fourteenth Amendment, U.S. House of Representatives Vote (June 13, 1866)

Party	Ayes	Nays	No Vote
Republican	130	0	6
Democratic	0	36	3
Union	8	0	1
Total	138	36	10

Table 6-2c Passage and Ratification of the Fourteenth Amendment, State Ratification (28 of 37 Needed)

Year	Ratify	Reject	Rescind
1866	6	4	
1867	16	4	
1868	6	0	2

5. *Congressional Globe*, 39th Cong., 1st Sess. (1866), 2538, 1088–91, 2768–69, 3148.

every State, the same political rights and privileges; and to all persons in every State equal protection in the enjoyment of life, liberty and property.

More conservative Republicans insisted that the federal Constitution and federal law not undermine the economic status quo in the South. They favored constitutional amendments and federal statutes that were limited to guaranteeing former slaves (and southern Unionists) formal legal equality.

The resulting Fourteenth Amendment was a compromise between more radical and more conservative Republican factions. The crucial provisions of that text declare:

1. *All persons born or naturalized in the United States, and subject to the jurisdiction thereof, are citizens of the United States and of the State wherein they reside. No State shall make or enforce any law which shall abridge the privileges or immunities of citizens of the United States; nor shall any State deprive any person of life, liberty, or property, without due process of law; nor deny to any person within its jurisdiction the equal protection of the laws.*

 . . .

5. *The Congress shall have power to enforce, by appropriate legislation, the provisions of this article.*

Section 2 of the Fourteenth Amendment penalizes states that deprive male citizens of the right to vote in a federal election for reasons other than participation in the rebellion or criminal offenses by reducing the offending state's representation in Congress in proportion to the percentage of men disenfranchised. Section 3 declares former state and federal officials who sided with the Confederacy ineligible to hold political office. Section 4 states that the United States is not liable for debts incurred by the Confederate government or states that joined the Confederacy.

The Fourteenth Amendment was proposed by Congress in June 1866, but the state ratification process was not completed until July 1868. Congress refused to acknowledge efforts by several states to rescind ratification, while accepting ratification votes from states that had previously voted down the amendment. Some southern legislatures were not allowed representation in Congress until the state legislature approved the Fourteenth Amendment.[6]

When reading the excerpts below, consider the relationship between the constitutional amendment proposed by the more radical Republicans and the final version of the Fourteenth Amendment. What rights did the most radical faction of the Republican Party seek to protect? What rights did the most conservative faction of the Republican Party seek to protect? To what extent did the persons who proposed different Fourteenth Amendments believe they were using different words to protect the same constitutional rights? To what extent do you believe the final language of the Fourteenth Amendment reflects a self-conscious decision to reject more radical Republican claims? To what extent does the final language of the Fourteenth Amendment reflect a self-conscious decision to not decide the precise constitutional status of persons of color and what constituted the fundamental rights of American citizens? Do you believe that the original and final versions of the Fourteenth Amendment are substantially different? Compare the final version of the Fourteenth Amendment with the most radical interpretation of the Thirteenth Amendment. Do any significant differences exist between the Thirteenth Amendment as interpreted by Charles Sumner and the Fourteenth Amendment? Did the Fourteenth Amendment narrow or broaden the more radical version of the Thirteenth Amendment?

The Thirteenth, Fourteenth, and Fifteenth Amendments include provisions that declare, "The Congress shall have power to enforce, by appropriate legislation, the provisions of this article." Future generations debated whether that language gives Congress authority to interpret the meaning of the post–Civil War Amendments. Do the excerpts below cast any light on how the framers of those amendments understood constitutional authority? Such Democrats as Andrew Rogers insisted that the Fourteenth Amendment radically altered the Constitution. Did Republicans agree?

REPRESENTATIVE JOHN BINGHAM (Republican, Ohio)

. . .

. . . I repel the suggestion made here in the heat of debate, that the committee or any of its members who favor the proposition seek in any form to mar the Constitution of the country or take away from any State any right that belongs to it, or from any citizen of any State any right that belongs to him under that Constitution. The proposition pending before the House is simply a proposition to arm the Congress of the United States, by consent of the people of the United States, with the power to enforce the bill of rights as it stands in the Constitution today. . . .

. . .

Gentlemen admit the force of the provisions in the bill of rights, that the citizens of the United States shall be entitled to all the privileges and immunities of

6. John William Burgess, *Reconstruction and the Constitution, 1866-1876* (New York: Charles Scribner's Sons, 1905), 198-199.

citizens of the United States in the several States, and that no person shall be deprived of life, liberty, or property without due process of law; but they say, "We are opposed to its enforcement by act of Congress under an amended Constitution, as proposed." That is the sum and substance of all the argument that we have heard on this subject. Why are gentlemen opposed to the enforcement of the bill of rights, as proposed? Because they aver it would interfere with the reserved rights of the States! Who ever before heard that any State had reserved to itself the right, under the Constitution of the United States, to withhold from any citizen within its limits, under any pretext whatever, any of the privileges of a citizen of the United States, or to impose upon him, no matter from what State he may have come, any burden contrary to that provision of the Constitution which declares that the citizen shall be entitled in the several States to all the immunities of a citizen of the United States?

What does the word immunity in your Constitution mean? Exemption from unequal burdens. Ah! Say the gentlemen who oppose this amendment, we are not opposed to equal rights; we are not opposed to the bill of rights that all shall be protected alike in life, liberty, and property; we are only opposed to enforcing it by national authority, even by the consent of the loyal people of all the States.

REPRESENTATIVE ANDREW J. ROGERS (Democrat, New Jersey)

. . .

. . . [T]he first section of this program of disunion is the most dangerous to liberty. It saps the foundation of the Government; it destroys the elementary principles of the States; it consolidates everything into one imperial despotism; it annihilates all the rights which lie at the foundation of the Union of the States, and which have characterized this Government and made it prosperous and great during the long period of its existence.

This section of the joint resolution is no more nor less than an attempt to embody in the Constitution of the United States that outrageous and miserable civil rights bill which passed both Houses of Congress and was vetoed by the President of the United States upon the ground that it was a direct attempt to consolidate the power of the States and to take away from them the elementary principles which lie at their foundation. It is only an attempt to ingraft upon the Constitution of the United States one of the most dangerous, most wicked, most intolerant, and most odious propositions ever introduced into this House or attempted to be ingrafted upon the fundamental law of the Federal Union.

. . . What are privileges and immunities? Why, sir, all the rights we have under the laws of the country are embraced under the definition of privileges and immunities. The right to marry is a privilege. The right to contract is a privilege. The right to be a juror is a privilege. The right to be a judge or President of the United States is a privilege. I hold if that ever becomes a part of the fundamental law of the land it will prevent any State from refusing to allow anything to anybody embraced under the term of privileges and immunities. If a negro is refused the right to be a juror, that will take away from him his privileges and immunities as a citizen of the United States, and the Federal Government will step in and interfere, and the result will be a contest between the powers of the Federal Government and the powers of the States. It will rock the earth like the throes of an earthquake until its tragedy will summon the inhabitants of the world to witness its dreadful shock.

. . .

Yes, gentlemen, it is but the negro again appearing in the background. The only object of the constitutional amendment is to drive the people of the South, ay, and even the people of the North, wherever there is much of a negro population, to allow that population not qualified but universal suffrage, without regard to intelligence or character, to allow them to come to the ballot-box and cast their votes equally with white men.

. . .

Sir, I want it distinctly understood that the American people believe that this Government was made for white men and white women. They do not believe, nor can you make them believe—the edict of God Almighty is stamped against it—that there is a social equality between the black race and the white.

I have no fault to find with the colored race. I have not the slightest antipathy to them. I wish them well, and if I were in a State where they exist in large numbers I would vote to give them every right enjoyed by the white people except the right of a negro man to marry a white woman and the right to vote. But, sir, this proposition goes further than any that has ever been attempted to be carried into effect. Why, sir, even in Rhode Island today there is a property qualification in regard to the white man's voting as well as the negro. And yet Representatives of the eastern, middle, western, and some of the border States come here and attempt in this indirect way to inflict upon the people of the South negro suffrage. God deliver this people from such a wicked, odious, pestilent despotism! God save the people of the South from the degradation by which they would be obliged to go to the polls and vote side by side with the negro!

. . .

REPRESENTATIVE ROGERS

. . . I only wish to know what you mean by "due process of law."

REPRESENTATIVE BINGHAM

I reply to the gentleman, the courts have settled that long ago, and the gentleman can go and read their decisions.

. . .

The question is, simply, whether you will give by this amendment to the people of the United States the power, by legislative enactment, to punish officials of the States for violation of the oaths enjoined upon them by their Constitution? That is the question, and the whole question. The adoption of the proposed amendment will take from the States no rights that belong to the States. They elect their Legislatures; they enact their laws for the punishment of crimes against life, liberty, or property; but in the event of the adoption of this amendment, if they conspire together to enact laws refusing the equal protection to life, liberty, or property, the Congress is thereby vested with power to hold them to answer before the bar of the national courts for the violation of their oaths and of the rights of their fellow-men. Why should it not be so? That is the question. Why should it not be so? Is the bill of rights to stand in our Constitution hereafter, as in the past five years within eleven States, a mere dead letter? It is absolutely essential to the safety of the people that it should be enforced. . . .

SENATOR BENJAMIN WADE (Republican, Ohio)

I move to amend the joint resolution by . . . substituting the proposition which I send to the Chair to be read.

. . .

> SEC. 2. No class of persons as to the right of any of whom to suffrage discrimination shall be made, by any State, shall be included in the basis of representation, unless such discrimination be in virtue of impartial qualifications founded on intelligence or property or because of alienage, or for participation in rebellion or other crime. . . .

. . . There are some reasons, and many believe there are good reasons, for restricting universal suffrage, and upon such principles as not to justify the inflicting of a punishment or penalty upon a State which adopts restricted suffrage. It is already done in some of the New England States. . . . I believe the constitution of [Massachusetts] restricts the right of suffrage to persons who can read the Constitution of the United States and write their names. I am not prepared to say that that is not a wise restriction. At all events, a State has the right to try that experiment; but if she tries it, under the report of the committee she must lose, in the proportion that she has such persons among her inhabitants, her representatives in Congress. I do not think that ought to be so. . . .

Under [my proposed] amendment you ascertain the classes of the population, and when any discrimination shall be made upon any of these subjects the whole of that particular class will be excluded. There is only one question to be determined. If the exclusion is because of race or color, the question is what amount of colored population is there in the State, and in exactly that proportion she is to lose representation. . . .

. . .

I have seen other suggested amendments which I would like to have prevail. . . . I am for the suffrage to our friends in the South, the men who have stood by us in this rebellion, the men who have hazarded their lives and all that they hold dear to defend our country. I think our friends, the colored people of the South, should not be excluded from the right of voting, and they shall not be if my vote with the votes of a sufficient number who agree with me in Congress shall be able to carry it. . . . My own opinion is that if you go down to the very foundation of justice, so far from weakening yourself with the people, you will strengthen yourself immensely by it; but I know that it is not the opinion of many here, and I suppose we must accommodate ourselves to the will of majorities, and if we cannot do all we would, do all we can. . . .

REPRESENTATIVE THADDEUS STEVENS (Republican, Pennsylvania)

. . .

In my youth, in my manhood, in my old age, I fondly dreamed that when any fortunate chance should have broken up for awhile the foundation of our institutions, and released us from obligations the most tyrannical that ever man imposed in the name of freedom, that the intelligent, pure and just men of this Republic, true to their professions and their consciences, would have so remodeled all our institutions as to have freed them from every vestige of human oppression, of inequality of rights, of the recognized degradation of the poor, and the superior caste of the rich. In short, that no distinction would be tolerated in this purified Republic but what arose from merit and conduct. This bright dream has vanished "like the baseless fabric of a vision." I find that we shall be obliged to be content with patching up the worst portions of the ancient edifice, and leaving it, in many of its parts, to be swept through by the tempests, the frosts, and the storms of despotism.

Do you inquire why, holding these views and possessing some will of my own, I accept so imperfect a proposition? I answer, because I live among men and not among angels; among men as intelligent, as determined, and as independent as myself, who, not agreeing with me, do not choose to yield, their opinions to mine. Mutual concession, therefore, is our only resort, or mutual hostilities.

. . .

The first section [of the proposed Fourteenth Amendment] is altered by defining who are citizens of the United States and of the States. This is an excellent amendment, long needed to settle conflicting decisions between the several States and the United States. It declares this great privilege to belong to every person born or naturalized in the United States.

The second section has received but slight alteration. I wish it had received more. It contains much less power than I could wish; it has not half the vigor of the amendment which was lost in the Senate. It . . . would have worked the enfranchisement of the colored man in half the time.

The third section has been wholly changed by substituting the ineligibility of certain high offenders for the disfranchisement of all rebels until 1870.

This I cannot look upon as an improvement. It opens the elective franchise to such as the States choose to admit. In my judgment, it endangers the Government of the country, both State and national; and may give the next Congress and President to the reconstructed rebels. With their enlarged basis of representation, and exclusion of the loyal men of color from the ballot-box, I see no hope of safety unless in the prescription of proper enabling acts, which shall do justice to the freedmen and enjoin enfranchisement as a condition precedent.

. . .

. . . [L]et us no longer delay; take what we can get now, and hope for better things in further legislation; in enabling acts or other provisions. . . .

B. Principles

The debates underlying secession and the Civil War were about slavery. Differences existed between more northern and more southern states over such questions as federal power to sponsor internal improvements, but the existence of slavery made those differences irreconcilable. Abraham Lincoln on the campaign trail repeatedly spoke of an original constitutional understanding that slavery was "in a course of ultimate extinction." His Gettysburg Address maintained that the United States was constitutionally "dedicated to the proposition that all men are created equal." Southerners offered an alternative to Lincoln's anti-slavery constitutional vision. Confederate Vice-President Alexander Stephens declared that the fundamental constitutional principle of the Confederate Constitution was "that the negro is not equal to the white man; that slavery—subordination to the superior race—is his natural and normal condition."[7]

The Thirteenth Amendment transformed constitutional debates over the place of slavery in the constitutional regime into constitutional controversies over the significance of emancipation. African-American leaders and more radical Republicans believed that the post–Civil War constitutional order fundamentally altered previous constitutional commitments. Frederick Douglass spoke for this constitutional vision when he declared,

> No war but an Abolition war; no peace but an Abolition peace; liberty for all, chains for none; the black man a soldier in war, a laborer in peace; a voter at the South as well as at the North; America his permanent home, and all Americans his fellow countrymen.[8]

Democrats, more conservative Republicans, and white southerners minimized the significance of the three new constitutional amendments. President Andrew

7. Alexander H. Stephens, *A Constitutional View of the Late War between the States* (Philadelphia: National Publishing Co., 1870), 2:705.

8. Frederick Douglass, *Frederick Douglass: Selected Speeches and Writings*, ed. Philip S. Foner (Chicago: Chicago Review Press, 1999), 566.

Johnson and his political allies interpreted the post–Civil War Constitution as abolishing only slavery and granting free blacks formal equality. Johnson's veto of the Civil Rights Act of 1866 maintained,

> The white race and the black race of the South have hitherto lived together under the relation of master and slave—capital owning labor. Now, suddenly, that relation is changed, and as to ownership capital and labor are divorced. They stand now each master of itself. In this new relation, one being necessary to the other, there will be a new adjustment, which both are deeply interested in making harmonious. Each has equal power in settling the terms, and if left to the laws that regulate capital and labor it is confidently believed that they will satisfactorily work out the problem. Capital, it is true, has more intelligence, but labor is never so ignorant as not to understand its own interests, not to know its own value, and not to see that capital must pay that value.

C. Scope

The post–Civil War Amendments reopened debate about the scope of the Bill of Rights. Most antebellum constitutional decisions makers agreed that the first eight amendments to the Constitution of the United States limited only federal power. The Supreme Court of the United States adopted this consensus view in *Barron v. Baltimore* (1833) when ruling that state legislatures were not bound by the takings clause of the Fifth Amendment. Whether *Barron* remained good law after the Fourteenth Amendment was initially uncertain. Section 1 of this amendment declared, "No State shall make or enforce any law which shall abridge the privileges or immunities of citizens of the United States." Prominent Republicans asserted that the liberties set out in the Bill of Rights were among the "privileges and immunities of the Citizens of the United States."

Americans have debated for more than 150 years whether the persons responsible for the Fourteenth Amendment intended to incorporate the Bill of Rights. The most recent commentary concludes that Reconstruction Republicans did intend to nationalize the Bill of Rights.[9] Conventional wisdom fifty years ago supported the opposite conclusion.[10] Both Representative John Bingham and Senator Jacob Howard, the legislators who led the floor fights for the Fourteenth Amendment, made speeches interpreting the Fourteenth Amendment as incorporating the Bill of Rights. How widely their interpretation was shared or known is not entirely clear.

The Supreme Court of the United States firmly rejected contentions that the Fourteenth Amendment nationalized the Bill of Rights. Justice Samuel Miller's majority opinion in the *Slaughter-House Cases* (1873) emphatically challenged assertions that "by the simple declaration that no State should make or enforce any law which shall abridge the privileges and immunities of citizens of the United States," the Fourteenth Amendment "transfer[red] the security and protection of all the civil rights . . . from the States to the Federal government." *United States v. Cruikshank* (1876) more explicitly stated that *Barron* remained the constitutional law of the land. The First Amendment, Chief Justice Waite's opinion stated, "like the other amendments proposed and adopted at the same time, was not intended to limit the powers of the State governments in respect to their own citizens, but to operate upon the National government alone."

Slaughter-House and *Cruikshank* raise both jurisprudential and political questions. The jurisprudential question is whether the Supreme Court correctly interpreted the Fourteenth Amendment. The political question is why the Republican majority on the Supreme Court more narrowly interpreted the Fourteenth Amendment than did many Republicans in Congress. Were Republican justices more conservative than Republicans in Congress? Did Republicans fail to make their intentions legally clear? Are these cases evidence that enthusiasm for civil rights waned among most Republicans during the 1870s?

Slaughter-House Cases, 83 U.S. 36 (1873)

The Republican-controlled state legislature of Louisiana in 1869 passed a law incorporating the Crescent City Live-Stock Landing and Slaughtering Company. The legislation required all butchers in New Orleans to use the "grand

9. The most influential recent works are Michael Kent Curtis, *No State Shall Abridge: The Fourteenth Amendment and the Bill of Rights* (Durham, NC: Duke University Press, 1987) and Akhil Reed Amar, *The Bill of Rights: Creation and Reconstruction* (New Haven, CT: Yale University Press, 2000).

10. See especially Charles Fairman, "Does the Fourteenth Amendment Incorporate the Bill of Rights? The Original Understanding," *Stanford Law Review* 2 (1949): 5.

slaughterhouse" controlled by the Crescent City Company. The state legislature claimed that moving animal slaughtering into one central, regulated location was a justifiable exercise of the state's "police power," which is the traditional legislative authority to pass laws that promote public health, safety, or morality. Dispossessed butchers disagreed. They believed that the Crescent City monopoly unconstitutionally deprived them of their right to make a living. That the Crescent City Company was controlled by a group of seventeen wealthy and politically influential individuals fed public antipathy. Southern Democrats charged that the "carpet bagging" Republican legislature responsible for the monopoly was more interested in conferring illegitimate special privileges on favored groups than in promoting the general interest.

The disgruntled butchers, acting as the Butchers' Benevolent Association of New Orleans, brought suit against the Crescent City Company and the state of New Orleans. John Campbell, a former associate justice of the Supreme Court,[11] *represented the dispossessed butchers. His brief claimed that the Louisiana monopoly violated the Thirteenth Amendment and three provisions of the Fourteenth Amendment. Campbell placed special emphasis on the provision in the Fourteenth Amendment that prohibited states from enforcing "any law which shall abridge the privileges and immunities of citizens of the United States." He argued that one of the privileges and immunities of U.S. citizens was the right to labor freely in an honest vocation. Campbell noted that the Fourteenth Amendment prohibits states from denying any person "equal protection of the law." In his view, this monopoly unequally bestowed artificial privileges on some butchers at the expense of others. Finally, Campbell noted that the Fourteenth Amendment declares that states shall not "deprive any person of life, liberty, or property, without due process of law." He argued that the legislature's interference with the ability of butchers to pursue an honest living deprived them of both their liberty to work and the value of their property. For good measure, this son of the Confederacy added that the Thirteenth Amendment prohibits the sort of "involuntary servitude" that would be created when butchers had to pay monopolists a set fee for the privilege of conducting their business. When the Supreme Court of Louisiana rejected these arguments, Campbell and the Butchers' Benevolent Association appealed to the Supreme Court of the United States.*

11. Campbell resigned from the Court in 1861, after Alabama seceded from the Union.

The Supreme Court of the United States by a 5-4 vote ruled that state-granted monopolies did not violate the Thirteenth or Fourteenth Amendments. Justice Samuel Miller's majority opinion insisted that states remained responsible for protecting the fundamental rights of citizens. Miller's controversial opinion sharply distinguished between the "privileges and immunities" of state citizens and the "privileges and immunities" of citizens of the United States. He narrowly interpreted the due process and equal protection clauses.

Slaughter-House *is one of the most important and contested decisions ever made by the Supreme Court of the United States. When reading the case, consider how Justice Miller interprets the privileges and immunities clause, the due process clause, and the equal protection clause of the Fourteenth Amendment. On what points do he and the dissenting opinion disagree? Why does Justice Miller insist that the post–Civil War Amendments do not create a substantial change in the institutions responsible for protecting fundamental freedoms? Why does Justice Field disagree? Who has the better argument?*

Slaughter-House *was the first case in which the Supreme Court discussed the meaning of the post–Civil War Amendments. This may seem surprising, given that the issues before the court directly concerned the rights of butchers, not the rights of former slaves. Nevertheless,* Slaughter-House *is often regarded as sharply curtailing the constitutional rights of persons of color. To what extent do you believe that John Campbell, who as a justice supported the* Dred Scott *decision, might have seen* Slaughter-House *as a vehicle for cabining the post–Civil War Amendments? Justice Miller's decision asserted that the primary purpose of these amendments was the protection of the freedmen. How, if at all, does his opinion nevertheless narrow constitutional protections for persons of color?*

JUSTICE MILLER delivered the opinion of the court.

. . .

The power here exercised by the legislature of Louisiana is, in its essential nature, one which has been, up to the present period in the constitutional history of this country, always conceded to belong to the States. . . .

This [police] power is, and must be from its very nature, incapable of any very exact definition or limitation. Upon it depends the security of social order, the life and health of the citizen, the comfort of an existence in a thickly populated community, the enjoyment of private and social life, and the beneficial use of property. . . . The regulation of the place and manner of conducting the slaughtering of animals, and the business of butchering within a city, and the inspection of the animals to be killed for meat, and of the meat afterwards, are among the most necessary and frequent exercises of this power. . . .

It cannot be denied that the statute under consideration is aptly framed to remove from the more densely populated part of the city, the noxious slaughter-houses, and large and offensive collections of animals necessarily incident to the slaughtering business of a large city, and to locate them where the convenience, health, and comfort of the people require they shall be located. And it must be conceded that the means adopted by the act for this purpose are appropriate, are stringent, and effectual. . . .

. . .

It may, therefore, be considered as established, that the authority of the legislature of Louisiana to pass the present statute is ample, unless some restraint in the exercise of that power be found in the constitution of that State or in the amendments to the Constitution of the United States, adopted since the date of the decisions we have already cited. . . .

. . .

The most cursory glance at [the Thirteenth and Fourteenth Amendments] discloses a unity of purpose, when taken in connection with the history of the times, which cannot fail to have an important bearing on any question of doubt concerning their true meaning. . . .

The institution of African slavery, as it existed in about half the States of the Union, and the contests pervading the public mind for many years, between those who desired its curtailment and ultimate extinction and those who desired additional safeguards for its security and perpetuation, culminated in the effort, on the part of most of the States in which slavery existed, to separate from the Federal government, and to resist its authority. This constituted the war of the rebellion, and whatever auxiliary causes may have contributed to bring about this war, undoubtedly the overshadowing and efficient cause was African slavery. . . .

. . .

We repeat, then, in the light of this recapitulation of events, almost too recent to be called history, but which are familiar to us all; and on the most casual examination of the language of these amendments, no one can fail to be impressed with the one pervading purpose found in them all, lying at the foundation of each, and without which none of them would have been even suggested; we mean the freedom of the slave race, the security and firm establishment of that freedom, and the protection of the newly-made freeman and citizen from the oppressions of those who had formerly exercised unlimited dominion over him. . . .

We do not say that no one else but the negro can share in this protection. Both the language and spirit of these articles are to have their fair and just weight in any question of construction. Undoubtedly while negro slavery alone was in the mind of the Congress which proposed the thirteenth article, it forbids any other kind of slavery, now or hereafter. If Mexican peonage or the Chinese coolie labor system shall develop slavery of the Mexican or Chinese race within our territory, this amendment may safely be trusted to make it void. And so if other rights are assailed by the States which properly and necessarily fall within the protection of these articles, that protection will apply, though the party interested may not be of African descent. . . .

. . . [T]he distinction between citizenship of the United States and citizenship of a State is clearly recognized and established [by the Fourteenth Amendment]. . . .

We think this distinction and its explicit recognition in this amendment of great weight in this argument, because the next paragraph of this same section, which is the one mainly relied on by the plaintiffs in error, speaks only of privileges and immunities of citizens of the United States, and does not speak of those of citizens of the several States.

The language is, "No State shall make or enforce any law which shall abridge the privileges or immunities of citizens of the United States." It is a little remarkable, if this clause was intended as a protection to the citizen of a State against the legislative power of his own State, that the word citizen of the State should be left out when it is so carefully used, and used in contradistinction to citizens of the United States, in the very sentence which precedes it. It is too clear for argument that the change in phraseology was adopted understandingly and with a purpose. . . . .

Fortunately we are not without judicial construction of this clause of the Constitution. The first and the leading case on the subject is that of *Corfield v. Coryell*, decided by Mr. Justice Washington in the Circuit Court for the District of Pennsylvania in 1823. "The inquiry," he says, "is, what are the privileges and immunities of citizens of the several States? We feel no hesitation in confining these expressions to those privileges and immunities which are fundamental; which belong of right to the citizens of all free governments, and which have at all times been enjoyed by citizens of the several States which compose this Union, from the time of their becoming free, independent, and sovereign. What these fundamental principles are, it would be more tedious than difficult to enumerate. They may all, however, be comprehended under the following general heads: protection by the government, with the right to acquire and possess property of every kind, and to pursue and obtain happiness and safety, subject, nevertheless, to such restraints as the government may prescribe for the general good of the whole." . . .

. . . Was it the purpose of the fourteenth amendment, by the simple declaration that no State should make or enforce any law which shall abridge the privileges and immunities of citizens of the United States, to transfer the security and protection of all the civil rights which we have mentioned, from the States to the Federal government? And where it is declared that Congress shall have the power to enforce that article, was it intended to bring within the power of Congress the entire domain of civil rights heretofore belonging exclusively to the States?

All this and more must follow, if the proposition of the plaintiffs in error be sound. For not only are these rights subject to the control of Congress whenever in its discretion any of them are supposed to be abridged by State legislation, but that body may also pass laws in advance, limiting and restricting the exercise of legislative power by the States, in their most ordinary and usual functions, as in its judgment it may think proper on all such subjects. . . . The argument we admit is not always the most conclusive which is drawn from the consequences urged against the adoption of a particular construction of an instrument. But when, as in the case before us, these consequences are so serious, so far-reaching and pervading, so great a departure from the structure and spirit of our institutions; when the effect is to fetter and degrade the State governments by subjecting them to the control of Congress, in the exercise of powers heretofore universally conceded to them of the most ordinary and fundamental character; when in fact it radically changes the whole theory of the relations of the State and Federal governments to each other and of both these governments to the people; the argument has a force that is irresistible, in the absence of language which expresses such a purpose too clearly to admit of doubt.

We are convinced that no such results were intended by the Congress which proposed these amendments, nor by the legislatures of the States which ratified them.

. . .

The argument has not been much pressed in these cases that the defendant's charter deprives the plaintiffs of their property without due process of law, or that it denies to them the equal protection of the law. . . .

We are not without judicial interpretation, . . . , both State and National, of the meaning of [the due process] clause. And it is sufficient to say that under no construction of that provision that we have ever seen, or any that we deem admissible, can the restraint imposed by the State of Louisiana upon the exercise of their trade by the butchers of New Orleans be held to be a deprivation of property within the meaning of that provision.

"Nor shall any State deny to any person within its jurisdiction the equal protection of the laws."

In the light of the history of these amendments, and the pervading purpose of them, which we have already discussed, it is not difficult to give a meaning to this clause. The existence of laws in the States where the newly emancipated negroes resided, which discriminated with gross injustice and hardship against them as a class, was the evil to be remedied by this clause, and by it such laws are forbidden.

. . . We doubt very much whether any action of a State not directed by way of discrimination against the negroes as a class, or on account of their race, will ever be held to come within the purview of this provision. It is so clearly a provision for that race and that emergency, that a strong case would be necessary for its application to any other. . . . .

. . .

JUSTICE FIELD, dissenting:

. . .

The act of Louisiana presents the naked case, unaccompanied by any public considerations, where a right to pursue a lawful and necessary calling, previously enjoyed by every citizen, and in connection with which a thousand persons were daily employed, is taken away and vested exclusively for twenty-five years, for an extensive district and a large population, in a single corporation, or its exercise is for that period restricted to the establishments of the corporation, and there allowed only upon onerous conditions. . . .

The question presented is, therefore, one of the gravest importance, not merely to the parties here, but to the whole country. It is nothing less than the question whether the recent amendments to the Federal Constitution protect the citizens of the United States against the deprivation of their common rights by State legislation. In my judgment the fourteenth amendment does afford such protection, and was so intended by the Congress which framed and the States which adopted it. . . .

The amendment does not attempt to confer any new privileges or immunities upon citizens, or to enumerate or define those already existing. It assumes that there are such privileges and immunities which belong of right to citizens as such, and ordains that they shall not be abridged by State legislation. If this inhibition has no reference to privileges and immunities of this character, but only refers, as held by the majority of the court in their opinion, to such privileges and immunities as were before its adoption specially designated in the Constitution or necessarily implied as belonging to citizens of the United States, it was a vain and idle enactment, which accomplished nothing, and most unnecessarily excited Congress and the people on its passage. With privileges and immunities thus designated or implied no State could ever have interfered by its laws, and no new constitutional provision was required to inhibit such interference. The supremacy of the Constitution and the laws of the United States always controlled any State legislation of that character. But if the amendment refers to the natural and inalienable rights which belong to all citizens, the inhibition has a profound significance and consequence.

What, then, are the privileges and immunities which are secured against abridgment by State legislation? . . .

The terms, privileges and immunities, are not new in the amendment; they were in the Constitution before the amendment was adopted. They are found in the second section of the fourth article, which declares that "the citizens of each State shall be entitled to all privileges and immunities of citizens in the several States," and they have been the subject of frequent consideration in judicial decisions. [*Justice Field then quoted the same passage from* Corfield v. Coryell *that Justice Miller had quoted.*] This appears to me to be a sound construction of the clause in question. The privileges and immunities designated are those which of right belong to the citizens of all free governments. Clearly among these must be placed the right to pursue a lawful employment in a lawful manner, without other restraint than such as equally affects all persons. . . .

. . . The privileges and immunities of citizens of the United States, of every one of them, is secured against abridgment in any form by any State. The fourteenth amendment places them under the guardianship of the National authority. All monopolies in any known trade or manufacture are an invasion of these privileges, for they encroach upon the liberty of citizens to acquire property and pursue happiness. . . .

. . .

This equality of right, with exemption from all disparaging and partial enactments, in the lawful pursuits of life, throughout the whole country, is the distinguishing privilege of citizens of the United States. To them, everywhere, all pursuits, all professions, all avocations are open without other restrictions than such as are imposed equally upon all others of the same age, sex, and condition. The State may prescribe such regulations for every pursuit and calling of life as will promote the public health, secure the good order and advance the general prosperity of society, but when once prescribed, the pursuit or calling must be free to be followed by every citizen who is within the conditions designated, and will conform to the regulations. This is the fundamental idea upon which our institutions rest, and unless adhered to in the legislation of the country our government will be a republic only in name. The fourteenth amendment, in my judgment, makes it essential to the validity of the legislation of every State that this equality of right should be respected. . . . That only is a free government, in the American sense of the term, under which the inalienable right of every citizen to pursue his happiness is unrestrained, except by just, equal, and impartial laws.

JUSTICE BRADLEY, dissenting. . . .
JUSTICE SWAYNE, dissenting. . . .

III. Individual Rights

MAJOR DEVELOPMENTS

- Some confiscation of property in both North and South
- Congress grants exemptions from the draft to religious pacifists
- National debates over the right to bear arms

The status of individual rights during the Civil War and Reconstruction confounds common claims that personal liberties are the first casualty of war. The American experience was far more complex. Both the Union and the Confederacy passed unprecedented measures to confiscate property. The Union measure, however, was scaled down considerably and only sporadically enforced. Americans also gained religious freedoms during the Civil War. For the first time, persons other than Protestants served as military chaplains, and Congress granted religious pacifists exemptions from military service. The Civil War had little influence on other rights. While the conflict raged, Americans rarely considered the right to bear arms or the right to marry. Little debate took place on the constitutionality of morals laws.

When reading the materials on property rights, religious freedom, guns rights, and personal liberties, consider possible relationships between the controversies over these rights. To what extent were all participants in these controversies influenced by broader political and constitutional developments? Did persons involved in one debate over personal rights rely on similar or different principles than persons involved in other debates over personal rights? How are these debates similar to or different from Jacksonian Era controversies over individual rights?

A. Property

Many important Civil War and Reconstruction measures raised questions about constitutional property rights. Critics claimed that the First and Second Confiscation Acts, the Emancipation Proclamation, the Legal Tender Act, and the Ironclad Oath violated the due process and takings clauses of the Fifth Amendment. Former Justice John Campbell urged the Supreme Court in the *Slaughter-House Cases* (1873) to declare that state-chartered monopolies violated the constitutional right to pursue an ordinary calling protected by the Thirteenth Amendment and various clauses of the Fourteenth Amendment. Proponents of these federal and state regulations claimed that each was a legitimate exercise of federal war powers or state police powers. Republicans in Congress stated that persons who supported the Confederacy forfeited their right to hold property and their right to practice various professions. State legislators maintained that loyalty oaths secured allegiance, and that state-chartered monopolies promoted the public welfare.

These debates over confiscation, emancipation, legal tender, test oaths, and monopolies nationalized constitutional controversies over economic rights. The most important disputes over property that arose before the Civil War concerned the proper interpretation of state constitutional provisions. State legislatures and judges determined when and whether public officials could condemn land to build railroads. The most important disputes over property that arose between 1861 and 1876 were over the proper interpretation of federal constitutional provisions. The president, members of Congress, and federal judges determined the conditions under which property could be confiscated and loyalty oaths imposed. Although Americans during the Civil War ended the national controversy over whether persons could hold property rights in other persons, many constitutional controversies over property debated in the 1860s remain vibrant today.

Partisanship influenced some, but not all, debates over property rights. Most Republicans agreed that slave owners should not be compensated for emancipated slaves. Radical Republicans proposed measures that would confiscate all property owned by persons supporting the Confederacy. Conservative Republicans preferred much weaker measures. Democrats opposed uncompensated emancipation, property confiscation, and loyalty oaths. Party played no role when the judges on the Supreme Court considered whether test oaths violated the right to practice various professions.

The constitutional status of many property rights was less settled politically than legally at the end of Reconstruction. Slavery was dead. Professionals had a constitutional right not to be forced to swear to their past loyalty. The Supreme Court ruled that government could print paper money and that state monopolies did not violate constitutional rights to practice a common calling. Nevertheless, *Knox v. Lee* (1871) and the *Slaughter-House Cases* (1873) were decided by narrow judicial majorities. Moreover, property claims during the Civil War and Reconstruction were asserted by Democrats or persons identified with Democratic causes. No one knew whether the Republican majority on the Supreme Court and in the national legislature would be more sympathetic when, in the future, Republicans or persons identified with Republican causes claimed that their constitutional property rights had been violated.

Contracts

The Legal Tender Act of 1863 raised questions about constitutional rights as well as questions about constitutional powers. That law required creditors to accept federally printed paper money as payment for all debts. In *Hepburn v. Griswold* (1870), the Supreme Court held by a 5-3 vote that Congress could not require creditors to accept "greenbacks" for debts acquired before the Legal Tender Act became law. Chief Justice Chase claimed that the Constitution did not vest the national government with the power to make paper currency legal tender throughout the United States. That was the constitutional powers issue. Chase then discussed constitutional rights when concluding that the Legal Tender Act was not "necessary and proper." Requiring creditors to take paper money as payment for preexisting debts, he stated, violated the spirit, if not the letter, of the contracts clause of Article I, section 10, the due process clause of the Fifth Amendment, and the takings clause of the Fifth Amendment:

> It is true that [the contracts clause] is not applied in terms to the government of the United States. . . .
>
> But we think it clear that those who framed and those who adopted the Constitution, intended that the spirit of this prohibition should pervade the entire body of legislation, and that the justice which the Constitution was ordained to establish was not thought by them to be compatible with legislation of an opposite tendency. In other words, we cannot doubt that a law not made in pursuance of an express power, which necessarily and in its direct operation impairs the obligation of contracts, is inconsistent with the spirit of the Constitution.
>
> Another provision, found in the fifth amendment, must be considered in this connection. We refer to that which ordains that private property shall not be taken for public use without compensation. . . . It does not, in terms, prohibit legislation which appropriates the private property of one class of citizens to the use of another class; but if such property cannot be taken for the benefit of all, without compensation, it is difficult to understand how it can be so taken for the benefit of a part without violating the spirit of the prohibition.
>
> . . .
>
> It is quite clear, that whatever may be the operation of such an act, due process of law makes no part of it. Does it deprive any person of property? A very large proportion of the property of civilized men exists in the form of contracts. These contracts almost invariably stipulate for the payment of money. And we have already seen that contracts in the United States, prior to the act under consideration, for the payment of money, were contracts to pay the sums specified in gold and silver coin. And it is beyond doubt that the holders of these contracts were and are as fully entitled to the protection of this constitutional provision as the holders of any other description of property.

One year later the Supreme Court in *Knox v. Lee* (1871) overruled *Hepburn*. Justice William Strong's majority opinion brushed aside claims that the Legal Tender Act violated the contracts clause or the due process clause. He wrote:

> We come next to the argument much used, and, indeed, the main reliance of those who assert the unconstitutionality of the legal tender acts. It is that they are prohibited by the spirit of the Constitution because they indirectly impair the obligation of contracts. . . . The argument assumes two things,—first, that the acts do, in effect, impair the obligation of contracts, and second, that Congress is prohibited from taking any action which may indirectly have that effect. . . . We have been asked whether Congress can declare that a contract to deliver a quantity of grain may be satisfied by the tender of a less quantity. Undoubtedly not. But this is a false analogy. There is a wide distinction between a tender of quantities, or of specific articles, and a tender of legal values. Contracts for the delivery of specific articles belong exclusively to the domain of State legislation, while contracts for the payment of money are subject to the authority of Congress, at least so far as relates to the means of payment. They are engagements to pay with lawful money of the United States, and Congress is empowered to regulate that money. It cannot, therefore, be maintained that the legal tender acts impaired the obligation of contracts.
>
> . . .
>
> Closely allied to the objection we have just been considering is the argument pressed upon us that the legal tender acts were prohibited by the spirit of the fifth amendment, which forbids taking private property for public use without just compensation or due process of law. That provision has always been understood as referring only to a direct appropriation, and not to consequential injuries resulting from the exercise of lawful power. It has never been supposed to have any bearing upon, or to inhibit laws that indirectly work harm and loss to individuals. A new tariff, an embargo, a draft, or a war may inevitably bring upon individuals great losses; may,

indeed, render valuable property almost valueless. They may destroy the worth of contracts.

Knox settled both the constitutionality of the Legal Tender Act and the status of the contracts clause as a restriction on federal power. Chief Justice Chase correctly noted that constitutional authorities had long considered the contracts clause a limit on both state and federal power. After *Knox*, the contracts clause limited only state power.

Takings

Radical Republicans believed confiscation to be crucial to their post–Civil War constitutional vision. Federal laws forfeiting the property of persons who supported the Confederacy, Senator Charles Sumner and his political allies believed, would deal a deathblow to slavery, punish disloyal Americans, and provide the federal government with substantial southern lands that could be distributed to freedmen. Proponents of confiscation insisted that both law and precedent supported congressional power to free slaves and seize the lands of those supporting the Confederacy. They note that the law of nations permits belligerents to confiscate any enemy property that may be used in the war effort. Nor was confiscation a novel proposal in 1861. Americans confiscated British property without substantial constitutional objection during the Revolutionary War.

The confiscation laws that Republicans passed had more bark than bite. The Second Confiscation Act authorized the president to seize the property of all citizens supporting the Confederacy. President Lincoln, conservative Republicans, and Democrats successfully insisted that the property be forfeited only after a judicial hearing, and that real estate be forfeited only for the lifetime of the property holder. Even as modified, the Second Confiscation Act received rough judicial treatment. The highest court of Kentucky in *Norris v. Doniphan* (KY 1863) declared the measure unconstitutional, with Judge Bullitt's majority opinion stating, "The constitution does not authorize the confiscation of the property of a rebel, because of his crime, without a trial by jury of the offender and his conviction 'by due process of law.'"[12] Seven years later, the Supreme Court of the United States reached a different conclusion in *Miller v. United States* (1870). Justice William Strong ruled that precedents from the American Revolution established "that aiders and abettors of the public enemy were themselves enemies, and hence that their property might lawfully be confiscated." The combination of cumbersome procedures and constitutional doubts nevertheless proved fatal to the radical hope for substantial confiscation and redistribution. The federal government rarely implemented the Second Confiscation Act. Little property was actually confiscated.

Emancipation also raised questions about the property rights of slaveholders. Many Americans thought that uncompensated emancipation violated the takings clause of the Fifth Amendment. Senator Edgar Cowan of Pennsylvania maintained that federal laws emancipating the slaves of Confederate supporters violated the due process rights of slaveholders. Representative Fernando Wood of New York declared that federal laws or constitutional amendments abolishing slavery "appropriate[d] private property without due compensation, or confiscate[d] it without the formality of trial and condemnation."[13] Lincoln and his political allies initially supported compensation. The federal law abolishing slavery in the District of Columbia compensated slaveholders. However, compensation schemes were abandoned as the Civil War dragged on. The Confiscation Act of 1862, the Emancipation Proclamation, and the Thirteenth Amendment freed slaves without offering any compensation to slaveholders.

Debate over the Second Confiscation Act (1861–62)[14]

The Second Confiscation Act permitted the president to seize all property of any person suspected of supporting the Confederacy. If a federal court found that property belonged to a Confederate supporter, the property was forfeited to the United States. After passing the Second Confiscation Act, Congress adopted a resolution declaring, "Nor shall any punishment or proceeding under said act be so construed to work a forfeiture of the real estate of the offender beyond his natural life." This meant that the federal government could seize the property of such persons as Jefferson Davis only

12. *Norris v. Doniphan*, 61 Ky. (4 Mete.) 385 (1863).

13. *Congressional Globe*, 38th Cong., 1st Sess. (1864), 2929.

14. *Congressional Globe*, 37th Cong., 2nd Sess. (1861–1862), 18–19, 1049–54, 1795, 2188–96.

as long as Davis was alive. When Davis died, ownership reverted to his heirs.

The Second Confiscation Act was a compromise between radical and conservative Republicans. Radical Republicans maintained that the Constitution did not require any judicial proceedings before the property of people who supported secession was confiscated. "Whoever lays violent hands upon the fabric of just civil government for the purpose of its overthrow," Representative John Bingham of Ohio declared, "should be deprived at once of property and life." Senator Lyman Trumbull of Illinois spoke for this faction when he proposed a confiscation bill providing "for the absolute and complete forfeiture . . . of every species of property, real and personal . . . belonging to persons . . . who, during its existence, shall take up arms against the United States, or in anywise aid or abet the rebellion." Democrats and conservative Republicans insisted that the U.S. Constitution required that property not on an actual battlefield be confiscated only after the property holder was convicted of treason in court. Senator Orville Browning of Illinois stated,

> *A state of war does not justify the civil power in abrogating constitutions, nor in violating the rights of persons or property. The right to life, liberty and the pursuit of happiness is as inalienable in the citizen in time of war as in time of peace; and the tenure by which he holds his property is the same and as inviolate . . . as in the hour of greatest tranquility.*[15]

President Lincoln supported conservative Republicans, insisting that forfeiture take place in civil courts and be limited to the life of the offender. This latter limitation was based on the treason clause of the Constitution, which declares, "No Attainder of Treason shall work Corruption of Blood, or Forfeiture except during the Life of the Person attainted."

Daniel Hamilton claims that the confiscation debates mark a shift in American thinking about property. Radical Republicans took the feudal view that "property rights were created and defined by the state and could be altered in the public interest." Conservative Republicans treated property as a natural right that could not be taken by government in the absence of judicial procedures.[16] *Based on the materials below, do you believe Hamilton's analysis correct? What else might explain the difference between proponents and opponents of legislative confiscation? Why was Abraham Lincoln a particularly vigorous opponent of legislative confiscation?*

SENATOR LYMAN TRUMBULL (Republican, Illinois)

. . .

. . . The right of seizure and confiscation of the property of the enemy as prize of war is a settled principle of international law which has been affirmed by our own Supreme Court. In the case of *Brown v. United States* (1814), . . . the court say

> Respecting the power of Government no doubt is entertained. That war gives to the sovereign full right to take the persons and confiscate the property of the enemy wherever found, is conceded. . . .[17]

. . .

Without special act of Congress, I presume no one questions that our military commanders, in the prosecution of the war in insurrectionary districts, may, for the time being, seize and make use of the property of the rebels and their slaves; but on the restoration of peace, the right of the owners would revive. Hence, if we would have uniformity of action among the commanders of our armies, and forfeit forever the property of rebels and their claims to the service of their fellow-men, it must be done by act of Congress. According to the modern usage of nations, private property of alien enemies on land has not generally been forfeited; but the right of forfeiture is unquestionable, and may be exercised, if necessary to secure the just ends of the war, or in retaliation for forfeitures by the enemy. The rebels, wherever they have the power, have seized and confiscated the property of loyal men,[18] and this, according even to modern usage as between independent nations, would give to the United States the right to confiscate in turn; much more would they possess that right as against rebels, who have causelessly taken up arms against the Government. The right to free the slaves of rebels would be equally clear with that to confiscate their property generally, for it is as property they profess to hold them; but as one of the most efficient means for attaining the end for which the armies of the Union have been called forth, the

15. Orville H. Browning, *Speech of Hon. O.H. Browning of Illinois on the Confiscation of Property* (Chicago: L. Towers & Co., 1862), 6.

16. Daniel Hamilton, *The Limits of Sovereignty* (Chicago: University of Chicago Press, 2007), 8. The introduction to this reading relies heavily on Hamilton's analysis.

17. The Supreme Court in *Brown v. United States* held that while Congress had the power to confiscate enemy property during times of war, confiscation could occur only by legislative decree.

18. For a discussion of confiscation policy in the Confederacy, see Hamilton, *Limits of Sovereignty*, 82–139.

right to restore to them the God-given liberty, of which they have been unjustly deprived, is doubly clear.

SENATOR EDGAR COWAN (Republican, Pennsylvania)

. . .

. . . Congress cannot forfeit the property of rebels for longer than their lives, by the enactment of any law whatever, for the following reasons:

1. Those persons now in rebellion, having levied war against the United States, are guilty of treason within the exact definition of that crime contained in the third section of the third article of the Constitution. . . .

2. Therefore any law made for the guidance of the courts must conform to this provision, and no other greater penalty could be imposed than it would warrant. If, therefore, the law was to enact an absolute forfeiture of the estates of the traitor, it would be bad for the excess, and the judges would be obliged to make the sentence constitutional, either by cutting down the statutory penalty to a forfeiture of his estates for life, or by omitting to forfeit them at all.

The power assumed in this bill is also obnoxious to the provisions of the Constitution, if it be assumed that Congress can legislate an effectual forfeiture of the estates of rebels, as such, without allowing them an opportunity or means of trial in the courts. . . .

Here, it is attempted to deprive a large class of persons of all their estates and property, without any arrest, without any presentment by a grand jury, without any trial by a petit jury, without, indeed, any trial at all in any court. This would be to deprive them of their property in the very face of the provision requiring that it shall only be done "by due process of law," means proceedings according to the course of the common law.

. . . Congress . . . has no power to punish anybody (except for contempts) and today, if we had half a dozen of the worst rebels caged here in this Chamber, we could inflict upon them no punishment. We could not order the Sergeant-at-Arms to hang or behead them, no matter how certain we might be of their guilt. Nay, more the President himself and all his Army could not lead them away from this Hall to execution. The only way they could be punished at all, would be to deliver them over the judges. . . .

A bill of attainder was a mode of proceeding resorted to in England, as well as in some of the United States during the Revolution, to condemn and punish traitors, by Parliament or the Legislature, in cases where they were out of the reach of the process of the courts; nay, indeed, in many cases even after they were dead. In such cases the law-making branch of the Government supplied the want of due process of law by blending together in one statute the law and the application of the law to particular persons named therein, or to a class of persons by description. Bills of attainder condemned the accused to death, if not dead already, forfeited their estates, and corrupted the inheritable blood of their children and heirs, so that no one could take any estate either from or through them. Bills, however, like the one under consideration, which does not propose to inflict capital punishment, or corrupt the blood of the offenders, but imposed other penalties of lesser grade, were called "bills of pains and penalties."

It may be said the latter are not within the prohibition, and therefore allowable here. It is true they are not within the letter of it, but being equally within the mischief, which was, that the legislature should in any case attempt to usurp and exercise the functions of the courts; and construing the fifth amendment in connection, I have no doubt they are also prohibited. Indeed, no one can come to any other conclusion but that the convention which framed the Constitution intended to remove every possibility of the usurpation, by Congress, of the power to punish anybody without "due process of law." . . .

SENATOR CHARLES SUMNER (Republican, Massachusetts)

. . .

The persons now arrayed for the overthrow of the Government of the United States are unquestionably criminals, subject to all the penalties of rebellion, which is of course treason under the Constitution of the United States.

The same persons now arrayed in war against the Government of the United States are unquestionably enemies, exposed to all the incidents of war, with its penalties, seizures, contributions, confiscations, captures, and prizes.

. . .

Therefore, sir, in determining our course, we may banish all question of power. The power is ample and indubitable, being regulated in the one case by the Constitution and in the other case by the rights of war. If we treat them as criminals, then we are under the restraints of the Constitution; if we treat them as enemies, then we have all the latitude sanctioned by the rights of war. If we treat them as both, then we combine our penalties from the double sources. What is done against them merely as criminals will naturally be in conformity with the Constitution; but what is done against them as enemies, will have no limitation except the rights of war.

. . .

. . . [W]hat are the rights against enemies which Congress may exercise in war.

. . .

Although there have been so many conventions granting exemption from the liabilities resulting from a state of war, the right to seize the property of enemies found in our territory when war breaks out, remains indisputable, according to the law of nations. . . .

. . .

Private property of an enemy on land may be taken as a penalty for the illegal acts of individuals, or of the community to which they belong.

Private property of an enemy on land may be taken for contributions to support the war.

Private property of an enemy on land may be taken on the field of battle, in the operations of a siege or in the storming of a place which refuses to capitulate. . . .

The pretended property of an enemy in slaves may be unquestionably taken; and, when taken, will of course be at the disposal of the captor. If slaves be regarded as property, then will their confiscation come precisely within the rule already stated. But since slaves are men, there is still another rule of public law applicable to them. It is clear that, where there is an intestine division in an enemy country, we may take advantage of it. . . . In giving freedom to the slaves, a nation in war simply takes advantage of the actual condition of things. . . .

The obligation is more certain and more extensive with regard to a people whom our enemy has unjustly oppressed. For a people thus spoiled of their liberty never renounce their hope of recovering it. If they have not voluntarily incorporated themselves with the State by which they have been subdued—if they have not freely aided her in the war against us—we ought certainly so to use our victory as not merely to give them a new master, but to break their chains. To deliver an oppressed people is a noble fruit of victory; it is a valuable advantage gained thus to acquire a faithful friend. . . .

. . .

Therefore, according to the rights of war, slaves, if regarded as property, may be declared free, or if regarded as men, they may also be declared free, under two acknowledged rules; first of self-interest, in order to procure an ally, and secondly of conscience and equity, in order to do an act of justice which shall ennoble victory. . . .

Abraham Lincoln, To the Senate and House of Representatives (July 17, 1862)

. . .

Before I was informed of the passage of the Resolution [limiting forfeitures to life estates], I had prepared the draft of a Message, stating objections to the bill becoming a law, a copy of which draft is herewith transmitted.

Fellow citizens of the House of Representatives

. . .

There is much in the bill to which I perceive no objection. It is wholly prospective; and it touches neither person or property, of any loyal citizen; in which particulars, it is just and proper. The first and second sections provide for the conviction and punishment of persons who shall be guilty of treason, and persons who shall "incite, set on foot, assist, or engage in any rebellion, or insurrection, against the authority of the United States, or the laws thereof, or shall give aid or comfort thereto, or shall engage in, or give aid and comfort to any such existing rebellion, or insurrection." By fair construction, persons within these sections are not to be punished without regular trials, in duly constituted courts, under the forms, and all the substantial provisions of law, and of the constitution, applicable to their several cases. To this I perceive no objection; especially as such persons would be within the general pardoning power, and also the special provision for pardon and amnesty, contained in this act. It is also provided, that the slaves of persons convicted under these sections shall be free. I think there is an unfortunate form of expression, rather than a substantial objection, in this. It is startling to say that Congress can free a slave within a state; and yet if it were said the ownership of the slave had first been transferred to the nation, and that Congress had then liberated, him, the difficulty would at once vanish. And this is the real case. The traitor against the general government forfeits his slave, at least as justly as he does any other property; and he forfeits both to the government against which he offends. The government, so far as there can be ownership, thus owns the . . . forfeited slaves; and the question for Congress, in regard to them is, "Shall they be made free, or be sold to new masters?" I perceive no objection to Congress deciding in advance that they shall be free. . . .

. . .

That to which I chiefly object, pervades most parts of the act, but more distinctly appears in the first, second, seventh and eighth sections. It is the sum of those provisions which results in the divesting of title forever. For the causes of treason, and the ingredients of treason, not amounting to the full crime, it declares forfeiture, extending beyond the lives of the guilty parties; whereas the Constitution of the United States declares that "no attainder of treason shall work corruption of blood, or forfeiture, except during the life of the person attainted." True, there is to be no formal attainder in this case; still I think the greater punishment can not be constitutionally inflicted, in a different form, for the same offence. With great respect, I am constrained to say I think this feature of the act is unconstitutional. It would not be difficult to modify it.

. . .

Again, this act, by proceedings *in rem*, forfeits property, for the ingredients of treason, without a conviction of the supposed criminal, or a personal hearing given him in any proceeding. That we may not touch property lying within our reach, because we can not give personal notice to an owner who is absent endeavoring to destroy the govern[ment,] is certainly not very satisfactory; still the owner may not be thus engaged, and I think a reasonable time should be provided for such parties to appear and have personal hearings. . . .

. . .

Due Process

Americans from 1861 to 1876 disputed whether the Constitution protected the right to practice certain professions or engage in certain callings. The *Slaughter-House Cases* (1873) ruled that a state monopoly did not violate the constitutional right of butchers to practice their trade. The *Test Oath Cases* (1867) declared unconstitutional federal and state laws that required lawyers and ministers to swear they had always been loyal to the United States.

Republicans insisted that persons occupying vital offices take loyalty oaths. The first loyalty oaths were demanded the week after Fort Sumter was attacked. That summer Congress passed a statute requiring every federal employee to swear that they would "support, protect and defend the Constitution and Government of the United States against all enemies." In 1862 Congress expanded the scope and depth of loyalty oaths. New federal statutes required that all federal government officeholders, elected or appointed, and all jurors in federal trials swear to past loyalty as well as future allegiance. Many northern states demanded similar oaths. California required all litigants in state courts to swear past, present, and future allegiance to the United States. The Missouri Test Oath Act required members of all professions to swear that they had not committed one of nearly a hundred acts.

The Supreme Court in *Ex parte Garland* (1867) and *Cummings v. Missouri* (1867) by 5-4 votes declared unconstitutional the ironclad oaths for attorneys practicing in federal courts and for members of various professions. Justice Field's majority opinion in *Cummings* emphasized a supposed constitutional right to practice a profession. He wrote,

> The theory upon which our political institutions rest is, that all men have certain inalienable rights; that among these are life, liberty, and the pursuit of happiness; and that, in the pursuit of happiness, all avocations, all honors, all positions are alike open to everyone, and that in the protection of these rights all are equal before the law.

Field, who six years later fought as a dissenter for the rights of butchers in the *Slaughter-House Cases*, insisted here that "any deprivation or suspension of any of these rights for past conduct is punishment, and can be in no other wise defined." Test oaths as punishment, he concluded, violated both the constitutional prohibition on bills of attainder and the ex post facto clause.

B. Religion

Americans became more tolerant of religious diversity during the Civil War and Reconstruction Era. Religious (and racial) prejudices weakened in the North when men of different religious faiths (and races) fought together in the Union Army. The federal government made two landmark decisions recognizing the rights of religious minorities. For the first time in history, Congress permitted non-Protestants to become military chaplains. For the first time, Congress granted religious pacifists exemptions from compulsory military service. The Supreme Court struck a blow for religious freedom when the judicial majority in *Cummings v. Missouri* (1867) ruled that ministers could not be required to swear that they had always been loyal to the United States.

Illustration 6-2 Augustus Hill Garland

Augustus Hill Garland was an Arkansas Whig who joined his state in secession and served as a member of both the House of Representatives and the Senate in the Confederate government. After the war, he received a pardon from President Andrew Johnson and sought to return to his practice as a member of the bar of the U.S. Supreme Court. *Ex parte Garland* (1866) tested the authority of Congress to ban former Confederates from practicing law.. He later served as a Democratic governor of Arkansas, a U.S. senator, and U.S. attorney general.

Source: Library of Congress, Prints and Photographs Division, Washington, DC 20540, USA.

Consider two different explanations for this greater recognition of religious diversity. First, the Civil War inspired a greater northern commitment to the rights of religious minorities. Persons of different faiths who fought together in a common cause gained greater appreciation for one another, particular when that cause was increasingly identified as a crusade for fundamental human rights. Second, Protestants during the Civil War were more tolerant of Jews and Protestant pacifists than they were of Catholics before the Civil War. Jews challenged the ban on non-Protestant chaplains. Quakers sought exemptions from military service during the Civil War. Republicans might have been less tolerant of these changes had Catholics demanded military chaplains or exemptions from military service.

Establishment

Jewish soldiers gained rights during the Civil War. In 1861 federal law required that all military chaplains be "regularly ordained minister[s] of some Christian denomination."[19] In practice, only Protestant clergy were appointed as military chaplains. When Arnold Fischel applied to be the chaplain for a New York military regiment with a majority of Jewish members, Secretary of War Simon Cameron rejected his application. Many leading northern newspapers protested that decision. Cameron's critics maintained that laws prohibiting Jews from becoming chaplains violated "those rights . . . for which the bones of many of our brethren in faith are now mouldering on the banks of the Potomac."[20] Senator Lyman Trumbull presented the Senate with a petition signed by seven thousand citizens urging that religious restrictions on chaplains be repealed. President Lincoln publicly supported repeal. On July 17, 1862, Congress passed a new law on military chaplains that declared, "No person shall be appointed a chaplain in the United States army who is not a regularly ordained minister of some religious denomination."[21]

Free Exercise

Most states and the federal government granted religious pacifists legal exemptions from draft laws during the Civil War. Twenty states in 1861 mandated exemptions in either the state constitution or state law. The constitution of Oregon declared, "Persons whose religious tenets, or conscientious scruples forbid them to bear arms shall not be compelled to do so." The federal Draft Act of 1863 made no exception for religious believers, although recruiters were told to follow state law. This practice meant that the federal government did not draft religious pacifists who had been granted state exemptions from military service. Many congressmen objected to the lack of a federal exemption for conscientious objection. In 1864 the Federal Draft

19. 12 U.S. Stat. 287, 288 (1861).

20. Isaac Markens, *Abraham Lincoln and the Jews* (New York: Isaac Markens, 1909), 8.

21. 12 U.S. Stat. 594, 595 (1862). For the full account of this incident, see Markens, *Abraham Lincoln and the Jews*, 8–10.

Act was amended to insert a new provision providing exemptions. That provision declared,

> That members of religious denominations, who shall, by oath or affirmation, declare that they are conscientiously opposed to the bearing of arms, and who are prohibited from doing so by the rules and articles of faith and practice of said religious denominations, shall, when drafted into the military service, be considered non-combatants, and shall be assigned by the Secretary of War to duty in the hospitals, or to the care of freedmen, or shall pay the sum of three hundred dollars to such person as the Secretary of War shall designate to receive it, to be applied to the benefit of the sick and wounded soldiers; Provided, That no person shall be entitled to the benefit of the provisions of this section unless his declaration of conscientious scruples against bearing arms shall be supported by satisfactory evidence that his deportment has been uniformly consistent with such declaration.

This was the first time that Congress had provided religious believers with an exemption from a federal law.[22]

C. Guns

Republicans aggressively championed the right of persons of color to bear arms. Anti-slavery advocates were outraged when unreconstructed southern legislatures forbade former slaves from joining the state militia or bearing arms. A memorial from colored citizens of South Carolina declared,

> We ask that, inasmuch as the Constitution of the United States explicitly declares that the right to keep and bear arms shall not be infringed—and the Constitution is the Supreme law of the land—that the late efforts of the Legislature of this State to pass an act to deprive us of arms be forbidden, as a plain violation of the Constitution, and unjust to many of us in the highest degree, who have been soldiers, and purchased our muskets from the United States Government when mustered out of service.[23]

Republicans in Congress supported such claims. Some identified the right to bear arms with a right to self-defense. In a speech discussing the "indispensable . . . safeguards of liberty under our form of government," Senator Samuel Pomeroy of Kansas asserted,

> Every man . . . should have the right to bear arms for the defense of himself and family and his homestead. And if the cabin door of the freedman is broken open and the intruder enters for purposes as vile as were known to slavery, then should a well-loaded musket be in the hand of the occupant to send the polluted wretch to another world, where his wretchedness will forever remain complete.[24]

Historians dispute whether Republicans during Reconstruction opposed only discriminatory restrictions on the right to bear arms or also racially neutral restrictions on the right to bear arms. Consider an incident that occurred early in Reconstruction. The unreconstructed legislature of South Carolina passed a law stating:

> That persons of color constitute no part of the militia of the State, and no one of them shall, without permission in writing from the district judge or magistrate, be allowed to keep a fire-arm, sword, or other military weapon, except that one of them, who is though owner of an arm, may keep a shot-gun or rifle, such as is ordinarily used in hunting, but not a pistol, musket, or other fire-arm or weapon appropriate for purposes of war.[25]

General Daniel Sickles, the local commander of Union forces, immediately issued an order voiding the entire law. With respect to the right to weapons, his order declared:

> The constitutional rights of all loyal and well-disposed inhabitants to bear arms will not be infringed; nevertheless this shall not be construed to sanction the unlawful practice of carrying concealed weapons, nor to authorize any person to enter with

22. 13 U.S. Stat. 6, 9 (1864). For more information, see Kurt T. Lash, "The Second Adoption of the Free Exercise Clause: Religious Exemptions under the Fourteenth Amendment," *Northwestern University Law Review* 88 (1994): 1141–46.

23. Stephen P. Halbrook, *Freedman, the Fourteenth Amendment, and the Right to Bear Arms, 1866-1876* (Westport, CT: Greenwood Publishing Group, 1998), 9.

24. *Congressional Globe*, 39th Cong., 1st Sess. (1866), 1182.

25. Edward McPherson, *The Political History of the United States during the Period of Reconstruction* (Washington, DC: Philip & Solomons, 1871), 35.

> arms on the premises of another against his consent. No one shall bear arms who has borne arms against the United States, unless he shall have taken [an] amnesty oath. . . . And no disorderly person, vagrant, or disturber of the peace, shall be allowed to bear arms.[26]

Contemporary proponents of a strong right to bear arms emphasize that Sickles spoke of "the constitutional right . . . to bear arms." Proponents of gun regulations emphasize that Sickles endorsed various limits on gun rights, as long as those limits did not include racial discriminations.

One incident suggests that Republicans were committed to a right to bear arms independent of militia service. In 1866 and 1867 Senator Henry Wilson of Massachusetts proposed legislation "disarming and disbanding" the militia forces in the vast majority of states that had seceded from the Union. Senator Wartman Willey of West Virginia raised a "constitutional objection against depriving men of the right to bear arms and the total disarming of men in times of peace." After a short debate Senator Wilson agreed to strike out the word "disarmed." Mollified, Senator Willey and a congressional majority voted for the revised bill. Congress, Reconstruction Republicans agreed, could disband state militias but could not normally disarm people who had not been convicted of crimes.[27]

Most legal scholars in the Reconstruction Era narrowly interpreted the right to bear arms. John Norton Pomeroy's *An Introduction to the Constitutional Law of the United States* yoked the right to bear arms to the militia. When commenting on "the right of the people to keep and bear arms," Pomeroy wrote:

> The object of this clause is to secure a well-armed militia. It has always been the policy of free governments to dispense, as far as possible, with standing armies, and to rely for their defence, both against foreign invasion and domestic turbulence, upon the militia. Regular armies have always been associated with despotism. But a militia would be useless unless the citizens were enabled to exercise themselves in the use of warlike weapons. To preserve this privilege, and to secure to the people the ability to oppose themselves in military force against the usurpations of government, as well as against enemies from without, that government is forbidden by any law or proceeding to invade or destroy the right to keep and bear arms. But all such provisions, all such guaranties, must be construed with reference to their intent and design. This constitutional inhibition is certainly not violated by laws forbidding persons to carry dangerous or concealed weapons, or laws forbidding the accumulation of quantities of arms with the design to use them in a riotous or seditious manner. The clause is analogous to the one securing freedom of speech and of the press. Freedom, not license, is secured; the fair use, not the libellous abuse, is protected.[28]

When constitutional commentators looked to state law, they emphasized the decision of the Supreme Court of Arkansas in *State v. Buzzard* (AR 1842), which linked arms bearing and militia service. Treatise writers thought the more individual rights holding of *Bliss v. Commonwealth* (KY 1822) to be less representative of American law.[29]

Federal courts, after some internal debate, rejected contentions that persons of color had a federal constitutional right to bear arms. Riding circuit, Justice William Woods sustained federal power to prosecute the perpetrators of a massacre against persons of color for, among other reasons, conspiring to deprive citizens of their constitutional right to bear arms. His opinion asserted, "A man who carries arms openly, and for his own protection, or for any other lawful purpose, has as clear a right to do so, as to carry his own watch or wear his own hat."[30] The Supreme Court in *United States v. Cruiskshank* (1876) reached a different conclusion when ruling that the perpetrators of the Colfax massacres could not be prosecuted for denying persons of color the right to bear arms. States, the justices declared, were constitutionally free to regulate arms bearing as they saw fit.

> The right there specified is that of "bearing arms for a lawful purpose." This is not a right granted by the Constitution. Neither is it in any manner dependent upon that instrument for its existence. The second

---

26. Ibid., 37.

27. For the debate in question, see *Congressional Globe*, 39th Cong., 2nd Sess. (1867), 1848–49.

28. John Norton Pomeroy, *An Introduction to the Constitutional Law of the United States* (New York: Hurd and Houghton, 1868), 152–53.

29. See Saul Cornell, *A Well Regulated Militia: The Founding Fathers and the Origins of Gun Control in America* (New York: Oxford University Press, 2006), 187–90.

30. Ibid., 193.

> amendment declares that it shall not be infringed; but this, as has been seen, means no more than that it shall not be infringed by Congress. This is one of the amendments that has no other effect than to restrict the powers of the national government, leaving the people to look for their protection against any violation by their fellow-citizens of the rights it recognizes, to . . . the "powers which relate to merely municipal legislation, or what was, perhaps, more properly called internal police," "not surrendered or restrained" by the Constitution of the United States.

Most states and state courts during Reconstruction linked the right to bear arms to the militia. The Supreme Court of Texas in *English v. State* (TX 1872) ruled that federal and state rights to bear arms protected "only the right to 'keep' such 'arms' as are used for purposes of war, in distinction from those which are employed in quarrels and broils, and fights between maddened individuals."[31] The Supreme Court of Arkansas in *Fife v. State* (AK 1876) concluded, "The arms which it guarantees American citizens the right to keep and to bear, are such as are needful to, and ordinarily used by a well regulated militia."[32] The Supreme Court of Tennessee elaborated at somewhat greater length on the connection between militia service and the right to bear arms. Judge Freeman's opinion in *Andrews v. State* (TN 1871) maintained,

> What, then, is [the citizen] protected in the right to keep and thus use? Not everything that may be useful for offense or defense; but what may properly be included or understood under the title of arms, taken in connection with the fact that the citizen is to keep them, as a citizen. Such, then, as are found to make up the usual arms of the citizen of the country, and the use of which will properly train and render him efficient in defense of his own liberties, as well as of the State. Under this head, with a knowledge of the habits of our people, and of the arms in the use of which a soldier should be trained, we would hold, that the rifle of all descriptions, the shot gun, the musket, and repeater, are such arms; and that under the Constitution the right to keep such arms, cannot be infringed or forbidden by the Legislature. Their use, however, to be subordinated to such regulations and limitations as are or may be authorized by the law of the land, passed to subserve the general good, so as not to infringe the right secured and the necessary incidents to the exercise of such right.[33]

31. *English v. State*, 35 Tex. 476 (1872).
32. *Fife v. State*, 31 Ark. 455 (1876).

During the Civil War and the Reconstruction Era, the more progressive factions in American politics were the most prominent supporters of a broad right to bear arms. At present the more conservative factions in American politics are the most prominent supporters of a broad right to bear arms. As you read later materials in this text, consider the reasons for this change in the constitutional politics of the Second Amendment. How might this history of the right to bear arms during the Civil War and Reconstruction influence the proper interpretation of the contemporary Constitution? Does this history strengthen the individual right to bear arms, or only the constitutional right to nondiscriminatory laws concerning the bearing of arms? Might one read this history as strengthening the right to official protection from criminals?

D. Personal Freedom and Public Morality

Anti-slavery advocates advanced three constitutional arguments that had enduring significance for government power to regulate individual behavior. First, abolitionists consistently asserted that the Declaration of Independence provided the foundational principles of American constitutionalism. To the extent that the post–Civil War Constitution incorporated the Declaration of Independence, that Constitution aimed to protect what Jefferson described as "unalienable rights" to "life, liberty, and the pursuit of happiness." That "pursuit" might justify constitutional rights to drink, bowl, and enjoy various intimate relationships. Second, the persons responsible for the Thirteenth Amendment defined the badges and incidents of slavery broadly. Senator James Harlan's speech defending the proposed Thirteenth Amendment stated that among the "incidents of slavery" were "abolit[ion] of the conjugal relationship," "annul[ment] [of] the law of God establishing the relation of man and wife," and "the abolition practically of the parental relation." So viewed, the constitutional prohibition on involuntary servitude

33. *Andrews v. State*, 50 Tenn. 165 (1871).

could be interpreted as guaranteeing family rights, as well as rights to property and free labor. Third, prominent Supreme Court justices interpreted the Fourteenth Amendment as protecting fundamental rights. Justice Field's dissent in the *Slaughter-House Cases* (1873) insisted that the privileges and immunities clause "refer[red] to the natural and inalienable rights which belong to all citizens" and emphasized "the right to pursue a lawful employment in a lawful manner." His opinion nevertheless created an opening for proponents of drinking, gambling, abortion, homosexuality, and related activities to assert that these behaviors were among "the natural and inalienable rights" protected by the Fourteenth Amendment.

IV. Democratic Rights

MAJOR DEVELOPMENTS

- Lincoln administration restricts criticism of war policies
- Many states require voters to take loyalty oaths
- Debates over the rights entailed by American citizenship

The Civil War was the first military conflict in American history in which the federal government restricted basic democratic rights. The Lincoln administration arrested prominent war critics and temporarily shut down newspapers hostile to the war effort. The Union Army interfered with voting in crucial border states. After the Civil War Republicans in Congress required all national representatives to swear that they had never been disloyal to the United States. Many states insisted that voters take similar oaths. Union military officials in the South interfered with elections and suppressed anti-Reconstruction speech.

These measures were bitterly contested at the time and remain controversial today. Supporters of the Lincoln administration and Reconstruction politics, then and now, claim that the federal suppression policies were relatively mild and aimed at persons who were providing material support to the Confederate Army or were conspiring to deny rights to newly freed persons of color. Politics for the most part proceeded normally. Democrats in 1864 suffered no official sanctions for running on a platform urging Americans to restore the Union "as it was." The military remained on the sidelines when Republicans lost control of the Reconstruction South. Critics of the Lincoln administration and Reconstruction politics, then and now, insist that Republicans in power reneged on their prewar commitments to democracy. Former Congressman Clement Vallandigham, the most vociferous critic of administration policies during the Civil War, was convicted by a military commission and banished. White supremacists who criticized Reconstruction policies were hauled before military commissions.

When reading the materials in this section, consider why the federal government made far more efforts to restrict speech and other democratic rights during the Civil War than during either the Mexican War or the War of 1812. To what extent were these different policies best explained by differences in these wars (all of which provoked substantial dissent)? To what extent was Abraham Lincoln, a former Whig, more willing to use federal power than the Jeffersonian (Madison) and Jacksonian (Polk) presidents in office during the previous wars? Consider the justification for such policies. What do you believe best explains restrictions on democratic rights? Was the federal government more interested in preventing illegal actions or in enforcing political conformity? What policies do you believe were justified? Might you have supported greater suppression of political rights in the Reconstruction South in order to better protect the rights of newly freed slaves?

A. Free Speech

Abraham Lincoln had a narrow conception of free speech rights in wartime. As president, he ordered subordinates to arrest persons whose speeches he believed interfered with the war effort. When suspending the writ of habeas corpus on September 24, 1862, Lincoln declared,

> Now, therefore, be it ordered, first, that during the existing insurrection and as a necessary measure for suppressing the same, all Rebels and Insurgents, their aiders and abettors within the United States, and all persons discouraging volunteer enlistments, resisting militia drafts, or guilty of any disloyal practice, affording aid and comfort to Rebels against the authority of the United States, shall be subject to

> martial law and liable to trial and punishment by Courts Martial or Military Commission.[34]

Lincoln claimed that these restrictions on free speech were necessary to maintain the morale of the army. In 1863, he wrote,

> Long experience has shown that armies cannot be maintained unless desertion shall be punished by the severe penalty of death. The case requires, and the law and the constitution, sanction this punishment. Must I shoot a simple-minded soldier boy who deserts, while I must not touch a hair of a wily agitator who induces him to desert? This is none the less injurious when effected by getting a father, or brother, or friend, into a public meeting, and there working upon his feeling, till he is persuaded to write the soldier boy, that he is fighting in a bad cause, for a wicked administration of a contemptible government, too weak to arrest and punish him if he shall desert. I think that in such a case, to silence the agitator, and save the boy, is not only constitutional, but, withal, a great mercy.[35]

Lincoln sometimes rescinded censorship orders issued by subordinates or military officials when he concluded that suppression was impolitic. Lincoln never asserted that suppression was unconstitutional. A letter to one overeager general declared, "I regret to hear of the arrest of the Democrat editor. . . . Please spare me the trouble this is likely to bring."[36]

Both Democrats and Republicans sharply condemned administration efforts to restrict political dissent. A meeting of Albany Democrats resolved:

> It is the ancient and undoubted prerogative of this people to canvass public measures and merits of public men. It is a "homebred right," a fireside privilege. It had been enjoyed in every house, cottage, and cabin in the nation. It is as undoubted as the right of breathing air or walking on the earth.[37]

Many of Lincoln's otherwise strongest political supporters shared this commitment to protecting First Amendment rights in wartime. Senator Lyman Trumbull of Illinois told a Chicago crowd that Republicans

> have been the advocate of free speech for the last forty years, and should not allow the party which during the whole time has been using the gag to usurp our place. We are fighting for the restoration of the Union, and the preservation of the Constitution, and all the liberties it guarantees to every citizen.[38]

Free Speech during Reconstruction. The best-known controversy involving free speech rights during Reconstruction occurred when William McCardle, the editor of the *Vicksburg Times*, was arrested for writing an editorial that condemned northern generals as "infamous, cowardly, and abandoned villains" who should be "lodged in a penitariary." McCardle applied for a writ of habeas corpus, claiming that he could not be tried before a military commission. After a lower federal court denied him the writ, McCardle appealed to the Supreme Court of the United States. While the Court was considering his appeal, Congress passed a law stripping the justices of the necessary jurisdiction. The Supreme Court in *Ex parte McCardle* (1869) promptly ruled that the case be dismissed. What might have been an important case on both habeas corpus and free speech became an important case on federal jurisdiction.

The Trial of Clement Vallandigham (1863)[39]

Clement Vallandigham (1820–71) was a three-term member of the House of Representatives (1856–62) and the most prominent northern defender of secession. His speeches caustically denounced Lincoln, Lincoln's war policies, and all policies aimed at freeing slaves. On April 13, 1863, General Ambrose Burnside, the Union commander in the Ohio region, issued a general order decreeing that all persons "declaring sympathies for the enemy" be tried as "spies or traitors" by a military court. Undeterred, Vallandigham on May 1 gave a public speech that depicted the Civil War as "a war for the purpose of crushing out liberty and erecting a depotism" and "a war for the freedom of the blacks and the enslavement of the whites." Four days later Vallandigham was arrested. A military court found him guilty. Abraham Lincoln ordered that he be exiled to the Confederacy.

34. Lincoln, *Collected Works*, 5:437.
35. Ibid., 6:266–67.
36. Ibid., 6:326.
37. Curtis, *No State Shall Abridge*, 323.
38. Ibid., 329.
39. Excerpted from *The Trial of Hon. Clement Vallandigham* (Cincinnati, OH: Bickey and Carroll, 1863).

Vallandigham sought a writ of habeas corpus. His claim was rejected by the local circuit court of the United States, and in 1864 the Supreme Court claimed not have jurisdiction to hear an appeal from that decision. Vallandigham escaped to Canada. While he was abroad, Ohio Democrats nominated him to be the party candidate for governor.

The following excerpts are from Vallandigham's military trial and his habeas corpus appeal. Consider the following questions when reading these materials. Was Vallandigham arrested because his speech was disloyal, or because his speech had a tendency to depress northern morale? Suppose Vallandigham had claimed that many northern generals were incompetent (many were). Would he have been arrested? Does George Pugh's argument for Vallandigham accept any government power to restrict speech in wartime? Few people have heard of Pugh's constitutional defense of free speech. Is that obscurity best explained by Pugh's client or by the quality of Pugh's defense?

Application for Habeas Corpus: Statement of Major General Burnside

. . .

If I were to indulge in wholesale criticisms of the policy of the Government, it would demoralize the army under my command, and every friend of his country would call me a traitor. If the officers or soldiers were to indulge in such criticisms, it would weaken the army to the extent of their influence; and if this criticism were universal in the army, it would cause it to be broken to pieces, the Government to be divided, our homes to be invaded, and anarchy to reign. My duty to my Government forbids me to indulge in such criticisms; officers and soldiers are not allowed so to indulge, and this course will be sustained by all honest men.

. . . If it is my duty and the duty of the troops to avoid saying anything that would weaken the army, by preventing a single recruit from joining the ranks, by bringing the laws of Congress into disrepute, or by causing dissatisfaction in the ranks, it is equally the duty of every citizen in the Department to avoid the same evil. If it is my duty to prevent the propagation of this evil in the army, or in a portion of my Department, it is equally my duty in all portions of it; and it is my duty to use all the force in my power to stop it.

If I were to find a man from the enemy's country distributing in my camps speeches of their public men that tended to demoralize the troops or to destroy their confidence in the constituted authorities of the Government, I would have him tried, and hung if found guilty, and all the rules of modern warfare would sustain me. Why should such speeches from our own public men be allowed?

The press and public men, in a great emergency like the present, should avoid the use of party epithets and bitter invectives, and discourage the organization of secret political societies, which are always undignified and disgraceful to a free people, but now they are absolutely wrong and injurious; they create dissensions and discord, which just now amount to treason. The simple names "Patriot" and "Traitor" are comprehensive enough.

. . .

It is said that the speeches which are condemned have been made in the presence of large bodies of citizens, who, if they thought them wrong, would have then and there condemned them. That is no argument. These citizens do not realize the effect upon the army of our country, who are its defenders. They have never been in the field; never faced the enemies of their country; never undergone the privations of our soldiers in the field; and, besides, they have been in the habit of hearing their public men speak, and, as a general thing, of approving of what they say; therefore, the greater responsibility rests upon the public men and upon the public press, and it behooves them to be careful as to what they say. They must not use license and plead that they are exercising liberty. In this Department it cannot be done. I shall use all the power I have to break down such license, and I am sure I will be sustained in this course by all honest men. At all events, I will have the consciousness, before God, of having done my duty to my country, and when I am swerved from the performance of that duty by any pressure, public or private, or by any prejudice, I will no longer be a man or a patriot.

. . . If the people do not approve th[e] [policy of the Lincoln administration], they can change the constitutional authorities of that Government, at the proper time and by the proper method. Let them freely discuss the policy in a proper tone; but my duty requires me to stop license and intemperate discussion, which tends to weaken the authority of the Government and army: whilst the latter is in the presence of the enemy, it is cowardly so to weaken it. This license could not be used in our camps—the man would be torn in pieces who would attempt it. There is no fear of the people losing their liberties; we all know that to be the cry of demagogues, and none but the ignorant will listen to it; all intelligent men know that our people are too far advanced in the scale of religion, civilization, education, and freedom, to allow any power on earth to interfere with their liberties; but this same advancement in these great characteristics of our people teaches them to make all necessary sacrifices for their country when an emergency requires. They will support the constituted authorities of the Government, whether they agree with them or not. Indeed, the army itself is a part of the people, and is so thoroughly educated in the love of civil liberty, which is the best guarantee for the permanence of our republican institutions, that it would itself be the first to oppose any attempt to continue the exercise of military authority after the establishment of peace by the overthrow of the rebellion. No man on earth can lead our citizen soldiery to the establishment of a military despotism, and no man living would have the folly to attempt it. To do so would be to seal his own doom. On this point there can be no ground for apprehension on the part of the people. . . .

Opening Argument of the Honorable George E. Pugh

. . .

. . . [T]he right of the American people to deliberate upon and freely to speak of what General Burnside calls the "Policy of the Government" at all times—whether of peace or of war, of safety or of peril, of ease or of difficulty—is a right supreme, and absolute, and unquestionable. They can exhort each other to impeach the President or any executive officer; to impeach any magistrate of judicial authority; to condemn Congressmen and legislators of every description. They can, at pleasure, indulge in criticism, by "wholesale" or otherwise, not only upon "the policy" adopted or proposed by their servants, military as well as civil, but upon the conduct of those servants in each and every particular, upon their actions, their words, their probable motives, their public characters. And, in speaking of such subjects, any citizen addressing his fellow-citizens, by their consent, in a peaceable assembly, may use invective, or sarcasm, or ridicule, or passionate apostrophe or appeal, or—what is, ordinarily, much better—plain, solid, unostentatious argument. There is no style of rhetoric to be prescribed for the people. They are the masters of every style, and of every art and form of utterance. General Burnside suggests that "the press and public men, in a great emergency like the present, should avoid the use of party epithets and bitter invectives." I esteem that as excellent advice on all occasions; but, unfortunately, the General and I must both succumb, with what grace we can, to the choice or fancy of the people. They will render his advice or my advice effectual, if they approve it, by not reading such papers and not listening to such orators as habitually violate or trifle with decorum. There is no other way; there can be no censorship, civil or military, in this regard. That would inevitably, and at once, destroy the liberty of speech and of the press: that presupposes an incapacity of the people to distinguish right from wrong, truth from falsehood, reason from intemperance, or decency from outrage. And, if we cannot confide in the good sense of the people as to these things, how can we confide in them at all?

I know that much is written and spoken every day, and in the most public manner, at which honorable men feel indignant, or, at least, annoyed. But does it really affect the people at large? Does it alienate them from the Government under which they live? Does it induce them to think less dearly of their kinsmen, their friends, their neighbors, in military service; or to be unmindful of the toils of any soldier in camp, or on the march, or of his sufferings in the awful day of battle? Does it palsy the ministering hand? Does it prevent the sympathizing tear? . . . General Burnside errs, and errs greatly, in supposing that our people are often excited by some false or foul word; but, by and by, assertion meets contradiction, violence encounters violence; and so, at length, slowly perhaps, but certainly, will justice achieve her victory, and conclude the contest.

. . .

. . . [B]ut the effect on the soldiers. Well, sir, let us inquire into that. The soldiers have been citizens; they have been in the habit of attending public meetings, and of listening to public speakers. They are not children, but grown men—stalwart, sensible, and gallant men—with their hearts in the right place, and with arms ready to strike whenever and wherever the cause of their country demands. The General assures us of more, even, than this: "No man on earth," he says, "can lead our citizen-soldiery to the establishment of a military despotism." And are these the men to be discouraged, and, especially, to feel weary in heart or limb—unable to cope with an enemy in the field—because Mr. Vallandigham, or any other public speaker, may have said something, at Mount Vernon or elsewhere, with which they do not agree? The soldiers have not chosen me for their eulogist; but I will say, of my own accord, that they are no such tender plants as General Burnside imagines. They know, exactly, for what they went into the field; they are not alarmed, nor dissatisfied, nor discouraged, because their fellow citizens, at home, attend public meetings, and listen to public speeches, as heretofore; they have no serious misgiving as to the estimation in which they are holden by the people of the Northern and Northwestern States, without any distinction of sects, parties, or factions.

. . .

Mr. Vallandigham said, furthermore, as the Judge-Advocate assures us, "that, if the Administration had so wished, the war could have been honorably terminated months ago." That allegation may be true; I have no means, except from what is alleged subsequently, of deciding whether it be true or false. Nor do I find myself much enlightened by the next sentence imputed to Mr. Vallandigham: that "peace might have been honorably obtained by listening to the proposed intermediation of France." I do not know what terms, if any, the Emperor of the French suggested; but they would have to be very advantageous, as well as unmistakably honorable, before I would consent to his interference, or the interference of any other monarch, with the affairs of our distracted republic. And yet, if Mr. Vallandigham thinks otherwise, he has the same right to declare and to maintain his opinion as I have to maintain or to declare mine. But he made another accusation, and of much more serious importance: he said "that propositions by which the Southern States could be won back, and the South be guaranteed their rights under the Constitution, had been rejected, the day before the late battle at Fredericksburg, by Lincoln and his minions"—"meaning thereby," as the Judge-Advocate kindly informs us, "the President of the United States and those under him in authority." I never heard that it was actionable, at common law, to say of one man, orally, that he was the minion of another; and, far less, that it could be a matter of State prosecution. As to the rest, the accusation is one of fact—positive, distinct, with addition of time and circumstances. Is it true, or is it false? Sir, I do not know; but I do know that *that* is a vital question to the American people. Was it for making such an accusation that Mr. Vallandigham has been arrested; and is it by imprisoning him, or otherwise stopping his mouth, that Mr. Lincoln would answer to such an accusation in the face of his countrymen, of the civilized world, of the tribunal of God and of history? As to General Burnside, whose personal sincerity in these proceedings, as well as at the battle of Fredericksburg, I do not intend to question, what living man is more interested to have the truth, or the falsehood, of that accusation publicly ascertained?

. . .

These are obviously conclusions of the speaker—correctly or incorrectly drawn—from premises of which little, very little indeed, is narrated by the specification. I do not undertake to say, and I cannot say, at present, whether such conclusions are correct or incorrect; but what are they—and, in asking this question, I would lay my hand, if possible, upon the heart of every freeman—what are they but the impassioned appeals of a sincere, conscientious, honorable, and, if you please, over-vigilant citizen? Granted—if you will have it so—that he is in error, and greatly in error: I do not ask you to approve his conclusions, or in any manner to accept his opinions; but I do ask you, in all truthfulness, whether these words bear any taint of treason or disloyalty? They were intended, most evidently, to arouse the people to a sense of the vast peril in which all of us now stand; and, although they are startling, and seem very bitter, should we not err upon the side of jealousy rather than upon the side of laxity and too much confidence in our rulers, at a time when, month by month, day by day, the Union of our fathers, the Constitution by which that Union was ordained, and the Liberty of which the Constitution and the Union were intended as perpetual guarantees, are fading into a dim, a broken, and a most sorrowful vision?

. . .

Since, what time, I would inquire, has it become an offense of such magnitude for any citizen to propose the cessation of a war which he believes to be unnecessary and injudicious. . . .

B. Voting

Americans eliminated some restrictions on voting rights while imposing new qualifications. The Fifteenth Amendment forbade states from making racial discriminations when determining who was eligible to vote. During the Civil War soldiers were permitted to vote by absentee ballot. Republicans were unwilling to abolish other restrictions on voting. Congress during the debate over the Fifteenth Amendment rejected language that would forbid states from imposing property or literacy qualifications. National legislators also repeatedly rejected calls for constitutional amendments or federal laws granting women to the right to vote. The U.S. Supreme Court in *Minor v. Happersett* (1874) held that the post–Civil War Amendments did not give women the right to vote.

Republicans often demanded test oaths for voting. Many states passed legislation requiring potential voters to swear that they had never been disloyal to the Union. State courts divided on the constitutionality of these measures. Courts in West Virginia, Tennessee, Maryland, and Missouri sustained those test oaths, with the Supreme Court of West Virginia in *Randolph v. Good* (WV 1869) bluntly declaring, "The legislature had the constitutional power to exclude the enemies of the State from the polls, and to continue them so excluded as long as it might be necessary to the public."[40] Courts in Arkansas, Nevada, and New York declared test oaths for voters unconstitutional. The Supreme Court of Arkansas in *Rison v. Farr* (AK 1865) held, "The right of suffrage in this state, if not an inherent, is at least a constitutional right, and whoever possesses the required qualification, cannot be restrained from the exercise of that right except by the alteration of the constitution, and any law infringing upon that right as vested by the constitution is null and void."[41] The Supreme Court of the United States divided 4-4 when adjudicating an appeal from the Missouri case sustaining the state test oath.

Congress in 1865 imposed test oaths for both representatives and senators. That qualification prevented persons who had been elected by the former slave states to office in the Confederacy from becoming representatives or senators. Democrats and more conservative Republicans condemned this use of the test oath. A House committee in 1866 issued a report urging that the test oath be maintained. Nevertheless, the test oath was modified in 1868 and 1871 before being abandoned in 1884.

40. *Randolph v. Good*, 3 W. Va. 551 (1869).

41. *Rison v. Farr*, 24 Ark. 161 (1865).

Congress Debates the Ironclad Oath (1866)[42]

Republicans insisted that all members of Congress swear that they had always been loyal to the Union. The Ironclad Test Oath of 1862 required persons to declare

> *I, A.B., do solemnly swear (or affirm) that I have never voluntarily borne arms against the United States since I have been a citizen thereof; that I have voluntarily given no aid, countenance, counsel or encouragement to persons engaged in armed hostilities thereto; that I have neither sought nor accepted nor attempted to exercise the functions of any office whatever under any authority or pretended authority hostile to the United States; that I have not yielded a voluntary support to any pretended government, authority, power or constitution within the United States, hostile or inimical thereto. And I do further swear (or affirm) that, to the best of my knowledge and ability, I will support and defend the Constitution of the United States, against all enemies, foreign and domestic. . . .*[43]

Controversy broke out when the 38th Congress was seated in December 1863. Senator James Bayard of Delaware refused to take the oath. The Senate, by a 28-11 vote, refused to budge. Bayard took the oath and then resigned his seat.

The conflict over the test oath intensified when the 39th Congress met in December 1865. Buoyed by President Andrew Johnson's modest Reconstruction goals, many former slave states elected former Confederate officeholders to the House and Senate. Republicans in Congress refused to seat them. Taking advantage of several procedural rules, the Republican majority in the House examined the past record of persons elected to Congress and determined who could take the oath in good faith. With rare exceptions, all persons elected from the former slave states were excluded.

The ironclad test oath remained controversial during Reconstruction. Johnson administration officials insisted that most southerners be asked to swear only to their future allegiance. This mild oath was necessary, in their view, for the federal government to operate in the South.

42. Excerpted from House Committee on the Judiciary, *Report on Modification of the Oath of Office*, 39th Cong., 1st Sess. (1866), H.R. Doc. No. 51. The introduction to this excerpt relies extensively on Harold Melvin Hyman, *Era of the Oath: Northern Loyalty Tests during the Civil War and Reconstruction* (Philadelphia: University of Pennsylvania Press, 1954).

43. 12 U.S. Stat. 502, 502-03 (1862).

Treasury Secretary Hugh McCulloch asserted, "It is impossible to procure the services of competent revenue officers to assess and collect taxes who can take the test oath." Republicans in Congress insisted that Reconstruction required a complete transformation of the southern political elite. Senator Charles Sumner of Massachusetts responded to McCulloch's practice by declaring, "The Administration, in defiance of Congress, is determined to employ rebels in reconstruction."[44]

Prodded by the Johnson administration, the House Judiciary Committee considered whether the test oath should be modified. On April 23 the committee counseled against modification by a 2-1 vote. Those test oath laws that survived judicial scrutiny were not officially repealed until 1884.

The materials below are from the 1865 House reports on the test oaths. What are the most important constitutional and political arguments for requiring government officials to swear that they have always been loyal to the Union? What are the most important constitutional and political arguments to the contrary? Suppose that Mississippi had elected Jefferson Davis to the Senate. Should he have been seated?

REPRESENTATIVE JAMES F. WILSON (Republican, Iowa)

. . .

The act prescribing this oath of office was passed when the nation was in the midst of a gigantic war, waged against it by its own citizens, and Congress intended to establish by it a permanent rule of public policy, which should exclude from the offices of the United States every citizen who had voluntarily abandoned his allegiance to the government, and joined in the mad attempt of traitors to destroy it. The official positions which many of the leading traitors held under the government while engaged in organizing the rebellion, were sources of power without which the war could not have been commenced. Those positions gave the conspirators a resistless influence over the people of the southern States, and supplied the means for organizing forces that converted one-half of the republic into battle-fields, on which loyalty and treason contended for four years. If every officer of the government had proved true to his trust the rebellion could not have occurred. . . .

. . .

44. Hyman, *Era of the Oath*, 55, 54.

. . . The treachery of 1861 may be repeated if those who participated in it should again be intrusted with power. Conspirators might profit by the experience of the past, and make future treason more successful than that which, overwhelming with disaster, now lies at our feet. Failure often begets wisdom. It is not uncommon for disaster to give birth to success. Give to the enemies of this republic another opportunity to wield the official power which they possessed in the past, and success in some form may come to and abide with them.

The committee understand that it is the deliberate purpose of Congress to maintain the policy of the act of July 2, 1862, which is to keep the offices of the government in the hands of loyal men. Treason is not to be made respectable by the robes of office. Places of honor, trust, power, and profit, should be bestowed on the loyal only. True men can be found in the insurrectionary States to fill all such places, and none other should be selected. . . .

. . .

. . . [T]he committee is of opinion that one of the most effective means of making treason odious is to close all official doors against traitors; fill the offices of the government with loyal men; put no traitors on guard. This, in the judgment of the committee, will surely make treason odious, and tend to produce harmony of action between the legislative and executive branches of the government.

. . .

There are thousands of loyal men in the southern States who can take the test oath, and to such should the offices in those States be given. Let the government recognize their claims in this regard, and loyalty and respect for the laws of the United States will soon be strong enough to overcome the social power which now frowns upon every Union man who stood by the flag of the republic throughout the whole course of the war.

Temporary inconveniences should not turn the government aside from this policy. The unhappy condition of the southern States cannot be improved by changing laws which may be opposed to the views and feelings of those citizens who fought for four years to destroy the government. They must learn that obedience to law is a duty not to be lightly regarded; and that loyalty to the government is a virtue which cannot be destroyed by the social power of the disloyal. When these ends are secured, it may be expedient to modify the test oath, but not until then.

REPRESENTATIVE ANDREW J. ROGERS (Democrat, New Jersey)

. . .

. . . It is but a small asking, simply to urge the modification of an oath unknown to the Constitution and established in time of war for the purposes of war and I am a little surprised that they did not recommend its entire repeal. The war is ended, and peace has been proclaimed.

The only question that ought to be raised is, are they loyal men, and if they can take the oath to support the Constitution. That is all that ought or really can be required of them. . . .

. . . Let us bury passion, hate, and revenge in the deep ocean of oblivion, and rise to the true standard of our country, forgiving our southern brethren, as we would that they, in like circumstances, should forgive us. . . .

. . .

This test oath must, at some time, and that is not far distant, be repealed. It cannot remain always, unless it is the determination of the people to deprive the present generation in the south from a voice in the affairs of the nation. This cannot be and this country remain a republic. The people of the south are ready and anxious to participate in the affairs of the government, and defend and support the Constitution of their country. The worst despotisms of the Old World have been established through the forms of test oaths; and to exclude seven millions of people from participating in federal affairs by the taking of an oath unknown to the Constitution, a condition precedent and one which they cannot take without false swearing, is despotism pure and simple. The Constitution provides in article six that executive and judicial officers of the United States shall be bound by oath to support it. This is the only oath that can be legally required of the persons who are to execute the offices of the Treasury and Post Office Departments, for they are clearly executive officers of the United States, within the meaning of the Constitution.

. . .

The masses of the people in the south had no hand in originating the rebellion and it was simply the result of the action of certain leading secessionists of the south and certain radicals and fanatics in the north. It is, therefore, uncharitable, anti-Christian, and unfair to visit punishment upon a whole people because of the sins of a few. . . .

C. Citizenship

The Fourteenth Amendment provides standards for determining federal citizenship. The first sentence declares, "All persons born or naturalized in the United States and subject to the jurisdiction thereof, are citizens of the United States." This clause overruled *Dred Scott v. Sandford* (1857), which held that free persons of color were not citizens of the United States. *Dred Scott* was politically abandoned before being constitutionally discarded. Attorney General Edward Bates in 1862 declared that the Lincoln administration was treating free blacks as American citizens. Republicans made that position the official law of the land when framing and ratifying the Fourteenth Amendment.

The Supreme Court limited the privileges and immunities of U.S. citizenship under the Fourteenth Amendment to those privileges and immunities that citizens of the United States enjoyed before the Fourteenth Amendment was ratified. In the *Slaughter-House Cases* (1873), Justice Miller's majority opinion emphatically rejected the proposition that "the purpose of the fourteenth amendment, by the simple declaration that no State should make or enforce any law which shall abridge the privileges and immunities of citizens of the United States," was "to transfer the security and protection of all the civil rights which we have mentioned, from the States to the Federal government." A Supreme Court decision to the contrary, he declared, would "radically change . . . the whole theory of the relations of the State and Federal governments to each other and of both these governments to the people." Four justices thought that citizenship bore far more privileges. Justice Field's dissent maintained, "The privileges and immunities designated are those which of right belong to the citizens of all free governments. Clearly among these must be placed the right to pursue a lawful employment in a lawful manner, without other restraint than such as equally affects all persons." The justices were more united the next year when rejecting claims that the privileges and immunities clause gave female citizens the right to vote. In *Minor v. Happersett* (1874), Chief Justice Waite ruled that voting was not a privilege or immunity of any citizen.

V. Equality

MAJOR DEVELOPMENTS

- Continued animus against class legislation
- Persons of color declared equal before the law
- Congress debates what legislation enforces the constitutional rights of persons of color
- Federal officials reject claims that new constitutional amendments give women the right to vote

Americans from 1861 to 1876 transformed some inherited understandings of constitutional equality while preserving others. The Fourteenth Amendment made explicit that all persons had a *federal* constitutional right to equality under the law. Section 1 declared, "No state . . . shall deny to any person within its jurisdiction the equal protection of the law." Section 5 gave Congress the power to enforce that guarantee. While the Fourteenth Amendment did not explicitly mention race, Americans understood that some previously accepted racial discriminations were now unconstitutional. Nevertheless, most constitutional authorities did not believe that they were making fundamental changes to longstanding constitutional practices. Legislatures could make distinctions when "real differences" existed between different persons. Gender discriminations survived intact, as did the constitutional status of Native Americans. Many Americans believed that some racial distinctions remained constitutional after the Fourteenth Amendment was ratified.

Justice Samuel Miller's influential opinion in the *Slaughter-House Cases* (1873) cabined the revolutionary possibility of the post–Civil War Amendments. Miller maintained that the new Constitution sharply limited state power to make racial discriminations. He wrote, "It is true that only the fifteenth amendment, in terms, mentions the negro by speaking of his color and his slavery. But it is just as true that each of the other articles was addressed to the grievances of that race, and designed to remedy them." Nevertheless, although Miller recognized that the Fourteenth Amendment states that government may not deny equal protection to "any person," he confined equality rights to persons of color, declaring, "We doubt very much whether any action of a State not directed by way of discrimination against the negroes as a class, or on account of their race, will ever be held to come within the purview of this provision." More subtly, by narrowly interpreting the rights protected by the privileges and immunities clause of the Fourteenth Amendment, Miller sharply limited judicial capacity to protect persons of color.

When reading the materials in this section, compare Jacksonian understandings of equality to the dominant strands of egalitarian thinking during the Civil War and Reconstruction. To what extent did Reconstruction Republicans ensure that persons of color enjoyed the same equality rights that Jacksonians limited to white people? Did the effort to extend equality rights to persons of color necessarily transform broader constitutional conceptions of equality? To what extent, as a matter of constitutional law or constitutional politics, did the effort to extend greater equality rights to persons of color make efforts to prevent other Americans from securing greater equality rights more difficult? To what extent did the effort to cabin equality rights to persons of color narrow the actual equality rights enjoyed by persons of color?

A. Equality Under Law

Republicans deliberately drafted constitutional provisions that spoke of general rights to equality rather than a specific right against racial discrimination. During the debates over the Fourteenth Amendment, congressmen rejected proposed versions that forbade "discrimination . . . as to the civil rights of persons because of race, color, or previous condition of servitude" in favor of language forbidding states to "deny to any person . . . the equal protection of the laws." Republicans favored the broader language partly because they were committed to a broader principle of equality. Senator Charles Sumner of Massachusetts insisted, "Equality [is] the master principle of our system, and the very frontispiece of our constitution."[45] Republicans were also concerned with the equality rights of specific white persons. Southern states before the Civil War repressed anti-slavery advocacy, and many southern Unionists feared reprisals from former Confederates. Union military commanders warned Congress that southern Republicans of all races were not "secure in the enjoyment of their rights . . . and could not rely upon the State Courts for justice."[46]

45. Charles Sumner, *The Works of Charles Sumner*, vol. IX (Boston: Lee and Shepard, 1875), 477.

46. William E. Nelson, *The Fourteenth Amendment: From Political Principle to Judicial Doctrine* (Cambridge, MA: Harvard University Press, 1988), 42.

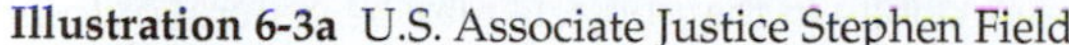

Illustration 6-3a U.S. Associate Justice Stephen Field

Illustration 6-3b Michigan Chief Justice Thomas Cooley

Stephen Field (6-3a) and Thomas M. Cooley (6-3b) were among the most influential jurists in post-Civil War America. Ironically, neither was partisan Republican. Stephen Field of California was an anti-slavery Democrat and Abraham Lincoln's only Democratic appointee to the U.S. Supreme Court. Thomas Cooley had been a Democrat in Michigan before joining the Free Soil movement but became a more independent "Liberal Republican" during Reconstruction. From his dissent in the *Slaughter-House Cases* (1873) through his concurrence in the *Income Tax Cases* (1895), Field vigorously defended property rights. Thomas Cooley had a more varied career, serving as chief justice of the Michigan Supreme Court, founding commissioner of the Interstate Commerce Commission, and professor at the University of Michigan law school, where he became a leading treatise writer. His views on the limited powers of the state and the expansive rights of individuals were highly influential with judges and lawyers across the country.

Sources: Library of Congress, Prints and Photographs Division, Washington, DC 20540, USA; Bentley Image Bank, Bentley Historical Library.

Constitutional amendments couched in general language promised to secure the rights of white southern Unionists as well as free blacks.

State constitutional decision makers insisted that state laws respect egalitarian principles. All legislative distinctions had to be based on real differences and serve the public good. Treatise writers and state court justices railed against class legislation. Citing John Locke's "On Civil Government" Thomas Cooley asserted, "Those who make the laws are to govern by promulgated, established laws, not to be varied in particular cases, but to have one rule for rich and poor, for the favorite at court and the countryman at plough." The Supreme Court of Maine in *In re Opinion of the Justices* (ME 1871) declared,

> There is nothing of a public nature any more entitling the manufacturer to public gifts than the sailor, the mechanic, the lumberman, or the farmer. Our government is based on the equality of rights. . . . The State cannot rightfully discriminate among occupations, for a discrimination in favor of one branch of industry is a discrimination adverse to all other branches. The State is equally to protect all,

giving no undue advantages or special and exclusive preferences to any.[47]

Justice William Barrows further spoke of "the cardinal principle that the State shall give all alike the benefit of equal laws without favoritism or partiality."[48]

Thomas Cooley, A Treatise of the Constitutional Limitations which Rest upon the Legislative Power of the States of the American Union (1868)[49]

Thomas McIntyre Cooley (1824-1898) was the chief justice of the Michigan Supreme Court, a professor of law at the University of Michigan School of Law, the first chairperson of the Interstate Commerce Commission, and the leading legal treatise writer of the post–Civil War period. His most important work, Constitutional Limitations, *was "written in full sympathy with all those restraints which the caution of the fathers has imposed upon the exercise of the powers of government" and is the most cited constitutional treatise of the era. Courts after the Civil War quoted extensively from Cooley when adjudicating various state constitutional questions, from the power of municipal corporations to the constitutional meaning of free speech.*

Cooley's analysis of "unequal and partial legislation" was particularly influential. The first edition of Constitutional Limitations *was published in 1868, the year the Fourteenth Amendment was ratified. In this work, Cooley emphasized equality as a master principle of American constitutional law. His treatise focused as much on general constitutional commitments as on specific constitutional provisions. Cooley and other constitutional commentators insisted that partial legislation was unconstitutional. On what basis does Cooley make that constitutional claim? How does he determine the constitutional status of special legislation? Notice how little attention Cooley paid to the equal protection rights of persons of color. Does he believe that the equal protection clause has any impact on free state policies?*

Judge Cooley practiced what Professor Cooley preached. In People ex rel. Detroit & H.R. Co. v. Salem Township Bd. *(MI 1870), the Supreme Court of Michigan considered whether a local town could constitutionally assist railroads. Cooley wrote the opinion declaring the measure to be unconstitutional class legislation. He stated,*

> *The discrimination by the State between different classes of occupations, and the favoring of one at the expense of the rest, whether that one be farming or banking, merchandising or milling, printing or railroading, is not legitimate legislation, and is an invasion of that equality of right and privilege which is a maxim in State government. . . . [I]t is not the business of the State to make discriminations in favor of one class against another, or in favor of one employment against another. The State can have no favorites. Its business is to protect the industry of all, and to give all the benefit of equal laws. It cannot compel an unwilling minority to submit to taxation in order that it may keep upon its feet any business that cannot stand alone.*[50]

Unequal and Partial Legislation.

. . .

Laws public in their objects may be general or local in their application; they may embrace many subjects or one, and they may extend to all the citizens or be confined to particular classes, as minors, or married women, bankers or traders, and the like. The power that legislates for the State at large must determine whether particular rules shall extend to the whole State and all its citizens, or to a part of the State or a class of its citizens only. The circumstances of a particular locality, or the prevailing public opinion in that section of the State, may require or make acceptable different police regulations from those demanded in another, or call for different taxation, and a different application of the public moneys. The legislature may, therefore, prescribe or authorize different laws of police, allow the right of eminent domain to be exercised in different cases and through different modes, and prescribe peculiar restrictions upon taxation in each distinct municipality, provided the State constitution does not forbid. This is done constantly, and the fact that the laws are local in their operation is not supposed to render them objectionable in principle. The legislature may also deem it desirable to establish peculiar

47. *In re Opinion of the Justices*, 58 Me. 590, (1871).

48. Ibid., 609.

49. Excerpted from Thomas M. Cooley, *A Treatise on the Constitutional Limitations which Rest upon the Legislation Power of the States of the American Union* (Boston: Little, Brown, and Company, 1874), 389–96.

50. *People ex rel. Detroit & H. R. Co. v. Salem Township Bd.*, 20 Mich. 452 (1870).

rules for the several occupations, and distinctions in the rights, obligations, and legal capacities of different classes of citizens. The business of common carriers, for instance, or of bankers, may require special statutory regulations for the general benefit, and it may be desirable to give one class of laborers a special lien for their wages, while it would be impracticable or impolitic to do the same by persons engaged in some other employments. If otherwise unobjectionable, all that can be required in these cases is, that they be general in their application to the class or the locality to which they apply, and they are then *general laws* in the constitutional sense.

But a statute would not be constitutional which should proscribe a class or a party for opinion's sake, or which should select particular individuals from a class or locality, and subject them to peculiar rules, or impose upon them special obligations or burdens, from which others in the same locality or class are exempt.

The legislature may suspend the operation of the general laws of the State; but when it does so, the suspension must be general, and cannot be made in individual cases, or for particular localities. Privileges may be granted to individuals, when by so doing the rights of other persons are not injuriously affected; disabilities may be removed; the legislature as *parens patrim* may grant authority to the guardians of incompetent persons to exercise a statutory authority over their estate for their assistance, comfort, or support, and for the discharge of legal or equitable liens upon it; but every one has a right to demand that he be governed by general rules, and a special statute that singles his case out as one to be regulated by a different law from that which is applied in all similar cases would not be legitimate legislation, but an arbitrary mandate, unrecognized in free government. Mr. Locke has said of those who make the laws: "They are to govern by promulgated, established laws, not to be varied in particular cases, but to have one rule for rich and poor, for the favorite at court and the countryman at plough"; and this may be justly said to have become a maxim in the law, by which may be tested the authority and binding force of legislative enactments.

Special courts could not be created for the trial of the rights and obligations of particular individuals; and those cases in which legislative acts granting new trials or other special relief in judicial proceedings, while they have been regarded as usurpations of judicial authority, have also been considered obnoxious to the objection that they undertook to suspend general laws in special cases. The doubt might also arise whether a regulation made for any one class of citizens, entirely arbitrary in its character, and restricting their rights, privileges, or legal capacities in a manner before unknown to the law, could be sustained, notwithstanding its generality. Distinctions in these respects should be based upon some reason which renders them important,—like the want of capacity in infants, and insane persons; but if the legislature should undertake to provide that persons following some specified lawful trade or employment should not have capacity to make contracts, or to receive conveyances, or to build such houses as others were allowed to erect, or in any other way to make such use of their property as was permissible to others, it can scarcely be doubted that the act would transcend the due bounds of legislative power, even if it did not come in conflict with express constitutional provisions. The man or the class forbidden the acquisition or enjoyment of property in the manner permitted to the community at large would be deprived of *liberty* in particulars of primary importance to his or their "pursuit of happiness."

Equality of rights, privileges, and capacities unquestionably should be the aim of the law; and if special privileges are granted, or special burdens or restrictions imposed in any case, it must be presumed that the legislature designed to depart as little as possible from this fundamental maxim of government. The State, it is to be presumed, has no favors to bestow, and designs to inflict no arbitrary deprivation of rights. Special privileges are obnoxious, and discriminations against persons or classes are still more so, and as a rule of construction are always to be leaned against as probably not contemplated or designed. It has been held that a statute requiring attorneys to render services in suits for poor persons without fee or reward was to be confined strictly to the cases therein prescribed; and if by its terms it expressly covered civil cases only, it could not be extended to embrace defences of criminal prosecutions. So where a constitutional provision confined the elective franchise to "*white* male citizens," and it appeared that the legislation of the State had always treated of negroes, mulattoes, and *other colored persons*, in contradistinction to white, it was held that although quadroons, being a recognized class of colored persons, must be excluded, yet that the rule of exclusion would not be carried further. . . .

There are unquestionably cases in which the State may grant privileges to specified individuals without violating any constitutional principle, because, from the nature of the case, it is impossible they should be possessed and enjoyed by all; and if it is important that they should exist, the proper State authority must be left to select the grantees. Of this class are grants of the franchise to be a corporation. Such grants, however, which confer upon a few persons what cannot be shared by the many, and which, though supposed to be made on public grounds, are nevertheless frequently of great value to the corporators and therefore sought with avidity, are never to be extended by construction beyond the plain terms in which they are conferred. No rule is better settled than that charters of incorporation are to be construed strictly against the corporators. . . .

. . .

[*The 3rd edition of* Constitutional Limitations, *published in 1874, added the following commentary on the equal protection clause to this section.*[51]]

. . . It was not within the power of the States before the adoption of the fourteenth amendment, to deprive citizens of the equal protection of the laws; but there were servile classes not thus shielded, and when these were made freemen, there were some who disputed their claim to citizenship, and some State laws were in force which established discriminations against them. To settle doubts and preclude all such laws, the fourteenth amendment was adopted; and the same securities which one citizen may demand, all others are now entitled to.

B. Race

The Civil War witnessed an unprecedented surge in the American constitutional commitment to racial equality. Slavery and white supremacy were central to the Jacksonian constitutional order and the early Civil War regime. Congress in 1861 proposed an amendment that forbade the federal government from emancipating slaves. Federal troops in 1863 were called into New York City to quell a riot by angry white citizens who did not want to fight in a war that they perceived as a fight for African-American rights. Constitutional commitments changed dramatically during and immediately after the Lincoln presidency. At the end of the Civil War Americans passed a constitutional amendment abolishing slavery. Within three years they ratified a constitutional amendment guaranteeing freed slaves "the equal protection of the laws." In 1872 Americans ratified the Fifteenth Amendment, which forbade states from making racial discriminations in voting laws.

Federal and state laws passed during the Civil War expressed broad commitments to this new racial egalitarianism. Congress in 1862 prohibited slavery in the territories, abolished slavery in the District of Columbia, and authorized the president to draft African-Americans. Two years later Congress mandated that black troops be paid the same wages as white troops. Many state legislatures in the free states revised legislative codes in response to reports of African-American heroism on the battlefield. Common legal discriminations against persons of color were repealed. During Reconstruction several northern courts declared that segregated schools violated the state constitution.

Republicans abandoned the Jacksonian racial regime in three stages. In the first stage, federal officials were content to ignore the Supreme Court's decision in *Dred Scott v. Sandford* (1857). Congress prohibited slavery in the territories and the Lincoln administration publicly announced that free blacks were American citizens. In the second stage, Lincoln declared all slaves in territories still controlled by the Confederacy to be free. The Emancipation Proclamation was based on presidential war powers. Lincoln made no reference to property rights, even though opponents insisted that emancipation violated the due process clause of the Fifth Amendment. In the third phase, the Thirteenth, Fourteenth, and Fifteenth Amendments were passed, as were federal laws implementing those provisions. These amendments and statutes made any return to the racial politics of the Jacksonian Era impossible.

The racial practices that Americans abandoned were far clearer than the racial practices they adopted. General agreement existed that the post–Civil War Constitution prohibited slavery and made persons of color American citizens. Controversies quickly developed, however, over what the abolition of slavery and equal citizenship meant in constitutional practice. One view, championed in such cases as *In re Turner* (1867) and by such congressional radicals as Charles Sumner, maintained that the new racial regime required both courts and elected officials to guarantee persons of color a wide array of political, economic, and civil rights. In another view, championed by President Andrew Johnson and most northern Democrats, the abolition of slavery

51. Thomas M. Cooley, *A Treatise on the Constitutional Limitations which Rest upon the Legislative Power of the States of the American Union*, 3rd ed. (Boston: Little, Brown, and Company, 1874), 466.

meant that persons of color were free to forge their own lives under whatever laws and discriminations localities believed promoted the public welfare. The Supreme Court, in such cases as *United States v. Cruikshank* (1876), articulated a constitutional vision closer to—although not identical with—the northern Democratic interpretation of the post–Civil War Amendments.

The Civil War and Reconstruction left a legal and political legacy. The legal legacy was egalitarian. When President Rutherford B. Hayes took his oaths of office in 1877, persons of color were protected by the Thirteenth, Fourteenth, and Fifteenth Amendments, as well as by numerous federal statutes, most notably the Civil Rights Act of 1866, the Enforcement Act of 1871, and the Civil Rights Act of 1875. The political legacy was less egalitarian. The American constitutional experience during Reconstruction suggested that racial equality could be promoted only by a president, a Congress, and a federal judiciary united by a strong commitment to racial equality. Whether persons of color could realize equal citizenship in the absence of this strong political consensus seemed an increasingly dubious proposition by the end of Reconstruction.

Implementing the Thirteenth Amendment

Immediately after the Civil War, Republicans in Congress sought to exercise federal power aggressively under Section 2 of the Thirteenth Amendment. That provision empowered the national legislature "to enforce" the constitutional prohibition on slavery "by appropriate legislation." Legislation was particularly necessary, Republicans believed, after southern states in the wake of the Civil War passed a series of Black Codes that sharply restricted the rights of former slaves and other persons of color. These codes limited the ability of former slaves to sell their labor, acquire property, testify in court, own weapons, and participate in political life. The Mississippi Black Code required persons of color to obtain written documentation of housing and employment. State law declared, "Every freedman, free Negro, and mulatto shall, on the second Monday of January 1866, and annually thereafter, have a lawful home or employment, and shall have a written evidence thereof." Many Black Codes imposed severe sentences for persons of color convicted of crimes.

Led by Lyman Trumbull (1813–96), the chair of the Senate Judiciary Committee, Republicans in Congress championed two bills designed to eradicate the badges and incidents of slavery in the south. The Freedman's Bureau Act of 1866 authorized federal agents to provide freedman with land, homes, jobs, and an education. The Civil Rights Act of 1866 declared that persons of color were citizens of the United States and prohibited states from passing contract, property, and criminal laws that discriminated on the basis of race. Both measures passed Congress only to be vetoed by President Andrew Johnson. Congress initially failed to override Johnson's veto of the Freedmen's Bureau Act, but did immediately override his veto of the Civil Rights Act. In the fall of 1866 Congress passed a revised version of the Freedmen's Bureau Act over another veto from President Johnson.

The participants in the debate over the Freedman's Bureau Act and the Civil Rights Act of 1866 disputed the constitutional meaning of emancipation. Republicans identified slavery with numerous legal deprivations that required positive federal legislation to cure. Senator Trumbull declared,

> Those laws that prevented the colored man going from home, that did not allow him to buy or to sell, or to make contracts; that did not allow him to own property; that did not allow him to enforce rights; that did not allow him to be educated, were all badges of servitude made in the interest of slavery and as a part of slavery. They never would have been thought of or enacted anywhere but for slavery, and when slavery falls they fall also. The policy of the States where slavery has existed has been to legislate in its interest; and out of deference to slavery, which was tolerated by the Constitution of the United States, even some of the non-slaveholding States passed laws abridging the rights of the colored man which were restraints upon liberty. When slavery goes, all this system of legislation, devised in the interests of slavery and for the purpose of degrading the colored race, of keeping the negro in ignorance, of blotting out from his very soul the light of reason, if that were possible, that he might not think, but know only, like the ox, to labor, go with it.[52]

Radical Republicans insisted that the Thirteenth Amendment authorized Congress to grant voting rights to persons of color. Charles Sumner asserted,

52. Alfred Avins, ed., *The Reconstruction Amendments Debate* (Richmond: Virginia Commission on Constitutional Government, 1967), 108.

> The ballot is protector. Perhaps, at the present moment, this is its highest function. Slavery has ceased in name; but this is all. The old master still asserts an inhuman power, and now by positive statutes seeks to bind his victim in new chains. . . . To save the freedman from this tyranny, with all its accumulated outrage, is a solemn duty. For this we are now devising guaranties; but, believe me, the only sufficient guaranty is the ballot. Let the freedman vote, and he will have in himself under the law a constant, ever-present, self-protecting power. The armor of citizenship will be his best security. The ballot will be to him sword and buckler,—sword with which to pierce his enemies, and buckler on which to receive their assault. Its possession will be a terror and a defense. The law, which is the highest reason, boasts that every man's house is his castle; but the freedman can have no castle without the ballot. When the master knows that he may be voted down, he will know that he must be just, and everything is contained in justice. . . . To him who has the ballot all other things shall be given,—protection, opportunity, education, a homestead.[53]

Democrats championed a far narrower construction of slavery and the Thirteenth Amendment. Senator Thomas Hendricks of Indiana asked,

> What is slavery? It is not a relation between the slave and the State; it is not a public relation; it is a relation between two persons whereby the conduct of the one is placed under the will of the other. It is purely and entirely a domestic relation, and is so classed by all law writers; the law regulates that relation as it regulates other domestic relations. This constitutional amendment broke asunder this private relation between the master and his slave, and the slave then, so far as the right of the master was concerned, became free; but did the slave, under that amendment, acquire any other right than to be free from the control of his master?[54]

The materials below also highlight disputes among Republicans over the best means for promoting racial equality. Moderate Republicans insisted that strong prohibitions on discrimination in property, contract, and criminal law were constitutionally sufficient. Some radicals, led by Representative Thaddeus Stevens of Pennsylvania, insisted that economic equality was a prerequisite to all other equalities. Stevens famously proposed laws that would require the federal government to confiscate the plantations of former slaveholders and provide all families of freedmen with forty acres. In a speech championing that bill, Stevens declared,

> Nothing is so likely to make a man a good citizen as to make him a freeholder. Nothing will so multiply the productions of the South as to divide [plantations] into small farms. Nothing will make men so industrious and moral as to let them feel that they are above want and are the owners of the soil which they till.[55]

Other radicals insisted that Congress first enfranchise persons of color. Representative James Ashley of Ohio declared, "If I were a black man, with the chains just stricken from my limbs . . . and you should offer me the ballot, or a cabin and forty acres of cotton land, I would take the ballot."[56] Suppose you were forced in 1866 to make the tragic choice between granting persons of color anti-discrimination rights, economic rights, or political rights. Which rights would be your highest priority?

Congressional Debates over the Second Freedmen's Bureau Act (1866)

The Second Freedmen's Bureau Act was a Republican effort to extend the life and expand the duties of the Freedmen's Bureau established by law in March 1865. Republicans hoped to provide persons of color with the economic and educational opportunities they thought necessary for equal citizenship. The constitutional debate over the measure was partisan. Republicans insisted that the Second Freedmen's Bureau Act was a legitimate exercise of both the war power and Section 2 of the Thirteenth Amendment. Democrats rejected both claims. President Andrew Johnson and other Democrats further insisted that the provisions in the bill authorizing the federal government to obtain land and use military commissions violated the due process clause of the Fifth Amendment and the right to a jury trial guaranteed

53. Ibid., 213.
54. Ibid., 107.
55. *Congressional Globe*, 40th Cong., 1st Sess. (1867), 205.
56. Eric Foner, *Reconstruction: America's Unfinished Revolution, 1863–1877* (New York: Harper & Row, 1988), 236.

by the Sixth Amendment. The Second Freedman's bill easily passed both houses of Congress but was vetoed by President Johnson on February 19, 1866. Congress failed to override that veto. Within six months Republicans passed a slightly revised version of the Second Freedmen's Bureau Act and successfully overrode President Johnson's veto.

The following excerpts focus on congressional power under Section 2 of the Thirteenth Amendment. Note that the Freedmen's Bureau Act refers to "refugees and freedmen." Eric Schnapper, a prominent contemporary proponent of affirmative action, maintains that these references demonstrate that Reconstruction Republicans approved those racial classifications that they believed promoted racial equality. He writes,

> *From the closing days of the Civil War until the end of civilian Reconstruction some five years later, Congress adopted a series of social welfare programs whose benefits were expressly limited to blacks. These programs were generally open to all blacks, not only to recently freed slaves, and were adopted over repeatedly expressed objections that such racially exclusive measures were unfair to whites. The race-conscious Reconstruction programs were enacted concurrently with the fourteenth amendment and were supported by the same legislators who favored the constitutional guarantee of equal protection. This history strongly suggests that the framers of the amendment could not have intended it generally to prohibit affirmative action for blacks or other disadvantaged groups.*[57]

Schnapper correctly claims that opponents of the Freedmen's Bureau bill repeatedly condemned that proposal for unconstitutionally giving special treatment to persons of color. Does he also correctly characterize proponents of the measure as championing race-conscious measures? Does the text of the Freedmen's Act rely on racial classifications? To what extent does Senator Trumbull interpret the bill as providing benefits to all persons of color, as opposed to all former slaves?

The Proposed Second Freedmen's Bill[58]

. . .

Sec. 3. *And be it further enacted,* That the Secretary of War may direct such issues of provisions, clothing, fuel, and other supplies, including medical stores and transportation, and afford such aid, medical or otherwise, as he may deem needful for the immediate and temporary shelter and supply of destitute and suffering refugees and freedmen, their wives and children, under such rules and regulations as he may direct: *Provided,* That no person shall be deemed "destitute," "suffering," or "dependent upon the government for support," within the meaning of this act, who, being able to find employment, could by proper industry and exertion avoid such destitution, suffering, or dependence.

Sec. 4. *And be it further enacted,* That the President is hereby authorized to reserve from sale or from settlement, under the homestead or pre-emption laws, and to set apart for the use of freedmen and loyal refugees, male or female, unoccupied public lands in Florida, Mississippi, Alabama, Louisiana, and Arkansas, not exceeding in all three millions of acres of good land; and the Commissioner, under the direction of the President, shall cause the same from time to time to be allotted and assigned, in parcels not exceeding forty acres each, to the loyal refugees and freedmen, who shall be protected in the use and enjoyment thereof for such term of time and at such annual rent as may be agreed on between the Commissioner and such refugees or freedmen. . . .

Sec. 6. *And be it further enacted,* That the Commissioner shall, under the direction of the President, procure in the name of the United States, by grant or purchase, such lands within the districts aforesaid as may be required for refugees and freedmen dependent on the government for support; and he shall provide or cause to be erected suitable buildings for asylums and schools. . . .

Sec. 7. *And be it further enacted,* That whenever in any State or district in which the ordinary course of judicial proceedings has been interrupted by the rebellion, and wherein, in consequence of any State or local law, ordinance, police or other regulation, custom, or prejudice, any of the civil rights or immunities belonging to white persons, including the right to make and enforce contracts, to sue, be parties, and give evidence, to inherit, purchase, lease, sell, hold and convey real and personal property, and to have full and equal benefit of all laws and proceedings for the security of person and estate, including the constitutional right of bearing arms, are refused or denied to negroes, mulattoes, freedmen, refugees, or any other persons, on account of race, color, or any previous condition of slavery or

---

57. Eric Schnapper, "Affirmative Action and the Legislative History of the Fourteenth Amendment," *Virginia Law Review* 71 (1985): 753.

58. Congressional Globe, 39th Cong., 1st Sess. (Feburary 3, 1866), App. 83.

involuntary servitude, or wherein they or any of them are subjected to any other or different punishment, pains, or penalties, for the commission of any act or offence, than are prescribed for white persons committing like acts or offences, it shall be the duty of the President of the United States, through the Commissioner, to extend military protection and jurisdiction over all cases affecting such persons so discriminated against.

The Senate Debate[59]

SENATOR THOMAS HENDRICKS (Democrat, Indiana)

. . .

. . . If they have been made free and brought into the class of citizens, upon what principle can you authorize the Government of the United States to buy homes for them? Upon what principle can you authorize the Government of the United States to buy lands for the poor people in any State in the Union? They may be very meritorious; their cases may appeal with great force to our sympathies; it may almost appear necessary to prevent suffering that we should buy a home for each poor person in the country; but where is the power of the General Government to do this thing? Is it true that by this revolution the persons and property of the people have been brought within the jurisdiction of Congress and taken from without the control and jurisdiction of the States? I have understood heretofore that it has never been disputed that the duty to provide for the poor, the insane, the blind, and all who are dependent upon society, rests upon the States, and that the power does not belong to the General Government. What has occurred, then, in this war that has changed the relation of the people to the General Government to so great an extent that Congress may become the purchaser of homes for them? If we can go so far, I know of no limit to the powers of Congress. . . .

. . .

It is claimed that under this second section Congress may do anything necessary, in its judgment, not only to secure the freedom of the negro, but to secure him all civil rights that are secured to white people. I deny that construction, and it will be a very dangerous construction to adopt. The first section abolishes slavery. The second section proves that Congress may enforce the abolition of slavery "by appropriate legislation." What is slavery? It is not a relation between the slave and the State; it is not a public relation; it is a relation between two persons whereby the conduct of the one is placed under the will of the other. It is purely and entirely a domestic relation, and is so classed by all law writers; the law regulates that relation as it regulates other domestic relations. This constitutional amendment broke asunder this private relation between the master and his slave, and the slave then, so far as the right of the master was concerned, became free; but did the slave, under that amendment, acquire any other right than to be free from the control of his master? The law of the State which authorized this relation is abrogated and annulled by this provision of the Federal Constitution, but no new rights are conferred upon the freedman.

Then, sir, to make a contract is a civil right which has ordinarily been regulated by the States. The form of that contract and the ceremonies that shall attend it are not to be regulated by Congress, but by the States. Suppose that it becomes the judgment of the State that a contract between a colored man and a white man shall be evidenced by other solemnities and instruments than are required between two white men, shall not the State be allowed to make such a provision? Is it a civil right to give evidence in courts? Is it a civil right to sit upon a jury? If it be a civil right to sit upon a jury, this bill will require that if any negro is refused the privilege of sitting upon a jury, he shall be taken under the military protection of the Government. Is the right to marry according to a man's choice a civil right? Marriage is a civil contract, and to marry according to one's choice is a civil right. Suppose a State shall deny the right of amalgamation, the right of a negro man to intermarry with a white woman, then that negro may be taken under the military protection of the Government; and what does that mean? . . .

. . .

My judgment is that under the second section of the [Thirteenth] amendment we may pass such a law as will secure the freedom declared in the first section, but that we cannot go beyond that limitation. If a man has been, by this provision of the Constitution, made free from his master, and that master undertakes to make him a slave again, we may pass such laws as are sufficient in our judgment to prevent that act; but if the Legislature of the State denies to the citizen as he is now called, the freedom, equal privileges with the white man, I want to know if that Legislature, and

59. *Congressional Globe*, 39th Cong., 1st Sess. (1866), 317–22.

each member of that Legislature, is responsible to the penalties prescribed in this bill? It is not an act of the old master; it is an act of the State government, which defines and regulates the civil rights of the people.

. . .

SENATOR LYMAN TRUMBULL (Republican, Illinois)

. . .

. . . [W]hat was the object of the Freedmen's Bureau, and why was it established? It was established to look after a large class of people who, as the results of the war, had been thrown upon the hands of the Government, and must have perished but for its fostering care and protection. Does the Senator mean to deny the power of this Government to protect people under such circumstances? . . .

. . . [W]e have thrown upon us four million people who have toiled all their lives for others; who, unlike the Indians, had no property at the beginning of the rebellion; who were never permitted to own anything, never permitted to eat the bread their own hands had earned; many of whom are without any means of support, in the midst of a prejudiced and hostile population who have been struggling to overthrow the Government. These four million people, made free by the acts of war and the constitutional amendment, have been, wherever they could, loyal and true to the Union; and the Senator seriously asks, what authority have we to appropriate money to take care of them? What would he do with them? Would he allow them to starve and die? Would he turn them over to the mercy of the men who, through their whole lives, have had their earnings, to be enslaved again? It is not the first time that money has been appropriated to take care of the destitute African. For years it has been the law that whenever persons of African descent were brought to our shores with the intention of reducing them to slavery, the Government should, if possible, rescue and restore them to their native land; and we have appropriated hundreds of thousands of dollars for this object. . . .

. . .

. . . [T]he Senator from Indiana says it extends all over the United States. Well, by its terms it does, though practically it can have little if any operation outside of the late slaveholding States. If freedmen should congregate in large numbers at Cairo, Illinois or at Evansville, Indiana, and become a charge upon the people of those States, the Freedmen's Bureau would have a right to extend its jurisdiction over them, provide for their wants, secure for them employment, and place them in situations where they could provide for themselves. . . .

. . .

. . . The cheapest way by which you can save this race from starvation and destruction is to educate them. They will soon become self-sustaining. The report of the Freedmen's Bureau shows that today more than seventy thousand black children are being taught in the schools which have been established in the South. We shall not long have to support any of these blacks out of the public Treasury if we educate and furnish them land upon which they can make a living for themselves.

. . .

. . . I think [the Thirteenth] amendment does confer authority to enact these provisions into law and execute them. . . . What was the object of the constitutional amendment abolishing slavery? It was not, as the Senator says, simply to take away the power of the master over the slave. Did we not mean something more than that? Did we mean that hereafter slavery should not exist, no matter whether the servitude was claimed as due to an individual or the State? The constitutional amendment abolishes just as absolutely all provisions of State or local law which make a man a slave as it takes away the power of his former master to control him.

If the construction put by the Senator from Indiana upon the amendment be the true one, and we have merely taken from the master the power to control the slave and left him at the mercy of the State to be deprived of his civil rights, the trumpet of freedom that we have been blowing throughout the land has given an "uncertain sound," and the promised freedom is a delusion. Such was not the intention of Congress, which proposed the constitutional amendment, nor is such the fair meaning of the amendment itself. With the destruction of slavery necessarily follows the destruction of the incidents to slavery. When slavery was abolished, slave codes in its support were abolished also.

Those laws that prevented the colored man going from home, that did not allow him to buy or to sell, or to make contracts; that did not allow him to own property; that did not allow him to enforce rights; that did not allow him to be educated, were all badges of servitude made in the interest of slavery and as a part of slavery. They never would have been thought of or enacted anywhere but for slavery, and when slavery falls they fall also. The policy of the States where slavery has existed has been to legislate in its interest; and out of deference to slavery, which was tolerated by the Constitution of the United States, even some of the non-slaveholding States passed laws abridging the rights of the colored man which were restraints upon liberty. When slavery goes, all this system of legislation, devised in the interests of slavery and for the purpose of degrading the colored race, of keeping the negro in ignorance, of blotting out from his very soul the light of reason, if that were possible, that he might not think, but know only, like the ox, to labor, go with it.

Now, when slavery no longer exists, the policy of the Government is to legislate in the interest of freedom. Now, our laws are to be enacted with a view to educate, improve, enlighten, and Christianize the negro; to make him an independent man; to teach him to think and to reason; to improve that principle which the great Author of all has implanted in every human breast, which is susceptible of the highest cultivation, and destined to go on enlarging and expanding through the endless ages of eternity.

I have no doubt that under this provision of the Constitution we may destroy all these discriminations in civil rights against the black man; and if we cannot, our constitutional amendments amount to nothing. It was for that purpose that the second clause of that amendment was adopted, which says that Congress shall have authority, by appropriate legislation, to carry into effect the article prohibiting slavery. Who is to decide what that appropriate legislation is to be? The Congress of the United States; and it is for Congress to adopt such appropriate legislation as it may think proper, so that it be a means to accomplish the end. If we believe a Freedmen's Bureau necessary, if we believe an act punishing any man who deprives a colored person of any civil rights on account of his color necessary—if that is one means to secure his freedom, we have the constitutional right to adopt it. If in order to prevent slavery Congress deem it necessary to declare null and void all laws which will not permit the colored man to contract, which will not permit him to testify, which will not permit him to buy and sell, and to go where he pleases, it has the power to do so, and not only the power, but the duty to do so. . . .

But, says the Senator from Indiana, we have laws in Indiana prohibiting black people from marrying whites, and are you going to disregard these laws? Are our laws enacted for the purpose of preventing amalgamation to be disregarded, and is a man to be punished because he undertakes to enforce them? I beg the Senator from Indiana to read the bill. One of its objects is to secure the same civil rights and subject to the same punishments persons of all races and colors. How does this interfere with the law of Indiana preventing marriages between whites and blacks? Are not both races treated alike by the law of Indiana? Does not the law make it just as much a crime for a white man to marry a black woman as for a black woman to marry a white man, and *vice versa*?

Implementing the Fourteenth Amendment

Congressional Debates over the Civil Rights Act of 1875

The Civil Rights Act of 1875 had a tortuous path to passage. In 1870 Senator Charles Sumner proposed prohibiting racial segregation in public schools, inns, common carriers, places of public amusement, cemeteries, and other institutions. The bill was debated and modified for the next three years, but opponents prevented the proposal from being brought to a vote. Sumner and Representative Benjamin Butler of Massachusetts introduced a similar bill in December 1873. This bill passed the Senate but was tabled by the House. The lame-duck Congress returned to the bill in the winter of 1874–75. Although Republicans had lost their majority in the House of Representatives in the November 1874 elections, the new majority would not be seated until March 1875. As a last-ditch effort to pass a civil rights act, Republicans scrapped the provision prohibiting school segregation and reworked certain procedural rules. As a result of this maneuvering the Civil Rights Act of 1875 became law in February.

Compare the debate over the Civil Rights Act of 1875 to the debates over the Second Freedmen's Bureau Act. To what extent do the proponents and opponents of these acts take similar positions? Does the nature of the debate over the meaning of the Fourteenth Amendment change from 1866 to 1875? Senator Matthew Carpenter was a Republican who had supported previous civil rights acts. What might explain his different position in 1875? Michael McConnell has maintained that Republican support for the original Sumner bill demonstrates that the framers of the Fourteenth Amendment believed that school segregation was unconstitutional.[60] *Do you agree with this analysis?*

60. Michael W. McConnell, "Originalism and the Desegregation

The Civil Rights Act of 1875[61]

Whereas it is essential to just government we recognize the equality of all men before the law, and hold that it is the duty of government in its dealings with the people to mete out equal and exact justice to all, of whatever nativity, race, color, or persuasion, religious or political; and it being the appropriate object of legislation to enact great fundamental principles into law: Therefore,

Sec. 1. Be it enacted by the Senate and House of Representatives of the United States of America in Congress assembled, That all persons within the jurisdiction of the United States shall be entitled to the full and equal enjoyment of the accommodations, advantages, facilities, and privileges of inns, public conveyances on land or water, theaters, and other places of public amusement; subject only to the conditions and limitations established by law, and applicable alike to citizens of every race and color, regardless of any previous condition of servitude. . . .

The Senate Debate[62]

SENATOR CHARLES SUMNER (Republican, Massachusetts)

. . .

. . . The denial of any right is a wrong that darkens the enjoyment of all the rest. Besides the right to testify and the right to vote, there are other rights without which Equality does not exist. The precise rule is Equality before the Law; nor more nor less; that is, the condition before the Law in which all are alike—being entitled without any discrimination to the equal enjoyment of all institutions, privileges, advantages, and conveniences created or regulated by law, among which are the right to testify and the right to vote. But this plain requirement is not satisfied, logically or reasonably, by these two concessions, so that when they are recognized all others are trifles. The court-house and ballot-box are not the only places for the rule. These two are not the only institutions for its operation. The rule is general; how then restrict it to two cases? It is, all are equal before the law—not merely before the law in two cases, but before the law in all cases without limitation or exception. Important as it is to testify and to vote, life is not all contained even in those possessions.

The new-made citizen is called to travel for business, for health, or for pleasure, but here his trials begin. The doors of the public hotel, which from the earliest days of our jurisprudence have always opened hospitality to the stronger, close against him, and the public conveyances, which the common law declares equally free to all alike, have no such freedom for him. He longs, perhaps, for respite and relaxation at some place of public amusement, and here also the same adverse discrimination is made. With the anxieties of a parent, seeking the welfare of his child, he strives to bestow upon him the inestimable blessings of education, and takes him affectionately to the common school, created by law and supported by the taxation to which he has contributed, but these doors slam rudely in the face of the child where is garnered up the parent's heart. . . . [L]ittle children are turned away and forbidden at the door of the common school, because of the skin. And the same insulting ostracism shows itself in other institutions of science and learning, also in the church and in the last resting place on earth.

. . .

. . . There is no colored person who does not resent the imputation that he is seeking to intrude himself socially anywhere. This is no question of society; no question of social life; no question of social equality, if anybody knows what that means. The object is simply Equality before the law, a term which explains itself. Now, as the law does not presume to create or regulate social relations, these are in no respect affected by the pending measure. Each person, whether Senator or citizen, is always free to choose who shall be his friend, his associate, his guest. . . . His house is his "castle;" and this very designation, borrowed from the common law, shows his absolute independence within its walls; nor is there any difference, whether it be palace or hovel, but when he leaves his "castle" and goes abroad, this independence is at an end. He walks the streets; but he is subject to the prevailing law of Equality; nor can he appropriate the sidewalk to his own exclusive use, driving into the gutter all whose skin is less white than his own. . . .

. . .

How vain to argue that there is no denial of Equal Rights when this separation is enforced. The substitute is invariably an inferior article. Does any Senator deny it? Therefore, it is not Equality. At best it is an

Decisions," *Virginia Law Review* 81 (1995): 947.

61. 18 U.S. Stat. 335, 335-36 (1875).

62. *Congressional Globe,* 42nd Cong., 2nd Sess. (1872), 381–84; *Congressional Record,* 43rd Cong., 2nd. Sess. (1875), 1861–63.

equivalent only; but no equivalent is an equality. Separation implies one thing for a white person and another thing for a colored person; but equality is where all have the same alike. There can be no substitute for equality; nothing but itself. Even if accommodations are the same, as notoriously they are not, there is no Equality. . . .

. . .

I begin with public hotels or inns, because the rule with regard to them may be traced to the earliest period of the common law. . . .

. . .

. . . [T]he innkeeper [is] under constraint of law, which he must obey; "bound to take in all travelers and wayfaring persons;" "nor can he impose unreasonable terms upon them;" and liable for an action and even to an indictment for refusal. Such is the law.

With this preemptory rule opening the doors of inns to all travelers, without distinction, to the extent of authorizing not only an action but an indictment for the refusal to receive a traveler, it is plain that the pending bill is only declaratory of existing law giving it the sanction of Congress.

Public conveyances, whether on land or water, are known to the law as common carriers, and they, too have obligations not unlike those of inns. . . .

. . .

Theaters and other places of public amusement, licensed by law, are kindred to inns or public conveyances, though less noticed by jurisprudence. But, like their prototypes, they undertake to provide for the public under sanction of law. They are public institutions, regulated if not created by law, enjoying privileges, and in consideration thereof, assuming duties not unlike those of the inn and the public conveyance. From essential reason, the rule should be the same with all. As the inn cannot close its doors, or the public conveyance refuse a seat to any paying traveler, decent in condition, so must it be with the theater and other places of public amusement. Here are institutions whose peculiar object is the "pursuit of happiness," which has been placed among the equal rights of all. How utterly irrational the pretension to outrage a large portion of the community. The law can lend itself to no such intolerable absurdity, and this, I insist, shall be declared by Congress.

The common school falls naturally into the same category. Like the others, it must be open to all or its designation is a misnomer and a mockery. It is not a school for whites or blacks, but a school for all; in other words a common school. Much is implied in this term, according to which the school harmonizes with the other institutions already mentioned. It is an inn where children rest on the road to knowledge. It is a public conveyance where children are passengers. It is a theater where children resort for enduring recreation. Like the others, it assumes to provide for the public; therefore it must be open to all; nor can there be any exclusion, except on grounds equally applicable to the inn, the public conveyance, and the theater.

But the common school has a higher character. Its object is the education of the young, and it is sustained by taxation to which all contribute. . . .

. . .

It is easy to see that the separate school founded on an odious discrimination and sometimes offered as an equivalent for the common school, is an ill-disguised violation of the principle of Equality, while as a pretended equivalent it is an utter failure and instead of a parent is only a churlish step-mother.

. . .

The separate school wants the first requisite of the common school, inasmuch as it is not equally open to all; and since this is inconsistent with the declared role of republican institutions, such a school is not republican in character. Therefore, it is not a preparation for the duties of life. The child is not trained in the way he should go; for he is trained under than ban of inequality. How can he grow up to the stature of equal citizenship? He is pinched and dwarfed while the stigma of color is stamped upon him. . . .

Nor is the separation without evil to the whites. The prejudice of color is nursed when it should be stifled. . . . Children learn by example more than by precept. How precious the example which teaches that all are equal in rights. But this can be only where all commingle in the common school as in common citizenship. There is no separate ballot-box. There should be no separate school. It is not enough that all should be taught alike; they must all be taught together. They are not only to receive equal quantities of knowledge, but all are to receive it in the same way. But they cannot be taught alike unless all are taught together; nor can they receive equal quantities of knowledge in the same way, except at the common school.

The common school is important to all; but to the colored child it is a necessity. Excluded from the common school, he finds himself too frequently without any substitute. Often there is no school. But even where a separate school is planted it is inferior in character. . . . For him there is no assurance of education except in the common school, where he will be under the safeguard of all. White parents will take care not only that the common school is not neglected, but that its teachers and means of instruction are the best possible, and the colored child will have the benefit of this watchfulness. This decisive consideration completes the irresistible argument for the common school as the equal parent of all without distinction of color.

. . .

Mr. President, against these conclusions there is but one argument, which, when considered, is nothing but a prejudice. . . . It is the prejudice of color which pursues its victim in the long pilgrimage from the cradle to the grave, closing the school, barring the hotel, excluding from the public conveyance, insulting at the theater, shutting the gates of science and playing its fantastic tricks even in the church where he kneels and the grave where his dust mingles with the surrounding earth . . . . This is the whole case. And shall those equal rights, promised by the great Declaration, be sacrificed to a prejudice? Shall that equality before the law, which is the best part of citizenship, be denied to those who do not happen to be white? Is this a white man's Government, or is it a Government of "all men," as declared by our fathers? Is it a Republic of equal laws, or an oligarchy of the skin? This is the question now presented.

SENATOR MATTHEW CARPENTER (Republican, Wisconsin)

. . .

Four million of human beings who were held in slavery at the commencement of the late civil war, have been emancipated and made citizens of the United States, and of the States in which they reside. This great and sudden change in the social condition of the States where slavery existed has created discontent, and inflamed the prejudice of those who belonged to the dominant race against their former slaves lately raised to legal and political equality. This bill is intended to repress all manifestations of this prejudice, and to secure to the colored man the rights he ought to enjoy. If it could go upon the statute-book and accomplish a complete eradication of the deep and long-existing prejudice of the white race against social contact with the race in whose favor it is proposed, it would be a signal triumph of humanity. And in this history of the colored race since the beginning of the war there is abundant reason for the desire to create, in lieu of this prejudice, a feeling of fraternity between the two races.

. . .

But haste is not always speed; and especially is this true of attempts to coerce sentiment or suppress prejudice. This can only be accomplished by time, kindly entreaty, reason, and argument. And all experience demonstrates that every unavailing attempt to force men into compliance with social, religious, or political dogmas has the effect to postpone the end desired. . . .

One provision of this bill declares that certain persons shall be entitled to equal accommodations and facilities of public conveyance on land or water. This might be sustained as a regulation of commerce if confined to the commerce over which Congress possesses the power of regulation—commerce with foreign nations, among the several States, or with the Indian tribes. But the bill does not purport to be a regulation of the particular branches of commerce over which Congress has control. It applies to every person or corporation engaged in transportation from point to point within a State as well as to those engaged in transporting among the several States.

It is well settled that no act of Congress can be valid under the Constitution unless it can fairly be referred to some head of Federal jurisdiction. For instance, in regulating commerce among the States, Congress might provide that every person engaged in such commerce should be entitled to accommodation of inns in the several States through which he might pass in the prosecution of his business; and perhaps, upon the theory that a cheerful mind is favorable to enterprise, might provide that he should be admitted to theaters and other places of public amusement in the States wherein he might be temporarily sojourning during the transaction of his business. Such provision in regard to theaters would be somewhat fantastic as a regulation of commerce; and yet, if Congress saw fit so to provide, such provision might be sustained as relating to a subject over which Congress has jurisdiction. But the bill under consideration does not rest upon this ground, because its provisions are not confined to persons engaged in such commerce.

. . .

It is manifest that the fourth clause [of the fourteenth amendment], that "no State shall deny to any person within its jurisdiction the equal protection of the laws," has no application to this subject, especially to the jury clause of this bill. It is equally evident that the third clause, "nor shall any State deprive any person of life, liberty, or property without due process of law" has no such application.

This is evident from the fact that women and infants are citizens of the United States, and the fact that they are excluded from serving as jurors in every State in the Union, and the fact that no one pretends or claims that, in consequence of such ineligibility they are deprived or life, liberty, or property, or of the equal protection of the laws.

. . .

I can conceive of no argument based upon the fourteenth amendment establishing the right to serve as a juror which does not also establish the right to serve in the Legislature and hold any State office. And this, in view of the fifteenth amendment, must be regarded as a perfect *reductio ad absurdum*.

. . .

From this consideration which I have briefly stated, I am compelled to vote against the bill. . . . I am consoled, however, by the confidence that, if it should become a law, the judicial courts will intervene to vindicate the Constitution.

Federal Courts

Federal judges quickly moved from initial support for broad congressional power to curb violence against newly freed slaves to imposing sharp limits on national authority to enforce the Thirteenth, Fourteenth, and Fifteenth Amendments. In an 1871 federal circuit court case Judge William Wood ruled that the post–Civil War Amendments permitted Congress to punish private conspiracies aimed at preventing persons from enjoying all the liberties set out in the Bill of Rights. His opinion in *U.S. v. Hall* declared:

> Denying includes inaction as well as action, and denying the equal protection of the laws includes the omission to protect, as well as the omission to pass laws for protection. . . . [A]s it would be unseemly for congress to interfere directly with state enactments . . . the only appropriate legislation it can make is that which will operate directly on offenders and offenses, and protect the rights which the amendment secures. . . . We think, therefore, that the right of freedom of speech, and the other rights enumerated in the first eight articles of amendment to the constitution of the United States, are the privileges and immunities of citizens of the United States, that they are secured by the constitution, that congress has the power to protect them by appropriate legislation.[63]

The Supreme Court over the next five years overruled or sharply narrowed each important ruling of *United States v. Hall*:

1. The *Slaughter-House Cases* (1873) ruled that the rights enumerated in the first eight amendments to the Constitution were not among the privileges and immunities of U.S. citizens protected by the United States.
2. *United States v. Cruikshank* (1876) ruled that white supremacists who massacred African-American voters could not be prosecuted, because voting was not a fundamental right and the indictment declared that "the wrong contemplated against the rights of these citizens was on account of their race or color."
3. *United States v. Reese* (1875) ruled that Sections 3 and 4 of the Enforcement Act of 1870 were unconstitutional because they prohibited state officials and private actors from interfering with voting and did not make explicit that the wrong had to be "on account of race, color, or previous condition of servitude."

The precise impact of these cases is controversial. Federal attorneys and national legislators strongly committed to securing racial equality could easily amend indictments and statutes to make clear that offenders had racial motivations for denying former slaves their rights. *Slaughter-House*, *Cruikshank*, and *Reese* were handed down, however, at a time when the national commitment to racial equality was waning. In this environment a significant risk existed that efforts to secure racial equality would founder when federal courts made that task more difficult.

The States and School Segregation

Struggles for racial equality took place in the states as well as in the national government. Many controversies concerned segregation in the public schools, the operation of which was becoming an important function of local government in the North. Numerous

63. *United States v. Hall*, 26 F. Cas. 79 (C. C. S. D. Ala. 1871).

states and state courts anticipated *Brown v. Board of Education* (1954) by almost one hundred years. During the 1860s and 1870s Americans passed constitutional amendments, enacted laws, and made judicial decisions that provided children of color with the right to attend desegregated schools. Minnesota, Maine, Massachusetts, New Hampshire, and Vermont desegregated schools before the Civil War. Rhode Island, Connecticut, Michigan, Illinois, and New Jersey passed laws desegregating schools after the Civil War. Other states, most notably Nevada, Kansas, Indiana, California, Kentucky, West Virginia, Maryland, and Missouri, passed new laws requiring segregation. Many African-Americans brought suits in state courts challenging these local decisions to segregate public schools. In Iowa, Michigan, and Illinois, those lawsuits were successful, although in Illinois justices left open the possibility that segregated classrooms might be constitutional. Courts sustained segregated public schools in New York, California, Nevada, Ohio, and Indiana. Partisanship mattered. State courts with Republican majorities more often declared segregated schools unconstitutional than did state courts with Democratic majorities.

Clark v. Board of School Directors, 24 Iowa 266 (1868)

Susan Clark was a 12-year old African-American who lived in Muscatine, Iowa. In 1867 the local school board refused to allow her to attend the school in her neighborhood, Grammar School No. 2, because that school was designated for white children only. Clark sued the board of school directors, claiming that school segregation violated Iowa law and the state constitution. The state district court agreed that school segregation in Iowa violated the state constitution. The school board appealed that decision to the Supreme Court of Iowa.

The Iowa Supreme Court sustained the lower court ruling, striking down school segregation. Judge Cole maintained that segregated schools were inconsistent with the provision in the Iowa Constitution that required communities to educate all children. Compare the opinion below with assertions of racial equality during Reconstruction and the Supreme Court's opinion in Brown v. Board of Education *(1954). To what extent does Judge Cole rely on enduring arguments about racial equality? To what extent does he rely on arguments distinctive to Reconstruction?*

JUDGE COLE delivered the opinion of the Court.

In view of the principle of equal rights to all, upon which our government is founded, it would seem necessary, in order to justify a denial of such equality of right to any one, that some express sovereign authority for such denial should be shown.

But it is claimed, that, since the board of directors are authorized and empowered to have as many schools in their district township as they may deem proper, and are charged with a discretion in their control and management, they may, therefore, establish schools for colored children, and require such to attend them, or none. And, in this particular case, the fact, that public sentiment is opposed to the intermingling of white and colored children in the same schools, is presented as a justification for the exercise of the discretion in the establishing and maintaining of a separate school for the colored children. . . .

. . .

The legislature, by enacting, as it did in 1846 *et seq*, that the common "schools" shall be open and free alike to all *white* children, as effectually excluded colored children, as if it had expressly enacted that they should be excluded.. . . . Under these laws, it is clear that the board of directors had no discretion intrusted to them to admit colored children into the common schools or to establish separate schools for them.

When the legislature enacted, as it did in 1858, that colored children should be admitted to the common schools only upon the "unanimous consent of the persons sending to the school," and, in case such consent was not given, then the education of colored youth should be provided for in separate schools, all discretion in relation to that matter was effectually denied to the board of school directors. And it would not have been competent for the board of directors, in their discretion, to have admitted colored children to the common schools, without the unanimous consent of the persons sending to the school.

Now, under our Constitution, which declares that provision shall be made "for the education of *all the youths of the State* through a system of common schools," which constitutional declaration has been effectuated by enactments providing for the "instruction of youth between the ages of five and twenty-one years," without regard to color or nationality, is it not equally clear that all discretion is denied to the board of school directors as to what *youths* shall be admitted? It seems to us that the proposition is too clear to admit of question.

. . .

We conclude, therefore, that the law makes no distinction whatever, as to the right of children between the ages of five and twenty-one years, to attend the common schools, and that there is no discretion left with, or given to, the board of school directors, to make any distinction in regard to children within the specified ages.

. . .

That the board of directors is clothed with certain discretionary powers as to the establishment, maintenance and management of schools within its district cannot be denied. Doubtless the board may, in its discretion, fix the boundaries within which children must reside, in order to be entitled to admission to a certain school; or may fix the grade of each school, and require certain qualifications, or proficiency in studies, or the like, before any pupil shall be entitled to admission therein.

But this discretion is limited by the line which fixes the *equality of right* in all the youths between the ages of five and twenty-one years. No discretion which disturbs that equality can be exercised; for the exercise of such a discretion would be a violation of the law, which expressly gives the same rights to *all* the youths. Therefore, it is not competent for the board of directors to require the children of Irish parents to attend one school, and the children of German parents another; the children of catholic parents to attend one school, and the children of protestant parents another. And if it should so happen, that there be one or more poorly clad or ragged children in the district, and public sentiment was opposed to the intermingling of such with the well dressed youths of the district, in the same school, it would not be competent for the board of directors, in their discretion, to pander to such false public sentiment, and require the poorly clothed children to attend a separate school.

The term "colored race" is but another designation, and in this country but a synonym for African. Now, it is very clear, that, if the board of directors are clothed with a discretion to exclude African children from our common schools, and require them to attend (if at all) a school composed wholly of children of that nationality, they would have the same power and right to exclude German children from our common schools, require them to attend (if at all) a school composed wholly of children of that nationality, and so of Irish, French, English and other nationalities, which together constitute the *American,* and which it is the tendency of our institutions and policy of the government to organize into one harmonious *people,* with a common country and stimulated with the common purpose to perpetuate and spread our free institutions for the development, elevation and happiness of *mankind.*

. . . For the courts to sustain a board of school directors or other subordinate board or officer in limiting the rights and privileges of persons by reason of their nationality, would be to sanction a plain violation of the spirit of our laws not only, but would tend to perpetuate the national differences of our people and stimulate a constant strife, if not a war of races.

. . .

In other words, all the youths are equal before the law, and there is no discretion vested in the board of directors or elsewhere, to interfere with or disturb that equality. The board of directors may exercise a uniform discretion equally operative upon all, as to the residence, or qualifications, or freedom from contagious disease, or the like, of children, to entitle them to admission to each particular school; but the board cannot, in their discretion, or otherwise, deny a youth admission to any particular school because of his or her nationality, religion, color, clothing or the like.

. . .

JUDGE WRIGHT, dissenting.

. . .

. . . [W]hile the Constitution provides for the education *of all the youths of the State,* by a system of common schools, and while, without regard to color, the legislature has provided, in obedience to the Constitution, for this instruction, I am not prepared to admit that the school directors have no discretion in arranging the schools, nor that they cannot direct where the children shall attend school, provided, of course, they are kept within their proper districts, and have furnished to them the necessary and proper instruction. I concede that the law makes no distinction as to the rights of children between the ages of five and twenty-one. All have a right to attend the common schools. And this is what the Constitution intended to secure. This right, the directors in this case recognized. The rule adopted by them was reasonable, and I cannot admit that the refusal to admit this scholar into this particular school was so wrongful as that the courts should interfere by mandamus. If she was allowed to attend a school in the proper district, having the suitable instruction furnished to others, then I know of no principle upon which she can complain. . . .

There is no absolute legal right in a colored child to attend a white school rather than one made up of children of African descent; just as there is no such right in a white child to attend a colored school. The school officers, in my opinion, are the appropriate judges in these matters. And, when they, to the extent of the means at their command, furnish to all alike the instruction contemplated by the Constitution and law, I would not compel them to admit the scholars into one rather than another school of the district.

If, in their opinion, the best interests of the schools require that particular families should be kept together, or should be separated; if they believe that scholars will more rapidly advance, and the harmony and welfare of the schools be promoted by having this child under this instruction, and that one under another; if, because of the actual condition of public sentiment for the time being, they deem it more advisable, and, in the exercise of a sound discretion, direct that colored children shall be taught by themselves; or, on the other hand, should direct that all should attend the same school,—I do not believe the courts should interfere. If this rule excludes the child from the benefit of the common schools within his or her district, just as fully, just as completely as all others, then there would be a violation of an imperative duty. . . . The principle of equal rights to all does not demand that all the children of the district should be taught in the same building, nor by the same teacher; nor that a colored child shall be transferred from one school to another, nor that this should be done for a white child. The true inquiry is: Have all equal school privileges? And, if so, being all children alike, and alike equal before the law, but no more, this equality is preserved by adopting the same rule as to all. This equality was in no sense disturbed, under the rule adopted by this board. So holding, I cannot concur in affirming the judgment below upon the point ruled in the foregoing opinion.

C. Gender

The women's rights movement was greatly disappointed in the course of American constitutionalism from 1861 to 1876. Proponents of women's suffrage before the Civil War often played important roles in the abolitionist movement. Many established cordial relationships with prominent anti-slavery Republicans. When the Civil War ended, such activists as Elizabeth Cady Stanton and Susan B. Anthony called for constitutional amendments endorsing gender as well as racial equality. They were quickly disenchanted. Republicans during Reconstruction repeatedly declared, "This was the negro's hour." While many Republican leaders favored women's suffrage, few were willing to jeopardize measures aimed at achieving greater racial equality by making efforts to be more inclusive. The *American Anti-Slavery Standard* expressed this conviction in an editorial declaring,

> We do not conceal our conviction that this is "the negro's hour"—an hour which, as it is improved or wasted, may crown with complete victory thirty years toil in his behalf, or once more commit him to the vindictive ferocity of the system from which he seems about to escape. It is an hour in which it is certainly perilous and may be fatal to relax any energy hitherto devoted to his emancipation, or to allow any fraction of our strength to be diverted to another issue. Hence, we cannot agree that the enfranchisement of women and the enfranchisement of the blacks stand on the same ground, or are entitled to equal effort at this moment. They certainly are not identified in the popular mind, and Mrs. Stanton must see that while there is a strong party in Congress who can be brought to vote directly or indirectly for putting the ballot in the hands of the blacks, no considerable portion of those votes could be carried now for an amendment to the Constitution which should include women.
>
> Thirty years of agitation and four years of war have created this costly opportunity. If we let it pass, it passes forever, or at any rate, for a generation. For that reason we have no right, from an anxiety for something besides justice to the negro, to throw away a single chance of securing it for him. Causes have their crises. That of the negro has come; that of the women's rights movement has not come.[64]

During the decade after the Civil War, Congress repeatedly defeated or tabled proposals for women's suffrage. Worse, from the perspective of the women's movement, Americans inserted the word "male" into the Constitution. Section 2 of the Fourteenth Amendment deprives states of representation only to the

64. "Women's Rights," *American Anti-Slavery Standard*, December 30, 1865.

extent that the state deprives male citizens of voting rights.

In the late 1860s some prominent feminists promoted litigation as a means for transforming what appeared to be political defeats into constitutional victories. Such proponents of this "New Departure" as Virginia Minor, Elizabeth Cady Stanton, and Susan B. Anthony asserted that Republicans had secured constitutional amendments that required states to enfranchise women. The text of the Fourteenth Amendment did not distinguish between racial and gender equality. Section 1 declares, "No state shall deny to any person the equal protection of the laws" and "No State shall make or enforce any law which shall abridge the privileges or immunities of citizens of the United States." Relying heavily on previous anti-slavery arguments that called for constitutions to be interpreted in light of fundamental constitutional principles, Minor, Stanton, and Anthony insisted that voting was one of the fundamental rights protected by the privileges and immunities clause of the Fourteenth Amendment. Because no one disputed that women were citizens of the United States, their argument concluded, the text of the Fourteenth Amendment enfranchised women.

The New Departure was not successful. Victoria Woodhull's memorial to Congress failed to persuade national legislators to pass a law declaring that gender discrimination violated the Fourteenth and Fifteenth Amendments. Susan B. Anthony failed to persuade a federal court that she was constitutionally entitled to vote in the 1872 national election. In *Bradwell v. State* (1873) and *Minor v. Happersett* (1874) the Supreme Court of the United States ruled that the privileges and immunities clause of the Fourteenth Amendment gave neither women nor anyone else the constitutional right to be an attorney or to vote. Justice Joseph Bradley, who thought that the privileges and immunities clause protected the right of men to become lawyers, claimed that woman were not constitutionally suited for the legal profession.

The Senate Debates Women's Suffrage (1866)[65]

Senator Edgar Cowan of Pennsylvania sparked a vigorous legislative debate over women's rights when he proposed that a bill granting men of color the right to vote in the District of Columbia should also grant women the ballot. Cowan was one of the most conservative Republicans in the Senate. He hoped that his amendment might divide moderate and radical Republicans in ways that prevented any change in the voting laws. Some Republicans took Cowan's bait, insisting that women had the same right to vote as did persons of color. Other Republicans, after announcing that they agreed with the principle of female suffrage, insisted that this was not the proper occasion for granting women the ballot. Still other Republicans insisted that the reasons for granting persons of color the ballot did not justify granting women the ballot. After three days of debate, Senator Cowan's amendment was voted down by a 37-9 vote.

Consider both the general principles and strategies adopted in the discussion of Senator Cowan's proposed amendment. What reasons do pro-suffrage Republicans give for granting women the right to vote? To what extent do they claim that the same principle justifies granting the ballot to persons of color and granting the ballot to women? On what grounds do other Republicans claim that differences exist between men of color and women that justify giving the ballot only to the former?

One hundred years later white supremacists repeated the Cowan gambit. During the debates over the Civil Rights Act of 1964, opponents of African-American rights supported a statutory amendment forbidding gender as well as race discrimination. They miscalculated. Racial liberals during the Great Society had the votes necessary to accept the clause prohibiting gender discrimination as well as the votes necessary to pass a bill outlawing both racial and gender discrimination. Pro-suffrage advocates were not as fortunate in 1866. Most Republicans, even those who supported women's rights, refused to support the statutory amendment enfranchising women. Might women have been granted the right to vote if proponents of women's suffrage held firm? What would you have done if you were a senator in 1866?

SENATOR EDGAR COWAN (Republican, Pennsylvania)

. . .

. . . I should like to hear even the most astute and learned Senator upon this floor give any better reason for the exclusion of females from the right of suffrage than there is for the exclusion of negroes. . . .

Now, for my part, I very much prefer, if the franchise is to be widened, if more people are to be admitted to the exercise of it, to allow females to participate than I would negroes; but certainly I shall never give my consent to the disfranchisement of females who

65. *Congressional Globe*, 39th Cong., 2nd Sess., (1866), 46–47, 55–66, 77–84, 107.

live in society, who pay taxes, who are governed by the laws, and who have a right, I think, even in that respect, at times to throw their weight in the balance for the purpose of correcting the corruptions and the viciousness to which the male portions of the family tend. I think they have a right to throw their influence into the scale; and I should like to hear any reason to be offered why this should not be so.

Taxation and representation ought to go hand in hand. That we have heard here until all ears have been wearied with it. If taxation and representation are to go hand in hand, why should they not go hand in hand with regard to the female as well as the male? Is there any reason why Mrs. Smith should be governed by a goatherd of a mayor any more than John Smith, if he could correct it. He is paid by taxes levied and assessed on her property just in the same way as he is paid out of taxes levied on the property of John. If she commits an offense she is subjected to be tried, convicted, and punished by the other sex alone; and she has no protection whatever in any way either as to her property, her person, or to her liberty very often.

. . .

Mr. President, if we are to adventure ourselves upon this wide sea of universal suffrage, I object to manhood suffrage. I do not know anything specially about manhood which dedicates it to this purpose more than exists about womanhood. Womanhood to me is rather the more exalted of the two. It is purer; it is higher; it is holier; and it is not purchasable at the same price that the other is, in my judgment. If you want to widen the franchise so as to purify your ballot-box, throw the virtue of the country into it; throw the temperance of the country into it; throw the angel element, if I may so express myself, into it. Let there be as little diabolism as possible, but as much of the divinity as you can get. . . .

SENATOR BENJAMIN WADE (Republican, Ohio)

. . . I have always been of the opinion that in a republican Government the right of voting ought to be limited only by the years of discretion. . . .

. . .

. . . I think it will puzzle any gentleman to draw a line of demarcation between the right of the male and the female on this subject. Both are liable to all the laws you pass; their property, their persons, and their lives are affected by the laws. Why, then, should not the females have a right to participate in their construction as well as the male part of the community? There is no argument that I can conceive of or that I have yet heard that makes any discrimination between the two on the question of right.

Why should there be any restriction? Is it because gentleman apprehend that the female portion of the community are not as virtuous, that they are not as well calculated to consider what laws and principles of the government will conduce to their welfare as men are? The great mass of our educated females understand all these great concerns of Government infinitely better than that great mass of ignorant population from other countries which you admit to the polls without hesitation.

But, sir, the right of suffrage in my judgment has bearings altogether beyond any rights of persons or property that are to be vindicated by it. I lay it down that in any free community, if any particular class of that community are excluded from this right they cannot maintain their dignity. . . . My judgment is that if this right is accorded to females you would find that they would be elevated in their minds and in their intellects. The best discipline you can offer them would be to permit and to require them to participate in these great concerns of Government, so that their rights and the rights of their children should depend in a manner upon the way in which they understand these great things.

. . .

I do not believe that it will have any unfavorable effect upon the female character if woman are permitted to come up to the polls and vote. I believe it would exercise a most humane and civilizing influence upon the roughness and rudeness with which men meet on those occasions if the polished ladies of the land would come up to the ballot-box clothed with these rights and participate in the exercise of the franchise. It has not been found that association with ladies is apt to make men rude and uncivilized and I do not think the reflex of it presents that lady-like character which we all prize so highly. I do not think it has that effect. On the other hand, in my judgment, if it was popular to-day for ladies to go to the polls, no man would regret their presence there, and the districts where their ballots were given would be harmonized, civilized, and rendered more gentlemanly, if I may say so, on the one side and on the other, and it would prevent the rude collisions that are apt to occur at these places, while it would reflect back no uncivilizing or unladylike influence upon the female part of the community. That is the way I judge it. Of course, as it has never been tried in this country, it is more or less of an experiment; but here in this District is the very place to try your experiment.

I know that the same things were said about the abolition of slavery. I was here. . . . I agree, however, that there is not the same pressing necessity for allowing females as there is for allowing the colored people to vote; because the ladies of the land are not under the ban of a hostile race grinding them to powder. They are in high fellowship with those that do govern, who, to a great extent, act as their agents, their friends, promoting their interests in every vote they give, and therefore communities get along very well without conferring this right upon the female. But when you speak of it as a right and as a great educational power in the hands of females, and I am called on to vote on the subject, I will vote that which I think under all circumstances is right, just, and proper. I shrink not from the question because I am told by gentlemen that it is unpopular. The question with me is, is it right? Show me that it is wrong, and then I will withhold my vote; but I have heard no argument that convinces me that the thing is not right.

. . . It seems to me there is a wrong done to those who are shut out from any participation in the Government, and that it is a violation of their rights; and what odds does it make whether you call it a natural or conventional or artificial right? I contend that when you set up a Government you shall call every man who has arrived at the years of discretion who has committed no crime, into your community and ask him to participate in setting up that Government; and if you shut him out without any reason, you do him a wrong, one of the greatest wrongs that you can inflict upon a man. . . .

SENATOR HENRY WILSON (Republican, Massachusetts)

. . .

. . . [W]hile I will vote now or at any time for woman suffrage . . . as a distinct separate measure, I am unalterably opposed to connecting that question with the pending question of negro suffrage. The question of negro suffrage is now an imperative necessity; a necessity that the negro should possess it for his own protection; a necessity that he should possess it that the nation may preserve its power, its strength, and its utility. . . .

. . .

. . . This bill, embodying pure manhood suffrage, is destined to become the law in spite of all opposition and all lamentations. I am opposed, therefore, to associating with this achieved measure the question of suffrage for women.

. . .

. . . I am for securing the needed suffrage for the colored race. I am for enfranchising the black man, and then if this other question shall come up in due time and I have a vote to give I shall be ready to give my vote for it. But to vote for it now is to couple it with the great measure now pressing upon us, to weaken that measure and to endanger its immediate triumph, and therefore I shall vote against the amendment proposed by the Senator from Pennsylvania, made, it is too apparent, not for the enfranchisement of woman, but against the enfranchisement of the black man.

SENATOR REVERDY JOHNSON (Democrat, Maryland)

. . .

Ladies have duties peculiar to themselves which cannot be discharged by anybody else; the nurture and education of the children; the demands upon them consequent upon the preservation of their household; and they are supposed to be more or less in their proper vocation when they are attending to those particular duties. But independent of that, I think that if it was submitted to the ladies—I mean the ladies in the true acceptation of the term—of the United States, the privilege would not only not be asked for, but would be rejected. I do not think the ladies of the United States would agree to enter into a canvass and to undergo what is often the degradation of seeking to vote, particularly in the cities, getting up to the polls, crowded out and crowded in. I rather think they would feel it, instead of a privilege, a dishonor.

There is another reason why the right should not be extended to them, unless it is the purpose of the honorable member and of the Senate to go a step further. The reason why the males are acceded the privilege, and why it was almost universal in the United States with reference to those of a certain age, is that they may be called upon to defend the country in time of war or in time of insurrection. I do not suppose it is pretended that the ladies should be included in the militia organization or be compelled to take up arms to defend the country. That must be done by the male sex, I hope.

. . .

The honorable member from Ohio seems to suppose that the right should be given as a means, if I understand him, of protecting themselves and as a means of elevating them intellectually. I had supposed the theory was that the woman was protected by the man. If she is insulted she is not expected to knock the man who insults her down, or, during the days of the duello to send him a challenge. She goes to her male friend, her husband or brother or acquaintance. Nature has not made her for the rough and tumble, so to speak, of life. She is intended to be delicate. She is intended to soften the asperities and roughness of the male sex. She is intended to comfort him in the days of his trial, not to participate herself actively in the contest either in the forum, in the council chamber, or on the battlefield. As to her not being protected, what lady has ever said that her rights were not protected because she had not the right of suffrage? There are women, respectable I have no doubt in point of character, moral and virtuous women no doubt, but they are called, and properly called, the "strong-minded": they are in the public estimation contradistinguished from the delicate; they are men in women's garb.

. . .

. . . I have seen elections in Baltimore, where they are just as orderly as they are in other cities; but we all know that in times of high party excitement it is impossible to preserve that order which would be sufficient to protect a delicate female from insult, and no lady would venture to run the hazard of being subjected to the insults that she would be almost certain to receive.

They do not want this privilege. As to protecting themselves, as to taking a part in the Government in order to protect themselves, if they govern those who govern, is not that protection enough? And who does not know that they govern us? Thank God they do. . . .

Bradwell v. Illinois, 83 U.S. 130 (1873)

Myra Bradwell (1831–94) applied for a license to practice law in Illinois. She had apprenticed for many years in a law

Illustration 6-4 Myra Bradwell
Source: Archive Photos/Getty Images

office, edited the Chicago Legal News, *the most important legal newspaper in the Midwest, and passed the Illinois bar examination. The Supreme Court of Illinois nevertheless denied her application on the ground that Bradwell was a married woman. Lawyers in Illinois, the justices pointed out, had obligations to make contracts with their clients, but married women in Illinois did not have the right to make contracts in their name. Hence, Bradwell could not be a lawyer. The Illinois justices also denied Bradwell's application because they believed "as an almost axiomatic truth" that "God designed the sexes to occupy different spheres of action, and that it belonged to men to make, apply, and execute the laws."[66] Bradwell appealed that decision to the Supreme Court of the United States.*

The Supreme Court ruled 8-1 that states could constitutionally prohibit woman from practicing law. Justice Miller's majority opinion declared that states were free to regulate the practice of law in any way. Miller reached this conclusion because he did not believe that the right to practice law was one of the privileges and immunities of American citizens. Justice Bradley rejected that ground for denying Bradwell's petition. His Slaughter-House *dissent, issued immediately before* Bradwell, *had stated that state laws forbidding persons from practicing law and other common callings violated the Fourteenth Amendment. Bradley concluded that states could forbid women from practicing law on the ground that women were not naturally suited to be lawyers.*

Charles Fairman, a prominent legal historian in the twentieth century, declared, "As a demonstration of man's superior fitness for the law, [Bradley's] opinion was not a shining example."[67] Why did Fairman make that assessment? Is Bradley's opinion incompetent because he holds nineteenth-century notions of gender roles or because, even by nineteenth-century standards, his opinion is deficient? How does Senator Matthew Carpenter of Wisconsin, Bradwell's lawyer, interpret the post–Civil War Amendments? Is his argument for gender equality consistent with the text and history of the Fourteenth Amendment? Contemporary lawyers treat Bradwell *as raising equal protection issues. Why did nineteenth-century lawyers and judges treat* Bradwell *as a privileges and immunities case?*

While Bradwell *was being litigated, Illinois repealed the state rule against women practicing law. In 1892, at the age of sixty-one, Myra Bradwell was admitted to the bar.*

---

66. *In re Bradwell*, 55 Ill. 535 (1869).

67. Charles Fairman, *Reconstruction and Reunion, Part One* (New York: Macmillan, 1971), 1366.

MATTHEW HALE CARPENTER for the plaintiff

. . .

. . . [T]he profession of the law, like the clerical profession and that of medicine, is an avocation open to every citizen of the United States. And while the legislature may prescribe qualifications for entering upon this pursuit, they cannot, under the guise of fixing qualifications, exclude a class of citizens from admission to the bar. The legislature may say at what age candidates shall be admitted; may elevate or depress the standard of learning required. But a qualification, to which a whole class of citizens never can attain, is not a regulation of admission to the bar, but is, as to such citizens, a prohibition. For instance, a State legislature could not, in enumerating the qualifications, require the candidate to be a white citizen. This would be the exclusion of all colored citizens, without regard to age, character, or learning. Yet no sound mind can draw a distinction between such an act and a custom, usage, or law of a State, which denies this privilege to all female citizens, without regard to age, character, or learning. If the legislature may, under pretence of fixing qualifications, declare that no female citizen shall be permitted to practice law, it may as well declare that no colored citizen shall practice law; for the only provision in the Constitution of the United States which secures to colored male citizens the privilege of admission to the bar, or the pursuit of the other ordinary avocations of life, is the provision that "no State shall make or enforce any law which shall abridge the privileges or immunities of a citizen." And if this provision does protect the colored citizen, then it protects every citizen, black or white, male or female.

. . .

. . . I maintain that the fourteenth amendment opens to every citizen of the United States, male or female, black or white, married or single, the honorable professions as well as the servile employments of life; and that no citizen can be excluded from any one of them. Intelligence, integrity, and honor are the only qualifications that can be prescribed as conditions precedent to an entry upon any honorable pursuit or profitable avocation, and all the privileges and immunities which I vindicate to a colored citizen, I vindicate to our mothers, our sisters, and our daughters. The inequalities of sex will undoubtedly have their influence, and be considered by every client desiring to employ counsel.

There may be cases in which a client's rights can only be rescued by an exercise of the rough qualities possessed by men. There are many causes in which the silver voice of woman would accomplish more than the severity and sternness of man could achieve. Of a bar composed of men and women of equal integrity and learning, women might be more or less frequently retained, as the taste or judgment of clients might dictate. But the broad shield of the Constitution is over them all, and protects each in that measure of success which his or her individual merits may secure.

JUSTICE MILLER delivered the opinion of the court.

. . .

. . . The opinion just delivered in the *Slaughter-House Cases* [1873] renders elaborate argument in the present case unnecessary; for, unless we are wholly and radically mistaken in the principles on which those cases are decided, the right to control and regulate the granting of license to practice law in the courts of a State is one of those powers which are not transferred for its protection to the Federal government, and its exercise is in no manner governed or controlled by citizenship of the United States in the party seeking such license.

JUSTICE BRADLEY (with JUSTICE SWAYNE and JUSTICE FIELD), concurring.

. . .

. . . [T]he civil law, as well as nature herself, has always recognized a wide difference in the respective spheres and destinies of man and woman. Man is, or should be, woman's protector and defender. The natural and proper timidity and delicacy which belongs to the female sex evidently unfits it for many of the occupations of civil life. The constitution of the family organization, which is founded in the divine ordinance, as well as in the nature of things, indicates the domestic sphere as that which properly belongs to the domain and functions of womanhood. The harmony, not to say identity, of interest and views which belong, or should belong, to the family institution is repugnant to the idea of a woman adopting a distinct and independent career from that of her husband. So firmly fixed was this sentiment in the founders of the common law that it became a maxim of that system of jurisprudence that a woman had no legal existence separate from her husband, who was regarded as her head and representative in the social state; and, notwithstanding some recent modifications of this civil status, many of the special rules of law flowing from and dependent upon this cardinal principle still exist in full force in most States. One of these is, that a married woman is incapable, without her husband's consent, of making contracts which shall be binding on her or him. This very incapacity was one circumstance which the Supreme Court of Illinois deemed important in rendering a married woman incompetent fully to perform the duties and trusts that belong to the office of an attorney and counsellor.

It is true that many women are unmarried and not affected by any of the duties, complications, and incapacities arising out of the married state, but these are exceptions to the general rule. The paramount destiny and mission of woman are to fulfill the noble and benign offices of wife and mother. This is the law of the Creator. And the rules of civil society must be adapted to the general constitution of things, and cannot be based upon exceptional cases.

The humane movements of modern society, which have for their object the multiplication of avenues for woman's advancement, and of occupations adapted to her condition and sex, have my heartiest concurrence. But I am not prepared to say that it is one of her fundamental rights and privileges to be admitted into every office and position, including those which require highly special qualifications and demanding special responsibilities. In the nature of things it is not every citizen of every age, sex, and condition that is qualified for every calling and position. It is the prerogative of the legislator to prescribe regulations founded on nature, reason, and experience for the due admission of qualified persons to professions and callings demanding special skill and confidence. This fairly belongs to the police power of the State; and, in my opinion, in view of the peculiar characteristics, destiny, and mission of woman, it is within the province of the legislature to ordain what offices, positions, and callings shall be filled and discharged by men, and shall receive the benefit of those energies and responsibilities, and that decision and firmness which are presumed to predominate in the sterner sex.

The CHIEF JUSTICE dissented from the judgment of the court, and from all the opinions.

D. Native Americans

Native Americans fared poorly during the Civil War and Reconstruction. The vast majority of Republicans believed that Native Americans, particularly those who maintained tribal affiliation, were not American citizens. Senator James Rood Doolittle expressed the convention wisdom when he stated, "I do not think [Native Americans] are yet in a condition to be incorporated as part of the citizens of the United States and made liable to be bound by the contracts which they make and to be sued upon their contracts."[68] The Fourteenth Amendment's declaration that "all persons born in the United States and subject to the jurisdiction thereof, are citizens of the United States" reflected a congressional consensus that members of Native American tribes, who were not fully subject to the jurisdiction of the United States, should not be citizens of the United States.

VI. Criminal Justice

MAJOR DEVELOPMENTS

- Supreme Court declares that martial law cannot be imposed when civilian courts are open
- Police and judges battle over confessions
- Greater emphasis on right to counsel than trial by jury

The constitutional politics of criminal justice was structured by two different wars. The first was the Civil War and the aftermath of the Union victory. From 1861 to 1865 the Lincoln administration suspended habeas corpus, declared martial law, and arrested numerous persons suspected of interfering with the Union military effort without first obtaining warrants. Congress in 1867 declared martial law throughout much of the South. The second war was the municipal war against crime fought by urban politicians and increasingly professionalized police forces. One commentator has observed,

> Professional police forces were created in a handful of American cities with military-style hierarchies, staffed with career officers who had incentives to aggressively investigate crime. Law enforcement became a career, and one that paid better-than-average wages. Ferreting out criminals led to retention and promotion. The legal rules that had prevented aggressive policing were also eliminated between 1850 and 1920. Officers were given broader search and arrest powers, [and] began to routinely (and roughly) interrogate suspects . . . with impunity.[69]

Remarkable parallels exist between the war against secession and the war against crime. Both represented sharp breaks from the constitutional past. The Civil War was the first military conflict in American history in which the federal government suspended habeas corpus throughout the nation, used military commissions to try civilians, and arrested thousands of citizens suspected of disloyalty. The 1850s, 1860s, and 1870s witnessed the rise of professional police forces, members of which insisted and often received novel constitutional protections when fighting crime. Executive officials concerned with secession and crime demanded greater powers to promote the public good. Lincoln administration officials maintained that the president had the power to suspend habeas corpus and impose martial law. Police officers maintained that they were constitutionally authorized to question persons suspected of crime without warning them that their confessions might be admitted as evidence in a court of law. Strong opposition to both demands existed. Northern Democrats and some northern Republicans insisted that civilians had a constitutional right to a civilian jury trial in all places where courts were open. Defense lawyers insisted that criminal suspects should be questioned by magistrates, who traditionally warned their subjects that confessions could be admitted as evidence in courts.

Courts during the war against secession and the war against crime often rejected executive demands for greater power. The Supreme Court in *Ex parte Milligan* (1866) ruled that citizens could not be tried by military commissions in places where courts were open. Many states judges exhibited a traditional antipathy to confessions. Courts were nevertheless largely ineffective in their struggle to curb executive behavior in either the war against secession or the war against crime. Shortly after *Milligan* was handed down, Congress passed the First Reconstruction Act, which imposed martial law throughout the South. Policemen continued to seek confessions, confident that in most cases the confessed criminal would not litigate the constitutionality of the means by which the confession was obtained.

68. *Congressional Globe*, 39th Cong., 1st Sess. (1866), 2892–4.

69. Wesley MacNeil Oliver, "The Neglected History of Criminal Procedure, 1850–1940," *Rutgers Law Review* 62 (2010): 459–60.

A. Due Process and Habeas Corpus

Federal and military officials frequently suspended habeas corpus and declared martial law. Less than two months after taking the oath of office, President Lincoln ordered that habeas corpus be suspended in Maryland to secure the safe transportation of troops from the northern states to the nation's capital. On September 24, 1862, Lincoln suspended habeas corpus and imposed martial law throughout the United States. Congress later authorized presidential suspensions by passing the Habeas Corpus Act of 1863. The Republican majority in Congress also sanctioned the use of military tribunals when passing the Conscription Act of 1863. Four years later Congress passed the First Reconstruction Act, which permitted Union military commanders in the South to use military commissions to try civilians. In no other period in American history was the writ of habeas corpus suspended so frequently or martial law declared within the territory of the United States.

Suspending habeas corpus and imposing martial law enabled the Lincoln administration and Reconstruction Republicans to move swiftly and decisively against persons they feared were disloyal, dangerous, or otherwise a threat to the general public. By suspending habeas corpus, the Lincoln administration could arrest and detain without trial persons suspected of assisting the Confederate cause. The best recent estimate is that government officials arrested and detained approximately fourteen thousand persons during the Civil War.[70] By imposing martial law, the Lincoln administration could have military commissions rather than juries try persons suspected of interfering with the war effort. Approximately 1,500 persons were tried by military commissions during the Civil War, and another 1,500 were tried by military commissions during Reconstruction.[71] Most persons detained and tried by military commissions were charged with such crimes as desertion, trading with the enemy, and selling liquor to soldiers. Others were suspected of more political offenses. Members of the Lincoln administration ordered or approved the detention of and military trials for leading administration critics, most notably former Congressman Clement Vallandigham. The persons who plotted with John Wilkes Booth to assassinate Lincoln were also tried by a military commission.[72]

Many prominent Americans challenged the constitutionality of official decisions to suspend habeas corpus and declare martial law. Some constitutional objections were based on the separation of powers. Chief Justice Roger Taney in *Ex parte Merryman* (1861) held that President Lincoln acted unconstitutionally when he suspended habeas corpus and declared martial law without congressional authorization. During the debate over the Habeas Corpus Act of 1863, Democrats asserted that only Congress could suspend habeas corpus, and that Congress could not delegate to the president the power to determine when suspending habeas corpus or declaring martial law was appropriate. Other constitutional objections were based on individual rights. Lincoln's critics as well as opponents of Reconstruction maintained that federal laws imposing martial law in places where the courts were open violated such constitutional liberties as the right to trial by jury.

The constitutional debates over habeas corpus and martial law were bipartisan during the Civil War. Leading Republicans opposed the Lincoln administration's efforts to restrict civil liberties during wartime. Senator Lyman Trumbull of Illinois, the main sponsor of the Habeas Corpus Act of 1863, was a moderate Republican and a vigorous critic of the Lincoln administration's attempts to suspend habeas corpus and impose martial law without congressional authorization. All five justices Lincoln appointed to the Supreme Court joined the decision in *Ex parte Milligan* (1865) that held that the president had no power to declare martial law where courts were open. Democrats also opposed Lincoln administration restrictions. Governor Horatio Seymour of New York and his political allies were particularly vigorous critics.

Partisan alliances strengthened during Reconstruction debates over habeas corpus and martial law. Republicans favored and Democrats opposed the First Reconstruction Act, which imposed martial law throughout the South. As time wore on, however, many Republicans wearied of military efforts to protect African-Americans' rights. The effort to police the South was consistently underfunded and was

70. Mark E. Neely, Jr., *The Fate of Liberty: Abraham Lincoln and Civil Liberties* (New York: Oxford University Press, 1991), 233–35.

71. Ibid., 176–77.

72. Booth was killed before he could be brought to trial.

eventually abandoned as part of the bargain that enabled Republican Rutherford B. Hayes to be declared the winner of the 1876 presidential election.

The Civil War

Ex Parte Milligan, 71 U.S. 2 (1866)

Lambdin P. Milligan, a Confederate sympathizer in Indiana, was arrested by military authorities in 1864 and accused of plotting to steal and provide weapons for the Confederate Army. The Habeas Corpus Act of 1863 required that persons denied habeas corpus be indicted by a grand jury and tried by a civilian court within a short period of time after their detention. Lincoln administration officials tried Milligan before a military tribunal, which sentenced him to death. Milligan appealed to a federal circuit court for a writ of habeas corpus on the ground that his imprisonment, trial, and sentence were unconstitutional. Although both justices on the circuit court probably agreed that Milligan was being illegally detained, they agreed to disagree, because the Supreme Court at that time was obligated to hear all cases whenever the two federal circuit justices hearing the appeal certified their disagreement on the legal issues. President Andrew Johnson assured judicial review by delaying Milligan's scheduled execution until after the Supreme Court determined whether Milligan had been legally convicted.

The Supreme Court decided Milligan *in a rapidly changing political environment. By the spring of 1865 few persons were deeply concerned with the status of persons detained for interfering with the Union war effort. Lincoln intimated that, after a Confederate surrender, he planned to release all detainees and pardon most people convicted of wartime offenses. Republicans in 1865 were far more concerned with how the decision in* Milligan *cast light on the constitutionality of martial law in the Reconstruction South.*

The Supreme Court unanimously declared that Milligan had been illegally convicted by a military commission. Judge David Davis's majority opinion insisted that neither Congress nor the president could impose martial law in places where the courts were open. Chief Justice Chase, in a concurring opinion, maintained that Milligan was illegally convicted because President Lincoln did not follow the procedures laid out in the Habeas Corpus Act of 1863. Unlike Justice Davis, Chief Justice Chase believed that Congress was free to impose martial law in places where courts were open.

The majority opinion in Milligan *was and is controversial. One Republican journal compared Justice Davis's effort to limit federal power to the* Dred Scott *decision. Republicans were particularly concerned with the broad scope of* Milligan *because Congress was debating legislation authorizing martial law in the Reconstruction South. Davis's opinion cast doubt on whether such legislation would be constitutional when southern courts were open. Justice Davis privately indicated surprise that his opinion in* Milligan *should have so troubled Republicans in Congress. Given that Justice Davis frequently indicated in "private" that much Reconstruction legislation was unconstitutional, was this profession sincere? Could Republicans impose martial law in the South if, as* Milligan *held, martial law may never be declared when the courts are open and functioning? If the judicial majority had no intention of commenting on martial law in the South, then why not decide the case on the statutory grounds on which Chief Justice Chase's opinion relied? Lincoln's judicial appointees split 3-2 in favor of congressional power to impose martial law. The Jacksonian holdovers on the Supreme Court split 4-1 in favor of denying congressional power. What do you think explains that division?*

Illustration 6-5 Lambdin P. Milligan

Source: Library of Congress Prints and Photographs Division Washington, D.C. 20540 USA.

Milligan *has been hailed as one of the greatest opinions for individual liberty issued by the Supreme Court. Is this characterization correct? How much courage was needed for a judge to assert a right to a civilian trial after the war was over? Does* Milligan *better stand for the proposition that those persons unconstitutionally deprived of liberty during a war are likely to be remedied only after the war?*

JUSTICE DAVIS delivered the opinion of the court.

. . .

. . . Milligan, not a resident of one of the rebellious states, or a prisoner of war, but a citizen of Indiana for twenty years past, and never in the military or naval service, is, while at his home, arrested by the military power of the United States, imprisoned, and, on certain criminal charges preferred against him, tried, convicted, and sentenced to be hanged by a military commission, organized under the direction of the military commander of the military district of Indiana. Had this tribunal the legal power and authority to try and punish this man?

No graver question was ever considered by this court, nor one which more nearly concerns the rights of the whole people; for it is the birthright of every American citizen when charged with crime, to be tried and punished according to law. The power of punishment is, alone through the means which the laws have provided for that purpose, and if they are ineffectual, there is an immunity from punishment, no matter how great an offender the individual may be, or how much his crimes may have shocked the sense of justice of the country, or endangered its safety. By the protection of the law human rights are secured; withdraw that protection, and they are at the mercy of wicked rulers, or the clamor of an excited people. If there was law to justify this military trial, it is not our province to interfere; if there was not, it is our duty to declare the nullity of the whole proceedings. . . . By th[e] Constitution and the laws authorized by it this question must be determined. The provisions of that instrument on the administration of criminal justice are too plain and direct, to leave room for misconstruction or doubt of their true meaning. Those applicable to this case are found in that clause of the original Constitution which says, "That the trial of all crimes, except in case of impeachment, shall be by jury"; and in the fourth, fifth, and sixth articles of the amendments. . . . These securities for personal liberty thus embodied, were such as wisdom and experience had demonstrated to be necessary for the protection of those accused of crime. And so strong was the sense of the country of their importance, and so jealous were the people that these rights, highly prized, might be denied them by implication, that when the original Constitution was proposed for adoption it encountered severe opposition; and but for the belief that it would be so amended as to embrace them, it would never have been ratified.

. . . The Constitution of the United States is a law for rulers and people, equally in war and in peace, and covers with the shield of its protection all classes of men, at all times, and under all circumstances. No doctrine, involving more pernicious consequences, was ever invented by the wit of man than that any of its provisions can be suspended during any of the great exigencies of government. Such a doctrine leads directly to anarchy or despotism, but the theory of necessity on which it is based is false; for the government, within the Constitution, has all the powers granted to it, which are necessary to preserve its existence; as has been happily proved by the result of the great effort to throw off its just authority.

Have any of the rights guaranteed by the Constitution been violated in the case of Milligan? and if so, what are they?

. . .

. . . [I]t is said that the jurisdiction is complete under the "laws and usages of war."

It can serve no useful purpose to inquire what those laws and usages are, whence they originated, where found, and on whom they operate; they can never be applied to citizens in states which have upheld the authority of the government, and where the courts are open and their process unobstructed. This court has judicial knowledge that in Indiana the Federal authority was always unopposed, and its courts always open to hear criminal accusations and redress grievances; and no usage of war could sanction a military trial there for any offence whatever of a citizen in civil life, in nowise connected with the military service. Congress could grant no such power; and to the honor of our national legislature be it said, it has never been provoked by the state of the country even to attempt its exercise. One of the plainest constitutional provisions was, therefore, infringed when Milligan was tried by a court not ordained and established by Congress, and not composed of judges appointed during good behavior.

. . .

Another guarantee of freedom was broken when Milligan was denied a trial by jury. The great minds of the country have differed on the correct interpretation to be given to various provisions of the Federal Constitution; and judicial decision has been often invoked to settle their true meaning; but until recently no one ever doubted that the right of trial by jury was fortified in the organic law against the power of attack. It is now assailed; but if ideas can be expressed in words, and language has any meaning, this right—one of the most valuable in a free country—is preserved to every one accused of crime who is not attached to the army, or navy, or militia in actual service. . . .

The discipline necessary to the efficiency of the army and navy, required other and swifter modes of trial than are furnished by the common law courts; and, in pursuance of the power conferred by the Constitution, Congress has declared the kinds of trial, and the manner in which they shall be conducted, for offences committed while the party is in the military or naval service. Every one connected with these branches of the public service is amenable to the jurisdiction which Congress has created for their government, and, while thus serving, surrenders his right to be tried by the civil courts. All other persons, citizens of states where the courts are open, if charged with crime, are guaranteed the inestimable privilege of trial by jury. This privilege is a vital principle, underlying the whole administration of criminal justice; it is not held by sufferance, and cannot be frittered away on any plea of state or political necessity. When peace prevails, and the authority of the government is undisputed, there is no difficulty of preserving the safeguards of liberty; for the ordinary modes of trial are never neglected, and no one wishes it otherwise; but if society is disturbed by civil commotion—if the passions of men are aroused and the restraints of law weakened, if not disregarded—these safeguards need, and should receive, the watchful care of those intrusted with the guardianship of the Constitution and laws. In no other way can we transmit to posterity unimpaired the blessings of liberty, consecrated by the sacrifices of the Revolution.

It is claimed that martial law covers with its broad mantle the proceedings of this military commission. The proposition is this: that in a time of war the commander of an armed force (if in his opinion the exigencies of the country demand it, and of which he is to judge), has the power, within the lines of his military district, to suspend all civil rights and their remedies, and subject citizens as well as soldiers to the rule of his will; and in the exercise of his lawful authority cannot be restrained, except by his superior officer or the President of the United States.

. . .

The statement of this proposition shows its importance; for, if true, republican government is a failure, and there is an end of liberty regulated by law. Martial law, established on such a basis, destroys every guarantee of the Constitution, and effectually renders the "military independent of and superior to the civil power"—the attempt to do which by the King of Great Britain was deemed by our fathers such an offence, that they assigned it to the world as one of the causes which impelled them to declare their independence. Civil liberty and this kind of martial law cannot endure together; the antagonism is irreconcilable; and, in the conflict, one or the other must perish.

. . .

It is essential to the safety of every government that, in a great crisis, like the one we have just passed through, there should be a power somewhere of suspending the writ of habeas corpus. In every war, there are men of previously good character, wicked enough to counsel their fellow-citizens to resist the measures deemed necessary by a good government to sustain its just authority and overthrow its enemies; and their influence may lead to dangerous combinations. In the emergency of the times, an immediate public investigation according to law may not be possible; and yet, the peril to the country may be too imminent to suffer such persons to go at large. Unquestionably, there is then an exigency which demands that the government, if it should see fit in the exercise of a proper discretion to make arrests, should not be required to produce the persons arrested in answer to a writ of habeas corpus. The Constitution goes no further. It does not say after a writ of habeas corpus is denied a citizen, that he shall be tried otherwise than by the course of the common law; if it had intended this result, it was easy by the use of direct words to have accomplished it. The illustrious men who framed that instrument were guarding the foundations of civil liberty against the abuses of unlimited power; they were full of wisdom, and the lessons of history informed them that a trial by an established court, assisted by an impartial jury, was the only sure way of protecting the citizen against oppression and wrong. Knowing this, they limited the suspension to one great right, and left the rest to remain forever inviolable. But, it is insisted that the safety of the country in time of war demands that this broad claim for martial law shall be sustained. If this were true, it could be well said that a country, preserved at the sacrifice of all the cardinal principles of liberty, is not worth the cost of preservation. Happily, it is not so.

. . .

It is difficult to see how the safety of the country required martial law in Indiana. If any of her citizens were plotting treason, the power of arrest could secure them, until the government was prepared for their trial, when the courts were open and ready to try them. It was as easy to protect witnesses before a civil as a military tribunal; and as there could be no wish to convict, except on sufficient legal evidence, surely an ordained and established court was better able to judge of this than a military tribunal composed of gentlemen not trained to the profession of the law.

It follows, from what has been said on this subject, that there are occasions when martial rule can be properly applied. If, in foreign invasion or civil war, the courts are actually closed, and it is impossible to administer criminal justice according to law, then, on the theatre of active military operations, where war really prevails, there is a necessity to furnish a substitute for the civil authority, thus overthrown, to preserve the safety of the army and society; and as no power is left but the military, it is allowed to govern by martial rule until the laws can have their free course. As necessity creates the rule, so it limits its duration; for, if this government is continued after the courts are reinstated, it is a gross usurpation of power. Martial rule can never exist where the courts are open, and in the proper and unobstructed exercise of their jurisdiction. It is also confined to the locality of actual war. Because, during the late Rebellion it could have been enforced in Virginia, where the national authority was overturned and the courts driven out, it does not follow that it should obtain in Indiana, where that authority was never disputed, and justice was always administered. And so in the case of a foreign invasion, martial rule may become a necessity in one state, when, in another, it would be "mere lawless violence."

The CHIEF JUSTICE (with JUSTICE SWAYNE, JUSTICE WAYNE, and JUSTICE MILLER), concurring.

. . .

The crimes with which Milligan was charged were of the gravest character, and the petition and exhibits in the record, which must here be taken as true, admit his guilt. But whatever his desert of punishment may be, it is more important to the country and to every citizen that he should not be punished under an illegal sentence, sanctioned by this court of last resort, than that he should be punished at all. The laws which protect the liberties of the whole people must not be violated or set aside in order to inflict, even upon the guilty, unauthorized though merited justice.

. . .

The holding of the Circuit and District Courts of the United States in Indiana had been uninterrupted. The administration of the laws in the Federal courts had remained unimpaired. Milligan was imprisoned under the authority of the President, and was not a prisoner of war. No list of prisoners had been furnished to the judges, either of the District or Circuit Courts, as required by the law. A grand jury had attended the Circuit Courts of the Indiana district, while Milligan was there imprisoned, and had closed its session without finding any indictment or presentment or otherwise proceeding against the prisoner.

His case was thus brought within the precise letter and intent of the act of Congress, unless it can be said that Milligan was not imprisoned by authority of the President; and nothing of this sort was claimed in argument on the part of the government.

. . .

And it is equally clear that he was entitled to the discharge prayed for.

. . .

But the opinion which has just been read goes further; and as we understand it, asserts not only that the military commission held in Indiana was not authorized by Congress, but that it was not in the power of Congress to authorize it; from which it may be thought to follow, that Congress has no power to indemnify the officers who composed the commission against liability in civil courts for acting as members of it.

We cannot agree to this.

. . .

We think that Congress had power, though not exercised, to authorize the military commission which was held in Indiana.

. . .

It is not denied that the power to make rules for the government of the army and navy is a power to provide for trial and punishment by military courts without a jury. It has been so understood and exercised from the adoption of the Constitution to the present time.

...

We think, therefore, that the power of Congress, in the government of the land and naval forces and of the militia, is not at all affected by the fifth or any other amendment. It is not necessary to attempt any precise definition of the boundaries of this power. But may it not be said that government includes protection and defence as well as the regulation of internal administration? And is it impossible to imagine cases in which citizens conspiring or attempting the destruction or great injury of the national forces may be subjected by Congress to military trial and punishment in the just exercise of this undoubted constitutional power? Congress is but the agent of the nation, and does not the security of individuals against the abuse of this, as of every other power, depend on the intelligence and virtue of the people, on their zeal for public and private liberty, upon official responsibility secured by law, and upon the frequency of elections, rather than upon doubtful constructions of legislative powers?

But we do not put our opinion, that Congress might authorize such a military commission as was held in Indiana, upon the power to provide for the government of the national forces.

Congress has the power not only to raise and support and govern armies but to declare war. It has, therefore, the power to provide by law for carrying on war. This power necessarily extends to all legislation essential to the prosecution of war with vigor and success, except such as interferes with the command of the forces and the conduct of campaigns. That power and duty belong to the President as commander-in-chief. Both these powers are derived from the Constitution, but neither is defined by that instrument. Their extent must be determined by their nature, and by the principles of our institutions.

...

Where peace exists the laws of peace must prevail. What we do maintain is, that when the nation is involved in war, and some portions of the country are invaded, and all are exposed to invasion, it is within the power of Congress to determine in what states or districts such great and imminent public danger exists as justifies the authorization of military tribunals for the trial of crimes and offences against the discipline or security of the army or against the public safety.

...

We cannot doubt that, in such a time of public danger, Congress had power, under the Constitution, to provide for the organization of a military commission, and for trial by that commission of persons engaged in this conspiracy. The fact that the Federal courts were open was regarded by Congress as a sufficient reason for not exercising the power; but that fact could not deprive Congress of the right to exercise it. Those courts might be open and undisturbed in the execution of their functions, and yet wholly incompetent to avert threatened danger, or to punish, with adequate promptitude and certainty, the guilty conspirators.

In Indiana, the judges and officers of the courts were loyal to the government. But it might have been otherwise. In times of rebellion and civil war it may often happen, indeed, that judges and marshals will be in active sympathy with the rebels, and courts their most efficient allies.

We have confined ourselves to the question of power. It was for Congress to determine the question of expediency. And Congress did determine it. That body did not see fit to authorize trials by military commission in Indiana, but by the strongest implication prohibited them. With that prohibition we are satisfied, and should have remained silent if the answers to the questions certified had been put on that ground, without denial of the existence of a power which we believe to be constitutional and important to the public safety,—a denial which, as we have already suggested, seems to draw in question the power of Congress to protect from prosecution the members of military commissions who acted in obedience to their superior officers, and whose action, whether warranted by law or not, was approved by that up-right and patriotic President under whose administration the Republic was rescued from threatened destruction. . . .

Reconstruction

Constitutional controversies over habeas corpus, martial law, and due process were partisan during Reconstruction. Republicans in Congress passed a series of acts authorizing Union military officials posted in the South to use military commissions to try various crimes. The First Reconstruction Act (1867) asserted that "no legal State governments or adequate protection for life or property now exists in the rebel States," divided the South into military districts, mandated that the president appoint military officials to govern those districts, and gave those military officials the option of using civil juries or military commissions. Section 3 of the act stated:

> That it shall be the duty of each officer assigned as aforesaid, to protect all persons in their rights of person and property, to suppress insurrection, disorder, and violence, and to punish, or cause to be punished, all disturbers of the public peace and criminals; and to this end he may allow local civil tribunals to take jurisdiction of and to try offenders, or, when in his judgment it may be necessary for the trial of offenders, he shall have power to organize military commissions or tribunals for that purpose.[73]

President Andrew Johnson vetoed the First Reconstruction Act, but his veto was overridden by overwhelming Republican majorities in both the House of Representatives and the Senate.

Republicans justified martial law in the South as a necessary measure to protect persons of color and Union supporters. Senator Lyman Trumbull of Illinois asserted,

> The State organizations . . . are not republican; . . . moreover, . . . the loyal men who assisted the Government to put down the rebellion are in the condition of a vanquished party; . . . murders and persecutions of loyal men are increasing in frequency and turpitude, and . . . they cannot obtain justice in the civil courts or adequate military protection.

Congress, Trumbull maintained, could secure fundamental rights only by "enter[ing] into those States and hurl[ing] from power the disloyal element which controls and governs them." He and other Republicans declared that the necessary and proper clause gave Congress the power to protect endangered rights in former confederate states. Trumbull stated,

> The Congress of the United States is vested with authority to pass all laws necessary to carry into execution all powers intrusted to this Government. . . . [I]t should exercise this power and pass the necessary laws to secure to Union men and loyal citizens their rights in these rebellious States, the necessary laws to place them in authority and control so that they may have protection, and secure to all republican liberty.[74]

73. 14 U.S. Stat. 428, 428 (1867).

74. *Congressional Globe*, 39th Cong., 2nd Sess. (1866), 159–60.

Democrats charged that martial law in the South was both unnecessary and unconstitutional. After pointing out that "the States in question have each of them an actual government . . . which properly belongs to a free state," President Andrew Johnson's message vetoing the First Reconstruction Act denied the necessity of interfering with southern legal processes and civilian jury trials.

> The provisions which [former slave state] governments have made for the preservation of order, the suppression of crime, and the redress of private injuries are in substance and principle the same as those which prevail in the Northern States and in other civilized countries. They certainly have not succeeded in preventing the commission of all crime, nor has this been accomplished anywhere in the world. . . . All the information I have on the subject convinces me that the masses of the Southern people and those who control their public acts, while they entertain diverse opinions on questions of Federal policy, are completely united in the effort to reorganize their society on the basis of peace and to restore their mutual prosperity as rapidly and as completely as their circumstances will permit.

Johnson cited the Supreme Court's decision in *Milligan* as supporting his claim that Congress could not impose martial law when southern courts were open. He concluded his veto message with a lengthy argument that imposing martial law violated fundamental constitutional rights.

> I need not say to the representatives of the American people that their Constitution forbids the exercise of judicial power in any way but one—that is, by the ordained and established courts. It is equally well known that in all criminal cases a trial by jury is made indispensable by the express words of that instrument. I will not enlarge on the inestimable value of the right thus secured to every freeman or speak of the danger to public liberty in all parts of the country which must ensue from a denial of it anywhere or upon any pretense. . . . It is in such a condition of things that an act of Congress is proposed which, if carried out, would deny a trial by the lawful courts and juries to 9,000,000 American citizens and to their posterity for an indefinite period. It seems to be scarcely possible that anyone should seriously believe this consistent with a

> Constitution which declares in simple, plain, and unambiguous language that all persons shall have that right and that no person shall ever in any case be deprived of it. The Constitution also forbids the arrest of the citizen without judicial warrant, grounded on probable cause. This bill authorizes an arrest without warrant, at the pleasure of a military commander. The Constitution declares that "no person shall be held to answer for a capital or otherwise infamous crime unless on presentment by a grand jury." This bill holds every person not a soldier answerable for all crimes and all charges without any presentment. The Constitution declares that "no person shall be deprived of life, liberty, or property without due process of law." This bill sets aside all process of law, and makes the citizen answerable in his person and property to the will of one man, and as to his life to the will of two. Finally, the Constitution declares that "the privilege of the writ of *habeas corpus* shall not be suspended unless when, in case of rebellion or invasion, the public safety may require it"; whereas this bill declares martial law (which of itself suspends this great writ) in time of peace, and authorizes the military to make the arrest, and gives to the prisoner only one privilege, and that is a trial "without unnecessary delay." He has no hope of release from custody, except the hope, such as it is, of release by acquittal before a military commission.

Prominent northern Democrats launched a litigation campaign aimed at securing a judicial decision that would declare unconstitutional the institution of martial law in the South. Initial efforts failed on jurisdictional grounds. The Supreme Court in *Mississippi v. Johnson* (1867) ruled that federal justices could not issue an injunction prohibiting the president from enforcing the Reconstruction Acts. *Georgia v. Stanton* (1867) held that states lacked the standing to make a general attack on Reconstruction measures. Democrats seemed more fortunate after military officers in Mississippi arrested and detained William McCardle, a racist newspaper editor from Mississippi. Rejecting pleas from congressional Republicans, the justices ruled that the Supreme Court had jurisdiction to determine whether McCardle could be tried by a military commission.

Faced with the strong probability that the Supreme Court would use McCardle's case as a vehicle for declaring the First Reconstruction Act unconstitutional, Republicans aggressively protected their legislative handiwork from judicial attack. First, they passed legislation shrinking the size of the Supreme Court. This measure prevented President Johnson from replacing Justice Catron, who died in 1865, and Justice Wayne, who died two years later, with justices who shared Johnson's hostility to Reconstruction. Second, Congress repealed the Habeas Corpus Act of 1867, the law that gave the Supreme Court jurisdiction to decide McCardle's case. The Repealer Act was passed after the Supreme Court heard arguments in McCardle's case but before the justices announced their decision. In *Ex parte McCardle* (1869) the justices sustained the Repealer Act and refused to determine the substance of McCardle's constitutional attack on martial law in the South.[75] The private correspondence of the justices suggests that they would have declared the First Reconstruction Act unconstitutional had Congress not stripped the Supreme Court of jurisdiction.

B. Search and Seizure

The ordinary constitutional politics of search and seizure was influenced by the increasing perception that professional police officers needed greater leeway to fight crime than the common law provided. Many state courts, building on precedents from the Jacksonian Era, provided professional police officers with constitutional immunities from lawsuits brought by innocent victims of police mistakes. State courts permitted unconstitutionally seized goods to be admitted in a criminal trial. The Supreme Judicial Court of Maine emphatically rejected the exclusion rule in *State v. McCann* (ME 1873). When rejecting Cornelius McCann's claim that the prosecutor could not introduce illegally seized liquors in his trial for violating prohibition laws, Judge Anderson tersely declared:

> It is objected that the seizure was illegal, the officer having proceeded to search without any warrant. Suppose it was so, that is no defense for the defendant's violation of law. If the sheriff has violated any law he is responsible for such violation, but that

75. The date for the *McCardle* case is sometimes reported as 1868, since it was the practice in the mid-nineteenth century to cite cases by the beginning date of the Supreme Court's term (in this case December 1868). Here we use the date when the case was actually handed down, which was April 12, 1869.

will not constitute any justification or excuse for the defendant.[76]

C. Interrogations

The official constitutional law of investigations and interrogations diverged sharply from unofficial constitutional practice. Official constitutional law was hostile to confessions, particularly when any suspicion existed that the confession was motivated by either coercion or the hope of leniency. *McGlothlin v. State* (TN 1865) articulated the traditional common law antipathy to confessions as the primary evidence used to convict persons suspected of crime. "A confession, to be received," the justices determined,

> must be freely and voluntarily made, and where the mind has been placed under restraints, by the flattery of hope or the terror of fear, for the purpose of forcing the accused to make a confession, it must appear that prior to the confession, it had become again free, and totally relieved from the influence of the hopes or fears, induced by the promises or threats which had been used, else the confession will not be admissible.[77]

Constitutional practice relied more heavily on confessions than opinions such as *McGlothlin* suggest. Police officers frequently beat suspects or otherwise induced confessions to prevent crime and obtain convictions. Superintendent George Walling of the New York police force bluntly declared that his officers routinely employed various strategies to induce confessions from criminal suspects.

Thomas Cooley summarized the common law hostility to confessions in his 1874 edition of *Constitutional Limitations*:

> The proceeding to establish guilt shall not be inquisitorial. A peculiar excellence of the common-law system of trial over that which has prevailed in other civilized countries, consists in the fact that the accused is never compelled to give evidence against himself. . . .
>
> It is the law in some of the States when a person is charged with crime, and is brought before an examining magistrate, and the witnesses in support of the charge have been heard, that the prisoner may also make a statement concerning the transaction charged against him, and that this may be used against him on the trial if supposed to have a tendency to establish guilt. But the prisoner is to be first cautioned that he is under no obligation to answer any question put to him unless he chooses, and that whatever he says and does must be entirely voluntary. He is also to be allowed the presence and advice of counsel; and if that privilege is denied him it may be sufficient reason for discrediting any damaging statements he may have made. When, however, the statute has been complied with, and no species of coercion appears to have been employed, the statement the prisoner may have made is evidence which can be used against him on his trial, and is generally entitled to great weight. . . .
>
> But to make it admissible in any case it ought to appear that it was made voluntarily, and that no motives of hope or fear were employed to induce the accused to confess. The evidence ought to be clear and satisfactory that the prisoner was neither threatened nor cajoled into admitting what very possibly was untrue. Under the excitement of a charge of crime, coolness and self-possession are to be looked for in very few persons; and however strongly we may reason with ourselves that no one will confess a heinous offense of which he is not guilty, the records of criminal courts bear abundant testimony to the contrary. If confessions could prove a crime beyond doubt, no act which was ever punished criminally would be better established than witchcraft. . . .
>
> A confession alone ought not to be sufficient evidence of the *corpus delicti*. There should be other proof that a crime has actually been committed; and the confession should only be allowed for the purpose of connecting the defendant with the offense. And if the party's hopes or fears are operated upon him to induce him to make it, this fact will be sufficient to preclude the confession being received; the rule upon this subject being so strict that even saying to the prisoner it will be better for him to confess, has been decided to be a holding out of such inducements to confession, especially when said by a person having a prisoner in custody, as should render the statement obtained by means of it inadmissible.[78]

76. *State v. McCann*, 61 Me. 116 (1873).
77. *McGlothlin v. State*, 2 Coldw. 223 (TN 1865).
78. Cooley, *Constitutional Limitations*, 3rd ed., 312–14.

Police officers nevertheless found inducing confessions a fruitful means for combating crime, even when their methods were constitutionally questionable. Owing to the widespread lack of attorneys, few poor persons or persons of color challenged unconstitutionally induced confessions. Most states did not exclude the fruits of unconstitutionally obtained confessions. In *Duffy v. People* (NY 1863), the Court of Appeals of New York admitted into evidence a watch allegedly stolen by the defendant, even though the police officer located the watch through an unconstitutionally extracted confession. Judge Selden's opinion asserted:

> The rule which excludes evidence of the confessions of persons charged with crimes, where such confessions have been made under the influence of threats or promises, has never been held to exclude evidence of any facts which were ascertained in consequence of such confessions. . . . The course pursued has usually been to admit proof of the words used by the prisoner with reference to the extraneous facts, and then to receive proof of the facts themselves.[79]

D. Juries and Lawyers

Criminal defendants enjoyed increased access to lawyers and decreased access to juries during the Civil War and Reconstruction. More states provided attorneys to persons accused of crime. Many constitutional authorities asserted or implied that poor persons had a right to a state-appointed attorney. Thomas Cooley in 1874 declared, "Perhaps the privilege most important to the person accused of crime . . . is that to be defended by counsel."[80] The jury came under increased attack. Presidential and congressional decisions to impose martial law denied jury trials to persons accused of supporting the Confederacy or opposing Reconstruction. In ordinary criminal trials, states began to experiment with alternatives to the jury trial.

E. Punishments

The Civil War and Reconstruction left the constitutional politics of punishment untouched. Few criminal defendants challenged the constitutionality of their sentences, and no state or federal court declared a criminal sanction unconstitutional. The Supreme Court of the Territory of New Mexico expressed the conventional wisdom of the time in *Garcia v. Territory of New Mexico* (NM 1869) when rejecting a constitutional attack on whipping. The cruel and unusual punishment clause, Chief Judge Watts asserted, "was never designed to abridge or limit the selection by the law-making power of such kind of punishment as was deemed most effective in the punishment and suppression of crime."[81]

American notions of what constituted cruel and unusual punishment were evolving. In the 1868 edition of *Constitutional Limitations*, Thomas Cooley made no mention of whipping. Six years later the third edition of that work suggested that some state constitutions prohibited that punishment. Cooley declared,

> Probably any punishment declared by statute for an offence which was punishable in the same way at the common law, could not be regarded as cruel or unusual in the constitutional sense. . . . But those degrading punishments which in any State had become obsolete before its existing constitution was adopted, we think may well be held forbidden by it as cruel and unusual. We may well doubt the right to establish the whipping-post and the pillory in States where they were never recognized as instruments of punishment, or in States whose constitutions, revised since public opinion had banished them, have forbidden cruel and unusual punishments. In such States the public sentiment must be regarded as having condemned them as "cruel," and any punishment which, if every employed at all, has become altogether obsolete, must certainly be looked upon as "unusual."[82]

The status of capital punishment in the United States also remained largely unchanged. Maine and Iowa abolished that sanction in the early 1870s but reinstituted the death penalty within the decade. Abraham Lincoln commuted many death sentences of soldiers who deserted during the Civil War. Nevertheless, Lincoln expressed no qualms about the constitutionality of executions. During the first year of his presidency Lincoln was asked to commute the death sentence of Nathaniel Gordon, a notorious slave trader. Many northerners urged Lincoln to halt the execution on the ground that no slave trader had ever been

79. *Duffy v. People*, 26 N.Y. 588 (1863).
80. Cooley, *Constitutional Limitations*, 3rd ed., 330.
81. *Garcia v. Territory of New Mexico*, 1 N.M. 415 (1869).
82. Cooley, *Constitutional Limitations*, 3rd ed., 329.

executed in the United States. Lincoln refused. On February 4, 1862, he wrote

> And whereas, a large number of respectable citizens have earnestly besought me to commute the said sentence of the said Nathaniel Gordon to a term of imprisonment for life, which application I have felt it to be my duty to refuse;
>
> And whereas, it has seemed to me probable that the unsuccessful application made for the commutation of his sentence may have prevented the said Nathaniel Gordon from making the necessary preparation for the awful change which awaits him:
>
> Now, therefore, be it known, that I, Abraham Lincoln, President of the United States of America, have granted and do hereby grant unto him, the said Nathaniel Gordon, a respite of the above recited sentence, until Friday the twenty-first day of February, A.D. 1862, between the hours of twelve o'clock at noon and three o'clock in the afternoon of the said day, when the said sentence shall be executed.
>
> In granting this respite, it becomes my painful duty to admonish the prisoner that, relinquishing all expectation of pardon by Human Authority, he refer himself alone to the mercy of the common God and Father of all men.[83]

Nathaniel Gordon was hanged on February 21, 1862.

Suggested Readings

Belz, Herman. *A New Birth of Freedom: The Republican Party and the Freedmen's Rights 1861 to 1866* (Westport, CT: Greenwood, 1976).

Benedict, Michael Les. *A Compromise of Principle: Congressional Republicans and Reconstruction, 1863–1869* (New York: Norton, 1974).

Benedict, Michael Les. *Preserving the Constitution: Essays on Politics and the Constitution in the Reconstruction Era* (New York: Fordham University Press, 2006).

Berger, Raoul. *Government by Judiciary: The Transformation of the Fourteenth Amendment* (Cambridge, MA: Harvard University Press, 1977).

Brandon, Mark. *Free in the World: American Slavery and Constitutional Failure* (Princeton, NJ: Princeton University Press, 1998).

Curtis, Michael Kent. *No State Shall Abridge: The Fourteenth Amendment and the Bill of Rights* (Durham, NC: Duke University Press, 1986).

83. Lincoln, *Collected Works*, 5:128.

Fairman, Charles. *Reconstruction and Reunion, 1864–88* (New York: Macmillan, 1971).

Farber, Daniel A. *Lincoln's Constitution* (Chicago: University of Chicago Press, 2003).

Foner, Eric, *Reconstruction: America's Unfinished Revolution, 1863–1877* (New York: Harper & Row, 1988).

Hamilton, Daniel W. *The Limits of Sovereignty: Property Confiscation in the Union and the Confederacy during the Civil War* (Chicago: University of Chicago Press, 2007).

Hyman, Harold M. *A More Perfect Union: The Impact of the Civil War and Reconstruction on the Constitution* (New York: Knopf, 1973).

Hyman, Harold M., and William M. Wiecek. *Equal Justice under Law: Constitutional Development, 1835–1875* (New York: Harper & Row, 1982).

Kaczorowski, Robert J. *The Politics of Judicial Interpretation: The Federal Courts, Department of Justice and Civil Rights, 1866–1876* (Dobbs Ferry, NY: Oceana, 1985).

Lane, Charles. *The Day Freedom Died: The Colfax Massacre, the Supreme Court, and the Betrayal of Reconstruction* (New York: Henry Holt and Co., 2008).

Lurie, Jonathan. *The* Slaughterhouse Cases*: Regulation, Reconstruction, and the Fourteenth Amendment* (Lawrence: University Press of Kansas, 2003).

McKitrick, Eric. *Andrew Johnson and Reconstruction* (Chicago: University of Chicago Press, 1960).

McPherson, James M. *Battle Cry of Freedom: The Civil War* (New York: Oxford University Press, 1988).

Neely, Mark E., Jr. *The Fate of Liberty: Abraham Lincoln and Civil Liberties* (New York: Oxford University Press, 1991).

Nelson, William E. *The Fourteenth Amendment: From Political Principle to Judicial Doctrine* (Cambridge, MA: Harvard University Press, 1988).

Randall, James G. *Constitutional Problems under Lincoln* (Urbana: University of Illinois Press, 1951).

Ross, Michael A. *Justice of Shattered Dreams: Samuel Freeman Miller and the Supreme Court during the Civil War Era* (Baton Rouge: Louisiana State University Press, 2003).

Streichler, Stuart. *Justice Curtis in the Civil War Era: At the Crossroads of American Constitutionalism* (Charlottesville: University of Virginia Press, 2005).

Tsesis, Alexander. *The Thirteenth Amendment and American Freedom: A Legal History* (New York: New York University Press, 2004).

Vorenberg, Michael. *Final Freedom: The Civil War, the Abolition of Slavery, and the Thirteenth Amendment* (New York: Cambridge University Press, 2001).

Wills, Garry. *Lincoln at Gettysburg: The Words that Remade America* (New York: Simon and Schuster, 1992).

Chapter 7

The Republican Era: 1877–1932

I. Introduction

Americans reconfigured the constitutional politics of rights and liberties during the Republican Era. For the first hundred years after the Constitution was ratified, debates over civil liberties (other than slavery) were either episodic or local. By the time that Franklin Roosevelt became president in 1932, the constitutional politics of rights and liberties was both systemic and national. These changes were triggered by larger trends as well as key events during the intervening years. The federal government's efforts to suppress political dissent during World War I inspired unprecedented debates over the meaning of the First Amendment. American imperialism raised questions about whether persons living in newly acquired territories had the same rights as persons living in New York City or Des Moines. Members of an emerging African-American middle class developed national strategies for challenging segregation. New organizations such as the American Civil Liberties Union (ACLU) and the National Association for the Advancement of Colored People (NAACP) became permanent participants in national struggles over rights and liberties.

Many new or invigorated debates over constitutional liberties raised issues associated with industrialization, immigration, and imperialism. Industrialization created a working class that many reformers believed needed far more state protection than had previously been the case. Constitutional controversies broke out over whether elected officials could pass laws establishing minimum wages or limiting working hours for certain vulnerable laborers. Immigration threatened to undermine the cultural, religious, and ideological homogeneity that many nineteenth-century thinkers thought essential for a constitutional republic. Nativists initiated constitutional controversies when they tightened requirements for American citizenship and passed laws suppressing such strange, dangerous, and un-American political ideas as socialism and anarchism. Imperialism forced Americans to confront whether the "Constitution followed the flag." Both Congress and the Supreme Court debated whether American officials in foreign countries had to respect the liberties enumerated in the Bill of Rights.

Parties. Democrats and Republicans competed as near equals during the late nineteenth century, with Republicans gaining the advantage after the election of 1896. Elections in the late nineteenth century were volatile. Democrats and Republicans took turns occupying the White House from 1876 until 1900. One-hundred-seat swings in the House of Representatives were not uncommon. Only the Senate remained a stable bulwark of Republican strength, ensuring that party's control over federal judicial appointments. Electoral politics stabilized in the first quarter of the twentieth century, with Republicans winning every presidential election held from 1896 until 1932, with the exception of the 1912 and 1916 elections. Democrat Woodrow Wilson gained office in 1912 only after a schism in the Republican Party resulted in William Howard Taft running on the Republican Party ticket and former Republican President Theodore Roosevelt campaigning on the Progressive Party ticket. Wilson was barely reelected in 1916, and Republicans easily won the next three presidential elections. Republicans also usually controlled at least one, if not both, houses of Congress. The vast majority of federal judges after 1900 were appointed by Republican presidents.

The Civil War both structured and increasingly confused partisan alignments. Republicans in the

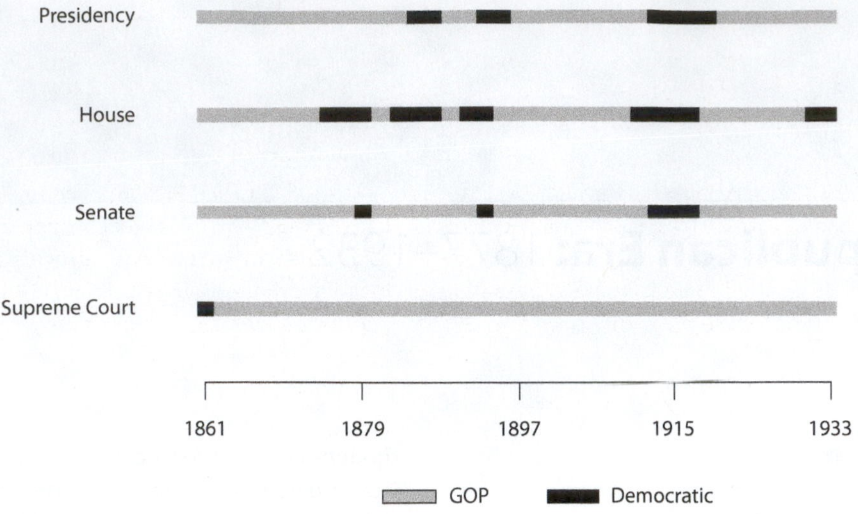

Figure 7-1 Partisan Control of the U.S. Government, 1861–1932

North often "waved the bloody shirt" to maintain voting allegiances. Once Reconstruction ended the South became solidly Democratic. Western states were often up for grabs. Partisan alignments rooted in the constitutional struggles of the 1860s and 1870s, however, often had difficulty incorporating new issues. By 1900 the Republican and Democratic label mattered less than at any previous time in the past fifty years. Prominent Democrats and Republicans in the Northeast favored business interests. Western and Southern Populists pushed Democrats more toward economic reform. Progressives from all regions of the country pushed Republicans in similar directions. Sectionalism often better explained constitutional positions than did partisan affiliation. Nevertheless, conservatives and liberals in both major parties were found in every region.

Race was the one major civil rights issue that consistently divided Republicans and Democrats. Republicans championed African-American voting rights. The Republican Party platform of 1888 spoke of the "the supreme and sovereign right of every lawful citizen, rich or poor, native or foreign born, white or black, to cast one free ballot in public elections, and to have that ballot duly counted." Democrats insisted that local governments should rule the South. The Democratic Party platform of 1892 asserted,

> The policy of Federal control of elections, to which the Republican party has committed itself, is fraught with the gravest dangers, scarcely less momentous than would result from a revolution practically establishing monarchy on the ruins of the Republic. It strikes at the North as well as at the South, and injures the colored citizen even more than the white; it means a horde of deputy marshals at every polling place, armed with Federal power; returning boards appointed and controlled by Federal authority, the outrage of the electoral rights of the people in the several States, the subjugation of the colored people to the control of the party in power.

Democrats were more successful on racial matters, even though Republicans won more national elections than Democrats. The Republican Party's formal commitment to African-American rights was not in practice strong or consistent enough to prevent southern Democrats from disenfranchising (often violently) persons of color and instituting a regime of Jim Crow. Pro-business Republicans in the late nineteenth century often joined with Democrats to defeat national legislation providing greater protections for voting rights. Republican presidents often found sustained enforcement of Reconstruction measures too expensive. By 1900 most Republicans spoke out only against lynching and other atrocities. Party elites abandoned the bloody shirt in order to promote a reconciliation with the South that might aid Republican commercial interests and gain white votes in the South.[1]

Third parties played a prominent role in constitutional politics. The Populist Party championed far

1. See Stanley P. Hirshson, *Farewell to the Bloody Shirt: Northern Republicans and the Southern Negro, 1877–1893* (Bloomington: Indiana University Press, 1962).

greater regulation of business enterprise than did either Democrats or Republicans. The 1896 Populist Party platform declared, "We believe that the power of government—in other words, of the people—should be expanded . . . as rapidly and as far as the good sense of an intelligent people and the teachings of experience shall justify, to the end that oppression, injustice and poverty, shall eventually cease in the land." The Progressive Party in 1912 called for federal laws mandating an eight-hour day and a six-day work week, requiring minimum wages, prohibiting child labor, and adopting health and safety standards for risky occupations. Neither Populists nor Progressives gained national power, but each major party had a significant faction that was committed to more moderate versions of populist or progressive reform. William Jennings Bryan, the three-time Democratic Party candidate for president, was also nominated for the presidency by the Populist Party in 1896. Herbert Hoover, the successful Republican candidate for the presidency in 1928, gained a reputation as a progressive reformer in the 1910s.

Interest Groups. The Republican Era witnessed the rise of permanent organized groups that relied on lobbying and litigation to achieve their constitutional visions. The elite lawyers who formed the American Bar Association in 1878 fought for a strong judiciary that would protect individual property rights and act as a bulwark against progressive legislation. The American Federation of Labor (AFL), founded in 1886, focused on using collective bargaining to secure higher wages, a shorter workday, and job security. The AFL also discriminated against black workers, opposed women's employment, and supported the exclusion of Chinese workers. Two women's groups, the National Woman Suffrage Association (NWSA) and the American Woman Suffrage Association, fought to secure gender equality. After the ratification of the Nineteenth Amendment the NWSA became the League of Women Voters. The NAACP, which quickly became the most important organization committed to racial equality, was founded in 1909. The ACLU was organized after World War I. The Anti-Saloon League, the largest interest group in the United States during the Republican Era, led the fight for Prohibition.

The Scopes Trial in Tennessee illustrates how organized interests influenced constitutional politics. In 1925 John Scopes was fined by a local court after he taught Darwin's theory of evolution in a public

Table 7-1 Percentage of Popular Vote in Presidential Election by Political Party, 1876–1932

Year	Republican	Democrat	Populist	Socialist	Progressive	Other
1876	**48**	51				1
1880	**48**	48				3
1884	48	**49**				3
1888	**48**	49				4
1892	43	**46**	9			2
1896	**51**	47				2
1900	**52**	46	0	1		2
1904	**56**	38	1	3		2
1908	**52**	43		3		3
1912	23	**42**		6	27	2
1916	46	**49**		3		1
1920	**60**	34		3		2
1924	**54**	29			17	1
1928	**58**	41		1		0
1932	40	**57**		2		1

Note: Winning party marked in bold.

school. Eager to have courts declare such laws unconstitutional, the ACLU arranged for Clarence Darrow, perhaps the leading litigator of the early twentieth century, to handle the Scopes defense. Conservative evangelical groups responded by arranging to have William Jennings Bryan assist the prosecution. The result was another "trial of the century," which garnered enough national attention to spawn a Broadway play, *Inherit the Wind*, and a hit movie of the same name starring Frederick March, Gene Kelly, and Spencer Tracy. Neither Scopes nor the town of Dayton, Tennessee, where Scopes taught, could have possibly afforded such legal talent. Their dispute became famous when interest groups contested the constitutional issue in order to advance their national political agendas.

Courts. State and federal courts were important and permanent institutional players in the constitutional politics of rights and liberties. Struggles over the proper interpretation of the post–Civil War Amendments, legislation expanding the jurisdiction of federal courts, the rise of the elite bar, and the mobilization of rights-based interest groups all empowered judges as constitutional decision makers. The Supreme Court of the United States was repeatedly called on to determine whether federal and state economic regulations interfered with the rights protected by the due process clauses of the Fifth and Fourteenth Amendments. *Lochner v. New York* (1905), the most famous civil liberties decision of the Republican Era, held unconstitutional a New York law that restricted bakers to a sixty-hour work week on the ground that the measure violated the freedom of workers to contract with their employers to work for longer hours. In other cases, the justices ruled that states were obligated to respect only a few provisions in the Bill of Rights, that Congress was limited only by the due process clause of the Fifth Amendment when governing overseas territories, that the Fourth and Fifth Amendments restricted congressional power to investigate and prosecute businesses, and that government could regulate free speech that had a tendency to produce harmful social consequences.

Supreme Court justices during the late nineteenth century struck down important national civil rights legislation, most notable the provisions in the Civil Rights Act of 1875 prohibiting discrimination in inns, public conveniences, and places of public amusement. *Plessy v. Ferguson* (1896) gave judicial blessing to state-mandated segregation. Proponents of racial equality enjoyed greater success in the early twentieth century, when the justices struck down some techniques that southern states used to disenfranchise persons of color and, in *Buchanan v. Warley* (1917), ruled that state-mandated residential segregation was unconstitutional. State courts played even greater roles in adjudicating claims of constitutional right. The basic principles underlying Supreme Court decisions on the freedom of contract and racial segregation were first articulated by state judges.

Constitutional Thought. Constitutional struggles between 1877 and 1932 focused on the threats that a more activist democracy posed to individual liberty and equality. Conservative constitutional decision makers worried that popular majorities might pass class legislation designed to benefit one group of people at the expense of another, perhaps by bestowing special privileges on workers or redistributing property. Late-nineteenth-century populists and early-twentieth-century progressives believed that elected officials could generally be trusted to pass regulations that promoted the public good. They justified expanded government power as a strong counterweight to powerful private economic interests.

Partisan alignments on civil liberties issues at the turn of the twentieth century were quite different than at present. Many progressives believed that government should have the power to restrict all liberties when doing so served the general welfare. Woodrow Wilson, a prominent progressive thinker before his election to the presidency, vigorously championed federal power to regulate the economy and restrict free speech. Many conservatives insisted that the same principles that justified the freedom of contract also supported constitutional protection for noneconomic liberties. Christopher G. Tiedeman, whose libertarian constitutional writings were often cited by courts in arguments for limiting government power to regulate commercial relationships, opposed state laws forbidding interracial marriage as unwarranted state interference with private relationships.[2]

For most of the Republican Era "civil rights and liberties" was not a distinctive area of constitutional

2. Christopher G. Tiedeman, *A Treatise on State and Federal Control of Persons and Property in the United States*, vol. II (St. Louis: The F.H. Thomas Law Book Co., 1900), 894-95.

Box 7-1 A Partial Cast of Characters of the Republican Era

Stephen J. Field	▪ Conservative Democrat ▪ Justice on California Supreme Court (1857–63) ▪ Appointed by Abraham Lincoln to the U.S. Supreme Court (1863–97) ▪ Known for his belief in a strong role for judicial review, strict limits on federal power, and broad protections for the rights of private property
Louis Brandeis	▪ Progressive Democrat ▪ Successful Boston lawyer and activist in Progressive, labor, and Zionist causes ▪ Leading defender of workplace regulation; developed the factually oriented "Brandeis brief" to support the constitutionality of such laws ▪ Appointed by Woodrow Wilson to the U.S. Supreme Court, leading to a contentious confirmation battle ▪ First Jew to serve on the U.S. Supreme Court (1916–39) ▪ Important advocate on the Court for free speech and a right to privacy
Oliver Wendell Holmes, Jr.	▪ Progressive Republican ▪ Influential Boston legal scholar and a precursor to the "legal realist" movement ▪ Served on the Supreme Judicial Court of Massachusetts (1882–1902) ▪ Appointed by Theodore Roosevelt to the U.S. Supreme Court (1902–32) ▪ Known for his view that the law evolved over time and that courts should generally be deferential to what political majorities decide
David J. Brewer	▪ Conservative Republican ▪ Served in a variety of judicial positions in Kansas, culminating in his election to the state supreme court (1870–84) ▪ Appointed by Chester Arthur to the U.S. Circuit Court (1884–89) ▪ Appointed by Benjamin Harrison to U.S. Supreme Court (1889–1910) ▪ Popular speaker and prominent Christian author ▪ Among the more conservative justices on the Court, but a frequent supporter of minority rights
John Marshall Harlan	▪ Whig and Republican ▪ Slaveholding unionist from Kentucky who joined the Union Army ▪ Kentucky attorney general (1863–67) ▪ Appointed by Rutherford B. Hayes to the U.S. Supreme Court (1877–1911) ▪ Critic of the Court's decisions on race and congressional power

law. Constitutional thinkers incorporated speech and other rights issues into existing conceptions of legitimate government power. State legislatures possessed "the police power," which authorized elected officials to pass any law that advanced the public welfare. Legislation that clearly promoted the health or morality of the public was constitutional, no matter what burden the law placed on the individual right. Laws that did not really promote the well being of the public or, worse, provided benefits to some people at the expense of others were unconstitutional. This conceptual framework helps explain why the Supreme Court in *Holden v. Hardy* (1898) declared that states could regulate the working hours of coal miners but in *Lochner v. New York* (1905) declared unconstitutional a state law regulating the hours that bakers worked. The burden such legislation placed on the individual right was the same. The difference between the cases was that the justices believed that limiting the hours that a miner could work promoted public health (because coal mining was considered dangerous and exhausting work), whereas restricting bakers served no purpose other than to enable bakers to make more favorable contracts with their employers.[3]

Whether the judicial practice in many cases corresponded with this theory seemed increasingly doubtful during the early twentieth century. Proponents of what became known as *sociological jurisprudence* maintained that such cases as *Lochner* were better explained by judicial willingness to wield rigid notions of individual rights to defeat the public good than by traditional police powers doctrine. Some progressives insisted that justices ought to extend greater protections to certain favored liberties or "preferred freedoms." In *Near v. Minnesota* (1931) Chief Justices Charles Evans Hughes ruled that government needed very powerful reasons for imposing a prior restraint on free speech. "The protection . . . as to previous restraint is not absolutely unlimited," he wrote, "but the limitation has been recognized only in exceptional cases." This

3. See Howard Gillman, *The Constitution Besieged: The Rise and Demise of Lochner Era Police Powers Jurisprudence* (Durham, NC: Duke University Press, 1993).

Table 7-2 Major Rights and Liberties Issues and Decisions of the Republican Era

Major Political Issues	Major Constitutional Issues	Major Court Decisions
Erosion of Federal Commitment to Black Civil Rights	Expansion of Federal Judicial Power	*Reynolds v. United States* (1878)
Jim Crow	Application of Fourteenth Amendment Against Exercises of State Police Powers	*Civil Rights Cases* (1883)
Industrialization	"State Action" Requirement	*In re Jacobs* (NY 1885)
Labor Unrest	Separate But Equal	*Mugler v. Kansas* (1887)
Populism and Progressivism	Debate Over "Incorporation" of Bill of Rights	*Fong Yue Ting v. United States* (1893)
Social Darwinism	The "Living" Constitution	*Plessy v. Ferguson* (1896)
Workplace Regulation	Application of Constitutional Protections to Overseas Territories	*Lochner v. New York* (1905)
Prohibition	Due Process Protections for Property Rights	*Twining v. New Jersey* (1908)
Creation of National Association for the Advancement of Colored People	Liberty of Contract	*Ex parte Young* (1908)
Founding of the American Civil Liberties Union	Free Speech and Advocacy of Unlawful Conduct	*Weeks v. United States* (1914)
Immigration and Nativism	Prior Restraints on the Press	*Buchanan v. Warley* (1917)
Spanish-American War	Prohibition Amendment	*Schenck v. United States* (1919)
World War I	Direct Democracy	*Balzac v. Porto Rico* (1922)
Women's Suffrage Movement	Women's Suffrage Amendment	*Adkins v. Children's Hospital* (1923)
Eugenics	Privacy Rights	*Meyer v. Nebraska* (1923)
	Sterilization Laws	*Buck v. Bell* (1927)
	Sunday Closing Laws	*Whitney v. California* (1927)
	Constitutional Protections for Members of the Mormon Church	*Olmstead v. United States* (1928)
	Rights to Citizenship	*Near v. Minnesota* (1931)
	Birth of the Exclusionary Rule	*Powell v. Alabama* (1932)
	Nationalization of the Right to Counsel	

shift from a traditional focus on the scope of government powers to a new focus on the importance of certain rights took on increased importance during the New Deal/Great Society Era.[4]

Legacies. The most important legacy of the Republican Era was a negative one. For the next eighty years a broad consensus existed that the Supreme Court abused the power of judicial review when protecting the freedom of contract and other economic rights. In this view, judges across the country, spurred on by a conservative elite bar, used the pretense of protecting individual freedom to promote conservative policy preferences for laissez-faire economics. *Lochner v. New York* (1905) became the primary example of justices substituting their personal views for constitutional law. "Lochnerizing" was the worst accusation that could be leveled against a judicial opinion or constitutional argument. Whenever justices have subsequently sought to protect constitutional rights and liberties they have had to self-consciously distinguish their decisions from Republican-Era decisions protecting the freedom of contract.

The Republican Era witnessed the gradual emergence of modern civil rights and liberties. The NAACP gained their first judicial victories during the 1910s and 1920s. Judicial liberals during the 1940s, 1950s, and 1960s relied heavily on the arguments for strong free speech protections that Justices Oliver Wendell Holmes and Louis Brandeis pioneered in a series of dissents written during and immediately after World War I. The Supreme Court first announced the exclusionary rule in *Weeks v. United States* (1914), holding that evidence obtained in violation of the Fourth Amendment could not be used in federal criminal proceedings. Other judicial opinions supported the privilege against self-incrimination and emphasized the importance of individual privacy against the expanding powers of government. In these and other matters constitutional decision makers established foundations for rights that later constitutional decision makers built on, modified, or decisively rejected.

4. See Howard Gillman, "Preferred Freedoms: The Progressive Expansion of State Power and the Rise of Modern Civil Liberties Jurisprudence," *Political Research Quarterly* 47 (1994): 623–53.

II. Foundations

MAJOR DEVELOPMENTS

- Women's suffrage and Prohibition amendments
- Supreme Court rules that federal officials governing overseas territories are not restricted by the Bill of Rights
- State officials required to respect certain fundamental rights but not most provisions in the Bill of Rights

Americans struggled with constitutional change. The meaning of the post–Civil War Amendments was unclear. Women, prohibitionists, and others proposed additional constitutional amendments. Constitutional issues arose in new circumstances. Technological changes that the framers had not foreseen raised questions about the constitutional status of wiretapping and whether noise from a new urban train line unconstitutionally took property from disturbed homeowners. The acquisition of Puerto Rico and the Philippines after the Spanish-American War raised questions about the constitutional limits on federal laws governing foreign territories. The combination of immigration, industrialization, and imperialism forced Americans to think about how a Constitution forged in the late eighteenth century should function at the turn of the twentieth century. Many commentators championed a living Constitution, with flexible standards that adjusted to changing political, economic, and social conditions.[5]

A. Sources

Americans added four new amendments to the Constitution during the Republican Era. The Sixteenth Amendment (1913) authorized a federal income tax. The Seventeenth Amendment (1913) mandated popular elections for the Senate. The Eighteenth Amendment (1919) prohibited the manufacture, sale, and transportation of intoxicating liquors. The Nineteenth Amendment (1920) prohibited states from denying the right to vote on the basis of gender.

Political developments explain why Americans ratified no constitutional amendments during the last quarter of the nineteenth century but four in the first

5. See Howard Gillman, "The Collapse of Constitutional Originalism and the Rise of the Notion of the 'Living Constitution' in the Course of American State-Building," *Studies in American Political Development* 11 (1997): 191–247.

years of the twentieth. During the late nineteenth century many elites promoted a cult of the Constitution. In this view, the post–Civil War Amendments perfected the Constitution. Progressives in the early twentieth century were more skeptical. These reformers believed that the Constitution, like all entities trying to thrive in changing circumstances, needed to adapt in order to keep up with the times. Charles Beard and other progressive historians claimed that crucial constitutional provisions reflected the interests of an economic elite rather than the desire to promote the well being of average people. These attitudes eased the passage of constitutional amendments, some of which had previously failed.

The Supreme Court at the turn of the century reaffirmed past commitments to customary international law as a source of individual rights. Justice Gray's majority opinion in *The Paquete Habana* (1900) asserted, "International law is part of our law." What that phrase means remains the subject of enduring controversy.

Constitutions and Amendments

Congressional Debate over Prohibition (1917)[6]

Prohibition was the reform cause of the Republican Era. More Americans at the turn of the twentieth century were members of such organizations as the Women's Christian Temperance Union (WCTU) and the Anti-Saloon League than of any other public interest group. Prohibitionists included among their ranks suffragettes, Boston Puritans, rural sharecroppers, and the Ku Klux Klan. During the nineteenth century members of this coalition fought for state and local laws banning the manufacture, sale, and use of intoxicating liquors. Experience demonstrated that state and local laws were easily circumvented when nearby communities remained "wet." Determined to fashion a "dry" America, Prohibition forces began an aggressive push for a constitutional amendment.

Participants in the debate over the proposed Eighteenth Amendment discussed both the powers of government and individual rights. Proponents of Prohibition insisted that federal power was necessary because drinking was a national problem that state laws could not adequately address. In their view drinking was a vice and a menace to the public good. Opponents of Prohibition raised concerns about police powers that had historically been reserved to the states. Many insisted that Americans had a fundamental right to drink, beer in particular.

Prohibition was more popular among the people than among elected officials. Many members of Congress voted for the Prohibition amendment, confident that the text would not be ratified by the required three-quarters of the states. They were wrong. The Senate approved the Eighteenth Amendment in August 1917. The House approved in December 1917. Thirteenth months later two-thirds of the states had approved. That most of the nation's brewers had Germanic surnames in the wake of World War I furthered the Prohibition cause.

When reading the excerpts of the debates below, consider the place of Prohibition in the constitutional politics of the Republican Era. What are the most important differences between supporters and opponents of Prohibition? To what extent do the debates over Prohibition replay other debates over police powers and the proper balance between federal and state power that took place from 1877 to 1932?

SENATOR BOIES PENROSE (Republican, Pennsylvania)

. . .

Serious doubt may be expressed whether any amendment to the Constitution may properly be placed in that instrument which, without the consent of all the States, would deprive any one of them of one or more of the several reserved powers. . . .

. . .

The police power is the most vital of all the reserved powers in the States, but under this proposed amendment certain States in the Union which did not, in 1789, and in all likelihood now, could never be made to surrender the police power to the Federal Government, will find a large part of that power wrenched from them, not only without their consent but in defiance of their wishes.

. . .

The proposition is intrinsically and radically vicious and intolerable. Legislation of this character, in my opinion, ought to be preeminently and primarily of strictly State concern. There are many States now having prohibition laws where the people acquiesce in them more or less willingly; but if these laws had been handed to them by a mandate from a central authority in Washington, the result in many cases would have been resentment and revolution.

6. 55 Congressional Record, 65th Cong., 1st Sess. (August 1, 1917), 5636–45.

The only practical way to establish prohibition or any other police proposition over an area of country is through the agencies of the States. Otherwise, it would take an American army to enforce it.

. . .

It, in my opinion, will be inevitable that our system of government will break down if we continue the course which has been followed during the last few years of centralizing everything in the Congress of the United States here in Washington. I believe that the doctrine of State rights, which was once so vigorously maintained by great men in the Senate, and concerning which a great civil war was fought, is more important today than at any other time in the history of the country, in view of our tremendous growth of population and resources and wealth and diversified interests.

SENATOR WILLIAM KENYON (Republican, Iowa)

. . .

No one rises on this floor or elsewhere to defend the American saloon directly.

The American saloon has no conscience. It never did a good act or failed to do a bad one. It is a trap for the youth; a destroyer for the old; a foul spawning place for crime; a corrupter of politics; knows no party; supports those men for office whom it thinks can be easiest influenced; has no respect for law or the courts; debauches city councils, juries and everyone it can reach in power in the unity of its vote, and creates cowards in office.

It flatters, tricks, cajoles, and deceives in order to accomplish its purpose; is responsible for more ruin and death than all the wars the nation has ever engaged in; has corrupted more politics, ruined more lives, widowed more women, orphaned more children, destroyed more homes, caused more tears to flow, broken more hearts, undermined more manhood, and sent more people to an early grave than any other influence in our land.

Its day has come. No subterfuge can long save it. It will be drafted into the open, the influences behind it stripped of their masks. A mighty public conscience is aroused, moving on rapidly, confidently, undismayed, and undeceived. Behind it are the churches of the Nation—Protestant and Catholic—schools, colleges, and homes. This public conscience is not discouraged by defeat or deceived by any cunning devices, by any shams or pretenses. Its cause is the cause of humanity, of righteousness, and God Almighty fights with it.

. . .

No denunciation, no slurs, no jests on the floor of the Senate, no hurling of epithet, no cheap ribaldry in the cloakrooms will stop this fight. It is going on in Congress, and it is going on in the Nation until the tear-producing, orphan-making, home-wrecking, manhood debauching, character-destroying, hell-filling saloon is just as certainly doomed as slavery was doomed.

A saloonless Nation means an efficient Nation, better able to cope with any problem threatening it from without or within.

SENATOR HENRY MYERS (Democrat, Montana)

. . .

There are many things which are now on the statute books of our country by virtue of national legislation which in the beginning of our history were not considered proper subjects of national legislation. Pure-food control, sanitation, child-labor regulation, limitation of hours of labor for men, women, and children—all these things were attained in the face of intense opposition. It took time and toilsome effort. The people in attaining them were fettered by traditions of the dark ages of the past, but by persistent effort they emerged and came out in the bright sunlight of a better day.

I believe that the people of this country, through an enlightened conscience and a sounder public opinion, have about arrived at a point where they are ready to adopt by a national constitutional amendment national prohibition of the manufacture and use of liquor. The time has come to strike for it. The people are ready to pass on it. They want a chance. It is the sense of an enlightened public, sustained by the best professional and scientific authorities, that the use of liquor has no merit in it, neither as food nor medicine. It is a palpable evil, socially, physically, morally, politically, economically. The progress in this reform has been slow, but steady and sure, and I believe the day for marking the milepost of that achievement is finally at hand.

. . .

SENATOR JOHN WEEKS (Republican, Massachusetts)

. . .

. . . [T]here is no attempt made by the proponents of this legislation to make provision for any compensation on account of the destruction of a business which has continued to exist during the entire life of the Republic by national license. I am opposed to confiscation of property in any form at any time, whether or not I entirely approve of the individuals engaged in this business or the character of the business conducted. When we propose confiscation we are inaugurating a policy which is likely to be most far-reaching in its effect. Some one may conclude that some other form of business is not entirely for the public interest, and the fact that we have established a confiscation precedent may result in its being extended to other fields.

Finally, it seems to me that the individual has rights which should be protected. The vast majority of those who indulge in stimulants, in these days especially, do so to a very moderate degree. I am not satisfied that the multitudinous statistics which are given out about the harm coming from wines and light beers are well founded. . . .

There are innumerable things in which we indulge which are undoubtedly more or less harmful to individuals, and I think that statement would be equally true in its application to food consumed in unreasonable quantities and at unreasonable times.

The Debate over the Nineteenth Amendment (1918)

Women in the Republican Era campaigned vigorously for the right to vote. As with Prohibition, the campaign began in the states. The state constitution of Wyoming in 1889 was amended to declare that "rights of citizens . . . to vote and hold office shall not be denied or abridged on account of sex. Both male and female citizens . . . shall equally enjoy all civil, political and religious rights and privileges." Other western states shortly followed suit. By the turn of the twentieth century, women in slightly more than half the states had a right to cast ballots in at least some elections. The suffrage campaign gained strength during the second decade of the twentieth century. Alice Paul and the National Woman's Party gained national attention when they picketed the White House, demanding that women be granted the right to vote. Woodrow Wilson's claim that World War I was being fought to "make the world safe for democracy" provided rhetorical

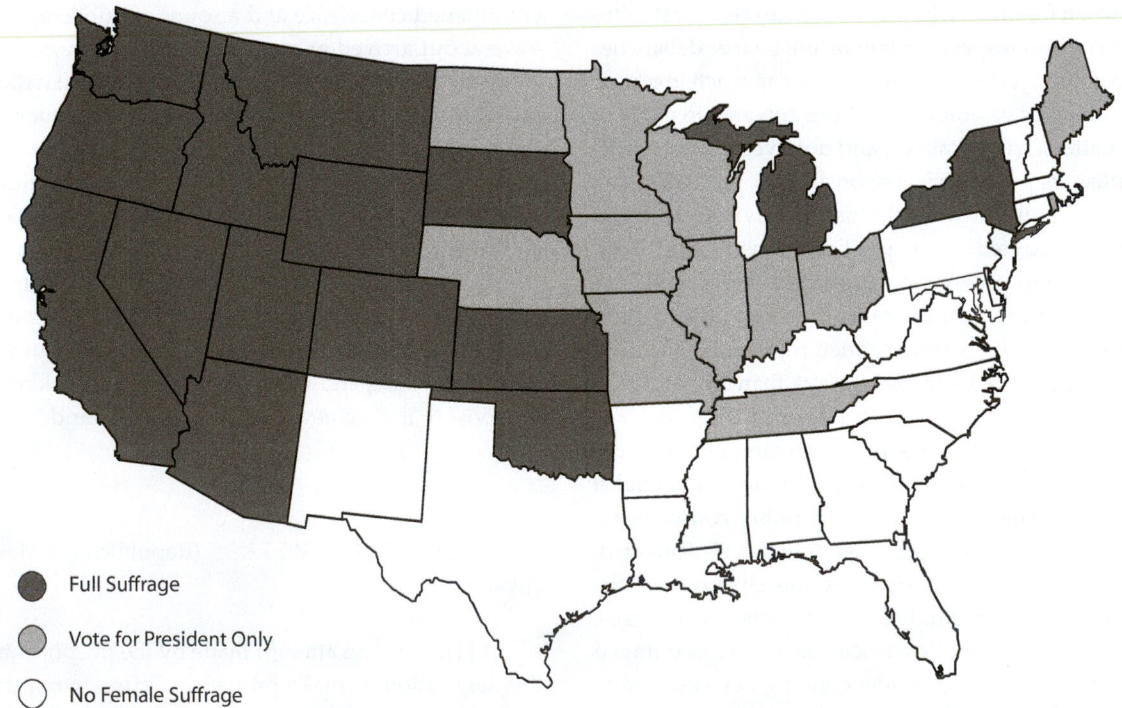

Figure 7-2 Female Suffrage in the States before Passage of Nineteenth Amendment, 1919

fuel for those who believed in an expanded suffrage. Wilson's conversion to the suffrage cause proved crucial. Both houses of Congress approved the Nineteenth Amendment in 1918. The amendment was ratified two years later.

The excerpts below are drawn from testimony taken at a congressional hearing on the Nineteenth Amendment and the speech Wilson that gave endorsing the amendment. What are the crucial differences between proponents and opponents of women's suffrage? To what extent do the debates over women's suffrage in the Republican Era differ from debates over women's rights in previous and subsequent eras?

Congressional Hearings on the Nineteenth Amendment[7]

Dr. ANNA HOWARD SHAW (National American Woman Suffrage Association)

. . .

I want to say in closing, gentlemen, that we are not asking for the Federal amendment for women because we are not loyal to our country, because we are not willing to do war work, and because we are not willing to sacrifice and to suffer, but because we want this measure passed for two reasons: One is that to fail to ask for it at this time would be treason to the fundamental cause for which we as a nation have entered the war. President Wilson declared that we are at war because of that which is dearest to our hearts, democracy, that those who submit to authority shall have a voice in their government. If that is the basic reason for entering the war, then those of us who have striven for this amendment and for our freedom and democracy in this country to yield to-day, to withdraw from the battle, would be to desert the men in the trenches and leave them to fight across the sea for not only democracy for the world but for democracy for our own country. We believe in that fundamental principle because we believe in the ideals of democracy. Because we are loyal to the men in the trenches, because we are loyal to ourselves, because we believe the word of the President of the United States, we are to-day, gentlemen, pleading for democracy, that those who submit to authority shall have a voice in their government. The war is not going to last forever. God pity us, it is lasting too long.

. . .

CARRIE CHAPMAN CATT (President, National American Woman's Suffrage Association)

. . .

As to the charge that women suffrage represents a vote which can not be trusted in time of war, I want to call your attention to certain facts in connection with our country. We have or had in 1910 2,000,000 more men in the country than we had women. We have had in this country a great increase in naturalization since the war began. There were a great many foreigners who were afraid that they would be conscripted by their home government who made haste to take out their citizenship papers. They are not patriotic. They are not loyal to this country. They are seeking protection for themselves. When an election is to be held, as it will be ere long, it must be remembered that we are taking a step which our allies have not taken. . . .

. . . When the election comes, who is going to do the voting? Every slacker has a vote. Every newly-made citizen will have a vote. Every pro-German who can not be trusted with any kind of military or war service will have a vote. Every peace-at-any-price man, every conscientious objector, and even the alien enemy will have a vote. You will not secure anything more than a majority at best of the soldiers in Europe. It is a test, a risk, which no other country has been asked to take.

The women here who belong to the families of the men on the other side can not be called disloyal. There actually is at least one and probably more than one women in a family of every man who goes on the other side who is going to use her vote to back every preparation of the war, every condition which is going to make it easier and safer for him, and every condition which is going to bring the war to a successful end, if she has the opportunity to cast a loyal vote. It is a risk, a danger to a country like ours to send 1,000,000 men out of the country who are loyal and not to replace those men by the loyal votes of the women they have left at home.

. . .

. . . So long as this Nation, by cooperation with the States, unites in giving the vote to every newcoming foreigner without any test, or much test, of education or fitness, and without ever raising the question of whether they would like the vote or not, women feel that an indignity is put upon them. . . .

7. Excerpted from House Committee on Woman Suffrage, *Extending the Right of Suffrage to Women: Hearings before the Committee on Woman Suffrage on H.J. Res. 200*, 65th Cong., 2nd Sess. (1918).

HENRY A. WISE WOOD (President, Aero Club of America)

. . .

Ours is a representative democracy, wherein the majority rule in the selection of its officials. Approximately one-half of the adult population of the United States is composed of women. Having the vote, there then is no legal obstacle in the way of the election of a Congress wherein one-half or more of its membership shall be of women, nor of the selection of a Cabinet similarly apportioned, nor of the election of a woman to the Presidency, nor of the apportionment of women, even in majority, upon the Supreme Court bench. Give woman the vote, and these become possibilities, probabilities, some of them eventually even certainties.

Let no man deceive himself; woman will insist upon holding office in full proportion to her numbers. To that her politicians may be expected to see.

. . .

War, indeed, is stern business. With its preparation, its declaration, its prosecution, its incidental and inevitable infliction of deaths innumerable, no mother, no woman, should have aught to do. As well make of a woman a public executioner. To the assertion that has been made, that to withhold these functions from the mothers of the Nation is preposterous, I unhesitatingly reply that it is preposterous that the mothers of the Nation should be permitted to sit in the halls of Congress where they may be required to decree the deaths of their own sons!

The belief that pacifism, the shrinking even from necessary war, is no more prevalent among women than among men is not borne out by the facts. . . .

. . .

For these weighty and fundamental reasons I am unalterably opposed to woman suffrage, although, as I have said, but three years ago I was its hearty advocate. These three years have taught me that a nation's freedom is to be safeguarded not by the display of gentleness, or love, or mercy, but solely by a nation's ability to crush with brute force whoever unjustly assails it. To create, direct, and deliver brute force is a man's, not a woman's, job.

. . .

EX-SENATOR JOSEPH W. BAILEY (Democrat, Texas)

. . .

As I sat here this morning and heard these ladies talk, no shadow of doubt entered my mind that they could intelligently perform the duties of an elector, nor do I doubt that these ladies on the suffrage side could do as well; but they constitute a very small per cent of the women in the United States. And what are we to expect from the uncounted millions who have not had the good fortune to be educated as highly as these ladies here and who have not enjoyed the leisure to improve themselves? I do not hesitate to say that we have too many ignorant voters in this country now [applause], and woman suffrage will enormously increase the number. When I say "ignorant" I do not mean that they can not read and write, but I mean that they do not understand the theory of this Government or the measures upon which they may be called to pass. . . .

. . .

. . . Our ideal woman is one of gentle speech, and her effort always is to make the world happier, even if she does not make it wiser. She goes about her mission in life with a smile on her lips and joy in her heart, oppressed with no sense of duty unperformed and perplexed by no duty unperformable. She chooses to sit at the bedside of the sick rather than in the seats of the mighty and delights more in training her children than in governing the country; that which she loves most is to point her boy to ambition's dazzling heights and tell him how difficult, but still how glorious, it is to attain them; or to teach her daughter to shun every man who does not believe in women and every woman who does not believe in God. That, sir, is our ideal woman. Such a woman was the wife of Thomas Jefferson; such a woman was the mother of George Washington; and if the God of nations would grant me one prayer above all others, that prayer would be that such a woman shall be the American wife and mother through all the years to come; for with her this Republic can not perish, and without her this Republic can not survive.

CHARLOTTE E. ROWE (National Association Opposed to Woman Suffrage)

. . .

Feminization is a much deeper thing than the mere casting of a ballot on election day. The leaders of the other side have recognized that fact. And we are opposing this feminization of government, and we are opposing this deeper thing to which the vote is merely a steppingstone.

. . .

. . . I believe that this terrible problem of war—all these terrible conditions to which civilization is heir—never will be destroyed until the power of womanhood is aroused. And that power of woman will be destroyed by political participation; because the moment you enfranchise your womanhood you make them Democrats, Republicans, or Socialists, all wrangling among themselves, duplicating the necessary work of men and also bringing into your electorate this feminine, absolutely incompetent vote, so far as any enforcement of the law goes.

. . .We say to you that the power of womanhood is the greatest force in the world; but we tell you also that woman's power is always by inspiration. A woman can only win by inspiring men. And when a woman says to you that she has no power without the ballot: when she says to you that she cannot impress her day and her generation without this physical weapon of manhood, I say to you that already she has lost her grip on womanhood, and the ballot can never in the world give it back to her.

. . .

Woodrow Wilson, Speech on Women's Suffrage[8]

. . . I regard the concurrence of the Senate in the constitutional amendment proposing the extension of the suffrage to women as vitally essential to the successful prosecution of the great war of humanity in which we are engaged. . . .

. . .

This is a peoples' war and the peoples' thinking constitutes its atmosphere and morale, not the predilections of the drawing room or the political considerations of the caucus. If we be indeed democrats and wish to lead the world to democracy, we can ask other peoples to accept in proof of our sincerity and our ability to lead them whither they wish to be led nothing less persuasive and convincing than our actions. Our professions will not suffice. Verification must be forthcoming when verification is asked for. And in this case verification is asked for,—asked for in this particular matter. You ask by whom? Not through diplomatic channels; not by Foreign Ministers. Not by the intimations of parliaments. It is asked for by the anxious, expectant, suffering peoples with whom we are dealing and who are willing to put their destinies in some measure in our hands, if they are sure that we wish the same things that they wish. . . . Through many, many channels I have been made aware what the plain, struggling, workaday folk are thinking upon whom the chief terror and suffering of this tragic war falls. They are looking to the great, powerful, famous Democracy of the West to lead them to the new day for which they have so long waited; and they think, in their logical simplicity, that democracy means that women shall play their part in affairs alongside men and upon an equal footing with them. If we reject measures like this, in ignorance or defiance of what a new age has brought forth, of what they have seen but we have not, they will cease to follow or to trust us. They have seen their own governments accept this interpretation of democracy,—seen old governments like Great Britain, which did not profess to be democratic, promise readily and as of course this justice to women, though they had before refused it, the strange revelations of this war having made many things new and plain, to governments as well as to peoples.

Are we alone to refuse to learn the lesson? Are we alone to ask and take the utmost that women can give, service and sacrifice of every kind, and still say that we do not see what title that gives them to stand by our sides in the guidance of the affairs of their nation and ours? We have made partners of the women in this war; shall we admit them only to a partnership of sacrifice and suffering and toil and not to a partnership of privilege and of right? This war could not have been fought, either by the other nations engaged or by America, if it had not been for the services of the women—services rendered in every sphere,—nor merely in the fields of effort in which we have been accustomed to see them work, but wherever men have worked and upon the very skirts and edges of the battle itself. We shall not only be distrusted but shall deserve to be distrusted if we do not enfranchise them with the fullest possible enfranchisement, as it is now certain that the other great free nations will enfranchise them. We cannot isolate our thought or our action in such a matter from the thought of the rest of the world. We must either conform or deliberately reject what they propose and resign the leadership of liberal minds to others.

. . .

And not to the winning of the war only. It is vital to the right solution of the great problems which we must settle, and settle immediately when the war is over. We shall need then a vision of affairs which is theirs, and,

8. *Congressional Record*, 65th Cong., 2nd Sess. (1918), 10, 928–29.

as we have never needed them before, the sympathy and insight and clear moral instinct of the women of the world. The problems of that time will strike to the roots of many things that we have not hitherto questioned, and I for one believe that our safety in those questioning days, as well as our comprehension of matters that touch society to the quick, will depend upon the direct and authoritative participation of women in our counsels. We shall need their moral sense to preserve what is right and fine and worthy to our system of life as well as to discover just what it is that ought to be purified and reformed. Without their counsellings we shall be only half wise. . . .

The Law of Nations

The Paquete Habana, 175 U.S. 677 (1900)

The Paquete Habana *was a Cuban fishing boat manned by two Cuban fishermen. On April 25, 1898, shortly after the Spanish-American War began, the* Paquete Habana *was captured by an American ship. The boat owners claimed that the capture was illegal. International law, they insisted, forbade states from treating as war prizes fishing boats that were not engaged in any hostilities. A federal district court disagreed with this contention and ordered the* Paquete Habana *condemned and sold. The boat owners appealed to the Supreme Court of the United States.*

The Supreme Court reversed the lower court's decision. Justice Gray's majority opinion ruled that international law forbade the capture of fishing boats and that the principles of international law were part of the law of the United States. On what basis does Justice Gray assert that international law is part of American law? Is the idea that international law matters only in the absence of a contrary constitutional rule, or is the influence more weighty than that? Do federal and state statutes trump customary international law? How does the dissenting opinion treat the legal status of international law? Which opinion do you think is correct? Under what conditions, if any, could the United States constitutionally defy customary international law?

MR. JUSTICE GRAY delivered the opinion of the Court.

. . .

By an ancient usage among civilized nations, beginning centuries ago and gradually ripening into a rule of international law, coast fishing vessels pursuing their vocation of catching and bringing in fresh fish have been recognized as exempt, with their cargoes and crews, from capture as prize of war.

. . .

The doctrine which exempts coast fishermen, with their vessels and cargoes, from capture as prize of war, has been familiar to the United States from the time of the War of Independence.

. . .

International law is part of our law, and must be ascertained and administered by the courts of justice of appropriate jurisdiction as often as questions of right depending upon it are duly presented for their determination. For this purpose, where there is no treaty and no controlling executive or legislative act or judicial decision, resort must be had to the customs and usages of civilized nations, and, as evidence of these, to the works of jurists and commentators who by years of labor, research, and experience have made themselves peculiarly well acquainted with the subjects of which they treat. . . .

. . .

[Our] review of the precedents and authorities on the subject appears to us abundantly to demonstrate that, at the present day, by the general consent of the civilized nations of the world, and independently of any express treaty or other public act, it is an established rule of international law, founded on considerations of humanity to a poor and industrious order of men, and of the mutual convenience of belligerent states, that coast fishing vessels, with their implements and supplies, cargoes and crews, unarmed and honestly pursuing their peaceful calling of catching and bringing in fresh fish, are exempt from capture as prize of war.

The exemption, of course, does not apply to coast fishermen or their vessels if employed for a warlike purpose, or in such a way as to give aid or information to the enemy, nor when military or naval operations create a necessity to which all private interests must give way.

Nor has the exemption been extended to ships or vessels employed on the high sea in taking whales or seals or cod or other fish which are not brought fresh to market, but are salted or otherwise cured and made a regular article of commerce.

This rule of international law is one which prize courts administering the law of nations are bound to take judicial notice of, and to give effect to, in the absence of any treaty or other public act of their own government in relation to the matter.

. . .

MR. CHIEF JUSTICE FULLER, with whom concurred MR. JUSTICE HARLAN and MR. JUSTICE McKENNA, dissenting:

The district court held these vessels and their cargoes liable because not "satisfied that, as a matter of law, without any ordinance, treaty, or proclamation, fishing vessels of this class are exempt from seizure."

This Court holds otherwise not because such exemption is to be found in any treaty, legislation, proclamation, or instruction granting it, but on the ground that the vessels were exempt by reason of an established rule of international law applicable to them which it is the duty of the court to enforce.

I am unable to conclude that there is any such established international rule, or that this Court can properly revise action which must be treated as having been taken in the ordinary exercise of discretion in the conduct of war.

. . .

In truth, the exemption of fishing craft is essentially an act of grace, and not a matter of right, and it is extended or denied as the exigency is believed to demand.

. . .

In my judgment, the rule is that exemption from the rigors of war is in the control of the Executive. He is bound by no immutable rule on the subject. It is for him to apply, or to modify, or to deny altogether such immunity as may have been usually extended.

Exemptions may be designated in advance or granted according to circumstances, but carrying on war involves the infliction of the hardships of war, at least to the extent that the seizure or destruction of enemy's property on sea need not be specifically authorized in order to be accomplished. . . .

B. Principles

Late-nineteenth-century Americans discovered that their newly amended Constitution had an uncertain mission. Many radical Republicans during Reconstruction insisted that the Thirteenth, Fourteenth, and Fifteenth Amendments revolutionized the constitutional politics of fundamental rights. They looked forward to a new regime in which the federal government would promote political and economic equality. Conservative Republicans and Democrats, in contrast, thought those amendments did little more than end slavery. They looked forward to "the Constitution as it was," minus human bondage. Prominent constitutional elites less concerned with racial issues championed the free labor constitutional commitments of the early Republican Party. They hoped that the end of slavery meant the end of discriminatory legislation intended to benefit some people at the expense of others.

Much constitutional thinking in the Republican Era was rooted in one of two schools of political thought, Social Darwinism or Pragmatism. Both reflected the influence of Charles Darwin, the scientist who formulated the theory of evolution or natural selection. Social Darwinists maintained that government should avoid economic regulation and let natural selection determine wages, prices, and other business practices. Herbert Spencer's *Social Statics* declared:

> Political economy says it is good that speculators should be allowed to operate on the food-markets as they see well: the law of equal freedom (contrary to the current notion) holds them justified in doing this, and condemns all interference with them as inequitable. . . . One of the settled conclusions of political economy is, that wages and prices cannot be artificially regulated: meanwhile it is an obvious inference from the law of equal freedom that no artificial regulation of them is morally permissible.[9]

Pragmatists insisted on a living Constitution, one that adjusted constitutional rules and principles in light of political and social changes. Woodrow Wilson, who was a prominent progressive thinker before becoming president of the United States, wrote,

> Living political constitutions must be Darwinian in structure and in practice. Society is a living organism and must obey the laws of life, not of mechanics; it must develop.
>
> All that progressives ask or desire is permission—in an era when "development," "evolution," is the scientific word—to interpret the Constitution according to the Darwinian principle; all they ask is

9. Herbert Spencer, *Social Statics* (New York: D. Appleton, 1871), 501.

recognition of the fact that a nation is a living thing and not a machine.[10]

C. Scope

Constitutional authorities rejected three distinct attempts to substantially broaden the scope of federal constitutional protections for civil rights. *Ross v. McIntyre* (1891) held that the Bill of Rights had no extraterritorial effect. American officials in foreign countries had to consult treaties, but not the Constitution, when determining whether their actions were legal. *Balzac v. Porto Rico* (1922) and other *Insular Cases*, most notably *Downes v. Bidwell* (1903) and *Hawaii v. Manhichi* (1903), concluded that Congress was limited by the Bill of Rights only when governing territories being prepared for statehood. Oklahoma residents had the right to trial by jury, but persons residing in Puerto Rico or the Philippines did not. A Supreme Court majority in *Hurtado v. California* (1884) ruled that state governments were not limited by any provision in the Bill of Rights. That position was modified after 1895. In a series of cases, judicial majorities determined that the due process clause of the Fourteenth Amendment had some overlap with the Bill of Rights. By 1932 the justices had ruled that states could not take property without compensation or to benefit private parties, could not deprive a person of the right to counsel, and could not violate free speech rights.

The state action requirement debuted in the Republican Era. The Supreme Court in the *Civil Rights Cases* (1883) held that the Fourteenth Amendment was a restriction only against the official actions of state government and thus did not prohibit purely private interference with individual rights. That ruling did not absolutely bar federal efforts to combat all private discrimination. The justices recognized that the Thirteenth Amendment has no state action requirement. Republican Era justices also recognized that private individuals could be held to constitutional standards when their discrimination had some connection to official action or law. Nevertheless, the state action requirement, combined with the continued vitality of *Barron v. Baltimore* (1833), sharply limited federal protection for individual rights in the states.

10. Woodrow Wilson, "What Is Progress?" in *The New Freedom*, ed. William Bayard Hale (New York: Doubleday, Page and Co., 1913), 48.

Incorporation

The post–Civil War Amendments provided potential constitutional foundations for expanding federal judicial authority. Federal courts before the Civil War had very few opportunities to supervise state behavior. Chief Justice Marshall ruled in *Barron v. Baltimore* (1833) that the Bill of Rights applied only to the federal government. Prominent Republicans during Reconstruction condemned *Barron*. Many insisted that the proposed Fourteenth Amendment required states to protect the same rights and follow the same procedures in criminal prosecutions that were required of the federal government under the first eight amendments. In the technical language of constitutional law, they claimed that the provisions of the federal Bill of Rights were "incorporated" into the Fourteenth Amendment via the privileges and immunities or due process clauses, thus making them enforceable by federal courts against the states.

The Supreme Court initially refused to incorporate any provision of the Bill of Rights. The *Slaughter-House Cases* (1873) rejected claims that the liberties set out in the first eight amendments were among the "privileges and immunities" of U.S. citizens that "no state could abridge." A judicial majority in *Hurtado v. California* (1884) ruled that the due process clause of the Fourteenth Amendment did not incorporate any clause in the Bill of Rights other than the due process clause of the Fifth Amendment. If such rights as the right to be indicted by a grand jury were guaranteed by the due process clause, Justice Stanley Matthews' majority opinion declared, the framers of the Fifth Amendment would have had no need to mention explicitly both the right to a grand jury and due process.

Judicial majorities became more receptive to incorporation over time. *Twining v. New Jersey* (1908) declared that the crucial due process issue was whether the right in question was "a fundamental principle of liberty and justice which inheres in the very idea of free government and is the inalienable right of a citizen of such a government." Most decisions that applied this standard rejected claims that states were prohibited from violating a particular provision of the Bill of Rights. *Twining* held that a state prosecutor did not violate the Fourteenth Amendment by commenting to the jury on a criminal defendant's failure to take the stand, even though identical comments by a federal prosecutor would violate the privilege against self-incrimination protected by the Fifth Amendment.

Nevertheless, by the end of the Republican Era the Supreme Court had ruled that the due process clause of the Fourteenth Amendment forbade states from violating the takings clause of the Fifth Amendment (*Chicago, Burlington & O.R. Co. v. Chicago* [1897]), the free speech clause of the First Amendment (*Gitlow v. United States* [1925]), and the right to counsel protected by the Sixth Amendment (*Powell v. Alabama* [1932]). As the justices embraced incorporation of the Bill of Rights, they also found more opportunities to exercise the power of judicial review. An increasing frequency in judicial invalidations in state and federal statutes marked the Republican Era.

Twining v. New Jersey, 211 U.S. 78 (1908)

Albert Twining and David Cornell were accused of deceiving the state of New Jersey about certain transactions in which they engaged as directors of the Monmouth Trust & Safe Deposit Company. In his closing arguments, the prosecutor made the following comments on Twining and Cornell's failure to testify in their defense:

> *[T]hat they stay off the stand, having heard testimony which might be prejudicial to them, without availing themselves of the right to go upon the stand and contradict it, is sometimes a matter of significance.*

When the judge charged the jury he remarked, "Because a man does not go upon the stand you are not necessarily justified in drawing an inference of guilt. But you have a right to consider the fact that he does not go upon the stand where a direct accusation is made against him." Twining and Cornell were found guilty and sentenced to six and four years in prison, respectively. Several appellate courts in New Jersey sustained their convictions under the provisions of the state constitution. Because federal courts interpreted the Fifth Amendment as prohibiting prosecutors from commenting on a failure to testify in the federal criminal justice system, Twining and Cornell appealed to the Supreme Court of the United States. They argued that their conviction violated the due process clause of the Fourteenth Amendment which incorporated the Fifth Amendment.

The Supreme Court by an 8-1 vote sustained the convictions. Justice Moody's majority opinion insisted that the right against self-incrimination was neither a privilege nor an immunity of citizens of the United States, nor was it an element of due process protected by the Fourteenth Amendment. Moody acknowledged that most Americans agreed that persons had a fundamental right against compelled incrimination. Why does he nevertheless claim that

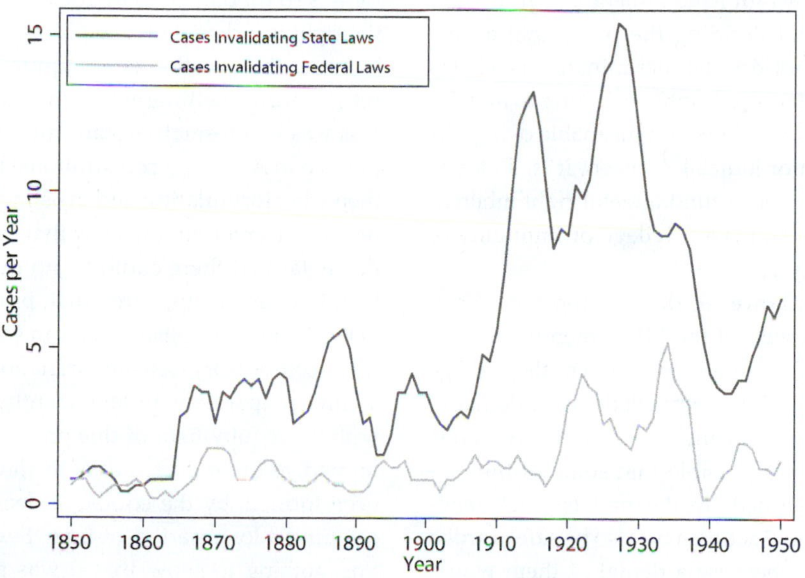

Figure 7-3 Supreme Court Invalidation of State and Federal Laws, 1850–1950

Note: Centered, five-year moving averages.

Source: Congressional Research Service, *The Constitution of the United States of America, Analysis and Interpretation* (Washington, DC: Government Printing Office, 2004); Keith E. Whittington, *The Judicial Review of Congress* [dataset].

the Fourteenth Amendment does not protect that right? Why does Justice Harlan disagree? Justice Harlan insists that Twining *permits states to extract confessions by torture. Could you write an opinion consistent with* Twining *asserting that torture does violate due process, or is Justice Harlan correct?*

JUSTICE MOODY delivered the opinion of the court

. . .

The exemption from testimonial compulsion, that is, from disclosure as a witness of evidence against oneself, forced by any form of legal process, is universal in American law, though there may be differences as to its exact scope and limits. At the time of the formation of the Union the principle that no person could be compelled to be a witness against himself had become embodied in the common law and distinguished it from all other systems of jurisprudence. It was generally regarded then, as now, as a privilege of great value, a protection to the innocent, though a shelter to the guilty, and a safeguard against heedless, unfounded, or tyrannical prosecutions.

. . .

. . . There can be no doubt, so far as the decision in the *Slaughter-House Cases* (1873) has determined the question, that the civil rights sometimes described as fundamental and inalienable, which, before the War Amendments, were enjoyed by state citizenship and protected by state government, were left untouched by this clause of the 14th Amendment. . . . If, then, it be assumed, without deciding the point, that an exemption from compulsory self-incrimination is what is described as a fundamental right belonging to all who live under a free government, and incapable of impairment by legislation or judicial decision, it is, so far as the states are concerned, a fundamental right inherent in state citizenship, and is a privilege or immunity of that citizenship only. . . .

The defendants, however, do not stop here. They appeal to another clause of the 14th Amendment, and insist that the self-incrimination which they allege the instruction to the jury compelled was a denial of due process of law. This contention requires separate consideration, for it is possible that some of the personal rights safeguarded by the first eight Amendments against national action may also be safeguarded against state action, because a denial of them would be a denial of due process of law. If this is so, it is not because those rights are enumerated in the first eight Amendments, but because they are of such a nature that they are included in the conception of due process of law. Few phrases of the law are so elusive of exact apprehension as this. . . .

. . . Is it a fundamental principle of liberty and justice which inheres in the very idea of free government and is the inalienable right of a citizen of such a government? If it is, and if it is of a nature that pertains to process of law, this court has declared it to be essential to due process of law. In approaching such a question it must not be forgotten that in a free representative government nothing is more fundamental than the right of the people, through their appointed servants, to govern themselves in accordance with their own will, except so far as they have restrained themselves by constitutional limits specifically established, and that, in our peculiar dual form of government, nothing is more fundamental than the full power of the state to order its own affairs and govern its own people, except so far as the Federal Constitution, expressly or by fair implication, has withdrawn that power. The power of the people of the states to make and alter their laws at pleasure is the greatest security for liberty and justice. . . . Under the guise of interpreting the Constitution we must take care that we do not import into the discussion our own personal views of what would be wise, just, and fitting rules of government to be adopted by a free people, and confound them with constitutional limitations. . . . We have to consider whether the right is so fundamental in due process that a refusal of the right is a denial of due process. One aid to the solution of the question is to inquire how the right was rated during the time when the meaning of due process was in a formative state, and before it was incorporated in American constitutional law. Did those who then were formulating and insisting upon the rights of the people entertain the view that the right was so fundamental that there could be no due process without it? It has already appeared that, prior to the formation of the American Constitutions, in which the exemption from compulsory self-incrimination was specifically secured, separately, independently, and side by side with the requirement of due process, the doctrine was formed, as other doctrines of the law of evidence have been formed, by the course of decision in the courts, covering a long period of time. Searching further, we find nothing to show that it was then thought to be other than a just and useful principle of law. None of the great instruments in which we are accustomed to look for the declaration of the fundamental rights made reference to it. . . .

. . .

. . . [F]our only of the thirteen original states insisted upon incorporating the privilege in the Constitution, and they separately and simultaneously with the requirement of due process of law, and . . . three states proposing amendments were silent upon this subject. . . . This survey does not tend to show that it was then in this country the universal or even general belief that the privilege ranked among the fundamental and inalienable rights of mankind; and what is more important here, it affirmatively shows that the privilege was not conceived to be inherent in due process of law, but, on the other hand, a right separate, independent, and outside of due process. . . .

. . .

Even if the historical meaning of due process of law and the decisions of this court did not exclude the privilege from it, it would be going far to rate it as an immutable principle of justice which is the inalienable possession of every citizen of a free government. Salutary as the principle may seem to the great majority, it cannot be ranked with the right to hearing before condemnation, the immunity from arbitrary power not acting by general laws, and the inviolability of private property. The wisdom of the exemption has never been universally assented to since the days of Bentham, many doubt it to-day, and it is best defended not as an unchangeable principle of universal justice, but as a law proved by experience to be expedient. It has no place in the jurisprudence of civilized and free countries outside the domain of the common law, and it is nowhere observed among our own people in the search for truth outside the administration of the law. It should, must, and will be rigidly observed where it is secured by specific constitutional safeguards, but there is nothing in it which gives it a sanctity above and before constitutions themselves. . . . The power of their people ought not to be fettered, their sense of responsibility lessened, and their capacity for sober and restrained self-government weakened, by forced construction of the Federal Constitution. If the people of New Jersey are not content with the law as declared in repeated decisions of their courts, the remedy is in their own hands. . . .

JUSTICE HARLAN, dissenting:

. . .

. . . In my judgment, immunity from self-incrimination is protected against hostile state action, not only by that clause in the 14th Amendment declaring that "no state shall make or enforce any law which shall abridge the privileges or immunities of citizens of the United States," but by the clause, in the same Amendment, "nor shall any state deprive any person of life, liberty, or property, without due process of law." . . .

. . .

Can there be any doubt that, at the opening of the War of Independence, the people of the colonies claimed as one of their birthrights the privilege of immunity from self-incrimination? This question can be answered in but one way. If, at the beginning of the Revolutionary War, any lawyer had claimed that one accused of crime could lawfully be compelled to testify against himself, he would have been laughed at by his brethren of the bar, both in England and America. . . . [W]hen the first Congress met, there was entire unanimity among statesmen of that day as to the necessity and wisdom of having a national Bill of Rights which would, beyond all question, secure against Federal encroachment all the rights, privileges, and immunities which, everywhere and by everybody in America, were then recognized as fundamental in Anglo-American liberty. . . . By the 5th Amendment, as already stated, it was expressly declared that no one should be compelled, in a criminal case, to be a witness against himself. Those Amendments being adopted by the nation, the people no longer feared that the United States or any Federal agency could exert power that was inconsistent with the fundamental rights recognized in those Amendments. . . .

. . . [The Fourteenth] Amendment declared that all persons born or naturalized in the United States and subject to its jurisdiction are citizens of the United States, "and of the state wherein they reside." Momentous as this declaration was, in its political consequences, it was not deemed sufficient for the complete protection of the essential rights of national citizenship and personal liberty. Although the nation was restrained by existing constitutional provisions from encroaching upon those rights, yet, so far as the Federal Constitution was concerned, the states could, at that time, have dealt with those rights upon the basis entirely of their own Constitution and laws. It was therefore deemed necessary that the 14th Amendment should, in the name of the United States, forbid, as it expressly does, any *state* from making or enforcing a law that will abridge the privileges or immunities of citizens of the United States, or deprive any person of life, liberty, or property without due process of law. The privileges and immunities mentioned in the original Amendments, and universally regarded as our heritage of liberty from the common law, were thus secured to every citizen of the United States, and placed beyond assault by any government, Federal or state; and due process of law, in all public proceedings affecting life, liberty, or property, was enjoined equally upon the nation and the states.

. . .

I will not attempt to enumerate all the privileges and immunities which *at that time* belonged to citizens of the United States. But I confidently assert that among such privileges was the privilege of immunity from self-incrimination which the people of the United States, by adopting the 5th Amendment, had placed beyond Federal encroachment. Can such a view be deemed unreasonable in the face of the fact, frankly conceded in the opinion of the court, that, at common law, as well at the time of the formation of the Union and when the 14th Amendment was adopted, immunity from self-incrimination was a privilege "universal in American law," was everywhere deemed "of great value, a protection to the innocent, though a shelter to the guilty, and a safeguard against heedless, unfounded, or tyrannical prosecutions?" Is it conceivable that a privilege or immunity of such a priceless character, one expressly recognized in the supreme law of the land, one thoroughly interwoven with the history of Anglo-American liberty, was not in the mind of the country when it declared, in the 14th Amendment, that no state shall abridge the privileges or immunities of citizens of the United States? The 14th Amendment would have been disapproved by every state in the Union if it had saved or recognized the right of a state to compel one accused of crime, in its courts, to be a witness against himself. We state the matter in this way because it is common knowledge that the compelling of a person to criminate himself shocks or ought to shock the sense of right and justice to everyone who loves liberty.

. . . [A]s I read the opinion of the court, it will follow from the general principles underlying it, or from the reasoning pursued therein, that the 14th Amendment would be no obstacle whatever in the way of a state law or practice under which, for instance, cruel or unusual punishments (such as the thumbscrew, or the rack, or burning at the stake) might be inflicted. So of a state law which infringed the right of free speech, or authorized unreasonable searches or seizures of persons, their houses, papers, or effects, or a state law under which one accused of crime could be put in jeopardy twice or oftener, at the pleasure of the prosecution, for the same offense. . . .

Extraterritoriality

Ross v. McIntyre, 140 U.S. 453 (1891)

John Ross was a crew member on the Bullion, *an American ship docked in Japan. On May 9, 1880, Ross was arrested and charged with the murder of Robert Kelly, a crewmate. He was tried by the American consul in Japan, found guilty, and sentenced to death. President Rutherford B. Hayes commuted that sentence to life in prison. Ten years later Ross filed a habeas corpus petition, claiming that the federal law authorizing the American consul in Japan to try American citizens without a jury for crimes committed in Japan was unconstitutional. The federal circuit court ruled that the federal law was constitutional. Ross appealed to the Supreme Court of the United States.*

The Supreme Court unanimously ruled that Ross was constitutionally convicted. Justice Field asserted that the rules of constitutional criminal procedure apply only to American citizens tried in the United States. Why does he reach that conclusion? Suppose the consul had flipped a coin to decide whether Ross was guilty. Would that have been constitutional? Ross *was decided when Americans were debating the merits of obtaining an overseas empire. Might that have influenced the judicial decision? Would John Marshall or Roger Taney have reached the same conclusion?*

JUSTICE FIELD delivered the opinion of the Court.

. . .

. . . By the constitution a government is ordained and established "for the United States of America," and not for countries outside of their limits. The guaranties it affords against accusation of capital or infamous crimes, except by indictment or presentment by a grand jury, and for an impartial trial by a jury when thus accused, apply only to citizens and others within the United States, or who are brought there for trial for alleged offenses committed elsewhere, and not to residents or temporary sojourners abroad. . . . The constitution can have no operation in another country. When, therefore, the representatives or officers of our government are permitted to exercise authority of any kind in another country, it must be on such conditions as the two countries may agree; the laws of neither one being obligatory upon the other. The deck of a private American vessel, it is true, is considered, for many purposes, constructively as territory of the United States; yet persons on board of such vessels, whether officers, sailors, or passengers, cannot invoke the protection of the provisions referred to until brought within the actual territorial boundaries of the United States. . . . The framers of the constitution, who were fully aware of the necessity of having judicial authority exercised by our consuls in non-Christian countries, if commercial intercourse was to be had with their people, never could have supposed that all the guaranties in the administration of the law upon criminals at home were to be transferred to such consular establishments, and applied before an American who had committed a felony there could be accused and tried. They must have known that such a requirement would defeat the main purpose of investing the consul with judicial authority. . . .

Illustration 7-1 "The Constitution Follows the Flag" Song Sheet

This 1901 patriotic song from the Spanish-American War reflected a popular phrase of the time.

Source: George Alexander and Jean Schwartz, "The Constitution Follows the Flag" [song sheet], 1901. Music Division, The New York Public Library for the Performing Arts, Astor, Lenox and Tilden Foundations.

Balzac v. Porto Rico, 258 U.S. 298 (1922)

Jesus Balzac was the editor of a local paper in Puerto Rico. In 1918 he was charged with criminal libel for publishing a series of articles critical of the territorial governor. At trial Balzac claimed that his conduct was protected by the First Amendment, and that the Sixth Amendment guaranteed him the right to a jury trial. Both contentions were overruled. Balzac was found guilty and sentenced to four months in prison. After the Supreme Court of Puerto Rico affirmed that decision, Balzac appealed to the Supreme Court of the United States.

The Supreme Court of the United States unanimously upheld Balzac's conviction. Chief Justice Taft's opinion declared that the Bill of Rights only limited federal power in incorporated territories being prepared for statehood. The parties to Balzac *agreed that all Puerto Rican residents were citizens of the United States under the Foraker Act of 1900. Why did Taft nevertheless conclude that Puerto Rico was an unincorporated territory? How does Taft distinguish between Puerto Rico and Texas, which was considered an incorporated territory? To what extent do you believe that the race of most inhabitants of a territory influenced judicial and legislative decisions on whether it was incorporated? Notice that Taft decided the First Amendment issue on the merits rather than claiming that Congress was not bound by that provision. Does this imply that persons living in unincorporated territories have the right to free speech?*

Balzac *was decided unanimously, but the claim that the Bill of Rights limited federal power only in incorporated territories had been heatedly contested in previous cases. Consider Justice Harlan's dissent in* Hawaii v. Mankichi *(1903), which declared,*

> *In my opinion, the Constitution of the United States became the supreme law of Hawaii immediately upon the acquisition by the United States of complete sovereignty over the Hawaiian Islands, and without any act of Congress formally extending the Constitution to those islands. . . . From the moment when the government of Hawaii accepted the joint resolution of 1898 by a formal transfer of its sovereignty to the United States, . . . every human being in Hawaii charged with the commission of crime there could have rightly insisted that neither his life nor his liberty could be taken, as punishment for crime, by any process or as the result of any mode of procedure that was inconsistent with the Constitution of the United States. Can it be that the Constitution is the supreme law in the states of the Union, in the organized territories of the United States, between the Atlan-*

tic and Pacific oceans, and in the District of Columbia, and yet was not . . . the supreme law in territories and among peoples situated as were the territory and people of Hawaii, and over which the United States had acquired all rights of sovereignty of whatsoever kind? A negative answer to this question, and a recognition of the principle that such an answer involves, would place Congress above the Constitution. It would mean that the benefit of the constitutional provisions designed for the protection of life and liberty may be claimed by some of the people subject to the authority and jurisdiction of the United States, but cannot be claimed by others equally subject to its authority and jurisdiction. It would mean that the will of Congress, not the Constitution, is the supreme law of the land for certain peoples and territories under our jurisdiction. It would mean that the United States may acquire territory by cession, conquest, or treaty, and that Congress may exercise sovereign dominion over it, outside of and in violation of the Constitution and under regulations that could not be applied to the organized territories of the United States and their inhabitants. It would mean that, under the influence and guidance of commercialism and the supposed necessities of trade, this country had left the old ways of the fathers, as defined by a written constitution, and entered upon a new way, in following which the American people will lose sight of, or become indifferent to, principles which had been supposed to be essential to real liberty. It would mean that, if the principles now announced should become firmly established, the time may not be far distant when, under the exactions of trade and commerce, and to gratify an ambition to become the dominant political power in all the earth, the United States will acquire territories in every direction, which are inhabited by human beings, over which territories, to be called "dependencies" or "outlying possessions," we will exercise absolute dominion, and whose inhabitants will be regarded as "subjects" or "dependent peoples," to be controlled as Congress may see fit, not as the Constitution requires nor as the people governed may wish. Thus, will be engrafted upon our republican institutions, controlled by the supreme law of a written Constitution, a colonial system entirely foreign to the genius of our government and abhorrent to the principles that underlie and pervade the Constitution.

CHIEF JUSTICE TAFT delivered the opinion of the Court.

. . .

It is well settled that these provisions for jury trial in criminal and civil cases apply to the Territories of the United States. *Webster v. Reid* (1850). But it is just as clearly settled that they do not apply to territory belonging to the United States which has not been incorporated into the Union. *Hawaii v. Mankichi* (1903). It was further settled in *Downes v. Bidwell* (1903) that neither the Philippines nor Porto Rico was territory which had been incorporated in the Union or become a part of the United States, as distinguished from merely belonging to it. . . .

. . .

. . . [T]he Porto Rican can not insist upon the right of trial by jury, except as his own representatives in his legislature shall confer it on him. The citizen of the United States living in Porto Rico cannot there enjoy a right of trial by jury under the federal Constitution, any more than the Porto Rican. It is locality that is determinative of the application of the Constitution, in such matters as judicial procedure, and not the status of the people who live in it.

. . .

The jury system needs citizens trained to the exercise of the responsibilities of jurors. In common-law countries centuries of tradition have prepared a conception of the impartial attitude jurors must assume. The jury system postulates a conscious duty of participation in the machinery of justice which it is hard for people not brought up in fundamentally popular government at once to acquire. One of its greatest benefits is in the security it gives the people that they, as jurors, actual or possible, being part of the judicial system of the country, can prevent its arbitrary use or abuse. Congress has thought that a people like the Filipinos, or the Porto Ricans, trained to a complete judicial system which knows no juries, living in compact and ancient communities, with definitely formed customs and political conceptions, should be permitted themselves to determine how far they wish to adopt this institution of Anglo-Saxon origin, and when. . . .

. . .

A second assignment of error is based on the claim that the alleged libels here did not pass the bounds of legitimate comment on the conduct of the Governor of the island, against whom they were directed, and that its prosecution is a violation of the First Amendment to the Constitution, securing free speech and a free press. A reading of the two articles removes the slightest doubt that they go far beyond the "exuberant expressions of meridional speech." . . . Indeed, they are so excessive and outrageous in their character that they suggest the query whether their superlative vilification has not overleaped itself and become unconsciously humorous. But this is not a defense.

JUSTICE HOLMES concurs in the result.

State Action

The post–Civil War Amendments raised a new concern about the scope of constitutional protection for fundamental rights—state action. The Fourteenth Amendment declares, "No State shall make or enforce any law which shall abridge the privileges or immunities of citizens of the United States; nor shall any State deprive any person of life, liberty, or property, without due process of law, nor deny to any person within its jurisdiction the equal protection of the laws." During the debates over the Civil Rights Act of 1875 prominent Democrats and some Republicans insisted that these provisions gave neither Congress nor the federal courts power to punish private discrimination or other private conduct that might prevent people from exercising various liberties. In their view the Fourteenth Amendment forbade only state laws and official conduct that sanctioned discrimination or violated fundamental rights.

The Supreme Court in the *Civil Rights Cases* (1883) endorsed the conservative claim that the Fourteenth Amendment forbade only official conduct that violated rights when declaring unconstitutional the provision in the Civil Rights Act of 1875 prohibiting places of public accommodation and amusement from discriminating on the basis of race. Constitutional decision makers in the Republican Era prohibited some private discrimination when they found some official sanction for the offending individual behavior. In *Nixon v. Condon* (1932) a judicial majority ruled that the state Democratic Party was a state actor for Fourteenth Amendment purposes when a state law authorized that party's executive committee to determine who would vote in primary elections and the party excluded persons of color. Justice Cardozo's majority opinion stated, "When those agencies are invested with an authority independent of the will of the association in whose name they undertake to speak, they become to that extent the organs of the state itself, the repositories of official power."

Civil Rights Cases, 109 U.S. 3 (1883)

Stanley, Nichols, Ryan, and Singleton were indicted in four separate cases for violating the Civil Rights Act of 1875, which forbade racial discrimination by "inns, public conveyances on land and water, theaters, and other places of public amusement." The local circuit courts divided evenly on whether that law was constitutional. Around the same time, Robinson brought a suit against the Memphis & Charleston Railroad for refusing to allow his wife to ride in the ladies car. A jury found for the railway company. The Supreme Court combined these five cases when considering the constitutionality of the Civil Rights Act of 1875.

The Supreme Court by an 8-1 vote declared the crucial provision of the Civil Rights Act unconstitutional. Justice Bradley's majority opinion ruled that the Fourteenth Amendment forbade only states from denying equal protection, not private parties. The Fourteenth Amendment, a judicial majority held, required plaintiffs alleging rights violations to prove "state action." Private discrimination was beyond the scope of the amendment and, by extension, beyond the scope of Congress' power to enforce the provisions of the amendment. How does Justice Bradley reach that conclusion? Why does he reject the claim that Congress does not have power under the Thirteenth Amendment to forbid some private discrimination? Why does Justice Harlan disagree with that conclusion? (Justice Harlan felt so strongly that the majority had erred that he decided to write his dissent with the same pen and inkwell that Chief Justice Taney used to write the Dred Scott *opinion.) If state officials decide not to protect blacks from hostile or discriminatory behavior by other people in the state, would that be a kind of "state action" that would fall under the scope of the equal protection clause? Shortly after passing the Civil Rights Act of 1875, national party leaders struck a bargain to end Reconstruction. Did that bargain influence the justices? Would the case have been decided differently if the issues had come before the justices in 1870?*

JUSTICE BRADLEY delivered the opinion of the Court.

. . .

The first section of the fourteenth amendment . . . declares that "no state shall make or enforce any law which shall abridge the privileges or immunities of citizens of the United States; nor shall any state deprive any person of life, liberty, or property without due process of law; nor deny to any person within its jurisdiction the equal protection of the laws." It is state action of a particular character that is prohibited. Individual invasion of individual rights is not the subject-matter of the amendment. It has a deeper and broader scope. It nullifies and makes void all state legislation, and state action of every kind, which impairs the privileges and immunities of citizens of the United States, or which injures them in life, liberty, or property without due process of law, or which denies to any of them the equal protection of the laws. It not only does this, but . . . the last section of the amendment invests congress with power to enforce it by appropriate legislation. To enforce what? To enforce the prohibition. To adopt appropriate legislation for correcting the effects of such prohibited state law and state acts, and thus to render them effectually null, void, and innocuous. This is the legislative power conferred upon congress, and this is the whole of it. It does not invest congress with power to legislate upon subjects which are within the domain of state legislation; but to provide modes of relief against state legislation, or state action, of the kind referred to. It does not authorize congress to create a code of municipal law for the regulation of private rights; but to provide modes of redress against the operation of state laws, and the action of state officers, executive or judicial, when these are subversive of the fundamental rights specified in the amendment. Positive rights and privileges are undoubtedly secured by the fourteenth amendment; but they are secured by way of prohibition against state laws and state proceedings affecting those rights and privileges, and by power given to congress to legislate for the purpose of carrying such prohibition into effect; and such legislation must necessarily be predicated upon such supposed state laws or state proceedings, and be directed to the correction of their operation and effect. . . .

. . .

And so in the present case, until some state law has been passed, or some state action through its officers or agents has been taken, adverse to the rights of citizens sought to be protected by the fourteenth amendment, no legislation of the United States under said amendment, nor any proceeding under such legislation, can be called into activity, for the prohibitions of the amendment are against state laws and acts done under state authority. . . .

An inspection of the law shows that it makes no reference whatever to any supposed or apprehended violation of the fourteenth amendment on the part of the states. It is not predicated on any such view. It proceeds *ex directo* to declare that certain acts committed by individuals shall be deemed offenses, and shall be prosecuted and punished by proceedings in the courts of the United States. It does not profess to be corrective of any constitutional wrong committed by the states; it does not make its operation to depend upon any such wrong committed. It applies equally to cases arising in states which have the justest laws respecting the personal rights of citizens, and whose authorities are ever ready to enforce such laws as to those which arise in states that may have violated the prohibition of the amendment. In other words, it steps into the domain of local jurisprudence, and lays down rules for the conduct of individuals in society towards each other, and imposes sanctions for the enforcement of those rules, without referring in any manner to any supposed action of the state or its authorities.

. . .

In this connection it is proper to state that civil rights, such as are guaranteed by the constitution against state aggression, cannot be impaired by the wrongful acts of individuals, unsupported by state authority in the shape of laws, customs, or judicial or executive proceedings. The wrongful act of an individual, unsupported by any such authority, is simply a private wrong, or a crime of that individual; an invasion of the rights of the injured party, it is true, whether they affect his person, his property, or his reputation; but if not sanctioned in some way by the state, or not done under state authority, his rights remain in full force, and may presumably be vindicated by resort to the laws of the state for redress. An individual cannot deprive a man of his right to vote, to hold property, to buy and to sell, to sue in the courts, or to be a witness or a juror; he may, by force or fraud, interfere with the enjoyment of the right in a particular case; he may commit an assault against the person, or commit murder, or use ruffian violence at the polls, or slander the good name of a fellow-citizen; but unless protected in these wrongful acts by some shield of state law or state authority, he cannot destroy or injure the right; he will only render himself amenable to satisfaction or punishment; and amenable therefor to the laws of the state where the wrongful acts are committed. Hence, in all those cases where the constitution seeks to protect the rights of the citizen against discriminative and unjust laws of the state by prohibiting such laws, it is not individual offenses, but abrogation and denial of rights, which it denounces, and for which it clothes the congress with power to provide a remedy. . . .

. . .

. . . Conceding . . . that congress has a right to enact all necessary and proper laws for the obliteration and prevention of slavery, with all its badges and incidents, is [it] also true, that the denial to any person of admission to the accommodations and privileges of an inn, a public conveyance, or a theater, does subject that person to any form of servitude, or tend to fasten upon him any badge of slavery? If it does not, then power to pass the law is not found in the thirteenth amendment.

. . .

After giving to these questions all the consideration which their importance demands, we are forced to the conclusion that such an act of refusal has nothing to do with slavery or involuntary servitude, and that if it is violative of any right of the party, his redress is to be sought under the laws of the state; or, if those laws are adverse to his rights and do not protect him, his remedy will be found in the corrective legislation which congress has adopted, or may adopt, for counteracting the effect of state laws, or state action, prohibited by the fourteenth amendment. It would be running the slavery argument into the ground to make it apply to every act of discrimination which a person may see fit to make as to the guests he will entertain, or as to the people he will take into his coach or cab or car, or admit to his concert or theater, or deal with in other matters of intercourse or business. Innkeepers and public carriers, by the laws of all the states, so far as we are aware, are bound, to the extent of their facilities, to furnish proper accommodation to all unobjectionable persons who in good faith apply for them. If the laws themselves make any unjust discrimination, amenable to the prohibitions of the fourteenth amendment, congress has full power to afford a remedy under that amendment and in accordance with it.

When a man has emerged from slavery, and by the aid of beneficent legislation has shaken off the inseparable concomitants of that state, there must be some stage in the progress of his elevation when he takes the rank of a mere citizen, and ceases to be the special favorite of the laws, and when his rights as a citizen, or a man, are to be protected in the ordinary modes by which other men's rights are protected. There were thousands of free colored people in this country before the abolition of slavery, enjoying all the essential rights of life, liberty, and property the same as white citizens; yet no one, at that time, thought that it was any invasion of their personal *status* as freemen because they were not admitted to all the privileges enjoyed by white citizens, or because they were subjected to discriminations in the enjoyment of accommodations in inns, public conveyances, and places of amusement. Mere discriminations on account of race or color were not regarded as badges of slavery. . . .

. . .

JUSTICE HARLAN, dissenting.

The opinion in these cases proceeds, as it seems to me, upon grounds entirely too narrow and artificial. The substance and spirit of the recent amendments of the constitution have been sacrificed by a subtle and ingenious verbal criticism. . . . Constitutional provisions, adopted in the interest of liberty, and for the purpose of securing, through national legislation, if need be, rights inhering in a state of freedom, and belonging to American citizenship, have been so construed as to defeat the ends the people desired to accomplish, which they attempted to accomplish, and which they supposed they had accomplished by changes in their fundamental law.

. . .

That there are burdens and disabilities which constitute badges of slavery and servitude, and that the express power delegated to congress to enforce, by appropriate legislation, the thirteenth amendment, may be exerted by legislation of a direct and primary character, for the eradication, not simply of the institution, but of its badges and incidents, are propositions which ought to be deemed indisputable. They lie at the very foundation of the civil rights act of 1866. . . . I do not contend that the thirteenth amendment invests congress with authority, by legislation, to regulate the entire body of the civil rights which citizens enjoy, or may enjoy, in the several states. But I do hold that since slavery, as the court has repeatedly declared, was the moving or principal cause of the adoption of that amendment, and since that institution rested wholly upon the inferiority, as a race, of those held in bondage, their freedom necessarily involved immunity from, and protection against, all discrimination against them, because of their race, in respect of such civil rights as belong to freemen of other races. Congress, therefore, under its express power to enforce that amendment, by appropriate legislation, may enact laws to protect that people against the deprivation, *on account of their race*, of any civil rights enjoyed by other freemen in the same state; and such legislation may be of a direct and primary character, operating upon states, their officers and agents, and also upon, at least, such individuals and corporations as exercise public functions and wield power and authority under the state.

. . .

It remains now to inquire what are the legal rights of colored persons in respect of the accommodations, privileges, and facilities of public conveyances, inns, and places of public amusement.

As to public conveyances on land and water. . . . [T]his court . . . said that a common carrier is "in the exercise of a sort of public office and has public duties to perform, from which he should not be permitted to exonerate himself without the assent of the parties concerned." To the same effect . . . , it was ruled that railroads are public highways, established, by authority of the state, for the public use; that they are none the less public highways because controlled and owned by private corporations; that it is a part of the function of government to make and maintain highways for the conveyance of the public; that no matter who is the agent, and what is the agency, the function performed is *that of the state;* that although the owners may be private companies, they may be compelled to permit the public to use these works in the manner in which they can be used. . . .

. . .

Such being the relations these corporations hold to the public, it would seem that the right of a colored person to use an improved public highway, upon the terms accorded to freemen of other races, is as fundamental in the state of freedom, established in this country, as are any of the rights which my brethren concede to be so far fundamental as to be deemed the essence of civil freedom. "Personal liberty consists," says Blackstone, "in the power of locomotion, of changing situation, or removing one's person to whatever place one's own inclination may direct, without restraint, unless by due course of law." But of what value is this right of locomotion, if it may be clogged by such burdens as congress intended by the act of 1875 to remove? . . .

. . .

. . . [A] keeper of an inn is in the exercise of a *quasi* public employment. The law gives him special privileges, and he is charged with certain duties and responsibilities to the public. The public nature of his employment forbids him from discriminating against any person asking admission as a guest on account of the race or color of that person.

As to places of public amusement. . . . [They] are established and maintained under direct license of the law. The authority to establish and maintain them comes from the public. The colored race is a part of that public. The local government granting the license represents them as well as all other races within its jurisdiction. A license from the public to establish a place of public amusement, imports, in law, equality of right, at such places, among all the members of that public. . . .

. . .

The assumption that [the fourteenth] amendment consists wholly of prohibitions upon state laws and state proceedings in hostility to its provisions, is unauthorized by its language. . . .

. . .

But what was secured to colored citizens of the United States—as between them and their respective states—by the grant to them of state citizenship? With what rights, privileges, or immunities did this grant from the nation invest them? There is one, if there be no others—exemption from race discrimination in respect of any civil right belonging to citizens of the white race in the same state. That, surely, is their constitutional privilege when within the jurisdiction of other states. And such must be their constitutional right, in their own state, unless the recent amendments be "splendid baubles," thrown out to delude those who deserved fair and generous treatment at the hands of the nation. Citizenship in this country necessarily imports equality of civil rights among citizens of every race in the same state. It is fundamental in American citizenship that, in respect of such rights, there shall be no discrimination by the state, or its officers, or by individuals, or corporations exercising public functions or authority, against any citizen because of his race or previous condition of servitude. . . .

. . .

If, then, exemption from discrimination in respect of civil rights is a new constitutional right, secured by the grant of state citizenship to colored citizens of the United States, why may not the nation, by means of its own legislation of a primary direct character, guard, protect, and enforce that right? It is a right and privilege which the nation conferred. It did not come from the states in which those colored citizens reside. It has been the established doctrine of this court during all its history, accepted as vital to the national supremacy, that congress, in the absence of a positive delegation of power to the state legislatures, may by legislation enforce and protect any right derived from or created by the national constitution.

. . .

. . . If the grant to colored citizens of the United States of citizenship in their respective states imports exemption from race discrimination, in their states, in respect of the civil rights belonging to citizenship, then, to hold that the amendment remits that right to the states for their protection, primarily, and stays the hands of the nation, until it is assailed by state laws or state proceedings, is to adjudge that the amendment, so far from enlarging the powers of congress,—as we have heretofore said it did,—not only curtails them, but reverses the policy which the general government has pursued from its very organization. Such an interpretation of the amendment is a denial to congress of the power, by appropriate legislation, to enforce one of its provisions. . . . I venture, with all respect for the opinion of others, to insist that the national legislature may, without transcending the limits of the constitution, do for human liberty and the fundamental rights of American citizenship, what it did, with the sanction of this court, for the protection of slavery and the rights of the masters of fugitive slaves. . . .

. . .

My brethren say that when a man has emerged from slavery, and by the aid of beneficient legislation has shaken off the inseparable concomitants of that state, there must be some stage in the progress of his elevation when he takes the rank of a mere citizen, and ceases to be the special favorite of the laws, and when his rights as a citizen, or a man, are to be protected in the ordinary modes by which other men's rights are protected. It is, I submit, scarcely just to say that the colored race has been the special favorite of the laws. What the nation, through congress, has sought to accomplish in reference to that race is, what had already been done in every state in the Union for the white race, to secure and protect rights belonging to them as freemen and citizens; nothing more. The one underlying purpose of congressional legislation has been to enable the black race to take the rank of mere citizens. The difficulty has been to compel a recognition of their legal right to take that rank, and to secure the enjoyment of privileges belonging, under the law, to them as a component part of the people for whose welfare and happiness government is ordained. At every step in this direction the nation has been confronted with class tyranny, which a contemporary English historian says is, of all tyrannies, the most intolerable, "for it is ubiquitous in its operation, and weighs, perhaps, most heavily on those whose obscurity or distance would withdraw them from the notice of a single despot." To-day it is the colored race which is denied, by corporations and individuals wielding public authority, rights fundamental in their freedom and citizenship. At some future time it may be some other race that will fall under the ban. If the constitutional amendments be enforced, according to the intent with which, as I conceive, they were adopted, there cannot be, in this republic, any class of human beings in practical subjection to another class, with power in the latter to dole out to the former just such privileges as they may choose to grant. . . .

III. Individual Rights

MAJOR DEVELOPMENTS

- Federal and state justices protect the freedom of contract
- Debates over whether the United States is a Christian country
- Judges provide due process protection to some noneconomic behaviors, including, in some states, drinking

Americans proposed numerous unprecedented regulations of individual behavior during the Republican Era. Populists insisted that government sharply limit the prices that railroads charged farmers and riders. Progressives championed minimum wage and maximum hour laws for workers. Protestants called on government to regulate drinking and birth control. Urban reformers advocated zoning laws. Doctors asked states to ban abortion.

Proponents made two related claims when defending the constitutionality of these proposals. Reformers frequently insisted that government was merely exercising traditional police powers in light of new conditions and social science research. That government had not previously regulated behavior did not mean that government could not regulate behavior when scientific examination of novel social conditions determined that the regulation served the public good. Many progressives celebrated a "living Constitution." Under living constitutionalism some forms of behavior that were constitutionally protected in the past became legitimate subjects for regulation in the present as social needs and practices changed. Roscoe Pound, a champion of sociological jurisprudence (that is, a jurisprudence that responds to changing social facts), declared, "It is felt that a law cannot be constitutional now if it would have been unconstitutional one hundred years ago. *In fact* it might have been an unreasonable deprivation of liberty as things were even fifty years ago, and yet be a reasonable regulation as things are now."[11]

Opponents claimed that proposed reforms violated individual and property rights. Many insisted that the due process clauses of the federal and state constitutions protected the "right of the citizen to be free in the enjoyment of all his faculties."[12] This right encompassed a freedom of contract and, often, such freedoms as the right to go to private school or the right to drink. Others critics invoked an inherited constitutional animus against class legislation. The Supreme Court in *Adair v. United States* (1908) declared unconstitutional a law prohibiting "yellow dog" contracts (contracts in which employees promised not to join a union) on the ground that

> the right of a person to sell his labor upon such terms as he deems proper is, in its essence, the same as the right of the purchaser of labor to prescribe the conditions upon which he will accept such labor from the person offering to sell it. . . . In all such particulars the employer and the employee have equality of right, and any legislation that disturbs that equality is an arbitrary interference with the liberty of contract which no government can legally justify in a free land.

Other commentators spoke of an "unwritten constitution." Some turned to natural law as a basis for judicial protection of individual liberty. In *The Unwritten Constitution of the United States,* Christopher Tiedeman declared,

> In these days of great social unrest, we applaud the disposition of the courts to seize hold of these general declarations of rights as an authority for them to lay their interdict upon all legislative acts which interfere with the individual's natural rights, even though these acts do not violate any specific or special provision of the Constitution.[13]

When reading the materials in this section, consider the following questions. To what extent did participants in Republican Era constitutional debates adjust inherited understandings of individual right to new circumstances? Were constitutional decisions good-faith efforts to apply traditional police powers doctrine and hostility to class legislation, or were constitutional decision makers substituting policy preferences for law? What is the significance of appeals to natural law or a living Constitution? Did participants in Republican Era constitutional debates privilege those rights that best promoted particular interests, or were many guided by more general philosophical principles that justified a broad range of liberties that transcended the interest of any political, economic, or social class?

A. Property

The Republican Era was the high-water mark for constitutional protection of property rights. *Lochner v. New York* (1905), the most famous constitutional decision of that period, held that maximum hour laws for bakers violated the freedom of contract protected by the due process clause of the Fourteenth Amendment. Other federal and state court decisions struck down regulations that provided various protections for workers and consumers. Some decisions spoke of the freedom of contract. Others emphasized traditional common law protections for liberty and property. William Howard Taft, who was president of the United States from 1909 to 1913 and chief justice of the United States from 1921 to 1930, spoke for many American elites when he maintained,

> You cannot conceive of a government of individual liberty in which the right of property is not secured—the destruction of the right of property is the beginning of the end of individual liberty, because the right of property is that right which secures to the individual the product of his labor and the ownership of his savings, the reward of his industry and self-restraint.[14]

Neither Americans as a whole nor judges as a class went on a rampage striking down legislation regulating economic and property rights. Even the most libertarian justices on federal and state courts sustained

11. Roscoe Pound, "Liberty of Contract," *Yale Law Journal* 18 (1909): 469.

12. *Allgeyer v. Louisiana,* 165 U.S. 578 (1897).

13. Christopher Gustavus Tiedeman, *The Unwritten Constitution of the United States* (New York: G. P. Putnam's Sons, 1890), 81.

14. Robert C. Post, "Mr. Taft Becomes Chief Justice," *University of Cincinnati Law Review* 76 (2008): 885n95.

the vast majority of federal and state laws. The same judicial majority that in *Lochner* declared maximum hour laws for bakers to be unconstitutional sustained maximum hour laws for coal miners (*Holden v. Hardy* [1898]), factory workers (*Bunting v. Oregon* [1917]), and women (*Muller v. Oregon* [1908]). Much evidence indicates that the justices were more concerned with striking down certain selective examples of unreasonable class legislation than with prohibiting all economic regulation in service of a sweeping commitment to laissez-faire economics. Federal and state court justices regularly sustained laws that prevented persons from selling unhealthy products, even though such measures involved the same degree of regulation as laws requiring employers to pay their employees minimum wages.

The due process clauses of the federal and state constitutions were the primary vehicle for protecting property rights. Many federal and state justices interpreted those provisions as protecting the freedom of contract or the more general "right of the citizen to be free in the enjoyment of all his faculties."[15] Other constitutional provisions protecting property received more narrow readings. The Supreme Court did not significantly expand previous interpretations of the takings clause. Federal justices limited the scope of the contracts clause. *Stone v. Mississippi* (1879) gave local government broad power to abrogate existing contracts when doing so advanced the public good.

Contracts

The contracts clause lost more bite during the Republican Era. The Supreme Court ruled that the states could not bargain away their police power. No matter the explicit terms of a corporate charter or contract with the government, future governing officials retained the power to make whatever laws they believed best promoted the health, safety, welfare, and morals of the citizenry.

Boston Beer Co. v. Massachusetts (1877) was an early example of this judicially imposed limit on rights under the contract clause. The Boston Beer Company obtained a corporate charter giving that business the right to manufacture and sell malt liquor. In 1869 Massachusetts passed the Prohibitory Liquor Law, which banned the manufacture and sale of that product, among other beverages. A unanimous Supreme Court sustained that measure. Justice Bradley's opinion asserted,

> Whatever differences of opinion may exist as to the extent and boundaries of the police power, and however difficult it may be to render a satisfactory definition of it, there seems to be no doubt that it does extend to the protection of the lives, health, and property of the citizens, and to the preservation of good order and the public morals. The legislature cannot, by any contract, divest itself of the power to provide for these objects. They belong emphatically to that class of objects which demand the application of the maxim, *salus populi suprema lex*; and they are to be attained and provided for by such appropriate means as the legislative discretion may devise. That discretion can no more be bargained away than the power itself.

Stone v. Mississippi (1879) held that a state could not contract away the right to ban lotteries. Chief Justice Waite bluntly stated, "All agree that the legislature cannot bargain away the police power of a State."

Takings

Litigants had more success invoking the takings clauses of the federal and state constitutions than invoking the contracts clause of the federal constitution. The Supreme Court in *Pumpelly v. Green Bay & Mississippi Canal Co.* (1871) ruled that a taking occurred when government physically invaded private land, even when the state did not actually take title. Wisconsin was required to pay for damage caused when a state dam flooded private property, Justice Miller maintained, because when "real estate is actually invaded by superinduced additions of water, earth, sand, or other material, or by having any artificial structure placed on it, so as to effectually destroy or impair its usefulness, it is a taking." The justices also found an unconstitutional taking in *Pennsylvania Coal Co. v. Mahon* (1922). That decision struck down a Pennsylvania law prohibiting coal companies from mining beneath homes, even after the company had explicitly reserved the right to mine beneath homes as part of their contracts giving surface rights to homeowners.

15. *Allgeyer*, 165 U.S. 578.

Most takings clause claims were rejected. *Mugler v. Kansas* (1887) sustained a Kansas law forbidding the manufacture of alcoholic beverages as a constitutional exercise of the police power. *Village of Euclid v. Ambler Realty Co.* (1926) upheld the creation of local zoning ordinances, with Justice Sutherland's majority opinion stating, "The exclusion of buildings devoted to business, trade, etc., from residential districts, bears a rational relation to the health and safety of the community." *Miller v. Schoene* (1928) sustained a Virginia decision to cut down private cedar trees in order to prevent a fungus from infecting private apple orchards. Justice Stone's opinion for the court held that states could decide that some forms of private property were more valuable than others when deciding what property to protect. He wrote,

> It would have been none the less a choice if, instead of enacting the present statute, the state, by doing nothing, had permitted serious injury to the apple orchards within its borders to go on unchecked. When forced to such a choice the state does not exceed its constitutional powers by deciding upon the destruction of one class of property in order to save another which, in the judgment of the legislature, is of greater value to the public.

Mugler v. Kansas, 123 U.S. 623 (1887)

Peter Mugler owned a brewery in Salina, Kansas. In 1881 Kansas enacted a law "prohibit[ing] the manufacture and sale of intoxicating liquors, except for medical, mechanical, and scientific purposes." Mugler continued to brew malt liquor until he was arrested, tried, convicted, and fined $100. The Supreme Court of Kansas sustained that conviction. Mugler, with financial backing from major brewing companies, appealed to the Supreme Court of the United States. He claimed that prohibition laws violated the Fourteenth Amendment right of citizens to drink, and that the Kansas law, by dramatically reducing the value of his brewery, took property without compensation.

The Supreme Court of the United States by an 8-1 vote ruled that the Kansas prohibition law was constitutional. Justice John Harlan's majority opinion asserted that prohibition laws were legitimate uses of the police power and that states did not take property when they imposed police power restrictions on private property. How does Justice Harlan define the police power? Under his definition, could the state ban diet sodas and fast food? Would such a law be constitutional in your judgment? Harlan's opinion insists that judges must carefully examine restrictions on private property to ensure that they are really necessary to promote the public interest and are not "mere pretenses" for arbitrary power. What are the implications for individual rights, and for democracy, if judges make independent determinations regarding the relationship between a particular regulation and the public welfare? Mugler *was the first judicial opinion that cited* Marbury v. Madison *(1803) for the proposition that courts had the power to declare laws unconstitutional. What explains the eighty-four years of silence? Why might Harlan have chosen this case to cite* Marbury?

JUSTICE HARLAN delivered the opinion of the court.

. . . That legislation by a state prohibiting the manufacture within her limits of intoxicating liquors, to be there sold or bartered for general use as a beverage, does not necessarily infringe any right, privilege, or immunity secured by the constitution of the United States, is made clear by the decisions of this court, rendered before and since the adoption of the fourteenth amendment. . . .

. . .

. . . [T]he right to manufacture drink for one's personal use is subject to the condition that such manufacture does not endanger or affect the rights of others. If such manufacture does prejudicially affect the rights and interests of the community, it follows, from the very premises stated, that society has the power to protect itself, by legislation, against the injurious consequences of that business. . . . But by whom, or by what authority, is it to be determined whether the manufacture of particular articles of drink, either for general use or for the personal use of the maker, will injuriously affect the public? Power to determine such questions, so as to bind all, must exist somewhere; else society will be at the mercy of the few, who, regarding only their own appetites or passions, may be willing to imperil the peace and security of the many, provided only they are permitted to do as they please. Under our system that power is lodged with the legislative branch of the government. It belongs to that department to exert what are known as the police powers of the state, and to determine, primarily, what measures are appropriate or needful for the protection of the public morals, the public health, or the public safety.

It does not at all follow that every statute enacted ostensibly for the promotion of these ends is to be accepted as a legitimate exertion of the police powers of the state. There are, of necessity, limits beyond which legislation cannot rightfully go. While every possible presumption is to be indulged in favor of the validity of a statute, the courts must obey the constitution rather than the law-making department of government, and must, upon their own responsibility, determine whether, in any particular case, these limits have been passed. "To what purpose," it was said in *Marbury v. Madison* (1803) "are powers limited, and to what purpose is that limitation committed to writing, if these limits may, at any time, be passed by those intended to be restrained? The distinction between a government with limited and unlimited powers is abolished, if those limits do not confine the persons on whom they are imposed, and if acts prohibited and acts allowed are of equal obligation." The courts are not bound by mere forms, nor are they to be misled by mere pretenses. They are at liberty, indeed, are under a solemn duty, to look at the substance of things, whenever they enter upon the inquiry whether the legislature has transcended the limits of its authority. If, therefore, a statute purporting to have been enacted to protect the public health, the public morals, or the public safety, has no real or substantial relation to those objects, or is a palpable invasion of rights secured by the fundamental law, it is the duty of the courts to so adjudge, and thereby give effect to the constitution.

Keeping in view these principles, as governing the relations of the judicial and legislative departments of government with each other, it is difficult to perceive any ground for the judiciary to declare that the prohibition by Kansas of the manufacture or sale, within her limits, of intoxicating liquors for general use there as a beverage, is not fairly adapted to the end of protecting the community against the evils which confessedly result from the excessive use of ardent spirits. There is no justification for holding that the state, under the guise merely of police regulations, is here aiming to deprive the citizen of his constitutional rights; for we cannot shut out of view the fact, within the knowledge of all, that the public health, the public morals, and the public safety, may be endangered by the general use of intoxicating drinks; nor the fact established by statistics accessible to every one, that the idleness, disorder, pauperism, and crime existing in the country, are, in some degree at least, traceable to this evil. If, therefore, a state deems the absolute prohibition of the manufacture and sale within her limits, of intoxicating liquors, for other than medical, scientific, and mechanical purposes, to be necessary to the peace and security of society, the courts cannot, without usurping legislative functions, override the will of the people as thus expressed by their chosen representatives. . . .

. . .

The principal that no person shall be deprived of life, liberty, or property without due process of law . . . has never been regarded as incompatible with the principle, equally vital, because essential to the peace and safety of society, that all property in this country is held under the implied obligation that the owner's use of it shall not be injurious to the community. . . .

. . .

As already stated, the present case must be governed by principles that do not involve the power of eminent domain, in the exercise of which property may not be taken for public use without compensation. A prohibition simply upon the use of property for purposes that are declared, by valid legislation, to be injurious to the health, morals, or safety of the community, cannot, in any just sense, be deemed a taking or an appropriation of property for the public benefit. Such legislation does not disturb the owner in the control or use of his property for lawful purposes, nor restrict his right to dispose of it, but is only a declaration by the state that its use by any one, for certain forbidden purposes, is prejudicial to the public interests. Nor can legislation of that character come within the fourteenth amendment, in any case, unless it is apparent that its real object is not to protect the community, or to promote the general well-being, but, under the guise of police regulation, to deprive the owner of his liberty and property, without due process of law. The power which the states have of prohibiting such use by individuals of their property, as will be prejudicial to the health, the morals, or the safety of the public, is not, and, consistently with the existence and safety of organized society, cannot be, burdened with the condition that the state must compensate such individual owners for pecuniary losses they may sustain, by reason of their not being permitted, by a noxious use of their property, to inflict injury upon the community. The exercise of the police power by the destruction of property which is itself a public nuisance, or the prohibition of its use in a particular way, whereby its value becomes depreciated, is very different from taking property for public use, or from depriving a person of his property without due process of law. In the one case, a nuisance only is abated; in the other, unoffending property is taken away from an innocent owner. It is true, when the defendants in these cases purchased or erected their breweries, the laws of the state did not forbid the manufacture of intoxicating liquors. But the state did not thereby give any assurance, or come under an obligation, that its legislation upon that subject would remain unchanged. . . .

. . .

JUSTICE FIELD, dissenting

. . . I agree to so much of the opinion as asserts that there is nothing in the constitution or laws of the United States affecting the validity of the act of Kansas prohibiting the sale of intoxicating liquors manufactured in the state, except for the purposes mentioned. But I am not prepared to say that the state can prohibit the manufacture of such liquors within its limits if they are intended for exportation, or forbid their sale within its limits, under proper regulations for the protection of the health and morals of the people, if congress has authorized their importation, though the act of Kansas is broad enough to include both such manufacture and sale. . . .

Pennsylvania Coal Co. v. Mahon, 260 U.S. 393 (1922)

H. J. Mahon owned a house in Pittston, Pennsylvania. When that property was purchased from the Pennsylvania Coal Company, the original buyer agreed that Pennsylvania Coal retained the right to mine under the surface of the land and that the company was not responsible for any damage done to the surface by those mining operations. In 1921 the Pennsylvania legislature passed the Kohler Act, which forbade companies from engaging in mining operations that might threaten the foundations of any dwelling. Mahon sought a judicial decree prohibiting Pennsylvania Coal from mining under his house. A lower Pennsylvania court rejected his claim. After that decision was reversed by the Supreme Court of Pennsylvania, Pennsylvania Coal appealed to the Supreme Court of the United States.

The Supreme Court by a 4-3 vote declared the Kohler Act unconstitutional. Justice Holmes's majority opinion insisted that government took property, even when the state did not actually take physical possession, when government regulations substantially reduced or destroyed the value of the property. Such actions became known as "regulatory takings." What is the constitutional foundation for regulatory takings? Is compensation for such takings inherent in the language of the takings clause, the original understanding of the framers, or the general principles underlying property rights? Pennsylvania Coal Company *is the only constitutional case in which Justice Holmes wrote the majority opinion and Justice Brandeis issued the dissent. In most other cases, whether the issue was the freedom of contract or the freedom of speech, the two justices voted together. Why do Holmes and Brandeis differ in this case? Why does Holmes think that regulation went "too far?" Why does Brandeis maintain that government can prevent Pennsylvania Coal from mining under the surface of Mahon's house, even though the company reserved that right when it first sold the land?*

JUSTICE HOLMES delivered the opinion of the Court.

. . .

Government hardly could go on if to some extent values incident to property could not be diminished without paying for every such change in the general law. As long recognized, some values are enjoyed under an implied limitation and must yield to the police power. But obviously the implied limitation must have its limits or the contract and due process clauses are gone. One fact for consideration in determining such limits is the extent of the diminution. When it reaches a certain magnitude, in most if not in all cases there must be an exercise of eminent domain and compensation to sustain the act. So the question depends upon the particular facts. The greatest weight is given to the judgment of the legislature but it always is open to interested parties to contend that the legislature has gone beyond its constitutional power.

This is the case of a single private house. No doubt there is a public interest even in this, as there is in every purchase and sale and in all that happens within the commonwealth. . . . But usually in ordinary private affairs the public interest does not warrant much of this kind of interference. A source of damage to such a house is not a public nuisance even if similar damage is inflicted on others in different places. The damage is not common or public. . . . Furthermore, it is not justified as a protection of personal safety. That could be provided for by notice. Indeed the very foundation of this bill is that the defendant gave timely notice of its intent to mine under the house. On the other hand the extent of the taking is great. It purports to abolish what is recognized in Pennsylvania as an estate in land—a very valuable estate—and what is declared by the Court below to be a contract hitherto binding the plaintiffs. If we were called upon to deal with the plaintiffs' position alone we should think it clear that the statute does not disclose a public interest sufficient to warrant so extensive a destruction of the defendant's constitutionally protected rights.

. . .

It is our opinion that the act cannot be sustained as an exercise of the police power, so far as it affects the mining of coal under streets or cities in places where the right to mine such coal has been reserved. . . . What makes the right to mine coal valuable is that it can be exercised with profit. To make it commercially impracticable to mine certain coal has very nearly the same effect for constitutional purposes as appropriating or destroying it. This we think that we are warranted in assuming that the statute does.

. . .

The rights of the public in a street purchased or laid out by eminent domain are those that it has paid for. If in any case its representatives have been so short sighted as to acquire only surface rights without the right of support we see no more authority for supplying the latter without compensation than there was for taking the right of way in the first place and refusing to pay for it because the public wanted it very much. The protection of private property in the Fifth Amendment presupposes that it is wanted for public use, but provides that it shall not be taken for such use without compensation. . . . When this seemingly absolute protection is found to be qualified by the police power, the natural tendency of human nature is to extend the qualification more and more until at last private property disappears. But that cannot be accomplished in this way under the Constitution of the United States.

The general rule at least is that while property may be regulated to a certain extent, if regulation goes too far it will be recognized as a taking. . . . In general it is not plain that a man's misfortunes or necessities will justify his shifting the damages to his neighbor's shoulders. . . . We are in danger of forgetting that a strong public desire to improve the public condition is not enough to warrant achieving the desire by a shorter cut than the constitutional way of paying for the change. As we already have said this is a question of degree—and therefore cannot be disposed of by general propositions. . . .

. . . So far as private persons or communities have seen fit to take the risk of acquiring only surface rights, we cannot see that the fact that their risk has become a danger warrants the giving to them greater rights than they bought.

JUSTICE BRANDEIS dissenting.

. . .

Every restriction upon the use of property imposed in the exercise of the police power deprives the owner of some right theretofore enjoyed, and is, in that sense, an abridgment by the state of rights in property without making compensation. But restriction imposed to protect the public health, safety or morals from dangers threatened is not a taking. The restriction here in question is merely the prohibition of a noxious use. The property so restricted remains in the possession of its owner. The state does not appropriate it or make any use of it. The state merely prevents the owner from making a use which interferes with paramount rights of the public. Whenever the use prohibited ceases to be noxious—as it may because of further change in local or social conditions—the restriction will have to be removed and the owner will again be free to enjoy his property as heretofore.

The restriction upon the use of this property cannot, of course, be lawfully imposed, unless its purpose is to protect the public. But the purpose of a restriction does not cease to be public, because incidentally some private persons may thereby receive gratuitously valuable special benefits. Thus, owners of low buildings may obtain, through statutory restrictions upon the height of neighboring structures, benefits equivalent to an easement of light and air. . . . Restriction upon use does not become inappropriate as a means, merely because it deprives the owner of the only use to which the property can then be profitably put. The liquor [*Mugler v. Kansas* (1887)] case[] settled that. . . . Nor is a restriction imposed through exercise of the police power inappropriate as a means, merely because the same end might be effected through exercise of the power of eminent domain, or otherwise at public expense. Every restriction upon the height of buildings might be secured through acquiring by eminent domain the right of each owner to build above the limiting height; but it is settled that the state need not resort to that power. . . . If by mining anthracite coal the owner would necessarily unloose poisonous gases, I suppose no one would doubt the power of the state to prevent the mining, without buying his coal fields. And why may not the state, likewise, without paying compensation, prohibit one from digging so deep or excavating so near the surface, as to expose the community to like dangers? In the latter case, as in the former, carrying on the business would be a public nuisance.

. . .

It is said that this is a case of a single dwelling house, that the restriction upon mining abolishes a valuable estate hitherto secured by a contract with the plaintiffs, and that the restriction upon mining cannot be justified as a protection of personal safety, since that could be provided for by notice. . . . May we say that notice would afford adequate protection of the public safety where the Legislature and the highest court of the state, with greater knowledge of local conditions, have declared, in effect, that it would not? If the public safety is imperiled, surely neither grant, nor contract, can prevail against the exercise of the police power. . . . The rule that the state's power to take appropriate measures to guard the safety of all who may be within its jurisdiction may not be bargained away was applied to compel carriers to establish grade crossings at their own expense, despite contracts to the contrary . . . .

Due Process

The most intense constitutional debates over property rights concerned how to interpret the due process clauses of the federal and state constitutions. Reformers insisted that modern industrial conditions justified far more regulation of business relationships in the public interest than had previously been the case. Conservatives insisted that such regulations promoted the interests of one class of people at the expense of another, not the public good. Debate centered on the "freedom of contract," the view that states should not ordinarily interfere with the bargaining process.

State courts were initially more willing than federal courts to impose substantive due process limitations on laws regulating economic bargains. State judges interpreting state due process clauses during the late nineteenth century declared unconstitutional laws limiting the hours women could work (*Ritchie v. People* [IL 1895]) and laws forbidding persons from manufacturing cigars in a tenement house (*In re Jacobs* [NY 1885]). The Supreme Court of Illinois in *Ritchie v. People* set out the basic constitutional principle underlying these decisions. "Liberty," Judge Magruder wrote, "includes the right to make contracts, as well with reference to the amount and duration of labor to be performed as concerning any other lawful matter. Hence the right to make contracts is an inherent and inalienable one, and any attempt to unreasonably abridge it is opposed to the constitution."[16] The U.S. Supreme Court under Chief Justice Morrison Waite (1873–88) was more reluctant. When sustaining laws regulating the prices that grain elevators could charge, Waite's majority opinion in *Munn v. Illinois* (1877) asserted,

> Property does become clothed with a public interest when used in a manner to make it of public consequence, and affect the community at large. When, therefore, one devotes his property to a use in which the public has an interest, he, in effect, grants to the public an interest in that use, and must submit to be controlled by the public for the common good, to the extent of the interest he has thus created.

Nevertheless, while *Munn* upheld state regulatory power, the opinion hinted at greater judicial protection for property that was not "clothed with a public interest."

The U.S. Supreme Court more strictly scrutinized laws regulating the bargaining process after Grover Cleveland appointed Melville Fuller to the chief justiceship in 1888. In *Chicago, M & St. P. Ry. Co. v. Minnesota* (1890) a Fuller Court majority insisted that the due process clause required judicial oversight whenever states sought to regulate the prices that railroads and other businesses charged for their services. Justice Blatchford's opinion stated,

> The question of the reasonableness of a rate of charge for transportation by a railroad company . . . is eminently a question for judicial investigation, requiring due process of law for its determination. If the company is deprived of the power of charging reasonable rates for the use of its property, and such deprivation takes place in the absence of an investigation by judicial machinery, it is deprived of the lawful use of its property, and thus, in substance and effect, of the property itself, without due process of law, and in violation of the constitution

16. *Ritchie v. People*, 40 N.E. 453 (Ill. 1895).

of the United States; and, in so far as it is thus deprived, while other persons are permitted to receive reasonable profits upon their invested capital, the company is deprived of the equal protection of the laws.

Over the next thirty years judicial majorities struck down many state and a few federal laws that opponents claimed violated the freedom of contract or otherwise unconstitutionally interfered with private bargains. *Lochner v. New York* (1905) is the most famous of these decisions. That decision declared unconstitutional a New York law that limited bakers to working ten hours a day and sixty hours a week. Other famous decisions include:

- *Allgeyer v. Louisiana* (1897), which declared unconstitutional a Louisiana law limiting contracts with out-of-state insurance companies.
- *Adair v. United States* (1908), which declared unconstitutional a federal law prohibiting "yellow dog" contracts, which are contracts that prohibit employees from joining a union.
- *Coppage v. Kansas* (1915), which declared unconstitutional a state law prohibiting yellow dog contracts.
- *Adkins v. Children's Hospital* (1923), which declared unconstitutional a minimum wage law for women.

The justices often disputed whether particular laws were good-faith legislative efforts to promote the public welfare or unconstitutional attempts to interfere with private bargains. Nevertheless, most Supreme Court justices during the first third of the twentieth century agreed that the due process clause normally prohibited states from favoring one class of citizens at the expense of another. Justice Harlan's majority opinion in *Adair* stated, "the employer and the employee have equality of right, and any legislation that disturbs that equality is an arbitrary interference with the liberty of contract which no government can legally justify in a free land." By contrast Justice Holmes, and later Justice Brandeis, insisted that elected officials were free to regulate all aspects of the bargaining process.

Courts sustained most state and federal regulations. Justice McKenna, when sustaining laws limiting the hours persons worked in factories, asserted, "In view of the well-known fact that the custom in our industries does not sanction a longer service than ten hours per day, it cannot be held, as a matter of law, that the legislative requirement is unreasonable or arbitrary as a matter of law."[17] The Supreme Court was particularly deferential to legislation restricting property rights passed during or in the wake of World War I. *Block v. Hirsh* (1921) sustained a federal law designed to prevent price gouging in the Washington, DC, housing market by permitting tenants to remain on the property after their lease expired, as long as they paid rent. Justice Holmes's majority opinion stated, "Circumstances have clothed the letting of buildings in the District of Columbia with a public interest so great as to justify regulation by law."

The freedom of contract cases divided Americans by ideology, not partisanship. Theodore Roosevelt, the Republican president from 1901 to 1909, ran for president in 1912 on a Progressive platform that condemned such judicial decisions as *Lochner*. William Howard Taft, the Republican president from 1909 to 1913, ran for president in 1912 on a platform that endorsed judicial protection of the freedom of contract. The two leading judicial proponents of the freedom of contract in the 1920s, Justices James McReynolds and George Sutherland, were a Democrat and a Republican, respectively. They were consistently opposed by Justice Holmes, a Republican, and Justice Brandeis, a Democrat.

In re Jacobs, 2 N.Y. Crim. R. 539 (1885)

Peter Jacobs made cigars in a New York tenement house. On May 14, 1884, he was arrested and charged with violating a state law that forbade "the manufacture of cigars or preparation of tobacco in any form on any floor, or in any part of any floor, in any tenement-house." Jacobs sought a petition of habeas corpus on the ground that his arrest was unconstitutional. He insisted that the New York statute violated his right to not have property or liberty taken away without due process of law. After the Supreme Court of New York rejected his claim, Jacobs appealed to the New York Court of Appeals. His case soon became a cause célèbre. William Evarts, a leading member of the bar, former secretary of state, and soon-to-be U.S. senator, represented Jacobs before the Court of Appeals in an effort to set an important precedent limiting legislative power.

The Court of Appeals of New York granted the writ of habeas corpus. In an influential opinion, Judge Earl asserted that the ban on manufacturing cigars in a tenement house

17. *Bunting v. Oregon*, 243 U.S. 426 (1917).

Table 7-3 Selection of U.S. Supreme Court Cases Reviewing State Laws under Due Process Clause

Case	Vote	Outcome	Decision
Slaughterhouse Cases, 83 U.S. 36 (1873)	5-4	Upheld	States may limit how butchers practice their profession and establish a monopoly slaughterhouse as a public health measure
Hurtado v. California, 110 U.S. 516 (1884)	8-1	Upheld	The use of a grand jury is not essential to the requirements of due process
Barbier v. Connolly, 113 U.S. 27 (1885)	9-0	Upheld	Cities may prohibit operation of commercial or public laundries at night as a public safety measure
Powell v. Pennsylvania, 127 U.S. 678 (1888)	8-1	Upheld	States may prohibit the manufacture or sale of oleomargarine as a public health measure
Smyth v. Ames, 169 U.S. 466 (1898)	9-0	Struck down	States may not impose a maximum rate on railroad charges that deprive corporations of a reasonable profit on their operations
Austin v. Tennessee, 179 U.S. 343 (1900)	5-4	Upheld	States may prohibit the sale of cigarettes as a public health measure
Lochner v. New York, 198 U.S. 45 (1905)	5-4	Struck down	States may not impose a maximum hours limitation on commercial bakers as a public health measure
Twining v. New Jersey, 211 U.S. 78 (1908)	8-1	Upheld	State criminal procedures must not violate fundamental principles of liberty and justice, but state courts may allow juries to draw conclusions about guilt from the defendant's refusal to testify
Murphy v. California, 225 U.S. 623 (1912)	9-0	Upheld	Nonuseful occupations, such as operating a pool hall, that have naturally pernicious tendencies may be regulated or prohibited even in the absence of demonstrated harms
Bunting v. Oregon, 243 U.S. 426 (1917)	5-3	Upheld	State may pass a general maximum hour law as a health measure for factory employees
Meyer v. Nebraska, 262 U.S. 390 (1923)	7-2	Struck down	States may not prohibit the teaching of foreign languages
Pierce v. Society of Sisters, 268 U.S. 510 (1925)	9-0	Struck down	States may not require parents to send children to public school rather than private school
Village of Euclid v. Ambler Realty Co., 272 U.S. 365 (1926)	6-3	Upheld	Cities may adopt comprehensive zoning plans detailing permitted land use and building restrictions
New State Ice Co. v. Liebmann, 285 U.S. 262 (1932)	7-2	Struck down	States may not require licenses before a new company can enter an industry
Nebbia v. New York, 291 U.S. 502 (1934)	5-4	Upheld	States may set a minimum retail price for milk
West Coast Hotel v. Parrish, 300 U.S. 379 (1937)	5-4	Upheld	States may require employers to pay a legal minimum wage
Williamson v. Lee Optical Co., 348 U.S. 483 (1955)	8-0	Upheld	States may prohibit nonlicensed individuals from fitting lenses into eyeglasses as a public health measure

(Continued)

Table 7-3 *(Continued)*

Case	Vote	Outcome	Decision
Griswold v. Connecticut, 381 U.S. 479 (1965)	7-2	Struck down	States may not prohibit the use of contraceptives by married couples
Loving v. Virginia, 388 U.S. 1 (1967)	9-0	Struck down	Individuals have a fundamental right to marry a person of another race that states cannot restrict
Roe v. Wade, 410 U.S. 113 (1973)	7-2	Struck down	Individuals have a fundamental right to choose whether to reproduce, and states cannot impose an absolute prohibition on abortion
Moore v. City of East Cleveland, 431 U.S. 494 (1977)	5-4	Struck down	House ordinances with restrictive definition of "family" for single-family units violate basic values recognized in substantive due process
Michael H. v. Gerald D, 491 U.S. 110 (1989)	5-4	Upheld	States may presume that children born within a marriage are the result of the marriage and deny visitation rights to a natural father
Bennis v. Michigan, 516 U.S. 442 (1996)	7-2	Upheld	States may seize a car used in the act of prostitution, regardless of the innocence of the owner of the car
Washington v. Glucksberg, 521 U.S. 702 (1997)	9-0	Upheld	States may prohibit doctor-assisted suicide
Lawrence v. Texas, 539 U.S. 558 (2003)	6-3	Struck down	States may not criminalize consensual homosexual sodomy

deprived Jacobs of both liberty and property in violation of the due process clause of both the New York and the federal constitutions. How does Judge Earl define liberty and property? How does he define the police power? Why does he believe the New York regulation is unconstitutional? Does the specter of "class legislation" play a role in his analysis? Suppose New York wanted to pass a narrower regulation. What language would you recommend that state lawmakers use?

JUDGE EARL delivered the opinion of the Court.

. . .

What does this act attempt to do? In form, it makes it a crime for a cigarmaker in New York and Brooklyn, the only cities in the State having a population exceeding 500,000, to carry on a perfectly lawful trade in his own home. Whether he owns the tenement-house or has hired a room therein for the purpose of prosecuting his trade, he cannot manufacture therein his own tobacco into cigars for his own use or for sale, and he will become a criminal for doing that which is perfectly lawful outside of the two cities named—everywhere else, so far as we are able to learn, in the whole world. He must either abandon the trade by which he earns a livelihood for himself and family, or, if able, procure a room elsewhere, or hire himself out to one who has a room upon such terms as, under the fierce competition of trade and the inexorable laws of supply and demand, he may be able to obtain from his employer. He may choose to do his work where he can have the supervision of his family and their help, and such choice is denied him. He may choose to work for himself rather than for a taskmaster, and he is left without freedom of choice. He may desire the advantage of cheap production in consequence of his cheap rent and family help, and of this he is deprived. In the unceasing struggle for success and existence which pervades all societies of men, he may be deprived of that which will enable him to maintain his hold, and to survive. . . . It is, therefore, plain that this law interferes with the profitable and free use of his property by the owner or lessee of a tenement-house who is a cigarmaker, and trammels him in the application of his industry and the disposition of his labor, and thus, in a strictly legitimate sense, it arbitrarily deprives him of his property and of some portion of his personal liberty.

The constitutional guaranty that no person shall be deprived of his property without due process of law may be violated without the physical taking of property for public or private use. Property may be destroyed, or its value may be annihilated; it is owned and kept for some useful purpose and it has no value unless it can be used. Its capability for enjoyment and adaptability to some use are essential characteristics and attributes without which property cannot be conceived; and hence any law which destroys it or its value, or takes away any of its essential attributes, deprives the owner of his property.

The constitutional guaranty would be of little worth, if the legislature could, without compensation, destroy property or its value, deprive the owner of its use, deny him the right to live in his own house, or to work at any lawful trade therein. If the legislature has the power under the Constitution to prohibit the prosecution of one lawful trade in a tenement-house, then it may prevent the prosecution of all trades therein. . . .

So, too, one may be deprived of his liberty and his constitutional rights thereto violated without the actual imprisonment or restraint of his person. Liberty, in its broad sense as understood in this country, means the right, not only of freedom from actual servitude, imprisonment or restraint, but the right of one to use his faculties in all lawful ways, to live and work where he will, to earn his livelihood in any lawful calling, and to pursue any lawful trade or avocation. All laws, therefore, which impair or trammel these rights, which limit one in his choice of a trade or profession, or confine him to work or live in a specified locality, or exclude him from his own house, or restrain his otherwise lawful movements . . . are infringements upon his fundamental rights of liberty, which are under constitutional protection. . . .

But the claim is made that the legislature could pass this act in the exercise of the police power which every sovereign State possesses. That power is very broad and comprehensive, and is exercised to promote the health, comfort, safety and welfare of society. Its exercise in extreme cases is frequently justified by the maxim *salus populi suprema lex est* ["let the welfare of the people be the supreme law"]. It is used to regulate the use of property by enforcing the maxim *sic utere tuo, ut alienum non lædas* ["so use your own so as not to harm that of another"]. Under it the conduct of an individual and the use of property may be regulated so as to interfere, to some extent, with the freedom of the one and the enjoyment of the other; and in cases of great emergency engendering overruling necessity, property may be taken or destroyed without compensation, and without what is commonly called due process of law. . . .

. . .

Generally it is for the legislature to determine what laws and regulations are needed to protect the public health and secure the public comfort and safety, and while its measures are calculated, intended, convenient and appropriate to accomplish these ends, the exercise of its discretion is not subject to review by the courts. But they must have some relation to these ends. Under the mere guise of police regulations, personal rights and private property cannot be arbitrarily invaded, and the determination of the legislature is not final or conclusive. If it passes an act ostensibly for the public health, and thereby destroys or takes away the property of a citizen, or interferes with his personal liberty, then it is for the courts to scrutinize the act and see whether it really relates to and is convenient and appropriate to promote the public health. . . .

We will now once more recur to the law under consideration. It does not deal with tenement-houses as such; it does not regulate the number of persons who may live in any one of them, or be crowded into one room, nor does it deal with the mode of their construction for the purpose of securing the health and safety of their occupants or of the public generally. It deals mainly with the preparation of tobacco and the manufacture of cigars, and its purpose obviously was to regulate them. We must take judicial notice of the nature and qualities of tobacco. It has been in general use among civilized men for more than two centuries. It is used in some form by a majority of the men in this State, by the good and bad, learned and unlearned, the rich and the poor. Its manufacture into cigars is permitted without any hindrance, except for revenue purposes, in all civilized lands. It has never been said, so far as we can learn, and it was not affirmed even on the argument before us, that its preparation and manufacture into cigars were dangerous to the public health. We are not aware, and are not able to learn, that tobacco is even injurious to the health of those who deal in it, or are engaged in its production or manufacture. We certainly know enough about it to be sure that its manipulation in one room can produce no harm to the health of the occupants of other rooms in the same house. . . . What possible relation can cigarmaking in any building have to the health of the general public? . . . What possible relation to the health of the occupants of a large tenement-house could cigarmaking in one of its remote rooms have? If the legislature had in mind the protection of the occupants of tenement-houses, why was the act confined in its operation to the two cities only? It is plain that this is not a health law, and that it has no relation whatever to the public health. Under the guise of promoting the public health the legislature might as well have banished cigarmaking from all the cities of the State, or confined it to a single city or town, or have placed under a similar ban the trade of a baker, of a tailor, of a shoemaker, of a woodcarver, or of any other of the innocuous trades carried on by artisans in their own homes. The power would have been the same, and its exercise, so far as it concerns fundamental, constitutional rights, could have been justified by the same arguments. Such legislation may invade one class of rights to-day and another to-morrow, and if it can be sanctioned under the Constitution, while far removed in time we will not be far away in practical statesmanship from those ages when governmental prefects supervised the building of houses, the rearing of cattle, the sowing of seed and the reaping of grain, and governmental ordinances regulated the movements and labor of artisans, the rate of wages, the price of food, the diet and clothing of the people, and a large range of other affairs long since in all civilized lands regarded as outside of governmental functions. Such governmental interferences disturb the normal adjustments of the social fabric, and usually derange the delicate and complicated machinery of industry and cause a score of ills while attempting the removal of one.

When a health law is challenged in the courts as unconstitutional on the ground that it arbitrarily interferes with personal liberty and private property without due process of law, the courts must be able to see that it has at least in fact some relation to the public health, that the public health is the end actually aimed at, and that it is appropriate and adapted to that end. This we have not been able to see in this law, and we must, therefore, pronounce it unconstitutional and void. . . .

Holden v. Hardy, 169 U.S. 366 (1898)

Holden owned the Old Jordan Mine in Bingham Canyon, Utah. His employees worked ten hours a day mining ore. Utah law declared, "The period of employment of workingmen in smelters and all other institutions for the reduction or refining of ores or metals shall be eight hours per day." For violating this law, Holden was arrested, convicted, fined $50, and sentenced to spend fifty-seven days in prison until the fine was paid. Holder asked for a writ of habeas corpus against Hardy, the local sheriff, on the ground that the Utah maximum hour law violated the due process clause of the Fourteenth Amendment. After the Supreme Court of Utah rejected his claim Holden appealed to the Supreme Court of the United States.

The Supreme Court of the United States by a 7-2 vote ruled that the Utah maximum hour law was constitutional. Justice Brown's majority opinion noted that such limitations on contract rights did not exist when the Constitution was ratified. Nevertheless, he insisted that this labor law and many other legal innovations were constitutional. Is Holden v. Hardy *an early example of living constitutionalism? Does Brown's opinion imply that federal courts might have reached a different result if the issue had been raised one hundred years earlier? Does his opinion maintain only that such laws had not previously been passed, or that they were always constitutional? On what basis does Justice Brown distinguish between legal innovations that are consistent with due process and those that are unconstitutional?*

JUSTICE BROWN delivered the opinion of the court.

. . .

. . . [I]n passing upon the validity of state legislation under [the Fourteenth Amendment], this court has not failed to recognize the fact that the law is, to a certain extent, a progressive science; that, in some of the States, methods of procedure, which at the time the Constitution was adopted were deemed essential to the protection and safety of the people or to the liberty of the citizen have been found to be no longer necessary; that restrictions which had formerly been laid upon the conduct of individuals or of classes of individuals had proved detrimental to their interests, while, upon the other hand, certain other classes of persons, particularly those engaged in dangerous or unhealthful employments, have been found to be in need of additional protection. . . .

. . . This case does not call for an expression of opinion as to the wisdom of these changes or their validity under the Fourteenth Amendment. . . . They are mentioned only for the purpose of calling attention to the probability that other changes of no less importance may be made in the future, and that, while the cardinal principles of justice are immutable, the methods by which justice is administered are subject to constant fluctuation, and that the Constitution of the

United States, which is necessarily and to a large extent inflexible and exceedingly difficult of amendment, should not be so construed as to deprive the States of the power to so amend their laws as to make them conform to the wishes of the citizens as they may deem best for the public welfare without bringing them into conflict with the supreme law of the land.

. . .

Recognizing the difficulty in defining with exactness the phrase "due process of law," it is certain that these words imply a conformity with natural and inherent principles of justice, and forbid that one man's property, or right to property, shall be taken for the benefit of another, or for the benefit of the State, without compensation; and that no one shall be condemned in his person or property without an opportunity of being heard in his own defence.

As the possession of property, of which a person cannot be deprived, doubtless implies that such property may be acquired, it is safe to say that a state law which undertakes to deprive any class of persons of the general power to acquire property would also be obnoxious to the same provision. Indeed, we may go a step further and say that, as property can only be legally acquired as between living persons by contract, a general prohibition against entering into contracts with respect to property, or having as their object the acquisition of property, should be equally invalid.

. . .

This right of contract, however, is itself subject to certain limitations which the State may lawfully impose in the exercise of its police powers. While this power is inherent in all governments, it has doubtless been greatly expanded in its application during the past century, owing to an enormous increase in the number of occupations which are dangerous, or so far detrimental to the health of employees as to demand special precautions for their wellbeing and protection, or the safety of adjacent property. While . . . the police power cannot be put forward as an excuse for oppressive and unjust legislation, it may be lawfully resorted to for the purpose of preserving the public health, safety or morals, or the abatement of public nuisances, and a large discretion "is necessarily vested in the legislature to determine not only what the interests of the public require, but what measures are necessary for the protection of such interests."

. . .

. . . While the business of mining coal and manufacturing iron began in Pennsylvania as early as 1716, and in Virginia, North Carolina and Massachusetts even earlier than this, both mining and manufacturing were carried on in such a limited way and by such primitive methods that no special laws were considered necessary, prior to the adoption of the Constitution, for the protection of the operatives; but, in the vast proportions which these industries have since assumed, it has been found that they can no longer be carried on with due regard to the safety and health of those engaged in them without special protection against the dangers necessarily incident to these employments. In consequence of this, laws have been enacted in most of the States designed to meet these exigencies and to secure the safety of persons peculiarly exposed to these dangers. . . . In States where manufacturing is carried on to a large extent, provision is made for the protection of dangerous machinery against accidental contact, for the cleanliness and ventilation of working rooms, for the guarding of well holes, stairways, elevator shafts, and for the employment of sanitary appliances. In others, where mining is the principal industry, special provision is made for the shoring up of dangerous walls, for ventilation shafts, bore holes, escapement shafts, means of signaling the surface, for the supply of fresh air and the elimination, as far as possible, of dangerous gases, for safe means of hoisting and lowering cages, for a limitation upon the number of persons permitted to enter a cage, that cages shall be covered, and that there shall be fences and gates around the top of shafts, besides other similar precautions. . . .

. . .

Upon the principles above stated, we think the act in question may be sustained as a valid exercise of the police power of the State. The enactment does not profess to limit the hours of all workmen, but merely those who are employed in underground mines or in the smelting, reduction or refining of ores or metals. These employments, when too long pursued, the legislature has judged to be detrimental to the health of the employees, and, so long as there are reasonable grounds for believing that this is so, its decision upon this subject cannot be reviewed by the Federal courts.

While the general experience of mankind may justify us in believing that men may engage in ordinary employment more than eight hours per day without injury to their health, it does not follow that labor for the same length of time is innocuous when carried on beneath the surface of the earth, where the operative is deprived of fresh air and sunlight and is frequently subjected to foul atmosphere and a very high temperature or to the influence of noxious gases generated by the processes of refining or smelting.

. . .

The legislature has also recognized the fact, which the experience of legislators in many States has corroborated, that the proprietors of these establishments and their operatives do not stand upon an equality, and that their interests are, to a certain extent, conflicting. The former naturally desire to obtain as much labor as possible from their employees, while the latter are often induced by the fear of discharge to conform to regulations which their judgment, fairly exercised, would pronounce to be detrimental to their health or strength. In other words, the proprietors lay down the rules and the laborers are practically constrained to obey them. In such cases, self-interest is often an unsafe guide, and the legislature may properly interpose its authority.

. . .

JUSTICE BREWER and JUSTICE PECKHAM dissented.

Lochner v. New York, 198 U.S. 45 (1905)

Joseph Lochner owned the Lochner Home Bakery. In 1899 and 1901 he was fined for allowing employees to work more than ten hours a day, or sixty hours a week. This violated the New York Bakeshop Act of 1895, which limited the hours that bakers could work. Proponents of the measure maintained that having bakers exposed to flour dust for many hours in poorly ventilated bakeries was dangerous. Opponents argued that the law violated "liberty of contract," did little to protect the health of bakers, and was primarily motivated by the desire to promote the interests of organized labor at the expense of "boss bakers" who owned small shops and operated on a small margin of profit. By a closely divided vote the Court of Appeals of New York sustained Lochner's fine. Lochner appealed that decision to the Supreme Court of the United States.

The Supreme Court by a 5-4 vote declared that the Bakeshop Act violated the due process clause of the Fourteenth Amendment. Justice Peckham's majority opinion ruled that the measure was neither a valid health law nor a valid labor law. Justice Harlan's dissent insisted that the law was a valid health law, even if not a valid labor law. Justice Holmes's dissent maintained that the law was both a valid health law and a valid labor law. Lochner v. New York *has a special place in the canon of constitutional history as the exemplar of justices abusing their power by deciding cases on the basis of their personal views. As you read the case, consider whether this accusation is fair—or, if fair, whether* Lochner *is an especially egregious example of this phenomenon. What standard of review do the various justices apply? Do they dispute the standard of review or the application of that standard to the facts in* Lochner*? Justice Holmes's* Lochner *dissent became a rallying cry for progressives. How consistent is that dissent with Republican Era constitutional jurisprudence? Would you be willing to apply the principles of that dissent to racial segregation or free speech? If not, why do those rights raise different issues?*

JUSTICE PECKHAM delivered the opinion of the court.

. . .

The statute necessarily interferes with the right of contract between the employer and employees concerning the number of hours in which the latter may labor in the bakery of the employer. The general right to make a contract in relation to his business is part of the liberty of the individual protected by the Fourteenth Amendment of the Federal Constitution. Under that provision, no State can deprive any person of life, liberty or property without due process of law. The right to purchase or to sell labor is part of the liberty protected by this amendment unless there are circumstances which exclude the right. There are, however, certain powers, existing in the sovereignty of each State in the Union, somewhat vaguely termed police powers, the exact description and limitation of which have not been attempted by the courts. Those powers, broadly stated and without, at present, any attempt at a more specific limitation, relate to the safety, health, morals and general welfare of the public. Both property and liberty are held on such reasonable conditions as may be imposed by the governing power of the State in the exercise of those powers, and with such conditions the Fourteenth Amendment was not designed to interfere.

. . .

It must, of course, be conceded that there is a limit to the valid exercise of the police power by the State. There is no dispute concerning this general proposition. Otherwise the Fourteenth Amendment would have no efficacy, and the legislatures of the States would have unbounded power, and it would be enough to say that any piece of legislation was enacted to conserve the morals, the health or the safety of the people; such legislation would be valid no matter how absolutely without foundation the claim might be. The claim of the police power would be a mere pretext—become another and delusive name for the supreme sovereignty of the State to be exercised free from constitutional restraint. This is not contended for. In every case that comes before this court, therefore, where legislation of this character is concerned and where the protection of the Federal Constitution is sought, the question necessarily arises: is this a fair, reasonable and appropriate exercise of the police power of the State, or is it an unreasonable, unnecessary and arbitrary interference with the right of the individual to his personal liberty or to enter into those contracts in relation to labor which may seem to him appropriate or necessary for the support of himself and his family? . . .

. . .

The question whether this act is valid as a labor law, pure and simple, may be dismissed in a few words. There is no reasonable ground for interfering with the liberty of person or the right of free contract by determining the hours of labor in the occupation of a baker. There is no contention that bakers as a class are not equal in intelligence and capacity to men in other trades or manual occupations, or that they are able to assert their rights and care for themselves without the protecting arm of the State, interfering with their independence of judgment and of action. They are in no sense wards of the State. Viewed in the light of a purely labor law, with no reference whatever to the question of health, we think that a law like the one before us involves neither the safety, the morals, nor the welfare of the public, and that the interest of the public is not in the slightest degree affected by such an act. The law must be upheld, if at all, as a law pertaining to the health of the individual engaged in the occupation of a baker. It does not affect any other portion of the public than those who are engaged in that occupation. Clean and wholesome bread does not depend upon whether the baker works but ten hours per day or only sixty hours a week. The limitation of the hours of labor does not come within the police power on that ground.

. . .

We think the limit of the police power has been reached and passed in this case. There is, in our judgment, no reasonable foundation for holding this to be necessary or appropriate as a health law to safeguard the public health or the health of the individuals who are following the trade of a baker. . . .

We think that there can be no fair doubt that the trade of a baker, in and of itself, is not an unhealthy one to that degree which would authorize the legislature to interfere with the right to labor, and with the right of free contract on the part of the individual, either as employer or employee. In looking through statistics regarding all trades and occupations, it may be true that the trade of a baker does not appear to be as healthy as some other trades, and is also vastly more healthy than still others. To the common understanding, the trade of a baker has never been regarded as an unhealthy one. . . . It is unfortunately true that labor, even in any department, may possibly carry with it the seeds of unhealthiness. But are we all, on that account, at the mercy of legislative majorities? A printer, a tinsmith, a locksmith, a carpenter, a cabinetmaker, a dry goods clerk, a bank's, a lawyer's or a physician's clerk, or a clerk in almost any kind of business, would all come under the power of the legislature on this assumption. No trade, no occupation, no mode of earning one's living could escape this all-pervading power, and the acts of the legislature in limiting the hours of labor in all employments would be valid although such limitation might seriously cripple the ability of the laborer to support himself and his family. . . . It might be said that it is unhealthy to work more than that number of hours in an apartment lighted by artificial light during the working hours of the day; that the occupation of the bank clerk, the lawyer's clerk, the real estate clerk, or the broker's clerk in such offices is therefore unhealthy, and the legislature, in its paternal wisdom, must therefore have the right to legislate on the subject of, and to limit the hours for, such labor, and, if it exercises that power and its validity be questioned, it is sufficient to say it has reference to the public health; it has reference to the health of the employees condemned to labor day after day in buildings where the sun never shines; it is a health law, and therefore it is valid, and cannot be questioned by the courts.

It is also urged, pursuing the same line of argument, that it is to the interest of the State that its population should be strong and robust, and therefore any legislation which may be said to tend to make people healthy must be valid as health laws, enacted under the police power. If this be a valid argument and a justification for this kind of legislation, it follows that the protection of the Federal Constitution from undue interference with liberty of person and freedom of contract is visionary wherever the law is sought to be justified as a valid exercise of the police power. Scarcely any law but might find shelter under such assumptions, and conduct, properly so called, as well as contract, would come under the restrictive sway of the legislature. Not only the hours of employees, but the hours of employers, could be regulated, and doctors, lawyers, scientists, all professional men, as well as athletes and artisans, could be forbidden to fatigue their brains and bodies by prolonged hours of exercise, lest the fighting strength of the State be impaired. We mention these extreme cases because the contention is extreme. We do not believe in the soundness of the views which uphold this law. On the contrary, we think that such a law as this, although passed in the assumed exercise of the police power, and as relating to the public health, or the health of the employees named, is not within that power, and is invalid. The act is not, within any fair meaning of the term, a health law, but is an illegal interference with the rights of individuals, both employers and employees, to make contracts regarding labor upon such terms as they may think best, or which they may agree upon with the other parties to such contracts. . . .

. . . In our judgment, it is not possible, in fact, to discover the connection between the number of hours a baker may work in the bakery and the healthful quality of the bread made by the workman. The connection, if any exists, is too shadowy and thin to build any argument for the interference of the legislature. If the man works ten hours a day, it is all right, but if ten and a half or eleven, his health is in danger and his bread may be unhealthful, and, therefore, he shall not be permitted to do it. This, we think, is unreasonable, and entirely arbitrary. When assertions such as we have adverted to become necessary in order to give, if possible, a plausible foundation for the contention that the law is a "health law," it gives rise to at least a suspicion that there was some other motive dominating the legislature than the purpose to subserve the public health or welfare.

. . .

JUSTICE HARLAN, with whom JUSTICE WHITE and JUSTICE DAY joined, dissenting.

. . .

Granting then that there is a liberty of contract which cannot be violated even under the sanction of direct legislative enactment, but assuming, as according to settled law we may assume, that such liberty of contract is subject to such regulations as the State may reasonably prescribe for the common good and the wellbeing of society, what are the conditions under which the judiciary may declare such regulations to be in excess of legislative authority and void? . . .

. . . If there be doubt as to the validity of the statute, that doubt must therefore be resolved in favor of its validity, and the courts must keep their hands off, leaving the legislature to meet the responsibility for unwise legislation. If the end which the legislature seeks to accomplish be one to which its power extends, and if the means employed to that end, although not the wisest or best, are yet not plainly and palpably unauthorized by law, then the court cannot interfere. In other words, when the validity of a statute is questioned, the burden of proof, so to speak, is upon those who assert it to be unconstitutional. . . .

. . .

It is plain that this statute was enacted in order to protect the physical wellbeing of those who work in bakery and confectionery establishments. It may be that the statute had its origin, in part, in the belief that employers and employees in such establishments were not upon an equal footing, and that the necessities of the latter often compelled them to submit to such exactions as unduly taxed their strength. Be this as it may, the statute must be taken as expressing the belief of the people of New York that, as a general rule, and in the case of the average man, labor in excess of sixty hours during a week in such establishments may endanger the health of those who thus labor. Whether or not this be wise legislation it is not the province of the court to inquire. Under our systems of government, the courts are not concerned with the wisdom or policy of legislation. So that, in determining the question of power to interfere with liberty of contract, the court may inquire whether the means devised by the State are germane to an end which may be lawfully accomplished and have a real or substantial relation to the protection of health, as involved in the daily work of the persons, male and female, engaged in bakery and confectionery establishments. But when this inquiry is entered upon, I find it impossible, in view of common experience, to say that there is here no real or substantial relation between the means employed by the State and the end sought to be accomplished by its legislation. Nor can I say that the statute has no appropriate or direct connection with that protection to health which each State owes to her citizens, or that it is not promotive of the health of the employees in question, or that the regulation prescribed by the State is utterly unreasonable and extravagant or wholly arbitrary. Still less can I say that the statute is, beyond question, a plain, palpable invasion of rights secured by the fundamental law. Therefore, I submit that this court will transcend its functions if it assumes to annul the statute of New York. It must be remembered that this statute does not apply to all kinds of business. . . .

. . .

. . . What the precise facts are it may be difficult to say. It is enough for the determination of this case, and it is enough for this court to know, that the question is one about which there is room for debate and for an honest difference of opinion. There are many reasons of a weighty, substantial character, based upon the experience of mankind, in support of the theory that, all things considered, more than ten hours' steady work each day, from week to week, in a bakery or confectionery establishment, may endanger the health, and shorten the lives of the workmen, thereby diminishing their physical and mental capacity to serve the State, and to provide for those dependent upon them.

. . .

JUSTICE HOLMES dissenting.

. . .

This case is decided upon an economic theory which a large part of the country does not entertain. If it were a question whether I agreed with that theory, I should desire to study it further and long before making up my mind. But I do not conceive that to be my duty, because I strongly believe that my agreement or disagreement has nothing to do with the right of a majority to embody their opinions in law. It is settled by various decisions of this court that state constitutions and state laws may regulate life in many ways which we, as legislators, might think as injudicious, or, if you like, as tyrannical, as this, and which, equally with this, interfere with the liberty to contract. Sunday laws and usury laws are ancient examples. A more modern one is the prohibition of lotteries. The liberty of the citizen to do as he likes so long as he does not interfere with the liberty of others to do the same, which has been a shibboleth for some well known writers, is interfered with by school laws, by the Post Office, by every state or municipal institution which takes his money for purposes thought desirable, whether he likes it or not. The Fourteenth Amendment does not enact Mr. Herbert Spencer's *Social Statics*. . . . [A] constitution is not intended to embody a particular economic theory, whether of paternalism and the organic relation of the citizen to the State or of laissez faire. It is made for people of fundamentally differing views, and the accident of our finding certain opinions natural and familiar or novel and even shocking ought not to conclude our judgment upon the question whether statutes embodying them conflict with the Constitution of the United States.

General propositions do not decide concrete cases. The decision will depend on a judgment or intuition more subtle than any articulate major premise. But I think that the proposition just stated, if it is accepted, will carry us far toward the end. Every opinion tends to become a law. I think that the word liberty in the Fourteenth Amendment is perverted when it is held to prevent the natural outcome of a dominant opinion, unless it can be said that a rational and fair man necessarily would admit that the statute proposed would infringe fundamental principles as they have been understood by the traditions of our people and our law. It does not need research to show that no such sweeping condemnation can be passed upon the statute before us. A reasonable man might think it a proper measure on the score of health. Men whom I certainly could not pronounce unreasonable would uphold it as a first instalment of a general regulation of the hours of work. Whether in the latter aspect it would be open to the charge of inequality I think it unnecessary to discuss.

Muller v. Oregon, 208 U.S. 412 (1908)

Curt Muller owned the Grand Laundry in Mulnomah County, Oregon. On September 4, 1905, he required a female employee, Mrs. E. Gotcher, to work more than ten hours. This violated an Oregon statute that declared, "No female (shall) be employed in any mechanical establishment, or factory, or laundry in this state more than ten hours during any one day." Muller was arrested, tried, convicted, and fined $10. The Supreme Court of Oregon sustained his conviction. Muller appealed to the Supreme Court of the United States.

The Supreme Court unanimously upheld the conviction. Justice Brewer's opinion declared that differences between men and women justified permitting states to pass regulations limiting the hours women worked. What does Justice Brewer believe are the differences between men and women? Why does he believe these differences have constitutional significance?

Table 7-4 A Selection of Legal Interest Groups and Their Signature Victories

Organization and Year of Founding	Notable U.S. Supreme Court Victories
National Consumers' League (1899)	*Muller v. Oregon* (1908) *Bunting v. Oregon* (1917)
American Jewish Congress (1918)	*McCollum v. Board of Education* (1948) *Shelley v. Kraemer* (1948)
American Civil Liberties Union (1920)	*Mapp v. Ohio* (1961) *Griswold v. Connecticut* (1965)
National Association for the Advancement of Colored People Legal Defense Fund (1939)[18]	*Brown v. Board of Education* (1954) *Furman v. Georgia* (1972)
Americans United for Separation of Church and State (1947)	*Flast v. Cohen* (1968) *Lemon v. Kurtzman* (1971)
National Center for Law and Economic Justice (1965)	*Goldberg v. Kelly* (1970) *Califano v. Westcott* (1979)
Lambda Legal (1973)	*Romer v. Evans* (1996) *Lawrence v. Texas* (2003)
Center for Individual Rights (1988)	*Rosenberger v. Rector and Visitors of University of Virginia* (1995) *Gratz v. Bollinger* (2003)
Institute for Justice (1991)	*Zelman v. Simmons-Harris* (2002) *Granholm v. Heald* (2005)

In 1908 Muller was considered a triumph for progressives. The National Consumers League assisted Oregon in defending this law by securing the services of one of the leading progressive lawyers in the country—future Supreme Court justice Louis D. Brandeis. Brandeis devised an innovative legal strategy. His brief offered only two short pages of legal argument but then included fifteen pages of excerpts from other state and foreign statutes regulating working hours for women (to establish that Oregon's judgment was supported by many other legislatures) and ninety-five pages of medical reports supporting the assertion that long working hours had a detrimental effect on women's health. As you read the opinion, consider whether the justices were more influenced by Brandeis's data or by their "general knowledge" of the role of women in society. Was Muller a liberal or conservative decision?

LOUIS D. BRANDEIS, "Brief for the State of Oregon"

The legal rules applicable to this case are few and are well established, namely:

First: The right to purchase or to sell labor is a part of the "liberty" protected by the Fourteenth Amendment of the Federal Constitution.

Second: This right to "liberty" is, however, subject to such reasonable restraint of action as the State may impose in the exercise of the police power for the protection of health, safety, morals, and the general welfare.

. . .

Fourth: Such a law will not be sustained if the Court can see that it has no real or substantial relation to public health, safety, or welfare, or that it is "an unreasonable, unnecessary and arbitrary interference with the right of the individual to his personal liberty or to enter into those contracts in relation to labor which may seem to him appropriate or necessary for the support of himself and his family."

But "If the end which the Legislature seeks to accomplish be one to which its power extends, and if the means employed to that end, although not the wisest or best, are yet not plainly and palpably unauthorized

18. The NAACP was founded in 1909. The Legal Defense Fund, which is now entirely independent of the NAACP, became a separate organization in 1939.

by law, then the Court cannot interfere. In other words, when the validity of a statute is questioned, the burden of proof, so to speak, is upon those who assail it.

Fifth: . . .

The facts of common knowledge of which the Court may take judicial notice . . . establish, we submit, conclusively, that there is reasonable ground for holding that to permit women in Oregon to work in a "mechanical establishment, or factory, or laundry" more than ten hours in one day is dangerous to the public health, safety, morals, or welfare.

These facts of common knowledge will be considered under the following heads:

Part I. Legislation (foreign and American), restricting the hours of labor for women.

Part II. The world's experience upon which the legislation limiting the hours of labor for women is based.

. . .

JUSTICE BREWER delivered the opinion of the Court.

. . .

. . . We held in *Lochner v. New York* (1905) that a law providing that no laborer shall be required or permitted to work in bakeries more than sixty hours in a week or ten hours in a day was not, as to men, a legitimate exercise of the police power of the State, but an unreasonable, unnecessary, and arbitrary interference with the right and liberty of the individual to contract in relation to his labor, and, as such, was in conflict with, and void under, the Federal Constitution. That decision is invoked by plaintiff in error as decisive of the question before us. But this assumes that the difference between the sexes does not justify a different rule respecting a restriction of the hours of labor.

. . .

The legislation and opinions referred to in the margin [of the Brandeis brief] may not be, technically speaking, authorities, and in them is little or no discussion of the constitutional question presented to us for determination, yet they are significant of a widespread belief that woman's physical structure, and the functions she performs in consequence thereof, justify special legislation restricting or qualifying the conditions under which she should be permitted to toil. Constitutional questions, it is true, are not settled by even a consensus of present public opinion, for it is the peculiar value of a written constitution that it places in unchanging form limitations upon legislative action, and thus gives a permanence and stability to popular government which otherwise would be lacking. At the same time, when a question of fact is debated and debatable, and the extent to which a special constitutional limitation goes is affected by the truth in respect to that fact, a widespread and long-continued belief concerning it is worthy of consideration. We take judicial cognizance of all matters of general knowledge.

. . .

That woman's physical structure and the performance of maternal functions place her at a disadvantage in the struggle for subsistence is obvious. This is especially true when the burdens of motherhood are upon her. Even when they are not, by abundant testimony of the medical fraternity, continuance for a long time on her feet at work, repeating this from day to day, tends to injurious effects upon the body, and, as healthy mothers are essential to vigorous offspring, the physical wellbeing of woman becomes an object of public interest and care in order to preserve the strength and vigor of the race.

Still again, history discloses the fact that woman has always been dependent upon man. He established his control at the outset by superior physical strength, and this control in various forms, with diminishing intensity, has continued to the present. As minors, though not to the same extent, she has been looked upon in the courts as needing especial care that her rights may be preserved. Education was long denied her, and while now the doors of the schoolroom are opened and her opportunities for acquiring knowledge are great, yet, even with that and the consequent increase of capacity for business affairs, it is still true that, in the struggle for subsistence, she is not an equal competitor with her brother. Though limitations upon personal and contractual rights may be removed by legislation, there is that in her disposition and habits of life which will operate against a full assertion of those rights. She will still be where some legislation to protect her seems necessary to secure a real equality of right. Doubtless there are individual exceptions, and there are many respects in which she has an advantage over him; but, looking at it from the viewpoint of the effort to maintain an independent position in life, she is not upon an equality. Differentiated by these matters from the other sex, she is properly placed in a class by herself, and legislation designed for her protection may be sustained even when like legislation is not necessary for men, and could not be sustained. It is impossible to close one's eyes to the fact that she still looks to her brother, and depends upon him. Even though all restrictions on political, personal, and contractual rights were taken away, and she stood, so far as statutes are concerned, upon an absolutely equal plane with him, it would still be true that she is so constituted that she will rest upon and look to him for protection; that her physical structure and a proper discharge of her maternal functions—having in view not merely her own health, but the wellbeing of the race—justify legislation to protect her from the greed, as well as the passion, of man. The limitations which this statute places upon her contractual powers, upon her right to agree with her employer as to the time she shall labor, are not imposed solely for her benefit, but also largely for the benefit of all. Many words cannot make this plainer. The two sexes differ in structure of body, in the functions to be performed by each, in the amount of physical strength, in the capacity for long-continued labor, particularly when done standing, the influence of vigorous health upon the future wellbeing of the race, the self-reliance which enables one to assert full rights, and in the capacity to maintain the struggle for subsistence. This difference justifies a difference in legislation, and upholds that which is designed to compensate for some of the burdens which rest upon her. . . .

Adkins v. Children's Hospital, 261 U.S. 525 (1923)

The Children's Hospital of the District of Columbia objected to a local law requiring that employers pay minimum wages to women and children. Lawyers for the hospital filed a lawsuit

Illustration 7-2 This Decision Affirms Your Constitutional Right to Starve
This cartoon was produced for the National Consumer's League in response to the U.S. Supreme Court's decision in *Adkins v. Children's Hospital* (1923), which struck down the federal minimum wage for women.

Source: By permission of the Estate of Rollin Kirby Post.

against Jesse Adkins and other members of the Wage Board of the District of Columbia asking the court to restrain those officials from implementing the minimum wage law. The lower federal court dismissed the suit, but that decision was reversed by the Court of Appeals for the District of Columbia. Adkins appealed to the Supreme Court of the United States.

The Supreme Court had previously split 4-4 in Stettler v. O'Hara *(1917) on whether the Fourteenth Amendment permitted Oregon to set a minimum wage for women working in private employment. The 4-4 split occurred because the recently appointed Louis Brandeis had worked on the initial litigation as an attorney. Had Brandeis not participated, or had President Wilson selected a different progressively-inclined appointee to the Court in 1916, the justices would have upheld the constitutionality of the minimum wage for women in 1917. By the time* Adkins *came before the Supreme Court, its conservative wing had been augmented. President Harding had appointed Chief Justice William Howard Taft, Justice George Sutherland, and Justice Pierce Butler, each of whom was more protective of property rights than their predecessors.*

The Supreme Court by a 5-3 vote declared unconstitutional minimum wage laws for women. Justice Sutherland's opinion asserted that minimum wage laws arbitrarily interfered with the bargaining process between female employees and (male) employers. Sutherland's opinion distinguishes between minimum hour laws and minimum wage laws. How does he make that distinction? Is the distinction sound? Sutherland also asserts that the Nineteenth Amendment supports his conclusion. On what basis does he make that argument? Why do Chief Justice Taft and Justice Holmes disagree? Who is correct? Should progressives applaud the decision for treating women and men in the same manner when regulating the work environment?

Adkins v. Children's Hospital *ushered in one of the most activist periods in the Court's history. The justices rarely employed freedom of contract rhetoric in the 1910s. Chief Justice Taft's dissent in* Adkins *assumed that* Lochner v. New York *(1905) was silently overruled by* Bunting v. Oregon *(1917). Justices appointed by Republican presidents Warren Harding and Calvin Coolidge during the 1920s more aggressively exercised judicial power than their predecessors, striking down an increasing number of state regulations as inconsistent with due process.*

JUSTICE SUTHERLAND delivered the opinion of the Court.

. . .

In *Muller v. Oregon* (1908), the validity of an Oregon statute, forbidding the employment of any female in certain industries more than ten hours during any one day was upheld. The decision proceeded upon the theory that the difference between the sexes may justify a different rule respecting hours of labor in the case of women than in the case of men. . . . But the ancient inequality of the sexes, otherwise than physical, as suggested in the *Muller* case has continued "with diminishing intensity." In view of the great—not to say revolutionary—changes which have taken place since that utterance, in the contractual, political and civil status of women, culminating in the Nineteenth Amendment, it is not unreasonable to say that these differences have now come almost, if not quite, to the vanishing point. In this aspect of the matter, while the physical differences must be recognized in appropriate cases, and legislation fixing hours or conditions of work may properly take them into account, we cannot accept the doctrine that women of mature age, *sui juris*, require or may be subjected to restrictions upon their liberty of contract which could not lawfully be imposed in the case of men under similar circumstances. To do so would be to ignore all the implications to be drawn from the present day trend of legislation, as well as that of common thought and usage, by which woman is accorded emancipation from the old doctrine that she must be given special protection or be subjected to special restraint in her contractual and civil relationships. In passing, it may be noted that the instant statute applies in the case of a woman employer contracting with a woman employee as it does when the former is a man.

The essential characteristics of the statute now under consideration, which differentiate it from the laws fixing hours of labor, will be made to appear as we proceed. It is sufficient now to point out that the latter . . . deal with incidents of the employment having no necessary effect upon the heart of the contract, that is, the amount of wages to be paid and received. A law forbidding work to continue beyond a given number of hours leaves the parties free to contract about wages, and thereby equalize whatever additional burdens may be imposed upon the employer as a result of the restrictions as to hours, by an adjustment in respect of the amount of wages. . . .

. . .

The law takes account of the necessities of only one party to the contract. It ignores the necessities of the employer by compelling him to pay not less than a certain sum not only whether the employee is capable of earning it, but irrespective of the ability of his business to sustain the burden, generously leaving him, of course, the privilege of abandoning his business as an alternative for going on at a loss. Within the limits of the minimum sum, he is precluded, under penalty of fine and imprisonment, from adjusting compensation to the differing merits of his employees. It compels him to pay at least the sum fixed in any event, because the employee needs it, but requires no service of equivalent value from the employee. . . . The law is not confined to the great and powerful employers, but embraces those whose bargaining power may be as weak as that of the employee. It takes no account of periods of stress and business depression, of crippling losses, which may leave the employer himself without adequate means of livelihood. To the extent that the sum fixed exceeds the fair value of the services rendered, it amounts to a compulsory exaction from the employer for the support of a partially indigent person, for whose condition there rests upon him no peculiar responsibility, and therefore, in effect, arbitrarily shifts to his shoulders a burden which, if it belongs to anybody, belongs to society as a whole.

. . .

It has been said that legislation of the kind now under review is required in the interest of social justice, for whose ends freedom of contract may lawfully be subjected to restraint. The liberty of the individual to do as he pleases, even in innocent matters, is not absolute. It must frequently yield to the common good, and the line beyond which the power of interference may not be pressed is neither definite nor unalterable, but may be made to move, within limits not well defined, with changing need and circumstance. Any attempt to fix a rigid boundary would be unwise, as well as futile. But, nevertheless, there are limits to the power, and when these have been passed, it becomes the plain duty of the courts in the proper exercise of their authority to so declare. To sustain the individual freedom of action contemplated by the Constitution is not to strike down the common good, but to exalt it, for surely the good of society as a whole cannot be better served than by the preservation against arbitrary restraint of the liberties of its constituent members.

. . .

CHIEF JUSTICE TAFT, dissenting.

. . .

Legislatures, in limiting freedom of contract between employee and employer by a minimum wage, proceed on the assumption that employees, in the class receiving least pay, are not upon a full level of equality of choice with their employer, and, in their necessitous circumstances, are prone to accept pretty much anything that is offered. They are peculiarly subject to the overreaching of the harsh and greedy employer. The evils of the sweating system and of the long hours and low wages which are characteristic of it are well known. Now I agree that it is a disputable question in the field of political economy how far a statutory requirement of maximum hours or minimum wages may be a useful remedy for these evils, and whether it may not make the case of the oppressed employee worse than it was before. But it is not the function of this Court to hold congressional acts invalid simply because they are passed to carry out economic views which the Court believes to be unwise or unsound.

. . .

The right of the legislature under the Fifth and Fourteenth Amendments to limit the hours of employment on the score of the health of the employee, it seems to me, has been firmly established. . . . In [*Bunting v. Oregon* (1917)], this Court sustained a law limiting the hours of labor of any person, whether man or woman, working in any mill, factory or manufacturing establishment to ten hours a day with a proviso as to further hours to which I shall hereafter advert. The law covered the whole field of industrial employment, and certainly covered the case of persons employed in bakeries. Yet the opinion in the *Bunting* case does not mention the *Lochner* case. No one can suggest any constitutional distinction between employment in a bakery and one in any other kind of a manufacturing establishment which should make a limit of hours in the one invalid and the same limit in the other permissible. It is impossible for me to reconcile the *Bunting* case and the *Lochner* case, and I have always supposed that the *Lochner* case was thus overruled *sub silentio*. . . .

However, the opinion herein does not overrule the *Bunting* case in express terms, and therefore I assume that the conclusion in this case rests on the distinction between a minimum of wages and a maximum of hours in the limiting of liberty to contract. I regret to be at variance with the Court as to the substance of this distinction. In absolute freedom of contract, the one term is as important as the other, for both enter equally into the consideration given and received, a restriction as to one is not any greater, in essence, than the other, and is of the same kind. One is the multiplier, and the other the multiplicand.

. . .

I am not sure from a reading of the opinion whether the Court thinks the authority of *Muller v. Oregon* is shaken by the adoption of the Nineteenth Amendment. The Nineteenth Amendment did not change the physical strength or limitations of women upon which the decision in *Muller v. Oregon* rests. The Amendment did give women political power, and makes more certain that legislative provisions for their protection will be in accord with their interests as they see them. But I don't think we are warranted in varying constitutional construction based on physical differences between men and women, because of the Amendment.

. . .

I am authorized to say that JUSTICE SANFORD concurs in this opinion.

JUSTICE HOLMES, dissenting.

. . . To me, notwithstanding the deference due to the prevailing judgment of the Court, the power of Congress seems absolutely free from doubt. The end, to remove conditions leading to ill health, immorality and the deterioration of the race, no one would deny to be within the scope of constitutional legislation. The means are means that have the approval of Congress, of many States, and of those governments from which we have learned our greatest lessons. When so many intelligent persons, who have studied the matter more than any of us can, have thought that the means are effective and are worth the price, it seems to me impossible to deny that the belief reasonably may be held by reasonable men. . . .

. . .

I confess that I do not understand the principle on which the power to fix a minimum for the wages of women can be denied by those who admit the power to fix a maximum for their hours of work. I fully assent to the proposition that here, as elsewhere, the distinctions of the law are distinctions of degree, but I perceive no difference in the kind or degree of interference with liberty, the only matter with which we have any concern, between the one case and the other. The bargain is equally affected whichever half you regulate. *Muller v. Oregon,* I take it, is as good law today as it was in 1908. It will need more than the Nineteenth Amendment to convince me that there are no differences between men and women, or that legislation cannot take those differences into account. . . .

B. Religion

Americans at the turn of the twentieth century debated whether the United States was a Christian nation. Justice David Brewer in *Church of the Holy Trinity v. United States* (1892) bluntly stated, "This is a Christian Nation." The National Reform Organization proposed that the Preamble to the Constitution be amended to read

> We, the People of the United States, recognizing the being and attributes of Almighty God, the Divine Authority of the Holy Scriptures, the law of God as the paramount rule, and Jesus, the Messiah, the Saviour and Lord of all, in order to form a more perfect union, establish justice, insure domestic tranquility, provide for the common defence, promote the general welfare, and secure the blessings of liberty to ourselves and to our posterity, do ordain and establish this Constitution for the United States of America.[19]

Other interest groups sought a sharper separation of church and state than had been practiced during the first hundred years of national existence. The National Liberal League, which represented the growing number of explicitly secular Americans, proposed a constitutional amendment that declared,

> Neither Congress nor any State shall make any law respecting an establishment of religion, or favoring any particular form of religion, or prohibiting the free exercise thereof; or permitting in any degree a union of Church and State, or granting any special privilege, immunity, or advantage to any sect or religious body, or to any number of sects or religious bodies; or taxing the people of any State, either directly or indirectly, for the support of any sect or religious body, or of any number of sects or religious bodies.[20]

The constitutional politics of religion varied by issue. Proponents and opponents of Christianity in public life tangled over laws banning work and other activities on Sunday. Protestants and Catholics debated the merits of Bible reading in public schools. Americans

19. Steven Keith Green, "The National Reform Association and the Religious Amendments to the Constitution, 1864-1876." Unpublished Masters thesis, University of North Carolina at Chapel Hill (1987), 1-2.

20. National Liberal League, *Equal Rights in Religion* (Boston, MA: National Liberal League, 1876), 16.

were more united when members of new religious movements claimed constitutional rights. Few constitutional commentators dissented when the Supreme Court in *Reynolds v. United States* (1878) asserted that religious freedom did not encompass plural marriage.

Establishment

Establishment clause debates became more secular. The National Liberal League, an organization of prominent secularists committed to a separation of church and state, insisted, "The Constitution of the United States is built on the principle that the State can be, and ought to be, totally independent of the Church." When opposing state funding for religious organizations, members of that interest group declared, "The natural reason and conscience of mankind are a sufficient guarantee of a happy, well-ordered, and virtuous religious community."[21] Proponents of state support for religious practices and religious institutions emphasized the secular benefits of such measures. Wilbur Crafts, a Presbyterian moral reformer, claimed to have entirely secular reasons for supporting legislation that declared Sunday a day of rest. "The Sabbath laws, like the marriage laws," he wrote, "can be justified on hygienic, social and moral grounds to those who reject the religious ones." The Supreme Court regularly sustained legislation that provided resources to religious groups on the ground that such laws served secular ends. In *Bradfield v. Roberts* (1899) Justice Peckham described as "wholly immaterial" the fact that a hospital receiving government funds was run by the Roman Catholic Church.

Wilbur F. Crafts, The Civil Sabbath: The Friend, Not the Foe, of Liberty (1889)[22]

Wilbur Crafts (1849–1922) was a prominent religious lecturer and essayist. His causes included Prohibition, restrictions on narcotics, bans on vampire movies, and legislation forbidding close dancing. Crafts also championed laws that promoted Sunday as a day of rest. The longtime editor of several religious publications, he delivered frequent lectures and wrote many essays urging that such Sunday amusements as baseball be banned by legislation.

"The Civil Sabbath: The Friend, Not the Foe, of Liberty" is Crafts' best-known defense of Sunday laws. Why does Crafts maintain that Sunday laws are not an establishment of religion? Suppose that the state of California declared Tuesday to be a day of rest. Would that be sufficient? Crafts emphasizes that Sunday laws are for the benefit of labor. Would you describe him as a liberal or a conservative? Or is Crafts something else?

. . .

. . . There is no instance of a stable, long continued popular government where the people have kept themselves in infancy by devoting their God-given Rest Day to Sunday dissipation and its twin, Sunday toil. . . . American institutions are the roots of the American Constitution, and the American Sabbath is the very taproot of them all, supplying the people with the physical, mental and moral vitality necessary to self-government.

. . .

The right arm, the most important part, of the Sabbath Reform is the promotion of the religious Sabbath; its left arm, the preservation of the civil Sabbath. These two things—the Christian Sabbath on the one hand, and the American Sabbath on the other—are as distinct as my two arms, that resemble and cooperate, and yet are by no means the same. This distinction is itself an answer to most of the objections to Sabbath laws, which rest chiefly on the false assumption that they are enforcements of a duty to God, punishments of a sin against God. . . . It is admitted, however, by our opponents that it is the province of civil law to enforce man's duties to man, and especially to punish crimes against man. It is exactly on this ground that Sabbath laws forbid Sunday work and Sunday dissipation, namely, as *crimes against man*. . . . To rob a poor man of his purse or coat is only petty larceny. But it is grand larceny to steal the poor man's weekly Rest day, his "Home day," his Independence day. Ceaseless toil is slow murder.

Sunday laws are not "religious legislation" because they come from the Bible any more than the laws against adultery, which are as distinctly a part of Biblical morality, in distinction from heathen morality, as Sabbath laws. Both the Bible and the codes of the most advanced governments forbid murder, theft, adultery,

21. "The Thirteen Principles: Platform of the National Liberty League," *The Index* (Boston: Free Religious Association), vol. 8, June 28, 1877 at 1.

22. Excerpted from Wilbur F. Crafts, *Addresses on the Civil Sabbath* (New York: Authors' Publishing Co., 1890), 17.

false witness, and work on the Sabbath. . . . "Legislation against crime is not religious legislation. It is legislation on morality *purely on a civil basis.*"

. . .

. . . The church exhorts men against Sunday work and Sunday dissipation because God sees and will punish; but the State forbids these things because they are unhealthy to the body politic physically, mentally, morally and politically. . . . The church says of Sabbath desecration: Such conduct is displeasing to God; but the State says of Sunday work: What is more to us, charged to protect not divine but human rights, we won't stand it—the perpetual treadmill of toil, labor without leisure. . . . [T]he Sabbath laws, like the marriage laws, can be justified on hygienic, social and moral grounds to those who reject the religious ones.

. . .

. . . The objectors always quote the first amendment of the United States Constitution, that prohibits Congress to set up "an establishment of religion." The word "establishment" is a historic word, of no doubtful interpretation. When it was written into the Constitution, there was in the Old World, as there is to-day, the custom of selecting a single religion or a single sect and supporting it by the State, which also appoints its officers. A Sabbath law, in order to come under this prohibition, would need to require the building of churches by taxation, the State support of ministers of religion, and their political appointment, which no advocate of Sabbath legislation proposes or desires.

I have shown that the reference to "an establishment of religion" in the first amendment to the Constitution has no application whatever to the American Sabbath; but the latter part of this amendment, which requires that Congress shall make no laws prohibiting the free exercise of religion, does have a bearing upon the case in hand. When Congress ordered Sunday work in the mail service, it broke this Constitutional provision, for it made it impossible, by this *irreligious* test, for millions devoted to the Church, and unwilling to give up its services, and conscientious about doing needless Sunday work, to hold positions in this largest department of public service. That Act of Congress was not a law but a crime. The most conscientious men, who are best adapted to handle the wealth of the people in the mail, are thus distinctly excluded from the post-offices of the country—a very serious interference with the "free exercise of religion." The petition against Sunday mails is, therefore, not a request that Congress will do something *for* religion, but that it will cease to do something *against* religion. The present status is not neutrality, but hostility. We do not believe in state *and* church, but neither do we believe in state *against* church. Our petition asks Congress to desist from breaking the Constitution.

. . .

In many places it has happened that the barbers have circulated among themselves a signed agreement for Sunday closing, knowing that Sunday work, like swearing, is serving Satan without pay; that the same profit is made by the barbers of a town or city when they work six days as when they work seven. One barber refuses to sign, and so all the others think they must keep up their Sunday work, lest some shiftless customer, on a cold or rainy Saturday, may not come to his usual barber, because he knows that another will be open on the morrow. So the liberty of one man or a few becomes the Sunday slavery of a whole trade. In such a case law comes in, and, by "Sunday-closing" of all the barber shops, proclaims what all sensible barbers *will do,* and the one foolish barber *must do,* for his own good and the good of others. What is here said of barbers might be said also of bakers, launders, grocers,—indeed of nearly all forms of Sunday work for gain. If it is foolish in the seller to spend seven days in making six days' sales, it is shiftless in the buyer to leave his Saturday buying over for the Sabbath, so making himself and others needless work on the Rest Day. . . .

Nathaniel C. Nash, **The Sunday Law: Unconstitutional and Unscriptural** (1868)[23]

Nathaniel Cushing Nash (1804–80) was a prominent Boston businessperson and occasional officeholder. He was an opponent of slavery before the Civil War and an influential member of the Republican Party. While serving in the lower house of the Massachusetts state legislature, Nash led the fight to open the Boston Public Library on Sunday.

"The Sunday Law: Unconstitutional and Unscriptural" is a speech that Nash gave in the state legislature protesting efforts to close libraries on Sunday. Although we have

23. Nathaniel C. Nash, *The Sunday Law, Unconstitutional and Unscriptural: An Argument Presented in Committee of the Whole in the Massachusetts Legislature* (Boston: Nathaniel C. Nash, 1868).

redacted parts of that section of the speech, Nash spent most of his energies asserting that the Bible did not command Sunday laws. Given the rest of his speech, what was the point of that claim? Was Nash merely trying to demonstrate that his Christian credentials were as good as his political opponents? Was his constitutional claim based on a belief that no religious consensus existed that Sunday was a day of rest?

. . . [N]o law enforcing the observance of Sunday in any particular on citizens in general is constitutional.

The observation of the Sabbath is a doctrine of some of the Christian sects; but even among them, great differences exist as to the method and obligation of this observance. To select some one or two sects, Methodist and Congregational, and elevate their peculiarities into statutes, is manifestly "subordinating one sect or denomination to another," which the 11th Amendment [of the Massachusetts Constitution] expressly forbids.

To say that men whose religion ignores the observance of the Sabbath shall surrender their freedom to the dogmas of their neighbors is a violation of that clause of that Amendment, which provides that "all sections, demeaning themselves peaceably, shall be *equally under the protection of the law.*"

To oblige any man to forego, on Sunday, a pleasure or business, innocent on other days, because his neighbor thinks he ought to forego it, is a palpable violation of the 2d Article of the first part of the Constitution, which provides that no subject shall be restrained from worshipping God according to the dictates of his own conscience, provided he does not obstruct others in their religious worship; since it obliges a citizen, in addition to his own chosen method of worship, to model his life in such way as to help the worship of his neighbor. This subordinating my peaceable and innocent freedom to the quiet domination of another's method of worship is elevating his into an established church, and degrading mine into a merely tolerated heresy; a proceeding at war with this whole Article, and subversive of the very first principle of religious equality established in our Constitution.

I do not hesitate to say that the Sabbath laws of this State are and have been a gross and insolent violation of its Constitution ever since 1780, to say nothing of earlier laws. It is time one or two overbearing sects should be put back into the limits of law. Nothing but the indifference with which these laws have been hitherto treated has enabled them to hold their place on the Statute book. Now that they are pushed to absurd and most injurious uses, as in closing libraries, etc., on Sunday, the clear sense and instinctive love of equality among us will soon sweep them from the Statutes.

. . .

. . . [T]he restrictions . . . upon the employments of Sunday, the first day of the week, were put into the civil code *because they were in the church creed*. Here was the worst sort of "union of Church and State," interfering with the rights of conscience, preventing the free expression of opinion, forbidding that open conflict of truth with error which soonest accomplishes the overthrow of error. The progress of civilization and Christianity, since that time, has taught us that the Church has no right to dictate rules to the State; but when the Church rules in question are proved flagrantly wrong, when the Bible, from which those rules purport to have been taken, is found to hold a position not only different, but *opposite*, it is surely time to discard these Sabbatical laws, the remains of a code that rested on Judaism far more than Christianity, and to follow Jesus and Paul, and the great reformers of Protestantism, in claiming the right of private judgment in regard to *all* "observance of days."

Moral laws cannot be repealed by any power of earth or any mandate of heaven. Nothing seems clearer than that compulsory Sabbath or Lord's-day observances are *persecution*, and hence a violation of the rights of man. . . .

Free Exercise

Protestants and Catholics continued to struggle over Bible readings in public schools. Most state courts sustained local and state laws requiring children to read from the King James Bible. The Supreme Court of Georgia in *Wilkerson v. City of Rome* (GA 1922) asserted,

> It would require a strained and unreasonable construction to find anything in the ordinance which interferes with the natural and inalienable right to worship God according to the dictates of one's own conscience. The mere listening to the reading of an extract from the Bible and a brief prayer at the opening of school exercises would seem far remote from such interference.[24]

24. *Wilkerson v. City of Rome*, 110 S.E. 895 (Ga. 1922).

A significant minority of state courts declared Bible reading unconstitutional. The Supreme Court of South Dakota in *State v. Weedman* (SD 1929) declared,

> This case involves the right of the Protestants to read their translation of the Bible and conduct their form of worship in the common schools, and to compel the Catholic children to attend upon such services over the objections of their parents. On the broad constitutional ground of an infringement of religious liberty, we must hold such action unlawful.[25]

Few elected officials, political activists, or judges believed that unpopular religious believers enjoyed much constitutional protection, particularly when their religious practices seemed inconsistent with accepted standards of morality. Constitutional decision makers in all branches of state government expressed little sympathy for demands for constitutionally based exemptions. The New York Court of Appeals in *People v. Pierson* (NY 1903) brusquely turned aside the plea of a man who sought to heal a sick child by prayer instead of seeing a doctor. "Full and free enjoyment of religious profession and worship is guarantied," the justices declared, "but acts which are not worship are not."[26]

Mormons were the main target of ostensibly neutral laws that burdened religious practices. The Republican Party repeatedly condemned that sect's commitment to plural marriage. The party's 1876 platform insisted,

> The constitution confers upon congress sovereign power over the territories of the United States for their government. And in the exercise of this power it is the right and duty of congress to prohibit and extirpate in the territories that relic of barbarism, polygamy; and we demand such legislation as will secure this end and the supremacy of American institutions in all the territories.

Congress passed numerous acts designed to achieve those goals. Some directly outlawed polygamy. Others attached civil penalties to persons who engaged in or advocated polygamy. All were sustained without dissent by the Supreme Court of the United States.

25. *State v. Weedman*, 226 N.W. 348 (S.D. 1929).

26. *People v. Pierson*, 68 N.E. 243 (N.Y. 1903).

Reynolds v. United States, 98 U.S. 145 (1878)

George Reynolds was a prominent member of the Mormon Church. Committed to following church decrees, he practiced polygamy. He first married Polly Ann Tuddenham and then Amelia Jane Schofield. The second marriage violated a federal law forbidding multiple marriages in American territories. At trial Reynolds was convicted, sentenced to two years in prison, and fined $500. He appealed to the Territorial Supreme Court. When his claims were rejected, Reynolds appealed to the Supreme Court of the United States.

Reynolds v. United States *was one episode in the lengthy conflict between the Mormon Church and the federal government over both polygamy and Mormon claims about revelations. Mainstream Christians during the late nineteenth century did not take kindly to religious leaders who claimed to be contemporary prophets. The conflict was also political. The Mormon leadership in Utah was committed to establishing a theocracy, which many Americans regarded as treasonous. Brigham Young, the spiritual leader of the Latter Day Saints and former territorial governor, declared, "If I am controlled by the Spirit of the Most High, I am a king." Such declarations were frowned upon by national political leaders. President Rutherford Hayes declared,*

> *The Territory [of Utah] is virtually under theocratic government of the Mormon Church. The Union of Church and State is complete. . . . Polygamy and every other evil sanctioned by the Church is safe. To destroy the temporal power of the Mormon Church is the end in view.*[27]

The Supreme Court unanimously ruled that Reynolds was constitutionally convicted. Chief Justice Waite's opinion for the Court is best known for the sharp distinction that he draws between religious beliefs and religious actions. What is that distinction and what is its constitutional justification? Does Waite insist that religious action may always be regulated? If so, what exactly does free exercise protect? Waite connects polygamy with "statutory despotism." Is he referring to the intrinsic qualities of multiple marriages or to the actual conflict between the Mormon Church and the United States? Might the Reynolds *opinion have been different had the Mormons merely been an obscure religious group? Do you believe that marriage laws and political*

27. Martha M. Ertman, "The Story of *Reynolds v. United States*: Federal 'Hell Hounds' Punishing Mormon Treason," in *Family Law Stories*, ed. Carol Sanger (Eagan, MN: Foundation Press, 2008), 68–69 (quoting Young and Hayes).

Illustration 7-3 What It Is Bound to Come To
Political cartoon depicting Mormon leader Brigham Young and his wives being forced into divorce court by a U.S. soldier.
Source: Library of Congress, Prints and Photographs Division, Washington, DC 20540, USA.

institutions are politically or constitutionally connected? What is the connection? Consider the following assertion:

> *The story of* Reynolds *demonstrates its limited relevance to same-sex marriage and gay rights. In contrast to the practice and preferences of nineteenth-century Mormons to separate, if not fully secede, from American law and culture, same-sex marriage is fundamentally an assimilationist move for gay people to further integrate into American life.*[28]

Is Professor Ertman correct to claim that same-sex marriage and plural marriage are disanalogous? Is the analogy correct on cultural, political, or constitutional grounds? How do your beliefs about the cultural and political fights over both practices influence your thinking about the constitutionality of both practices?

Mormons eventually abandoned the fight for polygamy. In 1890 the Mormon leadership claimed to have a revelation from God urging the sect to foreswear multiple marriages. Statehood followed in 1896. George Reynolds, however, remained unrepentant. After being released from prison he married a third wife, Mary Goold, and began living underground. By the time Reynolds died in 1909 he had fathered thirty-two children.

CHIEF JUSTICE WAITE delivered the opinion of the court.

. . .

Before the adoption of the Constitution, attempts were made in some of the colonies and States to legislate not only in respect to the establishment of religion, but in respect to its doctrines and precepts as well.

28. Ertman, "Story of *Reynolds*," 55.

The people were taxed, against their will, for the support of religion, and sometimes for the support of particular sects to whose tenets they could not and did not subscribe. Punishments were prescribed for a failure to attend upon public worship, and sometimes for entertaining heretical opinions. The controversy upon this general subject was animated in many of the States, but seemed at last to culminate in Virginia. In 1784, the House of Delegates of that State having under consideration "a bill establishing provision for teachers of the Christian religion," . . . directed that . . . the people be requested "to signify their opinion respecting the adoption of such a bill at the next session of assembly."

. . . Mr. Madison prepared a "Memorial and Remonstrance," . . . in which he demonstrated "that religion, or the duty we owe the Creator," was not within the cognizance of civil government. . . . At the next session the proposed bill was not only defeated, but another, "for establishing religious freedom," drafted by Mr. Jefferson, was passed. . . . In the preamble of this act. . . after a recital "that to suffer the civil magistrate to intrude his powers into the field of opinion, and to restrain the profession or propagation of principles on supposition of their ill tendency, is a dangerous fallacy which at once destroys all religious liberty," it is declared "that it is time enough for the rightful purposes of civil government for its officers to interfere when principles break out into overt acts against peace and good order." In these two sentences is found the true distinction between what properly belongs to the church and what to the State.

. . . [A]t the first session of the first Congress the amendment now under consideration was proposed with others by Mr. Madison. It met the views of the advocates of religious freedom, and was adopted. Mr. Jefferson afterwards, in reply to an address to him by a committee of the Danbury Baptist Association . . . took occasion to say:

> Believing with you that religion is a matter which lies solely between man and his God; that he owes account to none other for his faith or his worship; that the legislative powers of the government reach actions only, and not opinions,—I contemplate with sovereign reverence that act of the whole American people which declared that their legislature should "make no law respecting an establishment of religion or prohibiting the free exercise thereof," thus building a wall of separation between church and State. Adhering to this expression of the supreme will of the nation in behalf of the rights of conscience, I shall see with sincere satisfaction the progress of those sentiments which tend to restore man to all his natural rights, convinced he has no natural right in opposition to his social duties.

Coming as this does from an acknowledged leader of the advocates of the measure, it may be accepted almost as an authoritative declaration of the scope and effect of the amendment thus secured. Congress was deprived of all legislative power over mere opinion, but was left free to reach actions which were in violation of social duties or subversive of good order.

Polygamy has always been odious among the northern and western nations of Europe, and, until the establishment of the Mormon Church, was almost exclusively a feature of the life of Asiatic and of African people. At common law, the second marriage was always void . . . and from the earliest history of England polygamy has been treated as an offence against society. . . .

. . . [W]e think it may safely be said there never has been a time in any State of the Union when polygamy has not been an offence against society, cognizable by the civil courts and punishable with more or less severity. In the face of all this evidence, it is impossible to believe that the constitutional guaranty of religious freedom was intended to prohibit legislation in respect to this most important feature of social life. Marriage, while from its very nature a sacred obligation, is nevertheless, in most civilized nations, a civil contract, and usually regulated by law. Upon it society may be said to be built, and out of its fruits spring social relations and social obligations and duties, with which government is necessarily required to deal. In fact, according as monogamous or polygamous marriages are allowed, do we find the principles on which the government of the people, to a greater or less extent, rests. Professor Lieber says, polygamy leads to the patriarchal principle, and which, when applied to large communities, fetters the people in stationary despotism, while that principle cannot long exist in connection with monogamy. . . .

. . . Laws are made for the government of actions, and while they cannot interfere with mere religious belief and opinions, they may with practices. Suppose one believed that human sacrifices were a necessary part of religious worship, would it be seriously contended that the civil government under which he lived could not interfere to prevent a sacrifice? Or if a wife religiously believed it was her duty to burn herself upon the funeral pile of her dead husband, would it be beyond the power of the civil government to prevent her carrying her belief into practice?

So here, as a law of the organization of society under the exclusive dominion of the United States, it is provided that plural marriages shall not be allowed. Can a man excuse his practices to the contrary because of his religious belief? To permit this would be to make the professed doctrines of religious belief superior to the law of the land, and in effect to permit every citizen to become a law unto himself. Government could exist only in name under such circumstances. . . .

JUSTICE FIELD, concurring

. . . .

C. Guns

The right to bear arms faded from prominence after the Civil War and Reconstruction. The Supreme Court in a series of decisions including *United States v. Cruikshank* (1876), *Presser v. Illinois* (1886), and *Miller v. Texas* (1894) ruled that state laws restricting gun rights did not violate the federal Constitution. These decisions unanimously held that the right to bear arms was not one of the fundamental rights protected by the privileges and immunities or due process clauses of the Fourteenth Amendment. "The second amendment declares that [the right to bear arms] shall not be infringed," Justice William Woods declared in *Presser*, "but this, as has been seen, means no more than that it shall not be infringed by Congress."

Most constitutional commentators and state courts construed state constitutional protections for the right to bear arms narrowly. They considered the right to bear arms a "collective right of the people," not a liberty of the individual. An influential article in the *Harvard Law Review* asserted:

> The right guaranteed is not so much to the individual for his private quarrels or feuds as to the people collectively for the common defense against the common enemy, foreign or domestic. The guaranty is to insure the safety of the people, their "laws and liberties," against assaults from any source or quarter, but not to give individuals singly or in groups uncontrollable means of aggression against the rights of others. Granting that the individual may carry weapons when necessary for his personal defense or that of his family or property, it is submitted that he may be forbidden to carry dangerous weapons except in cases where he has reason to believe and does believe that it is necessary for such defense. In fine, I venture the opinion that, without violence to the constitutional guaranty of the right of the people to bear arms, the carrying of weapons by individuals may be regulated, restricted, and even prohibited according as conditions and circumstances may make it necessary for the protection of the people.[29]

The Supreme Court of Kansas in *City of Salina v. Blaksley* (KS 1905) reached the same conclusion. "The provision in question," Judge Greene wrote, "applies only to the right to bear arms as a member of the state militia."[30] This militia-based interpretation of the right to bear arms was not unanimous. *State v. Kerner* (NC 1921) emphasized the right of self-defense when declaring unconstitutional a state law requiring persons who wished to carry weapons outside of their homes to obtain a license. "In the case of a riot or mob violence, or other emergency requiring the defense of public order," the state justices in North Carolina maintained, the state law "would place law-abiding citizens entirely at the mercy of the lawless element."[31]

D. Personal Freedom and Public Morality

The turn of the twentieth century witnessed unprecedented demands for federal and state regulation of individual behavior. Americans joined crusades to restrict birth control, abortion, drinking, drug use, and, as fans of *The Music Man* may remember, pool. Some states required all persons to be vaccinated against disease. Others passed eugenic laws, sterilizing criminals and persons thought to be mentally unfit. Some laws were rooted in Protestant moral virtues. Others reflected new social science research on public health. Most progressive reformers combined appeals to moral virtue and social science. These demands for state regulation inspired new constitutional rights claims.

---

29. Lucilius A. Emery, "The Constitutional Right to Keep and Bear Arms," *Harvard Law Review* 28 (1915): 477.

30. *City of Salina v. Blaksley*, 72 Kan. 230 (1905).

31. *State v. Kerner*, 181 N.C. 574 (1921).

Novel exercises of the police power, opponents claimed, unreasonably restricted traditional individual rights.

Judges treated regulations of personal behavior in much the same way that they treated economic regulations. The vast majority of federal and state regulations passed judicial muster as legitimate exercises of the police power. The Supreme Court of Washington, when sustaining a ban on opium in *Territory v. Ah Lim* (WA 1890), asserted that "the state has an interest in the health of its citizens, and has a right to see to it that its citizens are self-supporting."[32] Justice Harlan in *Jacobson v. Commonwealth of Massachusetts* (1905) rejected a claim that persons had a constitutional right to not be vaccinated against small-pox. His majority opinion declared:

> The liberty secured by the Fourteenth Amendment, this court has said, consists, in part, in the right of a person "to live and work where he will," . . . and yet he may be compelled, by force if need be, against his will and without regard to his personal wishes or his pecuniary interests, or even his religious or political convictions, to take his place in the ranks of the army of his country and risk the chance of being shot down in its defense. It is not, therefore, true that the power of the public to guard itself against imminent danger depends in every case involving the control of one's body upon his willingness to submit to reasonable regulations established by the constituted authorities, under the sanction of the State, for the purpose of protecting the public collectively against such danger.

Justice Holmes in *Buck v. Bell* (1927) notoriously asserted, "Three generations of imbeciles are enough," when sustaining a Virginia law that permitted state officials to sterilize persons they believed to be "feebleminded."

Courts struck down some state regulations of personal behavior. These cases relied on the same rights principles the justices employed in such cases as *Lochner v. New York* (1905). The Supreme Court of the United States in *Meyer v. Nebraska* (1923) asserted that "liberty" in the Fourteenth Amendment

> denotes not merely freedom from bodily restraint, but also the right of the individual to contract, to engage in any of the common occupations of life, to acquire useful knowledge, to marry, establish a home and bring up children, to worship God according to the dictates of his own conscience, and generally to enjoy those privileges long recognized at common law as essential to the orderly pursuit of happiness by free men.

Meyer declared unconstitutional a state law forbidding persons to teach German. Two years later, the justices relied on the same principles in *Pierce v. Society of Sisters* when declaring unconstitutional an Oregon law requiring children to attend public schools. Several state courts found a constitutional right to drink. When striking down a state prohibition law in *Commonwealth v. Campbell* (KY 1909), the Court of Appeals of Kentucky asserted that "the question of what a man will drink, or eat, or wear, provided the others are not invaded, is one which addresses itself alone to the will of the citizen." Unlike *Lochner*, these individual rights cases were not discredited during the New Deal. Several became foundations for judicial decisions protecting the right to use birth control and obtain a legal abortion.

Commonwealth v. Campbell, 133 Ky. 50, 117 S.W. 383 (1909)

Peter Campbell brought a quart of malt liquor into Nicholasville, Kentucky. This action violated a local ordinance that declared, "It shall be unlawful for any person . . . to bring into . . . the town of Nicholasville, Kentucky, any spirituous, vinous, malt or other intoxicating liquor." Campbell was tried, convicted, and fined $100 by a local police court. After an appellate court reversed that sentence, Campbell appealed to the state Court of Appeals of Kentucky.

Commonwealth v. Campbell *was one of many cases testing the constitutionality of local prohibition measures. While most state courts had little difficulty with laws regulating the sale of alcohol, bans on consumption were frequently struck down. The Supreme Court of Appeals in West Virginia declared in* State v. Gillman *(WV 1889) that a state prohibition law violated the privileges and immunities clause of the Fourteenth Amendment. North Carolina reached a similar conclusion in* State v. Williams *(NC 1908).*

The Court of Appeals of Kentucky declared the town prohibition ordinance unconstitutional. Judge Barker's unanimous opinion ruled that persons had a state constitutional right in Kentucky to eat and drink as they saw fit.

32. *Territory v. Ah Lim*, 1 Wash. 156 (1890).

Illustration 7-4 Mr. Dry and "Thou Shalt Not!"
"Mr. Dry" was a popular characterization of the Prohibition forces in the early twentieth century. This cartoon was published in the *New York World*, a leading voice of the northern Democratic Party published by Joseph Pulitzer.
Source: The Granger Collection, New York.

Judge Barker makes a sharp distinction between the sale and use of alcoholic beverages. Is this distinction sound? If persons have a constitutional right to drink, must other persons have a constitutional right to produce alcohol? Would the same rules cover fatty foods?

JUDGE BARKER delivered the opinion of the Court.

. . .

. . . The history of our state from its beginning shows that there was never even the claim of a right on the part of the Legislature to interfere with the citizen using liquor for his own comfort, provided that in so doing he committed no offense against public decency by being intoxicated; and we are of opinion that it never has been within the competency of the Legislature to so restrict the liberty of the citizen, and certainly not since the adoption of the present Constitution. The Bill of Rights, which declares that among the inalienable rights possessed by the citizens is that of seeking and pursuing their safety and happiness, and that the absolute and arbitrary power over the lives, liberty, and property of freeman exists nowhere in a republic, not even in the largest majority, would be but an empty sound if the Legislature could prohibit the citizen the right of owning or drinking liquor, when in so doing he did not offend the laws of decency by being intoxicated in public. Man in his natural state has a right to do whatever he chooses and has the power to do. When he becomes a member of organized society, under governmental regulation, he surrenders, of necessity, all of his natural right the exercise of which is, or may be, injurious to his fellow citizens. This is the price that he pays for governmental protection, but it is not within the competency of a free government to invade the sanctity of the absolute rights of the citizen any further than the direct protection of society requires. Therefore the question of what a man will drink, or eat, or own, provided the rights of others are not invaded, is one which addresses itself alone to the will of the citizen. It is not within the competency of government to invade the privacy of a citizen's life and to regulate his conduct in matters in which he alone is concerned, or to prohibit him any liberty the exercise of which will not directly injure society.

. . .

. . . Nothing that we have said herein is in derogation of the power of the state under the Constitution to regulate the sale of liquor, or any other use of it which in itself is inimical to the public health, morals, or safety; but as spirituous liquor is a legitimate subject of property, its ownership and possession cannot be denied when that ownership and possession is not in itself injurious to the public. The right to use liquor for one's own comfort, if the use is without direct injury to the public, is one of the citizen's natural and inalienable rights, guaranteed to him by the Constitution, and cannot be abridged as long as the absolute power of a majority is limited by our present Constitution. The theory of our government is to allow the largest liberty to the individual commensurate with the public safety, or, as it has been otherwise expressed, that government is best which governs the least. Under our institutions there is no room for that inquisitorial and protective spirit which seeks to regulate the conduct of men in matters in themselves indifferent, and to make them conform to a standard, not of their own choosing, but the choosing of the lawgiver; that inquisitorial and protective spirit which seeks to prescribe what a man shall eat and wear, or drink or think, thus crushing out individuality and insuring Chinese inertia by the enforcement of the use of the Chinese shoe in the matter of the private conduct of mankind. We hold that the police power—vague and wide and undefined as it is—has limits, and in matters such as that we have in hand its utmost frontier is marked by the maxim: "Sic utere tuo ut alienum non lædas" [*"so use your own so as not to harm that of another"*].

Meyer v. Nebraska, 262 U.S. 390 (1923)

Robert T. Meyer taught at Zion Parochial School in Hamilton County, Nebraska. The children of German immigrants who attended the school received their religious instruction in German. This practice violated a Nebraska law that declared, "No person, individually or as a teacher, shall, in any private, denominational, parochial or public school, teach any subject to any person in any language than the English language." A trial court found Meyer guilty of violating this statute and fined him $25. After the Supreme Court of Nebraska sustained this sentence, Meyer appealed to the Supreme Court of the United States.

The Supreme Court by a 7-2 vote declared the Nebraska law unconstitutional. Justice James McReynolds asserted both that teaching German was a liberty protected by the Fourteenth Amendment and that the prohibition was supported by no legitimate rationale for the promotion of public health, safety, or morality. The Nebraska law prohibiting the use of German in schools was part of a national effort to assimilate immigrants by insisting on the English language. Does Justice McReynolds reject this goal or merely the law as a means to a goal? Compare Meyer *to* Lochner v. New York *(1905). Is* Meyer *a straightforward application of* Lochner, *complete with Justice Holmes's dissent? Do the justices debate the importance of protecting certain fundamental rights or dispute whether the law actually advances public health, safety, or morality? If the same lawsuit were brought today, the decision in* Meyer *would no doubt rely heavily on the freedom of religion. Is* Meyer *really a religious freedom case brought before the incorporation of the First Amendment? What would be the result if the same case came before the contemporary Supreme Court?*

JUSTICE McREYNOLDS delivered the opinion of the Court.

. . .

While this Court has not attempted to define with exactness the liberty . . . guaranteed [by the due process clause of the Fourteenth Amendment], the term has received much consideration and some of the included things have been definitely stated. Without doubt, it denotes not merely freedom from bodily restraint, but also the right of the individual to contract, to engage in any of the common occupations of life, to acquire useful knowledge, to marry, establish a home and bring up children, to worship God according to the dictates of his own conscience, and generally to enjoy those privileges long recognized at common law as essential to the orderly pursuit of happiness by free men. . . .

The American people have always regarded education and acquisition of knowledge as matters of supreme importance which should be diligently promoted. . . . Corresponding to the right of control, it is the natural duty of the parent to give his children education suitable to their station in life, and nearly all the States, including Nebraska, enforce this obligation by compulsory laws.

Practically, education of the young is only possible in schools conducted by especially qualified persons who devote themselves thereto. The calling always has been regarded as useful and honorable, essential, indeed, to the public welfare. Mere knowledge of the German language cannot reasonably be regarded as harmful. Heretofore it has been commonly looked upon as helpful and desirable. Plaintiff in error taught this language in school as part of his occupation. His right thus to teach and the right of parents to engage him so to instruct their children, we think, are within the liberty of the Amendment.

. . .

It is said the purpose of the legislation was to promote civic development by inhibiting training and education of the immature in foreign tongues and ideals before they could learn English and acquire American ideals, and "that the English language should be and become the mother tongue of all children reared in this State." It is also affirmed that the foreign born population is very large, that certain communities commonly use foreign words, follow foreign leaders, move in a foreign atmosphere, and that the children are thereby hindered from becoming citizens of the most useful type, and the public safety is imperiled.

That the State may do much, go very far, indeed, in order to improve the quality of its citizens, physically, mentally and morally, is clear; but the individual has certain fundamental rights which must be respected. The protection of the Constitution extends to all, to those who speak other languages as well as to those born with English on the tongue. Perhaps it would be highly advantageous if all had ready understanding of our ordinary speech, but this cannot be coerced by methods which conflict with the Constitution—a desirable end cannot be promoted by prohibited means.

. . .

The desire of the legislature to foster a homogeneous people with American ideals prepared readily to understand current discussions of civic matters is easy to appreciate. Unfortunate experiences during the late war and aversion toward every characteristic of truculent adversaries were certainly enough to quicken that aspiration. But the means adopted, we think, exceed the limitations upon the power of the State and conflict with rights assured to plaintiff in error. . . .

. . . [M]ere abuse incident to an occupation ordinarily useful is not enough to justify its abolition, although regulation may be entirely proper. No emergency has arisen which renders knowledge by a child of some language other than English so clearly harmful as to justify its inhibition with the consequent infringement of rights long freely enjoyed. We are constrained to conclude that the statute as applied is arbitrary and without reasonable relation to any end within the competency of the State.

. . .

JUSTICE HOLMES, dissenting.[33]

We all agree, I take it, that it is desirable that all the citizens of the United States should speak a common tongue, and therefore that the end aimed at by the statute is a lawful and proper one. The only question is whether the means adopted deprive teachers of the liberty secured to them by the Fourteenth Amendment. It is with hesitation and unwillingness that I differ from my brethren with regard to a law like this, but I cannot bring my mind to believe that, in some circumstances, and circumstances existing, it is said, in Nebraska, the statute might not be regarded as a reasonable or even necessary method of reaching the desired result. The part of the act with which we are concerned deals with the teaching of young children. Youth is the time when familiarity with a language is established and if there are sections in the state where a child would hear only Polish or French or German spoken at home, I am not prepared to say that it is unreasonable to provide that, in his early years, he shall hear and speak only English at school. But, if it is reasonable, it is not an undue restriction of the liberty either of teacher or scholar. No one would doubt that a teacher might be forbidden to teach many things, and the only criterion of his liberty under the Constitution that I can think of is "whether, considering the end in view, the statute passes the bounds of reason and assumes the character of a merely arbitrary fiat." . . . I think I appreciate the objection to the law, but it appears to me to present a question upon which men reasonably might differ, and therefore I am unable to say that the Constitution of the United States prevents the experiment's being tried.

. . .

33. This dissent was actually issued in a companion case, *Bartels v. Iowa*, 262 U.S. 404 (1923).

JUSTICE SUTHERLAND concurs in this opinion.

Buck v. Bell, 274 U.S. 200 (1927)

Carrie Buck was a nineteen-year-old rape victim who became pregnant. The family with whom she lived had her committed to the State Colony for Epileptics and Feeble-Minded. After she gave birth to her daughter, the superintendent of the colony recommended sterilization when he discovered that a revised Binet-Simon I.Q. test revealed Carrie Buck's mental age as nine and her mother's mental age as less than eight. Virginia law permitted forced sterilization of people considered "feebleminded." That law reflected Progressive Era enthusiasm for race improvement through eugenic sterilization.The Supreme Court of Appeals of the State of Virginia approved the sterilization order. Buck appealed to the Supreme Court of the United States.

The Supreme Court by an 8-1 vote sustained the Virginia forced sterilization law. Justice Holmes, an enthusiast for eugenics, insisted that state laws mandating sterilization were reasonable exercises of the police power. How does he reach that conclusion? Read Buck *in light of Holmes's dissents in freedom of contract and freedom of speech cases. How does the opinion influence your understanding of progressive constitutional thought before the New Deal?*

Subsequent investigations found that neither Carrie Buck nor her daughter Vivian were mentally handicapped.

JUSTICE HOLMES delivered the opinion of the Court.

. . .

. . . The judgment finds the facts that have been recited and that Carrie Buck "is the probable potential parent of socially inadequate offspring, likewise afflicted, that she may be sexually sterilized without detriment to her general health and that her welfare and that of society will be promoted by her sterilization," and thereupon makes the order. In view of the general declarations of the Legislature and the specific findings of the Court obviously we cannot say as matter of law that the grounds do not exist, and if they exist they justify the result. We have seen more than once that the public welfare may call upon the best citizens for their lives. It would be strange if it could not call upon those who already sap the strength of the State for these lesser sacrifices, often not felt to be such by those concerned, in order to prevent our being swamped with incompetence. It is better for all the world, if instead of waiting to execute degenerate offspring for crime, or to let them starve for their imbecility, society can prevent those who are manifestly unfit from continuing their kind. The principle that sustains compulsory vaccination is broad enough to cover cutting the Fallopian tubes. Three generations of imbeciles are enough. But, it is said, however it might be if this reasoning were applied generally, it fails when it is confined to the small number who are in the institutions named and is not applied to the multitudes outside. It is the usual last resort of constitutional arguments to point out shortcomings of this sort. But the answer is that the law does all that is needed when it does all that it can, indicates a policy, applies it to all within the lines, and seeks to bring within the lines all similarly situated so far and so fast as its means allow. Of course so far as the operations enable those who otherwise must be kept confined to be returned to the world, and thus open the asylum to others, the equality aimed at will be more nearly reached.

JUSTICE BUTLER dissents.

IV. Democratic Rights

MAJOR DEVELOPMENTS

- First federal laws restricting speech since 1798
- Justice Holmes introduces the "clear and present danger" test for free speech
- Ongoing debates over universal suffrage and laws regulating elections
- Efforts to tighten immigration and naturalization

The Republican Era witnessed sharp disputes over democracy and pluralism. Supreme Court opinions in the late nineteenth century insisted that the United States was a constitutional *republic*. Justice Louis Brandeis, appointed by President Wilson in 1915, wrote the first opinions in Supreme Court history that referred to the United States as a constitutional *democracy*. This debate transcended party labels. Members of the Republican Party had no greater tendency to claim the United States was a republic than members of the Democratic Party. Many constitutional decision makers commonly referred to the United States as a democratic republic. Still, more than a verbal quibble was taking place. Civic republicans in the eighteenth and nineteenth centuries emphasized the importance of cultural homogeneity and consensus on basic values. In contrast, a growing number of Americans at the turn of the twentieth century celebrated pluralism. Some clashes between civic republicans and pluralists took place over such individual rights issues as prohibition and eugenics. Others concerned free speech, voting, and citizenship.

Small-r republicans were far more fearful of immigration and social pluralism than small-d democrats. Small-r republicans worried about the increasing numbers of immigrants and citizens with "un-American" cultural, economic, and political values. They believed that these threats were best countered by restrictions on free speech, limits on suffrage, restrictions on immigration (particularly Chinese immigration), and the assimilation of "hyphenated Americans" (e.g., Irish-Americans, Russian-Americans). Small-d democrats were more welcoming of increased social pluralism. They believed that Americans should adopt speech, voting, and citizenship policies that encouraged a multiplicity of ideas and values.

Debates over the merits of cultural pluralism more often divided progressives than divided progressives from conservatives. Woodrow Wilson, who ran for president as a progressive, demanded legislation restricting free speech during World War I and frequently spoke about the threats presented by hyphenated Americans. Brandeis, a Wilson appointee to the Supreme Court, penned prominent dissents defending broad free speech rights and essays championing cultural pluralism.

A. Free Speech

The constitutional politics of free speech was reconfigured at the turn of the twentieth century. Conservative libertarians who regarded both free speech and the freedom of contract as aspects of "the right of the citizen to be free in the enjoyment of all his faculties"[34] were the leading proponents of expression rights during the first half of the Republican Era. Progressives who linked free speech to democratic governance were the leading proponents of free speech in the second half of the Republican Era. Most progressives, however, insisted that elected representatives had the power to regulate free speech and the liberty of contract whenever such regulation promoted the public good.

Events immediately before and during World War I transformed free speech debates in the United States.[35] Prominent Americans feared that the new wave of immigrants from eastern and southern Europe either retained loyalties to their place of birth or were committed to a Socialist revolution. These fears were heightened when individual anarchists at the turn of the century assassinated several heads of state (including President William McKinley), the Communist revolution in Russia toppled the Czar, the Socialist Party in the United States gained an increasing share of the vote in many urban communities, and militant labor leaders threatened mass strikes. Even before the United States entered World War I, many Americans were calling for legislation that would restrict "disloyal" utterances, usually associated with immigrants. Woodrow Wilson's State of the Union Address in 1915 asserted:

> I am sorry to say that the gravest threats against our national peace and safety have been uttered within our own borders. There are citizens of the United States, I blush to admit, born under other flags but welcomed under our generous naturalization laws to the full freedom and opportunity of America, who have poured the poison of disloyalty into the very arteries of our national life; who have sought to bring the authority and good name of our Government into contempt, to destroy our industries wherever they thought it effective for their vindictive purposes to strike at them, and to debase our politics to the uses of foreign intrigue. Their number is not great as compared with the whole number of those sturdy hosts by which our nation has been enriched in recent generations out of virile foreign stock; but it is great enough to have brought deep disgrace upon us and to have made it necessary that we should promptly make use of processes of law by which we may be purged of their corrupt distempers. . . . I urge you to enact such laws at the earliest possible moment and feel that in doing so I am urging you to do nothing less than save the honor and self-respect of the nation. Such creatures of passion, disloyalty,

34. *Allgeyer*, 165 U.S. 578.

35. See Mark A. Graber, *Transforming Free Speech: The Ambiguous Legacy of Civil Libertarianism* (Berkeley: University of California Press, 1992).

> and anarchy must be crushed out. They are not many, but they are infinitely malignant, and the hand of our power should close over them at once. They have formed plots to destroy property, they have entered into conspiracies against the neutrality of the Government, they have sought to pry into every confidential transaction of the Government in order to serve interests alien to our own. It is possible to deal with these things very effectually. I need not suggest the terms in which they may be dealt with.

These concerns inspired the passage of the Espionage Act of 1917, the Sedition Act of 1918, and many similar state statutes. The crucial provision of the Espionage Act of 1917 declared,

> Whoever, when the United States is at war, shall wilfully make or convey false reports or false statements with intent to interfere with the operation or success of the military or naval forces of the United States or to promote the success of its enemies and whoever when the United States is at war, shall wilfully cause or attempt to cause insubordination, disloyalty, mutiny, refusal of duty, in the military or naval forces of the United States, or shall wilfully obstruct the recruiting or enlistment service of the United States, to the injury of the service or of the United States, shall be punished by a fine of not more than $10,000 or imprisonment for not more than twenty years, or both.[36]

This was no idle, symbolic gesture. More than two thousand persons were arrested for violating federal restrictions on speech. More than one thousand were convicted.

The Supreme Court initially relied on traditional conceptions of the police powers when it unanimously sustained the convictions of persons found guilty of violating the Espionage Act or related restrictions on free speech. Judicial opinions in free speech cases emphasized that elected officials could restrict speech when reasonable persons might think the regulation served the public interest. In *Schenck v. United States* (1919), Justice Holmes asserted,

> The question in every case is whether the words used are used in such circumstances and are of such a nature as to create a clear and present danger that they will bring about the substantive evils that Congress has a right to prevent. It is a question of proximity and degree. When a nation is at war many things that might be said in time of peace are such a hindrance to its effort that their utterance will not be endured so long as men fight and that no Court could regard them as protected by any constitutional right.

One week later, when sustaining the conviction of prominent Socialist leader Eugene V. Debs, Holmes asserted that persons could be constitutionally convicted when "the words used had as their natural tendency and reasonably probable effect to obstruct the recruiting service."[37] This formulation, different in tone from "clear and present danger," is sometimes referred to as the "bad tendency test." This test permits government to regulate all speech that may cause some harm that the government has the authority to prevent (such as draft obstruction, or even litter).

The Red Scare that took place after World War I inspired continued restrictions on political dissent, but these restrictions were no longer unanimously sustained by the Supreme Court. In *Abrams v. United States* (1919), the justices ruled by a 7-2 vote that Jacob Abrams could be sentenced to ten years in prison for urging workers to protest American involvement in the Russian Revolution by a general strike. Justice Holmes, joined by Justice Brandeis, issued a sharp dissent. The most famous passage in that dissent asserted,

> But when men have realized that time has upset many fighting faiths, they may come to believe even more than they believe the very foundations of their own conduct that the ultimate good desired is better reached by free trade in ideas—that the best test of truth is the power of the thought to get itself accepted in the competition of the market, and that truth is the only ground upon which their wishes safely can be carried out. That, at any rate, is the theory of our Constitution. It is an experiment, as all life is an experiment. Every year, if not every day, we have to wager our salvation upon some prophecy based upon imperfect knowledge. While that experiment is part of our system, I think that we should be eternally vigilant against attempts to check the expression of opinions that we loathe and believe to be fraught with death, unless they so im-

36. 40 U.S. Stat. 553, 553 (1917).

37. *Debs v. United States*, 249 U.S. 211 (1919).

minently threaten immediate interference with the lawful and pressing purposes of the law that an immediate check is required to save the country.

Many scholars think that Holmes, perhaps influenced by District Court Judge Learned Hand's more libertarian opinion in *Masses Publishing Co. v. Patten* (D.C. N.Y. 1917) or Harvard Law Professor Zechariah Chafee's defense of free speech in *The New Republic*,[38] became more protective of free speech rights.[39] The Holmes dissent in *Abrams* could nevertheless be reconciled with traditional doctrine. Holmes noted that the statute in question did not specifically prohibit what Abrams said and that Abrams's "poor and puny anonymities" were highly unlikely to have any impact on the body politic.

By the end of the Republican Era the more progressive justices on the court were clearly imposing a higher standard in free speech cases than was called for by inherited police powers logic. Brandeis's concurring opinion in *Whitney v. California* (1927) rejected claims that elected officials could regulate speech as freely as he believed they could regulate property. He insisted that speech, unlike property, could be regulated only when persons incited imminent and serious violence. By a 5-4 vote in *Near v. Minnesota* (1931), the Supreme Court formally imposed a similarly high standard when declaring constitutional limits on legislation imposing prior restraints on speech. Chief Justice Hughes's majority opinion declared that elected officials could adopt prior restraints "only in exceptional cases."

38. Zechariah Chafee, Jr., "Freedom of Speech," *The New Republic* (November 16, 1918): 67.

39. Holmes corresponded with both Hand and Chafee in period between his *Schenck* opinion and *Abrams* dissent. See Gerald Gunther, "Learned Hand and the Origins of Modern First Amendment Doctrine: Some Fragments of History," *Stanford Law Review* 27 (1975): 719.

Table 7-5 Selection of U.S. Supreme Court Cases Reviewing State and Federal Laws Restricting Dangerous Speech

Case	Vote	Outcome	Decision
United States ex rel. Turner v. Williams, 194 U.S. 279 (1904)	9-0	Upheld	Anarchist aliens can be denied entry into the country because of their views
Fox v. Washington, 236 U.S. 273 (1915)	9-0	Upheld	Speech that "encourages and incites" illegal behavior can be prohibited
Schenck v. United States, 249 U.S. 47 (1919)	9-0	Upheld	Writers of pamphlets can be punished if the writings present a clear and present danger that military recruitment will be disrupted
Abrams v. United States, 250 U.S. 616 (1919)	7-2	Upheld	Writers of leaflets that have a tendency to obstruct the war effort may be punished
Gilbert v. Minnesota, 254 U.S. 325 (1920)	7-2	Upheld	States may also punish speech that has the tendency to obstruct the federal war effort
Gitlow v. New York, 268 U.S. 652 (1925)	7-2	Upheld	Writers of pamphlets with a tendency to produce industrial unrest and a threat to government stability can be prosecuted for criminal anarchism
Whitney v. California, 274 U.S. 357 (1927)	9-0	Upheld	States may punish those who use speech to produce a clear and present danger to society by, for example, forming a revolutionary Communist Party
Near v. Minnesota, 283 U.S. 697 (1931)	5-4	Struck down	State efforts to block the publication of "defamatory" newspaper was an unconstitutional prior restraint
DeJonge v. Oregon, 299 U.S. 353 (1937)	9-0	Struck down	Individuals have a right of association that encompasses the right to speak at a public meeting sponsored by the Communist Party

(*Continued*)

Table 7-5 *(Continued)*

Case	Vote	Outcome	Decision
Herndon v. Lowry, 301 U.S. 242 (1937)	5-4	Struck down	Membership in the Communist Party, and solicitation of a few members, fails to establish an attempt to incite others to insurrection
Chaplinsky v. New Hampshire, 315 U.S. 568 (1942)	9-0	Upheld	"Fighting words" or verbal insults are a type of speech, like libel and obscenity, with no social value that are not entitled to constitutional protection
Terminiello v. Chicago, 337 U.S. 1 (1949)	5-4	Struck down	Inflammatory speech is constitutionally protected, even if the audience reacts violently toward the speaker
Feiner v. New York, 340 U.S. 315 (1951)	6-4	Upheld	Speech that causes imminent public discord or incites a riot may be suppressed
Dennis v. United States, 341 U.S. 494 (1951)	6-2	Upheld	A leader of the revolutionary Communist Party may be charged with conspiracy that presents a clear and present danger to the government
Yates v. United States, 354 U.S. 298 (1957)	6-1	Struck down	Speech is protected if one advocates or teaches about forcible overthrow of the government as an abstract principle rather than as an incitement to concrete action
Sweezy v. New Hampshire, 354 U.S. 234 (1957)	6-2	Struck down	Legislative investigation into a college teacher's lectures on socialism and membership in the Progressive Party is unconstitutional
Brandenburg v. Ohio, 395 U.S. 444 (1969)	9-0	Struck down	Government may only punish speech that aims to produce imminent lawless action, not speech that merely advocates lawless action
R.A.V. v. City of St. Paul, 505 U.S. 377 (1992)	9-0	Struck down	Hate crimes ordinance held to be unconstitutional content based restriction on speech
Virginia v. Black, 538 U.S. 343 (2003)	7-2	Struck down	Cross-burning statutes are unconstitutional to the extent that jury may presume a threat merely from evidence of cross-burning
Holder v. Humanitarian Law Project, 130 S. Ct. 2705 (2010)	6-3	Upheld	Congress may prohibit individuals and groups from providing "material support," including "expert advice and assistance," to specified terrorist groups
Snyder v. Phelps, 131 S.Ct. 1207 (2011)	8-1	Struck down	Speech on a public sidewalk, about a public issue, cannot be liable for a tort of emotional distress, even if the speech is outside a memorial service and is found to be "outrageous"

Schenck v. United States, 249 U.S. 47 (1919)

Charles Schenck was the general secretary of the American Socialist Party. American Socialists opposed the government's decision in 1917 to declare war on Germany. During the week of August 13–20, 1917, Schenck and other Socialists distributed pamphlets to the general public and persons eligible for the draft that condemned the Wilson administration and insisted that the draft was unconstitutional. Schenck was promptly arrested, convicted, and sentenced to ten years in prison for violating the Espionage Act of 1917. He appealed to the Supreme Court of the United States.

The Supreme Court unanimously ruled that Schenck was constitutionally convicted. Justice Holmes's majority opinion declared that government may limit speech when there is "a clear and present danger" that the speaker "will bring about the substantive evils that Congress has a right to prevent." How protective of speech was this test in Schenck? *Suppose that Schenck had merely told persons eligible for the draft that they would be better off going to college and making money than volunteering for the army. Could he have been constitutionally convicted under the Espionage Act?*

JUSTICE HOLMES delivered the opinion of the Court.

...

The document in question upon its first printed side recited the first section of the Thirteenth Amendment, said that the idea embodied in it was violated by the conscription act and that a conscript is little better than a convict. In impassioned language it intimated that conscription was despotism in its worst form and a monstrous wrong against humanity in the interest of Wall Street's chosen few. It said, "Do not submit to intimidation," but in form at least confined itself to peaceful measures such as a petition for the repeal of the act. The other and later printed side of the sheet was headed "Assert Your Rights." It stated reasons for alleging that any one violated the Constitution when he refused to recognize "your right to assert your opposition to the draft," and went on, "If you do not assert and support your rights, you are helping to deny or disparage rights which it is the solemn duty of all citizens and residents of the United States to retain." It described the arguments on the other side as coming from cunning politicians and a mercenary capitalist press, and even silent consent to the conscription law as helping to support an infamous conspiracy. It denied the power to send our citizens away to foreign shores to shoot up the people of other lands, and added that words could not express the condemnation such cold-blooded ruthlessness deserves , &c., &c., winding up, "You must do your share to maintain, support and uphold the rights of the people of this country." Of course the document would not have been sent unless it had been intended to have some effect, and we do not see what effect it could be expected to have upon persons subject to the draft except to influence them to obstruct the carrying of it out. The defendants do not deny that the jury might find against them on this point.

But it is said, suppose that that was the tendency of this circular, it is protected by the First Amendment to the Constitution. . . . It well may be that the prohibition of laws abridging the freedom of speech is not confined to previous restraints, although to prevent them may have been the main purpose. . . . We admit that in many places and in ordinary times the defendants in saying all that was said in the circular would have been within their constitutional rights. But the character of every act depends upon the circumstances in which it is done. . . . The most stringent protection of free speech would not protect a man in falsely shouting fire in a theatre and causing a panic. . . . The question in every case is whether the words used are used in such circumstances and are of such a nature as to create a clear and present danger that they will bring about the substantive evils that Congress has a right to prevent. It is a question of proximity and degree. When a nation is at war many things that might be said in time of peace are such a hindrance to its effort that their utterance will not be endured so long as men fight and that no Court could regard them as protected by any constitutional right. It seems to be admitted that if an actual obstruction of the recruiting service were proved, liability for words that produced that effect might be enforced. . . . If the act, (speaking, or circulating a paper,) its tendency and the intent with which it is done are the same, we perceive no ground for saying that success alone warrants making the act a crime. . . .

Whitney v. California, 274 U.S. 357 (1927)

In 1919 Charlotte Anita Whitney helped to organize the California branch of the Communist Labor Party. The platform and declaration of principles of the national organization asserted:

> *The Communist Labor Party of the United States of America declares itself in full harmony with the revolutionary working class parties of all countries and stated by the Third International formed at Moscow.*
>
> *The most important means of capturing state power for the workers is the action of the masses, proceeding from the place where the workers are gathered together—in the shops and factories. The use of the political machinery of the capitalist state for this purpose is only secondary.*[40]

40. "Platform and Program of the Communist Labor Party of America," Adopted by its Founding Convention, Sept. 5, 1919, as published in *The Ohio Socialist*, Sept. 17, 1919 at 3.

Illustration 7-5 You and I Cannot Live in the Same Land
This 1916 cover illustration from the San Francisco anarchist magazine *The Blast* reflects the sense of conflict between the government and dissident political movements in the early twentieth century, as well as the growing interest in free speech arguments on the political left during World War I.

Source: The Blast, Volume. 1, Issue 15, July 1, 1916, page 1123. Republished in Alexander Berkman, ed., *The Blast* (Oakland, CA: AK Press, 2005).

Whitney believed that the California chapter should take a more moderate position. At the state organizing convention, she proposed the following resolution.

> *The C. L. P. of California fully recognizes the value of political action as a means of spreading communist propaganda; it insists that in proportion to the development of the economic strength of the working class, it, the working class, must also develop its political power. The C. L. P. of California proclaims and insists that the capture of political power, locally or nationally by the revolutionary working class can be of tremendous assistance to the workers in their struggle of emancipation. Therefore, we again urge the workers who are possessed of the right of franchise to cast their votes for the party which represents their immediate and final interest—the C. L. P.—at all elections, being fully convinced of the utter futility of obtaining any real measure of justice or freedom under officials elected by parties owned and controlled by the capitalist class.*[41]

Whitney was subsequently arrested and tried for criminal syndicalism, understood as "advocating, teaching or aiding and abetting the commission of crime, sabotage (which word is hereby defined as meaning willful and malicious physical damage or injury to physical property), or unlawful acts of force and violence or unlawful methods of terrorism as a means of accomplishing a change in industrial ownership or control or effecting any political change." She was convicted, even though she testified at trial that she only championed legal methods for promoting social change. The Supreme Court of California sustained her conviction. Whitney appealed those rulings to the Supreme Court of the United States.

The Supreme Court had reviewed a similar challenge to a state criminal anarchy statute two years earlier in Gitlow v. New York *(1925). The justices in that case incorporated the First Amendment. Justice Sanford's majority opinion agreed with the defense that "freedom of speech and of the press . . . are among the fundamental personal rights and 'liberties' protected by the due process clause of the Fourteenth Amendment from impairment by the States." That principle, however, did Benjamin Gitlow little good. The justices by a 7-2 vote sustained his conviction for publishing "The Left-Wing Manifesto." "That a State in the exercise of its police power may punish those who abuse this freedom by utterances inimical to the public welfare, tending to corrupt public morals, incite to crime, or disturb the public peace," Justice Sanford stated, "is not open to question." Justices Holmes and Brandeis dissented.*

The Supreme Court also sustained Whitney's conviction by the same 7-2 vote. Justice Sanford's majority opinion claimed that courts should defer to legislative findings that certain utterances tended to present a clear and present danger. Justice Brandeis insisted that convictions for speech were constitutional only if the particular speaker was guilty of inciting an audience to imminent and serious violence. As precedential support for this claim, Brandeis cited a series of cases in which the justices protected property rights. Was this citation correct? Did the justices in Lochner v. New York *(1905) worry about whether Joseph Lochner's actions threatened public harm, or did they conclude that baking as a whole was not an unhealthy trade? Suppose that in 1925 the Supreme Court had abandoned the freedom of contract. Could Brandeis have written the* Whitney *concurrence?*

The most famous passage of the Whitney *concurrence begins by asserting, "Those who won our independence." Does Brandeis accurately describe how the American revolutionaries or constitutional framers understood free speech? Does he accurately describe their more general principles? What, in your judgment, provides the foundation for Brandeis's theory of free speech? Is that theory sound?*

JUSTICE SANFORD delivered the opinion of the Court.

. . .

. . . [T]he freedom of speech which is secured by the Constitution does not confer an absolute right to speak, without responsibility, whatever one may choose, or an unrestricted and unbridled license giving immunity for every possible use of language and preventing the punishment of those who abuse this freedom; and [that] a State in the exercise of its police power may punish those who abuse this freedom by utterances inimical to the public welfare, tending to incite to crime, disturb the public peace, or endanger the foundations of organized government and threaten its overthrow by unlawful means, is not open to question. . . .

By enacting the provisions of the Syndicalism Act the State has declared, through its legislative body, that to knowingly be or become a member of or assist in organizing an association to advocate, teach or aid and abet the commission of crimes or unlawful acts of force, violence or terrorism as a means of

41. Haig A. Bosmajian, *Anita Whitney, Louis Brandeis, and the First Amendment* (Cranbury, NJ: Associated University Presses, 2010), 75.

accomplishing industrial or political changes, involves such danger to the public peace and the security of the State, that these acts should be penalized in the exercise of its police power. That determination must be given great weight. Every presumption is to be indulged in favor of the validity of the statute . . . and it may not be declared unconstitutional unless it is an arbitrary or unreasonable attempt to exercise the authority vested in the State in the public interest. . . .

The essence of the offense denounced by the Act is the combining with others in an association for the accomplishment of the desired ends through the advocacy and use of criminal and unlawful methods. It partakes of the nature of a criminal conspiracy. . . . That such united and joint action involves even greater danger to the public peace and security than the isolated utterances and acts of individuals is clear. . . .

. . .

JUSTICE BRANDEIS, concurring.

. . .

Despite arguments to the contrary which had seemed to me persuasive, it is settled that the due process clause of the Fourteenth Amendment applies to matters of substantive law as well as to matters of procedure. Thus all fundamental rights comprised within the term liberty are protected by the federal Constitution from invasion by the states. The right of free speech, the right to teach and the right of assembly are, of course, fundamental rights. . . . . These may not be denied or abridged. But, although the rights of free speech and assembly are fundamental, they are not in their nature absolute. Their exercise is subject to restriction, if the particular restriction proposed is required in order to protect the state from destruction or from serious injury, political, economic or moral. That the necessity which is essential to a valid restriction does not exist unless speech would produce, or is intended to produce, a clear and imminent danger of some substantive evil which the state constitutionally may seek to prevent has been settled. See *Schenck v. United States* (1918). . . .

. . . The Legislature must obviously decide, in the first instance, whether a danger exists which calls for a particular protective measure. But where a statute is valid only in case certain conditions exist, the enactment of the statute cannot alone establish the facts which are essential to its validity. Prohibitory legislation has repeatedly been held invalid, because unnecessary, where the denial of liberty involved was that of engaging in a particular business. The powers of the courts to strike down an offending law are no less when the interests involved are not property rights, but the fundamental personal rights of free speech and assembly.

. . .

Those who won our independence believed that the final end of the state was to make men free to develop their faculties, and that in its government the deliberative forces should prevail over the arbitrary. They valued liberty both as an end and as a means. They believed liberty to be the secret of happiness and courage to be the secret of liberty. They believed that freedom to think as you will and to speak as you think are means indispensable to the discovery and spread of political truth; that without free speech and assembly discussion would be futile; that with them, discussion affords ordinarily adequate protection against the dissemination of noxious doctrine; that the greatest menace to freedom is an inert people; that public discussion is a political duty; and that this should be a fundamental principle of the American government. They recognized the risks to which all human institutions are subject. But they knew that order cannot be secured merely through fear of punishment for its infraction; that it is hazardous to discourage thought, hope and imagination; that fear breeds repression; that repression breeds hate; that hate menaces stable government; that the path of safety lies in the opportunity to discuss freely supposed grievances and proposed remedies; and that the fitting remedy for evil counsels is good ones. Believing in the power of reason as applied through public discussion, they eschewed silence coerced by law—the argument of force in its worst form. Recognizing the occasional tyrannies of governing majorities, they amended the Constitution so that free speech and assembly should be guaranteed.

Fear of serious injury cannot alone justify suppression of free speech and assembly. Men feared witches and burnt women. It is the function of speech to free men from the bondage of irrational fears. To justify suppression of free speech there must be reasonable ground to fear that serious evil will result if free speech is practiced. There must be reasonable ground to believe that the danger apprehended is imminent. There must be reasonable ground to believe that the evil to be prevented is a serious one. Every denunciation of existing law tends in some measure to increase the probability that there will be violation of it. Condonation of a breach enhances the probability.

Expressions of approval add to the probability. Propagation of the criminal state of mind by teaching syndicalism increases it. Advocacy of lawbreaking heightens it still further. But even advocacy of violation, however reprehensible morally, is not a justification for denying free speech where the advocacy falls short of incitement and there is nothing to indicate that the advocacy would be immediately acted on. The wide difference between advocacy and incitement, between preparation and attempt, between assembling and conspiracy, must be borne in mind. In order to support a finding of clear and present danger it must be shown either that immediate serious violence was to be expected or was advocated, or that the past conduct furnished reason to believe that such advocacy was then contemplated.

Those who won our independence by revolution were not cowards. They did not fear political change. They did not exalt order at the cost of liberty. To courageous, self-reliant men, with confidence in the power of free and fearless reasoning applied through the processes of popular government, no danger flowing from speech can be deemed clear and present, unless the incidence of the evil apprehended is so imminent that it may befall before there is opportunity for full discussion. If there be time to expose through discussion the falsehood and fallacies, to avert the evil by the processes of education, the remedy to be applied is more speech, not enforced silence. Only an emergency can justify repression. Such must be the rule if authority is to be reconciled with freedom. Such, in my opinion, is the command of the Constitution. It is therefore always open to Americans to challenge a law abridging free speech and assembly by showing that there was no emergency justifying it.

Moreover, even imminent danger cannot justify resort to prohibition of these functions essential to effective democracy, unless the evil apprehended is relatively serious. Prohibition of free speech and assembly is a measure so stringent that it would be inappropriate as the means for averting a relatively trivial harm to society. A police measure may be unconstitutional merely because the remedy, although effective as means of protection, is unduly harsh or oppressive. Thus, a state might, in the exercise of its police power, make any trespass upon the land of another a crime, regardless of the results or of the intent or purpose of the trespasser. It might, also, punish an attempt, a conspiracy, or an incitement to commit the trespass. But it is hardly conceivable that this court would hold constitutional a statute which punished as a felony the mere voluntary assembly with a society formed to teach that pedestrians had the moral right to cross uninclosed, unposted, waste lands and to advocate their doing so, even if there was imminent danger that advocacy would lead to a trespass. The fact that speech is likely to result in some violence or in destruction of property is not enough to justify its suppression. There must be the probability of serious injury to the State. Among free men, the deterrents ordinarily to be applied to prevent crime are education and punishment for violations of the law, not abridgment of the rights of free speech and assembly.

. . .

[*Brandeis concurred rather than dissented only because Whitney did not raise these issues at trial.*]

Near v. Minnesota, 283 U.S. 697 (1931)

Jay Near was the owner of the Saturday Press, *a newspaper published in Minneapolis, Minnesota. In his paper, Near combined anti-Semitic diatribes with attacks on official corruption. The November 19, 1927, edition of the* Saturday Press *asserted,*

> *There have been too many men in this city and especially those in official life, who HAVE been taking orders and suggestions from JEW GANGSTERS, therefore we HAVE Jew Gangsters, practically ruling Minneapolis.*

Partly in response to the Saturday Press, *Minnesota passed a law permitting local officials to abate as a nuisance any "malicious, scandalous and defamatory newspaper, magazine or other periodical." Once a newspaper was declared a nuisance, further publication of scandalous material could be punished as contempt of court. Almost immediately after this law was passed, local officials in Minneapolis brought an action seeking to prevent further publication of the* Saturday Press. *The local trial court ruled that the* Press *was a malicious, scandalous and defamatory newspaper," and declared the journal a public nuisance. After the Supreme Court of Minnesota sustained that verdict, Near, with the financial and legal help of the more prestigious* Chicago Tribune, *appealed to the Supreme Court of the United States.*[42]

42. For a very readable and colorful account of the times and trials of Jay Near and *Near v. Minnesota*, see Fred W. Friendly, *Minnesota Rag: Corruption, Yellow Journalism, and the Case that Saved the Freedom of the Press* (New York: Vintage Books, 1982).

The Supreme Court declared by a 5-4 vote that Jay Near had a constitutional right to continue to publish the Saturday Press. *Chief Justice Hughes declared that the injunction against further publication violated the long-standing First Amendment ban on prior restraints. His opinion is cited today for the proposition that prior restraints on free speech are almost never constitutional. Would Hughes have agreed with this interpretation of his opinion? Notice that he emphasizes that under Minnesota law, Minnesota officials were not obligated to prove Near's publications false. Suppose, as Justice Butler claims, that Near's statements had been proven false. Would* Near *have been decided the same way? Should* Near *have been decided the same way? What is the special harm of prior restraints? Is Hughes correct when he asserts that subsequent libel suits provide sufficient protections for public figures who are accused of misdeeds? Is Justice Butler right to distinguish this case from the censorship practices in England?*

CHIEF JUSTICE HUGHES delivered the opinion of the Court.

. . .

The question is whether a statute authorizing such proceedings in restraint of publication is consistent with the conception of the liberty of the press as historically conceived and guaranteed. In determining the extent of the constitutional protection, it has been generally, if not universally, considered that it is the chief purpose of the guaranty to prevent previous restraints upon publication. The struggle in England, directed against the legislative power of the licenser, resulted in renunciation of the censorship of the press. The liberty deemed to be established was thus described by Blackstone:

> The liberty of the press is indeed essential to the nature of a free state; but this consists in laying no *previous* restraints upon publications, and not in freedom from censure for criminal matter when published. Every freeman has an undoubted right to lay what sentiments he pleases before the public; to forbid this is to destroy the freedom of the press; but if he publishes what is improper, mischievous or illegal, he must take the consequence of his own temerity.

. . . The criticism upon Blackstone's statement has not been because immunity from previous restraint upon publication has not been regarded as deserving of special emphasis, but chiefly because that immunity cannot be deemed to exhaust the conception of the liberty guaranteed by state and federal constitutions. . . . In the present case, we have no occasion to inquire as to the permissible scope of subsequent punishment. For whatever wrong the appellant has committed or may commit by his publications the State appropriately affords both public and private redress by its libel laws. . . . [T]he statute in question does not deal with punishments; it provides for no punishment, except in case of contempt for violation of the court's order, but for suppression and injunction, that is, for restraint upon publication.

The objection has also been made that the principle as to immunity from previous restraint is stated too broadly, if every such restraint is deemed to be prohibited. That is undoubtedly true; the protection even as to previous restraint is not absolutely unlimited. But the limitation has been recognized only in exceptional cases. . . . No one would question but that a government might prevent actual obstruction to its recruiting service or the publication of the sailing dates of transports or the number and location of troops. . . . These limitations are not applicable here. . . .

The exceptional nature of its limitations places in a strong light the general conception that liberty of the press, historically considered and taken up by the Federal Constitution, has meant, principally, although not exclusively, immunity from previous restraints or censorship. The conception of the liberty of the press in this country had broadened with the exigencies of the colonial period and with the efforts to secure freedom from oppressive administration. That liberty was especially cherished for the immunity it afforded from previous restraint of the publication of censure of public officers and charges of official misconduct. . . .

. . .

The fact that, for approximately one hundred and fifty years, there has been almost an entire absence of attempts to impose previous restraints upon publications relating to the malfeasance of public officers is significant of the deep-seated conviction that such restraints would violate constitutional right. Public officers, whose character and conduct remain open to debate and free discussion in the press, find their remedies for false accusations in actions under libel laws providing for redress and punishment, and not in proceedings to restrain the publication of newspapers and periodicals. The general principle that the constitutional guaranty of the liberty of the press gives immunity from previous restraints has been approved in many decisions under the provisions of state constitutions.

The importance of this immunity has not lessened. While reckless assaults upon public men, and efforts to bring obloquy upon those who are endeavoring faithfully to discharge official duties, exert a baleful influence and deserve the severest condemnation in public opinion, it cannot be said that this abuse is greater, and it is believed to be less, than that which characterized the period in which our institutions took shape. Meanwhile, the administration of government has become more complex, the opportunities for malfeasance and corruption have multiplied, crime has grown to most serious proportions, and the danger of its protection by unfaithful officials and of the impairment of the fundamental security of life and property by criminal alliances and official neglect, emphasizes the primary need of a vigilant and courageous press, especially in great cities. The fact that the liberty of the press may be abused by miscreant purveyors of scandal does not make any the less necessary the immunity of the press from previous restraint in dealing with official misconduct. Subsequent punishment for such abuses as may exist is the appropriate remedy consistent with constitutional privilege.

. . .

JUSTICE BUTLER (with JUSTICE VAN DEVANTER, JUSTICE McREYNOLDS, and JUSTICE SUTHERLAND), dissenting.

. . .

The record shows, and it is conceded, that defendants' regular business was the publication of malicious, scandalous and defamatory articles concerning the principal public officers, leading newspapers of the city, many private persons and the Jewish race. It also shows that it was their purpose at all hazards to continue to carry on the business. In every edition, slanderous and defamatory matter predominates to the practical exclusion of all else. Many of the statements are so highly improbable as to compel a finding that they are false. The articles themselves show malice.

. . .

The Act was passed in the exertion of the State's power of police, and this court is, by well established rule, required to assume, until the contrary is clearly made to appear, that there exists in Minnesota a state of affairs that justifies this measure for the preservation of the peace and good order of the State.

. . .

The Minnesota statute does not operate as a *previous* restraint on publication within the proper meaning of that phrase. It does not authorize administrative control in advance such as was formerly exercised by the licensers and censors but prescribes a remedy to be enforced by a suit in equity. In this case, there was previous publication made in the course of the business of regularly producing malicious, scandalous and defamatory periodicals. The business and publications unquestionably constitute an abuse of the right of free press. The statute denounces the things done as a nuisance on the ground, as stated by the state supreme court, that they threaten morals, peace and good order. There is no question of the power of the State to denounce such transgressions. . . .

There is nothing in the statute purporting to prohibit publications that have not been adjudged to constitute a nuisance. It is fanciful to suggest similarity between the granting or enforcement of the decree authorized by this statute to prevent *further* publication of malicious, scandalous and defamatory articles and the *previous* restraint upon the press by licensers as referred to by Blackstone and described in the history of the times to which he alludes. . . .

B. Voting

Immigration fostered fierce contests over voting rights. Many prominent Americans insisted that stern measures were needed to prevent the foreign born from introducing "un-American" ideas into the polity. In an essay entitled "The Failure of Universal Suffrage," Francis Parkman asserted, "When extensive districts and, notably, large portions of populous cities are filled by masses of imported ignorance and heredity ineptitude, the whole ferments together till the evil grows insufferable."[43] Other Americans insisted that all persons in a democracy were entitled to cast ballots. John Martin Luther Babcock declared, "The basis of the right of suffrage [is that] in the broad realm of natural rights, one man is essentially as good as another."[44] Proponents of restricted suffrage proposed voter

43. Francis Parkman, "The Failure of Universal Suffrage," *North American Review* 127 (July-Aug. 1888):1-20.

44. John Martin Luther Babcock, *The Right of the Ballot: A Reply to Francis Parkman and Others Who Have Asserted "The Failure of Universal Suffrage"* (Boston: Press of John Wilson & Son, 1879), 8.

registration laws, literacy tests, and the increased use of party primaries for fostering a more intelligent (and, in the South, a white) electorate. Many proponents of women's suffrage claimed that giving women the vote was a necessary means to counteract the influence of foreign-born voters and voters of color.

The Republican Era witnessed increased regulation of the electoral process. Legislatures required the secret ballot, imposed limits on campaign finance, and prohibited fusion (the practice of two parties nominating the same candidate in order to have that candidate mentioned twice on the ballot). Some reforms were aimed at restricting and regulating voter participation. Others reflected progressive antipathy to political parties and political machines. Many states and communities adopted the secret, or "Australian," ballot. Reformers believed that secret ballots reduced corrupt party influence on voters and required that the individual voter demonstrate a certain degree of intelligence.

Courts generally permitted elected officials to construct the electoral process as they saw fit. The Wisconsin Supreme Court in *State ex rel. Runge v. Anderson* (WI 1898) declared, "Manifestly, the right to vote, the secrecy of the vote, and the purity of elections, all essential to the success of our form of government, cannot be secured without legislative regulations. Such regulations, within reasonable limits, strengthen and make effective the constitutional guaranties instead of impairing or destroying them." Justices were also deferential when elected officials failed to act. When refusing to reapportion the state legislature, the Supreme Court of Illinois asserted in *Fergus v. Marks* (IL 1926) that "the duty to reapportion the State is a specific legislative duty imposed by the constitution solely upon the legislative department of the State, and it, alone, is responsible to the people for a failure to perform that duty."[45] Some state courts were less deferential. The Supreme Court of Indiana in *Parker v. State ex rel. Powell* (IN 1892) concluded that justices could review legislative apportionments. "The cardinal principle of free representative government," Justice Coffey's majority opinion declared, "that the electors shall have equal weight in exercising the right of suffrage is recognized and secured."[46] *Newberry v. United States* (1921) was the most important instance of judicial activism on voting matters. The U.S. Supreme Court in that case declared unconstitutional a federal law limiting campaign spending in primary elections. Significantly, the judicial majority ruled that Congress could not regulate state primaries. No justice found an independent constitutional problem with state regulations of campaign finance.

45. *Fergus v. Marks*, 321 Ill. 510 (1926).

46. *Parker v. State ex rel. Powell*, 133 Ind. 178 (1892).

State ex rel. Runge v. Anderson, 100 Wis. 523 (1898)

The Democratic Party and the People's Party in 1898 each chose Carl Runge as their nominee for city attorney of Milwaukee, Wisconsin. When composing the ballot, William Andersen, the city clerk, printed Runge's name only on the Democratic Party line. Andersen did so because Wisconsin law forbade printing a candidate's name twice for the same office. This measure was intended to prevent fusion, the decision by two parties to combine support for one candidate. Runge asked for a writ of mandamus on the ground that the Wisconsin anti-fusion law violated voting rights protected by the constitution of Wisconsin. The trial court rejected this claim. Runge appealed to the Supreme Court of Wisconsin.

The Supreme Court of Wisconsin sustained the Wisconsin election law. Judge Marshall's majority opinion asserted that the state legislature had the power to regulate the ballot. Why does Marshall believe that the Wisconsin anti-fusion law is a reasonable regulation? Why does Judge Winslow disagree? Do the rights at issue belong to individual voters or to members of the political parties? What is the appropriate degree of judicial scrutiny when elected officials regulate the election process? Runge v. Anderson *was one of numerous state cases on election regulation decided in the Republican Era. What do you believe explains the increased regulation of elections? Why were most justices deferential to elected officials?*

JUDGE MARSHALL delivered the opinion of the Court.

. . .

. . . [I]t is said that the law is not constitutional because it violates section 3, art. 3, of the constitution of Wisconsin, which provides that all votes shall be by ballot. To support that, it is argued that the law takes from the voter the constitutional privilege of making his own ballot and depositing it as so prepared. No reason for this contention is perceived. The word "ballot" and the expression "vote by ballot" had a well-understood and universal meaning at the time of the adoption of the constitution, and it must be taken

Table 7-6 Selection of U.S. Supreme Court Cases Reviewing State and Federal Laws Regulating Elections

Case	Vote	Outcome	Decision
Minor v. Happersett, 88 U.S. 162 (1875)	9-0	Upheld	State restriction of suffrage to male citizens is constitutional
Ex parte Yarbrough, 110 U.S. 651 (1884)	9-0	Upheld	Congress has power to regulate fraud or violence against voters in federal elections
Davis v. Beason, 133 U.S. 333 (1890)	8-0	Upheld	Territorial regulation that bars individuals who practiced or advocated the crime of bigamy from voting is constitutional
Williams v. Mississippi, 170 U.S. 213 (1898)	8-0	Upheld	A literacy test does not on its face impose a racially discriminatory qualification on voting
Mason v. Missouri, 179 U.S. 328 (1900)	9-0	Upheld	States may change voter registration laws and adopt different voter registration laws for different parts of the state without violating equal protection requirements
Newberry v. United States, 256 U.S. 232 (1921)	8-1	Struck down	Congress has no power to regulate state primaries
Grovey v. Townsend, 295 U.S. 45 (1935)	9-0	Upheld	The federal Constitution did not prohibit the Texas Democratic Party from organizing a "whites only" primary election
Breedlove v. Suttles, 302 U.S. 277 (1937)	9-0	Upheld	Poll taxes do not interfere with any federal constitutional privilege, and reasonable exemptions from a poll tax are consistent with equal protection requirements
United States v. Classic, 313 U.S. 299 (1941)	6-3	Struck down	The right of qualified voters to vote in a primary and have their votes counted is secured by the federal Constitution when state law makes the primary election an integral part of the procedure for choosing Representatives
Smith v. Allwright, 321 U.S. 649 (1944)	9-0	Struck down	Party primaries are part of the machinery of state government, and racially exclusive "white primaries" violate equal protection requirements
Mills v. Alabama, 384 U.S. 214 (1966)	9-0	Struck down	States may not prohibit "electioneering" on Election Day, as applied to newspaper editorial
Katzenbach v. Morgan, 384 U.S. 641 (1966)	7-2	Upheld	Congress may ban the use of literacy tests as a voter qualification even though the Supreme Court had not found such tests to be a violation of equal protection requirements
Williams v. Rhodes, 393 U.S. 23 (1968)	6-3	Struck down	Complex and high hurdles for new and minor parties to be listed on the ballot violate the equal protection clause
Kramer v. Union Free School District No. 15, 395 U.S. 621 (1969)	6-3	Struck down	Restriction of eligible voters in school board elections to real property owners or parents of schoolchildren violates the equal protection clause
Oregon v. Mitchell, 400 U.S. 112 (1970)	5-4	Struck down	Congress may impose an eighteen-year minimum-age requirement for federal elections but has no authority to set a minimum voting age for state and local elections
Buckley v. Valeo, 424 U.S. 1 (1976)	7-1	Struck down	Congress may restrict individual contributions to campaigns but may not limit independent expenditures

(*Continued*)

Table 7-6 *(Continued)*

Case	Vote	Outcome	Decision
Brown v. Hartlage, 456 U.S. 45 (1982)	9-0	Struck down	States may not prohibit candidates from making campaign promises as a means of preventing electoral corruption
Federal Election Commission v. Conservative Political Action Committee, 470 U.S. 480 (1985)	7-2	Struck down	Congress may not limit the amount of expenditures by an independent political action committee (PAC) in support of candidates
Burson v. Freeman, 504 U.S. 191 (1992)	5-3	Upheld	State may create a no-campaigning buffer zone around polling places
U.S. Term Limits v. Thornton, 514 U.S. 779 (1995)	5-4	Struck down	States may not impose term limits on incumbent members of Congress
Republican Party of Minnesota v. White, 536 U.S. 765 (2002)	5-4	Struck down	States may not prohibit judicial candidates from discussing issues that might come before the court
McConnell v. Federal Election Commission, 540 U.S. 93 (2003)	5-4	Upheld	Congress may regulate donations to political parties and may regulate corporate campaign expenditures close to primary and general elections
Citizens United v. Federal Election Commission, 558 U.S. 50 (2010)	5-4	Struck down	Congress may not impose a broad ban on corporate entities spending general funds on "electioneering communications"

as the law that the thought which was in the minds of the framers of the constitution was in harmony with such meaning. Any attempt to go outside of that would be usurpation, not interpretation or construction. . . . The word "ballot," means, in the election of public officers, and always meant, a paper so prepared by printing or writing thereon as to show the voter's choice, and "vote by ballot" the deposit of such paper in a box in such a way as to conceal the voter's choice if he so desires. In that sense and in no other the words were used in the constitution, and they secure to each person entitled to vote the rights which their meaning clearly conveys, and they are in no way interfered with by the act under consideration. . . .

. . .

. . . Manifestly, the right to vote, the secrecy of the vote, and the purity of elections, all essential to the success of our form of government, cannot be secured without legislative regulations. Such regulations, within reasonable limits, strengthen and make effective the constitutional guaranties instead of impairing or destroying them. Some interference with freedom of action is permissible and necessarily incident to the power to regulate at all, as some interference with personal liberty is necessary and incident to government; and so far as legislative regulations are reasonable and bear on all persons equally so far as practicable in view of the constitutional end sought, they cannot be rightfully said to contravene any constitutional right. . . . We are unable to see anything in the present ballot law which passes beyond the bounds of reasonable regulation in view of the end sought,—the right of all to vote in secrecy and upon the basis of political equality and purity. True, a political party cannot be represented as such on the official ballot unless it polled, at the preceding general election, at least two per cent. of the votes cast in the election district, but that does not in any manner prevent any voter from voting for any person he sees fit, for any office. The law requires blanks to be left under the name of each candidate, sufficient for the voter to write a name therein in place of the one printed. He is permitted thus to split his ticket as he sees fit, so that it will contain the names of some candidates of one party and some of another, according to his choice, and then he is permitted to vote the ticket so prepared by a single mark at the top in the place provided for that purpose, or he may designate the candidates of his choice by separate markings, and all reasonable safeguards are thrown around him to prevent his so marking his ticket as to lose his vote for any candidate he desires to vote for. . . . An inspection of all the so-called Australian ballot laws now in force in the several states, will not disclose a more perfect system for the protection of the voter in his constitutional right to vote on an equality with every other voter, and to designate in secrecy his choice, than is found in the Wisconsin law.

. . .

. . . Mere party fealty and party sentiment, which influences men to desire to be known as members of a particular organization, are not the subjects of constitutional care. It deals with the individual right of the citizen to vote for the candidates of his choice, and if that be not impaired, and reasonable opportunity be furnished for equal representation on the official ballot under a party designation, no unjust discrimination can successfully be claimed. . . . The confusion and uncertainty that would arise in such a case from the double printing of names, furnishes a strong reason for prohibiting it, and that, with the other reasons mentioned, strongly support the wisdom of the prohibition as a proper legislative regulation.

. . .

JUDGE WINSLOW, dissenting.

I regard the provision of the election law which is attacked in this case as an unwarrantable interference with the freedom of election, and hence void. Its only purpose is to prevent fusion between two parties. This is plain to the most casual reader. That it will quite effectively accomplish this purpose seems equally plain; that it is a laudable, or even lawful, purpose, I deny. If one party has named a worthy ticket, there is no reason, in law or morals, why another should be debarred from indorsing that ticket except on pain of surrendering its existence. It is easy to say that the rights of the elector are not infringed; that he may still vote for the men of his choice, because their names are on the official ballot; and that the party designation makes no difference in the result. This argument is, in my opinion, unsatisfactory. Political rights are universally exercised through party organizations, and such organizations are recognized by this very law. When the law interferes with the freedom of action of the party, it necessarily interferes with the freedom of action of the citizens who compose that party. This law says to the party, and through the party to the electors composing it: "You shall not indorse candidates of any other party, except on condition that you surrender your existence as a party and lose your right of representation upon the official ballot in the future." Knowing, as we do, the strength of party ties, and the practical necessity of party organizations, it seems to me that this threat is neither necessary nor reasonable. It cannot be claimed that this provision is aimed at any evil practices or wrongful act. It will prevent no illegal vote from being cast, nor will it stop any corrupt practice, nor in any way preserve the purity of the ballot. There is, in my judgment, no reason, in good morals or in the principles of republican government, for any such device. It is well to surround the ballot with reasonable regulations, and to adopt all precautions that will prevent corruption and illegal voting; but it is not well to make the ballot difficult for the honest voter, nor to adopt devices which tend only to hinder the full exercise of political rights.

C. Citizenship

Americans more heavily regulated immigration and naturalization during the Republican Era. The Chinese Exclusion Acts of 1882, 1892, and 1902 forbade most Chinese natives from entering the United States, forbade Chinese immigrants from becoming citizens of the United States, and permitted the deportation of all Chinese aliens who did not have a proper certificate of residency. The National Origins Act of 1924 set sharp limits on immigration from southern and eastern Europe, as well as non-European countries. The Supreme Court of the United States sustained these measures. The judicial majority in *Fong Yue Ting v. United States* (1893) stated, "It is an accepted maxim of international law that every sovereign nation has the power, as inherent in sovereignty, and essential to self-preservation, to forbid the entrance of foreigners within its dominions, or to admit them only in such cases and upon such conditions as it may see fit to prescribe." The justices drew the line, however, when federal authorities sought to deny citizenship to children of Chinese citizens residing in the United States. *United States v. Wong Kim Ark* (1898) held that all persons born in the United States were citizens of the United States, unless their parents were in the diplomatic service of another country or members of an invading army.

Citizenship requirements were otherwise tightened. Worried about immigrants with radical European ideas, Congress required that all persons wishing to be naturalized swear fidelity to the Constitution of the United States. *United States v. Schwimmer* (1929) tested the meaning of that obligation. The judicial majority on the Supreme Court ruled that Rosika Schwimmer could not be an American citizen because she was a pacifist who would not take up arms in defense of the United States. Justice Holmes was astounded, given that women in the United States did not have the legal right to take up arms to defend the country.

United States v. Wong Kim Ark, 169 U.S. 649 (1898)

Wong Kim Ark was born in San Francisco in 1873. His parents were Chinese citizens residing in the United States. In 1895 the collector of customs for San Francisco refused to allow him to return from a trip to China on the ground that he was not a citizen of the United States. The local federal district court issued a writ of habeas corpus on the ground that Wong Kim Ark was an American citizen. The United States appealed to the Supreme Court.

The Supreme Court by a 6-2 vote agreed that Wong Kim Ark was an American citizen. Justice Gray's majority opinion ruled that the Constitution of the United States adopted the common law principle that citizenship was determined by birth. Wong Kim Ark was born in the United States. His parents were not in the diplomatic service or foreign soldiers. Therefore, Wong Kim Ark enjoyed birthright citizenship. Chief Justice Fuller in dissent maintained that persons inherited citizenship from their parents, that the common law rule tying citizenship to the soil was a relic of feudalism. Who has the better argument? Does the text of the Constitution or constitutional history clarify this issue? If not, what principles are most consistent with fundamental constitutional commitments?

Wong Kim Ark's parents were legal aliens. The Supreme Court's decision in Wong Kim Ark *is, however, frequently cited for the proposition that the children of illegal aliens also enjoy birthright citizenship if they were born in the United States. Does that claim follow from the logic or spirit of Justice Gray's argument?*

JUSTICE GRAY . . . delivered the opinion of the court.

. . .

The constitution nowhere defines the meaning of [citizen], either by way of inclusion or of exclusion, except in so far as this is done by the affirmative declaration that "all persons born or naturalized in the United States, and subject to the jurisdiction thereof, are citizens of the United States." In this, as in other respects, it must be interpreted in the light of the common law, the principles and history of which were familiarly known to the framers of the constitution.

. . .

The fundamental principle of the common law with regard to English nationality was birth within the allegiance—also called "ligealty," "obedience," "faith," or "power"—of the king. The principle embraced all persons born within the king's allegiance, and subject to his protection. Such allegiance and protection were mutual . . . and were not restricted to natural-born subjects and naturalized subjects, or to those who had taken an oath of allegiance; but were predicable of aliens in amity, so long as they were within the kingdom. Children, born in England, of such aliens, were therefore natural-born subjects. But the children, born within the realm, of foreign ambassadors, or the children of alien enemies, born during and within their hostile occupation of part of the king's dominions, were not natural-born subjects, because not born within the allegiance, the obedience, or the power, or, as would be said at this day, within the jurisdiction, of the king.

. . .

The same rule was in force in all the English colonies upon this continent down to the time of the Declaration of Independence, and in the United States afterwards, and continued to prevail under the constitution as originally established.

. . .

. . . The fourteenth amendment affirms the ancient and fundamental rule of citizenship by birth within the territory, in the allegiance and under the protection of the country, including all children here born of resident aliens, with the exceptions or qualifications (as old as the rule itself) of children of foreign sovereigns or their ministers, or born on foreign public ships, or of enemies within and during a hostile occupation of part of our territory, and with the single additional exception of children of members of the Indian tribes owing direct allegiance to their several tribes. The amendment, in clear words and in manifest intent, includes the children born within the territory of the United States of all other persons, of whatever race or color, domiciled within the United States. Every citizen or subject of another country, while domiciled here, is within the allegiance and the protection, and consequently subject to the jurisdiction, of the

United States. His allegiance to the United States is direct and immediate, and, although but local and temporary, continuing only so long as he remains within our territory, is yet, in the words of Lord Coke in *Calvin's Case* (1608), "strong enough to make a natural subject, for, if he hath issue here, that issue is a natural-born subject"; and his child, . . . "If born in the country, is as much a citizen as the natural-born child of a citizen, and by operation of the same principle." It can hardly be denied that an alien is completely subject to the political jurisdiction of the country in which he resides, seeing that, as said by Mr. Webster, when secretary of state:

> Independently of a residence with intention to continue such residence; independently of any domiciliation; independently of the taking of any oath of allegiance, or of renouncing any former allegiance,—it is well known that by the public law an alien, or a stranger born, for so long a time as he continues within the dominions of a foreign government, owes obedience to the laws of that government, and may be punished for treason or other crimes as a native-born subject might be, unless his case is varied by some treaty stipulations.

To hold that the fourteenth amendment of the constitution excludes from citizenship the children born in the United States of citizens or subjects of other countries, would be to deny citizenship to thousands of persons of English, Scotch, Irish, German, or other European parentage, who have always been considered and treated as citizens of the United States.

. . .

During the debates in the senate in January and February, 1866, upon the civil rights bill, Mr. Trumbull, the chairman of the committee which reported the bill, moved to amend the first sentence thereof so as to read: "All persons born in the United States, and not subject to any foreign power, are hereby declared to be citizens of the United States, without distinction of color." Mr. Cowan, of Pennsylvania, asked "whether it will not have the effect of naturalizing the children of Chinese and Gypsies, born in this country?" Mr. Trumbull answered, "Undoubtedly;" . . .

The power of naturalization, vested in congress by the constitution, is a power to confer citizenship, not a power to take it away. "A naturalized citizen," said Chief Justice Marshall,

> becomes a member of the society, possessing all the rights of a native citizen, and standing, in the view of the constitution, on the footing of a native. The constitution does not authorize congress to enlarge or abridge those rights. The simple power of the national legislature is to prescribe a uniform rule of naturalization, and the exercise of this power exhausts it, so far as respects the individual. The constitution then takes him up, and, among other rights, extends to him the capacity of suing in the courts of the United States, precisely under the same circumstances under which a native might sue.

Congress having no power to abridge the rights conferred by the constitution upon those who have become naturalized citizens by virtue of acts of congress, a fortiori no act or omission of congress, as to providing for the naturalization of parents or children of a particular race, can affect citizenship acquired as a birthright, by virtue of the constitution itself, without any aid of legislation. The fourteenth amendment, while it leaves the power, where it was before, in congress, to regulate naturalization, has conferred no authority upon congress to restrict the effect of birth, declared by the constitution to constitute a sufficient and complete right to citizenship.

. . .

The fact, therefore, that acts of congress or treaties have not permitted Chinese persons born out of this country to become citizens by naturalization, cannot exclude Chinese persons born in this country from the operation of the broad and clear words of the constitution: "All persons born in the United States, and subject to the jurisdiction thereof, are citizens of the United States."

. . .

CHIEF JUSTICE FULLER, with whom concurred JUSTICE HARLAN, dissenting.

. . .

The [English common law] rule was the outcome of the connection in feudalism between the individual and the soil on which he lived, and the allegiance due was that of liege men to their liege lord. . . .

. . .

Obviously, where the constitution deals with common-law rights and uses common-law phraseology, its language should be read in the light of the common law; but when the question arises as to what constitutes citizenship of the nation, involving, as it does, international relations, and political as contradistinguished from civil status, international principles must be considered; and, unless the municipal law of England appears to have been affirmatively accepted, it cannot be allowed to control in the matter of construction.

. . .

Before the Revolution, the views of the publicists had been thus put by Vattel: ". . . The true bond which connects the child with the body politic is not the matter of an inanimate piece of land, but the moral relations of his parentage. * * * The place of birth produces no change in the rule that children follow the condition of their fathers, for it is not naturally the place of birth that gives rights, but extraction."

. . .

The framers of the constitution were familiar with the distinctions between the Roman law and the feudal law, between obligations based on territoriality and those based on the personal and invisible character of origin; and there is nothing to show that in the matter of nationality they intended to adhere to principles derived from regal government, which they had just assisted in overthrowing.

. . .

By the fifth clause of the first section of article 2 of the constitution it is provided that "no person except a natural-born citizen, or a citizen of the United States, at the time of the adoption of the constitution, shall be eligible to the office of president; neither shall any person be eligible to that office who shall not have attained to the age of thirty-five years, and been fourteen years a resident within the United States."

. . .

Considering the circumstances surrounding the framing of the constitution, I submit that it is unreasonable to conclude that "natural-born citizen" applied to everybody born within the geographical tract known as the United States, irrespective of circumstances; and that the children of foreigners, happening to be born to them while passing through the country, whether of royal parentage or not, or whether of the Mongolian, Malay, or other race, were eligible to the presidency, while children of our citizens, born abroad, were not.

. . .

The civil rights act became a law April 9, 1866, and provided "that all persons born in the United States, and not subject to any foreign power, excluding Indians not taxed, are hereby declared to be citizens of the United States." . . .

. . .

If the act of 1866 had not contained the words "and not subject to any foreign power," the children neither of public ministers nor of aliens in territory in hostile occupation would have been included within its terms on any proper construction, for their birth would not have subjected them to ties of allegiance, whether local and temporary, or general and permanent.

There was no necessity as to them for the insertion of the words, although they were embraced by them.

But there were others in respect of whom the exception was needed, namely, the children of aliens, whose parents owed local and temporary allegiance merely, remaining subject to a foreign power by virtue of the tie of permanent allegiance, which they had not severed by formal abjuration or equivalent conduct, and some of whom were not permitted to do so if they would.

And it was to prevent the acquisition of citizenship by the children of such aliens merely by birth within the geographical limits of the United States that the words were inserted.

Two months after the statute was enacted, on June 16, 1866, the fourteenth amendment was proposed, and declared ratified July 28, 1868. The first clause of the first section reads: "All persons born or naturalized in the United States and subject to the jurisdiction thereof, are citizens of the United States and of the state wherein they reside." The act was passed and the amendment proposed by the same congress, and it is not open to reasonable doubt that the words "subject to the jurisdiction thereof," in the amendment, were used as synonymous with the words "and not subject to any foreign power," of the act.

. . .

These considerations lead to the conclusion that the rule in respect of citizenship of the United States prior to the fourteenth amendment differed from the English common-law rule in vital particulars, and, among others, in that it did not recognize allegiance as indelible, and in that it did recognize an essential difference between birth during temporary and birth during permanent residence. If children born in the United States were deemed presumptively and generally citizens, this was not so when they were born of aliens whose residence was merely temporary, either in fact or in point of law.

. . .

In other words, the fourteenth amendment does not exclude from citizenship by birth children born in the

United States of parents permanently located therein, and who might themselves become citizens; nor, on the other hand, does it arbitrarily make citizens of children born in the United States of parents who, according to the will of their native government and of this government, are and must remain aliens.

United States v. Schwimmer, 279 U.S. 644 (1929)

Rosika Schwimmer emigrated from Hungary to the United States in 1921. Five years later she sought to become an American citizen. The Naturalization Act of 1906 required that all applicants "declare on oath in open court" that they "will support and defend the Constitution and laws of the United States against all enemies, foreign and domestic, and bear true faith and allegiance to the same." At her naturalization hearing Schwimmer testified, "I am willing to do everything that an American citizen has to do except fighting. If American women would be compelled to do that, I would not do that. I am an uncompromising pacifist." On this basis, the local federal district court declared that Schwimmer was ineligible for citizenship. That decision was reversed by the Court of Appeals for the Seventh Circuit. The United States appealed to the Supreme Court of the United States.

The Supreme Court ruled by a 6-3 vote that Schwimmer was ineligible for citizenship. Justice Butler's majority opinion maintained that bearing arms was a fundamental duty of citizens, and, as such, Schwimmer was insufficiently attached to constitutional principles. Schwimmer was a fifty-year-old woman who was not legally allowed to bear arms. Why does Justice Butler think that these facts have no bearing on the case? Was he right? Suppose that Schwimmer believed in an established church or that the federal government should not have the power to regulate bankruptcy. Would she be ineligible for American citizenship because she was insufficiently attached to constitutional principles? Would Justice Holmes deny citizenship to an anarchist?

JUSTICE BUTLER delivered the opinion of the Court.

. . .

Except for eligibility to the Presidency, naturalized citizens stand on the same footing as do native-born citizens. All alike owe allegiance to the government, and the government owes to them the duty of protection. These are reciprocal obligations, and each is a consideration for the other. But aliens can acquire such equality only by naturalization according to the uniform rules prescribed by the Congress. They have no natural right to become citizens, but only that which is by statute conferred upon them. Because of the great value of the privileges conferred by naturalization, the statutes prescribing qualifications and governing procedure for admission are to be construed with definite purpose to favor and support the government. And, in order to safeguard against admission of those who are unworthy, or who for any reason fail to measure up to required standards, the law puts the burden upon every applicant to show by satisfactory evidence that he has the specified qualifications.

. . .

That it is the duty of citizens by force of arms to defend our government against all enemies whenever necessity arises is a fundamental principle of the Constitution.

. . .

Whatever tends to lessen the willingness of citizens to discharge their duty to bear arms in the country's defense detracts from the strength and safety of the government. And their opinions and beliefs as well as their behavior indicating a disposition to hinder in the performance of that duty are subjects of inquiry under the statutory provisions governing naturalization and are of vital importance, for if all or a large number of citizens oppose such defense the "good order and happiness" of the United States cannot long endure. And it is evident that the views of applicants for naturalization in respect of such matters may not be disregarded. The influence of conscientious objectors against the use of military force in defense of the principles of our government is apt to be more detrimental than their mere refusal to bear arms. The fact that, by reason of sex, age or other cause, they may be unfit to serve does not lessen their purpose or power to influence others. . . .

. . .

A pacifist, in the general sense of the word, is one who seeks to maintain peace and to abolish war. Such purposes are in harmony with the Constitution and policy of our government. But the word is also used and understood to mean one who refuses or is unwilling for any purpose to bear arms because of conscientious considerations and who is disposed to encourage others in such refusal. And one who is without any sense of nationalism is not well bound or held by the ties of affection to any nation or government. Such persons are liable to be incapable of the attachment for and devotion to the principles of our Constitution that are required of aliens seeking naturalization.

It is shown by official records and everywhere well known that during the recent war there were found among those who described themselves as pacifists and conscientious objectors many citizens—though happily a minute part of all—who were unwilling to bear arms in that crisis and who refused to obey the laws of the United States and the lawful commands of its officers and encouraged such disobedience in others. Local boards found it necessary to issue a great number of noncombatant certificates, and several thousand who were called to camp made claim because of conscience for exemption from any form of military service. Several hundred were convicted and sentenced to imprisonment for offenses involving disobedience, desertion, propaganda and sedition. It is obvious that the acts of such offenders evidence a want of that attachment to the principles of the Constitution of which the applicant is required to give affirmative evidence by the Naturalization Act.

. . .

JUSTICE HOLMES (with JUSTICE BRANDEIS), dissenting.

The applicant seems to be a woman of superior character and intelligence, obviously more than ordinarily desirable as a citizen of the United States. . . . So far as the adequacy of her oath is concerned I hardly can see how that is affected by the statement, inasmuch as she is a woman over fifty years of age, and would not be allowed to bear arms if she wanted to. And as to the opinion the whole examination of the applicant shows that she holds none of the now-dreaded creeds but thoroughly believes in organized government and prefers that of the United States to any other in the world. Surely it cannot show lack of attachment to the principles of the Constitution that she thinks that it can be improved. I suppose that most intelligent people think that it might be. Her particular improvement looking to the abolition of war seems to me not materially different in its bearing on this case from a wish to establish cabinet government as in England, or a single house, or one term of seven years for the President. To touch a more burning question, only a judge mad with partisanship would exclude because the applicant thought that the Eighteenth Amendment should be repealed.

Of course the fear is that if a war came the applicant would exert activities such as were dealt with in *Schenck v. United States* (1919). But that seems to me unfounded. Her position and motives are wholly different from those of Schenck. She is an optimist and states in strong and, I do not doubt, sincere words her belief that war will disappear and that the impending destiny of mankind is to unite in peaceful leagues. I do not share that optimism nor do I think that a philosophic view of the world would regard war as absurd. But most people who have known it regard it with horror, as a last resort, and even if not yet ready for cosmopolitan efforts, would welcome any practicable combinations that would increase the power on the side of peace. The notion that the applicant's optimistic anticipations would make her a worse citizen is sufficiently answered by her examination which seems to me a better argument for her admission than any that I can offer. Some of her answers might excite popular prejudice, but if there is any principle of the Constitution that more imperatively calls for attachment than any other it is the principle of free thought—not free thought for those who agree with us but freedom for the thought that we hate. I think that we should adhere to that principle with regard to admission into, as well as to life within this country. And recurring to the opinion that bars this applicant's way, I would suggest that the Quakers have done their share to make the country what it is, that many citizens agree with the applicant's belief and that I had not supposed hitherto that we regretted our inability to expel them because they believed more than some of us do in the teachings of the Sermon on the Mount.

JUSTICE SANFORD, dissenting. . . .

V. Equality

MAJOR DEVELOPMENTS

- Attacks on administrative discretion that might lead to the unequal application of the laws
- The birth of Jim Crow and the NAACP
- Women gain the right to vote but dispute whether to pursue an equal rights amendment
- Native Americans who abandon tribes become citizens

Americans in the Republican Era tested the meaning of both the new equal protection clause in the federal constitution and the inherited equal protection clauses in state constitutions. White southerners adopted Jim Crow policies that rigidly segregated persons by race. Women demanded the right to vote and sit on juries.

Employers insisted that minimum wage laws gave their employees special advantages in the bargaining process. Other businesses complained that laws granting government bureaucrats discretion to determine whether businesses were upholding safety and other regulations denied equality under law. Native Americans explored whether various provisions in the post–Civil War Amendments changed their constitutional status.

The success of equality claims varied by forum and issue. Federal courts were generally unsympathetic to claims that persons had been denied equal protection of the laws. Justice Oliver Wendell Holmes, Jr., in *Buck v. Bell* (1927) described equal protection as the "last resort" for desperate litigators. The justices sustained racial segregation, declared that the Fourteenth Amendment did not make Native American citizens, gave no constitutional rights to women, and generally rejected equal protection claims brought by those who objected to state regulations or bureaucratic decisions. Federal courts did prove somewhat more sympathetic to African-American rights toward the end of the Republican Era and were far more willing to hear due process attacks on state regulations. Other constitutional decision makers were more sympathetic to a broad array of equal protection claims. While courts in the southern states sustained Jim Crow legislation, some northern state courts ruled that school districts could not overtly segregate by race. The Nineteenth Amendment granted women the right to vote and some state courts gave women the right to sit on juries. The Dawes Act declared that Native Americans who left their tribes were citizens of the United States. Many state court decisions found that laws granting too much bureaucratic discretion were inconsistent with state constitutional commitments to equality under law.

As you read the materials in this section, consider the following questions. What explains the pattern of judicial decisions and legislative responses to constitutional claims of equality? Were courts protecting the most powerful or the politically powerless? Which groups did constitutional decision makers conceive of as politically powerless? What other patterns, if any, do you see in the constitutional decisions made on equality during the Republican Era?

A. Equality Under Law

Government efforts to regulate an increasingly industrial state strained existing notions of equality under law. Opponents of labor regulations claimed that such measures were class legislation that favored employees at the expense of employers. The legislative habit of passing special legislation that provided benefits for specific persons or businesses often violated state constitutional provisions specifically designed to limit or eradicate that practice. One commentator notes,

> By the early twentieth century most states had by constitutional revision specifically prohibited a variety of special legislation and also constitutionally proscribed such legislation where general statutes could apply. Specific prohibitions typically proscribed special laws relating to the adoption and legitimation of minors; restoring civil rights to felons; chartering corporations; releasing or extinguishing debts; changing of the law of descent; removing the disabilities of age; granting divorces; granting relief available in courts of law; authorizing the creation, extension, enforcement, impairment, or release of liens; designating voting places; providing for special elections; affecting the estates of deceased persons; granting special or exclusive privileges; changing the names of persons; chartering cities, towns, villages or other subdivisions; changing county seats; creating local offices; prescribing the powers or duties of local officials; creating, increasing or decreasing the fees or salaries of public officials; fixing punishments; refunding monies; remitting fines; relating to local roads, bridges, and ferries; relating to local schools; granting tax exemptions; authorizing special taxes; regulating the jurisdiction of courts; changing the venue of civil or criminal trials; validating deeds; regulating rates of interest; protecting game and fish; and validating invalid acts of officials. However gradually, in most of the states these reforms substantially reduced the number of special laws enacted at each legislative session.[47]

Administrative discretion provided another challenge for inherited notions of equality under law. State governments at the turn of the century increased the number of civil servants and other officials with the authority to determine whether businesses were operating safely and in a manner consistent with legal

47. Robert M. Ireland, "The Problem of Local, Private, and Special Legislation in the Nineteenth Century United States," *American Journal of Legal History* 46 (2004): 283–84.

standards. Many persons complained that these standards permitted arbitrary and capricious treatment in violation of constitutional commitments to equality. The Supreme Court in both *Barbier v. Connolly* (1884) and *Yick Wo v. Hopkins* (1886) insisted that bureaucratic discretion uncabined by clear legal standards was unconstitutional. State courts expressed similar concern with bureaucratic discretion. *Mayor and City Council of Baltimore v. Radecke* (MD 1878) declared unconstitutional a law that permitted the mayor to rescind at will permits for steam engines, because the local ordinance "lays down no *rules* by which its *impartial execution* can be secured or partiality and oppression prevented."[48]

Yick Wo v. Hopkins, 118 U.S. 356 (1886)

Yick Wo was fined $10 by a San Francisco police court for operating a laundry in a wooden building without obtaining a license. The local ordinance declared, "It shall be unlawful . . . for any person or persons to establish, maintain, or carry on a laundry, . . . without having first obtained the consent of the board of supervisors, except the same be located in a building constructed either of brick or stone." Unable to pay the fee, Yick Wo was imprisoned for ten days. Yick Wo filed for a writ of habeas corpus against Hopkins, the local sheriff, claiming that his confinement was illegal. His petition pointed out that the local authorities had denied permits to all Chinese immigrants operating laundries in wooden buildings but gave permits to all but one of the non-Chinese persons who were operating similar laundries. The Supreme Court of California refused to issue the writ. Yick Wo appealed to the Supreme Court of the United States.

The Supreme Court unanimously ruled that Yick Wo was unconstitutionally imprisoned. Justice Matthews's opinion asserted that the offending law allowed city officials to make arbitrary distinctions among citizens and that city officials had arbitrarily discriminated against persons of Chinese descent. The case stands for the proposition that a law containing no overtly discriminatory provisions may nevertheless violate the equal protection clause if implemented in a discriminatory fashion. Was the main fault of the law the lack of standards for determining who could operate a laundry in a wooden building or the discriminatory enforcement? Yick Wo *was decided unanimously. What do you believe explains that unanimity?*

JUSTICE MATTHEWS delivered the opinion of the Court.

. . .

We are . . . constrained, at the outset, to differ from the supreme court of California upon the real meaning of the ordinances in question. That court considered these ordinances as vesting in the board of supervisors a not unusual discretion in granting or withholding their assent to the use of wooden buildings as laundries, to be exercised in reference to the circumstances of each case, with a view to the protection of the public against the dangers of fire. We are not able to concur in that interpretation of the power conferred upon the supervisors. There is nothing in the ordinances which points to such a regulation of the business of keeping and conducting laundries. They seem intended to confer, and actually to confer, not a discretion to be exercised upon a consideration of the circumstances of each case, but a naked and arbitrary power to give or withhold consent, not only as to places, but as to persons; so that, if an applicant for such consent, being in every way a competent and qualified person, and having complied with every reasonable condition demanded by any public interest, should, failing to obtain the requisite consent of the supervisors to the prosecution of his business, apply for redress by the judicial process of *mandamus* to require the supervisors to consider and act upon his case, it would be a sufficient answer for them to say that the law had conferred upon them authority to withhold their assent, without reason and without responsibility. The power given to them is not confided to their discretion in the legal sense of that term, but is granted to their mere will. It is purely arbitrary, and acknowledges neither guidance nor restraint.

. . .

The ordinance drawn in question . . . does not prescribe a rule and conditions, for the regulation of the use of property for laundry purposes, to which all similarly situated may conform. It allows, without restriction, the use for such purposes of buildings of brick or stone; but, as to wooden buildings, constituting nearly all those in previous use, it divides the owners or occupiers into two classes, not having respect to their personal character and qualifications for the business, nor the situation and nature and adaptation of the buildings themselves, but merely by an arbitrary line, on one side of which are those who are permitted to pursue their industry by the mere will and

48. *Mayor and City Council of Baltimore v. Radecke*, 49 Md. 217 (1878).

consent of the supervisors, and on the other those from whom that consent is withheld, at their mere will and pleasure. And both classes are alike only in this: that they are tenants at will, under the supervisors, of their means of living. . . .

The rights of the petitioners, as affected by the proceedings of which they complain, are not less because they are aliens and subjects of the emperor of China. . . . The fourteenth amendment to the constitution is not confined to the protection of citizens. It says: "Nor shall any state deprive any person of life, liberty, or property without due process of law; nor deny to any person within its jurisdiction the equal protection of the laws." These provisions are universal in their application, to all persons within the territorial jurisdiction, without regard to any differences of race, of color, or of nationality; and the equal protection of the laws is a pledge of the protection of equal laws. . . .

When we consider the nature and the theory of our institutions of government, the principles upon which they are supposed to rest, and review the history of their development, we are constrained to conclude that they do not mean to leave room for the play and action of purely personal and arbitrary power. . . . [T]he fundamental rights to life, liberty, and the pursuit of happiness, considered as individual possessions, are secured by those maxims of constitutional law which are the monuments showing the victorious progress of the race in securing to men the blessings of civilization under the reign of just and equal laws, so that, in the famous language of the Massachusetts bill of rights, the government of the commonwealth "may be a government of laws and not of men." For the very idea that one man may be compelled to hold his life, or the means of living, or any material right essential to the enjoyment of life, at the mere will of another, seems to be intolerable in any country where freedom prevails, as being the essence of slavery itself.

. . .

In the present cases, we are not obliged to reason from the probable to the actual, and pass upon the validity of the ordinances complained of, as tried merely by the opportunities which their terms afford, of unequal and unjust discrimination in their administration; for the cases present the ordinances in actual operation, and the facts shown establish an administration directed so exclusively against a particular class of persons as to warrant and require the conclusion that, whatever may have been the intent of the ordinances as adopted, they are applied by the public authorities charged with their administration, and thus representing the state itself, with a mind so unequal and oppressive as to amount to a practical denial by the state of that equal protection of the laws which is secured to the petitioners, as to all other persons, by the broad and benign provisions of the fourteenth amendment to the constitution of the United States. Though the law itself be fair on its face, and impartial in appearance, yet, if it is applied and administered by public authority with an evil eye and an unequal hand, so as practically to make unjust and illegal discriminations between persons in similar circumstances, material to their rights, the denial of equal justice is still within the prohibition of the constitution. . . .

B. Race

The promise of Reconstruction collapsed during the Republican Era. The federal government provided some protection for voting rights during the 1880s, but a coalition of Democrats and Republicans that was more interested in business first defeated proposals to strengthen voting rights and then in 1893 repealed several important Reconstruction measures aimed at securing racial equality in the South. Emboldened, southerners held constitutional conventions that enshrined white supremacy in the form of racial segregation as the fundamental law of the land. The Supreme Court in the first part of the Republican Era supported these efforts. The justices in *Plessy v. Ferguson* (1896) sustained a local law that segregated train passengers by race, in *Williams v. Mississippi* (1898) refused to look at the racial motivations underlying the adoption of constitutional rules disadvantaging African-Americans, and in *Giles v. Harris* (1903) conceded that courts could do little when southerners denied the ballot to persons of color.

Defenders of Jim Crow often justified their race-based decision making by differentiating between what they claimed were natural distinctions among the races and inappropriate acts of discrimination against particular races. Constitutional decision makers insisted that racial discriminations violated the Fourteenth Amendment. When declaring unconstitutional a law prohibiting persons of color from sitting on juries, the Supreme Court in *Strauder v. West Virginia* (1879) asserted that the post–Civil War Constitution required

> that the law in the States shall be the same for the black as for the white; that all persons, whether colored or white, shall stand equal before the laws of the States, and, in regard to the colored race, for whose protection the amendment was primarily designed, that no discrimination shall be made against them by law because of their color[.] The words of the amendment, it is true, are prohibitory, but they contain a necessary implication of a positive immunity, or right, most valuable to the colored race,—the right to exemption from unfriendly legislation against them distinctively as colored,—exemption from legal discriminations, implying inferiority in civil society, lessening the security of their enjoyment of the rights which others enjoy, and discriminations which are steps towards reducing them to the condition of a subject race.

Most constitutional commentators and decision makers believed, however, that laws reflecting "real" differences between the races were in the public interest. Gilbert Thomas Stephenson's influential *Race Distinctions in American Law* asserted,

> There is an essential difference between race distinctions and race discriminations. North Carolina, for example, has a law that white and Negro children shall not attend the same schools, but that separate schools shall be maintained. If the terms for all the public schools in the State are equal in length, if the teaching force is equal in numbers and ability, if the school buildings are equal in convenience, accommodations, and appointments, a race distinction exists but not a discrimination. Identity of accommodation is not essential to avoid the charge of discrimination. If there are in a particular school district twice as many white children as there are Negro children, the school building for the former should be twice as large as that for the latter. The course of study need not be the same. If scientific investigation and experience show that in the education of the Negro child emphasis should be placed on one course of study, and in the education of the white child, on another; it is not a discrimination to emphasize industrial training in the Negro school, if that is better suited to the needs of the Negro pupil, and classics in the white school if the latter course is more profitable to the white child. There is no discrimination so long as there is equality of opportunity, and this equality may often be attained only by a difference in methods.[49]

Government officials who implemented race distinctions often faced tricky problems in determining who was a person of color. In *United States v. Bhagat Singh Thind* (1923) the Supreme Court decided that the federal government would rely heavily on common understandings concerning who was white, not the "scientific" race studies of the day. Most southern constitutional decision makers regarded any person with any nonwhite ancestry as a person of color

The period between the end of Reconstruction and the New Deal was not entirely bleak for persons of color. Continuing a practice that began during Reconstruction, some northern state courts overturned local decisions to segregate public schools and, at the very least, strongly hinted that such policies were unconstitutional. The Supreme Court of Kansas, when declaring that local school boards had no power to separate public school children by race, asserted,

> If the board has the power, because of race, to establish separate schools for children of African descent, then the board has the power to establish separate schools for persons of Irish descent or German descent; and if it has the power, because of color, to establish separate schools for black children, then it has the power to establish separate schools for red-headed children and blondes. We do not think that the board has any such power.[50]

The U.S. Supreme Court after 1910 proved more willing to declare unconstitutional egregious forms of race discrimination. *Buchanan v. Warley* (1917) struck down laws compelling segregation in the housing market. More important, the Republican Era witnessed the birth of the NAACP. Founded by W. E. B. DuBois and other civil rights activists, the NAACP by the end of the Republican Era had become a powerful force for racial equality.

---

49. Gilbert Thomas Stephenson, *Race Distinctions in American Law* (New York: Association Press, 1910), 2–3.

50. *Board of Education of City of Ottawa v. Tinnon*, 26 Kan. 1 (1881). For a general survey of northern law law on school segregation, see Morgan Kousser, *Dead End: The Development of Nineteenth-Century Litigation in Racial Discrimination in Schools* (New York: Oxford University Press, 1986).

United States v. Bhagat Singh Thind, 261 U.S. 204 (1923)

Bhagat Singh Thind was granted American citizenship by a federal district court. The United States protested this decision on the ground that the Naturalization Act of 1917 was limited to "aliens being free white persons" or "aliens of African nativity." Thind, who was born in India, claimed to be a white person. The United States disagreed. Both the local federal district court and Court of Appeals for the Ninth Circuit ruled that Thind was eligible for American citizenship. The United States appealed to the Supreme Court.

The Supreme Court unanimously ruled that Thind was not eligible for citizenship. Justice Sutherland's unanimous opinion asserted that persons of Asian-Indian descent were not white persons under the legal definition of white. Sutherland insisted that "free white persons" should be interpreted in a manner consistent with common understandings. Why does he reach that conclusion? How does that conclusion influence his decision? To what extent was Sutherland merely interpreting a racist statute? To what extent was he augmenting the racism of his era?

JUSTICE SUTHERLAND delivered the opinion of the Court.

. . .

If the applicant is a white person, within the meaning of this section, he is entitled to naturalization; otherwise not. . . .

. . .

. . . It may be true that the blond Scandinavian and the brown Hindu have a common ancestor in the dim reaches of antiquity, but the average man knows perfectly well that there are unmistakable and profound differences between them to-day; and it is not impossible, if that common ancestor could be materialized in the flesh, we should discover that he was himself sufficiently differentiated from both of his descendants to preclude his racial classification with either. The question for determination is not, therefore, whether by the speculative processes of ethnological reasoning we may present a probability to the scientific mind that they have the same origin, but whether we can satisfy the common understanding that they are now the same or sufficiently the same to justify the interpreters of a statute—written in the words of common speech, for common understanding, by unscientific men—in classifying them together in the statutory category as white persons. . . .

. . .

. . . We are unable to agree with the District Court, or with other lower federal courts, in the conclusion that a native Hindu is eligible for naturalization under section 2169. The words of familiar speech, which were used by the original framers of the law, were intended to include only the type of man whom they knew as white. The immigration of that day was almost exclusively from the British Isles and Northwestern Europe, whence they and their forebears had come. When they extended the privilege of American citizenship to "any alien being a free white person" it was these immigrants—bone of their bone and flesh of their flesh—and their kind whom they must have had affirmatively in mind. The succeeding years brought immigrants from Eastern, Southern and Middle Europe, among them the Slavs and the dark-eyed, swarthy people of Alpine and Mediterranean stock, and these were received as unquestionably akin to those already here and readily amalgamated with them. It was the descendants of these, and other immigrants of like origin, who constituted the white population of the country when section 2169, re-enacting the naturalization test of 1790, was adopted, and, there is no reason to doubt, with like intent and meaning.

. . .

What we now hold is that the words "free white persons" are words of common speech, to be interpreted in accordance with the understanding of the common man, synonymous with the word "Caucasian" only as that word is popularly understood. As so understood and used, whatever may be the speculations of the ethnologist, it does not include the body of people to whom the appellee belongs. It is a matter of familiar observation and knowledge that the physical group characteristics of the Hindus render them readily distinguishable from the various groups of persons in this country commonly recognized as white. The children of English, French, German, Italian, Scandinavian, and other European parentage, quickly merge into the mass of our population and lose the distinctive hallmarks of their European origin. On the other hand, it cannot be doubted that the children born in this country of Hindu parents would retain indefinitely the clear evidence of their ancestry. It is very far from our thought to suggest the slightest question of racial superiority or inferiority. What we suggest is merely racial difference, and it is of such character and extent that the great body of our people instinctively recognize it and reject the thought of assimilation. . . .

The Rise of Jim Crow

Reconstruction efforts to secure racial equality collapsed during the first half of the Republican Era. Republican administrations made some effort to secure African-American voting rights in the late 1870s and 1880s. Attorney General Taft ordered local federal attorneys supervising federal elections to "secure voters against whatever in general hinders or prevents them from a free exercise of the elective franchise, extending that care alike to the registration lists, the act of voting, and the personal freedom and security of the voter."[51] The Supreme Court sustained some convictions obtained by Republican officials. The judicial majority in *Ex parte Yarbrough* (1884) asserted, "Can it be doubted that congress can, by law, protect the act of voting, the place where it is done, and the man who votes from personal violence or intimidation, and the election itself from corruption or fraud?" Nevertheless, voting laws were too weak and federal enforcement too sporadic to have any substantial effect on African-American voting. Republicans made one last-ditch effort during 1889–90 to pass a stronger voting rights act. That effort failed. Three years later, after the Democrats regained control of the House of Representatives, Congress repealed Reconstruction Era laws requiring federal supervision of elections. The House majority report urging that repeal stated,

> These statutes should be speedily repealed because they mix State and Federal authority and power in the control and regulation of popular elections, thereby causing jealousy and friction between the two governments; because they have been used and will be used in the future as a part of the machinery of a political party to reward friends and destroy enemies; because under the practical operations of them the personal rights of citizens have been taken from them and justice and freedom denied them; because their enactment shows a distrust of the States, and their inability or indisposition to properly guard the elections, which, if ever true, has now happily passed away; and last, but not least, because their repeal will eliminate the judiciary from the political arena, and restore somewhat, we trust, the confidence of the people in the integrity and impartiality of the Federal tribunals.[52]

The ongoing federal retreat on Reconstruction emboldened southern champions of white supremacy. Southern constitutional conventions in the late 1890s and early decades of the twentieth century aggressively sought to marginalize persons of color. The keynote speaker at the Alabama Constitutional Convention of 1901 bluntly declared that the purpose of the new state constitution was "within the limits imposed by the Federal Constitution, to establish white supremacy in this State." Such Supreme Court decisions as *Plessy v. Ferguson* (1896) and such state court decisions as *Ratcliffe v. Beale* (MS 1896) indicated that justices had no intention of interfering with race relations in the South. The Supreme Court in *Giles v. Harris* (1903) abandoned all efforts to ensure racial equality in this region. When rejecting a lawsuit claiming that Alabama officials were not registering persons of color to vote, Justice Holmes, a wounded veteran of the Army of the Potomac, raised the white flag of surrender by acknowledging the powerlessness of the federal government in the face of southern intransigence.

> The bill imports that the great mass of the white population intends to keep the blacks from voting. To meet such an intent something more than ordering the plaintiff's name to be inscribed upon the lists of 1902 will be needed. If the conspiracy and the intent exist, a name on a piece of paper will not defeat them. Unless we are prepared to supervise the voting in that state by officers of the court, it seems to us that all that the plaintiff could get from equity would be an empty form. Apart from damages to the individual, relief from a great political wrong, if done, as alleged, by the people of a state and the state itself, must be given by them or by the legislative and political department of the government of the United States.

Debates over the Lodge Federal Elections Bill (1890)[53]

The Lodge Federal Elections Bill was the last effort that the Republican Party made in the late nineteenth century to reconstruct southern politics. Republicans in 1888 ran on a platform committed to restoring democracy in the South. The first substantive paragraph of that platform declared,

51. Pamela Brandwein, *Rethinking the Judicial Settlement of Reconstruction* (New York: Cambridge University Press, 2011), 130.

52. House Report No. 18, 53rd Cong., 1st Sess. (1893), 8–9.

53. *Congressional Record*, House, 51st Cong., 1st Sess. (1890), 6544, 6728.

> *We hold the free and honest popular ballot and the just and equal representation of all the people to be the foundation of our Republican government and demand effective legislation to secure the integrity and purity of elections, which are the fountains of all public authority. We charge that the present Administration and the Democratic majority in Congress owe their existence to the suppression of the ballot by a criminal nullification of the Constitution and laws of the United States.*

The resulting campaign was successful. Republicans regained control of the White House and both houses of Congress. Newly elected president Benjamin Harrison called on Republicans in Congress to fulfill their commitment to African-American voting rights. Representative Henry Cabot Lodge crafted a federal elections bill that required federal supervision of federal elections in any district where a sufficient number of citizens petitioned for supervision. Those supervisors had the power to oversee the voter registration process, voting, and vote counting to ensure that the election process was fair and respected federal law. Republicans had two reasons for promoting this bill. Most obviously, the party was committed to granting all qualified persons the right to vote. Moreover, most, but not all, Republicans believed that the Republican Party would be competitive in the South only if persons of color could vote freely.

The Lodge Federal Elections bill failed to pass. The measure was repeatedly stalled while Congress considered other matters. In the late 1890s a coalition of Democrats and conservative Republicans finally killed the bill.

REPRESENTATIVE HENRY CABOT LODGE (Republican, Massachusetts)

. . .

The bill before us proposes to extend and perfect existing laws in regard to the supervision of the elections of members of this body, so that they will be effective throughout the United States, wherever the applications of the law is demanded. It is needless for me to say to the House that the power of the United States in regard to elections extends only to those at which members of this body are chosen. This bill proposes to exercise this power, when demanded, in such a way as to secure, as far as possible, fair and honest elections for Representatives in Congress, without disturbing or overthrowing in any way the State machinery employed for the same purpose.

. . .

The first principle in the bill, therefore, is to secure this absolute publicity in regard to everything connected with the election of a member of Congress. The second is to make sure that every man who is entitled to vote has an opportunity to cast his vote freely and have it counted, and that no man who is not entitled to vote shall be allowed to vote. To the qualified voter this bill aims to give full opportunity. If he is threatened it seeks to protect him; if he is ignorant it seeks to inform him. On the other hand, in order to prevent the man who is trying to vote in violation of the law or the officer who is fraudulent and corrupt from carrying out his wrongdoing, this bill offers the means of speedy punishment and of collecting the evidence necessary to conviction.

. . .

Such being the principles and purposes of the bill, two questions arise in regard to it: First, is it within the power of Congress to enact such a law; and second, if Congress has the power, is it necessary and expedient to exercise it? As to the first point, the constitutional power to enact such legislation, there is not, I think, much room for discussion. The language of the Constitution is so plain that it admits of but one interpretation, and if doubt ever could have existed, the decisions of the Supreme Court make doubt no longer position.

The necessary power is found in section 4, article I, of the Constitution, which is as follows:

> The times, places and manner of holding elections for Senators and Representatives, shall be prescribed in each State by the Legislature thereof; but the Congress may at times by law make or alter such regulations, except as to the places of choosing Senators.

The language employed in this section is so plain that it would seem almost superfluous to enter into argument or discussion as to its meaning. If words mean anything those just quoted mean that the power of Congress over the conduct of elections of members of that body is absolute and complete. . . .

. . .

In view of the language of the Constitution, of its intentions as explained by its framers, and of the full and elaborate decisions of the Supreme Court on every point which could be involved therein, there can be no need for your committee to offer further argument as to the constitutional powers of Congress to pass such a bill as that which they report herewith. This bill is only a partial exercise of the plenary power of Congress in regard to the election of Representatives. . . .

. . . If citizens of the United States entitled to vote for Representatives in Congress are deprived of their rights, it is the duty of Congress to see that they are protected. If Congressional elections anywhere are tainted with fraud or corruption, or are perverted by violence, it is the duty of Congress to interfere, and that duty is imperative, because the power of interference exists. If the people, or any considerable body of people, believe that Congressional elections anywhere are fraudulent or corrupt, it is the duty of Congress to interfere in order to restore public confidence.

. . .

. . . If any State thinks that any class of citizens is unfit to vote through ignorance it can disqualify them from voting for State officers or for members of this House. It has but to put an educational qualification into its constitution. But the disqualification like the qualification can not recognize color, and that is the reason that legal methods have never been tried. The negro is not thrust out from his rights merely because he is ignorant and unfit to use them, as is constantly charged, but because his skin is black. It is this distinction which gives the lie to every principle of American liberty that is at the bottom of the difficulty and of the problem which we all deplore.

The first step, then, toward the settlement of the negro problem and toward the elevation and protection of the race is to take it out of national party politics. This can be done in but one way. The United States must extend to every citizen equal rights. . . .

An honest vote lies at the bottom of our system of government. It is the only way we have to discover and assert the will of the majority, and the will of the majority governs in this country. If we do not ascertain that will honestly it will be determined by force. You may call these truisms, if you like, but truisms are more apt to be forgotten than anything else, and yet to disregard them is the road to ruin. Free elections are the safety of this Government. We here can interfere with none but those which concern the Congress itself, but it is our plain duty to see to it that those at least are preserved in their purity and integrity. So far as a party question enters into this it can be easily dealt with. If one party benefits by free elections it is because that party is cheated now. If neither party is cheated by fraud, then free and honest elections will affect neither. If both cheat, both will suffer.

. . .

HENRY ST. GEORGE TUCKER III (Democrat, Virginia)

. . .

This is a government of limited powers. There is no power which we have here except that which the Constitution gives us; and, unless this Constitution of the land shows, not doubtfully, but clearly, that this bill comes within it, it is the sworn duty of every member of the House to vote against it.

. . .

. . . [W]herever a bill impinges upon the right of a State to control her own affairs as secured to her in the Constitution there we must stop. The history of the Constitution and the instrument itself show the intent of the framers was that Federal and State powers should be separate and distinct, the Federal Government to be supreme in its powers as defined and limited to the Constitution, and outside or beyond them powerless to change, influence, or control all other governmental powers which were expressly "reserved to the States respectively, or to the people."

. . .

. . . The bill is sectional. It is aimed at the South. Is there anything anywhere in the bill to show that it is not? . . .

. . . [T]he [Speaker of the House] practically admits . . . that if the defense which he alleges is made by the Southern people, that they defraud the negro for the preservation of their own civilization, were true, that it would be proper and right and admissible. I say he admits practically that, for the preservation of State governments, property and life, the things that are charged against the people of the South might be proper; yet that when you come to national elections it would not do.

Why gentlemen, is it possible that the man who poses as the great friend of the negro would admit that it was proper to kill him or cheat him for one purpose, but very wicked, immoral, and improper to do so for another. . . .

. . .

Now, I say that the South is getting along first rate. We ask you to give us a free chance in the race of life. We know better how to attend to these social questions than you can possibly know, with all your professed patriotism. We know perfectly well that we have a serious problem before us; that we are educating the negro; that we are giving him those rights which make him prosperous and happy; that we are doing for him more than you can do for him and will continue to do it. We ask for our section what patriotic sons of Erin all over the civilized globe demand for their race, "Home rule for Ireland." Our cause is the same.

Now, I ask you where the demand for this bill comes from. Does it come from the negro? Does it come from the Southern Republicans? Where does it come from? The committee to which I have the honor to belong have had some advocates of this subject before it. Who were they? Most of them politicians, and negroes who live by politics, and one poor fellow who has gone crazy since, who is now in the asylum and who was crazy then, and that class of evidence is the basis of this bill. The business people of the country, North and South, do not want it, for they know that it will disorganize business in many portions of the country, endanger capital invested, and bring discontent and strife where now peace and happiness reign. . . .

Plessy v. Ferguson, 163 U.S. 537 (1896)

Homer Plessy was a person of color who on June 7, 1892, purchased a first-class ticket on the East Louisiana Railway to travel from New Orleans to Covington, Louisiana. Plessy sat down in a car reserved for white persons only. After refusing to obey the conductor's order to move, Plessy was removed from the train and arrested for violating state segregation laws. The Louisiana state legislature in 1890 had decreed "that all railway companies carrying passengers in their coaches in this state, shall provide equal but separate accommodations for the white, and colored races," and that "any passenger insisting on going into a coach or compartment to which by race he does not belong, shall be liable to a fine of twenty-five dollars, or in lieu thereof to imprisonment for a period of not more than twenty days in the parish prison." A trial court convicted Plessy, and that conviction was sustained by the Supreme Court of Louisiana. Plessy appealed to the Supreme Court of the United States.

Plessy v. Ferguson *is an early example of a test case. Homer Plessy did not act spontaneously on June 7. The Committee of Citizens, a group of prominent African-Americans in New Orleans, recruited Plessy to challenge the constitutionality of early segregation laws. Plessy was chosen because he had only one great-grandparent who was a person of color and could be identified as a person of color only by acquaintances. Given his complexion, Plessy would have been allowed to occupy the car reserved for white persons had the East Louisiana Railway not cooperated with the Committee of Citizens in bringing the test case. Eager to overturn the Louisiana law and similar ones being passed in the Jim Crow South, the Committee of Citizens recruited Albion Tourgee, a prominent Republican journalist and lawyer, to argue their case before the Supreme Court.*[54]

The Supreme Court rejected Plessy's appeal by a 7-1 vote. Justice Brown's majority opinion declared that racial segregation was a reasonable exercise of the police power. Compare the majority opinion in Plessy *to the opinions in* Lochner v. New York *(1905). Was the judicial majority in* Plessy *more deferential to the state legislature than was the judicial majority in* Lochner, *or were the same standards applied in both the race and the contract cases? Notice the majority's assumption that race is a fixed category that legislation is "powerless" to change. What is the point of that assertion? Louisiana was not attempting to force integration, but mandate segregation.*

Justice Harlan's dissent is most noted for the claim, "There is no caste here. Our constitution is color-blind, and neither knows nor tolerates classes among citizens." Many contemporary Americans cite this claim when asserting that affirmative action programs are unconstitutional. Others insist that such assertions read Harlan out of context. Based on your reading of the dissent, which reading do you think is correct? Consider in this context two other Harlan opinions issued shortly after Plessy. *In* Cumming v. Richmond County Board of Education *(1899) a unanimous Supreme Court found no problems with a local school board that, in a financial crisis, chose to close the high school for students of color while keeping open the high school for white students. After noting that the plaintiffs in the case had not challenged the segregation laws, but merely the allocation of funds between segregated schools, Harlan's opinion stated,*

> *The board had before it the question whether it should maintain, under its control, a high school for about 60 colored children or withhold the benefits of education in primary schools from 300 children of the same race. It was impossible, the board believed, to give educational facilities to the 300 colored children who were unprovided for, if it maintained a separate school for the 60 children who wished to have a high-school education. Its decision was in the interest of the greater number of colored children, leaving the smaller number to obtain a high-school education in existing private institutions at*

54. For a good case study of the Plessy litigation, see Charles A. Lofgren, *The Plessy Case: A Legal Historical Interpretation* (New York: Oxford University Press, 1987).

an expense not beyond that incurred in the high school discontinued by the board.

In Berea College v. Commonwealth of Kentucky *(1908) a judicial majority ruled that Kentucky could prohibit any association incorporated by the state from "teach[ing] white and negro children in a private school at the same time and place." Justice Harlan was the sole dissenter. He declared,*

> *The capacity to impart instruction to others is given by the Almighty for beneficent purposes; and its use may not be forbidden or interfered with by government,—certainly not, unless such instruction is, in its nature, harmful to the public morals or imperils the public safety. The right to impart instruction, harmless in itself or beneficial to those who receive it, is a substantial right of property,—especially, where the services are rendered for compensation. But even if such right be not strictly a property right, it is, beyond question, part of one's liberty as guaranteed against hostile state action by the Constitution of the United States. . . . If pupils, of whatever race,—certainly, if they be citizens,—choose, with the consent of their parents, or voluntarily, to sit together in a private institution of learning while receiving instruction which is not in its nature harmful or dangerous to the public, no government, whether Federal or state, can legally forbid their coming together, or being together temporarily, for such an innocent purpose.*

Harlan in both Cumming *and* Berea College *asserted that the constitutionality of segregated schools was not an issue in these cases. Did his dissent in* Plessy *commit him to declaring such measures unconstitutional in related cases? Does Harlan's refusal to commit on this issue in subsequent cases suggest that he regarded school segregation as an open question, perhaps because he may have thought the police powers case stronger?*

Many years later, at a memorial service for Justice Harlan, Justice Brown recanted his original opinion in Plessy.[55]

JUSTICE BROWN delivered the opinion of the court.

. . .

That [the Louisiana law] does not conflict with the thirteenth amendment . . . is too clear for argument. Slavery implies involuntary servitude,—a state of bondage; the ownership of mankind as a chattel, or, at least, the control of the labor and services of one man for the benefit of another, and the absence of a legal right to the disposal of his own person, property, and services. . . .

A statute which implies merely a legal distinction between the white and colored races—a distinction which is founded in the color of the two races, and which must always exist so long as white men are distinguished from the other race by color—has no tendency to destroy the legal equality of the two races, or re-establish a state of involuntary servitude. . . .

. . .

. . . The object of the [Fourteenth] amendment was undoubtedly to enforce the absolute equality of the two races before the law, but, in the nature of things, it could not have been intended to abolish distinctions based upon color, or to enforce social, as distinguished from political, equality, or a commingling of the two races upon terms unsatisfactory to either. Laws permitting, and even requiring, their separation, in places where they are liable to be brought into contact, do not necessarily imply the inferiority of either race to the other, and have been generally, if not universally, recognized as within the competency of the state legislatures in the exercise of their police power. The most common instance of this is connected with the establishment of separate schools for white and colored children, which have been held to be a valid exercise of the legislative power even by courts of states where the political rights of the colored race have been longest and most earnestly enforced.

. . .

It is claimed by the plaintiff in error that, in a mixed community, the reputation of belonging to the dominant race, in this instance the white race, is "property," in the same sense that a right of action or of inheritance is property. Conceding this to be so, for the purposes of this case, we are unable to see how this statute deprives him of, or in any way affects his right to, such property. If he be a white man, and assigned to a colored coach, he may have his action for damages against the company for being deprived of his so-called "property." Upon the other hand, if he be a colored man, and be so assigned, he has been deprived of no property, since he is not lawfully entitled to the reputation of being a white man.

In this connection, it is also suggested by the learned counsel for the plaintiff in error that the same argument that will justify the state legislature in requiring railways to provide separate accommodations for the

55. H. B. Brown, "The Dissenting Opinions of Mr. Justice Harlan," *American Law Review* 46 (1912): 321.

two races will also authorize them to require separate cars to be provided for people whose hair is of a certain color, or who are aliens, or who belong to certain nationalities, or to enact laws requiring colored people to walk upon one side of the street, and white people upon the other, or requiring white men's houses to be painted white, and colored men's black, or their vehicles or business signs to be of different colors, upon the theory that one side of the street is as good as the other, or that a house or vehicle of one color is as good as one of another color. The reply to all this is that every exercise of the police power must be reasonable, and extend only to such laws as are enacted in good faith for the promotion of the public good, and not for the annoyance or oppression of a particular class. . . .

So far, then, as a conflict with the fourteenth amendment is concerned, the case reduces itself to the question whether the statute of Louisiana is a reasonable regulation, and with respect to this there must necessarily be a large discretion on the part of the legislature. In determining the question of reasonableness, it is at liberty to act with reference to the established usages, customs, and traditions of the people, and with a view to the promotion of their comfort, and the preservation of the public peace and good order. Gauged by this standard, we cannot say that a law which authorizes or even requires the separation of the two races in public conveyances is unreasonable, or more obnoxious to the fourteenth amendment than the acts of congress requiring separate schools for colored children in the District of Columbia, the constitutionality of which does not seem to have been questioned, or the corresponding acts of state legislatures.

We consider the underlying fallacy of the plaintiff's argument to consist in the assumption that the enforced separation of the two races stamps the colored race with a badge of inferiority. If this be so, it is not by reason of anything found in the act, but solely because the colored race chooses to put that construction upon it. . . . The argument . . . assumes that social prejudices may be overcome by legislation, and that equal rights cannot be secured to the negro except by an enforced commingling of the two races. We cannot accept this proposition. If the two races are to meet upon terms of social equality, it must be the result of natural affinities, a mutual appreciation of each other's merits, and a voluntary consent of individuals. . . . Legislation is powerless to eradicate racial instincts, or to abolish distinctions based upon physical differences, and the attempt to do so can only result in accentuating the difficulties of the present situation. If the civil and political rights of both races be equal, one cannot be inferior to the other civilly or politically. If one race be inferior to the other socially, the constitution of the United States cannot put them upon the same plane.

. . .

JUSTICE BREWER did not hear the argument or participate in the decision of this case.

JUSTICE HARLAN, dissenting.

In respect of civil rights, common to all citizens, the constitution of the United States does not, I think, permit any public authority to know the race of those entitled to be protected in the enjoyment of such rights. . . . Indeed, such legislation as that here in question is inconsistent not only with that equality of rights which pertains to citizenship, national and state, but with the personal liberty enjoyed by every one within the United States.

. . .

. . . Every one knows that the statute in question had its origin in the purpose, not so much to exclude white persons from railroad cars occupied by blacks, as to exclude colored people from coaches occupied by or assigned to white persons. . . . No one would be so wanting in candor as to assert the contrary. . . .

. . . If a state can prescribe, as a rule of civil conduct, that whites and blacks shall not travel as passengers in the same railroad coach, why may it not so regulate the use of the streets of its cities and towns as to compel white citizens to keep on one side of a street, and black citizens to keep on the other? Why may it not, upon like grounds, punish whites and blacks who ride together in street cars or in open vehicles on a public road or street? Why may it not require sheriffs to assign whites to one side of a court room, and blacks to the other? And why may it not also prohibit the commingling of the two races in the galleries of legislative halls or in public assemblages convened for the consideration of the political questions of the day? Further, if this statute of Louisiana is consistent with the personal liberty of citizens, why may not the state require the separation in railroad coaches of native and naturalized citizens of the United States, or of Protestants and Roman Catholics?

. . .

The white race deems itself to be the dominant race in this country. And so it is, in prestige, in achievements, in education, in wealth, and in power. So, I doubt not, it will continue to be for all time, if it remains true to its great heritage, and holds fast to the principles of constitutional liberty. But in view of the constitution, in the eye of the law, there is in this country no superior, dominant, ruling class of citizens. There is no caste here. Our constitution is color-blind, and neither knows nor tolerates classes among citizens. In respect of civil rights, all citizens are equal before the law. The humblest is the peer of the most powerful. The law regards man as man, and takes no account of his surroundings or of his color when his civil rights as guarantied by the supreme law of the land are involved. It is therefore to be regretted that this high tribunal, the final expositor of the fundamental law of the land, has reached the conclusion that it is competent for a state to regulate the enjoyment by citizens of their civil rights solely upon the basis of race.

In my opinion, the judgment this day rendered will, in time, prove to be quite as pernicious as the decision made by this tribunal in the *Dred Scott* Case.

...The present decision, it may well be apprehended, will not only stimulate aggressions, more or less brutal and irritating, upon the admitted rights of colored citizens, but will encourage the belief that it is possible, by means of state enactments, to defeat the beneficent purposes which the people of the United States had in view when they adopted the recent amendments of the constitution, by one of which the blacks of this country were made citizens of the United States and of the states in which they respectively reside, and whose privileges and immunities, as citizens, the states are forbidden to abridge. Sixty millions of whites are in no danger from the presence here of eight millions of blacks. The destinies of the two races, in this country, are indissolubly linked together, and the interests of both require that the common government of all shall not permit the seeds of race hate to be planted under the sanction of law. What can more certainly arouse race hate, what more certainly create and perpetuate a feeling of distrust between these races, than state enactments which, in fact, proceed on the ground that colored citizens are so inferior and degraded that they cannot be allowed to sit in public coaches occupied by white citizens? That, as all will admit, is the real meaning of such legislation as was enacted in Louisiana.

. . .

I am of opinion that the state of Louisiana is inconsistent with the personal liberty of citizens, white and black, in that state, and hostile to both the spirit and letter of the constitution of the United States. If laws of like character should be enacted in the several states of the Union, the effect would be in the highest degree mischievous. Slavery, as an institution tolerated by law, would, it is true, have disappeared from our country; but there would remain a power in the states, by sinister legislation, to interfere with the full enjoyment of the blessings of freedom, to regulate civil rights, common to all citizens, upon the basis of race, and to place in a condition of legal inferiority a large body of American citizens, now constituting a part of the political community, called the "People of the United States," for whom, and by whom through representatives, our government is administered. Such a system is inconsistent with the guaranty given by the constitution to each state of a republican form of government, and may be stricken down by congressional action, or by the courts in the discharge of their solemn duty to maintain the supreme law of the land, anything in the constitution or laws of any state to the contrary notwithstanding....

John B. Knox, Address to the Alabama Constitutional Convention (1901)[56]

The Alabama Constitutional Convention of 1901 was one of many southern constitutional conventions that took place at the turn of the twentieth century. These conventions were devoted to promoting white supremacy, although delegates also considered other issues related to representation, state debts, industrialization, and various matters of more local interest. White supremacists in the South recognized that they could not pass laws that bluntly declared that persons of color could not vote. Nevertheless, such federal court decisions as Williams v. Mississippi *(1898) gave southerners confidence that measures designed to disenfranchise persons of color would pass judicial scrutiny, as long as they did not rely explicitly on racial classifications.*

John B. Knox, a local attorney, was elected to preside over the Alabama Constitutional Convention. The excerpt below is from his initial address to the delegates. Both Knox and the resulting Alabama Constitution focused primarily on laws disenfranchising persons of color. Why did white supremacists rely so heavily on disenfranchisement as opposed to other racist measures? Why were they so confident that

56. Excerpted from John Barnett Knox, *Address of Hon. John B. Knox* (Montgomery, AL: The Brown's Printing Co., 1901).

the Alabama Constitution would survive federal judicial review?

. . .

In my judgment, the people of Alabama have been called upon to face no more important situation than now confronts us, unless it be when they, in 1861, stirred by the momentous issue of impending conflict between the North and the South, were forced to decide whether they would remain in or withdraw from the Union.

Then, as now, the negro was the prominent factor in the issue.

. . .

And what is it that we want to do? Why it is within the limits imposed by the Federal Constitution, to establish white supremacy in this State.

This is our problem, and we should be permitted to deal with it, unobstructed by outside influences, with a sense of our responsibilities as citizens and our duty to posterity.

. . .

. . . [W]e may congratulate ourselves that this sectional feeling which has served to impair the harmony of our common country, and to limit the power and retard the development of the greatest government on earth, is fast yielding to reason.

. . .

The Southern man knows the negro, and the negro knows him. The only conflict which has, or is ever likely to arise, springs from the effort of ill-advised friends in the North to confer upon him, without previous training or preparation, places of power and responsibility, for which he is wholly unfitted, either by capacity or experience.

. . .

But if we would have white supremacy, we must establish it by law—not by force or fraud. If you teach your boy that it is right to buy a vote, it is an easy step for him to learn to use money to bribe or corrupt officials or trustees of any class. If you teach your boy that it is right to steal votes, it is an easy step for him to believe that it is right to steal whatever he may need or greatly desire. The results of such an influence will enter every branch of society, it will reach your bank cashiers, and affect positions of trust in every department; it will ultimately enter your courts, and affect the administrations of justice.

. . .

Mississippi is the pioneer State in this movement. In addition to the payment of a poll tax, there it is provided that only those can vote who have been duly registered, and only those can register who can read, or understand when read to them, any clause in the Constitution. The decision as to who are sufficiently intelligent to meet the requirements of the understanding clause is exclusively in the hands of the registrars.

. . .

In Louisiana and North Carolina, the methods of relief adopted are substantially the same, and require, in addition to the poll tax clause, that the voter shall register in accordance with the provisions of the Constitution, and only those are authorized to register who are able to read and write any section of the Constitution in the English language, with the further proviso, that no male person who was, on January 1st, 1867, or at any time prior thereto, entitled to vote under the laws of any State in the United States, wherein he then resided, and no lineal descendant of any such person, shall be denied the right to register and vote at any election, by reason of his failure to possess the educational qualifications prescribed, provided he registers within the time limited by the terms of the Constitution. . . .

. . .

These provisions are justified in law and in morals, because it is said that the negro is not discriminated against on account of his race, but on account of his intellectual and moral condition. There is a difference, it is claimed with great force, between the uneducated white man and the ignorant negro. There is in the white man an inherited capacity for government, which is wholly wanting in the negro. Before the art of reading and writing was known, the ancestors of the Anglo-Saxon had established an orderly system of government, the basis in fact of the one under which we now live. That the negro on the other hand, is descended from a race lowest in intelligence and moral perceptions of all the races of men. . . .

As stated by Judge [Thomas] Cooley, the right of suffrage is not a natural right, because it exists where it is allowed to be exercised only for the good of the State—to say that those whose participation in the affairs of the State would endanger and imperil the good of the State have nevertheless, the right to participate, is not only folly in itself, but it is to set the individual above the State.

The election laws in Massachusetts contain substantially the same provisions as are embodied in the Constitutions of Louisiana and North Carolina just referred to. The election law of that State, as it stands today, provides that the voter must be able to read the

Constitution of the Commonwealth in the English language, and to write his name, except that "no person who is prevented from reading and writing as aforesaid, by physical disability, or who had the right to vote on the first day of May in the year 1857, shall, if otherwise qualified, be deprived of the right to vote by reason of not being able so to read or write."

. . .

The exception in the Massachusetts law was, no doubt, directed against illiterate and incompetent immigrants, whereas the provisions in the Constitutions of Louisiana and North Carolina were directed against illiterate and incompetent negroes, as well as foreigners.

But it is beyond the province of courts . . . to inquire into the motives of the law-making power; their function is confined to ascertaining the meaning and effect of the law drawn in question. . . .

. . .

It has been urged in some quarters as a reason why this movement for a new Constitution should be defeated that we propose to adopt a suffrage plan which will offer to the negro an incentive to obtain an education, while the child of the white man will be without a like stimulus, because protected in his right to vote without regard to the density of his ignorance.

I do not understand that any delegate to the Convention is pledged to any such legislation. We are pledged, "not to deprive any white man of the right to vote," but this does not extend unless this Convention chooses to extend it beyond the right of voters now living. It is a question worthy of careful consideration, whether we would be warranted in pursuing any course which would have a tendency to condemn any part of our population to a condition of perpetual illiteracy. Provisions of the Constitution prescribing educational qualifications for voters as they affect those who now have no right to vote but in the course of time will acquire the right are wisely intended to serve not as a curse, but as a noble stimulus to the acquirement of an education and to a proper preparation for meeting and discharging the duties of a citizen. . . .

The Birth of the Civil Rights Movement

The modern civil rights movement was born in the first decades of the twentieth century. In 1905, W. E. B. DuBois and William Monroe Trotter founded the Niagara Movement. The Niagara Declaration of Principles stated,

Suffrage: . . . [W]e believe that this class of American citizens should protest emphatically and continually against the curtailment of their political rights. We believe in manhood suffrage; we believe that no man is so good, intelligent or wealthy as to be entrusted wholly with the welfare of his neighbor.

Civil Liberty: We believe also in protest against the curtailment of our civil rights. All American citizens have the right to equal treatment in places of public entertainment according to their behavior and deserts.

Economic Opportunity: We especially complain against the denial of equal opportunities to us in economic life; in the rural districts of the South this amounts to peonage and virtual slavery; all over the South it tends to crush labor and small business enterprises; and everywhere American prejudice, helped often by iniquitous laws, is making it more difficult for Negro-Americans to earn a decent living.

Education: Common school education should be free to all American children and compulsory. High school training should be adequately provided for all, and college training should be the monopoly of no class or race in any section of our common country. We believe that, in defense of our own institutions, the United States should aid common school education, particularly in the South, and we especially recommend concerted agitation to this end. We urge an increase in public high school facilities in the South, where the Negro-Americans are almost wholly without such provisions. We favor well-equipped trade and technical schools for the training of artisans, and the need of adequate and liberal endowment for a few institutions of higher education must be patent to sincere well-wishers of the race.

Courts: We demand upright judges in courts, juries selected without discrimination on account of color and the same measure of punishment and the same efforts at reformation for black as for white offenders. We need orphanages and farm schools for dependent children, juvenile reformatories for delinquents, and the abolition of the dehumanizing convict-lease system.[57]

---

57. W. E. B. DuBois, "Declaration of Principles," in *African American Political Thought, 1890–1930: Washington, DuBois, Garvey, and Randolph,* ed. Cary D. Wintz (Armonk, NY: M.E. Sharpe, 1996), 103–04.

Between 1909 and 1911 the Niagara Movement was reconstituted as the NAACP. The mission statement of that group declared that the NAACP would "promote equality of rights and eradicate caste or race prejudice among the citizens of the United States; advance the interest of colored citizens; secure for them impartial suffrage; and increase their opportunities for securing justice in the courts, education for the children, employment according to their ability and complete equality before law."[58] By the end of the Republican Era the NAACP was an influential voice in the fight against lynching, disenfranchisement, and segregation. John Parker, a Hoover nominee from North Carolina, failed to be confirmed by the Senate for seat on the Supreme Court in part because of NAACP opposition.

NAACP litigation campaigns and greater elite support for pruning the excesses of Jim Crow help explain why the Supreme Court became more receptive to constitutional claims raised by African-Americans in the last decades of the Republican Era. The justices from 1911 to 1932 declared unconstitutional peonage laws that essentially forced African-Americans to remain with their present employers (*Bailey v. Alabama* [1911], *United States v. Reynolds* [1914]), struck down laws mandating residential segregation (*Buchanan v. Warley* [1917]), put some teeth into the concept of "separate but equal" (*McCabe v. Atchison, Topeka & Santa Fe Railway Company* [1914]), and voided some state restrictions on African-American voting (*Guinn and Beal v. United States* [1915]). These decisions mostly influenced American race relations at the margin. Nevertheless, both the institutional and precedential foundations for the modern civil rights movement were in place when Franklin Delano Roosevelt became president.

Buchanan v. Warley, 245 U.S. 60 (1917)

Charles Buchanan, a white person, sold a house in Louisville, Kentucky, to William Warley, a person of color. Their contract required Warley to pay only if he had a legal right under local law to "occupy said property as a residence." Louisville law at the time forbade any person of color from moving into any block in which "a greater number of houses are occupied as residences . . . by white persons than are occupied as residences . . . by colored people." The next section of the legislation placed the same constraint on white persons moving into predominantly African-American neighborhoods. Buchanan claimed that Warley had to pay the purchase price because the Louisville ordinance violated the Fourteenth Amendment. A local trial court disagreed. The Court of Appeals of Kentucky sustained the ruling that the Louisville statute was constitutional. Buchanan appealed to the Supreme Court of the United States.

The Supreme Court unanimously declared unconstitutional the law mandating residential segregation in Louisville. Justice William Day's majority opinion ruled that states could not forbid persons from selling their property to a person of a different race. Day's majority opinion claims that Buchanan *raised different issues than* Plessy v. Ferguson *(1896), which permitted racial segregation in transportation. How does Day distinguish* Plessy*? What do you believe best explains the difference between the two cases? Are the Court's "liberty of contract" cases relevant here?*

White supremacists had more luck when private means for promoting racial segregation came before the Supreme Court. A unanimous Supreme Court in Corrigan v. Buckley *(1926) ruled that private agreements not to sell property to persons of color did not violate any constitutional rights. Justice Sanford's opinion stated, "none of [the post-Civil War] amendments prohibited private individuals from entering into contracts respecting the control and disposition of their own property."*

JUSTICE DAY delivered the opinion of the Court.

. . .

The Fourteenth Amendment protects life, liberty, and property from invasion by the states without due process of law. Property is more than the mere thing which a person owns. It is elementary that it includes the right to acquire, use, and dispose of it. The Constitution protects these essential attributes of property. . . . Property consists of the free use, enjoyment, and disposal of a person's acquisitions without control or diminution save by the law of the land.

True it is that dominion over property springing from ownership is not absolute and unqualified. The disposition and use of property may be controlled in the exercise of the police power in the interest of the public health, convenience, or welfare. Harmful occupations may be controlled and regulated. Legitimate business may also be regulated in the interest of the public. Certain uses of property may be confined to portions of the municipality other than the resident district, such as livery stables, brickyards and the like, because of the impairment of the health and comfort of

58. The Crisis 2 (1911), 193.

the occupants of neighboring property. Many illustrations might be given from the decisions of this court, and other courts, of this principle, but these cases do not touch the one at bar.

. . .

. . . While a principal purpose of the [Fourteenth] Amendment was to protect persons of color, the broad language used was deemed sufficient to protect all persons, white or black, against discriminatory legislation by the states. This is now the settled law. In many of the cases since arising the question of color has not been involved and the cases have been decided upon alleged violations of civil or property rights irrespective of the race or color of the complainant. . . .

. . .

The defendant in error insists that *Plessy v. Ferguson* (1896) is controlling in principle in favor of the judgment of the court below. . . . It is to be observed that in that case there was no attempt to deprive persons of color of transportation in the coaches of the public carrier, and the express requirements were for equal though separate accommodations for the white and colored races. In *Plessy v. Ferguson*, classification of accommodations was permitted upon the basis of equality for both races.

. . .

That there exists a serious and difficult problem arising from a feeling of race hostility which the law is powerless to control, and to which it must give a measure of consideration, may be freely admitted. But its solution cannot be promoted by depriving citizens of their constitutional rights and privileges.

. . .

It is the purpose of such enactments, and, it is frankly avowed it will be their ultimate effect, to require by law, at least in residential districts, the compulsory separation of the races on account of color. Such action is said to be essential to the maintenance of the purity of the races, although it is to be noted in the ordinance under consideration that the employment of colored servants in white families is permitted, and nearby residences of colored persons not coming within the blocks, as defined in the ordinance, are not prohibited.

The case presented does not deal with an attempt to prohibit the amalgamation of the races. The right which the ordinance annulled was the civil right of a white man to dispose of his property if he saw fit to do so to a person of color and of a colored person to make such disposition to a white person.

It is urged that this proposed segregation will promote the public peace by preventing race conflicts. Desirable as this is, and important as is the preservation of the public peace, this aim cannot be accomplished by laws or ordinances which deny rights created or protected by the federal Constitution.

It is said that such acquisitions by colored persons depreciate property owned in the neighborhood by white persons. But property may be acquired by undesirable white neighbors or put to disagreeable though lawful uses with like results.

We think this attempt to prevent the alienation of the property in question to a person of color was not a legitimate exercise of the police power of the state, and is in direct violation of the fundamental law enacted in the Fourteenth Amendment of the Constitution preventing state interference with property rights except by due process of law. That being the case, the ordinance cannot stand. . . .

C. Gender

The ratification of the Nineteenth Amendment in 1920 raised questions about whether women had a constitutional right to serve on juries. Most state constitutions mandated that jurors be chosen from among eligible voters. Some state courts interpreted these provisions as granting women the right to sit on juries once they were granted the right to vote. *People v. Bartlz* (MI 1920) declared, "It seems clear to us that by making a woman an elector she is thereby placed in a class which makes her eligible for jury duty."[59] Other state tribunals interpreted state constitutional provisions on jury service as prohibiting woman from service on juries because women were not voters when those constitutional provisions were ratified. *People ex rel. Fyfe v. Barnett* (IL 1925) stated, "While [the Nineteenth Amendment] had the effect of nullifying every expression in the Constitution and laws of the state denying or abridging the right of suffrage to women on account of their sex, it did not purport to have any effect whatever on the subject of liability or eligibility of citizens for jury service."[60]

Women debated the next steps toward gender equality. Alice Paul and other members of the National Woman's Party insisted on the Blanket Amendment, a constitutional provision that provided the same protection against gender discrimination as the Fourteenth Amendment provided against racial discrimination. Many progressive women opposed this amendment,

59. *People v. Bartlz*, 212 Mich. 580 (1920).
60. *People ex rel. Fyfe v. Barnett*, 319 Ill. 403 (1925).

believing that women needed special protections in industry that might be declared unconstitutional if the Blanket Amendment were ratified. This schism remained vibrant long after the Republican Era ended.

Debates over the Blanket Amendment (1924)[61]

Shortly after the Nineteenth Amendment was ratified, the National Woman's Party drafted and several members of Congress proposed the Blanket Amendment. The original version of this proposal, later known as the Equal Rights Amendment, declared, "Men and women shall have Equal Rights throughout the United States and every place subject to its jurisdiction." The Blanket Amendment sparked a sharp controversy among women's groups. Many women favored tearing down all laws that discriminated between men and women. Women associated with the labor movement, however, insisted that elected officials should be free to pass legislation that provided special protections to women in the work force.

The August 1924 edition of Forum *presented a debate between two prominent feminist activists. Doris Stevens (1892–1963) was a leader in the fight for women's suffrage and a founder of the National Woman's Party. Alice*

61. "The Blanket Amendment—A Debate," *The Forum* 72 (August 1924):148.

"Until Women Vote," by Rollin Kirby, from a 1915 issue of Woman's Journal.

Illustration 7-6 Until Women Vote

This 1915 political cartoon in a feminist journal reflects the close ties between the women's suffrage movement and the economic reform movement. Many feminists argued that voting rights for women would empower women economically and politically and lead to greater support for social reform legislation.

Source: The Granger Collection, New York.

Hamilton (1869–1970) was the first woman to be a professor of medicine at Harvard Medical School. On what points do Stevens and Hamilton agree? On what points do they disagree? Do they disagree on the consequences of the Blanket Amendment or on the principles embodied in the Blanket Amendment? Whose view would you have supported in 1924? Hamilton makes more generalizations about women than does Stevens. How do these generalizations influence her opinions? Do you believe that Hamilton would have taken a different position today? Would you?

Doris Stevens, "Suffrage Does Not Give Equality"

. . .

When women finally got the right to vote, after seventy-five years of agitation in the United States, many good citizens sighed with relief and said, "Now that's over. The woman problem is disposed of." But was it? Exactly what do women want now? Just this. They want the same rights, in law and in custom, with which every man is now endowed through the accident of being born a male. . . .

There is not a single State in the Union in which men and women live under equal protection of the law. There is not a State which does not in some respects still reflect toward women the attitude of either the old English Common Law or the Napoleonic Code. Woman is still conceived to be in subjection to, and under the control of the husband, if married, or of the male members of the family, if unmarried. In most of the States the father and mother have been made equal guardians of their children, but many of these States still deny the mother equal rights to the earnings and services of the children. . . . In forty States the husband owns the services of his wife in the home. In most of these States this means that the husband recovers the damages for the loss of her services to him. More than half the States do not permit women to serve on juries. Some legislators oppose jury service for women because of "moral hazard" of deliberating in a room with men. . . . In only a third of the States is prostitution a crime for the male as well as the female.

With the removal of all legal discriminations against women solely on account of sex, women will possess with men:

Equal control of their children
Equal control of their property
Equal control of their earnings
Equal right to make contracts
Equal citizenship rights
Equal inheritance rights
Equal control of national, state, and local government
Equal opportunities in schools and universities
Equal opportunities in government service
Equal opportunities in professions and industries
Equal pay for equal work

. . .

. . . The amendment under consideration will in no way affect [helpful maternal legislation], for the simple reason that it is not based on sex, but upon the special need of a given group under certain circumstances. The same is true of widows' pensions. Such pensions are written for the benefit of the child, and are being given more and more to whichever parent of the child survives, widow or widower. . . . The final objection says: Grant political, social, and civil equality to women, but do not give equality to women in industry.

Here lies the heart of the whole controversy. It is not astonishing, but very intelligent indeed, that the battle should center on the point of woman's right to sell her labor on the same terms as man. For unless she is able equally to compete, to earn, to control, and to invest her money, unless in short woman's economic position is made more secure, certainly she cannot establish equality in fact. She will have won merely the shadow of power without essential and authentic substance.

Those who would limit only women to certain occupations and to certain restricted hours of work, base their program of discrimination on two points, the "moral hazard" to women and their biological inferiority. It is a philosophy which would penalize all women because some women are morally frail and physically weak. It asks women to set their pace with the weakest members of their sex. All men are not strong. Happily it has not occurred to society to limit the development of all men because some are weak. Would these protectionists be willing to say that because some men-members of the Cabinet had been suspected of morality frailty, no men should henceforth serve as Cabinet Ministers? . . .

. . . Women will be quite as sensible and adroit at avoiding work beyond their strength as men have been, once they have a free choice. What reason is there to believe that if tomorrow the whole industrial field were opened to women on the same terms as men, women would insist on doing the most menial tasks in the world, the most difficult, the tasks for which they are least fitted? . . .

. . .

But, it is argued, women are more easily exploited in industry than men. There are reasons for that outside of sex, not the least of which is the shocking neglect by men's labor organizations to organize women in their trades. . . . Protection is a delusion. Protection, no matter how benevolent in motive, unless applied alike to both sexes, amounts to actual penalization.

The Woman's Party is not an industrial organization and therefore does not propose to say whether workers shall work eight or four hours a day, or what wages shall be paid for such work; whether more leisure for the masses shall be got by legislation or unionism. In the best interests of women, it stands against restrictions which are not alike for both sexes, and which, therefore, constantly limit the scope of women's entry into the field of more desirable and better paid work. It believes that no human being, man or woman, should be exploited by industry. As firmly it believes that just so long as sex is made the artificial barrier to labor-selling, merit can never become the criterion of an applicant for a job. . . .

Alice Hamilton, "Protection for Women Workers"

. . . I belong to the group which holds that the right method is to repeal or alter one by one the laws that now hamper women or work injustice to them, and which opposes the constitutional amendment sponsored by the Woman's Party on the ground that it is too dangerously sweeping and all-inclusive. If no legislation is to be permitted except it apply to both sexes, we shall find it impossible to regulate by law the hours of wages or conditions of work of women and that would be, in my opinion, a harm far greater than the good that might be accomplished by removing certain antiquated abuses and injustices, which, bad as they are, do not injure nearly as many women as would be affected if all protective laws for working women were rendered unconstitutional.

. . .

We are told by members of the Women's Party that if we "free" the working woman, allow her to "compete on equal terms with men," her industrial status will at once be raised. She is supposed now to be suffering from the handicap of laws regulating her working conditions and hours of labor and longing to be rid of them. . . . Will anyone say that it is better to be a woman wage earner in Indiana where hours are practically unrestricted than in Ohio where a woman is sure of a nine-hour day and a six-day week? Is the textile worker in Rhode Island freer and happier than her sister in Massachusetts because she is not handicapped by legal restrictions, except a ten-hour day, while the Massachusetts woman may work only nine hours, and that not without a break, must have time for her noonday meal, one day of rest in seven, no night work, and is not allowed to sell her work for less than a minimum living wage? . . . I should like to ask Kansas women if they envy the freedom of the women of Missouri and if they are ready to give up the laws which provide for an eight-hour day and a six-day week and a minimum wage and no night work.

One great source of weakness in the women's labor movement is the fact that so many of them are very young. . . .

. . . [Young women are] reckless of health and strength, individualistic, lacking the desire to organize, and quite powerless, without organization, to control in any way the conditions of their work.

On the other hand, the older women are as a rule even harder to bring together and more devoid of courage. They are usually mothers of families, widows, or deserted, or with sick or incompetent husbands; they carry the double burden of housework and factory work and they are recognized by all who know the labor world as the most hopeless material for the union organizer, incapable of rebellion, capable of endless submission. It is for these women that the laws prohibiting night work are most needed. The father of a family, if he works at night, can get his sleep during the day and yet have his meals served and his children cared for; the mother of a family cannot, even if her husband is there. . . .

. . .

The advocates of the blanket amendment say that they do not oppose laws designed to protect the child, that they are ready to favor protection of "pregnant persons" and "nursing persons." . . . But the damage done by an industrial poison may antedate pregnancy. Women who have worked in a lead trade before marriage and still more women who work in lead after marriage are more likely to be sterile than women who have worked in other trades; if they conceive they are less likely to carry the child to term; and if they do they are less likely to bear a living child and their living children are less able to survive the first weeks of life.

. . .

In Holland, I am told, the two sexes have recently been put on an equality in industry, not by taking privileges away from the women, but by extending them to the men. Holland is an old country, which has long been used to labor legislation. I cannot believe that we in the United States are nearing that point very fast, though I should like to think so. Meantime, until we reach it, I must, as a practical person, familiar with the great, inarticulate body of working women, reiterate my belief that they are largely helpless, that they have very special needs which unaided they cannot attain, and that it would be a crime for the country to pass legislation which would not only make it impossible to better their lot in the near future but would even deprive them of the small measure of protection they now enjoy.

D. Native Americans

Native Americans who abandoned their tribes were granted citizenship after a long legal and political struggle. The Supreme Court in *Elk v. Wilkins* (1884) rejected claims that the Fourteenth Amendment made Native American citizens. Justice Horace Gray's majority opinion ruled that only Congress could naturalize Native Americans. He wrote,

> The question whether any Indian tribes, or any members thereof, have become so far advanced in civilization that they should be let out of the state of pupilage, and admitted to the privileges and responsibilities of citizenship, is a question to be decided by the nation whose wards they are and whose citizens they seek to become, and not by each Indian for himself.

Congress swiftly responded to this invitation. The Dawes Act (1887) granted citizenship to Native Americans who "resided separate and apart from any tribe of Indians" and "adopted the habits of civilized life." The crucial provision of that federal statute declared:

> Every Indian born within the territorial limits of the United States who has voluntarily taken up, within said limits, his residence separate and apart from any tribe of Indians therein, and has adopted the habits of civilized life, is hereby declared to be a citizen of the United States, and is entitled to all the rights, privileges, and immunities of such citizens, whether said Indian has been or not, by birth or otherwise, a member of any tribe of Indians within the territorial limits of the United States without in any manner affecting the right of any such Indian to tribal or other property.[62]

Native Americans who remained tribal members were not U.S. citizens and were not protected by the Bill of Rights. *Talton v. Mayes* (1896) held that tribal courts could forgo the constitutional protections of the grand jury and due process clauses of the Fifth Amendment. Justice White's majority opinion maintained that tribunals that judged offenses against tribal laws were not federal courts subject to federal constitutional limitations. He wrote,

> The existence of the right in congress to regulate the manner in which the local powers of the Cherokee Nation shall be exercised does not render such local powers federal powers arising from and created by the constitution of the United States. It follows that, as the powers of local self-government enjoyed by the Cherokee Nation existed prior to the constitution, they are not operated upon by the fifth amendment, which, as we have said, had for its sole object to control the powers conferred by the constitution on the national government.

VI. CRIMINAL JUSTICE

MAJOR DEVELOPMENTS

- Birth of the modern exclusionary rule
- Nationalization of the right to counsel
- Supreme Court adopts more progressive notions of "cruel and unusual" punishments

Criminal justice varied according to the crime and the criminal. Many constitutional decision makers who championed the freedom of contract defended the right of businesses to be free from invasive investigations. Current understandings of the Fourth Amendment and the exclusionary rule date from constitutional decisions protecting business enterprises from undue government regulation. During the first quarter of the twentieth century, proponents of civil liberties became

62. 24 U.S. Stat. 388, 390 (1887).

concerned with how the police and courts treated persons of color and political dissidents. The National Popular Government League, a nonpartisan organization of leading progressive elites, complained in 1920 about "continued violation of [the] Constitution and breaking of . . . Laws by the Department of Justice." These complaints included "wholesale arrests . . . without warrant or any process of law; men and women . . . jailed and held *incomunicado* without access of friends or counsel; homes . . . entered without search-warrant. . . workingmen and workingwomen suspected of radical views shamefully abused and maltreated."[63] The foundational decisions on modern habeas corpus and right to counsel are Progressive Era responses to racism and criminal justice in the South. Prohibition also influenced constitutional criminal procedure. American courts in the 1920s were overwhelmed with the novel constitutional claims that arose when police officers used new technologies for detecting bootleggers and bootleggers used such new inventions as the car in attempting to evade capture.

A. Due Process and Habeas Corpus

The Republican Era initially witnessed a sharp curtailment of habeas corpus and due process rights. Reconstruction Era Republicans passed statutes that permitted persons of color to make aggressive use of federal habeas corpus. However, as the federal government retreated from commitments to racial equality, there was a concomitant erosion in the commitment to make the protections of habeas corpus available to defendants of color who believed that justice in the state courts was less than perfect. *Virginia v. Rives* (1879) held that defendants could remove their case to a federal court only when they claimed that a state law violated the federal Constitution, and not when they claimed prejudicial enforcement of state laws. *Ex parte Royall* (1886) ruled that federal courts could not hear habeas corpus claims unless the petitioner had first fully litigated his constitutional claims in a state court. Both rulings had the practical effect of closing the federal courthouse door to most poor litigants and litigants of color, who could not afford the arduous processes required to bring a habeas claim before federal justices.

The combination of race, religion, habeas corpus, and due process was combustible in the early twentieth century. Leo Frank's conviction and death sentence for murder sparked a national controversy, as northern Jews mobilized in response to the "blood libel," the claim that Leo Frank engaged in a Jewish ritual when he allegedly murdered a Christian virgin in order to use her blood to make matzah for Passover. The Supreme Court majority was unmoved by claims that Frank was a victim of mob justice. Justice Pitney's majority opinion in *Frank v. Mangum* (1915) maintained that habeas corpus relief was appropriate only when a state court lacked jurisdiction and that the Georgia trial court that convicted Frank had jurisdiction over murder. "Mere errors in point of law," he declared, "however serious, committed by a criminal court in the exercise of its jurisdiction over a case properly subject to its cognizance, cannot be reviewed by habeas corpus." Justice Holmes, who dissented in *Frank*, was more successful eight years later in *Moore v. Dempsey* (1923), in which his majority opinion insisted that a mob-dominated trial so lacked due process that it could oust the state court of jurisdiction.

Several cases in the 1920s suggested a developing bipartisan consensus on minimum due process standards. *Powell v. Alabama* (1932) ruled that persons had a due process right to counsel in all cases and a right to state-appointed counsel when necessary to achieve justice. *Connally v. General Construction Co.* (1926) declared unconstitutional a state law that required employers to pay "the current rate of per diem wages in the locality" on the ground that the measure was unconstitutionally vague. Justice Sutherland's opinion for the Court stated, "A statute which either forbids or requires the doing of an act in terms so vague that men of common intelligence must necessarily guess at its meaning and differ as to its application violates the first essential of due process of law."

Moore v. Dempsey, 261 U.S. 86 (1923)

Frank Moore and other African-Americans held a political meeting in a church on September 30, 1919. After one member of a white mob who attacked the meeting was killed, a race riot took place. Although numerous African-Americans were killed, local authorities indicted only Moore and four other African-Americans for the murder of Clinton Lee, the one white person killed in the melee. Moore and his

63. National Popular Government League, *Report upon the Illegal Practices by the United States Department Of Justice* (Washington, DC: National Popular Government League, 1920), 2–3.

Illustration 7-7 Prisoners from Elaine Massacre
The U.S. Army intervened in the 1919 race riots in Elaine, Arkansas, which left dozens dead and a large number of black residents under arrest. The U.S. Supreme Court overturned the conviction of some of those prisoners in *Moore v. Dempsey* (1923) at the request of the NAACP.

Source: From the Collections of the Arkansas History Commission.

co-defendants were convicted in a trial that last three-quarters of an hour, in part because a mob outside the courtroom demanded a capital verdict. Their conviction was sustained by the Supreme Court of Arkansas. With assistance from the NAACP, Moore appealed that decision to the Supreme Court of the United States.

The Supreme Court decided by a 7-2 vote that Moore had been unconstitutionally convicted. Justice Holmes's majority opinion ruled that a mob-dominated trial violated due process and justified habeas corpus relief. According to prevailing legal precedents, persons were allowed habeas corpus relief only when they were convicted by a court without jurisdiction. On what basis does Justice Holmes claim that the Arkansas court lacked jurisdiction in this case? Does Holmes insist that any due process violation or only egregious due process violations can oust courts of jurisdiction? On what basis does Justice McReynolds conclude that Moore did not have any due process claim?

JUSTICE HOLMES delivered the opinion of the Court.

. . .

Shortly after the arrest of the petitioners a mob marched to the jail for the purpose of lynching them but were prevented by the presence of United States troops and the promise of . . . leading officials that if the mob would refrain, as the petition puts it, they would execute those found guilty in the form of law. . . . According to affidavits of two white men and the colored witnesses on whose testimony the petitioners were convicted, . . . [local notables] made good their promise by calling colored witnesses and having them whipped and tortured until they would say what was wanted, among them being the two relied on to prove the petitioners' guilt. . . . On November 3 the petitioners were brought into Court, informed that a certain lawyer was appointed their counsel and were placed on trial before a white jury—blacks being systematically excluded from both grand and petit juries. The Court and neighborhood were thronged with an adverse crowd that threatened the most dangerous consequences to anyone interfering with the desired result. The counsel did not venture to demand delay or a change of venue, to challenge a juryman or to ask for separate trials. He had had no preliminary consultation with the accused, called no witnesses for the defence although they could have been produced, and did not put the defendants on the stand. The trial lasted about three-quarters of an hour and in less than five minutes the jury brought in a verdict of guilty of murder in the first degree. According to the allegations and affidavits there never was a chance for the petitioners to be acquitted; no juryman could have voted for an acquittal and continued to live in Phillips County and if any prisoner by any chance had been acquitted by a jury he could not have escaped the mob.

. . .

In *Frank v. Mangum* (1915), it was recognized of course that if in fact a trial is dominated by a mob so that there is an actual interference with the course of justice, there is a departure from due process of law; and that "if the State, supplying no corrective process, carries into execution a judgment of death or imprisonment based upon a verdict thus produced by mob domination, the State deprives the accused of his life or liberty without due process of law." We assume in accordance with that case that the corrective process supplied by the State may be so adequate that interference by habeas corpus ought not to be allowed. It certainly is true that mere mistakes of law in the course of a trial are not to be corrected in that way. But if the case is that the whole proceeding is a mask—that counsel, jury and judge were swept to the fatal end by an irresistible wave of public passion, and that the State Courts failed to correct the wrong, neither perfection in the machinery for correction nor the possibility that the trial court and counsel saw no other way of avoiding an immediate outbreak of the mob can prevent this Court from securing to the petitioners their constitutional rights.

. . .

JUSTICE McREYNOLDS (joined by JUSTICE SUTHERLAND), dissenting.

. . .

The matter is one of gravity. If every man convicted of crime in a state court may thereafter resort to the federal court and by swearing, as advised, that certain allegations of fact tending to impeach his trial are "true to the best of his knowledge and belief," and thereby obtain as of right further review, another way has been added to a list already unfortunately long to prevent prompt punishment. The delays incident to enforcement of our criminal laws have become a national scandal and give serious alarm to those who observe. Wrongly to decide the present cause probably will produce very unfortunate consequences.

. . .

Let us consider with some detail what was presented to the court below.

There was the complete record of the cause in the state courts—trial and Supreme—showing no irregularity. After indictment the defendants were arraigned for trial and eminent counsel appointed to defend them. He cross-examined the witnesses, made exceptions, and evidently was careful to preserve a full and complete transcript of the proceedings. The trial was unusually short but there is nothing in the record to indicate that it was illegally hastened. November 3, 1919, the jury returned a verdict of "guilty"; November 11th the defendants were sentenced to be executed on December 27th. . . .

. . .

It appears that during September, 1919, bloody conflicts took place between whites and blacks in Phillips County, Arkansas—"the Elaine riot." Many negroes and some whites were killed. A committee of seven prominent white men was chosen to direct operations in putting down the so-called insurrection and conduct investigation with a view of discovering and punishing the guilty. This committee published a statement, certainly not intemperate, about October 7th, wherein they stated the "ignorance and superstition of a race of children" was played upon for gain by a black swindler, and told of an organization to attack the whites. It urged all persons white or black, in possession of information which might assist in discovering those responsible for the insurrection, to confer with it, upon the understanding that such action would be for the public safety and the informant's identity carefully safeguarded. I find nothing in this statement which counsels lawlessness or indicates more than an honest effort by upstanding men to meet the grave situation.

. . .

The Supreme Court of the state twice reversed the conviction of other negroes charged with committing murder during the disorders of September, 1919. The first opinion came down on the very day upon which the judgment against petitioners was affirmed, and held the verdict so defective that no judgment could be entered upon it. The second directed a reversal because the trial court had refused to hear evidence on the motion to set aside the regular panel of the petit jury....

...Under the disclosed circumstances I cannot agree that the solemn adjudications by courts of a great state, which this court has refused to review, can be successfully impeached by the mere ex parte affidavits made upon information and belief of interested convicts joined by two white men—confessedly atrocious criminals. The fact that petitioners are poor and ignorant and black naturally arouses sympathy; but that does not release us from enforcing principles which are essential to the orderly operation of our federal system.

B. Search and Seizure

The Supreme Court provided some constitutional protection for businesses against intrusive government investigations. *Boyd v. United States* (1886) invoked both the Fourth and Fifth Amendments when declaring unconstitutional a federal attorney's effort to compel a business to turn over its records. *Gouled v. United States* (1921) articulated what became known as the "mere evidence" rule. Government may use search warrants to look for stolen property or dangerous objects, but not to recover incriminating papers. Justice Clarke stated,

> Although search warrants have thus been used in many cases ever since the adoption of the Constitution, and although their use has been extended from time to time to meet new cases within the old rules, nevertheless it is clear that . . . they may not be used as a means of gaining access to a man's house or office and papers solely for the purpose of making search to secure evidence to be used against him in a criminal or penal proceeding, but that they may be resorted to only when a primary right to such search and seizure may be found in the interest which the public or the complainant may have in the property to be seized, or in the right to the possession of it, or when a valid exercise of the police power renders possession of the property by the accused unlawful and provides that it may be taken.

Federal courts provided less protection to criminal suspects when considering the constitutional status of inventions or technologies unknown to the common law. In *Carroll v. United States* (1925) the Supreme Court ruled that police officers could search cars without a warrant as long as they had probable cause for thinking that the occupants were transporting illegal goods. In justifying less cumbersome access to cars, Chief Justice Taft's majority opinion pointed out that, unlike a house, a "vehicle can be quickly moved out of the locality or jurisdiction in which the warrant must be sought." A 5-4 judicial majority in *Olmstead v. United States* (1928) determined that police could wiretap a person without first obtaining a warrant. Chief Justice Taft's majority opinion asserted that the protections of the Fourth Amendment did not apply because "there was no searching. There was no seizure. The evidence was secured by the use of the sense of hearing and that only. There was no entry of the houses or offices of the defendants." Justice Brandeis's historic dissenting opinion is the first effort to apply the Fourth Amendment to the realm of electronic surveillance by equating the amendment with "the right most valued by civilized men": the "right to be let alone."

The Progressive Era witnessed the birth of the modern exclusionary rule. That rule requires courts in criminal cases to exclude any evidence that the prosecution has obtained illegally or unconstitutionally. By the beginning of the New Deal, the federal government and a significant minority of states had adopted the exclusionary rule. The Supreme Court in *Weeks v. United States* (1914) explained that the federal government should not "execute the criminal laws of the country . . . by means of unlawful seizures and enforced confessions," since the fruits of such actions would themselves be tainted by lawlessness.

Most state courts did not follow the lead of the U.S. Supreme Court when interpreting the requirements of their constitutions. "Courts in the administration of the criminal law," *Gindrat v. People* (IL 1891) stated, "are not accustomed to be over-sensitive in regard to the sources from which evidence comes, and will avail themselves of all evidence that is competent and pertinent."[64] When criticizing the exclusionary rule in *People v. Defore* (NY 1926), Judge Cardozo bluntly described the exclusionary rule as mandating "the criminal is to go free because the constable has blundered."[65]

---

64. *Gindrat v. Illinois*, 138 Ill. 103 (1891).

65. *People v. Defore*, 242 N.Y. 13 (1926).

Boyd v. United States, 116 U.S. 616 (1886)

E. A. Boyd and Sons made a contract to supply glass to the architect responsible for constructing a new federal building in Philadelphia. The federal government claimed that Boyd lied to the government when securing a duty-free permit to replace some glass that the company supplied to the architect. The local federal attorney insisted that Boyd supply the federal government with invoices for glass previously imported by that company. If Boyd refused to do so, federal law presumed that the glass had been illegally imported. Boyd refused to produce the invoices. The federal court then declared that the glass Boyd had imported was forfeited to the government. Boyd appealed this ruling to the Supreme Court of the United States, claiming that the court order to produce the invoices violated both the Fourth and Fifth Amendments.

The Supreme Court unanimously reversed the lower federal court. Justice Bradley's majority opinion declared that a judicial order requiring a person to supply private invoices to the government violated both the Fourth and Fifth Amendments. On what basis does Bradley conclude that the Fourth Amendment was violated? On what basis does he conclude that the Fifth Amendment was violated? Why does Justice Miller conclude that only the Fifth Amendment was violated? Consider how this case fits into the jurisprudence of the late nineteenth century. Was Boyd *motivated by a commitment to business enterprise, a commitment to limited government, or some other commitment? Was the decision a straightforward application of common law legal rules dating from* Entick v. Carrington *(1765)?*

JUSTICE BRADLEY delivered the opinion of the Court.

. . .

. . . Is a search and seizure, or, what is equivalent thereto, a compulsory production of a man's private papers, to be used in evidence against him in a proceeding to forfeit his property for alleged fraud against the revenue laws—is such a proceeding for such a purpose an "*unreasonable* search and seizure" within the meaning of the fourth amendment of the constitution? or is it a legitimate proceeding?. . . [W]e do not find any long usage or any contemporary construction of the constitution, which would justify any of the acts of congress now under consideration. As before stated, the act of 1863 was the first act in this country, and we might say, either in this country or in England, so far as we have been able to ascertain, which authorized the search and seizure of a man's private papers, or the compulsory production of them, for the purpose of using them in evidence against him in a criminal case, or in a proceeding to enforce the forfeiture of his property. Even the act under which the obnoxious writs of assistance were issued did not go as far as this, but only authorized the examination of ships and vessels, and persons found therein, for the purpose of finding goods prohibited to be imported or exported, or on which the duties were not paid, and to enter into and search any suspected vaults, cellars, or warehouses for such goods. The search for and seizure of stolen or forfeited goods, or goods liable to duties and concealed to avoid the payment thereof, are totally different things from a search for and seizure of a man's private books and papers for the purpose of obtaining information therein contained, or of using them as evidence against him. The two things differ *toto coelo*. In the one case, the government is entitled to the possession of the property; in the other it is not. The seizure of stolen goods is authorized by the common law; and the seizure of goods forfeited for a breach of the revenue laws, or concealed to avoid the duties payable on them, has been authorized by English statutes for at least two centuries past; and the like seizures have been authorized by our own revenue acts from the commencement of the government.

. . .

As every American statesman, during our revolutionary and formative period as a nation, was undoubtedly familiar with this monument of English freedom, and considered [*Entick v. Carrington* (1765)] as the true and ultimate expression of constitutional law, it may be confidently asserted that its propositions were in the minds of those who framed the fourth amendment to the constitution, and were considered as sufficiently explanatory of what was meant by unreasonable searches and seizures. . . . After describing the power claimed by the secretary of state for issuing general search-warrants, and the manner in which they were executed, Lord CAMDEN says:

. . .

> Papers are the owner's goods and chattels; they are his dearest property, and are so far from enduring a seizure, that they will hardly bear an inspection; and though the eye cannot by the laws of England be guilty of a trespass, yet where private papers are removed and carried away the secret nature of those

goods will be an aggravation of the trespass, and demand more considerable damages in that respect. Where is the written law that gives any magistrate such a power? I can safely answer, there is none; and therefore it is too much for us, without such authority, to pronounce a practice legal which would be subversive of all the comforts of society.

. . .

The principles laid down in this opinion affect the very essence of constitutional liberty and security. They reach further than the concrete form of the case then before the court, with its adventitious circumstances; they apply to all invasions on the part of the government and its employees of the sanctity of a man's home and the privacies of life. It is not the breaking of his doors, and the rummaging of his drawers, that constitutes the essence of the offense; but it is the invasion of his indefeasible right of personal security, personal liberty and private property, where that right has never been forfeited by his conviction of some public offense,—it is the invasion of this sacred right which underlies and constitutes the essence of Lord CAMDEN's judgment. Breaking into a house and opening boxes and drawers are circumstances of aggravation; but any forcible and compulsory extortion of a man's own testimony, or of his private papers to be used as evidence to convict him of crime, or to forfeit his goods, is within the condemnation of that judgment. In this regard the fourth and fifth amendments run almost into each other. Can we doubt that when the fourth and fifth amendments to the constitution of the United States were penned and adopted, the language of Lord CAMDEN was relied on as expressing the true doctrine on the subject of searches and seizures, and as furnishing the true *criteria* of the reasonable and "unreasonable" character of such seizures?. . . .

. . .

. . . [A]ny compulsory discovery by extorting the party's oath, or compelling the production of his private books and papers, to convict him of crime, or to forfeit his property, is contrary to the principles of a free government. It is abhorrent to the instincts of an Englishman; it is abhorrent to the instincts of an American. It may suit the purposes of despotic power, but it cannot abide the pure atmosphere of political liberty and personal freedom.

. . .

We have already noticed the intimate relation between the two amendments. They throw great light on each other. For the "unreasonable searches and seizures" condemned in the fourth amendment are almost always made for the purpose of compelling a man to give evidence against himself, which in criminal cases is condemned in the fifth amendment; and compelling a man "in a criminal case to be a witness against himself," which is condemned in the fifth amendment, throws light on the question as to what is an "unreasonable search and seizure" within the meaning of the fourth amendment. And we have been unable to perceive that the seizure of a man's private books and papers to be used in evidence against him is substantially different from compelling him to be a witness against himself. We think it is within the clear intent and meaning of those terms. . . .

JUSTICE MILLER (joined by the CHIEF JUSTICE), concurring.

. . . I am of opinion that this is a criminal case within the meaning of that clause of the fifth amendment to the constitution of the United States which declares that no person "shall be compelled in any criminal case to be a witness against himself." And I am quite satisfied that the effect of the act of congress is to compel the party on whom the order of the court is served to be a witness against himself. . . . But this being so, there is no reason why this court should assume that the action of the court below, in requiring a party to produce certain papers as evidence on the trial, authorizes an unreasonable search or seizure of the house, papers, or effects of that party. There is in fact no search and no seizure authorized by the statute. . . .

. . . [W]hat search does this statute authorize? If the mere service of a notice to produce a paper to be used as evidence, which the party can obey or not as he chooses, is a search, then a change has taken place in the meaning of words, which has not come within my reading, and which I think was unknown at the time the constitution was made. The searches meant by the constitution were such as led to seizure when the search was successful. But the statute in this case uses language carefully framed to forbid any seizure under it, as I have already pointed out.

While the framers of the constitution had their attention drawn, no doubt, to the abuses of this power of searching private houses and seizing private papers, as practiced in England, it is obvious that they only intended to restrain the abuse, while they did not abolish the power. Hence it is only *unreasonable* searches and seizures that are forbidden, and the means of securing this protection was by abolishing searches under warrants, which were called general warrants, because they authorized searches in any place, for any thing.

This was forbidden, while searches founded on affidavits, and made under warrants which described the thing to be searched for, the person and place to be searched, are still permitted.

I cannot conceive how a statute aptly framed to require the production of evidence in a suit by mere service of notice on the party, who has that evidence in his possession, can be held to authorize an unreasonable search or seizure, when no seizure is authorized or permitted by the statute.

I am requested to say that the chief justice concurs in this opinion.

Weeks v. United States, 232 U.S. 383 (1914)

Fremont Weeks was arrested and charged with selling lottery tickets through the mail. After he was arrested at his place of work, both local police officers and a federal marshal entered his house without a warrant, searched his rooms, and seized various incriminating papers. Before the trial Weeks demanded that the police return his property. The federal district court denied that motion and permitted the property to be introduced at the criminal trial. Weeks was convicted, fined, and sentenced to a jail term. He immediately appealed to the U.S. Supreme Court.

The Supreme Court held that Weeks was unconstitutionally convicted. Justice Day's unanimous opinion ruled that federal prosecutors could not introduce physical evidence at trial that had been obtained by an unconstitutional search. Weeks *is the first clear instance in which federal courts applied the exclusionary rule, the rule that unconstitutionally seized evidence may not be introduced at a criminal trial. What is the justification for that rule? What was the scope of that rule in 1914? Suppose that the police officers had returned the papers to Weeks but testified about their contents at trial. Would the Supreme Court have permitted that evidence?*

Weeks *is a Fifth Amendment case that limits the use of unconstitutionally seized evidence in federal trials. Justice Day made no effort to apply the decision to state criminal trials.*

JUSTICE DAY delivered the opinion of the court:

. . .

. . . The tendency of those who execute the criminal laws of the country to obtain conviction by means of unlawful seizures and enforced confessions, the latter often obtained after subjecting accused persons to unwarranted practices destructive of rights secured by the Federal Constitution, should find no sanction in the judgments of the courts, which are charged at all times with the support of the Constitution, and to which people of all conditions have a right to appeal for the maintenance of such fundamental rights.

. . .

The case in the aspect in which we are dealing with it involves the right of the court in a criminal prosecution to retain for the purposes of evidence the letters and correspondence of the accused, seized in his house in his absence and without his authority, by a United States marshal holding no warrant for his arrest and none for the search of his premises. The accused, without awaiting his trial, made timely application to the court for an order for the return of these letters, as well or other property. This application was denied, the letters retained and put in evidence, after a further application at the beginning of the trial, both applications asserting the rights of the accused under the 4th and 5th Amendments to the Constitution. If letters and private documents can thus be seized and held and used in evidence against a citizen accused of an offense, the protection of the 4th Amendment, declaring his right to be secure against such searches and seizures, is of no value, and, so far as those thus placed are concerned, might as well be stricken from the Constitution. The efforts of the courts and their officials to bring the guilty to punishment, praiseworthy as they are, are not to be aided by the sacrifice of those great principles established by years of endeavor and suffering which have resulted in their embodiment in the fundamental law of the land. The United States marshal could only have invaded the house of the accused when armed with a warrant issued as required by the Constitution, upon sworn information, and describing with reasonable particularity the thing for which the search was to be made. Instead, he acted without sanction of law, doubtless prompted by the desire to bring further proof to the aid of the government, and under color of his office undertook to make a seizure of private papers in direct violation of the constitutional prohibition against such action. Under such circumstances, without sworn information and particular description, not even an order of court would have justified such procedure; much less was it within the authority of the United States marshal to thus invade the house and privacy of the accused. . . . To sanction such proceedings would be to affirm by judicial decision a manifest neglect, if not an open defiance, of the prohibitions of the Constitution, intended for the protection of the people against such unauthorized action.

. . .

We therefore reach the conclusion that the letters in question were taken from the house of the accused by an official of the United States, acting under color of his office, in direct violation of the constitutional rights of the defendant; that having made a seasonable application for their return, which was heard and passed upon by the court, there was involved in the order refusing the application a denial of the constitutional rights of the accused, and that the court should have restored these letters to the accused. In holding them and permitting their use upon the trial, we think prejudicial error was committed. As to the papers and property seized by the policemen, it does not appear that they acted under any claim of Federal authority such as would make the amendment applicable to such unauthorized seizures. The record shows that what they did by way of arrest and search and seizure was done before the finding of the indictment in the Federal court; under what supposed right or authority does not appear. What remedies the defendant may have against them we need not inquire, as the 4th Amendment is not directed to individual misconduct of such officials. Its limitations reach the Federal government and its agencies. . . .

People v. Defore, 242 N.Y. 13 (1926)

John Defore was arrested by a police officer who believed that Defore had stolen an overcoat. The officer, who lacked either an arrest or a search warrant, searched the boardinghouse where Defore resided. The search revealed a blackjack, a weapon that was illegal under New York law. Defore was arrested and tried for possessing that weapon. His motion to have the weapon excluded was rejected and he was convicted. Defore appealed that decision to the Court of Appeals of New York.

The New York Court of Appeals rejected Defore's appeal. Judge Cardozo insisted that New York law did not require illegally obtained evidence to be excluded at a criminal trial. Benjamin Cardozo was considered one of the most progressive justices on the state bench. Why would a progressive judge in the 1920s reject the exclusionary rule?

JUDGE CARDOZO delivered the opinion of the Court.

. . .

We hold with the defendant that the evidence against him was the outcome of a trespass. The officer might have been resisted, or sued for damages, or even prosecuted for oppression. . . . He was subject to removal or other discipline at the hands of his superiors. These consequences are undisputed. The defendant would add another. We must determine whether evidence of criminality, procured by an act of trespass, is to be rejected as incompetent for the misconduct of the trespasser.

. . . *Weeks v. United States* (1914) held that articles wrongfully seized by agents of the federal government should have been returned to the defendant or excluded as evidence, if a timely motion to compel return had been made before the trial. . . . There has been no blinking the consequences. The criminal is to go free because the constable has blundered.

The new doctrine has already met the scrutiny of courts of sister states. The decisions have been brought together for our guidance through the industry of counsel. In 45 states (exclusive of our own) the subject has been considered. Fourteen states have adopted the rule of the *Weeks* case either as there laid down or as subsequently broadened. Thirty-one have rejected it.

. . .

The federal rule as it stands is either too strict or too lax. A federal prosecutor may take no benefit from evidence collected through the trespass of a federal officer. The thought is that, in appropriating the results, he ratifies the means. . . . He does not have to be so scrupulous about evidence brought to him by others. How finely the line is drawn is seen when we recall that marshals in the service of the nation are on one side of it, and police in the service of the states on the other. The nation may keep what the servants of the states supply. . . . We must go farther or not so far. The professed object of the trespass rather than the official character of the trespasser should test the rights of government. . . . The incongruity of other tests gains emphasis from the facts of the case before us. The complainant, the owner of the overcoat, co-operated with the officer in the arrest and the attendant search. Their powers were equal, since the charge was petit larceny, a misdemeanor. If one spoke or acted for the state, so also did the other. A government would be disingenuous, if, in determining the use that should be made of evidence drawn from such a source, it drew a line between them. This would be true whether they had acted in concert or apart. We exalt form above substance when we hold that the use is made lawful because the intruder is without a badge of office. We break with precedent altogether when we press the prohibition farther.

. . .

We are confirmed in this conclusion when we reflect how far-reaching in its effect upon society the new consequences would be. The pettiest peace officer would have it in his power, through overzeal or indiscretion, to confer immunity upon an offender for crimes the most flagitious. A room is searched against the law, and the body of a murdered man is found. If the place of discovery may not be proved, the other circumstances may be insufficient to connect the defendant with the crime. The privacy of the home has been infringed, and the murderer goes free. Another search, once more against the law, discloses counterfeit money or the implements of forgery. The absence of a warrant means the freedom of the forger. Like instances can be multiplied. We may not subject society to these dangers until the Legislature has spoken with a clearer voice. . . .

Olmstead v. United States, 277 U.S. 438 (1928)

Federal agents suspected that Roy Olmstead was the leader of a multi-million dollar conspiracy to import and sell intoxicating liquors in violation of federal Prohibition laws. In order to gain the necessary evidence to arrest and convict Olmstead, federal agents tapped his home and office phones. These wiretaps enabled the agents to overhear conversations in which Olmstead and his confederates engaged in illegal business transactions and bribed local police officers in Seattle, Washington. After five months, Olmstead was arrested, tried, and convicted of violating federal laws against "unlawfully possessing, transporting and importing intoxicating liquors." Olmstead appealed this conviction to the U.S. Supreme Court on two grounds. First, he claimed that the admission of the wiretaps at trial violated his Fourth and Fifth Amendment rights. Second, he claimed that federal agents could not use at trial evidence gathered in ways that violated local laws. Since wiretapping was illegal in Washington, evidence gained by wiretapping could not be used in federal courts in Washington.

The Supreme Court by a 5-4 vote sustained Olmstead's conviction. Chief Justice Taft's majority opinion ruled that the Fourth and Fifth Amendments prohibited only physical searches. Taft also ruled that federal courts could admit evidence obtained by means that violated local laws. Both the Taft majority opinion and the Brandeis dissent examine original understandings and recent precedents. How does each interpret these legal sources? Who has the better argument? Olmstead *is the first major case on constitutional criminal procedure in which the more liberal justices on the Supreme Court offer a more expansive reading of constitutional rights than do the more conservative justices. What might explain that change?*

CHIEF JUSTICE TAFT delivered the opinion of the Court.

. . .

The well-known historical purpose of the Fourth Amendment, directed against general warrants and writs of assistance, was to prevent the use of governmental force to search a man's house, his person, his papers, and his effects, and to prevent their seizure against his will. . . .

. . .

The amendment itself shows that the search is to be of material things—the person, the house, his papers, or his effects. The description of the warrant necessary to make the proceeding lawful is that it must specify the place to be searched and the person or things to be seized.

. . . The Fourth Amendment may have proper application to a sealed letter in the mail, because of the constitutional provision for the Postoffice Department and the relations between the government and those who pay to secure protection of their sealed letters. . . . It is plainly within the words of the amendment to say that the unlawful rifling by a government agent of a sealed letter is a search and seizure of the sender's papers or effects. The letter is a paper, an effect, and in the custody of a government that forbids carriage, except under its protection.

The United States takes no such care of telegraph or telephone messages as of mailed sealed letters. The amendment does not forbid what was done here. There was no searching. There was no seizure. The evidence was secured by the use of the sense of hearing and that only. There was no entry of the houses or offices of the defendants.

. . .

The language of the amendment cannot be extended and expanded to include telephone wires, reaching to the whole world from the defendant's house or office. The intervening wires are not part of his house or office, any more than are the highways along which they are stretched.

. . .

Neither the cases we have cited nor any of the many federal decisions brought to our attention hold the Fourth Amendment to have been violated as against a defendant, unless there has been an official search and seizure of his person or such a seizure of his papers or his tangible material effects or an actual physical invasion of his house "or curtilage" for the purpose of making a seizure.

. . .

What has been said disposes of the only question that comes within the terms of our order granting certiorari in these cases. But some of our number, departing from that order, have concluded that there is merit in the twofold objection, overruled in both courts below, that evidence obtained through intercepting of telephone messages by a government agent was inadmissible, because the mode of obtaining it was unethical and a misdemeanor under the law of Washington.

. . .

A standard which would forbid the reception of evidence, if obtained by other than nice ethical conduct by government officials, would make society suffer and give criminals greater immunity than has been known heretofore. In the absence of controlling legislation by Congress, those who realize the difficulties in bringing offenders to justice may well deem it wise that the exclusion of evidence should be confined to cases where rights under the Constitution would be violated by admitting it.

JUSTICE BRANDEIS, dissenting.

. . .

"We must never forget," said Mr. Chief Justice Marshall in *McCulloch v. Maryland* (1819) "that it is a Constitution we are expounding." Since then this court has repeatedly sustained the exercise of power by Congress, under various clauses of that instrument, over objects of which the fathers could not have dreamed. . . . We have likewise held that general limitations on the powers of government, like those embodied in the due process clauses of the Fifth and Fourteenth Amendments, do not forbid the United States or the states from meeting modern conditions by regulations which "a century ago, or even half a century ago, probably would have been rejected as arbitrary and oppressive." . . . Clauses guaranteeing to the individual protection against specific abuses of power, must have a similar capacity of adaptation to a changing world. . . .

When the Fourth and Fifth Amendments were adopted, "the form that evil had theretofore taken" had been necessarily simple. Force and violence were then the only means known to man by which a government could directly effect self-incrimination. It could compel the individual to testify—a compulsion effected, if need be, by torture. It could secure possession of his papers and other articles incident to his private life—a seizure effected, if need be, by breaking and entry. Protection against such invasion of "the sanctities of a man's home and the privacies of life" was provided in the Fourth and Fifth Amendments by specific language. . . . But "time works changes, brings into existence new conditions and purposes." Subtler and more far-reaching means of invading privacy have become available to the government. Discovery and invention have made it possible for the government, by means far more effective than stretching upon the rack, to obtain disclosure in court of what is whispered in the closet.

Moreover, "in the application of a Constitution, our contemplation cannot be only of what has been, but of what may be." The progress of science in furnishing the government with means of espionage is not likely to stop with wire tapping. Ways may some day be developed by which the government, without removing papers from secret drawers, can reproduce them in court, and by which it will be enabled to expose to a jury the most intimate occurrences of the home. Advances in the psychic and related sciences may bring means of exploring unexpressed beliefs, thoughts and emotions. . . . Can it be that the Constitution affords no protection against such invasions of individual security?

. . .

The evil incident to invasion of the privacy of the telephone is far greater than that involved in tampering with the mails. Whenever a telephone line is tapped, the privacy of the persons at both ends of the line is invaded, and all conversations between them upon any subject, and although proper, confidential, and privileged, may be overheard. Moreover, the tapping of one man's telephone line involves the tapping of the telephone of every other person whom he may call, or who may call him. As a means of espionage, writs of assistance and general warrants are but puny instruments of tyranny and oppression when compared with wire tapping.

. . .

. . . The makers of our Constitution undertook to secure conditions favorable to the pursuit of happiness. They recognized the significance of man's spiritual nature, of his feelings and of his intellect. They knew that only a part of the pain, pleasure and satisfactions of life are to be found in material things. They sought to protect Americans in their beliefs, their thoughts, their emotions and their sensations. They conferred, as against the government, the right to be let alone—the most comprehensive of rights and the right most valued by civilized men. To protect that right, every unjustifiable intrusion by the government upon the privacy of the individual, whatever the means employed, must be deemed a violation of the Fourth Amendment. And the use, as evidence in a criminal proceeding, of facts ascertained by such intrusion must be deemed a violation of the Fifth.

Applying to the Fourth and Fifth Amendments the established rule of construction, the defendants' objections to the evidence obtained by wire tapping must, in my opinion, be sustained. It is, of course, immaterial where the physical connection with the telephone wires leading into the defendants' premises was made. And it is also immaterial that the intrusion was in aid of law enforcement. Experience should teach us to be most on our guard to protect liberty when the government's purposes are beneficent. Men born to freedom are naturally alert to repel invasion of their liberty by evil-minded rulers. The greatest dangers to liberty lurk in insidious encroachment by men of zeal, well-meaning but without understanding.

. . .

Independently of the constitutional question, I am of opinion that the judgment should be reversed. By the laws of Washington, wire tapping is a crime. . . . To prove its case, the government was obliged to lay bare the crimes committed by its officers on its behalf. A federal court should not permit such a prosecution to continue.

. . .

Decency, security, and liberty alike demand that government officials shall be subjected to the same rules of conduct that are commands to the citizen. In a government of laws, existence of the government will be imperiled if it fails to observe the law scrupulously. Our government is the potent, the omnipresent teacher. For good or for ill, it teaches the whole people by its example. Crime is contagious. If the government becomes a lawbreaker, it breeds contempt for law; it invites every man to become a law unto himself; it invites anarchy. To declare that in the administration of the criminal law the end justifies the means—to declare that the government may commit crimes in order to secure the conviction of a private criminal—would bring terrible retribution. Against that pernicious doctrine this court should resolutely set its face.

JUSTICE HOLMES, dissenting.

My brother BRANDEIS has given this case so exhaustive an examination that I desire to add but a few words. While I do not deny it I am not prepared to say that the penumbra of the Fourth and Fifth Amendments covers the defendant, although I fully agree that courts are apt to err by sticking too closely to the words of a law where those words import a policy that goes beyond them. But I think . . . that apart from the Constitution the government ought not to use evidence obtained and only obtainable by a criminal act. There is no body of precedents by which we are bound, and which confines us to logical deduction from established rules. Therefore we must consider the two objects of desire, both of which we cannot have, and make up our minds which to choose. It is desirable that criminals should be detected, and to that end that all available evidence should be used. It also is desirable that the government should not itself foster and pay for other crimes, when they are the means by which the evidence is to be obtained. If it pays its officers for having got evidence by crime I do not see why it may not as well pay them for getting it in the same way, and I can attach no importance to protestations of disapproval if it knowingly accepts and pays and announces that in future it will pay for the fruits. We have to choose, and for my part I think it a less evil that some criminals should escape than that the government should play an ignoble part.

. . .

JUSTICE BUTLER, dissenting.

. . .

Telephones are used generally for transmission of messages concerning official, social, business and personal affairs including communications that are private and privileged—those between physician and patient, lawyer and client, parent and child, husband

and wife. The contracts between telephone companies and users contemplate the private use of the facilities employed in the service. The communications belong to the parties between whom they pass. During their transmission the exclusive use of the wire belongs to the persons served by it. Wire tapping involves interference with the wire while being used. Tapping the wires and listening in by the officers literally constituted a search for evidence. As the communications passed, they were heard and taken down. . . .

This court has always construed the Constitution in the light of the principles upon which it was founded. The direct operation or literal meaning of the words used do not measure the purpose or scope of its provisions. Under the principles established and applied by this court, the Fourth Amendment safeguards against all evils that are like and equivalent to those embraced within the ordinary meaning of its words. . . .

JUSTICE STONE, dissenting. . . .

C. Interrogations

Plea bargaining came of age during the Republican Era. Until the early twentieth century, many judges looked askance at the practice of obtaining confessions by reducing the criminal charge. The Supreme Court of Mississippi in *Deloach v. State* (MS 1900) expressed the conventional late-nineteenth-century wisdom when declaring,

> As the plea of guilty is often made because the defendant supposes that he will thereby receive some favor of the court in the sentence, it is the English practice not to receive such plea unless it is persisted in by the defendant after being informed that such plea will make no alteration in the punishment. By analogy, we think the defendant should be permitted to withdraw his plea of guilty, when unadvisedly given, where any reasonable ground is offered for going to the jury. . . . All courts should so administer the law and construe the rules of practice as to secure a hearing upon the merits, if possible.[66]

Thirty years later plea-bargaining was far more accepted. The Criminal Court of Appeals of Oklahoma in *Moseley v. State* (OK 1930) articulated the new conventional wisdom when ruling,

> While it is true that the county attorney could make no agreement to reduce the grade of the crime or to fix the punishment thereof without the consent of the trial court, yet such agreement should be approved where the defendant acts on it in good faith and surrenders statutory or constitutional rights to expedite the hearing of the case, and especially is that so where the agreement of the county attorney aids in the speedy administration of justice and the punishment agreed upon is adequate under all the circumstances surrounding the case.[67]

By the end of the Republican Era the vast majority of convictions were obtained through confessions induced by a plea bargain.[68] This remains a central reality of our current system of criminal justice.

D. Juries and Lawyers

The jury trial continued to decline in constitutional status. Most criminal suspects avoided a jury trial by pleading guilty to a lesser offense. More defendants chose to be tried by a single judge. State judges initially disfavored bench trials. The Supreme Court of Iowa in *State v. Carman* (IA 1884) ruled that a defendant did not have the constitutional right to waive a jury trial. Judge Adams declared, "Life and liberty are too sacred to be placed at the disposal of any one man, and always will be so long as man is fallible."[69] Other late-nineteenth-century courts began adopting the modern practice of giving the criminal defendant the right to be tried by a judge instead of a jury. In *State v. White* (LA 1881) the Supreme Court of Louisiana ruled that state laws permitting defendants to be tried by a judge were constitutional means "to secure the chances of a speedy trial to the accused, and to relieve the parishes of the enormous expense and great inconvenience of drawing, summoning and empanelling large numbers of jurors five or six times a year."[70] The Supreme Court similarly concluded in *Patton v. United States* (1930)

66. *Deloach v. State*, 77 Miss. 691 (1900).

67. *Moseley v. State*, 46 Okl.Cr. 435 (1930).

68. For more information, see Albert W. Alschuler, "Plea Bargaining and Its History," *Columbia Law Review* 79 (1979): 1.

69. *State v. Carman*, 63 Iowa 130 (1884).

70. *State v. White*, 33 La. Ann. 1218 (1881). See Susan C. Towne, "The Historical Origins of Bench Trial for Serious Crimes," *American Journal of Legal History* 26 (1982): 123.

that the jury trial was a right of the accused that could be waived and not a vital structure of government that ensured popular participation in the criminal process. Justice Sutherland's opinion for the Court asserted that constitutional protections for a jury trial were "meant to confer a right upon the accused which he may forego at his election."[71]

Constitutional decision makers were far more supportive of the practice of providing defendants with lawyers. Numerous state courts emphasized the central role of an attorney in the criminal process. The Supreme Court of California in *People v. Napthaly* (CA 1895) declared, "Under our law every person accused of a felony is entitled to the aid of counsel, whether imprisoned or admitted to bail; and a refusal of an opportunity to procure such counsel amounts to the deprivation of an important right, essential to his safety."[72] Many state courts ruled that in certain circumstances the right to counsel included the right of an indigent person to have a court-appointed counsel. The Court of Appeals of Kentucky reached this conclusion in *Williams v. Commonwealth* (KY 1908). Judge Nunn's unanimous opinion asserted,

> It has been the custom of the courts of this state, as well as most of the states, and is a commendable one, when a prisoner is unable to employ counsel, for the court to designate some one to defend him, and it is the duty of such counsel, which he owes to his profession, when so designated, not to withhold his assistance nor spare his best exertions in the defense of one who has the double misfortune to be stricken by poverty and accused of crime. We, however, do not understand the provision of the Constitution and the authorities cited to require the court to appoint counsel for a defendant charged with a felony when he does not desire the aid of counsel, and when the court can see that the person charged is a person of at least ordinary intelligence and can fully appreciate the position which he occupies; but in a case like this, when the defendant is without education, and has not mind enough to know when he was placed in jeopardy, we are of the opinion that it was the court's duty to interpose and see that he was properly represented.[73]

The U.S. Supreme Court in *Powell v. Alabama* (1932) relied heavily on these state constitutional decisions when holding that the due process clause of the Fourteenth Amendment protected the right to be represented by private defense counsel and required state-appointed counsel in certain circumstances.

Powell v. Alabama, 287 U.S. 45 (1932)

Ozie Powell was one of nine African-American teenagers, later known as the Scottsboro Boys, who travelled on the Southern Railroad from Chattanooga to Memphis. While the train was in Alabama, the African-American teenagers fought with several white teenagers. All but one of the white teenagers were thrown off the train. The white youths immediately reported what had happened to a stationmaster, who called a posse of men to stop the train. When the train was stopped, two white women on the train, Victoria Price and Ruby Bates, claimed that they had been raped by the African-American teenagers. Twelve days later all nine teenagers were put on trial for their lives. Counsel were appointed on the day of the trial and were not given any time to prepare. Eight of the nine boys were convicted and sentenced to death. The Supreme Court of Alabama affirmed that decision by a 6-1 vote (the justices did reverse one sentence). Powell appealed to the Supreme Court of the United States. The plight of the Scottsboro Boys received national attention, with both the NAACP and the American Communist Party offering to provide legal assistance. (The defendants chose the Communists.)[74]

The Supreme Court by a 7-2 vote reversed the convictions of the seven Scottsboro Boys still under a death sentence. Justice Sutherland's majority opinion ruled that the due process clause of the Fourteenth Amendment required counsel to be appointed in certain capital cases. Justice Sutherland noted that English common law did not recognize a right to counsel. Why does he nevertheless assume that due process entails the right to counsel and, in certain cases, the right to court-appointed counsel? Powell v. Alabama *is one of the most celebrated civil liberties cases in American history.*

---

71. For a survey of the history, see Stephen A. Siegel, "The Constitution on Trial: Article III's Jury Trial Provision, Originalism, and the Problem of Motivated Reasoning," *Santa Clara Law Review* 52 (2012): 373-455.

72. *People v. Napthaly*, 105 Cal. 641 (1895).

73. *Williams v. Commonwealth*, 110 S.W 339 (1908).

74. The story of the Scottsboro Boys is fascinating. For a good account, see James E. Goodman, *Stories of Scottsboro* (New York: Vintage, 1995).

The author, Justice Sutherland, was a firm proponent of the freedom of contract and other property rights. Do you see any connections between Justice Sutherland's commitment to the Lochner *line of decisions and his support for the Scottsboro Boys?*

JUSTICE SUTHERLAND delivered the opinion of the Court.

...

... [D]uring perhaps the most critical period of the proceedings against these defendants, that is to say, from the time of their arraignment until the beginning of their trial, when consultation, thorough-going investigation and preparation were vitally important, the defendants did not have the aid of counsel in any real sense, although they were as much entitled to such aid during that period as at the trial itself.

... The defendants, young, ignorant, illiterate, surrounded by hostile sentiment, haled back and forth under guard of soldiers, charged with an atrocious crime regarded with especial horror in the community where they were to be tried, were thus put in peril of their lives within a few moments after counsel for the first time charged with any degree of responsibility began to represent them.

It is not enough to assume that counsel thus precipitated into the case thought there was no defense, and exercised their best judgment in proceeding to trial without preparation. Neither they nor the court could say what a prompt and thorough-going investigation might disclose as to the facts. No attempt was made to investigate. No opportunity to do so was given. Defendants were immediately hurried to trial. ... Under the circumstances disclosed, we hold that defendants were not accorded the right of counsel in any substantial sense. To decide otherwise, would simply be to ignore actualities. ...

... The prompt disposition of criminal cases is to be commended and encouraged. But in reaching that result a defendant, charged with a serious crime, must not be stripped of his right to have sufficient time to advise with counsel and prepare his defense. To do that is not to proceed promptly in the calm spirit of regulated justice but to go forward with the haste of the mob.

...

If recognition of the right of a defendant charged with a felony to have the aid of counsel depended upon the existence of a similar right at common law as it existed in England when our Constitution was adopted, there would be great difficulty in maintaining it as necessary to due process. Originally, in England, a person charged with treason or felony was denied the aid of counsel, except in respect of legal questions which the accused himself might suggest. At the same time parties in civil cases and persons accused of misdemeanors were entitled to the full assistance of counsel. ...

...

The rule was rejected by the colonies. ...

...

It thus appears that in at least twelve of the thirteen colonies the rule of the English common law, in the respect now under consideration, had been definitely rejected and the right to counsel fully recognized in all criminal prosecutions, save that in one or two instances the right was limited to capital offenses or to the more serious crimes; and this court seems to have been of the opinion that this was true in all the colonies. ...

...

It never has been doubted by this court, or any other so far as we know, that notice and hearing are preliminary steps essential to the passing of an enforceable judgment, and that they, together with a legally competent tribunal having jurisdiction of the case, constitute basic elements of the constitutional requirement of due process of law. ...

What, then, does a hearing include? Historically and in practice, in our own country at least, it has always included the right to the aid of counsel when desired and provided by the party asserting the right. The right to be heard would be, in many cases, of little avail if it did not comprehend the right to be heard by counsel. Even the intelligent and educated layman has small and sometimes no skill in the science of law. If charged with crime, he is incapable, generally, of determining for himself whether the indictment is good or bad. He is unfamiliar with the rules of evidence. Left without the aid of counsel he may be put on trial without a proper charge, and convicted upon incompetent evidence, or evidence irrelevant to the issue or otherwise inadmissible. He lacks both the skill and knowledge adequately to prepare his defense, even though he have a perfect one. He requires the guiding hand of counsel at every step in the proceedings against him. Without it, though he be not guilty, he faces the danger of conviction because he does not know how to establish his innocence. If that be true of men of intelligence, how much more true is it of the ignorant and illiterate, or those of feeble intellect. If in any case, civil or criminal, a state or federal court were arbitrarily to refuse to hear a party by counsel, employed by and appearing for him, it reasonably may not be doubted that such a refusal would be a denial of a hearing, and, therefore, of due process in the constitutional sense.

...

In the light of the facts outlined in the forepart of this opinion—the ignorance and illiteracy of the defendants, their youth, the circumstances of public hostility, the imprisonment and the close surveillance of the defendants by the military forces, the fact that their friends and families were all in other states and communication with them necessarily difficult, and above all that they stood in deadly peril of their lives—we think the failure of the trial court to give them reasonable time and opportunity to secure counsel was a clear denial of due process.

But passing that, and assuming their inability, even if opportunity had been given, to employ counsel, as the trial court evidently did assume, we are of opinion that, under the circumstances just stated, the necessity of counsel was so vital and imperative that the failure of the trial court to make an effective appointment of counsel was likewise a denial of due process within the meaning of the Fourteenth Amendment. Whether this would be so in other criminal prosecutions, or under other circumstances, we need not determine. All that it is necessary now to decide, as we do decide, is that in a capital case, where the defendant is unable to employ counsel, and is incapable adequately of making his own defense because of ignorance, feeble-mindedness, illiteracy, or the like, it is the duty of the court, whether requested or not, to assign counsel for him as a necessary requisite of due process of law; and that duty is not discharged by an assignment at such a time or under such circumstances as to preclude the giving of effective aid in the preparation and trial of the case. To hold otherwise would be to ignore the fundamental postulate, already adverted to, "that there are certain immutable principles of justice which inhere in the very idea of free government which no member of the Union may disregard."...

...

JUSTICE BUTLER (joined by JUSTICE McREYNOLDS), dissenting.

...

If correct, the ruling that the failure of the trial court to give petitioners time and opportunity to secure counsel was denied of due process is enough, and with this the opinion should end. But the Court goes on to declare that "the failure of the trial court to make an effective appointment of counsel was likewise a denial of due process within the meaning of the Fourteenth Amendment." This is an extension of federal authority into a field hitherto occupied exclusively by the several States. Nothing before the Court calls for a consideration of the point. It was not suggested below and petitioners do not ask for its decision here. The Court, without being called upon to consider it, adjudges without a hearing an important constitutional question concerning criminal procedure in state courts. . . .

E. Punishments

Americans debated both the theory and the practice of cruel and unusual punishments. The main theoretical issue was whether cruel and unusual punishment clauses in the federal and state constitutions forbade only punishments that were considered barbaric in 1791 or whether some punishments might become cruel and unusual over time. The main practical issues were the constitutional status of whipping, sterilization, the death penalty, and specific forms of execution.

Constitutional decision makers took one of two different general approaches when determining whether a specific punishment was cruel and unusual. The deferential approach maintained that constitutional limitations on punishment forbade only particularly barbarous punishments such as torture. This approach focused entirely on the punishment and not at all on the crime. Burning at the stake was barbaric and could not be imposed for any crime. Prison was not barbaric, so a legislature could punish any crime with as long a sentence as elected officials thought appropriate. *Hobbs v. State* (IN 1893) was a leading case for the deferential position. The Supreme Court of Indiana brushed aside a claim that two years in prison for "riotous conspiracy" was unconstitutional. Judge Hackney wrote:

> The word "cruel," when considered in relation to the time when it found place in the bill of rights, meant, not a fine or imprisonment, or both, but such as that inflicted at the whipping post, in the pillory, burning at the stake, breaking on the wheel, etc. The word, according to modern interpretation, does not affect legislation providing imprisonment for life or for years, or the death penalty by hanging

> or electrocution. If it did, our laws for the punishment of crime would give no security to the citizen. Neither is punishment by fine or imprisonment "unusual."[75]

An increasing minority of states adopted a more progressive approach to constitutional limitations on punishment. Judges who adopted this approach were willing to consider whether punishments permitted at the founding could become unconstitutional, and whether the constitutionality of a punishment depended on the crime. A long prison term might be a constitutional punishment for armed robbery, but not for parking one's horse in the wrong stall. *McDonald v. Commonwealth* (MA 1899) was a leading state authority for the progressive approach. The Supreme Judicial Court of Massachusetts sustained a state law enhancing the sentences of repeat criminals but insisted that the state constitution limited prison sentences for certain crimes. Judge Morton wrote,

> It would be going too far to say that their power is unlimited in these respects. Ordinarily, the terms "cruel and unusual" imply something inhuman and barbarous in the nature of the punishment. But it is possible that imprisonment in the state prison for a long term of years might be so disproportionate to the offense as to constitute a cruel and unusual punishment.[76]

The Supreme Court of the United States took a deferential approach in the late nineteenth century but moved toward a more progressive approach during the twentieth century. When sustaining firing squads (*Wilkerson v. Utah* [1878]) and the electric chair (*In re Kemmler* [1890]) as constitutional modes of execution, Supreme Court justices limited application of the cruel and unusual punishment clause to "punishments of torture . . . and all others in the same line of unnecessary cruelty." The White Court took a different approach in *Weems v. United States* (1910). The judicial majority in that case declared that a prison term in chains that lasted more than a decade was a constitutionally disproportionate punishment for a financial crime. Nevertheless, *Weems* was the only case in which the Supreme Court before the New Deal Era ruled that a punishment was cruel and unusual.

75. *Hobbs v. State*, 32 N.E. 1019 (Ind. 1893).
76. *McDonald v. Commonwealth*, 173 Mass. 322 (1899).

Weems v. United States, 217 U.S. 349 (1910)

Paul Weems falsified official documents when serving as a Coast Guard officer in the Philippines. He was tried, convicted, and sentenced to fifteen years of cadena, which meant that he would be chained and required to perform hard and painful labors. The Supreme Territorial Court of the Philippines sustained the sentence. Weems appealed that decision to the Supreme Court of the United States.

The Supreme Court by a 6-2 vote declared that the cadena in this case was cruel and unusual punishment. Justice McKenna's majority opinion declared that fifteen years at hard labor was an unconstitutionally disproportionate punishment for a financial crime. McKenna notes that jail sentences were not considered cruel and unusual under common law. Why does he nevertheless find the cadena to be cruel and unusual punishment? Why does Justice White disagree? Who has the better argument? Note that Justice Holmes was the other dissenter in Weems. *How might you relate this Holmes dissent to his dissents in* Lochner v. New York *(1905) (opposing the freedom of contract) and* Abrams v. United States *(1919) (defending the freedom of speech)?*

JUSTICE McKENNA delivered the opinion of the court:

. . .

. . . With power in a legislature great, if not unlimited, to give criminal character to the actions of men, with power unlimited to fix terms of imprisonment with what accompaniments they might, what more potent instrument of cruelty could be put into the hands of power? And it was believed that power might be tempted to cruelty. This was the motive of the clause, and if we are to attribute an intelligent providence to its advocates we cannot think that it was intended to prohibit only practices like the Stuarts', or to prevent only an exact repetition of history. We cannot think that the possibility of a coercive cruelty being exercised through other forms of punishment was overlooked. We say "coercive cruelty," because there was more to be considered than the ordinary criminal laws. Cruelty might become an instrument of tyranny; of zeal for a purpose, either honest or sinister.

Legislation, both statutory and constitutional, is enacted, it is true, from an experience of evils but its general language should not, therefore, be necessarily confined to the form that evil had theretofore taken.

Time works changes, brings into existence new conditions and purposes. Therefore a principle, to be vital, must be capable of wider application than the mischief which gave it birth. This is peculiarly true of constitutions. They are not ephemeral enactments, designed to meet passing occasions. They are, to use the words of Chief Justice Marshall, "designed to approach immortality as nearly as human institutions can approach it." The future is their care, and provision for events of good and bad tendencies of which no prophecy can be made. In the application of a constitution, therefore, our contemplation cannot be only of what has been, but of what may be. Under any other rule a constitution would indeed be as easy of application as it would be deficient in efficacy and power. Its general principles would have little value, and be converted by precedent into impotent and lifeless formulas. Rights declared in words might be lost in reality. . . .

. . .

. . . [P]rominence is given to the power of the legislature to define crimes and their punishment. We concede the power in most of its exercises. We disclaim the right to assert a judgment against that of the legislature, of the expediency of the laws, or the right to oppose the judicial power to the legislative power to define crimes and fix their punishment, unless that power encounters in its exercise a constitutional prohibition. In such case, not our discretion, but our legal duty, strictly defined and imperative in its direction, is invoked. Then the legislative power is brought to the judgment of a power superior to it for the instant. And for the proper exercise of such power there must be a comprehension of all that the legislature did or could take into account,—that is, a consideration of the mischief and the remedy. However, there is a certain subordination of the judiciary to the legislature. The function of the legislature is primary, its exercise fortified by presumptions of right and legality, and is not to be interfered with lightly, nor by any judicial conception of its wisdom or propriety. They have no limitation, we repeat, but constitutional ones, and what those are the judiciary must judge. . . .

. . .

From this comment we turn back to the law in controversy. Its character and the contence in this case may be illustrated by examples even better than it can be represented by words. There are degrees of homicide that are not punished so severely, nor are the following crimes: misprision of treason, inciting rebellion, conspiracy to destroy the government by force, recruiting soldiers in the United States to fight against the United States, forgery of letters patent, forgery of bonds and other instruments for the purpose of defrauding the United States, robbery, larceny, and other crimes. Section 86 of the Penal Laws of the United States . . . provides that any person charged with the payment of any appropriation made by Congress, who shall pay to any clerk or other employee of the United States a sum less than that provided by law, and require a receipt for a sum greater than that paid to and received by him, shall be guilty of embezzlement, and shall be fined in double the amount so withheld, and imprisoned not more than two years. The offense described has similarity to the offense for which Weems was convicted, but the punishment provided for it is in great contrast to the penalties of *cadena temporal* and its "accessories." . . . And this contrast shows more than different exercises of legislative judgment. It is greater than that. It condemns the sentence in this case as cruel and unusual. It exhibits a difference between unrestrained power and that which is exercised under the spirit of constitutional limitations formed to establish justice. The state thereby suffers nothing and loses no power. The purpose of punishment is fulfilled, crime is repressed by penalties of just, not tormenting, severity, its repetition is prevented, and hope is given for the reformation of the criminal.

. . .

It follows from these views that, even if the minimum penalty of *cadena temporal* had been imposed, it would have been repugnant to the Bill of Rights. In other words, the fault is in the law; and, as we are pointed to no other under which a sentence can be imposed, the judgment must be reversed, with directions to dismiss the proceedings.

JUSTICE WHITE (joined by JUSTICE HOLMES), dissenting:

. . .

Of course, in every case where punishment is inflicted for the commission of crime, if the suffering of the punishment by the wrongdoer be alone regarded, the sense of compassion aroused would mislead and render the performance of judicial duty impossible. . . . Turning aside, therefore, from mere emotional tendencies, and guiding my judgment alone by the aid of the reason at my command, I am unable to agree with the ruling of the court. As, in my opinion, that ruling rests upon an interpretation of the cruel and unusual punishment clause of the 8th Amendment, never before announced, which is repugnant to the natural import of the language employed in the clause, and which interpretation curtails the legislative power of Congress to define and punish crime by asserting a right of judicial supervision over the exertion of that power, in disregard of the distinction between the legislative and judicial department of the government, I deem it my duty to dissent and state my reasons.

. . .

Whatever may be the difficulty, if any, in fixing the meaning of the prohibition at its origin, it may not be doubted, and indeed is not questioned by anyone, that the cruel punishments against which the Bill of Rights provided were the atrocious, sanguinary, and inhuman punishments which had been inflicted in the past upon the persons of criminals. This being certain, the difficulty of interpretation, if any, is involved in determining what was intended by the unusual punishments referred to and which were provided against. Light, however, on this subject, is at once afforded by observing that the unusual punishments provided against were responsive to and obviously considered to be the illegal punishments complained of. These complaints were, first, that customary modes of bodily punishments, such as whipping and the pillory, had, under the exercise of judicial discretion, been applied to so unusual a degree as to cause them to be illegal; and, second, that in some cases an authority to sentence to perpetual imprisonment had been exerted under the assumption that power to do so resulted from the existence of judicial discretion to sentence to imprisonment, when it was unusual, and therefore illegal, to inflict life imprisonment in the absence of express legislative authority. In other words, the prohibitions, although conjunctively stated, were really disjunctive, and embraced as follows: (a) Prohibitions against a resort to the inhuman bodily punishments of the past; (b) or, where certain bodily punishments were customary, a prohibition against their infliction to such an extent as to be unusual and consequently illegal; (c) or the infliction, under the assumption of the exercise of judicial discretion, of unusual punishments not bodily, which could not be imposed except by express statute, or which were wholly beyond the jurisdiction of the court to impose.

. . .

. . . [T]hat the 8th Amendment is in the precise words of the guaranty on that subject in the Virginia Bill of Rights [which adopted the language of the English Bill of Rights], would seem to make it perfectly clear that it was only intended by that Amendment to remedy the wrongs which had been provided against in the English Bill of Rights, and which were likewise provided against in the Virginia provision. . . . But this obvious result lends no support to the theory that the adoption of the Amendment operated or was intended to prevent the legislative branch of the government from prescribing, according to its conception of what public policy required, such punishments, severe or otherwise, as it deemed necessary for the prevention of crime, provided, only, resort was not had to the infliction of bodily punishments of a cruel and barbarous character, against which the Amendment expressly provided. . . .

. . .

From all the considerations which have been stated, I can deduce no ground whatever which, to my mind, sustains the interpretation now given to the cruel and unusual punishment clause. On the contrary, in my opinion, the review which has been made demonstrates that the word "cruel," as used in the Amendment, forbids only the lawmaking power, in prescribing punishment for crime, and the courts in imposing punishment, from inflicting unnecessary bodily suffering through a resort to inhuman methods for causing bodily torture, like or which are of the nature of the cruel methods of bodily torture which had been made use of prior to the Bill of Rights of 1689, and against the recurrence of which the word "cruel" was used in that instrument. To illustrate. Death was a well-known method of punishment, prescribed by law, and it was, of course, painful, and in that sense was cruel. But the infliction of this punishment was clearly not prohibited by the word "cruel," although that word manifestly was intended to forbid the resort to barbarous and unnecessary methods of bodily torture in executing even the penalty of death. . . .

Suggested Readings

Arkes, Hadley. *The Return of George Sutherland: Restoring a Jurisprudence of Natural Rights* (Princeton, NJ: Princeton University Press, 1994).

Baer, Judith A. *The Chains of Protection: The Judicial Response to Women's Labor Legislation* (Westport, CT: Greenwood Press, 1978).

Benedict, Michael Les. "Laissez-Faire and Liberty: A Re-evaluation of the Meaning and Origins of Laissez-Faire Constitutionalism." *Law and History* 3 (1985): 293–331.

Beth, Loren P. *The Development of the American Constitution, 1877–1917* (New York: Harper & Row, 1971).

Bickel, Alexander M., and Benno C. Schmidt, Jr. *The Judiciary and Responsible Government, 1910–21* (New York: Cambridge University Press, 2007).

Brandwein, Pamela. *Rethinking the Judicial Settlement of Reconstruction* (New York: Cambridge University Press, 2011).

Cardozo, Benjamin N. *The Nature of the Judicial Process* (New Haven, CT: Yale University Press, 1921).

Chafee, Zechariah. *Free Speech in the United States* (Cambridge, MA: Harvard University Press, 1941).

Cott, Nancy F. *The Grounding of Modern Feminism* (New Haven, CT: Yale University Press, 1987).

Fiss, Owen M. *The Troubled Beginnings of the Modern State* (New York: Macmillan, 1993).

Gillman, Howard. *The Constitution Besieged: The Rise and Demise of Lochner Era Police Power Jurisprudence* (Durham, NC: Duke University Press, 1993).

Gillman, Howard. "How Political Parties Can Use the Courts to Advance Their Agendas: Federal Courts in the United States, 1875–1891." *American Political Science Review* 96 (2002): 511–24.

Gordon, Sarah Barringer. *The Mormon Question: Polygamy and Constitutional Conflict in Nineteenth-Century America* (Chapel Hill: University of North Carolina Press, 2002).

Graber, Mark A. *Transforming Free Speech: The Ambiguous Legacy of Civil Libertarianism* (Berkeley: University of California Press, 1991).

Hamm, Richard F. *Shaping the Eighteenth Amendment: Temperance Reform, Legal Culture and the Polity, 1880–1920* (Chapel Hill: University of North Carolina Press, 1995).

Hirschon, Stanley P. *Farewell to the Bloody Shirt: Northern Republicans and the Southern Negro, 1877–1893* (Bloomington: Indiana University Press, 1962).

Hofstadter, Richard. *The Age of Reform* (New York: Random House, 1955).

Kens, Paul. *Judicial Power and Reform Poltiics: The Anatomy of* Lochner v. New York (Lawrence: University Press of Kansas, 1990).

Kens, Paul. *Justice Stephen Field: Shaping American Liberty from the Gold Rush to the Gilded Age* (Lawrence: University Press of Kansas, 1997).

Kull, Andrew. *The Color-Blind Constitution* (Cambridge, MA: Harvard University Press, 1992).

Lane, Charles. *The Day Freedom Died: The Colfax Massacre, the Supreme Court, and the Betrayal of Reconstruction* (New York: Henry Holt and Co., 2008).

Lofgren, Charles A. *The Plessy Case: A Legal-Historical Interpretation* (New York: Oxford University Press, 1987).

Mason, Alpheus T. *William Howard Taft: Chief Justice* (New York: Simon and Schuster, 1965).

Murphy, Paul L. *World War I and the Origins of Civil Liberties in the United States* (New York: Norton, 1979).

Novkov, Julie. *Racial Union: Law, Intimacy, and the White State in Alabama, 1865–1954* (Ann Arbor: University of Michigan Press, 2008).

Polenberg, Richard. *Fighting Faiths: The Abrams Case, the Supreme Court and Free Speech* (New York: Notable Trials Library, 1996).

Przybyszewski, Linda. *The Republic According to John Marshall Harlan* (Chapel Hill: University of North Carolina Press, 1999).

Rabban, David M. *Free Speech in Its Forgotten Years* (New York: Cambridge University Press, 1997).

Richardson, Heather Cox. *The Death of Reconstruction: Race, Labor, and Politics in the Post–Civil War North* (Cambridge, MA: Harvard University Press, 2001).

Ritter, Gretchen. *The Constitution as Social Design: Gender and Civic Membership in the American Constitutional Order* (Palo Alto, CA: Stanford University Press, 2006).

Siegel, Reva B. "She the People: The Nineteenth Amendment, Sex Equality, Federalism, and the Family." *Harvard Law Review* 115 (2002): 947–1046.

Sparrow, Bartholomew H. *The* Insular Cases *and the Emergence of American Empire* (Lawrence: University Press of Kansas, 2006).

Strum, Philippa. *Louis D. Brandeis: Justice for the People* (Cambridge, MA: Harvard University Press, 1984).

Sullivan, Kathleen S. *Constitutional Context: Women and Rights Discourse in Nineteenth-Century America* (Baltimore, MD: Johns Hopkins University Press, 2007).

Swisher, Carl B. *Stephen Field: Craftsman of the Law* (Chicago: University of Chicago Press, 1930).

Tamanaha, Brian Z. *Beyond the Formalist-Realist Divide: The Role of Politics in Judging* (Princeton, NJ: Princeton University Press, 2010).

Urofsky, Melvin I. *Louis D. Brandeis: A Life* (New York: Pantheon, 2009).

White, G. Edward. *Justice Oliver Wendell Holmes: Law and the Inner Self* (New York: Oxford University Press, 1993).

Woodward, C. Vann. *The Strange Career of Jim Crow*, rev. ed. (New York: Oxford University Press, 1966).

Chapter 8

The New Deal/Great Society Era: 1933–1968

I. Introduction

In the decades following the Great Depression liberals transformed the American constitutional landscape. These transformations included the complete abandonment of the freedom of contract, the abolition of Jim Crow, the nationalization of almost every provision in the Bill of Rights, the expansion of constitutional protections for persons accused of crime, the reapportioning of all congressional districts consistent with the principle of one person, one vote, and a dramatic expansion in free speech rights. The New Deal/Great Society Era witnessed such constitutional landmarks as *Brown v. Board of Education* (1954), the Voting Rights Act of 1965, and *Miranda* warnings. Much contemporary constitutional debate is over whether to expand, maintain, or abandon the constitutional heritage of the New Deal/Great Society Era.

Americans became more liberal during the mid-twentieth century for several reasons. The Great Depression increased popular support for labor unions and government programs designed to help people who had been disadvantaged or made vulnerable by industrialization. During the struggles against Nazi Germany and the Soviet Union, Americans emphasized the more liberal and egalitarian strands of their constitutional tradition in order to distinguish the United States from totalitarian regimes. Hitler revealed the ugliness of white supremacy and anti-Semitism. The Nazi effort to build a master race discredited eugenics. African- and Asian-Americans gained greater respect as a result of their heroics during World War II. Support for constitutional criminal procedure increased in response to increased attention to the way that southern courts treated blacks and to show trials and other violations of human rights that occurred in Joseph Stalin's Soviet Union. Many foreign policy hawks sought greater racial equality to combat Russian propaganda in the Third World. Americans became more racially liberal after the media exposed them to the inherent brutality of Jim Crow.

Liberal commitments unfolded in two stages. From 1933 until 1960 liberals debated what constitutional rights and liberties were entailed by political liberalism and the institutional responsibilities for securing those rights and liberties. New Dealers in the elected branches of government agreed that traditional property rights were subject to regulation by popular majorities but debated whether the same popular majorities should be able to regulate communist speech. New Dealers on the Supreme Court debated whether justices should strike down legislation restricting political dissent. Broad pronouncements were sometimes made without substantial implementation. The Truman administration and the early Warren Court declared a constitutional commitment to racial equality, but the United States in 1960 remained a largely segregated polity. From 1961 to 1968 all three branches of the national government became committed to modern liberal understandings of constitutional rights and liberties. The Supreme Court nationalized the Bill of Rights, struck down school prayer, ordered states to reapportion legislative districts, mandated both the exclusionary rule and *Miranda* warnings, and provided new protections for political dissenters. Great Society liberals in Congress passed such measures as the Civil Rights Act of 1964 and the Voting Rights Act of 1965. Great Society liberals in the executive branch vigorously enforced those measures, publicly championed liberal notions of racial equality, and submitted amicus briefs to the Supreme Court urging the justices to adopt liberal understandings of constitutional rights.

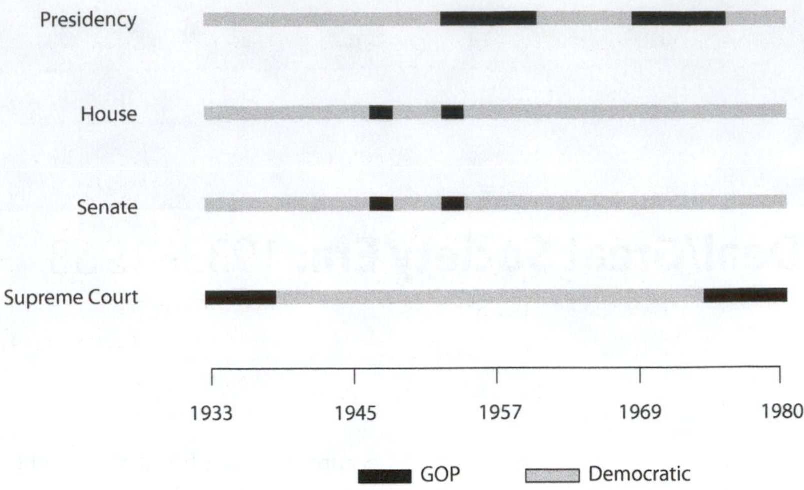

Figure 8-1 Partisan Control of the U.S. Government, 1933–80

Liberals in state government sometimes anticipated liberal national policies. The Supreme Court of California in 1947 struck down state laws prohibiting interracial marriages. Most states already provided counsel to indigent defendants accused of felonies before the Supreme Court in *Gideon v. Wainwright* (1963) ruled that the due process clause of the Fourteenth Amendment required that practice.

Parties. Liberals exercised more influence over constitutional development during the New Deal/Great Society Era than at any other time in American history. From 1933 until 1968 liberals either controlled or exercised significant power in all three branches of the national government and in many states. The liberal spirit in the United States was bipartisan, except in the South. Political liberalism found a congenial home among Democrats, despite the ongoing presence in the party of southern white supremacists. Liberal Democrats controlled the presidency for all but eight years of the New Deal/Great Society Era. Many Republicans, particularly those from the Northeast and the West Coast, supported liberal Democrats. Republicans such as Thomas Dewey, the GOP nominee for president in both 1944 and 1948; Herbert Brownell, the attorney general under President Eisenhower; and Nelson Rockefeller, the longtime Republican governor of New York, were as progressive as (if not more progressive than) their Democratic rivals. The Supreme Court was a bastion of bipartisan constitutional liberalism, particularly after Republican Earl Warren was appointed chief justice in 1954 and several very liberal justices joined the bench in the early 1960s. That liberalism can be partly traced to self-conscious decisions by the national executive. Aware that the federal judiciary could be a crucial ally in administrative struggles against conservatives in Congress and the states, members of the Justice Department in the Roosevelt, Truman, Eisenhower, Kennedy, and Johnson administrations frequently vetted judicial nominees on the basis of their progressive positions and commitment to racial equality.

Numerous incidents highlight the close cooperation among liberals in all three branches of the national government. Bipartisan majorities in 1964 passed legislation authorizing the Justice Department to challenge state laws requiring persons to pay poll taxes before voting. The Johnson administration supported lawsuits bringing that issue to the Supreme Court. In *Harper v. Virginia Board of Elections* (1966) the Supreme Court declared that the equal protection clause prohibited poll taxes. The Roosevelt administration in 1943 nominated court of appeals judge Wiley Rutledge rather than the more famous judge Learned Hand for a Supreme Court vacancy because Rutledge was thought more likely to protect civil rights and liberties.[1] Later that year the Supreme Court reversed a 1940 decision and declared in *Barnette v. West Virginia State Board of Education* (1943) that states could not require public school students to salute the flag.

Divisions among New Dealers initially hampered efforts to achieve liberal constitutional visions.

1. McMahon, Kevin J., *Reconsidering Roosevelt on Race: How the Presidency Paved the Road to* Brown (Chicago: University of Chicago Press, 2003).

Table 8-1 Major Rights and Liberties Issues and Decisions of the New Deal and Great Society Era

Major Political Issues	**Major Constitutional Issues**	**Major Court Decisions**
Great Depression	Abandonment of Freedom of Contract	*Home Building & Loan Ass'n v. Blaisdell* (1934)
New Deal	Decline of Protection for Property Rights	*West Coast Hotel Co. v. Parrish* (1937)
World War II	Nationalization of the Bill of Rights	*Palko v. Connecticut* (1937)
Cold War	Enhanced Judicial Protections for "Discrete and Insular Minorities"	*United States v. Carolene Products* (1938)
McCarthyism	Assault on "Separate But Equal"	*Skinner v. Oklahoma* (1942)
Civil Rights Movement	Increased Tendency to Find State Action	*Ex parte Quirin* (1942)
Police Brutality	Enhanced Scrutiny of Government Support for Religion	*Barnette v. West Virginia State Board of Education* (1943)
Little Rock Crisis	New Federal Rights Guarantees for Criminal Defendants	*Smith v. Allwright* (1944)
Civil Rights Act of 1964	One Person, One Vote	*Korematsu v. United States* (1944)
Voting Rights Act of 1965	New Protections for Privacy and Personal Liberty	*Shelley v. Kraemer* (1948)
Vietnam War	Enhanced Protections for Free Speech and Press	*Dennis v. United States* (1951)
War on Poverty		*Brown v. Board of Education* (1954)
Urban Rioting		*Mapp v. Ohio* (1961)
		Engle v. Vitale (1962)
		Sherbert v. Verner (1963)
		Gideon v. Wainwright (1963)
		Reynolds v. Sims (1964)
		New York Times v. Sullivan (1964)
		Griswold v. Connecticut (1965)
		Harper v. Virginia State Board of Elections (1966)
		Katzenbach v. Morgan (1966)
		Miranda v. Arizona (1966)
		Katz v. United States (1967)
		Duncan v. Louisiana (1968)
		Brandenburg v. Ohio (1969)

We presently think of liberals as being committed to economic redistribution, free speech, racial equality, and the rights of persons suspected of criminal offenses. Until the 1960s, however, few persons who thought of themselves as liberals shared all these values. Southern Democrats supported Social Security but not *Brown v. Board of Education* (1954). President Truman was a racial liberal who ordered that the military be desegregated, but he supported restricting free speech, especially for Communists. Liberals during the 1940s and 1950s disputed whether state officials ought to enjoy the same freedom from constitutional restrictions when catching criminals as they enjoyed when regulating the economy, or whether strict adherence to the rules of constitutional criminal procedure was necessary to protect the rights of African-Americans and other minorities. Prominent liberal law professors and judges, recalling how justices during the first part of the twentieth century struck down progressive legislation, were often ambivalent about empowering justices to declare more conservative laws unconstitutional. Few liberals expressed any opinion on abortion or gay rights before the 1970s.

Liberals efforts were also hampered by powerful conservatives in both Congress and the states. A conservative coalition in Congress composed of midwestern

Republicans and southern Democrats stalled proposed measures on racial equality, passed laws restricting free speech rights, and threatened to restrain a federal judiciary perceived as too soft on Communism, too internationalist, and, for southerners, too sympathetic to persons of color. State judges frequently condemned judicial decisions that nationalized federal policy.

Progressives in the elected branches of government fought back, using their power to maintain and augment the influence of progressives in the judiciary. Liberals in the Eisenhower Justice Department refused to support court-curbing proposals made in Congress. Congress was largely deaf to the pleas of state justices concerned with the nationalizing tendencies of the Warren Court.

Interest Groups. Public interest groups played an important role in bringing liberal constitutional complaints to public attention. Elite advocacy organizations such as the ACLU and the NAACP Legal Defense and Education Fund made major contributions to mid-twentieth-century constitutional liberalism. The ACLU and the NAACP provided legal support for persons claiming constitutional violations and lobbied sympathetic officials for favorable civil liberties and rights policies.[2] The Supreme Court handed down a series of decisions favoring the legal and constitutional rights of poor people only after the publicly funded Legal Services Corporation put those issues on the docket of the federal bench.[3] Liberal grassroots rights movements, most notably the Southern Christian Leadership Conference, also influenced the course of American constitutionalism. These groups achieved their goals by protest and, later, through the ballot box. President Roosevelt desegregated the federal workplace in order to prevent a mass civil rights march from taking place in Washington, DC, during World War II.[4] Martin Luther King's protests in Birmingham and Selma influenced the timing and content of the Civil Rights Act of 1964 and the Voting Rights Act of 1965.

Conservatives mobilized in response to these liberal efforts. The White Citizens Council organized massive resistance to *Brown v. Board of Education*. Robert Welch, concerned with perceived Communist influence in the national government and civil rights movement, founded the John Birch Society in 1958. In 1955 William Buckley published the first issue of *The National Review*, which became the leading voice for conservative intellectuals.

Courts. Liberals dominated the judiciary, but differences over liberal commitments and the proper role of the federal judiciary created both personal and professional tensions on the Stone, Vinson, and Warren Courts. Prominent liberals were ambivalent about the role of unelected justices in a democratic society. Alexander Bickel famously summed up what he coined as the "countermajoritarian difficulty" when he declared, "When the Supreme Court declares unconstitutional a legislative act or the action of an elected executive, it thwarts the will of the representatives of the actual people of the here and now."[5] Some liberals insisted that unelected justices had special roles to play in a liberal democracy. Justice Hugo Black in *Chambers v. Florida* (1940) maintained, "Under our constitutional system, courts stand against any winds that blow as havens of refuge for those who might otherwise suffer because they are helpless, weak, outnumbered, or because they are non-conforming victims of prejudice and public excitement." Other liberals insisted that the commitment to democracy entailed the constitutional right of popular majorities to adopt illiberal policies. In a famous series of lectures that criticized such instances of judicial activism as *Brown v. Board of Education*, Judge Learned Hand stated, "It would be most irksome to be ruled by a bevy of Platonic Guardians, even if I knew how to choose them, which I assuredly do not."[6]

Political liberals debated whether litigation was a practical means for securing liberal understandings of rights and liberties. Martin Luther King, Jr., believed in

2. Charles R. Epp, *The Rights Revolution: Lawyers, Activists, and Supreme Courts in Comparative Perspective* (Chicago: University of Chicago Press, 1998).

3. Susan E. Lawrence, *The Poor in Court: The Legal Services Program and Supreme Court Decision Making* (Princeton, NJ: Princeton University Press, 1990).

4. Philip A. Klinkner and Rogers M. Smith, *The Rise and Decline of Racial Equality in America* (Chicago: University of Chicago Press, 1999).

5. Alexander M. Bickel, *The Least Dangerous Branch: The Supreme Court at the Bar of Politics* (New Haven: Yale University Press, 1962), 16–17.

6. Learned Hand, *The Bill of Rights* (New York: Atheneum, 1972), 73.

mass action. In his view, white Americans responded more favorably to nonviolent protests in the streets of major cities than to judicial opinions. King's "Letter from the Birmingham Jail" asserted, "Nonviolent direct action seeks to create such a crisis and foster such a tension that a community which has constantly refused to negotiate is forced to confront the issue. It seeks to so dramatize the issue that it can no longer be ignored."[7] Thurgood Marshall had little interest in direct action. Litigation was his means for securing justice. At one point, frustrated by calls for student protest against Jim Crow, Marshall declared, "Desegregation [i]s men's work and should not be entrusted to children."[8]

The dispute between King and Marshall over the role of the federal judiciary remains vibrant today. Many law professors insist that the Supreme Court during the Great Society was the institution that most liberalized public life in the United States. Owen Fiss credits the justices with "a program of constitutional reform almost revolutionary in its aspiration and . . . in its achievement." In his view, "it was the Warren Court that spurred the great changes" in American civil rights and liberties and "inspired and protected those who sought to implement them."[9] Many political scientists are far more skeptical of the role that courts played during the mid-twentieth century. In his exceptionally detailed and controversial book *The Hollow Hope: Can the Courts Bring About Social Change?* Gerald Rosenberg concludes that *Brown v. Board of Education* did very little to desegregate schools. His bottom line is that "U.S. courts can almost never be effective producers of significant social reform," that judges can "at best . . . second the social reform acts of the other branches of government." Worse, Rosenberg believes, "not only does litigation steer activists to an institution that is constrained from helping them, but also it siphons off crucial resources and talent, and runs the risk of weakening political efforts." Finally, he points out that "funding a litigation campaign means that other strategic options are starved of funds."[10]

Constitutional Thought. Many explanations and justifications exist for the liberal direction that American constitutional politics took during the mid-twentieth century. One simplistic justification is that constitutional liberals were simply following clear constitutional mandates. Justice Hugo Black was the most vigorous proponent of this understanding of constitutional liberalism. Black, a justice from 1937 until 1971, repeatedly insisted that his votes for free speech, racial equality, and constitutional protections for persons suspected of crimes merely implemented preexisting rules that happened in many instances to coincide with liberal political values.[11] Another simplistic explanation is that constitutional liberals were simply making those constitutional rules that benefited political liberals. Professor Martin Shapiro suggests that the high constitutional rhetoric of the New Deal is best understood as little more than a means "to transfer [judicial] patronage from a Republican to a Democratic clientele."[12]

These pure law and pure politics explanations of constitutional liberalism fail to account for extremely important elements of New Deal/Great Society constitutional politics. Justice Black was a textualist no matter the political outcome. He supported liberal claims that governing officials could never regulate speech but opposed liberal claims that married people had a right to use birth control. Justices appointed by both Democrats and Republicans favored the idea of one person, one vote and opposed constitutional protections for property rights. The constitutional politics of the New Deal/Great Society Era are better understood in light of commitments to a living Constitution, the regionalization of American politics, perceived Cold War imperatives, and increased American commitments to democracy. These themes help explain why

7. Martin Luther King, Jr., "Letter from a Birmingham Jail," in *The Times Were a Changin': The Sixties Reader*, eds. Irwin Unger and Debi Unger (New York: Three Rivers Press, 1998), 130.

8. Mark V. Tushnet, *Making Civil Rights Law: Thurgood Marshall and the Supreme Court, 1936–1961* (New York: Oxford University Press, 1961), 305.

9. Owen M. Fiss, "A Life Twice Lived," *Yale Law Journal* 100 (1991): 1117, 1118.

10. Gerald N. Rosenberg, *The Hollow Hope: Can Courts Bring About Social Change?*, 2nd ed. (Chicago: University of Chicago Press, 2008), 422–23.

11. See, for example, the overview provided by Jeffrey D. Hockett, *New Deal Justice: The Constitutional Jurisprudence of Hugo L. Black, Felix Frankfurter, and Robert H. Jackson* (Lanham, Md.: Roman & Littlefield, 1996).

12. Martin Shapiro, "The Supreme Court: From Warren to Burger," in *The New American Political System*, ed. Anthony King (Washington, DC: American Enterprise Institute, 1978), 190–91.

Box 8-1 A Partial Cast of Characters of the New Deal/Great Society Era

Charles Evans Hughes	■ Republican ■ Governor of New York (1907–10) ■ Appointed by Taft to the Supreme Court (1910–16) ■ Resigned from the Court to run for president against Woodrow Wilson in 1916 ■ Secretary of state (1921–25) ■ Appointed by Hoover as chief justice of the U.S. Supreme Court (1930–41) ■ Started his career as a progressive reformer but later gained a more conservative reputation; guided the Supreme Court through the Court-packing challenge; wrote key decisions upholding the New Deal
Felix Frankfurter	■ Progressive who supported Teddy Roosevelt's Bull Moose Campaign but otherwise described himself as "politically homeless" ■ Helped found the American Civil Liberties Union and served as counsel for the National Consumers League ■ Professor at Harvard Law School (1914-1917, 1919-1939) ■ Like his mentor Oliver Wendell Holmes, Jr., criticized judicial review of progressive economic regulation ■ Advised Franklin Roosevelt on domestic policy ■ Appointed by Roosevelt to Supreme Court (1939-1962) ■ As a justice, known for his advocacy of judicial restraint when reviewing legislation and for his reluctance to apply the federal Constitution to the states
Hugo Black	■ Democrat ■ U.S. senator (1927–37) and, after 1932, a liberal New Dealer ■ Appointed by Roosevelt to Supreme Court (1937–71) ■ Supported the Court-packing plan while in the Senate ■ As a justice, known for his textualism, appeals to history, and a simultaneous emphasis on judicial restraint and firm defense of civil liberties
Earl Warren	■ Republican, although so popular in California that he was simultaneously nominated by the Republican, Democratic, and Progressive Parties for statewide office ■ California attorney general (1939–43) ■ California governor (1943–53) ■ Appointed by Eisenhower as chief justice of the U.S. Supreme Court (1953–69) ■ Led an increasingly liberal Court that supported congressional and presidential power and carved out new civil rights and civil liberties
Thurgood Marshall	■ Democrat ■ Lead litigator for the NAACP Legal Defense Fund ■ Appointed by Kennedy to U.S. Court of Appeals (1961–65) ■ U.S. solicitor general (1965–67) ■ Appointed by Johnson to U.S. Supreme Court (1967–91) ■ Major architect of the NAACP's school desegregation campaign, leading to *Brown v. Board of Education* (1954) ■ Known for his close alliance with Brennan as a defender of individual rights on the Supreme Court

(*Continued*)

Box 8-1 *(Continued)*

William Brennan	▪ Democrat ▪ Judge on New Jersey Supreme Court (1951–56) ▪ Appointed by Eisenhower to U.S. Supreme Court (1956–90); chosen as part of a reelection bid to appeal to Catholic Democrats ▪ Became one of the most significant justices of the twentieth century, writing many of the landmark decisions of the Warren Court and exerting a major influence in the Burger Court; known for his strong advocacy of active judicial review and expansive liberal interpretation of constitutional rights

constitutional liberals in the New Deal/Great Society Era championed certain values and the extent to which they thought constitutional law an appropriate vehicle for advancing those values.

Constitutional liberals were committed to a living Constitution. In this view, while the Constitution remained the foundation for rights and liberties, the content of those rights and liberties evolved in response to changing sociological, economic, and political conditions. Chief Justice Earl Warren articulated this commitment to living constitutionalism when he declared, "The words of the [Eighth] Amendment are not precise, and . . . their scope is not static. The Amendment must draw its meaning from the evolving standards of decency that mark the progress of a maturing society."[13] Sometimes these evolving standards limited the scope of preexisting constitutional rights. Many progressive thinkers insisted that nineteenth-century constitutional understandings of property rights were increasingly anachronistic in light of new industrial and political conditions. More often, the idea of a living Constitution provided grounds for expanding constitutional rights and liberties. *Brown v. Board of Education* provides a good example of this constitutional logic. Chief Justice Warren's opinion in this case began by noting that the original understanding of the Fourteenth Amendment was "inconclusive," in part because "the conditions of public education did not approximate those existing today." The status of separate but equal, he declared, had to be judged in light of contemporary conditions. Warren wrote, "We must consider public education in the light of its full development and its present place in American life throughout the Nation." His unanimous opinion highlighted contemporary social science research indicating that racial segregation harmed children of color. Past decisions sustaining Jim Crow policies were distinguished, determined not to be relevant to the issue before the Court, because previous generations of justices were unaware of modern research findings. "Whatever may have been the extent of psychological knowledge at the time of *Plessy v. Ferguson*," Warren wrote, "this finding is amply supported by modern authority." *Brown* did not reject the original constitutional commitment to equality. The justices, however, insisted on applying that commitment in light of modern conditions and knowledge.

Brown highlights the geography of constitutional transformation during the New Deal/Great Society Era. One "dominant motif of the Warren Court," Lucas Powe observes, was "an assault on the South as a unique legal and cultural region." He details how, with rare exception, Warren Court decisions were "directed exclusively at the South and [were] designed to force the South to conform to northern—that is, national—norms." Those decisions not directed at the South "were directed at Catholics or rural interests, neither of which played prominent roles in the governing coalitions of the mid-twentieth century."[14] Constitutional liberals between 1932 and 1968 rarely limited the power of the national government. Michael Klarman observes that many mid-twentieth-century constitutional criminal procedure decisions are best understood "as the Court imposing a national consensus on recalcitrant outliers."[15] The Voting Rights Act of 1965

13. *Trop v. Dulles*, 356 U.S. 86, 100 (1958).

14. Lucas A. Powe, Jr., *The Warren Court and American Politics* (Cambridge, MA: The Belknap Press of Harvard, 2000), 490.

15. Michael Klarman, "Scottsboro," *Marquette Law Review* 93 (2009): 379.

Illustration 8-1 Good Morning, Judge!
Source: Pittsburgh Press, January 9, 1937. Courtesy FDR Library.

banned literacy tests only in seven southern states. The Supreme Court in 1967 declared unconstitutional anti-miscegenation laws on the books in Virginia, Alabama, Arkansas, Delaware, Florida, Georgia, Kentucky, Louisiana, Mississippi, Missouri, North Carolina, Oklahoma, South Carolina, Tennessee, Texas, and West Virginia.

World War II and the Cold War exercised a complex influence on civil rights and liberties. On the one hand, both conflicts generated restrictions on constitutional rights. During World War II the government removed Japanese-Americans from the West Coast. The constitutionality of that removal was sustained by the Supreme Court in *Korematsu v. United States* (1944). During the McCarthy Era Congress passed measures limiting communist advocacy. The Supreme Court in *Dennis v. United States* (1951) permitted the government to prosecute Communist Party leaders. Both conflicts also inspired increased commitments to liberal freedoms. The need to mobilize American citizens and, during the Cold War, to gain approval from Third World countries led the United States to provide greater opportunities for persons of color. "As presidents and secretaries of state from 1946 to the mid-1960s worried about the impact of race discrimination on U.S. prestige abroad," Mary Dudziak notes, "civil rights reform came to be seen as crucial to U.S. foreign policy."[16] Constitutional decision makers frequently contrasted rights in the United States with their absence abroad. Justice Jackson in 1943 compared American rejection of "coerced uniformity" to the "fast failing efforts of our present totalitarian enemies" in an opinion striking down state laws mandating flag salutes in public schools.

Liberals during this period were small-d democrats. The Democratic Party platform of 1940 boasted that the Roosevelt administration had strengthened and would continue to strengthen democracy. President Johnson began his address urging Congress to pass the Voting Rights Act of 1965 by proclaiming, "I speak tonight for

16. Mary L. Dudziak, *Cold War Civil Rights: Race and the Image of American Democracy* (Princeton, NJ: Princeton University Press, 2000), 6.

the dignity of man and the destiny of democracy." The famous "Footnote Four" in *United States v. Carolene Products Co.* (1938) maintained that this commitment to democracy entailed a special judicial solicitude for two kinds of rights. The first were rights directly associated with democratic processes, the most important of which were the right to free speech and the right to vote. The second were the rights of "discrete and insular minorities" such as persons of color or Jehovah's Witnesses, who because of small size or prejudice were unable to use ordinary political processes to protect their rights and ordinary interests.

New Dealers transformed the rights commitments of an earlier liberalism. Liberalism for most of American history was identified with John Locke and a commitment to property rights. Most persons who identified as liberals by the mid-twentieth century were skeptical of the broad rights claims underlying traditional property rights. The philosopher John Dewey and Oliver Wendell Holmes based their Progressive Era challenges to the freedom of contract on a general skepticism of all natural rights. Chastened by Hitler and Stalin, many American liberals after World War II supported a robust set of universal human rights that transcended time, place, and culture. Franklin Roosevelt was reconceptualizing inherited constitutional and liberal understandings when he declared in 1941,

> We look forward to a world founded upon four essential human freedoms.
>
> The first is freedom of speech and expression—everywhere in the world.
>
> The second is freedom of every person to worship God in his own way—everywhere in the world.
>
> The third is freedom from want, which, translated into world terms, means economic understandings which will secure to every nation a healthy peacetime life for its inhabitants—everywhere in the world.
>
> The fourth is freedom from fear, which, translated into world terms, means a world-wide reduction of armaments to such a point and in such a thorough fashion that no nation will be in a position to commit an act of physical aggression against any neighbor—anywhere in the world.

Legacies. The New Deal/Great Society Era had a profound influence on American constitutionalism. Civil rights lawyers today need know hardly anything about constitutional decisions made before 1933, except that such decisions as *Lochner v. New York* (1905) were mistakes. Almost every area of constitutional civil rights practice, however, has been structured by decisions made between 1933 and 1968. *Brown* is the foundational decision for constitutional understandings of racial equality. State reapportionments must follow the one person, one vote rule announced in *Reynolds v. Sims* (1964). Public figures can win libel suits only if they meet the demanding standards of *New York Times Co. v. Sullivan* (1964). Police must still give *Miranda* (1965) warnings. Unconstitutionally seized evidence is still subject to the exclusionary rule announced in *Mapp v. Ohio* (1961). The New Deal/Great Society legacy is equally as clear when we examine statutes. Both the Civil Rights Act of 1964 and the Voting Rights Act of 1965 remain iconic. Both are part of the fundamental law of the United States even if both technically could be repealed by ordinary majorities.

The New Deal/Great Society Era continues to exert a powerful influence on constitutional understandings. Contemporary liberals bear a close family resemblance to the Great Society liberals of 1965 and some resemblance to the New Deal liberals of 1935, but have little more than the label "liberal" in common with persons who considered themselves liberal in 1875. Many Americans remain committed to the constitutional visions championed by Martin Luther King, Jr., Franklin Roosevelt, Earl Warren, and Lyndon Johnson. Many contemporary progressives insist that a newly empowered progressive regime need do little more than build on the legacy left by the progressive giants of the 1940s, 1950s, and 1960s. To a remarkable degree many constitutional conservatives are heirs to the tradition marked out by such liberal dissenters on the Warren Court as John Harlan and Felix Frankfurter rather than successors to the constitutional conservatism of the justices who opposed the New Deal.[17]

During the New Deal/Great Society Era liberals for the first time in American history regarded federal courts as a valued, preeminent, and often exclusive site for pursuing a progressive constitutional politics. Previously, progressives had sought to win the support of elected officials and avoid losing their legislative gains

17. See Thomas M. Keck, *The Most Activist Supreme Court in History: The Road to Modern Judicial Conservatism* (Chicago: University of Chicago Press, 2004).

in the courtroom. Judges during and immediately after Reconstruction did more to emasculate federal legislation promoting racial equality than to overturn state legislation promoting white supremacy. Labor unions at the turn of the twentieth century regarded courts as hostile terrain. Law professors who came of age during the 1960s, by comparison, taught their students that progressive courts were the norm and that the federal judiciary was the institution most likely to be sympathetic to liberal constitutional claims. One central question to think about throughout this chapter is whether the judiciary in the mid-twentieth century became a relatively enduring bastion of constitutional liberalism, or whether, as Powe insists, the tribunal led by Earl Warren was "a historically unique Court operating in an historically unique era."[18]

II. Foundations

MAJOR DEVELOPMENTS

- Special emphasis on democratic processes and rights of discrete and insular minorities
- Incorporation of most provisions in the Bill of Rights
- Increased tendency to find state action in cases alleging unconstitutional racial discrimination

New Deal and Great Society liberals expanded the scope of constitutional rights and liberties. When Richard Nixon became president in 1969 state officials had to respect most provisions of the Bill of Rights. Governing officials abroad and in the military had to respect due process rights when punishing other Americans. Private individuals were considered state actors for constitutional purposes when they were performing a public function or were significantly involved with the government.

The expanded scope of the Bill of Rights did not occur because Americans changed the constitutional text. Three constitutional amendments ratified between 1933 and 1968 altered constitutional rights and liberties, but none provided grounds for the increased scope of constitutional liberty. Americans in the mid-twentieth century also rejected claims that international human rights agreements provided legal limitations on state officials or federal officials acting on foreign soil.

Constitutional liberals took their constitutional bearings from crucial mid-twentieth-century judicial decisions. Americans debating the meaning of racial equality in 1968 looked to *Brown v. Board of Education* (1954). Liberal constitutionalists regarded the Constitutional Revolution of 1937 as the final word on the constitutional status of the freedom of contract. Progressives who championed the living Constitution celebrated a constitutional commitment to democratic conceptions of liberty and equality, even as they recognized that many political elites who framed the Constitution of 1787 scorned democracy. These constitutional decisions and commitments help explain why liberals insisted that American officials abroad, state officials domestically, and private persons with particular connections to state activities were constitutionally obligated to adhere to liberal understandings of democracy, equality, and fundamental rights.

A. Sources

The sources for constitutional rights remained largely the same. Americans ratified five constitutional amendments during the New Deal/Great Society Era. These provisions repealed prohibition, limited the president to two terms in office, permitted residents in the District of Columbia to vote for the president, abolished the poll tax in federal elections, and established procedures in case the president became disabled. Americans considered whether participation in the international human rights community significantly altered the constitutional landscape. After a brief debate a broad national consensus developed that such international agreements as the United Nations Charter (1945) and the Universal Declaration of Human Rights (1948) did not, without further legislation or constitutional amendment, influence the substance of domestic rights.

Constitutions and Amendments

Prohibition repeal was the first constitutional achievement of the New Deal. The Association against the Prohibition Amendment, a group of prominent industrialists, helped finance the Democratic Party during the 1928 and 1932 campaigns. The Democratic Party platform in 1932 called for the repeal of the Eighteenth Amendment. Immediately after Franklin Roosevelt

18. Powe, *The Warren Court and American Politics*, 486.

was elected Congress approved and a constitutional majority of states ratified the Twenty-First Amendment. Looking backward, the Twenty-First Amendment might be understood as returning to states their traditional power to regulate the health, safety, morals, and welfare of the citizenry. Many participants in state constitutional conventions who voted to repeal the Eighteenth Amendment relied heavily on Republican Era conceptions of the police power and individual rights. Looking forward, the repeal of Prohibition anticipated later constitutional resistance to morals legislation.

The Twenty-Third Amendment, which granted citizens in the District of Columbia the right to vote in presidential elections, and the Twenty-Fourth Amendment, which outlawed poll taxes in national elections, combined several themes dear to the heart of liberal constitutionalists. Both amendments made the United States more democratic by expanding access to the franchise. Both imposed national standards on the South. The states that failed to ratify the Twenty-Third Amendment were former members of the Confederate States of American plus Kentucky. By 1960 poll taxes were imposed only below the Mason-Dixon line. The Twenty-Fourth Amendment did not outlaw poll taxes in state elections. Constitutional liberals soon corrected that omission. In the Voting Rights Act of 1965, Congress authorized lawsuits challenging the constitutionality of state poll taxes. The Supreme Court in *Harper v. Virginia Board of Elections* (1966) declared unconstitutional state poll taxes.

Bruce Ackerman claims that Americans from 1933 to 1968 ratified de facto amendments to the Constitution. They first constitutionalized the basic principles underlying the New Deal, including national power to regulate all economic activities and the abandonment of the freedom of contract. "New Dealers," Ackerman writes, "us[ed] a series of national electoral victories as mandates that ultimately induced all three branches of the national government to recognize that the People had endorsed activist national government."[19] New Deal judicial appointees correctly refused to revive the freedom of contract, in this view, because of constitutional decisions made between 1933 and 1940, and not in 1787 or 1868. Ackerman views the civil rights revolution as a second constitutional moment. He writes,

> Johnson's landslide victory [in 1964], accompanied by decisive Democratic majorities in Congress, established a new institutional pattern. All three branches were now mutually supporting one another in asserting that the People of the United States had made a considered judgment about human rights.[20]

It was popular support for the Civil Rights Act of 1964 and the Voting Rights Act of 1965 that entrenched *Brown* as a constitutional decision, not the original intentions of the persons responsible for the equal protection clause of the Fourteenth Amendment.

Ackerman's views are controversial, but his writings accurately capture an important dimension of liberal constitutionalism. Liberals (and many conservatives) during the second half of the twentieth century did not ground their constitutional understandings in the original constitutional text or constitutional practices at the time those texts were ratified. Supreme Court decisions in the 1950s and 1960s pointed to judicial decisions in the 1930s as constitutional authorities justifying national power over the economy. Constitutional debate over racial equality during the twentieth century focused on the meaning of *Brown* and the Civil Rights Acts of the 1960s. Did these practices reflect popular beliefs that the Constitution had been amended outside of Article V, were they examples of reasoning from precedent, or do they suggest that the Constitutional Revolution of 1937 was illegitimate?

The Law of Nations

Many Americans touted international law as an independent source for fundamental rights and liberties. In the wake of World War II the United States became a leader of the international human rights community. Most Americans enthusiastically endorsed the United Nations (UN) and various UN resolutions spelling out fundamental rights. Article 55 of the UN Charter called for "universal respect for, and observance of human rights and fundamental freedoms for all without distinction as to race, sex, language, or religion." The Universal Declaration of Human Rights (1948)

19. Bruce Ackerman, *We the People: Transformations* (Cambridge, MA: Harvard University Press, 1998), 268.

20. Ibid., 110.

proclaimed universal rights to free speech, free exercise of religion, and due process of law, as well as such rights as "the right to work, to free choice of employment, to just and favourable conditions of work and to protection against unemployment" (Article 23), "the right to rest and leisure, including reasonable limitation of working hours and periodic holidays with pay" (Article 24), and the "right to a standard of living adequate for the health and well-being of [a person] and of his family, including food, clothing, housing and medical care and necessary social services" (Article 25). "All nations," the Universal Declaration insisted, "shall strive by teaching and education to promote respect for these rights and freedoms and by progressive measures, national and international, to secure their universal and effective recognition and observance."

Prominent liberals during the early Cold War believed that these UN proclamations provided new foundations for rights and liberties in the United States. President Truman's Commission on Civil Rights cited Article 55 of the UN Charter as providing a legal basis for declaring segregation in the United States unconstitutional. Several Supreme Court justices cited the UN Charter when striking down a California law that prevented American citizens from enjoying gifts of land from parents who were not eligible for citizenship. After noting "We have recently pledged ourselves to cooperate with the United Nations to 'promote . . . universal respect for, and observance of, human rights and fundamental freedoms for all without distinction as to race, sex, language, or religion,'" Justice Black's concurring opinion in *Oyama v. California* (1948) asked, "How can this nation be faithful to this international pledge if state laws which bar land ownership and occupancy by aliens on account of race are permitted to be enforced?" Justice Murphy's concurrence observed, "This nation has recently pledged itself, through the United Nations Charter, to promote respect for, and observance of, human rights and fundamental freedoms for all without distinction as to race, sex, language and religion. . . . The Alien Land Law['s] . . . inconsistency with the Charter . . . is but one more reason why the statute must be condemned."

Conservatives mobilized against these citations of international law. The American Bar Association repeatedly condemned efforts to make human rights treaties binding law. *Time* magazine informed readers that if the United States were constitutionally obligated to respect the liberties set out in the UN Declaration of Human Rights, the nation "would have to become even more totalitarian than, say, the Soviet Union."[21] Senator John Bricker and political allies in Congress proposed a series of amendments that would prevent any human rights treaty from becoming domestic law without congressional approval. The most popular version declared:

> Section 1: A provision of a treaty or other international agreement which conflicts with this Constitution shall not be of any force or effect.
>
> Section 2: An international agreement other than a treaty shall become effective as internal law in the United States only by an act of the Congress.

The Bricker Amendment failed to pass the Senate in 1954 by one vote. Liberals balked at restricting human rights. President Eisenhower's legislative allies balked at restricting the president.[22] Three years later, in *Reid v. Covert* (1957), liberals on the Supreme Court defused the debate by clearly stating that treaties and executive agreements could not empower the federal government to violate constitutional rights. "[N]o agreement with a foreign nation," Justice Black declared, "can confer power on the Congress, or on any other branch of Government, which is free from the restraints of the Constitution."[23]

B. Principles

Liberals were committed to democratic notions of liberty and equality. Liberty and equality are longstanding American constitutional commitments. Democracy is not. Many framers of the Constitution insisted that the United States was a republic. Prominent Americans for the next 150 years debated whether the United States was best thought of as a constitutional republic or as a constitutional democracy. A general consensus

---

21. *Time*, "The Bricker Amendment: A Cure Worse Than the Disease," July 13, 1953.

22. For more information on the Bricker Amendment, see Duane Tananbaum, *The Bricker Amendment Controversy: A Test of Eisenhower's Political Leadership* (Ithaca, NY: Cornell University Press, 1988). This section relies heavily on that work.

23. Black did not discuss treaties expanding civil rights and civil liberties, the real concern of persons who supported the Bricker Amendment. Whether an executive agreement to outlaw capital punishment was constitutional may have been an open question after *Reid v. Covert*.

that the Constitution should be understood primarily as a framework for democratic government did not develop until the New Deal. This consensus transformed inherited notions of constitutional liberty and equality.

New Dealers emphasized rights to democratic processes rather than freedoms from government regulation. Free speech and, later, voting rights became "preferred freedoms" because those liberties provided citizens with the means for adequately protecting more substantive rights and interests. The freedom of speech, Justice Cardozo declared in *Palko v. Connecticut* (1937), was "the matrix, the indispensable condition, of nearly every other form of freedom." Citizens able to articulate their policy preferences and freely cast ballots could determine for themselves what individual rights they thought fundamental.

The focus of constitutional equality turned from general prohibitions against so-called class legislation to prohibitions against laws that targeted "discrete and insular minorities." The principles underlying class legislation made little sense in a society increasingly committed to interest group liberalism. New Dealers thought legitimate private efforts to secure favorable legislation. They doubted whether any public interest existed independent of the interest of particular social groups. Virtually all legislation, the "pluralist" political science of the 1940s and 1950s maintained, provided special benefits to particular groups. In a constitutional regime characterized by bargaining over public policy, New Dealers concluded, constitutional equality rights turned on whether particular groups, most notably African-Americans, were participating as equals in electoral and legislative bargaining processes.

Palko v. Connecticut suggested that liberals might protect some fundamental freedoms distinct from democratic processes or equality. Justice Cardozo's opinion in that case maintained that the due process clause of the Fourteenth Amendment guaranteed those rights that were required by "the very essence of a scheme of ordered liberty" and were grounded in "a principle of justice so rooted in the traditions and conscience of our people as to be ranked as fundamental." Justices in subsequent years cited this or similar phrases when striking down laws sterilizing criminals in *Skinner v. Oklahoma* (1942), banning married people from using birth control in *Griswold v. Connecticut* (1965), and expanding the constitutional protections for persons accused of criminal offenses. These cases could nevertheless be explained as protections for discrete and insular minorities. The Connecticut law declared unconstitutional in *Griswold* was enforced only against birth control clinics that provided advice to poor persons. No private doctor was ever prosecuted for prescribing birth control to a private, more affluent patient.

These New Deal/Great Society conceptions of liberty and equality inspired a new two-tiered scheme of constitutional protection for rights. Constitutional decision makers before the 1930s relied on a "one-size-fits-all" approach to constitutional guarantees. Legislation limiting the exercise of a right or distinguishing between people was constitutional if the law plainly served a legitimate public purpose and if any distinction was based on real differences between people. Liberals distinguished among rights. Most legislative restrictions or classifications satisfied constitutional standards if they met a very undemanding rationality standard. Legislation that restricted such preferred freedoms as the freedom of speech or burdened such "discrete and insular minorities" as persons of color, however, required what became known as strict scrutiny. Such laws were ordinarily unconstitutional unless the measure was a necessary or narrowly tailored means for achieving a compelling government end.

When employing this two-tiered theory of constitutional right, New Deal and Great Society thinkers often placed emphasis on social science investigations. Karl Llewellyn, who led the call for a realist jurisprudence, asserted, "We need improved machinery for making the facts about [the effects of legal rules]—or about needs and conditions to be affected by a decision—available to courts."[24] Most proponents of legal realism during the 1930s employed social science research to justify judicial deference toward state and federal efforts to regulate property rights. By the 1950s, however, liberals were using social science evidence, particularly social science evidence refuting innate racial differences, to justify judicial protection for certain liberties. Chief Justice Warren's unanimous opinion in *Brown v. Board of Education* (1954) relied on social science evidence when famously concluded, "Segregation with the sanction of law . . . has a tendency to retard the education and mental development of Negro children. . . . Whatever may have been the extent of psychological knowledge

24. Karl N. Llewellyn, "Some Realism about Realism—Responding to Dean Pound," *Harvard Law Review* 44 (1931): 1222.

Table 8-2 Tiers of Scrutiny of Legislative Classifications

Level of Judicial Scrutiny	Trigger	Doctrinal Test to Uphold Classification
Strict scrutiny	Suspect classifications, such as race and nationality, or infringes on fundamental rights	Serves a compelling government interest and is the least restrictive necessary to serve that interest
Intermediate scrutiny	Quasi-suspect classifications, such as gender	Serves an important government interest and is substantially related to serving that interest
Rational basis test	All other classifications, economic classifications in particular	Serves a legitimate government interest and is rationally related to serving that interest

at the time of *Plessy v. Ferguson* (1896), this finding is amply supported by modern authority." Warren then cited seven works by social scientists.

Gunnar Myrdal's *An American Dilemma* (1944), one of the works that Warren cited, expressed the most optimistic version of the New Deal/Great Society constitutional vision. Myrdal, an exceptionally influential Swedish social scientist, believed that most citizens of the United States were committed to what he called the "American Creed." This Creed required "liberty, equality, justice, and fair opportunity to everybody." Myrdal recognized that few African-Americans enjoyed these rights. Nevertheless, he insisted that race prejudice was not inherent in constitutional principle, but was justified merely "in terms of tradition, expediency, or utility." As more Americans became aware of the conflict between racism and constitutional principle, Myrdal and other liberals hoped, Jim Crow practices would largely be abandoned.[25]

United States v. Carolene Products Co., 144 U.S. 304 (1938)

The Carolene Products Company shipped "Milnut" across state lines in violation of the Filled Milk Act of 1923. That law forbade companies from shipping in interstate commerce "skimmed milk compounded with any fat or oil other than milk fat, so as to resemble milk or cream." The Carolene Products Company insisted that the bill was an unconstitutional effort to protect dairy farmers, not a legitimate exercise of the federal power to regulate interstate commerce. The federal district court agreed and declared the Filled Milk Act unconstitutional. The United States appealed that ruling to the Supreme Court.

The Supreme Court by a 6-1 vote had little difficulty finding constitutional grounds for sustaining the federal law. Justice Stone's majority opinion declared that federal officials could prohibit the interstate shipment of any good that they believed was in some way harmful. "Congress," he declared, "is free to exclude from interstate commerce articles whose use in the states for which they are destined it may reasonably conceive to be injurious to the public health, morals, or welfare." Moreover, Stone continued, federal justices should not second-guess congressional judgments that certain milk products were unhealthy. His majority opinion emphasized that legislative fact-findings must normally be presumed correct unless they are utterly irrational. "The existence of facts supporting the legislative judgment is to be presumed," Stone declared, "for regulatory legislation affecting ordinary commercial transactions is not to be pronounced unconstitutional unless in the light of the facts made known or generally assumed it is of such a character as to preclude the assumption that it rests upon some rational basis within the knowledge and experience of the legislators." The justices relied on this very weak rational basis test when determining the constitutionality of most legislative restrictions or classifications. Stone appended a footnote to this assertion that indicated that the justices might not always be so deferential to legislatures. Stricter scrutiny was

25. Karl Gunnar Myrdal, *An American Dilemma* (New York: Harper & Row, 1944), lxxxi.

warranted, he suggested, when legislation was inconsistent with explicit constitutional text, interfered with democratic processes, or violated the rights of "discrete and insular minorities."

Footnote Four of United States v. Carolene Products Co. *is the most famous footnote in Supreme Court history. What is the underlying logic of the footnote? Is the logic of the first paragraph, which was added after a suggestion by Chief Justice Hughes, consistent with the logic of the more famous second and third paragraphs? Is Justice Stone suggesting that some constitutional rights or principles are more important than other constitutional rights or principles? Is he suggesting that the judiciary is institutionally better suited than the elected branches of government to protect rights to political processes and prevent discrimination against "discrete and insular minorities"? Does the fundamental logic of the* Carolene Products *footnote reflect developments in the political system? For many decades the Court nurtured a reputation for happily second-guessing the wisdom of economic regulation. In light of the Court's capitulation to the New Deal a year earlier, might the justices have been looking for a new job description?*

JUSTICE STONE delivered the opinion of the Court.

. . .

[Footnote 4:] There may be narrower scope for operation of the presumption of constitutionality when legislation appears on its face to be within a specific prohibition of the Constitution, such as those of the first ten Amendments, which are deemed equally specific when held to be embraced within the Fourteenth. . . . It is unnecessary to consider now whether legislation which restricts those political processes which can ordinarily be expected to bring about repeal of undesirable legislation, is to be subjected to more exacting judicial scrutiny under the general prohibitions of the Fourteenth Amendment than are most other types of legislation. [These include] restrictions upon the right to vote, . . . on restraints upon the dissemination of information, . . . on interferences with political organizations, [and] prohibition of peaceable assembly. Nor need we enquire whether similar considerations enter into the review of statutes directed at particular religious, . . . or national . . . or racial minorities; whether prejudice against discrete and insular minorities may be a special condition, which tends seriously to curtail the operation of those political processes ordinarily to be relied upon to protect minorities, and which may call for a correspondingly more searching judicial inquiry.

American Civil Liberties Union, **Policy Guide** (1976)[26]

The ACLU was the most prominent organization that championed civil rights and liberties during the New Deal/Great Society Era. The ACLU was founded in 1920 by Roger Nash Baldwin, a pacifist who had been arrested after he refused to be inducted into the Army during World War I. Unlike other civil liberties organizations at the time, the ACLU proclaimed a commitment to protecting free speech and related rights of all people. Over the next twenty years, the organization quickly evolved into a leading mainstream liberal bastion. Such prominent liberals as Eleanor Roosevelt and Harry Truman addressed ACLU conventions or publicly identified with the ACLU's mission of protecting free speech, the free exercise of religion, and the rights of persons of color. The ACLU's increasing prominence in the New Deal coalition created internal tensions between the more moderate and radical members of the organization, tensions that were almost always resolved in favor of the moderates. In 1939 the ACLU Board of Directors voted to expel Elizabeth Gurley Flynn on the ground that a member of the Communist Party could not be an ACLU board member.

The following are ACLU policy positions during the New Deal/Great Society Era. Consider the connections between these different assertions. Were the central commitments of the ACLU united by a common principle? What is that common principle? Many of these principles were or became constitutional law by 1968. As you read the materials in the rest of the chapter, consider why the ACLU was very successful on some matters (freedom of speech, racial equality) and moderately successful on others (government funding of parochial schools and abortion), but unsuccessful on still others (the draft, marijuana).[27]

Policy #1. Believing that pre-censorship is the most dangerous of all curtailments of the freedom of expression guaranteed by the First Amendment, the ACLU opposes any government restriction or punishment, prior to publication or exhibition, of any form of expression on grounds of obscenity. (1970. Similar policy announced in 1959.)

. . .

26. Excerpted from American Civil Liberties Union, *1976 Policy Guide of the American Civil Liberties Union* (New York: American Civil Liberties Union, 1976).

27. For more information about the ACLU, see Samuel Walker, *In Defense of American Liberties: A History of the ACLU* (New York: Oxford University Press, 1990).

Policy #23. In the spirit of its support for diversity on the air, the ACLU endorses the FCC's Fairness Doctrine. The doctrine, in essence, says that if broadcasters are to operate their publicly granted licenses in the "public interest, convenience and necessity," they must present important public issues, and offer opportunity for contrasting points of view for those issues. (1969. Similar policy announced in 1955.)

. . .

Policy #43. The Union agrees with the Supreme Court's long-standing interpretation of the Second Amendment that the individual's right to keep and bear arms applies only to the preservation of "a well-regulated militia." . . . Except for lawful police and military purposes, the possession of weapons by individuals is not constitutionally protected. (1968)

. . .

Policy #70. The ACLU believes that the "no establishment of religion" clause of the First Amendment bars public aid to parochial schools through the expenditure of government funds. (1958)

Policy #71. The ACLU believes that any program of religious indoctrination—direct or indirect—in the public schools or with public resources is a violation of the constitutional principle of separation of church and state. (1949)

. . .

Policy #90. Expressions of opinion, whether made in public or private, are protected by the First and Fourteenth Amendments, except when:

1. They become an integral part of conduct violating a valid law, or
2. They are a direct incitement to specific and immediate violation of law; or
3. They threaten a danger of unlawful acts so great and so immediate that time is lacking for answer. . . . (1949)

. . .

Policy #106. Military conscription is a severe infringement of individual liberties, at best the resort of a nation facing an imminent threat. . . . ACLU believes that government has the duty to prove to the public that so drastic a step as conscription is required today. No such showing has been made. (1969)

. . .

Policy #203. A person who has been arrested must have the aid and presence of counsel during police station interrogation. Any confession obtained when counsel is denied should be inadmissible at a criminal trial. (1965)

. . .

Policy #214. The use of marijuana involves protected constitutional rights, including the right to privacy. Intrusion by government on such a constitutionally protected right places a burden of justification on government. (1968)

. . .

Policy #233. The ACLU opposes capital punishment because the death penalty denies equal protection of the laws, is cruel and unusual punishment, and removes guarantees of due process of law. (1965)

. . .

Policy #256. The ACLU asserts that a woman has a right to have an abortion. (1968)

. . .

Policy #301. Discrimination in the rental, sale, or mortgaging of housing, public or private, based on race, color, sex, religion, national origin, political affiliation, alienage or illegitimacy, is a denial of basic civil rights. The ACLU believes that such discrimination should be challenged on constitutional grounds, when possible, and that it should be prohibited by legislation. (1975. Similar policies announced in 1947 and 1959.)

Policy #305. Racial segregation in public elementary and secondary schools violates the equal protection of the law guarantee of the Fourteenth Amendment. (1953–54)

. . .

In a community where non-whites are generally housed in racially segregated, consolidated areas, *de facto* school segregation cannot be justified either by officially ignoring race in administrative decisions on school districting or by adhering to the neighborhood school as the pre-eminent ideal. It is not sufficient for a school to be color blind. School boards and other appropriate local authorities have a constitutional and affirmative obligation to correct drastic racial imbalances in order that all children will enjoy equal protection of the laws under the Fourteenth Amendment. (1963)

. . .

Policy #317. The ACLU . . . will . . . support legislation, litigation, and educational programs to protect: (1) the right of privacy of the poor, by opposing such tactics as midnight visits to the homes of those receiving assistance . . . (2) the right to a hearing, with counsel if desired, for welfare applicants and recipients in connection with their right to assistance or respecting the reduction or termination of assistance. . . . (1969)

. . .

Policy #319. The equal protection clause of the Fourteenth Amendment is infringed by the dilution, as well as the denial, of the right to vote, and malapportionment by the states thus raises a civil liberties issue. (1961)

C. Scope

Americans broadened the scope of constitutional rights protections. By 1968 far more persons in more circumstances had to respect more constitutional provisions than was the case in 1933. State officials could no longer violate most provisions in the Bill of Rights. Federal officials could no longer violate the constitutional rights of American citizens residing in foreign countries. Private persons were far more likely to be considered state actors when they engaged in what had previously been thought to be private race discrimination.

Incorporation

Most provisions in the Bill of Rights were incorporated during the New Deal/Great Society years. When that era began the due process clause of the Fourteenth Amendment was understood as obligating states to respect only the free speech/free press clause of the First Amendment, the takings clause of the Fifth Amendment, and the right to counsel clause of the Sixth Amendment. Thirty-five years later states were bound by almost every provision of the Bill of Rights. The Supreme Court held both state and federal criminal trials to the same constitutional standards. The only provisions in the Bill of Rights not clearly incorporated when Earl Warren left the bench were the Second Amendment, the Third Amendment, the grand jury requirement of the Sixth Amendment, the Seventh Amendment, and, perhaps, the excessive bail clause of the Eight Amendment.

Many liberals in the early New Deal years opposed incorporation. They were skeptical of judicial power and opposed broad interpretation of constitutional provisions protecting criminal suspects. Justice Cardozo's majority opinion in *Palko v. Connecticut* suggested that the overlap between due process in the Fourteenth Amendment and the Bill of Rights was quite small. In his view,

> The right to trial by jury and the immunity from prosecution except as the result of an indictment may have value and importance. Even so, they are not of the very essence of a scheme of ordered liberty. To abolish them is not to violate a "principle of justice so rooted in the traditions and conscience of our people as to be ranked as fundamental." . . . Few would be so narrow or provincial as to maintain that a fair and enlightened system of justice would be impossible without them. What is true of jury trials and indictments is true also, as the cases show, of the immunity from compulsory self-incrimination. . . . This too might be lost, and justice still be done.

Justice Felix Frankfurter in *Adamson v. California* (1947) urged the justices to give states the same leeway to experiment with different criminal processes as the justices were giving state and federal officials to experiment with different economic regulations. "Due process was not restricted to rules fixed in the past," John Harlan wrote several decades later, "for that would be to deny every quality of the law but its age, and to render it incapable of progress or improvement."

New voices soon emerged. By the 1940s most constitutional liberals favored the nationalization of civil rights. Justice Black spoke for these liberals when he insisted that the due process clause of the Fourteenth Amendment required states to respect every provision in the first eight amendments to the Constitution. "I have never believed that under the guise of federalism," Black asserted, "the States should be able to experiment with the protections afforded our citizens through the Bill of Rights." Black and his judicial allies were particularly concerned with criminal trials in the former Confederate states. The judicial strategy of reversing only particularly egregious convictions no longer seemed adequate for dealing with Jim Crow justice. Instead, the Warren Court majority began imposing national standards on all local criminal trials.

Racial issues played a major role in decisions expanding the scope of the Bill of Rights. A high percentage of cases incorporating provisions in the Bill of Rights involved appeals from persons of color who had been convicted in a southern court. Some decisions incorporating a constitutional provision simply ensured that southern states followed the same norms as most northern states. *Gideon v. Wainwright* (1963), the decision holding that the due process clause of the Fourteenth Amendment incorporated the Sixth Amendment right to counsel, is a particularly good example of the regional bias of incorporation. In response to a request from the attorney general of Florida, the attorneys general of Alabama and North Carolina filed an amicus brief before the Supreme Court asserting that states should be free to determine when a criminal defendant was provided counsel. The attorneys general of Massachusetts, Minnesota, Colorado, Connecticut, Georgia, Hawaii, Idaho, Illinois, Indiana, Kentucky, Maine, Michigan, Missouri, Nevada, Ohio, North Dakota, South Dakota, Oregon, Rhode Island, Washington, West Virginia, and Alaska filed an amicus brief insisting that states be bound by the same rules as the federal government. The Supreme Court decision incorporating the Sixth Amendment required southern states to do what northern states were already doing.

"Selective incorporation" was the process by which most provisions of the Bill of Rights were incorporated by the due process clause of the Fourteenth Amendment. As described in *Duncan v. Louisiana* (1968), selective incorporation required the justices to determine whether a particular constitutional provision was central to "ordered liberty" or "fundamental fairness." If the provision was deemed an element of ordered liberty, then the entire provision was incorporated. If a comment by a federal prosecutor on a criminal defendant's failure to testify violates the Fifth Amendment, then the same comment by a state prosecutor violates the Fourteenth Amendment. The same is true of state police, state prosecutorial, or state judicial decisions that violate any other incorporated provision of the Bill of Rights.

Selective incorporation differs from the "fundamental fairness" test Justice Cardozo applied in *Palko*. Cardozo insisted that trials could be fundamentally fair even if they were inconsistent with federal standards under the Bill of Rights. Some overlap exists between due process and other provisions of the Bill of Rights. Confessions extracted by torture violate both the right against self-incrimination and fundamental fairness. Nevertheless, not every official action that violates the self-incrimination clause of the Fifth Amendment also violates due process. Cardozo believed that prosecutors who comment on an accused person's failure to testify at trial violate the Fifth Amendment, but that such practices are not so fundamentally unfair as to also violate due process.

In theory selective incorporation also differs from total incorporation. Justice Black and other proponents of total incorporation insisted that the due process clause requires states to honor every provision of the Bill of Rights, that justices have no business determining which provisions are more important than others. By the 1960s, however, selective incorporation resembled total incorporation, as every litigated provision was interpreted as central to ordered liberty. Although not every clause of the Bill of Rights has been officially incorporated, in no case decided after 1960 has the Supreme Court ruled that a state action is constitutional when the identical action by a federal official would violate the Bill of Rights.

Duncan v. Louisiana, 391 U.S. 145 (1968)

Gary Duncan, a nineteen-year-old African American, was arrested for battery after he allegedly slapped Herman Landry, a white boy. At trial Duncan's request for a jury trial was denied. The trial judge, accepting the account of the incident offered by the white witnesses who testified, sentenced Duncan to sixty days in prison and ordered him to pay a $150 fine. Federal law at that time required a jury trial in all criminal cases other than petty crimes with a maximum punishment of less than six months. The maximum punishment for simple battery in Louisiana was two years. Duncan appealed his conviction to the Supreme Court of the United States. He claimed that states were obligated by the due process clause of the Fourteenth Amendment to provide jury trials whenever a federal court would be obligated to provide a jury trial under the Sixth Amendment.

The Supreme Court by a 7-2 vote declared that Duncan was unconstitutionally convicted. Justice White's majority opinion ruled that the due process clause of the Fourteenth Amendment required states to respect the rights protected by the jury clause of the Sixth Amendment. Instead of determining whether Duncan's trial was fundamentally fair, White considered whether the jury trial provision of the Sixth Amendment was necessary for fundamental fairness.

Table 8-3 U.S. Supreme Court Cases Applying the Federal Bill of Rights to the States

Amendment	Right	Case
First Amendment	Establishment of religion	*Everson v. Board of Education Free* (1947)
	Exercise of religion	*Cantwell v. Connecticut* (1940)
	Freedom of speech	*Gitlow v. New York* (1925)
	Freedom of the press	*Near v. Minnesota* (1931)
	Freedom of assembly	*DeJonge v. Oregon* (1937)
Second Amendment	Right to keep and bear arms	*McDonald v. Chicago* (2010)
Fourth Amendment	Unreasonable searches	*Wolf v. Colorado* (1949)
	Exclusionary rule	*Mapp v. Ohio* (1961)
Fifth Amendment	Double jeopardy	*Benton v. Maryland* (1969)
	Self-incriminating	*Malloy v. Hogan* (1964)
	Taking without just compensation	*Chicago, B & Q.R. Co. v. Chicago* (1897)
Sixth Amendment	Speedy trial	*Klopfer v. North Carolina* (1967)
	Public trial	*In re Oliver* (1948)
	Jury trial	*Duncan v. Louisiana* (1968)
	Impartial jury	*Irvin v. Dowd* (1961)
	Notice of charges	*Cole v. Arkansas* (1948)
	Confrontation of witnesses	*Pointer v. Texas* (1965)
	Right to subpoena witnesses	*Washington v. Texas* (1967)
	Right to counsel	*Gideon v. Wainwright* (1963)
Eighth Amendment	Cruel and unusual punishment	*Robinson v. California* (1962)

After concluding that a jury trial was a necessary element of a fair trial, he ruled that any trial that violated the Sixth Amendment guarantee also violated the due process clause of the Fourteenth Amendment. Consider whether this reasoning is sound. In his concurring opinion Justice Black defended his long-standing commitment to the "total incorporation" of the Bill of Rights. Must Black's argument depend on the historical record, or may total incorporation rest on American traditions and that position's capacity to reduce judicial discretion? Justice Harlan's dissent asserts that many particulars of the Sixth Amendment are not necessary for fundamental fairness; for example, a trial by a jury of ten persons would not be unfair even though the Sixth Amendment requires a twelve-person jury. Is he correct? Harlan claimed that total incorporation, which insists that every provision of the Bill of Rights is fully incorporated, and fundamental fairness, which insists that due process is limited to basic fairness, are the only two intellectually coherent positions. Is this correct?

JUSTICE WHITE delivered the opinion of the Court.

. . .

The test for determining whether a right extended by the Fifth and Sixth Amendments with respect to federal criminal proceedings is also protected against state action by the Fourteenth Amendment has been phrased in a variety of ways in the opinions of this Court. The question has been asked whether a right is among those "fundamental principles of liberty and justice which lie at the base of all our civil and political institutions," . . . whether it is "'basic in our system of jurisprudence,'" . . . and whether it is "a fundamental right, essential to a fair trial. . . ." Because we believe that trial by jury in criminal cases is fundamental to the American scheme of justice, we hold that the Fourteenth Amendment guarantees a right of jury trial in all criminal cases which—were they to be tried in a federal court—would come within the Sixth Amendment's guarantee.[28]

28. [Footnote by Justice White] In one sense recent cases applying provisions of the first eight Amendments to the States represent a new approach to the "incorporation" debate. Earlier the Court can be seen as having asked, when inquiring into whether

. . .

The guarantees of jury trial in the Federal and State Constitutions reflect a profound judgment about the way in which law should be enforced and justice administered. A right to jury trial is granted to criminal defendants in order to prevent oppression by the Government. Those who wrote our constitutions knew from history and experience that it was necessary to protect against unfounded criminal charges brought to eliminate enemies and against judges too responsive to the voice of higher authority. . . . Providing an accused with the right to be tried by a jury of his peers gave him an inestimable safeguard against the corrupt or overzealous prosecutor and against the compliant, biased, or eccentric judge. If the defendant preferred the common-sense judgment of a jury to the more tutored but perhaps less sympathetic reaction of the single judge, he was to have it. Beyond this, the jury trial provisions in the Federal and State Constitutions reflect a fundamental decision about the exercise of official power—a reluctance to entrust plenary powers over the life and liberty of the citizen to one judge or to a group of judges. Fear of unchecked power, so typical of our State and Federal Governments in other respects, found expression in the criminal law in this insistence upon community participation in the determination of guilt or innocence. The deep commitment of the Nation to the right of jury trial in serious criminal cases as a defense against arbitrary law enforcement qualifies for protection under the Due Process Clause of the Fourteenth Amendment, and must therefore be respected by the States.

. . .

JUSTICE BLACK, with whom JUSTICE DOUGLAS joins, concurring.

. . . In [my *Adamson v. California* (1947)] dissent, . . . I took the position . . . that the Fourteenth Amendment made all of the provisions of the Bill of Rights applicable to the States. . . . I am very happy to support this selective process through which our Court has since the *Adamson* case held most of the specific Bill of Rights' protections applicable to the States to the same extent they are applicable to the Federal Government. Among these are the right to trial by jury decided today, the right against compelled self-incrimination, the right to counsel, the right to compulsory process for witnesses, the right to confront witnesses, the right to a speedy and public trial, and the right to be free from unreasonable searches and seizures.

. . . What I wrote [in *Adamson*] was the product of years of study and research. . . . My legislative experience has convinced me . . . to rely on what *was* said . . . by the men who actually sponsored the Amendment in the Congress. I know from my years in the United States Senate that it is to men like Congressman Bingham, who steered the Amendment through the House, and Senator Howard, who introduced it in the Senate, that members of Congress look when they seek the real meaning of what is being offered. And they vote for or against a bill based on what the sponsors of that bill and those who oppose it tell them it means. The historical appendix to my *Adamson* dissent leaves no doubt in my mind that both its sponsors and those who opposed it believed the Fourteenth Amendment made the first eight Amendments of the Constitution (the Bill of Rights) applicable to the States.

. . . [T]he dissent states that "the great words of the four clauses of the first section of the Fourteenth Amendment would have been an exceedingly peculiar way to say that 'The rights heretofore guaranteed against federal intrusion by the first eight Amendments are henceforth guaranteed against state intrusion as well.'" . . . In response to this I can say only that the words "No State shall make or enforce any law which

---

some particular procedural safeguard was required of a State, if a civilized system could be imagined that would not accord the particular protection. . . . The recent cases, on the other hand, have proceeded upon the valid assumption that state criminal processes are not imaginary and theoretical schemes but actual systems bearing virtually every characteristic of the common-law system that has been developing contemporaneously in England and in this country. The question thus is whether given this kind of system a particular procedure is fundamental—whether, that is, a procedure is necessary to an Anglo-American regime of ordered liberty. . . . Of each of these determinations that a constitutional provision originally written to bind the Federal Government should bind the States as well it might be said that the limitation in question is not necessarily fundamental to fairness in every criminal system that might be imagined but is fundamental in the context of the criminal processes maintained by the American States. . . . A criminal process which was fair and equitable but used no juries is easy to imagine. . . . Yet no American State has undertaken to construct such a system. Instead, every American State, including Louisiana, uses the jury extensively, and imposes very serious punishments only after a trial at which the defendant has a right to a jury's verdict. In every State, including Louisiana, the structure and style of the criminal process—the supporting framework and the subsidiary procedures—are of the sort that naturally complement jury trial, and have developed in connection with and in reliance upon jury trial.

shall abridge the privileges or immunities of citizens of the United States" seem to me an eminently reasonable way of expressing the idea that henceforth the Bill of Rights shall apply to the States. . . . What more precious "privilege" of American citizenship could there be than that privilege to claim the protections of our great Bill of Rights? I suggest that any reading of "privileges or immunities of citizens of the United States" which excludes the Bill of Rights' safeguards renders the words of this section of the Fourteenth Amendment meaningless. . . .

. . .

. . . I do want to point out what appears to me to be the basic difference between [Justice Harlan and me]. His view . . . is that "due process is an evolving concept" and therefore that it entails a "gradual process of judicial inclusion and exclusion" to ascertain those "immutable principles . . . of free government which no member of the Union may disregard." Thus the Due Process Clause is treated as prescribing no specific and clearly ascertainable constitutional command that judges must obey in interpreting the Constitution, but rather as leaving judges free to decide at any particular time whether a particular rule or judicial formulation embodies an "immutable principl[e] of free government" or is "implicit in the concept of ordered liberty," or whether certain conduct "shocks the judge's conscience" or runs counter to some other similar, undefined and undefinable standard. Thus due process, according to my Brother HARLAN, is to be a phrase with no permanent meaning, but one which is found to shift from time to time in accordance with judges' predilections and understandings of what is best for the country. If due process means this, the Fourteenth Amendment, in my opinion, might as well have been written that "no person shall be deprived of life, liberty or property except by laws that the judges of the United States Supreme Court shall find to be consistent with the immutable principles of free government." It is impossible for me to believe that such unconfined power is given to judges in our Constitution that is a written one in order to limit governmental power.

. . . [M]y Brother HARLAN [states] that "due process of law requires only fundamental fairness." But the "fundamental fairness" test is one on a par with that of shocking the conscience of the Court. Each of such tests depends entirely on the particular judge's idea of ethics and morals instead of requiring him to depend on the boundaries fixed by the written words of the Constitution. Nothing in the history of the phrase "due process of law" suggests that constitutional controls are to depend on any particular judge's sense of values. . . .

Finally I want to add that I am not bothered by the argument that applying the Bill of Rights to the States, "according to the same standards that protect those personal rights against federal encroachment," interferes with our concept of federalism in that it may prevent States from trying novel social and economic experiments. I have never believed that under the guise of federalism the States should be able to experiment with the protections afforded our citizens through the Bill of Rights. . . .

JUSTICE FORTAS, concurring. . . .

JUSTICE HARLAN, whom JUSTICE STEWART joins, dissenting.

. . .

The States have always borne primary responsibility for operating the machinery of criminal justice within their borders, and adapting it to their particular circumstances. In exercising this responsibility, each State is compelled to conform its procedures to the requirements of the Federal Constitution. The Due Process Clause of the Fourteenth Amendment requires that those procedures be fundamentally fair in all respects. It does not, in my view, impose or encourage nationwide uniformity for its own sake; it does not command adherence to forms that happen to be old; and it does not impose on the States the rules that may be in force in the federal courts except where such rules are also found to be essential to basic fairness.

. . .

I believe I am correct in saying that every member of the Court for at least the last 135 years has agreed that our Founders did not consider the requirements of the Bill of Rights so fundamental that they should operate directly against the States. . . . They were wont to believe rather that the security of liberty in America rested primarily upon the dispersion of governmental power across a federal system. . . . The Bill of Rights was considered unnecessary by some . . . but insisted upon by others in order to curb the possibility of abuse of power by the strong central government they were creating. . . .

A few members of the Court have taken the position that the intention of those who drafted the first section of the Fourteenth Amendment was simply, and exclusively, to make the provisions of the first eight Amendments applicable to state action. . . . This view has never been accepted by this Court. In my view, . . . the first section of the Fourteenth Amendment was meant neither to incorporate, nor to be limited to, the specific guarantees of the first eight Amendments. The overwhelming historical evidence marshalled by Professor Fairman[29] demonstrates, to me conclusively, that the Congressmen and state legislators who wrote, debated, and ratified the Fourteenth Amendment did not think they were "incorporating" the Bill of Rights and the very breadth and generality of the Amendment's provisions suggest that its authors did not suppose that the Nation would always be limited to mid-19th century conceptions of "liberty" and "due process of law" but that the increasing experience and evolving conscience of the American people would add new "intermediate premises." In short, neither history, nor sense, supports using the Fourteenth Amendment to put the States in a constitutional straitjacket with respect to their own development in the administration of criminal or civil law.

. . . Apart from the approach taken by the absolute incorporationists, I can see only one method of analysis that has any internal logic. That is to start with the words "liberty" and "due process of law" and attempt to define them in a way that accords with American traditions and our system of government. This approach, involving a much more discriminating process of adjudication than does "incorporation," is, albeit difficult, the one that was followed throughout the 19th and most of the present century. It entails a "gradual process of judicial inclusion and exclusion," . . . seeking, with due recognition of constitutional tolerance for state experimentation and disparity, to ascertain those "immutable principles . . . of free government which no member of the Union may disregard." . . . Due process was not restricted to rules fixed in the past, for that "would be to deny every quality of the law but its age, and to render it incapable of progress or improvement." . . . Nor did it impose nationwide uniformity in details. . . .

. . .

29. Charles Fairman, "Does the Fourteenth Amendment Incorporate the Bill of Rights? The Original Understanding," *Stanford Law Review* 2 (1949):5.

The relationship of the Bill of Rights to this "gradual process" seems to me to be twofold. In the first place it has long been clear that the Due Process Clause imposes some restrictions on state action that parallel Bill of Rights restrictions on federal action. Second, and more important than this accidental overlap, is the fact that the Bill of Rights is evidence, at various points, of the content Americans find in the term "liberty" and of American standards of fundamental fairness. . . . The logically critical thing, however, was not that the rights had been found in the Bill of Rights, but that they were deemed, in the context of American legal history, to be fundamental. . . .

. . . In sum, there is a wide range of views on the desirability of trial by jury, and on the ways to make it most effective when it is used; there is also considerable variation from State to State in local conditions such as the size of the criminal caseload, the ease or difficulty of summoning jurors, and other trial conditions bearing on fairness. . . .

This Court, other courts, and the political process are available to correct any experiments in criminal procedure that prove fundamentally unfair to defendants. That is not what is being done today: instead, and quite without reason, the Court has chosen to impose upon every State one means of trying criminal cases; it is a good means, but it is not the only fair means, and it is not demonstrably better than the alternatives States might devise.

Extraterritoriality

The Supreme Court during the New Deal/Great Society Era proved (nearly) as willing to impose Bill of Rights restrictions on the federal government acting overseas as it was to impose restrictions on state governments acting domestically. The increased and more permanent American presence in foreign countries after World War II led some liberals to rethink the rule in *Ross v. McIntyre* (1891) that constitutional practices do not travel outside of territories in which the United States is sovereign. In *Reid v. Covert* (1957) the justices declared that an American woman charged with murdering her husband was entitled to a jury trial, even though the crime and trial took place in England. Justice Black's plurality opinion for four justices asserted, "When the Government reaches out to punish a citizen who is abroad, the shield which the Bill of Rights and other parts of the Constitution provide to protect his life and liberty should not be stripped away just because he happens to be in another land." The Supreme Court later required civilian trials for active service members whose domestic crimes were not related to their military service. "We have concluded that the crime to be under military jurisdiction must be service connected," Justice Douglas concluded in *O'Callahan v. Parker* (1969), "lest 'cases arising in the land or naval forces, or in the Militia, when in actual service in time of War or public danger' . . . be expanded to deprive every member of the armed services of the benefits on an indictment by a grand jury and a trial by a jury of his peers."

Aliens were not as fortunate as American citizens. *In re Yamashita* (1946) held that the United States could use a military commission to try a Japanese general accused of committing atrocities during World War II. In *Johnson v. Eisentrager* (1950) a judicial majority rejected claims that Germans accused of spying during World War II were entitled to a writ of habeas corpus. Justice Jackson's majority opinion noted that Eisentrager

> (a) is an enemy alien; (b) has never been or resided in the United States; (c) was captured outside of our territory and there held in military custody as a prisoner of war; (d) was tried and convicted by a Military Commission sitting outside the United States; (e) for offenses against laws of war committed outside the United States; (f) and is at all times imprisoned outside the United States.

Reid v. Covert, 354 U.S. 1 (1957)

Clarice Covert murdered her husband, a sergeant in the Air Force, when he was stationed in the United Kingdom. Congressional law at the time authorized military trials for all persons who committed crimes on an army base overseas. Covert was tried by a military court, found guilty of murder, sentenced to life in prison, and shipped to the District of Columbia to serve her sentence. Upon entering the United States she petitioned the local federal district court for a writ of habeas corpus, claiming that her military trial violated her Fifth and Sixth Amendment rights. The district court granted the writ. The United States appealed to the Supreme Court.

The Supreme Court on June 11, 1956, rejected Covert's claims. Relying on Ross v. McIntyre *(1891), Justice Clark's majority opinion ruled "that the Constitution does not require trial before an Article III court in a foreign country for offenses committed there by an American citizen." Justice Clark's opinion was published before Chief Justice Warren, Justice Douglas, and Justice Frankfurter had finished writing their dissents. During the writing process Justice Harlan was convinced to rehear the case. Upon reargument, he joined the majority, along with Justice Brennan, who had replaced Justice Minton. With the retirement of Justice Reed a 5-4 majority to reject the habeas petition became a 6-2 majority in favor of Covert's claims.*

The Supreme Court in 1957 ruled that Covert had a constitutional right to a jury trial. Justice Black's plurality opinion declares that American officials who try Americans citizens have to respect all provisions in the Bill of Rights. Does Justice Black overrule Ross v. McIntyre, *or does he distinguish the case? As of 1957, under what conditions would a judicial majority insist that a person accused of a crime overseas had constitutional rights? The differences between Justice Black and Justice Harlan on the rights of Americans overseas mirror their differences over incorporation. Black insists that government officials cannot "pick and choose" among constitutional rights when conducting trials overseas. Harlan insists only that trials be fundamentally fair. Do incorporation and questions about the extraterritorial scope of the constitution present similar issues? Or might different rules apply for each?*

JUSTICE BLACK announced the judgment of the Court and delivered an opinion, in which THE CHIEF JUSTICE, JUSTICE DOUGLAS, and JUSTICE BRENNAN join.

. . .

. . . [W]e reject the idea that when the United States acts against citizens abroad it can do so free of the Bill of Rights. The United States is entirely a creature of the Constitution. Its power and authority have no other source. It can only act in accordance with all the limitations imposed by the Constitution. When the Government reaches out to punish a citizen who is abroad, the shield which the Bill of Rights and other parts of the Constitution provide to protect his life and liberty should not be stripped away just because he happens to be in another land. . . .

. . .

The language of Art. III, 2 manifests that constitutional protections for the individual were designed to restrict the United States Government when it acts outside of this country, as well as here at home. After declaring that all criminal trials must be by jury, the section states that when a crime is "not committed within any State, the Trial shall be at such Place or Places as the Congress may by Law have directed." If this language is permitted to have its obvious meaning, sec. 2 is applicable to criminal trials outside of the States as a group without regard to where the offense is committed or the trial held. . . .

. . . While it has been suggested that only those constitutional rights which are "fundamental" protect Americans abroad, we can find no warrant, in logic or otherwise, for picking and choosing among the remarkable collection of "Thou shalt nots" which were explicitly fastened on all departments and agencies of the Federal Government by the Constitution and its Amendments. Moreover, in view of our heritage and the history of the adoption of the Constitution and the Bill of Rights, it seems peculiarly anomalous to say that trial before a civilian judge and by an independent jury picked from the common citizenry is not a fundamental right. . . .

. . .

The *Ross [v. McIntyre]* approach that the Constitution has no applicability abroad has long since been directly repudiated by numerous cases. That approach is obviously erroneous if the United States Government, which has no power except that granted by the Constitution, can and does try citizens for crimes committed abroad. Thus the *Ross* case rested, at least in substantial part, on a fundamental misconception and the most that can be said in support of the result reached there is that the consular court jurisdiction had a long history antedating the adoption of the Constitution. The Congress has recently buried the consular system of trying Americans. We are not willing to jeopardize the lives and liberties of Americans by disinterring it. At best, the *Ross* case should be left as a relic from a different era.

. . .

The "*Insular Cases*" can be distinguished from the present cases in that they involved the power of Congress to provide rules and regulations to govern temporarily territories with wholly dissimilar traditions and institutions whereas here the basis for governmental power is American citizenship. None of these cases had anything to do with military trials and they cannot properly be used as vehicles to support an extension of military jurisdiction to civilians. Moreover, it is our judgment that neither the cases nor their reasoning should be given any further expansion. The concept that the Bill of Rights and other constitutional protections against arbitrary government are inoperative when they become inconvenient or when expediency dictates otherwise is a very dangerous doctrine and if allowed to flourish would destroy the benefit of a written Constitution and undermine the basis of our Government. If our foreign commitments become of such nature that the Government can no longer satisfactorily operate within the bounds laid down by the Constitution, that instrument can be amended by the method which it prescribes. But we have no authority, or inclination, to read exceptions into it which are not there.

. . .

JUSTICE FRANKFURTER, concurring in the result. . . .

JUSTICE HARLAN, concurring in the result.

I concur in the result, on the narrow ground that, where the offense is capital, Article 2(11) cannot constitutionally be applied to the trial of civilian dependents of members of the armed forces overseas in times of peace.

. . .

. . . I do not think that it can be said that these safeguards of the Constitution are never operative without the United States, regardless of the particular circumstances. On the other hand, I cannot agree with the suggestion that every provision of the Constitution must always be deemed automatically applicable to American citizens in every part of the world. For *Ross* and the *Insular Cases* do stand for an important proposition, one which seems to me a wise and necessary gloss on our Constitution. The proposition is, of course, not that the Constitution "does not apply" overseas, but that there are provisions in the Constitution which do not necessarily apply in all circumstances in every foreign place. . . .

On this basis, I cannot agree with the sweeping proposition that a full Article III trial, with indictment and trial by jury, is required in every case for the trial of a civilian dependent of a serviceman overseas. The Government, it seems to me, has made an impressive showing that, at least for the run-of-the-mill offenses committed by dependents overseas, such a requirement would be . . . impractical. . . .

So far as capital cases are concerned, I think they stand on quite a different footing than other offenses. In such cases, the law is especially sensitive to demands for that procedural fairness which inheres in a civilian trial where the judge and trier of fact are not responsive to the command of the convening authority. I do not concede that whatever process is "due" an offender faced with a fine or a prison sentence necessarily satisfies the requirements of the Constitution in a capital case. . . . In fact, the Government itself has conceded that one grave offense, treason, presents a special case:

> The gravity of this offense is such that we can well assume that, whatever difficulties may be involved in trial far from the scene of the offense . . . , the trial should be in our courts.

I see no reason for not applying the same principle to any case where a civilian dependent stands trial on pain of life itself. The number of such cases would appear to be so negligible that the practical problems of affording the defendant a civilian trial would not present insuperable problems.

JUSTICE CLARK, with whom JUSTICE BURTON joins, dissenting.

. . .

Historically, the military has always exercised jurisdiction by court-martial over civilians accompanying armies in time of war.

. . .

. . . [I]t is reasonable to provide that the military commander who bears full responsibility for the care and safety of those civilians attached to his command should also have authority to regulate their conduct. Moreover, all members of an overseas contingent should receive equal treatment before the law. In their actual day-to-day living, they are a part of the same unique communities, and the same legal considerations should apply to all. There is no reason for according to one class a different treatment than is accorded to another. . . .

. . .

Another alternative the Congress might have adopted was the establishment of federal courts pursuant to Article III of the Constitution. These constitutional courts would have to sit in each of the 63 foreign countries where American troops are stationed at the present time. Aside from the fact that the Constitution has never been interpreted to compel such an undertaking, it would seem obvious that it would be manifestly impossible. The problem of the use of juries in common law countries alone suffices to illustrate this. . . .

Likewise, trial of offenders by an Article III court in this country, perhaps workable in some cases, is equally impracticable as a general solution to the problem. The hundreds of petty cases involving black-market operations, narcotics, immorality, and the like, could hardly be brought here for prosecution even if the Congress and the foreign nation involved authorized such a procedure.

The only alternative remaining—probably the alternative that the Congress will now be forced to choose—is that Americans committing offenses on foreign soil be tried by the courts of the country in which the offense is committed. . . . It is clear that trial before an American court-martial in which the fundamentals of due process are observed is preferable to leaving American servicemen and their dependents to the widely varying standards of justice in foreign courts throughout the world. Under these circumstances, it is untenable to say that Congress could have exercised a lesser power adequate to the end proposed.

My brothers who are concurring in the result seem to find some comfort in that, for the present they void an Act of Congress only as to capital cases. I find no distinction in the Constitution between capital and other cases. . . .

State Action

New Deal and Great Society liberals often found government complicity with what justices in the Republican Era regarded as private race discrimination. *The Civil Rights Cases* (1883) held that the Fourteenth Amendment limited only state actors. Supreme Court majorities did not overrule that decision, but they often found state action behind what had previously been considered private behavior. Judicial decisions held:

1. Private parties performing a public function had to respect constitutional norms. Such public functions were performed by company towns, shopping centers, and, most important, political parties and organizations participating in primary elections.
2. Private parties had to respect constitutional norms whenever the state was significantly involved in their activities. Significant state involvement included enforcing restrictive racial covenants and leasing property to a restaurant that refused to serve persons of color.

3. State action was often present when southern businesses called on law enforcement officials to oust persons of color protesting segregation.
4. State action was not necessary when private parties in the housing market discriminated against persons of color, because denying contract or property rights on the basis of race was a badge or incident of slavery outlawed by the Thirteenth Amendment.

These constitutional decisions had significant policy consequences. *Smith v. Allwright* (1944) and other Supreme Court decisions largely abolished party primaries in the South that were restricted to white persons. African-American voting in Democratic primaries increased substantially in many states when political parties were no longer permitted to discriminate against persons of color when choosing candidates for general elections. Courts and elected officials eliminated many private barriers to integrated housing. *Shelley v. Kraemer* (1948) found state action when courts enforced restrictive covenants, housing contracts that prevent persons from reselling their homes to persons of color. In *Burton v. Wilmington Parking Authority* (1961) the justices held by a vote of 6-3 that because the Eagle Coffee Shoppe leased space within a parking garage operated by the city's Wilmington Parking Authority, the business was deemed a state actor bound by the Fourteenth Amendment and thus could not deny service to William Burton because of his race. "The State has so far insinuated itself into a position of interdependence with Eagle," Justice Clark wrote, "that it must be recognized as a joint participant in the challenged activity." *Jones v. Alfred H. Mayer Co.* (1968) held that private housing discrimination violated the Thirteenth Amendment, which does not have a state action requirement.

Federal court decisions on state action provided crucial support for civil rights protestors. Encouraged by amicus briefs from the federal government, the Warren Court found state action or some other excuse for reversing every conviction that came before the justices for trespass or disturbing the peace that resulted from sit-in protests conducted by members of the civil rights movement during the early 1960s. In *Lombard v. Louisiana* (1963) Chief Justice Earl Warren found state action when the proprietor of a segregated lunch counter claimed to have been influenced by a police announcement that protests against segregation would not be tolerated. Justice Black in *Robinson v. Florida* (1964) ruled that a state law requiring separate toilets in restaurants that hired persons of color provided sufficient grounds to find state involvement with Shell City Restaurant's refusal to serve persons of color. All told, for state action or other reasons, the justices overturned state court decisions convicting sit-in demonstrators in more than twenty cases. No conviction of a civil rights protestor was sustained before passage of the Civil Rights Act of 1964. In *Hamm v. Rock City* (1965) that act was interpreted as voiding all remaining state convictions not yet appealed to the Supreme Court.

Bell v. Maryland (1964) provoked a particularly vigorous debate over the state action doctrine. Justice Brennan's opinion for the Court reversed convictions for trespassing because, after the convictions became final, Baltimore prohibited segregation in public places. Justices Douglas and Goldberg wrote concurring opinions declaring that states had constitutional obligations to ban segregation in places of public accommodation. Douglas stated,

> Segregation of Negroes in the restaurants and lunch counters of parts of America is a relic of slavery. It is a badge of second-class citizenship. It is a denial of a privilege and immunity of national citizenship and of the equal protection guaranteed by the Fourteenth Amendment against abridgment by the States. When the state police, the state prosecutor, and the state courts unite to convict Negroes for renouncing that relic of slavery, the "State" violates the Fourteenth Amendment.

Justice Black disagreed. His dissent spoke of "the unchallenged right of a man who owns a business to run the business in his own way so long as some valid regulatory statute does not tell him to do otherwise."

Smith v. Allwright, 321 U.S. 649 (1944)

On July 27, 1940, Lonnie Smith, an African-American resident of Harris County, Texas, attempted to vote in the Texas Democratic Party primary. S. E. Allwright, the local election judge, refused to allow Smith to cast a ballot on the ground that membership in the Democratic Party in Texas was limited to white persons. Smith sued Allwright, claiming $5,000 in damages for violating his Fourteenth and Fifteenth Amendment rights. Allwright claimed that the Texas Democratic Party was a private organization and *hence constitutionally free to bar persons of color from party primaries. Both the federal district court and Court of Appeals of the Fifth Circuit rejected Smith's argument. Smith appealed to the Supreme Court of the United States.*

Smith *was the latest episode in the saga of the white primary. During the Republican Era the Supreme Court declared unconstitutional a Texas law prohibiting persons of color from voting in Democratic primaries (*Nixon v. Herndon *[1927]) and a Texas law that authorized the state executive committee of the Democratic Party to establish criteria for membership (*Nixon v. Condon *[1932]). The Texas legislature responded by repealing all state laws regulating party membership. The Texas Democratic Party then prohibited persons of color from being party members. A unanimous Supreme Court in* Grovey v. Townsend *(1935) declared that this practice did not violate the Fourteenth or Fifteenth Amendment because the Democratic Party was a private organization. Justice Roberts' opinion asserted, "We are unable to characterize the managers of the primary election as state officers in such sense that any action taken by them in obedience to the mandate of the state convention respecting eligibility to participate in the organization's deliberations, is state action."*

Six years after Grovey *was decided, the justices in* United States v. Classic *(1941) held that Congress had power under Article I, Section 2 to regulate state primaries. The crucial passage in Justice Stone's majority opinion declared,*

> *The right to participate in the choice of representatives for Congress includes, as we have said, the right to cast a ballot and to have it counted at the general election whether for the successful candidate or not. Where the state law has made the primary an integral part of the procedure of choice, or where in fact the primary effectively controls the choice, the right of the elector to have his ballot counted at the primary, is likewise included in the right protected by Article I, s 2. And this right of participation is protected just as is the right to vote at the election, where the primary is by law made an integral part of the election machinery.*

Thurgood Marshall, arguing his first case before the Supreme Court, relied heavily on Classic *when insisting that state action existed in* Smith. *If persons had a right to vote in primaries for Article I, Section 2 purposes, Marshall reasoned, then persons of color ought to have a right to vote in primaries for Fourteenth and Fifteenth Amendment purposes.*

The Supreme Court agreed with Marshall's contention by an 8-1 vote. Justice Stanley Reed, a New Deal Democrat from Kentucky, insisted that because states organized primary elections, parties in those primary elections could not discriminate on the basis of race. Are Classic *and* Grovey *inconsistent? If they are consistent, did other events between 1935 and 1944 explain the judicial reversal in the white primary cases?*

Texas Democrats made one last effort to retain the white primary. In Fort Bend County, the Jaybird Political Association, an organization restricted to white citizens, held a preprimary election that inevitably determined the winner of the Democratic primary in that county. The Supreme Court again found state action. Justice Black's plurality opinion in Terry v. Adams *(1953) concluded, "No election machinery could be sustained if its purpose or effect was to deny Negroes on account of their race an effective voice in the governmental affairs of their country, state, or community." Justice Clark pointed out that "the Jaybird Democratic Association operates as part and parcel of the Democratic Party," and that their primary was therefore as much state action as a Democratic Party primary.*[30]

JUSTICE REED delivered the opinion of the Court.

. . .

We . . . held [in *United States v. Classic* (1941)] that Section 4 of Article I of the Constitution authorized Congress to regulate primary as well as general elections, . . . "where the primary is by law made an integral part of the election machinery." . . . *Classic* bears upon *Grovey v. Townsend* (1935) not because exclusion of Negroes from primaries is any more or less state action by reason of the unitary character of the electoral process but because the recognition of the place of the primary in the electoral scheme makes clear that state delegation to a party of the power to fix the qualifications of primary elections is delegation of a state function that may make the party's action the action of the state. . . .

It may now be taken as a postulate that the right to vote in such a primary for the nomination of candidates without discrimination by the State, like the right to vote in a general election, is a right secured by the Constitution. . . . By the terms of the Fifteenth Amendment that right may not be abridged by any state on account of race. . . .

. . .

30. For more information on the white primary cases, see William M. Wiecek, *The Birth of the Modern Constitution: The United States Supreme Court, 1941–1953* (New York: Cambridge University Press, 2006), 236–43.

Primary elections are conducted by the party under state statutory authority. The county executive committee selects precinct election officials and the county, district or state executive committees, respectively, canvass the returns. These party committees or the state convention certify the party's candidates to the appropriate officers for inclusion on the official ballot for the general election. No name which has not been so certified may appear upon the ballot for the general election as a candidate of a political party. . . . The state courts are given exclusive original jurisdiction of contested elections and of mandamus proceedings to compel party officers to perform their statutory duties.

We think that this statutory system for the selection of party nominees for inclusion on the general election ballot makes the party which is required to follow these legislative directions an agency of the state in so far as it determines the participants in a primary election. The party takes its character as a state agency from the duties imposed upon it by state statutes; the duties do not become matters of private law because they are performed by a political party. . . . When primaries become a part of the machinery for choosing officials, state and national, as they have here, the same tests to determine the character of discrimination or abridgement should be applied to the primary as are applied to the general election. If the state requires a certain electoral procedure, prescribes a general election ballot made up of party nominees so chosen and limits the choice of the electorate in general elections for state offices, practically speaking, to those whose names appear on such a ballot, it endorses, adopts and enforces the discrimination against Negroes, practiced by a party entrusted by Texas law with the determination of the qualifications of participants in the primary. This is state action within the meaning of the Fifteenth Amendment. . . .

The United States is a constitutional democracy. Its organic law grants to all citizens a right to participate in the choice of elected officials without restriction by any state because of race. This grant to the people of the opportunity for choice is not to be nullified by a state through casting its electoral process in a form which permits a private organization to practice racial discrimination in the election. Constitutional rights would be of little value if they could be thus indirectly denied. . . .

. . . In constitutional questions, where correction depends upon amendment and not upon legislative action this Court throughout its history has freely exercised its power to reexamine the basis of its constitutional decisions. This has long been accepted practice, and this practice has continued to this day. . . . *Grovey v. Townsend* is overruled.

. . .

JUSTICE FRANKFURTER concurs in the result.

JUSTICE ROBERTS.

. . .

. . . [T]he instant decision, overruling that announced about nine years ago, tends to bring adjudications of this tribunal into the same class as a restricted railroad ticket, good for this day and train only. I have no assurance, in view of current decisions, that the opinion announced today may not shortly be repudiated and overruled by justices who deem they have new light on the subject. . . .

It is suggested that *Grovey v. Townsend* was overruled sub silentio in *United States v. Classic*. . . . [I]n the Classic case, *Grovey v. Townsend* was distinguished in brief and argument by the Government without suggestion that it was wrongly decided. . . . The case is not mentioned in either of the opinions in the *Classic* case.

Louisiana statutes [in *Classic*] required the primary to be conducted by State officials and made it a State election, whereas, under the Texas statute, the primary is a party election conducted at the expense of members of the party and by officials chosen by the party. If this court's opinion in the *Classic* case discloses its method of overruling earlier decisions, I can only protest that, in fairness, it should rather have adopted the open and frank way of saying what it was doing than, after the event, characterize its past action as overruling *Grovey v. Townsend* though those less sapient never realized the fact.

It is regrettable that in an era marked by doubt and confusion, an era whose greatest need is steadfastness of thought and purpose, this court, which has been looked to as exhibiting consistency in adjudication, and a steadiness which would hold the balance even in the face of temporary ebbs and flows of opinion, should now itself become the breeder of fresh doubt and confusion in the public mind as to the stability of our institutions.

Shelley v. Kraemer, 334 U.S. 1 (1948)

J. D. Shelley and his spouse, persons of color, on August 11 purchased from Josephine Fitzgerald a house on Labadie Avenue in St. Louis, Missouri. Thirty-four years prior, most homeowners on that block had signed a restrictive covenant. The crucial provision of that agreement prohibited each owner from selling or renting their plot to "people of the Negro or Mongolian Race." Louis Kraemer, a party to that agreement, brought a lawsuit asking that the Shelley family be required to leave the house and be divested of their title to the property. The state trial court rejected their lawsuit on the ground that the original restrictive covenant had not been validly made. That decision was reversed by the Supreme Court of Missouri, which concluded that the restrictive covenant was valid and did not violate the constitutional rights of the Shelleys. The Shelleys appealed that verdict to the Supreme Court of the United States, claiming that judicial enforcement of the restrictive covenant violated the Fourteenth Amendment. For the first time in American history, the United States submitted an amicus brief on behalf of the party claiming unconstitutional racial discrimination.

Restrictive covenants were a popular means for fostering residential segregation after the Supreme Court in Buchanan v. Warley *(1917) ruled that elected officials could not mandate racial segregation in the housing market. If people in an entire neighborhood agreed not to sell or rent their homes to persons of color, however, such covenants could keep neighborhoods segregated in perpetuity. The Supreme Court in* Buckley v. Corrigan *(1926) declared such private agreements did not violate the Fourteenth Amendment.*

The Supreme Court unanimously ruled that courts could not enforce restrictive covenants. Chief Justice Vinson's majority opinion declared that state action occurred when courts enforced a restrictive covenant. He did not declare restrictive covenants illegal. Had Fitzgerald in 1948 refused to sell to persons of color, the Vinson Court would not have found a constitutional wrong. This meant that the impact of Shelley *was quite limited. Persons of color would gain constitutional rights only when persons who signed a restrictive racial covenant either changed their mind or sold the property to someone who was later willing to sell to a person of color. Did the justices rule that states cannot prevent a willing seller from conveying property to a willing buyer of a different race? This was Chief Justice Vinson's understanding of* Shelley. *Five years later he insisted that persons who violated a restrictive racial covenant could be sued for damages by other parties to that agreement. His opinion in* Barrows v. Jackson *(1953) declared, "No non-Caucasian has been injured or could be injured if damages are assessed against respondent for breaching the promise which she willingly and voluntarily made to petitioners, a promise which neither the federal law nor the Constitution proscribes." That opinion was the lone dissent. Justice Minton's majority opinion declared that courts could not order any remedy when persons violated restrictive racial covenants. "This Court," he wrote, "will not permit or require California to coerce respondent to respond in damages for failure to observe a restrictive covenant that this Court would deny California the right to enforce in equity." This suggests that* Shelley *is based on the common law principle that contracts against public policy are not judicially enforceable. What is left of the requirement of "state action" after* Shelley? *Does* Shelley *permit police to enforce a restaurant's decision to not serve African-Americans or your decision to invite only members of your ethnic group to a party? Was* Shelley *rooted more in politics than in law? The justices abhorred restrictive racial covenants. The United States government and prominent interest groups wanted restrictive covenants declared judicially unenforceable. Under these circumstances, the Vinson Court might not have needed much of a legal excuse to rule against the Kraemers.*

Brief for the United States as Amicus Curiae

The Federal Government has a special responsibility for the protection of the fundamental civil rights guaranteed to the people by the Constitution and laws of the United States. . . . The Government is of the view that judicial enforcement of racial restrictive covenants on real property is incompatible with the spirit and letter of the Constitution and laws of the United States. It is fundamental that no agency of government should participate in any action which will result in depriving any person of essential rights because of race or color or creed. This Court has held that such discriminations are prohibited by the organic law of the land, and that no legislative body has power to create them. It must follow, therefore, that the Constitutional rights guaranteed to every person cannot be denied by private contracts enforced by the judicial branch of government—especially where the discrimination created by private contracts have grown to such proportions as to become detrimental to the public welfare and against public policy.

. . .

Racial restrictive covenants . . . are responsible for the creation of isolated areas in which over-crowded racial minorities are confined, and in which living conditions are steadily worsened. The avenues of escape are being narrowed and reduced. As to the people so trapped, there is no life in the accepted sense of the word; liberty is a mockery, and the right to pursue happiness a phrase without meaning, empty of hope and reality. This situation cannot be reconciled with the spirit of mutual tolerance and respect for the dignity and rights of the individual which give vitality to our democratic way of life. The time has come to destroy these evils which threaten the safety of our free institutions.

The fact that racial restrictive covenants are being enforced by instrumentalities of government has become a source of serious embarrassment to agencies of the Federal Government in the performance of many essential functions, including the programs relating to housing and home finance, to public health, to the protection of dependent native racial minorities in the United States and its territories, to the conduct of foreign affairs, and to the protection of civil rights.

CHIEF JUSTICE VINSON delivered the opinion of the Court.

. . .

It cannot be doubted that among the civil rights intended to be protected from discriminatory state action by the Fourteenth Amendment are the rights to acquire, enjoy, own and dispose of property. Equality in the enjoyment of property rights was regarded by the framers of that Amendment as an essential precondition to the realization of other basic civil rights and liberties which the Amendment was intended to guarantee. . . .

It is likewise clear that restrictions on the right of occupancy of the sort sought to be created by the private agreements in these cases could not be squared with the requirements of the Fourteenth Amendment if imposed by state statute or local ordinance. . . .

. . . Here the particular patterns of discrimination and the areas in which the restrictions are to operate, are determined, in the first instance, by the terms of agreements among private individuals. Participation of the State consists in the enforcement of the restrictions so defined. . . .

Since the decision of this Court in the *Civil Rights Cases* (1883), . . . the principle has become firmly embedded in our constitutional law that the action inhibited by the first section of the Fourteenth Amendment is only such action as may fairly be said to be that of the States. That Amendment erects no shield against merely private conduct, however discriminatory or wrongful.

We conclude, therefore, that the restrictive agreements standing alone cannot be regarded as a violation of any rights guaranteed to petitioners by the Fourteenth Amendment. So long as the purposes of those agreements are effectuated by voluntary adherence to their terms, it would appear clear that there has been no action by the State and the provisions of the Amendment have not been violated. . . .

But here there was more. These are cases in which the purposes of the agreements were secured only by judicial enforcement by state courts of the restrictive terms of the agreements. . . .

That the action of state courts and of judicial officers in their official capacities is to be regarded as action of the State within the meaning of the Fourteenth Amendment, is a proposition which has long been established by decisions of this Court. . . .

. . .

. . . We have no doubt that there has been state action in these cases in the full and complete sense of the phrase. The undisputed facts disclose that petitioners were willing purchasers of properties upon which they desired to establish homes. The owners of the properties were willing sellers; and contracts of sale were accordingly consummated. It is clear that but for the active intervention of the state courts, supported by the full panoply of state power, petitioners would have been free to occupy the properties in question without restraint.

These are not cases, as has been suggested, in which the States have merely abstained from action, leaving private individuals free to impose such discriminations as they see fit. Rather, these are cases in which the States have made available to such individuals the full coercive power of government to deny to petitioners, on the grounds of race or color, the enjoyment of property rights in premises which petitioners are willing and financially able to acquire and which the grantors are willing to sell. . . .

. . .

We hold that in granting judicial enforcement of the restrictive agreements in these cases, the States have denied petitioners the equal protection of the laws and that, therefore, the action of the state courts cannot stand. We have noted that freedom from discrimination by the States in the enjoyment of property rights was among the basic objectives sought to be effectuated by the framers of the Fourteenth Amendment. That such discrimination has occurred in these cases is clear. Because of the race or color of these petitioners they have been denied rights of ownership or occupancy enjoyed as a matter of course by other citizens of different race or color. . . . Only recently this Court has had occasion to declare that a state law which denied equal enjoyment of property rights to a designated class of citizens of specified race and ancestry, was not a legitimate exercise of the state's police power but violated the guaranty of the equal protection of the laws. . . .

. . .

JUSTICE REED, JUSTICE JACKSON, and JUSTICE RUTLEDGE took no part in the consideration or decision of these cases.

Jones v. Alfred H. Mayer Co., 392 U.S. 409 (1968)

Joseph Lee Jones and Barbara Jo Jones, two African-American citizens, sought to buy a house in the Paddock Woods community from the Alfred H. Mayer Company. The Mayer Company had a company policy to not sell to persons of color. The Jones family sued, claiming that the refusal to sell violated their federal statutory rights, the Fourteenth Amendment, and the Thirteenth Amendment. The Mayer Company asserted that, as a private business, their racial discrimination was not barred by the post–Civil War Amendments. The federal district court sided with the Mayer Company, finding no state action present in this case. After that decision was sustained by the Court of Appeals for the Eighth Circuit, Joseph and Barbara Jones appealed to the Supreme Court of the United States.

The Supreme Court ruled by a 7-2 vote that the Mayer Company had violated constitutional rights. Justice Stewart relied on federal statutes passed under the Thirteenth Amendment, rather than legislation implementing the Fourteenth Amendment. That substitution was crucial, because the Thirteenth Amendment has no state action requirement. At the same time, that clever substitution raised certain puzzles. The Mayer Company could not constitutionally have developed Paddock Woods with slave labor. The more complex question is whether their refusal to sell plots in that development to persons of color was a badge or incident of slavery. Under Justice Stewart's opinion, might all forms of race discrimination be considered badges and incidents of slavery? Is the same true for Justice Douglas's concurring opinion? Indeed, were Justice Douglas's opinion the law of the land, could a claim of race discrimination ever be dismissed for lack of state action? Does this interpretation amount to a resurrection of the analysis of the Thirteenth Amendment elaborated by Justice John Marshall Harlan (the first) in his dissenting opinion in the Civil Rights Cases *(1883)? Review the debates over the Thirteenth Amendment and the Freedmen's Bureau Act. Which judicial opinion best captures original understandings during Reconstruction?*

While the Supreme Court was considering Jones v. Alfred H. Mayer Co., *Congress passed the Fair Housing Act of 1968. The crucial provision of that statute makes it unlawful "to refuse to sell or rent after the making of a bona fide offer, or to refuse to negotiate for the sale or rental of, or otherwise make unavailable or deny, a dwelling to any person because of race, color, religion, sex, familial status, or national origin." Justices White and Harlan believed that no need existed to decide* Jones *in light of this statute. Do you agree?*

JUSTICE STEWART delivered the opinion of the Court.

In this case, we are called upon to determine the scope and the constitutionality of an Act of Congress, 42 U.S.C. § 1982, which provides that:

> All citizens of the United States shall have the same right, in every State and Territory, as is enjoyed by white citizens thereof to inherit, purchase lease, sell, hold, and convey real and personal property.

. . . We hold that § 1982 bars all racial discrimination, private as well as public, in the sale or rental of property, and that the statute, thus construed, is a valid exercise of the power of Congress to enforce the Thirteenth Amendment

. . .

It has never been doubted . . . , "that the power vested in Congress to enforce the [Thirteenth Amendment] by appropriate legislation," includes the power to enact laws "direct and primary, operating upon the acts of individuals, whether sanctioned by State legislation or not." . . .

Thus, the fact that § 1982 operates upon the unofficial acts of private individuals, whether or not sanctioned by state law, presents no constitutional problem. If Congress has power under the Thirteenth

Amendment to eradicate conditions that prevent Negroes from buying and renting property because of their race or color, then no federal statute calculated to achieve that objective can be thought to exceed the constitutional power of Congress simply because it reaches beyond state action to regulate the conduct of private individuals. The constitutional question in this case, therefore, comes to this: does the authority of Congress to enforce the Thirteenth Amendment "by appropriate legislation" include the power to eliminate all racial barriers to the acquisition of real and personal property? We think the answer to that question is plainly yes.

"By its own unaided force and effect," the Thirteenth Amendment "abolished slavery, and established universal freedom." . . . Whether or not the Amendment itself did any more than that—a question not involved in this case—it is at least clear that the Enabling Clause of that Amendment empowered Congress to do much more. For that clause clothed "Congress with power to pass *all laws necessary and proper for abolishing all badges and incidents of slavery in the United States.*"

Those who opposed passage of the Civil Rights Act of 1866 argued, in effect that the Thirteenth Amendment merely authorized Congress to dissolve the legal bond by which the Negro slave was held to his master. Yet many had earlier opposed the Thirteenth Amendment on the very ground that it would give Congress virtually unlimited power to enact laws for the protection of Negroes in every State. And the majority leaders in Congress—who were, after all, the authors of the Thirteenth Amendment—had no doubt that its Enabling Clause contemplated the sort of positive legislation that was embodied in the 1866 Civil Rights Act. Their chief spokesman, Senator Trumbull of Illinois, the Chairman of the Judiciary Committee, had brought the Thirteenth Amendment to the floor of the Senate in 1864. In defending the constitutionality of the 1866 Act, he argued that, if the narrower construction of the Enabling Clause were correct, then

> the trumpet of freedom that we have been blowing throughout the land has given an "uncertain sound," and the promised freedom is a delusion. Such was not the intention of Congress, which proposed the constitutional amendment, nor is such the fair meaning of the amendment itself. . . . I have no doubt that, under this provision . . . , we may destroy all these discriminations in civil rights against the black man, and if we cannot, our constitutional amendment amounts to nothing. It was for that purpose that the second clause of that amendment was adopted, which says that Congress shall have authority, by appropriate legislation, to carry into effect the article prohibiting slavery. Who is to decide what that appropriate legislation is to be? The Congress of the United States, and it is for Congress to adopt such appropriate legislation as it may think proper, so that it be a means to accomplish the end.

Surely Senator Trumbull was right. Surely Congress has the power under the Thirteenth Amendment rationally to determine what are the badges and the incidents of slavery, and the authority to translate that determination into effective legislation. Nor can we say that the determination Congress has made is an irrational one. For this Court recognized long ago that, whatever else they may have encompassed, the badges and incidents of slavery—its "burdens and disabilities"—included restraints upon

> those fundamental rights which are the essence of civil freedom, namely, the same right . . . to inherit, purchase, lease, sell and convey property, as is enjoyed by white citizens.

. . . Just as the Black Codes, enacted after the Civil War to restrict the free exercise of those rights, were substitutes for the slave system, so the exclusion of Negroes from white communities became a substitute for the Black Codes. And when racial discrimination herds men into ghettos and makes their ability to buy property turn on the color of their skin, then it too is a relic of slavery.

JUSTICE DOUGLAS, concurring.

. . .

Enabling a Negro to buy and sell real and personal property is a removal of one of many badges of slavery.

. . .

Some badges of slavery remain today. While the institution has been outlawed, it has remained in the minds and hearts of many white men. Cases which have come to this Court depict a spectacle of slavery unwilling to die. We have seen contrivances by States designed to thwart Negro voting, . . . Negroes have been excluded over and again from juries solely on account of their race, . . . or have been forced to sit in segregated seats in courtrooms. They have been made to attend segregated and inferior schools, or been denied entrance to colleges or graduate schools because of their color. Negroes have been prosecuted for marrying whites. They have been forced to live in segregated residential districts, . . . and residents of white neighborhoods have denied them entrance. . . . Negroes have been forced to use segregated facilities in going about their daily lives, having been excluded from railway coaches, . . . public parks, . . . restaurants, . . . public beaches, . . . municipal golf courses, . . . amusement parks, . . . buses, . . . public libraries. A state court judge in Alabama convicted a Negro woman of contempt of court because she refused to answer him when he addressed her as "Mary," although she had made the simple request to be called "Miss Hamilton." *Hamilton v. Alabama* (1964). . . .

. . .

Today the black is protected by a host of civil rights laws. But the forces of discrimination are still strong.

. . .

. . . [P]rejudices, once part and parcel of slavery, still persist. The men who sat in Congress in 1866 were trying to remove some of the badges or "customs" of slavery when they enacted § 1982. . . .

JUSTICE HARLAN, whom JUSTICE WHITE joins, dissenting.

. . .

. . . I believe that the Court's construction of § 1982 as applying to purely private action is almost surely wrong, and, at the least, is open to serious doubt. The issues of the constitutionality of § 1982, as construed by the Court, and of liability under the Fourteenth Amendment alone, also present formidable difficulties. Moreover, the political processes of our own era have, since the date of oral argument in this case, given birth to a civil rights statute [embodying "fair housing" provisions] which would, at the end of this year, make available to others, though apparently not to the petitioners themselves, the type of relief which the petitioners now seek. It seems to me that this latter factor so diminishes the public importance of this case that by far the wisest course would be for this Court to refrain from decision and to dismiss the writ as improvidently granted.

[Justice Harlan's dissent then asserted that the Civil Rights Act of 1866 did not prohibit private discrimination in the housing market.]

III. Individual Rights

MAJOR DEVELOPMENTS

- The Court abandons protection for the freedom of contract
- Public school prayer declared unconstitutional
- The Court protects the right to procreate, marry, and use birth control if married

Proponents of the New Deal and Great Society agreed on a hierarchy of individual constitutional rights. Religious freedom enjoyed constitutional protection from the very beginning of the New Deal, and that protection increased during the 1960s. Constitutional liberals during the 1960s began protecting constitutional rights to marriage and procreation within marriage. New Dealers insisted that economic matters were policy questions entrusted to elected officials. No prominent political party, political movement, or justice from 1933 until 1968 paid any significant attention to the Second Amendment. The Supreme Court's docket reflected these priorities, devoting increasing attention to civil liberties and exhibiting a declining interest in cases raising traditional property rights.

New Deal/Great Society liberals struggled to justify their commitment to preferred freedoms, the notion that some constitutional rights deserved greater judicial protection than others. Justice Douglas in *Griswold v. Connecticut* (1965) maintained that American constitutional history supported protecting some rights not explicitly protected by the Constitution, but not others. "Overtones of some arguments suggest that *Lochner v. New York* (1905) should be our guide," he asserted when defending the constitutional right of married people to use birth control.

> But we decline that invitation. . . . We do not sit as a super-legislature to determine the wisdom, need, and propriety of laws that touch economic problems, business affairs, or social conditions. This law, however, operates directly on an intimate relation of husband and wife and their physician's role in one aspect of that relation.

Justice Black scorned this logic. He accused Justice Douglas of making decisions on the basis of "natural justice," which "require[d] judges to determine what is or is not constitutional on the basis of their own appraisal of what laws are unwise or unnecessary." As you read the materials in this section, think about

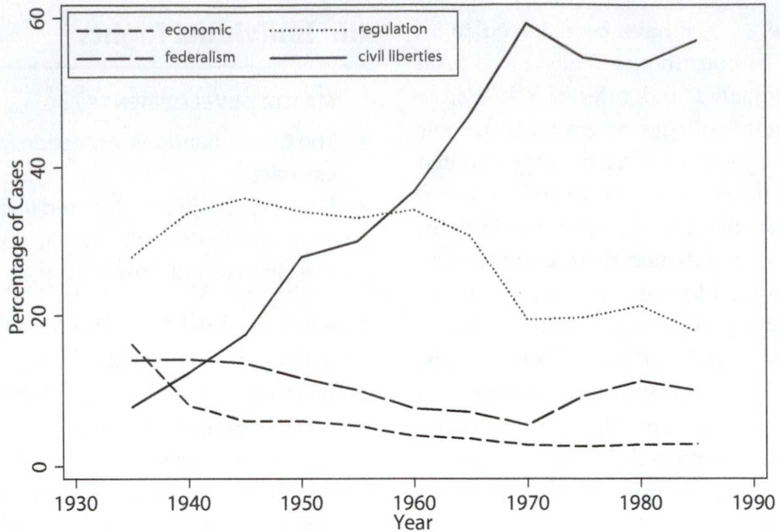

Figure 8-2 Agenda Change of the U.S. Supreme Court, 1933–88

Note: Five-year intervals averaged.

Source: Richard L. Pacelle, Jr., *The Transformation of the Supreme Court's Agenda* (Boulder, CO: Westview Press, 1991), table 3-1.

whether and how judicial protections for some rights but not others might be explained or justified.

A. Property

New Deal and Great Society liberals had a very narrow conception of constitutional property rights. Commercial and economic matters raised policy questions that were constitutionally entrusted to the elected branches of government. When making public policy, those institutions considered the public interest, broadly understood. Economic life was left free only when elected officials believed not regulating promoted the general good. The Constitution neither constrained action thought to be in the public interest nor mandated in advance what constituted the public interest.

Judicial activism on behalf of property or contract rights was inconsistent with New Deal constitutional liberalism. The New Deal Constitution provided few if any constraints on national and state efforts to regulate economic behavior. The freedom of contract was eviscerated entirely. The contracts clause and takings clause were interpreted as providing only minimal barriers to regulation in the public interest. The Warren Court made some feints at protecting welfare rights during the 1960s, but those doctrinal trends were soon sharply limited. Justices, who were not democratically accountable and who were less likely than elected officials to make intelligent economic policies, liberals insisted, should defer to whatever commercial policies legislators and administrators thought best.

Contracts

The contracts clause ceased to be of any constitutional significance. In *Home Building and Loan Ass'n v. Blaisdell* (1934) a divided Supreme Court ruled that state legislatures could adjust existing contract obligations when doing so was perceived to be necessary to limit the impact of an economic depression. For the next forty years the notion that government could impair the obligations of contract when doing so was in the public interest reduced the contracts clause to a legal nullity, at least in federal courtrooms. Few litigants raised contracts clause claims and those who did lost. *El Paso v. Simmons* (1965) illustrates the exceptionally narrow scope of contract clause rights when Earl Warren was chief justice. A Texas law permitted persons who purchased land from the state but failed to make the required payments to reestablish their interest in the property by paying their debt with interest, as long as the land had not been resold. In 1941 Texas passed a new law providing a five-year limit on when that property right could be asserted. The Supreme Court sustained that measure. Observing that "it is not every modification of a contractual promise that impairs the obligation of contract under federal law, any more than it is every alteration of existing remedies that violates the Contract Clause," Justice Byron White's majority opinion declared that the state interest in the "effective utilization of public lands" outweighed what he believed was the "mild" burden to the original purchaser.

Home Building & Loan Association v. Blaisdell, 290 U.S. 398 (1934)

John Blaisdell was one of many Minnesota homeowners who fell behind in their payments during the Depression. Fearful that the Home Building and Loan Association would foreclose, he applied to the Minnesota courts for relief under the Minnesota Moratorium Law of 1932. That statute extended the time period for overdue mortgages. Most properties covered by the law could not be foreclosed and sold by the lender until May 1, 1935, provided the owner continued to pay the fair rental value of the home. The trial court agreed to extend the period in which Blaisdell could redeem his mortgage. That decision was upheld by the Supreme Court of Minnesota. The Home Building and Loan Association appealed to the Supreme Court of the United States.

The Supreme Court sustained the Minnesota law by a 5-4 vote. Chief Justice Hughes insisted that the contracts clause did not prevent states from passing laws for the public welfare, provided those laws did not destroy the value of a contract. As you read the opinions, consider what each justice believes to be fundamental constitutional purposes and what theories of constitutional interpretation follow from their logic. What does Chief Justice Hughes mean when he declares, "While emergency does not create power, emergency may furnish the occasion for the exercise of power"? How does Justice Sutherland respond to this claim? If Chief Justice Hughes's notion of the police power were applied to other rights, would courts be able to protect any right? Does any good reason exist for thinking that the contracts clause ought to receive a more narrow interpretation than the First Amendment?

CHIEF JUSTICE HUGHES delivered the opinion of the Court.

. . .

Emergency does not create power. Emergency does not increase granted power or remove or diminish the restrictions imposed upon power granted or reserved. The Constitution was adopted in a period of grave emergency. Its grants of power to the federal government and its limitations of the power of the States were determined in the light of emergency, and they are not altered by emergency. . . .

While emergency does not create power, emergency may furnish the occasion for the exercise of power. . . . The constitutional question presented in the light of an emergency is whether the power possessed embraces the particular exercise of it in response to particular conditions. Thus, the war power of the federal government is not created by the emergency of war, but it is a power given to meet that emergency. It is a power to wage war successfully, and thus it permits the harnessing of the entire energies of the people in a supreme co-operative effort to preserve the nation. But even the war power does not remove constitutional limitations safeguarding essential liberties. When the provisions of the Constitution, in grant or restriction, are specific, so particularized as not to admit of construction, no question is presented. Thus, emergency would not permit a state to have more than two Senators in the Congress, or permit the election of President by a general popular vote without regard to the number of electors to which the States are respectively entitled, or permit the States to "coin money" or to "make anything but gold and silver coin a tender in payment of debts." But, where constitutional grants and limitations of power are set forth in general clauses, which afford a broad outline, the process of construction is essential to fill in the details. That is true of the contract clause. . . .

. . .

The obligation of a contract is the law which binds the parties to perform their agreement. . . . But this broad language cannot be taken without qualification. Chief Justice Marshall pointed out the distinction between obligation and remedy. . . . Said he: "The distinction between the obligation of a contract, and the remedy given by the legislature to enforce that obligation, has been taken at the bar, and exists in the nature of things. Without impairing the obligation of the contract, the remedy may certainly be modified as the wisdom of the nation shall direct."

. . .

Not only is the constitutional provision qualified by the measure of control which the state retains over remedial processes, but the state also continues to possess authority to safeguard the vital interests of its people. It does not matter that legislation appropriate to that end "has the result of modifying or abrogating contracts already in effect." . . . Not only are existing laws read into contracts in order to fix obligations as between the parties, but the reservation of essential attributes of sovereign power is also read into contracts as a postulate of the legal order. The policy of protecting contracts against impairment presupposes the maintenance of a government by virtue of which contractual relations are worthwhile,—a government which retains adequate authority to secure the peace and good order of society. This principle of harmonizing the constitutional prohibition with the necessary residuum of state power has had progressive recognition in the decisions of this Court.

. . . The Legislature cannot "bargain away the public health or the public morals." . . .

. . .

Undoubtedly, whatever is reserved of state power must be consistent with the fair intent of the constitutional limitation of that power. The reserved power cannot be construed so as to destroy the limitation, nor is the limitation to be construed to destroy the reserved power in its essential aspects. They must be construed in harmony with each other. This principle precludes a construction which would permit the state to adopt as its policy the repudiation of debts or the destruction of contracts or the denial of means to enforce them. But it does not follow that conditions may not arise in which a temporary restraint of enforcement may be consistent with the spirit and purpose of the constitutional provision and thus be found to be within the range of the reserved power of the state to protect the vital interests of the community. . . . It cannot be maintained that the constitutional prohibition should be so construed as to prevent limited and temporary interpositions with respect to the enforcement of contracts if made necessary by a great public calamity such as fire, flood, or earthquake. . . . The reservation of state power appropriate to such extraordinary conditions may be deemed to be as much a part of all contracts as is the reservation of state power to protect the public interest in the other situations to which we have referred. And, if state power exists to give temporary relief from the enforcement of contracts in the presence of disasters due to physical causes such as fire, flood, or earthquake, that power cannot be said to be nonexistent when the urgent public need demanding such relief is produced by other and economic causes.

. . .

In these cases of leases, it will be observed that the relief afforded was temporary and conditional; that it was sustained because of the emergency due to scarcity of housing; and that provision was made for reasonable compensation to the landlord during the period he was prevented from regaining possession. . . .

. . .

It is no answer to say that this public need was not apprehended a century ago, or to insist that what the provision of the Constitution meant to the vision of that day it must mean to the vision of our time. If by the statement that what the Constitution meant at the time of its adoption it means to-day, it is intended to say that the great clauses of the Constitution must be confined to the interpretation which the framers, with the conditions and outlook of their time, would have placed upon them, the statement carries its own refutation. It was to guard against such a narrow conception that Chief Justice Marshall uttered the memorable warning: "We must never forget, that it is a constitution we are expounding," . . . "a constitution intended to endure for ages to come, and, consequently, to be adapted to the various crises of human affairs. . . . The case before us must be considered in the light of our whole experience and not merely in that of what was said a hundred years ago."

Nor is it helpful to attempt to draw a fine distinction between the intended meaning of the words of the Constitution and their intended application. When we consider the contract clause and the decisions which have expounded it in harmony with the essential reserved power of the states to protect the security of their peoples, we find no warrant for the conclusion that the clause has been warped by these decisions from its proper significance or that the founders of our government would have interpreted the clause differently had they had occasion to assume that responsibility in the conditions of the later day. The vast body of law which has been developed was unknown to the fathers, but it is believed to have preserved the essential content and the spirit of the Constitution. With a growing recognition of public needs and the relation of individual right to public security, the court has sought to prevent the perversion of the clause through its use as an instrument to throttle the capacity of the states to protect their fundamental interests. . . .

An emergency existed in Minnesota which furnished a proper occasion for the exercise of the reserved power of the state to protect the vital interests of the community. . . .

The legislation was addressed to a legitimate end; that is, the legislation was not for the mere advantage of particular individuals but for the protection of a basic interest of society.

. . .

The conditions upon which the period of redemption is extended do not appear to be unreasonable. . . . [T]he integrity of the mortgage indebtedness is not impaired; interest continues to run; the validity of the sale and the right of a mortgagee-purchaser to title or to obtain a deficiency judgment, if the mortgagor fails to redeem within the extended period, are maintained; and the conditions of redemption, if redemption there be, stand as they were under the prior law. The mortgagor during the extended period is not ousted from possession, but he must pay the rental value of the premises as ascertained in judicial proceedings and this amount is applied to the carrying of the property and to interest upon the indebtedness. . . .

. . .

JUSTICE SUTHERLAND, with whom JUSTICE VAN DEVANTER, JUSTICE McREYNOLDS, and JUSTICE BUTLER join, dissenting.

. . .

A provision of the Constitution, it is hardly necessary to say, does not admit of two distinctly opposite interpretations. It does not mean one thing at one time and an entirely different thing at another time. If the contract impairment clause, when framed and adopted, meant that the terms of a contract for the payment of money could not be altered . . . by a state statute enacted for the relief of hardly pressed debtors to the end and with the effect of postponing payment or enforcement during and because of an economic or financial emergency, it is but to state the obvious to say that it means the same now. . . .

. . .

The provisions of the Federal Constitution, undoubtedly, are pliable in the sense that in appropriate cases they have the capacity of bringing within their grasp every new condition which falls within their meaning. . . . But, their meaning is changeless; it is only their application which is extensible. . . .

The whole aim of construction, as applied to a provision of the Constitution, is to discover the meaning, to ascertain and give effect to the intent of its framers and the people who adopted it. . . . The necessities which gave rise to the provision, the controversies which preceded, as well as the conflicts of opinion which were settled by its adoption, are matters to be considered to enable us to arrive at a correct result. . . . As nearly as possible we should place ourselves in the condition of those who framed and adopted it. . . . And, if the meaning be at all doubtful, the doubt should be resolved, wherever reasonably possible to do so, in a way to forward the evident purpose with which the provision was adopted. . . .

An application of these principles to the question under review removes any doubt, if otherwise there would be any, that the contract impairment clause denies to the several states the power to mitigate hard consequences resulting to debtors from financial or economic exigencies by an impairment of the obligation of contracts of indebtedness. A candid consideration of the history and circumstances which led up to and accompanied the framing and adoption of this clause will demonstrate conclusively that it was framed and adopted with the specific and studied purpose of preventing legislation designed to relieve debtors especially in time of financial distress. . . .

. . .

The present exigency is nothing new. From the beginning of our existence as a nation, periods of depression, of industrial failure, of financial distress, of unpaid and unpayable indebtedness, have alternated with years of plenty. The vital lesson that expenditure beyond income begets poverty, that public or private extravagance, financed by promises to pay, either must end in complete or partial repudiation or the promises be fulfilled by self-denial and painful effort, though constantly taught by bitter experience, seems never to be learned; and the attempt by legislative devices to shift the misfortune of the debtor to the shoulders of the creditor without coming into conflict with the contract impairment clause has been persistent and oft-repeated.

. . .

A statute which materially delays enforcement of the mortgagee's contractual right of ownership and possession does not modify the remedy merely; it destroys, for the period of delay, all remedy so far as the enforcement of that right is concerned. The phrase "obligation of a contract" in the constitutional sense imports a legal duty to perform the specified obligation of that contract, not to substitute and perform, against the will of one of the parties, a different, albeit equally valuable, obligation. And a state, under the contract impairment clause, has no more power to accomplish such a substitution than has one of the parties to the contract against the will of the other. It cannot do so either by acting directly upon the contract or by bringing about the result under the guise of a statute in form acting only upon the remedy. If it could, the efficacy of the constitutional restriction would, in large measure, be made to disappear. . . .

Takings

Justices supported some takings claims but insisted that any taking that served the public interest satisfied the "public purpose" element of the Fifth Amendment. After *Berman v. Parker* (1954) "public purpose" largely went the way of the freedom of contract. *Berman* arose after government officials in Washington, DC, attempted to reduce urban blight by condemning several city blocks, paying compensation, and turning the property over to a private developer. No justice expressed qualms about any public/private distinction that might limit constitutional takings to instances when the government took title to the condemned property. "When the legislature has spoken," Justice Douglas declared, "the public interest has been declared in terms well-nigh conclusive." The justices were more protective when persons claimed that their property had been taken without compensation. Government airports were particularly vulnerable to takings claims. In *United States v. Causby* (1946) Justice Douglas insisted that the government pay compensation when flights from the local airport that went less than one hundred feet above a farm killed chickens and prevented the owners from sleeping. More often than not the justices found reason for concluding that a state regulation was not a taking. A unanimous Court in *Goldblatt v. Town of Hempstead* (1962) sustained a local regulation forbidding additional excavation in a lot that had been used to mine sand and gravel for over thirty years. "If this ordinance is otherwise a valid exercise of the town's police powers," Justice Clark wrote, "the fact that it deprives the property of its most beneficial use does not render it unconstitutional."

Due Process

The freedom of contract was an early casualty of the New Deal. A 5-4 judicial majority in *Nebbia v. New York* (1934) abandoned the crucial public/private distinction when sustaining a state law regulating the price at which milk could be bought or sold. Such previous cases as *Munn v. Illinois* (1877) had held that government could regulate only "business affected with a public interest." This implied a class of private businesses beyond the scope of state regulation. Justice Roberts's majority opinion rejected that distinction when asserting,

> There is no closed class or category of businesses affected with a public interest, and the function of courts in the application of the Fifth and Fourteenth Amendments is to determine in each case whether circumstances vindicate the challenged regulation as a reasonable exertion of governmental authority or condemn it as arbitrary or discriminatory. . . . The phrase "affected with a public interest" can, in the nature of things, mean no more than that an industry, for adequate reason, is subject to control for the public good.

Libertarians detected a heartbeat in *Morehead v. People of State of New York ex rel. Tipaldo* (1936) when Justices Roberts joined the four most conservative justices in a decision declaring unconstitutional a New York law requiring employers to pay their female employees a wage determined to provide a "reasonable value" for their service. Roberts was willing to strike down the law, however, only because the lawyers for the state of New York did not ask the justices to overrule *Adkins v. Children's Hospital* (1923), a previous decision striking down minimum wage laws for women. When the same issue arose the next year in *West Coast Hotel v. Parrish* (1937), Roberts voted with the more liberal justices to sustain the law under constitutional attack. Chief Justice Hughes, writing for the majority, challenged the very existence of the freedom of contract. He declared,

> The Constitution does not speak of freedom of contract. It speaks of liberty and prohibits the deprivation of liberty without due process of law. . . . [T]he liberty safeguarded is liberty in a social organization which requires the protection of law against the evils which menace the health, safety, morals, and welfare of the people. Liberty under the Constitution is thus necessarily subject to the restraints of due process, and regulation which is reasonable in relation to its subject and is adopted in the interests of the community is due process.

Four years later, in *Wickard v. Filburn* (1941), a unanimous Supreme Court ruled that farmers did not have a constitutional right to grow more than their allotted acreage of wheat, even when their entire crop was consumed on their farm. Justice Robert Jackson's unanimous opinion for the Court did not even consider whether the Constitution protected the right to grow food on a farm for home consumption.

During the following years the justices divided only on whether due process claims in economic cases should be rejected outright or evaluated under a toothless rationality standard. Justice Black championed the position that economic regulations did not have to satisfy any due process standard. His majority opinion in *Ferguson v. Skrupa* (1963) sustaining a Kansas law that forbade nonlawyers from becoming "debt-adjusters" stated,

> The doctrine that prevailed in *Lochner* . . . and like cases—that due process authorizes courts to hold laws unconstitutional when they believe the legislature has acted unwisely—has long since been discarded. We have returned to the original constitutional proposition that courts do not substitute their social and economic beliefs for the judgment of legislative bodies, who are elected to pass laws. . . . It is now settled that States "have power to legislate against what are found to be injurious practices in their internal commercial and business affairs, so long as their laws do not run afoul of some specific federal constitutional prohibition, or of some valid federal law."

Justice Harlan's concurring opinion insisted that the state demonstrate economic regulations "bear a rational relation to a constitutionally permissible objective," and that the justices apply the rationality test previously laid out in *Williamson v. Lee Optical Co.* (1955). That test was hardly onerous. In *Williamson*, a unanimous Court sustained an Oklahoma law requiring persons purchasing new glasses to obtain a prescription from an ophthalmologist or optometrist. A prescription was necessary even when buying frames for lenses purchased the previous day or when the original frames were bent. Justice Douglas's unanimous opinion conceded that the measure under due process attack "may exact a needless, wasteful requirement in many cases." Nevertheless, he insisted, laws met due process standards if they had some rational applications. "The law," Douglas wrote, "need not be in every respect logically consistent with its aims to be constitutional. It is enough that there is an evil at hand for correction, and that it might be thought that the particular legislative measure was a rational way to correct it."

West Coast Hotel Co. v. Parrish, 300 U.S. 379 (1937)

Elise Parrish was employed as a chambermaid by the Cascadian Hotel in Wenatchee, Washington. After being discharged for unknown reasons, she sued the hotel for back pay. A Washington state law passed in 1913 declared that the weekly minimum wage for chambermaids was $14.50. Parrish, who had been paid 22 cents an hour, believed that she was owed $216.19. The local trial court disagreed, insisting that the Washington minimum wage law had been ruled unconstitutional in Adkins v. Children's Hospital *(1923). The Supreme Court of Washington reversed that finding. The West Coast Hotel immediately appealed to the Supreme Court of the United States.*[31]

Two months after the state court decision in Parrish, *the Supreme Court seemingly dealt a fatal blow to any effort to revive minimum wage laws for women. In* Morehead v. People of State of New York ex rel. Tipaldo *(1936), a 5-4 judicial majority declared unconstitutional a New York law requiring employers to pay their female employees a minimum wage. Convinced that the justices would not overrule* Adkins, *the lawyers for the state of New York emphasized what they believed was an important distinction between the law at issue in* Morehead *and measures previously declared unconstitutional. Congress had required employers in the District of Columbia to pay a "living wage." New York required employers to pay what a state board determined was the "reasonable value" of services. Justice Pierce Butler's majority opinion in* Morehead *rejected this distinction. The due process clause of the Fourteenth Amendment, in his view, prohibited almost all laws regulating wages. He declared,*

> *The right to make contracts about one's affairs is a part of the liberty protected by the due process clause. Within this liberty are provisions of contracts between employer*

31. For a detailed case study of the *Parrish* litigation, see William E. Leuchtenburg, *The Supreme Court Reborn: The Constitutional Revolution in the Age of Roosevelt* (New York: Oxford University Press, 1995), 163–79.

and employee fixing the wages to be paid. In making contracts of employment, generally speaking, the parties have equal right to obtain from each other the best terms they can by private bargaining. Legislative abridgement of that freedom can only be justified by the existence of exceptional circumstances. Freedom of contract is the general rule and restraint the exception. . . .

. . . [T]he state is without power by any form of legislation to prohibit, change or nullify contracts between employers and adult women workers as to the amount of wages to be paid.

The Supreme Court in Parrish *sustained by a 5-4 vote the state law mandating minimum wage laws. Chief Justice Hughes's majority opinion overruled* Adkins. *Did any vestige of the freedom of contract survive* Parrish? *Hughes treats state assistance to the poor as a "subsidy for unconscionable employers." Is this correct? Is the dissent correct that minimum wage laws require employers to provide welfare that should be provided by the public? The justices in* Parrish *disputed the significance of gender differences. The more radical feminists of the 1930s, led by Alice Paul, abhorred* Parrish *for permitting legislators to make gender classifications. Professor Julie Novkov makes the intriguing suggestion that the Court opened the door for regulating the wages of men and women only by implicitly treating all workers as having the diminished capacities that women were thought to have during the early twentieth century.*[32]

Justice Roberts was the only justice who voted differently in Parrish *than he did in* Morehead. *Observers initially believed that Roberts had switched in response to Roosevelt's Court-packing plan (discussed in Vol. 1). Subsequent evidence proved this wrong. Roberts voted to overrule* Adkins *during a judicial conference held in December 1936, before Roosevelt sought to increase the number of justices on the Supreme Court. Roberts claimed that he voted to declare the New York statute unconstitutional only because state lawyers had not argued that* Adkins *should be overruled. An ongoing debate exists over whether this justification can be taken at face value.*[33] *Given the political circumstances of 1936 and 1937, do you believe that a justice who sustained a law he believed unconstitutional because counsel had not advanced proper arguments was acting in the best traditions of the adversary system or was stubbornly refusing to acknowledge the constitutional environment?*

CHIEF JUSTICE HUGHES delivered the opinion of the Court.

. . .

. . . The Constitution does not speak of freedom of contract. It speaks of liberty and prohibits the deprivation of liberty without due process of law. In prohibiting that deprivation, the Constitution does not recognize an absolute and uncontrollable liberty. Liberty in each of its phases has its history and connotation. But the liberty safeguarded is liberty in a social organization which requires the protection of law against the evils which menace the health, safety, morals, and welfare of the people. Liberty under the Constitution is thus necessarily subject to the restraints of due process, and regulation which is reasonable in relation to its subject and is adopted in the interests of the community is due process.

. . .

It is manifest that this established principle is peculiarly applicable in relation to the employment of women in whose protection the state has a special interest. That phase of the subject received elaborate consideration in *Muller v. Oregon* (1908) . . . where the constitutional authority of the state to limit the working hours of women was sustained. We emphasized the consideration that "woman's physical structure and the performance of maternal functions place her at a disadvantage in the struggle for subsistence" and that her physical well being "becomes an object of public interest and care in order to preserve the strength and vigor of the race." . . .

With full recognition of the earnestness and vigor which characterize the prevailing opinion in [*Adkins v. Children's Hospital* (1923)], we find it impossible to reconcile that ruling with these well-considered declarations. What can be closer to the public interest than the health of women and their protection from unscrupulous and overreaching employers? And if the protection of women is a legitimate end of the exercise of state power, how can it be said that the requirement of the payment of a minimum wage fairly fixed in order to meet the very necessities of existence is not an admissible means to that end? The Legislature of the state

32. See Julie Novkov, *Constituting Workers, Protecting Women: Gender, Law, and Labor in the Progressive Era and New Deal Years* (Ann Arbor: University of Michigan Press, 2001).

33. For an excellent summary of this controversy, see Alan Brinkley, Laura Kalman, William W. Leuchtenburg, and G. Edward White, "The Debate over the Constitutional Revolution of 1937," *American Historical Review* 110 (2005): 1052.

was clearly entitled to consider the situation of women in employment, the fact that they are in the class receiving the least pay, that their bargaining power is relatively weak, and that they are the ready victims of those who would take advantage of their necessitous circumstances. The Legislature was entitled to adopt measures to reduce the evils of the "sweating system," the exploiting of workers at wages so low as to be insufficient to meet the bare cost of living, thus making their very helplessness the occasion of a most injurious competition. The Legislature had the right to consider that its minimum wage requirements would be an important aid in carrying out its policy of protection. The adoption of similar requirements by many states evidences a deep seated conviction both as to the presence of the evil and as to the means adapted to check it. Legislative response to that conviction cannot be regarded as arbitrary or capricious and that is all we have to decide. Even if the wisdom of the policy be regarded as debatable and its effects uncertain, still the Legislature is entitled to its judgment.

There is an additional and compelling consideration which recent economic experience has brought into a strong light. The exploitation of a class of workers who are in an unequal position with respect to bargaining power and are thus relatively defenseless against the denial of a living wage is not only detrimental to their health and well being, but casts a direct burden for their support upon the community. What these workers lose in wages the taxpayers are called upon to pay. The bare cost of living must be met. We may take judicial notice of the unparalleled demands for relief which arose during the recent period of depression and still continue to an alarming extent despite the degree of economic recovery which has been achieved. . . . The community is not bound to provide what is in effect a subsidy for unconscionable employers. The community may direct its law-making power to correct the abuse which springs from their selfish disregard of the public interest. . . .

JUSTICE SUTHERLAND, joined by JUSTICE VAN DEVANTER, JUSTICE McREYNOLDS, and JUSTICE BUTLER, dissenting.

. . .

In the *Adkins Case* we . . . said that while there was no such thing as absolute freedom of contract, but that it was subject to a great variety of restraints, nevertheless, freedom of contract was the general rule and restraint the exception; and that the power to abridge that freedom could only be justified by the existence of exceptional circumstances. . . .

We further pointed out four distinct classes of cases in which this court from time to time had upheld statutory interferences with the liberty of contract. They were, in brief, (1) statutes fixing rates and charges to be exacted by businesses impressed with a public interest; (2) statutes relating to contracts for the performance of public work; (3) statutes prescribing the character, methods, and time for payment of wages; and (4) statutes fixing hours of labor. It is the last class that has been most relied upon as affording support for minimum-wage legislation; and much of the opinion in the *Adkins Case* . . . is devoted to pointing out the essential distinction between fixing hours of labor and fixing wages. What is there said need not be repeated. It is enough for present purposes to say that statutes of the former class deal with an incident of the employment, having no necessary effect upon wages. The parties are left free to contract about wages, and thereby equalize such additional burdens as may be imposed upon the employer as a result of the restrictions as to hours by an adjustment in respect of the amount of wages. This court, wherever the question is adverted to, has been careful to disclaim any purpose to uphold such legislation as fixing wages, and has recognized an essential difference between the two.

. . .

. . . The common-law rules restricting the power of women to make contracts have, under our system, long since practically disappeared. Women today stand upon a legal and political equality with men. There is no longer any reason why they should be put in different classes in respect of their legal right to make contracts; nor should they be denied, in effect, the right to compete with men for work paying lower wages which men may be willing to accept. And it is an arbitrary exercise of the legislative power to do so. . . .

. . .

Since the contractual rights of men and women are the same, does the legislation here involved, by restricting only the rights of women to make contracts as to wages, create an arbitrary discrimination? We think it does. Difference of sex affords no reasonable ground for making a restriction applicable to the wage contracts of all working women from which like contracts of all working men are left free. Certainly a suggestion that the bargaining ability of the average woman is not equal to that of the average man would lack substance. The ability to make a fair bargain, as every one knows, does not depend upon sex.

Williamson v. Lee Optical, Inc., 348 U.S. 483 (1955)

The Lee Optical Company prepared lenses and frames for persons who needed glasses. In 1953, Oklahoma passed a law that prohibited opticians from providing lenses and frames without a prescription from a licensed ophthalmologist or optometrist. Opticians were required to obtain or have on hand these prescriptions, even when replacing lost glasses or repairing broken frames. The Lee Optical Company asked for an injunction against Mac Williamson, the attorney general of Oklahoma, claiming that the law was an unreasonable violation of the due process clause of the Fourteenth Amendment. Oklahoma insisted that the law was a reasonable means to ensure that persons had regular checkups. The local federal district court declared part of the law unconstitutional. Oklahoma appealed to the Supreme Court of the United States.

A unanimous Court had no difficulty finding this law constitutional. Justice Douglas's majority opinion ruled that economic regulations would have to satisfy a very toothless rational basis standard. Do you believe Justice Douglas's explanation for the law's purpose? What do you believe was the actual purpose of the measure? Should that matter? After Williamson, *can you imagine an economic regulation that a legislature might actually pass that New Deal/Great Society justices would find an unreasonable violation of due process?*

JUSTICE DOUGLAS delivered the opinion of the Court.

. . .

The Oklahoma law may exact a needless, wasteful requirement in many cases. But it is for the legislature, not the courts, to balance the advantages and disadvantages of the new requirement. It appears that, in many cases, the optician can easily supply the new frames or new lenses without reference to the old written prescription. It also appears that many written prescriptions contain no directive data in regard to fitting spectacles to the face. But in some cases the directions contained in the prescription are essential if the glasses are to be fitted so as to correct the particular defects of vision or alleviate the eye condition. The legislature might have concluded that the frequency of occasions when a prescription is necessary was sufficient to justify this regulation of the fitting of eyeglasses. Likewise, when it is necessary to duplicate a lens, a written prescription may or may not be necessary. But the legislature might have concluded that one was needed often enough to require one in every case. Or the legislature may have concluded that eye examinations were so critical, not only for correction of vision but also for detection of latent ailments or diseases, that every change in frames and every duplication of a lens should be accompanied by a prescription from a medical expert. To be sure, the present law does not require a new examination of the eyes every time the frames are changed or the lenses duplicated. For if the old prescription is on file with the optician, he can go ahead and make the new fitting or duplicate the lenses. But the law need not be in every respect logically consistent with its aims to be constitutional. It is enough that there is an evil at hand for correction, and that it might be thought that the particular legislative measure was a rational way to correct it.

The day is gone when this Court uses the Due Process Clause of the Fourteenth Amendment to strike down state laws, regulatory of business and industrial conditions because they may be unwise, improvident, or out of harmony with a particular school of thought. . . . "For protection against abuses by legislatures, the people must resort to the polls, not to the courts."

[In evaluating equal protection claims the] problem of legislative classification is a perennial one, admitting of no doctrinaire definition. Evils in the same field may be of different dimensions and proportions, requiring different remedies. Or so the legislature may think. . . . Or the reform may take one step at a time, addressing itself to the phase of the problem which seems most acute to the legislative mind. . . . The legislature may select one phase of one field and apply a remedy there, neglecting the others. . . . The prohibition of the Equal Protection Clause goes no further than the invidious discrimination. We cannot say that that point has been reached here. For all this record shows, the ready-to-wear branch of this business may not loom large in Oklahoma or may present problems of regulation distinct from the other branch.

Third, the District Court held unconstitutional, as violative of the Due Process Clause of the Fourteenth Amendment, that portion of § 3 which makes it unlawful "to solicit the sale of . . . frames, mountings . . . or any other optical appliances." . . .

An eyeglass frame, considered in isolation, is only a piece of merchandise. But an eyeglass frame is not used in isolation . . . ; it is used with lenses; and lenses, pertaining as they do to the human eye, enter the field of health. Therefore, the legislature might conclude that to regulate one effectively it would have to regulate the other. Or it might conclude that both the sellers of frames and the sellers of lenses were in a business where advertising should be limited, or even abolished, in the public interest. . . . The advertiser of frames may be using his ads to bring in customers who will buy lenses. If the advertisement of lenses is to be abolished or controlled, the advertising of frames must come under the same restraints—or so the legislature might think. We see no constitutional reason why a State may not treat all who deal with the human eye as members of a profession who should use no merchandising methods for obtaining customers. . . .

B. Religion

The constitutional status of religion changed sharply during the New Deal/Great Society Era. By 1969 the Supreme Court had incorporated the free exercise and establishment clauses of the First Amendment, ruled that states could burden the free exercise of religion only if they demonstrated a compelling interest, declared school prayer exercises unconstitutional, and struck down some, but not all, state assistance to religious schools and organizations. Official constitutional law as handed down by federal justices, however, often did not describe actual constitutional practice. Many local officials, particularly in rural districts, ignored judicial decisions prohibiting school prayer and other religious exercises.

World War II and the Cold War help explain this greater concern for religious freedom. Government officials during the 1930s, 1940s, and 1950s consistently sought to distinguish the United States from Hitler's Germany and Stalin's Soviet Union. One very obvious distinction was the lack of religious persecution in the United States. Franklin Roosevelt on the eve of World War II repeatedly emphasized religious freedom as a signature element of American constitutionalism. Roosevelt administration officials sharply condemned domestic violence against Jehovah's Witnesses and recruited justices who would support civil liberties on the bench. The anti-Semitism fashionable in much polite American society during the early twentieth century was discredited by the concentration camps.

Increasing religious diversity fostered greater religious freedom. During the Republican Era many conflicts over religion were between traditional Protestants, who favored what they believed were nonsectarian religious activities in public schools while opposing state aid to private religious schools, and Catholics, who favored state aid to private religious schools while opposing what they believed were quite sectarian religious activities in public schools. Members of less mainstream religious sects, most notably Mormons, enjoyed little political or judicial support when they claimed that their religious rights were violated. The constitutional politics of religion became more diverse during the twentieth century. Three new groups joined the fray—liberal Protestants, Jews, and secularists. All three opposed state programs that aided or accommodated religious education and voluntary prayer in public schools. On issues of religious exemptions from general laws, the alliance fractured. Liberal Protestant and Jewish organizations favored exemptions. Secularists opposed them.

America's religious identity reflected this increased religious diversity and secularism. By 1950 New Deal constitutional authorities no longer spoke of the United States as a "Christian nation." The United States became a "Judeo-Christian nation"[34] or simply a "religious nation." Justice Douglas probably spoke for most New Deal elites in the 1950s when he claimed in *Zorach v. Clauson* (1952), "We are a religious people whose institutions presuppose a Supreme Being." Great Society elites rarely spoke of the United States as a religious nation. Consider the difference between Franklin Roosevelt and John Kennedy. At crucial moments, most notably immediately before D-Day, Roosevelt led the nation in prayer. Kennedy informed the electorate in 1960,

> I believe in an America where the separation of church and state is absolute—where no Catholic prelate would tell the President (should he be a Catholic) how to act and no Protestant minister would tell his parishioners for whom to vote—where no church or church school is granted any public funds or political preference—and where no man is denied public office merely because his religion differs from the President who might appoint him or the people who might elect him.

---

34. See *United States v. Seeger*, 380 U.S. 163 (1965).

Establishment

Supreme Court decisions during the New Deal/Great Society Era erected a high wall between church and state. Justice Black spoke for every liberal New Dealer on the Supreme Court when, in *Everson v. Board of Education of Ewing Tp.* (1947), he stated,

> The "establishment of religion" clause of the First Amendment means at least this: Neither a state nor the Federal Government can set up a church. Neither can pass laws which aid one religion, aid all religions, or prefer one religion over another. Neither can force nor influence a person to go to or to remain away from church against his will or force him to profess a belief or disbelief in any religion. No person can be punished for entertaining or professing religious beliefs or disbeliefs, for church attendance or non-attendance. No tax in any amount, large or small, can be levied to support any religious activities or institutions, whatever they may be called, or whatever from they may adopt to teach or practice religion. Neither a state nor the Federal Government can, openly or secretly, participate in the affairs of any religious organizations or groups and vice versa.

Most justices agreed that voluntary religious exercises in public schools unconstitutionally breached that wall between church and state. Justice Black spoke for a 6-1 judicial majority in *Engel v. Vitale* (1962) when declaring a state prayer exercise unconstitutional. The justices immediately made clear that the constitutional problem in *Engel* was the state-sponsored religious exercise, not the state-written prayer. Pennsylvania law required that the school day begin with a reading of ten Biblical verses. Maryland law required that the school day begin with a recitation of the Lord's Prayer. Both were declared unconstitutional in *Abington School Dist. v. Schempp* (1963). Justice Clark's majority opinion declared, "[These] are religious exercises, required by the States in violation of the command of the First Amendment that the Government maintain strict neutrality, neither aiding nor opposing religion." Such rulings proved hard to implement, not least because many teachers and school boards remained committed to prayer in public schools.

The Supreme Court from 1933 until 1968 had more difficulty determining when the government had impermissibly assisted religion. A 5-4 majority in *Everson* concluded that school boards could constitutionally reimburse families for transportation expenses, even when the program included the costs of transporting children to religious school. "We must be careful, in protecting the citizens of New Jersey against state-established churches," Justice Black asserted, "to be sure that we do not inadvertently prohibit New Jersey from extending its general State law benefits to all its citizens without regard to their religious belief." The next year, in *McCollum v. Board of Education* (1948), an 8-1 judicial majority declared "release time" programs unconstitutional. Under these very popular local practices, religious teachers taught in public schools, although only with the consent of parents. Justice Black's majority opinion curtly dismissed state arguments.

> Pupils compelled by law to go to school for secular education are released in part from their legal duty upon the condition that they attend the religious classes. This is beyond all question a utilization of the tax-established and tax-supported public school system to aid religious groups to spread their faith.

The justices almost immediately muddied establishment clause waters in *Zorach v. Clauson* (1952) by finding a similar release time program constitutional. Under New York law parents could give permission for their children to leave school for religious education, while those without permission remained in their public school classrooms. Justice Douglas's majority opinion found an important constitutional distinction between *Zorach* and *McCollum*. "In the *McCollum* case," he wrote, "the classrooms were used for religious instruction and the force of the public school was used to promote that instruction. Here, as we have said, the public schools do no more than accommodate their schedules to a program of outside religious instruction." More generally, Douglas insisted that state efforts to provide assistance for religious activities had much constitutional merit. His conclusion asserted,

> We are a religious people whose institutions presuppose a Supreme Being. . . . When the state encourages religious instruction or cooperates with religious authorities by adjusting the schedule of public events to sectarian needs, it follows the best of our traditions. For it then respects the religious nature of our people and accommodates the public service to their spiritual needs.

Table 8-4 Public School Teacher Attitudes on Prayer in the Classroom, 1965

Statement	Percent of Teachers Agreeing with Statement				
	South	**New England**	**Midwest**	**Mid-Atlantic**	**Mountain West**
Prayer and Bible-reading decisions interfere with teacher freedom	69	73	54	58	53
Devotional services have no place in the public school	11	25	48	41	60
Should not stop prayers and Bible readings because of a few dissenters	94	89	71	70	65
Bible readings and prayers are beneficial to students	94	91	86	75	80
Public school is not the proper place to develop religious values	34	43	62	58	72

Source: H. Frank Way, Jr., "Survey Research on Judicial Decisions: The Prayer and Bible Reading Cases," *Western Political Quarterly* 21 (1968): 199.

Engel v. Vitale, 370 U.S. 421 (1962)

Steven Engel was a parent of a Jewish public school student in New Hyde Park, New York. At that time public school days in New York began with the following prayer, written by the New York Board of Regents: "Almighty God, we acknowledge our dependence upon Thee, and we beg Thy blessings upon us, our parents, our teachers and our Country." Students were not required to say these words if their parents objected. Engel and other parents insisted that state-mandated religious exercises in public schools violated the establishment clause of the First Amendment as incorporated by the Fourteenth Amendment, even if those exercises were voluntary. New York insisted that nonsectarian prayers were an American tradition and were consistent with religious freedom (and a vital bulwark against communist influence). A lower state court rejected the parents' claim, as did the New York Court of Appeals. Engel appealed to the Supreme Court of the United States.

The Supreme Court by a 6-1 vote declared unconstitutional the New York regents' prayer. Justice Black's majority opinion asserted that states could not sponsor religious exercises in public schools. To what extent do the justices in the majority object to state officials writing prayers? To what extent do the justices in the majority object to the state sponsoring a religious exercise? New York claimed their prayer was nonsectarian. Do you agree? Given the diversity of religion in the United States, is nonsectarian prayer possible? Is Justice Stewart nevertheless correct when he insists that, as an historical matter, Americans have endorsed the concept of nonsectarian prayer?

Engle v. Vitale *is one of the most politically controversial decisions in the history of the Supreme Court. President Kennedy at a press conference declared that the American people should "support the Constitution and the responsibility of the Supreme Court in interpreting it." The* Christian Century, *a liberal Protestant publication, stated that the court had "protect[ed] the integrity of the religious conscience and the proper function of religious and government institutions." Conservatives sharply disagreed. Cardinal Francis Spelling accused the Supreme Court of "strik[ing] at the heart of the Godly tradition in which America's children have for so long been raised." The* Wall Street Journal *described the outcome as a "violent wrecking of the Constitution's language."[35] Many rural school districts ignored the* Engel *decision. Regional resistance to this opinion continues to this day, especially in communities dominated by a Southern Baptist tradition.*

35. For these and other responses, see Powe, *The Warren Court,* 187–88.

JUSTICE BLACK delivered the opinion of the Court.

. . .

We think that by using its public school system to encourage recitation of the Regents' prayer, the State of New York has adopted a practice wholly inconsistent with the Establishment Clause. There can, of course, be no doubt that New York's program of daily classroom invocation of God's blessings as prescribed in the Regents' prayer is a religious activity. . . . [T]he constitutional prohibition against laws respecting an establishment of religion must at least mean that in this country it is no part of the business of government to compose official prayers for any group of the American people to recite as a part of a religious program carried on by government.

. . .

By the time of the adoption of the Constitution, our history shows that there was a widespread awareness among many Americans of the dangers of a union of Church and State. . . . The First Amendment was added to the Constitution to stand as a guarantee that neither the power nor the prestige of the Federal Government would be used to control, support or influence the kinds of prayer the American people can say—that the people's religions must not be subjected to the pressures of government for change each time a new political administration is elected to office. Under that Amendment's prohibition against governmental establishment of religion, as reinforced by the provisions of the Fourteenth Amendment, government in this country, be it state or federal, is without power to prescribe by law any particular form of prayer which is to be used as an official prayer in carrying on any program of governmentally sponsored religious activity.

. . . Neither the fact that the [New York] prayer may be denominationally neutral nor the fact that its observance on the part of the students is voluntary can serve to free it from the limitations of the Establishment Clause. . . . The Establishment Clause, unlike the Free Exercise Clause, does not depend upon any showing of direct governmental compulsion and is violated by the enactment of laws which establish an official religion whether those laws operate directly to coerce nonobserving individuals or not. . . . When the power, prestige and financial support of government is placed behind a particular religious belief, the indirect coercive pressure upon religious minorities to conform to the prevailing officially approved religion is plain. But the purposes underlying the Establishment Clause go much further than that. Its first and most immediate purpose rested on the belief that a union of government and religion tends to destroy government and to degrade religion. The history of governmentally established religion, both in England and in this country, showed that whenever government had allied itself with one particular form of religion, the inevitable result had been that it had incurred the hatred, disrespect and even contempt of those who held contrary beliefs. . . . The Establishment Clause thus stands as an expression of principle on the part of the Founders of our Constitution that religion is too personal, too sacred, too holy, to permit its "unhallowed perversion" by a civil magistrate. Another purpose of the Establishment Clause rested upon an awareness of the historical fact that governmentally established religions and religious persecutions go hand in hand. The Founders knew that . . . persecutions had received the sanction of law in several of the colonies in this country soon after the establishment of official religions in those colonies. It was in large part to get completely away from this sort of systematic religious persecution that the Founders brought into being our Nation, our Constitution, and our Bill of Rights with its prohibition against any governmental establishment of religion. The New York laws officially prescribing the Regents' prayer are inconsistent both with the purposes of the Establishment Clause and with the Establishment Clause itself.

. . . [T]he First Amendment, which tried to put an end to governmental control of religion and of prayer, was not written to destroy either. . . . [I]t was written to quiet well-justified fears . . . arising out of an awareness that governments of the past had shackled men's tongues to make them speak only the religious thoughts that government wanted them to speak and to pray only to the God that government wanted them to pray to. It is neither sacrilegious nor antireligious to say that each separate government in this country should stay out of the business of writing or sanctioning official prayers and leave that purely religious function to the people themselves and to those the people choose to look to for religious guidance.

. . .

JUSTICE DOUGLAS, concurring. . . .

JUSTICE STEWART, dissenting.

. . .

. . . I cannot see how an "official religion" is established by letting those who want to say a prayer say it.

On the contrary, I think that to deny the wish of these school children to join in reciting this prayer is to deny them the opportunity of sharing in the spiritual heritage of our Nation.

. . .

At the opening of each day's Session of this Court we stand, while one of our officials invokes the protection of God. Since the days of John Marshall our Crier has said, "God save the United States and this Honorable Court." Both the Senate and the House of Representatives open their daily Sessions with prayer. Each of our Presidents, from George Washington to John F. Kennedy, has upon assuming his Office asked the protection and help of God.

. . .

I do not believe that this Court, or the Congress, or the President has by the actions and practices I have mentioned established an "official religion" in violation of the Constitution. And I do not believe the State of New York has done so in this case. What each has done has been to recognize and to follow the deeply entrenched and highly cherished spiritual traditions of our Nation—traditions which come down to us from those who almost two hundred years ago avowed their "firm Reliance on the Protection of divine Providence" when they proclaimed the freedom and independence of this brave new world.

Free Exercise

New Deal/Great Society liberals concluded that strict scrutiny was the appropriate standard when states refused to grant persons exemptions from laws that significantly burdened their religious practice. "Any incidental burden on the free exercise of appellant's religion," Justice Brennan wrote in *Sherbert v. Verner* (1963), "may be justified by a 'compelling state interest in the regulation of a subject within the State's constitutional power to regulate.'" Sincerity of conviction was the only proper test for religious belief. "Men may believe what they cannot prove," Justice Douglas declared in *United States v. Ballard* (1944). He continued, "They may not be put to the proof of their religious doctrines or beliefs. Religious experiences

Table 8-5 Selection of State and Lower Federal Court Applications of *Engel v. Vitale*

Case	Decision
DeSpain v. DeKalb County Community School District, 384 F. 2d 836 (7th Cir., 1967)	Kindergarten "thank you" verse constitutes a prayer, even when stripped of explicit references to God, and is therefore unconstitutional
Lincoln v. Page, 109 N.H. 30 (NH 1968)	Prayer before town meeting is constitutional
Aronow v. United States, 432 F.2d 242 (9th Cir., 1970)	Use of "In God We Trust" is ceremonial, not religious
Mangold v. Albert Gallatin Area School District, 438 F.2d 1194 (3rd Cir., 1971)	Administration-initiated "voluntary" student Bible reading and mass prayer are unconstitutional
Fox v. Los Angeles, 22 Cal. 3d 792 (CA 1978)	Display of lighted cross at Christmas at city hall is unconstitutional
Collins v. Chandler Unified School District, 470 F. Supp. 959 (D. AZ, 1979)	Student council–initiated prayer before school assemblies is unconstitutional
Malnak v. Yogi, 592 F.2d 197 (3rd Cir., 1979)	Public school class in transcendental meditation is unconstitutional
Brandon v. Board of Education, 487 F. Supp. 1219 (D. NY, 1980)	Use of school facilities by student prayer group is unconstitutional
Breen v. Runkel, 614 F. Supp. 355 (D. MI, 1985)	Bible reading and classroom prayer by individual teachers without direction from school administrators is still unconstitutional state action
Jager v. Douglas County School District, 862 F.2d 824 (11th Cir., 1989)	Religious invocation before school football games is unconstitutional

which are as real as life to some may be incomprehensible to others."

Sherbert v. Verner, 374 U.S. 398 (1963)

Adell Sherbert was a Seventh-Day Adventist whose faith prohibited Saturday work. Shortly after she converted, the textile mill where she was employed adopted a six-day workweek. Sherbert was fired after refusing to work on Saturday. Her application for unemployment benefits was turned down. The South Carolina Employment Security Commission determined that she had refused "without good cause, to accept suitable work." Sherbert sued Charles Verner and other members of the Employment Security Commission, claiming that their refusal to give her benefits violated the First and Fourteenth Amendments. Both the local trial court and the Supreme Court of South Carolina rejected that claim. Sherbert appealed to the Supreme Court of the United States.

The Supreme Court in Braunfeld v. Brown *(1961) by a 6-3 vote had rejected a similar constitutional claim. In that case, Orthodox Jews objected to Sunday laws that required them to close their businesses on that day. Chief Justice Warren's plurality opinion declared,*

> *it cannot be expected, much less required, that legislators enact no law regulating conduct that may in some way result in an economic disadvantage to some religious sects and not to others because of the special practices of the various religions. We do not believe that such an effect is an absolute test for determining whether the legislation violates the freedom of religion protected by the First Amendment.*
>
> *. . . . If the purpose or effect of a law is to impede the observance of one or all religions or is to discriminate invidiously between religions, that law is constitutionally invalid even though the burden may be characterized as being only indirect. But if the State regulates conduct by enacting a general law within its power, the purpose and effect of which is to advance the State's secular goals, the statute is valid despite its indirect burden on religious observance unless the State may accomplish its purpose by means which do not impose such a burden.*

The Supreme Court ruled by a 7-2 vote that Sherbert was entitled to unemployment benefits. Justice Brennan's majority opinion insisted that states needed to demonstrate a compelling interest in order to enforce laws that burdened the free exercise of religion. Justice Brennan claimed that the decision in Sherbert *declaring the denial of unemployment unconstitutional was consistent with the Court's recent decision in* Braunfeld v. Brown *(1961) On what basis does he distinguish the two cases? Is the distinction sound? Given that Justice Brennan dissented in* Braunfeld, *do you believe the distinction was made in good faith? Justice Stewart claims that the Supreme Court's free exercise jurisprudence was on a collision course with that tribunal's establishment clause jurisprudence. Why does he make that claim? Is that claim correct? What is the correct reconciliation of the two clauses?*

JUSTICE BRENNAN delivered the opinion of the Court.

. . .

The door of the Free Exercise Clause stands tightly closed against any governmental regulation of religious beliefs as such. Government may neither compel affirmation of a repugnant belief, nor penalize or discriminate against individuals or groups because they hold religious views abhorrent to the authorities, . . . nor employ the taxing power to inhibit the dissemination of particular religious views. . . . On the other hand, the Court has rejected challenges under the Free Exercise Clause to governmental regulation of certain overt acts prompted by religious beliefs or principles, for "even when the action is in accord with one's religious convictions, [it] is not totally free from legislative restrictions." *Braunfeld v. Brown* (1961). . . . The conduct or actions so regulated have invariably posed some substantial threat to public safety, peace or order.

Plainly enough, appellant's conscientious objection to Saturday work constitutes no conduct prompted by religious principles of a kind within the reach of state legislation. If, therefore, the decision of the South Carolina Supreme Court is to withstand appellant's constitutional challenge, it must be either because her disqualification as a beneficiary represents no infringement by the State of her constitutional rights of free exercise, or because any incidental burden on the free exercise of appellant's religion may be justified by a "compelling state interest in the regulation of a subject within the State's constitutional power to regulate."

We turn first to the question whether the disqualification for benefits imposes any burden on the free exercise of appellant's religion. We think it is clear that it does. . . . [I]t is true that no criminal sanctions directly compel appellant to work a six-day week. But this is only the beginning, not the end, of our inquiry.

For "[i]f the purpose or effect of a law is to impede the observance of one or all religions or is to discriminate invidiously between religions, that law is constitutionally invalid even though the burden may be characterized as being only indirect." *Braunfeld v. Brown*. . . . Here not only is it apparent that appellant's declared ineligibility for benefits derives solely from the practice of her religion, but the pressure upon her to forego that practice is unmistakable. The ruling forces her to choose between following the precepts of her religion and forfeiting benefits, on the one hand, and abandoning one of the precepts of her religion in order to accept work, on the other hand. Governmental imposition of such a choice puts the same kind of burden upon the free exercise of religion as would a fine imposed against appellant for her Saturday worship.

. . .

We must next consider whether some compelling state interest enforced in the eligibility provisions of the South Carolina statute justifies the substantial infringement of appellant's First Amendment right. . . . No such abuse or danger has been advanced in the present case. The appellees suggest no more than a possibility that the filing of fraudulent claims by unscrupulous claimants feigning religious objections to Saturday work might not only dilute the unemployment compensation fund but also hinder the scheduling by employers of necessary Saturday work. . . . [E]ven if the possibility of spurious claims did threaten to dilute the fund and disrupt the scheduling of work, it would plainly be incumbent upon the appellees to demonstrate that no alternative forms of regulation would combat such abuses without infringing First Amendment rights. . . .

In these respects, then, the state interest asserted in the present case is wholly dissimilar to the interests which were found to justify the less direct burden upon religious practices in *Braunfeld v. Brown*. The Court recognized that the Sunday closing law which that decision sustained undoubtedly served "to make the practice of [the Orthodox Jewish merchants'] religious beliefs more expensive," . . . But the statute was nevertheless saved by a countervailing factor which finds no equivalent in the instant case—a strong state interest in providing one uniform day of rest for all workers. That secular objective could be achieved, the Court found, only by declaring Sunday to be that day of rest. Requiring exemptions for Sabbatarians, while theoretically possible, appeared to present an administrative problem of such magnitude, or to afford the exempted class so great a competitive advantage, that such a requirement would have rendered the entire statutory scheme unworkable. In the present case no such justifications underlie the determination of the state court that appellant's religion makes her ineligible to receive benefits.

. . .

JUSTICE DOUGLAS, concurring. . . .

JUSTICE STEWART, concurring in the result.

. . .

. . . [T]here are many situations where legitimate claims under the Free Exercise Clause will run into head-on collision with the Court's insensitive and sterile construction of the Establishment Clause. The controversy now before us is clearly such a case.

. . .

If the appellant's refusal to work on Saturdays were based on indolence, or on a compulsive desire to watch the Saturday television programs, no one would say that South Carolina could not hold that she was not "available for work" within the meaning of its statute. That being so, the Establishment Clause as construed by this Court not only permits but affirmatively requires South Carolina equally to deny the appellant's claim for unemployment compensation when her refusal to work on Saturdays is based upon her religious creed. For, as said in *Everson v. Board of Education* (1947) . . . the Establishment Clause bespeaks "a government . . . stripped of all power . . . to support, or otherwise to assist any or all religions. . ." and no State "can pass laws which aid one religion." . . . In the words of the Court in *Engel v. Vitale* (1962), . . . the Establishment Clause forbids the "financial support of government" to be "placed behind a particular religious belief."

To require South Carolina to so administer its laws as to pay public money to the appellant under the circumstances of this case is thus clearly to require the State to violate the Establishment Clause as construed by this Court. This poses no problem for me, because I think the Court's mechanistic concept of the Establishment Clause is historically unsound and constitutionally wrong. . . .

. . .

. . . I think it is the Court's duty to face up to the dilemma posed by the conflict between the Free Exercise Clause of the Constitution and the Establishment

Clause as interpreted by the Court. . . . For so long as the resounding but fallacious fundamentalist rhetoric of some of our Establishment Clause opinions remains on our books, to be disregarded at will as in the present case, . . . so long will the possibility of consistent and perceptive decision in this most difficult and delicate area of constitutional law be impeded and impaired. And so long, I fear, will the guarantee of true religious freedom in our pluralistic society be uncertain and insecure.

. . .

JUSTICE HARLAN, whom JUSTICE WHITE joins, dissenting.

Today's decision is disturbing both in its rejection of existing precedent and in its implications for the future. . . .

. . .

. . . [T]he appellant was "unavailable for work," and thus ineligible for benefits, when personal considerations prevented her from accepting employment on a full-time basis in the industry and locality in which she had worked. The fact that these personal considerations sprang from her religious convictions was wholly without relevance to the state court's application of the law. Thus in no proper sense can it be said that the State discriminated against the appellant on the basis of her religious beliefs or that she was denied benefits because she was a Seventh-day Adventist. She was denied benefits just as any other claimant would be denied benefits who was not "available for work" for personal reasons.

. . .

. . . [T]he [majority opinion] necessarily overrules *Braunfeld v. Brown*. . . , which held that it did not offend the "Free Exercise" Clause of the Constitution for a State to forbid a Sabbatarian to do business on Sunday. The secular purpose of the statute before us today is even clearer than that involved in *Braunfeld*. And just as in *Braunfeld*—where exceptions to the Sunday closing laws for Sabbatarians would have been inconsistent with the purpose to achieve a uniform day of rest and would have required case-by-case inquiry into religious beliefs—so here, an exception to the rules of eligibility based on religious convictions would necessitate judicial examination of those convictions and would be at odds with the limited purpose of the statute to smooth out the economy during periods of industrial instability. Finally, the indirect financial burden of the present law is far less than that involved in *Braunfeld*. Forcing a store owner to close his business on Sunday may well have the effect of depriving him of a satisfactory livelihood if his religious convictions require him to close on Saturday as well. Here we are dealing only with temporary benefits, amounting to a fraction of regular weekly wages and running for not more than 22 weeks. . . . Clearly, any differences between this case and *Braunfeld* cut against the present appellant.

. . . .

It has been suggested that such singling out of religious conduct for special treatment may violate the constitutional limitations on state action. . . . My own view, however, is that at least under the circumstances of this case it would be a permissible accommodation of religion for the State, if it chose to do so, to create an exception to its eligibility requirements for persons like the appellant. The constitutional obligation of "neutrality" . . . is not so narrow a channel that the slightest deviation from an absolutely straight course leads to condemnation. . . . The State violates its obligation of neutrality when, for example, it mandates a daily religious exercise in its public schools, with all the attendant pressures on the school children that such an exercise entails. . . . But there is, I believe, enough flexibility in the Constitution to permit a legislative judgment accommodating an unemployment compensation law to the exercise of religious beliefs such as appellant's.

For very much the same reasons, however, I cannot subscribe to the conclusion that the State is constitutionally compelled to carve out an exception to its general rule of eligibility in the present case. Those situations in which the Constitution may require special treatment on account of religion are, in my view, few and far between, and this view is amply supported by the course of constitutional litigation in this area. . . . Such compulsion in the present case is particularly inappropriate in light of the indirect, remote, and insubstantial effect of the decision below on the exercise of appellant's religion and in light of the direct financial assistance to religion that today's decision requires.

C. Guns

Gun rights were ignored during the New Deal/Great Society period. Democrats and Republicans did not mention gun rights or gun control in their national party platforms. No prominent interest group championed either gun rights or gun control. Legislation requiring gun registration, prohibiting concealed weapons, and forbidding convicted felons from owning weapons was constitutionally uncontroversial. Most persons assumed that constitutional provisions did not bar such regulations, either because gun rights were restricted to the militia or because legislative restrictions that reasonably promoted the public interest were consistent with constitutional rights to bear arms. The Senate Report on the Omnibus Crime Control and Safe Streets Act of 1968 bluntly declared, "The [second] amendment presents no obstacle to the enactment and enforcement of" gun control legislation.[36]

A general consensus formed by the middle of the twentieth century that the Second Amendment had no bearing on a private right to bear arms independent of a state militia. Justice McReynolds stated the conventional wisdom in *United States v. Miller* (1939) when he declared,

> In the absence of any evidence tending to show that possession or use of a "shotgun having a barrel of less than eighteen inches in length" at this time has some reasonable relationship to the preservation or efficiency of a well regulated militia, we cannot say that the Second Amendment guarantees the right to keep and bear such an instrument.

An occasional dissent aside, every lower federal and state court that discussed gun rights reached the same or similar conclusions.[37] In *Matthews v. State* (IN 1958) the Supreme Court of Indiana held that a state law prohibiting persons from carrying weapons in their homes or places of business unless they were licensed to do so was consistent with a state constitutional provision declaring, "The people shall have a right to bear arms, for the defense of themselves and the State." The judicial majority declared, "The Legislature has the power, in the interest of public safety and welfare to provide reasonable regulations for the use of firearms which may be readily concealed, such as pistols."[38]

36. Senate Report 90–1097, Omnibus Crime Control and Safe Streets Act of 1968, 90th Cong., 2nd Sess. (1968), 52.

37. See Adam Winkler, "Scrutinizing the Second Amendment," *Michigan Law Review* 105 (2007): 683.

38. *Matthews v. State*, 237 Ind. 677 (1958).

D. Personal Freedom and Public Morality

The New Deal/Great Society Era was marked by an apparent abandonment of and then a slow but steady increase in constitutional privacy rights. During the 1930s and early 1940s, businesses lost what had previously been some immunity to government investigations of private records. Beginning in the 1940s, however, a series of judicial decisions provided protection for different forms of privacy, procreation rights, the right of married couples to use birth control, and the right to marry. In retrospect, these cases provided crucial precedential support for the judicial decision in *Roe v. Wade* (1973) that protected the right to an abortion. From the perspective of the time, the justices may have been doing little more than removing statutory relics and extending well-established family rights to discrete and insular minorities.

The constitutional politics of personal morality during the New Deal/Great Society Era was largely state constitutional politics. National political parties took no stands on eugenics, birth control, or family law. Such public interest groups as Planned Parenthood, and later the ACLU, actively lobbied state legislatures to abandon restrictive policies. Most states abandoned sterilization before or immediately after World War II, after experience with the Nazis changed perspectives on the full implications of a government claim to have the power to sterilize people considered unfit. By the 1960s birth control was increasingly available to both married and unmarried couples. Many states were considering liberalizing bans on abortion, although the complete abandonment of restrictions garnered little political support. Most states outside of the South repealed bans on interracial marriage. The Supreme Court of California in *Perez v. Sharpe* (CA 1948) declared that state's prohibition of interracial marriage unconstitutional.

The three most important Supreme Court decisions on privacy handed down from 1933 to 1968—*Skinner v. Oklahoma* (1942) (the right not to be sterilized), *Griswold v. Connecticut* (1965) (the right of married people to use birth control), and *Loving v. Virginia* (1966) (the right to marry a person of a different race)—protected discrete and insular minorities or rejected positions identified with the Catholic Church. The offending restrictions on family and procreation had previously been abandoned by the vast majority of states. Judicial opinions, most notably those written by Justice Douglas, contained language that could be wielded in a broader judicial crusade against conservative family policies, but the justices did not elaborate on the meaning of those decisions before the Nixon presidency.

Skinner v. State of Oklahoma ex rel. Williamson, 316 U.S. 535 (1942)

Jack T. Skinner could not stay out of legal trouble. In 1926 he was arrested and convicted for stealing chickens. Three years later he was convicted for armed robbery. In 1934 he was again convicted of armed robbery. Two years later Mac Williamson, the attorney general of Oklahoma, sought to have Skinner sterilized. Oklahoma law at that time declared that "any person adjudged to be . . . an habitual criminal shall be rendered sexually sterile." Habitual criminals were defined as persons who had "been convicted two or more times to final judgment of the commission of crimes amounting to felonies involving moral turpitude." Skinner claimed that these laws imposed cruel and unusual punishments, violated the due process clause of the Constitution, and denied him equal protection of the laws. The state argued that this was a legitimate eugenics measure based on beliefs that criminal tendencies were heritable. The district court ruled in favor of the state. When the Supreme Court of Oklahoma affirmed that ruling, Skinner appealed to the Supreme Court of the United States.

Despite having upheld the use of sterilization just fifteen years earlier in Buck v. Bell *(1927), the Supreme Court unanimously declared Skinner's sentence unconstitutional. Justice Douglas claimed that mandatory sterilization violated the equal protection clause of the Fourteenth Amendment. Chief Justice Stone insisted that this was a due process case. On what clause would you rely? The justices made little effort to distinguish this case from such cases as* Lochner v. New York *(1905), in which courts were criticized for substituting their judgment for that of elected officials. What justified the decision to declare Oklahoma's law unconstitutional? Could the justices legitimately decide that eugenics was pseudoscience? Could they so decide because most scientists and states by 1940 opposed eugenics? If you are relying on scientific understandings, when did eugenic measures become unconstitutional? Are there any conditions under which you believe that state-mandated sterilization is constitutional? Note that* Skinner *was decided during World War II, when the United States was fighting totalitarian regimes that routinely used racialized eugenics and sterilizations. Was the experience with Nazism the sort of historical development that should lead us to change our views of what rights deserve special protection?*

JUSTICE DOUGLAS delivered the opinion of the Court.

. . . We are dealing here with legislation which involves one of the basic civil rights of man. Marriage and procreation are fundamental to the very existence and survival of the race. The power to sterilize, if exercised, may have subtle, far-reaching and devastating effects. In evil or reckless hands it can cause races or types which are inimical to the dominant group to wither and disappear. There is no redemption for the individual whom the law touches. Any experiment which the State conducts is to his irreparable injury. He is forever deprived of a basic liberty. We mention these matters not to reexamine the scope of the police power of the States. We advert to them merely in emphasis of our view that strict scrutiny of the classification which a State makes in a sterilization law is essential, lest unwittingly or otherwise invidious discriminations are made against groups or types of individuals in violation of the constitutional guaranty of just and equal laws. . . . When the law lays an unequal hand on those who have committed intrinsically the same quality of offense and sterilizes one and not the other, it has made as invidious a discrimination as if it had selected a particular race or nationality for oppressive treatment. . . . Sterilization of those who have thrice committed grand larceny with immunity for those who are embezzlers is a clear, pointed, unmistakable discrimination. Oklahoma makes no attempt to say that he who commits larceny by trespass or trick or fraud has biologically inheritable traits which he who commits embezzlement lacks. . . . The equal protection clause would indeed be a formula of empty words if such conspicuously artificial lines could be drawn. . . .

. . .

CHIEF JUSTICE STONE concurring.

I concur in the result, but I am not persuaded that we are aided in reaching it by recourse to the equal protection clause.

If Oklahoma may resort generally to the sterilization of criminals on the assumption that their propensities are transmissible to future generations by inheritance, I seriously doubt that the equal protection clause requires it to apply the measure to all criminals in the first instance, or to none. . . .

There are limits to the extent to which the presumption of constitutionality can be pressed, especially where the liberty of the person is concerned (see *United States v. Carolene Products Co.* . . . n.4 [1938]). . . . Although petitioner here was given a hearing to ascertain whether sterilization would be detrimental to his health, he was given none to discover whether his criminal tendencies are of an inheritable type. Undoubtedly a state may, after appropriate inquiry, constitutionally interfere with the personal liberty of the individual to prevent the transmission by inheritance of his socially injurious tendencies. . . . But until now we have not been called upon to say that it may do so without giving him a hearing and opportunity to challenge the existence as to him of the only facts which could justify so drastic a measure. . . .

JUSTICE JACKSON, concurring.

. . . I also think the present plan to sterilize the individual in pursuit of a eugenic plan to eliminate from the race characteristics that are only vaguely identified and which in our present state of knowledge are uncertain as to transmissibility presents other constitutional questions of gravity. . . .

. . . There are limits to the extent to which a legislatively represented majority may conduct biological experiments at the expense of the dignity and personality and natural powers of a minority—even those who have been guilty of what the majority define as crimes. . . .

Perez v. Sharp, 32 Cal. 2d 711 (1948)

W. G. Sharp, a county clerk in California, refused to marry Andrea Perez to Sylvester Davis because she was white and he was African-American. California law at the time declared, "All marriages of white persons with negroes, Mongolians, members of the Malay race, or mulattoes are illegal and void." With the assistance of the Catholic Interracial Council, Perez and Davis sought a writ of mandamus from the California Supreme Court that would compel the county clerk to marry them. They insisted that the California law violated religious freedom, equal protection rights, and the right to marry. California responded by claiming both that states had an absolute right to regulate marriage and that the state commitment to white supremacy justified the ban on interracial marriage.[39]

The Supreme Court of California by a 4-3 vote issued the writ of mandamus. Justice Roger Traynor's majority opinion declared unconstitutional the state ban on interracial marriage. Why do you think that state courts took the lead in this area of the law? The lawyers for Perez and Davis emphasized the free exercise of religion issue. What is the religious freedom issue? Was this a sound ground for the right to marry? The Supreme Court of California declares, "the right to marry is the right to join in marriage with the person of one's choice." Does this entail a commitment to same sex marriage? How would California have ruled on that issue in 1948? Nineteen years later the Supreme Court of the United States in Loving v. Virginia *(1967) declared that bans on interracial marriage violated the equal protection and due process clauses of the Fourteenth Amendment. Chief Justice Warren's opinion asserted,*

> *Marriage is one of the "basic civil rights of man," fundamental to our very existence and survival." To deny this fundamental freedom on so unsupportable a basis as the racial classifications embodied in these statutes, classifications so directly subversive of the principle of equality at the heart of the Fourteenth Amendment, is surely to deprive all the State's citizens of liberty without due process of law. The Fourteenth Amendment requires that the freedom of choice to marry not be restricted by invidious racial discriminations. Under our Constitution, the freedom to marry, or not marry, a person of another race resides with the individual and cannot be infringed by the State.*

JUSTICE TRAYNOR delivered the opinion of the Court.

. . .

The regulation of marriage is considered a proper function of the state. It is well settled that a legislature may declare monogamy to be the "law of social life under its dominion," even though such a law might inhibit the free exercise of certain religious practices. . . . If the miscegenation law under attack in the present proceeding is directed at a social evil and employs a reasonable means to prevent that evil, it is valid regardless of its incidental effect upon the conduct of particular religious groups. If, on the other hand, the law is discriminatory and irrational, it unconstitutionally restricts not only religious liberty but the liberty to marry as well.

. . .

The right to marry is as fundamental as the right to send one's child to a particular school or the right to

39. For more details on this case, see Phyl Newbeck, *Virginia Hasn't Always Been for Lovers: Interracial Marriage Bans and the Case of Richard and Mildred Loving* (Carbondale: Southern Illinois University Press, 2004), 75–78.

have offspring. . . . Legislation infringing such rights must be based upon more than prejudice and must be free from oppressive discrimination to comply with the constitutional requirements of due process and equal protection of the laws.

Since the right to marry is the right to join in marriage with the person of one's choice, a statute that prohibits an individual from marrying a member of a race other than his own restricts the scope of his choice and thereby restricts his right to marry. It must therefore be determined whether the state can restrict that right on the basis of race alone without violating the equal protection of the laws clause of the United States Constitution.

. . .

A state law prohibiting members of one race from marrying members of another race is not designed to meet a clear and present peril arising out of an emergency. In the absence of an emergency the state clearly cannot base a law impairing fundamental rights of individuals on general assumptions as to traits of racial groups. It has been said that a statute such as section 60 does not discriminate against any racial group, since it applies alike to all persons whether Caucasian, Negro, or members of any other race. . . . The decisive question, however, is not whether different races, each considered as a group, are equally treated. The right to marry is the right of individuals, not of racial groups. The equal protection clause of the United States Constitution does not refer to rights of the Negro race, the Caucasian race, or any other race, but to the rights of individuals. . . . Since the essence of the right to marry is freedom to join in marriage with the person of one's choice, a segregation statute for marriage necessarily impairs the right to marry.

. . .

. . . The categorical statement that non-Caucasians are inherently physically inferior is without scientific proof. In recent years scientists have attached great weight to the fact that their segregation in a generally inferior environment greatly increases their liability to physical ailments. In any event, generalizations based on race are untrustworthy in view of the great variations among members of the same race. The rationalization, therefore, that marriage between Caucasians and non-Caucasians is socially undesirable because of the physical disabilities of the latter, fails to take account of the physical disabilities of Caucasians and fails also to take account of variations among non-Caucasians. The Legislature is free to prohibit marriages that are socially dangerous because of the physical disabilities of the parties concerned. . . . The miscegenation statute, however, condemns certain races as unfit to marry with Caucasians on the premise of a hypothetical racial disability, regardless of the physical qualifications of the individuals concerned. If this premise were carried to its logical conclusion, non-Caucasians who are now precluded from marrying Caucasians on physical grounds would also be precluded from marrying among themselves on the same grounds. The concern to prevent marriages in the first category and the indifference about marriages in the second reveal the spuriousness of the contention that intermarriage between Caucasians and non-Caucasians is socially dangerous on physical grounds.

. . .

Respondent maintains that Negroes are socially inferior . . . and that the progeny of a marriage between a Negro and a Caucasian suffer not only the stigma of such inferiority but the fear of rejection by members of both races. If they do, the fault lies not with their parents, but with the prejudices in the community and the laws that perpetuate those prejudices by giving legal force to the belief that certain races are inferior. If miscegenous marriages can be prohibited because of tensions suffered by the progeny, mixed religious unions could be prohibited on the same ground.

There are now so many persons in the United States of mixed ancestry, that the tensions upon them are already diminishing and are bound to diminish even more in time. Already many of the progeny of mixed marriages have made important contributions to the community. In any event the contention that the miscegenation laws prohibit inter-racial marriage because of its adverse effects on the progeny is belied by the extreme racial intermixture that it tolerates.

. . .

Careful examination of the arguments in support of the legislation in question reveals that "there is absent the compelling justification which would be needed to sustain discrimination of that nature." . . .

JUSTICE CARTER, concurring.

It is my considered opinion that the statutes here involved . . . are the product of ignorance, prejudice and intolerance, and I am happy to join in the decision of this court holding that they are invalid and unenforceable. This decision is in harmony with the declarations contained in the Declaration of Independence which are guaranteed by the Bill of Rights and the Fourteenth Amendment to the Constitution of the United States and re-affirmed by the Charter of the United Nations . . . that all human beings have equal rights regardless of race, color or creed, and that the right to liberty and the pursuit of happiness is inalienable and may not be infringed because of race, color or creed. To say that these statutes may stand in the face of the concept of liberty and equality embraced within the ambit of the above-mentioned fundamental law is to make of that concept an empty, hollow mockery.

. . .

JUSTICE EDMONDS, concurring.

I agree with the conclusion that marriage is "something more than a civil contract subject to regulation by the State; it is a fundamental right of free men." Moreover, it is grounded in the fundamental principles of Christianity. The right to marry, therefore, is protected by the constitutional guarantee of religious freedom, and I place my concurrence in the judgment upon a broader ground than that the challenged statutes are discriminatory and irrational.

. . .

JUSTICE SHENK, with whom JUSTICE SCHAUER and JUSTICE SPENCE join, dissenting.

. . .

Our Constitution expressly provides that the free exercise of religion guaranteed "shall not be so construed as to justify practices inconsistent with the peace or safety of this State."

. . . [T]the right of the state to exercise extensive control over the marriage contract has always been recognized. The institution of matrimony is the foundation of society, and the community at large has an interest in the maintenance of its integrity and purity. . . .

. . .

In passing upon the validity of any statutory enactment the power of the courts is not unlimited. It is circumscribed by well recognized rules, some which as applicable to the case are: that all presumptions and intendments are in favor of the constitutionality of a statute; that all doubts are to be resolved in favor of and not against the validity of a statute; that before an act of a co-ordinate branch of our government can be declared invalid by the courts for the reason that it is in conflict with the Constitution, such conflict must be clear, positive and unquestionable; that in the case of any fair, reasonable doubt of its constitutionality the statute should be upheld, and the doubt be resolved in favor of the expressed will of the Legislature. . . .

. . .

On the biological phase there is authority for the conclusion that the crossing of the primary races leads gradually to retrogression and to eventual extinction of the resultant type unless it is fortified by reunion with the parent stock. . . .

. . .

. . . Here there is no lack of equal treatment. Sections 60 and 69 of our Civil Code do not discriminate against persons of either the white or Negro races. . . . Each petitioner has the right and the privilege of marrying within his or her own group. The regulation does not rest solely upon a difference in race. The question is not merely one of difference, nor of superiority or inferiority, but of consequence and result. The underlying factors that constitute justification for laws against miscegenation closely parallel those which sustain the validity of prohibitions against incest and incestuous marriages. . . . Moreover the argument based upon equal protection does not take into proper account the extensive control the state has always exercised over the marriage contract, nor of the further fact that at the very time the Constitution of the United States was being formulated miscegenation was considered inimical to the public good and was frowned upon by the colonies, and continued to be so regarded and prohibited in states having any substantial admixture of population at the time the 14th amendment was adopted. In view of this fact, and the unanimity of judicial decision sustaining such statutes, it seems impossible to believe that any constitutional guaranty was intended to prohibit this legislation. . . .

Griswold v. Connecticut, 381 U.S. 479 (1965)

Estelle Griswold, the executive director of Planned Parenthood in Connecticut, was arrested on November 10, 1961, for running a birth control clinic in New Haven. Connecticut law at that time forbade persons from "us[ing] any drug, medicinal article or instrument for the purpose of preventing conception." Griswold was charged with aiding and abetting that offense after she prescribed birth control for married couples. The trial court found her guilty and fined her $100. Griswold appealed, claiming that the Connecticut

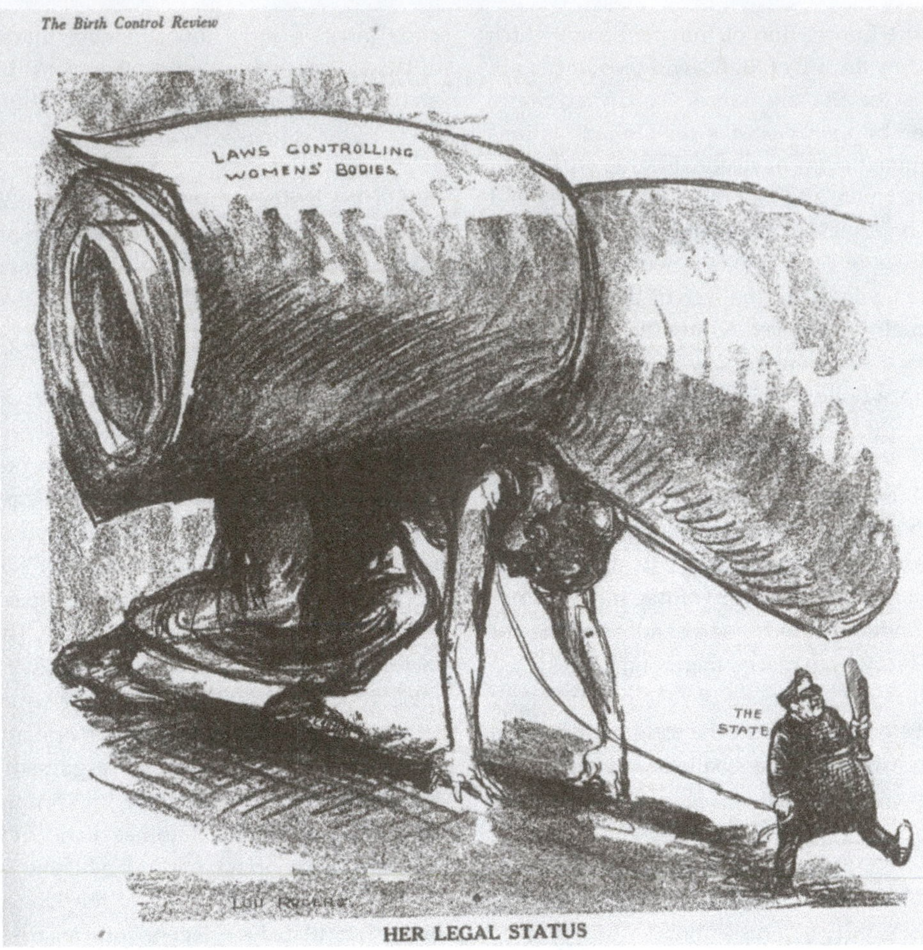

Illustration 8-2 Her Legal Status

Source: Cartoon in The Birth Control Review, May 1919. Margaret Sanger Papers. Photographer/creator: unknown. Copyright: unknown.

law unconstitutionally violated privacy rights protected by the Ninth and Fourteenth Amendments. Attorneys for the state of Connecticut insisted that the total ban on birth control helped discourage illicit sexual relations and promoted the view that procreation was the primary justification for sex. The Supreme Court of Connecticut rejected Griswold's claims. She appealed to the Supreme Court of the United States.

Griswold *culminated a long effort to have the Supreme Court make a decision on the constitutionality of birth control. Proponents of family planning targeted Connecticut because Connecticut and Massachusetts were the only states that banned all uses of birth control. The first effort failed when the Supreme Court in* Tileston v. Ullman *(1943) ruled that a doctor did not have standing to litigate the constitutional rights of his patients. The second effort failed when the Supreme Court in* Poe v. Ullman *(1961) ruled that litigants could not bring a case until after Connecticut enforced the statutory ban on birth control. Justices Harlan and Douglas issued dissents in that case, urging the justices to declare the Connecticut law unconstitutional (Justice Harlan's dissent is noted below). Finally, in 1965, Planned Parenthood designed a case that ensured standing. Because Ms. Griswold had been arrested and fined, she had standing to challenge the constitutionality of the Connecticut law. By the time* Griswold *reached the Supreme Court more than one million women were using the Pill, which had been approved by the Federal Drug Administration in 1960.*

The Supreme Court by a 7-2 vote reversed the Supreme Court of Connecticut. Justice Douglas's opinion for the court ruled that Connecticut could not constitutionally forbid married person from using birth control. What is the constitutional foundation of this right? To what extent is that foundation sound? The justices in Griswold *emphasized that the right they were protecting was a right of married couples to not be interrogated about their private use of contraception. Suppose you were asked to write a statute that would limit birth control as much as possible in light of* Griswold. *How much conduct could you restrict? Could you shut down Planned Parenthood of Connecticut by banning doctors from prescribing birth control for their patients?*

JUSTICE DOUGLAS delivered the opinion of the Court.

. . .

. . . Overtones of some arguments suggest that *Lochner v. New York* (1905) should be our guide. But we decline that invitation. . . . We do not sit as a super-legislature to determine the wisdom, need, and propriety of laws that touch economic problems, business affairs, or social conditions. This law, however, operates directly on an intimate relation of husband and wife and their physician's role in one aspect of that relation.

The association of people is not mentioned in the Constitution nor in the Bill of Rights. The right to educate a child in a school of the parents' choice—whether public or private or parochial—is also not mentioned. Nor is the right to study any particular subject or any foreign language. Yet the First Amendment has been construed to include certain of those rights.

. . .

. . . [S]pecific guarantees in the Bill of Rights have penumbras, formed by emanations from those guarantees that help give them life and substance. . . . Various guarantees create zones of privacy. The right of association contained in the penumbra of the First Amendment is one. . . . The Third Amendment in its prohibition against the quartering of soldiers "in any house" in time of peace without the consent of the owner is another facet of that privacy. The Fourth Amendment explicitly affirms the "right of the people to be secure in their persons, houses, papers, and effects, against unreasonable searches and seizures." The Fifth Amendment in its Self-Incrimination Clause enables the citizen to create a zone of privacy which government may not force him to surrender to his detriment. The Ninth Amendment provides: "The enumeration in the Constitution, of certain rights, shall not be construed to deny or disparage others retained by the people."

. . .

The present case concerns a relationship lying within the zone of privacy created by several fundamental constitutional guarantees. And it concerns a law which, in forbidding the use of contraceptives rather than regulating their manufacture or sale, seeks to achieve its goals by means having a maximum destructive impact upon that relationship. Such a law cannot stand in light of the familiar principle, so often applied by this Court, that a "governmental purpose to control or prevent activities constitutionally subject to state regulation may not be achieved by means which sweep unnecessarily broadly and thereby invade the area of protected freedoms." Would we allow the police to search the sacred precincts of marital bedrooms for telltale signs of the use of contraceptives? The very idea is repulsive to the notions of privacy surrounding the marriage relationship.

We deal with a right of privacy older than the Bill of Rights—older than our political parties, older than our school system. Marriage is a coming together for better or for worse, hopefully enduring, and intimate to the degree of being sacred. It is an association that promotes a way of life, not causes; a harmony in living, not political faiths; a bilateral loyalty, not commercial or social projects. Yet it is an association for as noble a purpose as any involved in our prior decisions.

JUSTICE GOLDBERG, whom THE CHIEF JUSTICE and JUSTICE BRENNAN join, concurring.

. . .

. . . This Court, in a series of decisions, has held that the Fourteenth Amendment absorbs and applies to the States those specifics of the first eight amendments which express fundamental personal rights. The language and history of the Ninth Amendment reveal that the Framers of the Constitution believed that there are additional fundamental rights, protected from governmental infringement, which exist alongside those fundamental rights specifically mentioned in the first eight constitutional amendments.

. . .

. . . To hold that a right so basic and fundamental and so deep-rooted in our society as the right of privacy in marriage may be infringed because that right is not guaranteed in so many words by the first eight amendments to the Constitution is to ignore the Ninth Amendment and to give it no effect whatsoever. . . .

. . . The Ninth Amendment simply shows the intent of the Constitution's authors that other fundamental personal rights should not be denied such protection or disparaged in any other way simply because they are not specifically listed in the first eight constitutional amendments. I do not see how this broadens the authority of the Court; rather it serves to support what this Court has been doing in protecting fundamental rights.

In determining which rights are fundamental, judges are not left at large to decide cases in light of their personal and private notions. Rather, they must look to the "traditions and [collective] conscience of our people" to determine whether a principle is "so rooted [there] . . . as to be ranked as fundamental." . . .

. . .

The entire fabric of the Constitution and the purposes that clearly underlie its specific guarantees demonstrate that the rights to marital privacy and to marry and raise a family are of similar order and magnitude as the fundamental rights specifically protected. Although the Constitution does not speak in so many words of the right of privacy in marriage, I cannot believe that it offers these fundamental rights no protection. The fact that no particular provision of the Constitution explicitly forbids the State from disrupting the traditional relation of the family—a relation as old and as fundamental as our entire civilization—surely does not show that the Government was meant to have the power to do so. Rather, as the Ninth Amendment expressly recognizes, there are fundamental personal rights such as this one, which are protected from abridgment by the Government though not specifically mentioned in the Constitution.

. . .

JUSTICE HARLAN, concurring in the judgment

[Justice Harlan concurred on the basis of his dissent in *Poe v. Ullman* (1961). The crucial passages of that dissent are below.]

. . .

In my view, the proper constitutional inquiry in this case is whether this Connecticut statute infringes the Due Process Clause of the Fourteenth Amendment because the enactment violates basic values "implicit in the concept of ordered liberty." . . .

. . . [A] statute making it a criminal offense for married couples to use contraceptives is an intolerable and unjustifiable invasion of privacy in the conduct of the most intimate concerns of an individual's personal life. . . .

. . .

Due process has not been reduced to any formula; its content cannot be determined by reference to any code. The best that can be said is that through the course of this Court's decisions it has represented the balance which our Nation, built upon postulates of respect for the liberty of the individual, has struck between that liberty and the demands of organized society. If the supplying of content to this Constitutional concept has of necessity been a rational process, it certainly has not been one where judges have felt free to roam where unguided speculation might take them. The balance of which I speak is the balance struck by this country, having regard to what history teaches are the traditions from which it developed as well as the traditions from which it broke. That tradition is a living thing. A decision of this Court which radically departs from it could not long survive, while a decision which builds on what has survived is likely to be sound. No formula could serve as a substitute, in this area, for judgment and restraint.

. . .

. . . [T]he very inclusion of the category of morality among state concerns indicates that society is not limited in its objects only to the physical well-being of the community, but has traditionally concerned itself with the moral soundness of its people as well. . . . The laws regarding marriage which provide both when the sexual powers may be used and the legal and societal context in which children are born and brought up, as well as laws forbidding adultery, fornication and homosexual practices which express the negative of the proposition, confining sexuality to lawful marriage, form a pattern so deeply pressed into the substance of our social life that any Constitutional doctrine in this area must build upon that basis. . . .

. . .

Precisely what is involved here is this: the State is asserting the right to enforce its moral judgment by intruding upon the most intimate details of the marital relation with the full power of the criminal law. . . . In sum, the statute allows the State to enquire into, prove and punish married people for the private use of their marital intimacy.

. . . This enactment involves what, by common understanding throughout the English-speaking world, must be granted to be a most fundamental aspect of "liberty," the privacy of the home in its most basic sense, and it is this which requires that the statute be subjected to "strict scrutiny." . . .

. . .

It is clear, of course, that this Connecticut statute does not invade the privacy of the home in the usual sense, since the invasion involved here may, and doubtless usually would, be accomplished without any physical intrusion whatever into the home. What the statute undertakes to do, however, is to create a crime which is grossly offensive to this privacy. . . .

. . .

. . . [I]f the physical curtilage of the home is protected, it is surely as a result of solicitude to protect the privacies of the life within. Certainly the safeguarding of the home does not follow merely from the sanctity of property rights. The home derives its pre-eminence as the seat of family life. . . .

Of this whole "private realm of family life" it is difficult to imagine what is more private or more intimate than a husband and wife's marital relations. . . .

. . .

Adultery, homosexuality and the like are sexual intimacies which the State forbids altogether, but the intimacy of husband and wife is necessarily an essential and accepted feature of the institution of marriage, an institution which the State not only must allow, but which always and in every age it has fostered and protected. It is one thing when the State exerts its power either to forbid extra-marital sexuality altogether, or to say who may marry, but it is quite another when, having acknowledged a marriage and the intimacies inherent in it, it undertakes to regulate by means of the criminal law the details of that intimacy.

. . .

JUSTICE WHITE, concurring in the judgment.

. . .

. . . I wholly fail to see how the ban on the use of contraceptives by married couples in any way reinforces the State's ban on illicit sexual relationships. . . .

. . . A statute limiting its prohibition on use to persons engaging in the prohibited relationship would serve the end posited by Connecticut in the same way, and with the same effectiveness, or ineffectiveness, as the broad anti-use statute under attack in this case. I find nothing in this record justifying the sweeping scope of this statute, with its telling effect on the freedoms of married persons, and therefore conclude that it deprives such persons of liberty without due process of law.

JUSTICE BLACK, with whom JUSTICE STEWART joins, dissenting.

. . .

The Court talks about a constitutional "right of privacy" as though there is some constitutional provision or provisions forbidding any law ever to be passed which might abridge the "privacy" of individuals. But there is not. There are, of course, guarantees in certain specific constitutional provisions which are designed in part to protect privacy at certain times and places with respect to certain activities. Such, for example, is the Fourth Amendment's guarantee against "unreasonable searches and seizures." But I think it belittles that Amendment to talk about it as though it protects nothing but "privacy." . . . [A] person can be just as much, if not more, irritated, annoyed and injured by an unceremonious public arrest by a policeman as he is by a seizure in the privacy of his office or home.

. . . For these reasons I get nowhere in this case by talk about a constitutional "right of privacy" as an emanation from one or more constitutional provisions. I like my privacy as well as the next one, but I am nevertheless compelled to admit that government has a right to invade it unless prohibited by some specific constitutional provision. . . .

. . .

The due process argument which my Brothers HARLAN and WHITE adopt here is based, as their opinions indicate, on the premise that this Court is vested with power to invalidate all state laws that it considers to be arbitrary, capricious, unreasonable, or oppressive, or on this Court's belief that a particular state law under scrutiny has no "rational or justifying" purpose, or is offensive to a "sense of fairness and justice." If these formulas based on "natural justice," or others which mean the same thing, are to prevail, they require judges to determine what is or is not constitutional on the basis of their own appraisal of what laws are unwise or unnecessary. The power to make such decisions is of course that of a legislative body. . . .

My Brother GOLDBERG has adopted the recent discovery that the Ninth Amendment as well as the Due Process Clause can be used by this Court as authority to strike down all state legislation which this Court thinks violates "fundamental principles of liberty and justice," or is contrary to the "traditions and [collective] conscience of our people." He also states, without proof satisfactory to me, that in making decisions on this basis judges will not consider "their personal and private notions." One may ask how they can avoid considering them. . . . That Amendment was passed, not to broaden the powers of this Court or any other department of "the General Government," but, as every student of history knows, to assure the people that the Constitution in all its provisions was intended to limit the Federal Government to the powers granted expressly or by necessary implication. . . . This fact is perhaps responsible for the peculiar phenomenon that for a period of a century and a half no serious suggestion was ever made that the Ninth Amendment, enacted to protect state powers against federal invasion, could be used as a weapon of federal power to prevent state legislatures from passing laws they consider appropriate to govern local affairs. . . .

. . .

I realize that many good and able men have eloquently spoken and written, sometimes in rhapsodical strains, about the duty of this Court to keep the Constitution in tune with the times. The idea is that the Constitution must be changed from time to time and that this Court is charged with a duty to make those changes. For myself, I must with all deference reject that philosophy. The Constitution makers knew the need for change and provided for it. Amendments suggested by the people's elected representatives can be submitted to the people or their selected agents for ratification. That method of change was good for our Fathers, and being somewhat old-fashioned I must add it is good enough for me. . . .

. . .

JUSTICE STEWART, whom JUSTICE BLACK joins, dissenting

. . . I think this is an uncommonly silly law. . . . But we are not asked in this case to say whether we think this law is unwise, or even asinine. We are asked to hold that it violates the United States Constitution. And that I cannot do.

. . .

What provision of the Constitution, then, does make this state law invalid? The Court says it is the right of privacy "created by several fundamental constitutional guarantees." With all deference, I can find no such general right of privacy in the Bill of Rights, in any other part of the Constitution, or in any case ever before decided by this Court. . . .

IV. Democratic Rights

MAJOR DEVELOPMENTS

- Increased commitment to the United States as a constitutional democracy
- Free speech protected in numerous circumstances
- Voting considered a fundamental right

"Mere legislative preferences or beliefs respecting matters of public convenience may well support regulation directed at other personal activities," Justice Owen Roberts declared in *Schneider v. State* (1939), "but be insufficient to justify such as diminishes the exercise of rights so vital to the maintenance of democratic institutions." This sentence marks the first time in American history that a Supreme Court justice in a majority opinion described the United States as a democracy. Justices during the nineteenth century routinely described the United States as a "republic." As late as 1926, in *Myers v. United States*, Chief Justice Taft spoke of "the evil genius of democracy." Constitutional liberals became democrats only in the middle of the twentieth century. Speech, voting, and citizenship rights were broadened during this transition from a constitutional republic to a constitutional democracy.

Free speech was the most important beneficiary of this democratic transition. The "freedom of speech and expression" was the first of the "essential human freedoms" that Roosevelt sought to ensure "everywhere in the world." *Thomas v. Collins* (1945) spoke of "the preferred place given in our scheme to the great, indispensable democratic freedoms secured by the First Amendment." By the time Richard Nixon took office, liberals in the national government and federal judiciary had established constitutional rights to speak in public forums, to advocate (but not incite) illegal activity, and to criticize public officials, as long as the criticisms were not reckless or intentionally false.

Voting rights became fundamental during the Great Society. Congressional majorities during the New Deal sought to make voting a fundamental constitutional right but were defeated by consistent filibusters in the Senate. The Supreme Court in *Breedlove v. Suttles* (1937) sustained poll taxes with little difficulty. The next generation of constitutional liberals was more successful. The Voting Rights Act of 1965 provided strong remedies to ensure that persons of color were able to exercise what Congress maintained was their constitutional right to vote. Chief Justice Warren in 1964 declared, "The right to vote freely for the candidate of one's choice is of the essence of a democratic society." The democratic right to vote was a right to an equal vote. Justice Black in *Wesberry v. Sanders* (1964) asserted, "To say that a vote is worth more in one district than another would . . . run counter to our fundamental ideas of democratic government."

Schneiderman v. United States (1943) made democratic commitments central to citizenship. The issue in this case was whether a professed Communist could swear to faithfully uphold the Constitution. Justice Murphy's opinion for the Court made clear that a good constitutional citizen need not be committed to any particular economic system or scheme of fundamental rights. Anyone willing to work within the democratic process to achieve any political change was sufficiently attached to constitutional principles to be an American citizen. "Whatever attitude we may individually hold toward persons and organizations that believe in or advocate extensive changes in our existing order," Murphy wrote," it should be our desire and concern at all times to uphold the right of free discussion and free thinking to which we as a people claim primary attachment."

A. Free Speech

The First Amendment occupied the center of the constitutional stage during the New Deal/Great Society Era. Justice Benjamin Cardozo, in *Palko v. Connecticut* (1937), described the freedom of speech as "the matrix, the indispensable condition, of nearly every other form of freedom." Labor unions, Jehovah's Witnesses, Nazis, African-Americans, and political radicals enjoyed far more constitutional protection than had previously been the case. Powerful forces remained committed to restricting speech, and anti-communists exercised considerable influence during the 1950s. Nevertheless, free speech enjoyed far more constitutional protection by the end of the New Deal/Great Society Era than at the beginning. By 1969 the Supreme Court had handed down decisions striking down mandatory flag salutes in schools; limiting the scope of obscenity statutes; giving protestors access to public streets and parks; permitting those protestors to freely condemn existing laws, unless they incited others to imminent violence; and forbidding libel suits by public officials, unless they could prove the publication was reckless or intentionally false.

No account of free speech during the New Deal/Great Society Era can omit the exploits of Senator Joe McCarthy, the House Un-American Affairs Committee, Roosevelt administration efforts to prosecute neo-Nazis during World War II, southern efforts to suppress the civil rights movements, and various efforts to suppress political dissent during the Vietnam War. Nevertheless, those who sought to restrict speech confronted far greater opposition than had previously been the case. During World War I and the Red Scare elected officials who sought to restrict free speech were opposed only by a few isolated politicians and fledgling political movements. McCarthy and other proponents of limited speech rights confronted powerful progressive congressmen in leadership positions, unsympathetic executive branch officials, well-funded interest groups, and liberals on the bench. The result was often pitched battles over free speech rights in which neither side fully realized its constitutional goals. By the end of the New Deal/Great Society Era these battles became a free speech rout.

During the 1960s, the federal judiciary with the full support of the national executive championed the free speech rights of civil rights protestors. This unprecedented protection included decisions striking down laws requiring the NAACP to reveal its membership to the general public, laws prohibiting certain protests, laws prohibiting NAACP attorneys from soliciting lawsuits against Jim Crow practices, and libel decisions that threatened to bankrupt the civil rights movement. The justices in *Brandenburg v. Ohio* (1969) announced that Justice Brandeis's libertarian concurrence in *Whitney v. California* (1927), which declared that government could restrict only incitement to imminent violence, was the constitutional law of the land.

Politics and law strengthened constitutional speech rights during the mid-twentieth century. The ACLU by the 1940s was a powerful, respectable organization. Many prominent New Dealers and proponents of the Great Society were either members of the ACLU or sympathized with mainstream ACLU positions. Several Roosevelt judicial appointees, most notably Wiley Rutledge and Robert Jackson, were selected in part because of their perceived commitment to free speech rights.

Justices interested in protecting free speech received assistance from the academy. Zechariah Chafee, Alexander Meiklejohn, and Thomas Emerson published exceptionally influential works championing broad protections for First Amendment freedoms. Chafee, whose first writings were published in the wake of World War I, became a tireless advocate for expression rights until his death in 1956. His *Free Speech in the United States* vigorously insisted on a special judicial obligation to protect political dissenters whose speech did not present a clear and present danger of serious harm.[40] Meiklejohn went further, claiming that the First Amendment should be taken literally. Developing a position also championed by Justices Hugo Black and William Douglas, Meiklejohn claimed that government could never regulate political expression and that the constitutional cure for bad speech was more speech.[41] In *Toward a General Theory of the First Amendment* Emerson synthesized almost forty years of free speech advocacy. Free speech could rarely, if ever, be regulated, Emerson believed, because expression rights were central to democratic government, a vital means for determining the truth about matters of public interest, a central facet of self-expression, and a far safer means for political change than revolution.[42] None of these scholars claimed to be promulgating the rules that were in force when the Bill of Rights was adopted in 1791 or when the Fourteenth Amendment was ratified in 1868. Rather, committed to a living Constitution, the free speech theorists of the New Deal/Great Society Era were interested in what standards protected expression rights under twentieth-century conditions. "That [the framers] were Blackstonians," an influential legal historian concluded, "does not mean that we cannot be Brandeisians."[43]

The justices considered free speech in many different contexts. Persons who claimed that their First Amendment rights had been violated included Jehovah's Witnesses, labor union organizers, employers, Nazis, Communists, members of the Ku Klux Klan, civil rights protestors, and opponents of the Vietnam War. When reading the materials below, consider how the justices reacted to these different claimants. To what extent do the justices and other constitutional decision makers rely on general constitutional principles or theories of judicial power? To what extent were constitutional developments influenced by the particular persons claiming free speech rights?

Jehovah's Witnesses. Many important free speech and religious liberty cases during the 1930s and 1940s concerned the rights of Jehovah's Witnesses. Members of that sect were often prosecuted after they aggressively proselytized on city streets or refused to salute the flag. The most famous cases concerning the rights of Jehovah's Witnesses involved local laws requiring public schoolchildren to salute the flag. In *Minersville School District v. Gobitis* (1940) the Supreme Court ruled that communities could require public schoolchildren to salute the flag. Three years later, in *West Virginia State Board of Education v. Barnette* (1943), the Supreme Court overruled *Gobitis*, holding that mandatory flag salutes violated constitutional free speech and religious rights.

Two other Supreme Court decisions involving Jehovah's Witnesses had enduring consequences for American law. *Lovell v. Griffin* (1938) declared unconstitutional a city ordinance that required all persons seeking to distribute literature to get a permit from the city manager. Chief Justice Hughes's unanimous opinion emphasized that the city manager was not guided by any legal standards and condemned official censorship. He wrote,

> Whatever the motive which induced its adoption, its character is such that it strikes at the very foundation of the freedom of the press by subjecting it to license and censorship. The struggle for the freedom of the press was primarily directed against the power of the licensor.

Chaplinsky v. New Hampshire (1942) declared that certain categories of speech were not constitutionally protected, most notably "fighting words." Justice Murphy stated,

> There are certain well-defined and narrowly limited classes of speech, the prevention and punishment of which has never been thought to raise any Constitutional problem. These include the lewd and obscene, the profane, the libelous, and the insulting or "fighting" words—those which by their very utterance inflict injury or tend to incite an immediate breach of the peace. It has been well observed that

40. Zechariah Chafee, Jr., *Free Speech in the United States* (Cambridge, MA: Harvard University Press, 1941).

41. Alexander Meiklejohn, *Free Speech and Its Relation to Self-Government* (New York: Harper Brothers, 1948).

42. Thomas Irwin Emerson, *Toward a General Theory of the First Amendment* (New York: Random House, 1966).

43. Leonard W. Levy, *Legacy of Suppression: Freedom of Speech and Press in Early American History* (Cambridge, MA: Harvard University Press, 1960), 309.

> such utterances are no essential part of any exposition of ideas, and are of such slight social value as a step to truth that any benefit that may be derived from them is clearly outweighed by the social interest in order and morality.

Later New Deal/Great Society decisions narrowed each category of "unprotected" speech.

Labor and Management. Much of Roosevelt's New Deal was premised on stabilizing industrial production by requiring owners and unions to commit to a regime of collective bargaining. Company officials and labor leaders worked out employment agreements and then worked together to ensure cooperation with the terms of the agreement. Given the important role played by labor unions in this system, the decision of justices during the New Deal to side with labor in the one major case in which free speech rights conflicted with the right of workers to organize may not be surprising. The liberal majority in *Associated Press v. National Labor Relations Board* (1937) brushed aside free speech issues when ruling that the Associated Press could not fire editorial workers who belonged to a union. Justice Roberts stated,

> The order of the Board in nowise circumscribes the full freedom and liberty of the petitioner to publish the news as it desires it published or to enforce policies of its own choosing with respect to the editing and rewriting of news for publication, and the petitioner is free at any time to discharge Watson or any editorial employee who fails to comply with the policies it may adopt.

The four most conservative justices on the Court objected vigorously. Justice Sutherland's dissent insisted, "It would seem to be an exercise of only reasonable prudence for an association engaged in part

Illustration 8-3 Elementary Schoolchildren Saluting the Flag, March 1943

Elementary school children starting the day by saluting the flag, March 1943, Rochester, New York. The hand-over-heart pledge style in the United States was not standardized until after World War II.

Source: Library of Congress Prints and Photographs Division Washington, D.C. 20540

in supplying the public with fair and accurate factual information with respect to the contests between labor and capital to see that those whose activities include that service are free from either extreme sympathy or extreme prejudice one way or the other."

Liberals during the New Deal were more protective of speech by union members and organizers. In *Hague v. Committee for Industrial Organization* (1939) the Supreme Court blocked Jersey City Mayor Frank Hague's efforts to prevent unions from holding local meetings. Hague's efforts included permit requirements for parades and prohibitions on distributing handbills. The justices declared these actions unconstitutional. Justice Roberts's majority opinion stated:

> Wherever the title of streets and parks may rest, they have immemorially been held in trust for the use of the public and, time out of mind, have been used for purposes of assembly, communicating thoughts between citizens, and discussing public questions. Such use of the streets and public places has, from ancient times, been a part of the privileges, immunities, rights, and liberties of citizens. The privilege of a citizen of the United States to use the streets and parks for communication of views on national questions may be regulated in the interest of all; it is not absolute, but relative, and must be exercised in subordination to the general comfort and convenience, and in consonance with peace and good order; but it must not, in the guise of regulation, be abridged or denied.

Hague established what is now known as the "public forum" doctrine, which provides that persons have a constitutional right to speak on public streets, in public parks, and in other places that have been traditionally been held open for expression.

Two other important decisions protected the speech rights of unions. *Thornhill v. Alabama* (1940) made clear that union members had a constitutional right to picket. When striking down an Alabama statute that banned picketing Justice Murphy asserted, "The dissemination of information concerning the facts of a labor dispute must be regarded as within that area of free discussion that is guaranteed by the Constitution." *Thomas v. Collins* (1945) protected the right of union organizers against state laws that required them to obtain a special license before they could recruit union members. Justice Rutledge's majority opinion asserted, "The right either of workmen or of unions . . . to assemble and discuss their own affairs is as fully protected by the Constitution as the right of businessmen, farmers, educators, political party members or others to assemble and discuss their affairs and to enlist the support of others."

World War II. New Deal liberals were remarkably receptive during World War II to the civil liberties of persons who sympathized with the Nazi cause in word but not in deed. Roosevelt sought to suppress domestic Nazis, but Justice Department prosecutions were far less frequent or enthusiastic than similar prosecutions during World War I. Federal courts were havens of speech protection. Six of the seven convictions that reached the Supreme Court were reversed. Each reversal was on statutory grounds. Nevertheless, the justices made clear that they would be far less willing to find Nazi activities illegal under federal law than courts had been during and immediately after World War I. "Men are not subject to criminal punishment because their conduct offends our patriotic emotions or thwarts a general purpose sought to be effected by specific commands which they have not disobeyed," the majority opinion in *Viereck v. United States* (1943) declared. The justices in *Keegan v. United States* (1945) ruled that persons could not be convicted of obstructing the draft for counseling others that the draft was unconstitutional, a claim nearly identical to assertions that sent Charles Schenck to jail in 1918. Justice Murphy in *Hartzel v. United States* (1944) cited Justice Holmes's dissent in *Abrams v. United States* (1919) as authority for interpreting federal law as requiring proof of a specific intent to interfere with military recruitment. Pamphlets that "depict[ed] the war as a gross betrayal of America, denounce[d] our English Allies and the Jews and assail[ed] in reckless terms the integrity and patriotism of the President of the United States," under this standard, were "not enough by [them]self to warrant a finding of criminal intent."

Communists. The liberalism of the New Deal/Great Society Era was substantially tempered by powerful efforts to suppress communism and perceived fellow travelers. The House of Representatives in 1938 established the House Un-American Activities Committee and authorized members to investigate

> (1) the extent, character, and objects of un-American propaganda activities in the United States, (2) the diffusion within the United States of subversive and un-American propaganda that is instigated from foreign countries or of a domestic origin and attacks the principle of the form of government guaranteed by our Constitution, and (3) all other questions in

relation thereto that would aid Congress in any necessary remedial legislation.[44]

During the late 1940s and early 1950s Senator Joseph McCarthy of Wisconsin and his political allies claimed that Communist spies and supporters had successfully infiltrated the federal government.

Congress passed numerous measures designed to alleviate the perceived Communist threat. The most important were the Smith Act of 1940 and the Internal Security Act of 1950. The Smith Act declared,

It shall be unlawful for any person—

(1) to knowingly or willfully advocate, abet, advise, or teach the duty, necessity, desirability, or propriety of overthrowing or destroying any government of the United States by force or violence, or by the assassination of any officer of any such government;

(2) with the intent to cause the overthrow or destruction of any government in the United States, to print, publish, edit, issue, circulate, sell, distribute, or publicly display any written or printed matter advocating, advising, or teaching the duty, necessity, desirability, or propriety of overthrowing or destroying any government in the United States by force or violence;

Shall be fined under this title or imprisoned not

(3) to organize or help to organize any society, group, or assembly of persons who teach, advocate, or encourage the overthrow or destruction of any government in the United States by force or violence; or to be or become a member of, or affiliate with, any such society, group, or assembly of persons, knowing the purposes thereof.[45]

The Internal Security Act, sometimes known as the McCarran Act, required all persons who were members of Communist groups or Communist "front organizations" to register with the national government as foreign agents and prohibited "any person knowingly to combine, conspire, or agree with any other person to perform any act which would substantially contribute to the establishment within the United States of a totalitarian dictatorship, the direction and control of which is to be vested in, or exercised by or under the domination or control of, any foreign government."[46]

44. 83 *Congressional Record*, 75th Cong., 3rd Sess. (1938), 7568.

45. 55 U.S. Stat. 670, 671 (1940).

46. 64 U.S. Stat. 987, 991 (1950).

The Supreme Court sustained the main anti-communist measures of the 1940s and 1950s but nibbled at the edges to limit prosecution of lesser Communist figures. *Dennis v. United States* (1951) affirmed convictions obtained under the Smith Act. *Communist Party of the United States v. Subversive Activities Control Board* (1961) sustained the Internal Security Act. Nevertheless, liberals on the court often found means for restricting government efforts to investigate and prosecute suspected Communists. *Yates v. United States* (1957) reversed the convictions of fourteen defendants under the Smith Act because the federal government failed to charge them with incitement to illegal action. *Pennsylvania v. Nelson* (1956) declared that the Smith Act and other federal laws preempted all state laws aimed at restricting communist advocacy.

The Civil Rights Movement. The civil rights movement sought and gained new free speech protections. Many southern communities sought to restrict African-American protests by making traditional use of longstanding practices that permitted government officials to identify members of political organizations, forbid lawyers from soliciting clients, and limit the access speakers enjoyed to public property. In a series of decisions, the Supreme Court declared such actions unconstitutional.

- *NAACP v. Alabama* (1958) forbade states from obtaining the names and addresses of NAACP members.
- *NAACP v. Button* (1963) declared that civil rights lawyers had a constitutional right to solicit clients for cases attacking the constitutionality of racial segregation.
- The Supreme Court in numerous cases found First Amendment or due process flaws with state efforts to convict civil rights protestors of disturbing the peace and related offenses.
- *New York Times Co. v. Sullivan* (1964) struck down a state libel award that might have bankrupted a major civil rights organization and curtailed news coverage of civil rights protests.

These decisions may have played as important a role as *Brown v. Board of Education* (1954) in dismantling Jim Crow. The civil rights movement relied on mass protests to change northern opinion on racial issues. By consistently protecting the rights of civil rights protestors, federal courts facilitated Martin Luther King, Jr.'s efforts to build the necessary national support for passing such laws as the Civil Rights Act of 1964 and the Voting Rights Act of 1965.

The Vietnam Era. The Supreme Court was remarkably protective of speech during the Vietnam Era, with the notable exception of *United States v. O'Brien* (1967). That case held that Congress could constitutionally forbid persons from burning draft cards on the somewhat questionable ground that the prohibition on burning draft cards was not aimed at speech (and the less dubious ground that federal justices should not make decisions on the basis of legislative motivations). The justices were more protective of speech in *Bond v. Floyd* (1966). The Georgia state legislature had refused to seat Julian Bond, a prominent civil rights activist, on the ground that Bond had publicly praised persons who refused to be drafted into the Army. Chief Justice Warren's opinion condemning that refusal asserted, "The manifest function of the First Amendment in a representative government requires that legislators be given the widest latitude to express their views on issues of policy." In *Tinker v. Des Moines Independent School District* (1969) the justices ruled that students who expressed their opposition to the Vietnam War by wearing a black armband could not be suspended from school in the absence of evidence that their protest disrupted the classroom. "When he is in the cafeteria, or on the playing field, or on the campus during the authorized hours, he may express his opinions, even on controversial subjects like the conflict in Vietnam," Justice Fortas's majority opinion contended, "if he does so without 'materially and substantially interfer(ing) with the requirements of appropriate discipline in the operation of the school' and without colliding with the rights of others."

West Virginia State Board of Education v. Barnette, 319 U.S. 624 (1943)

Walter Barnette was a Jehovah's Witness and the father of several children attending public schools in Charleston, West Virginia. On January 9, 1942, West Virginia mandated that all public children salute the flag of the United States during the school day. Barnette maintained that this decree violated his and his children's free speech and free exercise rights. Their faith regarded saluting the flag of any country as akin to worshiping false gods or idols. A federal district court agreed and ordered the West Virginia State Board of Education not to enforce the mandatory flag salute. The Board of Education appealed to the Supreme Court of the United States.

By an 8-1 vote in Minersville School District v. Gobitis *(1940) the Supreme Court had previously sustained a local policy mandating that public school students salute the flag. Justice Frankfurter's majority opinion in that case declared,*

> *We are dealing with an interest inferior to none in the hierarchy of legal values. National unity is the basis of national security. To deny the legislature the right to select appropriate means for its attainment presents a totally different order of problem from that of the propriety of subordinating the possible ugliness of littered streets to the free expression of opinion through distribution of handbills.*

Justice Stone was the lone dissenter.

Gobitis *provoked two intense reactions. The first was a mass assault on Jehovah's Witnesses. Members of that sect who refused to salute the flag found their children expelled from school, their property vandalized, and themselves victims of mob violence. The second was an elite assault on the Supreme Court. Prominent jurists and journalists excoriated the justices for failing to declare a constitutional right to refrain from saluting the flag. Two years after* Gobitis *was decided Justices Hugo Black, William O. Douglas, and Frank Murphy publicly confessed error in* Jones v. Opelika *(1942), writing, "We think this is an appropriate occasion to state that we now believe [*Gobitis*] was wrong decided," and "Our democratic form of government . . . has a high responsibility to accommodate itself to the religious views of minorities." The two justices appointed to the Supreme Court between 1940 and 1943, Robert Jackson and Wiley Rutledge, were chosen in part because they supported the civil rights and liberties of Jehovah's Witnesses.*

Gobitis *may have been overruled legislatively or by executive degree before the justices decided* Barnette. *Disturbed that the existing pledge of allegiance ceremony bore too close a resemblance to the Nazi salute, Congress in 1942 passed a new law regulating public displays of loyalty. One provision in the bill stated, "Citizens will always show full respect to the flag when the pledge is given merely by standing at attention." The executive branch interpreted this law as preempting all state and local decrees requiring students to salute the flag and recite the pledge of allegiance. "State and local regulations demanding a different standard of performance," Justice Department lawyers declared, "must give way entirely, or at least be made to conform." After 1942 Roosevelt administration officials mandated that "a school board order respecting flag salute exercises should not now be permitted to exact more of the pupil with religious scruples against the flag salute than that he should stand at attention while the exercise is being conducted."*[47]

The Supreme Court in Barnette *overruled* Gobitis *by a 6-3 vote. Justice Jackson's majority opinion held that persons could not be constitutionally compelled to salute the flag. What explains this support for free speech rights? Jehovah's Witnesses were not a politically powerful group. Did the Jewish and Catholic members of the New Deal coalition believe that strong protections for the speech and religious rights of other religious minorities would establish precedents that would protect them in the future? Did New Dealers value free speech and religious freedom even though they believed it unlikely that their religious freedom or speech rights would be threatened in the future? Justice Jackson's opinion in* Barnette *famously declares, "One's right to life, liberty, and property, to free speech, a free press, freedom of worship and assembly, and other fundamental rights may not be submitted to vote; they depend on the outcome of no elections." Is this correct? Suppose that Woodrow Wilson (or Abraham Lincoln) had been president in 1940 and had previously appointed a majority of the sitting Supreme Court justices. Would the Court have produced the same result? Is Justice Frankfurter right that judicial officials in a democracy should not second-guess decisions made by elected officials? Is Justice Jackson correct when he maintains that justices in a democracy must prevent political coercion by elected officials?*

JUSTICE JACKSON delivered the opinion of the Court.

. . .

. . . [C]ensorship or suppression of expression of opinion is tolerated by our Constitution only when the expression presents a clear and present danger of action of a kind the State is empowered to prevent and punish. It would seem that involuntary affirmation could be commanded only on even more immediate and urgent grounds than silence. But here the power of compulsion is invoked without any allegation that remaining passive during a flag salute ritual creates a clear and present danger that would justify an effort even to muffle expression. To sustain the compulsory flag salute we are required to say that a Bill of Rights which guards the individual's right to speak his own mind, left it open to public authorities to compel him to utter what is not in his mind.

. . .

The very purpose of a Bill of Rights was to withdraw certain subjects from the vicissitudes of political controversy, to place them beyond the reach of majorities and officials and to establish them as legal principles to be applied by the courts. One's right to life, liberty, and property, to free speech, a free press, freedom of worship and assembly, and other fundamental rights may not be submitted to vote; they depend on the outcome of no elections. . . . The right of a State to regulate, for example, a public utility may well include, so far as the due process test is concerned, power to impose all of the restrictions which a legislature may have a "rational basis" for adopting. But freedoms of speech and of press, of assembly, and of worship may not be infringed on such slender grounds. They are susceptible of restriction only to prevent grave and immediate danger to interests which the state may lawfully protect. . . .

. . .

Struggles to coerce uniformity of sentiment in support of some end thought essential to their time and country have been waged by many good as well as by evil men. Nationalism is a relatively recent phenomenon but at other times and places the ends have been racial or territorial security, support of a dynasty or regime, and particular plans for saving souls. As first and moderate methods to attain unity have failed, those bent on its accomplishment must resort to an ever-increasing severity. As governmental pressure toward unity becomes greater, so strife becomes more bitter as to whose unity it shall be. Probably no deeper division of our people could proceed from any provocation than from finding it necessary to choose what doctrine and whose program public educational officials shall compel youth to unite in embracing. Ultimate futility of such attempts to compel coherence is the lesson of every such effort from the Roman drive to stamp out Christianity as a disturber of its pagan unity, the Inquisition, as a means to religious and dynastic unity, the Siberian exiles as a means to Russian unity, down to the fast failing efforts of our present totalitarian enemies. Those who begin coercive elimination of dissent soon find themselves exterminating dissenters. Compulsory unification of opinion achieves only the unanimity of the graveyard.

. . .

47. This introduction relies heavily on Shawn Francis Peters, *Judging Jehovah's Witnesses: Religious Persecution and the Dawn of the Rights Revolution* (Lawrence: University Press of Kansas, 2000).

The case is made difficult not because the principles of its decision are obscure but because the flag involved is our own. Nevertheless, we apply the limitations of the Constitution with no fear that freedom to be intellectually and spiritually diverse or even contrary will disintegrate the social organization. To believe that patriotism will not flourish if patriotic ceremonies are voluntary and spontaneous instead of a compulsory routine is to make an unflattering estimate of the appeal of our institutions to free minds. We can have intellectual individualism and the rich cultural diversities that we owe to exceptional minds only at the price of occasional eccentricity and abnormal attitudes. When they are so harmless to others or to the State as those we deal with here, the price is not too great. But freedom to differ is not limited to things that do not matter much. That would be a mere shadow of freedom. The test of its substance is the right to differ as to things that touch the heart of the existing order.

If there is any fixed star in our constitutional constellation, it is that no official, high or petty, can prescribe what shall be orthodox in politics, nationalism, religion, or other matters of opinion or force citizens to confess by word or act their faith therein. If there are any circumstances which permit an exception, they do not now occur to us.

. . .

The decision of this Court in *Minersville School District v. Gobitis* (1940) [is] overruled.

JUSTICE ROBERTS and JUSTICE REED adhere to the views expressed by the Court in *Minersville School District v. Gobitis*. . . .

JUSTICE BLACK and JUSTICE DOUGLAS, concurring. . . .

JUSTICE MURPHY, concurring. . . .

JUSTICE FRANKFURTER, dissenting.

One who belongs to the most vilified and persecuted minority in history[48] is not likely to be insensible to the freedoms guaranteed by our Constitution. Were my purely personal attitude relevant I should wholeheartedly associate myself with the general libertarian views in the Court's opinion, representing as they do the thought and action of a lifetime. But as judges we are neither Jew nor Gentile, neither Catholic nor agnostic. We owe equal attachment to the Constitution and are equally bound by our judicial obligations whether we derive our citizenship from the earliest or the latest immigrants to these shores. As a member of this Court I am not justified in writing my private notions of policy into the Constitution, no matter how deeply I may cherish them or how mischievous I may deem their disregard. The duty of a judge who must decide which of two claims before the Court shall prevail, that of a State to enact and enforce laws within its general competence or that of an individual to refuse obedience because of the demands of his conscience, is not that of the ordinary person. It can never be emphasized too much that one's own opinion about the wisdom or evil of a law should be excluded altogether when one is doing one's duty on the bench. The only opinion of our own even looking in that direction that is material is our opinion whether legislators could in reason have enacted such a law. In the light of all the circumstances, including the history of this question in this Court, it would require more daring than I possess to deny that reasonable legislators could have taken the action which is before us for review. . . . I cannot bring my mind to believe that the "liberty" secured by the Due Process Clause gives this Court authority to deny to the State of West Virginia the attainment of that which we all recognize as a legitimate legislative end, namely, the promotion of good citizenship, by employment of the means here chosen.

. . .

. . . The Constitution does not give us greater veto power when dealing with one phase of "liberty" than with another. . . . Our power does not vary according to the particular provision of the Bill of Rights which is invoked. The right not to have property taken without just compensation has, so far as the scope of judicial power is concerned, the same constitutional dignity as the right to be protected against unreasonable searches and seizures, and the latter has no less claim than freedom of the press or freedom of speech or religious freedom. . . .

. . .

We are told that a flag salute is a doubtful substitute for adequate understanding of our institutions. The states that require such a school exercise do not have to justify it as the only means for promoting good citizenship in children, but merely as one of diverse

48. Justice Frankfurter was Jewish.

means for accomplishing a worthy end. We may deem it a foolish measure, but the point is that this Court is not the organ of government to resolve doubts as to whether it will fulfill its purpose. Only if there be no doubt that any reasonable mind could entertain can we deny to the states the right to resolve doubts their way and not ours.

...

One's conception of the Constitution cannot be severed from one's conception of a judge's function in applying it. The Court has no reason for existence if it merely reflects the pressures of the day. Our system is built on the faith that men set apart for this special function, freed from the influences of immediacy and from the deflections of worldly ambition, will become able to take a view of longer range than the period of responsibility entrusted to Congress and legislatures. We are dealing with matters as to which legislators and voters have conflicting views. Are we as judges to impose our strong convictions on where wisdom lies? That which three years ago had seemed to five successive Courts to lie within permissible areas of legislation is now outlawed by the deciding shift of opinion of two Justices. What reason is there to believe that they or their successors may not have another view a few years hence? . . . Of course, judicial opinions, even as to questions of constitutionality, are not immutable. As has been true in the past, the Court will from time to time reverse its position. But I believe that never before these Jehovah's Witnesses cases (except for minor deviations subsequently retraced) has this Court overruled decisions so as to restrict the powers of democratic government. Always heretofore, it has withdrawn narrow views of legislative authority so as to authorize what formerly it had denied.

...

Of course patriotism cannot be enforced by the flag salute. But neither can the liberal spirit be enforced by judicial invalidation of illiberal legislation. Our constant preoccupation with the constitutionality of legislation rather than with its wisdom tends to preoccupation of the American mind with a false value. The tendency of focusing attention on constitutionality is to make constitutionality synonymous with wisdom, to regard a law as all right if it is constitutional. Such an attitude is a great enemy of liberalism. Particularly in legislation affecting freedom of thought and freedom of speech much which should offend a free-spirited society is constitutional. Reliance for the most precious interests of civilization, therefore, must be found outside of their vindication in courts of law. Only a persistent positive translation of the faith of a free society into the convictions and habits and actions of a community is the ultimate reliance against unabated temptations to fetter the human spirit.

The Internal Security Act (1950)

The Internal Security Act (ISA) of 1950 sought to root out all Communists in the federal government and defense industry, as well as remove perceived loopholes in previous anti-communist measures. Proponents insisted that the measure constitutionally enabled the federal government to identify and arrest Communists who, aware of existing laws, did not openly advocate the overthrow of the national government. Opponents insisted that the measure was unnecessary and inconsistent with constitutional rights. After three years of debate the ISA passed both houses of Congress in 1950. President Truman vetoed the bill, but that veto was overridden by overwhelming margins in both the Senate and the House of Representatives.

Both Senator Patrick McCarran and President Truman agreed that Communist leaders were constitutionally convicted under the Smith Act. Is Senator McCarran correct that Communists might find a way of avoiding these decisions and therefore extra precautions are needed? Is President Truman correct that the existing law was more than sufficient? What, in your judgment, were the risks involved in applying the ISA to Communist-front organizations? Assume that Senator McCarran was correct that such organizations were prepared to do the will of the Communist Party. If you believed that assertion, would you support the ISA?

The Supreme Court in Communist Party of the United States v. Subversive Activities Control Board *(1961) sustained the registration portions of the ISA by a 5-4 margin. Justice Frankfurter's majority opinion emphasized the judicial obligation to defer to congressional fact-finding.*

Individual liberties fundamental to American institutions are not to be destroyed under pretext of preserving those institutions, even from the gravest external dangers. But where the problems of accommodating the exigencies of self-preservation and the values of liberty are as complex and intricate as they are in the situation described in the findings . . . of the Subversive Activities Control Act—when existing government is menaced by a world-wide integrated movement which employs every combination of possible means, peaceful and violent, domestic and foreign, overt and clandestine, to destroy the government itself—the legislative judgment as to how that threat may best be met consistently with the safeguarding of persons' freedom is not to be set aside merely because the judgment of judges would, in the first instance, have chosen other methods. Especially where Congress, in seeking to reconcile competing and urgently demanding values within our social institutions, legislates not to prohibit individuals from organizing for the effectuation of ends found to be menacing to the very existence of those institutions, but only to prescribe the conditions under which such organization is permitted, the legislative determination must be respected.

Patrick A. McCarran, The Internal Security Act of 1950 (1951)[49]

. . .

The Communist party of the United States constitutes a sizeable army dedicated to trickery, deceit, espionage, sabotage, and terrorism; but it must be pointed out that the strength of the Communist fifth column cannot be measured merely by the number of party members. J. Edgar Hoover, Chief of the Federal Bureau of Investigation, recently testified before a congressional subcommittee:

> Even though there are only 54,174 members in the party, the fact remains that the party leaders themselves boast that for every party member there are 10 others who follow the party line and who are ready, willing, and able to do the party's work. In other words, there is a potential fifth column of 540,000 people dedicated to this philosophy.

American communism is not, however, a home-grown product, but is a weed which has been deliberately transplanted in this country by foreign agents. It has been thoroughly established that this fifth column is a part of a world-wide network under the control and direction of the Kremlin, and that it stands ready to do the do the Kremlin's bidding.

. . . Communist organizations, together with certain officers and members thereof, should be required to register, and to identify their literature and broadcasts. We should make unlawful those overt acts (not thoughts or ideas) of the Communists which are designed to overthrow the Government of the United States. We must sever the pipe-line of infiltration of foreign agents who are the life blood of the Communist conspiracy in this country; and we must provide a procedure for detaining all persons, Communist as well as other subversives, who are likely to commit espionage or sabotage in time of war or other emergency. All our attacks on the Communist conspiracy must be in keeping with our constitutional procedures. We must not burn down the house to destroy the rats. . . .

. . .

In order to understand the need for [the criminal provisions], some reference should be made to the inadequacies of prior law. The Alien Registration Act of 1940 made it a crime to advocate the overthrow of the Government of the United States by force and violence. Although there is no doubt but that a basic principle of the Communist conspiracy in this country involves the use of force and violence, in order to evade this statute the present line of the Communist party is to avoid, wherever possible, the open advocacy of force and violence. It should be likewise pointed out that in the Smith Act under which the eleven Communist leaders were convicted in New York, there is an essential element of advocating the overthrow of the Government by force and violence. In view of this conviction, it is obvious that greater emphasis will henceforth by placed on an avoidance of any semblance of open advocacy of force and violence. Thus, it would be increasingly difficult to establish in particular cases the violation of that law.

. . .

A common error of zealous but misguided defenders of "constitutional rights" is their failure to perceive that while the freedoms guaranteed by the First Amendment . . . are fundamental, they are not in their nature absolute. This error is not confined to the guileless. There are many who maliciously seek to cloak their activities, directed against the general interest, with some immunity claimed to be derived from the First Amendment. The Communists are most prominent among these, and their bogus piety explains much of the opposition to the Act. . . .

Harry Truman, Veto of the Internal Security Bill (1950)

I return herewith, without my approval, H.R. 9490, the proposed "Internal Security Act of 1950."

. . .

49. Excerpted from Patrick A. McCarran, "The Internal Security Act of 1950," *University of Pittsburgh Law Review* 12 (1951): 481.

There would be no serious problem if the bill required proof that an organization was controlled and financed by the Communist Party before it could be classified as a communist-front organization. However, recognizing the difficulty of proving those matters, the bill would permit such a determination to be based solely upon "the extent to which the positions taken or advanced by it from time to time on matters of policy do not deviate from those" of the communist movement.

This provision could easily be used to classify as a communist-front organization any organization which is advocating a single policy or objective which is also being urged by the Communist Party or by a communist foreign government. In fact, this may be the intended result, since the bill defines "organization" to include "a group of persons . . . permanently or temporarily associated together for joint action on any subject or subjects." Thus, an organization which advocates low-cost housing for sincere humanitarian reasons might be classified as a communist-front organization because the communists regularly exploit slum conditions as one of their fifth-column techniques.

. . .

The basic error of these sections is that they move in the direction of suppressing opinion and belief. This would be a very dangerous course to take, not because we have any sympathy for communist opinions, but because any governmental stifling of the free expression of opinion is a long step toward totalitarianism.

There is no more fundamental axiom of American freedom than the familiar statement: In a free country, we punish men for the crimes they commit, but never for the opinions they have. And the reason this is so fundamental to freedom is not, as many suppose, that it protects the few unorthodox from suppression by the majority. To permit freedom of expression is primarily for the benefit of the majority, because it protects criticism, and criticism leads to progress.

. . .

And what kind of effect would these provisions have on the normal expression of political views? Obviously, if this law were on the statute books, the part of prudence would be to avoid saying anything that might be construed by someone as not deviating sufficiently from the current communist propaganda line. And since no one could be sure in advance what views were safe to express, the inevitable tendency would be to express no views on controversial subjects.

. . .

We need not fear the expression of ideas—we do need to fear their suppression.

Our position in the vanguard of freedom rests largely on our demonstration that the free expression of opinion, coupled with government by popular consent, leads to national strength and human advancement. Let us not, in cowering and foolish fear, throw away the ideals which are the fundamental basis of our free society. . . .

Dennis v. United States, 341 U.S. 494 (1951)

Eugene Dennis was the general secretary of the American Communist Party. In 1948 he and ten other party leaders were indicted for violating the Smith Act of 1940. They were charged with a conspiracy to

> *organize as the Communist Party of the United States, a society, group, and assembly of persons who teach and advocate the overthrow and destruction of the Government of the United States by force and violence, and knowingly and willfully to advocate and teach the duty and necessity of overthrowing and destroying the Government of the United States.*

After a trial marked by dubious behavior on the part of counsel for both sides and the trial judge, Dennis and nine of his peers were sentenced to five years in prison. (Additionally, every lawyer on the defense team was cited for contempt.) After Dennis's appeal was denied by the Court of Appeals for the District of Columbia Circuit he appealed to the Supreme Court of the United States.

The Supreme Court ruled by a 7-2 vote that Dennis was constitutionally convicted. Chief Justice Vinson's plurality opinion claimed that Dennis's activities presented a "clear and present danger." How do the various judicial opinions in Dennis *interpret the clear and present danger test? Which interpretation of the test do you believe is correct? Is Justice Jackson correct to note that the clear and present danger test is best applied to isolated speakers and that Communist Party leaders are best understood as criminal conspirators? Is Justice Douglas correct that the only conspiracy that occurred was an effort to persuade Americans to believe something? What evidence would you require before convicting the defendants in this case?*

CHIEF JUSTICE VINSON announced the judgment of the Court and an opinion in which JUSTICE REED, JUSTICE BURTON and JUSTICE MINTON join.

. . .

That it is within the power of the Congress to protect the Government of the United States from armed rebellion is a proposition which requires little discussion. Whatever theoretical merit there may be to the argument that there is a "right" to rebellion against dictatorial governments is without force where the existing structure of the government provides for peaceful and orderly change. We reject any principle of governmental helplessness in the face of preparation for revolution, which principle, carried to its logical conclusion, must lead to anarchy. No one could conceive that it is not within the power of Congress to prohibit acts intended to overthrow the Government by force and violence. The question with which we are concerned here is not whether Congress has such power, but whether the means which it has employed conflict with the First . . . Amendment . . . to the Constitution.

. . .

The . . . Smith Act . . . is directed at advocacy, not discussion. Thus, the trial judge properly charged the jury that they could not convict if they found that petitioners did "no more than pursue peaceful studies and discussions or teaching and advocacy in the realm of ideas." . . . Congress did not intend to eradicate the free discussion of political theories, to destroy the traditional rights of Americans to discuss and evaluate ideas without fear of governmental sanction. Rather Congress was concerned with the very kind of activity in which the evidence showed these petitioners engaged.

. . .

Although no case subsequent to *Whitney* [*v. California* (1927)] and *Gitlow* [*v. New York* (1925)] has expressly overruled the majority opinions in those cases, there is little doubt that subsequent opinions have inclined toward the Holmes-Brandeis rationale. . . . But . . . neither Justice Holmes nor Justice Brandeis ever envisioned that a shorthand phrase ["clear and present danger"] should be crystallized into a rigid rule to be applied inflexibly without regard to the circumstances of each case. Speech is not an absolute, above and beyond control by the legislature when its judgment, subject to review here, is that certain kinds of speech are so undesirable as to warrant criminal sanction. Nothing is more certain in modern society than the principle that there are no absolutes, that a name, a phrase, a standard has meaning only when associated with the considerations which gave birth to the nomenclature. . . . To those who would paralyze our Government in the face of impending threat by encasing it in a semantic straitjacket we must reply that all concepts are relative.

. . .

Obviously, the words cannot mean that before the Government may act, it must wait until the putsch is about to be executed, the plans have been laid and the signal is awaited. If Government is aware that a group aiming at its overthrow is attempting to indoctrinate its members and to commit them to a course whereby they will strike when the leaders feel the circumstances permit, action by the Government is required. The argument that there is no need for Government to concern itself, for Government is strong, it possesses ample powers to put down a rebellion, it may defeat the revolution with ease needs no answer. . . . Certainly an attempt to overthrow the Government by force, even though doomed from the outset because of inadequate numbers of power of the revolutionists, is a sufficient evil for Congress to prevent. The damage which such attempts create both physically and politically to a nation makes it impossible to measure the validity in terms of the probability of success, or the immediacy of a successful attempt. . . .

The situation with which Justices Holmes and Brandeis were concerned in *Gitlow* was a comparatively isolated event, bearing little relation in their minds to any substantial threat to the safety of the community. . . . They were not confronted with any situation comparable to the instant one—the development of an apparatus designed and dedicated to the overthrow of the Government, in the context of world crisis after crisis.

Chief Judge Learned Hand, writing for the majority below, interpreted the phrase as follows: "In each case [courts] must ask whether the gravity of the 'evil,' discounted by its improbability, justifies such invasion of free speech as is necessary to avoid the danger." . . . We adopt this statement of the rule. As articulated by Chief Judge Hand, it is as succinct and inclusive as any other we might devise at this time. It takes into consideration those factors which we deem relevant, and relates their significances. More we cannot expect from words.

. . .

. . . Petitioners intended to overthrow the Government of the United States as speedily as the circumstances would permit. Their conspiracy to organize the Communist Party and to teach and advocate the overthrow of the Government of the United States by force and violence created a "clear and present danger" of an attempt to overthrow the Government by force and violence. They were properly and constitutionally convicted for violation of the Smith Act. . . .

JUSTICE CLARK took no part in the consideration or decision of this case.

JUSTICE FRANKFURTER, concurring in affirmance of the judgment.

. . .

. . . The demands of free speech in a democratic society as well as the interest in national security are better served by candid and informed weighing of the competing interests, within the confines of the judicial process, than by announcing dogmas too inflexible for the non-Euclidian problems to be solved.

But how are competing interests to be assessed? Since they are not subject to quantitative ascertainment, the issue necessarily resolves itself into asking, who is to make the adjustment?—who is to balance the relevant factors and ascertain which interest is in the circumstances to prevail? Full responsibility for the choice cannot be given to the courts. Courts are not representative bodies. They are not designed to be a good reflex of a democratic society. Their judgment is best informed, and therefore most dependable, within narrow limits. Their essential quality is detachment, founded on independence. History teaches that the independence of the judiciary is jeopardized when courts become embroiled in the passions of the day and assume primary responsibility in choosing between competing political, economic and social pressures.

Primary responsibility for adjusting the interests which compete in the situation before us of necessity belongs to the Congress. . . . We are to set aside the judgment of those whose duty it is to legislate only if there is no reasonable basis for it.

. . .

On the one hand is the interest in security. The Communist Party was not designed by these defendants as an ordinary political party. . . . The jury found that the Party rejects the basic premise of our political system—that change is to be brought about by nonviolent constitutional process. The jury found that the Party advocates the theory that there is a duty and necessity to overthrow the Government by force and violence. It found that the Party entertains and promotes this view, not as a prophetic insight or as a bit of unworldly speculation, but as a program for winning adherents and as a policy to be translated into action.

. . . [I]n determining whether application of the statute to the defendants is within the constitutional powers of Congress, we are not limited to the facts found by the jury. . . . We may take judicial notice that the Communist doctrines which these defendants have conspired to advocate are in the ascendency in powerful nations who cannot be acquitted of unfriendliness to the institutions of this country. . . . In sum, it would amply justify a legislature in concluding that recruitment of additional members for the Party would create a substantial danger to national security.

On the other hand is the interest in free speech. The right to exert all governmental powers in aid of maintaining our institutions and resisting their physical overthrow does not include intolerance of opinions and speech that cannot do harm although opposed and perhaps alien to dominant, traditional opinion. . . .

. . . No matter how clear we may be that the defendants now before us are preparing to overthrow our Government at the propitious moment, it is self-delusion to think that we can punish them for their advocacy without adding to the risks run by loyal citizens who honestly believe in some of the reforms these defendants advance. It is a sobering fact that in sustaining the convictions before us we can hardly escape restriction on the interchange of ideas.

. . .

It is not for us to decide how we would adjust the clash of interests which this case presents were the primary responsibility for reconciling it ours. Congress has determined that the danger created by advocacy of overthrow justifies the ensuing restriction on freedom of speech. The determination was made after due deliberation, and the seriousness of the congressional purpose is attested by the volume of legislation passed to effectuate the same ends.

Civil liberties draw at best only limited strength from legal guaranties. Preoccupation by our people with the constitutionality, instead of with the wisdom, of legislation or of executive action is preoccupation with a false value. . . . Focusing attention on constitutionality tends to make constitutionality synonymous with wisdom. When legislation touches freedom of thought and freedom of speech, such a tendency is a formidable enemy of the free spirit. Much that should be rejected as illiberal, because repressive and envenoming, may well be not unconstitutional. The ultimate reliance for the deepest needs of civilization must be found outside their vindication in courts of law; apart from all else, judges, howsoever they may conscientiously seek to discipline themselves against it, unconsciously are too apt to be moved by the deep undercurrents of public feeling. A persistent, positive translation of the liberating faith into the feelings and thoughts and actions of men and women is the real protection against attempts to strait-jacket the human mind. Such temptations will have their way, if fear and hatred are not exorcized. The mark of a truly civilized man is confidence in the strength and security derived from the inquiring mind. We may be grateful for such honest comforts as it supports, but we must be unafraid of its incertitudes. Without open minds there can be no open society. And if society be not open the spirit of man is mutilated and becomes enslaved.

JUSTICE JACKSON, concurring.

. . .

I would save ["clear and present danger"], unmodified, for application as a "rule of reason" in the kind of case for which it was devised. When the issue is criminality of a hot-headed speech on a street corner, or circulation of a few incendiary pamphlets, or parading by some zealots behind a red flag, or refusal of a handful of school children to salute our flag, it is not beyond the capacity of the judicial process to gather, comprehend, and weigh the necessary materials for decision whether it is a clear and present danger of substantive evil or a harmless letting off of steam. It is not a prophecy, for the danger in such cases has matured by the time of trial or it was never present. . . . The formula in such cases favors freedoms that are vital to our society, and, even if sometimes applied too generously, the consequences cannot be grave. But its recent expansion has extended, in particular to Communists, unprecedented immunities. Unless we are to hold our Government captive in a judge-made verbal trap, we must approach the problem of a well-organized, nation-wide conspiracy, such as I have described, as realistically as our predecessors faced the trivialities that were being prosecuted until they were checked with a rule of reason.

. . .

The authors of the clear and present danger test never applied it to a case like this, nor would I. If applied as it is proposed here, it means that the Communist plotting is protected during its period of incubation; its preliminary stages of organization and preparation are immune from the law; the Government can move only after imminent action is manifest, when it would, of course, be too late.

. . .

JUSTICE BLACK, dissenting.

. . .

. . . [T]he only way to affirm these convictions is to repudiate directly or indirectly the established "clear and present danger" rule. . . . The opinions for affirmance indicate that the chief reason for jettisoning the rule is the expressed fear that advocacy of Communist doctrine endangers the safety of the Republic. Undoubtedly, a governmental policy of unfettered communication of ideas does entail dangers. To the Founders of this Nation, however, the benefits derived from free expression were worth the risk. . . . I have always believed that the First Amendment is the keystone of our Government, that the freedoms it guarantees provide the best insurance against destruction of all freedom. At least as to speech in the realm of public matters, I believe that the "clear and present danger" test does not "mark the furthermost constitutional boundaries of protected expression" but does "no more than recognize a minimum compulsion of the Bill of Rights."

So long as this Court exercises the power of judicial review of legislation, I cannot agree that the First Amendment permits us to sustain laws suppressing freedom of speech and press on the basis of Congress' or our own notions of mere "reasonableness." Such a doctrine waters down the First Amendment so that it amounts to little more than an admonition to Congress. The Amendment as so construed is not likely to protect any but those "safe" or orthodox views which rarely need its protection. . . .

. . .

JUSTICE DOUGLAS, dissenting.

. . .

. . . Free speech has occupied an exalted position because of the high service it has given our society. Its protection is essential to the very existence of a democracy. The airing of ideas releases pressures which otherwise might become destructive. When ideas compete in the market for acceptance, full and free discussion exposes the false and they gain few adherents. Full and free discussion even of ideas we hate encourages the testing of our own prejudices and preconceptions. Full and free discussion keeps a society from becoming stagnant and unprepared for the stresses and strains that work to tear all civilizations apart.

. . .

There comes a time when even speech loses its constitutional immunity. Speech innocuous one year may at another time fan such destructive flames that it must be halted in the interests of the safety of the Republic. That is the meaning of the clear and present danger test. When conditions are so critical that there will be no time to avoid the evil that the speech threatens, it is time to call a halt. Otherwise, free speech which is the strength of the Nation will be the cause of its destruction.

Yet free speech is the rule, not the exception. The restraint to be constitutional must be based on more than fear, on more than passionate opposition against the speech, on more than a revolted dislike for its contents. There must be some immediate injury to society that is likely if speech is allowed.

. . .

. . . If we are to take judicial notice of the threat of Communists within the nation, it should not be difficult to conclude that as a political party they are of little consequence. Communists in this country have never made a respectable or serious showing in any election. I would doubt that there is a village, let alone a city or county or state, which the Communists could carry. Communism in the world scene is no bogeyman; but Communism as a political faction or party in this country plainly is. Communism has been so thoroughly exposed in this country that it has been crippled as a political force. Free speech has destroyed it as an effective political party. . . .

How it can be said that there is a clear and present danger that this advocacy will succeed is, therefore, a mystery. . . . [I]n America they are miserable merchants of unwanted ideas; their wares remain unsold. The fact that their ideas are abhorrent does not make them powerful.

New York Times Co. v. Sullivan, 376 U.S. 254 (1964)

The New York Times *on March 29, 1960, published a full-page advertisement sponsored by the Committee to Defend Martin Luther King and the Struggle for Freedom in the South. Under the heading "Heed Their Rising Voices," the advertisement described the nonviolent struggle of civil rights activists and the often-violent responses of southern police officers to their protests. Harry Belafonte, Nat King Cole, Sammy Davis, Jr., Mahalia Jackson, John Lewis, Sidney Poitier, A. Philip Randolph, Jackie Robinson, and Eleanor Roosevelt were among the notables who signed the call for financial help. L. B. Sullivan, a city commissioner of Montgomery, Alabama, accurately claimed that the advertisement made several false statements about his conduct during several civil rights protests—for example, contrary to the claim made in the* Times, *Sullivan did not padlock the dining hall at Alabama State College in order to starve students into abandoning civil rights protests. Sullivan wrote a letter to the* Times *demanding that the false statements be retracted. When the* Times *refused Sullivan sued the newspaper and four Alabama ministers for libel. Other Alabama officials similarly sued the* Times, *the four ministers, and Martin Luther King, Jr., for libel on the basis of the statements made in the advertisement. The total damages asked for were $3 million, more than enough to bankrupt crucial civil rights organizations and seriously curtail newspaper coverage of the civil rights movement. An Alabama trial court awarded Sullivan $500,000 in damages, the highest libel award in the history of the state. The Supreme Court of Alabama sustained that appeal, and the* New York Times *appealed to the Supreme Court of the United States.*[50]

The Supreme Court unanimously overturned the Alabama decision. Justice Brennan's majority opinion declared that public officials could receive damages for libel only if the jury found actual malice. In law, this means that the speech was false and that the speaker either knew the speech was false or recklessly disregarded the truth. Consider whether New York Times v. Sullivan *is a free speech case or a civil rights case. Suppose that Martin Luther King, Jr., had won a $500,000 verdict in a New York court against an Alabama newspaper. Would the Supreme Court have issued the same ruling?* New York Times v. Sullivan *has been hailed as a great victory for freedom of the press and condemned as a license for sloppy reporting. Which assessment do you believe is correct? Does the actual malice standard chill a good deal of reporting, given that many small entrepreneurs cannot afford to fight an expensive lawsuit? Does the same standard give too much immunity to press magnates with large pockets? Is there any viable way to protect against vexatious lawsuits while promoting ethical journalism? Does the First Amendment have anything in particular to say about that subject?*

JUSTICE BRENNAN delivered the opinion of the Court.

. . .

. . . [W]e consider this case against the background of a profound national commitment to the principle

50. For a complete history, see Anthony Lewis, *Make No Law: The* Sullivan *Case and the First Amendment* (New York: Vintage, 1992).

that debate on public issues should be uninhibited, robust, and wide-open, and that it may well include vehement, caustic, and sometimes unpleasantly sharp attacks on government and public officials. . . . The present advertisement, as an expression of grievance and protest on one of the major public issues of our time, would seem clearly to qualify for the constitutional protection. The question is whether it forfeits that protection by the falsity of some of its factual statements and by its alleged defamation of respondent.

Authoritative interpretations of the First Amendment guarantees have consistently refused to recognize an exception for any test of truth—whether administered by judges, juries, or administrative officials—and especially one that puts the burden of proving truth on the speaker. . . . As Madison said, "Some degree of abuse is inseparable from the proper use of every thing; and in no instance is this more true than in that of the press." . . .

. . . [E]rroneous statement is inevitable in free debate, and . . . must be protected if the freedoms of expression are to have the "breathing space" that they "need . . . to survive." . . .

Injury to official reputation affords no more warrant for repressing speech that would otherwise be free than does factual error. . . . Criticism of their official conduct does not lose its constitutional protection merely because it is effective criticism and hence diminishes their official reputations.

If neither factual error nor defamatory content suffices to remove the constitutional shield from criticism of official conduct, the combination of the two elements is no less inadequate. This is the lesson to be drawn from the great controversy over the Sedition Act of 1798, . . . which first crystallized a national awareness of the central meaning of the First Amendment. . . . The Act allowed the defendant the defense of truth, and provided that the jury were to be judges both of the law and the facts. Despite these qualifications, the Act was vigorously condemned as unconstitutional in an attack joined in by Jefferson and Madison. . . . [Madison's] premise was that the Constitution created a form of government under which "The people, not the government, possess the absolute sovereignty." The structure of the government dispersed power in reflection of the people's distrust of concentrated power, and of power itself at all levels. This form of government was "altogether different" from the British form, under which the Crown was sovereign and the people were subjects. "Is it not natural and necessary, under such different circumstances," he asked, "that a different degree of freedom in the use of the press should be contemplated?" . . .

Although the Sedition Act was never tested in this Court, the attack upon its validity has carried the day in the court of history. Fines levied in its prosecution were repaid by Act of Congress on the ground that it was unconstitutional. . . . Calhoun, reporting to the Senate on February 4, 1836, assumed that its invalidity was a matter "which no one now doubts." . . . Jefferson, as President, pardoned those who had been convicted and sentenced under the Act and remitted their fines. . . .

. . .

A rule compelling the critic of official conduct to guarantee the truth of all his factual assertions—and to do so on pain of libel judgments virtually unlimited in amount—leads to . . . "self-censorship." Allowance of the defense of truth, with the burden of proving it on the defendant, does not mean that only false speech will be deterred. . . . Under such a rule, would-be critics of official conduct may be deterred from voicing their criticism, even though it is believed to be true and even though it is in fact true, because of doubt whether it can be proved in court or fear of the expense of having to do so. . . .

The constitutional guarantees require, we think, a federal rule that prohibits a public official from recovering damages for a defamatory falsehood relating to his official conduct unless he proves that the statement was made with "actual malice"—that is, with knowledge that it was false or with reckless disregard of whether it was false or not.

. . .

JUSTICE BLACK, with whom JUSTICE DOUGLAS joins, concurring.

. . . I base my vote to reverse on the belief that the First and Fourteenth Amendments not merely "delimit" a State's power to award damages to "public officials against critics of their official conduct" but completely prohibit a State from exercising such a power. The Court goes on to hold that a State can subject such critics to damages if "actual malice" can be proved against them. "Malice," even as defined by the Court, is an elusive, abstract concept, hard to prove and hard to disprove. The requirement that malice be proved provides at best an evanescent protection for the right critically to discuss public affairs and certainly does not measure up to the sturdy safeguard embodied in the First Amendment. . . .

. . .

. . . To punish the exercise of this right to discuss public affairs or to penalize it through libel judgments is to abridge or shut off discussion of the very kind most needed. This Nation, I suspect, can live in peace without libel suits based on public discussions of public affairs and public officials. But I doubt that a country can live in freedom where its people can be made to suffer physically or financially for criticizing their government, its actions, or its officials. . . . An unconditional right to say what one pleases about public affairs is what I consider to be the minimum guarantee of the First Amendment.

. . .

JUSTICE GOLDBERG, with whom JUSTICE DOUGLAS joins, concurring in the result.

. . .

In my view, the First and Fourteenth Amendments to the Constitution afford to the citizen and to the press an absolute, unconditional privilege to criticize official conduct despite the harm which may flow from excesses and abuses. . . . The right should not depend upon a probing by the jury of the motivation of the citizen or press. The theory of our Constitution is that every citizen may speak his mind and every newspaper express its view on matters of public concern and may not be barred from speaking or publishing because those in control of government think that what is said or written is unwise, unfair, false, or malicious. In a democratic society, one who assumes to act for the citizens in an executive, legislative, or judicial capacity must expect that his official acts will be commented upon and criticized. Such criticism cannot, in my opinion, be muzzled or deterred by the courts at the instance of public officials under the label of libel.

. . .

The conclusion that the Constitution affords the citizen and the press an absolute privilege for criticism of official conduct does not leave the public official without defenses against unsubstantiated opinions or deliberate misstatements. . . . The public official certainly has equal if not greater access than most private citizens to media of communication. In any event, despite the possibility that some excesses and abuses may go unremedied, we must recognize that "the people of this nation have ordained in the light of history, that, in spite of the probability of excesses and abuses, [certain] liberties are, in the long view, essential to enlightened opinion and right conduct on the part of the citizens of a democracy." . . .

United States v. O'Brien, 391 U.S. 367 (1967)

On March 31, 1966, David Paul O'Brien publicly burned his draft card when protesting the Vietnam War. He was immediately arrested for violating a 1965 federal law prohibiting any person from "forg[ing], alter[ing], knowingly destroy[ing], knowingly mutilat[ing], or in any other manner chang[ing]" a draft card. At trial, O'Brien asserted that the federal statute unconstitutionally abridged his free speech rights. The government insisted that laws prohibiting the destruction of draft cards were a reasonable exercise of the congressional power to raise armies. O'Brien was convicted and sentenced to six years in prison. The Court of Appeals for the First Circuit reversed that sentence on the ground that the main purpose of the federal law was to punish the act of burning draft cards as a form of political protest. The United States appealed to the Supreme Court.

The Supreme Court by a 7-1 vote declared that O'Brien was constitutionally convicted. Chief Justice Warren ruled that O'Brien had engaged in symbolic speech, but that the Court should defer when government had non-speech-related reasons for regulating such forms of expression. What test does the court use to determine whether a person has engaged in symbolic speech or expressive conduct? What standard does the Warren Court use for determining when government may regulate symbolic speech or expressive conduct? Are those standards consistent with First Amendment values? Is Warren correct when he claims that justices should rarely, if ever, examine the subjective motives of legislators? Does such a rule enable governing officials to ban a good deal of political protest under the guise of neutral rules? Does allowing judicial inquiry into motives inevitably require subjective decisions on the part of justices?

United States v. O'Brien *was one of the relatively rare cases in which the Supreme Court rejected the First Amendment claims of a person who was protesting the Vietnam War. The justices in* Bond v. Floyd *(1965) ruled that persons could not be sanctioned for praising draft resisters—the same sort of advocacy that sent Eugene Debs to prison during the Republican Era.* Tinker v. Des Moines Independent Community School District *(1969) protected the right of schoolchildren to engage in nondisruptive protest.*

That same year the Court determined that Robert Watts had been within his constitutional rights when he declared, "If they ever make me carry a rifle the first man I want to get in my sights is L. B. J." The judicial majority in Watts v. United States *(1969) "agree[d] with petitioner that his only offense here was 'a kind of very crude offensive method of stating a political opposition to the President.'" Two years later the judicial majority in* Cohen v. California *(1971) reversed a conviction against Paul Cohen for wearing a jacket with the words "FUCK THE DRAFT" emblazoned on the back. Justice Harlan's majority opinion maintained that "the Constitution leaves matters of taste and style so largely to the individual."* Hess v. Indiana *(1973) held that Indiana could not convict for disorderly conduct a Vietnam War protestor who, after police broke up a rally, declared, "We'll take the fucking street later." The per curiam opinion concluded, "Since there was no evidence or rational inference from the import of the language, that his words were intended to produce, and likely to produce, imminent disorder, those words could not be punished by the State on the ground that they had a 'tendency to lead to violence.'" In* Spence v. Washington *(1974) the Supreme Court sided with a Vietnam War protestor who had pasted a peace symbol over his flag. This, the per curiam opinion stated, "was a pointed expression of anguish by appellant about the then-current domestic and foreign affairs of his government."*

Consider this pattern of decisions in light of constitutional understandings during the Civil War, World War I, and World War II. Why were war protestors during the 1960s and 1970s more successful in federal courts than were war protestors in the early twentieth century? To what extent do you believe that these different patterns are a consequence of greater respect for free speech rights, or do they merely reflect less judicial support for the Vietnam War? What explains the particular pattern of decisions during the Vietnam War? Does a coherent theory of the First Amendment explain why the justices frequently supported the rights of Vietnam protestors, but not always? Why was O'Brien the main exception to this libertarian tendency?

CHIEF JUSTICE WARREN delivered the opinion of the Court.

. . .

We cannot accept the view that an apparently limitless variety of conduct can be labeled "speech" whenever the person engaging in the conduct intends thereby to express an idea. . . . This Court has held that when "speech" and "nonspeech" elements are combined in the same course of conduct, a sufficiently important governmental interest in regulating the nonspeech element can justify incidental limitations on First Amendment freedoms. . . . [W]e think it clear that a government regulation is sufficiently justified if it is within the constitutional power of the Government; if it furthers an important or substantial governmental interest; if the governmental interest is unrelated to the suppression of free expression; and if the incidental restriction on alleged First Amendment freedoms is no greater than is essential to the furtherance of that interest. . . .

The constitutional power of Congress to raise and support armies and to make all laws necessary and proper to that end is broad and sweeping. . . . The power of Congress to classify and conscript manpower for military service is "beyond question." . . . The issuance of certificates indicating the registration and eligibility classification of individuals is a legitimate and substantial administrative aid in the functioning of this system. And legislation to insure the continuing availability of issued certificates serves a legitimate and substantial purpose in the system's administration.

. . .

1. The registration certificate serves as proof that the individual described thereon has registered for the draft. . . . Voluntarily displaying the two certificates is an easy and painless way for a young man to dispel a question as to whether he might be delinquent in his Selective Service obligations. . . . Additionally, in a time of national crisis, reasonable availability to each registrant of the two small cards assures a rapid and uncomplicated means for determining his fitness for immediate induction, no matter how distant in our mobile society he may be from his local board.

2. The information supplied on the certificates facilitates communication between registrants and local boards, simplifying the system and benefiting all concerned. . . .

3. Both certificates carry continual reminders that the registrant must notify his local board of any change of address, and other specified changes in his status. . . .

. . .

The many functions performed by Selective Service certificates establish beyond doubt that Congress has a legitimate and substantial interest in preventing their wanton and unrestrained destruction and assuring their continuing availability by punishing people who knowingly and wilfully destroy or mutilate them. . . .

. . .

. . . [T]he 1965 Amendment specifically protects th[ese] substantial governmental interest[s]. We perceive no alternative means that would more precisely and narrowly assure the continuing availability of issued Selective Service certificates than a law which prohibits their wilful mutilation or destruction. . . . The governmental interest and the scope of the 1965 Amendment are limited to preventing harm to the smooth and efficient functioning of the Selective Service System. When O'Brien deliberately rendered unavailable his registration certificate, he wilfully frustrated this governmental interest. For this noncommunicative impact of his conduct, and for nothing else, he was convicted.

. . .

O'Brien finally argues that the 1965 Amendment is unconstitutional as enacted because what he calls the "purpose" of Congress was "to suppress freedom of speech." We reject this argument because under settled principles the purpose of Congress, as O'Brien uses that term, is not a basis for declaring this legislation unconstitutional.

It is a familiar principle of constitutional law that this Court will not strike down an otherwise constitutional statute on the basis of an alleged illicit legislative motive. . . .

Inquiries into congressional motives or purposes are a hazardous matter. . . . What motivates one legislator to make a speech about a statute is not necessarily what motivates scores of others to enact it, and the stakes are sufficiently high for us to eschew guesswork. We decline to void essentially on the ground that it is unwise legislation which Congress had the undoubted power to enact and which could be reenacted in its exact form if the same or another legislator made a "wiser" speech about it.

. . .

JUSTICE DOUGLAS, dissenting.

[Justice Douglas's dissented urged the justices to consider the constitutionality of the draft]

Brandenburg v. Ohio, 395 U.S. 444 (1969)

Clarence Brandenburg was a leader of a local Ku Klux Klan affiliate in Ohio. During a speech at a rally Brandenburg asserted,

> *The Klan has more members in the State of Ohio than does any other organization. We're not a revengent organization, but if our President, our Congress, our Supreme Court, continues to suppress the white, Caucasian race, it's possible that there might have to be some revengeance taken.*

For these and similar comments Brandenburg was convicted under an Ohio law that forbade "advocat[ing] . . . the duty, necessity, or propriety of crime, sabotage, violence, or unlawful methods of terrorism as a means of accomplishing industrial or political reform." The Supreme Court of Ohio sustained his conviction. Brandenburg appealed to the Supreme Court of the United States.

A unanimous Supreme Court reversed. The per curiam decision insisted that speakers could be convicted only if their words incited imminent illegal conduct. No justice made a distinction between advocacy of racial or ethnic hatred and advocacy of communist revolution. Does this demonstrate a principled commitment to the freedom of speech or a failure to make constitutionally relevant distinctions? The justices also claimed that the decision in Whitney v. California *(1927) was discredited in* Dennis v. United States *(1951). Is this accurate? Is the constitutional standard used in* Dennis *more consistent with* Whitney *than the constitutional standard used in* Brandenberg? *Justice Brandeis in his* Whitney *concurrence insisted that only serious evils justified restricting free speech. Does* Brandenbug *adopt this element of the Brandeis concurrence?*

PER CURIAM.

. . .

The Ohio Criminal Syndicalism Statute was enacted in 1919. From 1917 to 1920, identical or quite similar laws were adopted by 20 States and two territories. . . . In 1927, this Court sustained the constitutionality of California's Criminal Syndicalism Act, . . . the text of which is quite similar to that of the laws of Ohio. *Whitney v. California* (1927). . . . The Court upheld the statute on the ground that, without more, "advocating" violent means to effect political and economic change involves such danger to the security of the State that the State may outlaw it. But *Whitney* has been thoroughly discredited by later decisions. See *Dennis v. United States* (1951). . . . These later decisions have fashioned the principle that the constitutional guarantees of free speech and free press do not permit a State to forbid or proscribe advocacy of the use of force or of law violation except where such advocacy is directed to inciting or producing imminent lawless action and is likely to incite or produce such action. . . . A statute which fails to draw this distinction impermissibly intrudes upon the freedoms guaranteed by the

First and Fourteenth Amendments. It sweeps within its condemnation speech which our Constitution has immunized from governmental control....

Measured by this test, Ohio's Criminal Syndicalism Act cannot be sustained. The Act punishes persons who "advocate or teach the duty, necessity, or propriety" of violence "as a means of accomplishing industrial or political reform"; or who publish or circulate or display any book or paper containing such advocacy; or who "justify" the commission of violent acts "with intent to exemplify, spread or advocate the propriety of the doctrines of criminal syndicalism"; or who "voluntarily assemble" with a group formed "to teach or advocate the doctrines of criminal syndicalism." Neither the indictment nor the trial judge's instructions to the jury in any way refined the statute's bald definition of the crime in terms of mere advocacy not distinguished from incitement to imminent lawless action.

... The contrary teaching of *Whitney v. California* ... cannot be supported, and that decision is therefore overruled.

JUSTICE BLACK, concurring....

JUSTICE DOUGLAS, concurring.

...

... I see no place in the regime of the First Amendment for any "clear and present danger" test, whether strict and tight as some would make it, or free-wheeling as the Court in *Dennis* rephrased it.

The line between what is permissible and not subject to control and what may be made impermissible and subject to regulation is the line between ideas and overt acts.

The example usually given by those who would punish speech is the case of one who falsely shouts fire in a crowded theatre.

This is, however, a classic case where speech is brigaded with action. . . . They are indeed inseparable and a prosecution can be launched for the overt acts actually caused. Apart from rare instances of that kind, speech is, I think, immune from prosecution. . . . The quality of advocacy turns on the depth of the conviction; and government has no power to invade that sanctuary of belief and conscience.

Media

Broadcasting sparked constitutional debate in the New Deal/Great Society Era. The Federal Communications Commission (FCC) in "Editorializing by Broadcast Licensees" (1949) determined that radio and television should be regulated in the public interest. For "radio [and later television] to be maintained as a medium of free speech for the general public as a whole rather than as an outlet for the personal or private interests of the licensee," the FCC concluded, "licensees [must] devote a reasonable percentage of their broadcast time to the discussion of public issues of interest in the community served by their stations and that such programs be designed so that the public has a reasonable opportunity to hear different opposing positions on the public issues of interest and importance to the community."[51] The Supreme Court sustained what became known as the "Fairness Doctrine" in *Red Lion Broadcasting Co. v. Federal Communications Commission* (1969).

Red Lion Broadcasting Co. v. Federal Communications Commission, 395 U.S. 367 (1969)

The Red Lion Broadcasting Company owned and operated WGCB, a small radio station in Pennsylvania. On November 27, 1964, the Reverend Billy James Hargis accused Fred J. Cook of associating with Communists; being fired by a previous employer for making false statements; and defending Alger Hiss, a former State Department employee who had been convicted of spying for the Soviet Union.[52] *Cook demanded that WGCB permit him to reply to these charges. Cook based his demand on FCC regulations, known as the "Fairness Doctrine," that declared:*

> *When, during the presentation of views on a controversial issue of public importance, an attack is made upon the honesty, character, integrity or like personal qualities of an identified person or group, the licensee shall, within a reasonable time and in no event later than 1 week after*

51. "Report on Editorializing by Broadcast Licensees, 13 F.C.C. 1246 (1949).

52. The specific words were: "Who is Cook? Cook was fired from the *New York World Telegram* after he made a false charge publicly on television against an unnamed official of the New York City government.... After losing his job, Cook went to work for the left-wing publication, *The Nation*, one of the most scurrilous publications of the left which has championed many communist causes over many years.... Now, among other things Fred Cook wrote for *The Nation*, was an article absolving Alger Hiss of any wrong doing , . . . there was a 208 page attack on the FBI and J. Edgar Hoover; another attack by Mr. Cook was on the Central Intelligence Agency. . . ."

> *the attack, transmit to the person or group attacked . . . an offer of a reasonable opportunity to respond over the licensee's facilities.*

Red Lion refused, claiming that the Fairness Doctrine violated the First Amendment. The FCC rejected that claim and that ruling was sustained by the Court of Appeals for the District of Columbia Circuit. Red Lion appealed to the Supreme Court of the United States.

The Supreme Court by an 8-0 vote sustained the Fairness Doctrine. Justice White's opinion maintained that the federal government could impose restrictions on broadcasters that could not be imposed on ordinary speakers. Individual speakers have no constitutional obligation to be fair. Why does Justice White impose a contrary obligation on radio stations? Is his reasoning sound? Most liberal groups supported the Fairness Doctrine. Why did liberal groups in the 1960s support broadcast regulation? Was such support more consistent with liberal values? Was such support consistent with the interest of liberal interest groups?

Five years later, in Miami Herald Publishing Company v. Tornillo *(1974), the Supreme Court unanimously declared unconstitutional a Florida law that gave political candidates a right to reply to critical editorials. Had the* Miami Herald *been a radio station, such a law would have clearly have been constitutional under* Red Lion. *Nevertheless, without mentioning* Red Lion, *three judicial opinions had little difficulty finding the Florida statute inconsistent with the First Amendment. Chief Justice Burger's majority opinion declared:*

> *The Florida statute fails to clear the barriers of the First Amendment because of its intrusion into the function of editors. A newspaper is more than a passive receptacle or conduit for news, comment, and advertising. The choice of material to go into a newspaper, and the decisions made as to limitations on the size and content of the paper, and treatment of public issues and public officials—whether fair or unfair—constitute the exercise of editorial control and judgment. It has yet to be demonstrated how governmental regulation of this crucial process can be exercised consistent with First Amendment guarantees of a free press as they have evolved to this time.*

Does Red Lion *suggest any constitutional distinction between newspapers and radio stations? Do you believe that any constitutional distinctions exist?*

JUSTICE WHITE delivered the opinion of the Court

. . .

Before 1927, the allocation of frequencies was left entirely to the private sector, and the result was chaos. It quickly became apparent that broadcast frequencies constituted a scarce resource whose use could be regulated and rationalized only by the Government. Without government control, the medium would be of little use because of the cacophony of competing voices, none of which could be clearly and predictably heard. Consequently, the Federal Radio Commission was established to allocate frequencies among competing applicants in a manner responsive to the public "convenience, interest, or necessity."

. . .

Although broadcasting is clearly a medium affected by a First Amendment interest, . . . differences in the characteristics of new media justify differences in the First Amendment standards applied to them. . . . For example, the ability of new technology to produce sounds more raucous than those of the human voice justifies restrictions on the sound level, and on the hours and places of use, of sound trucks so long as the restrictions are reasonable and applied without discrimination. . . .

Just as the Government may limit the use of sound-amplifying equipment potentially so noisy that it drowns out civilized private speech, so may the Government limit the use of broadcast equipment. The right of free speech of a broadcaster, the user of a sound truck, or any other individual does not embrace a right to snuff out the free speech of others. . . .

When two people converse face to face, both should not speak at once if either is to be clearly understood. But the range of the human voice is so limited that there could be meaningful communications if half the people in the United States were talking and the other half listening. Just as clearly, half the people might publish and the other half read. But the reach of radio signals is incomparably greater than the range of the human voice and the problem of interference is a massive reality. . . . [O]nly a tiny fraction of those with resources and intelligence can hope to communicate by radio at the same time if intelligible communication is to be had, even if the entire radio spectrum is utilized in the present state of commercially acceptable technology.

. . .

Where there are substantially more individuals who want to broadcast than there are frequencies to allocate, it is idle to posit an unabridgeable First Amendment right to broadcast comparable to the right of every individual to speak, write, or publish. If 100 persons want broadcast licenses but there are only 10 frequencies to allocate, all of them may have the same "right" to a license; but if there is to be any effective communication by radio, only a few can be licensed and the rest must be barred from the airwaves. . . .

. . .

. . . A license permits broadcasting, but the licensee has no constitutional right to be the one who holds the license or to monopolize a radio frequency to the exclusion of his fellow citizens. There is nothing in the First Amendment which prevents the Government from requiring a licensee to share his frequency with others and to conduct himself as a proxy or fiduciary with obligations to present those views and voices which are representative of his community and which would otherwise, by necessity, be barred from the airwaves.

This is not to say that the First Amendment is irrelevant to public broadcasting. . . . Because of the scarcity of radio frequencies, the Government is permitted to put restraints on licensees in favor of others whose views should be expressed on this unique medium. But the people as a whole retain their interest in free speech by radio and their collective right to have the medium function consistently with the ends and purposes of the First Amendment. It is the right of the viewers and listeners, not the right of the broadcasters, which is paramount. . . . It is the right of the public to receive suitable access to social, political, esthetic, moral, and other ideas and experiences which is crucial here. That right may not constitutionally be abridged either by Congress or by the FCC.

. . .

Nor can we say that it is inconsistent with the First Amendment goal of producing an informed public capable of conducting its own affairs to require a broadcaster to permit answers to personal attacks occurring in the course of discussing controversial issues, or to require that the political opponents of those endorsed by the station be given a chance to communicate with the public. Otherwise, station owners and a few networks would have unfettered power to make time available only to the highest bidders, to communicate only their own views on public issues, people and candidates, and to permit on the air only those with whom they agreed. There is no sanctuary in the First Amendment for unlimited private censorship operating in a medium not open to all. . . .

. . .

It is strenuously argued, however, that if political editorials or personal attacks will trigger an obligation in broadcasters to afford the opportunity for expression to speakers who need not pay for time and whose views are unpalatable to the licensees, then broadcasters will be irresistibly forced to self-censorship and their coverage of controversial public issues will be eliminated or at least rendered wholly ineffective. Such a result would indeed be a serious matter, for should licensees actually eliminate their coverage of controversial issues, the purposes of the doctrine would be stifled.

At this point, however, as the Federal Communications Commission has indicated, that possibility is at best speculative. . . . [I]f experience with the administration of those doctrines indicates that they have the net effect of reducing rather than enhancing the volume and quality of coverage, there will be time enough to reconsider the constitutional implications. The fairness doctrine in the past has had no such overall effect.

That this will occur now seems unlikely, however, since if present licensees should suddenly prove timorous, the Commission is not powerless to insist that they give adequate and fair attention to public issues. It does not violate the First Amendment to treat licensees given the privilege of using scarce radio frequencies as proxies for the entire community, obligated to give suitable time and attention to matters of great public concern. To condition the granting or renewal of licenses on a willingness to present representative community views on controversial issues is consistent with the ends and purposes of those constitutional provisions forbidding the abridgment of freedom of speech and freedom of the press. . . .

. . .

Scarcity is not entirely a thing of the past. . . .

. . . The radio spectrum has become so congested that at times it has been necessary to suspend new applications. The very high frequency television spectrum is, in the country's major markets, almost entirely occupied, although space reserved for ultra high frequency television transmission, which is a relatively recent development as a commercially viable alternative, has not yet been completely filled.

The rapidity with which technological advances succeed one another to create more efficient use of spectrum space on the one hand, and to create new uses for that space by ever growing numbers of people on the other, makes it unwise to speculate on the future allocation of that space. It is enough to say that the resource is one of considerable and growing importance whose scarcity impelled its regulation by an agency authorized by Congress. . . .

Other Free Speech Issues

Obscenity. Obscenity became a national issue that presaged the culture wars of later eras. Many liberals worried about the tendency for great literature to be declared obscene and thought lesser works portraying nudity and sex to be harmless forms of entertainment that merited constitutional protection. Conservatives insisted that traditional bans on obscenity were proper means of instilling virtue and preventing crime. The Supreme Court, while nominally declaring obscenity constitutionally unprotected, defined obscenity very narrowly. Justice Brennan's opinion in *Roth v. United States* (1957) asserted,

> All ideas having even the slightest redeeming social importance—unorthodox ideas, controversial ideas, even ideas hateful to the prevailing climate of opinion—have the full protection of the guaranties, unless excludable because they encroach upon the limited area of more important interests. But implicit in the history of the First Amendment is the rejection of obscenity as utterly without redeeming social importance.

For the next decade the Supreme Court was flooded with obscenity cases. These cases yielded very little constitutional law, in part because the justices could rarely agree on a broad doctrine. Justice Stewart in *Jacobellis v. State of Ohio* (1964) declared in some frustration, "I shall not today attempt further to define the kinds of material I understand to be [hard-core pornography]. . . . But I know it when I see it."

B. Voting

Voting became a fundamental constitutional right during the New Deal/Great Society Era. By 1969 general agreement existed in all three branches of the national government that neither the national nor a state government could deny a person a right to vote in a general election unless there was a compelling reason to do so. Equally as important, Congress passed and the federal government actively enforced legislation ensuring that persons of color, the most common targets of laws denying the ballot, could exercise their constitutional right to vote. For the first time in American history, Americans enjoyed near-universal adult suffrage.

The recognition of a constitutional right to vote was bipartisan during the New Deal/Great Society Era. The 1960 Democratic Party platform asserted:

> The right to vote is the first principle of self-government. The Constitution also guarantees to all Americans the equal protection of the laws.
>
> . . .
>
> We will support whatever action is necessary to eliminate literacy tests and the payment of poll taxes as requirements for voting.

The 1960 Republican Party platform pledged:

> Continued vigorous enforcement of the civil rights laws to guarantee the right to vote to all citizens in all areas of the country.
>
> Legislation to provide that the completion of six primary grades in a state accredited school is conclusive evidence of literacy for voting purposes.

World War II provided the impetus for a national commitment to voting rights. When urging Congress to pass legislation enabling troops serving abroad to cast ballots, President Roosevelt insisted that voting was a constitutional right, not a legislative privilege. His 1944 State of the Union address declared, "The signers of the Constitution did not intend a document which, even in wartime, would be construed to take away the franchise of any of those who are fighting to preserve the Constitution itself." Congress responded by passing measures that provided soldiers with absentee ballots and exempted persons in the military from paying state poll taxes. Liberals in Congress during the 1940s spoke of a constitutional right to vote when proposing to abolish all polls taxes. "Can it be said, in view of the civilization of the present day that a man's poverty has anything to do with his qualification to vote?" a Senate majority report asked in 1942.[53]

The civil rights movement provided the impetus for the voting rights gains of the 1960s. Overwhelming majorities in both parties supported the Voting Rights Act of 1965. That measure outlawed all voting tests in districts in which less than half the adult population had voted in the 1964 presidential election. Congress required those districts to gain approval or preclear-

53. 88 *Congressional Record*, 77th Cong., 2nd Sess. (1942), 9029.

ance from either a federal court in the District of Columbia or the attorney general before making any changes to their voting laws. Before 1965, when the NAACP or national government secured a judicial ruling declaring a state literacy test unconstitutional (after a decade or so of litigation), the offending state usually responded by either adopting a different literacy test or switching to an "understanding" test—thus setting off another round of litigation. After 1965 offending states could adopt new tests only with permission of the federal government. The Supreme Court in *South Carolina v. Katzenbach* (1966) had little difficulty finding all these provisions constitutional. "As against the reserved powers of the States," Chief Justice Warren stated, "Congress may use any rational means to effectuate the constitutional prohibition of racial discrimination in voting." The Supreme Court in *Katzenbach v. Morgan* (1966) ruled that Congress could also prohibit otherwise constitutional state laws when doing so might prevent or deter unconstitutional practices. Results were immediate. A sharp increase in African-American voting and African-American elected officials occurred almost immediately after the Voting Rights Act of 1965 became law and withstood judicial scrutiny.

The Supreme Court proactively promoted voting rights. The justices in *Reynolds v. Sims* (1964) determined that all state and legislative districts were constitutionally required to be apportioned on the principle of one person, one vote. *Harper v. Virginia Board of Elections* (1966) declared poll taxes unconstitutional. Justice Douglas's majority opinion asserted, "Wealth, like race, creed, or color, is not germane to one's ability to participate intelligently in the electoral process. Lines drawn on the basis of wealth or property, like those of race . . . are traditionally disfavored." Three years after *Harper* the Supreme Court confirmed that statutes restricting the right to vote would receive the highest degree of judicial scrutiny. When invalidating a New York law limiting the franchise in school elections to persons with taxable property or children in the schools, Chief Justice Warren's majority opinion in *Kramer v. Union Free School Dist. No. 15* (1969) declared,

> The presumption of constitutionality and the approval given "rational" classifications in other types of enactments are based on an assumption that the institutions of state government are structured so as to represent fairly all the people. However, when the challenge to the statute is in effect a challenge of this basic assumption, the assumption can no longer serve as the basis for presuming constitutionality.

Exclusions, this decision held, must be "necessary to promote a compelling state interest."

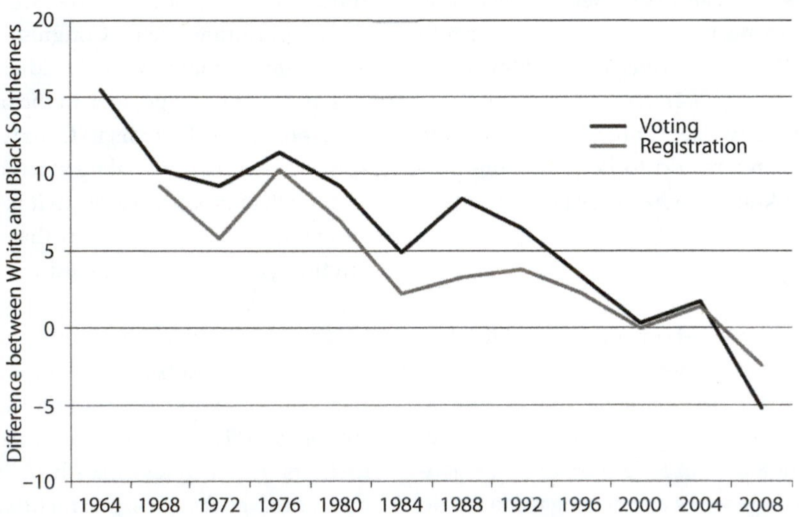

Figure 8-3 Difference between White and Black Southern Registration and Voting Rates, 1964–2008

Note: Voting registration and voter turnout numbers based on self-reports from surveys administered by the U.S. Census for presidential elections.

Source: U.S. Census Bureau, Historical Current Population Survey Time Series Tables A-9 and A-10.

Congressional Reports on the Voting Rights Act of 1965[54]

President Lyndon Johnson was determined to pass an effective voting rights bill. His State of the Union message on January 4, 1965, proposed that the nation "eliminate every remaining obstacle to the right and the opportunity to vote." Governor George Wallace of Alabama perversely contributed to national support for African-American voting when his state troopers attacked a civil rights march in Selma on March 7. Buttressed by increased popular support, Justice Department officials drafted a bill with three crucial features. First, all literacy and other voting tests were suspended in all jurisdictions where less than 50 percent of the adult population had voted in the 1964 election. Second, federal officials were sent to those jurisdictions and given the power to register qualified voters. Third, those jurisdictions were permitted to make changes in the voting laws only if those changes were approved (precleared) by the Justice Department or the Court of Appeals for the District of Columbia.

The resulting congressional debate focused on poll taxes and the preclearance provision. Liberals attempted to add a ban on state and local poll taxes but settled for a provision that authorized the attorney general to challenge the constitutionality of such measures in court. Conservatives sought to limit the preclearance provisions. They were unsuccessful. In early August the House approved the Voting Rights Act by a 328-74 vote and the Senate approved by a 79-18 vote. President Johnson signed the measure into law on August 6, 1965.

Majority Report

The bill as introduced and reported is primarily intended to enforce the 15th amendment to the Constitution of the United States. . . .

. . .

We all recognize the necessity to eradicate once and for all the chronic system of racial discrimination which has for so long excluded so many citizens from the electorate because of the color of their skins, contrary to the explicit command of the 15th amendment. . . .

. . .

Experience has shown that the case-by case litigation approach [adopted in the Civil Rights Acts of 1957, 1960, and 1964] will not solve the voting discrimination problem. The statistics alone are conclusive. In Alabama in 1964 only 19.4 percent of voting age Negroes were registered to vote, an increase of only 9.2 percent since 1958. In Mississippi approximately 6.4 percent of voting age Negroes were registered in 1964, compared to 4.4 percent 10 years earlier. And in Louisiana Negro registration appears to have increased only one-tenth of 1 percent between 1958 and 1965.

The inadequacy of existing laws is attributable to both the intransigence of local officials and dilatory tactics, two factors which have largely neutralized years of litigating effort by the Department of Justice. . . .

Dallas County, [Alabama,] with Selma as the county seat, has a voting-age population of approximately 29,500, of whom 14,500 are white persons and 15,000 are Negroes. In 1961, 9,195 of the whites—64 percent of the voting-age total—and 156 Negroes—1 percent of the total—were registered to vote in Dallas County.

On April 13, 1961, the Government filed a lawsuit against the county board of registrars under the Civil Rights Acts of 1957 and 1960. The district court and the court of appeals found that the registrars in office when the suit was filed had been engaging in a pattern and practice of discrimination against Negroes. But when the case came to trial 13 months later, those registrars had resigned and new ones had been appointed. Although there was proof of discrimination by prior registrars, including the misuse of the application form as a test, the court found that the present registrars were not discriminating and it declined to issue an injunction. . . .

. . .

Another example of the difference in treatment accorded whites and Negroes occurred in George County, Miss., where Negro college graduates were rejected while a white applicant [was accepted] who gave the following interpretation of a State constitutional provision that "there shall be no imprisonment for debt": "I think that a Neorger should have 2 years in college be fore voting be cause he don't understand." He also explained to the registrar's evident satisfaction that the duties and obligations of citizenship were "under Standing of pepper & Government ship blessing."

Often whites are not made to take the tests at all. . . .

. . .

. . . History has show that the suspension of the tests and devices alone would not assure access of all persons to voting and registration without regard to race

54. Senate Report 162, "Voting Rights Legislation," 89th Cong., 1st Sess. (1965), 2–26.

or color. The maladministration of tests and devices has been the major problem. Other tactics of discrimination, however, have been used and could readily be resorted to by State or local election officials where tests and devices have been suspended.

That this is so is demonstrated by two recent actions in Louisiana and Alabama. The registrars in East and West Feliciana Parishes were enjoined by the three-judge district court in *United States v. Louisiana* (1965). . . from using various State literacy tests. Their response was to close the registration office thus freezing the unlawful registration disparity in those parishes. In Dallas County, Ala., the registrars . . . slowed down the pace of registration so as to prevent any appreciable number of Negroes, qualified or not, from completing the registration process. . . .

. . .

The proposed statute implements the explicit command of the 15th amendment that "the right . . . to vote shall not be denied or abridged . . . by any State on account of race [or] color."

. . .

The factual background is always relevant in assessing the constitutional "appropriateness" of legislation. . . .

There can be no doubt about the present need for Federal legislation to correct widespread violations of the 15th amendment. The prevailing conditions in those areas where the bill will operate offer ample justification for congressional action because there is little basis for supposing that [without] action, the States and subdivisions affected will themselves remedy the present situation in view of the history of the adoption and administration of the several tests and devices reached by the bill.

The choice of the means to solve a problem within the legitimate concern of the Congress is largely a legislative question. What the Supreme Court said in sustaining the constitutionality of the Civil Rights Act of 1964 is fully applicable:

> . . . where we find that the legislators, in light of the facts and testimony before them, have a rational basis for finding a chosen regulatory scheme necessary to the protection of commerce, our investigation is at an end. . . .

In enforcing the 15th amendment Congress may forbid the use of voter qualification laws where necessary to meet the risk of continued or renewed violations of constitutional rights even though, in the absence of the course of illegal conduct predicated upon the use of such tests, the same State laws might be unobjectionable.

Minority Report[55]

Statement of CHARLES J. BLOCH

. . .

The sole power given to Congress by [the 15th] amendment . . . is to *prevent* the United States or any State from denying certain people the right to vote on account of their race or color.

That amendment does not confer the right upon Congress to confer upon anyone the right to vote.

. . .

The theory of this bill and of the Attorney General is that if in the opinion of Congress a State imposes standards which are discriminatory, or applies legal standards (test and devices) discriminatorily, Congress may by statute divest that State of its constitutional powers of determining the conditions upon which the right of suffrage may be exercised; may substitute its own conditions, and may do all of that retroactively.

This Constitution gives the Congress no such power over any State of this Union, North or South, East or West, Republican or Democrat.

. . .

. . . [T]he United States of America would be divided into two groups—the good and the bad—if you please.

The "good" the 41 States and a portion of 2 others, could go on exercising their rights and freedoms, and enforcing their statutes.

The "bad"—seven and a portion of those two others—could not.

[*Bloch then discussed the conditions for becoming a "covered jurisdiction"*]

The dates are purely arbitrary.

The percentage used is equally arbitrary.

The events are purely arbitrary.

The supposed result from the facts determined is purely arbitrary.

. . .

55. Rather than write a separate minority report, Senators Eastland, McClellan, and Ervin adopted statements made by the witnesses, attorneys Charles J. Bloch and Thomas H. Watkins, during the Senate hearings on the Voting Rights Act.

The *New York Times* of March 18 editorially said of the "drafters" of this bill in the Justice Department:

> . . . In the six Southern States where less than half the voting population participated in the last presidential election, *presumption of past discrimination will be automatic, and no literacy or other qualifying test will be allowed to bar anyone from the ballot box in Federal, State, or local elections.*

That same Constitution which is held to guarantee freedom to the owners of the *New York Times* to make money by printing what they please, guarantees to every State of this Union, the people of every State of this Union,—including the "six Southern States"—the right to be free from this tyrannical provision sought to be imposed on the basis of "presumptions."

. . .

. . . [T]here are 416 counties or political subdivisions as to which the Attorney General says "voting discrimination has unquestionable been widespread."

In how many of these countries has the Department of Justice instituted suits in the last 8 years? In how many of these suits has the Court found a pattern and practice" of discrimination authorizing the appointment of federal referees?

One of two states of facts is unquestionably true. There is no widespread discrimination forbidden by the 15th amendment, or the Department of Justice has, purposefully or neglectfully, been lax in the exercise of the processes at its disposal which would remedy such widespread discrimination if it in fact existed.

. . .

Statement of THOMAS WATKINS

. . .

In destroying the constitutional rights of Mississippi and other States to use literacy tests as a qualification of the privilege of voting, S. 1564 constitutes an undisguised frontal assault on the Constitution, as interpreted by the Supreme Court of the United States for more than 100 years. This bill flies squarely in the face of the same Constitution that every U.S. Senator has taken an oath to uphold.

The very first article of that Constitution authorizes the individual States to decide the qualifications of voters in both Federal and State elections, subject only to the proviso that whoever is deemed qualified to vote for "the most numerous branch of the State legislature" is automatically qualified to vote in Federal elections.

. . .

The 15th amendment did not give Congress the power to prohibit discrimination on grounds of education. This bill, in seeking to abolish literacy tests, does just that. . . .

It is clear that Congress and the States intended the 15th amendment to mean exactly what it said. The color of a man cannot be a reason to grant or deny him the right to vote. But all other qualifications are left entirely to the wisdom of the States.

. . .

The Attorney General states that the bill will deny the use of "onerous, vague, unfair tests and devices enacted for the purpose of disenfranchising Negroes." The bill, however, does not use this language. It prohibits the use of any literacy tests. If the bill prohibited onerous, vague, and unfair tests which tended to disenfranchise Negroes, it would be very much closer to the power granted Congress by the 15th amendment.

. . .

This act does not apply to all States or political subdivisions but is applicable only to a special class of States or political subdivisions. This classification violates the fifth amendment to the Constitution. The prohibition against denial of due process of law is, under this amendment, applicable to the United States. . . .

. . .

It is thoroughly established that any classification must rest always upon some difference, and *this difference must bear a reasonable and just relation to the purpose of the act in respect to which classification is proposed.*

The members of the class are determined by the Attorney General, based on findings of the Director of the Census, either: (1) That less than 50 percent of the persons of voting age residing therein were registered on November 1, 1964; *or* (2) that less than 50 percent of such persons voted in the presidential election of November 1964.

This classification is unrealistic, arbitrary, and unreasonable, as well as discriminatory. It does not pretend to prevent discriminatory use of tests except in approximately six States. Other States can have and use the tests as much as they please and yet not be within the class. . . .

. . .

. . . There is no such thing as a second-class State. Every State in this Union is equal to every other State and is guaranteed the rights and privileges enjoyed by every other State. . . .

. . .

The present emotionalism does not justify taking constitutional shortcuts. A desirable goal does not justify an unconstitutional means. If the accomplishments of this bill are desirable, let them be forthcoming in the only legal way—by constitutional amendment.

Katzenbach v. Morgan, 384 U.S. 641 (1966)

John P. Morgan and Christine Morgan were voters in New York who objected to a provision in the Voting Rights Act of 1965 that prohibited states from denying the vote to any person who had completed the sixth grade in Puerto Rico merely because that person could not read English. They filed a lawsuit in federal court asking for an injunction prohibiting the attorney general of the United States, Nicholas Katzenbach, from enforcing that provision. The local federal district court ruled that the provision was unconstitutional. The United States appealed to the Supreme Court.

A 7-2 judicial majority declared that Congress had acted constitutionally. Justice Brennan's majority opinion clearly held that Congress could prohibit otherwise constitutional laws when doing so might prevent unconstitutional action. Permitting Spanish speakers to vote, he observed, might prevent Puerto Ricans in New York from discrimination in violation of the equal protection clause. More controversially, Brennan's opinion suggested that Congress could interpret as well as enforce the post–Civil War Amendments—in other words, that Congress had the authority under Section 5 of the Fourteenth Amendment to determine whether the Constitution prohibited discrimination against non-English speakers. Does Justice Brennan make that claim? If so, is that claim correct?

Section 5 of the Fourteenth Amendment might permit Congress to exercise the following powers:

- *Provide remedies for judicially ascertained constitutional violations; e.g., determine that victims of unconstitutional discrimination should receive one-thousand dollars in damages*
- *Find the factual predicates of constitutional violations; e.g., if the Supreme Court has said that literacy tests do not necessarily discriminate against persons of color, Congress may conclude after an investigation that such tests are in fact consistently applied in ways that intentionally discriminate against persons of color, and on that basis ban literacy tests*
- *Forbid otherwise constitutional actions in order to prevent or deter unconstitutional behavior; e.g., require state police officers to have training in multiculturalism*
- *Independently interpret the rights protected by the Fourteenth Amendment; e.g., find that the equal protection clause forbids discrimination against the physically handicapped unless a compelling reason exists for the discrimination*

Which of these powers does Justice Brennan endorse? Which does Justice Harlan endorse? Which do you believe the Constitution sanctions?

JUSTICE BRENNAN delivered the opinion of the Court.

. . .

. . . A construction of § 5 that would require a judicial determination that the enforcement of the state law precluded by Congress violated the Amendment, as a condition of sustaining the congressional enactment, would depreciate both congressional resourcefulness and congressional responsibility for implementing the Amendment. It would confine the legislative power in this context to the insignificant role of abrogating only those state laws that the judicial branch was prepared to adjudge unconstitutional, or of merely informing the judgment of the judiciary by particularizing the "majestic generalities" of § 1 of the Amendment.

. . .

By including § 5 the draftsmen sought to grant to Congress, by a specific provision applicable to the Fourteenth Amendment, the same broad powers expressed in the Necessary and Proper Clause, Art. I, § 8, cl. 18. The classic formulation of the reach of those powers was established by Chief Justice Marshall in *McCulloch v. Maryland* (1819). . . .

> Let the end be legitimate, let it be within the scope of the constitution, and all means which are appropriate, which are plainly adapted to that end, which are not prohibited, but consistent with the letter and spirit of the constitution, are constitutional.

. . . There can be no doubt that § 4 (e) may be regarded as an enactment to enforce the Equal Protection Clause. Congress explicitly declared that it enacted § 4 (e) "to secure the rights under the fourteenth amendment of persons educated in American-flag schools in which the predominant classroom language was other than English." The persons referred to include those who have migrated from the Commonwealth of Puerto Rico to New York and who have been denied the right to vote because of their inability to read and write English, and the Fourteenth Amendment rights referred to include those emanating from the Equal Protection Clause. More specifically, § 4 (e) may be viewed as a measure to secure for the Puerto Rican community residing in New York nondiscriminatory treatment by government—both in the imposition of voting qualifications and the provision or administration of governmental services, such as public schools, public housing and law enforcement.

Section 4 (e) may be readily seen as "plainly adapted" to furthering these aims of the Equal Protection Clause. The practical effect of § 4 (e) is to prohibit New York from denying the right to vote to large segments of its Puerto Rican community. Congress has thus prohibited the State from denying to that community the right that is "preservative of all rights." . . . This enhanced political power will be helpful in gaining nondiscriminatory treatment in public services for the entire Puerto Rican community. Section 4 (e) thereby enables the Puerto Rican minority better to obtain "perfect equality of civil rights and the equal protection of the laws." It was well within congressional authority to say that this need of the Puerto Rican minority for the vote warranted federal intrusion upon any state interests served by the English literacy requirement. It was for Congress, as the branch that made this judgment, to assess and weigh the various conflicting considerations—the risk or pervasiveness of the discrimination in governmental services, the effectiveness of eliminating the state restriction on the right to vote as a means of dealing with the evil, the adequacy or availability of alternative remedies, and the nature and significance of the state interests that would be affected by the nullification of the English literacy requirement as applied to residents who have successfully completed the sixth grade in a Puerto Rican school. It is not for us to review the congressional resolution of these factors. It is enough that we be able to perceive a basis upon which the Congress might resolve the conflict as it did. There plainly was such a basis to support § 4 (e) in the application in question in this case. Any contrary conclusion would require us to be blind to the realities familiar to the legislators.

The result is no different if we confine our inquiry to the question whether § 4 (e) was merely legislation aimed at the elimination of an invidious discrimination in establishing voter qualifications. We are told that New York's English literacy requirement originated in the desire to provide an incentive for non-English speaking immigrants to learn the English language and in order to assure the intelligent exercise of the franchise. Yet Congress might well have questioned, in light of the many exemptions provided, and some evidence suggesting that prejudice played a prominent role in the enactment of the requirement, whether these were actually the interests being served. Congress might have also questioned whether denial of a right deemed so precious and fundamental in our society was a necessary or appropriate means of encouraging persons to learn English, or of furthering the goal of an intelligent exercise of the franchise. Finally, Congress might well have concluded that as a means of furthering the intelligent exercise of the franchise, an ability to read or understand Spanish is as effective as ability to read English for those to whom Spanish-language newspapers and Spanish-language radio and television programs are available to inform them of election issues and governmental affairs. Since Congress undertook to legislate so as to preclude the enforcement of the state law, and did so in the context of a general appraisal of literacy requirements for voting, . . . to which it brought a specially informed legislative competence, it was Congress' prerogative to weigh these competing considerations. Here again, it is enough that we perceive a basis upon which Congress might predicate a judgment that the application of New York's English literacy requirement to deny the right to vote to a person with a sixth grade education in Puerto Rican schools in which the language of instruction was other than English constituted an invidious discrimination in violation of the Equal Protection Clause.

. . .

JUSTICE HARLAN, whom JUSTICE STEWART joins, dissenting.

Worthy as its purposes may be thought by many, I do not see how § 4 (e) of the Voting Rights Act of 1965 can be sustained except at the sacrifice of fundamentals in the American constitutional system—the separation between the legislative and judicial function and the boundaries between federal and state political authority. . . .

. . .

When recognized state violations of federal constitutional standards have occurred, Congress is of course empowered by § 5 to take appropriate remedial measures to redress and prevent the wrongs. . . . But it is a judicial question whether the condition with which Congress has thus sought to deal is in truth an infringement of the Constitution, something that is the necessary prerequisite to bringing the § 5 power into play at all. . . .

A more recent Fifteenth Amendment case serves to illustrate this distinction. In *South Carolina v. Katzenbach* (1966), . . . decided earlier this Term, we held certain remedial sections of this Voting Rights Act of 1965 constitutional under the Fifteenth Amendment, which is directed against deprivations of the right to vote on account of race. In enacting those sections of the Voting Rights Act the Congress made a detailed investigation of various state practices that had been used to deprive Negroes of the franchise. . . . In passing upon the remedial provisions, we reviewed first the "voluminous legislative history" as well as judicial precedents supporting the basic congressional finding that the clear commands of the Fifteenth Amendment had been infringed by various state subterfuges. . . . Given the existence of the evil, we held the remedial steps taken by the legislature under the Enforcement Clause of the Fifteenth Amendment to be a justifiable exercise of congressional initiative.

Section 4 (e), however, presents a significantly different type of congressional enactment. The question here is not whether the statute is appropriate remedial legislation to cure an established violation of a constitutional command, but whether there has in fact been an infringement of that constitutional command, that is, whether a particular state practice or, as here, a statute is so arbitrary or irrational as to offend the command of the Equal Protection Clause of the Fourteenth Amendment. That question is one for the judicial branch ultimately to determine. Were the rule otherwise, Congress would be able to qualify this Court's constitutional decisions under the Fourteenth and Fifteenth Amendments, let alone those under other provisions of the Constitution, by resorting to congressional power under the Necessary and Proper Clause. . . . In effect the Court reads § 5 of the Fourteenth Amendment as giving Congress the power to define the *substantive* scope of the Amendment. If that indeed be the true reach of § 5, then I do not see why Congress should not be able as well to exercise its § 5 "discretion" by enacting statutes so as in effect to dilute equal protection and due process decisions of this Court. In all such cases there is room for reasonable men to differ as to whether or not a denial of equal protection or due process has occurred, and the final decision is one of judgment. Until today this judgment has always been one for the judiciary to resolve.

. . .

. . . [No] factual data provide a legislative record supporting § 4 (e) by way of showing that Spanish-speaking citizens are fully as capable of making informed decisions in a New York election as are English-speaking citizens. Nor was there any showing whatever to support the Court's alternative argument that § 4 (e) should be viewed as but a remedial measure designed to cure or assure against unconstitutional discrimination of other varieties, *e.g.*, in "public schools, public housing and law enforcement," . . . to which Puerto Rican minorities might be subject in such communities as New York.

Thus, we have here not a matter of giving deference to a congressional estimate, based on its determination of legislative facts, bearing upon the validity *vel non* of a statute, but rather what can at most be called a legislative announcement that Congress believes a state law to entail an unconstitutional deprivation of equal protection. Although this kind of declaration is of course entitled to the most respectful consideration, coming as it does from a concurrent branch and one that is knowledgeable in matters of popular political participation, I do not believe it lessens our responsibility to decide the fundamental issue of whether in fact the state enactment violates federal constitutional rights. . . .

Reapportionment

Reynolds v. Sims, 377 U.S. 533 (1964)

M.O. Sims and other members of a Birmingham business association sued Alabama officials responsible for conducting elections, claiming that the failure to apportion violated their Fourteenth Amendment rights. One of the officials sued was B. A. Reynolds, a judge of a county probate court. Sims based his claim in part on a provision in the constitution of Alabama requiring that the state legislature be reapportioned every ten years to reflect population changes and shifts. The Alabama legislation had failed to redistrict after 1900. The result by 1960 was significant inequalities in representation. Counties with more than half a million people were entitled to the same one senator as counties with barely over ten thousand persons. A three-judge panel on the federal district court declared the Alabama plan unconstitutional, as well as two similar substitutes that had just passed the Alabama state legislature. Alabama appealed to the Supreme Court of the United States.

The Supreme Court affirmed the lower court decision by an 8-1 vote. Chief Justice Earl Warren's majority opinion insisted that the Constitution required state legislatures to be apportioned in a manner consistent with the one person, one vote principle. Reynolds *and* Baker v. Carr *(1961), which held that courts could adjudicate conflicts over apportionment, are among the most important and controversial opinions handed down by the Supreme Court of the United States. Earl Warren, who also wrote* Brown, *believed that these decisions were his most important contributions to constitutional law. What is the constitutional foundation of one person, one vote? Is that foundation sound? Given that only one house in the national government is apportioned by population, on what basis does Warren determine that both houses in state legislatures must be apportioned by population? Is his analysis correct? Does Warren insist that all legislative districts must contain equal population or merely that states must make population equality their primary concern in apportioning legislative districts? Under what conditions does* Reynolds *suggest that states may deviate from population equality? How much deviation is constitutionally acceptable?*

The Supreme Court's decisions in the reapportionment cases caused an intense but short-lived political firestorm. One month after Reynolds *was handed down the Republican Party called for a constitutional amendment that would partly reverse the result of that decision. The Republican Party platform of 1964 committed the party "to a Constitutional amendment, as well as legislation, enabling States having bicameral legislatures to apportion one House on bases of their choosing, including factors other than population." Members of Congress proposed numerous bills that would either prevent federal courts from adjudicating apportionment controversies or mandate different decisions. A proposed constitutional amendment barely missed Senate passage in 1965.*

Efforts to reverse Reynolds *nevertheless failed and failed quickly. Most Democrats supported the decision. The Democratic Party platform of 1968 declared, "We fully recognize the principle of one man, one vote in all elections." That principle was reasonably popular among the general public. Finally, and perhaps most important, within a few years all national and state legislators were elected in districts apportioned consistently with the principles announced in* Reynolds. *The winners of these elections had little incentive to denounce the electoral system under which they had been elected.*

Substantial debate exists over the impact of the reapportionment decisions. General agreement exists that the Supreme Court changed electoral practice. The dramatic malapportionments that once dotted the political landscape no longer exist. Differences between congressional districts within states are now minimal and differences between state legislative districts are much smaller than was the case before Reynolds *was decided. Whether these electoral changes have made other differences is more controversial. Most political actors at the time believed that reapportionment would shift power from conservative rural districts to more liberal urban districts. Gerald Rosenberg's survey concludes that these hopes were not realized. He writes, "While there are studies both finding and not finding effects, an overall reading seems to be that any [policy] effects that can be traced to reapportionment are small."*[56] *One recent study found that reapportionment benefited Democrats and incumbents. Democrats benefited in part because previous districts had often resulted from Republican gerrymanders, in part because the Democratic landslide in 1964 increased the number of state legislators committed to Democratic gerrymanders after* Reynolds, *and in part because the majority of the justices who reapportioned districts after* Reynolds *were Democrats. Incumbents benefited because* Reynolds *increased opportunities for redistricting and incumbents were in a position to ensure that they would benefit from the new apportionments.*[57] *Many observers think the lasting legacy of* Reynolds *is the increased use of gerrymanders in state legislatures as each party seeks to maximize their seats in Congress and states legislatures.*

CHIEF JUSTICE WARREN delivered the opinion of the Court.

. . .

Undeniably the Constitution of the United States protects the right of all qualified citizens to vote, in state as well as in federal elections. A consistent line of decisions by this Court in cases involving attempts to deny or restrict the right of suffrage has made this indelibly clear. . . . The right to vote freely for the candidate of

56. Rosenberg, *The Hollow Hope*, 297.

57. See Gary W. Cox and Jonathan N. Katz, *The Electoral Consequences of the Reapportionment Revolution* (New York: Cambridge University Press, 2002).

one's choice is of the essence of a democratic society, and any restrictions on that right strike at the heart of representative government. And the right of suffrage can be denied by a debasement or dilution of the weight of a citizen's vote just as effectively as by wholly prohibiting the free exercise of the franchise. . . .

. . .

. . . [T]he fundamental principle of representative government in this country is one of equal representation for equal numbers of people, without regard to race, sex, economic status, or place of residence within a State. Our problem, then, is to ascertain, in the instant cases, whether there are any constitutionally cognizable principles which would justify departures from the basic standard of equality among voters in the apportionment of seats in state legislatures.

. . .

Legislators represent people, not trees or acres. Legislators are elected by voters, not farms or cities or economic interests. As long as ours is a representative form of government, and our legislatures are those instruments of government elected directly by and directly representative of the people, the right to elect legislators in a free and unimpaired fashion is a bedrock of our political system. . . . If a State should provide that the votes of citizens in one part of the State should be given two times, or five times, or 10 times the weight of votes of citizens in another part of the State, it could hardly be contended that the right to vote of those residing in the disfavored areas had not been effectively diluted. It would appear extraordinary to suggest that a State could be constitutionally permitted to enact a law providing that certain of the State's voters could vote two, five, or 10 times for their legislative representatives, while voters living elsewhere could vote only once. And it is inconceivable that a state law to the effect that, in counting votes for legislators, the votes of citizens in one part of the State would be multiplied by two, five, or 10, while the votes of persons in another area would be counted only at face value, could be constitutionally sustainable. Of course, the effect of state legislative districting schemes which give the same number of representatives to unequal numbers of constituents is identical. . . . Weighting the votes of citizens differently, by any method or means, merely because of where they happen to reside, hardly seems justifiable. . . .

. . .

Logically, in a society ostensibly grounded on representative government, it would seem reasonable that a majority of the people of a State could elect a majority of that State's legislators. To conclude differently, and to sanction minority control of state legislative bodies, would appear to deny majority rights in a way that far surpasses any possible denial of minority rights that might otherwise be thought to result. Since legislatures are responsible for enacting laws by which all citizens are to be governed, they should be bodies which are collectively responsive to the popular will. And the concept of equal protection has been traditionally viewed as requiring the uniform treatment of persons standing in the same relation to the governmental action questioned or challenged. With respect to the allocation of legislative representation, all voters, as citizens of a State, stand in the same relation regardless of where they live. Any suggested criteria for the differentiation of citizens are insufficient to justify any discrimination, as to the weight of their votes, unless relevant to the permissible purposes of legislative apportionment. Since the achieving of fair and effective representation for all citizens is concededly the basic aim of legislative apportionment, we conclude that the Equal Protection Clause guarantees the opportunity for equal participation by all voters in the election of state legislators. Diluting the weight of votes because of place of residence impairs basic constitutional rights under the Fourteenth Amendment just as much as invidious discriminations based upon factors such as race, *Brown v. Board of Education* (1954), or economic status, *Griffin v. Illinois* (1956). . . . Our constitutional system amply provides for the protection of minorities by means other than giving them majority control of state legislatures. And the democratic ideals of equality and majority rule, which have served this Nation so well in the past, are hardly of any less significance for the present and the future.

. . .

To the extent that a citizen's right to vote is debased, he is that much less a citizen. The fact that an individual lives here or there is not a legitimate reason for overweighting or diluting the efficacy of his vote. . . . The weight of a citizen's vote cannot be made to depend on where he lives. Population is, of necessity, the starting point for consideration and the controlling criterion for judgment in legislative apportionment controversies. A citizen, a qualified voter, is no more nor no less so because he lives in the city or on the farm. This is the clear and strong command of our Constitution's Equal Protection Clause. This is an essential part of the concept of a government of laws and not men. This is at the heart of Lincoln's vision of "government of the people, by the people, [and] for the people." The Equal Protection Clause demands no less than substantially equal state legislative representation for all citizens, of all places as well as of all races.

We hold that, as a basic constitutional standard, the Equal Protection Clause requires that the seats in both houses of a bicameral state legislature must be apportioned on a population basis. Simply stated, an individual's right to vote for state legislators is unconstitutionally impaired when its weight is in a substantial fashion diluted when compared with votes of citizens living in other parts of the State. Since, under neither the existing apportionment provisions nor either of the proposed plans was either of the houses of the Alabama Legislature apportioned on a population basis, the District Court correctly held that all three of these schemes were constitutionally invalid. . . .

. . .

The system of representation in the two Houses of the Federal Congress is one ingrained in our Constitution, as part of the law of the land. It is one conceived out of compromise and concession indispensable to the establishment of our federal republic. Arising from unique historical circumstances, it is based on the consideration that in establishing our type of federalism a group of formerly independent States bound themselves together under one national government. Admittedly, the original 13 States surrendered some of their sovereignty in agreeing to join together "to form a more perfect Union." But at the heart of our constitutional system remains the concept of separate and distinct governmental entities which have delegated some, but not all, of their formerly held powers to the single national government. . . . Political subdivisions of States—counties, cities, or whatever—never were and never have been considered as sovereign entities. Rather, they have been traditionally regarded as subordinate governmental instrumentalities created by the State to assist in the carrying out of state governmental functions. . . . The relationship of the States to the Federal Government could hardly be less analogous.

. . .

. . . So long as the divergences from a strict population standard are based on legitimate considerations incident to the effectuation of a rational state policy, some deviations from the equal-population principle are constitutionally permissible with respect to the apportionment of seats in either or both of the two houses of a bicameral state legislature. But neither history alone, nor economic or other sorts of group interests, are permissible factors in attempting to justify disparities from population-based representation. Citizens, not history or economic interests, cast votes. Considerations of area alone provide an insufficient justification for deviations from the equal-population principle. Again, people, not land or trees or pastures, vote. . . .

A consideration that appears to be of more substance in justifying some deviations from population-based representation in state legislatures is that of insuring some voice to political subdivisions, as political subdivisions. . . . Local governmental entities are frequently charged with various responsibilities incident to the operation of state government. . . . And a State may legitimately desire to construct districts along political subdivision lines to deter the possibilities of gerrymandering. However, permitting deviations from population-based representation does not mean that each local governmental unit or political subdivision can be given separate representation, regardless of population. . . . But if, even as a result of a clearly rational state policy of according some legislative representation to political subdivisions, population is submerged as the controlling consideration in the apportionment of seats in the particular legislative body, then the right of all of the State's citizens to cast an effective and adequately weighted vote would be unconstitutionally impaired.

. . .

JUSTICE CLARK, concurring in the affirmance.

It seems to me that all that the Court need say in this case is that each plan considered by the trial court is "a crazy quilt," clearly revealing invidious discrimination in each house of the Legislature and therefore violative of the Equal Protection Clause. . . .

. . .

JUSTICE STEWART. . . .

JUSTICE HARLAN, dissenting.

. . .

. . . [T]e Equal Protection Clause was never intended to inhibit the States in choosing any democratic method they pleased for the apportionment of their legislatures. This is shown by the language of the Fourteenth

Amendment taken as a whole, by the understanding of those who proposed and ratified it, and by the political practices of the States at the time the Amendment was adopted. It is confirmed by numerous state and congressional actions since the adoption of the Fourteenth Amendment, and by the common understanding of the Amendment as evidenced by subsequent constitutional amendments and decisions of this Court before *Baker v. Carr* (1961). . . .

. . .

. . . Of the 23 loyal States which ratified the Amendment before 1870, five had constitutional provisions for apportionment of at least one house of their respective legislatures which wholly disregarded the spread of population. Ten more had constitutional provisions which gave primary emphasis to population, but which applied also other principles, such as partial ratios and recognition of political subdivisions, which were intended to favor sparsely settled areas. Can it be seriously contended that the legislatures of these States, almost two-thirds of those concerned, would have ratified an amendment which might render their own States' constitutions unconstitutional?

. . .

. . . As of 1961, the Constitutions of all but 11 States, roughly 20% of the total, recognized bases of apportionment other than geographic spread of population. . . . [I]t is evident that the actual practice of the States is even more uniformly than their theory opposed to the Court's view of what is constitutionally permissible.

. . .

Generalities cannot obscure the cold truth that cases of this type are not amenable to the development of judicial standards. No set of standards can guide a court which has to decide how many legislative districts a State shall have, or what the shape of the districts shall be, or where to draw a particular district line. No judicially manageable standard can determine whether a State should have single-member districts or multimember districts or some combination of both. No such standard can control the balance between keeping up with population shifts and having stable districts. In all these respects, the courts will be called upon to make particular decisions with respect to which a principle of equally populated districts will be of no assistance whatsoever. Quite obviously, there are limitless possibilities for districting consistent with such a principle. Nor can these problems be avoided by judicial reliance on legislative judgments so far as possible. Reshaping or combining one or two districts, or modifying just a few district lines, is no less a matter of choosing among many possible solutions, with varying political consequences, than reapportionment broadside.

. . .

. . . [P]eople are not ciphers and . . . legislators can represent their electors only by speaking for their interests—economic, social, political—many of which do reflect the place where the electors live. The Court does not establish, or indeed even attempt to make a case for the proposition that conflicting interests within a State can only be adjusted by disregarding them when voters are grouped for purposes of representation.

. . .

These decisions also cut deeply into the fabric of our federalism. What must follow from them may eventually appear to be the product of state legislatures. Nevertheless, no thinking person can fail to recognize that the aftermath of these cases, however desirable it may be thought in itself, will have been achieved at the cost of a radical alteration in the relationship between the States and the Federal Government, more particularly the Federal Judiciary. Only one who has an overbearing impatience with the federal system and its political processes will believe that that cost was not too high or was inevitable.

Finally, these decisions give support to a current mistaken view of the Constitution and the constitutional function of this Court. This view, in a nutshell, is that every major social ill in this country can find its cure in some constitutional "principle," and that this Court should "take the lead" in promoting reform when other branches of government fail to act. The Constitution is not a panacea for every blot upon the public welfare, nor should this Court, ordained as a judicial body, be thought of as a general haven for reform movements. The Constitution is an instrument of government, fundamental to which is the premise that in a diffusion of governmental authority lies the greatest promise that this Nation will realize liberty for all its citizens. This Court, limited in function in accordance with that premise, does not serve its high purpose when it exceeds its authority, even to satisfy justified impatience with the slow workings of the political process. For when, in the name of constitutional interpretation, the Court adds something to the Constitution that was deliberately excluded from it, the Court in reality substitutes its view of what should be so for the amending process.

Table 8-6 Selection of U.S. Supreme Court Cases Reviewing State Apportionment of Legislative Districts

Case	Vote	Outcome	Decision
McPherson v. Blacker, 146 U.S. 1 (1892)	9-0	Upheld	At-large election of presidential electors does not violate federal Constitution
Richardson v. McChesney, 218 U.S. 487 (1910)	9-0	Dismissed	A case is moot when election results have already been certified
State of Ohio on Relation of Davis v. Hildebrant, 241 U.S. 565 (1916)	6-0	Upheld	States may reapportion by referendum
Smiley v. Holm, 285 U.S. 355 (1932)	8-0	Struck down	State legislatures exercise a regular lawmaking function when drawing congressional districts, which are potentially subject to gubernatorial veto
Colegrove v. Green, 328 U.S. 549 (1946)	4-3	Dismissed	Evaluation of whether congressional districts meet federal statutory requirements is a political question for Congress to assess
Baker v. Carr, 369 U.S. 186 (1962)	6-2	Remanded	Legislative districting is subject to equal protection scrutiny by courts
Gray v. Sanders, 372 U.S. 368 (1963)	8-1	Struck down	County-based voting system for primaries for statewide offices violates one-person, one-vote requirement
Wesberry v. Sanders, 376 U.S. 1 (1964)	6-3	Struck down	Congressional districts must be drawn so as to give equal representation to equal numbers
Reynolds v. Sims, 377 U.S. 533 (1964)	8-1	Struck down	Both chambers of a state legislature must be apportioned on the basis of population and equally sized districts
Gaffney v. Cummings, 412 U.S. 735 (1973)	6-3	Upheld	Minor variations in state legislative district size are acceptable, and districting plans may take into account partisanship of voters
White v. Regester, 412 U.S. 755 (1973)	6-3	Struck down	Minor variations in state legislative district size are acceptable, but multi-member districts are unconstitutional when they negatively impact the electoral chances of historicallly disadvantaged groups
United Jewish Organizations of Williamsburgh v. Carey, 430 U.S. 144 (1977)	7-1	Upheld	Districting plans may take into account the race of voters in order to positively impact the electoral changes of historically disadvantaged groups
Connor v. Finch, 431 U.S. 407 (1977)	7-1	Struck down	Preserving county boundaries is not an adequate justification for creating variations in district size
Karcher v. Daggett, 462 U.S. 725 (1983)	5-4	Struck down	Even trivial variations in congressional district size are unacceptable unless justified by a legitimate state interest
Thornburg v. Gingles, 478 U.S. 30 (1986)	9-0	Struck down	Districting plans that move a cohesive minority group into an electoral district such that their favored candidate will be consistently defeated are illegal

(*Continued*)

Table 8-6 *(Continued)*

Case	Vote	Outcome	Decision
Shaw v. Reno, 509 U.S. 630 (1993)	5-4	Remanded	Bizarrely drawn legislative districts that separate voters based on race may be unconstitutional
Bush v. Vera, 517 U.S. 952 (1996)	5-4	Struck down	Highly irregular legislative districts that separate voters based on race are unconstitutional
League of Latin American Citizens v. Perry, 548 U.S. 399 (2006)	5-4	Upheld	States may redraw legislative boundaries as often as they want and may draw "partisan gerrymanders"

Harper v. Virginia Board of Elections, 383 U.S. 663 (1966)

Annie Harper, a citizen of Virginia, was unable to vote because she could not pay the $1.50 poll tax mandated by state law. On March 17, 1964, she brought a lawsuit in federal court claiming that the poll tax deprived her of the equal protection of the laws. Virginia responded that the equal protection clause was concerned primarily with race discrimination, not disparities based on the ability to pay. Virginia's claim was supported by Breedlove v. Suttles *(1937), which unanimously held that "to make payment of poll taxes a prerequisite of voting is not to deny any privilege or immunity protected by the Fourteenth Amendment." The federal district court, on the basis of* Breedlove, *sustained the Virginia law. Harper appealed to the Supreme Court of the United States.*

The Supreme Court declared the Virginia poll tax unconstitutional by a 6-3 vote. Justice Douglas's majority opinion declared voting to be a fundamental right that could not be denied based on the ability to pay. To what extent does Justice Douglas focus on the inequality between more and less affluent citizens, and to what extent is he concerned with the substance of the inequality, the right to vote? Would Justice Douglas strike down fees to swim in a town pool? A literacy test for voting? Justice Douglas asserts "the equal protection clause is not shackled to the political theory of a particular era." What did he mean by that? Is this assertion correct or is Justice Black correct that such practices are inconsistent with the judicial obligation to interpret a written Constitution? Consider also the influence of the Voting Rights Act of 1965 on the judicial decision in Harper. *That law authorized the president to bring a lawsuit challenging the constitutionality of poll taxes. Could an argument be made that justices are freer to rely on broad principles of justice when governing officials consciously decide that the Supreme Court shall make policy on a particular issue? What other constitutional foundations do you find for Justice Douglas's opinion? Suppose that the Supreme Court had sustained the Virginia poll tax. Given the Voting Rights Act of 1965, would that have been a countermajoritarian decision?*

JUSTICE DOUGLAS delivered the opinion of the Court.

. . .

. . . [O]nce the franchise is granted to the electorate, lines may not be drawn which are inconsistent with the Equal Protection Clause of the Fourteenth Amendment. . . .

We conclude that a State violates the Equal Protection Clause of the Fourteenth Amendment whenever it makes the affluence of the voter or payment of any fee an electoral standard. Voter qualifications have no relation to wealth nor to paying or not paying this or any other tax. Our cases demonstrate that the Equal Protection Clause of the Fourteenth Amendment restrains the States from fixing voter qualifications which invidiously discriminate. Thus, without questioning the power of a State to impose reasonable residence restrictions on the availability of the ballot, . . . we held in *Carrington v. Rash* (1965) . . . that a State may not deny the opportunity to vote to a *bona fide* resident merely because he is a member of the armed services.

. . .

It is argued that a State may exact fees from citizens for many different kinds of licenses; that, if it can demand from all an equal fee for a driver's license, it can demand from all an equal poll tax for voting. But we must remember that the interest of the State, when it comes to voting, is limited to the power to fix qualifications. Wealth, like race, creed, or color, is not germane to one's ability to participate intelligently in the electoral process. Lines drawn on the basis of wealth or property, like those of race . . . are traditionally disfavored. . . .

. . . [T]he Equal Protection Clause is not shackled to the political theory of a particular era. In determining what lines are unconstitutionally discriminatory, we have never been confined to historic notions of equality, any more than we have restricted due process to a fixed catalogue of what was at a given time deemed to be the limits of fundamental rights. . . . Notions of what constitutes equal treatment for purposes of the Equal Protection Clause do change. . . .

. . .

We have long been mindful that, where fundamental rights and liberties are asserted under the Equal Protection Clause, classifications which might invade or restrain them must be closely scrutinized and carefully confined. . . .

Those principles apply here. For, to repeat, wealth or fee paying has, in our view, no relation to voting qualifications; the right to vote is too precious, too fundamental to be so burdened or conditioned.

JUSTICE BLACK, dissenting.

In *Breedlove v. Suttles* (1937), . . . we unanimously upheld the right of the State of Georgia to make payment of its state poll tax a prerequisite to voting in state elections. . . . Since the *Breedlove* . . . case . . . [was] decided, the Federal Constitution has not been amended. I would adhere to the holding of those cases. . . .

It should be pointed out at once that the Court's decision is to no extent based on a finding that the Virginia law as written or as applied is being used as a device or mechanism to deny Negro citizens of Virginia the right to vote on account of their color. Apparently the Court agrees with the District Court below and with my Brothers HARLAN and STEWART that this record would not support any finding that the Virginia poll tax law the Court invalidates has any such effect. If the record could support a finding that the law as written or applied has such an effect, the law would, of course, be unconstitutional as a violation of the Fourteenth and Fifteenth Amendments. . . .

. . . The mere fact that a law results in treating some groups differently from others does not, of course, automatically amount to a violation of the Equal Protection Clause. To bar a State from drawing any distinctions in the application of its laws would practically paralyze the regulatory power of legislative bodies. . . . Voting laws are no exception to this principle. All voting laws treat some persons differently from others in some respects. Some bar a person from voting who is under 21 years of age; others bar those under 18. Some bar convicted felons or the insane, and some have attached a freehold or other property qualification for voting.

. . . [U]nder a proper interpretation of the Equal Protection Clause, States are to have the broadest kind of leeway in areas where they have a general constitutional competence to act. In view of the purpose of the terms to restrain the courts from a wholesale invalidation of state laws under the Equal Protection Clause, it would be difficult to say that the poll tax requirement is "irrational," or "arbitrary," or works "invidious discriminations." State poll tax legislation can "reasonably," "rationally" and without an "invidious" or evil purpose to injure anyone be found to rest on a number of state policies, including (1) the State's desire to collect its revenue, and (2) its belief that voters who pay a poll tax will be interested in furthering the State's welfare when they vote. . . . Property qualifications existed in the Colonies and were continued by many States after the Constitution was adopted. Although I join the Court in disliking the policy of the poll tax, this is not, in my judgment, a justifiable reason for holding this poll tax law unconstitutional. Such a holding on my part would, in my judgment, be an exercise of power which the Constitution does not confer upon me.

Another reason for my dissent from the Court's judgment and opinion is that it seems to be using the old "natural law due process formula" to justify striking down state laws as violations of the Equal Protection Clause. . . .

The Court denies that it is using the "natural law due process formula." It says that its invalidation of the Virginia law "is founded not on what we think governmental policy should be, but on what the Equal Protection Clause requires." I find no statement in the Court's opinion, however, which advances even a plausible argument as to why the alleged discriminations which might possibly be effected by Virginia's poll tax law are "irrational," "unreasonable," "arbitrary," or "invidious," or have no relevance to a legitimate policy which the State wishes to adopt. . . . The Court's failure to give any reasons to show that these purposes of the poll tax are "irrational," "unreasonable," "arbitrary," or "invidious" is a pretty clear indication to me that none exist. I can only conclude that the primary, controlling, predominant, if not the exclusive, reason for declaring the Virginia law unconstitutional is the Court's deep-seated hostility and antagonism, which I share, to making payment of a tax a prerequisite to voting.

The Court's justification for consulting its own notions, rather than following the original meaning of the Constitution, as I would, apparently is based on the belief of the majority of the Court that for this Court to be bound by the original meaning of the Constitution is an intolerable and debilitating evil; that our Constitution should not be "shackled to the political theory of a particular era," and that, to save the country from the original Constitution, the Court must have constant power to renew it and keep it abreast of this Court's more enlightened theories of what is best for our society.

It seems to me that this is an attack not only on the great value of our Constitution itself, but also on the concept of a written constitution which is to survive through the years as originally written unless changed through the amendment process which the Framers wisely provided. Moreover, when a "political theory" embodied in our Constitution becomes outdated, it seems to me that a majority of the nine members of this Court are not only without constitutional power, but are far less qualified, to choose a new constitutional political theory than the people of this country proceeding in the manner provided by Article V.

. . .

JUSTICE HARLAN, whom JUSTICE STEWART joins, dissenting.

. . .

Property qualifications and poll taxes have been a traditional part of our political structure. . . . [I]t is only by fiat that it can be said, . . . that there can be no rational debate as to their advisability. Most of the early Colonies had them; many of the States have had them during much of their histories; and, whether one agrees or not, arguments have been and still can be made in favor of them. For example, it is certainly a rational argument that payment of some minimal poll tax promotes civic responsibility, weeding out those who do not care enough about public affairs to pay $1.50 or thereabouts a year for the exercise of the franchise. It is also arguable, indeed it was probably accepted as sound political theory by a large percentage of Americans through most of our history, that people with some property have a deeper stake in community affairs, and are consequently more responsible, more educated, more knowledgeable, more worthy of confidence, than those without means, and that the community and Nation would be better managed if the franchise were restricted to such citizens. . . .

. . .

Property and poll-tax qualifications . . . are not in accord with current egalitarian notions of how a modern democracy should be organized. It is, of course, entirely fitting that legislatures should modify the law to reflect such changes in popular attitudes. However, it is all wrong, in my view, for the Court to adopt the political doctrines popularly accepted at a particular moment of our history and to declare all others to be irrational and invidious, barring them from the range of choice by reasonably minded people acting through the political process. It was not too long ago that Mr. Justice Holmes felt impelled to remind the Court that the Due Process Clause of the Fourteenth Amendment does not enact the *laissez-faire* theory of society. . . . The times have changed, and perhaps it is appropriate to observe that neither does the Equal Protection Clause of that Amendment rigidly impose upon America an ideology of unrestrained egalitarianism.

C. Citizenship

Congressional power to strip persons of citizenship was hotly contested. The Supreme Court in 1958 rendered split decisions, both by 5-4 votes, holding that Congress could divest of citizenship a person who voted in a foreign election (*Perez v. Brownell*) but could not do so as a punishment for crime (*Trop v. Dulles*). Justice Frankfurter's majority opinion in *Perez* insisted that the federal power to regulate foreign affairs included the federal power to divest citizenship when appropriate. Quoting the executive branch committee that drafted the Nationality Act of 1940, he stated,

> Taking an active part in the political affairs of a foreign state by voting in a political election therein is believed to involve a political attachment and practical allegiance thereto which is inconsistent with continued allegiance to the United States, whether or not the person in question has or acquires the nationality of the foreign state. In any event it is not believed that an American national should be permitted to participate in the political affairs of a foreign state and at the same time retain his American

> nationality. The two facts would seem to be inconsistent with each other.

Perez was overruled nine years later in *Afroyim v. Rusk* (1967), again by a 5-4 vote. Justice Black's majority opinion insisted that democracies did not allow rulers to determine who was and who was not a citizen. He concluded,

> Citizenship in this Nation is a part of a cooperative affair. Its citizenry is the country and the country is its citizenry. The very nature of our free government makes it completely incongruous to have a rule of law under which a group of citizens temporarily in office can deprive another group of citizens of their citizenship. We hold that the Fourteenth Amendment was designed to, and does, protect every citizen of this Nation against a congressional forcible destruction of his citizenship, whatever his creed, color, or race. Our holding does no more than to give to this citizen that which is his own, a constitutional right to remain a citizen in a free country unless he voluntarily relinquishes that citizenship.

The New Deal Court also expanded access to citizenship. In *Schneiderman v. United States* (1943) the Court explored whether a member of the Communist Party had "demonstrated attachment to the principles of the Constitution of the United States" as required by federal law.[58] The judicial majority ruled that Schneiderman was qualified for American citizenship. Justice Murphy maintained,

> As Justice Holmes said [in dissent in *United States v. Schwimmer* (1931)], "Surely it cannot show lack of attachment to the principles of the Constitution that [one] thinks that it can be improved." Criticism of, and the sincerity of desires to improve the Constitution should not be judged by conformity to prevailing thought because, "if there is any principle of the Constitution that more imperatively calls for attachment than any other it is the principle of free thought—not free thought for those who agree with us but freedom for the thought that we hate.". . . . Whatever attitude we may individually hold toward persons and organizations that believe in or advocate extensive changes in our existing order, it should be our desire and concern at all times to uphold the right of free discussion and free thinking to which we as a people claim primary attachment. To neglect this duty in a proceeding in which we are called upon to judge whether a particular individual has failed to manifest attachment to the Constitution would be ironical indeed.

58. For one interesting rumination on the subject, see Sanford Levinson, *Constitutional Faith* (Princeton, NJ: Princeton University Press, 1989).

V. Equality

MAJOR DEVELOPMENTS

- Race-conscious measures required to meet strict scrutiny standard
- School segregation declared unconstitutional
- Indian Bill of Rights

The modern understanding of equal protection took shape during the New Deal/Great Society Era. Constitutional decision makers before the 1930s believed that legislation could distinguish among groups of people when doing so advanced the public good and was related to a real difference between the groups. In theory all groups were judged by the same standard. By the late 1960s, however, constitutional equality was bifurcated. In most circumstances government was free to make any distinction between most groups of people as long as the distinction satisfied a very weak rational basis test. When government discriminated on the basis of race or ethnicity or against other "discrete and insular minorities," however, elected officials had to demonstrate that their actions were necessary means to achieve compelling ends.

When reading the materials below, think about the reasons that might explain why constitutional authorities held government officials to a higher standard when they made racial distinctions than when they made other distinctions. The history of the equal protection clause provides legal reasons for treating race discrimination differently from any other form of discrimination. The *Carolene Products* footnote suggests another possibility. Racial discriminations merit greater scrutiny because persons of color have historically been politically powerless and frequently victimized by prejudiced white majorities. A third possibility is that racial discriminations are particularly odious in that discriminating on the basis of race is more inconsistent with fundamental moral and constitutional principles than discriminating between different businesses or between labor and management.

Table 8-7 Selection of U.S. Supreme Court Cases Reviewing State Laws under Equal Protection

Case	Vote	Result	Outcome
Slaughterhouse Cases, 83 U.S. 36 (1873)	5-4	Upheld	Equal protection clause has no application to laws not aimed at creating hardships for blacks as a class; state law restricting the ability of some butchers to practice their profession is constitutional
Strauder v. West Virginia, 100 U.S. 303 (1880)	7-2	Struck down	States may not categorically exclude blacks from juries
Yick Wo v. Hopkins, 118 U.S. 356 (1886)	9-0	Struck down	States may not systematically deny permits to operate wooden laundries to Chinese laundry owners
Plessy v. Ferguson, 163 U.S. 537 (1896)	7-1	Upheld	States may require separate accommodations on railway cars for blacks and whites
Connolly v. Union Sewer Pipe Co., 184 U.S. 540 (1902)	7-1	Struck down	Antitrust statute that exempts only farmers and ranchers unconstitutionally makes arbitrary distinctions among otherwise similar acts and vocations
Lindsley v. Natural Carbonic Gas Co., 220 U.S. 61 (1911)	9-0	Upheld	Legislative classifications are consistent with the equal protection clause so long as they are not wholly arbitrary and have some reasonable basis, and the courts should assume a reasonable factual situation that could support the classification; consequently, states may prohibit some methods of extracting natural gas while allowing others
Buck v. Bell, 274 U.S. 200 (1927)	8-1	Upheld	States may require the forced sterilization of patients at state institutions considered "feeble-minded"
Stewart Dry Goods Co. v. Lewis, 294 U.S. 550 (1935)	6-3	Struck down	A graduated tax on a business' sales that increases with the amount of total sales is arbitrary and unconstitutional
Brown v. Board of Education, 347 U.S. 483 (1954)	9-0	Struck down	Segregation of children in public schools on the basis of race is unconstitutional
Baker v. Carr, 369 U.S. 186 (1962)	6-2	Struck down	Malapportioned legislative districts raise equal protection concerns that may be addressed by courts
Peterson v. City of Greenville, 373 U.S. 244 (1963)	8-1	Struck down	Trespass convictions of black sit-in protesters violate the equal protection clause when state law exists requiring segregated lunch counters
Williamson v. Lee Optical Co., 348 U.S. 483 (1955)	9-0	Upheld	Law that limits persons who are not optometrists or ophthalmologists from fitting lenses to faces has a rational basis and does not represent the kind of invidious discrimination that requires more careful judicial scrutiny
Reed v. Reed, 404 U.S. 71 (1971)	9-0	Struck down	Mandatory preference of men over women as probate administrators is an arbitrary distinction and violates equal protection clause
San Antonio Independent School District v. Rodriguez, 411 U.S. 1 (1973)	5-4	Upheld	Equal protection clause does not require equal resources or advantages, and unequal funding of school districts is constitutional
Milliken v. Bradley, 418 U.S. 717 (1974)	5-4	Upheld	De facto racial segregation across school districts does not violate the equal protection clause

(*Continued*)

Table 8-7 *(Continued)*

Case	Vote	Result	Outcome
Craig v. Boren, 429 U.S. 190 (1976)	7-2	Struck down	Statute that prohibits the sale of beer to males under 21 but allows females over 18 to purchase is unconstitutional; gender classifications should be reviewed on the basis of an "intermediate" level of scrutiny
Regents of the University of California v. Bakke, 438 U.S. 265 (1978)	5-4	Struck down	Universities may consider race in admissions in order to achieve a diverse student body but may not establish a quota system
Plyler v. Doe, 457 U.S. 202 (1982)	5-4	Struck down	States may not deny public services such as education to illegal aliens
McCleskey v. Kemp, 481 U.S. 279 (1987)	5-4	Upheld	Racially disparate results from death penalty sentencing do not prove violation of the equal protection clause without a demonstration of racially discriminatory purpose
City of Richmond v. J. A. Croson Co., 488 U.S. 469 (1989)	6-3	Struck down	States may not use racial set-asides for public contracts on the basis of generalized assertions of past discrimination
Romer v. Evans, 517 U.S. 620 (1996)	6-3	Struck down	Colorado's "Amendment 2", preventing government offices throughout the state from prohibiting all forms of discrimination against gays and lesbians, is inexplicable by anything but animus toward the affected class and lacks a rational relationship to a legitimate state interest
United States v. Virginia, 518 U.S. 515 (1996)	7-1	Struck down	Virginia Military Institute's male-only admission policy denies women "full citizenship stature"
Grutter v. Bollinger, 539 U.S. 306 (2003)	5-4	Upheld	Universities may consider race in admissions in order to achieve a "critical mass" of minority students

Finally, government might be held to a higher standard when making racial classifications because far more laws making racial classifications are based on prejudice than are laws making other classifications.

Strict scrutiny was limited to distinctions of race and ethnicity. Some proponents of women's rights claimed that arguments for racial equality also supported greater gender equality. These arguments did not gain official sanction until the late 1970s. Warren Court opinions on gender equality resembled Waite Court opinions delivered in the late nineteenth century.

A. Equality Under Law

The Supreme Court abandoned inherited concerns with class legislation. Judicial opinions held that unless race or a related classification was at issue, elected officials could make any distinction between people or classes of people that might be thought rational. *Railway Express Agency v. People of State of New York* (1949) is a typical case. A New York City ordinance forbade any person from operating an "advertising vehicle" unless the vehicle was "engaged in the usual business or regular work of the owner." A unanimous Supreme Court quickly dismissed claims that the law violated the equal protection clause. Justice Douglas's opinion for the Court asserted,

> We cannot say that that judgment is not an allowable one. Yet if it is, the classification has relation to the purpose for which it is made and does not contain the kind of discrimination against which the Equal Protection Clause affords protection. It is by such practical considerations based on experience

> rather than by theoretical inconsistencies that the question of equal protection is to be answered. . . . And the fact that New York City sees fit to eliminate from traffic this kind of distraction but does not touch what may be even greater ones in a different category, such as the vivid displays on Times Square, is immaterial. It is no requirement of equal protection that all evils of the same genus be eradicated or none at all.

B. Race

The New Deal/Great Society Era witnessed dramatic changes in the constitutional status of African-Americans. Jim Crow reigned supreme when Franklin Roosevelt took office in 1933. By the time Lyndon Johnson left office in 1969 Americans were living in a new constitutional universe. *Plessy v. Ferguson* (1896) had been overruled by a series of decisions beginning with *Brown v. Board of Education* (1954). *Brown* was considered as central to the constitutional order as *Marbury v. Madison* (1803). Congress had passed such powerful anti-discrimination laws as the Civil Rights Act of 1964 and the Voting Rights Act of 1965. Racial equality had by no means been achieved, but a general consensus existed that Jim Crow was moribund.

The changing constitutional status of African Americans was in large part a consequence of changing partisan commitments, particularly those of the Democratic Party. The 1932 Democratic Party platform did not mention race. The Republican Party platform briefly stated, "Vindication of the rights of the Negro citizen to enjoy the full benefits of life, liberty and the pursuit of happiness is traditional in the Republican Party, and our party stands pledged to maintain equal opportunity and rights for Negro citizens." Beginning in 1940 each party platform included longer and stronger articulations of commitments to racial equality. By 1960 both parties were equally committed to both *Brown* and a frontal federal attack on Jim Crow. The Democratic Party platform that year asserted,

> We shall also seek to create an affirmative new atmosphere in which to deal with racial divisions and inequalities which threaten both the integrity of our democratic faith and the proposition on which our nation was founded—that all men are created equal. It is our faith in human dignity that distinguishes our open free society from the closed totalitarian society of the Communists.
>
> . . .
>
> The time has come to assure equal access for all Americans to all areas of community life, including voting booths, schoolrooms, jobs, housing, and public facilities.
>
> . . .
>
> A new Democratic Administration will also use its full powers—legal and moral—to ensure the beginning of good-faith compliance with the Constitutional requirement that racial discrimination be ended in public education.

The Republican Party platform of 1960 echoed that commitment to racial equality.

> We supported the position of the Negro school children before the Supreme Court. We believe the Supreme Court school decision should be carried out in accordance with the mandate of the Court.
>
> . . .
>
> The Department of Justice will continue its vigorous support of court orders for school desegregation. Desegregation suits now pending involve at least 39 school districts. Those suits and others already concluded will affect most major cities in which school segregation is being practiced.

All three branches of the national government participated in this assault on racial segregation. Beginning in 1957, Congress passed ever-tougher anti-discrimination laws. Members of the executive branch sought pro–civil rights jurists for the federal bench; submitted amicus briefs urging justices to declare Jim Crow practices unconstitutional; and, during the 1960s, proposed bold civil rights initiatives.[59] President Truman's "Special Message to Congress" in 1948 declared,

> The Federal Government has a clear duty to see that Constitutional guarantees of individual liberties and of equal protection under the laws are not denied or abridged anywhere in our Union. That duty is shared by all three branches of the Government, but it can be fulfilled only if the Congress enacts modern, comprehensive civil rights laws, adequate to the needs of the day, and demonstrating our continuing faith in the free way of life.

59. McMahon, *Reconsidering Roosevelt.*

The Supreme Court repeatedly sided with African-Americans, both in cases concerned with equal protection and on other constitutional matters. Thurgood Marshall by 1965 had become the most successful Supreme Court advocate in American history.

An increasingly powerful civil rights movement successfully prodded elected officials to promote racial equality. Charles Houston, Thurgood Marshall, and other lawyers from the NAACP Legal Defense Fund developed the litigation strategy responsible for first undermining and then overruling *Plessy v. Ferguson*. A. Philip Randolph and Martin Luther King, Jr., organized protest movements that induced governing officials to adopt anti-discrimination policies and increased support for such policies in the North. Violent southern responses to the peaceful civil rights protests organized by Martin Luther King, Jr., outraged many racial moderates in the North and led to the Civil Rights Act of 1964 and the Voting Rights Act of 1965.[60]

Contemporary scholars debate the extent to which litigation campaigns deserve the credit for abolishing Jim Crow. Conventional accounts maintain that it was judicial decisions that destroyed segregation in the South. "It was the Warren Court," a prominent Yale law professor writes, "that spurred the great changes to follow, and inspired and protected those who sought to implement them."[61] Gerald Rosenberg's *The Hollow Hope*, however, insists that the litigation campaign achieved little and that Americans moved toward racial equality only when the mass African-American protests organized by Randolph and King pushed the national government to pass and enforce civil rights legislation. In his view,

> The courts were ineffective in producing significant social reform in civil rights in the first decade after *Brown* [because] . . . political leadership at the national, state, and local levels was arrayed against civil rights, making implementation of judicial decisions nearly impossible, . . . the culture of the South was segregationist, leaving the courts with few public supporters . . . , [and] the American court system was itself designed to lack implementation powers, to move slowly, and to be strongly tied to local concerns.[62]

Michael Klarman suggests a fascinating third view. His "backlash" thesis asserts that *Brown* initially empowered the worst racists in the South, but their violent efforts to suppress the civil rights movement turned northern public opinion in favor of greater constitutional equality.[63]

The reasons for the substantial civil rights gains during the New Deal/Great Society Era are also controversial. The conventional account suggests that Americans recognized the immorality of racism and began living up to the commitments of the post–Civil War Amendments. These commitments were fueled by social science findings rejecting past claims of white genetic superiority, as well as by a sharp reaction to the racial practices of Nazi Germany. Other commentators insist that less noble reasons explain the frontal attack on Jim Crow. Derrick Bell maintains that "the interest of blacks in achieving racial equality will be accommodated only when it converges with the interests of whites."[64] American elites had two reasons for eliminating Jim Crow. First, the United States during the Cold War needed the support of third-world nations, whose population and leadership were repelled by American racial practices.[65] Second, as African-American moved north to states in which they had traditionally been allowed to vote, northern politicians had greater incentives to support African-American rights. More general social trends were also weakening Jim Crow. Urbanization, increased demographic mobility, and economic prosperity put pressure on the southern commitment to white supremacy.

Strict Scrutiny

Constitutional liberals insisted that racial classifications satisfy higher constitutional standards. By the end of the New Deal/Great Society Era federal courts

60. See Klarman, "Scottsboro."

61. Fiss, "A Life Twice Lived," 1118.

62. Rosenberg, *The Hollow Hope*, 93.

63. Michael J. Klarman, *From Jim Crow to Civil Rights: The Supreme Court and the Struggle for Racial Equality* (New York: Oxford University Press, 2006).

64. Derrick A. Bell, Jr., "*Brown v. Board of Education* and the Interest-Convergence Dilemma," *Harvard Law Review* 93 (1980): 523.

65. See especially Mary Dudziak, *Cold War Civil Rights: Race and the Image of American Democracy* (Princeton, NJ: Princeton University Press, 2000).

had determined that racial discriminations and distinctions were constitutional only if they satisfied a "strict scrutiny" test. This test required that the law be a necessary means (or narrowly tailored) to achieve a compelling government end. With one exception, no racial classification litigated during the New Deal/Great Society Era satisfied that standard. The one exception, *Korematsu v. United States* (1944), sustained President Roosevelt's decision to require Japanese-Americans on the West Coast to be removed to relocation camps during World War II. Remarkably, *Korematsu*, a case presently regarded as one of the most racist decisions in American history, was also the first case in which the Supreme Court used the strict scrutiny test.

Korematsu v. United States, 323 U.S. 214 (1944)

Fred Toyosaburo Korematsu was a Japanese-American citizen who lived and worked as a welder in San Leandro, California. On February 19, 1942, President Roosevelt issued an executive order authorizing military commanders to define "military areas" and exclude any or all persons from them. On May 3, 1942, Lieutenant General John DeWitt, the military commander of the Western Defense Command, issued "Exclusion Order No. 34," which declared that "from and after 12 o'clock noon, P. W. T., of Saturday, May 9, 1942, all persons of Japanese ancestry, both alien and non-alien, be excluded" from Alameda County, California. Overall, more than 100,000 Japanese-Americans were forced to leave their homes, often with no more than a week's notice, and become essentially prisoners of war for three years in relocation camps. Families were typically given one room with no private baths or kitchens. Korematsu, who lived in Alameda County, refused to leave his home and job. He was arrested for violating the ordinance, found guilty, and sentenced to five years on probation. After the Court of Appeals for the Ninth Circuit affirmed the conviction, Korematsu appealed to the Supreme Court of the United States.

The relocation orders sharply divided the Roosevelt War Department, which favored removing the Japanese, from prominent civil libertarians in the Roosevelt Justice Department. Justice Department lawyers were particularly concerned when they learned that General DeWitt's report justifying the relocation order contained many false or unproven facts. After noting that claims made in that report were "in conflict with information in the possession of the Department of Justice," an early draft of the federal government's brief in Korematsu *asserted, "In view of the contrariety of the reports on the matter we do not ask the Court to take judicial notice of the recital of those facts contained in the Report." War Department lawyers edited that passage to read that the report was based on "tendencies and probabilities as evidenced by attitudes, opinions, and slight experience, rather than a conclusion based upon objectively ascertainable facts."*

Korematsu's lawyers faced a steep challenge in light of the Supreme Court's decision in Hirabayashi v. United States *(1943). In that case the justices unanimously sustained a curfew that military commanders had imposed on persons of Japanese ancestry. Chief Justice Stone's opinion for the Court asserted,*

> *Distinctions between citizens solely because of their ancestry are by their very nature odious to a free people whose institutions are founded upon the doctrine of equality. For that reason, legislative classification or discrimination based on race alone has often been held to be a denial of equal protection. We may assume that these considerations would be controlling here were it not for the fact that the danger of espionage and sabotage, in time of war and of threatened invasion, calls upon the military authorities to scrutinize every relevant fact bearing on the loyalty of populations in the danger areas. Because racial discriminations are in most circumstances irrelevant and therefore prohibited, it by no means follows that, in dealing with the perils of war, Congress and the Executive are wholly precluded from taking into account those facts and circumstances which are relevant to measures for our national defense and for the successful prosecution of the war, and which may in fact place citizens of one ancestry in a different category from others. "We must never forget, that it is a constitution we are expounding," "a constitution intended to endure for ages to come, and, consequently, to be adapted to the various crises of human affairs." The adoption by Government, in the crisis of war and of threatened invasion, of measures for the public safety, based upon the recognition of facts and circumstances which indicate that a group of one national extraction may menace that safety more than others, is not wholly beyond the limits of the Constitution and is not to be condemned merely because in other and in most circumstances racial distinctions are irrelevant.*

The Supreme Court in Korematsu *sustained the relocation order by a 6-3 vote. Justice Black's majority opinion, while insisting that racial classifications are "immediately suspect," nevertheless found that military necessities justified removing Japanese-Americans from the West Coast.*

Why did Justice Black reach that decision? Did he share the popular sentiment that Japanese-Americans threatened the West Coast? Did he believe that the justices should defer to the president in wartime? What do you make of the view expressed by Justice (and former attorney general) Jackson that the Court should have stayed out of the dispute and not have given judicial sanction to the use of race? Support for Korematsu *vanished the day that World War II ended. Almost all constitutional scholars presently believe that the* Korematsu *case was a judicial "disaster."*[66] *Mark Tushnet has an interesting take on this consensus. He writes,* "Korematsu *was part of a process of social learning that . . . diminishes contemporary threats to civil liberties in our present situation."*[67] *In his view, having made the wrong decision in* Korematsu *and learned from that experience, Americans are less likely to engage in such acts as racial profiling in the future. Is this correct? To what extent do you believe that the general consensus that the Japanese internment was wrong has influenced public policy during the war on terror?*

The United States government in 1988 formally apologized to those Japanese-Americans who were forced to leave their homes during World War II. Ten years later Fred Korematsu received the Presidential Medal of Freedom.

JUSTICE BLACK delivered the opinion of the Court.

. . .

It should be noted, to begin with, that all legal restrictions which curtail the civil rights of a single racial group are immediately suspect. That is not to say that all such restrictions are unconstitutional. It is to say that courts must subject them to the most rigid scrutiny. Pressing public necessity may sometimes justify the existence of such restrictions; racial antagonism never can.

. . .

. . . [W]e are unable to conclude that it was beyond the war power of Congress and the Executive to exclude those of Japanese ancestry from the West Coast war area at the time they did. True, exclusion from the area in which one's home is located is a far greater deprivation than constant confinement to the home from 8 p.m. to 6 a.m. Nothing short of apprehension by the proper military authorities of the gravest imminent danger to the public safety can constitutionally justify either. But exclusion from a threatened area, no less than curfew, has a definite and close relationship to the prevention of espionage and sabotage. The military authorities, charged with the primary responsibility of defending our shores, concluded that curfew provided inadequate protection and ordered exclusion. They did so . . . in accordance with Congressional authority to the military to say who should, and who should not, remain in the threatened areas.

. . .

Like curfew, exclusion of those of Japanese origin was deemed necessary because of the presence of an unascertained number of disloyal members of the group, most of whom we have no doubt were loyal to this country. It was because we could not reject the finding of the military authorities that it was impossible to bring about an immediate segregation of the disloyal from the loyal that we sustained the validity of the curfew order as applying to the whole group. In the instant case, temporary exclusion of the entire group was rested by the military on the same ground. The judgment that exclusion of the whole group was for the same reason a military imperative answers the contention that the exclusion was in the nature of group punishment based on antagonism to those of Japanese origin. That there were members of the group who retained loyalties to Japan has been confirmed by investigations made subsequent to the exclusion. . . .

. . .

It is said that we are dealing here with the case of imprisonment of a citizen in a concentration camp solely because of his ancestry, without evidence or inquiry concerning his loyalty and good disposition towards the United States. Our task would be simple, our duty clear, were this a case involving the imprisonment of a loyal citizen in a concentration camp because of racial prejudice. Regardless of the true nature of the assembly and relocation centers—and we deem it unjustifiable to call them concentration camps with all the ugly connotations that term implies—we are dealing specifically with nothing but an exclusion order. To cast this case into outlines of racial prejudice, without reference to the real military dangers which were presented, merely confuses the issue. Korematsu was not excluded from the Military Area because of hostility to him or his race. He was excluded because we are at war with the Japanese Empire, because the properly constituted military authorities feared an invasion of our West Coast and felt constrained to take

66. The classic citation is Eugene Rostow, "The Japanese American Cases—A Disaster," *Yale Law Journal* 54 (1945): 489.

67. Mark Tushnet, "Defending *Korematsu*? Reflections on Civil Liberties in Wartime," *Wisconsin Law Review 2003* (2003): 274.

proper security measures, because they decided that the military urgency of the situation demanded that all citizens of Japanese ancestry be segregated from the West Coast temporarily, and finally, because Congress, reposing its confidence in this time of war in our military leaders—as inevitably it must—determined that they should have the power to do just this. There was evidence of disloyalty on the part of some, the military authorities considered that the need for action was great, and time was short. We cannot—by availing ourselves of the calm perspective of hindsight—now say that at that time these actions were unjustified.

JUSTICE FRANKFURTER, concurring.

. . .

The provisions of the Constitution which confer on the Congress and the President powers to enable this country to wage war are as much part of the Constitution as provisions looking to a nation at peace. . . . To find that the Constitution does not forbid the military measures now complained of does not carry with it approval of that which Congress and the Executive did. That is their business, not ours.

JUSTICE ROBERTS, dissenting.

. . . The liberty of every American citizen freely to come and to go must frequently, in the face of sudden danger, be temporarily limited or suspended. The civil authorities must often resort to the expedient of excluding citizens temporarily from a locality. The drawing of fire lines in the case of a conflagration, the removal of persons from the area where a pestilence has broken out, are familiar examples. . . . [But] the exclusion was but a part of an over-all plan for forceable detention. This case cannot, therefore, be decided on any such narrow ground as the possible validity of a Temporary Exclusion Order under which the residents of an area are given an opportunity to leave and go elsewhere in their native land outside the boundaries of a military area. To make the case turn on any such assumption is to shut our eyes to reality.

. . .

JUSTICE MURPHY, dissenting.

This exclusion of all persons of Japanese ancestry, both alien and non-alien, from the Pacific Coast area on a plea of military necessity in the absence of martial law ought not to be approved. Such exclusion goes over "the very brink of constitutional power" and falls into the ugly abyss of racism.

. . .

. . . The judicial test of whether the Government, on a plea of military necessity, can validly deprive an individual of any of his constitutional rights is whether the deprivation is reasonably related to a public danger that is so "immediate, imminent, and impending" as not to admit of delay and not to permit the intervention of ordinary constitutional processes to alleviate the danger. . . . Civilian Exclusion Order No. 34, banishing from a prescribed area of the Pacific Coast "all persons of Japanese ancestry, both alien and non-alien," clearly does not meet that test. Being an obvious racial discrimination, the order deprives all those within its scope of the equal protection of the laws as guaranteed by the Fifth Amendment. It further deprives these individuals of their constitutional rights to live and work where they will, to establish a home where they choose and to move about freely. In excommunicating them without benefit of hearings, this order also deprives them of all their constitutional rights to procedural due process. Yet no reasonable relation to an "immediate, imminent, and impending" public danger is evident to support this racial restriction which is one of the most sweeping and complete deprivations of constitutional rights in the history of this nation in the absence of martial law.

It must be conceded that the military and naval situation in the spring of 1942 was such as to generate a very real fear of invasion of the Pacific Coast, accompanied by fears of sabotage and espionage in that area. The military command was therefore justified in adopting all reasonable means necessary to combat these dangers. In adjudging the military action taken in light of the then apparent dangers, we must not erect too high or too meticulous standards; it is necessary only that the action have some reasonable relation to the removal of the dangers of invasion, sabotage and espionage. But the exclusion, either temporarily or permanently, of all persons with Japanese blood in their veins has no such reasonable relation. And that relation is lacking because the exclusion order necessarily must rely for its reasonableness upon the assumption that all persons of Japanese ancestry may have a dangerous tendency to commit sabotage and espionage and to aid our Japanese enemy in other ways. It is difficult to believe that reason, logic or experience could be marshaled in support of such an assumption.

. . .

. . . The reasons appear, instead, to be largely an accumulation of much of the misinformation, half-truths and insinuations that for years have been directed against Japanese Americans by people with racial and economic prejudices—the same people who have been among the foremost advocates of the evacuation. A military judgment based upon such racial and sociological considerations is not entitled to the great weight ordinarily given the judgments based upon strictly military considerations. . . .

. . . [T]o infer that examples of individual disloyalty prove group disloyalty and justify discriminatory action against the entire group is to deny that under our system of law individual guilt is the sole basis for deprivation of rights. Moreover, this inference, which is at the very heart of the evacuation orders, has been used in support of the abhorrent and despicable treatment of minority groups by the dictatorial tyrannies which this nation is now pledged to destroy. To give constitutional sanction to that inference in this case, however well-intentioned may have been the military command on the Pacific Coast, is to adopt one of the cruelest of the rationales used by our enemies to destroy the dignity of the individual and to encourage and open the door to discriminatory actions against other minority groups in the passions of tomorrow.

No adequate reason is given for the failure to treat these Japanese Americans on an individual basis by holding investigations and hearings to separate the loyal from the disloyal, as was done in the case of persons of German and Italian ancestry. . . .

. . .

I dissent, therefore, from this legalization of racism. Racial discrimination in any form and in any degree has no justifiable part whatever in our democratic way of life. It is unattractive in any setting but it is utterly revolting among a free people who have embraced the principles set forth in the Constitution of the United States. All residents of this nation are kin in some way by blood or culture to a foreign land. Yet they are primarily and necessarily a part of the new and distinct civilization of the United States. They must accordingly be treated at all times as the heirs of the American experiment and as entitled to all the rights and freedoms guaranteed by the Constitution.

JUSTICE JACKSON, dissenting.

. . .

. . . [I]f any fundamental assumption underlies our system, it is that guilt is personal and not inheritable. Even if all of one's antecedents had been convicted of treason, the Constitution forbids its penalties to be visited upon him, for it provides that "no Attainder of Treason shall work Corruption of Blood, or Forfeiture except during the Life of the Person attained." But here is an attempt to make an otherwise innocent act a crime merely because this prisoner is the son of parents as to whom he had no choice, and belongs to a race from which there is no way to resign. If Congress in peacetime legislation should enact such a criminal law, I should suppose this Court would refuse to enforce it.

. . .

It would be impracticable and dangerous idealism to expect or insist that each specific military command in an area of probable operations will conform to conventional tests of constitutionality. When an area is so beset that it must be put under military control at all, the paramount consideration is that its measures be successful, rather than legal. The armed services must protect a society, not merely its Constitution. The very essence of the military job is to marshal physical force, to remove every obstacle to its effectiveness, to give it every strategic advantage. . . . No court can require such a commander in such circumstances to act as a reasonable man; he may be unreasonably cautious and exacting. Perhaps he should be. But a commander in temporarily focusing the life of a community on defense is carrying out a military program; he is not making law in the sense the courts know the term. He issues orders, and they may have a certain authority as military commands, although they may be very bad as constitutional law.

But if we cannot confine military expedients by the Constitution, neither would I distort the Constitution to approve all that the military may deem expedient. This is what the Court appears to be doing, whether consciously or not. I cannot say, from any evidence before me, that the orders of General DeWitt were not reasonably expedient military precautions, nor could I say that they were. But even if they were permissible military procedures, I deny that it follows that they are constitutional. If, as the Court holds, it does follow, then we may as well say that any military order will be constitutional and have done with it.

. . .

In the very nature of things military decisions are not susceptible of intelligent judicial appraisal. . . .

Much is said of the danger to liberty from the Army program for deporting and detaining these citizens of Japanese extraction. But a judicial construction of the due process clause that will sustain this order is a far more subtle blow to liberty than the promulgation of the order itself. A military order, however unconstitutional, is not apt to last longer than the military emergency. Even during that period a succeeding commander may revoke it all. But once a judicial opinion rationalizes such an order to show that it conforms to the Constitution, or rather rationalizes the Constitution to show that the Constitution sanctions such an order, the Court for all time has validated the principle of racial discrimination in criminal procedure and of transplanting American citizens. The principle then lies about like a loaded weapon ready for the hand of any authority that can bring forward a plausible claim of an urgent need. Every repetition imbeds that principle more deeply in our law and thinking and expands it to new purposes. All who observe the work of courts are familiar with what Judge Cardozo described as "the tendency of a principle to expand itself to the limit of its logic." A military commander may overstep the bounds of constitutionality, and it is an incident. But if we review and approve, that passing incident becomes the doctrine of the Constitution. There it has a generative power of its own, and all that it creates will be in its own image. Nothing better illustrates this danger than does the Court's opinion in this case.

. . . I should hold that a civil court cannot be made to enforce an order which violates constitutional limitations even if it is a reasonable exercise of military authority. The courts can exercise only the judicial power, can apply only law, and must abide by the Constitution, or they cease to be civil courts and become instruments of military policy.

The Road to *Brown*

Nathan Margold, Preliminary Report to the Joint Committee Supervising the Expenditure of the 1930 Appropriation by the American Fund for Public Service to the N.A.A.C.P. (1931)[68]

In the late 1920s the NAACP received a $100,000 grant from the American Fund for Public Service to be used for litigation challenging Jim Crow. On the recommendation of Felix Frankfurter and Charles Hamilton Houston, Nathan Margold drafted a strategic plan. Margold's plan emphasized the need to rely on federal law and seek desegregation as the remedy for southern failures to provide equal school districts for persons of color. In 1935 Charles Houston implemented a modified version of this plan. Houston emphasized equalization lawsuits. He believed that southern school districts would prefer the cheaper alternative of running desegregated schools than having to provide the same funding for schools for children of different races. Hamilton and his young associate, Thurgood Marshall, also brought lawsuits equalizing teacher salaries, in part because inequalities could be objectively determined and in part to gain support from crucial members of the African-American community.[69]

Consider the following memorandum in light of the constitutional status of African-Americans in 1930. Do you agree with Margold's assessment of litigation priorities? Had you been asked to write the memo (for a salary of $20,000, in 1930 dollars), what changes would you have made in his approach to school litigation?

. . .

. . . The prevailing discrimination is due largely to a disproportionate allocation of school funds between white and colored schools, rather than to injudicious use of such funds as are made available for the latter. The factors establishing the unfair character of this discrimination are much more tangible and susceptible to convincing demonstration than those related to discrimination resulting from careless or unwise administration. The ascertainment and comparison of *per capita* expenditures involves no serious question of judgment on which [one] may reasonably differ. Nor should it be insurmountably difficult to make proper allowances, in specific cases, for geographical or other local factors which might render improper a precisely equal *per capita* allocation of school funds. Local complications could hardly explain the gross discrimination consistently practiced through the south, nor lead to a denial of judicial intervention if existing facts are convincingly proven.

. . .

It requires no comment to indicate the precise application of the language and decision in *Yick Wo v. Hopkins* (1886) to the case of a statute which separates

68. Nathan Margold, "Preliminary Report to the Joint Committee Supervising the Expenditure of the 1930 Appropriation by the American Fund for Public Service to the N.A.A.C.P.," 1931, National Association for the Advancement of Colored People Records, 1842–1999, Manuscript Division, Library of Congress, Washington, DC.

69. See Mark Tushnet, *Making Constitutional Law: Thurgood Marshall and the Supreme Court, 1961-1991* (New York: Oxford University Press, 1997) and Richard Kluger, *Simple Justice: The History of Brown v. Board of Education and Black America's Struggle for Equality* (New York: Vintage, 2004).

whites and Negroes into different schools and vests arbitrary and unlimited power on a state officer to divide the general school fund between them. Such statutes, at least in southern states, bear the stamp of invalidity both on their face and in their ultimate actual operation.

. . .

Assuming that effective remedies exist to compel each division to be made without discrimination, the very multiplicity of suits which would have to be brought is itself appalling. A separate suit would be required against each officer charged with the duty of making the divisions. In practice, the worst discrimination undoubtedly occurs in the final division between white and colored schools, where the most numerous suits must be brought, while the least discrimination is possible in the division between counties, where only one suit per state would suffice. . . . The seven suits contemplated for all seven states in the American Fund memorandum would barely cause a ripple on the surface of the vast sea of litigation really required.

. . .

This vicious situation . . . represents the very heart of the evils in education against which our campaign should be directed. It would be a great mistake to fritter away our limited funds on sporadic attempts to force the making of equal divisions of school funds in the few instances where such attempts might be expected to succeed. At the most, we could do no more than to eliminate a very minor part of the discrimination during the year our suits are commenced. We should not be establishing any new principles, nor bringing any sort of pressure to bear which can reasonably be expected to retain the slightest force beyond that exerted by the specific judgment or order that we might obtain. And we should be leaving wholly untouched the very essence of the existing evils.

On the other hand, if we boldly challenge the constitutional validity of segregation if and when accompanied irremediably by discrimination, we can strike directly at the most prolific sources of discrimination. We can transform into an authoritative adjudication the principle of law, now only theoretically inferable from *Yick Wo v. Hopkins*, that segregation coupled with discrimination resulting from administrative action permitted but not required by state statute, is just as much a denial of equal protection of the laws as is segregation coupled with discrimination required by express statutory enactment. And the threat of using this adjudication as a means of destroying segregation itself, would always exert a very real and powerful force at least to complete enormous improvement in the Negro schools through voluntary official action.

There remains for consideration only the danger of stirring up intense opposition, ill-will, and strife as a result of any attack upon a custom so deeply entrenched in popular prejudice as is the segregation of races in public schools. A similar danger would be entailed by any sort of effective action which we can hope to take in our campaign. In the case of the large majority of white southerners, inequality in the division of funds is just as deeply entrenched as segregation. That, indeed, is why it is extensively practiced and why a campaign like ours is necessary at all. It is not an exaggeration to say that a really effective campaign to force equal if separate accommodations, resulting as it necessarily would, either in a heavy increase in taxation or an appreciable decrease in the efficiency of white schools, would entail just as much intensity of feeling as will the course of action which I earnestly recommend to the committee for approval. It is not as though we were striking at all segregation under any and all circumstances. We are attacking segregation only because it is the only means now open to us of fighting the disgraceful discrimination that is being practiced against the Negro race. We are not trying to deprive southern states of their acknowledged privilege of providing separate accommodations for the two races. We are trying only to force them to comply with their equally acknowledged duty to provide "equal if separate" accommodations in white and colored schools. The state law now affords us no real opportunity to fight the disgraceful discrimination that is being practiced under it. We must attack the practice of segregation, as *now provided for and administered*, or permit the discrimination to go on for the most part unimpaired. In choosing to attack it, we are in effect seeking only to compel the states which desire segregation to provide for it in a form which will render equality imperative and provide Negro parents with effective, practicable means of forcing derelict educational officers to perform their duties properly. Approached from this point of view, and accompanied by extensive, carefully supervised publicity, I feel certain the danger of inciting ill-will and alienating enlightened public opinion can be reduced far below the point where it is outweighed by the ultimate good to be accomplished.

. . .

. . . [T]he Fourteenth Amendment is contravened, not though the maintenance of a school at which white

Illustration 8-4 Thurgood Marshall and Spottswood W. Robinson III

Thurgood Marshall (right) and Spottswood W. Robinson III, lead attorneys for the NAACP in *Brown v. Board of Education* (1954). Robinson became the first African-American to serve on the U.S. Court of Appeals for the District of Columbia when he was appointed by President Lyndon Johnson in 1964. Marshall became the first African-American to serve on the U.S. Supreme Court when Johnson appointed him to that office in 1967.

Source: Library of Congress Prints and Photographs Division Washington, D.C. 20540

children are taught; but through the failure to provide equal facilities for colored children either by admitting them to the only school there is, or by providing them with a school similar to the one maintained exclusively for the whites. Where a similar school is not provided, it is the exclusion of the Negroes from the white school which contravenes the Fourteenth Amendment, and it is that exclusion which can be said to compel the admission of colored children into the white school despite invalid provisions in the state constitution or statutes to the contrary.

. . .

There is no distinction between a case where no school at all is available and one where an inferior one is provided. The Negro children are entitled to equal accommodations. Where the only way they can get such accommodations is by admission to the white school, their exclusion from that school under color of state law contravenes the Fourteenth Amendment and can be corrected by mandamus.

Civil Rights Advocates Debate Strategy (1935)

The Journal of Negro Education *in 1935 ran a special edition on "The Courts and the Separate Negro School." Many prominent African-American intellectuals contributed essays analyzing and critiquing efforts to eradicate a Jim Crow system of education through litigation. The most famous and controversial article was written by W. E. B. Du Bois, the leading African-American scholar during the first third of the twentieth century and a founding member of the NAACP. Vigorously opposed to the litigation campaign outlined by Nathan Margold and implemented by*

Charles Houston, DuBois resigned from the NAACP in the 1930s.

The Du Bois and Thompson essays highlight significant disagreements within the African-American community over how to best achieve racial equality in the United States. Suppose that the NAACP had adopted Du Bois's arguments. What would have been the probable consequences for the constitutional status of race relationships in the United States?

W. E. B. Du Bois, Does the Negro Need Separate Schools? (1935)[70]

. . .

. . . I know that race prejudice in the United States today is such that most Negroes cannot receive proper education in white institutions. If the public schools of Atlanta, Nashville, New Orleans and Jacksonville were thrown open to all races tomorrow, the education that colored children would get in them would be worse than pitiable. It would not be education. And in the same way, there are many public school systems in the North where Negroes are admitted and tolerated, but they are not educated; they are crucified. There are certain Northern universities where Negro students, no matter what their ability, desert, or accomplishment, cannot get fair recognition, either in classroom or on the campus, in dining halls and student activities, or in common human courtesy. . . .

Under such circumstances, there is no room for argument as to whether the Negro needs separate schools or not. The plain fact faces us, that either he will have separate schools or he will not be educated.

. . .

. . . There are times when one must stand up for principle at the cost of discomfort, harm, and death. But in the case of the education of the young, you must consider not simply yourself but the children and the relation of children to life. It is difficult to think of anything more important for the development of a people than proper training for their children; and yet I have repeatedly seen wise and loving colored parents take infinite pains to force their little children into schools where the white children, white teachers, and white parents despised and resented the dark child, made a mock of it, neglected or bullied it, and literally rendered its life a living hell. . . . Therefore, in evaluating the advantage and disadvantage of accepting race hatred as a brutal but real fact, or of using a little child as a battering ram upon which its nastiness can be thrust, we must give greater value and greater emphasis to the rights of the child's own soul. We shall get a finer, better balance of spirit; an infinitely more capable and rounded personality by putting children in schools where they are wanted, and where they are happy and inspired, than in thrusting them into halls where they are ridiculed and hated.

. . .

. . . Negroes must know the history of the Negro race in America, and this they will seldom get in white institutions. . . . Negroes who celebrate the birthdays of Washington and Lincoln and the worthy, but colorless and relatively unimportant "founders" of various Negro colleges, ought not to forget the 5th of March—that first national holiday of this country, which commemorates the martyrdom of Crispus Attucks. They ought to celebrate Negro Health Week and Negro History Week. They ought to study intelligently and from their own point of view, the slave trade, slavery, emancipation, Reconstruction, and present economic development.

. . .

To sum up this; theoretically, the Negro needs neither segregated schools nor mixed schools. What he needs is Education. What he must remember is that there is no magic, either in mixed schools or in segregated schools. A mixed school with poor and unsympathetic teachers, with hostile public opinion, and no teaching of truth concerning black folk, is bad. A segregated school with ignorant placeholders, inadequate equipment, poor salaries, and wretched housing, is equally bad. Other things being equal, the mixed school is the broader, more natural basis for the education of all youth. It gives wider contacts; it suppresses the inferiority complex. But other things seldom are equal, and in that case, Sympathy, Knowledge, and the Truth, outweigh all that the mixed school can offer.

Chas. H. Thompson, Court Action the Only Reasonable Alternative to Remedy Immediate Abuses of the Negro Separate School (1935)[71]

. . .

In the first instance, I think most of us would agree that to *segregate* is to *stigmatize*, however much we

70. Excerpted from W. E. B. DuBois, "Does the Negro Need Separate Schools?" *Journal of Negro Education* 4 (1935): 328–35.

71. Excerpted from Chas H. Thompson, "Court Action the Only Reasonable Alternative to Remedy Immediate Abuses of the Negro Separate School," *Journal of Negro Education* 4 (1935): 419–34.

may try to rationalize it. We segregate the criminal, the insane, pupils with low I.Q.'s, Negroes, and other undesirables. To argue that Negroes are no more stigmatized than white people who are also segregated is, and should be recognized, as sheer sophistry. For we all know that segregation is practically always initiated on the basis that Negroes are inferior and undesirable. Thus, when Negroes allow themselves to be cajoled into accepting the status defined by the separate school, they do something to their personalities which is infinitely worse than any of the discomforts *some* of them *may* experience in a mixed school.

In the second instance, the separate school is generally uneconomical, and frequently financially burdensome. Except in very large cities where the Negro population is fairly dense, separate schools mean costly duplication of facilities and an unreasonable increase in school expenditures. Consequently, where sufficient funds are not available to support decent schools for both whites and Negroes, and even in many cases where they are sufficient, it is the Negro school that suffers, and there is very little that is done about it. . . .

In the third instance, and finally, not only is the separate school uneconomical and undemocratic but it results in the *mis*-education of both races. Separation of the two racial groups, at an early age, when they should be learning to know and respect each other, develops anti-racial and provincial attitudes in both, and necessitates, in adulthood, re-education against tremendous odds. The net results of such an educational policy are that the Negro develops an almost ineradicable inferiority complex and evolves a set of Jim Crow standards and values; the white child develops an unwarranted sense of superiority—if not an actual contempt for or indifference towards the Negro. And both races develop a misunderstanding of each other that necessitates all of the expensive and ineffective race-relations machinery that we have in this country at the present time. . . .

Brown v. Board of Education of Topeka (Brown I), 347 U.S. 483 (1954)

Linda Brown was a young girl who attended the Monroe School, an all-black school in Topeka, Kansas. When she was seven her father attempted to enroll her in the Summer School, which by local ordinance was restricted to white children. The Summer School was attractive to the Brown family because it had better facilities and was closer to their house than the Monroe School. When the Summer School refused to enroll Linda Brown, her father, assisted by the local NAACP, filed a lawsuit claiming that the segregation law violated the equal protection clause of the Fourteenth Amendment. The federal district court in Kansas rejected the lawsuit and the Brown family appealed to the Supreme Court of the United States. In 1952 the Supreme Court announced that the justices would adjudicate that appeal, along with similar suits filed in South Carolina, Virginia, Delaware, and the District of Columbia. The Truman administration submitted a legal brief supporting the NAACP that included a long passage inserted by the State Department emphasizing the difficulties that segregation posed for America's diplomatic efforts to win the hearts and minds of the "Third World" in the Cold War. The Court was unable to reach an agreement after the initial arguments and scheduled a second hearing, asking the parties to focus particularly on the original meaning of the Fourteenth Amendment in regard to racially segregated public schools. By then Dwight Eisenhower had been inaugurated and his nomination of California's former Republican governor Earl Warren as chief justice had been confirmed. The Eisenhower Justice Department reaffirmed the federal government's support for judicial action against segregation.

Brown v. Board of Education *was the culmination of a long litigation campaign aimed at overturning the ruling in* Plessy v. Ferguson *(1896) that the Fourteenth Amendment did not prohibit "separate but equal" facilities for blacks and whites. By the early 1950s the NAACP had won a string of victories that either put bite into or chipped away at the concept of "separate but equal" in the context of segregated schools. In* State of Missouri ex rel. Gaines v. Canada *(1938) the Supreme Court ruled that states had to provide legal education to persons of color within the state.* Sipuel v. Board of Regents of University of Oklahoma *(1948) held that qualified persons of color were entitled to immediate admission into a formerly all-white law school and did not have to wait for the state to establish a separate institution for students of color.* McLaurin v. Oklahoma State Regents *(1950) added that African-American students attending formerly all-white graduate programs could not be segregated from white students when doing so might interfere with their ability to obtain an equal education.* Sweatt v. Painter *(1950) established that a separate school for students of color had to be equal in all respects to a school restricted to white students. A crucial passage in the* Sweatt *opinion raised questions about whether, in a society in which white persons held all the positions of influence, a separate institution for students of color could ever be the equal of a white institution. Chief Justice Vinson observed,*

> *The University of Texas Law School possesses to a far greater degree those qualities which are incapable of objective measurement but which make for greatness in a law school. Such qualities, to name but a few, include reputation of the faculty, experience of the administration, position and influence of the alumni, standing in the community, traditions and prestige. It is difficult to believe that one who had a free choice between these law schools would consider the question close.*

Public primary and secondary education posed a tougher challenge. Because those schools affected far more people and involved young children, they were much more politically sensitive. Case-by-case litigation was a prohibitively expensive and time-consuming proposition. Hopes that southern states would abolish separate schools rather than fund them adequately had proven futile. Such states as South Carolina were willing to commit the substantial funds perceived necessary to salvage the separate schools. Many black parents and teachers were far more interested in improving the resources flowing into black schools than in eliminating these schools in favor of integrated facilities. Persons who challenged segregated schools ran exceptional personal risks. Consider the fate of Joseph DeLaine, the person responsible for the South Carolina lawsuit against segregated schools:

> *Before it was over, they fired him from the little schoolhouse at the church he had taught devotedly for ten years. And they fired his wife and two of his sisters and a niece. And they threatened him with bodily harm. And they sued him on trumped-up charges and convicted him in a kangaroo court and left him with a judgment that denied him credit from any bank. And they burned his house to the ground while the fire department stood around watching the flames consume the night. And they stoned the church at which he pastored. And fired shotguns at him out of the dark.*[72]

The Supreme Court in Brown *unanimously declared public school segregation unconstitutional. Chief Justice Earl Warren's opinion maintained that Jim Crow education deprived children of color of an equal education. No prominent (or even not-so-prominent) commentator at present would overrule the decision, but disagreement exists on the proper basis for declaring school segregation unconstitutional. On what basis did the Justice Department and Chief Justice Warren believe segregated schools to be unconstitutional? Do you believe that either justification is correct? Are the arguments in the* Brown *opinion even legally credible, or are they better explained by Warren's determination to rally a unanimous Court and not offend southern sensibilities any more than necessary? What is the best constitutional justification for* Brown?

72. Kluger, *Simple Justice*, 3.

Brief for the United States, Amicus Curiae, *Brown v. Board of Education*

. . .

[These cases raise] questions of the first importance in our society. For racial discriminations imposed by law, or having the sanction or support of government, inevitably tend to undermine the foundations of a society dedicated to freedom, justice, and equality. The proposition that all men are created equal is not mere rhetoric. It implies a rule of law—an indispensable condition to a civilized society—under which all men stand equal and alike in the rights and opportunities secured to them by their government. Under the Constitution every agency of government, national and local, legislative, executive, and judicial, must treat each of our people as an *American,* and not as a member of a particular group classified on the basis of race or some other constitutional irrelevancy. The color of a man's skin—like his religious beliefs, or his political attachments, or the country from which he or his ancestors came to the United States—does not diminish or alter his legal status or constitutional rights. "Our Constitution is color-blind, and neither knows nor tolerates classes among citizens."

. . .

It is in the context of the present world struggle between freedom and tyranny that the problem of racial discrimination must be viewed. The United States is trying to prove to the people of the world, of every nationality, race, and color, that a free democracy is the most civilized and most secure form of government yet devised by man. We must set an example for others by showing firm determination to remove existing flaws in our democracy.

The existence of discrimination against minority groups in the United States has an adverse effect upon our relations with other countries. Racial discrimination furnishes grist for the Communist propaganda mills, and it raises doubts even among friendly nations as to the intensity of our devotion to the democratic faith. . . .

The Government submits that compulsory racial segregation is itself, without more, an unconstitutional discrimination. "Separate but equal" is a contradiction in terms. Schools or other public facilities where persons are segregated by law, solely on the basis of race or color, cannot in any circumstances be regarded as equal. The constitutional requirement is that of equality, not merely in one sense of the word but in every sense. Nothing in the language or history of the Fourteenth Amendment supports the notion that facilities need be equal only in a physical sense.

People who are compelled by law to live in a ghetto do not enjoy equality, even though their houses are as good as, or better than, those on the outside. . . . The same is true of children who know that because of their color the law sets them apart from others, and requires them to attend separate schools specially established for members of their race. The facts of everyday life confirm the finding of the district court in the Kansas case that segregation has a "detrimental effect" on colored children; that it affects their motivation to learn; and that it has a tendency to retard their educational and mental development and to deprive them of benefits they would receive in an integrated school system. . . .

. . .

In these days, when the free world must conserve and fortify the moral as well as the material sources of its strength, it is especially important to affirm that the Constitution of the United States places no limitation, express or implied, on the principle of the equality of all men before the law. Mr. Justice Harlan said in his dissent in the *Plessy* case,

> We boast of the freedom enjoyed by our people above all other peoples. But it is difficult to reconcile that boast with a state of the law which, practically, puts the brand of servitude and degradation upon a large class of our fellow-citizens, our equals before the law.

The Government and people of the United States must prove by their actions that the ideals expressed in the Bill of Rights are living realities, not literary abstractions. As the President has stated:

> If we wish to inspire the people of the world whose freedom is in jeopardy, if we wish to restore hope to those who have already lost their civil liberties, if we wish to fulfill the promise that is ours, we must correct the remaining imperfections in our practice of democracy.

We know the way. We need only the Will.

CHIEF JUSTICE WARREN delivered the opinion of the Court.

. . .

The plaintiffs contend that segregated public schools are not "equal" and cannot be made "equal," and that hence they are deprived of the equal protection of the laws. . . .

Reargument was largely devoted to the circumstances surrounding the adoption of the Fourteenth Amendment in 1868. . . . This discussion and our own investigation convince us that, although these sources cast some light, it is not enough to resolve the problem with which we are faced. At best, they are inconclusive. The most avid proponents of the post-War Amendments undoubtedly intended them to remove all legal distinctions among "all persons born or naturalized in the United States." Their opponents, just as certainly, were antagonistic to both the letter and the spirit of the Amendments and wished them to have the most limited effect. What others in Congress and the state legislatures had in mind cannot be determined with any degree of certainty.

An additional reason for the inconclusive nature of the Amendment's history, with respect to segregated schools, is the status of public education at that time. In the South, the movement toward free common schools, supported by general taxation, had not yet taken hold. Education of white children was largely in the hands of private groups. Education of Negroes was almost nonexistent, and practically all of the race were illiterate. In fact, any education of Negroes was forbidden by law in some states. Today, in contrast, many Negroes have achieved outstanding success in the arts and sciences as well as in the business and professional world. It is true that public school education at the time of the Amendment had advanced further in the North, but the effect of the Amendment on Northern States was generally ignored in the congressional debates. . . . As a consequence, it is not surprising that there should be so little in the history of the Fourteenth Amendment relating to its intended effect on public education.

. . .

. . . [T]here are findings below that the Negro and white schools involved have been equalized, or are being equalized, with respect to buildings, curricula, qualifications and salaries of teachers, and other "tangible" factors. Our decision, therefore, cannot turn on merely a comparison of these tangible factors in the Negro and white schools involved in each of the cases. We must look instead to the effect of segregation itself on public education.

In approaching this problem, we cannot turn the clock back to 1868 when the Amendment was adopted, or even to 1896 when *Plessy v. Ferguson* was written. We must consider public education in the light of its full development and its present place in American life throughout the Nation. Only in this way can it be determined if segregation in public schools deprives these plaintiffs of the equal protection of the laws.

Today, education is perhaps the most important function of state and local governments. Compulsory school attendance laws and the great expenditures for education both demonstrate our recognition of the importance of education to our democratic society. It is required in the performance of our most basic public responsibilities, even service in the armed forces. It is the very foundation of good citizenship. Today it is a principal instrument in awakening the child to cultural values, in preparing him for later professional training, and in helping him to adjust normally to his environment. In these days, it is doubtful that any child may reasonably be expected to succeed in life if he is denied the opportunity of an education. Such an opportunity, where the state has undertaken to provide it, is a right which must be made available to all on equal terms.

We come then to the question presented: Does segregation of children in public schools solely on the basis of race, even though the physical facilities and other "tangible" factors may be equal, deprive the children of the minority group of equal educational opportunities? We believe that it does.

In *Sweatt v. Painter* (1950), in finding that a segregated law school for Negroes could not provide them equal educational opportunities, this Court relied in large part on "those qualities which are incapable of objective measurement but which make for greatness in a law school." In *McLaurin v. Oklahoma State Regents* (1950), the Court, in requiring that a Negro admitted to a white graduate school be treated like all other students, again resorted to intangible considerations: ". . . his ability to study, to engage in discussions and exchange views with other students, and, in general, to learn his profession." Such considerations apply with added force to children in grade and high schools. To separate them from others of similar age and qualifications solely because of their race generates a feeling of inferiority as to their status in the community that may affect their hearts and minds in a way unlikely ever to be undone. . . . Whatever may have been the extent of psychological knowledge at the time of *Plessy v. Ferguson*, this finding is amply supported by modern authority.[73] Any language in *Plessy v. Ferguson* contrary to this finding is rejected.

We conclude that in the field of public education the doctrine of "separate but equal" has no place. Separate educational facilities are inherently unequal. Therefore, we hold that the plaintiffs and others similarly situated for whom the actions have been brought are, by reason of the segregation complained of, deprived of the equal protection of the laws guaranteed by the Fourteenth Amendment. This disposition makes unnecessary any discussion whether such segregation also violates the Due Process Clause of the Fourteenth Amendment.

Because these are class actions, because of the wide applicability of this decision, and because of the great variety of local conditions, the formulation of decrees in these cases presents problems of considerable complexity. On reargument, the consideration of appropriate relief was necessarily subordinated to the primary question—the constitutionality of segregation in public education. We have now announced that such segregation is a denial of the equal protection of the laws. In order that we may have the full assistance of the parties in formulating decrees, the cases will be restored to the docket, and the parties are requested to present further argument. . . .

---

73. [Footnote by the Court] K. B. Clark, *Effect of Prejudice and Discrimination on Personality Development* (Midcentury White House Conference on Children and Youth, 1950); Witmer and Kotinsky, *Personality in the Making* (1952), c. VI; Deutscher and Chein, The Psychological Effects of Enforced Segregation: A Survey of Social Science Opinion, 26 *J. Psychol.* 259 (1948); Chein, What are the Psychological Effects of Segregation Under Conditions of Equal Facilities?, 3 *Int. J. Opinion and Attitude Res.* 229 (1949); Brameld, Educational Costs, in *Discrimination and National Welfare* (MacIver, ed., 1949), 44–48; Frazier, *The Negro in the United States* (1949), 674–681. And see generally Myrdal, *An American Dilemma* (1944).

Bolling v. Sharpe, 347 U.S. 497 (1954)

Spottswood Thomas Bolling was one of several African-American parents who sought to have their children attend Sousa Junior High School in Washington, DC. Their children were denied admission solely because Sousa Junior High was restricted to white pupils. Bolling sued C. Melvin Sharpe, the president of the Board of Education for the District of Columbia. A federal district court dismissed the lawsuit. Bolling appealed that decision to the Supreme Court of the United States.

Segregation in the District of Columbia raised different constitutional issues than segregation in the states. The equal protection clause of the Fourteenth Amendment limits only state governments. No such restriction on the federal government explicitly appears in the Bill of Rights.

The Supreme Court unanimously ordered that schools in Washington, DC, be desegregated. Chief Justice Warren's opinion asserted that the due process clause of the Fifth Amendment contained an equal protection component and that Jim Crow education in the District of Columbia violated that constitutional commitment. Was this a sound interpretation of the Constitution or did Bolling *reflect the political impossibility of declaring that only the federal government could segregate by race?* Bolling, *but not* Brown, *asserts that "classifications based solely upon race must be scrutinized with particular care" and that "segregation in public education is not reasonably related to any proper governmental objective." Both statements could have been made with respect to segregation in the states. Why does the* Bolling *opinion make these assertions, but not the* Brown *opinion? Might the justices have believed that they could be more forthright when declaring a federal law unconstitutional because the executive branch of the national government was on record as calling for an end to segregation in the District of Columbia?*

CHIEF JUSTICE WARREN delivered the opinion of the Court.

. . .

We have this day held that the Equal Protection Clause of the Fourteenth Amendment prohibits the states from maintaining racially segregated public schools. The legal problem in the District of Columbia is somewhat different, however. The Fifth Amendment, which is applicable in the District of Columbia, does not contain an equal protection clause as does the Fourteenth Amendment which applies only to the states. But the concepts of equal protection and due process, both stemming from our American ideal of fairness, are not mutually exclusive. The "equal protection of the laws" is a more explicit safeguard of prohibited unfairness than "due process of law," and, therefore, we do not imply that the two are always interchangeable phrases. But, as this Court has recognized, discrimination may be so unjustifiable as to be violative of due process.

Classifications based solely upon race must be scrutinized with particular care, since they are contrary to our traditions and hence constitutionally suspect. . . .

Although the Court has not assumed to define "liberty" with any great precision, that term is not confined to mere freedom from bodily restraint. Liberty under law extends to the full range of conduct which the individual is free to pursue, and it cannot be restricted except for a proper governmental objective. Segregation in public education is not reasonably related to any proper governmental objective, and thus it imposes on Negro children of the District of Columbia a burden that constitutes an arbitrary deprivation of their liberty in violation of the Due Process Clause.

In view of our decision that the Constitution prohibits the states from maintaining racially segregated public schools, it would be unthinkable that the same Constitution would impose a lesser duty on the Federal Government. We hold that racial segregation in the public schools of the District of Columbia is a denial of the due process of law guaranteed by the Fifth Amendment to the Constitution.

Brown v. Board of Education of Topeka (Brown II), 349 U.S. 294 (1955)

The Supreme Court in Brown I *ordered the parties to return the next year and argue the appropriate remedy. The NAACP insisted that the justices order an immediate end to all state-mandated segregation. Southern states disagreed. Both the briefs for the states involved in the initial* Brown *litigation and amicus briefs submitted by Arkansas, Maryland, North Carolina, Oklahoma, and Florida insisted that the Court had demanded the impossible. If the justices would not modify their position in* Brown I, *they should certainly not provide firm standards for the desegregation process. The United States took an intermediate position. The Eisenhower administration insisted on "an immediate and substantial start toward desegregation." The Justice Department's brief noted that "popular hostility, where found to exist, is a problem that needs to be recognized and faced with understanding, but it can afford no legal justification for a failure to end school segregation."*

The Supreme Court in Brown II *unanimously adopted the position advocated by the United States. Chief Justice Warren's opinion either paraphrased or adopted wholesale passages from the Justice Department's brief, including the crucial claim that schools be desegregated with "all deliberate speed." Traditionally, winning parties in lawsuits are entitled to their remedy the instant the judicial decision is final. A person whom the Supreme Court determines has been unconstitutionally convicted normally must be immediately released from jail. Certainly, states cannot continue enforcing a ban on flag burning after the statute has been declared unconstitutional. Why did Chief Justice Warren nevertheless insist that states could continue enforcing unconstitutional segregation laws? Was his reasoning valid? Was the* Brown II *decision sound constitutional politics in light of southern resistance or did the failure to order immediate desegregation encourage that resistance?*

CHIEF JUSTICE WARREN delivered the opinion of the Court.

These cases were decided on May 17, 1954. The opinions of that date, declaring the fundamental principle that racial discrimination in public education is unconstitutional, are incorporated herein by reference. All provisions of federal, state, or local law requiring or permitting such discrimination must yield to this principle. There remains for consideration the manner in which relief is to be accorded.

. . .

Full implementation of these constitutional principles may require solution of varied local school problems. School authorities have the primary responsibility for elucidating, assessing, and solving these problems; courts will have to consider whether the action of school authorities constitutes good faith implementation of the governing constitutional principles. Because of their proximity to local conditions and the possible need for further hearings, the courts which originally heard these cases can best perform this judicial appraisal. Accordingly, we believe it appropriate to remand the cases to those courts.

In fashioning and effectuating the decrees, the courts will be guided by equitable principles. Traditionally, equity has been characterized by a practical flexibility in shaping its remedies and by a facility for adjusting and reconciling public and private needs. These cases call for the exercise of these traditional attributes of equity power. At stake is the personal interest of the plaintiffs in admission to public schools as soon as practicable on a nondiscriminatory basis. To effectuate this interest may call for elimination of a variety of obstacles in making the transition to school systems operated in accordance with the constitutional principles set forth in our May 17, 1954, decision. Courts of equity may properly take into account the public interest in the elimination of such obstacles in a systematic and effective manner. But it should go without saying that the vitality of these constitutional principles cannot be allowed to yield simply because of disagreement with them.

While giving weight to these public and private considerations, the courts will require that the defendants make a prompt and reasonable start toward full compliance with our May 17, 1954, ruling. Once such a start has been made, the courts may find that additional time is necessary to carry out the ruling in an effective manner. The burden rests upon the defendants to establish that such time is necessary in the public interest and is consistent with good faith compliance at the earliest practicable date. To that end, the courts may consider problems related to administration, arising from the physical condition of the school plant, the school transportation system, personnel, revision of school districts and attendance areas into compact units to achieve a system of determining admission to the public schools on a nonracial basis, and revision of local laws and regulations which may be necessary in solving the foregoing problems. They will also consider the adequacy of any plans the defendants may propose to meet these problems and to effectuate a transition to a racially nondiscriminatory school system. During this period of transition, the courts will retain jurisdiction of these cases.

Implementing *Brown*

The Reaction to *Brown*. The reaction to *Brown* was paradoxically mixed and one-sided. Public opinion polls indicated that a slight majority of Americans supported the judicial decision striking down legally segregated schools. Outside of the African-American

Illustration 8-5 Elementary School Desegregation Protest in New Orleans, November 1960
Source: Times-Picayune

community, however, few persons in the North danced in the streets when federal courts began ordering the desegregation of southern schools. By comparison, opposition in the South was intense. The Southern Manifesto, issued in 1956 and signed by almost every southerner in Congress, was a relatively mild expression of southern opposition to *Brown*. That Manifesto asserted,

> We regard the decisions of the Supreme Court in the school cases as a clear abuse of judicial power. It climaxes a trend in the Federal Judiciary undertaking to legislate, in derogation of the authority of Congress, and to encroach upon the reserved rights of the States and the people.
>
> . . .
>
> This unwarranted exercise of power by the Court, contrary to the Constitution, is creating chaos and confusion in the States principally affected. It is destroying the amicable relations between the white and Negro races that have been created through 90 years of patient effort by the good people of both races. It has planted hatred and suspicion where there has been heretofore friendship and understanding.
>
> . . .
>
> We pledge ourselves to use all lawful means to bring about a reversal of this decision which is contrary to the Constitution and to prevent the use of force in its implementation.[74]

More typical was a claim made by George Wallace, who, after losing an election to an even more racially

74. 102 *Congressional Record*, 84th Cong., 2nd Sess. (1956), 4515–16.

extreme opponent, swore that he would never be "out-niggered" again. Wallace kept that promise.[75]

The Eisenhower administration temporized after *Brown*. Administration officials abroad celebrated *Brown* as a demonstration of the American commitment to racial equality. Domestically, neither the president nor executive branch officials had much to say, at least publicly, about the Warren Court decision. Eisenhower broke silence only when the Governor of Arkansas, Orville Farbus, called out the state national guard to prevent federal courts from desegregating schools in Little Rock. Eisenhower's speech to the nation on September 24, 1957, asserted,

> It is important that the reasons for my action be understood by all our citizens. As you know, the Supreme Court of the United States has decided that separate public educational facilities for the races are inherently unequal and therefore compulsory school segregation laws are unconstitutional.
>
> Our personal opinions about the decision have no bearing on the matter of enforcement; the responsibility and authority of the Supreme Court to interpret the Constitution are very clear. Local Federal Courts were instructed by the Supreme Court to issue such orders and decrees as might be necessary to achieve admission to public schools without regard to race—and with all deliberate speed.
>
> . . . The very basis of our individual rights and freedoms rests upon the certainty that the President and the Executive Branch of Government will support and insure the carrying out of the decisions of the Federal Courts, even, when necessary with all the means at the President's command.

Brown provoked a surprising controversy among a prominent group of northern jurists. Many New Dealers had difficulty distinguishing judicial decisions declaring school segregation unconstitutional from what they perceived as the "infamous" judicial decisions declaring Roosevelt's economic program unconstitutional. Judge Learned Hand in 1958 informed a Harvard Law School audience that the Supreme Court in *Brown* had "assume[ed] the role of a third legislative chamber" by conducting "its own reappraisal of the relative values at stake" in ways not compelled by the Constitution.[76] The next year Herbert Wechsler, possibly the most distinguished constitutional law professor of the time, sharply criticized the reasoning of *Brown*. Wechsler regarded *Brown* as a freedom of association case in which the balance of equities favored neither party. "For me," he declared,

> assuming equal facilities, the question posed by state-enforced segregation is not one of discrimination at all. Its human and its constitutional dimensions lie entirely elsewhere, in the denial by the state of freedom to associate, a denial that impinges in the same way on any groups or races that may be involved. . . .
>
> . . . Given a situation where the state must practically choose between denying the association to those individuals who wish it or imposing it on those who would avoid it, is there a basis in neutral principles for holding that the Constitution demands that the claims for association should prevail? I should like to think there is, but I confess that I have not yet written the opinion. To write it is for me the challenge of the school-segregation cases.[77]

Other law professors rose to Wechsler's challenge. Louis Pollak emphasized the stigmatic harms of segregation. "We see little doubt," he wrote, "that it is a function of Jim Crow laws to make identification as a Negro a matter of stigma. Such government denigration is a form of injury the Constitution recognizes and will protect against."[78] Charles Black more bluntly stated that no competent constitutional decision maker could take "separate but equal seriously." He pointed out,

> If a whole race of people finds itself confined within a system which is set up and continued for the very purpose of keeping it in an inferior station, and if the question is then solemnly propounded whether such a race is being treated "equally," I think we ought to exercise one of the sovereign prerogatives of philosophers—that of laughter.[79]

---

75. Dan T. Carter, *The Politics of Rage: George Wallace, the Origins of the New Conservatism, and the Transformation of American Politics* (New York: Simon & Schuster, 1995).

76. Learned Hand, *The Bill of Rights* (New York: Atheneum, 1972), 54–55.

77. Herbert Wechsler, "Toward Neutral Principles of Constitutional Law," *Harvard Law Review* 73 (1959): 34.

78. Louis H. Pollak, "Racial Discrimination and Judicial Integrity: A Reply to Professor Wechsler," *University of Pennsylvania Law Review* 108 (1959): 28.

79. Charles L. Black, Jr., "The Lawfulness of the Segregation Decisions," *Yale Law Journal* 69 (1960): 424.

"All Deliberate Speed." During the late 1950s and early 1960s Americans experienced deliberation but no speed in desegregating public schools, except in the border states. A few federal district court justices aggressively sought to abolish dual school systems. Judge J. Skelley Wright in 1960 issued an injunction against the entire Louisiana legislature, threatening them with prison should they interfere with school desegregation in New Orleans. More federal judges were satisfied with school plans that enabled a few children of color to attend formerly all-white schools. Judge Frank Hooper of the federal district court in Georgia informed the school board in Atlanta that he would accept any plan that allowed for "token integration." He proved a person of his word when Atlanta adopted a program permitting high school seniors to request transfers to different high schools, with a commitment to extending the program one grade per year. Some judges engaged in outright resistance. Judge T. Whitfield Davison of Dallas rejected a plan that would desegregate the first grade and then add a grade every year thereafter. Mixing six-year-olds, he claimed, "would lead, in the opinion and the light of history and unquestionable sources to an amalgamation of the races."[80]

The Supreme Court largely took a hands-off approach during the first decade after *Brown II.* The justices occasionally intervened to tell governing officials what they could not do. Most notably, in *Cooper v. Aaron* (1958), the justices gave a lecture to the governor of Arkansas on his duty to obey a court order mandating that a few children of color be allowed to attend formerly all-white schools in Little Rock, Arkansas. *Goss v. Board of Education* (1963) declared unconstitutional a Tennessee law permitting all children to transfer into a school in which a majority of students were of their race. *Griffin v. County School Board of Prince Edward County* (1964) struck down an effort to evade *Brown* by closing down public schools and giving state funds to segregated private schools. What the justices did not do during these years was inform school districts and lower federal court justices what they had to do to comply with *Brown.* One consequence of this inaction was that in 1964, less than 2 percent of all African-American students in former Confederate states were attending even marginally desegregated schools.

The Civil Rights Act of 1964 dramatically changed the constitutional politics of school desegregation. That measure contained two provisions that spurred desegregation. First, Congress cut off all federal funds to school districts not in compliance with *Brown,* and compliance was determined by the executive branch of the federal government. Second, Congress authorized the Justice Department to bring lawsuits that would desegregate public schools, thus extending the constitutional attack beyond the limited budgets and staffs of civil rights organizations. Two results were immediate. First, the number of African-American children in desegregated schools increased dramatically after 1965. Second, the Warren Court became markedly more aggressive when ruling on school desegregation cases.

80. This paragraph relies on J. W. Peltason, *58 Lonely Men: Southern Justices and School Desegregation* (Urbana: University of Illinois Press, 1971), 221–43, 130–31, 121.

Green v. County School Board of New Kent County, 391 U.S. 430 (1968)

Charles Green was an African-American child who attended public school in New Kent County, Virginia. When Green first entered the public school system New Kent County law required children to attend whatever school had previously been reserved for students of their race, unless their parents asked for a transfer. As of 1964 no student of either race had requested a transfer. In 1965 Green and other African-American families sued the school board, claiming that the assignment system perpetuated the racial policies declared unconstitutional in Brown v. Board of Education *(1954). The school board responded by adopting a freedom of choice plan. Under this scheme for assigning pupils, parents could choose which school their children would attend. All white children chose the school previously reserved for all-white children. Eighty-five percent of the African-American parents chose the school previously reserved for children of color. The Greens renewed their lawsuit, insisting that New Kent County had still not complied with* Brown. *Their lawsuit was rejected by both the federal district court and the Court of Appeals for the Fourth Circuit. The Greens appealed to the Supreme Court of the United States.*

The Supreme Court unanimously declared the freedom of choice plan unconstitutional. Justice Brennan's opinion for the Court insisted that school districts must immediately desegregate. Green *marks the end of "all deliberate speed" and the shift toward integration rather than desegregation*

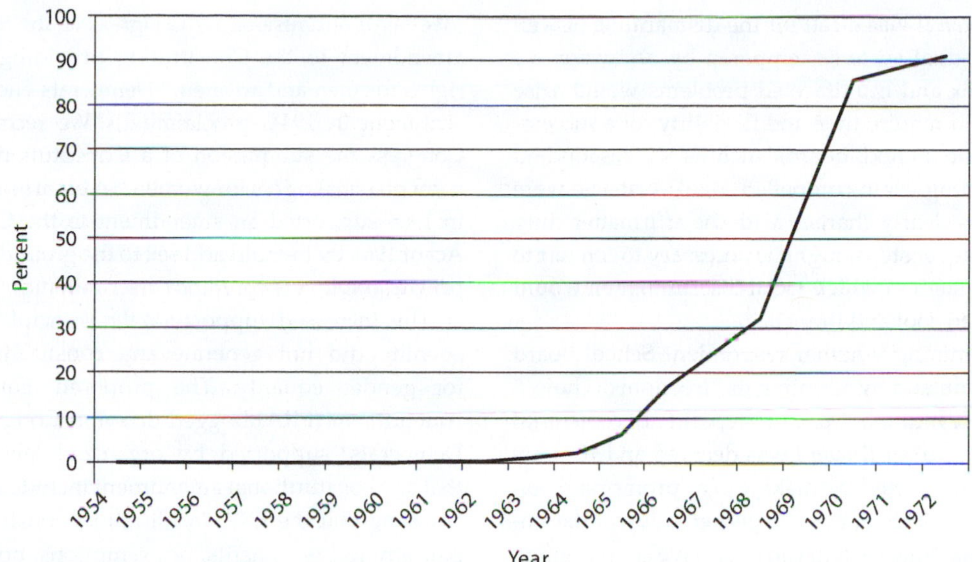

Figure 8-4 Percentage of All Black Southern Schoolchildren Attending School with Whites
Source: Gerald N. Rosenberg, *The Hollow Hope*, rev. ed. (Chicago: University of Chicago Press, 2008), 50. Missing data interpolated in figure.

as the remedy for Brown *violations. How does Justice Brennan explain this decision? Do you think his explanation is correct? Is* Green *merely an application or an extension of* Brown?

JUSTICE BRENNAN delivered the opinion of the Court.

. . .

The pattern of separate "white" and "Negro" schools in the New Kent County school system established under compulsion of state laws is precisely the pattern of segregation to which *Brown I* and *Brown II* were particularly addressed, and which *Brown I* declared unconstitutionally denied Negro school children equal protection of the laws. Racial identification of the system's schools was complete, extending not just to the composition of student bodies at the two schools, but to every facet of school operations—faculty, staff, transportation, extracurricular activities and facilities. . . .

It was such dual systems that, 14 years ago, *Brown I* held unconstitutional. . . . It is, of course, true that, for the time immediately after *Brown II*, the concern was with making an initial break in a long-established pattern of excluding Negro children from schools attended by white children. . . . Under *Brown II*, that immediate goal was only the first step, however. The transition to a unitary, nonracial system of public education was and is the ultimate end to be brought about. . . .

It is against this background that 13 years after *Brown II* commanded the abolition of dual systems we must measure the effectiveness of respondent School Board's "freedom of choice" plan to achieve that end. The School Board contends that it has fully discharged its obligation by adopting a plan by which every student, regardless of race, may "freely" choose the school he will attend. The Board attempts to cast the issue in its broadest form by arguing that its "freedom of choice" plan may be faulted only by reading the Fourteenth Amendment as universally requiring "compulsory integration," a reading it insists the wording of the Amendment will not support. But that argument ignores the thrust of *Brown II*. In the light of the command of that case, what is involved here is the question whether the Board has achieved the "racially nondiscriminatory school system" *Brown II* held must be effectuated in order to remedy the established unconstitutional deficiencies of its segregated system. In the context of the state-imposed segregated pattern of long standing, the fact that, in 1965, the Board opened the doors of the former "white" school to Negro children and of the "Negro" school to white children merely begins, not ends, our inquiry whether the Board has taken steps adequate to abolish its dual, segregated system. *Brown II* was a call for the dismantling of well entrenched dual systems tempered by an awareness that complex and multifaceted problems would arise which would require time and flexibility for a successful resolution. School boards such as the respondent then operating state-compelled dual systems were nevertheless clearly charged with the affirmative duty to take whatever steps might be necessary to convert to a unitary system in which racial discrimination would be eliminated root and branch. . . .

In determining whether respondent School Board met that command by adopting its "freedom of choice" plan, it is relevant that this first step did not come until some 11 years after *Brown I* was decided and 10 years after *Brown II* directed the making of a "prompt and reasonable start." This deliberate perpetuation of the unconstitutional dual system can only have compounded the harm of such a system. Such delays are no longer tolerable. . . . Moreover, a plan that, at this late date, fails to provide meaningful assurance of prompt and effective disestablishment of a dual system is also intolerable. "The time for mere deliberate speed has run out," . . . The burden on a school board today is to come forward with a plan that promises realistically to work, and promises realistically to work now. . . .

C. Gender

American women from 1933 to 1968 gained many legal rights but no additional constitutional rights. Legislatures repealed or stopped enforcing traditional restrictions on women's economic and social liberties. A small but steadily increasing number of women became lawyers, doctors, members of other professions, and elected officials. Still, although many barriers had been broken down, constitutional law remained largely the same. States less often passed laws that made gender distinctions or otherwise discriminated on the basis of gender, but most constitutional decisions makers thought those laws that were passed or remained on the books were consistent with the Fourteenth Amendment.

Most liberals during the New Deal/Great Society Era were committed to the basic principle of gender equality.[81] The Republican Party platform in 1940 asserted, "We favor submission by Congress to the States of an amendment to the Constitution providing for equal rights for men and women." Democrats endorsed that sentiment in 1944, proclaiming, "We recommend to Congress the submission of a Constitutional amendment on equal rights for women." A bipartisan coalition in 1964 supported an amendment to the Civil Rights Act of 1964 that would add sex to the grounds on which private employers could not discriminate.

This increased support for the principle of gender equality did not generate any constitutional gains for gender equality. The proposed Equal Rights Amendment (ERA) bogged down in Congress. Many Democrats, supported by organized labor, insisted that any constitutional amendment include a provision asserting that the ERA "shall not be construed to impair any rights, benefits, or exemptions, now or hereinafter by law upon persons of the female sex."[82] This provision was unacceptable to most women's groups. Federal courts proved unwilling to bestow rights upon women in advance of congressional action. In several decisions, most notably *Goesaert v. Cleary* (1948) and *Hoyt v. Florida* (1961), the Supreme Court insisted that gender distinctions and classifications merited no special protection. In *Hoyt*, Justice Harlan, speaking for a unanimous Court, asserted,

> Despite the enlightened emancipation of women from the restrictions and protections of bygone years, and their entry into many parts of community life formerly considered to be reserved to men, woman is still regarded as the center of home and family life. We cannot say that it is constitutionally impermissible for a State, acting in pursuit of the general welfare, to conclude that a woman should be relieved from the civic duty of jury service unless she herself determines that such service is consistent with her own special responsibilities.

A few state courts were more intrepid. The New Jersey Superior Court in *Gallagher v. City of Bayonne* (NJ 1968) struck down a state law requiring women at bars to sit at tables. Justice Matthews wrote,

> I cannot accept, however, as a general assumption that mere sexual difference is a viable classification

81. For a good short history of the Equal Rights Amendment, see Jane J. Mansbridge, *Why We Lost the ERA* (Chicago: University of Chicago Press, 1986), 7–19.

82. This was the so-called "Hayden Rider," added by the Senate during a 1953 debate over a version of an Equal Rights Amendment; 99 *Congressional Record*, 83rd Cong., 1st Sess. (1953), 8955.

> under equal protection concepts. I am sure that there are specific instances when such a basis may be used, especially those relating to gonadic reasons. In the majority of instances, however, we are dealing with the application of laws to humanity generally, and humanity quite clearly is comprised of both masculine and feminine elements.[83]

D. Native Americans

Native Americans continued to occupy a distinctive place in the American constitutional order. Federal courts continued to rule that neither Congress when governing Native Americans nor tribal governments were constitutionally required to respect the limitations placed on congressional and state power by the Bill of Rights. *Tee-Hit-Ton Indians v. United States* (1955) declared, "No case in this Court has ever held that taking of Indian title or use by Congress required compensation." The Court of Appeals for the Tenth Circuit in *Native American Church of America v. Navajo Tribal Council* (1959) held that tribal governments need not respect the Bill of Rights. Judge Huxman emphasized that Indian tribes are essentially sovereign states. Their "external powers" (the power to enter into treaties with foreign nations) may have been limited by conquest, but their "internal powers" of self-governance are presumed not to be constrained by the laws of the United States, except where Congress has clearly expressed its intent to thus limit tribal sovereignty. For this reason the court concluded that tribal governments were not bound by the First Amendment. Indian tribes, Huxman asserted,

> have a status higher than that of states. They are subordinate and dependent nations possessed of all powers as such only to the extent that they have expressly been required to surrender them by the superior sovereign, the United States. The Constitution is, of course, the supreme law of the land, but it is nonetheless a part of the laws of the United States. Under the philosophy of the decisions, it, as any other law, is binding upon Indian nations only where it expressly binds them, or is made binding by treaty or some act of Congress. No provision in the Constitution makes the First Amendment applicable to Indian nations nor is there any law of Congress doing so. It follows that neither, under the Constitution or the laws of Congress, do the Federal courts have jurisdiction of tribal laws or regulations, even though they may have an impact to some extent on forms of religious worship.[84]

In 1968 Congress passed the Indian Civil Rights Act (ICRA), informally known as the Indian Bill of Rights. In language that closely mirrors that of the Bill of Rights, ICRA imposes many limits on tribal governments' power that are similar, but not identical, to the limits that the Constitution imposes on federal and state governments. The crucial provision of that statute asserts

> No Indian tribe in exercising powers of self-government shall—
>
> (1) make or enforce any law prohibiting the free exercise of religion, or abridging the freedom of speech, or of the press, or the right of the people peaceably to assemble and to petition for a redress of grievances;
>
> (2) violate the right of the people to be secure in their persons, houses, papers, and effects against unreasonable search and seizures, nor issue warrants, but upon probable cause, supported by oath or affirmation, and particularly describing the place to be searched and the person or thing to be seized;
>
> (3) subject any person for the same offense to be twice put in jeopardy;
>
> (4) compel any person in any criminal case to be a witness against himself;
>
> (5) take any private property for a public use without just compensation;
>
> (6) deny to any person in a criminal proceeding the right to a speedy and public trial, to be informed of the nature and cause of the accusation, to be confronted with the witnesses against him, to have compulsory process for obtaining witnesses in his favor, and at his own expense to have the assistance of counsel for his defense;
>
> (7) require excessive bail, impose excessive fines, inflict cruel and unusual punishments, and in no event impose for conviction of any one offense any penalty or punishment greater than imprisonment for a term of one year and a fine of $5,000, or both;

83. *Gallgher v. City of Bayonne*, 55 N.J. 159 (1969).

84. *Native American Church of America v. Navajo Tribal Council*, 272 F.2d. 131 (10th Cir. 1959).

(8) deny to any person within its jurisdiction the equal protection of its laws or deprive any person of liberty or property without due process of law;
(9) pass any bill of attainder or ex post facto law; or
(10) deny to any person accused of an offense punishable by imprisonment the right, upon request, to a trial by jury of not less than six persons.[85]

Reactions to the ICRA have been mixed. Some scholars suggest that the act unduly restricts tribal sovereignty. They argue that Euro-American notions of individual rights may be incompatible with American Indian societies that have traditionally understood themselves "as a complex of responsibilities and duties."[86] Others maintain that the act insufficient protects civil liberties. They note that the ICRA leaves the enforcement of its provisions to tribal governments and does not (except in the case of habeas corpus petitions) provide for recourse to federal courts.[87]

VI. Criminal Justice

MAJOR DEVELOPMENTS

- The Supreme Court begins to impose national standards on the criminal justice system in what has become known as the "Due Process Revolution"
- The Supreme Court excludes unconstitutionally obtained evidence from state criminal trials
- The Supreme Court requires police officers to read suspects in custody their *Miranda* warnings before beginning interrogations

The New Deal/Great Society Era witnessed the Due Process Revolution. Federal and state courts dramatically expanded the constitutional rights of criminal suspects. During the 1930s and 1940s the Supreme Court aggressively protected victims of particularly egregious police practices, most notably persons of color in the Jim Crow South. During the 1950s and 1960s the justices nationalized almost all constitutional protections for criminal suspects in the Bill of Rights. The Warren Court handed down decisions that significantly expanded the constitutional protections offered by the Fourth, Fifth, Sixth, and Eighth Amendments. By the time Richard Nixon took office persons accused of crimes enjoyed unprecedented constitutional protections from the moment that the police first suspected they had broken the law until all the collateral consequences of their criminal sentences were removed. As Figure 8-5 suggests, however, the liberal justices of the post–New Deal period were not united on these developments. The justices of the Warren Court were more supportive of the claims of criminal defendants than were the justices of the 1940s. Liberal New Deal justices were often more supportive of civil liberties claims than of the claims of criminal defendants and criminal suspects. The replacement of New Dealers such as Justice Reed with a new generation of Great Society liberals such as Justice Brennan proved crucial to the Due Process Revolution.

These developments were fueled by particular justices, not political parties. Party platforms said little or nothing about either crime policy or the constitutional rights of criminal suspects. Such Warren Court decisions as *Mapp v. Ohio* (1961) initially did little to place constitutional criminal procedure on the national agenda. Republicans in 1964 attacked the Court in speeches, but not in their party platform. State court justices, by comparison, regularly held meetings that issued statements lambasting the Warren Court. The Conference of State Supreme Court Justices in 1958 complained, "The Supreme Court too often has tended to adopt the role of policy-maker without proper judicial restraint."[88] Legal scholars concerned with judicial activism wrote law review articles ridiculing the reasoning underlying the incorporation cases and judicial decisions expanding the rights of criminal suspects. Still, very little national opposition to the trend of constitutional decision making in criminal process cases existed before the mid-1960s. To the extent that the major political parties sent messages to the justices, those messages indicated that most American elites tolerated rulings that gradually increased the rights of poor persons and persons of color accused of crime.

The due process and civil rights revolutions were closely connected. Prominent elites expressed concern with local practices that discriminated against poor

85. 82 US Stat. 73, 77-78 (1968).

86. Vine Deloria, Jr., and Clifford Lytle, *The Nations Within: The Past and Future of American Indian Sovereignty* (Austin: University of Texas Press, 1984), 213.

87. For a more in-depth discussion of ICRA and the tension between individual rights and tribal sovereignty, see Carole E. Goldberg, "Individual Rights and Tribal Revitalization," *Arizona State Law Journal* 35 (2003): 889–90.

88. Charles S. Hyneman, *The Supreme Court on Trial* (New York: Atherton Press, 1963), 23.

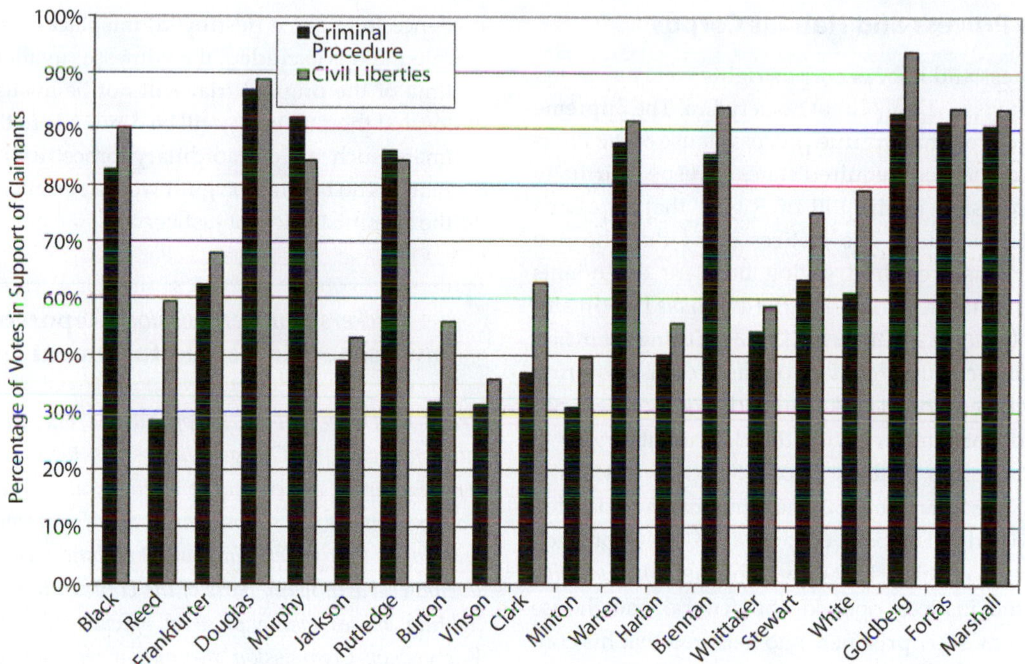

Figure 8-5 Individual Justice Support for Claimants in Criminal Procedure and Civil Liberties Cases on the Vinson and Warren Courts

Notes: Justices listed in order of appointment. Category of civil liberties cases excludes criminal justice cases.

Source: Supreme Court Database, www.scdb.wustl.edu.

persons and persons of color. The Wickersham Commission of 1931 was the first of many blue-ribbon panels that condemned police use of "third-degree" methods against powerless minorities. Many prominent Warren Court decisions protecting the rights of criminal suspects concerned persons of color who were victims of racist practices. Chief Justice Warren's initial draft of *Miranda v. Arizona* (1966) asserted,

> In a series of cases decided by this Court . . . Negro defendants were subjected to physical brutality—beatings, hanging, whipping—employed to extort confessions. In 1947, the President's Committee on Civil Rights probed further into police violence upon minority groups. The files of the Justice Department, in the words of the Committee, abounded "with evidence of illegal official action in southern states."[89]

Quite frequently the Supreme Court insisted that southern law enforcement officials adopt practices already implemented by federal law enforcement officials. Decisions such as *Miranda v. Arizona* (1965), Lucas Powe suggests, were intended "to force state systems to behave like [the justices] assumed the FBI, United States attorneys, and the federal courts behaved."[90]

The strong procedural protections found in Supreme Court opinions do not describe actual practice. Persons of color whose cases became *cause célèbres* sometimes had their convictions reversed and, after extensive struggles, became free persons. The vast majority of persons accused of crime, particularly in the South, experienced practices that Supreme Court opinions dutifully intoned were unconstitutional. Even in the North the most frequent impact of many Supreme Court decisions was to increase the practice of police perjury and enable suspect criminals to obtain more favorable plea bargains.[91]

89. Louis Michael Seidman, "Brown *and* Miranda," *California Law Review* 80 (1992): 751n254.

90. Powe, *The Warren Court*, 492.

91. See Rosenberg, *The Hollow Hope*; Myron W. Orfield, Jr., "Deterrence, Perjury, and the Heater Factor: An Exclusionary Rule in the Chicago Criminal Courts," *University of Colorado Law Review* 63 (1992): 75.

A. Due Process and Habeas Corpus

Due process and habeas corpus rights were expanded during the New Deal/Great Society Era. The Supreme Court declared that the due process clause of the Fourteenth Amendment required states to respect virtually every provision in the Bill of Rights that regulated criminal procedure. The justices ruled that the due process clause required giving indigent defendants access to state transcripts (*Griffin v. Illinois* [1956]) and lawyers (*Douglas v. California* [1963]) during their first appeal of a criminal conviction, as well as requiring states to take steps to make sure adverse pretrial publicity did not interfere with the defendant's right to a fair trial (*Estes v. Texas* [1965]; *Sheppard v. Maxwell* [1966]). The Warren Court dramatically expanded access to federal habeas corpus. In a series of decisions, the most important of which was *Brown v. Allen* (1953), the justices opened the federal courthouse doors to any state prisoner who believed that his constitutional rights had been violated at trial. *Fay v. Noia* (1963) ruled that federal courts could sometimes hear constitutional claims that had not first been raised in state courts. *Townsend v. Sain* (1963) permitted federal courts to hold factual hearings on those claims, and, as every civil rights lawyer knew, federal courts in the 1960s were far more likely than state courts to find facts favorable to the defendant. Congress codified these decisions when passing the Federal Habeas Corpus Act of 1966.

The constitutional politics of due process and habeas corpus did not move uniformly in a liberal direction. Two decisions suggested important limits to constitutional liberalism. *Ex parte Quirin* (1942) sustained President Roosevelt's decision to try alleged German saboteurs before a military tribunal. When sustaining the decision, the unanimous Supreme Court treated as dicta language in *Ex parte Milligan* (1866) suggesting that civilian trials must be held whenever courts are open. *Linkletter v. Walker* (1965) held that the *Mapp v. Ohio* (1961) decision could not apply retroactively in habeas corpus appeals. This meant that persons sentenced before 1961 on the basis of unconstitutionally obtained evidence could not have their convictions reversed. Justice Clark's majority opinion asserted,

> To make the rule of *Mapp* retrospective would tax the administration of justice to the utmost. Hearings would have to be held on the excludability of evidence long since destroyed, misplaced or deteriorated. If it is excluded, the witnesses available at the time of the original trial will not be available or if located their memory will be dimmed. To thus legitimate such an extraordinary procedural weapon that has no bearing on guilt would seriously disrupt the administration of justice.

Wickersham Commission, **Report on Lawlessness in Law Enforcement** (1931)[92]

President Hoover in 1929 appointed a blue-ribbon commission headed by George Wickersham to investigate the criminal justice system in the United States. The National Commission on Law Observance and Enforcement spent much of its energy detailing how Prohibition was becoming unenforceable in many parts of the United States and highlighting abuses taking place in official enforcement. The Wickersham Commission also authorized three prominent lawyers—Zechariah Chafee, Jr., Walter H. Pollak, and Carl S. Stern—to conduct a more general survey of law enforcement practices. Their final report detailed how the "third degree—the inflicting of pain, physical, or mental, to extract confessions or statements—is widespread throughout the country." "Third-degree practices," another section of the report asserted, "were particularly used against Negroes" and more generally "against the poor and uninfluential." Liberal reformers regarded the Wickersham Commission report as providing the blueprint for reforming the criminal justice system. Many Supreme Court decisions in the following years cited the findings and recommendations of the commission. Think about the practices documented in the Wickersham Report. Which are consequences of discrimination against the poor and racial minorities? Which are consequences of (over)aggressive police efforts to fight crime? Should these different motivations make a constitutional difference?

. . .

It is a fundamental principle of our law, constantly reaffirmed by courts and almost as constantly disregarded by many law-enforcement officers, that everyone is presumed to be innocent of crime until convicted. . . .

---

92. Excerpted from Wickersham Commission Reports, *No. 11 Report on Lawlessness in Law Enforcement* (Montclair, NJ: Patterson Smith, 1968), 153, 158–59, 1–8.

. . .

That [constitutional] rights have been very generally disregarded by the police has been asserted in print and in current discussion. The constitutional privilege that no man shall be compelled to be a witness against himself in a criminal case, often is a serious obstacle to the detection of crime. There is much evidence that despite this constitutional declaration and because of the obstacles thus presented, confessions of guilt frequently are unlawfully extorted by the police from prisoners by means of cruel treatment, colloquially known as the third degree. . . .

. . .

The practice of the third degree involves violation of such fundamental rights as those of (1) personal liberty; (2) bail; (3) protection from personal assault and battery; (4) the presumption of innocence until conviction of guilty by due process of law; and (5) the right to employ counsel, who shall have access to him at reasonable hours. Holding prisoners *incommunicado* in order to persuade or extort confessions is all too frequently resorted to by the police. As the report shows, courts give no approval to any of these practices, and convictions of crime based upon confessions of guilt secured by such methods are very generally set aside.

After reviewing the evidence obtainable the authors of the report reach the conclusion that the third degree—that is, the use of physical brutality, or other forms of cruelty, to obtain involuntary confessions or admissions—is widespread. Protracted questioning of prisoners is commonly employed. Threats and methods of intimidation, adjusted to the age or mentality of the victim, are frequently used, either by themselves or in combination with some of the other practices mentioned. Physical brutality, illegal detention, and refusal to allow access of counsel to the prisoner is common. Even where the law requires prompt production of a prisoner before a magistrate, the police not infrequently delay doing so and employ the time in efforts to compel confession. The practice of holding the accused *incommunicado*, unable to get in touch with their family or friends or counsel, is so frequent that in places there are cells called "*incommunicado* cells." Brutality and violence in making an arrest also are employed at times, before the prisoner reaches the jail, in order to put him in a frame of mind which makes him more amenable to questioning afterwards. . . . On the other hand, they found little evidence of the practice among Federal officials. . . .

While the third degree is used mainly against arrested persons suspected of having committed a crime, it also sometimes is employed against other persons for the purpose of getting information about an offense from persons who are not suspected of having committed it, but only of knowing about it. While third-degree methods are most frequently practiced by policemen and detectives, there are cases in which prosecuting officers and their assistants participate in them. To the contention that the third degree is necessary to get the facts, the reporters aptly reply in the language of the present Lord Chancellor of England (Lord Sankey): "It is not admissible to do a great right by doing a little wrong. . . . It is not sufficient to do justice by obtaining a proper result by irregular or improper means." Not only does the use of the third degree involve a flagrant violation of the law by the officers of the law, but it involves also the dangers of false confessions, and it tends to make police and prosecutors less zealous in the search for objective evidence. . . . We agree with the conclusion expressed in the report, that "The third degree brutalizes the police, hardens the prisoner against society, and lowers the esteem in which the administration of justice is held by the public." Probably the best remedy for this evil would be the enforcement of the rule that every person arrested charged with crime should be forthwith taken before a magistrate, advised of the charge against him, given the right to have counsel and then interrogated by the magistrate. His answers should be recorded and should be admissible in evidence against him in all subsequent proceedings. If he choose not to answer, it should be permissible for counsel for the prosecution and for the defense, as well as for the trial judge, to comment on his refusal. The existing rule in many jurisdictions which forbids counsel or court to comment on the failure of the accused to testify in his own behalf should be abolished. . . .

Griffin v. Illinois, 351 U.S. 12 (1956)

Judson Griffin was found guilty of armed robbery by a trial court in Cook County, Illinois. Illinois law granted all persons convicted at trial the right to appeal their sentence. In order to exercise that right, persons not sentenced to death had to purchase a certified copy of the trial record. Griffin could not afford the cost. He filed a petition for habeas corpus, insisting that the failure to provide him with a free copy of the trial record violated the equal protection and due process clauses of the Fourteenth Amendment. The Illinois courts rejected that contention. Griffin appealed to the Supreme Court of the United States.

The Supreme Court by a 5-4 vote reversed the Illinois courts. Justice Black's plurality opinion maintained that once a state gave persons a right to appeal, the state could not condition that right on the ability to pay for a trial transcript. The justices in Griffin *agreed that money can buy criminal defendants high-priced lawyers but cannot buy them acquittals. On what constitutional basis do Justices Black, Frankfurter, and Harlan determine whether money ought to be able to buy persons an appeal from a criminal conviction? Which opinion do you believe is constitutionally correct? What more generally should money be allowed and not allowed to buy in the criminal process?*

JUSTICE BLACK announced the judgment of the Court and an opinion in which THE CHIEF JUSTICE, JUSTICE DOUGLAS, and JUSTICE CLARK join.

Providing equal justice for poor and rich, weak and powerful alike is an age-old problem. People have never ceased to hope and strive to move closer to that goal. . . . [O]ur own constitutional guaranties of due process and equal protection both call for procedures in criminal trials which allow no invidious discriminations between persons and different groups of persons. Both equal protection and due process emphasize the central aim of our entire judicial system—all people charged with crime must, so far as the law is concerned, "stand on an equality before the bar of justice in every American court." . . .

Surely no one would contend that either a State or the Federal Government could constitutionally provide that defendants unable to pay court costs in advance should be denied the right to plead not guilty or to defend themselves in court. Such a law would make the constitutional promise of a fair trial a worthless thing. Notice, the right to be heard, and the right to counsel would under such circumstances be meaningless promises to the poor. In criminal trials a State can no more discriminate on account of poverty than on account of religion, race, or color. Plainly the ability to pay costs in advance bears no rational relationship to a defendant's guilt or innocence and could not be used as an excuse to deprive a defendant of a fair trial. . . .

There is no meaningful distinction between a rule which would deny the poor the right to defend themselves in a trial court and one which effectively denies the poor an adequate appellate review accorded to all who have money enough to pay the costs in advance. It is true that a State is not required by the Federal Constitution to provide appellate courts or a right to appellate review at all. . . . But that is not to say that a State that does grant appellate review can do so in a way that discriminates against some convicted defendants on account of their poverty. Appellate review has now become an integral part of the Illinois trial system for finally adjudicating the guilt or innocence of a defendant. Consequently at all stages of the proceedings the Due Process and Equal Protection Clauses protect persons like petitioners from invidious discriminations. . . .

All of the States now provide some method of appeal from criminal convictions, recognizing the importance of appellate review to a correct adjudication of guilt or innocence. Statistics show that a substantial proportion of criminal convictions are reversed by state appellate courts. Thus to deny adequate review to the poor means that many of them may lose their life, liberty or property because of unjust convictions which appellate courts would set aside. Many States have recognized this and provided aid for convicted defendants who have a right to appeal and need a transcript but are unable to pay for it. A few have not. Such a denial is a misfit in a country dedicated to affording equal justice to all and special privileges to none in the administration of its criminal law. There can be no equal justice where the kind of trial a man gets depends on the amount of money he has. Destitute defendants must be afforded as adequate appellate review as defendants who have money enough to buy transcripts.

. . .

JUSTICE FRANKFURTER, concurring in the judgment.

. . .

. . . [N]either the fact that a State may deny the right of appeal altogether nor the right of a State to make an appropriate classification, based on differences in crimes and their punishment, nor the right of a State to lay down conditions it deems appropriate for criminal appeals, sanctions differentiations by a State that have no relation to a rational policy of criminal appeal or authorizes the imposition of conditions that offend the deepest presuppositions of our society. Surely it would not need argument to conclude that a State could not, within its wide scope of discretion in these matters, allow an appeal for persons convicted of crimes punishable by imprisonment of a year or more, only on payment of a fee of $500. Illinois, of course, has done nothing so crude as that. But Illinois has said, in effect, that the Supreme Court of Illinois can consider alleged errors occurring in a criminal trial only if the basis for determining whether there were errors is brought before it by a bill of exceptions and not otherwise. From this it follows that Illinois has decreed that only defendants who can afford to pay for the stenographic minutes of a trial may have trial errors reviewed on appeal by the Illinois Supreme Court. . . . It has thereby shut off means of appellate review for indigent defendants.

. . .

. . . Of course a State need not equalize economic conditions. A man of means may be able to afford the retention of an expensive, able counsel not within reach of a poor man's purse. Those are contingencies of life which are hardly within the power, let alone the duty, of a State to correct or cushion. But when a State deems it wise and just that convictions be susceptible to review by an appellate court, it cannot by force of its exactions draw a line which precludes convicted indigent persons, forsooth erroneously convicted, from securing such a review merely by disabling them from bringing to the notice of an appellate tribunal errors of the trial court which would upset the conviction were practical opportunity for review not foreclosed.

. . .

JUSTICE BURTON and JUSTICE MINTON, whom JUSTICE REED and JUSTICE HARLAN join, dissenting.

. . .

. . . [C]ertainly Illinois does not deny equal protection to convicted defendants when the terms of appeal are open to all, although some may not be able to avail themselves of the full appeal because of their poverty. Illinois is not bound to make the defendants economically equal before its bar of justice. For a State to do so may be a desirable social policy, but what may be a good legislative policy for a State is not necessarily required by the Constitution of the United States. Persons charged with crimes stand before the law with varying degrees of economic and social advantage. Some can afford better lawyers and better investigations of their cases. Some can afford bail, some cannot. Why fix bail at any reasonable sum if a poor man can't make it?

The Constitution requires the equal protection of the law, but it does not require the States to provide equal financial means for all defendants to avail themselves of such laws.

JUSTICE HARLAN, dissenting.

. . .

. . . All that Illinois has done is to fail to alleviate the consequences of differences in economic circumstances that exist wholly apart from any state action.

The Court thus holds that, at least in this area of criminal appeals, the Equal Protection Clause imposes on the States an affirmative duty to lift the handicaps flowing from differences in economic circumstances. That holding produces the anomalous result that a constitutional admonition to the States to treat all persons equally means in this instance that Illinois must give to some what it requires others to pay for. Granting that such a classification would be reasonable, it does not follow that a State's failure to make it can be regarded as discrimination. . . .

. . . [N]o economic burden attendant upon the exercise of a privilege bears equally upon all, and in other circumstances the resulting differentiation is not treated as an invidious classification by the State, even though discrimination against "indigents" by name would be unconstitutional. Thus, while the exclusion of "indigents" from a free state university would deny them equal protection, requiring the payment of tuition fees surely would not, despite the resulting exclusion of those who could not afford to pay the fees. And if imposing a condition of payment is not the equivalent of a classification by the State in one case, I fail to see why it should be so regarded in another. Thus if requiring defendants in felony cases to pay for a transcript constitutes a discriminatory denial to indigents of the right of appeal available to others, why is it not a similar denial in misdemeanor cases or, for that matter, civil cases?

. . .

. . . [W]hatever else may be said of Illinois' reluctance to expend public funds in perfecting appeals for indigents, it can hardly be said to be arbitrary. A policy of economy may be unenlightened, but it is certainly not capricious. And that it has never generally been so regarded is evidenced by the fact that our attention has been called to no State in which in forma pauperis appeals were established contemporaneously with the right of appeal. I can find nothing in the past decisions of this Court justifying a holding that the Fourteenth Amendment confines the States to a choice between allowing no appeals at all or undertaking to bear the cost of appeals for indigents, which is what the Court in effect now holds.

It is argued finally that, even if it cannot be said to be "arbitrary," the failure of Illinois to provide petitioners with the means of exercising the right of appeal that others are able to exercise is simply so "unfair" as to be a denial of due process. I have some question whether the non-arbitrary denial of a right that the State may withhold altogether could ever be so characterized. In any event, however, to so hold it is not enough that we consider free transcripts for indigents to be a desirable policy or that we would weigh the competing social values in favor of such a policy were it our function to distribute Illinois' public funds among alternative uses. Rather the question is whether some method of assuring that an indigent is able to exercise his right of appeal is "implicit in the concept of ordered liberty." Such an equivalence between persons in the means with which to exercise a right of appeal has not, however, traditionally been regarded as an essential of "fundamental fairness," and the reforms extending such aid to indigents have only recently gained widespread acceptance.

Fay v. Noia, 372 U.S. 391 (1963)

Charles Noia and two co-defendants in 1942 were convicted of felony murder and sentenced to life in prison. Noia's co-defendants appealed their convictions. Noia did not. A federal appeals court in 1955 declared that every confession in the case was unconstitutionally coerced. As a result of that decision, the two co-defendants who had appealed were set free. Noia immediately filed a petition for habeas corpus on the ground that he had been convicted on the basis of an unconstitutionally coerced confession. A lower New York court granted the writ, but the New York Court of Appeals reversed that judgment on the ground that, under New York criminal procedure law, Noia had waived his constitutional rights by failing to appeal his 1942 conviction in a timely fashion. Noia promptly filed a petition for habeas corpus in federal court. A lower federal court refused to issue the writ on the ground that Noia had failed to take advantage of state court proceedings in 1942. That decision was reversed by the Court of Appeals for the Second Circuit. New York appealed to the Supreme Court of the United States.

The Supreme Court by a 6-3 vote sustained the grant of habeas corpus. Justice Brennan's majority opinion ruled that federal courts in habeas cases could hear constitutional claims not raised at the state trial as long as the petitioner had not intentionally withheld the claim. What constitutional and statutory arguments does Justice Brennan make in support of independent federal review of constitutional claims? Do you find these claims plausible? What prudential claims does Justice Clark make in his dissenting opinion? How strong are his arguments? Is Justice Harlan correct that the judicial decision in Fay *is inconsistent with constitutional commitments to federalism? What are the constitutional and prudential vices and virtues of "adequate and independent state grounds"—the doctrine that a prisoner may normally only raise constitutional claims in a federal habeas corpus procedure if he or she has complied with all state procedural rules for raising that claim? Do you think that requiring a deliberate, conscious waiver best balances respect for constitutional rights and respect for state courts or should federal courts normally refuse to hear any claim that could have been raised in a state proceeding but was not?*

JUSTICE BRENNAN delivered the opinion of the Court.

. . .

. . . We hold: (1) Federal courts have power under the federal habeas statute to grant relief despite the applicant's failure to have pursued a state remedy not available to him at the time he applies; the doctrine under which state procedural defaults are held to constitute an adequate and independent state law ground barring direct Supreme Court review is not to be extended to limit the power granted the federal courts under the federal habeas statute. . . . (3) Noia's failure to appeal cannot under the circumstances be deemed an intelligent and understanding waiver of his right to appeal such as to justify the withholding of federal habeas corpus relief.

. . .

We do well to bear in mind the extraordinary prestige of the Great Writ, habeas corpus ad subjiciendum, in Anglo-American jurisprudence: "the most celebrated writ in the English law. . . ." These are not extravagant expressions. Behind them may be discerned the unceasing contest between personal liberty and government oppression. It is no accident that habeas corpus has time and again played a central role in national crises, wherein the claims of order and of liberty clash most acutely, not only in England in the seventeenth century, but also in America from our very beginnings, and today. Although in form the Great Writ is simply a mode of procedure, its history is inextricably intertwined with the growth of fundamental rights of personal liberty. For its function has been to provide a prompt and efficacious remedy for whatever society deems to be intolerable restraints. Its root principle is that in a civilized society, government must always be accountable to the judiciary for a man's imprisonment: if the imprisonment cannot be shown to conform with the fundamental requirements of law, the individual is entitled to his immediate release. Thus there is nothing novel in the fact that today habeas corpus in the federal courts provides a mode for the redress of denials of due process of law. . . .

. . .

. . . Under the conditions of modern society, Noia's imprisonment, under a conviction procured by a confession . . . to have been coerced, and which the State here concedes was obtained in violation of the Fourteenth Amendment, is no less intolerable than was Bushell's under the conditions of a very different society; and habeas corpus is no less the appropriate remedy.

. . .

. . . [H]abeas corpus has traditionally been regarded as governed by equitable principles. . . . Among them is the principle that a suitor's conduct in relation to the matter at hand may disentitle him to the relief he seeks. Narrowly circumscribed, in conformity to the historical role of the writ of habeas corpus as an effective and imperative remedy for detentions contrary to fundamental law, the principle is unexceptionable. We therefore hold that the federal habeas judge may in his discretion deny relief to an applicant who has deliberately bypassed the orderly procedure of the state courts and in so doing has forfeited his state court remedies.

But we wish to make very clear that this grant of discretion is not to be interpreted as a permission to introduce legal fictions into federal habeas corpus. . . . If a habeas applicant, after consultation with competent counsel or otherwise, understandingly and knowingly forewent the privilege of seeking to vindicate his federal claims in the state courts, whether for strategic, tactical, or any other reasons that can fairly be described as the deliberate by-passing of state procedures, then it is open to the federal court on habeas to deny him all relief if the state courts refused to entertain his federal claims on the merits—though of course only after the federal court has satisfied itself, by holding a hearing or by some other means, of the facts bearing upon the applicant's default. . . .

. . .

. . . Our decision today swings open no prison gates. Today as always few indeed is the number of state prisoners who eventually win their freedom by means of federal habeas corpus. Those few who are ultimately successful are persons whom society has grievously wronged and for whom belated liberation is little enough compensation. Surely no fair-minded person will contend that those who have been deprived of their liberty without due process of law ought nevertheless to languish in prison. . . . If the States withhold effective remedy, the federal courts have the power and the duty to provide it. Habeas corpus is one of the precious heritages of Anglo-American civilization. We do no more today than confirm its continuing efficacy.

JUSTICE CLARK, dissenting.

. . . The short of it is that Noia's incarceration rests entirely on an adequate and independent state ground—namely, that he knowingly failed to perfect any appeal from his conviction of murder. While it may be that the Court's "decision today swings open no prison gates," the Court must admit in all candor that it effectively swings closed the doors of justice in the face of the State, since it certainly cannot prove its case twenty years after the fact. . . .

First, there can be no question but that a rash of new applications from state prisoners will pour into the federal courts, and 98 percent of them will be frivolous, if history is any guide. This influx will necessarily have an adverse effect upon the disposition of meritorious applications, for, as my Brother Jackson said, they will "be buried in a flood of worthless ones." . . .

Second, the effective administration of criminal justice in state courts receives a staggering blow. Habeas corpus is in effect substituted for appeal, seriously disturbing the orderly disposition of state prosecutions and jeopardizing the finality of state convictions in disregard of the States' comprehensive procedural safeguards which, until today, have been respected by the federal courts. . . .

. . .

JUSTICE HARLAN, whom JUSTICE CLARK and JUSTICE STEWART join, dissenting.

I dissent from the Court's opinion and judgment for the reason that the federal courts have no power, statutory or constitutional, to release the respondent Noia from state detention. This is because his custody by New York does not violate any federal right, since it is pursuant to a conviction whose validity rests upon an adequate and independent state ground which the federal courts are required to respect.

. . .

. . . It is clear that a State may not preclude Supreme Court review of federal claims by discriminating against or evading the assertion of a federal right, and indeed that state procedural grounds for refusal to consider a federal claim must rest on a "fair or substantial basis." Occasionally this means that a state procedural rule which may properly preclude the raising of state claims in a state court cannot thwart review of federal claims in this Court. These principles are inherent in the concept that a state ground, to be of sufficient breadth to support the judgment, must be both "adequate" and "independent."

But determination of the adequacy and independence of the state ground, I submit, marks the constitutional limit of our power in this sphere. . . . For this Court to go beyond the adequacy of the state ground and to review and determine the correctness of that ground on its merits would, in our hypothetical case, be to assume full control over a State's procedures for the administration of its own criminal justice. This is and must be beyond our power if the federal system is to exist in substance as well as form. The right of the State to regulate its own procedures governing the conduct of litigants in its courts, and its interest in supervision of those procedures, stand on the same constitutional plane as its right and interest in framing "substantive" laws governing other aspects of the conduct of those within its borders.

. . .

Under the circumstances here—particularly the fact that Noia was represented by counsel whose competence is not challenged—is this a reasonable ground for barring collateral assertion of the federal claim? Certainly the State has a vital interest in requiring that appeals be taken on the basis of facts known at the time, since the first assertion of a claim many years later might otherwise require release long after it was feasible to hold a new trial. . . .

. . . I recognize that Noia's predicament may well be thought one that strongly calls for correction. But the proper course to that end lies with the New York Governor's powers of executive clemency, not with the federal courts. Since Noia is detained pursuant to a state judgment whose validity rests on an adequate and independent state ground, the judgment below should be reversed.

Ex parte Quirin, 317 U.S. 1 (1942)

The FBI during the summer of 1942 captured Richard Quirin and seven other German agents sent to the United States to sabotage American defense plants. One of the persons captured, Herbert Haupt, was arguably an American citizen. President Roosevelt wanted all eight to be court-martialed and executed. After consulting with his cabinet, Roosevelt settled for a military commission. On July 28 all the Germans were found guilty. Counsel immediately asked the Supreme Court for a writ of habeas corpus, claiming that the president had no power to establish a military commission and that the trials violated the Fifth and Sixth Amendments. The Court heard arguments on July 29 and July 30. The unanimous decision rejecting habeas corpus was announced on July 31. The petitioners were sentenced to death on August 3. President Roosevelt commuted the sentences of the two who turned themselves in. The others were executed on August 8.

Ex parte Quirin *had a disturbing aftermath. The justices on July 31 merely announced their decision without giving reasons. Writing an opinion proved more difficult. The justices quickly discovered that they lacked a common rationale for not granting habeas corpus. Worse, some evidence exists that Chief Justice Stone began to question whether the initial decision was correct—a troubling matter, given that six petitioners had already been executed. As you read the opinion, consider the extent to which those doubts may have influenced his rationale.* Ex parte Milligan *(1866) held that martial law could not be suspended on American soil when courts were open. The Justice Department urged the justices to overrule that part of* Milligan. *Stone did not. How does he distinguish* Quirin *from* Milligan? *Do you find that distinction convincing?*

CHIEF JUSTICE STONE delivered the opinion of the Court.

. . .

Petitioners' main contention is that the President is without any statutory or constitutional authority to order the petitioners to be tried by military tribunal for offenses with which they are charged; that in consequence they are entitled to be tried in the civil courts with the safeguards, including trial by jury, which the Fifth and Sixth Amendments guarantee to all persons charged in such courts with criminal offenses. . . .

. . .

The Constitution . . . invests the President, as Commander in Chief, with the power to wage war which Congress has declared, and to carry into effect all laws passed by Congress for the conduct of war and for the government and regulation of the Armed Forces, and all laws defining and punishing offenses against the law of nations, including those which pertain to the conduct of war.

. . .

. . . It is unnecessary for present purposes to determine to what extent the President as Commander in Chief has constitutional power to create military commissions without the support of Congressional legislation. For here Congress has authorized trial of offenses against the law of war before such commissions. We are concerned only with the question whether it is within the constitutional power of the National Government to place petitioners upon trial before a military commission for the offenses with which they are charged. We must therefore first inquire whether any of the acts charged is an offense against the law of war cognizable before a military tribunal, and if so whether the Constitution prohibits the trial. . . . [T]hese petitioners were charged with an offense against the law of war which the Constitution does not require to be tried by jury.

. . .

By universal agreement and practice, the law of war draws a distinction between the armed forces and the peaceful populations of belligerent nations and also between those who are lawful and unlawful combatants. Lawful combatants are subject to capture and detention as prisoners of war by opposing military forces. Unlawful combatants are likewise subject to capture and detention, but in addition they are subject to trial and punishment by military tribunals for acts which render their belligerency unlawful. The spy who secretly and without uniform passes the military lines of a belligerent in time of war, seeking to gather military information and communicate it to the enemy, or an enemy combatant who without uniform comes secretly through the lines for the purpose of waging war by destruction of life or property, are familiar examples of belligerents who are generally deemed not to be entitled to the status of prisoners of war, but to be offenders against the law of war subject to trial and punishment by military tribunals. . . .

. . .

Our Government, by thus defining lawful belligerents entitled to be treated as prisoners of war, has recognized that there is a class of unlawful belligerents not entitled to that privilege, including those who, though combatants, do not wear "fixed and distinctive emblems." And by Article 15 of the Articles of War Congress has made provision for their trial and punishment by military commission, according to "the law of war."

By a long course of practical administrative construction by its military authorities, our Government has likewise recognized that those who during time of war pass surreptitiously from enemy territory into our own, discarding their uniforms upon entry, for the commission of hostile acts involving destruction of life or property, have the status of unlawful combatants punishable as such by military commission. . . .

. . .

Citizenship in the United States of an enemy belligerent does not relieve him from the consequences of a belligerency which is unlawful because in violation of the law of war. Citizens who associate themselves with the military arm of the enemy government, and with its aid, guidance and direction enter this country bent on hostile acts, are enemy belligerents within the meaning of the Hague Convention and the law of war. . . .

. . .

But petitioners insist that, even if the offenses with which they are charged are offenses against the law of war, their trial is subject to the requirement of the Fifth Amendment that no person shall be held to answer for a capital or otherwise infamous crime unless on a presentment or indictment of a grand jury, and that such trials by Article III, [Section] 2, and the Sixth Amendment must be by jury in a civil court. Before the Amendments, . . . the Judiciary Article, had provided, "The Trial of all Crimes, except in Cases of Impeachment, shall be by Jury," and had directed that "such Trial shall be held in the State where the said Crimes shall have been committed."

Presentment by a grand jury and trial by a jury of the vicinage where the crime was committed were at the time of the adoption of the Constitution familiar parts of the machinery for criminal trials in the civil courts. But they were procedures unknown to military tribunals, which are not courts in the sense of the Judiciary Article. . . . As this Court has often recognized, it was not the purpose or effect of [Section] 2 of

Article III, read in the light of the common law, to enlarge the then existing right to a jury trial. . . .

The Fifth and Sixth Amendments, while guaranteeing the continuance of certain incidents of trial by jury which Article III, [Section] 2 had left unmentioned, did not enlarge the right to jury trial as it had been established by that Article. . . .

. . .

. . . An express exception from Article III, [Section] 2, and from the Fifth and Sixth Amendments, of trials of petty offenses and of criminal contempts has not been found necessary in order to preserve the traditional practice of trying those offenses without a jury. It is no more so in order to continue the practice of trying, before military tribunals without a jury, offenses committed by enemy belligerents against the law of war.

. . .

Since the Amendments, like [Section] 2 of Article III, do not preclude all trials of offenses against the law of war by military commission without a jury when the offenders are aliens not members of our Armed Forces, it is plain that they present no greater obstacle to the trial in like manner of citizen enemies who have violated the law of war applicable to enemies. Under the original statute authorizing trial of alien spies by military tribunals, the offenders were outside the constitutional guaranty of trial by jury, not because they were aliens but only because they had violated the law of war by committing offenses constitutionally triable by military tribunal.

. . .

Petitioners, and especially petitioner Haupt, stress the pronouncement of this Court in the *Milligan* case . . . that the law of war "can never be applied to citizens in states which have upheld the authority of the government, and where the courts are open and their process unobstructed." Elsewhere in its opinion, . . . the Court was at pains to point out that Milligan, a citizen twenty years resident in Indiana, who had never been a resident of any of the states in rebellion, was not an enemy belligerent either entitled to the status of a prisoner of war or subject to the penalties imposed upon unlawful belligerents. We construe the Court's statement as to the inapplicability of the law of war to Milligan's case as having particular reference to the facts before it. From them the Court concluded that Milligan, not being a part of or associated with the armed forces of the enemy, was a non-belligerent, not subject to the law of war save as—in circumstances found not there to be present, and not involved here—martial law might be constitutionally established.

It is enough that petitioners here, upon the conceded facts, were plainly within those boundaries, and were held in good faith for trial by military commission, charged with being enemies who, with the purpose of destroying war materials and utilities, entered, or after entry remained in, our territory without uniform—an offense against the law of war. We hold only that those particular acts constitute an offense against the law of war which the Constitution authorizes to be tried by military commission. . . .

B. Search and Seizure

New Deal liberals were initially inclined to limit constitutional protections against official searches. In *Oklahoma Press Publishing Company v. Walling* (1946) the Supreme Court unanimously brushed aside a claim that federal officials had no right to search corporate books to see whether a corporation was acting in a manner consistent with the Federal Labor Standards Act. Justice Wiley Rutledge's majority opinion bluntly asserted, "The Fifth Amendment affords no protection by virtue of the self-incrimination provision, whether for the corporation or for its officers; and the Fourth, if applicable, at the most guards against abuse only by way of too much indefiniteness or breadth in the things required to be 'particularly described.'" The judicial majority in *Wolf v. People of the State of Colorado* (1949) held that states were not required to adhere to the federal exclusionary rule established in *Weeks v. United States* (1914). Justice Frankfurter's majority opinion asserted,

> The exclusion of evidence is a remedy which directly serves only to protect those upon whose person or premises something incriminating has been found. We cannot, therefore, regard it as a departure from basic standards to remand such persons, together with those who emerge scatheless from a search, to the remedies of private action and such protection as the internal discipline of the police, under the eyes of an alert public opinion, may afford. Granting that in practice the exclusion of evidence may be an effective way of deterring unreasonable searches, it is not for this Court to condemn as falling below the minimal standards assured by the Due Process Clause a State's reliance upon other methods which, if consistently enforced, would be equally effective.

The combination of *Wolf* and *Weeks* led to the "silver platter" doctrine. While federal prosecutors could not use evidence illegally obtained by federal agents, the Supreme Court permitted federal prosecutors to use evidence obtained by state police by means that would have violated the Fourth Amendment if used by a federal agent.

Great Society liberals had a more expansive interpretation of constitutional rights against search and seizure. A 5-4 judicial majority in *Elkins v. United States* (1960) abandoned the silver platter doctrine. After noting the many states that had adopted the exclusionary rule, Justice Stewart noted,

> The very essence of a healthy federalism depends upon the avoidance of needless conflict between state and federal courts. Yet when a federal court sitting in an exclusionary state admits evidence lawlessly seized by state agents, it not only frustrates state policy, but frustrates that policy in a particularly inappropriate and ironic way. For by admitting the unlawfully seized evidence the federal court serves to defeat the state's effort to assure obedience to the Federal Constitution.

In 1961 the Supreme Court ruled that the due process clause of the Fourteenth Amendment forbade states from introducing unconstitutionally obtained evidence during criminal trials. When nationalizing the exclusionary rule in *Mapp v. Ohio* (1961), Justice Clark's majority opinion stated, "Having once recognized that the right to privacy embodied in the Fourth Amendment is enforceable against the States, and that the right to be secure against rude invasions of privacy by state officers is, therefore, constitutional in origin, we can no longer permit that right to remain an empty promise." Six years later the Supreme Court overruled *Olmstead v. United States* (1928). *Katz v. United States* (1967) determined that police must normally obtain a warrant before wiretapping. Justice Stewart's majority opinion declared that the Fourth and Fourteenth Amendments protect areas and matters where people have "a reasonable expectation of privacy" and that warrantless searches, no matter how reasonable, are presumptively unconstitutional.

Warren Court majorities did not always hand down pro-defendant rulings in search and seizure cases. *Terry v. Ohio* (1968) held that police had a right to stop and frisk a suspect, even when they did not have probable cause to believe the person being frisked had committed a crime. Chief Justice Warren's majority opinion asserted,

> We cannot blind ourselves to the need for law enforcement officers to protect themselves and other prospective victims of violence in situations where they may lack probable cause for an arrest. When an officer is justified in believing that the individual whose suspicious behavior he is investigating at close range is armed and presently dangerous to the officer or to others, it would appear to be clearly unreasonable to deny the officer the power to take necessary measures to determine whether the person is in fact carrying a weapon and to neutralize the threat of physical harm.

Mapp v. Ohio, 367 U.S. 643 (1961)

Several Cleveland police officers forcibly entered the home of Dollree Mapp on May 23, 1957. Despite having no search warrant, the officers searched the house and found obscene material. On the basis of that evidence, Ms. Mapp was tried, convicted, and sentenced to an indeterminate prison term. The Supreme Court of Ohio sustained the conviction on the ground that the evidence was not unconstitutionally obtained and, even if unconstitutionally obtained, was admissible at trial under Ohio constitutional law. Mapp appealed that decision to the Supreme Court of the United States primarily on the ground that her conviction for obscenity violated the First Amendment.

The Supreme Court by a 6-3 vote ruled that Mapp's Fourth and Fourteenth Amendment rights were violated when unconstitutionally obtained evidence was introduced at her trial. Justice Clark's Mapp *opinion overruled* Wolf v. People of the State of Colorado *(1949), which held that evidence seized in violation of the Fourth Amendment could be introduced in a state or federal criminal trial. Clark stated that the "factual considerations" underlying* Wolf *had changed. What were those factual considerations? How had they changed? Did those changes make a constitutional difference? How does Justice Clark justify the exclusionary rule? Does he claim that the exclusionary rule deters unconstitutional searches? Does he insist that the government should not profit by its own wrongdoing? Does either justification explain satisfactorily why courts must exclude reliable evidence of guilt from a criminal trial?*

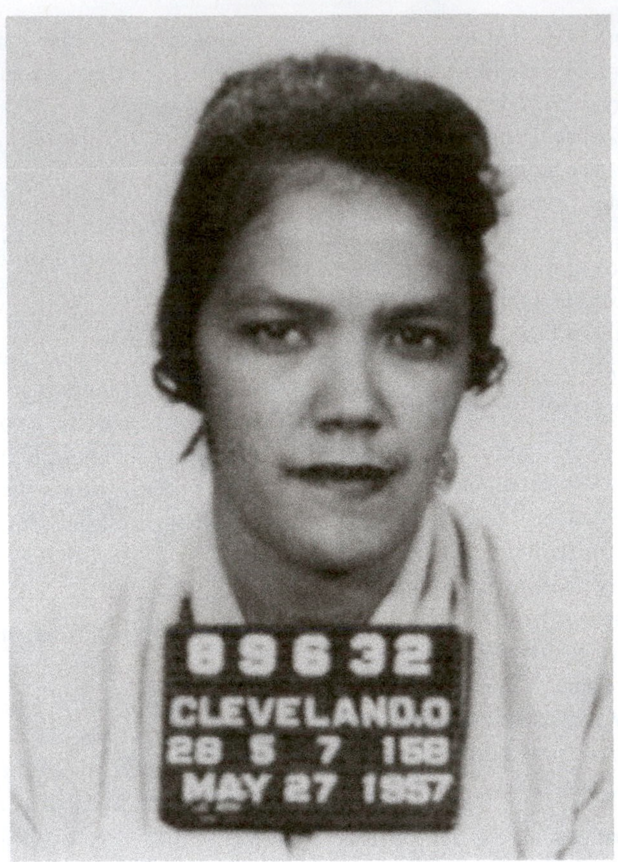

Illustration 8-6 Mugshot of Dollree Mapp
Source: AP Photo

JUSTICE CLARK delivered the opinion of the Court.

. . .

The Court in *Wolf v. Colorado* (1949) first stated that "[t]he contrariety of views of the States" on the adoption of the exclusionary rule of *Weeks v. United States* (1914) was "particularly impressive." . . . While in 1949, prior to the *Wolf* case, almost two-thirds of the States were opposed to the use of the exclusionary rule, now, despite the *Wolf* case, more than half of those since passing upon it, by their own legislative or judicial decision, have wholly or partly adopted or adhered to the *Weeks* rule. . . . Significantly, among those now following the rule is California, which, according to its highest court, was "compelled to reach that conclusion because other remedies have completely failed to secure compliance with the constitutional provisions. . . ." In connection with this California case, we note that the second basis elaborated in *Wolf* in support of its failure to enforce the exclusionary doctrine against the States was that "other means of protection" have been afforded "the right to privacy." The experience of California that such other remedies have been worthless and futile is buttressed by the experience of other States. The obvious futility of relegating the Fourth Amendment to the protection of other remedies has, moreover, been recognized by this Court since *Wolf*. . . .

. . .

It, therefore, plainly appears that the factual considerations supporting the failure of the *Wolf* Court to include the *Weeks* exclusionary rule when it recognized the enforceability of the right to privacy against the States in 1949, while not basically relevant to the constitutional consideration, could not, in any analysis, now be deemed controlling.

. . .

Since the Fourth Amendment's right of privacy has been declared enforceable against the States through the Due Process Clause of the Fourteenth, it is enforceable against them by the same sanction of exclusion as is used against the Federal Government.

Were it otherwise, then just as without the *Weeks* rule the assurance against unreasonable federal searches and seizures would be "a form of words," valueless and undeserving of mention in a perpetual charter of inestimable human liberties, so too, without that rule the freedom from state invasions of privacy would be so ephemeral and so neatly severed from its conceptual nexus with the freedom from all brutish means of coercing evidence as not to merit this Court's high regard as a freedom "implicit in the concept of ordered liberty." At the time that the Court held in *Wolf* that the Amendment was applicable to the States through the Due Process Clause, the cases of this Court, as we have seen, had steadfastly held that as to federal officers the Fourth Amendment included the exclusion of the evidence seized in violation of its provisions. Even *Wolf* "stoutly adhered" to that proposition. . . . Therefore, in extending the substantive protections of due process to all constitutionally unreasonable searches—state or federal—it was logically and constitutionally necessary that the exclusion doctrine—an essential part of the right to privacy—be also insisted upon as an essential ingredient of the right newly recognized by the *Wolf* case. In short, the admission of the new constitutional right by *Wolf* could not consistently tolerate denial of its most important constitutional privilege, namely, the exclusion of the evidence which an accused had been forced to give by reason of the unlawful seizure. To hold otherwise is to grant the right but in reality to withhold its privilege and enjoyment. . . .

. . .

. . . [O]ur holding that the exclusionary rule is an essential part of both the Fourth and Fourteenth Amendments is not only the logical dictate of prior cases, but it also makes very good sense. There is no war between the Constitution and common sense. Presently, a federal prosecutor may make no use of evidence illegally seized, but a State's attorney across the street may, although he supposedly is operating under the enforceable prohibitions of the same Amendment. Thus the State, by admitting evidence unlawfully seized, serves to encourage disobedience to the Federal Constitution which it is bound to uphold.

. . .

There are those who say, as did Justice (then Judge) Cardozo, that under our constitutional exclusionary doctrine "[t]he criminal is to go free because the constable has blundered." *People v. Defore* (1926). . . . In some cases this will undoubtedly be the result. But . . . "there is another consideration—the imperative of judicial integrity." . . . The criminal goes free, if he must, but it is the law that sets him free. Nothing can destroy a government more quickly than its failure to observe its own laws, or worse, its disregard of the charter of its own existence. . . . Nor can it lightly be assumed that, as a practical matter, adoption of the exclusionary rule fetters law enforcement. Only last year this Court expressly considered that contention and found that "pragmatic evidence of a sort" to the contrary was not wanting. *Elkins v. United States* (1960). . . . The Court noted that

> The federal courts themselves have operated under the exclusionary rule of *Weeks* for almost half a century; yet it has not been suggested either that the Federal Bureau of Investigation has thereby been rendered ineffective, or that the administration of criminal justice in the federal courts has thereby been disrupted. . . .

The ignoble shortcut to conviction left open to the State tends to destroy the entire system of constitutional restraints on which the liberties of the people rest. Having once recognized that the right to privacy embodied in the Fourth Amendment is enforceable against the States, and that the right to be secure against rude invasions of privacy by state officers is, therefore, constitutional in origin, we can no longer permit that right to remain an empty promise. Because it is enforceable in the same manner and to like effect as other basic rights secured by the Due Process Clause, we can no longer permit it to be revocable at the whim of any police officer who, in the name of law enforcement itself, chooses to suspend its enjoyment. Our decision, founded on reason and truth, gives to the individual no more than that which the Constitution guarantees him, to the police officer no less than that to which honest law enforcement is entitled, and, to the courts, that judicial integrity so necessary in the true administration of justice.

JUSTICE BLACK, concurring.

. . .

. . . [W]hen the Fourth Amendment's ban against unreasonable searches and seizures is considered together with the Fifth Amendment's ban against compelled self-incrimination, a constitutional basis emerges which not only justifies but actually requires the exclusionary rule.

The close interrelationship between the Fourth and Fifth Amendments, as they apply to this problem, has long been recognized and, indeed, was expressly made the ground for this Court's holding in *Boyd v. United States* (1886). There the Court fully discussed this relationship and declared itself "unable to perceive that the seizure of a man's private books and papers to be used in evidence against him is substantially different from compelling him to be a witness against himself." . . . [I]t seems to me that the *Boyd* doctrine, though perhaps not required by the express language of the Constitution strictly construed, is amply justified from an historical standpoint, soundly based in reason, and entirely consistent with what I regard to be the proper approach to interpretation of our Bill of Rights. . . .

. . .

JUSTICE DOUGLAS, concurring.

. . .

When we allowed States to give constitutional sanction to the "shabby business" of unlawful entry into a home, . . . we did indeed rob the Fourth Amendment of much meaningful force. There are, of course, other theoretical remedies. One is disciplinary action within the hierarchy of the police system, including prosecution of the police officer for a crime. Yet . . . , "Self-scrutiny is a lofty ideal, but its exaltation reaches new heights if we expect a District Attorney to prosecute himself or his associates for well-meaning violations of the search and seizure clause during a raid the District Attorney or his associates have ordered."

The only remaining remedy, if exclusion of the evidence is not required, is an action of trespass by the homeowner against the offending officer. . . . The truth is that trespass actions against officers who make unlawful searches and seizures are mainly illusory remedies.

. . .

Memorandum of JUSTICE STEWART.

[*Justice Stewart insisted that Ms. Mapp's conviction violated the First Amendment and did not discuss the Fourth Amendment issue.*]

JUSTICE HARLAN, whom JUSTICE FRANKFURTER and JUSTICE WHITTAKER join, dissenting.

. . .

I would not impose upon the States this federal exclusionary remedy. The reasons given by the majority for now suddenly turning its back on *Wolf* seem to me notably unconvincing.

. . . [I]t is said that "the factual grounds upon which *Wolf* was based" have since changed, in that more States now follow the *Weeks* exclusionary rule than was so at the time *Wolf* was decided. While that is true, a recent survey indicates that at present one-half of the States still adhere to the common-law non-exclusionary rule, and one, Maryland, retains the rule as to felonies. . . . But in any case surely all this is beside the point, as the majority itself indeed seems to recognize. Our concern here, as it was in *Wolf*, is not with the desirability of that rule but only with the question whether the States are constitutionally free to follow it or not as they may themselves determine, and the relevance of the disparity of views among the States on this point lies simply in the fact that the judgment involved is a debatable one. Moreover, the very fact on which the majority relies, instead of lending support to what is now being done, points away from the need of replacing voluntary state action with federal compulsion.

. . .

An approach which regards the issue as one of achieving procedural symmetry or of serving administrative convenience surely disfigures the boundaries of this Court's functions in relation to the state and federal courts. Our role in promulgating the *Weeks* rule . . . was quite a different one than it is here. There, in implementing the Fourth Amendment, we occupied the position of a tribunal having the ultimate responsibility for developing the standards and procedures of judicial administration within the judicial system over which it presides. Here we review state procedures whose measure is to be taken not against the specific substantive commands of the Fourth Amendment but under the flexible contours of the Due Process Clause. I do not believe that the Fourteenth Amendment empowers this Court to mould state remedies effectuating the right to freedom from "arbitrary intrusion by the police" to suit its own notions of how things should be done. . . .

I regret that I find so unwise in principle and so inexpedient in policy a decision motivated by the high purpose of increasing respect for Constitutional rights. But in the last analysis I think this Court can increase respect for the Constitution only if it rigidly respects the limitations which the Constitution places upon it, and respects as well the principles inherent in its own processes. In the present case I think we exceed both, and that our voice becomes only a voice of power, not of reason.

Katz v. United States, 389 U.S. 347 (1967)

The FBI suspected that Charles Katz was involved in illegal gambling and placed him under surveillance on February 4, 1965. During the next few days, federal agents noticed that Katz always used a public phone on Sunset Boulevard at the same time of day. After learning that those calls were made to a gambler in Massachusetts, FBI agents, acting without a warrant, placed a listening device in the public phone booth. Over the next days, agents heard Katz providing gambling information. Katz was arrested and charged with violating federal laws that prohibited the interstate transmission of bets or wagers. Katz objected to the use of information obtained by the listening device, but that objection was overruled. He was found guilty as charged and ordered to pay a $300 fine. After the Court of Appeals for the Ninth Circuit affirmed the district court decision, Katz appealed to the Supreme Court of the United States.

The Supreme Court by a 7-1 vote declared that Katz was unconstitutionally convicted, overruling Olmstead v. United States *(1928). Justice Stewart's majority opinion maintained that the Fourth Amendment protects areas and matters where people have "a reasonable expectation of privacy" and that warrantless searches, no matter how reasonable, are presumptively unconstitutional. Justice Harlan joined the majority in imposing constitutional limitations on the state, while Justice Black dissented. What constitutional reasons does each give for his position? Given that in most areas of constitutional law Harlan was far more conservative than Black, why did their positions reverse in this case? Notice that the justices do not dispute that the FBI had good reason to think that Katz was committing a crime. Why do they nevertheless insist that the agents should have obtained a warrant? Is this a correct interpretation of the Fourth Amendment?*

JUSTICE STEWART delivered the opinion of the Court.

. . .

. . . [T]he Fourth Amendment protects people, not places. What a person knowingly exposes to the public, even in his own home or office, is not a subject of Fourth Amendment protection. . . . But what he seeks to preserve as private, even in an area accessible to the public, may be constitutionally protected. . . .

The Government stresses the fact that the telephone booth from which the petitioner made his calls was constructed partly of glass, so that he was as visible after he entered it as he would have been if he had remained outside. But what he sought to exclude when he entered the booth was not the intruding eye—it was the uninvited ear. He did not shed his right to do so simply because he made his calls from a place where he might be seen. No less than an individual in a business office, in a friend's apartment, or in a taxicab, a person in a telephone booth may rely upon the protection of the Fourth Amendment. One who occupies it, shuts the door behind him, and pays the toll that permits him to place a call is surely entitled to assume that the words he utters into the mouthpiece will not be broadcast to the world. To read the Constitution more narrowly is to ignore the vital role that the public telephone has come to play in private communication.

The Government contends, however, that the activities of its agents in this case should not be tested by Fourth Amendment requirements, for the surveillance technique they employed involved no physical penetration of the telephone booth from which the petitioner placed his calls. It is true that the absence of such penetration was at one time thought to foreclose further Fourth Amendment inquiry, *Olmstead v. United States* (1928) . . . for that Amendment was thought to limit only searches and seizures of tangible property. But "[t]he premise that property interests control the right of the Government to search and seize has been discredited." . . . [O]nce it is recognized that the Fourth Amendment protects people—and not simply "areas"—against unreasonable searches and seizures, it becomes clear that the reach of that Amendment cannot turn upon the presence or absence of a physical intrusion into any given enclosure.

. . . The Government's activities in electronically listening to and recording the petitioner's words violated the privacy upon which he justifiably relied while using the telephone booth, and thus constituted a "search and seizure" within the meaning of the Fourth Amendment. The fact that the electronic device employed to achieve that end did not happen to penetrate the wall of the booth can have no constitutional significance.

. . .

. . . [T]his Court has never sustained a search upon the sole ground that officers reasonably expected to find evidence of a particular crime and voluntarily confined their activities to the least intrusive means consistent with that end. Searches conducted without warrants have been held unlawful "notwithstanding facts unquestionably showing probable cause," . . . for the Constitution requires "that the deliberate, impartial judgment of a judicial officer . . . be interposed between the citizen and the police. . . ." . . . [S]earches conducted outside the judicial process, without prior approval by judge or magistrate, are *per se* unreasonable under the Fourth Amendment—subject only to a few specifically established and well delineated exceptions.

It is difficult to imagine how any of those exceptions could ever apply to the sort of search and seizure involved in this case. Even electronic surveillance substantially contemporaneous with an individual's arrest could hardly be deemed an "incident" of that arrest.

Nor could the use of electronic surveillance without prior authorization be justified on grounds of "hot pursuit." And, of course, the very nature of electronic surveillance precludes its use pursuant to the suspect's consent.

. . .

Wherever a man may be, he is entitled to know that he will remain free from unreasonable searches and seizures. The government agents here ignored "the procedure of antecedent justification . . . that is central to the Fourth Amendment," a procedure that we hold to be a constitutional precondition of the kind of electronic surveillance involved in this case. Because the surveillance here failed to meet that condition, and because it led to the petitioner's conviction, the judgment must be reversed.

JUSTICE DOUGLAS, with whom JUSTICE BRENNAN joins, concurring.

. . .

Neither the President nor the Attorney General is a magistrate. In matters where they believe national security may be involved, they are not detached, disinterested, and neutral as a court or magistrate must be. Under the separation of powers created by the Constitution, the Executive Branch is not supposed to be neutral and disinterested. Rather it should vigorously investigate and prevent breaches of national security and prosecute those who violate the pertinent federal laws. The President and Attorney General are properly interested parties, cast in the role of adversary, in national security cases. They may even be the intended victims of subversive action. Since spies and saboteurs are as entitled to the protection of the Fourth Amendment as suspected gamblers like petitioner, I cannot agree that, where spies and saboteurs are involved adequate protection of Fourth Amendment rights is assured when the President and Attorney General assume both the position of "adversary and prosecutor" and disinterested, neutral magistrate.

. . .

JUSTICE HARLAN, concurring.

I join the opinion of the Court, which I read to hold only (a) that an enclosed telephone booth is an area where, like a home, . . . and unlike a field, . . . a person has a constitutionally protected reasonable expectation of privacy; (b) that electronic, as well as physical, intrusion into a place that is in this sense private may constitute a violation of the Fourth Amendment, and (c) that the invasion of a constitutionally protected area by federal authorities is, as the Court has long held, presumptively unreasonable in the absence of a search warrant.

As the Court's opinion states, "the Fourth Amendment protects people, not places." The question, however, is what protection it affords to those people. Generally, as here, the answer to that question requires reference to a "place." My understanding of the rule that has emerged from prior decisions is that there is a twofold requirement, first that a person have exhibited an actual (subjective) expectation of privacy and, second, that the expectation be one that society is prepared to recognize as "reasonable." Thus, a man's home is, for most purposes, a place where he expects privacy, but objects, activities, or statements that he exposes to the "plain view" of outsiders are not "protected," because no intention to keep them to himself has been exhibited. On the other hand, conversations in the open would not be protected against being overheard, for the expectation of privacy under the circumstances would be unreasonable. . . .

. . .

JUSTICE WHITE, concurring.

. . .

In joining the Court's opinion, I note the Court's acknowledgment that there are circumstances in which it is reasonable to search without a warrant. . . . Wiretapping to protect the security of the Nation has been authorized by successive Presidents. . . . We should not require the warrant procedure and the magistrate's judgment if the President of the United States or his chief legal officer, the Attorney General, has considered the requirements of national security and authorized electronic surveillance as reasonable.

JUSTICE BLACK, dissenting.

. . .

While I realize that an argument based on the meaning of words lacks the scope, and no doubt the appeal, of broad policy discussions and philosophical discourses on such nebulous subjects as privacy, for me, the language of the Amendment is the crucial place to look in construing a written document such as our Constitution. . . . The first clause [of the Fourth Amendment] protects "persons, houses, papers, and effects against unreasonable searches and seizures. . . ." These words connote the idea of tangible things with size, form, and weight, things capable of being searched, seized, or both. The second clause of the Amendment still further establishes its Framers' purpose to limit its protection to tangible things by providing that no warrants shall issue but those "particularly describing the place to be searched, and the persons or things to be seized." A conversation overheard by eavesdropping, whether by plain snooping or wiretapping, is not tangible and, under the normally accepted meanings of the words, can neither be searched nor seized. In addition the language of the second clause indicates that the Amendment refers not only to something tangible so it can be seized, but to something already in existence, so it can be described. Yet the Court's interpretation would have the Amendment apply to overhearing future conversations, which, by their very nature, are nonexistent until they take place. How can one "describe" a future conversation, and, if one cannot, how can a magistrate issue a warrant to eavesdrop one in the future? It is argued that information showing what is expected to be said is sufficient to limit the boundaries of what later can be admitted into evidence; but does such general information really meet the specific language of the Amendment, which says "particularly describing"? Rather than using language in a completely artificial way, I must conclude that the Fourth Amendment simply does not apply to eavesdropping.

Tapping telephone wires, of course, was an unknown possibility at the time the Fourth Amendment was adopted. But eavesdropping (and wiretapping is nothing more than eavesdropping by telephone) was. . . . There can be no doubt that the Framers were aware of this practice, and, if they had desired to outlaw or restrict the use of evidence obtained by eavesdropping, I believe that they would have used the appropriate language to do so in the Fourth Amendment. They certainly would not have left such a task to the ingenuity of language-stretching judges. . . .

I do not deny that common sense requires, and that this Court often has said, that the Bill of Rights' safeguards should be given a liberal construction. This principle, however, does not justify construing the search and seizure amendment as applying to eavesdropping or the "seizure" of conversations. The Fourth Amendment was aimed directly at the abhorred practice of breaking in, ransacking and searching homes and other buildings and seizing people's personal belongings without warrants issued by magistrates. . . .

. . .

The Fourth Amendment protects privacy only to the extent that it prohibits unreasonable searches and seizures of "persons, houses, papers, and effects." No general right is created by the Amendment so as to give this Court the unlimited power to hold unconstitutional everything which affects privacy. Certainly the Framers, well acquainted as they were with the excesses of governmental power, did not intend to grant this Court such omnipotent lawmaking authority as that. The history of governments proves that it is dangerous to freedom to repose such powers in courts.

C. Interrogations

Warren Court decisions on the right against self-incrimination permanently altered the constitutional politics of criminal justice. Before 1960 judicial decisions expanding the rights of persons suspected of crimes usually reversed convictions of persons of color in the South who were victims of third-degree police practices. *Brown v. Mississippi* (1936) was a typical example. In that case the Supreme Court unanimously overturned a death sentence in which the prosecutor relied on confessions obtained only after the defendant was repeatedly beaten. Chief Justice Hughes's opinion asserted, "It would be difficult to conceive of methods more revolting to the sense of justice than those taken to procure the confessions of these petitioners, and the use of the confessions thus obtained as the basis for conviction and sentence was a clear denial of due process." Such decisions caused few political ripples outside of the South. Constitutional politics changed dramatically when the Supreme Court in a series of cases culminating in *Miranda v. Arizona* (1966) aggressively moved against police efforts to obtain confessions. By the end of the New Deal/Great Society Era, Richard Nixon, George Wallace, and others were vigorously conducting national political campaigns against *Miranda* and other decisions that they believed showed more sympathy for criminals than their victims.

Three decisions handed down between 1964 and 1966 moved American constitutional law from concerns with whether a confession in a particular case was reliable to a concern with taking the prophylactic steps necessary to ensure that defendants were aware of their right to not confess. In *Massiah v. United States* (1964) the justices ruled that federal agents could not interrogate a criminal suspect in the absence of counsel after the suspect had been indicted. *Esobedo v. State of Illinois* (1964) held that criminal suspects could not be interrogated by police after they had requested to speak with an attorney. Justice Goldberg's majority opinion declared,

> Where, as here, the investigation is no longer a general inquiry into an unsolved crime but has begun to focus on a particular suspect, the suspect has been taken into police custody, the police carry out a process of interrogations that lends itself to eliciting incriminating statements, the suspect has requested and been denied an opportunity to consult with his lawyer, and the police have not effectively warned him of his absolute constitutional right to remain silent, the accused has been denied "The Assistance of Counsel" in violation of the Sixth Amendment to the Constitution as "made obligatory upon the States by the Fourteenth Amendment," . . . and that no statement elicited by the police during the interrogation may be used against him at a criminal trial.

Miranda required that police provide criminal suspects in custody with four pieces of information before beginning an interrogation.

- They had the right to remain silent.
- If they did not remain silent, the information they provided could be used in a court of law.
- They had a right to an attorney.
- If they could not afford an attorney, one would be provided for them.

Should an accused wish to exercise those rights, interrogation had to stop.

Massiah, Esobedo, and *Miranda* focused constitutional attention on whether the criminal suspect was aware of his constitutional right to counsel and had a meaningful opportunity to exercise that right, not on whether the confession was voluntary. The justices suggested two reasons for this new conception of the constitutional right against self-incrimination. First, the justices often had great difficulty determining whether a confession obtained in a secret interrogation was coerced. Eliminating secret interrogations where counsel was not present ensured that confessions obtained were voluntary. Second, the Warren Court majority opposed interrogations as a means for solving crimes. "We have learned the lesson of history," Justice Goldberg wrote in *Esobedo*, "that a system of criminal law enforcement which comes to depend on the 'confession' will, in the long run, be less reliable and more subject to abuses than a system which depends on extrinsic evidence independently secured through skillful investigation."

Miranda v. Arizona, 384 U.S. 436 (1966)

On March 13, 1963, Ernesto Miranda was arrested for kidnapping and raping an eighteen-year-old woman. At the time of his arrest Miranda was a twenty-three-year-old junior high school dropout. At the station house Miranda was questioned for two hours until he confessed. All parties agreed that he had not been informed of his right to have a lawyer present, but there was no evidence that Miranda was beaten or threatened in any way during the interrogation. That confession was admitted into evidence at a jury trial over defense counsel's objections. Miranda was found guilty and sentenced to twenty to thirty years in prison. The Supreme Court of Arizona affirmed the conviction. Miranda appealed to the Supreme Court of the United States.

The Supreme Court by a 5-4 vote declared that Miranda's confession was unconstitutionally obtained. Chief Justice Warren's majority opinion held that confessions could not normally be introduced at criminal trials unless suspects had been advised that they had a right to remain silent, that any confession could be used against them, that they had a right to an attorney, and that, if indigent, the court would appoint an attorney to represent them. Should the Supreme Court have made prophylactic rules aimed at reducing the number of coerced confessions or simply determined whether a confession in a particular case was voluntary? If constitutionality had to be determined on a case-by-case basis then would the Supreme Court have to review the specific circumstances of every challenged confession? Assuming that the Court was justified in making prophylactic rules, does Miranda *establish the correct rules? Chief Justice Warren's opinion maintains that pursuit of confessions distracts police from actually investigating the crime. Does this comment express the American commitment to an adversarial (as opposed to an inquisitorial) criminal process, or does the* Miranda *opinion seriously underestimate the role of interrogations and confessions?*

Whether and how Miranda *has influenced police practices remains controversial. One dispute concerns the Warren Court's degree of interference with law enforcement. Paul Cassell in 1996 claimed to have demonstrated statistically that "*Miranda *has significantly harmed law enforcement efforts in this country." He estimated that the* Miranda *decision has prevented a confession in one out of every six criminal cases, freeing about 28,000 "serious violent offenders" and 79,000 "property offenders."*[93] *Other scholars, most notably Stephen Schulhofer, question Cassell's data. Schulhofer insists that the statistical impact of* Miranda *is closer to zero.*[94]*A related controversy is over the extent to which* Miranda *warnings actually reduce confessions. Summarizing many studies on the subject, Gerald Rosenberg concludes that "warnings are given because . . . they don't affect police work very much." He notes that "while the police may give the warnings, they do so in a way calculated to diminish or disparage their impact," and that most criminal suspects, even after being warned, do "not appreciate the reasons for remaining silent."*[95]

Miranda *had a clearer influence on constitutional politics. For much of the New Deal/Great Society Era, constitutional criminal procedure was often part of a civil rights or anti-poverty agenda.* Miranda *was decided at a time when crime rates were increasing substantially and riots were taking place in many inner cities, including south-central Los Angeles (Watts), Newark, Cleveland, Chicago, Atlanta, and Detroit. President Johnson responded by creating a commission to study the underlying causes. The most famous passage of the resultant Kerner Commission report warned that the United States was "moving toward two societies, one black, one white—separate and unequal."*[96] *Rather than focus on underlying causes, many Americans, with encouragement from more conservative political entrepreneurs, made connections between these events and liberal Supreme Court decisions on constitutional criminal procedure. A strong backlash developed against justices who were perceived as caring more about the rights of criminals than their victims. Richard Nixon rode this backlash to power in 1968.*

CHIEF JUSTICE WARREN delivered the opinion of the Court.

. . .

. . . [T]he modern practice of in-custody interrogation is psychologically rather than physically oriented. As we have stated before, "Since *Chambers v. Florida* (1940) . . . , this Court has recognized that coercion can be mental as well as physical, and that the blood of the accused is not the only hallmark of an unconstitutional inquisition." . . . Interrogation still takes place in privacy. Privacy results in secrecy and this in turn results in a gap in our knowledge as to what in fact goes on in the interrogation rooms.

. . .

. . . [T]he setting prescribed by [police] manuals and observed in practice [is] clear. In essence, it is this: To be alone with the subject is essential to prevent distraction and to deprive him of any outside support. The aura of confidence in his guilt undermines his will to resist. He merely confirms the preconceived story the police seek to have him describe. Patience and persistence, at times relentless questioning, are employed. To obtain a confession, the interrogator must "patiently maneuver himself or his quarry into a position from which the desired objective may be attained." When normal procedures fail to produce the needed result, the police may resort to deceptive stratagems such as giving false legal advice. It is important to keep the subject off balance, for example, by trading on his insecurity about himself or his surroundings. The police then persuade, trick, or cajole him out of exercising his constitutional rights.

93. Paul G. Cassell, "Miranda's Social Costs: An Empirical Reassessment," *Northwestern Law Review* 90 (1996):387.

94. Stephen J. Schulhofer, "Miranda's Practical Effect: Substantial Benefits and Vanishingly Small Social Costs," *Northwestern Law Review* 90 (1996):500.

95. Gerald N. Rosenberg, *The Hollow Hope: Can Courts Bring About Social Change?* (Chicago: University of Chicago Press, 1991), 327–29.

96. Kerner Commission, *Report of the National Advisory Commission on Civil Disorders* (Washington, D.C.: U.S. Government Printing Office, 1968).

. . .

It is obvious that such an interrogation environment is created for no purpose other than to subjugate the individual to the will of his examiner. This atmosphere carries its own badge of intimidation. To be sure, this is not physical intimidation, but it is equally destructive of human dignity. The current practice of incommunicado interrogation is at odds with one of our Nation's most cherished principles—that the individual may not be compelled to incriminate himself. Unless adequate protective devices are employed to dispel the compulsion inherent in custodial surroundings, no statement obtained from the defendant can truly be the product of his free choice.

. . .

. . . [T]he constitutional foundation underlying the privilege is the respect a government—state or federal—must accord to the dignity and integrity of its citizens. To maintain a "fair state-individual balance," to require the government "to shoulder the entire load," . . . to respect the inviolability of the human personality, our accusatory system of criminal justice demands that the government seeking to punish an individual produce the evidence against him by its own independent labors, rather than by the cruel, simple expedient of compelling it from his own mouth. . . . In sum, the privilege is fulfilled only when the person is guaranteed the right "to remain silent unless he chooses to speak in the unfettered exercise of his own will." . . .

. . .

It is impossible for us to foresee the potential alternatives for protecting the privilege which might be devised by Congress or the States in the exercise of their creative rule-making capacities. Therefore we cannot say that the Constitution necessarily requires adherence to any particular solution for the inherent compulsions of the interrogation process as it is presently conducted. . . . We encourage Congress and the States to continue their laudable search for increasingly effective ways of protecting the rights of the individual while promoting efficient enforcement of our criminal laws. However, unless we are shown other procedures which are at least as effective in apprising accused persons of their right of silence and in assuring a continuous opportunity to exercise it, the following safeguards must be observed.

At the outset, if a person in custody is to be subjected to interrogation, he must first be informed in clear and unequivocal terms that he has the right to remain silent. For those unaware of the privilege, the warning is needed simply to make them aware of it—the threshold requirement for an intelligent decision as to its exercise. More important, such a warning is an absolute prerequisite in overcoming the inherent pressures of the interrogation atmosphere. It is not just the subnormal or woefully ignorant who succumb to an interrogator's imprecations, whether implied or expressly stated, that the interrogation will continue until a confession is obtained or that silence in the face of accusation is itself damning and will bode ill when presented to a jury. Further, the warning will show the individual that his interrogators are prepared to recognize his privilege should he choose to exercise it.

. . .

The warning of the right to remain silent must be accompanied by the explanation that anything said can and will be used against the individual in court. This warning is needed in order to make him aware not only of the privilege, but also of the consequences of forgoing it. It is only through an awareness of these consequences that there can be any assurance of real understanding and intelligent exercise of the privilege. Moreover, this warning may serve to make the individual more acutely aware that he is faced with a phase of the adversary system—that he is not in the presence of persons acting solely in his interest.

The circumstances surrounding in-custody interrogation can operate very quickly to overbear the will of one merely made aware of his privilege by his interrogators. Therefore, the right to have counsel present at the interrogation is indispensable to the protection of the Fifth Amendment privilege under the system we delineate today. Our aim is to assure that the individual's right to choose between silence and speech remains unfettered throughout the interrogation process. . . . Thus, the need for counsel to protect the Fifth Amendment privilege comprehends not merely a right to consult with counsel prior to questioning, but also to have counsel present during any questioning if the defendant so desires.

. . .

. . . No effective waiver of the right to counsel during interrogation can be recognized unless specifically made after the warnings we here delineate have been given. . . .

. . .

Once warnings have been given, the subsequent procedure is clear. If the individual indicates in any manner, at any time prior to or during questioning, that he wishes to remain silent, the interrogation must cease. . . . If the individual states that he wants an attorney, the interrogation must cease until an attorney is present. . . .

. . .

In announcing these principles, we are not unmindful of the burdens which law enforcement officials must bear, often under trying circumstances. We also fully recognize the obligation of all citizens to aid in enforcing the criminal laws. This Court, while protecting individual rights, has always given ample latitude to law enforcement agencies in the legitimate exercise of their duties. The limits we have placed on the interrogation process should not constitute an undue interference with a proper system of law enforcement. As we have noted, our decision does not in any way preclude police from carrying out their traditional investigatory functions. Although confessions may play an important role in some convictions, the cases before us present graphic examples of the overstatement of the "need" for confessions. In each case authorities conducted interrogations ranging up to five days in duration despite the presence, through standard investigating practices, of considerable evidence against each defendant. . . .

. . .

Over the years the Federal Bureau of Investigation has compiled an exemplary record of effective law enforcement while advising any suspect or arrested person, at the outset of an interview, that he is not required to make a statement, that any statement may be used against him in court, that the individual may obtain the services of an attorney of his own choice and, more recently, that he has a right to free counsel if he is unable to pay.

. . .

The practice of the FBI can readily be emulated by state and local enforcement agencies. The argument that the FBI deals with different crimes than are dealt with by state authorities does not mitigate the significance of the FBI experience.

. . .

JUSTICE CLARK, dissenting

. . .

Custodial interrogation has long been recognized as "undoubtedly an essential tool in effective law enforcement." . . . Recognition of this fact should put us on guard against the promulgation of doctrinaire rules.

Under the "totality of circumstances" rule . . . , I would consider in each case whether the police officer prior to custodial interrogation added the warning that the suspect might have counsel present at the interrogation and, further, that a court would appoint one at his request if he was too poor to employ counsel. In the absence of warnings, the burden would be on the State to prove that counsel was knowingly and intelligently waived or that in the totality of the circumstances, including the failure to give the necessary warnings, the confession was clearly voluntary.

. . .

JUSTICE HARLAN, whom JUSTICE STEWART and JUSTICE WHITE join, dissenting.

. . .

. . . The Fifth Amendment has never been thought to forbid all pressure to incriminate one's self in the situations covered by it. . . .

. . .

Without at all subscribing to the generally black picture of police conduct painted by the Court, I think it must be frankly recognized at the outset that police questioning allowable under due process precedents may inherently entail some pressure on the suspect and may seek advantage in his ignorance or weaknesses. The atmosphere and questioning techniques, proper and fair though they be, can in themselves exert a tug on the suspect to confess, and in this light "[t]o speak of any confessions of crime made after arrest as being 'voluntary' or 'uncoerced' is somewhat inaccurate, although traditional. A confession is wholly and incontestably voluntary only if a guilty person gives himself up to the law and becomes his own accuser." . . . Until today, the role of the Constitution has been only to sift out undue pressure, not to assure spontaneous confessions.

What the Court largely ignores is that its rules impair, if they will not eventually serve wholly to frustrate, an instrument of law enforcement that has long and quite reasonably been thought worth the price paid for it. There can be little doubt that the Court's new code would markedly decrease the number of confessions. . . .

. . .

JUSTICE WHITE, with whom JUSTICE HARLAN and JUSTICE STEWART join, dissenting.

The proposition that the privilege against self-incrimination forbids in-custody interrogation without the warnings specified in the majority opinion and without a clear waiver of counsel has no significant support in the history of the privilege or in the language of the Fifth Amendment. As for the English authorities and the common-law history, the privilege, firmly established in the second half of the seventeenth century, was never applied except to prohibit compelled judicial interrogations. The rule excluding coerced confessions matured about one hundred years later, "[b]ut there is nothing in the reports to suggest that the theory has its roots in the privilege against self-incrimination. And so far as the cases reveal, the privilege, as such, seems to have been given effect only in judicial proceedings, including the preliminary examinations by authorized magistrates." . . .

. . .

The obvious underpinning of the Court's decision is a deep-seated distrust of all confessions. As the Court declares that the accused may not be interrogated without counsel present, absent a waiver of the right to counsel, and as the Court all but admonishes the lawyer to advise the accused to remain silent, the result adds up to a judicial judgment that evidence from the accused should not be used against him in any way, whether compelled or not. . . . I see nothing wrong or immoral, and certainly nothing unconstitutional, in the police's asking a suspect whom they have reasonable cause to arrest whether or not he killed his wife or in confronting him with the evidence on which the arrest was based, at least where he has been plainly advised that he may remain completely silent. . . . Until today, "the admissions or confessions of the prisoner, when voluntarily and freely made, have always ranked high in the scale of incriminating evidence." . . . Particularly when corroborated, as where the police have confirmed the accused's disclosure of the hiding place of implements or fruits of the crime, such confessions have the highest reliability and significantly contribute to the certitude with which we may believe the accused is guilty. Moreover, it is by no means certain that the process of confessing is injurious to the accused. To the contrary it may provide psychological relief and enhance the prospects for rehabilitation.

This is not to say that the value of respect for the inviolability of the accused's individual personality should be accorded no weight or that all confessions should be indiscriminately admitted. This Court has long read the Constitution to proscribe compelled confessions, a salutary rule from which there should be no retreat. But I see no sound basis, factual or otherwise, and the Court gives none, for concluding that the present rule against the receipt of coerced confessions is inadequate for the task of sorting out inadmissible evidence and must be replaced by the per se rule which is now imposed. . . .

. . .

The rule announced today will measurably weaken the ability of the criminal law to perform these tasks. It is a deliberate calculus to prevent interrogations, to reduce the incidence of confessions and pleas of guilty and to increase the number of trials. . . . There is, in my view, every reason to believe that a good many criminal defendants who otherwise would have been convicted on what this Court has previously thought to be the most satisfactory kind of evidence will now under this new version of the Fifth Amendment, either not be tried at all or will be acquitted if the State's evidence, minus the confession, is put to the test of litigation. . . .

D. Juries and Lawyers

Twentieth-century liberals regarded the right to an attorney, rather than the right to trial by jury, as the most important constitutional protection for persons accused of crime. *Gideon v. Wainwright* (1963), the decision that held that persons accused of felonies have a right to a state-appointed attorney, is the rare judicial decision favoring the rights of criminal defendants that is presently celebrated by most Americans. By comparison, federal courts during the mid-twentieth century did not hand down any major decisions on the right to a jury that are either celebrated or vilified. The justices did hand down numerous decisions condemning racial discrimination in the jury selection process. In *Norris v. Alabama* (1935) Chief Justice Hughes's unanimous opinion asserted,

> We think that the evidence that for a generation or longer no negro had been called for service on any jury in Jackson county, that there were negroes qualified for jury service, that according to the practice of the jury commission their names would normally appear on the preliminary list of male citizens of the requisite age but that no names of negroes were placed on the jury roll, and the testimony with respect to the lack of appropriate consideration of the qualifications of negroes, established the discrimination which the Constitution forbids.

Nevertheless, liberal justices moved less aggressively against racial discrimination in jury selection than they did against racial discrimination in other facets of the criminal process. In *Swain v. Alabama* (1965) a divided Warren Court ruled that an African-American convicted of raping a white woman was not entitled to a new trial merely because the prosecutor had peremptorily challenged every prospective African-American juror. Judge White's opinion stated,

> We cannot hold that the Constitution requires an examination of the prosecutor's reasons for the exercise of his challenges in any given case. The presumption in any particular case must be that the prosecutor is using the State's challenges to obtain a fair and impartial jury to try the case before the court. The presumption is not overcome, and the prosecutor therefore subjected to examination, by allegations that, in the case at hand, all Negroes were removed from the jury, or that they were removed because they were Negroes.

Gideon v. Wainwright, 372 U.S. 335 (1963)

Clarence Gideon was arrested and charged with the burglary of a pool hall in Panama City, Florida. Gideon could not afford a lawyer. The trial judge rejected his request that a lawyer be appointed for him on the ground that defense counsel was constitutionally required only in capital cases. After being convicted and sentenced to five years in prison, Gideon brought a habeas corpus proceeding against the director of the Florida Division of Corrections, Louis Wainwright. Both the trial court and the Supreme Court of Florida rejected this contention on the basis of the Supreme Court's decision in Betts v. Brady *(1942). Justice Roberts's majority opinion in that case held that the constitutional right to counsel depended on the particular circumstances before the court. He wrote,*

> *The Fourteenth Amendment prohibits the conviction and incarceration of one whose trial is offensive to the common and fundamental ideas of fairness and right, and while want of counsel in a particular case may result in a conviction lacking in such fundamental fairness, we cannot say that the amendment embodies an inexorable command that no trial for any offense, or in any court, can be fairly conducted and justice accorded a defendant who is not represented by counsel.*

Gideon appealed the Florida decisions to the Supreme Court of the United States.

The Supreme Court unanimously overruled Betts v. Brady. *Justice Black's opinion for the Court declared that the right to counsel was fundamental and could not ordinarily be denied. On what basis does Justice Black reach that conclusion? Does* Gideon *give persons accused of any crime a right to government-appointed counsel? After* Gideon, *do you have a right to counsel when contesting a parking ticket? Does* Gideon *indicate when counsel must be appointed? Does* Gideon *require that counsel be appointed immediately after arrest, or is counsel required only when the actual trial begins?* Gideon *was decided at a time when Democrats were announcing a war on poverty. Might the justices have seen the right to a government-appointed counsel as the judicial contribution to that national effort?*

United States v. Wade *(1967) cleared up some of those issues. Justice Brennan's majority opinion asserted, "The Sixth Amendment guarantee . . . appl[ies] to 'critical' stages of the proceedings." These critical stages included arraignments, interrogations with the defendant after indictment, and line-ups. With respect to the latter,* Wade *asserted,*

> *Since it appears that there is grave potential for prejudice, intentional or not, in the pretrial lineup . . . and since presence of counsel itself can often avert prejudice and assure a meaningful confrontation at trial, there can be little doubt that for Wade the postindictment lineup was a critical stage of the prosecution at which he was "as much entitled to such aid (of counsel) . . . as at the trial itself."*

JUSTICE BLACK delivered the opinion of the Court.

. . . [R]eason and reflection require us to recognize that in our adversary system of criminal justice, any person haled into court, who is too poor to hire a lawyer, cannot be assured a fair trial unless counsel is provided for him. This seems to us to be an obvious truth. Governments, both state and federal, quite properly spend vast sums of money to establish machinery to try defendants accused of crime. Lawyers to prosecute are everywhere deemed essential to protect the public's interest in an orderly society. Similarly, there are few defendants charged with crime, few indeed, who fail to hire the best lawyers they can get to prepare and present their defenses. That government hires lawyers to prosecute and defendants who have the money hire lawyers to defend are the strongest indications of the wide-spread belief that lawyers in criminal courts are necessities, not luxuries. The right of one charged with crime to counsel may not be deemed fundamental and essential to fair trials in some countries, but it is in ours. From the very beginning, our state and national constitutions and laws have laid great emphasis on procedural and substantive safeguards designed to assure fair trials before impartial tribunals in which every defendant stands equal before the law. This noble ideal cannot be realized if the poor man charged with crime has to face his accusers without a lawyer to assist him. . . .

. . . Florida, supported by two other States, has asked that *Betts v. Brady* (1942) be left intact. Twenty-two States, as friends of the Court, argue that *Betts* was "an anachronism when handed down" and that it should now be overruled. We agree.

. . .

JUSTICE DOUGLAS. . . .

JUSTICE CLARK, concurring in the result. . . .

JUSTICE HARLAN, concurring.

. . .

I cannot subscribe to the view that *Betts v. Brady* represented "an abrupt break with its own well-considered precedents." . . . In 1932, in *Powell v. Alabama*, a capital case, this Court declared that under the particular facts there presented—"the ignorance and illiteracy of the defendants, their youth, the circumstances of public hostility . . . and above all that they stood in deadly peril of their lives" . . . —the state court had a duty to assign counsel for the trial as a necessary requisite of due process of law. . . .

Thus when this Court, a decade later, decided *Betts v. Brady*, it did no more than to admit of the possible existence of special circumstances in noncapital as well as capital trials, while at the same time insisting that such circumstances be shown in order to establish a denial of due process. . . .

The principles declared in *Powell* and in *Betts*, however, have had a troubled journey throughout the years that have followed first the one case and then the other. . . .

In noncapital cases, the "special circumstances" rule has continued to exist in form while its substance has been substantially and steadily eroded. In the first decade after *Betts*, there were cases in which the Court found special circumstances to be lacking, but usually by a sharply divided vote. However, no such decision has been cited to us, and I have found none, after . . . 1950. At the same time, there have been not a few cases in which special circumstances were found in little or nothing more than the "complexity" of the legal questions presented, although those questions were often of only routine difficulty. The Court has come to recognize, in other words, that the mere existence of a serious criminal charge constituted in itself special circumstances requiring the services of counsel at trial. In truth the *Betts v. Brady* rule is no longer a reality. . . .

E. Punishments

During the New Deal/Great Society Era, debates over capital punishment took center stage. Constitutional liberals in the 1930s and 1940s expressed concern that persons of color were being sentenced to death after unfair trials. Lawyers from the NAACP Legal Defense Fund sought to overturn death sentences when the defendant had not had effective assistance of counsel or was indicted by a racially biased grand jury.

The constitutional controversies over capital punishment during the 1930s, 1940s, and 1950s were over whether the imposition of capital punishment in particular cases violated constitutional norms. Consider *State of Louisiana ex rel. Francis v. Resweber* (1947). Louisiana's first effort to electrocute Willie Francis failed when a mechanical error resulted in an electric shock insufficient for death. A new death warrant was issued authorizing electrocution a week later. Five justices on the Supreme Court insisted that no constitutional problems existed with the second attempt at execution. Justice Stanley Reed's majority opinion declared:

> The cruelty against which the Constitution protects a convicted man is cruelty inherent in the method of punishment, not the necessary suffering involved in any method employed to extinguish life humanely. The fact that an unforeseeable accident prevented the prompt consummation of the sentence cannot, it seems to us, add an element of cruelty to a subsequent execution.

Four justices dissented. Noting that Francis had suffered substantial pain during the first attempt at electrocution, Justice Harold Burton wrote, "The all-important consideration is that the execution shall be so instantaneous and substantially painless that the punishment shall be reduced, as nearly as possible, to no more than that of death itself." When asserting that any further attempt to execute Willie Francis would be cruel and unusual, Burton and the other justices in the dissent assumed that no constitutional problems existed with the first attempt.

Rudolph v. Alabama (1963) dramatically changed the constitutional politics of capital punishment. Dissenting from the Supreme Court's decision not to hear that case, Justices Goldberg, Douglas, and Brennan suggested that lawyers might make Eighth Amendment attacks on the death penalty per se, rather than point to constitutional violations peculiar to the particular defendant before the Court. "I would grant certiorari in the case," Goldberg wrote, "to consider whether the Eighth and Fourteen Amendments to the United States Constitution permit the imposition of the death penalty on a convicted rapist who has neither taken nor endangered human life." Such groups as the NAACP Legal Defense Fund immediately took up and expanded this challenge. Rather than simply attack the constitutionality of executing persons for rape, civil rights lawyers began claiming that capital punishment was an unconstitutional sanction for all crimes.

The legal campaign against capital punishment bore fruit in *Witherspoon v. Illinois* (1968). The Supreme Court in that case prohibited prosecutors from challenging for cause jurors who were morally opposed to capital punishment or had moral qualms about capital punishment. Justice Stewart's majority opinion suggested that proper application of constitutional norms required death cases to be argued before juries extremely unlikely to impose capital punishment.

> A man who opposes the death penalty, no less than one who favors it, can make the discretionary judgment entrusted to him by the State and can thus obey the oath he takes as a juror. But a jury from which all such men have been excluded cannot perform the task demanded of it. Guided by neither rule nor standard, "free to select or reject as it (sees) fit," a jury that must choose between life imprisonment and capital punishment can do little more—and must do nothing less—than express the conscience of the community on the ultimate question of life or death. Yet, in a nation less than half of whose people believe in the death penalty, a jury composed exclusively of such people cannot speak for the community. Culled of all who harbor doubts about the wisdom of capital punishment—of all who would be reluctant to pronounce the extreme penalty—such a jury can speak only for a distinct and dwindling minority.

The constitutional attack on capital punishment enjoyed even greater successes outside of the Supreme Court. Increased public opposition to capital punishment, increased unwillingness of juries to impose death sentences, increased unwillingness of prosecutors to seek death sentences, and increased unwillingness of state courts to sustain death sentences resulted in a national moratorium on executions that began during the late 1960s.

The Supreme Court's commitment to a living Constitution fueled attacks on capital punishment. In *Trop v. Dulles* (1958) a 5-4 judicial majority held that a federal law stripping soldiers of citizenship as a punishment for desertion violated the Eighth Amendment. Chief Justice Warren's majority opinion asserted that the "[Eighth] Amendment must draw its meaning from the evolving standards of decency that mark the progress of a maturing society." If, as *Trop* indicated, common punishments at the time that the Bill of Rights was ratified could become cruel and unusual over time, then, opponents of capital punishment by 1968 were convinced, the time had come to declare capital punishment cruel and unusual.

Suggested Readings

Brown-Nagin, Tomiko. *Courage to Dissent: Atlanta and the Long History of the Civil Rights Movement* (New York: Oxford University Press, 2011).

Cortner, Richard C. *The Supreme Court and the Second Bill of Rights: The Fourteenth Amendment and the Nationalization of Civil Liberties* (Madison: University of Wisconsin Press, 1981).

Cray, Ed. *Chief Justice: A Biography of Earl Warren* (New York: Simon & Schuster, 1997).

Cushman, Barry. *Rethinking the New Deal Court: The Structure of a Constitutional Revolution* (New York: Oxford University Press, 1998).

Dudziak, Mary L. *Cold War Civil Rights: Race and the Image of American Democracy* (Princeton, NJ: Princeton University Press, 2002).

Emerson, Thomas Irwin. *The System of Freedom of Expression* (New York: Random House, 1970).

Feldman, Noah. *Scorpions: The Battles and Triumphs of FDR's Great Supreme Court Justices* (New York: Hachette, 2010).

Goluboff, Risa Lauren. *The Lost Promise of Civil Rights* (Cambridge, MA: Harvard University Press, 2007).

Graham, Hugh Davis. *The Civil Rights Era: Origins and Development of National Policy* (New York: Oxford University Press, 1990).

Hirsch, H. N. *The Enigma of Felix Frankfurter* (New York: Basic, 1981).

Horwitz, Morton J. *The Warren Court and the Pursuit of Justice* (New York: Hill and Wang, 1998).

Irons, Peter H. *Justice at War* (New York: Oxford University Press, 1983).

Kalman, Laura. *Abe Fortas: A Biography* (New Haven, CT: Yale University Press, 1990).

Kluger, Richard. *Simple Justice: The History of* Brown v. Board of Education *and Black America's Struggle for Equality* (New York: Knopf, 1984).

Lawrence, Susan E. *The Poor in Court: The Legal Services Program and Supreme Court Decision Making* (Princeton, NJ: Princeton University Press, 1990).

Leuchtenburg, William Edward. *The Supreme Court Reborn: The Constitutional Revolution in the Age of Roosevelt* (New York: Oxford University Press, 1995).

Lewis, Anthony. *Gideon's Trumpet* (New York: Random House, 1964).

Lovell, George. *This Is Not Civil Rights: Discovering Rights Talk in 1939 America* (Chicago: University of Chicago Press, 2012).

Mason, Alpheus Thomas. *Harlan Fiske Stone: Pillar of the Law* (New York: Viking Press, 1956).

McMahon, Kevin J. *Reconsidering Roosevelt on Race: How the Presidency Paved the Road to* Brown (Chicago: University of Chicago Press, 2003).

Meiklejohn, Alexander. *Political Freedom: The Constitutional Powers of the People* (New York: Oxford University Press, 1965).

Murphy, Bruce Allen. *Wild Bill: The Legend and Life of William O. Douglas* (New York: Random House, 2003).

Newman, Roger K. *Hugo Black: A Biography* (New York: Pantheon, 1994).

Novkov, Julie. *Constituting Workers, Protecting Women: Gender, Law and Labor in the Progressive Era and New Deal Years* (Ann Arbor: University of Michigan Press, 2001).

Peters, Shawn Francis. *Judging Jehovah's Witnesses: Religious Persecution and the Dawn of the Rights Revolution* (Lawrence: University Press of Kansas, 2000).

Powe, Lucas A. *The Warren Court and American Politics* (Cambridge, MA: Harvard University Press, 2000).

Tushnet, Mark V. *Making Civil Rights Law: Thurgood Marshall and the Supreme Court, 1936–61* (New York: Oxford University Press, 1994).

Tushnet, Mark V. *Making Constitutional Law: Thurgood Marshall and the Supreme Court, 1961–1991* (New York: Oxford University Press, 1997).

Tushnet, Mark V. *The Warren Court in Historical and Political Perspective* (Charlottesville: University of Virginia Press, 1999).

Vose, Clement E. *Caucasians Only: The Supreme Court, the NAACP, and the Restrictive Covenant Cases* (Berkeley: University of California Press, 1959).

Wiecek, William M. *The Birth of the Modern Constitution: The United States Supreme Court, 1941–1953* (New York: Cambridge University Press, 2006).

Chapter 9

Liberalism Divided: 1969–1980

I. Introduction

The three presidential candidates in 1968 were committed New Dealers with sharply diverging beliefs about the Great Society. Hubert Humphrey, George Wallace, and Richard Nixon had no significant quarrel with the Constitutional Revolution of 1937. Each aspirant for the presidency had a very different perspective on constitutional developments during the Great Society. Humphrey, who had championed racial liberalism in the Senate for twenty years, promised to maintain and expand the legacy of the 1960s. Wallace, the former pro-segregation governor of Alabama, promised to roll back virtually every major constitutional decision of the previous decade. Richard Nixon, who was endorsed in 1960 by both Martin Luther King, Sr., and Senator Strom Thurmond of South Carolina, favored some Great Society policies but not others. When Nixon barely eked out a victory over Humphrey, with Wallace gaining more votes than any third-party candidate in American history, the electorate's message was unclear, particularly in light of continued Democratic majorities in the Senate and House. The best that could be said was that American constitutional politics had not generated a working majority committed to expanding, maintaining, or abandoning the constitutional developments of the 1960s.

Americans remained committed to New Deal liberalism for the next twelve years but did not decisively affirm or repudiate either the Great Society or the New Deal Democratic coalition that dominated politics from 1932 to 1968. The 1970s were characterized by divided government and internal divisions within both major parties. Voters elected both Democrats and Republicans (including conservative Democrats and liberal Republicans) in sufficient numbers to give no clear message to governing officials. Presidents Richard Nixon and Jimmy Carter reflected this ambivalence. Nixon vigorously opposed busing while expanding affirmative action. Carter pushed for women's rights while opposing federal funding for abortion.

Constitutional law matched the erratic development of constitutional politics. Women gained rights during the 1970s. The rights of persons suspected of crime were narrowed. The Supreme Court in *Roe v. Wade* (1973) held that abortion was a fundamental constitutional right, but in *San Antonio Independent School District v. Rodriguez* (1973) ruled that education was not. The justices in 1976 announced a stricter constitutional standard for gender distinctions (*Craig v. Boren*) and permitted states to impose capital punishment (*Gregg v. Georgia*). More generally, constitutional developments during the late 1960s and 1970s did not reflect any jurisprudential theory, the platform of any political party, or the positions championed by any particular interest group.

Parties. Partisan competition during this period was between political actors who agreed on the basic constitutional principles underlying the New Deal but bitterly disputed the constitutional achievements and merits of the Great Society. Democrats running for the presidency promised to maintain and expand the legacy of the 1960s. The Democratic Party platform of 1968 declared, "The Civil Rights Act of 1964 and 1968 and the Voting Rights Act of 1965 . . . are basic to America's long march toward full equality under the law," and promised that if existing civil rights laws "prove inadequate, or if their compliance provisions fail to serve their purposes, we will propose new laws." Republicans endorsed some constitutional developments during the Great Society, but not others.

Richard Nixon on the campaign trail in 1968 was sharply critical of Warren Court decisions on school prayer and the rights of criminal suspects, but he either supported or did not comment on other liberal constitutional commitments. The Republican Party platform of 1968 pledged "concern for the unique problems of citizens long disadvantaged in our total society by race, color, national origin, creed, or sex" but neither endorsed nor opposed the Civil Rights Act of 1964 or the Voting Rights Act of 1965. George Wallace condemned the most important legislative and judicial decisions of the 1960s. His American Independent Party declared,

> The Federal Government has in the past three decades seized and usurped many powers not delegated to it, such as, among others: the operation and control of the public school system of the several states; [and] the power to prescribe the eligibility and qualifications of those who would vote in our state and local elections. . . . The Federal Government has forced the states to reapportion their legislatures, a prerogative of the states alone.
>
> . . . [T]he Federal Government has adopted so-called "Civil Rights Acts," particularly the one adapted in 1964, which have set race against race and class against class.

Divided government and divided parties structured American constitutional politics. For eight of the twelve years between 1969 and 1980 Republicans controlled the presidency while Democrats controlled both houses of Congress. Democrats were, on average, more liberal than Republicans, but neither party presented a united front to voters. Southern Democrats such as Senator Sam Ervin of North Carolina and Senator James Eastland of Mississippi remained the leading opponents of the Great Society. Such Republican liberals as Senator Jacob Javits of New York and Attorney General Eliot Richardson remained leading enthusiasts for an expanded Great Society. Controversies over social issues created additional political cleavages. The formerly solid Democratic South became a political battleground as Richard Nixon's southern strategy sought to take advantage of southern conservative opposition to Great Society programs and liberal judicial decisions on constitutional criminal procedure, school prayer, and abortion. Abortion, obscenity, and women's rights divided political elites from the more religious lower-middle class, rather than Republicans from Democrats.

Interest Groups. Interest group activity was divided. The ACLU lost many members after supporting the rights of Nazis to march in Skokie, Illinois. The African-American/Jewish alliance that was a pillar of the civil rights movement during the 1960s frayed when concerns over affirmative action replaced concerns over

Table 9-1 Major Rights and Liberties Issues and Decisions of the Era of Liberalism Divided

Major Political Issues	Major Constitutional Issues	Major Court Decisions
Vietnam War	Welfare Rights	*Dandridge v. Williams* (1970)
Extending or Contracting the Great Society	Busing	*New York Times v. United States* (1971)
Crime Control	Affirmative Action	*Swann v. Charlotte-Meckleburg Board of Education* (1971)
Aftermath of Black Civil Rights Movement	Free Exercise of Religion	*Wisconsin v. Yoder* (1972)
Minority Rights Revolution	Level of Judicial Scrutiny for Gender Classification	*Roe v. Wade* (1973)
Women's Movement	Death Penalty	*San Antonio Independent School District v. Rodriguez* (1973)
Environmental Movement	Access to Federal Habeas Corpus	*Buckley v. Valeo* (1976)
Sexual Revolution	Scope of *Mapp* and *Miranda*	*Gregg v. Georgia* (1976)
Moral Majority	Abortion	*Craig v. Boren* (1976)
Money in Elections	Free Speech	*Wainwright v. Sykes* (1977)
		Regents of the University of California v. Bakke (1978)

desegregation. Free exercise and establishment clause controversies broke out between liberal and conservative members of the same religion rather than along the traditional Protestant/Catholic/Jewish divide. Interest groups also became more specialized. During the New Deal/Great Society Era the ACLU was the leading liberal voice across a wide spectrum of constitutional issues. By 1980 every group and every right seemed to have an organization dedicated to lobbying and litigating on its behalf.

Conservative interest groups mobilized during the 1970s. Evangelicals entered politics in order to restore what they believed were traditional American social values. Libertarian activists launched litigation campaigns to restore what they believed were traditional property rights. These conservative interest groups often augmented and sometimes replaced the state governments, businesses, and churches that had opposed liberal interest group lobbying and litigation during the New Deal/Great Society Era. No conservative interest group in 1980 rivaled the ACLU or NAACP in influence, but both evangelical and libertarian associations had an increasing influence on American constitutional politics.

Courts. Political stalemates empowered federal and state justices. Sometimes, as in the Federal Election Campaign Act of 1974, Congress explicitly invited the justices to make constitutional policy. More often, as was the case with abortion, Americans could not muster lawmaking majorities that either approved or disapproved of controversial judicial decisions. Politicians on the conservative side of the aisle condemned judicial activism, while politicians on the liberal side celebrated judicial independence. Judicial nominations became more contentious, as Richard Nixon sought to move the Supreme Court in a more conservative direction and liberals in Congress sought to preserve Warren Court activism. In this contentious environment judges had a fair degree of freedom to act on their distinctive vision, as long as that vision was acceptable to some strong fragment in electoral politics.

The Burger Court reflected the broader divisions in American politics. Two of Richard Nixon's judicial appointees, Justice William Rehnquist and, to a lesser extent, Chief Justice Warren Burger, fought to reverse many constitutional decisions made during the Great Society. Justices Thurgood Marshall and William Brennan, members of previous Warren Court majorities, enthusiastically endorsed new liberal constitutional commitments. The other five justices, three of whom were appointed by Presidents Nixon and Gerald Ford, had more idiosyncratic perspectives on the constitutional issues of the day. The Burger Court's decision in *Roe v. Wade,* striking down bans on abortion in forty-six states, was stunningly activist even by Warren Court standards. More conservative majorities rejected constitutional welfare rights in *Dandridge v. Williams* (1970) and curtailed access to federal habeas corpus in *Wainwright v. Sykes* (1977). Frequently the centrist justices on the Burger Court split the difference, handing down decisions in gender discrimination, capital punishment, and affirmation action cases that were less liberal than the Warren Court would have made, but not as conservative as Nixon and many of his supporters would have liked. As Figure 9-1 indicates, the Burger Court was far more conservative than the Warren Court of the late 1960s, but the large bloc of centrist justices kept the Court generally in line with the Democratic Congress through the 1970s and 1980s. Professor Vincent Blasi has suggested that "rootless activism" was the defining characteristic of the Supreme Court during the 1970s.[1]

Constitutional Thought. Political divisions were largely over the extent to which the work of the Great Society was unfinished, the particular aspects of the Great Society that were unfinished, and which governing institutions were primarily responsible for finishing the work of the Great Society. Most mainstream Democrats and Republicans were horrified when George Wallace and a growing number of conservative intellectuals called for overturning landmark constitutional decisions of the 1960s as well as the Civil Rights Act of 1964. Richard Nixon, by comparison, limited his complaints about an activist judiciary to the constitutional criminal procedure decisions of the 1960s and the school busing decisions of the 1970s.[2] Nixon celebrated *Brown v. Board of Education* (1954) and endorsed legislative efforts to expand the Voting Rights Act of 1965. He was more concerned with the future direc-

1. Vincent Blasi, "The Rootless Activism of the Burger Court," in *The Burger Court: The Counter-Revolution That Wasn't*, ed. Vincent Blasi (New Haven, CT: Yale University Press, 1983), 198.

2. See Kevin J. McMahon, *Nixon's Court: His Challenge to Judicial Liberalism and Its Political Consequences* (Chicago: University of Chicago Press, 2011).

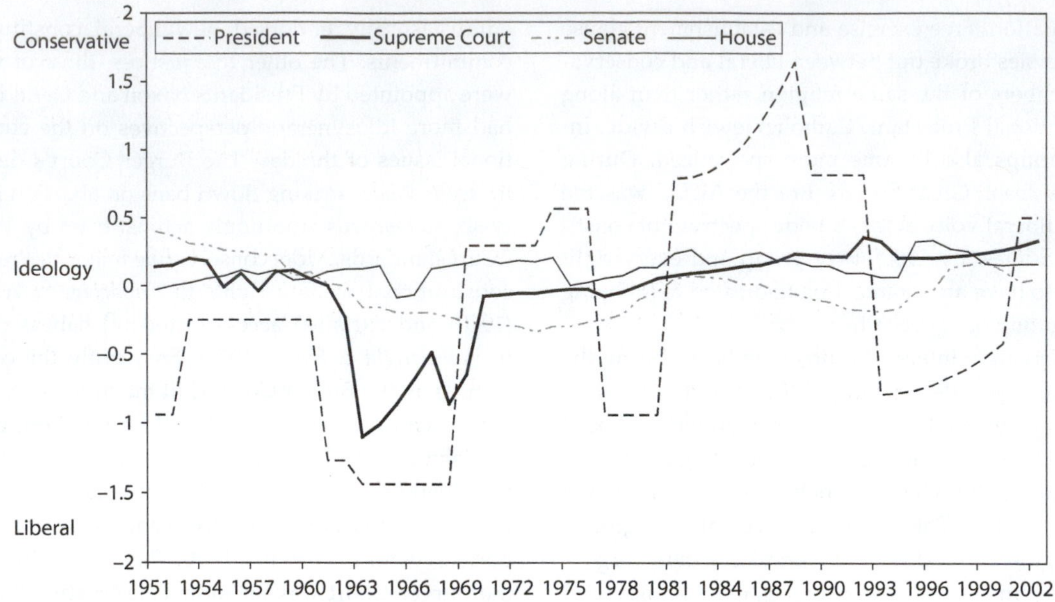

Figure 9-1 Left-Right Location of Supreme Court Relative to Other Branches, 1950–2002

Note: Median member of each institution placed on common ideological scale based on actual individual votes on cases (Court), bills (Congress), or individual statements about the actions taken by other institutions.

Source: Michael Bailey, "Comparable Preference Estimates across Time and Institutions for the Court, Congress and Presidency," http://www9.georgetown.edu/faculty/baileyma/Data.htm.

tion of constitutional rights and liberties than with returning the United States to the constitutional status quo of the 1950s.

The judicial tendency in the 1970s to measure time by counting the years between *Brown v. Board of Education* and the case before the Court illustrates key differences between Americans regarding the future of civil rights and liberties. Progressives regarded the Great Society as the beginning step in the long process of making the United States a more egalitarian society. They interpreted that passage of time as evidence that more extensive remedies were needed to realize the racial equality promised by the Great Society. A frustrated Justice Marshall in 1971 commented on how the "devastating, often irreparable, injury to those children who experience segregation and isolation was noted seventeen years ago in *Brown*."[3] Nixon and his political allies, in contrast, regarded the Great Society largely as finishing the process of making the United States a more egalitarian society. They interpreted the same passage of time as justifying an end to judicial supervision of public schools. "A quarter of a century after *Brown*," Justice Powell moaned in *Columbus Board of Education v. Penick* (1979), "the federal judiciary should be limiting rather than expanding the extent to which courts are operating the public school systems of our country." Whether constitutional decision makers thought that affirmative action promoted or betrayed the egalitarian principles of the Great Society depended in large part on whether they believed the effects of Jim Crow had largely been eradicated by the 1970s.

Many progressives advanced constitutional arguments more rooted in philosophical claims about fundamental rights than in democratic theory. The New Deal/Great Society commitments to democracy and fundamental rights were mutually reinforcing. Liberals from 1933 until 1968 could justify commitments to racial equality, freedom of religion, the nationalization of the Bill of Rights, and broad rights for political and cultural dissenters as making the United States more democratic or as goals consistent with universal human rights. Differences between democratic and fundamental rights as foundations for judicial activism became more acute during the 1970s. The democratic

3. *Dandridge v. Jefferson Parish School Board*, 404 U.S. 1219 (1971).

theory underlying Footnote Four in *Carolene Products* (1938) emphasized history and political practice when determining whose rights needed special solicitude. Persons of color merited special constitutional protection because they were politically powerless and had historically been victims of discrimination. By the 1970s many progressives were more inspired by such works as John Rawls's *A Theory of Justice* (1971), which looked to moral philosophy as the proper source of rights and liberties. Persons of color and women merited special constitutional protection because race and gender were arbitrary bases for distinguishing people. American progressives placed greater emphasis on autonomy rights, such as the right to a legal abortion, than the democratic theory rights that liberals had championed during the New Deal and Great Society Era.

More conservative thinkers challenged the liberal consensus of the 1960s. Robert Bork in 1971 published "Neutral Principles and Some First Amendment Problems," an influential essay that criticized numerous Warren Court decisions as inconsistent with the original meaning of constitutional provisions. Alexander Bickel's *The Morality of Consent* (1975) urged justices to pay greater heed to the eighteenth century English conservative Edmund Burke than the more liberal John Locke. Richard Posner and other libertarian scholars published works in law and economics that called for greater judicial protection for property rights.[4] By 1980 conservative constitutional thought was far more respectable than it had been for a generation, even if that school of thought had not yet exerted substantial influence on the federal judiciary.

Under pressure from both the left and the right, the "preferred freedoms" structure of constitutional doctrine began to break down. New Deal liberals insisted that government needed a compelling interest to restrict such rights as free speech and the right to racial equality but needed only a rational basis to limit most property rights. The Burger Court provided greater doctrinal flexibility to handle such controversies by introducing a new intermediate standard of review. *Craig v. Boren* (1976) ruled that government could make gender distinctions when those distinctions were an important means to a substantial government interest. Several justices suggested that the Court replace this two- or three-tiered scrutiny with a sliding scale that considered the importance of the right, the offensiveness of the classification, and the value of the state interest.

Legacies. The constitutional politics of the 1970s entrenched the constitutional liberalism of the New Deal/Great Society Era. When Richard Nixon was first elected president many Americans realistically hoped or feared that the constitutional developments of the previous decades would be abandoned or reversed. That did not happen. Parochial schools obtained a few more state resources and persons suspected of crimes enjoyed fewer procedural protections than might have been expected from the Warren Court. Nevertheless, most major Warren Court precedents and Great Society measures were less controversial in 1980 than they were in 1968. On the eve of the Reagan presidency no prominent party or political movement in the United States challenged claims that the Fourteenth Amendment incorporated most provisions in the Bill of Rights, that adults had the right to marry and use birth control, that government could not restrict speech that did not present an imminent danger of harm, and that state legislative apportionments had to approximate one person, one vote. *Brown v. Board of Education* (1954) was celebrated as the best judicial decision in American history. The Civil Rights Act of 1964 and the Voting Rights Act of 1965 were near-sacred texts, no more subject to revision than the principle of state equality in the Senate. Americans were also committed to some degree of gender equality by the start of the Reagan years. Americans might debate whether the Equal Rights Amendment was necessary, but a broad consensus existed that most traditional gender distinctions were unconstitutional.

The 1970s introduced the constitutional questions that continue to excite and divide Americans. Abortion, affirmative action, and campaign finance reform first enjoyed substantial national prominence during the Nixon presidency. Constitutional decision makers did not resolve these problems, but they provided the constitutional ground rules for future debates. The next generation of campaign finance cases, following *Buckley v. Valeo* (1976), focused on the government interest to prevent corruption rather than political equality. Affirmative action debates after *Bakke v. Regents of*

4. See Robert H. Bork, "Neutral Principles and Some First Amendment Problems," *Indiana Law Review* 47 (1971): 29; Alexander Bickel, *The Morality of Consent* (New Haven, CT: Yale University Press, 1975); and Richard A. Posner, *Economic Analysis of Law* (Boston: Little, Brown and Company, 1973).

Box 9-1 A Partial Cast of Characters of the Era of Liberalism Divided

Warren Burger	▪ Republican ▪ Minnesota lawyer ▪ Appointed by Dwight Eisenhower to the federal circuit court (1956–69) ▪ Appointed by Richard Nixon as chief justice of the United States (1969–86) ▪ Public critic of the Warren Court while serving as a circuit court judge ▪ Conservative on social issues and emphasized checks and balances on separation of powers issues; developed a reputation as a weak chief justice
Harry Blackmun	▪ Republican ▪ Minnesota lawyer ▪ Appointed by Dwight Eisenhower to the federal circuit court (1959–1970) ▪ Appointed by Richard Nixon to Supreme Court (1970–94) ▪ Known as one of "Minnesota Twins" for his close support of Warren Burger early in tenure on Court but later became closely allied with William Brennan ▪ Best known for authoring majority opinion in *Roe v. Wade* (1973)
Lewis F. Powell	▪ Democrat ▪ Virginia lawyer ▪ Presided over desegregation of public schools as chair of Richmond school board (1952–61) ▪ Facilitated the creation of the Legal Services Program as president of the American Bar Association (1964–65) but also encouraged more active efforts by business to build public and political support for the "free enterprise system" ▪ Appointed by Richard Nixon to the Supreme Court (1972–87), where he became an important swing vote on the Burger Court and developed a reputation as a moderate
Byron White	▪ Democrat ▪ Rhodes Scholar and star professional football player from Colorado before World War II ▪ Attended law school after serving in naval intelligence; clerked for Chief Justice Fred Vinson ▪ Deputy attorney general (1961–62) ▪ Appointed by John F. Kennedy to Supreme Court (1962–93) ▪ Known as a pragmatic jurist and a swing vote on the Warren and Burger Courts

the University of California (1978) focused on diversity rather than national obligations to alleviate harms for past societal discrimination.

Liberals became increasingly wedded to judicial power. Liberals during the New Deal/Great Society Era celebrated the achievements of Franklin Roosevelt, Lyndon Johnson, and Martin Luther King, Jr., as well as Earl Warren, William Douglas, and, at least before 1965, Hugo Black. Thurgood Marshall and William Brennan stood alone as progressive constitutional heroes during the 1970s. At a time when Richard Nixon won two consecutive elections and conservatives gained power in many congressional elections, courts that protected abortion rights, outlawed much gender discrimination, curtailed capital punishment, and permitted the *New York Times* to publish the Pentagon Papers seemed the best institutional site for progressive constitutional politics to move forward. Frank Michelman spoke for many liberals when he observed that justices have a unique capacity to "listen . . . for voices from the margins."[5] Liberal commitments to judicial

5. Frank Michelman, "Law's Republic," *Yale Law Journal* 97 (1988): 1537.

activism influenced progressive electoral politics. Congressional liberals did not aggressively oppose bans on federal funding for medically necessary abortions because they were confident that the Hyde Amendment would be declared unconstitutional by federal justices. Such legislators were bitterly disappointed when the Supreme Court in *Harris v. McRae* (1980) sustained that measure. Even with this and other disappointments, many liberals remained judicial supremacists long after federal courts ceased to be bastions of liberalism. Many progressives at present retain commitments to judicial power first forged in the 1960s and 1970s.

II. Foundations

MAJOR DEVELOPMENTS

- Failure to ratify the Equal Rights Amendment
- More emphasis on substantive rights than democratic rights
- State action doctrine narrowed

Americans did not significantly alter the constitutional text or the scope of constitutional rights and liberties during the 1970s. Political divisions doomed the ERA. Persons who agreed on the general principle of gender equality could not agree sufficiently on the actual impact of the ERA to generate the supermajority needed under Article V. The Supreme Court did not tinker with Warren Court precedents that incorporated almost every provision of the Bill of Rights against the states and insisted that American governing officials abroad respect the basic due process rights of American citizens. The Supreme Court did significantly narrow the state action doctrine, particularly when the rights of African-Americans were not at issue.

Constitutional decision makers acted more often on socially liberal than on economically liberal principles. The Supreme Court declared that the due process clause protected the right to an abortion and required heightened, but not strict, scrutiny when government officials made gender discriminations. Proponents of economic liberalism did not enjoy the same success. The Supreme Court decisively rejected claims that poor persons had a right to basic necessities.

A. Sources

The sources of constitutional rights and liberties did not change significantly. The Twenty-Sixth Amendment forbade federal and state officials from denying the ballot to citizens "eighteen years of age or older . . . on account of age." Divided liberals could not, however, produce a constitutional majority to pass the ERA, even though both major parties endorsed the amendment and most Americans rejected nineteenth-century rulings on the constitutional status of women. Constitutional understandings first articulated during the New Deal and Great Society became further entrenched during the 1970s as Republicans in the executive branch pledged fidelity to New Deal understandings of property rights, the gains made by the civil rights movement in the 1960s, and other (but not all) aspects of Great Society constitutionalism.

Constitutions and Amendments

College students and their age peers gained the right to vote when the Twenty-Sixth Amendment was ratified in 1971. That provision declared, "The right of citizens of the United States, who are eighteen years of age or older, to vote shall not be denied or abridged by the United States or by any State on account of age." The sponsors of the Twenty-Sixth Amendment were concerned with protest movements on college campuses and convinced that young persons who served in the Vietnam War had a right to cast ballots. The Voting Rights Act of 1965 had included a provision enfranchising persons eighteen and older. The Supreme Court in *Oregon v. Mitchell* (1971) by a 5-4 vote declared that Congress had the power to determine qualifications for voters in federal elections, but not in state elections. No one but Justice Black, the only justice who distinguished between federal and state elections, thought this state of affairs constitutionally coherent. The Twenty-Sixth Amendment was immediately approved by Congress and two-thirds of the states.

Proponents of gender equality had more difficulty obtaining a constitutional amendment. In 1968 and 1972 both major political parties endorsed the ERA. The House in 1971 approved the ERA by a 354-24 vote. The Senate vote in 1972 was 84-8. Within two years thirty states had agreed that "equality of Rights under the law shall not be denied or abridged by the United States or any state on account of sex." Then the ERA stalled. Proponents gained five additional states (of the thirty-eight needed for ratification) during the 1970s, but no more.

Scholars still debate why the ERA failed,[6] but several reasons seem important. Liberals were internally divided over what policies the ERA forbade. More progressive liberals insisted that the ERA supported women serving in military units and, perhaps, constitutional rights to abortion. An article in the 1971 *Yale Law Journal* declared, "The principle of the Amendment must be applied comprehensively and without exception." After noting that "all combat is dangerous, degrading and dehumanizing," the authors insisted that there "is little to choose . . . between brutalizing our young men and brutalizing our young women."[7] Moderates responded that the ERA would not produce these controversial consequences. Professor William Van Alstyne stated, "It is extraordinarily implausible . . . to suppose that if the Congress and the President were mutually of the view that the insertion of women into combat infantry was not appropriate . . . that the Supreme Court would nonetheless presume to 'overrule' their combined judgment."[8] By the mid-1970s legislative and judicial reforms had achieved most of the goals sought by moderate proponents of the ERA. The federal government and most states had passed laws prohibiting many gender classifications. In a series of opinions culminating in *Craig v. Boren* (1976), the Supreme Court ruled that ordinary gender distinctions violated the equal protection clause of the Fourteenth Amendment. When more progressive and more moderate proponents of the ERA were unable to agree on language establishing that the constitutional amendment did not make more dramatic changes in gender relationships than most people wanted, enough moderates in crucial states joined with social conservatives to prevent the ERA from being ratified.[9]

Some differences between proponents of more egalitarian and proponents of more deferentialist interpretations of the ERA were over political strategy. Many egalitarians, confident that the ERA would pass, attempted to develop a record that would justify judicial decisions interpreting that amendment as providing very broad protections for women. With the benefit of hindsight, what would you have advised them? Should egalitarians have modified their rhetoric to facilitate passage of the ERA, or should they have stood on principle? Should any of this rhetoric have influenced subsequent interpretation of the ERA?

The failure of the ERA did not leave American constitutionalism unchanged. By the time that Ronald Reagan was elected president no substantial opposition existed to Supreme Court decisions that heightened the level of scrutiny that gender distinctions received. A strong political consensus had formed that the equal protection clause required states to scrutinize gender classifications more carefully than ordinary legislative classifications but less carefully than racial classifications. Reagan, while opposed to the ERA, kept a campaign promise when he nominated Sandra Day O'Connor as the first woman justice on the Supreme Court. More specifics about gender discrimination were unclear. As frequently occurred during the 1970s, Americans could neither agree wholeheartedly with champions of constitutional liberalism nor completely reject their norms.

B. Principles

Constitutional liberalism subtly changed during the period between the Great Society and the Reagan Era. The constitutional liberalism of the New Deal/Great Society Era emphasized democratic principles. Free speech and voting rights merited special constitutional protection because both were necessary conditions of a democracy. Persons of color merited special constitutional protection because they were a "discrete and insular minority" that lacked a fair share of democratic political power. Progressives during the 1970s placed greater emphasis on liberal principles that imposed substantive limits on government. In a series of lectures revealingly entitled "The Unfinished Business of the Warren Court," Professor Charles Black of the Yale Law School insisted that the promise of the Great Society would be fulfilled only when the Supreme Court developed "a *corpus juris* of human rights." According to Black, the central principles underlying the Warren Court and the Great Society were "the positive content and worth of American citizenship" and the right to enjoy citizenship "in all its parts without respect to race." Some elements of citizenship were procedural.

6. A particularly good account, on which we rely heavily here, is Jane J. Mansbridge, *Why We Lost the ERA* (Chicago: University of Chicago Press, 1986).

7. Barbara A. Brown, Thomas I. Emerson, Gail Falk, and Ann E. Freedman, "The Equal Rights Amendment: A Constitutional Basis for Equal Rights of Women," *Yale Law Journal* 80 (1971): 890, 977.

8. William W. Van Alstyne, "The Proposed Twenty-Seventh Amendment: A Brief Supportive Comment," *Washington University Law Quarterly* 65, no. 8 (1979): 189, 194–95 n.10

9. See Mansbridge, *Why We Lost the ERA*, 78.

"Citizenship," Black wrote, "is the right to be heard and counted on public affairs, the right to vote on equal terms, to speak, and to hold office when legitimately chosen," as well as "the right to be treated fairly when one is the object of action by . . . government." Black also insisted that citizenship had a substantive component, conferring "the broad right to lead a *private* life—for without this all dignity and happiness are impossible."[10]

Liberals during the 1970s turned to Harvard philosopher John Rawls (1921–2002) when elaborating what they believed were the appropriate government principles and fundamental rights for a constitutional democracy. Rawls's most influential work, *A Theory of Justice* (1971), claimed that constitutional government should be committed to the following norms:

> First: each person is to have an equal right to the most extensive basic liberty compatible with a similar liberty for others.
>
> Second: social and economic inequalities are to be arranged so that they are both (a) reasonably expected to be to everyone's advantages, and (b) attached to positions and offices open to all.[11]

Prominent progressive theorists during the 1970s and afterward tinkered with these principles and conclusions, but most agreed with three central tenets of Rawlsian liberalism. First, unlike New Deal liberals who emphasized "discrete and insular minorities," liberal constitutionalists after 1969 placed increased weight on "arbitrary contingencies."[12] Whether discrimination against persons of color or women was wrong depended more on whether race or gender was a morally relevant characteristic and less on whether persons of color or women had historically enjoyed their fair share of political power. Second, the new generation of liberal constitutionalists treated conceptions of the good life as arbitrary. From this premise they deduced that governing officials had no business passing morals legislation or other measures based on particular conceptions of the good life. Persons had a right to use birth control, regardless of whether most people favored birth control laws or those restrictions were evenhandedly enforced. Finally, the most progressive strand of constitutional liberalism proposed replacing classic liberal property rights with constitutional rights to redistribution. Some prominent liberals contended that all persons had a right to the basic necessities of life that would enable them to pursue their private conceptions of the good.

Several liberal law professors called for the Supreme Court to integrate Rawlsian logic into constitutional law. Professor Frank Michelman of Harvard Law School urged constitutional decision makers to "take [their] cue from Professor Rawls' idea of 'justice as fairness.'"[13] Ronald Dworkin, when calling for "a fusion of constitutional law and moral theory," described *A Theory of Justice* as "an abstract and complex book about justice which no constitutional lawyer will be able to ignore."[14]

The precise influence of this liberal turn is unclear. If influence is measured by citation, Rawls had no influence on Supreme Court decision making. Many commentators continued insisting that democratic principles justified rights to abortion, basic necessities, and other progressive constitutional goals.[15] Still, a reasonable argument can be made that Justices Brennan and Marshall, the two most prominent liberals on the Supreme Court, over time voted more consistently with the principles articulated in *A Theory of Justice* than with the principles underlying the *Carolene Products* footnote.

Persons who favored the democratic principles underlying Great Society constitutionalism criticized the new generation of liberal thinkers for belittling the constitutional commitment to majoritarianism. "Our society does not . . . accept the notion of a discoverable and objectively valid set of morals," John Hart Ely declared "at least not a set that could plausibly serve to overturn the decisions of our elected representatives."[16] Justice William Rehnquist declared that living constitutionalism

---

10. Charles L. Black, Jr., "The Unfinished Business of the Warren Court," *Washington Law Review* 46 (1970): 44, 8, 9.

11. John Rawls, *A Theory of Justice*, (Cambridge, MA: Harvard University Press, 1971), 60.

12. Ibid., 141.

13. Frank I. Michelman, "Foreword: On Protecting the Poor through the Fourteenth Amendment," *Harvard Law Review* 83 (1969): 7, 14–15.

14. Ronald M. Dworkin, *Taking Rights Seriously* (Cambridge, MA: Harvard University Press, 1977), 149.

15. For a later effort to rely on democratic principles to justify the liberal decisions of the 1970s, see Guido Calabresi, "Foreword: Antidiscrimination and Constitutional Accountability (What the Bork-Brennan Debate Ignores)," *Harvard Law Review* 105 (1991): 77.

16. John Hart Ely, *Democracy and Distrust: A Theory of Judicial Review* (Cambridge, MA: Harvard University Press, 1980), 54.

"misconceives the nature of the Constitution, which was designed to enable the popularly elected branches of government, not the judicial branch, to keep the country abreast of the times."[17] Sharply rejecting a central premise of Rawlsian liberalism, both the conservative Rehnquist and more politically liberal Ely challenged claims that persons could prove the existence of particular liberal values. "There is no conceivable way," Rehnquist wrote, "in which I can logically demonstrate to you that the judgments of my conscience are superior to the judgments of your conscience and vice versa."[18] Noting that the more libertarian Harvard philosopher Robert Nozick's *Anarchy, State and Utopia* (1974) reached very different conclusions than did Rawls, Ely stated, "There simply does not exist *a* method of moral philosophy." He imagined a Supreme Court opinion that read, "We like Rawls, you like Nozick. We win, 6-3."[19]

C. Scope

Constitutional decision makers during the Nixon and Carter years accepted inherited conceptions of incorporation and the extraterritorial force of the Constitution. Americans did not witness any substantial changes in the constitutional obligations of governing officials outside of the United States. American citizens who lived abroad and military personnel who committed nonservice offenses were constitutionally entitled to civilian trials when tried by American governing officials, but governing officials abroad had no obligation to provide the same treatment to foreigners under their jurisdiction. Divided liberals accepted the incorporation doctrine passed down from the New Deal/Great Society years. After Justice Harlan retired in 1971 questions about whether states had to respect most provisions laid out in the Bill of Rights gradually disappeared. By 1980 the justices on the Supreme Court, when reviewing criminal convictions, routinely assumed that federal and state officials were bound by the same constitutional rules.

The constitutional politics of state action and the direction of judicial decision making, however, changed after Richard Nixon was elected to the presidency. Fewer cases involved claims that the state should be held responsible for private race discrimination. Judicial majorities in nonrace cases modified existing precedents in ways that made state action more difficult to prove.[20]

By 1969 the most important state action decisions of the previous generation were irrelevant. The Civil Rights Act of 1964 barred racial discrimination in restaurants, hotels, and other places of public accommodation. The Civil Rights Act of 1968 barred racial discrimination in the housing market. These measures relied on the commerce clause of Article I, Section 8. This use of the commerce power meant that victims of race discrimination in the 1970s did not have to prove the state action required by the Fourteenth Amendment. All they had to demonstrate was that the individual behavior being regulated affected interstate commerce. This proved easy to demonstrate, particularly because the prevailing doctrine at the time required justices to give extraordinary deference to legislative claims that a regulation of individual behavior promoted interstate commerce. *Heart of Atlanta Motel, Inc. v. United States* (1964), the decision that sustained the Civil Rights Act of 1964, declared,

> The power of Congress to promote interstate commerce also includes the power to regulate the local incidents thereof, including local activities in both the States of origin and destination, which might have a substantial and harmful effect upon that commerce. One need only examine the evidence which we have discussed above to see that Congress may—as it has—prohibit racial discrimination by motels serving travelers, however "local" their operations may appear.

Burger Court justices in nonracial cases usually distinguished rather than overruled past precedents finding state action. Warren Court justices found state action whenever they determined that a nominally private entity played a "public function" or found "significant state involvement." By 1980 "public function" has been transformed into "exclusive public function," and "significant state involvement" had become "significant state encouragement." In *Moose Lodge No. 107 v. Irvis* (1972) the Supreme Court considered whether a private club with a state liquor license could refuse to serve African-Americans. Justice Rehnquist's

17. William H. Rehnquist, "The Notion of a Living Constitution," *Texas Law Review* 54 (1976): 699.

18. Rehnquist, "The Notion," 704.

19. Ely, *Democracy and Distrust*, 58.

20. See Terri Peretti, "Constructing the State Action Doctrine, 1940–1990," *Law and Social Inquiry* 35 (2010): 273.

majority opinion looked for active state support. He found none. "However detailed this type of regulation may be in some particulars," his majority decision affirming a right to discriminate declared, "it cannot be said to in any way foster or encourage racial discrimination."

Jackson v. Metropolitan Edison Co. (1974) illustrates both of these changes in the constitutional law of state action. The issue was whether a privately owned utility company that was granted a monopoly on electric services could terminate service without providing notice and a hearing. Justice Rehnquist's majority opinion rejected this claim of constitutional wrong. He first concluded that although the utility performed a public function, state action was not present because states had no obligation to provide citizens with electricity. Hence, the Metropolitan Edison was not performing a function that was "traditionally the exclusive prerogative of the State." Rehnquist then observed that although Pennsylvania regulated utility companies, the state had not in any way encouraged Metropolitan Edison to adopt its procedures for terminating service. In his words,

> Approval by a state utility commission of such a request from a regulated utility, where the commission has not put its own weight on the side of the proposed practice by ordering it, does not transmute a practice initiated by the utility and approved by the commission into "state action."

State Action

Moose Lodge No. 107 v. Irvis, 407 U.S. 163 (1972)

K. Leroy Irvis, an African-American man, was denied dining room service by Moose Lodge No. 107, the Harrisburg, Pennsylvania, affiliate of a national fraternal organization. Moose Lodge did not admit persons of color as members and did not serve food to persons of color who, like Irvis, were guests of white members. Irvis sued Moose Lodge, claiming that their discriminatory policies violated the equal protection clause of the Fourteenth Amendment. His petition for relief asked Pennsylvania to withdraw the state's liquor license until Moose Lodge abandoned its racial practices. Moose Lodge responded that, as a private club, they were free to discriminate and that their state liquor license was an insufficient basis to find state action. The district court found for Irvis and invalidated Moose Lodge's liquor license. Moose Lodge appealed to the Supreme Court of the United States.

The Supreme Court by a 6-3 vote found no state action. Justice Rehnquist's majority opinion maintained that Pennsylvania did not encourage or participate in racial discrimination merely by giving the Moose Lodge a liquor license. Justice Rehnquist regards the license as analogous to police protection, a state service available to (almost) all citizens. Justices Douglas and Brennan regard the license as a scarce commodity. Which characterization do you believe is most appropriate? How does the proper characterization influence your understanding of the decision? What sort of state involvement does Justice Rehnquist demand for state action? Under what conditions would Justice Douglas permit a private club to discriminate against persons of color?

JUSTICE REHNQUIST delivered the opinion of the Court.

. . .

The Court has never held . . . that discrimination by an otherwise private entity would be violative of the Equal Protection Clause if the private entity receives any sort of benefit or service at all from the State, or if it is subject to state regulation in any degree whatever. Since state-furnished services include such necessities of life as electricity, water, and police and fire protection, such a holding would utterly emasculate the distinction between private, as distinguished from state, conduct. . . . Our holdings indicate that, where the impetus for the discrimination is private, the State must have "significantly involved itself with invidious discriminations," . . . in order for the discriminatory action to fall within the ambit of the constitutional prohibition.

. . .

Here, there is nothing approaching the symbiotic relationship between lessor and lessee that was present in *Burton v. Wilmington Parking Authority* (1961), where the private lessee obtained the benefit of locating in a building owned by the state-created parking authority, and the parking authority was enabled to carry out its primarily public purpose of furnishing parking space by advantageously leasing portions of the building constructed for that purpose to commercial lessees such as the owner of the Eagle Restaurant. Unlike *Burton*, the Moose Lodge building is located on land owned by it, not by any public authority. Far from apparently holding itself out as a place of public accommodation, Moose Lodge quite ostentatiously proclaims the fact that it is not open to the public at large. Nor is it located and operated in such surroundings that, although private in name, it discharges a function or performs a service that would otherwise in all likelihood be performed by the State. In short, while Eagle was a public restaurant in a public building, Moose Lodge is a private social club in a private building.

. . . [T]he Pennsylvania Liquor Control Board plays absolutely no part in establishing or enforcing the membership or guest policies of the club that it licenses to serve liquor. There is no suggestion in this record that Pennsylvania law, either as written or as applied, discriminates against minority groups either in their right to apply for club licenses themselves or in their right to purchase and be served liquor in places of public accommodation. The only effect that the state licensing of Moose Lodge to serve liquor can be said to have on the right of any other Pennsylvanian to buy or be served liquor on premises other than those of Moose Lodge is that, for some purposes, club licenses are counted in the maximum number of licenses that may be issued in a given municipality. . . .

The District Court was at pains to point out in its opinion what it considered to be the "pervasive" nature of the regulation of private clubs by the Pennsylvania Liquor Control Board. As that court noted, an applicant for a club license must make such physical alterations in its premises as the board may require, must file a list of the names and addresses of its members and employees, and must keep extensive financial records. The board is granted the right to inspect the licensed premises at any time when patrons, guests, or members are present.

However detailed this type of regulation may be in some particulars, it cannot be said to in any way foster or encourage racial discrimination. Nor can it be said to make the State in any realistic sense a partner or even a joint venturer in the club's enterprise. The limited effect of the prohibition against obtaining additional club licenses when the maximum number of retail licenses allotted to a municipality has been issued, when considered together with the availability of liquor from hotel, restaurant, and retail licensees, falls far short of conferring upon club licensees a monopoly in the dispensing of liquor in any given municipality or in the State as a whole. We therefore hold that . . . the operation of the regulatory scheme enforced by the Pennsylvania Liquor Control Board does not sufficiently implicate the State in the discriminatory guest policies of Moose Lodge to make the latter "state action" within the ambit of the Equal Protection Clause of the Fourteenth Amendment.

. . .

JUSTICE DOUGLAS, with whom JUSTICE MARSHALL joins, dissenting.

. . .

. . . Liquor licenses in Pennsylvania, unlike driver's licenses, or marriage licenses, are not freely available to those who meet racially neutral qualifications. There is a complex quota system. . . . What the majority neglects to say is that the quota for Harrisburg, where Moose Lodge No. 107 is located, has been full for many years. No more club licenses may be issued in that city.

This state-enforced scarcity of licenses restricts the ability of blacks to obtain liquor, for liquor is commercially available only at private clubs for a significant portion of each week. Access by blacks to places that serve liquor is further limited by the fact that the state quota is filled. A group desiring to form a nondiscriminatory club which would serve blacks must purchase a license held by an existing club, which can exact a monopoly price for the transfer. The availability of such a license is speculative, at best, however, for, as Moose Lodge itself concedes, without a liquor license, a fraternal organization would be hard-pressed to survive.

Thus, the State of Pennsylvania is putting the weight of its liquor license, concededly a valued and important adjunct to a private club, behind racial discrimination.

. . .

JUSTICE BRENNAN, with whom JUSTICE MARSHALL joins, dissenting.

When Moose Lodge obtained its liquor license, the State of Pennsylvania became an active participant in the operation of the Lodge bar. Liquor licensing laws are only incidentally revenue measures; they are primarily pervasive regulatory schemes under which the State dictates and continually supervises virtually every detail of the operation of the licensee's business. Very few, if any, other licensed businesses experience such complete state involvement. Yet the Court holds that such involvement does not constitute "state action" making the Lodge's refusal to serve a guest liquor solely because of his race a violation of the

Fourteenth Amendment. The vital flaw in the Court's reasoning is its complete disregard of the fundamental value underlying the "state action" concept. . . .

The state action doctrine reflects the profound judgment that denials of equal treatment, and particularly denials on account of race or color, are singularly grave when government has or shares responsibility for them. Government is the social organ to which all in our society look for the promotion of liberty, justice, fair and equal treatment, and the setting of worthy norms and goals for social conduct. Therefore something is uniquely amiss in a society where the government, the authoritative oracle of community values, involves itself in racial discrimination. . . .

. . .

However it may deal with its licensees in exercising its great and untrammeled power over liquor traffic, the state may not discriminate against others or disregard the operation of the Equal Protection Clause of the Fourteenth Amendment as it affects personal rights. Here, the state has used its great power to license the liquor traffic in a manner which has no relation to the traffic in liquor itself, but instead permits it to be exploited in the pursuit of a discriminatory practice. . . .

III. INDIVIDUAL RIGHTS

MAJOR DEVELOPMENTS

- Supreme Court protects abortion rights
- Struggles between more liberal and more conservative religious groups replace traditional struggles between Protestants and Catholics
- Little or no protection for property or gun rights

Americans modified only slightly the constitutional priorities respecting individual rights of the New Deal and Great Society. *Roe v. Wade* (1973) vaulted family rights and rights to procreation to the top of the constitutional food chain, but liberal justices during the 1970s also maintained a fairly high wall between church and state. The justices in the late 1970s demonstrated that the contracts clause was not entirely moribund as a source for constitutional rights, but no constitutional decision maker made any effort to even partly restore pre–New Deal constitutional protections for property rights. Constitutional decision makers during the Nixon and Carter presidencies continued to ignore the Second Amendment.

A. Property

Political activists from 1969 to 1980 raised two very different challenges to the New Deal consensus that economic and social questions raised policy questions constitutionally entrusted exclusively to elected officials. Progressive advocacy groups claimed that the due process and equal protection clauses of the Fourteenth Amendment obligated states to provide certain welfare services for poorer citizens. Conservative advocacy groups claimed that environmental and other government regulations took property without compensation. Neither more progressive nor more conservative activists had much success changing the constitutional status quo during the 1970s. The Supreme Court refused to find a constitutional right to basic necessities. The freedom of contract remained moribund. The contracts clause was revived only as a marginal limit on state power. Takings clause law continued to be highly favorable to government regulation.

Divided liberals in the elected branches of government from 1969 to 1980 were more concerned with economic policy than economic rights. A broad consensus existed among most Democrats and Republicans that government was constitutionally entitled to pursue almost every regulatory policy that a reasonable person might think advanced the public good. Democrats and Republicans during these years competed over which party offered the mix of government regulations and redistributive policies that would best promote economic prosperity and alleviate poverty. No party championed measures or litigation that sought to revive the freedom of contract, the contracts clause, or substantial taking clause restrictions on government power.

Contracts

Court watchers were surprised when the Supreme Court breathed some life into the constitutional obligation to not "impair the obligation of contract." In 1974 New Jersey repealed a law that forbade the Port Authority from using bond revenues to subsidize railroads that were regularly losing money. When bondholders sued to have the original law enforced, the Supreme Court in *United States Trust Co. v. New Jersey* (1977) supported the bondholders. Justice Blackmun's majority opinion concluded that when state laws impair the obligations of government contracts, the "impairment" must be "both reasonable and necessary to serve the . . . important purposes claimed by the State." Justice Brennan's dissent accused the majority of ignoring the established "principle that lawful exercises of a State's police powers stand paramount to private rights held under contract." The next year the judicial majority imposed a constitutional limit on state power to impair the obligation of private contracts. A 5-3 majority in *Allied Structural Steel Co. v. Spannaus* (1978) struck down a Minnesota law that imposed pension obligations on businesses, even when no employees had vested rights to a pension. Laws that "impose a completely unexpected liability," Justice Stewart's majority opinion declared, are subject to strict contract clause scrutiny, particularly when the beneficiaries are a fairly narrow class of citizens.

The significance of *United States Trust Co.* and *Allied Structural Steel* was unclear at the time. Some commentators believed that a revival of judicial protection for contract and property rights was in the works as more conservatives were appointed to the federal bench. Others wondered whether these were isolated judicial decisions based on unique facts and judicial quirks. The latter turned out to be correct.

Takings

The constitutional law of takings largely remained the same during the 1970s, even as conservative public interest groups championed doctrines that required stricter judicial scrutiny. Libertarian legal scholars associated with the burgeoning law and economics movement provided intellectual foundations for constitutional attacks on many forms of government regulation. Ronald Coase, Richard Posner, and Richard Epstein insisted that the market was more efficient than government regulation and that costly regulation violated Fifth and Fourteenth Amendment rights.[21] By end of the decade several conservative political interest groups were actively lobbying and litigating for the constitutional rights of property owners. The Pacific Legal Foundation (PLF), a libertarian public interest group, played a notable role urging justices to find that many regulations took property without compensation. "Under a system where an individual's property is subject to excessive governmental restrictions," the PLF amicus brief in *Penn Central Transportation Co v. City of New York* (1978) declared,

> ownership of land constitutes an exceedingly high risk. The increasing risks incident to property ownership have the potential to make investment in land less attractive, with the ultimate result of higher development costs and higher prices imposed by those who have assumed such risks. The risk is ultimately passed on to consumers whether it be the retailer seeking commercial space in a shopping center or the individual in search of affordable housing.

Such claims fell on deaf judicial ears before Ronald Reagan became president. A 6-3 judicial majority found that no constitutional taking had occurred when New York City designated the Penn Central terminal an historic landmark and forbade the owners from making certain changes. Justice Brennan's majority opinion declared that federal courts would rarely conclude that constitutional violations had occurred when ruling on a "public program adjusting the benefits and burdens of economic life to promote the common good."

Penn Central Transportation Co. v. City of New York, 438 U.S. 104 (1978)

On August 21, 1967, the Landmark Preservation Commission of New York City designated the Grand Central Terminal as an historic landmark. The owner of an historic landmark had an obligation to keep the property in "good repair" and could not make changes to the exterior without obtaining the permission of the Landmarks Preservation Commission. In return owners of historic landmarks could obtain some exemptions from zoning laws for other properties. In 1968 the Commission refused to give the Penn Central Transportation Company permission to construct an office building on top of the Terminal. Penn Central sued, claiming that the Landmark Preservation Law took property in violation of the Fifth and Fourteenth Amendments. New York City claimed that aesthetic regulations did not take property, and, if so, the right to exemptions from other zoning laws provided reasonable compensation. A lower New York Court sided with Penn Central, but that decision was reversed by the New York Supreme Court. After the New York Court of

21. See Richard A. Posner, *Economic Analysis of Law* (Boston: Little, Brown and Co., 1973); R.H. Coase, *The Firm, the Market, and the Law* (Chicago: University of Chicago Press, 1988); Richard Epstein, *Takings: Private Property and the Power of Eminent Domain* (Cambridge, MA: Harvard University Press, 1985).

Appeals affirmed that decision. Penn Central appealed to the Supreme Court of the United States.

The Supreme Court by a 6-3 vote ruled that no compensable taking had occurred. Justice Brennan's majority opinion balanced various factors when concluding that New York City could constitutionally declare Penn Central an historical landmark. What were those factors? Why does Brennan conclude that they did not justify compensation? As was increasingly the case during the 1970s, the justices divided largely along ideological lines when considering when an unconstitutional taking had occurred. Why did this division occur in the 1970s and not earlier? Does Justice Brennan's opinion demonstrate adequate respect for property rights, or did constitutional liberals during the 1970s retreat a bit from the principles underlying property decisions in the New Deal/Great Society Era? On what grounds does Justice Rehnquist justify his ruling to reverse a decision made by elected officials, given his reluctance to do so in other areas of constitutional law? Do you see any relationship between the ideological divisions in this case and the ideological divisions that began to take shape in individual rights cases concerning religion and abortion?

JUSTICE BRENNAN delivered the opinion of the Court.

. . .

. . . [T]his Court, quite simply, has been unable to develop any "set formula" for determining when "justice and fairness" require that economic injuries caused by public action be compensated by the government, rather than remain disproportionately concentrated on a few persons. . . . Indeed, we have frequently observed that whether a particular restriction will be rendered invalid by the government's failure to pay for any losses proximately caused by it depends largely "upon the particular circumstances [in that] case." . . .

In engaging in these essentially ad hoc, factual inquiries, the Court's decisions have identified several factors that have particular significance. The economic impact of the regulation on the claimant and, particularly, the extent to which the regulation has interfered with distinct investment-backed expectations are, of course, relevant considerations. . . . So, too, is the character of the governmental action. A "taking" may more readily be found when the interference with property can be characterized as a physical invasion by government . . . than when interference arises from some public program adjusting the benefits and burdens of economic life to promote the common good.

More importantly for the present case, in instances in which a state tribunal reasonably concluded that "the health, safety, morals, or general welfare" would be promoted by prohibiting particular contemplated uses of land, this Court has upheld land-use regulations that destroyed or adversely affected recognized real property interests. . . .

. . .

. . . [T]he submission that appellants may establish a "taking" simply by showing that they have been denied the ability to exploit a property interest that they heretofore had believed was available for development is quite simply untenable. Were this the rule, this Court would have erred not only in upholding laws restricting the development of air rights, . . . but also in approving those prohibiting both the subjacent . . . and the lateral . . . development of particular parcels. "Taking" jurisprudence does not divide a single parcel into discrete segments and attempt to determine whether rights in a particular segment have been entirely abrogated. In deciding whether a particular governmental action has effected a taking, this Court focuses rather both on the character of the action and on the nature and extent of the interference with rights in the parcel as a whole. . . .

. . .

. . . [A]ppellants' repeated suggestions that they are solely burdened and unbenefited is factually inaccurate. This contention overlooks the fact that the New York City law applies to vast numbers of structures in the city in addition to the Terminal—all the structures contained in the 31 historic districts and over 400 individual landmarks, many of which are close to the Terminal. Unless we are to reject the judgment of the New York City Council that the preservation of landmarks benefits all New York citizens and all structures, both economically and by improving the quality of life in the city as a whole—which we are unwilling to do—we cannot conclude that the owners of the Terminal have in no sense been benefited by the Landmarks Law. Doubtless appellants believe they are more burdened than benefited by the law, but that must have been true, too, of the property owners in [other cases].

. . .

. . . [T]he New York City law does not interfere in any way with the present uses of the Terminal. Its designation as a landmark not only permits but contemplates that appellants may continue to use the property precisely as it has been used for the past 65 years: as a railroad terminal containing office space and concessions. So the law does not interfere with what must be regarded as Penn Central's primary expectation concerning the use of the parcel. More importantly, on this record, we must regard the New York City law as permitting Penn Central not only to profit from the Terminal but also to obtain a "reasonable return" on its investment.

. . .

On this record, we conclude that the application of New York City's Landmarks Law has not effected a "taking" of appellants' property. The restrictions imposed are substantially related to the promotion of the general welfare and not only permit reasonable beneficial use of the landmark site but also afford appellants opportunities further to enhance not only the Terminal site proper but also other properties.

JUSTICE REHNQUIST, with whom THE CHIEF JUSTICE and JUSTICE STEVENS join, dissenting.

. . . Where a relatively few individual buildings, all separated from one another, are singled out and treated differently from surrounding buildings, no . . . reciprocity exists. The cost to the property owner which results from the imposition of restrictions applicable only to his property and not that of his neighbors may be substantial—in this case, several million dollars—with no comparable reciprocal benefits. And the cost associated with landmark legislation is likely to be of a completely different order of magnitude than that which results from the imposition of normal zoning restrictions. Unlike the regime affected by the latter, the landowner is not simply prohibited from using his property for certain purposes, while allowed to use it for all other purposes. Under the historic-landmark preservation scheme adopted by New York, the property owner is under an affirmative duty to preserve his property as a landmark at his own expense. To suggest that because traditional zoning results in some limitation of use of the property zoned, the New York City landmark preservation scheme should likewise be upheld, represents the ultimate in treating as alike things which are different. The rubric of "zoning" has not yet sufficed to avoid the well-established proposition that the Fifth Amendment bars the "Government from forcing some people alone to bear public burdens which, in all fairness and justice, should be borne by the public as a whole." . . .

. . .

The Fifth Amendment provides in part: "nor shall private property be taken for public use, without just compensation." In a very literal sense, the actions of appellees violated this constitutional prohibition. Before the city of New York declared Grand Central Terminal to be a landmark, Penn Central could have used its "air rights" over the Terminal to build a multistory office building, at an apparent value of several million dollars per year. Today, the Terminal cannot be modified in any form, including the erection of additional stories, without the permission of the Landmark Preservation Commission, a permission which appellants, despite good-faith attempts, have so far been unable to obtain. Because the Taking Clause of the Fifth Amendment has not always been read literally, however, the constitutionality of appellees' actions requires a closer scrutiny of this Court's interpretation of the three key words in the Taking Clause—"property," "taken," and "just compensation."

Appellees do not dispute that valuable property rights have been destroyed. And the Court has frequently emphasized that the term "property" as used in the Taking Clause includes the entire "group of rights inhering in the citizen's [ownership]." . . .

Appellees have thus destroyed—in a literal sense, "taken"—substantial property rights of Penn Central. While the term "taken" might have been narrowly interpreted to include only physical seizures of property rights, "the construction of the phrase has not been so narrow. . . .

. . .

Appellees in response would argue that a taking only occurs where a property owner is denied all reasonable value of his property. The Court has frequently held that, even where a destruction of property rights would not otherwise constitute a taking, the inability of the owner to make a reasonable return on his property requires compensation under the Fifth Amendment. . . . But the converse is not true. A taking does not become a noncompensable exercise of police power simply because the government in its grace allows the owner to make some "reasonable" use of his property. "[I]t is the character of the invasion, not the amount of damage resulting from it, so long as the damage is substantial, that determines the question whether it is a taking." . . .

Due Process

During the 1960s and 1970s some liberal scholars and activists asserted that persons had constitutional rights to certain basic necessities. Charles Reich's "The New Property" argued that government was constitutionally obligated to provide the services that impecunious citizens needed to survive.[22] Frank Michelman claimed that persons have a constitutional right to "minimum protection against economic hazard." This "minimum protection" entails "constitutional rights to provision for certain basic ingredients of individual welfare, such as food, shelter, health care, and education."[23] Assisted significantly by federal funding, such public interest groups as the Legal Services Organization and the Center on Social Welfare Policy were able to place the rights of poor people on the agenda of the Supreme Court and win several important victories that were initially thought to put a right to basic necessities within reach.[24]

Social welfare activists who hoped that the 1970s would witness a judicial declaration that welfare was a constitutional right were disappointed. The Supreme Court ruled that poor persons had no federal constitutional right to housing, no right to welfare, and no right to anything more than a minimal education. Social welfare policy, Justice Stewart's majority opinion in *Dandridge v. Williams* (1970) claimed, was as much a matter of legislative discretion as any other social or economic policy. Justice White's majority opinion in *Lindsey v. Normet* (1972) asserted that "the assurance of adequate housing . . . is a legislative not a judicial function." The next year Justice Powell denied that education was a fundamental right. Summarizing five years of judicial decisions rejecting claims that the Constitution guaranteed basic necessities, his majority opinion in *San Antonio Independent School District v. Rodriguez* (1973) asserted, "It is not the province of this Court to create substantive constitutional rights in the name of guaranteeing equal protection of the laws."

Burger Court majorities did find that welfare recipients had some constitutional procedural rights with respect to those benefits that states granted by statute. In *Goldberg v. Kelly* (1970) Justice Brennan's majority opinion ruled that governing officials could not stop welfare payments without giving recipients a formal opportunity to demonstrate that they had a *statutory* entitlement to those benefits. Rather than assert that poor persons had a constitutional right to welfare, the litigants asserted that their statutory right under New York law was "property," which under the Fourteenth Amendment could not be taken from them without due process of law. "Welfare," Brennan agreed,

> by meeting the basic demands of subsistence, can help bring within the reach of the poor the same opportunities that are available to others to participate meaningfully in the life of the community. At the same time, welfare guards against the societal malaise that may flow from a widespread sense of unjustified frustration and insecurity. Public assistance, then, is not mere charity, but a means to "promote the general Welfare, and secure the Blessings of Liberty to ourselves and our Posterity." The same governmental interests that counsel the provision of welfare, counsel as well its uninterrupted provision to those eligible to receive it; pre-termination evidentiary hearings are indispensable to that end.

This welfare right was limited to instances in which state or local law explicitly provided benefits. By 1980 American constitutional law had clearly established that no one had a constitutional right to any government assistance.

The Burger Court narrowed the circumstances in which certain government benefits, ranging from welfare to government employment, could create property or liberty interests for due process purposes. *Arnett v. Kennedy* (1974) ruled that a police officer fired for cause had no right to a hearing before an impartial decision maker when the rules for retaining police officers did not require such a procedure. Justice Rehnquist's majority opinion stated, "Where the grant of a substantive right is inextricably intertwined with the limitations on the procedures which are to be employed in determining that right, a litigant in the position of appellee must take the bitter with the sweet." *Paul v. Davis* (1976) indicated that the Burger Court would rarely, if ever, find a constitutional property interest that was not explicitly articulated in state law. The issue in that case was whether a person was entitled to a hearing before a local police officer branded him as an "active

22. Charles Reich, "The New Property," *Yale Law Journal* 73 (1964): 733.

23. Frank I. Michelman, "Foreword: On Protecting the Poor through the Fourteenth Amendment," *Harvard Law Review* 83 (1969): 7; Frank I. Michelman, "Welfare Rights in a Constitutional Democracy," *Washington University Law Quarterly* 1979 (1979): 659.

24. See Susan E. Lawrence, *The Poor in Court* (Princeton, NJ: Princeton University Press, 1990); Martha F. Davis, *Brutal Need: Lawyers and the Welfare Rights Movement, 1960–1973* (New Haven, CT: Yale University Press, 1993).

shoplifter" in a poster sent to all local businesses. Justice Rehnquist's majority opinion ruled that no federal constitutional interests were invoked, although he did not rule out the possibility of lawsuits for defamation in state court. Past precedents, Rehnquist insisted, did not compel the Court to find that "reputation alone, apart from some more tangible interests such as employment, is either 'liberty' or 'property' by itself sufficient to invoke the procedural protection of the Due Process Clause."

Dandridge v. Williams, 397 U.S. 471 (1970)

Linda Williams was a poor mother of eight children who lived in Baltimore County, Maryland. The Maryland Department of Public Welfare provided poor families with no more than $250 a month under the Aid to Families with Dependent Children (AFDC) program. This was almost $50 less than what Maryland estimated the Williams family needed to purchase basic necessities. Williams sued Edmund Dandridge, the chairman of the Maryland State Board of Public Welfare, claiming that the state's refusal to adjust maximum grants for large families violated the equal protection clause. Dandridge responded that the state had made a reasonable decision about how to allocate scarce public funds. A local federal district court declared the maximum grant policy unconstitutional. Maryland appealed to the Supreme Court of the United States.

The Supreme Court by a 6-3 vote sustained the Maryland welfare law. Justice Stewart insisted that courts had no more business scrutinizing welfare laws than they would the maximum hour law at issue in Lochner v. New York *(1905). Is he correct? Why does Justice Marshall think that the Constitution provides a basis for treating programs providing basic necessities to poor persons differently from programs providing subsidies for local transportation? Imagine that* Dandridge *had been decided differently and that Maryland responded by abandoning all welfare. Would that have violated any of Ms. Williams's constitutional rights? Three years after* Dandridge, *the Supreme Court in* Roe v. Wade *(1973) declared that the Fourteenth Amendment protected abortion rights. Why were moderate liberals in the 1970s more willing to strike down bans on reproductive choice than restrictive welfare policies? Were these priorities implicit in the Constitution, in past precedents, or in centrist 1970 values?*

JUSTICE STEWART delivered the opinion of the Court.

. . .

. . . [H]ere we deal with state regulation in the social and economic field, not affecting freedoms guaranteed by the Bill of Rights, and claimed to violate the Fourteenth Amendment only because the regulation results in some disparity in grants of welfare payments to the largest AFDC families. For this Court to approve the invalidation of state economic or social regulation as "overreaching" would be far too reminiscent of an era when the Court thought the Fourteenth Amendment gave it power to strike down state laws "because they may be unwise, improvident, or out of harmony with a particular school of thought." . . . That era long ago passed into history. . . .

In the area of economics and social welfare, a State does not violate the Equal Protection Clause merely because the classifications made by its laws are imperfect. If the classification has some "reasonable basis," it does not offend the Constitution simply because the classification "is not made with mathematical nicety or because in practice it results in some inequality."

To be sure, the cases cited . . . enunciating this fundamental standard under the Equal Protection Clause, have in the main involved state regulation of business or industry. The administration of public welfare assistance, by contrast, involves the most basic economic needs of impoverished human beings. We recognize the dramatically real factual difference between the cited cases and this one, but we can find no basis for applying a different constitutional standard. . . . [I]t is a standard that is true to the principle that the Fourteenth Amendment gives the federal courts no power to impose upon the States their views of what constitutes wise economic or social policy.

Under this long-established meaning of the Equal Protection Clause, it is clear that the Maryland Maximum grant regulation is constitutionally valid. . . . [A] solid foundation for the regulation can be found in the State's legitimate interest in encouraging employment and in avoiding discrimination between welfare families and the families of the working poor. By combining a limit on the recipient's grant with permission to retain money earned, without reduction in the amount of the grant, Maryland provides an incentive to seek gainful employment. And by keying the maximum family AFDC grants to the minimum wage a steadily employed head of a household receives, the State maintains some semblance of an equitable balance between families on welfare and those supported by an employed breadwinner.

. . .

JUSTICE BLACK, with whom THE CHIEF JUSTICE joins, concurring....

JUSTICE HARLAN, concurring....

JUSTICE DOUGLAS, dissenting....

JUSTICE MARSHALL, whom JUSTICE BRENNAN joins, dissenting.

...

In the instant case, the only distinction between those children with respect to whom assistance is granted and those children who are denied such assistance is the size of the family into which the child permits himself to be born. The class of individuals with respect to whom payments are actually made (the first four or five eligible dependent children in a family), is grossly underinclusive in terms of the class that the AFDC program was designed to assist, namely, all needy dependent children. Such underinclusiveness manifests "a prima facie violation of the equal protection requirement of reasonable classification," compelling the State to come forward with a persuasive justification for the classification.

Under the so-called "traditional test," a classification is said to be permissible under the Equal Protection Clause unless it is "without any reasonable basis." ... On the other hand, if the classification affects a "fundamental right," then the state interest in perpetuating the classification must be "compelling" in order to be sustained....

In my view, equal protection analysis of this case is not appreciably advanced by the a priori definition of a "right," fundamental or otherwise. Rather, concentration must be placed upon the character of the classification in question, the relative importance to individuals in the class discriminated against of the governmental benefits that they do not receive, and the asserted state interests in support of the classification....

It is the individual interests here at stake that, as the Court concedes, most clearly distinguish this case from the "business regulation" equal protection cases. AFDC support to needy dependent children provides the stuff that sustains those children's lives: food, clothing, shelter. And this Court has already recognized several times that when a benefit, even a "gratuitous" benefit, is necessary to sustain life, stricter constitutional standards, both procedural and substantive, are applied to the deprivation of that benefit.

...

... [I]t should be noted that, to the extent there is a legitimate state interest in encouraging heads of AFDC households to find employment, application of the maximum grant regulation is also grossly underinclusive because it singles out and affects only large families. No reason is suggested why this particular group should be carved out for the purpose of having unusually harsh "work incentives" imposed upon them....

In the final analysis, Maryland has set up an AFDC program structured to calculate and pay the minimum standard of need to dependent children. Having set up that program, however, the State denies some of those needy children the minimum subsistence standard of living, and it does so on the wholly arbitrary basis that they happen to be members of large families. One need not speculate too far on the actual reason for the regulation, for in the early stages of this litigation the State virtually conceded that it set out to limit the total cost of the program along the path of least resistance....

...

... [I]t cannot suffice merely to invoke the spectre of the past and to recite from ... *Williamson v. Lee Optical of Oklahoma, Inc.* (1955) to decide the case. Appellees are not a gas company or an optical dispenser; they are needy dependent children and families who are discriminated against by the State. The basis of that discrimination—the classification of individuals into large and small families—is too arbitrary and too unconnected to the asserted rationale, the impact on those discriminated against—the denial of even a subsistence existence—too great, and the supposed interests served too contrived and attenuated to meet the requirements of the Constitution. In my view Maryland's maximum grant regulation is invalid under the Equal Protection Clause of the Fourteenth Amendment.

B. Religion

The constitutional politics of religious freedom took contemporary shape during the Nixon administration. Political debates over religious exercises in the public sphere and state assistance to religious organizations became struggles between more liberal and more conservative religious groups. Public debates over funding for parochial schools that once pitted Protestants against Catholics now pitted more liberal Protestants, Catholics, and Jews against more conservative Protestants, Catholics, and Jews. The very names of the leading contests in these fights reflected the changing cleavages in the constitutional politics of religion. "Protestants United for Separation of Church and State" became "Americans United for Separation of Church and State." The "Moral Majority" became a leading voice for school prayer and state assistance to church-supported schools. Those fights became increasingly politicized as the Nixon administration sought judicial rulings that would enable more public moneys to support religious activities.

While controversies over the relationship between church and state intensified, constitutional law in 1980 remained similar to constitutional law in 1969. States could burden the free exercise of religion only if they demonstrated a compelling interest. The judicial ban on nonsectarian school prayer remained the law of the land. The establishment clause forbade most, but not all, state assistance to religious schools and organizations. Newly appointed Justice William Rehnquist and, to a lesser extent, Chief Justice Warren Burger favored weakening the wall of separation between church and state, but Ford appointee John Stevens was, if anything, more committed to preventing funds from going to religious organizations than were traditional New Dealers. Liberals won most of the constitutional battles, but these wins produced a backlash that promised increased political support for conservative politicians in the future.

Establishment

The Burger Court during the 1970s rejected state and local efforts to provide financial assistance to religious schools. In *Lemon v. Kurtzman* (1971) the Supreme Court announced an important three-part test for determining when state programs that assisted religious institutions were constitutional. Chief Justice Burger's majority opinion asserted, "First, the statute must have a secular legislative purpose; second, its principal or primary effect must be one that neither advances nor inhibits religion, . . . finally, the statute must not foster 'an excessive government entanglement with religion.'" Few state laws survived this test before Ronald Reagan became president. *Lemon* struck down a Pennsylvania statute allowing local officials to reimburse private schools for teaching secular subjects, using secular textbooks, and providing other secular instructional materials. Burger's opinion asserted,

> The Pennsylvania statute has the further defect of providing state financial aid directly to the church-related school. . . . The government cash grants before us now provide no basis for predicting that comprehensive measures of surveillance and controls will not follow. In particular the government's post-audit power to inspect and evaluate a church-related school's financial records and to determine which expenditures are religious and which are secular creates an intimate and continuing relationship between church and state.

Committee for Public Education and Religious Liberty v. Nyquist (1973) declared unconstitutional a state law giving income tax credits to parents whose children attended private schools. Justice Powell's majority opinion declared, "By reimbursing parents for a portion of their tuition bill, the State seeks to relieve their financial burdens sufficiently to assure that they continue to have the option to send their children to religion-oriented schools."

Burger Court majorities rejected religious activities and symbols on public grounds. The 6-3 majority in *Stone v. Graham* (1980) declared unconstitutional a Kentucky law mandating that the Ten Commandments be posted in public law classrooms. The per curiam opinion stated:

> The Ten Commandments are undeniably a sacred text in the Jewish and Christian faiths, and no legislative recitation of a supposed secular purpose can blind us to that fact. The Commandments do not confine themselves to arguably secular matters, such as honoring one's parents, killing or murder, adultery, stealing, false witness, and covetousness. Rather, the first part of the Commandments concerns the religious duties of believers: worshipping the Lord God alone, avoiding idolatry, not using the Lord's name in vain, and observing the Sabbath Day.

Free Exercise

The Supreme Court continued to insist that states provide exemptions for religious believers from neutral state laws that burdened religious practice, unless a compelling interest justified the failure to provide an exemption. *Wisconsin v. Yoder* (1972) held that the Amish should enjoy an exemption from mandatory schooling laws. Justice Douglas dissented in part, but only because he thought that the justices had not adequately considered the free exercise rights of Amish teenagers who might want to attend public schools.

Table 9-2 Selection of U.S. Supreme Court Cases Reviewing State Actions under Establishment Clause

Case	Vote	Outcome	Decision
Everson v. Board of Education, 330 U.S. 1 (1947)	5-4	Upheld	State reimbursement for transportation expenses for children attending private religious schools does not violate establishment clause
McCollum v. Board of Education, 333 U.S. 203 (1948)	8-1	Struck down	"Release time" program allowing voluntary religion classes during school day on school grounds violates establishment clause
McGowan v. Maryland, 366 U.S. 420 (1961)	8-1	Upheld	State restriction on commercial activities on Sunday does not violate establishment clause
Engel v. Vitale, 370 U.S. 421 (1962)	6-1	Struck down	Nondenominational, government-directed school prayer violates establishment clause
Epperson v. Arkansas, 393 U.S. 97 (1968)	9-0	Struck down	State ban on the teaching of human evolution violates establishment clause
Lemon v. Kurtzman, 403 U.S. 602 (1971)	8-0	Struck down	State financial support for teacher salaries, textbooks, and secular instructional materials in parochial schools is unconstitutional
Widmar v. Vincent, 454 U.S. 263 (1981)	8-1	Struck down	University exclusion of student religious groups from facilities violates free speech, and granting equal access to religious groups would not violate establishment clause
Marsh v. Chambers, 463 U.S. 783 (1983)	6-3	Upheld	State legislative chaplain and prayer do not violate the establishment clause
Aguilar v. Felton, 473 U.S. 402 (1985)	5-4	Struck down	State program providing remedial instruction to parochial schoolchildren violates establishment clause
Lee v. Weisman, 505 U.S. 577 (1992)	5-4	Struck down	Government-directed, clergy-led prayer at high school graduation violates establishment clause
Agnostini v. Felton, 521 U.S. 203 (1997)	5-4	Upheld	Overruled *Aguilar,* holding that state program providing remedial instruction to parochial school children does not violate establishment clause
Sante Fe Independent School District v. Doe, 530 U.S. 290 (2000)	6-3	Struck down	Student-led but government-supervised prayer at high school football games violates establishment clause
Zelman v. Simmons-Harris, 536 U.S. 639 (2002)	5-4	Upheld	States may use a system of educational tuition vouchers to help parents pay for private religious schools
Van Orden v. Perry, 545 U.S. 677 (2005)	5-4	Upheld	Monument of Ten Commandments may be displayed at state capitol if message is secular

A series of cases requiring the justices to determine conscientious objector status during the Vietnam War proved more complicated. Federal law exempted from the draft "any person . . . who, by reason of religious training and belief, is conscientiously opposed to participation in war in any form." Congress did not define what constituted religious belief. In *United States v. Seeger* (1965) the justices indicated that persons seeking conscientious objector status need not believe that pacifism was commanded by a Supreme Being in the traditional sense. The test, Justice Clark claimed, was whether "a given belief . . . occupies a place in the life of its possessor parallel to that filled by the orthodox belief in God." Although Justice Clark claimed only to be interpreting the federal statute, Justice Douglas's concurring opinion suggested that any other interpretation violated the religion clauses of the First Amendment. Five years later, in *Welsh v. United States* (1970), a judicial majority granted a religious exemption to a person who declared, "I believe that human life is valuable in and of itself; in its living; therefore I will not injure or kill another human being." The federal statute, Justice Black declared, "exempts from military service all those whose consciences, spurred by deeply held moral, ethical, or religious beliefs, would give them no rest or peace if they allowed themselves to become a part of an instrument of war." Justice Harlan's concurring opinion stated that, as was the case in *Seeger,* any other interpretation would violate the religion clauses of the First Amendment. Guy Gillette was less fortunate when he claimed to be conscientiously opposed only to the Vietnam War. Justice Marshall's majority opinion in *Gillette v. United States* (1971) pointed out that the federal statute exempted only persons "opposed to participation in war in any form." He quickly brushed aside claims of religious discrimination. Marshall declared that the federal law "says that anyone who is conscientiously opposed to all war shall be relieved of military service. The specified objection must have a grounding in 'religious training and belief,' but no particular sectarian affiliation or theological position is required."[25]

Wisconsin v. Yoder, 406 U.S. 205 (1972)

Jonas Yoder and his Old Order Amish neighbors refused to enroll their children in either a public or a private high school. Enrollment, Yoder and others insisted, threatened their children's salvation and the integrity of the Amish community. Wisconsin law at this time required children to attend public or approved private schools until they were sixteen years old. Yoder was found guilty of violating this statute and fined $5. On appeal, the Supreme Court of Wisconsin ruled that the mandatory schooling statute violated the free exercise rights of religious believers. Wisconsin appealed that decision to the Supreme Court of the United States.

The Supreme Court by a 6-1 vote ruled that Yoder had a constitutional right to have his children exempted from the state mandatory education law. Chief Justice Burger's majority opinion places great weight on evidence that the Amish are a successful, law-abiding community that "rejects public welfare in any of its usual modern forms." Is Justice Douglas correct that such considerations should have no bearing on the case? Is the key issue whether the religious group has praiseworthy qualities or the extent of the harm to the community imposed by the state mandate? Is Justice Douglas correct that the children in this case had constitutional rights also in need of protection? Did you have a constitutional right to not attend the Sunday school of your parents' designation? Notice the interesting judicial alignment in Yoder. *Chief Justice Burger, generally thought of as conservative, was very supportive of the Amish claim. Justice Douglas, the most liberal member of the Court, had significant reservations. What might explain the alignment in* Yoder? *Does support for* Yoder *make one a liberal, a conservative, or something else?*

CHIEF JUSTICE BURGER delivered the opinion of the Court.

. . .

Amish objection to formal education beyond the eighth grade is firmly grounded in the[ir] central religious concepts. They object to the high school, and higher education generally, because the values they teach are in marked variance with Amish values and the Amish way of life; they view secondary school

25. Heavyweight boxing champion Muhammad Ali was the most famous conscientious objector whose case came before the Supreme Court. The justices in *Clay v. United States* (1971) ruled that the local federal draft board and district court had failed to acknowledge that his objections to war were rooted in his Black Muslim faith. Ali's experience demonstrates how persons are rarely made whole, even after winning Supreme Court cases. During the four years in which his draft status was litigated Ali was stripped of his heavyweight title and barred from boxing. Although he later regained that title, most observers believe that his skills diminished significantly during that layoff.

education as an impermissible exposure of their children to a "worldly" influence in conflict with their beliefs. The high school tends to emphasize intellectual and scientific accomplishments, self-distinction, competitiveness, worldly success, and social life with other students. Amish society emphasizes informal learning-through-doing; a life of "goodness," rather than a life of intellect; wisdom, rather than technical knowledge; community welfare, rather than competition; and separation from, rather than integration with, contemporary worldly society.

. . .

. . . [I]n order for Wisconsin to compel school attendance beyond the eighth grade against a claim that such attendance interferes with the practice of a legitimate religious belief, it must appear either that the State does not deny the free exercise of religious belief by its requirement, or that there is a state interest of sufficient magnitude to override the interest claiming protection under the Free Exercise Clause. . . .

. . . [O]nly those interests of the highest order and those not otherwise served can overbalance legitimate claims to the free exercise of religion. We can accept it as settled, therefore, that, however strong the State's interest in universal compulsory education, it is by no means absolute to the exclusion or subordination of all other interests. E.g., *Sherbert v. Verner* (1963). . . .

. . .

. . . [W]e see that the record in this case abundantly supports the claim that the traditional way of life of the Amish is not merely a matter of personal preference, but one of deep religious conviction, shared by an organized group, and intimately related to daily living. That the Old Order Amish daily life and religious practice stem from their faith is shown by the fact that it is in response to their literal interpretation of the Biblical injunction from the Epistle of Paul to the Romans, "be not conformed to this world." . . .

. . .

. . . The conclusion is inescapable that secondary schooling, by exposing Amish children to worldly influences in terms of attitudes, goals, and values contrary to beliefs, and by substantially interfering with the religious development of the Amish child and his integration into the way of life of the Amish faith community at the crucial adolescent stage of development, contravenes the basic religious tenets and practice of the Amish faith, both as to the parent and the child.

. . .

. . . [T]his case cannot be disposed of on the grounds that Wisconsin's requirement for school attendance to age 16 applies uniformly to all citizens of the State and does not, on its face, discriminate against religions or a particular religion, or that it is motivated by legitimate secular concerns. A regulation neutral on its face may, in its application, nonetheless offend the constitutional requirement for governmental neutrality if it unduly burdens the free exercise of religion. *Sherbert*. . . .

. . .

The State advances two primary arguments in support of its system of compulsory education. It notes . . . that some degree of education is necessary to prepare citizens to participate effectively and intelligently in our open political system if we are to preserve freedom and independence. Further, education prepares individuals to be self-reliant and self-sufficient participants in society. We accept these propositions.

However, the evidence adduced by the Amish in this case is persuasively to the effect that an additional one or two years of formal high school for Amish children in place of their long-established program of informal vocational education would do little to serve those interests. . . .

. . . Whatever their idiosyncrasies as seen by the majority, this record strongly shows that the Amish community has been a highly successful social unit within our society, even if apart from the conventional "mainstream." Its members are productive and very law-abiding members of society; they reject public welfare in any of its usual modern forms. . . .

. . .

Insofar as the State's claim rests on the view that a brief additional period of formal education is imperative to enable the Amish to participate effectively and intelligently in our democratic process, it must fall. The Amish alternative to formal secondary school education has enabled them to function effectively in their day-to-day life under self-imposed limitations on relations with the world, and to survive and prosper in contemporary society as a separate, sharply identifiable and highly self-sufficient community for more than 200 years in this country. In itself this is strong evidence that they are capable of fulfilling the social and political responsibilities of citizenship without compelled attendance beyond the eighth grade at the price of jeopardizing their free exercise of religious belief. . . .

. . .

Indeed it seems clear that if the State is empowered, as *parens patriae*, to "save" a child from himself or his Amish parents by requiring an additional two years of compulsory formal high school education, the State will in large measure influence, if not determine, the religious future of the child. . . . The history and culture of Western civilization reflect a strong tradition of parental concern for the nurture and upbringing of their children. This primary role of the parents in the upbringing of their children is now established beyond debate as an enduring American tradition. . . .

. . . Aided by a history of three centuries as an identifiable religious sect and a long history as a successful and self-sufficient segment of American society, the Amish in this case have convincingly demonstrated the sincerity of their religious beliefs, the interrelationship of belief with their mode of life, the vital role that belief and daily conduct play in the continued survival of Old Order Amish communities and their religious organization, and the hazards presented by the State's enforcement of a statute generally valid as to others. Beyond this, they have carried the even more difficult burden of demonstrating the adequacy of their alternative mode of continuing informal vocational education in terms of precisely those overall interests that the State advances in support of its program of compulsory high school education. In light of this convincing showing, one that probably few other religious groups or sects could make, and weighing the minimal difference between what the State would require and what the Amish already accept, it was incumbent on the State to show with more particularity how its admittedly strong interest in compulsory education would be adversely affected by granting an exemption to the Amish. *Sherbert*. . . .

. . .

JUSTICE POWELL and JUSTICE REHNQUIST took no part in the consideration or decision of this case.

JUSTICE STEWART, with whom JUSTICE BRENNAN joins, concurring. . . .

JUSTICE WHITE, with whom JUSTICE BRENNAN and JUSTICE STEWART join, concurring.

. . .

In the present case, the State is not concerned with the maintenance of an educational system as an end in itself, it is rather attempting to nurture and develop the human potential of its children, whether Amish or non-Amish: to expand their knowledge, broaden their sensibilities, kindle their imagination, foster a spirit of free inquiry, and increase their human understanding and tolerance. It is possible that most Amish children will wish to continue living the rural life of their parents, in which case their training at home will adequately equip them for their future role. Others, however, may wish to become nuclear physicists, ballet dancers, computer programmers, or historians, and for these occupations, formal training will be necessary. There is evidence in the record that many children desert the Amish faith when they come of age. A State has a legitimate interest not only in seeking to develop the latent talents of its children but also in seeking to prepare them for the life style that they may later choose, or at least to provide them with an option other than the life they have led in the past. In the circumstances of this case, although the question is close, I am unable to say that the State has demonstrated that Amish children who leave school in the eighth grade will be intellectually stultified or unable to acquire new academic skills later. The statutory minimum school attendance age set by the State is, after all, only 16.

. . .

JUSTICE DOUGLAS, dissenting in part

It is the future of the student, not the future of the parents, that is imperiled by today's decision. If a parent keeps his child out of school beyond the grade school, then the child will be forever barred from entry into the new and amazing world of diversity that we have today. The child may decide that that is the preferred course, or he may rebel. It is the student's judgment, not his parents', that is essential if we are to give full meaning to what we have said about the Bill of Rights and of the right of students to be masters of their own destiny. If he is harnessed to the Amish way of life by those in authority over him and if his education is truncated, his entire life may be stunted and deformed. The child, therefore, should be given an opportunity to be heard before the State gives the exemption which we honor today.

. . .

I think the emphasis of the Court on the "law and order" record of this Amish group of people is quite irrelevant. A religion is a religion irrespective of what the misdemeanor or felony records of its members might be. I am not at all sure how the Catholics, Episcopalians, the Baptists, Jehovah's Witnesses, the

Unitarians, and my own Presbyterians would make out if subjected to such a test. . . . [T]he Amish, whether with a high or low criminal record, certainly qualify by all historic standards as a religion within the meaning of the First Amendment.

C. Guns

The constitutional politics of the right to bear arms changed more than the constitutional law of the Second Amendment. The same legal principles that governed federal and state rights to bear arms during the New Deal/Great Society Era remained in force. Constitutional decision makers maintained that the right to bear arms either referred to the militia or was subject to reasonable regulation. This consensus, however, began to fray. As demands for gun control increased, opponents of regulation began articulating possible constitutional limits on state and federal crime control legislation.

In the wake of several political assassinations and inner-city riots, gun control gained a larger place on the national agenda during the Nixon and Carter presidencies. Initially both major political parties supported regulation. Democrats in 1968 boasted that "Democratic leadership [had] secured the enactment of a new gun control law as a step toward putting the weapons of wanton violence beyond the reach of criminal and irresponsible hands." Republicans called for "enactment of legislation to control indiscriminate availability of firearms, safeguarding the right of responsible citizens to collect, own and use firearms for legitimate purposes, retaining primary responsibility at the state level, with such federal laws as necessary to better enable the states to meet their responsibilities." After the Black Panthers staged a protest by carrying shotguns into the California state capitol, Governor Ronald Reagan signed a state law banning individuals from carrying loaded weapons in a city. Reagan emphasized that he was against any "restrictive gun law" but that this weapons ban would be welcomed by any "true sportsman or gun lover."[26]

Eight years later, both parties were more supportive of gun rights. Republicans in 1976 asserted, "We support the right of citizens to keep and bear arms. We oppose federal registration of firearms. Mandatory sentences for crimes committed with a lethal weapon are the only effective solution to this problem." Democrats adopted a platform combining commitments to regulation and rights:

> Handguns simplify and intensify violent crime. Ways must be found to curtail the availability of these weapons. The Democratic Party must provide the leadership for a coordinated federal and state effort to strengthen the presently inadequate controls over the manufacture, assembly, distribution and possession of handguns and to ban Saturday night specials.
>
> The Democratic Party, however, affirms the right of sportsmen to possess guns for purely hunting and target-shooting purposes.

Both parties were responding to important changes in the broader political environment. Public opinion polls taken during the 1970s showed increased support for tougher sentences on criminals who used guns and less support for gun control. Powerful interests began aggressively promoting the constitutional right to bear arms. Political activists committed to fighting for broad Second Amendment rights seized control of the National Rifle Association (NRA) from moderates who had historically been willing to accept some gun control measures. This new generation of NRA leadership saw their role as championing "the political, civil and inalienable rights of the American people to keep and bear arms as a common law and Constitutional right both of the individual citizen and of the collective militia."[27]

This increased political support for Second Amendment rights did not immediately increase legal support for Second Amendment rights. The Supreme Court had no occasion from 1969 until 1980 to revisit past precedents. The overwhelming number of lower federal and state court decisions held that constitutional gun rights were restricted to the militia or subject to reasonable state regulation. The Eighth Circuit in *United States v. Synnes* (1971) quickly disposed of an argument that the firearms restrictions in the Omnibus Crime Control and Safe Street Act of 1968 violated the Second Amendment. "While the Court in [*United States*

26. "Reagan Signs Curb on Loaded Weapons," *New York Times* (July 29, 1967), 16.

27. Reva B. Siegel, "Dead or Alive: Originalism as Popular Constitutionalism in *Heller*," *Harvard Law Review* 122 (2008): 211. This paragraph relies heavily on Siegel's paper.

v.] *Miller* (1939) dealt with the prohibited possession of a sawed-off shotgun," Judge Heaney wrote,

> the reasoning and conclusion of that case has carried forward to other federal gun legislation. . . . Although [the Omnibus Crime Control Act] is the broadest federal gun legislation to date, we see no conflict between it and the Second Amendment since there is no showing that prohibiting possession of firearms by felons obstructs the maintenance of a "well regulated militia."[28]

Gun rights activists did break a long losing streak when the Court of Appeals of New Mexico in *City of Las Vegas v. Moberg* (1971) declared unconstitutional a local ordinance that forbade persons from carrying "deadly weapons, concealed or otherwise." While asserting that bans on concealed weapons "do not deprive citizens of the right to bear arms," a unanimous tribunal insisted that a complete prohibition "den[ied] the people the constitutionally guaranteed right to bear arms."[29] Both the highest courts in Kansas and Colorado declared similar laws unconstitutional.[30] Other state judiciaries did not adopt the principles of these decisions. When sustaining a state law forbidding persons from carrying pistols, the Texas Court of Criminal Appeals declared in *Collins v. State* (TX 1973),

> Art. 483, . . . which makes it unlawful to "carry on or about his person . . . any pistol . . ." is not violative of the constitutional right of every citizen to keep and bear arms in the lawful defense of himself or the state, the Legislature having the power by law to enact such law with a view to prevent crime.[31]

With the exception of total bans on carrying weapons, no other constitutional attack on state gun control laws between 1969 and 1980 was successful.[32]

28. *United States v. Synnes*, 438 F.2d 764 (8th Cir. 1971).

29. *City of Las Vegas v. Moberg*, 82 N.M. 626 (N.M. App. 1971).

30. See *City of Lakewood v. Pillow*, 501 P.2d 744 (1972); *City of Junction City v. Mevis*, 601 P.2d 1145 (1979).

31. *Collins v. State*, S.W.2d 876 (1973)

32. See Adam Winkler, "Scrutinizing the Second Amendment," *Michigan Law Review* 105 (2007): 683.

D. Personal Freedom and Public Morality

The 1970s witnessed the intensification and partial restructuring of the culture wars in American constitutional politics. Nineteenth-century culture wars were often fought between Catholics and Protestants and centered on such issues as Prohibition and Protestant religious practices in public schools. During the twentieth century, some cultural issues, most notably temperance, were largely resolved, while new cultural divides emerged. *Roe v. Wade* (1973), the decision striking down bans on abortion in forty-six states, accelerated political struggles over gender roles, the sexual revolution, and morals legislation. Over time, Republicans became committed to a pro-life policy, stating in 1976, "The Republican Party favors a continuance of the public dialogue on abortion and supports the efforts of those who seek enactment of a constitutional amendment to restore protection of the right to life for unborn children." Democrats became the party committed to pro-choice policies, declaring in 1976, "We fully recognize the religious and ethical nature of the concerns which many Americans have on the subject of abortion. We feel, however, that it is undesirable to attempt to amend the U.S. Constitution to overturn the Supreme Court decision in this area." Intense debates over abortion and related policies took place in both the national and state legislatures. New interest groups emerged that reshaped constitutional understandings about the place of abortion and the role of courts in the American constitutional order. As Figure 9-2 indicates, general public opinion has been consistently supportive of abortion rights with some restrictions, but partisan polarization on this issue has increased since the *Roe* decision.

The Supreme Court ignited a constitutional firestorm when ruling in *Roe* that the "right of privacy" first announced in *Griswold v. Connecticut* (1965) "is broad enough to encompass a woman's decision whether or not to terminate her pregnancy." The judicial majority in *Roe* divided pregnancy into three trimesters. States could not restrict abortion at all in the first trimester. Second-trimester restrictions were constitutional only if they promoted maternal health. During the third trimester a state could ban abortion, as long as such bans included a maternal health exception.

During the following years the justices considered various restrictions on abortion and birth control on almost an annual basis. Every funding restriction was

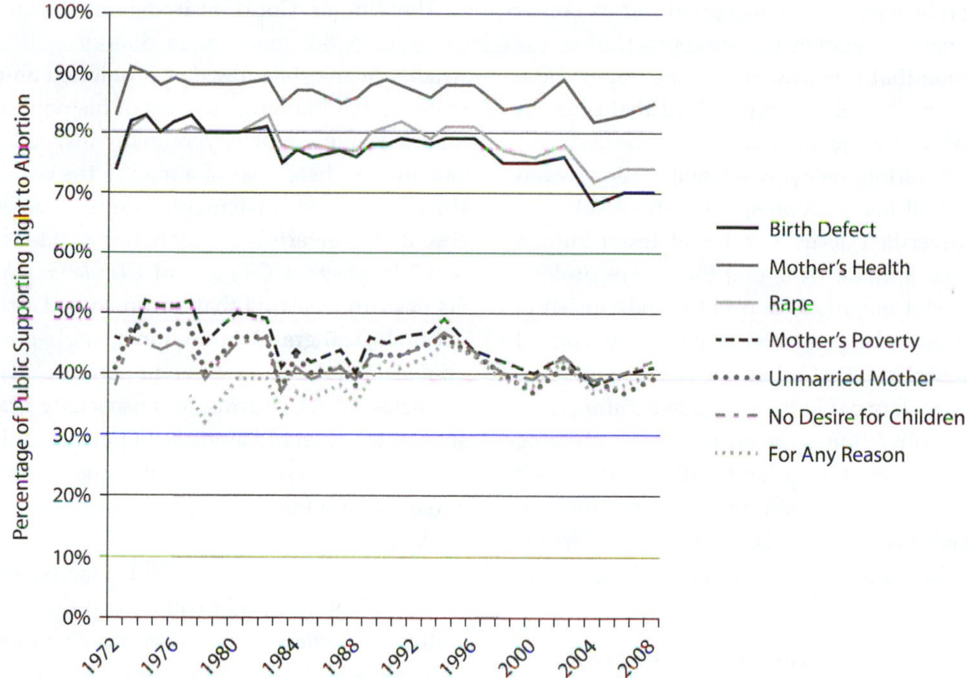

Figure 9-2 Public Support for Abortion Rights, 1972–2008
Source: General Social Survey

sustained. "The financial constraints that restrict an indigent woman's ability to enjoy the full range of constitutionally protected freedom of choice," Justice Stewart wrote in *Harris v. McRae* (1980), "are the product not of governmental restrictions on access to abortions, but rather of her indigency." Almost every other restriction on abortion and birth control was declared unconstitutional. "'Compelling' is . . . the key word," Justice Brennan declared in *Carey v. Population Services International* (1975) when declaring unconstitutional a law prohibiting persons from giving contraception to teenagers. In his view, which was adopted by the judicial majority in the years immediately after *Roe*, "where a decision as fundamental as that of whether to bear or beget a child is involved, regulations imposing a burden on it may be justified only by compelling state interests, and must be narrowly drawn to express only those interests."

Roe contributed to two important changes in constitutional politics. During the 1950s and 1960s abortion reformers were most often associated with public health organizations or organizations committed to limiting population growth. Proponents of reproductive rights during the Great Society typically condemned policies that denied poorer Americans access to birth control and abortion services that were readily obtainable by more affluent Americans. During the late 1960s and 1970s women's groups became the leading champion of abortion rights. The National Abortion Rights Action League (NARAL) emphasized that "women cannot take advantage of opportunities . . . if they cannot control their fertility."[33] Pro-life activism also changed shape during the 1970s. Before *Roe*, opposition to abortion was led largely by Catholic organizations. During the 1970s Catholics joined forces with conservative Protestants to form powerful interest groups dedicated to promoting a conservative understanding of constitutional family rights. The National Right to Life Committee, originally a Catholic organization, became nonsectarian and assumed a role as the leading political force for abortion restrictions.

Supreme Court decisions made clear that the justices were protecting liberal privacy and autonomy rights, not merely striking down laws that in practice discriminated against the poor or persons of color. Standing

33. Mary Ziegler, "The Framing of a Right to Choose: *Roe v. Wade* and the Changing Debate on Abortion Law," *Law and History Review* 27 (2009): 313, 315.

alone, *Roe* might have been conceptualized as securing less fortunate Americans the same practical access to legal abortion that was available to the upper class. The lawyers for "Jane Roe" emphasized that point in oral argument, and the justices seemed concerned with equality issues during their private deliberations, even though the actual *Roe* opinion spoke only of substantive right. Nevertheless, in a series of lesser-known cases, the justices made clear that they were protecting rights against majorities and not merely insisting that poorer persons be given access to the birth control and abortion services that most doctors provided for more affluent private patients. *Eisenstadt v. Baird* (1972) overturned a conviction of a birth-control advocate who publicly gave contraception to college students.[34] Justice Brennan's majority opinion found no constitutional difference between the rights of married persons at stake in *Griswold* and the issue before the Court in *Eisenstadt*.

> It is true that in *Griswold* the right of privacy in question inhered in the marital relationship. Yet the marital couple is not an independent entity with a mind and heart of its own, but an association of two individuals each with a separate intellectual and emotional makeup. If the right of privacy means anything, it is the right of the individual, married or single, to be free from unwarranted governmental intrusion into matters so fundamentally affecting a person as the decision whether to bear or beget a child.

In *Zablocki v. Redhail* (1978) an 8-1 judicial majority struck down a Wisconsin law requiring persons who had outstanding child support obligations to obtain judicial approval before being allowed to marry. Justice Marshall's majority opinion stated, "It would make little sense to recognize a right of privacy with respect to other matters of family life and not with respect to the decision to enter the relationship that is the foundation of the family in our society." Over the lone dissent of Justice Black, the Supreme Court in *Boddie v. Connecticut* (1971) ruled that state courts were obligated to waive fees when poor persons sought divorce.

The Burger Court also defended rights to rear children. A 5-2 majority in *Stanley v. Illinois* (1972) struck down a state law that prohibited an unmarried father from obtaining custody of his natural children. Justice White's majority opinion insisted, "The private interest here, that of a man in the children he has sired and raised, undeniably warrants deference and, absent a powerful countervailing interest, protection." In *Moore v. City of East Cleveland, Ohio* (1977) a 5-4 majority declared that a woman had a right to rear her biological grandchildren in a single-family household, even if they had different parents. "The tradition of uncles, aunts, cousins, and especially grandparents sharing a household along with parents and children," Justice Powell wrote, "has roots equally venerable and equally deserving of constitutional recognition" as the nuclear family.

This judicial solicitude for marriage and child rearing did not extend to other forms of intimacy. The justices in *Hollenbaugh v. Carnegie Free Library* (1978) let stand a lower court opinion permitting local officials to discharge a librarian and a janitor who were having an adulterous affair. The proverbial "ménage à trois" enjoyed no constitutional protection. "Once a married couple admits strangers as onlookers," the Court of Appeals for the Fourth Circuit in *Lovisi v. Slayton* (1976) stated, "federal protection of privacy dissolves."[35] Gay rights barely registered on the judicial docket. Several lower federal court decisions sustained state bans on homosexual activities. A federal district judge in *Doe v. Commonwealth's Attorney for City of Richmond* (1975) dismissed a claim that homosexual intimacy enjoyed constitutional protection, noting that privacy rights were prohibitions against "trespasses upon the privacy of the incidents of marriage, upon the sanctity of the home, or upon the nurture of family life."[36] State courts routinely dismissed claims about same-sex marriage. "Marriage," the Ohio Supreme Court declared in *Irwin v. Lupardus* (OH 1980), "is by definition a heterosexual relationship which cannot exist between persons of the same sex."[37]

---

34. William (Bill) Baird was a leading proponent of birth control and abortion rights during the 1960s and 1970s. He frequently publicly violated laws against providing such services to minors. For this reason he was a named party to many cases on these matters in this era.

35. *Lovisi v. Slayton*, 535 F.2d 349 (1976).

36. *Doe v. Commonwealth's Attorney for City of Richmond*, 403 F. Supp. 1199 (E.D. Va. 1975).

37. *Irwin v. Lupardus*, 1980 WL 355015 (Ohio App., 8 Dist., 1980).

Illustration 9-1 Alternative to *Roe v. Wade*

Source: Paul Conrad, "Alternative to *Roe v. Wade*," *Los Angeles Times*, November 21, 1988, II5. © Copyright, Paul Conrad Estate.

Abortion

Roe v. Wade, 410 U.S. 113 (1973)

Norma McCorvey was a young unmarried woman who claimed that she became pregnant after being raped. McCorvey sought an abortion, but Texas law at the time permitted pregnancies to be terminated only for the "purpose of saving the life of the mother." Using the pseudonym Jane Roe, McCorvey sought an injunction against Henry Wade, the state attorney for Dallas County, Texas, that would forbid him from enforcing the state laws against abortion on the ground that they were unconstitutional. A three-judge panel declared the Texas law void for vagueness. Texas appealed to the Supreme Court of the United States.

The Supreme Court by a 7-2 vote ruled the Texas ban on abortion unconstitutional. Justice Blackmun's majority opinion maintained that the right of privacy discussed in Griswold v. Connecticut *(1965) encompassed the right to terminate a pregnancy. The majority opinions in* Roe *assume that the crucial question is whether the fetus is a person. Is this correct? States may ban animal sacrifices, even though no one thinks dogs are protected by the Fourteenth Amendment. Conversely, no state requires people to donate kidneys to needy persons. Is either of these analogies helpful in thinking about abortion? What is the source of the constitutional right in the opinions that follow? Does* Roe *follow from* Griswold *as easily as Justice Stewart suggests? Might* Griswold *be right and* Roe *wrong? On what logic? Justice Blackmun, who in the*

1950s served as resident counsel for the Mayo Clinic in Rochester, Minnesota, divides pregnancy into trimesters. What is the significance of the trimester system? Does this system have sound constitutional roots, or is the trimester system further proof that Roe *is illegitimate judicial legislation?*

In Doe v. Bolton *(1973), a companion case to* Roe v. Wade, *the Supreme Court considered Georgia laws that limited abortion to circumstances involving a serious health threat to the mother, required the woman seeking an abortion to be a Georgia resident, mandated that three doctors certify that the reason for the abortion was legitimate, and required that the abortion be performed in a hospital. These provisions were typical of abortion reform laws passed during the 1960s.All were declared unconstitutional by the same 7-2 majority. Justice Blackmum's majority opinion declared, "The woman's right to receive medical care in accordance with her licensed physician's best judgment and the physician's right to administer it are substantially limited by this statutorily imposed overview."*

JUSTICE BLACKMUN delivered the opinion of the Court.

...

Three reasons have been advanced to explain historically the enactment of criminal abortion laws in the 19th century and to justify their continued existence.

It has been argued occasionally that these laws were the product of a Victorian social concern to discourage illicit sexual conduct. Texas, however, does not advance this justification in the present case, and it appears that no court or commentator has taken the argument seriously....

A second reason is concerned with abortion as a medical procedure. When most criminal abortion laws were first enacted, the procedure was a hazardous one for the woman.... Thus, it has been argued that a State's real concern in enacting a criminal abortion law was to protect the pregnant woman, that is, to restrain her from submitting to a procedure that placed her life in serious jeopardy.

Modern medical techniques have altered this situation.... Mortality rates for women undergoing early abortions, where the procedure is legal, appear to be as low as or lower than the rates for normal childbirth. Consequently, any interest of the State in protecting the woman from an inherently hazardous procedure, except when it would be equally dangerous for her to forgo it, has largely disappeared....

The third reason is the State's interest—some phrase it in terms of duty—in protecting prenatal life. Some of the argument for this justification rests on the theory that a new human life is present from the moment of conception. The State's interest and general obligation to protect life then extends, it is argued, to prenatal life. Only when the life of the pregnant mother herself is at stake, balanced against the life she carries within her, should the interest of the embryo or fetus not prevail. Logically, of course, a legitimate state interest in this area need not stand or fall on acceptance of the belief that life begins at conception or at some other point prior to life birth. In assessing the State's interest, recognition may be given to the less rigid claim that as long as at least potential life is involved, the State may assert interests beyond the protection of the pregnant woman alone.

...

The Constitution does not explicitly mention any right of privacy. In a line of decisions, however, ... the Court has recognized that a right of personal privacy, or a guarantee of certain areas or zones of privacy, does exist under the Constitution.... These decisions make it clear that only personal rights that can be deemed "fundamental" or "implicit in the concept of ordered liberty," *Palko v. Connecticut* (1937), are included in this guarantee of personal privacy. They also make it clear that the right has some extension to activities relating to marriage, procreation, contraception, family relationships, and child rearing and education. This right of privacy, whether it be founded in the Fourteenth Amendment's concept of personal liberty and restrictions upon state action, as we feel it is, or in the Ninth Amendment's reservation of rights to the people, is broad enough to encompass a woman's decision whether or not to terminate her pregnancy. The detriment that the State would impose upon the pregnant woman by denying this choice altogether is apparent. Specific and direct harm medically diagnosable even in early pregnancy may be involved. Maternity, or additional offspring, may force upon the woman a distressful life and future. Psychological harm may be imminent. Mental and physical health may be taxed by child care. There is also the distress, for all concerned, associated with the unwanted child, and there is the problem of bringing a child into a family already unable, psychologically and otherwise, to care for it. In other cases, as in this one, the additional difficulties and continuing stigma of unwed motherhood may be involved.

All these are factors the woman and her responsible physician necessarily will consider in consultation.

On the basis of elements such as these, appellant and some amici argue that the woman's right is absolute and that she is entitled to terminate her pregnancy at whatever time, in whatever way, and for whatever reason she alone chooses. With this we do not agree. . . . [A] State may properly assert important interests in safeguarding health, in maintaining medical standards, and in protecting potential life. At some point in pregnancy, these respective interests become sufficiently compelling to sustain regulation of the factors that govern the abortion decision. . . .

. . .

Where certain "fundamental rights" are involved, the Court has held that regulation limiting these rights may be justified only by a "compelling state interest," . . . and that legislative enactments must be narrowly drawn to express only the legitimate state interests at stake. . . .

. . .

The appellee and certain amici argue that the fetus is a "person" within the language and meaning of the Fourteenth Amendment. . . . If this suggestion of personhood is established, the appellant's case, of course, collapses, for the fetus' right to life would then be guaranteed specifically by the Amendment. . . .

The Constitution does not define "person" in so many words. . . . But in nearly all [constitutional references to "person" in] these instances, the use of the word is such that it has application only postnatally. None indicates, with any assurance, that it has any possible prenatal application.

All this, together with our observation that throughout the major portion of the 19th century prevailing legal abortion practices were far freer than they are today, persuades us that the word "person," as used in the Fourteenth Amendment, does not include the unborn.

. . .

Texas urges that, apart from the Fourteenth Amendment, life begins at conception and is present throughout pregnancy, and that, therefore, the State has a compelling interest in protecting that life from and after conception. We need not resolve the difficult question of when life begins. When those trained in the respective disciplines of medicine, philosophy, and theology are unable to arrive at any consensus, the judiciary, at this point in the development of man's knowledge, is not in a position to speculate as to the answer.

. . .

With respect to the State's important and legitimate interest in the health of the mother, the "compelling" point, in the light of present medical knowledge, is at approximately the end of the first trimester. This is so because of the now-established medical fact . . . that until the end of the first trimester mortality in abortion may be less than mortality in normal childbirth. It follows that, from and after this point, a State may regulate the abortion procedure to the extent that the regulation reasonably relates to the preservation and protection of maternal health. . . .

With respect to the State's important and legitimate interest in potential life, the "compelling" point is at viability. This is so because the fetus then presumably has the capability of meaningful life outside the mother's womb. State regulation protective of fetal life after viability thus has both logical and biological justifications. If the State is interested in protecting fetal life after viability, it may go so far as to proscribe abortion during that period, except when it is necessary to preserve the life or health of the mother.

. . .

JUSTICE STEWART, concurring.

. . . *Griswold* stands as one in a long line of . . . cases decided under the doctrine of substantive due process, and I now accept it as such.

. . .

Several decisions of this Court make clear that freedom of personal choice in matters of marriage and family life is one of the liberties protected by the Due Process Clause of the Fourteenth Amendment. *Loving v. Virginia* (1967) . . . ; *Griswold v. Connecticut* (1965) . . . ; *Pierce v. Society of Sister* (1925) . . . ; *Meyer v. Nebraska* (1923). . . . As recently as last Term, in *Eisenstadt v. Baird* (1972), we recognized "the right of the individual, married or single, to be free from unwarranted governmental intrusion into matters so fundamentally affecting a person as the decision whether to bear or beget a child." That right necessarily includes the right of a woman to decide whether or not to terminate her pregnancy. . . .

. . .

JUSTICE DOUGLAS, concurring

. . .

The Ninth Amendment obviously does not create federally enforceable rights. It merely says, "The enumeration in the Constitution, of certain rights, shall not be construed to deny or disparage others retained by the people." But a catalogue of these rights includes customary, traditional, and time-honored rights, amenities, privileges, and immunities that come within the sweep of "the Blessings of Liberty" mentioned in the preamble to the Constitution. Many of them, in my view, come within the meaning of the term "liberty" as used in the Fourteenth Amendment.

First is the autonomous control over the development and expression of one's intellect, interests, tastes, and personality.

. . .

Second is freedom of choice in the basic decisions of one's life respecting marriage, divorce, procreation, contraception, and the education and upbringing of children.

. . .

Third is the freedom to care for one's health and person, freedom from bodily restraint or compulsion, freedom to walk, stroll, or loaf.

. . .

. . . The "liberty" of the mother, though rooted as it is in the Constitution, may be qualified by the State. . . . But where fundamental personal rights and liberties are involved, the corrective legislation must be "narrowly drawn to prevent the supposed evil." . . .

. . .

The right to seek advice on one's health and the right to place reliance on the physician of one's choice are basic to Fourteenth Amendment values. We deal with fundamental rights and liberties, which, as already noted, can be contained or controlled only by discretely drawn legislation that preserves the "liberty" and regulates only those phases of the problem of compelling legislative concern. The imposition by the State of group controls over the physician-patient relationship is not made on any medical procedure apart from abortion, no matter how dangerous the medical step may be. The oversight imposed on the physician and patient in abortion cases denies them their "liberty," viz., their right of privacy, without any compelling, discernible state interest.

. . .

CHIEF JUSTICE BURGER, concurring.

. . .

I do not read the Court's holdings today as having the sweeping consequences attributed to them by the dissenting Justices; the dissenting views discount the reality that the vast majority of physicians observe the standards of their profession, and act only on the basis of carefully deliberated medical judgments relating to life and health. Plainly, the Court today rejects any claim that the Constitution requires abortions on demand.

JUSTICE WHITE, with whom JUSTICE REHNQUIST joins, dissenting.

. . .

With all due respect, I dissent. I find nothing in the language or history of the Constitution to support the Court's judgments. The Court simply fashions and announces a new constitutional right for pregnant women and, with scarcely any reason or authority for its action, invests that right with sufficient substance to override most existing state abortion statutes. The upshot is that the people and the legislatures of the 50 States are constitutionally disentitled to weigh the relative importance of the continued existence and development of the fetus, on the one hand, against a spectrum of possible impacts on the mother, on the other hand. As an exercise of raw judicial power, the Court perhaps has authority to do what it does today; but in my view its judgment is an improvident and extravagant exercise of the power of judicial review that the Constitution extends to this Court.

The Court apparently values the convenience of the pregnant woman more than the continued existence and development of the life or potential life that she carries. Whether or not I might agree with that marshaling of values, I can in no event join the Court's judgment because I find no constitutional warrant for imposing such an order of priorities on the people and legislatures of the States. In a sensitive area such as this, involving as it does issues over which reasonable men may easily and heatedly differ, I cannot accept the Court's exercise of its clear power of choice by interposing a constitutional barrier to state efforts to protect human life and by investing women and doctors with the constitutionally protected right to exterminate it. This issue, for the most part, should be left with the people and to the political processes the people have devised to govern their affairs.

. . .

JUSTICE REHNQUIST, dissenting.

. . .

If the Court means by the term "privacy" no more than that the claim of a person to be free from unwanted state regulation of consensual transactions may be a form of "liberty" protected by the Fourteenth Amendment, there is no doubt that similar claims have been upheld in our earlier decisions on the basis of that liberty. . . . The test traditionally applied in the area of social and economic legislation is whether or not a law such as that challenged has a rational relation to a valid state objective. *Williamson v. Lee Optical Co.* (1955). . . . The Due Process Clause of the Fourteenth Amendment undoubtedly does place a limit, albeit a broad one, on legislative power to enact laws such as this. If the Texas statute were to prohibit an abortion even where the mother's life is in jeopardy, I have little doubt that such a statute would lack a rational relation to a valid state objective. . . . But the Court's sweeping invalidation of any restrictions on abortion during the first trimester is impossible to justify under that standard, and the conscious weighing of competing factors that the Court's opinion apparently substitutes for the established test is far more appropriate to a legislative judgment than to a judicial one.

. . .

The decision here to break pregnancy into three distinct terms and to outline the permissible restrictions the State may impose in each one, for example, partakes more of judicial legislation than it does of a determination of the intent of the drafters of the Fourteenth Amendment.

The fact that a majority of the States reflecting, after all the majority sentiment in those States, have had restrictions on abortions for at least a century is a strong indication, it seems to me, that the asserted right to an abortion is not "so rooted in the traditions and conscience of our people as to be ranked as fundamental." . . .

To reach its result, the Court necessarily has had to find within the scope of the Fourteenth Amendment a right that was apparently completely unknown to the drafters of the Amendment. As early as 1821, the first state law dealing directly with abortion was enacted by the Connecticut Legislature. . . . By the time of the adoption of the Fourteenth Amendment in 1868, there were at least 36 laws enacted by state or territorial legislatures limiting abortion. . . .

There apparently was no question concerning the validity of this provision or of any of the other state statutes when the Fourteenth Amendment was adopted. The only conclusion possible from this history is that the drafters did not intend to have the Fourteenth Amendment withdraw from the States the power to legislate with respect to this matter.

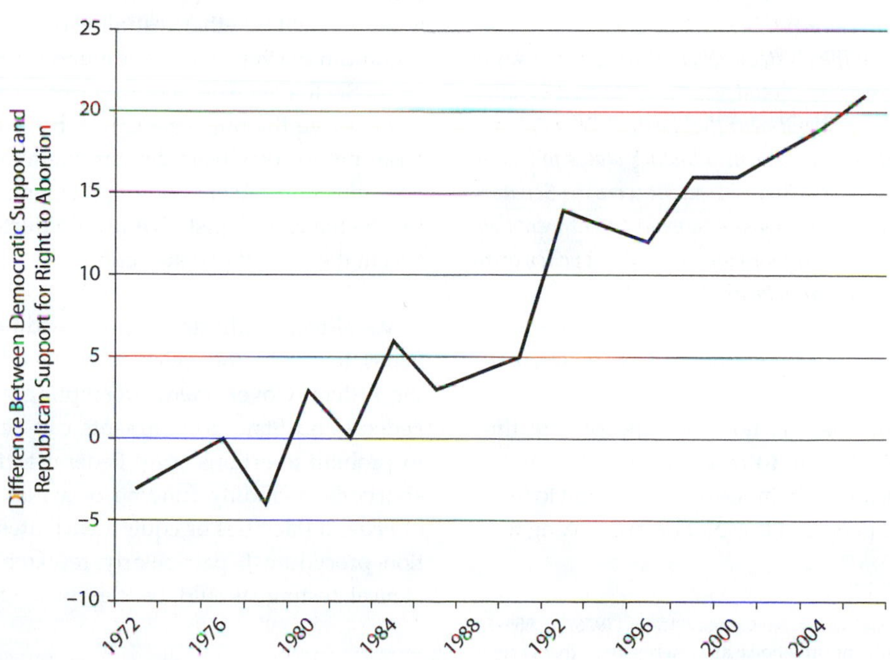

Figure 9-3 Partisan Divergence in Public Support for Abortion Rights, 1972–2008

Source: American National Election Studies.

Debate over the Human Life Amendment (1976)[38]

Opponents of legal abortion immediately sought constitutional amendments that would overturn Roe v. Wade *(1973). The Human Life Amendment was the most popular effort. That proposal asserted that genetic humans had a right to life from conception, fertilization, or implantation. Given that the Supreme Court in* Roe *emphasized that the unborn were not constitutional persons under the Fourteenth Amendment, such an amendment would undercut an important foundation of the decision declaring abortion a fundamental right.*[39] *Senator Jesse Helms of North Carolina in 1976 proposed the most popular version of the Human Rights Amendment:*

> *SECTION 1. With respect to the right of life guaranteed in this Constitution, every human being subject to the jurisdiction of the United States, or of any State, shall be deemed, from the moment of fertilization, to be a person and entitled to the right of life.*
>
> *SECTION 2. Congress and the several States shall have concurrent power to enforce this article by appropriate legislation.*

The Senate Subcommittee on Constitutional Amendments rejected this proposal by a 5-2 vote. The Senate rejected by a 47-40 vote Senator Helms's motion to have a full debate on the Human Life Amendment.

Consider the pro-life strategy when reading the excerpts from that Senate debate. Would you have advised Senator Helms to propose the amendment that he did? Why not propose a constitutional amendment allowing states to choose whether to ban abortions? To what extent were the Senators trying to make abortion policy and to what extent were they trying to foist responsibility for making abortion policy on to the states or the federal judiciary?

SENATOR JESSE HELMS (Republican, North Carolina)

. . .

Mr. President, there is no more appropriate time than now for the Senate to take the initiative, and to exercise moral leadership in restoring the right to life of the unborn. The people of this Nation are looking to us for leadership because they recognize the simple fact that only Congress—not the President, not the several States, and certainly not the Federal judiciary—can put an end to this wholesale destruction of human life.

The main thrust of any human life amendment must be to insure that all human beings enjoy the protection of the right to life. This can be done by insuring that all human beings are considered "persons" under the protection of the fifth and fourth[40] amendments. . . .

. . .

It is most important . . . that the beginning of life, and therefore, the beginning of the constitutional protection of that life, be defined with precision and clarity. Our scientific knowledge today is sufficient to provide such a definition; and the language must not be so loose or general that the way is opened for arguments that the period of protected life should be shortened for the sake of convenience. On the other hand, it is not necessary to encumber the unborn child with all the constitutional rights of an adult; our concern can be limited to the right to life.

. . .

Although the right to life can be made a constitutional right, the Federal Government should not preempt the rights of the States to prohibit abortion, prescribe penalties, and regulate the implementation of abortion. This is especially important, because there is some doubt whether restraints on Federal and State action can reach private action under the 14th amendment. Such a doctrine has been put forward in certain cases before the Supreme Court, but I think that it is wise and prudent, from the standpoint of the Constitution and the problems of enforcement, to leave room for the States to legislative prohibitions against abortion in the field of private action.

. . .

As already indicated, this amendment allows the States to act in the fields of State interest, without the Federal Government preempting all action. Both Federal and State governments can act concurrently to prohibit abortions. Any Federal action promoting abortions, including funding of actual abortions, use of Federal [facilities or equipment] intended [for abortion procedures], particularly research that involves clinical testing, would be clearly a violation of the

38. 132 *Congressional Record*, 94th Cong., 2nd Sess. (1976), 11, 555–61.

39. Several prominent pro-choice arguments insist that women have rights to terminate pregnancies, even if the fetus has a right to life. See Judith Jarvis Thomson, "A Defense of Abortion," *Philosophy and Public Affairs* 1 (1971): 47-66.

40. We suspect that Senator Helms misspoke or else this is a mistranscription. No doubt he meant to say "Fifth and Fourteenth Amendments."

constitutional rights of the unborn. The Federal Government could act to outlaw interstate commerce in abortions, and in drugs, instruments, and equipment intended to [be used in abortion procedures]. The States would have similar powers within their jurisdictions. The States, particularly, could delineate the spheres of culpability with respect to participating in abortions, prescribe penalties, and enforcement powers of local jurisdictions. . . .

. . .

The real evil of abortion is the distorted mentality in the living that is created when social convenience, pleasure, or utility is preferred to human life; or when the quality of life as a value supplants life itself as a value. We cannot allow our society to cross the line which allows the ultimate abrogation of the rights of an individual. We can debate the proper social measures that must be taken to alleviate the problems of human life; but there should be no debate about life itself.

SENATOR HUGH SCOTT (Republican, Pennsylvania)

. . . I believe a question of abortion should be decided by the State government under its police power. . . .

We live in a very diverse and large Nation, where people of various sections of the country have different points of view on a matter of this nature.

. . .

I shall read my amendment in the nature of a substitute to the joint resolution. . . .

. . .

> Except as otherwise provided in this Constitution the power to regulate the circumstances under which pregnancy may or may not be terminated is reserved to the States, except within the District of Columbia, Federal territory, or other area of exclusive Federal jurisdiction.

. . . My proposal places the responsibility where I believe it belongs and permits each State to decide for itself whether or not it wants any laws on abortion; and if a State wants a law on abortion, what type of law it favors.

. . .

SENATOR BIRCH BAYH (Democrat, Indiana)

. . .

I point out, as the chairman of the subcommittee, never before in my experience in the Senate, nor my 8 years in the Indiana State Legislature, have I been involved in an issue which involved this unique combination of moral and philosophical and religious beliefs commingled with political-legal-medical questions. It is an issue that has caused the Senator from Indiana a great deal of anguish regarding the position I should assume personally, on the other hand, and what position I should assume as a Senator, on the other. After a great deal of thought—and, indeed, some prayer—the Senator from Indiana came to the conclusion, personally, that abortion is wrong.

. . . I did not feel it would be right for me to take the personal moral decision that I was prepared to make and to impose that standard, on every other citizen of this country.

. . .

It is easy enough for me to say that I am opposed to abortion and that I think it is wrong. It is also wrong for me to impose my moral conviction on others who may well be faced with an entirely different set of circumstances from that of the Senator from Indiana.

. . .

I fear greatly that adoption of any of the proposed amendments regarding abortion would be far more in line with the unfortunate experience encountered with the 18th amendment [Prohibition] than with the rest of the Constitution. Without arguing the merits, can anyone seriously doubt that adoption of any of the proposed amendments would result in tens of thousands of women seeking abortion through illicit channels? Can there be doubt that if any of the proposed amendments were adopted that there would immediately be unleashed active political forces designed to repeal the amendment?

. . .

The means by which the Supreme Court decision in *Roe* . . . would be overturned under three of the proposed constitutional amendments, those introduced by Senators HELMS and BUCKLEY[,] is by establishing as part of the Constitution legal protection for a fetus at all stages of biological development. In other words, the language of the amendment nullifies the Court's distinction of viability, and establishes "life" as beginning at the moment of fertilization. No matter what one's personal views are as to when life begins, there can be no disagreement as to the clear fact that we have been unable to establish to everyone's satisfaction exactly when this mysterious transformation takes place. It is at the time of conception? Or fertilization? Is it only after "quickening" or viability? By amending the Constitution to establish one view as to when life begins at a time when there is no clear agreement among people in general, appears to me a serious misreading of the nature of the Constitution itself. The very term Constitution implies a document of a permanent and abiding nature. As one who has great faith in this durable document, I feel that we cannot and must not use the Constitution as an instrument for moral preference. We cannot and should not presume to provide for the people of this country, people with widely varying opinions on such fundamental issues, a definitive answer to a question that is clearly not open to certitude.

. . .

While I am deeply disturbed by the concept of abortion for convenience sake, I find that I cannot support an amendment which would not allow a woman who has been brutalized by the crime of rape the option of terminating a pregnancy that resulted against her will. . . .

Similarly, I feel that I cannot support an amendment which is so absolute as to prevent a woman who is carrying a fetus with a detectable and deadly genetic disease—[such] as Tay-Sachs or [D]own's syndrome—the option of terminating her pregnancy. . . .

. . . [O]ne of the possible effects of the proposed amendments would be to prohibit the use of certain forms of contraceptive devices in use by millions of Americans. Because the amendments define life as beginning at fertilization, the use of many contraceptive devices, such as the intrauterine device used by almost 9 million women, would no longer be permitted since medical testimony indicated there is evidence that such devices may work by preventing implantation after fertilization. . . .

. . . The question is whether we, as elected representatives, feel that amending the Constitution to impose one conception of life on all our citizens, is indeed the most responsible course of action. I have concluded it is not a responsible course of action. Each of us must make that important choice for himself or herself.

IV. Democratic Rights

MAJOR DEVELOPMENTS

- Voting Rights Act extended and expanded
- Judicial protection extended for the publication of the top-secret *Pentagon Papers*
- Supreme Court declares unconstitutional some constitutional limits on campaign finance

The democratic revolution that took place during the New Deal/Great Society Era became entrenched during the 1970s. No significant political or legal challenges were posed to the most important constitutional decisions on speech or voting rights. More often than not national institutions expanded democratic rights. *New York Times Co. v. United States* (1971) announced a strong constitutional barrier against government censorship of what many thought was the publication of top-secret government information. The Voting Rights Acts of 1970 and 1975 prohibited all literacy and understanding tests and banned residency requirements for presidential elections.

Unlike the Warren Court, which tended to declare only state laws unconstitutional, Burger Court majorities were often willing to impose constitutional limits on federal action. The Supreme Court in *New York Times Co. v. United States* (1971) declared that President Nixon had no constitutional right to obtain an injunction preventing the *New York Times* from publishing the Pentagon Papers. *Buckley v. Valeo* (1976) declared unconstitutional major sections of the Federal Election Campaign Act of 1974. In neither instance did the justices act against the dominant national coalition. By 1971 the Democratic majority in Congress had clearly turned against the Vietnam War. A badly divided Congress in 1974 enacted campaign finance reform only by including measures promising expedited judicial review of constitutionally controversial provisions.

A. Free Speech

A general consensus developed by the mid-1970s that many traditional restrictions on free speech were unconstitutional. No serious challenges were raised to either the holding in *Brandenburg v. Ohio* (1969) that government could punish speech criminally only if the speaker incited imminent criminal violence or the rule in *New York Times Co. v. Sullivan* (1964) that persons who criticized public officials could be sued for libel only if they spoke with reckless disregard for the truth or intentionally lied. The holding in *New York Times Co. v. United States* (1971) that speech could be censored only if the harm threatened was the equivalent of imperiling a ship at sea during wartime also enjoyed wide support. By the late 1970s most governing officials had abandoned traditional prosecutions for sedition or related offenses.

The constitutional politics of free speech shifted during the late 1960s and 1970s. Throughout most of the New Deal/Great Society Era free speech issues pitted liberal proponents of expression rights against conservative advocates of restriction. The new free speech issues of the 1970s cross-cut existing political cleavages. Campaign finance produced a bewildering series of political alignments. The plaintiffs in *Buckley v. Valeo* (1976) included James Buckley, one of the most conservative members of the U.S. Senate, and Eugene McCarthy, whose 1968 campaign for the presidency attacked President Lyndon Johnson from the political left. Many observers described campaign finance as a war between the ACLU, which by the 1970s was clearly aligned with the Democratic left, and Common Cause, a progressive interest group dedicated to regulating the political process. The Supreme Court split the difference. *Buckley* held that Congress could regulate campaign contributions in order to prevent corruption or the appearance of corruption, but could not regulate campaign expenditures or independent expenditures. Most significant, the judicial majority determined that the political use of money was constitutionally protected speech and that government had no constitutional business leveling the political playing field

Obscenity became a greater public concern. In 1970 the bipartisan Presidential Commission on Obscenity and Pornography reached the politically surprising conclusion that obscenity and pornography were not major social problems. "Empirical research designed to clarify the question," the Commission's report concluded, "has found no evidence to date that exposure to explicit sexual materials plays a significant role in the causation of delinquent or criminal behavior among youths or adults."[41] Rather than ban most erotic literature, the Commission recommended more sex education and more frank talk about sex. Both President Nixon and the Senate (by a 60-5 vote) condemned the Commission's report. Nixon "categorically reject[ed] [the Commission's] morally bankrupt conclusions and major recommendations." The Supreme Court in the 1970s sided more often with politicians than social scientists. Chief Justice Burger, when sustaining a ban on obscenity in *Miller v. California* (1973), asserted,

> The First Amendment protects works which, taken as a whole, have serious literary, artistic, political, or scientific value, regardless of whether the government or a majority of the people approve of the ideas these works represent. . . . But the public portrayal of hard-core sexual conduct for its own sake, and for the ensuing commercial gain, is a different matter.

Justice Douglas's dissent insisted that obscenity was no exception to First Amendment principles. He wrote,

> The First Amendment was designed "to invite dispute," to induce "a condition of unrest," to "create dissatisfaction with conditions as they are," and even to stir "people to anger." . . . The idea that the First Amendment permits punishment for ideas that are "offensive" to the particular judge or jury sitting in judgment is astounding.

The Burger Court also provided greater protection to commercial advertisements. *Virginia State Board of Pharmacy v. Virginia Citizens Consumer Council, Inc.* (1976) declared unconstitutional a state ban on advertising the price for prescription drugs. Justice Blackmun's majority opinion insisted, "As to the particular consumer's interest in the free flow of commercial information, that interest may be as keen, if not keener by far, than his interest in the day's most urgent political debate." Justice Rehnquist, the lone dissenter, charged that the decision "elevates commercial intercourse between a seller hawking his wares and a buyer seeking to strike a bargain to the same plane as has been previously reserved for the free marketplace of ideas."

New York Times Co. v. United States, 403 U.S. 713 (1971)

In the winter of 1971 Daniel Ellsberg delivered to the New York Times *a forty-seven volume secret study that former defense secretary Robert McNamara had commissioned on the history of the Vietnam War.*[42] *Ellsberg, a former employee of the Defense Department, had become convinced that publication of this study might turn American public*

41. The Report of the Commission on Obscenity and Pornography (New York: Random House, 1971), 32.

42. For a more detailed history of the *Pentagon Papers* case, see David Rudenstine, *The Day the Presses Stopped: A History of the* Pentagon Papers *Case* (Berkeley: University of California Press, 1996).

Illustration 9-2a Chief Justice Warren Burger

Illustration 9-2b Associate Justice William Brennan

Chief Justice Burger led the effort in the 1970s and early 1980s to modify many of the liberal precedents written by Justice Brennan during the Warren Court years of the late 1950s and 1960s.

Source: Library of Congress, Prints and Photographs Division, Washington, DC 20540, USA.

opinion decisively against the war effort. The Times, *after deliberating for three months, decided to publish selections from the papers in a ten-part series beginning on Sunday, June 13, 1971. Three days after the first installment was published, the Nixon administration obtained a temporary restraining order forbidding the* Times *from further publication. An evidentiary hearing was held on Friday, June 18. The injunction was removed the next day. Meanwhile, the* Washington Post *had obtained a copy of the Pentagon Papers and begun publication. On Monday, June 21, a federal district judge refused a Nixon administration request to enjoin publication of the* Post. *Two days later the Court of Appeals for the Second Circuit ordered the federal district court in New York to hold additional hearings on the* Times *publication, while the Court of Appeals for the District of Columbia Circuit affirmed the judicial order refusing to enjoin the* Washington Post. *The ink was hardly dry on these orders when the Supreme Court on June 25 declared that both cases would be reviewed and informed the parties that briefs were due and oral argument would take place the next day. Four days later the justices handed down their decision in* New York Times Co. v. United States.

As you read these opinions, compare the standards the individual justices use when determining whether a prior restraint is constitutional to the standards those justices use when determining whether speech may be sanctioned after publication. What reason do the justices give for imposing higher standards for prior restraints? Is the historical bias against prior restraints sufficient? Do other good constitutional reasons exist for permitting publication of materials that threaten the sort of harms that government may constitutionally regulate after publication? Consider the speed at which the case was decided. Is Justice Black right when he indicates that immediate resolution is necessary, because every passing day aggravates the evil of censorship? Is Justice Harlan right to suggest that free speech cases should be resolved in the same orderly manner as other constitutional issues? Under what conditions, if any, should the Court expedite rulings on constitutional issues?

Determined to prevent further leaks of classified information, President Nixon formed a special surveillance unit in the White House. That group, which became known as the Plumbers, was initially formed to stop leaks but soon began to conduct espionage against Nixon's political opponents. Their burglary of the Democratic Party headquarters at the Watergate Hotel and the subsequent efforts by the White House to obstruct investigations of that crime eventually led to Nixon's resignation.

PER CURIAM.

. . .

Any system of prior restraints of expression comes to this Court bearing a heavy presumption against its constitutional validity. . . . The Government "thus carries a heavy burden of showing justification for the imposition of such a restraint." . . . The District Court for the Southern District of New York in the *New York Times* case, . . . and the District Court for the District of Columbia and the Court of Appeals for the District of Columbia Circuit, . . . in the *Washington Post* case held that the Government had not met that burden. We agree.

. . .

JUSTICE BLACK, with whom JUSTICE DOUGLAS joins, concurring.

. . . [T]he Government's case against the *Washington Post* should have been dismissed and . . . the injunction against the *New York Times* should have been vacated without oral argument when the cases were first presented to this Court. I believe that every moment's continuance of the injunctions against these newspapers amounts to a flagrant, indefensible, and continuing violation of the First Amendment. . . . In my view it is unfortunate that some of my Brethren are apparently willing to hold that the publication of news may sometimes be enjoined. Such a holding would make a shambles of the First Amendment.

. . . [F]or the first time in the 182 years since the founding of the Republic, the federal courts are asked to hold that the First Amendment does not mean what it says, but rather means that the Government can halt the publication of current news of vital importance to the people of this country.

. . . [T]he Executive Branch seems to have forgotten the essential purpose and history of the First Amendment. . . . Both the history and language of the First Amendment support the view that the press must be left free to publish news, whatever the source, without censorship, injunctions, or prior restraints.

In the First Amendment, the Founding Fathers gave the free press the protection it must have to fulfill its essential role in our democracy. The press was to serve the governed, not the governors. The Government's power to censor the press was abolished so that the press would remain forever free to censure the Government. The press was protected so that it could bare the secrets of government and inform the people. Only a free and unrestrained press can effectively expose deception in government. And paramount among the responsibilities of a free press is the duty to prevent any part of the government from deceiving the people and sending them off to distant lands to die of foreign fevers and foreign shot and shell. In my view, far from deserving condemnation for their courageous reporting, the *New York Times*, the *Washington Post*, and other newspapers should be commended for serving the purpose that the Founding Fathers saw so clearly. In revealing the workings of government that led to the Vietnam war, the newspapers nobly did precisely that which the Founders hoped and trusted they would do.

. . .

JUSTICE DOUGLAS, with whom JUSTICE BLACK joins, concurring.

. . .

The dominant purpose of the First Amendment was to prohibit the widespread practice of governmental suppression of embarrassing information. It is common knowledge that the First Amendment was adopted against the widespread use of the common law of seditious libel to punish the dissemination of material that is embarrassing to the powers-that-be. . . . The present cases will, I think, go down in history as the most dramatic illustration of that principle. A debate of large proportions goes on in the Nation over our posture in Vietnam. That debate antedated the disclosure of the contents of the present documents. The latter are highly relevant to the debate in progress.

Secrecy in government is fundamentally anti-democratic, perpetuating bureaucratic errors. Open debate and discussion of public issues are vital to our national health. On public questions there should be "uninhibited, robust, and wide-open" debate. . . .

JUSTICE BRENNAN, concurring.

. . .

. . . [T]he First Amendment tolerates absolutely no prior judicial restraints of the press predicated upon surmise or conjecture that untoward consequences may result. Our cases, it is true, have indicated that there is a single, extremely narrow class of cases in which the First Amendment's ban on prior judicial restraint may be overridden. . . . [O]nly governmental allegation and proof that publication must inevitably, directly, and immediately cause the occurrence of an event kindred to imperiling the safety of a transport already at sea can support even the issuance of an interim restraining order. . . .

. . .

JUSTICE STEWART, with whom JUSTICE WHITE joins, concurring.

. . .

. . . [I]n the cases before us we are asked neither to construe specific regulations nor to apply specific laws. We are asked, instead, to perform a function that the Constitution gave to the Executive, not the Judiciary. We are asked, quite simply, to prevent the publication by two newspapers of material that the Executive Branch insists should not, in the national interest, be published. I am convinced that the Executive is correct with respect to some of the documents involved. But I cannot say that disclosure of any of them will surely result in direct, immediate, and irreparable damage to our Nation or its people. That being so, there can under the First Amendment be but one judicial resolution of the issues before us. I join the judgments of the Court.

JUSTICE WHITE, with whom JUSTICE STEWART joins, concurring.

I concur in today's judgments, but only because of the concededly extraordinary protection against prior restraints enjoyed by the press under our constitutional system. I do not say that in no circumstances would the First Amendment permit an injunction against publishing information about government plans or operations. Nor, after examining the materials the Government characterizes as the most sensitive and destructive, can I deny that revelation of these documents will do substantial damage to public interests. Indeed, I am confident that their disclosure will have that result. But I nevertheless agree that the United States has not satisfied the very heavy burden that it must meet to warrant an injunction against publication in these cases, at least in the absence of express and appropriately limited congressional authorization for prior restraints in circumstances such as these.

. . .

The Criminal Code contains numerous provisions potentially relevant to these cases. . . . Section 798 . . . proscribes knowing and willful publication of any classified information concerning the cryptographic systems or communication intelligence activities of the United States as well as any information obtained from communication intelligence operations. If any of the material here at issue is of this nature, the newspapers are presumably now on full notice of the position of the United States and must face the consequences if they publish. I would have no difficulty in sustaining convictions under these sections on facts that would not justify the intervention of equity and the imposition of a prior restraint.

It is thus clear that Congress has addressed itself to the problems of protecting the security of the country and the national defense from unauthorized disclosure of potentially damaging information. . . . It has not, however, authorized the injunctive remedy against threatened publication. . . .

JUSTICE MARSHALL, concurring.

. . .

In these cases we are not faced with a situation where Congress has failed to provide the Executive with broad power to protect the Nation from disclosure of damaging state secrets. Congress has on several occasions given extensive consideration to the problem of protecting the military and strategic secrets of the United States. This consideration has resulted in the enactment of statutes making it a crime to receive, disclose, communicate, withhold, and publish certain documents, photographs, instruments, appliances, and information. . . .

. . .

Either the Government has the power under statutory grant to use traditional criminal law to protect the country or, if there is no basis for arguing that Congress has made the activity a crime, it is plain that Congress has specifically refused to grant the authority the Government seeks from this Court. In either case this Court does not have authority to grant the requested relief. It is not for this Court to fling itself into every breach perceived by some Government official nor is it for this Court to take on itself the burden of enacting law, especially a law that Congress has refused to pass.

. . .

CHIEF JUSTICE BURGER, dissenting.

. . . In these cases, the imperative of a free and unfettered press comes into collision with another imperative, the effective functioning of a complex modern government and specifically the effective exercise of certain constitutional powers of the Executive. Only those who view the First Amendment as an absolute in all circumstances—a view I respect, but reject—can find such cases as these to be simple or easy.

These cases are not simple for another and more immediate reason. We do not know the facts of the cases. No District Judge knew all the facts. No Court of Appeals Judge knew all the facts. No member of this Court knows all the facts.

Why are we in this posture, in which only those judges to whom the First Amendment is absolute and permits of no restraint in any circumstances or for any reason, are really in a position to act?

I suggest we are in this posture because these cases have been conducted in unseemly haste. . . .

. . .

. . . An issue of this importance should be tried and heard in a judicial atmosphere conducive to thoughtful, reflective deliberation, especially when haste, in terms of hours, is unwarranted in light of the long period the *Times*, by its own choice, deferred publication.

It is not disputed that the *Times* has had unauthorized possession of the documents for three to four months, during which it has had its expert analysts studying them, presumably digesting them and preparing the material for publication. . . .

Would it have been unreasonable, since the newspaper could anticipate the Government's objections to release of secret material, to give the Government an opportunity to review the entire collection and determine whether agreement could be reached on publication? . . . With such an approach—one that great newspapers have in the past practiced and stated editorially to be the duty of an honorable press—the newspapers and Government might well have narrowed the area of disagreement as to what was and was not publishable, leaving the remainder to be resolved in orderly litigation, if necessary. . . .

. . .

The consequence of all this melancholy series of events is that we literally do not know what we are acting on. As I see it, we have been forced to deal with litigation concerning rights of great magnitude without an adequate record, and surely without time for adequate treatment either in the prior proceedings or in this Court. . . . I agree generally with Mr. Justice HARLAN and Mr. Justice BLACKMUN but I am not prepared to reach the merits.

. . .

JUSTICE HARLAN, with whom THE CHIEF JUSTICE and JUSTICE BLACKMUN join, dissenting.

. . .

. . . It is plain to me that the scope of the judicial function in passing upon the activities of the Executive Branch of the Government in the field of foreign affairs is very narrowly restricted. This view is, I think, dictated by the concept of separation of powers upon which our constitutional system rests.

In a speech on the floor of the House of Representatives, Chief Justice John Marshall, then a member of that body, stated: "The President is the sole organ of the nation in its external relations, and its sole representative with foreign nations." . . . From that time, shortly after the founding of the Nation, to this, there has been no substantial challenge to this description of the scope of executive power. . . .

. . .

The power to evaluate the "pernicious influence" of premature disclosure is not, however, lodged in the Executive alone. I agree that, in performance of its duty to protect the values of the First Amendment against political pressures, the judiciary must review the initial Executive determination to the point of satisfying itself that the subject matter of the dispute does lie within the proper compass of the President's foreign relations power. Constitutional considerations forbid "a complete abandonment of judicial control." . . . Moreover the judiciary may properly insist that the determination that disclosure of the subject matter would irreparably impair the national security be made by the head of the Executive Department concerned—here the Secretary of State or the Secretary of Defense—after actual personal consideration by that officer. . . .

But in my judgment the judiciary may not properly go beyond these two inquiries and redetermine for itself the probable impact of disclosure on the national security.

. . .

JUSTICE BLACKMUN, dissenting.

. . .

The First Amendment . . . is only one part of an entire Constitution. Article II of the great document vests in the Executive Branch primary power over the conduct of foreign affairs and places in that branch the responsibility for the Nation's safety. Each provision of the Constitution is important, and I cannot subscribe to a doctrine of unlimited absolutism for the First Amendment at the cost of downgrading other provisions. . . . What is needed here is a weighing, upon properly developed standards, of the broad right of the press to print and of the very narrow right of the Government to prevent. Such standards are not yet developed. . . .

I therefore would remand these cases to be developed expeditiously, of course, but on a schedule permitting the orderly presentation of evidence from both sides, with the use of discovery, if necessary, as authorized by the rules, and with the preparation of briefs, oral argument, and court opinions of a quality better than has been seen to this point. . . .

Campaign Finance

Buckley v. Valeo, 424 U.S. 1 (1976)

Americans of all political persuasions complained about campaign finance during the 1960s and 1970s. Democrats in 1968 were "alarmed at the growing costs of political participation in our country and the consequent reliance of political parties and candidates on large contributors." Republicans that year "favor[ed] a new Election Reform Act that will apply clear, reasonable restraints to political spending and fund-raising, whether by business, labor or individuals." The Watergate scandals intensified public demand for reform. "Shocked" by the fundraising techniques of Nixon's Committee to Re-Elect the President (CREEP), which included pressure on corporations to provide millions of dollars in secret campaign donations in exchange for government benefits (such as milk price supports), Congress was determined to bring under control the country's campaign financing system. The crucial provisions of the Federal Election Campaign Act of 1974 (FECA)

- *Prohibited persons from contributing more than $1,000 to a particular candidate and more than $25,000 to candidates in any particular election.*
- *Limited independent expenditures on behalf of a candidate to $1,000.*[43]
- *Limited the amount that candidates could contribute to their campaigns.*
- *Limited the amount that candidates could spend on their campaigns.*
- *Established a system of public financing for campaigns that distinguished between major parties that had received more than 25 percent of the vote in the most recent presidential election, minor parties that had received between 5 and 25 percent of the vote, and other parties that had received less than 5 percent of the vote.*

Numerous national officials raised constitutional objections to these provisions. President Ford, when signing the FECA stated, "I had some strong reservations about one version or one provision or another of the legislation and I suspect some of the people here on both sides of the aisle have the same." Many national officials allayed their constitutional doubts by placing a provision in the FECA that guaranteed swift judicial review of the bill's most important provisions.

A remarkably diverse group of plaintiffs challenged the constitutionality of these provisions. The named plaintiff, James L. Buckley, was the junior senator from New York, elected on the Conservative Party ticket. Other plaintiffs included Eugene McCarthy, the former Democratic senator from Minnesota; Stewart Mott, a multimillionaire who had spent a fortune financing opposition to the Vietnam War; and William Steiger, who was seeking a Republican congressional nomination in Wisconsin. Organizational plaintiffs included the New York Civil Liberties Union, the Mississippi Republican Party, the American Conservative Party, and the Libertarian Party. The named defendant, Francis Valeo, was the secretary of the Senate and a member of the Federal Elections Commission created by the FECA. After some complex jurisdictional maneuvering, the lower federal courts declared virtually every provision of the FECA constitutional. Plaintiffs appealed to the Supreme Court of the United States.

The Supreme Court by a 5-3 vote sustained most contribution limits, but by a 7-1 vote struck down all the expenditure limits. The limit on how much candidates could contribute to their campaigns was declared unconstitutional by a 6-2 vote. The per curiam opinion insisted that campaign contributions and expenditures were considered speech for constitutional purposes, that contributions could

43. An independent expenditure occurs when a person spends money on behalf of a candidate without consulting the candidate. If, for example, you were to make a commercial urging persons to vote for Jones in the next presidential election without contacting Jones or anyone on his or her campaign staff, that would be an independent expenditure. Unsurprisingly, the line between independent expenditures and contributions is often easily skirted.

be regulated to prevent corruption, but that elected officials could not regulate expenditures to ensure a level political playing field. The per curiam opinion insisted that political contributions are as much constitutionally protected speech as a public address by a political candidate. Why do the justices equate political contributions with speech? Are they correct? What justifies restricting campaign finance? Are these justifications sound or should courts also permit laws that "level the playing field"? Is Justice White correct that the per curiam opinion demonstrates little knowledge of the actual working of political campaigns or might Justice White underestimate the extent to which campaign finance laws are likely to be incumbent protection acts? On what basis do the justices distinguish contributions and expenditures? Are these distinctions constitutionally sound? If not, should the justices have upheld the whole FECA or struck the whole statute down? Does the split decision make political sense? FECA was based on a series of compromises and complex assumptions about the way that campaign financing works. Even if striking down some provisions while retaining others made constitutional sense, a good argument might be made that the totality was unworkable.[44]

PER CURIAM.

. . .

The Act's contribution and expenditure limitations operate in an area of the most fundamental First Amendment activities. Discussion of public issues and debate on the qualifications of candidates are integral to the operation of the system of government established by our Constitution. . . .

. . .

A restriction on the amount of money a person or group can spend on political communication during a campaign necessarily reduces the quantity of expression by restricting the number of issues discussed, the depth of their exploration, and the size of the audience reached. This is because virtually every means of communicating ideas in today's mass society requires the expenditure of money. The distribution of the humblest handbill or leaflet entails printing, paper, and circulation costs. Speeches and rallies generally necessitate hiring a hall and publicizing the event. The electorate's increasing dependence on television, radio, and other mass media for news and information has made these expensive modes of communication indispensable instruments of effective political speech.

The expenditure limitations contained in the Act represent substantial rather than merely theoretical restraints on the quantity and diversity of political speech. The $1,000 ceiling on spending "relative to a clearly identified candidate" . . . would appear to exclude all citizens and groups except candidates, political parties, and the institutional press from any significant use of the most effective modes of communication. . . .

By contrast with a limitation upon expenditures for political expression, a limitation upon the amount that any one person or group may contribute to a candidate or political committee entails only a marginal restriction upon the contributor's ability to engage in free communication. A contribution serves as a general expression of support for the candidate and his views, but does not communicate the underlying basis for the support. . . . At most, the size of the contribution provides a very rough index of the intensity of the contributor's support for the candidate. A limitation on the amount of money a person may give to a candidate or campaign organization thus involves little direct restraint on his political communication, for it permits the symbolic expression of support evidenced by a contribution but does not in any way infringe the contributor's freedom to discuss candidates and issues. While contributions may result in political expression if spent by a candidate or an association to present views to the voters, the transformation of contributions into political debate involves speech by someone other than the contributor.

. . .

It is unnecessary to look beyond the Act's primary purpose—to limit the actuality and appearance of corruption resulting from large individual financial contributions—in order to find a constitutionally sufficient justification for the $1,000 contribution limitation. Under a system of private financing of elections, a candidate lacking immense personal or family wealth must depend on financial contributions from others to provide the resources necessary to conduct a successful campaign. The increasing importance of the communications media and sophisticated mass-mailing and polling operations to effective campaigning make the raising of large sums of money an ever more essential ingredient of an effective candidacy. To the extent that large contributions are given to secure a political quid pro quo from current and potential office holders,

44. For an argument to that effect, see Gordon Silverstein, *Law's Allure: How Law Shapes, Constrains, Saves, and Kills Politics* (New York: Cambridge University Press, 2009), 152–74.

the integrity of our system of representative democracy is undermined. Although the scope of such pernicious practices can never be reliably ascertained, the deeply disturbing examples surfacing after the 1972 election demonstrate that the problem is not an illusory one.

Of almost equal concern as the danger of actual quid pro quo arrangements is the impact of the appearance of corruption stemming from public awareness of the opportunities for abuse inherent in a regime of large individual financial contributions. . . .

. . .

The Act's expenditure ceilings impose direct and substantial restraints on the quantity of political speech. . . . It is clear that a primary effect of these expenditure limitations is to restrict the quantity of campaign speech by individuals, groups, and candidates. . . .

. . .

. . . [T]he independent advocacy restricted by the provision does not presently appear to pose dangers of real or apparent corruption comparable to those identified with large campaign contributions. . . . Unlike contributions, such independent expenditures may well provide little assistance to the candidate's campaign and indeed may prove counterproductive. The absence of prearrangement and coordination of an expenditure with the candidate or his agent not only undermines the value of the expenditure to the candidate, but also alleviates the danger that expenditures will be given as a quid pro quo for improper commitments from the candidate. . . .

. . .

It is argued, however, that the ancillary governmental interest in equalizing the relative ability of individuals and groups to influence the outcome of elections serves to justify the limitation on express advocacy of the election or defeat of candidates imposed by 608 (e) (1)'s expenditure ceiling. But the concept that government may restrict the speech of some elements of our society in order to enhance the relative voice of others is wholly foreign to the First Amendment. . . . The First Amendment's protection against governmental abridgment of free expression cannot properly be made to depend on a person's financial ability to engage in public discussion. . . .

. . .

The ceiling on personal expenditures by candidates on their own behalf . . . imposes a substantial restraint on the ability of persons to engage in protected First Amendment expression. The candidate, no less than any other person, has a First Amendment right to engage in the discussion of public issues and vigorously and tirelessly to advocate his own election and the election of other candidates. Indeed, it is of particular importance that candidates have the unfettered opportunity to make their views known so that the electorate may intelligently evaluate the candidates' personal qualities and their positions on vital public issues before choosing among them on election day. . . .

The primary governmental interest served by the Act—the prevention of actual and apparent corruption of the political process—does not support the limitation on the candidate's expenditure of his own personal funds. . . .

. . .

No governmental interest that has been suggested is sufficient to justify the restriction on the quantity of political expression imposed by . . . campaign expenditure limitations. The major evil associated with rapidly increasing campaign expenditures is the danger of candidate dependence on large contributions. The interest in alleviating the corrupting influence of large contributions is served by the Act's contribution limitations and disclosure provisions. . . .

The interest in equalizing the financial resources of candidates competing for federal office is no more convincing a justification for restricting the scope of federal election campaigns. Given the limitation on the size of outside contributions, the financial resources available to a candidate's campaign, like the number of volunteers recruited, will normally vary with the size and intensity of the candidate's support. There is nothing invidious, improper, or unhealthy in permitting such funds to be spent to carry the candidate's message to the electorate. Moreover, the equalization of permissible campaign expenditures might serve not to equalize the opportunities of all candidates, but to handicap a candidate who lacked substantial name recognition or exposure of his views before the start of the campaign.

. . .

JUSTICE STEVENS took no part in the consideration or decision of these cases.

CHIEF JUSTICE BURGER, concurring in part and dissenting in part.

. . .

Congress intended to regulate all aspects of federal campaign finances, but what remains after today's holding leaves no more than a shadow of what Congress contemplated. I question whether the residue leaves a workable program.

. . .

. . . For me contributions and expenditures are two sides of the same First Amendment coin.

. . . By limiting campaign contributions, the Act restricts the amount of money that will be spent on political activity—and does so directly. . . . Limiting contributions, as a practical matter, will limit expenditures and will put an effective ceiling on the amount of political activity and debate that the Government will permit to take place. The argument that the ceiling is not, after all, very low as matters now stand gives little comfort for the future, since the Court elsewhere notes the rapid inflation in the cost of political campaigning. . . .

. . .

. . . In my view Congress can no more ration political expression than it can ration religious expression; and limits on political or religious contributions and expenditures effectively curb expression in both areas. There are many prices we pay for the freedoms secured by the First Amendment; the risk of undue influence is one of them, confirming what we have long known: Freedom is hazardous, but some restraints are worse.

JUSTICE WHITE, concurring in part and dissenting in part.

. . .

. . . I dissent from the Court's view that the expenditure limitations . . . violate the First Amendment.

. . .

Since the contribution and expenditure limitations are neutral as to the content of speech and are not motivated by fear of the consequences of the political speech of particular candidates or of political speech in general, this case depends on whether the nonspeech interests of the Federal Government in regulating the use of money in political campaigns are sufficiently urgent to justify the incidental effects that the limitations visit upon the First Amendment interests of candidates and their supporters.

. . . Congress was plainly of the view that [independent] expenditures . . . have corruptive potential; but the Court strikes down the provision, strangely enough claiming more insight as to what may improperly influence candidates than is possessed by the majority of Congress that passed this bill and the President who signed it. Those supporting the bill undeniably included many seasoned professionals who have been deeply involved in elective processes and who have viewed them at close range over many years.

. . .

As an initial matter, the argument that money is speech and that limiting the flow of money to the speaker violates the First Amendment proves entirely too much. . . . Federal and state taxation directly removes from company coffers large amounts of money that might be spent on larger and better newspapers. . . . But it has not been suggested, nor could it be successfully, that these laws, and many others, are invalid because they siphon off or prevent the accumulation of large sums that would otherwise be available for communicative activities.

. . . [M]oney is not always equivalent to or used for speech, even in the context of political campaigns. I accept the reality that communicating with potential voters is the heart of an election campaign and that widespread communication has become very expensive. There are, however, many expensive campaign activities that are not themselves communicative or remotely related to speech. Furthermore, campaigns differ among themselves. Some seem to spend much less money than others and yet communicate as much as or more than those supported by enormous bureaucracies with unlimited financing. The record before us no more supports the conclusion that the communicative efforts of congressional and Presidential candidates will be crippled by the expenditure limitations than it supports the contrary. The judgment of Congress was that reasonably effective campaigns could be conducted within the limits established by the Act and that the communicative efforts of these campaigns would not seriously suffer. . . .

. . . [E]xpenditure ceilings reinforce the contribution limits and help eradicate the hazard of corruption. . . . Without limits on total expenditures, campaign costs will inevitably and endlessly escalate. Pressure to raise funds will constantly build and with it the temptation to resort in "emergencies" to those sources of large sums, who, history shows, are sufficiently confident of not being caught to risk flouting contribution limits. Congress would save the candidate from this predicament by establishing a reasonable ceiling on all candidates. . . . It should be added that many successful candidates will also be saved from large, overhanging campaign debts which must be paid off with money raised while holding public office and at a time when they are already preparing or thinking about the next campaign. The danger to the public interest in such situations is self-evident.

. . .

It is also important to restore and maintain public confidence in federal elections. It is critical to obviate or dispel the impression that federal elections are purely and simply a function of money, that federal offices are bought and sold or that political races are reserved for those who have the facility—and the stomach—for doing whatever it takes to bring together those interests, groups, and individuals that can raise or contribute large fortunes in order to prevail at the polls.

. . .

I also disagree with the Court's judgment that [the provision] which limits the amount of money that a candidate or his family may spend on his campaign, violates the Constitution. Although it is true that this provision does not promote any interest in preventing the corruption of candidates, the provision does, nevertheless, serve salutary purposes related to the integrity of federal campaigns. By limiting the importance of personal wealth [the Federal Election Campaign Act] helps to assure that only individuals with a modicum of support from others will be viable candidates. This in turn would tend to discourage any notion that the outcome of elections is primarily a function of money. Similarly, the statute tends to equalize access to the political arena, encouraging the less wealthy, unable to bankroll their own campaigns, to run for political office.

. . .

JUSTICE MARSHALL, concurring in part and dissenting in part.

I join in all of the Court's opinion except [the decision to declare unconstitutional limitations on how much candidates may personally contribution to their campaigns].

. . .

. . . In my view the interest is more precisely the interest in promoting the reality and appearance of equal access to the political arena. . . .

One of the points on which all Members of the Court agree is that money is essential for effective communication in a political campaign. It would appear to follow that the candidate with a substantial personal fortune at his disposal is off to a significant "headstart." Of course, the less wealthy candidate can potentially overcome the disparity in resources through contributions from others. But ability to generate contributions may itself depend upon a showing of a financial base for the campaign or some demonstration of pre-existing support, which in turn is facilitated by expenditures of substantial personal sums. . . . And even if the advantage can be overcome, the perception that personal wealth wins elections may not only discourage potential candidates without significant personal wealth from entering the political arena, but also undermine public confidence in the integrity of the electoral process.

The concern that candidacy for public office not become, or appear to become, the exclusive province of the wealthy assumes heightened significance when one considers the impact of [the contribution limits] which the Court today upholds. . . . While the limitations on contributions are neutral in the sense that all candidates are foreclosed from accepting large contributions, there can be no question that large contributions generally mean more to the candidate without a substantial personal fortune to spend on his campaign. Large contributions are the less wealthy candidate's only hope of countering the wealthy candidate's immediate access to substantial sums of money. With that option removed, the less wealthy candidate is without the means to match the large initial expenditures of money of which the wealthy candidate is capable. In short, the limitations on contributions put a premium on a candidate's personal wealth.

JUSTICE BLACKMUN, concurring in part and dissenting in part. . . .

JUSTICE REHNQUIST, concurring in part and dissenting in part. . . .

B. Voting

Americans during the late 1960s and 1970s could not decide whether to continue, maintain, or modify the crucial principles underlying the voting rights revolution of the previous decades. A broad consensus existed that the Voting Rights Act of 1965 was constitutionally sacred, that voting was a fundamental right protected by the Fourteenth Amendment, and that this protection included the principle of one person, one vote. Nevertheless, controversies arose over the application of these principles, as progressives committed to universal adult suffrage sought to have more and more federal and state voting restrictions declared unconstitutional. The Supreme Court required congressional election districts to be as mathematically equal as possible, but states were permitted greater deviations from one person, one vote when apportioning state legislative districts. Residency requirements were held to unconstitutionally abridge the right to vote, but states were permitted to disenfranchise felons.

Voting rights initially enjoyed broad bipartisan support outside of the South. Democratic majorities in both houses of Congress passed and Republican presidents enthusiastically signed the Voting Rights Acts of 1970 and 1975. Those measures outlawed literacy tests throughout the nation, prohibited state residency requirements for presidential elections, provided additional protections for non-English-speaking voters, and gave eighteen-year-olds the right to cast a ballot in federal and state elections. The Supreme Court sustained all of these measures, with the exception of the provision in the Voting Rights Act of 1970 that extended the right to vote in state elections to eighteen-year-olds, which the Court declared unconstitutional in *Oregon v. Mitchell* (1970). Congress immediately proposed and the states quickly ratified a constitutional amendment granting eighteen-year-olds this right.

By the end of the decade Democrats were more enthusiastic about voting rights than were Republicans. The Democratic Party platform of 1976 stated,

> We support the right of all Americans to vote for President no matter where they live; vigorous enforcement of voting rights legislation to assure the constitutional rights of minority and language-minority citizens; the passage of legislation providing for registration by mail in federal elections to erase existing barriers to voter participation; and full home rule for the District of Columbia.

The Republican Party platform that year was far more restrained on voting rights, stating, "We encourage full participation in our electoral process. We further recognize the sanctity and value of the ballot. In that regard, we oppose 'federal post card registration.'"

The main difference between the constitutional politics of voting rights during the New Deal/Great Society Era and these politics during the 1970s was institutional. Elected officials made the most important decisions on voting rights from 1940 until 1965. Federal justices assumed the burden of decision making on voting rights during the 1970s. The increasing importance of litigation stemmed from two sources. First, many cases arose in which the crucial question was the proper interpretation of voting rights provisions passed by Congress. Second, judicial decisions during the Great Society nationalized voting issues that had previously been resolved by state constitutional decision makers. The Burger Court was increasingly occupied with concerns about how to implement the one person, one vote principle announced in *Reynolds v. Sims* (1964), how far to extend the right to vote recognized in *Harper v. State Board of Elections* (1966), and the constitutionality of various state laws that entrenched two-party politics.

During the late 1970s constitutional decision makers first confronted the majority-minority districts that would become constitutionally explosive in the Reagan Era. These districts, drawn in response to *Reynolds v. Sims* or the Voting Rights Acts, were structured to ensure that the majority of voters were persons of color who would likely elect persons of color to office. The Supreme Court first confronted the constitutional issues that majority-minority districts raised in *United Jewish Organizations v. Carey* (1977) after the New York legislature split a traditional Jewish community in order to create a predominantly African-American legislative district. Justice White's majority opinion contended that under certain conditions, state officials could use race as a criterion when apportioning legislative seats. He wrote, "The Constitution does not prevent a State subject to the Voting Rights Act from deliberately creating or preserving black majorities in particular districts in order to ensure that its reapportionment plan complies with § 5" of that act. Chief Justice Burger disagreed, asserting that the "drawing of political boundary lines with the sole, explicit objective of reaching a predetermined racial result cannot ordinarily be squared with the Constitution."

Congressional Debate on the Voting Rights Act of 1970[45]

In 1970 and 1975 Congress passed important amendments to the Voting Rights Act of 1965. While many provisions in

45. 116 *Congressional Record*, 91st Cong., 2nd Sess. (1970), 5517–23, 5542–48.

each measure were aimed at eliminating ongoing discrimination against persons of color, both included provisions directed at other forms of discrimination. Both were rooted in congressional recognition that voting was a fundamental constitutional right. Both measures enjoyed substantial bipartisan support, with opposition based almost exclusively in the South. When signing the Voting Rights Act of 1970, President Nixon declared that the measure was of "great importance" and was "dramatic evidence that the American system works." President Ford, when mustering Republican support for the Voting Rights Act of 1975, declared that "the right to vote is the foundation of freedom, and . . . this right must be protected."

Title I of the Voting Rights Act of 1970 declared that the provisions of the 1965 Voting Rights Act would be maintained until 1975 and that districts where less than 50 percent of the voting-age population had voted in the 1968 presidential election would be required to obtain preclearance for any change in voting laws. For the first time, the legislation covered some northern electoral districts. Title II outlawed literacy or understanding tests for five years throughout the nation, abolished residency requirements for presidential elections, and mandated that states establish procedures for absentee voting in presidential elections. Title III prohibited states from denying persons ages eighteen or older a right to vote if they were otherwise qualified.

The Voting Rights Act of 1975 extended all the provisions of the Voting Rights Act of 1965 until 1982 and required political subdivisions where less than half the eligible population had voted in the 1972 presidential election to seek preclearance from the Justice Department or a panel of three federal district court judges on the District of Columbia Circuit before changing their voting rules. Title II of that measure placed a permanent ban on literacy and understanding tests. Title III provided language minorities with greater access to the ballot. Section 203 declared,

> *The Congress finds that voting discrimination against citizens of language minorities is pervasive and national in scope. Such minority citizens are from environments in which the dominant language is other than English. In addition they have been denied equal educational opportunities by State and local governments, resulting in severe disabilities and continuing illiteracy in the English language. The Congress further finds that, where State and local officials conduct elections only in English, language minority citizens are excluded from participation in the electoral process. In many areas of the country, this exclusion is aggravated by acts of physical, economic, and political intimidation. The Congress declares that, in order to enforce the guarantees of the fourteenth and fifteenth amendments to the United States Constitution, it is necessary to eliminate such discrimination by prohibiting English only elections, and by prescribing other remedial devices.*

The excerpts below are from the debates over the Voting Rights Act of 1970. To what extent do these debates repeat themes from the debate over the Voting Rights Act of 1965? Do you detect important new developments that took place in the intervening five years? What changes might you have made to the Voting Rights Act of 1965 in light of the experiences of the late 1960s and 1970s?

The Supreme Court in Oregon v. Mitchell *(1970) unanimously sustained every provision in the Voting Rights Act of 1970 except the provision granting eighteen-years olds the right to vote in federal and state elections. A 5-4 majority sustained congressional power to grant younger Americans the right to vote in federal elections. A 5-4 majority rejected congressional power to grant younger Americans the right to vote in state elections.* Oregon v. Mitchell *exhibits a common pattern in Burger Court opinions. Eight justices believed that no good constitutional distinction existed between federal laws regulating the right to vote in state elections and federal laws regulating the right to vote in federal elections. Justice Douglas, speaking for four justices, maintained that Congress could lower the voting age in all elections, arguing, "Congress might well conclude that a reduction in the voting age from 21 to 18 was needed in the interest of equal protection. The Act itself brands the denial of the franchise to 18-year-olds as 'a particularly unfair treatment of such citizens in view of the national defense responsibilities imposed' on them." Justice Harlan, speaking for four justices, maintained that Congress could not lower the voting age in any election, writing, "I am of the opinion that the Fourteenth Amendment was never intended to restrict the authority of the States to allocate their political power as they see fit, and therefore that it does not authorize Congress to set voter qualifications, in either state or federal elections." Justice Black split the difference. He maintained that the provision lowering the age limit in national elections was constitutional because "Congress has ultimate supervisory power over congressional elections." He voted to strike the legislative attempt to lower the age limit in state elections because Congress was invading an area that he believed the Constitution of 1789 had reserved to the states and was not warranted by congressional power to enforce the post–Civil War Amendments' ban on racial discrimination.*

Justice Black's view that Congress could lower the voting age to eighteen for federal but not state elections temporarily became the law of the land (until Americans ratified the Twenty-Sixth Amendment), even though Black was the only justice who believed that a constitutional distinction existed between federal power to regulate state and federal elections.

. . .

During the hearings on the Voting Rights Act before the Senate Judiciary Committee . . . extensive facts were presented which compel the conclusion that the Voting Rights Act of 1965 must be extended for an additional five years. The Voting Rights Act of 1965 has been the most effective civil rights legislation ever enacted by the Congress. It is the only federal legislation that has proven effective in implementing the 15th Amendment and making real the rights to register and vote which that Amendment secures on paper. The success of the 1965 Act is directly traceable to its distinguishing feature in comparison to prior civil rights legislation; its immediate and automatic application, without the need for lengthy and repeated litigation in jurisdictions which fall within the formula provided in section 4 of the Act. . . . Negroes have registered and voted in record numbers in areas where before 1965 they had been systemically denied the franchise. Discriminatory devices to deny the franchise have been struck down or deferred.

. . .

In Alabama, the nonwhite population registered to vote increased from 19.3 in 1964 to 56.7 percent in the late summer of 1968; in Georgia, from 27.4 to 56.1 percent; in Louisiana, from 31.6 to 59.3 percent; in Mississippi, from 6.7 to 59.9 percent; in South Carolina, from 37.3 to 50.8 percent.

In addition to the large numbers of black citizens registering and voting, many are now running for office in Southern states to help assure adequate representation of all interests.

While progress has been significant, it should not obscure the pressing needs which remain. Negro registration is still well below that of whites in [m]any areas covered by the Act—and less than one-half in many counties. The continuing resistance to equal voting rights and risk of back-sliding should the protections of the Act be weakened are amply demonstrated in the instances in which the Attorney General has found it necessary to send in observers to assure that all persons were able to vote and have their votes counted regardless of race and to initiate legal actions to set aside elections and voting changes infected by racial discrimination.

If the 1965 Act is not extended, states and countries presently covered by the Act will be able to petition the court for their removal in August 1970—five years after the statute's enactment. . . .That means that sections 4 and 5, which have made the Voting Right Act of 1965 so successful, will cease to be effective this year and we will again be relegated to piecemeal judicial remedies which proved so unsuccessful in the past in keeping up with a rapid succession of ingenious roadblocks.

. . . The last five years has provided ample evidence that if these key provisions of the Act are permitted to expire, the procedural protections for voter registration will stop, thereby freeing—indeed, inviting—the resurgence of the discriminatory forces which operated so effectively prior to enactment of the law. . . .

. . .

While a great many citizens in the South have shown a commendable effort to comply with and help implement the Voting Rights Act of 1965, the intent and desire shown by others to circumvent the Act indicates that the dangers which necessitated the statute in the first place have not been eliminated. A wide range of obstructionist weapons have been experienced. Decided court cases demonstrate that boundary lines have been gerrymandered, elections have been switched to an at-large basis, elective offices have been abolished where Negroes had a chance of winning, the appointments process has been substituted for the elective process, election officials have withheld the necessary information for voting and running for office, and both physical and economic intimidation have been employed.

. . .

Even though other areas have no recent history of discriminatory abuses like that which prompted enactment of the 1965 Act, this extension is justified for two reasons; (1) because of the discriminatory impact which the requirement of literacy as a precondition to voting may have on minority groups and the poor; and (2) because there is insufficient relationship between literacy and responsible, interested voting to justify such a broad restriction of the franchise.

In the subcommittee hearings, the Commission on Civil Rights submitted a memorandum based on a study made by the Bureau of the Census, which suggests that the suspension of literacy tests in all States will result in significant increases in registration of educationally disadvantaged blacks and whites, Mexican Americans, Puerto Ricans, Cuban Americans and other members of the Spanish-speaking and Spanish-surname community in America, and American Indians. The report of the Commission on Civil Rights also suggests that literacy tests in all states deprive a greater proportion of minority citizens of the right to vote than of whites.

Professed state interests which are advanced to support restrictions on the franchise require close scrutiny. And as Father Hesburgh, Chairman of the Civil Rights Commission, stated in his letter of March 28, 1969, to the President: "the lives and fortunes of illiterates are no less affected by the actions of local, State and Federal governments than those of their more fortunate brethren. . . . Today, with television so widely available," he continued, "it is possible for one with little formal education to be a well-informed and intelligent member of the electorate." Thus, literacy tests not only abridge the right to suffrage on account of race and color, but also constitute an unreasonable classification against educationally disadvantaged persons in violation of the equal protection clause of the 14th Amendment.

Second, we propose to limit residency requirements in presidential elections. . . .

The main rational for a residency requirement in statewide or local elections—to ensure that the new resident has sufficient time to familiarize himself with state or local issues—has little relevance to presidential elections because the issues tend to be nationwide in scope and receive nationwide dissemination by the communications media.

SENATOR SAM ERVIN (Democrat, North Carolina)

. . .

I have searched in vain for the constitutional justification for the 1965 act. Any person who can read and understand the English language can see that the Federal Constitution grants to the States the power to prescribe voter qualifications. . . . Until very recently neither the Congress nor the Federal courts has had difficulty understanding this plain language in the Constitution.

. . .

Regretfully, the Supreme Court in *South Carolina v. Katzenbach* (1966) departed from this old and wise view of the 15th amendment. According to this expansive view of congressional power under the 15th amendment, Congress can and has nullified state power to set voter qualifications without any judicial or reasonable determination that such qualifications violate the 15th amendment. If literacy tests, constitutional on their face and as applied, can be prohibited by Congress as in the 1965 act, then what is left of State power over voter qualifications?

. . .

The Supreme Court in *Katzenbach v. Morgan* (1966) . . . asserted that section 5 of the 14th amendment in effect grants Congress the power to define the equal protection clause. This new theory of congressional power to "enact appropriate legislation" to secure equal protection of the law is a theory which can be employed to eliminate all State legislative and judicial power over any matter. The constitutional theory set forth in *Katzenbach v. Morgan* could quite literally establish the basis for dismantling completely the federal system provided for in the Constitution.

. . .

Mr. President, the Constitution was written to put restraints on government. The Founders rejected the theory that the liberty of a free people should depend on the self-restraint of the Governors. Yet, under Justice Brennan's theory, Congress can legislate on all matters from before the cradle to after the grave. And the only protection we now have for the preservation of our liberties is the hope that Congress will exercise self-restraint.

. . .

The formula used to bring six Southern States and 39 counties of North Carolina under the provisions of the act contains no reference whatever to a denial or abridgment of the right to vote on account of race, color, or previous condition of servitude. It arbitrarily and illogically assumes a violation of the 15th amendment whenever but only when States and counties with literacy tests had less than 50 percent of their voting age population registered or actually voting in the 1964 presidential election.

. . .

One of the particularly onerous forms of discriminatory treatment is incorporated in section 5 of the 1965 act. Under that section a State or political subdivision condemned under the trigger device of the act must submit any changes to the Attorney General or the three-judge district court for the District of Columbia. The State of North Carolina, which, in this century, has never been proven guilty of denying a single person the right to vote on account of race, must, hat-in-hand, take every change in its election laws to Washington for approval by persons who have no constitutional authority whatsoever over voter qualifications.

...

The legislative condemnation of the 1965 act of Southern States and election officials constitutes a bill of attainder expressly forbidden by the U.S. Constitution. The people of seven States and parts of other States, and more particularly the State election officials in those areas, are convicted under the formula of the 1965 act of violating the 15th amendment without any semblance of judicial trial....

The 1965 act violates another one of the most fundamental doctrines of our federal system of government, the equality of the States. The act operates to deny to certain Southern States the constitutional authority given all States to prescribe voting qualifications. While I believe that in the absence of proof of racial discrimination, any restriction by Congress on the States' power to set voting qualifications violates the Constitution, certainly a restriction on the power of only certain States constitutes an even greater disregard of constitutional principles....

The Right to Vote

The Supreme Court, with one notable exception, expanded the holding of *Harper v. Virginia State Board Elections* (1966) that the right to vote was fundamental under the equal protection clause of the Fourteenth Amendment. *Dunn v. Blumstein* (1972) held that states may not forbid bona fide residents who have only resided in the state for a short period of time from voting in state elections. Justice Marshall's majority opinion stated,

> Durational residence requirements in this case founder because of their crudeness as a device for achieving the articulated state goal of assuring the knowledgeable exercise of the franchise. The classifications created by durational residence requirements obviously permit any longtime resident to vote regardless of his knowledge of the issues—and obviously many longtime residents do not have any. On the other hand, the classifications bar from the franchise many other, admittedly new, residents who have become at least minimally, and often fully, informed about the issues.... There is simply nothing in the record to support the conclusive presumption that residents who have lived in the State for less than a year and their county for less than three months are uninformed about elections.

Richardson v. Ramirez (1974), which sustained state laws forbidding convicted felons from voting, was the only prominent Burger Court decision that upheld a state decision to limit access to the ballot.

Richardson v. Ramirez, 418 U.S. 24 (1974)

In 1952 Abran Ramirez was convicted of robbery by assault, a felony in the state of Texas. He served three months in prison and successfully completed parole in 1962. Ten years later Viola Richardson, a California election official, refused to allow Ramirez to register to vote on the ground that California law declared that "no ... person convicted of an infamous crime ... shall exercise the privileges of an elector in this state." Ramirez sued Richardson, claiming that the California ban on felons voting was unconstitutional. The Supreme Court of California declared unconstitutional the state law denying convicted felons the right to vote. Richardson appealed that decision to the Supreme Court of the United States.

The Supreme Court by a 6-3 vote declared that states could prohibit convicted felons from voting. Justice Rehnquist's majority opinion relies heavily on the language of the Fourteenth Amendment and the widespread nineteenth-century practice of disenfranchising felons. Justice Marshall in dissent points out that numerous Supreme Court decisions on voting rights during the 1960s and 1970s struck down practices that were widespread when the Fourteenth Amendment was ratified. Does either justice really engage the central contentions of the other, or is this a case in which historical arguments conflict with doctrinal arguments? On what basis would you resolve that conflict? Note that by the 1970s most former felons, who were disproportionately poor and persons of color, were likely to cast ballots for Democrats. How if at all has that influenced the constitutional politics of felon disenfranchisement?

JUSTICE REHNQUIST delivered the opinion of the Court.

...

... [R]espondents' claim implicates not merely the language of the Equal Protection Clause of [Section 1 of the Fourteenth Amendment, but also the provisions of the less familiar [Section] 2 of the Amendment:

> . . . [W]hen the right to vote at any [federal or state] election is denied to any of the male inhabitants of such State, being twenty-one years of age, and citizens of the United States, or in any way abridged, except for participation in rebellion, or other crime, the basis of representation therein shall be reduced in the proportion which the number of such male citizens shall bear to the whole number of male citizens twenty-one years of age in such State. . . .

Petitioner contends that . . . [Section] 2 expressly exempts from the sanction of that section disenfranchisement grounded on prior conviction of a felony. She goes on to argue that those who framed and adopted the Fourteenth Amendment could not have intended to prohibit outright in [Section] 1 of that Amendment that which was expressly exempted from the lesser sanction of reduced representation imposed by [Section] 2 of the Amendment. This argument seems to us a persuasive one unless it can be shown that the language of [Section] 2, "except for participation in rebellion, or other crime," was intended to have a different meaning than would appear from its face.

. . .

Throughout the floor debates in both the House and the Senate, in which numerous changes of language in [Section] 2 were proposed, the language "except for participation in rebellion, or other crime" was never altered. . . . What little comment there was on the phrase in question here supports a plain reading of it.

. . .

Further light is shed on the understanding of those who framed and ratified the Fourteenth Amendment, and thus on the meaning of [Section] 2, by the fact that at the time of the adoption of the Amendment, 29 States had provisions in their constitutions which prohibited, or authorized the legislature to prohibit, exercise of the franchise by persons convicted of felonies or infamous crimes.

. . .

. . . Although the Court has never given plenary consideration to the precise question of whether a State may constitutionally exclude some or all convicted felons from the franchise, we have indicated approval of such exclusions on a number of occasions. . . . In *Lassiter v. Northampton County Board of Elections* (1959), the Court said, . . .

> Residence requirements, age, previous criminal record . . . are obvious examples indicating factors which a State may take into consideration in determining the qualifications of voters.

. . .

As we have seen, . . . the exclusion of felons from the vote has an affirmative sanction in [Section] 2 of the Fourteenth Amendment, a sanction which was not present in the case of the other restrictions on the franchise which were invalidated in the cases on which respondents rely. We hold that the understanding of those who adopted the Fourteenth Amendment, as reflected in the express language of [Section] 2 and in the historical and judicial interpretation of the Amendment's applicability to state laws disenfranchising felons, is of controlling significance in distinguishing such laws from those other state limitations on the franchise which have been held invalid under the Equal Protection Clause by this Court. . . .

Pressed upon us by the respondents, and by amici curia, are contentions that these notions are outmoded, and that the more modern view is that it is essential to the process of rehabilitating the exfelon that he be returned to his role in society as a fully participating citizen when he has completed the serving of his term. We would by no means discount these arguments if addressed to the legislative forum which may properly weigh and balance them against those advanced in support of California's present constitutional provisions. But it is not for us to choose one set of values over the other. If respondents are correct, and the view which they advocate is indeed the more enlightened and sensible one, presumably the people of the State of California will ultimately come around to that view. And if they do not do so, their failure is some evidence, at least, of the fact that there are two sides to the argument.

. . .

JUSTICE MARSHALL, with whom JUSTICE BRENNAN joins, dissenting.

. . .

It is clear that [Section] 2 was not intended and should not be construed to be a limitation on the other sections of the Fourteenth Amendment. Section 2 provides a special remedy—reduced representation—to cure a particular form of electoral abuse—the disenfranchisement of Negroes. There is no indication that the framers of the provisions intended that special penalty to be the exclusive remedy for all forms of electoral discrimination. . . .

Rather, a discrimination to which the penalty provision of [Section] 2 is inapplicable must still be judged against the Equal Protection Clause of [Section] 1 to determine whether judicial or congressional remedies should be invoked. That conclusion is compelled by this Court's holding in *Oregon v. Mitchell* (1970). Although [Section] 2 excepts from its terms denial of the franchise not only to ex-felons but also to persons under 21 years of age, we held that the Congress, under [Section] 2, had the power to implement the Equal Protection Clause by lowering the voting age to 18 in federal elections. . . .

The Court's references to congressional enactments contemporaneous to the adoption of the Fourteenth Amendment . . . are inapposite. They do not explain the purpose for the adoption of [Section] 2 of the Fourteenth Amendment. They merely indicate that disenfranchisement for participation in crime was not uncommon in the States at the time of the adoption of the Amendment. . . . But "constitutional concepts of equal protection are not immutably frozen like insects trapped in Devonian amber." . . . We have repeatedly observed:

> "[T]he Equal Protection Clause is not shackled to the political theory of a particular era. In determining what lines are unconstitutionally discriminatory, we have never been confined to historic notions of equality, any more than we have restricted due process to a fixed catalogue of what was at a given time deemed to be the limits of fundamental rights." *Harper v. Virginia Board of Elections* (1966). . . .

Accordingly, neither the fact that several States had ex-felon disenfranchisement laws at the time of the adoption of the Fourteenth Amendment, nor that such disenfranchisement was specifically excepted from the special remedy of [Section] 2, can serve to insulate such disenfranchisement from equal protection scrutiny.

In my view, the disenfranchisement of ex-felons must be measured against the requirements of the Equal Protection Clause of [Section] 1 of the Fourteenth Amendment. That analysis properly begins with the observation that because the right to vote "is of the essence of a democratic society, and any restrictions on that right strike at the heart of representative government." . . .

. . .

I think it clear that the State has not met its burden of justifying the blanket disenfranchisement of former felons presented by this case. There is certainly no basis for asserting that ex-felons have any less interest in the democratic process than any other citizen. Like everyone else, their daily lives are deeply affected and changed by the decisions of government. . . .

. . .

The disenfranchisement of ex-felons had "its origin in the fogs and fictions of feudal jurisprudence and doubtless has been brought forward into modern statutes without fully realizing either the effect of its literal significance or the extent of its infringement upon the spirit of our system of government." I think it clear that measured against the standards of this Court's modern equal protection jurisprudence, the blanket disenfranchisement of ex-felons cannot stand.

I respectfully dissent.

JUSTICE DOUGLAS, dissenting. . . .

Reapportionment

Gaffney v. Cummings, 412 U.S. 735 (1973)

Theodore Cummings asked a federal district court to issue an injunction prohibiting the secretary of state in Connecticut from implementing an apportionment plan for the state legislature that had been devised in the fall of 1971. Under the plan the average deviation from perfect equality for the state senate was 0.45 percent, and the maximum deviation (the deviation between the most and least numerous districts) was 1.81 percent. The respective figures for the state assembly were 1.9 percent and 7.83 percent. These deviations resulted from efforts to ensure that Democrats and Republicans received legislative seats proportional to their vote. Cummings proposed a redistricting plan with substantially less deviation from perfect equality than the plan proposed by the apportionment board. The federal district court issued the injunction. J. Brian Gaffney, the chair of the state Republican Party, appealed that decision to the Supreme Court of the United States.

The Supreme Court by a 6-3 vote declared the apportionment plan constitutional. Justice White's majority opinion held that state apportionments need not strive to obtain perfect equality and that deviations of less than 10 percent would not be considered prima facie evidence of constitutional wrong. That same year the Supreme Court in White v. Weiser *(1973) ruled that states must strive to obtain perfect equality when apportioning congressional districts. How does Justice White distinguish federal from state apportionments? Does he rely on the Fourteenth Amendment, some other constitutional provision, or* Reynolds v. Sims *(1964)? Is his distinction constitutionally correct?*

JUSTICE WHITE delivered the opinion of the Court.

. . .

The requirement of Art. I, section 2, of the Constitution, that representatives be chosen "by the People of the several States," mandates that "one man's vote in a congressional election is to be worth as much as another's." . . . This standard "permits only the limited population variances which are unavoidable despite a good-faith effort to achieve absolute equality, or for which justification is shown." In [previous cases], the Court found inconsistent with this standard state statutes creating congressional districts having total maximum deviations of 5.97% and 13.1%, respectively. It is the standard of these cases which is the prevailing rule under Art. I and which we confirm in *White v. Weiser* (1973) . . . today for the purposes of congressional reapportionment.

. . . [T]here are fundamental differences between congressional districting under Art. I . . . and . . . state legislative reapportionments governed by the Fourteenth Amendment and *Reynolds v. Sims* (1964). . . . [D]istricts in state reapportionments [must] be "as nearly of equal population as is practicable," . . . and that "[s]o long as the divergences from a strict population standard are based on legitimate considerations incident to the effectuation of a rational state policy, some deviations from the equal-population principle are constitutionally permissible with respect to the apportionment of seats in either or both of the two houses of a bicameral state legislature." . . .

. . .

. . . Fair and effective representation may be destroyed by gross population variations among districts, but it is apparent that such representation does not depend solely on mathematical equality among district populations. There are other relevant factors to be taken into account and other important interests that States may legitimately be mindful of. . . . An unrealistic overemphasis on raw population figures, a mere nose count in the districts, may submerge these other considerations and itself furnish a ready tool for ignoring factors that in day-to-day operation are important to an acceptable representation and apportionment arrangement.

. . .

. . . We have repeatedly recognized that state reapportionment is the task of local legislatures or of those organs of state government selected to perform it. Their work should not be invalidated under the Equal Protection Clause when only minor population variations among districts are proved. . . .

. . .

We are quite unconvinced that the reapportionment plan offered by the three-member Board violated the Fourteenth Amendment because it attempted to reflect the relative strength of the parties in locating and defining election districts. It would be idle, we think, to contend that any political consideration taken into account in fashioning a reapportionment plan is sufficient to invalidate it. . . . The very essence of districting is to produce a different—a more "politically fair"—result than would be reached with elections at large, in which the winning party would take 100% of the legislative seats. Politics and political considerations are inseparable from districting and apportionment. The political profile of a State, its party registration, and voting records are available precinct by precinct, ward by ward. These subdivisions may not be identical with census tracts, but, when overlaid on a census map, it requires no special genius to recognize the political consequences of drawing a district line along one street rather than another. It is not only obvious, but absolutely unavoidable, that the location and shape of districts may well determine the political complexion of the area. District lines are rarely neutral phenomena. They can well determine what district will be predominantly Democratic or predominantly Republican, or make a close race likely. Redistricting may pit incumbents against one another or make very difficult the election of the most experienced legislator. The reality is that districting inevitably has and is intended to have substantial political consequences.

. . . [J]udicial interest should be at its lowest ebb when a State purports fairly to allocate political power to the parties in accordance with their voting strength and, within quite tolerable limits, succeeds in doing so. There is no doubt that there may be other reapportionment plans for Connecticut that would have different political consequences and that would also be constitutional.

Perhaps any of appellees' plans would have fallen into this category, as would the court's, had it propounded one. But neither we nor the district courts have a constitutional warrant to invalidate a state plan, otherwise within tolerable population limits, because it undertakes, not to minimize or eliminate the political strength of any group or party, but to recognize it and, through districting, provide a rough sort of proportional representation in the legislative halls of the State.

JUSTICE BRENNAN, with whom JUSTICE DOUGLAS and JUSTICE MARSHALL join, dissenting.

. . .

. . . The Court reasons that even in the absence of any explanation for the failure to achieve equality, the showing of a total deviation of almost 8% does not make out a prima facie case of invidious discrimination under the Fourteenth Amendment. Deviations no greater than 8% are, in other words, to be deemed de minimis, and the State need not offer any justification at all for the failure to approximate more closely the ideal of *Reynolds v. Sims*. . . .

. . . Since the Court expresses no misgivings about our recent decision in *Abate v. Mundt* (1971) . . . where we held that a total deviation of 11.9% must be justified by the State, one can reasonably surmise that a line has been drawn at 10%—deviations in excess of that amount are apparently acceptable only on a showing of justification by the State; deviations less than that amount require no justification whatsoever.

The proposition that certain deviations from equality of district population are so small as to lack constitutional significance, while repeatedly urged on this Court by States that failed to achieve precise equality, has never before commanded a majority of the Court. . . .

. . .

. . . [I]t is important to understand that the demand for precise mathematical equality rests neither on a scholastic obsession with abstract numbers nor a rigid insensitivity to the political realities of the reapportionment process. Our paramount concern has remained an individual and personal right—the right to an equal vote. . . . We have demanded equality in district population precisely to insure that the weight of a person's vote will not depend on the district in which he lives. The conclusion that a State may, without any articulated justification, deliberately weight some persons' votes more heavily than others, seems to me fundamentally at odds with the purpose and rationale of our reapportionment decisions. Regrettably, today's decisions are likely to jeopardize the very substantial gains that have been made during the last four years. . . .

Regulating Elections

The Burger Court adjudicated far more constitutional challenges to state regulations of political parties and access to the ballot than the justices had at any other time in history. Many cases raised challenges to state laws that strengthened the major political parties. Conservative and progressive reformers saw the two major parties as obstacles to their political and policy ambitions. They sought to weaken the control that Democrats and Republicans exercised over national and state elections, as well as the power that party elites wielded to determine party nominees. Frustrated by state laws that entrenched the major parties, third parties and independent candidates turned to the judiciary.

The liberal members of the Burger Court were more willing than the conservative members to strike down state laws regulating elections and political parties. Justice Marshall articulated the case for judicial intervention in *Illinois State Board of Elections v. Socialist Workers Party* (1979) when declaring unconstitutional a state law requiring independent candidates to obtain more signatures to be placed on the ballot in local elections than were necessary to be placed on the ballot in state elections. "Restrictions on access to the ballot," he stated,

> burden two distinct and fundamental rights, "the right of individuals to associate for the advancement of political beliefs, and the right of qualified voters, regardless of their political persuasion, to cast their votes effectively." . . . When such vital individual rights are at stake, a State must establish that its classification is necessary to serve a compelling interest. . . . To be sure, the Court has previously acknowledged that States have a legitimate interest in regulating the number of candidates on the ballot. . . . The States' interest in screening out frivolous candidates must be considered in light of the significant role that third parties have played in the political development of the Nation.

The conservative justices on the Burger Court were more deferential to state officials. Justice White's majority opinion in *Storer v. Brown* (1974) maintained,

"As a practical matter, there must be a substantial regulation of elections if they are to be fair and honest and if some sort of order, rather than chaos, is to accompany the democratic processes." *Storer* sustained a California law that forbade a candidate from appearing on the ballot as an independent if he or she had been a member of a major political party the previous year. Justice White asserted,

> California apparently believes with the Founding Fathers that splintered parties and unrestrained factionalism may do significant damage to the fabric of government. . . . It appears obvious to us that the one-year disaffiliation provision furthers the State's interest in the stability of its political system. We also consider that interest as not only permissible, but compelling and as outweighing the interest the candidate and his supporters may have in making a late rather than an early decision to seek independent ballot status.

As was the case with many questions of constitutional law during the 1970s, crucial votes were cast by centrist justices who made fine distinctions not perceived by either the more liberal or the more conservative members of the Burger Court. In *Rosario v. Rockefeller* (1973) the justices sustained a New York law forbidding persons from voting in a party primary if they had not registered as a party member before the last election. That same year, in *Kuspers v. Pontikes*, the justices overturned an Illinois law forbidding persons from voting in a party primary if they had voted in the other party's primary the year before. Six justices could not perceive a distinction between the two laws. Justices Powell, Brennan, Marshall, and Douglas thought both restrictions unconstitutional. Justices Rehnquist and Blackmun voted to sustain both. The actual decisions in both reflected the opinions of Justices White, Stewart, and Chief Justice Burger, the three justices who thought the cases constitutionally different.

C. Citizenship

Americans debated the constitutional status of laws discriminating against aliens. Supreme Court decisions, as Justice Powell admitted in *Ambach v. Norwick* (1979), did not always "form an unwavering line." The justices during the 1970s concluded that states could not discriminate against aliens when making welfare payments, enact general bans on aliens in the civil service, prohibit aliens from becoming attorneys or civil engineers, or discriminate against aliens when disbursing financial assistance for higher education. In *Foley v. Connelie* (1978), however, a 5-4 judicial majority declared that states could prohibit aliens from becoming police officers. Chief Justice Burger's majority opinion asserted,

> [A] democratic society is ruled by its people. Thus, it is clear that a State may deny aliens the right to vote, or to run for elective office, for these lie at the heart of our political institutions. . . . Likewise, we have recognized that citizenship may be a relevant qualification for fulfilling those "important nonelective executive, legislative, and judicial positions," held by "officers who participate directly in the formulation, execution, or review of broad public policy." . . . This is not because our society seeks to reserve the better jobs to its members. Rather, it is because this country entrusts many of its most important policy responsibilities to these officers, the discretionary exercise of which can often more immediately affect the lives of citizens than even the ballot of a voter or the choice of a legislator. In sum, then, it represents the choice, and right, of the people to be governed by their citizen peers.

Justice Marshall's dissent agreed with the broad principle but disagreed with the application. He maintained,

> Thus the phrase "execution of broad public policy" . . . cannot be read to mean simply the carrying out of government programs, but rather must be interpreted to include responsibility for actually setting government policy pursuant to a delegation of substantial authority from the legislature. The head of an executive agency for example, charged with promulgating complex regulations under a statute, executes broad public policy in a sense that file clerks in the agency clearly do not. In short, . . . those "elective or important nonelective" positions that involve broad policymaking responsibilities are the only state jobs from which aliens as a group may constitutionally be excluded. . . . In my view, the job of state trooper is not one of those positions.

The next year a similarly divided Court in *Ambach v. Norwick* (1979) determined that public school teachers carried out the sort of government function that justified the position's restriction to citizens.

The Supreme Court scrutinized federal laws discriminating against aliens less carefully. Nevertheless, an absolute ban on aliens holding federal jobs was declared unconstitutional in *Hampton v. Mow Sun Wong* (1976).

V. Equality

MAJOR DEVELOPMENTS

- Fights over busing and affirmative action
- Gender discrimination subject to heightened judicial scrutiny
- Supreme Court declines to treat education as a fundamental right for equal protection purposes

The movement for racial equality during the New Deal/Great Society Era inspired numerous other constitutional demands for equality. Constitutional decision makers were asked to consider whether legislation discriminating against women, aliens, illegitimate children, the poor, and various other persons was presumptively unconstitutional. The lawyers and political activists involved in these campaigns borrowed heavily from the NAACP's campaign against Jim Crow. Proponents of women's rights asserted that gender and race classifications were equally suspect because gender and race are immutable characteristics, African Americans and women were relatively powerless politically, and both had experienced a long history of discrimination. Organizations following the path blazed by the NAACP Legal Defense Fund even adopted such names as the National Organization for Women Legal Defense Fund or the Mexican American Legal Defense Fund. Many of these movements were successful. John Skrentny speaks of a "minority rights revolution" that included, often as a matter of claimed constitutional right, "bilingual education for Latinos, equal rights for women in education, and equal rights for the disabled," as well as the expansion of affirmative action programs to non-African-Americans.[46]

The new constitutional politics of equal rights splintered both liberals and equal protection clause doctrine. Progressives in Congress and on the Supreme Court maintained that state and federal laws discriminated against numerous groups and that such discriminations warranted the highest or at least a high degree of constitutional scrutiny. Proponents of gender equality urged that the ERA be ratified and that, regardless of its ratification, the Fourteenth Amendment be interpreted as requiring strict scrutiny of gender classifications. Other constitutional decision makers agreed that members of many groups had characteristics or a history that justified some degree of heightened judicial protection. Moderates worried that the ERA might unsettle traditional practices, such as all-male combat forces, and thought the Fourteenth Amendment should be interpreted as requiring intermediate scrutiny for gender classifications. More conservative Americans rejected the central premises of both progressive and moderate understandings of constitutional equality. History, in their view, sanctioned heightened judicial scrutiny only for racial classifications. Real differences between men and women justified many traditional gender classifications.

Moderates carried the day while Richard Nixon, Gerald Ford, and Jimmy Carter held the presidency. Officially, the justices announced three levels of scrutiny:

- Strict scrutiny for racial distinctions. Official distinctions must be a necessary means to a compelling government end.
- Intermediate scrutiny for gender distinctions. Official distinctions must be a substantial means to an important government end.
- Rational scrutiny for most other distinctions. Official distinctions must be a rational means to a legitimate government end.

Unofficially, many more levels existed. Both Justices Marshall and Stevens insisted that constitutional decision makers had, in practice, adopted a continuum in which the degree of judicial scrutiny reflected the obnoxiousness of the classification, the importance of the good being distributed, and the fit between the government purpose and the discrimination under constitutional attack.

Affirmative action furthered muddied the waters. Liberals divided over whether classifications ostensibly designed to benefit members of historically disadvantaged groups merited the same constitutional scrutiny as classifications clearly designed to harm members of those groups. A very tenuous compromise was reached in *Bakke v. Regents of the University of California* (1978). Justice Powell's crucial fifth vote in this decision created a majority for the principle that affirmative action

46. John D. Skrentny, *The Minority Rights Revolution* (Cambridge, MA: Harvard University Press, 2002), 2.

was a constitutional means for seeking diversity but not for ameliorating social disadvantage.

A. Equality Under Law

Constitutional decision makers confronted an extraordinary variety of demands for equality. Initially the Supreme Court of the United States seemed sympathetic. When striking down a Louisiana law that declared that only legitimate children be compensated under workmen's compensation for the death of a parent, Justice Powell's majority opinion in *Weber v. Aetna Casualty & Surety Co.* (1972) justified heightened judicial scrutiny for laws that discriminated against the children of unmarried parents.,

> The status of illegitimacy has expressed through the ages society's condemnation of irresponsible liaisons beyond the bonds of marriage. But visiting this condemnation on the head of an infant is illogical and unjust. Moreover, imposing disabilities on the illegitimate child is contrary to the basic concept of our system that legal burdens should bear some relationship to individual responsibility or wrongdoing. Obviously, no child is responsible for his birth and penalizing the illegitimate child is an ineffectual—as well as an unjust—way of deterring the parent. Courts are powerless to prevent the social opprobrium suffered by these hapless children, but the Equal Protection Clause does enable us to strike down discriminatory laws relating to status of birth where—as in this case—the classification is justified by no legitimate state interest, compelling or otherwise.

U.S. Department of Agriculture v. Moreno (1973) ruled unconstitutional a federal law prohibiting households of unrelated persons from using food stamps. While purporting to use rational scrutiny, Justice Brennan's majority opinion maintained that the law "was intended to prevent so-called 'hippies' and 'hippie communes' from participating in the food stamp program." Brennan concluded, "A bare congressional desire to harm a politically unpopular group cannot constitute a legitimate government interest."

The Supreme Court became less solicitous of equality claims as the decade wore on. *San Antonio Independent School District v. Rodriguez* (1973) ruled that using local property taxes to fund public education neither discriminated against the class of persons who lived in property-poor school districts nor denied a fundamental right to the children who resided in those districts. That decision put a practical halt, for the most part, to efforts to expand both the suspect class and fundamental rights strands of equal protection analysis. In *United States Railroad Retirement Board v. Fritz* (1980) the justices reemphasized that a very deferential rationality standard was appropriate for virtually all equal protection claims. Justice Rehnquist's majority opinion asserted, "Where, as here, there are plausible reasons for Congress' action, our inquiry is at an end. It is, of course, constitutionally irrelevant whether this reasoning in fact underlay the legislative decision, . . . because this Court has never insisted that a legislative body articulate its reasons for enacting a statute."

San Antonio Independent School District v. Rodriguez, 411 U.S. 1 (1973)

Demetrio Rodriguez was a child who lived in the Edgewood Independent School District. Edgewood was an urban, residential, and relatively poor area in San Antonio, Texas, with a student population that was 90 percent Mexican-American and 6 percent African-American. Per-pupil spending in Edgewood in the 1967–68 academic year was $356, of which $26 was raised locally. Children in the Alamo Heights School District were more fortunate. Alamo Heights, whose students were mostly white, spent $594 per pupil. The disparity was largely explained by differences in revenue from local property taxes. Although Edgewood assessed property at a higher rate, the more affluent Alamo Heights District raised substantially more school funds from a lesser tax rate. In 1968 Rodriguez was among the children and parents living in the Edgewood Independent School District who filed suit against state and county government officials, arguing that public school funding in Texas violated the equal protection clause of the Fourteenth Amendment. A three-judge panel in the local federal district court found the public school system in Texas to violate the Fourteenth Amendment. Texas appealed to the Supreme Court of the United States.

While Rodriguez *was being litigated, the Supreme Court of California in* Serrano v. Priest *(CA 1971) declared that a similar scheme for funding public education violated the state constitution. Justice Sullivan's majority opinion concluded,*

> *The California public school financing system, . . . since it deals intimately with education, obviously touches upon*

a fundamental interest. . . . [T]his system conditions the full entitlement to such interest on wealth, classifies its recipients on the basis of their collective affluence and makes the quality of a child's education depend upon the resources of his school district and ultimately upon the pocketbook of his parents. We find that such financing system as presently constituted is not necessary to the attainment of any compelling state interest. Since it does not withstand the requisite "strict scrutiny," it denies to the plaintiffs and others similarly situated the equal protection of the laws.[47]

The plaintiffs in Rodriguez *hoped that the Supreme Court of the United States would similarly conclude that, under the equal protection clause, wealth was a suspect classification, education was a fundamental interest, and the Texas scheme for financing public education was unconstitutional.*

The Supreme Court reversed the district court by a 5-4 vote. Justice Powell's majority opinion insists that school finance raises the economic and social policy questions that require, in the post–New Deal world, substantial judicial deference. Is Powell as deferential as the justices in the Williamson v. Lee Optical *line of cases, or does* Rodriguez *suggest circumstances in which wealth and education might trigger greater judicial scrutiny? Justice Marshall's dissent rejects the claim that justices should either strictly scrutinize legislation or passively defer to the legislature. Instead, he insists that justices should use a sliding scale when evaluating equal protection claims. Does Marshall's account correctly identify what the Burger Court was doing? Does this account correctly identify what the justices should do?* Rodriguez *marked a continued retreat by the Burger Court from previous decisions expanding the number of suspect classes and fundamental interests under the equal protection clause. To what extent is that retreat explained by constitutional politics or constitutional law? How do the various opinions identify suspect classes and fundamental interests? What is the best understanding of suspect classes and fundamental interests under the equal protection clause?*

JUSTICE POWELL delivered the opinion of the Court.

. . .

The precedents of this Court provide the proper starting point. The individuals, or groups of individuals, who constituted the class discriminated against in our prior cases shared two distinguishing characteristics: because of their impecunity they were completely unable to pay for some desired benefit, and as a consequence, they sustained an absolute deprivation of a meaningful opportunity to enjoy that benefit.

. . .

. . . [I]n support of their charge that the system discriminates against the "poor," appellees have made no effort to demonstrate that it operates to the peculiar disadvantage of any class fairly definable as indigent, or as composed of persons whose incomes are beneath any designated poverty level. Indeed, there is reason to believe that the poorest families are not necessarily clustered in the poorest property districts. . . .

. . . [L]ack of personal resources has not occasioned an absolute deprivation of the desired benefit. The argument here is not that the children in districts having relatively low assessable property values are receiving no public education; rather, it is that they are receiving a poorer quality education than that available to children in districts having more assessable wealth. Apart from the unsettled and disputed question whether the quality of education may be determined by the amount of money expended for it, a sufficient answer to appellees' argument is that, at least where wealth is involved, the Equal Protection Clause does not require absolute equality or precisely equal advantages. Nor, indeed, in view of the infinite variables affecting the educational process, can any system assure equal quality of education except in the most relative sense. . . .

. . .

However described, it is clear that appellees' suit asks this Court to extend its most exacting scrutiny to review a system that allegedly discriminates against a large, diverse, and amorphous class, unified only by the common factor of residence in districts that happen to have less taxable wealth than other districts. The system of alleged discrimination and the class it defines have none of the traditional indicia of suspectness: the class is not saddled with such disabilities, or subjected to such a history of purposeful unequal treatment, or relegated to such a position of political powerlessness as to command extraordinary protection from the majoritarian political process.

. . .

Nothing this Court holds today in any way detracts from our historic dedication to public education. We are in complete agreement with the conclusion of the three-judge panel below that "the grave significance of education both to the individual and to our society" cannot be doubted. But the importance of a service

47. *Serrano v. Priest*, 5 Cal. 3rd 584 (1971)

performed by the State does not determine whether it must be regarded as fundamental for purposes of examination under the Equal Protection Clause. . . .

. . .

. . . It is not the province of this Court to create substantive constitutional rights in the name of guaranteeing equal protection of the laws. Thus, the key to discovering whether education is "fundamental" is not to be found in comparisons of the relative societal significance of education as opposed to subsistence or housing. Nor is it to be found by weighing whether education is as important as the right to travel. Rather, the answer lies in assessing whether there is a right to education explicitly or implicitly guaranteed by the Constitution.

Education, of course, is not among the rights afforded explicit protection under our Federal Constitution. Nor do we find any basis for saying it is implicitly so protected. As we have said, the undisputed importance of education will not alone cause this Court to depart from the usual standard for reviewing a State's social and economic legislation. . . .

. . .

. . . [W]e stand on familiar ground when we continue to acknowledge that the Justices of this Court lack both the expertise and the familiarity with local problems so necessary to the making of wise decisions with respect to the raising and disposition of public revenues. Yet, we are urged to direct the States either to alter drastically the present system or to throw out the property tax altogether in favor of some other form of taxation. No scheme of taxation, whether the tax is imposed on property, income, or purchases of goods and services, has yet been devised which is free of all discriminatory impact. In such a complex arena in which no perfect alternatives exist, the Court does well not to impose too rigorous a standard of scrutiny lest all local fiscal schemes become subjects of criticism under the Equal Protection Clause.

. . .

. . . One also must remember that the system here challenged is not peculiar to Texas or to any other State. In its essential characteristics, the Texas plan for financing public education reflects what many educators for a half century have thought was an enlightened approach to a problem for which there is no perfect solution. We are unwilling to assume for ourselves a level of wisdom superior to that of legislators, scholars, and educational authorities in 50 States, especially where the alternatives proposed are only recently conceived and nowhere yet tested. The constitutional standard under the Equal Protection Clause is whether the challenged state action rationally furthers a legitimate state purpose or interest. We hold that the Texas plan abundantly satisfies this standard.

. . .

JUSTICE STEWART, concurring. . . .

JUSTICE BRENNAN, dissenting. . . .

JUSTICE WHITE, with whom JUSTICE DOUGLAS and JUSTICE BRENNAN join, dissenting.

. . .

The difficulty with the Texas system is that it provides a meaningful option to Alamo Heights and like school districts but almost none to Edgewood and those other districts with a low per-pupil real estate tax base. In these latter districts, no matter how desirous parents are of supporting their schools with greater revenues, it is impossible to do so through the use of the real estate property tax. . . .

The Equal Protection Clause permits discriminations between classes but requires that the classification bear some rational relationship to a permissible object sought to be attained by the statute. It is not enough that the Texas system before us seeks to achieve the valid, rational purpose of maximizing local initiative; the means chosen by the State must also be rationally related to the end sought to be achieved. . . .

Neither Texas nor the majority heeds this rule. If the State aims at maximizing local initiative and local choice, by permitting school districts to resort to the real property tax if they choose to do so, it utterly fails in achieving its purpose in districts with property tax bases so low that there is little if any opportunity for interested parents, rich or poor, to augment school district revenues. . . .

. . .

JUSTICE MARSHALL, with whom JUSTICE DOUGLAS concurs, dissenting

. . .

I must once more voice my disagreement with the Court's rigidified approach to equal protection analysis. The Court apparently seeks to establish today that equal protection cases fall into one of two neat categories which dictate the appropriate standard of review—strict scrutiny or mere rationality. But this

Court's decisions in the field of equal protection defy such easy categorization. A principled reading of what this Court has done reveals that it has applied a spectrum of standards in reviewing discrimination allegedly violative of the Equal Protection Clause. This spectrum clearly comprehends variations in the degree of care with which the Court will scrutinize particular classifications, depending, I believe, on the constitutional and societal importance of the interest adversely affected and the recognized invidiousness of the basis upon which the particular classification is drawn. . . .

. . .

. . . [I]t seems to me inescapably clear that this Court has consistently adjusted the care with which it will review state discrimination in light of the constitutional significance of the interests affected and the invidiousness of the particular classification. In the context of economic interests, we find that discriminatory state action is almost always sustained, for such interests are generally far removed from constitutional guarantees. . . . But the situation differs markedly when discrimination against important individual interests with constitutional implications and against particularly disadvantaged or powerless classes is involved. The majority suggests, however, that a variable standard of review would give this Court the appearance of a "superlegislature." I cannot agree. Such an approach seems to me a part of the guarantees of our Constitution and of the historic experiences with oppression of and discrimination against discrete, powerless minorities which underlie that document. In truth, the Court itself will be open to the criticism raised by the majority so long as it continues on its present course of effectively selecting in private which cases will be afforded special consideration without acknowledging the true basis of its action. . . .

. . .

Since the Court now suggests that only interests guaranteed by the Constitution are fundamental for purposes of equal protection analysis, and since it rejects the contention that public education is fundamental, it follows that the Court concludes that public education is not constitutionally guaranteed. It is true that this Court has never deemed the provision of free public education to be required by the Constitution. . . . [but] [e]ducation directly affects the ability of a child to exercise his First Amendment rights, both as a source and as a receiver of information and ideas, whatever interests he may pursue in life. . . . The opportunity for formal education may not necessarily be the essential determinant of an individual's ability to enjoy throughout his life the rights of free speech and association guaranteed to him by the First Amendment. But such an opportunity may enhance the individual's enjoyment of those rights, not only during but also following school attendance. . . . Education serves the essential function of instilling in our young an understanding of and appreciation for the principles and operation of our governmental processes. Education may instill the interest and provide the tools necessary for political discourse and debate. Indeed, it has frequently been suggested that education is the dominant factor affecting political consciousness and participation. . . .

. . .

The Court seeks solace for its action today in the possibility of legislative reform. The Court's suggestions of legislative redress and experimentation will doubtless be of great comfort to the schoolchildren of Texas' disadvantaged districts, but considering the vested interests of wealthy school districts in the preservation of the status quo, they are worth little more. The possibility of legislative action is, in all events, no answer to this Court's duty under the Constitution to eliminate unjustified state discrimination. . . .

B. Race

The political coalitions responsible for *Brown v. Board of Education* (1954) and the Civil Rights Act of 1964 splintered during the 1970s. General agreement existed that the liberal decisions striking down Jim Crow were constitutionally correct. By the middle of the 1970s attacks on *Brown* and the Civil Rights Act had disappeared from both public and private discourse. In practice both were treated as being as sacred constitutionally as the commerce clause. Constitutional fights now took place over the meaning of *Brown*. More conservative liberals insisted that Great Society measures had largely cured racial problems in the United States. As long as Americans remained committed to the antidiscrimination principles set out in *Brown* and the Civil Rights Act of 1964, racial equality would be achieved shortly. More progressive liberals insisted that *Brown* and the Civil Rights Act of 1964 merely began the process by which the United States might become a more egalitarian society. Aggressive, often race-conscious measures were necessary to eradicate the legacy of Jim Crow.

These racial issues slowly began to realign American politics. Progressive Democrats insisted that racial matters were getting worse, not better. Hubert Humphrey in 1975 informed the Senate that "segregation is spreading out over more and more central cities and even some inner suburbs are being absorbed into growing ghettos."[48] The 1976 Democratic Party platform endorsed strong measures for securing desegregation:

> The Supreme Court decision of 1954 and the aftermath were based on the recognition that separate educational facilities are inherently unequal. It is clearly our responsibility as a party and as citizens to support the principles of our Constitution.
>
> The Democratic Party pledges its concerted help through special consultation, matching funds, incentive grants and other mechanisms to communities which seek education, integrated both in terms of race and economic class, through equitable, reasonable and constitutional arrangements. Mandatory transportation of students beyond their neighborhoods for the purpose of desegregation remains a judicial tool of the last resort for the purpose of achieving school desegregation. . . . We encourage a variety of other measures, including the redrawing of attendance lines, pairing of schools, use of the "magnet school" concept, strong fair housing enforcement, and other techniques for the achievement of racial and economic integration.

The Nixon administration maintained that the civil rights decisions of the 1960s had largely ended the reign of Jim Crow and that only a few mopping-up operations were necessary to complete that process. Nixon in 1972 declared that "dismantling the old dual school system . . . has now been substantially completed." Republican platforms in the 1970s emphatically rejected the practice of busing schoolchildren to public schools in neighborhoods with different racial balances as a means of further integrating public schools.

> We believe that segregated schools are morally wrong and unconstitutional. However, we oppose forced busing to achieve racial balances in our schools. We believe there are educational advantages for children in attending schools in their own neighborhoods and that the Democrat-controlled Congress has failed to enact legislation to protect this concept. The racial composition of many schools results from decisions by people about where they choose to live. If Congress continues to fail to act, we would favor consideration of an amendment to the Constitution forbidding the assignment of children to schools on the basis of race.
>
> Our approach is to work to eradicate the root causes of segregated schools, such as housing discrimination and gerrymandered school districts. We must get on with the education of all our children.

The gradual hardening of party positions influenced the composition of each political coalition. By 1980 African Americans had become the most loyal Democratic Party members in the country. The once solidly Democratic South was now badly divided between African-American Democrats and an increasing number of white Republicans. Many working-class white Democrats in the North frequently crossed party lines to support Republicans who attacked affirmative action or welfare programs whose primary beneficiaries were perceived, usually incorrectly, as being persons of color.

The Supreme Court increasingly became the institution of choice for determining the constitutional meaning of racial equality during the 1970s. The Voting Rights Acts of 1970 and 1975 aside, the combination of partisan divisions, sectional divisions, and divided government largely prevented the national government from passing legislation with remotely the same impact on American race relations as the Civil Rights Acts of the previous decade. Congress occasionally protested school busing programs and passed legislation that seemed to require some affirmative action. More crucial issues were left to the courts to determine.

The liberals on the Supreme Court proved just as divided as the liberals in politics. The result was a series of judicial decisions that broadly reflected the general ambivalence of the American public, but in terms of specific detail typically reflected little more than the peculiar vision of one or two Supreme Court justices. *Swann v. Charlotte-Mecklenburg Board of Education* (1971) permitted federal courts to order wide-ranging intradistrict remedies for any past violations of *Brown*, but *Milliken v. Bradley* (1974) prohibited courts from busing students between school districts. A badly divided Court in *Regents of the University of California v. Bakke* (1978) determined that universities could institute race-conscious programs to achieve diversity, but

48. 121 *Congressional Record*, 94th Cong., 1st Sess. (1975), 30443.

not to remedy general societal discrimination. *Fullilove v. Kliznick* (1980) suggested that, unlike state race-conscious policies that were constitutionally required to meet a strict scrutiny standard, federal affirmative action policies were required to satisfy only an intermediate scrutiny standard.

Implementing *Brown*

The constitutional politics of race became national and partisan when NAACP lawyers attempted to integrate northern schools and federal judges attempted to implement *Brown* by busing students across metropolitan areas. During the Great Society Republicans and northern Democrats generally supported efforts to abolish Jim Crow in the South. Many northerners did not display the same enthusiasm for racial equality when courts found *Brown* violations in their school districts. Bitter controversies broke out, particularly when district judges ordered busing when implementing the Supreme Court's directive in *Green v. County School Board of New Kent County* (1968) to actively integrate schools. Busing plans were particularly common in and around cities. Patterns of residential segregation in urban America usually reinforced school segregation, even after the legal supports for school segregation had been removed. Some white Americans objected to busing because they objected to racially integrated schools. Others expressed less-racist concerns with the integrity of the local neighborhood school. Many complained that courts drew plans that wreaked havoc on lower-middle-class white communities while largely immunizing more affluent communities from the costs of desegregation. President Nixon, in a special message to Congress on March 17, 1972, spoke for many Americans when he asserted, "A remedy for the historic evil of racial discrimination has often created a new evil of disrupting communities and imposing hardship on children—both black and white—who are themselves wholly innocent of the wrongs that the plan seeks to set right."

The Supreme Court in the 1970s made a series of decisions that both sanctioned and limited busing as a tool for integrating school districts. The initial judicial decisions suggested that courts were prepared to make aggressive use of busing to secure racial equality. *Swann v. Charlotte-Mecklenburg Board of Education* (1971) ruled that federal courts could remedy *Brown* violations by busing children to any school within the offending school district. *Keyes v. School District No. 1, Denver, Colorado* (1973), the first northern school desegregation case the justices considered, held that courts could order busing throughout a large metropolitan school district after finding evidence of intentional segregation in one part of a school district. The more moderate justices on the Burger Court, however, almost immediately began restraining lower federal court justices. *Milliken v. Bradley* (1974) ruled that courts could not order an interdistrict remedy for *Brown* violations unless those violations took place in both school districts. *Pasadena City Board of Education v. Spangler* (1976) held that remedies for school segregation need not be adjusted for demographic changes that recreated racial imbalances, as long as these demographic changes were not caused by *Brown* violations. Significantly, the Supreme Court from *Brown* to *Swann* spoke with one voice. Beginning with *Keyes*, race cases divided the liberal justices from the conservative justices, with a changing alliance of centrist justices casting the crucial votes.

As many northern white families fled the cities for the suburbs, the combination of *Milliken* and *Pasadena* meant that federal judges could order busing only between inner-city public schools, an increasing number of which had very few white students. As Justice Marshall's dissent in *Milliken* noted, "Because of the already high and rapidly increasing percentage of Negro students in the Detroit system, as well as the prospect of white flight, a Detroit-only plan simply has no hope of achieving actual desegregation." Opponents of busing responded that these decisions returned control over education to local communities. Chief Justice Burger's majority opinion in *Milliken* asserted, "No single tradition in public education is more deeply rooted than local control over the operation of schools; local autonomy has long been thought essential both to the maintenance of community concern and support for public schools and to quality of the educational process."

Busing decisions reflected the distinction that the justices drew between de jure and de facto discrimination. De jure discrimination occurs when government officials pass laws or make decisions that explicitly separate children by race. Burger Court majorities ruled that federal courts could impose a variety of intrusive and creative remedies within any school district that had engaged in de jure segregation. De facto segregation occurs when private citizens choose not to associate with members of other races. Burger Court majorities ruled that federal courts had no authority to interfere with the consequences of de facto segregation. While the theoretical difference between de jure and de facto discrimination may be clear, distinguishing between them in practice is difficult. Most school cases in the 1970s required lengthy and expensive hearings in which lower court justices attempted to figure out whether the unbalanced racial composition of a school was the result of state practices or private prejudices. When reading the excerpts in this section, consider the extent to which segregation by 1980 was de jure or de facto, and whether, given the history of race in the United States, that distinction should matter for constitutional purposes.

Swann v. Charlotte-Mecklenburg Board of Education, 402 U.S. 1 (1971)

The Charlotte-Mecklenburg school system was segregated by race prior to Brown. *The system remained largely racially segregated during the first decade after* Brown, *despite various court orders. The majority of the district's black students attended nearly all-black schools. Most of the black student population and the all-black schools were located inside the city of Charlotte. Most of the white population and the all-white schools were located in the outlying suburbs. Dissatisfied with the pace of desegregation, James E. Swann and other African-American parents in 1965 brought a lawsuit against the Charlotte-Mecklenburg Board of Education. While the litigation was pending in the federal courts, the Supreme Court decided* Green v. County School Board of New Kent County *(1968). In light of that case's holding that formally segregated schools districts must "convert to a unitary system in which racial discrimination [is] eliminated root and branch," U.S. District Judge James McMillan adopted a plan that redrew the attendance zones for each school, reassigned teachers to achieve a racial balance across schools, and bused students to achieve more equal racial balances in individual schools. Most controversially, Judge McMillan paired schools in all-white neighborhoods with schools in virtually all-black neighborhoods, with the result being that many children had lengthy bus rides before reaching their assigned school. The Court of Appeals for the Fourth Circuit sustained Judge McMillan's plan to desegregate high schools but rejected his plan to desegregate elementary schools. Both Swann and the Charlotte-Mecklenburg Board of Education appealed to the Supreme Court.*

The Supreme Court unanimously sustained Judge's McMillan's plan to desegregate schools in Charlotte-Mecklenburg. Chief Justice Burger's unanimous opinion cautiously approved the busing of children and the use of race in determining school assignments as a means for integrating schools that had been unconstitutionally segregated. The deliberations within the Court revealed important latent divisions that soon became public. Chief Justice Burger thought that Swann *limited busing. Other justices endorsed the* Swann *opinion because they approved busing and race classifications as a remedy for past segregation. What limits, if any, do you believe that* Swann *places on remedies designed to desegregate schools? What limits do you believe the Constitution places on that process?*

The Court in Swann *was willing to bus schoolchildren between cities and suburbs only because all were part of one large school district. Three years later, the Supreme Court rejected a similar remedy because the city of Detroit and Detroit suburbs had separate school districts. Chief Justice Burger declared, "The constitutional right of the Negro respondents residing in Detroit is to attend a unitary school system in that district. Unless petitioners drew the district lines in a discriminatory fashion, or arranged for white students residing in the Detroit District to attend schools in Oakland and Macomb Counties, they were under no constitutional duty to make provisions for Negro students to do so."*

CHIEF JUSTICE BURGER delivered the opinion of the Court.

. . .

The objective today remains to eliminate from the public schools all vestiges of state-imposed segregation. Segregation was the evil struck down by *Brown I* (1954) as contrary to the equal protection guarantees of the Constitution. That was the violation sought to be corrected by the remedial measures of *Brown II* (1955) . That was the basis for the holding in *Green* (1968) that school authorities are "clearly charged with the affirmative duty to take whatever steps might be necessary to convert to a unitary system in which racial discrimination would be eliminated root and branch."

. . .

. . . In addition to the classic pattern of building schools specifically intended for Negro or white students, school authorities have sometimes, since *Brown*, closed schools which appeared likely to become racially mixed through changes in neighborhood residential patterns. This was sometimes accompanied by building new schools in the areas of white suburban expansion farthest from Negro population centers in order to maintain the separation of the races with a minimum departure from the formal principles of "neighborhood zoning." Such a policy does more than simply influence the short-run composition of the student body of a new school. It may well promote segregated residential patterns which, when combined with "neighborhood zoning," further lock the school system into the mold of separation of the races. Upon a proper showing a district court may consider this in fashioning a remedy.

In ascertaining the existence of legally imposed school segregation, the existence of a pattern of school construction and abandonment is thus a factor of great weight. In devising remedies where legally imposed segregation has been established, it is the responsibility of local authorities and district courts to see to it that future school construction and abandonment are not used and do not serve to perpetuate or re-establish the dual system. When necessary, district courts should retain jurisdiction to assure that these responsibilities are carried out.

. . .

Our objective in dealing with the issues presented by these cases is to see that school authorities exclude no pupil of a racial minority from any school, directly or indirectly, on account of race; it does not and cannot embrace all the problems of racial prejudice, even when those problems contribute to disproportionate racial concentrations in some schools.

. . .

. . . If we were to read the holding of the District Court to require, as a matter of substantive constitutional right, any particular degree of racial balance or mixing, that approach would be disapproved and we would be obliged to reverse. The constitutional command to desegregate schools does not mean that every school in every community must always reflect the racial composition of the school system as a whole.

. . .

As we said in *Green*, a school authority's remedial plan or a district court's remedial decree is to be judged by its effectiveness. Awareness of the racial composition of the whole school system is likely to be a useful starting point in shaping a remedy to correct past constitutional violations. In sum, the very limited use made of mathematical ratios [for assignments of students to individual schools] was within the equitable remedial discretion of the District Court.

. . .

The record in this case reveals the familiar phenomenon that in metropolitan areas minority groups are often found concentrated in one part of the city. In some circumstances certain schools may remain all or largely of one race until new schools can be provided or neighborhood patterns change. Schools all or predominately of one race in a district of mixed population will require close scrutiny to determine that school assignments are not part of state-enforced segregation.

In light of the above, it should be clear that the existence of some small number of one-race, or virtually one-race, schools within a district is not in and of itself the mark of a system that still practices segregation by law. . . .

An optional majority-to-minority transfer provision has long been recognized as a useful part of every desegregation plan. Provision for optional transfer of those in the majority racial group of a particular school to other schools where they will be in the minority is an indispensable remedy for those students willing to transfer to other schools in order to lessen the impact on them of the state-imposed stigma of segregation. . . .

. . .

Absent a constitutional violation there would be no basis for judicially ordering assignment of students on a racial basis. All things being equal, with no history of discrimination, it might well be desirable to assign pupils to schools nearest their homes. But all things are not equal in a system that has been deliberately constructed and maintained to enforce racial segregation. The remedy for such segregation may be administratively awkward, inconvenient, and even bizarre in some situations and may impose burdens on some; but all awkwardness and inconvenience cannot be avoided in the interim period when remedial adjustments are being made to eliminate the dual school systems.

No fixed or even substantially fixed guidelines can be established as to how far a court can go, but it must be recognized that there are limits. The objective is to dismantle the dual school system. "Racially neutral" assignment plans proposed by school authorities to a district court may be inadequate; such plans may fail to counteract the continuing effects of past school segregation resulting from discriminatory location of school sites or distortion of school size in order to achieve or maintain an artificial racial separation. . . .

. . .

The decree provided that the buses used to implement the plan would operate on direct routes. Students would be picked up at schools near their homes and transported to the schools they were to attend. The trips for elementary school pupils average about seven miles and the District Court found that they would take "not over 35 minutes at the most." This system compares favorably with the transportation plan previously operated in Charlotte under which each day 23,600 students on all grade levels were transported an average of 15 miles one way for an average trip requiring over an hour. In these circumstances, we find no basis for holding that the local school authorities may not be required to employ bus transportation as one tool of school desegregation. Desegregation plans cannot be limited to the walk-in school.

An objection to transportation of students may have validity when the time or distance of travel is so great as to either risk the health of the children or significantly impinge on the educational process. . . .

. . .

At some point, these school authorities and others like them should have achieved full compliance with this Court's decision in *Brown I*. The systems would then be "unitary" in the sense required by our decision in *Green*. . . .

It does not follow that the communities served by such systems will remain demographically stable, for in a growing, mobile society, few will do so. Neither school authorities nor district courts are constitutionally required to make year-by-year adjustments of the racial composition of student bodies once the affirmative duty to desegregate has been accomplished and racial discrimination through official action is eliminated from the system. This does not mean that federal courts are without power to deal with future problems; but in the absence of a showing that either the school authorities or some other agency of the State has deliberately attempted to fix or alter demographic patterns to affect the racial composition of the schools, further intervention by a district court should not be necessary. . . .

Executive and Legislative Attacks on Busing

Judicial decisions mandating busing as a remedy for desegregation were unpopular. Working-class whites, upset by both the prospect of desegregation and the class bias of many busing orders, fought court orders by rioting, removing their children from public schools, and supporting conservative politicians who promised to stand up to liberal justices. Massive resistance occurred on a national scale. Some of the most violent protests over busing took place in Boston, the capital of the only state to vote for George McGovern in 1972.[49] *President Nixon proposed that Congress prohibit courts from ordering busing as a remedy for segregation except under extraordinary circumstances. Congressional liberals, concerned with the establishment of precedents that would limit judicial power, defeated these measures. Instead, elected officials concerned with existing remedies for desegregation frequently united on such measures as the Eagleton-Biden Amendment, which forbade the Department of Health, Education, and Welfare from using federal funds to facilitate busing.* Brown v. Califano *(1980) sustained that measure.*

President Nixon and Senator Humphrey of Minnesota had very different beliefs about race relations in the United States. Nixon insists that Jim Crow has largely been abolished. Humphrey claims that segregation is on the rise. Do these differences explain their different perspectives on busing and congressional power, or does each have a fundamentally different constitutional understanding of race?

Richard Nixon, Special Message to the Congress on Equal Educational Opportunities and School Busing (March 17, 1972)

. . .

There is no escaping the fact that some people oppose busing because of racial prejudice. But to go on from this to conclude that "anti-busing" is simply a code word for prejudice is an exercise in arrant unreason. There are right reasons for opposing busing, and there are wrong reasons—and most people, including large and increasing numbers of blacks and other minorities, oppose it for reasons that have little or nothing to do with race. It would compound an injustice to persist in massive busing simply because some people oppose it for the wrong reasons.

. . .

If we are to be realists, we must recognize that in a free society there are limits to the amount of

49. See J. Harvie Wilkinson III, *From* Brown *to* Bakke*: The Supreme Court and School Integration: 1954–1978* (New York: Oxford University Press, 1979), 131–249.

Government coercion that can reasonably be used; that in achieving desegregation we must proceed with the least possible disruption of the education of the Nation's children; and that our children are highly sensitive to conflict, and highly vulnerable to lasting psychic injury.

. . .

. . . [I]n the past 3 years, progress toward eliminating the vestiges of the dual system has been phenomenal—and so too has been the shift in public attitudes in those areas where dual systems were formerly operated. In State after State and community after community, local civic, business and educational leaders of all races have come forward to help make the transition peacefully and successfully. Few voices are now raised urging a return to the old patterns of enforced segregation.

. . .

At the same time, there has been a marked shift in the focus of concerns by blacks and members of other minorities. Minority parents have long had a deep and special concern with improving the quality of their children's education. For a number of years, the principal emphasis of this concern—and of the Nation's attention—was on desegregating the schools. Now that the dismantling of the old dual system has been substantially completed there is once again a far greater balance of emphasis on improving schools, on convenience, on the chance for parental involvement—in short, on the same concerns that motivate white parents—and, in many communities, on securing a greater measure of control over schools that serve primarily minority-group communities. Moving forward on desegregation is still important but the principal concern is with preserving the principle, and with ensuring that the great gains made since *Brown*, and particularly in recent years, are not rolled back in a reaction against excessive busing. Many black leaders now express private concern, moreover, that a reckless extension of busing requirements could bring about precisely the results they fear most: a reaction that would undo those gains, and that would begin the unraveling of advances in other areas that also are based on newly expanded interpretations of basic Constitutional rights.

Also, it has not escaped their notice that those who insist on system-wide racial balance insist on a condition in which, in most communities, every school would be run by whites and dominated by whites, with blacks in a permanent minority—and without escape from that minority status. The result would be to deny blacks the right to have schools in which they are the majority.

. . .

As we cut through the clouds of emotionalism that surround the busing question, we can begin to identify the legitimate issues.

Concern for the quality of education a child gets is legitimate.

Concern that there be no retreat from the principle of ending racial discrimination is legitimate.

Concern for the distance a child has to travel to get to school is legitimate.

Hubert Humphrey, Senate Retreats from Equal Opportunity (1975)[50]

Mr. President, the U.S. Senate has dealt a severe blow to the hopes of millions of fellow Americans by its action to limit and curtail the use of Federal funds for the transportation of students by reason of race.

. . .

Students are not transported "by reason of race" in desegregation plans. They are transported to disestablish de jure segregation, and busing assignments are often made on the basis of residence, not race. In many plans few additional students are actually transported although existing buses are rerouted. . . .

. . .

. . . Congress is saying that the only available way to integrate most urban schools is wrong and illegitimate. The action can only encourage supporters of segregation and increase the already immense pressures on the Federal courts.

Instead of providing aid to help make a difficult transition work better, Congress is taking the posture of State legislatures in the 1950s, striking out in every possible way to remove financial and administrative resources to support the process. This will not stop the courts from implementing constitutional requirements, but will intensify the atmosphere of racial polarization surrounding the change and minimize the chances of carefully planned desegregation.

. . .

While Congress rails against school desegregation, no one gives much notice to the fact that the grim predictions of the "[Kerner] Commission" about 7 years

50. 121 *Congressional Record*, 94th Cong., 1st Sess. (1975), 30, 542–43.

ago[51] are coming true, perhaps even faster than the Commission foresaw in some of the largest metropolitan areas. Segregation is spreading out over more and more central cities and even some inner suburbs are being absorbed into growing ghettos. . . . In the face of these powerful segregating trends and the growing evidence that State action played a major role in setting them in motion, a decision to prohibit administrative enforcement of desegregation is a decision for intensifying segregation. Our cities are moving steadily toward a level of segregation and inequality that can only have terrifying consequences for American Society. . . .

Affirmative Action

Great Society liberals combined strong anti-discrimination rhetoric with the belief that vague forms of "affirmative action" should be taken to promote increased representation of persons of color in education, employment, and politics. During the 1970s this concern for affirmative action hardened into various policies that specifically required admissions officers and employers to take race into account when making decisions. The Nixon administration often aggressively insisted that employers hire targeted numbers of minorities. In part this reflected the continued commitment among many Republicans to a strong version of racial equality. Cynics pointed out that the Nixon administration was using affirmative action to divide traditional white, ethnic, Democratic voters from persons of color. White ethnic groups and trade groups became key opponents of affirmative action in the 1970s but were later replaced by more ideologically motivated organizations.

The Supreme Court was initially reluctant to become involved in the constitutional debate over affirmative action. A 5-4 majority in *DeFunis v. Odegaard* (1974) dismissed a challenge to a law school affirmative action program on the ground that the plaintiff, who had been allowed to matriculate pending the outcome of the litigation, was about to graduate. Justice Douglas sharply criticized the University of Washington's use of race in the law school admissions process. His dissent, which also condemned the Law School Admission Test (LSAT) as racially biased, asserted,

> There is no constitutional right for any race to be preferred. The years of slavery did more than retard the progress of blacks. Even a greater wrong was done the whites by creating arrogance instead of humility and by encouraging the growth of the fiction of a superior race. There is no superior person by constitutional standards. A DeFunis who is white is entitled to no advantage by reason of that fact; nor is he subject to any disability, no matter what his race or color. Whatever his race, he had a constitutional right to have his application considered on its individual merits in a racially neutral manner.

Four years later the Supreme Court by a series of 5-4 votes in *Regents of the University of California v. Bakke* (1978) ruled:

- State affirmative action plans had to satisfy the same strict scrutiny standard as discrimination against persons of color.
- Educational diversity was a compelling government interest that justified affirmative action, but affirmative action was not justified as a remedy for general societal discrimination.
- Affirmative action plans could give applicants of color a "plus" but could not establish strict quotas.

The justices in *Fullilove v. Klutznick* (1980) further muddied the affirmative action waters by suggesting that federal affirmative action plans might have to satisfy a lesser, not well defined constitutional standard. When sustaining a federal program that required contractors doing business with the government to employ a certain percentage of persons of color, Chief Justice Burger's plurality opinion asserted,

> A program that employs racial or ethnic criteria, even in a remedial context, calls for close examination; yet we are bound to approach our task with appropriate deference to the Congress, a co-equal branch charged by the Constitution with the power to "provide for the . . . general Welfare of the United States" and "to enforce, by appropriate legislation," the equal protection guarantees of the Fourteenth Amendment.

Regents of the University of California v. Bakke, 438 U.S. 265 (1978)

Alan Bakke was a Marine captain in Vietnam and an engineer. His lifelong ambition was to be a doctor. In 1973 he was

51. This report warned that the nation was "moving toward two societies, one black, one white—separate and unequal." National Advisory Commission on Civil Disorders, *Report of the National Advisory Commission on Civil Disorders* (Washington, DC: Government Printing Office, 1968).

Table 9-3 Amicus Filings on Affirmative Action in University Admissions, *Bakke* and *Grutter*

Stance	***Regents of the University of California v. Bakke* (1978)**	***Grutter v. Bollinger* (2003)**
Favoring affirmative action	Total: 40	Total: 62
	Association of American Medical Colleges	Association of American Medical Colleges
	American Bar Association	Association of American Law Schools
	American Association of University Professors	American Sociological Association
	NAACP Legal Defense Fund	NAACP Legal Defense Fund
	Legal Services Corporation	ACLU
	NOW	General Motors Corporation
	National Association of Affirmative Action Officers	American Federation of Labor
		Retired Military Officers
Opposing affirmative action	Total: 14	Total: 15
	American Subcontractors Association	Pacific Legal Foundation
	Chamber of Commerce of the United States of America	National Association of Scholars
	American Federation of Teachers	Cato Institute
	Fraternal Order of Police	United States
	American Jewish Committee	
	Polish American Congress	

rejected by all twelve medical schools to which he applied. One of those institutions was the University of California, Davis. Davis had just instituted a program in which sixteen of the one hundred seats in the entering class were committed to students of color. Bakke, whose grades and board scores were considerably higher than the average of those persons admitted under the special program, sued the university, claiming that the special program violated the Fourteenth Amendment. The trial court rejected his contentions, but that decision was reversed by the Supreme Court of California. The university appealed to the Supreme Court of the United States.

The Supreme Court by a 5-4 vote declared that Davis had unconstitutionally discriminated against Bakke. Justice Powell's crucial opinion for the Court insisted that all racial classifications must satisfy a strict scrutiny standard, that diversity was the only government interest in Bakke *that met that standard, and that diversity could justify only racial preferences as opposed to racial quotas. No other justice on the court drew these fine distinctions. Four justices insisted that "benign" racial classifications that were designed to assist previously disadvantaged groups rather than harm discrete and insular minorities need meet only a lesser judicial standard. The other four justices limited their analysis to a statutory question. Powell's opinion nevertheless became the official law of the land because he was the median justice on all issues. Powell maintains that all race conscious laws must meet strict scrutiny. Why does he make that claim? Why do other justices disagree? Who is correct? Powell also maintains that diversity is the best and only justification for affirmative action. Is that correct? Given the pervasiveness of racial discrimination in the United States, could any public institution make a good case that past practices had skewed their admissions or hiring processes, leaving them with some obligation to compensate for past practices? Do all or the overwhelming majority of white persons in the United States benefit from these processes because they are white? Does affirmative action ignore the numerous ways in which many persons are disadvantaged? What does the Constitution have to say about these issues? Why does*

Powell differentiate between quotas and the "plus" system? Is that distinction sound in theory? Is that distinction sound in practice or will schools adjust pluses to obtain a fairly fixed number of students of color?

JUSTICE POWELL announced the judgment of the Court.

...

The guarantees of the Fourteenth Amendment extend to all persons. Its language is explicit: "No State shall . . . deny to any person within its jurisdiction the equal protection of the laws." It is settled beyond question that the rights created by the first section of the Fourteenth Amendment are, by its terms, guaranteed to the individual. . . . The guarantee of equal protection cannot mean one thing when applied to one individual and something else when applied to a person of another color. If both are not accorded the same protection, then it is not equal.

Nevertheless, petitioner argues that the court below erred in applying strict scrutiny to the special admissions program because white males, such as respondent, are not a "discrete and insular minority" requiring extraordinary protection from the majoritarian political process. . . . This rationale, however, has never been invoked in our decisions as a prerequisite to subjecting racial or ethnic distinctions to strict scrutiny. . . . Racial and ethnic classifications . . . are subject to stringent examination without regard to these additional characteristics. . . .

...

Although many of the Framers of the Fourteenth Amendment conceived of its primary function as bridging the vast distance between members of the Negro race and the white "majority," . . . the Amendment itself was framed in universal terms, without reference to color, ethnic origin, or condition of prior servitude. . . .[T]he 39th Congress was intent upon establishing in the federal law a broader principle than would have been necessary simply to meet the particular and immediate plight of the newly freed Negro slaves. . . .

...

. . . [T]he difficulties entailed in varying the level of judicial review according to a perceived "preferred" status of a particular racial or ethnic minority are intractable. The concepts of "majority" and "minority" necessarily reflect temporary arrangements and political judgments. . . . [T]he white "majority" itself is composed of various minority groups, most of which can lay claim to a history of prior discrimination at the hands of the State and private individuals. . . . There is no principled basis for deciding which groups would merit "heightened judicial solicitude" and which would not. . . .

. . . [T]here are serious problems of justice connected with the idea of preference itself. First, it may not always be clear that a so-called preference is, in fact, benign. . . . Nothing in the Constitution supports the notion that individuals may be asked to suffer otherwise impermissible burdens in order to enhance the societal standing of their ethnic groups. Second, preferential programs may only reinforce common stereotypes holding that certain groups are unable to achieve success without special protection based on a factor having no relationship to individual worth. . . . Third, there is a measure of inequity in forcing innocent persons in respondent's position to bear the burdens of redressing grievances not of their making.

...

We have held that, in order to justify the use of a suspect classification, a State must show that its purpose or interest is both constitutionally permissible and substantial and that its use of the classification is "necessary . . . to the accomplishment" of its purpose or the safeguarding of its interest. . . . The special admissions program purports to serve the purposes of: (i) "reducing the historic deficit of traditionally disfavored minorities in medical schools and in the medical profession". . . ; (ii) countering the effects of societal discrimination; (iii) increasing the number of physicians who will practice in communities currently underserved; and (iv) obtaining the educational benefits that flow from an ethnically diverse student body. It is necessary to decide which, if any, of these purposes is substantial enough to support the use of a suspect classification.

If petitioner's purpose is to assure within its student body some specified percentage of a particular group merely because of its race or ethnic origin, such a preferential purpose must be rejected not as insubstantial, but as facially invalid. Preferring members of any one group for no reason other than race or ethnic origin is discrimination for its own sake. This the Constitution forbids. . . .

...

We have never approved a classification that aids persons perceived as members of relatively victimized groups at the expense of other innocent individuals in the absence of judicial, legislative, or administrative findings of constitutional or statutory violations. . . . After such findings have been made, the governmental interest in preferring members of the injured groups at the expense of others is substantial, since the legal rights of the victims must be vindicated. . . . Without such findings of constitutional or statutory violations, it cannot be said that the government has any greater interest in helping one individual than in refraining from harming another. Thus, the government has no compelling justification for inflicting such harm.

. . .

Petitioner identifies, as another purpose of its program, improving the delivery of health care services to communities currently underserved. It may be assumed that, in some situations, a State's interest in facilitating the health care of its citizens is sufficiently compelling to support the use of a suspect classification. But there is virtually no evidence in the record indicating that petitioner's special admissions program is either needed or geared to promote that goal. . . .

. . .

The fourth goal asserted by petitioner is the attainment of a diverse student body. This clearly is a constitutionally permissible goal for an institution of higher education. Academic freedom, though not a specifically enumerated constitutional right, long has been viewed as a special concern of the First Amendment. . . .

The atmosphere of "speculation, experiment and creation"—so essential to the quality of higher education—is widely believed to be promoted by a diverse student body. . . . [I]t is not too much to say that the "nation's future depends upon leaders trained through wide exposure" to the ideas and mores of students as diverse as this Nation of many peoples.

. . .

Physicians serve a heterogeneous population. An otherwise qualified medical student with a particular background—whether it be ethnic, geographic, culturally advantaged or disadvantaged—may bring to a professional school of medicine experiences, outlooks, and ideas that enrich the training of its student body and better equip its graduates to render with understanding their vital service to humanity.

. . .

It may be assumed that the reservation of a specified number of seats in each class for individuals from the preferred ethnic groups would contribute to the attainment of considerable ethnic diversity in the student body. But petitioner's argument that this is the only effective means of serving the interest of diversity is seriously flawed. . . . The diversity that furthers a compelling state interest encompasses a far broader array of qualifications and characteristics, of which racial or ethnic origin is but a single, though important, element. Petitioner's special admissions program, focused solely on ethnic diversity, would hinder, rather than further, attainment of genuine diversity.

. . . The experience of other university admissions programs, which take race into account in achieving the educational diversity valued by the First Amendment, demonstrates that the assignment of a fixed number of places to a minority group is not a necessary means toward that end. . . . In such an admissions program, race or ethnic background may be deemed a "plus" in a particular applicant's file, yet it does not insulate the individual from comparison with all other candidates for the available seats. The file of a particular black applicant may be examined for his potential contribution to diversity without the factor of race being decisive when compared, for example, with that of an applicant identified as an Italian-American if the latter is thought to exhibit qualities more likely to promote beneficial educational pluralism. Such qualities could include exceptional personal talents, unique work or service experience, leadership potential, maturity, demonstrated compassion, a history of overcoming disadvantage, ability to communicate with the poor, or other qualifications deemed important. In short, an admissions program operated in this way is flexible enough to consider all pertinent elements of diversity in light of the particular qualifications of each applicant, and to place them on the same footing for consideration, although not necessarily according them the same weight. . . .

This kind of program treats each applicant as an individual in the admissions process. The applicant who loses out on the last available seat to another candidate receiving a "plus" on the basis of ethnic background will not have been foreclosed from all consideration for that seat simply because he was not the right color or had the wrong surname. It would mean only that his combined qualifications, which may have included similar nonobjective factors, did not outweigh those of the other applicant. . . .

. . .

JUSTICE BRENNAN, JUSTICE WHITE, JUSTICE MARSHALL, and JUSTICE BLACKMUN, concurring in the judgment in part and dissenting in part.

. . . Government may take race into account when it acts not to demean or insult any racial group, but to remedy disadvantages cast on minorities by past racial prejudice, at least when appropriate findings have been made by judicial, legislative, or administrative bodies with competence to act in this area.

. . .

The Fourteenth Amendment, the embodiment in the Constitution of our abiding belief in human equality, has been the law of our land for only slightly more than half its 200 years. And for half of that half, the Equal Protection Clause of the Amendment was largely moribund. . . . Worse than desuetude, the Clause was early turned against those whom it was intended to set free, condemning them to a "separate but equal" status before the law, a status always separate but seldom equal. Not until 1954—only 24 years ago—was this odious doctrine interred by our decision in *Brown v. Board of Education* (1954). . . . Even then, inequality was not eliminated with "all deliberate speed." . . . Against this background, claims that law must be "colorblind" or that the datum of race is no longer relevant to public policy must be seen as aspiration, rather than as description of reality. This is not to denigrate aspiration; for reality rebukes us that race has too often been used by those who would stigmatize and oppress minorities. Yet we cannot—and, as we shall demonstrate, need not under our Constitution . . . let color blindness become myopia which masks the reality that many "created equal" have been treated within our lifetimes as inferior both by the law and by their fellow citizens.

. . .

Unquestionably we have held that a government practice or statute which restricts "fundamental rights" or which contains "suspect classifications" is to be subjected to "strict scrutiny," and can be justified only if it furthers a compelling government purpose and, even then, only if no less restrictive alternative is available. . . . But no fundamental right is involved here. . . . Nor do whites, as a class, have any of the traditional indicia of suspectness: the class is not saddled with such disabilities, or subjected to such a history of purposeful unequal treatment, or relegated to such a position of political powerlessness as to command extraordinary protection from the majoritarian political process. . . . Nor has anyone suggested that the University's purposes contravene the cardinal principle that racial classifications that stigmatize—because they are drawn on the presumption that one race is inferior to another or because they put the weight of government behind racial hatred and separatism—are invalid without more. . . .

. . .

. . . [A] number of considerations . . . lead us to conclude that racial classifications designed to further remedial purposes " 'must serve important governmental objectives, and must be substantially related to achievement of those objectives.'" . . . First, race, like, "gender-based classifications, too often [has] been inexcusably utilized to stereotype and stigmatize politically powerless segments of society." While a carefully tailored statute designed to remedy past discrimination could avoid these vices, . . . we nonetheless have recognized that the line between honest and thoughtful appraisal of the effects of past discrimination and paternalistic stereotyping is not so clear, and that a statute based on the latter is patently capable of stigmatizing all women with a badge of inferiority. . . . State programs designed ostensibly to ameliorate the effects of past racial discrimination obviously create the same hazard of stigma, since they may promote racial separatism and reinforce the views of those who believe that members of racial minorities are inherently incapable of succeeding on their own. . . .

Second, race, like gender and illegitimacy . . . is an immutable characteristic which its possessors are powerless to escape or set aside. . . . [S]uch divisions are contrary to our deep belief that "legal burdens should bear some relationship to individual responsibility or wrongdoing," . . . and that advancement sanctioned, sponsored, or approved by the State should ideally be based on individual merit or achievement, or at the least on factors within the control of an individual. . . .

. . .

Davis' articulated purpose of remedying the effects of past societal discrimination is, under our cases, sufficiently important to justify the use of race-conscious admissions programs where there is a sound basis for concluding that minority underrepresentation is substantial and chronic, and that the handicap of past discrimination is impeding access of minorities to the Medical School.

. . .

Certainly, on the basis of the undisputed factual submissions before this Court, Davis had a sound basis for believing that the problem of underrepresentation of minorities was substantial and chronic, and that the problem was attributable to handicaps imposed on minority applicants by past and present racial discrimination. Until at least 1973, the practice of medicine in this country was, in fact, if not in law, largely the prerogative of whites. In 1950, for example, while Negroes constituted 10% of the total population, Negro physicians constituted only 2.2% of the total number of physicians. The overwhelming majority of these, moreover, were educated in two predominantly Negro medical schools, Howard and Meharry. By 1970, the gap between the proportion of Negroes in medicine and their proportion in the population had widened: the number of Negroes employed in medicine remained frozen at 2.2%, while the Negro population had increased to 11.1%. The number of Negro admittees to predominantly white medical schools, moreover, had declined in absolute numbers during the years 1955 to 1964.

. . .

Davis clearly could conclude that the serious and persistent underrepresentation of minorities in medicine depicted by these statistics is the result of handicaps under which minority applicants labor as a consequence of a background of deliberate, purposeful discrimination against minorities in education and in society generally, as well as in the medical profession. From the inception of our national life, Negroes have been subjected to unique legal disabilities impairing access to equal educational opportunity. Under slavery, penal sanctions were imposed upon anyone attempting to educate Negroes. After enactment of the Fourteenth Amendment the States continued to deny Negroes equal educational opportunity, enforcing a strict policy of segregation that itself stamped Negroes as inferior, . . . that relegated minorities to inferior educational institutions, and that denied them intercourse in the mainstream of professional life necessary to advancement. . . . [M]assive official and private resistance [to *Brown* and related decisions] prevented, and to a lesser extent still prevents, attainment of equal opportunity in education at all levels and in the professions. The generation of minority students applying to Davis Medical School since it opened in 1968—most of whom were born before or about the time *Brown I* was decided—clearly have been victims of this discrimination. . . . [T]he conclusion is inescapable that applicants to medical school must be few indeed who endured the effects of *de jure* segregation, the resistance to *Brown I*, or the equally debilitating pervasive private discrimination fostered by our long history of official discrimination, . . . and yet come to the starting line with an education equal to whites.

. . .

JUSTICE WHITE, concurring. . . .

JUSTICE MARSHALL, concurring.

. . . [I]t must be remembered that, during most of the past 200 years, the Constitution, as interpreted by this Court, did not prohibit the most ingenious and pervasive forms of discrimination against the Negro. Now, when a State acts to remedy the effects of that legacy of discrimination, I cannot believe that this same Constitution stands as a barrier.

. . .

. . . It is plain that the Fourteenth Amendment was not intended to prohibit measures designed to remedy the effects of the Nation's past treatment of Negroes. The Congress that passed the Fourteenth Amendment is the same Congress that passed the 1866 Freedmen's Bureau Act, an Act that provided many of its benefits only to Negroes. . . .

. . .

While I applaud the judgment of the Court that a university may consider race in its admissions process, it is more than a little ironic that, after several hundred years of class-based discrimination against Negroes, the Court is unwilling to hold that a class-based remedy for that discrimination is permissible. In declining to so hold, today's judgment ignores the fact that, for several hundred years, Negroes have been discriminated against not as individuals, but rather solely because of the color of their skins. It is unnecessary in 20th-century America to have individual Negroes demonstrate that they have been victims of racial discrimination; the racism of our society has been so pervasive that none, regardless of wealth or position, has managed to escape its impact. The experience of Negroes in America has been different in kind, not just in degree, from that of other ethnic groups. It is not merely the history of slavery alone, but also that a whole people were marked as inferior by the law. And that mark has endured. The dream of America as the great melting pot has not been realized for the Negro; because of his skin color, he never even made it into the pot.

. . . It is because of a legacy of unequal treatment that we now must permit the institutions of this society to give consideration to race in making decisions about who will hold the positions of influence, affluence, and prestige in America. For far too long, the doors to those positions have been shut to Negroes. If we are ever to become a fully integrated society, one in which the color of a person's skin will not determine the opportunities available to him or her, we must be willing to take steps to open those doors. . . .

. . .

JUSTICE BLACKMUN, concurring. . . .

JUSTICE STEVENS, with whom THE CHIEF JUSTICE, JUSTICE STEWART, and JUSTICE REHNQUIST join, concurring in the judgment in part and dissenting in part.

[*Justices Stevens concluded that the affirmative action program violated Title VI of the Civil Rights Act. He did not discuss the constitutional issue.*]

Racial Discrimination

Constitutional decision makers in the 1970s were willing to find race discrimination only when states either explicitly made race-based classifications or when an ostensibly neutral state law had both a racial purpose and a racially disparate effect. *Palmer v. Thompson* (1971) ruled that a racial purpose was not sufficient to find discrimination in the absence of a racially disparate effect. This case arose after Jackson, Mississippi, closed all public pools rather than obey a court order requiring integration. Justice Black's majority opinion asserted, "[This is] not a case where a city is maintaining different sets of facilities for blacks and whites and forcing the races to remain separate in recreational or educational activities." *Washington v. Davis* (1976) ruled that a racially disparate effect was not sufficient to find discrimination in the absence of a racial purpose. Justice White maintained that "discriminatory impact" could be used to prove discriminatory purpose, but only when the state could not provide a race-neutral justification for the disparate result. This requirement is difficult to meet. In *Village of Arlington Heights v. Metropolitan Housing Development Corp.* (1977) a Burger Court majority indicated that persons of color would have trouble proving that long-standing single-family zoning regulations violated the equal protection clause. After noting that "official action will not be held unconstitutional solely because it results in a racially disproportionate impact," Justice Powell's majority opinion concluded that "the Village originally adopted its buffer policy long before [plaintiffs] entered the picture and has applied the policy too consistently for us to infer discriminatory purpose from its application in this case."

Washington v. Davis, 426 U.S. 229 (1976)

George Harley and John Dugan Sellers were African-American men who were not hired as police officers in the District of Columbia because they failed a civil service examination known as Test 21. Harley and Sellers, along with Alfred E. Davis, an African-American police officer who had been denied promotion on the basis of the exam, sued Mayor Walter Washington and the Metropolitan Police Department (MPD). They claimed that the test discriminated against persons of color because persons of color were far more likely to fail the examination than white persons and that the test had not been demonstrated to correlate with job performance. The federal district court ruled that the MPD's hiring and promotion policies did not violate the equal protection clause. The Circuit Court of Appeals for the District of Columbia Circuit, however, found that the use of Test 21 in the hiring process was unconstitutional. Mayor Washington and the MPD appealed to the Supreme Court of the United States.

The Supreme Court by a 7-2 vote ruled that the test was constitutional. Justice White's opinion for the Court in Washington *holds that persons who make equal protection claims must prove discriminatory intent as well as discriminatory impact. What reason does Justice White give for this conclusion? Should plaintiffs have to prove either discriminatory intent or discriminatory impact, but not both? One, but not the other? Why did Justice White fail to find discriminatory intent in this case? Consider two possible reasons. First, White concluded that the test was fair. Second, White concluded that the MPD's overall hiring process was fair. Both of these reasons are noted in the opinion. Do you agree with both or either? Suppose that someone wanted to sue a public university that used the LSAT. Does* Washington v. Davis *foreclose that possibility, or can you think of a way to distinguish that claim?*

JUSTICE WHITE delivered the opinion of the Court.

. . .

The central purpose of the Equal Protection Clause of the Fourteenth Amendment is the prevention of official conduct discriminating on the basis of race. . . . But our cases have not embraced the proposition that a law or other official act, without regard to whether it reflects a racially discriminatory purpose, is unconstitutional solely because it has a racially disproportionate impact.

Almost 100 years ago, *Strauder v. West Virginia* . . . (1880), established that the exclusion of Negroes from grand and petit juries in criminal proceedings violated the Equal Protection Clause, but the fact that a particular jury or a series of juries does not statistically reflect the racial composition of the community does not in itself make out an invidious discrimination forbidden by the Clause. "A purpose to discriminate must be present which may be proven by systematic exclusion of eligible jurymen of the proscribed race or by unequal application of the law to such an extent as to show intentional discrimination." . . .

The school desegregation cases have also adhered to the basic equal protection principle that the invidious quality of a law claimed to be racially discriminatory must ultimately be traced to a racially discriminatory purpose. That there are both predominantly black and predominantly white schools in a community is not alone violative of the Equal Protection Clause. The essential element of de jure segregation is "a current condition of segregation resulting from intentional state action." . . .

This is not to say that the necessary discriminatory racial purpose must be express or appear on the face of the statute, or that a law's disproportionate impact is irrelevant in cases involving Constitution-based claims of racial discrimination. A statute, otherwise neutral on its face, must not be applied so as invidiously to discriminate on the basis of race. . . . It is also clear from the cases dealing with racial discrimination in the selection of juries that the systematic exclusion of Negroes is itself such an "unequal application of the law . . . as to show intentional discrimination." . . . A prima facie case of discriminatory purpose may be proved as well by the absence of Negroes on a particular jury combined with the failure of the jury commissioners to be informed of eligible Negro jurors in a community . . . or with racially non-neutral selection procedures. . . . With a prima facie case made out, "the burden of proof shifts to the State to rebut the presumption of unconstitutional action by showing that permissible racially neutral selection criteria and procedures have produced the monochromatic result." . . .

Necessarily, an invidious discriminatory purpose may often be inferred from the totality of the relevant facts, including the fact, if it is true, that the law bears more heavily on one race than another. It is also not infrequently true that the discriminatory impact—in the jury cases for example, the total or seriously disproportionate exclusion of Negroes from jury venires—may for all practical purposes demonstrate unconstitutionality because in various circumstances the discrimination is very difficult to explain on nonracial grounds. Nevertheless, we have not held that a law, neutral on its face and serving ends otherwise within the power of government to pursue, is invalid under the Equal Protection Clause simply because it may affect a greater proportion of one race than of another. Disproportionate impact is not irrelevant, but it is not the sole touchstone of an invidious racial discrimination forbidden by the Constitution. . . .

There are some indications to the contrary in our cases. . . . Accepting the finding [in *Palmer v. Thompson* (1971)] that the pools were closed to avoid violence and economic loss, this Court rejected the argument that the abandonment of this service was inconsistent with the outstanding desegregation decree and that the otherwise seemingly permissible ends served by the ordinance could be impeached by demonstrating that racially invidious motivations had prompted the city council's action. . . . The opinion warned against grounding decision on legislative purpose or motivation, thereby lending support for the proposition that the operative effect of the law rather than its purpose is the paramount factor. But the holding of the case was that the legitimate purposes of the ordinance—to preserve peace and avoid deficits—were not open to impeachment by evidence that the council-men were actually motivated by racial considerations. . . .

. . .

As an initial matter, we have difficulty understanding how a law establishing a racially neutral qualification for employment is nevertheless racially discriminatory and denies "any person . . . equal protection of the laws" simply because a greater proportion of Negroes fail to qualify than members of other racial or ethnic groups. . . . Test 21, which is administered generally to prospective Government employees, concededly seeks to ascertain whether those who take it have acquired a particular level of verbal skill; and it is untenable that the Constitution prevents the Government from seeking modestly to upgrade the communicative abilities of its employees rather than to be satisfied with some lower level of competence, particularly where the job requires special ability to communicate orally and in writing. . . .

Nor on the facts of the case before us would the disproportionate impact of Test 21 warrant the conclusion that it is a purposeful device to discriminate against Negroes and hence an infringement of the constitutional rights of respondents as well as other black applicants. As we have said, the test is neutral on its face and rationally may be said to serve a purpose the Government is constitutionally empowered to pursue. Even agreeing with the District Court that the differential racial effect of Test 21 called for further inquiry, we think the District Court correctly held that the affirmative efforts of the Metropolitan Police Department to recruit black officers, the changing racial composition of the recruit classes and of the force in general, and the relationship of the test to the training program negated any inference that the Department discriminated on the basis of race or that "a police officer qualifies on the color of his skin rather than ability." . . .

. . . A rule that a statute designed to serve neutral ends is nevertheless invalid, absent compelling justification, if in practice it benefits or burdens one race more than another would be far reaching and would raise serious questions about, and perhaps invalidate, a whole range of tax, welfare, public service, regulatory, and licensing statutes that may be more burdensome to the poor and to the average black than to the more affluent white. . . .

. . .

JUSTICE STEVENS, concurring.

. . .

Frequently the most probative evidence of intent will be objective evidence of what actually happened rather than evidence describing the subjective state of mind of the actor. For normally the actor is presumed to have intended the natural consequences of his deeds. This is particularly true in the case of governmental action which is frequently the product of compromise, of collective decisionmaking, and of mixed motivation. It is unrealistic, on the one hand, to require the victim of alleged discrimination to uncover the actual subjective intent of the decisionmaker or, conversely, to invalidate otherwise legitimate action simply because an improper motive affected the deliberation of a participant in the decisional process. A law conscripting clerics should not be invalidated because an atheist voted for it.

My point in making this observation is to suggest that the line between discriminatory purpose and discriminatory impact is not nearly as bright, and perhaps not quite as critical, as the reader of the Court's opinion might assume. I agree, of course, that a constitutional issue does not arise every time some disproportionate impact is shown. On the other hand, when the disproportion is as dramatic as in . . . *Yick Wo v. Hopkins* (1886), it really does not matter whether the standard is phrased in terms of purpose or effect. . . .

There are two reasons why I am convinced that the challenge to Test 21 is insufficient. First, the test serves the neutral and legitimate purpose of requiring all applicants to meet a uniform minimum standard of literacy. Reading ability is manifestly relevant to the police function, there is no evidence that the required passing grade was set at an arbitrarily high level, and there is sufficient disparity among high schools and high school graduates to justify the use of a separate uniform test. Second, the same test is used throughout the federal service. The applicants for employment in the District of Columbia Police Department represent such a small fraction of the total number of persons who have taken the test that their experience is of minimal probative value in assessing the neutrality of the test itself. That evidence, without more, is not sufficient to overcome the presumption that a test which is this widely used by the Federal Government is in fact neutral in its effect as well as its "purpose" as that term is used in constitutional adjudication.

. . .

JUSTICE BRENNAN, with whom JUSTICE MARSHALL joins, dissenting.

[Justices Brennan and Marshall claimed that Test 21 violated federal statutory law. The dissent did not discuss the constitutional issues, although they did express the view that "petitioners should have been required to prove that the police training examinations either measure job-related skills or predict job performance."]

C. Gender

Divided liberals believed that men and women were constitutional equals in some general sense but could not agree on what this commitment to constitutional equality entailed in practice. More progressive liberals believed that men and women ought to be held to the same standards in virtually all areas of public life. Both the Fourteenth Amendment and the proposed ERA, in their view, ought to be interpreted in ways that altered the place of women in American society. More conservative liberals believed that while women should no longer be excluded from most areas of public life, natural differences between men and women provided a sound basis for limiting combat to men and maintaining many traditional family practices. Such persons supported judicial decisions striking down particularly offensive sex classifications and an ERA limited to prohibiting consensually unjust discriminations, but opposed constitutional practices that threatened more substantial changes in the status of men and women.

No consensus formed behind either constitutional vision. Governing officials failed to ratify the ERA but they also repealed or failed to enforce many laws that reinforced traditional gender roles. The Supreme Court, at first implicitly and then explicitly, held government officials to higher constitutional standards when making gender classifications than when making ordinary classifications, but not as high a standard as was required for racial classifications. Congress, but not the Supreme Court, forbade discrimination on the basis of pregnancy. The Court of Appeals for the Third Circuit in *Vorchheimer v. School District of Philadelphia* (1976) divided evenly when adjudicating the constitutionality of all-male and all-female public high schools.[52]

Americans across the political spectrum endorsed gender equality. Presidents Nixon, Ford, and Carter all championed the ERA. The Democratic and Republican Party platforms in 1972 and 1976 urged ratification. The Republican platform in 1976 declared, "The Republican Party reaffirms its support for ratification of the Equal Rights Amendment. Our Party was the first national party to endorse the E.R.A. in 1940. . . . The Platform stated then, and repeats now, that the Republican Party 'fully endorses the principle of equal rights, equal opportunities and equal responsibilities for women.'" Democrats asserted, "We seek ratification of the Equal Rights Amendment, to insure that sex discrimination in all its forms will be ended, implementation of Title IX, and elimination of discrimination against women in all federal programs." Public opinion polls demonstrated broad support for a general ban on laws discriminating against women.

Liberals did not agree on how a general principle of gender equality should be implemented. After legislative and judicial decisions removed the most offensive gender classifications from public life, public attention focused on such serious matters as women in combat and such less serious concerns as unisex bathrooms. Consensus on abstract norms collapsed as these specifics took center stage. The more the ERA was perceived as mandating substantive change in gender roles, the greater the public opposition became. Thirty-five states eventually ratified the amendment, three short of the constitutionally mandated three-fifths.

The constitutional politics of gender equality from 1968 to 1980 was marked by greater public interest group participation. The most important of these groups, NOW, was committed "to bring[ing] women into full participation in the mainstream of American society now, exercising all the privileges and responsibilities thereof in truly equal partnership with men."[53] The newly formed Women's Rights Project of the ACLU, headed by future Supreme Court justice Ruth Bader Ginsburg, lobbied for the passage of the ERA and sponsored litigation aimed at having courts declare gender a suspect classification, a ruling that would require all laws distinguishing between men and women to be necessary means to compelling government interests. These groups were not strong enough to achieve their ultimate goals, but NOW and the Women's Rights Project did help bring about laws and judicial decisions that substantially changed the status of women in the United States.

Divisions over gender rights during the 1970s were exacerbated by the increased visibility of two additional perspectives on the constitutional rights of men and women. Many religious men and women insisted that traditionally legal distinctions between the sexes were more natural and appropriate than even more conservative liberals were willing to acknowledge. Led by Phyllis Schlafly, cultural conservatives claimed that laws based on long-standing gender roles were constitutionally sound. More radical feminists insisted that liberal conceptions of equality rooted in the civil rights

52. *Vorchheimer v. School District of Philadelphia*, 532 F.2d 880 (1976).

53. The National Organization for Women, "Statement of Purpose," in *From Many, One: Readings in American Political and Social Thought*, ed. Richard C. Sinopoli (Washington, DC: Georgetown University Press, 1997), 150.

Illustration 9-3 Equal Rights Amendment Rally with Eleanor Smeall, Betty Ford, and Lady Bird Johnson

NOW President Eleanor Smeall (L) and former first ladies Betty Ford (C), and Lady Bird Johnson (R) kick off a rally for equal rights on October 12, 1981, at the Lincoln Memorial in Washington.

Source: UPI Photo/Files.

movement could not achieve equality for women. Led by Catharine MacKinnon, these feminists asserted that the constitutional requirement that women be judged by the same standards used to judge men devalued distinctively female perspectives by treating inherently male norms as universal.

National Organization for Women, Bill of Rights (1968)[54]

NOW was founded in 1966. Convinced that women's issues would be placed on the national agenda only if a mass organization of women pressured public officials, Professor Pauli Murray of Yale University and Betty Friedan, the author of The Feminine Mystique, *organized a meeting of concerned men and women in October of that year. Although the organization they formed initially consisted of only three hundred persons, NOW immediately grew into the nation's foremost advocate for women's rights across numerous policy and constitutional areas.*

The following declaration was adopted by NOW at their national convention in 1967. How do these demands compare with the demands that women made in previous historical eras? How do they compare with demands for racial equality made in the mid-twentieth century?

. . .

We Demand:

I. That the United States Congress immediately pass the Equal Rights Amendment to the Constitution to provide that "Equality of rights under the law shall not be denied or abridged by the United States or by any State on account of sex" and that such then be immediately ratified by the several States.

II. That equal employment opportunity be guaranteed to all women, as well as men by insisting that

54. Excerpted from National Organization for Women, *NOW Bill of Rights for 1968* (Washington, DC: National Organization for Women, 1968).

the Equal Employment Opportunity Commission enforce the prohibitions against sex discrimination in employment under Title VII of the Civil Rights Act of 1964 with the same vigor as it enforces the prohibitions against racial discrimination.

III. That women be protected by law to insure their rights to return to their jobs within a reasonable time after childbirth without loss of seniority or other accrued benefits and be paid maternity leave as a form of social security and/or employee benefit.

. . .

V. That child care facilities be established by law on the same basis as parks, libraries and public schools adequate to the needs of children, from the pre-school years through adolescence, as a community resource to be used by all citizens from all income levels.

VI. That the right of women to be educated to their full potential equally with men be secured by Federal and State legislation, eliminating all discrimination and segregation by sex, written and unwritten, at all levels of education including college, graduate and professional schools, loans and fellowships and Federal and State training programs, such as the job Corps.

VII. The right of women in poverty to secure job training, housing and family allowances on equal terms with men, but without prejudice to a parent's right to remain at home to care for his or her children; revision of welfare legislation and poverty programs which deny women dignity, privacy and self respect.

VIII. The right of women to control their own reproductive lives by removing from penal codes the laws limiting access to contraceptive information and devices and laws governing abortion.

Debate over the Equal Rights Amendment

The ERA proved surprisingly contentious. After sailing through both houses of Congress by overwhelming majorities and being ratified immediately by more than half the states, the process stalled. Several issues bedeviled the amendment's sponsors. First, in light of legislative decisions providing for a greater degree of gender equality and Supreme Court decisions striking down gender classifications, many Americans wondered what difference the ERA made in practice. Second, many Americans feared that while the ERA might no longer be necessary to remove offensive gender classifications from American life, more liberal justices might use that text to promote gender practices popular majorities thought undesirable.

The following two readings are from two leading participants in the debate over the ERA. Ruth Bader Ginsburg in 1977 was a professor at Columbia Law School and the head of the Women's Rights Project of the ACLU. Phyllis Schlafly was a prominent conservative activist and head of the Eagle Forum. To what extent do Ginsburg and Schlafly dispute the probable impact of the ERA? To what extent do they dispute whether those consequences are desirable? Suppose you agreed with Schlafly's account of the ERA. Would that make you more or less likely to support ratification?

Ruth Bader Ginsburg and Brenda Feigen Fasteau, Sex Bias in the U.S. Code (1977)[55]

. . .

Equalization of the treatment of women and men under Federal law is an overdue task which should command priority attention of the President and Congress. . . . [A] myriad of unwarranted differentials clutter the U.S. Code. While many are obsolete or of minor importance when viewed in isolation, the cumulative effect is reflective of a society that assigns to women, solely on the basis of their sex, a subordinate or dependent role.

. . . As America enters the closing quarter of the 20th century . . . , Federal laws should not portray women as "the second sex," but as persons with rights, responsibilities and opportunities fully equal to those of men.

. . .

Underlying the recommendations made in this report is the fundamental point that allocation of responsibilities within the family is a matter properly determined solely by the individuals involved. Government should not steer individual decisions concerning household or breadwinning roles by casting the law's weight on the side of (or against) a particular method of ordering private relationships. Rather, a policy of strict neutrality should be pursued. That policy would accommodate both traditional and innovative patterns. At the same time, it should assure removal of artificial constraints so that women and men willing to explore their full potential as human beings may create new traditions by their actions.

55. Excerpted from Ruth Bader Ginsburg and Brenda Feigen Fasteau, *Sex Bias in the U.S. Code: A Report of the U.S. Commission on Civil Rights* (Washington, DC: Government Printing Office, 1977), 204-220.

. . .

The main rule the Commission proposes . . . calls for sex-neutral terminology except in the rare instance where no suitable sex-neutral substitute term exists, or the reference is to a physical characteristic unique to some or all members of one sex, or the constitutional right to privacy necessitates a sex-specific reference.

. . .

Provision of payments for wives and widows, but not for similarly situated husbands and widowers, has been characteristic of Federal social and employment benefit legislation. Increased female participation in the paid labor force has impelled reassessment of the quality of this differential. Once thought to operate benignly in women's favor, the differential perpetuates invidious discrimination against women who are gainfully employed, whether by choice, or, as is more often the case, necessity. Withholding from a woman's spouse benefits paid to a man's spouse in effect denies the woman equal compensation. A scheme built upon the breadwinning husband–dependent homemaking wife concept inevitably treats the woman's efforts or aspirations in the economic sector as less important than the man's.

. . .

. . . Women temporarily unable to work due to childbirth or pregnancy-related physical disability should not be treated as labor force outcasts. Job security, income protection, and health insurance coverage during such physical disability is essential if equal opportunity in the job market is to become a reality for women. . . . [T[he increasingly common two-earner family pattern should impel development of a comprehensive program of government-supported child care.

. . .

. . . [A] spouse's or former marriage partner's alimony should be based on financial ability.

. . .

Current provisions dealing with statutory rape, rape, and prostitution are discriminatory on their face. With respect to prostitution, enforcement practices compound the discrimination. . . . There is a growing national movement recommending unqualified decriminalization as sound policy, implementing equal rights and individual privacy principles. . . .

Sex-segregated penal institutions are separate and, in a variety of ways, unequal. Preparation for return to a community in which men and women have equal rights, responsibilities, and opportunities is not fostered by the present arrangement. While the personal privacy principle permits maintenance of separate sleeping and bathroom facilities, no other facilities, e.g. work, school, cafeteria, should be maintained for one sex only.

. . .

Supporters of the equal rights principle firmly reject draft or combat exemption for women, as Congress did when it refused to qualify the equal rights amendment by incorporating any military service exemption. The equal rights principle implies that women must be subject to the draft if men are, that military assignments must be made on the basis of individual capacity rather than sex, and that a woman must have the same opportunity as a man to qualify for any position to which she aspires in the uniformed services.

. . .

Societies established by Congress to aid and educate young people on their way to adulthood [i.e., Boy and Girl Scouts] should be geared toward a world in which equal opportunity for men and women is a fundamental principle. In some cases, separate clubs under one umbrella unit might be a suitable solution, at least for a transition period. In other cases, the educational purpose would be served best by immediately extending membership to both sexes in a single organization. . . .

Phyllis Schlafly, A Short History of E.R.A. (1986)[56]

The Equal Rights Amendment was presented to the American public as something that would benefit women, "put women in the U.S. Constitution," and lift women out of their so-called "second-class citizenship." However, in thousands of debates, the ERA advocates were unable to show any way that ERA would benefit women or end any discrimination against them. The fact is that women already enjoy every constitutional right that men enjoy and have enjoyed equal employment opportunity since 1964.

. . .

The opponents of ERA were able to show many harms that ERA would cause.

56. Excerpted from Phyllis Schlafly, "A Short History of E.R.A.," *Phyllis Schlafly Report* 20 (1986).

1. ERA would take away legal rights that women possessed—*not* confer any new rights on women.
   A. ERA would take away women's traditional exemption from military conscription and also from military combat duty. . . .
   B. . . . ERA would make unconstitutional the laws, which then existed in every state, that impose on a husband the obligation to support his wife.
2. ERA would take away important rights and powers of the states and confer these on other branches of government which are farther removed from the people.
   A. ERA would give enormous power to the Federal courts to decide the definitions of the words in ERA, "sex" and "equality of rights." . . .
3. Section II of ERA would give enormous new powers to the Federal Government that now belong to the states. . . .
4. ERA's impact on education would take away rights from women students, upset many customs and practices, and bring government intrusion into private schools.
   A. ERA would make unconstitutional all the current exceptions in Title IX which allow for single-sex schools and colleges and for separate treatment of the sexes for certain activities. ERA would mean the end of single-sex colleges. ERA would force the sex integration of fraternities, sororities, Boy Scouts, Girl Scouts, YMCA, YWCA, Boys State and Girls State conducted by the American Legion, and mother-daughter and father-son school events.
5. ERA would put abortion rights into the U.S. Constitution, and make abortion funding a new constitutional right.
6. ERA would put "gay rights" into the U.S. Constitution, because the word in the Amendment is "sex" not women.

The Standard of Constitutional Protection

Judicial majorities debated the proper standard for laws that made gender distinctions before settling on a standard of intermediate scrutiny. The justices in *Reed v. Reed* (1971) for the first time in Supreme Court history ruled that a state law unconstitutionally discriminated against women. Chief Justice Burger ostensibly used a rational scrutiny standard when striking down a state law preferring men to women when determining the administrator of a will. His opinion asserted, "To give a mandatory preference to members of either sex over members of the other, merely to accomplish the elimination of hearings on the merits, is to make the very kind of arbitrary legislative choice forbidden by the Equal Protection Clause of the Fourteenth Amendment." Given that administrative convenience had historically been considered a legitimate government purpose, many commentators believed that the justices were moving toward a higher standard for judging the constitutionality of gender discriminations and distinctions. Four justices in *Frontiero v. Richardson* (1973) proposed that gender discrimination be as strictly scrutinized as race discrimination. Unable to obtain a fifth vote for strict scrutiny, the justices compromised in *Craig v. Boren* (1976) on an intermediate scrutiny standard. Justice Brennan's majority opinion asserted, "To withstand constitutional challenge, previous cases establish that classifications by gender must serve important governmental objectives and must be substantially related to achievement of those objectives."

Frontiero v. Richardson, 411 U.S. 677 (1973)

Lieutenant Sharron Frontiero of the United States Air Force was turned down when she applied to obtain housing and medical benefits for her husband, Joseph Frontiero, because she did not provide half the support for the family. Male officers could obtain benefits for their spouses without having to prove any dependency. Frontiero brought a lawsuit against Elliott Richardson, the Secretary of Defense, claiming that this military policy violated the equal protection component of the due process clause of the Fifth Amendment. A federal district court denied relief. Frontiero appealed to the Supreme Court of the United States.

The Supreme Court by an 8-1 vote ruled that Frontiero had a right to the same benefits that were available to similarly situated male officers. Justice Brennan and three other members of the Court applied the strict scrutiny test, which required laws making gender classifications be necessary means to compelling government ends. On what basis do they apply that standard? Do you think their analysis is compelling? Four other justices insist that the law in this case did not even satisfy the rational scrutiny test. Do you think that this assertion is correct, or were the justices smuggling in a higher standard? Was Justice Powell correct in thinking that justices should not have changed the law at this point in time, in light of what most persons thought was the impending ratification of the ERA? Might a justice thinking strategically deny Frontiero's claim, thus strengthening the case for ERA? Notice that Justice Brennan analogizes sex discrimination to racial discrimination. What are the merits and demerits of that analogy?

JUSTICE BRENNAN announced the judgment of the Court and an opinion in which JUSTICE DOUGLAS, JUSTICE WHITE, and JUSTICE MARSHALL join.

. . .

There can be no doubt that our Nation has had a long and unfortunate history of sex discrimination. Traditionally, such discrimination was rationalized by an attitude of "romantic paternalism" which, in practical effect, put women, not on a pedestal, but in a cage. . . . As a result of [such] notions . . . , our statute books gradually became laden with gross, stereotyped distinctions between the sexes and, indeed, throughout much of the 19th century the position of women in our society was, in many respects, comparable to that of blacks under the pre–Civil War slave codes. Neither slaves nor women could hold office, serve on juries, or bring suit in their own names, and married women traditionally were denied the legal capacity to hold or convey property or to serve as legal guardians of their own children. . . . And although blacks were guaranteed the right to vote in 1870, women were denied even that right—which is itself "preservative of other basic civil and political rights"—until adoption of the Nineteenth Amendment half a century later.

It is true, of course, that the position of women in America has improved markedly in recent decades. Nevertheless, it can hardly be doubted that, in part because of the high visibility of the sex characteristic, women still face pervasive, although at times more subtle, discrimination in our educational institutions, in the job market and, perhaps most conspicuously, in the political arena.

Moreover, since sex, like race and national origin, is an immutable characteristic determined solely by the accident of birth, the imposition of special disabilities upon the members of a particular sex because of their sex would seem to violate "the basic concept of our system that legal burdens should bear some relationship to individual responsibility. . . ." . . . And what differentiates sex from such nonsuspect statuses as intelligence or physical disability, and aligns it with the recognized suspect criteria, is that the sex characteristic frequently bears no relation to ability to perform or contribute to society. As a result, statutory distinctions between the sexes often have the effect of invidiously relegating the entire class of females to inferior legal status without regard to the actual capabilities of its individual members.

We might also note that, over the past decade, Congress has itself manifested an increasing sensitivity to sex-based classifications. In Title VII of the Civil Rights Act of 1964, for example, Congress expressly declared that no employer, labor union, or other organization subject to the provisions of the Act shall discriminate against any individual on the basis of "race, color, religion, sex, or national origin." . . . Thus, Congress itself has concluded that classifications based upon sex are inherently invidious, and this conclusion of a coequal branch of Government is not without significance to the question presently under consideration. . . .

With these considerations in mind, we can only conclude that classifications based upon sex, like classifications based upon race, alienage, or national origin, are inherently suspect, and must therefore be subjected to strict judicial scrutiny. . . .

. . .

. . . [A]ny statutory scheme which draws a sharp line between the sexes, solely for the purpose of achieving administrative convenience, necessarily commands "dissimilar treatment for men and women who are . . . similarly situated," and therefore involves the "very kind of arbitrary legislative choice forbidden by the [Constitution]. . . ." We therefore conclude that, by according differential treatment to male and female members of the uniformed services for the sole purpose of achieving administrative convenience, the challenged statutes violate the Due Process Clause of the Fifth Amendment insofar as they require a female member to prove the dependency of her husband.

JUSTICE STEWART concurs in the judgment, agreeing that the statutes before us work an invidious discrimination in violation of the Constitution. *Reed v. Reed* (1971). . . .

JUSTICE POWELL, with whom THE CHIEF JUSTICE and JUSTICE BLACKMUN join, concurring in the judgment.

I agree that the challenged statutes constitute an unconstitutional discrimination against servicewomen in violation of the Due Process Clause of the Fifth Amendment, but I cannot join the opinion of MR. JUSTICE BRENNAN, which would hold that all classifications based upon sex, "like classifications based upon race, alienage, and national origin," are "inherently suspect and must therefore be subjected to close judicial scrutiny." . . . It is unnecessary for the Court in this case to characterize sex as a suspect classification, with all of the far-reaching implications of such a holding. . . . In my view, we can and should decide this case on the authority of *Reed v. Reed* (1971) and reserve for the future any expansion of its rationale.

There is another, and I find compelling, reason for deferring a general categorizing of sex classifications as invoking the strictest test of judicial scrutiny. The Equal Rights Amendment, which if adopted will resolve the substance of this precise question, has been approved by the Congress and submitted for ratification by the States. If this Amendment is duly adopted, it will represent the will of the people accomplished in the manner prescribed by the Constitution. By acting prematurely and unnecessarily, as I view it, the Court has assumed a decisional responsibility at the very time when state legislatures, functioning within the traditional democratic process, are debating the proposed Amendment. It seems to me that this reaching out to pre-empt by judicial action a major political decision which is currently in process of resolution does not reflect appropriate respect for duly prescribed legislative processes.

. . .

JUSTICE REHNQUIST, dissenting.

[*Justice Rehnquist adopted the opinion of the lower federal court. The crucial section of that opinion is excerpted below.*]

. . .

Congress apparently reached the conclusion that it would be more economical to require married female members claiming husbands to prove actual dependency than to extend the presumption of dependency to such members. Such a presumption made to facilitate administration of the law does not violate the equal protection guarantee of the Constitution if it does not unduly burden or oppress one of the classes upon which it operates. Nothing in the instant statutory classification jeopardizes the ability of a female member to obtain the benefits intended to be bestowed upon her by the statutes. The classification is burdensome for a female member who is not actually providing over one-half the support for her claimed husband only to the extent that were she a man she could receive dependency benefits in spite of the fact that her spouse might not be actually dependent, as that term has been defined by Congress. In other words, the alleged injustice of the distinction lies in the possibility that some married service men are getting "windfall" payments, while married service women are denied them. Sharron Frontiero is one of the service women thus denied a windfall.

All dependency benefits are unquestionably valuable, windfalls are not, but we are of the opinion that the incidental bestowal of some undeserved benefits on male members of the uniformed services does not so unreasonably burden female members that the administrative classification should be ruled unconstitutional.

Military Service

Americans maintained traditional restrictions against women in the military. Responding to the Soviet Union's invasion of Afghanistan in 1980, the Carter administration urged that both men and women be required to register for the draft. President Carter's proposal to Congress declared, "Equity is achieved when both men and women are asked to serve in proportion to the ability of the Armed Forces to use them effectively."[57] Congress chose to require only men to register for the draft. The Senate report claimed, "the arguments for treating men and women equally—so compelling in many areas of our national life—simply cannot overcome the judgment of our military leaders and of the congress itself that a male-only system best serves our national security."[58] The Supreme Court in *Rostker v. Goldberg* (1981) sustained the congressional decision to register only males. Justice Rehnquist's majority opinion asserted, "That Congress and the Executive have decided that women should not serve in combat fully justifies Congress in not authorizing their registration, since the purpose of registration is to develop a pool of potential combat troops."

57. 126 *Congressional Record*, 96th Cong., 2nd Sess. (1980), E1602.

58. 126 *Congressional Record*, 96th Cong., 2nd Sess. (1980), 13,881.

Rostker was one of three decisions handed down by the Supreme Court between 1975 and 1981 that sustained the constitutionality of various gender discriminations associated with military service. In *Schlesinger v. Ballard* (1975) a 5-4 judicial majority ruled that the military could give women a longer time than men to achieve promotion before a mandatory discharge. Justice Stewart's majority opinion indicated that because women were not eligible for numerous Navy missions, "women line officers had less opportunity for promotion than did their male counterparts, and . . . a longer period of tenure for women officers would, therefore, be consistent with the goal to provide women officers with 'fair and equitable career advancement programs.'" *Personnel Administrator of Massachusetts v. Feeney* (1979) ruled that Massachusetts could give preference to military veterans for civil service positions, even though over 98 percent of the people eligible for that benefit were men. Justice Stewart's majority opinion sustained the statute on the ground that Massachusetts had enacted "a preference for veterans of either sex over nonveterans of either sex, not for men over women."

Pregnancy

Congress was more sympathetic than the Supreme Court to claims that excluding pregnancy from health benefits discriminated against women. In *Gedulig v. Aiello* (1974) a 6-3 judicial majority ruled that California did not violate the equal protection clause by adopting a state insurance program that did not provide benefits to persons suffering disabilities resulting from pregnancy. Justice Stewart's majority opinion asserted, "There is no risk from which men are protected and women are not. Likewise, there is no risk from which women are protected and men are not." Congress responded by passing the Pregnancy Discrimination Act of 1978. Although the national legislature relied on the commerce power when adopting that measure, the House report criticized the justices for failing to recognize that excluding pregnancy from coverage discriminated against women, stating, "The plan included comprehensive coverage for males, and failed to provide comprehensive coverage for females."[59]

D. Native Americans

Constitutional decision makers did not interpret the Indian Civil Rights Act of 1968 as providing Native Americans with the same rights against tribal councils as state citizens had against state governments. *Santa Clara Pueblo v. Martinez* (1978) concerned a Pueblo rule that granted tribal citizenship to children of Pueblo fathers, but not to children of Pueblo mothers. The local federal court ruled that tribal councils could discriminate against women. Judge Mechem's opinion stated, "The equal protection guarantee of the Indian Civil Rights Act should not be construed in a manner which would require or authorize this Court to determine which traditional values will promote cultural survival and therefore should be preserved and which of them are inimical to cultural survival and should therefore be abrogated." That decision was reversed by the Court of Appeals for the Tenth Circuit. After noting, "The Fourteenth Amendment standards do not . . . apply with full force," Judge Doyle continued, "They do, nevertheless, serve as a persuasive guide to the decision. The history and decisions teach us that the Indian Bill of Rights is modeled after the Constitution of the United States and is to be interpreted in the light of constitutional law decisions." The Supreme Court reversed the Tenth Circuit on jurisdictional grounds. Justice Marshall's majority opinion nevertheless displayed more sympathy to the district court's position that courts not interfere with tribal culture than it did to the circuit court's opinion that Native Americans should enjoy the same rights as other Americans. Marshall stated, "Efforts by the federal judiciary to apply the statutory prohibitions of [the ICRA] in a civil context may substantially interfere with a tribe's ability to maintain itself as a culturally and politically distinct entity." Is this the correct balance between tribal autonomy and the rights of woman? How would you do the balance?[60]

VI. Criminal Justice

MAJOR DEVELOPMENTS

- Crime becomes a national political issue
- *Mapp* and *Miranda* are narrowed but remain the law of the land

59. H. Rep. 95–948, "Pregnancy Discrimination Act of 1978," in *Legislative History of the Pregnancy Discrimination Act of 1978*, 95th Cong., 2nd Sess. (1978), 148.

60. For a good discussion of these issues, see Sarah Song, *Justice, Gender, and the Poltiics of Multiculturalism* (New York: Cambridge University Press, 2007).

- **All capital punishment statutes declared unconstitutional in 1972, but states subsequently adopt revised statutes, and these statutes are sustained by the Supreme Court in 1976**

Crime became a national issue during the late 1960s. Many liberals insisted that increases in violent offenses demonstrated the importance of expanding Great Society programs to eliminate the economic causes of criminal activity. More Americans were convinced that the crime wave was rooted in permissive politicians and judges. Critics charged the Warren Court with handcuffing the police and permitting hardened criminals to escape justice on petty technicalities. In one influential essay, Judge Henry Friendly asked, "Is Innocence Irrelevant?" This article complained that convicted criminals often raised numerous constitutional issues in habeas corpus that had no bearing on their guilt. The end result was "abuse by prisoners, a waste of the precious and limited resources available for the criminal process, and public disrespect for the judgment of criminal courts."[61]

Party platforms marked the emergence of crime as a major national issue that divided Republicans from Democrats. After charging that "lawlessness is crumbling the foundations of American society," Republicans in 1968 promised to "[s]ecure . . . the enactment of laws enabling law enforcement officials to obtain and use evidence needed to prosecute criminals." Under the banner, "Justice and Law," Democrats declared, "In fighting crime we must not foster injustice. Lawlessness cannot be ended by curtailing the hard-won liberties of all Americans."

Richard Nixon repeatedly emphasized his opposition to Warren Court decisions protecting the rights of persons suspected and convicted of crime. Warren Burger, the judge who Nixon chose to replace Earl Warren, gained public attention for his vocal criticisms of Supreme Court decisions expanding Fourth, Fifth, and Sixth Amendment rights. When nominating Justices Lewis Powell and William Rehnquist to the Supreme Court, Nixon asserted, "I believe some court decisions have gone too far in the past in weakening the peace forces as against the criminal forces in our society. I believe the peace forces must not be denied the legal tools they need to protect the innocent from criminal elements."

Nixon achieved some of his goals, but neither he nor his judicial appointments reversed the Due Process Revolution. Compared to the 1960s, criminal defendants won fewer cases in the Supreme Court after Nixon's election, as illustrated in Figure 9-4. The Burger Court narrowly interpreted such decisions as *Mapp v. Ohio* (1961) and *Miranda v. Arizona* (1966). *United States v. Calandra* (1974) held that prosecutors could use unconstitutionally obtained evidence in grand jury proceedings. *Harris v. New York* (1971) ruled that statements obtained in violation of *Miranda* could be used to impeach witnesses. *Stone v. Powell* (1976) declared that federal courts in habeas corpus cases would not normally consider Fourth Amendment claims. Nevertheless, the basic landmarks of the Due Process Revolution remained standing. *Miranda* and *Mapp* did not survive the 1970s unscathed, but when President Reagan assumed office, they "appear[ed] more secure they ha[d] been for a number of years."[62] Burger Court decisions built on the liberalism of the Warren Court on such matters as the right to counsel, juries, and capital punishment. In 1972 a 5-4 judicial majority declared unconstitutional all state procedures used to impose the death penalty. Although the justices in *Gregg v. Georgia* (1976) found a new set of procedures constitutional, the end result was that capital punishment by 1980 was subject to far more constitutional restraints than it was when Richard Nixon took office in 1969.

Liberals concerned with the more conservative trend of Burger Court decisions began to look to state courts and state constitutions as sources of legal protection against what they believed to be illegal searches, coerced confessions, and cruel and unusual punishments. State court decisions endorsing liberal constitutional understandings, constitutionalists of all political persuasions recognized, are immune from federal reversal, provided that their state constitutional foundations are clearly articulated. This is a liberal application of adequate and independent grounds, the doctrine that the Supreme Court cannot consider a question of federal constitutional law if the case can be resolved

61. Henry J. Friendly, "Is Innocence Irrelevant? Collateral Attack on Criminal Judgments," *University of Chicago Law Review* 38 (1970):172.

62. Yale Kamisar, "The Warren Court (Was It Really So Defense-Minded?), the Burger Court (Is It Really So Prosecution-Oriented?), and Police Investigatory Practices," in *The Burger Court: The Counter-Revolution That Wasn't*, ed. Vincent Blasi (New Haven, CT: Yale University Press, 1983), 90.

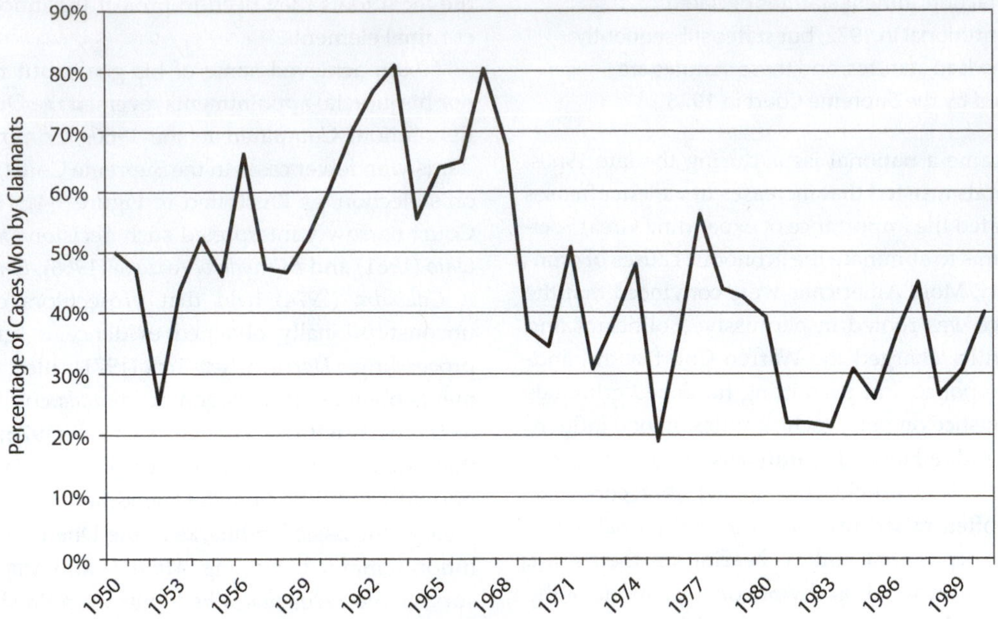

Figure 9-4 Percentage of Victories in U.S. Supreme Court by Claimants in Criminal Justice Cases, 1950–90

on the basis of a constitutionally permitted state law. Justice William Brennan became a leading champion of the new judicial federalism as he increasingly found himself in dissent on the Burger Court. In an influential article, he asserted,

> State courts cannot rest when they have afforded their citizens the full protections of the federal Constitution. State constitutions, too, are a font of individual liberties, their protections often extending beyond those required by the Supreme Court's interpretation of federal law. The legal revolution which has brought federal law to the fore must not be allowed to inhibit the independent protective force of state law—for without it, the full realization of our liberties cannot be guaranteed.[63]

Some state courts did provide protections for persons suspected of crime under state constitutional law on grounds that had been rejected under federal constitutional law. Nevertheless, studies suggest that the new judicial federalism had very little impact, particularly in constitutional criminal procedure. State courts tended to interpret state constitutional provisions in the same way that they interpreted the corresponding federal constitutional provisions. When state courts became decidedly more liberal than the national government, as was the case in California and Florida, voters passed constitutional amendments restoring the federal status quo.[64]

A. Due Process and Habeas Corpus

The Burger Court exhibited what many thought was a surprising concern with due process rights before and during trials. A judicial majority in *In re Winship* (1970) asserted that due process required the prosecution to prove all elements of a crime beyond a reasonable doubt, even in proceedings for juvenile delinquency. The justices in another series of decisions aggressively policed the plea-bargaining process. Chief Justice Burger's majority opinion in *Santobello v. New York* (1971) asserted that "'plea bargaining,' is an essential component of the administration of justice," but that judges

63. William J. Brennan, Jr., "State Constitutions and the Protection of Individual Rights" *Harvard Law Review* 90 (1977): 489, 491.

64. See G. Alan Tarr, "The New Judicial Federalism in Perspective," *Notre Dame Law Review* 72 (1997): 1097; Barry Latzer, *State Constitutions and Criminal Justice* (Santa Barbara, CA: ABC-Clio, 1991).

must ensure that (a) the defendant has adequate counsel, (b) the plea is "voluntary and knowing," (c) "if it [is] induced by promises, the essence of those promises must in some ways be known," and (d) the plea bargain be kept. The Supreme Court in *Bordenkircher v. Hayes* (1978), however, found no due process problem when a prosecutor threatened a criminal suspect with a more severe offense if that person refused to accept a plea bargain.

The justices were less accommodating to constitutional claims on habeas corpus matters. Two decisions sharply limited access to that writ. *Stone v. Powell* (1976) held that federal courts may not hear habeas corpus claims based on the exclusionary rule whenever the state court had held a full and fair hearing on the matter, even if the state court had reached an erroneous legal conclusion. After noting that "[a]pplication of the [exclusionary] rule deflects the truthfinding process and often frees the guilty," Justice Powell's majority opinion stated, "There is no reason to believe that the overall educative effect of the exclusionary rule would be appreciably diminished if search-and-seizure claims could not be raised in federal habeas corpus review of state convictions." *Wainwright v. Sykes* (1977) declared that federal habeas petitioners could ordinarily raise only those constitutional claims that they had first raised at trial. Overruling *Fay v. Noia* (1963), the Burger Court adopted a presumption that defense lawyers—even overworked and inexperienced public defenders—had strategic reasons for failing to make constitutional objections to the trial judge. This is a conservative application of adequate and state grounds. The constitutional state law which requires a criminal defendant to make a timely objection to some alleged constitutional wrong may prevent federal courts from considering whether the conviction was, in fact, unconstitutional. State judges did not necessarily believe that their increased autonomy and responsibility would alter their behavior in such cases, but they did recognize the Burger Court's greater willingness to trust the state courts.

In re Winship, 397 U.S. 358 (1970)

A family court judge in New York found that Samuel Winship, a twelve-year-old boy, had stolen $112 from a pocketbook. The judge admitted that the evidence did not support a finding that Winship was guilty beyond a reasonable doubt, but chose to rely on New York law that required delinquency

Table 9-4 State Judges' Views on *Stone v. Powell*, by Percentage

Viewpoint	Strongly Agree	Agree	No Opinion	Disagree	Strongly Disagree
State cases will now be better prepared and argued	3.3	17.4	35.9	33.7	9.8
Cases will now be scrutinized more carefully in state courts	2.2	20.7	16.3	46.7	14.1
State courts are being given more latitude	4.3	50.0	16.3	26.1	3.3
Burger Court is not quick to interfere with state courts	7.6	66.3	9.8	15.2	1.1
Burger Court has more confidence in state courts	6.5	52.2	21.7	16.3	3.3
Warren Court had less confidence in state courts	12.0	66.3	13.0	7.6	1.1

Source: G. Larry Mays, "*Stone v. Powell*: The Impact on State Appellate Court Judges' Perceptions," *Journal of Criminal Justice* 11 (1983): 32.

determinations to be made on "a preponderance of the evidence." Winship was placed in a training school for a period between eighteen months and six years. Winship appealed this verdict, claiming that he could be constitutionally adjudged a delinquent only if there was no reasonable doubt that he had committed a criminal offense. Several New York appellate courts rejected this claim. Winship appealed to the Supreme Court of the United States.

The Supreme Court by a 6-3 vote ruled that Winship was unconstitutionally convicted. Justice Brennan's majority opinion held that due process required that both adults and juveniles be found guilty of a crime only if all elements were proven beyond a reasonable doubt. On what constitutional foundation does the "beyond reasonable doubt" rule rest? What reasons do the justices give for insisting that the "beyond reasonable doubt" requirement is one of the "essentials of due process" that must structure a juvenile court proceeding? Does the case shed any light on the earlier "incorporation" debate? Justice Black, a liberal on incorporation, dissented in Winship *because that Bill of Rights does not include a provision requiring proof beyond a reasonable doubt. Justice Harlan, who opposed incorporation, was in the majority because the requirement of reasonable doubt, in his view, was an element of fundamental fairness. Is reasonable doubt an element of fundamental fairness in the juvenile system? Does the Bill of Rights not require reasonable doubt?*

JUSTICE BRENNAN delivered the opinion of the Court.

. . .

The requirement that guilt of a criminal charge be established by proof beyond a reasonable doubt dates at least from our early years as a Nation. . . . Although virtually unanimous adherence to the reasonable-doubt standard in common-law jurisdictions may not conclusively establish it as a requirement of due process, such adherence does "reflect a profound judgment about the way in which law should be enforced and justice administered." . . .

Expressions in many opinions of this Court indicate that it has long been assumed that proof of a criminal charge beyond a reasonable doubt is constitutionally required. . . . Mr. Justice Frankfurter stated that "[i]t [is] the duty of the Government to establish . . . guilt beyond a reasonable doubt. This notion—basic in our law and rightly one of the boasts of a free society—is a requirement and a safeguard of due process of law in the historic, procedural content of due process." . . .

The reasonable-doubt standard plays a vital role in the American scheme of criminal procedure. It is a prime instrument for reducing the risk of convictions resting on factual error. The standard provides concrete substance for the presumption of innocence—that bedrock "axiomatic and elementary" principle whose "enforcement lies at the foundation of the administration of our criminal law." . . .

The requirement of proof beyond a reasonable doubt has this vital role in our criminal procedure for cogent reasons. The accused during a criminal prosecution has at stake interest of immense importance, both because of the possibility that he may lose his liberty upon conviction and because of the certainty that he would be stigmatized by the conviction. Accordingly, a society that values the good name and freedom of every individual should not condemn a man for commission of a crime when there is reasonable doubt about his guilt. . . .

Moreover, use of the reasonable-doubt standard is indispensable to command the respect and confidence of the community in applications of the criminal law. It is critical that the moral force of the criminal law not be diluted by a standard of proof that leaves people in doubt whether innocent men are being condemned. It is also important in our free society that every individual going about his ordinary affairs have confidence that his government cannot adjudge him guilty of a criminal offense without convincing a proper factfinder of his guilt with utmost certainty.

Lest there remain any doubt about the constitutional stature of the reasonable-doubt standard, we explicitly hold that the Due Process Clause protects the accused against conviction except upon proof beyond a reasonable doubt of every fact necessary to constitute the crime with which he is charged.

. . . The same considerations that demand extreme caution in factfinding to protect the innocent adult apply as well to the innocent child. . . . [C]ivil labels and good intentions do not themselves obviate the need for criminal due process safeguards in juvenile courts, for " [a] proceeding where the issue is whether the child will be found to be 'delinquent' and subjected to the loss of his liberty for years is comparable in seriousness to a felony prosecution." . . .

. . .

. . . It is true, of course, that the juvenile may be engaging in a general course of conduct inimical to his welfare that calls for judicial intervention. But that intervention cannot take the form of subjecting the child to the stigma of a finding that he violated a criminal law and to the possibility of institutional confinement on proof insufficient to convict him were he an adult.

. . .

JUSTICE HARLAN, concurring.

. . .

. . . [T]he reason for different standards of proof in civil as opposed to criminal litigation becomes apparent. In a civil suit between two private parties for money damages, for example, we view it as no more serious in general for there to be an erroneous verdict in the defendant's favor than for there to be an erroneous verdict in the plaintiff's favor. . . .

. . .

. . . I view the requirement of proof beyond a reasonable doubt in a criminal case as bottomed on a fundamental value determination of our society that it is far worse to convict an innocent man than to let a guilty man go free. It is only because of the nearly complete and long-standing acceptance of the reasonable-doubt standard by the States in criminal trials that the Court has not before today had to hold explicitly that due process, as an expression of fundamental procedural fairness, requires a more stringent standard for criminal trials than for ordinary civil litigation.

When one assesses the consequences of an erroneous factual determination in a juvenile delinquency proceeding in which a youth is accused of a crime, I think it must be concluded that, while the consequences are not identical to those in a criminal case, the differences will not support a distinction in the standard of proof. First, and of paramount importance, a factual error here, as in a criminal case, exposes the accused to a complete loss of his personal liberty through a state-imposed confinement away from his home, family, and friends. And, second, a delinquency determination, to some extent at least, stigmatizes a youth in that it is by definition bottomed on a finding that the accused committed a crime. Although there are no doubt costs to society (and possibly even to the youth himself) in letting a guilty youth go free, I think here, as in a criminal case, it is far worse to declare an innocent youth a delinquent. I therefore agree that a juvenile court judge should be no less convinced of the factual conclusion that the accused committed the criminal act with which he is charged than would be required in a criminal trial.

. . .

CHIEF JUSTICE BURGER, with whom JUSTICE STEWART joins, dissenting.

. . . What the juvenile court system needs is not more but less of the trappings of legal procedure and judicial formalism; the juvenile court system requires breathing room and flexibility in order to survive, if it can survive the repeated assaults from this Court.

. . .

My hope is that today's decision will not spell the end of a generously conceived program of compassionate treatment intended to mitigate the rigors and trauma of exposing youthful offenders to a traditional criminal court; each step we take turns the clock back to the pre-juvenile-court era. I cannot regard it as a manifestation of progress to transform juvenile courts into criminal courts, which is what we are well on the way to accomplishing. We can only hope the legislative response will not reflect our own by having these courts abolished.

JUSTICE BLACK, dissenting.

. . . The Bill of Rights . . . does by express language provide for, among other things, a right to counsel in criminal trials, a right to indictment, and the right of a defendant to be informed of the nature of the charges against him. And in two places the Constitution provides for trial by jury, but nowhere in that document is there any statement that conviction of crime requires proof of guilt beyond a reasonable doubt. The Constitution thus goes into some detail to spell out what kind of trial a defendant charged with crime should have, and I believe the Court has no power to add to or subtract from the procedures set forth by the Founders. I realize that it is far easier to substitute individual judges' ideas of "fairness" for the fairness prescribed by the Constitution, but I shall not at any time surrender my belief that that document itself should be our guide, not our own concept of what is fair, decent, and right. . . . As I have said time and time again, I prefer to put my faith in the words of the written Constitution itself rather than to rely on the shifting, day-to-day standards of fairness of individual judges.

. . .

I admit a strong, persuasive argument can be made for a standard of proof beyond a reasonable doubt in criminal cases—and the majority has made that argument well—but it is not for me as a judge to say for that reason that Congress or the States are without constitutional power to establish another standard that the Constitution does not otherwise forbid. It is quite true that proof beyond a reasonable doubt has long been required in federal criminal trials. It is also true that this requirement is almost universally found in the governing laws of the States. And as long as a particular jurisdiction requires proof beyond a reasonable doubt, then the Due Process Clause commands that every trial in that jurisdiction must adhere to that standard. . . . But when, as here, a State through its duly constituted legislative branch decides to apply a different standard, then that standard, unless it is otherwise unconstitutional, must be applied to insure that persons are treated according to the "law of the land." The State of New York has made such a decision, and in my view nothing in the Due Process Clause invalidates it.

Wainwright v. Sykes, 433 U.S. 72 (1977)

John Sykes was arrested for the murder of Willie Gilbert on January 8, 1972. After being taken to the police station and read his Miranda *rights, he told the police that he had committed the crime. Defense counsel raised no objection when this confession was introduced at trial. The jury found Sykes guilty of third-degree murder and sentenced him to ten years in prison. While serving that sentence Sykes filed a petition of habeas corpus in the Florida courts. The petition claimed that his confession was unconstitutionally admitted into evidence because he was drunk when he confessed, he did not understand the* Miranda *warnings, and the police officers were aware of his condition. After that petition was rejected by state justices Sykes filed a federal habeas petition. The federal district court ruled that under* Fay v. Noia *(1963) Sykes had a right to a hearing on whether his confession was voluntary. That decision was affirmed by the Court of Appeals for the Fifth Circuit. Florida appealed to the Supreme Court of the United States.*

The Supreme Court by a 7-2 vote overruled Fay v. Noia *and rejected Sykes's habeas corpus petition. Justice Rehnquist ruled that persons who failed to make constitutional objections at trial may not raise those issues on habeas corpus unless they demonstrate "cause and prejudice." What is "cause and prejudice"? Justice Rehnquist appeals to federalism. Does federalism support the "cause and prejudice" standard? What other values support that standard? What are the contrary values? Both the Rehnquist majority opinion and the Brennan dissent make prudential arguments. Rehnquist worries about lawyers who "sandbag," foregoing constitutional claims at trial in order to raise them later in federal habeas corpus. Brennan insists that the failure to raise a constitutional claim is often due to ignorance or inexperience. Who is right? To what extent do you believe that such procedural decisions as* Wainwright v. Sykes *sharply curtail the substantive rights declared during the due process revolution?*

JUSTICE REHNQUIST delivered the opinion of the Court.

. . .

We think that the rule of *Fay v. Noia* (1963), broadly stated, may encourage "sandbagging" on the part of defense lawyers, who may take their chances on a verdict of not guilty in a state trial court with the intent to raise their constitutional claims in a federal habeas court if their initial gamble does not pay off. The refusal of federal habeas courts to honor contemporaneous-objection rules may also make state courts themselves less stringent in their enforcement. Under the rule of *Fay v. Noia*, state appellate courts know that a federal constitutional issue raised for the first time in the proceeding before them may well be decided in any event by a federal habeas tribunal. Thus, their choice is between addressing the issue notwithstanding the petitioner's failure to timely object, or else face the prospect that the federal habeas court will decide the question without the benefit of their views.

The failure of the federal habeas courts generally to require compliance with a contemporaneous-objection rule tends to detract from the perception of the trial of a criminal case in state court as a decisive and portentous event. A defendant has been accused of a serious crime, and this is the time and place set for him to be tried by a jury of his peers and found either guilty or not guilty by that jury. To the greatest extent possible all issues which bear on this charge should be determined in this proceeding: the accused is in the courtroom, the jury is in the box, the judge is on the bench, and the witnesses, having been subpoenaed and duly sworn, await their turn to testify. Society's resources have been concentrated at that time and place in order to decide, within the limits of human fallibility, the question of guilt or innocence of one of its citizens. Any procedural rule which encourages the result that those proceedings be as free of error as possible is thoroughly desirable, and the contemporaneous-objection rule surely falls within this classification.

. . .

The "cause"-and-"prejudice" exception . . . will afford an adequate guarantee, we think, that the rule will not prevent a federal habeas court from adjudicating for the first time the federal constitutional claim of a defendant who in the absence of such an adjudication will be the victim of a miscarriage of justice. Whatever precise content may be given those terms by later cases, we feel confident in holding without further elaboration that they do not exist here. Respondent has advanced no explanation whatever for his failure to object at trial, and, as the proceeding unfolded, the trial judge is certainly not to be faulted for failing to question the admission of the confession himself. The other evidence of guilt presented at trial, moreover, was substantial to a degree that would negate any possibility of actual prejudice resulting to the respondent from the admission of his inculpatory statement.

. . .

CHIEF JUSTICE BURGER, concurring. . . .

JUSTICE STEVENS, concurring. . . .

JUSTICE WHITE, concurring in the judgment. . . .

JUSTICE BRENNAN, with whom JUSTICE MARSHALL joins, dissenting.

. . .

. . . [A]ny realistic system of federal habeas corpus jurisdiction must be premised on the reality that the ordinary procedural default is born of the inadvertence, negligence, inexperience, or incompetence of trial counsel. . . . The case under consideration today is typical. The Court makes no effort to identify a tactical motive for the failure of Sykes' attorney to challenge the admissibility or reliability of a highly inculpatory statement. . . . Indeed, there is no basis for inferring that Sykes or his state trial lawyer was even aware of the existence of his claim under the Fifth Amendment. . . . Rather, any realistic reading of the record demonstrates that we are faced here with a lawyer's simple error.

. . .

. . . *Fay*'s commitment to enforcing intentional but not inadvertent procedural defaults offers a realistic measure of protection for the habeas corpus petitioner seeking federal review of federal claims that were not litigated before the State. The threatened creation of a more "airtight system of forfeitures" would effectively deprive habeas petitioners of the opportunity for litigating their constitutional claims before any forum and would disparage the paramount importance of constitutional rights in our system of government. Such a restriction of habeas corpus jurisdiction should be countenanced, I submit, only if it fairly can be concluded that *Fay*'s focus on knowing and voluntary forfeitures unduly interferes with the legitimate interests of state courts or institutions. The majority offers no suggestion that actual experience has shown that *Fay*'s bypass test can be criticized on this score. . . .

. . .

Punishing a lawyer's unintentional errors by closing the federal courthouse door to his client is both a senseless and misdirected method of deterring the slighting of state rules. It is senseless because unplanned and unintentional action of any kind generally is not subject to deterrence; and, to the extent that it is hoped that a threatened sanction addressed to the defense will induce greater care and caution on the part of trial lawyers, thereby forestalling negligent conduct or error, the potential loss of all valuable state remedies would be sufficient to this end. And it is a misdirected sanction because even if the penalization of incompetence or carelessness will encourage more thorough legal training and trial preparation, the habeas applicant, as opposed to his lawyer, hardly is the proper recipient of such a penalty. . . . This is especially true when so many indigent defendants are without any realistic choice in selecting who ultimately represents them at trial. Indeed, if responsibility for error must be apportioned between the parties, it is the State, through its attorney's admissions and certification policies, that is more fairly held to blame for the fact that practicing lawyers too often are ill-prepared or ill-equipped to act carefully and knowledgeably when faced with decisions governed by state procedural requirements. . . .

B. Search and Seizure

The exclusionary rule announced in *Mapp v. Ohio* (1961) remained the law of the land, but the Nixon appointees to the Supreme Court, often joined by Justice White, carved out numerous exceptions or limitations to the principle that prosecutors may not rely on unconstitutionally obtained evidence to secure criminal convictions:

- Unconstitutionally obtained evidence may be used in a criminal trial when the defendant was not the victim of the unconstitutional search. *Alderman v. United States* (1969).
- Unconstitutionally obtained evidence may be introduced in a grand jury proceeding. *United States v. Calandra* (1974).
- Claims that persons were convicted of a crime on the basis of unconstitutionally obtained evidence may not be heard in habeas corpus procedures if the state court held a full and fair hearing on the underlying Fourth Amendment issue. *Stone v. Powell* (1976).
- Unconstitutionally obtained evidence may be introduced in civil tax proceedings. *United States v. Janis* (1976).
- Unconstitutionally obtained evidence may be used at trial to impeach a criminal defendant's testimony. *United States v. Havens* (1980).

Proponents of these exceptions insisted that the sole purpose of the exclusionary rule was to deter unconstitutional behavior and that the deterrent effect in the particular situation before the court was minimal. Proponents insisted that the exclusionary rule reflected the principle that state actors should not benefit from state wrongs. As was often the case with Burger Court decisions, the power of decision rested with centrist judges who often made fine distinctions that appeared obscure to both such conservatives as Justice Rehnquist, who preferred to overrule *Mapp*, and such progressives as Justices Brennan and Marshall, who thought that *Mapp* should be extended.

The Supreme Court was more liberal in determining when a search violated the Fourth and Fourteenth Amendments. *United States v. United States District Court* (1972) rejected claims that the president had the power to order wiretaps without a warrant. Justice Powell's opinion for the Court asserted,

> The Government's concerns do not justify departure in this case from the customary Fourth Amendment requirement of judicial approval prior to initiation of a search or surveillance.... A prior warrant establishes presumptive validity of the surveillance and will minimize the burden of justification in post-surveillance judicial review. By no means of least importance will be the reassurance of the public generally that indiscriminate wiretapping and bugging of law-abiding citizens cannot occur.

Payton v. New York (1980) held that warrantless home arrests are normally unconstitutional. The "basic principle of Fourth Amendment law that searches and seizures inside a home without a warrant are presumptively unreasonable," Justice Stevens stated, "has equal force when the seizure of a person is involved."

United States v. Calandra, 414 U.S. 338 (1974)

A federal grand jury in Ohio investigating loan sharking sought to ask John Calandra questions about documents seized from his place of business by federal agents. Calandra refused to answer, claiming that the search was unconstitutional and that the exclusionary rule announced in Mapp v. Ohio *(1961) prohibited grand juries from considering the fruits of an unconstitutional search. A federal district court agreed with Calandra's claims. That ruling was sustained by the Court of Appeals for the Sixth Circuit. The United States appealed to the Supreme Court of the United States.*

The Supreme Court by a 6-3 vote ruled that Calandra had to answer the grand jury questions. Justice Powell's majority opinion asserted that the exclusionary rule did not apply to grand jury proceedings. Justices Powell and Justice Brennan dispute the purpose of the exclusionary rule. What purpose does each believe the exclusionary rule serves? Which opinion is more faithful to precedent? Which is more faithful to the Constitution? To what extent might some justices in the majority have been more interested in overruling Mapp *than faithfully following that precedent? Why did the centrist judges on the Burger Court prefer creating exceptions to the exclusionary rule to overruling* Mapp?

JUSTICE POWELL delivered the opinion of the Court.

...

The purpose of the exclusionary rule is not to redress the injury to the privacy of the search victim. . . . Instead, the rule's prime purpose is to deter future unlawful police conduct and thereby effectuate the guarantee of the Fourth Amendment against unreasonable searches and seizures. . . .

Despite its broad deterrent purpose, the exclusionary rule has never been interpreted to proscribe the use of illegally seized evidence in all proceedings or against all persons. As with any remedial device, the application of the rule has been restricted to those areas where its remedial objectives are thought most efficaciously served. . . .

In deciding whether to extend the exclusionary rule to grand jury proceedings, we must weigh the potential injury to the historic role and functions of the grand jury against the potential benefits of the rule as applied in this context. It is evident that this extension of the exclusionary rule would seriously impede the grand jury. Because the grand jury does not finally adjudicate guilt or innocence, it has traditionally been allowed to pursue its investigative and accusatorial functions unimpeded by the evidentiary and procedural restrictions applicable to a criminal trial. Permitting witnesses to invoke the exclusionary rule before a grand jury would precipitate adjudication of issues hitherto reserved for the trial on the merits and would delay and disrupt grand jury proceedings. Suppression hearings would halt the orderly progress of an investigation and might necessitate extended litigation of issues only tangentially related to the grand jury's primary objective. . . .

Against this potential damage to the role and functions of the grand jury, we must weigh the benefits to be derived from this proposed extension of the exclusionary rule. Suppression of the use of illegally seized evidence against the search victim in a criminal trial is thought to be an important method of effectuating the Fourth Amendment. But it does not follow that the Fourth Amendment requires adoption of every proposal that might deter police misconduct. . . .

Any incremental deterrent effect which might be achieved by extending the rule to grand jury proceedings is uncertain at best. Whatever deterrence of police misconduct may result from the exclusion of illegally seized evidence from criminal trials, it is unrealistic to assume that application of the rule to grand jury proceedings would significantly further that goal. Such an extension would deter only police investigation consciously directed toward the discovery of evidence solely for use in a grand jury investigation. The incentive to disregard the requirement of the Fourth Amendment solely to obtain an indictment from a grand jury is substantially negated by the inadmissibility of the illegally seized evidence in a subsequent criminal prosecution of the search victim. For the most part, a prosecutor would be unlikely to request an indictment where a conviction could not be obtained. We therefore decline to embrace a view that would achieve a speculative and undoubtedly minimal advance in the deterrence of police misconduct at the expense of substantially impeding the role of the grand jury.

. . .

The purpose of the Fourth Amendment is to prevent unreasonable governmental intrusions into the privacy of one's person, house, papers, or effects. The wrong condemned is the unjustified governmental invasion of these areas of an individual's life. That wrong, committed in this case, is fully accomplished by the original search without probable cause. Grand jury questions based on evidence obtained thereby involve no independent governmental invasion of one's person, house, papers, or effects, but rather the usual abridgment of personal privacy common to all grand jury questioning. Questions based on illegally obtained evidence are only a derivative use of the product of a past unlawful search and seizure. They work no new Fourth Amendment wrong. Whether such derivative use of illegally obtained evidence by a grand jury should be proscribed presents a question, not of rights, but of remedies.

. . .

JUSTICE BRENNAN, with whom JUSTICE DOUGLAS and JUSTICE MARSHALL join, dissenting.

. . . This downgrading of the exclusionary rule to a determination whether its application in a particular type of proceeding furthers deterrence of future police misconduct reflects a startling misconception, unless it is a purposeful rejection, of the historical objective and purpose of the rule.

The commands of the Fourth Amendment are, of course, directed solely to public officials. Necessarily, therefore, only official violations of those commands could have created the evil that threatened to make the Amendment a dead letter. But curtailment of the evil, if a consideration at all, was at best only a hoped-for effect of the exclusionary rule, not its ultimate objective. Indeed, there is no evidence that the possible deterrent effect of the rule was given any attention by the judges chiefly responsible for its formulation. Their concern as guardians of the Bill of Rights was to fashion an enforcement tool to give content and meaning to the Fourth Amendment's guarantees. . . .

. . . The exclusionary rule, if not perfect, accomplished the twin goals of enabling the judiciary to avoid the taint of partnership in official lawlessness and of assuring the people—all potential victims of unlawful government conduct—that the government would not profit from its lawless behavior, thus minimizing the risk of seriously undermining popular trust in government.

. . .

The judges who developed the exclusionary rule were well aware that it embodied a judgment that it is better for some guilty persons to go free than for the police to behave in forbidden fashion. . . . In reversing the judgment of convictions in [*Silverthrone Lumber Co. v. United States* (1920)], the Court, speaking through Mr. Justice Holmes, held that the Government was barred from utilizing any fruits of its forbidden act, stating that "[t]he essence of a provision forbidding the acquisition of evidence in a certain way is that not merely evidence so acquired shall not be used before the Court but that it shall not be used at all." . . .

. . .

To be sure, the exclusionary rule does not "provide that illegally seized evidence is inadmissible against anyone for any purpose." But clearly there is a crucial distinction between withholding its cover from individuals whose Fourth Amendment rights have not been violated—as has been done in the "standing" cases . . . and withdrawing its cover from persons whose Fourth Amendment rights have in fact been abridged.

. . .

In *Mapp v. Ohio* (1961), the Court thought it had "close[d] the only courtroom door remaining open to evidence secured by official lawlessness" in violation of Fourth Amendment rights. . . . The door is again ajar. As a consequence, I am left with the uneasy feeling that today's decision may signal that a majority of my colleagues have positioned themselves to reopen the door still further and abandon altogether the exclusionary rule in search-and-seizure cases; for surely they cannot believe that application of the exclusionary rule at trial furthers the goal of deterrence, but that its application in grand jury proceedings will not "significantly" do so. Unless we are to shut our eyes to the evidence that crosses our desks every day, we must concede that official lawlessness has not abated and that no empirical data distinguishes trials from grand jury proceedings. I thus fear that when next we confront a case of a conviction rested on illegally seized evidence, today's decision will be invoked to sustain the conclusion in that case also, that "it is unrealistic to assume" that application of the rule at trial would "significantly further" the goal of deterrence—though, if the police are presently undeterred, it is difficult to see how removal of the sanction of exclusion will induce more lawful official conduct.

C. Interrogations

The temptation exists to repeat verbatim the first paragraph of the introduction to the previous section, substituting only *Miranda v. Arizona* (1966) for *Mapp v. Ohio* (1961). As was the case with *Mapp, Miranda* bent during this period but did not break. Nixon appointees were willing to make exceptions to the rule that prosecutors could not introduce confessions at trial unless the persons arrested had been given *Miranda* warnings. *Harris v. New York* (1971) permitted prosecutors to use such confessions when cross-examining the defendant, and many state courts embraced that greater leniency toward prosecutors. Nevertheless, the centrist judges on the Burger Court were unwilling to overrule *Miranda*.

The Burger Court had a more mixed record when determining what constituted a custodial confession. Many cases turned on slight changes in the fact pattern. Both *Brewer v. Williams* (1977) and *Rhode Island v. Innis* (1980) concerned confessions obtained in squad cars after the suspect had invoked the right to remain silent. In *Brewer* the police officers struck up a conversation with the defendant in which they commented that the victim's family really wanted to find the body in order to have a proper Christian burial. In *Innis* the police officers struck up a conversation with themselves in which they expressed concern that children might find and use the loaded gun used in the murder. *Brewer*, by a 5-4 vote, tossed the subsequent confession. *Innis*, by a 6-3 vote, declared the confession constitutionally obtained. Few persons other than Justices Stewart and Powell perceived any significant differences in the cases.

Harris v. New York, 401 U.S. 222 (1971)

Viven Harris was arrested for selling heroin to an undercover police officer. During an interrogation that day Harris made several incriminating statements. The state prosecutor, aware that Harris was not given proper Miranda *warnings, did not introduce those statements during the direct examination of the arresting officer. When cross-examining Harris,*

Table 9-5 State Supreme Court Treatment of Confessions after *Harris v. New York*

Ruling	Number of States	Percentage of States
Adopt *Harris* rule for state courts	35	81
Reject *Harris* rule for state courts	8	19
Total	43	100

Source: John Gruhl, "State Supreme Courts and the U.S. Supreme Court's Post-*Miranda* Rulings," *Journal of Criminal Law and Criminology* 72 (1981): 895.

the prosecutor introduced the incriminating statements into evidence after Harris declared that he could not remember what he said after being arrested. The trial judge instructed the jury that they could use the incriminating statements when considering whether Harris's testimony was credible, but not when considering whether he had committed the crime. The jury found Harris guilty of selling narcotics. He was sentenced to prison for six to eight years. The Supreme Court, Appellate Division of New York and the New York Court of Appeals affirmed the trial court's ruling that the incriminating statements were admissible. Harris appealed to the Supreme Court of the United States.

The Supreme Court by a 5-4 vote ruled the confessions admissible. Chief Justice Burger's majority opinion declared that confessions obtained in violation of Miranda *could be used to impeach a criminal defendant. Why does the chief justice claim that a prosecutor can introduce evidence of a confession secured without* Miranda *warnings on cross-examination, even though such evidence could not be admitted on direct examination? Do you believe that* Harris *exploits a legal ambiguity in* Miranda, *or was this case a first step toward overruling that decision? If you were a defense attorney after* Harris, *would you ever allow your client to take the stand if the client had made a confession without proper* Miranda *warnings*

CHIEF JUSTICE BURGER delivered the opinion of the Court.

. . .

Some comments in the *Miranda* opinion can indeed be read as indicating a bar to use of an uncounseled statement for any purpose, but discussion of that issue was not at all necessary to the Court's holding and cannot be regarded as controlling. *Miranda* barred the prosecution from making its case with statements of an accused made while in custody prior to having or effectively waiving counsel. It does not follow from *Miranda* that evidence inadmissible against an accused in the prosecution's case in chief is barred for all purposes, provided of course that the trustworthiness of the evidence satisfies legal standards.

. . .

. . . Petitioner's testimony in his own behalf . . . contrasted sharply with what he told the police shortly after his arrest. The impeachment process here undoubtedly provided valuable aid to the jury in assessing petitioner's credibility, and the benefits of this process should not be lost, in our view, because of the speculative possibility that impermissible police conduct will be encouraged thereby. Assuming that the exclusionary rule has a deterrent effect on proscribed police conduct, sufficient deterrence flows when the evidence in question is made unavailable to the prosecution in its case in chief.

Every criminal defendant is privileged to testify in his own defense, or to refuse to do so. But that privilege cannot be construed to include the right to commit perjury. . . . Having voluntarily taken the stand, petitioner was under an obligation to speak truthfully and accurately, and the prosecution here did no more than utilize the traditional truth-testing devices of the adversary process. . . .

The shield provided by *Miranda* cannot be perverted into a license to use perjury by way of a defense, free from the risk of confrontation with prior inconsistent utterances. We hold, therefore, that petitioner's credibility was appropriately impeached by use of his earlier conflicting statements.

JUSTICE BLACK dissents.

JUSTICE BRENNAN, with whom JUSTICE DOUGLAS and JUSTICE MARSHALL join, dissenting.

[The privilege against self-incrimination] is fulfilled only when an accused is guaranteed the right "to remain silent unless he chooses to speak in the unfettered exercise of his own will." . . . The choice of whether to testify in one's own defense must therefore be "unfettered," since that choice is an exercise of the constitutional privilege. . . . [T]he accused is denied an "unfettered" choice when the decision whether to take the stand is burdened by the risk that an illegally obtained prior statement may be introduced to impeach his direct testimony denying complicity in the crime charged against him. We settled this proposition in *Miranda* where we said:

> The privilege against self-incrimination protects the individual from being compelled to incriminate himself in any manner. . . . [S]tatements merely intended to be exculpatory by the defendant are often used to impeach his testimony at trial. . . . These statements are incriminating in any meaningful sense of the word and may not be used without the full warnings and effective waiver required for any other statement.

. . .

The objective of deterring improper police conduct is only part of the larger objective of safeguarding the integrity of our adversary system. The "essential mainstay" of that system . . . is the privilege against self-incrimination, which for that reason has occupied a central place in our jurisprudence since before the Nation's birth. Moreover, "we may view the historical development of the privilege as one which groped for the proper scope of governmental power over the citizen. . . . All these policies point to one overriding thought: the constitutional foundation underlying the privilege is the respect a government . . . must accord to the dignity and integrity of its citizens." . . . These values are plainly jeopardized if an exception against admission of tainted statements is made for those used for impeachment purposes. . . . The Court today tells the police that they may freely interrogate an accused incommunicado and without counsel and know that although any statement they obtain in violation of *Miranda* cannot be used on the State's direct case, it may be introduced if the defendant has the temerity to testify in his own defense. This goes far toward undoing much of the progress made in conforming police methods to the Constitution. I dissent.

People v. Disbrow, 16 Cal. 3rd 101 (1976)

Robert Disbrow informed a California police officer that he was shot in the leg five times while killing his estranged wife and a friend of his wife in self-defense. Disbrow was taken to a hospital, where he was interviewed by Detective Yost. After Disbrow told Yost that he wished to remain silent, Yost informed him that no subsequent statement could be used against him. Disbrow then made some incriminating statements that were inconsistent with his self-defense claim. During Disbrow's trial the prosecutor used these statements solely to impeach Disbrow's credibility on cross-examination. After Disbrow's first trial ended in a mistrial, he agreed to a bench trial solely on the basis of the transcript of his first trial. The presiding judge found him guilty of voluntary manslaughter and sentenced him to prison. Disbrow appealed that verdict, claiming that the use of his confession violated his rights under the constitutions of California and the United States.

The Supreme Court of California by a 4-3 vote ruled that Disbrow was unconstitutionally convicted. Justice Mosk claimed that the self-incrimination provision of the California Constitution barred any use of confessions obtained without proper warning, even though the Supreme Court in United States v. Harris *(1971) had just interpreted the identical language of the federal Constitution to permit such confessions to be used for impeachment purposes. Does Justice Mosk give any reason for rejecting* Harris *other than his belief that* Harris *was wrongly decided? Is that a sufficient basis for interpreting the California Constitution? Justice Richardson insists that states should adopt a presumption that similar language in state and federal constitutions has the same meaning. What is the basis of that presumption? Is that presumption sound?*

JUSTICE MOSK delivered the opinion of the Court.

. . .

In *Harris v. New York* (1971), the Supreme Court held that statements which were inadmissible as affirmative evidence because of a failure to comply with *Miranda* could nevertheless be used for impeachment purposes to attack the credibility of a defendant's trial testimony, as long as the statements were not "coerced" or "involuntary." . . .

. . .

. . . [O]ur principal objection to the *Harris* rule lies in the considerable potential that a jury, even with the benefit of a limiting instruction, will view prior inculpatory statements as substantive evidence of guilt rather than as merely reflecting on the declarant's veracity. The theory of a limiting instruction loses meaning in this context. It is to be recalled that we are here dealing with extrajudicial inculpatory admissions. To instruct a jury that they are not to consider expressions of complicity in the charged crime as evidence that the speaker in fact committed the charged crime, but only for the purpose of demonstrating that he was probably lying when he denied committing the charged crime, would be to require, in the words of Learned Hand, "a mental gymnastic which is beyond, not only [the jury's] power, but anybody's else." . . .

. . .

. . . [W]e are further convinced of the impropriety of receipt of this evidence by a significant rationale of the exclusionary rule itself. In *People v. Cahan* (CA 1955), . . . the landmark case in which this court adopted the rule for California two decades ago, we said, "the success of the lawless venture depends entirely on the court's lending its aid by allowing the evidence to be introduced. . . . Out of regard for its own dignity as an agency of justice and custodian of liberty the court should not have a hand in such 'dirty business.'" In the case at bar, accordingly, exclusion of the statements illegally extracted from defendant by Detective Yost would "relieve the courts from being compelled to participate in such illegal conduct." . . .

We therefore hold that the privilege against self-incrimination of article I, section 15, of the California Constitution precludes use by the prosecution of any extrajudicial statement by the defendant, whether inculpatory or exculpatory, either as affirmative evidence or for purposes of impeachment, obtained during custodial interrogation in violation of the standards declared in *Miranda v. Arizona* (1966) and its California progeny. Accordingly, we . . . declare that *Harris* is not persuasive authority in any state prosecution in California.

We pause finally to reaffirm the independent nature of the California Constitution and our responsibility to separately define and protect the rights of California citizens despite conflicting decisions of the United States Supreme Court interpreting the federal Constitution. . . . [I]n light of recent erosion of *Miranda* standards as a matter of federal constitutional law, it is appropriate to observe that no State is precluded by the decision from adhering to higher standards under state law. Each State has power to impose higher standards governing police practices under state law than is required by the Federal Constitution. . . .

. . .

JUSTICE TOBRINER and JUSTICE SULLIVAN, concurring.

CHIEF JUSTICE WRIGHT, concurring. . . .

JUSTICE RICHARDSON, with whom JUSTICE McCOMB and JUSTICE CLARK join, dissenting.

. . .

It is both readily apparent and significant that the self-incrimination clauses of the Fifth Amendment to the United States Constitution and of article I, section 15, of the state Constitution contain virtually identical language. Also, the Fourth Amendment and article I, section 13, of the state Constitution employ similar language in prohibiting unreasonable searches and seizures. The very obvious and substantial identity of phrasing in the two Constitutions strongly suggests to me the wisdom, insofar as possible, of identity of interpretation of those clauses. The same considerations of policy, need for uniformity and avoidance of confusion apply with equal force to the Fourth and Fifth Amendment protections contained in article I of our state Constitution.

These important factors of deference and of policy have been recently well expressed in Justice Clark's dissenting opinion in *People v. Norman* (CA 1975) . . . wherein he quotes the following language. . . :

> Decisions of the United States Supreme Court construing constitutional phraseology are highly persuasive. . . . The persuasion of the United States Supreme Court decisions is particularly strong in the area of search and seizure and the exclusionary rule. California courts have for years spoken of the basis of the exclusionary rule as the Fourth Amendment. A sudden switch to a California ground to avoid the impact of federal high court decision invites the successful use of the initiative process to overrule the California decision with its concomitant harm to the prestige, influence, and function of the judicial branch of state government. . . . The more courts feel free to adopt ground rules unpersuaded by contrary decisions of other courts, the greater the likelihood there is of uncertainty in those ground rules. The uncertainty is mitigated if proper deference is paid United States Supreme Court holdings. . . .

I believe the foregoing reasoning is eminently sound, equally applicable to self-incrimination language that is nearly identical in the two Constitutions, and that no special, unique, or distinctive California conditions exist which justify a departure from a general principle favoring uniformity. In my view, in the absence of very strong countervailing circumstances we should defer to the leadership of the nation's highest court in its interpretation of nearly identical constitutional language, rather than attempt to create a separate echelon of state constitutional interpretations to which we will advert whenever a majority of this court differ from a particular high court interpretation. The reason for the foregoing principle is that it promotes uniformity and harmony in an area of the law which peculiarly and uniquely requires them. The alternative required by the majority must inevitably lead to the growth of a shadow tier of dual constitutional interpretations state by state which, with temporal variances, will add complexity to an already complicated body of law.

. . .

The case before us presents a classic example, in my opinion, of the fallacy of the majority approach. Here the majority propose to rely on and encourage development of a separate California self-incrimination privilege notwithstanding the near identity of language in the Fifth Amendment to the federal Constitution and article I, section 15, of the California Constitution. The inevitable result is two rules or standards of interpretation of single constitutional language. Furthermore, the majority blithely ignore what has long been recognized, namely, that the privilege against self-incrimination is a single common law privilege which existed long before its incorporation into either the United States or California Constitution.... On principle, even in situations of varying constitutional expressions of a single common law privilege uniform interpretation should normally be required and expected.... A fortiori, as in the matters before us when constitutional language approaches identity, the compulsion toward uniformity of interpretation should be even greater. That being so, on what basis do the majority hold that the language of our state Constitution should be construed in a different manner than the substantially identical language of the Fifth Amendment privilege as construed in *Harris*? What circumstance peculiar to California requires that we do so? I can think of none. The majority have suggested none....

D. Juries and Lawyers

Judicial decisions emphasized the right to a jury that represented a fair cross-sample of the community. *Peters v. Kiff* (1972) held that white defendants had a right to a jury from which persons of color were not unconstitutionally excluded. *Duren v. Missouri* (1979) held that men had a right to a jury from which women were not unconstitutionally excluded.

This right to a jury composed of a fair cross-section of the community did not entail the right to a twelve-person jury or a unanimous jury verdict. In *Williams v. Florida* (1970) Justice White asserted,

> The number should probably be large enough to promote group deliberation, free from outside attempts at intimidation, and to provide a fair possibility for obtaining a representative cross-section of the community. But we find little reason to think that these goals are in any meaningful sense less likely to be achieved when the jury numbers six, than when it numbers 12—particularly if the requirement of unanimity is retained.

Justice White repeated this assertion verbatim in *Apodaca v. Oregon* (1972) when holding that juries need not be unanimous. Six proved to be the bottom limit in jury size. The justices in *Ballew v. Georgia* (1978) held that five-person juries were unconstitutional and in *Burch v. Louisiana* (1979) held that six-person juries had to be unanimous. As was the case with the *Peters* line of cases, the need for a representative cross-sample provided a crucial foundation for the Sixth Amendment right. Justice Blackmun declared in *Ballew*,

> Because of the fundamental importance of the jury trial to the American system of criminal justice, any further reduction that promotes inaccurate and possibly biased decisionmaking, that causes untoward differences in verdicts, and that prevents juries from truly representing their communities, attains constitutional significance.

Judicial decisions on the right to an attorney broke very little ground. *Argensinger v. Hamlin* (1972) ruled that the right to counsel in *Gideon v. Wainwright* (1963) entailed that "no imprisonment may be imposed... unless the accused is represented by counsel." Justice Douglas wrote:

> The requirement of counsel may well be necessary for a fair trial even in a petty-offense prosecution. We are by no means convinced that legal and constitutional questions involved in a case that actually leads to imprisonment even for a brief period are any less complex than when a person can be sent off for six months or more.

In 1979 the justices limited *Gideon* and *Argensinger* to cases in which a prison sentence was actually imposed.

A 5-4 judicial majority in *Scott v. Illinois* determined that criminal defendants who were merely fined had no right to counsel, even if they could have been sentenced to prison for the offense they were found guilty of committing. Justice Rehnquist's majority opinion asserted, "Actual imprisonment is a penalty different in kind from fines or the mere threat of imprisonment."

Peters v. Kiff, 407 U.S. 493 (1972)

Dean Peters was tried for burglary in December 1966, convicted, and sentenced to ten years in a Georgia penitentiary. While in prison Peters sought a writ of habeas corpus on the ground that African-Americans had unconstitutionally been discriminated against in the selection of the grand jury that indicted him and the petit jury that convicted him. Both the federal district and the Court of Appeals for the Fifth Circuit ruled that a white man had no constitutional right to a biracial jury. Peters appealed to the U.S. Supreme Court.

The Supreme Court by a 6-3 vote held that Peters had been unconstitutionally convicted. Justice Marshall's opinion for the court ruled that excluding persons of color from juries violates both the equal protection rights of persons of color and the defendant's right to a jury composed of a fair cross-section of community. Why does Justice Marshall think that this discrimination violates the rights of white defendants as well as persons of color? Why does Justice Rehnquist disagree? Who has the better constitutional argument?

JUSTICE MARSHALL announced the judgment of the Court and an opinion in which JUSTICE DOUGLAS and JUSTICE STEWART join.

. . .

. . . The exclusion of Negroes from jury service, like the arbitrary exclusion of any other well defined class of citizens, offends a number of related constitutional values.

. . .

. . . In *Strauder v. West Virginia* (1880), the Court observed that the exclusion of Negroes from jury service injures not only defendants, but also other members of the excluded class: it denies the class of potential jurors the "privilege of participating equally . . . in the administration of justice," and it stigmatizes the whole class, even those who do not wish to participate, by declaring them unfit for jury service, and thereby putting "a brand upon them, affixed by law, an assertion of their inferiority." . . .

Moreover, the Court has also recognized that the exclusion of a discernible class from jury service injures not only those defendants who belong to the excluded class, but other defendants as well, in that it destroys the possibility that the jury will reflect a representative cross-section of the community. . . .

Long before this Court held that the Constitution imposes the requirement of jury trial on the States, it was well established that the Due Process Clause protects a defendant from jurors who are actually incapable of rendering an impartial verdict, based on the evidence and the law. Thus, a defendant cannot, consistent with due process, be subjected to trial by an insane juror, by jurors who are intimidated by the threat of mob violence, or by jurors who have formed a fixed opinion about the case from newspaper publicity. Moreover, even if there is no showing of actual bias in the tribunal, this Court has held that due process is denied by circumstances that create the likelihood or the appearance of bias. . . .

These principles compel the conclusion that a State cannot, consistent with due process, subject a defendant to indictment or trial by a jury that has been selected in an arbitrary and discriminatory manner, in violation of the Constitution and laws of the United States. Illegal and unconstitutional jury selection procedures cast doubt on the integrity of the whole judicial process.

. . .

. . . [T]he exclusion from jury service of a substantial and identifiable class of citizens has a potential impact that is too subtle and too pervasive to admit of confinement to particular issues or particular cases. First, if we assume that the exclusion of Negroes affects the fairness of the jury only with respect to issues presenting a clear opportunity for the operation of race prejudice, that assumption does not provide a workable guide for decision in particular cases. For the opportunity to appeal to race prejudice is latent in a vast range of issues, cutting across the entire fabric of our society.

Moreover, we are unwilling to make the assumption that the exclusion of Negroes has relevance only for issues involving race. When any large and identifiable segment of the community is excluded from jury service, the effect is to remove from the jury room qualities of human nature and varieties of human experience the range of which is unknown, and perhaps unknowable. It is not necessary to assume that the excluded group will consistently vote as a class in order to conclude, as we do, that its exclusion deprives the jury of a perspective on human events that may have unsuspected importance in any case that may be presented.

...

JUSTICE WHITE, with whom JUSTICE BRENNAN and JUSTICE POWELL join, concurring in the judgment....

CHIEF JUSTICE BURGER, with whom JUSTICE BLACKMUN and JUSTICE REHNQUIST join, dissenting.

...

... [I]n order for petitioner's conviction to be set aside, it is not enough to show merely that there has been some unconstitutional or unlawful action at the trial level. It must be established that petitioner's conviction has resulted from the denial of federally secured rights properly asserted by him.... The Court has held in a long line of cases that a Negro defendant is denied equal protection by the systematic exclusion of Negroes from jury service.... These decisions have been predicated from the beginning on the judicially noticeable fact

> that prejudices often exist against particular classes in the community, which sway the judgment of jurors, and which, therefore, operate in some cases to deny to persons of those classes the full enjoyment of that protection which others enjoy.

... This presumption of prejudice derives from the fact that the defendant is a member of the excluded class, but the Court has never intimated that a defendant is the victim of unconstitutional discrimination if he does not claim that members of his own race have been excluded....

...

... I completely agree that juries should not be deprived of the insights of the various segments of the community. . . . [Nevertheless,] [t]he question of a jury's bias or prejudice is totally factual in nature. If the possibility of prejudice is too remote or speculative to support a finding of unconstitutionality, a different result cannot be justified by relying on the element of illegality. The constitutional and statutory prohibition against such conduct is extraneous to the due process question, for it in no way renders the possibility of prejudice less remote or less speculative. If this were a borderline case on the facts, it might conceivably be appropriate to resolve the doubt against the State due to its complicity in the alleged unlawful discrimination. But, judging from all existing authority, this is not a close case at all.

E. Punishments

No executions took place in the United States in the years between 1968 and 1976. Governors refused to issue death warrants. Winthrop Rockefeller, the governor of Arkansas, commuted every person on death row, asserting that the death penalty was "cruel and unusual punishment" and maintaining that "the exercise of executive clemency has provided a form of moral leadership that has brought about substantive changes in the law."[65] The Supreme Court by a 5-4 vote in *Furman v. Georgia* (1972) put what many thought was a permanent halt to executions by declaring unconstitutional every state statute authorizing capital punishment. Justices Brennan and Marshall insisted that capital punishment in any circumstance was cruel and unusual. Justice Douglas leaned toward a similar conclusion, although his opinion was unclear. Justices White and Stewart, while maintaining that the death penalty in the abstract might be constitutional, insisted that capital punishment in the United States was too arbitrarily imposed to withstand constitutional scrutiny. Justice Stewart's opinion asserted,

> These death sentences are cruel and unusual in the same way that being struck by lightning is cruel and unusual. For, of all the people convicted of rapes and murders in 1967 and 1968, many just as reprehensible as these, the petitioners are among a capriciously selected random handful upon whom the sentence of death has in fact been imposed. My concurring Brothers have demonstrated that, if any basis can be discerned for the selection of these few to be sentenced to die, it is the constitutionally impermissible basis of race. . . . But racial discrimination has not been proved, and I put it to one side. I simply conclude that the Eighth and Fourteenth Amendments cannot tolerate the infliction of a sentence of death under legal systems that permit this

65. Winthrop Rockefeller, "Executive Clemency and the Death Penalty," *Catholic University Law Review* 21 (1971), 94, 99, 100.

> unique penalty to be so wantonly and so freakishly imposed.

The reaction to *Furman* was swift. Thirty-five states and the federal government immediately passed new capital punishment statutes. Most were based on recommendations made by the authors of the Model Penal Code (MPC). The MPC urged states to adopt a bifurcated process: a trial on guilt followed by a trial on punishment. The jury during the penalty phase would be guided by a series of statutory aggravating and mitigating factors. Aggravating factors included previous convictions, the murder of a police officer, and whether a murder was particularly heinous. Mitigating factors included the lack of previous convictions, any mental incapacity, and evidence of remorse. Persons could be sentenced to death only if the jury found beyond a reasonable doubt at least one aggravating factor and determined that the aggravating factors outweighed the mitigating factors. A few states responded to *Furman* by passing mandatory death statutes. Under such measures, anyone convicted of a particular crime—for example, murder of a police officer—would automatically be sentenced to death.

The Burger Court in *Gregg v. Georgia* (1976) and *Woodson v. North Carolina* (1976) split the difference. Justices Brennan and Marshall repeated their claim in *Furman* that the death penalty was always unconstitutional. Chief Justice Burger and Justices Rehnquist, White, and Blackmun insisted that the new statutes cured whatever defects had doomed pre-*Furman* measures. Justices Stevens, Powell, and Stewart cast the crucial votes declaring constitutional in *Gregg* the statutes based on the MPC, but declaring unconstitutional in *Woodson* the mandatory death penalty statutes. Remarkably, these centrist judges concluded that mandatory death penalties resulted in more arbitrary death sentences than did a regime of guided jury discretion. In their view, juries faced with a mandatory death scheme tended for idiosyncratic reasons to find some defendants guilty of only second-degree murder. For this reason, the plurality concluded, guided discretion would actually result in less variation in death sentences than laws that only superficially gave juries no discretion at all. Justice Stewart's opinion striking down a mandatory death sentence in *Woodson v. North Carolina* (1976) declared,

> The history of mandatory death penalty statutes in the United States thus reveals that the practice of sentencing to death all persons convicted of a particular offense has been rejected as unduly harsh and unworkably rigid. The two crucial indicators of evolving standards of decency respecting the imposition of punishment in our society—jury determinations and legislative enactments—both point conclusively to the repudiation of automatic death sentences. At least since the Revolution, American jurors have, with some regularity, disregarded their oaths and refused to convict defendants where a death sentence was the automatic consequence of a guilty verdict.

Most constitutional decision makers cheered the restoration of capital punishment. After *Gregg*, state executions rose to levels not seen since the 1950s.

A few state judges dissented from the pro–capital punishment consensus. The Supreme Judicial Court of Massachusetts repeatedly found that state legislative attempts to reintroduce the death penalty violated the state constitution. One opinion declared,

> [A]rt. 26 of the Declaration of Rights "No magistrate or court of law, shall . . . inflict cruel or unusual punishments" forbids the imposition of a death penalty in this Commonwealth in the absence of a showing on the part of the Commonwealth that the availability of that penalty contributes more to the achievement of a legitimate State purpose—for example, the purpose of deterring criminal conduct—than the availability in like cases of the penalty of life imprisonment. Existing studies of the entire subject have provided no such demonstration regarding any of the situations of murder that would be covered by the proposed legislation, nor has the Legislature made findings resulting from investigation that might furnish the demonstration.[66]

This strategy proved politically risky. California Chief Justice Rose Bird was defeated for reelection in 1986 after consistently blocking the implementation of the death penalty in that state.

66. *Opinion of the Justices*, 372 Mass. 912 (1977). See also *District Attorney for Suffolk District v. Watson*, 381 Mass. 648 (1980).

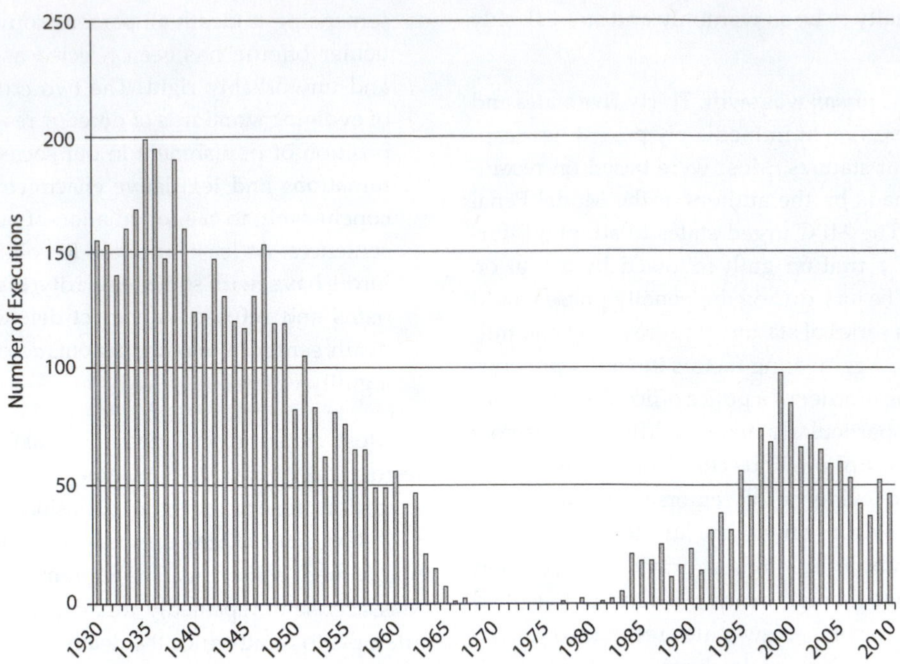

Figure 9-5 Executions in the United States, 1930–2010

Source: Hugo Adam Bedau, ed., *The Death Penalty in America*, 3rd ed. (New York: Oxford University Press, 1982), 25. The Death Penalty Information Center (http://www.deathpenaltyinfo.org).

Gregg v. Georgia, 428 U.S. 153 (1976)

Troy Gregg and Floyd Allen were hitchhiking in northern Florida when they were picked up by Fred Simmons and Bob Moore. At a rest stop just outside of Atlanta, Georgia, Gregg and Allen robbed and murdered their benefactors. A jury rejected Gregg's claim of self-defense. He was convicted of two counts of armed robbery and two counts of murder. Consistent with Georgia law, the trial judge convened a penalty hearing to determine whether Gregg would be sentenced to death. At that hearing the jury found two aggravating factors sufficient to justify capital punishment: the murder was committed while Gregg was engaged in armed robbery, another capital felony, and the murder was committed for pecuniary gain. The Supreme Court of Georgia affirmed the death sentence. Although the justices rejected the first aggravating factor on the ground that defendants in Georgia were not being sentenced to death for armed robbery, the judges found the other factor sufficient to impose capital punishment. Gregg appealed to the Supreme Court of the United States.

The Supreme Court by a 7-2 vote sustained the death sentence. Justice Stewart's plurality opinion declared that the Georgia procedure for imposing capital punishment would reduce the arbitrary infliction of the sentence that offended the justices in Furman v. Georgia *(1972). On what basis do the justices claim that bifurcated trials are more likely to reduce arbitrariness than mandatory death sentences? Note that only three of the nine justices on the Court believed that mandatory death schemes were constitutionally different from guided jury discretion. Do you believe that distinction sound? What is the constitutional significance of the response to* Furman*? Do you believe that any justice changed his mind on the constitutionality of capital punishment between 1972 and 1976? Do you believe that the outpouring of support for capital punishment had constitutional significance, or do you agree with Justice Marshall that the evidence still demonstrated that the death penalty was inconsistent with informed public opinion? Did the* Furman *precedent influence any justice? Why did Justice White, a member of the* Furman *majority, vote to sustain both mandatory and discretionary death penalties, while Justice Stewart, a dissenter in* Furman*, voted to strike down mandatory death penalty laws?*

Judgment of the Court, and opinion of JUSTICE STEWART, JUSTICE POWELL, and JUSTICE STEVENS, announced by JUSTICE STEWART.

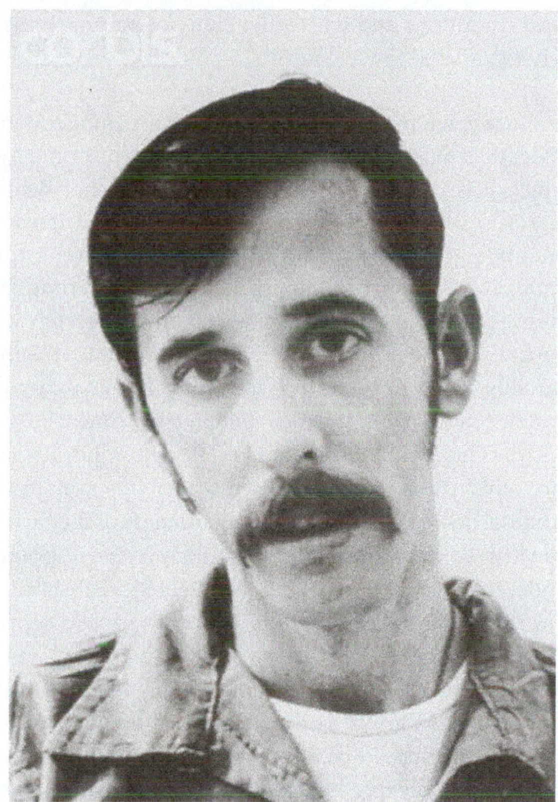

Illustration 9-4 Troy Leon Gregg

Troy Leon Gregg on Georgia death row, July 2, 1976. He died in a bar fight in North Carolina on the night of his escape from the Georgia State Prison in Reidsville in 1980.
Source: © Bettmann/CORBIS.

. . .

. . . We . . . hold that the punishment of death does not invariably violate the Constitution.

. . .

. . . [T]he Court has not confined the prohibition embodied in the Eighth Amendment to "barbarous" methods that were generally outlawed in the 18th century. Instead, the Amendment has been interpreted in a flexible and dynamic manner. . . . [T]he Clause forbidding "cruel and unusual" punishments "is not fastened to the obsolete but may acquire meaning as public opinion becomes enlightened by a humane justice."

. . .

. . . [O]ur cases also make clear that public perceptions of standards of decency with respect to criminal sanctions are not conclusive. A penalty also must accord with "the dignity of man," which is the "basic concept underlying the Eighth Amendment." . . . This means, at least, that the punishment not be "excessive." . . . [T]he inquiry into "excessiveness" has two aspects. First, the punishment must not involve the unnecessary and wanton infliction of pain. . . . Second, the punishment must not be grossly out of proportion to the severity of the crime. . . .

. . .

. . . [I]n assessing a punishment selected by a democratically elected legislature against the constitutional measure, we presume its validity. We may not require the legislature to select the least severe penalty possible so long as the penalty selected is not cruelly inhumane or disproportionate to the crime involved. And a heavy burden rests on those who would attack the judgment of the representatives of the people.

. . .

The imposition of the death penalty for the crime of murder has a long history of acceptance both in the United States and in England. The common-law rule imposed a mandatory death sentence on all convicted murderers. . . . And the penalty continued to be used into the 20th century by most American States, although the breadth of the common-law rule was diminished, initially by narrowing the class of murders to be punished by death and subsequently by widespread adoption of laws expressly granting juries the discretion to recommend mercy. . . .

It is apparent from the text of the Constitution itself that the existence of capital punishment was accepted by the Framers. At the time the Eighth Amendment was ratified, capital punishment was a common sanction in every State. Indeed, the First Congress of the United States enacted legislation providing death as the penalty for specified crimes. . . . The Fifth Amendment, adopted at the same time as the Eighth, contemplated the continued existence of the capital sanction by imposing certain limits on the prosecution of capital cases. . . . [T]he Fourteenth Amendment, adopted over three-quarters of a century later, similarly contemplates the existence of the capital sanction in providing that no State shall deprive any person of "life, liberty, or property" without due process of law.

. . .

The most marked indication of society's [continued] endorsement of the death penalty for murder is the legislative response to *Furman v. Georgia* (1972). The legislatures of at least 35 States have enacted new statutes that provide for the death penalty for at least some crimes that result in the death of another person. And the Congress of the United States, in 1974, enacted a statute providing the death penalty for aircraft piracy that results in death. . . . [A]ll of the post-*Furman* statutes make clear that capital punishment itself has not been rejected by the elected representatives of the people.

. . .

. . . [T]he actions of juries in many States since *Furman* are fully compatible with the legislative judgments, reflected in the new statutes, as to the continued utility and necessity of capital punishment in appropriate cases. At the close of 1974 at least 254 persons had been sentenced to death since *Furman*, and by the end of March 1976, more than 460 persons were subject to death sentences.

. . .

The death penalty is said to serve two principal social purposes: retribution and deterrence of capital crimes by prospective offenders.

In part, capital punishment is an expression of society's moral outrage at particularly offensive conduct. This function may be unappealing to many, but it is essential in an ordered society that asks its citizens to rely on legal processes rather than self-help to vindicate their wrongs.

. . . [T]he decision that capital punishment may be the appropriate sanction in extreme cases is an expression of the community's belief that certain crimes are themselves so grievous an affront to humanity that the only adequate response may be the penalty of death.

Statistical attempts to evaluate the worth of the death penalty as a deterrent to crimes by potential offenders have occasioned a great deal of debate. The results simply have been inconclusive. . . . We may nevertheless assume safely that there are murderers, such as those who act in passion, for whom the threat of death has little or no deterrent effect. But for many others, the death penalty undoubtedly is a significant deterrent. There are carefully contemplated murders, such as murder for hire, where the possible penalty of death may well enter into the cold calculus that precedes the decision to act. And there are some categories of murder, such as murder by a life prisoner, where other sanctions may not be adequate.

The value of capital punishment as a deterrent of crime is a complex factual issue the resolution of which properly rests with the legislatures, which can evaluate the results of statistical studies in terms of their own local conditions and with a flexibility of approach that is not available to the courts. . . .

. . .

Finally, we must consider whether the punishment of death is disproportionate in relation to the crime for which it is imposed. There is no question that death as a punishment is unique in its severity and irrevocability. . . . But we are concerned here only with the imposition of capital punishment for the crime of murder, and when a life has been taken deliberately by the offender, we cannot say that the punishment is invariably disproportionate to the crime. It is an extreme sanction, suitable to the most extreme of crimes.

. . . [T]he penalty of death is different in kind from any other punishment imposed under our system of criminal justice. Because of the uniqueness of the death penalty, *Furman* held that it could not be imposed under sentencing procedures that created a substantial risk that it would be inflicted in an arbitrary and capricious manner. . . .

. . . [W]here discretion is afforded a sentencing body on a matter so grave as the determination of whether a human life should be taken or spared, that discretion must be suitably directed and limited so as to minimize the risk of wholly arbitrary and capricious action.

. . .

The . . . [Georgia] procedures require the jury to consider the circumstances of the crime and the criminal before it recommends sentence. No longer can a Georgia jury do as *Furman*'s jury did: reach a finding of the defendant's guilt and then, without guidance or direction, decide whether he should live or die. Instead, the jury's attention is directed to the specific circumstances of the crime: Was it committed in the course of another capital felony? Was it committed for money? Was it committed upon a peace officer or judicial officer? Was it committed in a particularly heinous way or in a manner that endangered the lives of many persons? In addition, the jury's attention is focused on the characteristics of the person who committed the crime: Does he have a record of prior convictions for capital offenses? Are there any special facts about this defendant that mitigate against imposing capital punishment (e. g., his youth, the extent of his cooperation with the police, his emotional state at the time of the crime). As a result, while some jury discretion still exists, "the discretion to be exercised is controlled by clear and objective standards so as to produce non-discriminatory application." . . .

As an important additional safeguard against arbitrariness and caprice, the Georgia statutory scheme provides for automatic appeal of all death sentences to the State's Supreme Court. That court is required by statute to review each sentence of death and determine whether it was imposed under the influence of passion or prejudice, whether the evidence supports the jury's finding of a statutory aggravating circumstance, and whether the sentence is disproportionate compared to those sentences imposed in similar cases. . . .

. . .

The basic concern of *Furman* centered on those defendants who were being condemned to death capriciously and arbitrarily. . . . The new Georgia sentencing procedures . . . focus the jury's attention on the particularized nature of the crime and the particularized characteristics of the individual defendant. While the jury is permitted to consider any aggravating or mitigating circumstances, it must find and identify at least one statutory aggravating factor before it may impose a penalty of death. In this way the jury's discretion is channeled. No longer can a jury wantonly and freakishly impose the death sentence; it is always circumscribed by the legislative guidelines. In addition, the review function of the Supreme Court of Georgia affords additional assurance that the concerns that prompted our decision in *Furman* are not present to any significant degree in the Georgia procedure applied here.

. . .

JUSTICE WHITE, with whom THE CHIEF JUSTICE and JUSTICE REHNQUIST join, concurring in the judgment.

. . .

. . . Petitioner has argued in effect that no matter how effective the death penalty may be as a punishment, government, created and run as it must be by humans, is inevitably incompetent to administer it. This cannot be accepted as a proposition of constitutional law. Imposition of the death penalty is surely an awesome responsibility for any system of justice and those who participate in it. Mistakes will be made and discriminations will occur which will be difficult to explain. However, one of society's most basic tasks is that of protecting the lives of its citizens and one of the most basic ways in which it achieves the task is through criminal laws against murder. I decline to interfere with the manner in which Georgia has chosen to enforce such laws on what is simply an assertion of lack of faith in the ability of the system of justice to operate in a fundamentally fair manner.

. . .

Statement of THE CHIEF JUSTICE and JUSTICE REHNQUIST. . . .

JUSTICE BLACKMUN, concurring in the judgment. . . .

JUSTICE BRENNAN, dissenting.

. . .

The fatal constitutional infirmity in the punishment of death is that it treats "members of the human race as nonhumans, as objects to be toyed with and discarded. [It is] thus inconsistent with the fundamental premise of the Clause that even the vilest criminal remains a human being possessed of common human dignity." . . . As such it is a penalty that "subjects the individual to a fate forbidden by the principle of civilized treatment guaranteed by the [Clause]." I therefore would hold, on that ground alone, that death is today a cruel and unusual punishment prohibited by the Clause. . . .

. . .

JUSTICE MARSHALL, dissenting.

. . .

Since the decision in *Furman*, the legislatures of 35 States have enacted new statutes authorizing the imposition of the death sentence for certain crimes, and Congress has enacted a law providing the death penalty for air piracy resulting in death. . . . I would be less than candid if I did not acknowledge that these developments have a significant bearing on a realistic assessment of the moral acceptability of the death penalty to the American people. But if the constitutionality of the death penalty turns, as I have urged, on the opinion of an informed citizenry, then even the enactment of new death statutes cannot be viewed as conclusive. In *Furman*, I observed that the American people are largely unaware of the information critical to a judgment on the morality of the death penalty, and concluded that if they were better informed they would consider it shocking, unjust, and unacceptable. . . . A recent study, conducted after the enactment of the post-*Furman* statutes, has confirmed that the American people know little about the death penalty, and that the opinions of an informed public would differ significantly from those of a public unaware of the consequences and effects of the death penalty.[67]

Even assuming, however, that the post-*Furman* enactment of statutes authorizing the death penalty renders the prediction of the views of an informed citizenry an uncertain basis for a constitutional decision, the enactment of those statutes has no bearing whatsoever on the conclusion that the death penalty is unconstitutional because it is excessive. . . .

. . .

The death penalty, unnecessary to promote the goal of deterrence or to further any legitimate notion of retribution, is an excessive penalty forbidden by the Eighth and Fourteenth Amendments. I respectfully dissent from the Court's judgment upholding the sentences of death imposed upon the petitioners in these cases.

Suggested Readings

Baer, Judith A. *Equality under the Constitution: Reclaiming the Fourteenth Amendment* (Ithaca, NY: Cornell University Press, 1983).

Belz, Herman. *Equality Transformed: A Quarter-Century of Affirmative Action* (New Brunswick, NJ: Transaction, 1991).

Blasi, Vincent, ed. *The Burger Court: The Counter-Revolution That Wasn't* (New Haven, CT: Yale University Press, 1983).

Burgess, Susan A. *Contest for Constitutional Authority* (Lawrence: University Press of Kansas, 1992).

Bussiere, Elizabeth. *Disentitling the Poor: The Warren Court, Welfare Rights, and the American Political Tradition* (University Park: Pennsylvania State University Press, 1997)

Carmines, Edward G., and James A. Stimson. *Issue Evolution: Race and the Transformation of American Politics* (Princeton, NJ: Princeton University Press, 1989).

Craig, Barbara Hinkson, and David M. O'Brien. *Abortion and American Politics* (Chatham, NJ: Chatham House, 1993).

Devins, Neal. *Shaping Constitutional Values: Elected Government, the Supreme Court, and the Abortion Debate* (Baltimore, MD: Johns Hopkins University Press, 1996).

Epp, Charles R. *Making Rights Right: Activists, Bureaucrats, and the Creation of the Legalistic State* (Chicago: University of Chicago Press, 2010).

Epstein, Lee, and Joseph Fiske Kobylka. *The Supreme Court and Legal Change: Abortion and the Death Penalty* (Chapel Hill: University of North Carolina Press, 1992).

Frymer, Paul. *Black and Blue: African Americans, the Labor Movement, and the Decline of the Democratic Party* (Princeton, NJ: Princeton University Press, 2008).

Garrow, David J. *Liberty and Sexuality: The Right to Privacy and the Making of* Roe v. Wade (Berkeley: University of California Press, 1994).

Jeffries, John Calvin. *Justice Lewis F. Powell, Jr.* (New York: C. Scribner's Sons, 1994).

Luker, Kristin. *Abortion and the Politics of Motherhood* (Berkeley: University of California Press, 1984).

Mansbridge, Jane J. *Why We Lost the ERA* (Chicago: University of Chicago Press, 1986).

Mayeri, Serena. *Reasoning from Race: Feminism, Law, and the Civil Rights Revolution* (Cambridge, MA: Harvard University Press, 2011).

McGirr, Lisa. *Suburban Warriors: The Origins of the New American Right* (Princeton, NJ: Princeton University Press, 2001).

McMahon, Kevin J. *Nixon's Court: His Challenge to Judicial Liberalism and Its Political Consequences* (Chicago: University of Chicago Press, 2011).

Michelman, Frank I. *Brennan and Democracy* (Princeton, NJ: Princeton University Press, 1999).

O'Neill, Timothy J. Bakke *and the Politics of Equality: Friends and Foes in the Classroom of Litigation* (Middleton, CT: Wesleyan University Press, 1985).

Rudenstine, David. *The Day the Presses Stopped: A History of the* Pentagon Papers *Case* (Berkeley: University of California Press, 1996).

Schwartz, Bernard. *The Ascent of Pragmatism: The Burger Court in Action* (Reading, MA: Addison Wesley, 1990).

Silverstein, Mark. *Judicious Choices: The New Politics of Supreme Court Confirmations* (New York: W.W. Norton & Co., 1994).

Strentny, John D. *The Minority Rights Revolution* (Cambridge, MA: Harvard University Press, 2004).

Wermiel, Stephen. *Justice Brennan: Liberal Champion* (New York: Houghton Mifflin Harcourt, 2010).

Woodward, Bob, and Scott Armstrong. *The Brethren: Inside the Supreme Court* (New York: Simon and Schuster, 1979).

67. Austin Sarat and Neil Vidmar, "Public Opinion, the Death Penalty, and the Eighth Amendment: Testing the Marshall Hypothesis," *Wisconsin Law Review* 1 (1976): 171–206.

Part 3 **Contemporary Issues**

Chapter 10

The Reagan Era: 1981–1993

I. Introduction

The 1980 national election shocked liberals. Ronald Reagan, a former actor, won a landslide victory in the presidential election, Republicans gained control of the Senate, and the Democratic margin in the House of Representatives was substantially reduced. Reagan, the new Republicans in the Senate, the working majority in the House of Representatives established after 1980, and the eventual Republican judicial majority on the federal courts were more conservative on economic and social matters than any other governing coalition in the past generation. Republican Party platforms in 1980, 1984, 1988, and 1992 championed policies and the appointment of federal justices that would reverse liberal rights and liberties decisions.

Liberal Democrats fought back. The 1982 midterm elections eroded the gains that Republicans had made in Congress during the 1980 election. In 1986 the control of the Senate slipped back into Democratic hands, despite Reagan's own overwhelming reelection in 1984. Nevertheless, liberals during the 1980s more often sought to slow conservative inroads into American constitutionalism than to blaze new progressive trails.

Reagan Era constitutional debates were distinctly post–New Deal. Members of the Reagan coalition opposed political and social developments that had occurred in the 1960s and 1970s. They sought to overturn such liberal constitutional decisions as *Roe v. Wade* (1973)(abortion rights), *Engel v. Vitale* (1962) (school prayer), and *Mapp v. Ohio* (1961) (exclusionary rule). Few challenged earlier liberal decisions such as *West Coast Hotel v. Parrish* (1937) (no constitutional protection for the freedom of contract) or *Brown v. Board of Education* (1954) (desegregation of schools). Some conservative politicians, lawyers, and judges raised questions about the scope and legitimacy of government powers that had been regarded as settled for fifty years. Nevertheless, more radical challenges to the New Deal constitutional order were usually on the intellectual margins. The constitutional order that conservatives wished to preserve looked more like the United States in 1955 than the United States in 1925.

Parties. The Republican Party of Ronald Reagan was far more conservative on constitutional matters than the Republican Party of Dwight Eisenhower. Reagan repeatedly condemned both liberals and liberal justices for legalizing abortion, prohibiting prayer in schools, tolerating pornography, and championing the rights of criminal suspects. Under the banner "Our Constitutional System," the Republican Party platform of 1984 declared,

> We commend the President for appointing federal judges committed to the rights of law-abiding citizens and traditional family values. We share the public's dissatisfaction with an elitist and unresponsive federal judiciary. If our legal institutions are to regain respect, they must respect the people's legitimate interests in a stable, orderly society. In his second term, President Reagan will continue to appoint Supreme Court and other federal judges who share our commitment to judicial restraint.

Judicial restraint, other provisions in the platform made clear, would enable conservatives to restore voluntary prayer in school, ban abortion, and prevent criminals from going free on constitutional technicalities. Individual Republicans had previously championed many of these constitutional positions. What was new in 1980 was the central place that all of these positions occupied in the official constitutional vision of the Republican Party.

Democrats became more conservative on economic matters during the 1980s but held the liberal line on most constitutional rights. The party excoriated the measures that Republicans thought necessary for restoring fundamental constitutional commitments as an abandonment of constitutional rights. The 1984 Democratic Party platform asserted,

> The hard truth is that if Mr. Reagan is reelected our most vigorous defender of the rule of law—the United States Supreme Court—could be lost to the cause of equal justice for another generation. Today, five of the nine members of that Court are over 75. Our next President will likely have the opportunity to shape that Court, not just for his own term—or even for his own lifetime—but for the rest of ours, and for our children's too.
>
> There can be little doubt that a Supreme Court chosen by Ronald Reagan would radically restrict constitutional rights and drastically reinterpret existing laws.

Abortion was the most contentious rights issue to badly divided the parties. Republicans sought to prohibit abortion throughout the United States. The 1984 platform asserted,

> The unborn child has a fundamental individual right to life which cannot be infringed. We therefore reaffirm our support for a human life amendment

Table 10-1 Major Rights and Liberties Issues and Decisions of the Reagan Era

Major Political Issues	**Major Constitutional Issues**	**Major Court Decisions**
Partisan Polarization	Legitimacy of Controversial Warren Court Precedents	*Plyler v. Doe* (1982)
Partisan Transformation of Federal Judiciary	Original Meaning	*United States v. Leon* (1984)
Christian Conservatism	Property Rights	*Bowers v. Hardwick* (1986)
Rise of Conservative Public Interest Groups	Abortion	*Batson v. Kentucky* (1986)
Assault Weapons Ban	Public Funds and Parochial Schools	*Johnson v. Transportation Agency, Santa Clara County* (1987)
War on Drugs	School Prayer	*McCleskey v. Kemp* (1987)
Gay Rights Movement	Exemptions for Religious Believers	*City of Richmond v. J.A. Croson* (1989)
Second-Wave Feminism	Flag Burning	*Doe v. University of Michigan* (1989)
Campus Speech Codes and Hate Speech	Second Amendment	*Skinner v. Railway Labor Executives Association* (1989)
Fairness Doctrine	Criminalization of Homosexual Sodomy	*Employment Division v. Smith* (1990)
Voting Rights	Affirmative Action	*Lee v. Weisman* (1992)
Crime Control	Gender Discrimination	*Planned Parenthood of Southeastern Pennsylvania v. Casey* (1992)
	Majority-Minority Districts	*Lucas v. South Carolina Coastal Council* (1992)
	Limits on Speech Considered Harmful to Discrete and Insular Minorities	*Shaw v. Reno* (1993)
	Good-Faith Exception to Fourth Amendment	
	Interrogations	
	Jury Selection	
	Death Penalty	
	Exclusionary Rule	

> to the Constitution, and we endorse legislation to make clear that the Fourteenth Amendment's protections apply to unborn children. We oppose the use of public revenues for abortion and will eliminate funding for organizations which advocate or support abortion.

Democrats championed legal abortion. The 1984 party platform asserted, "The fundamental right of a woman to reproductive freedom rests on the votes of six members of the Supreme Court—five of whom are over 75. That right could easily disappear during a second Reagan term."

The two parties offered sharply divergent understandings of constitutional equality. Democrats saw the United States as a society wracked by unconstitutional discrimination. The party platform in 1984 asserted,

> A new Democratic Administration will understand that the age-old scourge of discrimination and prejudice against many groups in American society is still rampant and very much a part of the reason for the debilitating circumstances in which disadvantaged peoples are forced to live. Although strides have been made in combating discrimination and defamation against Americans of various ethnic groups, much remains to be done. Therefore, we pledge an end to the Reagan Administration's punitive policy toward women, minorities, and the poor and support the reaffirmation of the principle that the government is still responsible for protecting the civil rights of all citizens. Government has a special responsibility to those whom society has historically prevented from enjoying the benefits of full citizenship for reasons of race, religion, sex, age, national origin and ethnic heritage, sexual orientation, or disability.

Republicans called for a public policy that was color-blind and sex-blind. Their party platform maintained,

> Americans demand a civil rights policy premised on the letter of the Civil Rights Act of 1964. That law requires equal rights; and it is our policy to end discrimination on account of sex, race, color, creed, or national origin. . . .
>
> Just as we must guarantee opportunity, we oppose attempts to dictate results. We will resist efforts to replace equal rights with discriminatory quota systems and preferential treatment. Quotas are the most insidious form of discrimination: reverse discrimination against the innocent. We must always remember that, in a free society, different individual goals will yield different results.

Democrats became increasingly committed to feminist perspectives on public policy. Republicans in 1980 dropped from the party platform their coalition's longstanding commitment to ratifying the ERA. As a candidate, however, Reagan promised to make a woman his first appointment to the Supreme Court of the United States.

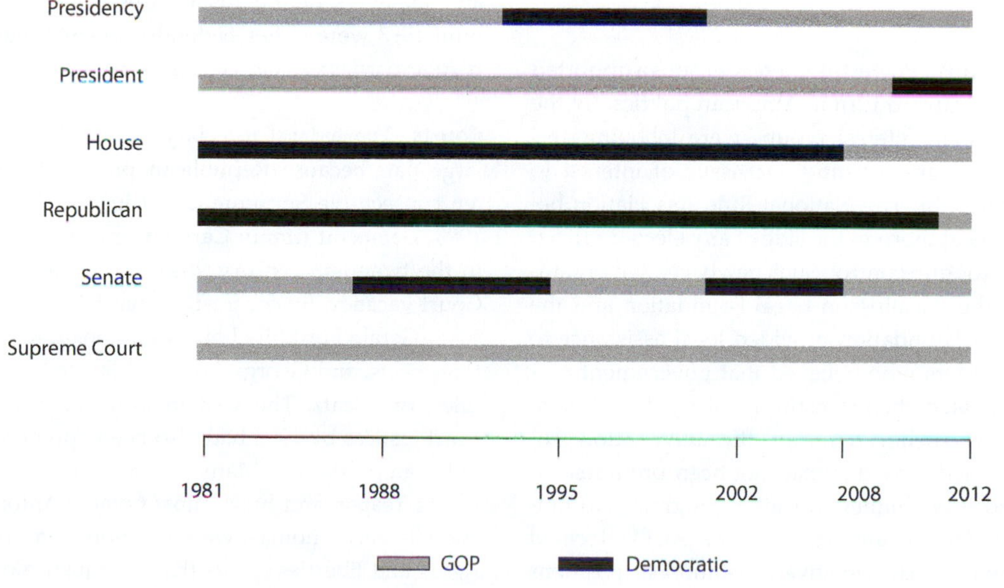

Figure 10-1 Partisan Control of the U.S. Government, 1981–2012

All elected branches of the national government moved to the right during the Reagan Era. Ronald Reagan had long been a darling of the conservative movement. His successor, George Bush, championed far more conservative positions as president than he had as a Nixon Republican during the 1960s and 1970s. The new Republicans elected to the Senate during the Reagan Era were also far more conservative than previous Republicans. By the mid-1980s liberal Republicans were becoming extinct. The small Democratic margins in the House of Representatives often left practical power in the hands of senior southern Democrats who, while more liberal than southern Republicans, had never accepted much of the Great Society rights and liberties agenda. The Voting Rights Act did bring to power a new generation of southern Democrats who were far more liberal than the more veteran Democrats from Dixie. Nevertheless, liberal successes in the 1980s were largely limited to defeating conservative civil rights proposals and refusing to confirm some of Reagan's more conservative judicial nominees. With rare exceptions, liberals could not pass new federal legislation, object to conservative executive actions, or force Republican presidents to appoint liberals to the federal bench. While congressional liberals prevented Congress from passing legislation banning abortion, they could not reverse Reagan and Bush administration policies that interpreted existing federal law as permitting the federal government to deny federal funds to any family-planning service that advised clients about abortion.

Interest Groups. Powerful interest groups supported the strong rightward turn in American politics. By the 1980s prominent interest groups were lobbying and litigating on every constitutional issue of interest to the political right. The National Rifle Association became a political thorn in the side of any elected official who voted for gun control. Such newly created organizations as the Washington Legal Foundation and the Pacific Legal Foundation provided legal assistance to property holders who believed that government regulations violated their constitutional rights or white applicants who believed that an affirmative action program explained why they had not been promoted or accepted to some higher education program. No umbrella organization analogous to the ACLU formed that championed conservative constitutional positions on all questions of rights and liberties. The conservative movement in the Reagan Era was instead an often uneasy alliance between religious conservatives who opposed the secularist bent of Great Society liberalism, libertarians who opposed the redistributive bent of Great Society liberalism, and foreign policy hawks who opposed the internationalist trends of Great Society liberalism.

Two associations played particularly important roles in conservative constitutional politics. The first was the Moral Majority and its associated evangelical movement. Such preachers as Jerry Falwell and Pat Robertson helped organize conservative Christians into politically active coalitions. Evangelicals by the late 1980s were solid Republican voters. They wielded powerful influence, particularly in the South and Midwest, in support of candidates who proposed banning abortion, permitting voluntary school prayer, and allowing state funding for church-affiliated parochial schools. The second was the Federalist Society, an association formed by law students, lawyers, and law professors who opposed the dominant New Deal liberalism of the legal academy and legal profession. Federalist Society members did not agree on a common conservative agenda. Many were libertarians far more committed to limiting government regulation than banning abortion. Others were social conservatives more concerned with cutting pornography than taxes. Nevertheless, the Federalist Society soon became a clearinghouse for conservative constitutional ideas and activism. Numerous conservative justices and members of the Justice Department from 1981 until 1993 were either Federalist Society members or regular participants in Federalist Society meetings.

Courts. The federal judiciary moved to the right in large part because Republican presidents appointed ten consecutive Supreme Court justices from 1969 to 1993. Democrat Jimmy Carter was the only president in the twentieth century who did not a fill Supreme Court vacancy. By contrast, Richard Nixon filled four seats, Gerald Ford filled one seat, Ronald Reagan filled three seats, and George Bush in his one term in office filled two seats. The vast majority of lower federal court justices by 1992 had also been appointed by Republican presidents. Many justices appointed by Presidents Reagan and Bush, most notable Antonin Scalia and Clarence Thomas, were far more conservative on rights and liberties issues than any justice other than William Rehnquist appointed between 1933 and 1980.

Box 10-1 A Partial Cast of Characters of the Reagan Era

Ronald Reagan	■ Republican ■ California conservative ■ Actor who made his political debut in Barry Goldwater's 1964 presidential campaign ■ Governor of California (1967–75) ■ President of the United States (1981–89) ■ United social conservatives, economic conservatives, and foreign-policy hawks into a single coalition ■ Emphasized a constitutional philosophy that combined traditional morality, law and order, small government, and judicial restraint
Sandra Day O'Connor	■ Republican ■ Arizona moderate conservative ■ Arizona state senator (1969–74) ■ Arizona state judge (1975–81) ■ Appointed to the U.S. Supreme Court by Ronald Reagan ■ Served on the U.S. Supreme Court (1981–2006) ■ First female Supreme Court justice ■ Became a swing vote on the Burger and Rehnquist Courts, often joining the conservatives on federalism and separation of powers issues, but with liberals on abortion
William Rehnquist	■ Republican ■ Arizona conservative ■ Goldwater supporter who joined the Nixon Justice Department ■ Deputy attorney general in Office of Legal Counsel (1969–71) ■ Associate justice on the U.S. Supreme Court (1971–86) ■ Chief justice on the U.S. Supreme Court (1986–2005) ■ Went from a lone dissenter in the 1970s to a leader of the conservative wing of the Court in the 1980s ■ Advocate of federalism and judicial deference to the exercise of government power
John Paul Stevens	■ Republican ■ Chicago antitrust lawyer ■ Appointed by Richard Nixon to the federal circuit court (1970–75) ■ Appointed by Gerald Ford to the U.S. Supreme Court (1975–2010) ■ A consensus, nonpolitical choice for the Court after Watergate, Stevens was not known for a distinctive judicial philosophy but became a vocal member of the liberal wing as the Court became more conservative over time

In 1985 President Reagan elevated Rehnquist to the chief justiceship. By 1993 the median justices on the Rehnquist Court were Reagan appointees Anthony Kennedy and Sandra Day O'Connor. The two most liberal justices, Harry Blackmun and John Paul Stevens, were pre-Reagan Republican judicial appointees.

The new conservative majority pushed constitutional law rightward. While neither the Burger nor the early Rehnquist Court overruled such decisions as *Mapp v. Ohio* (1961), *Miranda v. Arizona* (1965), or other landmark liberal decisions, judicial majorities carved out numerous exceptions to the exclusionary rule,

Miranda warnings, and other cherished liberal rulings. *United States v. Leon* (1984) held that prosecutors could introduce unconstitutionally obtained evidence at trial if the police officer who obtained the evidence had acted in "good faith." Other judicial decisions eased constitutional restrictions on the flow of government money to parochial schools. The justices in *Mueller v. Allen* (1983) ruled that states could permit parents to deduct private school tuition on their income taxes, even if the vast majority of parents eligible for the full deduction had enrolled their children in religious schools. Economic rights returned to the judicial agenda. Supreme Court decisions interpreting the takings clause of the Fifth Amendment enabled landowners to challenge government restrictions that rendered their property or parts of their property economically useless.

Conservative Republicans had more difficulty reversing Great Society rights policies. Liberals in Congress retained the votes necessary to defeat constitutional amendments permitting elected officials to regulate abortion, sanction prayer in public schools, and ban flag burning. Conservatives could not cobble together a legislative majority willing to limit the federal judicial power to better integrate schools by busing schoolchildren. Conservative efforts to place more conservatives on the federal bench were limited by the infrequency with which openings occurred on the Supreme Court, as well as by vigorous liberal opposition to particularly conservative appointees. After Democrats regained control of the Senate in 1986 liberals successfully defeated the proposed Supreme Court nomination of Robert Bork, a lower federal court judge who was on record as opposing almost all important liberal Warren Court decisions. The result was a judiciary far more conservative than the Warren Court, but not nearly as conservative as the Reagan and Bush administrations.

After a decade of steady movement to the right the Reagan Revolution hit surprising roadblocks in 1992. The Supreme Court decisions in *Lee v. Weisman* (1992) and *Planned Parenthood v. Casey* (1992) refused to overrule previous decisions outlawing school prayer and legalizing abortion, respectively. Both *Lee* and *Casey* suggested that the more moderate Republican Justices Sandra Day O'Connor and Anthony Kennedy thought that the Reagan Revolution had gone far enough. While these justices would not expand the liberal precedents of the past, they were not willing to abandon the central constitutional precedents of the New Deal and Great Society. That November Democrats won their first presidential election in sixteen years. William Jefferson Clinton was elected to the presidency on a platform committed to the traditional liberal vision of the constitutional order. The Democratic return to power in the executive branch meant that even if the liberal constitutional vision was not to be revived, that vision was unlikely to be substantially weakened for the foreseeable future.

Constitutional Thought. Most conservatives during the 1980s championed some version of originalism. Such originalists as Robert Bork and Antonin Scalia insisted that justices should interpret constitutional provisions in light of what those provisions meant at the time they were ratified. In this view, the phrase "cruel and unusual punishment" in the Eighth Amendment meant exactly what "cruel and unusual punishment" meant in 1791. Originalists during the 1970s and early 1980s generally employed originalist arguments when criticizing liberal judicial activism. *Roe v. Wade* (1973) wrongly held that the due process clause of the Fourteenth Amendment protected abortion, originalists asserted, because Americans did not believe "due process" entailed the right to terminate a pregnancy when the Fourteenth Amendment was ratified in 1868. Voluntary prayer in public school was constitutional because a long tradition supported that practice.

As conservatives gained more control over the federal courts, some originalists championed greater judicial activism on behalf of conservative causes. Such originalists as Richard Epstein insisted that the Constitution limited federal and state power to redistribute property. Other conservatives looked to the past when constructing arguments against affirmative action and in favor of exempting religious believers from various secular policies. Many of these arguments influenced American constitutional politics at the turn of the twenty-first century.

Constitutional doctrine became more complex. Supreme Court justices, Justice O'Connor in particular, employed the very deferential rational basis test or the very strict compelling interest test in fewer rights and liberties cases. New tests emerged that seemed hybrids of the old tests. When determining whether state regulations of abortion were constitutional, the plurality opinion in *Planned Parenthood v. Casey* (1992) substituted an "undue burden" test for the compelling interest test employed after *Roe v. Wade*. The majority opinion in *Dolan v. City of Tigard* (1994) preferred a "rough proportionality" standard to the rational basis test that many state courts used when determining the constitutionality of land-use restrictions. Multipart tests for constitutional violations multiplied, particularly in First Amendment cases. *Clark v. Community for Creative Non-Violence* (1984) held that time, place, and manner restrictions on speech in public parks and other public fora were constitutional if the restrictions were "justified without reference to the content of the regulated speech," "narrowly tailored to serve a significant state interest," and left "open ample alternative channels for communication of the information." By the end of the Reagan Era the requirement that police give *Miranda* warnings seemed to contain more exceptions than applications.

Legacies. Ronald Reagan and his political allies accomplished a great deal from 1981 until 1993, even if they did not entirely transform the American constitutional regime. For most of the twentieth century constitutional debate was over whether Americans should retain the status quo or move constitutional politics to the left. After 1981 constitutional debate focused just as often on the merits of adopting more conservative constitutional commitments. Liberal constitutional campaigns were abandoned or at least modified. Litigants stopped asking the Supreme Court to declare that capital punishment violates the Eighth and Fourteenth Amendments. Instead, contemporary liberals argue that the execution of a particular individual or small class of persons violates constitutional standards.

Reagan and his political allies established a new long-standing conservative presence in American constitutional politics. Conservatives did not win every constitutional struggle during the Reagan years or after, but they have played major roles in every constitutional controversy that has roiled the public since 1980. Constitutional debates would never again be contests between different liberals. Rather, from 1980 until the present, liberals and conservatives have debated on relatively equal terms the constitutional meaning of free speech, cruel and unusual punishment, and the due process clause.

II. Foundations

MAJOR DEVELOPMENTS

- Increased emphasis on the original meaning of constitutional provisions protecting civil liberties
- Defeat of amendments overturning Supreme Court decisions on school prayer, flag burning, and abortion
- Bill of Rights held to not limit searches of foreign citizens residing outside the United States

Reagan Republicans believed that the Great Society had perverted the American constitutional regime. Reagan and his political allies condemned courts, in particular, for hamstringing legislative efforts to fight crime, improve education, secure public morality, and assert American power abroad. The dominant theme of the leading Reagan conservatives was that unelected justices were seizing power from elected officials. The campaign to return constitutional authority to elected officials included the proposal of a series of constitutional amendments that would overturn liberal judicial decisions; self-conscious efforts to staff federal courts with conservatives committed to overruling liberal precedents; and a public constitutional philosophy, originalism, which clearly explained why past liberal decisions were illegitimate. Robert Bork, the most visible proponent of Reagan constitutional conservatism, condemned such judicial decisions as *Roe v. Wade* (1973) as inconsistent with the original intention of the persons responsible for the Bill of Rights and Fourteenth Amendment. Most originalists in the 1980s emphasized the need for greater judicial restraint. Bork's writings immediately before and during the Reagan Era rarely discussed instances in which justices who applied the original intentions of the framers would need to strike down laws passed by popular majorities.

Conservatives enjoyed mixed success in their efforts to reshape constitutional foundations. Originalism gained respectability and prominence as a method of constitutional interpretation. Conservative judicial majorities narrowed the conditions in which private parties were considered state actors and the circumstances in which federal officials were bound by the Bill of Rights when acting outside the United States. Nevertheless, almost all pillars of constitutional liberalism remained standing. Conservative efforts to secure constitutional amendments overruling decisions that had struck down abortion bans and voluntary school prayer failed. No Supreme Court justice accepted Reagan administration invitations to reconsider the incorporation of the Bill of Rights.

A. Sources

The textual and extratextual sources of constitutional rights and liberties remained the same. Conservatives proposed, but Congress did not approve, constitutional amendments that would reverse liberal judicial rights decisions. Federal judges maintained the traditional practice of treating customary international law, including the customary international law of human rights, as part of the law of the United States. A lower federal court, however, ruled that courts were bound to respect the customary international law of human rights only in the absence of a federal statute or executive decree.

Constitutions and Amendments

Conservative Republicans proposed several constitutional amendments to overturn Supreme Court decisions protecting civil liberties. The Republican Party platform of 1980 called for a "constitutional amendment to restore protection of the right to life for unborn children" and called on Congress "to restore the right of individuals to participate in voluntary, non-denominational prayer in schools and other public facilities." Shortly after winning the 1980 presidential election President Reagan proposed a constitutional amendment to permit voluntary prayer in public schools. His message to Congress declared, "The public expression through prayer of our faith in God is a fundamental part of our American heritage and a privilege which should not be excluded by law from any American school, public or private." Prominent congressmen at the same time proposed a constitutional amendment permitting states and Congress to ban abortion. Shortly after the Supreme Court in *Texas v. Johnson* (1989) declared that the First Amendment protected the right to burn the American flag, President George Bush proposed a constitutional amendment to overturn that decision.

These amendments enjoyed broad support, but all were defeated. The Senate in 1982 rejected a proposed constitutional amendment that would overturn *Roe v. Wade* (1973). The proposed amendment restoring voluntary prayer died the same year in the Senate. The proposed amendment permitting Congress and the states to prohibit flag burning came closer to passage. Congressional Democrats first stalled a constitutional amendment by passing a new federal law prohibiting flag burning. When the Supreme Court declared that law unconstitutional in *United States v. Eichman* (1990), the flag protection amendment was reintroduced. The resulting 58-42 vote in the Senate and 254-177 vote in the House fell just short of the required two-thirds majority.

The debates over these constitutional amendments were similar. Republicans and some conservative Democrats insisted that amendments were necessary to correct Supreme Court decisions that misinterpreted the Constitution. Democrats and some liberal Republicans maintained that the Supreme Court should retain the final word over the meaning of constitutional provisions protecting civil liberties and that elected officials ought not challenge those decisions, even by constitutional amendment. This liberal commitment to a particularly powerful form of judicial supremacy stemmed from the ideological belief that courts had special capacities to protect rights and powerless minorities; the pragmatic assessment that the Supreme Court, even augmented by Reagan appointees, was likely to be more liberal on rights issues than the Reagan administration; and the political calculation that foisting responsibility for such issues as abortion on the courts was a good political tactic in a badly divided polity.

Debate over the Flag Protection Amendment (1989–90)

Americans reacted sharply when the Supreme Court in Texas v. Johnson *(1989) by a 5-4 vote declared unconstitutional a Texas law prohibiting burning the flag of the United States. President George Bush almost immediately called for a constitutional amendment stating, "The Congress and the states shall have the power to prohibit the physical desecration of the flag of the United States." The Democratic Party leadership in Congress temporarily diverted the proposed constitutional amendment by passing the Flag Protection Act of 1990. That measure declared that "whoever knowingly mutilates, defaces, burns, maintains on the floor or ground, or tramples upon any flag of the United States" would be imprisoned for one year and fined $1000. President Bush and his allies renewed their demands for a constitutional amendment after the Supreme Court in* United States v. Eichman *(1990) declared the Flag Protection Act unconstitutional. Proponents of the amendment insisted that they were correcting mistaken judicial decisions. Opponents maintained that the Bill of Rights should not be altered. After a sharp debate, neither the Senate nor the House could muster the necessary two-thirds majority to pass the amendment on to the states.*

When reading the excerpts from the debate over the flag protection amendment, consider the following questions.

Illustration 10-1 Flag Burning on the Steps of the U.S. Capitol

Persian Gulf war protestor Dave Blalock and others, including Shawn Eichman, gathered on the steps of the U.S. Capitol to burn the American flag as soon as the Flag Protection Act of 1989 went into effect. Their convictions for violating the statute were thrown out when the law was ruled unconstitutional in *United States v. Eichman* (1990).

Source: UPI Photo/Files.

What was the significance of the flag-burning amendment? Were proponents correct that the amendment had no influence on constitutional civil liberties other than to permit elected officials to prohibit people from burning the flag? How might that amendment influence the interpretation of the First Amendment in other circumstances? Were opponents of the amendment correct to declare that the Constitution should not be tampered with? If, as some opponents of the amendment believed, the Supreme Court decision in Texas v. Johnson *was wrong, why was the passage of a correcting amendment not an appropriate remedy? Do you need to read* Texas v. Johnson *(see Section IV) before reaching a judgment about the congressional debate?*

George Bush, Remarks Announcing the Proposed Constitutional Amendment on Desecration of the Flag (June 30, 1989)

. . .

. . . Our flag represents freedom and the unity of our nation. And our flag flies in peace, thanks to the sacrifices of so many Americans.

. . . And we feel in our hearts, and we know from our experience, that the surest way to preserve liberty is to protect the spirit that sustains it. And this flag sustains that spirit, and it's one of our most powerful ideas. And like all powerful ideas, if it is not defended, it is defamed. To the touch, this flag is merely fabric.

But to the heart, the flag represents and reflects the fabric of our nation—our dreams, our destiny, our very fiber as a people.

. . . Free speech is a right that is dear and close to all. It is in defense of that right, and the others enshrined in our Constitution, that so many have sacrificed. But before we accept dishonor to our flag, we must ask ourselves how many have died following the order to "Save the Colors!" We must ask how many have fought for the ideals it represents. And we must honor those who have been handed the folded flag from the casket at Arlington.

. . . [T]oday I am grateful to the leaders here and the leaders of the Congress with us in this audience who have proposed a constitutional amendment to protect the flag. Its language is stark, and it's simple and to the point: "The Congress and the States shall have power to prohibit the physical desecration of the flag of the United States." Simple and to the point, this amendment preserves the widest conceivable range of options for free expression. It applies only to the flag, the unique symbol of our nation.

Senate Committee on the Judiciary, Measures to Protect the American Flag (June 21, 1990)[1]

SENATOR JOSEPH BIDEN (Democrat, Delaware)

. . .

While the debate over the flag protection amendment is an old one, the question of how to reconcile flag protection with the First Amendment is not. Because for the most of our history, most of our preeminent constitutional scholars have seen no tension between the two, have seen no tension between protecting the flag and the first amendment.

. . .

I spent a great deal of time last year discussing, why, to me, at least, the flag is so vitally important to this country. The flag symbolizes the bond that unites one of the most heterogeneous nations, heterogeneous people in the world—because that is what we are, a heterogeneous community. Little or no homogeneity exists.

This Nation does not have the ethnicity that binds other nations of the world. What this Nation has is people of different races, backgrounds, and religions, who are fundamentally different and, in my view, need symbols, as well as substance to bind us. The flag is binding and, in my view, warrants protection, if not by statute, by a constitutional amendment, assuming one can be drawn that does not do violence to the first amendment.

. . .

There are those who are willing to protect the flag regardless of the cost, that are willing to pass a flag amendment even if the price of that amendment is doing fundamental violence to the first amendment. This is a price that I personally am not willing to pay, a price that I believe the President's proposed amendment . . . would exact. I believe the flag should be protected but not at the cost of infringing the core values of the first amendment.

. . .

SENATOR STROM THURMOND (Republican, South Carolina)

. . .

President Bush and other proponents of a constitutional amendment seek to restore to the Congress and the States the power to protect the integrity of the flag. Prior to the *Texas v. Johnson* (1989) decision, the Congress and 48 States believed they were on sound constitutional ground when they passed statutes prohibiting the desecration of the flag.

. . .

However, I believe this debate will not be concluded until the American people have had the opportunity to decide on a proposed constitutional amendment. The Supreme Court is not infallible nor the final arbiter for determining a constitutional right. Under our democracy, the American people are sovereign and have the ultimate authority to govern themselves. The Constitution provides, under Article V, the means for the American people to amend the Constitution when necessary. It is my firm belief that Congress should pass our proposed constitutional amendment and send it to the States where the citizens of this great country can decide if they want to prohibit the physical desecration of the American flag.

. . .

More than any other symbol in our history, the American flag represents our ideals, our values, and

1. Hearing Before the Committee on the Judiciary, United States Senate on Proposing an Amendment to the Constitution Authorizing the Congress and the States to Prohibit the Physical Desecration of the American Flag, 101st Cong., 2nd Sess. (1990), 1-6.

identity as a nation. We should not be hesitant in protecting the most profound emblem of this democracy.

. . .

It is not the President's intention, nor that of the proponents of this amendment, to restrict free and unfettered debate on public policy. A free exchange of ideas and opinion will go on unimpeded. Free speech is a fundamental right protected under the Constitution. Flag burning is not. The first amendment has never been construed as protecting any and all means of expression. There are restrictions on the use of utterly obscene and pornographic material as a means of expression. There are restrictions on destroying American currency even if it is an expression against Government expenditures. Similarly, if a citizen is opposed to the U.S. Postal Service, he is not free to express his opposition by blowing up mail-boxes. The first amendment has not been stricken from the Constitution because of these limitations. Likewise, the first amendment will not be in jeopardy if the Congress and the States are allowed to prohibit the physical desecration of the American flag.

. . .

SENATOR EDWARD KENNEDY (Democrat, Massachusetts)

Today the U.S. Congress is not the only legislature in the world considering a ban on the desecration of its country's flag. The totalitarian regime in China is about to outlaw burning, tarnishing, tearing, treading on, and other acts harming the Chinese flag.

The United States, with its honorable tradition of tolerance of dissent, should not emulate the brutal dictatorship in China. Our country, our Constitution, and our flag stand for something far better than the enforced obedience that the Chinese Government demands.

True, we cherish our flag for its design, its colors, and its fabric; but we cherish it most because of what it stands for—the ideals of liberty and tolerance and justice written into the Constitution and enshrined in the hearts of our country.

These ideas are secured by the Bill of Rights, which protects the fundamental freedoms that the flag represents, and for which the American Revolution was fought. For two centuries, nothing has caused the Nation to amend the Bill of Rights.

. . .

We all agree that flag burning is a despicable act. It expresses unthinking hatred for America, and it casts contempt on the symbol under which so many Americans have fought and died in service to their country. Flag burning sends a deeply offensive message—that the protester loathes the great Nation that we all hold so dear.

But the first amendment protects not only speech we admire, but also speech we abhor. No constitutional guarantee is more central to our democracy than freedom of speech. If the Government can censor its critics, then the ideal of free and open debate—so indispensable to our democracy and to our freedom—becomes an empty promise.

Any amendment to remove the constitutional protection for flag desecration—no matter how well-meaning or carefully drawn—would irreparably damage our remaining liberties. If we adopt such an amendment and make an exception to the first amendment because of our concern over a single act of flag burning, what will we say the next time a majority is offended by some other form of protest? If we yield to the temptation to stifle unpopular, offensive views today, there is no fair way to draw the line against banning other unpopular views tomorrow.

. . .

A constitutional amendment would also damage the separation of powers that has protected our constitutional freedoms throughout our history. For more than 200 years, we have trusted the courts to determine when expression is protected by the Constitution, because the judges insulated from public pressure can best evaluate the claims of unpopular minorities. But adopting a constitutional amendment will upset this separation of powers; elected officials will decide when minority views are worthy of protection. Once we adopt this precedent, no unpopular minority can safely assume its rights will be preserved tomorrow.

The Law of Nations

Americans agreed that customary international law was a source of individual rights, but the precise constitutional status of the law of nations remained unclear. The Court of Appeals for the Second Circuit in *Filártiga v. Peña-Irala* (1980) adopted a broad interpretation of federal judicial power to enforce international human rights law when ruling that federal courts could adjudicate a lawsuit brought by a Paraguayan citizen charging members of the Paraguayan government with torturing his son. Judge Kaufmann's unanimous opinion held that Article III gave Congress the power to authorize federal courts to hear a lawsuit between Paraguayan citizens over human rights violations that occurred in Paraguay because "the Laws of the United States" included customary international law. "The law of nations forms an integral part of the common law," Kaufmann declared, "and a review of the history surrounding the adoption of the Constitution demonstrates that it became a part of the common law of the United States upon the adoption of the Constitution."[2]

President Reagan and his political allies did not question assertions that international law was part of the law of the United States. Administration officials claimed that international law permitted the United States to mine Nicaraguan harbors in response to charges that such actions violated the law of nations and did not deny the authority of the law of nations. Nevertheless, conservatives insisted that American constitutional authorities were the only persons authorized to determine whether American policy was consistent with the law of nations, and that, for constitutional purposes, international law was merely a default rule or a rule of statutory interpretation. No administration accepted the authority of the International Court of Justice (ICJ) or any ICJ ruling on whether American actions violated international law. The Court of Appeals for the Eleventh Circuit in *Garcia-Mir v. Meese* (1986) articulated the Reagan administration position that an executive decree is a higher source of legal authority than customary international law. The issue in that case concerned the conditions under which the United States could detain Cuban refugees who had not legally entered the country. The Cuban refugees asserted that their continued detention violated international law. Judge Johnson agreed that "courts must construe American law so as to avoid violating principles of public international law." Nevertheless, he maintained that the Constitution required courts to follow international law only when no other conflicting legal authority existed. Noting that Attorney General Meese had approved the detention, Judge Johnson rejected the petition because "public international law is controlling only where there is no treaty and no controlling executive or legislative act or judicial decision."[3]

2. *Filártiga v. Peña-Irala*, 630 F.2d 876 (2d. Cir. 1980).

3. *Garcia-Mir v. Meese*, 788 F.2d 1446 (11th Cir. 1986).

B. Principles

Reagan conservatives regarded originalism as the only legitimate means for interpreting constitutional provisions protecting civil liberties. In this view, the First Amendment's declaration that "Congress shall make no law respecting an establishment of religion" means exactly what those words meant when the First Amendment was ratified in 1791. If no one in 1791 questioned the power of public officials to sponsor voluntary prayer exercises, then the establishment clause did not prohibit government officials from sponsoring prayer. Robert Bork declared, "Only by limiting themselves to the historic intentions underlying each clause of the Constitution can judges avoid becoming legislators, avoid enforcing their own moral predilections, and ensure the Constitution is law."[4] Reagan administration officials in the Justice Department enthusiastically adopted this jurisprudential principle. The Reagan Justice Department's *Guidelines on Constitutional Litigation* proclaimed, "Government attorneys should attempt to construct arguments based solely on the ordinary use of the words at the time the provision at issue was ratified."

When Ronald Reagan took office conservatives believed that justices committed to originalism supported traditional values and rarely engaged in judicial activism. Richard Viguerie, a prominent New Right activist, identified core conservative commitments as "a moral order, based on God" and "the Constitution of the United States, as originally conceived by the Founding Fathers."[5] In 1986 Ronald Reagan, at the investiture of Chief Justice William Rehnquist and Associate Justice Antonin Scalia, claimed that originalism was the only legitimate means of interpreting the Constitution because "the principle of judicial restraint has had an honored place in our tradition."

Two tensions soon emerged within this conservative effort to unite originalism, judicial restraint, and support for traditional values. The first was jurisprudential. Americans during the late twentieth century confronted circumstances in which originalism, judicial restraint, and support for traditional values diverged.

4. Judge Robert H. Bork, "The Constitution, Original Intent, and Economic Rights," *University of San Diego Law Review* 23 (1986): 823.

5. Richard A. Viguerie, *The New Right: We're Ready to Lead* (Falls Church, VA: Viguerie Co., 1980), 11.

Consider the concerns of evangelical Christians who wished to homeschool their children or not have their children be assigned certain books in the public schools. Courts could protect their "traditional" values only by actively striking down mandatory schooling laws and curriculum policies approved by elected officials. Whether originalism supported such decisions was at least open to question. Some conservative interest groups, most notably the Institute for Justice, openly championed judicial activism in service of what they believed were the natural rights foundations of the Constitution. Others temporized. The second tension was both political and jurisprudential. Prominent liberals charged that originalism as practiced by Reagan conservatives was no more constraining than any other principle of constitutional interpretation. When opposing affirmative action or campaign finance reform, they charged, conservative constitutional decision makers either ignored history or cherry-picked the quotes that supported their positions, ignoring the substantial historical evidence on the other side.

Consider these tensions when reading the materials below. To what extent did Reagan administration officials acknowledge possible tensions between originalism, judicial restraint, and support for traditional moral values? How did they resolve the tensions they perceived?

Office of Legal Policy, Guidelines on Constitutional Litigation (1988)[6]

The Reagan administration aggressively advanced a conservative constitutional vision. Led by Attorney General Edwin Meese, conservatives carefully scrutinized all potential Justice Department appointees and candidates for federal judicial nominations to ensure a commitment to originalism and opposition to such liberal judicial precedents as Roe v. Wade *(1973). Justice Department officials made numerous speeches and produced many position papers detailing and justifying their conservative commitments.* The Constitution in the Year 2000: Choices Ahead in Constitutional Interpretation *(1988) and* Guidelines on Constitutional Litigation *(1988) were two particularly influential expositions of the constitutional philosophy of the Reagan administration.* The Constitution in the Year 2000 *sharply contrasts conservative and liberal constitutional visions. While the report was ostensibly written to "communicat[e] to the public, the media, and members of Congress the growing importance of the judicial selection process," the text makes the case for such Reagan administration priorities as eliminating the exclusionary rule and restoring voluntary prayer in public schools.* Guidelines on Constitutional Litigation *is a more explicitly partisan document designed "to guide the government's litigating attorneys."[7] That manual sets forth a particular theory of constitutional interpretation, originalism, and the constitutional positions that Reagan administration officials believed followed from originalism.*

When reading the following excerpts from the Guidelines on Constitutional Litigation, *consider the following questions. Many critics of the Reagan administration believed that conservatives had politicized the Justice Department. On what basis was that claim made? Was that claim correct? What was the difference between the Reagan administration Justice Department and past Justice Departments that had actively promoted such decisions as* Brown v. Board of Education *(1954)? Was the Reagan administration more ideological, more thorough, or simply more conservative? To what extent did the Reagan administration correctly capture the original meaning of constitutional provisions? To what extent was originalism merely a pretext for justifying politically conservative stances?*

As Robert Bork reminds us, "constitutional adjudication starts from the proposition that the Constitution is law" and thus "constrain[s] judgment." . . . Consequently, constitutional language should be construed as it was publicly understood at the time of its drafting and ratification and government attorneys should advance constitutional arguments based solely on this "original meaning." To do this, government attorneys should attempt to construct arguments based solely on the ordinary use of the words at the time the provision at issue was ratified. . . .

. . .

6. Excerpted from Office of Legal Policy, U.S. Department of Justice, *Guidelines for Constitutional Litigation* (Washington, D.C.: Government Printing Office, 1988).

7. Office of Legal Policy, U.S. Department of Justice, *The Constitution in the Year 2000: Choices Ahead in Constitutional Interpretation* (Washington, D.C.: Government Printing Office, 1988).

Decisions Inconsistent With These Principles of Interpretation

The so-called "right of privacy" cases provide examples of judicial creation of rights not reasonably found in the Constitution. The Supreme Court first articulated a constitutional right to privacy in *Griswold v. Connecticut* (1965). In that case, the Court held that a state statute forbidding contraceptive use was unconstitutional because it violated a "right of privacy" which, although not explicitly mentioned in the Constitution, was implicitly created by the First, Third, Fourth, Fifth, and Ninth Amendments. . . . Justice Douglas writing for the plurality in essence created a new and unspecified right out of a series of specified rights, without explaining how a series of specified rights can combine to form some other, unspecified right. . . . Eight years later, in *Roe v. Wade* (1973), the Court held unconstitutional state laws prohibiting abortions under this so-called "right of privacy." In the words of [John Hart Ely], "[w]hat is frightening about *Roe* is that this super-protected right is not inferable from the language of the Constitution, the framers' thinking respecting the specific problem in issue, any general value derivable from the provisions they included, or the nation's government structure." . . . Ironically, as is often attempted with legitimate constitutional rights, the "right of privacy"—which by its terms protects an individual from government action—was later asserted to require the government to take action (i.e., to subsidize abortions performed on indigents). Here, the Supreme Court correctly refused to change this so-called right into an entitlement. *Harris v. McRae* (1980). . . .

In *Sherbert v. Verner* (1963), the Supreme Court ruled unconstitutional, under the Free Exercise Clause of the First Amendment applied through the Fourteenth Amendment, a state law denying unemployment compensation to those who refused without good cause to accept a job, which law resulted in denying benefits to a Seventh Day Adventist who for religious reasons refused to accept Saturday work. The opinion nowhere cited the actual language of the First Amendment, which reads "Congress shall make no law respecting an establishment of religion, or *prohibiting* the free exercise thereof. . . ." The Supreme Court turned a distinction of kind into a distinction of degree by talking in terms of "burden" instead of "prohibition." . . .

In *Miranda v. Arizona* (1966), the Court, overturning numerous precedents, created hitherto unknown rights in suspects to prevent questioning and to have counsel present at interrogations. While the Court ostensibly relied on the Fifth Amendment, the language of that Amendment only protects persons from being compelled to answer incriminating questions. The Court further created a detailed code of procedures for police interrogations that in no way can be derived from the prohibition against actual coercion, stipulating that suspects must be advised of these newly devised rights—the so-called "*Miranda* warnings"—and must "knowingly and intelligently" waive them before any questioning can take place. As Justice White wrote in dissent, the *Miranda* decision "is neither compelled nor even strongly suggested by the language of the Fifth Amendment, is at odds with American and English legal history, and involves a departure from a long line of precedent." . . .

. . .

The Constitution protects numerous individual liberties against government infringement. . . . Fidelity to the Constitution requires that these individual liberties be vigorously defended. . . . On the other hand, expanding an express constitutional right beyond its legitimate scope is as improper as creating additional constitutional rights out of whole cloth. . . .

. . .

In *Skinner v. Oklahoma* (1942), the Supreme Court first suggested the concept of fundamental rights that invites courts to undertake a stricter scrutiny of the inherently legislative task of line drawing. In that case the Court held that a statute requiring compulsory sterilization for "habitual criminals" was unconstitutional because the legislation "involves one of the basic civil rights of man"—procreation. One would be hard-pressed to defend the wisdom or morality of such a law. Nevertheless, the Court's analysis, resting on a fundamental right to procreate, is troublesome. The Court made no mention of where in the Constitution such a right is found, and did not analyze the case according to clauses actually in the Constitution. Rather, it simply asserted that "[m]arriage and procreation are fundamental to the very existence and survival of the race." . . .

Chip Mellor, Natural Rights and the Future of Public Interest Law (1991)[8]

William "Chip" Mellor was the founder, along with Clint Bolick, of the Institute for Justice. Both were former

8. Excerpted from William H. Mellor III and Clint Bolick, *The Quest for Justice: Natural Rights and the Future of Public Interest Law,*

members of the Reagan administration. Chip Mellor had worked in the Department of Energy, which President Reagan unsuccessfully attempted to dismantle. Clint Bolick had worked in the Equal Employment Opportunity Commission under Clarence Thomas. When they left the administration they formed a new libertarian public interest law firm that litigated against government interference with property rights, free speech, and school choice. Unlike previous conservative litigation efforts, which were often orchestrated by business interests to serve immediate financial interests, the Institute for Justice had an ideological and policy agenda. Mellor and Bolick sought to inspire judicial activism based on libertarian commitments rather than on the more egalitarian principles that animated the Warren Court.

The following excerpt is taken from a speech that Mellor gave at the founding of the Institute for Justice. How does Mellor distinguish conservative judicial activism from liberal judicial activism? Does he maintain that the framers were libertarians, that the constitutional tradition is libertarian, or that libertarian principles are just? Are there legitimate constitutional differences between liberal and conservative judicial activism?

. . . Clint Bolick and I vowed that one day we would join forces to pursue a vision of public interest advocacy devoted to individual rights and economic liberty. We had witnessed first hand the graphic difference between pro-business and pro-free enterprise litigation. We saw the tragic consequences of expedient, ad hoc case selection with a public interest veneer. Clint and I concluded that a very different approach was necessary—a long-term, philosophically and tactically consistent litigation program based on natural rights and the Constitution. We believed this new approach was essential if the courts were to play their designated role as guarantors of liberty. The rule of law so necessary to a free society was too often twisted into a force that destroyed not only isolated individuals, but also the very fabric of community upon which our society is based. Court-ordered busing as neighborhood schools failed, open-ended protection of criminals while the pain of crime victims was ignored, expansion of welfare entitlements while government closed avenues for initiative and upward mobility—all these and more were among the policies that our legal system fostered and protected.

. . . The theory of judicial restraint, that is, the notion that judges are to apply the written law and not attempt to create it, was the jurisprudential touchstone of the Reagan administration. Conservatives vehemently opposed judicial activism that led to sweeping changes wrought by judges accountable to no one. . . .

. . . While abhorring many results of liberal judicial activism, we believed that emphasis on judicial restraint as an end in itself gave insufficient hope for protecting crucial rights. And for those rights already emasculated by judicial edict, judicial restraint simply enshrines bad law.

For example, the Constitution states that private property shall be protected from government expropriation. Yet decades of court-made law removed much of this protection. Is one wrong in calling for judicial activism that urges courts to strike down wrongful government takings? The Constitution protects economic liberty, but this right was nullified through a single Supreme Court case a hundred years ago. Is one a proponent of improper judicial activism in calling for the reversal of such intolerable precedent? . . .

The Institute of Justice will meet this challenge [of solving real world problems] through systematic litigation designed to take us, step by step, closer to a modern jurisprudence based on natural rights. In doing so we will be guided by two overriding principles. First, a recognition that our system of law is based upon inalienable individual rights to life, liberty, and the pursuit of happiness. Second, a belief that in every instance where government activity adversely affects these rights a court should begin its inquiry with a presumption of liberty. This presumption should only give way upon showing that a law is actually necessary and proper to the exercise of a constitutionally delegated power. These two principles are crucial because they recognize and seek to restore the fundamental relationship of the individual to the state envisioned by the Founders.

C. Scope

Ronald Reagan and his political allies sought to narrow both the scope and the meaning of constitutional protections for rights and liberties. Prominent conservatives rejected claims that the Fourteenth Amendment required states to respect the liberties enumerated in the Bill of Rights, sought to narrow the circumstances in which private persons could be considered state

Heritage Lectures No. 342 (Washington, DC: Heritage Foundation, 1991).

actors for constitutional purposes, and argued that federal officials were not bound by the Bill of Rights when acting overseas. The first argument failed. The incorporation doctrine remained vibrant in the 1980s. Conservatives were more successful when they proposed narrowing state action and limiting federal obligations to respect the civil rights of persons residing outside the United States.

Prominent members of the Reagan administration tried without success to convince the Supreme Court to rethink such cases as *Duncan v. Louisiana* (1968), which interpreted the Fourteenth Amendment as requiring state officials to respect in full almost every provision in the Bill of Rights. In a speech before the American Bar Association Edwin Meese declared, "Nothing can be done to shore up the intellectually shaky foundation" of incorporation, and "Nowhere else has the principle of federalism been dealt so politically violent and constitutionally suspect a blow as by the theory of incorporation."[9] Federal courts were unresponsive. No judicial opinion even hinted at possible retrenchment.

Conservatives fared better when proposing limits on the state action doctrine, the constitutional rules that determine when an ostensibly private actor is required to act in a manner consistent with the Bill of Rights. Two cases illustrate the increasingly narrow scope of this doctrine. In *Blum v. Yaretsky* (1982) the Supreme Court held that nursing homes that received more than 90 percent of their funding from the government were not state actors unless the state used funding to encourage the private decision under constitutional attack. Justice Rehnquist declared, "That programs undertaken by the State result in substantial funding of the activities of a private entity is no more persuasive than the fact of regulation of such an entity in demonstrating that the State is responsible for decisions made by the entity in the course of its business." In *DeShaney v. Winnebago County Department of Social Services* (1989) a conservative majority ruled that states had no constitutional obligation to protect persons from private violence. Rejecting a lawsuit claiming that social workers had negligently remained passive when confronted with overwhelming evidence of child abuse, now Chief Justice Rehnquist declared, "A State's failure to protect an individual against private violence simply does not constitute a violation of the Due Process Clause."

Conservative majorities on the Supreme Court ruled that federal officials had no obligation to respect the rights of foreign residents when acting in foreign countries. When upholding the warrantless search of the home of a Mexican citizen, Chief Justice Rehnquist's opinion for the Court in *United States v. Verdugo-Urquidez* (1990) stated, "The purpose of the Fourth Amendment was to protect the people of the United States against arbitrary action by their own Government; it was never suggested that the provision was intended to restrain the actions of the Federal Government against aliens outside of the United States territory."

State Action

DeShaney v. Winnebago County Department of Social Services, 489 U.S. 189 (1989)

Joshua DeShaney, a four-year-old boy, suffered severe brain damage after being beaten by his father, Randy DeShaney. The Winnebago County Department of Social Services had substantial evidence that Randy DeShaney was abusing his son. Nevertheless, state officials did not remove Joshua from Randy DeShaney's house, even after a caseworker documented that Randy DeShaney had violated a previous agreement with the Department of Social Services. After the final beating Joshua's mother, Melody DeShaney, sued the Department of Social Services on his behalf. She claimed that state officials violated Joshua DeShaney's due process rights when they failed to remove him from what they should have known was an abusive home. The Department of Social Services responded that they had no constitutional responsibility to protect Joshua from harms inflicted by private persons. The local federal district court rejected the DeShaney argument. That decision was sustained by the Court of Appeals for the Second Circuit. DeShaney appealed to the Supreme Court of the United States.

The Supreme Court by a 6-3 vote held that the Department of Social Services was not liable for Joshua DeShaney's injuries. Chief Justice Rehnquist's majority opinion maintained that Wisconsin had no obligation under the due process clause to protect persons from private violence unless the person was in state custody. On what basis does he reach that conclusion? Justice Brennan agrees that the state is not

9. Edwin Meese, "Before the American Bar Association, July 9, 1985," in *The Great Debate* (Washington, DC: Federalist Society, 1986), 8.

obligated to provide child protection services. Why does he conclude that the Department of Social Services was constitutionally responsible for Joshua DeShaney's injuries? All the justices agree that Joshua DeShaney is an unusually sympathetic plaintiff. How does that influence their analysis? How should that influence their analysis?

CHIEF JUSTICE REHNQUIST delivered the opinion of the Court.

. . .

. . . [N]othing in the language of the Due Process Clause itself requires the State to protect the life, liberty, and property of its citizens against invasion by private actors. The Clause is phrased as a limitation on the State's power to act, not as a guarantee of certain minimal levels of safety and security. It forbids the State itself to deprive individuals of life, liberty, or property without "due process of law," but its language cannot fairly be extended to impose an affirmative obligation on the State to ensure that those interests do not come to harm through other means. Nor does history support such an expansive reading of the constitutional text. Like its counterpart in the Fifth Amendment, the Due Process Clause of the Fourteenth Amendment was intended to prevent government "from abusing [its] power, or employing it as an instrument of oppression." . . . Its purpose was to protect the people from the State, not to ensure that the State protected them from each other. The Framers were content to leave the extent of governmental obligation in the latter area to the democratic political processes.

Consistent with these principles, our cases have recognized that the Due Process Clauses generally confer no affirmative right to governmental aid, even where such aid may be necessary to secure life, liberty, or property interests of which the government itself may not deprive the individual. . . . If the Due Process Clause does not require the State to provide its citizens with particular protective services, it follows that the State cannot be held liable under the Clause for injuries that could have been averted had it chosen to provide them. As a general matter, then, we conclude that a State's failure to protect an individual against private violence simply does not constitute a violation of the Due Process Clause.

. . .

. . . It is true that in certain limited circumstances the Constitution imposes upon the State affirmative duties of care and protection with respect to particular individuals. . . . [T]he Eighth Amendment's prohibition against cruel and unusual punishment . . . requires the State to provide adequate medical care to incarcerated prisoners. . . .

But these cases afford petitioners no help. Taken together, they stand only for the proposition that when the State takes a person into its custody and holds him there against his will, the Constitution imposes upon it a corresponding duty to assume some responsibility for his safety and general well-being. . . . The rationale for this principle is simple enough: when the State by the affirmative exercise of its power so restrains an individual's liberty that it renders him unable to care for himself, and at the same time fails to provide for his basic human needs—e.g., food, clothing, shelter, medical care, and reasonable safety—it transgresses the substantive limits on state action set by the Eighth Amendment and the Due Process Clause. . . . The affirmative duty to protect arises not from the State's knowledge of the individual's predicament or from its expressions of intent to help him, but from the limitation which it has imposed on his freedom to act on his own behalf. . . .

. . . Petitioners concede that the harms Joshua suffered occurred not while he was in the State's custody, but while he was in the custody of his natural father, who was in no sense a state actor. While the State may have been aware of the dangers that Joshua faced in the free world, it played no part in their creation, nor did it do anything to render him any more vulnerable to them. That the State once took temporary custody of Joshua does not alter the analysis, for when it returned him to his father's custody, it placed him in no worse position than that in which he would have been had it not acted at all; the State does not become the permanent guarantor of an individual's safety by having once offered him shelter. Under these circumstances, the State had no constitutional duty to protect Joshua.

. . .

JUSTICE BRENNAN, with whom JUSTICE MARSHALL and JUSTICE BLACKMUN join, dissenting.

. . .

. . . I would focus first on the action that Wisconsin has taken with respect to Joshua and children like him, rather than on the actions that the State failed to take. . . .

. . .

Wisconsin has established a child-welfare system specifically designed to help children like Joshua.

Wisconsin law places upon the local departments of social services such as respondent (DSS [Department of Social Services] or Department) a duty to investigate reported instances of child abuse. . . . While other governmental bodies and private persons are largely responsible for the reporting of possible cases of child abuse, . . . Wisconsin law channels all such reports to the local departments of social services for evaluation and, if necessary, further action. . . . In this way, Wisconsin law invites—indeed, directs—citizens and other governmental entities to depend on local departments of social services such as respondent to protect children from abuse.

The specific facts before us bear out this view of Wisconsin's system of protecting children. Each time someone voiced a suspicion that Joshua was being abused, that information was relayed to the Department for investigation and possible action. When Randy DeShaney's second wife told the police that he had "'hit the boy causing marks and [was] a prime case for child abuse,'" the police referred her complaint to DSS. When, on three separate occasions, emergency room personnel noticed suspicious injuries on Joshua's body, they went to DSS with this information. . . .

. . .

In these circumstances, a private citizen, or even a person working in a government agency other than DSS, would doubtless feel that her job was done as soon as she had reported her suspicions of child abuse to DSS. Through its child-welfare program, in other words, the State of Wisconsin has relieved ordinary citizens and governmental bodies other than the Department of any sense of obligation to do anything more than report their suspicions of child abuse to DSS. If DSS ignores or dismisses these suspicions, no one will step in to fill the gap. Wisconsin's child-protection program thus effectively confined Joshua DeShaney within the walls of Randy DeShaney's violent home until such time as DSS took action to remove him. Conceivably, then, children like Joshua are made worse off by the existence of this program when the persons and entities charged with carrying it out fail to do their jobs.

. . .

. . . My disagreement with the Court arises from its failure to see that inaction can be every bit as abusive of power as action, that oppression can result when a State undertakes a vital duty and then ignores it. Today's opinion construes the Due Process Clause to permit a State to displace private sources of protection and then, at the critical moment, to shrug its shoulders and turn away from the harm that it has promised to try to prevent. Because I cannot agree that our Constitution is indifferent to such indifference, I respectfully dissent.

JUSTICE BLACKMUN, dissenting.

Like the antebellum judges who denied relief to fugitive slaves, . . . the Court today claims that its decision, however harsh, is compelled by existing legal doctrine. On the contrary, the question presented by this case is an open one, and our Fourteenth Amendment precedents may be read more broadly or narrowly depending upon how one chooses to read them. Faced with the choice, I would adopt a "sympathetic" reading, one which comports with dictates of fundamental justice and recognizes that compassion need not be exiled from the province of judging. . . .

Poor Joshua! Victim of repeated attacks by an irresponsible, bullying, cowardly, and intemperate father, and abandoned by respondents who placed him in a dangerous predicament and who knew or learned what was going on, and yet did essentially nothing except, as the Court revealingly observes, "dutifully recorded these incidents in [their] files." It is a sad commentary upon American life, and constitutional principles—so full of late of patriotic fervor and proud proclamations about "liberty and justice for all"—that this child, Joshua DeShaney, now is assigned to live out the remainder of his life profoundly retarded. Joshua and his mother, as petitioners here, deserve—but now are denied by this Court—the opportunity to have the facts of their case considered in the light of the constitutional protection that [federal law] is meant to provide.

III. INDIVIDUAL RIGHTS

MAJOR DEVELOPMENTS

- Some judicial protection for property rights under the takings clause
- Courts reaffirm the constitutional right to an abortion and the prohibition on state-sponsored prayer exercises in public schools
- Greater judicial solicitude for state assistance to religious organizations
- No right to homosexual conduct

The constitutional politics of individual rights was subtly transformed during the Reagan Era. At the dawn of the 1980s most conservatives championed judicial restraint on almost all individual rights issues, from the right to bear arms to the right to terminate a pregnancy. As Reagan conservatism matured and conservatives established a foothold in the judiciary, many political actors on the right demanded constitutional protection for a different set of individual rights. This conservative rights agenda included judicial protection for property rights, the rights of evangelical Christians, and the rights of gun holders. By the mid-1990s constitutional politics had become a struggle between liberal and conservative conceptions of constitutional rights rather than a contest between liberal proponents of judicial activism and conservative proponents of judicial restraint.

When reading the materials in this section, consider two different explanations for increased conservative calls for judicial activism (and corresponding liberal calls for judicial restraint). The first is political. By 1990 the majority of the justices on the Supreme Court and federal bench were conservatives appointed by Republican presidents. These justices were often sympathetic to property rights and the right to bear arms. The second is jurisprudential. Warren Court activism helped fashion a constitutional culture committed to judicial protection for fundamental rights. Conservatives socialized in this culture were more inclined to change the ideological direction of activist decisions than to abandon judicial rights protection, becoming, as one Reagan judicial appointed declared, little more than "potted plant[s]."[10]

A. Property

Reagan Republicans had an ambivalent attitude toward due process protections for property rights. Conservatives celebrated economic liberty. Ronald Reagan consistently spoke of "economic freedom." The 1984 Republican Party platform declared, "Our society provides both a ladder of opportunity on which all can climb to success and a safety net of assistance for those who need it. To safeguard both, government must protect property rights, provide a sound currency, and minimize its intrusions into individual decisions to work, save, invest, and take risks." Nevertheless, the Reagan years saw few efforts to revive the constitutional protection for the freedom of contract asserted in *Lochner v. New York* (1905). Most prominent conservative constitutional thinkers scorned *Lochner*. In a speech criticizing conservatives who favored reviving *Lochner*, Robert Bork declared, "Judicial review of economic regulations . . . works a massive shift away from democracy and toward judicial role."[11] The Reagan Justice Department worked up some enthusiasm for broader interpretations of the contracts clause and takings clause. *The Constitution in the Year 2000* called for constitutional decision makers to use those provisions to "shield . . . the liberty of private property from governmental interference much the same way as the First Amendment shields the liberty of speech."[12] The *Guidelines on Constitutional Litigation* said nothing about property rights.

Conservative politicians had legal and political reasons to refrain from aggressively championing property rights, particularly the freedom of contract. The Reagan administration was committed to overruling *Roe v. Wade* (1973). Reviving *Lochner* undermined the central premise of the attack on judicial protection for abortion—namely, that the due process clause of the Fourteenth Amendment did not protect unenumerated rights. Moreover, as conservatives gained control of electoral institutions, they had less need for a judicial crusade on behalf of private property. Judicial restraint on economic policy left conservative elected officials free to reject or repeal measures that trenched on economic liberty.

Libertarian public interest groups and some conservatives in the legal academy more aggressively promoted such explicit constitutional protections for private property as the takings clause of the Fifth Amendment and the contracts clause of Article I. In the mid-1980s a new generation of conservative public interest law firms emerged. Such firms as the Institute for Justice and the Rocky Mountains Legal Foundation stood ready to assist property owners and others aggrieved by federal and state regulations. The conservative legal leadership that emerged in the 1980s and 1990s also recognized that the courts were an important policymaking arena and that litigation could be used as an offensive tool in policy making. Learning

10. Richard A. Posner, "What Am I, a Potted Plant? The Case against Strict Constructionism," *New Republic* (September 28, 1987), 23. See also Thomas Moylan Keck, *The Most Activist Supreme Court in History: The Road to Modern Judicial Conservatism* (Chicago: University of Chicago Press, 2004).

11. Bork, "The Constitution, Original Intent, and Economic Rights," 829.

12. Office of Legal Policy, *The Constitution in the Year 2000*, 117.

lessons from well-established liberal interest groups like the ACLU and the NAACP Legal Defense Fund, these new conservative groups mounted strategic litigation campaigns.

These campaigns soon influenced constitutional law. The Supreme Court in the late 1980s revived the takings clause as a limit on government power. Conservative litigators had less luck with the contracts clause and freedom of contract. Neither influenced the constitutional politics of the Reagan Era.

Contracts

After a brief reemergence, the contracts clause returned to oblivion. *Allied Structural Steel Co. v. Spannaus* (1978) and *United Trust Co. of New York v. New Jersey* (1977) suggested that conservative justices might impose significant contract clause limits on state power to impair existing contractual relationships without sufficient justification. The justices did not, however, expand those precedents. The Supreme Court decided very few contract clause cases and almost always upheld the state regulation being constitutionally challenged. *Energy Reserves Group, Inc., v. Kansas Power and Light Co.* (1983) sustained a Kansas law that altered the price at which suppliers could purchase natural gas. Justice Blackmun's majority opinion claimed that the parties should have expected legal changes because the natural gas industry was "heavily regulated," and that the Kansas law rested on a "significant and legitimate state interest" in "protect[ing] consumers from the escalation of natural gas prices caused by deregulation." *General Motors Corp. v. Romein* (1992) declared that the Michigan legislature could give retroactive effect to a law overturning a state judicial decision that permitted companies to withhold disability payments. Justice O'Connor's unanimous opinion declared, "Petitioners' suggestion that we should read every workplace regulation into the private contractual arrangements of employers and employees would expand the definition of contract so far that the constitutional provision would lose its anchoring purpose, *i.e.*, 'enabl[ing] individuals to order their personal and business affairs according to their particular needs and interests.'"

Takings

Conservative intellectuals, public interest groups, and justices enjoyed increasing success in their campaign to impose takings clause limitations on various environment laws and land-use regulations. Professor Richard Epstein of the University of Chicago led the fight for property rights in the academy. His influential book *Takings* asserted that the Fifth and Fourteenth Amendments were violated any time that state regulations lowered the value of property. That work concluded, "First, the eminent domain logic allows forced exchanges only for the public use, which excluded naked transfers from one person to another. Second, it requires compensation, so everyone receives something of greater value in exchange for the *rights* surrendered."[13] Such libertarian public interest groups as the Rocky Mountain Legal Foundation, the Washington Legal Foundation, and the Institute for Justice supported hundreds of lawsuits claiming takings violations, some of which found their way to the Supreme Court. Justices divided on ideological lines, with the more conservative justices voting to declare that the state regulation violated constitutional property rights and the more liberal justices voting to sustain the government decision. More frequently than in the recent past, the Supreme Court found takings clause violations.

During the early 1980s liberals sometimes joined conservatives in requiring compensation for a taking. A 6-3 majority in *Loretto v. Teleprompter Manhattan CATV Corp.* (1982) struck down a state measure that required landowners to allow cable television wires on their rental property. Justice Marshall, the most liberal justice on the Burger Court, wrote the majority opinion rejecting the application of the *Penn Central* (1978) balancing test to the situation before the Court. "[W]hen the physical intrusion reaches the extreme form of a permanent physical occupation," Marshall declared, "a taking has occurred." Compensation was due no matter the social benefit or harm to the landowner. Permanent physical occupations violated the takings clause "whether the action achieves an important public benefit or has only minimal economic impact on the owner."

Ideological divisions soon emerged. A 5-4 judicial majority in *Lucas v. South Carolina Coastal Council* (1992) ruled that a regulation could take property even when the government did not physically invade the land in

13. Richard A. Epstein, *Takings: Private Property and the Power of Eminent Domain* (Cambridge, MA: Harvard University Press, 1985), 332.

question. Speaking for the five most conservative justices on the Rehnquist Court, Justice Scalia declared that a compensable taking occurred whenever a regulation deprived persons of "all economically beneficial use" of their holdings. In both *Nollan v. California Coastal Commission* (1987) and *Dolan v. City of Tigard* (1994) 5-4 conservative judicial majorities ruled that legislative conditions on development had to satisfy Fifth and Fourteenth Amendment standards. Chief Justice Rehnquist's majority opinion in *Dolan* announced a two-part test for determining when conditions on development were constitutional. He declared that courts "must first determine whether the 'essential nexus' exists between the legitimate state interest and the permit condition exacted by the city," and then determine "the required degree of connection between the exactions and the projected impact of the proposed development." "Rough proportionality," Rehnquist insisted, was required. He maintained that governing officials "must make some sort of individualized determination that the required dedication is related both in nature and extent to the impact of the proposed development." The city of Tigard failed this test. City officials sought to condition a permit to double the size of an electrical supply store on the petitioner's willingness to dedicate part of her property for flood drainage and part of her property for a bicycle path. The judicial majority in *Dolan* concluded that the city's interest in flood control could be as well secured by a private as a public greenway and that local officials had not sufficiently demonstrated that the increased traffic that might result if the store was expanded justified creating an easement for a public bicycle path.

The Supreme Court was more deferential to elected officials when interpreting the constitutional requirement that private property "be taken for public use." *Hawaii Housing Authority v. Midkiff* (1984) sustained a law that required major landowners in Hawaii to sell parcels to their tenants. Justice O'Connor's unanimous opinion employed a traditional rational basis test when permitting Hawaii to exercise the power of eminent domain to transfer title from large property holders to smaller property holders. She asserted,

> The people of Hawaii have attempted . . . to reduce the perceived social and economic evils of a land oligopoly traceable to their monarchs. The land oligopoly has, according to the Hawaii Legislature, created artificial deterrents to the normal functioning of the State's residential land market and forced thousands of individual homeowners to lease, rather than buy, the land underneath their homes. Regulating oligopoly and the evils associated with it is a classic exercise of a State's police powers.

State courts reached similar conclusions. The Supreme Court of Michigan in *Poletown Neighborhood Council v. City of Detroit* (MI 1981) sustained the city of Detroit's condemnation of property in a local neighborhood in order to help General Motors build a plant that the automobile manufacturer insisted was necessary to prevent them from moving to another state. The per curiam opinion declared, "The power of eminent domain is to be used in this instance primarily to accomplish the essential public purposes of alleviating unemployment and revitalizing the economic base of the community. The benefit to a private interest is merely incidental."[14]

Lucas v. South Carolina Coastal Council, 505 U.S. 1003 (1992)

David Lucas was a real estate developer. In 1986 he paid nearly $1 million for two residential lots on the Isle of Palms, a barrier island near Charleston, South Carolina. Lucas intended to build single-family houses on his newly acquired property. His plans were thwarted when the South Carolina legislature in 1988 passed the Beachfront Management Act, which prohibited all construction (other than small decks or wooden walkways) within designated areas near beaches, including the lots owned by Lucas. Lucas challenged the constitutionality of the government's action in state court. The trial court agreed that Lucas's land had been rendered "valueless" by the government's action and that he was entitled to compensation. The Supreme Court of South Carolina reversed that decision, arguing that the construction would cause a public harm that could be prohibited under the state's police powers. Lucas appealed to the Supreme Court of the United States.

The Supreme Court by a 5-4 vote ruled that a compensable taking had occurred. Justice Scalia's majority opinion maintained that the takings clause required states to provide compensation when a regulation made private property worthless, unless the owner had no preexisting right to use

14. *Poletown Neighborhood Council v. City of Detroit*, 410 Mich. 616 (1981).

the property in the prohibited way. What is the constitutional foundation of that rule? Does Scalia refer to history, precedent, or general constitutional principles? What differences do you perceive between judicial activism on behalf of property rights and such cases as Roe v. Wade *(1973)? Justice Scalia notes that no compensation is required if the new restriction is consistent with previously existing property law or the common law of nuisance. South Carolina can forbid people from mining on their property if such an action is likely to cause poison gas to rise to the surface. What is the constitutional foundation of that rule? Under what conditions do the dissenting judges believe that South Carolina could pass regulations that would destroy the entire value of Lucas's property? What is the correct constitutional rule?*

JUSTICE SCALIA delivered the opinion of the Court.

. . .

. . . We have described at least two discrete categories of regulatory action as compensable without case-specific inquiry into the public interest advanced in support of the restraint. The first encompasses regulations that compel the property owner to suffer a physical "invasion" of his property. In general (at least with regard to permanent invasions), no matter how minute the intrusion, and no matter how weighty the public purpose behind it, we have required compensation. . . . The second situation in which we have found categorical treatment appropriate is where regulation denies all economically beneficial or productive use of land. . . . As we have said on numerous occasions, the Fifth Amendment is violated when land-use regulation "does not substantially advance legitimate state interests *or denies an owner economically viable use of his land.*"

. . .

. . . [T]he *functional* basis for permitting the government, by regulation, to affect property values without compensation—that "Government hardly could go on if to some extent values incident to property could not be diminished without paying for every such change in the general law,"—does not apply to the relatively rare situations where the government has deprived a landowner of all economically beneficial uses. . . . [R]egulations that leave the owner of land without economically beneficial or productive options for its use—typically, as here, by requiring land to be left substantially in its natural state—carry with them a heightened risk that private property is being pressed into some form of public service under the guise of mitigating serious public harm. . . .

. . .

Where the State seeks to sustain regulation that deprives land of all economically beneficial use, we think it may resist compensation only if the logically antecedent inquiry into the nature of the owner's estate shows that the proscribed use interests were not part of his title to begin with. This accords, we think, with our "takings" jurisprudence, which has traditionally been guided by the understandings of our citizens regarding the content of, and the State's power over, the "bundle of rights" that they acquire when they obtain title to property. It seems to us that the property owner necessarily expects the uses of his property to be restricted, from time to time, by various measures newly enacted by the State in legitimate exercise of its police powers; "as long recognized, some values are enjoyed under an implied limitation and must yield to the police power." And in the case of personal property, by reason of the State's traditionally high degree of control over commercial dealings, he ought to be aware of the possibility that new regulation might even render his property economically worthless (at least if the property's only economically productive use is sale or manufacture for sale). In the case of land, however, we think the notion pressed by the Council that title is somehow held subject to the "implied limitation" that the State may subsequently eliminate all economically valuable use is inconsistent with the historical compact recorded in the Takings Clause that has become part of our constitutional culture.

Where "permanent physical occupation" of land is concerned, we have refused to allow the government to decree it anew (without compensation), no matter how weighty the asserted "public interests" involved, though we assuredly *would* permit the government to assert a permanent easement that was a pre-existing limitation upon the land owner's title. We believe similar treatment must be accorded confiscatory regulations, *i.e.,* regulations that prohibit all economically beneficial use of land: Any limitation so severe cannot be newly legislated or decreed (without compensation), but must inhere in the title itself, in the restrictions that background principles of the State's law of property and nuisance already place upon land ownership. A law or decree with such an effect must, in other words, do no more than duplicate the result that could have been achieved in the courts—by adjacent landowners (or other uniquely affected persons) under the State's law of private nuisance, or by the State under its complementary power to abate nuisances that affect the public generally, or otherwise.

. . .

It seems unlikely that common-law principles would have prevented the erection of any habitable or productive improvements on petitioner's land; they rarely support prohibition of the "essential use" of land. The question, however, is one of state law to be dealt with on remand. . . .

JUSTICE KENNEDY, concurring in the judgment.

. . .

. . . Where a taking is alleged from regulations which deprive the property of all value, the test must be whether the deprivation is contrary to reasonable, investment-backed expectations. . . .

In my view, reasonable expectations must be understood in light of the whole of our legal tradition. The common law of nuisance is too narrow a confine for the exercise of regulatory power in a complex and interdependent society. The State should not be prevented from enacting new regulatory initiatives in response to changing conditions, and courts must consider all reasonable expectations whatever their source. The Takings Clause does not require a static body of state property law; it protects private expectations to ensure private investment. I agree with the Court that nuisance prevention accords with the most common expectations of property owners who face regulation, but I do not believe this can be the sole source of state authority to impose severe restrictions. Coastal property may present such unique concerns for a fragile land system that the State can go further in regulating its development and use than the common law of nuisance might otherwise permit.

. . . The promotion of tourism [however] ought not to suffice to deprive specific property of all value without a corresponding duty to compensate. . . .

JUSTICE BLACKMUN, dissenting.

. . .

The Court creates its new takings jurisprudence based on the trial court's finding that the property had lost all economic value. This finding is almost certainly erroneous. Petitioner still can enjoy other attributes of ownership, such as the right to exclude others, "one of the most essential sticks in the bundle of rights that are commonly characterized as property." Petitioner can picnic, swim, camp in a tent, or live on the property in a movable trailer. State courts frequently have recognized that land has economic value where the only residual economic uses are recreation or camping. Petitioner also retains the right to alienate the land, which would have value for neighbors and for those prepared to enjoy proximity to the ocean without a house.

. . .

. . . [T]he State has full power to prohibit an owner's use of property if it is harmful to the public. "Since no individual has a right to use his property so as to create a nuisance or otherwise harm others, the State has not 'taken' anything when it asserts its power to enjoin the nuisance-like activity." It would make no sense under this theory to suggest that an owner has a constitutionally protected right to harm others, if only he makes the proper showing of economic loss.

. . .

Until today, the Court explicitly had rejected the contention that the government's power to act without paying compensation turns on whether the prohibited activity is a common-law nuisance. The brewery closed in *Mugler v. Kansas* (1887) itself was not a common-law nuisance, and the Court specifically stated that it was the role of the legislature to determine what measures would be appropriate for the protection of public health and safety. . . .

. . .

Even more perplexing, however, is the Court's reliance on common-law principles of nuisance in its quest for a value-free takings jurisprudence. In determining what is a nuisance at common law, state courts make exactly the decision that the Court finds so troubling when made by the South Carolina General Assembly today: They determine whether the use is harmful. Common-law public and private nuisance law is simply a determination whether a particular use causes harm. . . .

. . .

JUSTICE STEVENS, dissenting.

. . .

In addition to lacking support in past decisions, the Court's new rule is wholly arbitrary. A landowner whose property is diminished in value 95% recovers nothing, while an owner whose property is diminished 100% recovers the land's full value. The case at hand illustrates this arbitrariness well. The Beachfront Management Act not only prohibited the building of new dwellings in certain areas, it also prohibited the rebuilding of houses that were "destroyed beyond repair by natural causes or by fire." . . . Thus, if the homes adjacent to Lucas' lot were destroyed by a hurricane one day after the Act took effect, the owners would not be able to rebuild, nor would they be assured recovery. Under the Court's categorical approach, Lucas (who has lost the opportunity to build) recovers, while his neighbors (who have lost *both* the opportunity to build *and* their homes) do not recover. The arbitrariness of such a rule is palpable.

. . .

Viewed more broadly, the Court's new rule and exception conflict with the very character of our takings jurisprudence. We have frequently and consistently recognized that the definition of a taking cannot be reduced to a "set formula" and that determining whether a regulation is a taking is "essentially [an] ad hoc, factual inquiry." *Penn Central Transportation Co. v. New York City* (1978). The rigid rules fixed by the Court today clash with this enterprise: "fairness and justice" are often disserved by categorical rules. . . .

Due Process

Due process protection for property rights was the proverbial dog that did not bark in the night. Conservatives did not revive the freedom of contract. Liberals largely abandoned campaigns to fashion a due process right to basic necessities. Constitutional commentators of all political persuasions often pointed to their restraint on those due process issues as establishing vital constitutional credentials. Liberal proponents of constitutional abortion rights confessed that Reagan Era welfare spending cuts were constitutional when responding to charges that their constitutional theories were designed to promote judicial activism on all matters that the left believed were bad policy. Conservatives emphasized their criticisms of such cases as *Lochner v. New York* (1905) as establishing the principled foundation for their commitment to judicial activism on campaign finance and other property rights cases.

B. Religion

Ronald Reagan helped solidify the new constitutional politics of religion. The traditional constitutional politics of religion pitted Protestants, who favored public expressions of religion but opposed providing state funds for sectarian institutions, against Catholics, who took the opposite position on both matters. Richard Nixon created a new alliance of conservative Protestants and Catholics (as well as orthodox Jews) who favored public expressions of religion and the provision of state aid to sectarian institutions. Ronald Reagan and the Republican Party appealed to that coalition. The Republican Party promised to adopt policies and appoint judges that would permit some public funding for private religious schools and restore voluntary prayer in public schools.

Republicans enjoyed substantial political and some constitutional success. By the end of the 1980s most evangelical Christians were reliable Republican voters. The party made substantial inroads into the Catholic vote. Government provided more aid to private schools. The late Burger and Rehnquist Courts usually sustained the provision of such aid. Conservatives failed, however, to obtain their highest public priority. Congress refused to approve a school prayer amendment. In *Lee v. Weisman* (1992) a 6-3 majority ruled that public officials had no constitutional business sponsoring a prayer ceremony at a middle-school graduation.

Establishment

Reagan conservatives sought to provide greater financial support to sectarian institutions and religious practices. In *The Constitution in the Year 2000* the Reagan Department of Justice urged federal courts to

> be less willing to find Establishment Clause violations in non-discriminatory programs of aid to private, religious schools. . . . This view of the First Amendment would basically leave to the representative branches of government the questions of whether and to what extent public funds should be spent on private, religious education. Under this approach, private education would likely survive as a viable alternative to public education, for many states undoubtedly would welcome the opportunity to experiment with various types of aid.[15]

Reagan administration officials urged the Supreme Court to overrule *Engle v. Vitale* (1962), the decision

15. Office of Legal Policy, *Constitution in the Year 2000*, 80.

holding that public schools could not sponsor voluntary prayer exercises. "God should never have been expelled from America's classrooms in the first place," Reagan declared in his 1983 State of the Union address when asking Congress for "a constitutional amendment to permit voluntary school prayer."

Private religious schools and religious institutions gained more access to public funds during the Reagan years. Supreme Court doctrine focused on whether the government aid discriminated between religious and nonreligious institutions and individuals, rather than on whether government money was financing religious activities or organizations. In *Mueller v. Allen* (1983) the Supreme Court sustained a Minnesota law that permitted taxpayers to deduct school expenses from their taxes, including expenses incurred sending children to private schools. *Bowen v. Kendrick* (1988) permitted the federal government to give grants to religious organizations that urged teenagers to abstain from sexual relationships. Both laws provided benefits for both secular and religious choices. Chief Justice Rehnquist's majority opinion in *Bowen* declared, "Nothing in our previous cases prevents Congress from . . . recognizing the important part religion or religious organizations may play in resolving certain secular problems," most notably those problems associated with "adolescent sexual activity and adolescent pregnancy." The justices drew a line, however, when New York State drew a school district boundary for the purpose of creating a special program for Satmar Hasidic children with special educational needs. Justice Souter's opinion in *Board of Education of Kiryas Joel Village School v. Grumet* (1984) stated that the legislature's act was "substantially equivalent to defining a political subdivision and hence the qualification for its franchise by a religious test, resulting in a purposeful and forbidden fusion of governmental and religious functions."

Reagan conservatives were far less successful when seeking to restore voluntary school prayer. The Supreme Court in *Wallace v. Jaffree* (1985) declared unconstitutional an Alabama statute requiring a moment of silence for prayer or meditation. Justice Stevens's majority opinion maintained that state law could not privilege prayer over other activities, declaring, "The addition of 'or voluntary prayer' indicates that the State intended to characterize prayer as a favored practice. Such an endorsement is not consistent with the established principle that the government must pursue a course of complete neutrality toward religion."

Social conservatives were particularly disappointed when in *Lee v. Weisman* (1992) two of Ronald Reagan's judicial appointees, Justices Kennedy and O'Connor, joined with four other justices to form a majority supporting the ruling that public officials could not constitutionally authorize a nonsectarian prayer at a middle-school graduation ceremony. Kennedy's majority opinion maintained that the establishment clause forbids both direct and subtle coercion, and that middle-school-aged children were subtly coerced into participating in prayer exercises at their graduation. Although doctrinally ambiguous, *Lee v. Wiseman* practically ended the conservative quest to restore voluntary prayer to public schools. The early Rehnquist Court consistently rejected perceived attempts to bring religion more directly into the public school classroom. *Edwards v. Aguillard* (1987) declared unconstitutional a Louisiana law that required public schools to teach the theory of creation science along with the theory of evolution or refrain from teaching anything about human origins.

Conservatives gained a small victory when the Supreme Court in *Marsh v. Chambers* (1983) ruled that states could sponsor prayer before the opening of the state legislature. Chief Justice Burger's majority opinion maintained,

> In light of the unambiguous and unbroken history of more than 200 years, there can be no doubt that the practice of opening legislative sessions with prayer has become part of the fabric of our society. To invoke Divine guidance on a public body entrusted with making the laws is not, in these circumstances, an "establishment" of religion or a step toward establishment; it is simply a tolerable acknowledgment of beliefs widely held among the people of this country.

Ronald Reagan, Speech to National Religious Broadcasters (1984)

The Reagan coalition actively cultivated conservative Christians. The Republican Party offered religious conservatives such policy initiatives as bans on abortion and funding for parochial schools, as well as reassurance that the government shared their fundamental commitments. President Reagan consistently invoked God in his speeches and indicated that he supported conservative religious causes.

Conservative evangelicals, in return, supported the Reagan administration, voting in overwhelming numbers for Republican candidates during the 1980s and early 1990s. Religious broadcasters were particularly influential. Such evangelicals as Pat Robertson, Tammy Faye Bakker, and Jim Bakker reached millions of Americans through their broadcasts championing conservative religion, conservative lifestyles, and conservative politics.

The following speech highlights the close association between the Reagan Revolution and evangelical Christians. How does Reagan understand the fundamental commitments of religious Americans? Do these commitments describe all religious Americans or only a subset of religious Americans? Reagan has no difficulty talking about his belief in Jesus Christ. Is this constitutionally appropriate? On the one hand, presidents have as much right to practice, share, and promote their religious beliefs as other persons. On the other hand, the separation of church and state might suggest a constitutional ethic that discourages presidents from speaking of their personal faith so explicitly in public.

. . .

Let me set the record straight on your account: The spectacular growth of CBN [Christian Broadcasting Network] and PTL [Praise the Lord] and Trinity [Trinity Broadcasting Network], of organizations that produce religious programs for radio and television, not to mention the booming industry in Christian books, underlines a far-reaching change in our country.

Americans yearn to explore life's deepest truths. And to say their entertainment—their idea of entertainment is sex and violence and crime is an insult to their goodness and intelligence. We are people who believe love can triumph over hate, creativity over destruction, and hope over despair. And that's why so many millions hunger for your product—God's good news.

I was pleased last year to proclaim 1983 the Year of the Bible. But, you know, a group called the ACLU severely criticized me for doing that.

Well I wear their indictment like a badge of honor.

I believe I stand in pretty good company. Abraham Lincoln called the Bible "the best gift God has given to man." "But for it," he said, "we wouldn't know right from wrong." Like that image of George Washington kneeling in prayer in the snow at Valley Forge, Lincoln described a people who knew it was not enough to depend on their own courage and goodness; they must also look to God their Father and Preserver. And their faith to walk with Him and trust in His Word brought them the blessings of comfort, power, and peace that they sought.

. . .

My experience in this office I hold has only deepened a belief I've held for many years: Within the covers of that single Book are all the answers to all the problems that face us today, if we'd only read and believe.

. . .

God's most blessed gift to His family is the gift of life. He sent us the Prince of Peace as a babe in a manger. I've said that we must be cautious in claiming God is on our side. I think the real question we must answer is, are we on His side?

I know what I'm about to say now is controversial, but I have to say it. This nation cannot continue turning a blind eye and a deaf ear to the taking of some 4,000 unborn children's lives every day. That's one every 21 seconds. . . .

. . .

Let me assure you of something else: We want parents to know their children will not be victims of child pornography. I look forward to signing a new bill now awaiting final action in a conference committee that will tighten our laws against child pornography. And we're concerned about enforcement of all the Federal antiobscenity laws.

. . .

I know one thing I'm sure most of us agree on: God, source of all knowledge, should never have been expelled from our children's classrooms. The great majority of our people support voluntary prayer in schools.

We hear of [cases] where courts say it is dangerous to allow students to meet in Bible study or prayer clubs. And then there was the case of that kindergarten class that was reciting a verse. They said, "We thank you for the flowers so sweet. We thank you for the food we eat. We thank you for the birds that sing. We thank you, God, for everything." A court order of—a court of appeals ordered them to stop. They were supposedly violating the Constitution of the United States.

. . .

During the last decade, we've seen people's commitment to religious liberty expressed by the establishment of thousands of new religious schools. These schools were built by the sacrifices of parents determined to provide a quality education for their children in an environment that permits traditional values to flourish.

. . .

If the Lord—If the Lord is our light, our strength, and our salvation, whom shall we fear? Of whom shall we be afraid? No matter where we live, we have a promise that can make all the difference, a promise from Jesus to soothe our sorrows, heal our hearts, and drive away our fears. He promised there will never be a dark night that does not end. Our "weeping may endure for a night, but joy cometh in the morning." He promised if our hearts are true, His love will be as sure as sunlight. And, by dying for us, Jesus showed how far our love should be ready to go: all the way.

Mueller v. Allen, 463 U.S. 388 (1983)

Van D. Mueller was a taxpayer residing in Minnesota. He objected to a 1978 state law permitting Minnesota residents to deduct from their taxable income $500 for "tuition, textbooks and transportation" expenses incurred for each dependent attending kindergarten through the sixth grade and $700 for similar expenses incurred for each dependent attending seventh grade through twelfth grade. In 1981 Mueller sued Clyde Allen, the Minnesota Commissioner of the Department of Revenue. He claimed that by permitting parents to take a tax deduction for expenses incurred in sending their children to religious schools, Minnesota violated the establishment clause of the First Amendment (as incorporated by the due process clause of the Fourteenth Amendment). Both the local federal district court and the Court of Appeals for the Eighth Circuit sustained the Minnesota law. Mueller appealed to the Supreme Court of the United States.

The Supreme Court by a 5-4 vote sustained the Minnesota law. Justice Rehnquist's majority opinion emphasized that the establishment clause permitted state assistance to religion when the tax benefit was available to all parents and any benefit to religion resulted from private parental choices. Justice Rehnquist and Justice Brennan agree that Committee for Public Education v. Nyquist *(1973) is the relevant precedent. In* Nyquist, *the Supreme Court declared unconstitutional a New York law providing tuition reimbursement to parents who sent their children to private schools. How does Justice Rehnquist, who dissented in* Nyquist, *distinguish the Minnesota law at issue in* Mueller? *Is his distinction convincing? Should the Court have overruled* Nyquist?

Many conservative proponents of government support for religious education charge liberals with inconsistency for insisting that government must fund a woman's constitutionally protected choice to terminate a pregnancy but not a parent's constitutionally protected choice to send a child to a private religious school. Michael McConnell, a law professor, former judge, and former member of the Reagan Justice Department, declares,

> *These two issues, abortion funding and religious education funding, seem to pose the same question of constitutional law: when is the government's refusal to fund a constitutionally protected choice an impermissible "burden" on the exercise of the right? In both cases, the Constitution protects the right to decide for oneself—whether to have an abortion or to carry the child to term, and whether to obtain a religious or a secular education for one's children. And in both cases, the government funds one alternative and not the other: the Hyde Amendment to the Medicaid Act prohibits the use of federal funds to perform abortions, and a series of Supreme Court decisions . . . effectively prohibit the use of government funds for religious schools.*[16]

Is this analogy sound?

JUSTICE REHNQUIST delivered the opinion of the Court.

. . .

The general nature of our inquiry in this area has been guided, since the decision in *Lemon v. Kurtzman* (1971), by the "three-part" test laid down in that case:

"First, the statute must have a secular legislative purpose; second, its principal or primary effect must be one that neither advances nor inhibits religion . . . ; finally, the statute must not foster 'an excessive government entanglement with religion.'"

. . .

Little time need be spent on the question of whether the Minnesota tax deduction has a secular purpose. . . .

A State's decision to defray the cost of educational expenses incurred by parents—regardless of the type of schools their children attend—evidences a purpose that is both secular and understandable. An educated populace is essential to the political and economic health of any community, and a State's efforts to assist parents in meeting the rising cost of educational

16. Michael W. McConnell, "The Selective Funding Problem: Abortions and Religious Schools," *Harvard Law Review* 104 (1991): 989.

expenses plainly serves this secular purpose of ensuring that the State's citizenry is well educated. Similarly, Minnesota, like other States, could conclude that there is a strong public interest in assuring the continued financial health of private schools, both sectarian and nonsectarian. . . .

. . .

We turn therefore to the more difficult but related question whether the Minnesota statute has "the primary effect of advancing the sectarian aims of the nonpublic schools." . . .

. . . [T]he deduction is available for educational expenses incurred by all parents, including those whose children attend public schools and those whose children attend nonsectarian private schools or sectarian private schools. . . . "[T]he provision of benefits to so broad a spectrum of groups is an important index of secular effect."

. . . Unlike the assistance at issue in *Committee for Public Education v. Nyquist* (1973), [Minnesota] permits all parents—whether their children attend public school or private—to deduct their children's educational expenses. . . . [A] program . . . that neutrally provides state assistance to a broad spectrum of citizens is not readily subject to challenge under the Establishment Clause.

We also agree with the Court of Appeals that, by channeling whatever assistance it may provide to parochial schools through individual parents, Minnesota has reduced the Establishment Clause objections to which its action is subject. . . . Where, as here, aid to parochial schools is available only as a result of decisions of individual parents no "imprimatur of state approval" can be deemed to have been conferred on any particular religion, or on religion generally.

. . .

If parents of children in private schools choose to take especial advantage of the relief provided by [the tax deduction] it is no doubt due to the fact that they bear a particularly great financial burden in educating their children. More fundamentally, whatever unequal effect may be attributed to the statutory classification can fairly be regarded as a rough return for the benefits . . . provided to the State and all taxpayers by parents sending their children to parochial schools. In the light of all this, we believe it wiser to decline to engage in the type of empirical inquiry into those persons benefited by state law which petitioners urge.

. . .

Turning to the third part of the *Lemon* inquiry, we have no difficulty in concluding that the Minnesota statute does not "excessively entangle" the State in religion. . . .

JUSTICE MARSHALL, with whom JUSTICE BRENNAN, JUSTICE BLACKMUN, and JUSTICE STEVENS join, dissenting.

The Establishment Clause of the First Amendment prohibits a State from subsidizing religious education, whether it does so directly or indirectly. In my view, this principle of neutrality forbids . . . the tax deduction at issue here, which subsidizes tuition payments to sectarian schools. I also believe that the Establishment Clause prohibits the tax deductions that Minnesota authorizes for the cost of books and other instructional materials used for sectarian purposes.

. . .

. . . [D]irect government subsidization of parochial school tuition is impermissible because "the effect of the aid is unmistakably to provide desired financial support for nonpublic, sectarian institutions." "[A]id to the educational function of [parochial] schools . . . necessarily results in aid to the sectarian school enterprise as a whole" because "[t]he very purpose of many of those schools is to provide an integrated secular and religious education." . . . While "services such as police and fire protection, sewage disposal, highways, and sidewalks," may be provided to parochial schools in common with other institutions, because this type of assistance is clearly "'marked off from the religious function'" of those schools, unrestricted financial assistance, such as grants for the maintenance and construction of parochial schools, may not be provided. "In the absence of an effective means of guaranteeing that the state aid derived from public funds will be used exclusively for secular, neutral, and nonideological purposes, it is clear from our cases that direct aid in whatever form is invalid."

Indirect assistance in the form of financial aid to parents for tuition payments is similarly impermissible because it is not "subject to . . . restrictions" which "'guarantee the separation between secular and religious educational functions and . . . ensure that State financial aid supports only the former.'" By ensuring that parents will be reimbursed for tuition payments they make, the Minnesota statute requires that taxpayers in general pay for the cost of parochial education and extends a financial "incentive to parents to send their children to sectarian schools." . . .

That parents receive a reduction of their tax liability, rather than a direct reimbursement, is of no greater significance here than it was in *Nyquist*. . . . What is of controlling significance is not the form but the "substantive impact" of the financial aid. "[I]nsofar as such benefits render assistance to parents who send their children to sectarian schools, their purpose and inevitable effect are to aid and advance those religious institutions."

. . .

That the Minnesota statute makes some small benefit available to all parents cannot alter the fact that the most substantial benefit provided by the statute is available only to those parents who send their children to schools that charge tuition. It is simply undeniable that the single largest expense that may be deducted under the Minnesota statute is tuition. The statute is little more than a subsidy of tuition masquerading as a subsidy of general educational expenses. The other deductible expenses are de minimis in comparison to tuition expenses.

. . . In this case, it is undisputed that well over 90% of the children attending tuition-charging schools in Minnesota are enrolled in sectarian schools. History and experience likewise instruct us that any generally available financial assistance for elementary and secondary school tuition expenses mainly will further religious education because the majority of the schools which charge tuition are sectarian. Because Minnesota, like every other State, is committed to providing free public education, tax assistance for tuition payments inevitably redounds to the benefit of nonpublic, sectarian schools and parents who send their children to those schools.

. . .

For the first time, the Court has upheld financial support for religious schools without any reason at all to assume that the support will be restricted to the secular functions of those schools and will not be used to support religious instruction. This result is flatly at odds with the fundamental principle that a State may provide no financial support whatsoever to promote religion. . . .

Edwards v. Aguillard, 482 U.S. 578 (1987)

Don Aguillard was the parent of a child who attended public school in Louisiana. In 1982 the Louisiana legislature passed the Balanced Treatment for Creation-Science and Evolution-Science in Public-School Instruction Act, which required public school teachers to either give equal time to evolution and creation science or teach neither. Aguillard and others filed a lawsuit against Edwin Edwards, the governor of Louisiana, asking the court to issue an injunction against implementation of the Balanced Treatment Act on the ground that the law violated the establishment clause of the First Amendment as incorporated by the due process clause of the Fourteenth Amendment. Both the district court and the Court of Appeals for the Fifth Circuit agreed that the Balanced Treatment Act was unconstitutional. Louisiana appealed to the Supreme Court of the United States.

The Supreme Court by a 7-2 vote ruled that the Balanced Treatment Act violated the establishment clause. Justice Brennan's majority opinion insisted that the measure had no secular purpose and that the primary effect of the Balanced Treatment Act was to advance religion. Justice Scalia's dissent insists that the law was designed to prevent indoctrination. Why does Justice Brennan reject the evidence on which Scalia relies to reach this conclusion? Is Brennan able to identify legislative motivations, or is Scalia right that courts should not make this attempt? On what basis should a nonscientist determine whether creation science is a legitimate theory or a mask for introducing religious beliefs into a classroom? Will clever religious majorities always be able to find a pretense for imposing their religious views on the public if judges do not scrutinize allegedly sectarian lawmaking? If Scalia is right, would Jewish legislators be able to ban pork and cheeseburgers from school cafeterias on the basis of one study in an obscure journal that concludes that nonkosher food is not healthy?

JUSTICE BRENNAN delivered the opinion of the Court

. . .

. . . The Court has applied a three-pronged test to determine whether legislation comports with the Establishment Clause. First, the legislature must have adopted the law with a secular purpose. Second, the statute's principal or primary effect must be one that neither advances nor inhibits religion. Third, the statute must not result in an excessive entanglement of government with religion. *Lemon v. Kurtzman* (1971). . . .

. . .

Lemon's first prong focuses on the purpose that animated adoption of the Act. A governmental intention to promote religion is clear when the State enacts a law to serve a religious purpose. . . . In this case, appellants have identified no clear secular purpose for the Louisiana Act.

True, the Act's stated purpose is to protect academic freedom. . . . The Court of Appeals, however, correctly concluded that the Act was not designed to further that goal. . . . Even if "academic freedom" is read to mean "teaching all of the evidence" with respect to the origin of human beings, the Act does not further this purpose. The goal of providing a more comprehensive science curriculum is not furthered either by outlawing the teaching of evolution or by requiring the teaching of creation science.

. . .

It is clear from the legislative history that the purpose of the legislative sponsor, Senator Bill Keith, was to narrow the science curriculum. During the legislative hearings, Senator Keith stated: "My preference would be that neither [creationism nor evolution] be taught." Such a ban on teaching does not promote—indeed, it undermines—the provision of a comprehensive scientific education.

It is equally clear that requiring schools to teach creation science with evolution does not advance academic freedom. The Act does not grant teachers a flexibility that they did not already possess to supplant the present science curriculum with the presentation of theories, besides evolution, about the origin of life. . . .

Furthermore, the goal of basic "fairness" is hardly furthered by the Act's discriminatory preference for the teaching of creation science and against the teaching of evolution. While requiring that curriculum guides be developed for creation science, the Act says nothing of comparable guides for evolution. . . . The Act forbids school boards to discriminate against anyone who "chooses to be a creation-scientist" or to teach "creationism," but fails to protect those who choose to teach evolution or any other noncreation science theory, or who refuse to teach creation science.

. . .

. . . [W]e need not be blind in this case to the legislature's preeminent religious purpose in enacting this statute. There is a historic and contemporaneous link between the teachings of certain religious denominations and the teaching of evolution. . . .

. . .

. . . The legislative history documents that the Act's primary purpose was to change the science curriculum of public schools in order to provide persuasive advantage to a particular religious doctrine that rejects the factual basis of evolution in its entirety. The sponsor of the Creationism Act, Senator Keith, explained during the legislative hearings that his disdain for the theory of evolution resulted from the support that evolution supplied to views contrary to his own religious beliefs. . . .

In this case, the purpose of the Creationism Act was to restructure the science curriculum to conform with a particular religious viewpoint. Out of many possible science subjects taught in the public schools, the legislature chose to affect the teaching of the one scientific theory that historically has been opposed by certain religious sects. . . .

. . .

The Louisiana Creationism Act advances a religious doctrine by requiring either the banishment of the theory of evolution from public school classrooms or the presentation of a religious viewpoint that rejects evolution in its entirety. The Act violates the Establishment Clause of the First Amendment because it seeks to employ the symbolic and financial support of government to achieve a religious purpose. . . .

JUSTICE POWELL, with whom JUSTICE O'CONNOR joins, concurring.

. . .

. . . "Academic freedom" does not encompass the right of a legislature to structure the public school curriculum in order to advance a particular religious belief. . . .

. . .

Here, it is clear that religious belief is the Balanced Treatment Act's "reason for existence." The tenets of creation science parallel the Genesis story of creation, and this is a religious belief. "[N]o legislative recitation of a supposed secular purpose can blind us to that fact." . . .

That the statute is limited to the scientific evidences supporting [creationism] . . . does not render its purpose secular. In reaching its conclusion that the Act is unconstitutional, the Court of Appeals "[did] not deny that the underpinnings of creationism may be supported by scientific evidence." And there is no need to do so. Whatever the academic merit of particular subjects or theories, the Establishment Clause limits the discretion of state officials to pick and choose among them for the purpose of promoting a particular religious belief. The language of the statute and its legislative history convince me that the Louisiana Legislature exercised its discretion for this purpose in this case.

. . .

JUSTICE WHITE, concurring in the judgment. . . .

JUSTICE SCALIA, with whom THE CHIEF JUSTICE joins, dissenting.

. . .

. . . Our cases in no way imply that the Establishment Clause forbids legislators merely to act upon their religious convictions. We surely would not strike down a law providing money to feed the hungry or shelter the homeless if it could be demonstrated that, but for the religious beliefs of the legislators, the funds would not have been approved. Also, political activism by the religiously motivated is part of our heritage. Notwithstanding the majority's implication to the contrary, we do not presume that the sole purpose of a law is to advance religion merely because it was supported strongly by organized religions or by adherents of particular faiths. . . .

Similarly, we will not presume that a law's purpose is to advance religion merely because it "'happens to coincide or harmonize with the tenets of some or all religions.'" Thus, the fact that creation science coincides with the beliefs of certain religions, a fact upon which the majority relies heavily, does not itself justify invalidation of the Act.

. . .

. . . Had the Court devoted to this central question of the meaning of the legislatively expressed purpose a small fraction of the research into legislative history that produced its quotations of religiously motivated statements by individual legislators, it would have discerned quite readily what "academic freedom" meant: students' freedom from indoctrination. The legislature wanted to ensure that students would be free to decide for themselves how life began, based upon a fair and balanced presentation of the scientific evidence—that is, to protect "the right of each [student] voluntarily to determine what to believe (and what not to believe) free of any coercive pressures from the State." The legislature did not care whether the topic of origins was taught; it simply wished to ensure that when the topic was taught, students would receive "'all of the evidence.'"

. . .

. . . Living up to its title of "Balanced Treatment for Creation-Science and Evolution-Science Act," it treats the teaching of creation the same way. It does not mandate instruction in creation science, forbids teachers to present creation science "as proven scientific fact," and bans the teaching of creation science unless the theory is (to use the Court's terminology) "discredit[ed] '. . . at every turn'" with the teaching of evolution.

. . . The Louisiana legislators had been told repeatedly that creation scientists were scorned by most educators and scientists, who themselves had an almost religious faith in evolution. It is hardly surprising, then, that in seeking to achieve a balanced, "non-indoctrinating" curriculum, the legislators protected from discrimination only those teachers whom they thought were suffering from discrimination. . . . The two provisions respecting the development of curriculum guides are also consistent with "academic freedom" as the Louisiana Legislature understood the term. Witnesses had informed the legislators that, because of the hostility of most scientists and educators to creation science, the topic had been censored from or badly misrepresented in elementary and secondary school texts. In light of the unavailability of works on creation science suitable for classroom use . . . and the existence of ample materials on evolution, it was entirely reasonable for the legislature to conclude that science teachers attempting to implement the Act would need a curriculum guide on creation science, but not on evolution, and that those charged with developing the guide would need an easily accessible group of creation scientists. Thus, the provisions of the Act of so much concern to the Court support the conclusion that the legislature acted to advance "academic freedom."

. . .

I have to this point assumed the validity of the *Lemon* "purpose" test. In fact, . . . it is "a constitutional theory [that] has no basis in the history of the amendment it seeks to interpret, is difficult to apply and yields unprincipled results. . . ."

. . .

. . . [W]hile it is possible to discern the objective "purpose" of a statute (i.e., the public good at which its provisions appear to be directed), or even the formal motivation for a statute where that is explicitly set forth (as it was, to no avail, here), discerning the subjective motivation of those enacting the statute is, to be honest, almost always an impossible task. The number of possible motivations, to begin with, is not binary, or indeed even finite. In the present case, for example, a particular legislator need not have voted for the Act either because he wanted to foster religion or because he wanted to improve education. He may have thought the bill would provide jobs for his district, or may have wanted to make amends with a faction of his party he had alienated on another vote, or he may have been a close friend of the bill's sponsor, or he may have been repaying a favor he owed the majority leader, or he may have hoped the Governor would appreciate his vote and make a fundraising appearance for him, or he may have been pressured to vote for a bill he disliked by a wealthy contributor or by a flood of constituent mail, or he may have been seeking favorable publicity, or he may have been reluctant to hurt the feelings of a loyal staff member who worked on the bill, or he may have been settling an old score with a legislator who opposed the bill, or he may have been mad at his wife who opposed the bill, or he may have been intoxicated and utterly unmotivated when the vote was called, or he may have accidentally voted "yes" instead of "no," or, of course, he may have had (and very likely did have) a combination of some of the above and many other motivations. To look for the sole purpose of even a single legislator is probably to look for something that does not exist.

. . .

Having achieved, through these simple means, an assessment of what individual legislators intended, we must still confront the question (yet to be addressed in any of our cases) how many of them must have the invalidating intent. If a state senate approves a bill by vote of 26 to 25, and only one of the 26 intended solely to advance religion, is the law unconstitutional? What if 13 of the 26 had that intent? What if 3 of the 26 had the impermissible intent, but 3 of the 25 voting against the bill were motivated by religious hostility or were simply attempting to "balance" the votes of their impermissibly motivated colleagues? Or is it possible that the intent of the bill's sponsor is alone enough to invalidate it—on a theory, perhaps, that even though everyone else's intent was pure, what they produced was the fruit of a forbidden tree?

. . .

Given the many hazards involved in assessing the subjective intent of governmental decisionmakers, the first prong of *Lemon* is defensible, I think, only if the text of the Establishment Clause demands it. That is surely not the case. The Clause states that "Congress shall make no law respecting an establishment of religion." . . . It is . . . far from an inevitable reading of the Establishment Clause that it forbids all governmental action intended to advance religion; and if not inevitable, any reading with such untoward consequences must be wrong. . . .

Lee v. Weisman, 505 U.S. 577 (1992)

Deborah Weisman was a student at Nathan Bishop Middle School in Providence, Rhode Island. The principal at Nathan Bishop regularly asked a member of the Providence clergy to offer an invocation and benediction at graduation. The Weisman family insisted that the practice was unconstitutional, but to no avail. In June 1989 the principal, Robert Lee, asked a local rabbi to offer prayers, and that offer was accepted. The Weismans filed a lawsuit against Lee, claiming that prayer at graduation violated the First and Fourteenth Amendments. The local district court refused to issue a temporary injunction barring the prayer exercise but later issued an injunction prohibiting similar prayer exercises during future graduations. The United States Court of Appeals for the First Circuit affirmed that decision. Lee appealed to the Supreme Court of the United States.

The Supreme Court by a 5-4 vote ruled that prayer exercises during middle-school graduation ceremonies violated the establishment clause. Justice Kennedy's majority opinion maintained that the constitutional violation occurred because middle-school students were "indirectly" coerced by the state into participating in a religious exercise. What was that coercion? Why does Justice Scalia claim that no coercion took place? Does the establishment clause require coercion, or is state sponsorship of a religious exercise sufficient? What might explain why Justices O'Connor and Kennedy, Reagan judicial appointees, were more willing to support funding for religious institutions than voluntary school prayer?

JUSTICE KENNEDY delivered the opinion of the Court.

. . .

These dominant facts mark and control the confines of our decision: State officials direct the performance of a formal religious exercise at promotional and graduation ceremonies for secondary schools. Even for those students who object to the religious exercise, their attendance and participation in the state-sponsored religious activity are, in a fair and real sense, obligatory, though the school district does not require attendance as a condition for receipt of the diploma.

. . .

. . . It is beyond dispute that, at a minimum, the Constitution guarantees that government may not coerce anyone to support or participate in religion or its exercise, or otherwise act in a way which "establishes a [state] religion or religious faith, or tends to do so." . . . The State's involvement in the school prayers challenged today violates these central principles.

That involvement is as troubling as it is undenied. A school official, the principal, decided that an invocation and a benediction should be given; this is a choice attributable to the State, and, from a constitutional perspective, it is as if a state statute decreed that the prayers must occur. The principal chose the religious participant, here a rabbi, and that choice is also attributable to the State. The reason for the choice of a rabbi is not disclosed by the record, but the potential for divisiveness over the choice of a particular member of the clergy to conduct the ceremony is apparent.

. . .

The State's role did not end with the decision to include a prayer and with the choice of clergyman. Principal Lee provided Rabbi Gutterman with a copy of the "Guidelines for Civic Occasions" and advised him that his prayers should be nonsectarian. Through these means, the principal directed and controlled the content of the prayers. . . . It is a cornerstone principle of our Establishment Clause jurisprudence that it is no part of the business of government to compose official prayers for any group of the American people to recite as a part of a religious program carried on by government, *Engel v. Vitale* (1962), and that is what the school officials attempted to do.

. . .

Our decision . . . in *Engel v. Vitale* . . . recognize[d], among other things, that prayer exercises in public schools carry a particular risk of indirect coercion. . . . What to most believers may seem nothing more than a reasonable request that the nonbeliever respect their religious practices, in a school context may appear to the nonbeliever or dissenter to be an attempt to employ the machinery of the State to enforce a religious orthodoxy.

We need not look beyond the circumstances of this case to see the phenomenon at work. The undeniable fact is that the school district's supervision and control of a high school graduation ceremony places public pressure, as well as peer pressure, on attending students to stand as a group or, at least, maintain respectful silence during the invocation and benediction. This pressure, though subtle and indirect, can be as real as any overt compulsion. . . . [F]or the dissenter of high school age, who has a reasonable perception that she is being forced by the State to pray in a manner her conscience will not allow, the injury is no less real. There can be no doubt that for many, if not most, of the students at the graduation, the act of standing or remaining silent was an expression of participation in the rabbi's prayer. That was the very point of the religious exercise. It is of little comfort to a dissenter, then, to be told that, for her, the act of standing or remaining in silence signifies mere respect, rather than participation. What matters is that, given our social conventions, a reasonable dissenter in this milieu could believe that the group exercise signified her own participation or approval of it.

Finding no violation under these circumstances would place objectors in the dilemma of participating, with all that implies, or protesting. We do not address whether that choice is acceptable if the affected citizens are mature adults, but we think the State may not, consistent with the Establishment Clause, place primary and secondary school children in this position. Research in psychology supports the common assumption that adolescents are often susceptible to pressure from their peers towards conformity, and that the influence is strongest in matters of social convention. . . .

. . .

. . . Law reaches past formalism. And to say a teenage student has a real choice not to attend her high school graduation is formalistic in the extreme. True, Deborah could elect not to attend commencement without renouncing her diploma; but we shall not allow the case to turn on this point. Everyone knows that, in our society and in our culture, high school graduation is one of life's most significant occasions. . . . Graduation is a time for family and those closest to the student to celebrate success and express mutual wishes of gratitude and respect, all to the end of impressing upon the young person the role that it is his or her right and duty to assume in the community and all of its diverse parts.

. . .

JUSTICE BLACKMUN, with whom JUSTICE STEVENS and JUSTICE O'CONNOR join, concurring.

. . .

The mixing of government and religion can be a threat to free government, even if no one is forced to participate. When the government puts its imprimatur on a particular religion, it conveys a message of exclusion to all those who do not adhere to the favored beliefs. A government cannot be premised on the belief that all persons are created equal when it asserts that God prefers some. . . .

. . .

JUSTICE SOUTER, with whom JUSTICE STEVENS and JUSTICE O'CONNOR join, concurring.

. . .

. . . [T]he Establishment Clause forbids state-sponsored prayers in public school settings no matter how nondenominational the prayers may be. In barring the State from sponsoring generically theistic prayers where it could not sponsor sectarian ones, we hold true to a line of precedent from which there is no adequate historical case to depart.

Since *Everson v. Board of Education* (1947), we have consistently held the Clause applicable no less to governmental acts favoring religion generally than to acts favoring one religion over others. . . .

. . .

. . . [T]he Framers meant the Establishment Clause's prohibition to encompass nonpreferential aid to religion. . . . The House . . . persuad[ed] the Senate to accept this as the final text of the Religion Clauses: "Congress shall make no law respecting an establishment of religion, or prohibiting the free exercise thereof." What is remarkable is that, unlike the earliest House drafts or the final Senate proposal, the prevailing language is not limited to laws respecting an establishment of "a religion," "a national religion," "one religious sect," or specific "articles of faith." The Framers repeatedly considered and deliberately rejected such narrow language, and instead extended their prohibition to state support for "religion" in general.

Implicit in their choice is the distinction between preferential and nonpreferential establishments, which the weight of evidence suggests the Framers appreciated. . . .

While these considerations are, for me, sufficient to reject the nonpreferentialist position, one further concern animates my judgment. In many contexts, including this one, nonpreferentialism requires some distinction between "sectarian" religious practices and those that would be, by some measure, ecumenical enough to pass Establishment Clause muster. Simply by requiring the enquiry, nonpreferentialists invite the courts to engage in comparative theology. I can hardly imagine a subject less amenable to the competence of the federal judiciary, or more deliberately to be avoided where possible.

. . .

Petitioners contend that, because the early Presidents included religious messages in their inaugural and Thanksgiving Day addresses, the Framers could not have meant the Establishment Clause to forbid noncoercive state endorsement of religion. The argument ignores the fact, however, that Americans today find such proclamations less controversial than did the founding generation, whose published thoughts on the matter belie petitioners' claim. President Jefferson, for example, steadfastly refused to issue Thanksgiving proclamations of any kind, in part because he thought they violated the Religion Clauses. . . .

During his first three years in office, James Madison also refused to call for days of thanksgiving and prayer, though later, amid the political turmoil of the War of 1812, he did so on four separate occasions. . . .

To be sure, the leaders of the young Republic engaged in some of the practices that separationists like Jefferson and Madison criticized. The First Congress did hire institutional chaplains, . . . and Presidents Washington and Adams unapologetically marked days of "'public thanksgiving and prayer.'" Yet in the face of the separationist dissent, those practices prove, at best, that the Framers simply did not share a common understanding of the Establishment Clause, and, at worst, that they, like other politicians, could raise constitutional ideals one day and turn their backs on them the next. . . .

. . .

JUSTICE SCALIA, with whom THE CHIEF JUSTICE, JUSTICE WHITE, and JUSTICE THOMAS join, dissenting.

. . .

. . . The history and tradition of our Nation are replete with public ceremonies featuring prayers of thanksgiving and petition. . . .

. . . The Declaration of Independence, the document marking our birth as a separate people, "appeal[ed] to the Supreme Judge of the world for the rectitude of our intentions" and avowed "a firm reliance on the protection of divine Providence." In his first inaugural address, after swearing his oath of office on a Bible, George Washington deliberately made a prayer a part of his first official act as President. . . .

. . .

The other two branches of the Federal Government also have a long-established practice of prayer at public events. . . . Congressional sessions have opened with a chaplain's prayer ever since the First Congress. . . .

In addition to this general tradition of prayer at public ceremonies, there exists a more specific tradition of invocations and benedictions at public school graduation exercises. By one account, the first public high school graduation ceremony took place in Connecticut in July, 1868—the very month, as it happens, that the Fourteenth Amendment (the vehicle by which the Establishment Clause has been applied against the States) was ratified—when "15 seniors from the Norwich Free Academy marched in their best Sunday suits and dresses into a church hall and waited through majestic music and long prayers." . . .

. . .

. . . [T]he Court's notion that a student who simply sits in "respectful silence" during the invocation and benediction (when all others are standing) has somehow joined—or would somehow be perceived as having joined—in the prayers is nothing short of ludicrous. . . . [S]urely "our social conventions" have not coarsened to the point that anyone who does not stand on his chair and shout obscenities can reasonably be deemed to have assented to everything said in his presence. . . .

. . . [I]f it is a permissible inference that one who is standing is doing so simply out of respect for the prayers of others that are in progress, then how can it possibly be said that a "reasonable dissenter . . . could believe that the group exercise signified her own participation or approval"? Quite obviously, it cannot. I may add, moreover, that maintaining respect for the religious observances of others is a fundamental civic virtue that government (including the public schools) can and should cultivate—so that, even if it were the case that the displaying of such respect might be mistaken for taking part in the prayer, I would deny that the dissenter's interest in avoiding even the false appearance of participation constitutionally trumps the government's interest in fostering respect for religion generally.

. . .

The other "dominant fac[t]" identified by the Court is that "[s]tate officials direct the performance of a formal religious exercise" at school graduation ceremonies. . . . All the record shows is that principals of the Providence public schools, acting within their delegated authority, have invited clergy to deliver invocations and benedictions at graduations; and that Principal Lee invited Rabbi Gutterman, provided him a two-page pamphlet, prepared by the National Conference of Christians and Jews, giving general advice on inclusive prayer for civic occasions, and advised him that his prayers at graduation should be nonsectarian. How these facts can fairly be transformed into the charges that Principal Lee "directed and controlled the content of [Rabbi Gutterman's] prayer," . . . that school officials "monitor prayer," . . . and attempted to "'compose official prayers,'" . . . and that the "government involvement with religious activity in this case is pervasive," . . . is difficult to fathom. . . .

. . .

The coercion that was a hallmark of historical establishments of religion was coercion of religious orthodoxy and of financial support by force of law and threat of penalty. Typically, attendance at the state church was required; only clergy of the official church could lawfully perform sacraments; and dissenters, if tolerated, faced an array of civil disabilities. . . .

. . .

I must add one final observation: the Founders of our Republic knew the fearsome potential of sectarian religious belief to generate civil dissension and civil strife. And they also knew that nothing, absolutely nothing, is so inclined to foster among religious believers of various faiths a toleration—no, an affection—for one another than voluntarily joining in prayer together, to the God whom they all worship and seek. Needless to say, no one should be compelled to do that, but it is a shame to deprive our public culture of the opportunity, and indeed the encouragement, for people to do it voluntarily. The Baptist or Catholic who heard and joined in the simple and inspiring prayers of Rabbi Gutterman on this official and patriotic occasion was inoculated from religious bigotry and prejudice in a manner that cannot be replicated. To deprive our society of that important unifying mechanism in order to spare the nonbeliever what seems to me the minimal inconvenience of standing, or even sitting in respectful nonparticipation, is as senseless in policy as it is unsupported in law.

Free Exercise

The main conflicts over free exercise rights were waged between elected officials and judges. Congress passed legislation reversing two important Supreme Court decisions. After the Supreme Court in *Goldman v. Weinberger* (1986) ruled that an air force chaplain had no constitutional right to wear a yarmulke, bipartisan majorities in Congress passed legislation permitting military chaplains to dress as their religion commanded. After the Supreme Court in *Employment Division v. Smith* (1990) ruled that the free exercise clause did not grant religious believers exemptions from generally applicable laws that burdened their religious practices, bipartisan majorities in Congress passed the Religious Freedom Restoration Act. That measure required states and the federal government to grant religious believers exemptions unless there was a compelling interest not to do so. Liberals in Congress and the courts both tended to support free exercise rights. Many conservatives in Congress, however, supported the compelling state interest test to determine free exercise rights that the most conservative justices on the Supreme Court rejected.

Conservative elected officials and political activists interpreted free exercise rights broadly. As conservative Christians played greater roles in Republican politics, Republican politicians became more sensitive to evangelicals who sought exemptions from more liberal state rules, particularly state policies concerning public education. The Reagan Justice Department endorsed the liberal position in the 1960s that elected officials must provide accommodation for religious believers "unless the government could show that it was pursuing a compelling interest in the least restrictive manner possible." "By following this direction," the Justice Department continued, "the Court would acknowledge both the role of religion as a mediating institution in society and the potential threat that the expansion of government poses to that role. Moving in this direction would reflect the view that religion has a special place, which government must recognize, in our constitutional structure."[17]

Reagan administration officials became embroiled in controversy when supporting Bob Jones University. The Internal Revenue Service refused to grant that institution tax-exempt status because university rules maintained that God forbade interracial dating and marriage. The Supreme Court in *Bob Jones University v. United States* (1983) disagreed with both the administration and the university. Chief Justice Burger's majority opinion asserted, "The Government has a fundamental, overriding interest in eradicating racial discrimination in education" that "substantially outweighs whatever burden denial of tax benefits places on petitioners' exercise of their religious beliefs."

Bob Jones reflected both judicial commitments to racial equality and the traditional conservative judicial hostility to broad interpretations of the free exercise clause. The more conservative justices on the Warren Court dissented from the decision in *Sherbert v. Verner* (1963) that required states to provide a compelling reason for not exempting religious believers from state laws that burdened their religious practice. As Richard Nixon and Ronald Reagan increased the number of conservatives on the federal bench, the Supreme Court supported fewer and fewer free exercise claims. *United States v. Lee* (1982) unanimously rejected the free exercise claim of an Amish employer who refused to pay Social Security taxes. Chief Justice Burger believed that the compelling state interest test announced in *Sherbert v. Verner* (1963) was satisfied because "it would be difficult to accommodate the comprehensive social security system with myriad exceptions flowing from a wide variety of religious beliefs." *Goldman v. Weinberger* by a 5-4 vote ruled that the compelling interest test should not be applied when determining whether military uniform rules should be applied to a Jewish military chaplain who wished to wear a yarmulke. Given the military's need to "foster instinctive obedience, unity, commitment, and esprit de corps," Justice Rehnquist declared, "our review of military regulations challenged on First Amendment grounds is far more deferential than constitutional review of similar laws or regulations designed for civil society." Conservatives on the lower court were unsympathetic to free exercise claims raised by conservative Christians. In *Mozert v. Hawkins County Board of Education* (1987) the Sixth Circuit unanimously rejected a lawsuit by evangelical parents who wished to have their children exempted from their public school's required readings that violated their religious beliefs. Judge Danny Boggs, a recent Reagan judicial appointee, asserted, "School boards may set curricula bounded only by the Establishment Clause."[18] In 1990 the more conservative justices on the Rehnquist Court, joined by Justice Stevens, scuttled the compelling interest test altogether. Justice Scalia's majority opinion in *Employment Division v. Smith* stated, "The right of free exercise does not relieve an individual of the obligation to comply

17. Office of Legal Policy, *The Constitution in the Year 2000*, 87.

18. *Mozert v. Hawkins County Board of Education*, 827 F.2d 1058 (6th Cir. 1987).

with a valid and neutral law of general applicability on the ground that the law proscribes (or prescribes) conduct that his religion prescribes (or proscribes)."

The Rehnquist Court was more supportive of free exercise claims when they perceived that state laws were directed against a religion or a religious practice. The justices in *Church of the Babalu Aye v. Hialeah* (1993) unanimously agreed that the city of Hialeah could not pass ordinances prohibiting animal sacrifice when the rules in question were clearly gerrymandered to outlaw only the religious practices of the local Santerian sect. Justice Kennedy's opinion for the Court maintained that government could not discriminate "against some or all religious beliefs or regulate . . . or prohibit . . . conduct because it is undertaken for religious reasons."

Employment Division v. Smith, 494 U.S. 872 (1990)

Alfred Smith and Galen Black were fired from their jobs as drug counselors after they used peyote for sacramental purposes during a Native American religious ceremony. Their firing was consistent with Oregon law, which forbade the knowing or intentional possession of a "controlled substance," classified peyote as a controlled substance, and denied benefits to persons discharged for work-related reasons. Smith and Black sued Oregon, claiming that their firing and subsequent denial of unemployment violated their free exercise rights. Both the Oregon Court of Appeals and the Oregon Supreme Court ruled that Smith and Black had a constitutional right to an exemption from the state ban on peyote. Oregon appealed to the Supreme Court of the United States.

The Supreme Court by a 6-3 vote ruled that Oregon had not violated constitutional rights. Justice Scalia and four other justices maintained that religious believers had no free exercise right to exemptions from generally applicable state laws. Justice O'Connor insisted that religious believers ordinarily had rights to exemptions, but that Oregon had a compelling reason not to exempt Smith and Black from state drug laws. All justices in Smith *claimed to be following precedent, but each opinion interprets precedent differently. On what grounds does Justice Scalia distinguish* Sherbert v. Verner *(1963) and* Wisconsin v. Yoder *(1972) from* Smith*? Is his distinction convincing? Does Justice O'Connor offer a convincing interpretation of the line of cases between* Yoder *and* Smith *in which the Court almost*

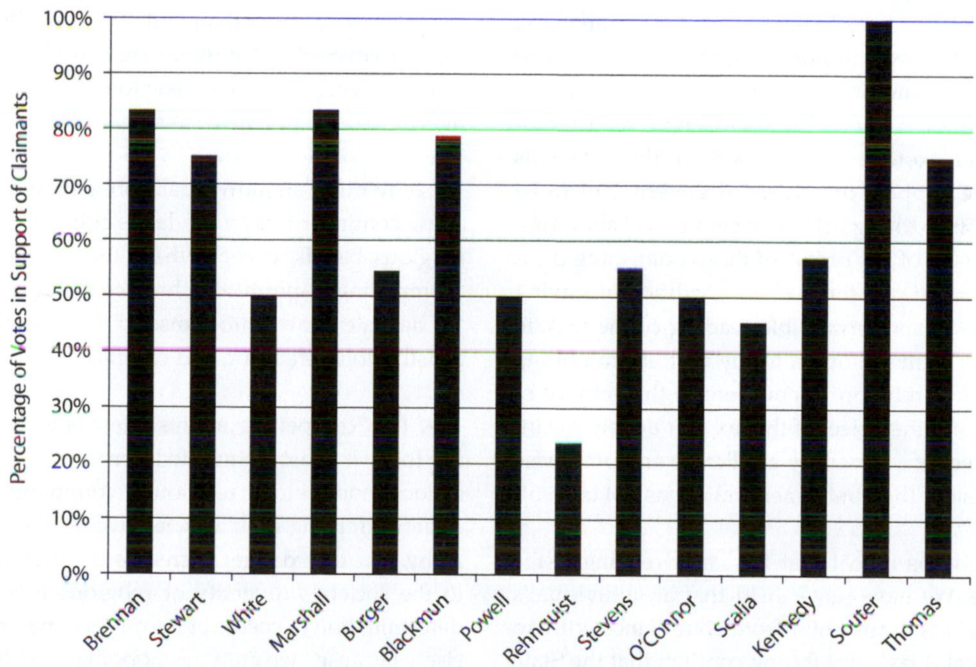

Figure 10-2 Individual Justice Support for Claimants in Religious Liberty Cases on Burger and Rehnquist Courts

Notes: Justices listed in order of appointment. Minimum of three votes in religious free exercise cases during chief justice tenure of Warren Burger and William Rehnquist.

always rejected free exercise claims? Is Justice O'Connor correct when she insists that Oregon law has a compelling interest in not exempting religious believers from drug laws? Justices Scalia and O'Connor dispute the extent to which minority religions are capable of politically defending their rights and interests. Based on what you have read and your experience, who has the better argument?

JUSTICE SCALIA delivered the opinion of the Court.

. . .

. . . The free exercise of religion means, first and foremost, the right to believe and profess whatever religious doctrine one desires. . . . The government may not compel affirmation of religious belief, . . . punish the expression of religious doctrines it believes to be false, . . . impose special disabilities on the basis of religious views or religious status, . . . or lend its power to one or the other side in controversies over religious authority or dogma. . . .

. . .

Respondents in the present case, however, seek to carry the meaning of "prohibiting the free exercise [of religion]" one large step further. . . . They assert . . . that "prohibiting the free exercise [of religion]" includes requiring any individual to observe a generally applicable law that requires (or forbids) the performance of an act that his religious belief forbids (or requires). As a textual matter, we do not think the words must be given that meaning. It is no more necessary to regard the collection of a general tax, for example, as "prohibiting the free exercise [of religion]" by those citizens who believe support of organized government to be sinful than it is to regard the same tax as "abridging the freedom . . . of the press" of those publishing companies that must pay the tax as a condition of staying in business. It is a permissible reading of the text, in the one case as in the other, to say that, if prohibiting the exercise of religion (or burdening the activity of printing) is not the object of the tax, but merely the incidental effect of a generally applicable and otherwise valid provision, the First Amendment has not been offended. . . .

Our decisions reveal that the latter reading is the correct one. We have never held that an individual's religious beliefs excuse him from compliance with an otherwise valid law prohibiting conduct that the State is free to regulate. On the contrary, the record of more than a century of our free exercise jurisprudence contradicts that proposition. . . . We first had occasion to assert that principle in *Reynolds v. United States* (1878), . . . where we rejected the claim that criminal laws against polygamy could not be constitutionally applied to those whose religion commanded the practice. . . .

. . .

The only decisions in which we have held that the First Amendment bars application of a neutral, generally applicable law to religiously motivated action have involved not the Free Exercise Clause alone, but the Free Exercise Clause in conjunction with other constitutional protections, such as . . . the right of parents . . . to direct the education of their children, see *Wisconsin v. Yoder* (1972). . . .

. . .

Respondents argue that, even though exemption from generally applicable criminal laws need not automatically be extended to religiously motivated actors, at least the claim for a religious exemption must be evaluated under the balancing test set forth in *Sherbert v. Verner* (1963). . . . Under the *Sherbert* test, governmental actions that substantially burden a religious practice must be justified by a compelling governmental interest. . . . We have never invalidated any governmental action on the basis of the *Sherbert* test except the denial of unemployment compensation. Although we have sometimes purported to apply the *Sherbert* test in contexts other than that, we have always found the test satisfied. . . . In recent years we have abstained from applying the *Sherbert* test (outside the unemployment compensation field) at all. . . .

. . .

. . . To make an individual's obligation to obey such a law contingent upon the law's coincidence with his religious beliefs, except where the State's interest is "compelling"—permitting him, by virtue of his beliefs, "to become a law unto himself," . . . contradicts both constitutional tradition and common sense.

. . .

If the "compelling interest" test is to be applied at all, then, it must be applied across the board, to all actions thought to be religiously commanded. . . . Any society adopting such a system would be courting anarchy, but that danger increases in direct proportion to the society's diversity of religious beliefs, and its determination to coerce or suppress none of them. Precisely because "we are a cosmopolitan nation made up of people of almost every conceivable religious preference," . . . and precisely because we value and protect that religious divergence, we cannot afford the luxury of deeming presumptively invalid, as applied to the religious objector, every regulation of conduct that does not protect an interest of the highest order. . . .

Values that are protected against government interference through enshrinement in the Bill of Rights are not thereby banished from the political process. Just as a society that believes in the negative protection accorded to the press by the First Amendment is likely to enact laws that affirmatively foster the dissemination of the printed word, so also a society that believes in the negative protection accorded to religious belief can be expected to be solicitous of that value in its legislation as well. It is therefore not surprising that a number of States have made an exception to their drug laws for sacramental peyote use. . . . But to say that a nondiscriminatory religious practice exemption is permitted, or even that it is desirable, is not to say that it is constitutionally required, and that the appropriate occasions for its creation can be discerned by the courts. It may fairly be said that leaving accommodation to the political process will place at a relative disadvantage those religious practices that are not widely engaged in; but that unavoidable consequence of democratic government must be preferred to a system in which each conscience is a law unto itself or in which judges weigh the social importance of all laws against the centrality of all religious beliefs.

. . .

JUSTICE O'CONNOR . . . concurring.

. . .

. . . [A] law that prohibits certain conduct—conduct that happens to be an act of worship for someone—manifestly does prohibit that person's free exercise of his religion. A person who is barred from engaging in religiously motivated conduct is barred from freely exercising his religion. Moreover, that person is barred from freely exercising his religion regardless of whether the law prohibits the conduct only when engaged in for religious reasons, only by members of that religion, or by all persons. It is difficult to deny that a law that prohibits religiously motivated conduct, even if the law is generally applicable, does not at least implicate First Amendment concerns.

The Court responds that generally applicable laws are "one large step" removed from laws aimed at specific religious practices. The First Amendment, however, does not distinguish between laws that are generally applicable and laws that target particular religious practices. Indeed, few States would be so naive as to enact a law directly prohibiting or burdening a religious practice as such. Our free exercise cases have all concerned generally applicable laws that had the effect of significantly burdening a religious practice. If the First Amendment is to have any vitality, it ought not be construed to cover only the extreme and hypothetical situation in which a State directly targets a religious practice. . . .

To say that a person's right to free exercise has been burdened, of course, does not mean that he has an absolute right to engage in the conduct. Under our established First Amendment jurisprudence, we have recognized that the freedom to act, unlike the freedom to believe, cannot be absolute. . . . Instead, we have respected both the First Amendment's express textual mandate and the governmental interest in regulation of conduct by requiring the Government to justify any substantial burden on religiously motivated conduct by a compelling state interest and by means narrowly tailored to achieve that interest. . . .

. . .

The Court endeavors to escape from our decision . . . in *Yoder* by labeling [it a] "hybrid" decision . . . but there is no denying that [*Yoder*] expressly relied on the Free Exercise Clause. . . . [W]e have never distinguished between cases in which a State conditions receipt of a benefit on conduct prohibited by religious beliefs and cases in which a State affirmatively prohibits such conduct. The *Sherbert* compelling interest test applies in both kinds of cases. . . .

. . .

. . . [T]he Court today suggests that the disfavoring of minority religions is an "unavoidable consequence" under our system of government, and that accommodation of such religions must be left to the political process. . . . In my view, however, the First Amendment was enacted precisely to protect the rights of those whose religious practices are not shared by the majority and may be viewed with hostility. The history of our free exercise doctrine amply demonstrates the harsh impact majoritarian rule has had on unpopular or emerging religious groups such as the Jehovah's Witnesses and the Amish. . . .

The Court's holding today not only misreads settled First Amendment precedent; it appears to be unnecessary to this case. I would reach the same result applying our established free exercise jurisprudence.

There is no dispute that Oregon's criminal prohibition of peyote places a severe burden on the ability of respondents to freely exercise their religion. Peyote is a sacrament of the Native American Church, and is regarded as vital to respondents' ability to practice their religion. . . .

There is also no dispute that Oregon has a significant interest in enforcing laws that control the possession and use of controlled substances by its citizens. . . . As we recently noted, drug abuse is "one of the greatest problems affecting the health and welfare of our population" and thus "one of the most serious problems confronting our society today." . . . In light of our recent decisions holding that the governmental interests in the collection of income tax, . . . a comprehensive social security system, . . . and military conscription, . . . are compelling, respondents do not seriously dispute that Oregon has a compelling interest in prohibiting the possession of peyote by its citizens.

. . . Although the question is close, I would conclude that uniform application of Oregon's criminal prohibition is "essential to accomplish," . . . its overriding interest in preventing the physical harm caused by the use of a Schedule I controlled substance. Oregon's criminal prohibition represents that State's judgment that the possession and use of controlled substances, even by only one person, is inherently harmful and dangerous. Because the health effects caused by the use of controlled substances exist regardless of the motivation of the user, the use of such substances, even for religious purposes, violates the very purpose of the laws that prohibit them. . . . Moreover, in view of the societal interest in preventing trafficking in controlled substances, uniform application of the criminal prohibition at issue is essential to the effectiveness of Oregon's stated interest in preventing any possession of peyote. . . .

. . .

JUSTICE BLACKMUN, with whom JUSTICE BRENNAN and JUSTICE MARSHALL join, dissenting.

. . .

In weighing respondents' clear interest in the free exercise of their religion against Oregon's asserted interest in enforcing its drug laws, it is important to articulate in precise terms the state interest involved. It is not the State's broad interest in fighting the critical "war on drugs" that must be weighed against respondents' claim, but the State's narrow interest in refusing to make an exception for the religious, ceremonial use of peyote. . . .

The State's interest in enforcing its prohibition, in order to be sufficiently compelling to outweigh a free exercise claim, cannot be merely abstract or symbolic. The State cannot plausibly assert that unbending application of a criminal prohibition is essential to fulfill any compelling interest if it does not, in fact, attempt to enforce that prohibition. In this case, the State actually has not evinced any concrete interest in enforcing its drug laws against religious users of peyote. Oregon has never sought to prosecute respondents, and does not claim that it has made significant enforcement efforts against other religious users of peyote. The State's asserted interest thus amounts only to the symbolic preservation of an unenforced prohibition. . . .

. . .

The State also seeks to support its refusal to make an exception for religious use of peyote by invoking its interest in abolishing drug trafficking. There is, however, practically no illegal traffic in peyote. . . . Peyote simply is not a popular drug; its distribution for use in religious rituals has nothing to do with the vast and violent traffic in illegal narcotics that plagues this country. . . .

House Committee on the Judiciary, Report on the Religious Freedom Restoration Act (1993)[19]

The Religious Freedom Restoration Act (RFRA) was passed by a bipartisan coalition outraged by the Supreme Court's decision in Employment Division v. Smith *(1990). Great Society liberals historically favored granting exemptions to religious believers. Many conservatives touted the virtues of exemptions as evangelical Christians faced challenges practicing their faith in more liberal communities. Such traditional rivals as the ACLU and the Christian Legal Society joined forces in lobbying Congress to reverse* Smith. *Congress needed little prodding. The RFRA passed the House by a unanimous vote and the Senate with only three dissenting votes.*

19. Excerpted from House Committee on the Judiciary, *Religious Freedom Restoration Act of 1993*, 103rd Cong., 1st Sess. (1993), H. Rep. 103–88.

Compare the House report on RFRA to the dissents in Smith. *Did the legislative sponsors of RFRA enshrine Justice O'Connor's opinion? Why did national legislators believe that they were authorized to overturn a Supreme Court decision? Does the near-unanimous vote suggest that Justice Scalia was right to think that religious minorities do not need special judicial protection? While attempting to overturn a Supreme Court decision, Congress also provided federal courts with a powerful tool to strike down state laws. To what extent does RFRA empower or disempower justices?*[20]

H.R. 1308, the Religious Freedom Restoration Act of 1993, responds to the Supreme Court's decision in *Employment Division, Department of Human Resources of Oregon v. Smith* (1990) by creating a statutory right requiring that the compelling governmental interest test be applied in cases in which the free exercise of religion has been burdened by a law of general applicability.

. . .

The Free Exercise Clause of the First Amendment states in relevant part that "Congress shall make no law . . . prohibiting the free exercise (of religion)." However, the clarity of the Constitution has not prevented government from burdening religiously inspired action. Though laws directly targeting religious practices have become increasingly rare, facially neutral laws of general applicability have nefariously burdened the free exercise of religion in the United States throughout American history. Such laws, often upheld by the courts, undermined the exercise of religion by various groups.

. . .

The effect of the *Smith* decision has been to subject religious practices forbidden by laws of general applicability to the lowest level of scrutiny employed by the courts. Because the "rational relationship test" only requires that a law must be rationally related to a legitimate state interest, the *Smith* decision has created a climate in which the free exercise of religion is continually in jeopardy; facially neutral and generally applicable laws have and will, unless the Religious Freedom Restoration Act is passed, continue to burden religion. After *Smith*, claimants will be forced to convince courts that an inappropriate legislative motive created statutes and regulations. However, legislative motive often cannot be determined and courts have been reluctant to impute bad motives to legislators.

It is not feasible to combat the burdens of generally applicable laws on religion by relying upon the political process for the enactment of separate religious exemptions in every Federal, State, and local statute. As the Supreme Court itself said:

> The very purpose of a Bill of Rights was to withdraw certain subjects from the vicissitudes of political controversy, to place them beyond the reach of majorities and officials and to establish them as legal principles to be applied by the courts. One's right to life, liberty, and property, to free speech, a free press, freedom of worship and assembly, and other fundamental rights may not be submitted to vote; they depend on the outcome of no elections.

The Committee believes that the compelling governmental interest test must be restored. As Justice O'Connor stated in *Smith*, "[t]he compelling interest test reflects the First Amendment's mandate of preserving religious liberty to the fullest extent possible in a pluralistic society. For the Court to deem this command a luxury, is to denigrate the very purpose of a Bill of Rights."

. . .

. . . [T]he Committee believes that Congress has the constitutional authority to enact H.R. 1308. Pursuant to Section 5 of the Fourteenth Amendment and the Necessary and Proper Clause embodied in Article I, Section 8 of the Constitution, the legislative branch has been given the authority to provide statutory protection for a constitutional value when the Supreme Court has been unwilling to assert its authority. The Supreme Court has repeatedly upheld such congressional action after declining to find a constitutional protection itself. However, limits to congressional authority do exist. Congress may not (1) create a statutory right prohibited by some other provision of the Constitution, (2) remove rights granted by the Constitution, or (3) create a right inconsistent with an objective of a constitutional provision. Because H.R. 1308 is well within these limits, the Committee believes that in passing the Religious Freedom Restoration Act, Congress appropriately creates a statutory right within the perimeter of its power.

---

20. As discussed in Chapter 11, the Supreme Court declared RFRA unconstitutional in *Boerne v. Flores* (1997).

Additional Views of Hon. Henry J. Hyde, Hon. F. James Sensenbrenner, Hon. Bill McCollum, Hon. Howard Coble, Hon. Charles T. Canady, Hon. Bob Inglis, Hon. Robert W. Goodlatte

. . .

When this legislation was considered by the Subcommittee on Civil and Constitutional Rights and the full Judiciary Committee in the 102nd Congress, Congressman Henry J. Hyde (Ill.) offered several amendments. These amendments were designed to alleviate concerns that had been raised with respect to (1) abortion-related claims, (2) third-party challenges to government-funded social service programs run by religious institutions and (3) third-party challenges to the tax-exempt status of religious institutions. Since that time, each of these concerns has been resolved either through explicit statutory language or has been addressed in the Committee report.

In justification of the need for this legislation, proponents have provided the Committee with long lists of cases in which free exercise claims have failed since *Smith* was decided. Unfortunately, however, even prior to *Smith*, it is well known that the "compelling state interest" test had proven an unsatisfactory means of providing protection for individuals trying to exercise their religion in the face of government regulations. Restoration of the pre-*Smith* standard, although politically practical, will likely prove, over time, to be an insufficient remedy. It would have been preferable, given the unique opportunity presented by this legislation, to find a solution that would give solid protection to religious claimants against unnecessary government intrusion.

An attempt was made to cure these deficiencies through an amendment offered in the Subcommittee markup in the 102nd Congress. The amendment would have focused the attention of courts on those interests which are truly "compelling." The amendment defined the term "compelling state interest" as, "an interest in the nondiscriminatory enforcement of generally applicable and otherwise valid civil or criminal law directed to: (a) the protection of an individual from death or serious bodily harm, (b) the protection of the public health from identifiable risks of infection or other public health hazards, (c) the protection of private or public property, (d) the protection of individuals from abuse or neglect, or discrimination on the basis of race or national origin, or (e) the protection of national security, including the maintenance of discipline in the Armed Forces of the United States."

. . . The amendment was not adopted by the Subcommittee.

In reality, the Act will not guarantee that religious claimants bringing free exercise challenges will win, but only that they have a chance to fight. It will perpetuate, by statute, both the benefits and frustrations faced by religious claimants prior to the Supreme Court's decision in *Smith*. Although we have this remaining concern, we support enactment of the legislation.

C. Guns

Guns were a late-developing but important battleground for the culture wars that wracked American politics.[21] For most of the twentieth century the NRA played little role in constitutional politics. During the late 1970s a new generation of NRA leaders began aggressively challenging gun control legislation as inconsistent with the Second Amendment. Ronald Reagan and his political allies supported this new movement for the right to bear arms. The Republican Party platform in 1980 declared, "We believe the right of citizens to keep and bear arms must be preserved. Accordingly, we oppose federal registration of firearms. We therefore support Congressional initiatives to remove those provisions of the [federal law] that do not significantly impact on crime but serve rather to restrain the law-abiding citizen in his legitimate use of firearms." Prominent scholars provided substantial support for the individual rights interpretation of the Second Amendment. In a particularly influential article entitled "The Embarrassing Second Amendment," Professor Sanford Levinson questioned how liberals such as himself could interpret most provisions of the Bill of Rights broadly while adopting the most cribbed interpretation of constitutional gun rights. He chided "most members of the legal academy [for] treat[ing] the Second Amendment as the equivalent of an embarrassing relative, whose mention brings a quick change of subject to other, more respectable family members."[22]

---

21. For a good account of these constitutional politics, see Reva Siegel, "Dead or Alive: Originalism as Popular Constitutionalism in *Heller*," *Harvard Law Review* 122 (2008): 191.

22. Sanford Levinson, "The Embarrassing Second Amendment," *Yale Law Journal* 99 (1989): 658.

The imbroglio over the Clinton administration's attempt to ban assault weapons highlighted the new ferocity of constitutional debates over gun rights. Democrats in 1992 promised new gun control laws:

> It is time to shut down the weapons bazaars in our cities. We support a reasonable waiting period to permit background checks for purchases of handguns, as well as assault weapons controls to ban the possession, sale, importation and manufacture of the most deadly assault weapons. We do not support efforts to restrict weapons used for legitimate hunting and sporting purposes. We will work for swift and certain punishment of all people who violate the country's gun laws and for stronger sentences for criminals who use guns. We will also seek to shut down the black market for guns and impose severe penalties on people who sell guns to children.

Few were prepared for the vigorous attack of the NRA and other proponents of gun rights on Clinton's effort to prohibit semi-automatic weapons. The Federal Assault Weapons Ban became law, but many of its proponents were defeated in the 1994 national elections.

Debate over the Federal Assault Weapons Ban (1994)[23]

Many Americans were stunned by the intensity of debates over gun control during the 1980s and early 1990s. Gun control provisions in crime bills debated before 1980 were not constitutionally or even politically controversial. By the mid-1990s Second Amendment issues were on the national agenda. The controversy over whether to include a ban on semi-automatic weapons in the Violent Crime Control and Law Enforcement Act of 1994 was particularly fierce. Conservative congressmen and the NRA maintained that the proposed ban violated the constitutional right to bear arms. Proponents of gun control rallied their forces. The bill passed the House by a 235-195 vote and the Senate by a 61-38 vote. President Clinton signed the measure on September 13, 1994. Nevertheless, opponents may have had the last laugh. Republicans in November 1994 gained control of both houses of Congress partly as a result of backlash from the assault weapons ban in crucial states and legislative districts.

When reading the materials below, consider the following questions. What explains the sudden constitutional controversy over gun control in the late twentieth century? To what extent do opponents of the assault weapons ban object to the specific ban and to what extent do they object to the precedent for gun control? Are they right that banning some weapons creates a precedent that can be used to ban others? To what extent do proponents of the ban think that government can ban all weapons? Do they draw a sound constitutional line between weapons that can and cannot be constitutionally prohibited?

REPRESENTATIVE GERALD SOLOMON (Republican, New York)

If this bill is passed, there will soon be another one cutting away a little more of the right to bear arms provided under the second amendment to the Constitution.

The ironic part of this is that many of the same people who are cutting away our rights under the second amendment, are the ones who would be most insistent about protecting rights under the first amendment, like free speech. All of our rights under the U.S. Constitution should be protected, not just the ones the current President happens to favor.

REPRESENTATIVE JIM BUNNING (Republican, Kentucky)

If we pass this bill today, we will be setting a dangerous precedent that could lead us down a very slippery slope. Once Congress adopts the theory that limiting access to firearms reduces crime, there will be tremendous pressure to ban more and more of them until the right to bear arms is effectively nullified.

REPRESENTATIVE SIDNEY YATES (Democrat, Illinois)

. . . Nowhere in the basic document of the United States is there a constitutional right, written or implied, giving an individual a separate right to bear arms. Many have made arguments to the contrary, stating the second amendment gives an individual a right to bear arms. This is untrue. The entire provision reads as follows: "A well-regulated militia, being necessary to the security of a free state, the right of the people to keep and bear arms, shall not be infringed." This legislation will not infringe on the rights of any law-abiding American. The right to bear arms is not absolute. The second amendment relates to the organization of a militia; not the organization of thugs and gangsters.

23. 139 *Congressional Record,* 103rd Cong., 1st Sess. (1993), 9339, 9344, 9363, 9368, 18,528, 21,512, 23,808, 23,820, 24,070, 24,107.

REPRESENTATIVE THOMAS MANTON (Democrat, New York)

This bill would ban 10 specific semiautomatic assault weapons. And nothing in the Constitution guarantees the right of a drug lord or a street punk to possess a grenade launcher or an AK-47.

SENATOR LARRY CRAIG (Republican, Idaho)

. . . [T]he right to bear arms is not some abstract notion of the Founding Fathers. It is based on human experience in combating tyranny. An armed citizen has the power to resist threats from other citizens or the Government.

It is no surprise that the Federal Government is uneasy even about guns in the hands of law-abiding citizens. That is exactly what the Founding Fathers wanted: a very real check on the power of the Government over the people.

REPRESENTATIVE JOHN DOOLITTLE (Republican, California)

I believe the right to bear arms, protected by the U.S. Constitution, carries the same constitutional authority as any of the individual liberties found in the Constitution. Just as the first amendment doesn't preclude speech the Founding Founders might have deemed objectionable, the second amendment is not limited to firearms Washington deems appropriate. The burden is on the government, not law-abiding citizens, to justify abrogation of the individual liberties protected by the second amendment. In my mind, the ban on assault-style semi-automatic weapons is a clear violation of the Constitution.

SENATOR JOHN GLENN (Democrat, Ohio)

. . . We hear a lot about the right to bear arms. The Supreme Court has ruled repeatedly that the right to bear arms does not mean that every single citizen in this country can be armed to the teeth to whatever degree they desire. That is not the meaning of the right to bear arms.

. . .

. . . [A]t what level do they propose to keep this right to bear arms? If we are to have these AK-47–type assault weapons, what are they to be used for? They say, "Well, we want to use them for hunting." I do not know how many times you have to hit a deer or a rabbit or a quail or a duck with a multifiring weapon like that to make sure that it is dead.

Now, going down the ladder of destructiveness, at what level do we say we have a right to bear arms? If it is not nuclear, if it is not a Stinger, if it is not bazooka, then where is it below that, in which we say destructive power in the hands of one individual is so frightening that for the public good that we want to limit this, and you should not have something that can kill 500 people at one time out there on the street.

It just seems to me that makes common sense. To me, you reach the cutoff point with weapons that were designed for war. . . .

SENATOR THOMAS HARKIN (Democrat, Iowa)

As we all know, the framers to the Constitution were very much opposed to a standing army. They had experiences with the British army, and they did not want a standing army here. Instead, they wanted a militia, people in their own homes to be called out like the National Guard in times of emergency. But they wanted them regulated—"A well-regulated Militia." They did not say a rag-tag group of people each having their own gun. The second amendment says, "A well-regulated Militia, being necessary to the security of a free State, the right of the people to keep and bear arms shall not be infringed."

SENATOR ORRIN HATCH (Republican, Utah)

The second amendment protects the individual's right to bear arms—to bear arms to protect the family, to hunt, to engage in sporting activities. The so-called assault weapons ban violates that right. It is based on hysterical fear and is unjustified in both law and in fact.

SENATOR TED STEVENS (Republican, Alaska)

I warn those responsible gun owners in my State and throughout the United States to beware of what has happened here today under the guise of an assault weapons ban. We are making steps that will threaten sports gun owners, responsible hunters, those who use guns in target practice, the sport-based sporting goods stores, manufacturers, and the National Rifle Association.

. . .

Finally, let me again warn responsible owners of guns that a major step backward has been taken today on the right to bear arms. I would hope that those on the other side would reflect on the real difference between what they classify as an assault weapon, which has a horrifying name, and a legitimate semiautomatic shotgun, which I am going to be carrying in my hand on September 1.

D. Personal Freedom and Public Morality

Reagan conservatives made reversing *Roe v. Wade* (1973) their highest public priority. Republican Party platforms in 1980, 1984, 1988, and 1992 adopted strong pro-life positions. President Reagan repeatedly made speeches condemning abortion. Members of the Justice Department strategized on the best means for obtaining a judicial decision that would overrule *Roe*. Solicitor generals in the Reagan and Bush administration wrote Supreme Court briefs urging the justices to rethink constitutional protections for abortion. All federal judicial nominees were scrutinized to ensure that they supported the administration position on reproductive choice. The five justices appointed from 1980 to 1992—Sandra Day O'Connor, Antonin Scalia, Anthony Kennedy, David Souter, and Clarence Thomas—were all less supportive of abortion rights than the justices they replaced.

Administration efforts to overrule *Roe v. Wade* made steady progress. Justice O'Connor, who joined the Court in 1981, voted to sustain every abortion regulation before the Court during the 1980s. Justices Scalia and Kennedy, who joined the Court in the mid-1980s, voted similarly. By 1989 the judicial majority seemed poised to abandon judicial protection for reproductive choice. Chief Justice William Rehnquist's majority opinion in *Webster v. Reproductive Health Services* (1989) found no constitutional problem with a Missouri law that declared "the life of each human being begins at conception" and banned any public funds from being used to support abortion. He asserted, "The key elements of the *Roe* framework—trimesters and viability—are not found in the text of the Constitution or in any place else one would expect to find a constitutional principle. Since the bounds of the inquiry are essentially indeterminate, the result has been a web of legal rules that have become increasingly intricate, resembling a code of regulations rather than a body of constitutional doctrine." Rehnquist concluded that reproductive choice was better described as "a liberty interest protected by the Due Process Clause" than a "fundamental right." Liberals on and off the Court despaired. Justice Blackmun's dissent moaned, "Not with a bang, but a whimper, the plurality discards a landmark case of the last generation, and casts into darkness the hopes and visions of every woman in this country who had come to believe that the Constitution guaranteed her the right to exercise some control over her unique ability to bear children."

The Supreme Court by 1990 seemed prepared to abandon or at least sharply curtail all judicial activism on behalf of substantive rights under the due process clause. Conservative majorities maintained that the due process clause of the Fourteenth Amendment did not protect gays and lesbians. Justice White's opinion in *Bowers v. Hardwick* (1986) asserted that history clearly foreclosed a "fundamental right . . . to engage in acts of consensual sodomy." *Cruzan v. Director, Missouri Dept. of Health* (1990) sustained a Missouri judicial decision requiring clear and convincing evidence that a person in a vegetative state would not wish to be administered life-sustaining treating. Chief Justice Rehnquist emphasized the state "interest in the protection and preservation of human life" as justifying the Missouri decision to "place an increased risk of an erroneous decision on those seeking to terminate an incompetent individual's life-sustaining treatment." Conservatives on the court announced a method for interpreting the due process clause that cabined judicial activism. In *Michael H. v. Gerald D.* (1989) Justice Scalia declared, "We refer to the most specific level at which a relevant tradition protecting, or denying protection to, the asserted right can be identified." Scalia's opinion for the Court concluded that an adulterous father had no rights with respect to children conceived and born when the mother was married to another man. Justice Brennan's dissent in *Michael H.* sharply disputed Justice Scalia's approach to interpreting the due process clause. He wrote,

> In construing the Fourteenth Amendment to offer shelter only to those interests specifically protected by historical practice, moreover, the plurality ignores the kind of society in which our Constitution exists. We are not an assimilative, homogeneous society, but a facilitative, pluralistic one, in which we must be willing to abide someone else's unfamiliar or even repellent practice because the same tolerant impulse protects our own idiosyncrasies.

Closer inspection suggested that liberals were holding their own in the culture wars, even as they were losing particular skirmishes. Justice O'Connor gave conservatives particular concern. During her first years on the Court, although she consistently voted to sustain regulations on abortion, her opinions provided far narrower grounds for rejecting pro-choice arguments than those penned by Chief Justice Rehnquist or Justice Scalia. Her separate opinion in *Webster* pointedly refused to overrule *Roe*. In other cases Justice O'Connor expressed some support for using the due process clause to protect substantive freedoms. In *Turner v. Safley* (1987) O'Connor spoke for a unanimous Court when ruling that inmates had a constitutional right to marry. Her concurring opinion in *Cruzan* interpreted the due process clause as granting persons the right to refuse life-sustaining treatment under certain conditions. Justice O'Connor's one-paragraph concurrence in *Michael H.* declared that Justice Scalia's "mode of historical analysis" was "somewhat inconsistent with our past decisions," and that she "would not foreclose the unanticipated by the prior imposition of a single mode of historical analysis."

Conservative fears were realized when the Supreme Court decided *Planned Parenthood v. Casey* (1992). Justices O'Connor, Kennedy, and Souter formed a three-judge plurality that, while narrowing the scope of *Roe*, reaffirmed its basic principle. Justice Blackmun celebrated the plurality decision to keep abortion legal even as he disputed the decision to sustain various laws regulating abortion. Justice Scalia was apoplectic. When the Democrats returned to the White House after the 1992 national election and President Clinton appointed two new members of the Supreme Court, the conservative goal of overturning *Roe* seemed more distant than ever.

Abortion

The Reagan Administration on Roe v. Wade (1986)[24]

The Reagan administration was publicly dedicated to reversing Roe v. Wade *(1973). The Justice Department made a concerted effort to place anti-*Roe *justices on the federal bench and support anti-*Roe *litigation. The Reagan administration's* Guidelines on Constitutional Litigation *described both* Griswold v. Connecticut *(1965) and* Roe *as "examples of judicial creation of 'fundamental' rights not found in the Constitution."*[25] The Constitution in the Year 2000 *stated, "Roe is invalid because it is not supported by any values legitimately derivable from the text, history, or structure of the Constitution."*[26] *In* Thornburgh v. American College of Obstetricians and Gynecologists *(1986) the Reagan administration officially asked the Supreme Court to overrule* Roe. *The Bush Justice Department repeated this request in subsequent cases.*

The following excerpts are from the amicus brief that the Reagan Administration submitted in Thornburgh. *Compare the administration's arguments against* Roe *to the dissents in* Roe *and* Casey. *What are the most important differences and similarities? Do institutional perspectives explain any differences you might spot? Several reasons have been proposed for the failure of the administration's efforts to overrule* Roe:

- *The Reagan and Bush Justice Departments failed to predict the behavior of their judicial nominees in office.*
- *Pro-choice senators prevented the nomination of such persons as Judge Robert Bork, a reliable vote against* Roe. *As a result, conservatives had to select judges whose predilections in this area were not as well known.*
- *The campaign against* Roe *was internally handicapped by such persons as Reagan's Chief of Staff Howard Baker, who were either not militantly anti-*Roe *or believed that for political reasons Republicans were likely to gain more votes if* Roe *remained the law.*
- *Conservative justices gained new perspectives on* Roe *and precedent once they sat on the Supreme Court.*

Why do you think that the effort to overrule Roe *failed?*

...

... *Roe v. Wade* (1973) is not easy for courts to conduct in a principled fashion. The key factors in the equation—viability, trimesters, the right to terminate one's pregnancy—have no moorings in the text of our Constitution or in familiar constitutional doctrine. Because the parameters of the inquiry are indeterminate, courts are disposed to indulge in a free-ranging, essentially legislative, process of devising regulatory schemes that reflect their notions of morality and social justice. The result has been a set of judicially-crafted rules that has become increasingly more intricate and complex, taking courts further away from what they do best and into the realm of what legislatures do best.

---

24. Excerpted from "Brief for the United States as Amicus Curiae in Support of Appellants," *Thornburgh v. American College of Obstetricians and Gynecologists*, 476 U.S. 747 (1986).

25. Office of Legal Policy, *Guidelines*, 82.

26. Office of Legal Policy, *Constitution in the Year 2000*, 18.

Table 10-2 Selection of U.S. Supreme Court Cases On Abortion Rights

Case	Vote	Outcome	Decision
United States v. Vuitch, 402 U.S. 62 (1971)	5-4	Upheld	Health exception to criminal abortion statute not unconstitutionally vague
Roe v. Wade, 410 U.S. 113 (1973)	7-2	Struck down	State may not criminalize the provision of abortions in the first two trimesters of pregnancy and may only regulate abortions in the second trimester in the interest of maternal health
Doe v. Bolton, 410 U.S. 179 (1973)	7-2	Struck down	State may not require use of hospitals or hospital review committees to obtain an abortion
Planned Parenthood of Central Missouri v. Danforth, 428 U.S. 52 (1976)	5-4	Struck down	States may not require spousal consent to obtain abortion, and parent consent laws must have a judicial bypass
Maher v. Roe, 432 U.S. 464 (1977)	6-3	Upheld	States may limit use of Medicaid to pay for abortion services
Harris v. McRae, 448 U.S. 297 (1980)	5-4	Upheld	Congress may limit the use of federal funds to pay for abortion services
Akron v. Akron Center for Reproductive Health, 462 U.S. 416 (1983)	6-3	Struck down	State does not have an adequate interest to impose a waiting period, require that doctors dispose of aborted fetuses in a "humane" manner, require that doctors counsel patients on alternatives to abortion, require parental consent, or require that abortions after the first trimester be performed in a hospital
Webster v. Reproductive Health Services, 492 U.S. 490 (1989)	5-4	Upheld	States may require viability tests on fetuses late in pregnancies and may restrict the use of public facilities for the performance of abortions
Hodgson v. Minnesota, 497 U.S. 417 (1990)	5-4	Struck down	Requiring notification of both parents for minors seeking abortions does not serve a legitimate state interest
Planned Parenthood of Southeastern Pennsylvania v. Casey, 505 U.S. 883 (1992)	5-4	Struck down	State may not impose an undue burden on the right to an abortion, and a spousal-notification requirement imposes such a burden; waiting periods and parental consent requirements are constitutional
Stenberg v. Carhart, 530 U.S. 914 (2000)	5-4	Struck down	State ban on "partial-birth abortions" unconstitutional to the extent that it bans a medically necessary procedure
Gonzalez v. Carhart, 550 U.S. 124 (2007)	5-4	Upheld	Federal ban on "partial-birth abortions" not unconstitutional on its face

We recognize that the principle of *stare decisis*, furthering as it does the policies of continuity and consistency of adjudication, weighs against reconsidering recent precedents. This principle, however, does not count so strongly in constitutional litigation, where, short of a constitutional amendment, this Court is the only body capable of effecting a needed change. . . . Where a judicial formulation affecting the allocation of constitutional powers has proven "unsound in principle and unworkable in practice," where it "leads to inconsistent results at the same time that it disserves principles of democratic self-governance," this Court has not hesitated to reconsider a prior decision. . . .

. . .

There is no explicit textual warrant in the Constitution for a right to an abortion. It is true, of course, that words, and certainly the words of general constitutional provisions, do not interpret themselves. That being said, the further afield interpretation travels from its point of departure in the text, the greater the danger that constitutional adjudication will be like a picnic to which the framers bring the words and the judges the meaning. Constitutional interpretation retains the fullest measure of legitimacy when it is disciplined by fidelity to the framers' intention as revealed by history, or, failing sufficient help from history, by the interpretive tradition of the legal community. . . .

. . .

The ultimate textual source for *Roe v. Wade* is the Fourteenth Amendment's guarantee: "nor shall any State deprive any person of . . . liberty . . . without due process of law." . . . The expansive possibilities of "due process," however, early offered temptations which by all accounts led to one of the most troubled and demoralizing episodes in our constitutional history, during which the Court repeatedly frustrated the workings of the ordinary democratic process by imposing its own debatable and parochial view of appropriate social policy [*Lochner v. New York* (1905)]. . . . The now prevailing doctrine that the Due Process Clause incorporates particular protections of the Bill of Rights, however controversial on historical grounds, was plainly intended to have the function of reining in such judicial extravagance and reanchoring the interpretation of that Clause in the constitutional text—though somewhat downstream of its historical starting point.

Viewed in this context, *Roe v. Wade* seems particularly ill-founded. Due process analysis, while it must recognize the need to go beyond scrutiny of the few relevant words of the Clause, must nevertheless seek a connection with the intentions of those who framed and ratified the constitutional text. As this Court acknowledged in *Roe v. Wade*, however, . . . state laws condemning or limiting abortion were very general at the time the Fourteenth Amendment was adopted. . . . Nor does the tenor and contemporaneous understanding of those laws leave much doubt that they were directed, not only at protecting maternal health, but also at what was widely viewed as a moral evil comprehending the destruction of actual or potential human life and the undermining of family values in whose definition and reenforcement the state has always had a significant stake. It is fair to conclude that those who drafted and voted for the Fourteenth Amendment would have been surprised indeed to learn that they had put any part of such subjects beyond the pale of state legislative regulation. . . .

Planned Parenthood of Southeastern Pennsylvania v. Casey, 505 U.S. 833 (1992)

Planned Parenthood of Southeastern Pennsylvania, other abortion clinics, and a physician sought an injunction prohibiting Governor Robert Casey from enforcing the Pennsylvania Abortion Control Act of 1982. That measure required that a woman seeking an abortion (1) give informed consent prior to the procedure after being provided certain information about abortion and alternatives to abortion; (2) wait at least twenty-four hours after receiving that information before having the abortion; (3) obtain informed consent from one parent if the woman seeking the abortion was a minor (although the statute provided for a judicial bypass); and (4) if married, sign a statement indicating that she had notified her husband of her decision to obtain an abortion. The district court granted the plaintiffs' requests, holding that the provisions violated their constitutional rights. The Court of Appeals for the Third Circuit struck down the spousal notification provision but reversed the district court's rulings as to the rest of the provisions. All parties appealed to the Supreme Court

The Supreme Court by a 7-2 vote sustained every provision in the Pennsylvania Abortion Control Act except the spousal notification requirement. Justices O'Connor, Kennedy, and Souter issued a crucial plurality opinion that abandoned the trimester semester adopted in Roe v. Wade *(1973) but reaffirmed* Roe's *holding that the due process clause protected the right to terminate a pregnancy. Henceforth, the plurality declared, all restrictions on abortion would have to satisfy an "undue burden" standard, not a compelling interest test. The plurality opinion in* Casey *has been hailed as an example of judicial statesmanship and condemned for judicial arrogance. Which characterization do you think is best? To what extent do Justices O'Connor, Kennedy, and Souter maintain* Roe *because they believe the case correctly decided and to what extent do you believe that their opinion rests on the judicial duty to act consistently with precedent? Does the plurality opinion give too much deference to precedent by following* Roe *or too little by abandoning the trimester system detailed in* Roe*? Are the concurrences and dissenting opinions correct when they insist that strict scrutiny and the trimester system are central to the abortion right protected in* Roe*? The plurality emphasizes fundamental differences between the judicial decisions to overrule* Lochner v. New York *(1905) and* Plessy v. Ferguson *(1896). What are those differences? Do you agree with the plurality? Justice Scalia's dissent ridicules many assertions made by the plurality. Do you find his ridicule merited or inappropriate? Can justices settle controversies in the manner suggested by the plurality opinion? Did* Casey *settle the constitutional controversy over abortion?*

Lawyers for Planned Parenthood vigorously challenged any effort to find a middle position that would weaken, but not overrule, constitutional protections for abortion. Kathryn Kolbert, their lawyer, refused to suggest any standard other than strict scrutiny for evaluating the Pennsylvania statute. "To abandon strict scrutiny for a less protective standard," she bluntly declared, "would be the same as overruling Roe*."*[27] *What strategy would you have adopted had you been asked to defend your preferred position before the Supreme Court? If you are strongly pro-life or pro-choice, would you defend that position to the hilt or would you offer the Court a middle ground somewhat more favorable to your preferred position than the state quo when* Casey *was being litigated?*

JUSTICE O'CONNOR, JUSTICE KENNEDY, and JUSTICE SOUTER announced the judgment of the Court.

Liberty finds no refuge in a jurisprudence of doubt. Yet 19 years after our holding that the Constitution protects a woman's right to terminate her pregnancy in its early stages, *Roe v. Wade* (1973), . . . that definition of liberty is still questioned. . . .

. . .

After considering the fundamental constitutional questions resolved by *Roe,* principles of institutional integrity, and the rule of *stare decisis,* we are led to conclude this: the essential holding of *Roe v. Wade* should be retained and once again reaffirmed.

. . .

Constitutional protection of the woman's decision to terminate her pregnancy derives from the Due Process Clause of the Fourteenth Amendment. It declares that no State shall "deprive any person of life, liberty, or property, without due process of law." The controlling word in the cases before us is "liberty." Although a literal reading of the Clause might suggest that it governs only the procedures by which a State may deprive persons of liberty, for at least 105 years, since *Mugler v. Kansas* (1887), the Clause has been understood to contain a substantive component as well, one "barring certain government actions regardless of the fairness of the procedures used to implement them."

. . .

Our law affords constitutional protection to personal decisions relating to marriage, procreation, contraception, family relationships, child rearing, and education. . . . Our cases recognize "the right of the *individual,* married or single, to be free from unwarranted governmental intrusion into matters so fundamentally affecting a person as the decision whether to bear or beget a child." *Eisenstadt v. Baird* (1972). . . . Our precedents "have respected the private realm of family life which the state cannot enter." . . . These matters, involving the most intimate and personal choices a person may make in a lifetime, choices central to personal dignity and autonomy, are central to the liberty protected by the Fourteenth Amendment. At the heart of liberty is the right to define one's own concept of existence, of meaning, of the universe, and of the mystery of human life. Beliefs about these matters could not define the attributes of personhood were they formed under compulsion of the State.

. . . Though abortion is conduct, it does not follow that the State is entitled to proscribe it in all instances. That is because the liberty of the woman is at stake in a sense unique to the human condition and so unique to the law. The mother who carries a child to full term is subject to anxieties, to physical constraints, to pain that only she must bear. That these sacrifices have from the beginning of the human race been endured by woman with a pride that ennobles her in the eyes of others and gives to the infant a bond of love cannot alone be grounds for the State to insist she make the sacrifice. Her suffering is too intimate and personal for the State to insist, without more, upon its own vision of the woman's role, however dominant that vision has been in the course of our history and our culture. The destiny of the woman must be shaped to a large extent on her own conception of her spiritual imperatives and her place in society.

. . .

27. Linda Greenhouse, "Abortion and the Law: Court Gets Stark Argument on Abortion," *The New York Times* (April 23, 1992), A1, A17.

. . . [W]hen this Court reexamines a prior holding, its judgment is customarily informed by a series of prudential and pragmatic considerations designed to test the consistency of overruling a prior decision with the ideal of the rule of law, and to gauge the respective costs of reaffirming and overruling a prior case. Thus, for example, we may ask whether the rule has proven to be intolerable simply in defying practical workability . . . ; whether the rule is subject to a kind of reliance that would lend a special hardship to the consequences of overruling and add inequity to the cost of repudiation . . . ; whether related principles of law have so far developed as to have left the old rule no more than a remnant of abandoned doctrine . . . ; or whether facts have so changed, or come to be seen so differently, as to have robbed the old rule of significant application or justification. . . .

Although *Roe* has engendered opposition, it has in no sense proven "unworkable," . . . representing as it does a simple limitation beyond which a state law is unenforceable. . . .

. . .

. . . [F]or two decades of economic and social developments, people have organized intimate relationships and made choices that define their views of themselves and their places in society, in reliance on the availability of abortion in the event that contraception should fail. The ability of women to participate equally in the economic and social life of the Nation has been facilitated by their ability to control their reproductive lives. . . . The Constitution serves human values, and while the effect of reliance on *Roe* cannot be exactly measured, neither can the certain cost of overruling *Roe* for people who have ordered their thinking and living around that case be dismissed.

No evolution of legal principle has left *Roe* 's doctrinal footings weaker than they were in 1973. No development of constitutional law since the case was decided has implicitly or explicitly left *Roe* behind as a mere survivor of obsolete constitutional thinking.

. . .

In a less significant case, *stare decisis* analysis could, and would, stop at the point we have reached. But the sustained and widespread debate *Roe* has provoked calls for some comparison between that case and others of comparable dimension that have responded to national controversies and taken on the impress of the controversies addressed. . . .

The first example is that line of cases identified with *Lochner v. New York* (1905), which imposed substantive limitations on legislation limiting economic autonomy in favor of health and welfare regulation, adopting, in Justice Holmes's view, the theory of laissez-faire. . . . *West Coast Hotel Co. v. Parrish* (1937), signaled the demise of *Lochner*. . . . In the meantime, the Depression had come and, with it, the lesson that seemed unmistakable to most people by 1937, that the interpretation of contractual freedom protected in [*Lochner* and related cases] rested on fundamentally false factual assumptions about the capacity of a relatively unregulated market to satisfy minimal levels of human welfare. . . .

The second comparison that 20th century history invites is with the cases employing the separate-but-equal rule for applying the Fourteenth Amendment's equal protection guarantee. They began with *Plessy v. Ferguson* (1896). . . .

The Court in *Brown v. Board of Education* (1954) . . . observ[ed] that whatever may have been the understanding in *Plessy* 's time of the power of segregation to stigmatize those who were segregated with a "badge of inferiority," it was clear by 1954 that legally sanctioned segregation had just such an effect, to the point that racially separate public educational facilities were deemed inherently unequal. . . . Society's understanding of the facts upon which a constitutional ruling was sought in 1954 was thus fundamentally different from the basis claimed for the decision in 1896. . . .

. . .

. . . Because neither the factual underpinnings of *Roe* 's central holding nor our understanding of it has changed (and because no other indication of weakened precedent has been shown), the Court could not pretend to be reexamining the prior law with any justification beyond a present doctrinal disposition to come out differently from the Court of 1973. To overrule prior law for no other reason than that would run counter to the view repeated in our cases, that a decision to overrule should rest on some special reason over and above the belief that a prior case was wrongly decided. . . .

. . .

. . . [T]he Court's legitimacy depends on making legally principled decisions under circumstances in which their principled character is sufficiently plausible to be accepted by the Nation.

. . .

Where, in the performance of its judicial duties, the Court decides a case in such a way as to resolve the sort of intensely divisive controversy reflected in *Roe* and those rare, comparable cases, its decision has a dimension that the resolution of the normal case does not carry. It is the dimension present whenever the Court's interpretation of the Constitution calls the contending sides of a national controversy to end their national division by accepting a common mandate rooted in the Constitution.

The Court is not asked to do this very often, having thus addressed the Nation only twice in our lifetime, in the decisions of *Brown* and *Roe*. But when the Court does act in this way, its decision requires an equally rare precedential force to counter the inevitable efforts to overturn it and to thwart its implementation. . . . But whatever the premises of opposition may be, only the most convincing justification under accepted standards of precedent could suffice to demonstrate that a later decision overruling the first was anything but a surrender to political pressure, and an unjustified repudiation of the principle on which the Court staked its authority in the first instance. So to overrule under fire in the absence of the most compelling reason to reexamine a watershed decision would subvert the Court's legitimacy beyond any serious question. . . .

. . .

. . . A decision to overrule *Roe*'s essential holding under the existing circumstances would address error, if error there was, at the cost of both profound and unnecessary damage to the Court's legitimacy, and to the Nation's commitment to the rule of law. It is therefore imperative to adhere to the essence of *Roe*'s original decision, and we do so today.

. . . [T]he basic decision in *Roe* was based on a constitutional analysis which we cannot now repudiate. The woman's liberty is not so unlimited, however, that from the outset the State cannot show its concern for the life of the unborn, and at a later point in fetal development the State's interest in life has sufficient force so that the right of the woman to terminate the pregnancy can be restricted.

. . .

We conclude the line should be drawn at viability, so that before that time the woman has a right to choose to terminate her pregnancy. We adhere to this principle for two reasons. First, as we have said, is the doctrine of *stare decisis*. . . .

The second reason is that the concept of viability, as we noted in *Roe*, is the time at which there is a realistic possibility of maintaining and nourishing a life outside the womb, so that the independent existence of the second life can in reason and all fairness be the object of state protection that now overrides the rights of the woman. . . .

. . .

We reject the trimester framework, which we do not consider to be part of the essential holding of *Roe*. . . . Measures aimed at ensuring that a woman's choice contemplates the consequences for the fetus do not necessarily interfere with the right recognized in *Roe*, although those measures have been found to be inconsistent with the rigid trimester framework announced in that case. A logical reading of the central holding in *Roe* itself, and a necessary reconciliation of the liberty of the woman and the interest of the State in promoting prenatal life, require, in our view, that we abandon the trimester framework as a rigid prohibition on all previability regulation aimed at the protection of fetal life. The trimester framework suffers from these basic flaws: in its formulation it misconceives the nature of the pregnant woman's interest; and in practice it undervalues the State's interest in potential life, as recognized in *Roe*.

. . .

. . . Only where state regulation imposes an undue burden on a woman's ability to make this decision does the power of the State reach into the heart of the liberty protected by the Due Process Clause.

. . .

A finding of an undue burden is a shorthand for the conclusion that a state regulation has the purpose or effect of placing a substantial obstacle in the path of a woman seeking an abortion of a nonviable fetus. A statute with this purpose is invalid because the means chosen by the State to further the interest in potential life must be calculated to inform the woman's free choice, not hinder it. And a statute which, while furthering the interest in potential life or some other valid state interest, has the effect of placing a substantial obstacle in the path of a woman's choice cannot be considered a permissible means of serving its legitimate ends. . . .

. . .

[*Informed Consent*.] To the extent [past precedents] find a constitutional violation when the government requires, as it does here, the giving of truthful, nonmisleading information about the nature of the procedure, the attendant health risks and those of childbirth, and the "probable gestational age" of the fetus, those cases go too far, are inconsistent with *Roe*'s acknowledgment of an important interest in potential life, and are overruled. . . .

. . .

[*Twenty-Four-Hour Waiting Law.*] . . . The idea that important decisions will be more informed and deliberate if they follow some period of reflection does not strike us as unreasonable, particularly where the statute directs that important information become part of the background of the decision. . . .

. . .

[*Spousal Notification.*] In well-functioning marriages, spouses discuss important intimate decisions such as whether to bear a child. But there are millions of women in this country who are the victims of regular physical and psychological abuse at the hands of their husbands. Should these women become pregnant, they may have very good reasons for not wishing to inform their husbands of their decision to obtain an abortion. . . .

The spousal notification requirement is thus likely to prevent a significant number of women from obtaining an abortion. It does not merely make abortions a little more difficult or expensive to obtain; for many women, it will impose a substantial obstacle. We must not blind ourselves to the fact that the significant number of women who fear for their safety and the safety of their children are likely to be deterred from procuring an abortion as surely as if the Commonwealth had outlawed abortion in all cases.

. . .

[*Parental Consent.*] Our cases establish, and we reaffirm today, that a State may require a minor seeking an abortion to obtain the consent of a parent or guardian, provided that there is an adequate judicial bypass procedure. . . .

. . .

Our Constitution is a covenant running from the first generation of Americans to us and then to future generations. It is a coherent succession. Each generation must learn anew that the Constitution's written terms embody ideas and aspirations that must survive more ages than one. We accept our responsibility not to retreat from interpreting the full meaning of the covenant in light of all of our precedents. We invoke it once again to define the freedom guaranteed by the Constitution's own promise, the promise of liberty.

JUSTICE STEVENS, concurring in part and dissenting in part.

. . .

. . . A state-imposed burden on the exercise of a constitutional right is measured both by its effects and by its character: A burden may be "undue" either because the burden is too severe or because it lacks a legitimate, rational justification.

The 24-hour delay requirement fails both parts of this test. The findings of the District Court establish the severity of the burden that the 24-hour delay imposes on many pregnant women. Yet even in those cases in which the delay is not especially onerous, it is, in my opinion, "undue" because there is no evidence that such a delay serves a useful and legitimate purpose. . . .

The counseling provisions are similarly infirm. Whenever government commands private citizens to speak or to listen, careful review of the justification for that command is particularly appropriate. . . . The statute requires that this information be given to *all* women seeking abortions, including those for whom such information is clearly useless, such as those who are married, those who have undergone the procedure in the past and are fully aware of the options, and those who are fully convinced that abortion is their only reasonable option. Moreover, the statute requires physicians to inform all of their patients of "[t]he probable gestational age of the unborn child." . . . This information is of little decisional value in most cases, because 90% of all abortions are performed during the first trimester when fetal age has less relevance than when the fetus nears viability. Nor can the information required by the statute be justified as relevant to any "philosophic" or "social" argument, . . . either favoring or disfavoring the abortion decision in a particular case. In light of all of these facts, I conclude that the information requirements . . . do not serve a useful purpose and thus constitute an unnecessary—and therefore undue—burden on the woman's constitutional liberty to decide to terminate her pregnancy.

JUSTICE BLACKMUN, concurring in part, concurring in the judgment in part, and dissenting in part.

. . .

State restrictions on abortion violate a woman's right of privacy in two ways. First, compelled continuation of a pregnancy infringes upon a woman's right to bodily integrity by imposing substantial physical intrusions and significant risks of physical harm. . . .

Further, when the State restricts a woman's right to terminate her pregnancy, it deprives a woman of the right to make her own decision about reproduction and family planning—critical life choices that this Court long has deemed central to the right to privacy. . . . Because motherhood has a dramatic impact on a woman's educational prospects, employment opportunities, and self-determination, restrictive abortion laws deprive her of basic control over her life. . . .

A State's restrictions on a woman's right to terminate her pregnancy also implicate constitutional guarantees of gender equality. State restrictions on abortion compel women to continue pregnancies they otherwise might terminate. By restricting the right to terminate pregnancies, the State conscripts women's bodies into its service, forcing women to continue their pregnancies, suffer the pains of childbirth, and in most instances, provide years of maternal care. The State does not compensate women for their services; instead, it assumes that they owe this duty as a matter of course. This assumption—that women can simply be forced to accept the "natural" status and incidents of motherhood—appears to rest upon a conception of women's role that has triggered the protection of the Equal Protection Clause. . . .

. . .

Roe's requirement of strict scrutiny as implemented through a trimester framework should not be disturbed. No other approach has gained a majority, and no other is more protective of the woman's fundamental right. Lastly, no other approach properly accommodates the woman's constitutional right with the State's legitimate interests.

Application of the strict scrutiny standard results in the invalidation of all the challenged provisions. Indeed, as this Court has invalidated virtually identical provisions in prior cases, *stare decisis* requires that we again strike them down.

. . .

CHIEF JUSTICE REHNQUIST, with whom JUSTICE WHITE, JUSTICE SCALIA, and JUSTICE THOMAS join, concurring in the judgment in part and dissenting in part.

We believe that *Roe* was wrongly decided, and that it can and should be overruled consistently with our traditional approach to *stare decisis* in constitutional cases.

. . .

In *Roe v. Wade,* the Court recognized a "guarantee of personal privacy" which "is broad enough to encompass a woman's decision whether or not to terminate her pregnancy." . . . We are now of the view that, in terming this right fundamental, the Court in *Roe* read the earlier opinions upon which it based its decision much too broadly. Unlike marriage, procreation, and contraception, abortion "involves the purposeful termination of a potential life." . . . The abortion decision must therefore "be recognized as *sui generis,* different in kind from the others that the Court has protected under the rubric of personal or family privacy and autonomy."

Nor do the historical traditions of the American people support the view that the right to terminate one's pregnancy is "fundamental." The common law which we inherited from England made abortion after "quickening" an offense. At the time of the adoption of the Fourteenth Amendment, statutory prohibitions or restrictions on abortion were commonplace; in 1868, at least 28 of the then-37 States and 8 Territories had statutes banning or limiting abortion. . . . By the turn of the century virtually every State had a law prohibiting or restricting abortion on its books. By the middle of the present century, a liberalization trend had set in. But 21 of the restrictive abortion laws in effect in 1868 were still in effect in 1973 when *Roe* was decided, and an overwhelming majority of the States prohibited abortion unless necessary to preserve the life or health of the mother.

. . .

. . . [T]he opinion asserts that the Court could justifiably overrule its decision in *Lochner* only because the Depression had convinced "most people" that constitutional protection of contractual freedom contributed to an economy that failed to protect the welfare of all. . . . Surely the joint opinion does not mean to suggest that people saw this Court's failure to uphold minimum wage statutes as the cause of the Great Depression! In any event, the *Lochner* Court did not base its rule upon the policy judgment that an unregulated market was fundamental to a stable economy; it simply believed, erroneously, that "liberty" under the Due Process Clause protected the "right to make a contract." . . .

. . .

The joint opinion also agrees that the Court acted properly in rejecting the doctrine of "separate but equal" in *Brown*. . . . This is strange, in that under the opinion's "legitimacy" principle the Court would seemingly have been forced to adhere to its erroneous decision in *Plessy* because of its "intensely divisive" character. . . . Fortunately, the Court did not choose that option in *Brown,* and instead frankly repudiated *Plessy.* . . . The rule of *Brown* is not tied to popular opinion about the evils of segregation; it is a judgment that the Equal Protection Clause does not permit racial segregation, no matter whether the public might come to believe that it is beneficial. On that ground it stands, and on that ground alone the Court was justified in properly concluding that the *Plessy* Court had erred.

. . .

. . . The joint opinion asserts that, in order to protect its legitimacy, the Court must refrain from overruling a controversial decision lest it be viewed as favoring those who oppose the decision. But a decision to *adhere* to prior precedent is subject to the same criticism, for in such a case one can easily argue that the Court is responding to those who have demonstrated in favor of the original decision. . . .

The end result of the joint opinion's paeans of praise for legitimacy is the enunciation of a brand new standard for evaluating state regulation of a woman's right to abortion—the "undue burden" standard. . . . *Roe v. Wade* adopted a "fundamental right" standard under which state regulations could survive only if they met the requirement of "strict scrutiny." While we disagree with that standard, it at least had a recognized basis in constitutional law at the time *Roe* was decided. The same cannot be said for the "undue burden" standard, which is created largely out of whole cloth by the authors of the joint opinion. . . .

In evaluating abortion regulations under that standard, judges will have to decide whether they place a "substantial obstacle" in the path of a woman seeking an abortion. . . . In that this standard is based even more on a judge's subjective determinations than was the trimester framework. . . .

. . .

We have stated above our belief that the Constitution does not subject state abortion regulations to heightened scrutiny. . . . A woman's interest in having an abortion is a form of liberty protected by the Due Process Clause, but States may regulate abortion procedures in ways rationally related to a legitimate state interest.

. . .

[*Informed Consent.*] . . . [T]his required presentation of "balanced information" is rationally related to the State's legitimate interest in ensuring that the woman's consent is truly informed, . . . and in addition furthers the State's interest in preserving unborn life. . . .

[*Waiting Periods.*] . . . We are of the view that, in providing time for reflection and reconsideration, the waiting period helps ensure that a woman's decision to abort is a well-considered one, and reasonably furthers the State's legitimate interest in maternal health and in the unborn life of the fetus.

. . .

[*Parental Consent.*] We think it beyond dispute that a State "has a strong and legitimate interest in the welfare of its young citizens, whose immaturity, inexperience, and lack of judgment may sometimes impair their ability to exercise their rights wisely." A requirement of parental consent to abortion, like myriad other restrictions placed upon minors in other contexts, is reasonably designed to further this important and legitimate state interest. . . .

. . .

[*Spousal Notification.*] . . . In our view, the spousal notice requirement is a rational attempt by the State to improve truthful communication between spouses and encourage collaborative decisionmaking, and thereby fosters marital integrity. . . . The spousal notice provision will admittedly be unnecessary in some circumstances, and possibly harmful in others, but "the existence of particular cases in which a feature of a statute performs no function (or is even counterproductive) ordinarily does not render the statute unconstitutional or even constitutionally suspect." . . . The Pennsylvania Legislature was in a position to weigh the likely benefits of the provision against its likely adverse effects, and presumably concluded, on balance, that the provision would be beneficial. Whether this was a wise decision or not, we cannot say that it was irrational. . . .

. . .

JUSTICE SCALIA, with whom THE CHIEF JUSTICE, JUSTICE WHITE, and JUSTICE THOMAS join, concurring in the judgment in part and dissenting in part.

. . . The States may, if they wish, permit abortion on demand, but the Constitution does not *require* them to do so. The permissibility of abortion, and the limitations upon it, are to be resolved like most important questions in our democracy: by citizens trying to persuade one another and then voting. . . .

. . . I reach that conclusion not because of anything so exalted as my views concerning the "concept of existence, of meaning, of the universe, and of the mystery of human life." . . . Rather, I reach it for the same reason I reach the conclusion that bigamy is not constitutionally protected—because of two simple facts: (1) the Constitution says absolutely nothing about it, and (2) the longstanding traditions of American society have permitted it to be legally proscribed. . . .

. . .

. . . I must, however, respond to a few of the more outrageous arguments in today's opinion, which it is beyond human nature to leave unanswered. . . .

. . .

While we appreciate the weight of the arguments . . . that Roe *should be overruled, the reservations any of us may have in reaffirming the central holding of* Roe *are outweighed by the explication of individual liberty we have given combined with the force of* stare decisis.

. . .

The Court's reliance upon *stare decisis* can best be described as contrived. It insists upon the necessity of adhering not to all of *Roe,* but only to what it calls the "central holding." It seems to me that *stare decisis* ought to be applied even to the doctrine of *stare decisis,* and I confess never to have heard of this new, keep-what-you-want-and-throw-away-the-rest version. . . .

. . . I must confess . . . that I have always thought . . . the arbitrary trimester framework, which the Court today discards, was quite as central to *Roe* as the arbitrary viability test, which the Court today retains. . . .

. . .

Where, in the performance of its judicial duties, the Court decides a case in such a way as to resolve the sort of intensely divisive controversy reflected in Roe *. . . , its decision has a dimension that the resolution of the normal case does not carry. It is the dimension present whenever the Court's interpretation of the Constitution calls the contending sides of a national controversy to end their national division by accepting a common mandate rooted in the Constitution.*

The Court's description of the place of *Roe* in the social history of the United States is unrecognizable. Not only did *Roe* not, as the Court suggests, *resolve* the deeply divisive issue of abortion; it did more than anything else to nourish it, by elevating it to the national level where it is infinitely more difficult to resolve. National politics were not plagued by abortion protests, national abortion lobbying, or abortion marches on Congress before *Roe v. Wade* was decided. Profound disagreement existed among our citizens over the issue—as it does over other issues, such as the death penalty—but that disagreement was being worked out at the state level. . . .

. . .

. . . *"[T]o overrule under fire . . . would subvert the Court's legitimacy. . . ."*

. . .

The Imperial Judiciary lives. . . .

. . .

. . . [T]he American people love democracy and the American people are not fools. As long as this Court thought (and the people thought) that we Justices were doing essentially lawyers' work up here—reading text and discerning our society's traditional understanding of that text—the public pretty much left us alone. Texts and traditions are facts to study, not convictions to demonstrate about. But if in reality our process of constitutional adjudication consists primarily of making *value judgments;* if we can ignore a long and clear tradition clarifying an ambiguous text, . . . if, as I say, our pronouncement of constitutional law rests primarily on value judgments, then a free and intelligent people's attitude towards us can be expected to be (*ought* to be) quite different. The people know that their value judgments are quite as good as those taught in any law school—maybe better. If, indeed, the "liberties" protected by the Constitution are, as the Court says, undefined and unbounded, then the people *should* demonstrate, to protest that we do not implement *their* values instead of *ours.* Not only that, but confirmation hearings for new Justices *should* deteriorate into question-and-answer sessions in which Senators go through a list of their constituents' most favored and most disfavored alleged constitutional rights, and seek the nominee's commitment to support or oppose them. Value judgments, after all, should be voted on, not dictated; and if our Constitution has somehow accidently committed them to the Supreme Court, at least we can have a sort of plebiscite each time a new nominee to that body is put forward.

. . .

We should get out of this area, where we have no right to be, and where we do neither ourselves nor the country any good by remaining.

Gay Rights

Bowers v. Hardwick, 478 U.S. 186 (1986)

An Atlanta police officer on August 3, 1982, had a warrant to arrest Michael Hardwick for failing to appear in court after Hardwick was given a summons for public drinking. The officer entered Hardwick's bedroom and observed him engaging in oral sex with another man. The officer arrested Hardwick for violating a Georgia law that declared, "A person commits the offense of sodomy when he performs or submits to any sexual act involving the sex organs of one person and the mouth or anus of another." Although the local district attorney elected not to press charges, Hardwick brought a lawsuit in federal court against Michael Bowers, the attorney general of Georgia, claiming that he was in imminent danger of being arrested under an unconstitutional statute. Bowers responded that no one had a constitutional right to practice sodomy. The district court dismissed Hardwick's complaint, but that decision was reversed by the Court of Appeals for the Eleventh Circuit. Bowers appealed to the Supreme Court.

The Supreme Court by a 5-4 vote declared that states could regulate homosexual sodomy. Justice White's majority opinion emphasized that states had historically regulated same-sex intimacy and that the right to sodomy bore no resemblance to the privacy rights the court had protected. Why did White reject the analogy between homosexuality and abortion? Why does Justice Blackmun disagree? Who has the better argument? Was the method of finding fundamental rights in Bowers *consistent with* Roe v. Wade*? If not, what explains the difference?*

In 1990, after his retirement, Justice Powell told students at New York University Law School, "I think I probably made a mistake in [Bowers].[28]

JUSTICE WHITE delivered the opinion of the Court.

. . .

. . . [N]one of the rights announced in [previous substantive due process] cases bears any resemblance to the claimed constitutional right of homosexuals to engage in acts of sodomy that is asserted in this case. No connection between family, marriage, or procreation on the one hand and homosexual activity on the other has been demonstrated, either by the Court of Appeals or by respondent. Moreover, any claim that these cases nevertheless stand for the proposition that any kind of private sexual conduct between consenting adults is constitutionally insulated from state proscription is unsupportable. . . .

. . .

Striving to assure itself and the public that announcing rights not readily identifiable in the Constitution's text involves much more than the imposition of the Justices' own choice of values on the States and the Federal Government, the Court has sought to identify the nature of the rights qualifying for heightened judicial protection. In *Palko v. Connecticut* (1937), it was said that this category includes those fundamental liberties that are "implicit in the concept of ordered liberty," such that "neither liberty nor justice would exist if [they] were sacrificed." A different description of fundamental liberties appeared in *Moore v. East Cleveland* (1977) where they are characterized as those liberties that are "deeply rooted in this Nation's history and tradition."

It is obvious to us that neither of these formulations would extend a fundamental right to homosexuals to engage in acts of consensual sodomy. Proscriptions against that conduct have ancient roots. . . . Sodomy was a criminal offense at common law and was forbidden by the laws of the original thirteen States when they ratified the Bill of Rights. In 1868, when the Fourteenth Amendment was ratified, all but 5 of the 37 States in the Union had criminal sodomy laws. In fact, until 1961, all 50 States outlawed sodomy, and today, 24 States and the District of Columbia continue to provide criminal penalties for sodomy performed in private and between consenting adults. Against this background, to claim that a right to engage in such conduct is "deeply rooted in this Nation's history and tradition" or "implicit in the concept of ordered liberty" is, at best, facetious.

Nor are we inclined to take a more expansive view of our authority to discover new fundamental rights imbedded in the Due Process Clause. The Court is most vulnerable and comes nearest to illegitimacy when it deals with judge-made constitutional law having little or no cognizable roots in the language or design of the Constitution. . . .

. . .

. . . [I]llegal conduct is not always immunized whenever it occurs in the home. Victimless crimes, such as the possession and use of illegal drugs, do not escape the law where they are committed at home. . . . And

28. John C. Jeffries Jr., *Justice Lewis F. Powell, Jr.* (New York: Charles Scribner's Sons, 1994), 528.

if respondent's submission is limited to the voluntary sexual conduct between consenting adults, it would be difficult, except by fiat, to limit the claimed right to homosexual conduct while leaving exposed to prosecution adultery, incest, and other sexual crimes even though they are committed in the home. We are unwilling to start down that road.

. . . The law is constantly based on notions of morality, and if all laws representing essentially moral choices are to be invalidated under the Due Process Clause, the courts will be very busy indeed. . . .

CHIEF JUSTICE BURGER, concurring.

. . .

. . . [T]the proscriptions against sodomy have very "ancient roots." Decisions of individuals relating to homosexual conduct have been subject to state intervention throughout the history of Western civilization. Condemnation of those practices is firmly rooted in Judeao-Christian moral and ethical standards. . . . Blackstone described "the infamous crime against nature" as an offense of "deeper malignity" than rape, a heinous act "the very mention of which is a disgrace to human nature," and "a crime not fit to be named." The common law of England, including its prohibition of sodomy, became the received law of Georgia and the other Colonies. In 1816 the Georgia Legislature passed the statute at issue here, and that statute has been continuously in force in one form or another since that time. To hold that the act of homosexual sodomy is somehow protected as a fundamental right would be to cast aside millennia of moral teaching.

. . .

JUSTICE POWELL, concurring.

. . . I agree with the Court that there is no fundamental right. . . . This is not to suggest, however, that respondent may not be protected by the Eighth Amendment of the Constitution. The Georgia statute at issue in this case, authorizes a court to imprison a person for up to 20 years for a single private, consensual act of sodomy. In my view, a prison sentence for such conduct—certainly a sentence of long duration—would create a serious Eighth Amendment issue. . . .

. . .

JUSTICE BLACKMUN, with whom JUSTICE BRENNAN, JUSTICE MARSHALL, and JUSTICE STEVENS join, dissenting.

This case is no more about "a fundamental right to engage in homosexual sodomy" than *Stanley v. Georgia* (1969) was about a fundamental right to watch obscene movies or *Katz v. United States* (1967) was about a fundamental right to place interstate bets from a telephone booth. Rather, this case is about "the most comprehensive of rights and the right most valued by civilized men," namely, "the right to be let alone."

. . . I believe we must analyze Hardwick's claim in the light of the values that underlie the constitutional right to privacy. If that right means anything, it means that, before Georgia can prosecute its citizens for making choices about the most intimate aspects of their lives, it must do more than assert that the choice they have made is an "'abominable crime not fit to be named among Christians.'"

. . .

"Our cases long have recognized that the Constitution embodies a promise that a certain private sphere of individual liberty will be kept largely beyond the reach of government." In construing the right to privacy, the Court has proceeded along two somewhat distinct, albeit complementary, lines. First, it has recognized a privacy interest with reference to certain decisions that are properly for the individual to make. . . . Second, it has recognized a privacy interest with reference to certain places without regard for the particular activities in which the individuals who occupy them are engaged. . . . The case before us implicates both the decisional and the spatial aspects of the right to privacy.

. . .

Only the most willful blindness could obscure the fact that sexual intimacy is "a sensitive, key relationship of human existence, central to family life, community welfare, and the development of human personality." . . . The fact that individuals define themselves in a significant way through their intimate sexual relationships with others suggests, in a Nation as diverse as ours, that there may be many "right" ways of conducting those relationships, and that much of the richness of a relationship will come from the freedom an individual has to choose the form and nature of these intensely personal bonds. . . .

. . . The Court claims that its decision today merely refuses to recognize a fundamental right to engage in homosexual sodomy; what the Court really has refused to recognize is the fundamental interest all individuals have in controlling the nature of their intimate associations with others.

The behavior for which Hardwick faces prosecution occurred in his own home, a place to which the Fourth Amendment attaches special significance. The Court's treatment of this aspect of the case is symptomatic of its overall refusal to consider the broad principles that have informed our treatment of privacy in specific cases. Just as the right to privacy is more than the mere aggregation of a number of entitlements to engage in specific behavior, so too, protecting the physical integrity of the home is more than merely a means of protecting specific activities that often take place there. . . .

. . .

The assertion that "traditional Judeo-Christian values proscribe" the conduct involved cannot provide an adequate justification. That certain, but by no means all, religious groups condemn the behavior at issue gives the State no license to impose their judgments on the entire citizenry. The legitimacy of secular legislation depends instead on whether the State can advance some justification for its law beyond its conformity to religious doctrine.

This case involves no real interference with the rights of others, for the mere knowledge that other individuals do not adhere to one's value system cannot be a legally cognizable interest, let alone an interest that can justify invading the houses, hearts, and minds of citizens who choose to live their lives differently.

. . . I can only hope that . . . the Court soon will reconsider its analysis and conclude that depriving individuals of the right to choose for themselves how to conduct their intimate relationships poses a far greater threat to the values most deeply rooted in our Nation's history than tolerance of nonconformity could ever do. . . .

JUSTICE STEVENS, with whom JUSTICE BRENNAN and JUSTICE MARSHALL join, dissenting.

. . .

Our prior cases make two propositions abundantly clear. First, the fact that the governing majority in a State has traditionally viewed a particular practice as immoral is not a sufficient reason for upholding a law prohibiting the practice; neither history nor tradition could save a law prohibiting miscegenation from constitutional attack. Second, individual decisions by married persons, concerning the intimacies of their physical relationship, even when not intended to produce offspring, are a form of "liberty" protected by the Due Process Clause of the Fourteenth Amendment. Moreover, this protection extends to intimate choices by unmarried as well as married persons. . . .

. . .

Although the meaning of the principle that "all men are created equal" is not always clear, it surely must mean that every free citizen has the same interest in "liberty" that the members of the majority share. From the standpoint of the individual, the homosexual and the heterosexual have the same interest in deciding how he will live his own life, and, more narrowly, how he will conduct himself in his personal and voluntary associations with his companions. State intrusion into the private conduct of either is equally burdensome. . . .

IV. Democratic Rights

MAJOR DEVELOPMENTS

- Supreme Court protects the constitutional right to burn the flag
- Supreme Court rejects some federal and state efforts to create black-majority legislative districts
- States not permitted to discriminate against the children of illegal aliens

Reagan conservatives transformed the constitutional politics of democracy. For most of the twentieth century constitutional struggles over political processes pitted liberals, who favored judicial activism on behalf of expanded free speech and voting rights, against conservatives, who supported restricting expression and the franchise. The constitutional politics of democracy during the 1980s and early 1990s often pitted conservative champions of judicial activism against liberal proponents of legislation regulating expression and voting. Conservatives raised constitutional objections to campus hate speech restrictions, broadcast regulations, campaign finance laws, and efforts to create election districts where a majority of voters were persons of color. Most liberals defended all these measures as consistent with the constitutional commitment to democracy.

Conservatives accepted many Warren Court precedents when criticizing liberal efforts to regulate speech and voting. By the end of the Reagan Era Americans of all political persuasions endorsed the principle of one person, one vote. Federal and state justices agreed that free speech could be restricted only when government demonstrated a compelling interest. Disputes raged over the application of these shared constitutional commitments. Campus debates over speech codes addressed whether proposed regulations prohibited the expression of ideas protected by the First Amendment or fighting words that enjoyed no constitutional protection. Lani Guinier and her critics fought over whether creating black-majority congressional districts realized or perverted the principles underlying the Voting Rights Acts.

The Supreme Court neither fully endorsed nor rejected conservative claims that government officials were unconstitutionally regulating the democratic process. The various laws and practices that the Court declared unconstitutional included prohibitions on burning the flag, state restrictions on campaign finance, the drawing of bizarrely shaped black-majority districts, and a state law that permitted Jerry Falwell to sue *Hustler Magazine* for intentional infliction of emotional distress. The justices permitted Democrats and Republicans to engage in partisan gerrymanders but forbade the use of race in the legislative districting process. The latter decisions relied on conservative antipathy to race-conscious measures but may have benefited Democrats politically.

A. Free Speech

The partisan structure of free speech debates shifted during this period. Political liberals by the 1980s were as inclined to regulate the marketplace of ideas as political conservatives. The controversy over whether the Constitution protected flag burning pitted conservative proponents of restriction against liberal proponents of free speech. Proposals to prohibit hate speech on college campuses pitted liberal proponents of restriction against conservative proponents of free speech. An unusual alliance of radical feminists and conservative Christians championed bans on pornography. More traditional liberals and more conservative libertarians often joined forces to fight these proposed limits on free speech. The Supreme Court typically sided with more traditional liberals and more libertarian conservatives when defeating efforts from both the left and the right to prohibit various forms of expression.

The subject matter of free speech debates shifted. The classical free speech controversy was over whether government could ban advocacy of such doctrines as communism or anarchism. During the 1980s and 1990s the most important free speech controversies concerned the conditions under which persons could champion communism, anarchism, or the doctrine of their choice. Subsidiary categories of First Amendment law took center stage and proliferated. Constitutional controversies raged over speech on public property, subsidized speech, the speech rights of government employees, expressive association, broadcast regulation, commercial speech, and campaign finance. The Supreme Court generally sustained government power to regulate speech on public property, speech that used public funds, and the speech of government employees. Private speech was subject to less regulation. Reagan administration officials abolished the Fairness Doctrine, which regulated speech on radio and television. The Supreme Court provided some protections for commercial speech and campaign contributions while sustaining other regulations.

Consider these shifts in the constitutional politics of free speech as you read the materials in this section. Is there a principled difference between the restrictions on speech championed by many conservatives and the restrictions on speech championed by many liberals? Notice how many free speech issues became intertwined with welfare state policies. Can such issues as the constitutional status of subsidized speech be resolved using principles dating from the Brandeis and Holmes dissents in the Republican Era, or do they require a rethinking of the First Amendment?

Advocacy

A general consensus existed during the 1980s that the main Warren Court precedents on free speech were correctly decided. Americans accepted the principle stated in *Brandenburg v. Ohio* (1969) that "the constitutional guarantees of free speech and free press do not permit a State to forbid or proscribe advocacy of the use of force or of law violation except where such advocacy is directed to inciting or producing imminent lawless action and is likely to incite or produce such action." Constitutional decision makers abided by *New York Times Co. v. Sullivan* (1964), which prohibited "a public official from recovering damages for a defamatory falsehood relating to his official conduct unless he proves that the statement was made with 'actual malice'—that is, with knowledge that it was false or with reckless disregard of whether it was false or not." When finding that public figures could not normally collect damages for intentional infliction of emotional distress, Chief Justice Rehnquist's unanimous opinion in *Hustler Magazine v. Falwell* (1988) stated, "The First Amendment recognizes no such thing as a 'false' idea." The Reagan Justice Department's *Guidelines on Constitutional Litigation* celebrated Justice Holmes's dissent in *Abrams v. United States* (1919) and informed federal attorneys that *Brandenburg v. Ohio* was rightly decided.[29]

Both liberals and conservatives tested the boundaries of these libertarian principles. President George Bush, Republicans in Congress, and many Democrats insisted that elected officials could prohibit flag burning, even as they contended that Americans were free to express hatred for the United States. Prominent liberals who sought to prohibit hate speech on college campuses and in the workplace claimed that insults were not constitutionally protected speech. Many conservatives maintained that obscenity did not advance any ideas. Radical feminists insisted that pornography subordinated woman in violation of the constitutional commitment to equality.

Proponents of these restrictions enjoyed more success in nonjudicial arenas than in the courts. Congress enthusiastically banned flag burning. Many colleges prohibited hate speech. Indianapolis passed an ordinance based on the feminist critique of pornography. Judges proved more committed to libertarian understandings of free speech. The Supreme Court in *Texas v. Johnson* (1989) and *United States v. Eichman* (1990) declared unconstitutional prohibitions on flag burning. Federal judges declared unconstitutional several university attempts to ban hate speech. The Supreme Court in *R.A.V. v. St. Paul* (1992) struck down a local ordinance that forbade placing symbols on property that "arouse . . . anger, alarm or resentment in others on the basis of race, color, creed, religion or gender." A federal appeals court in *American Booksellers Association, Inc. v. Hudnut* (1985) declared unconstitutional the Indianapolis ordinance prohibiting pornography.

Texas v. Johnson, 491 U.S. 397 (1989)

Gregory Johnson burned an American flag during a protest outside the Republican Party's 1984 national convention in Dallas, Texas. He was arrested and charged with violating a Texas law forbidding "desecrating . . . a state or national flag." Johnson was found guilty by the trial court, sentenced to a year in prison, and fined $2,000. That conviction was reversed by the Texas Court of Criminal Appeals. Texas appealed to the Supreme Court of the United States.

The Supreme Court by a 5-4 vote ruled that Johnson was unconstitutionally convicted. Justice Brennan's majority opinion asserts that burning the flag is an expressive activity protected by the First Amendment. Consider the unusual line-up of the justices. Justices Scalia and Kennedy provided crucial votes for the judicial decision. What might explain the judicial voting pattern in this case? The majority and dissenting opinions dispute whether the flag has partisan content. Why does Brennan believe that laws banning flag burning prohibit the expression of ideas? Why does Chief Justice Rehnquist disagree? What does Justice Kennedy mean when he declares, "Sometimes we must make decisions we do not like"? Does Kennedy believe that a better Constitution would permit elected officials to burn flags?

Congress responded to Texas v. Johnson *by passing the Flag Protection Act of 1989. The crucial provision of that legislation declared, "Whoever knowingly mutilates, defaces, physically defiles, burns, maintains on the floor or ground, or tramples upon any flag of the United States shall be fined under this title or imprisoned for not more than one year, or both." No justice altered his or her position when deciding the constitutionality of that measure. Justice Brennan's majority opinion in* United States v. Eichman *(1990) declared, "Government may create national symbols, promote them, and encourage their respectful treatment. But the Flag Protection Act of 1989 goes well beyond this by criminally proscribing expressive conduct because of its likely communicative impact."*

JUSTICE BRENNAN delivered the opinion of the Court.

. . .

Johnson was convicted of flag desecration for burning the flag rather than for uttering insulting words. This fact somewhat complicates our consideration of his conviction under the First Amendment. We must first determine whether Johnson's burning of the flag constituted expressive conduct, permitting him to invoke the First Amendment in challenging his conviction. . . .

. . .

In deciding whether particular conduct possesses sufficient communicative elements to bring the First

29. Office of Legal Policy, *Guidelines on Constitutional Litigation*, 76.

Amendment into play, we have asked whether "[a]n intent to convey a particularized message was present, and [whether] the likelihood was great that the message would be understood by those who viewed it." . . .

. . .

Johnson burned an American flag as part—indeed, as the culmination—of a political demonstration that coincided with the convening of the Republican Party and its renomination of Ronald Reagan for President. The expressive, overtly political nature of this conduct was both intentional and overwhelmingly apparent. . . . In these circumstances, Johnson's burning of the flag was conduct "sufficiently imbued with elements of communication" . . . to implicate the First Amendment.

. . .

. . . The State offers two separate interests to justify this conviction: preventing breaches of the peace and preserving the flag as a symbol of nationhood and national unity. We hold that the first interest is not implicated on this record and that the second is related to the suppression of expression.

Texas claims that its interest in preventing breaches of the peace justifies Johnson's conviction for flag desecration. However, no disturbance of the peace actually occurred or threatened to occur because of Johnson's burning of the flag. . . .

The State's position, therefore, amounts to a claim that an audience that takes serious offense at particular expression is necessarily likely to disturb the peace and that the expression may be prohibited on this basis. Our precedents do not countenance such a presumption. On the contrary, they recognize that a principal "function of free speech under our system of government is to invite dispute. It may indeed best serve its high purpose when it induces a condition of unrest, creates dissatisfaction with conditions as they are, or even stirs people to anger." . . .

. . .

Nor does Johnson's expressive conduct fall within that small class of "fighting words" that are "likely to provoke the average person to retaliation, and thereby cause a breach of the peace." . . . No reasonable onlooker would have regarded Johnson's generalized expression of dissatisfaction with the policies of the Federal Government as a direct personal insult or an invitation to exchange fisticuffs. . . .

. . .

The State also asserts an interest in preserving the flag as a symbol of nationhood and national unity. . . . The State, apparently, is concerned that such conduct will lead people to believe either that the flag does not stand for nationhood and national unity, but instead reflects other, less positive concepts, or that the concepts reflected in the flag do not in fact exist, that is, that we do not enjoy unity as a Nation. These concerns blossom only when a person's treatment of the flag communicates some message, and thus are related "to the suppression of free expression." . . .

. . .

If there is a bedrock principle underlying the First Amendment, it is that the government may not prohibit the expression of an idea simply because society finds the idea itself offensive or disagreeable. . . .

. . .

Texas' focus on the precise nature of Johnson's expression . . . misses the point of our prior decisions: their enduring lesson, that the government may not prohibit expression simply because it disagrees with its message, is not dependent on the particular mode in which one chooses to express an idea. If we were to hold that a State may forbid flag burning wherever it is likely to endanger the flag's symbolic role, but allow it wherever burning a flag promotes that role—as where, for example, a person ceremoniously burns a dirty flag—we would be saying that when it comes to impairing the flag's physical integrity, the flag itself may be used as a symbol—as a substitute for the written or spoken word or a "short cut from mind to mind"—only in one direction. We would be permitting a State to "prescribe what shall be orthodox" by saying that one may burn the flag to convey one's attitude toward it and its referents only if one does not endanger the flag's representation of nationhood and national unity.

. . .

We are tempted to say, in fact, that the flag's deservedly cherished place in our community will be strengthened, not weakened, by our holding today. Our decision is a reaffirmation of the principles of freedom and inclusiveness that the flag best reflects, and of the conviction that our toleration of criticism such as Johnson's is a sign and source of our strength. Indeed, one of the proudest images of our flag, the one immortalized in our own national anthem, is of the bombardment it survived at Fort McHenry. It is the Nation's resilience, not its rigidity, that Texas sees reflected in the flag—and it is that resilience that we reassert today.

. . .

JUSTICE KENNEDY, concurring.

. . .

The hard fact is that sometimes we must make decisions we do not like. We make them because they are right, right . . . in the sense that the law and the Constitution, as we see them, compel the result. And so great is our commitment to the process that, except in the rare case, we do not pause to express distaste for the result, perhaps for fear of undermining a valued principle that dictates the decision. This is one of those rare cases.

. . .

CHIEF JUSTICE REHNQUIST, with whom JUSTICE WHITE and JUSTICE O'CONNOR join, dissenting.

. . .

The American flag throughout more than 200 years of our history, has come to be the visible symbol embodying our Nation. It does not represent the views of any particular political party, and it does not represent any particular political philosophy. The flag is not simply another "idea" or "point of view" competing for recognition in the marketplace of ideas. Millions and millions of Americans regard it with an almost mystical reverence regardless of what sort of social, political, or philosophical beliefs they may have. I cannot agree that the First Amendment invalidates the Act of Congress, and the laws of 48 of the 50 States, which make criminal the public burning of the flag.

. . .

But the Court insists that the Texas statute prohibiting the public burning of the American flag infringes on respondent Johnson's freedom of expression. Such freedom, of course, is not absolute. . . .

. . . [T]he public burning of the American flag by Johnson was no essential part of any exposition of ideas, and at the same time it had a tendency to incite a breach of the peace. Johnson was free to make any verbal denunciation of the flag that he wished; indeed, he was free to burn the flag in private. He could publicly burn other symbols of the Government or effigies of political leaders. He did lead a march through the streets of Dallas, and conducted a rally in front of the Dallas City Hall. He engaged in a "die-in" to protest nuclear weapons. He shouted out various slogans during the march, including: "Reagan, Mondale which will it be? Either one means World War III"; "Ronald Reagan, killer of the hour, Perfect example of U.S. power"; and "red, white and blue, we spit on you, you stand for plunder, you will go under." . . . For none of these acts was he arrested or prosecuted; it was only when he proceeded to burn publicly an American flag stolen from its rightful owner that he violated the Texas statute.

. . . [Johnson's] act . . . conveyed nothing that could not have been conveyed and was not conveyed just as forcefully in a dozen different ways. As with "fighting words," so with flag burning, for purposes of the First Amendment: It is "no essential part of any exposition of ideas, and [is] of such slight social value as a step to truth that any benefit that may be derived from [it] is clearly outweighed" by the public interest in avoiding a probable breach of the peace. . . .

. . . The Texas statute deprived Johnson of only one rather inarticulate symbolic form of protest—a form of protest that was profoundly offensive to many—and left him with a full panoply of other symbols and every conceivable form of verbal expression to express his deep disapproval of national policy. Thus, in no way can it be said that Texas is punishing him because his hearers—or any other group of people—were profoundly opposed to the message that he sought to convey. Such opposition is no proper basis for restricting speech or expression under the First Amendment. It was Johnson's use of this particular symbol, and not the idea that he sought to convey by it or by his many other expressions, for which he was punished.

. . .

JUSTICE STEVENS, dissenting.

. . .

A country's flag is a symbol of more than "nationhood and national unity." . . . It also signifies the ideas that characterize the society that has chosen that emblem as well as the special history that has animated the growth and power of those ideas. . . .

. . .

The value of the flag as a symbol cannot be measured. Even so, I have no doubt that the interest in preserving that value for the future is both significant and legitimate. Conceivably that value will be enhanced by the Court's conclusion that our national commitment to free expression is so strong that even the United States as ultimate guarantor of that freedom is without power to prohibit the desecration of its unique symbol. But I am unpersuaded. The creation of a federal right to post bulletin boards and graffiti on the Washington Monument might enlarge the market for free expression, but at a cost I would not pay. Similarly, in my considered judgment, sanctioning the public desecration of the flag will tarnish its value—both for those who cherish the ideas for which it waves and for those who desire to don the robes of martyrdom by burning it. That tarnish is not justified by the trivial burden on free expression occasioned by requiring that an available, alternative mode of expression—including uttering words critical of the flag . . . be employed.

. . .

. . . The content of respondent's message has no relevance whatsoever to the case. The concept of "desecration" does not turn on the substance of the message the actor intends to convey, but rather on whether those who view the act will take serious offense. Accordingly, one intending to convey a message of respect for the flag by burning it in a public square might nonetheless be guilty of desecration if he knows that others—perhaps simply because they misperceive the intended message—will be seriously offended. Indeed, even if the actor knows that all possible witnesses will understand that he intends to send a message of respect, he might still be guilty of desecration if he also knows that this understanding does not lessen the offense taken by some of those witnesses. . . .

The Hate Speech Debate

Liberals engaged in heated controversies over the merits and constitutionality of restricting racist and related invective on college campuses.[30] The University of Michigan's "Policy on Discrimination and Discriminatory Harassment" was a prominent example of such policies. Enacted after a series of severe racist incidents occurred on campus, that policy prohibited

1. Any behavior, verbal or physical, that stigmatizes or victimizes an individual on the basis of race, ethnicity, religion, sex, sexual orientation, creed, national origin, ancestry, age, marital status, handicap or Vietnam-era veteran status, and that
   a. Involves an express or implied threat to an individual's academic efforts, employment, participation in University sponsored extra-curricular activities or personal safety; or
   b. Has the purpose or reasonably foreseeable effect of interfering with an individual's academic efforts, employment, participation in University sponsored extra-curricular activities or personal safety; or
2. Sexual advances, requests for sexual favors, and verbal or physical conduct that stigmatizes or victimizes an individual on the basis of sex or sexual orientation where such behavior:
   a. Involves an express or implied threat to an individual's academic efforts, employment, participation in University sponsored extra-curricular activities or personal safety; or
   b. Has the purpose or reasonably foreseeable effect of interfering with an individual's academic efforts, employment, participation in University sponsored extra-curricular activities or personal safety; or
   c. Creates an intimidating, hostile, or demeaning environment for educational pursuits, employment or participation in University sponsored extra-curricular activities.[31]

Proponents of such measures emphasized the frequency of racist invective on campus (and elsewhere) and the real harms that such invective inflicted on victims. Professor Mari Matsuda maintained,

> When victims of racist speech are left to assuage their own wounds, we burden a limited class: the traditional victims of discrimination. This class already experiences diminished access to private remedies such as effective counterspeech, and this diminished access is exacerbated by hate messages. Debasing speech discredits targets, further reducing their ability to have their speech taken seriously. The application of absolutist free speech principles to hate speech, then, is a choice to burden one group with a disproportionate share of the costs of speech promotion. The principle of equality is violated by such allocation. The more progressive principle of rectification or reparation—the obligation to repair effects of historical wrongs—is even more grossly violated.

---

30. Restrictions on speech in the workplace may raise similar issues. See David E. Bernstein, *You Can't Say That! The Growing Threat to Civil Liberties from Antidiscrimination Laws* (Washington, DC: Cato Institute, 2003).

31. *Doe v. University of Michigan*, 721 F. Supp. 852, 856 (E.D. Mich., 1989).

> The failure to hear the victim's story results in an inability to give weight to competing values of constitutional dimension. The competing values recognized under international law are equality, liberty, and personality. Each person under that scheme is entitled to basic dignity, to nondiscrimination, and to the freedom to participate fully in society. If there is any central principle to the Bill of Rights, surely that is it. . . . [T]he underlying first amendment values of self-fulfillment, knowledge, participation, and stable community recognized by first amendment theorists are sacrificed when hate speech is protected. The constitutional commitment to equality and the promise to abolish the badges and incidents of slavery are emptied of meaning when target-group members must alter their behavior, change their choice of neighborhood, leave their jobs, and warn their children off the streets because of hate group activity.[32]

Opponents emphasized that restrictions on campus speech can often silence constitutionally protected speech and weaken more vital constitutional protections for less-powerful citizens. Nadine Strossen, general counsel to the ACLU, asserted,

> Censorship traditionally has been the tool of people who seek to subordinate minorities, not those who seek to liberate them. . . . [T]he civil rights movement of the 1960s depended upon free speech principles. These principles allowed protestors to carry their message to audiences who found such messages highly offensive and threatening to their most cherished views of themselves and their way of life. . . . Only strong principles of free speech and association could—and did—protect the drive for desegregation. Martin Luther King, Jr, wrote his historic letter from a Birmingham jail, but the Birmingham parade ordinance that King and other demonstrators had violated eventually was declared an unconstitutional invasion of their free speech rights. . . .
>
> The more disruptive, militant forms of civil rights protest. . .—such as marches, sit-ins, and kneel-ins—were especially dependent on the Warren Court's generous constructions of the First Amendment. . . . The insulting and often racist language that some militant black activists hurled at police officers and other government officials was also protected under the same principles and precedents.[33]

Proposed restrictions on hate speech fared better in constitutional politics than in constitutional law. Courts in California and Michigan struck down restrictions adopted by Stanford University and the University of Michigan. *Corry v. Stanford* (CA 1995) concluded, "The Speech Code prohibits speech based on the content of the underlying expression and is not directed at conduct. It punishes those who express views on the disfavored subjects of race, gender and the like, yet permits fighting words which do not address these topics."[34] Nevertheless, many colleges and universities maintained—and continue to maintain—such rules. Those policies are rarely, if ever, enforced, but they serve as a symbolic expression of the institution's strong commitment to equality and, no doubt, chill what some regard as racial or sexist invective and others believe is constitutionally protected speech.[35]

The Supreme Court of the United States considered a related matter when declaring unconstitutional in *R.A.V. v. St. Paul* (1992) a Minneapolis statute that prohibited placing "on public or private property a symbol . . . which one knows . . . arouses anger, alarm or resentment in others on the basis of race, color, creed, religion or gender." The justices agreed that the states could constitutionally prohibit "fighting words" that threatened a breach of the peace, but that the Minneapolis statute prohibited constitutionally protected speech. They disputed whether a better-drafted measure might pass constitutional muster. The main controversy was over whether the Minneapolis statute was content neutral. Content neutrality forbids government when passing otherwise constitutional regulations from discriminating against people who hold certain ideas or speak on certain subjects. Government may ban murder, but public officials may not ban murder by proponents of progressive taxation or scholars who have published articles discussing the income tax. Justice Scalia's opinion in *R.A.V.* maintained

32. Mari Matsuda, "Public Response to Racist Speech: Considering the Victims Story," *Michigan Law Review* 87 (1989):2320, 2376–77

33. Nadine Strossen, "Regulating Racist Speech on Campus: A Modest Proposal," *Duke Law Journal* 1990 (1990):484, 567-68.

34. *Corry v. Stanford*, No.740309 (Cal. Super. Ct. Feb. 27, 1995).

35. For good discussions of the constitutional politics of hate speech regulations on campus, see Jon B. Gould, *Speak No Evil: The Triumph of Hate Speech Regulation* (Chicago: University of Chicago Press, 2005) and Donald Alexander Downs, *Restoring Free Speech and Liberty on Campus* (New York: Cambridge University Press, 2004).

that hate speech laws violate this constitutional commitment to content neutrality. He wrote:

> [T]he ordinance applies only to "fighting words" that insult, or provoke violence, "on the basis of race, color, creed, religion or gender." Displays containing abusive invective, no matter how vicious or severe, are permissible unless they are addressed to one of the specified disfavored topics. Those who wish to use "fighting words" in connection with other ideas—to express hostility, for example, on the basis of political affiliation, union membership, or homosexuality—are not covered. The First Amendment does not permit St. Paul to impose special prohibitions on those speakers who express views on disfavored subjects.

Justice Blackmun's concurrence insisted that hate speech laws prohibited the most dangerous fighting words and did not unconstitutionally discriminate against speech on disfavored topics. He declared,

> Just as Congress may determine that threats against the President entail more severe consequences than other threats, so St. Paul's City Council may determine that threats based on the target's race, religion, or gender cause more severe harm to both the target and to society than other threats. This latter judgment—that harms caused by racial, religious, and gender-based invective are qualitatively different from that caused by other fighting words—seems to me eminently reasonable and realistic.

Doe v. University of Michigan, 721 F. Supp. 852 (E.D. Mich., 1989)

John Doe was the pseudonym of a University of Michigan graduate student who wished to discuss controversial biological theories suggesting significant racial and gender differences. Doe claimed that he did not raise these issues in class because he feared that such assertions as "biological differences explain why more men than women are engineers" violated the University of Michigan's Policy on Discrimination and Discriminatory Harassment. With the assistance of several public interest groups, Doe asked a federal district court to declare the offending university policy unconstitutional.

The federal district court in Doe v. University of Michigan *issued a permanent injunction barring enforcement of the speech provisions in the Michigan Policy on Discrimination and Discriminatory Harassment. Judge Cohn ruled that the prohibitions were overbroad and vague. The Michigan policy, he maintained, could be interpreted as banning constitutionally protected speech, and reasonable persons could not determine what was prohibited. Suppose you were asked to rewrite the Michigan policy. What regulations do you believe Judge Cohn would find constitutional? What regulations do you believe are constitutional? Under what conditions, if any, should members of a university community be able to assert the following:*

1. *There is only one true religion and nonadherents will go to Hell.*
2. *Specific gender roles or sexual practices are unnatural (or disgusting).*
3. *Members of one sex, race, ethnic group, or religion have certain capacities that members of other races, ethnic groups, religions, or the other sex lack.*

JUDGE COHN delivered the following opinion.

. . .

. . . It is clear that so-called "fighting words" are not entitled to First Amendment protection. *Chaplinsky v. New Hampshire* (1942). These would include "the lewd and obscene, the profane, the libelous, and the insulting or 'fighting words'—those which by their very utterance inflict injury or tend to incite an immediate breach of the peace." Under certain circumstances racial and ethnic epithets, slurs, and insults might fall within this description and could constitutionally be prohibited by the University. In addition, such speech may also be sufficient to state a claim for common law intentional infliction of emotional distress. Credible threats of violence or property damage made with the specific intent to harass or intimidate the victim because of his race, sex, religion, or national origin is punishable both criminally and civilly under state law. Similarly, speech which has the effect of inciting imminent lawless action and which is likely to incite such action may also be lawfully punished. Civil damages are available for speech which creates a hostile or abusive working environment on the basis of race or sex. . . . If the Policy had the effect of only regulating in these areas, it is unlikely that any constitutional problem would have arisen.

What the University could not do, however, was establish an anti-discrimination policy which had the effect of prohibiting certain speech because it disagreed with ideas or messages sought to be conveyed. As the Supreme Court stated in *West Virginia State Board of Education v. Barnette* (1943): "If there is any star fixed in our constitutional constellation, it is that no official, high or petty, can prescribe what shall be orthodox in politics, nationalism, religion, or other matters of opinion or force citizens to confess by word or act their faith therein." Nor could the University proscribe speech simply because it was found to be offensive, even gravely so, by large numbers of people. . . .

These principles acquire a special significance in the university setting, where the free and unfettered interplay of competing views is essential to the institution's educational mission.

. . .

. . . [T]he state may not prohibit broad classes of speech, some of which may indeed be legitimately regulable, if in so doing a substantial amount of constitutionally protected conduct is also prohibited. This was the fundamental infirmity of the Policy.

The University repeatedly argued that the Policy did not apply to speech that is protected by the First Amendment. . . . However, as applied by the University over the past year, the Policy was consistently applied to reach protected speech.

On December 7, 1988, a complaint was filed against a graduate student in the School of Social Work alleging that he harassed students based on sexual orientation and sex. The basis for the sexual orientation charge was apparently that in a research class, the student openly stated his belief that homosexuality was a disease and that he intended to develop a counseling plan for changing gay clients to straight. . . . A formal hearing on the charges was held on January 28, 1989. The hearing panel unanimously found that the student was guilty of sexual harassment but refused to convict him of harassment on the basis of sexual orientation.

. . . Although the student was not sanctioned over the allegations of sexual orientation harassment, the fact remains that the Policy Administrator—the authoritative voice of the University on these matters—saw no First Amendment problem in forcing the student to a hearing to answer for allegedly harassing statements made in the course of academic discussion and research. . . .

. . .

Doe also urges that the policy be struck down on the grounds that it is impermissibly vague. A statute is unconstitutionally vague when "men of common intelligence must necessarily guess at its meaning." A statute must give adequate warning of the conduct which is to be prohibited and must set out explicit standards for those who apply it. . . . These considerations apply with particular force where the challenged statute acts to inhibit freedoms affirmatively protected by the constitution. However, the chilling effect caused by an overly vague statute must be both real and substantial and a narrowing construction must be unavailable before a court will set it aside.

Looking at the plain language of the Policy, it was simply impossible to discern any limitation on its scope or any conceptual distinction between protected and unprotected conduct. . . . The operative words in the cause section required that language must "stigmatize" or "victimize" an individual. However, both of these terms are general and elude precise definition. Moreover, it is clear that the fact that a statement may victimize or stigmatize an individual does not, in and of itself, strip it of protection under the accepted First Amendment tests.

The first of the "effects clauses" stated that in order to be sanctionable, the stigmatizing and victimizing statements had to "involve an express or implied threat to an individual's academic efforts, employment, participation in University sponsored extra-curricular activities or personal safety." It is not clear what kind of conduct would constitute a "threat" to an individual's academic efforts. It might refer to an unspecified threat of future retaliation by the speaker. Or it might equally plausibly refer to the threat to a victim's academic success because the stigmatizing and victimizing speech is so inherently distracting. Certainly the former would be unprotected speech. However, it is not clear whether the latter would.

Moving to the second "effect clause," a stigmatizing or victimizing comment is sanctionable if it has the purpose or reasonably foreseeable effect of interfering with an individual's academic efforts, etc. Again, the question is what conduct will be held to "interfere" with an individual's academic efforts. The language of the policy alone gives no inherent guidance. . . .

. . .

While the Court is sympathetic to the University's obligation to ensure equal educational opportunities for all of its students, such efforts must not be at the expense of free speech. Unfortunately, this was precisely what the University did. . . . [T]here is no evidence in the record that any officials at the University ever seriously attempted to reconcile their efforts to combat discrimination with the requirements of the First Amendment. . . .

Public Property, Subsidies, Employees, and Schools

The American welfare state generated new free speech controversies. Most previous free speech controversies involved private persons speaking on private property or a public thoroughfare or using private resources to communicate some message. By the 1980s many free speech controversies involved a person who wished to speak on public property, a beneficiary of government funds, or a public employee. With the decline of the traditional town green as a site for speech, speakers aiming to reach the public sought access to various public properties. Such government programs as the National Endowment for the Arts provided millions of dollars to subsidize speech. Far more Americans than ever before were employed by the federal, state, and local governments. These changes in the broader environment forced constitutional decision makers to consider more often and more deeply the constitutional rules for speech on public property, speech subsidized by public money, and speech by public employees.

The Supreme Court gave elected officials broad power to regulate speech on public property, subsidized speech, the speech of public employees, and speech in public schools. When sustaining a state law banning solicitations in airport terminals, the Court in *International Society for Krishna Consciousness v. Lee* (1992) largely confined "public forums" to parks and public streets. This is significant, because restrictions on speech in public fora, defined as a "government property that has traditionally been available for public expression," are "subject to the highest scrutiny." Rehnquist, by placing particular emphasis on the words "traditionally been available," concluded that most new forms or uses of government property do not create public forums. "Given the lateness with which the modern air terminal has made its appearance," he wrote, "it hardly qualifies for the description of having immemorially . . . [,] time out of mind[,] been held in the public trust and used for purposes of expressive activity." *Clark v. Community for Creative Non-Violence* (1984) showed great deference to official decisions regulating speech in public forums, as long as the regulation was viewpoint and subject-matter neutral. Past precedents required state officials to demonstrate that state regulations on the time, manner, and place of speech are narrowly tailored to restrict only as much speech as is necessary to serve a legitimate state purpose. Justice White, when permitting the National Park Service to forbid persons protesting homelessness to sleep in Lafayette Park, insisted that courts accept any reasonable assertion that state regulations meet that standard. "We do not believe," he wrote, that past First Amendment cases "assign to the judiciary the authority to replace the Park Service as the manager of the Nation's parks or endow the judiciary with the competence to judge how much protection of park lands is wise and how that level of conservation is to be attained." The justices were as accommodating when public authorities restricted the expression rights of schoolchildren. *Bethel School District No. 403 v. Fraser* (1986) deferred to a principal's judgment about appropriate speech in public schools. When sustaining the suspension of a student who used sexual innuendo when making a speech during an assembly, Chief Justice Burger declared, "The undoubted freedom to advocate unpopular and controversial views in schools and classrooms must be balanced against the society's countervailing interest in teaching students the boundaries of socially appropriate behavior."

Four other important cases involving public employees, publicly subsidized public property, or public schools rejected First Amendment claims.

- *Connick v. Myers* (1983) held that government employees had no First Amendment right to speak on matters of private concern. Justice White's opinion for the Court declared that an assistant district attorney could be fired for complaining about office policy.
- *Rust v. Sullivan* (1991) ruled that the federal government could forbid doctors and associations receiving public funds from giving patients advice about abortion.
- *Madsen v. Women's Health Center* (1994) sustained the major provisions of an injunction restricting anti-abortion speech on streets and sidewalks within thirty-six feet of an abortion clinic.
- *Hazelwood School District v. Kuhlmeier* (1988) permitted a school principle to forbid the publication in a student newspaper of an article that described the experiences of pregnant students.

The justices did not reflexively side with the government when public property, public subsidies, public employment, or public schools were involved. *Connick* reaffirmed *Pickering v. Board of Education* (1968), which held that public employees did have some First Amendment rights to speak on matters of public concern. *Madsen* declared unconstitutional a three-hundred-foot no-approach zone around the abortion clinic. Nevertheless, the general trend of decisions gave government a great deal of control over public property, public funds, public employees, and public schools.

Rust v. Sullivan, 500 U.S. 173 (1991)

Dr. Irving Rust was the medical director of the Bronx Center, a facility owned by Planned Parenthood. For many years, Planned Parenthood received federal funds under Title X of the Public Health Service Act (1970). One provision of that act declared, "None of the funds appropriated under this subchapter shall be used in programs where abortion is a method of family planning." In 1988 the Reagan administration interpreted that provision as forbidding any program receiving federal funds under Title X from referring a client to an abortion provider. If asked about abortion by a client, federally funded programs were required to assert, "The project does not consider abortion an appropriate method of family planning and therefore does not counsel or refer for abortion." This policy became known as the gag rule. Dr. Rust filed a lawsuit against Louis Sullivan, the secretary of health and human services, claiming that the gag rule violated the free speech rights of doctors and the due process rights of their patients. Both the local federal district court and the Court of Appeals for the Second Circuit declared that the rules were constitutional. Rust appealed to the Supreme Court of the United States.

The Supreme Court by a 5-4 vote sustained the gag rule.[36] *Chief Justice Rehnquist's majority opinion asserted that the Constitution permitted the federal government to fund particular viewpoints without providing financial support for alternative perspectives. Presidents may forbid their press secretaries from criticizing their State of the Union address. Does this analogy hold for anyone who accepts public funds? What limits does Chief Justice Rehnquist place on federal subsidies? When would the dissent permit funding to be tied to conditions limiting speech? Chief Justice Rehnquist makes clear that Dr. Rust could say whatever he wanted to his private patients. Does this rule provide sufficient protection to doctors? Justices Souter and Kennedy voted to sustain the gag rule. On this basis could you in 1991 assume that both justices were probably ready to overrule* Roe v. Wade*?*

Days after taking office President Clinton directed the Department of Health and Human Services to eliminate the gag rule.[37]

CHIEF JUSTICE REHNQUIST delivered the opinion of the Court.

. . .

There is no question but that the statutory prohibition . . . is constitutional. In *Maher v. Roe*, . . . (1977) we upheld a state welfare regulation under which Medicaid recipients received payments for services related to childbirth, but not for nontherapeutic abortions. The Court rejected the claim that this unequal subsidization worked a violation of the Constitution. We held that the government may "make a value judgment favoring childbirth over abortion, and . . . implement that judgment by the allocation of public funds." . . . Here the Government is exercising the authority it possesses under *Maher* and *Harris v. McRae* . . . (1980), to subsidize family planning services which will lead to conception and childbirth, and declining to "promote or encourage abortion." The Government can, without violating the Constitution, selectively fund a program to encourage certain activities it believes to be in the public interest, without at the same time funding an alternative program which seeks to deal with the problem in another way. In so doing, the Government has not discriminated on the basis of viewpoint; it has merely chosen to fund one activity to the exclusion of the other. "[A] legislature's decision not to subsidize the exercise of a fundamental right does not infringe the right." . . .

. . .

To hold that the Government unconstitutionally discriminates on the basis of viewpoint when it chooses to fund a program dedicated to advance certain permissible goals, because the program in advancing those goals necessarily discourages alternative goals, would render numerous Government programs constitutionally suspect. When Congress established a National Endowment for Democracy to encourage other countries to adopt democratic principles, . . . it was not

36. Justice O'Connor's dissent did not discuss the constitutional issue. She concluded that Reagan administration officials improperly interpreted Title X.

37. Office of the President, *Memorandum: Title X "Gag Rule"* (February 5, 1993), 58 Fed. Reg. 7,455.

constitutionally required to fund a program to encourage competing lines of political philosophy such as communism and fascism. . . .

. . .

. . . [T]he Government is not denying a benefit to anyone, but is instead simply insisting that public funds be spent for the purposes for which they were authorized. The Secretary's regulations do not force the Title X grantee to give up abortion-related speech; they merely require that the grantee keep such activities separate and distinct from Title X activities. . . . The Title X grantee can continue to perform abortions, provide abortion-related services, and engage in abortion advocacy; it simply is required to conduct those activities through programs that are separate and independent from the project that receives Title X funds. . . .

. . . [O]ur "unconstitutional conditions" cases involve situations in which the Government has placed a condition on the recipient of the subsidy rather than on a particular program or service, thus effectively prohibiting the recipient from engaging in the protected conduct outside the scope of the federally funded program. In *FCC v. League of Women Voters of Cal.* (1984), we invalidated a federal law providing that noncommercial television and radio stations that receive federal grants may not "engage in editorializing." . . . The effect of the law was that "a noncommercial educational station that receives only 1% of its overall income from [federal] grants is barred absolutely from all editorializing" and "barred from using even wholly private funds to finance its editorial activity." . . . We expressly recognized, however, that were Congress to permit the recipient stations to "establish 'affiliate' organizations which could then use the station's facilities to editorialize with nonfederal funds, such a statutory mechanism would plainly be valid." . . .

. . .

. . . [T]he Title X program regulations do not significantly impinge upon the doctor-patient relationship. Nothing in them requires a doctor to represent as his own any opinion that he does not in fact hold. Nor is the doctor-patient relationship established by the Title X program sufficiently all encompassing so as to justify an expectation on the part of the patient of comprehensive medical advice. The program does not provide post conception medical care, and therefore a doctor's silence with regard to abortion cannot reasonably be thought to mislead a client into thinking that the doctor does not consider abortion an appropriate option for her. The doctor is always free to make clear that advice regarding abortion is simply beyond the scope of the program. In these circumstances, the general rule that the Government may choose not to subsidize speech applies with full force.

. . .

JUSTICE BLACKMUN, with whom JUSTICE MARSHALL joins, . . . dissenting.

. . .

Until today, the Court never has upheld viewpoint-based suppression of speech simply because that suppression was a condition upon the acceptance of public funds. Whatever may be the Government's power to condition the receipt of its largess upon the relinquishment of constitutional rights, it surely does not extend to a condition that suppresses the recipient's cherished freedom of speech based solely upon the content or viewpoint of that speech. . . .

It cannot seriously be disputed that the counseling and referral provisions at issue in the present cases constitute content-based regulation of speech. Title X grantees may provide counseling and referral regarding any of a wide range of family planning and other topics, save abortion. . . .

The regulations are also clearly viewpoint based. While suppressing speech favorable to abortion with one hand, the Secretary compels antiabortion speech with the other. For example, the Department of Health and Human Services' own description of the regulations makes plain that "Title X projects are required to facilitate access to prenatal care and social services, including adoption services, that might be needed by the pregnant client to promote her well-being and that of her child, while making it abundantly clear that the project is not permitted to promote abortion by facilitating access to abortion through the referral process."

. . .

Remarkably, the majority concludes that "the Government has not discriminated on the basis of viewpoint; it has merely chosen to fund one activity to the exclusion of the other." But the majority's claim that the regulations merely limit a Title X project's speech to preventive or preconceptional services rings hollow in light of the broad range of nonpreventive services that the regulations authorize Title X projects to provide. By refusing to fund those family-planning projects that advocate abortion because they advocate abortion, the

Government plainly has targeted a particular viewpoint. . . .

. . .

The Court concludes that the challenged regulations do not violate the First Amendment rights of Title X staff members because any limitation of the employees' freedom of expression is simply a consequence of their decision to accept employment at a federally funded project. But it has never been sufficient to justify an otherwise unconstitutional condition upon public employment that the employee may escape the condition by relinquishing his or her job. It is beyond question "that a government may not require an individual to relinquish rights guaranteed him by the First Amendment as a condition of public employment." . . .

. . .

In the cases at bar, the speaker's interest in the communication is both clear and vital. In addressing the family-planning needs of their clients, the physicians and counselors who staff Title X projects seek to provide them with the full range of information and options regarding their health and reproductive freedom. Indeed, the legitimate expectations of the patient and the ethical responsibilities of the medical profession demand no less. "The patient's right of self-decision can be effectively exercised only if the patient possesses enough information to enable an intelligent choice. . . . The physician has an ethical obligation to help the patient make choices from among the therapeutic alternatives consistent with good medical practice." . . .

The Government's articulated interest in distorting the doctor-patient dialogue—ensuring that federal funds are not spent for a purpose outside the scope of the program—falls far short of that necessary to justify the suppression of truthful information and professional medical opinion regarding constitutionally protected conduct. . . .

Finally, it is of no small significance that the speech the Secretary would suppress is truthful information regarding constitutionally protected conduct of vital importance to the listener. One can imagine no legitimate governmental interest that might be served by suppressing such information. . . .

. . .

JUSTICE STEVENS, dissenting. . . .

JUSTICE O'CONNOR, dissenting. . . .

Campaign Finance

Many, but not all, restrictions on campaign finance did not survive the 1980s. *Citizens Against Rent Control v. City of Berkeley* (1981) declared unconstitutional laws restricting contributions to campaigns for and against ballot measures. Chief Justice Burger's majority opinion asserted, "Contributions by individuals to support concerted action by a committee advocating a position on a ballot measure is beyond question a very significant form of political expression." The Supreme Court was more supportive of regulation in *Austin v. Michigan Chamber of Commerce* (1990), in which a 6-3 majority sustained a state law prohibiting corporations from making independent expenditures during state elections. Justice Marshall's majority opinion noted how "state created advantages . . . permit [corporations] to use resources amassed in the economic marketplace to obtain an unfair advantage in the political marketplace."

Media

Conservatives in the executive branch and federal judiciary provided broader constitutional protection for broadcast media than had previously been the case. The Reagan administration abandoned the Fairness Doctrine and other policies that the Supreme Court in *Red Lion Broadcast Co. v. FCC* (1969) had ruled were constitutional regulations of radio and television. *Sable Communications of California, Inc. v. F.C.C.* (1989) held that dial-up-telephone services, even services that enabled callers to hear sexually explicit speech, were subject to the highest degree of constitutional protection. The justices unanimously agreed that telephone services were unlike those broadcast media that *Red Lion* concluded were subject to more extensive government regulation. "Unlike an unexpected outburst on a radio broadcast," Justice White asserted, "the message received by one who places a call to a dial-a-porn service is not so invasive or surprising that it prevents an unwilling listener from avoiding exposure to it." Five years later, in *Turner Broadcasting System, Inc. v. F.C.C.* (1994), the justices concluded that cable television services were also unlike those broadcast media that *Red Lion* held were subject to more extensive government regulation. Justice Kennedy's opinion for the Court stated,

> Cable television does not suffer from the inherent limitations that characterize the broadcast medium. . . .

[S]oon there may be no practical limitation on the number of speakers who may use the cable medium. Nor is there any danger of physical interference between two cable speakers attempting to share the same channel. In light of these fundamental technological differences between broadcast and cable transmission, application of the more relaxed standard of scrutiny adopted in Red Lion and the other broadcast cases is inapt when determining the First Amendment validity of cable regulation.

The Fairness Doctrine

Ronald Reagan and other prominent conservatives believed that the Fairness Doctrine violated the constitutional rights of broadcasters. These regulations, which were promulgated by the FCC in 1949, required broadcasters to present diverse views on controversial issues. Although the Supreme Court in Red Lion Broadcasting Co. v. FCC *(1969) ruled that the Fairness Doctrine was constitutional, Reagan appointees on the FCC after conducting a series of hearings in the mid-1980s repealed the offending regulations. Congress almost immediately passed the Fairness in Broadcasting Act of 1987, which restored the Fairness Doctrine. President Reagan vetoed that measure. The national legislature lacked the votes to override.*

The excerpts below are from the FCC's 1985 Report on the Fairness Doctrine *[i.e., Section 73.1910], the resulting congressional debate over the Fairness Doctrine, and the Reagan veto of the Fairness Doctrine. What are the best constitutional justifications of the original FCC rule? Why did the FCC and President Reagan come to believe these rules inadequate? Who has the better argument? Think about the influence of law and politics on the debate over the Fairness Doctrine. Did the Fairness Doctrine benefit some political actors at the expense of others? Did those perceived political benefits explicitly or implicitly influence the constitutional debate over that policy?*

Federal Communications Commission, Inquiry into Section 73.1910," 102 F.C.C2d 142 (1985)

. . .

On the basis of the voluminous factual record compiled in this proceeding, our experience in administering the doctrine and our general expertise in broadcast regulation, we no longer believe that the fairness doctrine, as a matter of policy, serves the public interest. In making this determination, we do not question the interest of the listening and viewing public in obtaining access to diverse and antagonistic sources of information. Rather, we conclude that the fairness doctrine is no longer a necessary or appropriate means by which to effectuate this interest. We believe that the interest of the public in viewpoint diversity is fully served by the multiplicity of voices in the marketplace today and that the intrusion by government into the content of programming occasioned by the enforcement of the doctrine unnecessarily restricts the journalistic freedom of broadcasters. Furthermore, we find that the fairness doctrine, in operation, actually inhibits the presentation of controversial issues of public importance to the detriment of the public and in degradation of the editorial prerogatives of broadcast journalists.

. . .

We believe that there are serious questions raised with respect to the constitutionality of the fairness doctrine whether or not the Supreme Court chooses to continue to apply the less exacting standard which it has traditionally employed in assessing the constitutionality of broadcast regulation. . . . [T]he compelling evidence in this proceeding demonstrates that the fairness doctrine, in operation, inhibits the presentation of controversial issues of public importance. As a consequence, even under a standard of review short of the strict scrutiny standard applied to test the constitutionality of restraints on the press, we believe that the fairness doctrine can no longer be justified on the grounds that it is necessary to promote the First Amendment rights of the viewing and listening public. Indeed, the chilling effect on the presentation of controversial issues of public importance resulting from our regulatory policies affirmatively disserves the interest of the public in obtaining access to diverse viewpoints. In addition, we believe that the fairness doctrine, as a regulation which directly affects the content of speech aired over broadcast frequencies, significantly impairs the journalistic freedom of broadcasters. . . . [I]n light of the substantial increase in the number and types of information sources, we believe that the artificial mechanism of interjecting the government into an affirmative role of overseeing the content of speech is unnecessary to vindicate the interest of the public in obtaining access to the marketplace of ideas. . . .

. . .

. . . [T]he fairness doctrine in its operation encourages broadcasters to air only the minimal amount of controversial issue programming sufficient to comply with the first prong [obligation to cover matters of public importance]. By restricting the amount and type of controversial programming aired, a broadcaster minimizes the potentially substantial burdens associated with the second prong of the doctrine [equal time and right to reply] while remaining in compliance with the strict letter of its regulatory obligations. . . .

. . .

. . . [T]he record is replete with descriptions from broadcasters who have candidly recounted specific instances in which they decided not to air controversial matters of public importance because such broadcasts might trigger fairness doctrine obligations. For example, fearing the imposition of onerous regulatory burdens, Meredith Corporation states that one of its stations elected not to air a paid program on the nuclear arms race. . . .

. . .

. . . [I]t is only "major" or "significant" opinions which are within the scope of the regulatory obligation to provide contrasting viewpoints. . . . While the broadcaster in the first instance is responsible for evaluating the "viewpoints and shades of opinion which are to be presented," we are obligated to review the reasonableness of the broadcaster's evaluation. As a consequence, the fairness doctrine in operation inextricably involves the Commission in the dangerous task of evaluating the merits of particular viewpoints. This evaluation has serious First Amendment ramifications. . . .

Broadcasters who have been denied or threatened with a denial of the renewal of their licenses due to fairness doctrine violations have generally not been those which have provided only minimal coverage of controversial and important public issues. Indeed, some licensees that we have not renewed or threatened with non-renewal have presented controversial issue programming far in excess of that aired by the typical licensee. In a number of situations it was the licenses of broadcasters who aired opinions which many in society found to be abhorrent or extreme which were placed in jeopardy due to allegations of fairness doctrine violations. . . .

. . .

. . . [W]e find the information marketplace of today different from that which existed in 1974 [when the last FCC Fairness Report was issued], as many of the "future" electronic technologies have now become contributors to the marketplace of ideas. . . . [T]he growth of traditional broadcast facilities, as well as the development of new electronic information technologies, provides the public with suitable access to the marketplace of ideas so as to render the fairness doctrine unnecessary. Moreover, we find that the dynamics of the information services marketplace overall insures that the public will be sufficiently exposed to controversial issues of public importance. Accordingly, we no longer believe it appropriate to continue a system of government imposed obligations requiring licensees to discover and "fairly" address controversial issues of public importance. We believe that elimination of the fairness doctrine would not only promote discussion of such issues, but also pay greater fidelity to fundamental First Amendment values.

. . .

. . . Our experience with industry performance persuades us that radio and television broadcasters would be sufficiently motivated to provide coverage to controversial issues of public importance in the absence of fairness doctrine obligations. Indeed, assuming arguendo that television is the most relied upon information source, then there is a strong market incentive to cover such issues in response to the demand. . . . [M]arketplace forces are the primary determinants of information oriented programming. Moreover, given our previous analysis regarding the chilling effect of the fairness doctrine, we believe it reasonable to expect an increase in the coverage of these types of issues. In any event, there is no reason to believe that there will be a decline in the coverage of controversial issues of public importance.

. . .

We take issue with the assumption that intrusive governmental regulation is necessary to "protect" broadcasters from groups which allegedly attempt to influence their programming decisions. The First Amendment forbids governmental intervention in order to "protect" print journalists and we believe that broadcast journalists are in no greater need of "protection" than their counterparts in the print media. We think it telling, in this regard, that broadcasters themselves are not seeking this protection. . . .

Balance may be a laudable editorial goal, but there are grave dangers when the government tries to strike that balance. First, as we have just noted above, determining what constitutes balanced programming is a very subjective endeavor. Second, as we have described, having the government attempt to achieve balance by means of enforcing the fairness doctrine results in a chilling effect to the ultimate detriment of the listening public. Third, there are the inherent dangers of an arm of the federal government influencing the content of programming in an attempt to guarantee balance. Further, the First Amendment does not require and may well not permit a neat apportionment, dictated by the government, in the marketplace of ideas, with equal space assigned to every viewpoint. . . .

Ronald Reagan, Message to the Senate Returning without Approval the Fairness in Broadcasting Bill (1987)

. . .

In any other medium besides broadcasting, federal policing of the editorial judgment of journalists would be unthinkable. The framers of the First Amendment, confident that public debate would be freer and healthier without the kind of interference represented by the "fairness doctrine," chose to forbid such regulations in the clearest terms: "Congress shall make no law . . . abridging the freedom of speech, or of the press." . . .

I recognize that 18 years ago the Supreme Court indicated that the fairness doctrine as then applied to a far less technologically advanced broadcast industry did not contravene the First Amendment. *Red Lion Broadcasting Co. v. FCC* (1969). The Red Lion decision was based on the theory that usable broadcast frequencies were then so inherently scarce that government regulation of broadcasters was inevitable and the FCC's "fairness doctrine" seemed to be a reasonable means of promoting diverse and vigorous debate of controversial issues.

The Supreme Court indicated in *Red Lion* a willingness to reconsider the appropriateness of the fairness doctrine if it reduced rather than enhanced broadcast coverage. . . . It may now be fairly concluded that the growth in the number of available media outlets does indeed outweigh whatever justifications may have seemed to exist at the period during which the doctrine was developed. The FCC itself has concluded that the doctrine is an unnecessary and detrimental regulatory mechanism. . . .

Quite apart from these technological advances, we must not ignore the obvious intent of the First Amendment, which is to promote vigorous public debate and a diversity of viewpoints in the public forum as a whole, not in any particular medium, let alone in any particular journalistic outlet. History has shown that the dangers of an overly timid or biased press cannot be averted through bureaucratic regulation, but only through the freedom and competition that the First Amendment sought to guarantee.

S. 742 simply cannot be reconciled with the freedom of speech and the press secured by our Constitution. It is, in my judgment, unconstitutional. Well-intentioned as S. 742 may be, it would be inconsistent with the First Amendment and with the American tradition of independent journalism. Accordingly, I am compelled to disapprove this measure.

Ernest Hollings, Speech in Response to Reagan Veto (1987)[38]

. . .

The President claims here that his veto is based on the infringement now due to the technological development of the first amendment. Such a claim we have demonstrated time and time again is incorrect and misguided for in fact the fairness doctrine enhances freedom of speech, and gives our citizens a greater variety of information. It permits those who do not own broadcast stations to use the airwaves, the public's airwaves to participate in important public debate and in doing so the doctrine places only a minimal burden on the broadcasters and a tremendous blessing upon the broadcasters, namely has given them not only balance in the presentation of important, public issues, but more, their credibility.

. . .

The Government's oversight of the broadcast industry and the establishment of the fairness doctrine rests on four fundamental conclusions:

First. A valuable public resource, the electromagnetic spectrum, remains scarce relative to demand; broadcast channels are limited, despite the introduction of new video and audio services.

Second. Congress in the Communications Act has chosen a system where a select few are licensed to utilize the broadcast spectrum in exchange for a commitment to operate in the public interest as public trustees.

38. 135 *Congressional Record*, 100th Cong., 1st Sess., (1987), 16, 990–93.

Third. The doctrine has permitted those who do not own broadcast stations to have an opportunity to participate in important public debate and has provided the public with a greater range of views upon which to make informed decisions; and

Fourth. The doctrine is no more than good journalistic practice that does not chill the speech of broadcasters.

. . .

With the FCC's elimination of many of the public trust requirements of broadcasters, there has been a tremendous turnover in the ownership of broadcast stations. . . . As a result of this great change in ownership, the industry is no longer dominated by those who have had a commitment to serve the public. Many of the new owners are faceless corporations who have regard only for the value of the license and the ability to turn it over for profit, not for the service responsibilities that are entailed. . . .

Other Free Speech Issues

Obscenity and Pornography. Many radical feminists joined the social conservative crusade against obscenity and pornography. Conservatives objected to obscenity on the ground that too-explicit depictions of sexual conduct debased the culture and had no intellectual value. A presidential Commission on Pornography, chaired by Attorney General Edwin Meese, reported,

> The special power of the First Amendment ought, in our opinion, to be reserved for the conveying of arguments and information in a way that surpasses some admittedly low threshold of cognitive appeal, whether that appeal be emotive, intellectual, aesthetic, or informational. We have no doubt that this low threshold will be surpassed by a wide range of sexually explicit material conveying unpopular ideas about sex in a manner that is offensive to most people, and we accept that this is properly part of a vision of the First Amendment that is designed substantially to protect unpopular ways of saying unpopular things. But we also have little doubt that most of what we have seen that to us qualifies as hard-core material falls below this minimal threshold of cognitive or similar appeal.
>
> . . .
>
> . . . The manner of presentation and distribution of most standard pornography confirms the view that at bottom the predominant use of such material is as a masturbatory aid. We do not say that there is anything necessarily wrong with that for that reason. But once the predominant use, and the appeal to that predominant use, becomes apparent, what emerges is that much of what this material involves is not so much portrayal of sex, or discussion of sex, but simply sex itself.[39]

During the last decades of the twentieth century, radical feminist theorists, most notably Catharine MacKinnon and Andrea Dworkin, pioneered a new attack on pornography. They concluded that pornography was not constitutionally protected by the First Amendment because "the graphically sexually explicit subordination of women" served to foster attitudes that contributed to violence against women and sexual discrimination. In one very influential article, MacKinnon asserted,

> Pornography constructs the social reality of gender, the force behind sexism, the subordination in gender inequality, is made invisible; dissent from it becomes inaudible as well as rare. What a woman is, is defined in pornographic terms; this is what pornography does. If the law then looks neutrally on the reality of gender so produced, the harm that has been done will not be perceptible as harm. It becomes just the way things are. Refusing to look at what has been substantively done will institutionalize inequality in law and it will look just like principle.
>
> . . . If women's freedom is as incompatible with pornography's construction of our freedom as our equality is incompatible with pornography's construction of our equality, we get neither freedom nor equality under the liberal calculus. Equality for women is incompatible with a definition of men's freedom that is at our expense. What can freedom for women mean, so long as we remain unequal? Why should men's freedom to use us in this way be purchased with our second-class civil status?[40]

MacKinnon's critique divided the feminist community. Many feminists defended more traditional libertarian views, insisting that MacKinnon's attack on por-

39. U.S. Department of Justice, *Attorney General's Commission on Pornography: Final Report* (Washington, D.C.: Government Printing Office, 1986), 20.

40. Catharine A. MacKinnon, "Pornography, Civil Rights, and Speech," *Harvard Civil Rights and Civil Liberties Law Review* 20 (1985): 7.

nography, if anything, reinforced traditional gender notions.

> Laws which would increase the state's regulation of sexual images present many dangers for women. Although these proposals draw much of their feminist support from women's anger at the market for images of sexual violence, they are aimed not at violence, but at sexual explicitness. Far-right elements recognize the possibility of using the full potential of the ordinances to enforce their sexually conservative world view, and have supported them for that reason. Feminists should therefore look carefully at the text of these "model" laws in order to understand why many believe them to be a useful tool in anti-feminist moral crusades.
>
> The proposed ordinances are dangerous because they seek to embody in law an analysis of the role of sexuality and sexual images in the oppression of women with which even all feminists do not agree. Underlying virtually every section of the proposed laws there is an assumption that sexuality is a realm of unremitting, unequaled victimization for women. . . . But this analysis is not the only feminist perspective on sexuality. Feminist theorists have also argued that the sexual terrain, however power-laden, is actively contested. Women are agents, and not merely victims, who make decisions and act on them, and who desire, seek out, and enjoy sexuality.[41]

Anti-pornography activists enjoyed some political success, but constitutional decision makers eventually rejected all their proposals. An alliance of radical feminists and conservative opponents of obscenity in 1983 convinced the Minneapolis city council to pass an ordinance based on a model anti-pornography ordinance that MacKinnon had drafted, but that measure was vetoed by Mayor Donald Fraser. The next year the same alliance successfully passed a similar measure in Indianapolis. That measure outlawed pornography, which it defined as "the graphic sexually explicit subordination of women, whether in pictures or in words," that "includes one or more of the following:

> (1) Women are presented as sexual objects who enjoy pain or humiliation; or
> (2) Women are presented as sexual objects who experience sexual pleasure in being raped; or
> (3) Women are presented as sexual objects tied up or cut up or mutilated or bruised or physically hurt, or as dismembered or truncated or fragmented or severed into body parts; or
> (4) Women are presented as being penetrated by objects or animals; or
> (5) Women are presented in scenarios of degradation, injury, abasement, torture, shown as filthy or inferior, bleeding, bruised, or hurt in a context that makes these conditions sexual; or
> (6) Women are presented as sexual objects for domination, conquest, violation, exploitation, possession, or use, or through postures or positions of servility or submission or display.

The Seventh Circuit Court of Appeals in *American Booksellers Association, Inc. v. Hudnut* (1985) declared that measure unconstitutional on the ground that Indianapolis had prohibited constitutionally protected speech. Judge Easterbrook wrote,

> Racial bigotry, anti-semitism, violence on television, reporters' biases—these and many more influence the culture and shape our socialization. None is directly answerable by more speech, unless that speech too finds its place in the popular culture. Yet all is protected as speech, however insidious. Any other answer leaves the government in control of all of the institutions of culture, the great censor and director of which thoughts are good for us.
>
> . . .
>
> Indianapolis seeks to prohibit certain speech because it believes this speech influences social relations and politics on a grand scale, that it controls attitudes at home and in the legislature. This precludes a characterization of the speech as low value. True, pornography and obscenity have sex in common. But Indianapolis left out of its definition any reference to literary, artistic, political, or scientific value.[42]

41. Lisa Duggan, Nan D. Hunter, and Carole C. Vance, "False Promises: Feminist Anti-Pornography Legislation," *New York Law School Law Review* 38 (1993): 162–63.

42. *American Booksellers Association, Inc. v. Hudnut*, 771 F.2d 323 (7th Cir., 1985). For a good study of the Minneapolis and Indianapolis struggles over pornography, see Donald Alexander Downs, *The New Politics of Pornography* (Chicago: University of Chicago Press, 1989).

Federal judges were more willing to sustain more traditional morals laws regulating erotic conduct and pornography. *Barnes v. Glen Theatre* (1991) ruled that states could require dancers at adult clubs to wear pasties and G-strings, even if nude dancing was expressive conduct. Chief Justice Rehnquist's majority opinion stated, "Public indecency statutes such as the one before us reflect moral disapproval of people appearing in the nude among strangers in public places." A unanimous Supreme Court in *New York v. Ferber* (1982) authorized states to prohibit child pornography. Justice White asserted, "The prevention of sexual exploitation and abuse of children constitutes a government objective of surpassing importance."

Child pornography and bans on nudity aside, efforts to ban obscenity and pornography fell victim to constitutional culture as much as constitutional law. By the early 1990s depictions of sex had become common fare in the movies and on cable television. Characters on major network series talked about sex in ways that might have been banned during the first half of the twentieth century. The emerging Internet promised to make access to sexually explicit materials universal. In this environment anti-obscenity crusades seemed as antiquated as Prohibition.

Commercial Speech. Commercial speech enjoyed substantial constitutional protection by the mid-1990s. Justice Blackmun urged the justices to protect all "truthful, nonmisleading, noncoercive" advertisements. While that view did not yet command a majority, judicial majorities heightened the standard of constitutional protection. *Central Hudson Gas v. Public Service Commission* (1980) announced a four-part test for assessing the constitutionality of such speech. Justice Powell wrote,

> For commercial speech to come within [the First Amendment], it at least must concern lawful activity and not be misleading. Next we ask whether the asserted governmental interest is substantial. If both inquiries yield positive answers, we must determine whether the regulation directly advances the governmental interest asserted, and whether it is not more extensive than is necessary to serve that interest.

Prohibitions on advertisements for legal services were among the many state regulations that failed to meet this standard.

Expressive Associations. Expressive associations did not fare as well as broadcasters, commercial speakers, and campaign contributors. *Roberts v. U.S. Jaycees* (1984) assessed whether Minnesota could require a private civic organization to accept women as equal members. Justice Brennan's majority opinion recognized that persons had a constitutional right to organize in order to pursue activities protected by the First Amendment. He concluded, however, that the Jaycees were not an expressive organization. He wrote, "The local chapters of the Jaycees are large and basically unselective groups. . . . Apart from age and sex, neither the national organization nor the local chapters employ any criteria for judging applicants for membership, and new members are routinely recruited and admitted with no inquiry into their backgrounds."

B. VOTING

The constitutional politics of voting rights during the Great Society was better for conservatives than Republicans. Many conservatives had principled objections to the provisions in the Voting Rights Acts that interfered with state prerogatives, to Warren Court decisions that announced an unenumerated fundamental right to vote, and to the increased use of racial classifications when apportioning legislative districts. Many Republicans welcomed the large number of white southerners who had abandoned the Democratic Party once persons of color gained access to the ballot and the high probability that majority-minority districts increased the number of both African-American and Republican elected officials. Republicans who gained control of more state legislatures during the 1980s learned that they could gerrymander with the best of the Democrats.

These differences in constitutional politics and constitutional law explain why partisan divisions during the voting rights debates of the 1980s and early 1990s often diverged from judicial divisions. Judicial decisions were structured by ideology. Conservative justices interpreted the Voting Rights Act narrowly, insisted that race could not be the predominant factor when apportioning legislative districts, and rejected judicial power to correct gerrymanders. Many Republican-elected officials supported legislation broadening the Voting Rights Act endorsed efforts to increase the number of majority-minority legislative districts, and gerrymandered whenever they were the majority party in the state legislature. Democrats in both the judiciary and the legislature supported broad readings of the Voting Rights Act, but liberal justices supported the majority-minority legislative districts that Democrat-elected officials often opposed. The result of the sometimes strange alliances between judges identified with one party and elected officials identified with the other was that by the mid-1990s the Voting Rights Act had been slightly strengthened, the federal judiciary had declared unconstitutional several efforts to increase the number of majority-minority legislative districts, and the constitutional status of legislative gerrymanders was unclear.

The Voting Rights Acts

The Supreme Court initially sent mixed signals on the Voting Rights Acts of 1965, 1970 and 1975. *City of Rome v. United States* (1980) ruled that the attorney general had power under the Voting Rights Acts to reject a proposed change in local voting practices that would have a discriminatory effect on persons of color, even if those changes did not have a discriminatory purpose. Justice Marshall's majority opinion declared, "The Act's ban on electoral changes that are discriminatory in effect is an appropriate method of promoting the purposes of the Fifteenth Amendment, even if it is assumed that § 1 of the Amendment prohibits only intentional discrimination in voting," because "Congress could rationally have concluded that, because electoral changes by jurisdictions with a demonstrable history of intentional racial discrimination in voting create the risk of purposeful discrimination, it was proper to prohibit changes that have a discriminatory impact." *City of Mobile v. Bolden* (1980) reached a more conservative result, ruling that Mobile, Alabama, violated neither the Fifteenth Amendment nor the Voting Rights Act by maintaining an at-large system for voting for city commissions, even though no member of the city's African-American population had ever been elected to office. Justice Stewart's plurality opinion declared, "Our decisions have made clear that action by a State that is racially neutral on its face violates the Fifteenth Amendment only if motivated by a discriminatory purpose." *Rome* and *Mobile* reached different conclusions solely because Rome adopted an election procedure that had a discriminatory effect while Mobile maintained a procedure that had a discriminatory effect.

Over strong opposition from the Reagan administration, a coalition of Democrats and moderate Republicans amended the Voting Rights Act to empower federal courts to prohibit all election and voting laws that had discriminatory effects. The Voting Rights Act Amendments of 1982 declared,

> (a) No voting qualification or prerequisite to voting or standard, practice, or procedure shall be imposed or applied by any State or political subdivision in a manner which results in a denial or abridgement of the right of any citizen of the United States to vote on account of race or color. . . .
>
> (b) A violation of subsection (a) is established if, based on the totality of circumstances, it is shown that the political processes leading to nomination or election in the State or political subdivision are not equally open to participation by members of a class of citizens protected by subsection (a) in that its members have less opportunity than other members of the electorate to participate in the political process and to elect representatives of their choice. The extent to which members of a protected class have been elected to office in the State or political subdivision is one circumstance which may be considered: *Provided,* That nothing in this section establishes a right to have members of a protected class elected in numbers equal to their proportion in the population.

The Supreme Court incorporated this statutory change into its voting rights jurisprudence. In *Gingles v. Thornburg* (1986) all nine justices on the Burger Court acknowledged that persons of color could demonstrate a rights violation if the "totality of circumstances" demonstrated that they could not elect the candidates of their choice. The justices did not agree on precisely what encompassed that "totality of circumstances," but they agreed that the focus of litigation under the Voting Rights Act would be how voting systems actually affected the political power of persons of color, and not primarily whether local voting laws had a discriminatory purpose.

Senate Committee on the Judiciary, Senate Report on the Voting Rights Act Amendments of 1982 (1982)[43]

The Voting Rights Act Amendments of 1982 extended the temporary preclearance provisions of the Voting Rights Act of 1965 for twenty-five years, modified the legal conditions for "bailing out" of the preclearance procedures, and reversed the ruling in City of Mobile v. Bolden *(1980) that plaintiffs must prove purposeful discrimination to demonstrate a voting rights violation. The Voting Rights Act Amendments of 1982 substituted an effects test for a motives test. Plaintiffs had to prove only that they had "less opportunity than other members of the electorate to participate in the political process and to elect representatives of their choice."*

The debate over the amendments was largely limited to the "effects" provision. The Democratic majority in the House of Representatives passed a bill explicitly reversing the decision in City of Mobile. *A very conservative Senate subcommittee issued a report defending the purpose requirement. The Reagan administration strongly supported the Senate subcommittee's version of the Voting Rights Act. President Reagan in November 1981 stated, "I believe that the act should retain the 'intent' test under existing law, rather than changing to a new and untested 'effects' standard." Senator Bob Dole brokered a compromise when he proposed adding the following disclaimer to the House proposal: "That nothing in this section establishes a right to have members of a protected class elected in numbers equal to their proportion in the population." So amended, the Voting Rights Act Amendments passed the House and Senate with overwhelming majorities. President Reagan signed the bill on June 29, 1982.*

Consider the following questions when reading the excerpts below from the Senate report. Why do you believe that a bipartisan consensus formed on the need to jettison the purpose test? Was this a matter of principle? What was the role of partisan advantage? What are the strengths and weaknesses of the results test? What test would you require that plaintiffs in voting rights cases meet? The Judiciary Committee claimed that they were not reversing a Supreme Court decision, but merely amending a federal statute. Is that what the Senate was doing? Was the decision to reverse City of Mobile *constitutional?*

43. Excerpted from Senate Committee on the Judiciary, *Senate Report on the Voting Rights Act Amendments of 1982,* 97th Cong., 2d Sess. (1982), S. Rep. 97–417.

. . .

Although we have come a long way since 1965, the nation's task in securing voting rights is not finished. Continued progress toward equal opportunity in the electoral process will be halted if we abandon the act's crucial safeguards now.

The committee is equally concerned about the risk of losing what progress has already been won. The gains are fragile. Without the preclearance of new laws, many of the advances of the past decade could be wiped out overnight with new schemes and devices.

. . .

A review of the kinds of proposed changes that have been objected to by the Attorney General in recent years reveals the types of impediments that still face minority voters in the covered jurisdictions. Among the types of changes that have been objected to most frequently in the period from 1975–1980 are annexations; the use of at-large elections, majority vote requirements, or numbered posts; and the redistricting of boundary lines. This reflects the fact that, since the adoption of the voting rights act, covered jurisdictions have substantially moved from the direct impediments to the right to vote to more sophisticated devices that dilute minority voting.

. . . In January 1980, the De Kalb County Georgia board of registration adopted a policy that it would no longer approve community groups' requests to conduct voter registration drives, even though only 24 percent of black eligible voters were registered, compared to 81 percent of whites. A lawsuit was required to make the county submit the change, and the attorney general objected.

. . .

In the three years following passage of the voting rights act, the city of Indianola, Mississippi reduced the proportion of its black population by more than 30 percent through annexation of outlying white areas while refusing contemporaneous request to annex 11 adjoining predominantly black subdivisions. These predominantly black subdivisions receive city services but are excluded from voting for city officials. Not one of the annexations was ever submitted for preclearance.

. . .

The amendment to the language of section 2 is designed to make clear that plaintiffs need not prove a discriminatory purpose in the adoption or maintenance of the challenged system of practice in order to establish a violation. Plaintiffs must either prove such intent, or, alternatively, must show that the challenged system or practice, in the context of all the circumstances in the jurisdiction in question, results in minorities being denied equal access to the political process.

. . .

. . . To establish a violation, plaintiffs could show a variety of factors, depending upon the kind of rule, practice, or procedure called into question.

Typical factors include:

1. The extent of any history of official discrimination in the state or political subdivision that touched the right of the members of the minority group to register, to vote, or otherwise to participate in the democratic process;
2. The extent to which voting in the elections of the state or political subdivision is racially polarized;
3. The extent to which the state or political subdivision has used unusually large election districts, majority vote requirements, anti-single shot provisions, or other voting practices or procedures that may enhance the opportunity for discrimination against the minority group;
4. If there is a candidate slating process, whether the members of the minority group have been denied access to that process;
5. The extent to which members of the minority group in the state or political subdivision bear the effects of discrimination in such areas as education, employment and health, which hinder their ability to participate effectively in the political process;
6. Whether political campaigns have been characterized by overt or subtle racial appeals;
7. The extent to which members of the minority group have been elected to public office in the jurisdiction.

Additional factors that in some cases have had probative value as part of plaintiffs' evidence to establish a violation are:

Whether there is a significant lack of responsiveness on the part of elected officials to the particularized needs of the members of the minority group.

Whether the policy underlying the state or political subdivision's use of such voting qualification, prerequisite to voting, or standard, practice or procedure is tenuous.

While these enumerated factors will often be the most relevant ones, in some cases other factors will be indicative of the alleged dilution.

. . .

When a federal judge is called upon to determine the validity of a practice challenged under section 2, as amended, he or she is required to act in full accordance with the disclaimer in section 2 which reads as follows:

> The extent to which members of a protected class have been elected to office in the state or political subdivision is one "circumstance" which may be considered, provided that nothing in this section establishes a right to have members of a protected class elected in numbers equal to their proportion in the population.

. . . [T]his provision is both clear and straightforward. . . . It puts to rest any concerns that have been voiced about racial quotas.

. . .The intent test is inappropriate as the exclusive standard for establishing a violation of section 2. . . . The main reason is that, simply put, the test asks the wrong question. . . . [I]f an electoral system operates today to exclude blacks or hispanics from a fair chance to participate, then the matter of what motives were in an official's mind 100 years ago is of the most limited relevance. The standard under the committee amendment is whether minorities have equal access to the process of electing their representatives. If they are denied a fair opportunity to participate, the committee believes that the system should be changed, regardless of what may or may not be provable about events which took place decades ago.

Second, the committee has heard persuasive testimony that the intent test is unnecessarily divisive because it involves charges of racism on the part of individual officials or entire communities. . . .

. . .

Third, the intent test will be an inordinately difficult burden for plaintiffs in most cases. In the case of laws enacted many decades ago, the legislators cannot be subpoenaed from their graves for testimony about the motives behind their actions. . . .

...

The proposed amendment modifying a results test to section 2 is a clearly constitutional exercise of congressional power under Article 1 and the Fourteenth and Fifteenth Amendments. By now the breadth of congressional power to enforce these provisions is hornbook law.

...

Congress may enact measures going beyond the direct requirements of the Fifteenth Amendment, if such measures are appropriate and reasonably adapted to protect citizens against the risk that the right to vote will be denied in violation of the Fifteenth Amendment. That point, clearly established in [*South Carolina v. Katzenbach* (1966)], has not been seriously challenged in subsequent years.

...

The committee has concluded that to enforce fully the Fourteenth and Fifteenth Amendments, it is necessary that section 2 ban election procedures and practices that result in a denial or abridgment of the right to vote. In reaching this conclusion, we find (1) that the difficulties faced by plaintiffs forced to prove discriminatory intent through case-by-case adjudication create a substantial risk that intentional discrimination barred by the Fourteenth and Fifteenth Amendments will go undetected, uncorrected and undeterred unless the results test proposed for section 2 is adopted; and (2) that voting practices and procedures that have discriminatory results perpetuate the effects of past purposeful discrimination.

...

Congress cannot alter the judicial interpretations in [*City of Mobile v. Bolden* (1980)] of the Fourteenth and Fifteenth Amendments by simple statute. But the proposed amendment to Section 2 does not seek to reverse the court's constitutional interpretation. Rather, the proposal is a proper statutory exercise of congress' enforcement power described above and it is not a redefinition of the scope of the constitutional provisions. . . .

...

Additional Views of SENATOR ORRIN G. HATCH (Republican, Utah)

...

The objectives of these amendments are vastly different than those of the original Act. In place of the traditional focus upon equal access to registration and the ballot, the amendments would focus upon equal outcome in the electoral process. Instead of aiming ultimately at the nonconsideration of race in the electoral process as did the original act, the amendments would make race the over-riding factor in public decisions in this area. Instead of directing its protections toward the individual citizen as did the original act—and as does the constitution—the amendments would make racial and ethnic groups the basic unit of protection. Instead of reinforcing the great constitutional principle of equal protection as did the original act, the amendments would substitute a totally alien principle of equal results.

...

There is no core value under the results test other than election results. There is no core value that can lead anywhere other than toward proportional representation by race and ethnic group. There is no ultimate or threshold question that a court must ask under the results test that will lead in any other direction. . . .

...

. . . [T]he concept of a process "equally open to participation" brings to the fore what is perhaps the major defect to the results test. To the extent that it leads anywhere other than to pure proportional representation (and I do not believe that it does), the test provides absolutely no intelligible guidance to courts in determining whether or not a section 2 violation has been established or to communities in determining whether or not their electoral structures and policies are in conformity with the law. What is an "equally open" political process? How can it be identified in terms other than statistical or results-oriented analysis? Under what circumstances is an "objective factor of discrimination," such as an at-large system, a barrier to such an "open" political process and when is it not? What would a totally "open" political process look like? How would a community effectively overcome evidence that their elected representative bodies lacked proportional representation?

...

Perhaps most importantly, the proposed "compromise" suffers from the defects of the House provision in that it attempts statutorily to overturn the Supreme Court's decision in *City of Mobile* interpreting the Fifteenth Amendment. . . . [T]he Congress simply cannot overturn a constitutional decision of the Supreme Court through a mere statute. The Court has held that the Fifteenth Amendment requires a demonstration of intentional or purposeful discrimination. To the extent that the voting rights act generally and Section 2 specifically are predicated upon this amendment—and they are—there is no authority with congress to reinterpret its requirements and to impose greater restrictions upon the states in the conduct of their own affairs. There is no power within congress to act outside the boundaries of the Fifteenth Amendment, as interpreted by the court, at least so long as the federal government remains a government of delegated powers.

. . .

The new voting rights act will also enhance enormously the role of the federal judiciary in the state and municipal governmental process. Race-neutral or ethnic-neutral decisions affecting countless aspects of this process will suddenly be subject to new scrutiny by the courts on the basis of whether such aspects are "tenuous," whether they contribute to an "equal opportunity to participate," whether they permit protected minorities to "elect representatives of their choice," and so forth. As the committee report accurately states, the new section 2 requires, above all, the application of "the court's overall judgment." There is, in fact, little more to the test than this.

Above all, the present measure plays havoc with traditional notions of civil rights and discrimination, and distorts these concepts beyond all recognition. In the process, it can only contribute toward undermining the virtually-realized consensus in this nation in behalf of equality and civil rights in their traditional form—equality of opportunity and equality of access, not equality of result and equality of outcome. The historical evolution of this nation away from the consideration of race in public policy decisions will be halted. The present amendments in the voting rights act represent nothing less than a full retreat from the color-blind principles of law fostered by *Brown v. Board of Education* (1954), the Civil Rights Act of 1964, and the original Voting Rights Act itself. . . .

Majority-Minority Districts

Majority-minority districts are legislative districts apportioned to ensure that members of a racial minority, typically either African-Americans or Hispanic-Americans, constitute a majority of voters. Such districts increased dramatically during the 1980s for legal and partisan reasons. The Supreme Court in *Thornburg v. Gingles* (1986) ruled that the elements of a vote dilution claim under the Voting Rights Act of 1982 included whether "the minority group . . . is politically cohesive" and whether "the white majority votes sufficiently as a bloc to . . . usually defeat the minority's preferred candidate." Many state legislatures interpreted this language as requiring them to create legislative districts in which the majority of voters were either African-American or Hispanic-American. Republican Party leaders and at least some Republicans in the Department of Justice interpreted this language as an opportunity to disrupt relationships between white Democratic incumbents and voters of color. During the late 1980s, one commentator observes, "the Republican National Committee undertook a campaign of guerilla warfare, working with black Democrats against white Democrats in legislatures throughout the South."[44] By 1992 state legislatures had created at least twenty-five majority-minority congressional districts.

Legislative efforts to create majority-minority districts were controversial. The constitutional controversy concerned the use of race in the legislative districting process. The Supreme Court in *Shaw v. Reno* (1993) declared that racial gerrymanders were constitutional only if they were narrowly tailored to serve compelling ends, such as compliance with the Voting Rights Act. The political controversy erupted when President Clinton nominated Professor Lani Guinier to be assistant attorney general for civil rights. Guinier, who as a scholar proposed various electoral schemes designed in part to increase representatives of color, eventually withdrew after a bitter debate that included charges that she was a "Quota Queen." An ongoing scholarly controversy concerns the electoral consequences of majority-minority districts. Most studies conclude that the existence of majority-minority districts in a state increases the number of Republicans elected statewide, but no agreement exists on whether that increase is substantial or slight.

Shaw v. Reno, 509 U.S. 630 (1993)

Ruth Shaw was a white resident of North Carolina. After the 1990 census North Carolina gained a twelfth seat in the

44. David T. Canon, *Race, Redistricting, and Representation: The Unintended Consequences of Black Majority Districts* (Chicago: University of Chicago Press, 1999), 57. This section relies heavy on Canon's study.

Figure 10-3 North Carolina Congressional District 12, 1992

House of Representatives. With strong support from the Bush administration, the state legislature used that opportunity to carve a second black-majority district. The resulting legislative district was irregularly shaped. One state legislator quoted in the majority opinion observed, "If you drove down the interstate with both car doors open, you'd kill most of the people in the district." Shaw objected to being moved from the Second Congressional District to the newly formed Twelfth Congressional District. She filed a lawsuit against the attorney general of the United States, who by the time the case reached the Supreme Court was Janet Reno. The local district court rejected the lawsuit. Shaw appealed to the Supreme Court of the United States.

The Supreme Court by a 5-4 vote ruled that the United States and North Carolina had engaged in an unconstitutional racial gerrymander. Justice O'Connor's majority opinion insisted that race-conscious electoral districting had to meet the same strict scrutiny standard as other race-conscious programs. Why does Justice O'Connor reach that conclusion? Why do the dissents disagree? Who has the better argument? The 5-4 split in Shaw *pit the more conservative justices on the early Rehnquist Court against the more liberal justices. Republican elected officials, by comparison, were at least as supportive of the Twelfth District as Democrats. How do you explain the differences between elected officials and judges on racial gerrymanders?*

JUSTICE O'CONNOR delivered the opinion of the Court.

. . .

Classifications of citizens solely on the basis of race "are by their very nature odious to a free people whose institutions are founded upon the doctrine of equality." They threaten to stigmatize individuals by reason of their membership in a racial group and to incite racial hostility. Accordingly, we have held that the Fourteenth Amendment requires state legislation that expressly distinguishes among citizens because of their race to be narrowly tailored to further a compelling governmental interest.

. . .

Appellants contend that redistricting legislation that is so bizarre on its face that it is "unexplainable on grounds other than race," demands the same close scrutiny that we give other state laws that classify citizens by race. Our voting rights precedents support that conclusion.

. . .

The difficulty of proof . . . does not mean that a racial gerrymander, once established, should receive less scrutiny under the Equal Protection Clause than other state legislation classifying citizens by race. Moreover, it seems clear to us that proof sometimes will not be difficult at all. In some exceptional cases, a reapportionment plan may be so highly irregular that, on its face, it rationally cannot be understood as anything other than an effort to "segregat[e] . . . voters" on the basis of race. *Gomillion v. Lightfoot* (1960), in which a tortured municipal boundary line was drawn to exclude black voters, was such a case. . . .

Put differently, we believe that reapportionment is one area in which appearances do matter. A reapportionment plan that includes in one district individuals who belong to the same race, but who are otherwise widely separated by geographical and political boundaries, and who may have little in common with one another but the color of their skin, bears an uncomfortable resemblance to political apartheid. It reinforces the perception that members of the same racial group—regardless of their age, education, economic status, or the community in which they live—think alike, share the same political interests, and will prefer the same candidates at the polls. We have rejected such perceptions elsewhere as impermissible racial stereotypes. . . . By perpetuating such notions, a racial gerrymander may exacerbate the very patterns of racial bloc voting that majority-minority districting is sometimes said to counteract.

The message that such districting sends to elected representatives is equally pernicious. When a district obviously is created solely to effectuate the perceived common interests of one racial group, elected officials are more likely to believe that their primary obligation is to represent only the members of that group, rather than their constituency as a whole. This is altogether antithetical to our system of representative democracy. . . .

For these reasons, we conclude that a plaintiff challenging a reapportionment statute under the Equal Protection Clause may state a claim by alleging that the legislation, though race-neutral on its face, rationally cannot be understood as anything other than an effort to separate voters into different districts on the basis of race, and that the separation lacks sufficient justification. . . .

. . .

The state appellees suggest that a covered jurisdiction may have a compelling interest in creating majority-minority districts in order to comply with the Voting Rights Act. The States certainly have a very strong interest in complying with federal antidiscrimination laws that are constitutionally valid as interpreted and as applied. But in the context of a Fourteenth Amendment challenge, courts must bear in mind the difference between what the law permits and what it requires.

For example, on remand North Carolina might claim that it adopted the revised plan in order to comply with the § 5 "nonretrogression" principle. Under that principle, a proposed voting change cannot be precleared if it will lead to "a retrogression in the position of racial minorities with respect to their effective exercise of the electoral franchise." . . .

. . . [W]e do not read . . . any of our . . . § 5 cases to give covered jurisdictions carte blanche to engage in racial gerrymandering in the name of nonretrogression. A reapportionment plan would not be narrowly tailored to the goal of avoiding retrogression if the State went beyond what was reasonably necessary to avoid retrogression. . . .

. . .

Racial classifications of any sort pose the risk of lasting harm to our society. They reinforce the belief, held by too many for too much of our history, that individuals should be judged by the color of their skin. Racial classifications with respect to voting carry particular dangers. Racial gerrymandering, even for remedial purposes, may balkanize us into competing racial factions; it threatens to carry us further from the goal of a political system in which race no longer matters—a goal that the Fourteenth and Fifteenth Amendments embody, and to which the Nation continues to aspire. It is for these reasons that race-based districting by our state legislatures demands close judicial scrutiny.

. . .

JUSTICE WHITE, with whom JUSTICE BLACKMUN and JUSTICE STEVENS join, dissenting.

. . .

The grounds for my disagreement with the majority are simply stated: Appellants have not presented a cognizable claim, because they have not alleged a cognizable injury. To date, we have held that only two types of state voting practices could give rise to a constitutional claim. The first involves direct and outright deprivation of the right to vote, for example by means of a poll tax or literacy test. . . . Plainly, this variety is not implicated by appellants' allegations and need not detain us further. The second type of unconstitutional practice is that which "affects the political strength of various groups" in violation of the Equal Protection Clause. As for this latter category, we have insisted that members of the political or racial group demonstrate that the challenged action have the intent and effect of unduly diminishing their influence on the political process.

. . .

. . . [W]e have limited such claims by insisting upon a showing that "the political processes . . . were not equally open to participation by the group in question—that its members had less opportunity than did other residents in the district to participate in the political processes and to elect legislators of their choice." . . .

. . .

. . . [I]t strains credulity to suggest that North Carolina's purpose in creating a second majority-minority district was to discriminate against members of the majority group by "impair[ing] or burden[ing their] opportunity . . . to participate in the political process." . . . Whites constitute roughly 76% of the total population and 79% of the voting age population in North Carolina. Yet, under the State's plan, they still constitute a voting majority in 10 (or 83%) of the 12 congressional districts. Though they might be dissatisfied at the prospect of casting a vote for a losing candidate—a lot shared by many, including a disproportionate number of minority voters—surely they cannot complain of discriminatory treatment.

. . .

The other part of the majority's explanation of its holding is related to its simultaneous discomfort and fascination with irregularly shaped districts. Lack of compactness or contiguity, like uncouth district lines, certainly is a helpful indicator that some form of gerrymandering (racial or other) might have taken place and that "something may be amiss." . . .

But while district irregularities may provide strong indicia of a potential gerrymander, they do no more than that. In particular, they have no bearing on whether the plan ultimately is found to violate the Constitution. Given two districts drawn on similar, race-based grounds, the one does not become more injurious than the other simply by virtue of being snake-like, at least so far as the Constitution is concerned and absent any evidence of differential racial impact. . . . It is shortsighted as well, for a regularly shaped district can just as effectively effectuate racially discriminatory gerrymandering as an odd-shaped one. By focusing on looks rather than impact, the majority "immediately casts attention in the wrong direction—toward superficialities of shape and size, rather than toward the political realities of district composition." . . .

. . .

JUSTICE BLACKMUN, dissenting. . . .

JUSTICE STEVENS, dissenting.

. . .

I believe that the Equal Protection Clause is violated when the State creates . . . uncouth district boundaries . . . for the sole purpose of making it more difficult for members of a minority group to win an election. The duty to govern impartially is abused when a group with power over the electoral process defines electoral boundaries solely to enhance its own political strength at the expense of any weaker group. That duty, however, is not violated when the majority acts to facilitate the election of a member of a group that lacks such power because it remains underrepresented in the state legislature—whether that group is defined by political affiliation, by common economic interests, or by religious, ethnic, or racial characteristics. The difference between constitutional and unconstitutional gerrymanders has nothing to do with whether they are based on assumptions about the groups they affect, but whether their purpose is to enhance the power of the group in control of the districting process at the expense of any minority group, and thereby to strengthen the unequal distribution of electoral power.

. . . If it is permissible to draw boundaries to provide adequate representation for rural voters, for union members, for Hasidic Jews, for Polish Americans, or for Republicans, it necessarily follows that it is permissible to do the same thing for members of the very minority group whose history in the United States gave birth to the Equal Protection Clause.

JUSTICE SOUTER, dissenting.

. . .

. . . Unlike other contexts in which we have addressed the State's conscious use of race, electoral districting calls for decisions that nearly always require some consideration of race for legitimate reasons where there is a racially mixed population. As long as members of racial groups have the commonality of interest implicit in our ability to talk about concepts like "minority voting strength," and "dilution of minority votes," and as long as racial bloc voting takes place, legislators will have to take race into account in order to avoid dilution of minority voting strength in the districting plans they adopt. One need look no further than the Voting Rights Act to understand that this may be required. . . .

In districting, . . . the mere placement of an individual in one district instead of another denies no one a right or benefit provided to others. All citizens may register, vote, and be represented in whatever district, the individual voter has a right to vote in each election, and the election will result in the voter's representation. . . . It is true, of course, that one's vote may be more or less effective depending on the interests of the other individuals who are in one's district, and our cases recognize the reality that members of the same race often have shared interests. "Dilution" thus refers to the effects of districting decisions not on an individual's political power viewed in isolation, but on the political power of a group. . . .

. . . [B]ecause there frequently will be a constitutionally permissible use of race in electoral districting, as exemplified by the consideration of race to comply with the Voting Rights Act . . . , it has seemed more appropriate for the Court to identify impermissible uses by describing particular effects sufficiently serious to justify recognition under the Fourteenth Amendment. Under our cases there is in general a requirement that in order to obtain relief under the Fourteenth Amendment, the purpose and effect of the districting must be to devalue the effectiveness of a voter compared to what, as a group member, he would otherwise be able to enjoy. . . .

The Lani Guinier Nomination Fight

President Bill Clinton launched a political free-for-all when in April 1993 he nominated Lani Guinier, a University of Pennsylvania law professor and former lawyer for the NAACP Legal Defense Fund, as assistant attorney general for civil rights. Guinier in a series of controversial articles had previously championed cumulative voting and

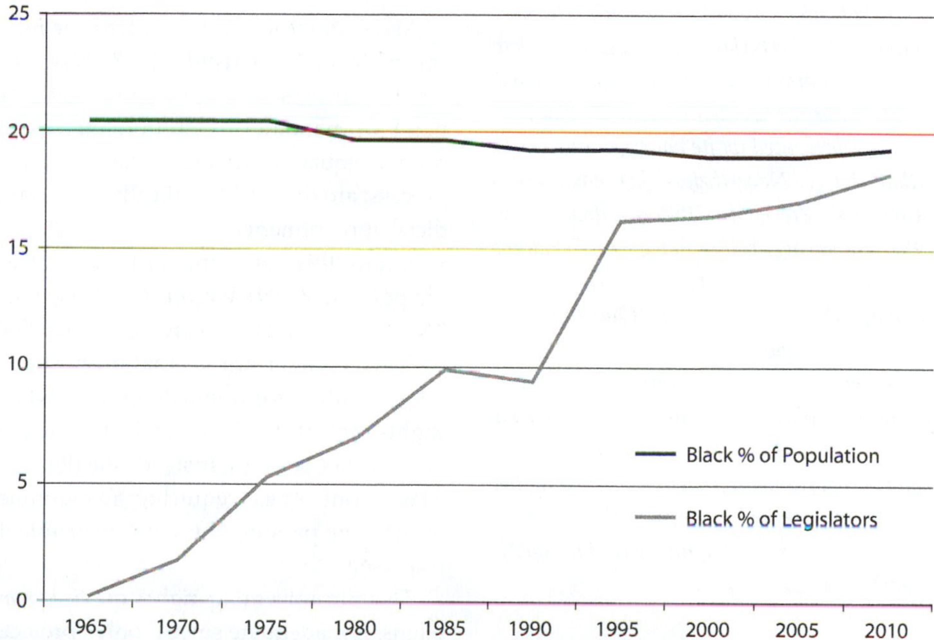

Figure 10-4 Black State Legislators as a Percentage of All Legislators in the South

Source: Bernard Grofman and Lisa Handley, "The Impact of the Voting Rights Act on Black Representation in Southern State Legislatures," *Legislative Studies Quarterly* 16 (1991):111, 113; National Conference of State Legislatures. This material is reproduced with permission of John Wiley & Sons, Inc.

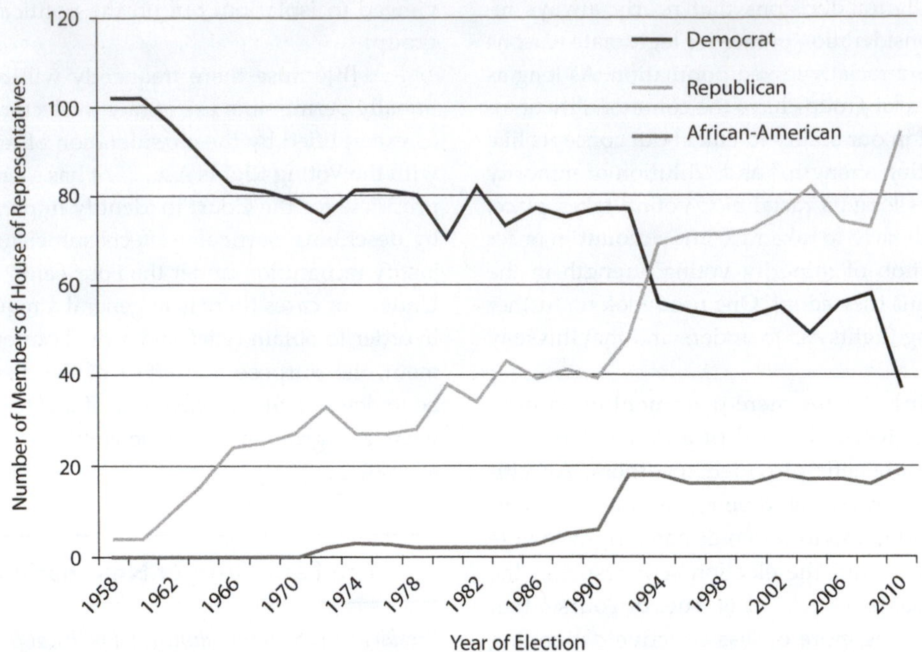

Figure 10-5 Partisan and Racial Composition of Southern Delegation to the U.S. House of Representatives, 1959–2013

proportional representation both as remedies for voting rights violations and on their merits.[45] *Some of these articles spoke of authentic black representation. Such critics as Clint Bolick, a prominent libertarian activist, claimed that Guinier favored representation schemes in which a fixed number of persons of color represented persons of color and white representatives represented white voters. Guinier vigorously denied that charge. Nevertheless, her nomination proved too controversial. President Clinton withdrew the nomination in the late spring, before Senate confirmation hearings could be held.*

Consider the charge that Guinier was a "Quota Queen" when reading the materials below. Is the charge accurate? If not accurate, is the charge nevertheless within the ambit of legitimate constitutional politics? How does Guinier defend her preferred electoral schemes? Many European countries have some version of proportional representation. Should the United States consider proportional representation schemes, or is the idea un-American (or at least antithetical to constitutional principles)?

Clint Bolick, Clinton's Quota Queens (1993)[46]

. . .

Ms. Guinier sets the standard for innovative radicalism. In a 1989 *Harvard Civil Rights-Civil Liberties Law Review* article, she . . . proclaims that anti-discrimination laws mandate "a result-oriented inquiry, in which roughly equal outcomes, not merely an apparently fair process, are the goal," and calls for racial quotas in judicial appointments.

But for this new vanguard, quotas are only a starting point. In a 1991 *Virginia Law Review* article entitled "No Two Seats: The Elusive Quest for Political Equality," Ms. Guinier argues that proportional legislative representation for minority groups, which the Voting Rights Act of 1965 presently is construed to guarantee, is not enough. Instead, she demands equal legislative outcomes, requiring abandonment not only of the "one person, one vote" principle, but majority rule itself.

The current voting rights quota system, she complains, is inadequate since it only "protects the right to

45. See Lani Guiner, *Tyranny of the Majority: Fundamental Fairness in Representative Democracy* (New York: Free Press, 1994).

46. Excerpted from Clint Bolick, "Clinton's Quota Queens," *Wall Street Journal*, April 30, 1993.

be 'present,' whereas the right to control government policy is reserved to those who can organize a majority." The solution, she urges, is to eliminate the "'winner-take-all' features of any majoritarian electoral or legislative voting process in which the minority is identifiable, racially homogenous, insular, and permanent."

Ms. Guinier would invoke the Voting Rights Act in such circumstances to eliminate "one person, one vote" procedures and the requirement of winning electoral or legislative majorities. Instead, she would create an "aggregating device" with which "voluntary minority interest constituencies could choose to cumulate their votes to express the intensity of their distinctive groups interests."

. . .

In the legislative arena, "simpleminded notions of majority rule," Ms. Guinier asserts, "interact with racial block voting to make statutorily protected groups perennial legislative losers." Wherever this is true, she contends, the Voting Rights Act should require new procedures to ensure "a fairer distribution of political power." Though her proposals in this context are amorphous, they include cumulative voting and elimination of majority thresholds to ensure "each group has a right to have its interests satisfied a fair proportion of the time."

Whether or not these proposals have merit as public policy, Ms. Guinier clearly believes they are compelled by the Voting Rights Act, which she would be charged with enforcing as assistant attorney general. Ms. Guinier would graft onto the existing system a complex racial spoils system that would further polarize an already divided nation.

. . .

Mr. Clinton owes his election in no small part to the disappearance of the "Q" word from the political lexicon in 1992. If he persists in entrusting the civil rights law enforcement apparatus to the likes of Ms. Guinier . . . , the in-your-face civil rights agenda they no doubt will promote may ultimately prove the most incendiary of political miscalculations.

Lani Guinier, What I Would Have Told the Senate (1993)[47]

. . .

. . . [T]he Voting Rights Act has not yet completely succeeded in giving all Americans an equally effective voice in their government.

. . .

In my work, I have argued that when voters are denied the ability to choose for themselves candidates who conscientiously represent their interests, those representatives are not "authentic." Contrary to the distortions of conservative critics, I have never suggested that only blacks can be authentic representatives. Again and again, I have focused on giving voters the choice as to what attributes should matter in picking a representative.

For myself, I believe in a politics of like minds, not one of like bodies, and I firmly believe that white candidates of good will can authentically represent black voters, just as I believe that black candidates can authentically represent white voters. . . .

. . .

Let me give just two examples of the sorts of recommendations I have made in my work: cumulative voting and legislative supermajority requirements. . . .

. . .

To understand how cumulative voting works, let's look at one place that has tried it; Chilton County, Alabama. . . .

When the at-large election system was struck down by a federal court as intentionally discriminatory, the county adopted a cumulative system in which each voter can cast seven votes to fill the seven commission seats. What makes cumulative voting work so well is that a voter who feels very strongly about a candidate can give that candidate more than one vote. So if Voter A really wants candidate Z to win, she can throw all seven of her votes behind him. On the other hand, if Voter B feels strongly about more than one candidate, he can spread out his votes. It's up to each voter to choose for himself or herself the strategy that best serves his or her interests.

. . . Cumulative voting does not assign voters to groups according to any predetermined assumptions. Nor does it require voters to vote as part of a group. The only groups that are recognized by cumulative voting are those that voters choose to join by the way they cast their ballots.

Cumulative voting makes it impossible for any one bloc of voters to capture an unfairly high number of seats. Under the old system, 51 percent of Chilton County's voters could capture all the seats all the time,

47. Lani Guinier, "What I Would Have Told the Senate," *Washington Post*, June 13, 1993.

completely shutting out the other 49 percent of the voters. Under the cumulative system, however, many more voters can elect the candidates they want. A majority of the voters still elects a majority of commission, but smaller groups get some representation too. This is not minority rule; it's democratic fair play.

The results of cumulative voting in Chilton County have been quite encouraging. As a result of the system, the first black commissioner in the county's history was elected. And other groups (like Republicans) also elected representatives for the first time. This means that the commission better reflects the views and priorities of the county's citizens, and these diverse representatives can build coalitions and alliances on the commission that will result in fairer treatment for all county residents.

. . .

The purpose of supermajority rules is to encourage broad-based consensus before certain decisions are made and to oblige the majority to consult with and take into account the viewpoint of a substantial minority. As George Will wrote . . . in defending the Republican minority veto in the Senate, "Democracy is trivialized when reduced to simple majoritarianism—government by adding machine. A mature, nuanced democracy makes provision for respecting not mere numbers but also intensity of feeling."

. . .

Here's one example of how well a supermajority requirement has worked. Ten years ago, a federal court found that the election system for the Mobile, Ala., city government was set up in an intentionally discriminatory manner: It was designed to make sure that black voters could not elect anyone, and the government was unresponsive to the needs of blacks. As part of the remedy, the Alabama legislature agreed to require that decisions of the new city council receive at least five votes from the seven-member council. (This is a supermajority requirement because a 4 to 3 vote is not good enough.) This meant biracial coalitions: The four members of the council elected from majority-white districts cannot run the council without the active support of at least one of the members elected from a majority-black district. Community activists report that this supermajority voting rule has fostered coalition building and dialogue. . . .

Gerrymandering

The Supreme Court showed far more deference to partisan gerrymanders than racial gerrymanders. A badly divided Court in *Davis v. Bandemer* (1986) suggested that federal courts would rarely interfere when state legislators drew electoral districts in ways that enabled the majority party to gain more representatives than were merited by their statewide percentage of the vote. Four justices demanded that plaintiffs challenging a partisan gerrymander demonstrate long-standing problems with the operation of state elections. Justice White wrote,

> An equal protection violation may be found only where the electoral system substantially disadvantages certain voters in their opportunity to influence the political process effectively. In this context, such a finding of unconstitutionality must be supported by evidence of continued frustration of the will of a majority of the voters or effective denial to a minority of voters of a fair chance to influence the political process.

Three justices maintained that partisan gerrymanders raised no justiciable issues. Justice O'Connor declared, "The Equal Protection Clause does not supply judicially manageable standards for resolving purely political gerrymandering claims, and no group right to an equal share of political power was ever intended by the Framers of the Fourteenth Amendment." Justice Powell and Justice Stevens were more open to striking down partisan gerrymanders. They maintained that an examination of such factors as "the shapes of voting districts" and "established political subdivision boundaries" could demonstrate that "a districting plan purposefully discriminates against political opponents."

Regulating Elections

The Supreme Court cast a suspicious eye on state laws regulating the electoral process. *Tashjian v. Republican Party* (1986) ruled that parties had a constitutional right to allow independents to vote in party primaries. Justice Marshall's majority opinion asserted that a political party's "attempt to broaden the base of public participation in and support for its activities is conduct undeniably central to the exercise of the right of association." *Anderson v. Celebrezze* (1983) by a 5-4 vote struck down special rules that burdened efforts by independent candidates to be placed on the ballot. Justice Steven's majority opinion contended,

> A burden that falls unequally on new or small political parties or on independent candidates impinges,

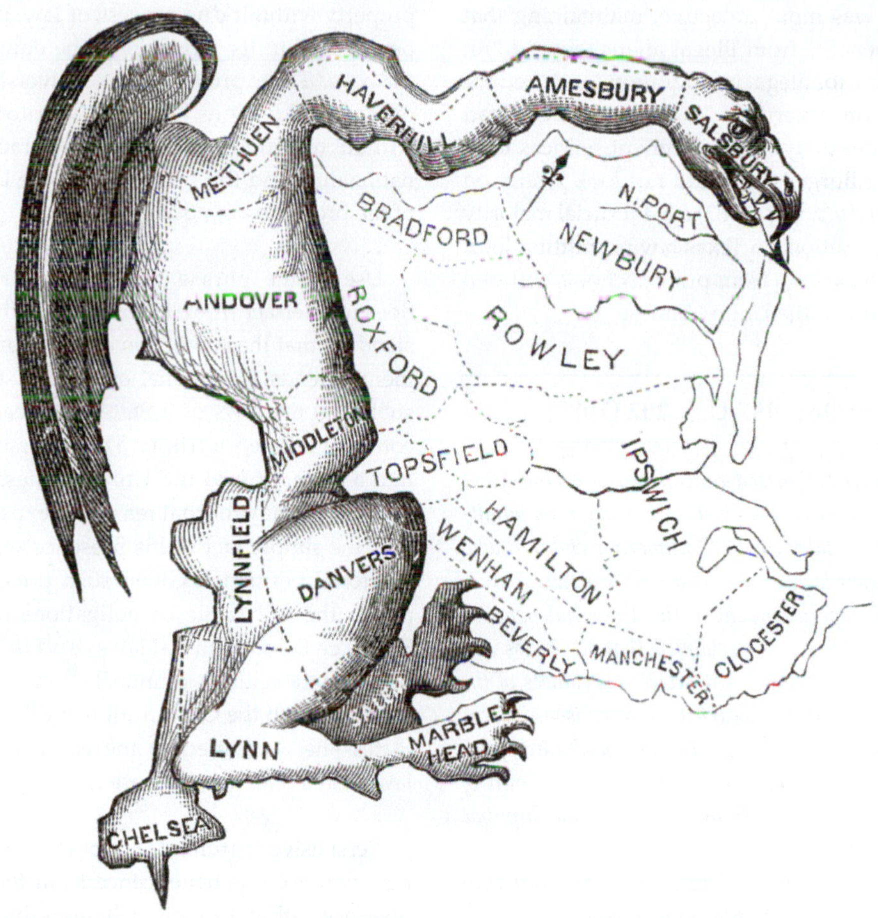

Illustration 10-2 The Gerry-Mander, A New Species of Monster

In 1812, the Republican majority in the Massachusetts legislature drew up a new map for state senate districts that seemed biased against the Federalists. The Federalists loudly complained. The legislative district for a portion of Essex County was said to resemble a salamander, and one Federalist paper named the district after the Republican governor, Elbridge Gerry. Strategically drawn legislative districts became known as "gerrymanders." Many, most notably the legislative district at issue in *Shaw v. Reno* (1989), are even less compact.

Source: Elkanah Tisdale (1771–1835). Originally published in the Boston Centinel, 1812.

by its very nature, on associational choices protected by the First Amendment. It discriminates against those candidates and—of particular importance—against those voters whose political preferences lie outside the existing political parties. . . . In short, the primary values protected by the First Amendment, "a profound national commitment to the principle that debate on public issues should be uninhibited, robust, and wide-open," are served when election campaigns are not monopolized by the existing political parties.

C. Citizenship

Americans debated whether persons illegally in the United States have any legal or constitutional rights. National parties were slow to take strong positions. The Republican Party platform in 1980 did not mention the issue. Republicans in 1992 promised only to "seek stiff penalties for those who smuggle illegal aliens into the country." The Democratic platform that year said nothing about illegal immigration, only promising "immigration policies that promote fairness, non-discrimination and family reunification." The Reagan administration was more proactive, maintaining that "withholding benefits from illegal aliens" would "reduce the incentive for illegal immigration" and "reduce the tax burden on Americans."[48] States took the lead in passing statutes denying government services to illegal aliens. The Burger Court did not look kindly on those laws. In *Plyler v. Doe* (1982) a 5-4 judicial majority declared unconstitutional a Texas law permitting local school boards to exclude from public schools children who were illegally in the United States.

Plyler v. Doe, 457 U.S. 202 (1982)

The Texas legislature authorized local officials to exclude from public schools all children who had not legally been admitted into the United States. In 1977 numerous children who could not prove their legal status filed a class action against James Plyler, the superintendent of the Tyler Independent School District in Texas. They claimed that the Texas law violated the due process and equal protection clauses of the Fourteenth Amendment. The local federal court issued an injunction forbidding Plyler from excluding the children from public schools. That decision was sustained by the Court of Appeals for the Fifth Circuit. Texas appealed to the Supreme Court of the United States.

The Supreme Court by a 5-4 vote declared unconstitutional the Texas law banning undocumented children from public schools. Justice Brennan's majority opinion insisted that no good reason existed to deprive these children of an education. Brennan insisted that laws discriminating against the children of illegal aliens merited heightened constitutional scrutiny. Why does he make this claim? Why do the dissenters disagree? Who has the better argument? Chief Justice Burger's dissent concludes, "The solution to this seemingly intractable problem is to defer to the political processes, unpalatable as that may be to some." Is he correct? Which governing institution should be responsible for determining the status of illegal aliens and their children?

JUSTICE BRENNAN delivered the opinion of the Court.

. . .

"The Fourteenth Amendment to the Constitution is not confined to the protection of citizens. It says: 'Nor shall any state deprive any person of life, liberty, or property without due process of law; nor deny to any person within its jurisdiction the equal protection of the laws.' These provisions are universal in their application, to all persons within the territorial jurisdiction, without regard to any differences of race, of color, or of nationality; and the protection of the laws is a pledge of the protection of equal laws."

. . .

Use of the phrase "within its jurisdiction" thus does not detract from, but rather confirms, the understanding that the protection of the Fourteenth Amendment extends to anyone, citizen or stranger, who is subject to the laws of a State, and reaches into every corner of a State's territory. That a person's initial entry into a State, or into the United States, was unlawful, and that he may for that reason be expelled, cannot negate the simple fact of his presence within the State's territorial perimeter. Given such presence, he is subject to the full range of obligations imposed by the State's civil and criminal laws. And until he leaves the jurisdiction—either voluntarily, or involuntarily in accordance with the Constitution and laws of the United States—he is entitled to the equal protection of the laws that a State may choose to establish.

. . .

Persuasive arguments support the view that a State may withhold its beneficence from those whose very presence within the United States is the product of their own unlawful conduct. These arguments do not apply with the same force to classifications imposing disabilities on the minor children of such illegal entrants. At the least, those who elect to enter our territory by stealth and in violation of our law should be prepared to bear the consequences, including, but not limited to, deportation. But the children of those illegal entrants are not comparably situated. Their "parents have the ability to conform their conduct to societal norms," and presumably the ability to remove themselves from the State's jurisdiction; but the children who are plaintiffs in these cases "can affect neither their parents' conduct nor their own status." . . .

Of course, undocumented status is not irrelevant to any proper legislative goal. Nor is undocumented status an absolutely immutable characteristic since it is the product of conscious, indeed unlawful, action. But [the Texas law] is directed against children, and imposes its discriminatory burden on the basis of a legal characteristic over which children can have little control. It is thus difficult to conceive of a rational

48. Office of Legal Policy, *The Constitution in the Year 2000*, 166.

justification for penalizing these children for their presence within the United States. . . .

Public education is not a "right" granted to individuals by the Constitution. But neither is it merely some governmental "benefit" indistinguishable from other forms of social welfare legislation. Both the importance of education in maintaining our basic institutions, and the lasting impact of its deprivation on the life of the child, mark the distinction. . . . We have recognized "the public schools as a most vital civic institution for the preservation of a democratic system of government." . . . In addition, education provides the basic tools by which individuals might lead economically productive lives to the benefit of us all. In sum, education has a fundamental role in maintaining the fabric of our society. We cannot ignore the significant social costs borne by our Nation when select groups are denied the means to absorb the values and skills upon which our social order rests.

. . .

These well-settled principles allow us to determine the proper level of deference. . . . Undocumented aliens cannot be treated as a suspect class because their presence in this country in violation of federal law is not a "constitutional irrelevancy." Nor is education a fundamental right; a State need not justify by compelling necessity every variation in the manner in which education is provided to its population. But more is involved in these cases than the abstract question whether § 21.031 discriminates against a suspect class, or whether education is a fundamental right. Section 21.031 imposes a lifetime hardship on a discrete class of children not accountable for their disabling status. The stigma of illiteracy will mark them for the rest of their lives. By denying these children a basic education, we deny them the ability to live within the structure of our civic institutions, and foreclose any realistic possibility that they will contribute in even the smallest way to the progress of our Nation. In determining the rationality of § 21.031, we may appropriately take into account its costs to the Nation and to the innocent children who are its victims. In light of these countervailing costs, the discrimination contained in § 21.031 can hardly be considered rational unless it furthers some substantial goal of the State.

. . .

. . . [A]ppellants appear to suggest that the State may seek to protect itself from an influx of illegal immigrants. While a State might have an interest in mitigating the potentially harsh economic effects of sudden shifts in population, § 21.031 hardly offers an effective method of dealing with an urgent demographic or economic problem. There is no evidence in the record suggesting that illegal entrants impose any significant burden on the State's economy. To the contrary, the available evidence suggests that illegal aliens underutilize public services, while contributing their labor to the local economy and tax money to the state fisc. . . .

. . . [W]hile it is apparent that a State may "not . . . reduce expenditures for education by barring [some arbitrarily chosen class of] children from its schools," appellants suggest that undocumented children are appropriately singled out for exclusion because of the special burdens they impose on the State's ability to provide high-quality public education. But the record in no way supports the claim that exclusion of undocumented children is likely to improve the overall quality of education in the State. . . .

. . . The State has no assurance that any child, citizen or not, will employ the education provided by the State within the confines of the State's borders. In any event, the record is clear that many of the undocumented children disabled by this classification will remain in this country indefinitely, and that some will become lawful residents or citizens of the United States. It is difficult to understand precisely what the State hopes to achieve by promoting the creation and perpetuation of a subclass of illiterates within our boundaries, surely adding to the problems and costs of unemployment, welfare, and crime. It is thus clear that whatever savings might be achieved by denying these children an education, they are wholly insubstantial in light of the costs involved to these children, the State, and the Nation.

If the State is to deny a discrete group of innocent children the free public education that it offers to other children residing within its borders, that denial must be justified by a showing that it furthers some substantial state interest. . . .

JUSTICE MARSHALL, concurring.

. . . It continues to be my view that a class-based denial of public education is utterly incompatible with the Equal Protection Clause of the Fourteenth Amendment.

JUSTICE BLACKMUN, concurring.

. . .

. . . [W]hen the State provides an education to some and denies it to others, it immediately and inevitably creates class distinctions of a type fundamentally inconsistent with . . . the Equal Protection Clause. . . . [C]lassifications involving the complete denial of education are in a sense unique, for they strike at the heart of equal protection values by involving the State in the creation of permanent class distinctions. In a sense, then, denial of an education is the analogue of denial of the right to vote: the former relegates the individual to second-class social status; the latter places him at a permanent political disadvantage.

This conclusion is fully consistent with [*San Antonio Independent School District v. Rodriguez* (1973)]. The Court there reserved judgment on the constitutionality of a state system that "occasioned an absolute denial of educational opportunities to any of its children," noting that "no charge fairly could be made that the system [at issue in *Rodriguez*] fails to provide each child with an opportunity to acquire . . . basic minimal skills." . . . Here, however, the State has undertaken to provide an education to most of the children residing within its borders. And, in contrast to the situation in *Rodriguez*, it does not take an advanced degree to predict the effects of a complete denial of education upon those children targeted by the State's classification. In such circumstances, the voting decisions suggest that the State must offer something more than a rational basis for its classification.

JUSTICE POWELL, concurring.

. . .

Our review in a case such as these is properly heightened. . . . The classification at issue deprives a group of children of the opportunity for education afforded all other children simply because they have been assigned a legal status due to a violation of law by their parents. These children thus have been singled out for a lifelong penalty and stigma. A legislative classification that threatens the creation of an underclass of future citizens and residents cannot be reconciled with one of the fundamental purposes of the Fourteenth Amendment. In these unique circumstances, the Court properly may require that the State's interests be substantial and that the means bear a "fair and substantial relation" to these interests.

. . .

CHIEF JUSTICE BURGER, with whom JUSTICE WHITE, JUSTICE REHNQUIST, and JUSTICE O'CONNOR join, dissenting.

The dispositive issue in these cases, simply put, is whether, for purposes of allocating its finite resources, a state has a legitimate reason to differentiate between persons who are lawfully within the state and those who are unlawfully there. The distinction the State of Texas has drawn—based not only upon its own legitimate interests but on classifications established by the Federal Government in its immigration laws and policies—is not unconstitutional.

. . .

The Court first suggests that these illegal alien children, although not a suspect class, are entitled to special solicitude under the Equal Protection Clause because they lack "control" over or "responsibility" for their unlawful entry into this country. . . . However, the Equal Protection Clause does not preclude legislators from classifying among persons on the basis of factors and characteristics over which individuals may be said to lack "control." Indeed, in some circumstances persons generally, and children in particular, may have little control over or responsibility for such things as their ill health, need for public assistance, or place of residence. Yet a state legislature is not barred from considering, for example, relevant differences between the mentally healthy and the mentally ill, or between the residents of different counties, simply because these may be factors unrelated to individual choice or to any "wrongdoing." The Equal Protection Clause protects against arbitrary and irrational classifications, and against invidious discrimination stemming from prejudice and hostility; it is not an all-encompassing "equalizer" designed to eradicate every distinction for which persons are not "responsible."

. . .

The importance of education is beyond dispute. Yet we have held repeatedly that the importance of a governmental service does not elevate it to the status of a "fundamental right" for purposes of equal protection analysis. . . . Moreover, the Court points to no meaningful way to distinguish between education and other governmental benefits in this context. Is the Court suggesting that education is more "fundamental" than food, shelter, or medical care?

. . .

Once it is conceded—as the Court does—that illegal aliens are not a suspect class, and that education is not a fundamental right, our inquiry should focus on and be limited to whether the legislative classification at issue bears a rational relationship to a legitimate state purpose.

The State contends primarily that § 21.031 serves to prevent undue depletion of its limited revenues available for education, and to preserve the fiscal integrity of the State's school-financing system against an ever-increasing flood of illegal aliens—aliens over whose entry or continued presence it has no control. Of course such fiscal concerns alone could not justify discrimination against a suspect class or an arbitrary and irrational denial of benefits to a particular group of persons. Yet I assume no Member of this Court would argue that prudent conservation of finite state revenues is per se an illegitimate goal. . . .

Without laboring what will undoubtedly seem obvious to many, it simply is not "irrational" for a state to conclude that it does not have the same responsibility to provide benefits for persons whose very presence in the state and this country is illegal as it does to provide for persons lawfully present. By definition, illegal aliens have no right whatever to be here, and the state may reasonably, and constitutionally, elect not to provide them with governmental services at the expense of those who are lawfully in the state.

. . .

The Constitution does not provide a cure for every social ill, nor does it vest judges with a mandate to try to remedy every social problem. Moreover, when this Court rushes in to remedy what it perceives to be the failings of the political processes, it deprives those processes of an opportunity to function. When the political institutions are not forced to exercise constitutionally allocated powers and responsibilities, those powers, like muscles not used, tend to atrophy. Today's cases, I regret to say, present yet another example of unwarranted judicial action which in the long run tends to contribute to the weakening of our political processes.

. . .

The solution to this seemingly intractable problem is to defer to the political processes, unpalatable as that may be to some.

V. EQUALITY

MAJOR DEVELOPMENTS

- Fierce battles in states over funding for public schools
- Strict curbs on affirmative action
- Emergence of strong gender gaps in American constitutional politics

Reagan conservatives sought to preserve what they believed was the constitutional status quo on equality issues before the late 1960s. Reagan and his allies celebrated *Brown v. Board of Education* (1954). Conservatives endorsed the bans on racial and gender discrimination decreed by the Civil Rights Act of 1964. Many, however, thought that success had spoiled the civil rights movement. Civil rights activists, Reagan and others complained, were now seeking special privileges rather than equal treatment. More generally, conservatives insisted that new demands for equality by persons of color, women, and others often ignored real differences between people, imposed racial and gender classifications that repeated the odious policies of the past, and called on judges to substitute their elite perspectives for those of democratically elected officials.

Many liberals claimed that this conservative willingness to endorse the constitutional status quo was based less on sincere commitments to racial and gender equality than on a pragmatic concession that the constitutional clock could not be turned further back than 1964. Noting the strong appeals that Republicans made to southern whites, civil rights activists insisted that opposition to such policies as affirmative action, comparative worth, and the rights of other historically disadvantaged groups was the most recent manifestation of the same prejudices that had underpinned Jim Crow. Liberals in the 1980s maintained that *Brown* was about anti-subordination, not anti-classification, and that the decision was certainly not limited to racial classifications. Achieving the promise of *Brown* required a broad-scale attack on numerous status-based inequalities, the abandonment of "neutral" policies that in practice favored white men, and the creation of strong affirmative action programs that would bring members of historically disadvantaged groups into positions of political, economic, and educational influence.

A. Equality Under Law

Reagan conservatives sought to narrow the equal protection clause to only apply to intentional race discrimination and some intentional gender discriminations. The 1988 *Guidelines on Constitutional Litigation* informed federal attorneys that, "with exception of racial equality, which under the Fourteenth Amendment is entitled to special scrutiny," they "should avoid making arguments, and should attack arguments advanced by opposing counsel, for creating new suspect classes not found in the Constitution."[49] Reagan and his political allies also sought to narrow the fundamental rights strand of equal protection jurisprudence. Federal attorneys were similarly informed that they "should avoid making arguments, and should attack arguments advanced by opposing counsel, for creating new fundamental rights not found in the Constitution."[50]

This effort to cabin the equal protection clause was mostly successful. No new suspect classifications were created. The late Burger and early Rehnquist Courts did not find any new fundamental rights that warranted heightened scrutiny. Nevertheless, in *City of Cleburne, Texas v. Cleburne Living Center* (1985), the Supreme Court ignored an amicus brief from the Reagan administration and unanimously declared unconstitutional a city ordinance banning a group home for the mentally retarded. Justice White's majority opinion claimed to use rational scrutiny. He asserted, "Requiring the permit in this case appears to us to rest on an irrational prejudice against the mentally retarded." Justice Marshall was skeptical. Insisting that laws discriminating against the mentally handicapped be subject to heightened scrutiny, he wrote, "Cleburne's ordinance surely would be valid under the traditional rational-basis test applicable to economic and commercial regulation."

State courts more aggressively used state equal protection clauses to create new suspect classes and fundamental rights, particularly when adjudicating attacks on public school funding. "The reluctance of the U.S. Supreme Court to declare school finance equity a constitutional right," Douglas Reed notes, "created a decentralized, state-by state litigation effort."[51] Some state courts rejected such claims, interpreting state equality clauses as protecting no more rights than the federal equal protection clauses protected. Many state courts insisted that their state constitution demanded far more egalitarian school funding policies than the federal constitution. The Supreme Court of Kentucky in *Rose, et al. v. Council for Better Education* (KY 1989), when ordering the state legislature to provide more funds for schools and allocate those funds more equitably, asserted, "The children of the poor and the children of the rich, the children who live in the poor districts and the children who live in the rich districts must be given the same opportunity and access to an adequate education." By the mid-1990s many state judiciaries were engaged in protracted battles with state legislatures over the constitutionally appropriate means for financing public education.

Congress was also more willing to expand equality rights beyond traditional suspect classes. In 1990 both houses passed and President Bush enthusiastically signed the Americans with Disabilities Act (ADA). This law prohibited discrimination against persons with disabilities; required employees, educational institutions, and places of public accommodation to provide reasonable accommodations for disabled persons; and mandated that communications services accommodate persons with hearing and speech disabilities. Significantly, the national legislature prefaced the ADA with findings indicating that the disabled had many indicia of traditional suspect classes. These findings included the following claims:

- Historically, society has tended to isolate and segregate individuals with disabilities, and, despite some improvements, such forms of discrimination against individuals with disabilities continue to be a serious and pervasive social problem.
- Discrimination against individuals with disabilities persists in such critical areas as employment, housing, public accommodations, education, transportation, communication, recreation, institutionalization, health services, voting, and access to public services.
- Individuals with disabilities continually encounter various forms of discrimination, including outright intentional exclusion; the discriminatory effects of architectural, transportation, and communication barriers; overprotective rules and policies; failure to make modifications to existing facilities and practices; exclusionary qualification standards and criteria; segregation; and relegation to lesser services, programs, activities, benefits, jobs, or other opportunities.
- Census data, national polls, and other studies have documented that people with disabilities, as a group, occupy an inferior status in our society, and

---

49. Office of Legal Policy, *Guidelines on Constitutional Litigation*, 77.
50. Ibid., 78.
51. Douglas S. Reed, *On Equal Terms: The Constitutional Politics of Educational Opportunity* (Princeton, NJ: Princeton University Press, 2001), xix. For another excellent study of the constitutional politics of public school finance, see Michael Paris, *Framing Equal Opportunity: Law and the Politics of School Reform* (Stanford, CA: Stanford University Press, 2010).

are severely disadvantaged socially, vocationally, economically, and educationally.

- Individuals with disabilities are a discrete and insular minority who have been faced with restrictions and limitations, subjected to a history of purposeful unequal treatment, and relegated to a position of political powerlessness in our society, based on characteristics that are beyond the control of such individuals and resulting from stereotypic assumptions not truly indicative of the individual ability of such individuals to participate in and contribute to society.
- The nation's proper goals regarding individuals with disabilities are to assure equality of opportunity, full participation, independent living, and economic self-sufficiency for such individuals.
- The continuing existence of unfair and unnecessary discrimination and prejudice denies people with disabilities the opportunity to compete on an equal basis and pursue those opportunities for which our free society is justifiably famous and costs the United States billions of dollars in unnecessary expenses resulting from dependency and nonproductivity.[52]

The ADA had strong partisan support. Senator Edward Kennedy of Massachusetts described the bill as "an historic step in the long journey to complete the unfinished business of America and bring full civil rights and fair opportunity to all our citizens."[53] President George Bush praised the ADA for "keeping faith with the spirit of our courageous forefathers who wrote in the Declaration of Independence: 'We hold these truths to be self-evident, that all men are created equal, that they are endowed by their Creator with certain unalienable rights.'"

How do you explain the strong Republican support for the ADA, given the conservative desire to not create new suspect classes? Were conservative Republicans opposed to claims that the equal protection clause mandated protections for a variety of suspect classes, or did conservatives object only to the federal judiciary creating new suspect classes?[54]

52. 104 U.S. Stat. 327, 328-29 (1990).

53. 135 *Congressional Record*, 101st Cong., 1st Sess. (1989), 19888.

54. As discussed in Chapter 11, the Supreme Court in *Board of Trustees for the University of Alabama v. Garrett* (2001) declared some provisions of the ADA unconstitutional.

Rose, et al. v. Council for Better Education, 1989 Ky. 55 (1989)

Sixty-six school districts in Kentucky, joining together as the Council for Better Education (CBE), filed a lawsuit claiming that the use of state revenue and local taxes to support public education violated Section 183 of the Kentucky Constitution, which required the Kentucky General Assembly to provide for an "efficient" system of public schools. The complaint was lodged against the president pro tempore of the state senate, John Rose. State laws that funded public education through a combination of state revenue and local taxes, the CBE alleged, resulted in unconstitutional disparities in the money available for public schooling in individual districts. The state denied that the school system was unconstitutionally funded and claimed that public school financing raised nonjusticiable "political questions." The trial judge found that the state failure to provide an "efficient" school violated a "fundamental right" to education under the state constitution. The judge ordered the legislature to raise and allocate additional funds for education that ensured a state school system that was "substantial[ly]" uniform. State officials appealed to the Supreme Court of Kentucky.

The Supreme Court of Kentucky by a 5-2 decision declared that the existing state system was unconstitutional. Chief Justice Stephens maintained that the state constitution made education a fundamental right and required the state legislature to provide all children in the state with equal access to public schools. On what basis does he reach that conclusion? Do the dissents dispute how Stephens interprets the state constitution or his conception of the judicial role? Stephens did not issue a specific order equalizing education in Kentucky. Instead, he ordered the state legislature to develop policies consistent with his opinion. Does this demonstrate a proper understanding of the separation of powers or judicial unwillingness to ensure that important rights are protected?

CHIEF JUSTICE STEPHENS delivered the opinion of the Court.

. . .

Several conclusions readily appear from a reading of this section [183 of the Kentucky Constitution]. First, it is the obligation, the sole obligation, of the General Assembly to provide for a system of common schools in Kentucky. The obligation to so provide is clear and unequivocal and is, in effect, a constitutional mandate. Next, the school system must be provided throughout the entire state, with no area (or its children) being omitted. The creation, implementation and maintenance of the school system must be achieved by appropriate legislation. Finally, the system must be an efficient one.

. . .

Comments of Delegate Beckner on the report which led to the selection of the language in Section 183 reflect the framers' cognizance of the importance of education and, emphasized that the educational system in Kentucky must be improved. . . .

. . . Delegate Beckner . . . told [his] fellow delegates . . . what this section means.

- The providing of public education through a system of common schools by the General Assembly is the most "vital question" presented to them.
- Education of children must not be minimized to the "slightest degree."
- Education must be provided to the children of the rich and poor alike.
- Education of children is essential to the prosperity of our state.
- Education of children should be supervised by the State.
- There must be a constant and continuing effort to make our schools more efficient.
- We must not finance our schools in a *de minimis* fashion.
- All schools and children stand upon one level in their entitlement to equal state support.

. . .

In *City of Louisville v. Commonwealth* (KY 1909), the Court held:

> In this state the subject of public education has always been regarded and treated as a matter of state concern. In the last Constitution, as well as in the one preceding it, *the most explicit care was evinced to promote public education as a duty of the state*. . . .
>
> In obedience to that requirement, the General Assembly has provided a system of public schools. . . . All [schools throughout the state] have the one main essential—that they are free schools, open to all the children of proper school age residing in the locality, *and affording equal opportunity for all* to acquire the learning taught in the various common school branches . . . (emphasis added).

The decision, specifically relying on Section 183, postulated: public education in the common schools is a duty of the state; that the General Assembly attempted to obey the mandate (as it certainly has attempted to do now); and although there are certain different provisions for different localities, *all* common schools must be free, open to all students, and provide equal opportunities for all students to acquire the same education. In other words, although by accident of birth and residence, a student lives in a poor, financially deprived area, he or she is still entitled to the same educational opportunities that those children in the wealthier districts obtain. . . .

. . .

The system of common schools must be adequately funded to achieve its goals. The system of common schools must be substantially uniform throughout the state. Each child, *every child*, in this Commonwealth must be provided with an equal opportunity to have an adequate education. Equality is the key word here. The children of the poor and the children of the rich, the children who live in the poor districts and the children who live in the rich districts must be given the same opportunity and access to an adequate education. This obligation cannot be shifted to local counties and local school districts.

. . .

We do not instruct the General Assembly to enact any specific legislation. We do not direct the members of the General Assembly to raise taxes. It is their decision how best to achieve efficiency. We only decide the nature of the constitutional mandate. We only determine the intent of the framers. Carrying-out that intent is the duty of the General Assembly.

. . .

Our job is to determine the constitutional validity of the system of common schools within the meaning of the Kentucky Constitution, Section 183. We have done so. We have declared the system of common schools to be unconstitutional. It is now up to the General Assembly to re-create, and re-establish a system of common schools within this state which will be in compliance with the Constitution. We have no doubt they will proceed with their duty.

. . .

JUSTICE GANT, concurring. . . .

JUSTICE WINTERSHEIMER, concurring. . . .

JUSTICE VANCE, dissenting.

I do not concur with the majority that the present system of common schools has, on the basis of the record before us, been shown to be *constitutionally* under-funded or inadequate.

. . .

Section 183 of the Constitution of Kentucky leaves to the legislative discretion the best method of providing for an efficient system of common schools. . . . Legislative discretion cannot be extended to such limits as to allow the legislature, in its discretion, to fail to meet its constitutional mandate, but I do not believe it is within the province of this court to interfere with legislative discretion as to the level of school funding unless it clearly appears from the record that the level of funding is so low that it cannot reasonably accomplish basic educational necessities. Not all academic failure is the result of under-funding.

. . .

Whether the General Assembly will provide a system of common schools of the highest order or one which barely meets the minimum requirements is a burden which must be placed squarely upon the shoulders of the General Assembly, where the constitution places it. It does not rest with the courts, and indeed the doctrine of separation of powers prohibits judicial interference with legislative prerogative. If we do not exercise restraint in this matter, I fear that every theoretical defect in the educational system will be escalated into litigation to determine the constitutional efficiency of the system.

. . .

JUSTICE LEIBSON, dissenting.

Respectfully, I dissent. I agree in principle with the majority's opinion that the General Assembly has failed thus far to, "by appropriate legislation, provide for an efficient system of common schools throughout the State." Nevertheless, this case should be reversed and dismissed because it does not present an "actual" or "justiciable" controversy. . . .

. . .

We were only asked to decide one issue in this lawsuit: whether the General Assembly has responded adequately to its constitutional responsibility. This is a political question, pure and simple. We have undertaken to "enter upon policy determinations for which judicially manageable standards are lacking." Without such standards, a case is not justiciable. It is not enough to decide that Kentucky does not have an "efficient system of common schools throughout the State," as Section 183 of the Constitution requires, without specifying what statutes are unconstitutional, and why. Yet, the former is not asked, and the latter is not possible. I repeat, this case is not justiciable. . . .

B. Race

The constitutional politics of racial equality witnessed struggles over the legacy of *Brown v. Board of Education* (1954). All prominent political actors celebrated *Brown* as a landmark statement of fundamental American values. Constitutional arguments about equality often referred to *Brown* instead of the text or history of the Fourteenth Amendment. Nevertheless, this celebratory consensus masked bitter disputes over what *Brown* meant and what *Brown* achieved.

Reagan conservatives regarded *Brown* as resting on the principle that racial and related classifications were constitutionally odious. Racial classifications were wrong because no real difference existed between persons of different races. This anti-classification logic explains why Reagan conservatives vigorously opposed state- and federally mandated affirmative action programs, at least those that explicitly relied on race when making admissions or employment decisions. "Discrimination on the basis of race," Justice Scalia wrote in *City of Richmond v. J. A. Croson Co.* (1989), "is illegal, immoral, unconstitutional, inherently wrong, and destructive of democratic society." Anti-classification arguments frequently maintained that the promise of *Brown* had largely been achieved. They observed that Americans by 1980 had abandoned laws that explicitly granted rights to persons of one race but not another. While government needed to be vigilant to prevent backsliding, such policies as continued federal court efforts to integrate schools and affirmative action were both unnecessary and destructive, unless they were efforts to remedy the particular victims of racial discrimination or specific acts of past race discrimination. Conservatives remained committed to eradicating de jure segregation, segregation clearly rooted in state decisions. They opposed efforts to combat de facto segregation, segregation rooted in private decisions by individuals to associate with members of their race.

Many progressive liberals regarded *Brown* as resting on the principle that no group of persons should have a subordinate status in the United States. So understood, *Brown* was a precedent that supported the rights of woman, aliens, homosexuals, and other historically disadvantaged groups. Anti-subordinationists insisted that Jim Crow and affirmative action policies were fundamentally different. The former were intended to create a subordinate class. The latter were aimed at achieving greater social equality. Persons committed to the anti-subordination interpretation of *Brown* maintained that the promise of that decision was largely unfulfilled. Too many African-Americans, women, and members of historically disadvantaged groups were poorly educated,remained in poverty and were outside the corridors of power. Justice Marshall's dissent in *Croson* spoke of "the tragic and indelible fact that discrimination against blacks and other racial minorities in this Nation has pervaded our Nation's history and continues to scar our society." Affirmative action and continued judicial efforts to integrate public schools were among the many policies necessary for the United States to become a truly racially egalitarian society. Progressive liberals did not sharply distinguish between de jure and de facto discrimination. What conservatives claimed were private decisions to associate with members of one's race, progressives insisted were another baneful consequence of past state-mandated race discrimination.

The constitutional law of racial equality was often at odds with actual practice. Local race-conscious policies often flourished, even as the Supreme Court in *Croson* insisted that such policies satisfy the same strict scrutiny standard as laws discriminating against persons of color. Cities interested in establishing minority set-asides (programs that required a certain percentage of public contracts be given to persons of color) simply commissioned an expensive disparity study that demonstrated that past racial prejudice in their community explained the lack of minority contractors or subcontractors.[55] Many American public schools and schools systems exhibited considerable segregation, even as Supreme Court opinions proclaimed that the last vestiges of state-mandated segregation had disappeared. Gary Orfield's study of public schooling in the early 1990s concluded, "More than forty years after *Brown*, racial separation both between and within school districts is an ordinary, unnoticed fixture in K–12 education."[56]

55. See Martin J. Sweet, *Merely Judgment: Ignoring, Evading, and Trumping the Supreme Court* (Charlottesville: University of Virginia Press, 2010).

56. Gary Orfield, Susan E. Eaton, and the Harvard Project on School Desegregation, *Dismantling Desegregation: The Quiet Reversal of Brown v. Board of Education* (New York: New Press, 1996), xiv.

Implementing *Brown*

Federal judges began relinquishing control over school districts previously found in violation of the principles announced in *Brown v. Board of Education* (1954). The early Rehnquist Court established standards that encouraged lower federal courts to end their oversight over the desegregation process. *Board of Education of Oklahoma City Public Schools v. Dowell* (1991) declared, "Dissolving a desegregation decree after the local authorities have operated in compliance with it for a reasonable period of time properly recognizes that necessary concern for the important values of local control of public school systems dictates that a federal court's regulatory control of such systems not extend beyond the time required to remedy the effects of past intentional discrimination." *Freeman v. Pitts* (1992) permitted the justices to return control to the local school district even if public schools remained highly segregated, as long as the trial judge concluded that present segregation was de facto, better explained by recent demographic trends than by past de jure official discrimination.

The early Rehnquist Court did continue monitoring some public school systems. The justices in *United States v. Fordice* (1992) ruled that Mississippi had not fully cured past racial segregation in public colleges, even though state laws discriminating by race had been repealed. Justice White's majority opinion declared,

> If the State perpetuates policies and practices traceable to its prior system that continue to have segregative effects—whether by influencing student enrollment decisions or by fostering segregation in other facets of the university system—and such policies are without sound educational justification and can be practicably eliminated, the State has not satisfied its burden of proving that it has dismantled its prior system. Such policies run afoul of the Equal Protection Clause, even though the State has abolished the legal requirement that whites and blacks be educated separately and has established racially neutral policies not animated by a discriminatory purpose.

The judges then faulted Mississippi for, among other failings, requiring standardized test scores for formerly all-white schools that were higher than those required for admission to formerly all-black schools. *Missouri v. Jenkins* (1989) held that federal courts could order communities to pay for desegregation by increasing taxes, although the justices unanimously agreed that federal judges could not directly impose that levy. Justice White's majority opinion maintained that federal courts had the power to order local school districts "to pay [their] share of the cost of the remedy for a *Brown* violation," even if the tax increase violated a state law. Six years later, however, the justices in *Missouri v. Jenkins II* (1995) ruled that district courts attempting to cure *Brown* violations could not order salary increases for teachers and new magnet programs to attract white students who lived outside of the district. Chief Justice Rehnquist asserted, "The District Court's pursuit of the goal of 'desegregative attractiveness' results . . . is so far removed from the task of eliminating the racial identifiability of the schools within [the district] that we believe it is beyond the admittedly broad discretion of the District Court."

Freeman v. Pitts, 503 U.S. 467 (1992)

Willie Pitts and other African-Americans living in DeKalb County, Georgia, in 1968 filed a class action against the DeKalb County School System (DCSS). The suit claimed that public schools in the system remained unconstitutionally segregated, violating Brown v. Board of Education *(1954). In 1969 the district court entered an order mandating that the DCSS take specific steps to become a unitary school system. While those steps were being implemented, the district court retained jurisdiction over the lawsuit. In 1986 the DCSS asked the district court to dismiss the lawsuit on the ground that DeKalb County was now operating a unitary school system that had eliminated all vestiges of past segregation. The district court found that DCSS was operating a unitary system with respect to student assignments, transportation, physical facilities, and extracurricular activities, but not with respect to teacher and principal assignments, resource allocation, and quality of education. The court announced that its judicial supervision would be limited to those areas in which vestiges of segregation remained. The Court of Appeals for the Eleventh Circuit reversed that decision, insisting that the district court supervise all educational matters as long as any vestiges of segregation had not been removed. The DCSS appealed to the Supreme Court of the United States.*

The Supreme Court unanimously reversed,, but the justices disputed the precise order to be given to the lower courts. Justice Kennedy's opinion for the Court maintained that the district court should no longer supervise those matters on which the district court judge determined that the DSCC had removed all vestiges of past segregation. The justices in the majority recognized that many schools in DeKalb County were de facto segregated. Although half the schoolchildren in the district were African-American, more than one-third of all public schools were either 90 percent black or 90 percent white. How did this information influence judicial opinions? Why does Justice Kennedy discount the actual racial composition of most DeKalb County schools? Why does Justice Blackmun disagree? Do you believe that Freeman *should be celebrated for fulfilling the promise of* Brown *or condemned for abandoning the promise of* Brown*?*

JUSTICE KENNEDY delivered the opinion of the Court.

. . .

The duty and responsibility of a school district once segregated by law is to take all steps necessary to eliminate the vestiges of the unconstitutional de jure system. This is required in order to ensure that the principal wrong of the de jure system, the injuries and stigma inflicted upon the race disfavored by the violation, is no longer present. This was the rationale and the objective of *Brown* I (1954) and *Brown* II (1955).

The objective of *Brown* I was made more specific by our holding in *Green v. School Bd. of New Kent County* (1968) that the duty of a former de jure district is to "take whatever steps might be necessary to convert to a unitary system in which racial discrimination would be eliminated root and branch."

. . .

As we have long observed, "local autonomy of school districts is a vital national tradition." Returning schools to the control of local authorities at the earliest practicable date is essential to restore their true accountability in our governmental system. When the school district and all state entities participating with it in operating the schools make decisions in the absence of judicial supervision, they can be held accountable to the citizenry, to the political process, and to the courts in the ordinary course. . . .

We hold that, in the course of supervising desegregation plans, federal courts have the authority to relinquish supervision and control of school districts in incremental stages, before full compliance has been achieved in every area of school operations. While retaining jurisdiction over the case, the court may determine that it will not order further remedies in areas where the school district is in compliance with the decree. . . . In particular, the district court may determine that it will not order further remedies in the area of student assignments where racial imbalance is not traceable, in a proximate way, to constitutional violations.

A court's discretion to order the incremental withdrawal of its supervision in a school desegregation case must be exercised in a manner consistent with the purposes and objectives of its equitable power. Among the factors which must inform the sound discretion of the court in ordering partial withdrawal are the following: whether there has been full and satisfactory compliance with the decree in those aspects of the system where supervision is to be withdrawn; whether retention of judicial control is necessary or practicable to achieve compliance with the decree in other facets of the school system; and whether the school district has demonstrated, to the public and to the parents and students of the once disfavored race, its good-faith commitment to the whole of the court's decree and to those provisions of the law and the Constitution that were the predicate for judicial intervention in the first instance.

In considering these factors, a court should give particular attention to the school system's record of compliance. A school system is better positioned to demonstrate its good-faith commitment to a constitutional course of action when its policies form a consistent pattern of lawful conduct directed to eliminating earlier violations. . . .

. . .

. . . In the case before us the District Court designed a comprehensive plan for desegregation of DCSS in 1969, one that included racial balance in student assignments. The desegregation decree was designed to achieve maximum practicable desegregation. Its central remedy was the closing of black schools and the reassignment of pupils to neighborhood schools, with attendance zones that achieved racial balance. The plan accomplished its objective in the first year of operation, before dramatic demographic changes altered residential patterns. . . .

That there was racial imbalance in student attendance zones was not tantamount to a showing that the school district was in noncompliance with the decree or with its duties under the law. Racial balance is not to be achieved for its own sake. It is to be pursued when racial imbalance has been caused by a constitutional violation. Once the racial imbalance due to the de jure violation has been remedied, the school district is under no duty to remedy imbalance that is caused by demographic factors. . . .

The findings of the District Court that the population changes which occurred in DeKalb County were not caused by the policies of the school district, but rather by independent factors, are consistent with the mobility that is a distinct characteristic of our society. . . .

Where resegregation is a product not of state action but of private choices, it does not have constitutional implications. It is beyond the authority and beyond the practical ability of the federal courts to try to counteract these kinds of continuous and massive demographic shifts. To attempt such results would require ongoing and never-ending supervision by the courts of school districts simply because they were once de jure segregated. Residential housing choices, and their attendant effects on the racial composition of schools, present an ever-changing pattern, one difficult to address through judicial remedies.

. . .

As the de jure violation becomes more remote in time and these demographic changes intervene, it becomes less likely that a current racial imbalance in a school district is a vestige of the prior de jure system. The causal link between current conditions and the prior violation is even more attenuated if the school district has demonstrated its good faith. In light of its finding that the demographic changes in DeKalb County are unrelated to the prior violation, the District Court was correct to entertain the suggestion that DCSS had no duty to achieve system-wide racial balance in the student population. . . .

. . .

JUSTICE THOMAS took no part in the consideration or decision of this case.

JUSTICE SCALIA, concurring.

. . .

Racially imbalanced schools are the product of a blend of public and private actions, and any assessment that they would not be segregated, or would not be as segregated, in the absence of a particular one of those factors is guesswork. It is similarly guesswork, of course, to say that they would be segregated, or would be as segregated, in the absence of one of those factors. . . . Thus, allocation of the burden of proof foreordains the result in almost all of the "vestige of past discrimination" cases. . . .

. . .

. . . Our post- *Green* cases provide that, once state-enforced school segregation is shown to have existed in a jurisdiction in 1954, there arises a presumption, effectively irrebuttable (because the school district cannot prove the negative), that any current racial imbalance is the product of that violation, at least if the imbalance has continuously existed.

. . .

. . . [G]ranting the merits of this approach at the time of *Green*, it is now 25 years later. "From the very first, federal supervision of local school systems was intended as a temporary measure to remedy past discrimination." We envisioned it as temporary partly because "[n]o single tradition in public education is more deeply rooted than local control over the operation of schools," and because no one's interest is furthered by subjecting the Nation's educational system to "judicial tutelage for the indefinite future." But we also envisioned it as temporary, I think, because the rational basis for the extraordinary presumption of causation simply must dissipate as the de jure system and the school boards who produced it recede further into the past. Since a multitude of private factors has shaped school systems in the years after abandonment of de jure segregation—normal migration, population growth (as in this case), "white flight" from the inner cities, increases in the costs of new facilities—the percentage of the current makeup of school systems attributable to the prior, government-enforced discrimination has diminished with each passing year, to the point where it cannot realistically be assumed to be a significant factor.

At some time, we must acknowledge that it has become absurd to assume, without any further proof, that violations of the Constitution dating from the days when Lyndon Johnson was President, or earlier, continue to have an appreciable effect upon current operation of schools. . . . We must soon revert to the ordinary principles of our law, of our democratic heritage, and of our educational tradition: that plaintiffs alleging equal protection violations must prove intent and causation and not merely the existence of racial disparity, that public schooling, even in the South, should be controlled by locally elected authorities acting in conjunction with parents, and that it is "desirable" to permit pupils to attend "schools nearest their homes."

JUSTICE SOUTER, concurring. . . .

JUSTICE BLACKMUN, with whom JUSTICE STEVENS and JUSTICE O'CONNOR join, concurring in the judgment.

It is almost 38 years since this Court decided *Brown v. Board of Education*, (1954). In those 38 years the students in DeKalb County, Ga., never have attended a desegregated school system even for one day. The majority of "black" students never have attended a school that was not disproportionately black. . . .

. . .

That the District Court's jurisdiction should continue until the school board demonstrates full compliance with the Constitution follows from the reasonable skepticism that underlies judicial supervision in the first instance. . . . "A district court need not accept at face value the profession of a school board which has intentionally discriminated that it will cease to do so in the future." It makes little sense, it seems to me, for the court to disarm itself by renouncing jurisdiction in one aspect of a school system, while violations of the Equal Protection Clause persist in other aspects of the same system. . . .

. . .

DCSS claims that it need not remedy the segregation in DeKalb County schools because it was caused by demographic changes for which DCSS has no responsibility. It is not enough, however, for DCSS to establish that demographics exacerbated the problem; it must prove that its own policies did not contribute. Such contribution can occur in at least two ways: DCSS may have contributed to the demographic changes themselves, or it may have contributed directly to the racial imbalance in the schools.

To determine DCSS' possible role in encouraging the residential segregation, the court must examine the situation with special care. . . . Close examination is necessary because what might seem to be purely private preferences in housing may in fact have been created, in part, by actions of the school district. . . . This interactive effect between schools and housing choices may occur because many families are concerned about the racial composition of a prospective school and will make residential decisions accordingly. Thus, schools that are demonstrably black or white provide a signal to these families, perpetuating and intensifying the residential movement.

In addition to exploring the school district's influence on residential segregation, the District Court here should examine whether school-board actions might have contributed to school segregation. Actions taken by a school district can aggravate or eliminate school segregation independent of residential segregation. School-board policies concerning placement of new schools and closure of old schools and programs such as magnet classrooms and majority-to-minority (M-to-M) transfer policies affect the racial composition of the schools. . . .

. . .

A review of the record suggests that from 1969 until 1975, DCSS failed to desegregate its schools. During that period, the number of students attending racially identifiable schools actually increased, and increased more quickly than the increase in black students. By 1975, 73% of black elementary students and 56% of black high school students were attending majority black schools, although the percentages of black students in the district population were just 20% and 13%, respectively.

. . .

Thus, in 1976, before most of the demographic changes, the District Court found that DCSS had not complied with the 1969 order to eliminate the vestiges of its former de jure school system. Indeed, the 1976 order found that DCSS had contributed to the growing racial imbalance of its schools. Given these determinations in 1976, the District Court, at a minimum, should have required DCSS to prove that, but for the demographic changes between 1976 and 1985, its actions would have been sufficient to "convert promptly to a system without a 'white' school and a 'Negro' school, but just schools." The available evidence suggests that this would be a difficult burden for DCSS to meet.

. . .

The District Court apparently has concluded that DCSS should be relieved of the responsibility to desegregate because such responsibility would be burdensome. To be sure, changes in demographic patterns aggravated the vestiges of segregation and made it more difficult for DCSS to desegregate. But an integrated school system is no less desirable because it is difficult to achieve, and it is no less a constitutional imperative because that imperative has gone unmet for 38 years.

Affirmative Action

Affirmative action replaced busing as the most contentious racial issue dividing Americans. Reagan Republicans insisted that race-conscious employment and university admissions policies were unconstitutional unless they were narrowly tailored to remedy identifiable victims of discrimination. The Republican Party platform of 1984 asserted, "We will resist efforts to replace equal rights with discriminatory quota systems and preferential treatment. Quotas are the most insidious form of discrimination: reverse discrimination against the innocent." Liberal Democrats as vigorously defended affirmative action policies. The 1984 Democratic Party platform "reaffirm[ed] [a] longstanding commitment to the eradication of discrimination in all aspects of American life through the use of affirmative action, goals, timetables and other verifiable measures to overturn historic patterns and historic burdens of discrimination in hiring, training, promotions, contract procurement, education and the administration of all Federal programs."

The Supreme Court consistently sided with conservatives when adjudicating state and local affirmation action programs. *Wygant v. Jackson Board of Education* (1986) struck down a contract that gave teachers of color special protections against layoffs during recessions. *City of Richmond v. J.A. Croson* (1989) declared unconstitutional a set-aside program that required contractors doing business with the city to give at least 30 percent of their subcontracts to minority-owned businesses. The opinions for the Court in both cases insisted that affirmative action programs were subject to the same constitutional standards as Jim Crow segregation. After noting that the justices had "consistently repudiated distinctions between citizens solely because of their ancestry as being odious to a free people whose institutions are founded upon the doctrine of equality," Justice Powell's plurality opinion in *Wygant* asserted, "The level of scrutiny does not change merely because the challenged classification operates against a group that historically has not been subject to government discrimination." *Croson* more clearly stated that strict scrutiny was the appropriate standard for reviewing state and local affirmative action programs.

Liberals fared better when the Supreme Court examined a federal affirmative action policy. By a 5-4 vote the Supreme Court in *Metro Broadcasting, Inc. v. FCC* (1990) sustained an administrative decision to consider race when awarding broadcast licenses. Justice Brennan's majority opinion insisted that intermediate scrutiny was the appropriate standard of review in light of the special congressional responsibility to enforce the equal protection clause. He stated, "Benign race-conscious measures mandated by Congress . . . are constitutionally permissible to the extent that they serve important governmental objectives within the power of Congress and are substantially related to achievement of those objectives." The FCC's minority enhancement policy, Brennan concluded, was a constitutional means to "promote programming diversity."

Two Presidents on Affirmative Action

Republican and Democratic leaders sharply disputed the merits of affirmative action. Republican presidents and candidates for the presidency maintained that affirmative action violated the constitutional commitment to equal justice. Democratic presidents and candidates for the presidency maintained that affirmative action was necessary to realize the constitutional commitment to equal justice. When reading the following brief excerpts from Presidents Reagan and Clinton, consider their different understandings of constitutional equality. How does each understand the constitutional commitment to equality? Whose vision is correct? How do these presidential statements on affirmative action differ from the judicial opinions in the next excerpt from City of Richmond v. J.A. Croson *(1989)?*

Ronald Reagan, Radio Address to the Nation on Civil Rights (1985)

The principle that guides us and the principle embodied in the law is one of nondiscrimination. I'm sure that you have all seen the statue representing justice that presides in many of our courtrooms—the woman with the blindfold covering her eyes. Her eyes are covered because true justice should never depend on whether you're rich or poor, or black or white, or if you're Hispanic or Asian, or if your ancestors came from Italy, Poland, Latvia, or any other country, including Ireland, where some of my family's from.

Equal treatment and equality before the law—these are the foundations on which a just and free society is built. But there are some today who, in the name of equality, would have us practice discrimination. They have turned our civil rights laws on their head, claiming they mean exactly the opposite of what they say. These people tell us that the Government should enforce discrimination in favor of some groups through hiring quotas, under which people get or lose particular jobs or promotions solely because of their race or sex. Some bluntly assert that our civil rights laws only apply to special groups and were never intended to protect every American.

. . .

The truth is, quotas deny jobs to many who would have gotten them otherwise, but who weren't born a specified race or sex. That's discrimination pure and simple and is exactly what the civil rights laws were designed to stop. Quotas also cast a shadow on the real achievements of minorities, which makes quotas a double tragedy.

William J. Clinton, Remarks on Affirmative Action (1995)

The purpose of affirmative action is to give our Nation a way to finally address the systemic exclusion of individuals of talent on the basis of their gender or race, from opportunities to develop, perform, achieve, and contribute. Affirmative action is an effort to develop a systematic approach to open the doors of education, employment, and business development opportunities to qualified individuals who happen to be members of groups that have experienced long-standing and persistent discrimination.

. . .

The unemployment rate for African-Americans remains about twice that of whites. The Hispanic rate is still much higher. Women have narrowed the earnings gap, but still make only 72 percent as much as men do for comparable jobs. The average income for an Hispanic woman with a college degree is still less than the average income of a white man with a high school diploma.

. . . [O]nly six-tenths of one percent of senior management positions are held by African-Americans, four-tenths of a percent by Hispanic-Americans, three-tenths of a percent by Asian-Americans. Women hold between 3 and 5 percent of these positions. White males make up 43 percent of our work force but hold 95 percent of these jobs.

. . .

The job of ending discrimination in this country is not over. That should not be surprising. We had slavery for centuries before the passage of the 13th, 14th, and 15th amendments. We waited another 100 years for the civil rights legislation. Women have had the vote less than 100 years. We have always had difficulty with these things, as most societies do. But we are making more progress than many people.

Based on the evidence, the job is not done. So here is what I think we should do. We should reaffirm the principle of affirmative action and fix the practices. We should have a simple slogan: Mend it, but don't end it.

City of Richmond v. J. A. Croson Co., 488 U.S. 469 (1989)

The Richmond City Council in 1983 passed an ordinance requiring contractors who did business with the city to give at least 30 percent of their subcontracts to minority-owned businesses. This policy was partly based on evidence that although the community was 50 percent African-American, less than 1 percent of all city contracts went to persons of color. That fall the J. A. Croson Company was denied a contract to install plumbing fixtures at a city jail because the company failed to abide by the set-aside policy, believing that the only minority-owned businesses that they could subcontract with to supply fixtures were either unqualified or too expensive. Croson sued the City of Richmond, claiming that the minority set-aside program was unconstitutional. After a series of decisions, appeals, and remands the Court of Appeals for the Fourth Circuit declared the Richmond ordinance unconstitutional. Richmond appealed to the Supreme Court of the United States.

The Supreme Court by a 6-3 vote declared the minority set-aside unconstitutional. Justice O'Connor's opinion for the Court insisted that Richmond's race-conscious policy did not satisfy the strict scrutiny standard. Why does Justice O'Connor insist that the policy meet this standard? Why does Justice Marshall disagree? In Fullilove v. Klutznick *(1980) the Supreme Court sustained a similar federal minority set-aside program. How does O'Connor distinguish* Croson *from* Fullilove? *Is that distinction sound? Is that distinction sincere? How do you explain increasing judicial hostility to race-conscious programs?*

JUSTICE O'CONNOR announced the judgment of the Court.

. . .

. . . Congress, unlike any State or political subdivision, has a specific constitutional mandate to enforce the dictates of the Fourteenth Amendment. The power to "enforce" may at times also include the power to define situations which *Congress* determines threaten principles of equality and to adopt prophylactic rules to deal with those situations. . . .

That Congress may identify and redress the effects of society-wide discrimination does not mean that, *a fortiori,* the States and their political subdivisions are free to decide that such remedies are appropriate. Section 1 of the Fourteenth Amendment is an explicit *constraint* on state power, and the States must undertake any remedial efforts in accordance with that provision. To hold otherwise would be to cede control over the content of the Equal Protection Clause to the 50 state legislatures and their myriad political subdivisions. The mere recitation of a benign or compensatory purpose for the use of a racial classification would essentially entitle the States to exercise the full power of Congress under § 5 of the Fourteenth Amendment and insulate any racial classification from judicial scrutiny under § 1. We believe that such a result would be contrary to the intentions of the Framers of the Fourteenth Amendment, who desired to place clear limits on the States' use of race as a criterion for legislative action, and to have the federal courts enforce those limitations. . . .

It would seem equally clear, however, that a state or local subdivision (if delegated the authority from the State) has the authority to eradicate the effects of private discrimination within its own legislative jurisdiction. This authority must, of course, be exercised within the constraints of § 1 of the Fourteenth Amendment. . . . As a matter of state law, the city of Richmond has legislative authority over its procurement policies, and can use its spending powers to remedy private discrimination, if it identifies that discrimination with the particularity required by the Fourteenth Amendment.

Thus, if the city could show that it had essentially become a "passive participant" in a system of racial exclusion practiced by elements of the local construction industry, we think it clear that the city could take affirmative steps to dismantle such a system. It is beyond dispute that any public entity, state or federal, has a compelling interest in assuring that public dollars, drawn from the tax contributions of all citizens, do not serve to finance the evil of private prejudice.

. . . The Richmond Plan denies certain citizens the opportunity to compete for a fixed percentage of public contracts based solely upon their race. To whatever racial group these citizens belong, their "personal rights" to be treated with equal dignity and respect are implicated by a rigid rule erecting race as the sole criterion in an aspect of public decisionmaking.

Absent searching judicial inquiry into the justification for such race-based measures, there is simply no way of determining what classifications are "benign" or "remedial" and what classifications are in fact motivated by illegitimate notions of racial inferiority or simple racial politics. Indeed, the purpose of strict scrutiny is to "smoke out" illegitimate uses of race by assuring that the legislative body is pursuing a goal important enough to warrant use of a highly suspect tool. The test also ensures that the means chosen "fit" this compelling goal so closely that there is little or no possibility that the motive for the classification was illegitimate racial prejudice or stereotype.

Classifications based on race carry a danger of stigmatic harm. Unless they are strictly reserved for remedial settings, they may in fact promote notions of racial inferiority and lead to a politics of racial hostility. We thus reaffirm the view . . . that the standard of review under the Equal Protection Clause is not dependent on the race of those burdened or benefited by a particular classification.

. . .

In this case, blacks constitute approximately 50% of the population of the city of Richmond. Five of the nine seats on the city council are held by blacks. The concern that a political majority will more easily act to the disadvantage of a minority based on unwarranted assumptions or incomplete facts would seem to militate for, not against, the application of heightened judicial scrutiny in this case. . . .

. . .

. . . [A] generalized assertion that there has been past discrimination in an entire industry provides no guidance for a legislative body to determine the precise scope of the injury it seeks to remedy. It "has no logical stopping point." "Relief" for such an ill-defined wrong could extend until the percentage of public contracts awarded to MBE's [minority business enterprises] in Richmond mirrored the percentage of minorities in the population as a whole.

. . .

. . . The 30% quota cannot in any realistic sense be tied to any injury suffered by anyone. . . .

. . .

Reliance on the disparity between the number of prime contracts awarded to minority firms and the minority population of the city of Richmond is similarly misplaced. There is no doubt that "[w]here gross statistical disparities can be shown, they alone in a proper case may constitute prima facie proof of a pattern or practice of discrimination" under Title VII. But it is equally clear that "[w]hen special qualifications are required to fill particular jobs, comparisons to the general population (rather than to the smaller group of individuals who possess the necessary qualifications) may have little probative value."

In this case, the city does not even know how many MBE's in the relevant market are qualified to undertake prime or subcontracting work in public construction projects. . . .

Without any information on minority participation in subcontracting, it is quite simply impossible to evaluate overall minority representation in the city's construction expenditures.

. . .

. . . To accept Richmond's claim that past societal discrimination alone can serve as the basis for rigid racial preferences would be to open the door to competing claims for "remedial relief" for every disadvantaged group. The dream of a Nation of equal citizens in a society where race is irrelevant to personal opportunity and achievement would be lost in a mosaic of shifting preferences based on inherently unmeasurable claims of past wrongs. "Courts would be asked to evaluate the extent of the prejudice and consequent harm suffered by various minority groups. Those whose societal injury is thought to exceed some arbitrary level of tolerability then would be entitled to preferential classifications. . . ." We think such a result would be contrary to both the letter and spirit of a constitutional provision whose central command is equality.

The foregoing analysis applies only to the inclusion of blacks within the Richmond set-aside program. There is *absolutely no evidence* of past discrimination against Spanish-speaking, Oriental, Indian, Eskimo, or Aleut persons in any aspect of the Richmond construction industry. The District Court took judicial notice of the fact that the vast majority of "minority" persons in Richmond were black. It may well be that Richmond has never had an Aleut or Eskimo citizen. The random inclusion of racial groups that, as a practical matter, may never have suffered from discrimination in the construction industry in Richmond suggests that perhaps the city's purpose was not in fact to remedy past discrimination.

. . .

JUSTICE STEVENS, concurring in part and concurring in the judgment.

. . .

. . . [T]his litigation involves an attempt by a legislative body, rather than a court, to fashion a remedy for a past wrong. Legislatures are primarily policymaking bodies that promulgate rules to govern future conduct. . . . It is the judicial system, rather than the legislative process, that is best equipped to identify past wrongdoers and to fashion remedies that will create the conditions that presumably would have existed had no wrong been committed. Thus, in cases involving the review of judicial remedies imposed against persons who have been proved guilty of violations of law, I would allow the courts in racial discrimination cases the same broad discretion that chancellors enjoy in other areas of the law.

. . .

The justification for the ordinance is the fact that in the past white contractors—and presumably other white citizens in Richmond—have discriminated against black contractors. The class of persons benefited by the ordinance is not, however, limited to victims of such discrimination—it encompasses persons who have never been in business in Richmond as well as minority contractors who may have been guilty of discriminating against members of other minority groups. . . .

. . . [T]he composition of the disadvantaged class of white contractors presumably includes some who have been guilty of unlawful discrimination, some who practiced discrimination before it was forbidden by law, and some who have never discriminated against anyone on the basis of race. Imposing a common burden on such a disparate class merely because each member of the class is of the same race stems from reliance on a stereotype rather than fact or reason.

JUSTICE KENNEDY, concurring in part and concurring in the judgment. . . .

JUSTICE SCALIA, concurring in the judgment.

. . . The benign purpose of compensating for social disadvantages, whether they have been acquired by reason of prior discrimination or otherwise, can no more be pursued by the illegitimate means of racial discrimination than can other assertedly benign purposes we have repeatedly rejected. The difficulty of overcoming the effects of past discrimination is as nothing compared with the difficulty of eradicating from our society the source of those effects, which is the tendency—fatal to a Nation such as ours—to classify and judge men and women on the basis of their country of origin or the color of their skin. . . . [D]iscrimination on the basis of race is illegal, immoral, unconstitutional, inherently wrong, and destructive of democratic society.

. . .

A sound distinction between federal and state (or local) action based on race rests not only upon the substance of the Civil War Amendments, but upon social reality and governmental theory. It is a simple fact that . . . "the dispassionate objectivity [and] the flexibility that are needed to mold a race-conscious remedy around the single objective of eliminating the effects of past or present discrimination"—political qualities already to be doubted in a national legislature,—are substantially less likely to exist at the state or local level. The struggle for racial justice has historically been a struggle by the national society against oppression in the individual States. . . .

In my view there is only one circumstance in which the States may act *by race* to "undo the effects of past discrimination": where that is necessary to eliminate their own maintenance of a system of unlawful racial classification. . . .

. . .

It is plainly true that in our society blacks have suffered discrimination immeasurably greater than any directed at other racial groups. But those who believe that racial preferences can help to "even the score" display, and reinforce, a manner of thinking by race that was the source of the injustice and that will, if it endures within our society, be the source of more injustice still. The relevant proposition is not that it was blacks, or Jews, or Irish who were discriminated against, but that it was individual men and women, "created equal," who were discriminated against. And the relevant resolve is that that should never happen again. Racial preferences appear to "even the score" (in some small degree) only if one embraces the proposition that our society is appropriately viewed as divided into races, making it right that an injustice rendered in the past to a black man should be compensated for by discriminating against a white. Nothing is worth that embrace. Since blacks have been disproportionately disadvantaged by racial discrimination, any race-neutral remedial program aimed at the disadvantaged *as such* will have a disproportionately beneficial impact on blacks.

Only such a program, and not one that operates on the basis of race, is in accord with the letter and the spirit of our Constitution.

. . .

JUSTICE MARSHALL, with whom JUSTICE BRENNAN and JUSTICE BLACKMUN join, dissenting.

. . .

. . . As much as any municipality in the United States, Richmond knows what racial discrimination is; a century of decisions by this and other federal courts has richly documented the city's disgraceful history of public and private racial discrimination. In any event, the Richmond City Council *has* supported its determination that minorities have been wrongly excluded from local construction contracting. Its proof includes statistics showing that minority-owned businesses have received virtually no city contracting dollars and rarely if ever belonged to area trade associations; testimony by municipal officials that discrimination has been widespread in the local construction industry; and exhaustive and widely publicized federal studies . . . which showed that pervasive discrimination in the Nation's tight-knit construction industry had operated to exclude minorities from public contracting. These are precisely the types of statistical and testimonial evidence which, until today, this Court had credited in cases approving of race-conscious measures designed to remedy past discrimination.

. . .

. . . My view has long been that race-conscious classifications designed to further remedial goals "must serve important governmental objectives and must be substantially related to achievement of those objectives" in order to withstand constitutional scrutiny. Analyzed in terms of this two-pronged standard, Richmond's set-aside, like the federal program on which it was modeled, is "plainly constitutional."

Richmond has two powerful interests in setting aside a portion of public contracting funds for minority-owned enterprises. The first is the city's interest in eradicating the effects of past racial discrimination. It is far too late in the day to doubt that remedying such discrimination is a compelling, let alone an important, interest. . . . Richmond has a second compelling interest in setting aside, where possible, a portion of its contracting dollars. That interest is the prospective one of preventing the city's own spending decisions from reinforcing and perpetuating the exclusionary effects of past discrimination.

. . .

. . . When government channels all its contracting funds to a white-dominated community of established contractors whose racial homogeneity is the product of private discrimination, it does more than place its *imprimatur* on the practices which forged and which continue to define that community. It also provides a measurable boost to those economic entities that have thrived within it, while denying important economic benefits to those entities which, but for prior discrimination, might well be better qualified to receive valuable government contracts. In my view, the interest in ensuring that the government does not reflect and reinforce prior private discrimination in dispensing public contracts is every bit as strong as the interest in eliminating private discrimination—an interest which this Court has repeatedly deemed compelling. . . .

. . .

. . . [W]here the issue is not present discrimination but rather whether *past* discrimination has resulted in the *continuing exclusion* of minorities from a historically tight-knit industry, a contrast between population and work force is entirely appropriate to help gauge the degree of the exclusion. . . . This contrast is especially illuminating in cases like this, where a main avenue of introduction into the work force—here, membership in the trade associations whose members presumably train apprentices and help them procure subcontracting assignments—is itself grossly dominated by nonminorities. The majority's assertion that the city "does not even know how many MBE's in the relevant market are qualified" is thus entirely beside the point. If Richmond indeed has a monochromatic contracting community, this most likely reflects the lingering power of past exclusionary practices. . . .

. . .

In my judgment, Richmond's set-aside plan also comports with the second prong of the equal protection inquiry, for it is substantially related to the interests it seeks to serve in remedying past discrimination and in ensuring that municipal contract procurement does not perpetuate that discrimination. . . . Like the federal provision [at issue in *Fullilove v. Klutznick* (1980)], Richmond's is limited to five years in duration, and was not renewed when it came up for reconsideration in 1988. Like the federal provision, Richmond's contains a waiver provision freeing from its subcontracting requirements those nonminority firms that demonstrate that they cannot comply with its provisions.

Like the federal provision, Richmond's has a minimal impact on innocent third parties. While the measure affects 30% of *public* contracting dollars, that translates to only 3% of overall Richmond area contracting.

. . .

Today, for the first time, a majority of this Court has adopted strict scrutiny as its standard of Equal Protection Clause review of race-conscious remedial measures. This is an unwelcome development. A profound difference separates governmental actions that themselves are racist and governmental actions that seek to remedy the effects of prior racism or to prevent neutral governmental activity from perpetuating the effects of such racism.

Racial classifications "drawn on the presumption that one race is inferior to another or because they put the weight of government behind racial hatred and separatism" warrant the strictest judicial scrutiny because of the very irrelevance of these rationales. By contrast, racial classifications drawn for the purpose of remedying the effects of discrimination that itself was race based have a highly pertinent basis: the tragic and indelible fact that discrimination against blacks and other racial minorities in this Nation has pervaded our Nation's history and continues to scar our society. . . .

In concluding that remedial classifications warrant no different standard of review under the Constitution than the most brutal and repugnant forms of state-sponsored racism, a majority of this Court signals that it regards racial discrimination as largely a phenomenon of the past, and that government bodies need no longer preoccupy themselves with rectifying racial injustice. I, however, do not believe this Nation is anywhere close to eradicating racial discrimination or its vestiges. In constitutionalizing its wishful thinking, the majority today does a grave disservice not only to those victims of past and present racial discrimination in this Nation whom government has sought to assist, but also to this Court's long tradition of approaching issues of race with the utmost sensitivity.

. . .

Congress' concern in passing the Reconstruction Amendments, and particularly their congressional authorization provisions, was that States would *not* adequately respond to racial violence or discrimination against newly freed slaves. To interpret any aspect of these Amendments as proscribing state remedial responses to these very problems turns the Amendments on their heads. The Amendments specifically empowered the Federal Government to combat discrimination at a time when the breadth of federal power under the Constitution was less apparent than it is today. But nothing in the Amendments themselves, or in our long history of interpreting or applying those momentous charters, suggests that States, exercising their police power, are in any way constitutionally inhibited from working alongside the Federal Government in the fight against discrimination and its effects.

. . .

JUSTICE BLACKMUN, with whom JUSTICE BRENNAN joins, dissenting. . . .

C. Gender

The Reagan Era witnessed the rise of several gender gaps in American constitutional politics. Democratic and Republican Party platforms adopted different positions on women's rights. Democrats strongly favored the ERA and legal abortion. Republicans abandoned previous support for the ERA and opposed legal abortion. Such feminist groups as NOW became influential partners in the Democratic Party coalition. Such conservative groups as Concerned Women of American cast their lot with the Republican Party. In every national election held during the 1980s and afterward, women were more inclined than men to vote for candidates nominated by the Democratic Party. Remarkably, this gender gap in voting is not strongly related to the different positions that the major parties take on women's rights. Public opinion suggests that support for ERA and legal abortion more often divide better- and lesser-educated Americans than they divide men from women. Other surveys suggest that women vote more Democratic than men because women are more likely than men to favor Democratic Party positions on such issues as health care and foreign military interventions.[57]

Neither Reagan conservatives nor social liberals were pleased with the trend of constitutional decisions on gender equality in the 1980s and early 1990s. By the end of Ronald Reagan's first term the ERA was dead, but a fair degree of gender equality was incorporated into American constitutional law. Many states

57. Carole Kennedy Chaney, R. Michael Alvarez, and Jonathan Nagler, "Explaining the Gender Gap in U.S. Presidential Elections, 1980–1992," *Political Research Quarterly* 51 (1998): 311.

ratified state equal rights amendments containing language identical or nearly identical to the language of the failed federal ERA. The Supreme Court in *Mississippi University for Women v. Hogan* (1982) reaffirmed and sharpened previous decisions holding all official gender distinctions to a higher constitutional standard. When declaring unconstitutional a state law maintaining an all-women school of nursing, Justice O'Connor wrote,

> A statute that classifies individuals on the basis of their gender must carry the burden of showing an "exceedingly persuasive justification" for the classification. The burden is met only by showing at least that the classification serves "important governmental objectives and that the discriminatory means employed" are "substantially related to the achievement of those objectives."

The Supreme Court in *Johnson v. Transportation Agency* (1987) ruled that affirmative action programs for woman did not violate either Title VII or the Civil Rights Act of 1964 (and, implicitly, did not violate the equal protection clause). Claims based on more radical understandings of gender equality failed. State and federal judges consistently rejected "comparable worth" arguments, that asserted that employers violated equality rights by paying workers in traditional male jobs a higher salary than workers in traditional female jobs.[58]

National Party Platforms on Women's Rights (1980)

1980 was a crucial turning point in the constitutional politics of women's rights. National political parties during the mid-twentieth century were not sharply divided on women's issues. Historically, Republicans more strongly favored women's rights than Democrats. Reagan Republicans charted a new course. While the 1980 Democratic Party adopted a ringing endorsement of the ERA, the Republican Party took no position on the matter.

When reading the excerpts from these party platforms, consider the reasons for and the nature of new divisions between the parties on gender issues. Why did Democrats become the party of choice for feminists and Republicans the party of choice for more traditional women? How great were the actual differences between the parties? What, in addition to the ERA, divided Democrats from Republicans on gender issues in 1980?

Democratic Party Platform (1980)

The Democratic Party commits itself to strong steps to close the wage gap between men and women, to expand child care opportunities for families with working parents, to end the tax discrimination that penalizes married working couples, and to ensure that women can retire in dignity.

We will strictly enforce existing anti-discrimination laws with respect to hiring, pay and promotions. We will adopt a full employment policy, with increased possibilities for part-time work. Vocational programs for young women in our high schools and colleges will be equalized and expanded. Fields traditionally reserved for men . . . from construction to engineering . . . must be opened to women, a goal which must be promoted through government incentives and federally sponsored training programs.

Perhaps most important, the Democratic Party is committed to the principle of equal pay for work of comparable value. . . . [W]e will ensure that women in both the public and private sectors are not only paid equally for work which is identical to that performed by men, but are also paid equally for work which is of comparable value to that performed by men.

. . .

In the 1980s, the Democratic Party commits itself to a Constitution, economy, and society open to women on an equal basis with men.

The primary route to that new horizon is ratification of the Equal Rights Amendment. A Democratic Congress, working with women's leaders, labor, civil and religious organizations, first enacted ERA in Congress and later extended the deadline for ratification. Now, the Democratic Party must ensure that ERA at last becomes the 27th Amendment to the Constitution. We oppose efforts to rescind ERA in states which have already ratified the amendment, and we shall insist that past recessions are invalid.

In view of the high priority which the Democratic Party places on ratification of the ERA, the Democratic National Committee renews its commitment not to hold

58. For a good study of the comparable worth movement, see Michael W. McCann, *Rights at Work: Pay Equity Reform and the Politics of Legal Mobilization* (Chicago: University of Chicago Press, 1994).

national or multi-state meetings, conferences, or conventions in states which have not yet ratified the ERA. The Democratic Party shall withhold financial support and technical campaign assistance from candidates who do not support the ERA. The Democratic Party further urges all national organizations to support the boycott of the unratified states by not holding national meetings, conferences, or conventions in those states.

Furthermore, the Democratic Party shall seek to eliminate sex-based discrimination and inequities from all aspects of our society.

Republican Party Platform (1980)

We acknowledge the legitimate efforts of those who support or oppose ratification of the Equal Rights Amendment.

We reaffirm our Party's historic commitment to equal rights and equality for women.

We support equal rights and equal opportunities for women, without taking away traditional rights of women such as exemption from the military draft. We support the enforcement of all equal opportunity laws and urge the elimination of discrimination against women. We oppose any move which would give the federal government more power over families.

Ratification of the Equal Rights Amendment is now in the hands of state legislatures, and the issues of the time extension and rescission are in the courts. The states have a constitutional right to accept or reject a constitutional amendment without federal interference or pressure. At the direction of the White House, federal departments launched pressure against states which refused to ratify ERA. Regardless of one's position on ERA, we demand that this practice cease.

. . . [T]he following urgent problems must be resolved.

Total integration of the work force (not separate but equal) is necessary to bring women equality in pay;

Girls and young women must be given improved early career counseling and job training to widen the opportunities for them in the world of work;

Women's worth in the society and in the jobs they hold, at home or in the workplace, must be re-evaluated to improve the conditions of women workers concentrated in low-status, low-paying jobs;

Equal opportunity for credit and other assistance must be assured to women in small businesses; . . .

One of the most critical problems in our nation today is that of inadequate child care for the working mother. As champions of the free enterprise system, of the individual, and of the idea that the best solutions to most problems rest at the community level, Republicans must find ways to meet this, the working woman's need. The scope of this problem is fully realized only when it is understood that many female heads of households are at the poverty level and that they have a very large percentage of the nation's children.

. . .

. . . The Social Security system is still biased against women, and non-existent pension plans combine with that to produce a bereft elderly woman. The Republican Party must not and will not let this continue.

We reaffirm our belief in the traditional role and values of the family in our society. The damage being done today to the family takes its greatest toll on the woman. Whether it be through divorce, widowhood, economic problems, or the suffering of children, the impact is greatest on women. The importance of support for the mother and homemaker in maintaining the values of this country cannot be over-emphasized.

American Nurses Association v. State of Illinois, 783 F.2d 716 (1986)

Illinois paid state workers in predominately male occupations a higher salary than state workers in predominantly female occupations. The American Nurses Association (ANA) filed a class action suit in federal court, claiming that this practice violated the Civil Rights Act of 1964 and the equal protection clause of the Fourteenth Amendment. A lower district court dismissed the lawsuit. The ANA appealed to the Court of Appeals for the Eighth Circuit.

The court of appeals reversed the federal district court on narrow grounds. Judge Posner rejected the ANA's claim that Illinois had a legal and constitutional obligation to pay workers in traditionally female jobs the same as workers in traditionally male jobs of similar value to society. He ruled, however, that persons making comparable worth claims might be able to demonstrate intentional gender discrimination. Why does Judge Posner reject comparative worth claims? What does he believe the ANA had to demonstrate to prove its case? What standard would you impose?

JUDGE POSNER delivered the opinion of the Court.

. . .

Comparable worth is not a legal concept, but a shorthand expression for the movement to raise the ratio of wages in traditionally women's jobs to wages in traditionally men's jobs. Its premises are both historical and cognitive. The historical premise is that a society politically and culturally dominated by men steered women into certain jobs and kept the wages in those jobs below what the jobs were worth, precisely because most of the holders were women. The cognitive premise is that analytical techniques exist for determining the relative worth of jobs that involve different levels of skill, effort, risk, responsibility, etc. These premises are vigorously disputed on both theoretical and empirical grounds. Economists point out that unless employers forbid women to compete for the higher-paying, traditionally men's jobs—which would violate federal law—women will switch into those jobs until the only difference in wages between traditionally women's jobs and traditionally men's jobs will be that necessary to equate the supply of workers in each type of job to the demand. Economists have conducted studies which show that virtually the entire difference in the average hourly wage of men and women, including that due to the fact that men and women tend to be concentrated in different types of job, can be explained by the fact that most women take considerable time out of the labor force in order to take care of their children. As a result they tend to invest less in their "human capital" (earning capacity); and since part of any wage is a return on human capital, they tend therefore to be found in jobs that pay less. Consistently with this hypothesis, the studies find that women who have never married earn as much as men who have never married. To all this the advocates of comparable worth reply that although there are no longer explicit barriers to women's entering traditionally men's jobs, cultural and psychological barriers remain as a result of which many though not all women internalize men's expectations regarding jobs appropriate for women and therefore invest less in their human capital.

On the cognitive question economists point out that the ratio of wages in different jobs is determined by the market rather than by any a priori conception of relative merit, in just the same way that the ratio of the price of caviar to the price of cabbage is determined by relative scarcity rather than relative importance to human welfare. Upsetting the market equilibrium by imposing such a conception would have costly consequences, some of which might undercut the ultimate goals of the comparable worth movement. If the movement should cause wages in traditionally men's jobs to be depressed below their market level and wages in traditionally women's jobs to be jacked above their market level, women will have less incentive to enter traditionally men's fields and more to enter traditionally women's fields. Analysis cannot stop there, because the change in relative wages will send men in the same direction: fewer men will enter the traditionally men's jobs, more the traditionally women's jobs. As a result there will be more room for women in traditionally men's jobs and at the same time fewer opportunities for women in traditionally women's jobs—especially since the number of those jobs will shrink as employers are induced by the higher wage to substitute capital for labor inputs (e.g., more word processors, fewer secretaries). Labor will be allocated less efficiently; men and women alike may be made worse off.

. . .

It should be clear from this brief summary that the issue of comparable worth . . . is not of the sort that judges are well equipped to resolve intelligently or that we should lightly assume has been given to us to resolve by Title VII or the Constitution. An employer (private or public) that simply pays the going wage in each of the different types of job in its establishment, and makes no effort to discourage women from applying for particular jobs or to steer them toward particular jobs, would be justifiably surprised to discover that it may be violating federal law because each wage rate and therefore the ratio between them have been found to be determined by cultural or psychological factors attributable to the history of male domination of society; that it has to hire a consultant to find out how it must, regardless of market conditions, change the wages it pays, in order to achieve equity between traditionally male and traditionally female jobs; and that it must pay backpay, to boot. . . .

The next question is whether a failure to achieve comparable worth . . . might permit an inference of deliberate and therefore unlawful discrimination, as distinct from passive acceptance of a market-determined disparity in wages. . . .

. . .

The plaintiffs can get no mileage out of casting a comparable worth case as an equal protection case. The Supreme Court held in *Washington v. Davis* (1976), that the equal protection clause is violated only by intentional discrimination; the fact that a law or official practice adopted for a lawful purpose has a racially differential impact is not enough....

... Knowledge of a disparity is not the same thing as an intent to cause or maintain it; if for example the state's intention was to pay market wages, its knowledge that the consequence would be that men got higher wages on average than women and that the difference might exceed any premium attributable to a difference in relative worth would not make it guilty of intentionally discriminating against women. Similarly, even if the failure to act on the comparable worth study could be regarded as "reaffirming" the state's commitment to pay market wages, this would not be enough to demonstrate discriminatory purpose. To demonstrate such a purpose the failure to act would have to be motivated at least in part by a desire to benefit men at the expense of women.

...

... If the "use of a sex-biased system for pay and classification which results in and perpetuates discrimination in compensation against women employed in historically female-dominated sex-segregated job classifications," just means that the state is paying wages determined by the market rather than by the principle of comparable worth, it states no claim. But if it means to allege that the state has departed from the market measure on grounds of sex—not only paying higher than market wages in predominantly male job classifications and only market wages in predominantly female classifications, but keeping women from entering the predominantly male jobs ("sex-segregated")—it states a claim....

...

... Suppose the state has declined to act on the results of the comparable worth study not because it prefers to pay (perhaps is forced by labor-market or fiscal constraints to pay) market wages but because it thinks men deserve to be paid more than women. This would be the kind of deliberate sex discrimination that Title VII forbids, once the statute is understood to allow wage disparities between dissimilar jobs to be challenged....

Johnson v. Transportation Agency, Santa Clara County, 480 U.S. 616 (1987)

Paul Johnson and Diane Joyce were employees of the Transportation Agency of Santa Clara County, California. Both applied for promotion to road dispatcher. Agency supervisors concluded that both were qualified for the position but recommended Johnson for promotion. The agency's affirmative action coordinator disagreed, contending that promoting Joyce was more consistent with the agency's affirmative action program. James Graebner, the director of the agency, promoted Joyce. Johnson filed a lawsuit, claiming that this decision violated his rights under Title VII of the Civil Rights Act of 1964. The crucial provision of that statute declares that employers may not "discriminate against any individual with respect to his compensation, terms, conditions, or privileges of employment, because of such individual's race, color, religion, sex or national origin." The local federal district court ruled that unlawful discrimination had taken place. The Court of Appeals for the Ninth Circuit reversed that ruling. Johnson appealed to the Supreme Court of the United States.[59]

The Supreme Court by a 6-3 vote declared that Paul Johnson was not legally entitled to the promotion. Justice Brennan's majority opinion declared that employers could legally adopt affirmative action plans to correct "manifest" racial and gender "imbalances" in the workplace. What reasons does he give for reaching that conclusion? Why does Justice Scalia disagree? Who has the better argument? The majority opinion does not discuss whether the Transportation Agency violated the equal protection clause of the Constitution (a claim that Johnson did not make). If that was their concern, what standard should the justices have used? During the Reagan Era courts maintained that discrimination against persons of color had to satisfy a stricter standard than discrimination against women. Does this mean that affirmative action programs for women had to satisfy a lesser constitutional standard than affirmative action programs for persons of color?

JUSTICE BRENNAN delivered the opinion of the Court.

...

The first issue is whether consideration of the sex of applicants for Skilled Craft jobs was justified by the existence of a "manifest imbalance" that reflected underrepresentation of women in "traditionally segregated job categories." ... The requirement that the "manifest imbalance" relate to a "traditionally segregated job category" provides assurance both that sex or race will be

---

59. For a good account of the case, see Melvin I. Urofsky, *Affirmative Action on Trial: Sex Discrimination in Johnson v. Santa Clara* (Lawrence: University Press of Kansas, 1997).

taken into account in a manner consistent with Title VII's purpose of eliminating the effects of employment discrimination, and that the interests of those employees not benefiting from the plan will not be unduly infringed.

. . .

It is clear that the decision to hire Joyce was made pursuant to an Agency plan that directed that sex or race be taken into account for the purpose of remedying underrepresentation. The Agency Plan acknowledged the "limited opportunities that have existed in the past" for women to find employment in certain job classifications "where women have not been traditionally employed in significant numbers." As a result, observed the Plan, women were concentrated in traditionally female jobs in the Agency, and represented a lower percentage in other job classifications than would be expected if such traditional segregation had not occurred. Specifically, 9 of the 10 Para-Professionals and 110 of the 145 Office and Clerical Workers were women. By contrast, women were only 2 of the 28 Officials and Administrators, 5 of the 58 Professionals, 12 of the 124 Technicians, none of the Skilled Craft Workers, and 1—who was Joyce—of the 110 Road Maintenance Workers. The Plan sought to remedy these imbalances through "hiring, training and promotion of . . . women throughout the Agency in all major job classifications where they are underrepresented."

. . .

The Agency's Plan emphatically did not authorize blind hiring. It expressly directed that numerous factors be taken into account in making hiring decisions, including specifically the qualifications of female applicants for particular jobs. . . .

. . . Given the obvious imbalance in the Skilled Craft category, and given the Agency's commitment to eliminating such imbalances, it was plainly not unreasonable for the Agency to determine that it was appropriate to consider as one factor the sex of Ms. Joyce in making its decision. The promotion of Joyce thus satisfies the first requirement . . . , since it was undertaken to further an affirmative action plan designed to eliminate Agency work force imbalances in traditionally segregated job categories.

We next consider whether the Agency Plan unnecessarily trammeled the rights of male employees or created an absolute bar to their advancement. . . . [T]he Plan sets aside no positions for women. . . . As the Agency Director testified, the sex of Joyce was but one of numerous factors he took into account in arriving at his decision. The Plan thus resembles the "Harvard Plan" approvingly noted by Justice POWELL in *Regents of University of California v. Bakke* (1978), which considers race along with other criteria in determining admission to the college. . . . No persons are automatically excluded from consideration; all are able to have their qualifications weighed against those of other applicants.

. . .

. . . The Agency has identified a conspicuous imbalance in job categories traditionally segregated by race and sex. It has made clear from the outset, however, that employment decisions may not be justified solely by reference to this imbalance, but must rest on a multitude of practical, realistic factors. It has therefore committed itself to annual adjustment of goals so as to provide a reasonable guide for actual hiring and promotion decisions. The Agency earmarks no positions for anyone; sex is but one of several factors that may be taken into account in evaluating qualified applicants for a position. As both the Plan's language and its manner of operation attest, the Agency has no intention of establishing a work force whose permanent composition is dictated by rigid numerical standards.

. . .

JUSTICE STEVENS, concurring.

. . .

. . . I see no reason why the employer has any duty, prior to granting a preference to a qualified minority employee, to determine whether his past conduct might constitute an arguable violation of Title VII. Indeed, in some instances the employer may find it more helpful to focus on the future. Instead of retroactively scrutinizing his own or society's possible exclusions of minorities in the past to determine the outer limits of a valid affirmative-action program—or indeed, any particular affirmative-action decision—in many cases the employer will find it more appropriate to consider other legitimate reasons to give preferences to members of under-represented groups. Statutes enacted for the benefit of minority groups should not block these forward-looking considerations.

. . .

JUSTICE O'CONNOR, concurring in the judgment.

. . .

In my view, the proper initial inquiry in evaluating the legality of an affirmative action plan by a public employer under Title VII is no different from that required by the Equal Protection Clause. In either case, consistent with the congressional intent to provide some measure of protection to the interests of the employer's nonminority employees, the employer must have had a firm basis for believing that remedial action was required. An employer would have such a firm basis if it can point to a statistical disparity sufficient to support a prima facie claim under Title VII by the employee beneficiaries of the affirmative action plan of a pattern or practice claim of discrimination.

. . .

In this case, I am also satisfied that respondents had a firm basis for adopting an affirmative action program. Although the District Court found no discrimination against women in fact, at the time the affirmative action plan was adopted, there were no women in its skilled craft positions. Petitioner concedes that women constituted approximately 5% of the local labor pool of skilled craft workers in 1970. Thus, when compared to the percentage of women in the qualified work force, the statistical disparity would have been sufficient for a prima facie Title VII case brought by unsuccessful women job applicants. . . .

JUSTICE WHITE, dissenting. . . .

JUSTICE SCALIA, with whom THE CHIEF JUSTICE joins, and with whom JUSTICE WHITE joins in part, dissenting.

. . . The Court today completes the process of converting [Title VII of the Civil Rights Act of 1964] from a guarantee that race or sex will not be the basis for employment determinations, to a guarantee that it often will. Ever so subtly, . . . we effectively replace the goal of a discrimination-free society with the quite incompatible goal of proportionate representation by race and by sex in the workplace. . . .

. . .

. . . [T]he plan's purpose was assuredly not to remedy prior sex discrimination by the Agency. It could not have been, because there was no prior sex discrimination to remedy. The majority, in cataloging the Agency's alleged misdeeds, neglects to mention the District Court's finding that the Agency "has not discriminated in the past, and does not discriminate in the present against women in regard to employment opportunities in general and promotions in particular." . . .

Not only was the plan not directed at the results of past sex discrimination by the Agency, but its objective was not to achieve the state of affairs that this Court has dubiously assumed would result from an absence of discrimination—an overall work force "more or less representative of the racial and ethnic composition of the population in the community." Rather, the oft-stated goal was to mirror the racial and sexual composition of the entire county labor force, not merely in the Agency work force as a whole, but in each and every individual job category at the Agency. In a discrimination-free world, it would obviously be a statistical oddity for every job category to match the racial and sexual composition of even that portion of the county work force qualified for that job; it would be utterly miraculous for each of them to match, as the plan expected, the composition of the entire work force. Quite obviously, the plan did not seek to replicate what a lack of discrimination would produce, but rather imposed racial and sexual tailoring that would, in defiance of normal expectations and laws of probability, give each protected racial and sexual group a governmentally determined "proper" proportion of each job category.

. . .

The most significant proposition of law established by today's decision is that racial or sexual discrimination is permitted under Title VII when it is intended to overcome the effect, not of the employer's own discrimination, but of societal attitudes that have limited the entry of certain races, or of a particular sex, into certain jobs. Even if the societal attitudes in question consisted exclusively of conscious discrimination by other employers, this holding would contradict a decision of this Court rendered only last Term. *Wygant v. Jackson Board of Education* (1986), held that the objective of remedying societal discrimination cannot prevent remedial affirmative action from violating the Equal Protection Clause. . . .

. . .

. . . It is absurd to think that the nationwide failure of road maintenance crews, for example, to achieve the Agency's ambition of 36.4% female representation is attributable primarily, if even substantially, to systematic exclusion of women eager to shoulder pick and shovel. It is a "traditionally segregated job category" . . . in the sense that, because of longstanding social attitudes, it has not been regarded by women themselves as desirable work. . . . There are, of course, those who believe that the social attitudes which cause women themselves to avoid certain jobs and to favor others are as nefarious as conscious, exclusionary discrimination. Whether or not that is so (and there is assuredly no consensus on the point equivalent to our national consensus against intentional discrimination), the two phenomena are certainly distinct. And it is the alteration of social attitudes, rather than the elimination of discrimination, which today's decision approves as justification for state-enforced discrimination. This is an enormous expansion, undertaken without the slightest justification or analysis.

. . .

. . . [W]hat the Court means by "taking distinctions in qualifications into account" consists of no more than eliminating from the applicant pool those who are not even minimally qualified for the job. Once that has been done, once the promoting officer assures himself that all the candidates before him are "M.Q.'s" (minimally qualifieds), he can then ignore, as the Agency Director did here, how much better than minimally qualified some of the candidates may be, and can proceed to appoint from the pool solely on the basis of race or sex, until the affirmative-action "goals" have been reached. The requirement that the employer "take distinctions in qualifications into account" thus turns out to be an assurance, not that candidates' comparative merits will always be considered, but only that none of the successful candidates selected over the others solely on the basis of their race or sex will be utterly unqualified. That may be of great comfort to those concerned with American productivity; and it is undoubtedly effective in reducing the effect of affirmative-action discrimination upon those in the upper strata of society, who (unlike road maintenance workers, for example) compete for employment in professional and semiprofessional fields where, for many reasons, including most notably the effects of past discrimination, the numbers of "M.Q." applicants from the favored groups are substantially less. But I fail to see how it has any relevance to whether selecting among final candidates solely on the basis of race or sex is permissible under Title VII, which prohibits discrimination on the basis of race or sex.

D. Native Americans

The constitutional status and rights of Native Americans did not change significantly during the Reagan Era. Native Americans living off the reservation enjoyed the same constitutional and legal rights as other Americans. Tribal governments determined the rights of Native Americans on reservations, subject to such congressional measures as the Indian Bill of Rights, which limited the power of tribal governments to violate some, but not all, of the rights set out in the Constitution of the United States. The Supreme Court ratified this arrangement in *Duro v. Reina* (1990). The issue in that case was whether a tribal government had the power to prosecute a member of a different tribe for a crime committed on a reservation. The justices by a 7-2 vote rejected that authority. Justice Kennedy's majority opinion asserted, "Tribal power does not extend beyond internal relations among members." Furthermore, he wrote, "We hesitate to adopt a view of tribal sovereignty that would single out another group of citizens, nonmember Indians, for trial by political bodies that do not include them." Kennedy recognized that tribal members did not enjoy the same protections as state residents. He noted that the Indian Bill of Rights did not protect the right "to appointed counsel for those unable to afford a lawyer." This lack of protection, he claimed, was "justified by the voluntary character of tribal membership and the concomitant right of participation in a tribal government, the authority of which rests on consent."

Congress expanded the rights of Native Americans when passing the American Indian Religious Freedom Act of 1978. That measure declared "the policy of the United States to protect and preserve for American Indians their inherent right of freedom to believe, express, and exercise the traditional religions of the American Indian . . . including but not limited to access to sites, use and possession of sacred objects, and the freedom to worship through ceremonials and traditional rites."[60] The Supreme Court in *Lyng v. Northwest Indian Cemetery Protective Association* (1988) declared the measure nonjusticiable. Rejecting an attempt by a Native American tribe to prevent the federal government from building a road through a sacred burial ground, Justice O'Connor's majority opinion stated, "Nowhere in the law is there so much as a hint of any intent to create a cause of action or any judicially enforceable individual rights." Justice Brennan's dissent asserted,

> This refusal essentially leaves Native Americans with absolutely no constitutional protection against perhaps the gravest threat to their religious practices. . . . I find it difficult to imagine conduct more

60. 92 U.S. Stat. 469 (1978).

insensitive to religious needs than the Government's determination to build a marginally useful road in the face of uncontradicted evidence that the road will render the practice of respondents' religion impossible.

In response to the Court's decision, Congress designated the area a "wilderness" under the Wilderness Act. The road was not built.

VI. CRIMINAL JUSTICE

MAJOR DEVELOPMENTS

- Increased limits on federal habeas corpus petitions
- Good-faith exception to the exclusionary rule
- Increased use of capital punishment

Reagan conservatives inherited from Richard Nixon a commitment to reversing liberal decisions that they believed hampered police efforts to fight crime. Liberals, the 1984 Republican Party platform complained, were "more concerned for abstract criminal rights than for victims of crime." That platform promised to "restore a constitutionally valid federal death penalty," "modify the exclusionary rule," and "curtail abuses by prisoners of federal habeas corpus procedures." The Reagan Justice Department bluntly declared, "Neither the search and seizure exclusionary rule nor the procedural rules for custodial interrogations established by *Miranda v. Arizona* (1966) are required by the Constitution."[61] Democrats were decidedly more ambivalent about constitutional criminal procedure and the death penalty. Democratic Party platforms said little or nothing about the constitutional rights of persons accused or convicted of criminal offenses.

The Reagan Revolution in criminal justice enjoyed far more success in courts than in Congress. Liberals in Congress consistently blocked proposed laws that would curb the rights of criminal suspects and persons convicted of crimes. President George Bush, when signing the Crime Control Act of 1990, expressed "deep disappointment" that Congress had rejected many administration proposals, including "a death penalty for the most heinous Federal crimes . . ., comprehensive reform of habeas corpus proceedings that continue to nullify State death penalty laws through repetitive hearings and endless delays, [and] reform of the exclusionary rule to allow juries to consider all evidence gathered by law enforcement officers acting in good faith." The Supreme Court was more receptive than Congress to many of these proposals. Reagan's four judicial appointees often formed a judicial majority with Nixon judicial appointees (and Justice Byron White) on questions of constitutional criminal procedure. By 1994 the Supreme Court had declared that unconstitutionally seized evidence could be admitted at a criminal trial if the police had acted on a "good faith" belief that the search was constitutional (*United States v. Leon* [1984]); established important exceptions to the rule that confessions could be admitted only if preceded by *Miranda* warnings (*New York v. Quarles* [1984]); sharply narrowed access to habeas corpus (*McCleskey v.* Zant [1991]), even when capitally sentenced prisoners made claims of actual innocence (*Herrera v. Collins* [1993]); and rejected challenges to capital punishment based on statistical evidence that murderers whose victims were white were far more likely to be executed than those who murdered persons of color (*McCleskey v. Kemp* [1987]).

Despondent liberals experienced a few rays of light. The Supreme Court did not actually overrule such liberal pillars as *Mapp v. Ohio* (1961) (exclusionary rule) and *Miranda v. Arizona* (1966). Some death sentences were reversed. The judicial majority in *Batson v. Kentucky* (1986) ruled that prosecutors could not use preemptory challenges to remove persons of color from juries. Finally, Justices Blackmun and Justice Stevens, Republican appointees in the 1970s, took more liberal positions in cases concerned with constitutional criminal procedure. By the end of the Reagan Era Stevens, Blackmun, and eventually Justice Sandra Day O'Connor had forming a nascent majority committed to preventing further erosion of liberal constitutional decisions handed down during the 1960s and 1970s.

A. Due Process and Habeas Corpus

Reagan conservatives were committed to a crime-control model of constitutional criminal procedure. Proponents of this model insist that constitutional provisions protecting the rights of persons suspected of crime be interpreted to enable law enforcement officials to identify, arrest, and punish criminals. Conservatives in the 1980s combined this appeal for crime control with concerns for federalism and finality. They maintained that

61. Office of Legal Policy, *Guidelines on Constitutional Litigation*, 86.

the federal government should not routinely intervene in state criminal proceedings. Chief Justice Rehnquist combined appeals to federalism and finality in *Herrera v. Collins* (1993) when denying a person under a sentence of death the right to a new trial on the basis of newly discovered evidence suggesting the petitioner was not guilty. His opinion declared, "But because of the very disruptive effect that entertaining claims of actual innocence would have on the need for finality in capital cases, and the enormous burden that having to retry cases based on often stale evidence would place on the States, the threshold showing for such an assumed right would necessarily be extraordinarily high."

The Bail Reform Act of 1984 illustrates the conservative commitment to crime control. That law focused more on preventing bad acts than making sure that criminal defendants appeared at trial. The Senate report on this legislation declared,

> Federal bail laws must address the alarming problem of crimes committed by persons on release and must give the courts adequate authority to make release decisions that give appropriate recognition to the danger a person may pose to others if released. The adoption of these changes marks a significant departure from the basic philosophy of the Bail Reform Act [of 1966], which is that the sole purpose of bail laws must be to assure the appearance of the defendant at judicial proceedings.[62]

The Bail Reform Act sought to reduce crime by permitting courts to deny bail to criminal suspects whenever judges determined that the person was a potential threat to the community. The Supreme Court in *United States v. Salerno* (1987) declared the Bail Reform Act constitutional. Chief Justice Rehnquist's majority opinion stated, "The Government's regulatory interest in community safety can, in appropriate circumstances, outweigh an individual's liberty interest."

President Reagan and his political allies enjoyed mixed success when promoting greater solicitude for federalism in constitutional criminal procedure. No Supreme Court justice displayed any interest in overruling or even narrowing past decisions holding that the due process clause of the Fourteenth Amendment required states to respect the protections set out in the Bill of Rights for persons suspected and convicted of crime. The Burger and Rehnquist Courts, however, were more sympathetic to claims that expansive federal habeas corpus rights interfered with the sovereign power of states to punish crimes. Several decisions placed sharp limits on federal habeas corpus rights in the name of federalism (and finality). *Teague v. Lane* (1989) held that persons convicted in state courts could not base federal habeas corpus petitions on judicial decisions handed down after their initial round of appeals, even if a judicial majority might think those rules mandated by the Constitution. If the Supreme Court in 1990 expanded the scope of *Miranda* rights, a person whose conviction became final in 1989 could not base a habeas corpus claim on that decision. In *McCleskey v. Zant* (1991) the justices placed sharp curbs on second or successive habeas corpus petitions. The judicial majority, invoking federalism and finality, ruled that federal courts should only hear a second habeas corpus petition if the convicted prisoner could demonstrate that the constitutional claim could not possibly have been known when the first petition was filed.

Herrera v. Collins, 506 U.S. 390 (1993)

Lionel Torres Herrera in 1982 was convicted by a Texas jury of murdering Officers David Rucker and Enrique Carrisalez. He was subsequently sentenced to death. The Texas Court of Criminal Appeals affirmed the sentence and the Supreme Court of Texas denied certiorari. Herrera's first habeas corpus petition was unsuccessful. In 1990 Herrera filed a second habeas corpus petition in state court, claiming that newly discovered evidence proved that he was not the murderer. That evidence consisted of affidavits from the lawyer who represented his brother, Raul Herrera, Sr., and Raul Herrera's former cellmate. Both claimed that Raul confessed to the murders before dying in 1984. After the Texas courts denied relief, Herrera filed a federal habeas corpus claim in federal court. Herrera's petition included additional affidavits from persons who swore that Raul confessed the murder to them and an affidavit from Raul Herrera, Jr., who claimed that he saw his father commit the murders. Both the federal district court and the Court of Appeals for the Fifth Circuit rejected Herrera's claim on the ground that "actual innocence" does not state a claim for relief in federal habeas corpus. Herrera appealed to the Supreme Court of the United States.

The Supreme Court by a 6-3 vote rejected Herrera's claim. Chief Justice Rehnquist's majority opinion ruled that

62. Senate Committee on the Judiciary, *Comprehensive Crime Control Act of 1984*, 98th Cong., 2nd Sess. (1984), S. Rep. 98-225.

the due process clause does not give persons the right to a new trial based on newly discovered evidence of actual innocence. He also maintained that Herrera did not make an adequate showing of innocence even if such a right existed. On what basis does the Chief Justice deny that persons have due process right to a new trial? Why does Justice Blackmun disagree? Under what conditions, if any, do you think that a new trial is constitutionally required? Are the standards different in death cases? The Chief Justice insists that executive clemency is the appropriate vehicle when prisoners raise claims of actual innocence. What institution do you believe is best suited for making the judgment that a person constitutionally convicted at trial may actually be innocent? Suppose you agreed with Justice Rehnquist that black-letter law provided no remedy, but you were convinced that the petitioner before you was innocent. As a justice of the Supreme Court, what would you do?

CHIEF JUSTICE REHNQUIST delivered the opinion of the Court.

. . .

Once a defendant has been afforded a fair trial and convicted of the offense for which he was charged, the presumption of innocence disappears. . . . Here, it is not disputed that the State met its burden of proving at trial that petitioner was guilty of the capital murder of Officer Carrisalez beyond a reasonable doubt. Thus, in the eyes of the law, petitioner does not come before the Court as one who is "innocent," but, on the contrary, as one who has been convicted by due process of law of two brutal murders.

. . .

Claims of actual innocence based on newly discovered evidence have never been held to state a ground for federal habeas relief absent an independent constitutional violation occurring in the underlying state criminal proceeding. . . . This rule is grounded in the principle that federal habeas courts sit to ensure that individuals are not imprisoned in violation of the Constitution—not to correct errors of fact.

. . .

This is not to say that our habeas jurisprudence casts a blind eye toward innocence. . . . [W]e have held that a petitioner otherwise subject to defenses of abusive or successive use of the writ may have his federal constitutional claim considered on the merits if he makes a proper showing of actual innocence. . . . But this body of our habeas jurisprudence makes clear that a claim of "actual innocence" is not itself a constitutional claim, but instead a gateway through which a habeas petitioner must pass to have his otherwise barred constitutional claim considered on the merits.

Petitioner in this case is simply not entitled to habeas relief based on the reasoning of this line of cases. For he does not seek excusal of a procedural error so that he may bring an independent constitutional claim challenging his conviction or sentence, but rather argues that he is entitled to habeas relief because newly discovered evidence shows that his conviction is factually incorrect. . . .

Petitioner asserts that this case is different because he has been sentenced to death. But we have "refused to hold that the fact that a death sentence has been imposed requires a different standard of review on federal habeas corpus." . . .

. . .

. . . [W]e cannot say that Texas' refusal to entertain petitioner's newly discovered evidence eight years after his conviction transgresses a principle of fundamental fairness "rooted in the traditions and conscience of our people." This is not to say, however, that petitioner is left without a forum to raise his actual innocence claim. For under Texas law, petitioner may file a request for executive clemency. Clemency is deeply rooted in our Anglo-American tradition of law, and is the historic remedy for preventing miscarriages of justice where judicial process has been exhausted.

. . .

Executive clemency has provided the "fail safe" in our criminal justice system. It is an unalterable fact that our judicial system, like the human beings who administer it, is fallible. But history is replete with examples of wrongfully convicted persons who have been pardoned in the wake of after-discovered evidence establishing their innocence. . . . Recent authority confirms that over the past century clemency has been exercised frequently in capital cases in which demonstrations of "actual innocence" have been made.

. . .

We may assume, for the sake of argument in deciding this case, that in a capital case a truly persuasive demonstration of "actual innocence" made after trial would render the execution of a defendant unconstitutional, and warrant federal habeas relief if there were no state avenue open to process such a claim. But because of the very disruptive effect that entertaining claims of actual innocence would have on the need for finality in capital cases, and the enormous burden that having to retry cases based on often stale evidence would place on the States, the threshold showing for such an assumed right would necessarily be extraordinarily high. The showing made by petitioner in this case falls far short of any such threshold.

Petitioner's newly discovered evidence consists of affidavits. In the new trial context, motions based solely upon affidavits are disfavored because the affiants' statements are obtained without the benefit of cross-examination and an opportunity to make credibility determinations. Petitioner's affidavits are particularly suspect in this regard because, with the exception of Raul Herrera, Jr.'s affidavit, they consist of hearsay. . . .

The affidavits filed in this habeas proceeding were given over eight years after petitioner's trial. No satisfactory explanation has been given as to why the affiants waited until the 11th hour—and, indeed, until after the alleged perpetrator of the murders himself was dead—to make their statements. . . .

. . . Finally, the affidavits must be considered in light of the proof of petitioner's guilt at trial—proof which included two eyewitness identifications, numerous pieces of circumstantial evidence, and a handwritten letter in which petitioner apologized for killing the officers and offered to turn himself in under certain conditions. . . .

. . .

JUSTICE O'CONNOR, with whom JUSTICE KENNEDY joins, concurring.

. . .

Ultimately, two things about this case are clear. First is what the Court does not hold. Nowhere does the Court state that the Constitution permits the execution of an actually innocent person. Instead, the Court assumes for the sake of argument that a truly persuasive demonstration of actual innocence would render any such execution unconstitutional and that federal habeas relief would be warranted if no state avenue were open to process the claim. Second is what petitioner has not demonstrated. Petitioner has failed to make a persuasive showing of actual innocence. . . . Accordingly, the Court has no reason to pass on, and appropriately reserves, the question whether federal courts may entertain convincing claims of actual innocence. That difficult question remains open. If the Constitution's guarantees of fair procedure and the safeguards of clemency and pardon fulfill their historical mission, it may never require resolution at all.

JUSTICE SCALIA, with whom JUSTICE THOMAS joins, concurring.

. . . There is no basis in text, tradition, or even in contemporary practice (if that were enough) for finding in the Constitution a right to demand judicial consideration of newly discovered evidence of innocence brought forward after conviction. In saying that such a right exists, the dissenters apply nothing but their personal opinions to invalidate the rules of more than two-thirds of the States, and a Federal Rule of Criminal Procedure for which this Court itself is responsible. If the system that has been in place for 200 years (and remains widely approved) "shock[s]" the dissenters' consciences, perhaps they should doubt the calibration of their consciences, or, better still, the usefulness of "conscience shocking" as a legal test.

. . .

JUSTICE WHITE, concurring in the judgment.

In voting to affirm, I assume that a persuasive showing of "actual innocence" made after trial, even though made after the expiration of the time provided by law for the presentation of newly discovered evidence, would render unconstitutional the execution of petitioner in this case. To be entitled to relief, however, petitioner would at the very least be required to show that based on proffered newly discovered evidence and the entire record before the jury that convicted him, "no rational trier of fact could [find] proof of guilt beyond a reasonable doubt." For the reasons stated in the Court's opinion, petitioner's showing falls far short of satisfying even that standard, and I therefore concur in the judgment.

JUSTICE BLACKMUN, with whom JUSTICE STEVENS and JUSTICE SOUTER join dissenting.

Nothing could be more contrary to contemporary standards of decency or more shocking to the conscience than to execute a person who is actually innocent.

. . .

This Court has ruled that punishment is excessive and unconstitutional if it is "nothing more than the purposeless and needless imposition of pain and suffering," or if it is "grossly out of proportion to the severity of the crime." If it is violative of the Eighth Amendment to execute someone who is guilty of those crimes, then it plainly is violative of the Eighth Amendment to execute a person who is actually innocent. Executing an innocent person epitomizes "the purposeless and needless imposition of pain and suffering."

. . .

The Court also suggests that allowing petitioner to raise his claim of innocence would not serve society's interest in the reliable imposition of the death penalty because it might require a new trial that would be less accurate than the first. This suggestion misses the point entirely. The question is not whether a second trial would be more reliable than the first but whether, in light of new evidence, the result of the first trial is sufficiently reliable for the State to carry out a death sentence. Furthermore, it is far from clear that a State will seek to retry the rare prisoner who prevails on a claim of actual innocence. . . .

. . .

Execution of the innocent is equally offensive to the Due Process Clause of the Fourteenth Amendment. . . .

. . . Execution of an innocent person is the ultimate "'arbitrary impositio[n].'" It is an imposition from which one never recovers and for which one can never be compensated. Thus, I also believe that petitioner may raise a substantive due process challenge to his punishment on the ground that he is actually innocent.

. . .

The majority's discussion of petitioner's constitutional claims is even more perverse when viewed in the light of this Court's recent habeas jurisprudence. Beginning with a trio of decisions in 1986, this Court shifted the focus of federal habeas review of successive, abusive, or defaulted claims away from the preservation of constitutional rights to a fact-based inquiry into the habeas petitioner's guilt or innocence. The Court sought to strike a balance between the State's interest in the finality of its criminal judgments and the prisoner's interest in access to a forum to test the basic justice of his sentence. In striking this balance, the Court adopted the view . . . that there should be an exception to the concept of finality when a prisoner can make a colorable claim of actual innocence. . . .

Having adopted an "actual-innocence" requirement for review of abusive, successive, or defaulted claims, however, the majority would now take the position that "a claim of 'actual innocence' is not itself a constitutional claim, but instead a gateway through which a habeas petitioner must pass to have his otherwise barred constitutional claim considered on the merits." In other words, having held that a prisoner who is incarcerated in violation of the Constitution must show he is actually innocent to obtain relief, the majority would now hold that a prisoner who is actually innocent must show a constitutional violation to obtain relief. The only principle that would appear to reconcile these two positions is the principle that habeas relief should be denied whenever possible.

. . .

. . . The possibility of executive clemency is not sufficient to satisfy the requirements of the Eighth and Fourteenth Amendments. . . . The vindication of rights guaranteed by the Constitution has never been made to turn on the unreviewable discretion of an executive official or administrative tribunal. . . .

. . .

. . . I would hold that, to obtain relief on a claim of actual innocence, the petitioner must show that he probably is innocent. This standard is supported by several considerations. First, new evidence of innocence may be discovered long after the defendant's conviction. Given the passage of time, it may be difficult for the State to retry a defendant who obtains relief from his conviction or sentence on an actual-innocence claim. The actual-innocence proceeding thus may constitute the final word on whether the defendant may be punished. In light of this fact, an otherwise constitutionally valid conviction or sentence should not be set aside lightly. Second, conviction after a constitutionally adequate trial strips the defendant of the presumption of innocence. . . . When a defendant seeks to challenge the determination of guilt after he has been validly convicted and sentenced, it is fair to place on him the burden of proving his innocence, not just raising doubt about his guilt. . . .

I do not understand why the majority so severely faults petitioner for relying only on affidavits. It is common to rely on affidavits at the preliminary-consideration stage of a habeas proceeding. The opportunity for cross-examination and credibility determinations comes at the hearing, assuming that the petitioner is entitled to one. It makes no sense for this Court to impugn the reliability of petitioner's evidence on the ground that its credibility has not been tested when the reason its credibility has not been tested is that petitioner's habeas proceeding has been truncated by the Court of Appeals and now by this Court. In its haste to deny petitioner relief, the majority seems to confuse the question whether the petition may be dismissed summarily with the question whether petitioner is entitled to relief on the merits of his claim.

B. Search and Seizure

Conservatives enjoyed two important successes. *United States v. Leon* (1984) adopted what many conservatives believed was the second-best position on the exclusionary rule. While not overruling *Mapp v. Ohio* (1961), as Reagan administration officials wished, the justices ruled that unconstitutionally obtained evidence could be admitted at trial when the police had acted on a good-faith belief that their actions were consistent with constitutional norms. Justice White's majority opinion claimed that *Mapp* should not apply because the exclusionary rule would not deter police officers who were unknowingly violating the Constitution. Conservatives (and liberals committed to the war on drugs) also cheered Supreme Court decisions in *Skinner v. Railway Labor Executives Association* (1989) and *National Treasury Employees Union v. Von Raab* (1989) sustaining government power to test railway employees and customs officials for drugs and alcohol, even if no reason existed for suspecting them of any wrongdoing. Justice Kennedy's majority opinion in *Skinner* asserted that suspicionless searches were constitutional when conditions "present . . . special needs beyond normal law enforcement that may justify departures from the usual warrant and probable-cause requirements."

The Supreme Court was not implacably hostile to claims that government officials had violated Fourth and Fourteenth Amendment rights. *Arizona v. Hicks* (1987) held that police officers lawfully in a house to investigate a shooting could not conduct a search to discover evidence of other crimes unless they had a warrant or probable cause to justify that search. Justice Scalia's majority opinion asserted, "Taking action, unrelated to the objectives of the authorized intrusion, which exposed to view concealed portions of the apartment or its contents, did produce a new invasion of respondent's privacy unjustified by the exigent circumstance that validated the entry." Still, liberals lost far more ground than they gained, with respect to both the percentage of cases rejecting claims of constitutional right and the breadth of judicial opinions in those cases. *United States v. Sokolow* (1989) was a more typical early Rehnquist Court case. Federal agents stopped Andrew Sokolow at the Honolulu Airport because his behavior matched the profile of a drug courier. Chief Justice Rehnquist's majority opinion found that the search was reasonable under the circumstances. "A court sitting to determine the existence of reasonable suspicion must require the agent to articulate the factors leading to that conclusion," he wrote, "but the fact that these factors may be set forth in a 'profile' does not somehow detract from their evidentiary significance as seen by a trained agent."

United States v. Leon, 468 U.S. 897 (1984)

Officer Cyril Rombach of the Burbank Police Department obtained a tip from an informant that Alberto Leon had illegal drugs in his house and car. Based on this information, Rombach obtained a search warrant from a California judge. The search was successful. Leon was arrested and charged by federal prosecutors with conspiracy to possess and distribute cocaine. At trial Leon claimed that the search was unconstitutional. The judge lacked probable cause to issue the warrant, Leon claimed, because Rombach's informant was not reliable. The federal district court agreed with Leon. The evidence obtained by Officer Rombach's search was suppressed. The United States appealed, claiming both that probable cause existed for the search warrant and that the Fourth Amendment did not require that evidence be suppressed when police officers had a good-faith belief that they were acting on the basis of a constitutional search warrant. The Court of Appeals for the Ninth Circuit rejected both claims. The United States appealed to the Supreme Court.

The Supreme Court by a 6-3 vote ruled that admitting the seized drugs into trial was constitutional. Justice White's majority opinion held that prosecutors may introduce unconstitutionally obtained evidence at trial when the police officers acted on a good faith belief that their search was constitutional. Why does he claim that the exclusionary rule is not essential to the Fourth Amendment? Does the dissent effectively criticize this position? What do you believe are the likely consequences of the good-faith exception? Will fewer criminals go free, as Justice White believes, because police officers made good faith mistakes? Or, as the dissents maintain, will Leon *encourage ignorance of the law?*

JUSTICE WHITE delivered the opinion of the Court.

. . .

The Fourth Amendment contains no provision expressly precluding the use of evidence obtained in violation of its commands, and an examination of its origin and purposes makes clear that the use of fruits of a past unlawful search or seizure "work[s] no new Fourth Amendment wrong." . . . The rule . . . operates as "a judicially created remedy designed to safeguard

Fourth Amendment rights generally through its deterrent effect, rather than a personal constitutional right of the party aggrieved." . . .

. . .

The substantial social costs exacted by the exclusionary rule for the vindication of Fourth Amendment rights have long been a source of concern. . . . An objectionable collateral consequence of this interference with the criminal justice system's truth-finding function is that some guilty defendants may go free or receive reduced sentences as a result of favorable plea bargains. Particularly when law enforcement officers have acted in objective good faith or their transgressions have been minor, the magnitude of the benefit conferred on such guilty defendants offends basic concepts of the criminal justice system. . . . Indiscriminate application of the exclusionary rule, therefore, may well "generat[e] disrespect for the law and administration of justice." . . . Accordingly, "[a]s with any remedial device, the application of the rule has been restricted to those areas where its remedial objectives are thought most efficaciously served." . . .

. . .

As yet, we have not recognized any form of good-faith exception to the Fourth Amendment exclusionary rule. But the balancing approach that has evolved during the years of experience with the rule provides strong support for the modification currently urged upon us. As we discuss below, our evaluation of the costs and benefits of suppressing reliable physical evidence seized by officers reasonably relying on a warrant issued by a detached and neutral magistrate leads to the conclusion that such evidence should be admissible in the prosecution's case in chief.

. . .

To the extent that proponents of exclusion rely on its behavioral effects on judges and magistrates . . . , their reliance is misplaced. First, the exclusionary rule is designed to deter police misconduct rather than to punish the errors of judges and magistrates. Second, there exists no evidence suggesting that judges and magistrates are inclined to ignore or subvert the Fourth Amendment or that lawlessness among these actors requires application of the extreme sanction of exclusion.

. . . [W]e discern no basis, and are offered none, for believing that exclusion of evidence seized pursuant to a warrant will have a significant deterrent effect on the issuing judge or magistrate. Many of the factors that indicate that the exclusionary rule cannot provide an effective "special" or "general" deterrent for individual offending law enforcement officers apply as well to judges or magistrates. And, to the extent that the rule is thought to operate as a "systemic" deterrent on a wider audience, it clearly can have no such effect on individuals empowered to issue search warrants. Judges and magistrates are not adjuncts to the law enforcement team; as neutral judicial officers, they have no stake in the outcome of particular criminal prosecutions. The threat of exclusion thus cannot be expected significantly to deter them. Imposition of the exclusionary sanction is not necessary meaningfully to inform judicial officers of their errors, and we cannot conclude that admitting evidence obtained pursuant to a warrant while at the same time declaring that the warrant was somehow defective will in any way reduce judicial officers' professional incentives to comply with the Fourth Amendment, encourage them to repeat their mistakes, or lead to the granting of all colorable warrant requests.

. . .

We have frequently questioned whether the exclusionary rule can have any deterrent effect when the offending officers acted in the objectively reasonable belief that their conduct did not violate the Fourth Amendment. "No empirical researcher, proponent or opponent of the rule, has yet been able to establish with any assurance whether the rule has a deterrent effect. . . ." . . . But even assuming that the rule effectively deters some police misconduct and provides incentives for the law enforcement profession as a whole to conduct itself in accord with the Fourth Amendment, it cannot be expected, and should not be applied, to deter objectively reasonable law enforcement activity.

. . .

This is particularly true, we believe, when an officer acting with objective good faith has obtained a search warrant from a judge or magistrate and acted within its scope. In most such cases, there is no police illegality and thus nothing to deter. It is the magistrate's responsibility to determine whether the officer's allegations establish probable cause and, if so, to issue a warrant comporting in form with the requirements of the Fourth Amendment. In the ordinary case, an officer cannot be expected to question the magistrate's probable-cause determination or his judgment that the form of the warrant is technically sufficient. . . . Penalizing the officer for the magistrate's error, rather than his own, cannot logically contribute to the deterrence of Fourth Amendment violations.

. . .

JUSTICE BLACKMUN, concurring. . . .

JUSTICE BRENNAN, with whom JUSTICE MARSHALL joins, dissenting.

. . . That today's decisions represent the pièce de résistance of the Court's past efforts cannot be doubted, for today the Court sanctions the use in the prosecution's case in chief of illegally obtained evidence against the individual whose rights have been violated—a result that had previously been thought to be foreclosed.

. . .

The majority ignores the fundamental constitutional importance of what is at stake here. While the machinery of law enforcement and indeed the nature of crime itself have changed dramatically since the Fourth Amendment became part of the Nation's fundamental law in 1791, what the Framers understood then remains true today—that the task of combating crime and convicting the guilty will in every era seem of such critical and pressing concern that we may be lured by the temptations of expediency into forsaking our commitment to protecting individual liberty and privacy. It was for that very reason that the Framers of the Bill of Rights insisted that law enforcement efforts be permanently and unambiguously restricted in order to preserve personal freedoms. In the constitutional scheme they ordained, the sometimes unpopular task of ensuring that the government's enforcement efforts remain within the strict boundaries fixed by the Fourth Amendment was entrusted to the courts. . . .

. . .

At bottom, the Court's decision turns on the proposition that the exclusionary rule is merely a "'judicially created remedy designed to safeguard Fourth Amendment rights generally through its deterrent effect, rather than a personal constitutional right.'" . . . This view of the scope of the Amendment relegates the judiciary to the periphery. Because the only constitutionally cognizable injury has already been "fully accomplished" by the police by the time a case comes before the courts, the Constitution is not itself violated if the judge decides to admit the tainted evidence. . . .

. . .

Because seizures are executed principally to secure evidence, and because such evidence generally has utility in our legal system only in the context of a trial supervised by a judge, it is apparent that the admission of illegally obtained evidence implicates the same constitutional concerns as the initial seizure of that evidence. Indeed, by admitting unlawfully seized evidence, the judiciary becomes a part of what is in fact a single governmental action prohibited by the terms of the Amendment. Once that connection between the evidence-gathering role of the police and the evidence-admitting function of the courts is acknowledged, the plausibility of the Court's interpretation becomes more suspect. Certainly nothing in the language or history of the Fourth Amendment suggests that a recognition of this evidentiary link between the police and the courts was meant to be foreclosed. . . . The Amendment therefore must be read to condemn not only the initial unconstitutional invasion of privacy—which is done, after all, for the purpose of securing evidence—but also the subsequent use of any evidence so obtained.

. . .

. . . [S]eizures are generally executed for the purpose of bringing "proof to the aid of the Government," . . . that the utility of such evidence in a criminal prosecution arises ultimately in the context of the courts, and that the courts therefore cannot be absolved of responsibility for the means by which evidence is obtained. . . . [T]he obligations cast upon government by the Fourth Amendment are not confined merely to the police. In the words of Justice Holmes: "If the search and seizure are unlawful as invading personal rights secured by the Constitution those rights would be infringed yet further if the evidence were allowed to be used."

. . .

. . . [T]he deterrence theory is both misguided and unworkable. First, the Court has frequently bewailed the "cost" of excluding reliable evidence. In large part, this criticism rests upon a refusal to acknowledge the function of the Fourth Amendment itself. If nothing else, the Amendment plainly operates to disable the government from gathering information and securing evidence in certain ways. In practical terms, of course, this restriction of official power means that some incriminating evidence inevitably will go undetected if the government obeys these constitutional restraints. It is the loss of that evidence that is the "price" our society pays for enjoying the freedom and privacy safeguarded by the Fourth Amendment. Thus, some criminals will go free not, in Justice (then Judge) Cardozo's misleading epigram, "because the constable has blundered," . . . but rather because official compliance with Fourth Amendment requirements makes it more difficult to catch criminals. Understood in this way, the Amendment directly contemplates that some reliable and incriminating evidence will be lost to the government; therefore, it is not the exclusionary rule, but the Amendment itself that has imposed this cost.

In addition, the Court's decisions over the past decade have made plain that the entire enterprise of attempting to assess the benefits and costs of the exclusionary rule in various contexts is a virtually impossible task for the judiciary to perform honestly or accurately. . . .

. . .

To be sure, the [exclusionary] rule operates to some extent to deter future misconduct by individual officers who have had evidence suppressed in their own cases. But what the Court overlooks is that the deterrence rationale for the rule is not designed to be, nor should it be thought of as, a form of "punishment" of individual police officers for their failures to obey the restraints imposed by the Fourth Amendment. . . . Instead, the chief deterrent function of the rule is its tendency to promote institutional compliance with Fourth Amendment requirements on the part of law enforcement agencies generally. Thus, as the Court has previously recognized, "over the long term, [the] demonstration [provided by the exclusionary rule] that our society attaches serious consequences to violation of constitutional rights is thought to encourage those who formulate law enforcement policies, and the officers who implement them, to incorporate Fourth Amendment ideals into their value system." . . . It is only through such an institution wide mechanism that information concerning Fourth Amendment standards can be effectively communicated to rank-and-file officers.

. . .

. . . A chief consequence of today's decisions will be to convey a clear and unambiguous message to magistrates that their decisions to issue warrants are now insulated from subsequent judicial review. Creation of this new exception for good-faith reliance upon a warrant implicitly tells magistrates that they need not take much care in reviewing warrant applications, since their mistakes will from now on have virtually no consequence: If their decision to issue a warrant was correct, the evidence will be admitted; if their decision was incorrect but the police relied in good faith on the warrant, the evidence will also be admitted. Inevitably, the care and attention devoted to such an inconsequential chore will dwindle. Although the Court is correct to note that magistrates do not share the same stake in the outcome of a criminal case as the police, they nevertheless need to appreciate that their role is of some moment in order to continue performing the important task of carefully reviewing warrant applications. Today's decisions effectively remove that incentive.

. . . Moreover, the good-faith exception will encourage police to provide only the bare minimum of information in future warrant applications. The police will now know that if they can secure a warrant, so long as the circumstances of its issuance are not "entirely unreasonable," . . . all police conduct pursuant to that warrant will be protected from further judicial review. The clear incentive that operated in the past to establish probable cause adequately because reviewing courts would examine the magistrate's judgment carefully, . . . has now been so completely vitiated that the police need only show that it was not "entirely unreasonable" under the circumstances of a particular case for them to believe that the warrant they were issued was valid. . . . The long-run effect unquestionably will be to undermine the integrity of the warrant process.

. . .

When the public, as it quite properly has done in the past as well as in the present, demands that those in government increase their efforts to combat crime, it is all too easy for those government officials to seek expedient solutions. In contrast to such costly and difficult measures as building more prisons, improving law enforcement methods, or hiring more prosecutors and judges to relieve the overburdened court systems in the country's metropolitan areas, the relaxation of Fourth Amendment standards seems a tempting, costless means of meeting the public's demand for better law enforcement. In the long run, however, we as a society pay a heavy price for such expediency, because as Justice Jackson observed, the rights guaranteed in the Fourth Amendment "are not mere second-class rights but belong in the catalog of indispensable freedoms." . . . Once lost, such rights are difficult to recover. There is hope, however, that in time this or some later Court will restore these precious freedoms to their rightful place as a primary protection for our citizens against overreaching officialdom.

JUSTICE STEVENS . . . dissenting.

. . .

. . . Today, for the first time, this Court holds that although the Constitution has been violated, no court should do anything about it at any time and in any proceeding. In my judgment, the Constitution requires more. Courts simply cannot escape their responsibility for redressing constitutional violations if they admit evidence obtained through unreasonable searches and seizures, since the entire point of police conduct that violates the Fourth Amendment is to obtain evidence for use at trial. If such evidence is admitted, then the courts become not merely the final and necessary link in an unconstitutional chain of events, but its actual motivating force. . . . Nor should we so easily concede the existence of a constitutional violation for which there is no remedy. To do so is to convert a Bill of Rights into an unenforced honor code that the police may follow in their discretion. The Constitution requires more; it requires a remedy. If the Court's new rule is to be followed, the Bill of Rights should be renamed.

Skinner v. Railway Labor Executives Association, 489 U.S. 602 (1989)

The Railway Labor Executives Association (RLEA) objected to Federal Railroad Administration (FRA) rules mandating that railroad employees take blood and urine tests when they were involved in train accidents or violated safety rules. The rules for accidents permitted the government to test employees even when no reason existed for suspecting that the employee was responsible for the accident, violated safety rules or was under the influence of drugs or alcohol. The RLEA sought an injunction against Samuel Skinner, the secretary of transportation, and the FRA prohibiting them from implementing the blood and urine tests. The federal district court rejected their claim, but that decision was reversed by the Court of Appeals for the Ninth Circuit. The United States appealed to the Supreme Court of the United States.

The Supreme Court by a 7-2 vote declared that the FRA could authorize suspicionless searches of railroad employees. Justice Kennedy's majority opinion maintained that such searches were reasonable means to prevent serious accidents. Why does Kennedy think that the government may test people without any suspicion that they have engaged in wrongdoing? Does Justice Marshall dispute that drug testing may save lives? On what basis does he disagree with Kennedy's conclusion? Who has the better argument? To what extent do you agree with Marshall that the Court was adopting a "drug exception" to the Fourth Amendment? Is such an exception warranted?

On the same day that Skinner *was decided, the Supreme Court by a 5-4 vote in* National Treasury Employees Union v. Von Raab *(1989) ruled that the federal government could require members of the U.S. Customs Service seeking certain promotions to take urine tests. Justice Kennedy's majority opinion asserted, "The public interest demands effective measures to bar drug users from positions directly involving the interdiction of illegal drugs." Justice Brennan and Marshall repeated their assertion in* Skinner *that "the Court's abandonment of the Fourth Amendment's express requirement that searches of the person rest on probable cause is unprincipled and unjustifiable." Justice Scalia and Stevens, who joined the* Skinner *majority, also dissented. Scalia wrote,*

> *I joined the Court's opinion [in* Skinner*] because the demonstrated frequency of drug and alcohol use by the targeted class of employees, and the demonstrated connection between such use and grave harm, rendered the search a reasonable means of protecting society. I decline to join the Court's opinion in the present case because neither frequency of use nor connection to harm is demonstrated or even likely. In my view the Customs Service rules are a kind of immolation of privacy and human dignity in symbolic opposition to drug use.*

Does a constitutional difference exist between drug testing train employees after accidents and drug testing customs officials who apply for certain promotions?

JUSTICE KENNEDY delivered the opinion of the Court.

. . .

We have long recognized that a "compelled intrusio[n] into the body for blood to be analyzed for alcohol content" must be deemed a Fourth Amendment search. See *Schmerber v. California* (1966). In light of our society's concern for the security of one's person, it is obvious that this physical intrusion, penetrating beneath the skin, infringes an expectation of privacy that society is prepared to recognize as reasonable. The ensuing chemical analysis of the sample to obtain physiological data is a further invasion of the tested employee's privacy interests. Much the same is true of the breath-testing procedures required under . . . the regulations. Subjecting a person to a breathalyzer test, which generally requires the production of alveolar or "deep lung" breath for chemical analysis implicates similar concerns about bodily integrity and, like the blood-alcohol test we considered in *Schmerber*, should also be deemed a search.

Unlike the blood-testing procedure at issue in *Schmerber*, the procedures prescribed by the FRA regulations for collecting and testing urine samples do not entail a surgical intrusion into the body. It is not disputed, however, that chemical analysis of urine, like that of blood, can reveal a host of private medical facts about an employee, including whether he or she is epileptic, pregnant, or diabetic. Nor can it be disputed that the process of collecting the sample to be tested, which may in some cases involve visual or aural monitoring of the act of urination, itself implicates privacy interests. . . . Because it is clear that the collection and testing of urine intrudes upon expectations of privacy that society has long recognized as reasonable, . . . these intrusions must be deemed searches under the Fourth Amendment.

. . .

. . . Except in certain well-defined circumstances, a search or seizure . . . is not reasonable unless it is accomplished pursuant to a judicial warrant issued upon probable cause. We have recognized exceptions to this rule, however, "when 'special needs, beyond the normal need for law enforcement, make the warrant and probable-cause requirement impracticable.'" When faced with such special needs, we have not hesitated to balance the governmental and privacy interests to assess the practicality of the warrant and probable-cause requirements in the particular context. . . .

The Government's interest in regulating the conduct of railroad employees to ensure safety . . . "presents 'special needs' beyond normal law enforcement that may justify departures from the usual warrant and probable-cause requirements." . . . It is undisputed that these and other covered employees are engaged in safety-sensitive tasks. . . .

The FRA has prescribed toxicological tests, not to assist in the prosecution of employees, but rather "to prevent accidents and casualties in railroad operations that result from impairment of employees by alcohol or drugs." This governmental interest in ensuring the safety of the traveling public and of the employees themselves plainly justifies prohibiting covered employees from using alcohol or drugs on duty, or while subject to being called for duty. . . . The question that remains, then, is whether the Government's need to monitor compliance with these restrictions justifies the privacy intrusions at issue absent a warrant or individualized suspicion.

An essential purpose of a warrant requirement is to protect privacy interests by assuring citizens subject to a search or seizure that such intrusions are not the random or arbitrary acts of government agents. A warrant assures the citizen that the intrusion is authorized by law, and that it is narrowly limited in its objectives and scope. A warrant also provides the detached scrutiny of a neutral magistrate, and thus ensures an objective determination whether an intrusion is justified in any given case. In the present context, however, a warrant would do little to further these aims. Both the circumstances justifying toxicological testing and the permissible limits of such intrusions are defined narrowly and specifically in the regulations that authorize them, and doubtless are well known to covered employees. Indeed, in light of the standardized nature of the tests and the minimal discretion vested in those charged with administering the program, there are virtually no facts for a neutral magistrate to evaluate.

. . .

We have recognized, moreover, that the government's interest in dispensing with the warrant requirement is at its strongest when, as here, "the burden of obtaining a warrant is likely to frustrate the governmental purpose behind the search." As the FRA recognized, alcohol and other drugs are eliminated from the bloodstream at a constant rate, and blood and breath samples taken to measure whether these substances were in the bloodstream when a triggering event occurred must be obtained as soon as possible. Although the metabolites of some drugs remain in the urine for longer periods of time and may enable the FRA to estimate whether the employee was impaired by those drugs at the time of a covered accident, incident, or rule violation, the delay necessary to procure a warrant nevertheless may result in the destruction of valuable evidence.

. . .

. . . [T]he expectations of privacy of covered employees are diminished by reason of their participation in an industry that is regulated pervasively to ensure safety, a goal dependent, in substantial part, on the health and fitness of covered employees. . . .

. . . Though some of the privacy interests implicated by the toxicological testing at issue reasonably might be viewed as significant in other contexts, logic and history show that a diminished expectation of privacy attaches to information relating to the physical condition of covered employees and to this reasonable means of procuring such information. We conclude, therefore, that the testing procedures . . . pose only limited threats to the justifiable expectations of privacy of covered employees.

By contrast, the Government interest in testing without a showing of individualized suspicion is compelling. Employees subject to the tests discharge duties fraught with such risks of injury to others that even a momentary lapse of attention can have disastrous consequences. Much like persons who have routine access to dangerous nuclear power facilities, employees who are subject to testing under the FRA regulations can cause great human loss before any signs of impairment become noticeable to supervisors or others. . . . Indeed, while respondents posit that impaired employees might be detected without alcohol or drug testing, the premise of respondents' lawsuit is that even the occurrence of a major calamity will not give rise to a suspicion of impairment with respect to any particular employee.

. . .

The testing procedures . . . also help railroads obtain invaluable information about the causes of major accidents and to take appropriate measures to safeguard the general public. Positive test results would point toward drug or alcohol impairment on the part of members of the crew as a possible cause of an accident, and may help to establish whether a particular accident, otherwise not drug related, was made worse by the inability of impaired employees to respond appropriately. Negative test results would likewise furnish invaluable clues, for eliminating drug impairment as a potential cause or contributing factor would help establish the significance of equipment failure, inadequate training, or other potential causes, and suggest a more thorough examination of these alternatives. . . .

A requirement of particularized suspicion of drug or alcohol use would seriously impede an employer's ability to obtain this information, despite its obvious importance. Experience confirms the FRA's judgment that the scene of a serious rail accident is chaotic. Investigators who arrive at the scene shortly after a major accident has occurred may find it difficult to determine which members of a train crew contributed to its occurrence. Obtaining evidence that might give rise to the suspicion that a particular employee is impaired, a difficult endeavor in the best of circumstances, is most impracticable in the aftermath of a serious accident. . . . It would be unrealistic, and inimical to the Government's goal of ensuring safety in rail transportation, to require a showing of individualized suspicion in these circumstances.

. . .

JUSTICE STEVENS, concurring in part and concurring in the judgment. . . .

JUSTICE MARSHALL, with whom JUSTICE BRENNAN joins, dissenting.

. . .

Until recently, an unbroken line of cases had recognized probable cause as an indispensable prerequisite for a full-scale search, regardless of whether such a search was conducted pursuant to a warrant or under one of the recognized exceptions to the warrant requirement. . . . Only where the government action in question had a "substantially less intrusive" impact on privacy, and thus clearly fell short of a full-scale search, did we relax the probable-cause standard. Even in this class of cases, we almost always required the government to show some individualized suspicion to justify the search. . . .

. . .

. . . There is no drug exception to the Constitution, any more than there is a communism exception or an exception for other real or imagined sources of domestic unrest. Because abandoning the explicit protections of the Fourth Amendment seriously imperils "the right to be let alone—the most comprehensive of rights and the right most valued by civilized men," I reject the majority's "special needs" rationale as unprincipled and dangerous.

The proper way to evaluate the FRA's testing regime is to use the same analytic framework which we have traditionally used to appraise Fourth Amendment claims involving full-scale searches, at least until the recent "special needs" cases. Under that framework, we inquire, serially, whether a search has taken place, whether the search was based on a valid warrant or undertaken pursuant to a recognized exception to the warrant requirement, whether the search was based on probable cause or validly based on lesser suspicion because it was minimally intrusive, and, finally, whether the search was conducted in a reasonable manner.

. . .

It is the probable-cause requirement, that the FRA's testing regime most egregiously violates, a fact which explains the majority's ready acceptance and expansion of the countertextual "special needs" exception. By any measure, the FRA's highly intrusive collection and testing procedures qualify as full-scale personal searches. Under our precedents, a showing of probable cause is therefore clearly required. But even if these searches were viewed as entailing only minimal intrusions on the order, say, of a police stop-and-frisk, the FRA's program would still fail to pass constitutional muster, for we have, without exception, demanded that even minimally intrusive searches of the person be founded on individualized suspicion. . . .

. . .

Compelling a person to produce a urine sample on demand intrudes deeply on privacy and bodily integrity. Urination is among the most private of activities. It is generally forbidden in public, eschewed as a matter of conversation, and performed in places designed to preserve this tradition of personal seclusion. . . . The majority's characterization of the privacy interests implicated by urine collection as "minimal" is nothing short of startling.

. . .

I recognize that invalidating the full-scale searches involved in the FRA's testing regime for failure to comport with the Fourth Amendment's command of probable cause may hinder the Government's attempts to make rail transit as safe as humanly possible. But constitutional rights have their consequences, and one is that efforts to maximize the public welfare, no matter how well intentioned, must always be pursued within constitutional boundaries. Were the police freed from the constraints of the Fourth Amendment for just one day to seek out evidence of criminal wrongdoing, the resulting convictions and incarcerations would probably prevent thousands of fatalities. Our refusal to tolerate this specter reflects our shared belief that even beneficent governmental power—whether exercised to save money, save lives, or make the trains run on time—must always yield to "a resolute loyalty to constitutional safeguards."

. . .

The majority's trivialization of the intrusions on worker privacy posed by the FRA's testing program is matched at the other extreme by its blind acceptance of the Government's assertion that testing will "dete[r] employees engaged in safety-sensitive tasks from using controlled substances or alcohol," and "help railroads obtain invaluable information about the causes of major accidents." With respect to deterrence, it is simply implausible that testing employees after major accidents occur will appreciably discourage them from using drugs or alcohol. . . . Under the majority's deterrence rationale, people who skip school or work to spend a sunny day at the zoo will not taunt the lions because their truancy or absenteeism might be discovered in the event they are mauled. It is, of course, the fear of the accident, not the fear of a postaccident revelation, that deters. . . .

C. Interrogations

Miranda v. Arizona (1966) barely survived the Reagan Era. The Reagan and Bush administrations were determined to reverse the Supreme Court's ruling that confessions could normally not be admitted into evidence unless the persons in custody were informed that they had a right to remain silent, that their comments could be used against them in a court of law, that they had a right to an attorney, and that an attorney would be appointed for them if they could not afford counsel. "Because there is no constitutional or statutory basis for these rules, and because they have a detrimental effect on the search for truth in criminal investigations and adjudication," the 1988 *Guidelines on Constitutional Litigation* declared, "government lawyers should seek to convince the courts to construe these rules narrowly and, where possible, to limit further their scope or abandon them entirely."[63] Conservatives enjoyed considerable success in employing this litigation strategy. *Miranda* was not overruled, but the Supreme Court carved out numerous exceptions to the constitutional rule that confessions could not be admitted into evidence unless *Miranda* warnings were given.

New York v. Quarles (1984) exemplifies how the Supreme Court narrowed *Miranda*. In response to questions asked after his arrest before *Miranda* warnings were given, Benjamin Quarles informed police officers where he had stashed a gun in a supermarket. The justices found the confession admissible. Justice Rehnquist's majority opinion treated *Miranda* warnings as a means to a constitutional end rather than as a constitutional right. "The prophylactic *Miranda* warn-

63. Office of Legal Policy, *Guidelines on Constitutional Litigation*, 87.

ings," he wrote, "are not themselves rights protected by the Constitution but [are] instead measures to insure that the right against compulsory self-incrimination [is] protected." Rehnquist concluded, "There is a 'public safety' exception to the requirement that *Miranda* warnings be given before a suspect's answers may be admitted into evidence." The more liberal Justice Marshall was appalled. "Without establishing that interrogations concerning the public's safety are less likely to be coercive than other interrogations," his dissent declared, "the majority cannot endorse the 'public-safety' exception and remain faithful to the logic of *Miranda v. Arizona*."

Other Supreme Court decisions further narrowed *Miranda*:

- *Davis v. United States* (1994) held that police may question a suspect after *Miranda* warnings unless the suspect clearly asserts a right to remain silent.
- *Illinois v. Perkins* (1990) held that undercover police agents posing as cellmates to persons in prison are not required to give *Miranda* warnings.
- *Michigan v. Harvey* (1990) held that statements otherwise inadmissible under *Miranda* may be admitted to impeach a witness.
- *Pennsylvania v. Bruder* (1988) held that an ordinary traffic stop is not an arrest for *Miranda* purposes.
- *Arizona v. Mauro* (1987) held that *Miranda* warnings are not necessary when a defendant speaks with his spouse and is tape-recorded by a police officer.
- *Colorado v. Spring* (1987) held that suspects may knowingly waive their right to remain silent even if they are unaware of the crimes of which they are suspected.
- *Colorado v. Connelly* (1986) held that statements made to police officers by persons not in custody are admissible, even if no *Miranda* warnings were given.
- *Morn v. Burbine* (1986) held that *Miranda* does not require police to inform a suspect that an attorney hired by a family member is trying to reach him.
- *Oregon v. Elstad* (1985) held that police need not inform a suspect that a custodial confession given before *Miranda* warnings is not admissible in court before asking the suspect to repeat the confession after giving *Miranda* warnings.
- *Nix v. Williams* (1984) held that evidence obtained by a confession made before *Miranda* warnings is admissible if the evidence would have inevitably been discovered by the police.

Miranda retained some bite. *Michigan v. Jackson* (1986) held that once a suspect asserted the right to remain silent, any confession gained by subsequent police questioning was inadmissible. Nevertheless, most persons by the early 1990s predicted that *Miranda* would not survive the appointment of one or two additional judicial conservatives.

D. Juries And Lawyers

The right to a jury and an attorney bucked the conservative trend of constitutional criminal justice. Republican Party platforms and Reagan Justice Department manifestos were indifferent to the constitutional status of *Gideon v. Wainwright* (1963), the decision that interpreted the Sixth Amendment as requiring states to provide counsel for indigent criminal defendants. Conservatives raised few strong objections to past judicial decisions expanding the constitutional right to a jury trial. Ideological divisions on the Supreme Court were less rigid when litigants claimed that Sixth Amendment rights had been violated. The resulting decisions were more liberal than those in other areas of constitutional justice. *Batson v. Kentucky* (1986), which limited the use of race-based peremptory challenges to prospective jurors, is the only instance during the 1980s when the Supreme Court overruled a Warren Court decision that had *rejected* a rights claim made by a defendant in a criminal trial.

Juries. *Batson v. Kentucky* was the most important case on jury trials decided during the Reagan Era. That case overruled *Swain v. Alabama* (1965) and held that defendants could prove that prosecutors were using their peremptory challenges to exclude persons of a particular race from a jury solely by examining prosecutorial behavior at their trial. The Rehnquist Court almost immediately expanded *Batson* to cover civil trials and other uses of preemptory challenges to exclude members of suspect or quasi-suspect classes from juries. *Edmonson v. Leesville Concrete Co. Inc.* (1991) held that civil litigants could not use peremptory challenges to strike members of a particular race from a jury. *Georgia v. McCollum* (1992) ruled that the *Batson* rule prohibited both prosecutors and defense lawyers from using peremptory challenges to exclude members of a particular race from a jury. "Be it at the hands of the State or the defense," Justice Blackmun declared, if a court allows jurors to be excluded because of group bias, "[it] is [a] willing participant in a scheme that could only undermine the very foundation of our system of justice—our citizens' confidence in it." *J. E. B. v. Alabama ex. rel. T. B.* (1994) ruled that Batson prohibited peremptory challenges that excluded jurors based solely on gender. Justice Blackmun's majority opinion asserted, "When state actors exercise peremptory challenges in reliance on gender stereotypes, they ratify and reinforce prejudicial views of the relative abilities of men and women."

Lawyers (and Other Forms of Assistance). The Supreme Court made two important decisions on the rights of indigent criminal defendants. *Strickland v. Washington* (1984) established tough standards for determining when counsel's poor performance at trial violated the Sixth and Fourteenth Amendments. Justice O'Connor's majority opinion declared, "The defendant must show that there is a reasonable probability that, but for counsel's unprofessional errors, the result of the proceeding would have been different." Rarely did judges find counsel's performance to be below that standard. *Ake v. Oklahoma* (1985) ruled that indigent defendants sometimes had a right to psychiatric services, in addition to a right to counsel. Justice Marshall's majority opinion stated, "When a defendant demonstrates to the trial judge that his sanity at the time of the offense is to be a significant factor at trial, the State must, at a minimum, assure the defendant access to a competent psychiatrist who will conduct an appropriate examination and assist in evaluation, preparation, and presentation of the defense."

Both *Strickland* and *Ake* were decided by 8-1 votes. Justice Marshall was the only dissenter in *Strickland*. Justice Rehnquist was the only dissenter in *Ake*.

Illustration 10-3 Race and Jury Selection

Source: Illustration by Harry Campbell.

This was a far higher degree of consensus than occurred in the other constitutional criminal procedure decisions handed down during the Reagan Era. What explains that consensus? What explains the more liberal (or less conservative) direction of decisions on the right to a jury and the right to counsel?

Batson v. Kentucky, 476 U.S. 79 (1986)

James Kirkland Batson, an African-American man, was arrested for second-degree burglary and receipt of stolen goods. At his trial the prosecutor used peremptory challenges to strike all four members of the jury venire who were black. Traditionally both sides at trial have a certain number of peremptory challenges that may used for any reason. For example, defendants may challenge a prospective juror for cause when they have a hunch that the juror does not like them based on the juror's body language. Batson's defense counsel objected to the prosecutor's actions but was unsuccessful. The all-white jury convicted Batson on all charges. Batson appealed, claiming that allowing the prosecutor to strike all African-Americans from the jury violated his right to a fair jury trial. The Supreme Court of Kentucky rejected that plea. Batson appealed to the Supreme Court of the United States.

The Supreme Court by a 7-2 vote declared that Batson had been deprived of a fair jury trial. Justice Powell's majority opinion ruled that defendants in a criminal trial had a right to prove racial discrimination solely on evidence concerning how the prosecutor exercised peremptory challenges in their cases. Batson *overruled* Swain v. Alabama *(1965), which required defendants to demonstrate that a prosecutor or prosecutors from the same office consistently struck all African-Americans from trial juries. Why does Justice Powell believe that* Swain *should be overruled? Why does Justice Rehnquist disagree? Who has the better argument? What explains why the Supreme Court in the conservative Reagan Era reversed a conservative precedent from the liberal New Deal/Great Society Era?*

JUSTICE POWELL delivered the opinion of the Court.

. . .

More than a century ago, the Court decided that the State denies a black defendant equal protection of the laws when it puts him on trial before a jury from which members of his race have been purposefully excluded. *Strauder v. West Virginia* (1880). . . .

In holding that racial discrimination in jury selection offends the Equal Protection Clause, the Court in *Strauder* recognized, however, that a defendant has no right to a "petit jury composed in whole or in part of persons of his own race." . . .

Purposeful racial discrimination in selection of the venire violates a defendant's right to equal protection because it denies him the protection that a trial by jury is intended to secure. . . . Those on the venire must be "indifferently chosen," to secure the defendant's right under the Fourteenth Amendment to "protection of life and liberty against race or color prejudice."

Racial discrimination in selection of jurors harms not only the accused whose life or liberty they are summoned to try. Competence to serve as a juror ultimately depends on an assessment of individual qualifications and ability impartially to consider evidence presented at a trial. . . . A person's race simply "is unrelated to his fitness as a juror." . . .

The harm from discriminatory jury selection extends beyond that inflicted on the defendant and the excluded juror to touch the entire community. Selection procedures that purposefully exclude black persons from juries undermine public confidence in the fairness of our system of justice. . . .

. . .

. . . [T]he State's privilege to strike individual jurors through peremptory challenges is subject to the commands of the Equal Protection Clause. Although a prosecutor ordinarily is entitled to exercise permitted peremptory challenges "for any reason at all, as long as that reason is related to his view concerning the outcome" of the case to be tried, . . . the Equal Protection Clause forbids the prosecutor to challenge potential jurors solely on account of their race or on the assumption that black jurors as a group will be unable impartially to consider the State's case against a black defendant.

. . .

The standards for assessing a prima facie case in the context of discriminatory selection of the venire have been fully articulated since *Swain v. Alabama* (1965). . . . These principles support our conclusion that a defendant may establish a prima facie case of purposeful discrimination in selection of the petit jury solely on evidence concerning the prosecutor's exercise of peremptory challenges at the defendant's trial. To establish such a case, the defendant first must show that he is a member of a cognizable racial group, . . . and that the prosecutor has exercised peremptory challenges to remove from the venire members of the defendant's race. Second, the defendant is entitled to rely on the fact, as to which there can be no dispute, that peremptory challenges constitute a jury selection practice that permits "those to discriminate who are of a mind to discriminate." . . . Finally, the defendant must show that these facts and any other relevant circumstances raise an inference that the prosecutor used that practice to exclude the veniremen from the petit jury on account of their race. This combination of factors in the empaneling of the petit jury, as in the selection of the venire, raises the necessary inference of purposeful discrimination.

. . .

Once the defendant makes a prima facie showing, the burden shifts to the State to come forward with a neutral explanation for challenging black jurors. Though this requirement imposes a limitation in some cases on the full peremptory character of the historic challenge, we emphasize that the prosecutor's explanation need not rise to the level justifying exercise of a challenge for cause. . . . But the prosecutor may not rebut the defendant's prima facie case of discrimination by stating merely that he challenged jurors of the defendant's race on the assumption—or his intuitive judgment—that they would be partial to the defendant because of their shared race. . . . Just as the Equal Protection Clause forbids the States to exclude black persons from the venire on the assumption that blacks as a group are unqualified to serve as jurors . . . , so it forbids the States to strike black veniremen on the assumption that they will be biased in a particular case simply because the defendant is black. The core guarantee of equal protection, ensuring citizens that their State will not discriminate on account of race, would be meaningless were we to approve the exclusion of jurors on the basis of such assumptions, which arise solely from the jurors' race. Nor may the prosecutor rebut the defendant's case merely by denying that he had a discriminatory motive or "affirm[ing] [his] good faith in making individual selections." . . . The prosecutor therefore must articulate a neutral explanation related to the particular case to be tried. The trial court then will have the duty to determine if the defendant has established purposeful discrimination.

. . .

While we recognize, of course, that the peremptory challenge occupies an important position in our trial procedures, we do not agree that our decision today will undermine the contribution the challenge generally makes to the administration of justice. The reality of practice, amply reflected in many state—and federal—court opinions, shows that the challenge may be, and unfortunately at times has been, used to discriminate against black jurors. By requiring trial courts to be sensitive to the racially discriminatory use of peremptory challenges, our decision enforces the mandate of equal protection and furthers the ends of justice. In view of the heterogeneous population of our Nation, public respect for our criminal justice system and the rule of law will be strengthened if we ensure that no citizen is disqualified from jury service because of his race.

. . .

JUSTICE WHITE, concurring. . . .

JUSTICE MARSHALL, concurring.

. . .

Misuse of the peremptory challenge to exclude black jurors has become both common and flagrant. Black defendants rarely have been able to compile statistics showing the extent of that practice, but the few cases setting out such figures are instructive. . . . An instruction book used by the prosecutor's office in Dallas County, Texas, explicitly advised prosecutors that they conduct jury selection so as to eliminate "'any member of a minority group.'" In 100 felony trials in Dallas County in 1983–1984, prosecutors peremptorily struck 405 out of 467 eligible black jurors; the chance of a qualified black sitting on a jury was 1 in 10, compared to 1 in 2 for a white.

. . .

I wholeheartedly concur in the Court's conclusion that use of the peremptory challenge to remove blacks from juries, on the basis of their race, violates the Equal Protection Clause. I would go further, however, in fashioning a remedy adequate to eliminate that discrimination. Merely allowing defendants the opportunity to challenge the racially discriminatory use of peremptory challenges in individual cases will not end the illegitimate use of the peremptory challenge.

Evidentiary analysis similar to that set out by the Court . . . has been adopted as a matter of state law in States including Massachusetts and California. Cases from those jurisdictions illustrate the limitations of the approach. First, defendants cannot attack the discriminatory use of peremptory challenges at all unless the challenges are so flagrant as to establish a prima facie case. This means, in those States, that where only one or two black jurors survive the challenges for cause, the prosecutor need have no compunction about striking them from the jury because of their race. . . .

Second, when a defendant can establish a prima facie case, trial courts face the difficult burden of assessing prosecutors' motives. . . . Any prosecutor can easily assert facially neutral reasons for striking a juror, and trial courts are ill equipped to second-guess those reasons. How is the court to treat a prosecutor's statement that he struck a juror because the juror had a son about the same age as defendant, . . . or seemed "uncommunicative," . . . or "never cracked a smile" and, therefore "did not possess the sensitivities necessary to realistically look at the issues and decide the facts in this case?" If such easily generated explanations are sufficient to discharge the prosecutor's obligation to justify his strikes on nonracial grounds, then the protection erected by the Court today may be illusory.

Nor is outright prevarication by prosecutors the only danger here. . . . A prosecutor's own conscious or unconscious racism may lead him easily to the conclusion that a prospective black juror is "sullen," or "distant," a characterization that would not have come to his mind if a white juror had acted identically. . . .

The inherent potential of peremptory challenges to distort the jury process by permitting the exclusion of jurors on racial grounds should ideally lead the Court to ban them entirely from the criminal justice system. . . .

. . .

JUSTICE STEVENS, with whom JUSTICE BRENNAN joins, concurring. . . .

JUSTICE O'CONNOR, concurring. . . .

CHIEF JUSTICE BURGER, joined by JUSTICE REHNQUIST, dissenting.

. . .

Today the Court sets aside the peremptory challenge, a procedure which has been part of the common law for many centuries and part of our jury system for nearly 200 years. It does so on the basis of a constitutional argument that was rejected, without a single dissent, in *Swain v. Alabama*. . . .

. . .

A moment's reflection quickly reveals the vast differences between the racial exclusions involved in *Strauder* and the allegations before us today:

> Exclusion from the venire summons process implies that the government (usually the legislative or judicial branch) . . . has made the general determination that those excluded are unfit to try *any* case. Exercise of the peremptory challenge, by contrast, represents the discrete decision, made by one of two or more opposed *litigants* in the trial phase of our adversary system of justice, that the challenged venireperson will likely be more unfavorable to that litigant in that *particular case* than others on the same venire.

. . .

Unwilling to rest solely on jury venire cases such as *Strauder*, the Court also invokes general equal protection principles in support of its holding. But peremptory challenges are often lodged, of necessity, for reasons "normally thought irrelevant to legal proceedings or official action, namely, the race, religion, nationality, occupation or affiliations of people summoned for jury duty." . . . Moreover, in making peremptory challenges, both the prosecutor and defense attorney necessarily act on only limited information or hunch. The process cannot be indicted on the sole basis that such decisions are made on the basis of "assumption" or "intuitive judgment." . . . As a result, unadulterated equal protection analysis is simply inapplicable to peremptory challenges exercised in any particular case. . . .

. . .

. . . Our system permits two types of challenges: challenges for cause and peremptory challenges. Challenges for cause obviously have to be explained; by definition, peremptory challenges do not. "It is called a peremptory challenge, because the prisoner may challenge peremptorily, on his own dislike, *without showing of any cause*." . . . Analytically, there is no middle ground: A challenge either has to be explained or it does not. It is readily apparent, then, that to permit inquiry into the basis for a peremptory challenge would force "the peremptory challenge [to] collapse into the challenge for cause." . . .

. . .

JUSTICE REHNQUIST, with whom THE CHIEF JUSTICE joins, dissenting.

. . .

I cannot subscribe to the Court's unprecedented use of the Equal Protection Clause to restrict the historic scope of the peremptory challenge, which has been described as "a necessary part of trial by jury." . . . In my view, there is simply nothing "unequal" about the State's using its peremptory challenges to strike blacks from the jury in cases involving black defendants, so long as such challenges are also used to exclude whites in cases involving white defendants, Hispanics in cases involving Hispanic defendants, Asians in cases involving Asian defendants, and so on. This case-specific use of peremptory challenges by the State does not single out blacks, or members of any other race for that matter, for discriminatory treatment. Such use of peremptories is at best based upon seat-of-the-pants instincts, which are undoubtedly crudely stereotypical and may in many cases be hopelessly mistaken. But as long as they are applied across-the-board to jurors of all races and nationalities, I do not see—and the Court most certainly has not explained—how their use violates the Equal Protection Clause.

. . .

The use of group affiliations, such as age, race, or occupation, as a "proxy" for potential juror partiality, based on the assumption or belief that members of one group are more likely to favor defendants who belong to the same group, has long been accepted as a legitimate basis for the State's exercise of peremptory challenges. . . . Indeed, given the need for reasonable limitations on the time devoted to *voir dire,* the use of such "proxies" by both the State and the defendant may be extremely useful in eliminating from the jury persons who might be biased in one way or another. The Court today holds that the State may not use its peremptory challenges to strike black prospective jurors on this basis without violating the Constitution. But I do not believe there is anything in the Equal Protection Clause, or any other constitutional provision, that justifies such a departure from the substantive holding . . . of *Swain.* Petitioner in the instant case failed to make a sufficient showing to overcome the presumption announced in *Swain* that the State's use of peremptory challenges was related to the context of the case. I would therefore affirm the judgment of the court below. . . .

E. Punishments

Ronald Reagan and his political allies sought to restore capital punishment. The Republican Party platform in 1980 declared, "We believe that the death penalty serves as an effective deterrent to capital crime and should be applied by the federal government and by states which approve it as an appropriate penalty for certain major crimes." President Reagan's State of the Union address in 1985 called on Congress to pass legislation that "in keeping with the will of the overwhelming majority of Americans, [mandates] the use of the death penalty where necessary."

Many moderate and conservative Democrats supported these pro–capital punishment initiatives, particularly after Democratic presidential candidate Michael Dukaskis's anti–capital punishment response to a question in the 1988 presidential debates was seen as detrimental to his campaign. Public support for the death penalty had ebbed in the 1960s but had surged back in the 1970s and 1980s. When campaigning for the presidency in 1992, Governor Bill Clinton of Arkansas recognized this change in public opinion when he very publically demonstrated his commitment to capital punishment by returning to his home state to oversee the execution of Ricky Ray Rector.

The Supreme Court of the United States was in step with the rest of constitutional politics on the death penalty. *McCleskey v. Kemp* (1987) rejected a broad challenge to capital punishment statutes as administered. McCleskey's lawyers relied on statistics demonstrating that persons who murdered white victims were far more likely to be sentenced to death than murderers whose victims were persons of color. Justice Powell's majority opinion rejected this use of statistics because McCleskey had not demonstrated that racial prejudice specifically influenced the jury decision to sentence him to death. Many important decisions curtailed access to federal habeas corpus, the process that during the 1970s and early 1980s enabled many capitally sentenced persons to avoid execution. *McCleskey v. Zant* (1991) sharply restricted the use of successive habeas corpus petitions in death cases. *Herrera v. Collins* (1993) ruled that federal habeas corpus proceedings could rarely consider new evidence that a capitally sentenced prison was innocent. In *Butler v. McKellar* (1990) and *Penry v. Lynaugh* (1989) a 5-4 judicial majority extended *Teague v. Lane* (1989) to death cases. Persons sentenced to death could not normally have their conviction or sentence reversed in habeas corpus, even when a judicial majority believed that the trial court had made a constitutional mistake, unless the judicial majority maintained that previous precedents so clearly dictated the right constitutional rule that the trial court decision was an unreasonable interpretation of the constitutional law.

The Supreme Court's changing stance on victim impact statements (VIS) in capital trials demonstrated the importance of the judicial appointment process. In *Booth v. Maryland* (1987) a 5-4 majority ruled such statements inadmissible. Justice Powell's majority opinion asserted,

> The focus of a VIS is not on the defendant, but on the character and reputation of the victim and the effect on his family. These factors may be wholly unrelated to the blameworthiness of a particular defendant. As our cases have shown, the defendant often will not know the victim, and therefore will have no knowledge about the existence or characteristics of the victim's family. Moreover, defendants rarely select their victims based on whether the murder will have an effect on anyone other than the person murdered. Allowing the jury to rely on a VIS therefore could result in imposing the death sentence because of factors about which the defendant was unaware, and that were irrelevant to the decision to kill.

The Supreme Court reconsidered *Booth* in *Payne v. Tennessee* (1991). By then two members of the *Booth* majority, Justices Powell and Brennan, had retired and been replaced by two Republican appointees, Justices Kennedy and Souter. The result was a 6-3 decision permitting states to introduce victim impact statements. Chief Justice Rehnquist's majority opinion declared,

> We are now of the view that a State may properly conclude that for the jury to assess meaningfully the defendant's moral culpability and blameworthiness, it should have before it at the sentencing phase evidence of the specific harm caused by the defendant. The State has a legitimate interest in counteracting the mitigating evidence which the defendant is entitled to put in, by reminding the sentencer that just as the murderer should be considered as an individual, so too the victim is an individual whose death represents a unique loss to society and in particular to his family.

Justices Blackmun and Stevens rethought their original support for capital punishment in light of the Supreme Court's increased willingness to sustain death sentences. Before retiring, Blackmun recanted completely. His dissent from the denial of certiorari in *Callins v. Collins* (1994) stated, "Experience has taught us that the constitutional goal of eliminating arbitrariness and discrimination from the administration of death can never be achieved without compromising an equally essential component of fundamental fairness—individualized sentencing." Justice Scalia blasted this attack on the capital sentencing process. His opinion in *Callins* called on the Supreme Court to reverse the past precedents imposing significant limits on state capacity to execute vicious criminals. In his view, if popular majorities "merely conclude that justice requires such brutal deaths to be avenged by capital punishment[,] the creation of false, untextual, and unhistorical contradictions within the Court's Eighth Amendment jurisprudence should not prevent them."

Liberals had more luck when they made Eighth and Fourteenth Amendment attacks on criminal sanctions outside the context of capital punishment. For the first time in American history the Supreme Court ruled in favor of a prisoner's claim that prison conditions violated constitutional norms. Justice O'Connor's majority opinion in *Hudson v. McMillian* (1992) stated, "When prison officials maliciously and sadistically use force to cause harm, contemporary standards of decency always are violated." Judicial majorities imposed some limits on popular "three strikes and you're out" laws" that imposed harsh sentences on repeat offenders. *Solem v. Helm* (1983) overturned a trial court decision to sentence a repeat offender to life in prison without parole for passing a bad $100 check. Justice Powell's majority opinion stated,

> We find that Helm has received the penultimate sentence for relatively minor criminal conduct. He has been treated more harshly than other criminals in the State who have committed more serious crimes. He has been treated more harshly than he would have been in any other jurisdiction, with the possible exception of a single State. We conclude that his sentence is significantly disproportionate to his crime, and is therefore prohibited by the Eighth Amendment.

The justices were not as tenderhearted when drug offenders made cruel and unusual punishment claims. *Harmelin v. Michigan* (1991) sustained a mandatory life sentence for possessing a substantial amount of cocaine. Justice Kennedy's plurality opinion stated,

Possession, use, and distribution of illegal drugs represent "one of the greatest problems affecting the health and welfare of our population." Petitioner's suggestion that his crime was nonviolent and victimless, is false to the point of absurdity. To the contrary, petitioner's crime threatened to cause grave harm to society.

McCleskey v. Kemp, 481 U.S. 279 (1987)

Warren McCleskey shot and killed a white police officer during a robbery. He was convicted of murder and sentenced to death after a Georgia jury found two aggravating circumstances beyond a reasonable doubt: first, that McCleskey had murdered a police officer, and second, that the murder was committed during an armed robbery. The Supreme Court of Georgia affirmed the sentence and the Supreme Court of the United States rejected McCleskey's request for a writ of certiorari. McCleskey then instituted an action for habeas corpus, insisting that Georgia's procedures for imposing capital punishment discriminated against persons of color. McCleskey, an African-American man, claimed that Georgia disproportionately sentenced to death persons who murdered white victims, even when the aggravating and mitigating circumstances were identical.[64] *After Georgia state courts and lower federal courts rejected this claim, McCleskey appealed to the Supreme Court of the United States.*

The Supreme Court rejected McCleskey's petition by a 5-4 vote. Justice Powell's majority opinion held that McCleskey had failed to demonstrate that he was a victim of race discrimination. Justice Powell worried that if the Court accepted McCleskey's claim, the justices would soon face claims that race and other forms of discrimination influenced other aspects of the criminal justice system. Is this a legitimate prudential argument? Is there a basis for distinguishing between race discrimination in the capital sentencing process and race discrimination in the criminal justice system more generally? The evidence that McCleskey presented to the Supreme Court of the United States differed from the evidence that opponents of capital punishment presented to the Supreme Court in Furman v. Georgia *(1972). Before 1970 persons of color were far more likely to be sentenced to death than white persons, even when the circumstances of their crimes were similar. McCleskey's claim focused on the race*

64. See David C. Baldus, Charles Pulaski, and George Woodworth, "Comparative Review of Death Sentences: An Empirical Study of the Georgia Experience," *Journal of Criminal Law and Criminology* 74 (1983): 661.

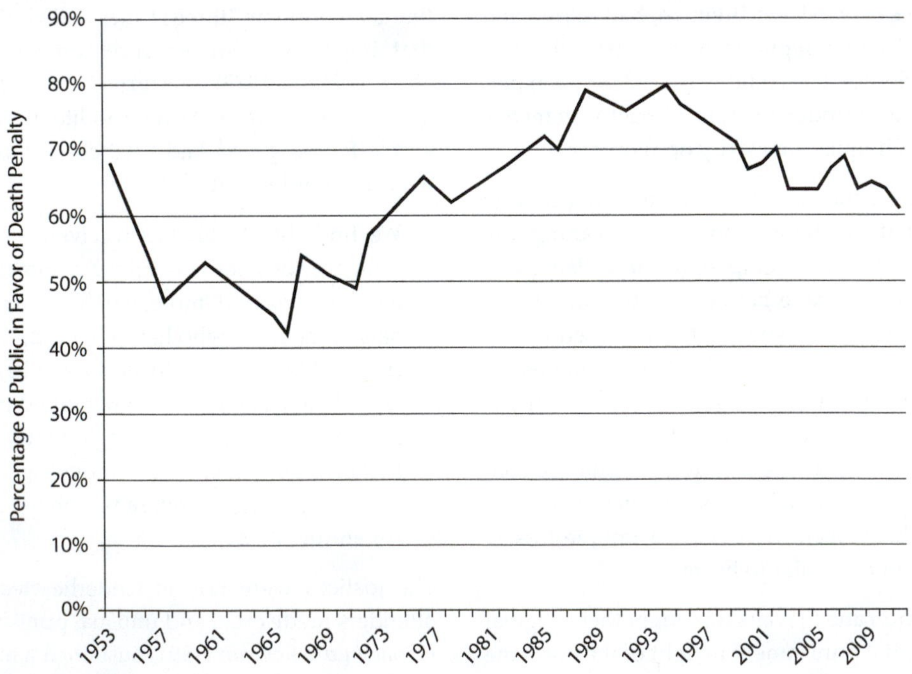

Figure 10-6 Public Support for the Death Penalty, 1953–2011

Source: Copyright © Gallup, Inc. All rights reserved. The content is used with permission; however, Gallup retains all rights of republication.

of murder victims. The studies he presented indicated that criminal defendants who murdered whites had a far greater chance of being sentenced to death than criminal defendants who murdered persons of color. Do you believe that a constitutional difference exists between discrimination on the basis of the race of the defendant and discrimination on the basis of the race of the victim?[65] *Did any of the justices see a distinction? How did the justices treat the evidence that McCleskey presented?*

McCleskey *was the last major effort that opponents of capital punishment made to strike a serious blow against the practice. Lawyers still attacked the constitutionality of individual death sentences or small categories of death-sentenced persons, but in no subsequent case was the constitutionality of most death sentences in the United States seriously questioned. While proponents of capital punishment cheered this development and the increase in executions that took place during the 1980s and 1990s, Justice Powell did not. Shortly after retiring from the bench, Powell recanted his* McCleskey *opinion.*[66]

JUSTICE POWELL delivered the opinion of the Court.

. . .

Our analysis begins with the basic principle that a defendant who alleges an equal protection violation has the burden of proving "the existence of purposeful discrimination." . . . A corollary to this principle is that a criminal defendant must prove that the purposeful discrimination "had a discriminatory effect" on him. . . . Thus, to prevail under the Equal Protection Clause, McCleskey must prove that the decisionmakers in *his* case acted with discriminatory purpose. He offers no evidence specific to his own case that would support an inference that racial considerations played a part in his sentence. Instead, he relies solely on the Baldus study. McCleskey argues that the Baldus study compels an inference that his sentence rests on purposeful discrimination. McCleskey's claim that these statistics are sufficient proof of discrimination, without regard to the facts of a particular case, would extend to all capital cases in Georgia, at least where the victim was white and the defendant is black.

The Court has accepted statistics as proof of intent to discriminate in certain limited contexts. First, this Court has accepted statistical disparities as proof of an equal protection violation in the selection of the jury venire in a particular district. . . . Second, this Court has accepted statistics in the form of multiple-regression analysis to prove statutory violations under Title VII of the Civil Rights Act of 1964. . . .

But the nature of the capital sentencing decision, and the relationship of the statistics to that decision, are fundamentally different from the corresponding elements in the venire-selection or Title VII cases. Most importantly, each particular decision to impose the death penalty is made by a petit jury selected from a properly constituted venire. Each jury is unique in its composition, and the Constitution requires that its decision rest on consideration of innumerable factors that vary according to the characteristics of the individual defendant and the facts of the particular capital offense. . . . Thus, the application of an inference drawn from the general statistics to a specific decision in a trial and sentencing simply is not comparable to the application of an inference drawn from general statistics to a specific venire-selection or Title VII case. In those cases, the statistics relate to fewer entities, and fewer variables are relevant to the challenged decisions.

Another important difference between the cases in which we have accepted statistics as proof of discriminatory intent and this case is that, in the venire-selection and Title VII contexts, the decisionmaker has an opportunity to explain the statistical disparity. . . . Here, the State has no practical opportunity to rebut the Baldus study. "[C]ontrolling considerations of . . . public policy," . . . dictate that jurors "cannot be called . . . to testify to the motives and influences that led to their verdict." . . . Similarly, the policy considerations behind a prosecutor's traditionally "wide discretion" suggest the impropriety of our requiring prosecutors to defend their decisions to seek death penalties, "often years after they were made." . . . Moreover, absent far stronger proof, it is unnecessary to seek such a rebuttal, because a legitimate and unchallenged explanation for the decision is apparent from the record: McCleskey committed an act for which the United States Constitution and Georgia laws permit imposition of the death penalty.

. . .

. . . Even Professor Baldus does not contend that his statistics *prove* that race enters into any capital sentencing decisions or that race was a factor in McCleskey's

---

65. For a good discussion of these issues, see Randall L Kennedy, "*McCleskey v. Kemp*: Race, Capital Punishment, and the Supreme Court," *Harvard Law Review* 101 (1988): 1388.

66. See Mark Graber, "Judicial Recantations: Two Thoughts about Second Thoughts," *Syracuse Law Review* 45 (1995): 807.

particular case. Statistics at most may show only a likelihood that a particular factor entered into some decisions. There is, of course, some risk of racial prejudice influencing a jury's decision in a criminal case. There are similar risks that other kinds of prejudice will influence other criminal trials. . . . The question "is at what point that risk becomes constitutionally unacceptable." . . .

. . .

At most, the Baldus study indicates a discrepancy that appears to correlate with race. Apparent disparities in sentencing are an inevitable part of our criminal justice system. The discrepancy indicated by the Baldus study is "a far cry from the major systemic defects identified in *Furman*." . . . "[T]here can be 'no perfect procedure for deciding in which cases governmental authority should be used to impose death.'" . . . Despite these imperfections, our consistent rule has been that constitutional guarantees are met when "the mode [for determining guilt or punishment] itself has been surrounded with safeguards to make it as fair as possible." . . . Where the discretion that is fundamental to our criminal process is involved, we decline to assume that what is unexplained is invidious. In light of the safeguards designed to minimize racial bias in the process, the fundamental value of jury trial in our criminal justice system, and the benefits that discretion provides to criminal defendants, we hold that the Baldus study does not demonstrate a constitutionally significant risk of racial bias affecting the Georgia capital sentencing process.

. . .

. . . McCleskey's claim, taken to its logical conclusion, throws into serious question the principles that underlie our entire criminal justice system. The Eighth Amendment is not limited in application to capital punishment, but applies to all penalties. . . . Thus, if we accepted McCleskey's claim that racial bias has impermissibly tainted the capital sentencing decision, we could soon be faced with similar claims as to other types of penalty. Moreover, the claim that his sentence rests on the irrelevant factor of race easily could be extended to apply to claims based on unexplained discrepancies that correlate to membership in other minority groups, and even to gender. . . . If arbitrary and capricious punishment is the touchstone under the Eighth Amendment, such a claim could—at least in theory—be based upon any arbitrary variable, such as the defendant's facial characteristics, or the physical attractiveness of the defendant or the victim. . . . The Constitution does not require that a State eliminate any demonstrable disparity that correlates with a potentially irrelevant factor in order to operate a criminal justice system that includes capital punishment. As we have stated specifically in the context of capital punishment, the Constitution does not "plac[e] totally unrealistic conditions on its use."

McCleskey's arguments are best presented to the legislative bodies. It is not the responsibility—or indeed even the right—of this Court to determine the appropriate punishment for particular crimes. It is the legislatures, the elected representatives of the people, that are "constituted to respond to the will and consequently the moral values of the people." Legislatures also are better qualified to weigh and "evaluate the results of statistical studies in terms of their own local conditions and with a flexibility of approach that is not available to the courts."

JUSTICE BRENNAN, with whom JUSTICE MARSHALL joins, and with whom JUSTICE BLACKMUN and JUSTICE STEVENS join . . . dissenting.

. . .

At some point in this case, Warren McCleskey doubtless asked his lawyer whether a jury was likely to sentence him to die. A candid reply to this question would have been disturbing. First, counsel would have to tell McCleskey that few of the details of the crime or of McCleskey's past criminal conduct were more important than the fact that his victim was white. . . . Furthermore, counsel would feel bound to tell McCleskey that defendants charged with killing white victims in Georgia are 4.3 times as likely to be sentenced to death as defendants charged with killing blacks. . . . In addition, frankness would compel the disclosure that it was more likely than not that the race of McCleskey's victim would determine whether he received a death sentence: 6 of every 11 defendants convicted of killing a white person would not have received the death penalty if their victims had been black, . . . while, among defendants with aggravating and mitigating factors comparable to McCleskey's, 20 of every 34 would not have been sentenced to die if their victims had been black. . . .

. . .

It is important to emphasize at the outset that the Court's observation that McCleskey cannot prove the influence of race on any particular sentencing decision is irrelevant in evaluating his Eighth Amendment claim. Since *Furman v. Georgia* (1972), . . . the Court has been concerned with the *risk* of the imposition of an arbitrary sentence, rather than the proven fact of one. *Furman* held that the death penalty "may not be imposed under sentencing procedures that create a substantial risk that the punishment will be inflicted in an arbitrary and capricious manner." . . . This emphasis on risk acknowledges the difficulty of divining the jury's motivation in an individual case. In addition, it reflects the fact that concern for arbitrariness focuses on the rationality of the system as a whole, and that a system that features a significant probability that sentencing decisions are influenced by impermissible considerations cannot be regarded as rational. . . .

. . .

The Baldus study indicates that, after taking into account some 230 nonracial factors that might legitimately influence a sentencer, the jury *more likely than not* would have spared McCleskey's life had his victim been black. The study distinguishes between those cases in which (1) the jury exercises virtually no discretion because the strength or weakness of aggravating factors usually suggests that only one outcome is appropriate; and (2) cases reflecting an "intermediate" level of aggravation, in which the jury has considerable discretion in choosing a sentence. McCleskey's case falls into the intermediate range. In such cases, death is imposed in 34% of white-victim crimes and 14% of black-victim crimes, a difference of 139% in the rate of imposition of the death penalty. . . . In other words, just under 59%—almost 6 in 10—defendants comparable to McCleskey would not have received the death penalty if their victims had been black.

. . .

. . . Furthermore, blacks who kill whites are sentenced to death at nearly 22 *times* the rate of blacks who kill blacks, and more than 7 *times* the rate of whites who kill blacks. . . . In addition, prosecutors seek the death penalty for 70% of black defendants with white victims, but for only 15% of black defendants with black victims, and only 19% of white defendants with black victims. . . . Since our decision upholding the Georgia capital sentencing system in *Gregg*, the State has executed seven persons. All of the seven were convicted of killing whites, and six of the seven executed were black. . . . Such execution figures are especially striking in light of the fact that, during the period encompassed by the Baldus study, only 9.2% of Georgia homicides involved black defendants and white victims, while 60.7% involved black victims.

. . . Georgia's legacy of a race-conscious criminal justice system . . . indicates that McCleskey's claim is not a fanciful product of mere statistical artifice.

For many years, Georgia operated openly and formally precisely the type of dual system the evidence shows is still effectively in place. The criminal law expressly differentiated between crimes committed by and against blacks and whites, distinctions whose lineage traced back to the time of slavery.

. . .

The discretion afforded prosecutors and jurors in the Georgia capital sentencing system creates . . . opportunities [for continued discrimination]. No guidelines govern prosecutorial decisions to seek the death penalty, and Georgia provides juries with no list of aggravating and mitigating factors, nor any standard for balancing them against one another. . . . The Georgia sentencing system therefore provides considerable opportunity for racial considerations, however subtle and unconscious, to influence charging and sentencing decisions.

. . .

In fairness, the Court's fear that McCleskey's claim is an invitation to descend a slippery slope also rests on the realization that any humanly imposed system of penalties will exhibit some imperfection. Yet to reject McCleskey's powerful evidence on this basis is to ignore both the qualitatively different character of the death penalty and the particular repugnance of racial discrimination, considerations which may properly be taken into account in determining whether various punishments are "cruel and unusual."

. . .

JUSTICE BLACKMUN, with whom JUSTICE MARSHALL and JUSTICE STEVENS join, and with whom JUSTICE BRENNAN joins in part, dissenting.

. . .

Under *Batson v. Kentucky* (1986) . . . , McCleskey must meet a three-factor standard. First, he must establish that he is a member of a group "that is a recognizable, distinct class, singled out for different treatment." Second, he must make a showing of a substantial degree of differential treatment. Third, he must establish that the allegedly discriminatory procedure is susceptible to abuse or is not racially neutral. . . .

. . . The Baldus study demonstrates that black persons are a distinct group that are singled out for different treatment in the Georgia capital sentencing system. . . .

. . .

McCleskey demonstrated the degree to which his death sentence was affected by racial factors by introducing multiple-regression analyses that explain how much of the statistical distribution of the cases analyzed is attributable to the racial factors. . . . The most persuasive evidence of the constitutionally significant effect of racial factors in the Georgia capital sentencing system is McCleskey's proof that the race of the victim is more important in explaining the imposition of a death sentence than is the factor whether the defendant was a prime mover in the homicide. Similarly, the race-of-victim factor is nearly as crucial as the statutory aggravating circumstance whether the defendant had a prior record of a conviction for a capital crime. . . .

McCleskey produced evidence concerning the role of racial factors at the various steps in the decision-making process, focusing on the prosecutor's decision as to which cases merit the death sentence. McCleskey established that the race of the victim is an especially significant factor at the point where the defendant has been convicted of murder and the prosecutor must choose whether to proceed to the penalty phase of the trial and create the possibility that a death sentence may be imposed or to accept the imposition of a sentence of life imprisonment. McCleskey demonstrated this effect at both the statewide level . . . and in Fulton County where he was tried and sentenced. . . .

. . .

. . . The issue in this case is the extent to which the constitutional guarantee of equal protection limits the discretion in the Georgia capital sentencing system. As the Court concedes, discretionary authority can be discriminatory authority. . . . Prosecutorial decisions may not be "'deliberately based upon an unjustifiable standard such as race, religion, or other arbitrary classification.'" . . .

. . .

JUSTICE STEVENS, with whom JUSTICE BLACKMUN joins, dissenting.

. . .

The Court's decision appears to be based on a fear that the acceptance of McCleskey's claim would sound the death knell for capital punishment in Georgia. If society were indeed forced to choose between a racially discriminatory death penalty (one that provides heightened protection against murder "for whites only") and no death penalty at all, the choice mandated by the Constitution would be plain. . . . But the Court's fear is unfounded. One of the lessons of the Baldus study is that there exist certain categories of extremely serious crimes for which prosecutors consistently seek, and juries consistently impose, the death penalty without regard to the race of the victim or the race of the offender. If Georgia were to narrow the class of death-eligible defendants to those categories, the danger of arbitrary and discriminatory imposition of the death penalty would be significantly decreased, if not eradicated. As Justice BRENNAN has demonstrated in his dissenting opinion, such a restructuring of the sentencing scheme is surely not too high a price to pay.

The First Presidential Debate *(1988)*

The 1988 national election was a contest between Vice President George Bush, who promised to continue Ronald Reagan's legacy, and Governor Michael Dukakis of Massachusetts, one of the nation's leading liberals. Dukakis held an early lead in much of the polling, but Bush ran a far more effective campaign. On November 6, 1988, Bush captured 426 electoral votes to Dukakis's 111. Bush won the popular vote by nearly 8 percentage points.

Many commentators regard the first presidential debate as an important turning point in the campaign. In response to a question by reporter Bernard Shaw about capital punishment, Dukakis appeared wooden and unfeeling. As you read that exchange, consider how you would have advised an anti–capital punishment candidate to respond. Did Dukakis have a better response, or, given the climate of the late 1980s, were Democrats better off abandoning opposition to the death penalty?

Bernard Shaw

. . . Governor, if Kitty Dukakis were raped and murdered, would you favor an irrevocable death penalty for the killer?

Michael Dukakis

No, I don't, Bernard. And I think you know that I've opposed the death penalty during all of my life. I don't

Table 10-3 Selection of U.S. Supreme Court Cases Reviewing the Constitutionality of the Death Penalty

Case	Vote	Outcome	Decision
Wilkerson v. Utah, 99 U.S. 130 (1879)	9-0	Upheld	Execution by firing squad not cruel and unusual punishment
Francis v. Resweber, 329 U.S. 459 (1947)	5-4	Upheld	Attempting a second execution after the first attempt failed is constitutional
Witherspoon v. Illinois, 391 U.S. 510 (1968)	6-3	Struck down	States may not strike potential jurors simply because they have moral objections to the death penalty
Furman v. Georgia, 408 U.S. 238 (1972)	5-4	Struck down	All existing applications of the death penalty are arbitrary and capricious and are unconstitutional
Woodson v. North Carolina, 428 U.S. 280 (1976)	5-4	Struck down	Mandatory death penalty for all first-degree murder convictions is unconstitutional
Gregg v. Georgia, 428 U.S. 153 (1976)	7-2	Upheld	Death penalty may be constitutionally applied if juries are given standards that limit their sentencing discretion
Coker v. Georgia, 433 U.S. 584 (1977)	7-2	Struck down	Death penalty may not be applied to cases of rape that do not result in the death of the victim
Glass v. Louisiana, 471 U.S. 1080 (1985)	7-2	Upheld	Electrocution is a constitutional means of execution
Ford v. Wainwright, 477 U.S. 399 (1986)	5-4	Struck down	States may not execute the insane
McCleskey v. Kemp, 481 U.S. 279 (1987)	5-4	Upheld	Racially disparate results from death penalty sentencing does not violate the equal protection clause without a showing of racially discriminatory purpose
Thompson v. Oklahoma, 487 U.S. 815 (1988)	5-3	Struck down	States may not impose the death penalty on those who were under the age of sixteen when they committed their offense
Herrera v. Collins, 506 U.S. 390 (1993)	6-3	Upheld	A claim of actual innocence on newly discovered evidence is not by itself sufficient for federal review of death penalty conviction
Atkins v. Virginia, 536 U.S. 304 (2002)	6-3	Struck down	States may not execute the mentally handicapped
Roper v. Simmons, 543 U.S. 551 (2005)	5-4	Struck down	States may not impose the death penalty on those who were under the age of eighteen when they committed their offense
Baze v. Rees, 553 U.S. 35 (2008)	7-2	Upheld	Lethal injection is a constitutional means of execution
Kennedy v. Louisiana, 554 U.S. 407 (2008)	5-4	Struck down	Eighth amendment does not permit a state to punish the rape of a child with the death penalty

see any evidence that it's a deterrent, and I think there are better and more effective ways to deal with violent crime. We've done so in my own state. And it's one of the reasons why we have had the biggest drop in crime of any industrial state in America; why we have the lowest murder rate of any industrial state in America. But we have work to do in this nation. We have work to do to fight a real war, not a phony war, against drugs. And that's something I want to lead, something we haven't had over the course of the past many years, even though the Vice President has been at least allegedly in charge of that war. We have much to do to step up that war, to double the number of drug enforcement agents, to fight both here and abroad, to work with our neighbors in this hemisphere. And I want to call a hemispheric summit just as soon after the 20th of January as possible to fight that war. But we also have to deal with drug education prevention here at home. And that's one of the things that I hope I can lead personally as the President of the United States. We've had great success in my own state. And we've reached out to young people and their families and been able to help them by beginning drug education and prevention in the early elementary grades. So we can fight this war, and we can win this war. And we can do so in a way that marshals our forces, that provides real support for state and local law enforcement officers who have not been getting that support, and do it in a way which will bring down violence in this nation, will help our youngsters to stay away from drugs, will stop this avalanche of drugs that's pouring into the country, and will make it possible for our kids and our families to grow up in safe and secure and decent neighborhoods.

Shaw

Mr. Vice President, your one-minute rebuttal.

George Bush

Well, a lot of what this campaign is about, it seems to me Bernie, goes to the question of values. And here I do have, on this particular question, a big difference with my opponent. You see, I do believe that some crimes are so heinous, so brutal, so outrageous, and I'd say particularly those that result in the death of a police officer, for those real brutal crimes, I do believe in the death penalty, and I think it is a deterrent, and I believe we need it. And I'm glad that the Congress moved on this drug bill and have finally called for that related to these narcotics drug kingpins. And so we just have an honest difference of opinion: I support it and he doesn't.

Suggested Readings

Bell, Derrick. *And We Are Not Saved: The Elusive Quest for Racial Justice* (New York: Basic, 1987).

Bork, Robert H. *The Tempting of America: The Political Seduction of the Law* (New York: Free Press, 1990).

Choper, Jesse H. *Securing Religious Liberty: Principles for Judicial Interpretation of the Religion Clauses* (Chicago: University of Chicago Press, 1995).

Davis, Sue. *Justice Rehnquist and the Constitution* (Princeton, NJ: Princeton University Press, 1989).

Downs, Donald Alexander. *The New Politics of Pornography* (Chicago: University of Chicago Press, 1989).

Epps, Garrett. *To an Unknown God: Religious Freedom on Trial* (New York: St. Martin's, 2001).

Epstein, Richard. *Takings: Private Property and the Power of Eminent Domain* (Cambridge, MA: Harvard University Press, 1985).

Graber, Mark A. *Rethinking Abortion: Equal Choice, the Constitution, and Reproductive Politics* (Princeton, NJ: Princeton University Press, 1996).

Guinier, Lani. *The Tyranny of the Majority: Fundamental Fairness in Representative Democracy* (New York: Free Press, 1994).

Kahn, Ronald. *The Supreme Court and Constitutional Theory, 1953–1993* (Lawrence: University Press of Kansas, 1994).

Karst, Kenneth L. *Belonging to America: Equal Citizenship and the Constitution* (New Haven, CT: Yale University Press, 1989).

Lazarus, Edward. *Closed Chambers: The First Eyewitness Account of the Epic Struggles Inside the Supreme Court* (New York: Times, 1998).

MacKinnon, Catherine A. *Feminism Unmodified: Discourses on Life and Law* (Cambridge, MA: Harvard University Press, 1987).

Matsuda, Mari J., Charles R. Lawrence III, Richard Delgado, and Kimberle Williams Crenshaw. *Words that Wound: Critical Race Theory, Assaultive Speech, and the First Amendment* (Boulder, CO: Westview, 1993).

McCann, Michael W. *Rights at Work: Pay Equity Reform and the Politics of Legal Mobilization* (Chicago: University of Chicago Press, 1994).

Minow, Martha. *Making All the Difference: Inclusion, Exclusion, and American Law* (Ithaca, NY: Cornell University Press, 1990).

O'Neill, Johnathan G. *Originalism in American Law and Politics: A Constitutional History* (Baltimore, MD: Johns Hopkins University Press, 2005).

Perry, Michael J. *The Constitution, the Courts, and Human Rights: An Inquiry into the Legitimacy of Constitutional Policymaking by the Judiciary* (New Haven, CT: Yale University Press, 1982).

Savage, David G. *Turning Right: The Making of the Rehnquist Court* (New York: Wiley, 1992).

Thernstrom, Abigail M. *Whose Votes Count? Affirmative Action and Minority Voting Rights* (Cambridge, MA: Harvard University Press, 1987).

Tribe, Laurence H. *Constitutional Choices* (Cambridge, MA: Harvard University Press, 1985).

Chapter 11

The Contemporary Era: 1994–Present

I. Introduction

Contemporary constitutional politics is frequently structured by polarized national parties and surprisingly centrist judicial decisions. Republican and Democratic elites take sharply different positions on such issues as abortion, capital punishment, and the role of religion in public life. When such matters are adjudicated by the Supreme Court, the justices by increasingly narrow margins often adopt moderate positions that fail to satisfy the most important constituencies on both the political left and the political right. This period of polarized parties and more centrist courts has led to the following series of constitutional decisions and practices. Abortion may be heavily regulated but not completely prohibited. Campaign contributions may be limited, but campaign expenditures may not. States may constitutionally impose capital punishment, but not for crimes committed by persons who are mentally retarded or younger than eighteen years old. The Supreme Court declared that the University of Michigan had adopted constitutional race-conscious policies for law school admissions but unconstitutional race-conscious admissions policies for undergraduate admissions. Frequently, liberals and conservatives bitterly condemn the same judicial ruling as abandoning vital constitutional principles.

The course of contemporary constitutional politics has been erratic. A list of contemporary constitutional winners might include gays and lesbians, parents who send their children to religious schools, persons subject to the death penalty (the execution rate has been cut in half since 2000), proponents of an individual right to bear arms, and multimillionaires who wish to make very large independent campaign expenditures. What these groups have in common is for the reader to determine. Some Supreme Court decisions have had substantial impacts on the course of constitutional politics. *Bush v. Gore* (2000) played a major role in deciding the 2000 presidential election. Other Supreme Court decisions, despite the overheated rhetoric from both sides of the political spectrum, were of far less consequence. American policy on the War on Terror barely changed after the Supreme Court in three cases—*Hamdi v. Rumsfeld* (2004), *Hamdan v. Rumsfeld* (2006), and *Boumediene v. Bush* (2008)—declared unconstitutional various Bush administration policies on detaining suspected terrorists.

Parties. The constitutional politics of civil liberties is more polarized than at any previous time in American history. The Republican Party is presently the home for persons committed to the constitutional rights of gun holders, property owners, religious conservatives, and white Americans aggrieved by affirmative action. The Democratic Party is presently the home for persons committed to the rights associated with nontraditional lifestyles, reproductive choice, and persons of color. The Democratic Party is also home to the decreasing number of persons committed to the rights of persons suspected of crimes, although President Clinton, President Obama, and many Democrats in Congress frequently reject positions on constitutional criminal procedure taken by such groups as the ACLU.[1] Party platforms reflect these differences. The Republican

1. See Geoffrey C. Layman and Thomas M. Carsey, "Party Polarization and 'Conflict Extension' in the American Electorate," *American Journal of Political Science* 46 (2002): 786-802.

Table 11-1 Major Rights and Liberties Issues and Decisions of the Contemporary Era

Major Political Issues	**Major Constitutional Issues**	**Major Court Decisions**
Partisan Polarization and Divided Government	Second Amendment	*Romer v. Evans* (1996)
Crime Control	Takings Clause	*Bush v. Gore* (2000)
War on Terror	Due Process and Habeas Corpus	*Kyllo v. United States* (2001)
Iraq War	Regulation of Abortion	*Lawrence v. Texas* (2003)
Property Rights	Homosexual Rights and Same-Sex Marriage	*Grutter v. Bollinger* (2003)
Money in Elections	Majority-Minority Districts	*Hamdi v. Rumsfeld* (2004)
Bans on Handguns	Campaign Finance Reform	*Kelo v. City of New London* (2005)
Culture Wars	Religious Liberty	*Boumediene v. Bush* (2008)
Disputed Presidential Election	Equal Protection	*District of Columbia v. Heller* (2008)
Voting Rights	Fourth Amendment and New Technologies	*Citizens United v. Federal Election Commission* (2010)
		McDonald v. City of Chicago (2010)

platform in 2000 emphasized a commitment to judicial restraint and public order.

> In the federal courts, scores of judges with activist backgrounds in the hard-left now have lifetime tenure. . . . Whom do the American people trust to restore the rule of law, not just in our streets and playgrounds, not just in boardrooms and on Wall Street, but in our courts and in the Justice Department itself? The answer is clear. Governor Bush is determined to name only judges who have demonstrated respect for the Constitution and the processes of our republic.

Democrats in 2000 celebrated activist justices who broadly interpreted certain constitutional rights and liberties.

> Democrats oppose efforts to strip the federal courts of jurisdiction to decide critical issues affecting workers, immigrants, veterans and others of access to justice. And, unlike Republicans, Al Gore will appoint justices to the Supreme Court who have a demonstrated concern for and commitment to the individual rights protected by our Constitution, including the right to privacy.

On some issues Democrats and Republicans have reverse inherited positions on judicial restraint and activism. The Republican Party Platform in 2012 called for Supreme Court judges to impose sharp limitations on federal power to enact national health care laws and other measures inconsistent with a broad interpretation of state authority under the Tenth Amendment, as well as strike down state and federal campaign finance laws, affirmative action politics, gun control measures, uses of eminent domain that transferred property from one private owner to another, and laws that required religious employers to provide employees with health plans that covered contraception. Unsurprisingly, the Democratic Party platform in 2012 exhibited little or no "concern and commitment to" any of the individual rights that Republicans would have federal judges protect.

Neither political party gained the political control over national institutions necessary to make either distinctively conservative or liberal constitutional visions the official law of the land. Liberal Democrats briefly appeared to have established national domination after the election of 1992, when they gained control of the White House, Senate, and House of Representatives. That majority quickly dissipated. A far more conservative Republican party captured both houses of Congress in 1994 and retained that control until 2006. When President George W. Bush was elected president in 2000 and 2004, many commentators believed that the United States was in an enduring period of conservative domination.[2] The combination

---

2. Including one co-editor of this text. See Mark A. Graber, "Does it Really Matter? Conservative Courts in a Conservative Era," *Fordham Law Review* 75 (2006): 675. See also Stephen Skowronek, "Leadership by Definition: First Term Reflections on George W. Bush's Political Stance," *Perspectives on Politics* 3(2005): 817.

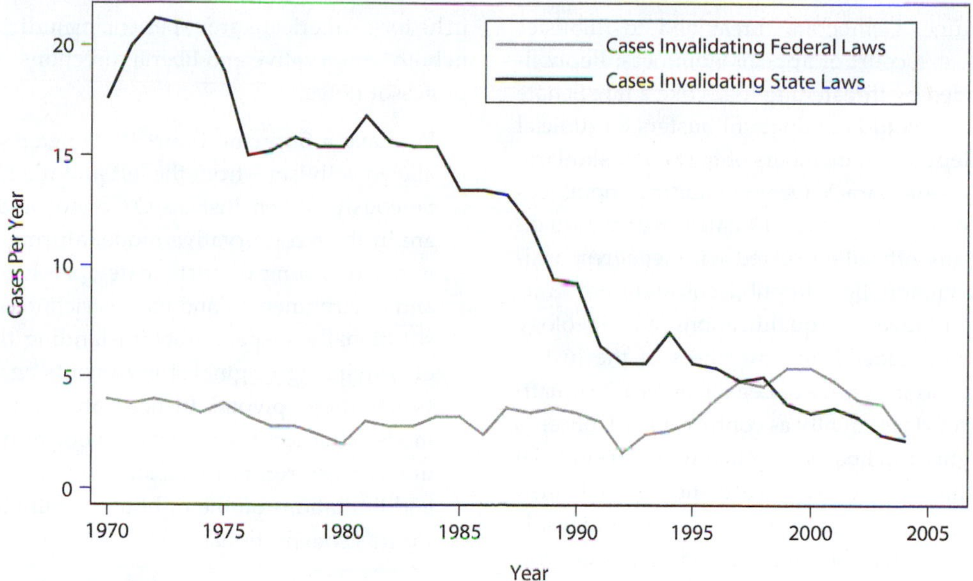

Figure 11-1 Supreme Court Invalidation of State and Federal Laws, 1970–2004

Note: Cases represented by centered, five-year moving average.

of Hurricane Katrina, the Iraq War, and an economic downturn enabled Democrats to regain control of Congress in 2006 and the White House in 2008. That complete control lasted two years before Republicans regained control of the House of Representatives and substantially reduced the Democratic Senate majority in 2010. Republican gains in state legislatures have resulted in new attacks on abortion rights and ongoing controversies over gerrymandering.

Interest Groups. Interest groups remain active in the constitutional politics of rights. More than one hundred interest groups participate when Congress considers revising campaign finance laws or contribute amicus briefs when courts consider the constitutional status of same-sex marriage. Many interest groups pour substantial resources into political and constitutional contests. Whether liberal and conservative associations cancel each other out or bias American constitutional politics in particular directions is controversial.

Many contemporary rights-oriented interest groups are closely identified with and sometimes connected to a particular political party. One recent study observed, "Electoral competition among interest groups . . . appears polarized along partisan lines."[3] The NRA usually supports Republicans. Americans United for the Separation of Church and State is composed largely of Democrats. The Tea Party is presently seeking to push the Republican Party to the right. MoveOn continually seeks to push Democrats to the left. The relative power of interest groups is also changing. Pro-choice and gay rights organizations have gained influence in the Democratic Party at the expense of organized labor. The 2012 Republican primary witnessed intense struggles between Christian conservatives, businesspersons, and libertarians for the soul of the party.

Courts. Political polarization helps explain the increasingly bitter tone of debates over the staffing of the federal judiciary and executive offices charged with the responsibility for making constitutional decisions. Ideological voting in judicial confirmations began to rise in the late 1960s, but most senators from one party did not routinely vote against every person nominated to the Supreme Court by a president from the other party. By comparison, almost half of all Democratic senators voted against confirming Bush nominee John Roberts as chief justice and more than two-thirds voted against confirming Samuel Alito. Similarly, more than two-thirds of Senate Republicans voted against Obama's two judicial nominees, Sonya Sotomayor and Elena Kagan. Contests over the appointments of lower federal court justices, once unheard of, are be-

3. Matt Grossmann and Casey B. K. Dominguez, "Party Coalitions and Interest Group Networks," *American Politics Research* 37 (2009): 794.

coming routine. Democrats threatened to filibuster President Bush's court of appeals nominees. Republicans responded by threatening to invoke a rare Senate procedure that would eliminate filibusters for judicial nominees. Republican members of the Senate similarly delayed votes on Barack Obama's judicial nominees for the lower federal courts. Debates over the qualifications of any official entrusted with legal responsibilities are common. Both Republicans and Democrats routinely scrutinize the qualifications and ideology of the attorney general and members of the Justice Department and the Office of Legal Counsel. The staffing of state courts is equally as controversial. Concerns over civil rights and liberties explain why state judicial elections, which once drew less attention in the United States than the average program on a local cable channel, now often become heated contests over gay marriage, capital punishment, and campaign spending.

The division among Supreme Court justices on numerous constitutional issues reflects the polarization of the polity at large, with one very important institutional exception. Justices Souter, Stevens, Ginsburg, and Breyer consistently adopt the more liberal position. Chief Justice Rehnquist, Justice Scalia, and Justice Thomas consistently take the more conservative position. Chief Justice John Roberts and Justice Samuel Alito, who replaced Rehnquist and O'Connor, are reliable conservative voters on most civil liberties issues. Justices Sonya Sotomayor and Elena Kagan, who replaced Justices Souter and Stevens, are reliable liberals. This has left the outcome of almost all politically salient civil liberties cases in the hands of Justices O'Connor and Kennedy, and after Justice O'Connor left the bench in 2005, solely in the hands of Justice Kennedy. Significantly, because justices on the Supreme Court cannot prevent decisions by filibusters or hold up decisions in committee, the two centrist justices on the late Rehnquist and early Roberts Courts probably exercise more power than does the median senator or representative. At the very least, Kennedy and O'Connor's votes have determined which party wins a case. O'Connor in particular often wrote crucial concurring opinions that reached constitutional middle grounds on the basis of distinctions that seven, and sometimes eight, members of the Court maintained were constitutionally indefensible.

These divisions between the liberal, conservative, and centrist judges help explain why, for the first time in history, Americans are experiencing judicial activism in both conservative and liberal directions. As one law professor notes,

> We have a Supreme Court that engages in unparalleled activism—from the left and the right simultaneously! When Justices O'Connor and Kennedy are in their conservative mode, affirmative action, minority voting districts, hate speech regulations, and environmental land use restrictions are all constitutionally suspect, notwithstanding the absence of convincing originalist arguments against them. When these pivotal Justices are in their liberal mode, abortion restrictions, school prayer, restrictions on gay rights, exclusion of women from VMI, and limitations on the right to die fall victim to the Court's constitutional axe.[4]

Most commentators have difficulty discerning any reason to this pattern, other than a general commitment to judicial activism on the part of all members of the federal bench. Thomas Keck points out, "Supreme Court Justices appointed by Republican presidents have been no more restrained than those appointed by Democrats. They exercise judicial review just as frequently, and they are no more reluctant to enter political thickets."[5] One might note a slight drift toward libertarianism. Justice Kennedy, whose appointment came only after Senate Democrats fought a bitter battle against President Reagan's more conservative appointee Robert Bork, is particularly inclined to take libertarian positions on flag burning, campaign finance reform, gun rights, and gay rights. Still, the drift is slight when compared to the constitutional politics at the turn of the twentieth century or during the New Deal. On some issues, gun rights and gay rights being good examples, clear conservative and liberal trends, respectively, are emerging. On others ranging from abortion to affirmative action, both the justices on the Supreme Court and elected officials in the national government seem locked in a constitutional trench warfare in which each side expends great resources for very little gain.

---

4. Michael J. Klarman, "Majoritarian Judicial Review: The Entrenchment Problem," *Georgetown Law Journal* 85 (1997): 548.

5. Thomas M. Keck, *The Most Activist Supreme Court in History: The Road to Modern Judicial Conservatism* (Chicago: University of Chicago Press, 2004), 286.

Box 11-1 A Partial Cast of Characters of the Contemporary Era

Ruth Bader Ginsburg	■ Democrat ■ Moderate liberal ■ Co-founded the *Women's Rights Law Reporter*, the first law journal in the U.S. to focus on women's rights (1970), and co-authored the first law school casebook on sex discrimination ■ First woman to receive tenure at Columbia University Law School (1972) ■ Co-founded the Women's Rights Project at the ACLU (1972); ACLU's general counsel (1973) ■ Argued several landmark Supreme Court cases, including *Reed v. Reed* (1971) and *Frontiero v. Richardson* (1973) ■ Appointed by Jimmy Carter to federal circuit court (1980-1993) ■ Appointed by Bill Clinton to U.S. Supreme Court (1993-present) ■ A reliable member of the Court's liberal wing, demonstrating consistent support for abortion rights, sexual equality, and affirmative action
Anthony Kennedy	■ Republican ■ Moderate conservative ■ California lawyer and lobbyist ■ Appointed by Gerald Ford to federal circuit court (1975–88) ■ Appointed by Ronald Reagan to U.S. Supreme Court (1988–present) after Robert Bork's nomination failed ■ Became pivotal swing vote on late Rehnquist and Roberts Courts; often votes with conservatives on government powers issues and with liberals on rights and liberties issues
Theodore Olson	■ Republican ■ Lawyer ■ Assistant attorney general in the Reagan administration (1981-1984) ■ Was a party to the Supreme Court case *Morrison v. Olson*, which upheld the constitutionality of the law authorizing creation of so-called "independent counsels" ■ Successfully represented presidential candidate George W. Bush before the Supreme Court during the disputed election in 2000 ■ Solicitor general of the United States in the George W. Bush administration (2001-2004) ■ Joined with David Boies, his opposing counsel in *Bush v. Gore*, to bring a federal lawsuit challenging California's state constitutional amendment banning same-sex marriage (2009-present)
Antonin Scalia	■ Republican ■ Conservative law professor ■ Assistant attorney general and head of the Office of Legal Counsel in the Nixon and Ford administrations (1974–77) ■ Appointed to the D.C. Circuit Court by Ronald Reagan (1982–86) and to the U.S. Supreme Court (1986–present) ■ First Italian-American appointed to the Court ■ An influential leader of the conservative legal movement since the 1970s; since joining the Court a vocal advocate for "originalism" and a proponent of a formalistic approach to the separation of powers

(Continued)

Box 11-1 *(Continued)*

David Souter	■ Republican ■ Moderate New Hampshire prosecutor and judge ■ New Hampshire attorney general (1976–78) and justice on state supreme court (1983–90) ■ Appointed by George H. W. Bush to the federal circuit court (1990) and to the U.S. Supreme Court (1990–2009) ■ Known as a "stealth nominee" with little public record on national or constitutional issues, he was easily confirmed by a Democratic Senate to replace liberal icon William Brennan; emphasizing caution and respect for precedent in his opinions, he soon joined the liberal wing of the Court
Clarence Thomas	■ Republican ■ Conservative lawyer, assistant secretary of education (1981), and director of the Equal Employment Opportunity Commission (1981–90) during the Reagan and Bush administrations ■ Appointed by George H. W. Bush to the D.C. Circuit Court (1990–91) and to the U.S. Supreme Court (1991–present) ■ After a bruising battle in the Senate ended in one of the closest successful confirmation votes in history, Thomas became the second African-American to serve on the Court ■ He soon emerged as one of the most conservative members of the Court and as a strong advocate for a less deferential brand of originalism than that favored by some of the other conservative justices

Constitutional Thought. Neither conservative Republicans nor liberal Democrats bring new ideological weapons to bear on this constitutional trench warfare. Republicans retain constitutional commitments from the Reagan Era. Conservative constitutional commentators insist more strongly than at any previous post–New Deal period that the Constitution be interpreted in light of the original meaning of constitutional provisions. Originalists at the turn of the twenty-first century, however, are more inclined to wield originalism in service of an activist agenda than the previous generation of originalists, who were more committed to judicial deference to elected officials.[6] Democrats retain their constitutional commitments from the New Deal/Great Society Era. Liberal constitutional commentators either insist on a living Constitution or devise an originalism that requires constitutional interpreters to understand the original meaning of constitutional language in terms of contemporary understandings of the principles laid down in 1791 or 1868.[7] Some liberals advance a popular constitutionalism rooted in a greater constitutional role for elected officials.[8] Whether popular constitutionalism is a good-faith position or a reaction to increased conservative control of the federal courts is a fair question. "A broad generalization, inaccurate only at the margins," one skeptic maintains, "is that nearly every constitutional theorist urges minimal judicial review and vigorous democratic dialogue on issues on which the theorist believes her preferred position is likely to prevail in the democratic dialogue and more-than-minimal review on issues on which the theorist believes her preferred position is unlikely to prevail there."[9]

6. See Keith E. Whittington, "The New Originalism," *Georgetown Journal of Law and Policy* 2 (2004): 599.

7. See Jack M. Balkin, *Living Originalism* (Cambridge, MA: Harvard University Press, 2011).

8. See Larry D. Kramer, *The People Themselves: Popular Constitutionalism and Judicial Review* (Oxford: Oxford University Press, 2005).

9. Mark Tushnet, "Policy Distortion and Democratic Debilitation: Comparative Illumination of the Countermajoritarian Difficulty," *Michigan Law Review* 94 (1995): 245n4.

Legacies. Determining the legacy of constitutional politics over the last twenty years is impossible. We cannot even determine whether Americans are locked in an enduring era of polarized politics or whether a new constitutional regime is dawning. Many liberals hope that the elections of 2006 and 2008 mark a new constitutional era, one that will be characterized by far more progressive constitutional commitments than has recently been the case. Republicans hope that 2010 marks either a return to power of the previous Republican coalition or, perhaps, a new and more conservative constitutional regime. It will not be known for some time whether recent elections were the beginning of a new progressive era, mark no change from the increased polarization of American politics that began in the late 1960s, or are merely a short-term deviation from the period of conservative Republican hegemony that began with the election of George W. Bush in 2000.

II. Foundations

MAJOR DEVELOPMENTS

- Sharp partisan disagreement on the meaning of almost all constitutional protections for civil liberties
- Judicial protection for detainees at Guantanamo Bay in Cuba
- Incorporation of the Second Amendment

Contemporary constitutional struggles over the foundations of civil liberties are structured by unprecedented agreements that a strong judiciary should protect constitutional rights and unprecedented partisan disagreements over the sources, underlying principles, and scope of the constitutional rights the judiciary should protect. Almost all Americans presently support aggressive use of the judicial power to declare laws unconstitutional, while as aggressively disputing how justices should wield that authority. Liberal Democrats want courts to protect abortion rights and strike down laws that permit government money to flow to private religious schools. Conservative Republicans want courts to protect property rights and declare gun control laws unconstitutional. Neither the Democratic nor Republican Party, nor any justice on the Supreme Court, champions judicial restraint across a wide range of rights issues. The voting blocs on the Supreme Court and in Congress on such matters of high political salience as abortion, gun control, and capital punishment are frequently the same.

Never before in American history have both political parties and the Supreme Court been so divided on such a wide variety of rights and liberties issues. Should either Republicans or Democrats gain more permanent control of the national government, or should either liberals or conservatives gain decisive control over the federal judiciary, the consequences for the sources, underlying principles, and scope and substance of constitutional rights are likely to be significant.

A. Sources

Struggles over the sources of constitutional rights moved to different arenas. Disputes over constitutional amendments moved from the national government to the states. Social conservatives responded to liberal state court decisions declaring a constitutional right to same-sex marriage by proposing and, in many states, ratifying state constitutional amendments that restricted marriage to heterosexual couples. New disputes broke out over the constitutional status of constitutional decisions in other countries. Conservatives concerned with Supreme Court opinions in gay rights and capital punishment cases that cited foreign sources demanded that constitutional rights be based exclusively on distinctively American sources. International law provided another site for conservative and liberal disagreements over the proper sources for rights and liberties, as liberals advocated various legal doctrines that required judicial protection for certain rights set out in several international human rights agreements.

Constitutions and Amendments

Passions for federal constitutional amendments protecting or limiting civil liberties have cooled. Political parties and movements in a polarized era face near-insuperable difficulties obtaining the supermajorities necessary for ratifying formal constitutional changes. Most Republicans, Democrats, conservatives, and liberals are convinced that the civil liberties provisions of the Constitution do not need amending. All that is necessary for virtue to triumph is five Supreme Court justices who will interpret the Constitution correctly. These partisan disputes over the best interpretation of constitutional rights help explain why struggles over judicial nominations (discussed in Vol. I) now evoke passions once evoked by efforts to pass a constitutional amendment enfranchising woman or prohibiting abortion.

Political activists promoting constitutional amendments turned to the states after the Supreme Judicial Court of Massachusetts in *Goodridge v. Department of Public Health* (MA 2004) declared that bans on same-sex marriage violated the state constitution. Their efforts were often successful, in part because all state constitutions are easier to amend than the federal constitution. More than half the states ratified constitutional amendments limiting marriage to one man and one woman. Many of these amendments were ratified by overwhelming majorities. Utah voters in 2004 passed a constitutional amendment declaring, "Marriage consists only of the legal union between a man and a woman. No other domestic union, however denominated, may be recognized as a marriage or given the same or substantially equivalent legal effect."[10] Florida in 2008 adopted a constitutional amendment declaring, "Inasmuch as marriage is the legal union of one man and one woman as husband and wife, no other legal union that is treated as marriage or the substantial equivalent thereof shall be valid or recognized."[11] Some observers believe that by increasing conservative turnout in the 2004 national election, proposed constitutional amendments banning same-sex marriage explain why George Bush defeated John Kerry in crucial states.

Comparative Constitutional Law

The constitutional status of comparative constitutional law is a bone of contention among some justices and many constitutional commentators. Justice Kennedy ignited the contemporary debate over the place of comparative constitutionalism in American law when in *Lawrence v. Texas* (2003) he commented on European constitutional decisions striking down bans on sodomy. The majority opinions in *Bowers v. Hardwick* (1986) pointed to the universal condemnation of homosexual behavior when sustaining a Georgia ban on such conduct. Kennedy looked abroad to refute that claim. "Almost five years before *Bowers* was decided," he wrote,

> the European Court of Human Rights considered a case with parallels to *Bowers* and to today's case. An adult male resident in Northern Ireland alleged he was a practicing homosexual who desired to engage in consensual homosexual conduct. . . . The court held that the laws proscribing the conduct were invalid under the European Convention on Human Rights. . . . Authoritative in all countries that are members of the Council of Europe (21 nations then, 45 nations now), the decision is at odds with the premise in *Bowers* that the claim put forward was insubstantial in our Western civilization.

While this passage might be read as merely refuting claims that *Bowers* was consistent with universal practice, Kennedy sometimes uses comparative constitutional practice as evidence of the contemporary standards that he believes are relevant to interpreting such provisions as the "cruel and unusual punishment" clause of the Eighth Amendment. When ruling in *Roper v. Simmons* (2005) that states could not constitutionally execute persons whose crimes were committed before they turned eighteen, he stated,

> Our determination that the death penalty is disproportionate punishment for offenders under 18 finds confirmation in the stark reality that the United States is the only country in the world that continues to give official sanction to the juvenile death penalty. This reality does not become controlling, for the task of interpreting the Eighth Amendment remains our responsibility. Yet at least from the time of the Court's decision in *Trop*, the Court has referred to the laws of other countries and to international authorities as instructive for its interpretation of the Eighth Amendment's prohibition of "cruel and unusual punishments."

Justice Scalia vehemently objected to this use of comparative sources. His dissent in *Roper* declared, "The basic premise of the Court's argument—that American law should conform to the laws of the rest of the world—ought to be rejected out of hand." In his view, "It is beyond comprehension why we should look" for American "standards of decency" to countries with "a legal, political, and social culture quite different from our own."

The Law of Nations

The constitutional status of customary international law remains contested. Many prominent conserva-

10. Utah Const., Art. I, sec. 29 (2004).
11. Florida Const., Art. I, sec 27 (2008).

tives maintain that giving the law of nations any independent legal status violates popular sovereignty. Curtis Bradley and Jack Goldsmith declare, "The modern position that CIL [customary international law] is federal common law is in tension with basic notions of American representative democracy." This tension exists because "when a federal court applies CIL as federal common law, it is not applying law generated by U.S. lawmaking processes. Rather, it is applying law derived from the views and practices of the international community."[12] Prominent liberals who defend the independent legal status of customary international law emphasize American participation and leadership in the international human rights regime. "The capacity of federal courts to incorporate customary international law into federal law," Harold Koh insists, "is absolutely critical to maintaining the coherence of federal law in areas of international concern." Otherwise, state governments would have "no domestic legal obligation to obey customary norms against genocide" in the absence of a treaty explicitly declaring those norms to be binding law."[13]

The Supreme Court limited treaties as a source of rights. The issue in *Sanchez-Llamas v. Oregon* (2006) was whether confessions obtained in violation of the Vienna Convention on Consular Relations could be admitted into evidence in a criminal trial. Article 36 of that treaty grants any foreign national detained by the police a right to have the consular post of his country informed. A 6-3 judicial majority ruled that no suppression was required when state police officers failed to fulfill American treaty obligations. Chief Justice Roberts declared, "The failure to inform a defendant of his Article 36 rights is unlikely, with any frequency, to produce unreliable confessions." The justices further ruled that persons who failed to make Article 36 claims at trial could not raise those claims in a habeas corpus appeal, even though the International Court of Justice (ICJ) had ruled that American procedural default rules could not be used to prevent adjudication of rights protected by the Vienna Convention. "Nothing in the structure or purpose of the ICJ," Roberts stated, "suggests that its interpretations were intended to be conclusive on our courts."

B. Principles

Contemporary Americans are governed by three constitutions: the constitution of liberal Democrats, the constitution of conservative Republicans, and the muddled set of constitutional rules that result in most cases when neither political faction has the power necessary to make its constitutional vision the official law of the land. H. W. Perry and Lucas Powe in 2004 described the contemporary battle over constitutional principle as follows:

> The Republicans have frozen their constitution at *Brown*. It is the bygone world of small-town America, with the decided improvement that racial discrimination is prohibited. Religion can be a part of the schools, abortion may be criminalized, and police practices are largely invisible to judicial scrutiny. Courts know their subordinate place and stay there, though activism may be required to get back to the right status quo.
>
> By contrast, the rights-oriented Democratic position requires a return to the Warren Court and a judiciary actively willing to place certain values into the Constitution because that is what right-thinkingpeople would have in a good constitution. Democrats look to a Court with the immodesty of Antonin Scalia and the jurisprudence of William J. Brennan. The "Great Court" is then coupled with an unacknowledged hostility to elections. Whatever their rhetoric about facilitating voting and voters, Democrats are unwilling to let elections decide the federal or state policies on affirmative action, criminal justice, abortion, and religion.
>
> At least compared to the Republican and the Democratic visions, the Court's doctrines look like bipartisanship personified. The Warren Court's legendary criminal procedure decisions still stand, but not for all they were worth. Affirmative action has been tamed rather than eliminated (or left to run riot). Women retain their right to an abortion, but the public need not fund it, and children need parents. State sponsored prayer is unconstitutional, but it has been almost a generation since the last funding program was struck down on establishment clause grounds. Not all the Court's positions

12. Curtis A. Bradley and Jack L. Goldsmith, "Customary International Law and Federal Common Law: A Critique of the Modern Position," *Harvard Law Review* 110 (1997): 857.

13. Harold Hongju Koh, "Is International Law Really State Law?" *Harvard Law Review* 111 (1998): 1840.

have been popular, but its middle ground may approximate public attitudes better than either of the two parties.[14]

These three constitutions are still engaged in what almost seems like a death struggle. The only major change that occurred in the past decade is that, inspired by a more conservative judiciary, conservative Republicans have become more enamored and liberal Democrats less enamored of judicial activism.

Two organizations, the Federalist Society and the American Constitutional Society, are crucial players in the contemporary battle over constitutional principle. The Federalist Society caters to conservatives and libertarians. Its mission statement declares,

> Law schools and the legal profession are currently strongly dominated by a form of orthodox liberal ideology which advocates a centralized and uniform society. While some members of the academic community have dissented from these views, by and large they are taught simultaneously with (and indeed as if they were) the law.
>
> The Federalist Society for Law and Public Policy Studies is a group of conservatives and libertarians interested in the current state of the legal order. It is founded on the principles that the state exists to preserve freedom, that the separation of governmental powers is central to our Constitution, and that it is emphatically the province and duty of the judiciary to say what the law is, not what it should be. The Society seeks both to promote an awareness of these principles and to further their application through its activities.
>
> This entails reordering priorities within the legal system to place a premium on individual liberty, traditional values, and the rule of law. It also requires restoring the recognition of the importance of these norms among lawyers, judges, law students and professors. In working to achieve these goals, the Society has created a conservative and libertarian intellectual network that extends to all levels of the legal community.[15]

Most prominent conservative law professors either belong to the Federalist Society or frequently speak at its meetings. Numerous Bush administration officials and judicial appointees have Federalist Society backgrounds.

The less effective American Constitutional Society is the organization of choice for liberal constitutional thinkers, particularly those with judicial ambitions. While less established and prominent than the Federalist Society, many members of the Obama Justice Department and Obama judicial appointees have American Constitutional Society connections. The mission statement of that organization declares:

> The American Constitution Society (ACS) believes that law should be a force to improve the lives of all people. ACS works for positive change by shaping debate on vitally important legal and constitutional issues through development and promotion of high-impact ideas to opinion leaders and the media; by building networks of lawyers, law students, judges and policymakers dedicated to those ideas; and by countering the activist conservative legal movement that has sought to erode our enduring constitutional values. By bringing together powerful, relevant ideas and passionate, talented people, ACS makes a difference in the constitutional, legal and public policy debates that shape our democracy.
>
> *Shaping Debate.* The American Constitution Society brings together many of the country's best legal minds to articulate a progressive vision of our Constitution and laws. Through its public programs (over 1,100 debates, conferences and press briefings across America each year), publications, and active on-line presence, ACS generates "intellectual capital" for ready use by progressive allies and shapes debates on key legal and public policy issues.
>
> The American Constitution Society is also debunking conservative buzzwords such as "originalism" and "strict construction" that use neutral-sounding language but all too often lead to conservative policy outcomes. Using both traditional and new media to communicate with policymakers, judges, lawyers and the public at large, ACS presents a compelling vision of core constitutional values such as genuine equality, liberty, justice and the rule of law.[16]

14. H. W. Perry, Jr., and L. A. Powe, Jr., "The Political Battle for the Constitution," *Constitutional Commentary* 21 (2004): 688–89.

15. The Federalist Society, "About Us," http://www.fed-soc.org/aboutus/.

16. American Constitution Society, "About ACS," http://www.acslaw.org/about.

Other organizations concerned with broad issues of constitutional principle exist, but they do not command the membership or influence of either the Federalist Society or the American Constitutional Society. In the polarized constitutional politics of the Contemporary Era, the general view is that you are either with us or against us.

C. Scope

Contemporary Americans experience polarization with a slight twist when they consider the scope of constitutional protection for civil liberties. The same sharp liberal and conservative divides that occur on other constitutional issues take place during debates over incorporation, state action, and the extraterritorial scope of the constitutional provisions protecting civil liberties. Justices O'Connor and Kennedy cast swing votes when these issues came before the Supreme Court. Unsurprisingly, liberals are more inclined than conservatives to find state action and insist that federal officials respect constitutional norms when acting outside the United States. In sharp contrast to the debates over incorporation that took place during the twentieth century, however, twenty-first-century conservatives are far more enthusiastic than twenty-first-century liberals when requiring state officials to respect the provisions of the Bill of Rights.

Liberals won the most important state action case decided in recent years. In *Brentwood Academy v. Tennessee Secondary School Athletic Association* (2001) a 5-4 majority found a high school athletic board to be a state actor when the overwhelming majority of participants were public school employees. Justice Souter's majority opinion declared, "The nominally private character of the Association is overborne by the pervasive entwinement of public institutions and public officials in its composition and workings." Liberals successfully convinced the Supreme Court to require federal officials acting outside the territory of the United States to respect constitutional norms when their actions took place in a location where the United States was exercising de facto sovereignty. In *Boumediene v. Bush* (2008) a 5-4 Supreme Court majority ruled that persons detained in Guantanamo Bay could petition federal courts for habeas corpus. Justice Kennedy's majority opinion emphasized that the United States was the de facto sovereign over the territory, even if not the de jure sovereign. He observed, "By surrendering formal sovereignty over any unincorporated territory to a third party, while at the same time entering into a lease that grants total control over the territory back to the United States, it would be possible for the political branches to govern without legal constraint."

McDonald v. City of Chicago (2010) was the most interesting and consequential recent case on the scope of constitutional protections for civil liberties. The 5-4 majority in that case ruled that the due process clause of the Fourteenth Amendment incorporated the Second Amendment. State officials, *McDonald* held, had to respect the same gun rights as federal officials did. Political actors on and off the court abandoned their previous attitudes toward incorporation when considering the incorporation of the Second Amendment. Conservatives, who had once regarded incorporation as an assault against federalism, championed *McDonald*'s sharp restrictions on states. Justice Alito's majority opinion declared, "Incorporated Bill of Rights protections are all to be enforced against the States under the Fourteenth Amendment according to the same standards that protect those personal rights against federal encroachment." Liberals in *McDonald* harkened back to doctrines previously championed byconservative opponents of incorporation. Justice Stevens in dissent stated, "The rights protected against state infringement by the Fourteenth Amendment's Due Process Clause need not be identical in shape or scope to the rights protected against Federal Government infringement by the various provisions of the Bill of Rights."

Think about this role reversal when reading the materials in this subsection. What explains the conservative embrace and liberal retreat from a broad understanding of incorporation? Under what conditions might similar developments occur with respect to state action or the extraterritorial application of the Constitution?

Incorporation

McDonald v. City of Chicago, 130 S. Ct. 3020 (2010)

Otis McDonald was an elderly community activist in Chicago who wished to keep a handgun in his house for protection against local drug dealers. Chicago law prohibited most persons from keeping a handgun in their home. In 2008 the Supreme Court in District of Columbia v. Heller *ruled that the Second Amendment protected an individual right to keep guns for self-defense and not merely a collective right connected to the state militia. McDonald and others immediately filed suit against Chicago. They claimed that the Chicago ban on handguns violated the Fourteenth Amendment, which, in their view, incorporated the Second Amendment. Relying heavily on recent scholarship, lawyers for McDonald and the NRA urged the court to reverse the holding in the* Slaughter-House Cases *(1873) and hold that the privileges and immunities clause of the Fourteenth Amendment incorporated the Bill of Rights. Both the local federal district court and the Court of Appeals for the Seventh Circuit rejected McDonald's lawsuit on the ground that the Fourteenth Amendment did not incorporate the Second Amendment right to bear arms. McDonald appealed to the Supreme Court of the United States.*

The Supreme Court in McDonald *ruled that the due process clause of the Fourteenth Amendment incorporated the Second Amendment. This was the first provision of the Bill of Rights to be selectively incorporated since the Supreme Court in* Benton v. Maryland *(1969) incorporated the double jeopardy clause of the Fifth Amendment. Justice Alito's majority opinion maintained that the right to bear arms was a fundamental right that state officials could not violate. The vote in* McDonald *was identical to the vote in* Heller *(see Section IIIC). To what extent does* McDonald *replay* Heller*? If you believe that* Heller *was correctly decided, then is* McDonald *also correctly decided? Notice how broadly conservatives interpret incorporation and how narrowly liberals interpret it. Did both sides flip from earlier positions? What is the significance of those flips? Justice Thomas insists that the privileges and immunities clause is the correct hook for incorporation. Why does he make that claim? Why do the justices reject that hook? What difference might a reliance on privileges and immunities make? Prominent professors submitted amicus briefs on both sides of* McDonald*. Do the various judicial opinions acknowledge disagreement among historians? How does that disagreement influence their analysis?*

JUSTICE ALITO announced the judgment of the Court

. . . We have previously held that most of the provisions of the Bill of Rights apply with full force to both the Federal Government and the States. Applying the standard that is well established in our case law, we hold that the Second Amendment right is fully applicable to the States.

. . .

Petitioners argue . . . that we should overrule [such decisions as *Slaughterhouse* (1873)] and hold that the right to keep and bear arms is one of the "privileges or immunities of citizens of the United States.". . .

We see no need to reconsider that interpretation here. For many decades, the question of the rights protected by the Fourteenth Amendment against state infringement has been analyzed under the Due Process Clause of that Amendment and not under the Privileges or Immunities Clause. We therefore decline to disturb the *Slaughter-House* holding.

. . .

. . . [W]e now turn directly to the question whether the Second Amendment right to keep and bear arms is incorporated in the concept of due process. In answering that question, . . . we must decide whether the right to keep and bear arms is fundamental to our scheme of ordered liberty, . . . or as we have said in a related context, whether this right is "deeply rooted in this Nation's history and tradition." . . .

Our decision in *Heller* (2008) points unmistakably to the answer. Self-defense is a basic right, recognized by many legal systems from ancient times to the present day, and in *Heller*, we held that individual self-defense is "the central component" of the Second Amendment right. . . .

Heller makes it clear that this right is "deeply rooted in this Nation's history and tradition." *Heller* explored the right's origins, noting that the 1689 English Bill of Rights explicitly protected a right to keep arms for self-defense, and that by 1765, Blackstone was able to assert that the right to keep and bear arms was "one of the fundamental rights of Englishmen."

. . .

The right to keep and bear arms was considered no less fundamental by those who drafted and ratified the Bill of Rights. "During the 1788 ratification debates, the fear that the federal government would disarm the people in order to impose rule through a standing army or select militia was pervasive in Antifederalist rhetoric." . . . Federalists responded, not by arguing that the right was insufficiently important to warrant protection but by contending that the right was adequately protected by the Constitution's assignment of only limited powers to the Federal Government. . . . Thus, Antifederalists and Federalists alike agreed that the right to bear arms was fundamental to the newly formed system of government....

...

The Civil Rights Act of 1866 . . . sought to protect the right of all citizens to keep and bear arms. Section 1 of the Civil Rights Act guaranteed the "full and equal benefit of all laws and proceedings for the security of person and property, as is enjoyed by white citizens."... Representative Bingham believed that the Civil Rights Act protected the same rights as enumerated in the Freedmen's Bureau bill, which of course explicitly mentioned the right to keep and bear arms. The unavoidable conclusion is that the Civil Rights Act, like the Freedmen's Bureau Act, aimed to protect "the constitutional right to bear arms" and not simply to prohibit discrimination.

...

Congress, however, ultimately deemed these legislative remedies insufficient. Southern resistance, Presidential vetoes, and this Court's pre-Civil-War precedent persuaded Congress that a constitutional amendment was necessary to provide full protection for the rights of blacks. Today, it is generally accepted that the Fourteenth Amendment was understood to provide a constitutional basis for protecting the rights set out in the Civil Rights Act of 1866....

...

In sum, it is clear that the Framers and ratifiers of the Fourteenth Amendment counted the right to keep and bear arms among those fundamental rights necessary to our system of ordered liberty.

...

... [W]e have never held that a provision of the Bill of Rights applies to the States only if there is a "popular consensus" that the right is fundamental, and we see no basis for such a rule. But in this case, as it turns out, there is evidence of such a consensus. An amicus brief submitted by 58 Members of the Senate and 251 Members of the House of Representatives urges us to hold that the right to keep and bear arms is fundamental. Another brief submitted by 38 States takes the same position.

... [P]etitioners and many others who live in high-crime areas dispute the proposition that the Second Amendment right does not protect minorities and those lacking political clout. . . . If, as petitioners believe, their safety and the safety of other law-abiding members of the community would be enhanced by the possession of handguns in the home for self-defense, then the Second Amendment right protects the rights of minorities and other residents of high-crime areas whose needs are not being met by elected public officials.

...

JUSTICE SCALIA, concurring....

JUSTICE THOMAS, concurring in part and concurring in the judgment.

...

... [T]he right to keep and bear arms is a privilege of American citizenship that applies to the States through the Fourteenth Amendment's Privileges or Immunities Clause.

...

. . . The notion that a constitutional provision that guarantees only "process" before a person is deprived of life, liberty, or property could define the substance of those rights [presently protected by the due process clause] strains credulity for even the most casual user of words. Moreover, this fiction is a particularly dangerous one. The one theme that links the Court's substantive due process precedents together is their lack of a guiding principle to distinguish "fundamental" rights that warrant protection from nonfundamental rights that do not....

...

Section 1 [of the Fourteenth Amendment] protects the rights of citizens "of the United States" specifically. The evidence overwhelmingly demonstrates that the privileges and immunities of such citizens included individual rights enumerated in the Constitution, including the right to keep and bear arms.

...

Commentators of the time explained that the rights and immunities of "citizens of the United States" recognized in [American] treaties "undoubtedly mean[t] those privileges that are common to all citizens of this republic." . . . It is therefore altogether unsurprising that several of these treaties identify liberties enumerated in the Constitution as privileges and immunities common to all United States citizens.

...

. . . Representative John Bingham, the principal draftsman of § 1 [of the Fourteenth Amendment], delivered a speech on the floor of the House in February 1866 introducing his first draft of the provision. Bingham began by discussing *Barron v. Baltimore* (1833) and its holding that the Bill of Rights did not apply to the States. He then argued that a constitutional amendment was necessary to provide "an express grant of power in Congress to enforce by penal enactment these great canons of the supreme law, securing to all the citizens in every State all the privileges and immunities of citizens, and to all the people all the sacred rights of person." . . . Bingham emphasized that § 1 was designed "to arm the Congress of the United States, by the consent of the people of the United States, with the power to enforce the bill of rights as it stands in the Constitution today. It 'hath that extent-no more.'"

. . .

This history confirms what the text of the Privileges or Immunities Clause most naturally suggests: Consistent with its command that "[n]o State shall . . . abridge" the rights of United States citizens, the Clause establishes a minimum baseline of federal rights, and the constitutional right to keep and bear arms plainly was among them.

. . .

JUSTICE STEVENS, dissenting.

. . .

I agree with the plurality's refusal to accept petitioners' primary submission. . . . Their briefs marshal an impressive amount of historical evidence for their argument that the Court interpreted the Privileges or Immunities Clause too narrowly in the *Slaughter-House Cases*. But the original meaning of the Clause is not as clear as they suggest and not nearly as clear as it would need to be to dislodge 137 years of precedent. The burden is severe for those who seek radical change in such an established body of constitutional doctrine. Moreover, the suggestion that invigorating the Privileges or Immunities Clause will reduce judicial discretion, strikes me as implausible, if not exactly backwards. "For the very reason that it has so long remained a clean slate, a revitalized Privileges or Immunities Clause holds special hazards for judges who are mindful that their proper task is not to write their personal views of appropriate public policy into the Constitution."

. . .

. . . [T]he right to possess a firearm of one's choosing is different in kind from the liberty interests we have recognized under the Due Process Clause. Despite the plethora of substantive due process cases that have been decided in the post-*Lochner* (1905) century, I have found none that holds, states, or even suggests that the term "liberty" encompasses either the common-law right of self-defense or a right to keep and bear arms. I do not doubt for a moment that many Americans feel deeply passionate about firearms, and see them as critical to their way of life as well as to their security. Nevertheless, it does not appear to be the case that the ability to own a handgun, or any particular type of firearm, is critical to leading a life of autonomy, dignity, or political equality. . . .

. . .

. . . [T]he Second Amendment differs in kind from the Amendments that surround it, with the consequence that its inclusion in the Bill of Rights is not merely unhelpful but positively harmful to petitioners' claim. Generally, the inclusion of a liberty interest in the Bill of Rights points toward the conclusion that it is of fundamental significance and ought to be enforceable against the States. But the Second Amendment plays a peculiar role within the Bill, as announced by its peculiar opening clause. Even accepting the *Heller* Court's view that the Amendment protects an individual right to keep and bear arms disconnected from militia service, it remains undeniable that "the purpose for which the right was codified" was "to prevent elimination of the militia." . . . It was the States, not private persons, on whose immediate behalf the Second Amendment was adopted. Notwithstanding the *Heller* Court's efforts to write the Second Amendment's preamble out of the Constitution, the Amendment still serves the structural function of protecting the States from encroachment by an overreaching Federal Government.

. . .

. . . [A]lthough it may be true that Americans' interest in firearm possession and state-law recognition of that interest are "deeply rooted" in some important senses, it is equally true that the States have a long and unbroken history of regulating firearms. . . .

. . .

. . . [T]he Court's imposition of a national standard is still more unwise because the elected branches have shown themselves to be perfectly capable of safeguarding the interest in keeping and bearing arms. The strength of a liberty claim must be assessed in connection with its status in the democratic process. And in this case, no one disputes "that opponents of [gun] control have considerable political power and do not seem to be at a systematic disadvantage in the democratic process," or that "the widespread commitment to an individual right to own guns . . . operates as a safeguard against excessive or unjustified gun control laws." . . .

. . .

JUSTICE BREYER, with whom JUSTICE GINSBURG and JUSTICE SOTOMAYOR join, dissenting.

. . .

I think it proper, above all where history provides no clear answer, to look to other factors in considering whether a right is sufficiently "fundamental" to remove it from the political process in every State. I would include among those factors the nature of the right; any contemporary disagreement about whether the right is fundamental; the extent to which incorporation will further other, perhaps more basic, constitutional aims; and the extent to which incorporation will advance or hinder the Constitution's structural aims, including its division of powers among different governmental institutions (and the people as well). Is incorporation needed, for example, to further the Constitution's effort to ensure that the government treats each individual with equal respect? Will it help maintain the democratic form of government that the Constitution foresees? In a word, will incorporation prove consistent, or inconsistent, with the Constitution's efforts to create governmental institutions well suited to the carrying out of its constitutional promises?

. . .

. . . [T]here is no popular consensus that the private self-defense right described in *Heller* is fundamental. . . . One side believes the right essential to protect the lives of those attacked in the home; the other side believes it essential to regulate the right in order to protect the lives of others attacked with guns. It seems unlikely that definitive evidence will develop one way or the other. And the appropriate level of firearm regulation has thus long been, and continues to be, a hotly contested matter of political debate. . . .

Moreover, there is no reason here to believe that incorporation of the private self-defense right will further any other or broader constitutional objective. We are aware of no argument that gun-control regulations target or are passed with the purpose of targeting "discrete and insular minorities." . . . Nor will incorporation help to assure equal respect for individuals. Unlike the First Amendment's rights of free speech, free press, assembly, and petition, the private self-defense right does not comprise a necessary part of the democratic process that the Constitution seeks to establish. . . . Unlike the First Amendment's religious protections, the Fourth Amendment's protection against unreasonable searches and seizures, the Fifth and Sixth Amendments' insistence upon fair criminal procedure, and the Eighth Amendment's protection against cruel and unusual punishments, the private self-defense right does not significantly seek to protect individuals who might otherwise suffer unfair or inhumane treatment at the hands of a majority. . . .

. . .

. . . [T]he incorporation of the right recognized in *Heller* would amount to a significant incursion on a traditional and important area of state concern, altering the constitutional relationship between the States and the Federal Government. Private gun regulation is the quintessential exercise of a State's "police power"—i.e., the power to "protec [t] . . . the lives, limbs, health, comfort, and quiet of all persons, and the protection of all property within the state," by enacting "all kinds of restraints and burdens" on both "persons and property." . . .

In sum, the police power, the superiority of legislative decisionmaking, the need for local decisionmaking, the comparative desirability of democratic decisionmaking, the lack of a manageable judicial standard, and the life-threatening harm that may flow from striking down regulations all argue against incorporation. Where the incorporation of other rights has been at issue, some of these problems have arisen. But in this instance all these problems are present, all at the same time, and all are likely to be present in most, perhaps nearly all, of the cases in which the constitutionality of a gun regulation is at issue. . . .

. . .

. . . [T]he very evidence that [the Court majority] advances in support of the conclusion that Reconstruction-era Americans strongly supported a private self-defense right shows with equal force that Americans wanted African-American citizens to have the same rights to possess guns as did white citizens. Here, for example is what Congress said when it enacted a Fourteenth Amendment predecessor, the Second Freedman's Bureau Act. It wrote that the statute, in order to secure "the constitutional right to bear arms . . . for all citizens," would assure that each citizen: "shall have . . . full and equal benefit of all laws and proceedings concerning personal liberty, personal security, and the acquisition, enjoyment, and disposition of estate, real and personal, including the constitutional right to bear arms, [by securing] . . . to . . . all the citizens of [every] . . . State or district without respect to race or color, or previous condition of slavery." This sounds like an antidiscrimination provision. . . .

. . .

. . . [N]othing in 18th-, 19th-, 20th-, or 21st-century history shows a consensus that the right to private armed self-defense, as described in *Heller*, is "deeply rooted in this Nation's history or tradition" or is otherwise "fundamental." Indeed, incorporating the right recognized in *Heller* may change the law in many of the 50 States. Read in the majority's favor, the historical evidence is at most ambiguous. And, in the absence of any other support for its conclusion, ambiguous history cannot show that the Fourteenth Amendment incorporates a private right of self-defense against the States.

Extraterritoriality

Boumediene v. Bush, 553 U.S. 723 (2008)

Lakhdar Boumediene was born in Algeria and acquired Bosnian citizenship during the 1990s. In 2001 he and five other persons were arrested by the Bosnian police, who suspected them of international terrorism. On January 17 the Supreme Court of Bosnia and Herzegovina ordered them released on the ground that no evidence supported that accusation. That night Bosnian police transferred custody of Boumediene and his alleged confederates to the United States. They were immediately shipped to the detention center in Guantanamo Bay, Cuba. According to their brief, from 2002 to 2008 the six men were subject to the following conditions:

> *They are confined to individual 8′ x 6′ cells consisting of concrete walls and steel mesh. Above each man's steel bunk, a fluorescent light remains on 24 hours a day. Petitioners have been subject to, among other things, up to 15 consecutive months of solitary confinement, sleep deprivation, and extreme temperature conditions. In 2004, for example, rogue soldiers crushed Mr. Ait Idir's face into a gravel courtyard and broke one of his fingers, even though he was restrained and posed no threat. Each Petitioner suffers from serious medical ailments caused or exacerbated by the conditions of his detention.*

Sometime during 2004 each man appeared before a Combatant Status Review Tribunal (CSRT). Each was determined to be an enemy combatant. Each asked for a writ of habeas corpus. Two separate proceedings were held. One federal district judge determined that aliens had no constitutional right to the writ. The other federal district judge determined that aliens had a constitutional right to the writ. Before the appeals could be heard by the federal circuit court, Congress passed the Detainee Treatment Act (DTA), which declared that "no court, justice, or judge shall have jurisdiction to hear or consider . . . an application for a writ of habeas corpus filed by or on behalf of an alien detained by the Department of Defense at Guantanamo Bay, Cuba." The Court of Appeals for the District of Columbia consolidated all cases and determined that the DTA was constitutional. Boumediene and others appealed to the Supreme Court of the United States.

The Supreme Court by a 5-4 vote determined that Congress could not deprive Guantanamo Bay detainees of their right to habeas corpus. Justice Kennedy's majority opinion ruled that aliens being held in areas where Americans had de facto sovereignty had a right to habeas corpus and that Congress had not provided an adequate substitute. Kennedy claims that the majority opinion is supported both by past precedents and by basic constitutional principles. How do the majority and dissent characterize those precedents and principles? Which side has the better argument? When Boumediene *was decided in 2008, support for President Bush and the Iraq War had fallen to new lows. Do you think that the political environment influenced the justices? Would the case have been decided similarly had President Bush enjoyed a 70 percent approval rating?*

JUSTICE KENNEDY delivered the opinion of the Court.

. . .

. . . [T]he parties in these cases have examined historical sources to construct a view of the common-law writ as it existed in 1789. . . . Diligent search by all parties reveals no certain conclusions. In none of the cases cited do we find that a common-law court would or would not have granted, or refused to hear for lack of jurisdiction, a petition for a writ of habeas corpus brought by a prisoner deemed an enemy combatant, under a standard like the one the Department of Defense has used in these cases, and when held in a territory, like Guantanamo, over which the Government has total military and civil control.

. . .

The Government argues . . . that Guantanamo is more closely analogous to Scotland and Hanover, territories that were not part of England but nonetheless controlled by the English monarch (in his separate capacities as King of Scotland and Elector of Hanover). . . . Lord Mansfield can be cited for the proposition that, at the time of the founding, English courts lacked the "power" to issue the writ to Scotland and Hanover, territories Lord Mansfield referred to as "foreign." But what matters for our purposes is why common-law courts lacked this power. Given the English Crown's delicate and complicated relationships with Scotland and Hanover in the 1700's, we cannot disregard the possibility that the common-law courts' refusal to issue the writ to these places was motivated not by formal legal constructs but by what we would think of as prudential concerns. This appears to have been the case with regard to other British territories where the writ did not run. . . .

. . .

We do not question the Government's position that Cuba, not the United States, maintains sovereignty, in the legal and technical sense of the term, over Guantanamo Bay. But this does not end the analysis. Our cases do not hold it is improper for us to inquire into the objective degree of control the Nation asserts over foreign territory. . . . Cuba, and not the United States, retains de jure sovereignty over Guantanamo Bay. . . . [T]he United States, by virtue of its complete jurisdiction and control over the base, maintains de facto sovereignty over this territory. . . .

. . .

True, the Court in [*Johnson v.*] *Eisentrager* (1950) denied access to the writ, and it noted the prisoners "at no relevant time were within any territory over which the United States is sovereign, and [that] the scenes of their offense, their capture, their trial and their punishment were all beyond the territorial jurisdiction of any court of the United States." . . . The Government seizes upon this language as proof positive that the *Eisentrager* Court adopted a formalistic, sovereignty-based test for determining the reach of the Suspension Clause. . . . We reject this reading. . . .

. . .

. . . Nothing in *Eisentrager* says that de jure sovereignty is or has ever been the only relevant consideration in determining the geographic reach of the Constitution or of habeas corpus. Were that the case, there would be considerable tension between *Eisentrager*, on the one hand, and the *Insular Cases* (1901-04) and *Reid* [*v. Covert*] (1957), on the other. . . .

The Government's formal sovereignty-based test raises troubling separation-of-powers concerns as well. . . . [A]lthough it recognized, by entering into the 1903 Lease Agreement, that Cuba retained "ultimate sovereignty" over Guantanamo, the United States continued to maintain the same plenary control it had enjoyed since 1898. Yet the Government's view is that the Constitution had no effect there, at least as to non-citizens, because the United States disclaimed sovereignty in the formal sense of the term. The necessary implication of the argument is that by surrendering formal sovereignty over any unincorporated territory to a third party, while at the same time entering into a lease that grants total control over the territory back to the United States, it would be possible for the political branches to govern without legal constraint.

Our basic charter cannot be contracted away like this. The Constitution grants Congress and the President the power to acquire, dispose of, and govern territory, not the power to decide when and where its terms apply. Even when the United States acts outside its borders, its powers are not "absolute and unlimited" but are subject "to such restrictions as are expressed in the Constitution." . . . Abstaining from questions involving formal sovereignty and territorial governance is one thing. To hold the political branches have the power to switch the Constitution on or off at will is quite another. The former position reflects this Court's recognition that certain matters requiring political judgments are best left to the political branches. The latter would permit a striking anomaly in our tripartite system of government, leading to a regime in which Congress and the President, not this Court, say "what the law is." *Marbury v. Madison* (1803).

. . .

Based on . . . *Eisentrager*, and the reasoning in our other extraterritoriality opinions, we conclude that at least three factors are relevant in determining the reach of the Suspension Clause: (1) the citizenship and status of the detainee and the adequacy of the process through which that status determination was made; (2) the nature of the sites where apprehension and then detention took place; and (3) the practical obstacles inherent in resolving the prisoner's entitlement to the writ.

Applying this framework, we note at the onset that the status of these detainees is a matter of dispute. . . .

As to the second factor relevant to this analysis, the detainees here are similarly situated to the *Eisentrager* petitioners in that the sites of their apprehension and detention are technically outside the sovereign territory of the United States. As noted earlier, this is a factor that weighs against finding they have rights under the Suspension Clause. But there are critical differences between Landsberg Prison, circa 1950, and the United States Naval Station at Guantanamo Bay in 2008. Unlike its present control over the naval station, the United States' control over the prison in Germany was neither absolute nor indefinite. Like all parts of occupied Germany, the prison was under the jurisdiction of the combined Allied Forces. . . .

As to the third factor, . . . [t]he Government presents no credible arguments that the military mission at Guantanamo would be compromised if habeas corpus courts had jurisdiction to hear the detainees' claims. And in light of the plenary control the United States asserts over the base, none are apparent to us.

. . .

We hold that Art. I, § 9, cl. 2, of the Constitution has full effect at Guantanamo Bay. If the privilege of habeas corpus is to be denied to the detainees now before us, Congress must act in accordance with the requirements of the Suspension Clause. . . .

In light of this holding the question becomes whether the statute stripping jurisdiction to issue the writ avoids the Suspension Clause mandate because Congress has provided adequate substitute procedures for habeas corpus. . . .

. . .

. . . [T]he privilege of habeas corpus entitles the prisoner to a meaningful opportunity to demonstrate that he is being held pursuant to "the erroneous application or interpretation" of relevant law. . . . And the habeas court must have the power to order the conditional release of an individual unlawfully detained—though release need not be the exclusive remedy and is not the appropriate one in every case in which the writ is granted. . . .

. . .

Petitioners identify what they see as myriad deficiencies in the CSRTs. The most relevant for our purposes are the constraints upon the detainee's ability to rebut the factual basis for the Government's assertion that he is an enemy combatant. . . . He does not have the assistance of counsel and may not be aware of the most critical allegations that the Government relied upon to order his detention. . . . The detainee can confront witnesses that testify during the CSRT proceedings. But given that there are in effect no limits on the admission of hearsay evidence—the only requirement is that the tribunal deem the evidence "relevant and helpful,". . .—the detainee's opportunity to question witnesses is likely to be more theoretical than real.

. . .

Although we make no judgment as to whether the CSRTs, as currently constituted, satisfy due process standards, we agree with petitioners that, even when all the parties involved in this process act with diligence and in good faith, there is considerable risk of error in the tribunal's findings of fact. . . . And given that the consequence of error may be detention of persons for the duration of hostilities that may last a generation or more, this is a risk too significant to ignore.

. . .

Although we hold that the DTA is not an adequate and effective substitute for habeas corpus, it does not follow that a habeas corpus court may disregard the dangers the detention in these cases was intended to prevent. . . . [T]he Suspension Clause does not resist innovation in the field of habeas corpus. Certain accommodations can be made to reduce the burden habeas corpus proceedings will place on the military without impermissibly diluting the protections of the writ.

. . .

Our opinion does not undermine the Executive's powers as Commander in Chief. On the contrary, the exercise of those powers is vindicated, not eroded, when confirmed by the Judicial Branch. Within the Constitution's separation-of-powers structure, few exercises of judicial power are as legitimate or as necessary as the responsibility to hear challenges to the authority of the Executive to imprison a person. Some of these petitioners have been in custody for six years with no definitive judicial determination as to the legality of their detention. Their access to the writ is a necessity to determine the lawfulness of their status, even if, in the end, they do not obtain the relief they seek.

. . .

It bears repeating that our opinion does not address the content of the law that governs petitioners' detention. That is a matter yet to be determined. We hold that petitioners may invoke the fundamental procedural protections of habeas corpus. The laws and Constitution are designed to survive, and remain in force, in extraordinary times. Liberty and security can be reconciled; and in our system they are reconciled within the framework of the law. The Framers decided that habeas corpus, a right of first importance, must be a part of that framework, a part of that law.

. . .

JUSTICE SOUTER, with whom JUSTICE GINSBURG and JUSTICE BREYER join, concurring.

. . .

A . . . fact insufficiently appreciated by the dissents is the length of the disputed imprisonments, some of the prisoners represented here today having been locked up for six years. . . . Hence the hollow ring when the dissenters suggest that the Court is somehow precipitating the judiciary into reviewing claims that the military (subject to appeal to the Court of Appeals for the District of Columbia Circuit) could handle within some reasonable period of time. . . .

. . .

CHIEF JUSTICE ROBERTS, with whom JUSTICE SCALIA, JUSTICE THOMAS, and JUSTICE ALITO join, dissenting.

. . .

I believe the system the political branches constructed adequately protects any constitutional rights aliens captured abroad and detained as enemy combatants may enjoy. I therefore would dismiss these cases on that ground. With all respect for the contrary views of the majority, I must dissent.

. . .

. . . Step back and consider what, in the real world, Congress and the Executive have actually granted aliens captured by our Armed Forces overseas and found to be enemy combatants:

- The right to hear the bases of the charges against them, including a summary of any classified evidence.
- The ability to challenge the bases of their detention before military tribunals modeled after Geneva Convention procedures. Some 38 detainees have been released as a result of this process. . . .
- The right, before the CSRT, to testify, introduce evidence, call witnesses, question those the Government calls, and secure release, if and when appropriate.
- The right to the aid of a personal representative in arranging and presenting their cases before a CSRT.
- Before the D.C. Circuit, the right to employ counsel, challenge the factual record, contest the lower tribunal's legal determinations, ensure compliance with the Constitution and laws, and secure release, if any errors below establish their entitlement to such relief.

In sum, the DTA satisfies the majority's own criteria for assessing adequacy. This statutory scheme provides the combatants held at Guantanamo greater procedural protections than have ever been afforded alleged enemy detainees—whether citizens or aliens—in our national history.

. . .

JUSTICE SCALIA, with whom THE CHIEF JUSTICE, JUSTICE THOMAS, and JUSTICE ALITO join, dissenting.

. . . The writ of habeas corpus does not, and never has, run in favor of aliens abroad; the Suspension Clause thus has no application, and the Court's intervention in this military matter is entirely ultra vires.

. . .

. . . A mere two Terms ago in *Hamdan v. Rumsfeld* (2006) . . . when the Court held (quite amazingly) that the Detainee Treatment Act of 2005 had not stripped habeas jurisdiction over Guantanamo petitioners' claims, four Members of today's five-Justice majority joined an opinion saying the following: "Nothing prevents the President from returning to Congress to seek the authority [for trial by military commission] he believes necessary. . . ." Turns out they were just kidding. For in response, Congress, at the President's request, quickly enacted the Military Commissions Act, emphatically reasserting that it did not want these prisoners filing habeas petitions. It is therefore clear that Congress and the Executive—both political branches—have determined that limiting the role of civilian courts in adjudicating whether prisoners captured abroad are properly detained is important to success in the war that some 190,000 of our men and women are now fighting. . . .

But it does not matter. The Court today decrees that no good reason to accept the judgment of the other two branches is "apparent." . . . "The Government," it declares, "presents no credible arguments that the military mission at Guantanamo would be compromised if habeas corpus courts had jurisdiction to hear the detainees' claims." . . . What competence does the Court have to second-guess the judgment of Congress and the President on such a point? None whatever. But the Court blunders in nonetheless. Henceforth, as today's opinion makes unnervingly clear, how to handle enemy prisoners in this war will ultimately lie with the branch that knows least about the national security concerns that the subject entails.

. . .

The Court would have us believe that *Eisentrager* rested on "[p]ractical considerations," such as the "difficulties of ordering the Government to produce the prisoners in a habeas corpus proceeding." . . . Formal sovereignty, says the Court, is merely one consideration "that bears upon which constitutional guarantees apply" in a given location. . . . This is a sheer rewriting of the case. *Eisentrager* mentioned practical concerns, to be sure—but not for the purpose of determining under what circumstances American courts could issue writs of habeas corpus for aliens abroad. It cited them to support its holding that the Constitution does not empower courts to issue writs of habeas corpus to aliens abroad in any circumstances.

. . .

The category of prisoner comparable to these detainees are not the *Eisentrager* criminal defendants, but the more than 400,000 prisoners of war detained in the United States alone during World War II. Not a single one was accorded the right to have his detention validated by a habeas corpus action in federal court—and that despite the fact that they were present on U.S. soil. . . . The Court's analysis produces a crazy result: Whereas those convicted and sentenced to death for war crimes are without judicial remedy, all enemy combatants detained during a war, at least insofar as they are confined in an area away from the battlefield over which the United States exercises "absolute and indefinite" control, may seek a writ of habeas corpus in federal court. And, as an even more bizarre implication from the Court's reasoning, those prisoners whom the military plans to try by full-dress Commission at a future date may file habeas petitions and secure release before their trials take place.

. . .

What drives today's decision is neither the meaning of the Suspension Clause, nor the principles of our precedents, but rather an inflated notion of judicial supremacy. The Court says that if the extraterritorial applicability of the Suspension Clause turned on formal notions of sovereignty, "it would be possible for the political branches to govern without legal constraint" in areas beyond the sovereign territory of the United States. . . . That cannot be, the Court says, because it is the duty of this Court to say what the law is. . . . It would be difficult to imagine a more question-begging analysis. "The very foundation of the power of the federal courts to declare Acts of Congress unconstitutional lies in the power and duty of those courts to decide cases and controversies properly before them." . . . Our power "to say what the law is" is circumscribed by the limits of our statutorily and constitutionally conferred jurisdiction. . . . And that is precisely the question in these cases: whether the Constitution confers habeas jurisdiction on federal courts to decide petitioners' claims. It is both irrational and arrogant to say that the answer must be yes, because otherwise we would not be supreme.

. . .

It is entirely clear that, at English common law, the writ of habeas corpus did not extend beyond the sovereign territory of the Crown. To be sure, the writ had an "extraordinary territorial ambit," because it was a so-called "prerogative writ," which, unlike other writs, could extend beyond the realm of England to other places where the Crown was sovereign. . . .

But prerogative writs could not issue to foreign countries, even for British subjects; they were confined to the King's dominions—those areas over which the Crown was sovereign. . . . Thus, the writ has never extended to Scotland, which, although united to England when James I succeeded to the English throne in 1603, was considered a foreign dominion under a different Crown—that of the King of Scotland. . . .

. . .

The Court dismisses the example of Scotland on the grounds that Scotland had its own judicial system and that the writ could not, as a practical matter, have been enforced there. . . . Those explanations are totally unpersuasive. The existence of a separate court system was never a basis for denying the power of a court to issue the writ. . . . And as for logistical problems, the same difficulties were present for places like the Channel Islands, where the writ did run. . . .

. . .

Today the Court warps our Constitution in a way that goes beyond the narrow issue of the reach of the Suspension Clause, invoking judicially brainstormed separation-of-powers principles to establish a manipulable "functional" test for the extraterritorial reach of habeas corpus (and, no doubt, for the extraterritorial reach of other constitutional protections as well). It blatantly misdescribes important precedents, most conspicuously Justice Jackson's opinion for the Court in *Johnson v. Eisentrager*. It breaks a chain of precedent as old as the common law that prohibits judicial inquiry into detentions of aliens abroad absent statutory authorization. And, most tragically, it sets our military commanders the impossible task of proving to a civilian court, under whatever standards this Court devises in the future, that evidence supports the confinement of each and every enemy prisoner.

III. Individual Rights

MAJOR DEVELOPMENTS

- Supreme Court recognizes an individual right to bear arms
- Several states recognize a constitutional right to same-sex marriage
- States permitted to adopt school-choice programs that subsidize tuition at private religious schools

The contemporary constitutional politics of individual rights is structured by unprecedented range, polarization, and the influence of one or two centrist justices. With the exception of the contracts clause, controversies swirl around virtually every constitutional right. Americans fight over takings, punitive damages, vouchers for religious schools, creationism, abortion, same-sex marriage, the right to die, and gun control. Most controversies pit Republicans against Democrats and more conservative justices against more liberal justices. Democrats and liberals favor abortion rights, same-sex marriage, the right to die, and bans on government support for religious activities. Republicans and conservatives favor property rights, granting religious groups access on equal terms to public benefits, and the right to bear arms. Justices dispute the proper occasions for judicial activism. The Supreme Court decides numerous rights cases by 5-4 margins, with Justice Kennedy (formerly Justices Kennedy and O'Connor) almost always casting the deciding vote. No member of the Rehnquist or Roberts Court champions judicial restraint on all or most issues of individual rights.

A. Property

Conservatives, libertarians, and Republicans are seeking to revive some but not all the traditional constitutional protections for property rights. The contracts clause remains moribund. Efforts to resurrect the freedom of contract are largely limited to the legal academy.[17] Both Republicans and conservatives, however, promote the takings clause as a bulwark against what they believe is overreaching government regulation. When the Republican Party in 2008 asserted, "At the center of a free economy is the right of citizens to be secure in their property," the emphasis was on what party members believed were unjust takings. The party's platforms in 2008 and 2012 condemned the Supreme Court's decision in *Kelo v. City of New London* (2005) for "allowing local governments to seize a person's home or land, not for vital public use, but for transfer to private developers." Republicans "call[ed] on state legislatures to moot the *Kelo* decision by appropriate legislation or constitutional amendments" and "pledge[d] on the federal level to pass legislation to protect against unjust federal takings."

Conservatives have yet to build on successful litigation campaigns during the 1980s and early 1990s that imposed stricter takings clause limits on government regulation. *Kelo* ruled that economic development was a legitimate use of eminent domain, even when the condemned property was given to a private business. *Stop the Beach Renourishment, Inc. v. Florida Dept. of Environmental Protection* (2010) avoided to decide whether judicial decisions could take property in violation of the Fifth and Fourteenth Amendments. A more ideologically diverse coalition of justices did impose constitutional limits on punitive damages in *BMW of North America, Inc. v. Gore* (1996) and *Philip Morris USA*

17. See David Bernstein, *Rehabilitating* Lochner: *Defending Individual Rights against Progressive Reform* (Chicago: University of Chicago Press, 2011). Very few liberals in the academy defend constitutional protection for welfare rights.

v. Williams (2007). No justice has suggested that the Constitution protects basic welfare rights.

Contracts

The contracts clause in the Supreme Court has either disappeared or is in deep hibernation. A leading constitutional commentator in 1996 asserted that the contracts clause "is interpreted to reach the narrowest range of cases that it could reach without being effectively read out of the Constitution."[18] Subsequent events suggest that this assertion exaggerated the influence of the contracts clause on contemporary Supreme Court jurisprudence. The justices, to the delight of constitutional law professors who do not like revising their lecture notes, have not resolved a contracts clause case in more than fifteen years.

Some contracts issues are bubbling up in state and lower federal courts. Many deal with state and local efforts to modify public employee benefits. Most challenges to state retrenchment policies have failed. The Court of Appeals for the Fourth Circuit in *Fraternal Order of Police Lodge No. 89 v. Prince George's County, MD* (2010) rejected a claim that county-mandated furloughs violated the contracts clause. Although county law specified that the terms of any collective bargaining agreement overrode contrary provisions in the local Personnel Law, the Fourth Circuit ruled that county rules permitting furloughs were in force unless the collective bargaining agreement included specific language to the contrary. "The Unions are simply asking for the benefit of a contract provision that was left on the bargaining table," Judge King concluded.[19] Litigants were more successful in *American Federation of State, County and Municipal Employees v. City of Benton, Arkansas* (2008), in which the Court of Appeals for the Eighth Circuit ruled that a city effort to reduce health insurance benefits for some retired public employees violated the contracts clause. Judge Doty imposed a relatively high standard of constitutional protection when he declared that "the City had not demonstrated a significant economic interest . . . related to 'unprecedented emergencies,' such as mass foreclosures caused by the Great Depression" that might justify any modification of the collective bargaining agreement between the city and public employees."[20]

Takings

The takings clause is the main front in contemporary battles over constitutional protection for property rights. Supported by conservative politicians and libertarian public interest groups, homeowners and small businesses are challenging environmental laws and land-use regulations that they believe impair or destroy property rights. Many challenges have been successful, particularly in the states. Often, local officials who are fearful of lawsuits either alter land-use regulations or make exceptions when faced with a potential takings claim.

Liberals have held the line in national constitutional politics. The Supreme Court in the two most important recent takings clause cases sustained state policies under constitutional attack. In *Kelo v. City of New London* (2005) a 5-4 judicial majority ruled that promoting economic development satisfied the "public use" prong of the takings clause when government used the power of eminent domain to transfer property from one private owner to another private owner who promised to create more jobs for the community. *Stop the Beach Renourishment, Inc. v. Florida Dept. of Environmental Protection* (2010) unanimously rejected a takings clause attack on Florida's effort to restore beaches eroded by hurricanes. The justices divided ideologically on whether a judicial decision could violate the takings clause. The more conservative justices on the Roberts Court insisted that judicial decisions could take property, but that the Florida Supreme Court had not taken property in this instance. Justice Kennedy and the four more liberal justices on the Roberts Court insisted that no need existed to resolve that question.

Proponents of property rights in the states are enjoying more success.[21] In the wake of *Kelo* forty-two states passed laws limiting the circumstances in which elected officials could exercise the power of

18. David Strauss, "Common Law Constitutional Interpretation," *University of Chicago Law Review* 63 (1996): 904.

19. *Fraternal Order of Police Lodge No. 89 v. Prince George's County, MD*, 608 F. 2d 183 (4th Cir. 2010).

20. *American Federation of State, County and Municipal Employees v. City of Benton, Arkansas*, 513 F.3d 874 (8th Cir., 2008). See also Joseph E. Slater, "Public-Sector Labor in the Age of Obama," *Indiana Law Journal* 87 (2012): 217–19.

21. See Ilya Somin, "The Judicial Reaction to *Kelo*," *Albany Government Law Review* 4 (2011): 1; and R. Benjamin Lingle, "Post-*Kelo* Eminent Domain Reform: A Double-Edged Sword for Historic Preservation," *Florida Law Review* 63 (2011): 985.

Illustration 11-1 Life, Liberty, and the Pursuit of Tax Revenue
Source: Cox & Forkum Editorial Cartoons.

eminent domain. While many laws are vague, some clearly limit legislative discretion. The Kansas legislature in 2007 declared, "The taking of private property by eminent domain for the purpose of selling, leasing or otherwise transferring such property to any private entity is prohibited except [in certain narrowly defined circumstances]."[22] Several state courts interpreted the takings clause of the state constitution as providing greater restrictions on state officials than did the takings clause of the national constitution. The Supreme Court of Oklahoma in *Board of County Commissioners of Muskogee County v. Lowery* (OK 2006) stated, "As a matter of Oklahoma constitutional and statutory law, economic development alone is not a public purpose to justify the exercise of county's power of eminent domain."[23] State decisions to provide additional constitutional rights are legitimate and common in other areas of state constitutional law. While a state court may not interpret a state constitution as permitting behavior forbidden by the national constitution, state officials are free to interpret or amend a state constitution to forbid behavior permitted by the national constitution.

22. Kan. Stat. Ann. § 26-501b (2009).

23. *Board of County Commissioners of Muskogee County v. Lowery*, 136 P.3d 639 (Okla. 2006).

Kelo v. City of New London, 545 U.S. 469 (2005)

Susette Kelo owned a home in the Fort Trumbull area of New London, Connecticut. In 1990 a state agency declared New London to be a "distressed municipality" in light of decades of job and population losses. In order to revitalize the city New London officials authorized an economic redevelopment plan that gave a significant parcel of land to the Pfizer Corporation. Pfizer, in turn, promised to build a pharmaceutical research facility, which was expected to substantially increase the number of jobs in the area. The land targeted for redevelopment included privates homes occupied by Susette Kelo and others. New London offered a fair market price for those homes, but Kelo and some other long-time residents did not want to leave communities in which they had lived for most of their lives. When New London began condemnation proceedings against these residents' property, Kelo filed a lawsuit in state court, claiming that the condemnation violated the takings clause of the Fifth and Fourteenth Amendments because government action transferring property from one private owner to another is not a "public use" for constitutional purposes. The trial court ruled that Connecticut could condemn some properties, but not others. On appeal the Supreme Court of Connecticut upheld all the proposed takings as a valid public use. Kelo appealed to the Supreme Court of the United States.

The Supreme Court by a 5-4 vote sustained New London's use of eminent domain. Justice Stevens's majority opinion declared that the public use requirement of the Fifth Amendment was satisfied any time a taking had a public benefit. Why does he reach that conclusion? Does Justice O'Connor successfully reconcile cases in which she thinks that the eminent domain power was illegitimate with casesin which she thinks that the power was legitimate? Alternatively, are both Justices Stevens and Thomas correct in thinking that either government is free to give condemned land to a private owner whenever doing so might advance a public interest or else government can never give condemned land to a private owner? Property rights activists protesting the Kelo *decision urged New Hampshire to condemn Justice Souter's farmhouse and convert the property into the Lost Liberty Inn, which might provide greater tax revenues for the state. If New Hampshire decided that the Lost Liberty Inn would provide an economic boon to the community, could they constitutionally condemn Justice Souter's property?*

In 2010 Pfizer announced they were closing down operations in New London.

JUSTICE STEVENS delivered the opinion of the Court.

. . .

Two polar propositions are perfectly clear. On the one hand, it has long been accepted that the sovereign may not take the property of *A* for the sole purpose of transferring it to another private party *B*, even though *A* is paid just compensation. On the other hand, it is equally clear that a State may transfer property from one private party to another if future "use by the public" is the purpose of the taking; the condemnation of land for a railroad with common-carrier duties is a familiar example. . . .

. . .

The disposition of this case turns on the question whether the City's development plan serves a "public purpose." Without exception, our cases have defined that concept broadly, reflecting our longstanding policy of deference to legislative judgments in this field.

In *Berman v. Parker* (1954), this Court upheld a redevelopment plan targeting a blighted area of Washington, D. C., in which most of the housing for the area's 5,000 inhabitants was beyond repair. Under the plan, the area would be condemned and part of it utilized for the construction of streets, schools, and other public facilities. The remainder of the land would be leased or sold to private parties for the purpose of redevelopment, including the construction of low-cost housing. . . . Writing for a unanimous Court, Justice Douglas refused to evaluate this claim in isolation, deferring instead to the legislative and agency judgment that the area "must be planned as a whole" for the plan to be successful. . . .

In *Hawaii Housing Authority v. Midkiff* (1984), the Court considered a Hawaii statute whereby fee title was taken from lessors and transferred to lessees (for just compensation) in order to reduce the concentration of land ownership. We unanimously upheld the statute and rejected the Ninth Circuit's view that it was "a naked attempt on the part of the state of Hawaii to take the property of A and transfer it to B solely for B's private use and benefit." Reaffirming *Berman's* deferential approach to legislative judgments in this field, we concluded that the State's purpose of eliminating the "social and economic evils of a land oligopoly" qualified as a valid public use. . . .

. . .

Those who govern the City were not confronted with the need to remove blight in the Fort Trumbull area, but their determination that the area was sufficiently distressed to justify a program of economic rejuvenation is entitled to our deference. The City has carefully formulated an economic development plan that it believes will provide appreciable benefits to the community, including—but by no means limited to—new jobs and increased tax revenue. As with other exercises in urban planning and development, the City is endeavoring to coordinate a variety of commercial, residential, and recreational uses of land, with the hope that they will form a whole greater than the sum of its parts. To effectuate this plan, the City has invoked a state statute that specifically authorizes the use of eminent domain to promote economic development. Given the comprehensive character of the plan, the thorough deliberation that preceded its adoption, and the limited scope of our review, it is appropriate for us, as it was in *Berman*, to resolve the challenges of the individual owners, not on a piecemeal basis, but rather in light of the entire plan. Because that plan unquestionably serves a public purpose, the takings challenged here satisfy the public use requirement of the Fifth Amendment.

. . .

. . . In affirming the City's authority to take petitioners' properties, we do not minimize the hardship that condemnations may entail, notwithstanding the payment of just compensation. We emphasize that nothing in our opinion precludes any State from placing further restrictions on its exercise of the takings power. Indeed, many States already impose "public use" requirements that are stricter than the federal baseline. Some of these requirements have been established as a matter of state constitutional law, while others are expressed in state eminent domain statutes that carefully limit the grounds upon which takings may be exercised. As the submissions of the parties and their *amici* make clear, the necessity and wisdom of using eminent domain to promote economic development are certainly matters of legitimate public debate. This Court's authority, however, extends only to determining whether the City's proposed condemnations are for a "public use" within the meaning of the Fifth Amendment to the Federal Constitution. Because over a century of our case law interpreting that provision dictates an affirmative answer to that question, we may not grant petitioners the relief that they seek.

JUSTICE KENNEDY, concurring.

. . .

This Court has declared that a taking should be upheld as consistent with the Public Use Clause as long as it is "rationally related to a conceivable public purpose." This deferential standard of review echoes the rational-basis test used to review economic regulation under the Due Process and Equal Protection Clauses. The determination that a rational-basis standard of review is appropriate does not, however, alter the fact that transfers intended to confer benefits on particular, favored private entities, and with only incidental or pretextual public benefits, are forbidden by the Public Use Clause.

A court applying rational-basis review under the Public Use Clause should strike down a taking that, by a clear showing, is intended to favor a particular private party, with only incidental or pretextual public benefits, just as a court applying rational-basis review under the Equal Protection Clause must strike down a government classification that is clearly intended to injure a particular class of private parties, with only incidental or pretextual public justifications.

. . .

JUSTICE O'CONNOR, with whom THE CHIEF JUSTICE, JUSTICE SCALIA, and JUSTICE THOMAS join, dissenting.

. . .

While the Takings Clause presupposes that government can take private property without the owner's consent, the just compensation requirement spreads the cost of condemnations and thus "prevents the public from loading upon one individual more than his just share of the burdens of government." . . . The public use requirement, in turn, imposes a more basic limitation, circumscribing the very scope of the eminent domain power: Government may compel an individual to forfeit her property for the *public's* use, but not for the benefit of another private person. This requirement promotes fairness as well as security. . . .

. . .

Our cases have generally identified three categories of takings that comply with the public use requirement, though it is in the nature of things that the boundaries between these categories are not always firm. Two are relatively straightforward and uncontroversial. First, the sovereign may transfer private property to public ownership—such as for a road, a hospital, or a military base. . . . Second, the sovereign may transfer private property to private parties, often common carriers, who make the property available for the public's use—such as with a railroad, a public utility, or a stadium. . . . But "public ownership" and "use-by-the-public" are sometimes too constricting and impractical ways to define the scope of the Public Use Clause. Thus we have allowed that, in certain circumstances and to meet certain exigencies, takings that serve a public purpose also satisfy the Constitution even if the property is destined for subsequent private use. See, *e.g.*, *Berman* v. *Parker* (1954); *Hawaii Housing Authority* v. *Midkiff* (1984).

. . .

The Court's holdings in *Berman* and *Midkiff* were true to the principle underlying the Public Use Clause. In both those cases, the extraordinary, precondemnation use of the targeted property inflicted affirmative harm on society—in *Berman* through blight resulting from extreme poverty and in *Midkiff* through oligopoly resulting from extreme wealth. And in both cases, the relevant legislative body had found that eliminating the existing property use was necessary to remedy the harm. . . . Thus a public purpose was realized when the harmful use was eliminated. Because each taking *directly* achieved a public benefit, it did not matter that the property was turned over to private use. Here, in contrast, New London does not claim that Susette Kelo's and Wilhelmina Dery's well-maintained homes are the source of any social harm. Indeed, it could not so claim without adopting the absurd argument that any single-family home that might be razed to make way for an apartment building, or any church that might be replaced with a retail store, or any small business that might be more lucrative if it were instead part of a national franchise, is inherently harmful to society and thus within the government's power to condemn.

In moving away from our decisions sanctioning the condemnation of harmful property use, the Court today significantly expands the meaning of public use. It holds that the sovereign may take private property currently put to ordinary private use, and give it over for new, ordinary private use, so long as the new use is predicted to generate some secondary benefit for the public—such as increased tax revenue, more jobs, maybe even aesthetic pleasure. But nearly any lawful use of real private property can be said to generate some incidental benefit to the public. Thus, if predicted (or even guaranteed) positive side-effects are enough to render transfer from one private party to another constitutional, then the words "for public use" do not realistically exclude *any* takings, and thus do not exert any constraint on the eminent domain power.

. . .

JUSTICE THOMAS, dissenting.

. . .

The most natural reading of the Clause is that it allows the government to take property only if the government owns, or the public has a legal right to use, the property, as opposed to taking it for any public purpose or necessity whatsoever. At the time of the founding, dictionaries primarily defined the noun "use" as "the act of employing any thing to any purpose." The term "use," moreover, "is from the Latin *utor*, which means 'to use, make use of, avail one's self of, employ, apply, enjoy, etc.'" . . . When the government takes property and gives it to a private individual, and the public has no right to use the property, it strains language to say that the public is "employing" the property, regardless of the incidental benefits that might accrue to the public from the private use. . . .

. . .

Tellingly, the phrase "public use" contrasts with the very different phrase "general Welfare" used elsewhere in the Constitution. . . . The Framers would have used some such broader term if they had meant the Public Use Clause to have a similarly sweeping scope. Other founding-era documents made the contrast between these two usages still more explicit. . . .

. . .

The public purpose interpretation of the Public Use Clause also unnecessarily duplicates a similar inquiry required by the Necessary and Proper Clause. The Takings Clause is a prohibition, not a grant of power: The Constitution does not expressly grant the Federal Government the power to take property for any public purpose whatsoever. Instead, the Government may take property only when necessary and proper to the exercise of an expressly enumerated power. . . . In other words, a taking is permissible under the Necessary and Proper Clause only if it serves a valid public purpose. Interpreting the Public Use Clause likewise to limit the government to take property only for sufficiently public purposes replicates this inquiry. If this is all the Clause means, it is, once again, surplusage. . . .

. . .

The "public purpose" test applied by *Berman* and *Midkiff* also cannot be applied in principled manner. "When we depart from the natural import of the term 'public use,' and substitute for the simple idea of a public possession and occupation, that of public utility, public interest, common benefit, general advantage or convenience . . . we are afloat without any certain principle to guide us." Once one permits takings for public purposes in addition to public uses, no coherent principle limits what could constitute a valid public use—at least, none beyond JUSTICE O'CONNOR's (entirely proper) appeal to the text of the Constitution itself. I share the Court's skepticism about a public use standard that requires courts to second-guess the policy wisdom of public works projects. The "public purpose" standard this Court has adopted, however, demands the use of such judgment, for the Court concedes that the Public Use Clause would forbid a purely private taking. It is difficult to imagine how a court could find that a taking was purely private except by determining that the taking did not, in fact, rationally advance the public interest. . . .

. . .

The consequences of today's decision are not difficult to predict, and promise to be harmful. So-called "urban renewal" programs provide some compensation for the properties they take, but no compensation is possible for the subjective value of these lands to the individuals displaced and the indignity inflicted by uprooting them from their homes. Allowing the government to take property solely for public purposes is bad enough, but extending the concept of public purpose to encompass any economically beneficial goal guarantees that these losses will fall disproportionately on poor communities. Those communities are not only systematically less likely to put their lands to the highest and best social use, but are also the least politically powerful. If ever there were justification for intrusive judicial review of constitutional provisions that protect "discrete and insular minorities," *United States v. Carolene Products Co.* (1938), surely that principle would apply with great force to the powerless groups and individuals the Public Use Clause protects. The deferential standard this Court has adopted for the Public Use Clause is therefore deeply perverse. . . .

Due Process

The Contemporary Era has witnessed one surprising nondevelopment and one surprising development in due process protections for economic and property rights. Despite efforts by some law professors to revive interest in the *Lochner* line of cases,[24] most conservative constitutional decision makers still treat the "liberty of contract" cases as canonical examples of illegitimate judicial activism. Justice Scalia's dissent in *Lawrence v. Texas* (2003) asserted that legislatures were as free to prohibit homosexual sodomy as they were to prohibit "working more than 60 hours per week in a bakery." Contemporary justices have been more receptive to claims that excessive punitive damages violate the due process clause of the Fifth and Fourteenth Amendments. Punitive damages are damages assessed in civil trials in addition to compensatory damages, which focus on actual economic loss. If I trespass on your land and maliciously kick over your little brother's sandcastle, your family may not suffer severe economic loss. Nevertheless, many people think that I should pay far more than the actual damages I have caused in order to deter such conduct in the future. Those additional damages are punitive damages. Quite frequently, juries award punitive damages far in excess of the actual damages given.

In *BMW of North America v. Gore* (1996) a 5-4 judicial majority overturned a jury decision that awarded $4 million in punitive damages but only $4,000 in actual damages. Justice Stevens's majority opinion declared, "Elementary notions of fairness enshrined in our constitutional jurisprudence dictate that a person receive fair notice not only of the conduct that will subject him to punishment but also of the severity of the penalty that a State may impose." Eleven years later the Supreme Court overturned a $79.5 million punitive damage award against Philip Morris, a cigarette manufacturer. Justice Breyer's majority decision in *Philip Morris USA v. Williams* (2007) declared, "The Constitution's Due Process Clause forbids a State to use a punitive damages award to punish a defendant for injury that it inflicts upon nonparties." The votes in these cases were less ideological than those that occurred in cases considering other constitutional property rights. Justices Ginsburg and Scalia, for example, agreed that courts should normally not interfere with punitive damage awards.

B. Religion

Religious freedom in the United States is presently structured by a series of complex relationships between interest groups, parties, elected officials, and judges. The constitutional politics of establishment is different than the constitutional politics of free exercise. The differences between most Democrats and most Republicans on religious freedom issues are not the same as the differences between the more liberal and more conservative justices on the Supreme Court.

Religious groups divide on establishment issues but are united on free exercise issues. Conservative religious groups favor government policies that accommodate religious belief. Liberal religious groups and more secular Americans support a greater separation between church and state. Virtually all religious groups favor granting religious groups exemptions from neutral state laws that burden religious practice, unless a strong state reason exists for not granting the exemption. When conversations turn to specifics, such as whether religious apartment owners must be required to rent to gay couples or whether Catholic organizations must offer employees health plans that pay for contraceptive services, the divide between conservative and liberal religious groups reemerges.

24. See Bernstein, *Rehabilitating* Lochner.

The Republican and Democratic Parties both favor accommodating religious belief, but Republicans do so more strongly and over a broader range of issues. The Republican Party platform in 2012 asserted,

> We support the public display of the Ten Commandments as a reflection of our history and of our country's Judeo-Christian heritage, and we affirm the right of students to engage in prayer at public school events in public schools and to have equal access to public schools and other public facilities to accommodate religious freedom in the public square. We assert every citizen's right to apply religious values to public policy and the right of faith-based organizations to participate fully in public programs without renouncing their beliefs, removing religious symbols, or submitting to government-imposed hiring practices. We oppose government discrimination against businesses due to religious views. We support the First Amendment right of freedom of association of the Boy Scouts of America and other service organizations whose values are under assault and condemn the State blacklisting of religious groups which decline to arrange adoptions by same-sex couples.

The Democratic Party platform was much shorter and more tepid, and failed to discuss numerous constitutional questions. That platform asserted,

> Faith-based organizations will always be critical allies in meeting the challenges that face our nation and our world - from domestic and global poverty, to climate change and human trafficking. People of faith and religious organizations do amazing work in communities across this country and the world, and we believe in lifting up and valuing that good work, and finding ways to support it where possible. We believe in constitutionally sound, evidence-based partnerships with faith-based and other non-profit organizations to serve those in need and advance our shared interests. There is no conflict between supporting faith-based institutions and respecting our Constitution, and a full commitment to both principles is essential for the continued flourishing of both faith and country.

Federal justices do not fully replicate the divisions between either interest groups or political parties. The divisions between liberal and conservative justices on such establishment clause issues as whether public funds can assist religious schools, the posting of the Ten Commandments in public places, and school prayer are identical to the divisions between liberal and conservative religious groups. Liberal justices favor a stricter separation between church and state than that expressed by the Democratic Party platform. Conservatives favor policies that accommodate religious belief. On free exercise issues, however, conservative justices reject constitutional entitlements to exemptions favored by conservative religious groups and many Republicans. Justice Stevens aside, the more liberal members of the Supreme Court support those exemptions.

When reading the materials in this section, think about the relationships between interest groups, parties, elected officials, and justices. What are the similarities? What are the differences? What explains those similarities and differences?

Establishment

Conservatives retain the initiative gained in the Reagan years. While liberals are merely trying to hold on to New Deal and Great Society precedents sharply separating church and state, conservatives continue to press for more accommodations for religion. Depending on your perspective Republicans and conservative religious groups have made considerable progress in either reducing discrimination against religious institutions in public aid programs or funneling more money to religious institutions. The Supreme Court has also shown greater tolerance for the placement of religious symbols in public places. Liberals have, however, held the line on school prayer. *Engle v. Vitale* (1962), which declared state-mandated prayer exercises unconstitutional, remains the law of the land, even as prayer continues in public school districts throughout rural America.[25]

Many judicial opinions in establishment cases rely heavily on the "endorsement" test, a test formulated by Justice O'Connor and the more liberal justices on the Rehnquist/Roberts Court. The test of constitutionality of government practices under the establishment clause, O'Connor claimed in numerous cases, was whether "the reasonable observer would view a government practice as endorsing religion."[26] When

---

25. See Kevin T. McGuire, "Public Schools, Religious Establishments, and the U.S. Supreme Court: An Examination of Policy Compliance," *American Politics Research* 37 (2009): 50.

26. *Capitol Square Review and Advisory Board v. Pinette*, 515 U.S. 753 (1995) (O'Connor, J., concurring).

reading the materials in this section, consider whether endorsement provides clear standards to guide constitutional decision makers and whether that test correctly captures the issues at stake in establishment clause debates.

Aid to Religious Institutions. Americans vigorously debate the extent to which religious schools and religious institutions may secure public funds. One controversy is over school-choice programs that give parents vouchers to help pay tuition at private schools, including private religious schools. Such programs were highly touted by the Bush administration, prominent social scientists, and many religious groups. They also receive substantial support from African-Americans in inner cities who were eager to accept any program that might improve public schooling in urban America. Teachers' unions and more liberal groups insist that state support for religious school tuition violates the establishment clause, even if parents could use the public benefit to send their child to a secular school. President Bush's "Faith-Based Initiatives" spawned a related controversy. Such programs fund religious groups that provide social services. President Bush asserted that such programs recognize the vital role that religious groups play in communal affairs.

> Government will never be replaced by charities and community groups. Yet when we see social needs in America, my administration will look first to faith-based programs and community groups, which have proven their power to save and change lives. We will not fund the religious activities of any group, but when people of faith provide social services, we will not discriminate against them.

Critics insist that such measures lower the barrier between church and state. Americans United for the Separation of Church and State maintains:

> The so-called "faith-based" initiative is a euphemism for taxpayer-supported religion. The initiative funnels taxpayer dollars to religious social service providers without adequate safeguards to prevent proselytism. In addition, these groups seek to discriminate in hiring based on religion even though their programs are publicly funded.[27]

27. Americans United, "The Faith-Based Initiative and Government Subsidies of Religious Institutions," http://www.au.org/issues/faith-based-initiative-government-subsidies-religious-institutions-other-schools.

The central constitutional issue in the debate over when public money may be directed to a religious institution is whether government officials are providing special benefits to religion or structuring programs in ways that encourage persons to put government benefits to religious use. Proponents insist that such programs facilitate private choice, including the private choice to be religious. If persons may constitutionally donate a tax refund to their church, supporters of these programs insist, then persons ought to be free to direct other government benefits to religious institutions as long as they do so as a result of "true private choice." Religion is discriminated against when persons can use public benefits for any purpose other than religion. Opponents claim that such programs unconstitutionally direct aid to religious organizations and that the incentives are often skewed to direct aid to religious institutions. When government provides funds for parents who send children to private schools and most private schools are religious schools, they point out, the state has stacked the deck in favor of diverting public money to religious institutions.

The Supreme Court in four important contemporary cases found that public moneys were being directed to religious schools only as a result of private choices. In *Zobrest v. Catalina Foothills School District* (1993) a 5-4 judicial majority ruled that Congress under the Individuals with Disabilities Act could provide a sign interpreter for a deaf child who was attending a Catholic school. After noting that the federal law entitled any disabled child to take advantage of the same benefit, Chief Justice Rehnquist declared, "Government programs that neutrally provide benefits to a broad class of citizens defined without reference to religion are not readily subject to an Establishment Clause challenge just because sectarian institutions may also receive an attenuated financial benefit." Four years later, in *Agostini v. Felton* (1997), a 5-4 judicial majority permitted public schoolteachers to provide remedial educational services to disadvantaged children on the grounds of a religious school. Citing *Zobrest*, Justice O'Connor's majority opinion announced that the justices had "abandoned the presumption . . . that the placement of public employees on parochial school grounds inevitably results in the impermissible effect of state-sponsored indoctrination or constitutes a symbolic union between government and religion." *Mitchell v. Helms* (2002) loosened the conditions under which the federal government and states could provide instructional materials to religious schools as part of a general program of aid to education. Justice Thomas's opinion for the judicial plurality insisted, "If the religious, irreligious, and areligious are all alike eligible for governmental aid, no one would conclude that any indoctrination that any particular recipient conducts has been done at the behest of the government." Finally, in *Zelman v. Simmons-Harris* (2003) the Supreme Court by a 5-4 vote sustained an Ohio law that provided financial assistance to parents who sent their children to private schools, the vast majority of which are religious.

Zelman v. Simmons-Harris, 536 U.S. 639 (2002)

Doris Simmons-Harris was a parent of a minor child in the Cleveland, Ohio, school district. In 1999 and 2000 the Ohio legislation enacted a comprehensive spending program designed to improve the exceptionally low performance of children in the Cleveland public schools. Elected officials increased the number of community and magnet schools in the Cleveland school district. They provided tutorial aid for students who chose to remain in the public school system. Finally, the state provided tuition grants of up to $2,250 to students who enrolled in either private schools or public schools in districts near Cleveland (although no school outside of Cleveland agreed to take any students). Schools accepting the money had to agree not to discriminate on the basis of religion or "advocate or foster unlawful behavior or teach hatred of any person or group on the basis of race, ethnicity, national origin, or religion." Fifty-six private schools agreed to accept public school students. Forty-six of those schools were sectarian. Simmons-Harris and other Cleveland residents who opposed the tuition grants filed a lawsuit against Susan Zelman, the superintendent of public instruction in Ohio. They claimed that government could not pay tuition for students to attend religious schools. Both the local federal district court and the Court of Appeals for the Sixth Circuit agreed with this contention. Zelman appealed to the Supreme Court of the United States.

The Supreme Court by a 5-4 vote sustained the voucher program. Chief Justice Rehnquist's opinion for the Court asserted that the establishment clause requirement that prgrams be neutral between religion and nonreligion was met because money flowed to religious schools only as a consequence of private choices made by parents. How do each of the opinions interpret neutrality, and how do these interpretations influence voting in Zelman*? What is more relevant to the constitutional analysis: that religious schools were not singled out as special beneficiaries, or that because of the extensive preexisting network of religious schools in Cleveland religious schools were the primary financial beneficiaries of this government program? The dissenting opinions in* Zelman *worry that public officials may use funding as a way to influence religious indoctrination. Is this a legitimate fear? Consider that many religions teach that their adherents are a "chosen people" or that only adherents will enjoy the afterlife. Could this be said to foster the hatred on the basis of religion prohibited by Ohio law? What restrictions on state funding might you insist upon? Are those restrictions neutral with respect to different religions?*

CHIEF JUSTICE REHNQUIST delivered the opinion of the Court.

. . .

. . . [W]here a government aid program is neutral with respect to religion, and provides assistance directly to a broad class of citizens who, in turn, direct government aid to religious schools wholly as a result of their own genuine and independent private choice, the program is not readily subject to challenge under the Establishment Clause. A program that shares these features permits government aid to reach religious institutions only by way of the deliberate choices of numerous individual recipients. The incidental advancement of a religious mission, or the perceived endorsement of a religious message, is reasonably attributable to the individual recipient, not to the government, whose role ends with the disbursement of benefits. . . . It is precisely for these reasons that we have never found a program of true private choice to offend the Establishment Clause.

We believe that the program challenged here is a program of true private choice . . . and thus constitutional. . . . [T]he Ohio program is neutral in all respects toward religion. It is part of a general and multifaceted undertaking by the State of Ohio to provide educational opportunities to the children of a failed school district. It confers educational assistance directly to a broad class of individuals defined without reference to religion, *i.e.*, any parent of a school-age child who resides in the Cleveland City School District. The program permits the participation of *all* schools within the district, religious or nonreligious. Adjacent public schools also may participate and have a financial incentive to do so. Program benefits are available to participating families on neutral terms, with no reference to religion. The only preference stated anywhere in the program is a preference for low-income families, who receive greater assistance and are given priority for admission at participating schools.

There are no "financial incentive[s]" that "ske[w]" the program toward religious schools.... The program here in fact creates financial *dis*incentives for religious schools, with private schools receiving only half the government assistance given to community schools and one-third the assistance given to magnet schools. Adjacent public schools, should any choose to accept program students, are also eligible to receive two to three times the state funding of a private religious school. Families too have a financial disincentive to choose a private religious school over other schools. Parents that choose to participate in the scholarship program and then to enroll their children in a private school (religious or nonreligious) must copay a portion of the school's tuition. Families that choose a community school, magnet school, or traditional public school pay nothing....

...

There also is no evidence that the program fails to provide genuine opportunities for Cleveland parents to select secular educational options for their school-age children. Cleveland schoolchildren enjoy a range of educational choices: They may remain in public school as before, remain in public school with publicly funded tutoring aid, obtain a scholarship and choose a religious school, obtain a scholarship and choose a nonreligious private school, enroll in a community school, or enroll in a magnet school. That 46 of the 56 private schools now participating in the program are religious schools does not condemn it as a violation of the Establishment Clause. The Establishment Clause question is whether Ohio is coercing parents into sending their children to religious schools, and that question must be answered by evaluating *all* options Ohio provides Cleveland schoolchildren, only one of which is to obtain a program scholarship and then choose a religious school.

... Cleveland's preponderance of religiously affiliated private schools certainly did not arise as a result of the program; it is a phenomenon common to many American cities.... It is true that 82% of Cleveland's participating private schools are religious schools, but it is also true that 81% of private schools in Ohio are religious schools.... To attribute constitutional significance to this figure, moreover, would lead to the absurd result that a neutral school-choice program might be permissible in some parts of Ohio, such as Columbus, where a lower percentage of private schools are religious schools, ... but not in inner-city Cleveland, where Ohio has deemed such programs most sorely needed, but where the preponderance of religious schools happens to be greater....

...

JUSTICE O'CONNOR, concurring.

...

... The share of public resources that reach religious schools is not as significant as respondents suggest.... Data from the 1999–2000 school year indicate that 82 percent of schools participating in the voucher program were religious and that 96 percent of participating students enrolled in religious schools.... These statistics do not take into account all of the reasonable educational choices that may be available to students in Cleveland public schools. When one considers the option to attend community schools, the percentage of students enrolled in religious schools falls to 62.1 percent. If magnet schools are included in the mix, this percentage falls to 16.5 percent....

Even these numbers do not paint a complete picture. The Cleveland program provides voucher applicants from low-income families with up to $2,250 in tuition assistance and provides the remaining applicants with up to $1,875 in tuition assistance.... In contrast, the State provides community schools $4,518 per pupil and magnet schools, on average, $7,097 per pupil.... Even if one assumes that all voucher students came from low-income families and that each voucher student used up the entire $2,250 voucher, at most $8.2 million of public funds flowed to religious schools under the voucher program in 1999–2000.... [T]he amount spent on religious private schools is minor compared to the $114.8 million the State spent on students in the Cleveland magnet schools.

...

Against this background, the support that the Cleveland voucher program provides religious institutions is neither substantial nor atypical of existing government programs. While this observation is not intended to justify the Cleveland voucher program under the Establishment Clause, ... it places in broader perspective alarmist claims about implications of the Cleveland program and the Court's decision in these cases. . . .

. . .

In my view the more significant finding in these cases is that Cleveland parents who use vouchers to send their children to religious private schools do so as a result of true private choice. The Court rejects, correctly, the notion that the high percentage of voucher recipients who enroll in religious private schools necessarily demonstrates that parents do not actually have the option to send their children to nonreligious schools. . . . Likewise, the mere fact that some parents enrolled their children in religious schools associated with a different faith than their own . . . says little about whether these parents had reasonable nonreligious options. Indeed, no voucher student has been known to be turned away from a nonreligious private school participating in the voucher program. . . .

. . .

JUSTICE THOMAS, concurring.

. . .

. . . There would be a tragic irony in converting the Fourteenth Amendment's guarantee of individual liberty into a prohibition on the exercise of educational choice.

The wisdom of allowing States greater latitude in dealing with matters of religion and education can be easily appreciated in this context. Respondents advocate using the Fourteenth Amendment to handcuff the State's ability to experiment with education. But without education one can hardly exercise the civic, political, and personal freedoms conferred by the Fourteenth Amendment. Faced with a severe educational crisis, the State of Ohio enacted wide-ranging educational reform that allows voluntary participation of private and religious schools in educating poor urban children otherwise condemned to failing public schools. The program does not force any individual to submit to religious indoctrination or education. It simply gives parents a greater choice as to where and in what manner to educate their children. This is a choice that those with greater means have routinely exercised.

. . .

While the romanticized ideal of universal public education resonates with the cognoscenti who oppose vouchers, poor urban families just want the best education for their children, who will certainly need it to function in our high-tech and advanced society. . . . The failure to provide education to poor urban children perpetuates a vicious cycle of poverty, dependence, criminality, and alienation that continues for the remainder of their lives. If society cannot end racial discrimination, at least it can arm minorities with the education to defend themselves from some of discrimination's effects.

JUSTICE STEVENS, dissenting. . . .

JUSTICE SOUTER, with whom JUSTICE STEVENS, JUSTICE GINSBURG, and JUSTICE BREYER join, dissenting.

. . .

. . . In the city of Cleveland the overwhelming proportion of large appropriations for voucher money must be spent on religious schools if it is to be spent at all, and will be spent in amounts that cover almost all of tuition. The money will thus pay for eligible students' instruction not only in secular subjects but in religion as well, in schools that can fairly be characterized as founded to teach religious doctrine and to imbue teaching in all subjects with a religious dimension. Public tax money will pay at a systemic level for teaching the covenant with Israel and Mosaic law in Jewish schools, the primacy of the Apostle Peter and the Papacy in Catholic schools, the truth of reformed Christianity in Protestant schools, and the revelation to the Prophet in Muslim schools, to speak only of major religious groupings in the Republic.

. . .

. . . If regular, public schools (which can get no voucher payments) "participate" in a voucher scheme with schools that can, and public expenditure is still predominantly on public schools, then the majority's reasoning would find neutrality in a scheme of vouchers available for private tuition in districts with no secular private schools at all. "Neutrality" as the majority employs the term is, literally, verbal and nothing more. This, indeed, is the only way the majority can gloss over the very nonneutral feature of the total scheme covering "*all* schools": public tutors may receive from the State no more than $324 per child to support extra tutoring (that is, the State's 90% of a total amount of $360), . . . whereas the tuition voucher schools (which turn out to be mostly religious) can receive up to $2,250. . . .

. . .

If . . . we ask the right question about genuine choice to use the vouchers, the answer shows that something is influencing choices in a way that aims the money in a religious direction: of 56 private schools in the district participating in the voucher program (only 53 of which accepted voucher students in 1999–2000), 46 of them are religious; 96.6% of all voucher recipients go to religious schools, only 3.4% to nonreligious ones. . . .

Even so, the fact that some 2,270 students chose to apply their vouchers to schools of other religions . . . might be consistent with true choice if the students "chose" their religious schools over a wide array of private nonreligious options, or if it could be shown generally that Ohio's program had no effect on educational choices and thus no impermissible effect of advancing religious education. But both possibilities are contrary to fact. First, even if all existing nonreligious private schools in Cleveland were willing to accept large numbers of voucher students, only a few more than the 129 currently enrolled in such schools would be able to attend, as the total enrollment at all nonreligious private schools in Cleveland for kindergarten through eighth grade is only 510 children and there is no indication that these schools have many open seats. Second, the $2,500 cap that the program places on tuition for participating low-income pupils has the effect of curtailing the participation of nonreligious schools: "nonreligious schools with higher tuition (about $4,000) stated that they could afford to accommodate just a few voucher students." By comparison, the average tuition at participating Catholic schools in Cleveland in 1999–2000 was $1,592, almost $1,000 below the cap.

. . .

In paying for practically the full amount of tuition for thousands of qualifying students . . . the scholarships purchase everything that tuition purchases, be it instruction in math or indoctrination in faith. The consequences of "substantial" aid . . . are realized here: the majority makes no pretense that substantial amounts of tax money are not systematically underwriting religious practice and indoctrination.

. . .

. . . [I]n the 21st century, the risk [of state aid corrupting religion] is one of "corrosive secularism" to religious schools, . . . and the specific threat is to the primacy of the schools' mission to educate the children of the faithful according to the unaltered precepts of their faith. . . .

. . .

Increased voucher spending is not, however, the sole portent of growing regulation of religious practice in the school, for state mandates to moderate religious teaching may well be the most obvious response to the third concern behind the ban on establishment, its inextricable link with social conflict. . . .

. . . Religious teaching at taxpayer expense simply cannot be cordoned from taxpayer politics, and every major religion currently espouses social positions that provoke intense opposition. Not all taxpaying Protestant citizens, for example, will be content to underwrite the teaching of the Roman Catholic Church condemning the death penalty. Nor will all of America's Muslims acquiesce in paying for the endorsement of the religious Zionism taught in many religious Jewish schools, which combines "a nationalistic sentiment" in support of Israel with a "deeply religious" element. Nor will every secular taxpayer be content to support Muslim views on differential treatment of the sexes, or, for that matter, to fund the espousal of a wife's obligation of obedience to her husband, presumably taught in any schools adopting the articles of faith of the Southern Baptist Convention. . . .

. . .

JUSTICE BREYER, with whom JUSTICE STEVENS and JUSTICE SOUTER join, dissenting.

. . . I write separately to emphasize the risk that publicly financed voucher programs pose in terms of religiously based social conflict. I do so because I believe that the Establishment Clause concern for protecting the Nation's social fabric from religious conflict poses an overriding obstacle to the implementation of this well-intentioned school voucher program. . . .

. . .

. . . [A]n "equal opportunity" approach [is] not workable. With respect to religious activities in the public schools, how could the Clause require public primary and secondary school teachers, when reading prayers or the Bible, *only* to treat all religions alike? In many places there were too many religions, too diverse a set of religious practices, too many whose spiritual beliefs denied the virtue of formal religious training. This diversity made it difficult, if not impossible, to devise meaningful forms of "equal treatment" by providing an "equal opportunity" for all to introduce their own religious practices into the public schools.

. . . The upshot is the development of constitutional doctrine that reads the Establishment Clause as avoiding religious strife, *not* by providing every religion with an *equal opportunity* (say, to secure state funding or to pray in the public schools), but by drawing fairly clear lines of *separation* between church and state—at least where the heartland of religious belief, such as primary religious education, is at issue.

. . .

. . . School voucher programs finance the religious education of the young. And, if widely adopted, they may well provide billions of dollars that will do so. Why will different religions not become concerned about, and seek to influence, the criteria used to channel this money to religious schools? Why will they not want to examine the implementation of the programs that provide this money—to determine, for example, whether implementation has biased a program toward or against particular sects, or whether recipient religious schools are adequately fulfilling a program's criteria? If so, just how is the State to resolve the resulting controversies without provoking legitimate fears of the kinds of religious favoritism that, in so religiously diverse a Nation, threaten social dissension?

Consider the voucher program here at issue. That program insists that the religious school accept students of all religions. Does that criterion treat fairly groups whose religion forbids them to do so? The program also insists that no participating school "advocate or foster unlawful behavior or teach hatred of any person or group on the basis of race, ethnicity, national origin, or religion." . . . As one *amicus* argues, "it is difficult to imagine a more divisive activity" than the appointment of state officials as referees to determine whether a particular religious doctrine "teaches hatred or advocates lawlessness." . . .

. . .

I do not believe that the "parental choice" aspect of the voucher program sufficiently offsets the concerns I have mentioned. Parental choice cannot help the taxpayer who does not want to finance the religious education of children. It will not always help the parent who may see little real choice between inadequate nonsectarian public education and adequate education at a school whose religious teachings are contrary to his own. It will not satisfy religious minorities unable to participate because they are too few in number to support the creation of their own private schools. It will not satisfy groups whose religious beliefs preclude them from participating in a government-sponsored program, and who may well feel ignored as government funds primarily support the education of children in the doctrines of the dominant religions. . . .

Religion in the Public Sphere. Americans and the Supreme Court had difficulty determining the place of religion, religious monuments in particular, in the public sphere. Two cases decided in 2005 illustrate the fine line between monuments that the judicial majority believed reflect the nation's heritage and monuments that unconstitutionally established religion. *McCreary County v. ACLU of Kentucky* by a 5-4 vote declared unconstitutional several efforts by a local government to display the Ten Commandments in the local courthouse. Justice Souter's majority opinion stated, "The display's unstinting focus was on religious passages, showing that the Counties were posting the Commandments precisely because of their sectarian content." That same day the justices by a 5-4 vote in *Van Orden v. Perry* decided that Texas could include a monument displaying the Ten Commandments in a collection of other monuments displaying facets of state history. Chief Justice Rehnquist declared, "Texas has treated its Capitol grounds monuments as representing the several strands in the State's political and legal history. The inclusion of the Ten Commandments monument in this group has a dual significance, partaking of both religion and government." Eight justices could find no difference between the two cases. Justice Breyer, who could, cast the deciding votes.

Whether the Roberts Court would reach the same conclusions is open to question. In *Salazar v. Buono* (2010) the Supreme Court by a 5-4 vote permitted the United States to transfer federal land to the Veterans of Foreign Wars (VFW) after a court ordered the removal of a large Latin cross memorializing soldiers killed in action. *Buono* was decided after Justice O'Connor left the Court and was replaced by Justice Alito. O'Connor voted against the display of the Ten Commandments in both *McCreary County* and *Van Orden*. Alito joined the majority in *Buono*. His concurrence asserted, "I see no reason to doubt that Congress' consistent goal, in legislating with regard to the Sunrise Rock monument, has been to commemorate our Nation's war dead and to avoid the disturbing symbolism that would have been created by the destruction of the monument."

Religion in Schools. Neither the Supreme Court nor the lower federal courts showed any inclination to revisit previous decisions forbidding public schools from conducting prayer exercises (*Lee v. Weisman* [1993]) or teaching religious alternatives to evolution (*Edwards v. Aguillard* [1987]). *Santa Fe Independent School District v. Doe* (2000) declared unconstitutional a policy that allowed students to determine by election whether prayers would be said before football games. Justice Stevens's majority opinion declared, "An objective Santa Fe High School student will unquestionably perceive the inevitable pregame prayer as stamped with her school's seal of approval." Federal courts rebuffed efforts to have public schools teach "intelligent design," the view that the universe was created by an intelligent entity. A federal district court in *Kitzmiller v. Dover Area School District* (2005) maintained that intelligent design was no different than the creationist theories that the Supreme Court in *Edwards* declared violated the establishment clause when taught in public schools.

Kitzmiller v. Dover Area School District, 400 F.Supp.2d 707 (M.D.Pa., 2005)

Tammy Kitzmiller was the parent of two children who attended Dover High School in Dover, Pennsylvania. On October 18, 2004, the Dover Board of Education passed the following resolution: "Students will be made aware of gaps/problems in Darwin's theory and of other theories of evolution including, but not limited to, intelligent design. Note: Origins of Life is not taught." The next month the board ordered ninth-grade science teachers to read the following statements to their students:

> *Because Darwin's Theory is a theory, it continues to be tested as new evidence is discovered. The Theory is not a fact. Gaps in the Theory exist for which there is no evidence. A theory is defined as a well-tested explanation that unifies a broad range of observations.*
>
> *Intelligent Design is an explanation of the origin of life that differs from Darwin's view. The reference book,* Of Pandas and People, *is available for students who might be interested in gaining an understanding of what Intelligent Design actually involves.*
>
> *With respect to any theory, students are encouraged to keep an open mind. The school leaves the discussion of the Origins of Life to individual students and their families.*

Kitzmiller and other parents who objected to these statements filed a lawsuit in the local federal district court, claiming that this policy violated the religion clauses of the Constitution of the United States and the Pennsylvania Constitution. They noted that the "reference book" mentioned by the board was created by a nonprofit organization founded by an ordained minister for the purpose of "proclaiming, publishing, preaching, [and] teaching . . . the Christian Gospel."

The federal district court in Kitzmiller *declared that the Dover policy violated the establishment clause of the First Amendment. Judge Jones ruled that efforts to integrate intelligent design into the public school curriculum stood on no better constitutional footing than the prior efforts to integrate creation science into the curriculum that the Supreme Court rejected in* Edwards v. Aguillard *(1987) and* Epperson v. Arkansas *(1968). Is Judge Jones correct that no difference exists between creation science and intelligent design? Consider that at least some persons with Ph.D.s in biology support intelligent design. Should that provide sufficient reasonable grounds for the Dover policy? Read* Dover *in light of* Gonzales v. Carhart *(2007). In that case Justice Kennedy permitted Congress to ban partial-birth abortions, even though an overwhelming majority of doctors claimed that partial-birth abortions were sometimes necessary to preserve maternal health. How do the scientific claims in* Dover *and* Gonzales *differ?*

JUDGE JONES delivered the following opinion.

. . .

The endorsement test recognizes that when government transgresses the limits of neutrality and acts in ways that show religious favoritism or sponsorship, it violates the Establishment Clause. . . .

As the endorsement test developed through application, it is now primarily a lens through which to view "effect," with purpose evidence being relevant to the inquiry derivatively. . . . The test consists of the reviewing court determining what message a challenged governmental policy or enactment conveys to a reasonable, objective observer who knows the policy's language, origins, and legislative history, as well as the history of the community and the broader social and historical context in which the policy arose. . . .

. . .

. . . [W]e conclude that the religious nature of ID (Intelligent Design) would be readily apparent to an objective observer, adult or child.

We initially note that John Haught, a theologian who testified as an expert witness for Plaintiffs and who has written extensively on the subject of evolution and religion, succinctly explained to the Court that the argument for ID is not a new scientific argument, but is rather an old religious argument for the existence of God. He traced this argument back to at least Thomas Aquinas in the 13th century, who framed the argument as a syllogism: Wherever complex design exists, there must have been a designer; nature is complex; therefore nature must have had an intelligent designer. . . .

Although proponents of the IDM [Intelligent Design Movement] occasionally suggest that the designer could be a space alien or a time-traveling cell biologist, no serious alternative to God as the designer has been proposed by members of the IDM, including Defendants' expert witnesses.

. . .

A "hypothetical reasonable observer," adult or child, who is "aware of the history and context of the community and forum" is also presumed to know that ID is a form of creationism. . . . The evidence at trial demonstrates that ID is nothing less than the progeny of creationism.

As Plaintiffs meticulously and effectively presented to the Court, *Pandas* went through many drafts, several of which were completed prior to and some after the Supreme Court's decision in *Edwards*, which held that the Constitution forbids teaching creationism as science. By comparing the pre and post *Edwards* drafts of *Pandas*, three astonishing points emerge: (1) the definition for creation science in early drafts is identical to the definition of ID; (2) cognates of the word creation (creationism and creationist), which appeared approximately 150 times were deliberately and systematically replaced with the phrase ID; and (3) the changes occurred shortly after the Supreme Court held that creation science is religious and cannot be taught in public school science classes in *Edwards*. This word substitution is telling, significant, and reveals that a purposeful change of words was effected without any corresponding change in content, which directly refutes [the publisher's] argument that by merely disregarding the words "creation" and "creationism," [they] expressly rejected creationism in *Pandas*.

. . .

An objective student is also presumed to know that the Dover School Board advocated for the curriculum change and disclaimer in expressly religious terms, that the proposed curriculum change prompted massive community debate over the Board's attempts to inject religious concepts into the science curriculum, and that the Board adopted the ID Policy in furtherance of an expressly religious agenda. . . . Importantly, the historical context that the objective student is presumed to know consists of a factor that weighed heavily in the Supreme Court's decision to strike down the balanced-treatment law in *Edwards*, specifically that "[o]ut of many possible science subjects taught in the public schools, the legislature chose to affect the teaching of the one scientific theory that historically has been opposed by certain religious sects." . . . Moreover, the objective student is presumed to know that encouraging the teaching of evolution as a theory rather than as a fact is one of the latest strategies to dilute evolution instruction employed by anti-evolutionists with religious motivations. . . .

In summary, the disclaimer singles out the theory of evolution for special treatment, misrepresents its status in the scientific community, causes students to doubt its validity without scientific justification, presents students with a religious alternative masquerading as a scientific theory, directs them to consult a creationist text as though it were a science resource, and instructs students to forego scientific inquiry in the public school classroom and instead to seek out religious instruction elsewhere. . . .

. . .

An objective adult member of the Dover community would also be presumed to know that ID and teaching about supposed gaps and problems in evolutionary theory are creationist religious strategies that evolved from earlier forms of creationism. . . . The objective observer is therefore aware of the social context in which the ID Policy arose and considered in light of this history, the challenged ID Policy constitutes an endorsement of a religious view.

. . .

The 225 letters to the editor and sixty-two editorials from the *York Daily Record* and *York Dispatch* that Plaintiffs offered at trial and which we have admitted for consideration in our analysis of the endorsement test and *Lemon*'s effect prong, show that hundreds of individuals in this small community felt it necessary to publish their views on the issues presented in this case for the community to see. Moreover, a review of the letters and editorials at issue reveals that in letter after letter and editorial after editorial, community members postulated that ID is an inherently religious concept, that the writers viewed the decision of whether to incorporate it into the high school biology curriculum as one which implicated a religious concept, and therefore that the curriculum change has the effect of placing the government's imprimatur on the Board's preferred religious viewpoint. These exhibits are thus probative of the fact that members of the Dover community perceived the Board as having acted to promote religion, with many citizens lined up as either for the curriculum change, on religious grounds, or against the curriculum change, on the ground that religion should not play a role in public school science class. Accordingly, the letters and editorials are relevant to, and provide evidence of, the Dover community's collective social judgment about the curriculum change because they demonstrate that "[r]egardless of the listener's support for, or objection to," the curriculum change, the community and hence the objective observer who personifies it, cannot help but see that the ID Policy implicates and thus endorses religion.

. . .

. . . [W]hile ID arguments may be true, a proposition on which the Court takes no position, ID is not science. We find that ID fails on three different levels, any one of which is sufficient to preclude a determination that ID is science. They are: (1) ID violates the centuries-old ground rules of science by invoking and permitting supernatural causation; (2) the argument of irreducible complexity, central to ID, employs the same flawed and illogical contrived dualism that doomed creation science in the 1980's; and (3) ID's negative attacks on evolution have been refuted by the scientific community. . . . ID has failed to gain acceptance in the scientific community, it has not generated peer-reviewed publications, nor has it been the subject of testing and research.

. . .

[The National Association of Scientists], the "most prestigious" scientific association in this country, views ID as follows:

> Creationism, intelligent design, and other claims of supernatural intervention in the origin of life or of species are not science because they are not testable by the methods of science. These claims subordinate observed data to statements based on authority, revelation, or religious belief. Documentation offered in support of these claims is typically limited to the special publications of their advocates. These publications do not offer hypotheses subject to change in light of new data, new interpretations, or demonstration of error. This contrasts with science, where any hypothesis or theory always remains subject to the possibility of rejection or modification in the light of new knowledge.

. . .

The evidence presented in this case demonstrates that ID is not supported by any peer-reviewed research, data or publications. Both Drs. Padian and Forrest testified that recent literature reviews of scientific and medical-electronic databases disclosed no studies supporting a biological concept of ID. . . .

. . .

. . . Although Defendants have consistently asserted that the ID Policy was enacted for the secular purposes of improving science education and encouraging students to exercise critical thinking skills, the Board took none of the steps that school officials would take if these stated goals had truly been their objective. The Board consulted no scientific materials. The Board contacted no scientists or scientific organizations. The Board failed to consider the views of the District's science teachers. The Board relied solely on legal advice from two organizations with demonstrably religious, cultural, and legal missions, the Discovery Institute and the TMLC [Thomas More Law Center]. . . .

Accordingly, we find that the secular purposes claimed by the Board amount to a pretext for the Board's real purpose, which was to promote religion in the public school classroom, in violation of the Establishment Clause.

. . .

To be sure, Darwin's theory of evolution is imperfect. However, the fact that a scientific theory cannot yet render an explanation on every point should not be used as a pretext to thrust an untestable alternative hypothesis grounded in religion into the science classroom or to misrepresent well-established scientific propositions. . . .

Free Exercise

Elected officials and justices dispute whether Congress can legislatively require states to give religious believers exemptions from generally valid laws unless a compelling interest requires uniform coverage. As noted in Chapter 10, a bipartisan congressional majority passed the Religious Freedom Restoration Act (RFRA), which mandated that states grant exemptions to religious believers. The Supreme Court in *Boerne v. Flores* (1997) unanimously declared that measure unconstitutional. Even those justices who insisted that the First and Fourteenth Amendments normally require exemptions for religious believers maintained that this rule could be mandated only by the Supreme Court, not by Congress.

The justices nevertheless unanimously sustained narrower congressional efforts to grant exemptions to religious believers. *Gonzales v. O Centro Espirita Beneficiente Uniao Do Ve* (2006) upheld the constitutionality of the RFRA as applied to the federal government. *Cutter v. Wilkinson* (2005) sustained the provision in the Religious Land Use and Institutionalized Persons Act (RLUIPA) requiring the compelling interest test for laws burdening the free exercise rights of prisoners. Justice Ginsburg's opinion for the Court noted that, unlike RFRA, RLUIPA focused on a limited set of circumstances in which a substantial risk existed of state constitutional violations. She wrote, "RLUIPA thus protects institutionalized persons who are unable freely to attend to their religious needs and are therefore dependent on the government's permission and accommodation for exercise of their religion." The justices unanimously ruled that religious groups could fire religious leaders for any reason, even if that reason was inconsistent with federal anti-discrimination laws. Chief Justice Roberts's opinion in *Hosanna-Tabor Evangelical Lutheran Church and School v. E.E.O.C* (2012) asserted, "Requiring a church to accept or retain an unwanted minister, or punishing a church for failing to do so, . . . interferes with the internal governance of the church, depriving the church of control over the selection of those who will personify its beliefs."

Recent years suggest a sharp shift in the constitutional politics of the free exercise clause. The most politically salient constitutional claims are presently made by evangelical Christians and other religious conservatives. Many maintain that they have a constitutional right to exceptions from mandatory school requirements, particular reading assignments in public schools, laws mandating that personnel in public hospitals provide reproductive services such as abortion, and laws that require that they not discriminate against gays and lesbians. In 2012 the U.S. Conference of Catholic Bishops denounced the Obama administration for requiring all nonchurch employers to provide their employees with health plans that included benefits for contraception. Although some states have passed statutes recognizing religious exemptions from these and similar decrees, most judges refuse to give those claims constitutional sanction.[28] In *Parker v. Hurley* (2008) the Court of Appeals for the First Circuit rejected a claim that parents had a free exercise right to prevent teachers from reading certain books to their children. Judge's Lynch's unanimous opinion asserted, "While parents can choose between public and private schools, they do not have a constitutional right to direct how a public school teaches their child."[29]

Same-sex marriage has raised particularly heated free exercise controversies. As an increasing number of states recognize same-sex marriage, religious conservatives are insisting that they have a constitutional right to treat such persons as not married. Many state laws authorizing same-sex marriage contain provisions that provide exemptions to persons who think such unions sinful. New York has declared,

> Nothing in this article shall be deemed or construed to prohibit any religious or denominational institution or organization, or any organization operated for charitable or educational purposes, which is operated, supervised or controlled by or in connection with a religious organization from limiting employment or sales or rental of housing accommodations or admission to or giving preference to persons of the same religion or denomination or from taking such action as is calculated by such organization to promote the religious principles for which it is established or maintained.[30]

Some proponents of same-sex marriage think this is a good compromise. They regard religious exemptions as an acceptable price to pay for achieving gay marriage or maintain that religious believers are entitled to exemptions as a matter of principle. Robin Fretwell Wilson maintains, "Forcing a public employee with a religious objection to facilitate a same-sex marriage would be intolerant in the extreme when little is to be

---

28. For a good summary, see Laura Underkuffler, "Odious Discrimination and the Religious Exemption Question," *Cardozo Law Review* 32 (2011): 2087.

29. *Parker v. Hurley*, 514 F. 3d 87 (1st Cir. 2008).

30. McKinney's Consolidated Laws of New York, § 10-b (2011).

gained by such rigid demands."[31] Others find offensive the notion that religious believers are entitled to exemptions from laws they believe protect basic human rights. Laura Underkuffler writes, "Why should religiously grounded discrimination be tolerated against gay and lesbian citizens when, regarding racial, religious, gender, national-origin, and other groups, it is not?"[32]

City of Boerne v. Flores, 521 U.S. 507 (1997)

P. F. Flores, the archbishop of San Antonio, sought to expand St. Peter Catholic Church, which was located in Boerne, Texas. The City of Boerne denied the archbishop's request for a permit on the ground that expansion was inconsistent with a recently enacted historical preservation plan. Flores challenged this decision in federal court, claiming that the permit denial was inconsistent with the Religious Freedom Restoration Act (RFRA). That statute sought to restore the rule of Sherbert v. Verner *(1963), which held that individuals could claim a constitutional exemption from laws that substantially burden religious practice unless the law served a compelling government interest. The district court ruled that Congress had no constitutional authority to extend RFRA to the states and that the case was governed by* Employment Division v. Smith *(1990). That decision held that the free exercise clause of the First Amendment, as incorporated by the Fourteenth Amendment, did not require states to exempt religious believers and organizations from generally applicable laws. The Court of Appeals for the Fifth Circuit reversed the lower federal court. Boerne appealed to the Supreme Court.*

The Supreme Court by a 6-3 vote declared RFRA unconstitutional. Justice Kennedy's majority opinion held that Section 5 of the Fourteenth Amendment did not give Congress the power to reverse Smith *or otherwise determine the meaning of constitutional rights provisions. The three dissenters agreed that the Section 5 power to "enforce" the Fourteenth Amendment did not include the power to determine the meaning of constitutional provisions, but they insisted that* Smith *was wrongly decided.*

Kennedy's opinion for the Court leans on John Marshall's language from Marbury v. Madison *(1803) when emphasizing the primacy of the Court's role in interpreting the Constitution. Does* Marbury *determine the result here? Reread the materials on the drafting of the Fourteenth Amendment. To what extent do they support Kennedy's conclusions?*

Justice Kennedy recognized that Congress could forbid otherwise constitutional state behavior when doing so might prevent or deter unconstitutional actions. Although the Constitution does not require police officers to take a class on the Fourth Amendment, such a class might reduce official violations of the equal protection clause. Kennedy insisted, however, that the Court apply a congruence and proportionality test to determine whether Congress has constitutionally exercised Section 5 powers. What is that test? What are the constitutional foundations of that test? Why does Justice Kennedy believe that RFRA fails that test?

JUSTICE KENNEDY delivered the opinion of the Court.

. . .

Legislation which deters or remedies constitutional violations can fall within the sweep of Congress' enforcement power even if in the process it prohibits conduct which is not itself unconstitutional and intrudes into "legislative spheres of autonomy previously reserved to the States." . . . For example, the Court upheld a suspension of literacy tests and similar voting requirements under Congress' parallel power to enforce the provisions of the Fifteenth Amendment . . . as a measure to combat racial discrimination in voting . . . despite the facial constitutionality of the tests. . . .

. . .

Congress' power under Section Five, however, extends only to "enforcing" the provisions of the Fourteenth Amendment. . . . The design of the Amendment and the text of Section Five are inconsistent with the suggestion that Congress has the power to decree the substance of the Fourteenth Amendment's restrictions on the States. Legislation which alters the meaning of the Free Exercise Clause cannot be said to be enforcing the Clause. Congress does not enforce a constitutional right by changing what the right is. It has been given the power "to enforce," not the power to determine what constitutes a constitutional violation. Were it not so, what Congress would be enforcing would no longer be, in any meaningful sense, the "provisions of [the Fourteenth Amendment]."

. . .

If Congress could define its own powers by altering the Fourteenth Amendment's meaning, no longer

31. Robin Fretwell Wilson, "Insubstantial Burdens: The Case for Government Exemptions to Same-Sex Marriage," *Northwestern Journal of Law & Social Policy* 5 (2010): 360.

32. Underkuffler, "Odious Discrimination," 2087.

would the Constitution be "superior paramount law, unchangeable by ordinary means." It would be "on a level with ordinary legislative acts, and, like other acts, . . . alterable when the legislature shall please to alter it." *Marbury v. Madison* (1803). . . . Under this approach, it is difficult to conceive of a principle that would limit congressional power. . . . Shifting legislative majorities could change the Constitution and effectively circumvent the difficult and detailed amendment process contained in Article V.

. . .

Respondent contends that RFRA is a proper exercise of Congress' remedial or preventive power. The Act, it is said, is a reasonable means of protecting the free exercise of religion as defined by *Smith*. It prevents and remedies laws which are enacted with the unconstitutional object of targeting religious beliefs and practices. To avoid the difficulty of proving such violations, it is said, Congress can simply invalidate any law which imposes a substantial burden on a religious practice unless it is justified by a compelling interest and is the least restrictive means of accomplishing that interest. If Congress can prohibit laws with discriminatory effects in order to prevent racial discrimination in violation of the Equal Protection Clause, then it can do the same, respondent argues, to promote religious liberty.

. . .

While preventive rules are sometimes appropriate remedial measures, there must be a congruence between the means used and the ends to be achieved. The appropriateness of remedial measures must be considered in light of the evil presented. . . .

. . .

. . . RFRA cannot be considered remedial, preventive legislation, if those terms are to have any meaning. RFRA is so out of proportion to a supposed remedial or preventive object that it cannot be understood as responsive to, or designed to prevent, unconstitutional behavior. It appears, instead, to attempt a substantive change in constitutional protections. Preventive measures prohibiting certain types of laws may be appropriate when there is reason to believe that many of the laws affected by the congressional enactment have a significant likelihood of being unconstitutional. . . .

. . .

The stringent test RFRA demands of state laws reflects a lack of proportionality or congruence between the means adopted and the legitimate end to be achieved. If an objector can show a substantial burden on his free exercise, the State must demonstrate a compelling governmental interest and show that the law is the least restrictive means of furthering its interest. Claims that a law substantially burdens someone's exercise of religion will often be difficult to contest. Requiring a State to demonstrate a compelling interest and show that it has adopted the least restrictive means of achieving that interest is the most demanding test known to constitutional law. If "'compelling interest' really means what it says . . . , many laws will not meet the test. . . . [The test] would open the prospect of constitutionally required religious exemptions from civic obligations of almost every conceivable kind." Laws valid under *Smith* would fall under RFRA without regard to whether they had the object of stifling or punishing free exercise. We make these observations not to reargue the position of the majority in *Smith* but to illustrate the substantive alteration of its holding attempted by RFRA. Even assuming RFRA would be interpreted in effect to mandate some lesser test, say, one equivalent to intermediate scrutiny, the statute nevertheless would require searching judicial scrutiny of state law with the attendant likelihood of invalidation. This is a considerable congressional intrusion into the States' traditional prerogatives and general authority to regulate for the health and welfare of their citizens.

. . . Simply put, RFRA is not designed to identify and counteract state laws likely to be unconstitutional because of their treatment of religion. In most cases, the state laws to which RFRA applies are not ones which will have been motivated by religious bigotry. If a state law disproportionately burdened a particular class of religious observers, this circumstance might be evidence of an impermissible legislative motive. RFRA's substantial-burden test, however, is not even a discriminatory effects or disparate-impact test. It is a reality of the modern regulatory state that numerous state laws, such as the zoning regulations at issue here, impose a substantial burden on a large class of individuals. When the exercise of religion has been burdened in an incidental way by a law of general application, it does not follow that the persons affected have been burdened any more than other citizens, let alone burdened because of their religious beliefs. In addition, the Act imposes in every case a least restrictive means requirement—a requirement that was not used in the pre-*Smith* jurisprudence RFRA purported to codify—which also indicates that the legislation is broader than is appropriate if the goal is to prevent and remedy constitutional violations.

. . .

Our national experience teaches that the Constitution is preserved best when each part of the government respects both the Constitution and the proper actions and determinations of the other branches. When the Court has interpreted the Constitution, it has acted within the province of the Judicial Branch, which embraces the duty to say what the law is. . . . When the political branches of the Government act against the background of a judicial interpretation of the Constitution already issued, it must be understood that in later cases and controversies the Court will treat its precedents with the respect due them under settled principles, including *stare decisis*, and contrary expectations must be disappointed. RFRA was designed to control cases and controversies, such as the one before us; but as the provisions of the federal statute here invoked are beyond congressional authority, it is this Court's precedent, not RFRA, which must control.

JUSTICE STEVENS, concurring.

It is my opinion, the Religious Freedom Restoration Act of 1993 (RFRA) is a "law respecting an establishment of religion" that violates the First Amendment to the Constitution.

. . .

JUSTICE SCALIA, with whom JUSTICE STEVENS joins, concurring in part. . . .

JUSTICE O'CONNOR, with whom JUSTICE BREYER joins, dissenting.

. . .

I agree with much of the reasoning set forth in . . . the Court's opinion. Indeed, if I agreed with the Court's standard in *Smith*, I would join the opinion. As the Court's careful and thorough historical analysis shows, Congress lacks the "power to decree the substance of the Fourteenth Amendment's restrictions on the States." Rather, its power under Section Five of the Fourteenth Amendment extends only to enforcing the Amendment's provisions. In short, Congress lacks the ability independently to define or expand the scope of constitutional rights by statute. . . .

Stare decisis concerns should not prevent us from revisiting our holding in *Smith*. "[S]tare decisis is a principle of policy and not a mechanical formula of adherence to the latest decision, however recent and questionable, when such adherence involves collision with a prior doctrine more embracing in its scope, intrinsically sounder, and verified by experience." . . . This principle is particularly true in constitutional cases where—as this case plainly illustrates—"correction through legislative action is practically impossible." . . . I believe that, in light of both our precedent and our Nation's tradition of religious liberty, *Smith* is demonstrably wrong. Moreover, it is a recent decision. As such, it has not engendered the kind of reliance on its continued application that would militate against overruling it. Cf. *Planned Parenthood of Southeastern Pennsylvania v. Casey* (1992).

. . .

I respectfully dissent from the Court's disposition of this case.

JUSTICE SOUTER, dissenting. . . .

JUSTICE BREYER, dissenting. . . .

Debate over Exemptions from the Affordable Care Act (2012)

The Obama administration initiated a controversy over religious freedom when the Department of Health and Human Services issued a regulation requiring all employers, other than churches, to provide employees with health care plans that covered contraception. Administration officials insisted that the mandate provided crucial health services to women. Opponents accused the administration of violating the rights of religious employees, such as Catholic hospitals, that were providing nondevotional services to the general public. The controversy did not die down when President Obama modified the plan so that no religious institution would be required to pay directly for birth control and related services.

When reading President Obama's defense of his compromise plan and the U.S. Conference of Catholic Bishops' criticism of that compromise, consider the following questions. Is the Obama plan a compromise, or does the plan violate the free exercise rights of Catholic employers? Are there any differences between the way in which the president handled the free exercise issues and how a court might adjudicate this controversy? To what extent should religious employers or service providers engaged in public commercial activity be given exemptions from secular laws that impinge on their religious conscience? Should Catholic pharmacists be permitted to refuse to fill a birth control prescription? Should an orthodox Jewish apartment owner be permitted to refuse to rent to a gay couple? Could an employer who is a Jehovah's Witness refuse to offer health insurance to employees?

Barack Obama, Remarks on Preventive Health Care Insurance Coverage and an Exchange with Reporters (February 10, 2012)

I know that some religious institutions, particularly those affiliated with the Catholic Church, have a religious objection to directly providing insurance that covers contraceptive services for their employees. And that's why we originally exempted all churches from this requirement. . . .

. . .

. . . Today we've reached a decision on how to move forward. Under the rule, women will still have access to free preventive care that includes contraceptive services, no matter where they work. So that core principle remains. But if a woman's employer is a charity or a hospital that has a religious objection to providing contraceptive services as part of their health plan, the insurance company—not the hospital, not the charity—will be required to reach out and offer the woman contraceptive care free of charge, without copays and without hassles.

The result will be that religious organizations won't have to pay for these services, and no religious institution will have to provide these services directly. Let me repeat: These employers will not have to pay for or provide contraceptive services. But women who work at these institutions will have access to free contraceptive services just like other women, and they'll no longer have to pay hundreds of dollars a year that could go towards paying the rent or buying groceries. . . . Religious liberty will be protected, and a law that requires free preventive care will not discriminate against women.

United States Conference of Catholic Bishops, Bishops Renew Call to Legislative Action on Religious Liberty (February 10, 2012)[33]

First, we objected to the rule forcing private health plans—nationwide, by the stroke of a bureaucrat's pen—to cover sterilization and contraception, including drugs that may cause abortion. All the other mandated "preventive services" prevent disease,and pregnancy is not a disease. Moreover, forcing plans to cover abortifacients violates existing federal conscience laws. Therefore, we called for the rescission of the mandate altogether.

33. http://www.usccb.org/news/2012/12-026.cfm.

Second, we explained that the mandate would impose a burden of unprecedented reach and severity on the consciences of those who consider such "services" immoral: insurers forced to write policies including this coverage; employers and schools forced to sponsor and subsidize the coverage; and individual employees and students forced to pay premiums for the coverage. We therefore urged HHS, if it insisted on keeping the mandate, to provide a conscience exemption for all of these stakeholders—not just the extremely small subset of "religious employers" that HHS proposed to exempt initially.

. . .

[The changes proposed by President Obama] require careful moral analysis, and moreover, appear subject to some measure of change. But we note at the outset that the lack of clear protection for key stakeholders—for self-insured religious employers; for religious and secular for-profit employers; for secular non-profit employers; for religious insurers; and for individuals—is unacceptable and must be corrected. And in the case where the employee and insurer agree to add the objectionable coverage, that coverage is still provided as a part of the objecting employer's plan, financed in the same way as the rest of the coverage offered by the objecting employer. This, too, raises serious moral concerns.

. . . [W]e note that today's proposal continues to involve needless government intrusion in the internal governance of religious institutions, and to threaten government coercion of religious people and groups to violate their most deeply held convictions. In a nation dedicated to religious liberty as its first and founding principle, we should not be limited to negotiating within these parameters. The only complete solution to this religious liberty problem is for HHS to rescind the mandate of these objectionable services. . . .

Establishment and Free Exercise (and Free Speech)

The American welfare state has spawned new controversies that combine establishment and free exercise concerns. Consider the plight of a town official faced with ten applications, one from a religious group, for the use of five softball fields in a public park on Sunday afternoon. The local ordinance declares that the town will provide umpires (paid for by taxpayers) and should allocate the fields to those organizations that make the greatest contribution to the community.

If the town official permits the religious group to use the softball field, critics might claim that tax money is going to a religious group in violation of the establishment clause. If the town official does not permit the religious group to use the field, critics might claim that religious groups are being discriminated against in violation of the free exercise clause.

With one very important exception the Supreme Court permits elected officials to choose whether to include religious groups in various benefits programs. A 7-2 majority in *Locke v. Davey* (2004) sustained a Washington law that excluded students studying devotional theology from a state scholarship program. Chief Justice Rehnquist's opinion emphasized the "play in the joints" between the free exercise and establishment clause. While he declared that a state could "permit Promise Scholars to pursue a degree in devotional theology," consistent with the establishment clause, Rehnquist added that a state's law that "deal(s) differently with religious education for the ministry than with education for other callings is . . . not evidence of hostility toward religion" that would violate the free exercise clause. The exceptional case when state officials have no choice is when states create a limited public forum, a forum for speech on certain subjects. In such circumstances judicial majorities, inspired by such interest groups as the Center for Individual Rights, have ruled that the free speech clause of the First Amendment forbids discrimination against religious perspectives. In *Rosenberger v. Rector and Visitors of University of Virginia* (1995) a 5-4 judicial majority ruled that the University of Virginia had to pay the printing costs for a student-run religious newspaper when the university paid the printing costs for all other student newspapers. Justice Kennedy's majority opinion asserted that state officials had "select[ed] for disfavored treatment those student journalistic efforts with religious editorial viewpoints." For a public university to grant access to its facilities "on a religion-neutral basis to a wide spectrum of student groups," he continued, "does not violate the Establishment Clause." A 6-3 majority in *Good News Club v. Milford Central School* (2001) applied these principles when ruling that public schools could not forbid Christian groups from meeting in public schools when secular groups were routinely granted access to those facilities. Justice Thomas's majority opinion stated, "When Milford denied the Good News Club access to the school's limited public forum on the ground that the Club was religious in nature, it discriminated against the Club because of its religious viewpoint in violation of the Free Speech Clause of the First Amendment."

C. Guns

The trend toward increased support for an individual right to bear arms, which began in the Reagan Era, is accelerating. The Republican Party has adopted an ever-stronger stance on Second Amendment rights. The party platform in 2012 declared:

> We uphold the right of individuals to keep and bear arms, a right which antedated the Constitution and was solemnly confirmed by the Second Amendment. We acknowledge, support, and defend the lawabiding citizen's God-given right of self-defense. . . . We support the fundamental right to self-defense wherever a lawabiding citizen has a legal right to be, and we support federal legislation that would expand the exercise of that right by allowing those with state-issued carry permits to carry firearms in any state that issues such permits to its own residents. Gun ownership is responsible citizenship, enabling Americans to defend their homes and communities. We condemn frivolous lawsuits against gun manufacturers and oppose federal licensing or registration of law-abiding gun owners. We oppose legislation that is intended to restrict our Second Amendment rights by limiting the capacity of clips or magazines or otherwise restoring the ill considered Clinton gun ban.

Democrats, who previously never discussed Second Amendment rights, now combine support for an individual right to bear arms with calls for gun control. The national party platform in 2012 declared,

> We recognize that the individual right to bear arms is an important part of the American tradition, and we will preserve Americans' Second Amendment right to own and use firearms. We believe that the right to own firearms is subject to reasonable regulation. We understand the terrible consequences of gun violence; it serves as a reminder that life is fragile, and our time here is limited and precious. We believe in an honest, open national conversation about firearms. We can focus on effective enforcement of existing laws, especially strengthening our background check system, and we can work together to enact commonsense improvements - like reinstating the assault weapons ban and closing the

gun show loophole - so that guns do not fall into the hands of those irresponsible, law-breaking few.

The Supreme Court in two pathbreaking cases supported constitutional gun rights. The justices in *District of Columbia v. Heller* (2008) by a 5-4 vote held that the Second Amendment protected an individual right to bear arms. *McDonald v. City of Chicago* (2010)[34] by the same 5-4 vote held that the due process clause of the Fourteenth Amendment incorporated this individual right to bear arms.

Contemporary constitutional debates over the Second Amendment revolve around two issues. The first is the relationship between the prefatory clause, "a well regulated Militia, being necessary to a free state," and the declaration that "the right of the people to keep and bear arms, shall not be infringed." Proponents of the standard or collective interpretation insist that Americans have no rights independent of the militia. Individuals may have a right to belong to existing state militias, but they have no right to bear arms for individual protection or hunting. Given that militias no longer exist or do not exist in their original form, the Second Amendment in this view has almost no practical implications for contemporary constitutional politics.[35] Proponents of the individual rights model assert that the preface declares one reason for the right to bear arms but does not exhaust the scope of the right. As championed by such scholars as Professor Eugene Volokh and Randy Barnett, this constitutional understanding insists that citizens have a constitutional right to bear arms for their protection and recreational use, even when their actions are not affiliated with a state militia.[36]

Americans also dispute the extent to which government may regulate an individual right to bear arms. No one thinks that the Second Amendment protects a private right to own tanks. Still, as *District of Columbia v. Heller* demonstrates, no agreement exists on the weapons the Constitution protects and the nature of that protection. Those who interpret the Second Amendment in light of the First Amendment suggest that a compelling interest may be necessary for the government to regulate gun rights. Those who see the Second Amendment as more similar to the Fourth Amendment believe that any regulation that might promote public safety is constitutional.

The lower federal courts are in the process of assessing the proper application of *Heller* to other assertions of an individual right to bear arms. The Court of Appeals for the District of Columbia in *Heller v. District of Columbia* II (2011) sustained most aspects of the registration requirements and the ban on assault weapons that the District of Columbia passed in the wake of the Supreme Court's *Heller* decision. The judges upheld "the requirement of mere registration" because that requirement was "longstanding." Judge Douglas Ginsburg asserted, "a regulation that is 'longstanding' . . . has long been accepted by the public" and "is not likely to burden a constitutional right." Applying intermediate scrutiny, Ginsburg then sustained the ban on semi-automatic rifles and similar weapons. That ban, he asserted, serves "important interests in protecting police officers and controlling crime," and does not "prevent a person from keeping a suitable and commonly used weapon in the home or for hunting."[37] A federal district court in Maryland was more solicitous of gun rights when declaring unconstitutional a state law requiring persons to demonstrate "good and substantial reason" why they should be given a permit to carry a handgun. Judge Legg's opinion in *Wollard v. Sheridan* (2012), after declaring that intermediate scrutiny was an appropriate standard of review, asserted, "Maryland's goal of 'minimizing the proliferation of handguns among those who do not have a demonstrated need for them,' is not a permissible method of preventing crime or ensuring public safety; it burdens the right too broadly."[38]

John Ashcroft, Letter to National Rifle Association (May 17, 2001)[39]

Prominent Justice Department officials in the Reagan, first Bush, and second Bush administrations publicly sup-

34. *McDonald* is exceprted in Section II.

35. See H. Richard Uviller and William G. Merkel, *The Militia and the Right to Bear Arms, or, How the Second Amendment Fell Silent* (Durham, NC: Duke University Press, 2002).

36. See Eugene Volokh, "The Commonplace Second Amendment," *New York University Law Review* 73 (1998): 793 and Randy E. Barnett and Don B. Kates, "Under Fire: The New Consensus on the Second Amendment," *Emory L.J.* 45 (1996): 1139.

37. *Heller v. District of Columbia*, 670 F.3d 1244 (C.A. D.C. 2011).

38. Woollard v. Sheridan, 2012 U.S. Dist. LEXIS 28498, *33 (D. Md. 2012).

39. John Ashcroft to James J. Baker, Executive Director of the NRA, http://wmsa.net/ashcroft.htm

ported the individual rights interpretation of the Second Amendment and aggressively took steps to make their position the constitutional law of the land. Within months of taking office in 2001 Attorney General John Ashcroft publicly announced that the Bush II administration was committed to upholding the individual right to bear arms. As you read the following letter, ask yourself what commitments the Bush administration was actually making. What letter do you believe Attorney General Eric Holder of the Obama administration might write?

. . . While I cannot comment on any pending litigation, let me state unequivocally my view that the text and the original intent of the Second Amendment clearly protect the right of individuals to keep and bear firearms. While some have argued that the Second Amendment guarantees only a "collective" right of the States to maintain militias, I believe the Amendment's plain meaning and original intent prove otherwise. Like the First and Fourth Amendments, the Second Amendment protects the rights of "the people" which the Supreme Court has noted is a term of art that should be interpreted consistently throughout the Bill of Rights.

. . . Just as the First and Fourth Amendment secure individual rights of speech and security respectively, the Second Amendment protects an individual's right to keep and bear arms. This view of the text comports with the all but unanimous understanding of the Founding Fathers. . . .

This is not a novel position. In early decisions, the United States Supreme Court routinely indicated that the right protected by the Second Amendment applied to individuals. See, *e.g.*, *Logan v. United States* (1892); *Miller v. Texas* (1893). . . . Justice Story embraced the same view in his influential *Commentaries on the Constitution*. . . . It is the view that was adopted by United States Attorney General Homer Cummings before Congress in testifying about the constitutionality of the first federal gun control statute, the National Firearms Act of 1934. . . . As recently as 1986, the United States Congress and President Ronald Reagan explicitly adopted this view in the Firearms Owners Protection Act. . . . Significantly, the individual's rights view is embraced by the preponderance of legal scholarship on the subject, which, I note, includes articles by academics on both ends of the political spectrum. . . .

In light of this vast body of evidence, I believe it is clear that the Constitution protects the private ownership of firearms for lawful purposes. As I was reminded during my confirmation hearing, some hold a different view and would, in effect, read the Second Amendment out of the Constitution. I must respectfully disagree with this view, for when I was sworn in as Attorney General of the United States, I took an oath to uphold and defend the Constitution. That responsibility applies to all parts of the constitution, including the Second Amendment. . . .

District of Columbia v. Heller, 554 U.S. 570 (2008)

Dick Heller, a special police officer in Washington, DC, applied for a license to keep a handgun in his home. The District of Columbia at the time banned all handguns but permitted the chief of police to issue a license for one year. When Heller was denied a permit he and several other citizens of the District challenged the constitutionality of the prohibition in federal court. The local district court dismissed their appeal, but that dismissal was reversed by the Court of Appeals for the District of Columbia. The appellate court decision found that Heller had an individual right to carry a gun for self-defense and that the total ban on handguns violated the Second Amendment. The District of Columbia appealed to the Supreme Court of the United States.

The Supreme Court by a 5-4 vote affirmed the Court of Appeals' decision that Heller had a Second Amendment right to have a handgun in his home. Justice Scalia's majority opinion maintained that both the text and the history of the Second Amendment support an individual right to bear arms. Both Justice Scalia and Justice Stevens rely heavily on the original meaning of constitutional provisions. Are they the same kind of originalists who simply interpret the same materials differently, or are they different kinds of originalists who place different emphasis on different materials? To what extent do you believe that historical materials, rather than policy preferences, drive each analysis? Consider also the implications of Heller. *What gun regulations would you predict would be unconstitutional after* Heller? *To what extent are you basing those predictions on your beliefs about judicial policy preferences or the language in the judicial opinions?*

JUSTICE SCALIA delivered the opinion of the Court.

. . .

The Second Amendment is naturally divided into two parts: its prefatory clause and its operative clause. The former does not limit the latter grammatically, but rather announces a purpose. The Amendment could be rephrased, "Because a well regulated Militia is necessary to the security of a free State, the right of the people to keep and bear Arms shall not be infringed." . . .

Logic demands that there be a link between the stated purpose and the command. . . . But apart from [a] clarifying function, a prefatory clause does not limit or expand the scope of the operative clause. . . .

. . .

The first salient feature of the operative clause is that it codifies a "right of the people." The unamended Constitution and the Bill of Rights use the phrase "right of the people" two other times, in the First Amendment's Assembly-and-Petition Clause and in the Fourth Amendment's Search-and-Seizure Clause. The Ninth Amendment uses very similar terminology ("The enumeration in the Constitution, of certain rights, shall not be construed to deny or disparage others retained by the people"). All three of these instances unambiguously refer to individual rights, not "collective" rights, or rights that may be exercised only through participation in some corporate body.

. . .

This contrasts markedly with the phrase "the militia" in the prefatory clause. As we will describe below, the "militia" in colonial America consisted of a subset of "the people"—those who were male, able bodied, and within a certain age range. Reading the Second Amendment as protecting only the right to "keep and bear Arms" in an organized militia therefore fits poorly with the operative clause's description of the holder of that right as "the people."

. . .

At the time of the founding, as now, to "bear" meant to "carry." . . . When used with "arms," however, the term has a meaning that refers to carrying for a particular purpose—confrontation. . . . Although the phrase implies that the carrying of the weapon is for the purpose of "offensive or defensive action," it in no way connotes participation in a structured military organization.

From our review of founding-era sources, we conclude that this natural meaning was also the meaning that "bear arms" had in the 18th century. In numerous instances, "bear arms" was unambiguously used to refer to the carrying of weapons outside of an organized militia. The most prominent examples are those most relevant to the Second Amendment: Nine state constitutional provisions written in the 18th century or the first two decades of the 19th, which enshrined a right of citizens to "bear arms in defense of themselves and the state" or "bear arms in defense of himself and the state." It is clear from those formulations that "bear arms" did not refer only to carrying a weapon in an organized military unit. . . .

. . .

Putting all of these textual elements together, we find that they guarantee the individual right to possess and carry weapons in case of confrontation.

. . .

It is therefore entirely sensible that the Second Amendment's prefatory clause announces the purpose for which the right was codified: to prevent elimination of the militia. The prefatory clause does not suggest that preserving the militia was the only reason Americans valued the ancient right; most undoubtedly thought it even more important for self-defense and hunting. But the threat that the new Federal Government would destroy the citizens' militia by taking away their arms was the reason that right—unlike some other English rights—was codified in a written Constitution. . . .

. . .

Our interpretation is confirmed by analogous arms-bearing rights in state constitutions that preceded and immediately followed adoption of the Second Amendment. Four States adopted analogues to the Federal Second Amendment in the period between independence and the ratification of the Bill of Rights. Two of them—Pennsylvania and Vermont—clearly adopted individual rights unconnected to militia service. Pennsylvania's Declaration of Rights of 1776 said: "That the people have a right to bear arms *for the defence of themselves,* and the state. . . ." . . . In 1777, Vermont adopted the identical provision, except for inconsequential differences in punctuation and capitalization. . . .

. . .

That . . . of the nine state constitutional protections for the right to bear arms enacted immediately after 1789 at least seven unequivocally protected an individual citizen's right to self-defense is strong evidence that that is how the founding generation conceived of the right. . . .

. . .

. . . [V]irtually all interpreters of the Second Amendment in the century after its enactment interpreted the amendment as we do.

. . .

St. George Tucker's version of *Blackstone's Commentaries* . . . conceived of the Blackstonian arms right as necessary for self-defense. . . . Tucker elaborated on the Second Amendment: "This may be considered as the true palladium of liberty. . . . The right to self-defence is the first law of nature: in most governments it has been the study of rulers to confine the right within the narrowest limits possible. Wherever standing armies are kept up, and the right of the people to keep and bear arms is, under any colour or pretext whatsoever, prohibited, liberty, if not already annihilated, is on the brink of destruction." . . . He believed that the English game laws had abridged the right by prohibiting "keeping a gun or other engine for the destruction of game."

. . .

Antislavery advocates routinely invoked the right to bear arms for self-defense. Joel Tiffany, for example, citing Blackstone's description of the right, wrote that "the right to keep and bear arms, also implies the right to use them if necessary in self defence; without this right to use the guaranty would have hardly been worth the paper it consumed." . . .

. . .

Like most rights, the right secured by the Second Amendment is not unlimited. From Blackstone through the 19th-century cases, commentators and courts routinely explained that the right was not a right to keep and carry any weapon whatsoever in any manner whatsoever and for whatever purpose. . . . For example, the majority of the 19th-century courts to consider the question held that prohibitions on carrying concealed weapons were lawful under the Second Amendment or state analogues. . . . [N]othing in our opinion should be taken to cast doubt on longstanding prohibitions on the possession of firearms by felons and the mentally ill, or laws forbidding the carrying of firearms in sensitive places such as schools and government buildings, or laws imposing conditions and qualifications on the commercial sale of arms.

. . .

. . . [T]he inherent right of self-defense has been central to the Second Amendment right. The handgun ban amounts to a prohibition of an entire class of "arms" that is overwhelmingly chosen by American society for that lawful purpose. The prohibition extends, moreover, to the home, where the need for defense of self, family, and property is most acute. Under any of the standards of scrutiny that we have applied to enumerated constitutional rights, banning from the home "the most preferred firearm in the nation to 'keep' and use for protection of one's home and family," . . . would fail constitutional muster.

. . .

We know of no other enumerated constitutional right whose core protection has been subjected to a freestanding "interest-balancing" approach. The very enumeration of the right takes out of the hands of government—even the Third Branch of Government—the power to decide on a case-by-case basis whether the right is *really worth* insisting upon. A constitutional guarantee subject to future judges' assessments of its usefulness is no constitutional guarantee at all. Constitutional rights are enshrined with the scope they were understood to have when the people adopted them, whether or not future legislatures or (yes) even future judges think that scope too broad. . . .

In sum, we hold that the District's ban on handgun possession in the home violates the Second Amendment, as does its prohibition against rendering any lawful firearm in the home operable for the purpose of immediate self-defense. Assuming that Heller is not disqualified from the exercise of Second Amendment rights, the District must permit him to register his handgun and must issue him a license to carry it in the home.

. . .

JUSTICE STEVENS, with whom JUSTICE SOUTER, JUSTICE GINSBURG, and JUSTICE BREYER join, dissenting.

. . .

The Second Amendment was adopted to protect the right of the people of each of the several States to maintain a well-regulated militia. It was a response to concerns raised during the ratification of the Constitution that the power of Congress to disarm the state militias and create a national standing army posed an intolerable threat to the sovereignty of the several States. Neither the text of the Amendment nor the arguments advanced by its proponents evidenced the slightest interest in limiting any legislature's authority to regulate private civilian uses of firearms. Specifically, there is no indication that the Framers of the Amendment intended to enshrine the common-law right of self-defense in the Constitution.

. . .

The preamble to the Second Amendment makes three important points. It identifies the preservation of the militia as the Amendment's purpose; it explains that the militia is necessary to the security of a free State; and it recognizes that the militia must be "well regulated." In all three respects it is comparable to provisions in several State Declarations of Rights that were adopted roughly contemporaneously with the Declaration of Independence. Those state provisions highlight the importance members of the founding generation attached to the maintenance of state militias; they also underscore the profound fear shared by many in that era of the dangers posed by standing armies. While the need for state militias has not been a matter of significant public interest for almost two centuries, that fact should not obscure the contemporary concerns that animated the Framers.

. . .

The parallels between the Second Amendment and these state declarations, and the Second Amendment's omission of any statement of purpose related to the right to use firearms for hunting or personal self-defense, is especially striking in light of the fact that the Declarations of Rights of Pennsylvania and Vermont *did* expressly protect such civilian uses at the time. . . . The contrast between those two declarations and the Second Amendment reinforces the clear statement of purpose announced in the Amendment's preamble. It confirms that the Framers' single-minded focus in crafting the constitutional guarantee "to keep and bear arms" was on military uses of firearms, which they viewed in the context of service in state militias.

. . .

The Court . . . overlooks the significance of the way the Framers used the phrase "the people." . . . In the First Amendment, no words define the class of individuals entitled to speak, to publish, or to worship; in that Amendment it is only the right peaceably to assemble, and to petition the Government for a redress of grievances, that is described as a right of "the people." These rights contemplate collective action. . . . Likewise, although the act of petitioning the Government is a right that can be exercised by individuals, it is primarily collective in nature. For if they are to be effective, petitions must involve groups of individuals acting in concert.

Similarly, the words "the people" in the Second Amendment refer back to the object announced in the Amendment's preamble. They remind us that it is the collective action of individuals having a duty to serve in the militia that the text directly protects and, perhaps more importantly, that the ultimate purpose of the Amendment was to protect the States' share of the divided sovereignty created by the Constitution.

. . .

The term "bear arms" is a familiar idiom; when used unadorned by any additional words, its meaning is "to serve as a soldier, do military service, fight." . . . Had the Framers wished to expand the meaning of the phrase "bear arms" to encompass civilian possession and use, they could have done so by the addition of phrases such as "for the defense of themselves," as was done in the Pennsylvania and Vermont Declarations of Rights. The *unmodified* use of "bear arms," by contrast, refers most naturally to a military purpose, as evidenced by its use in literally dozens of contemporary texts. The absence of any reference to civilian uses of weapons tailors the text of the Amendment to the purpose identified in its preamble.

. . .

Until today, it has been understood that legislatures may regulate the civilian use and misuse of firearms so long as they do not interfere with the preservation of a well-regulated militia. The Court's announcement of a new constitutional right to own and use firearms for private purposes upsets that settled understanding, but leaves for future cases the formidable task of defining the scope of permissible regulations. Today judicial craftsmen have confidently asserted that a policy choice that denies a "law-abiding, responsible citize[n]" the right to keep and use weapons in the home for self-defense is "off the table." . . . Given the presumption that most citizens are law abiding, and the reality that the need to defend oneself may suddenly arise in a host of locations outside the home, I fear that the District's policy choice may well be just the first of an unknown number of dominoes to be knocked off the table.

. . .

JUSTICE BREYER, with whom JUSTICE STEVENS, JUSTICE SOUTER, and JUSTICE GINSBURG join, dissenting.

. . .

. . . [T]he protection the Amendment provides is not absolute. The Amendment permits government to regulate the interests that it serves. Thus, irrespective of what those interests are—whether they do or do not include an independent interest in self-defense—the majority's view cannot be correct unless it can show that the District's regulation is unreasonable or inappropriate in Second Amendment terms. This the majority cannot do.

. . .

. . . [A] legislature could reasonably conclude that the law will advance goals of great public importance, namely, saving lives, preventing injury, and reducing crime. The law is tailored to the urban crime problem in that it is local in scope and thus affects only a geographic area both limited in size and entirely urban; the law concerns handguns, which are specially linked to urban gun deaths and injuries, and which are the overwhelmingly favorite weapon of armed criminals; and at the same time, the law imposes a burden upon gun owners that seems proportionately no greater than restrictions in existence at the time the Second Amendment was adopted. In these circumstances, the District's law falls within the zone that the Second Amendment leaves open to regulation by legislatures.

. . .

. . . The majority is wrong when it says that the District's law is unconstitutional "[u]nder any of the standards of scrutiny that we have applied to enumerated constitutional rights." . . . How could that be? It certainly would not be unconstitutional under, for example, a "rational basis" standard, which requires a court to uphold regulation so long as it bears a "rational relationship" to a "legitimate governmental purpose."

. . .

I would simply adopt an interest-balancing inquiry explicitly. The fact that important interests lie on both sides of the constitutional equation suggests that review of gun-control regulation is not a context in which a court should effectively presume either constitutionality (as in rational-basis review) or unconstitutionality (as in strict scrutiny). Rather, "where a law significantly implicates competing constitutionally protected interests in complex ways," the Court generally asks whether the statute burdens a protected interest in a way or to an extent that is out of proportion to the statute's salutary effects upon other important governmental interests. . . . Any answer would take account both of the statute's effects upon the competing interests and the existence of any clearly superior less restrictive alternative. . . .

In applying this kind of standard the Court normally defers to a legislature's empirical judgment in matters where a legislature is likely to have greater expertise and greater institutional factfinding capacity. . . .

. . .

No one doubts the constitutional importance of the statute's basic objective, saving lives. . . .

[Justice Breyer then discussed the evidence that the District relied on when imposing the handgun ban and the evidence indicating whether such bans are effective in practice. On the basis of this evidence, he concluded:]

. . .

The upshot is a set of studies and counterstudies that, at most, could leave a judge uncertain about the proper policy conclusion. But from respondent's perspective any such uncertainty is not good enough. That is because legislators, not judges, have primary responsibility for drawing policy conclusions from empirical fact. And, given that constitutional allocation of decisionmaking responsibility, the empirical evidence presented here is sufficient to allow a judge to reach a firm *legal* conclusion.

. . .

In weighing needs and burdens, we must take account of the possibility that there are reasonable, but less restrictive alternatives. . . . Here I see none.

The reason there is no clearly superior, less restrictive alternative to the District's handgun ban is that the ban's very objective is to reduce significantly the number of handguns in the District, say, for example, by allowing a law enforcement officer immediately to assume that *any* handgun he sees is an *illegal* handgun. And there is no plausible way to achieve that objective other than to ban the guns.

. . .

. . . [A]ny measure less restrictive in respect to the use of handguns for self-defense will, to that same extent, prove less effective in preventing the use of handguns for illicit purposes. If a resident has a handgun in the home that he can use for self-defense, then he has a handgun in the home that he can use to commit suicide or engage in acts of domestic violence. . . . If it is indeed the case, as the District believes, that the number of guns contributes to the number of gun-related crimes, accidents, and deaths, then, although there may be less restrictive, *less effective* substitutes for an outright ban, there is no less restrictive *equivalent* of an outright ban.

. . .

. . . [T]]he District law is tailored to the life-threatening problems it attempts to address. The law concerns one class of weapons, handguns, leaving residents free to possess shotguns and rifles, along with ammunition. The area that falls within its scope is totally urban. . . . That urban area suffers from a serious handgun-fatality problem. The District's law directly aims at that compelling problem. And there is no less restrictive way to achieve the problem-related benefits that it seeks.

. . .

. . . [T]he majority's decision threatens severely to limit the ability of more knowledgeable, democratically elected officials to deal with gun-related problems. The majority says that it leaves the District "a variety of tools for combating" such problems. It fails to list even one seemingly adequate replacement for the law it strikes down. I can understand how reasonable individuals can disagree about the merits of strict gun control as a crime-control measure, even in a totally urbanized area. But I cannot understand how one can take from the elected branches of government the right to decide whether to insist upon a handgun-free urban populace in a city now facing a serious crime problem and which, in the future, could well face environmental or other emergencies that threaten the breakdown of law and order. . . .

D. Personal Freedom and Public Morality

The main front of the constitutional culture wars began to change at the turn of the twenty-first century. The constitutional politics and law of abortion were relatively static from *Planned Parenthood v. Casey* (1993) to the 2010 midterm elections. Public attention turned to gay rights—in particular, federal and state constitutional protections for same-sex marriage. Important skirmishes are also currently taking place over the constitutional right to die. After the 2010 election, however, many state legislatures made renewed attempts to ban most if not all abortions. During the 2012 Republican primary prominent conservatives even challenged the constitutional rights to birth control many thought were firmly established by *Griswold v. Connecticut* (1965) and *Eisenstadt v. Baird* (1972).

Until recently fundamental rights analysis seemed entrenched in contemporary American constitutionalism. Constitutional debates were more often over the precise contours of rights to reproductive choice, same-sex intimacy, and a dignified death. Neither political liberals nor political conservatives gained the political power necessary to fashion a firm majority in both electoral institutions and the judiciary in favor of either a robust set of rights or the abandonment of modern protections for certain individual choices. Whether more recent attacks on abortion and birth control are largely symbolic gestures or the beginning of a new round in the culture wars will only become clear after the completion of a few more election cycles.

Troxel v. Granville (2000) illustrates fundamental rights analysis in contemporary American constitutional law. The issue in this case was whether a single mother could refuse to allow paternal grandparents visitation rights. When ruling for the mother, Justice O'Connor's plurality opinion asserted, "The liberty interest at issue in this case—the interest of parents in the care, custody, and control of their children—is perhaps the oldest of the fundamental liberty interests recognized by this Court." Justice Thomas, after noting that no party to the case seemed interested in overruling the long line of cases recognizing certain autonomy and family rights, agreed that case law recognized "a fundamental right of parents to direct the upbringing of their children." Justices Stevens and Kennedy in their dissents maintained that parents had a constitutional right to raise their children, but that a child might have a constitutional right or interest in maintaining preestablished relationships with other relatives. Justice Scalia was the only member of the Rehnquist Court who refused to engage in fundamental rights analysis.

Abortion

The abortion wars cooled during the late 1990s and the first decade of the twenty-first century. Neither liberal Democrats nor conservative Republicans have had the opportunity in the past twenty years to appoint a justice who would either cast a fifth vote for striking down most restrictions on abortion or overrule *Roe v. Wade* (1973). The rule of *Casey v. Planned Parenthood* (1993) that abortion be legal and, if states wish, heavily regulated seems likely to endure for the foreseeable future. Public opinion polls suggest that most Americans prefer the present middle-ground position of the Supreme Court to either the strongly pro-choice

Democratic Party platform[40] or the strongly pro-life Republican platform.[41]

The most important constitutional struggle over reproductive choice during most of the Contemporary Era was over partial-birth abortions. Consistent with the general pro-choice commitment of most Democrats, President Clinton opposed legislation that did not contain what he believed was the constitutionally mandated health exception. His veto of a 1996 bill declared,

> I cannot sign H.R. 1833, as passed, because it fails to protect women in such dire circumstances because by treating doctors who perform the procedure in these tragic cases as criminals, the bill poses a danger of serious harm to women. This bill, in curtailing the ability of women and their doctors to choose the procedure for sound medical reasons, violates the constitutional command that any law regulating abortion protect both the life and the health of the woman. The bill's overbroad criminal prohibition risks that women will suffer serious injury.
>
> The life exception in the current bill only covers cases where the doctor believes that the woman will die. It fails to cover cases where, absent the procedure, serious physical harm, often including losing the ability to have more children, is very likely to occur.

President Bush reversed this practice upon taken office. When signing the Partial Birth Act of 2003, he declared,

> In passing this legislation, members of the House and Senate made a studied decision based upon compelling evidence. The best case against partial birth abortion is a simple description of what happens and to whom it happens. It involves the partial delivery of a live boy or girl, and a sudden, violent end of that life. Our nation owes its children a different and better welcome. The bill I am about to sign protecting innocent new life from this practice reflects the compassion and humanity of America.
>
> In the course of the congressional debate, the facts became clear. Each year, thousands of partial birth abortions are committed. As Doctor C. Everett Koop, the pediatrician and former Surgeon General has pointed out, the majority of partial birth abortions are not required by medical emergency. As Congress has found, the practice is widely regarded within the medical profession as unnecessary, not only cruel to the child, but harmful to the mother, and a violation of medical ethics.

The Supreme Court also reversed course on the constitutionality of laws banning partial-birth abortions. In *Sternberg v. Carhart* (2000) the Supreme Court declared a state ban on partial-birth abortion unconstitutional. Quoting *Casey*, Justice Breyer's majority opinion declared, "First, the law lacks any exception 'for the preservation of the . . . health of the mother.' Second, it 'imposes an undue burden on a woman's ability' to choose a D & E [dilation and evacuation] abortion, thereby unduly burdening the right to choose abortion itself." In *Gonzales v. Carhart* (2007) the Supreme Court sustained a nearly identical federal ban. Justice Kennedy's majority opinion asserted, "A premise central to [*Casey*'s] conclusion—that the government has a legitimate and substantial interest in preserving and promoting fetal life—would be repudiated" should the justices strike down bans on partial-birth abortion. The major difference between the two cases was that Justice O'Connor, who cast the fifth vote in *Sternberg*, had retired and was replaced by the more pro-life Chief Justice Roberts.

The 2010 midterm elections, which resulted in substantial gains for Republicans in Congress and state legislatures, has revived, at least temporarily, the abortion wars. Popular pro-life proposals include laws requiring woman to have ultrasounds before being allowed to have an abortion, sharp limits on insurance coverage for abortion, further restrictions on abortion clinics, and bans on abortion after twenty weeks. Texas in 2011 passed a law requiring that before performing an abortion a physician inform the pregnant women

40. The Democratic party platform in 2012 asserted: "The Democratic Party strongly and unequivocally supports *Roe v. Wade* and a woman's right to make decisions regarding her pregnancy, including a safe and legal abortion, regardless of ability to pay. We oppose any and all efforts to weaken or undermine that right."

41. The Republican Party platform in 2012 asserted: "We support a human life amendment to the Constitution and endorse legislation to make clear that the Fourteenth Amendment's protections apply to unborn children. We oppose using public revenues to promote or perform abortion or fund organizations which perform or advocate it and will not fund or subsidize health care which includes abortion coverage. . . . We also salute the many States that have passed laws for informed consent, mandatory waiting periods prior to an abortion, and health-protective clinic regulation. We seek to protect young girls from exploitation through a parental consent requirement."

of "the possibility of increased risk of breast cancer following an induced abortion,"[42] perform a sonogram, and, unless the women declares she is uninterested, provide her with "a verbal explanation of the results of the sonogram images" as well as "make . . . audible the heart auscultation for the pregnant women to hear." The Court of Appeals for the Fifth Circuit sustained that law in *Texas Medical Providers Performing Abortion Services v. Lakey* (2012). Judge Jones stated, "The required disclosures of a sonogram, the fetal heartbeat, and their medical descriptions are the epitome of truthful, non-misleading information. They are not different in kind, although more graphic and scientifically up-to-date, than the disclosures discussed in *Casey*—probable gestational age of the fetus and printed material showing a baby's general prenatal development stages."[43] Not all justices have reached the same conclusion. A local court in Oklahoma struck down a state law requiring women seeking abortions to be exposed to a sonogram of their fetus before the doctor could perform the procedure. Judge Bryan Dixon asserted that the Oklahoma measure was an "unconstitutional special law" that "improperly is addressed only to patients, physicians and sonographers concerning abortions and does not address all patients, physicians and sonographers concerning other medical care where a general law could clearly be made applicable."[44] In the summer of 2012 a Mississippi judge issued an injunction prohibiting state officials from enforcing a law that required all persons performing abortions to have admitting privileges at the local hospital. "The threatened injury," a state judge noted, "the closure of the state's only clinic, create[s] a substantial obstacle to the right to choose." Governor Phil Bryant, when signing that bill, had declared that the legislation was designed to make Mississippi "abortion-free."[45]

The national constitutional politics of reproductive rights may also be heating up. Two Republican candidates for the 2012 presidential nomination, Rick Santorum and Mitt Romney, asserted that the Supreme Court in *Griswold v. Connecticut* (1965) had wrongly concluded that married people had the right to use birth control. What these events signify is not yet clear. Pro-life politicians may be posturing to score partisan points or, depending on the result of the next national elections and next series of judicial appointments, *Roe v. Wade* may come under renewed attack.

Gay Rights

Same-sex intimacy is the main front in contemporary constitutional culture wars. The Supreme Court intensified constitutional struggles when in *Lawrence v. Texas* (2003) the justices ruled that consenting adults had the right to engage in homosexual (and heterosexual) sodomy. Gay rights activists almost immediately saw *Lawrence* as a precedential vehicle for a constitutional right to same-sex marriage. Opponents of gay rights immediately mobilized to place constitutional and statutory barriers in the way of same-sex marriage.

Recently proponents of same-sex marriage appear to have some momentum. Polls suggest that a slim majority of Americans present believe the government officials should permit same sex couples to marry. Maryland and Washington became the seventh and eighth states to legalize same-sex marriage. Maine voters in November 2012 will decide whether to permit same sex couples to marry. The Court of Appeals for the Ninth Circuit in *Perry v. Brown* (2012) declared unconstitutional an amendment to the California Constitution declaring that marriage in that state is between one man and one woman.[46] The Obama Administration declared that the Justice Department would no longer defend in court the Defense against Marriage Act, which permits states to refuse to recognize out of state same-sex marriages. On May 9, 2012, President Obama on ABC News declared that he personally favored extending marriage rights to same-sex couples. "I think same-sex couples should be able to get married," he told reporter Robin Roberts. President Obama continued,

42. The National Cancer Institution at the National Institutes of Health reports that the most recent studies "consistently show . . . no association between induced and spontaneous abortions and breast cancer risk." National Cancer Institute, "Abortion, Miscarriage, and Breast Cancer Risk," http://www.cancer.gov/cancertopics/factsheet/Risk/abortion-miscarriage.

43. *Texas Medical Providers Performing Abortion Services v. Lakey*, 667 F.3d 570 (5th Cir. 2012)

44. *Nova Health Sys. v. Pruitt*, No. CV-2010-533 (Okla. Dist. Ct. Mar. 28, 2012).

45. *Jackson Women's Health Org. v. Currier*, No. 3:12cv436-DPJ-FKB, 2012 U.S. Dist. LEXIS 97272 (S.D. Miss. July 13, 2012); Phil Bryant, "State of the State," speech, Jackson, Mississippi, January 24, 2012. Available at http://www.governorbryant.com/governor-phil-bryant-gives-his-first-state-of-the-state-address/

46. *Perry v. Brown*, 671 F.3d 1052 (9th Circ. 2012).

Table 11-2 State-Level LGBT Rights Policies, 1993–2008

Policy	Number of States with Policy	
	May 1993	**November 2008**
Statutory prohibitions on same-sex marriage	3	45
Constitutional prohibitions on same-sex marriage	0	27
Constitutional prohibitions on same-sex marriage that do or may prohibit recognition of domestic partnerships and the like	0	17
Criminal prohibitions on consensual sodomy	23	0
Hate crimes statutes that cover sexual orientation	11	32
Anti-discrimination statutes that cover sexual orientation	8	20
Provision of domestic partnership benefits to public employees	0	15
Provision of some legal rights to nonemployee same-sex couples	0	11
Provision of substantial legal equality to same-sex couples	0	7
Issuance of marriage licenses to same-sex couples	0	2

Source: Thomas M. Keck, "Beyond Backlash: Assessing the Impact of Judicial Decisions on LGBT Rights," *Law and Society Review* 43 (2009): 174.

> if you look at the underlying values that we care so deeply about when we describe family, commitment, responsibility, lookin' after one another, teaching our kids to be responsible citizens and caring for one another, I actually think that it's consistent with our best and in some cases our most conservative values, sort of the foundation of what made this country great.[47]

The Democratic Party platform in 2012 followed Obama's lead, "support[ing] marriage equality" and calling for the "full repeal of the so-called Defense of Marriage Act."

Red America did not react passively to these developments. Most states still refuse to recognize same-sex marriage. On May 8, 2012, North Carolina became the 30th state to pass a constitutional amendment limiting marriage to a man and a woman. A small majority of the state courts that have considered the issue have ruled that neither federal nor the state constitution give same-sex couples the right to marry. The Republican Party in 2012 called for "a [federal] Constitutional amendment defining marriage as the union of one man and one woman," and described same-sex marriage as "an assault on the foundations of our society, challenging the institution which, for thousands of years . . . has been entrusted with the rearing of children and transmission of cultural values."

The cause of gay rights has advanced over the past twenty years, but the constitutional politics responsible for that advance remain controversial. Many commentators believe that the courts played a vital role in promoting rights to same-sex intimacy. Dan Pinello asserts that such cases as *Goodridge v. Board of Health* (MA 2004) "brought about enormous social change. . . . With nearly all other state and national policy makers at odds with its goal, the Massachusetts [high court] nonetheless achieved singular success in expanding the ambit of who receives the benefits of getting married in America, in inspiring political elites elsewhere in the country to follow suit, and in mobilizing grass-roots supporters to entrench their legal victory politically."[48] Other commentators insist that judicial victories are responsible for the conservative countermobilization and backlash that has had more costs than benefits for proponents of same-same intimacy. "The most significant short-term

47. "Transcript: Robin Roberts ABC News Interview with President Obama," May 9, 2012, at http://abcnews.go.com/Politics/transcript-robin-roberts-abc-news-interview-president-obama/story?id=16316043#.UBQoOEQ1bgE.

48. Daniel Pinello, *America's Struggle for Same-Sex Marriage* (New York: Cambridge University Press, 2006), 192–92. See also Thomas M. Keck, "Beyond Backlash: Assessing the Impact of Judicial Decisions on LGBT Rights," *Law and Society Review* 43 (2009): 151.

consequence of *Goodridge*," Michael Klarman writes, "may have been the political backlash that it inspired. By outpacing public opinion on issues of social reform, such rulings mobilize opponents, undercut moderates, and retard the cause they purport to advance."[49]

Keep these issues in mind when reading the materials below. What institutions do you believe are most responsible for the gains that proponents of same-sex intimacy have made in the past twenty years? What strategies have been most successful in changing constitutional norms? What strategies have been least successful?

Lawrence v. Texas, 539 U.S. 558 (2003)

Houston police entered John Lawrence's apartment in response to a complaint about gunfire. While in the apartment one police officer reported seeing Lawrence and Tyron Garner engaging in anal sex, a second reported seeing them engaging in oral sex, and the other two officers did not report seeing the pair engaging in any sexual activity. A leading scholarly account maintains that Lawrence and Garner were clothed and in separate rooms when the police entered Lawrence's apartment.[50] Whatever the actual facts, both men were arrested, convicted, and fined $200 under a Texas law that prohibited persons from "engag[ing] in deviate sexual intercourse with another individual of the same sex." After the Texas appellate courts denied their appeals, Lawrence and Garner appealed to the Supreme Court of the United States.

The Supreme Court by a 6-3 vote declared the Texas law unconstitutional. Justice Kennedy's opinion held that states could not criminalize intimate relationships between consenting adults. What is the source of this constitutional right? What is the scope of this constitutional right? Does Lawrence *commit the Court to recognizing same-sex marriages? What is the difference between the Kennedy opinion and the O'Connor concurrence? The* Lawrence *decision did not inspire nearly the backlash that occurred after* Roe v. Wade *(1973). Why might that have been the case?* Lawrence *overruled* Bowers v. Hardwick *(1986). Why did Justice Kennedy think overruling appropriate in this case, but not in* Planned Parenthood v. Casey *(1993)? Is there a principled difference between the two cases?*

JUSTICE KENNEDY delivered the opinion of the Court.

. . .

Liberty protects the person from unwarranted government intrusions into a dwelling or other private places. In our tradition the State is not omnipresent in the home. And there are other spheres of our lives and existence, outside the home, where the State should not be a dominant presence. Freedom extends beyond spatial bounds. Liberty presumes an autonomy of self that includes freedom of thought, belief, expression, and certain intimate conduct. The instant case involves liberty of the person both in its spatial and in its more transcendent dimensions.

. . .

The Court began its substantive discussion in *Bowers v. Hardwick* (1986) as follows: "The issue presented is whether the Federal Constitution confers a fundamental right upon homosexuals to engage in sodomy and hence invalidates the laws of the many States that still make such conduct illegal and have done so for a very long time." . . . That statement, we now conclude, discloses the Court's own failure to appreciate the extent of the liberty at stake. To say that the issue in *Bowers* was simply the right to engage in certain sexual conduct demeans the claim the individual put forward, just as it would demean a married couple were it to be said marriage is simply about the right to have sexual intercourse. The laws involved in *Bowers* and here are, to be sure, statutes that purport to do no more than prohibit a particular sexual act. Their penalties and purposes, though, have more far-reaching consequences, touching upon the most private human conduct, sexual behavior, and in the most private of places, the home. The statutes do seek to control a personal relationship that, whether or not entitled to formal recognition in the law, is within the liberty of persons to choose without being punished as criminals.

This, as a general rule, should counsel against attempts by the State, or a court, to define the meaning of the relationship or to set its boundaries absent injury to a person or abuse of an institution the law protects. It suffices for us to acknowledge that adults may choose to enter upon this relationship in the confines of their homes and their own private lives and still retain their dignity as free persons. When sexu-

49. Michael Klarman, "*Brown* and *Lawrence* (and *Goodridge*)," *Michigan Law Review* 104 (2005): 482. See also Gerald N. Rosenberg, *The Hollow Hope: Can Courts Bring about Social Change?*, rev. ed. (Chicago: University of Chicago Press, 2008).

50. Dale Carpenter, *Flagrant Conduct: The Story of* Lawrence v. Texas (New York: Norton, 2012).

ality finds overt expression in intimate conduct with another person, the conduct can be but one element in a personal bond that is more enduring. The liberty protected by the Constitution allows homosexual persons the right to make this choice.

. . .

. . . [F]ar from possessing "ancient roots," . . . American laws targeting same-sex couples did not develop until the last third of the 20th century. . . .

It was not until the 1970's that any State singled out same-sex relations for criminal prosecution, and only nine States have done so. . . . Post-*Bowers* even some of these States did not adhere to the policy of suppressing homosexual conduct. Over the course of the last decades, States with same-sex prohibitions have moved toward abolishing them. . . . In summary, the historical grounds relied upon in *Bowers* are more complex than the majority opinion and the concurring opinion by Chief Justice Burger indicate. Their historical premises are not without doubt and, at the very least, are overstated.

. . .

. . . [W]e think that our laws and traditions in the past half century are of most relevance here. These references show an emerging awareness that liberty gives substantial protection to adult persons in deciding how to conduct their private lives in matters pertaining to sex. . . .

. . .

. . [A]lmost five years before *Bowers* was decided the European Court of Human Rights considered a case with parallels to *Bowers* and to today's case. An adult male resident in Northern Ireland alleged he was a practicing homosexual who desired to engage in consensual homosexual conduct. The laws of Northern Ireland forbade him that right. He alleged that he had been questioned, his home had been searched, and he feared criminal prosecution. Thecourt held that the laws proscribing the conduct were invalid under the European Convention on Human Rights. . . . Authoritative in all countries that are members of the Council of Europe . . . the decision is at odds with the premise in *Bowers* that the claim put forward was insubstantial in our Western civilization.

In our own constitutional system the deficiencies in *Bowers* became even more apparent in the years following its announcement. The 25 States with laws prohibiting the relevant conduct referenced in the *Bowers* decision are reduced now to 13, of which 4 enforce their laws only against homosexual conduct. In those States where sodomy is still proscribed, whether for same-sex or heterosexual conduct, there is a pattern of nonenforcement with respect to consenting adults acting in private. The State of Texas admitted in 1994 that as of that date it had not prosecuted anyone under those circumstances.

Two principal cases decided after *Bowers* cast its holding into even more doubt. In *Planned Parenthood of Southeastern Pa. v. Casey* (1992), the Court . . . confirmed that our laws and tradition afford constitutional protection to personal decisions relating to marriage, procreation, contraception, family relationships, child rearing, and education. . . . The second post-*Bowers* case of principal relevance is *Romer v. Evans* (1996). There the Court struck down class-based legislation directed at homosexuals as a violation of the Equal Protection Clause. . . .

. . .

When homosexual conduct is made criminal by the law of the State, that declaration in and of itself is an invitation to subject homosexual persons to discrimination both in the public and in the private spheres. The central holding of *Bowers* has been brought in question by [*Romer*], and it should be addressed. Its continuance as precedent demeans the lives of homosexual persons.

. . .

To the extent *Bowers* relied on values we share with a wider civilization, it should be noted that the reasoning and holding in *Bowers* have been rejected elsewhere. The European Court of Human Rights has followed not *Bowers* but its own decision in *Dudgeon v. United Kingdom* (1981). . . . The right the petitioners seek in this case has been accepted as an integral part of human freedom in many other countries. There has been no showing that in this country the governmental interest in circumscribing personal choice is somehow more legitimate or urgent.

The doctrine of *stare decisis* is essential to the respect accorded to the judgments of the Court and to the stability of the law. It is not, however, an inexorable command. . . . The holding in *Bowers* . . . has not induced detrimental reliance comparable to some instances where recognized individual rights are involved.

. . .

Bowers was not correct when it was decided, and it is not correct today. It ought not to remain binding precedent. *Bowers v. Hardwick* should be and now is overruled.

The present case does not involve minors. It does not involve persons who might be injured or coerced or who are situated in relationships where consent might not easily be refused. It does not involve public conduct or prostitution. It does not involve whether the government must give formal recognition to any relationship that homosexual persons seek to enter. The case does involve two adults who, with full and mutual consent from each other, engaged in sexual practices common to a homosexual lifestyle. The petitioners are entitled to respect for their private lives. The State cannot demean their existence or control their destiny by making their private sexual conduct a crime. Their right to liberty under the Due Process Clause gives them the full right to engage in their conduct without intervention of the government. . . . The Texas statute furthers no legitimate state interest which can justify its intrusion into the personal and private life of the individual.

. . .

JUSTICE O'CONNOR, concurring in the judgment.

The Court today overrules *Bowers v. Hardwick* (1986). I joined *Bowers,* and do not join the Court in overruling it. Nevertheless, I agree with the Court that Texas' statute banning same-sex sodomy is unconstitutional. . . . Rather than relying on the substantive component of the Fourteenth Amendment's Due Process Clause, as the Court does, I base my conclusion on the Fourteenth Amendment's Equal Protection Clause.

. . .

This case raises a different issue than *Bowers:* whether, under the Equal Protection Clause, moral disapproval is a legitimate state interest to justify by itself a statute that bans homosexual sodomy, but not heterosexual sodomy. It is not. Moral disapproval of this group, like a bare desire to harm the group, is an interest that is insufficient to satisfy rational basis review under the Equal Protection Clause. . . . Indeed, we have never held that moral disapproval, without any other asserted state interest, is a sufficient rationale under the Equal Protection Clause to justify a law that discriminates among groups of persons.

. . .

Whether a sodomy law that is neutral both in effect and application, . . . would violate the substantive component of the Due Process Clause is an issue that need not be decided today. I am confident, however, that so long as the Equal Protection Clause requires a sodomy law to apply equally to the private consensual conduct of homosexuals and heterosexuals alike, such a law would not long stand in our democratic society. . . .

JUSTICE SCALIA, with whom THE CHIEF JUSTICE and JUSTICE THOMAS join, dissenting.

"Liberty finds no refuge in a jurisprudence of doubt." *Planned Parenthood of Southeastern Pa. v. Casey* . . . (1992). That was the Court's sententious response, barely more than a decade ago, to those seeking to overrule *Roe v. Wade* . . . (1973). The Court's response today, to those who have engaged in a 17-year crusade to overrule *Bowers v. Hardwick* (1986), is very different. The need for stability and certainty presents no barrier.

. . .

It seems to me that the "societal reliance" on the principles confirmed in *Bowers* and discarded today has been overwhelming. Countless judicial decisions and legislative enactments have relied on the ancient proposition that a governing majority's belief that certain sexual behavior is "immoral and unacceptable" constitutes a rational basis for regulation. . . . State laws against bigamy, same-sex marriage, adult incest, prostitution, masturbation, adultery, fornication, bestiality, and obscenity are likewise sustainable only in light of *Bowers'* validation of laws based on moral choices. Every single one of these laws is called into question by today's decision; the Court makes no effort to cabin the scope of its decision to exclude them from its holding. . . .

. . .

The Court today does not . . . describe homosexual sodomy as a "fundamental right" or a "fundamental liberty interest," nor does it subject the Texas statute to strict scrutiny. Instead, having failed to establish that the right to homosexual sodomy is "'deeply rooted in this Nation's history and tradition,'" the Court concludes that the application of Texas's statute to petitioners' conduct fails the rational-basis test, and overrules *Bowers'* holding to the contrary. . . .

It is (as *Bowers* recognized) entirely irrelevant whether the laws in our long national tradition criminalizing homosexual sodomy were "directed at homosexual conduct as a distinct matter." . . . Whether homosexual sodomy was prohibited by a law targeted at same-sex sexual relations or by a more general law prohibiting both homosexual and heterosexual sodomy, the only relevant point is that it *was* criminalized—which suffices to establish that homosexual sodomy is not a right "deeply rooted in our Nation's history and tradition." The Court today agrees that homosexual sodomy was criminalized and thus does not dispute the facts on which *Bowers actually* relied.

. . .

. . . [T]he Court says: "[W]e think that our laws and traditions in the past half century are of most relevance here. These references show *an emerging awareness* that liberty gives substantial protection to adult persons in deciding how to conduct their private lives *in matters pertaining to sex*." . . . Apart from the fact that such an "emerging awareness" does not establish a "fundamental right," the statement is factually false. States continue to prosecute all sorts of crimes by adults "in matters pertaining to sex": prostitution, adult incest, adultery, obscenity, and child pornography. Sodomy laws, too, have been enforced "in the past half century," in which there have been 134 reported cases involving prosecutions for consensual, adult, homosexual sodomy. . . .

In any event, an "emerging awareness" is by definition not "deeply rooted in this Nation's history and tradition[s]," as we have said "fundamental right" status requires. Constitutional entitlements do not spring into existence because some States choose to lessen or eliminate criminal sanctions on certain behavior. Much less do they spring into existence, as the Court seems to believe, because *foreign nations* decriminalize conduct. . . .

. . .

Today's opinion is the product of a Court, which is the product of a law-profession culture, that has largely signed on to the so-called homosexual agenda, by which I mean the agenda promoted by some homosexual activists directed at eliminating the moral opprobrium that has traditionally attached to homosexual conduct. . . .

. . . It is clear . . . that the Court has taken sides in the culture war, departing from its role of assuring, as neutral observer, that the democratic rules of engagement are observed. Many Americans do not want persons who openly engage in homosexual conduct as partners in their business, as scoutmasters for their children, as teachers in their children's schools, or as boarders in their home. They view this as protecting themselves and their families from a lifestyle that they believe to be immoral and destructive. The Court views it as "discrimination" which it is the function of our judgments to deter. So imbued is the Court with the law profession's anti-anti-homosexual culture, that it is seemingly unaware that the attitudes of that culture are not obviously "mainstream"; that in most States what the Court calls "discrimination" against those who engage in homosexual acts is perfectly legal; that proposals to ban such "discrimination" under Title VII have repeatedly been rejected by Congress, . . . that in some cases such "discrimination" is *mandated* by federal statute . . . ; and that in some cases such "discrimination" is a constitutional right, see *Boy Scouts of America v. Dale* . . . (2000).

Let me be clear that I have nothing against homosexuals, or any other group, promoting their agenda through normal democratic means. . . . I would no more *require* a State to criminalize homosexual acts—or, for that matter, display *any* moral disapprobation of them—than I would *forbid* it to do so. What Texas has chosen to do is well within the range of traditional democratic action, and its hand should not be stayed through the invention of a brand-new "constitutional right" by a Court that is impatient of democratic change. . . . [I]t is the premise of our system that those judgments are to be made by the people, and not imposed by a governing caste that knows best.

. . .

JUSTICE THOMAS, dissenting. . . .

Goodridge v. Department of Public Health, 440 Mass. 309 (2003)

Hillary Goodridge and Julie Goodridge had been a lesbian couple for thirteen years. The Goodridges in 2001 sought and were denied a marriage license on the ground that Massachusetts law did not permit same-sex couples to marry. The Goodridges promptly sued the Department of Health, claiming that limiting marriages to heterosexual couples violated numerous provisions of the Massachusetts Constitution. A lower court rejected their lawsuit. The Goodridges appealed to the Supreme Judicial Court of Massachusetts.

The Supreme Judicial Court of Massachusetts by a 4-3 vote declared the state marriage laws unconstitutional. Chief Justice Marshall's opinion asserted that bans on same-sex marriage do not even satisfy a rational basis standard. On what basis does Marshall choose the rational basis test? Would some stricter form of scrutiny be appropriate? Why does Marshall think that the ban on same-sex marriage does not satisfy rational scrutiny? Why do the dissents disagree?

Illustration 11-2 Massachusetts Chief Justice Margaret Marshall
Source: AP Photo/George Rizer, Pool.

The dissents insist that elected officials should determine whether same-sex marriages should be recognized. Is this claim correct?

CHIEF JUSTICE MARSHALL delivered the opinion of the Court.

Marriage is a vital social institution. The exclusive commitment of two individuals to each other nurtures love and mutual support; it brings stability to our society. For those who choose to marry, and for their children, marriage provides an abundance of legal, financial, and social benefits. In return it imposes weighty legal, financial, and social obligations. The question before us is whether, consistent with the Massachusetts Constitution, the Commonwealth may deny the protections, benefits, and obligations conferred by civil marriage to two individuals of the same sex who wish to marry. We conclude that it may not. The Massachusetts Constitution affirms the dignity and equality of all individuals. It forbids the creation of second-class citizens. In reaching our conclusion we have given full deference to the arguments made by the Commonwealth. But it has failed to identify any constitutionally adequate reason for denying civil marriage to same-sex couples.

. . .

. . . [In *Lawrence v. Texas* (2003), the Supreme Court of the United States] affirmed that the core concept of common human dignity protected by the Fourteenth Amendment to the United States Constitution precludes government intrusion into the deeply personal realms of consensual adult expressions of intimacy and one's choice of an intimate partner. The Court also reaffirmed the central role that decisions whether to marry or have children bear in shaping one's identity. The Massachusetts Constitution is, if anything, more protective of individual liberty and equality than the Federal Constitution; it may demand broader protection for fundamental rights; and it is less tolerant of government intrusion into the protected spheres of private life.

Barred access to the protections, benefits, and obligations of civil marriage, a person who enters into an intimate, exclusive union with another of the same sex is arbitrarily deprived of membership in one of our community's most rewarding and cherished institutions. That exclusion is incompatible with the constitutional principles of respect for individual autonomy and equality under law.

. . .

Marriage bestows enormous private and social advantages on those who choose to marry. Civil marriage is at once a deeply personal commitment to another human being and a highly public celebration of the ideals of mutuality, companionship, intimacy, fidelity, and family. "It is an association that promotes a way of life, not causes; a harmony in living, not political faiths; a bilateral loyalty, not commercial or social projects." Because it fulfils yearnings for security, safe haven, and connection that express our common humanity, civil marriage is an esteemed institution, and the decision whether and whom to marry is among life's momentous acts of self-definition.

. . .

For decades, indeed centuries, in much of this country (including Massachusetts) no lawful marriage was possible between white and black Americans. That long history availed not when the Supreme Court of California held in 1948 that a legislative prohibition against interracial marriage violated the due process and equality guarantees of the Fourteenth Amendment, *Perez v. Sharp* (CA 1948), or when, nineteen years later, the United States Supreme Court also held that a statutory bar to interracial marriage violated the Fourteenth Amendment, *Loving v. Virginia* (1967). As both *Perez* and *Loving* make clear, the right to marry means little if it does not include the right to marry the person of one's choice, subject to appropriate government restrictions in the interests of public health, safety, and welfare. In this case, as in *Perez* and *Loving*, a statute deprives individuals of access to an institution of fundamental legal, personal, and social significance—the institution of marriage—because of a single trait: skin color in *Perez* and *Loving*, sexual orientation here. As it did in *Perez* and *Loving*, history must yield to a more fully developed understanding of the invidious quality of the discrimination.

. . .

The individual liberty and equality safeguards of the Massachusetts Constitution protect both "freedom from" unwarranted government intrusion into protected spheres of life and "freedom to" partake in benefits created by the State for the common good. Both freedoms are involved here. Whether and whom to marry, how to express sexual intimacy, and whether and how to establish a family—these are among the most basic of every individual's liberty and due process rights. . . . And central to personal freedom and security is the assurance that the laws will apply equally to persons in similar situations. "Absolute equality before the law is a fundamental principle of our own Constitution. The liberty interest in choosing whether and whom to marry would be hollow if the Commonwealth could, without sufficient justification, foreclose an individual from freely choosing the person with whom to share an exclusive commitment in the unique institution of civil marriage.

. . .

. . . Our laws of civil marriage do not privilege procreative heterosexual intercourse between married people above every other form of adult intimacy and every other means of creating a family. [The Massachusetts marriage statute] contains no requirement that the applicants for a marriage license attest to their ability or intention to conceive children by coitus. Fertility is not a condition of marriage, nor is it grounds for divorce. . . . While it is certainly true that many, perhaps most, married couples have children together (assisted or unassisted), it is the exclusive and permanent commitment of the marriage partners to one another, not the begetting of children, that is the sine qua non of civil marriage.

. . .

The department has offered no evidence that forbidding marriage to people of the same sex will increase the number of couples choosing to enter into opposite-sex marriages in order to have and raise children. There is thus no rational relationship between the marriage statute and the Commonwealth's proffered goal of protecting the "optimal" child rearing unit. Moreover, the department readily concedes that people in same-sex couples may be "excellent" parents. . . . Given the wide range of public benefits reserved only for married couples, we do not credit the department's contention that the absence of access to civil marriage amounts to little more than an inconvenience to same-sex couples and their children. Excluding same-sex couples from civil marriage will not make children of opposite-sex marriages more secure, but it does prevent children of same-sex couples from enjoying the immeasurable advantages that flow from the assurance of "a stable family structure in which children will be reared, educated, and socialized." . . .

. . .

Here, the plaintiffs seek only to be married, not to undermine the institution of civil marriage. They do not want marriage abolished. They do not attack the binary nature of marriage, the consanguinity provisions, or any of the other gate-keeping provisions of the marriage licensing law. Recognizing the right of an individual to marry a person of the same sex will not diminish the validity or dignity of opposite-sex marriage, any more than recognizing the right of an individual to marry a person of a different race devalues the marriage of a person who marries someone of her own race. If anything, extending civil marriage to same-sex couples reinforces the importance of marriage to individuals and communities. That same-sex couples are willing to embrace marriage's solemn obligations of exclusivity, mutual support, and commitment to one another is a testament to the enduring place of marriage in our laws and in the human spirit.

. . .

JUDGE GREANEY, concurring.

. . . The withholding of relief from the plaintiffs, who wish to marry, and are otherwise eligible to marry, on the ground that the couples are of the same gender, constitutes a categorical restriction of a fundamental right. The restriction creates a straightforward case of discrimination that disqualifies an entire group of our citizens and their families from participation in an institution of paramount legal and social importance. . . .

. . .

Because our marriage statutes intend, and state, the ordinary understanding that marriage under our law consists only of a union between a man and a woman, they create a statutory classification based on the sex of the two people who wish to marry. . . .

A classification may be gender based whether or not the challenged government action apportions benefits or burdens uniformly along gender lines. This is so because constitutional protections extend to individuals and not to categories of people. Thus, when an individual desires to marry, but cannot marry his or her chosen partner because of the traditional opposite-sex restriction, a [state constitutional] violation has occurred. . . .

. . .

A comment is in order with respect to the insistence of some that marriage is, as a matter of definition, the legal union of a man and a woman. To define the institution of marriage by the characteristics of those to whom it always has been accessible, in order to justify the exclusion of those to whom it never has been accessible, is conclusory and bypasses the core question we are asked to decide. This case calls for a higher level of legal analysis. Precisely, the case requires that we confront ingrained assumptions with respect to historically accepted roles of men and women within the institution of marriage and requires that we reexamine these assumptions in light of the unequivocal language of [the state constitution], in order to ensure that the governmental conduct challenged here conforms to the supreme charter of our Commonwealth. . . . I do not doubt the sincerity of deeply held moral or religious beliefs that make inconceivable to some the notion that any change in the common-law definition of what constitutes a legal civil marriage is now, or ever would be, warranted. But, as matter of constitutional law, neither the mantra of tradition, nor individual conviction, can justify the perpetuation of a hierarchy in which couples of the same sex and their families are deemed less worthy of social and legal recognition than couples of the opposite sex and their families.

. . .

JUDGE SPINA, with whom JUDGE SOSMAN and JUDGE CORDY join, dissenting.

. . . The power to regulate marriage lies with the Legislature, not with the judiciary. Today, the court has transformed its role as protector of individual rights into the role of creator of rights, and I respectfully dissent.

. . . General Laws c. 207 enumerates certain qualifications for obtaining a marriage license. It creates no distinction between the sexes, but applies to men and women in precisely the same way. It does not create any disadvantage identified with gender, as both men and women are similarly limited to marrying a person of the opposite sex. . . .

Similarly, the marriage statutes do not discriminate on the basis of sexual orientation. As the court correctly recognizes, constitutional protections are extended to individuals, not couples. The marriage statutes do not disqualify individuals on the basis of sexual orientation from entering into marriage. All individuals, with certain exceptions not relevant here, are free to marry. Whether an individual chooses not to marry because of sexual orientation or any other reason should be of no concern to the court.

. . .

The marriage statutes do not impermissibly burden a right protected by our constitutional guarantee of due process implicit in art. 10 of our Declaration of Rights. There is no restriction on the right of any plaintiff to enter into marriage. Each is free to marry a willing person of the opposite sex. . . .

. . . Same-sex marriage, or the "right to marry the person of one's choice" as the court today defines that right, does not fall within the fundamental right to marry. Same-sex marriage is not "deeply rooted in this Nation's history," and the court does not suggest that it is. . . . In this Commonwealth and in this country, the roots of the institution of marriage are deeply set in history as a civil union between a single man and a single woman. There is no basis for the court to recognize same-sex marriage as a constitutionally protected right.

. . .

JUDGE SOSMAN, with whom JUDGE SPINA and JUDGE CORDY join, dissenting.

. . .

. . . [T]he [majority] opinion ultimately opines that the Legislature is acting irrationally when it grants benefits to a proven successful family structure while denying the same benefits to a recent, perhaps promising, but essentially untested alternate family structure. Placed in a more neutral context, the court would never find any irrationality in such an approach. For example, if the issue were government subsidies and tax benefits promoting use of an established technology for energy efficient heating, the court would find no equal protection or due process violation in the Legislature's decision not to grant the same benefits to an inventor or manufacturer of some new, alternative technology who did not yet have sufficient data to prove that that new technology was just as good as the established technology. . . .

The issue is whether it is rational to reserve judgment on whether this change can be made at this time without damaging the institution of marriage or adversely affecting the critical role it has played in our society. Absent consensus on the issue (which obviously does not exist), or unanimity amongst scientists studying the issue (which also does not exist), or a more prolonged period of observation of this new family structure (which has not yet been possible), it is rational for the Legislature to postpone any redefinition of marriage that would include same-sex couples until such time as it is certain that that redefinition will not have unintended and undesirable social consequences. . . .

. . .

JUDGE CORDY, with whom JUDGE SPINA and JUDGE SOSMAN join, dissenting.

. . . Although it may be desirable for many reasons to extend to same-sex couples the benefits and burdens of civil marriage (and the plaintiffs have made a powerfully reasoned case for that extension), that decision must be made by the Legislature, not the court.

. . .

The Massachusetts marriage statute does not impair the exercise of a recognized fundamental right, or discriminate on the basis of sex in violation of the equal rights amendment to the Massachusetts Constitution. Consequently, it is subject to review only to determine whether it satisfies the rational basis test. Because a conceivable rational basis exists upon which the Legislature could conclude that the marriage statute furthers the legitimate State purpose of ensuring, promoting, and supporting an optimal social structure for the bearing and raising of children, it is a valid exercise of the State's police power.

. . .

While the institution of marriage is deeply rooted in the history and traditions of our country and our State, the right to marry someone of the same sex is not. No matter how personal or intimate a decision to marry someone of the same sex might be, the right to make it is not guaranteed by the right of personal autonomy.

. . .

The marriage statute, in limiting marriage to heterosexual couples, does not constitute discrimination on the basis of sex in violation of the Equal Rights Amendment to the Massachusetts Constitution.

The Massachusetts marriage statute does not subject men to different treatment from women; each is equally prohibited from precisely the same conduct. . . .

. . . [H]ere there is no evidence that limiting marriage to opposite-sex couples was motivated by sexism in general or a desire to disadvantage men or women in particular. Moreover, no one has identified any harm, burden, disadvantage, or advantage accruing to either gender as a consequence of the Massachusetts marriage statute. In the absence of such effect, the statute limiting marriage to couples of the opposite sex does not violate the ERA's prohibition of sex discrimination.

. . .

The institution of marriage provides the important legal and normative link between heterosexual intercourse and procreation on the one hand and family responsibilities on the other. The partners in a marriage are expected to engage in exclusive sexual relations, with children the probable result and paternity presumed. Whereas the relationship between mother and child is demonstratively and predictably created and recognizable through the biological process of pregnancy and childbirth, there is no corresponding process for creating a relationship between father and child. Similarly, aside from an act of heterosexual intercourse nine months prior to childbirth, there is no process for creating a relationship between a man and a woman as the parents of a particular child. The institution of marriage fills this void by formally binding the husband-father to his wife and child, and imposing on him the responsibilities of fatherhood. The alternative, a society without the institution of marriage, in which heterosexual intercourse, procreation, and child care are largely disconnected processes, would be chaotic.

. . .

We must assume that the Legislature (1) might conclude that the institution of civil marriage has successfully and continually provided this structure over several centuries; (2) might consider and credit studies that document negative consequences that too often follow children either born outside of marriage or raised in households lacking either a father or a mother figure, and scholarly commentary contending that children and families develop best when mothers and fathers are partners in their parenting; and (3) would be familiar with many recent studies that variously support the proposition that children raised in intact families headed by same-sex couples fare as well on many measures as children raised in similar families headed by opposite-sex couples; support the proposition that children of same-sex couples fare worse on some measures; or reveal notable differences between the two groups of children that warrant further study.

. . .

. . .That the State does not preclude different types of families from raising children does not mean that it must view them all as equally optimal and equally deserving of State endorsement and support. For example, single persons are allowed to adopt children, but the fact that the Legislature permits single-parent adoption does not mean that it has endorsed single parenthood as an optimal setting in which to raise children or views it as the equivalent of being raised by both of one's biological parents. The same holds true with respect to same-sex couples—the fact that they may adopt children means only that the Legislature has concluded that they may provide an acceptable setting in which to raise children who cannot be raised by both of their biological parents.

. . .

So long as marriage is limited to opposite-sex couples who can at least theoretically procreate, society is able to communicate a consistent message to its citizens that marriage is a (normatively) necessary part of their procreative endeavor; that if they are to procreate, then society has endorsed the institution of marriage as the environment for it and for the subsequent rearing of their children; and that benefits are available explicitly to create a supportive and conducive atmosphere for those purposes. If society proceeds similarly to recognize marriages between same-sex couples who cannot procreate, it could be perceived as an abandonment of this claim, and might result in the mistaken view that civil marriage has little to do with procreation: just as the potential of procreation would not be necessary for a marriage to be valid, marriage would not be necessary for optimal procreation and child rearing to occur. In essence, the Legislature could conclude that the consequence of such a policy shift would be a diminution in society's ability to steer the acts of procreation and child rearing into their most optimal setting. . . .

The Defense of Marriage Act

The Defense of Marriage Act of 1996 (DOMA) was passed after the Supreme Court of Hawaii in Baehr v. Lewin *(HI 1993) declared unconstitutional a state law limiting marriage to a man and a woman. DOMA declared that no state was required to recognize an out-of-state marriage between two persons of the same sex and stated that federal law would not recognize same-sex marriages. The crucial Section 3 of DOMA declared, "In determining the meaning of any Act of Congress, or of any ruling, regulation, or interpretation of the various administrative bureaus and agencies of the United States, the word 'marriage' means only a legal union between one man and one woman as husband and wife, and the word 'spouse' refers only to a person of the opposite sex who is a husband or a wife."*

We have excerpted the majority and minority congressional reports on DOMA, as well as the Obama administration's claim that Section 3 is unconstitutional. Why did the congressional majority believe DOMA necessary? What reasons do they give for thinking DOMA constitutional? Why do the minority and the Obama administration disagree? Attorney General Holder claims that the Obama administration will continue to implement DOMA but will not defend that law in court. Is that view consistent with the president's obligation to execute federal law? Should a president who believes a law unconstitutional enforce that law? If so, should the president also defend that law in court?

House Committee on the Judiciary, Report on the Defense of Marriage Act (1996)[51]

The Defense of Marriage Act, has two primary purposes. The first is to defend the institution of traditional heterosexual marriage. The second is to protect the right of the States to formulate their own public policy regarding the legal recognition of same-sex unions, free from any federal constitutional implications that might attend the recognition by one State of the right for homosexual couples to acquire marriage licenses.

. . .

Simply stated, the gay rights organizations and lawyers driving the Hawaiian lawsuit have made plain that they consider Hawaii to be only the first step in a national effort to win by judicial fiat the right to same-sex "marriage." And the primary mechanism for nationalizing their break-through in Hawaii will be the Full Faith and Credit Clause of the U.S. Constitution.

. . .

The general rule for determining the validity of a marriage is "lex celebrationis" that is, a marriage is valid if it is valid according to the law of the place where it was celebrated. States observing that rule would, of course, presumptively recognize as valid a same-sex "marriage" license from Hawaii. There is, however, an important exception to the general rule. . . .

"A marriage which satisfies the requirements of the state where the marriage was contracted will everywhere be recognized as valid unless it violates the strong public policy of another state which had the most significant relationship to the spouses and the marriage at the time of the marriage."

. . .

Because no State in the United States has ever recognized same-sex "marriages," it would seem that courts in other States would be justified in invoking this exception. The matter is somewhat more complicated, however, as the U.S. Constitution speaks to this issue. The first sentence of the Full Faith and Credit Clause provides: "Full Faith and Credit shall be given in each State to the public Acts, Records, and judicial Proceedings of every other State."

Notwithstanding the seemingly mandatory terms of the Full Faith and Credit Clause, the U.S. Supreme Court has recognized a public policy exception that, in certain circumstances, would permit a State to decline to give effect to another State's laws. Indeed, despite the presumption created by lex celebrationis and reinforced by the Full Faith and Credit Clause, the Committee believes that a court conscientiously applying the relevant legal principles would be amply justified in refusing to give effect to a same-sex "marriage" license from another State.

But even as the Committee believes that States currently possess the ability to avoid recognizing a same-sex "marriage" license from another State, it recognizes that that conclusion is far from certain. For example, there is a burgeoning body of legal scholarship some of it inspired directly by the Hawaiian lawsuit to the effect that the Full Faith and Credit Clause does mandate extraterritorial recognition of "marriage" licenses given to homosexual couples. . . .

. . .

Recognition of same-sex "marriages" in Hawaii could also have profound implications for federal law as well. The word "marriage" appears in more than 800 sections of federal statutes and regulations, and the word "spouse" appears more than 3,100 times. With very limited exceptions, these terms are not defined in federal law.

. . . [T]o the extent that federal law has simply accepted state law determinations of who is married, a redefinition of marriage in Hawaii to include homosexual couples could make such couples eligible for a whole range of federal rights and benefits. . . .

51. House Committee on the Judiciary, Report in the Defense of Marriage Act, 104th Cong., 2nd Sess. (1996), H.R. Rep. 104–664.

. . .

We are, each of us, born a man or a woman. The committee needs no testimony from an expert witness to decode this point: Our engendered existence, as men and women, offers the most unmistakable, natural signs of the meaning and purpose of sexuality. And that is the function and purpose of begetting. At its core, it is hard to detach marriage from what may be called the "natural teleology of the body": namely, the inescapable fact that only two people, not three, only a man and a woman, can beget a child.

At bottom, civil society has an interest in maintaining and protecting the institution of heterosexual marriage because it has a deep and abiding interest in encouraging responsible procreation and child-rearing. Simply put, government has an interest in marriage because it has an interest in children.

. . .

Closely related to this interest in protecting traditional marriage is a corresponding interest in promoting heterosexuality. While there is controversy concerning how sexual "orientation" is determined, "there is good reason to think that a very substantial number of people are born with the potential to live either gay or straight lives." . . . "Maintaining a preferred societal status of heterosexual marriage thus will also serve to encourage heterosexuality."

. . .

Dissenting Views on H.R. 3396

. . .

The legal history of the full faith and credit clause which is central to this dispute is a sparse one, and no one can speak with absolute certainly about all aspects of this matter. But one thing is quite clear: whatever powers states have to reject a decision by another state to legalize same sex marriage, and to refuse to recognize such marriages within its own borders, derives directly from the Constitution and nothing Congress can do by statute either adds to or detracts from that power.

. . .

Section three of the bill, ironically for legislation which has been hailed as a defender of states rights, represents for the first time in our history a Congressional effort, if successful, to deny states full discretion over their own marriage laws. Section three of this bill says that no matter what an individual state says, and no matter by what procedure it does it, Congress will refuse to recognize same sex marriages. In debating against an amendment by Congresswoman Schroeder, one of the Senior Republicans on the Committee said that her amendment would make certain marriages "second class marriages" by denying them federal recognition. This acknowledgment that denying a marriage federal recognition substantially diminishes its legal force applies to this bill. If Hawaii or any other state were to allow people of the same sex who were deeply and emotionally attached to each other to regularize that relationship in a marriage, this bill says that the federal government would refuse to recognize it. Note that this is the case whether such decision is made by a State Supreme Court, a referendum of the state's population, a vote of the state's legislature, or some combination thereof. Thus, the bill is exactly the opposite of a states rights measure: the only real force it will have will be to deny a state and the people of that state the right to make decisions on the question of same sex marriage.

Our final ground for opposing this bill is our vehement disagreement with the notion that same sex marriages are a threat to marriage. By far the weakest part of this bill logically is its title, but its title is not simply accidental, but rather reflects the calculated political judgment that went into introducing this bill at this time, months before a national election, and rushing it through with inadequate analysis of its impact. . . .

The notion that allowing two people who are in love to become legally responsible to and for each other threatens heterosexual marriage is without factual basis. Indeed, when pressed during Subcommittee and Committee debate, majority Members could give no specific content to this assertion. The attraction that a man and a woman feel for each other, which leads them to wish to commit emotionally and legally to each other for life, obviously could not be threatened in any way, shape or form by the love that two other people feel for each other, whether they be people of the same sex or opposite sexes. There are of course problems which men and women who seek to marry, or seek to maintain a marriage, confront in our society. No one anywhere has produced any evidence, or even argued logically, that the existence of same sex couples is one of those difficulties. And to prove that this is simply an effort to capitalize on the public dislike of the notion of same sex marriages, as noted below, when Congresswoman Schroeder attempted to offer amendments that deal more directly with threats to existing heterosexual marriages, the majority unanimously and vehemently objected. . . .

Eric Holder, Letter from the Attorney General to Congress on Litigation Involving the Defense of Marriage Act (February 23, 2011)[52]

Dear Mr. Speaker:

. . .

. . . [T]he President and I have concluded that classifications based on sexual orientation warrant heightened scrutiny and that, as applied to same-sex couples legally married under state law, Section 3 of DOMA is unconstitutional.

The Supreme Court has yet to rule on the appropriate level of scrutiny for classifications based on sexual orientation. It has, however, rendered a number of decisions that set forth the criteria that should inform this and any other judgment as to whether heightened scrutiny applies: (1) whether the group in question has suffered a history of discrimination; (2) whether individuals "exhibit obvious, immutable, or distinguishing characteristics that define them as a discrete group"; (3) whether the group is a minority or is politically powerless; and (4) whether the characteristics distinguishing the group have little relation to legitimate policy objectives or to an individual's "ability to perform or contribute to society."

Each of these factors counsels in favor of being suspicious of classifications based on sexual orientation. First and most importantly, there is, regrettably, a significant history of purposeful discrimination against gay and lesbian people, by governmental as well as private entities, based on prejudice and stereotypes that continue to have ramifications today. . . .

Second, while sexual orientation carries no visible badge, a growing scientific consensus accepts that sexual orientation is a characteristic that is immutable; it is undoubtedly unfair to require sexual orientation to be hidden from view to avoid discrimination. . . .

Third, the adoption of laws like those at issue in *Romer v. Evans* (1996), and *Lawrence* [*v. Texas* (2003)], the longstanding ban on gays and lesbians in the military, and the absence of federal protection for employment discrimination on the basis of sexual orientation show the group to have limited political power and "ability to attract the [favorable] attention of the lawmakers." And while the enactment of the Matthew Shepard Act and pending repeal of Don't Ask, Don't Tell indicate that the political process is not closed *entirely* to gay and lesbian people, that is not the standard by which the Court has judged "political powerlessness." Indeed, when the Court ruled that gender-based classifications were subject to heightened scrutiny, women already had won major political victories such as the Nineteenth Amendment (right to vote) and protection under Title VII (employment discrimination).

Finally, there is a growing acknowledgment that sexual orientation "bears no relation to ability to perform or contribute to society." Recent evolutions in legislation (including the pending repeal of Don't Ask, Don't Tell), in community practices and attitudes, in case law . . . , and in social science regarding sexual orientation all make clear that sexual orientation is not a characteristic that generally bears on legitimate policy objectives.

. . .

In reviewing a legislative classification under heightened scrutiny, the government must establish that the classification is "substantially related to an important government objective." Under heightened scrutiny, "a tenable justification must describe actual state purposes, not rationalizations for actions in fact differently grounded." "The justification must be genuine, not hypothesized or invented post hoc in response to litigation."

. . . [T]he legislative record underlying DOMA's passage contains discussion and debate that undermines any defense under heightened scrutiny. The record contains numerous expressions reflecting moral disapproval of gays and lesbians and their intimate and family relationships—precisely the kind of stereotype-based thinking and animus the Equal Protection Clause is designed to guard against.

After careful consideration, including a review of my recommendation, the President has concluded that

52. Excerpted from U.S. Department of Justice, Office of Public Affairs, "Letter from the Attorney General to Congress on Litigation Involving the Defense of Marriage Act," http://www.justice.gov/opa/pr/2011/February/11-ag-223.html.

given a number of factors, including a documented history of discrimination, classifications based on sexual orientation should be subject to a heightened standard of scrutiny. The President has also concluded that Section 3 of DOMA, as applied to legally married same-sex couples, fails to meet that standard and is therefore unconstitutional. Given that conclusion, the President has instructed the Department not to defend the statute.

Notwithstanding this determination, the President has informed me that Section 3 will continue to be enforced by the Executive Branch. To that end, the President has instructed Executive agencies to continue to comply with Section 3 of DOMA, consistent with the Executive's obligation to take care that the laws be faithfully executed, unless and until Congress repeals Section 3 or the judicial branch renders a definitive verdict against the law's constitutionality. This course of action respects the actions of the prior Congress that enacted DOMA, and it recognizes the judiciary as the final arbiter of the constitutional claims raised.

States Debate Same-Sex Marriage

Many states are currently debating the status of same-sex marriage under state statutory and state constitutional law. As noted in Section IIA, numerous states passed constitutional amendments limiting marriage to one man and one woman. A few state legislatures passed bills legalizing same-sex marriage. The Maryland, New York, and Washington laws were signed by the governor. Governor Chris Christie of New Jersey vetoed legislation authorizing same-sex marriage. A Maine law authorizing same-sex marriage was rejected in a statewide initiative by a close vote (but will be reconsidered in November 2012). We have excerpted below the statement of purpose from the New York same-sex marriage law; Governor Christie's message vetoing the New Jersey same-sex marriage law; and the statement of principles by Protect Marriage Maine (formerly known as Stand for Marriage Maine), the interest group that promoted the initiative overturning the Maine same-sex marriage law and is fighting against the most recent state same-sex marriage initiative. Why does the New York legislature believe same-sex marriage to be a fundamental right? Why does Stand for Marriage Maine think that same-sex marriage threatens traditional marriage? Does Governor Christie propose an adequate compromise? What do you believe are the main differences that explain why some states allow gay marriage, some have civil unions, and some provide almost no benefits for enduring same-sex relationships?

New York Same-Sex Marriage Law, "Statement in Support"[53]

The "freedom to marry" is, in the words of the United States Supreme Court, "one of the vital personal rights essential to the orderly pursuit of happiness by free people." In New York, however, certain couples who seek to exercise this personal right may not do so solely because they are of the same sex. The bar against same-sex couples entering into marriages exists regardless of whether they are committed to each other, whether they have lived together for six months or 30 years, whether they have joined their finances or purchased property together, or whether they have conceived or adopted children. Rather, same-sex couples are simply unable to marry in this State and therefore denied the equal freedom to enter into a state-created and legally secured bond of personal, social and economic significance. This bill removes the barriers in New York law that currently deprive individuals of the equal right to marry the person of their choice.

Civil marriage provides a comprehensive structure of state-sanctioned protections, benefits and mutual responsibilities for couples who are permitted to marry. In such areas as health care, hospital visitation, child custody, pension benefits, property ownership, inheritance, taxation, insurance coverage, and testimonial privileges, married couples receive important safeguards against the loss or injury of a spouse, and crucial assurances against legal intrusion into their marital privacy. New York's more than 50,000 same-sex couples and their families confront many of the same life challenges as their different-sex counterparts, but are denied these basic protections. Further, couples who are denied the State's recognition are denoted, by force of law and policy, as not equal to couples in other comparable relationships. Couples who are excluded from marriage are told by the institutions of the State, in essence, that their solemn commitment to one another has no legal weight.

Just as the right to marry confers important benefits on individuals, the institution of marriage produces

53. "Statement in Support of A. 8354 (N.Y. 2011-2012)," http://assembly.state.ny.us/leg/?default_fld=&bn=A08354&term=2011&Memo=Y

incalculable benefits for society, by fostering stable familial relationships. Same-sex couples who wish to marry are not simply looking to obtain additional rights, they are seeking out substantial responsibilities as well: to undertake significant and binding obligations to one another, and to lives of "shared intimacy and mutual financial and emotional support." Granting legal recognition to these relationships can only strengthen New York's families, by extending the ability to participate in this crucial social institution to all New Yorkers.

. . .

To ensure that the bill does not improperly intrude into matters of conscience or religious belief, the bill affirms that no member of the clergy can be compelled to solemnize any marriage. In short, this bill grants equal access to the government-created legal institution of civil marriage, while leaving the religious institution of marriage to its own separate, and fully autonomous, sphere.

Beyond the freedom that clergy will retain over marriage decisions, the bill also ensures that the statutory protections for religious organizations found in the New York Human Rights law remains intact, including, guaranteeing that religious institutions remain free to choose who may use their facilities and halls for marriage ceremonies and celebrations, to whom they rent their housing accommodations, or to whom they provide religious services, consistent with their religious principles. Further, the bill contains language to ensure that benevolent organizations, like the Knights of Columbus, remain exempt from New York prohibitions against discrimination in public accommodations, and are not be required to rent social halls to weddings of same-sex or other couples it chooses not to accommodate.

Chris Christie, Veto Message (February 21, 2012)[54]

. . .

Neither the United States Constitution nor the New Jersey State Constitution contain a right to same-sex marriage. In 2006, in *Lewis v. Harris*, while holding that there is no fundamental constitutional right to same-sex marriage, the New Jersey Supreme Court ruled that same-sex couples must be afforded the same rights and benefits that are statutorily given to their heterosexual counterparts. While there is no fundamental constitutional right for individuals of the same sex to marry, same-sex couples now have the rights and benefits enjoyed by, and burdens and obligations borne by, married couples. . . .

Now, just five years later, Senate Bill No. 1 seeks to eliminate civil unions and allow couples of the same gender to be married. While the wisdom of, or need for, same-sex marriage can be debated, it is beyond dispute that such a step represents a profoundly significant societal change. The framers of our State Constitution created the referendum process in Article IX as the sole mechanism by which the Constitution can be amended to consider precisely such important issues. I have repeatedly encouraged, and continue to ask that, the Legislature trust the people of New Jersey and seek their input by allowing our citizens to vote on the question of same-sex marriage. This path of amending the State Constitution, which embraces our most cherished democratic ideals and is enshrined in our guiding legal document, is the only way to amend our Constitution and the best way to resolve the issue of same-sex marriage in our State.

It is also important to understand the nature of the problems with the State's civil union law that Senate Bill No. 1 seeks to remedy. Since 2007, the New Jersey Division on Civil Rights has received over 1,300 complaints related to disability, over 1,200 complaints related to race, and hundreds of complaints in each of the protected areas of national origin, age, and sex. During this same time period, the Division on Civil Rights received only 13 complaints related to civil unions. To be clear, discrimination in the law's application must not be tolerated, and any complaint alleging a violation of a citizen's rights is unacceptable. However, the limited number of complaints regarding civil unions confirms that New Jersey's civil union law has been effective.

Protect Marriage Maine, Why Marriage Matters[55]

. . . [M]arriage is not political. It is the foundation of society, a pre-political institution that has existed since the dawn of mankind in every civilization throughout the world.

54. Excerpted from Governor Chris Christie, "Senate Bill No. 1: Conditional Veto Message," http://www.njleg.state.nj.us/2012/Bills/S0500/1_V1.PDF.

55. Excerpted from http://protectmarriagemaine.com/marriage.php (visited July 27, 2012)

Many people mistakenly believe that allowing same-sex marriage would not threaten their own traditional marriages. The thought being that all marriages can simply coexist. However, the reality is, if the initiative to redefine marriage were to pass there would be only one definition of marriage in Maine, and it would apply to everyone. The law would view gender as meaningless in defining marriage. This would violate how the vast majority of nations and cultures have understood marriage throughout history—the union of one man and one woman. Moreover, it will result in profound consequences for society.

It is important to note that marriage is more than a religious institution. It plays a vital role in supporting a flourishing and loving society and clearly supports the public good. Marriage unites the couple to each other, and provides the ideal environment for a husband and wife's biological children to develop into well-adjusted adults that thrive and succeed. Children need, and have the right to experience, the unique and irreplaceable role of both a father and a mother. When a child is born, her mother is almost always actively involved in her life, but the same cannot always be said of her father. A well-functioning society encourages marriage so children will be born and raised by the two people responsible for bringing them into the world: their mother and father.

Marriage is society's first institution. Moreover, it is the only societal institution that is focused on the best interest of children by providing a structure to connect them to their own parents. The social science evidence is overwhelming that children do best on virtually every measurement of health, happiness and attainment when they are raised in an intact family with a mother and a father. While death and divorce too often prevent this ideal, that is the environment in which children thrive.

Same-sex marriage advocates propose moving away from a system that is best for society—especially for children—and focus only on the desires of individual adults. Under this selfish, genderless definition of marriage, the interests of Maine's children would not be considered, and as a result society as a whole would suffer.

Same-sex marriage advocates often maintain that a redefinition of marriage is needed so everyone has equal legal protection. Under current law, however, Maine already affords same-sex couples full legal equality. The initiative being advanced by gay advocates isn't, therefore, about equality. It is a political exercise to force their will on society so that society issues a stamp of approval on homosexual relationships.

By changing the law, legal experts warn that there will be serious and widespread consequences for society. Those people who refuse to accept this new definition of marriage as genderless could be punished, and churches and religious organizations could lose their tax exemptions and be forced to discard their core moral principles in order to be compliant with the law. Also, individuals, small businesses and groups will be subjected to lawsuits and cumbersome regulatory procedures. Those who disagree with the law for moral or personal reasons would be treated as bigots and purveyors of hate.

In short, the proposed ballot initiative to redefine marriage in Maine will undermine the entire institution of marriage for all of society, will strip the interests of children from our marriage laws, and will leave society without the only institution it has to connect men and women to each other, and to any children born of their union.

Right to Die (and Right to Life)

The right to die is a newly opened front in the culture wars. Proponents of physician-assisted suicide have besieged state legislatures and courts seeking to gain statutory or constitutional rights to end life under certain conditions. Some states have responded. Oregon in 1997 passed the "Death with Dignity Act," which permitted physicians to administer lethal drugs if requested by certain terminally ill patients. The Supreme Court in *Gonzales v. Oregon* (2006) by a 6-3 vote ruled that this assisted suicide law was not preempted by federal law. The justices were not, however, willing to find a constitutional right to die when such a right was not recognized by state law. *Washington v. Glucksberg* (1997) and *Vacco v. Quill* (1997) unanimously sustained state laws prohibiting physicians from providing life-ending assistance to terminally ill patients. Chief Justice Rehnquist's opinion in *Washington v. Glucksberg* declared, "The history of the law's treatment of assisted suicide in this country has been and continues to be one of the rejection of nearly all efforts to permit it." Five justices suggested that terminally ill patients might have a constitutional right to palliative care aimed at easing their pain and suffering, even if that care hastened their death. Justice O'Connor's concurrence left open the possibility that "suffering patients have a constitutionally cognizable interest in obtaining relief from the suffering that they may experience in the last days of their lives."

The skirmishes over the right to die (or remain alive) turned into a politically deadly conflict when in 2003 the Supreme Court of Florida ordered that feeding tubes be removed from Terri Schiavo, a woman who had long been in a persistent vegetative state. President Bush and the Republican majority in Congress condemned that decision. After a bitter partisan debate Congress passed a federal law ordering federal judicial review of the case. Federal courts found no constitutional violation of Ms. Schiavo's right to life. Her feeding tubes were removed and Ms. Schiavo was allowed to die.

The Terri Schiavo Affair

Theresa (Terri) Marie Schiavo collapsed in her home on the morning of February 25, 1990. She remained in a coma for over two months before doctors diagnosed her as being in a persistent vegetative state. After several failed therapies and treatments, her husband, Michael Schiavo, entered a "do not resuscitate order" for his wife. In 1998 Michael Schiavo petitioned the court to remove Terri Schiavo's feeding tube. That petition sparked a seven-year legal battle between Mr. Schiavo and Ms. Schiavo's parents, Robert and Mary Schindler, who bitterly opposed removing the feeding tube.

Michael Schiavo and the Schindlers were in Florida courts for more than five years litigating whether Terri Schiavo's feeding tube could be removed. Finally, in 2003, the Florida judiciary issued what appeared to be a decisive ruling. In In re Guardianship of Schiavo *the Supreme Court of Florida ruled that clear and convincing evidence demonstrated that Terri Schiavo would not have wanted to live in a persistent vegetative state. The court ordered the feeding tube removed.*

State and federal elected officials immediately rushed to aid the Schindler family. The Florida legislature acted first. State officials passed "Terri's Law," which gave Governor Jeb Bush authority to intervene in the case. The Florida Supreme Court in Bush v. Schiavo *(FL 2004) ruled this law unconstitutional on separation of powers grounds. Again, the justices ordered the feeding tube removed. Congress then passed a special bill mandating federal judicial oversight of the Schiavo case. President Bush flew back from vacation in Texas to sign the bill.*

This attempt to obtain federal judicial relief failed. A federal district court found no constitutional violation; that decision was sustained by the Court of Appeals for the Eleventh Circuit in Schiavo ex rel. Schindler v. Schiavo *(2005). The Supreme Court declined to grant certiorari. With all possible appeals exhausted, Ms. Schiavo's feeding tube was removed. She died on March 31, 2005.*

The tragic Schiavo case is an excellent example of American constitutional politics. All governing institutions were involved in determining whether to remove Terri Schiavo's feeding tube. As you read the excerpts below, consider the following questions. Did members of different institutions behave differently? Did state officials behave differently than federal officials? Did elected officials behave differently than judicial officials? What does the Constitution say about the issues raised by this case?

In re Guardianship of Schiavo, 851 So. 2d 182 (Fla. 2003)

. . .

In *Schiavo I* [2000], we affirmed the trial court's decision ordering Mrs. Schiavo's guardian to withdraw life-prolonging procedures. In so doing, we affirmed the trial court's rulings that (1) Mrs. Schiavo's medical condition was the type of end-stage condition that permits the withdrawal of life-prolonging procedures, (2) she did not have a reasonable medical probability of recovering capacity so that she could make her own decision to maintain or withdraw life-prolonging procedures, (3) the trial court had the authority to make such a decision when a conflict within the family prevented a qualified person from effectively exercising the responsibilities of a proxy, and (4) clear and convincing evidence at the time of trial supported a determination that Mrs. Schiavo would have chosen in February 2000 to withdraw the life-prolonging procedures.

. . .

The guardianship court determined that Mrs. Schiavo remained in a permanent vegetative state. The guardianship court concluded that there was no evidence of a treatment in existence that offered such promise of increased cognitive function in Mrs. Schiavo's cerebral cortex that she herself would elect to undergo it at this time. Having concluded that the parents had failed to meet their burden to establish, by a preponderance of evidence, that the judgment was no longer equitable, the guardianship court denied the motion for relief from judgment and rescheduled the removal of the hydration and nutrition tube. . . .

. . .

In the final analysis, the difficult question that faced the trial court was whether Theresa Marie Schindler Schiavo, not after a few weeks in a coma, but after ten years in a persistent vegetative state that has robbed her of most of her cerebrum and all but the most instinctive of neurological functions, with no hope of a medical cure but with sufficient money and strength of body to live indefinitely, would choose to continue the constant nursing care and the supporting tubes in hopes that a miracle would somehow recreate her missing brain tissue, or whether she would wish to permit a natural death process to take its course and for her family members and loved ones to be free to continue their lives. After due consideration, we conclude that the trial judge had clear and convincing evidence to answer this question as he did.

Congressional Debate over the Bill for the Relief of the Parents of Terri Schiavo (2005)[56]

A Bill for the Relief of the Parents of Terri Schiavo

Section 1: The United States District Court for the Middle District of Florida shall have jurisdiction to hear, determine, and render judgment on a suit or claim by or on behalf of Theresa Marie Schiavo for the alleged violation of any right of Theresa Marie Schiavo under the Constitution or laws of the United States relating to the withholding or withdrawal of feed, fluids, or medical treatment necessary to maintain her life.

Section 2: Any parent of Theresa Marie Schiavo shall have standing to bring a suit under this Act. . . . In such a suit, the District Court shall determine de novo any claim of a violation of any right of Theresa Marie Schiavo within the scope of this Act, not withstanding any prior State court determination and regardless of whether such a claim has previously been raised considered, or decided in State court proceedings. The District Court shall entertain and determine the suit without any delay or abstention in favor of State court proceedings, and regardless of whether remedies available in the State courts have been exhausted.

REPRESENTATIVE JAMES SENSENBRENNER (Republican, Wisconsin)

. . .

Terri Schiavo, a person whose humanity is as undeniable as her emotional responses to her family's tender care-giving, has committed no crime and has done nothing wrong. Yet the Florida courts have brought Terri and the Nation to an ugly crossroads by commanding medical professionals sworn to protect life to end Terri's life. This Congress must reinforce the law's commitment to justice and compassion for all Americans particularly the most vulnerable.

. . .

. . . [W]hile our federal structure reserves broad authority to the States, America's federal courts have played a historic role in defending the constitutional rights of all Americans including the disenfranchised, disabled, and dispossessed. Among the God-Given rights protected by the Constitution, no right is more sacred than the right to life.

. . .

Mr. Speaker, the measure of a Nation's commitment to the sanctity of life is reflected in its laws to the extent those laws honor and defend its most vulnerable citizens. When a person's intentions regarding whether to receive lifesaving treatment are unclear, the responsibility of a compassionate Nation is to affirm that person's right to life. In our deeds and in our public actions, we must build a culture of life that welcomes and defends all human life. The compassionate traditions and highest values of our country command us to action.

We must work diligently to not only help Terri Schiavo continue her own fight for life, but to join the fight of all those who have lost capacity to fight on their own. As millions of Americans observe the beginning of Holy Week this Palm Sunday, we are reminded that every life has purpose, and none is without meaning. The battle to defend the preciousness of every life in a culture that respects and defends life is not only Terri's fight, but it is America's fight.

REPRESENTATIVE DEBBIE WASSERMAN SCHULTZ (Democrat, Florida)

. . .

This very personal matter should not be politicized as it is being here today. . . .

. . .

56. Excerpted from 151 *Congressional Record*, 109th Cong., 1st Sess. (2005), 5447–54.

Do we really want to set the precedent of this great body, the United States Congress, to insert ourselves in the middle of families' private matters all across America?

If we do this, we will end up throwing end-of-life decisions into utter and complete chaos; and we cannot and should not do that. We are Members of Congress. We are not doctors. We are not medical experts. We are not bioethicists. We are Members of Congress.

. . .

We do not have the expertise or the facts in enough detail to get into these kinds of decisions and make decisions in those kind of cases. We are not God and we are not Terri Schiavo's husband, sister, brother, uncle or relation. We are Members of Congress. We make laws and we uphold the law and we swore to uphold and protect the Constitution and we are thumbing our noses at the Constitution if we do this here tonight.

. . .

Ms. Schiavo make it clear . . . that she would not have wished to remain in a persistent vegetative state.

. . .

The court heard that testimony, not from Terri Schiavo's husband, not from her parents, but from other family members and friends who heard her say these things. They said there was enough evidence to render the belief that she had made those statements. She made it clear that she wished not to remain in a persistent vegetative state, which she is in today. And this U.S. Government should not step in to circumvent the wishes of one dying woman.

George W. Bush, Statement on the Signing of Legislation for the Relief of the Parents of Theresa Marie Schiavo (March 21, 2005)

Today I signed into law a bill that will allow federal courts to hear a claim by or on behalf of Terri Schiavo for violation of her rights relating to the withholding or withdrawal of food, fluids, or medical treatment necessary to sustain her life. In cases like this one, where there are serious questions and substantial doubts, our society, our laws, and our courts should have a presumption in favor of life. This presumption is especially critical for those like Terri Schiavo who live at the mercy of others. I appreciate the bipartisan action by the Members of Congress to pass this bill. I will continue to stand on the side of those defending life for all Americans, including those with disabilities.

Schiavo ex rel. Schindler v. Schiavo, 403 F.23d 1289 (11th Cir. 2005)

Cruzan [*v. Missouri Department of Health* (1990)] did not establish that the Constitution requires application of a clear and convincing evidence standard before termination of care. The Supreme Court held in *Cruzan* only that a state could, if it wished, require that evidence of the incompetent's wishes be proven by clear and convincing evidence. . . .

. . .

. . . [E]ven if constitutional law did work the way the plaintiffs want, contrary to the explicit teaching of the Supreme Court in the *Cruzan* opinion itself, they would still not have a substantial case on this claim. Plaintiffs would not, because Florida has adopted the very requirement that they say the Constitution mandates, a clear and convincing evidence standard. The plaintiffs argue that the state courts should have concluded that the clear and convincing evidence standard was not met in this case, but a quarrel with the result of a proceeding does not state a claim that due process was not afforded. Stated differently, procedural due process does not guarantee a particular result.

The claim that the defendants' actions violate the Eighth Amendment's prohibition against cruel and unusual punishment, is plainly without merit. That constitutional provision applies only to punishments inflicted after conviction for crimes, not to life support or medical treatment decisions.

To the extent plaintiffs claim a substantive due process right [to life], there is no authority to support their position. We are mindful that the Supreme Court has described itself as having "always been reluctant to expand the concept of substantive due process because guideposts for responsible decisionmaking in this unchartered area are scarce and open-ended." The Court has specifically held that the substantive due process component of the Due Process Clause does not require a state to protect its citizens against injury by non-state actors. *DeShaney v. Winnebago County Dep't of Social Serv.* (1989). As we have already explained, the defendants are not state actors for present purposes.

IV. Democratic Rights

MAJOR DEVELOPMENTS

- Supreme Court declares corporations have rights to make independent expenditures
- *Bush v. Gore* (2000) resolves presidential election
- Controversy over the rights of illegal aliens

The contemporary politics of constitutional democracy is about the application of New Deal/Great Society principles rather than a struggle over whether those principles should be superseded by a different constitutional conception of democracy. The Brandeis/Holmes dissents in the World War I free speech cases and the Voting Rights Act of 1965 today have canonical status. When the Supreme Court debated the Florida recount in *Bush v. Gore* (2000), the issue was whether the means for counting ballots was consistent with the one person, one vote standard announced in *Reynolds v. Sims* (1964). When the Supreme Court considers constitutional attacks on campaign finance regulation, all parties to the debate agree that speech can be regulated only when government demonstrates a compelling interest.

While liberals and conservatives agree that free speech and voting rights are fundamental, they dispute the circumstances under which government regulation might improve the marketplace of ideas, promote democracy, or protect citizenship. Political liberals are inclined to favor campaign finance reform, restrictions on hate speech (although many liberals oppose such regulations), regulations on commercial speech, greater access to public property for speech, granting students free speech rights, fewer restrictions on federal funding for speech, majority-minority election districts, judicial oversight of partisan gerrymanders, and policies granting illegal aliens basic rights. Political conservatives are far more inclined to think unconstitutional laws regulating hate speech, commercial advertising, campaign finance reform, and laws creating majority-minority districts. They do not believe that judges should interfere when elected officials limit the use of public property for speech, selectively fund different speakers, engage in partisan gerrymanders, or restrict the rights of illegal aliens. With important exceptions, the Supreme Court generally supports more conservative notions of constitutional democracy.

Whether these diverse issue positions cohere into a principled whole is controversial. All parties claim that their preferred policies are rooted in principle and that their opponents seek only political advantage. Liberals insist that they are committed to diversity and the principle that all persons should have an equal influence on the official decisions that affect their lives. Conservatives note that this commitment to diversity often excludes evangelical Christians and speakers who sharply challenge perceived liberal orthodoxies on race and gender. Conservatives claim to be committed to the original understanding of the Constitution and government neutrality, but liberals note that the persons responsible for crucial constitutional provisions said nothing about campaign finance and the legitimacy of majority-minority districts. Stephen Feldman suggests that struggles over constitutional democracy are between liberal proponents of pluralist democracy, who insist that Americans must incorporate diverse perspectives on the public good, and proponents of republican democracy, who insist on respect for traditional virtues.[57] Another possible distinction between contemporary liberals and conservatives is that liberals are more inclined to consider historical and social context when evaluating regulations of constitutional democracy, while conservatives distrust government capacity to distinguish between better and worse speech or better and worse democratic behaviors.

A. Free Speech

Most contemporary free speech fights concern the circumstances under which persons can champion particular ideas rather what ideas are constitutionally protected. The most important free speech issues of the mid-twentieth century are settled. General agreement exists that government can restrict particular viewpoints only if elected officials demonstrate a compelling interest. A general consensus also exists that government can almost never demonstrate that compelling interest. Applying these and related principles, the Supreme Court has struck down a federal law prohibiting persons from lying about having military declarations (*United States v. Alvarez* [2012]), a state ban on violent video games (*Brown v. Entertainment Merchants Association* [2011]), a state rule of evidence for determining when cross burning is a true threat (*Virginia v. Black* [2003]), and a jury verdict award-

57. Stephen M. Feldman, *Free Expression and Democracy in America: A History* (Chicago: University of Chicago Press, 2008).

ing substantial damages against a group that, when picketing military funerals, claims that the death is divine retribution for liberal policies toward gays and lesbians (*Snyder v. Phelps* [2011]). Far more often government regulators insist that while a direct ban on advocacy is unconstitutional, government can regulate the conditions of advocacy as long as those restrictions are content-neutral and the state interest is sufficient to warrant some burden on speakers. Everyone agrees that you have a right to claim that government should spend more money on bicycle paths. Debate exists over how much you may spend when making this claim, whether the Automobile Club of America has a constitutional right to exclude persons who champion greater government spending on bicycle paths, whether students opposed to more bicycle paths have a right to ensure their mandatory student dues are not spent on advocating for more paths, whether you may use government funds to champion better bicycle paths, whether proponents of bicycle paths have a right to hold an all-night vigil in the local park, whether students in school have the same right as adults to champion government support for bicycles, and whether different free speech rules apply to the conversations about bicycles that take place in different media.

The Supreme Court has not reached decisive conclusions on these questions. The justices are gradually becoming more opposed to campaign finance reform, supportive of the right of union members to not have their dues be spent on partisan political causes, very sympathetic to the rights of expressive associations and commercial speakers, and generally supportive of free speech rights on the Internet. Rehnquist and early Roberts Court majorities are less sympathetic to persons who wish to speak on public property, oppose speech conditions on the receipt of public funds, or are engaged in abortion clinic protests. This overall pattern may reflect a drift toward mild libertarianism. The court no longer polices boundaries between political and private speech, but the justices permit government to use public resources as the people's elected representatives see fit. The pattern of decisions may also reflect the idiosyncratic preferences of Justices O'Connor and Kennedy.

Advocacy

Champions of unpopular or dangerous ideas enjoy more freedom than at any previous point in American history. Recent Supreme Court decisions have protected the rights of persons who wish to sell violent video games to children (*Brown v. Entertainment Merchants Association*), make videos portraying cruelty to animals (*United States v. Stevens* [2010]), lie about their military service (*United States v. Alvarez*), and disrupt military funerals (*Snyder v. Phelps*). Rejecting claims that "depictions of animal cruelty . . . are categorically unprotected by the First Amendment," Chief Justice Roberts's majority opinion in *Stevens* asserted, "The First Amendment itself reflects a judgment by the American people that the benefits of its restrictions on the Government outweigh the costs. Our Constitution forecloses any attempt to revise that judgment simply on the basis that some speech is not worth it." When declaring the Stolen Valor Act unconstitutional in *United States v. Alvarez,* Justice Kennedy asserted, "Our constitutional tradition stands against the idea that we need Oceania's Ministry of Truth." Persons had a right to claim falsely that they had won military honors because "absent any evidence that the speech was used to gain a material advantage," permitting regulation "would give government a broad censorial power unprecedented in this Court's cases or in our constitutional tradition." The justices are also sensitive to the possibility of compelled speech. A 7-2 majority in *Knox v. Service Employees International Union, Local 1000* (2012) held that the First Amendment requires public service unions to permit persons to "opt out" whenever any change takes place in the percentage or amount of union dues being used to fund political activities. Justice Alito's majority opinion asserted that "nonmembers should not be required to fund a union's political and ideological projects unless they choose to do so after having 'a fair opportunity' to assess the impact of paying for nonchargeable union activities."

Contemporary legislators ban advocacy only in specific contexts that suggest particular dangers. In *Holder v. Humanitarian Law Project* (2010) several advocacy organizations were charged with providing material support to terrorist groups. Chief Justice Roberts's majority opinion, while sustaining the statute, emphasized that "plaintiffs may say anything they wish on any topic." The federal law merely forbade groups from providing any training to terrorist groups, even training limited to securing demands peaceably. "Foreign organizations that engage in terrorist activity," Roberts insisted, "are so tainted by their criminal conduct that any contribution to such an organization facilitates that conduct."

In *Virginia v. Black* (2003) the justices declared unconstitutional a state law that permitted juries to presume from evidence that persons had burned a cross that they intended to threaten local persons of color. All nine justices agreed that "true threats" were not constitutionally protected. Only Justice Thomas would categorically ban cross burning. The issue dividing the other justices was the connection between cross burning and threats. Justice O'Connor's crucial plurality opinion insisted that the state had to demonstrate something more than the fact of a cross burning to demonstrate that a true threat was made. She observed that the Virginia statute "does not distinguish between a cross burning done with the purpose of creating anger or resentment and a cross burning done with the purpose of threatening or intimidating a victim."

Candidates for judicial office were another beneficiary of the strong libertarian bent of Supreme Court free speech jurisprudence, although their cases were decided by a far closer vote than most other First Amendment decisions handed down during the Contemporary Era. The justices in *Republican Party of Minnesota v. White* (2002), by a 5-4 vote, declared unconstitutional a state law prohibiting persons running for judicial office to take positions on contested political or legal issues. Justice Scalia's majority opinion insisted that if states (unwisely) held judicial elections, those elections were subject to the same constitutional principles as were all other elections. "The greater power to dispense with elections altogether does not include the lesser power to conduct elections under conditions of state-imposed voter ignorance," he wrote. "If the State chooses to tap the energy and the legitimizing power of the democratic process, it must accord the participants in that process the First Amendment rights that attach to their roles."

Illustration 11-3 Westboro Baptist Church Demonstration at Military Funeral, December 2005

Members of the Westboro Baptist Church demonstrating outside church services for the funeral of U.S. Army Private Peter Navarro, who was killed by an improvised explosive device in Iraq. The Westboro Church primarily consists of Fred Phelps and his family. This demonstration was held in Missouri on December 23, 2005. In 2010 the Missouri county where the funeral was held passed an ordinance banning protests near funerals.

Source: UPI/Bill Greenblatt.

Snyder v. Phelps, 131 S. Ct. 1207 (2011)

Albert Snyder is the father of Matthew Snyder, a soldier killed in Iraq. On March 10, 2006, Matthew Snyder's funeral was held in Westminster, Maryland. Before and during the funeral service Fred Phelps and other members of the Westboro Baptist Church picketed on public property approximately one thousand feet from the church where Snyder was laid to rest. As they had done at numerous other funerals for fallen soldiers, members of the Westboro Church held placards condemning the United States, Catholics, and homosexuals. Fallen soldiers, Phelps and his followers wish to communicate, are divine punishment for the fallen state of the country. After the service Snyder sued Phelps for defamation and intentional infliction of emotional damage (IIED). A jury in a federal district court awarded Snyder $2.9 million in compensatory damages and $8 million in punitive damages. The district judge reduced the award to $2.1 million. That decision was reversed by the Court of Appeals for the Fourth Circuit, which ruled that Phelps was protected by the First Amendment. Snyder appealed to the Supreme Court of the United States.

The Supreme Court by an 8-1 vote agreed that Fred Phelps was protected by the First Amendment. Chief Justice Roberts's majority opinion declared that Phelps was speaking on public affairs and that such speech received the highest degree of protection. Both the Chief Justice and Justice Alito in dissent agreed that Phelps deliberately targeted the funerals of soldiers to gain publicity and that his speech was highly offensive. They nevertheless reached different conclusions on whether that speech was protected. Why do they reach those different conclusions? Whose conclusions are correct? What might explain why the two Bush nominees to the Court disputed the best result in this case? What facts about the case would have to change for there to be a different result? Could government officials ban more conventional anti-war protestors from military funerals? Could family members sue photographers for publishing pictures of crime victims, the military dead, or autopsy photos of deceased racecar drivers?

CHIEF JUSTICE ROBERTS delivered the opinion of the Court.

. . .

Whether the First Amendment prohibits holding Westboro liable for its speech in this case turns largely on whether that speech is of public or private concern, as determined by all the circumstances of the case. . . . The First Amendment reflects "a profound national commitment to the principle that debate on public issues should be uninhibited, robust, and wide-open." *New York Times Co. v. Sullivan* (1964). That is because "speech concerning public affairs is more than self-expression; it is the essence of self-government." . . .

. . .

The "content" of Westboro's signs plainly relates to broad issues of interest to society at large, rather than matters of "purely private concern." The placards read "God Hates the USA/Thank God for 9/11," "America is Doomed," "Don't Pray for the USA," "Thank God for IEDs," "Fag Troops," "Semper Fi Fags," "God Hates Fags," "Maryland Taliban," "Fags Doom Nations," "Not Blessed Just Cursed," "Thank God for Dead Soldiers," "Pope in Hell," "Priests Rape Boys," "You're Going to Hell," and "God Hates You." While these messages may fall short of refined social or political commentary, the issues they highlight—the political and moral conduct of the United States and its citizens, the fate of our Nation, homosexuality in the military, and scandals involving the Catholic clergy—are matters of public import. The signs certainly convey Westboro's position on those issues, in a manner designed . . . to reach as broad a public audience as possible. . . .

. . . The fact that Westboro spoke in connection with a funeral cannot by itself transform the nature of Westboro's speech. Westboro's signs, displayed on public land next to a public street, reflect the fact that the church finds much to condemn in modern society. Its speech is "fairly characterized as constituting speech on a matter of public concern" and the funeral setting does not alter that conclusion.

. . .

Westboro's choice to convey its views in conjunction with Matthew Snyder's funeral made the expression of those views particularly hurtful to many, especially to Matthew's father. The record makes clear that the applicable legal term—"emotional distress"—fails to capture fully the anguish Westboro's choice added to Mr. Snyder's already incalculable grief. But Westboro conducted its picketing peacefully on matters of public concern at a public place adjacent to a public street. Such space occupies a "special position in terms of First Amendment protection."

. . .

Simply put, the church members had the right to be where they were. Westboro alerted local authorities to its funeral protest and fully complied with police guidance on where the picketing could be staged. The picketing was conducted under police supervision some 1,000 feet from the church, out of the sight of those at the church. The protest was not unruly; there was no shouting, profanity, or violence.

The record confirms that any distress occasioned by Westboro's picketing turned on the content and viewpoint of the message conveyed, rather than any interference with the funeral itself. A group of parishioners standing at the very spot where Westboro stood, holding signs that said "God Bless America" and "God Loves You," would not have been subjected to liability. It was what Westboro said that exposed it to tort damages.

Given that Westboro's speech was at a public place on a matter of public concern, that speech is entitled to "special protection" under the First Amendment. Such speech cannot be restricted simply because it is upsetting or arouses contempt. "If there is a bedrock principle underlying the First Amendment, it is that the government may not prohibit the expression of an idea simply because society finds the idea itself offensive or disagreeable." *Texas v. Johnson* (1989). . . .

The jury here was instructed that it could hold Westboro liable for intentional infliction of emotional distress based on a finding that Westboro's picketing was "outrageous." "Outrageousness," however, is a highly malleable standard with "an inherent subjectiveness about it which would allow a jury to impose liability on the basis of the jurors' tastes or views, or perhaps on the basis of their dislike of a particular expression." In a case such as this, a jury is "unlikely to be neutral with respect to the content of [the] speech," posing "a real danger of becoming an instrument for the suppression of . . . 'vehement, caustic, and sometimes unpleasan[t]'" expression. Such a risk is unacceptable; "in public debate [we] must tolerate insulting, and even outrageous, speech in order to provide adequate 'breathing space' to the freedoms protected by the First Amendment." What Westboro said, in the whole context of how and where it chose to say it, is entitled to "special protection" under the First Amendment, and that protection cannot be overcome by a jury finding that the picketing was outrageous.

. . .

JUSTICE BREYER, concurring. . . .

JUSTICE ALITO, dissenting.

. . .

[The Westboro Church does not have a First Amendment right to] intentionally inflict severe emotional injury on private persons at a time of intense emotional sensitivity by launching vicious verbal attacks that make no contribution to public debate. To protect against such injury, "most if not all jurisdictions" permit recovery in tort for the intentional infliction of emotional distress (or IIED). . . .

. . .

This Court has recognized that words may "by their very utterance inflict injury" and that the First Amendment does not shield utterances that form "no essential part of any exposition of ideas, and are of such slight social value as a step to truth that any benefit that may be derived from them is clearly outweighed by the social interest in order and morality." . . . When grave injury is intentionally inflicted by means of an attack like the one at issue here, the First Amendment should not interfere with recovery.

. . .

Since respondents chose to stage their protest at Matthew Snyder's funeral and not at any of the other countless available venues, a reasonable person would have assumed that there was a connection between the messages on the placards and the deceased. Moreover, since a church funeral is an event that naturally brings to mind thoughts about the afterlife, some of respondents' signs—e.g., "God Hates You," "Not Blessed Just Cursed," and "You're Going to Hell"—would have likely been interpreted as referring to God's judgment of the deceased.

Other signs would most naturally have been understood as suggesting—falsely—that Matthew was gay. Homosexuality was the theme of many of the signs. There were signs reading "God Hates Fags," "Semper Fi Fags," "Fags Doom Nations," and "Fag Troops." . . .

. . .

In light of this evidence, it is abundantly clear that respondents, going far beyond commentary on matters of public concern, specifically attacked Matthew Snyder because (1) he was a Catholic and (2) he was a member of the United States military. Both Matthew and petitioner were private figures, and this attack was not speech on a matter of public concern. While commentary on the Catholic Church or the United States military constitutes speech on matters of public concern, speech regarding Matthew Snyder's purely private conduct does not.

. . .

The Court concludes that respondents' speech was protected by the First Amendment for [several] reasons, but none is sound.

. . . [T]he Court finds that "the overall thrust and dominant theme of [their] demonstration spoke to" broad public issues. . . . I fail to see why actionable speech should be immunized simply because it is interspersed with speech that is protected. The First Amendment allows recovery for defamatory statements that are interspersed with nondefamatory statements on matters of public concern, and there is no good reason why respondents' attack on Matthew Snyder and his family should be treated differently.

. . .

. . . [T]he Court finds it significant that respondents' protest occurred on a public street, but this fact alone should not be enough to preclude IIED liability. To be sure, statements made on a public street may be less likely to satisfy the elements of the IIED tort than statements made on private property, but there is no reason why a public street in close proximity to the scene of a funeral should be regarded as a free-fire zone in which otherwise actionable verbal attacks are shielded from liability. . . .

. . .

. . . Allowing family members to have a few hours of peace without harassment does not undermine public debate. I would therefore hold that, in this setting, the First Amendment permits a private figure to recover for the intentional infliction of emotional distress caused by speech on a matter of private concern.

Public Property, Subsidies, Employees, and Schools

The Supreme Court currently permits substantial regulation when speakers claim rights to speak on public property, in public schools, or with public moneys. Cases frequently turn on the extent to which speech is seen as purely private or entwined with some public largess. While the Court in *Boy Scouts of America v. Dale* (2000) ruled that states could not require a private expressive organization to accept members whose beliefs or habits were inconsistent with the message the organization wished to communicate, the justices in *Christian Legal Society Chapter of the University of California, Hastings College of Law v. Martinez* (2010) sustained a university rule that required official law school groups, including the Christian Legal Society (CLS), to not "discriminate unlawfully on the basis of race, color, religion, national origin, ancestry, disability, age, sex, or sexual orientation." Justice Ginsburg's plurality opinion stated, "CLS may exclude any person for any reason if it forgoes the benefits of official recognition. The expressive-association precedents on which CLS relies, in contrast, involved regulations that *compelled* a group to include unwanted members, with no choice to opt out."

The late Rehnquist and Roberts Courts continue to narrowly define what constitute public fora, or places that are traditionally held open for speech. *United States v. American Library Association* (2003) reaffirmed previous decisions rejecting claims that libraries were public fora. When sustaining a federal law requiring libraries receiving federal money to block Internet access to obscenity and indecent material, Chief Justice Rehnquist declared, "A public library does not acquire Internet terminals in order to create a public forum for Web publishers to express themselves." *Arkansas Educational Television Commission v. Forbes* (1998) rejected claims that political debates sponsored by public television were obligated to include all candidates listed on the ballot. Justice Kennedy's majority opinion maintained that "the debate was a nonpublic forum, for which [the television station] could exclude Forbes in the reasonable, viewpoint-neutral exercise of its journalistic discretion."

The justices in three cases—*Madsen v. Women's Health Center, Inc.* (1994), *Schenck v. Pro-Choice Network of Western New York* (1997), and *Hill v. Colorado* (2000)—sustained most provisions in injunctions limiting pro-life protests outside of abortion clinics. Chief Justice Rehnquist's majority opinion in *Madsen* rejected claims that the ban on pro-life protests violated content neutrality, the principle that time, place, and manner restrictions on speech must not discriminate on the basis of particular viewpoints or subject matters. He wrote,

> The fact that the injunction in the present case did not prohibit activities of those demonstrating in favor of abortion is justly attributable to the lack of any similar demonstrations by those in favor of abortion, and of any consequent request that their demonstrations be regulated by injunction. There is no suggestion in this record that Florida law would not equally restrain similar conduct directed at a

target having nothing to do with abortion; none of the restrictions imposed by the court were directed at the contents of petitioner's message.

Watchtower Bible and Tract Society of New York v. Village of Stratton (2002) is a rare example of a contemporary case in which the Supreme Court declared unconstitutional a law restricting speech on public property. Stratton required that persons engaged in door-to-door advocacy obtain a permit. Justice Stevens declared this requirement "offensive—not only to the values protected by the First Amendment, but to the very notion of a free society—that in the context of everyday public discourse a citizen must first inform the government of her desire to speak to her neighbors and then obtain a permit to do so."

The Supreme Court narrowly defined the constitutional rights of public employees and public school students. *Garcetti v. Ceballos* (2005) held that an assistant district attorney may be fired for writing a memo suggesting that a prosecution be dropped because the police engaged in misrepresentation. Writing for the 5-4 majority Justice Kennedy declared, "When public employees make statements pursuant to their official duties, the employees are not speaking as citizens for First Amendment purposes, and the Constitution does not insulate their communications from employer discipline." Three years later the same 5-4 majority ruled that a high school principle did not violate the First and Fourteenth Amendments when she suspended a student for displaying a banner with the words "BONG HiTS 4 JESUS" at a school outing to witness the 2002 Olympic Torch Relay. Chief Justice Roberts asserted, "A principal may, consistent with the First Amendment, restrict student speech at a school event, when that speech is reasonably viewed as promoting illegal drug use."[58]

The justices have been more conflicted when considering free speech rights in cases concerned with public subsidies. *National Endowment for the Arts v. Finley* (1998) ruled that Congress could require federal officials to consider "general standards of decency and respect for the diverse beliefs and values of the American public" when awarding grants to artists. Justice O'Connor's majority opinion stated,

> Although the First Amendment certainly has application in the subsidy context, we note that the Government may allocate competitive funding according to criteria that would be impermissible were direct regulation of speech or a criminal penalty at stake. So long as legislation does not infringe on other constitutionally protected rights, Congress has wide latitude to set spending priorities. And as we held in *Rust v. Sullivan* (1991), Congress may "selectively fund a program to encourage certain activities it believes to be in the public interest, without at the same time funding an alternative program which seeks to deal with the problem in another way."

The justices distinguished *Rust v. Sullivan,* the decision that permitted the federal government to forbid doctors accepting federal funds to discuss abortion with their patients, in *Legal Services Corporation v. Velazquez* (2001), a case concerned with the free speech rights of federally funded lawyers. A 5-4 judicial majority declared unconstitutional a federal law that forbade the Legal Services Corporation from funding litigation aimed at changing welfare laws. Justice Kennedy's majority opinion asserted, "The advice from the attorney to the client and the advocacy by the attorney to the courts cannot be classified as governmental speech even under a generous understanding of that concept." Readers may wonder whether a court composed of doctors would similarly conclude that the lawyer-client relationship is constitutionally different from and merits more constitutional protection than the doctor-patient relationship.

Hill v. Colorado, 530 U.S. 703 (2000)

Leila Jeanne Hill regularly engaged in sidewalk counseling outside of abortion clinics in Colorado. Her counseling consisted of making signs, handing out leaflets, and attempting to talk to pregnant women in an effort to persuade them not to have an abortion. In 1993 Colorado passed a law that restricted speech outside of health facilities, including abortion clinics. The relevant provision of the statute declared, "No person shall knowingly approach another person within eight feet of such person, unless such other person consents, for the purpose of passing a leaflet or handbill to, displaying a sign to, or engaging in oral protest, education, or counseling with such other person in the public way or sidewalk

58. *Morse v. Frederick,* 551 U.S. 393 (2007).

area within a radius of one hundred feet from any entrance door to a health care facility." After a lengthy litigation process in which Colorado courts sustained the Colorado law on four separate occasions, Hill appealed to the Supreme Court of the United States.

The Supreme Court by a 6-3 vote ruled that the Colorado law was an appropriate time, place, and manner restriction. Justice Stevens's majority opinion maintained that state law may grant women seeking abortions the right to avoid unwanted speech. The dissents insist that abortion clinics are particularly appropriate sites for speech about abortion. Which perspective do you believe is most consistent with constitutional values? In many time, place, and manner cases liberal justices accuse conservative justices of weakening the principle that time, place, and manner restrictions must be narrowly tailored. They claim that the government interest is far too insubstantial or tenuous to restrict speech or that petitioners are being deprived of a vital means for communicating their ideas. In Hill *the conservative justices make the same charge against the liberal justices. To what extent might each wing of the Rehnquist Court be accused of strengthening or weakening narrow tailoring depending on the interests at stake? Is there a principled justification for the judicial decision that the Colorado regulation in* Hill *was constitutional but other restrictions on speech in public places are unconstitutional? Is there a principled justification for the opposite conclusion?*

JUSTICE STEVENS delivered the opinion of the Court.

. . .

The right to free speech, of course, includes the right to attempt to persuade others to change their views, and may not be curtailed simply because the speaker's message may be offensive to his audience. But the protection afforded to offensive messages does not always embrace offensive speech that is so intrusive that the unwilling audience cannot avoid it. . . .

The recognizable privacy interest in avoiding unwanted communication varies widely in different settings. It is far less important when "strolling through Central Park" than when "in the confines of one's own home," or when persons are "powerless to avoid" it. . . . More specific to the facts of this case, we have recognized that "[t]he First Amendment does not demand that patients at a medical facility undertake Herculean efforts to escape the cacophony of political protests." . . .

. . .

All four of the state court opinions upholding the validity of this statute concluded that it is a content-neutral time, place, and manner regulation. . . .

. . .

The Colorado statute passes that test for three independent reasons. First, it is not a "regulation of speech." Rather, it is a regulation of the places where some speech may occur. Second, it was not adopted "because of disagreement with the message it conveys." . . . [T]he statute's "restrictions apply equally to all demonstrators, regardless of viewpoint, and the statutory language makes no reference to the content of the speech." Third, the State's interests in protecting access and privacy, and providing the police with clear guidelines, are unrelated to the content of the demonstrators' speech. . . .

. . .

The Colorado statute's regulation of the location of protests, education, and counseling . . . places no restrictions on—and clearly does not prohibit—either a particular viewpoint or any subject matter that may be discussed by a speaker. Rather, it simply establishes a minor place restriction on an extremely broad category of communications with unwilling listeners. Instead of drawing distinctions based on the subject that the approaching speaker may wish to address, the statute applies equally to used car salesmen, animal rights activists, fundraisers, environmentalists, and missionaries. Each can attempt to educate unwilling listeners on any subject, but without consent may not approach within eight feet to do so.

. . . [T]he statute's restriction seeks to protect those who enter a health care facility from the harassment, the nuisance, the persistent importuning, the following, the dogging, and the implied threat of physical touching that can accompany an unwelcome approach within eight feet of a patient by a person wishing to argue vociferously face-to-face and perhaps thrust an undesired handbill upon her. The statutory phrases, "oral protest, education, or counseling," distinguish speech activities likely to have those consequences from speech activities (such as Justice Scalia's "happy speech". . .) that are most unlikely to have those consequences. . . .

. . .

Justice Kennedy suggests that a speaker who approaches a patient and "chants in praise of the Supreme Court and its abortion decisions, or hands out a simple leaflet saying, 'We are for abortion rights,'" would not be subject to the statute.... But what reason is there to believe the statute would not apply to that individual? She would be engaged in "oral protest" and "education," just as the abortion opponent who expresses her view that the Supreme Court decisions were incorrect would be "protest[ing]" the decisions and "educat[ing]" the patient on the issue....

...

Persons who are attempting to enter health care facilities—for any purpose—are often in particularly vulnerable physical and emotional conditions. The State of Colorado has responded to its substantial and legitimate interest in protecting these persons from unwanted encounters, confrontations, and even assaults by enacting an exceedingly modest restriction on the speakers' ability to approach.

...

JUSTICE SOUTER, with whom JUSTICE O"CONNOR, JUSTICE GINSBURG, and JUSTICE BREYER join, concurring.

...

... There is always a correlation with subject and viewpoint when the law regulates conduct that has become the signature of one side of a controversy. But that does not mean that every regulation of such distinctive behavior is content based as First Amendment doctrine employs that term. The correct rule, rather, is captured in the formulation that a restriction is content based only if it is imposed because of the content of the speech....

...

[Colorado] does not forbid the statement of any position on any subject. It does not declare any view as unfit for expression within the 100-foot zone or beyond it. What it forbids, and all it forbids, is approaching another person closer than eight feet (absent permission) to deliver the message. Anyone (let him be called protester, counselor, or educator) may take a stationary position within the regulated area and address any message to any person within sight or hearing. The stationary protester may be quiet and ingratiating, or loud and offensive; the law does not touch him, even though in some ways it could....

... The fact that speech by a stationary speaker is untouched by this statute shows that the reason for its restriction on approaches goes to the approaches, not to the content of the speech of those approaching. What is prohibited is a close encounter when the person addressed does not want to get close. So, the intended recipient can stay far enough away to prevent the whispered argument, mitigate some of the physical shock of the shouted denunciation, and avoid the unwanted handbill. But the content of the message will survive on any sign readable at eight feet and in any statement audible from that slight distance. Hence the implausibility of any claim that an anti-abortion message, not the behavior of protesters, is what is being singled out.

...

JUSTICE SCALIA, with whom JUSTICE THOMAS joins, dissenting

...

... [T]he regulation as it applies to oral communications is obviously and undeniably content-based. A speaker wishing to approach another for the purpose of communicating any message except one of protest, education, or counseling may do so without first securing the other's consent. Whether a speaker must obtain permission before approaching within eight feet—and whether he will be sent to prison for failing to do so—depends entirely on what he intends to say when he gets there. I have no doubt that this regulation would be deemed content-based in an instant if the case before us involved antiwar protesters, or union members seeking to "educate" the public about the reasons for their strike....

The Court asserts that this statute is not content-based for purposes of our First Amendment analysis because it neither (1) discriminates among viewpoints nor (2) places restrictions on "any subject matter that may be discussed by a speaker." ... But we have never held that the universe of content-based regulations is limited to those two categories, and such a holding would be absurd. Imagine, for instance, special place-and-manner restrictions on all speech except that which "conveys a sense of contentment or happiness." This "happy speech" limitation would not be "viewpoint-based"—citizens would be able to express their joy in equal measure at either the rise or fall of the NASDAQ, at either the success or the failure of the Republican Party—and would not discriminate on the basis of subject matter, since gratification could be expressed about anything at all....

... The Court's confident assurance that the statute poses no special threat to First Amendment freedoms because it applies alike to "used car salesmen, animal rights activists, fundraisers, environmentalists, and missionaries" . . . is a wonderful replication (except for its lack of sarcasm) of Anatole France's observation that "[t]he law, in its majestic equality, forbids the rich as well as the poor to sleep under bridges. . . ." This Colorado law is no more targeted at used car salesmen, animal rights activists, fund raisers, environmentalists, and missionaries than French vagrancy law was targeted at the rich. We know what the Colorado legislators, by their careful selection of content ("protest, education, and counseling"), were taking aim at, for they set it forth in the statute itself: the "right to protest or counsel against certain medical procedures" on the sidewalks and streets surrounding health care facilities. . . .

. . .

The burdens this law imposes upon the right to speak are substantial. . . . I have certainly held conversations at a distance of eight feet seated in the quiet of my chambers, but I have never walked along the public sidewalk—and have not seen others do so—"conversing" at an 8-foot remove. . . . The availability of a powerful amplification system will be of little help to the woman who hopes to forge, in the last moments before another of her sex is to have an abortion, a bond of concern and intimacy that might enable her to persuade the woman to change her mind and heart. The counselor may wish to walk alongside and to say, sympathetically and as softly as the circumstances allow, something like: "My dear, I know what you are going through. I've been through it myself. You're not alone and you do not have to do this. There are other alternatives. Will you let me help you? May I show you a picture of what your child looks like at this stage of her human development?" The Court would have us believe that this can be done effectively—yea, perhaps even more effectively—by shouting through a bullhorn at a distance of eight feet.

. . .

. . . A proper regard for the "place" involved in this case should result in, if anything, a commitment by this Court to adhere to and rigorously enforce our speech-protective standards. The public forum involved here—the public spaces outside of health care facilities—has become, by necessity and by virtue of this Court's decisions, a forum of last resort for those who oppose abortion. . . . For those who share an abiding moral or religious conviction (or, for that matter, simply a biological appreciation) that abortion is the taking of a human life, there is no option but to persuade women, one by one, not to make that choice. And as a general matter, the most effective place, if not the only place, where that persuasion can occur, is outside the entrances to abortion facilities. By upholding these restrictions on speech in this place the Court ratifies the State's attempt to make even that task an impossible one.

. . .

JUSTICE KENNEDY, dissenting.

. . .

The statute . . . restricts speech on particular topics. Of course, the enactment restricts "oral protest, education, or counseling" on any subject; but a statute of broad application is not content neutral if its terms control the substance of a speaker's message. If oral protest, education, or counseling on every subject within an 8-foot zone present a danger to the public, the statute should apply to every building entrance in the State. It does not. It applies only to a special class of locations: entrances to buildings with health care facilities. We would close our eyes to reality were we to deny that "oral protest, education, or counseling" outside the entrances to medical facilities concern a narrow range of topics—indeed, one topic in particular. By confining the law's application to the specific locations where the prohibited discourse occurs, the State has made a content-based determination. The Court ought to so acknowledge. Clever content-based restrictions are no less offensive than censoring on the basis of content. . . . If, just a few decades ago, a State with a history of enforcing racial discrimination had enacted a statute like this one, regulating "oral protest, education, or counseling" within 100 feet of the entrance to any lunch counter, our predecessors would not have hesitated to hold it was content based or viewpoint based. It should be a profound disappointment to defenders of the First Amendment that the Court today refuses to apply the same structural analysis when the speech involved is less palatable to it.

. . .

After the Court errs in finding the statute content neutral, it compounds the mistake by finding the law viewpoint neutral. Viewpoint-based rules are invidious speech restrictions, yet the Court approves this one. The purpose and design of the statute—as everyone ought to know and as its own defenders urge in attempted justification—are to restrict speakers on one side of the debate: those who protest abortions. The statute applies only to medical facilities, a convenient yet obvious mask for the legislature's true purpose and for the prohibition's true effect. One need read no further than the statute's preamble to remove any doubt about the question. The Colorado Legislature sought to restrict "a person's right to protest or counsel against certain medical procedures." . . . The word "against" reveals the legislature's desire to restrict discourse on one side of the issue regarding "certain medical procedures." . . .

. . .

The Court now strikes at the heart of the reasoned, careful balance I had believed was the basis for the joint opinion in *Casey*. The vital principle of the opinion was that in defined instances the woman's decision whether to abort her child was in its essence a moral one, a choice the State could not dictate. Foreclosed from using the machinery of government to ban abortions in early term, those who oppose it are remitted to debate the issue in its moral dimensions. In a cruel way, the Court today turns its back on that balance. It in effect tells us the moral debate is not so important after all and can be conducted just as well through a bullhorn from an 8-foot distance as it can through a peaceful, face-to-face exchange of a leaflet. The lack of care with which the Court sustains the Colorado statute reflects a most troubling abdication of our responsibility to enforce the First Amendment. . . .

Campaign Finance

Campaign finance reform is the central battleground for the contemporary constitutional politics of free speech. Government rarely restricts advocacy. The more crucial issue for many speakers is whether they can find a way to be heard. The Internet and government funding provide one set of avenues for participating in the marketplace of ideas. They are discussed in the next section. Spending one's money to promote one's ideas or a candidate is the other method for participating in contemporary democratic politics.

The contemporary struggle over campaign finance began in 1995 when Senators John McCain (R-AZ) and Russell Feingold (D-WI) introduced what became known as the Bipartisan Campaign Reform Act (BCRA). The BCRA forbade corporations and unions from using their general treasury funds to make independent expenditures for "electioneering communication," defined as "any broadcast, cable, or satellite communication" that "refers to a clearly identified candidate for Federal office" and is made within thirty days of a primary election. Another provision placed sharp limits on soft money, contributions that nominally go for party-building activities, but are in fact used to support particular candidates. After a long debate both houses of Congress passed the BCRA in 2002. President Bush signed the bill, although he expressed significant constitutional reservations. His signing statement praised the provisions in the bill "prevent[ing] unions and corporations from making unregulated, 'soft' money contributions," and "creat[ing] new disclosure requirements." Bush nevertheless criticized those provisions in the BCRA "preventing all individuals, not just unions and corporations, from making donations to political parties in connection with Federal elections" and questioned "the constitutionality of the broad ban on issue advertising, which restrains the speech of a wide variety of groups on issues of public import in the months closest to an election."

A 5-4 Supreme Court majority in *McConnell v. Federal Election Commission* (2003) sustained most of the constitutionally controversial provisions in the BCRA, applying the "less rigorous scrutiny" the justices believed applicable to legislation imposing limits on campaign contributions. The soft money prohibitions, Justices Stevens and O'Connor concluded, were constitutional means for combating "the danger that officeholders will decide issues not on the merits or the desires of their constituencies, but according to the wishes of those who have made large, financial contributions valued by the officeholder." Congress, the majority opinion continued, had the right "to prohibit corporations and unions from using funds in their treasuries to finance advertisements expressly advocating the election or defeat of candidates in federal elections." Besides, Justices O'Connor and Stevens reasoned, corporations and unions interested in express advocacy could simply create a separate, segregated fund for that purpose.

The Supreme Court began scrutinizing campaign finance laws more strictly when Justice O'Connor left the bench. Numerous decisions exhibited increased judicial hostility to federal laws restricting or regulating the use of money in political campaigns.

- *Randall v. Sorrell* (2006) declared unconstitutional a Vermont law limiting campaign contributions in state elections to $200 or $400 per candidate.

- *Federal Election Commission v. Wisconsin Right to Life* (2007) ruled that political advertisements violate the BCRA ban on electoral communications only "if the ad is susceptible of no reasonable interpretation other than as an appeal to vote for or against a specific candidate."
- *Citizens United v. Federal Election Commission* (2008) partly overruled *McConnell* and overruled completely *Austin v. Michigan Chamber of Commerce* (1990) when holding that corporations had the right to make independent expenditures on behalf of named candidates.
- *Arizona Free Enterprise Club's Freedom Club PAC v. Bennett* (2011) declared unconstitutional a state law that provided public funds to candidates when their electoral rival exceeded certain spending limits.
- *American Tradition Partnership, Inc. v. Bullock* (2012) summarily reversed a Montana Supreme Court decision that held that, because of the unique influence of corporate wealth on Montana politics, the Montana legislature could restrict independent corporate expenditures during political campaigns.

When deciding these cases the justices "repeatedly rejected the argument that the government has a compelling state interest in leveling the playing field that can justify undue burdens on political speech." As Chief Justice Roberts declared in *Arizona Free Enterprise*, "The First Amendment embodies our choice as a Nation that, when it comes to [campaigning for office], the guiding principle is freedom—the 'unfettered interchange of ideas'—not whatever the State may view as fair."

The impact of the Supreme Court's campaign finance decisions is controversial. Some commentators believe that the justices are responsible for unleashing a tidal wave of corporate spending in political campaigns. Others insist that the judges did little more than permit affluent Americans to spend money in one way rather than another. Before *Citizens United*, wealthy contributors relied on "527 groups" that were nominally engaged in issue advocacy but in practice, as the "Swift Boat Veteran" attacks on John Kerry in 2004 illustrate, were often more concerned with endorsing or defeating candidates. After *Citizens United* the same contributors directly advocated for and against candidates. The dramatic increase in corporate contributions to super-PACs during the first part of the 2012 presidential campaign can be attributed to *Citizens United*, but whether that money would have found a different outlet remains unclear.

Citizens United v. Federal Election Commission, 558 U.S. 310 (2010)

The nonprofit corporation Citizens United in January 2008 released a documentary entitled Hillary. *The movie was critical of then-senator Hillary Clinton, a candidate for her party's presidential nomination. Citizens United wanted to make the movie available on cable television through video-on-demand in the hope that they could influence the primary elections. The Federal Election Commission prohibited airing* Hillary *on the ground that the BCRA forbade corporations from broadcasting within thirty days of a primary election any advertisement that advocated the election or defeat of a specific candidate. That decision was supported by a federal district court. Citizens United appealed to the Supreme Court of the United States.*

The Supreme Court by a 5-4 vote reversed. In an opinion that overruled Austin v. Michigan Chamber of Commerce *(1990) and partially overruled* McConnell v. Federal Election Commission *(2003) Justice Kennedy ruled that corporations had the same right as individuals to make independent expenditures during political campaigns. Why does Justice Kennedy conclude that corporations have the same rights as individuals to make independent expenditures? Why do the dissents disagree? Who has the better argument? Compare the judicial line-up in* Citizens United *to the judicial line-up in* Buckley v. Valeo *(1976). Why has judicial voting in campaign finance cases become more ideological over the past thirty years?*

In his second State of the Union address President Barack Obama declared, "Last week, the Supreme Court reversed a century of law to open the floodgates for special interests—including foreign corporations—to spend without limit in our elections. Well, I don't think American elections should be bankrolled by America's most powerful interests, or worse, by foreign entities." Television coverage of the address caught Justice Alito wincing at the accusation and muttering, "Not true." What was true and not true about President Obama's assertions? Were these assertions appropriate presidential comments on constitutional issues or inappropriate efforts to interfere with judicial decisions? What steps could President Obama constitutionally take to limit or reverse the impact of Citizens United?

JUSTICE KENNEDY delivered the opinion of the Court.

The law before us is an outright ban, backed by criminal sanctions. Section 441b makes it a felony for all corporations—including nonprofit advocacy corporations—either to expressly advocate the election or defeat of candidates or to broadcast electioneering communications within 30 days of a primary election and 60 days of a general election. Thus, the following acts would all be felonies under §441b: The Sierra Club runs an ad, within the crucial phase of 60 days before the general election, that exhorts the public to disapprove of a Congressman who favors logging in national forests; the National Rifle Association publishes a book urging the public to vote for the challenger because the incumbent U. S. Senator supports a handgun ban; and the American Civil Liberties Union creates a Web site telling the public to vote for a Presidential candidate in light of that candidate's defense of free speech. These prohibitions are classic examples of censorship.

. . .

Section 441b's prohibition on corporate independent expenditures is thus a ban on speech. As a "restriction on the amount of money a person or group can spend on political communication during a campaign," that statute "necessarily reduces the quantity of expression by restricting the number of issues discussed, the depth of their exploration, and the size of the audience reached." *Buckley v. Valeo* (1976). Were the Court to uphold these restrictions, the Government could repress speech by silencing certain voices at any of the various points in the speech process. . . .

. . .

Premised on mistrust of governmental power, the First Amendment stands against attempts to disfavor certain subjects or viewpoints. . . . [I]t is inherent in the nature of the political process that voters must be free to obtain information from diverse sources in order to determine how to cast their votes. . . .

We find no basis for the proposition that, in the context of political speech, the Government may impose restrictions on certain disfavored speakers. Both history and logic lead us to this conclusion.

. . .

Austin v. Michigan Chamber of Commerce (1990) "uph[eld] a direct restriction on the independent expenditure of funds for political speech for the first time in [this Court's] history." . . . . [T]he *Austin* Court identified a new governmental interest in limiting political speech: an antidistortion interest. *Austin* found a compelling governmental interest in preventing "the corrosive and distorting effects of immense aggregations of wealth that are accumulated with the help of the corporate form and that have little or no correlation to the public's support for the corporation's political ideas."

. . .

If the First Amendment has any force, it prohibits Congress from fining or jailing citizens, or associations of citizens, for simply engaging in political speech. If the antidistortion rationale were to be accepted, however, it would permit Government to ban political speech simply because the speaker is an association that has taken on the corporate form. . . . If *Austin* were correct, the Government could prohibit a corporation from expressing political views in media beyond those presented here, such as by printing books. . . .

. . . The rule that political speech cannot be limited based on a speaker's wealth is a necessary consequence of the premise that the First Amendment generally prohibits the suppression of political speech based on the speaker's identity.

. . . All speakers, including individuals and the media, use money amassed from the economic marketplace to fund their speech. The First Amendment protects the resulting speech, even if it was enabled by economic transactions with persons or entities who disagree with the speaker's ideas.

Austin's antidistortion rationale would produce the dangerous, and unacceptable, consequence that Congress could ban political speech of media corporations. Media corporations are now exempt from §441b's ban on corporate expenditures. Yet media corporations accumulate wealth with the help of the corporate form, the largest media corporations have "immense aggregations of wealth," and the views expressed by media corporations often "have little or no correlation to the public's support" for those views. Thus, under the Government's reasoning, wealthy media corporations could have their voices diminished to put them on par with other media entities. There is no precedent for permitting this under the First Amendment.

. . .

The Government contends further that corporate independent expenditures can be limited because of its interest in protecting dissenting shareholders from being compelled to fund corporate political speech. This asserted interest . . . would allow the Government to ban the political speech even of media corporations. Assume, for example, that a shareholder of a corporation that owns a newspaper disagrees with the political views the newspaper expresses. Under the Government's view, that potential disagreement could give the Government the authority to restrict the media corporation's political speech. The First Amendment does not allow that power. There is, furthermore, little evidence of abuse that cannot be corrected by shareholders "through the procedures of corporate democracy."

. . .

Due consideration leads to this conclusion: *Austin* should be and now is overruled. We return to the principle established in *Buckley* and *First National Bank of Boston v. Bellotti* (1978) that the Government may not suppress political speech on the basis of the speaker's corporate identity. No sufficient governmental interest justifies limits on the political speech of nonprofit or for-profit corporations.

. . .

CHIEF JUSTICE ROBERTS, with whom JUSTICE ALITO joins, concurring.

The Government urges us in this case to uphold a direct prohibition on political speech. It asks us to embrace a theory of the First Amendment that would allow censorship not only of television and radio broadcasts, but of pamphlets, posters, the Internet, and virtually any other medium that corporations and unions might find useful in expressing their views on matters of public concern. Its theory, if accepted, would empower the Government to prohibit newspapers from running editorials or opinion pieces supporting or opposing candidates for office, so long as the newspapers were owned by corporations—as the major ones are. First Amendment rights could be confined to individuals, subverting the vibrant public discourse that is at the foundation of our democracy.

The Court properly rejects that theory, and I join its opinion in full. The First Amendment protects more than just the individual on a soapbox and the lonely pamphleteer. . . .

. . .

JUSTICE SCALIA, with whom JUSTICE ALITO joins, and with whom JUSTICE THOMAS joins in part, concurring.

. . .

The dissent says that when the Framers "constitutionalized the right to free speech in the First Amendment, it was the free speech of individual Americans that they had in mind." That is no doubt true. All the provisions of the Bill of Rights set forth the rights of individual men and women—not, for example, of trees or polar bears. But the individual person's right to speak includes the right to speak *in association with other individual persons*. Surely the dissent does not believe that speech by the Republican Party or the Democratic Party can be censored because it is not the speech of "an individual American." It is the speech of many individual Americans, who have associated in a common cause, giving the leadership of the party the right to speak on their behalf. The association of individuals in a business corporation is no different—or at least it cannot be denied the right to speak on the simplistic ground that it is not "an individual American."

But to return to, and summarize, my principal point, which is the conformity of today's opinion with the original meaning of the First Amendment. The Amendment is written in terms of "speech," not speakers. Its text offers no foothold for excluding any category of speaker, from single individuals to partnerships of individuals, to unincorporated associations of individuals, to incorporated associations of individuals—and the dissent offers no evidence about the original meaning of the text to support any such exclusion. We are therefore simply left with the question whether the speech at issue in this case is "speech" covered by the First Amendment. No one says otherwise. A documentary film critical of a potential Presidential candidate is core political speech, and its nature as such does not change simply because it was funded by a corporation. Nor does the character of that funding produce any reduction whatever in the "inherent worth of the speech" and "its capacity for informing the public." Indeed, to exclude or impede corporate speech is to muzzle the principal agents of the modern free economy. We should celebrate rather than condemn the addition of this speech to the public debate.

JUSTICE STEVENS, with whom JUSTICE GINSBURG, JUSTICE BREYER, and JUSTICE SOTOMAYOR join, concurring in part and dissenting in part.

. . . Neither Citizens United's nor any other corporation's speech has been "banned." All that the parties dispute is whether Citizens United had a right to use the funds in its general treasury to pay for broadcasts during the 30-day period. The notion that the First Amendment dictates an affirmative answer to that question is, in my judgment, profoundly misguided....

...

In the context of election to public office, the distinction between corporate and human speakers is significant. Although they make enormous contributions to our society, corporations are not actually members of it. They cannot vote or run for office. Because they may be managed and controlled by nonresidents, their interests may conflict in fundamental respects with the interests of eligible voters. The financial resources, legal structure, and instrumental orientation of corporations raise legitimate concerns about their role in the electoral process. Our lawmakers have a compelling constitutional basis, if not also a democratic duty, to take measures designed to guard against the potentially deleterious effects of corporate spending in local and national races.

...

The election context is distinctive in many ways, and the Court, of course, is right that the First Amendment closely guards political speech. But in this context the authority of legislatures to enact viewpoint-neutral regulations based on content and identity is well settled. We have, for example, allowed state-run broadcasters to exclude independent candidates from televised debates. We have upheld statutes that prohibit the distribution or display of campaign materials near a polling place. Although we have not reviewed them directly, we have never cast doubt on laws that place special restrictions on campaign spending by foreign nationals. And we have consistently approved laws that bar Government employees, but not others, from contributing to or participating in political activities. These statutes burden the political expression of one class of speakers, namely, civil servants. Yet we have sustained them on the basis of longstanding practice and Congress' reasoned judgment that certain regulations which leave "untouched full participation . . . in political decisions at the ballot box," help ensure that public officials are "sufficiently free from improper influences," and that "confidence in the system of representative Government is not . . . eroded to a disastrous extent".

The same logic applies to this case with additional force because it is the identity of corporations, rather than individuals, that the Legislature has taken into account. . . . Campaign finance distinctions based on corporate identity tend to be less worrisome . . . because the "speakers" are not natural persons, much less members of our political community, and the governmental interests are of the highest order. Furthermore, when corporations, as a class, are distinguished from noncorporations, as a class, there is a lesser risk that regulatory distinctions will reflect invidious discrimination or political favoritism.

...

The Framers took it as a given that corporations could be comprehensively regulated in the service of the public welfare. Unlike our colleagues, they had little trouble distinguishing corporations from human beings, and when they constitutionalized the right to free speech in the First Amendment, it was the free speech of individual Americans that they had in mind. While individuals might join together to exercise their speech rights, business corporations, at least, were plainly not seen as facilitating such associational or expressive ends. Even "the notion that business corporations could invoke the First Amendment would probably have been quite a novelty," given that "at the time, the legitimacy of every corporate activity was thought to rest entirely in a concession of the sovereign." . . . In light of these background practices and understandings, it seems to me implausible that the Framers believed "the freedom of speech" would extend equally to all corporate speakers, much less that it would preclude legislatures from taking limited measures to guard against corporate capture of elections.

...

... [I]n *Austin* , we considered whether corporations . . . could be barred from using general treasury funds to make independent expenditures in support of, or in opposition to, candidates. We held they could be. Once again recognizing the importance of "the integrity of the marketplace of political ideas" in candidate elections, we noted that corporations have "special advantages—such as limited liability, perpetual life, and favorable treatment of the accumulation and distribution of assets"—that allow them to spend prodigious general treasury sums on campaign messages that have "little or no correlation" with the beliefs held by actual persons. In light of the corrupting effects such spending might have on the political process, we permitted the State of Michigan to limit corporate expenditures on candidate elections to corporations'

PACs, which rely on voluntary contributions and thus "reflect actual public support for the political ideals espoused by corporations." . . .

. . .

On numerous occasions we have recognized Congress' legitimate interest in preventing the money that is spent on elections from exerting an "'undue influence on an officeholder's judgment'" and from creating "'the appearance of such influence,'" beyond the sphere of *quid pro quo* relationships. . . . Corruption operates along a spectrum, and the majority's apparent belief that *quid pro quo* arrangements can be neatly demarcated from other improper influences does not accord with the theory or reality of politics. It certainly does not accord with the record Congress developed in passing BCRA, a record that stands as a remarkable testament to the energy and ingenuity with which corporations, unions, lobbyists, and politicians may go about scratching each other's backs—and which amply supported Congress' determination to target a limited set of especially destructive practices.

. . .

. . . The legislative and judicial proceedings relating to BCRA generated a substantial body of evidence suggesting that, as corporations grew more and more adept at crafting "issue ads" to help or harm a particular candidate, these nominally independent expenditures began to corrupt the political process in a very direct sense. The sponsors of these ads were routinely granted special access after the campaign was over. . . . Many corporate independent expenditures, it seemed, had become essentially interchangeable with direct contributions in their capacity to generate *quid pro quo* arrangements. In an age in which money and television ads are the coin of the campaign realm, it is hardly surprising that corporations deployed these ads to curry favor with, and to gain influence over, public officials.

. . .

The fact that corporations are different from human beings might seem to need no elaboration, except that the majority opinion almost completely elides it. *Austin* set forth some of the basic differences. Unlike natural persons, corporations have "limited liability" for their owners and managers, "perpetual life," separation of ownership and control, "and favorable treatment of the accumulation and distribution of assets . . . that enhance their ability to attract capital and to deploy their resources in ways that maximize the return on their shareholders' investments." Unlike voters in U. S. elections, corporations may be foreign controlled. Unlike other interest groups, business corporations have been "effectively delegated responsibility for ensuring society's economic welfare"; they inescapably structure the life of every citizen. "'[T]he resources in the treasury of a business corporation,'" furthermore, "'are not an indication of popular support for the corporation's political ideas.'" . . .

It might also be added that corporations have no consciences, no beliefs, no feelings, no thoughts, no desires. Corporations help structure and facilitate the activities of human beings, to be sure, and their "personhood" often serves as a useful legal fiction. But they are not themselves members of "We the People" by whom and for whom our Constitution was established.

. . .

In a democratic society, the longstanding consensus on the need to limit corporate campaign spending should outweigh the wooden application of judge-made rules. The majority's rejection of this principle "elevate[s] corporations to a level of deference which has not been seen at least since the days when substantive due process was regularly used to invalidate regulatory legislation thought to unfairly impinge upon established economic interests." At bottom, the Court's opinion is thus a rejection of the common sense of the American people, who have recognized a need to prevent corporations from undermining self-government since the founding, and who have fought against the distinctive corrupting potential of corporate electioneering since the days of Theodore Roosevelt. It is a strange time to repudiate that common sense. While American democracy is imperfect, few outside the majority of this Court would have thought its flaws included a dearth of corporate money in politics.

JUSTICE THOMAS, concurring in part and dissenting in part. . . .

Media

Contemporary Americans apply First Amendment principles to an array of media and technologies that would have been as bewildering to the framers as they often are for many parents. Consider *Bartnicki v. Vopper* (2001). The issue in this case was whether a newspaper had a First Amendment right to publish illegally intercepted cell phone conversations in which a union official suggested "blow[ing] off their front porches" might be an appropriate negotiating tactic. The Supreme Court by a 6-3 vote found a constitutional right to publish. Justice Steven's majority opinion concluded, "A stranger's illegal conduct does not suffice to remove the First Amendment shield from speech about a matter of public concern." Justice Breyer agreed with the result in the case but indicated that new technologies posed challenges for constitutional doctrine. He called for judicial opinions that recognized that "the Constitution permits legislatures to respond flexibly to the challenges future technology may pose to the individual's interest in basic personal privacy." Chief Justice Rehnquist's dissent thought technologies that enable persons to intercept cell phone messages were a threat to free speech values. In his view, "the Court's decision diminishes, rather than enhances, the purposes of the First Amendment, thereby chilling the speech of the millions of Americans who rely upon electronic technology to communicate each day."

The contemporary Supreme Court applies different First Amendment standards to different media and speech technologies.

- Print journalism enjoys the same high degree of constitutional protection as ordinary speakers.
- Broadcasters enjoy a lesser degree of constitutional protection, because government owns the airways, facilities are scarce, and broadcast media can be intrusive (*Red Lion Broadcasting Co. v. FCC* [1969]; *FCC v. Pacifica Foundation* [1978]).
- Dial-up telephone services enjoy the same high degree of constitutional protection as newspapers and ordinary speakers (*Sable Communications of California v. FCC* [1989]).
- Cable television operators enjoy more protection than broadcast media (*Turner Broadcasting System v. FCC* [1994]), but not the same protections as ordinary speakers, newspapers, and dial-up telephone services (*Denver Area Educational Telecommunications Consortium v. FCC* [1996]).
- Internet services enjoy the same high degree of constitutional protection as ordinary speakers, print journalists, and dial-up telephone services (*Reno v. ACLU* [1997]).

Two factors complicate this fairly neat summary. First, elected officials sometimes disagree with Supreme Court doctrine. The Reagan administration abandoned the "Fairness Doctrine" (see Chapter 10) because officials believed that broadcasters had the same constitutional rights as print journalists. Second, substantial disagreement exists in the present federal judiciary over the precise First Amendment standards that ought to govern particular media. Consider the judicial line-up in *Turner Broadcasting Systems, Inc: v. FCC* (1994):

> KENNEDY, J., announced the judgment of the Court and delivered the opinion for a unanimous Court with respect to Part I, the opinion of the Court with respect to Parts II-A and II-B, in which REHNQUIST, C.J., and BLACKMUN, O'CONNOR, SCALIA, SOUTER, THOMAS, and GINSBURG, JJ., joined, the opinion of the Court with respect to Parts II-C, II-D, and III-A, in which REHNQUIST, C.J., and BLACKMUN, STEVENS, and SOUTER, J., joined, and an opinion with respect to Part III-B, in which REHNQUIST, C.J., and BLACKMUN and SOUTER, JJ., joined. BLACKMUN, J., filed a concurring opinion. STEVENS, J., filed an opinion concurring in part and concurring in the judgment. O'CONNOR, J., filed an opinion concurring in part and dissenting in part, in which SCALIA and GINSBURG, JJ., joined, and in Parts I and III of which THOMAS, J., joined. GINSBURG, J., filed an opinion concurring in part and dissenting in part.

Whether justices who reach maturity in age of the Internet, cable television, and iPhones will reach greater consensus is for the future to determine.

Other Free Speech Issues

Commercial Speech. The late Rehnquist Court increased constitutional protections for commercial speech, even though no major political party or mass movement is presently championing the First Amendment rights of commercial advertisers. The justices continued employing the *Central Hudson Gas v. Public Service Commission of New York* (1980) standards, which require them to examine whether commercial speech "concern(s) lawful activity" and is "not misleading," whether "the asserted government interest is substantial," "whether the regulation directly advances the government interest," and "whether it is not more extensive than is necessary to serve that interest." The unanimous decision in *44 Liquormart, Inc. v. Rhode Island* (1996) suggests that justices who followed *Central Hudson* will rarely sustain legislation banning "truthful, nonmisleading commercial speech." Justice Stevens wrote, "Bans that target truthful, nonmisleading commercial messages rarely protect consumers," but frequently "rest solely on the offensive assumption that the public will respond irrationally to the truth." The justices were more divided in *Lorillard Tobacco Co. v. Reilly* (2001). A 5-4 judicial majority declared unconstitutional a ban on outdoor advertising of cigarettes near schools or playgrounds. Justice O'Connor, speaking for the more conservative justices on the Rehnquist Court asserted, "Tobacco retailers and manufacturers have an interest in conveying truthful information about their products to adults, and adults have a corresponding interest in receiving truthful information about tobacco products."

Expressive Association. The late Rehnquist Court ruled that the First Amendment gave certain expressive associations the right to exclude nonbelievers. *Hurley v. Irish-American Gay, Lesbian and Bisexual Group of Boston* (1995) held that the organizers of the St. Patrick's Day parade in Boston had a right to exclude gay and lesbian groups. Justice Souter's unanimous opinion stated, "Dissemination of a view contrary to one's own is forced upon a speaker intimately connected with the communication advanced, the speaker's right to autonomy over the message is compromised." The justices were more divided when considering whether states could require the Boy Scouts to maintain an openly gay troop leader. Chief Justice Rehnquist, speaking for the five most conservative justices in *Boy Scouts of America v. Dale* (2000), insisted that such rules violated expressive association rights. In *Rumsfeld v. Forum for Academic and Institutional Rights, Inc.* (2006), however, the justices unanimously held that Congress did not violate rights of expressive association when requiring universities that accepted federal funds to allow the military to recruit on campus. "Unlike a parade organizer's choice of parade contingents," Chief Justice Roberts wrote, "a law school's decision to allow recruiters on campus is not inherently expressive."

Obscenity. The obscenity debates that wracked American constitutional politics during the late nineteenth century have cooled a bit. While social conservatives still call for bans on sexually expressive speech, violent pornography in particular, more energy is now devoted to overturning *Roe v. Wade* (1973) and preventing same-sex marriage. Congress did pass several laws that attempted to restrict the access children enjoyed to pornography on the Internet. The Communications Decency Act forbade Internet services from knowingly transmitting obscenity to minors. The Child Online Protection Act of 1998 (COPA) forbade making "any [obscene] communication for commercial purposes that is available to any minor." The Supreme Court declared both measures unconstitutional. *Reno v. ACLU* (1997) held that the Communications Decency Act "effectively suppresses a large amount of speech that adults have a constitutional right to receive and address to one another." *Ashcroft v. ACLU* (2004) found that "blocking and filtering software is an alternative less restrictive than COPA, and, in addition, likely more effective as a means of restricting children's access to materials harmful to them." In *F.C.C. v. Fox Television Stations, Inc.* (2012), the justices unanimously reversed an FCC decision to sanction broadcasters when fleeting and spontaneous expletives occurred on their shows on the ground that the FCC guidelines were unconstitutionally vague. Justice Kennedy's majority opinion asserted, "The Commission policy in place at the time of the broadcasts gave no notice to Fox or ABC that a fleeting expletive or a brief shot of nudity could be actionably indecent." Cable television characters frequently utter the sort of curses that thirty years ago might have resulted in the offending station being sanctioned.

Boy Scouts of America et al. v. Dale, 530 U.S. 640 (2000)

James Dale was a Cub Scout, a Boy Scout, an Eagle Scout, and, when he reached the age of eighteen, an assistant scoutmaster. On July 19, 1990, the Boy Scouts of America (BSA) revoked his membership because they learned he was a gay man. BSA leaders claimed that the Boy Scout oath, which declared that members must be "morally straight," entailed an obligation to be a heterosexual. Dale filed a lawsuit claiming his exclusion was inconsistent with a New Jersey law that forbade places of public accommodation from discriminating on the basis of sexual orientation. After a lengthy litigation process the New Jersey Supreme Court ruled that the Boy Scouts were a place of public accommodation and that their exclusion of Dale violated state law. The Boy Scouts appealed to the Supreme Court on the ground that this decision violated their rights of expressive association protected by the First Amendment.

The Supreme Court by a 5-4 vote reversed the Supreme Court of New Jersey. Chief Justice Rehnquist's majority opinion held that the Boy Scouts were an expressive association and that requiring them to include homosexuals violated the organization's First Amendment rights. Why does Chief Justice Rehnquist think that the Boy Scouts are an expressive organization? Why does Justice Stevens disagree? If Justice Rehnquist is right, could any organization exclude persons of color simply by stating that, in addition to other values, group members were committed to white supremacy? If Justice Stevens is right, could New Jersey prohibit the Klan from excluding persons of color?

CHIEF JUSTICE REHNQUIST delivered the opinion of the Court.

. . .

In *Roberts v. United States Jaycees* (1984) we observed that "implicit in the right to engage in activities protected by the First Amendment" is "a corresponding right to associate with others in pursuit of a wide variety of political, social, economic, educational, religious, and cultural ends." This right is crucial in preventing the majority from imposing its views on groups that would rather express other, perhaps unpopular, ideas. . . . Forcing a group to accept certain members may impair the ability of the group to express those views, and only those views, that it intends to express. Thus, "freedom of association . . . plainly presupposes a freedom not to associate."

The forced inclusion of an unwanted person in a group infringes the group's freedom of expressive association if the presence of that person affects in a significant way the group's ability to advocate public or private viewpoints. But the freedom of expressive association, like many freedoms, is not absolute. We have held that the freedom could be overridden "by regulations adopted to serve compelling state interests, unrelated to the suppression of ideas, that cannot be achieved through means significantly less restrictive of associational freedoms."

. . .

. . . [T]he general mission of the Boy Scouts is clear: "[T]o instill values in young people." The Boy Scouts seeks to instill these values by having its adult leaders spend time with the youth members, instructing and engaging them in activities like camping, archery, and fishing. During the time spent with the youth members, the scoutmasters and assistant scoutmasters inculcate them with the Boy Scouts' values—both expressly and by example. It seems indisputable that an association that seeks to transmit such a system of values engages in expressive activity.

. . .

The values the Boy Scouts seeks to instill are "based on" those listed in the Scout Oath and Law. The Boy Scouts explains that the Scout Oath and Law provide "a positive moral code for living; they are a list of 'do's' rather than 'don'ts.'" The Boy Scouts asserts that homosexual conduct is inconsistent with the values embodied in the Scout Oath and Law, particularly with the values represented by the terms "morally straight" and "clean."

. . .

The Boy Scouts asserts that it "teach[es] that homosexual conduct is not morally straight" and that it does "not want to promote homosexual conduct as a legitimate form of behavior." We accept the Boy Scouts' assertion.

We must then determine whether Dale's presence as an assistant scoutmaster would significantly burden the Boy Scouts' desire to not "promote homosexual conduct as a legitimate form of behavior." As we give deference to an association's assertions regarding the nature of its expression, we must also give deference to an association's view of what would impair its expression. That is not to say that an expressive association can erect a shield against antidiscrimination laws simply by asserting that mere acceptance of a member from a particular group would impair its message. But here Dale, by his own admission, is one of a group of gay Scouts who have "become leaders in their community and are open and honest about their sexual orientation." Dale was the copresident of a gay and lesbian organization at college and remains a gay rights activist. Dale's presence in the Boy Scouts would, at the very least, force the organization to send a message, both to the youth members and the world, that the Boy Scouts accepts homosexual conduct as a legitimate form of behavior.

. . .

. . . [A]ssociations do not have to associate for the "purpose" of disseminating a certain message in order to be entitled to the protections of the First Amendment. An association must merely engage in expressive activity that could be impaired in order to be entitled to protection.

. . . [E]ven if the Boy Scouts discourages Scout leaders from disseminating views on sexual issues—a fact that the Boy Scouts disputes with contrary evidence—the First Amendment protects the Boy Scouts' method of expression. If the Boy Scouts wishes Scout leaders to avoid questions of sexuality and teach only by example, this fact does not negate the sincerity of its belief discussed above.

. . . Dale makes much of the claim that the Boy Scouts does not revoke the membership of heterosexual Scout leaders that openly disagree with the Boy Scouts' policy on sexual orientation. But if this is true, it is irrelevant. The presence of an avowed homosexual and gay rights activist in an assistant scoutmaster's uniform sends a distinctly different message from the presence of a heterosexual assistant scoutmaster who is on record as disagreeing with Boy Scouts policy. The Boy Scouts has a First Amendment right to choose to send one message but not the other. The fact that the organization does not trumpet its views from the housetops, or that it tolerates dissent within its ranks, does not mean that its views receive no First Amendment protection.

. . .

JUSTICE STEVENS, with whom JUSTICE SOUTER, JUSTICE GINSBURG, and JUSTICE BREYER join, dissenting.

The majority holds that New Jersey's law violates BSA's right to associate and its right to free speech. But that law does not "impos[e] any serious burdens" on BSA's "collective effort on behalf of [its] shared goals" nor does it force BSA to communicate any message that it does not wish to endorse. New Jersey's law, therefore, abridges no constitutional right of BSA.

. . .

It is plain as the light of day that neither one of these principles—"morally straight" and "clean"—says the slightest thing about homosexuality. Indeed, neither term in the Boy Scouts' Law and Oath expresses any position whatsoever on sexual matters.

BSA's published guidance on that topic underscores this point. Scouts, for example, are directed to receive their sex education at home or in school, but not from the organization: "Your parents or guardian or a sex education teacher should give you the facts about sex that you must know." To be sure, Scouts are not forbidden from asking their Scoutmaster about issues of a sexual nature, but Scoutmasters are, literally, the last person Scouts are encouraged to ask: "If you have questions about growing up, about relationships, sex, or making good decisions, ask. Talk with your parents, religious leaders, teachers, or Scoutmaster." . . .

. . .

In light of BSA's self-proclaimed ecumenism, furthermore, it is even more difficult to discern any shared goals or common moral stance on homosexuality. Insofar as religious matters are concerned, BSA's bylaws state that it is "absolutely nonsectarian in its attitude toward . . . religious training." Because a number of religious groups do not view homosexuality as immoral or wrong and reject discrimination against homosexuals, it is exceedingly difficult to believe that BSA nonetheless adopts a single particular religious or moral philosophy when it comes to sexual orientation. This is especially so in light of the fact that Scouts are advised to seek guidance on sexual matters from their religious leaders (and Scoutmasters are told to refer Scouts to them); BSA surely is aware that some religions do not teach that homosexuality is wrong.

. . .

The Court seeks to fill the void by pointing to a statement of "policies and procedures relating to homosexuality and Scouting," signed by BSA's President and Chief Scout Executive in 1978 and addressed to the members of the Executive Committee of the national organization. The letter says that the BSA does "not believe that homosexuality and leadership in Scouting are appropriate."

. . .

. . . [T]he 1978 statement simply says that homosexuality is not "appropriate." It makes no effort to connect that statement to a shared goal or expressive activity of the Boy Scouts. Whatever values BSA seeks to instill in Scouts, the idea that homosexuality is not "appropriate" appears entirely unconnected to, and is mentioned nowhere in, the myriad of publicly declared values and creeds of the BSA. That idea does not appear to be among any of the principles actually taught to Scouts. Rather, the 1978 policy appears to be no more than a private statement of a few BSA executives that the organization wishes to exclude gays—and that wish has nothing to do with any expression BSA actually engages in.

. . .

. . . [T]he right to associate does not mean "that in every setting in which individuals exercise some discrimination in choosing associates, their selective process of inclusion and exclusion is protected by the Constitution." . . . In fact, until today, we have never once found a claimed right to associate in the selection of members to prevail in the face of a State's antidiscrimination law. To the contrary, we have squarely held that a State's antidiscrimination law does not violate a group's right to associate simply because the law conflicts with that group's exclusionary membership policy.

. . .

Surely there are instances in which an organization that truly aims to foster a belief at odds with the purposes of a State's antidiscrimination laws will have a First Amendment right to association that precludes forced compliance with those laws. But that right is not a freedom to discriminate at will, nor is it a right to maintain an exclusionary membership policy simply out of fear of what the public reaction would be if the group's membership were opened up. It is an implicit right designed to protect the enumerated rights of the First Amendment, not a license to act on any discriminatory impulse. To prevail in asserting a right of expressive association as a defense to a charge of violating an antidiscrimination law, the organization must at least show it has adopted and advocated an unequivocal position inconsistent with a position advocated or epitomized by the person whom the organization seeks to exclude. . . .

Even if BSA's right to associate argument fails, it nonetheless might have a First Amendment right to refrain from including debate and dialogue about homosexuality as part of its mission to instill values in Scouts. It can, for example, advise Scouts who are entering adulthood and have questions about sex to talk "with your parents, religious leaders, teachers, or Scoutmaster," and, in turn, it can direct Scoutmasters who are asked such questions "not undertake to instruct Scouts, in any formalized manner, in the subject of sex and family life" because "it is not construed to be Scouting's proper area." Dale's right to advocate certain beliefs in a public forum or in a private debate does not include a right to advocate these ideas when he is working as a Scoutmaster. And BSA cannot be compelled to include a message about homosexuality among the values it actually chooses to teach its Scouts, if it would prefer to remain silent on that subject.

. . .

BSA has not contended, nor does the record support, that Dale had ever advocated a view on homosexuality to his troop before his membership was revoked. . . . The Scoutmaster Handbook instructs Dale, like all Scoutmasters, that sexual issues are not their "proper area," and there is no evidence that Dale had any intention of violating this rule. Indeed, from all accounts Dale was a model Boy Scout and Assistant Scoutmaster up until the day his membership was revoked. . . .

. . .

Dale's inclusion in the Boy Scouts is nothing like the case in *Hurley*. His participation sends no cognizable message to the Scouts or to the world. Unlike GLIB, Dale did not carry a banner or a sign; he did not distribute any factsheet; and he expressed no intent to send any message. If there is any kind of message being sent, then, it is by the mere act of joining the Boy Scouts. Such an act does not constitute an instance of symbolic speech under the First Amendment.

. . .

The State of New Jersey has decided that people who are open and frank about their sexual orientation are entitled to equal access to employment as schoolteachers, police officers, librarians, athletic coaches, and a host of other jobs filled by citizens who serve as role models for children and adults alike. Dozens of Scout units throughout the State are sponsored by public agencies, such as schools and fire departments, that employ such role models. BSA's affiliation with numerous public agencies that comply with New Jersey's law against discrimination cannot be understood to convey any particular message endorsing or condoning the activities of all these people.

JUSTICE SOUTER, with whom JUSTICE GINSBURG and JUSTICE BREYER join, dissenting. . . .

B. Voting

The contemporary constitutional politics of voting is polarized on two different dimensions: constitutional principle and political advantage. Some divisions between conservatives and liberals are best explained in terms of different constitutional principles. The more conservative Supreme Court justices vote to strike down and the more liberal Supreme Court justices vote to sustain majority-minority legislative districts that most scholars believe advance Republican Party interests in the long run. *Bush v. Gore* (2000) is generally regarded as an instance where political advantage better explained the difference between conservatives and liberals, as well as Republicans and Democrats. In that case, the five most conservative justices on the Supreme Court, supported by Republicans in elected office, declared unconstitutional efforts to recount presidential ballots in Florida. This decision in effect gave the White House to the Republican candidate, Texas governor George W. Bush. Although both the majority and dissenting opinions declared that enduring constitutional principles supported their voting decisions, few observers can detect in other cases substantial commitment to the principles announced in that decision.

The constitutional politics of voting encompasses numerous issues, including whether ex-felons have a right to vote, whether the Supreme Court should review partisan gerrymanders, the constitutionality of various state voter registration laws, whether states may regulate the primary process, and the continued vitality of the Voting Rights Act. The stakes are high. Given the sharp divisions between Democrats and Republicans, as well as increasingly tight struggles for control of national and state institutions, slight changes in voting laws may alter partisan and ideological control of governing institutions.

One Person, One Vote

The Supreme Court's decision in *Reynolds v. Sims* (1964) requiring legislative districting to adhere to the one person, one vote principle touched off intense partisan struggles that remain vibrant today. *Bush v. Gore* (2000) was decided in part on the principle that different procedures for recounting ballots create the possibility that one citizen's ballot might be counted differently than another person's ballot. Gerrymandering is the more frequent consequence of *Reynolds*, as Democrats and Republicans struggle to draw congressional and state legislative district lines in ways that maximize partisan advantage. The Supreme Court has so far insisted that these struggles are not justiciable. Justice Scalia and three other justices in *Vieth v. Jubelirer* (2004) maintained that courts should not adjudicate claims that partisan gerrymanders are unconstitutional, because no judicially manageable standards exist for evaluating such claims. Scalia noted, "The fact that partisan districting is a lawful and common practice means that there is almost always room for an election-impeding lawsuit contending that partisan advantage was the predominant motivation." Justice Kennedy's concurring opinion suggested that some standards might exist, but that he had not yet discovered them. *League of United Latin American Citizens v. Perry* (2006) similarly held nonjusticiable a mid-decennial political gerrymander by the Republican Party dominated Texas legislature that was not necessitated by either demographic shifts or changes in the number of state congressional seats. Justice Kennedy wrote, "The text and structure of the Constitution and our case law indicate there is nothing inherently suspect about a legislature's decision to replace mid-decade a court-ordered plan with one of its own."

Bush v. Gore, 531 U.S. 98 (2000)

The 2000 national presidential election between Democratic Vice President Albert Gore and Republican Governor George Bush was extraordinarily close. Democrats celebrated prematurely when networks called Florida, a crucial swing state for Gore, in their favor. Several hours later many networks reversed their original projection and indicated that Bush was likely to win Florida's crucial electoral votes. By early morning all that was clear was that Governor Bush had a razor-thin margin, pending recounts. After an initial machine recount found that Governor Bush retained a 327-vote lead, Vice President Gore asked for a manual recount of the vote in four Florida counties: Broward, Miami-Dade, Volusia, and Palm Beach. Under Florida law all such recounts were subject to the reasonable discretion of the Florida secretary of state. That office in 2000 was held by Katherine Harris, a strong Bush supporter. She refused to order a recount, but her decision was unanimously overruled by the Supreme Court of Florida. When that recount found that Governor Bush had won by 537 votes Vice President Gore brought another lawsuit, claiming that the canvassing boards of a few heavily-Democratic counties failed to count a number of ballots for which the intent of the voter could be clearly discerned. The crucial counties used punch-card ballots, which required the voter to dislodge a "chad" in order to cast a legal vote. Gore insisted that many ballots demonstrated that the voter had attempted to vote for him, even though the voter had not fully dislodged the "chad" from the punch-card ballot. A divided Florida Supreme Court agreed that long-standing precedents in state law required that "every citizen's vote be counted whenever possible"; however, rather than order a selective recount of a small number of Democratic counties, the state justices ordered a state-wide recount as a way of ensuring equal treatment of all ballots. Bush appealed to the Supreme Court of the United States.

The Supreme Court first ordered that the recount be stayed and then issued a 7-2 decision declaring unconstitutional the Florida court decision ordering the recount. The five most conservative members of the Rehnquist Court ruled that the recount ordered by the Florida Supreme Court might allow for variations in the way that ballots were counted in different counties. The possibility that a ballot in one county might be counted and an identical ballot in other county discarded, the judicial majority concluded, violated the principle of "one person, one vote." This concern, combined with the disputed view that no time existed for organizing a better recount, led a bare majority of the most conservative justices to rule that no recount was possible. The decision effectively decided the presidential election.

Bush v. Gore *raises important questions about the relationship between law and politics. Consider whether the justices were relying on neutral principles of law or voting in favor of the candidate they preferred to occupy the presidency. Are the majority opinions inconsistent with the way the conservative majority normally adjudicates federalism, voting rights, and equal protection issues, as some of the dissenters charge? Is the dissenting claim that the Supreme Court should not have adjudicated this issue consistent with liberal understandings of judicial power in other areas of the law? If we treat the majority's equal protection concerns as a serious point of law, then how might these principles apply in other cases in which states allow counties to use different methods for counting votes? Why would the majority (famously) write, "Our consideration is limited to the present circumstances, for the problem of equal protection in election processes generally presents many complexities"? Is it significant that, in the decade following the decision, no serious changes have been made to an election system based on counties using different methods of counting votes? While the Supreme Court of the United States divided on seemingly ideological grounds in* Bush v. Gore, *state and lower federal court decisions during the 2000 election crisis demonstrated a less partisan pattern. Democratic appointees on lower federal courts rejected some legal claims made by the Gore campaign, while Republican appointees supported some of these claims. How might you explain this difference?*[59]

59. See Howard Gillman, *The Votes that Counted: How the Court Decided the 2000 Presidential Election* (Chicago: University of Chicago Press, 2001).

PER CURIAM

. . .

The individual citizen has no federal constitutional right to vote for electors for the President of the United States unless and until the state legislature chooses a statewide election as the means to implement its power to appoint members of the electoral college. . . . When the state legislature vests the right to vote for President in its people, the right to vote as the legislature has prescribed is fundamental; and one source of its fundamental nature lies in the equal weight accorded to each vote and the equal dignity owed to each voter. . . .

The right to vote is protected in more than the initial allocation of the franchise. Equal protection applies as well to the manner of its exercise. Having once granted the right to vote on equal terms, the State may not, by later arbitrary and disparate treatment, value one person's vote over that of another. See, e.g., *Harper v. Virginia Bd. of Elections* (1966). . . .

. . .

The recount mechanisms implemented in response to the decisions of the Florida Supreme Court do not satisfy the minimum requirement for nonarbitrary treatment of voters necessary to secure the fundamental right. Florida's basic command for the count of legally cast votes is to consider the "intent of the voter." . . . This is unobjectionable as an abstract proposition and a starting principle. The problem inheres in the absence of specific standards to ensure its equal application. The formulation of uniform rules to determine intent based on these recurring circumstances is practicable and, we conclude, necessary.

The want of those rules here has led to unequal evaluation of ballots in various respects. . . . As seems to have been acknowledged at oral argument, the standards for accepting or rejecting contested ballots might vary not only from county to county but indeed within a single county from one recount team to another.

. . .

The question before the Court is not whether local entities, in the exercise of their expertise, may develop different systems for implementing elections. Instead, we are presented with a situation where a state court with the power to assure uniformity has ordered a statewide recount with minimal procedural safeguards. When a court orders a statewide remedy, there must be at least some assurance that the rudimentary requirements of equal treatment and fundamental fairness are satisfied.

. . .

Upon due consideration of the difficulties identified to this point, it is obvious that the recount cannot be conducted in compliance with the requirements of equal protection and due process without substantial additional work. It would require not only the adoption (after opportunity for argument) of adequate statewide standards for determining what is a legal vote, and practicable procedures to implement them, but also orderly judicial review of any disputed matters that might arise. In addition, the Secretary has advised that the recount of only a portion of the ballots requires that the vote tabulation equipment be used to screen out undervotes, a function for which the machines were not designed. If a recount of overvotes were also required, perhaps even a second screening would be necessary. Use of the equipment for this purpose, and any new software developed for it, would have to be evaluated for accuracy by the Secretary, as required by [Florida law].

The Supreme Court of Florida has said that the legislature intended the State's electors to "participat[e] fully in the federal electoral process," as provided by [federal law]. [Federal law], in turn, requires that any controversy or contest that is designed to lead to a conclusive selection of electors be completed by December 12. That date is upon us, and there is no recount procedure in place under the State Supreme Court's order that comports with minimal constitutional standards. Because it is evident that any recount seeking to meet the December 12 date will be unconstitutional for the reasons we have discussed, we reverse the judgment of the Supreme Court of Florida ordering a recount to proceed.

. . .

CHIEF JUSTICE REHNQUIST, with whom JUSTICE SCALIA and JUSTICE THOMAS join, concurring.

. . .

In most cases, comity and respect for federalism compel us to defer to the decisions of state courts on issues of state law. That practice reflects our understanding that the decisions of state courts are definitive pronouncements of the will of the States as sovereigns. . . . Of course, in ordinary cases, the distribution of powers among the branches of a State's government raises no questions of federal constitutional law, subject to the requirement that the government be republican in character. . . . But there are a few exceptional cases in which the Constitution imposes a duty or confers a power on a particular branch of a State's government. This is one of them. Article II, § 1, cl. 2, provides that "[e]ach State shall appoint, in such Manner as the *Legislature* thereof may direct," electors for President and Vice President. (Emphasis added.) Thus, the text of the election law itself, and not just its interpretation by the courts of the States, takes on independent significance.

In *McPherson v. Blacker* (1892), . . . we explained that Art. II, § 1, cl. 2, "convey[s] the broadest power of determination" and "leaves it to the legislature exclusively to define the method" of appointment. . . . A significant departure from the legislative scheme for appointing Presidential electors presents a federal constitutional question.

. . .

In Florida, the legislature has chosen to hold statewide elections to appoint the State's 25 electors. Importantly, the legislature has delegated the authority to run the elections and to oversee election disputes to the Secretary of State (Secretary). . . . Isolated sections of the code may well admit of more than one interpretation, but the general coherence of the legislative scheme may not be altered by judicial interpretation so as to wholly change the statutorily provided apportionment of responsibility among these various bodies. In any election but a Presidential election, the Florida Supreme Court can give as little or as much deference to Florida's executives as it chooses, so far as Article II is concerned, and this Court will have no cause to question the court's actions. But, with respect to a Presidential election, the court must be both mindful of the legislature's role under Article II in choosing the manner of appointing electors and deferential to those bodies expressly empowered by the legislature to carry out its constitutional mandate.

Acting pursuant to its constitutional grant of authority, the Florida Legislature has created a detailed, if not perfectly crafted, statutory scheme that provides for appointment of Presidential electors by direct election. . . . Under the statute, "[v]otes cast for the actual candidates for President and Vice President shall be counted as votes cast for the presidential electors supporting such candidates." The legislature has designated the Secretary as the "chief election officer," with the responsibility to "[o]btain and maintain uniformity in the application, operation, and interpretation of the election laws." . . . The state legislature has delegated to county canvassing boards the duties of administering elections. . . . Those boards are responsible for providing results to the state Elections Canvassing Commission, comprising the Governor, the Secretary of State, and the Director of the Division of Elections. . . .

. . .

The [Supreme Court of Florida] determined that canvassing boards' decisions regarding whether to recount ballots past the certification deadline . . . are to be reviewed *de novo,* although the Election Code clearly vests discretion whether to recount in the boards, and sets strict deadlines subject to the Secretary's rejection of late tallies and monetary fines for tardiness. . . . Moreover, the Florida court held that all late vote tallies arriving during the contest period should be automatically included in the certification regardless of the certification deadline . . . thus virtually eliminating both the deadline and the Secretary's discretion to disregard recounts that violate it.

. . .

Given all these factors, and in light of the legislative intent identified by the Florida Supreme Court to bring Florida within the "safe harbor" provision of 3 U.S.C. § 5, the remedy prescribed by the Supreme Court of Florida cannot be deemed an "appropriate" one as of December 8. It significantly departed from the statutory framework in place on November 7, and authorized open-ended further proceedings which could not be completed by December 12, thereby preventing a final determination by that date.

. . .

JUSTICE STEVENS, with whom JUSTICE GINSBURG and JUSTICE BREYER join, dissenting.

The Constitution assigns to the States the primary responsibility for determining the manner of selecting the Presidential electors. . . . When questions arise about the meaning of state laws, including election laws, it is our settled practice to accept the opinions of the highest courts of the States as providing the final answers. On rare occasions, however, either federal statutes or the Federal Constitution may require federal judicial intervention in state elections. This is not such an occasion.

. . .

. . . The legislative power in Florida is subject to judicial review pursuant to Article V of the Florida Constitution, and nothing in Article II of the Federal Constitution frees the state legislature from the constraints in the State Constitution that created it. Moreover, the Florida Legislature's own decision to employ a unitary code for all elections indicates that it intended the Florida Supreme Court to play the same role in Presidential elections that it has historically played in resolving electoral disputes. The Florida Supreme Court's exercise of appellate jurisdiction therefore was wholly consistent with, and indeed contemplated by, the grant of authority in Article II.

. . .

Admittedly, the use of differing substandards for determining voter intent in different counties employing similar voting systems may raise serious concerns. Those concerns are alleviated—if not eliminated—by the fact that a single impartial magistrate will ultimately adjudicate all objections arising from the recount process. Of course, as a general matter, "[t]he interpretation of constitutional principles must not be too literal. We must remember that the machinery of government would not work if it were not allowed a little play in its joints." . . . If it were otherwise, Florida's decision to leave to each county the determination of what balloting system to employ—despite enormous differences in accuracy—might run afoul of equal protection. So, too, might the similar decisions of the vast majority of state legislatures to delegate to local authorities certain decisions with respect to voting systems and ballot design.

. . .

In the interest of finality, . . . the majority effectively orders the disenfranchisement of an unknown number of voters whose ballots reveal their intent—and are therefore legal votes under state law—but were for some reason rejected by ballot-counting machines. It does so on the basis of the deadlines set forth in Title 3 of the United States Code. . . . But, as I have already noted, those provisions merely provide rules of decision for Congress to follow when selecting among conflicting slates of electors. . . . They do not prohibit a State from counting what the majority concedes to be legal votes until a bona fide winner is determined. . . .

. . .

What must underlie petitioners' entire federal assault on the Florida election procedures is an unstated lack of confidence in the impartiality and capacity of the state judges who would make the critical decisions if the vote count were to proceed. Otherwise, their position is wholly without merit. The endorsement of that position by the majority of this Court can only lend credence to the most cynical appraisal of the work of judges throughout the land. It is confidence in the men and women who administer the judicial system that is the true backbone of the rule of law. Time will one day heal the wound to that confidence that will be inflicted by today's decision. One thing, however, is certain. Although we may never know with complete certainty the identity of the winner of this year's Presidential election, the identity of the loser is perfectly clear. It is the Nation's confidence in the judge as an impartial guardian of the rule of law.

JUSTICE SOUTER, with whom JUSTICE BREYER joins, and with whom JUSTICE STEVENS and JUSTICE GINSBURG join in part.

. . .

Petitioners have raised an equal protection claim (or, alternatively, a due process claim . . .) in the charge that unjustifiably disparate standards are applied in different electoral jurisdictions to otherwise identical facts. It is true that the Equal Protection Clause does not forbid the use of a variety of voting mechanisms within a jurisdiction, even though different mechanisms will have different levels of effectiveness in recording voters' intentions; local variety can be justified by concerns about cost, the potential value of innovation, and so on. But evidence in the record here suggests that a different order of disparity obtains under rules for determining a voter's intent that have been applied. . . . I can conceive of no legitimate state interest served by these differing treatments of the expressions of voters' fundamental rights. The differences appear wholly arbitrary.

In deciding what to do about this, we should take account of the fact that electoral votes are due to be cast in six days. I would therefore remand the case to the courts of Florida with instructions to establish uniform standards for evaluating the several types of ballots that have prompted differing treatments, to be applied within and among counties when passing on such identical ballots in any further recounting (or successive recounting) that the courts might order.

Unlike the majority, I see no warrant for this Court to assume that Florida could not possibly comply with this requirement before the date set for the meeting of electors, December 18. . . . There is no justification for denying the State the opportunity to try to count all disputed ballots now.

I respectfully dissent.

JUSTICE GINSBURG. . . .

JUSTICE BREYER, with whom JUSTICE STEVENS, JUSTICE GINSBURG, and JUSTICE SOUTER join in part.

. . .

. . . Those who caution judicial restraint in resolving political disputes have described the quintessential case for that restraint as a case marked, among other things, by the "strangeness of the issue," its "intractability to principled resolution," its "sheer momentousness, . . . which tends to unbalance judicial judgment," and "the inner vulnerability, the self-doubt of an institution which is electorally irresponsible and has no earth to draw strength from." Those characteristics mark this case.

At the same time, . . . the Court is not acting to vindicate a fundamental constitutional principle, such as the need to protect a basic human liberty. No other strong reason to act is present. Congressional statutes tend to obviate the need. And, above all, in this highly politicized matter, the appearance of a split decision runs the risk of undermining the public's confidence in the Court itself. That confidence is a public treasure. It has been built slowly over many years, some of which were marked by a Civil War and the tragedy of segregation. It is a vitally necessary ingredient of any successful effort to protect basic liberty and, indeed, the rule of law itself. We run no risk of returning to the days when a President (responding to this Court's efforts to protect the Cherokee Indians) might have said, "John Marshall has made his decision; now let him enforce it!" But we do risk a self-inflicted wound—a wound that may harm not just the Court, but the Nation. . . .

The Voting Rights Acts

The contemporary constitutional politics of the Voting Rights Act threatens to pit elected officials against judges, rather than liberal Democrats against conservative Republicans. A bipartisan congressional majority in 2006 voted to reauthorize crucial provisions of past

Voting Rights Acts, most notably those provisions that require covered districts to preclear all changes in voting laws with the Department of Justice or Court of Appeals for the District of Columbia. The House Committee report supporting reauthorization stated, "Forty years has been an insufficient amount of time to address the century during which racial minorities were denied the full rights of citizenship. While substantial strides have been made toward racial equality, the attitudes and actions of some States and political subdivisions continue to fall short."[60] President George W. Bush, when signing the Fannie Lou Hamer, Rosa Parks, and Coretta Scott King Voting Rights Act Reauthorization and Amendments Act of 2006 declared, "Today we renew a bill that helped bring a community on the margins into the life of American democracy."

The continued constitutional vitality of the Voting Rights Act is unclear. Chief Justice Roberts's opinion in *Northwest Austin Municipal Utility District No. One v. Holder* (2009), while not deciding that issue, raised questions about the continued constitutionality of requiring states to preclear election procedures. Justice Thomas was the only judge who did not sign that opinion; he voted to declare unconstitutional continued preclearance. The Court of Appeals for the District of Columbia in *Shelby County, Alabama v. Holder* (2012) insisted that important provisions of the Voting Rights Act still pass constitutional muster. Judge Tatel's opinion sustaining the preclearance requirements of that law pointed to Congressional fact-findings in support of that practice:

- 626 Attorney General objections that blocked discriminatory voting changes;
- 653 successful section 2 cases;
- over 800 proposed voting changes withdrawn or modified
- tens of thousands of observers sent to covered jurisdictions;
- 105 successful section 5 enforcement actions;
- 25 unsuccessful judicial preclearance actions;
- section 5's strong deterrent effect, i.e., "the number of voting changes that have never gone forward as a result of Section 5."[61]

60. House Committee on the Judiciary, "Fannie Lou Hamer, Rose Parks and Coretta Scott King Voting Rights Act Reauthorization and Amendments Act of 2006," 109th Cong., 2nd Sess. (2006), H.R. Rep 109-478, 56.

61. *Shelby County, Alabama v. Holder*, 679 F.3d 848 (C.A.D.C., 2012).

The Supreme Court is expected to consider an appeal from this or a similar case in the near future.

Northwest Austin Municipal Utility District No. One v. Holder, 557 U.S. 193 (2009).

The Northwest Austin Municipal Utility District (NAMUD) provides services to some residents of Travis County, Texas. Although the district is governed by distinct elected officials, Travis County runs its elections. In the summer of 2006 NAMUD asked for a declaratory judgment against the attorney general of the United States[62] *that the district no longer had to comply with the preclearance provisions of the Voting Rights Act. That judgment was denied by a federal district court on the ground that, under federal law, only counties could obtain a statutory bailout. NAMUD appealed this decision to the Supreme Court, claiming both that the district court misread the Voting Rights Act and that the continued existence of the preclearance provisions was unconstitutional.*

The Supreme Court unanimously ruled that NAMUD could bail out. Chief Justice Roberts decided the case on statutory grounds, but his opinion cast doubt on the continued constitutionality of the preclearance provisions of the Voting Rights Act. Was this a warning shot to Congress or an unnecessary dictum? Justice Thomas would declare the preclearance provisions unconstitutional. What reasons does he give? Thomas claims that the provisions of the Fifteenth Amendment should be balanced against the Tenth Amendment's commitment to state sovereignty. Might one argue that the Fifteenth Amendment, as the later enactment, always trumps the Tenth Amendment? None of the more liberal justices on the Roberts Court defended the 2006 extension of the Voting Rights Act. What might explain that judicial silence?

CHIEF JUSTICE ROBERTS delivered the opinion of the Court.

. . .

As enacted, [the preclearance and bail out provisions] of the Voting Rights Act were temporary provisions. They were expected to be in effect for only five years. . . . We upheld the temporary Voting Rights Act of 1965 as an appropriate exercise of congressional power in *Katzenbach v. Morgan* (1966), explaining

62. Eric Holder was the attorney general when the case was decided by the Supreme Court.

that "[t]he constitutional propriety of the Voting Rights Act of 1965 must be judged with reference to the historical experience which it reflects." . . . We concluded that the problems Congress faced when it passed the Act were so dire that "exceptional conditions [could] justify legislative measures not otherwise appropriate." . . .

. . .

The historic accomplishments of the Voting Rights Act are undeniable. When it was first passed, unconstitutional discrimination was rampant and the "registration of voting-age whites ran roughly 50 percentage points or more ahead" of black registration in many covered States. . . . Today, the registration gap between white and black voters is in single digits in the covered States; in some of those States, blacks now register and vote at higher rates than whites. . . .

At the same time, § 5, "which authorizes federal intrusion into sensitive areas of state and local policymaking, imposes substantial 'federalism costs.'" . . .

Section 5 goes beyond the prohibition of the Fifteenth Amendment by suspending *all* changes to state election law—however innocuous—until they have been precleared by federal authorities in Washington, D.C. . . .

Some of the conditions that we relied upon in upholding this statutory scheme in *Katzenbach* and *City of Rome v. United States* (1980) have unquestionably improved. Things have changed in the South. Voter turnout and registration rates now approach parity. Blatantly discriminatory evasions of federal decrees are rare. And minority candidates hold office at unprecedented levels. . . .

These improvements are no doubt due in significant part to the Voting Rights Act itself, and stand as a monument to its success. Past success alone, however, is not adequate justification to retain the preclearance requirements. . . . It may be that these improvements are insufficient and that conditions continue to warrant preclearance under the Act. But the Act imposes current burdens and must be justified by current needs.

The Act also differentiates between the States, despite our historic tradition that all the States enjoy "equal sovereignty." . . . Distinctions can be justified in some cases. "The doctrine of the equality of States . . . does not bar . . . remedies for *local* evils which have subsequently appeared." *Katzenbach*. . . . But a departure from the fundamental principle of equal sovereignty requires a showing that a statute's disparate geographic coverage is sufficiently related to the problem that it targets.

. . .

The evil that § 5 is meant to address may no longer be concentrated in the jurisdictions singled out for preclearance. The statute's coverage formula is based on data that is now more than 35 years old, and there is considerable evidence that it fails to account for current political conditions. For example, the racial gap in voter registration and turnout is lower in the States originally covered by § 5 than it is nationwide. . . .

The parties do not agree on the standard to apply in deciding whether, in light of the foregoing concerns, Congress exceeded its Fifteenth Amendment enforcement power in extending the preclearance requirements. The district argues that "'[t]here must be a congruence and proportionality between the injury to be prevented or remedied and the means adopted to that end'" . . . ; the Federal Government asserts that it is enough that the legislation be a "'rational means to effectuate the constitutional prohibition'" . . . . That question has been extensively briefed in this case, but we need not resolve it. The Act's preclearance requirements and its coverage formula raise serious constitutional questions under either test.

. . .

[*Chief Justice Roberts then concluded that "all political subdivisions . . . are eligible to file a bailout suit."*]

JUSTICE THOMAS, concurring in the judgment in part and dissenting in part.

. . . § 5 exceeds Congress' power to enforce the Fifteenth Amendment.

. . .

State autonomy with respect to the machinery of self-government defines the States as sovereign entities rather than mere provincial outposts subject to every dictate of a central governing authority. . . . In the main, the "Framers of the Constitution intended the States to keep for themselves, as provided in the Tenth Amendment, the power to regulate elections." . . .

To be sure, state authority over local elections is not absolute under the Constitution. The Fifteenth Amendment guarantees that the "right of citizens of the United States to vote shall not be denied or abridged by the United States or by any State on account of race, color, or previous condition of servitude," § 1, and it grants Congress the authority to "enforce" these rights "by appropriate legislation," § 2. . . . Nonetheless, because States still retain sovereign authority over their election systems, any measure enacted in furtherance of the Fifteenth Amendment must be closely examined to ensure that its encroachment on state authority in this area is limited to the appropriate enforcement of this ban on discrimination.

. . .

The extensive pattern of discrimination that led the Court to previously uphold § 5 as enforcing the Fifteenth Amendment no longer exists. Covered jurisdictions are not now engaged in a systematic campaign to deny black citizens access to the ballot through intimidation and violence. And the days of "grandfather clauses, property qualifications, 'good character' tests, and the requirement that registrants 'understand' or 'interpret' certain matter" . . . are gone. There is thus currently no concerted effort in these jurisdictions to engage in the "unremitting and ingenious defiance of the Constitution" that served as the constitutional basis for upholding the "uncommon exercise of congressional power" embodied in § 5. . . .

The lack of sufficient evidence that the covered jurisdictions currently engage in the type of discrimination that underlay the enactment of § 5 undermines any basis for retaining it. Punishment for long past sins is not a legitimate basis for imposing a forward-looking preventative measure that has already served its purpose. Those supporting § 5's reenactment argue that without it these jurisdictions would return to the racially discriminatory practices of 30 and 40 years ago. But there is no evidence that public officials stand ready, if given the chance, to again engage in concerted acts of violence, terror, and subterfuge in order to keep minorities from voting. Without such evidence, the charge can only be premised on outdated assumptions about racial attitudes in the covered jurisdictions. Admitting that a prophylactic law as broad as § 5 is no longer constitutionally justified based on current evidence of discrimination is not a sign of defeat. It is an acknowledgment of victory.

. . .

Indeed, when reenacting § 5 in 2006, Congress evidently understood that the emergency conditions which prompted § 5's original enactment no longer exist. . . . Instead of relying on the kind of evidence that the *Katzenbach* Court had found so persuasive, Congress instead based reenactment on evidence of what it termed "second generation barriers constructed to prevent minority voters from fully participating in the electoral process." . . . But such evidence is not probative of the type of purposeful discrimination that prompted Congress to enact § 5 in 1965. For example, Congress relied upon evidence of racially polarized voting within the covered jurisdictions. But racially polarized voting is not evidence of unconstitutional discrimination . . . is not state action, . . . and is not a problem unique to the South. . . .

This is not to say that voter discrimination is extinct. . . . But the existence of discrete and isolated incidents of interference with the right to vote has never been sufficient justification for the imposition of § 5's extraordinary requirements. From its inception, the statute was promoted as a measure needed to neutralize a coordinated and unrelenting campaign to deny an entire race access to the ballot. . . . Perfect compliance with the Fifteenth Amendment's substantive command is not now—nor has it ever been—the yardstick for determining whether Congress has the power to employ broad prophylactic legislation to enforce that Amendment. The burden remains with Congress to prove that the extreme circumstances warranting § 5's enactment persist today. A record of scattered infringement of the right to vote is not a constitutionally acceptable substitute.

In 1870, the Fifteenth Amendment was ratified in order to guarantee that no citizen would be denied the right to vote based on race, color, or previous condition of servitude. Congress passed § 5 of the VRA in 1965 because that promise had remained unfulfilled for far too long. But now—more than 40 years later—the violence, intimidation, and subterfuge that led Congress to pass § 5 and this Court to uphold it no longer remains. An acknowledgment of § 5's unconstitutionality represents a fulfillment of the Fifteenth Amendment's promise of full enfranchisement and honors the success achieved by the VRA.

Majority-Minority Districts

Constitutional controversies over majority-minority districts have temporarily abated. The Supreme Court in *Shaw v. Reno* (1993) declared unconstitutional a highly irregularly shaped congressional district in North Carolina that was structured to create an African-American majority. In *Miller v. Johnson* (1995) the five most conservative justices made clear that racial motivation was the problem in *Shaw*, not the shape of the district. "Parties alleging that a State has assigned voters on the basis of race are neither confined in their proof to evidence regarding the district's geometry and makeup nor required to make a threshold showing of bizarreness," Justice Kennedy wrote. He continued,

> The plaintiff's burden is to show, either through circumstantial evidence of a district's shape and demographics or more direct evidence going to legislative purpose, that race was the predominant factor motivating the legislature's decision to place a significant number of voters within or without a particular district. To make this showing, a plaintiff must prove that the legislature subordinated traditional race-neutral districting principles, including but not limited to compactness, contiguity, and respect for political subdivisions or communities defined by actual shared interests, to racial considerations.

The force of both *Shaw* and *Miller* was substantially blunted by *Easley v. Cromartie* (2001). The justices by a 5-4 vote ruled that the district court made a clear error when concluding that North Carolina was motivated by racial considerations rather than a desire to create a safe Democratic district. Legislatures were interested in race, Justice Breyer claimed, only because African-American Democrats in North Carolina voted more reliably Democrat than did white Democrats. He wrote, "A legislature may, by placing reliable Democratic precincts within a district without regard to race, end up with a district containing more heavily African-American precincts, but the reasons would be political rather than racial." After *Easley v. Cromartie* may any good lawyer mask the use of race in the districting process by insisting that the legislature was seeking only to group reliable Democrats?

Regulating Elections

Partisanship and ideology matter when Americans debate laws regulating voting and elections. Republicans insist that strict voting regulations are necessary to prevent fraud. The party platform in 2012 asserted,

> We applaud legislation to require photo identification for voting and to prevent election fraud, particularly with regard to registration and absentee ballots. We support State laws that require proof of citizenship at the time of voter registration to protect our electoral system against a significant and growing form of voter fraud. Every time that a fraudulent vote is cast, it effectively cancels out a vote of a legitimate voter.

Democrats seek to maximize the number of persons who vote. The party platform in 2012 stated,

> We believe the right to vote and to have your vote counted is an essential American freedom, and we oppose laws that place unnecessary restrictions on those seeking to exercise that freedom. Democrats have a proud history of standing up for the right to vote. During the Obama administration, the Justice Department has initiated careful, thorough, and independent reviews of proposed voting changes, and it has prevented states from implementing voter identification laws that would be harmful to minority voters. Democrats know that voter identification laws can disproportionately burden young voters, people of color, low-income families, people with disabilities, and the elderly, and we refuse to allow the use of political pretexts to disenfranchise American citizens.

Interest groups are active in voting rights debates.In December 2011 the NAACP Legal Defense and Education Fund criticized "the rising tide of legislative measures designed to block access to the polls for voters of color" and accused some political leaders of launching "a coordinated and comprehensive assault . . . against our voting rights." They noted that in recent years, "14 states have passed 25 various measures designed to restrict or limit ballot access" through "new and enhanced voter identification requirements" and other steps that "curtail voter access to registration, inhibit critical voter registration drives, limit voting periods, and tighten the ability to cast ballots."[63] Members of the conservative interest group Judicial Watch applaud those efforts that the NAACP condemns, contending that voting reform is necessary because "there appear to be more individuals on voter registration lists in [at least four] states than there are individuals eligible to vote, including individuals who are deceased." They claim that "allowing

63. NAACP Legal Defense and Education Fund, Inc., and the NAACP, *Defending Democracy: Confronting Modern Barriers to Voting Rights in America*, December 5, 2011, http://naacp.3cdn.net/67065c25be9ae43367_mlbrsy48b.pdf.

the names of ineligible voters to remain on the voting rolls harms the integrity of the electoral process and undermines voter confidence in the legitimacy of elections."[64]

The Supreme Court sometimes divides on partisan or ideological lines when adjudicating laws regulating voting. The five most conservative justices on the Roberts Court, joined by Justice Stevens, in *Crawford v. Marion County Election Board* (2008) sustained an Indiana law requiring persons to present a government-issued photo identification in order to cast a ballot. Partisanship played a lesser role in *California Democratic Party v. Jones* (2000), in which the Supreme Court considered the constitutionality of the blanket primary. Both the Democratic and Republican parties urged the justices to declare unconstitutional a California law that mandated one primary election with all candidates running on a single ballot. The Supreme Court complied with these partisan wishes in a 7-2 decision that celebrated the constitutional significance of parties. Justice Scalia's opinion stated, "Our cases vigorously affirm the special place the First Amendment reserves for, and the special protection it accords, the process by which a political party select[s] a standard bearer who best represents the party's ideologies and preferences."

Crawford v. Marion County Election Board, 553 U.S. 181 (2008)

William Crawford was a state legislator who represented one of the poorest districts in Indiana. In 2005 the Indiana legislature adopted a recommendation by a national bipartisan commission, chaired by former Democratic president James Carter and former Republican secretary of state James Baker, that states use photo identification cards, such as drivers' licenses, to prevent unlawful voting.[65] The Republican legislative majority omitted several commission recommendations that would help poor citizens, most of whom vote for Democrats, obtain the relevant documents. As soon as the law, SEA 483, was passed, Crawford filed a lawsuit against the Marion County Election Board, claiming that the Indiana law violated the voting rights of his constituents. Both the federal district court and the Court of Appeals for the Seventh Circuit sustained the Indiana law. Crawford appealed to the Supreme Court of the United States.

The Supreme Court by a vote of 6-3 declared the Indiana law constitutional. Three justices—Justice Stevens, Justice Kennedy, and Chief Justice Roberts—rejected only the facial attack on the constitutionality of the Indiana voting law. Their opinion ruled that the law was a legitimate means to prevent voting fraud, but they left open the possibility that individual citizens could prove that the law was unconstitutional as applied to them. Three justices—Justice Scalia, Justice Thomas, and Justice Alito—insisted that the law was constitutional as applied to all Indiana citizens. Three justices—Justice Souter, Justice Ginsburg, and Justice Breyer—claimed that the law was unconstitutional.

When reading the Crawford *case, consider the different discussions you might have on the Indiana policy in a class on American politics and a class on American constitutional law. Good reasons exist for thinking that the law was in part a Republican effort to prevent some Democrats from voting. Nevertheless, a reasonable person might think that photo identification cards might prevent some voting fraud. Is this a sufficient reason for a court to sustain the Indiana law? Does Justice Souter adequately demonstrate that Indiana was clearly not interested in voting fraud? Professor Heather Gerken of Yale Law School insists that such "shadow institutions" as the Commission on Federal Election Reform may provide guidelines for courts that will enable them to distinguish reasonable election laws from naked efforts to promote partisan goals.[66] Did the Carter/Baker Commission help the justices evaluate whether the Indiana law was constitutional? Should the report of a private commission have any influence on constitutional decisions? When should we expect courts to hand down nonpartisan decisions on election regulations?*

JUSTICE STEVENS announced the judgment of the Court and delivered an opinion in which THE CHIEF JUSTICE and JUSTICE KENNEDY join.

. . . [U]nder the standard applied in *Harper v. Virginia Board of Elections* (1966), even rational restrictions on the right to vote are invidious if they are unrelated to voter qualifications. In *Anderson v. Celebrezze* (1983), however, we confirmed the general rule that "evenhanded restrictions that protect the

64. Judicial Watch, "2012 Election Integrity Project: Judicial Watch Announces Legal Campaign to Force Clean Up of Voter Registration Rolls," February 9, 2012.

65. The full report of the commission can be found at http://www.american.edu/ia/cfer/report/report.html.

66. Heather Gerken, "Out of the Shadows," *Legal Times* (May 5, 2008).

integrity and reliability of the electoral process itself" are not invidious and satisfy the standard set forth in *Harper*. . . . Rather than applying any "litmus test" that would neatly separate valid from invalid restrictions, we concluded that a court must identify and evaluate the interests put forward by the State as justifications for the burden imposed by its rule, and then make the "hard judgment" that our adversary system demands.

. . .

The State has identified several state interests that arguably justify the burdens that SEA 483 imposes on voters and potential voters. While petitioners argue that the statute was actually motivated by partisan concerns and dispute both the significance of the State's interests and the magnitude of any real threat to those interests, they do not question the legitimacy of the interests the State has identified. Each is unquestionably relevant to the State's interest in protecting the integrity and reliability of the electoral process.

The first is the interest in deterring and detecting voter fraud. The State has a valid interest in participating in a nationwide effort to improve and modernize election procedures that have been criticized as antiquated and inefficient. The State also argues that it has a particular interest in preventing voter fraud in response to a problem that is in part the product of its own maladministration—namely, that Indiana's voter registration rolls include a large number of names of persons who are either deceased or no longer live in Indiana. Finally, the State relies on its interest in safeguarding voter confidence. . . .

. . .

. . . That conclusion is also supported by a report issued . . . by the Commission on Federal Election Reform chaired by former President Jimmy Carter and former Secretary of State James A. Baker III, which is a part of the record in these cases. In the introduction to their discussion of voter identification, they made these pertinent comments:

> A good registration list will ensure that citizens are only registered in one place, but election officials still need to make sure that the person arriving at a polling site is the same one that is named on the registration list. In the old days and in small towns where everyone knows each other, voters did not need to identify themselves. But in the United States, where 40 million people move each year, and in urban areas where some people do not even know the people living in their own apartment building let alone their precinct, some form of identification is needed.
>
> There is no evidence of extensive fraud in U.S. elections or of multiple voting, but both occur, and it could affect the outcome of a close election. The electoral system cannot inspire public confidence if no safeguards exist to deter or detect fraud or to confirm the identity of voters. Photo identification cards currently are needed to board a plane, enter federal buildings, and cash a check. Voting is equally important.

. . .

The only kind of voter fraud that SEA 483 addresses is in-person voter impersonation at polling places. The record contains no evidence of any such fraud actually occurring in Indiana at any time in its history. Moreover, petitioners argue that provisions of the Indiana Criminal Code punishing such conduct as a felony provide adequate protection against the risk that such conduct will occur in the future. It remains true, however, that flagrant examples of such fraud in other parts of the country have been documented throughout this Nation's history by respected historians and journalists, that occasional examples have surfaced in recent years, and that Indiana's own experience with fraudulent voting in the 2003 Democratic primary for East Chicago Mayor—though perpetrated using absentee ballots and not in-person fraud—demonstrate that not only is the risk of voter fraud real but that it could affect the outcome of a close election.

. . .

The burdens that are relevant to the issue before us are those imposed on persons who are eligible to vote but do not possess a current photo identification. . . . The fact that most voters already possess a valid driver's license, or some other form of acceptable identification, would not save the statute under our reasoning in *Harper*, if the State required voters to pay a tax or a fee to obtain a new photo identification. But just as other States provide free voter registration cards, the photo identification cards issued by Indiana's BMV [Bureau of Motor Vehicles] are also free. For most voters who need them, the inconvenience of making a trip to the BMV, gathering the required documents, and posing for a photograph surely does not qualify as a substantial burden on the right to vote, or even represent a significant increase over the usual burdens of voting.

Both evidence in the record and facts of which we may take judicial notice, however, indicate that a somewhat heavier burden may be placed on a limited number of persons. They include elderly persons born out-of-state, who may have difficulty obtaining a birth certificate; persons who because of economic or other personal limitations may find it difficult either to secure a copy of their birth certificate or to assemble the other required documentation to obtain a state-issued identification; homeless persons; and persons with a religious objection to being photographed. If we assume, as the evidence suggests, that some members of these classes were registered voters when SEA 483 was enacted, the new identification requirement may have imposed a special burden on their right to vote.

The severity of that burden is, of course, mitigated by the fact that, if eligible, voters without photo identification may cast provisional ballots that will ultimately be counted. To do so, however, they must travel to the circuit court clerk's office within 10 days to execute the required affidavit. It is unlikely that such a requirement would pose a constitutional problem unless it is wholly unjustified. And even assuming that the burden may not be justified as to a few voters, that conclusion is by no means sufficient to establish petitioners' right to the relief they seek in this litigation.

Given the fact that petitioners have advanced a broad attack on the constitutionality of SEA 483, seeking relief that would invalidate the statute in all its applications, they bear a heavy burden of persuasion. . . .

Petitioners ask this Court, in effect, to perform a unique balancing analysis that looks specifically at a small number of voters who may experience a special burden under the statute and weighs their burdens against the State's broad interests in protecting election integrity. Petitioners urge us to ask whether the State's interests justify the burden imposed on voters who cannot afford or obtain a birth certificate and who must make a second trip to the circuit court clerk's office after voting. But on the basis of the evidence in the record it is not possible to quantify either the magnitude of the burden on this narrow class of voters or the portion of the burden imposed on them that is fully justified.

. . .

In their briefs, petitioners stress the fact that all of the Republicans in the General Assembly voted in favor of SEA 483 and the Democrats were unanimous in opposing it. In her opinion rejecting petitioners' facial challenge, Judge Barker noted that the litigation was the result of a partisan dispute that had "spilled out of the state house into the courts." . . . It is fair to infer that partisan considerations may have played a significant role in the decision to enact SEA 483. If such considerations had provided the only justification for a photo identification requirement, we may also assume that SEA 483 would suffer the same fate as the poll tax at issue in *Harper*.

But if a nondiscriminatory law is supported by valid neutral justifications, those justifications should not be disregarded simply because partisan interests may have provided one motivation for the votes of individual legislators. The state interests identified as justifications for SEA 483 are both neutral and sufficiently strong to require us to reject petitioners' facial attack on the statute. The application of the statute to the vast majority of Indiana voters is amply justified by the valid interest in protecting "the integrity and reliability of the electoral process." . . .

JUSTICE SCALIA, with whom JUSTICE THOMAS and JUSTICE ALITO join, concurring in the judgment.

. . .

The Indiana photo-identification law is a generally applicable, nondiscriminatory voting regulation, and our precedents refute the view that individual impacts are relevant to determining the severity of the burden it imposes. . . .

. . .

Insofar as our election-regulation cases rest upon the requirements of the Fourteenth Amendment . . . weighing the burden of a nondiscriminatory voting law upon each voter and concomitantly requiring exceptions for vulnerable voters would effectively turn back decades of equal-protection jurisprudence. A voter complaining about such a law's effect on him has no valid equal-protection claim because, without proof of discriminatory intent, a generally applicable law with disparate impact is not unconstitutional. . . . The Fourteenth Amendment does not regard neutral laws as invidious ones, even when their burdens purportedly fall disproportionately on a protected class. A fortiori it does not do so when, as here, the classes complaining of disparate impact are not even protected.

. . .

. . . It is for state legislatures to weigh the costs and benefits of possible changes to their election codes, and their judgment must prevail unless it imposes a severe and unjustified overall burden upon the right to vote, or is intended to disadvantage a particular class. Judicial review of their handiwork must apply an objective, uniform standard that will enable them to determine, ex ante, whether the burden they impose is too severe.

. . . The universally applicable requirements of Indiana's voter-identification law are eminently reasonable. The burden of acquiring, possessing, and showing a free photo identification is simply not severe, because it does not "even represent a significant increase over the usual burdens of voting." . . . And the State's interests . . . are sufficient to sustain that minimal burden. That should end the matter. That the State accommodates some voters by permitting (not requiring) the casting of absentee or provisional ballots, is an indulgence—not a constitutional imperative that falls short of what is required.

JUSTICE SOUTER, with whom JUSTICE GINSBURG joins, dissenting.

Indiana's "Voter ID Law" threatens to impose nontrivial burdens on the voting right of tens of thousands of the State's citizens . . . and a significant percentage of those individuals are likely to be deterred from voting. . . . The statute is unconstitutional under the balancing standard of *Burdick v. Takushi* (1992): a State may not burden the right to vote merely by invoking abstract interests, be they legitimate, . . . or even compelling, but must make a particular, factual showing that threats to its interests outweigh the particular impediments it has imposed. The State has made no such justification here, and as to some aspects of its law, it has hardly even tried. I therefore respectfully dissent from the Court's judgment sustaining the statute.

. . .

The first set of burdens shown in these cases is the travel costs and fees necessary to get one of the limited variety of federal or state photo identifications needed to cast a regular ballot under the Voter ID Law. The travel is required for the personal visit to a license branch of the Indiana Bureau of Motor Vehicles (BMV), which is demanded of anyone applying for a driver's license or nondriver photo identification. . . . The need to travel to a BMV branch will affect voters according to their circumstances, with the average person probably viewing it as nothing more than an inconvenience. Poor, old, and disabled voters who do not drive a car, however, may find the trip prohibitive, witness the fact that the BMV has far fewer license branches in each county than there are voting precincts. . . .

For those voters who can afford the roundtrip, a second financial hurdle appears: in order to get photo identification for the first time, they need to present "'a birth certificate, a certificate of naturalization, U.S. veterans photo identification, U.S. military photo identification, or a U.S. passport.'" . . . [T]he two most common of these documents come at a price: Indiana counties charge anywhere from $3 to $12 for a birth certificate (and in some other States the fee is significantly higher), . . . and that same price must usually be paid for a first-time passport, since a birth certificate is required to prove U.S. citizenship by birth. The total fees for a passport, moreover, are up to about $100. So most voters must pay at least one fee to get the ID necessary to cast a regular ballot. As with the travel costs, these fees are far from shocking on their face, but in the *Burdick* analysis it matters that both the travel costs and the fees are disproportionately heavy for, and thus disproportionately likely to deter, the poor, the old, and the immobile.

. . .

The law allows these voters who lack the necessary ID to sign the poll book and cast a provisional ballot. . . . [T]hat is only the first step; to have the provisional ballot counted, a voter must then appear in person before the circuit court clerk or county election board within 10 days of the election, to sign an affidavit attesting to indigency or religious objection to being photographed (or to present an ID at that point). . . . Unlike the trip to the BMV (which, assuming things go smoothly, needs to be made only once every four years for renewal of nondriver photo identification), this one must be taken every time a poor person or religious objector wishes to vote, because the State does not allow an affidavit to count in successive elections. And unlike the trip to the BMV (which at least has a handful of license branches in the more populous counties), a county has only one county seat. Forcing these people to travel to the county seat every time they try to vote is particularly onerous for the reason noted already, that most counties in Indiana either lack public transportation or offer only limited coverage.

. . .

There is no denying the abstract importance, the compelling nature, of combating voter fraud. . . . But it takes several steps to get beyond the level of abstraction here.

To begin with, requiring a voter to show photo identification before casting a regular ballot addresses only one form of voter fraud: in-person voter impersonation. The photo ID requirement leaves untouched the problems of absentee-ballot fraud, which (unlike in-person voter impersonation) is a documented problem in Indiana. . . .

And even the State's interest in deterring a voter from showing up at the polls and claiming to be someone he is not must, in turn, be discounted for the fact that the State has not come across a single instance of in-person voter impersonation fraud in all of Indiana's history. . . .

. . .

Nothing else the State has to say does much to bolster its case. The State argues, for example, that even without evidence of in-person voter impersonation in Indiana, it is enough for the State to show that "opportunities [for such fraud] are transparently obvious in elections without identification checks" . . . . Of course they are, but Indiana elections before the Voter ID Law were not run "without identification checks"; on the contrary, as the Marion County Election Board informs us, "[t]ime-tested systems were in place to detect in-person voter impersonation fraud before the challenged statute was enacted" . . . . These included hiring poll workers who were precinct residents familiar with the neighborhood, and making signature comparisons, each effort being supported by the criminal provisions mentioned before. . . .

. . .

Although Indiana claims to have adopted its ID requirement relying partly on the Carter-Baker Report, . . . the State conspicuously rejected the Report's phase-in recommendation aimed at reducing the burdens on the right to vote, and just as conspicuously fails even to try to explain why.

. . .

Without a shred of evidence that in-person voter impersonation is a problem in the State, much less a crisis, Indiana has adopted one of the most restrictive photo identification requirements in the country. The State recognizes that tens of thousands of qualified voters lack the necessary federally issued or state-issued identification, but it insists on implementing the requirement immediately, without allowing a transition period for targeted efforts to distribute the required identification to individuals who need it. The State hardly even tries to explain its decision to force indigents or religious objectors to travel all the way to their county seats every time they wish to vote, and if there is any waning of confidence in the administration of elections it probably owes more to the State's violation of federal election law than to any imposters at the polling places. It is impossible to say, on this record, that the State's interest in adopting its signally inhibiting photo identification requirement has been shown to outweigh the serious burdens it imposes on the right to vote.

JUSTICE BREYER, dissenting. . . .

C. Citizenship

The Supreme Court partly reinvigorated the privileges and immunities clause in *Saenz v. Roe* (1999). The justices by a 7-2 vote declared that a California law mandating lower welfare benefits to new state residents violated the right to travel, a privilege and immunity of American citizenship. Justice Stevens's opinion for the Court asserted, "Citizens of the United States, whether rich or poor, have the right to choose to be citizens 'of the State wherein they reside.' The States, however, do not have any right to select their citizens." The justices have so far not elaborated on what other rights might follow from *Saenz*. No justice joined Justice Thomas's concurrence in *McDonald v. City of Chicago* (2010), which claimed that the privileges and immunities clause of the Fourteenth Amendment incorporates the Bill of Rights.

The rights of persons who are illegally in the United States is a burning issue in American constitutional politics. During the Reagan Era neither party said much about immigration. In 2008 and 2012 both national party platforms talked prominently and at some length about what to do about illegal immigration and persons illegally in the United States. Republicans call for measures sharply limiting the access to government services that persons illegally in the United States enjoy.

> The rule of law means guaranteeing to law enforcement the tools and coordination to deport criminal aliens without delay—and correcting court decisions that have made deportation so difficult. It means enforcing the law against those who overstay their visas, rather than letting millions flout

> the generosity that gave them temporary entry. It means imposing maximum penalties on those who smuggle illegal aliens into the U.S., both for their lawbreaking and for their cruel exploitation. It means requiring cooperation among federal, state and local law enforcement and real consequences, including the denial of federal funds, for self-described sanctuary cities, which stand in open defiance of the federal and state statutes that expressly prohibit such sanctuary policies, and which endanger the lives of U.S. citizens. It does not mean driver's licenses for illegal aliens, nor does it mean that states should be allowed to flout the federal law barring them from giving in-state tuition rates to illegal aliens, nor does it mean that illegal aliens should receive social security benefits, or other public benefits, except as provided by federal law.

Democrats call for measures that punish those who benefit from illegal immigration, but seek means for integrating people illegally in the United States into the American community.

> It's a problem when we only enforce our laws against the immigrants themselves, with raids that are ineffective, tear apart families, and leave people detained without adequate access to counsel. We realize that employers need a method to verify whether their employees are legally eligible to work in the United States, and we will ensure that our system is accurate, fair to legal workers, safeguards people's privacy, and cannot be used to discriminate against workers.
>
> For the millions living here illegally but otherwise playing by the rules, we must require them to come out of the shadows and get right with the law. We support a system that requires undocumented immigrants who are in good standing to pay a fine, pay taxes, learn English, and go to the back of the line for the opportunity to become citizens. They are our neighbors, and we can help them become full tax-paying, law-abiding, productive members of society.

Birthright citizenship is a particular bone of contention. The first sentence of the Fourteenth Amendment declares that "all persons born or naturalized in the United States, and subject to the jurisdiction thereof, are citizens of the United States." The Supreme Court in *United States v. Wong Kim Ark* (1898) interpreted that language to cover all persons in the United States who are not employed by or representing a foreign power. This has meant that for the past 150 years, the children of illegal aliens born in the United States have been considered citizens of the United States. Many Americans believe that the rule of *Wong Kim Ark* should be altered by judicial decree, legislation, or constitutional amendment. Peter Schuck, a prominent opponent of birthright citizenship, asserts that citizenship is "a mutual relationship to which both the nation and the individual must consent." The children of undocumented aliens, he continues, "are here as a result of an illegal act and thus have no claim to membership in a country built on the ideal of mutual consent."[67] Proponents of birthright citizenship insist that granting citizenship to the children of illegal aliens is both constitutionally mandated and just. Walter Dellinger, while in the Office of Legal Counsel in the Clinton administration, declared,

> Since the Civil War, America has thrived as a republic of free and equal citizens. This would no longer be true if we were to amend our Constitution in a way that would create a permanent caste of aliens, generation after generation after generation born in America but never to be among its citizens. To have citizenship in one's own right, by birth upon this soil, is fundamental to our liberty as we understand it.[68]

Struggles in California over the rights of illegal aliens have been particularly intense. In 1994 California voters passed Proposition 187, a ballot initiative that denied persons illegally in the United States health care, other social services, and public education. A lower federal court in 1995 declared those provisions unconstitutional. District Judge Pfaelzer's opinion in *League of United Latin American Citizens* (1995) ruled that crucial provisions of Proposition 187 either conflicted with federal law or with the Supreme Court's decision

67. Peter Schuck, "Birthright of a Nation," *New York Times* (August 13, 2010).

68. Walter Dellinger, "Statement Before the Subcommittees on Immigration and Claims and on the Constitution of the House Committee on the Judiciary," 104th Cong., 1st Sess. December 13, 1995 Available at http://www.justice.gov/olc/deny.tes.31.htm. (1995), 82.

in *Plyler v. Doe* (1982).[69] California judges proved more willing to sustain state legislation granting rights to illegal aliens. *Martinez v. Regents of the University of California* (CA 2010) ruled that illegal aliens could enjoy in-state tuition under a state law that granted such benefits to anyone who attended high school for three years in California. Judge Chin's majority opinion maintained that while "aliens, lawful or unlawful, cannot claim benefits under the [privileges and immunities clause of the Fourteenth Amendment], . . . no authority suggests the clause prohibits states from ever giving resident aliens (again, lawful or unlawful) benefits they do not also give to all American citizens."[70]

Arizona provided an occasion for a political imbroglio when passing the Support Our Law Enforcement and Safe Neighborhoods Act. The most controversial provision of that measure asserted,

> For any lawful stop, detention or arrest made by [an Arizona] law enforcement official or a law enforcement agency . . . in the enforcement of any other law or ordinance of a county, city or town [of] this state where reasonable suspicion exists that the person is an alien and is unlawfully present in the United States, a reasonable attempt shall be made, when practicable, to determine the immigration status of the person, except if the determination may hinder or obstruct an investigation.[71]

The Supreme Court in *Arizona v United States* (2012) by a 5-3 vote held that most provisions in the Arizona law were preempted by federal immigration laws. The justices sustained the requirement that state law officials determine the immigration status of detained persons they have reason to believe are illegal aliens, but only on the ground that the challenge was premature. Justice Kennedy wrote,

> The Federal Government has brought suit against a sovereign State to challenge the provision even before the law has gone into effect. There is a basic uncertainty about what the law means and how it will be enforced. At this stage, without the benefit of a definitive interpretation from the state courts, it would be inappropriate to assume §2(B) will be construed in a way that creates a conflict with federal law.

V. Equality

MAJOR DEVELOPMENTS

- Ongoing controversies over affirmative action
- Increased constitutional protection against gender discrimination
- Congress and the Court dispute the proper standard of constitutional protection for people with disabilities

Americans are both committed to and conflicted about constitutional equality. No prominent political movement champions the status inequalities of the past. Neither Democrats nor Republicans maintain that persons are entitled to special privileges or ought to shoulder particular burdens because of their race, gender, ethnicity, religion, or social class. Native Americans who choose to live on reservations aside, no political movement champions the notion that nominal equals may nevertheless have very different legal rights and obligations. Nevertheless, controversies rage over the legacy of the civil rights movement. Liberals and conservatives dispute whether persons of color and women have achieved actual equality, what other groups continue to be victims of inegalitarian social policies, what social policies best rectify past inequalities, and when real differences between different classes of persons justify laws that provide special benefits and burdens to only some people or groups. New disputes over whether communities may adopt zoning and other regulations designed to prevent superstores from taking business away from local shops have emerged while ongoing disputes over affirmative action rage.

Democrats and Republicans dispute what equality means. Prominent Democrats insist that the concerns that animated the civil rights revolution remain vibrant. Liberal Democrats support affirmative action programs for persons of color and women, believe that other Americans suffer from status inequalities, and champion anti-subordination conceptions of equality that focus on the actual condition of persons of different races, genders, and groups. The Democratic Party platform of 2008 asserted:

> Democrats will fight to end discrimination based on race, sex, ethnicity, national origin, language,

---

69. *League of United Latin American Citizens v. Wilson*, 908 F.Supp. 755 (C.D.Cal. 1995).

70. *Martinez v. Regents of the University of California*, 241 3.Pd 855 (Cal. 2010).

71. Ariz. Rev. Stat. Ann. § 11-1051(B) (2010).

> religion, sexual orientation, gender identity, age, and disability in every corner of our country, because that's the America we believe in.
>
> . . .
>
> We are committed to ensuring full equality for women: we reaffirm our support for the Equal Rights Amendment. . . . We will restore and support the White House Initiative on Asian-American and Pacific Islanders, including enforcement on disaggregation of Census data. We will make the Census more culturally sensitive, including outreach, language assistance, and increased confidentiality protections to ensure accurate counting of the growing Latino and Asian American, and Pacific Islander populations, and continue working on efforts to be more inclusive. We will sign the U.N. Convention on the Rights of Persons with Disabilities and restore the original intent of the Americans with Disabilities Act.
>
> We support the full inclusion of all families, including same-sex couples, in the life of our nation, and support equal responsibility, benefits, and protections. . . .
>
> . . . We support affirmative action, including in federal contracting and higher education, to make sure that those locked out of the doors of opportunity will be able to walk through those doors in the future.

Republicans are more inclined to think that the civil rights revolution has strayed from proper egalitarian paths. Conservatives oppose affirmative action policies, are more inclined than liberals to limit the beneficiaries of anti-discriminatory policies, and champion anti-classification conceptions of equality that emphasize the value of formal legal equality. The Republican Party platform of 2008 stated,

> Our commitment to equal opportunity extends from landmark school-choice legislation for the students of Washington D.C. to historic appointments at the highest levels of government. We consider discrimination based on sex, race, age, religion, creed, disability, or national origin to be immoral, and we will strongly enforce anti-discrimination statutes. We ask all to join us in rejecting the forces of hatred and bigotry and in denouncing all who practice or promote racism, anti-Semitism, ethnic prejudice, or religious intolerance. As a matter of principle, Republicans oppose any attempts to create race-based governments within the United States, as well as any domestic governments not bound by the Constitution or the Bill of Rights.
>
> Precisely because we oppose discrimination, we reject preferences, quotas, and set-asides, whether in education or in corporate boardrooms. The government should not make contracts on this basis, and neither should corporations. We support efforts to help low-income individuals get a fair shot based on their potential and merit, and we affirm the commonsense approach of the Chief Justice of the United States: that the way to stop discriminating on the basis of race is to stop discriminating.

The Supreme Court has reflected these partisan divisions. The more liberal justices on the Rehnquist and early Roberts Courts supported affirmative action, stricter scrutiny for gender discrimination, and more aggressive policing of other status inequalities. The more conservative justices opposed affirmative action, urged lesser scrutiny for gender discriminations, and opposed the creation of heightened scrutiny for new classes. Justices Kennedy and O'Connor, who held the balance of power, tended to favor the liberal position on women, the conservative position on heightened scrutiny for new classes, and split the difference on affirmative action. Interestingly, the standard partisan divisions on the Court did not occur in the few cases in which the justices considered the constitutional rights of Native Americans, which were generally decided in favor of tribal sovereignty.

A. Equality Under Law

A remarkable array of contemporary citizens maintain that they are not being treated as constitutional equals. Americans with disabilities, Wal-Mart stores, children in poorer school districts, gay rights activists, and numerous others have lobbied and litigated for policies that they believe promote equality under the law. Federal courts have been unsympathetic to these claims. No new suspect class has been announced in the past three decades. With the exception of rights associated with civil and criminal trials, the Supreme Court has not announced a new fundamental interest that requires heightened scrutiny. Indeed, the Supreme Court declared unconstitutional several congressional efforts to use Section 5 of the Fourteenth Amendment to expand equal protection rights outside of race and gender. *Board of Trustees of the University of Alabama v. Garrett* (2001) declared unconstitutional Title I of the Americans with Disabilities Act. The judicial majority insisted that Congress could protect handicapped Americans only from state discrimination that did not satisfy the rational basis test. Chief Justice Rehnquist's majority opinion asserted, "Congress had failed to identify a history and pattern of unconstitutional employment discrimination by the States against the disabled adequate to show that the states had engaged in irrational discrimination." The justices were more supportive of Congress and the disabled in *Tennessee v. Lane* (2004). In that case the justices ruled that Congress could require states to ensure that the handicapped had adequate access to courthouses as a means of implementing the constitutional "right to be present at all stages of a [criminal] trial."

Romer v. Evans (1996) was the important exception to the judicial tendency to restrict equal protection to race and gender. That case arose after Colorado voters passed an amendment to the state constitution forbidding localities from passing laws prohibiting discrimination against gays and lesbians. The justices by a 6-3 vote declared the amendment unconstitutional. The Court of Appeals for the Ninth Circuit in *Perry v. Brown* (2012) relied heavily on *Romer* when declaring unconstitutional a state constitutional amendment prohibiting same-sex marriage. Judge Reinhardt's majority opinion declared,

> Although the Constitution permits communities to enact most laws they believe to be desirable, it requires that there be at least a legitimate reason for the passage of a law that treats different classes of people differently. There was no such reason that Proposition 8 could have been enacted. Because under California statutory law, same-sex couples had all the rights of opposite-sex couples, regardless of their marital status, all parties agree that Proposition 8 had one effect only. It stripped same-sex couples of the ability they previously possessed to obtain from the State, or any other authorized party, an important right—the right to obtain and use the designation of 'marriage' to describe their relationships. Nothing more, nothing less. Proposition 8 therefore could not have been enacted to advance California's interests in childrearing or responsible procreation, for it had no effect on the rights of same-sex couples to raise children or on the procreative practices of other couples. Nor did Proposition 8 have any effect on religious freedom or on parents' rights to control their children's education; it could not have been enacted to safeguard these liberties.
>
> All that Proposition 8 accomplished was to take away from same-sex couples the right to be granted marriage licenses and thus legally to use the designation of "marriage," which symbolizes state legitimization and societal recognition of their committed relationships. Proposition 8 serves no purpose, and has no effect, other than to lessen the status and human dignity of gays and lesbians in California, and to officially reclassify their relationships and families as inferior to those of opposite-sex couples. The Constitution simply does not allow for "laws of this sort." *Romer v. Evans*.[72]

State courts have been more sympathetic to various claims of constitutional equality under the state constitution. One commentary notes,

> Many states have seen fit in cases involving equality to reconstitute the multi-tier system of review developed in the federal courts. In some instances, this has been done by expanding the scope of strict or intermediate scrutiny to encompass classifications or rights; which in the federal courts are assigned to lower regions. State courts have upgraded gender classifications from intermediate to strict scrutiny and have ruled that classifications based on sexual orientation are subject to heightened scrutiny. State courts have taken the position that education is a fundamental right; therefore, public school financing schemes are to be reviewed with strict scrutiny. And state courts have held that strict scrutiny should be applied to determine the constitutionality of laws that deny funding for abortions. In other instances, the tiers of review have been reconstituted by intensifying rationality review to give it an edge lacking under the federal approach. State courts may sharpen rationality review to assess the constitutionality of economic legislation that denies benefits for no apparent reason, interferes with fair competition, or grants special entitlements to a favored few. On occasion, state courts may enhance rationality review to examine the constitutionality

72. *Perry v. Brown*, 704 F. Supp. 2d 921 (N.D. Cal., 2010).

of criminal laws that provide differential penalties or treatment for similar offenses. One state court even used a sharpened version of rationality review to invalidate a statute that discriminated against adopted persons.[73]

Romer v. Evans, 517 U.S 620 (1996)

Richard Evans was a gay man who served as an aide to the mayor of Denver, Colorado. Denver and many other cities in Colorado passed ordinances in the late 1980s and early 1990s forbidding many forms of discrimination against homosexuals. In 1992 Colorado voters eliminated these protections (or preferences) by approving Amendment 2 to the state constitution. That amendment declared:

> *Neither the State of Colorado, through any of its branches or departments, nor any of its agencies, political subdivisions, municipalities or school districts, shall enact, adopt or enforce any statute, regulation, ordinance or policy whereby homosexual, lesbian or bisexual orientation, conduct, practices or relationships shall constitute or otherwise be the basis of or entitle any person or class of persons to have or claim any minority status, quota preferences, protected status or claim of discrimination.*

Evans and other gay and lesbian activists (including tennis star Martina Navratilova) immediately filed a lawsuit against Colorado governor Roy Romer, claiming that Amendment 2 violated their rights under the equal protection clause of the Constitution. A local trial court issued an injunction against enforcing the amendment; that decision was sustained by the Supreme Court of Colorado. Romer, who personally opposed the amendment, appealed to the Supreme Court of the United States.

The Supreme Court by a 6-3 vote declared Amendment 2 unconstitutional. Justice Kennedy's majority opinion claimed that the law was based on unconstitutional animus against gay and lesbian citizens. Kennedy purports to apply the rational basis test in Romer. *Does he in fact do so?* Williamson v. Lee Optical *(1955) held that a statute passes rational basis scrutiny if some applications are reasonable. Does Justice Kennedy insist that all applications of Amendment 2 are unreasonable? Note the emphasis his opinion places on laws that express hostility against a particular social group. Why is that relevant? Is Justice Scalia correct when he asserts that the majority has "mistaken a Kulturkampf for a fit of spite." or does Justice Scalia's opinion manifest the very prejudices against gays and lesbians that Justice Kennedy insists cannot be legitimate bases for public laws? Justice Scalia insists that Amendment 2 merely denies gays and lesbians special preferences. Is that correct? Would he claim that the Civil Rights Act of 1964 grants persons of color special preferences? If not, what is the difference between laws prohibiting discrimination against gays and lesbians and laws prohibiting discrimination against persons of color?*

JUSTICE KENNEDY delivered the opinion of the Court.

One century ago, the first Justice Harlan admonished this Court that the Constitution "neither knows nor tolerates classes among citizens." *Plessy v. Ferguson* (1896) (dissenting opinion). Unheeded then, those words now are understood to state a commitment to the law's neutrality where the rights of persons are at stake. The Equal Protection Clause enforces this principle and today requires us to hold invalid a provision of Colorado's Constitution.

. . .

Sweeping and comprehensive is the change in legal status effected by this law. . . . Homosexuals, by state decree, are put in a solitary class with respect to transactions and relations in both the private and governmental spheres. The amendment withdraws from homosexuals, but no others, specific legal protection from the injuries caused by discrimination, and it forbids reinstatement of these laws and policies.

. . .

Amendment 2 bars homosexuals from securing protection against the injuries that public accommodations laws address. That in itself is a severe consequence, but there is more. Amendment 2, in addition, nullifies specific legal protections for this targeted class in all transactions in housing, sale of real estate, insurance, health and welfare services, private education, and employment. . . .

. . .

Amendment 2's reach may not be limited to specific laws passed for the benefit of gays and lesbians. It is a fair, if not necessary, inference from the broad language of the amendment that it deprives gays and lesbians even of the protection of general laws and policies that prohibit arbitrary discrimination in governmental and private settings. . . . At some point in

73. Jeffrey M. Shaman, "The Evolution of Equality in State Constitutional Law," *Rutgers Law Journal* 34 (2003): 1013.

the systematic administration of these laws, an official must determine whether homosexuality is an arbitrary and thus forbidden basis for decision. Yet a decision to that effect would itself amount to a policy prohibiting discrimination on the basis of homosexuality, and so would appear to be no more valid under Amendment 2 than the specific prohibitions against discrimination the state court held invalid.

. . . [E]ven if, as we doubt, homosexuals could find some safe harbor in laws of general application, we cannot accept the view that Amendment 2's prohibition on specific legal protections does no more than deprive homosexuals of special rights. To the contrary, the amendment imposes a special disability upon those persons alone. Homosexuals are forbidden the safeguards that others enjoy or may seek without constraint. They can obtain specific protection against discrimination only by enlisting the citizenry of Colorado to amend the state constitution or perhaps, on the State's view, by trying to pass helpful laws of general applicability. This is so no matter how local or discrete the harm, no matter how public and widespread the injury. We find nothing special in the protections Amendment 2 withholds. These are protections taken for granted by most people either because they already have them or do not need them; these are protections against exclusion from an almost limitless number of transactions and endeavors that constitute ordinary civic life in a free society.

The Fourteenth Amendment's promise that no person shall be denied the equal protection of the laws must coexist with the practical necessity that most legislation classifies for one purpose or another, with resulting disadvantage to various groups or persons. . . . We have attempted to reconcile the principle with the reality by stating that, if a law neither burdens a fundamental right nor targets a suspect class, we will uphold the legislative classification so long as it bears a rational relation to some legitimate end. . . .

Amendment 2 fails, indeed defies, even this conventional inquiry. First, the amendment has the peculiar property of imposing a broad and undifferentiated disability on a single named group, an exceptional and, as we shall explain, invalid form of legislation. Second, its sheer breadth is so discontinuous with the reasons offered for it that the amendment seems inexplicable by anything but animus toward the class that it affects; it lacks a rational relationship to legitimate state interests.

Amendment 2 . . . is at once too narrow and too broad. It identifies persons by a single trait and then denies them protection across the board. The resulting disqualification of a class of persons from the right to seek specific protection from the law is unprecedented in our jurisprudence. . . .

It is not within our constitutional tradition to enact laws of this sort. Central both to the idea of the rule of law and to our own Constitution's guarantee of equal protection is the principle that government and each of its parts remain open on impartial terms to all who seek its assistance. . . . Respect for this principle explains why laws singling out a certain class of citizens for disfavored legal status or general hardships are rare. A law declaring that in general it shall be more difficult for one group of citizens than for all others to seek aid from the government is itself a denial of equal protection of the laws in the most literal sense. . . .

. . .

A second and related point is that laws of the kind now before us raise the inevitable inference that the disadvantage imposed is born of animosity toward the class of persons affected. . . . Amendment 2 . . . in making a general announcement that gays and lesbians shall not have any particular protections from the law, inflicts on them immediate, continuing, and real injuries that outrun and belie any legitimate justifications that may be claimed for it. . . .

The primary rationale the State offers for Amendment 2 is respect for other citizens' freedom of association, and in particular the liberties of landlords or employers who have personal or religious objections to homosexuality. Colorado also cites its interest in conserving resources to fight discrimination against other groups. The breadth of the Amendment is so far removed from these particular justifications that we find it impossible to credit them. . . .

. . .

JUSTICE SCALIA, with whom THE CHIEF JUSTICE and JUSTICE THOMAS join, dissenting.

The Court has mistaken a Kulturkampf for a fit of spite. The constitutional amendment before us here is not the manifestation of a "'bare . . . desire to harm'" homosexuals, . . . but is rather a modest attempt by seemingly tolerant Coloradans to preserve traditional sexual mores against the efforts of a politically powerful minority to revise those mores through use of the laws. That objective, and the means chosen to achieve it, are not only unimpeachable under any constitutional doctrine hitherto pronounced (hence the opinion's heavy reliance upon principles of righteousness rather than judicial holdings); they have been specifically approved by the Congress of the United States and by this Court.

In holding that homosexuality cannot be singled out for disfavorable treatment, the Court contradicts a decision, unchallenged here, pronounced only 10 years ago, see *Bowers v. Hardwick* (1986), and places the prestige of this institution behind the proposition that opposition to homosexuality is as reprehensible as racial or religious bias. Whether it is or not is *precisely* the cultural debate that gave rise to the Colorado constitutional amendment (and to the preferential laws against which the amendment was directed). Since the Constitution of the United States says nothing about this subject, it is left to be resolved by normal democratic means, including the democratic adoption of provisions in state constitutions. This Court has no business imposing upon all Americans the resolution favored by the elite class from which the Members of this institution are selected, pronouncing that "animosity" toward homosexuality . . . is evil. I vigorously dissent.

. . .

. . . The amendment prohibits *special treatment* of homosexuals, and nothing more. It would not affect, for example, a requirement of state law that pensions be paid to all retiring state employees with a certain length of service; homosexual employees, as well as others, would be entitled to that benefit. But it would prevent the State or any municipality from making death benefit payments to the "life partner" of a homosexual when it does not make such payments to the long time roommate of a nonhomosexual employee. . . .

Despite all of its hand wringing about the potential effect of Amendment 2 on general antidiscrimination laws, the Court's opinion ultimately does not dispute all this, but assumes it to be true. . . . The only denial of equal treatment it contends homosexuals have suffered is this: They may not obtain *preferential* treatment without amending the state constitution. . . .

The central thesis of the Court's reasoning is that any group is denied equal protection when, to obtain advantage (or, presumably, to avoid disadvantage), it must have recourse to a more general and hence more difficult level of political decisionmaking than others. The world has never heard of such a principle, which is why the Court's opinion is so long on emotive utterance and so short on relevant legal citation. And it seems to me most unlikely that any multilevel democracy can function under such a principle. For *whenever* a disadvantage is imposed, or conferral of a benefit is prohibited, at one of the higher levels of democratic decisionmaking (*i.e.*, by the state legislature rather than local government, or by the people at large in the state constitution rather than the legislature), the affected group has (under this theory) been denied equal protection. . . .

. . .

. . . The case most relevant to the issue before us today is not even mentioned in the Court's opinion: In *Bowers v. Hardwick*, we held that the Constitution does not prohibit what virtually all States had done from the founding of the Republic until very recent years—making homosexual conduct a crime. . . . If it is constitutionally permissible for a State to make homosexual conduct criminal, surely it is constitutionally permissible for a State to enact other laws merely *disfavoring* homosexual conduct. . . . And *a fortiori* it is constitutionally permissible for a State to adopt a provision *not even* disfavoring homosexual conduct, but merely prohibiting all levels of state government from bestowing *special protections* upon homosexual conduct. . . .

. . .

. . . The Court's opinion contains grim, disapproving hints that Coloradans have been guilty of "animus" or "animosity" toward homosexuality, as though that has been established as Unamerican. Of course it is our moral heritage that one should not hate any human being or class of human beings. But I had thought that one could consider certain conduct reprehensible—murder, for example, or polygamy, or cruelty to animals—and could exhibit even "animus" toward such conduct. Surely that is the only sort of "animus" at issue here: moral disapproval of homosexual conduct, the same sort of moral disapproval that produced the centuries old criminal laws that we held constitutional in *Bowers*. . . .

. . .

The problem (a problem, that is, for those who wish to retain social disapprobation of homosexuality) is that, because those who engage in homosexual conduct tend to reside in disproportionate numbers in certain communities, . . . have high disposable income, . . . and of course care about homosexual rights issues much more ardently than the public at large, they possess political power much greater than their numbers, both locally and statewide. Quite understandably, they devote this political power to achieving not merely a grudging social toleration, but full social acceptance, of homosexuality. . . .

. . .

That is where Amendment 2 came in. It sought to counter both the geographic concentration and the disproportionate political power of homosexuals by (1) resolving the controversy at the statewide level, and (2) making the election a single issue contest for both sides. It put directly, to all the citizens of the State, the question: Should homosexuality be given special protection? They answered no. The Court today asserts that this most democratic of procedures is unconstitutional. . . .

. . .

When the Court takes sides in the culture wars, it tends to be with the knights rather than the villains—and more specifically with the Templars, reflecting the views and values of the lawyer class from which the Court's Members are drawn. How that class feels about homosexuality will be evident to anyone who wishes to interview job applicants at virtually any of the Nation's law schools. The interviewer may refuse to offer a job because the applicant is a Republican; because he is an adulterer; because he went to the wrong prep school or belongs to the wrong country club; because he eats snails; because he is a womanizer; because she wears real animal fur; or even because he hates the Chicago Cubs. But if the interviewer should wish not to be an associate or partner of an applicant because he disapproves of the applicant's homosexuality, *then* he will have violated the pledge which the Association of American Law Schools requires all its member schools to exact from job interviewers: "assurance of the employer's willingness" to hire homosexuals. . . .

Retail Industry Leaders Association v. Fielder, 435 F. Supp. 2d 481 (D. Md. 2006)

Wal-Mart, a prominent superstore, is a member of the Retail Industry Leaders Association (RILA). Both Wal-Mart and the RILA objected to the Fair Share Health Care Fund Act of 2006 that was passed by the Maryland legislature. The crucial provision of that statute declared that all private employers who employed more than ten thousand persons and did "not spend up to 8% of the total wages paid to employees in the State on health insurance costs shall pay to the Secretary an amount equal to the difference between what the employer spends for health insurance costs and an amount equal to 8% of the total wages paid to employees in the State." Wal-Mart was the only employer in Maryland that employed more than ten thousand persons and spent less than 8 percent of total wages on health care costs. After the law was passed the RILA sued James D. Fielder, Jr., the Maryland secretary of labor, licensing, and regulation. The lawsuit claimed that Maryland violated the equal protection clause of the Constitution by passing a law that only affected Wal-Mart.[74]

The federal district court ruled that the Fair Share Health Care Fund Act of 2006 was constitutional. Judge Motz asserted that Maryland had a rational basis for targeting private employees who employed more than ten thousand persons. What was that reason? In your opinion, was that the real justification for the act, or was the Maryland legislature targeting Wal-Mart, a superstore that liberals complain pays low wages and provides limited benefits? Suppose that Maryland passed a similar law targeting a few family-owned bookstores. Would the federal district court have reached the same result? Should the federal district court have reached the same result?

JUDGE MOTZ delivered the following opinion.

. . .

The final question to be addressed is whether the Act violates the Equal Protection Clause. Because the Act relates to economic and social policy that does not create a suspect classification or infringe upon fundamental interests, it is presumed constitutional and "must be upheld against equal protection challenge if there is any reasonably conceivable state of facts that could provide a rational basis for the classification."

. . .

. . . [U]nder existing law RILA's equal protection challenge is unavailing. The Supreme Court has made it clear that "equal protection is not a license for courts to judge the wisdom, fairness, or logic of legislative choices." A necessary corollary of this principle is that legislatures are permitted the "leeway to approach a perceived problem incrementally." . . .

. . . [T]he distinctions drawn by the General Assembly are not necessarily irrational in and of themselves. What is lacking is any supporting information for the distinctions in the legislative record. Under current

74. The Court of Appeals for the Fourth Circuit reversed the district court on grounds unrelated to the equal protection claim.

Supreme Court law, this difference is one of constitutional significance and undermines RILA's equal protection challenge.

RILA makes a secondary argument that the Act violates the Equal Protection Clause because it was intentionally targeted at Wal-Mart. In support of this argument, RILA cites Justice Jackson's eloquent statement in his concurring opinion in *Railway Express Agency Inc. v. New York* (1949), that "nothing opens the door to arbitrary action so effectively as to allow . . . officials to pick and choose only a few to whom they will apply legislation and thus to escape the political retribution that might be visited upon them if larger numbers were affected."

Here, the legislation enacted by the General Assembly may well have been more thoughtfully considered (and the members of the Assembly more politically accountable) if it had subjected more than a single employer to its spending requirement. However, unless there is a reason to "infer antipathy" from the targeting of a particular group or person, "[t]he Constitution presumes that . . . even improvident decisions will eventually be rectified by the democratic process and that judicial intervention is generally unwarranted no matter how unwisely we may think a political branch has acted." It is only in cases involving politically vulnerable groups that the Supreme Court has appeared to rely, at least in part, on legislative antipathy when invalidating a law under the rational basis test.

B. Race

Many commentators claim that the United States has entered a "postracial era." The president is an African-American. Mass civil rights demonstrations are no longer a regular occurrence on city streets and college campuses. Neither the Democratic nor Republican Parties have specific sections in party platforms detailing their positions on race issues. Major Supreme Court decisions on race issues now occur only once every five years or so.

Americans dispute the significance of the reduced salience of racial issues in constitutional politics. Many believe that the United States has successfully become a color-blind nation. With the unfortunate exception of affirmative action and isolated instances of racial-discrimination, they claim, official policies reflect a national commitment to formal racial equality. Others insist that the low salience of race is better interpreted as an abandonment of the quest for racial equality. While official policies no longer explicitly discriminate against persons of color, they point out that the life chances of the average person of color remain substantially less than the life chances of the average white person.

The conditions under which government may consider race are vigorously disputed. Many progressives insist that government should consider race in order to achieve diversity and compensate for past injustices. Others think that race is sometimes a legitimate consideration when police are seeking to apprehend criminals and terrorists. These issues are fought in almost every setting, from state referenda on affirmative action to the law school admissions process to executive decisions about the conditions under which racial profiling is legitimate.

Affirmative Action

Affirmative action remains the main lightning rod for racial issues in the contemporary United States. Republicans condemn the use of race in school assignments, college admissions, and employment decisions. The amicus brief filed by the Bush II administration in *Parents Involved in Community Schools v. Seattle School District No. 1* (2007) asserted "race-conscious measures . . . are not only at odds with *Brown*'s ultimate objective of 'achiev[ing] a system of determining admission to the public schools on a nonracial basis,' but contravene the fundamental liberties guaranteed to each citizen by the Equal Protection Clause."[75] Democrats, sometimes with less enthusiasm, insist that affirmative action policies are legitimate means for achieving greater racial equality. The amicus brief submitted by the Obama Administration in *Fisher v. University of Texas at Austin* (2012) declares, "The educational benefits of diversity . . . are of critical importance to the United States. Careers in a range of fields that are vital to the national interest-such as the military officer corps, science, law, medicine, finance, education, and other professions . . . must be open to all segments of American society, regardless of race and ethnicity. That is not simply a matter of civic responsibility; it is a pressing necessity in an era of intense competition in the global economy and ever-evolving worldwide

75. Brief for the United States as Amicus Curiae Supporting Petitioner, Parents Involved in Community Schools v. Seattle School District No. 1, 551 U.S. 701 (2007), 7

national-security threats. For this reason, the Obama Justice Department concluded, "a university may institute a narrowly tailed policy that considers race as part of a holistic, individualized admissions process, when doing so is necessary to achieve the educational benefits of diversity."[76]

The U.S. Supreme Court in *Adarand Constructors, Inc. v. Peña* (1995) sent confusing signals on the constitutionality of affirmative action. Justice Scalia's opinion clearly stated that race-conscious measures were never or, perhaps, hardly ever constitutional unless designed to remedy specific victims of past discrimination. He wrote, "Under our Constitution there can be no such thing as either a creditor or a debtor race." The four more liberal justices on the Rehnquist Court insisted that Congress had broad powers to use race-conscious measures. Justice Ginsburg stated, "Congress [has] authority to act affirmatively, not only to end discrimination, but also to counter discrimination's lingering effects." Justice O'Connor's crucial plurality opinion split the difference. She insisted that affirmative action programs must meet three tough constitutional conditions:

- "Skepticism: Any preference based on racial or ethnic criteria must necessarily receive a most searching examination."
- "Consistency: The standard of review under the Equal Protection clause is not dependent on the race of those burdened or benefitted by a particular classification."
- "Congruence: Equal protection analysis in the Fifth Amendment area is the same as that under the Fourteenth Amendment."

"Taken together," O'Connor stated, "these three presumptions lead to the conclusion that any person, of whatever race, has the right to demand that any government actor subject to the Constitution justify any racial classification subjecting that person to unequal treatment under the strictest judicial scrutiny." Justice O'Connor concluded her opinion, however, by mitigating the apparent force of skepticism, consistency and congruence. "We wish to dispel the notion that strict scrutiny is 'strict in theory, but fatal in fact,'" she wrote. "The unhappy persistence of both the practice and the lingering effects of racial discrimination against minority groups in this country is an unfortunate reality, and government is not disqualified from acting in response to it."

O'Connor again took an intermediate position eight years later when litigants challenged admissions policies at the University of Michigan. She provided the crucial fifth vote in *Grutter v. Bollinger* (2003), which sustained the use of race in the admissions policy at Michigan Law School, while voting in *Gratz v. Bollinger* (2003) with the *Grutter* dissenters and Justice Breyer to strike down the use of race for determining undergraduate admissions at the University of Michigan. The policies were different. The law school required students to write an essay detailing their contributions to diversity, thus making all students in theory eligible for diversity consideration. The undergraduate admissions process gave a fixed number of points to persons of color. Nevertheless, only Justices Breyer and O'Connor believed that this difference made a constitutional difference. Significantly, this 1–1 "tie" strongly favored proponents of affirmative action. Universities committed to affirmative action programs simply adopted the Michigan Law School policy that the court sustained in *Grutter*.

Justice O'Connor's retirement has cast doubt on the future of affirmative action. The Roberts Court by 5-4 votes declared unconstitutional or illegal two-race conscious policies. *Parents Involved in Community Schools v. Seattle School District No. 1* (2007) held that school boards could not use race when assigning students to public schools unless they were complying with a court order to remedy the effects of past legal segregation. *Ricci v. DeStefano* (2009) ruled that New Haven violated the Civil Rights Act of 1964 when the city refused to promote firefighters on the basis of an exam on which white applicants scored substantially higher than applicants of color. Justice Kennedy's majority opinion stated, "Many of the candidates had studied for months, at considerable personal and financial expense, and thus the injury caused by the City's reliance on raw racial statistics at the end of the process was all the more severe."

The constitutional politics of affirmative action often moved from the courthouse to the voting booth. Led by Ward Connerly, a prominent African-American businessperson, opponents of affirmative action sponsored a series of ballot initiatives aimed at passing state constitutional amendments prohibiting the use of race in college admissions and state employment decisions. California voters in 1996 passed proposition 209. That measure added a provision to the state constitution

76. Brief for the United States as Amicus Curiae Supporting Respondents, *Fisher v. University of Texas at Austin* (2012), 5–6.

declaring, "The state shall not discriminate against, or grant preferential treatment to, any individual or group on the basis of race, sex, color, ethnicity, or national origin in the operation of public employment, public education, or public contracting."[77] Shortly after the Supreme Court decided *Grutter*, Connerly and his allies began a campaign to pass the Michigan Civil Rights Initiative (MCRI). The MCRI asserted,

> 1. The University of Michigan, Michigan State University, Wayne State University, and any other public college or university, community college, or school district shall not discriminate against, or grant preferential treatment to, any individual or group on the basis of race, sex, color, ethnicity, or national origin in the operation of public employment, public education, or public contracting.
> 2. The state shall not discriminate against, or grant preferential treatment to, any individual or group on the basis of race, sex, color, ethnicity, or national origin in the operation of public employment, public education, or public contracting.

In a speech defending the MCRI, Connerly stated,

> Do we have so little confidence in the American spirit and in yet unborn Americans of African and Mexican descent that we consign them to another generation of presumed inadequacy? Is it fair to say to a black parent: your child to be born eight years from now will still need a preference when he or she applies to college in the year 2028?
>
> I cannot describe to you the anger and humiliation that fills me as a "black" man to be viewed with such misplaced pity and misguided patronization.
>
> . . .
>
> This is not 1963. There is no governor blocking the school house door. There is no Sheriff Bull Connor with snarling dogs straining to attack black people. This is not about simple access to college. None of those circumstances exist, thanks to the Almighty and to an American spirit that embraces the principle of "equal treatment for every person."[78]

The Michigan Civil Rights Commission vigorously opposed the MCRI and adopted a resolution declaring:

> Whereas, the Michigan Civil Rights Commission recognizes the valuable contributions made to society by women and men of various cultures and ethnic groups and persons with disabilities; and
>
> Whereas, affirmative action has proven its value as an effective tool in the removal of barriers for women and men of various ethnic cultural groups who have been denied equal access to participation in education, employment, housing, and contracts on an equal basis. . . .
>
> . . .
>
> *Therefore, be it resolved* that the Michigan Civil Rights Commission will continue to act to eliminate discrimination and to ensure fair and equal access to employment, education and economic opportunities for all citizens in the State of Michigan; and
>
> *Further, be it resolved*, that the Michigan Civil Rights Commission vigorously opposes the Michigan Civil Rights Initiative designed to eliminate and undermine the basic principles of equal treatment under the law as set forth in the Michigan Constitution.[79]

The MCRI ballot initiative passed in 2006 by a nearly three-to-two ratio. Five years later a federal appeals court declared the measure unconstitutional. A panel for the Court of Appeals for the Sixth Circuit in *Coalition to Defend Affirmative Action v. Regents of the University of Michigan* (2011) concluded that the MCRI "targets a program that inures primarily to the benefit of the minority and reorders the political process in Michigan in such a way as to place special burdens on racial minorities."[80]

The constitutional law of affirmative action is changing. When this volume went to press the entire Sixth Circuit was reviewing the panel opinion in *Coalition to Defend Affirmative Action v. Regents of the University of Michigan* and the Supreme Court had just taken certiorari in *Fisher v. University of Texas at Austin*. The University of Texas relies on two means to achieve a critical mass of persons of color. First, all students in the top 10 percent of their class are admitted to any state university. Second, the university uses an

77. Cal. Const. art. I, §31(a) (1996).

78. Excerpted from Ward Connerly, "Taking it to Michigan: Announcing the 'Michigan Civil Rights Act'," speech delivered at the University of Michigan, July 8, 2003. Available at http://www.nationalreview.com/articles/207428/taking-it-michigan/ward-connerly.

79. State of Michigan, Department of Civil Rights, "Michigan Civil Rights Commission Adopts Resolution Opposing Michigan Civil Rights Initiative," March 11, 2004.

80. *Coalition to Defend Affirmative Action v. Regents of the University of Michigan*, 652 F. 3d 607 (6th Cir. 2011).

Illustration 11-4 Diversity and College Admissions
Source: Signe Wilkinson Editorial Cartoon used with the permission of Signe Wilkinson, the Washington Post Writers Group and the Cartoonist Group. All rights reserved.

evaluation system similar to that used by the University of Michigan School of Law in *Grutter* to fill remaining class seats. The Court of Appeals for the Fifth Circuit unanimously sustained this admissions process on the ground that the Texas race-conscious admissions program was identical to the Michigan Law School race-conscious admission program. The main difference between *Fisher* and *Grutter* may be that Justice Kennedy, who dissented in *Grutter,* is likely to cast the decisive vote in *Fisher*. Kennedy's opinions in *Grutter* and in *Parents Involved* indicate that he generally opposes explicit race-conscious measures but is more open to considering their constitutionality in narrow circumstances than the four more conservative justices on the Roberts Court.

Grutter v. Bollinger, 539 U.S. 306 (2003)

In 1996 Barbara Grutter was denied admission to the University of Michigan School of Law. The admissions policy of the law school at the time sought to "achieve that diversity which has the potential to enrich everyone's education and thus make a law school class stronger than the sum of its parts." The law school sought to achieve this objective partly through personal examination of all applications and partly by requiring each applicant to submit an essay on how they would diversify the institution. While the admissions policy recognized "many possible bases for diversity admissions," the law school explicitly emphasized "one particular type of diversity"—"racial and ethnic diversity with special reference to the inclusion of students from groups which have been historically discriminated against, like African Americans, Hispanics and Native Americans, who without this commitment might not be represented in our student body in meaningful numbers." Michigan claimed not to have fixed quotas, but the law school did seek to enroll a "critical mass" of African-American and other students of color. Grutter claimed that this policy discriminated against her in violation of the equal protection clause of the Fourteenth Amendment. A federal district court declared that the law school's policy was unconstitutional, but that decision was reversed by the Court of Appeals for the Sixth Circuit. Grutter appealed to the Supreme Court of the United States.

Justice O'Connor's majority opinion sustained the Michigan race/diversity policy. Her majority opinion declared that diversity was a compelling state interest and that the Michigan policy was narrowly tailored to achieve that goal. Why does Justice O'Connor declare that the policy was narrowly tailored? Why do the dissents disagree? Was her scrutiny as strict as that used in strict scrutiny cases where laws have discriminated against persons of color? Notice the emphasis the majority opinion places on the amicus briefs submitted by retired military officers and major corporations in favor of affirmative action. The military and major corporations are normally thought to be conservative organizations. Why did they support affirmative action? Do you think that these briefs influenced the result in Grutter*?*

On the same day that Grutter *was decided the Supreme Court by a 6-3 vote declared unconstitutional in* Gratz v. Bollinger *the use of race in undergraduate admissions at the University of Michigan. Michigan evaluated candidates on a 150-point scale. Up to 110 points could be gained through grades and test scores. Michigan awarded students twenty points for being a member of an historically underrepresented group. Persons might also receive twenty points for athletic skills or sociological disadvantage, but such characteristics as leadership skills or demonstrated artistic talent were given far fewer points. Justice O'Connor's crucial concurring opinion in* Gratz *asserted,*

> *[This] selection index, by setting up automatic, predetermined point allocations for the soft variables, ensures that the diversity contributions of applicants cannot be individually assessed. This policy stands in sharp contrast to the law school's admissions plan, which enables admissions officers to make nuanced judgments with respect to the contributions each applicant is likely to make to the diversity of the incoming class.*

Does Justice O'Connor provide a persuasive distinction between constitutional and unconstitutional affirmative action plans? Are the two Michigan plans likely to operate very differently in practice? What affirmative action plans do you believe will pass constitutional muster after Grutter *and* Gratz*? What affirmative action plans do you believe should pass constitutional muster?*

JUSTICE O'CONNOR delivered the opinion of the Court.

. . .

The Equal Protection Clause provides that no State shall "deny to any person within its jurisdiction the equal protection of the laws." Because the Fourteenth Amendment "protects *persons*, not *groups*," all "governmental action based on race—a *group* classification long recognized as in most circumstances irrelevant and therefore prohibited—should be subjected to detailed judicial inquiry to ensure that the *personal* right to equal protection of the laws has not been infringed." *Adarand Constructors, Inc. v. Peña* (1995). . . .

We have held that all racial classifications imposed by government "must be analyzed by a reviewing court under strict scrutiny." This means that such classifications are constitutional only if they are narrowly tailored to further compelling governmental interests. "Absent searching judicial inquiry into the justification for such race-based measures," we have no way to determine what "classifications are 'benign' or 'remedial' and what classifications are in fact motivated by illegitimate notions of racial inferiority or simple racial politics." *Richmond v. J. A. Croson Co.* (1989). We apply strict scrutiny to all racial classifications to "'smoke out' illegitimate uses of race by assuring that [government] is pursuing a goal important enough to warrant use of a highly suspect tool."

Strict scrutiny is not "strict in theory, but fatal in fact." *Adarand Constructors*. Although all governmental uses of race are subject to strict scrutiny, not all are invalidated by it. . . .

. . .

We have long recognized that, given the important purpose of public education and the expansive freedoms of speech and thought associated with the university environment, universities occupy a special niche in our constitutional tradition. . . . Our conclusion that the Law School has a compelling interest in a diverse student body is informed by our view that attaining a diverse student body is at the heart of the Law School's proper institutional mission, and that "good faith" on the part of a university is "presumed" absent "a showing to the contrary."

. . .

These benefits are substantial. As the District Court emphasized, the Law School's admissions policy promotes "cross-racial understanding," helps to break down racial stereotypes, and "enables [students] to better understand persons of different races." These benefits are "important and laudable," because "classroom discussion is livelier, more spirited, and simply more enlightening and interesting" when the students have "the greatest possible variety of backgrounds."

. . . These benefits are not theoretical but real, as major American businesses have made clear that the skills needed in today's increasingly global marketplace can only be developed through exposure to widely diverse people, cultures, ideas, and viewpoints. What is more, high-ranking retired officers and civilian leaders of the United States military assert that, "based on [their] decades of experience," a "highly qualified, racially diverse officer corps . . . is essential to the military's ability to fulfill its principle mission to provide national security." . . . At present, "the military cannot achieve an officer corps that is *both* highly qualified *and* racially diverse unless the service academies and the ROTC used limited race-conscious recruiting and admissions policies." . . .

. . .

In order to cultivate a set of leaders with legitimacy in the eyes of the citizenry, it is necessary that the path to leadership be visibly open to talented and qualified individuals of every race and ethnicity. All members of our heterogeneous society must have confidence in the openness and integrity of the educational institutions that provide this training. As we have recognized, law schools "cannot be effective in isolation from the individuals and institutions with which the law interacts." Access to legal education (and thus the legal profession) must be inclusive of talented and qualified individuals of every race and ethnicity, so that all members of our heterogeneous society may participate in the educational institutions that provide the training and education necessary to succeed in America.

. . .

To be narrowly tailored, a race-conscious admissions program cannot use a quota system—it cannot "insulate each category of applicants with certain desired qualifications from competition with all other applicants." Instead, a university may consider race or ethnicity only as a "'plus' in a particular applicant's file," without "insulating the individual from comparison with all other candidates for the available seats." In other words, an admissions program must be "flexible enough to consider all pertinent elements of diversity in light of the particular qualifications of each applicant, and to place them on the same footing for consideration, although not necessarily according them the same weight."

We find that the Law School's admissions program bears the hallmarks of a narrowly tailored plan. As Justice Powell made clear in *Regents of the University of California v. Bakke* (1978), truly individualized consideration demands that race be used in a flexible, nonmechanical way. It follows from this mandate that universities cannot establish quotas for members of certain racial groups or put members of those groups on separate admissions tracks. Nor can universities insulate applicants who belong to certain racial or ethnic groups from the competition for admission. Universities can, however, consider race or ethnicity more flexibly as a "plus" factor in the context of individualized consideration of each and every applicant.

. . .

Here, the Law School engages in a highly individualized, holistic review of each applicant's file, giving serious consideration to all the ways an applicant might contribute to a diverse educational environment. The Law School affords this individualized consideration to applicants of all races. There is no policy, either *de jure* or *de facto*, of automatic acceptance or rejection based on any single "soft" variable. Unlike the program at issue in *Gratz v. Bollinger* (2003), the Law School awards no mechanical, predetermined diversity "bonuses" based on race or ethnicity. . . .

. . .

. . . All applicants have the opportunity to highlight their own potential diversity contributions through the submission of a personal statement, letters of recommendation, and an essay describing the ways in which the applicant will contribute to the life and diversity of the Law School. What is more, the Law School actually gives substantial weight to diversity factors besides race. The Law School frequently accepts nonminority applicants with grades and test scores lower than underrepresented minority applicants (and other nonminority applicants) who are rejected. . . .

. . .

We take the Law School at its word that it would "like nothing better than to find a race-neutral admissions formula" and will terminate its race-conscious admissions program as soon as practicable. It has been 25 years since Justice Powell first approved the use of race to further an interest in student body diversity in the context of public higher education. Since that time, the number of minority applicants with high grades and test scores has indeed increased. We expect that 25 years from now, the use of racial preferences will no longer be necessary to further the interest approved today.

JUSTICE GINSBURG, with whom JUSTICE BREYER joins, concurring.

. . .

. . . [I]t remains the current reality that many minority students encounter markedly inadequate and unequal educational opportunities. Despite these inequalities, some minority students are able to meet the high threshold requirements set for admission to the country's finest undergraduate and graduate educational institutions. As lower school education in minority communities improves, an increase in the number of such students may be anticipated. From today's vantage point, one may hope, but not firmly forecast, that over the next generation's span, progress toward nondiscrimination and genuinely equal opportunity will make it safe to sunset affirmative action.

CHIEF JUSTICE REHNQUIST, with whom JUSTICE SCALIA, JUSTICE KENNEDY, and JUSTICE THOMAS join, dissenting.

. . .

In practice, the Law School's program bears little or no relation to its asserted goal of achieving "critical mass." Respondents explain that the Law School seeks to accumulate a "critical mass" of *each* underrepresented minority group. But the record demonstrates that the Law School's admissions practices with respect to these groups differ dramatically and cannot be defended under any consistent use of the term "critical mass."

From 1995 through 2000, the Law School admitted between 1,130 and 1,310 students. Of those, between 13 and 19 were Native American, between 91 and 108 were African-Americans, and between 47 and 56 were Hispanic. If the Law School is admitting between 91 and 108 African-Americans in order to achieve "critical mass," thereby preventing African-American students from feeling "isolated or like spokespersons for their race," one would think that a number of the same order of magnitude would be necessary to accomplish the same purpose for Hispanics and Native Americans. Similarly, even if all of the Native American applicants admitted in a given year matriculate, which the record demonstrates is not at all the case, how can this possibly constitute a "critical mass" of Native Americans in a class of over 350 students? In order for this pattern of admission to be consistent with the Law School's explanation of "critical mass," one would have to believe that the objectives of "critical mass" offered by respondents are achieved with only half the number of Hispanics and one-sixth the number of Native Americans as compared to African-Americans. But respondents offer no race-specific reasons for such disparities. Instead, they simply emphasize the importance of achieving "critical mass," without any explanation of why that concept is applied differently among the three underrepresented minority groups.

. . .

But the correlation between the percentage of the Law School's pool of applicants who are members of the three minority groups and the percentage of the admitted applicants who are members of these same groups is far too precise to be dismissed as merely the result of the school paying "some attention to [the] numbers." . . . [F]rom 1995 through 2000 the percentage of admitted applicants who were members of these minority groups closely tracked the percentage of individuals in the school's applicant pool who were from the same groups. . . .

. . .

JUSTICE KENNEDY, dissenting. . . .

JUSTICE SCALIA, with whom JUSTICE THOMAS joins, concurring in part and dissenting in part. . . .

JUSTICE THOMAS, with whom JUSTICE SCALIA joins [in part], concurring in part and dissenting in part.

Frederick Douglass, speaking to a group of abolitionists almost 140 years ago, delivered a message lost on today's majority:

> In regard to the colored people, there is always more that is benevolent, I perceive, than just, manifested towards us. What I ask for the negro is not benevolence, not pity, not sympathy, but simply *justice.* The American people have always been anxious to know what they shall do with us. . . . I have had but one answer from the beginning. Do nothing with us! Your doing with us has already played the mischief with us. Do nothing with us! If the apples will not remain on the tree of their own strength, if they are worm-eaten at the core, if they are early ripe and disposed to fall, let them fall! . . . And if the negro cannot stand on his own legs, let him fall also. All I ask is, give him a chance to stand on his own legs! Let him alone! . . .

Like Douglass, I believe blacks can achieve in every avenue of American life without the meddling of university administrators. Because I wish to see all students succeed whatever their color, I share, in some respect, the sympathies of those who sponsor the type of discrimination advanced by the University of Michigan Law School. The Constitution does not, however, tolerate institutional devotion to the status quo in admissions policies when such devotion ripens into racial discrimination. Nor does the Constitution countenance the unprecedented deference the Court gives to the Law School, an approach inconsistent with the very concept of "strict scrutiny."

. . .

The Constitution abhors classifications based on race, not only because those classifications can harm favored races or are based on illegitimate motives, but also because every time the government places citizens on racial registers and makes race relevant to the provision of burdens or benefits, it demeans us all.

. . .

The interest in remaining elite and exclusive that the majority thinks so obviously critical requires the use of admissions "standards" that, in turn, create the Law School's "need" to discriminate on the basis of race. The Court validates these admissions standards by concluding that alternatives that would require "a dramatic sacrifice of . . . the academic quality of all admitted students." . . . The majority errs, however, because race-neutral alternatives must only be "workable," and do "about as well" *in vindicating the compelling state interest.* The Court never explicitly holds that the Law School's desire to retain the status quo in "academic selectivity" is itself a compelling state interest, and . . . it is not. Therefore, the Law School should be forced to choose between its classroom aesthetic and its exclusionary admissions system—it cannot have it both ways.

. . .

Putting aside the absence of any legal support for the majority's reflexive deference, there is much to be said for the view that the use of tests and other measures to "predict" academic performance is a poor substitute for a system that gives every applicant a chance to prove he can succeed in the study of law. The rallying cry that in the absence of racial discrimination in admissions there would be a true meritocracy ignores the fact that the entire process is poisoned by numerous exceptions to "merit." For example, in the national debate on racial discrimination in higher education admissions, much has been made of the fact that elite institutions utilize a so-called "legacy" preference to give the children of alumni an advantage in admissions. This, and other, exceptions to a "true" meritocracy give the lie to protestations that merit admissions are in fact the order of the day at the Nation's universities. The Equal Protection Clause does not, however, prohibit the use of unseemly legacy preferences or many other kinds of arbitrary admissions procedures. What the Equal Protection Clause does prohibit are classifications made on the basis of race. So while legacy preferences can stand under the Constitution, racial discrimination cannot. I will not twist the Constitution to invalidate legacy preferences or otherwise impose my vision of higher education admissions on the Nation. The majority should similarly stay its impulse to validate faddish racial discrimination the Constitution clearly forbids.

. . .

It is uncontested that each year, the Law School admits a handful of blacks who would be admitted in the absence of racial discrimination. Who can differentiate between those who belong and those who do not? The majority of blacks are admitted to the Law School because of discrimination, and because of this policy all are tarred as undeserving. This problem of stigma does not depend on determinacy as to whether those stigmatized are actually the "beneficiaries" of racial discrimination. When blacks take positions in the highest places of government, industry, or academia, it is an open question today whether their skin color played a part in their advancement. The question itself is the stigma—because either racial discrimination did play a role, in which case the person may be deemed "otherwise unqualified," or it did not, in which case asking the question itself unfairly marks those blacks who would succeed without discrimination. Is this what the Court means by "visibly open"?

. . .

For the immediate future, however, the majority has placed its *imprimatur* on a practice that can only weaken the principle of equality embodied in the Declaration of Independence and the Equal Protection Clause. "Our Constitution is color-blind, and neither knows nor tolerates classes among citizens." *Plessy v. Ferguson* (1896) (Harlan, J., dissenting). It has been nearly 140 years since Frederick Douglass asked the intellectual ancestors of the Law School to "[d]o nothing with us!" and the Nation adopted the Fourteenth Amendment. Now we must wait another 25 years to see this principle of equality vindicated. I therefore respectfully dissent from the remainder of the Court's opinion and the judgment.

Parents Involved in Community Schools v. Seattle School District No. 1, 551 U.S. 701 (2007)

Parents Involved in Community Schools was an organization of parents who had children attending public schools in Seattle, Washington. Seattle had long been plagued with controversy over the racial composition of city schools. Lawsuits led to settlements requiring mandatory busing and race-conscious school assignments to achieve integration. In 1996 the Seattle School Board adopted a new plan to promote integration. Students were allowed to choose which high school they wished to attend. If a high school was oversubscribed, several tiebreakers were used to determine the final assignment. The first was whether a sibling of the applicant was already attending the school. The second was whether assigning an application to a particular school would "serve to bring the school into [racial] balance." At the time three-fifths of the children attending Seattle public schools were children of color. Under the tiebreaker rules, if a high school had fewer than 50 percent students of color, applicants of color would receive preference. If a high school had more than 70 percent students of color, white applicants would receive preference. Parents Involved filed a lawsuit claiming that this policy violated the equal protection clause of the Fourteenth Amendment. The school board responded that race-conscious policies were both a legitimate means for remedying past racial segregation and, if not, that achieving diversity in the public schools was a compelling state interest. The local federal district court sustained the Seattle policy. That decision was reversed by a three-judge panel on the Court of Appeals for the Ninth Circuit. The Ninth Circuit then held an en banc hearing, a hearing in which every justice on the circuit participates, and reinstated the original district court decision sustaining the Seattle law. Parents Involved appealed to the Supreme Court of the United States.

Crystal Meredith was the parent of a school-age child in Louisville, Kentucky. In 2000 the local federal district court declared the Louisville schools fully desegregated. The local federal judge then returned complete control over local decision making to the Board of Education. The next year the Jefferson County Board of Education, in an effort to preserve racial balance in elementary schools, adopted a racial tiebreaker similar to that implemented in Seattle. Meredith sued the school board, claiming that the tiebreaker violated the equal protection clause of the Fourteenth Amendment. Both the local federal district court and the Court of Appeals for the Sixth Circuit sustained the Louisville use of race. Meredith appealed to the Supreme Court of the United States.

Chief Justice Roberts's plurality opinion held that both the Seattle and Louisville plans were unconstitutional. Neither, in his view, served the compelling interest required by Grutter v. Bollinger *(2003). Why does the chief justice reach that conclusion? Why does Justice Breyer disagree? Justice Kennedy filed a concurring opinion. How does his opinion differ from that of the chief justice? Can you outline a policy for integrating schools that Justice Kennedy would think constitutional but the chief justice would not? All the justices claim to be following* Brown v. Board of Education *(1954), but they dispute the core meaning of that case. How do the different justices interpret* Brown*? What is the correct interpretation? How would you apply* Brown *in this case?*

CHIEF JUSTICE ROBERTS announced the judgment of the Court

. . .

It is well established that when the government distributes burdens or benefits on the basis of individual racial classifications, that action is reviewed under strict scrutiny. . . . In order to satisfy this searching standard of review, the school districts must demonstrate that the use of individual racial classifications in the assignment plans here under review is "narrowly tailored" to achieve a "compelling" government interest. . . .

. . . [O]ur prior cases, in evaluating the use of racial classifications in the school context, have recognized two interests that qualify as compelling. The first is the compelling interest of remedying the effects of past intentional discrimination. . . .Yet the Seattle public schools have not shown that they were ever segregated by law, and were not subject to court-ordered desegregation decrees. The Jefferson County public schools were previously segregated by law and were subject to a desegregation decree entered in 1975. In 2000, the District Court that entered that decree dissolved it, finding that Jefferson County had "eliminated the vestiges associated with the former policy of segregation and its pernicious effects," and thus had achieved "unitary" status. . . . Jefferson County accordingly does not rely upon an interest in remedying the effects of past intentional discrimination in defending its present use of race in assigning students. . . .. . .

The second government interest we have recognized as compelling for purposes of strict scrutiny is the interest in diversity in higher education upheld in *Grutter v. Bollinger* (2003). . . .

. . .

In the present cases, by contrast, race is not considered as part of a broader effort to achieve "exposure to widely diverse people, cultures, ideas, and viewpoints" . . . ; race, for some students, is determinative standing alone. . . . It is not simply one factor weighed with others in reaching a decision, as in *Grutter*; it is the factor. . . .

Even when it comes to race, the plans here employ only a limited notion of diversity, viewing race exclusively in white/nonwhite terms in Seattle and black/"other" terms in Jefferson County. . . . But under the Seattle plan, a school with 50 percent Asian-American students and 50 percent white students but no African-American, Native-American, or Latino students would qualify as balanced, while a school with 30 percent Asian-American, 25 percent African-American, 25 percent Latino, and 20 percent white students would not. It is hard to understand how a plan that could allow these results can be viewed as being concerned with achieving enrollment that is "'broadly diverse.'" . . .

. . .

The plans are tied to each district's specific racial demographics, rather than to any pedagogic concept of the level of diversity needed to obtain the asserted educational benefits. In Seattle, the district seeks white enrollment of between 31 and 51 percent (within 10 percent of "the district white average" of 41 percent), and nonwhite enrollment of between 49 and 69 percent (within 10 percent of "the district minority average" of 59 percent). . . . In Jefferson County, by contrast, the district seeks black enrollment of no less than 15 or more than 50 percent, a range designed to be "equally above and below Black student enrollment systemwide." . . .

. . .

Accepting racial balancing as a compelling state interest would justify the imposition of racial proportionality throughout American society, contrary to our repeated recognition that "[a]t the heart of the Constitution's guarantee of equal protection lies the simple command that the Government must treat citizens as individuals, not as simply components of a racial, religious, sexual or national class." . . . Allowing racial balancing as a compelling end in itself would "effectively assur[e] that race will always be relevant in American life, and that the 'ultimate goal' of 'eliminating entirely from governmental decision-making such irrelevant factors as a human being's race' will never be achieved.". . .

. . .

The parties and their amici debate which side is more faithful to the heritage of *Brown*, but the position of the plaintiffs in *Brown* (1954) was spelled out in their brief and could not have been clearer: "[T]he Fourteenth Amendment prevents states from according differential treatment to American children on the basis of their color or race." . . . What do the racial classifications at issue here do, if not accord differential treatment on the basis of race? As counsel who appeared before this Court for the plaintiffs in *Brown* put it: "We have one fundamental contention which we will seek to develop in the course of this argument, and that contention is that no State has any authority under the equal-protection clause of the Fourteenth Amendment to use race as a factor in affording educational opportunities among its citizens." . . . There is no ambiguity in that statement. And it was that position that prevailed in this Court, which emphasized in its remedial opinion that what was "[a]t stake is the personal interest of the plaintiffs in admission to public schools as soon as practicable on a nondiscriminatory basis," and what was required was "determining admission to the public schools on a nonracial basis." . . . What do the racial classifications do in these cases, if not determine admission to a public school on a racial basis?

Before *Brown*, schoolchildren were told where they could and could not go to school based on the color of their skin. The school districts in these cases have not carried the heavy burden of demonstrating that we should allow this once again—even for very different reasons. For schools that never segregated on the basis of race, such as Seattle, or that have removed the vestiges of past segregation, such as Jefferson County, the way "to achieve a system of determining admission to the public schools on a nonracial basis" . . . is to stop assigning students on a racial basis. The way to stop discrimination on the basis of race is to stop discriminating on the basis of race.

JUSTICE THOMAS, concurring.

. . .

Even supposing it mattered to the constitutional analysis, the race-based student assignment programs before us are not as benign as the dissent believes. . . . As these programs demonstrate, every time the government uses racial criteria to "bring the races together,". . . someone gets excluded, and the person excluded suffers an injury solely because of his or her race. The petitioner in the Louisville case received a letter from the school board informing her that her kindergartener would not be allowed to attend the school of petitioner's choosing because of the child's race. . . . This type of exclusion, solely on the basis of race, is precisely the sort of government action that pits the races against one another, exacerbates racial tension, and "provoke[s] resentment among those who believe that they have been wronged by the government's use of race." . . .

. . .

. . . [I]t is far from apparent that coerced racial mixing has any educational benefits, much less that integration is necessary to black achievement. Scholars have differing opinions as to whether educational benefits arise from racial balancing. Some have concluded that black students receive genuine educational benefits. . . . Others have been more circumspect. . . . And some have concluded that there are no demonstrable educational benefits. . . .

. . .

Furthermore, it is unclear whether increased interracial contact improves racial attitudes and relations. One researcher has stated that "the reviews of desegregation and intergroup relations were unable to come to any conclusion about what the probable effects of desegregation were . . . [;] virtually all of the reviewers determined that few, if any, firm conclusions about the impact of desegregation on intergroup relations could be drawn." . . . Some studies have even found that a deterioration in racial attitudes seems to result from racial mixing in schools. . . .

Most of the dissent's criticisms of today's result can be traced to its rejection of the color-blind Constitution. . . . The dissent attempts to marginalize the notion of a color-blind Constitution by consigning it to me and Members of today's plurality. . . . But I am quite comfortable in the company I keep. My view of the Constitution is Justice Harlan's view in *Plessy*: "Our Constitution is color-blind, and neither knows nor tolerates classes among citizens." . . . And my view was the rallying cry for the lawyers who litigated *Brown*. . . .

. . .

The segregationists in *Brown* embraced the arguments the Court endorsed in *Plessy*. Though *Brown* decisively rejected those arguments, today's dissent replicates them to a distressing extent. Thus, the dissent argues that "[e]ach plan embodies the results of local experience and community consultation." . . . Similarly, the segregationists made repeated appeals to societal practice and expectation. . . . The dissent argues that "weight [must be given] to a local school board's knowledge, expertise, and concerns." . . . The dissent argues that today's decision "threatens to substitute for present calm a disruptive round of race-related litigation," . . . and claims that today's decision "risks serious harm to the law and for the Nation." . . . The segregationists also relied upon the likely practical consequences of ending the state-imposed system of racial separation. . . . And foreshadowing today's dissent, the segregationists most heavily relied upon judicial precedent. . . .

. . .

What was wrong in 1954 cannot be right today. Whatever else the Court's rejection of the segregationists' arguments in *Brown* might have established, it certainly made clear that state and local governments cannot take from the Constitution a right to make decisions on the basis of race by adverse possession. The fact that state and local governments had been discriminating on the basis of race for a long time was irrelevant to the *Brown* Court. The fact that racial discrimination was preferable to the relevant communities was irrelevant to the *Brown* Court. And the fact that the state and local governments had relied on statements in this Court's opinions was irrelevant to the *Brown* Court. The same principles guide today's decision. None of the considerations trumpeted by the dissent is relevant to the constitutionality of the school boards' race-based plans because no contextual detail—or collection of contextual details . . . can "provide refuge from the principle that under our Constitution, the government may not make distinctions on the basis of race." . . .

. . .

JUSTICE KENNEDY, concurring in part and concurring in the judgment.

. . .

. . . The plurality opinion is too dismissive of the legitimate interest government has in ensuring all people have equal opportunity regardless of their race. The plurality's postulate that "[t]he way to stop discrimination on the basis of race is to stop discriminating on the basis of race" . . . is not sufficient to decide these cases. Fifty years of experience since *Brown v. Board of Education* . . . should teach us that the problem before us defies so easy a solution. School districts can seek to reach *Brown*'s objective of equal educational opportunity. The plurality opinion is at least open to the interpretation that the Constitution requires school districts to ignore the problem of de facto resegregation in schooling. I cannot endorse that conclusion. To the extent the plurality opinion suggests the Constitution mandates that state and local school authorities must accept the status quo of racial isolation in schools, it is, in my view, profoundly mistaken.

. . .

In the administration of public schools by the state and local authorities it is permissible to consider the racial makeup of schools and to adopt general policies to encourage a diverse student body, one aspect of which is its racial composition. . . . If school authorities are concerned that the student-body compositions of certain schools interfere with the objective of offering an equal educational opportunity to all of their students, they are free to devise race-conscious measures to address the problem in a general way and without treating each student in different fashion solely on the basis of a systematic, individual typing by race.

School boards may pursue the goal of bringing together students of diverse backgrounds and races through other means, including strategic site selection of new schools; drawing attendance zones with general recognition of the demographics of neighborhoods; allocating resources for special programs; recruiting students and faculty in a targeted fashion; and tracking enrollments, performance, and other statistics by race. These mechanisms are race conscious but do not lead to different treatment based on a classification that tells each student he or she is to be defined by race, so it is unlikely any of them would demand strict scrutiny to be found permissible. . . . Executive and legislative branches, which for generations now have considered these types of policies and procedures, should be permitted to employ them with candor and with confidence that a constitutional violation does not occur whenever a decisionmaker considers the impact a given approach might have on students of different races. Assigning to each student a personal designation according to a crude system of individual racial classifications is quite a different matter; and the legal analysis changes accordingly.

. . .

As to the dissent, the general conclusions upon which it relies have no principled limit and would result in the broad acceptance of governmental racial classifications in areas far afield from schooling. The dissent's permissive strict scrutiny (which bears more than a passing resemblance to rational-basis review) could invite widespread governmental deployment of racial classifications. There is every reason to think that, if the dissent's rationale were accepted, Congress, assuming an otherwise proper exercise of its spending authority or commerce power, could mandate either the Seattle or the Jefferson County plans nationwide. There seems to be no principled rule, moreover, to limit the dissent's rationale to the context of public schools. The dissent emphasizes local control, . . . the unique history of school desegregation, . . . and the fact that these plans make less use of race than prior plans, . . . but these factors seem more rhetorical than integral to the analytical structure of the opinion.

. . .

JUSTICE STEVENS, dissenting.

. . .

There is a cruel irony in the chief justice's reliance on our decision in *Brown v. Board of Education*. The first sentence in the concluding paragraph of his opinion states: "Before *Brown*, schoolchildren were told where they could and could not go to school based on the color of their skin." . . . This sentence reminds me of Anatole France's observation: "[T]he majestic equality of the la[w], forbid[s] rich and poor alike to sleep under bridges, to beg in the streets, and to steal their bread." The chief justice fails to note that it was only black schoolchildren who were so ordered; indeed, the history books do not tell stories of white children struggling to attend black schools.

. . .

JUSTICE BREYER, with whom JUSTICE STEVENS, JUSTICE SOUTER, and JUSTICE GINSBURG join, dissenting.

. . . In both Seattle and Louisville, the local school districts began with schools that were highly segregated in fact. In both cities plaintiffs filed lawsuits claiming unconstitutional segregation. . . . In Louisville, a federal court entered a remedial decree. In Seattle, the parties settled after the school district pledged to undertake a desegregation plan. In both cities, the school boards adopted plans designed to achieve integration by bringing about more racially diverse schools. In each city the school board modified its plan several times in light of, for example, hostility to busing, the threat of resegregation, and the desirability of introducing greater student choice. And in each city, the school boards' plans have evolved over time in ways that progressively diminish the plans' use of explicit race-conscious criteria.

. . .

No one here disputes that Louisville's segregation was de jure. But what about Seattle's? Was it de facto? De jure? A mixture? Opinions differed. Or is it that a prior federal court had not adjudicated the matter? Does that make a difference? Is Seattle free on remand to say that its schools were de jure segregated, just as in 1956 a memo for the School Board admitted? . . .

A court finding of de jure segregation cannot be the crucial variable. After all, a number of school districts in the South that the Government or private plaintiffs challenged as segregated by law voluntarily desegregated their schools without a court order—just as Seattle did. . . .

Moreover, Louisville's history makes clear that a community under a court order to desegregate might submit a race-conscious remedial plan before the court dissolved the order, but with every intention of following that plan even after dissolution. How could such a plan be lawful the day before dissolution but then become unlawful the very next day? . . .

. . .

Compelling Interest

. . .

First, there is a historical and remedial element: an interest in setting right the consequences of prior conditions of segregation. This refers back to a time when public schools were highly segregated, often as a result of legal or administrative policies that facilitated racial segregation in public schools. It is an interest in continuing to combat the remnants of segregation caused in whole or in part by these school-related policies, which have often affected not only schools, but also housing patterns, employment practices, economic conditions, and social attitudes. It is an interest in maintaining hard-won gains. And it has its roots in preventing what gradually may become the de facto resegregation of America's public schools. . . .

Second, there is an educational element: an interest in overcoming the adverse educational effects produced by and associated with highly segregated schools. . . . Studies suggest that children taken from those schools and placed in integrated settings often show positive academic gains. . . .

. . .

Third, there is a democratic element: an interest in producing an educational environment that reflects the "pluralistic society" in which our children will live. . . . It is an interest in helping our children learn to work and play together with children of different racial backgrounds. It is an interest in teaching children to engage in the kind of cooperation among Americans of all races that is necessary to make a land of three hundred million people one Nation.

. . .

. . . If we are to insist upon unanimity in the social science literature before finding a compelling interest, we might never find one. I believe only that the Constitution allows democratically elected school boards to make up their own minds as to how best to include people of all races in one America.

Narrow Tailoring

First, the race-conscious criteria at issue only help set the outer bounds of broad ranges. . . . They constitute but one part of plans that depend primarily upon other, nonracial elements.

. . .

Indeed, the race-conscious ranges at issue in these cases often have no effect, either because the particular school is not oversubscribed in the year in question, or because the racial makeup of the school falls within the broad range, or because the student is a transfer applicant or has a sibling at the school.

Second, broad-range limits on voluntary school choice plans are less burdensome, and hence more narrowly tailored . . . than other race-conscious restrictions this Court has previously approved. . . . Here, race becomes a factor only in a fraction of students' non-merit-based assignments—not in large numbers of students' merit-based applications. Moreover, the effect of applying race-conscious criteria here affects potentially disadvantaged students less severely, not more severely, than the criteria at issue in *Grutter*. Disappointed students are not rejected from a State's flagship graduate program; they simply attend a different one of the district's many public schools, which in aspiration and in fact are substantially equal. . . . And, in Seattle, the disadvantaged student loses at most one year at the high school of his choice. . . .

. . .

The wide variety of different integration plans that school districts use throughout the Nation suggests that the problem of racial segregation in schools, including de facto segregation, is difficult to solve. The fact that many such plans have used explicitly racial criteria suggests that such criteria have an important, sometimes necessary, role to play. The fact that the controlling opinion would make a school district's use of such criteria often unlawful (and the plurality's "colorblind" view would make such use always unlawful) suggests that today's opinion will require setting aside the laws of several States and many local communities. . . .

Racial Profiling

Over the last two decades constitutional concerns with racial profiling have heightened. African-American motorists complain about being pulled over for "driving while black." Studies demonstrate that police are far more likely to suspect racial minorities than white persons of committing crime. Incidents of famous African-Americans targeted by police for simply being in affluent neighborhoods exacerbate racial tensions. President Obama held a "beer summit" to ease the racial controversy ignited when Massachusetts police officer James Crowley arrested Harvard Professor Henry Gates, an African-American, for disorderly conduct after Crowley responded to a suspected burglary that turned out to be nothing more than Gates breaking into his residence in posh Cambridge, Massachusetts, after accidentally locking himself out.

A general consensus exists that ordinary racial profiling is both wrong and unconstitutional. Most Americans agree with a 2003 Department of Justice report that asserted, "Racial profiling sends the dehumanizing message to our citizens that they are judged by the color of their skin and harms the criminal justice system by eviscerating the trust that is necessary if law enforcement is to effectively protect our communities." Nevertheless, while most Americans oppose racial profiling in ordinary circumstances, many support racial or religious profiling of Muslims and persons from the Middle East during the War on Terror. The Department of Justice report expressed this concern when stating, "Given the incalculably high stakes involved in such investigations, federal law enforcement officers who are protecting national security or preventing catastrophic events (as well as airport security screeners) may consider race, ethnicity, alienage, and other relevant factors," although the administration officials then narrowed the circumstances in which such profiling could be done.

Proving racial profiling is difficult. In *Whren v. United States* (1996) a unanimous Supreme Court ruled that when police officials had objective reasons for searching a criminal suspect, courts should not consider whether the search was actually motivated by such subjective considerations as the race of the person under suspicion. Justice Scalia's unanimous opinion asserted that past precedents

> foreclose any argument that the constitutional reasonableness of traffic stops depends on the actual motivations of the individual officers involved. . . . [T]he Constitution prohibits selective enforcement of the law based on considerations such as race. But the constitutional basis for objecting to intentionally discriminatory application of laws is the Equal Protection Clause, not the Fourth Amendment. Subjective intentions play no role in ordinary, probable-cause Fourth Amendment analysis.[81]

Some plaintiffs have successfully raised racial-profiling claims in state court. The Superior Court of New Jersey in *State v. Soto* (NJ 1996) suppressed evidence seized by state police officers after finding that "defendants have proven at least a *de facto* policy on the part of the State Police out of the Moorestown Station of targeting blacks for investigation and arrest between April 1988 and May 1991 both south of exit 3 and between exits 1 and 7A of the [New Jersey] Turnpike."[82] Most allega-

81. For more information on racial profiling, see Kevin R. Johnson, "How Racial Profiling in America Became the Law of the Land: *United States v. Brignoni-Ponce* and *Whren v. United States* and the Need for Truly Rebellious Lawyering," *Georgetown Law Journal* 98 (2010): 1005.

82. *State v. Soto*, 734 A. 2d 350 (N.J., 1996).

tions of racial profiling are rejected. The Supreme Judicial Court of Massachusetts in *Commonwealth v. Lora* (MA 2008) articulated the majority view in state courts when asserting,

> The standard must be sufficiently rigorous that its imposition does not unnecessarily intrude on the exercise of powers constitutionally delegated to other branches of government. . . . [T]he initial burden rests on the defendant to produce evidence that similarly situated persons were treated differently because of their race. The practical weight of this burden is admittedly daunting in some cases, but not impossible.[83]

Department of Justice, Fact Sheet: Racial Profiling (June 17, 2003)[84]

The terrorist attacks of September 11, 2001, challenged the growing consensus in the United States against racial profiling by law enforcement officials. Before September 11 prominent liberals and conservatives agreed that, in the words of the second President Bush, racial profiling "was wrong and we will end it in America." After September 11 public opinion polls suggested that most Americans favored special screening at airports of anyone who looked like they hailed from the Middle East or seemed to be a Muslim. The Bush administration was accused of targeting Arab and Muslims noncitizens for special detention and deportment.

The Department of Justice Fact Sheet on Racial Profiling was the Bush administration's effort to reconcile administration behavior after September 11 with previous claims that racial profiling was wrong and unconstitutional. How does the Department of Justice draw the line between constitutional and unconstitutional uses of race? Under what conditions is the Justice Department willing to use race during the War on Terror? Should the Justice Department have made greater or lesser use of race?[85]

Racial Profiling Is Wrong and Will Not Be Tolerated

Racial profiling sends the dehumanizing message to our citizens that they are judged by the color of their skin and harms the criminal justice system by eviscerating the trust that is necessary if law enforcement is to effectively protect our communities.

America Has a Moral Obligation to Prohibit Racial Profiling. Race-based assumptions in law enforcement perpetuate negative racial stereotypes that are harmful to our diverse democracy, and materially impair our efforts to maintain a fair and just society. As Attorney General John Ashcroft said, racial profiling creates a "lose-lose" situation because it destroys the potential for underlying trust that "should support the administration of justice as a societal objective, not just as a law enforcement objective."

Racial Profiling Is Discrimination, and It Taints the Entire Criminal Justice System. Racial profiling rests on the erroneous assumption that any particular individual of one race or ethnicity is more likely to engage in misconduct than any particular individual of other races or ethnicities.

Taking Steps to Ban Racial Profiling:

President Bush Has Directed that Racial Profiling Be Formally Banned. In his February 27, 2001, Address to a Joint Session of Congress, President George W. Bush declared that racial profiling is "wrong and we will end it in America." He directed the Attorney General to review the use by federal law enforcement authorities of race as a factor in conducting stops, searches and other law enforcement investigative procedures. The Attorney General, in turn, instructed the Civil Rights Division to develop guidance for federal officials to ensure an end to racial profiling in federal law enforcement.

. . .

Prohibiting Racial Profiling in Routine or Spontaneous Activities in Domestic Law Enforcement: In making routine or spontaneous law enforcement decisions, such as ordinary traffic stops, federal law enforcement officers may not use race or ethnicity to any degree, except that officers may rely on race and ethnicity if a specific suspect description exists. This prohibition applies even where the use of race or ethnicity might otherwise be lawful.

Routine Patrol Duties Must Be Carried Out Without Consideration of Race. Federal law enforcement agencies

83. *Commonwealth v. Lora*, 451 Mass. 425 (2008).

84. Excerpted from U.S. Department of Justice, "Fact Sheet: Racial Profiling" (June 17, 2003).

85. See Kevin R. Johnson, "Racial Profiling after September 11: The Department of Justice's 2003 Guidelines," *Loyola Law Review* 50 (2004): 67.

and officers sometimes engage in law enforcement activities, such as traffic and foot patrols, that generally do not involve either the ongoing investigation of specific criminal activities or the prevention of catastrophic events or harm to the national security. Rather, their activities are typified by spontaneous action in response to the activities of individuals whom they happen to encounter in the course of their patrols and about whom they have no information other than their observations. These general enforcement responsibilities should be carried out without any consideration of race or ethnicity.

. . .

Stereotyping Certain Races as Having a Greater Propensity to Commit Crimes Is Absolutely Prohibited. Some have argued that overall discrepancies in crime rates among racial groups could justify using race as a factor in general traffic enforcement activities and would produce a greater number of arrests for non-traffic offenses (e.g., narcotics trafficking). We emphatically reject this view. It is patently unacceptable and thus prohibited under this guidance for federal law enforcement officers to engage in racial profiling.

Acting on Specific Suspect Identification Does Not Constitute Impermissible Stereotyping. The situation is different when a federal officer acts on the personal identifying characteristics of potential suspects, including age, sex, ethnicity or race. Common sense dictates that when a victim or witness describes the assailant as being of a particular race, authorities may properly limit their search for suspects to persons of that race. In such circumstances, the federal officer is not acting based on a generalized assumption about persons of different races; rather, the officer is helping locate a specific individual previously identified as involved in crime.

. . .

Taking Steps to Balance National Security Concerns:

Federal Law Enforcement Will Continue Terrorist Identification. Since the terrorist attacks on September 11, 2001, the President has emphasized that federal law enforcement personnel must use every legitimate tool to prevent future attacks, protect our nation's borders, and deter those who would cause devastating harm to our country and its people through the use of biological or chemical weapons, other weapons of mass destruction, suicide hijackings, or any other means.

Therefore, the racial profiling guidance recognizes that race and ethnicity may be used in terrorist identification, but only to the extent permitted by the nation's laws and the Constitution. The policy guidance emphasizes that, even in the national security context, the constitutional restriction on use of generalized stereotypes remains.

. . .

The Constitution Prohibits Consideration of Race or Ethnicity in Law Enforcement Decisions in All But the Most Exceptional Instances. Given the incalculably high stakes involved in such investigations, federal law enforcement officers who are protecting national security or preventing catastrophic events (as well as airport security screeners) may consider race, ethnicity, alienage, and other relevant factors. Constitutional provisions limiting government action on the basis of race are wide-ranging and provide substantial protections at every step of the investigative and judicial process. Accordingly, this policy will honor the rule of law and promote vigorous protection of our national security.

Federal Law Enforcement Must Guard Against Uncertain Threats of Terrorism. Because terrorist organizations might aim to engage in unexpected acts of catastrophic violence in any available part of the country (indeed, in multiple places simultaneously, if possible), there can be no expectation that the information must be specific to a particular locale or even to a particular identified scheme.

Even in the National Security Context, Reliance Upon Generalized Stereotypes Is Restricted by the Constitution. For example, at the security entrance to a federal courthouse, a man who appears to be of a particular ethnicity properly submits his briefcase for x-ray screening and passes through the metal detector. The inspection of the briefcase reveals nothing amiss. The man does not activate the metal detector, and there is nothing suspicious about his activities or appearance. Absent any threat warning or other particular reason to suspect that those of the man's apparent ethnicity pose a heightened danger to the courthouse, the federal security screener may not order the man to undergo a further inspection solely because of his apparent ethnicity.

C. Gender

Most Americans are committed to some form of gender equality. The Democratic Party platform in 2008 and 2012 included specific provisions endorsing women's rights. After declaring, "We believe that our daughters should have the same opportunities as our sons," Democrats in 2008 declared, "We will pass the 'Lilly Ledbetter' Act, which will make it easier to combat pay discrimination; we will pass the Fair Pay Act; and we will modernize the Equal Pay Act." Contemporary Republican Party platforms announce a commitment to equality under law that included women. The party platform in 2008 declared, "We consider discrimination based on sex, race, age, religion, creed, disability, or national origin to be immoral, and we will strongly enforce anti-discrimination statutes."

Contemporary controversies over gender equality have shifted from constitutional questions to the interpretation of federal anti-discrimination law. The "Lilly Ledbetter Act" in the Democratic Party platform referred to proposed legislation reversing the Supreme Court's decision in *Ledbetter v. Goodyear Tire & Rubber Co.* (2007). That decision held that federal law required victims of gender discrimination to file suit within 180 days after the discrimination occurred, even if they were unaware of the discrimination. After President Obama was elected, Congress almost immediately revised the federal code so that persons were excused from timely filing when they were unaware that discrimination was taking place. In *Oncale v. Sundowner Offshore Services, Inc.* (1998) both women and gay Americans gained rights when the Supreme Court interpreted federal anti-discrimination law as prohibiting sexual harassment.

Fewer struggles are taking place over federal constitutional law. *United States v. Virginia* (1996) is the most important decision on gender rights handed down in the Contemporary Era. A 7-1 majority declared that women had a constitutional right to be admitted to the Virginia Military Institute. Justice Ginsburg's majority opinion insisted that laws providing different treatment on the basis of gender required "an exceedingly persuasive justification" to pass constitutional muster, a standard some thought tougher than the previous requirement that such laws be a substantial means to an important government end. The Supreme Court has sustained some gender classifications. *Tuan Anh Nguyen v. I.N.S.* (2001) upheld federal laws that provide more onerous requirements for fathers to establish paternity than are required for mothers to establish maternity when a child is born out of wedlock and the other parent is not a citizen of the United States. Justice Kennedy's majority opinion asserted, "The critical importance of the Government's interest in ensuring some opportunity for a tie between citizen father and foreign born child . . . is a reasonable substitute for the opportunity manifest between mother and child at the time of birth."

The justices have become increasingly skeptical of congressional legislation enforcing gender equality. In *Nevada Department of Human Resources v. Hibbs* (2003) the Court, by a 6-3 vote, sustained the provisions in the Family Medical Leave Act (FMLA) that entitled state employees to take time off to care for sick relatives. Chief Justice Rehnquist asserted, "The impact of the discrimination targeted by the FMLA, which is based on mutually reinforcing stereotypes that only women are responsible for family caregiving and that men lack domestic responsibility, is significant." *Coleman v. Court of Appeals of Maryland* (2012), however, declared unconstitutional the provision in the FMLA that permitted state employees to have up to twelve weeks of leave when they were seriously ill. Justice Kennedy's majority opinion asserted, "To the extent, then, that the self-care provision addresses neutral leave policies with a disparate impact on women, it is not directed at a pattern of constitutional violations." The more important difference between *Hibbs* and *Coleman* may be that two justices in the *Hibbs* majority (Chief Justice Rehnquist and Justice O'Connor) had left the bench and been replaced by two justices (Chief Justice Roberts and Justice Alito) more skeptical of federal power.

State courts are confronting a wider variety of constitutional issues, particularly issues applying state equal rights amendments. The vast majority of state constitutions contain recently adopted provisions prohibiting gender discrimination. Most, but not all, state courts interpret these amendments as requiring strict scrutiny for laws that distinguish between men and women. Nevertheless, important differences exist. Several state courts interpret state equal rights amendments as requiring that states fund medically necessary abortions. The Supreme Court of New Mexico in *New Mexico Right to Choose/NARAL v. Johnson* (NM 1998) held that a state law restricting funding for abortion "undoubtedly singles out for less favorable treatment a gender-linked condition that is unique to women," and for that reason is "presumptively unconstitutional."[86] Others state courts insist that funding restrictions do not violate state constitutional bans on gender discrimination. The Supreme Court of Texas in *Bell v. Low*

86. *New Mexico Right to Choose/NARAL v. Johnson*, 986 P.2d 450 (NM 1998).

Income Women of Texas (TX 2002) stated, "To say that the State's funding restriction discriminates on the basis of pregnancy, which in turn is gender based, misses the mark. The classification here is not so much directed at women as a class as it is abortion as a medical treatment, which, because it involves a potential life, has no parallel as a treatment method."[87]

United States v. Virginia, 518 U.S 515 (1996)

The United States in 1990 brought a lawsuit against Virginia on behalf of several women who wished to attend Virginia Military Institute (VMI), a public, all-male university. The local federal district court sided with Virginia, concluding that single-sex education benefited both sexes and that women could not be admitted to VMI without severely disrupting the educational mission of that institution. After a federal circuit court reversed that decision on the ground that diversity was not promoted by restricting military education to men, Virginia established a parallel all-women's program, Virginia Women's Institute for Leadership (VWIL), at Mary Baldwin College. The all-women program was similar in some respects to the education offered at VMI but did not include the military environment. Nor, as all parties agreed, did VWIL enjoy the same reputation and alumni network as VMI. Despite these differences, the federal district court again sided with Virginia. This time, a divided Court of Appeals for the Fourth Circuit declared that Virginia had adequately provided diverse educational choices for state men and women. The United States appealed to the Supreme Court.

The Supreme Court by a 7-1 vote declared that VMI was constitutionally required to admit women. Justice Ginsburg's majority opinion insisted that all-male education at VMI was not intended to promote diverse educational choices, that co-education would not disrupt educational practices at VMI, and that VWIL was not an adequate substitute for the educational experience offered at the all-male military academy. Justice Ginsburg claimed that gender distinctions required "an exceedingly persuasive justification" to pass constitutional muster. Is this standard identical to intermediate scrutiny, more like strict scrutiny, or somewhere in between? The majority opinion places great emphasis on historical practices that barred women from higher education, often on the basis of pseudoscientific claims that higher education would damage female reproductive organs. Both the concurring and dissenting opinions insist that only contemporary history should be considered when evaluating the purpose of all-male universities. Who has the better argument? A fairly high probability exists that more women would prefer the program at VWIL than the program at VMI. If this is correct, why does Justice Ginsburg, a champion of women's rights and gender equality, insist that women must be admitted to VMI? Is Justice Scalia correct that the principles she advances, if followed consistently, will require abandoning all public single-sex schools and probably prohibit under present federal law any federal financial aid to private single-sex colleges? Is that a constitutional good or wrong?

JUSTICE GINSBURG delivered the opinion of the Court.

. . .

Parties who seek to defend gender-based government action must demonstrate an "exceedingly persuasive justification" for that action. Without equating gender classifications, for all purposes, to classifications based on race or national origin, the Court . . . has carefully inspected official action that closes a door or denies opportunity to women (or to men). . . . To summarize the Court's current directions for cases of official classification based on gender: Focusing on the differential treatment or denial of opportunity for which relief is sought, the reviewing court must determine whether the proffered justification is "exceedingly persuasive." The burden of justification is demanding and it rests entirely on the State. . . . The State must show "at least that the [challenged] classification serves 'important governmental objectives and that the discriminatory means employed' are 'substantially related to the achievement of those objectives.'" . . . The justification must be genuine, not hypothesized or invented *post hoc* in response to litigation. And it must not rely on overbroad generalizations about the different talents, capacities, or preferences of males and females. . . .

. . .

"Inherent differences" between men and women, we have come to appreciate, remain cause for celebration, but not for denigration of the members of either

87. *Bell v. Low Income Women of Texas*, 95 S.W.3d 253 (TX 2002). For good surveys of the status of gender rights in contemporary federal and state constitutional law, see Martha F. Davis, "The Equal Rights Amendment: Then and Now," *Columbia Journal of Gender and Law* 17 (2008): 419; and Lisa Baldez, Lee Epstein, and Andrew D. Martin, "Does the U.S. Constitution Need an Equal Rights Amendment? *Journal of Legal Studies* 35 (2006): 243.

sex or for artificial constraints on an individual's opportunity. Sex classifications may be used to compensate women "for particular economic disabilities [they have] suffered," . . . to advance full development of the talent and capacities of our Nation's people. But such classifications may not be used, as they once were . . . to create or perpetuate the legal, social, and economic inferiority of women.

. . .

. . . Virginia . . . asserts two justifications in defense of VMI's exclusion of women. First, the Commonwealth contends, "single-sex education provides important educational benefits," . . . and the option of single-sex education contributes to "diversity in educational approaches." . . . Second, the Commonwealth argues, "the unique VMI method of character development and leadership training," the school's adversative approach, would have to be modified were VMI to admit women. . . .

. . .

Neither recent nor distant history bears out Virginia's alleged pursuit of diversity through single-sex educational options. In 1839, when the Commonwealth established VMI, a range of educational opportunities for men and women was scarcely contemplated. . . . In admitting no women, VMI followed the lead of the Commonwealth's flagship school, the University of Virginia, founded in 1819.

. . .

Virginia describes the current absence of public single-sex higher education for women as "an historical anomaly." . . . But the historical record indicates action more deliberate than anomalous: First, protection of women against higher education; next, schools for women far from equal in resources and stature to schools for men; finally, conversion of the separate schools to coeducation.

. . .

The District Court forecast from expert witness testimony, and the Court of Appeals accepted, that coeducation would materially affect "at least these three aspects of VMI's program—physical training, the absence of privacy, and the adversative approach." . . . And it is uncontested that women's admission would require accommodations, primarily in arranging housing assignments and physical training programs for female cadets. . . . It is also undisputed, however, that "the VMI methodology could be used to educate women." . . . [S]ome women may prefer it to the methodology a women's college might pursue. . . . In sum, . . . "neither the goal of producing citizen soldiers," VMI's *raison d'être,* "nor VMI's implementing methodology is inherently unsuitable to women."

. . .

It may be assumed, for purposes of this decision, that most women would not choose VMI's adversative method. . . . The issue, however, is not whether "women—or men—should be forced to attend VMI"; rather, the question is whether the Commonwealth can constitutionally deny to women who have the will and capacity, the training and attendant opportunities that VMI uniquely affords.

The notion that admission of women would downgrade VMI's stature, destroy the adversative system and, with it, even the school, is a judgment hardly proved, a prediction hardly different from other "self-fulfilling prophec[ies]," . . . once routinely used to deny rights or opportunities. When women first sought admission to the bar and access to legal education, concerns of the same order were expressed. . . .

Women's successful entry into the federal military academies, and their participation in the Nation's military forces, indicate that Virginia's fears for the future of VMI may not be solidly grounded. The Commonwealth's justification for excluding all women from "citizen-soldier" training for which some are qualified, in any event, cannot rank as "exceedingly persuasive," as we have explained and applied that standard.

. . .

Virginia proposed a separate program, different in kind from VMI and unequal in tangible and intangible facilities. . . .

. . .

Virginia Women's Institution for Leadership (VWIL) students participate in ROTC and a "largely ceremonial" Virginia Corps of Cadets, . . . but Virginia deliberately did not make VWIL a military institute. The VWIL House is not a military-style residence and VWIL students need not live together throughout the 4-year program, eat meals together, or wear uniforms during the schoolday. . . . VWIL students thus do not experience the "barracks" life "crucial to the VMI experience," the spartan living arrangements designed to foster an "egalitarian ethic." . . .

VWIL students receive their "leadership training" in seminars, externships, and speaker series, . . . episodes and encounters lacking the "[p]hysical rigor, mental stress, . . . minute regulation of behavior, and indoctrination in desirable values" made hallmarks of VMI's citizen-soldier training. . . . Kept away from the pressures, hazards, and psychological bonding characteristic of VMI's adversative training, . . . VWIL students will not know the "feeling of tremendous accomplishment" commonly experienced by VMI's successful cadets. . . .

Virginia maintains that these methodological differences are "justified pedagogically," based on "important differences between men and women in learning and developmental needs," "psychological and sociological differences" Virginia describes as "real" and "not stereotypes." . . .

. . .

In myriad respects other than military training, VWIL does not qualify as VMI's equal. VWIL's student body, faculty, course offerings, and facilities hardly match VMI's. Nor can the VWIL graduate anticipate the benefits associated with VMI's 157-year history, the school's prestige, and its influential alumni network.

. . .

A prime part of the history of our Constitution, is the story of the extension of constitutional rights and protections to people once ignored or excluded. VMI's story continued as our comprehension of "We the People" expanded. . . . There is no reason to believe that the admission of women capable of all the activities required of VMI cadets would destroy the Institute rather than enhance its capacity to serve the "more perfect Union."

JUSTICE THOMAS took no part in the consideration or decision of these cases.

CHIEF JUSTICE REHNQUIST, concurring in the judgment.

. . .

While terms like "important governmental objective" and "substantially related" are hardly models of precision, they have more content and specificity than does the phrase "exceedingly persuasive justification." That phrase is best confined, as it was first used, as an observation on the difficulty of meeting the applicable test, not as a formulation of the test itself. . . .

. . .

Before this Court, Virginia has sought to justify VMI's single-sex admissions policy primarily on the basis that diversity in education is desirable, and that while most of the public institutions of higher learning in the Commonwealth are coeducational, there should also be room for single-sex institutions. I agree with the Court that there is scant evidence in the record that this was the real reason that Virginia decided to maintain VMI as men only. But, unlike the majority, I would consider only evidence that postdates our [contemporary decisions on gender classifications] and would draw no negative inferences from the Commonwealth's actions before that time. . . .

Even if diversity in educational opportunity were the Commonwealth's actual objective, the Commonwealth's position would still be problematic. The difficulty with its position is that the diversity benefited only one sex; there was single-sex public education available for men at VMI, but no corresponding single-sex public education available for women. . . .

. . .

Accordingly, the remedy should not necessarily require either the admission of women to VMI or the creation of a VMI clone for women. An adequate remedy in my opinion might be a demonstration by Virginia that its interest in educating men in a single-sex environment is matched by its interest in educating women in a single-sex institution. To demonstrate such, the Commonwealth does not need to create two institutions with the same number of faculty Ph.D.'s, similar SAT scores, or comparable athletic fields. . . . Nor would it necessarily require that the women's institution offer the same curriculum as the men's; one could be strong in computer science, the other could be strong in liberal arts. It would be a sufficient remedy, I think, if the two institutions offered the same quality of education and were of the same overall caliber.

. . .

In the end, the women's institution Virginia proposes, VWIL, fails as a remedy, because it is distinctly inferior to the existing men's institution and will continue to be for the foreseeable future. VWIL simply is not, in any sense, the institution that VMI is. In particular, VWIL is a program appended to a private college, not a self-standing institution; and VWIL is substantially underfunded as compared to VMI. I therefore ultimately agree with the Court that Virginia has not provided an adequate remedy.

JUSTICE SCALIA, dissenting.

Today the Court shuts down an institution that has served the people of the Commonwealth of Virginia with pride and distinction for over a century and a half.

To achieve that desired result, it rejects (contrary to our established practice) the factual findings of two courts below, sweeps aside the precedents of this Court, and ignores the history of our people. As to facts: It explicitly rejects the finding that there exist "gender-based developmental differences" supporting Virginia's restriction of the "adversative" method to only a men's institution, and the finding that the all-male composition of the Virginia Military Institute (VMI) is essential to that institution's character. As to precedent: It drastically revises our established standards for reviewing sex-based classifications. And as to history: It counts for nothing the long tradition, enduring down to the present, of men's military colleges supported by both States and the Federal Government.

. . .

. . . [I]n my view the function of this Court is to *preserve* our society's values regarding (among other things) equal protection, not to *revise* them; to prevent backsliding from the degree of restriction the Constitution imposed upon democratic government, not to prescribe, on our own authority, progressively higher degrees. For that reason it is my view that, whatever abstract tests we may choose to devise, they cannot supersede—and indeed ought to be crafted *so as to reflect*—those constant and unbroken national traditions that embody the people's understanding of ambiguous constitutional texts. More specifically, it is my view that "when a practice not expressly prohibited by the text of the Bill of Rights bears the endorsement of a long tradition of open, widespread, and unchallenged use that dates back to the beginning of the Republic, we have no proper basis for striking it down."

The all-male constitution of VMI comes squarely within such a governing tradition. Founded by the Commonwealth of Virginia in 1839 and continuously maintained by it since, VMI has always admitted only men. And in that regard it has not been unusual. For almost all of VMI's more than a century and a half of existence, its single-sex status reflected the uniform practice for government-supported military colleges. . . . [T]he tradition of having government-funded military schools for men is as well rooted in the traditions of this country as the tradition of sending only men into military combat. The people may decide to change the one tradition, like the other, through democratic processes; but the assertion that either tradition has been unconstitutional through the centuries is not law, but politics-smuggled-into-law.

. . .

Only the amorphous "exceedingly persuasive justification" phrase, and not the standard elaboration of intermediate scrutiny, can be made to yield this conclusion that VMI's single-sex composition is unconstitutional because there exist several women (or, one would have to conclude under the Court's reasoning, a single woman) willing and able to undertake VMI's program. Intermediate scrutiny has never required a least-restrictive-means analysis, but only a "substantial relation" between the classification and the state interests that it serves. . . . There is simply no support in our cases for the notion that a sex-based classification is invalid unless it relates to characteristics that hold true in every instance.

. . .

. . . [I]f the question of the applicable standard of review for sex-based classifications were to be regarded as an appropriate subject for reconsideration, the stronger argument would be not for elevating the standard to strict scrutiny, but for reducing it to rational-basis review. The latter certainly has a firmer foundation in our past jurisprudence: Whereas no majority of the Court has ever applied strict scrutiny in a case involving sex-based classifications, we routinely applied rational-basis review until the 1970's. . . . It is hard to consider women a "discrete and insular minorit[y]" unable to employ the "political processes ordinarily to be relied upon," when they constitute a majority of the electorate. And the suggestion that they are incapable of exerting that political power smacks of the same paternalism that the Court so roundly condemns. . . .

. . . As an initial matter, Virginia demonstrated at trial that "[a] substantial body of contemporary scholarship and research supports the proposition that, although males and females have significant areas of developmental overlap, they also have differing developmental needs that are deep-seated. . . . This finding alone, which even this Court cannot dispute, should be sufficient to demonstrate the constitutionality of VMI's all-male composition.

. . .

The Court's analysis at least has the benefit of producing foreseeable results. Applied generally, it means that whenever a State's ultimate objective is "great enough to accommodate women" (as it always will be), then the State will be held to have violated the Equal Protection Clause if it restricts to men even one means by which it pursues that objective—no matter how few women are interested in pursuing the objective by that means, no matter how much the single-sex program will have to be changed if both sexes are admitted, and no matter how beneficial that program has theretofore been to its participants.

The Court argues that VMI would not have to change very much if it were to admit women. . . . The principal response to that argument is that it is irrelevant: If VMI's single-sex status is substantially related to the government's important educational objectives, as I have demonstrated above and as the Court refuses to discuss, that concludes the inquiry. There should be no debate in the federal judiciary over "how much" VMI would be required to change if it admitted women and whether that would constitute "too much" change.

But if such a debate were relevant, the Court would certainly be on the losing side. The District Court found as follows: "[T]he evidence establishes that key elements of the adversative VMI educational system, with its focus on barracks life, would be fundamentally altered, and the distinctive ends of the system would be thwarted, if VMI were forced to admit females and to make changes necessary to accommodate their needs and interests." . . . Changes that the District Court's detailed analysis found would be required include new allowances for personal privacy in the barracks, such as locked doors and coverings on windows, which would detract from VMI's approach of regulating minute details of student behavior, "contradict the principle that everyone is constantly subject to scrutiny by everyone else," and impair VMI's "total egalitarian approach" under which every student must be "treated alike"; changes in the physical training program, which would reduce "[t]he intensity and aggressiveness of the current program"; and various modifications in other respects of the adversative training program that permeates student life. . . .

. . .

VWIL was carefully designed by professional educators who have long experience in educating young women. The program *rejects* the proposition that there is a "difference in the respective spheres and destinies of man and woman" . . . and is designed to "provide an all-female program that will achieve substantially similar outcomes [to VMI's] in an all-female environment." . . .

. . .

Under the constitutional principles announced and applied today, single-sex public education is unconstitutional.

. . . This is especially regrettable because, as the District Court here determined, educational experts in recent years have increasingly come to "suppor[t] [the] view that substantial educational benefits flow from a single-gender environment, be it male or female, *that cannot be replicated in a coeducational setting*." . . .

D. Native Americans

The constitutional politics of Native American rights is relatively quiet. Native Americans who do not live on reservations enjoy the same rights as other Americans. Native Americans who live on reservations are protected by the Indian Bill of Rights (1968), which requires tribal governments to respect many, but not all, provisions in the first ten amendments. State courts have ruled that the provisions in the Indian Bill of Rights should be interpreted in a manner identical to interpretation of the corresponding provisions in the Constitution of the United States. The Supreme Court of South Dakota in *State v. Madsen* (SD 2009) ruled that tribal courts were obligated to exclude illegally obtained evidence whenever a federal or state court under the Fourth Amendment would be obligated to exclude illegally obtained evidence. Chief Justice Gilbertson asserted, "The enactment of the Indian Civil Rights Act against the backdrop of *Mapp v. Ohio* (1961) evidences congressional intent to graft the Fourth Amendment exclusionary rule onto [that measure]."[88] *United States v. Lara* (2004) held that tribal courts were independent authorities and did not exercise delegated federal power. For this reason, the judicial majority concluded that the double jeopardy clause in the Fifth Amendment was not violated when a person convicted of a crime by a tribal court was subsequently charged with committing a federal crime for the same offense. Justice Breyer's opinion also concluded that the equal protection clause was not violated when Congress permitted tribal courts to try nonmember Native Americans for crimes committed on their lands.

88. *State v. Madsen*, 760 N.W.2d 370 (SC 2009).

VI. Criminal Justice

MAJOR DEVELOPMENTS

- Supreme Court protects rights of suspected terrorists detained by the United States
- Exclusionary rule and *Miranda* warnings remain the law of the land
- Narrow judicial majorities cut back on capital punishment and life sentences without parole for juveniles

Contemporary liberals and conservatives are engaged in trench warfare over domestic constitutional criminal procedure. Neither liberal proponents of due process models of constitutional criminal procedure, which emphasize protecting rights, nor conservative proponents of crime-control models of constitutional criminal procedure, which emphasize reducing crime, have moved the constitutional status quo more than a few legal feet. Capital punishment remains constitutional, even as narrow judicial majorities rule that the mentally retarded and minors may not be executed. The exclusionary rule and *Miranda* warnings remain the law of the land, although the Supreme Court often narrows the precise circumstances in which either is required. The Anti-Terrorism and Effective Death Penalty Act of 1996, which severely limited postconviction appeals, is the only major decision that arguably significantly altered constitutional understandings about criminal constitutional procedure inherited from the Reagan Era.

Several factors explain the relative stasis of contemporary constitutional criminal procedure. Neither liberal Democrats nor conservative Republicans have gained the control over national institutions necessary to make a due process or criminal-control model the official law of the land. As Figure 11-2 indicates, the contemporary justices differ dramatically in their willingness to support claimants in criminal justice cases. Justices Kennedy and O'Connor, the swing votes on the Rehnquist and Roberts Courts, vote as if they believe the conservative Reagan Revolution has gone far enough but are rarely willing to make liberal decisions that have far-reaching consequences. The legal profession and perhaps American constitutional culture accept the landmark cases decided during the Great Society. Many judges take *Mapp v. Ohio* (1961) and *Miranda v. Arizona* (1966) for granted. Constitutional debate is limited to more narrow questions about the precise circumstances in which the exclusionary rule and *Miranda* warnings should apply. The war on drugs, however, sometimes moves more moderate justices to narrow constitutional protections. In *Board of Education of Independent School District No. 92 of Pottawatomie County v. Earls* (2002) a 5-4 majority ruled that the Fourth Amendment did not bar random drug testing of all students participating in extracurricular activities. Other decisions cast doubt on the scope of any "drug exception" to the rights of persons suspected of crime. *Kyllo v. United States* (2001) ruled that prosecutors could not introduce drugs found after a thermal imager revealed the probable use of heat lamps used to grow marijuana.

The War on Terror is the lead story for contemporary constitutional criminal procedure. Both the Bush and Obama administrations have insisted that federal authorities have broad powers to investigate, detain, and punish suspected terrorists. Congress generally supports executive claims that constitutional rights provisions should be interpreted narrowly when the federal government is seeking to prevent terrorist activity. The USA Patriot Act of 2001 limited rights and expanded federal power to investigate terrorist activities. The Detainee Treatment Act of 2005 sharply curtailed habeas corpus rights for persons detained in the War on Terror. The Supreme Court was less supportive of Bush administration policies. The justices in *Hamdi v. Rumsfeld* (2004), *Hamdan v. Rumsfeld* (2006), and *Boumediene v. Bush* (2008) placed limits on national capacity to detain persons suspected of terrorism or try them before military tribunals. These decisions were hailed by civil libertarians but did little to change American policy. Justices played almost no role on other matters, most notably enhanced interrogation techniques and targeted assassinations, whose constitutionality continues to be debated solely in the elected branches of government and general media.

A. Due Process and Habeas Corpus

The domestic constitutional politics and law of due process and habeas corpus has not changed substantially since the end of the Reagan Era. State laws and constitutional decisions giving defendants rights to DNA testing under certain circumstances aside, persons accused of crime have neither gained nor lost significant due process rights. Much to the annoyance of conservatives and many state officials, federal courts

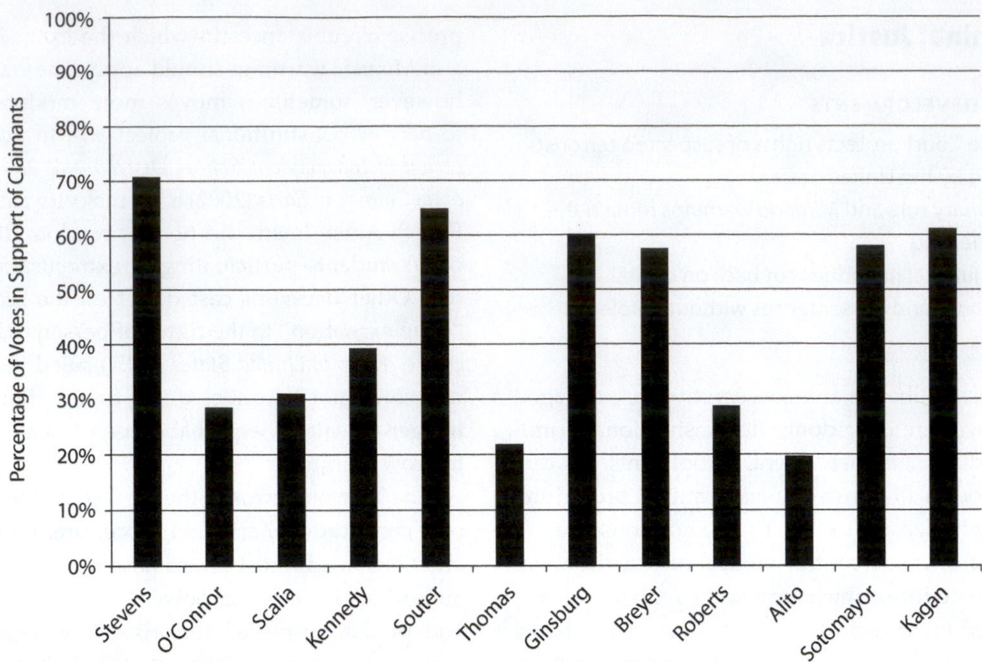

Figure 11-2 Individual Justice Support for Claimants in Criminal Procedure Cases before the Roberts Court
Note: Justices listed in order of appointment.

continue to correct numerous constitutional errors in habeas corpus proceedings. Much to the annoyance of liberals, habeas petitioners must typically have objected to the alleged constitutional error at trial (*Wainwright v. Sykes* [1977]), included all their habeas claims in their first habeas corpus petition (*McCleskey v. Zant* [1991]), and cannot allege new rules of law (*Teague v. Lane* [1989]).

Congress did significantly restrict habeas corpus rights when passing the Antiterrorism and Effective Death Penalty Act of 1996 (AEDPA). That measure, originally designed to counter domestic terrorism, focused far more on habeas corpus procedures in capital cases. Congress, with the blessing of President Clinton, placed time limits on when persons could file habeas corpus petitions, limited relief to cases in which the state court decision "was contrary to, or involved an unreasonable application of, clearly established Federal law" or "an unreasonable determination of the facts in light of the evidence," sharply limited the circumstances under which persons in prison could present second or successive habeas corpus presentations, and provided special procedures designed to streamline the death penalty process. The Supreme Court in *Felker v. Turpin* (1996) sustained the AEDPA.

New scientific technologies are confounding constitutional criminal procedure. Persons accused of crime are asserting a due process right to access DNA testing and claiming that states violate due process when potential DNA evidence is destroyed. Many prosecutors complain of the "CSI effect." Jurors, reared on television crime lab shows, are often unwilling to convict unless the state provides scientific tests linking the defendant to the crime.

The present law on DNA evidence is in a state of flux. The vast majority of states and the federal government have passed laws permitting DNA evidence and other scientific tests to be introduced into evidence under specific conditions. The Federal Innocence Protection Act of 2004 entitles defendants to have access to "DNA testing of specific evidence" when the tests are likely to be reliable and might "establish the actual innocence of the applicant of the Federal or State offense."[89]

Whether defendants currently have a constitutional right to DNA testing depends on the court and the proceeding. The Supreme Court in *District Attorney's*

89. 118 U.S. Stat. 2278, 2279–80 (2004).

Office for the Third Judicial District v. Osborne (2009) ruled that persons in postconviction hearings did not have a federal constitutional right to obtain DNA evidence. That ruling, however, was limited to postconviction hearings and may even have been limited by the peculiar facts of the case. The Supreme Court of South Dakota in *Jenner v. Dooley* (SD 2009) adopted more liberal rules under the state constitution. The justices asserted,

> Punishment of the innocent may be the worst of all injustices. To avoid such a grievous outcome courts should solemnly consider reopening a case if a "truly persuasive" showing of actual innocence lies close at hand. . . . When newly developed scientific procedures can establish innocence in a conviction laden with doubt, then elementary fairness may compel the new testing. . . . Yet, not every convict who cries innocence will be able to reopen a case to analyze old evidence. Our system of justice will hold little respect if its judgments are never final. Only in extraordinary circumstances should a court allow post-conviction scientific testing.
>
> After careful consideration, we have formulated the following guidelines for when post-conviction scientific analysis may be authorized: First, the evidence and test results must meet the [constitutional] standard for scientific reliability. A showing must be made that if the matter were presently tried the defendant would be entitled to the testing and the results would be admissible. Second, because convicted defendants may not obtain reconsideration of their cases whenever some new technology promises to reveal another angle on the evidence against them, it must be shown that a favorable result using the latest scientific procedures would most likely produce an acquittal in a new trial. An exorbitant cost may be grounds for denial, for example, especially if anticipated test results promise to be less than definite. If testing is allowed, the court should impose reasonable safeguards to ensure the preservation and integrity of the evidence. With biological evidence, courts have generally found post-conviction testing most suitable when (a) identity of a single perpetrator is at issue; (b) evidence against the defendant is so weak as to suggest real doubt of guilt; (c) the scientific evidence, if any, used to obtain the conviction has been impugned; and, (d) the nature of the biological evidence makes testing results on the issue of identity virtually dispositive.[90]

The Antiterrorism and Effective Death Penalty Act (1996)

American constitutional politics took a sharp turn toward crime-control models of criminal procedure after Timothy McVeigh detonated an explosion outside a federal office building in Oklahoma City, Oklahoma, killing 168 people. Although the original purpose of the AEDPA was to combat terrorism, debate soon turned to habeas corpus and streamlining capital punishment procedures. The most important provisions in the bill codified the Supreme Court's decision in Teague v. Lane *(1989) to grant habeas corpus only if the state court had failed to follow established federal law. The measure also sharply limited second or successive habeas corpus proceedings, and streamlined the appeals process for capitally sentenced prisoners. Other provisions of the AEDPA prohibited persons from providing any material support to identified terrorist organizations, placed new restrictions on immigration designed to prevent foreign terrorists from entering or remaining in the United States, and loosened some restrictions on federal investigations of suspected terrorists. The AEDPA passed the Senate by a 91-8 vote and the House by a 293-133 vote. President Clinton signed the bill into law on April 24, 1996.*

The debate over the AEDPA exhibited the new constitutional politics of criminal procedure. A few libertarians aside, Republicans overwhelmingly favored restricting habeas corpus and death penalty appeals. Some Democrats upheld their party's past commitment to due process models of criminal procedure when insisting that proposed restrictions on habeas corpus violated constitutional rights. President Clinton and other New Democrats, however, were often more concerned with crime control than due process. Indeed, President Clinton's signing statement criticized Congress for failing to grant federal agents broader powers to investigate terrorists.

Consider the following questions when reading the excerpts from the congressional debate, President Clinton's signing statement, and Felker v. Turpin *(1996), which unanimously sustained crucial provisions of the AEDPA. What is the connection between the habeas provisions and preventing terrorism? What balance do the different participants in the debate strike between the need to impose criminal sanc-*

90. *Jenner v. Dooley*, 590 N.W.2d 463 (SD 1990).

tions in a timely fashion and the need to ensure that capital trials meet constitutional standards? What is the correct balance? While contemporary Democrats are divided between proponents of the due process model and proponents of the crime-control model, most Democratic appointees on the federal bench retain traditional liberal commitments to the due process model. Why have many Democrats in public office become "tougher" on crime? If the reason is simple politics, what explains why other Democrats fought so hard against the AEDPA? Why are Democratic judicial appointees as a group more liberal on crime issues than Democrats in public office?

Congressional Debate over the AEDPA (April 18, 1996)[91]

REPRESENTATIVE HENRY HYDE (Republican, Illinois)

Now, habeas corpus reform, that is the Holy Grail. We have pursued that for 14 years, in my memory. The absurdity, the obscenity of 17 years from the time a person has been sentenced till that sentence is carried out through endless appeals, up and down the State court system, and up and down the Federal court system, makes a mockery of the law. It also imposes a cruel punishment on the victims, the survivors' families, and we seek to put an end to that.

We are not shredding the Constitution. We are shaping a process to keep it within the ambit of the Constitution, but to bring justice to the American people. That is what we have done with habeas corpus reform, and I simply direct attention to quotations from President Bill Clinton, who has said in death penalty cases, it normally takes 8 years to exhaust the appeals. It is ridiculous, 8 years is ridiculous; 15 and 17 years is even more so. So heed the words of our President on this subject.

REPRESENTATIVE BOB BARR (Republican, Georgia)

That is the importance of this legislation, and there is no clearer link, no stronger link, Mr. Speaker, between effective antiterrorism legislation and deterring criminal acts of violence in this country than habeas and death penalty reform. The American people are demanding it. Future generations who will have to face the constant problem of terrorism demand it. They know that it will work. They know we must have it.

. . . [T]he essence described as that crown jewel of this bill is the reform of habeas corpus for an effective death penalty. The bill sets time limits on the application and considerations of habeas writs; I think that is extremely important. No longer will petition after petition be filed with the courts, delaying endlessly the carrying out of sentences handed down by judges or juries.

We have a paradox in our society whereby someone serves on death row for life. If, in fact, we are going to have a strong deterrence, retribution so that the victim can actually feel as though they have been vindicated, we need an effective death penalty. This bill will give it for America.

REPRESENTATIVE HOWARD BERMAN (Democrat, California)

Let me point out that according to reliable data, since 1978, 40 percent of the habeas petitions heard by Federal judges in capital cases resulted in the reversal of the conviction or death sentence because of constitutional violations. One can be dismayed by the number of State court trials impaired by constitutional error, as reflected in this statistic, but heretofore, we could be heartened that life-tenured Federal judges, shielded by constitutional design from local political pressures, could restore constitutional rights.

In this bill, in an action ill-befitting Members of Congress sworn to uphold the Constitution, we are about to obliterate the only effective means of vindicating those rights. It is not the bill's accelerated deadlines or limits on second or successive applications with which I differ. I believe that meritorious objections have been raised to protracted appeals which deprive families and communities of closure in heinous criminal cases. But to require deference by the Federal courts to State court determinations of Federal constitutional law, I cannot countenance.

Shame on those who invoke the names of innocents slaughtered in Oklahoma City and over the skies of Lockerbie in their quest to effectively abolish the writ of habeas corpus. We know that those charged with terrorism will invariably be tried in Federal court. Extinguishing the right to a writ of habeas corpus will have no bearing whatsoever on these cases.

91. 142 *Congressional Record,* 104th Cong., 2nd Sess. (1996), 7961–69.

REPRESENTATIVE NANCY PELOSI (Democrat, California)

. . . To many people, habeas corpus sounds like an obscure legal phrase with minimal relevance to their lives. This misunderstanding could not be further from the truth. Habeas corpus is the mechanism by which a citizen in this Nation who is deprived of liberty can petition an independent court to test the legality of his or her detention. Habeas corpus safeguards our individual liberty and the bill before us today restricts habeas corpus appeals.

The habeas corpus provisions in this bill are dangerous to ordinary citizens. They increase the risk that innocent persons could be held in prison in violation of the constitution, or even executed. For the first time, a use it or lose it approach is being applied to a basic constitutional right. Constitutional rights are not time-bound, they are timeless or they are worthless.

The bill before us mandates strict habeas corpus filing deadlines that ordinary citizens, especially those lacking financial resources, may not be able to meet. It limits their right in almost all cases to only one round of Federal review, and severely limits the power that Federal courts have to correct unconstitutional incarceration. It cuts off most opportunities for incarcerated citizens to appeal to higher courts for relief. . . .

William J. Clinton, Statement on Signing the Antiterrorism and Effective Death Penalty Act of 1996 (April 24, 1996)

. . .

. . . [A]s strong as this bill is, it should have been stronger. For example, I asked the Congress to give U.S. law enforcement increased wiretap authority in terrorism cases, including the power to seek multipoint wiretaps, enabling police to follow a suspected terrorist from phone to phone, and authority for the kind of emergency wiretaps available in organized crime cases. But the Congress refused.

. . .

I asked that law enforcement be given increased access to hotel, phone and other records in terrorism cases. I asked for a mandatory penalty for those who knowingly transfer a firearm for use in a violent felony. I asked for a longer statute of limitations to allow law enforcement more time to prosecute terrorists who use weapons such as machine guns, sawed-off shotguns, and explosive devices. But the Congress stripped each of these provisions out of the bill. . . .

. . .

. . . I have long sought to streamline Federal appeals for convicted criminals sentenced to the death penalty. For too long, and in too many cases, endless death row appeals have stood in the way of justice being served. Some have expressed the concern that two provisions of this important bill could be interpreted in a manner that would undercut meaningful Federal habeas corpus review. I have signed this bill because I am confident that the Federal courts will interpret these provisions to preserve independent review of Federal legal claims and the bedrock constitutional principle of an independent judiciary.

Section 104(3) provides that a Federal district court may not issue a writ of habeas corpus with respect to any claim adjudicated on the merits in State court unless the decision reached was contrary to, or involved an unreasonable application of, clearly established Federal law, as determined by the Supreme Court. Some have suggested that this provision will limit the authority of the Federal courts to bring their own independent judgment to bear on questions of law and mixed questions of law and fact that come before them on habeas corpus.

In the great 1803 case of *Marbury v. Madison*, Chief Justice John Marshall explained for the Supreme Court that "[i]t is emphatically the province and duty of the judicial department to say what the law is." Section 104(3) would be subject to serious constitutional challenge if it were read to preclude the Federal courts from making an independent determination about "what the law is" in cases within their jurisdiction. I expect that the courts, following their usual practice of construing ambiguous statutes to avoid constitutional problems, will read section 104 to permit independent Federal court review of constitutional claims based on the Supreme Court's interpretation of the Constitution and Federal laws.

Section 104(4) limits evidentiary hearings in Federal habeas corpus cases when "the applicant has failed to develop the factual basis of a claim in State court proceedings." If this provision were read to deny litigants a meaningful opportunity to prove the facts necessary to vindicate Federal rights, it would raise serious constitutional questions. I do not read it that way. The provision applies to situations in which "the *applicant* has failed to develop the factual basis" of his or her claim. Therefore, section 104(4) is not triggered when some factor that is not fairly attributable to the applicant prevented evidence from being developed in State court.

. . .

This bill also makes a number of major, ill-advised changes in our immigration laws having nothing to do with fighting terrorism. These provisions eliminate most remedial relief for long-term legal residents and restrict a key protection for battered spouses and children. The provisions will produce extraordinary administrative burdens on the Immigration and Naturalization Service. The Administration will urge the Congress to correct them in the pending immigration reform legislation.

Felker v. Turpin, 518 U.S. 651 (1991)

CHIEF JUSTICE REHNQUIST delivered the opinion of the Court.

. . .

The Act requires a habeas petitioner to obtain leave from the court of appeals before filing a second habeas petition in the district court. But this requirement simply transfers from the district court to the court of appeals a screening function which would previously have been performed by the district court. . . . The Act also codifies some of the pre-existing limits on successive petitions, and further restricts the availability of relief to habeas petitioners. But we have long recognized that "the power to award the writ by any of the courts of the United States, must be given by written law," and we have likewise recognized that judgments about the proper scope of the writ are "normally for Congress to make."

The new restrictions on successive petitions constitute a modified res judicata rule, a restraint on what is called in habeas corpus practice "abuse of the writ." In *McCleskey v. Zant* (1991), we said that "the doctrine of abuse of the writ refers to a complex and evolving body of equitable principles informed and controlled by historical usage, statutory developments, and judicial decisions." The added restrictions which the Act places on second habeas petitions are well within the compass of this evolutionary process, and we hold that they do not amount to a "suspension" of the writ. . . .

B. Search and Seizure

Constitutional decision makers face difficult challenges when attempting to apply constitutional rules for search and seizure written during the late eighteenth century to twenty-first-century technologies. *Kyllo v. United States* (2001) considered the constitutionality of thermal imagers that can be used to detect different levels of heat in a house. *United States v. Jones* (2012) discussed the constitutionality of using a GPS device to track a suspect's movements. Trying to think of a late-eighteenth-century analogy to a GPS device, Justice Alito imaged "a constable secret[ing] himself in a coach . . . [and] remain[ing] there for a period of time in order to monitor the movements of the coach's owner," which he observed "would have required either a gigantic coach, a very tiny constable, or both, not to mention a constable with incredible fortitude and patience."

More often than not, the justices have not allowed police to use new technologies to conduct searches that would have been unconstitutional had they attempted to procure the same information by more traditional means. *Kyllo* declared unconstitutional the warrantless use of a thermal imager device to determine whether a suspect was growing marijuana (which requires heat lamps) in his garage. *Jones* declared unconstitutional the warrantless installation of a GPS device in a car. Justice Scalia's majority opinion asserted, "The Government physically occupied private property for the purpose of obtaining information. We have no doubt that such a physical intrusion would have been considered a "search" within the meaning of the Fourth Amendment when it was adopted." The justices are also considering whether police may make novel use of ancient technologies to investigate crime. The justices have scheduled for argument *Florida v. Jardines*, a case that explores whether police may without a warrant use dogs with a heightened sense of smell who are trained to detect certain illegal substances in a house.

The constitutional law of more traditional searches and seizures remains hotly contested, with the justices handing down both more liberal and more conservative decisions that frequently depend on particular facts. A 5-4 judicial majority in *Florence v. Board of Chosen Freeholders of County of Burlington* (2012) ruled that persons arrested for minor criminal offenses could be strip-searched if they were in a general jail population, but left open whether a different result might be constitutionally required for persons arrested for really minor offenses who were not being detained in a jail with more serious offenders. Other important Fourth Amendment cases include:

- *Herring v. United States* (2009), which held that the exclusionary rule applies only when the police recklessly or intentionally violate the Fourth Amendment.
- *Knowles v. Iowa* (1998), which held that police may not rely on the "search incident to arrest" exception to the warrant requirement to justify searches of persons given traffic citations.
- *Atwater v. City of Lago Vista* (2001), which held that police may arrest a person without a warrant for such minor offenses as a failure to use seatbelts.
- *Arizona v. Gant* (2009), which held that police may only search a car after arresting the occupant when the person arrested can reach the passenger compartment or the police believe the car contains evidence of the crime for which the occupant was arrested.
- *Bond v. United States* (2001), which held that bus passengers have a reasonable privacy expectation that their luggage will not be squeezed by police officers without a warrant.
- *Board of Education of Independent School District No. 92 of Pottawatomie County v. Earls* (2002), which held that schools could require suspicionless drug tests for all students who participate in extracurricular activities.
- *Safford Unified School District No. 1 v. Redding* (2009), which held that schools could not ordinarily strip-search teenage students.

One pattern in these cases might be a judicial tendency to slightly expand the substance of Fourth Amendment rights while expanding the application of both the good-faith exception in *United States v. Leon* (1984) and cases that restrict access to federal habeas corpus. The end result is that Americans have more Fourth Amendment rights but fewer opportunities to vindicate those rights.

Kyllo v. United States, 533 U.S. 27 (2001)

Federal agent William Elliott used an Agema Thermovision 210 thermal imager to scan the home of Danny Kyllo, whom he suspected was growing marijuana. The search, which took place without a warrant, revealed that portions of Kyllo's house were substantially hotter than others. A local magistrate then issued Elliott a warrant to search Kyllo's home, because growing marijuana indoors requires high-heat lamps. The search revealed that Kyllo was growing a substantial amount of marijuana. Both the local federal district court and the Court of Appeals for the Ninth Circuit rejected Kyllo's claim that the use of the thermal imager violated the Fourth Amendment. Kyllo appealed to the Supreme Court of the United States.

The Supreme Court by a 5-4 vote declared that the warrantless use of thermal imagers in this instance violated the Fourth Amendment. Justice Scalia's majority opinion held that technologies that enabled government agents to determine what is taking place inside a private home violate reasonable expectations of privacy. Why does Justice Scalia find a reasonable expectation of privacy? Why does Justice Stevens insist that no reasonable expectation of privacy exists? Justices Scalia and Thomas in this case joined three more liberal members of the Roberts Court. What might explain differences among the more conservative justices?

JUSTICE SCALIA delivered the opinion of the Court.

. . .

"At the very core" of the Fourth Amendment "stands the right of a man to retreat into his own home and there be free from unreasonable governmental intrusion." With few exceptions, the question whether a warrantless search of a home is reasonable and hence constitutional must be answered no.

On the other hand, the antecedent question whether or not a Fourth Amendment "search" has occurred is not so simple under our precedent. The permissibility of ordinary visual surveillance of a home used to be clear because, well into the 20th century, our Fourth Amendment jurisprudence was tied to common-law trespass. Visual surveillance was unquestionably lawful because "'the eye cannot by the laws of England be guilty of a trespass.'" . . .

. . . But in fact we have held that visual observation is no "search" at all—perhaps in order to preserve somewhat more intact our doctrine that warrantless searches are presumptively unconstitutional. In assessing when a search is not a search, we have applied somewhat in reverse the principle first enunciated in *Katz v. United States* (1967). . . . As Justice Harlan's oft-quoted concurrence described it, a Fourth Amendment search occurs when the government violates a subjective expectation of privacy that society recognizes as reasonable. We have subsequently applied this principle to hold that a Fourth Amendment search does *not* occur—even when the explicitly protected location of a *house* is concerned—unless "the individual manifested a subjective expectation of privacy in the object of the challenged search," and "society [is] willing to recognize that expectation as reasonable." . . .

. . .

The *Katz* test—whether the individual has an expectation of privacy that society is prepared to recognize as reasonable—has often been criticized as circular, and hence subjective and unpredictable. While it may be difficult to refine *Katz* when the search of areas such as telephone booths, automobiles, or even the curtilage and uncovered portions of residences is at issue, in the case of the search of the interior of homes—the prototypical and hence most commonly litigated area of protected privacy—there is a ready criterion, with roots deep in the common law, of the minimal expectation of privacy that *exists,* and that is acknowledged to be *reasonable.* To withdraw protection of this minimum expectation would be to permit police technology to erode the privacy guaranteed by the Fourth Amendment. We think that obtaining by sense-enhancing technology any information regarding the interior of the home that could not otherwise have been obtained without physical "intrusion into a constitutionally protected area," constitutes a search—at least where (as here) the technology in question is not in general public use. This assures preservation of that degree of privacy against government that existed when the Fourth Amendment was adopted. On the basis of this criterion, the information obtained by the thermal imager in this case was the product of a search.

The Government maintains, however, that the thermal imaging must be upheld because it detected "only heat radiating from the external surface of the house." The dissent makes this its leading point, contending that there is a fundamental difference between what it calls "off-the-wall" observations and "through-the-wall surveillance." But just as a thermal imager captures only heat emanating from a house, so also a powerful directional microphone picks up only sound emanating from a house—and a satellite capable of scanning from many miles away would pick up only visible light emanating from a house. We rejected such a mechanical interpretation of the Fourth Amendment in *Katz,* where the eavesdropping device picked up only sound waves that reached the exterior of the phone booth. Reversing that approach would leave the homeowner at the mercy of advancing technology—including imaging technology that could discern all human activity in the home.

. . .

We have said that the Fourth Amendment draws "a firm line at the entrance to the house." That line, we think, must be not only firm but also bright—which requires clear specification of those methods of surveillance that require a warrant. . . . Where, as here, the Government uses a device that is not in general public use, to explore details of the home that would previously have been unknowable without physical intrusion, the surveillance is a "search" and is presumptively unreasonable without a warrant.

. . .

JUSTICE STEVENS, with whom THE CHIEF JUSTICE, JUSTICE O'CONNOR, and JUSTICE KENNEDY join, dissenting.

There is, in my judgment, a distinction of constitutional magnitude between "through-the-wall surveillance" that gives the observer or listener direct access to information in a private area, on the one hand, and the thought processes used to draw inferences from information in the public domain, on the other hand. The Court has crafted a rule that purports to deal with direct observations of the inside of the home, but the case before us merely involves indirect deductions from "off-the-wall" surveillance, that is, observations of the exterior of the home. Those observations were made with a fairly primitive thermal imager that gathered data exposed on the outside of petitioner's home but did not invade any constitutionally protected interest in privacy. Moreover, I believe that the supposedly "bright-line" rule the Court has created in response to its concerns about future technological developments is unnecessary, unwise, and inconsistent with the Fourth Amendment.

. . . [S]earches and seizures of property in plain view are presumptively reasonable. Whether that property is residential or commercial, the basic principle is the same: "'What a person knowingly exposes to the public, even in his own home or office, is not a subject of Fourth Amendment protection.'"

. . . [T]his case involves nothing more than off-the-wall surveillance by law enforcement officers to gather information exposed to the general public from the outside of petitioner's home. . . . Unlike an x-ray scan, or other possible "through-the-wall" techniques, the detection of infrared radiation emanating from the home did not accomplish "an unauthorized physical penetration into the premises," nor did it "obtain information that it could not have obtained by observation from outside the curtilage of the house."

Indeed, the ordinary use of the senses might enable a neighbor or passerby to notice the heat emanating from a building, particularly if it is vented, as was the case here. Additionally, any member of the public might notice that one part of a house is warmer than another part or a nearby building if, for example, rainwater evaporates or snow melts at different rates across its surfaces. Such use of the senses would not convert into an unreasonable search if, instead, an adjoining neighbor allowed an officer onto her property to verify her perceptions with a sensitive thermometer. Nor, in my view, does such observation become an unreasonable search if made from a distance with the aid of a device that merely discloses that the exterior of one house, or one area of the house, is much warmer than another. Nothing more occurred in this case.

Thus, the notion that heat emissions from the outside of a dwelling are a private matter implicating the protections of the Fourth Amendment . . . is not only unprecedented but also quite difficult to take seriously. Heat waves, like aromas that are generated in a kitchen, or in a laboratory or opium den, enter the public domain if and when they leave a building. A subjective expectation that they would remain private is not only implausible but also surely not "one that society is prepared to recognize as 'reasonable.'"

. . .

. . . [The] privacy interest is at best trivial. After all, homes generally are insulated to keep heat in, rather than to prevent the detection of heat going out, and it does not seem to me that society will suffer from a rule requiring the rare homeowner who both intends to engage in uncommon activities that produce extraordinary amounts of heat, and wishes to conceal that production from outsiders, to make sure that the surrounding area is well insulated. The interest in concealing the heat escaping from one's house pales in significance to "the chief evil against which the wording of the Fourth Amendment is directed," the "physical entry of the home," and it is hard to believe that it is an interest the Framers sought to protect in our Constitution.

. . .

. . . I would not erect a constitutional impediment to the use of sense-enhancing technology unless it provides its user with the functional equivalent of actual presence in the area being searched. . . .

Florence v. Board of Chosen Freeholders of County of Burlington, 132 S. Ct. 1510 (2012)

Albert Florence was arrested by New Jersey police officers who mistakenly believed that he was behind on his obligation to pay a previous criminal fine. Upon his arrival at both the Burlington County Detention Center and the Essex County Correctional Facility, Florence was strip-searched by correctional authorities. These searches were conducted routinely and were unrelated to any suspicion that detainees were concealing contraband. After being released Florence sued the Board of Chosen Freeholders, the government entity that operated the prisons, claiming that the strip searches violated his Fourth and Fourteenth Amendment rights. The federal district court ruled that the strip searches were unconstitutional, but that decision was overturned by the Court of Appeals for the Third Circuit. Florence appealed to the Supreme Court of the United States.

The Supreme Court by a 5-4 vote ruled that the search was constitutional. Justice Kennedy's opinion held that corrections officials could conduct strip searches of all members of a general jail population without individualized suspicion. What constitutional interests do strip searches serve? Why does Justice Kennedy believe that the Court should not create an exception for persons arrested for minor offenses? Why does Justice Breyer disagree? Who has the better argument?

JUSTICE KENNEDY delivered the opinion of the Court

. . .

. . . [C]orrectional officials must be permitted to devise reasonable search policies to detect and deter the possession of contraband in their facilities. The task of determining whether a policy is reasonably related to legitimate security interests is "peculiarly within the province and professional expertise of corrections officials." This Court has repeated the admonition that, "'in the absence of substantial evidence in the record to indicate that the officials have exaggerated their response to these considerations courts should ordinarily defer to their expert judgment in such matters.'"

. . .

The question here is whether undoubted security imperatives involved in jail supervision override the assertion that some detainees must be exempt from the more invasive search procedures at issue absent reasonable suspicion of a concealed weapon or other contraband. The Court has held that deference must be given to the officials in charge of the jail unless there is "substantial evidence" demonstrating their response to the situation is exaggerated. Petitioner has not met this standard, and the record provides full justifications for the procedures used.

Correctional officials have a significant interest in conducting a thorough search as a standard part of the intake process. The admission of inmates creates numerous risks for facility staff, for the existing detainee population, and for a new detainee himself or herself. The danger of introducing lice or contagious infections, for example, is well documented. Persons just arrested may have wounds or other injuries requiring immediate medical attention. It may be difficult to identify and treat these problems until detainees remove their clothes for a visual inspection.

Jails and prisons also face grave threats posed by the increasing number of gang members who go through the intake process. . . . These considerations provide a reasonable basis to justify a visual inspection for certain tattoos and other signs of gang affiliation as part of the intake process. The identification and isolation of gang members before they are admitted protects everyone in the facility.

Detecting contraband concealed by new detainees, furthermore, is a most serious responsibility. Weapons, drugs, and alcohol all disrupt the safe operation of a jail. Correctional officers have had to confront arrestees concealing knives, scissors, razor blades, glass shards, and other prohibited items on their person, including in their body cavities. They have also found crack, heroin, and marijuana. The use of drugs can embolden inmates in aggression toward officers or each other; and, even apart from their use, the trade in these substances can lead to violent confrontations.

. . .

It is not surprising that correctional officials have sought to perform thorough searches at intake for disease, gang affiliation, and contraband. Jails are often crowded, unsanitary, and dangerous places. There is a substantial interest in preventing any new inmate, either of his own will or as a result of coercion, from putting all who live or work at these institutions at even greater risk when he is admitted to the general population.

. . .

People detained for minor offenses can turn out to be the most devious and dangerous criminals. . . . One of the terrorists involved in the September 11 attacks was stopped and ticketed for speeding just two days before hijacking. Reasonable correctional officials could conclude these uncertainties mean they must conduct the same thorough search of everyone who will be admitted to their facilities.

Experience shows that people arrested for minor offenses have tried to smuggle prohibited items into jail, sometimes by using their rectal cavities or genitals for the concealment. They may have some of the same incentives as a serious criminal to hide contraband. A detainee might risk carrying cash, cigarettes, or a penknife to survive in jail. Others may make a quick decision to hide unlawful substances to avoid getting in more trouble at the time of their arrest. . . .

Even if people arrested for a minor offense do not themselves wish to introduce contraband into a jail, they may be coerced into doing so by others. This could happen any time detainees are held in the same area, including in a van on the way to the station or in the holding cell of the jail. If, for example, a person arrested and detained for unpaid traffic citations is not subject to the same search as others, this will be well known to other detainees with jail experience. A hardened criminal or gang member can, in just a few minutes, approach the person and coerce him into hiding the fruits of a crime, a weapon, or some other contraband. . . . Exempting people arrested for minor offenses from a standard search protocol thus may put them at greater risk and result in more contraband being brought into the detention facility. This is a substantial reason not to mandate the exception petitioner seeks as a matter of constitutional law.

It also may be difficult, as a practical matter, to classify inmates by their current and prior offenses before the intake search. Jails can be even more dangerous than prisons because officials there know so little about the people they admit at the outset. An arrestee may be carrying a false ID or lie about his identity. The officers who conduct an initial search often do not have access to criminal history records. And those records can be inaccurate or incomplete. . . . In the absence of reliable information it would be illogical to require officers to assume the arrestees in front of them do not pose a risk of smuggling something into the facility.

. . . Even if they had accurate information about a detainee's current and prior arrests, officers, under petitioner's proposed regime, would encounter serious implementation difficulties. They would be required, in a few minutes, to determine whether any of the underlying offenses were serious enough to authorize the more invasive search protocol. Other possible classifications based on characteristics of individual detainees also might prove to be unworkable or even give rise to charges of discriminatory application. Most officers would not be well equipped to make any of these legal determinations during the pressures of the intake process. . . .

. . .

The circumstances before the Court, however, do not present the opportunity to consider a narrow exception of the sort Justice ALITO describes, which might restrict whether an arrestee whose detention has not yet been reviewed by a magistrate or other judicial officer, and who can be held in available facilities removed from the general population, may be subjected to the types of searches at issue here.

. . .

CHIEF JUSTICE ROBERTS, concurring. . . .

JUSTICE ALITO, concurring.

. . .

Undergoing such an inspection is undoubtedly humiliating and deeply offensive to many, but there are reasonable grounds for strip searching arrestees before they are admitted to the general population of a jail. As the Court explains, there is a serious danger that some detainees will attempt to smuggle weapons, drugs, or other contraband into the jail. Some detainees may have lice, which can easily spread to others in the facility, and some detainees may have diseases or injuries for which the jail is required to provide medical treatment. In addition, if a detainee with gang-related tattoos is inadvertently housed with detainees from a rival gang, violence may ensue.

Petitioner and the dissent would permit corrections officers to conduct the visual strip search at issue here only if the officers have a reasonable basis for thinking that a particular arrestee may present a danger to other detainees or members of the jail staff. But as the Court explains, corrections officers are often in a very poor position to make such a determination, and the threat to the health and safety of detainees and staff, should the officers miscalculate, is simply too great.

It is important to note, however, that the Court does not hold that it is always reasonable to conduct a full strip search of an arrestee whose detention has not been reviewed by a judicial officer and who could be held in available facilities apart from the general population. Most of those arrested for minor offenses are not dangerous, and most are released from custody prior to or at the time of their initial appearance before a magistrate. In some cases, the charges are dropped. In others, arrestees are released either on their own recognizance or on minimal bail. In the end, few are sentenced to incarceration. For these persons, admission to the general jail population, with the concomitant humiliation of a strip search, may not be reasonable, particularly if an alternative procedure is feasible. . . .

. . .

JUSTICE BREYER, with whom JUSTICE GINSBURG, JUSTICE SOTOMAYOR, and JUSTICE KAGAN join, dissenting.

. . .

In my view, such a search of an individual arrested for a minor offense that does not involve drugs or violence—say a traffic offense, a regulatory offense, an essentially civil matter, or any other such misdemeanor—is an "unreasonable searc[h]" forbidden by the Fourth Amendment, unless prison authorities have reasonable suspicion to believe that the individual possesses drugs or other contraband. And I dissent from the Court's contrary determination.

. . .

A strip search that involves a stranger peering without consent at a naked individual, and in particular at the most private portions of that person's body, is a serious invasion of privacy. We have recently said, in respect to a schoolchild (and a less intrusive search), that the "meaning of such a search, and the degradation its subject may reasonably feel, place a search that intrusive in a category of its own demanding its own specific suspicions." *Safford Unified School Dist. # 1 v. Redding* (2009). The Courts of Appeals have more directly described the privacy interests at stake, writing, for example, that practices similar to those at issue here are "demeaning, dehumanizing, undignified, humiliating, terrifying, unpleasant, embarrassing, [and] repulsive, signifying degradation and submission." . . . And the harm to privacy interests would seem particularly acute where the person searched may well have no expectation of being subject to such a search, say, because she had simply received a traffic ticket for failing to buckle a seatbelt, because he had not previously paid a civil fine, or because she had been arrested for a minor trespass.

. . .

. . . I have found no convincing reason indicating that, in the absence of reasonable suspicion, involuntary strip searches of those arrested for minor offenses are necessary in order to further the penal interests mentioned [by the majority]. And there are strong reasons to believe they are not justified.

The lack of justification is fairly obvious with respect to the first two penological interests advanced. The searches already employed at Essex and Burlington include: (a) pat-frisking all inmates; (b) making inmates go through metal detectors (including the Body Orifice Screening System (BOSS) chair used at Essex County Correctional Facility that identifies metal hidden within the body); (c) making inmates shower and use particular delousing agents or bathing supplies; and (d) searching inmates' clothing. No one here has offered any reason, example, or empirical evidence suggesting the inadequacy of such practices for detecting injuries, diseases, or tattoos. In particular, there is no connection between the genital lift and the "squat and cough" that Florence was allegedly subjected to and health or gang concerns.

The lack of justification for such a strip search is less obvious but no less real in respect to the third interest, namely that of detecting contraband. The information demonstrating the lack of justification is of three kinds. First, there are empirically based conclusions reached in specific cases. The New York Federal District Court, to which I have referred, conducted a study of 23,000 persons admitted to the Orange County correctional facility between 1999 and 2003. . . . The court [noted] that in four of these five instances [when drugs were found] there may have been "reasonable suspicion" to search, leaving only one instance in 23,000 in which the strip search policy "arguably" detected additional contraband. . . .

Second, there is the plethora of recommendations of professional bodies, such as correctional associations, that have studied and thoughtfully considered the matter. The American Correctional Association (ACA)—an association that informs our view of "what is obtainable and what is acceptable in corrections philosophy," has promulgated a standard that forbids suspicionless strip searches. And it has done so after consultation with the American Jail Association, National Sheriff's Association, National Institute of Corrections of the Department of Justice, and Federal Bureau of Prisons.

Third, there is general experience in areas where the law has forbidden here-relevant suspicionless searches. Laws in at least 10 States prohibit suspicionless strip searches. At the same time at least seven Courts of Appeals have considered the question and have required reasonable suspicion that an arrestee is concealing weapons or contraband before a strip search of one arrested for a minor offense can take place. Respondents have not presented convincing grounds to believe that administration of these legal standards has increased the smuggling of contraband into prison.

Indeed, neither the majority's opinion nor the briefs set forth any clear example of an instance in which contraband was smuggled into the general jail population during intake that could not have been discovered if the jail was employing a reasonable suspicion standard. . . .

C. Interrogations

The law of confessions remains a site for constitutional trench warfare. Conservatives are unable to form the majorities in politics or on the Supreme Court to reverse the Supreme Court's decision in *Miranda v. Arizona* (1966). Liberals are unable to form the majorities in politics or on the Supreme Court to overturn past decisions carving numerous exceptions to the rule that a confession may not be admitted into evidence unless the person under arrest was given *Miranda* warnings. Much legal talent has been employed in a series of cases that do little more than move the status quo a few legal feet to the left or right.

Dickerson v. United States (2000) was the most significant conservative challenge to *Miranda*. After a thirty year hiatus, the Court of Appeals for the Fourth Circuit revived the provision in the Omnibus Crime Control and Safe Streets Act of 1968 that permitted federal courts to admit all voluntary confessions, whether given after warnings or not. Supported by the Clinton administration, a 7-2 judicial majority quickly reversed the circuit court's decision. Chief Justice Rehnquist declared, "*Miranda* announced a constitutional rule that Congress may not supersede legislatively." Rehnquist's newfound support for *Miranda* may have been influenced by a long period of incremental conservative adjustment to the basic doctrine and the increasing number of police officers who accept *Miranda*.

The next decade witnessed skirmishes over precisely what interrogation practices are consistent with *Miranda*. The more liberal justices almost always find constitutional violations. The more conservative justices almost always find the police behavior constitutional. Justice Kennedy usually casts the deciding vote. In *Missouri v. Siebert* (2004) Kennedy declared that police could not withhold *Miranda* warnings, obtain a confession, give *Miranda* warnings, and then ask the suspect to repeat the confession. "The interrogation technique used in this case," he declared, "is designed to circumvent *Miranda v. Arizona*." In *Berghuis v. Thompkins* (2010) Kennedy found no constitutional violation when a suspect, after not responding to police questions for nearly three hours, made one incriminating statement. In his view, "If an accused makes a statement concerning the right to counsel that is ambiguous or equivocal or makes no statement, the police are not required to end the interrogation." Justice Kennedy finds principled differences between these cases. His fellow justices and many commentators do not perceive that principle.

Dickerson v. United States, 530 U.S. 428 (2000)

Before he was given Miranda *warnings Charles Thomas Dickerson made incriminating statements to the FBI about his participation in a bank robbery. His lawyer moved to suppress those statements on the ground that they were unconstitutionally obtained. The federal district court agreed, but that decision was reversed by the Court of Appeals for the Fourth Circuit. The Fourth Circuit majority insisted that Dickerson's case was governed by the Omnibus Crime Control and Safe Streets Act of 1968, which had not been enforced for thirty years. Section 3501 of that federal law declared, "If the trial judge determines that the confession was voluntarily made it shall be admitted in evidence." When justifying the decision to follow Congress rather than the Supreme Court's decision in* Miranda, *Judge Williams wrote,*

> *Congress has the power to overrule judicially created rules of evidence and procedure that are not required by the Constitution. Thus, whether Congress has the authority to enact § 3501 turns on whether the rule set forth by the Supreme Court in* Miranda *is required by the Constitution. Clearly it is not. At no point did the Supreme Court in* Miranda *refer to the warnings as constitutional rights. Indeed, the Court acknowledged that the Constitution did not require the warnings, disclaimed any intent to create a "constitutional straightjacket," referred to the warnings as "procedural safeguards," and invited Congress and the States "to develop their own safeguards for [protecting] the privilege." Since deciding* Miranda, *the Supreme Court has consistently referred to the Miranda warnings as "prophylactic,"* New York v. Quarles *(1984), and "not themselves rights protected by the Constitution." We have little difficulty concluding, therefore, that § 3501, enacted at the invitation of the Supreme Court and pursuant to Congress's unquestioned power to establish the rules of procedure and evidence in*

Table 11-3 Police Chief Attitudes on *Miranda* Warnings, by Percentage, 2005

Opinion	Strongly Disagree	Disagree	Agree	Strongly Agree
Court should have abolished *Miranda* warnings in *Dickerson*	10.3	77.3	10.3	2.1
In order to prevent dismissal of a case, arresting officers must routinely read *Miranda* warnings	16.5	23.7	34.0	25.8
Courts are too cautious with regard to *Miranda* warnings	2.0	70.7	23.3	4.0
Miranda warnings are useful in principle but ineffective in practice	9.4	76.0	13.5	1.0
Miranda requirement makes it difficult for people to do their job	18.2	68.7	11.1	2.0

Source: Marvin Zalman and Brad W. Smith, "The Attitudes of Police Executives toward *Miranda* and Interrogation Policies," *Journal of Criminal Law and Criminology* 97 (2007): 906, 908–909.

the federal courts, is constitutional. As a consequence, we hold that the admissibility of confessions in federal court is governed by § 3501, rather than the judicially created rule of Miranda.

Dickerson appealed to the Supreme Court of the United States.

The Supreme Court by a 7-2 vote declared that Dickerson's confession could not be constitutionally admitted as evidence at his trial. Chief Justice Rehnquist's majority opinion insisted that Miranda *was a constitutional decision that could not be overruled by Congress. How do you explain Rehnquist's decision to uphold* Miranda*? Did Rehnquist think* Miranda *correctly decided? Was he convinced that past precedent compelled the Court to sustain* Miranda*? Did crucial justices on the Rehnquist Court regard the assertion of judicial supremacy as more important than making what they might have thought were more desirable rules for constitutional criminal procedure? Suppose if instead of reinstituting "the totality of the circumstances" test, Congress had mandated a different verbal formula for giving warnings or required that attorneys be present whenever a confession was made. Would the result in* Dickerson *have been different?*

CHIEF JUSTICE REHNQUIST delivered the opinion of the Court.

. . .

Congress may not legislatively supersede our decisions interpreting and applying the Constitution. This case therefore turns on whether the *Miranda* Court announced a constitutional rule or merely exercised its supervisory authority to regulate evidence in the absence of congressional direction.

. . .

. . . [F]irst and foremost of the factors on the . . . side that *Miranda v. Arizona* (1966) is a constitutional decision is that both *Miranda* and two of its companion cases applied the rule to proceedings in state courts—to wit, Arizona, California, and New York. . . . It is beyond dispute that we do not hold a supervisory power over the courts of the several states. With respect to proceedings in state courts, our "authority is limited to enforcing the commands of the United States Constitution."

The *Miranda* opinion itself begins by stating that the Court granted certiorari "to explore some facets of the problems . . . of applying the privilege against self-incrimination to in-custody interrogation, *and to give concrete constitutional guidelines for law enforcement agencies and courts to follow.*" In fact, the majority opinion is replete with statements indicating that the majority thought it was announcing a constitutional rule. Indeed, the Court's ultimate conclusion was that the unwarned confessions obtained in the four cases before the Court in *Miranda* "were obtained from the defendant under circumstances that did not meet constitutional standards for protection of the privilege."

Additional support for our conclusion that *Miranda* is constitutionally based is found in the *Miranda* Court's invitation for legislative action to protect the constitutional right against coerced self-incrimination. . . . [T]he Court emphasized that it could not foresee "the potential alternatives for protecting the privilege which might be devised by Congress or the States," and it accordingly opined that the Constitution would not preclude legislative solutions that differed from the prescribed *Miranda* warnings but which were "at least as effective in apprising accused persons of their right of silence and in assuring a continuous opportunity to exercise it."

The Court of Appeals relied on the fact that we have, after our *Miranda* decision, made exceptions from its rule in cases such as . . . *Harris v. New York* (1971). These decisions illustrate the principle—not that *Miranda* is not a constitutional rule—but that no constitutional rule is immutable. No court laying down a general rule can possibly foresee the various circumstances in which counsel will seek to apply it, and the sort of modifications represented by these cases are as much a normal part of constitutional law as the original decision.

. . .

. . . In *Miranda,* the Court noted that reliance on the traditional totality-of-the-circumstances test raised a risk of overlooking an involuntary custodial confession, a risk that the Court found unacceptably great when the confession is offered in the case in chief to prove guilt. The Court therefore concluded that something more than the totality test was necessary. § 3501 reinstates the totality test as sufficient. Section 3501 therefore cannot be sustained if *Miranda* is to remain the law.

Whether or not we would agree with *Miranda's* reasoning and its resulting rule, were we addressing the issue in the first instance, the principles of *stare decisis* weigh heavily against overruling it now. . . .

We do not think there is such justification for overruling *Miranda. Miranda* has become embedded in routine police practice to the point where the warnings have become part of our national culture. . . . If anything, our subsequent cases have reduced the impact of the *Miranda* rule on legitimate law enforcement while reaffirming the decision's core ruling that unwarned statements may not be used as evidence in the prosecution's case in chief.

The disadvantage of the *Miranda* rule is that statements which may be by no means involuntary, made by a defendant who is aware of his "rights," may nonetheless be excluded and a guilty defendant go free as a result. But experience suggests that the totality-of-the-circumstances test which § 3501 seeks to revive is more difficult than *Miranda* for law enforcement officers to conform to, and for courts to apply in a consistent manner. . . .

In sum, we conclude that *Miranda* announced a constitutional rule that Congress may not supersede legislatively. Following the rule of *stare decisis*, we decline to overrule *Miranda* ourselves. . . .

JUSTICE SCALIA, with whom JUSTICE THOMAS joins, dissenting.

. . .

It takes only a small step to bring today's opinion out of the realm of power-judging and into the mainstream of legal reasoning: The Court need only go beyond its carefully couched iterations that "*Miranda* is a constitutional decision," that "*Miranda* is constitutionally based," that *Miranda* has "constitutional underpinnings," and come out and say quite clearly: "We reaffirm today that custodial interrogation that is not preceded by *Miranda* warnings or their equivalent violates the Constitution of the United States." It cannot say that, because a majority of the Court does not believe it. The Court therefore acts in plain violation of the Constitution when it denies effect to this Act of Congress.

. . .

Miranda was objectionable for innumerable reasons, not least the fact that cases spanning more than 70 years had rejected its core premise that, absent the warnings and an effective waiver of the right to remain silent and of the (thitherto unknown) right to have an attorney present, a statement obtained pursuant to custodial interrogation was necessarily the product of compulsion. Moreover, history and precedent aside, the decision in *Miranda*, if read as an explication of what the Constitution *requires*, is preposterous. There is, for example, simply no basis in reason for concluding that a response to the very first question asked, by a suspect who already *knows* all of the rights described in the *Miranda* warning, is anything other than a volitional act. And even if one assumes that the elimination of compulsion absolutely requires informing even the most knowledgeable suspect of his right to remain silent, it cannot conceivably require the right to have *counsel* present. There is a world of difference, which the Court recognized under the traditional voluntariness test but ignored in *Miranda*, between compelling a suspect to incriminate himself and preventing him from foolishly doing so of his own accord. . . .

. . . Thus, what is most remarkable about the *Miranda* decision—and what made it unacceptable as a matter of straightforward constitutional interpretation in the *Marbury* [*v. Madison*] (1803) tradition—is its palpable hostility toward the act of confession *per se*, rather than toward what the Constitution abhors, *compelled* confession. The Constitution is not, unlike the *Miranda* majority, offended by a criminal's commendable qualm of conscience or fortunate fit of stupidity.

. . .

The Court has squarely concluded that it is possible—indeed not uncommon—for the police to violate *Miranda* without also violating the Constitution. *Michigan v. Tucker* (1974), an opinion for the Court written by then-Justice REHNQUIST, rejected the true-to-*Marbury*, failure-to-warn-as-constitutional-violation interpretation of *Miranda*. It held that exclusion of the "fruits" of a *Miranda* violation—the statement of a witness whose identity the defendant had revealed while in custody—was not required. The opinion explained that the question whether the "police conduct complained of directly infringed upon respondent's right against compulsory self-incrimination" was a "separate question" from "whether it instead violated only the prophylactic rules developed to protect that right." The "procedural safeguards" adopted in *Miranda*, the Court said, "were not themselves rights protected by the Constitution but were instead measures to insure that the right against compulsory self-incrimination was protected," and to "provide practical reinforcement for the right." . . .

. . .

. . . [I]t is simply no longer possible for the Court to conclude, even if it wanted to, that a violation of *Miranda's* rules is a violation of the Constitution. But as I explained at the outset, that is what is required before the Court may disregard a law of Congress governing the admissibility of evidence in federal court. . . . [W]hat makes a decision "constitutional" in the only sense relevant here—in the sense that renders it impervious to supersession by congressional legislation such as § 3501—is the determination that the Constitution *requires* the result that the decision announces and the statute ignores. By disregarding congressional action that concededly does not violate the Constitution, the Court flagrantly offends fundamental principles of separation of powers, and arrogates to itself prerogatives reserved to the representatives of the people.

. . .

Thus, while I agree with the Court that § 3501 cannot be upheld without also concluding that *Miranda* represents an illegitimate exercise of our authority to review state-court judgments, I do not share the Court's hesitation in reaching that conclusion. . . . Despite the Court's Orwellian assertion to the contrary, it is undeniable that later cases have "undermined [*Miranda's*] doctrinal underpinnings," denying constitutional violation and thus stripping the holding of its only constitutionally legitimate support. . . .

. . .

I am not convinced by petitioner's argument that *Miranda* should be preserved because the decision occupies a special place in the "public's consciousness." As far as I am aware, the public is not under the illusion that we are infallible. I see little harm in admitting that we made a mistake in taking away from the people the ability to decide for themselves what protections (beyond those required by the Constitution) are reasonably affordable in the criminal investigatory process. . . .

D. Juries and Lawyers

The right to a jury and an attorney are among the most litigated but least politically explosive issues in contemporary constitutional criminal procedure. Intense political debates exist over whether *Mapp* and *Miranda* will be overruled and over who can constitutionally be executed. By comparison, a broad consensus exists that indigent criminal defendants have a right to have a defense lawyer and that jury selection should not be infected by racial prejudice. Contemporary federal and state cases raising Sixth Amendment questions typically feature long factual battles over whether counsel was adequate or whether racial prejudice actually infected the jury selection process.

Miller-El v. Dretke (2005) and *Burdine v. Johnson* (2001) illustrate the nature of much contemporary constitutional debate over jury trials and assistance of counsel. The majority and dissenting opinions in both cases agreed on certain basic principles. In *Miller-El* Justice Souter (majority) and Justice Thomas (dissent) agreed that prosecutors could not base peremptory challenges on the race of prospective jurors. Judge Benavides (majority) and Judge Barksdale (dissent) in *Burdine* agreed that persons claiming ineffective assistance of counsel must demonstrate prejudice. The dispute in both cases was over facts or inferences from the facts. Were the prosecutorial decisions at issue in *Miller-El* motivated by an unconstitutional desire to reduce the number of African-Americans on the jury or a constitutional desire to secure a pro–capital punishment jury? Was Burdine's lawyer unconscious for major portions of the capital trial or merely dozing while unimportant testimony was elicited? Both cases demonstrate the difficulties that defendants have proving racial prejudice and ineffective assistance of counsel. Strong presumptions exist that prosecutors have race-neutral motivations for challenging African-American jurors and that counsel's decisions are strategic rather than the result of incompetence or inattention.

Miller-El and *Burdine* are atypical in one important respect: the defendant won in each. The Supreme Court in *Miller-El* concluded that prosecutorial decisions to exercise peremptory challenges for ten of the eleven African-Americans eligible to sit on the jury were motivated by racial prejudice. Justice Souter's majority opinions stated, "The State's attempts to explain the prosecutors' questioning of particular witnesses on nonracial grounds fit the evidence less well than the racially discriminatory hypothesis." More often, lower federal court justices credit prosecutorial claims that they had race-neutral reasons for challenging prospective African-American jurors. The Fifth Circuit in *Burdine* concluded that defendants had a constitutional right to an attorney who was awake during the trial. In other cases, state and federal courts have failed to find prejudice when defense council was drunk or impaired by drugs during trial. In some cases, sleeping counsel has been deemed to provide a constitutionally acceptable level of representation.

The Supreme Court in two cases decided in 2012 ruled that persons accused of crime had the right to the effective assistance of counsel during the plea-bargaining process. In *Lafler v. Cooper*, the defendant rejected a plea bargain after defense counsel incorrectly informed him that the prosecution could not possibly prove a crucial element in his murder case. In *Missouri v. Frye*, defense counsel failed to communicate a plea bargain offer. Justice Kennedy's majority opinion in both cases asserted, "The right to adequate assistance of counsel cannot be defined or enforced without taking account of the central role plea bargaining plays in securing convictions and determining sentences."

Criminal defendants in the twenty-first century sometimes have the right to assistance beyond an attorney. Following *Ake v. Oklahoma* (1985), many states recognize that indigent defendants have a state constitutional right to have the state provide them with psychiatrists, investigators, and experts when doing so is necessary to assure a fair trial. *Husske v. Commonwealth* (VA 1996) declared, "The accused must demonstrate that the expert is required to address a critical issue and that the expert's assistance will contribute to the formulation and perfection of a viable defense."[92]

Burdine v. Johnson, 262 F. 3d 336 (5th Cir. 2001)

Calvin Burdine was convicted of the capital murder of W.T. Wise and sentenced to death in January 1984. His court-appointed counsel, Joe F. Cannon, appealed the decision, but both the conviction and the sentence were affirmed by the Texas Court of Criminal Appeals. In 1994 Burdine filed a second habeas corpus application in which he presented evidence that Cannon had repeatedly fallen asleep during his original trial. The state habeas court, after finding that "defense counsel repeatedly dozed and/or actually slept during substantial portions of [Burdine's] capital murder trial," concluded that Burdine had been denied his constitutional right under the Sixth and Fourteenth Amendments to the effective assistance of counsel. The Texas Court of Criminal Appeals reversed that ruling because Burdine did not demonstrate that he was prejudiced by counsel's sleeping at trial. Burdine then filed a habeas appeal in federal court. A federal district court concluded that prejudice should automatically be presumed whenever counsel sleeps for substantial portions of a trial. That decision was reversed by a three-judge panel on the Court of Appeals for the Fifth Circuit. The entire Fifth Circuit then agreed to determine the extent to which a sleeping attorney prejudiced a criminal defendant.

The Fifth Circuit by a 9-5 vote ruled that Burdine was denied his constitutional right to an attorney. Judge Benavides' majority opinion maintained, "Unconscious counsel equates to no counsel at all." Compare the majority opinion and the main dissent. On what points of law do they agree and disagree? On what facts do they agree and disagree? Who has the better legal argument? Who has the better factual argument? Both opinions recognize that courts have not presumed prejudice when counsel was drunk or under the influence of drugs. Why does Judge Benavides think that the occasional nap is different? Is he right? Should courts presume prejudice whenever an attorney is not fully awake or alert?

JUDGE BENAVIDES delivered the opinion of the Court.

. . .

The factual findings made during Burdine's state habeas proceedings demonstrate that Burdine's counsel was repeatedly asleep, and hence unconscious, as witnesses adverse to Burdine were examined and other evidence against Burdine was introduced. This unconsciousness extended through a not insubstantial portion of the 12 hour and 51 minute trial. Unconscious counsel equates to no counsel at all. Unconscious counsel does not analyze, object, listen or in any way exercise judgment on behalf of a client. . . .

The State suggests that because Cannon was physically present in the courtroom, his dozing constituted a form of performance that should be subjected to prejudice analysis. The State maintains that it is impossible to distinguish between sleeping counsel and other impairments that nevertheless have been subjected to prejudice analysis. We disagree. An unconscious attorney does not, indeed cannot, perform at all. This fact distinguishes the sleeping lawyer from the drunk or drugged one. Even the intoxicated attorney exercises judgment, though perhaps impaired, on behalf of his client at all times during a trial. Yet, the attorney that is unconscious during critical stages of a trial is simply not capable of exercising judgment. The unconscious attorney is in fact no different from an attorney that is physically absent from trial since both are equally unable to exercise judgment on behalf of their clients. Such absence of counsel at a critical stage of a proceeding makes the adversary process unreliable, and thus a presumption of prejudice is warranted.

92. *Husske v. Commonwealth*, 252 Va. 203 (1996).

. . .

JUDGE PATRICK E. HIGGINBOTHAM, joined by JUDGE KING, CHIEF JUDGE, JUDGE W. EUGENE DAVIS, and JUDGE WIENER, concurring:

. . .

. . . That sleeping counsel is absent counsel is elementary. Burdine's slumbering counsel presents us with a new factual situation, hopefully rare, but not a difficult question of the application of law to fact. The novelty of this case stems not from the implausibility of applying the rule to these facts, but from the stunning image of an attorney sleeping in the courtroom while his client is on trial for his life. We are not asked to stretch to conclude that counsel was absent in every relevant sense.

. . .

Surely the presentation of the evidence of guilt is a critical phase. Nor is it an answer that Burdine "freely and voluntarily confessed to his crime" (and hence that his lawyer slept didn't matter). This ignores both the record in this case and the reality that the effort to persuade a jury not to vote for death often runs, as here, throughout the guilt phase of the trial. The phrasing of the questions, their sequence and rhythm set tone and paint a picture. They become the platform for presenting the penalty case and final argument. The search for the precise evidence that came in as Burdine's counsel slept rests upon a view of trial dynamics and reality that confounds my forty years in the courtroom. With respect to my colleagues, that is not the way it works, and for the same reasons it is not the law. We presume prejudice because experience tells us that an occurrence presents both a high probability of prejudice and a difficulty of "proving it" in any finite sense. The law speaks of presumption not to supply a missing ingredient, but rather to recognize its inevitable presence. Right to counsel at critical stages is only an example of this principle. We simply will not put a person on trial for his life in the absence of counsel.

. . .

JUDGE E. GRADY JOLLY, joined by JUDGE JERRY E. SMITH, dissenting:

Because the record in this case makes clear that Burdine is plainly guilty of capital murder beyond a reasonable doubt; because Burdine voluntarily confessed to his crime; because, even though Burdine was fully aware that his counsel had slept at points during the trial, he repeatedly heaped post-trial compliments on his counsel for his performance at trial and continually has expressed confidence in his counsel after trial; because the record fairly establishes that Burdine's counsel actually provided competent representation throughout the course of the trial; because there is no suggestion in the record that Burdine suffered any prejudice on account of counsel's alleged sleeping, that is, there is no suggestion that the outcome in this case would have been any different on account of the allegations now made; because Burdine waited eleven years before he ever raised the "sleeping lawyer" claim; because there is no evidence in the record that shows that counsel's sleeping occurred at a critical stage in the trial, and because the now silent Burdine apparently could have offered testimony on this point but has chosen not to do so; and finally, because I am led to believe by these facts that the "sleeping lawyer" claim is in large part a diverting tactic to create the impression of a miscarriage of justice in a case in which substantial justice has been done, I respectfully dissent from the granting of habeas relief on the basis of the "sleeping lawyer" claim. . . .

JUDGE RHESA HAWKINS BARKSDALE, joined by JUDGE EDITH H. JONES, JUDGE JERRY E. SMITH and JUDGE EMILIO M. GARZA, dissenting:

. . .

. . . I would hold that, under the circumstances of this case, prejudice must be proved. Accordingly, I would remand. . . .

. . .

At trial, Cannon's theory of defense was: [an accomplice] instigated the murder; Burdine, who was recovering from lung-removal surgery, was too weak to have participated in the stabbing (Cannon had Burdine exhibit his surgical scars to the jury); and Wise [the victim] had taken advantage of Burdine, stealing his money, harassing and threatening him, including putting out contracts to physically harm him, and attempting to force him to prostitute himself.

An examination of the state court record reveals that, despite Cannon's sleeping during unidentified portions of the trial, there was a meaningful adversarial testing of the State's case. Cannon filed pre-trial motions, including for discovery, inspection, and production of evidence, such as Wise's criminal and employment records and photo albums of nude boys allegedly found in Wise's residence after the murder.

At trial, Cannon cross-examined the State's witnesses, made objections, and presented witnesses on behalf of Burdine. Most importantly, Cannon vigorously contested the admissibility of Burdine's confession—obviously, the key evidence of his guilt. . . .

. . .

. . . [F]or circumstances where, as here, counsel sleeps for unidentified portions of a trial, prejudice is not so likely that case-by-case inquiry into prejudice is not worth the cost. Again, the majority states that its rule "is limited to the egregious facts found by the state habeas court in this case." But, as noted, the state habeas court made no finding that Cannon's dozing and sleeping rose to the level of unconsciousness, and, in any event, no finding quantifying the amount of sleeping or what evidence was then being presented.Had the state habeas court actually found that Cannon was repeatedly unconscious during a substantial portion of trial, presumed-prejudice might well be warranted.

. . .

. . . [I]t is possible that unobjectionable evidence (or evidence which Cannon was already anticipating) may have been introduced while Cannon slept, without having a substantial effect on the reliability or fairness of Burdine's trial. Notwithstanding Cannon's sleep episodes, he provided at least some—indeed, as noted, a great deal of—meaningful assistance to Burdine and more than subjected the prosecution's case to "meaningful adversarial testing."

Along this line, and as discussed, although he ultimately was unsuccessful, Cannon vigorously contested the admissibility of Burdine's confession. Once the confession was admitted, Burdine's guilt was, for all intents and purposes, firmly established. In the light of Burdine's admissions in that confession and in his subsequent trial testimony that he was present during the robbery, knew it would occur, and witnessed part of Wise's murder, much of the evidence introduced by the State, especially evidence of the robbery, was essentially duplicative. Moreover, Cannon still sought to establish, through Burdine's testimony, that the confession, although already admitted in evidence, was coerced and inaccurate. He continued to press that point on direct appeal, again unsuccessfully.

In sum, Cannon's sleeping during unidentified portions of Burdine's trial did not result in its losing its character as a confrontation between adversaries, nor did it render the trial fundamentally unfair. Because Cannon provided meaningful assistance to Burdine, prejudice vel non to Burdine's defense, resulting from Cannon's sleeping, should be established under *Strickland v. Washington*'s (1984) two-prong test: Burdine should be required to demonstrate a reasonable probability that the outcome of the trial would have been different if, during the periods in which the transcript reflects no activity by Cannon, he had taken some action. . . .

E. Punishments

The constitutional law of punishment is moving in a slightly liberal direction. The number of persons executed each year in the United States is steadily decreasing. The Supreme Court has ruled that the Eighth and Fourteenth Amendments forbid executing the mentally retarded (*Atkins v. Virginia* [2002]), teenagers aged seventeen or younger at the time of their offense (*Roper v. Simmons* [2005]), and criminals who commit offenses other than murder (*Kennedy v. Louisiana* [2008]). The justices held that juvenile offenders may not be sentenced to life in prison without parole (*Miller v. Alabama* [2012]) and that juveniles guilty of crimes other than homicide may not constitutionally be sentenced to life in prison (*Graham v. Florida* [2010]). In *Brown v. Plata* (2011) a 5–4 judicial majority ordered California to release 46,000 prisoners on the ground that the health conditions in overcrowded state prisons violated the Eighth and Fourteenth Amendments. Justice Kennedy's majority opinion asserted, "A prison that deprives prisoners of basic sustenance, including adequate medical care, is incompatible with the concept of human dignity and has no place in civilized society."

Brown v. Plata aside, liberal Supreme Court decisions have influenced punitive practices at the margins. The present judicial majority seems willing to declare particular criminal sanctions unconstitutional only when the federal government and most states (and perhaps most Western nations) do not impose that punishment for that crime or for that offender. The justices have left standing such precedents as *McCleskey v. Kemp* (1987), which sharply limit claims that racial discrimination is affecting the capital sentencing process. *Ewing v. California* (2003) sustained California's controversial three-strikes law. That law mandated life in prison for any person convicted of three felonies. Justice O'Connor's majority opinion asserted,

When the California Legislature enacted the three strikes law, it made a judgment that protecting the public safety requires incapacitating criminals who have already been convicted of at least one serious or violent crime. Nothing in the Eighth Amendment prohibits California from making that choice. To the contrary, our cases establish that States have a valid interest in deterring and segregating habitual criminals.

Party platforms suggest that the constitutional politics of punishment is moving slightly rightwards. Republicans endorse capital punishment and stricter sentences for criminal offenders. The 2008 Republican Party platform asserted,

> We support mandatory sentencing provisions for gang conspiracy crimes, violent or sexual offenses against children, rape, and assaults resulting in serious bodily injury.
>
> Gang rape, child rape, and rape committed in the course of another felony deserve, at the least, mandatory life imprisonment.
>
> We oppose the granting of parole to dangerous or repeat felons.
>
> Courts must have the option of imposing the death penalty in capital murder cases and other instances of heinous crime, while federal review of those sentences should be streamlined to focus on claims of innocence and to prevent delaying tactics by defense attorneys.

Democrats now endorse capital punishment while insisting that the capital sentencing process include numerous safeguards. The 2008 Democratic Party platform stated, "We believe that the death penalty must not be arbitrary. DNA testing should be used in all appropriate circumstances, defendants should have effective assistance of counsel. In all death row cases, and thorough post-conviction reviews should be available."[93]

When reading the materials in this section, consider why the constitutional law of punishment is moving slightly leftward at a time when the constitutional politics of punishment is moving slightly to the right.

Roper v. Simmons, 543 U.S. 551 (2005)

Christopher Simmons, a seventeen-year-old, was arrested and charged with the brutal murder of Shirley Cook. Simmons was found guilty at trial and sentenced to death. After exhausting his direct appeals, Simmons sought post-conviction relief. His habeas corpus petition claimed that the Eighth and Fourteenth Amendments forbade states from executing any person who was less than eighteen years old when the criminal offense was committed. That claim was inconsistent with Stanford v. Kentucky *(1989). Justice Scalia's majority opinion in that case concluded that petitioners had "failed to establish a consensus against capital punishment for 16- and 17-year old offenders." Simmons insisted that such a consensus had developed in the subsequent fifteen years. The Supreme Court of Missouri agreed with Simmons and ruled that his execution would violate the Eighth and Fourteenth Amendments. Missouri appealed to the Supreme Court of the United States.*

The Supreme Court by a 5-4 vote declared that Simmons could not be constitutionally executed. Justice Kennedy's majority opinion held that the Eighth and Fourteenth Amendments prohibited states from executing persons who were younger than eighteen years old when their offense was committed. Following Justice Stevens's opinion in Atkins v. Virginia *(2002), which declared executing the mentally retarded unconstitutional, Justice Kennedy first found a national consensus against executing youthful offenders and then determined that such executions were inconsistent with legitimate penological goals. What reasons does Justice Kennedy give for reaching these conclusions? What does he believe changed in the sixteen years between* Stanford *and* Simmons*? Why do the dissenting justices disagree? What influence, if any, do you believe international law had on the decision in* Simmons*? What influence, if any, should international law have had on these decisions?*

JUSTICE KENNEDY delivered the opinion of the Court.

. . .

. . . [W]e now reconsider the issue decided in *Stanford v. Kentucky* (1989). The beginning point is a review of objective indicia of consensus, as expressed in particular by the enactments of legislatures that have addressed the question. These data give us essential instruction. We then must determine, in the exercise of our own independent judgment, whether the death penalty is a disproportionate punishment for juveniles.

The evidence of national consensus against the death penalty for juveniles is similar, and in some respects parallel, to the evidence [*Atkins v. Virginia* (2002)] held sufficient to demonstrate a national consensus against the death penalty for the mentally

93. The 2012 platforms of both major parties repeat these previous commitments.

Illustration 11-5 Juveniles and the Death Penalty

Source: Jeff Parker, Florida Today, 2005, http://www.cagle.com/news/deathpenaltyjuveniles/main.asp. © Copyright 2005 Parker–All Rights Reserved.

retarded. When *Atkins* was decided, 30 States prohibited the death penalty for the mentally retarded. This number comprised 12 that had abandoned the death penalty altogether, and 18 that maintained it but excluded the mentally retarded from its reach. By a similar calculation in this case, 30 States prohibit the juvenile death penalty, comprising 12 that have rejected the death penalty altogether and 18 that maintain it but, by express provision or judicial interpretation, exclude juveniles from its reach. *Atkins* emphasized that even in the 20 States without formal prohibition, the practice of executing the mentally retarded was infrequent. In the present case, too, even in the 20 States without a formal prohibition on executing juveniles, the practice is infrequent. Since *Stanford*, six States have executed prisoners for crimes committed as juveniles. In the past 10 years, only three have done so: Oklahoma, Texas, and Virginia.

. . .

Three general differences between juveniles under 18 and adults demonstrate that juvenile offenders cannot with reliability be classified among the worst offenders. First, as any parent knows and as the scientific and sociological studies respondent and his *amici* cite tend to confirm, "[a] lack of maturity and an underdeveloped sense of responsibility are found in youth more often than in adults and are more understandable among the young. These qualities often result in impetuous and ill-considered actions and decisions." . . . In recognition of the comparative immaturity and irresponsibility of juveniles, almost every State prohibits those under 18 years of age from voting, serving on juries, or marrying without parental consent.

The second area of difference is that juveniles are more vulnerable or susceptible to negative influences and outside pressures, including peer pressure. . . .

The third broad difference is that the character of a juvenile is not as well formed as that of an adult. The personality traits of juveniles are more transitory, less fixed.

These differences render suspect any conclusion that a juvenile falls among the worst offenders. The susceptibility of juveniles to immature and irresponsible behavior means "their irresponsible conduct is not as morally reprehensible as that of an adult." Their own vulnerability and comparative lack of control over their immediate surroundings mean juveniles have a greater claim than adults to be forgiven for failing to escape negative influences in their whole environment. . . .

. . .

. . . Whether viewed as an attempt to express the community's moral outrage or as an attempt to right the balance for the wrong to the victim, the case for retribution is not as strong with a minor as with an adult. Retribution is not proportional if the law's most severe penalty is imposed on one whose culpability or blameworthiness is diminished, to a substantial degree, by reason of youth and immaturity.

As for deterrence, it is unclear whether the death penalty has a significant or even measurable deterrent effect on juveniles, as counsel for petitioner acknowledged at oral argument. . . . [T]he same characteristics that render juveniles less culpable than adults suggest as well that juveniles will be less susceptible to deterrence. . . .

. . .

Our determination that the death penalty is disproportionate punishment for offenders under 18 finds confirmation in the stark reality that the United States is the only country in the world that continues to give official sanction to the juvenile death penalty. This reality does not become controlling, for the task of interpreting the Eighth Amendment remains our responsibility. Yet at least from the time of the Court's decision in *Trop v. Dulles* (1958), the Court has referred to the laws of other countries and to international authorities as instructive for its interpretation of the Eighth Amendment's prohibition of "cruel and unusual punishments."

. . .

JUSTICE STEVENS, with whom JUSTICE GINSBURG joins, concurring.

Perhaps even more important than our specific holding today is our reaffirmation of the basic principle that informs the Court's interpretation of the Eighth Amendment. If the meaning of that Amendment had been frozen when it was originally drafted, it would impose no impediment to the execution of 7-year-old children today. . . . In the best tradition of the common law, the pace of that evolution is a matter for continuing debate; but that our understanding of the Constitution does change from time to time has been settled since John Marshall breathed life into its text. . . .

JUSTICE O'CONNOR, dissenting.

. . .

It is by now beyond serious dispute that the Eighth Amendment's prohibition of "cruel and unusual punishments" is not a static command. Its mandate would be little more than a dead letter today if it barred only those sanctions—like the execution of children under the age of seven—that civilized society had already repudiated in 1791. . . .

. . .

In determining whether the juvenile death penalty comports with contemporary standards of decency, our inquiry begins with the "clearest and most reliable objective evidence of contemporary values"—the actions of the Nation's legislatures. . . .

. . . [A]t least seven States have current statutes that specifically set 16 or 17 as the minimum age at which commission of a capital crime can expose the offender to the death penalty. Five of these seven States presently have one or more juvenile offenders on death row (six if respondent is included in the count), and four of them have executed at least one under-18 offender in the past 15 years. In all, there are currently over 70 juvenile offenders on death row in 12 different States (13 including respondent). This evidence suggests some measure of continuing public support for the availability of the death penalty for 17-year-old capital murderers.

. . .

. . . [T]he Court adduces no evidence whatsoever in support of its sweeping conclusion, that it is only in "rare" cases, if ever, that 17-year-old murderers are sufficiently mature and act with sufficient depravity to warrant the death penalty. The fact that juveniles are generally *less* culpable for their misconduct than adults does not necessarily mean that a 17-year-old murderer cannot be *sufficiently* culpable to merit the death penalty. At most, the Court's argument suggests that the average 17-year-old murderer is not as culpable as the average adult murderer. But an especially depraved juvenile offender may nevertheless be just as culpable as many adult offenders considered bad enough to deserve the death penalty. Similarly, the fact that the availability of the death penalty may be *less* likely to deter a juvenile from committing a capital crime does not imply that this threat cannot *effectively* deter some 17-year-olds from such an act. . . .

. . .

For purposes of proportionality analysis, 17-year-olds as a class are qualitatively and materially different from the mentally retarded. "Mentally retarded" offenders, as we understood that category in *Atkins,* are *defined* by precisely the characteristics which render death an excessive punishment. A mentally retarded person is, "by definition," one whose cognitive and behavioral capacities have been proved to fall below a certain minimum. . . . Moreover, it defies common sense to suggest that 17-year-olds as a class are somehow equivalent to mentally retarded persons with regard to culpability or susceptibility to deterrence. Seventeen-year-olds may, on average, be less mature than adults, but that lesser maturity simply cannot be equated with the major, lifelong impairments suffered by the mentally retarded.

The proportionality issues raised by the Court clearly implicate Eighth Amendment concerns. But these concerns may properly be addressed not by means of an arbitrary, categorical age-based rule, but rather through individualized sentencing in which juries are required to give appropriate mitigating weight to the defendant's immaturity, his susceptibility to outside pressures, his cognizance of the consequences of his actions, and so forth. In that way the constitutional response can be tailored to the specific problem it is meant to remedy. . . .

. . .

Nevertheless, I disagree with Justice SCALIA's contention that foreign and international law have no place in our Eighth Amendment jurisprudence. Over the course of nearly half a century, the Court has consistently referred to foreign and international law as relevant to its assessment of evolving standards of decency. . . . [T]his Nation's evolving understanding of human dignity certainly is neither wholly isolated from, nor inherently at odds with, the values prevailing in other countries. On the contrary, we should not be surprised to find congruence between domestic and international values, especially where the international community has reached clear agreement—expressed in international law or in the domestic laws of individual countries—that a particular form of punishment is inconsistent with fundamental human rights. At least, the existence of an international consensus of this nature can serve to confirm the reasonableness of a consonant and genuine American consensus. The instant case presents no such domestic consensus, however, and the recent emergence of an otherwise global consensus does not alter that basic fact.

JUSTICE SCALIA, with whom THE CHIEF JUSTICE and JUSTICE THOMAS join, dissenting.

. . . What a mockery today's opinion makes of Hamilton's expectation [in *Federalist* 78 that the judges will never exercise "will,"] announcing the Court's conclusion that the meaning of our Constitution has changed over the past 15 years—not, mind you, that this Court's decision 15 years ago was *wrong,* but that the Constitution *has changed.* The Court reaches this implausible result by purporting to advert, not to the original meaning of the Eighth Amendment, but to "the evolving standards of decency," of our national society. It then finds, on the flimsiest of grounds, that a national consensus which could not be perceived in our people's laws barely 15 years ago now solidly exists. . . . The Court thus proclaims itself sole arbiter of our Nation's moral standards—and in the course of discharging that awesome responsibility purports to take guidance from the views of foreign courts and legislatures. Because I do not believe that the meaning of our Eighth Amendment, any more than the meaning of other provisions of our Constitution, should be determined by the subjective views of five Members of this Court and like-minded foreigners, I dissent.

. . .

Words have no meaning if the views of less than 50% of death penalty States can constitute a national consensus. . . .

. . . *None* of our cases dealing with an alleged constitutional limitation upon the death penalty has counted, as States supporting a consensus in favor of that limitation, States that have eliminated the death penalty entirely. And with good reason. Consulting States that bar the death penalty concerning the necessity of making an exception to the penalty for offenders under 18 is rather like including old-order Amishmen in a consumer-preference poll on the electric car. . . . That 12 States favor *no* executions says something about consensus against the death penalty, but nothing—absolutely nothing—about consensus that offenders under 18 deserve special immunity from such a penalty. In repealing the death penalty, those 12 States considered *none* of the factors that the Court puts forth as determinative of the issue before us today—lower culpability of the young, inherent recklessness, lack of capacity for considered judgment, etc. What might be relevant, perhaps, is how many of those States permit 16- and 17-year-old offenders to be treated as adults with respect to noncapital offenses. (They all do. . . .) . . .

. . .

The Court's reliance on the infrequency of executions for under-18 murderers credits an argument that this Court considered and explicitly rejected in *Stanford.* That infrequency is explained, we accurately said, both by "the undisputed fact that a far smaller percentage of capital crimes are committed by persons under 18 than over 18," and by the fact that juries are required at sentencing to consider the offender's youth as a mitigating factor. Thus, "it is not only possible, but overwhelmingly probable, that the very considerations which induce [respondent] and [his] supporters to believe that death should *never* be imposed on offenders under 18 cause prosecutors and juries to believe that it should *rarely* be imposed."

Of course, the real force driving today's decision is not the actions of four state legislatures, but the Court's ""'own judgment"'" that murderers younger than 18 can never be as morally culpable as older counterparts. . . . On the evolving-standards hypothesis, the only legitimate function of this Court is to identify a moral consensus of the American people. By what conceivable warrant can nine lawyers presume to be the authoritative conscience of the Nation?

. . .

We need not look far to find studies contradicting the Court's conclusions. As petitioner points out, the American Psychological Association (APA), which claims in this case that scientific evidence shows persons under 18 lack the ability to take moral responsibility for their decisions, has previously taken precisely the opposite position before this very Court. In its brief in *Hodgson v. Minnesota* (1990), the APA found a "rich body of research" showing that juveniles are mature enough to decide whether to obtain an abortion without parental involvement. Given the nuances of scientific methodology and conflicting views, courts—which can only consider the limited evidence on the record before them—are ill equipped to determine which view of science is the right one. Legislatures "are better qualified to weigh and 'evaluate the results of statistical studies in terms of their own local conditions and with a flexibility of approach that is not available to the courts.'"

Even putting aside questions of methodology, the studies cited by the Court offer scant support for a categorical prohibition of the death penalty for murderers under 18. At most, these studies conclude that, *on average,* or *in most cases,* persons under 18 are unable to take moral responsibility for their actions. Not one of the cited studies opines that all individuals under 18 are unable to appreciate the nature of their crimes.

. . .

In other contexts where individualized consideration is provided, we have recognized that at least some minors will be mature enough to make difficult decisions that involve moral considerations. For instance, we have struck down abortion statutes that do not allow minors deemed mature by courts to bypass parental notification provisions. It is hard to see why this context should be any different. Whether to obtain an abortion is surely a much more complex decision for a young person than whether to kill an innocent person in cold blood.

. . .

. . . [T]he basic premise of the Court's argument—that American law should conform to the laws of the rest of the world—ought to be rejected out of hand. In fact the Court itself does not believe it. In many significant respects the laws of most other countries differ from our law—including not only such explicit provisions of our Constitution as the right to jury trial and grand jury indictment, but even many interpretations of the Constitution prescribed by this Court itself. The Court-pronounced exclusionary rule, for example, is distinctively American. . . .

. . . Most other countries—including those committed to religious neutrality—do not insist on the degree of separation between church and state that this Court requires. For example, whereas "we have recognized special Establishment Clause dangers where the government makes direct money payments to sectarian institutions," countries such as the Netherlands, Germany, and Australia allow direct government funding of religious schools on the ground that "the state can only be truly neutral between secular and religious perspectives if it does not dominate the provision of so key a service as education, and makes it possible for people to exercise their right of religious expression within the context of public funding." . . .

And let us not forget the Court's abortion jurisprudence, which makes us one of only six countries that allow abortion on demand until the point of viability. . . .

. . .

The Court should either profess its willingness to reconsider all these matters in light of the views of foreigners, or else it should cease putting forth foreigners' views as part of the reasoned basis of its decisions. To invoke alien law when it agrees with one's own thinking, and ignore it otherwise, is not reasoned decisionmaking, but sophistry. . . .

F. Infamous Crimes and Criminals

The War on Terror

The Bush administration and Congress responded sharply to the September 11, 2001, terrorist attacks on the United States. Numerous suspected terrorists were detained at an American military base in Guantanamo Bay, Cuba, and at undisclosed sites in Europe. Some suspected terrorists were subjected to "enhanced interrogation," the precise nature of which is not known to any degree of certainty but which certainly included the use of sleep deprivation, controlled fear (muzzled dogs), stress positions, hypothermia, and waterboarding. The Bush administration insisted that these detainees, a few of whom were American citizens, had no rights to any hearings on their status, no right to habeas corpus, and could be tried by military commissions as unlawful combatants. Administrative officials, supported by the USA Patriot Act of 2001, engaged in extensive wiretapping in order to gain knowledge about terrorist activity. Many persons suspected that the Bush administration was also engaged in racial profiling. Federal officials made use of a federal law that permitted the government to detain for an indefinite period of time persons suspected of having material information about possible terrorist attacks. The Obama administration has engaged in some of these activities, abandoned others, and proposed new constitutionally controversial means for fighting the War on Terror.[94] Most notably, the Obama administration in 2011 ordered a drone attack in Yemen that killed Anwar al-Awlaki, an American citizen suspected of being an al-Qaeda leader. Harold Koh, the legal advisor to the State Department, justified that policy by maintaining that "individuals who are part of such an armed group are belligerent and, therefore, lawful targets under international law."[95]

Bush and Obama administration policies raise many constitutional questions. The first is the proper constitutional categories to use when thinking about the rights of suspected terrorists and suspected terrorist organizations.

- They might be common criminals, to be treated in the same manner as persons suspected of murder and other particularly despicable crimes.
- They might be enemy combatants, to be treated in the same manner as German and Japanese soldiers during World War II.
- They might be unlawful combatants, to be treated in the same manner as the German saboteurs tried in *In re Quirin* (1942).
- They might merit an entirely new classification.

The second series of questions concern how to apply existing rules of constitutional criminal procedure to the War on Terror. Preventing terrorism is a compelling interest. Whether that compelling interest justifies such actions as indefinite detention of material witnesses, extensive wiretapping, "enhanced methods of interrogation," or targeting persons for assassination is a more difficult question. A third series of questions concern constitutional authority for resolving these controversies.

- Congress may have the power as part of the congressional power to punish crimes against the United States and determine the laws of war.
- The president may have the power as part of the president's authority as commander-in-chief.

94. Jack Goldsmith, *Power and Constraint: The Accountable Presidency after 9/11* (New York: Norton, 2012), 3–22.

95. Harold Hongju Koh, "The Obama Administration and International Law," speech at the Annual Meeting of the American Society of International Law, Washington, D.C. (March 25, 2010). Available at http://www.state.gov/s/l/releases/remarks/139119.htm

- The Supreme Court may have the power as part of the judicial authority to interpret the Constitution (and existing federal laws).

A fair bipartisan consensus supports many actions taken against terrorists. Most Americans support giving government extensive powers to investigate suspected terrorists. The Obama administration supported legislation extending the Patriot Act's authorization of "roving wiretaps" and other related intrusions on privacy. The Obama administration also insisted on military trials for some suspected terrorists and, as of the publication of this book, has not shut down the detainee center at Guantanamo Bay. Both the Bush and Obama administrations have ordered and defended targeted assassinations of al-Qaeda leaders.

The sharpest partisan divisions exist on the treatment of persons being detained as suspected terrorists. Most Democrats believe that Bush administration policies violated numerous constitutional rights. The Democratic Party platform in 2008 stated,

> To build a freer and safer world, we will lead in ways that reflect the decency and aspirations of the American people. We will not ship away prisoners in the dead of night to be tortured in far-off countries, or detain without trial or charge prisoners who can and should be brought to justice for their crimes, or maintain a network of secret prisons to jail people beyond the reach of the law. We will respect the time-honored principle of habeas corpus, the seven century-old right of individuals to challenge the terms of their own detention that was recently reaffirmed by our Supreme Court. We will close the detention camp in Guantanamo Bay, the location of so many of the worst constitutional abuses in recent years. With these necessary changes, the attention of the world will be directed where it belongs: on what terrorists have done to us, not on how we treat suspects.

Republicans are more divided. Most oppose giving suspected terrorists habeas corpus rights. Most defended the provisions in the Detainee Treatment Act denying habeas corpus rights to persons detained in Guantanamo Bay. Republican presidential candidates sharply disputed when enhanced methods of interrogation were warranted. Led by Senator John McCain of Arizona, many Republicans in Congress supported placing restrictions on intelligence methods. Section 102 of a defense spending measure proposed in 2007 stated, "No person in the custody or under the effective control of the United States Government shall be subject to any treatment or technique of interrogation not authorized by and listed in the United States Army Field Manual."[96] President Bush indicated that enhanced methods of interrogation might nevertheless be legally employed in some circumstances. His letter to Congress objecting to that provision asserted,

> This bill would jeopardize the safety of the American people by undermining the CIA's enhanced interrogation program, which has helped the United States capture senior al Qaeda leaders and disrupt multiple attacks against the homeland, thus saving American lives. Section 102 has no place in an emergency wartime appropriations bill that should be focused on ensuring that the men and women of our Armed Forces have the funding they need to complete their mission.

The Supreme Court ruled in favor of detainee rights in three important cases. *Hamdi v. Rumsfeld* (2004) held that American citizens could not be held as unlawful combatants unless they were given a hearing to contest that status. *Hamdan v. Rumsfeld* (2006) held that Congress had not authorized military trials for suspected terrorists. *Boumediene v. Bush* (2008) ruled that detainees in Guantanamo Bay had the right to petition for a writ of habeas corpus. While civil libertarians hailed each decision as a triumph for fundamental rights, these decisions' effect on policy has been minimal. Guantanamo Bay remains open. While many detainees have been released, the releases seem to have been for reasons other than Supreme Court decisions.

Other Supreme Court and lower federal court decisions supported administration policies. In *Ashcroft v. Al-Kidd* (2011) four justices declared that persons could be detained as material witnesses against suspected terrorists, even though the material witness statute may have been used as a pretense to justify the detention. Four justices refused to discuss the constitutionality of the detention, although their opinions expressed significant doubts as to whether the government had acted constitutionally. The Court of Appeals for the Second Circuit in *Awadallah v. United States* (2003) declared that federal agents could detain for purposes of grand

96. 153 *Congressional Record*, 110th Cong., 2nd Sess. (2007), 24561. H.R. 4165 did not pass.

jury testimony persons believed to have material information about terrorists.[97] The Court of Appeals for the Seventh Circuit in *Tabbaa v. Chertoff* (2007) declared constitutional a customs search of all persons who had attended a prominent Islamic conference in Toronto.[98]

The USA Patriot Act

The USA Patriot Act of 2001 was the main congressional response to the terrorist attacks of September 11, 2001. Within days of that attack the Bush administration proposed that law enforcement agencies be given new powers to conduct searches, share information, detain and deport immigrants suspected of terrorist involvement, and freeze financial assets of suspected terrorists. Many Democrats insisted that Bush administration proposals violated the Constitution. After intense negotiations between the House, Senate, and White House, a modified bill passed Congress by overwhelming majorities. President Bush signed the bill into law on October 26, 2001.

The most constitutionally controversial provisions in the USA Patriot Act permit the government to not inform persons for a period of time that their houses have been searched (so-called sneak-and-peek warrants), permit various intelligence agencies to share information, and permit intelligence agencies to get wiretaps for reasons that would not justify a wiretap in a criminal investigation. Why does Senator Feingold criticize these practices? How do Senator Hatch and President Bush respond to those criticisms? Senator Leahy notes the many compromises that occurred during the debate over the Patriot Act. Were these compromises reasonable accommodations, or did one party give away the store (and, if so, which party and why)? Notice the emphasis placed on the four-year sunset provision. Was that provision wise? Could a court place a four-year sunset provision on a constitutionally borderline practice?

Senate Debate over the Patriot Act (October 25, 2001)[99]

SENATOR PATRICK LEAHY (Democrat, Vermont)

The bill we are passing today makes potentially sweeping changes in the relationships between the law enforcement and intelligence agencies. In the current crisis, there is justification for expanding authority specifically for counterintelligence to detect and prevent international terrorism. I support the FBI request for broader authority under FISA [Foreign Intelligence Surveillance Act] for pen registers and access to records without having to meet the statutory "agent of a foreign power" standard, because the Fourth Amendment does not normally apply to such techniques and the FBI has comparable authority in its criminal investigations. However, I have insisted that this authority to investigate U.S. persons be limited to counterintelligence investigations conducted to protect against international terrorism and spying activities and that such investigations may not be based solely on activities protected by the First Amendment. . . .

The gravest departure from that framework, and the one with most potential for abuses, is the new and unprecedented statutory authority for sharing of "foreign intelligence" from criminal investigations with "any other Federal law enforcement, intelligence, protective, immigration, national defense, or national security official."

. . .

The new authority to disseminate "foreign intelligence" from criminal investigations, including grand juries and law enforcement wiretaps, is an invitation to abuse without special safeguards. Fortunately, the final bill includes a provision, which was not in the Administration's original proposal, to maintain some degree of judicial oversight of the dissemination of grand jury information. Within a "reasonable time" after the disclosure of grand jury information, a government attorney "shall file under seal a notice with the court stating the fact that such information was disclosed and the departments, agencies, or entities to which the disclosure was made." No such judicial role is provided for the disclosure of information from wiretaps and other criminal investigative techniques including the infiltration of organizations with informants. However, that authority to disclose without judicial review is subject to the sunset in four years.

. . .

Another issue that has caused serious concern relates to the Administration's proposal for so-called "sneak and peek" search warrants. . . . Normally, when law enforcement officers execute a search warrant, they must leave a copy of the warrant and a receipt for all property seized at the premises searched.

97. *Awadallah v. United States*, 349 F.3d 42 (2d Cir. 2003).

98. *Tabbaa v. Chertoff*, 509 F.3d 89 (7th Cir. 2007).

99. Excerpted from *Congressional Record*, 107th Cong., 1st Sess. (2001), 20,673–705.

Thus, even if the search occurs when the owner of the premises is not present, the owner will receive notice that the premises have been lawfully searched pursuant to a warrant rather than, for example, burglarized.

. . .

I was able to make significant improvements in the Administration's original proposal that will help to ensure that the government's authority to obtain sneak and peek warrants is not abused. First, the provision that is now in section 213 of the bill prohibits the government from seizing any tangible property or any wire or electronic communication or stored electronic information unless it makes a showing of reasonable necessity for the seizure. . . . Second, the provision now requires that notice be given within a reasonable time of the execution of the warrant rather than giving a blanket authorization for up to a 90-day delay. What constitutes a reasonable time, of course, will depend upon the circumstances of the particular case. But I would expect courts to be guided by the teachings of the Second and the Ninth Circuits that, in the ordinary case, a reasonable time is no more than seven days.

. . .

Among the more controversial changes in FISA requested by the Administration was the proposal to allow surveillance and search when "a purpose" is to obtain foreign intelligence information. Current law requires that the secret procedures and different probable cause standards under FISA be used only if a high-level executive official certifies that "the purpose" is to obtain foreign intelligence information. The Administration's aim was to allow FISA surveillance and search for law enforcement purposes, so long as there was at least some element of a foreign intelligence purpose. This proposal raised constitutional concerns. . . .

. . . .

Section 218 of the bill adopts "significant purpose," and it will be up to the courts to determine how far law enforcement agencies may use FISA for criminal investigation and prosecution beyond the scope of the statutory definition of "foreign intelligence information."

. . .

We have done our utmost to protect Americans against abuse of these new law enforcement tools, and there are new law enforcement tools involved. In granting these new powers, the American people but also we, their representatives in Congress, grant the administration our trust that they are not going to be misused. It is a two way street. We are giving powers to the administration; we will have to extend some trust that they are not going to be misused.

The way we guarantee that is congressional oversight. . . .

Interestingly enough, the 4-year sunset provision included in this final agreement will be an enforcement mechanism for adequate oversight. We did not have a sunset provision in the Senate bill. The House included a 5-year provision. The administration wanted even 10 years. We compromised on 4. It makes sense. It makes sense because with everybody knowing there is that sunset provision, everybody knows they are going to have to use these powers carefully and in the best way. If they do that, then they can have extensions. If they don't, they won't. It also enhances our power for oversight.

SENATOR ORIN HATCH (Republican, Utah)

Another troublesome change concerns the 4-year sunset provision. . . . In my opinion, a sunset will undermine the effectiveness of the tools we are creating here and send the wrong message to the American public that somehow these tools are extraordinary.

One hardly understands the need to sunset legislation that both provides critically necessary tools and protects our civil liberties. Furthermore, as the Attorney General stated, how can we sunset these tools when we know full well that the terrorists will not sunset their evil intentions? I sincerely hope we undertake a thorough review and further extend the legislation once the 4-year period expires. At least, we will have 4 years of effective law enforcement against terrorism that we currently do not have.

SENATOR RUSSELL FEINGOLD (Democrat, Wisconsin)

As it seeks to combat terrorism, the Justice Department is making extraordinary use of its power to arrest and detain individuals, jailing hundreds of people on immigration violations and arresting more than a dozen "material witnesses" not charged with any crime. Although the Government has used these authorities before, it has not done so on such a broad scale. Judging from Government announcements, the Government has not brought any criminal charges related to the attacks with regard to the overwhelming majority of these detainees.

. . .

Of course, there is no doubt that if we lived in a police state, it would be easier to catch terrorists.

If we lived in a country that allowed the police to search your home at any time for any reason; if we lived in a country that allowed the government to open your mail, eavesdrop on your phone conversations, or intercept your email communications; if we lived in a country that allowed the government to hold people in jail indefinitely based on what they write or think, or based on mere suspicion that they are up to no good, then the government would no doubt discover and arrest more terrorists.

But that probably would not be a country in which we would want to live. And that would not be a country for which we could, in good conscience, ask our young people to fight and die. In short, that would not be America.

Preserving our freedom is one of the main reasons we are now engaged in this new war on terrorism. We will lose that war without firing a shot if we sacrifice the liberties of the American people.

. . .

. . . [T]he bill contains some very significant changes in criminal procedure that will apply to every federal criminal investigation in this country, not just those involving terrorism. One provision would greatly expand the circumstances in which law enforcement agencies can search homes and offices without notifying the owner prior to the search. The longstanding practice under the fourth amendment of serving a warrant prior to executing a search could be easily avoided in virtually every case, because the government would simply have to show that it had "reasonable cause to believe" that providing notice "'may' seriously jeopardize an investigation." This is a significant infringement on personal liberty.

Notice is a key element of fourth amendment protections. It allows a person to point out mistakes in a warrant and to make sure that a search is limited to the terms of a warrant. Just think about the possibility of the police showing up at your door with a warrant to search your house. You look at the warrant and say, "yes, that's my address, but the name on the warrant isn't me." And the police realize a mistake has been made and go away. If you're not home, and the police have received permission to do a "sneak and peek" search, they can come in your house, look around, and leave, and may never have to tell you that ever happened. That bothers me. I bet it bothers most Americans.

. . .

I am also very troubled by the broad expansion of Government power under the Foreign Intelligence Surveillance Act, known as FISA. When Congress passed FISA in 1978, it granted to the executive branch the power to conduct surveillance in foreign intelligence investigations without having to meet the rigorous probable cause standard under the fourth amendment that is required for criminal investigations.

There is a lower threshold for obtaining a wiretap order from the FISA court because the FBI is not investigating a crime, it is investigating foreign intelligence activities. But the law currently requires that intelligence gathering be the primary purpose of the investigation in order for this much lower standard to apply. The bill changes that requirement. The Government now will only have to show that intelligence is a "significant purpose" of the investigation. So even if the primary purpose is a criminal investigation, the heightened protections of the fourth amendment will not apply.

. . .

SENATOR HATCH

. . . [W]hat [Senator Feingold] called a "sneak and peek" search warrant, these warrants are already used throughout the United States, throughout our whole country. The bill simply codifies and clarifies the practice making certain that only a Federal court, not an agent or prosecutor, can authorize such a warrant.

Let me be clear. Courts already allow warrants under our fourth amendment. It is totally constitutional. It has been held so almost from the beginning of this country; some will say from the beginning of this country. Together with Senator Leahy, we carefully drafted a provision that standardizes this widely accepted practice.

Second, to respond to the suggestion that the legislation is not properly mindful of our constitutional liberties—my friend from Wisconsin talks theoretically about maybe the loss of some civil liberties—I would like to talk concretely about the loss of liberty of almost 6,000 people because of the terrorist acts on September 11. I am a little bit more concerned right now about their loss of life. I am even more concerned now that they have lost their lives that thousands of other Americans don't lose their lives because we fail to act and fail to give law enforcement the tools that are essential.

It is a nice thing to talk about theory. But we have to talk about reality. We have written this bill so the constitutional realities are that the Constitution is not infringed upon and civil liberties are not infringed upon except to the extent that the Constitution permits law enforcement to correct difficulties.

. . .

The tools we are promoting in this legislation have been carefully crafted to protect civil liberties. In addition to protecting civil liberties, give law enforcement the tools they need so we, to the extent we possibly can, will be able to protect our citizens from events and actions such as happened on September 11 of this year.

. . .

I think most people in this country would be outraged to know that various agencies of Government, the intelligence community, and law enforcement community, under current law— until this bill is passed—cannot exchange information that might help interdict and stop terrorism. People are outraged when they hear this. And they ought to be.

The fact is that that is the situation. I know the heads of the Criminal Division of the Justice Department have said that: Unless we can share this information, we cannot pick up the people who are terrorists, whom we need to stop, in time to stop them. I think they would be outraged to know that, under title III, you cannot electronically surveil a terrorist unless there is some underlying criminal predicate. In many cases, there is no underlying criminal predicate, so you can't do to terrorists what we can do for health care fraud, or for sexual exploitation of children, or for the Mafia, or for drug dealers.

People would be amazed to know we treat terrorism with kid gloves in the current criminal code. This bill stops that. I think most people would be amazed to know that pen register trap-and-trace devices are not permitted against terrorists under provisions of the law today. You can't get the numbers called out of the phone and you can't get the numbers called into the phone. That is what that means. This bill remedies that so we can get these numbers and do what has to be done.

I think most people are shocked to find out that you can't electronically surveil the terrorists. You have to go after the phone, and then you have to get a warrant in every jurisdiction where that phone shows up. Terrorists don't pay any attention to those antiquated laws. They just buy 10 cell phones, talk for a while, and throw it out the window. We have to be able to track terrorists. Under current law, we cannot do that with the efficiency that needs to be used here. I don't see any civil liberties violated there, but I see some of them protected. I think of the civil liberties of those approximately 6,000 people who lost their lives, and potentially many others if we don't give law enforcement the tools they need to do the job. . . .

George W. Bush, Remarks on Signing the USA Patriot Act of 2001 (October 26, 2001)

Good morning and welcome to the White House. Today we take an essential step in defeating terrorism, while protecting the constitutional rights of all Americans. With my signature, this law will give intelligence and law enforcement officials important new tools to fight a present danger.

. . .

Surveillance of communications is another essential tool to pursue and stop terrorists. The existing law was written in the era of rotary telephones. This new law that I sign today will allow surveillance of all communications used by terrorists, including e-mails, the Internet, and cell phones. As of today, we'll be able to better meet the technological challenges posed by this proliferation of communications technology.

Investigations are often slowed by limit on the reach of Federal search warrants. Law enforcement agencies have to get a new warrant for each new district they investigate, even when they're after the same suspect. Under this new law, warrants are valid across all districts and across all States.

And finally, the new legislation greatly enhances the penalties that will fall on terrorists or anyone who helps them. Current statutes deal more severely with drug traffickers than with terrorists. That changes today. We are enacting new and harsh penalties for possession of biological weapons. We're making it easier to seize the assets of groups and individuals involved in terrorism. The Government will have wider latitude in deporting known terrorists and their supporters. The statute of limitations on terrorist acts will be lengthened, as will prison sentences for terrorists.

This bill was carefully drafted and considered. Led by the Members of Congress on this stage and those seated in the audience, it was crafted with skill and care, determination and a spirit of bipartisanship for which the entire Nation is grateful. This bill met with an overwhelming—overwhelming—agreement in Congress because it upholds and respects the civil liberties guaranteed by our Constitution. . . .

Hamdi v. Rumsfeld, 542 U.S. 507 (2004)

Yaser Esam Hamdi was an American citizen who was born in Louisiana but raised in Saudi Arabia. In 2001 he was captured by Northern Alliance forces in Afghanistan and turned over to the American military. The military transferred Hamdi to a detention facility in Guantanamo Bay, Cuba. Once governing officials determined that Hamdi was an American citizen, he was transferred to a naval brig in Norfolk, Virginia, and later to Charleston, South Carolina. The U.S. government designated Hamdi as an "enemy combatant" to be held indefinitely and without trial. The government based this classification on a report submitted by Defense Department official Michael Mobbs that stated that Hamdi had received military training from the Taliban, carried a rifle, and was captured with his unit on the battlefield. Hamdi's father petitioned for a writ of habeas corpus on his son's behalf. He contended that Hamdi was a relief worker in Afghanistan, not a combatant for the Taliban or al-Qaeda. Equally as important, Hamdi's father insisted that the due process clause of the Constitution entitled American citizens to a full evidentiary hearing before they could be detained as enemy combatants. The federal district court ordered the government to produce more evidence that Hamdi was an enemy combatant, but that order was reversed by the Court of Appeals for the Fourth Circuit. Hamdi appealed to the Supreme Court of the United States.

The Supreme Court by an 8-1 vote declared Hamdi's detention illegal. Justice O'Connor, Justice Souter, and four other justices insisted that Hamdi's detention was inconsistent with federal law. Justices Stevens and Scalia insisted that Hamdi's detention was inconsistent with the Constitution. Justice Thomas maintained that the president had the power to detain American citizens as enemy combatants. As you read these opinions, consider the extent to which they depend on federal law or constitutional provisions. What do the various justices think are the constitutional rules for detaining American citizens as enemy combatants? What do you believe are the constitutional rules? Many observers were surprised when the Rehnquist Court declared that Hamdi was being illegally detained. What do you think explains the 8-1 decision rejecting Bush administration policy?

JUSTICE O'CONNOR announced the judgment of the Court and delivered an opinion, in which the CHIEF JUSTICE, JUSTICE KENNEDY, and JUSTICE BREYER join.

. . .

The [Authorization to Use Military Force] AUMF authorizes the President to use "all necessary and appropriate force" against "nations, organizations, or persons" associated with the September 11, 2001, terrorist attacks. There can be no doubt that individuals who fought against the United States in Afghanistan as part of the Taliban, an organization known to have supported the al Qaeda terrorist network responsible for those attacks, are individuals Congress sought to target in passing the AUMF. We conclude that detention of individuals falling into the limited category we are considering, for the duration of the particular conflict in which they were captured, is so fundamental and accepted an incident to war as to be an exercise of the "necessary and appropriate force" Congress has authorized the President to use.

The capture and detention of lawful combatants and the capture, detention, and trial of unlawful combatants, by "universal agreement and practice," are "important incident[s] of war." *Ex parte Quirin* (1942). The purpose of detention is to prevent captured individuals from returning to the field of battle and taking up arms once again. . . .

There is no bar to this Nation's holding one of its own citizens as an enemy combatant. In *Quirin*, one of the detainees, Haupt, alleged that he was a naturalized United States citizen. We held that "[c]itizens who associate themselves with the military arm of the enemy government, and with its aid, guidance and direction enter this country bent on hostile acts, are enemy belligerents within the meaning of . . . the law of war." . . . A citizen, no less than an alien, can be "part of or supporting forces hostile to the United States or coalition partners" and "engaged in an armed conflict against the United States" . . . ; such a citizen, if released, would pose the same threat of returning to the front during the ongoing conflict.

. . .

Ex parte Milligan (1866) . . . does not undermine our holding about the Government's authority to seize enemy combatants, as we define that term today. In that case, the Court made repeated reference to the fact that its inquiry into whether the military tribunal had jurisdiction to try and punish Milligan turned in large part on the fact that Milligan was not a prisoner of war, but a resident of Indiana arrested while at home there. That fact was central to its conclusion. Had Milligan been captured while he was assisting Confederate soldiers by carrying a rifle against Union troops on a Confederate battlefield, the holding of the Court might well have been different. . . .

. . .

Even in cases in which the detention of enemy combatants is legally authorized, there remains the question of what process is constitutionally due to a citizen who disputes his enemy-combatant status. Hamdi argues that he is owed a meaningful and timely hearing and that "extra-judicial detention [that] begins and ends with the submission of an affidavit based on third-hand hearsay" does not comport with the Fifth and Fourteenth Amendments. The Government counters that any more process than was provided below would be both unworkable and "constitutionally intolerable." . . .

. . .

. . . The ordinary mechanism that we use for balancing such serious competing interests, and for determining the procedures that are necessary to ensure that a citizen is not "deprived of life, liberty, or property, without due process of law" is the test that we articulated in *Mathews* v. *Eldridge* (1976). . . . *Mathews* dictates that the process due in any given instance is determined by weighing "the private interest that will be affected by the official action" against the Government's asserted interest, "including the function involved" and the burdens the Government would face in providing greater process. . . .

It is beyond question that substantial interests lie on both sides of the scale in this case. Hamdi's "private interest . . . affected by the official action," is the most elemental of liberty interests—the interest in being free from physical detention by one's own government. . . . Moreover, as critical as the Government's interest may be in detaining those who actually pose an immediate threat to the national security of the United States during ongoing international conflict, history and common sense teach us that an unchecked system of detention carries the potential to become a means for oppression and abuse of others who do not present that sort of threat. . . . We reaffirm today the fundamental nature of a citizen's right to be free from involuntary confinement by his own government without due process of law, and we weigh the opposing governmental interests against the curtailment of liberty that such confinement entails.

. . .

We hold that a citizen-detainee seeking to challenge his classification as an enemy combatant must receive notice of the factual basis for his classification, and a fair opportunity to rebut the Government's factual assertions before a neutral decisionmaker.

At the same time, the exigencies of the circumstances may demand that, aside from these core elements, enemy combatant proceedings may be tailored to alleviate their uncommon potential to burden the Executive at a time of ongoing military conflict. Hearsay, for example, may need to be accepted as the most reliable available evidence from the Government in such a proceeding. Likewise, the Constitution would not be offended by a presumption in favor of the Government's evidence, so long as that presumption remained a rebuttable one and fair opportunity for rebuttal were provided. . . .

We think it unlikely that this basic process will have the dire impact on the central functions of warmaking that the Government forecasts. The parties agree that initial captures on the battlefield need not receive the process we have discussed here; that process is due only when the determination is made to *continue* to hold those who have been seized. . . . While we accord the greatest respect and consideration to the judgments of military authorities in matters relating to the actual prosecution of a war, and recognize that the scope of that discretion necessarily is wide, it does not infringe on the core role of the military for the courts to exercise their own time-honored and constitutionally mandated roles of reviewing and resolving claims like those presented here. . . .

. . .

In so holding, we necessarily reject the Government's assertion that separation of powers principles mandate a heavily circumscribed role for the courts in such circumstances. Indeed, the position that the courts must forgo any examination of the individual case and focus exclusively on the legality of the broader detention scheme cannot be mandated by any reasonable view of separation of powers, as this approach serves only to *condense* power into a single branch of government. We have long since made clear that a state of war is not a blank check for the President when it comes to the rights of the Nation's citizens. *Youngstown Sheet & Tube*

(1951). Whatever power the United States Constitution envisions for the Executive in its exchanges with other nations or with enemy organizations in times of conflict, it most assuredly envisions a role for all three branches when individual liberties are at stake. . . .

. . .

JUSTICE SCALIA, with whom JUSTICE STEVENS joins, dissenting.

. . .

Where the Government accuses a citizen of waging war against it, our constitutional tradition has been to prosecute him in federal court for treason or some other crime. Where the exigencies of war prevent that, the Constitution's Suspension Clause allows Congress to relax the usual protections temporarily. Absent suspension, however, the Executive's assertion of military exigency has not been thought sufficient to permit detention without charge. No one contends that the congressional Authorization for Use of Military Force, on which the Government relies to justify its actions here, is an implementation of the Suspension Clause. Accordingly, I would reverse the decision below. . . .

JUSTICE O'CONNOR, writing for a plurality of this Court, asserts that captured enemy combatants (other than those suspected of war crimes) have traditionally been detained until the cessation of hostilities and then released. That is probably an accurate description of wartime practice with respect to enemy *aliens*. The tradition with respect to American citizens, however, has been quite different. Citizens aiding the enemy have been treated as traitors subject to the criminal process.

. . .

There are times when military exigency renders resort to the traditional criminal process impracticable. English law accommodated such exigencies by allowing legislative suspension of the writ of habeas corpus for brief periods. . . .

. . .

President Lincoln, when he purported to suspend habeas corpus without congressional authorization during the Civil War, apparently did not doubt that suspension was required if the prisoner was to be held without criminal trial. In his famous message to Congress on July 4, 1861, he argued only that he could suspend the writ, not that even without suspension, his imprisonment of citizens without criminal trial was permitted.

. . .

. . . In *Ex parte Quirin* (1942) it was uncontested that the petitioners were members of enemy forces. They were "*admitted* enemy invaders," (emphasis added), and it was "undisputed" that they had landed in the United States in service of German forces. . . . But where those jurisdictional facts are *not* conceded—where the petitioner insists that he is *not* a belligerent—*Quirin* left the pre-existing law in place: Absent suspension of the writ, a citizen held where the courts are open is entitled either to criminal trial or to a judicial decree requiring his release.

It follows from what I have said that Hamdi is entitled to a habeas decree requiring his release unless (1) criminal proceedings are promptly brought, or (2) Congress has suspended the writ of habeas corpus. . . .

. . .

JUSTICE THOMAS, dissenting.

. . .

The Founders intended that the President have primary responsibility—along with the necessary power—to protect the national security and to conduct the Nation's foreign relations. They did so principally because the structural advantages of a unitary Executive are essential in these domains. "Energy in the executive is a leading character in the definition of good government. It is essential to the protection of the community against foreign attacks." *The Federalist* No. 70. . . .

Congress, to be sure, has a substantial and essential role in both foreign affairs and national security. But it is crucial to recognize that *judicial* interference in these domains destroys the purpose of vesting primary responsibility in a unitary Executive. . . .

For these institutional reasons and because "Congress cannot anticipate and legislate with regard to every possible action the President may find it necessary to take or every possible situation in which he might act," it should come as no surprise that "[s]uch failure of Congress . . . does not, 'especially . . . in the areas of foreign policy and national security,' imply 'congressional disapproval' of action taken by the Executive." Rather, in these domains, the fact that Congress has provided the President with broad authorities does not imply—and the Judicial

Branch should not infer—that Congress intended to deprive him of particular powers not specifically enumerated. . . .

. . .

I acknowledge that the question whether Hamdi's executive detention is lawful is a question properly resolved by the Judicial Branch, though the question comes to the Court with the strongest presumptions in favor of the Government. The plurality agrees that Hamdi's detention is lawful if he is an enemy combatant. But the question whether Hamdi is actually an enemy combatant is "of a kind for which the Judiciary has neither aptitude, facilities nor responsibility and which has long been held to belong in the domain of political power not subject to judicial intrusion or inquiry." That is, although it is appropriate for the Court to determine the judicial question whether the President has the asserted authority, we lack the information and expertise to question whether Hamdi is actually an enemy combatant, a question the resolution of which is committed to other branches. . . .

. . .

The Government's asserted authority to detain an individual that the President has determined to be an enemy combatant, at least while hostilities continue, comports with the Due Process Clause. As these cases also show, the Executive's decision that a detention is necessary to protect the public need not and should not be subjected to judicial second-guessing. Indeed, at least in the context of enemy-combatant determinations, this would defeat the unity, secrecy, and dispatch that the Founders believed to be so important to the warmaking function. . . .

. . .

JUSTICE SOUTER, with whom JUSTICE GINSBURG joins, concurring in part, dissenting in part, and concurring in the judgment.

. . .

The defining character of American constitutional government is its constant tension between security and liberty, serving both by partial helpings of each. In a government of separated powers, deciding finally on what is a reasonable degree of guaranteed liberty whether in peace or war (or some condition in between) is not well entrusted to the Executive Branch of Government, whose particular responsibility is to maintain security. For reasons of inescapable human nature, the branch of the Government asked to counter a serious threat is not the branch on which to rest the Nation's entire reliance in striking the balance between the will to win and the cost in liberty on the way to victory; the responsibility for security will naturally amplify the claim that security legitimately raises. A reasonable balance is more likely to be reached on the judgment of a different branch, just as Madison said in remarking that "the constant aim is to divide and arrange the several offices in such a manner as that each may be a check on the other—that the private interest of every individual may be a sentinel over the public rights." *The Federalist* No. 51. Hence the need for an assessment by Congress before citizens are subject to lockup, and likewise the need for a clearly expressed congressional resolution of the competing claims.

Under this principle of reading [the AUMF] robustly to require a clear statement of authorization to detain, none of the Government's arguments suffices to justify Hamdi's detention.

. . .

. . . [T]he need to give practical effect to the conclusions of eight members of the Court rejecting the Government's position calls for me to join with the plurality in ordering remand on terms closest to those I would impose.

Republican Presidential Candidates Debate Enhanced Interrogation (May 15, 2007)

Shortly after the United States invaded Afghanistan in 2002, rumors circulated that the Bush administration had ordered intelligence agencies to use such "enhanced methods of interrogation" on suspected terrorists as waterboarding. Rumors that members of the Bush administration sanctioned torture intensified when photographs released from Abu Ghraib Prison in Iraq indicated that detainees had been badly abused. Other unofficial accounts indicated that detainees in Guantanamo Bay and in secret locations in Europe were either being subject to "enhanced interrogation" (if you favored the policy) or torture (if you did not).

The Bush administration repeatedly denied that administration officials were violating any constitutional or international prohibitions on torture. Nevertheless, Bush administration officials refused to provide details on exactly what was taking place in detention centers. Such administration officials as Jay Bybee and John Yoo wrote memos justifying as legitimate methods of interrogation practices that administration critics maintained were torture.

Some passages in John Yoo's memo to the State Department suggested that almost anything government officials might do would pass constitutional muster. "We believe it is beyond question that there can be no more compelling government interest than that which is presented here," he wrote, "and depending upon the precise factual circumstances of an interrogation, e.g., where there was credible information that the enemy combatant had information that could avert a threat, deprivations that may be caused would not be wanton or unnecessary."[100]

Bush administration interrogation policies united Democrats and divided Republicans. All major Democratic Party candidates for the presidency in 2008 asserted that they would ban enhanced interrogation if elected. Some Republicans, most notably John McCain, the eventual Republican Party nominee, took the same position. Others defended enhanced interrogation.

The excerpts below are from the Republican Party presidential debate in South Carolina that was held on May 15, 2007. What different positions do Republican presidential candidates take on enhanced interrogation or torture? How do they justify those positions? Which positions do you believe are most consistent with the Constitution? Do you believe that this is an instance where a president should ignore the Constitution? What explains the greater diversity in Republican positions on torture or enhanced interrogation?

BRIT HUME (MODERATOR): The questions in this round will be premised on a fictional, but we think plausible scenario involving terrorism and the response to it. Here is the premise: Three shopping centers near major U.S. cities have been hit by suicide bombers. Hundreds are dead, thousands injured. A fourth attack has been averted when the attackers were captured off the Florida coast and taken to Guantanamo Bay, where they are being questioned. U.S. intelligence believes that another larger attack is planned and could come at any time.

First question to you, Senator McCain. How aggressively would you interrogate those being held at Guantanamo Bay for information about where the next attack might be?

SENATOR JOHN MCCAIN (REPUBLICAN, ARIZONA): . . . The use of torture—we could never gain as much we would gain from that torture as we lose in world opinion. We do not torture people.

When I was in Vietnam, one of the things that sustained us, as we went—underwent torture ourselves, is the knowledge that if we had our positions reversed and we were the captors, we would not impose that kind of treatment on them.

It's not about the terrorists, it's about us. It's about what kind of country we are. And a fact: The more physical pain you inflict on someone, the more they're going to tell you what they think you want to know.

It's about us as a nation. We have procedures for interrogation in the Army Field Manual. Those, I think, would be adequate in 999,999 of cases, and I think that if we agree to torture people, we will do ourselves great harm in the world.

FORMER NEW YORK CITY MAYOR RUDY GIULIANI: In the hypothetical that you gave me, which assumes that we know there's going to be another attack and these people know about it, I would tell the people who had to do the interrogation to use every method they could think of. It shouldn't be torture, but every method they can think of—

MR. HUME: Water-boarding?

MR. GIULIANI: —and I would—and I would—well, I'd say every method they could think of, and I would support them in doing that because I've seen what can happen when you make a mistake about this, and I don't want to see another 3,000 people dead in New York or any place else.

FORMER MASSACHUSETTS GOVERNMENT MITT ROMNEY: . . . Some people have said, we ought to close Guantanamo. My view is, we ought to double Guantanamo. We ought to make sure that the terrorists—and there's no question but that in a setting like that where you have a ticking bomb that the president of the United States—not the CIA interrogator, the president of the United States—has to make the call. And enhanced interrogation techniques have to be used—not torture but enhanced interrogation techniques, yes.

MR. HUME: I'm going to come to the others in a moment, but I want to circle back to you, Senator

100. Memorandum from John Yoo, Deputy Assistant Attorney General, to William J. Haynes, General Counsel of the Department of Defense (March 14, 2003), 61.

McCain. You've heard reference here from me and others of the—what the administration calls the enhanced interrogation techniques. I may have misunderstood you, but it sounded to me as if you regard those techniques, or from what you know about them, as torture. Do you?

SENATOR MCCAIN: Yes, and the interesting thing about that aspect is that during the debate, when we had the detainee treatment act, there was a sharp division between those who had served in the military and those who hadn't. Virtually every senior officer, retired or active-duty, starting with Colin Powell, General Vessey and everyone else, agreed with my position that we should not torture people.

One of the reasons is, is because if we do it, what happens to our military people when they're captured? And also, they realize there's more to war than the battlefield.

So yes, literally every retired military person and active duty military person who has actually been in battle and served for extended times in the military supported my position, and I'm glad of it.

REPRESENTATIVE RON PAUL (REPUBLICAN, TEXAS): . . . I think it's interesting talking about torture here in that it's become enhanced interrogation technique. It sounds like Newspeak.

Nobody's for the torture, and I think that's important. But as far as taking care of a problem like this, the president has the authority to do that. If we're under imminent attack, the president can take that upon himself to do it.

REPRESENTATIVE TOM TANCREDO (REPUBLICAN, COLORADO): Well, let me just say that it's almost unbelievable to listen to this in a way. We're talking about—we're talking about it in such a theoretical fashion. You say that—that nuclear devices have gone off in the United States, more are planned, and we're wondering about whether waterboarding would be a—a bad thing to do? I'm looking for "Jack Bauer" at that time, let me tell you.

And—and there is—there is nothing—if you are talking about—I mean, we are the last best hope of Western civilization. And so all of the theories that go behind our activities subsequent to these nuclear attacks going off in the United States, they go out the window because when—when we go under, Western civilization goes under. So you better take that into account, and you better do every single thing you can as president of the United States to make sure, number one, it doesn't happen—that's right—but number two, you better respond in a way that makes them fearful of you because otherwise you guarantee something like this will happen.

Suggested Readings

Baer, Judith A. *Our Lives Before the Law: Constructing a Feminist Jurisprudence* (Princeton, NJ: Princeton University Press, 1999).

Balkin, Jack M., and Sanford A. Levinson. "Understanding the Constitutional Revolution," *Virginia Law Review* 87 (2001): 1045-1109.

Balkin, Jack M., and Reva B. Siegel. *The Constitution in 2020* (New York: Oxford University Press, 2009).

Brisbin, Richard A., Jr. *Justice Antonin Scalia and the Conservative Revival* (Baltimore, MD: Johns Hopkins University Press, 1997).

Carpenter, Dale. *Flagrant Conduct: The Story of* Lawrence v. Texas (New York: Norton, 2012).

Colucci, Frank J. *Justice Kennedy's Jurisprudence: The Full and Necessary Meaning of Liberty* (Lawrence: University Press of Kansas, 2009).

Gerber, Scott Douglas. *First Principles: The Jurisprudence of Clarence Thomas* (New York: New York University Press, 1999).

Gillman, Howard. *The Votes that Counted: How the Court Decided the 2000 Presidential Election* (Chicago: University of Chicago Press, 2000).

Hamilton, Marci A. *God vs. the Gavel: Religion and the Rule of Law* (New York: Cambridge University Press, 2005).

Keck, Thomas M. *The Most Activist Court in History: The Road to Modern Judicial Conservatism* (Chicago: University of Chicago Press, 2004).

King, Desmond S., and Rogers M. Smith. *Still a House Divided: Race and Politics in Obama's America* (Princeton, NJ: Princeton University Press, 2011).

Knowles, Helen J. *The Tie Goes to Freedom: Justice Anthony M. Kennedy on Liberty* (Lanham, MD: Rowman & Littlefield, 2009).

Koppelman, Andrew. *The Gay Rights Question in Contemporary American Law* (Chicago: University of Chicago Press, 2002).

Maltz, Earl M. *Rehnquist Justice: Understanding the Court Dynamic* (Lawrence: University Press of Kansas, 2003).

Maveety, Nancy. *Queen's Court: Judicial Power in the Rehnquist Era* (Lawrence: University Press of Kansas, 2008).

Pinello, Daniel R. *Gay Rights and American Law* (New York: Cambridge University Press, 2003).

Siegel, Reva B. "Dead or Alive: Originalism as Popular Constitutionalism in *Heller*," *Harvard Law Review* 122 (2008): 191–245.

Sweet, Martin J. *Merely Judgment: Ignoring, Evading, and Trumping the Supreme Court* (Charlottesville: University of Virginia Press, 2010).

Teles, Steven M. *The Rise of the Conservative Legal Movement: The Battle for the Control of the Law* (Princeton, NJ: Princeton University Press, 2008).

Tushnet, Mark. *A Court Divided* (New York: Norton, 2005).

Tushnet, Mark. *The New Constitutional Order* (Princeton, NJ: Princeton University Press, 2003).

Tushnet, Mark, ed. *The Constitution in Wartime: Beyond Alarmism and Complacency* (Durham, NC: Duke University Press, 2005).

Winkler, Adam. *Gunfight: The Battle over the Right to Bear Arms in America* (New York: Norton, 2011).

Yarbrough, Tinsley E. *The Rehnquist Court and the Constitution* (New York: Oxford University Press, 2000).

Yarbrough, Tinsley E. *David Hackett Souter: Traditional Republican on the Supreme Court* (New York: Oxford University Press, 2005).

Constitution of the United States of America

We the People of the United States, in Order to form a more perfect Union, establish Justice, insure domestic Tranquility, provide for the common defense, promote the general Welfare, and secure the Blessings of Liberty to ourselves and our Posterity, do ordain and establish this Constitution for the United States of America.

Article. I.

Section. 1. All legislative Powers herein granted shall be vested in a Congress of the United States, which shall consist of a Senate and House of Representatives.

Section. 2. The House of Representatives shall be composed of Members chosen every second Year by the People of the several States, and the Electors in each State shall have the Qualifications requisite for Electors of the most numerous Branch of the State Legislature.

No Person shall be a Representative who shall not have attained to the Age of twenty five Years, and been seven Years a Citizen of the United States, and who shall not, when elected, be an Inhabitant of that State in which he shall be chosen.

[Representatives and direct Taxes shall be apportioned among the several States which may be included within this Union, according to their respective Numbers, which shall be determined by adding to the whole Number of free Persons, including those bound to Service for a Term of Years, and excluding Indians not taxed, three fifths of all other Persons.][1] The actual Enumeration shall be made within three Years after the first Meeting of the Congress of the United States, and within every subsequent Term of ten Years, in such Manner as they shall by Law direct. The number of Representatives shall not exceed one for every thirty Thousand, but each State shall have at Least one Representative; and until such enumeration shall be made, the State of New Hampshire shall be entitled to choose three, Massachusetts eight, Rhode-Island and Providence Plantations one, Connecticut five, New-York six, New Jersey four, Pennsylvania eight, Delaware one, Maryland six, Virginia ten, North Carolina five, South Carolina five, and Georgia three.

When vacancies happen in the Representation from any State, the Executive Authority thereof shall issue Writs of Election to fill such Vacancies.

The House of Representatives shall choose their Speaker and other Officers; and shall have the sole Power of Impeachment.

Section. 3. The Senate of the United States shall be composed of two Senators from each State, [chosen by the Legislature thereof,][2] for six Years; and each Senator shall have one Vote.

Immediately after they shall be assembled in Consequence of the first Election, they shall be divided as equally as may be into three Classes. The Seats of the Senators of the first Class shall be vacated at the Expiration of the second Year, of the second Class at the Expiration of the fourth Year, and of the third Class at the Expiration of the sixth Year, so that one third may be chosen every second Year; [and if Vacancies happen by Resignation, or otherwise, during the Recess of the Legislature of any State, the Executive thereof may make temporary Appointments until the next Meeting of the Legislature, which shall then fill such Vacancies.][3]

1. Changed by Section 2 of the Fourteenth Amendment.

2. Changed by the Seventeenth Amendment.

3. Changed by the Seventeenth Amendment.

No Person shall be a Senator who shall not have attained to the Age of thirty Years, and been nine Years a Citizen of the United States, and who shall not, when elected, be an Inhabitant of that State for which he shall be chosen.

The Vice President of the United States shall be President of the Senate, but shall have no Vote, unless they be equally divided.

The Senate shall choose their other Officers, and also a President pro tempore, in the Absence of the Vice President, or when he shall exercise the Office of President of the United States.

The Senate shall have the sole Power to try all Impeachments. When sitting for that Purpose, they shall be on Oath or Affirmation. When the President of the United States is tried, the Chief Justice shall preside: And no Person shall be convicted without the Concurrence of two thirds of the Members present.

Judgment in Cases of Impeachment shall not extend further than to removal from Office, and disqualification to hold and enjoy any Office of honor, Trust or Profit under the United States: but the Party convicted shall nevertheless be liable and subject to Indictment, Trial, Judgment and Punishment, according to Law.

Section. 4. The Times, Places and Manner of holding Elections for Senators and Representatives, shall be prescribed in each State by the Legislature thereof; but the Congress may at any time by Law make or alter such Regulations, except as to the Places of choosing Senators.

The Congress shall assemble at least once in every Year, and such Meeting shall be [on the first Monday in December,][4] unless they shall by Law appoint a different Day.

Section. 5. Each House shall be the Judge of the Elections, Returns and Qualifications of its own Members, and a Majority of each shall constitute a Quorum to do Business; but a smaller Number may adjourn from day to day, and may be authorized to compel the Attendance of absent Members, in such Manner, and under such Penalties as each House may provide.

Each House may determine the Rules of its Proceedings, punish its Members for disorderly Behavior, and, with the Concurrence of two thirds, expel a Member.

Each House shall keep a Journal of its Proceedings, and from time to time publish the same, excepting such Parts as may in their Judgment require Secrecy; and the Yeas and Nays of the Members of either House on any question shall, at the Desire of one fifth of those Present, be entered on the Journal.

Neither House, during the Session of Congress, shall, without the Consent of the other, adjourn for more than three days, nor to any other Place than that in which the two Houses shall be sitting.

Section. 6. The Senators and Representatives shall receive a Compensation for their Services, to be ascertained by Law, and paid out of the Treasury of the United States. They shall in all Cases, except Treason, Felony and Breach of the Peace, be privileged from Arrest during their Attendance at the Session of their respective Houses, and in going to and returning from the same; and for any Speech or Debate in either House, they shall not be questioned in any other Place.

No Senator or Representative shall, during the Time for which he was elected, be appointed to any civil Office under the Authority of the United States, which shall have been created, or the Emoluments whereof shall have been increased during such time; and no Person holding any Office under the United States, shall be a Member of either House during his Continuance in Office.

Section. 7. All Bills for raising Revenue shall originate in the House of Representatives; but the Senate may propose or concur with Amendments as on other Bills.

Every Bill which shall have passed the House of Representatives and the Senate, shall, before it becomes a Law, be presented to the President of the United States; If he approve he shall sign it, but if not he shall return it, with his Objections to that House in which it shall have originated, who shall enter the Objections at large on their Journal, and proceed to reconsider it. If after such Reconsideration two thirds of that House shall agree to pass the Bill, it shall be sent, together with the Objections, to the other House, by which it shall likewise be reconsidered, and if approved by two thirds of that House, it shall become a Law. But in all such Cases the Votes of both Houses shall be determined by yeas and Nays, and the Names of the Persons voting for and against the Bill shall be entered on the Journal of each House respectively. If any Bill shall not be returned by

4. Changed by the Twentieth Amendment.

the President within ten Days (Sundays excepted) after it shall have been presented to him, the Same shall be a Law, in like Manner as if he had signed it, unless the Congress by their Adjournment prevent its Return, in which Case it shall not be a Law.

Every Order, Resolution, or Vote to which the Concurrence of the Senate and House of Representatives may be necessary (except on a question of Adjournment) shall be presented to the President of the United States; and before the Same shall take Effect, shall be approved by him, or being disapproved by him, shall be repassed by two thirds of the Senate and House of Representatives, according to the Rules and Limitations prescribed in the Case of a Bill.

Section. 8. The Congress shall have Power To lay and collect Taxes, Duties, Imposts and Excises, to pay the Debts and provide for the common Defense and general Welfare of the United States; but all Duties, Imposts and Excises shall be uniform throughout the United States;

To borrow Money on the credit of the United States;

To regulate Commerce with foreign Nations, and among the several States, and with the Indian Tribes;

To establish an uniform Rule of Naturalization, and uniform Laws on the subject of Bankruptcies throughout the United States;

To coin Money, regulate the Value thereof, and of foreign Coin, and fix the Standard of Weights and Measures;

To provide for the Punishment of counterfeiting the Securities and current Coin of the United States;

To establish Post Offices and post Roads;

To promote the Progress of Science and useful Arts, by securing for limited Times to Authors and Inventors the exclusive Right to their respective Writings and Discoveries;

To constitute Tribunals inferior to the supreme Court;

To define and punish Piracies and Felonies committed on the high Seas, and Offenses against the Law of Nations;

To declare War, grant Letters of Marque and Reprisal, and make Rules concerning Captures on Land and Water;

To raise and support Armies, but no Appropriation of Money to that Use shall be for a longer Term than two Years;

To provide and maintain a Navy;

To make Rules for the Government and Regulation of the land and naval Forces;

To provide for calling forth the Militia to execute the Laws of the Union, suppress Insurrections and repel Invasions;

To provide for organizing, arming, and disciplining, the Militia, and for governing such Part of them as may be employed in the Service of the United States, reserving to the States respectively, the Appointment of the Officers, and the Authority of training the Militia according to the discipline prescribed by Congress;

To exercise exclusive Legislation in all Cases whatsoever, over such District (not exceeding ten Miles square) as may, by Cession of particular States, and the Acceptance of Congress, become the Seat of the Government of the United States, and to exercise like Authority over all Places purchased by the Consent of the Legislature of the State in which the Same shall be, for the Erection of Forts, Magazines, Arsenals, dock-Yards and other needful Buildings;—And

To make all Laws which shall be necessary and proper for carrying into Execution the foregoing Powers, and all other Powers vested by this Constitution in the Government of the United States or in any Department or Officer thereof.

Section. 9. The Migration or Importation of such Persons as any of the States now existing shall think proper to admit, shall not be prohibited by the Congress prior to the Year one thousand eight hundred and eight, but a Tax or duty may be imposed on such Importation, not exceeding ten dollars for each Person.

The Privilege of the Writ of Habeas Corpus shall not be suspended, unless when in Cases of Rebellion or Invasion the public Safety may require it.

No Bill of Attainder or ex post facto Law shall be passed.

No Capitation, or other direct, Tax shall be laid, [unless in Proportion to the Census or Enumeration herein before directed to be taken.][5]

No Tax or Duty shall be laid on Articles exported from any State.

No Preference shall be given by any Regulation of Commerce or Revenue to the Ports of one State over

5. Changed by Sixteenth Amendment.

those of another: nor shall Vessels bound to, or from, one State, be obliged to enter, clear, or pay Duties in another.

No Money shall be drawn from the Treasury, but in Consequence of Appropriations made by Law; and a regular Statement and Account of the Receipts and Expenditures of all public Money shall be published from time to time.

No Title of Nobility shall be granted by the United States: And no Person holding any Office of Profit or Trust under them, shall, without the Consent of the Congress, accept of any present, Emolument, Office, or Title, of any kind whatever, from any King, Prince, or foreign State.

Section. 10. No State shall enter into any Treaty, Alliance, or Confederation; grant Letters of Marque and Reprisal; coin Money; emit Bills of Credit; make any Thing but gold and silver Coin a Tender in Payment of Debts; pass any Bill of Attainder, ex post facto Law, or Law impairing the Obligation of Contracts, or grant any Title of Nobility.

No State shall, without the Consent of the Congress, lay any Imposts or Duties on Imports or Exports, except what may be absolutely necessary for executing it's inspection Laws: and the net Produce of all Duties and Imposts, laid by any State on Imports or Exports, shall be for the Use of the Treasury of the United States; and all such Laws shall be subject to the Revision and Control of the Congress.

No State shall, without the Consent of Congress, lay any Duty of Tonnage, keep Troops, or Ships of War in time of Peace, enter into any Agreement or Compact with another State, or with a foreign Power, or engage in War, unless actually invaded, or in such imminent Danger as will not admit of delay.

Article. II.

Section. 1. The executive Power shall be vested in a President of the United States of America. He shall hold his Office during the Term of four Years, and, together with the Vice President, chosen for the same Term, be elected, as follows.

Each State shall appoint, in such Manner as the Legislature thereof may direct, a Number of Electors, equal to the whole Number of Senators and Representatives to which the State may be entitled in the Congress: but no Senator or Representative, or Person holding an Office of Trust or Profit under the United States, shall be appointed an Elector.

[The Electors shall meet in their respective States, and vote by Ballot for two Persons, of whom one at least shall not be an Inhabitant of the same State with themselves. And they shall make a List of all the Persons voted for, and of the Number of Votes for each; which List they shall sign and certify, and transmit sealed to the Seat of the Government of the United States, directed to the President of the Senate. The President of the Senate shall, in the Presence of the Senate and House of Representatives, open all the Certificates, and the Votes shall then be counted. The Person having the greatest Number of Votes shall be the President, if such Number be a Majority of the whole Number of Electors appointed; and if there be more than one who have such Majority, and have an equal Number of Votes, then the House of Representatives shall immediately choose by Ballot one of them for President; and if no Person have a Majority, then from the five highest on the List the said House shall in like Manner choose the President. But in choosing the President, the Votes shall be taken by States, the Representation from each State having one Vote; A quorum for this Purpose shall consist of a Member or Members from two thirds of the States, and a Majority of all the States shall be necessary to a Choice. In every Case, after the Choice of the President, the Person having the greatest Number of Votes of the Electors shall be the Vice President. But if there should remain two or more who have equal Votes, the Senate shall choose from them by Ballot the Vice President.][6]

The Congress may determine the Time of choosing the Electors, and the Day on which they shall give their Votes; which Day shall be the same throughout the United States.

No Person except a natural born Citizen, or a Citizen of the United States, at the time of the Adoption of this Constitution, shall be eligible to the Office of President; neither shall any person be eligible to that Office who shall not have attained to the Age of thirty five Years, and been fourteen Years a Resident within the United States.

[In Case of the Removal of the President from Office, or of his Death, Resignation, or Inability to

6. Changed by Twelfth Amendment.

discharge the Powers and Duties of the said Office, the Same shall devolve on the Vice President, and the Congress may by Law provide for the Case of Removal, Death, Resignation or Inability, both of the President and Vice President, declaring what Officer shall then act as President, and such Officer shall act accordingly, until the Disability be removed, or a President shall be elected.][7]

The President shall, at stated Times, receive for his Services, a Compensation, which shall neither be increased nor diminished during the Period for which he shall have been elected, and he shall not receive within that Period any other Emolument from the United States, or any of them.

Before he enter on the Execution of his Office, he shall take the following Oath or Affirmation:—"I do solemnly swear (or affirm) that I will faithfully execute the Office of President of the United States, and will to the best of my Ability, preserve, protect and defend the Constitution of the United States."

Section. 2. The President shall be Commander in Chief of the Army and Navy of the United States, and of the Militia of the several States, when called into the actual Service of the United States; he may require the Opinion, in writing, of the principal Officer in each of the executive Departments, upon any Subject relating to the Duties of their respective Offices, and he shall have Power to grant Reprieves and Pardons for Offenses against the United States, except in Cases of Impeachment.

He shall have Power, by and with the Advice and Consent of the Senate, to make Treaties, provided two thirds of the Senators present concur; and he shall nominate, and by and with the Advice and Consent of the Senate, shall appoint Ambassadors, other public Ministers and Consuls, Judges of the supreme Court, and all other Officers of the United States, whose Appointments are not herein otherwise provided for, and which shall be established by Law: but the Congress may by Law vest the Appointment of such inferior Officers, as they think proper, in the President alone, in the Courts of Law, or in the Heads of Departments.

The President shall have Power to fill up all Vacancies that may happen during the Recess of the Senate, by granting Commissions which shall expire at the End of their next Session.

Section. 3. He shall from time to time give to the Congress Information of the State of the Union, and recommend to their Consideration such Measures as he shall judge necessary and expedient; he may, on extraordinary Occasions, convene both Houses, or either of them, and in Case of Disagreement between them, with Respect to the Time of Adjournment, he may adjourn them to such Time as he shall think proper; he shall receive Ambassadors and other public Ministers; he shall take Care that the Laws be faithfully executed, and shall Commission all the Officers of the United States.

Section. 4. The President, Vice President and all civil Officers of the United States, shall be removed from Office on Impeachment for, and Conviction of, Treason, Bribery, or other high Crimes and Misdemeanors.

Article. III.

Section. 1. The judicial Power of the United States shall be vested in one supreme Court, and in such inferior Courts as the Congress may from time to time ordain and establish. The Judges, both of the supreme and inferior Courts, shall hold their Offices during good Behavior, and shall, at stated Times, receive for their Services, a Compensation, which shall not be diminished during their Continuance in Office.

Section. 2. The judicial Power shall extend to all Cases, in Law and Equity, arising under this Constitution, the Laws of the United States, and Treaties made, or which shall be made, under their Authority;—to all Cases affecting Ambassadors, other public Ministers and Consuls;—to all Cases of admiralty and maritime Jurisdiction;—to Controversies to which the United States shall be a Party;—to Controversies between two or more States;—[between a State and Citizens of another State;—][8] between Citizens of different States,—between Citizens of the same State claiming Lands under Grants of different States, and between a State, or the Citizens thereof, and foreign States, Citizens or Subjects.

In all Cases affecting Ambassadors, other public Ministers and Consuls, and those in which a State shall be Party, the supreme Court shall have original

7. Changed by Twenty-Fifth Amendment.

8. Changed by Eleventh Amendment.

Jurisdiction. In all the other Cases before mentioned, the supreme Court shall have appellate Jurisdiction, both as to Law and Fact, with such Exceptions, and under such Regulations as the Congress shall make.

The Trial of all Crimes, except in Cases of Impeachment; shall be by Jury; and such Trial shall be held in the State where the said Crimes shall have been committed; but when not committed within any State, the Trial shall be at such Place or Places as the Congress may by Law have directed.

Section. 3. Treason against the United States, shall consist only in levying War against them, or in adhering to their Enemies, giving them Aid and Comfort. No Person shall be convicted of Treason unless on the Testimony of two Witnesses to the same overt Act, or on Confession in open Court.

The Congress shall have Power to declare the Punishment of Treason, but no Attainder of Treason shall work Corruption of Blood, or Forfeiture except during the Life of the Person attainted.

Article. IV.

Section. 1. Full Faith and Credit shall be given in each State to the public Acts, Records, and judicial Proceedings of every other State; And the Congress may by general Laws prescribe the Manner in which such Acts, Records and Proceedings shall be proved, and the Effect thereof.

Section. 2. The Citizens of each State shall be entitled to all Privileges and Immunities of Citizens in the several States.

A Person charged in any State with Treason, Felony, or other Crime, who shall flee from Justice, and be found in another State, shall on Demand of the executive Authority of the State from which he fled, be delivered up, to be removed to the State having Jurisdiction of the Crime.

[No Person held to Service or Labor in one State, under the Laws thereof, escaping into another, shall, in Consequence of any Law or Regulation therein, be discharged from such Service or Labor, but shall be delivered up on Claim of the Party to whom such Service or Labor may be due.][9]

Section. 3. New States may be admitted by the Congress into this Union; but no new State shall be formed or erected within the Jurisdiction of any other State; nor any State be formed by the Junction of two or more States, or Parts of States, without the Consent of the Legislatures of the States concerned as well as of the Congress.

The Congress shall have Power to dispose of and make all needful Rules and Regulations respecting the Territory or other Property belonging to the United States; and nothing in this Constitution shall be so construed as to Prejudice any Claims of the United States, or of any particular State.

Section. 4. The United States shall guarantee to every State in this Union a Republican Form of Government, and shall protect each of them against Invasion; and on Application of the Legislature, or of the Executive (when the Legislature cannot be convened) against domestic Violence.

Article. V.

The Congress, whenever two thirds of both Houses shall deem it necessary, shall propose Amendments to this Constitution, or, on the Application of the Legislatures of two thirds of the several States, shall call a Convention for proposing Amendments, which, in either Case, shall be valid to all Intents and Purposes, as Part of this Constitution, when ratified by the Legislatures of three fourths of the several States, or by Conventions in three fourths thereof, as the one or the other Mode of Ratification may be proposed by the Congress; Provided that no Amendment which may be made prior to the Year One thousand eight hundred and eight shall in any Manner affect the first and fourth Clauses in the Ninth Section of the first Article; and that no State, without its Consent, shall be deprived of it's equal Suffrage in the Senate.

Article. VI.

All Debts contracted and Engagements entered into, before the Adoption of this Constitution, shall be as valid against the United States under this Constitution, as under the Confederation.

This Constitution, and the Laws of the United States which shall be made in Pursuance thereof; and

9. Changed by Thirteenth Amendment.

all Treaties made, or which shall be made, under the Authority of the United States, shall be the supreme Law of the Land; and the Judges in every State shall be bound thereby, any Thing in the Constitution or Laws of any State to the Contrary notwithstanding.

The Senators and Representatives before mentioned, and the Members of the several State Legislatures, and all executive and judicial Officers, both of the United States and of the several States, shall be bound by Oath or Affirmation, to support this Constitution; but no religious Test shall ever be required as a Qualification to any Office or public Trust under the United States.

Article. VII.

The Ratification of the Conventions of nine States, shall be sufficient for the Establishment of this Constitution between the States so ratifying the Same.

Done in Convention by the Unanimous Consent of the States present the Seventeenth Day of September in the Year of our Lord one thousand seven hundred and Eighty seven and of the Independence of the United States of America the Twelfth In Witness whereof We have hereunto subscribed our Names,

George Washington—President and deputy from Virginia

New Hampshire	John Langdon Nicholas Gilman
Massachusetts	Nathaniel Gorham Rufus King
Connecticut	William Samuel Johnson Roger Sherman
New York	Alexander Hamilton
New Jersey	William Livingston David Brearley William Paterson Jonathan Dayton
Pennsylvania	Benjamin Franklin Thomas Mifflin Robert Morris George Clymer Thomas FitzSimons Jared Ingersoll James Wilson Gouverneur Morris
Delaware	George Read Gunning Bedford, Jr. John Dickinson Richard Bassett Jacob Broom
Maryland	James McHenry Daniel of St. Thomas Jenifer Daniel Carroll
Virginia	John Blair James Madison, Jr.
North Carolina	William Blount Richard Dobbs Spaight Hugh Williamson
South Carolina	John Rutledge Charles Cotesworth Pinckney Charles Pinckney Pierce Butler
Georgia	William Few Abraham Baldwin

Attest William Jackson, Secretary

In Convention Monday
September 17th 1787.

Present
The States of

New Hampshire, Massachusetts, Connecticut, Mr. Hamilton from New York, New Jersey, Pennsylvania, Delaware, Maryland, Virginia, North Carolina, South Carolina and Georgia.

Resolved,

That the preceding Constitution be laid before the United States in Congress assembled, and that it is the Opinion of this Convention, that it should afterwards be submitted to a Convention of Delegates, chosen in each State by the People thereof, under the Recommendation of its Legislature, for their Assent and Ratification; and that each Convention assenting to, and ratifying the Same, should give Notice thereof to the United States in Congress assembled. Resolved, That it is the Opinion of this Convention, that as soon as the Conventions of nine States shall have ratified this Constitution, the United States in Congress assembled should fix a Day on which Electors should be appointed by the States which shall have ratified the same, and a Day on which the Electors should assemble to vote for the President, and the Time and Place for commencing Proceedings under this Constitution.

That after such Publication the Electors should be appointed, and the Senators and Representatives elected: That the Electors should meet on the Day fixed for the Election of the President, and should transmit their Votes certified, signed, sealed and directed, as the Constitution requires, to the Secretary of the United States in Congress assembled, that the Senators and Representatives should convene at the Time and Place assigned; that the Senators should appoint a President of the Senate, for the sole Purpose of receiving, opening and counting the Votes for President; and, that after he shall be chosen, the Congress, together with the President, should, without Delay, proceed to execute this Constitution.

By the unanimous Order of the Convention
George WASHINGTON—President

William JACKSON Secretary.

[Adding the Bill of Rights][10]

Congress of the United States begun and held at the City of New-York, on Wednesday the fourth of March, one thousand seven hundred and eighty nine:

THE Conventions of a number of the States, having at the time of their adopting the Constitution, expressed a desire, in order to prevent misconstruction or abuse of its powers, that further declaratory and restrictive clauses should be added: And as extending the ground of public confidence in the Government, will best ensure the beneficent ends of its institution:

10. On September 25, 1789, Congress transmitted to the state legislatures twelve proposed amendments, the first two of which, having to do with Congressional representation and congressional pay, were not adopted. The remaining ten amendments became the Bill of Rights. The amendment regarding congressional pay was later ratified and became the Twenty-Seventh Amendment.

RESOLVED by the Senate and House of Representatives of the United States of America, in Congress assembled, two thirds of both Houses concurring, that the following Articles be proposed to the Legislatures of the several States, as Amendments to the Constitution of the United States, all or any of which Articles, when ratified by three fourths of the said Legislatures, to be valid to all intents and purposes, as part of the said Constitution; viz.

ARTICLES in addition to, and Amendment of the Constitution of the United States of America, proposed by Congress, and ratified by the Legislatures of the several States, pursuant to the fifth Article of the original Constitution....

FREDERICK AUGUSTUS MUHLENBERG
Speaker of the House of Representatives.
JOHN ADAMS, Vice-President of the United States and President of the Senate.

ATTEST,
JOHN BECKLEY, Clerk of the House of Representatives.
SAMUEL A. OTIS, Secretary of the Senate.

AMENDMENTS
TO THE CONSTITUTION
OF THE
UNITED STATES OF AMERICA

Amendment I.[11]

Congress shall make no law respecting an establishment of religion, or prohibiting the free exercise thereof; or abridging the freedom of speech, or of the press, or the right of the people peaceably to assemble, and to petition the Government for a redress of grievances.

Amendment II.

A well regulated Militia, being necessary to the security of a free State, the right of the people to keep and bear Arms, shall not be infringed.

11. The first ten Amendments (Bill of Rights) were ratified effective December 15, 1791.

Amendment III.

No Soldier shall, in time of peace be quartered in any house, without the consent of the Owner, nor in time of war, but in a manner to be prescribed by law.

Amendment IV.

The right of the people to be secure in their persons, houses, papers, and effects, against unreasonable searches and seizures, shall not be violated, and no Warrants shall issue, but upon probable cause, supported by Oath or affirmation, and particularly describing the place to be searched, and the persons or things to be seized.

Amendment V.

No person shall be held to answer for a capital, or otherwise infamous crime, unless on a presentment or indictment of a Grand Jury, except in cases arising in the land or naval forces, or in the Militia, when in actual service in time of War or public danger; nor shall any person be subject for the same offence to be twice put in jeopardy of life or limb, nor shall be compelled in any criminal case to be a witness against himself, nor be deprived of life, liberty, or property, without due process of law; nor shall private property be taken for public use without just compensation.

Amendment VI.

In all criminal prosecutions, the accused shall enjoy the right to a speedy and public trial, by an impartial jury of the State and district wherein the crime shall have been committed; which district shall have been previously ascertained by law, and to be informed of the nature and cause of the accusation; to be confronted with the witnesses against him; to have compulsory process for obtaining witnesses in his favor, and to have the assistance of counsel for his defense.

Amendment VII.

In Suits at common law, where the value in controversy shall exceed twenty dollars, the right of trial by jury shall be preserved, and no fact tried by a jury shall be otherwise re-examined in any Court of the United States, than according to the rules of the common law.

Amendment VIII.

Excessive bail shall not be required, nor excessive fines imposed, nor cruel and unusual punishments inflicted.

Amendment IX.

The enumeration in the Constitution of certain rights shall not be construed to deny or disparage others retained by the people.

Amendment X.

The powers not delegated to the United States by the Constitution, nor prohibited by it to the States, are reserved to the States respectively, or to the people.

Amendment XI.[12]

The Judicial power of the United States shall not be construed to extend to any suit in law or equity, commenced or prosecuted against one of the United States by Citizens of another State, or by Citizens or Subjects of any Foreign State.

Amendment XII.[13]

The Electors shall meet in their respective states, and vote by ballot for President and Vice President, one of whom, at least, shall not be an inhabitant of the same state with themselves; they shall name in their ballots the person voted for as President, and in distinct ballots the person voted for as Vice-President, and they shall make distinct lists of all persons voted for as President, and of all persons voted for as Vice-President, and of the number of votes for each, which lists they shall sign and certify, and transmit sealed to the seat of the government of the United States, directed to the President of the Senate;—The President of the Senate shall, in the presence of the Senate and House of Representatives, open all the certificates and the votes shall then be counted;—The person having the greatest number of votes for President, shall be the

12. The Eleventh Amendment was ratified February 7, 1795.
13. The Twelfth Amendment was ratified June 15, 1804.

President, if such number be a majority of the whole number of Electors appointed; and if no person have such majority, then from the persons having the highest numbers not exceeding three on the list of those voted for as President, the House of Representatives shall choose immediately, by ballot, the President. But in choosing the President, the votes shall be taken by states, the representation from each state having one vote; a quorum for this purpose shall consist of a member or members from two-thirds of the states, and a majority of all the states shall be necessary to a choice. [And if the House of Representatives shall not choose a President whenever the right of choice shall devolve upon them, before the fourth day of March next following, then the Vice President shall act as President, as in the case of the death or other constitutional disability of the President—].[14] The person having the greatest number of votes as Vice-President, shall be the Vice-President, if such number be a majority of the whole number of Electors appointed, and if no person have a majority, then from the two highest numbers on the list, the Senate shall choose the Vice-President; a quorum for the purpose shall consist of two-thirds of the whole number of Senators, and a majority of the whole number shall be necessary to a choice. But no person constitutionally ineligible to the office of President shall be eligible to that of Vice President of the United States.

Amendment XIII.[15]

Section 1. Neither slavery nor involuntary servitude, except as a punishment for crime whereof the party shall have been duly convicted, shall exist within the United States, or any place subject to their jurisdiction.

Section 2. Congress shall have power to enforce this article by appropriate legislation.

Amendment XIV.[16]

Section 1. All persons born or naturalized in the United States and subject to the jurisdiction thereof, are citizens of the United States and of the State wherein they reside. No State shall make or enforce any law which shall abridge the privileges or immunities of citizens of the United States; nor shall any State deprive any person of life, liberty, or property, without due process of law; nor deny to any person within its jurisdiction the equal protection of the laws.

Section 2. Representatives shall be apportioned among the several States according to their respective numbers, counting the whole number of persons in each State, excluding Indians not taxed. But when the right to vote at any election for the choice of electors for President and Vice President of the United States, Representatives in Congress, the Executive and Judicial officers of a State, or the members of the Legislature thereof, is denied to any of the male inhabitants of such State, being twenty-one years of age, and citizens of the United States, or in any way abridged, except for participation in rebellion, or other crime, the basis of representation therein shall be reduced in the proportion which the number of such male citizens shall bear to the whole number of male citizens twenty-one years of age in such State.

Section 3. No person shall be a Senator or Representative in Congress, or elector of President and Vice President, or hold any office, civil or military, under the United States, or under any State, who, having previously taken an oath, as a member of Congress, or as an officer of the United States, or as a member of any State legislature, or as an executive or judicial officer of any State, to support the Constitution of the United States, shall have engaged in insurrection or rebellion against the same, or given aid or comfort to the enemies thereof. But Congress may by a vote of two-thirds of each House, remove such disability.

Section 4. The validity of the public debt of the United States, authorized by law, including debts incurred for payment of pensions and bounties for services in suppressing insurrection or rebellion, shall not be questioned. But neither the United States nor any State shall assume or pay any debt or obligation incurred in aid of insurrection or rebellion against the United States, or any claim for the loss or emancipation of any slave; but all such debts, obligations and claims shall be held illegal and void.

Section 5. The Congress shall have power to enforce, by appropriate legislation, the provisions of this article.

14. Changed by the Twentieth Amendment.
15. The Thirteenth Amendment was ratified December 6, 1865.
16. The Fourteenth Amendment was ratified July 9, 1868.

Amendment XV.[17]

Section 1. The right of citizens of the United States to vote shall not be denied or abridged by the United States or by any State on account of race, color, or previous condition of servitude.

Section 2. The Congress shall have power to enforce this article by appropriate legislation.

Amendment XVI.[18]

The Congress shall have power to lay and collect taxes on incomes, from whatever source derived, without apportionment among the several States, and without regard to any census or enumeration.

Amendment XVII.[19]

The Senate of the United States shall be composed of two Senators from each State, elected by the people thereof, for six years; and each Senator shall have one vote. The electors in each State shall have the qualifications requisite for electors of the most numerous branch of the State legislatures.

When vacancies happen in the representation of any State in the Senate, the executive authority of such State shall issue writs of election to fill such vacancies: Provided, That the legislature of any State may empower the executive thereof to make temporary appointments until the people fill the vacancies by election as the legislature may direct.

This amendment shall not be so construed as to affect the election or term of any Senator chosen before it becomes valid as part of the Constitution.

Amendment XVIII.[20]

[Section 1. After one year from the ratification of this article the manufacture, sale, or transportation of intoxicating liquors within, the importation thereof into, or the exportation thereof from the United States and all territory subject to the jurisdiction thereof for beverage purposes is hereby prohibited.

Section 2. The Congress and the several States shall have concurrent power to enforce this article by appropriate legislation.

Section 3. This article shall be inoperative unless it shall have been ratified as an amendment to the Constitution by the legislatures of the several States, as provided in the Constitution, within seven years from the date of the submission hereof to the States by the Congress.]

Amendment XIX.[21]

The right of citizens of the United States to vote shall not be denied or abridged by the United States or by any State on account of sex.

Congress shall have power to enforce this article by appropriate legislation.

Amendment XX.[22]

Section 1. The terms of the President and Vice President shall end at noon on the 20th day of January, and the terms of Senators and Representatives at noon on the 3d day of January, of the years in which such terms would have ended if this article had not been ratified; and the terms of their successors shall then begin.

Section 2. The Congress shall assemble at least once in every year, and such meeting shall begin at noon on the 3d day of January, unless they shall by law appoint a different day.

Section 3. If, at the time fixed for the beginning of the term of the President, the President elect shall have died, the Vice President elect shall become President. If a President shall not have been chosen before the time fixed for the beginning of his term, or if the President elect shall have failed to qualify, then the Vice President elect shall act as President until a President shall have qualified; and the Congress may by law provide for the case wherein neither a President elect nor a Vice President elect shall have qualified, declaring who shall then act as President, or the manner in which one

17. The Fifteenth Amendment was ratified February 3, 1870.

18. The Sixteenth Amendment was ratified February 3, 1913.

19. The Seventeenth Amendment was ratified April 8, 1913.

20. The Eighteenth Amendment was ratified January 16, 1919. Repealed by the Twenty-First Amendment, December 5, 1933.

21. The Nineteenth Amendment was ratified August 18, 1920.

22. The Twentieth Amendment was ratified January 23, 1933.

who is to act shall be selected, and such person shall act accordingly until a President or Vice President shall have qualified.

Section 4. The Congress may by law provide for the case of the death of any of the persons from whom the House of Representatives may choose a President whenever the right of choice shall have devolved upon them, and for the case of the death of any of the persons from whom the Senate may choose a Vice President whenever the right of choice shall have devolved upon them.

Section 5. Sections 1 and 2 shall take effect on the 15th day of October following the ratification of this article.

Section 6. This article shall be inoperative unless it shall have been ratified as an amendment to the Constitution by the legislatures of three-fourths of the several States within seven years from the date of its submission.

Amendment XXI.[23]

Section 1. The eighteenth article of amendment to the Constitution of the United States is hereby repealed.

Section 2. The transportation or importation into any State, Territory, or possession of the United States for delivery or use therein of intoxicating liquors, in violation of the laws thereof, is hereby prohibited.

Section 3. This article shall be inoperative unless it shall have been ratified as an amendment to the Constitution by conventions in the several States, as provided in the Constitution, within seven years from the date of the submission hereof to the States by the Congress.

Amendment XXII.[24]

Section 1. No person who has held the office of President, or acted as President, for more than two years of a term to which some other person was elected President shall be elected to the office of the President more than once. But this Article shall not apply to any person holding the office of President when this Article was proposed by the Congress, and shall not prevent any person who may be holding the office of President, or acting as President, during the term within which this Article becomes operative from holding the office of President or acting as President during the remainder of such term.

Section 2. This article shall be inoperative unless it shall have been ratified as an amendment to the Constitution by the legislatures of three-fourths of the several States within seven years from the date of its submission to the States by the Congress.

Amendment XXIII.[25]

Section 1. The District constituting the seat of Government of the United States shall appoint in such manner as the Congress may direct:

A number of electors of President and Vice President equal to the whole number of Senators and Representatives in Congress to which the District would be entitled if it were a State, but in no event more than the least populous State; they shall be in addition to those appointed by the States, but they shall be considered, for the purposes of the election of President and Vice President, to be electors appointed by a State; and they shall meet in the District and perform such duties as provided by the twelfth article of amendment.

Section 2. The Congress shall have power to enforce this article by appropriate legislation.

Amendment XXIV.[26]

Section 1. The right of citizens of the United States to vote in any primary or other election for President or Vice President, for electors for President or Vice President, or for Senator or Representative in Congress, shall not be denied or abridged by the United States or any State by reason of failure to pay any poll tax or other tax.

Section 2. The Congress shall have power to enforce this article by appropriate legislation.

23. The Twenty-First Amendment was ratified December 5, 1933.

24. The Twenty-Second Amendment was ratified February 27, 1951.

25. The Twenty-Third Amendment was ratified March 29, 1961.

26. The Twenty-Fourth Amendment was ratified January 23, 1964.

Amendment XXV.[27]

Section 1. In case of the removal of the President from office or of his death or resignation, the Vice President shall become President.

Section 2. Whenever there is a vacancy in the office of the Vice President, the President shall nominate a Vice President who shall take office upon confirmation by a majority vote of both Houses of Congress.

Section 3. Whenever the President transmits to the President pro tempore of the Senate and the Speaker of the House of Representatives his written declaration that he is unable to discharge the powers and duties of his office, and until he transmits to them a written declaration to the contrary, such powers and duties shall be discharged by the Vice President as Acting President.

Section 4. Whenever the Vice President and a majority of either the principal officers of the executive departments or of such other body as Congress may by law provide, transmit to the President pro tempore of the Senate and the Speaker of the House of Representatives their written declaration that the President is unable to discharge the powers and duties of his office, the Vice President shall immediately assume the powers and duties of the office as Acting President.

Thereafter, when the President transmits to the President pro tempore of the Senate and the Speaker of the House of Representatives his written declaration that no inability exists, he shall resume the powers and duties of his office unless the Vice President and a majority of either the principal officers of the executive department or of such other body as Congress may by law provide, transmit within four days to the President pro tempore of the Senate and the Speaker of the House of Representatives their written declaration that the President is unable to discharge the powers and duties of his office. Thereupon Congress shall decide the issue, assembling within forty-eight hours for that purpose if not in session. If the Congress, within twenty-one days after receipt of the latter written declaration, or, if Congress is not in session, within twenty-one days after Congress is required to assemble, determines by two-thirds vote of both Houses that the President is unable to discharge the powers and duties of his office, the Vice President shall continue to discharge the same as Acting President; otherwise, the President shall resume the powers and duties of his office.

Amendment XXVI.[28]

Section 1. The right of citizens of the United States, who are eighteen years of age or older, to vote shall not be denied or abridged by the United States or by any State on account of age.

Section 2. The Congress shall have power to enforce this article by appropriate legislation.

Amendment XXVII.[29]

No law, varying the compensation for the services of the Senators and Representatives, shall take effect, until an election of Representatives shall have intervened.

27. The Twenty-Fifth Amendment was ratified February 10, 1967.

28. The Twenty-Sixth Amendment was ratified July 1, 1971.

29. Congress submitted the text of the Twenty-Seventh Amendment to the States as part of the proposed Bill of Rights on September 25, 1789. The Amendment was not ratified together with the first ten Amendments, which became effective on December 15, 1791. The Twenty-Seventh Amendment was ratified May 7, 1992, by the vote of Michigan.

Appendix 2

Researching and Reading Government Documents

This volume contains a variety of government documents, as well as other types of materials such as political speeches and newspaper articles. Each type of document has its own peculiarities of form and serves its own purposes. Here we provide a brief guide to these sources.

U.S. Supreme Court Opinions

Although the relative importance of the U.S. Supreme Court as an interpreter of the U.S. Constitution has varied over the course of American history, the opinions of the Court are one of the primary sources for understanding how the Constitution has been read and applied over time. Judicial opinions are not always easy to read, even for those who are familiar with their particular style and the technical issues that they discuss. They are unlike any other text that you are likely to encounter in school or in life. You should expect to read and reread them carefully, but the reading becomes easier as you become practiced at it.

The U.S. Supreme Court is primarily an appellate court. It rarely exercises its "original jurisdiction" and serves as the trial court in which the issues of a case are first raised and the facts evaluated (and when it does hear such cases, it usually assigns them to a special master to hear the evidence and make a report to the justices). Instead, the Supreme Court generally hears cases after a trial has already been conducted and most of the issues in the case have already been resolved. The Supreme Court, like other appellate courts, exists to hear disagreements about the meaning and application of the law. The concern with the justices is with setting and clarifying the legal rules that courts will be applying in future cases, not necessarily with doing justice to the parties immediately in front of them.

After accepting a case for its consideration, the Supreme Court issues a decision that specifies how the legal question at issue in the case has been answered and an order that disposes of the case. The opinion in the case supplements these basic elements of the decision, explaining the reasoning of the justices in reaching that outcome. The Supreme Court decides many cases without an opinion, usually because the issues raised in those cases are relatively easy and do not have broader significance beyond that individual case. The Court provides opinions for all of its important decisions, and these opinions both provide a justification for what the Court has done and provides further guidance to lawyers and judges as to how they should understand what the Court has done and what they should do in similar cases in the future.

The decisions and opinions of the U.S. Supreme Court are available from a variety of sources. Initially, Supreme Court opinions were collected and published by private reporters. Because these early private efforts were not always profitable, Congress eventually stepped in to arrange that the official reports of the Court be published at government expense. Opinions in cases are first printed individually as "slip opinions" and later published in bound volumes of the *United States Reports*. The ninety volumes issued before 1875 were often cited by the name of the reporter who produced them (Dallas, Cranch, Wheaton, Peters, Howard, Black, Wallace, and Otto). Since then, they have been known simply as the *U.S. Reports*. Cases are cited by the volume of the *U.S. Reports* in which they appear, the page on which the case starts, and the year in which the case was decided. Thus, the case of *Marbury v. Madison* is cited as *Marbury v. Madison*, 5 U.S.

137 (1803), indicating that the case was decided in 1803 and can be found at page 137 of volume 5 of the *U.S. Reports*. Since the cases reported in the first 90 volumes of the *U.S. Reports* are also known by the individual reporter, *Marbury* can also be cited as 1 Cr. 137 (1803), indicating that the case can be found in the first volume of Cranch's reports (which is the same as volume 5 of the *U.S. Reports*). Both numbering systems can be cited together as 5 U.S. (1 Cr.) 137 (1803).

Besides the official *U.S. Reports*, Supreme Court decisions can also be found in other sources. The *Lawyers' Edition* of the *U.S. Reports* is published by the Lawyers' Cooperative Publishing Company and includes additional notes about the case. These versions are also cited by volume and page number with the abbreviation "L.Ed." indicating the *Lawyers' Edition* ("L.Ed. 2d" for the second series of the *Lawyers' Edition*, which began in 1957). Thus, *Marbury* can be found at 2 L.Ed. 60 (1803). For modern cases, the West Publishing Company also produces the *Supreme Court Reporter*, which is known by the initials "S.Ct.," which appears in print before the slip opinions are collected into the *U.S. Reports* (e.g., *City of Boerne v. Flores*, 117 S.Ct. 2157 [1997]). Three commercial, electronic services also reproduce these Supreme Court cases: Lexis-Nexis, Westlaw, and HeinOnline (the last provides electronic images of the *U.S. Reports* pages). Less complete sets of Supreme Court opinions can also be found on the Internet. The Supreme Court itself provides an electronic version of recent cases at http://www.supremecourtus.gov. Cases are also collected at FindLaw at http://www.findlaw.com/casecode/supreme.html and at Cornell Law School's Legal Information Institute at http://lii.law.cornell.edu. *Shepard's United States Citations* is a reference source that tracks the citation of Supreme Court cases in other opinions written by the Supreme Court and other courts. "Shepardizing" a case by tracking how a decision has been used by subsequent courts provides both a history of the use of that decision and an indication of the current state of the law. A similar service is provided by Westlaw's "KeyCite" system.

When the Supreme Court schedules a case for decision, it will typically accept written briefs from the parties in the case and will often schedule oral arguments as well. The oral arguments were once free-wheeling affairs that could last for days for a single case. They are now tightly regulated by the Court. At oral argument, lawyers are typically allowed thirty minutes to present their side of the case, with the chief justice immediately cutting off the argument when the time has expired. The justices typically ask questions at oral argument, and so the arguments often take the form of an exchange among the justices and the presenting lawyer rather than a monologue by the attorney. The justices also allow some interested parties who are not directly involved in a case to submit amicus curia ("friend of the court") briefs in order to supplement the record and highlight additional features of the case. On occasion, the justices will also allow an amicus to participate in oral arguments (often the U.S. government when the interpretation of a federal law or the Constitution is at issue but the United States is not an official party to the case). Some arguments and attorney briefs can be found in published sources, including Lexis-Nexis and *Landmark Briefs and Arguments of the Supreme Court of the United States*. Early volumes of the *U.S. Reports* often included summaries of the arguments of the attorneys in the case, and they are sometimes excerpted in this volume before the beginning of the Court's opinion. Audio files of some Supreme Court oral arguments can be found at Northwestern University's OYEZ website at http://www.oyez.org.

There are several elements in a typical appellate court decision. It usually begins with a *statement of the facts* in the case and an outline of the *prior history* of the case and how and why it reached the Supreme Court (in this volume, this information is frequently provided in the introductory headnote to the case). It then describes the *legal issue* raised by the case and the question to be resolved by the Court. It then explains the law that is relevant to deciding the case. It is here that the Court will provide its interpretation of the Constitution or other relevant laws that are necessary for deciding the case at hand. It is also here where the Court will describe or articulate the *doctrine* that encapsulates the Court's understanding of the law and that is to guide its application to individual cases. The opinion will then *apply the law* so understood to the particular facts of the case to resolve the questions raised by the case. Finally, the Court will conclude with an *order* disposing of the case.

The form of the order depends on how the case has reached the Court and what the justices have done. Earlier in its history, the judges on a lower court that found themselves divided on some legal question relevant to a case could "certify" those questions for Supreme Court review before a judgment was rendered. In those cases, the Court would answer the questions and send them back to the lower court for it to complete its work and issue a final judgment in the case. More typically, cases reach the Supreme Court after a final judgment has already been rendered in the lower courts, and the appellant in the case wants the Supreme Court to review and revise that judgment. The current route by which cases typically reach the Supreme Court is outlined in Figure A-1. Most cases reach the U.S. Supreme Court from the federal courts, but a significant number come from the state supreme courts. The appellate jurisdiction of the U.S. Supreme Court has been expanded by federal statute over time. Cases may be appealed from the state courts if they raise a "federal question," a question of the interpretation of federal law, treaties, or the U.S. Constitution, or if the parties are from different jurisdictions. The Court will typically "affirm" what the lower court has done or "reverse" it. In some cases, the order might "remand," or send back, the case to the court in which it originated for a final judgment that takes into account what the Supreme Court has done. If the Court finds that it does not have proper jurisdiction to hear and decide the case, it will dismiss the case. The consequence of a dismissal is that the judgment of the lower court will continue to stand. When cases come to the Supreme Court through a petition (e.g., a prisoner's petition for a writ of habeas corpus) or original jurisdiction (e.g., one state bringing suit against another state in a dispute over the location of the state boundary), rather than through an appeal, then the Court will rule directly on the case (e.g., granting or denying the petition) and not simply review the record of the lower court. Since the early twentieth century, the Court's docket has primarily been discretionary. The Court now receives thousands of requests each year that it issue a writ of certiorari (or "cert") scheduling a case to be heard on appeal. As Figure A-2 shows, the Court reached a peak of hearing nearly 300 cases per year in the late nineteenth century, before Congress began to reduce the number of cases that the Court had to hear on mandatory appeal. In recent years, the Court has granted cert in around a hundred cases per year. Thus, not only does the Court review only a tiny fraction of the total number of cases decided each year by the lower federal appellate courts and the state supreme courts, but it agrees to hear only a very small percentage of the cases that it is actively asked to review by the parties involved. Only four justices are needed to grant cert, a practice known as the Rule of Four. When the Court refuses to grant cert, then the justices are not making a decision on the merits of the case and the denial sets no new law for later cases.

In deciding cases on the merits, the Supreme Court operates on the basis of majority rule. The justices vote on what the judgment of the Court should be in each case, and a majority determines the Court's action. If the Court is equally divided (if, for example, one of the justices does not participate in the case due to illness or

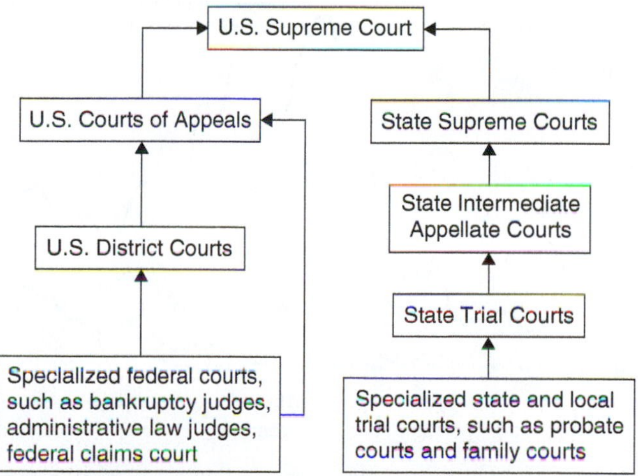

Figure A-1 Getting to the U.S. Supreme Court

Note: In some less common circumstances, cases can reach the U.S. Supreme Court by other routes.

a conflict of interest), then the judgment of the lower court stands. The justices discuss each case and vote in private conference after the case has been briefed and argued. By tradition, if the chief justice is a member of the majority, he may assign which of the members of the majority will write the official opinion of the Court. If the chief justice is a dissenter in the case, then the justice voting with the majority having the most seniority on the Court makes the assignment. After the opinions are drafted, they are circulated to the other justices for comments and revisions. Justices may, and sometimes do, change their votes after the opinions are drafted, and it is possible for enough justices to change their positions to change the outcome in the case. Once the opinions and votes are finalized, then the decision is publicly announced and the slip opinions are published. The decisions are typically announced by the justices orally from the bench, and occasionally the opinions will be read aloud by the justices from the bench (this was once the routine practice, but it is now very rare).

Judicial decisions may be announced in several ways. A unanimous opinion is one in which all the judges agree with the decision and reasoning. A majority opinion is one in which at least five justices agree with the decision and reasoning (or less than five if fewer than eight justices voted). An opinion might announce the judgment of the court but gives reasons that only a minority of justices support. A per curiam opinion ("by the court") is an unsigned opinion. These sometimes reflect a judicial consensus, but are sometimes used when there is significant disagreement among the justices (for example in Bush v. Gore [2000]).

Justices write concurring opinions when they agree with the result in the opinion announcing the judgment of the court, but not the reasoning. Justices write dissenting opinions when they disagree with the result in the opinion announcing the judgment of the court. When a case involves more than one issue (was the petitioner at trial denied the right to jury and/or the right to counsel), a justice may write an opinion that concurs in part and dissents in part. Justices may also sign part of another justice's opinion, but write a concurrence or dissent that only covers some aspect of the judicial reasoning. In cases with no majority opinions, the holding consists of any proposition that at least five justices seem to support. Lawyers are paid a good deal of money to identify and argue for the interpretation of such decisions that best help their client or cause. At earlier points in the Court's history, justices frequently refrained from writing separate opinions and often refrained from announcing their disagreement with the majority. Since the early twentieth century, however, the justices have proven very willing to voice their individual opinions in the Court's cases. Figure A-2 shows the number of cases with separate opinions produced by the justices on the Supreme Court over time. Until

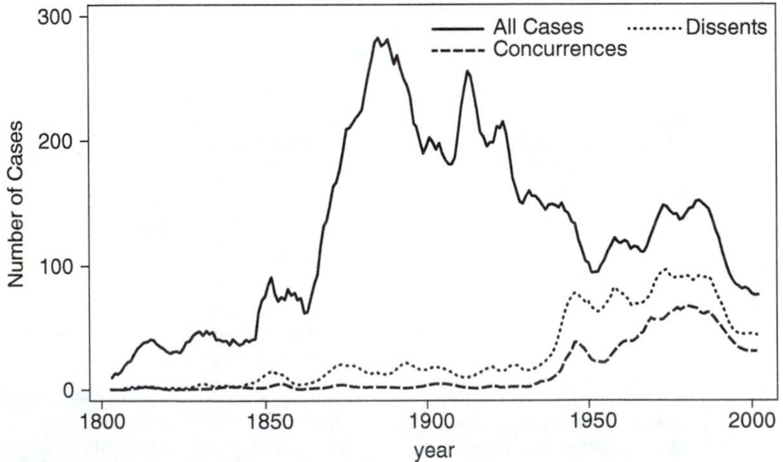

Figure A-2: Number of Supreme Court Cases with Separate Opinions

Note: Centered five-year moving averages.

Source: Lee Epstein, Jeffrey A. Segal, Harold J. Spaeth, Thomas G. Walker, *The Supreme Court Compendium*, 4th ed. (Washington, DC: CQ Press, 2007), Tables 3.2, 3.3.

the late 1930s, a steady 10 percent of the Court cases included a separately authored opinion. Since then, however, the justices have routinely produced dissenting and concurring opinions to supplement the majority opinion. Well over half of all cases decided since World War II include at least one dissenting opinion, and nearly half the cases decided since the mid-1960s include a concurring opinion. Concurring and dissenting opinions have no official standing, and the practice of producing such opinions has been criticized for weakening the authority of the Court and for muddying the state of the law. But separate opinions can be influential either by their own persuasive power or by signaling the possible future trajectory of the Court's majority.

Briefing a Case

Students often find it helpful to "brief" the cases that they read. This is not writing a lawyer's brief, such as those submitted to the Supreme Court. Briefing a case for study is a process of note-taking that identifies and summarizes the key elements in a judicial decision. Some basic elements of a brief are provided next, along with an explanation and an example (in italics) from *United States v. E.C. Knight Company* (1895).

Name of the case—This identifies the parties in the case (some cases also become known by their subject matter, such as *The Legal Tender Cases*). The first party listed is usually the appellant, the party that lost in the lower court and brought the case to the Supreme Court for review. The second party listed is usually the appellee, the party that won in the lower court and is responding to the appeal to the Supreme Court.

U.S. v. E. C. Knight Company

Citation of the case—The citation provides the specific location where the opinion can be found, preferably in the *U.S. Reports*.

156 U.S. 1

Year of the case—The year the case was decided provides important information about the context in which the decision was made.

1895

Vote in the case—The public vote in the case can be determined by identifying the justices who sign on to any dissenting opinions and subtracting them from the total number of justices who participated in the case (giving you the number of justices who must have voted with the majority). Remember that the publicly revealed vote is not necessarily the same as the vote of the justices in their private conference, and note that the decision will usually indicate if any of the sitting justices did not participate in the case.

8–1

Factual circumstances of the case—What are the key factual details that identify what the dispute is and what triggered the litigation? Note that the Court's opinions often provide more information than is essential for understanding the case. One challenge for the student is learning to identify which facts are critical to the case and help explain the legal and political significance of the case.

The American Sugar Refining Company of New Jersey tried to acquire E. C. Knight Company of Pennsylvania, which would have given the combined company control of 98 percent of the national market in refined sugar. The United States Department of Justice intervened under the authority of the Sherman Anti-Trust Act, petitioning the Court of Appeals for the Third Circuit to void the sale as an illegal restraint of trade.

Legal issue or question raised by the case—What are the legal questions being addressed by the Court in the case? (Note that there may be more than one.) What statutory or constitutional provisions are at issue?

Does Congress have authority under the interstate commerce clause of the U.S. Constitution to prohibit monopolies in the manufacturing of goods?

Outcome of the case—How did the Court dispose of the case, and who won? It is often useful also to know what subsequently happened to the parties and the issue in the case, though this will not of course appear in the Court's own decision.

Affirmed the circuit court. The appellee, E. C. Knight, won.

Legal holding of the case—How did the Court answer the legal question raised in the case?

Congress cannot directly regulate manufacturing.

Doctrine announced or applied in the case—What is the rule for decision that the Court used to resolve the case? This may be a doctrine that the Court invented in this same case, or it may be a doctrine that had been previously announced by the Court and is being used in the case. When the Court is using a previously announced doctrine, you will want to be aware of whether the justices are subtly altering or elaborating that rule as they are deciding this case.

The interstate commerce clause only authorizes Congress to regulate actions that directly affect interstate commerce, not actions that indirectly affect interstate commerce.

Author and legal reasoning of the majority opinion—Even though the majority opinion is formally the opinion of the Court and reflects the input of all the justices in the majority, the core reasoning of the decision will still reflect the particular ideas, commitments and style of the individual justice who wrote the opinion. The legal reasoning used in the majority opinion is frequently the most important aspect of a case, for it will guide future judges seeking to understand what the Court has done and how future cases should be decided. You will want to be able to provide a concise summary of the explanation that the Court offered for its decision and the interpretation of the relevant law that the Court provided.

Fuller. Sherman Anti-Trust Act must be interpreted in light of the constitutional limits on the power of Congress, and therefore cannot be understood to encroach on the police powers of the states. The states have the exclusive authority to regulate manufacturing and prohibit monopolies. Manufacturing affects interstate commerce only "incidentally and indirectly." Federal power extends only to the actual "articles of interstate commerce," and not to goods that are merely intended for interstate commerce. Commerce is the buying, selling and transportation of goods. Manufacturing is the production of goods, and the sale of one sugar refining company to another is a contract relating to manufacturing of sugar, not the interstate sale of sugar.

Author and legal reasoning of any concurring opinions—Concurring opinions are more individual efforts of the justices who write them than are majority opinions, and they provide an alternative legal explanation of how the case was decided. Note that a concurring opinion may attract as many or more justices than the official opinion of the court, meaning that more members of the Court agree with the legal reasoning of the concurring opinion than agree with the legal reasoning of the "court" opinion even though it is the majority opinion that has official status and announces the outcome of the case. Concurring opinions influence the holding of a case when there is no majority opinion. In such cases, the holding is any proposition that five justices arguably agree upon.

None.

Author and legal reasoning of any dissenting opinions—Like concurring opinions, dissenting opinions tend to be much more individualistic than the majority opinion. Justices often write dissenting opinions "for the future," in the hopes that a majority of the Court will eventually change its mind and in some future case adopt the reasoning of the dissent as its own. But dissenting opinions can also be written with a more immediate goal in mind, of attempting to persuade wavering members of the majority to change their votes before the decision is announced. Since the published dissents remain mere dissents, those particular efforts at persuasion were obviously unsuccessful.

Harlan. As decided in Gibbons v. Ogden *(1824) and other decisions, Congress has the authority to regulate "intercourse and traffic" among the states and things that are "incidental" to the interstate buying, selling and transportation of goods. Manufacturing, like transportation, is "incidental" to the buying and selling of goods, and is therefore covered by the interstate commerce clause. Any combination that "disturbs or unreasonably obstructs" interstate commerce directly affects the nation as a whole and can be prohibited by Congress. Prohibiting monopolies in manufacturing is an "appropriate" means for preventing the obstruction of interstate commerce (see* McCulloch v. Maryland *[1819]). Matters that "directly and injuriously affects" national commerce and "cannot be adequately controlled by any one State" can be regulated by Congress.*

Significance of case for American constitutional development—Unlike the other elements of the brief, this will not be obvious within the decision itself; but when reading the case, students should be thinking about why the case was included in the volume and is being taught in this course. Answering this question will often require thinking beyond the case itself and considering the context in which it was decided and its implications for subsequent politics. How did the case clarify or change the meaning of the law? What new issues or ideas were reflected in the case? What disputes or forces does the case reflect? How did the dispute and the outcome in the case fit into the political and social context of the time? How might the case have affected the politics, economy and society of the time? How might it have affected subsequent developments in those fields?

The case significantly limited one of the first and most important efforts of the federal government to regulate the national economy and imposed significant limits on the ability of the federal government to make future economic policy. The case bolstered conservatives in the Democratic and Republican parties and the emerging interstate corporations, but frustrated populists and their constituencies among farmers, workers, and small businesses. The decision reflected bipartisan conservative commitments (only one dis-

senter, and opinion author was a Democratic appointee), but came on the eve of the populist takeover of the Democratic Party in the elections of 1896, which also ended Democratic competitiveness in national elections until the 1930s.

Other Court Opinions

This volume contains decisions by a number of other courts besides the U.S. Supreme Court, and other courts are certainly relevant to American constitutionalism and to legal research. Decisions from other courts excerpted here come from elsewhere in the federal judicial system or from the state judicial systems.

The decisions of federal courts below the U.S. Supreme Court are not reported in the *U.S. Reports*, and as a consequence have a different citation system. Most significant decisions from the federal district courts (trial courts at the lowest level of the modern federal judicial system) are reported in the *Federal Supplement*. Those decisions are cited by the volume and page number in which they appear in the *Federal Supplement*, abbreviated as "F.Supp." Early district court cases were reported in *Federal Cases*, abbreviated as "F.Cas." Before the year in which the case was decided in the parenthesis after the page cite, the specific court is identified by "D," meaning district court, and an abbreviation for the state in which the court sits. If there is more than one federal district court in a state, the specific court will be identified by geography; e.g., "E.D. Mass." refers to the federal district court in the eastern district of Massachusetts. Thus the citation for *United States v. The William*, an early district court case from Massachusetts, is *United States v. The William*, 28 F. Cas. 614 (D. Mass. 1808). Although there is more than one judge assigned to each federal district, usually only one sits on any given case (and therefore, there can be no concurring or dissenting opinions). In certain important cases, Congress may require a three-judge panel to hear the case initially. One of those judges is expected to be from the circuit court, and appeals from such panels go directly to the U.S. Supreme Court. Since district courts are trial courts where cases start, cases decided there generally have no prior history in the judiciary. District court opinions are binding only in the district in which they are issued, and are good law until they are reversed by the same district court, by the circuit court that oversees that district, or by the U.S. Supreme Court.

Significant decisions from the federal circuit courts (the intermediate courts between the district courts and the U.S. Supreme Court, which now operate only as appellate courts but once also operated as trial courts) are reported in the *Federal Reporter*. The *Federal Reporter* is abbreviated as "Fed." or "F.," followed by "2d" or "3d" in the case of the second or third series of that reporter. Instead of "D." and a state, circuit courts are now identified by their circuit number (e.g., 3d Cir.). Early circuit court cases were also reported in *Federal Cases* and were known by the district of the state in which the circuit court was sitting rather than by number (e.g., Cir. Ct. Dist. So. Car., or CCDSC). Thus, *Elkison v. Deliesseline*, an early circuit court case from South Carolina, is *Elkison v. Deliesseline*, 8 F. Cas. 493 (Cir. Ct. Dist. So. Car. 1823). Circuit courts sit in panels of more than one judge, and thus there is a potential for dissenting and concurring opinions (though individual opinions are far more rare in these courts than in the Supreme Court). Circuit court cases are binding law only within the circuits in which they are handed down, and they are good law until overturned by that same circuit court or by the U.S. Supreme Court. Both types of federal cases, district and circuit, can also be found in Lexis-Nexis and Westlaw.

Biographical information about those who have served as federal judges, as well as other information about the federal courts, has been made available on the Internet by the Federal Judicial Center at http://www.fjc.gov.

State judicial systems have a similar structure to the federal judicial system, with trial courts and multi-member appellate courts capped by a highest appellate court for that type of case (some states create separate tracks, and separate supreme courts, for different kinds of cases, such as criminal and civil cases). State court decisions are published in reports maintained within each individual state, and those state reporting systems have sometimes changed over time. Thus, the Pennsylvania Supreme Court case of *Sharpless v. Mayor of Philadelphia*, published in the *Pennsylvania State Reports*, is cited as *Sharpless v. Mayor of Philadelphia*, 21 Pa. 147 (1853). Modern state cases are also collected and published in several regional reporters, such as the *Atlantic Reporter* and the *North Western Reporter*. State court decisions can also be found in Lexis-Nexis and Westlaw. State supreme court decisions are binding only within the state in which they are issued. State supreme courts are the highest authority on the laws and constitutions of their own states, just as the U.S. Supreme Court is the highest authority on federal laws and the U.S. Constitution. Federal laws and the U.S. Constitution are binding within each state and must also be interpreted and applied by state courts when they are relevant to deciding cases that arise within the state judicial systems. When interpreting federal laws or the U.S. Constitution, the state supreme courts can be reviewed and corrected by the U.S. Supreme Court (or any federal court, in the case of habeas petitions).

Congressional Documents

The most important documents produced by Congress are federal laws. Private laws are legislation intended to benefit particular individuals, such as laws waiving any financial claims that the government might have against an individual or excepting an individual from the usual application of immigration laws. Public laws are legislation that affect the general public. Once a bill becomes a law, it is assigned a public law number reflecting the Congress that passed it and its place in the sequence of laws passed by that Congress (e.g., PL 104–1 was the first law passed by the 104th Congress). Public laws and private laws and resolutions (pronouncements of one or both chambers of Congress that do not have the force of law) are collected and published in the *U.S. Statutes at Large*, which is cited by volume and page number, and year; e.g. PL 104-1 is printed at 109 U.S. Stat. 109 (1995). As laws are revised and amended over time, the still valid laws have been consolidated and codified, first in two editions of the *Revised Statutes* in the 1870s and since in several editions of the *United States Code*. The code is cited by subject-matter "title" number, section, and edition (e.g., PL 104–1 was incorporated into 2 USC 1301 [2000]).

Congress also produces a variety of other documents besides statutes and resolutions. The official actions of each chamber of Congress are recorded in constitutionally mandated journals. The debates on the floor of the House of Representatives and the Senate are reported in the *Congressional Record* and its predecessors (*Annals of Congress*, *Register of Debates*, and the *Congressional Globe*). Congressional committees, where most of the work of Congress is done, produce Documents (a wide range of materials that Congress has ordered published, including executive-branch reports and records), Reports (official reports by House and Senate committees to their parent chambers, usually explaining bills being recommended by the committee), and Transcripts of Hearings (transcripts of public testimony and discussion that committees gather on topics of interest). These are published separately by the committees. Early Documents and Reports were bound together in the *American State Papers*. Since 1817, Documents and Reports have been collected and published in the *United States Serial Set*. Committee Reports may include reports from both the majority and the minority (from the committee members who disagree with the majority report or the legislative action being recommended). All of these documents are commonly cited by the body that produced it, the title, the type of document, the number of the Congress that produced it, the session number, and the date; e.g., House Committee on the Judiciary, Apportionment Bill, 27th Cong., 2nd Sess. (1842), H.R. Rep. 27–909. Bill sponsors and the chairmen of the committees reporting legislation are understood to have a privileged voice in explaining the meaning and purpose of a bill, but Congress votes only on the text of the legislation itself, and the body as a whole does not have to approve or agree to anything that is said during legislative debate, written in committee reports, or contained in similar documents created during the legislative process.

Many of these documents are available in the CongressionalUniverse service of Lexis-Nexis and on HeinOnline. Many congressional documents produced through Reconstruction have been placed on the Internet by the Library of Congress at http://lcweb2.loc.gov/ammem/amlaw/lawhome.html. Very recent materials are available at the THOMAS website at http://thomas.loc.gov. Useful biographical information on individuals who have served in Congress can be found in the *Biographical Directory of the U.S. Congress*, available on the Internet at http://bioguide.congress.gov.

Executive Branch Documents

The various components of the federal executive branch produce a vast number and variety of documents.

The president himself produces a variety of documents, all of which have political significance but only some of which have immediate legal effect. The Constitution recognizes only two types of presidential documents. The first are general purpose presidential messages to Congress, the most famous of which is the annual message, or "State of the Union address." The second is the veto message to Congress, explaining the president's reasons for vetoing a proposed law.

These two constitutionally mandated forms of communication have been supplemented by other formal messages, most notably the inaugural address and the signing statement (remarking on a law being signed by the president, sometimes simply to commemorate the occasion, sometimes to note interpretations of, qualifications to, or concerns about the legislation being signed). Of course, the president also delivers a large number of informal speeches and public statements. Formal messages to Congress have routinely been published in the *Congressional Record*. The messages and speeches of the presidents through the early twentieth century were collected and published in *A Compilation of the Messages and Papers of the Presidents*. Franklin Roosevelt's speeches were published privately in *The Public Papers and Addresses of Franklin Delano Roosevelt*. Those of subsequent presidents have been published by the government in *Public Papers of the Presidents of the United States* and more frequently in *The Weekly Compilation of Presidential Documents*.

The president also produces documents with more immediate legal effect. Executive orders are directives from the president to members of the executive branch (military orders are their counterpart directed to the armed forces). So long as they do not contradict a constitutionally valid statute, these instructions are understood to be binding on subordinate executive officers, directing how they will implement laws and perform executive functions. Presidential proclamations are directed to the general public. Proclamations are often innocuous, declaring days of celebration and the like, but they are sometimes momentous, such as Abraham Lincoln's proclamation calling forth the state militias to put down secession and his Emancipation Proclamation. Executive orders through the early twentieth century were compiled in *Presidential Executive Orders*. They have subsequently been published in the *Federal Register* and compiled in the *Codification of Presidential Executive Orders and Proclamations*. Much of this material is available in HeinOnline. Some of it (along with press conference transcripts, party platforms, and other materials) has been made available on the Internet by the University of California at Santa Barbara's The American Presidency Project at http://www.presidency.ucsb.edu and through the National Archives at http://www.archives.gov/federal-register/index.html.

More routine are regulations and orders produced by executive branch agencies, primarily in the course of interpreting and implementing statutes. These regulations have the immediate force of law and receive substantial deference from the courts. They are published in the *Federal Register* and compiled in the *Code of Federal Regulations*.

Of particular significance to American constitutionalism are the legal opinions of the attorney general. These opinions derive from the constitutional authority of the president to command the written opinion of principal officers of the executive departments upon subjects relating to their office and from the statute originally creating the office of attorney general. The attorney general now routinely provides advisory opinions on legal issues, including constitutional issues. Attorney general opinions have more recently been supplemented by the legal opinions of the Office of Legal Counsel (OLC), which advises the attorney general. Attorney general opinions are compiled in *The Official Opinions of the Attorneys General of the United States*, which is cited by volume, the abbreviation "Op. Att'y Gen.," the page, and the date. A selection of the OLC opinions are published in *Opinions of the Office of Legal Counsel*, which is cited in the same fashion with the abbreviation "Op. O.L.C." These formal opinions guide the executive branch in its interpretation and application of the law, including constitutional law, and frequently guide private actors and other government officials, including judges, in their understandings of the law.

State-level executive branch officials perform many of these same functions in the state government. Such state documents are often compiled in equivalent state publications, but they are not always readily accessible and have not generally been collected in the same comprehensive fashion as the federal documents.

Legal Literature

Commentaries on the law produced by private citizens such as law professors or government officials writing in a private capacity have no official status, but they can reflect the currents of legal thinking at the time and exert substantial persuasive power on their own and future generations. As such, they can influence and be cited as authority by government actors who do have formal power, such as judges. Before the twentieth century, scholarly legal treatises that seek to critically synthesize the state of the law have had the greatest influence. Relevant examples of these include St. George Tucker's American edition of William Blackstone's *Commentaries on the Laws of England*

(1803), Joseph Story's *Commentaries on the Constitution of the United States* (1833), John Alexander Jameson's *A Treatise on Constitutional Conventions* (1866), Thomas Cooley's *Constitutional Limitations* (1868), and, more recently, Laurence H. Tribe's *American Constitutional Law* (1978). More diverse is the law review literature, scholarly articles in legal periodicals. An important guide to legal journals is the *Index to Legal Periodicals*. This venerable guide has recently been supplemented by various less comprehensive guides, including LegalTrac. The content of many law reviews is available through services such as Lexis-Nexis, Westlaw, and (with greater historical depth but somewhat less breadth) HeinOnline.

Citation guides for government and legal documents include *The Chicago Manual of Style* (most commonly used in the humanities and social sciences) and *The Bluebook: A Uniform System of Citation* (the most commonly used citation guide in the law schools). A generally helpful resource is the Law Library of Congress's Guide to Law Online, available at http://www.loc.gov/law/public/law-guide.html.

Appendix 3

Chronological Table of Presidents, Congress, and the Supreme Court

Years	President	House of Representatives	U.S. Senate	Supreme Court[1]
1789–1791	G. Washington (F)	Federalist	Federalist	Federalist
1791–1793	G. Washington (F)	Federalist	Federalist	Federalist
1793–1795	G. Washington (F)	Republican[2]	Federalist	Federalist
1795–1797	G. Washington (F)	Federalist	Federalist	Federalist
1797–1799	J. Adams (F)	Federalist	Federalist	Federalist
1799–1801	J. Adams (F)	Federalist	Federalist	Federalist
1801–1803	T. Jefferson (R)	Republican	Republican	Federalist
1803–1805	T. Jefferson (R)	Republican	Republican	Federalist
1805–1807	T. Jefferson (R)	Republican	Republican	Federalist
1807–1809	T. Jefferson (R)	Republican	Republican	Federalist
1809–1811	J. Madison (R)	Republican	Republican	Federalist
1811–1813	J. Madison (R)	Republican	Republican	Federalist
1813–1815	J. Madison (R)	Republican	Republican	Republican
1815–1817	J. Madison (R)	Republican	Republican	Republican
1817–1819	J. Monroe (R)	Republican	Republican	Republican
1819–1821	J. Monroe (R)	Republican	Republican	Republican
1821–1823	J. Monroe (R)	Republican	Republican	Republican
1823–1825	J. Monroe (R)	Republican	Republican[3]	Republican
1825–1827	J. Q. Adams (R)	Republican	Democrat	Republican
1827–1829	J. Q. Adams (R)	Democrat	Democrat	Republican
1829–1831	A. Jackson (D)	Democrat	Democrat	Republican
1831–1833	A. Jackson (D)	Democrat	Democrat	Republican
1833–1835	A. Jackson (D)	Democrat	Whig	Republican

(Continued)

1. Party control of Supreme Court represented by party affiliation of median member.
2. An "Anti-administration" majority that predates the formation of an organized political party.
3. Majority formed from coalition of states' rights Republicans and supporters of Andrew Jackson.

Years	President	House of Representatives	U.S. Senate	Supreme Court
1835–1837	A. Jackson (D)	Democrat	Democrat	Republican
1837–1839	M. Van Buren (D)	Democrat	Democrat	Democrat
1839–1841	M. Van Buren (D)	Democrat	Democrat	Democrat
1841–1843	W. H. Harrison/J. Tyler (W)	Whig	Whig	Democrat
1843–1845	J. Tyler (W)	Democrat	Whig	Democrat
1845–1847	J. Polk (D)	Democrat	Democrat	Democrat
1847–1849	J. Polk (D)	Whig	Democrat	Democrat
1849–1851	Z. Taylor/M. Fillmore (W)	Democrat	Democrat	Democrat
1851–1853	M. Fillmore (W)	Democrat	Democrat	Democrat
1853–1855	F. Pierce (D)	Democrat	Democrat	Democrat
1855–1857	F. Pierce (D)	Republican[4]	Democrat	Democrat
1857–1859	J. Buchanan (D)	Democrat	Democrat	Democrat
1859–1861	J. Buchanan (D)	Democrat	Democrat	Democrat
1861–1863	A. Lincoln (R)	Republican	Republican	Democrat
1863–1865	A. Lincoln (R)	Republican	Republican	Republican
1865–1867	A. Lincoln/A. Johnson (R)	Republican	Republican	Republican
1867–1869	A. Johnson (R)	Republican	Republican	Republican
1869–1871	U. S. Grant (R)	Republican	Republican	Republican
1871–1873	U. S. Grant (R)	Republican	Republican	Republican
1873–1875	U. S. Grant (R)	Republican	Republican	Republican
1875–1877	U. S. Grant (R)	Democrat	Republican	Republican
1877–1879	R. Hayes (R)	Democrat	Republican	Republican
1879–1881	R. Hayes (R)	Democrat	Republican	Republican
1881–1883	J. Garfield/C. Arthur (R)	Republican	Republican	Republican
1883–1885	C. Arthur (R)	Democrat	Republican	Republican
1885–1887	G. Cleveland (D)	Democrat	Republican	Republican
1887–1889	G. Cleveland (D)	Democrat	Republican	Republican
1889–1891	B. Harrison (R)	Republican	Republican	Republican
1891–1893	B. Harrison (R)	Democrat	Republican	Republican
1893–1895	G. Cleveland (D)	Democrat	Democrat	Republican
1895–1897	G. Cleveland (D)	Republican	Republican	Republican
1897–1899	W. McKinley (R)	Republican	Republican	Republican
1899–1901	W. McKinley (R)	Republican	Republican	Republican
1901–1903	W. McKinley/T. Roosevelt (R)	Republican	Republican	Republican
1903–1905	T. Roosevelt (R)	Republican	Republican	Republican
1905–1907	T. Roosevelt (R)	Republican	Republican	Republican
1907–1909	T. Roosevelt (R)	Republican	Republican	Republican

(Continued)

4. Majority formed from coalition of Republican and American (or "Know Nothing") Party members.

Years	President	House of Representatives	U.S. Senate	Supreme Court
1909–1911	W. H. Taft (R)	Republican	Republican	Republican
1911–1913	W. H. Taft (R)	Democrat	Republican	Republican
1913–1915	W. Wilson (D)	Democrat	Democrat	Republican
1915–1917	W. Wilson (D)	Democrat	Democrat	Republican
1917–1919	W. Wilson (D)	Democrat	Democrat	Republican
1919–1921	W. Wilson (D)	Republican	Republican	Republican
1921–1923	W. Harding/C. Coolidge (R)	Republican	Republican	Republican
1923–1925	C. Coolidge (R)	Republican	Republican	Republican
1925–1927	C. Coolidge (R)	Republican	Republican	Republican
1927–1929	C. Coolidge (R)	Republican	Republican	Republican
1929–1931	H. Hoover (R)	Republican	Republican	Republican
1931–1933	H. Hoover (R)	Democrat	Republican	Republican
1933–1935	F. D. Roosevelt (D)	Democrat	Democrat	Republican
1935–1937	F. D. Roosevelt (D)	Democrat	Democrat	Republican
1937–1939	F. D. Roosevelt (D)	Democrat	Democrat	Republican
1939–1941	F. D. Roosevelt (D)	Democrat	Democrat	Democrat
1941–1943	F. D. Roosevelt (D)	Democrat	Democrat	Democrat
1943–1945	F. D. Roosevelt/H. Truman (D)	Democrat	Democrat	Democrat
1945–1947	H. Truman (D)	Democrat	Democrat	Democrat
1947–1949	H. Truman (D)	Republican	Republican	Democrat
1949–1951	H. Truman (D)	Democrat	Democrat	Democrat
1951–1953	H. Truman (D)	Democrat	Democrat	Democrat
1953–1955	D. Eisenhower (R)	Republican	Republican	Democrat
1955–1957	D. Eisenhower (R)	Democrat	Democrat	Democrat
1957–1959	D. Eisenhower (R)	Democrat	Democrat	Democrat
1959–1961	D. Eisenhower (R)	Democrat	Democrat	Democrat
1961–1963	J. Kennedy (D)	Democrat	Democrat	Democrat
1963–1965	J. Kennedy/L. B. Johnson (D)	Democrat	Democrat	Democrat
1965–1967	L. B. Johnson (D)	Democrat	Democrat	Democrat
1967–1969	L. B. Johnson (D)	Democrat	Democrat	Democrat
1969–1971	R. Nixon (R)	Democrat	Democrat	Democrat
1971–1973	R. Nixon (R)	Democrat	Democrat	Democrat
1973–1975	R. Nixon/G. Ford (R)	Democrat	Democrat	Democrat
1975–1977	G. Ford (R)	Democrat	Democrat	Republican
1977–1979	J. Carter (D)	Democrat	Democrat	Republican
1979–1981	J. Carter (D)	Democrat	Democrat	Republican
1981–1983	R. Reagan (R)	Democrat	Republican	Republican
1983–1985	R. Reagan (R)	Democrat	Republican	Republican
1985–1987	R. Reagan (R)	Democrat	Republican	Republican

(Continued)

Years	President	House of Representatives	U.S. Senate	Supreme Court
1987–1989	R. Reagan (R)	Democrat	Democrat	Republican
1989–1991	G. Bush (R)	Democrat	Democrat	Republican
1991–1993	G. Bush (R)	Democrat	Democrat	Republican
1993–1995	W. Clinton (D)	Democrat	Democrat	Republican
1995–1997	W. Clinton (D)	Republican	Republican	Republican
1997–1999	W. Clinton (D)	Republican	Republican	Republican
1999–2001	W. Clinton (D)	Republican	Republican	Republican
2001–2003	G. W. Bush (R)	Republican	Democrat[5]	Republican
2003–2005	G. W. Bush (R)	Republican	Republican	Republican
2005–2007	G. W. Bush (R)	Republican	Republican	Republican
2007–2009	G. W. Bush (R)	Democrat	Democrat	Republican
2009–2011	B. Obama (D)	Democrat	Democrat	Republican
2011–2013	B. Obama (D)	Republican	Democrat	Republican

5. Majority control of the Senate changed three times during the 107th Congress, with the Democrats holding the majority most of the term.

Glossary

acquittal A legal declaration than the accused is not guilty.

adjudicate To preside over, as in a court presiding over a case.

advisory opinion A court statement on the constitutionality of a matter, such as a law or government action, outside the context of a civil or criminal trial. Not accepted in most court systems in the United States.

affidavit A written, sworn statement of fact.

affirm To uphold, as in the decision of a lower court.

affirmative action The giving of preference to members of historically oppressed groups in hiring or school admittance policies.

amicus (or amici) curiae Literally "friend of the court"; a person or entity who is not a party to the case but provides information to the court, whether in a brief or testimony, on behalf of one side.

annul To declare void, to eliminate.

anti-Federalists Those who opposed the ratification of the U.S. Constitution in the late eighteenth century.

appeal To contest the decision of a court before a higher authority, such as a higher court or an executive official.

appellant The party who contests a court's decisions after losing a case by bringing an appeal. Also called the petitioner.

appellate jurisdiction A court's authority to hear and decide challenges to the decisions of lower courts; the range of issues and cases that a court can hear on appeal.

appellee The party who responds to the appeal of a court decision that was in their favor. Also called the respondent.

arraignment A hearing in which the court reads the charges against a criminal defendant from the indictment, and the defendant enters a formal plea (i.e., guilty or not guilty).

Articles of Confederation The supreme law that governed the union of the original thirteen states of the United States from 1781 to 1789, predating the Constitution. The Articles of Confederation established a highly federated system in which the states, not the national government, were sovereign.

attitudinal model The theory that one can describe and predict a judge's legal decisions based on one's knowledge of the judge's policy preferences.

balancing test A tool used by courts to decide between competing rights and/or powers. Balancing tests establish frameworks or sets of criteria that take into account multiple factors that must be considered by a judge in determining the resolution of a dispute in which both sides have some claim to legal authority.

bicameral Two-chambered, as in the U.S. Congress divided between the House of Representatives and the Senate.

bill A piece of proposed legislation.

brief A written statement presented to the court that lays out the argument for one party.

briefing a case A summary and analysis of a case or judicial opinion

case A dispute brought before a court.

case law The body of cases that make up legal precedent.

case or controversy rule The requirement in Article III that the business of courts be limited to resolving active disputes between parties, prohibiting, for example, court involvement in speculative questions of legal interpretation.

certiorari (writ of) An appellate court's order to an inferior court to send it the records from a case that the appellate court has agreed to review. Appellants generally ask the U.S. Supreme Court to take a case by asking it to grant this writ.

checks and balances The legal structures that limit the power of government by granting each branch enough power to prevent the tyranny of other branches.

chilling effect A person's or entity's reluctance to act within its constitutional rights and powers due to a law or court ruling punishing similar (but not identical) behavior.

civil law Law pertaining to the relationships among individuals or organizations.

civil right Behavior and government action to which people are legally entitled, such as free speech and equal protection.

class action lawsuit A dispute brought before a court on behalf of a group, members of whom have sustained a common injury or harm.

comity Respect for the decisions of other political entities, especially respect by federal courts for the decisions of state courts.

common law Laws and procedures which are not formally codified in written constitutions or statutes but are instead built through judicial precedent.

compensatory damages Reparations granted to a winning plaintiff in a civil suit that cover the monetary value of losses or injury caused by the defendant.

concurrent powers Jurisdiction shared by national and state governments.

concurring opinion A judge's (or several judges') written statement(s) agreeing with the outcome arrived at by the majority of the court in a case but disagreeing with or adding to the majority's reasoning.

confrontation A defendant's right to hear testimony from and cross-examine the prosecution's witnesses in court.

constitutional law The body of legal decisions pertaining to matters arising under the constitution.

constitutionalism Constitutional interpretation and practice, concerned with the structure of and limitations on government.

contempt Disrespect to or failure to comply with the authority of a court.

contract A legally binding agreement between parties.

criminal law Law pertaining to the regulation of the interaction between individuals and the community or state, and the punishment of infractions thereof.

de facto Literally "in point of fact." As a situation or condition appears in reality, irrespective of legal conditions.

de jure Literally "as a matter of law." As a situation or condition is codified in law.

decree A legal order.

defamation Slander, libel, injury to a person's or an entity's reputation.

defendant The person accused in a criminal suit or sued in a civil suit.

delegation The act of one entity granting its powers to another.

deposition A witness' sworn statement taken out-of-court.

dicta; obiter dicta Language in a judge's opinion that goes beyond what is necessary to reach the judgment and is therefore not considered a part of legal precedent.

direct effects In pre-New Deal commerce clause jurisprudence, local actions are subject to federal regulation only if they directly affect interstate commerce.

dissenting opinion A judge's (or several judges') written statement(s) disagreeing with the outcome arrived at by the majority of the court in a case.

diversity jurisdiction Cases that the federal courts can hear because the parties involved are from two different jurisdictions, even though the case may not raise issues of federal law.

docket The list of cases to be heard by a court.

dormant commerce power The implicit prohibition on state governments from regulating interstate commerce even in the absence of conflicting federal regulations.

double jeopardy Trying a party more than once in the same jurisdiction for the same offense. Unconstitutional in the United States.

due process The legal rights and procedures to which individuals are constitutionally entitled before being subjected to legal constraints or disabilities. As outlined in the Fifth, Sixth, and Fourteenth Amendments and in decisions by the Supreme Court, these include (but are not limited to) the right to an attorney, the right to a jury trial, and freedom from double jeopardy.

eminent domain The power of the government to confiscate private property without the owner's consent, provided just compensation is paid.

enjoin To prohibit or demand the performance of certain acts.

enumerated powers Those powers of the government that are specifically listed in the Constitution.

equity Principles developed by courts based on fairness and equality that go beyond positive law.

ex post facto law A law that applies retroactively, subjecting parties to criminal sanctions for actions that were not illegal at the time they were committed. Unconstitutional in the United States.

exclusionary rule The prohibition against illegally obtained evidence being used at trial.

exclusive powers Jurisdiction retained by national or state governments and not shared with the other.

federal question jurisdiction Power of federal courts to hear cases that raise issues under federal law, regardless of who are the parties to the case.

federalism The principle that governing authority is divided between independent national and state governments.

felony A serious crime (in contrast to a misdemeanor), usually punishable by at least a year's incarceration.

gerrymander To design political boundaries in order to intentionally favor a certain political party or interest.

grand jury A body of citizens who decide whether to issue an indictment based on evidence presented to them by a prosecutor.

habeas corpus (writ of) Literally "you have the body." An order brought by or on behalf of a prisoner commanding a review of the lawfulness of the prisoner's detention.

hearsay An out-of-court statement by someone other than the witnessed introduced for the truth of the matter.

immunity Protection from prosecution for a party's criminal activity, often in exchange for their cooperation with prosecutors.

In re In regard to.

incorporation The process of defining the scope of the due process clause of the Fourteenth Amendment. The debate over incorporation specifically addresses which parts of the federal Bill of Rights are to be applied against the states.

indictment The formal, written charges against a criminal defendant presented by a grand jury.

indirect effects In pre-New Deal commerce clause jurisprudence, local actions are not subject to federal regulation if they only indirectly affect interstate commerce.

injunction A court order prohibiting or commanding the performance of certain acts.

intermediate scrutiny The amount of suspicion with which a court examines a regulation that impinges on some constitutional rights. To pass intermediate scrutiny, a regulation must further a substantial government interest and the restriction on constitutional rights must be no greater than necessary to the pursuit of that interest. Most notably applied to laws that make sex-based distinctions.

judgment of the court The official decision reached by a court specifying the legal outcome in a case.

judicial activism The philosophy that judges should frequently review and, when necessary, use constitutional grounds to strike down decisions by elected officials or other political figures. Usually has a negative connotation.

judicial restraint The philosophy that judges should show deference to the decisions of political figures, particularly those of elected officials.

judicial review The power of courts to find acts of executive and legislative officials unconstitutional and declare them void.

judicial supremacy The theory that the judiciary can determine how all governing officials must interpret the Constitution.

jurisdiction A government, branch of government, legal body, or person's authority over a certain territory or type of matter or dispute.

jurisprudential Concerning the court system.

justiciable Able to be reviewed and resolved by a court, as in a dispute.

legislative veto The power of the legislature, or portion of the legislature, to nullify an executive or administrative action.

libel Published defamation of a party's character or reputation.

line-item veto The power of a chief executive to reject part of a bill while approving the larger piece of legislation.

litigant A party to a lawsuit.

majority opinion The written statement detailing the official decision and reasoning of a court in a case.

mandamus (writ of) A court order demanding the performance of a duty by a public official or government body.

merits The facts of a case or argument, as opposed to the legal or procedural points.

***Miranda* warning** The rights of the accused with which police must acquaint suspects at the time of their arrest.

misdemeanor A minor crime (in contrast to a felony), usually punishable by fine, penalty, or confiscation, but little to no jail time.

mistrial A trial that the presiding judge declares void before its completion due to miscarriages of justice.

moot Already-resolved or irrelevant, as in a dispute. Courts will not hear cases in which the controversy between the parties has already been resolved or in which the parties involved no longer have a direct stake.

motion A request made to the court on behalf of one party in a suit.

natural law The rights of humans that are presumed to exist independent of government.

nonjusticiable Unable to be decided in court.

opinion of the court A written statement detailing the court's decision in a case and its reasoning.

oral argument The hearing before an appellate court during which lawyers for each side in a case present their spoken legal arguments before the judges and the judges ask questions.

original jurisdiction A government, branch of government, legal body, or person's authority to be the first to decide a matter, as opposed to hearing an appeal.

partisan Pertaining to a political party.

penumbra Rights and powers that are not enumerated in a constitution but are implied by enumerated rights and powers.

per curiam opinion Literally "by the court." An opinion by the court acting as a whole, as opposed to an opinion written by individual judges.

petitioner A party who appeals to a court to resolve a dispute. In the appeals process, the party filing the appeal is called the petitioner; the party against whom the appeal is filed is called the respondent.

plaintiff The party who brings suit in a civil case.

plenary Whole or complete, leaving no residuum; as in plenary power.

plurality opinion A written statement detailing the decision supported by the greatest number of judges in a case in which no majority is reached.

police power A government's power to regulate the health, safety, and morality of people within its territory.

political questions doctrine The legal view that certain matters are the exclusive domain of the legislative and executive branches of government and should therefore remain free of interference from the judiciary.

popular sovereignty The principle that the ultimate authority in a system of government rests with the people.

precedent A previous court decision on an issue.

preemption State laws are preempted or overriden when a federal law is intended to be the sole regulation or the state law is inconsistent with the federal law.

prima facie Literally "on the face of it." Assumed to be true unless effectively disproven.

prior restraint Censorship of speech or publications before their publication or airing.

public forum Places that, according to the Supreme Court, "by long tradition or by government fiat have been devoted to assembly and debate."

punitive damages Reparations granted to a winning plaintiff in a civil dispute that cover no specific costs or losses but are instead intended to punish the respondent and deter similar actions.

rational basis test The lowest level of scrutiny a court will give to a challenged regulation, which presumes the constitutionality of government action. To pass a rational basis test, a regulation must be rationally related to a legitimate public purpose. Generally applied when the law does not infringe on any fundamental rights or make use of any suspect classifications.

remand To send back, as in to send a case back to a lower court for review or to send a defendant back to jail pending sentencing.

respondent A party against whom legal action is taken. In the appeals process, the party against whom the appeal is filed is called the respondent; the party filing the appeal is called the petitioner.

reverse To overturn, as in the decision of a lower court.

ripe Ready to be decided by a court. A dispute's "ripeness" is determined by the court based on a number of criteria, including but not limited to level of controversy surrounding the issue at hand and the predicted ability of a legal remedy to resolve the dispute.

selective incorporation The application of individual clauses of the Bill of Rights against the states through the Fourteenth Amendment on a case-by-case basis.

separation of powers The functional division of government powers among independent branches of government in order to prevent any one government official from accumulating too much power and to take advantage of specialization.

solicitor general The Justice Department official who argues cases on behalf of the United States government before the Supreme Court.

sovereign immunity Protection from civil liability for sovereign governments.

standing to sue The right of a party to bring a dispute before a court. In order to have standing, parties must demonstrate that that they have suffered harm due to actions which may be remedied by the court.

stare decisis Literally "to stand by things decided." The judicial principle that courts should respect precedent.

state action Conduct by a state government or official; conduct performed under state law or state authorization, or a private party with a sufficient connection to the state.

state courts Courts established under state authority that hear disputes and controversies.

statute of limitations A law limiting the period of time that some action may form the basis of a lawsuit.

stay A temporary suspension of court action, for example, a stay of execution.

strategic model The theory that one can describe and predict a judge's legal decisions based on one's knowledge of the judge's policy preferences and the institutional circumstances that constrain the ability of a judge to act on those preferences.

strict construction The narrow reading of constitutional and statutory law.

strict scrutiny The greatest amount of suspicion with which a court examines a regulation that restricts a constitutional right, which presumes that a government action is unconstitutional. To pass strict scrutiny, a regulation must be a narrowly tailored or least restrictive means to achieving a compelling governmental interest. Generally applied when a government action interferes with fundamental rights or employs a suspect classification (such as race).

subpoena An order to give information to a court.

substantive due process Rights that are so fundamental they cannot be infringed without violating the constitutional protection against wrongful and arbitrary government coercion. Often applied to "unenumerated" rights to property or sexual liberty.

test A set of criteria used by courts to determine if actions are legal.

tort A civil wrong.

vacate To annul or eliminate; for example the decision of a lower court by a higher court.

warrant A legal authorization for law enforcement officials to perform a search or make an arrest.

writ A legal order.

Index

Note: *t* refers to table, *f* refers to figure, and *b* refers to box.

Cases